P9-CKF-255

LEADING CONSTITUTIONAL CASES

ON

CRIMINAL JUSTICE

Edited by

LLOYD L. WEINREB

Dane Professor of Law, Harvard University

1995 Edition

Westbury, New York
THE FOUNDATION PRESS, INC.
1995

COPYRIGHT © 1973–1994 THE FOUNDATION PRESS, INC.

————————

COPYRIGHT © 1995

By

THE FOUNDATION PRESS, INC.

All rights reserved

ISBN 1–56662–304–9

TEXT IS PRINTED ON 10% POST CONSUMER RECYCLED PAPER

PRINTED WITH SOY INK

PREFACE

This book provides in a simple format the texts of leading constitutional cases about the investigation and prosecution of crime. The continuing development of constitutional principles in this area makes it worthwhile to consider the cases explicitly as constitutional law and not only as aspects, more or less important, of the whole structure of the administration of criminal justice. The rhetoric of many of the opinions resounds remote from the "street" or the police station or the courthouse; some of the doctrine elaborated in them is not substantial enough to control practices that depend on more than legal doctrine. If constitutional law is not the whole or from every perspective the most important part of criminal justice, it is nonetheless an important part, and in its constitutional aspect it is distinctive. While I should not look only to the Supreme Court to learn about the criminal process, therefore, I do not believe that the significance of the cases contained here lies entirely in their immediate, concrete consequences.

I use these cases as they are presented here in a first-year law school course on Criminal Law, in which it seems appropriate to emphasize the constitutional aspect of criminal justice. In order to make the book more usable to others, who have their own ideas about which cases are most important, I have included more cases than I use myself. The book may also serve as an unadorned reference source for people who are professionally engaged in the work of criminal justice. The format has been designed for annual inclusion of significant cases decided in the current term of the Supreme Court (and exclusion of some that lose significance).

The cases are edited only for economy of space (and, sometimes, the reader's time), as neutrally as I was able. For the most part I have eliminated material that is largely irrelevant to criminal justice; material that is repetitious within a case or too much so within a line of connected cases reproduced here; historical material that does not currently have importance for the constitutional development; analyses of prior cases that serve mostly as a polite bow to the past; and separate opinions of the Justices that do not shed light on prevailing constitutional doctrine or (appear to) have much chance of prevailing themselves. I have included concurring and dissenting opinions that make a substantial contribution to discussion of the issue at stake; I have, I believe, applied that standard generously. Separate opinions that are not reproduced are indicated in a footnote at the end of the case, along with the votes of Justices who did not join one of the reproduced opinions.

The arrangement of cases is guided by the constitutional focus so far as that made sense. I could not always accept the Supreme Court's own statement about what constitutional rubric was at issue lest more important patterns disappear. The lineup decisions, *Wade* and *Kirby*, for example, "go off" on the right to counsel; but they are about lineups and have been so arranged. Rather than separate pieces of cases that deal significantly with more than one issue, such as *Schmerber*, I have placed the whole case where it seemed most usable. In the end, I adopted the arrangement that seemed least likely to intrude on the cases. Rearrangement for the needs of a particular course will not be difficult.

Most footnotes have been deleted without indication. The original numbers are used for those that have been retained. Since the Justices have increasingly relied on footnotes for citations and similar supporting material that was once included in the body of an opinion, readers should consult the official report if they want to be sure that nothing of that kind is missed. That should not be necessary for most purposes. Citations have been omitted freely, but dots have been inserted to indicate their omission as well as all other omissions in the body of an opinion.

The length of the book has increased substantially since the first edition was published in 1973. As I have prepared succeeding editions, I have felt increasingly the need to shorten opinions, omit concurring or dissenting opinions, or omit cases altogether, lest the book become heavy, unwieldy, and expensive. The more of such choices that I have had to make, the more often probably will my omissions surprise and disappoint some of the book's users. I have tried to include the material most likely to be useful to the largest number of readers.

Some new cases that are included in the year after they were decided may prove not to be important enough to be included thereafter. Since I review and edit cases a second time after the opinion appears in final form (usually about two years after the decision is announced), I have an opportunity then to reconsider its inclusion. Users may find it helpful to have new cases included while they are new, even if they are not leading cases. With that in mind, I expect hereafter to include cases liberally in the first two editions after the term in which the decision is announced and then to make a second, more restrictive judgment.

This 1995 edition includes two cases from the term of the Supreme Court just ended. Wilson v. Arkansas (1995) affirms that the "knock and announce" rule for searches of a dwelling is of constitutional dimension, and United States v. Witte (1995) discusses the application of the Double Jeopardy Clause to provisions of the United States Sentencing Guidelines for enhancement of a sentence because of related criminal conduct. In addition, two older cases have been added, at the suggestion of a professor who uses the book in a law school course on advanced criminal procedure. Nix v. Whiteside (1984) concerns the obligation of defense counsel who believes that the defendant intends to commit perjury if he testifies. Bordenkircher v. Hayes (1978) explores the range of a prosecutor's bargaining power in negotiations over a plea of guilty.

As in the past, I should be glad to hear from users of the book about omitted material that they would like to have included in future editions, as well as included material that might be omitted.

LLOYD L. WEINREB

July 1995

TABLE OF CONTENTS

TABLE OF CONTENTS

Page

TABLE OF CASES

Cases that are summarized in a note are indicated by an "n." following the page number.

TABLE OF CASES

*

LEADING CONSTITUTIONAL CASES

ON

CRIMINAL JUSTICE

*

1. THE CONSTITUTION OF THE UNITED STATES: SELECTED PROVISIONS

The Bill of Rights (Amendments 1–10) and the Fourteenth Amendment §§ 1, 5

AMENDMENT I

Congress shall make no law respecting an establishment of religion, or prohibiting the free exercise thereof; or abridging the freedom of speech, or of the press; or the right of the people peaceably to assemble, and to petition the Government for a redress of grievances.

AMENDMENT II

A well regulated Militia, being necessary to the security of a free State, the right of the people to keep and bear Arms, shall not be infringed.

AMENDMENT III

No Soldier shall, in time of peace be quartered in any house, without the consent of the Owner, nor in time of war, but in a manner to be prescribed by law.

AMENDMENT IV

The right of the people to be secure in their persons, houses, papers, and effects, against unreasonable searches and seizures, shall not be violated, and no Warrants shall issue, but upon probable cause, supported by Oath or affirmation, and particularly describing the place to be searched, and the persons or things to be seized.

AMENDMENT V

No person shall be held to answer for a capital, or otherwise infamous crime, unless on a presentment or indictment of a Grand Jury, except in cases arising in the land or naval forces, or in the Militia, when in actual service in time of War or public danger; nor shall any person be subject for the same offence to be twice put in jeopardy of life or limb; nor shall be compelled in any criminal case to be a witness against himself, nor be deprived of life, liberty, or property, without due process of law; nor shall private property be taken for public use, without just compensation.

AMENDMENT VI

In all criminal prosecutions, the accused shall enjoy the right to a speedy and public trial, by an impartial jury of the State and district wherein the crime shall have been committed, which district shall have been previously ascertained by law, and to be informed of the nature and cause of the accusation; to be confronted with the witnesses against him; to have compulsory process for obtaining witnesses in his favor, and to have the Assistance of Counsel for his defence.

AMENDMENT VII

In Suits at common law, where the value in controversy shall exceed twenty dollars, the right of trial by jury shall be preserved, and no fact tried by jury, shall be otherwise re-examined in any Court of the United States, than according to the rules of the common law.

AMENDMENT VIII

Excessive bail shall not be required, nor excessive fines imposed, nor cruel and unusual punishments inflicted.

AMENDMENT IX

The enumeration in the Constitution, of certain rights, shall not be construed to deny or disparage others retained by the people.

AMENDMENT X

The powers not delegated to the United States by the Constitution, nor prohibited by it to the States, are reserved to the States respectively, or to the people.

AMENDMENT XIV

Section 1. All persons born or naturalized in the United States, and subject to the jurisdiction thereof, are citizens of the United States and of the State wherein they reside. No State shall make or enforce any law which shall abridge the privileges or immunities of citizens of the United States; nor shall any State deprive any person of life, liberty, or property, without due process of law; nor deny to any person within its jurisdiction the equal protection of the laws.

. . .

Section 5. The Congress shall have power to enforce, by appropriate legislation, the provisions of this article.

2. DUE PROCESS OF LAW

PALKO v. CONNECTICUT

302 U.S. 319, 58 S.Ct. 149, 82 L.Ed. 288 (1937).

MR. JUSTICE CARDOZO delivered the opinion of the Court.

A statute of Connecticut permitting appeals in criminal cases to be taken by the state is challenged by appellant as an infringement of the Fourteenth Amendment of the Constitution of the United States. Whether the challenge should be upheld is now to be determined.

Appellant was indicted in Fairfield County, Connecticut, for the crime of murder in the first degree. A jury found him guilty of murder in the second degree, and he was sentenced to confinement in the state prison for life. Thereafter the State of Connecticut, with the permission of the judge presiding at the trial, gave notice of appeal to the Supreme Court of Errors. This it did pursuant to an act adopted in 1886 which is printed in the margin.[1] Public Acts, 1886, p. 560; now § 6494 of the General Statutes. Upon such appeal, the Supreme Court of Errors reversed the judgment and ordered a new trial. State v. Palko, 121 Conn. 669; 186 Atl. 657. It found that there had been error of law to the prejudice of the state (1) in excluding testimony as to a confession by defendant; (2) in excluding testimony upon cross-examination of defendant to impeach his credibility, and (3) in the instructions to the jury as to the difference between first and second degree murder.

Pursuant to the mandate of the Supreme Court of Errors, defendant was brought to trial again. Before a jury was impaneled and also at later stages of the case he made the objection that the effect of the new trial was to place him twice in jeopardy for the same offense, and in so doing to violate the Fourteenth Amendment of the Constitution of the United States. Upon the overruling of the objection the trial proceeded. The jury returned a verdict of murder in the first degree, and the court sentenced the defendant to the punishment of death. The Supreme Court of Errors affirmed the judgment of conviction, 122 Conn. 529; 191 Atl. 320 .... The case is here upon appeal. 28 U.S.C. § 344.

---

1. Sec. 6494. *Appeals by the state in criminal cases.* Appeals from the rulings and decisions of the superior court or of any criminal court of common pleas, upon all questions of law arising on the trial of criminal cases, may be taken by the state, with the permission of the presiding judge, to the supreme court of errors, in the same manner and to the same effect as if made by the accused.

. . .

1.   The execution of the sentence will not deprive appellant of his life without the process of law assured to him by the Fourteenth Amendment of the Federal Constitution.

The argument for appellant is that whatever is forbidden by the Fifth Amendment is forbidden by the Fourteenth also.   The Fifth Amendment, which is not directed to the states, but solely to the federal government, creates immunity from double jeopardy.   No person shall be "subject for the same offense to be twice put in jeopardy of life or limb."   The Fourteenth Amendment ordains, "nor shall any State deprive any person of life, liberty, or property, without due process of law."   To retry a defendant, though under one indictment and only one, subjects him, it is said, to double jeopardy in violation of the Fifth Amendment, if the prosecution is one on behalf of the United States.   From this the consequence is said to follow that there is a denial of life or liberty without due process of law, if the prosecution is one on behalf of the People of a State.   ...

We do not find it profitable to mark the precise limits of the prohibition of double jeopardy in federal prosecutions.   The subject was much considered in Kepner v. United States, 195 U.S. 100, decided in 1904 by a closely divided court.   The view was there expressed for a majority of the court that the prohibition was not confined to jeopardy in a new and independent case.   It forbade jeopardy in the same case if the new trial was at the instance of the government and not upon defendant's motion.   Cf. Trono v. United States, 199 U.S. 521.   All this may be assumed for the purpose of the case at hand, though the dissenting opinions (195 U.S. 100, 134, 137) show how much was to be said in favor of a different ruling. Right-minded men, as we learn from those opinions, could reasonably, even if mistakenly, believe that a second trial was lawful in prosecutions subject to the Fifth Amendment, if it was all in the same case.   Even more plainly, right-minded men could reasonably believe that in espousing that conclusion they were not favoring a practice repugnant to the conscience of mankind.   Is double jeopardy in such circumstances, if double jeopardy it must be called, a denial of due process forbidden to the states?   The tyranny of labels, Snyder v. Massachusetts, 291 U.S. 97, 114, must not lead us to leap to a conclusion that a word which in one set of facts may stand for oppression or enormity is of like effect in every other.

We have said that in appellant's view the Fourteenth Amendment is to be taken as embodying the prohibitions of the Fifth.   His thesis is even broader.   Whatever would be a violation of the original bill of rights (Amendments I to VIII) if done by the federal government is now equally unlawful by force of the Fourteenth Amendment if done by a state.   There is no such general rule.

The Fifth Amendment provides, among other things, that no person shall be held to answer for a capital or otherwise infamous crime unless on presentment or indictment of a grand jury. This court has held that, in prosecutions by a state, presentment or indictment by a grand jury may give way to informations at the instance of a public officer. ... The Fifth Amendment provides also that no person shall be compelled in any criminal case to be a witness against himself. This court has said that, in prosecutions by a state, the exemption will fail if the state elects to end it. Twining v. New Jersey, 211 U.S. 78, 106, 111, 112. ... The Sixth Amendment calls for a jury trial in criminal cases and the Seventh for a jury trial in civil cases at common law where the value in controversy shall exceed twenty dollars. This court has ruled that consistently with those amendments trial by jury may be modified by a state or abolished altogether. ... As to the Fourth Amendment, one should refer to Weeks v. United States, 232 U.S. 383, 398, and as to other provisions of the Sixth, to West v. Louisiana, 194 U.S. 258.

On the other hand, the due process clause of the Fourteenth Amendment may make it unlawful for a state to abridge by its statutes the freedom of speech which the First Amendment safeguards against encroachment by the Congress ... or the like freedom of the press ... or the free exercise of religion ... or the right of peaceable assembly, without which speech would be unduly trammeled ... or the right of one accused of crime to the benefit of counsel .... In these and other situations immunities that are valid as against the federal government by force of the specific pledges of particular amendments [2] have been found to be implicit in the concept of ordered liberty, and thus, through the Fourteenth Amendment, become valid as against the states.

The line of division may seem to be wavering and broken if there is a hasty catalogue of the cases on the one side and the other. Reflection and analysis will induce a different view. There emerges the perception of a rationalizing principle which gives to discrete instances a proper order and coherence. The right to trial by jury and the immunity from prosecution except as the result of an indictment may have value and importance. Even so, they are not of the very essence of a scheme of ordered liberty. To abolish them is not to violate a "principle of justice so rooted in the traditions and conscience of our people as to be ranked as fundamental." Snyder v. Massachusetts, supra, p. 105 .... Few would be so narrow or provincial as to maintain that a fair and enlightened system of justice would be impossible without them. What is true of jury trials and indictments is true also, as the cases show, of the immunity from compulsory self-incrimination. Twining v. New

---

2. First Amendment: "Congress shall make no law respecting an establishment of religion, or prohibiting the free exercise thereof; or abridging the freedom of speech, or of the press; or the right of the people peaceably to assemble, and to petition the Government for a redress of grievances."

Sixth Amendment: "In all criminal prosecutions, the accused shall enjoy the right ... to have the assistance of counsel for his defence."

Jersey, supra. This too might be lost, and justice still be done. Indeed, today as in the past there are students of our penal system who look upon the immunity as a mischief rather than a benefit, and who would limit its scope, or destroy it altogether. No doubt there would remain the need to give protection against torture, physical or mental. . . . Justice, however, would not perish if the accused were subject to a duty to respond to orderly inquiry. The exclusion of these immunities and privileges from the privileges and immunities protected against the action of the states has not been arbitrary or casual. It has been dictated by a study and appreciation of the meaning, the essential implications, of liberty itself.

We reach a different plane of social and moral values when we pass to the privileges and immunities that have been taken over from the earlier articles of the federal bill of rights and brought within the Fourteenth Amendment by a process of absorption. These in their origin were effective against the federal government alone. If the Fourteenth Amendment has absorbed them, the process of absorption has had its source in the belief that neither liberty nor justice would exist if they were sacrificed. Twining v. New Jersey, supra, p. 99. This is true, for illustration, of freedom of thought, and speech. Of that freedom one may say that it is the matrix, the indispensable condition, of nearly every other form of freedom. With rare aberrations a pervasive recognition of that truth can be traced in our history, political and legal. So it has come about that the domain of liberty, withdrawn by the Fourteenth Amendment from encroachment by the states, has been enlarged by latter-day judgments to include liberty of the mind as well as liberty of action. The extension became, indeed, a logical imperative when once it was recognized, as long ago it was, that liberty is something more than exemption from physical restraint, and that even in the field of substantive rights and duties the legislative judgment, if oppressive and arbitrary, may be overridden by the courts. . . . Fundamental too in the concept of due process, and so in that of liberty, is the thought that condemnation shall be rendered only after trial. . . . The hearing, moreover, must be a real one, not a sham or a pretense. . . . For that reason, ignorant defendants in a capital case were held to have been condemned unlawfully when in truth, though not in form, they were refused the aid of counsel. Powell v. Alabama [287 U.S. 45 (1932)], pp. 67, 68. The decision did not turn upon the fact that the benefit of counsel would have been guaranteed to the defendants by the provisions of the Sixth Amendment if they had been prosecuted in a federal court. The decision turned upon the fact that in the particular situation laid before us in the evidence the benefit of counsel was essential to the substance of a hearing.

Our survey of the cases serves, we think, to justify the statement that the dividing line between them, if not unfaltering throughout its course, has been true for the most part to a unifying principle.

On which side of the line the case made out by the appellant has appropriate location must be the next inquiry and the final one. Is that kind of double jeopardy to which the statute has subjected him a hardship so acute and shocking that our polity will not endure it? Does it violate those "fundamental principles of liberty and justice which lie at the base of all our civil and political institutions"? Hebert v. Louisiana [272 U.S. 312, 316 (1926)]. The answer surely must be "no." What the answer would have to be if the state were permitted after a trial free from error to try the accused over again or to bring another case against him, we have no occasion to consider. We deal with the statute before us and no other. The state is not attempting to wear the accused out by a multitude of cases with accumulated trials. It asks no more than this, that the case against him shall go on until there shall be a trial free from the corrosion of substantial legal error. State v. Felch, 92 Vt. 477; 105 Atl. 23; State v. Lee, supra. This is not cruelty at all, nor even vexation in any immoderate degree. If the trial had been infected with error adverse to the accused, there might have been review at his instance, and as often as necessary to purge the vicious taint. A reciprocal privilege, subject at all times to the discretion of the presiding judge, State v. Carabetta, 106 Conn. 114; 127 Atl. 394, has now been granted to the state. There is here no seismic innovation. The edifice of justice stands, its symmetry, to many, greater than before.

2. The conviction of appellant is not in derogation of any privileges or immunities that belong to him as a citizen of the United States.

There is argument in his behalf that the privileges and immunities clause of the Fourteenth Amendment as well as the due process clause has been flouted by the judgment.

Maxwell v. Dow [176 U.S. 581 (1900)], p. 584, gives all the answer that is necessary.

The judgment is

Affirmed.[*]

[*] Justice Butler noted his dissent.

Palko v. Connecticut was overruled in Benton v. Maryland, 395 U.S. 784, 794 (1969), in which the Supreme Court declared "that the double jeopardy prohibition of the Fifth Amendment represents a fundamental ideal in our constitutional heritage, and that it should apply to the States through the Fourteenth Amendment."

ADAMSON v. CALIFORNIA

332 U.S. 46, 67 S.Ct. 1672, 91 L.Ed. 1903 (1947).

MR. JUSTICE REED delivered the opinion of the Court.

The appellant, Adamson, a citizen of the United States, was convicted, without recommendation for mercy, by a jury in a Superior Court of the State of California of murder in the first degree. After considering the same objections to the conviction that are pressed here, the sentence of death was affirmed by the Supreme Court of the state. 27 Cal.2d 478, 165 P.2d 3. Review of that judgment by this Court was sought and allowed under Judicial Code § 237; 28 U.S.C. § 344. The provisions of California law which were challenged in the state proceedings as invalid under the Fourteenth Amendment to the Federal Constitution are those of the state constitution and penal code in the margin. They permit the failure of a defendant to explain or to deny evidence against him to be commented upon by court and by counsel and to be considered by court and jury.[3] The defendant did not testify. As the trial court gave its instructions and the District Attorney argued the case in accordance with the constitutional and statutory provisions just referred to, we have for decision the question of their constitutionality in these circumstances under the limitations of § 1 of the Fourteenth Amendment.

The appellant was charged in the information with former convictions for burglary, larceny and robbery and pursuant to § 1025, California Penal Code, answered that he had suffered the previous convictions. This answer barred allusion to these charges of convictions on the trial.[5] Under California's interpretation of § 1025 of the Penal Code and § 2051 of the Code of Civil Procedure, however, if the defendant, after answering affirmatively charges alleging prior convictions, takes the witness stand to deny

---

3. Constitution of California, Art. I, § 13: ". . . No person shall be twice put in jeopardy for the same offense; nor be compelled, in any criminal case, to be a witness against himself; nor be deprived of life, liberty, or property without due process of law; but in any criminal case, whether the defendant testifies or not, his failure to explain or to deny by his testimony any evidence or facts in the case against him may be commented upon by the court and by counsel, and may be considered by the court or the jury. . . ."

Penal Code of California, § 1323: "A defendant in a criminal action or proceeding cannot be compelled to be a witness against himself; but if he offers himself as a witness, he may be cross-examined by the counsel for the people as to all matters about which he was examined in chief. The failure of the defendant to explain or to deny by his testimony any evidence or facts in the case against him may be commented upon by counsel."

5. Penal Code of California, § 1025:

". . . In case the defendant pleads not guilty, and answers that he has suffered the previous conviction, the charge of the previous conviction must not be read to the jury, nor alluded to on the trial."

or explain away other evidence that has been introduced "the commission of these crimes could have been revealed to the jury on cross-examination to impeach his testimony." People v. Adamson, 27 Cal.2d 478, 494, 165 P.2d 3, 11; People v. Braun, 14 Cal.2d 1, 6, 92 P.2d 402, 405. This forces an accused who is a repeated offender to choose between the risk of having his prior offenses disclosed to the jury or of having it draw harmful inferences from uncontradicted evidence that can only be denied or explained by the defendant.

In the first place, appellant urges that the provision of the Fifth Amendment that no person "shall be compelled in any criminal case to be a witness against himself" is a fundamental national privilege or immunity protected against state abridgment by the Fourteenth Amendment or a privilege or immunity secured, through the Fourteenth Amendment, against deprivation by state action because it is a personal right, enumerated in the federal Bill of Rights.

Secondly, appellant relies upon the due process of law clause of the Fourteenth Amendment to invalidate the provisions of the California law, set out in note 3 supra, and as applied (a) because comment on failure to testify is permitted, (b) because appellant was forced to forego testimony in person because of danger of disclosure of his past convictions through cross-examination, and (c) because the presumption of innocence was infringed by the shifting of the burden of proof to appellant in permitting comment on his failure to testify.

We shall assume, but without any intention thereby of ruling upon the issue,[6] that permission by law to the court, counsel and jury to comment upon and consider the failure of defendant "to explain or to deny by his testimony any evidence or facts in the case against him" would infringe defendant's privilege against self-incrimination under the Fifth Amendment if this were a trial in a court of the United States under a similar law. Such an assumption does not determine appellant's rights under the Fourteenth Amendment. It is settled law that the clause of the Fifth Amendment, protecting a person against being compelled to be a witness against himself, is not made effective by the Fourteenth Amendment as a protection against state action on the ground that freedom from testimonial compulsion is a right of national citizenship, or because it is a

6. The California law protects a defendant against compulsion to testify, though allowing comment upon his failure to meet evidence against him. The Fifth Amendment forbids compulsion on a defendant to testify. Boyd v. United States, 116 U.S. 616, 631, 632; cf. Davis v. United States, 328 U.S. 582, 587, 593. A federal statute that grew out of the extension of permissible witnesses to include those charged with offenses negatives a presumption against an accused for failure to avail himself of the right to testify in his own defense. 28 U.S.C. § 632; Bruno v. United States, 308 U.S. 287. It was this statute which is interpreted to protect the defendant against comment for his claim of privilege. Wilson v. United States, 149 U.S. 60, 66; Johnson v. United States, 318 U.S. 189, 199.

personal privilege or immunity secured by the Federal Constitution as one of the rights of man that are listed in the Bill of Rights.

The reasoning that leads to those conclusions starts with the unquestioned premise that the Bill of Rights, when adopted, was for the protection of the individual against the federal government and its provisions were inapplicable to similar actions done by the states. Barron v. Baltimore, 7 Pet. 243; Feldman v. United States, 322 U.S. 487, 490. With the adoption of the Fourteenth Amendment, it was suggested that the dual citizenship recognized by its first sentence secured for citizens federal protection for their elemental privileges and immunities of state citizenship. The *Slaughter-House* Cases[8] decided, contrary to the suggestion, that these rights, as privileges and immunities of state citizenship, remained under the sole protection of the state governments. This Court, without the expression of a contrary view upon that phase of the issues before the Court, has approved this determination. Maxwell v. Bugbee, 250 U.S. 525, 537; Hamilton v. Regents, 293 U.S. 245, 261. The power to free defendants in state trials from self-incrimination was specifically determined to be beyond the scope of the privileges and immunities clause of the Fourteenth Amendment in Twining v. New Jersey, 211 U.S. 78, 91–98. "The privilege against self-incrimination may be withdrawn and the accused put upon the stand as a witness for the state."[9] The *Twining* case likewise disposed of the contention that freedom from testimonial compulsion, being specifically granted by the Bill of Rights, is a federal privilege or immunity that is protected by the Fourteenth Amendment against state invasion. This Court held that the inclusion in the Bill of Rights of this protection against the power of the national government did not make the privilege a federal privilege or immunity secured to citizens by the Constitution against state action. Twining v. New Jersey, supra, at 98–99; Palko v. Connecticut, supra, at 328. After declaring that state and national citizenship co-exist in the same person, the Fourteenth Amendment forbids a state from abridging the privileges and immunities of citizens of the United States. As a matter of words, this leaves a state free to abridge, within the limits of the due process clause, the privileges and immunities flowing from state citizenship. This reading of the Federal Constitution has heretofore found favor with the majority of this Court as a natural and logical interpretation. It accords with the constitutional doctrine of federalism by leaving to the states the responsibility of dealing with the privileges and immunities of their citizens except those inherent in national citizenship. It is the construction placed upon the amendment by justices whose own experience had given them contemporaneous knowledge of the purposes that led to the adoption of the Fourteenth Amendment.

---

8. 16 Wall. 36. ...

9. Snyder v. Massachusetts, 291 U.S. 97, 105; Palko v. Connecticut, 302 U.S. 319, 324; Twining v. New Jersey, supra, 114.

This construction has become embedded in our federal system as a functioning element in preserving the balance between national and state power. We reaffirm the conclusion of the *Twining* and *Palko* cases that protection against self-incrimination is not a privilege or immunity of national citizenship.

Appellant secondly contends that if the privilege against self-incrimination is not a right protected by the privileges and immunities clause of the Fourteenth Amendment against state action, this privilege, to its full scope under the Fifth Amendment, inheres in the right to a fair trial. A right to a fair trial is a right admittedly protected by the due process clause of the Fourteenth Amendment. Therefore, appellant argues, the due process clause of the Fourteenth Amendment protects his privilege against self-incrimination. The due process clause of the Fourteenth Amendment, however, does not draw all the rights of the federal Bill of Rights under its protection. That contention was made and rejected in Palko v. Connecticut, 302 U.S. 319, 323. It was rejected with citation of the cases excluding several of the rights, protected by the Bill of Rights, against infringement by the National Government. Nothing has been called to our attention that either the framers of the Fourteenth Amendment or the states that adopted intended its due process clause to draw within its scope the earlier amendments to the Constitution. *Palko* held that such provisions of the Bill of Rights as were "implicit in the concept of ordered liberty," p. 325, became secure from state interference by the clause. But it held nothing more.

Specifically, the due process clause does not protect, by virtue of its mere existence, the accused's freedom from giving testimony by compulsion in state trials that is secured to him against federal interference by the Fifth Amendment. Twining v. New Jersey, 211 U.S. 78, 99–114; Palko v. Connecticut, supra, p. 323. For a state to require testimony from an accused is not necessarily a breach of a state's obligation to give a fair trial. Therefore, we must examine the effect of the California law applied in this trial to see whether the comment on failure to testify violates the protection against state action that the due process clause does grant to an accused. The due process clause forbids compulsion to testify by fear of hurt, torture or exhaustion. It forbids any other type of coercion that falls within the scope of due process. California follows Anglo-American legal tradition in excusing defendants in criminal prosecutions from compulsory testimony. Cf. VIII Wigmore on Evidence (3d ed.) § 2252. That is a matter of legal policy and not because of the requirements of due process under the Fourteenth Amendment. So our inquiry is directed, not at the broad question of the constitutionality of compulsory testimony from the accused under the due process clause, but to the constitutionality of the provision of the California law that permits comment upon his failure to testify. It is, of course, logically possible that while an accused might be required, under appropriate penalties, to submit himself as a witness without a violation of due process, comment by judge or jury on inferences to be drawn from his failure to testify, in jurisdictions where an accused's privilege against self-incrimination is protected, might deny due process. For example, a statute might declare that a permitted refusal to testify would compel an acceptance of the truth of the prosecution's evidence.

Generally, comment on the failure of an accused to testify is forbidden in American jurisdictions. This arises from state constitutional or statutory provisions similar in character to the federal provisions. Fifth Amendment and 28 U.S.C. § 632. California, however, is one of a few states that permit limited comment upon a defendant's failure to testify. That permission is narrow. The California law is set out in note 3 and authorizes comment by court and counsel upon the "failure of the defendant to explain or to deny by his testimony any evidence or facts in the case against him." This does not involve any presumption, rebuttable or irrebuttable, either of guilt or of the truth of any fact, that is offered in evidence. Compare Tot v. United States, 319 U.S. 463, 470. It allows inferences to be drawn from proven facts. Because of this clause, the court can direct the jury's attention to whatever evidence there may be that a defendant could deny and the prosecution can argue as to inferences that may be drawn from the accused's failure to testify. . . . There is here no lack of power in the trial court to adjudge and no denial of a hearing. California has prescribed a method for advising the jury in the search for truth. However sound may be the legislative conclusion that an accused should not be compelled in any criminal case to be a witness against himself, we see no reason why comment should not be made upon his silence. It seems quite natural that when a defendant has opportunity to deny or explain facts and determines not to do so, the prosecution should bring out the strength of the evidence by commenting upon defendant's failure to explain or deny it. The prosecution evidence may be of facts that may be beyond the knowledge of the accused. If so, his failure to testify would have little if any weight. But the facts may be such as are necessarily in the knowledge of the accused. In that case a failure to explain would point to an inability to explain.

Appellant sets out the circumstances of this case, however, to show coercion and unfairness in permitting comment. The guilty person was not seen at the place and time of the crime. There was evidence, however, that entrance to the place or room where the crime was committed might have been obtained through a small door. It was freshly broken. Evidence showed that six fingerprints on the door were petitioner's. Certain diamond rings were missing from the deceased's possession. There was evidence that appellant, sometime after the crime, asked an unidentified person whether the latter would be interested in purchasing a diamond ring. As has been stated, the information charged other crimes to appellant and he admitted them. His argument here is that he could not take the stand to deny the evidence against him because he would be subjected to a cross-examination as to former crimes to impeach his veracity and the evidence so produced might well bring about his conviction. Such cross-examination is allowable in California. People v. Adamson, 27 Cal.2d 478, 494, 165 P.2d 3, 11. Therefore, appellant contends the California statute permitting comment denies him due process.

It is true that if comment were forbidden, an accused in this situation could remain silent and avoid evidence of former crimes and comment upon his failure to testify. We are of the view, however, that a state may control such a situation in accordance with its own ideas of the most efficient administration of criminal justice. The purpose of due process is not to protect an accused against a proper conviction but against an unfair conviction. When evidence is before a jury that threatens conviction, it does not seem unfair to require him to choose between leaving the adverse evidence unexplained and subjecting himself to impeachment through disclosure of former crimes. Indeed, this is a dilemma with which any defendant may be faced. If facts, adverse to the defendant, are proven by the prosecution, there may be no way to explain them favorably to the accused except by a witness who may be vulnerable to impeachment on cross-examination. The defendant must then decide whether or not to use such a witness. The fact that the witness may also be the defendant makes the choice more difficult but a denial of due process does not emerge from the circumstances.

There is no basis in the California law for appellant's objection on due process or other grounds that the statutory authorization to comment on the failure to explain or deny adverse testimony shifts the burden of proof or the duty to go forward with the evidence. Failure of the accused to testify is not an admission of the truth of the adverse evidence. Instructions told the jury that the burden of proof remained upon the state and the presumption of innocence with the accused. Comment on failure to deny proven facts does not in California tend to supply any missing element of proof of guilt. People v. Adamson, 27 Cal.2d 478, 489–95, 165 P.2d 3, 9–12. It only directs attention to the strength of the evidence for the prosecution or to the weakness of that for the defense. The Supreme Court of California called attention to the fact that the prosecutor's argument approached the borderline in a statement that might have been construed as asserting "that the jury should infer guilt solely from defendant's silence." That court felt that it was improbable the jury was misled into such an understanding of their power. We shall not interfere with such a conclusion. People v. Adamson, 27 Cal.2d 478, 494–95, 165 P.2d 3, 12.

. . .

We find no other error that gives ground for our intervention in California's administration of criminal justice.

Affirmed.[*]

MR. JUSTICE FRANKFURTER, concurring.

Less than ten years ago, Mr. Justice Cardozo announced as settled constitutional law that while the Fifth Amendment, "which is not directed to the states, but solely to the federal government," provides that no person shall be compelled in any criminal case to be a witness against himself, the process of law assured by the Fourteenth Amendment does not require such immunity from self-crimination: "in prosecutions by a state, the exemption will fail if the state elects to end it." Palko v. Connecticut, 302 U.S. 319, 322, 324. Mr. Justice Cardozo spoke for the Court, consisting of Mr. Chief Justice Hughes, and McReynolds, Brandeis, Sutherland, Stone, Roberts, Black, JJ. (Mr. Justice Butler dissented.) The matter no longer called for discussion; a reference to Twining v. New Jersey, 211 U.S. 78, decided thirty years before the *Palko* case, sufficed.

Decisions of this Court do not have equal intrinsic authority. The *Twining* case shows the judicial process at its best—comprehensive briefs and powerful arguments on both sides, followed by long deliberation, resulting in an opinion by Mr. Justice Moody which at once gained and has ever since retained recognition as one of the outstanding opinions in the history of the Court. After enjoying unquestioned prestige for forty years, the *Twining* case should not now be diluted, even unwittingly, either in its judicial philosophy or in its particulars. As the surest way of keeping the *Twining* case intact, I would affirm this case on its authority.

The circumstances of this case present a minor variant from what was before the Court in Twining v. New Jersey, supra. The attempt to inflate the difference into constitutional significance was adequately dealt with by Mr. Justice Traynor in the court below. People v. Adamson, 27 Cal.2d 478, 165 P.2d 3. The matter lies within a very narrow compass. The point is made that a defendant who has a vulnerable record would, by taking the stand, subject himself to having his credibility impeached thereby. ... Accordingly, under California law, he is confronted with the dilemma, whether to testify and perchance have his bad record prejudice him in the minds of the jury, or to subject himself to the unfavorable inference which the jury might draw from his silence. And so, it is argued, if he chooses the latter alternative, the jury ought not to be allowed to attribute his silence to a consciousness of guilt when it might be due merely to a desire to escape damaging cross-examination.

---

[*] The privilege against self-incrimination was made applicable to the states in Malloy v. Hogan, 378 U.S. 1 (1964). The specific holding of Adamson v. California, concerning the rule allowing comment on a defendant's failure to testify, was overruled in Griffin v. California, 380 U.S. 609 (1965).

This does not create an issue different from that settled in the *Twining* case. Only a technical rule of law would exclude from consideration that which is relevant, as a matter of fair reasoning, to the solution of a problem. Sensible and just-minded men, in important affairs of life, deem it significant that a man remains silent when confronted with serious and responsible evidence against himself which it is within his power to contradict. The notion that to allow jurors to do that which sensible and right-minded men do every day violates the "immutable principles of justice" as conceived by a civilized society is to trivialize the importance of "due process." Nor does it make any difference in drawing significance from silence under such circumstances that an accused may deem it more advantageous to remain silent than to speak, on the nice calculation that by taking the witness stand he may expose himself to having his credibility impugned by reason of his criminal record. Silence under such circumstances is still significant. A person in that situation may express to the jury, through appropriate requests to charge, why he prefers to keep silent. A man who has done one wrong may prove his innocence on a totally different charge. To deny that the jury can be trusted to make such discrimination is to show little confidence in the jury system. The prosecution is frequently compelled to rely on the testimony of shady characters whose credibility is bound to be the chief target of the defense. It is a common practice in criminal trials to draw out of a vulnerable witness' mouth his vulnerability, and then convince the jury that nevertheless he is telling the truth in this particular case. This is also a common experience for defendants.

For historical reasons a limited immunity from the common duty to testify was written into the Federal Bill of Rights, and I am prepared to agree that, as part of that immunity, comment on the failure of an accused to take the witness stand is forbidden in federal prosecutions. It is so, of course, by explicit act of Congress. 20 Stat. 30; see Bruno v. United States, 308 U.S. 287. But to suggest that such a limitation can be drawn out of "due process" in its protection of ultimate decency in a civilized society is to suggest that the Due Process Clause fastened fetters of unreason upon the States. (This opinion is concerned solely with a discussion of the Due Process Clause of the Fourteenth Amendment. I put to one side the Privileges or Immunities Clause of that Amendment. For the mischievous uses to which that clause would lend itself if its scope were not confined to that given it by all but one of the decisions beginning with the Slaughter-House Cases, 16 Wall. 36, see the deviation in Colgate v. Harvey, 296 U.S. 404, overruled by Madden v. Kentucky, 309 U.S. 83.)

Between the incorporation of the Fourteenth Amendment into the Constitution and the beginning of the present membership of the Court—a period of seventy years—the scope of that Amendment was passed upon by forty-three judges. Of all these judges, only one, who may respectfully be called an eccentric exception, ever indicated the belief that the Fourteenth Amendment was a shorthand summary of the first eight Amendments theretofore limiting only the Federal Government, and that due process incorporated those eight Amendments as restrictions upon the powers of the States. Among these judges were not only those who would have to be included among the greatest in the history of the Court, but—it is especially relevant to note—they included those whose services in the cause of human rights and the spirit of freedom are the most conspicuous in our history. It is not invidious to single out Miller, Davis, Bradley, Waite, Matthews, Gray, Fuller, Holmes, Brandeis, Stone and Cardozo (to speak only of the dead) as judges who were alert in safeguarding and promoting the interests of liberty and human dignity through law. But they were also judges mindful of the relation of our federal system to a progressively democratic society and therefore duly regardful of the scope of authority that was left to the States even after the Civil War. And so they did not find that the Fourteenth Amendment, concerned as it was with matters fundamental to the pursuit of justice, fastened upon the States procedural arrangements which, in the language of Mr. Justice Cardozo, only those who are "narrow or provincial" would deem essential to "a fair and enlightened system of justice." Palko v. Connecticut, 302 U.S. 319, 325. To suggest that it is inconsistent with a truly free society to begin prosecutions without an indictment, to try petty civil cases without the paraphernalia of a common law jury, to take into consideration that one who has full opportunity to make a defense remains silent is, in de Tocqueville's phrase, to confound the familiar with the necessary.

The short answer to the suggestion that the provision of the Fourteenth Amendment, which ordains "nor shall any State deprive any person of life, liberty, or property, without due process of law," was a way of saying that every State must thereafter initiate prosecutions through indictment by a grand jury, must have a trial by a jury of twelve in criminal cases, and must have trial by such a jury in common law suits where the amount in controversy exceeds twenty dollars, is that it is a strange way of saying it. It would be extraordinarily strange for a Constitution to convey such specific commands in such a roundabout and inexplicit way. After all, an amendment to the Constitution should be read in a " 'sense most obvious to the common understanding at the time of its adoption.' ... For it was for public adoption that it was proposed." See Mr. Justice Holmes in Eisner v. Macomber, 252 U.S. 189, 220. Those reading the English language with the meaning which it ordinarily conveys, those conversant with the political and legal history of the concept of due process, those sensitive to the relations of the States to the central government as well as the relation of some of the provisions of the Bill of Rights to the process of justice, would hardly recognize the Fourteenth Amendment as a cover for the various explicit provisions of the first eight Amendments. Some of these are enduring reflections of experience with human nature while some express the restricted views of Eighteenth-Century England regarding the best methods for the ascertainment of facts. The notion that the Fourteenth Amendment was a covert way of imposing upon the States all the rules which it seemed important to Eighteenth Century statesmen to write into the Federal Amendments, was rejected by judges who were themselves witnesses of the process by which the Fourteenth Amendment became part of the Constitution. Arguments that may now be adduced to prove that the first eight Amendments were concealed within the historic phrasing of the Fourteenth Amendment were not unknown at the time of its adoption. A surer estimate of their bearing was possible for judges at the time than distorting distance is likely to vouchsafe. Any evidence of design or purpose not contemporaneously known could hardly have influenced those who ratified the Amendment. Remarks of a particular proponent of the Amendment, no matter how influential, are not to be deemed part of the Amendment. What was submitted for ratification was his proposal, not his speech. Thus, at the time of the ratification of the Fourteenth Amendment the constitutions of nearly half of the ratifying States did not have the rigorous requirements of the Fifth Amendment for instituting criminal proceedings through a grand jury. It could hardly have occurred to these States that by ratifying the Amendment they uprooted their established methods for prosecuting crime and fastened upon themselves a new prosecutorial system.

Indeed, the suggestion that the Fourteenth Amendment incorporates the first eight Amendments as such is not unambiguously urged. Even the boldest innovator would shrink from suggesting to more than half the States that they may no longer initiate prosecutions without indictment by grand jury, or that thereafter all the States of the Union must furnish a jury of twelve for every case involving a claim above twenty dollars. There is suggested merely a selective incorporation of the first eight Amendments into the Fourteenth Amendment. Some are in and some are out, but we are left in the dark as to which are in and which are out. Nor are we given the calculus for determining which go in and which stay out. If the basis of selection is merely that those provisions of the first eight Amendments are incorporated which commend themselves to individual justices as indispensable to the dignity and happiness of a free man, we are thrown back to a merely subjective test. The protection against unreasonable search and seizure might have primacy for one judge, while trial by a jury of twelve for every claim above twenty dollars might appear to another as an ultimate need in a free society. In the history of thought "natural law" has a much longer and much better founded meaning and justification than such subjective selection of the first eight Amendments for incorporation into the Fourteenth. If all that is meant is that due process contains within itself certain minimal standards which are "of the very essence of a scheme of ordered liberty," Palko v. Connecticut, 302 U.S. 319, 325, putting upon this Court the duty of applying these standards from time to time, then we have merely arrived at the insight which our predecessors long ago expressed. We are called upon to apply to the difficult issues of our own day the wisdom afforded by the great opinions in this field, such as those in Davidson v. New Orleans, 96 U.S. 97; Missouri v. Lewis, 101 U.S. 22; Hurtado v. California, 110 U.S. 516; Holden v. Hardy, 169 U.S. 366; Twining v. New Jersey, 211 U.S. 78, and Palko v. Connecticut, 302 U.S. 319. This guidance bids us to be duly mindful of the heritage of the past, with its great lessons of how liberties are won and how they are lost. As judges charged with the delicate task of subjecting the government of a continent to the Rule of Law we must be particularly mindful that it is "*a constitution* we are expounding," so that it should not be imprisoned in what are merely legal forms even though they have the sanction of the Eighteenth Century.

It may not be amiss to restate the pervasive function of the Fourteenth Amendment in exacting from the States observance of basic liberties. See Malinski v. New York, 324 U.S. 401, 412 et seq.; Louisiana v. Resweber, 329 U.S. 459, 466 et seq. The Amendment neither comprehends the specific provisions by which the founders deemed it appropriate to restrict the federal government nor is it confined to them. The Due Process Clause of the Fourteenth Amendment has an independent potency, precisely as does the Due Process Clause of the Fifth Amendment in relation to the Federal Government. It ought not to require argument to reject the notion that due process of law meant one thing in the Fifth Amendment and another in the Fourteenth. The Fifth Amendment specifically prohibits prosecution of an "infamous crime" except upon indictment; it forbids double jeopardy; it bars compelling a person to be a witness against himself in any criminal case; it precludes deprivation of "life, liberty, or property, without due process of law . . . ." Are Madison and his contemporaries in the framing of the Bill of Rights to be charged with writing into it a meaningless clause? To consider "due process of law" as merely a shorthand statement of other specific clauses in the same amendment is to attribute to the authors and proponents of this Amendment ignorance of, or indifference to, a historic conception which was one of the great instruments in the arsenal of constitutional freedom which the Bill of Rights was to protect and strengthen.

A construction which gives to due process no independent function but turns it into a summary of the specific provisions of the Bill of Rights would, as has been noted, tear up by the roots much of the fabric of law in the several States, and would deprive the States of opportunity for reforms in legal process designed for extending the area of freedom. It would assume that no other abuses would reveal themselves in the course of time than those which had become manifest in 1791. Such a view not only disregards the historic meaning of "due process." It leads inevitably to a warped construction of specific provisions of the Bill of Rights to bring within their scope conduct clearly condemned by due process but not easily fitting into the pigeon-holes of the specific provisions. It seems pretty late in the day to suggest that a phrase so laden with historic meaning should be given an improvised content consisting of some but not all of the provisions of the first eight Amendments, selected on an undefined basis, with improvisation of content for the provisions so selected.

And so, when, as in a case like the present, a conviction in a State court is here for review under a claim that a right protected by the Due Process Clause of the Fourteenth Amendment has been denied, the issue is not whether an infraction of one of the specific provisions of the first eight Amendments is disclosed by the record. The relevant question is whether the criminal proceedings which resulted in conviction deprived the accused of the due process of law to which the United States Constitution entitled him. Judicial review of that guaranty of the Fourteenth Amendment inescapably imposes upon this Court an exercise of judgment upon the whole course of the proceedings in order to ascertain whether they offend those canons of decency and fairness which express the notions of justice of English-speaking peoples even toward those charged with the most heinous offenses. These standards of justice are not authoritatively formulated anywhere as though they were prescriptions in a pharmacopoeia. But neither does the application of the Due Process Clause imply that judges are wholly at large. The judicial judgment in applying the Due Process Clause must move within the limits of accepted notions of justice and is not to be based upon the idiosyncrasies of a merely personal judgment. The fact that judges among themselves may differ whether in a particular case a trial offends accepted notions of justice is not disproof that general rather than idiosyncratic standards are applied. An important safeguard against such merely individual judgment is an alert deference to the judgment of the State court under review.

MR. JUSTICE BLACK, dissenting.

. . .

This decision reasserts a constitutional theory spelled out in Twining v. New Jersey, 211 U.S. 78, that this Court is endowed by the Constitution with boundless power under "natural law" periodically to expand and contract constitutional standards to conform to the Court's conception of what at a particular time constitutes "civilized decency" and "fundamental liberty and justice." Invoking this *Twining* rule, the Court concludes that although comment upon testimony in a federal court would violate the Fifth Amendment, identical comment in a state court does not violate today's fashion in civilized decency and fundamentals and is therefore not prohibited by the Federal Constitution as amended.

The *Twining* case was the first, as it is the only, decision of this Court which has squarely held that states were free, notwithstanding the Fifth and Fourteenth Amendments, to extort evidence from one accused of crime. I agree that if *Twining* be reaffirmed, the result reached might appropriately follow. But I would not reaffirm the *Twining* decision. I think that decision and the "natural law" theory of the Constitution upon which it relies degrade the constitutional safeguards of the Bill of Rights and simultaneously appropriate for this Court a broad power which we are not authorized by the Constitution to exercise. Furthermore, the *Twining* decision rested on previous cases and broad hypotheses which have been undercut by intervening decisions of this Court. See Corwin, The Supreme Court's Construction of the Self-Incrimination Clause, 29 Mich. L.Rev. 1, 191, 202. My reasons for believing that the *Twining* decision should not be revitalized can best be understood by reference to the constitutional, judicial, and general history that preceded and followed the case. That reference must be abbreviated far more than is justified but for the necessary limitations of opinion-writing.

The first ten amendments were proposed and adopted largely because of fear that Government might unduly interfere with prized individual liberties. The people wanted and demanded a Bill of Rights written into their Constitution. The amendments embodying the Bill of Rights were intended to curb all branches of the Federal Government in the fields touched by the amendments—Legislative, Executive, and Judicial. The Fifth, Sixth, and Eighth Amendments were pointedly aimed at confining exercise of power by courts and judges within precise boundaries, particularly in the procedure used for the trial of criminal cases. Past history provided strong reasons for the apprehensions which brought these procedural amendments into being and attest the wisdom of their adoption. For the fears of arbitrary court action sprang largely from the past use of courts in the imposition of criminal punishments to suppress speech, press, and religion. Hence the constitutional limitations of courts' powers were, in the view of the Founders, essential supplements to the First Amendment, which was itself designed to protect the widest scope for all people to believe and to express the most divergent political, religious, and other views.

But these limitations were not expressly imposed upon state court action. In 1833, Barron v. Baltimore [7 Pet. 243], was decided by this Court. It specifically held inapplicable to the states that provision of the Fifth Amendment which declares: "nor shall private property be taken for public use, without just compensation." In deciding the particular point raised, the Court there said that it could not hold that the first eight amendments applied to the states. This was the controlling constitutional rule when the Fourteenth Amendment was proposed in 1866.

My study of the historical events that culminated in the Fourteenth Amendment, and the expressions of those who sponsored and favored, as well as those who opposed its submission and passage, persuades me that one of the chief objects that the provisions of the Amendment's first section, separately, and as a whole, were intended to accomplish was to make the Bill of Rights, applicable to the states. With full knowledge of the import of the *Barron* decision, the framers and backers of the Fourteenth Amendment proclaimed its purpose to be to overturn the constitutional rule that case had announced. This historical purpose has never received full consideration or exposition in any opinion of this Court interpreting the Amendment.

. . .

. . . I am attaching to this dissent an appendix which contains a résumé, by no means complete, of the Amendment's history. In my judgment that history conclusively demonstrates that the language of the first section of the Fourteenth Amendment, taken as a whole, was thought by those responsible for its submission to the people, and by those who opposed its submission, sufficiently explicit to guarantee that thereafter no state could deprive its citizens of the privileges and protections of the Bill of Rights. Whether this Court ever will, or whether it now should, in the light of past decisions, give full effect to what the Amendment was intended to accomplish is not necessarily essential to a decision here. However that may be, our prior decisions, including *Twining*, do not prevent our carrying out that purpose, at least to the extent of making applicable to the states, not a mere part, as the Court has, but the full protection of the Fifth Amendment's provision against compelling evidence from an accused to convict him of crime. And I further contend that the ''natural law'' formula which the Court uses to reach its conclusion in this case should be abandoned as an incongruous excrescence on our Constitution. I believe that formula to be itself a violation of our Constitution, in that it subtly conveys to courts, at the expense of legislatures, ultimate power over public policies in fields where no specific provision of the Constitution limits legislative power. . . .

. . .

I cannot consider the Bill of Rights to be an outworn 18th Century ''strait jacket'' as the *Twining* opinion did. Its provisions may be thought outdated abstractions by some. And it is true that they were designed to meet ancient evils. But they are the same kind of human evils that have emerged from century to century wherever excessive power is sought by the few at the expense of the many. In my judgment the people of no nation can lose their liberty so long as a Bill of Rights like ours survives and its basic purposes are conscientiously interpreted, enforced and respected so as to afford continuous protection against old, as well as new, devices and practices which might thwart those purposes. I fear to see the consequences of the Court's practice of substituting its own concepts of decency and fundamental justice for the language of the Bill of Rights as its point of departure in interpreting and enforcing that Bill of Rights. If the choice must be between the selective process of the *Palko* decision applying some of the Bill of Rights to the States, or the *Twining* rule applying none of them, I would choose the *Palko* selective process. But rather than accept either of these choices, I would follow what I believe was the original purpose of the Fourteenth Amendment—to extend to all the people of the nation the complete protection of the Bill of Rights. To hold that this Court can determine what, if any, provisions of the Bill of Rights will be enforced, and if so to what degree, is to frustrate the great design of a written Constitution.

Conceding the possibility that this Court is now wise enough to improve on the Bill of Rights by substituting natural law concepts for the Bill of Rights, I think the possibility is entirely too speculative to agree to take that course. I would therefore hold in this case that the full protection of the Fifth Amendment's proscription against compelled testimony must be afforded by California. This I would do because of reliance upon the original purpose of the Fourteenth Amendment.

It is an illusory apprehension that literal application of some or all of the provisions of the Bill of Rights to the States would unwisely increase the sum total of the powers of this Court to invalidate state legislation. The Federal Government has not been harmfully burdened by the requirement that enforcement of federal laws affecting civil liberty conform literally to the Bill of Rights. Who would advocate its repeal? It must be conceded, of course, that the natural-law-due-process formula, which the Court today reaffirms, has been interpreted to limit substantially this Court's power to prevent state violations of the individual civil liberties guaranteed by the Bill of Rights. But this formula also has been used in the past, and can be used in the future, to license this Court, in considering regulatory legislation, to roam at large in the broad expanses of policy and morals and to trespass, all too freely, on the legislative domain of the States as well as the Federal Government.

Since Marbury v. Madison, 1 Cranch 137, was decided, the practice has been firmly established, for better or worse, that courts can strike down legislative enactments which violate the Constitution. This process, of course, involves interpretation, and since words can have many meanings, interpretation obviously may result in contraction or extension of the original purpose of a constitutional provision, thereby affecting policy. But to pass upon the constitutionality of statutes by looking to the particular standards enumerated in the Bill of Rights and other parts of the Constitution is one thing; to invalidate statutes because of application of "natural law" deemed to be above and undefined by the Constitution is another. "In the one instance, courts proceeding within clearly marked constitutional boundaries seek to execute policies written into the Constitution; in the other, they roam at will in the limitless area of their own beliefs as to reasonableness and actually select policies, a responsibility which the Constitution entrusts to the legislative representatives of the people." Federal Power Commission v. Pipeline Co., 315 U.S. 575, 599, 601, n. 4.

... [Appendix to opinion of Black, J., omitted.]

MR. JUSTICE MURPHY, with whom MR. JUSTICE RUTLEDGE concurs, dissenting.

While in substantial agreement with the views of Mr. Justice Black, I have one reservation and one addition to make.

I agree that the specific guarantees of the Bill of Rights should be carried over intact into the first section of the Fourteenth Amendment. But I am not prepared to say that the latter is entirely and necessarily limited by the Bill of Rights. Occasions may arise where a proceeding falls so far short of conforming to fundamental standards of procedure as to warrant constitutional condemnation in terms of a lack of due process despite the absence of a specific provision in the Bill of Rights.

That point, however, need not be pursued here inasmuch as the Fifth Amendment is explicit in its provision that no person shall be compelled in any criminal case to be a witness against himself. That provision, as Mr. Justice Black demonstrates, is a constituent part of the Fourteenth Amendment.

Moreover, it is my belief that this guarantee against self-incrimination has been violated in this case. Under California law, the judge or prosecutor may comment on the failure of the defendant in a criminal trial to explain or deny any evidence or facts introduced against him. As interpreted and applied in this case, such a provision compels a defendant to be a witness against himself in one of two ways:

1. If he does not take the stand, his silence is used as the basis for drawing unfavorable inferences against him as to matters which he might reasonably be expected to explain. Thus he is compelled, through his silence, to testify against himself. And silence can be as effective in this situation as oral statements.

2. If he does take the stand, thereby opening himself to cross-examination, so as to overcome the effects of the provision in question, he is necessarily compelled to testify against himself. In that case, his testimony on cross-examination is the result of the coercive pressure of the provision rather than his own volition.

Much can be said pro and con as to the desirability of allowing comment on the failure of the accused to testify. But policy arguments are to no avail in the face of a clear constitutional command. This guarantee of freedom from self-incrimination is grounded on a deep respect for those who might prefer to remain silent before their accusers. To borrow language from Wilson v. United States, 149 U.S. 60, 66: "It is not every one who can safely venture on the witness stand though entirely innocent of the charge against him. Excessive timidity, nervousness when facing others and attempting to explain transactions of a suspicious character, and offences charged against him, will often confuse and embarrass him to such a degree as to increase rather than remove prejudices against him. It is not every one, however honest, who would, therefore, willingly be placed on the witness stand."

We are obliged to give effect to the principle of freedom from self-incrimination. That principle is as applicable where the compelled testimony is in the form of silence as where it is composed of oral statements. Accordingly, I would reverse the judgment below.[*]

---

[*] Justice Douglas joined the opinion of Justice Black.

ROCHIN v. CALIFORNIA

342 U.S. 165, 72 S.Ct. 205, 96 L.Ed. 183 (1952).

MR. JUSTICE FRANKFURTER delivered the opinion of the Court.

Having "some information that [the petitioner here] was selling narcotics," three deputy sheriffs of the County of Los Angeles, on the morning of July 1, 1949, made for the two-story dwelling house in which Rochin lived with his mother, common-law wife, brothers and sisters. Finding the outside door open, they entered and then forced open the door to Rochin's room on the second floor. Inside they found petitioner sitting partly dressed on the side of the bed, upon which his wife was lying. On a "night stand" beside the bed the deputies spied two capsules. When asked "Whose stuff is this?" Rochin seized the capsules and put them in his mouth. A struggle ensued, in the course of which the three officers "jumped upon him" and attempted to extract the capsules. The force they applied proved unavailing against Rochin's resistance. He was handcuffed and taken to a hospital. At the direction of one of the officers a doctor forced an emetic solution through a tube into Rochin's stomach against his will. This "stomach pumping" produced vomiting. In the vomited matter were found two capsules which proved to contain morphine.

Rochin was brought to trial before a California Superior Court, sitting without a jury, on the charge of possessing "a preparation of morphine" in violation of the California Health and Safety Code, 1947, § 11,500. Rochin was convicted and sentenced to sixty days' imprisonment. The chief evidence against him was the two capsules. They were admitted over petitioner's objection, although the means of obtaining them was frankly set forth in the testimony by one of the deputies, substantially as here narrated.

On appeal, the District Court of Appeal affirmed the conviction, despite the finding that the officers "were guilty of unlawfully breaking into and entering defendant's room and were guilty of unlawfully assaulting and battering defendant while in the room," and "were guilty of unlawfully assaulting, battering, torturing and falsely imprisoning the defendant at the alleged hospital." 101 Cal.App.2d 140, 143, 225 P.2d 1, 3. One of the three judges, while finding that "the record in this case reveals a shocking series of violations of constitutional rights," concurred only because he felt bound by decisions of his Supreme Court. These, he asserted, "have been looked upon by law enforcement officers as an encouragement, if not an invitation, to the commission of such lawless acts." Id. The Supreme Court of California denied without opinion Rochin's petition for a hearing. Two justices dissented from this denial, and in doing so expressed themselves thus: "... a conviction which rests upon evidence of incriminating objects obtained from the body of the accused by physical abuse is as invalid as a conviction which rests upon a verbal confession extracted from him by such abuse. ... Had the evidence forced from the defendant's lips consisted of an oral confession that he illegally possessed a drug ... he would have the protection of the rule of law which excludes coerced confessions from evidence. But because the evidence forced from his lips consisted of real objects the People of this state are permitted to base a conviction upon it. [We] find no valid ground of distinction between a verbal confession extracted by physical abuse and a confession wrested from defendant's body by physical abuse." 101 Cal.App.2d 143, 149–150, 225 P.2d 913, 917–918.

This Court granted certiorari, 341 U.S. 939, because a serious question is raised as to the limitations which the Due Process Clause of the Fourteenth Amendment imposes on the conduct of criminal proceedings by the States.

In our federal system the administration of criminal justice is predominantly committed to the care of the States. The power to define crimes belongs to Congress only as an appropriate means of carrying into execution its limited grant of legislative powers. U.S.Const., Art. I, § 8, cl. 18. Broadly speaking, crimes in the United States are what the laws of the individual States make them, subject to the limitations of Art. I, § 10, cl. 1, in the original Constitution, prohibiting bills of attainder and *ex post facto* laws, and of the Thirteenth and Fourteenth Amendments.

These limitations, in the main, concern not restrictions upon the powers of the States to define crime, except in the restricted area where federal authority has pre-empted the field, but restrictions upon the manner in which the States may enforce their penal codes. Accordingly, in reviewing a State criminal conviction under a claim of right guaranteed by the Due Process Clause of the Fourteenth Amendment, from which is derived the most far-reaching and most frequent federal basis of challenging State criminal justice, "we must be deeply mindful of the responsibilities of the States for the enforcement of criminal laws, and exercise with due humility our merely negative function in subjecting convictions from state courts to the very narrow scrutiny which the Due Process Clause of the Fourteenth Amendment authorizes." Malinski v. New York, 324 U.S. 401, 412, 418. Due process of law, "itself a historical product," Jackman v. Rosenbaum Co., 260 U.S. 22, 31, is not to be turned into a destructive dogma against the States in the administration of their systems of criminal justice.

However, this Court too has its responsibility. Regard for the requirements of the Due Process Clause "inescapably imposes upon this Court an exercise of judgment upon the whole course of the proceedings [resulting in a conviction] in order to ascertain whether they offend those canons of decency and fairness which express the notions of justice of English-speaking peoples even toward those charged with the most heinous offenses." Malinski v. New York, *supra*, at 416–417. These standards of justice are not authoritatively formulated anywhere as though they were specifics. Due process of law is a summarized constitutional guarantee of respect for those personal immunities which, as Mr. Justice Cardozo twice wrote for the Court, are "so rooted in the traditions and conscience of our people as to be ranked as fundamental," Snyder v. Massachusetts, 291 U.S. 97, 105, or are "implicit in the concept of ordered liberty." Palko v. Connecticut, 302 U.S. 319, 325.

The Court's function in the observance of this settled conception of the Due Process Clause does not leave us without adequate guides in subjecting State criminal procedures to constitutional judgment. In dealing not with the machinery of government but with human rights, the absence of formal exactitude, or want of fixity of meaning, is not an unusual or even regrettable attribute of constitutional provisions. Words being symbols do not speak without a gloss. On the one hand the gloss may be the deposit of history, whereby a term gains technical content. Thus the requirements of the Sixth and Seventh Amendments for trial by jury in the federal courts have a rigid meaning. No changes or chances can alter the content of the verbal symbol of "jury"—a body of twelve men who must reach a unanimous conclusion if the verdict is to go against the defendant. On the other hand, the gloss of some of the verbal symbols of the Constitution does not give them a fixed technical content. It exacts a continuing process of application.

When the gloss has thus not been fixed but is a function of the process of judgment, the judgment is bound to fall differently at different times and differently at the same time through different judges. Even more specific provisions, such as the guaranty of freedom of speech and the detailed protection against unreasonable searches and seizures, have inevitably evoked as sharp divisions in this Court as the least specific and most comprehensive protection of liberties, the Due Process Clause.

The vague contours of the Due Process Clause do not leave judges at large. We may not draw on our merely personal and private notions and disregard the limits that bind judges in their judicial function. Even though the concept of due process of law is not final and fixed, these limits are derived from considerations that are fused in the whole nature of our judicial process. See Cardozo, The Nature of the Judicial Process; The Growth of the Law; The Paradoxes of Legal Science. These are considerations deeply rooted in reason and in the compelling traditions of the legal profession. The Due Process Clause places upon this Court the duty of exercising a judgment, within the narrow confines of judicial power in reviewing State convictions, upon interests of society pushing in opposite directions.

Due process of law thus conceived is not to be derided as resort to a revival of "natural law." To believe that this judicial exercise of judgment could be avoided by freezing "due process of law" at some fixed stage of time or thought is to suggest that the most important aspect of constitutional adjudication is a function for inanimate machines and not for judges, for whom the independence safeguarded by Article III of the Constitution was designed and who are presumably guided by established standards of judicial behavior. Even cybernetics has not yet made that haughty claim. To practice the requisite detachment and to achieve sufficient objectivity no doubt demands of judges the habit of self-discipline and self-criticism, incertitude that one's own views are incontestable and alert tolerance toward views not shared. But these are precisely the presuppositions of our judicial process. They are precisely the qualities society has a right to expect from those entrusted with ultimate judicial power.

Restraints on our jurisdiction are self-imposed only in the sense that there is from our decisions no immediate appeal short of impeachment or constitutional amendment. But that does not make due process of law a matter of judicial caprice. The faculties of the Due Process Clause may be indefinite and vague, but the mode of their ascertainment is not self-willed. In each case "due process of law" requires an evaluation based on a disinterested inquiry pursued in the spirit of science, on a balanced order of facts exactly and fairly stated, on the detached consideration of conflicting claims, see Hudson County Water Co. v. McCarter, 209 U.S. 349, 355, on a judgment not *ad hoc* and episodic but duly mindful of reconciling the needs both of continuity and of change in a progressive society.

Applying these general considerations to the circumstances of the present case, we are compelled to conclude that the proceedings by which this conviction was obtained do more than offend some fastidious squeamishness or private sentimentalism about combatting crime too energetically. This is conduct that shocks the conscience. Illegally breaking into the privacy of the petitioner, the struggle to open his mouth and remove what was there, the forcible extraction of his stomach's contents—this course of proceeding by agents of government to obtain evidence is bound to offend even hardened sensibilities. They are methods too close to the rack and the screw to permit of constitutional differentiation.

It has long since ceased to be true that due process of law is heedless of the means by which otherwise relevant and credible evidence is obtained. This was not true even before the series of recent cases enforced the constitutional principle that the States may not base convictions upon confessions, however much verified, obtained by coercion. These decisions are not arbitrary exceptions to the comprehensive right of States to fashion their own rules of evidence for criminal trials. They are not sports in our constitutional law but applications of a general principle. They are only instances of the general requirement that States in their prosecutions respect certain decencies of civilized conduct. Due process of law, as a historic and generative principle, precludes defining, and thereby confining, these standards of conduct more precisely than to say that convictions cannot be brought about by methods that offend "a sense of justice." See Mr. Chief Justice Hughes, speaking for a unanimous Court in Brown v. Mississippi, 297 U.S. 278, 285–286. It would be a stultification of the responsibility which the course of constitutional history has cast upon this Court to hold that in order to convict a man the police cannot extract by force what is in his mind but can extract what is in his stomach.

To attempt in this case to distinguish what lawyers call "real evidence" from verbal evidence is to ignore the reasons for excluding coerced confessions. Use of involuntary verbal confessions in State criminal trials is constitutionally obnoxious not only because of their unreliability. They are inadmissible under the Due Process Clause even though statements contained in them may be independently established as true. Coerced confessions offend the community's sense of fair play and decency. So here, to sanction the brutal conduct which naturally enough was condemned by the court whose judgment is before us, would be to afford brutality the cloak of law. Nothing would be more calculated to discredit law and thereby to brutalize the temper of a society.

In deciding this case we do not heedlessly bring into question decisions in many States dealing with essentially different, even if related, problems. We therefore put to one side cases which have arisen in the State courts through use of modern methods and devices for discovering wrongdoers and bringing them to book. It does not fairly represent these decisions to suggest that they legalize force so brutal and so offensive to human dignity in securing evidence from a suspect as is revealed by this record. Indeed the California Supreme Court has not sanctioned this mode of securing a conviction. It merely exercised its discretion to decline a review of the conviction. All the California judges who have expressed themselves in this case have condemned the conduct in the strongest language.

We are not unmindful that hypothetical situations can be conjured up, shading imperceptibly from the circumstances of this case and by gradations producing practical differences despite seemingly logical extensions. But the Constitution is "intended to preserve practical and substantial rights, not to maintain theories." Davis v. Mills, 194 U.S. 451, 457.

On the facts of this case the conviction of the petitioner has been obtained by methods that offend the Due Process Clause. The judgment below must be

Reversed.

MR. JUSTICE BLACK, concurring.

Adamson v. California, 332 U.S. 46, 68–123, sets out reasons for my belief that state as well as federal courts and law enforcement officers must obey the Fifth Amendment's command that "No person ... shall be compelled in any criminal case to be a witness against himself." I think a person is compelled to be a witness against himself not only when he is compelled to testify, but also when as here, incriminating evidence is forcibly taken from him by a contrivance of modern science. ... California convicted this petitioner by using against him evidence obtained in this manner, and I agree with Mr. Justice Douglas that the case should be reversed on this ground.

In the view of a majority of the Court, however, the Fifth Amendment imposes no restraint of any kind on the states. They nevertheless hold that California's use of this evidence violated the Due Process Clause of the Fourteenth Amendment. Since they hold as I do in this case, I regret my inability to accept their interpretation without protest. But I believe that faithful adherence to the specific guarantees in the Bill of Rights insures a more permanent protection of individual liberty than that which can be afforded by the nebulous standards stated by the majority.

What the majority hold is that the Due Process Clause empowers this Court to nullify any state law if its application "shocks the conscience," offends "a sense of justice" or runs counter to the "decencies of civilized conduct." The majority emphasize that these statements do not refer to their own consciences or to their senses of justice and decency. For we are told that "we may not draw on our merely personal and private notions"; our judgment must be grounded on "considerations deeply rooted in reason and in the compelling traditions of the legal profession." We are further admonished to measure the validity of state practices, not by our reason, or by the traditions of the legal profession, but by "the community's sense of fair play and decency"; by the "traditions and conscience of our people"; or by "those canons of decency and fairness which express the notions of justice of English-speaking peoples." These canons are made necessary, it is said, because of "interests of society pushing in opposite directions."

If the Due Process Clause does vest this Court with such unlimited power to invalidate laws, I am still in doubt as to why we should consider only the notions of English-speaking peoples to determine what are immutable and fundamental principles of justice. Moreover, one may well ask what avenues of investigation are open to discover "canons" of conduct so universally favored that this Court should write them into the Constitution? All we are told is that the discovery must be made by an "evaluation based on a disinterested inquiry pursued in the spirit of science, on a balanced order of facts."

Some constitutional provisions are stated in absolute and unqualified language such, for illustration, as the First Amendment stating that no law shall be passed prohibiting the free exercise of religion or abridging the freedom of speech or press. Other constitutional provisions do require courts to choose between competing policies, such as the Fourth Amendment which, by its terms, necessitates a judicial decision as to what is an "unreasonable" search or seizure. There is, however, no express constitutional language granting judicial power to invalidate *every* state law of *every* kind deemed "unreasonable" or contrary to the Court's notion of civilized decencies; yet the constitutional philosophy used by the majority has, in the past, been used to deny a state the right to fix the price of gasoline, Williams v. Standard Oil Co., 278 U.S. 235; and even the right to prevent bakers from palming off smaller for larger loaves of bread, Jay Burns Baking Co. v. Bryan, 264 U.S. 504. These cases, and others, show the extent to which the evanescent standards of the majority's philosophy have been used to nullify state legislative programs passed to suppress evil economic practices. What paralyzing role this same philosophy will play in the future economic affairs of this country is impossible to predict. Of even graver concern, however, is the use of the philosophy to nullify the Bill of Rights. I long ago concluded that the accordion-like qualities of this philosophy must inevitably imperil all the individual liberty safeguards specifically enumerated in the Bill of Rights. Reflection and recent decisions [3] of this Court sanctioning abridgement of the freedom of speech and press have strengthened this conclusion.

MR. JUSTICE DOUGLAS, concurring.

The evidence obtained from this accused's stomach would be admissible in the majority of states where the question has been raised. So far as the reported cases reveal, the only states which would probably exclude the evidence would be Arkansas, Iowa, Michigan, and Missouri. Yet the Court now says that the rule which the majority of the states have fashioned violates the "decencies of civilized conduct." To that I cannot agree. It is a rule formulated by responsible courts with judges as sensitive as we are to the proper standards for law administration.

As an original matter it might be debatable whether the provision in the Fifth Amendment that no person "shall be compelled in any criminal case to be a witness against himself" serves the ends of justice. Not all civilized legal procedures recognize it. But the

---

3. American Communications Assn. v. Douds, 339 U.S. 382; Feiner v. New York, 340 U.S. 315; Dennis v. United States, 341 U.S. 494.

choice was made by the Framers, a choice which sets a standard for legal trials in this country. The Framers made it a standard of due process for prosecutions by the Federal Government. If it is a requirement of due process for a trial in the federal courthouse, it is impossible for me to say it is not a requirement of due process for a trial in the state courthouse. That was the issue recently surveyed in Adamson v. California, 332 U.S. 46. The Court rejected the view that compelled testimony should be excluded and held in substance that the accused in a state trial can be forced to testify against himself. I disagree. Of course an accused can be compelled to be present at the trial, to stand, to sit, to turn this way or that, and to try on a cap or a coat. See Holt v. United States, 218 U.S. 245, 252–253. But I think that words taken from his lips, capsules taken from his stomach, blood taken from his veins are all inadmissible provided they are taken from him without his consent. They are inadmissible because of the command of the Fifth Amendment.

That is an unequivocal, definite and workable rule of evidence for state and federal courts. But we cannot in fairness free the state courts from that command and yet excoriate them for flouting the "decencies of civilized conduct" when they admit the evidence. That is to make the rule turn not on the Constitution but on the idiosyncrasies of the judges who sit here.

The damage of the view sponsored by the Court in this case may not be conspicuous here. But it is part of the same philosophy that produced Betts v. Brady, 316 U.S. 455, denying counsel to an accused in a state trial against the command of the Sixth Amendment, and Wolf v. Colorado, 338 U.S. 25, allowing evidence obtained as a result of a search and seizure that is illegal under the Fourth Amendment to be introduced in a state trial. It is part of the process of erosion of civil rights of the citizen in recent years.

GRISWOLD v. CONNECTICUT

381 U.S. 479, 85 S.Ct. 1678, 14 L.Ed.2d 510 (1965).

MR. JUSTICE DOUGLAS delivered the opinion of the Court.

Appellant Griswold is Executive Director of the Planned Parenthood League of Connecticut. Appellant Buxton is a licensed physician and a professor at the Yale Medical School who served as Medical Director for the League at its Center in New Haven—a center open and operating from November 1 to November 10, 1961, when appellants were arrested.

They gave information, instruction, and medical advice to married persons as to the means of preventing conception. They examined the wife and prescribed the best contraceptive device or material for her use. Fees were usually charged, although some couples were serviced free.

The statutes whose constitutionality is involved in this appeal are §§ 53–32 and 54–196 of the General Statutes of Connecticut (1958 rev.). The former provides:

"Any person who uses any drug, medicinal article or instrument for the purpose of preventing conception shall be fined not less than fifty dollars or imprisoned not less than sixty days nor more than one year or be both fined and imprisoned."

Section 54–196 provides:

"Any person who assists, abets, counsels, causes, hires or commands another to commit any offense may be prosecuted and punished as if he were the principal offender."

The appellants were found guilty as accessories and fined $100 each, against the claim that the accessory statute as so applied violated the Fourteenth Amendment. The Appellate Division of the Circuit Court affirmed. The Supreme Court of Errors affirmed that judgment. 151 Conn. 544, 200 A.2d 479. We noted probable jurisdiction. 379 U.S. 926.

We think that appellants have standing to raise the constitutional rights of the married people with whom they had a professional relationship...

. . .

Coming to the merits, we are met with a wide range of questions that implicate the Due Process Clause of the Fourteenth Amendment. Overtones of some arguments suggest that Lochner v. New York, 198 U.S. 45, should be our guide. But we decline that invitation .... We do not sit as a super-legislature to determine the

33

wisdom, need, and propriety of laws that touch economic problems, business affairs, or social conditions. This law, however, operates directly on an intimate relation of husband and wife and their physician's role in one aspect of that relation.

The association of people is not mentioned in the Constitution nor in the Bill of Rights. The right to educate a child in a school of the parents' choice—whether public or private or parochial—is also not mentioned. Nor is the right to study any particular subject or any foreign language. Yet the First Amendment has been construed to include certain of those rights.

By Pierce v. Society of Sisters, [268 U.S. 510 (1925)], the right to educate one's children as one chooses is made applicable to the States by the force of the First and Fourteenth Amendments. By Meyer v. Nebraska, [262 U.S. 390 (1923)] the same dignity is given the right to study the German language in a private school. In other words, the State may not, consistently with the spirit of the First Amendment, contract the spectrum of available knowledge. The right of freedom of speech and press includes not only the right to utter or to print, but the right to distribute, the right to receive, the right to read ... and freedom of inquiry, freedom of thought, and freedom to teach ...—indeed the freedom of the entire university community. ... Without those peripheral rights the specific rights would be less secure. And so we reaffirm the principle of the *Pierce* and the *Meyer* cases.

In NAACP v. Alabama, 357 U.S. 449, 462, we protected the "freedom to associate and privacy in one's associations," noting that freedom of association was a peripheral First Amendment right. Disclosure of membership lists of a constitutionally valid association, we held, was invalid "as entailing the likelihood of a substantial restraint upon the exercise by petitioner's members of their right to freedom of association." Ibid. In other words, the First Amendment has a penumbra where privacy is protected from governmental intrusion. In like context, we have protected forms of "association" that are not political in the customary sense but pertain to the social, legal, and economic benefit of the members. ... In Schware v. Board of Bar Examiners, 353 U.S. 232, we held it not permissible to bar a lawyer from practice, because he had once been a member of the Communist Party. The man's "association with that Party" was not shown to be "anything more than a political faith in a political party" (id., at 244) and was not action of a kind proving bad moral character. ...

Those cases involved more than the "right of assembly"—a right that extends to all irrespective of their race or ideology. ... The right of "association," like the right of belief ... is more than the right to attend a meeting; it includes the right to express one's attitudes or philosophies by membership in a group or by affiliation with it or by other lawful means. Association in that context is a form of expression of opinion; and while it is not expressly included in the First Amendment its existence is necessary in making the express guarantees fully meaningful.

The foregoing cases suggest that specific guarantees in the Bill of Rights have penumbras, formed by emanations from those guarantees that help give them life and substance. . . . Various guarantees create zones of privacy. The right of association contained in the penumbra of the First Amendment is one, as we have seen. The Third Amendment in its prohibition against the quartering of soldiers "in any house" in time of peace without the consent of the owner is another facet of that privacy. The Fourth Amendment explicitly affirms the "right of the people to be secure in their persons, houses, papers, and effects, against unreasonable searches and seizures." The Fifth Amendment in its Self-Incrimination Clause enables the citizen to create a zone of privacy which government may not force him to surrender to his detriment. The Ninth Amendment provides: "The enumeration in the Constitution, of certain rights, shall not be construed to deny or disparage others retained by the people."

The Fourth and Fifth Amendments were described in Boyd v. United States, 116 U.S. 616, 630, as protection against all governmental invasions "of the sanctity of a man's home and the privacies of life." We recently referred in Mapp v. Ohio, 367 U.S. 643, 656, to the Fourth Amendment as creating a "right to privacy, no less important than any other right carefully and particularly reserved to the people." . . .

We have had many controversies over these penumbral rights of "privacy and repose." . . . These cases bear witness that the right of privacy which presses for recognition here is a legitimate one.

The present case, then, concerns a relationship lying within the zone of privacy created by several fundamental constitutional guarantees. And it concerns a law which, in forbidding the *use* of contraceptives rather than regulating their manufacture or sale, seeks to achieve its goals by means having a maximum destructive impact upon that relationship. Such a law cannot stand in light of the familiar principle, so often applied by this Court, that a "governmental purpose to control or prevent activities constitutionally subject to state regulation may not be achieved by means which sweep unnecessarily broadly and thereby invade the area of protected freedoms." NAACP v. Alabama, 377 U.S. 288, 307. Would we allow the police to search the sacred precincts of marital bedrooms for telltale signs of the use of contraceptives? The very idea is repulsive to the notions of privacy surrounding the marriage relationship.

We deal with a right of privacy older than the Bill of Rights— older than our political parties, older than our school system. Marriage is a coming together for better or for worse, hopefully enduring, and intimate to the degree of being sacred. It is an association that promotes a way of life, not causes; a harmony in living, not political faiths; a bilateral loyalty, not commercial or social projects. Yet it is an association for as noble a purpose as any involved in our prior decisions.

Reversed.

MR. JUSTICE GOLDBERG, whom THE CHIEF JUSTICE and MR. JUSTICE BRENNAN join, concurring.

I agree with the Court that Connecticut's birth-control law unconstitutionally intrudes upon the right of marital privacy, and I join in its opinion and judgment. Although I have not accepted the view that "due process" as used in the Fourteenth Amendment incorporates all of the first eight Amendments ... I do agree that the concept of liberty protects those personal rights that are fundamental, and is not confined to the specific terms of the Bill of Rights. My conclusion that the concept of liberty is not so restricted and that it embraces the right of marital privacy though that right is not mentioned explicitly in the Constitution is supported both by numerous decisions of this Court, referred to in the Court's opinion, and by the language and history of the Ninth Amendment. In reaching the conclusion that the right of marital privacy is protected, as being within the protected penumbra of specific guarantees of the Bill of Rights, the Court refers to the Ninth Amendment .... I add these words to emphasize the relevance of that Amendment to the Court's holding.

. . .

This Court, in a series of decisions, has held that the Fourteenth Amendment absorbs and applies to the States those specifics of the first eight amendments which express fundamental personal rights. The language and history of the Ninth Amendment reveal that the Framers of the Constitution believed that there are additional fundamental rights, protected from governmental infringement, which exist alongside those fundamental rights specifically mentioned in the first eight constitutional amendments.

The Ninth Amendment reads, "The enumeration in the Constitution, of certain rights, shall not be construed to deny or disparage others retained by the people."...

. . .

... To hold that a right so basic and fundamental and so deep-rooted in our society as the right of privacy in marriage may be infringed because that right is not guaranteed in so many words by the first eight amendments to the Constitution is to ignore the Ninth Amendment and to give it no effect whatsoever. Moreover, a judicial construction that this fundamental right is not protected by the Constitution because it is not mentioned in explicit terms by one of the first eight amendments or elsewhere in the Constitution would violate the Ninth Amendment, which specifically states that "[t]he enumeration in the Constitution, of certain rights, shall not be *construed* to deny or disparage others retained by the people." (Emphasis added.)

. . . I do not take the position of my Brother Black in his dissent in Adamson v. California, 332 U.S. 46, 68, that the entire Bill of Rights is incorporated in the Fourteenth Amendment, and I do not mean to imply that the Ninth Amendment is applied against the States by the Fourteenth. Nor do I mean to state that the Ninth Amendment constitutes an independent source of rights protected from infringement by either the States or the Federal Government. Rather, the Ninth Amendment shows a belief of the Constitution's authors that fundamental rights exist that are not expressly enumerated in the first eight amendments and an intent that the list of rights included there not be deemed exhaustive. . . . The Ninth Amendment simply shows the intent of the Constitution's authors that other fundamental personal rights should not be denied such protection or disparaged in any other way simply because they are not specifically listed in the first eight constitutional amendments. I do not see how this broadens the authority of the Court; rather it serves to support what this Court has been doing in protecting fundamental rights.

. . .

In sum, I believe that the right of privacy in the marital relation is fundamental and basic—a personal right "retained by the people" within the meaning of the Ninth Amendment. Connecticut cannot constitutionally abridge this fundamental right, which is protected by the Fourteenth Amendment from infringement by the States. I agree with the Court that petitioners' convictions must therefore be reversed.

MR. JUSTICE HARLAN, concurring in the judgment.

I fully agree with the judgment of reversal, but find myself unable to join the Court's opinion. The reason is that it seems to me to evince an approach to this case very much like that taken by my Brothers Black and Stewart in dissent, namely: the Due Process Clause of the Fourteenth Amendment does not touch this Connecticut statute unless the enactment is found to violate some right assured by the letter or penumbra of the Bill of Rights.

In other words, what I find implicit in the Court's opinion is that the "incorporation" doctrine may be used to *restrict* the reach of Fourteenth Amendment Due Process. For me this is just as unacceptable constitutional doctrine as is the use of the "incorporation" approach to *impose* upon the States all the requirements of the Bill of Rights as found in the provisions of the first eight amendments and in the decisions of this Court interpreting them. . . .

In my view, the proper constitutional inquiry in this case is whether this Connecticut statute infringes the Due Process Clause of the Fourteenth Amendment because the enactment violates basic values "implicit in the concept of ordered liberty," Palko v. Connecticut, 302 U.S. 319, 325. For reasons stated at length in my dissenting opinion in Poe v. Ullman, [367 U.S. 497 (1961)], I believe that it does. While the relevant inquiry may be aided by resort to one or more of the provisions of the Bill of Rights, it is not dependent on them or any of their radiations. The Due Process Clause of the Fourteenth Amendment stands, in my opinion, on its own bottom.

A further observation seems in order respecting the justification of my Brothers Black and Stewart for their "incorporation" approach to this case. Their approach does not rest on historical reasons, which are of course wholly lacking (see Fairman, Does the Fourteenth Amendment Incorporate the Bill of Rights? The Original Understanding, 2 Stan.L.Rev. 5 (1949)), but on the thesis that by limiting the content of the Due Process Clause of the Fourteenth Amendment to the protection of rights which can be found elsewhere in the Constitution, in this instance in the Bill of Rights, judges will thus be confined to "interpretation" of specific constitutional provisions, and will thereby be restrained from introducing their own notions of constitutional right and wrong into the "vague contours of the Due Process Clause." Rochin v. California, 342 U.S. 165, 170.

While I could not more heartily agree that judicial "self restraint" is an indispensable ingredient of sound constitutional adjudication, I do submit that the formula suggested for achieving it is more hollow than real. "Specific" provisions of the Constitution, no less than "due process," lend themselves as readily to "personal" interpretations by judges whose constitutional outlook is simply to keep the Constitution in supposed "tune with the times" (post, p. 522). ...

Judicial self-restraint will not, I suggest, be brought about in the "due process" area by the historically unfounded incorporation formula long advanced by my Brother Black, and now in part espoused by my Brother Stewart. It will be achieved in this area, as in other constitutional areas, only by continual insistence upon respect for the teachings of history, solid recognition of the basic values that underlie our society, and wise appreciation of the great roles that the doctrines of federalism and separation of powers have played in establishing and preserving American freedoms. ... Adherence to these principles will not, of course, obviate all constitutional differences of opinion among judges, nor should it. Their continued recognition will, however, go farther toward keeping most judges from roaming at large in the constitutional field than will the interpolation into the Constitution of an artificial and largely illusory restriction on the content of the Due Process Clause.

MR. JUSTICE BLACK, with whom MR. JUSTICE STEWART joins, dissenting.

I agree with my Brother Stewart's dissenting opinion. And like him I do not to any extent whatever base my view that this Connecticut law is constitutional on a belief that the law is wise or that its policy is a good one. In order that there may be no room at all to doubt why I vote as I do, I feel constrained to add that the law is every bit as offensive to me as it is to my Brethren of the majority and my Brothers Harlan, White and Goldberg who, reciting reasons why it is offensive to them, hold it unconstitutional. There is no single one of the graphic and eloquent strictures and criticisms fired at the policy of this Connecticut law either by the Court's opinion or by those of my concurring Brethren to which I cannot subscribe—except their conclusion that the evil qualities they see in the law make it unconstitutional.

. . .

The Court talks about a constitutional "right of privacy" as though there is some constitutional provision or provisions forbidding any law ever to be passed which might abridge the "privacy" of individuals. But there is not. There are, of course, guarantees in certain specific constitutional provisions which are designed in part to protect privacy at certain times and places with respect to certain activities. Such, for example, is the Fourth Amendment's guarantee against "unreasonable searches and seizures." But I think it belittles that Amendment to talk about it as though it protects nothing but "privacy." To treat it that way is to give it a niggardly interpretation, not the kind of liberal reading I think any Bill of Rights provision should be given. The average man would very likely not have his feelings soothed any more by having his property seized openly than by having it seized privately and by stealth. He simply wants his property left alone. And a person can be just as much, if not more, irritated, annoyed and injured by an unceremonious public arrest by a policeman as he is by a seizure in the privacy of his office or home.

One of the most effective ways of diluting or expanding a constitutionally guaranteed right is to substitute for the crucial word or words of a constitutional guarantee another word or words, more or less flexible and more or less restricted in meaning. This fact is well illustrated by the use of the term "right of privacy" as a comprehensive substitute for the Fourth Amendment's guarantee against "unreasonable searches and seizures." "Privacy" is a broad, abstract and ambiguous concept which can easily be shrunken in meaning but which can also, on the other hand, easily be interpreted as a constitutional ban against many things other than searches and seizures. I have expressed the view many times that First Amendment freedoms, for example, have suffered from a failure of the courts to stick to the simple language of the First Amendment in construing it, instead of invoking multitudes of words substituted for those the Framers used. . . . For these reasons I get nowhere in this case by talk about a constitutional "right of privacy" as an emanation from one or more constitutional provisions. I like my privacy as well as the next one, but I am nevertheless compelled to admit that government has a right to invade it unless prohibited by some specific constitutional provision. For these reasons I cannot agree with the Court's judgment and the reasons it gives for holding this Connecticut law unconstitutional.

. . .

I realize that many good and able men have eloquently spoken and written, sometimes in rhapsodical strains, about the duty of this Court to keep the Constitution in tune with the times. The idea is that the Constitution must be changed from time to time and that this Court is charged with a duty to make those changes. For myself, I must with all deference reject that philosophy. The Constitution makers knew the need for change and provided for it. Amendments suggested by the people's elected representatives can be submitted to the people or their selected agents for ratification. That method of change was good for our Fathers, and being somewhat old-fashioned I must add it is good enough for me. And so, I cannot rely on the Due Process Clause or the Ninth Amendment or any mysterious and uncertain natural law concept as a reason for striking down this state law. The Due Process Clause with an "arbitrary and capricious" or "shocking to the conscience" formula was liberally used by this Court to strike down economic legislation in the early decades of this century, threatening, many people thought, the tranquility and stability of the Nation. See, e.g., Lochner v. New York, 198 U.S. 45. That formula, based on subjective considerations of "natural justice," is no less dangerous when used to enforce this Court's views about personal rights than those about economic rights. I had thought that we had laid that formula, as a means for striking down state legislation, to rest once and for all in cases like West Coast Hotel Co. v. Parrish, 300 U.S. 379; Olsen v. Nebraska ex rel. Western Reference & Bond Assn., 313 U.S. 236, and many other opinions. See also Lochner v. New York, 198 U.S. 45, 74 (Holmes, J., dissenting).

. . .

. . . So far as I am concerned, Connecticut's law as applied here is not forbidden by any provision of the Federal Constitution as that Constitution was written, and I would therefore affirm.

MR. JUSTICE STEWART, whom MR. JUSTICE BLACK joins, dissenting.

Since 1879 Connecticut has had on its books a law which forbids the use of contraceptives by anyone. I think this is an uncommonly silly law. As a practical matter, the law is obviously unenforceable, except in the oblique context of the present case.

As a philosophical matter, I believe the use of contraceptives in the relationship of marriage should be left to personal and private choice, based upon each individual's moral, ethical, and religious beliefs. As a matter of social policy, I think professional counsel about methods of birth control should be available to all, so that each individual's choice can be meaningfully made. But we are not asked in this case to say whether we think this law is unwise, or even asinine. We are asked to hold that it violates the United States Constitution. And that I cannot do.

In the course of its opinion the Court refers to no less than six Amendments to the Constitution: the First, the Third, the Fourth, the Fifth, the Ninth, and the Fourteenth. But the Court does not say which of these Amendments, if any, it thinks is infringed by this Connecticut law.

We *are* told that the Due Process Clause of the Fourteenth Amendment is not, as such, the "guide" in this case. With that much I agree. There is no claim that this law, duly enacted by the Connecticut Legislature, is unconstitutionally vague. There is no claim that the appellants were denied any of the elements of procedural due process at their trial, so as to make their convictions constitutionally invalid. And, as the Court says, the day has long passed since the Due Process Clause was regarded as a proper instrument for determining "the wisdom, need, and propriety" of state laws. . . .

As to the First, Third, Fourth, and Fifth Amendments, I can find nothing in any of them to invalidate this Connecticut law, even assuming that all those Amendments are fully applicable against the States. It has not even been argued that this is a law "respecting an establishment of religion, or prohibiting the free exercise thereof." And surely, unless the solemn process of constitutional adjudication is to descend to the level of a play on words, there is not involved here any abridgment of "the freedom of speech, or of the press; or the right of the people peaceably to assemble, and to petition the Government for a redress of grievances." No soldier has been quartered in any house. There has been no search, and no seizure. Nobody has been compelled to be a witness against himself.

. . .

What provision of the Constitution, then, does make this state law invalid? The Court says it is the right of privacy "created by several fundamental constitutional guarantees." With all deference, I can find no such general right of privacy in the Bill of Rights, in any other part of the Constitution, or in any case ever before decided by this Court.

At the oral argument in this case we were told that the Connecticut law does not "conform to current community standards." But it is not the function of this Court to decide cases on the basis of community standards. We are here to decide cases "agreeably to the Constitution and laws of the United States." It is the essence of judicial duty to subordinate our own personal views, our own ideas of what legislation is wise and what is not. If, as I should surely hope, the law before us does not reflect the standards of the people of Connecticut, the people of Connecticut can freely exercise their true Ninth and Tenth Amendment rights to persuade their elected representatives to repeal it. That is the constitutional way to take this law off the books.

DUNCAN v. LOUISIANA

391 U.S. 145, 88 S.Ct. 1444, 20 L.Ed.2d 491 (1968).

MR. JUSTICE WHITE delivered the opinion of the Court.

Appellant, Gary Duncan, was convicted of simple battery in the Twenty-fifth Judicial District Court of Louisiana. Under Louisiana law simple battery is a misdemeanor, punishable by a maximum of two years' imprisonment and a $300 fine. Appellant sought trial by jury, but because the Louisiana Constitution grants jury trials only in cases in which capital punishment or imprisonment at hard labor may be imposed,[1] the trial judge denied the request. Appellant was convicted and sentenced to serve 60 days in the parish prison and pay a fine of $150. Appellant sought review in the Supreme Court of Louisiana, asserting that the denial of jury trial violated rights guaranteed to him by the United States Constitution. The Supreme Court, finding "[n]o error of law in the ruling complained of," denied appellant a writ of certiorari. Pursuant to 28 U.S.C. § 1257(2) appellant sought review in this Court, alleging that the Sixth and Fourteenth Amendments to the United States Constitution secure the right to jury trial in state criminal prosecutions where a sentence as long as two years may be imposed. . . .

Appellant was 19 years of age when tried. While driving on Highway 23 in Plaquemines Parish on October 18, 1966, he saw two younger cousins engaged in a conversation by the side of the road with four white boys. Knowing his cousins, Negroes who had recently transferred to a formerly all-white high school, had reported the occurrence of racial incidents at the school, Duncan stopped the car, got out, and approached the six boys. At trial the white boys and a white onlooker testified, as did appellant and his cousins. The testimony was in dispute on many points, but the witnesses agreed that appellant and the white boys spoke to each other, that appellant encouraged his cousins to break off the encounter and enter his car, and that appellant was about to enter the car himself for the purpose of driving away with his cousins.

---

1. La. Const., Art. VII, § 41:

"All cases in which the punishment may not be at hard labor shall ... be tried by the judge without a jury. Cases, in which the punishment may be at hard labor, shall be tried by a jury of five, all of whom must concur to render a verdict; cases, in which the punishment is necessarily at hard labor, by a jury of twelve, nine of whom must concur to render a verdict; cases in which the punishment may be capital, by a jury of twelve, all of whom must concur to render a verdict."

La.Rev.Stat. § 14:35 (1950):

"Simple battery is a battery, without the consent of the victim, committed without a dangerous weapon.

"Whoever commits a simple battery shall be fined not more than three hundred dollars, or imprisoned for not more than two years, or both."

43

The whites testified that just before getting in the car appellant slapped Herman Landry, one of the white boys, on the elbow. The Negroes testified that appellant had not slapped Landry, but had merely touched him. The trial judge concluded that the State had proved beyond a reasonable doubt that Duncan had committed simple battery, and found him guilty.

I.

The Fourteenth Amendment denies the States the power to "deprive any person of life, liberty, or property, without due process of law." In resolving conflicting claims concerning the meaning of this spacious language, the Court has looked increasingly to the Bill of Rights for guidance; many of the rights guaranteed by the first eight Amendments to the Constitution have been held to be protected against state action by the Due Process Clause of the Fourteenth Amendment. That clause now protects the right to compensation for property taken by the State;[4] the rights of speech, press, and religion covered by the First Amendment;[5] the Fourth Amendment rights to be free from unreasonable searches and seizures and to have excluded from criminal trials any evidence illegally seized;[6] the right guaranteed by the Fifth Amendment to be free of compelled self-incrimination;[7] and the Sixth Amendment rights to counsel,[8] to a speedy[9] and public[10] trial, to confrontation of opposing witnesses,[11] and to compulsory process for obtaining witnesses.[12]

The test for determining whether a right extended by the Fifth and Sixth Amendments with respect to federal criminal proceedings is also protected against state action by the Fourteenth Amendment has been phrased in a variety of ways in the opinions of this Court. The question has been asked whether a right is among those " 'fundamental principles of liberty and justice which lie at the base of all our civil and political institutions,' " Powell v. Alabama, 287 U.S. 45, 67 (1932);[13] whether it is "basic in our system of jurisprudence," In re Oliver, 333 U.S. 257, 273 (1948); and whether it is "a fundamental right, essential to a fair trial," Gideon v. Wainwright, 372 U.S. 335, 343–344 (1963); Malloy v. Hogan, 378 U.S. 1, 6 (1964); Pointer v. Texas, 380 U.S. 400, 403 (1965). The claim before us is that the right to trial by jury guaranteed by the Sixth Amendment meets these tests. The position of Louisiana, on the other hand, is that the Constitution imposes upon the States no

4. Chicago, B. & Q.R. Co. v. Chicago, 166 U.S. 226 (1897).

5. See, e.g., Fiske v. Kansas, 274 U.S. 380 (1927).

6. See Mapp v. Ohio, 367 U.S. 643 (1961).

7. Malloy v. Hogan, 378 U.S. 1 (1964).

8. Gideon v. Wainwright, 372 U.S. 335 (1963).

9. Klopfer v. North Carolina, 386 U.S. 213 (1967).

10. In re Oliver, 333 U.S. 257 (1948).

11. Pointer v. Texas, 380 U.S. 400 (1965).

12. Washington v. Texas, 388 U.S. 14 (1967).

13. Quoting from Hebert v. Louisiana, 272 U.S. 312, 316 (1926).

duty to give a jury trial in any criminal case, regardless of the seriousness of the crime or the size of the punishment which may be imposed. Because we believe that trial by jury in criminal cases is fundamental to the American scheme of justice, we hold that the Fourteenth Amendment guarantees a right of jury trial in all criminal cases which—were they to be tried in a federal court—would come within the Sixth Amendment's guarantee.[14] Since we consider the appeal before us to be such a case, we hold that the Constitution was violated when appellant's demand for jury trial was refused.

The history of trial by jury in criminal cases has been frequently told. It is sufficient for present purposes to say that by the time our Constitution was written, jury trial in criminal cases had been in existence in England for several centuries and carried impressive credentials traced by many to Magna Carta. . . .

. . .

. . . The Constitution itself, in Art. III, § 2, commanded:

14. In one sense recent cases applying provisions of the first eight Amendments to the States represent a new approach to the "incorporation" debate. Earlier the Court can be seen as having asked, when inquiring into whether some particular procedural safeguard was required of a State, if a civilized system could be imagined that would not accord the particular protection. For example, Palko v. Connecticut, 302 U.S. 319, 325 (1937), stated: "The right to trial by jury and the immunity from prosecution except as the result of an indictment may have value and importance. Even so, they are not of the very essence of a scheme of ordered liberty. . . . Few would be so narrow or provincial as to maintain that a fair and enlightened system of justice would be impossible without them." The recent cases, on the other hand, have proceeded upon the valid assumption that state criminal processes are not imaginary and theoretical schemes but actual systems bearing virtually every characteristic of the common-law system that has been developing contemporaneously in England and in this country. The question thus is whether given this kind of system a particular procedure is fundamental—whether, that is, a procedure is necessary to an Anglo-American regime of ordered liberty. It is this sort of inquiry that can justify the conclusions that state courts must exclude evidence seized in violation of the Fourth Amendment, Mapp v. Ohio, 367 U.S. 643 (1961); that state prosecutors may not comment on a defendant's failure to testify, Griffin v. California, 380 U.S. 609 (1965); and that criminal punishment may not be imposed for the status of narcotics addiction, Robinson v. California, 370 U.S. 660 (1962). Of immediate relevance for this case are the Court's holdings that the States must comply with certain provisions of the Sixth Amendment, specifically that the States may not refuse a speedy trial, confrontation of witnesses, and the assistance, at state expense if necessary, of counsel. See cases cited in nn. 8–12, supra. Of each of these determinations that a constitutional provision originally written to bind the Federal Government should bind the States as well it might be said that the limitation in question is not necessarily fundamental to fairness in every criminal system that might be imagined but is fundamental in the context of the criminal processes maintained by the American States.

When the inquiry is approached in this way the question whether the States can impose criminal punishment without granting a jury trial appears quite different from the way it appeared in the older cases opining that States might abolish jury trial. See, e.g., Maxwell v. Dow, 176 U.S. 581 (1900). A criminal process which was fair and equitable but used no juries is easy to imagine. It would make use of alternative guarantees and protections which would serve the purposes that the jury serves in the English and American systems. Yet no American State has undertaken to construct such a system. Instead, every American State, including Louisiana, uses the jury extensively, and imposes very serious punishments only after a trial at which the defendant has a right to a jury's verdict. In every State, including Louisiana, the structure and style of the criminal process—the supporting framework and the subsidiary procedures—are of the sort that naturally complement jury trial, and have developed in connection with and in reliance upon jury trial.

"The Trial of all Crimes, except in Cases of Impeachment, shall be by Jury; and such Trial shall be held in the State where the said Crimes shall have been committed."

Objections to the Constitution because of the absence of a bill of rights were met by the immediate submission and adoption of the Bill of Rights. Included was the Sixth Amendment which, among other things, provided:

"In all criminal prosecutions, the accused shall enjoy the right to a speedy and public trial, by an impartial jury of the State and district wherein the crime shall have been committed."

The constitutions adopted by the original States guaranteed jury trial. Also, the constitution of every State entering the Union thereafter in one form or another protected the right to jury trial in criminal cases.

Even such skeletal history is impressive support for considering the right to jury trial in criminal cases to be fundamental to our system of justice, an importance frequently recognized in the opinions of this Court. ...

Jury trial continues to receive strong support. The laws of every State guarantee a right to jury trial in serious criminal cases; no State has dispensed with it; nor are there significant movements underway to do so. Indeed, the three most recent state constitutional revisions, in Maryland, Michigan, and New York, carefully preserved the right of the accused to have the judgment of a jury when tried for a serious crime.

We are aware of prior cases in this Court in which the prevailing opinion contains statements contrary to our holding today that the right to jury trial in serious criminal cases is a fundamental right and hence must be recognized by the States as part of their obligation to extend due process of law to all persons within their jurisdiction. ... None of these cases, however, dealt with a State which had purported to dispense entirely with a jury trial in serious criminal cases. ... Respectfully, we reject the prior dicta regarding jury trial in criminal cases.

The guarantees of jury trial in the Federal and State Constitutions reflect a profound judgment about the way in which law should be enforced and justice administered. A right to jury trial is granted to criminal defendants in order to prevent oppression by the Government. Those who wrote our constitutions knew from history and experience that it was necessary to protect against unfounded criminal charges brought to eliminate enemies and against judges too responsive to the voice of higher authority. The framers of the constitutions strove to create an independent judiciary but insisted upon further protection against arbitrary action. Providing an accused with the right to be tried by a jury of his peers gave him an inestimable safeguard against the corrupt or overzealous prosecutor and against the compliant, biased, or eccentric judge. If the defendant preferred the common-sense judgment of a jury to the more tutored but perhaps less sympathetic reaction of the single judge, he was to have it. Beyond this, the jury trial provisions in the Federal and State Constitutions reflect a fundamental decision about the exercise of official power—a reluctance to entrust plenary powers over the life and liberty of the citizen to one judge or to a group of judges. Fear of unchecked power, so typical of our State and Federal Governments in other respects, found expression in the criminal law in this insistence upon community participation in the determination of guilt or innocence. The deep commitment of the Nation to the right of jury trial in serious criminal cases as a defense against arbitrary law enforcement qualifies for protection under the Due Process Clause of the Fourteenth Amendment, and must therefore be respected by the States.

Of course jury trial has "its weaknesses and the potential for misuse," Singer v. United States, 380 U.S. 24, 35 (1965). We are aware of the long debate, especially in this century, among those who write about the administration of justice, as to the wisdom of permitting untrained laymen to determine the facts in civil and criminal proceedings. Although the debate has been intense, with powerful voices on either side, most of the controversy has centered on the jury in civil cases. Indeed, some of the severest critics of civil juries acknowledge that the arguments for criminal juries are much stronger. In addition, at the heart of the dispute have been express or implicit assertions that juries are incapable of adequately understanding evidence or determining issues of fact, and that they are unpredictable, quixotic, and little better than a roll of dice. Yet, the most recent and exhaustive study of the jury in criminal cases concluded that juries do understand the evidence and come to sound conclusions in most of the cases presented to them and that when juries differ with the result at which the judge would have arrived, it is usually because they are serving some of the very purposes for which they were created and for which they are now employed.[26]

The State of Louisiana urges that holding that the Fourteenth Amendment assures a right to jury trial will cast doubt on the integrity of every trial conducted without a jury. Plainly, this is not the import of our holding. Our conclusion is that in the American States, as in the federal judicial system, a general grant of jury trial for serious offenses is a fundamental right, essential for preventing miscarriages of justice and for assuring that fair trials are provided for all defendants. We would not assert, however, that every criminal trial—or any particular trial—held before a judge alone is unfair or that a defendant may never be as fairly treated by a judge as he would be by a jury. Thus we hold no constitutional doubts

26. [H.] Kalven [Jr.] & [H.] Zeisel, [The American Jury (1966)].

about the practices, common in both federal and state courts, of accepting waivers of jury trial and prosecuting petty crimes without extending a right to jury trial. However, the fact is that in most places more trials for serious crimes are to juries than to a court alone; a great many defendants prefer the judgment of a jury to that of a court. Even where defendants are satisfied with bench trials, the right to a jury trial very likely serves its intended purpose of making judicial or prosecutorial unfairness less likely.

II.

Louisiana's final contention is that even if it must grant jury trials in serious criminal cases, the conviction before us is valid and constitutional because here the petitioner was tried for simple battery and was sentenced to only 60 days in the parish prison. We are not persuaded. It is doubtless true that there is a category of petty crimes or offenses which is not subject to the Sixth Amendment jury trial provision and should not be subject to the Fourteenth Amendment jury trial requirement here applied to the States. Crimes carrying possible penalties up to six months do not require a jury trial if they otherwise qualify as petty offenses .... But the penalty authorized for a particular crime is of major relevance in determining whether it is serious or not and may in itself, if severe enough, subject the trial to the mandates of the Sixth Amendment. District of Columbia v. Clawans, 300 U.S. 617 (1937). The penalty authorized by the law of the locality may be taken "as a gauge of its social and ethical judgments," 300 U.S., at 628, of the crime in question. In *Clawans* the defendant was jailed for 60 days, but it was the 90-day authorized punishment on which the Court focused in determining that the offense was not one for which the Constitution assured trial by jury. In the case before us the Legislature of Louisiana has made simple battery a criminal offense punishable by imprisonment for up to two years and a fine. The question, then, is whether a crime carrying such a penalty is an offense which Louisiana may insist on trying without a jury.

We think not. So-called petty offenses were tried without juries both in England and in the Colonies and have always been held to be exempt from the otherwise comprehensive language of the Sixth Amendment's jury trial provisions. There is no substantial evidence that the Framers intended to depart from this established common-law practice, and the possible consequences to defendants from convictions for petty offenses have been thought insufficient to outweigh the benefits to efficient law enforcement and simplified judicial administration resulting from the availability of speedy and inexpensive nonjury adjudications. These same considerations compel the same result under the Fourteenth Amendment. Of course the boundaries of the petty offense category have always been ill-defined, if not ambulatory. In the absence of an explicit constitutional provision, the definitional task necessarily falls on the courts, which must either pass upon the validity of legislative attempts to identify those petty offenses which are exempt from jury trial or, where the legislature has not addressed itself to the problem, themselves face the question in the first instance. In either case it is necessary to draw a line in the spectrum of crime, separating petty from serious infractions. This process, although essential, cannot be wholly satisfactory, for it requires attaching different consequences to events which, when they lie near the line, actually differ very little.

In determining whether the length of the authorized prison term or the seriousness of other punishment is enough in itself to require a jury trial, we are counseled by District of Columbia v. Clawans, supra, to refer to objective criteria, chiefly the existing laws and practices in the Nation. In the federal system, petty offenses are defined as those punishable by no more than six months in prison and a $500 fine.[32] In 49 of the 50 States crimes subject to trial without a jury, which occasionally include simple battery, are punishable by no more than one year in jail. Moreover, in the late 18th century in America crimes triable without a jury were for the most part punishable by no more than a six-month prison term, although there appear to have been exceptions to this rule. We need not, however, settle in this case the exact location of the line between petty offenses and serious crimes. It is sufficient for our purposes to hold that a crime punishable by two years in prison is, based on past and contemporary standards in this country, a serious crime and not a petty offense. Consequently, appellant was entitled to a jury trial and it was error to deny it.

The judgment below is reversed and the case is remanded for proceedings not inconsistent with this opinion.

MR. JUSTICE BLACK, with whom MR. JUSTICE DOUGLAS joins, concurring.

The Court today holds that the right to trial by jury guaranteed defendants in criminal cases in federal courts by Art. III of the United States Constitution and by the Sixth Amendment is also guaranteed by the Fourteenth Amendment to defendants tried in state courts. With this holding I agree for reasons given by the Court. I also agree because of reasons given in my dissent in Adamson v. California, 332 U.S. 46, 68. . . .

. . .

MR. JUSTICE HARLAN, whom MR. JUSTICE STEWART joins, dissenting.

Every American jurisdiction provides for trial by jury in criminal cases. The question before us is not whether jury trial is an ancient institution, which it is; nor whether it plays a significant role in the administration of criminal justice, which it does; nor whether it will

32. 18 U.S.C. § 1.

endure, which it shall.   The question in this case is whether the
State of Louisiana, which provides trial by jury for all felonies, is
prohibited by the Constitution from trying charges of simple battery
to the court alone.   In my view, the answer to that question,
mandated alike by our constitutional history and by the longer
history of trial by jury, is clearly "no."

The States have always borne primary responsibility for operating the machinery of criminal justice within their borders, and
adapting it to their particular circumstances.   In exercising this
responsibility, each State is compelled to conform its procedures to
the requirements of the Federal Constitution.   The Due Process
Clause of the Fourteenth Amendment requires that those procedures be fundamentally fair in all respects.   It does not, in my view,
impose or encourage nationwide uniformity for its own sake; it
does not command adherence to forms that happen to be old; and
it does not impose on the States the rules that may be in force in
the federal courts except where such rules are also found to be
essential to basic fairness.

The Court's approach to this case is an uneasy and illogical
compromise among the views of various Justices on how the Due
Process Clause should be interpreted.   The Court does not say that
those who framed the Fourteenth Amendment intended to make
the Sixth Amendment applicable to the States.   And the Court
concedes that it finds nothing unfair about the procedure by which
the present appellant was tried.   Nevertheless, the Court reverses
his conviction: it holds, for some reason not apparent to me, that
the Due Process Clause incorporates the particular clause of the
Sixth Amendment that requires trial by jury in federal criminal
cases—including, as I read its opinion, the sometimes trivial accompanying baggage of judicial interpretation in federal contexts.   I
have raised my voice many times before against the Court's continuing undiscriminating insistence upon fastening on the States federal
notions of criminal justice, and I must do so again in this instance.
With all respect, the Court's approach and its reading of history are
altogether topsy-turvy.

I.

I believe I am correct in saying that every member of the Court
for at least the last 135 years has agreed that our Founders did not
consider the requirements of the Bill of Rights so fundamental that
they should operate directly against the States.   They were wont to
believe rather that the security of liberty in America rested primarily
upon the dispersion of governmental power across a federal system.
The Bill of Rights was considered unnecessary by some but insisted
upon by others in order to curb the possibility of abuse of power by
the strong central government they were creating.

The Civil War Amendments dramatically altered the relation of
the Federal Government to the States.   The first section of the

Fourteenth Amendment imposes highly significant restrictions on state action. But the restrictions are couched in very broad and general terms: citizenship; privileges and immunities; due process of law; equal protection of the laws. Consequently, for 100 years this Court has been engaged in the difficult process Professor Jaffe has well called "the search for intermediate premises."[6] The question has been, Where does the Court properly look to find the specific rules that define and give content to such terms as "life, liberty, or property" and "due process of law"?

A few members of the Court have taken the position that the intention of those who drafted the first section of the Fourteenth Amendment was simply, and exclusively, to make the provisions of the first eight Amendments applicable to state action. This view has never been accepted by this Court. In my view, often expressed elsewhere, the first section of the Fourteenth Amendment was meant neither to incorporate, nor to be limited to, the specific guarantees of the first eight Amendments. The overwhelming historical evidence marshalled by Professor Fairman demonstrates, to me conclusively, that the Congressmen and state legislators who wrote, debated, and ratified the Fourteenth Amendment did not think they were "incorporating" the Bill of Rights[9] and the very breadth and generality of the Amendment's provisions suggest that its authors did not suppose that the Nation would always be limited to mid-19th century conceptions of "liberty" and "due process of law" but that the increasing experience and evolving conscience of the American people would add new "intermediate premises." In short, neither history, nor sense, supports using the Fourteenth Amendment to put the States in a constitutional straitjacket with respect to their own development in the administration of criminal or civil law.

Although I therefore fundamentally disagree with the total incorporation view of the Fourteenth Amendment, it seems to me that such a position does at least have the virtue, lacking in the Court's selective incorporation approach, of internal consistency: we look to the Bill of Rights, word for word, clause for clause, precedent for precedent because, it is said, the men who wrote the Amendment wanted it that way. For those who do not accept this "history," a different source of "intermediate premises" must be found. The Bill of Rights is not necessarily irrelevant to the search for guidance in interpreting the Fourteenth Amendment, but the reason for and the nature of its relevance must be articulated.

Apart from the approach taken by the absolute incorporationists, I can see only one method of analysis that has any internal

6. Jaffe, Was Brandeis an Activist? The Search for Intermediate Premises, 80 Harv. L.Rev. 986 (1967).

9. Fairman, Does the Fourteenth Amendment Incorporate the Bill of Rights? The Original Understanding, 2 Stan.L.Rev. 5 (1949). ...

. . .

logic. That is to start with the words "liberty" and "due process of law" and attempt to define them in a way that accords with American traditions and our system of government. This approach, involving a much more discriminating process of adjudication than does "incorporation," is, albeit difficult, the one that was followed throughout the 19th and most of the present century. It entails a "gradual process of judicial inclusion and exclusion," [10] seeking, with due recognition of constitutional tolerance for state experimentation and disparity, to ascertain those "immutable principles . . . of free government which no member of the Union may disregard." [11] Due process was not restricted to rules fixed in the past, for that "would be to deny every quality of the law but its age, and to render it incapable of progress or improvement." [12] Nor did it impose nationwide uniformity in details, for

> "[t]he Fourteenth Amendment does not profess to secure to all persons in the United States the benefit of the same laws and the same remedies. Great diversities in these respects may exist in two States separated only by an imaginary line. On one side of this line there may be a right of trial by jury, and on the other side no such right. Each State prescribes its own modes of judicial proceeding." [13]

Through this gradual process, this Court sought to define "liberty" by isolating freedoms that Americans of the past and of the present considered more important than any suggested countervailing public objective. The Court also, by interpretation of the phrase "due process of law," enforced the Constitution's guarantee that no State may imprison an individual except by fair and impartial procedures.

The relationship of the Bill of Rights to this "gradual process" seems to me to be twofold. In the first place it has long been clear that the Due Process Clause imposes some restrictions on state action that parallel Bill of Rights restrictions on federal action. Second, and more important than this accidental overlap, is the fact that the Bill of Rights is evidence, at various points, of the content Americans find in the term "liberty" and of American standards of fundamental fairness.

. . .

In all of these instances, the right guaranteed against the States by the Fourteenth Amendment was one that had also been guaranteed against the Federal Government by one of the first eight Amendments. The logically critical thing, however, was not that the rights had been found in the Bill of Rights, but that they were deemed, in the context of American legal history, to be fundamen-

---

10. Davidson v. New Orleans, 96 U.S. 97, 104.

11. Holden v. Hardy, 169 U.S. 366, 389.

12. Hurtado v. California, 110 U.S. 516, 529.

13. Missouri v. Lewis, 101 U.S. 22, 31.

tal. This was perhaps best explained by Mr. Justice Cardozo, speaking for a Court that included Chief Justice Hughes and Justices Brandeis and Stone, in Palko v. Connecticut, 302 U.S. 319 ....

Today's Court still remains unwilling to accept the total incorporationists' view of the history of the Fourteenth Amendment. This, if accepted, would afford a cogent reason for applying the Sixth Amendment to the States. The Court is also, apparently, unwilling to face the task of determining whether denial of trial by jury in the situation before us, or in other situations, is fundamentally unfair. Consequently, the Court has compromised on the ease of the incorporationist position, without its internal logic. It has simply assumed that the question before us is whether the Jury Trial Clause of the Sixth Amendment should be incorporated into the Fourteenth, jot-for-jot and case-for-case, or ignored. Then the Court merely declares that the clause in question is "in" rather than "out."

The Court has justified neither its starting place nor its conclusion. If the problem is to discover and articulate the rules of fundamental fairness in criminal proceedings, there is no reason to assume that the whole body of rules developed in this Court constituting Sixth Amendment jury trial must be regarded as a unit. The requirement of trial by jury in federal criminal cases has given rise to numerous subsidiary questions respecting the exact scope and content of the right. It surely cannot be that every answer the Court has given, or will give, to such a question is attributable to the Founders; or even that every rule announced carries equal conviction of this Court; still less can it be that every such subprinciple is equally fundamental to ordered liberty.

Examples abound. I should suppose it obviously fundamental to fairness that a "jury" means an "impartial jury."[19] I should think it equally obvious that the rule, imposed long ago in the federal courts, that "jury" means "jury of exactly twelve,"[20] is not fundamental to anything: there is no significance except to mystics in the number 12. Again, trial by jury has been held to require a unanimous verdict of jurors in the federal courts,[21] although unanimity has not been found essential to liberty in Britain, where the requirement has been abandoned.[22]

---

19. The Court has so held in, e.g., Irvin v. Dowd, 366 U.S. 717. Compare Dennis v. United States, 339 U.S. 162.

20. E.g., Rassmussen v. United States, 197 U.S. 516.

21. E.g., Andres v. United States, 333 U.S. 740. With respect to the common-law number and unanimity requirements, the Court suggests that these present no problem because "our decisions interpreting the Sixth Amendment are always subject to reconsideration ...." Ante, at 158, n. 30. These examples illustrate a major danger of the "incorporation" approach—that provisions of the Bill of Rights may be watered down in the needless pursuit of uniformity. Cf. my concurring opinion in Ker v. California, 374 U.S. 23, 44. Mr. Justice White alluded to this problem in his dissenting opinion in Malloy v. Hogan, supra, at 38.

22. Criminal Justice Act of 1967, § 13.

One further example is directly relevant here. The co-existence of a requirement of jury trial in federal criminal cases and a historic and universally recognized exception for "petty crimes" has compelled this Court, on occasion, to decide whether a particular crime is petty, or is included within the guarantee. Individual cases have been decided without great conviction and without reference to a guiding principle. The Court today holds, for no discernible reason, that if and when the line is drawn its exact location will be a matter of such fundamental importance that it will be uniformly imposed on the States. This Court is compelled to decide such obscure borderline questions in the course of administering federal law. This does not mean that its decisions are demonstrably sounder than those that would be reached by state courts and legislatures, let alone that they are of such importance that fairness demands their imposition throughout the Nation.

Even if I could agree that the question before us is whether Sixth Amendment jury trial is totally "in" or totally "out," I can find in the Court's opinion no real reasons for concluding that it should be "in." The basis for differentiating among clauses in the Bill of Rights cannot be that only some clauses are in the Bill of Rights or that only some are old and much praised, or that only some have played an important role in the development of federal law. These things are true of all. The Court says that some clauses are more "fundamental" than others, but it turns out to be using this word in a sense that would have astonished Mr. Justice Cardozo and which, in addition, is of no help. The word does not mean "analytically critical to procedural fairness" for no real analysis of the role of the jury in making procedures fair is even attempted. Instead, the word turns out to mean "old," "much praised," and "found in the Bill of Rights." The definition of "fundamental" thus turns out to be circular.

II.

Since, as I see it, the Court has not even come to grips with the issues in this case, it is necessary to start from the beginning. When a criminal defendant contends that his state conviction lacked "due process of law," the question before this Court, in my view, is whether he was denied any element of fundamental procedural fairness. Believing, as I do, that due process is an evolving concept and that old principles are subject to re-evaluation in light of later experience, I think it appropriate to deal on its merits with the question whether Louisiana denied appellant due process of law when it tried him for simple assault without a jury.

The obvious starting place is the fact that this Court has, in the past, *held* that trial by jury is not a requisite of criminal due process.
. . .

.   .   .

The argument that jury trial is not a requisite of due process is quite simple. The central proposition of *Palko,* supra, a proposition to which I would adhere, is that "due process of law" requires only that criminal trials be fundamentally fair. As stated above, apart from the theory that it was historically intended as a mere shorthand for the Bill of Rights, I do not see what else "due process of law" can intelligibly be thought to mean. If due process of law requires only fundamental fairness, then the inquiry in each case must be whether a state trial process was a fair one. The Court has held, properly I think, that in an adversary process it is a requisite of fairness, for which there is no adequate substitute, that a criminal defendant be afforded a right to counsel and to cross-examine opposing witnesses. But it simply has not been demonstrated, nor, I think, can it be demonstrated, that trial by jury is the only fair means of resolving issues of fact.

The jury is of course not without virtues. It affords ordinary citizens a valuable opportunity to participate in a process of government, an experience fostering, one hopes, a respect for law. It eases the burden on judges by enabling them to share a part of their sometimes awesome responsibility. A jury may, at times, afford a higher justice by refusing to enforce harsh laws (although it necessarily does so haphazardly, raising the questions whether arbitrary enforcement of harsh laws is better than total enforcement, and whether the jury system is to be defended on the ground that jurors sometimes disobey their oaths). And the jury may, or may not, contribute desirably to the willingness of the general public to accept criminal judgments as just.

It can hardly be gainsaid, however, that the principal original virtue of the jury trial—the limitations a jury imposes on a tyrannous judiciary—has largely disappeared. We no longer live in a medieval or colonial society. Judges enforce laws enacted by democratic decision, not by regal fiat. They are elected by the people or appointed by the people's elected officials, and are responsible not to a distant monarch alone but to reviewing courts, including this one.

The jury system can also be said to have some inherent defects, which are multiplied by the emergence of the criminal law from the relative simplicity that existed when the jury system was devised. It is a cumbersome process, not only imposing great cost in time and money on both the State and the jurors themselves, but also contributing to delay in the machinery of justice. Untrained jurors are presumably less adept at reaching accurate conclusions of fact than judges, particularly if the issues are many or complex. And it is argued by some that trial by jury, far from increasing public respect for law, impairs it: the average man, it is said, reacts favorably neither to the notion that matters he knows to be complex are being decided by other average men, nor to the way the jury system distorts the process of adjudication.

That trial by jury is not the only fair way of adjudicating criminal guilt is well attested by the fact that it is not the prevailing way, either in England or in this country. For England, one expert makes the following estimates. Parliament generally provides that new statutory offenses, unless they are of "considerable gravity" shall be tried to judges; consequently, summary offenses now outnumber offenses for which jury trial is afforded by more than six to one. Then, within the latter category, 84% of all cases are in fact tried to the court. Over all, "the ratio of defendants actually tried by jury becomes in some years little more than 1 per cent." [40]

In the United States, where it has not been as generally assumed that jury waiver is permissible, the statistics are only slightly less revealing. Two experts have estimated that, of all prosecutions for crimes triable to a jury, 75% are settled by guilty plea and 40% of the remainder are tried to the court. [42] In one State, Maryland, which has always provided for waiver, the rate of court trial appears in some years to have reached 90%. The Court recognizes the force of these statistics in stating,

> "We would not assert, however, that every criminal trial—or any particular trial—held before a judge alone is unfair or that a defendant may never be as fairly treated by a judge as he would be by a jury." Ante, at 158.

I agree. I therefore see no reason why this Court should reverse the conviction of appellant, absent any suggestion that his particular trial was in fact unfair, or compel the State of Louisiana to afford jury trial in an as yet unbounded category of cases that can, without unfairness, be tried to a court.

Indeed, even if I were persuaded that trial by jury is a fundamental right in some criminal cases, I could see nothing fundamental in the rule, not yet formulated by the Court, that places the prosecution of appellant for simple battery within the category of "jury crimes" rather than "petty crimes." . . .

    . . .

In sum, there is a wide range of views on the desirability of trial by jury, and on the ways to make it most effective when it is used; there is also considerable variation from State to State in local conditions such as the size of the criminal caseload, the ease or difficulty of summoning jurors, and other trial conditions bearing on fairness. We have before us, therefore, an almost perfect example of a situation in which the celebrated dictum of Mr. Justice Brandeis should be invoked. It is, he said,

> "one of the happy incidents of the federal system that a single courageous State may, if its citizens choose, serve as a laborato-

---

40. [G.] Williams, [The Proof of Guilt], at 302.

42. [H.] Kalven & [H.] Zeisel, [The American Jury], at 12–32.

ry ...."   New State Ice Co. v. Liebmann, 285 U.S. 262, 280, 311 (dissenting opinion).

This Court, other courts, and the political process are available to correct any experiments in criminal procedure that prove fundamentally unfair to defendants.   That is not what is being done today: instead, and quite without reason, the Court has chosen to impose upon every State one means of trying criminal cases; it is a good means, but it is not the only fair means, and it is not demonstrably better than the alternatives States might devise.

I would affirm the judgment of the Supreme Court of Louisiana.[*] [**]

[*] Justice Fortas wrote a concurring opinion.

[**] The Sixth Amendment does not require that a jury be composed of 12 members. Williams v. Florida, 399 U.S. 78 (1970) (8–1). In *Williams*, the defendant was tried for robbery before a six-person jury; the conviction was upheld.

In a state criminal case, a jury verdict of guilty is not required to be unanimous. John-son v. Louisiana, 406 U.S. 356 (1972) (5–4); Apodaca v. Oregon, 406 U.S. 404 (1972) (5–4). In *Johnson*, the defendant was convicted by a 9–3 verdict.   In *Apodaca*, two of the defendants were convicted by an 11–1 verdict, one defendant by a 10–2 verdict.

In a federal criminal case, a jury verdict of guilty is required to be unanimous. *Johnson*, above (5–4) (opinion of Justice Powell).

3. THE FOURTH AMENDMENT: ARREST AND SEARCH AND SEIZURE

DRAPER v. UNITED STATES

358 U.S. 307, 79 S.Ct. 329, 3 L.Ed.2d 327 (1959).

MR. JUSTICE WHITTAKER delivered the opinion of the Court.

Petitioner was convicted of knowingly concealing and transporting narcotic drugs in Denver, Colorado, in violation of 35 Stat. 614, as amended, 21 U.S.C. § 174. His conviction was based in part on the use in evidence against him of two "envelopes containing [865 grains of] heroin" and a hypodermic syringe that had been taken from his person, following his arrest, by the arresting officer. Before the trial, he moved to suppress that evidence as having been secured through an unlawful search and seizure. After hearing, the District Court found that the arresting officer had probable cause to arrest petitioner without a warrant and that the subsequent search and seizure were therefore incident to a lawful arrest, and overruled the motion to suppress. 146 F.Supp. 689. At the subsequent trial, that evidence was offered and, over petitioner's renewed objection, was received in evidence, and the trial resulted, as we have said, in petitioner's conviction. The Court of Appeals affirmed the conviction, 248 F.2d 295, and certiorari was sought on the sole ground that the search and seizure violated the Fourth Amendment and therefore the use of the heroin in evidence vitiated the conviction. We granted the writ to determine that question. 357 U.S. 935.

The evidence offered at the hearing on the motion to suppress was not substantially disputed. It established that one Marsh, a federal narcotic agent with 29 years' experience, was stationed at Denver; that one Hereford had been engaged as a "special employee" of the Bureau of Narcotics at Denver for about six months, and from time to time gave information to Marsh regarding violations of the narcotic laws, for which Hereford was paid small sums of money, and that Marsh had always found the information given by Hereford to be accurate and reliable. On September 3, 1956, Hereford told Marsh that James Draper (petitioner) recently had taken up abode at a stated address in Denver and "was peddling narcotics to several addicts" in that city. Four days later, on September 7, Hereford told Marsh "that Draper had gone to Chicago the day before [September 6] by train [and] that he was going to bring back three ounces of heroin [and] that he would return to Denver either on the morning of the 8th of September or the morning of the 9th of September also by train." Hereford also gave

Marsh a detailed physical description of Draper and of the clothing he was wearing,[2] and said that he would be carrying "a tan zipper bag," and that he habitually "walked real fast."

On the morning of September 8, Marsh and a Denver police officer went to the Denver Union Station and kept watch over all incoming trains from Chicago, but they did not see anyone fitting the description that Hereford had given. Repeating the process on the morning of September 9, they saw a person, having the exact physical attributes and wearing the precise clothing described by Hereford, alight from an incoming Chicago train and start walking "fast" toward the exit. He was carrying a tan zipper bag in his right hand and the left was thrust in his raincoat pocket. Marsh, accompanied by the police officer, overtook, stopped and arrested him. They then searched him and found the two "envelopes containing heroin" clutched in his left hand in his raincoat pocket, and found the syringe in the tan zipper bag. Marsh then took him (petitioner) into custody. Hereford died four days after the arrest and therefore did not testify at the hearing on the motion.

26 U.S.C. (Supp. V) § 7607, added by § 104(a) of the Narcotic Control Act of 1956, 70 Stat. 570, provides, in pertinent part:

"The Commissioner ... and agents, of the Bureau of Narcotics ... may—

"(2) make arrests without warrant for violations of any law of the United States relating to narcotic drugs ... where the violation is committed in the presence of the person making the arrest or where such person has reasonable grounds to believe that the person to be arrested has committed or is committing such violation."

The crucial question for us then is whether knowledge of the related facts and circumstances gave Marsh "probable cause" within the meaning of the Fourth Amendment, and "reasonable grounds" within the meaning of § 104(a), supra,[3] to believe that petitioner had committed or was committing a violation of the narcotic laws. If it did, the arrest, though without a warrant, was lawful and the subsequent search of petitioner's person and the seizure of the found heroin were validly made incident to a lawful arrest, and therefore the motion to suppress was properly overruled and the heroin was competently received in evidence at the trial. ...

Petitioner does not dispute this analysis of the question for decision. Rather he contends (1) that the information given by

2. Hereford told Marsh that Draper was a Negro of light brown complexion, 27 years of age, 5 feet 8 inches tall, weighed about 160 pounds, and that he was wearing a light colored raincoat, brown slacks and black shoes.

3. The terms "probable cause" as used in the Fourth Amendment and "reasonable grounds" as used in § 104(a) of the Narcotic Control Act, 70 Stat. 570, are substantial equivalents of the same meaning. United States v. Walker, 246 F.2d 519, 526 (C.A.7th Cir.); cf. United States v. Bianco, 189 F.2d 716, 720 (C.A.3d Cir.)

Hereford to Marsh was "hearsay" and, because hearsay is not legally competent evidence in a criminal trial, could not legally have been considered, but should have been put out of mind, by Marsh in assessing whether he had "probable cause" and "reasonable grounds" to arrest petitioner without a warrant, and (2) that, even if hearsay could lawfully have been considered, Marsh's information should be held insufficient to show "probable cause" and "reasonable grounds" to believe that petitioner had violated or was violating the narcotic laws and to justify his arrest without a warrant.

Considering the first contention, we find petitioner entirely in error. Brinegar v. United States, 338 U.S. 160, 172–173, has settled the question the other way. There, in a similar situation, the convict contended "that the factors relating to inadmissibility of the evidence [for] *purposes of proving guilt at the trial,* deprive[d] the evidence as a whole of sufficiency to show probable cause for the search ...." Id., at 172. (Emphasis added.) But this Court, rejecting that contention, said: "[T]he so-called distinction places a wholly unwarranted emphasis upon the criterion of admissibility in evidence, to prove the accused's guilt, of the facts relied upon to show probable cause. That emphasis, we think, goes much too far in confusing and disregarding the difference between what is required to prove guilt in a criminal case and what is required to show probable cause for arrest or search. It approaches requiring (if it does not in practical effect require) proof sufficient to establish guilt in order to substantiate the existence of probable cause. There is a large difference between the two things to be proved [guilt and probable cause], as well as between the tribunals which determine them and therefore a like difference in the *quanta* and modes of proof required to establish them." 338 U.S., at 172–173.

Nor can we agree with petitioner's second contention that Marsh's information was insufficient to show probable cause and reasonable grounds to believe that petitioner had violated or was violating the narcotic laws and to justify his arrest without a warrant. The information given to narcotic agent Marsh by "special employee" Hereford may have been hearsay to Marsh, but coming from one employed for that purpose and whose information had always been found accurate and reliable, it is clear that Marsh would have been derelict in his duties had he not pursued it. And when, in pursuing that information, he saw a man, having the exact physical attributes and wearing the precise clothing and carrying the tan zipper bag that Hereford had described, alight from one of the very trains from the very place stated by Hereford and start to walk at a "fast" pace toward the station exit, Marsh had personally verified every facet of the information given him by Hereford except whether petitioner had accomplished his mission and had the three ounces of heroin on his person or in his bag. And surely, with every other bit of Hereford's information being thus personally verified, Marsh had "reasonable grounds" to believe that the remaining unverified bit of Hereford's information—that Draper would have the heroin with him—was likewise true.

"In dealing with probable cause, . . . as the very name implies, we deal with probabilities. These are not technical; they are the factual and practical considerations of everyday life on which reasonable and prudent men, not legal technicians, act." Brinegar v. United States, supra, at 175. Probable cause exists where "the facts and circumstances within [the arresting officers'] knowledge and of which they had reasonably trustworthy information [are] sufficient in themselves to warrant a man of reasonable caution in the belief that" an offense has been or is being committed. Carroll v. United States, 267 U.S. 132, 162.

We believe that, under the facts and circumstances here, Marsh had probable cause and reasonable grounds to believe that petitioner was committing a violation of the laws of the United States relating to narcotic drugs at the time he arrested him. The arrest was therefore lawful, and the subsequent search and seizure, having been made incident to that lawful arrest, were likewise valid. It follows that petitioner's motion to suppress was properly denied and that the seized heroin was competent evidence lawfully received at the trial.

Affirmed.[*]

[*] Justice Douglas wrote a dissenting opinion.

UNITED STATES v. WATSON

423 U.S. 411, 96 S.Ct. 820, 46 L.Ed.2d 598 (1976).

MR. JUSTICE WHITE delivered the opinion of the Court.

This case presents questions under the Fourth Amendment as to the legality of a warrantless arrest and of an ensuing search of the arrestee's automobile carried out with his purported consent.

I

The relevant events began on August 17, 1972, when an informant, one Khoury, telephoned a postal inspector informing him that respondent Watson was in possession of a stolen credit card and had asked Khoury to cooperate in using the card to their mutual advantage. On five to 10 previous occasions Khoury had provided the inspector with reliable information on postal inspection matters, some involving Watson. Later that day Khoury delivered the card to the inspector. On learning that Watson had agreed to furnish additional cards, the inspector asked Khoury to arrange to meet with Watson. Khoury did so, a meeting being scheduled for August 22. Watson cancelled that engagement, but at noon on August 23, Khoury met with Watson at a restaurant designated by the latter. Khoury had been instructed that if Watson had additional stolen credit cards, Khoury was to give a designated signal. The signal was given, the officers closed in, and Watson was forthwith arrested. He was removed from the restaurant to the street where he was given the warnings required by Miranda v. Arizona, 384 U.S. 436 (1966). A search having revealed that Watson had no credit cards on his person, the inspector asked if he could look inside Watson's car, which was standing within view. Watson said, "Go ahead," and repeated these words when the inspector cautioned that "[i]f I find anything, it is going to go against you." Using keys furnished by Watson, the inspector entered the car and found under the floor mat an envelope containing two credit cards in the names of other persons. These cards were the basis for two counts of a four-count indictment charging Watson with possessing stolen mail in violation of 18 U.S.C. § 1708.

Prior to trial, Watson moved to suppress the cards, claiming that his arrest was illegal for want of probable cause and an arrest warrant and that his consent to search the car was involuntary and ineffective because he had not been told that he could withhold consent. The motion was denied, and Watson was convicted of illegally possessing the two cards seized from his car.

A divided panel of the Court of Appeals for the Ninth Circuit reversed, 504 F.2d 849 (1974), ruling that the admission in evidence

62

of the two credit cards found in the car was prohibited by the Fourth Amendment. In reaching this judgment, the court decided two issues in Watson's favor. First, notwithstanding its agreement with the District Court that Khoury was reliable and that there was probable cause for arresting Watson, the court held the arrest unconstitutional because the postal inspector had failed to secure an arrest warrant although he concededly had time to do so. Second, based on the totality of the circumstances, one of which was the illegality of the arrest, the court held Watson's consent to search had been coerced and hence was not a valid ground for the warrantless search of the automobile. We granted certiorari. 420 U.S. 924 (1975).

II

A major part of the Court of Appeals' opinion was its holding that Watson's warrantless arrest violated the Fourth Amendment. Although it did not expressly do so, it may have intended to overturn the conviction on the independent ground that the two credit cards were the inadmissible fruits of an unconstitutional arrest. ... However that may be, the Court of Appeals treated the illegality of Watson's arrest as an important factor in determining the voluntariness of his consent to search his car. We therefore deal first with the arrest issue.

Contrary to the Court of Appeals' view, Watson's arrest was not invalid because executed without a warrant. Title 18 U.S.C. § 3061(a)(3) expressly empowers the Board of Governors of the Postal Service to authorize Postal Service officers and employees "performing duties related to the inspection of postal matters" to

"(3) make arrests without warrant for felonies cognizable under the laws of the United States if they have reasonable grounds to believe that the person to be arrested has committed or is committing such a felony."

By regulation, 39 CFR § 232.5(a)(3) (1975), and in identical language, the Board of Governors has exercised that power and authorized warrantless arrests. Because there was probable cause in this case to believe that Watson had violated § 1708, the inspector and his subordinates, in arresting Watson, were acting strictly in accordance with the governing statute and regulations. The effect of the judgment of the Court of Appeals was to invalidate the statute as applied in this case and as applied to all the situations where a court fails to find exigent circumstances justifying a warrantless arrest. We reverse that judgment.

Under the Fourth Amendment, the people are to be "secure in their persons, houses, papers, and effects, against unreasonable searches and seizures, ... and no Warrants shall issue, but upon probable cause ...." Section 3061 represents a judgment by Congress that it is not unreasonable under the Fourth Amendment for postal inspectors to arrest without a warrant provided they have probable cause to do so. This was not an isolated or quixotic judgment of the legislative branch. Other federal law enforcement officers have been expressly authorized by statute for many years to make felony arrests on probable cause but without a warrant. This is true of United States marshals, 18 U.S.C. § 3053, and of agents of the Federal Bureau of Investigation, 18 U.S.C. § 3052; the Drug Enforcement Administration, 84 Stat. 1273, 21 U.S.C. § 878; the Secret Service, 18 U.S.C. § 3056(a); and the Customs Service, 26 U.S.C. § 7607.

Because there is a "strong presumption of constitutionality due to an Act of Congress, especially when it turns on what is 'reasonable,' " "[o]bviously the Court should be reluctant to decide that a search thus authorized by Congress was unreasonable and that the Act was therefore unconstitutional." United States v. Di Re, 332 U.S. 581, 585 (1948). Moreover, there is nothing in the Court's prior cases indicating that under the Fourth Amendment a warrant is required to make a valid arrest for a felony. Indeed, the relevant prior decisions are uniformly to the contrary.

. . .

The cases construing the Fourth Amendment thus reflect the ancient common-law rule that a peace officer was permitted to arrest without a warrant for a misdemeanor or felony committed in his presence as well as for a felony not committed in his presence if there was reasonable grounds for making the arrest. . . . This has also been the prevailing rule under state constitutions and statutes. . . .

. . .

The balance struck by the common law in generally authorizing felony arrests on probable cause, but without a warrant, has survived substantially intact. It appears in almost all of the States in the form of express statutory authorization. . . .

This is the rule Congress has long directed its principal law enforcement officers to follow. Congress has plainly decided against conditioning warrantless arrest power on proof of exigent circumstances. Law enforcement officers may find it wise to seek arrest warrants where practicable to do so, and their judgments about probable cause may be more readily accepted where backed by a warrant issued by a magistrate. . . . But we decline to transform this judicial preference into a constitutional rule when the judgment of the Nation and Congress has for so long been to authorize warrantless public arrests on probable cause rather than to encumber criminal prosecutions with endless litigation with respect to the existence of exigent circumstances, whether it was practicable to get a warrant, whether the suspect was about to flee, and the like.

Watson's arrest did not violate the Fourth Amendment, and the Court of Appeals erred in holding to the contrary.[*]

. . .

In consequence, we reverse the judgment of the Court of Appeals.

So ordered.[**]

[*] The Court concluded also that under the standard of Schneckloth v. Bustamonte, 412 U.S. 218 (1973), below, the defendant's consent to the search of his car was given voluntarily.

[**] Justice Powell wrote a concurring opinion. Justice Stewart wrote a brief opinion concurring in the result. Justice Marshall wrote a dissenting opinion, which Justice Brennan joined.

CALIFORNIA v. HODARI D.

499 U.S. 621, 111 S.Ct. 1547, 113 L.Ed.2d 690 (1991).

JUSTICE SCALIA delivered the opinion of the Court.

Late one evening in April 1988, Officers Brian McColgin and Jerry Pertoso were on patrol in a high-crime area of Oakland, California. They were dressed in street clothes but wearing jackets with "Police" embossed on both front and back. Their unmarked car proceeded west on Foothill Boulevard, and turned south onto 63rd Avenue. As they rounded the corner, they saw four or five youths huddled around a small red car parked at the curb. When the youths saw the officers' car approaching they apparently panicked, and took flight. The respondent here, Hodari D., and one companion ran west through an alley; the others fled south. The red car also headed south, at a high rate of speed.

The officers were suspicious and gave chase. McColgin remained in the car and continued south on 63rd Avenue; Pertoso left the car, ran back north along 63rd, then west on Foothill Boulevard, and turned south on 62nd Avenue. Hodari, meanwhile, emerged from the alley onto 62nd and ran north. Looking behind as he ran, he did not turn and see Pertoso until the officer was almost upon him, whereupon he tossed away what appeared to be a small rock. A moment later, Pertoso tackled Hodari, handcuffed him, and radioed for assistance. Hodari was found to be carrying $130 in cash and a pager; and the rock he had discarded was found to be crack cocaine.

In the juvenile proceeding brought against him, Hodari moved to suppress the evidence relating to the cocaine. The court denied the motion without opinion. The California Court of Appeal reversed, holding that Hodari had been "seized" when he saw Officer Pertoso running towards him, that this seizure was unreasonable under the Fourth Amendment, and that the evidence of cocaine had to be suppressed as the fruit of that illegal seizure. The California Supreme Court denied the State's application for review. We granted certiorari. 498 U.S. 807 (1990).

As this case comes to us, the only issue presented is whether, at the time he dropped the drugs, Hodari had been "seized" within the meaning of the Fourth Amendment.[1] If so, respondent argues,

1. California conceded below that Officer Pertoso did not have the "reasonable suspicion" required to justify stopping Hodari, see Terry v. Ohio, 392 U.S. 1 (1968). That it would be unreasonable to stop, for brief inquiry, young men who scatter in panic upon the mere sighting of the police is not self-evident, and arguably contradicts proverbial common sense. See Proverbs 28:1 ("The wicked flee when no man pursueth"). We do not decide that point here, but rely entirely upon the State's concession.

the drugs were the fruit of that seizure and the evidence concerning them was properly excluded. If not, the drugs were abandoned by Hodari and lawfully recovered by the police, and the evidence should have been admitted. (In addition, of course, Pertoso's seeing the rock of cocaine, at least if he recognized it as such, would provide reasonable suspicion for the unquestioned seizure that occurred when he tackled Hodari. ...

We have long understood that the Fourth Amendment's protection against "unreasonable ... seizures" includes seizure of the person .... From the time of the founding to the present, the word "seizure" has meant a "taking possession," 2 N. Webster, An American Dictionary of the English Language 67 (1828) .... For most purposes at common law, the word connoted not merely grasping, or applying physical force to, the animate or inanimate object in question, but actually bringing it within physical control. A ship still fleeing, even though under attack, would not be considered to have been seized as a war prize. ... A *res* capable of manual delivery was not seized until "tak[en] into custody." Pelham v. Rose, 9 Wall. 103, 106 (1870). To constitute an arrest, however—the quintessential "seizure of the person" under our Fourth Amendment jurisprudence—the mere grasping or application of physical force with lawful authority, whether or not it succeeded in subduing the arrestee, was sufficient. ...

To say that an arrest is effected by the slightest application of physical force, despite the arrestee's escape, is not to say that for Fourth Amendment purposes there is a *continuing* arrest during the period of fugitivity. If, for example, Pertoso had laid his hands upon Hodari to arrest him, but Hodari had broken away and had *then* cast away the cocaine, it would hardly be realistic to say that that disclosure had been made during the course of an arrest. ... The present case, however, is even one step further removed. It does not involve the application of any physical force; Hodari was untouched by Officer Pertoso at the time he discarded the cocaine. His defense relies instead upon the proposition that a seizure occurs "when the officer, by means of physical force *or show of authority*, has in some way restrained the liberty of a citizen." Terry v. Ohio, 392 U.S. 1, 19, n. 16 (1968) (emphasis added). Hodari contends (and we accept as true for purposes of this decision) that Pertoso's pursuit qualified as a "show of authority" calling upon Hodari to halt. The narrow question before us is whether, with respect to a show of authority as with respect to application of physical force, a seizure occurs even though the subject does not yield. We hold that it does not.

The language of the Fourth Amendment, of course, cannot sustain respondent's contention. The word "seizure" readily bears the meaning of a laying on of hands or application of physical force to restrain movement, even when it is ultimately unsuccessful. ("She seized the purse-snatcher, but he broke out of her grasp.") It does not remotely apply, however, to the prospect of a policeman yelling "Stop, in the name of the law!" at a fleeing form that continues to flee. That is no seizure. Nor can the result respondent wishes to achieve be produced—indirectly, as it were—by suggesting that Pertoso's uncomplied-with show of authority was a common-law arrest, and then appealing to the principle that all common-law arrests are seizures. An arrest requires *either* physical force (as described above) *or*, where that is absent, *submission* to the assertion of authority. ...

We do not think it desirable, even as a policy matter, to stretch the Fourth Amendment beyond its words and beyond the meaning of arrest, as respondent urges. Street pursuits always place the public at some risk, and compliance with police orders to stop should therefore be encouraged. Only a few of those orders, we must presume, will be without adequate basis, and since the addressee has no ready means of identifying the deficient ones it almost invariably is the responsible course to comply. Unlawful orders will not be deterred, moreover, by sanctioning through the exclusionary rule those of them that are *not* obeyed. Since policemen do not command "Stop!" expecting to be ignored, or give chase hoping to be outrun, it fully suffices to apply the deterrent to their genuine, successful seizures.

Respondent contends that his position is sustained by the so-called *Mendenhall* test, formulated by Justice Stewart's opinion in United States v. Mendenhall, 446 U.S. 544, 554 (1980), and adopted by the Court in later cases...: "A person has been 'seized' within the meaning of the Fourth Amendment only if, in view of all the circumstances surrounding the incident, a reasonable person would have believed that he was not free to leave." 446 U.S., at 554. ... In seeking to rely upon that test here, respondent fails to read it carefully. It says that a person has been seized "only if," not that he has been seized "whenever"; it states a *necessary*, but not a *sufficient* condition for seizure—or, more precisely, for seizure effected through a "show of authority." *Mendenhall* establishes that the test for existence of a "show of authority" is an objective one: not whether the citizen perceived that he was being ordered to restrict his movement, but whether the officer's words and actions would have conveyed that to a reasonable person. Application of this objective test was the basis for our decision in the other case principally relied upon by respondent, [Michigan v.] Chesternut [486 U.S. 567 (1988)], where we concluded that the police cruiser's slow following of the defendant did not convey the message that he was not free to disregard the police and go about his business. We did not address in *Chesternut*, however, the question whether, if the *Mendenhall* test was met—if the message that the defendant was not free to leave *had* been conveyed—a Fourth Amendment seizure would have occurred. ...

.   .   .

In sum, assuming that Pertoso's pursuit in the present case constituted a "show of authority" enjoining Hodari to halt, since Hodari did not comply with that injunction he was not seized until he was tackled. The cocaine abandoned while he was running was in this case not the fruit of a seizure, and his motion to exclude evidence of it was properly denied. We reverse the decision of the California Court of Appeal, and remand for further proceedings not inconsistent with this opinion.

It is so ordered.

JUSTICE STEVENS, with whom JUSTICE MARSHALL joins, dissenting.

The Court's narrow construction of the word "seizure" represents a significant, and in my view, unfortunate, departure from prior case law construing the Fourth Amendment. ... In particular, the Court now adopts a definition of "seizure" that is unfaithful to a long line of Fourth Amendment cases. Even if the Court were defining seizure for the first time, which it is not, the definition that it chooses today is profoundly unwise. In its decision, the Court assumes, without acknowledging, that a police officer may now fire his weapon at an innocent citizen and not implicate the Fourth Amendment—as long as he misses his target.

For the purposes of decision, the following propositions are not in dispute. First, when Officer Pertoso began his pursuit of respondent, the officer did not have a lawful basis for either stopping or arresting respondent. ... Second, the officer's chase amounted to a "show of authority" as soon as respondent saw the officer nearly upon him. ... Third, the act of discarding the rock of cocaine was the direct consequence of the show of authority. ... Fourth, as the Court correctly demonstrates, no common-law arrest occurred until the officer tackled respondent. ... Thus, the Court is quite right in concluding that the abandonment of the rock was not the fruit of a common-law arrest.

It is equally clear, however, that if the officer had succeeded in touching respondent before he dropped the rock—even if he did not subdue him—an arrest would have occurred. ... In that event (assuming the touching precipitated the abandonment), the evidence would have been the fruit of an unlawful common-law arrest. The distinction between the actual case and the hypothetical case is the same as the distinction between the common-law torts of assault and battery—a touching converts the former into the latter. Although the distinction between assault and battery was important for pleading purposes ... the distinction should not take on constitutional dimensions. The Court mistakenly allows this common-law distinction to define its interpretation of the Fourth Amendment.

At the same time, the Court fails to recognize the existence of another, more telling, common-law distinction—the distinction between an arrest and an attempted arrest. As the Court teaches us, the distinction between battery and assault was critical to a correct understanding of the common law of arrest. ... However, the facts of this case do not describe an actual arrest, but rather, an unlawful *attempt* to take a presumptively innocent person into custody. Such an attempt was unlawful at common law. Thus, if the Court wants to define the scope of the Fourth Amendment based on the common law, it should look, not to the common law of arrest, but to the common law of attempted arrest, according to the facts of this case.

The first question, then, is whether the common law should define the scope of the outer boundaries of the constitutional protection against unreasonable seizures. Even if, contrary to settled precedent, traditional common-law analysis were controlling, it would still be necessary to decide whether the unlawful attempt to make an arrest should be considered a seizure within the meaning of the Fourth Amendment, and whether the exclusionary rule should apply to unlawful attempts.

. . .

In United States v. Mendenhall, 446 U.S. 544 (1980), the Court "adhere[d] to the view that a person is 'seized' only when, by means of physical force or a show of authority, his freedom of movement is restrained." Id., at 553. The Court looked to whether the citizen who is questioned "remains free to disregard the questions and walk away," and if she is able to do so, then "there has been no intrusion upon that person's liberty or privacy" that would require some "particularized and objective justification" under the Constitution. Id., at 554. The test for a "seizure," as formulated by the Court in *Mendenhall*, was whether, "in view of all of the circumstances surrounding the incident, a reasonable person would have believed that he was not free to leave." Ibid. Examples of seizures include "the threatening presence of several officers, the display of a weapon by an officer, some physical touching of the person of the citizen, or the use of language or tone of voice indicating that compliance with the officer's request might be compelled." Ibid. The Court's unwillingness today to adhere to the "reasonable person" standard, as formulated by Justice Stewart in *Mendenhall*, marks an unnecessary departure from Fourth Amendment case law.

The Court today draws the novel conclusion that even though no seizure can occur *unless* the *Mendenhall* reasonable person standard is met ... the fact that the standard has been met does not necessarily mean that a seizure has occurred. ...

... [I]n Florida v. Royer, 460 U.S. 491 (1983), a plurality of the Court adopted Justice Stewart's formulation in *Mendenhall* as the appropriate standard for determining when police questioning crosses the threshold from a consensual encounter to a forcible stop. In *Royer*, the Court held that an illegal seizure had occurred. As a predicate for that holding, Justice White, in his opinion for the plurality, explained that the citizen "may not be detained *even momentarily* without reasonable, objective grounds for doing so; and his refusal to listen or answer does not, without more, furnish those grounds. United States v. Mendenhall, supra, at 556 (opinion of Stewart, J.)." 460 U.S., at 498 (emphasis added). The rule looks, not to the subjective perceptions of the person questioned, but rather, to the objective characteristics of the encounter that may suggest whether a reasonable person would have felt free to leave.

Even though momentary, a seizure occurs whenever an objective evaluation of a police officer's show of force conveys the message that the citizen is not entirely free to leave—in other words, that his or her liberty is being restrained in a significant way.

. . .

Finally, it is noteworthy that in Michigan v. Chesternut, 486 U.S. 567 (1988), the State asked us to repudiate the reasonable person standard developed in Terry [v. Ohio, 392 U.S. 1 (1968)], *Mendenhall*, [INS v.] *Delgado*, [466 U.S. 210 (1984)], and *Royer*. We decided, however, to "adhere to our traditional contextual approach," 486 U.S., at 573. In our opinion, we described Justice Stewart's analysis in *Mendenhall* as "a test to be applied in determining whether 'a person has been "seized" within the meaning of the Fourth Amendment' " and noted that "[t]he Court has since embraced this test." Ibid. Moreover, in commenting on the virtues of the test, we explained that it focused on the police officer's conduct:

> "The test's objective standard—looking to the reasonable man's interpretation of the conduct in question—allows the police to determine in advance whether the conduct contemplated will implicate the Fourth Amendment." Id., at 574.

Expressing his approval of the Court's rejection of Michigan's argument in *Chesternut*, Professor LaFave observed:

> "The 'free to leave' concept, in other words, has nothing to do with a particular suspect's choice to flee rather than submit or with his assessment of the probability of successful flight. Were it otherwise, police would be encouraged to utilize a very threatening but sufficiently slow chase as an evidence-gathering technique whenever they lack even the reasonable suspicion needed for a *Terry* stop." 3 W. LaFave, Search and Seizure § 9.2, p. 61 (2d ed. 1987, Supp.1991).

Whatever else one may think of today's decision, it unquestionably represents a departure from earlier Fourth Amendment case law. The notion that our prior cases contemplated a distinction between seizures effected by a touching on the one hand, and those effected by a show of force on the other hand, and that all of our repeated descriptions of the *Mendenhall* test stated only a necessary, but not a sufficient, condition for finding seizures in the latter category, is nothing if not creative lawmaking. Moreover, by narrowing the definition of the term seizure, instead of enlarging the scope of reasonable justifications for seizures, the Court has significantly limited the protection provided to the ordinary citizen by the Fourth Amendment. As we explained in *Terry* :

> "The danger in the logic which proceeds upon distinctions between a 'stop' and an 'arrest,' or 'seizure' of the person, and between a 'frisk' and a 'search' is twofold. It seeks to isolate from constitutional scrutiny the initial stages of the contact between the policeman and the citizen. And by suggesting a rigid all-or-nothing model of justification and regulation under the Amendment, it obscures the utility of limitations upon the scope, as well as the initiation, of police action as a means of constitutional regulation." Terry v. Ohio, 392 U.S., at 17.

III

In this case the officer's show of force—taking the form of a head-on chase—adequately conveyed the message that respondent was not free to leave. Whereas in *Mendenhall*, there was "nothing in the record [to] sugges[t] that the respondent had any objective reason to believe that she was not free to end the conversation in the concourse and proceed on her way," 446 U.S., at 555, here, respondent attempted to end "the conversation" before it began and soon found himself literally "not free to leave" when confronted by an officer running toward him head-on who eventually tackled him to the ground. There was an interval of time between the moment that respondent saw the officer fast approaching and the moment when he was tackled, and thus brought under the control of the officer. The question is whether the Fourth Amendment was implicated at the earlier or the later moment.

Because the facts of this case are somewhat unusual, it is appropriate to note that the same issue would arise if the show of force took the form of a command to "freeze," a warning shot, or the sound of sirens accompanied by a patrol car's flashing lights. In any of these situations, there may be a significant time interval between the initiation of the officer's show of force and the complete submission by the citizen. At least on the facts of this case, the Court concludes that the timing of the seizure is governed by the citizen's reaction, rather than by the officer's conduct. ... One consequence of this conclusion is that the point at which the interaction between citizen and police officer becomes a seizure occurs, not when a reasonable citizen believes he or she is no longer free to go, but rather, only after the officer exercises control over the citizen.

In my view, our interests in effective law enforcement and in personal liberty would be better served by adhering to a standard that "allows the police to determine in advance whether the conduct contemplated will implicate the Fourth Amendment." *Chesternut*, 486 U.S., at 574. The range of possible responses to a police show of force, and the multitude of problems that may arise in determining whether, and at which moment, there has been "submission," can only create uncertainty and generate litigation.

In some cases, of course, it is immediately apparent at which moment the suspect submitted to an officer's show of force. For example, if the victim is killed by an officer's gunshot, as in Tennessee v. Garner, 471 U.S. 1, 11 (1985) ("A police officer may not seize an unarmed, nondangerous suspect by shooting him dead"), or by a hidden roadblock, as in Brower v. Inyo County, 489 U.S. 593 (1989), the submission is unquestionably complete. But what if, for example, William James Caldwell (Brower) had just been wounded before being apprehended? Would it be correct to say that no seizure had occurred and therefore the Fourth Amendment was not implicated even if the pursuing officer had no justification whatsoever for initiating the chase? The Court's opinion in *Brower* suggests that the officer's responsibility should not depend on the character of the victim's evasive action. The Court wrote:

> "Brower's independent decision to continue the chase can no more eliminate respondents' responsibility for the termination of his movement effected by the roadblock than Garner's independent decision to flee eliminated the Memphis police officer's responsibility for the termination of his movement effected by the bullet." Id., at 595.

It seems equally clear to me that the constitutionality of a police officer's show of force should be measured by the conditions that exist at the time of the officer's action. A search must be justified on the basis of the facts available at the time it is initiated; the subsequent discovery of evidence does not retroactively validate an unconstitutional search. The same approach should apply to seizures; the character of the citizen's response should not govern the constitutionality of the officer's conduct.

If an officer effects an arrest by touching a citizen, apparently the Court would accept the fact that a seizure occurred, even if the arrestee should thereafter break loose and flee. In such a case, the constitutionality of the seizure would be evaluated as of the time the officer acted. That category of seizures would then be analyzed in the same way as searches, namely, was the police action justified when it took place? It is anomalous, at best, to fashion a different rule for the subcategory of "show of force" arrests.

In cases within this new subcategory, there will be a period of time during which the citizen's liberty has been restrained, but he or she has not yet completely submitted to the show of force. A motorist pulled over by a highway patrol car cannot come to an immediate stop, even if the motorist intends to obey the patrol car's signal. If an officer decides to make the kind of random stop forbidden by Delaware v. Prouse, 440 U.S. 648 (1979), and, after flashing his lights, but before the vehicle comes to a complete stop, sees that the license plate has expired, can he justify his action on the ground that the seizure became lawful after it was initiated but before it was completed? In an airport setting, may a drug enforcement agent now approach a group of passengers with his gun drawn, announce a "baggage search," and rely on the passengers' reactions to justify his investigative stops? The holding of today's majority fails to recognize the coercive and intimidating nature of such behavior and creates a rule that may allow such behavior to go unchecked.

The deterrent purposes of the exclusionary rule focus on the conduct of law enforcement officers, and on discouraging improper behavior on their part, and not on the reaction of the citizen to the show of force. In the present case, if Officer Pertoso had succeeded in tackling respondent before he dropped the rock of cocaine, the rock unquestionably would have been excluded as the fruit of the officer's unlawful seizure. Instead, under the Court's logic-chopping analysis, the exclusionary rule has no application because an attempt to make an unconstitutional seizure is beyond the coverage of the Fourth Amendment, no matter how outrageous or unreasonable the officer's conduct may be.

It is too early to know the consequences of the Court's holding. If carried to its logical conclusion, it will encourage unlawful displays of force that will frighten countless innocent citizens into surrendering whatever privacy rights they may still have. It is not too soon, however, to note the irony in the fact that the Court's own justification for its result is its analysis of the rules of the common law of arrest that antedated our decisions in Katz [v. United States, 389 U.S. 347 (1967)] and *Terry*. Yet, even in those days the common law provided the citizen with protection against an attempt to make an unlawful arrest. . . . The central message of *Katz* and *Terry* was that the protection the Fourth Amendment provides to the average citizen is not rigidly confined by ancient common-law precept. The message that today's literal-minded majority conveys is that the common law, rather than our understanding of the Fourth Amendment as it has developed over the last quarter of a century, defines, and limits, the scope of a seizure. The Court today defines a seizure as commencing, not with egregious police conduct, but rather, with submission by the citizen. Thus, it both delays the point at which "the Fourth Amendment becomes relevant"[19] to an encounter and limits the range of encounters that will come under the heading of "seizure." Today's qualification of the Fourth Amendment means that innocent citizens may remain "secure in their persons . . . against unreasonable searches and seizures" only at the discretion of the police.

19. Terry v. Ohio, 392 U.S., at 16.

Some sacrifice of freedom always accompanies an expansion in the executive's unreviewable law enforcement powers. A court more sensitive to the purposes of the Fourth Amendment would insist on greater rewards to society before decreeing the sacrifice it makes today. Alexander Bickel presciently wrote that "many actions of government have two aspects: their immediate, necessarily intended, practical effects, and their perhaps unintended or unappreciated bearing on values we hold to have more general and permanent interest." [22] The Court's immediate concern with containing criminal activity poses a substantial, though unintended, threat to values that are fundamental and enduring.

I respectfully dissent.

22. The Least Dangerous Branch 24 (1962).

445 U.S. 573, 100 S.Ct. 1371, 63 L.Ed.2d 639 (1980).

MR. JUSTICE STEVENS delivered the opinion of the Court.

These appeals challenge the constitutionality of New York statutes that authorize police officers to enter a private residence without a warrant and with force, if necessary, to make a routine felony arrest.

. . .

... We ... hold that the Fourth Amendment to the United States Constitution, made applicable to the States by the Fourteenth Amendment ... prohibits the police from making a warrantless and nonconsensual entry into a suspect's home in order to make a routine felony arrest.

We first state the facts of both cases in some detail and put to one side certain related questions that are not presented by these records. We then explain why the New York statutes are not consistent with the Fourth Amendment and why the reasons for upholding warrantless arrests in a public place do not apply to warrantless invasions of the privacy of the home.

I

On January 14, 1970, after two days of intensive investigation, New York detectives had assembled evidence sufficient to establish probable cause to believe that Theodore Payton had murdered the manager of a gas station two days earlier. At about 7:30 a.m. on January 15, six officers went to Payton's apartment in the Bronx, intending to arrest him. They had not obtained a warrant. Although light and music emanated from the apartment, there was no response to their knock on the metal door. They summoned emergency assistance and, about 30 minutes later, used crowbars to break open the door and enter the apartment. No one was there. In plain view, however, was a .30-caliber shell casing that was seized and later admitted into evidence at Payton's murder trial.

In due course Payton surrendered to the police, was indicted for murder, and moved to suppress the evidence taken from his apartment. The trial judge held that the warrantless and forcible entry was authorized by the New York Code of Criminal Procedure, and that the evidence in plain view was properly seized. He found that exigent circumstances justified the officers' failure to announce their purpose before entering the apartment as required by the statute. He had no occasion, however, to decide whether those circumstances also would have justified the failure to obtain a warrant, because he concluded that the warrantless entry was adequately supported by the statute without regard to the circumstances. The Appellate Division, First Department, summarily affirmed.

On March 14, 1974, Obie Riddick was arrested for the commission of two armed robberies that had occurred in 1971. He had been identified by the victims in June of 1973, and in January 1974 the police had learned his address. They did not obtain a warrant for his arrest. At about noon on March 14, a detective, accompanied by three other officers, knocked on the door of the Queens house where Riddick was living. When his young son opened the door, they could see Riddick sitting in bed covered by a sheet. They entered the house and placed him under arrest. Before permitting him to dress, they opened a chest of drawers two feet from the bed in search of weapons and found narcotics and related paraphernalia. Riddick was subsequently indicted on narcotics charges. At a suppression hearing, the trial judge held that the warrantless entry into his home was authorized by the revised New York statute, and that the search of the immediate area was reasonable under Chimel v. California, 395 U.S. 752. The Appellate Division, Second Department, affirmed the denial of the suppression motion.

The New York Court of Appeals, in a single opinion, affirmed the convictions of both Payton and Riddick. 45 N.Y.2d 300, 380 N.E.2d 224 (1978). . . .

. . .

Before addressing the narrow question presented by these appeals, we put to one side other related problems that are *not* presented today. Although it is arguable that the warrantless entry to effect Payton's arrest might have been justified by exigent circumstances, none of the New York courts relied on any such justification. The Court of Appeals majority treated both Payton's and Riddick's cases as involving routine arrests in which there was ample time to obtain a warrant, and we will do the same. Accordingly, we have no occasion to consider the sort of emergency or dangerous situation, described in our cases as "exigent circumstances," that would justify a warrantless entry into a home for the purpose of either arrest or search.

Nor do these cases raise any question concerning the authority of the police, without either a search or arrest warrant, to enter a third party's home to arrest a suspect. The police broke into Payton's apartment intending to arrest Payton and they arrested Riddick in his own dwelling. We also note that in neither case is it argued that the police lacked probable cause to believe that the suspect was at home when they entered. Finally, in both cases we are dealing with entries into homes made without the consent of any occupant. In *Payton,* the police used crowbars to break down

the door and in *Riddick,* although his three-year-old son answered
the door, the police entered before Riddick had an opportunity
either to object or to consent.

II

It is familiar history that indiscriminate searches and seizures
conducted under the authority of "general warrants" were the
immediate evils that motivated the framing and adoption of the
Fourth Amendment. Indeed, as originally proposed in the House
of Representatives, the draft contained only one clause, which
directly imposed limitations on the issuance of warrants, but imposed no express restrictions on warrantless searches or seizures.
As it was ultimately adopted, however, the Amendment contained
two separate clauses, the first protecting the basic right to be free
from unreasonable searches and seizures and the second requiring
that warrants be particular and supported by probable cause. . . .

It is thus perfectly clear that the evil the Amendment was
designed to prevent was broader than the abuse of a general
warrant. Unreasonable searches or seizures conducted without any
warrant at all are condemned by the plain language of the first
clause of the Amendment. Almost a century ago the Court stated in
resounding terms that the principles reflected in the Amendment
"reached farther than the concrete form" of the specific cases that
gave it birth, and "apply to all invasions on the part of the
Government and its employés of the sanctity of a man's home and
the privacies of life." Boyd v. United States, 116 U.S. 616, 630.
Without pausing to consider whether that broad language may
require some qualification, it is sufficient to note that the warrantless arrest of a person is a species of seizure required by the
Amendment to be reasonable. . . . Indeed, as Mr. Justice Powell
noted in his concurrence in United States v. Watson, [423 U.S. 411
(1976)] the arrest of a person is "quintessentially a seizure." 423
U.S., at 428.

The simple language of the Amendment applies equally to
seizures of persons and to seizures of property. Our analysis in this
case may therefore properly commence with rules that have been
well established in Fourth Amendment litigation involving tangible
items. As the Court reiterated just a few years ago, the "physical
entry of the home is the chief evil against which the wording of the
Fourth Amendment is directed." United States v. United States
District Court, 407 U.S. 297, 313. And we have long adhered to the
view that the warrant procedure minimizes the danger of needless
intrusions of that sort.

It is a "basic principle of Fourth Amendment law" that searches
and seizures inside a home without a warrant are presumptively
unreasonable. Yet it is also well settled that objects such as
weapons or contraband found in a public place may be seized by
the police without a warrant. The seizure of property in plain view

involves no invasion of privacy and is presumptively reasonable, assuming that there is probable cause to associate the property with criminal activity. The distinction between a warrantless seizure in an open area and such a seizure on private premises was plainly stated in G. M. Leasing Corp. v. United States, 429 U.S. 338, 354:

> "It is one thing to seize without a warrant property resting in an open area or seizable by levy without an intrusion into privacy, and it is quite another thing to effect a warrantless seizure of property, even that owned by a corporation, situated on private premises to which access is not otherwise available for the seizing officer."

As the late Judge Leventhal recognized, this distinction has equal force when the seizure of a person is involved. Writing on the constitutional issue now before us for the United States Court of Appeals for the District of Columbia Circuit sitting en banc, Dorman v. United States, 140 U.S.App.D.C. 313, 435 F.2d 385 (1970), Judge Leventhal first noted the settled rule that warrantless arrests in public places are valid. He immediately recognized, however, that

> "[a] greater burden is placed . . . on officials who enter a home or dwelling without consent. Freedom from intrusion into the home or dwelling is the archetype of the privacy protection secured by the Fourth Amendment." Id., at 317, 435 F.2d, at 389. (Footnote omitted.)

His analysis of this question then focused on the long-settled premise that, absent exigent circumstances, a warrantless entry to search for weapons or contraband is unconstitutional even when a felony has been committed and there is probable cause to believe that incriminating evidence will be found within. He reasoned that the constitutional protection afforded to the individual's interest in the privacy of his own home is equally applicable to a warrantless entry for the purpose of arresting a resident of the house; for it is inherent in such an entry that a search for the suspect may be required before he can be apprehended. Judge Leventhal concluded that an entry to arrest and an entry to search for and to seize property implicate the same interest in preserving the privacy and the sanctity of the home, and justify the same level of constitutional protection.

This reasoning has been followed in other circuits. . . . We find this reasoning to be persuasive and in accord with this Court's Fourth Amendment decisions.

The majority of the New York Court of Appeals, however, suggested that there is a substantial difference in the relative intrusiveness of an entry to search for property and an entry to search for a person. . . . It is true that the area that may legally be searched is broader when executing a search warrant than when executing an arrest warrant in the home. . . . This difference may be more theoretical than real, however, because the police may need to check the entire premises for safety reasons, and sometimes they ignore the restrictions on searches incident to arrest.

But the critical point is that any differences in the intrusiveness of entries to search and entries to arrest are merely ones of degree rather than kind. The two intrusions share this fundamental characteristic: the breach of the entrance to an individual's home. The Fourth Amendment protects the individual's privacy in a variety of settings. In none is the zone of privacy more clearly defined than when bounded by the unambiguous physical dimensions of an individual's home—a zone that finds its roots in clear and specific constitutional terms: "The right of the people to be secure in their ... houses ... shall not be violated." That language unequivocally establishes the proposition that "[a]t the very core [of the Fourth Amendment] stands the right of a man to retreat into his own home and there be free from unreasonable governmental intrusion." *Silverman v. United States*, 365 U.S. 505, 511. In terms that apply equally to seizures of property and to seizures of persons, the Fourth Amendment has drawn a firm line at the entrance to the house. Absent exigent circumstances, that threshold may not reasonably be crossed without a warrant.

III

Without contending that United States v. Watson, 423 U.S. 411, decided the question presented by these appeals, New York argues that the reasons that support the *Watson* holding require a similar result here. In *Watson* the Court relied on (a) the well-settled common-law rule that a warrantless arrest in a public place is valid if the arresting officer had probable cause to believe the suspect is a felon; (b) the clear consensus among the States adhering to that well settled common-law rule; and (c) the expression of the judgment of Congress that such an arrest is "reasonable." We consider each of these reasons as it applies to a warrantless entry into a home for the purpose of making a routine felony arrest.

A

An examination of the common-law understanding of an officer's authority to arrest sheds light on the obviously relevant, if not entirely dispositive, consideration of what the Framers of the Amendment might have thought to be reasonable. ...

. . .

It is obvious that the common-law rule on warrantless home arrests was not as clear as the rule on arrests in public places. ... [T]he weight of authority as it appeared to the Framers was to the effect that a warrant was required, or at the minimum that there were substantial risks in proceeding without one. The common-law sources display a sensitivity to privacy interests that could not have been lost on the Framers. The zealous and frequent repetition of the adage that a "man's house is his castle," made it abundantly clear that both in England and in the Colonies "the freedom of one's house" was one of the most vital elements of English liberty.[45]

Thus, our study of the relevant common law does not provide the same guidance that was present in *Watson.* Whereas the rule concerning the validity of an arrest in a public place was supported by cases directly in point and by the unanimous views of the commentators, we have found no direct authority supporting forcible entries into a home to make a routine arrest and the weight of the scholarly opinion is somewhat to the contrary. Indeed, the absence of any 17th or 18th century English cases directly in point, together with the unequivocal endorsement of the tenet that "a man's house is his castle," strongly suggests that the prevailing practice was not to make such arrests except in hot pursuit or when authorized by a warrant. ... In all events, the issue is not one that can be said to have been definitively settled by the common law at the time the Fourth Amendment was adopted.

B

A majority of the States that have taken a position on the question permit warrantless entry into the home to arrest even in the absence of exigent circumstances. At this time, 24 States permit such warrantless entries; 15 States clearly prohibit them, though 3 States do so on federal constitutional grounds alone; and 11 States have apparently taken no position on the question.

But these current figures reflect a significant decline during the last decade in the number of States permitting warrantless entries for arrest. ...

A longstanding, widespread practice is not immune from constitutional scrutiny. But neither is it to be lightly brushed aside. This is particularly so when the constitutional standard is as amorphous as the word "reasonable," and when custom and contemporary norms necessarily play such a large role in the constitutional analysis. In this case, although the weight of state-law authority is clear, there is by no means the kind of virtual unanimity on this question that was present in United States v. Watson, with regard to warrantless arrests in public places. See 423 U.S., at 422–423. Only 24 of the 50 States currently sanction warrantless entries into the home to arrest ... and there is an obvious declining trend. Further, the strength of the trend is greater than the numbers alone indicate. Seven state courts have recently held that warrantless home arrests violate their respective *State* constitutions. ... That is significant because by invoking a state constitutional provision, a state court immunizes its decision from review by this Court. This heightened degree of immutability underscores the depth of the principle underlying the result.

45. ... 2 Legal Papers of John Adams 142 (L. Wroth and H. Zobel ed. 1965). ...

C

No congressional determination that warrantless entries into the home are "reasonable" has been called to our attention. None of the federal statutes cited in the *Watson* opinion reflects any such legislative judgment. Thus, that support for the *Watson* holding finds no counterpart in this case.

Mr. Justice Powell, concurring in United States v. Watson, supra, at 429, stated: "But logic sometimes must refer to history and experience. The Court's opinion emphasizes the historical sanction accorded warrantless felony arrests [in public places]." In this case, however, neither history nor this Nation's experience requires us to disregard the overriding respect for the sanctity of the home that has been embedded in our traditions since the origins of the Republic.

IV

The parties have argued at some length about the practical consequences of a warrant requirement as a precondition to a felony arrest in the home. In the absence of any evidence that effective law enforcement has suffered in those States that already have such a requirement ... we are inclined to view such arguments with skepticism. More fundamentally, however, such arguments of policy must give way to a constitutional command that we consider to be unequivocal.

Finally, we note the State's suggestion that only a search warrant based on probable cause to believe the suspect is at home at a given time can adequately protect the privacy interests at stake, and since such a warrant requirement is manifestly impractical, there need be no warrant of any kind. We find this ingenious argument unpersuasive. It is true that an arrest warrant requirement may afford less protection than a search warrant requirement, but it will suffice to interpose the magistrate's determination of probable cause between the zealous officer and the citizen. If there is sufficient evidence of a citizen's participation in a felony to persuade a judicial officer that his arrest is justified, it is constitutionally reasonable to require him to open his doors to the officers of the law. Thus, for Fourth Amendment purposes, an arrest warrant founded on probable cause implicitly carries with it the limited authority to enter a dwelling in which the suspect lives when there is reason to believe the suspect is within.

Because no arrest warrant was obtained in either of these cases, the judgments must be reversed and the cases remanded to the New York Court of Appeals for further proceedings not inconsistent with this opinion.

It is so ordered.

MR. JUSTICE WHITE, with whom THE CHIEF JUSTICE and MR. JUSTICE REHNQUIST join, dissenting.

The Court today holds that absent exigent circumstances officers may never enter a home during the daytime to arrest for a dangerous felony unless they have first obtained a warrant. This hard-and-fast rule, founded on erroneous assumptions concerning the intrusiveness of home arrest entries, finds little or no support in the common law or in the text and history of the Fourth Amendment. I respectfully dissent.

. . .

II

A

Today's decision rests, in large measure, on the premise that warrantless arrest entries constitute a particularly severe invasion of personal privacy. I do not dispute that the home is generally a very private area or that the common law displayed a special "reverence . . . for the individual's right of privacy in his house." Miller v. United States [357 U.S. 301 (1958)] at 313. However, the Fourth Amendment is concerned with protecting people, not places, and no talismanic significance is given to the fact that an arrest occurs in the home rather than elsewhere. . . . It is necessary in each case to assess realistically the actual extent of invasion of constitutionally protected privacy. Further . . . all arrests involve serious intrusions onto an individual's privacy and dignity. Yet we settled in *Watson* that the intrusiveness of a public arrest is not enough to mandate the obtaining of a warrant. The inquiry in the present case, therefore, is whether the incremental intrusiveness that results from an arrest's being made *in the dwelling* is enough to support an inflexible constitutional rule requiring warrants for such arrests whenever exigent circumstances are not present.

Today's decision ignores the carefully crafted restrictions on the common-law power of arrest entry and thereby overestimates the dangers inherent in that practice. At common law, absent exigent circumstances, entries to arrest could be made only for felony. Even in cases of felony, the officers were required to announce their presence, demand admission, and be refused entry before they were entitled to break doors. Further, it seems generally accepted that entries could be made only during daylight hours. And, in my view, the officer entering to arrest must have reasonable grounds to believe, not only that the arrestee has committed a crime, but also that the person suspected is present in the house at the time of the entry.

These four restrictions on home arrests—felony, knock and announce, daytime, and stringent probable cause—constitute powerful and complementary protections for the privacy interests associated with the home. The felony requirement guards against abusive or arbitrary enforcement and ensures that invasions of the home occur only in case of the most serious crimes. The knock-and-announce and daytime requirements protect individuals against the fear, humiliation, and embarrassment of being roused from the beds in states of partial or complete undress. And these requirements allow the arrestee to surrender at his front door, thereby maintaining his dignity and preventing the officers from entering other rooms of the dwelling. The stringent probable-cause requirement would help ensure against the possibility that the police would enter when the suspect was not home, and, in searching for him, frighten members of the family or ransack parts of the house, seizing items in plain view. In short, these requirements, taken together, permit an individual suspected of a serious crime to surrender at the front door of his dwelling and thereby avoid most of the humiliation and indignity that the Court seems to believe necessarily accompany a house arrest entry. Such a front door arrest, in my view, is no more intrusive on personal privacy than the public warrantless arrests which we found to pass constitutional muster in [United States v.] *Watson* [423 U.S. 411 (1976)].

All of these limitations on warrantless arrest entries are satisfied on the facts of the present cases. The arrests here were for serious felonies—murder and armed robbery—and both occurred during daylight hours. The authorizing statutes required that the police announce their business and demand entry; neither Payton nor Riddick makes any contention that these statutory requirements were not fulfilled. And it is not argued that the police had no probable cause to believe that both Payton and Riddick were in their dwellings at the time of the entries. Today's decision, therefore, sweeps away any possibility that warrantless home entries might be permitted in some limited situations other than those in which exigent circumstances are present. The Court substitutes, in one sweeping decision, a rigid constitutional rule in place of the common-law approach, evolved over hundreds of years, which achieved a flexible accommodation between the demands of personal privacy and the legitimate needs of law enforcement.

A rule permitting warrantless arrest entries would not pose a danger that officers would use their entry power as a pretext to justify an otherwise invalid warrantless search. A search pursuant to a warrantless arrest entry will rarely, if ever, be as complete as one under authority of a search warrant. If the suspect surrenders at the door, the officers may not enter other rooms. Of course, the suspect may flee or hide, or may not be at home, but the officers cannot anticipate the first two of these possibilities and the last is unlikely given the requirement of probable cause to believe that the suspect is at home. Even when officers are justified in searching other rooms, they may seize only items within the arrestee's possession or immediate control or items in plain view discovered during the course of a search reasonably directed at discovering a hiding suspect. Hence a warrantless home entry is likely to uncover far less evidence than a search conducted under authority of a search warrant. Furthermore, an arrest entry will inevitably tip off the suspects and likely result in destruction or removal of evidence not uncovered during the arrest. I therefore cannot believe that the police would take the risk of losing valuable evidence through a pretextual arrest entry rather than applying to a magistrate for a search warrant.

B

While exaggerating the invasion of personal privacy involved in home arrests, the Court fails to account for the danger that its rule will "severely hamper effective law enforcement," United States v. Watson, 423 U.S., at 431 (Powell, J., concurring) .... The policeman on his beat must now make subtle discriminations that perplex even judges in their chambers. ... [P]olice will sometimes delay making an arrest, even after probable cause is established, in order to be sure that they have enough evidence to convict. Then, if they suddenly have to arrest, they run the risk that the subsequent exigency will not excuse their prior failure to obtain a warrant. This problem cannot effectively be cured by obtaining a warrant as soon as probable cause is established because of the chance that the warrant will go stale before the arrest is made.

Further, police officers will often face the difficult task of deciding whether the circumstances are sufficiently exigent to justify their entry to arrest without a warrant. This is a decision that must be made quickly in the most trying of circumstances. If the officers mistakenly decide that the circumstances are exigent, the arrest will be invalid and any evidence seized incident to the arrest or in plain view will be excluded at trial. On the other hand, if the officers mistakenly determine that exigent circumstances are lacking, they may refrain from making the arrest, thus creating the possibility that a dangerous criminal will escape into the community. The police could reduce the likelihood of escape by staking out all possible exits until the circumstances become clearly exigent or a warrant is obtained. But the costs of such a stakeout seem excessive in an era of rising crime and scarce police resources.

The uncertainty inherent in the exigent circumstances determination burdens the judicial system as well. In the case of searches, exigent circumstances are sufficiently unusual that this Court has determined that the benefits of a warrant outweigh the burdens imposed, including the burdens on the judicial system. In contrast, arrests recurringly involve exigent circumstances, and this Court has heretofore held that a warrant can be dispensed with without undue sacrifice in Fourth Amendment values. The situation should be no different with respect to arrests in the home. Under today's decision, whenever the police have made a warrantless home arrest there will be the possibility of "endless litigation with respect to the existence of exigent circumstances, whether it was practicable to get a warrant, whether the suspect was about to flee, and the like," United States v. Watson, supra, at 423–424.

Our cases establish that the ultimate test under the Fourth Amendment is one of "reasonableness." ... I cannot join the Court in declaring unreasonable a practice which has been thought entirely reasonable by so many for so long. It would be far preferable to adopt a clear and simple rule: after knocking and announcing their presence, police may enter the home to make a daytime arrest without a warrant when there is probable cause to believe that the person to be arrested committed a felony and is present in the house. This rule would best comport with the common-law background, with the traditional practice in the States, and with the history and policies of the Fourth Amendment. Accordingly, I respectfully dissent.[*] [**]

---

[*] Justice Blackmun wrote a concurring opinion. Justice Rehnquist wrote a dissenting opinion.

[**] "... [I]t is difficult to conceive of a warrantless home arrest that would not be unreasonable under the Fourth Amendment when the underlying offense is extremely minor." Welsh v. Wisconsin, 466 U.S. 740, 753 (1984). In Welsh, the defendant was arrested for drunk driving, a noncriminal violation. In view of the nature of the offense, the Court said, it was immaterial that evidence, the alcohol content of the defendant's blood, might imminently be lost. "... [A]n important factor to be considered when determining whether any exigency exists is the gravity of the underlying offense for which the arrest is being made. Moreover, although no exigency is created simply because there is probable cause to believe that a serious crime has been committed ... application of the exigent-circumstances exception in the context of a home entry should rarely be sanctioned when there is probable cause to believe that only a minor offense has been committed." Id. at 753.

In the absence of an emergency or consent to the entry, the Fourth Amendment requires a search warrant to enter the home of a third person in order to arrest a person for whom the police have an arrest warrant. Steagald v. United States, 451 U.S. 204 (1981) (7–2). The Court said: "... [W]hile an arrest warrant and a search warrant both serve to subject the probable cause determination of the police to judicial review, the interests protected by the two warrants differ. An arrest warrant is issued by a magistrate upon a showing that probable cause exists to believe that the subject of the warrant has committed an offense and thus the warrant primarily serves to protect an individual from an unreasonable seizure. A search warrant, in contrast, is issued upon a showing of probable cause to believe that the legitimate object of a search is located in a particular place and therefore safeguards an individual's interest in the privacy of his home and possessions against the unjustified intrusion of the police." 451 U.S. at 212–213.

"... Because an arrest warrant authorizes the police to deprive a person of his liberty, it necessarily also authorizes a limited invasion of that person's privacy interest when it is necessary to arrest him in his home. This analysis, however, is plainly inapplicable when the police seek to use an arrest warrant as legal authority to enter the home of a third party to conduct a search. Such a warrant embodies no judicial determination whatsoever regarding the person whose home is to be searched. Because it does not authorize the police to deprive the third person of his liberty, it cannot embody any derivative authority to deprive this person of his interest in the privacy of his home. Such a deprivation must instead be based on an independent showing that a legitimate object of a search is located in the third party's home. We have consistently held however, that such a determination is the province of the magistrate, and not that of the police." 451 U.S. at 214–215 n. 7.

ILLINOIS v. GATES

462 U.S. 213, 103 S.Ct. 2317, 76 L.Ed.2d 527 (1983).

JUSTICE REHNQUIST delivered the opinion of the Court.

Respondents Lance and Susan Gates were indicted for violation of state drug laws after police officers, executing a search warrant, discovered marihuana and other contraband in their automobile and home. Prior to trial the Gateses moved to suppress evidence seized during this search. The Illinois Supreme Court affirmed the decisions of lower state courts granting the motion. ... It held that the affidavit submitted in support of the State's application for a warrant to search the Gateses' property was inadequate under this Court's decisions in Aguilar v. Texas, 378 U.S. 108 (1964) and Spinelli v. United States, 393 U.S. 410 (1969).

We granted certiorari to consider the application of the Fourth Amendment to a magistrate's issuance of a search warrant on the basis of a partially corroborated anonymous informant's tip. ...

. . .

II

We now turn to the question presented in the State's original petition for certiorari, which requires us to decide whether respondents' rights under the Fourth and Fourteenth Amendments were violated by the search of their car and house. A chronological statement of events usefully introduces the issues at stake. Bloomingdale, Ill., is a suburb of Chicago located in Du Page County. On May 3, 1978, the Bloomingdale Police Department received by mail an anonymous handwritten letter which read as follows:

"This letter is to inform you that you have a couple in your town who strictly make their living on selling drugs. They are Sue and Lance Gates, they live on Greenway, off Bloomingdale Rd. in the condominiums. Most of their buys are done in Florida. Sue his wife drives their car to Florida, where she leaves it to be loaded up with drugs, then Lance flys down and drives it back. Sue flys back after she drops the car off in Florida. May 3 she is driving down there again and Lance will be flying down in a few days to drive it back. At the time Lance drives the car back he has the trunk loaded with over $100,000.00 in drugs. Presently they have over $100,000.00 worth of drugs in their basement.

"They brag about the fact they never have to work, and make their entire living on pushers.

"I guarantee if you watch them carefully you will make a big catch. They are friends with some big drugs dealers, who visit their house often.

"Lance & Susan Gates

"Greenway

"in Condominiums"

The letter was referred by the Chief of Police of the Bloomingdale Police Department to Detective Mader, who decided to pursue the tip. Mader learned, from the office of the Illinois Secretary of State, that an Illinois driver's license had been issued to one Lance Gates, residing at a stated address in Bloomingdale. He contacted a confidential informant, whose examination of certain financial records revealed a more recent address for the Gateses, and he also learned from a police officer assigned to O'Hare Airport that "L. Gates" had made a reservation on Eastern Airlines flight 245 to West Palm Beach, Fla., scheduled to depart from Chicago on May 5 at 4:15 p.m.

Mader then made arrangements with an agent of the Drug Enforcement Administration for surveillance of the May 5 Eastern Airlines flight. The agent later reported to Mader that Gates had boarded the flight, and that federal agents in Florida had observed him arrive in West Palm Beach and take a taxi to the nearby Holiday Inn. They also reported that Gates went to a room registered to one Susan Gates and that, at 7 o'clock the next morning, Gates and an unidentified woman left the motel in a Mercury bearing Illinois license plates and drove northbound on an interstate frequently used by travelers to the Chicago area. In addition, the DEA agent informed Mader that the license plate number on the Mercury was registered to a Hornet station wagon owned by Gates. The agent also advised Mader that the driving time between West Palm Beach and Bloomingdale was approximately 22 to 24 hours.

Mader signed an affidavit setting forth the foregoing facts, and submitted it to a judge of the Circuit Court of Du Page County, together with a copy of the anonymous letter. The judge of that court thereupon issued a search warrant for the Gateses' residence and for their automobile. The judge, in deciding to issue the warrant, could have determined that the *modus operandi* of the Gateses had been substantially corroborated. As the anonymous letter predicted, Lance Gates had flown from Chicago to West Palm Beach late in the afternoon of May 5th, had checked into a hotel room registered in the name of his wife, and, at 7 o'clock the following morning, had headed north, accompanied by an unidentified woman, out of West Palm Beach on an interstate highway used by travelers from South Florida to Chicago in an automobile bearing a license plate issued to him.

At 5:15 a.m. on March 7th, only 36 hours after he had flown out of Chicago, Lance Gates, and his wife, returned to their home in Bloomingdale, driving the car in which they had left West Palm Beach some 22 hours earlier. The Bloomingdale police were awaiting them, searched the trunk of the Mercury, and uncovered approximately 350 pounds of marihuana. A search of the Gateses' home revealed marihuana, weapons, and other contraband. The Illinois Circuit Court ordered suppression of all these items, on the ground that the affidavit submitted to the Circuit Judge failed to support the necessary determination of probable cause to believe that the Gateses' automobile and home contained the contraband in question. This decision was affirmed in turn by the Illinois Appellate Court ... and by a divided vote of the Supreme Court of Illinois. ...

The Illinois Supreme Court concluded—and we are inclined to agree—that, standing alone, the anonymous letter sent to the Bloomingdale Police Department would not provide the basis for a magistrate's determination that there was probable cause to believe contraband would be found in the Gateses' car and home. The letter provides virtually nothing from which one might conclude that its author is either honest or his information reliable; likewise, the letter gives absolutely no indication of the basis for the writer's predictions regarding the Gateses' criminal activities. Something more was required, then, before a magistrate could conclude that there was probable cause to believe that contraband would be found in the Gateses' home and car. ...

The Illinois Supreme Court also properly recognized that Detective Mader's affidavit might be capable of supplementing the anonymous letter with information sufficient to permit a determination of probable cause. ... In holding that the affidavit in fact did not contain sufficient additional information to sustain a determination of probable cause, the Illinois court applied a "two-pronged test," derived from our decision in Spinelli v. United States, 393 U.S. 410 (1969). The Illinois Supreme Court, like some others, apparently understood *Spinelli* as requiring that the anonymous letter satisfy each of two independent requirements before it could be relied on. ... According to this view, the letter, as supplemented by Mader's affidavit, first had to adequately reveal the "basis of Knowledge" of the letterwriter—the particular means by which he came by the information given in his report. Second, it had to provide facts sufficiently establishing either the "veracity" of the affiant's informant, or, alternatively, the "reliability" of the informant's report in this particular case.

The Illinois court, alluding to an elaborate set of legal rules that have developed among various lower courts to enforce the "two-pronged test," found that the test had not been satisfied. First, the "veracity" prong was not satisfied because, "[t]here was simply no basis [for] conclud[ing] that the anonymous person [who wrote the

letter to the Bloomingdale Police Department] was credible." ...
The court indicated that corroboration by police of details contained in the letter might never satisfy the "veracity" prong, and in
any event, could not do so if, as in the present case, only "innocent" details are corroborated. ... In addition, the letter gave no
indication of the basis of its writer's knowledge of the Gateses'
activities. The Illinois court understood *Spinelli* as permitting the
detail contained in a tip to be used to infer that the informant had a
reliable basis for his statements, but it thought that the anonymous
letter failed to provide sufficient detail to permit such an inference.
Thus, it concluded that no showing of probable cause had been
made.

We agree with the Illinois Supreme Court that an informant's
"veracity," "reliability," and "basis of knowledge" are all highly
relevant in determining the value of his report. We do not agree,
however, that these elements should be understood as entirely
separate and independent requirements to be rigidly exacted in
every case, which the opinion of the Supreme Court of Illinois
would imply. Rather, as detailed below, they should be understood
simply as closely intertwined issues that may usefully illuminate the
commonsense, practical question whether there is "probable cause"
to believe that contraband or evidence is located in a particular
place.

III

This totality-of-the-circumstances approach is far more consistent with our prior treatment of probable cause than is any rigid
demand that specific "tests" be satisfied by every informant's tip.
Perhaps the central teaching of our decisions bearing on the probable cause standard is that it is a "practical, nontechnical conception." Brinegar v. United States, 338 U.S. 160, 176 (1949). "In
dealing with probable cause, ... as the very name implies, we deal
with probabilities. These are not technical; they are the factual and
practical considerations of everyday life on which reasonable and
prudent men, not legal technicians, act." Id., at 175. Our observation in United States v. Cortez, 449 U.S. 411, 418 (1981), regarding
"particularized suspicion," is also applicable to the probable cause
standard:

> "The process does not deal with hard certainties, but with
> probabilities. Long before the law of probabilities was articu-
> lated as such, practical people formulated certain common-
> sense conclusions about human behavior; jurors as factfinders
> are permitted to do the same—and so are law enforcement
> officers. Finally, the evidence thus collected must be seen and
> weighed not in terms of library analysis by scholars, but as
> understood by those versed in the field of law enforcement."

As these comments illustrate, probable cause is a fluid concept—turning on the assessment of probabilities in particular factual

contexts—not readily, or even usefully, reduced to a neat set of legal rules. Informants' tips doubtless come in many shapes and sizes from many different types of persons. As we said in Adams v. Williams, 407 U.S. 143, 147 (1972): "Informants' tips, like all other clues and evidence coming to a policeman on the scene may vary greatly in their value and reliability." Rigid legal rules are ill-suited to an area of such diversity. "One simple rule will not cover every situation." Ibid.

Moreover, the "two-pronged test" directs analysis into two largely independent channels—the informant's "veracity" or "reliability" and his "basis of knowledge." . . . There are persuasive arguments against according these two elements such independent status. Instead, they are better understood as relevant considerations in the totality-of-the-circumstances analysis that traditionally has guided probable cause determinations: a deficiency in one may be compensated for, in determining the overall reliability of a tip, by a strong showing as to the other, or by some other indicia of reliability. . . .

If, for example, a particular informant is known for the unusual reliability of his predictions of certain types of criminal activities in a locality, his failure, in a particular case, to thoroughly set forth the basis of his knowledge surely should not serve as an absolute bar to a finding of probable cause based on his tip. . . . Likewise, if an unquestionably honest citizen comes forward with a report of criminal activity—which if fabricated would subject him to criminal liability—we have found rigorous scrutiny of the basis of his knowledge unnecessary. . . . Conversely, even if we entertain some doubt as to an informant's motives, his explicit and detailed description of alleged wrongdoing, along with a statement that the event was observed first-hand, entitles his tip to greater weight than might otherwise be the case. Unlike a totality-of-the-circumstances analysis, which permits a balanced assessment of the relative weights of all the various indicia of reliability (and unreliability) attending an informant's tip, the "two-pronged test" has encouraged an excessively technical dissection of informants' tips, with undue attention being focused on isolated issues that cannot sensibly be divorced from the other facts presented to the magistrate.

. . .

If the affidavits submitted by police officers are subjected to the type of scrutiny some courts have deemed appropriate, police might well resort to warrantless searches, with the hope of relying on consent or some other exception to the Warrant Clause that might develop at the time of the search. In addition, the possession of a warrant by officers conducting an arrest or search greatly reduces the perception of unlawful or intrusive police conduct, by assuring "the individual whose property is searched or seized of the lawful authority of the executing officer, his need to search, and the limits of his power to search." United States v. Chadwick, 433 U.S. 1, 9 (1977). Reflecting this preference for the warrant process, the traditional standard for review of an issuing magistrate's probable cause determination has been that so long as the magistrate had a "substantial basis for . . . conclud[ing]" that a search would uncover evidence of wrongdoing, the Fourth Amendment requires no more. Jones v. United States, 362 U.S. 257, 271 (1960). . . . We think reaffirmation of this standard better serves the purpose of encouraging recourse to the warrant procedure and is more consistent with our traditional deference to the probable cause determinations of magistrates than is the "two-pronged test."

Finally, the direction taken by decisions following *Spinelli* poorly serves "the most basic function of any government": "to provide for the security of the individual and of his property." Miranda v. Arizona, 384 U.S. 436, 539 (1966) (White, J., dissenting). The strictures that inevitably accompany the "two-pronged test" cannot avoid seriously impeding the task of law enforcement. . . . If, as the Illinois Supreme Court apparently thought, that test must be rigorously applied in every case, anonymous tips would be of greatly diminished value in police work. Ordinary citizens, like ordinary witnesses . . . generally do not provide extensive recitations of the basis of their everyday observations. Likewise, as the Illinois Supreme Court observed in this case, the veracity of persons supplying anonymous tips is by hypothesis largely unknown, and unknowable. As a result, anonymous tips seldom could survive a rigorous application of either of the *Spinelli* prongs. Yet, such tips, particularly when supplemented by independent police investigation, frequently contribute to the solution of otherwise "perfect crimes." While a conscientious assessment of the basis for crediting such tips is required by the Fourth Amendment, a standard that leaves virtually no place for anonymous citizen informants is not.

For all these reasons, we conclude that it is wiser to abandon the "two-pronged test" established by our decisions in *Aguilar* and *Spinelli*. In its place we reaffirm the totality-of-the-circumstances analysis that traditionally has informed probable cause determinations. . . . The task of the issuing magistrate is simply to make a practical, common-sense decision whether, given all the circumstances set forth in the affidavit before him, including the "veracity" and "basis of knowledge" of persons supplying hearsay information, there is a fair probability that contraband or evidence of a crime will be found in a particular place. And the duty of a reviewing court is simply to ensure that the magistrate had a "substantial basis for . . . conclud[ing]" that probable cause existed. Jones v. United States, supra, 362 U.S., at 271. We are convinced that this flexible, easily applied standard will better achieve the accommodation of public and private interests that the Fourth Amendment requires than does the approach that has developed from *Aguilar* and *Spinelli*.

Our earlier cases illustrate the limits beyond which a magistrate may not venture in issuing a warrant. A sworn statement of an affiant that "he has cause to suspect and does believe" that liquor illegally brought into the United States is located on certain premises will not do. Nathanson v. United States, 290 U.S. 41 (1933). An affidavit must provide the magistrate with a substantial basis for determining the existence of probable cause, and the wholly conclusory statement at issue in *Nathanson* failed to meet this requirement. An officer's statement that "[a]ffiants have received reliable information from a credible person and believe" that heroin is stored in a home, is likewise inadequate. Aguilar v. Texas, 378 U.S. 108 (1964). As in *Nathanson*, this is a mere conclusory statement that gives the magistrate virtually no basis at all for making a judgment regarding probable cause. Sufficient information must be presented to the magistrate to allow that official to determine probable cause; his action cannot be a mere ratification of the bare conclusions of others. In order to ensure that such an abdication of the magistrate's duty does not occur, courts must continue to conscientiously review the sufficiency of affidavits on which warrants are issued. But when we move beyond the "bare bones" affidavits present in cases such as *Nathanson* and *Aguilar*, this area simply does not lend itself to a prescribed set of rules, like that which had developed from *Spinelli*. Instead, the flexible, common-sense standard articulated in *Jones, Ventresca*, and *Brinegar* better serves the purposes of the Fourth Amendment's probable cause requirement.

. . .

IV

Our decisions applying the totality-of-the-circumstances analysis outlined above have consistently recognized the value of corroboration of details of an informant's tip by independent police work. In Jones v. United States, 362 U.S., at 269, we held that an affidavit relying on hearsay "is not to be deemed insufficient on that score, so long as a substantial basis for crediting the hearsay is presented." We went on to say that even in making a warrantless arrest an officer "may rely upon information received through an informant, rather than upon his direct observations, so long as the informant's statement is reasonably corroborated by other matters within the officer's knowledge." Ibid. Likewise, we recognized the probative value of corroborative efforts of police officials in *Aguilar*—the source of the "two-pronged test"—by observing that if the police had made some effort to corroborate the informant's report at issue, "an entirely different case" would have been presented. *Aguilar*, 378 U.S., at 109, n. 1.

Our decision in Draper v. United States, 358 U.S. 307 (1959), however, is the classic case on the value of corroborative efforts of police officials. There, an informant named Hereford reported that Draper would arrive in Denver on a train from Chicago on one of two days, and that he would be carrying a quantity of heroin. The informant also supplied a fairly detailed physical description of Draper, and predicted that he would be wearing a light colored raincoat, brown slacks and black shoes, and would be walking "real fast." Id. at 309. Hereford gave no indication of the basis for his information.

On one of the stated dates police officers observed a man matching this description exit a train arriving from Chicago; his attire and luggage matched Hereford's report and he was walking rapidly. We explained in *Draper* that, by this point in his investigation, the arresting officer "had personally verified every facet of the information given him by Hereford except whether petitioner had accomplished his mission and had the three ounces of heroin on his person or in his bag. And surely, with every other bit of Hereford's information being thus personally verified, [the officer] had 'reasonable grounds' to believe that the remaining unverified bit of Hereford's information—that Draper would have the heroin with him—was likewise true," id., at 313.

The showing of probable cause in the present case was fully as compelling as that in *Draper*. Even standing alone, the facts obtained through the independent investigation of Mader and the DEA at least suggested that the Gateses were involved in drug trafficking. In addition to being a popular vacation site, Florida is well-known as a source of narcotics and other illegal drugs. ... Lance Gates' flight to Palm Beach, his brief, overnight stay in a motel, and apparent immediate return north to Chicago in the family car, conveniently awaiting him in West Palm Beach, is as suggestive of a prearranged drug run, as it is of an ordinary vacation trip.

In addition, the magistrate could rely on the anonymous letter, which had been corroborated in major part by Mader's efforts—just as had occurred in *Draper*.[13] The Supreme Court of Illinois reasoned that *Draper* involved an informant who had given reliable

13. The Illinois Supreme Court thought that the verification of details contained in the anonymous letter in this case amounted only to "[t]he corroboration of innocent activity," 85 Ill.2d 376, 390, 423 N.E.2d 887, 893 (1981), and that this was insufficient to support a finding of probable cause. We are inclined to agree, however, with the observation of Justice Moran in his dissenting opinion that "[i]n this case, just as in *Draper*, seemingly innocent activity became suspicious in light of the initial tip." Id., at 396, 423 N.E.2d, at 896. And it bears noting that *all* of the corroborating detail established in *Draper*, supra, was of entirely innocent activity—a fact later pointed out by the Court ....

This is perfectly reasonable. As discussed previously, probable cause requires only a probability or substantial chance of criminal activity, not an actual showing of such activity. By hypothesis, therefore, innocent behavior frequently will provide the basis for a showing of probable cause; to require otherwise would be to *sub silentio* impose a drastically more rigorous definition of probable cause than the security of our citizens demands. We think the Illinois court attempted a too rigid classification of the types of conduct that may be relied upon in seeking to demonstrate probable cause. ... In making a determination of probable cause the relevant inquiry is not whether particular conduct is "innocent" or "guilty," but the degree of suspicion that attaches to particular types of noncriminal acts.

information on previous occasions, while the honesty and reliability of the anonymous informant in this case were unknown to the Bloomingdale police. While this distinction might be an apt one at the time the Police Department received the anonymous letter, it became far less significant after Mader's independent investigative work occurred. The corroboration of the letter's predictions that the Gateses' car would be in Florida, that Lance Gates would fly to Florida in the next day or so, and that he would drive the car north toward Bloomingdale all indicated, albeit not with certainty, that the informant's other assertions also were true. "[B]ecause an informant is right about some things, he is more probably right about other facts," *Spinelli*, 393 U.S., at 427 (White, J., concurring)—including the claim regarding the Gateses' illegal activity. This may well not be the type of "reliability" or "veracity" necessary to satisfy some views of the "veracity prong" of *Spinelli*, but we think it suffices for the practical, common-sense judgment called for in making a probable-cause determination. It is enough, for purposes of assessing probable cause, that "[c]orroboration through other sources of information reduced the chances of a reckless or prevaricating tale," thus providing "a substantial basis for crediting the hearsay." Jones v. United States, 362 U.S., at 269, 271.

Finally, the anonymous letter contained a range of details relating not just to easily obtained facts and conditions existing at the time of the tip, but to future actions of third parties ordinarily not easily predicted. The letterwriter's accurate information as to the travel plans of each of the Gateses was of a character likely obtained only from the Gateses themselves, or from someone familiar with their not entirely ordinary travel plans. If the informant had access to accurate information of this type a magistrate could properly conclude that it was not unlikely that he also had access to reliable information of the Gateses' alleged illegal activities. Of course, the Gateses' travel plans might have been learned from a talkative neighbor or travel agent; under the "two-pronged test" developed from *Spinelli,* the character of the details in the anonymous letter might well not permit a sufficiently clear inference regarding the letterwriter's "basis of knowledge." But, as discussed previously, supra, at 235, probable cause does not demand the certainty we associate with formal trials. It is enough that there was a fair probability that the writer of the anonymous letter had obtained his entire story either from the Gateses or someone they trusted. And corroboration of major portions of the letter's predictions provides just this probability. It is apparent, therefore, that the judge issuing the warrant had a "substantial basis for ... conclud[ing]" that probable cause to search the Gateses' home and

car existed.   The judgment of the Supreme Court of Illinois therefore must be reversed.[*]

[*] Justice White wrote an opinion concurring in the judgment.   Justice Brennan wrote
a dissenting opinion, which Justice Marshall
joined.   Justice Stevens wrote a dissenting
opinion, which Justice Brennan joined.

WILSON v. ARKANSAS

___ U.S. ___, 115 S.Ct. 1914, ___ L.Ed.2d ___ (1995).

JUSTICE THOMAS delivered the opinion of the Court.

At the time of the framing, the common law of search and seizure recognized a law enforcement officer's authority to break open the doors of a dwelling, but generally indicated that he first ought to announce his presence and authority. In this case, we hold that this common-law "knock and announce" principle forms a part of the reasonableness inquiry under the Fourth Amendment.

I

During November and December 1992, petitioner Sharlene Wilson made a series of narcotics sales to an informant acting at the direction of the Arkansas State Police. In late November, the informant purchased marijuana and methamphetamine at the home that petitioner shared with Bryson Jacobs. On December 30, the informant telephoned petitioner at her home and arranged to meet her at a local store to buy some marijuana. According to testimony presented below, petitioner produced a semiautomatic pistol at this meeting and waved it in the informant's face, threatening to kill her if she turned out to be working for the police. Petitioner then sold the informant a bag of marijuana.

The next day, police officers applied for and obtained warrants to search petitioner's home and to arrest both petitioner and Jacobs. Affidavits filed in support of the warrants set forth the details of the narcotics transactions and stated that Jacobs had previously been convicted of arson and firebombing. The search was conducted later that afternoon. Police officers found the main door to petitioner's home open. While opening an unlocked screen door and entering the residence, they identified themselves as police officers and stated that they had a warrant. Once inside the home, the officers seized marijuana, methamphetamine, valium, narcotics paraphernalia, a gun, and ammunition. They also found petitioner in the bathroom, flushing marijuana down the toilet. Petitioner and Jacobs were arrested and charged with delivery of marijuana, delivery of methamphetamine, possession of drug paraphernalia, and possession of marijuana.

Before trial, petitioner filed a motion to suppress the evidence seized during the search. Petitioner asserted that the search was invalid on various grounds, including that the officers had failed to "knock and announce" before entering her home. The trial court summarily denied the suppression motion. After a jury trial, petitioner was convicted of all charges and sentenced to 32 years in prison.

The Arkansas Supreme Court affirmed petitioner's conviction on appeal. 317 Ark. 548, 878 S.W.2d 755 (1994). The court noted that "the officers entered the home *while they were identifying themselves,*" but it rejected petitioner's argument that "the Fourth Amendment requires officers to knock and announce prior to entering the residence." *Id.,* at 553, 878 S.W.2d, at 758 (emphasis added). Finding "no authority for [petitioner's] theory that the knock and announce principle is required by the Fourth Amendment," the court concluded that neither Arkansas law nor the Fourth Amendment required suppression of the evidence. Ibid.

We granted certiorari to resolve the conflict among the lower courts as to whether the common-law knock-and-announce principle forms a part of the Fourth Amendment reasonableness inquiry. 513 U.S. ___ (1995). We hold that it does, and accordingly reverse and remand.

II

The Fourth Amendment to the Constitution protects "[t]he right of the people to be secure in their persons, houses, papers, and effects, against unreasonable searches and seizures." In evaluating the scope of this right, we have looked to the traditional protections against unreasonable searches and seizures afforded by the common law at the time of the framing.... "Although the underlying command of the Fourth Amendment is always that searches and seizures be reasonable," New Jersey v. T.L.O., 469 U.S. 325, 337 (1985), our effort to give content to this term may be guided by the meaning ascribed to it by the Framers of the Amendment. An examination of the common law of search and seizure leaves no doubt that the reasonableness of a search of a dwelling may depend in part on whether law enforcement officers announced their presence and authority prior to entering.

Although the common law generally protected a man's house as "his castle of defence and asylum," 3 W. Blackstone, Commentaries * 288 (hereinafter Blackstone), common-law courts long have held that "when the King is party, the sheriff (if the doors be not open) may break the party's house, either to arrest him, or to do other execution of the K[ing]'s process, if otherwise he cannot enter." Semayne's Case, 5 Co.Rep. 91a, 91b, 77 Eng.Rep. 194, 195 (K.B. 1603). To this rule, however, common-law courts appended an important qualification:

> "But before he breaks it, he ought to signify the cause of his coming, and to make request to open doors ..., for the law without a default in the owner abhors the destruction or breaking of any house (which is for the habitation and safety of man) by which great damage and inconvenience might ensue to

the party, when no default is in him; for perhaps he did not know of the process, of which, if he had notice, it is to be presumed that he would obey it. . . ."   Ibid., 77 Eng.Rep., at 195–196.

. . .

Several prominent founding-era commentators agreed on this basic principle. According to Sir Matthew Hale, the "constant practice" at common law was that "the officer may break open the door, if he be sure the offender is there, if after acquainting them of the business, and demanding the prisoner, he refuses to open the door." See 1 M. Hale, Pleas of the Crown * 582. William Hawkins propounded a similar principle: "the law doth never allow" an officer to break open the door of a dwelling "but in cases of necessity," that is, unless he "first signify to those in the house the cause of his coming, and request them to give him admittance." 2 W. Hawkins, Pleas of the Crown, ch. 14, § 1, p. 138 (6th ed. 1787). Sir William Blackstone stated simply that the sheriff may "justify breaking open doors, if the possession be not quietly delivered." 3 Blackstone * 412.

The common-law knock-and-announce principle was woven quickly into the fabric of early American law. Most of the States that ratified the Fourth Amendment had enacted constitutional provisions or statutes generally incorporating English common law . . . and a few States had enacted statutes specifically embracing the common-law view that the breaking of the door of a dwelling was permitted once admittance was refused. . . . Early American courts similarly embraced the common-law knock-and-announce principle. . . .

Our own cases have acknowledged that the common-law principle of announcement is "embedded in Anglo–American law," Miller v. United States, 357 U.S. 301, 313 (1958), but we have never squarely held that this principle is an element of the reasonableness inquiry under the Fourth Amendment. We now so hold. Given the longstanding common-law endorsement of the practice of announcement, we have little doubt that the Framers of the Fourth Amendment thought that the method of an officer's entry into a dwelling was among the factors to be considered in assessing the reasonableness of a search or seizure. Contrary to the decision below, we hold that in some circumstances an officer's unannounced entry into a home might be unreasonable under the Fourth Amendment.

This is not to say, of course, that every entry must be preceded by an announcement. The Fourth Amendment's flexible requirement of reasonableness should not be read to mandate a rigid rule of announcement that ignores countervailing law enforcement interests. As even petitioner concedes, the common-law principle of announcement was never stated as an inflexible rule requiring announcement under all circumstances. . . .

Indeed, at the time of the framing, the common-law admonition that an officer "ought to signify the cause of his coming," Semayne's Case, 5 Co.Rep., at 91b, 77 Eng.Rep., at 195, had not been extended conclusively to the context of felony arrests. . . . The common-law principle gradually was applied to cases involving felonies, but at the same time the courts continued to recognize that under certain circumstances the presumption in favor of announcement necessarily would give way to contrary considerations.

Thus, because the common-law rule was justified in part by the belief that announcement generally would avoid "the destruction or breaking of any house . . . by which great damage and inconvenience might ensue," Semayne's Case, supra, at 91b, 77 Eng.Rep., at 196, courts acknowledged that the presumption in favor of announcement would yield under circumstances presenting a threat of physical violence. . . . Similarly, courts held that an officer may dispense with announcement in cases where a prisoner escapes from him and retreats to his dwelling. . . . Proof of "demand and refusal" was deemed unnecessary in such cases because it would be a "senseless ceremony" to require an officer in pursuit of a recently escaped arrestee to make an announcement prior to breaking the door to retake him. . . . Finally, courts have indicated that unannounced entry may be justified where police officers have reason to believe that evidence would likely be destroyed if advance notice were given. . . .

We need not attempt a comprehensive catalog of the relevant countervailing factors here. For now, we leave to the lower courts the task of determining the circumstances under which an unannounced entry is reasonable under the Fourth Amendment. We simply hold that although a search or seizure of a dwelling might be constitutionally defective if police officers enter without prior announcement, law enforcement interests may also establish the reasonableness of an unannounced entry.

III

Respondent contends that the judgment below should be affirmed because the unannounced entry in this case was justified for two reasons. First, respondent argues that police officers reasonably believed that a prior announcement would have placed them in peril, given their knowledge that petitioner had threatened a government informant with a semiautomatic weapon and that Mr. Jacobs had previously been convicted of arson and firebombing. Second, respondent suggests that prior announcement would have produced an unreasonable risk that petitioner would destroy easily disposable narcotics evidence.

These considerations may well provide the necessary justification for the unannounced entry in this case. Because the Arkansas Supreme Court did not address their sufficiency, however, we remand to allow the state courts to make any necessary findings of fact and to make the determination of reasonableness in the first instance. The judgment of the Arkansas Supreme Court is reversed, and the case is remanded for further proceedings not inconsistent with this opinion.

It is so ordered.

CHIMEL v. CALIFORNIA

395 U.S. 752, 89 S.Ct. 2034, 23 L.Ed.2d 685 (1969).

MR. JUSTICE STEWART delivered the opinion of the Court.

This case raises basic questions concerning the permissible scope under the Fourth Amendment of a search incident to a lawful arrest.

The relevant facts are essentially undisputed. Late in the afternoon of September 13, 1965, three police officers arrived at the Santa Ana, California, home of the petitioner with a warrant authorizing his arrest for the burglary of a coin shop. The officers knocked on the door, identified themselves to the petitioner's wife, and asked if they might come inside. She ushered them into the house, where they waited 10 or 15 minutes until the petitioner returned home from work. When the petitioner entered the house, one of the officers handed him the arrest warrant and asked for permission to "look around." The petitioner objected, but was advised that "on the basis of the lawful arrest," the officers would nonetheless conduct a search. No search warrant had been issued.

Accompanied by the petitioner's wife, the officers then looked through the entire three-bedroom house, including the attic, the garage, and a small workshop. In some rooms the search was relatively cursory. In the master bedroom and sewing room, however, the officers directed the petitioner's wife to open drawers and "to physically move contents of the drawers from side to side so that [they] might view any items that would have come from [the] burglary." After completing the search, they seized numerous items—primarily coins, but also several medals, tokens, and a few other objects. The entire search took between 45 minutes and an hour.

At the petitioner's subsequent state trial on two charges of burglary, the items taken from his house were admitted into evidence against him, over his objection that they had been unconstitutionally seized. He was convicted, and the judgments of conviction were affirmed by both the California Court of Appeal, 61 Cal.Rptr. 714, and the California Supreme Court, 68 Cal.2d 436, 439 P.2d 333. Both courts accepted the petitioner's contention that the arrest warrant was invalid because the supporting affidavit was set out in conclusory terms, but held that since the arresting officers had procured the warrant "in good faith," and since in any event they had had sufficient information to constitute probable cause for the petitioner's arrest, that arrest had been lawful. From this conclusion the appellate courts went on to hold that the search of

102

the petitioner's home had been justified, despite the absence of a search warrant, on the ground that it had been incident to a valid arrest. We granted certiorari in order to consider the petitioner's substantial constitutional claims. 393 U.S. 958.

Without deciding the question, we proceed on the hypothesis that the California courts were correct in holding that the arrest of the petitioner was valid under the Constitution. This brings us directly to the question whether the warrantless search of the petitioner's entire house can be constitutionally justified as incident to that arrest. The decisions of this Court bearing upon that question have been far from consistent, as even the most cursory review makes evident.

Approval of a warrantless search incident to a lawful arrest seems first to have been articulated by the Court in 1914 as dictum in Weeks v. United States, 232 U.S. 383, in which the Court stated:

> "What then is the present case? Before answering that inquiry specifically, it may be well by a process of exclusion to state what it is not. It is not an assertion of the right on the part of the Government, always recognized under English and American law, to search the person of the accused when legally arrested to discover and seize the fruits or evidences of crime." Id., at 392.

That statement made no reference to any right to search the *place* where an arrest occurs, but was limited to a right to search the "person." Eleven years later the case of Carroll v. United States, 267 U.S. 132, brought the following embellishment of the *Weeks* statement:

> "When a man is legally arrested for an offense, whatever is found upon his person *or in his control* which it is unlawful for him to have and which may be used to prove the offense may be seized and held as evidence in the prosecution." Id., at 158. (Emphasis added.)

Still, that assertion too was far from a claim that the "place" where one is arrested may be searched so long as the arrest is valid. Without explanation, however, the principle emerged in expanded form a few months later in Agnello v. United States, 269 U.S. 20—although still by way of dictum:

> "The right without a search warrant contemporaneously to search persons lawfully arrested while committing crime and to search the place where the arrest is made in order to find and seize things connected with the crime as its fruits or as the means by which it was committed, as well as weapons and other things to effect an escape from custody, is not to be doubted. See Carroll v. United States, 267 U.S. 132, 158; Weeks v. United States, 232 U.S. 383, 392." 269 U.S., at 30.

And in Marron v. United States, 275 U.S. 192, two years later, the
dictum of *Agnello* appeared to be the foundation of the Court's
decision. In that case federal agents had secured a search warrant
authorizing the seizure of liquor and certain articles used in its
manufacture. When they arrived at the premises to be searched,
they saw "that the place was used for retailing and drinking
intoxicating liquors." Id., at 194. They proceeded to arrest the
person in charge and to execute the warrant. In searching a closet
for the items listed in the warrant they came across an incriminating
ledger, concededly not covered by the warrant, which they also
seized. The Court upheld the seizure of the ledger by holding that
since the agents had made a lawful arrest, "[t]hey had a right
without a warrant contemporaneously to search the place in order
to find and seize the things used to carry on the criminal enterprise." Id., at 199.

That the *Marron* opinion did not mean all that it seemed to say
became evident, however, a few years later in Go-Bart Importing Co.
v. United States, 282 U.S. 344, and United States v. Lefkowitz, 285
U.S. 452. In each of those cases the opinion of the Court was
written by Mr. Justice Butler, the author of the opinion in *Marron*.
In *Go-Bart*, agents had searched the office of persons whom they
had lawfully arrested, and had taken several papers from a desk, a
safe, and other parts of the office. The Court noted that no crime
had been committed in the agents' presence, and that although the
agent in charge "had an abundance of information and time to
swear out a valid [search] warrant, he failed to do so." 282 U.S., at
358. In holding the search and seizure unlawful, the Court stated:

> "Plainly the case before us is essentially different from
> Marron v. United States, 275 U.S. 192. There, officers execut-
> ing a valid search warrant for intoxicating liquors found and
> arrested one Birdsall who in pursuance of a conspiracy was
> actually engaged in running a saloon. As an incident to the
> arrest they seized a ledger in a closet where the liquor or some
> of it was kept and some bills beside the cash register. These
> things were visible and accessible and in the offender's immedi-
> ate custody. There was no threat or force or general search or
> rummaging of the place." 282 U.S., at 358.

This limited characterization of *Marron* was reiterated in *Lefkowitz*,
a case in which the Court held unlawful a search of desk drawers
and a cabinet despite the fact that the search had accompanied a
lawful arrest. 285 U.S., at 465.

The limiting views expressed in *Go-Bart* and *Lefkowitz* were
thrown to the winds, however, in Harris v. United States, 331 U.S.
145, decided in 1947. In that case, officers had obtained a warrant
for Harris' arrest on the basis of his alleged involvement with the
cashing and interstate transportation of a forged check. He was
arrested in the living room of his four-room apartment, and in an

attempt to recover two canceled checks thought to have been used in effecting the forgery, the officers undertook a thorough search of the entire apartment. Inside a desk drawer they found a sealed envelope, marked "George Harris, personal papers." The envelope, which was then torn open, was found to contain altered Selective Service documents, and those documents were used to secure Harris' conviction for violating the Selective Training and Service Act of 1940. The Court rejected Harris' Fourth Amendment claim, sustaining the search as "incident to arrest." Id., at 151.

Only a year after *Harris,* however, the pendulum swung again. In Trupiano v. United States, 334 U.S. 699, agents raided the site of an illicit distillery, saw one of several conspirators operating the still, and arrested him, contemporaneously "seiz[ing] the illicit distillery." Id., at 702. The Court held that the arrest and others made subsequently had been valid, but that the unexplained failure of the agents to procure a search warrant—in spite of the fact that they had had more than enough time before the raid to do so—rendered the search unlawful. The opinion stated:

> "It is a cardinal rule that, in seizing goods and articles, law enforcement agents must secure and use search warrants wherever reasonably practicable. ... This rule rests upon the desirability of having magistrates rather than police officers determine when searches and seizures are permissible and what limitations should be placed upon such activities. ... To provide the necessary security against unreasonable intrusions upon the private lives of individuals, the framers of the Fourth Amendment required adherence to judicial processes wherever possible. And subsequent history has confirmed the wisdom of that requirement.

> "A search or seizure without a warrant as an incident to a lawful arrest has always been considered to be a strictly limited right. It grows out of the inherent necessities of the situation at the time of the arrest. But there must be something more in the way of necessity than merely a lawful arrest." Id., at 705, 708.

In 1950, two years after *Trupiano,* came United States v. Rabinowitz, 339 U.S. 56, the decision upon which California primarily relies in the case now before us. In *Rabinowitz,* federal authorities had been informed that the defendant was dealing in stamps bearing forged overprints. On the basis of that information they secured a warrant for his arrest, which they executed at his one-room business office. At the time of the arrest, the officers "searched the desk, safe, and file cabinets in the office for about an hour and a half," id., at 59, and seized 573 stamps with forged overprints. The stamps were admitted into evidence at the defendant's trial, and this Court affirmed his conviction, rejecting the contention that the warrantless search had been unlawful. The Court held that the search in its entirety fell within the principle giving law enforcement authorities "[t]he right 'to search the place where the arrest is made in order to find and seize things connected with the crime ....'" Id., at 61. *Harris* was regarded as "ample authority" for that conclusion. Id., at 63. The opinion rejected the rule of *Trupiano* that "in seizing goods and articles, law enforcement agents must secure and use search warrants wherever reasonably practicable." The test, said the Court, "is not whether it is reasonable to procure a search warrant, but whether the search was reasonable." Id., at 66.

Rabinowitz has come to stand for the proposition, *inter alia,* that a warrantless search "incident to a lawful arrest" may generally extend to the area that is considered to be in the "possession" or under the "control" of the person arrested. And it was on the basis of that proposition that the California courts upheld the search of the petitioner's entire house in this case. That doctrine, however, at least in the broad sense in which it was applied by the California courts in this case, can withstand neither historical nor rational analysis.

Even limited to its own facts, the *Rabinowitz* decision was, as we have seen, hardly founded on an unimpeachable line of authority. As Mr. Justice Frankfurter commented in dissent in that case, the "hint" contained in *Weeks* was, without persuasive justification, "loosely turned into dictum and finally elevated to a decision." 339 U.S., at 75. And the approach taken in cases such as *Go-Bart, Lefkowitz,* and *Trupiano* was essentially disregarded by the *Rabinowitz* Court.

Nor is the rationale by which the State seeks here to sustain the search of the petitioner's house supported by a reasoned view of the background and purpose of the Fourth Amendment. Mr. Justice Frankfurter wisely pointed out in his *Rabinowitz* dissent that the Amendment's proscription of "unreasonable searches and seizures" must be read in light of "the history that gave rise to the words"—a history of "abuses so deeply felt by the Colonies as to be one of the potent causes of the Revolution ...." 339 U.S., at 69. The Amendment was in large part a reaction to the general warrants and warrantless searches that had so alienated the colonists and had helped speed the movement for independence. In the scheme of the Amendment, therefore, the requirement that "no Warrants shall issue, but upon probable cause," plays a crucial part. As the Court put it in McDonald v. United States, 335 U.S. 451:

> "We are not dealing with formalities. The presence of a search warrant serves a high function. Absent some grave emergency, the Fourth Amendment has interposed a magistrate between the citizen and the police. This was done not to

shield criminals nor to make the home a safe haven for illegal activities. It was done so that an objective mind might weigh the need to invade that privacy in order to enforce the law. The right of privacy was deemed too precious to entrust to the discretion of those whose job is the detection of crime and the arrest of criminals. . . . And so the Constitution requires a magistrate to pass on the desires of the police before they violate the privacy of the home. We cannot be true to that constitutional requirement and excuse the absence of a search warrant without a showing by those who seek exemption from the constitutional mandate that the exigencies of the situation made that course imperative.'' Id., at 455–456.

Even in the *Agnello* case the Court relied upon the rule that "[b]elief, however well founded, that an article sought is concealed in a dwelling house furnishes no justification for a search of that place without a warrant. And such searches are held unlawful notwithstanding facts unquestionably showing probable cause." 269 U.S., at 33. Clearly, the general requirement that a search warrant be obtained is not lightly to be dispensed with, and "the burden is on those seeking [an] exemption [from the requirement] to show the need for it . . . ." United States v. Jeffers, 342 U.S. 48, 51.

Only last Term in Terry v. Ohio, 392 U.S. 1, we emphasized that "the police must, whenever practicable, obtain advance judicial approval of searches and seizures through the warrant procedure," id., at 20, and that "[t]he scope of [a] search must be 'strictly tied to and justified by' the circumstances which rendered its initiation permissible." Id., at 19. The search undertaken by the officer in that "stop and frisk" case was sustained under that test, because it was no more than a "protective . . . search for weapons." Id., at 29. But in a companion case, Sibron v. New York, 392 U.S. 40, we applied the same standard to another set of facts and reached a contrary result, holding that a policeman's action in thrusting his hand into a suspect's pocket had been neither motivated by nor limited to the objective of protection. Rather, the search had been made in order to find narcotics, which were in fact found.

A similar analysis underlies the "search incident to arrest" principle, and marks its proper extent. When an arrest is made, it is reasonable for the arresting officer to search the person arrested in order to remove any weapons that the latter might seek to use in order to resist arrest or effect his escape. Otherwise, the officer's safety might well be endangered, and the arrest itself frustrated. In addition, it is entirely reasonable for the arresting officer to search for and seize any evidence on the arrestee's person in order to prevent its concealment or destruction. And the area into which an arrestee might reach in order to grab a weapon or evidentiary items must, of course, be governed by a like rule. A gun on a table or in a drawer in front of one who is arrested can be as dangerous to the arresting officer as one concealed in the clothing of the person arrested. There is ample justification, therefore, for a search of the arrestee's person and the area "within his immediate control"— construing that phrase to mean the area from within which he might gain possession of a weapon or destructible evidence.

There is no comparable justification, however, for routinely searching any room other than that in which an arrest occurs—or, for that matter, for searching through all the desk drawers or other closed or concealed areas in that room itself. Such searches, in the absence of well-recognized exceptions, may be made only under the authority of a search warrant. The "adherence to judicial processes" mandated by the Fourth Amendment requires no less.

This is the principle that underlay our decision in Preston v. United States, 376 U.S. 364. In that case three men had been arrested in a parked car, which had later been towed to a garage and searched by police. We held the search to have been unlawful under the Fourth Amendment, despite the contention that it had been incidental to a valid arrest. Our reasoning was straightforward:

> "The rule allowing contemporaneous searches is justified, for example, by the need to seize weapons and other things which might be used to assault an officer or effect an escape, as well as by the need to prevent the destruction of evidence of the crime—things which might easily happen where the weapon or evidence is on the accused's person or under his immediate control. But these justifications are absent where a search is remote in time or place from the arrest." Id., at 367.[9]

The same basic principle was reflected in our opinion last Term in *Sibron.* That opinion dealt with Peters v. New York, No. 74, as well as with Sibron's case, and *Peters* involved a search that we upheld as incident to a proper arrest. We sustained the search, however, only because its scope had been "reasonably limited" by the "need to seize weapons" and "to prevent the destruction of evidence," to which *Preston* had referred. We emphasized that the arresting officer "did not engage in an unrestrained and thoroughgoing examination of Peters and his personal effects. He seized him to cut short his flight, and he searched him primarily for weapons." 392 U.S., at 67.

It is argued in the present case that it is "reasonable" to search a man's house when he is arrested in it. But that argument is founded on little more than a subjective view regarding the acceptability of certain sorts of police conduct, and not on considerations

9. Our holding today is of course entirely consistent with the recognized principle that, assuming the existence of probable cause, automobiles and other vehicles may be searched without warrants "where it is not practicable to secure a warrant because the vehicle can be quickly moved out of the locality or jurisdiction in which the warrant must be sought." Carroll v. United States, 267 U.S. 132, 153: see Brinegar v. United States, 338 U.S. 160.

relevant to Fourth Amendment interests. Under such an uncon-
fined analysis, Fourth Amendment protection in this area would
approach the evaporation point. It is not easy to explain why, for
instance, it is less subjectively "reasonable" to search a man's house
when he is arrested on his front lawn—or just down the street—
than it is when he happens to be in the house at the time of arrest.
As Mr. Justice Frankfurter put it:

> "To say that the search must be reasonable is to require some
> criterion of reason. It is no guide at all either for a jury or for
> district judges or the police to say that an 'unreasonable search'
> is forbidden—that the search must be reasonable. What is the
> test of reason which makes a search reasonable?

> The test is the reason underlying and expressed by the Fourth
> Amendment: the history and the experience which it embodies
> and the safeguards afforded by it against the evils to which it
> was a response." United States v. Rabinowitz, 339 U.S., at 83
> (dissenting opinion).

Thus, although "[t]he recurring questions of the reasonableness of
searches" depend upon "the facts and circumstances—the total
atmosphere of the case," id., at 63, 66 (opinion of the Court), those
facts and circumstances must be viewed in the light of established
Fourth Amendment principles.

It would be possible, of course, to draw a line between
Rabinowitz and *Harris* on the one hand, and this case on the other.
For *Rabinowitz* involved a single room, and *Harris* a four-room
apartment, while in the case before us an entire house was
searched. But such a distinction would be highly artificial. The
rationale that allowed the searches and seizures in *Rabinowitz* and
Harris would allow the searches and seizures in this case. No
consideration relevant to the Fourth Amendment suggests any point
of rational limitation, once the search is allowed to go beyond the
area from which the person arrested might obtain weapons or
evidentiary items. The only reasoned distinction is one between a
search of the person arrested and the area within his reach on the
one hand, and more extensive searches on the other.[12]

---

12. It is argued in dissent that so long as
there is probable cause to search the place
where an arrest occurs, a search of that place
should be permitted even though no search
warrant has been obtained. This position
seems to be based principally on two premises: first, that once an arrest has been made,
the additional invasion of privacy stemming
from the accompanying search is "relatively
minor"; and second, that the victim of the
search may "shortly thereafter" obtain a judicial determination of whether the search was
justified by probable cause. With respect to
the second premise, one may initially question
whether all of the States in fact provide the
speedy suppression procedures the dissent
assumes. More fundamentally, however, we
cannot accept the view that Fourth Amendment interests are vindicated so long as "the
rights of the criminal" are "protect[ed] . . .
against introduction of evidence seized without probable cause." The Amendment is designed to prevent, not simply to redress, unlawful police action. In any event, we cannot
join in characterizing the invasion of privacy
that results from a top-to-bottom search of a
man's house as "minor." And we can see no
reason why, simply because some interference with an individual's privacy and freedom
of movement has lawfully taken place, further

The petitioner correctly points out that one result of decisions such as *Rabinowitz* and *Harris* is to give law enforcement officials the opportunity to engage in searches not justified by probable cause, by the simple expedient of arranging to arrest suspects at home rather than elsewhere. We do not suggest that the petitioner, is necessarily correct in his assertion that such a strategy was utilized here, but the fact remains that had he been arrested earlier in the day, at his place of employment rather than at home, no search of his house could have been made without a search warrant. In any event, even apart from the possibility of such police tactics, the general point so forcefully made by Judge Learned Hand in United States v. Kirschenblatt, 16 F.2d 202, remains:

> "After arresting a man in his house, to rummage at will among his papers in search of whatever will convict him, appears to us to be indistinguishable from what might be done under a general warrant; indeed, the warrant would give more protection, for presumably it must be issued by a magistrate. True, by hypothesis the power would not exist, if the supposed offender were not found on the premises; but it is small consolation to know that one's papers are safe only so long as one is not at home." Id., at 203.

Rabinowitz and *Harris* have been the subject of critical commentary for many years, and have been relied upon less and less in our own decisions. It is time, for the reasons we have stated, to hold that on their own facts, and insofar as the principles they stand for are inconsistent with those that we have endorsed today, they are no longer to be followed.

Application of sound Fourth Amendment principles to the facts of this case produces a clear result. The search here went far beyond the petitioner's person and the area from within which he might have obtained either a weapon or something that could have been used as evidence against him. There was no constitutional justification, in the absence of a search warrant, for extending the search beyond that area. The scope of the search was, therefore, "unreasonable" under the Fourth and Fourteenth Amendments, and the petitioner's conviction cannot stand.

Reversed.

MR. JUSTICE WHITE, with whom MR. JUSTICE BLACK joins, dissenting.

Few areas of the law have been as subject to shifting constitutional standards over the last 50 years as that of the search "incident to an arrest." There has been a remarkable instability in this whole area, which has seen at least four major shifts in emphasis. Today's

intrusions should automatically be allowed despite the absence of a warrant that the Fourth Amendment would otherwise require.

opinion makes an untimely fifth. In my view, the Court should not now abandon the old rule.

       . . .

II

The rule which has prevailed, but for very brief or doubtful periods of aberration, is that a search incident to an arrest may extend to those areas under the control of the defendant and where items subject to constitutional seizure may be found. The justification for this rule must, under the language of the Fourth Amendment, lie in the reasonableness of the rule. ... The Amendment does not proscribe "warrantless searches" but instead it proscribes "unreasonable searches" and this Court has never held nor does the majority today assert that warrantless searches are necessarily unreasonable.

Applying this reasonableness test to the area of searches incident to arrests, one thing is clear at the outset. Search of an arrested man and of the items within his immediate reach must in almost every case be reasonable. There is always a danger that the suspect will try to escape, seizing concealed weapons with which to overpower and injure the arresting officers, and there is a danger that he may destroy evidence vital to the prosecution. Circumstances in which these justifications would not apply are sufficiently rare that inquiry is not made into searches of this scope, which have been considered reasonable throughout.

The justifications which make such a search reasonable obviously do not apply to the search of areas to which the accused does not have ready physical access. This is not enough, however, to prove such searches unconstitutional. The Court has always held, and does not today deny, that when there is probable cause to search and it is "impracticable" for one reason or another to get a search warrant, then a warrantless search may be reasonable. E.g., even Trupiano v. United States, 334 U.S. 699 (1948). This is the case whether an arrest was made at the time of the search or not.

This is not to say that a search can be reasonable without regard to the probable cause to believe that seizable items are on the premises. But when there are exigent circumstances, and probable cause, then the search may be made without a warrant, reasonably. An arrest itself may often create an emergency situation making it impracticable to obtain a warrant before embarking on a related search. Again assuming that there is probable cause to search premises at the spot where a suspect is arrested, it seems to me unreasonable to require the police to leave the scene in order to obtain a search warrant when they are already legally there to make a valid arrest, and when there must almost always be a strong possibility that confederates of the arrested man will in the meanwhile remove the items for which the police have probable cause to search.   This must so often be the case that it seems to me as unreasonable to require a warrant for a search of the premises as to require a warrant for search of the person and his very immediate surroundings.

This case provides a good illustration of my point that it is unreasonable to require police to leave the scene of an arrest in order to obtain a search warrant when they already have probable cause to search and there is a clear danger that the items for which they may reasonably search will be removed before they return with a warrant.   Petitioner was arrested in his home after an arrest whose validity will be explored below, but which I will now assume was valid.   There was doubtless probable cause not only to arrest petitioner, but also to search his house.   He had obliquely admitted, both to a neighbor and to the owner of the burglarized store, that he had committed the burglary.   In light of this, and the fact that the neighbor had seen other admittedly stolen property in petitioner's house, there was surely probable cause on which a warrant could have issued to search the house for the stolen coins. Moreover, had the police simply arrested petitioner, taken him off to the station house, and later returned with a warrant,[5] it seems very likely that petitioner's wife, who in view of petitioner's generally garrulous nature must have known of the robbery, would have removed the coins.   For the police to search the house while the evidence they had probable cause to search out and seize was still there cannot be considered unreasonable.

III

This line of analysis, supported by the precedents of this Court, hinges on two assumptions.   One is that the arrest of petitioner without a valid warrant was constitutional as the majority assumes; the other is that the police were not required to obtain a search warrant in advance, even though they knew that the effect of the arrest might well be to alert petitioner's wife that the coins had better be removed soon.   Thus it is necessary to examine the constitutionality of the arrest since if it was illegal, the exigent circumstances which it created may not, as the consequences of a lawless act, be used to justify the contemporaneous warrantless search.   But for the arrest, the warrantless search may not be justified.   And if circumstances can justify the warrantless arrest, it would be strange to say that the Fourth Amendment bars the warrantless search, regardless of the circumstances, since the inva-

---

5. There were three officers at the scene of the arrest, one from the city where the coin burglary had occurred, and two from the city where the arrest was made. Assuming that one policeman from each city would be needed to bring the petitioner in and obtain a search warrant, one policeman could have been left to guard the house. However, if he not only could have remained in the house against petitioner's wife's will, but followed her about to assure that no evidence was being tampered with, the invasion of her privacy would be almost as great as that accompanying an actual search. Moreover, had the wife summoned an accomplice, one officer could not have watched them both.

sion and disruption of a man's life and privacy which stem from his arrest are ordinarily far greater than the relatively minor intrusions attending a search of his premises.

Congress has expressly authorized a wide range of officials to make arrests without any warrant in criminal cases. United States Marshals have long had this power, which is also vested in the agents of the Federal Bureau of Investigation, and in the Secret Service and the narcotics law enforcement agency. That warrantless arrest power may apply even when there is time to get a warrant without fear that the suspect may escape is made perfectly clear by the legislative history of the statute granting arrest power to the FBI.

. . .

The judgment of Congress is that federal law enforcement officers may reasonably make warrantless arrests upon probable cause, and no judicial experience suggests that this judgment is infirm. Indeed, past cases suggest precisely the contrary conclusion. . . .

In light of the uniformity of judgment of the Congress, past judicial decisions, and common practice rejecting the proposition that arrest warrants are essential wherever it is practicable to get them, the conclusion is inevitable that such arrests and accompanying searches are reasonable, at least until experience teaches the contrary. It must very often be the case that by the time probable cause to arrest a man is accumulated, the man is aware of police interest in him or for other good reasons is on the verge of flight. Moreover, it will likely be very difficult to determine the probability of his flight. Given this situation, it may be best in all cases simply to allow the arrest if there is probable cause, especially since that issue can be determined very shortly after the arrest.

Nor are the stated assumptions at all fanciful. It was precisely these facts which moved the Congress to grant to the FBI the power to arrest without a warrant without any showing of probability of flight. . . . Some weight should be accorded this factual judgment by law enforcement officials, adopted by the Congress.

IV

If circumstances so often require the warrantless arrest that the law generally permits it, the typical situation will find the arresting officers lawfully on the premises without arrest or search warrant. Like the majority, I would permit the police to search the person of a suspect and the area under his immediate control either to assure the safety of the officers or to prevent the destruction of evidence. And like the majority, I see nothing in the arrest alone furnishing probable cause for a search of any broader scope. However, where as here the existence of probable cause is independently established and would justify a warrant for a broader search for evidence, I would follow past cases and permit such a search to be carried out without a warrant, since the fact of arrest supplies an exigent circumstance justifying police action before the evidence can be removed, and also alerts the suspect to the fact of the search so that he can immediately seek judicial determination of probable cause in an adversary proceeding, and appropriate redress.

This view, consistent with past cases, would not authorize the general search against which the Fourth Amendment was meant to guard, nor would it broaden or render uncertain in any way whatsoever the scope of searches permitted under the Fourth Amendment. The issue in this case is not the breadth of the search, since there was clearly probable cause for the search which was carried out. No broader search than if the officers had a warrant would be permitted. The only issue is whether a search warrant was required as a precondition to that search. It is agreed that such a warrant would be required absent exigent circumstances. I would hold that the fact of arrest supplies such an exigent circumstance, since the police had lawfully gained entry to the premises to effect the arrest and since delaying the search to secure a warrant would have involved the risk of not recovering the fruits of the crime.

The majority today proscribes searches for which there is probable cause and which may prove fruitless unless carried out immediately. This rule will have no added effect whatsoever in protecting the rights of the criminal accused at trial against intro- duction of evidence seized without probable cause. Such evidence could not be introduced under the old rule. Nor does the majority today give any added protection to the right of privacy of those whose houses there is probable cause to search. A warrant would still be sworn out for those houses, and the privacy of their owners invaded. The only possible justification for the majority's rule is that in some instances arresting officers may search when they have no probable cause to do so and that such unlawful searches might be prevented if the officers first sought a warrant from a magistrate. Against the possible protection of privacy in that class of cases, in which the privacy of the house has already been invaded by entry to make the arrest—an entry for which the majority does not assert that any warrant is necessary—must be weighed the risk of destruc- tion of evidence for which there is probable cause to search, as a result of delays in obtaining a search warrant. Without more basis for radical change than the Court's opinion reveals, I would not upset the balance of these interests which has been struck by the former decisions of this Court.

In considering searches incident to arrest, it must be remem- bered that there will be immediate opportunity to challenge the probable cause for the search in an adversary proceeding. The suspect has been apprised of the search by his very presence at the scene, and having been arrested, he will soon be brought into contact with people who can explain his rights. As Mr. Justice Brennan noted in a dissenting opinion, joined by The Chief Justice and Justices Black and Douglas, in Abel v. United States, 362 U.S. 217, 249–250 (1960), a search contemporaneous with a warrantless arrest is specially safeguarded since "[s]uch an arrest may constitutionally be made only upon probable cause, the existence of which is subject to judicial examination, see Henry v. United States, 361 U.S. 98, 100; and such an arrest demands the prompt bringing of the person arrested before a judicial officer, where the existence of probable cause is to be inquired into. Fed.Rules Crim.Proc. 5(a) and (c). ... Mallory v. United States, 354 U.S. 449; McNabb v. United States, 318 U.S. 332." And since that time the Court has imposed on state and federal officers alike the duty to warn suspects taken into custody, before questioning them, of their right to a lawyer. Miranda v. Arizona, 384 U.S. 436 (1966); Orozco v. Texas, 394 U.S. 324 (1969).

An arrested man, by definition conscious of the police interest in him, and provided almost immediately with a lawyer and a judge, is in an excellent position to dispute the reasonableness of his arrest and contemporaneous search in a full adversary proceeding. I would uphold the constitutionality of this search contemporaneous with an arrest since there were probable cause both for the search and for the arrest, exigent circumstances involving the removal or destruction of evidence, and satisfactory opportunity to dispute the issues of probable cause shortly thereafter. In this case, the search was reasonable.[*] [**]

[*] Justice Harlan wrote a concurring opinion.

[**] See the reference to New York v. Belton, 453 U.S. 454 (1981), in the note following Chambers v. Maroney, below.

MARYLAND v. BUIE

494 U.S. 325, 110 S.Ct. 1093, 108 L.Ed.2d 276 (1990).

JUSTICE WHITE delivered the opinion of the Court.

A "protective sweep" is a quick and limited search of a premises, incident to an arrest and conducted to protect the safety of police officers or others. It is narrowly confined to a cursory visual inspection of those places in which a person might be hiding. In this case we must decide what level of justification is required by the Fourth and Fourteenth Amendments before police officers, while effecting the arrest of a suspect in his home pursuant to an arrest warrant, may conduct a warrantless protective sweep of all or part of the premises. The Court of Appeals of Maryland held that a running suit seized in plain view during such a protective sweep should have been suppressed at respondent's armed robbery trial because the officer who conducted the sweep did not have probable cause to believe that a serious and demonstrable potentiality for danger existed. 314 Md. 151, 166, 550 A.2d 79, 86 (1988). We conclude that the Fourth Amendment would permit the protective sweep undertaken here if the searching officer "possesse[d] a reasonable belief based on 'specific and articulable facts which, taken together with the rational inferences from those facts, reasonably warrant[ed]' the officer in believing," Michigan v. Long, 463 U.S. 1032, 1049–1050 (1983) (quoting Terry v. Ohio, 392 U.S. 1, 21 (1968)), that the area swept harbored an individual posing a danger to the officer or others. We accordingly vacate the judgment below and remand for application of this standard.

I

On February 3, 1986, two men committed an armed robbery of a Godfather's Pizza restaurant in Prince George's County, Maryland. One of the robbers was wearing a red running suit. That same day, Prince George's County police obtained arrest warrants for respondent Jerome Edward Buie and his suspected accomplice in the robbery, Lloyd Allen. Buie's house was placed under police surveillance.

On February 5, the police executed the arrest warrant for Buie. They first had a police department secretary telephone Buie's house to verify that he was home. The secretary spoke to a female first, then to Buie himself. Six or seven officers proceeded to Buie's house. Once inside, the officers fanned out through the first and second floors. Corporal James Rozar announced that he would "freeze" the basement so that no one could come up and surprise the officers. With his service revolver drawn, Rozar twice shouted into the basement, ordering anyone down there to come out. When a voice asked who was calling, Rozar announced three times: "this is the police, show me your hands." App. 5. Eventually, a pair of hands appeared around the bottom of the stairwell and Buie emerged from the basement. He was arrested, searched, and handcuffed by Rozar. Thereafter, Detective Joseph Frolich entered the basement "in case there was someone else" down there. Id., at 14. He noticed a red running suit lying in plain view on a stack of clothing and seized it.

The trial court denied Buie's motion to suppress the running suit, stating in part: "The man comes out from a basement, the police don't know how many other people are down there. He is charged with a serious offense." Id., at 19. The State introduced the running suit into evidence at Buie's trial. A jury convicted Buie of robbery with a deadly weapon and using a handgun in the commission of a felony.

The Court of Special Appeals of Maryland affirmed the trial court's denial of the suppression motion. The court stated that Detective Frolich did not go into the basement to search for evidence, but to look for the suspected accomplice or anyone else who might pose a threat to the officers on the scene. 72 Md.App. 562, 571–572, 531 A.2d 1290, 1295 (1987).

> "Traditionally, the sanctity of a person's home—his castle—requires that the police may not invade it without a warrant except under the most exigent of circumstances. But once the police are lawfully within the home, their conduct is measured by a standard of reasonableness. . . . [I]f there is reason to believe that the arrestee had accomplices who are still at large, something less than probable cause—reasonable suspicion—should be sufficient to justify a *limited additional intrusion* to investigate the *possibility* of their presence." Id., at 575–576, 531 A.2d, at 1297 (emphasis in original).

The Court of Appeals of Maryland reversed by a 4 to 3 vote. 314 Md. 151, 550 A.2d 79 (1988). The court acknowledged that "when the intrusion is slight, as in the case of a brief stop and frisk on a public street, and the public interest in prevention of crime is substantial, reasonable articulable suspicion may be enough to pass constitutional muster," id., at 159, 550 A.2d, at 83. The court, however, stated that when the sanctity of the home is involved, the exceptions to the warrant requirement are few, and held: "[T]o justify a protective sweep of a home, the government must show that there is probable cause to believe that ' "a serious and demonstrable potentiality for danger" ' exists." Id., at 159–160, 550 A.2d, at 83 (citation omitted). The court went on to find that the State had not satisfied that probable-cause requirement. Id., at 165–166, 550 A.2d, at 86. We granted certiorari, 490 U.S. 1097 (1989).

II

It is not disputed that until the point of Buie's arrest the police had the right, based on the authority of the arrest warrant, to search anywhere in the house that Buie might have been found, including the basement. ... There is also no dispute that if Detective Frolich's entry into the basement was lawful, the seizure of the red running suit, which was in plain view and which the officer had probable cause to believe was evidence of a crime, was also lawful under the Fourth Amendment. ... The issue in this case is what level of justification the Fourth Amendment required before Detective Frolich could legally enter the basement to see if someone else was there.

Petitioner, the State of Maryland, argues that, under a general reasonableness balancing test, police should be permitted to conduct a protective sweep whenever they make an in-home arrest for a violent crime. As an alternative to this suggested bright-line rule, the State contends that protective sweeps fall within the ambit of the doctrine announced in Terry v. Ohio, 392 U.S. 1 (1968), and that such sweeps may be conducted in conjunction with a valid in-home arrest whenever the police reasonably suspect a risk of danger to the officers or others at the arrest scene. The United States, as *amicus curiae* supporting the State, also argues for a *Terry*-type standard of reasonable, articulable suspicion of risk to the officer, and contends that that standard is met here. Respondent argues that a protective sweep may not be undertaken without a warrant unless the exigencies of the situation render such warrantless search objectively reasonable. According to Buie, because the State has shown neither exigent circumstances to immediately enter Buie's house nor an unforeseen danger that arose once the officers were in the house, there is no excuse for the failure to obtain a search warrant to search for dangerous persons believed to be on the premises. Buie further contends that, even if the warrant requirement is inapplicable, there is no justification for relaxing the probable-cause standard. If something less than probable cause is sufficient, respondent argues that it is no less than individualized suspicion—specific, articulable facts supporting a reasonable belief that there are persons on the premises who are a threat to the officers. According to Buie, there were no such specific, articulable facts to justify the search of his basement.

III

It goes without saying that the Fourth Amendment bars only unreasonable searches and seizures.... Our cases show that in determining reasonableness, we have balanced the intrusion on the individual's Fourth Amendment interests against its promotion of legitimate governmental interests.... Under this test, a search of the house or office is generally not reasonable without a warrant issued on probable cause. There are other contexts, however,

where the public interest is such that neither a warrant nor probable cause is required. . . .

The *Terry* case is most instructive for present purposes.   There
we held that an on-the-street "frisk" for weapons must be tested by
the Fourth Amendment's general proscription against unreasonable
searches because such a frisk involves "an entire rubric of police
conduct—necessarily swift action predicated upon the on-the-spot
observations of the officer on the beat—which historically has not
been, and as a practical matter could not be, subjected to the
warrant procedure."   *Ibid.*   We stated that there is " 'no ready test
for determining reasonableness other than by balancing the need to
search . . . against the invasion which the search . . . entails.' "   Id.,
at 21 (quoting Camara v. Municipal Court of San Francisco, 387 U.S.
523, 536–537 (1967)).   Applying that balancing test, it was held that
although a frisk for weapons "constitutes a severe, though brief,
intrusion upon cherished personal security," 392 U.S., at 24–25,
such a frisk is reasonable when weighed against the "need for law
enforcement officers to protect themselves and other prospective
victims of violence in situations where they may lack probable cause
for an arrest."   Id., at 24.   We therefore authorized a limited
patdown for weapons where a reasonably prudent officer would be
warranted in the belief, based on "specific and articulable facts," id.,
at 21, and not on a mere "inchoate and unparticularized suspicion
or 'hunch,' " id., at 27, "that he is dealing with an armed and
dangerous individual."   Ibid.

In Michigan v. Long, 463 U.S. 1032 (1983), the principles of
Terry were applied in the context of a roadside encounter: "[T]he
search of the passenger compartment of an automobile, limited to
those areas in which a weapon may be placed or hidden, is
permissible if the police officer possesses a reasonable belief based
on 'specific and articulable facts which, taken together with the
rational inferences from those facts, reasonably warrant' the officer
in believing that the suspect is dangerous and the suspect may gain
immediate control of weapons."   Id., at 1049–1050 (quoting *Terry,*
supra, at 21).   The *Long* Court expressly rejected the contention
that *Terry* restricted preventative searches to the person of a detained suspect.   463 U.S., at 1047.   In a sense, *Long* authorized a
"frisk" of an automobile for weapons.

The ingredients to apply the balance struck in *Terry* and *Long*
are present in this case.   Possessing an arrest warrant and probable
cause to believe Buie was in his home, the officers were entitled to
enter and to search anywhere in the house in which Buie might be
found.   Once he was found, however, the search for him was over,
and there was no longer that particular justification for entering any
rooms that had not yet been searched.

That Buie had an expectation of privacy in those remaining
areas of his house, however, does not mean such rooms were

immune from entry.   In *Terry* and *Long* we were concerned with
the immediate interest of the police officers in taking steps to assure
themselves that the persons with whom they were dealing were not
armed with, or able to gain immediate control of, a weapon that
could unexpectedly and fatally be used against them.   In the instant
case, there is an analogous interest of the officers in taking steps to
assure themselves that the house in which a suspect is being or has
just been arrested is not harboring other persons who are dangerous and who could unexpectedly launch an attack.   The risk of
danger in the context of an arrest in the home is as great as, if not
greater than, it is in an on-the-street or roadside investigatory
encounter.   A *Terry* or *Long* frisk occurs before a police-citizen
confrontation has escalated to the point of arrest.   A protective
sweep, in contrast, occurs as an adjunct to the serious step of taking
a person into custody for the purpose of prosecuting him for a
crime.   Moreover, unlike an encounter on the street or along a
highway, an in-home arrest puts the officer at the disadvantage of
being on his adversary's "turf."   An ambush in a confined setting of
unknown configuration is more to be feared than it is in open,
more familiar surroundings.

We recognized in *Terry* that "[e]ven a limited search of the
outer clothing for weapons constitutes a severe, though brief,
intrusion upon cherished personal security, and it must surely be an
annoying, frightening, and perhaps humiliating experience." *Terry,*
supra at 24–25.   But we permitted the intrusion, which was no
more than necessary to protect the officer from harm.   Nor do we
here suggest, as the State does, that entering rooms not examined
prior to the arrest is a *de minimis* intrusion that may be disregarded.   We are quite sure, however, that the arresting officers are
permitted in such circumstances to take reasonable steps to ensure
their safety after, and while making, the arrest.   That interest is
sufficient to outweigh the intrusion such procedures may entail.

We agree with the State, as did the court below, that a warrant
was not required.[1]   We also hold that as an incident to the arrest
the officers could, as a precautionary matter and without probable
cause or reasonable suspicion, look in closets and other spaces
immediately adjoining the place of arrest from which an attack
could be immediately launched.   Beyond that, however, we hold
that there must be articulable facts which, taken together with the
rational inferences from those facts, would warrant a reasonably
prudent officer in believing that the area to be swept harbors an
individual posing a danger to those on the arrest scene.   This is no

---

1.   Buie suggests that because the police
could have sought a warrant to search for
dangerous persons in the house, they were
constitutionally required to do so.   But the
arrest warrant gave the police every right to
enter the home to search for Buie.   Once
inside, the potential for danger justified a
standard of less than probable cause for conducting a limited protective sweep.

more and no less than was required in *Terry* and *Long,* and as in those cases, we think this balance is the proper one.

We should emphasize that such a protective sweep, aimed at protecting the arresting officers, if justified by the circumstances, is nevertheless not a full search of the premises, but may extend only to a cursory inspection of those spaces where a person may be found. The sweep lasts no longer than is necessary to dispel the reasonable suspicion of danger and in any event no longer than it takes to complete the arrest and depart the premises.

IV

Affirmance is not required by Chimel v. California, 395 U.S. 752 (1969), where it was held that in the absence of a search warrant, the justifiable search incident to an in-home arrest could not extend beyond the arrestee's person and the area from within which the arrestee might have obtained a weapon. First, *Chimel* was concerned with a full-blown search of the entire house for evidence of the crime for which the arrest was made, see id., at 754, 763, not the more limited intrusion contemplated by a protective sweep. Second, the justification for the search incident to arrest considered in *Chimel* was the threat posed by the arrestee, not the safety threat posed by the house, or more properly by unseen third parties in the house. To reach our conclusion today, therefore, we need not disagree with the Court's statement in *Chimel,* id., at 766–767, n. 12, that "the invasion of privacy that results from a top-to-bottom search of a man's house [cannot be characterized] as 'minor,'" nor hold that "simply because some interference with an individual's privacy and freedom of movement has lawfully taken place, further intrusions should automatically be allowed despite the absence of a warrant that the Fourth Amendment would otherwise require," ibid. The type of search we authorize today is far removed from the "top-to-bottom" search involved in *Chimel;* moreover, it is decidedly not "automati[c]," but may be conducted only when justified by a reasonable, articulable suspicion that the house is harboring a person posing a danger to those on the arrest scene.

V

We conclude that by requiring a protective sweep to be justified by probable cause to believe that a serious and demonstrable potentiality for danger existed, the Court of Appeals of Maryland applied an unnecessarily strict Fourth Amendment standard. The Fourth Amendment permits a properly limited protective sweep in conjunction with an in-home arrest when the searching officer possesses a reasonable belief based on specific and articulable facts that the area to be swept harbors an individual posing a danger to those on the arrest scene. We therefore vacate the judgment below and remand this case to the Court of Appeals of Maryland for further proceedings not inconsistent with this opinion.

It is so ordered.

. . .

JUSTICE BRENNAN, with whom JUSTICE MARSHALL joins, dissenting.

Today the Court for the first time extends Terry v. Ohio, 392 U.S. 1 (1968), into the home, dispensing with the Fourth Amendment's general requirements of a warrant and probable cause and carving a "reasonable suspicion" exception for protective sweeps in private dwellings. . . .

. . .

While the Fourth Amendment protects a person's privacy interests in a variety of settings, "physical entry of the home is the chief evil against which the wording of the Fourth Amendment is directed." United States v. United States District Court, Eastern District of Michigan, 407 U.S. 297, 313 (1972). The Court discounts the nature of the intrusion because it believes that the scope of the intrusion is limited. The Court explains that a protective sweep's scope is "narrowly confined to a cursory visual inspection of those places in which a person might be hiding," ante, at 327, and confined in duration to a period "no longer than is necessary to dispel the reasonable suspicion of danger and in any event no longer than it takes to complete the arrest and depart the premises." Ante, at 335–336. But these spatial and temporal restrictions are not particularly limiting. A protective sweep would bring within police purview virtually all personal possessions within the house not hidden from view in a small enclosed space. Police officers searching for potential ambushers might enter every room including basements and attics; open up closets, lockers, chests, wardrobes, and cars; and peer under beds and behind furniture. The officers will view letters, documents and personal effects that are on tables or desks or are visible inside open drawers; books, records, tapes, and pictures on shelves; and clothing, medicines, toiletries and other paraphernalia not carefully stored in dresser drawers or bathroom cupboards. While perhaps not a "full-blown" or "top-to-bottom" search, ante, at 336, a protective sweep is much closer to it than to a "limited patdown for weapons" or a " 'frisk' of an automobile." Ante, at 332. Because the nature and scope of the intrusion sanctioned here are far greater than those upheld in *Terry* and *Long,* the Court's conclusion that "[t]he ingredients to apply the balance struck in *Terry* and *Long* are present in this case," ibid., is unwarranted. The "ingredient" of a minimally intrusive search is absent, and the Court's holding today therefore unpalatably deviates from *Terry* and its progeny.

In light of the special sanctity of a private residence and the highly intrusive nature of a protective sweep, I firmly believe that police officers must have probable cause to fear that their personal safety is threatened by a hidden confederate of an arrestee before they may sweep through the entire home. Given the state-court determination that the officers searching Buie's home lacked probable cause to perceive such a danger and therefore were not lawfully present in the basement, I would affirm the state court's decision to suppress the incriminating evidence. I respectfully dissent.[*]

[*] Justice Stevens and Justice Kennedy wrote concurring opinions.

CHAMBERS v. MARONEY

399 U.S. 42, 90 S.Ct. 1975, 26 L.Ed.2d 419 (1970).

MR. JUSTICE WHITE delivered the opinion of the Court.

The principal question in this case concerns the admissibility of evidence seized from an automobile, in which petitioner was riding at the time of his arrest, after the automobile was taken to a police station and was there thoroughly searched without a warrant. The Court of Appeals for the Third Circuit found no violation of petitioner's Fourth Amendment rights. We affirm.

I

During the night of May 20, 1963, a Gulf service station in North Braddock, Pennsylvania, was robbed by two men each of whom carried and displayed a gun. The robbers took the currency from the cash register; the service station attendant, one Stephen Kovacich, was directed to place the coins in his right hand glove, which was then taken by the robbers. Two teen-agers, who had earlier noticed a blue compact station wagon circling the block in the vicinity of the Gulf station, then saw the station wagon speed away from a parking lot close to the Gulf station. About the same time, they learned that the Gulf station had been robbed. They reported to police, who arrived immediately, that four men were in the station wagon and one was wearing a green sweater. Kovacich told the police that one of the men who robbed him was wearing a green sweater and the other was wearing a trench coat. A description of the car and the two robbers was broadcast over the police radio. Within an hour, a light blue compact station wagon answering the description and carrying four men was stopped by the police about two miles from the Gulf station. Petitioner was one of the men in the station wagon. He was wearing a green sweater and there was a trench coat in the car. The occupants were arrested and the car was driven to the police station. In the course of a thorough search of the car at the station, the police found concealed in a compartment under the dashboard two .38-caliber revolvers (one loaded with dumdum bullets), a right-hand glove containing small change, and certain cards bearing the name of Raymond Havicon, the attendant at a Boron service station in McKeesport, Pennsylvania, who had been robbed at gunpoint on May 13, 1963. In the course of a warrant-authorized search of petitioner's home the day after petitioner's arrest, police found and seized certain .38-caliber ammunition, including some dumdum bullets similar to those found in one of the guns taken from the station wagon.

124

Petitioner was indicted for both robberies. His first trial ended in a mistrial but he was convicted of both robberies at the second trial. Both Kovacich and Havicon identified petitioner as one of the robbers. The materials taken from the station wagon were introduced into evidence, Kovacich identifying his glove and Havicon the cards taken in the May 13 robbery. The bullets seized at petitioner's house were also introduced over objections of petitioner's counsel. Petitioner was sentenced to a term of four to eight years' imprisonment for the May 13 robbery and to a term of two to seven years' imprisonment for the May 20 robbery, the sentences to run consecutively. Petitioner did not take a direct appeal from these convictions. In 1965, petitioner sought a writ of habeas corpus in the state court, which denied the writ after a brief evidentiary hearing; the denial of the writ was affirmed on appeal in the Pennsylvania appellate courts. Habeas corpus proceedings were then commenced in the United States District Court for the Western District of Pennsylvania. An order to show cause was issued. Based on the State's response and the state court record, the petition for habeas corpus was denied without a hearing. The Court of Appeals for the Third Circuit affirmed, 408 F.2d 1186, and we granted certiorari, 396 U.S. 900 (1969).

II

We pass quickly the claim that the search of the automobile was the fruit of an unlawful arrest. Both the courts below thought the arresting officers had probable cause to make the arrest. We agree. Having talked to the teen-age observers and to the victim Kovacich, the police had ample cause to stop a light blue compact station wagon carrying four men and to arrest the occupants, one of whom was wearing a green sweater, and one of whom had a trench coat with him in the car.[6]

Even so, the search which produced the incriminating evidence was made at the police station some time after the arrest and cannot be justified as a search incident to an arrest: "Once an accused is under arrest and in custody, then a search made at another place, without a warrant, is simply not incident to the arrest." Preston v. United States, 376 U.S. 364, 367 (1964). Dyke v. Taylor Implement Mfg. Co., 391 U.S. 216 (1968), is to the same effect; the reasons that have been thought sufficient to justify warrantless searches carried out in connection with an arrest no longer obtain when the accused is safely in custody at the station house.

There are, however, alternative grounds arguably justifying the search of the car in this case. In *Preston*, supra, the arrest was for vagrancy; it was apparent that the officers had no cause to believe

---

6. In any event, as we point out below, the validity of an arrest is not necessarily determinative of the right to search a car if there is probable cause to make the search. Here, as will be true in many cases, the circumstances justifying the arrest are also those furnishing probable cause for the search.

that evidence of crime was concealed in the auto. In *Dyke,* supra, the Court expressly rejected the suggestion that there was probable cause to search the car, 391 U.S., at 221–222. Here the situation is different, for the police had probable cause to believe that the robbers, carrying guns and the fruits of the crime, had fled the scene in a light blue compact station wagon which would be carrying four men, one wearing a green sweater and another wearing a trench coat. As the state courts correctly held, there was probable cause to arrest the occupants of the station wagon that the officers stopped; just as obviously was there probable cause to search the car for guns and stolen money.

In terms of the circumstances justifying a warrantless search, the Court has long distinguished between an automobile and a home or office. In Carroll v. United States, 267 U.S. 132 (1925), the issue was the admissibility in evidence of contraband liquor seized in a warrantless search of a car on the highway. After surveying the law from the time of the adoption of the Fourth Amendment onward, the Court held that automobiles and other conveyances may be searched without a warrant in circumstances that would not justify the search without a warrant of a house or an office, provided that there is probable cause to believe that the car contains articles that the officers are entitled to seize. The Court expressed its holding as follows:

> "We have made a somewhat extended reference to these statutes to show that the guaranty of freedom from unreasonable searches and seizures by the Fourth Amendment has been construed, practically since the beginning of the Government, as recognizing a necessary difference between a search of a store, dwelling house or other structure in respect of which a proper official warrant readily may be obtained, and a search of a ship, motor boat, wagon or automobile, for contraband goods, where it is not practicable to secure a warrant because the vehicle can be quickly moved out of the locality or jurisdiction in which the warrant must be sought.

> "Having thus established that contraband goods concealed and illegally transported in an automobile or other vehicle may be searched for without a warrant, we come now to consider under what circumstances such search may be made. . . . [T]hose lawfully within the country, entitled to use the public highways, have a right to free passage without interruption or search unless there is known to a competent official authorized to search, probable cause for believing that their vehicles are carrying contraband or illegal merchandise. . . .

> .   .   .   .

> "The measure of legality of such a seizure is, therefore, that the seizing officer shall have reasonable or probable cause for

believing that the automobile which he stops and seizes has contraband liquor therein which is being illegally transported." 267 U.S., at 153–154, 155–156.

The Court also noted that the search of an auto on probable cause proceeds on a theory wholly different from that justifying the search incident to an arrest:

"The right to search and the validity of the seizure are not dependent on the right to arrest. They are dependent on the reasonable cause the seizing officer has for belief that the contents of the automobile offend against the law." 267 U.S., at 158–159.

Finding that there was probable cause for the search and seizure at issue before it, the Court affirmed the convictions.

. . .

Neither *Carroll,* supra, nor other cases in this Court require or suggest that in every conceivable circumstance the search of an auto even with probable cause may be made without the extra protection for privacy that a warrant affords. But the circumstances that furnish probable cause to search a particular auto for particular articles are most often unforeseeable; moreover, the opportunity to search is fleeting since a car is readily movable. Where this is true, as in *Carroll* and the case before us now, if an effective search is to be made at any time, either the search must be made immediately without a warrant or the car itself must be seized and held without a warrant for whatever period is necessary to obtain a warrant for the search.[9]

In enforcing the Fourth Amendment's prohibition against un-reasonable searches and seizures, the Court has insisted upon probable cause as a minimum requirement for a reasonable search permitted by the Constitution. As a general rule, it has also required the judgment of a magistrate on the probable-cause issue and the issuance of a warrant before a search is made. Only in exigent circumstances will the judgment of the police as to probable cause serve as a sufficient authorization for a search. *Carroll,* supra, holds a search warrant unnecessary where there is probable cause to search an automobile stopped on the highway; the car is movable, the occupants are alerted, and the car's contents may never be found again if a warrant must be obtained. Hence an immediate search is constitutionally permissible.

Arguably, because of the preference for a magistrate's judg-ment, only the immobilization of the car should be permitted until a search warrant is obtained; arguably, only the "lesser" intrusion is permissible until the magistrate authorizes the "greater." But

---

9. Following the car until a warrant can be obtained seems an impractical alternative since, among other things, the car may be taken out of the jurisdiction. Tracing the car and searching it hours or days later would of course permit instruments or fruits of crime to be removed from the car before the search.

which is the "greater" and which the "lesser" intrusion is itself a debatable question and the answer may depend on a variety of circumstances. For constitutional purposes, we see no difference between on the one hand seizing and holding a car before presenting the probable cause issue to a magistrate and on the other hand carrying out an immediate search without a warrant. Given probable cause to search, either course is reasonable under the Fourth Amendment.

On the facts before us, the blue station wagon could have been searched on the spot when it was stopped since there was probable cause to search and it was a fleeting target for a search. The probable cause factor still obtained at the station house and so did the mobility of the car unless the Fourth Amendment permits a warrantless seizure of the car and the denial of its use to anyone until a warrant is secured. In that event there is little to choose in terms of practical consequences between an immediate search without a warrant and the car's immobilization until a warrant is obtained.[10] The same consequences may not follow where there is unforeseeable cause to search a house. Compare Vale v. Louisiana, *ante*, at 30. But as *Carroll*, supra, held, for the purposes of the Fourth Amendment there is a constitutional difference between houses and cars.

. . .

Affirmed.

MR. JUSTICE HARLAN, concurring in part and dissenting in part.

. . .

In sustaining the search of the automobile I believe the Court ignores the framework of our past decisions circumscribing the scope of permissible search without a warrant. The Court has long read the Fourth Amendment's proscription of "unreasonable" searches as imposing a general principle that a search without a warrant is not justified by the mere knowledge by the searching officers of facts showing probable cause. The "general requirement that a search warrant be obtained" is basic to the Amendment's protection of privacy, and " 'the burden is on those seeking [an] exemption . . . to show the need for it.' " E.g., Chimel v. California, 395 U.S. 752, 762 (1969) . . . .

Fidelity to this established principle requires that, where exceptions are made to accommodate the exigencies of particular situations, those exceptions be no broader than necessitated by the circumstances presented. . . .

---

10. It was not unreasonable in this case to take the car to the station house. All occupants in the car were arrested in a dark parking lot in the middle of the night. A careful search at that point was impractical and perhaps not safe for the officers, and it would serve the owner's convenience and the safety of his car to have the vehicle and the keys together at the station house.

Where officers have probable cause to search a vehicle on a public way, a further limited exception to the warrant requirement is reasonable because "the vehicle can be quickly moved out of the locality or jurisdiction in which the warrant must be sought." Carroll v. United States, 267 U.S. 132, 153 (1925). Because the officers might be deprived of valuable evidence if required to obtain a warrant before effecting any search or seizure, I agree with the Court that they should be permitted to take the steps necessary to preserve evidence and to make a search possible. ... The Court holds that those steps include making a warrantless search of the entire vehicle on the highway—a conclusion reached by the Court in *Carroll* without discussion—and indeed appears to go further and to condone the removal of the car to the police station for a warrantless search there at the convenience of the police. I cannot agree that this result is consistent with our insistence in other areas that departures from the warrant requirement strictly conform to the exigency presented.

The Court concedes that the police could prevent removal of the evidence by temporarily seizing the car for the time necessary to obtain a warrant. It does not dispute that such a course would fully protect the interests of effective law enforcement; rather it states that whether temporary seizure is a "lesser" intrusion than warrantless search "is itself a debatable question and the answer may depend on a variety of circumstances." Ante, at 51–52. I believe it clear that a warrantless search involves the greater sacrifice of Fourth Amendment values.

The Fourth Amendment proscribes, to be sure, unreasonable "seizures" as well as "searches." However, in the circumstances in which this problem is likely to occur the lesser intrusion will almost always be the simple seizure of the car for the period—perhaps a day—necessary to enable the officers to obtain a search warrant. In the first place, as this case shows, the very facts establishing probable cause to search will often also justify arrest of the occupants of the vehicle. Since the occupants themselves are to be taken into custody, they will suffer minimal further inconvenience from the temporary immobilization of their vehicle. Even where no arrests are made, persons who wish to avoid a search—either to protect their privacy or to conceal incriminating evidence—will almost certainly prefer a brief loss of the use of the vehicle in exchange for the opportunity to have a magistrate pass upon the justification for the search. To be sure, one can conceive of instances in which the occupant, having nothing to hide and lacking concern for the privacy of the automobile, would be more deeply offended by a temporary immobilization of his vehicle than by a prompt search of it. However, such a person always remains free to consent to an immediate search, thus avoiding any delay. Where consent is not forthcoming, the occupants of the car have an interest in privacy that is protected by the Fourth Amendment even where the circumstances justify a temporary seizure. Terry v. Ohio, supra. The Court's endorsement of a warrantless invasion of that privacy where another course would suffice is simply inconsistent with our repeated stress on the Fourth Amendment's mandate of " 'adherence to judicial processes.' " E.g., Katz v. United States, 389 U.S., at 357.[9]

. . .

The Court now ... creates a special rule for automobile searches that is seriously at odds with generally applied Fourth Amendment principles.

[*] [**]

. . .

9. Circumstances might arise in which it would be impracticable to immobilize the car for the time required to obtain a warrant—for example, where a single police officer must take arrested suspects to the station, and has no way of protecting the suspects' car during his absence. In such situations it might be wholly reasonable to perform an on-the-spot search based on probable cause. However, where nothing in the situation makes impracticable the obtaining of a warrant, I cannot join the Court in shunting aside that vital Fourth Amendment safeguard.

[*] Justice Stewart wrote a brief concurring opinion.

[**] The "automobile exception" to the requirement of a search warrant, as described in *Chambers,* allows police officers who have legitimately stopped an automobile and have probable cause to believe that items subject to seizure are being carried in it to search the automobile without a search warrant. In United States v. Ross, 456 U.S. 798 (1982) (6–3), the Supreme Court held that a search authorized on this basis can be as broad as a search pursuant to a warrant. "The scope of a warrantless search based on probable cause is no narrower—and no broader—than the scope of a search authorized by a warrant supported by probable cause. Only the prior approval of the magistrate is waived; the search otherwise is as the magistrate could authorize." 456 U.S. at 823. More particularly, the Court said that containers within the automobile that might hold the items to be seized can be opened and searched. "When a legitimate search is under way, and when its purpose and its limits have been precisely defined, nice distinctions between closets, drawers, and containers, in the case of a home, or between glove compartments, upholstered seats, trunks, and wrapped packages, in the case of a vehicle, must give way to the interest in the prompt and efficient completion of the task at hand." 456 U.S. at 821.

In New York v. Belton, 453 U.S. 454 (1981) (6–3), the Court held that a search incident to a lawful arrest, see Chimel v. California, 395 U.S. 752 (1969), above, of the occupant of an automobile can extend to the entire passenger compartment of the automobile, including all containers within it. "Container," the Court said, includes "any object capable of holding another object": glove compartment, luggage boxes, clothing, etc., 453 U.S. at 460 n. 4.

SOUTH DAKOTA v. OPPERMAN

428 U.S. 364, 96 S.Ct. 3092, 49 L.Ed.2d 1000 (1976).

MR. CHIEF JUSTICE BURGER delivered the opinion of the Court.

We review the judgment of the Supreme Court of South Dakota, holding that local police violated the Fourth Amendment to the Federal Constitution, as applicable to the States under the Fourteenth Amendment, when they conducted a routine inventory search of an automobile lawfully impounded by police for violations of municipal parking ordinances.

(1)

Local ordinances prohibit parking in certain areas of downtown Vermillion, S.D., between the hours of 2 a.m. and 6 a.m. During the early morning hours of December 10, 1973, a Vermillion police officer observed respondent's unoccupied vehicle illegally parked in the restricted zone. At approximately 3 a.m., the officer issued an overtime parking ticket and placed it on the car's windshield. The citation warned:

> "Vehicles in violation of any parking ordinance may be towed from the area."

At approximately 10 o'clock on the same morning, another officer issued a second ticket for an overtime parking violation. These circumstances were routinely reported to police headquarters, and after the vehicle was inspected, the car was towed to the city impound lot.

From outside the car at the impound lot, a police officer observed a watch on the dashboard and other items of personal property located on the back seat and back floorboard. At the officer's direction, the car door was then unlocked and, using a standard inventory form pursuant to standard police procedures, the officer inventoried the contents of the car, including the contents of the glove compartment, which was unlocked. There he found marihuana contained in a plastic bag. All items, including the contraband, were removed to the police department for safekeeping. During the late afternoon of December 10, respondent appeared at the police department to claim his property. The marihuana was retained by police.

Respondent was subsequently arrested on charges of possession of marihuana. His motion to suppress the evidence yielded by the inventory search was denied; he was convicted after a jury trial and sentenced to a fine of $100 and 14 days' incarceration in the

131

county jail. On appeal, the Supreme Court of South Dakota re-versed the conviction. The court concluded that the evidence had been obtained in violation of the Fourth Amendment prohibition against unreasonable searches and seizures. We granted certiorari, 423 U.S. 923 (1975), and we reverse.

(2)

This Court has traditionally drawn a distinction between auto-mobiles and homes or offices in relation to the Fourth Amendment. Although automobiles are "effects" and thus within the reach of the Fourth Amendment, ... warrantless examinations of automobiles have been upheld in circumstances in which a search of a home or office would not. ...

The reason for this well-settled distinction is twofold. First, the inherent mobility of automobiles creates circumstances of such exigency that, as a practical necessity, rigorous enforcement of the warrant requirement is impossible. ... But the Court has also upheld warrantless searches where no immediate danger was pre-sented that the car would be removed from the jurisdiction. ... Besides the element of mobility, less rigorous warrant requirements govern because the expectation of privacy with respect to one's automobile is significantly less than that relating to one's home or office. In discharging their varied responsibilities for ensuring the public safety, law enforcement officials are necessarily brought into frequent contact with automobiles. Most of this contact is distinctly noncriminal in nature. ... Automobiles, unlike homes, are sub-jected to pervasive and continuing governmental regulation and controls, including periodic inspection and licensing requirements. As an everyday occurrence, police stop and examine vehicles when license plates or inspection stickers have expired, or if other viola-tions, such as exhaust fumes or excessive noise, are noted, or if headlights or other safety equipment are not in proper working order.

The expectation of privacy as to autos is further diminished by the obviously public nature of automobile travel. Only two Terms ago, the Court noted:

> "One has a lesser expectation of privacy in a motor vehicle because its function is transportation and it seldom serves as one's residence or as the repository of personal effects. ... It travels public thoroughfares where both its occupants and its contents are in plain view." Cardwell v. Lewis, [417 U.S. 583 (1974)] at 590.

In the interests of public safety and as part of what the Court has called "community caretaking functions," Cady v. Dombrowski, [413 U.S. 433 (1973)], at 441, automobiles are frequently taken into police custody. Vehicle accidents present one such occasion. To permit the uninterrupted flow of traffic and in some circum-stances to preserve evidence, disabled or damaged vehicles will often be removed from the highways or streets at the behest of police engaged solely in caretaking and traffic-control activities. Police will also frequently remove and impound automobiles which violate parking ordinances and which thereby jeopardize both the public safety and the efficient movement of vehicular traffic. The authority of police to seize and remove from the streets vehicles impeding traffic or threatening public safety and convenience is beyond challenge.

When vehicles are impounded, local police departments generally follow a routine practice of securing and inventorying the automobiles' contents. These procedures developed in response to three distinct needs: the protection of the owner's property while it remains in police custody . . .; the protection of the police against claims or disputes over lost or stolen property . . .; and the protection of the police from potential danger . . . . The practice has been viewed as essential to respond to incidents of theft or vandalism. . . . In addition, police frequently attempt to determine whether a vehicle has been stolen and thereafter abandoned.

These caretaking procedures have almost uniformly been upheld by the state courts, which by virtue of the localized nature of traffic regulation have had considerable occasion to deal with the issue. Applying the Fourth Amendment standard of "reasonableness," [5] the state courts have overwhelmingly concluded that, even if an inventory is characterized as a "search," the intrusion is constitutionally permissible. . . .

The majority of the federal Courts of Appeals have likewise sustained inventory procedures as reasonable police intrusions. . . . These cases have recognized that standard inventories often include an examination of the glove compartment, since it is a customary place for documents of ownership and registration . . . as well as a place for the temporary storage of valuables.

(3)

The decisions of this Court point unmistakably to the conclusion reached by both federal and state courts that inventories pursuant to standard police procedures are reasonable. . . .

---

5. In analyzing the issue of reasonableness *vel non,* the courts have not sought to determine whether a protective inventory was justified by "probable cause." The standard of probable cause is peculiarly related to criminal investigations, not routine, noncriminal procedures. . . . The probable-cause approach is unhelpful when analysis centers upon the reasonableness of routine administrative caretaking functions, particularly when no claim is made that the protective procedures are a subterfuge for criminal investigations.

In view of the noncriminal context of inventory searches, and the inapplicability in such a setting of the requirement of probable cause, courts have held—and quite correctly—that search warrants are not required, linked as the warrant requirement textually is to the probable-cause concept. We have frequently observed that the warrant requirement assures that legal inferences and conclusions as to probable cause will be drawn by a neutral magistrate unrelated to the criminal investigative-enforcement process. With respect to noninvestigative police inventories of automobiles lawfully within governmental custody, however, the policies underlying the warrant requirement . . . are inapplicable.

In applying the reasonableness standard adopted by the Framers, this Court has consistently sustained police intrusions into automobiles impounded or otherwise in lawful police custody where the process is aimed at securing or protecting the car and its contents.　...

　. . .

The Vermillion police were indisputably engaged in a caretaking search of a lawfully impounded automobile.　...　The inventory was conducted only after the car had been impounded for multiple parking violations.　The owner, having left his car illegally parked for an extended period, and thus subject to impoundment, was not present to make other arrangements for the safekeeping of his belongings.　The inventory itself was prompted by the presence in plain view of a number of valuables inside the car.　...　[T]here is no suggestion whatever that this standard procedure, essentially like that followed throughout the country, was a pretext concealing an investigatory police motive.

On this record we conclude that in following standard police procedures, prevailing throughout the country and approved by the overwhelming majority of courts, the conduct of the police was not "unreasonable" under the Fourth Amendment.

The judgment of the South Dakota Supreme Court is therefore reversed and the case is remanded for further proceedings not inconsistent with this opinion.

Reversed and remanded.

MR. JUSTICE MARSHALL, with whom MR. JUSTICE BRENNAN and MR. JUSTICE STEWART join, dissenting.

The Court holds that the Fourth Amendment permits a routine police inventory search of the closed glove compartment of a locked automobile impounded for ordinary traffic violations.　Under the Court's holding, such a search may be made without attempting to secure the consent of the owner and without any particular reason to believe the impounded automobile contains contraband, evidence, or valuables or presents any danger to its custodians or the public.　Because I believe this holding to be contrary to sound elaboration of established Fourth Amendment principles, I dissent.

　...　[T]he requirement of a warrant aside, resolution of the question whether an inventory search of closed compartments inside a locked automobile can ever be justified as a constitutionally "reasonable" search depends upon a reconciliation of the owner's constitutionally protected privacy interests against governmental intrusion, and legitimate governmental interests furthered by securing the car and its contents.　...　The Court fails clearly to articulate the reasons for its reconciliation of these interests in this case, but it is at least clear to me that the considerations alluded to by the Court ... are insufficient to justify the Court's result in this case.

To begin with, the Court appears to suggest by reference to a "diminished" expectation of privacy, ante, at 368, that a person's constitutional interest in protecting the integrity of closed compartments of his locked automobile may routinely be sacrificed to governmental interests requiring interference with that privacy that are less compelling than would be necessary to justify a search of similar scope of the person's home or office. This has never been the law. The Court correctly observes that some prior cases have drawn distinctions between automobiles and homes or offices in Fourth Amendment cases; but even as the Court's discussion makes clear, the reasons for distinction in those cases are not present here. Thus, Chambers v. Maroney, 399 U.S. 42 (1970), and Carroll v. United States, 267 U.S. 132 (1925), permitted certain probable cause searches to be carried out without warrants in view of the exigencies created by the mobility of automobiles, but both decisions reaffirmed that the standard of probable cause necessary to authorize such a search was no less than the standard applicable to search of a home or office. ... In other contexts the Court has recognized that automobile travel sacrifices some privacy interests to the publicity of plain view .... But this recognition, too, is inapposite here, for there is no question of plain view in this case. Nor does this case concern intrusions of the scope that the Court apparently assumes would ordinarily be permissible in order to insure the running safety of a car. While it may be that privacy expectations associated with automobile travel are in some regards less than those associated with a home or office ... it is equally clear that "[t]he word 'automobile' is not a talisman in whose presence the Fourth Amendment fades away ...." Coolidge v. New Hampshire, 403 U.S. 443, 461 (1971). Thus, we have recognized that "[a] *search*, even of an automobile, is a substantial invasion of privacy," United States v. Ortiz, 422 U.S. 891, 896 (1975) (emphasis added), and accordingly our cases have consistently recognized that the nature and substantiality of interest required to justify a *search* of private areas of an automobile is no less than that necessary to justify an intrusion of similar scope into a home or office. ...[6]

The Court's opinion appears to suggest that its result may in any event be justified because the inventory search procedure is a "reasonable" response to

"three distinct needs: the protection of the owner's property while it remains in police custody ...; the protection of the

---

6. It would be wholly unrealistic to say that there is no reasonable and actual expectation in maintaining the privacy of closed compartments of a locked automobile, when it is customary for people in this day to carry their most personal and private papers and effects in their automobiles from time to time. ... Indeed, this fact is implicit in the very basis of the Court's holding—that such compartments may contain valuables in need of safeguarding.

police against claims or disputes over lost or stolen property
...; and the protection of the police from potential danger."
Ante, at 369.

This suggestion is flagrantly misleading, however, because the record of this case explicitly belies any relevance of the last two
concerns. In any event it is my view that none of these "needs,"
separately or together, can suffice to justify the inventory search
procedure approved by the Court.

First, this search cannot be justified in any way as a safety
measure, for—though the Court ignores it—the sole purpose given
by the State for the Vermillion police's inventory procedure was to
secure *valuables*, Record 75, 98. Nor is there any indication that
the officer's search in this case was tailored in any way to safety
concerns, or that ordinarily it is so circumscribed. Even aside from
the actual basis for the police practice in this case, however, I do
not believe that any blanket safety argument could justify a program
of routine searches of the scope permitted here. As Mr. Justice
Powell recognizes, ordinarily "there is little danger associated with
impounding unsearched automobiles," ante, at 378. Thus, while
the safety rationale may not be entirely discounted when it is
actually relied upon, it surely cannot justify the search of every car
upon the basis of undifferentiated possibility of harm; on the
contrary, such an intrusion could ordinarily be justified only in
those individual cases where the officer's inspection was prompted
by specific circumstances indicating the possibility of a particular
danger....

Second, the Court suggests that the search for valuables in the
closed glove compartment might be justified as a measure to protect
the police against lost property claims. Again, this suggestion is
belied by the record, since—although the Court declines to discuss
it—the South Dakota Supreme Court's interpretation of state law
explicitly absolves the police, as "gratuitous depositors," from any
obligation beyond inventorying objects in plain view and locking
the car. State v. Opperman, 228 N.W.2d 152, 159 (1975). Moreover ... it may well be doubted that an inventory procedure would
in any event work significantly to minimize the frustrations of false
claims.

Finally, the Court suggests that the public interest in protecting
valuables that may be found inside a closed compartment of an
impounded car may justify the inventory procedure. I recognize
the genuineness of this governmental interest in protecting property
from pilferage. But even if I assume that the posting of a guard
would be fiscally impossible as an alternative means to the same
protective end, I cannot agree with the Court's conclusion. The
Court's result authorizes—indeed it appears to require—the routine
search of nearly every car impounded. In my view, the Constitution
does not permit such searches as a matter of routine; absent

specific consent, such a search is permissible only in exceptional circumstances of particular necessity.

It is at least clear that any owner might prohibit the police from executing a protective search of his impounded car, since by hypothesis the inventory is conducted for the owner's benefit. Moreover, it is obvious that not everyone whose car is impounded would want it to be searched. Respondent himself proves this; but one need not carry contraband to prefer that the police not examine one's private possessions. Indeed, that preference is the premise of the Fourth Amendment. Nevertheless, according to the Court's result the law may presume that each owner in respondent's position consents to the search. I cannot agree. In my view, the Court's approach is squarely contrary to the law of consent; it ignores the duty, in the absence of consent, to analyze in each individual case whether there is a need to search a particular car for the protection of its owner which is sufficient to outweigh the particular invasion. It is clear to me under established principles that in order to override the absence of explicit consent, such a search must at least be conditioned upon the fulfillment of two requirements. First, there must be specific cause to believe that a search of the scope to be undertaken is necessary in order to preserve the integrity of particular valuable property threatened by the impoundment:

> "[I]n justifying the particular intrusion the police officer must be able to point to specific and articulable facts which ... reasonably warrant that intrusion." Terry v. Ohio, 392 U.S. [1 (1968)], at 21.

Such a requirement of "specificity in the information upon which police action is predicated is the central teaching of this Court's Fourth Amendment jurisprudence," id., at 21 n. 18, for "[t]he basic purpose of this Amendment, as recognized in countless decisions of this Court, is to safeguard the privacy and security of individuals against arbitrary invasions by governmental officials." Camara v. Municipal Court, 387 U.S. [523 (1967)], at 528. ... Second, even where a search might be appropriate, such an intrusion may only follow the exhaustion and failure of reasonable efforts under the circumstances to identify and reach the owner of the property in order to facilitate alternative means of security or to obtain his consent to the search, for in this context the right to refuse the search remains with the owner.... [16]

---

16. Additionally, although not relevant on this record, since the inventory procedure is premised upon benefit to the owner, it cannot be executed in any case in which there is reason to believe the owner would prefer to forego it. This principle, which is fully consistent with the Court's result today, requires, for example, that when the police harbor suspicions (amounting to less than probable cause) that evidence or contraband may be found inside the automobile, they may not inventory it, for they must presume that the owner would refuse to permit the search.

Because the record in this case shows that the procedures followed by the Vermillion police in searching respondent's car fall far short of these standards, in my view the search was impermissible and its fruits must be suppressed. First, so far as the record shows, the police in this case had no reason to believe that the glove compartment of the impounded car contained particular property of any substantial value. Moreover, the owner had apparently thought it adequate to protect whatever he left in the car overnight on the street in a business area simply to lock the car, and there is nothing in the record to show that the impoundment lot would prove a less secure location against pilferage ... particularly when it would seem likely that the owner would claim his car and its contents promptly, at least if it contained valuables worth protecting. Even if the police had cause to believe that the impounded car's glove compartment contained particular valuables, however, they made no effort to secure the owner's consent to the search. Although the Court relies, as it must, upon the fact that respondent was not present to make other arrangements for the care of his belongings, ante, at 375, in my view that is not the end of the inquiry. Here the police readily ascertained the ownership of the vehicle, Record, at 98–99, yet they searched it immediately without taking any steps to locate respondent and procure his consent to the inventory or advise him to make alternative arrangements to safeguard his property, id., at 32, 72, 73, 79. Such a failure is inconsistent with the rationale that the inventory procedure is carried out for the benefit of the owner.

The Court's result in this case elevates the conservation of property interests—indeed mere possibilities of property interests—above the privacy and security interests protected by the Fourth Amendment. For this reason I dissent. On the remand it should be clear in any event that this Court's holding does not preclude a contrary resolution of this case or others involving the same issues under any applicable state law. ... [*]

[*] Justice Powell wrote a concurring opinion. Justice White wrote a brief dissenting statement indicating his agreement with most of Justice Marshall's opinion.

UNITED STATES v. ROBINSON

414 U.S. 218, 94 S.Ct. 467, 38 L.Ed.2d 427 (1973).

MR. JUSTICE REHNQUIST delivered the opinion of the Court.

Respondent Robinson was convicted in United States District Court for the District of Columbia of the possession and facilitation of concealment of heroin in violation of 26 U.S.C. § 4704(a) (1964 ed.), and 21 U.S.C. § 174 (1964 ed.). He was sentenced to concurrent terms of imprisonment for these offenses. On his appeal to the Court of Appeals for the District of Columbia Circuit, that court first remanded the case to the District Court for evidentiary hearing concerning the scope of the search of respondent's person which had occurred at the time of his arrest. 145 U.S.App. D.C. 46, 447 F.2d 1215 (1971). The District Court made findings of fact and conclusions of law adverse to respondent, and he again appealed. This time the Court of Appeals en banc reversed the judgment of conviction, holding that the heroin introduced in evidence against respondent had been obtained as a result of a search which violated the Fourth Amendment to the United States Constitution. 153 U.S.App.D.C. 114, 471 F.2d 1082 (1972). We granted certiorari, 410 U.S. 982 (1973), and set the case for argument together with Gustafson v. Florida, No. 71–1669, post, p. 260 also decided today.

On April 23, 1968, at approximately 11 p.m., Officer Richard Jenks, a 15-year veteran of the District of Columbia Metropolitan Police Department, observed the respondent driving a 1965 Cadillac near the intersection of 8th and C Streets, N.E., in the District of Columbia. Jenks, as a result of previous investigation following a check of respondent's operator's permit four days earlier, determined there was reason to believe that respondent was operating a motor vehicle after the revocation of his operator's permit. This is an offense defined by statute in the District of Columbia which carries a mandatory minimum jail term, a mandatory minimum fine, or both. 40 D.C.Code § 40–302(d) (1967).

Jenks signaled respondent to stop the automobile, which respondent did, and all three of the occupants emerged from the car. At that point Jenks informed respondent that he was under arrest for "operating after revocation and obtaining a permit by misrepresentation." It was assumed by the Court of Appeals, and is conceded by the respondent here, that Jenks had probable cause to arrest respondent, and that he effected a full-custody arrest.

In accordance with procedures prescribed in police department instructions, Jenks then began to search respondent. He explained

139

at a subsequent hearing that he was "face-to-face" with the respondent, and "placed [his] hands on [the respondent], my right-hand to his left breast like this (demonstrating) and proceeded to pat him down thus (with the right hand)." During this patdown, Jenks felt an object in the left breast pocket of the heavy coat respondent was wearing, but testified that he "couldn't tell what it was" and also that he "couldn't actually tell the size of it." Jenks then reached into the pocket and pulled out the object, which turned out to be a "crumpled up cigarette package." Jenks testified that at this point he still did not know what was in the package:

> "As I felt the package I could feel objects in the package but I couldn't tell what they were . . . . I knew they weren't cigarettes."

The officer then opened the cigarette pack and found 14 gelatin capsules of white powder which he thought to be, and which later analysis proved to be, heroin. Jenks then continued his search of respondent to completion, feeling around his waist and trouser legs, and examining the remaining pockets. The heroin seized from the respondent was admitted into evidence at the trial which resulted in his conviction in the District Court.

The opinion for the plurality judges of the Court of Appeals, written by Judge Wright, the concurring opinion of Chief Judge Bazelon, and the dissenting opinion of Judge Wilkey, concurred in by three judges, gave careful and comprehensive treatment to the authority of a police officer to search the person of one who has been validly arrested and taken into custody. We conclude that the search conducted by Jenks in this case did not offend the limits imposed by the Fourth Amendment, and we therefore reverse the judgment of the Court of Appeals.

I

It is well settled that a search incident to a lawful arrest is a traditional exception to the warrant requirement of the Fourth Amendment. This general exception has historically been formulated into two distinct propositions. The first is that a search may be made of the *person* of the arrestee by virtue of the lawful arrest. The second is that a search may be made of the area within the control of the arrestee.

Examination of this Court's decisions in the area show that these two propositions have been treated quite differently. The validity of the search of a person incident to a lawful arrest has been regarded as settled from its first enunciation, and has remained virtually unchallenged until the present case. The validity of the second proposition, while likewise conceded in principle, has been subject to differing interpretations as to the extent of the area which may be searched.

.   .   .

Throughout the series of cases in which the Court has addressed the second proposition relating to a search incident to a lawful arrest—the permissible area beyond the person of the arrestee which such a search may cover—no doubt has been expressed as to the unqualified authority of the arresting authority to search the person of the arrestee. . . .

. . .

Thus the broadly stated rule, and the reasons for it, have been repeatedly affirmed in the decisions of this Court . . . . Since the statements in the cases speak not simply in terms of an exception to the warrant requirement, but in terms of an affirmative authority to search, they clearly imply that such searches also meet the Fourth Amendment's requirement of reasonableness.

II

In its decision of this case, the majority of the Court of Appeals decided that even after a police officer lawfully places a suspect under arrest for the purpose of taking him into custody, he may not ordinarily proceed to fully search the prisoner. He must instead conduct a limited frisk of the outer clothing and remove such weapons that he may, as a result of that limited frisk, reasonably believe and ascertain that the suspect has in his possession. While recognizing that Terry v. Ohio, 392 U.S. 1 (1968), dealt with a permissible "frisk" incident to an investigative stop based on less than probable cause to arrest, the Court of Appeals felt that the principles of that case should be carried over to this probable-cause arrest for driving while one's license is revoked. Since there would be no further evidence of such a crime to be obtained in a search of the arrestee, the Court held that only a search for weapons could be justified.

Terry v. Ohio, supra, did not involve an arrest for probable cause, and it made quite clear that the "protective frisk" for weapons which it approved might be conducted without probable cause. 392 U.S., at 21–22, 24–25. The Court's opinion explicitly recognized that there is a "distinction in purpose, character, and extent between a search incident to an arrest and a limited search for weapons" . . . . *Terry,* therefore, affords no basis to carry over to a probable cause arrest the limitations this Court placed on a stop-and-frisk search permissible without probable cause.

. . .

III

Virtually all of the statements of this Court affirming the existence of an unqualified authority to search incident to a lawful arrest are dicta. We would not therefore be foreclosed by principles of *stare decisis* from further examination into history and practice in order to see whether the sort of qualifications imposed by the Court of Appeals in this case were in fact intended by the Framers of the Fourth Amendment or recognized in [prior] cases .... Unfortunately such authorities as exist are sparse. ...

. . .

While these earlier authorities are sketchy, they tend to support the broad statement of the authority to search incident to arrest found in the successive decisions of this Court, rather than the restrictive one which was applied by the Court of Appeals in this case. ...

The Court of Appeals in effect determined that the *only* reason supporting the authority for a *full* search incident to lawful arrest was the possibility of discovery of evidence or fruits. Concluding that there could be no evidence or fruits in the case of an offense such as that with which respondent was charged, it held that any protective search would have to be limited by the conditions laid down in *Terry* for a search upon less than probable cause to arrest. Quite apart from the fact that *Terry* clearly recognized the distinction between the two types of searches, and that a different rule governed one than governed the other, we find additional reason to disagree with the Court of Appeals.

The justification or reason for the authority to search incident to a lawful arrest rests quite as much on the need to disarm the suspect in order to take him into custody as it does on the need to preserve evidence on his person for later use at trial. ... The standards traditionally governing a search incident to lawful arrest are not, therefore, commuted to the stricter *Terry* standards by the absence of probable fruits or further evidence of the particular crime for which the arrest is made.

Nor are we inclined, on the basis of what seems to us to be a rather speculative judgment, to qualify the breadth of the general authority to search incident to a lawful custodial arrest on an assumption that persons arrested for the offense of driving while their license has been revoked are less likely to be possessed of dangerous weapons than are those arrested for other crimes. It is scarcely open to doubt that the danger to an officer is far greater in the case of the extended exposure which follows the taking of a suspect into custody and transporting him to the police station than in the case of the relatively fleeting contact resulting from the typical *Terry*-type stop. This is an adequate basis for treating all custodial arrests alike for purposes of search justification.

But quite apart from these distinctions, our more fundamental disagreement with the Court of Appeals arises from its suggestion that there must be litigated in each case the issue of whether or not there was present one of the reasons supporting the authority for a search of the person incident to a lawful arrest. We do not think the long line of authorities of this Court dating back to Weeks [v. United States, 232 U.S. 383 (1914)], or what we can glean from the history of practice in this country and in England, requires such a case by case adjudication. A police officer's determination as to how and where to search the person of a suspect whom he has arrested is necessarily a quick *ad hoc* judgment which the Fourth Amendment does not require to be broken down in each instance into an analysis of each step in the search. The authority to search the person incident to a lawful custodial arrest, while based upon the need to disarm and to discover evidence, does not depend on what a court may later decide was the probability in a particular arrest situation that weapons or evidence would in fact be found upon the person of the suspect. A custodial arrest of a suspect based on probable cause is a reasonable intrusion under the Fourth Amendment; that intrusion being lawful, a search incident to the arrest requires no additional justification. It is the fact of the lawful arrest which establishes the authority to search, and we hold that in the case of a lawful custodial arrest a full search of the person is not only an exception to the warrant requirement of the Fourth Amendment, but is also a "reasonable" search under that Amendment.

IV

The search of respondent's person conducted by Officer Jenks in this case and the seizure from him of the heroin, were permissible under established Fourth Amendment law. While thorough, the search partook of none of the extreme or patently abusive characteristics which were held to violate the Due Process Clause of the Fourteenth Amendment in Rochin v. California, 342 U.S. 165 (1952). Since it is the fact of custodial arrest which gives rise to the authority to search,[6] it is of no moment that Jenks did not indicate any subjective fear of the respondent or that he did not himself suspect that respondent was armed. Having in the course of a lawful search come upon the crumpled package of cigarettes, he was entitled to inspect it; and when his inspection revealed the heroin capsules, he was entitled to seize them as "fruits, instrumentalities, or contraband" probative of criminal conduct. ... The judgment of the Court of Appeals holding otherwise is

Reversed.

MR. JUSTICE POWELL, concurring.[*]

6. The majority opinion of the Court of Appeals also discussed its understanding of the law where the police officer makes what the court characterized as "a routine traffic stop," i.e., where the officer would simply issue a notice of violation and allow the offender to proceed. Since in this case the officer did make a full custody arrest of the violator, we do not reach the question discussed by the Court of Appeals.

[*] Applicable also to Gustafson v. Florida, 414 U.S. 260, 94 S.Ct. 488 (1973), a companion case.

In a concurring opinion in *Gustafson,* Justice Stewart observed: "... [A] persuasive claim might have been made in this case that the custodial arrest of the petitioner for a minor traffic offense violated his rights under the Fourth and Fourteenth Amendments. But no such claim has been made. Instead, the petitioner has fully conceded the constitutional validity of his custodial arrest. That being so, it follows that the incidental search of his person was also constitutionally valid." 414 U.S. at 266.

Although I join the opinions of the Court, I write briefly to emphasize what seems to me to be the essential premise of our decisions.

The Fourth Amendment safeguards the right of "the people to be secure in their persons, houses, papers, and effects, against unreasonable searches and seizures . . . ." These are areas of an individual's life about which he entertains legitimate expectations of privacy. I believe that an individual lawfully subjected to a custodial arrest retains no significant Fourth Amendment interest in the privacy of his person. Under this view the custodial arrest is the significant intrusion of state power into the privacy of one's person. If the arrest is lawful, the privacy interest guarded by the Fourth Amendment is subordinated to a legitimate and overriding governmental concern. No reason then exists to frustrate law enforcement by requiring some independent justification for a search incident to a lawful custodial arrest. This seems to me the reason that a valid arrest justifies a full search of the person, even if that search is not narrowly limited by the twin rationales of seizing evidence and disarming the arrestee. The search incident to arrest is reasonable under the Fourth Amendment because the privacy interest protected by that constitutional guarantee is legitimately abated by the fact of arrest.

MR. JUSTICE MARSHALL, with whom MR. JUSTICE DOUGLAS and MR. JUSTICE BRENNAN join, dissenting.

Certain fundamental principles have characterized this Court's Fourth Amendment jurisprudence over the years. Perhaps the most basic of these was expressed by Mr. Justice Butler, speaking for a unanimous Court in GoBart Co. v. United States, 282 U.S. 344 (1931): "There is no formula for the determination of reasonableness. Each case is to be decided on its own facts and circumstances." Id., at 357. As we recently held, "The constitutional validity of a warrantless search is preeminently the sort of question which can only be decided in the concrete factual context of the individual case." Sibron v. New York, 392 U.S. 40, 59 (1968). And the intensive, at times painstaking, case-by-case analysis characteristic of our Fourth Amendment decisions bespeaks our "jealous regard for maintaining the integrity of individual rights." Mapp v. Ohio, 367 U.S. 643, 647 (1961). . . .

In the present case, however, the majority turns its back on these principles, holding that "the fact of the lawful arrest" always establishes the authority to conduct a full search of the arrestee's person, regardless of whether in a particular case "there was present one of the reasons supporting the authority for a search of the person incident to a lawful arrest." Ante, at 235. The majority's approach represents a clear and marked departure from our long tradition of case-by-case adjudication of the reasonableness of searches and seizures under the Fourth Amendment. I continue to believe that "[t]he scheme of the Fourth Amendment becomes meaningful only when it is assured that at some point the conduct of those charged with enforcing the laws can be subjected to the more detached, neutral scrutiny of a judge who must evaluate the reasonableness of a particular search or seizure in light of the particular circumstances." Terry v. Ohio, 392 U.S. 1, 21 (1968). Because I find the majority's reasoning to be at odds with these fundamental principles, I must respectfully dissent.

. . .

The majority's attempt to avoid case-by-case adjudication of Fourth Amendment issues is not only misguided as a matter of principle, but is also doomed to fail as a matter of practical application. As the majority itself is well aware, see ante, at 221 n. 1, the powers granted the police in this case are strong ones, subject to potential abuse. Although, in this particular case, Officer Jenks was required by Police Department regulation to make an in-custody arrest rather than to issue a citation, in most jurisdictions and for most traffic offenses the determination of whether to issue a citation or effect a full arrest is discretionary with the officer. There is always the possibility that a police officer, lacking probable cause to obtain a search warrant, will use a traffic arrest as a pretext to conduct a search. . . . I suggest this possibility not to impugn the integrity of our police, but merely to point out that case-by-case adjudication will always be necessary to determine whether a full arrest was effected for purely legitimate reasons or, rather, as a pretext for searching the arrestee. . . .

III

The majority states that "[a] police officer's determination as to how and where to search the person of a suspect whom he has arrested is necessarily a quick *ad hoc* judgment which the Fourth Amendment does not require to be broken down in each instance into an analysis of each step in the search." Ante, at 235. No precedent is cited for this broad assertion—not surprisingly, since there is none. Indeed, we only recently rejected such "a rigid all-or-nothing model of justification and regulation under the Amendment, [for] it obscures the utility of limitations upon the scope, as well as the initiation, of police action as a means of constitutional regulation. This Court has held in the past that a search which is reasonable at its inception may violate the Fourth Amendment by virtue of its intolerable intensity and scope." Terry v. Ohio, 392 U.S., at 17–18. As we there concluded, "in determining whether the seizure and search were 'unreasonable' our inquiry is a dual one—whether the officer's action was justified at its inception, and whether it was reasonably related in scope to the circumstances which justified the interference in the first place." Id., at 19–20.

As I view the matter, the search in this case divides into three distinct phases: the patdown of respondent's coat pocket; the

removal of the unknown object from the pocket; and the opening
of the crumpled up cigarette package.

A

No question is raised here concerning the lawfulness of the
patdown of respondent's coat pocket. The Court of Appeals unani-
mously affirmed the right of a police officer to conduct a limited
frisk for weapons when making an in-custody arrest, regardless of
the nature of the crime for which the arrest was made. . . .

B

With respect to the removal of the unknown object from the
coat pocket, the first issue presented is whether that aspect of the
search can be sustained as part of the limited frisk for weapons.
The weapons search approved by the Court of Appeals was modeled
upon the narrowly drawn protective search for weapons authorized
in *Terry,* which consists "of a limited patting of the outer clothing of
the suspect for concealed objects which might be used as instruments of assault." See Sibron v. New York, supra, 392 U.S., at 65.
See also *Terry,* 391 U.S., at 30.

It appears to have been conceded by the Government below
that the removal of the object from respondent's coat pocket
exceeded the scope of a *Terry* frisk for weapons, since under *Terry,*
an officer may not remove an object from the suspect's pockets
unless he has reason to believe it to be a dangerous weapon. . . .

In the present case, however, Officer Jenks had no reason to
believe and did not in fact believe that the object in respondent's
coat pocket was a weapon. He admitted later that the object did
not feel like a gun. . . . In fact, he did not really have any thoughts
one way or another about what was in the pocket. As Jenks himself
testified, "I just searched him. I didn't think about what I was
looking for. I just searched him." Since the removal of the object
from the pocket cannot be justified as part of a limited *Terry*
weapons frisk, the question arises whether it is reasonable for a
police officer, when effecting an in-custody arrest of a traffic offender, to make a fuller search of the person than is permitted pursuant
to *Terry.*

The underlying rationale of a search incident to arrest of a
traffic offender initially suggests as reasonable a search whose scope
is similar to the protective weapons frisk permitted in *Terry.* A
search incident to arrest, as the majority indicates, has two basic
functions: the removal of weapons the arrestee might use to resist
arrest or effect an escape, and the seizure of evidence or fruits of
the crime for which the arrest is made, so as to prevent its
concealment or destruction. . . .

The Government does not now contend that the search of
respondent's pocket can be justified by any need to find and seize

evidence in order to prevent its concealment or destruction, for as the Court of Appeals found, there are no evidence or fruits of the offense with which respondent was charged. The only rationale for a search in this case, then, is the removal of weapons which the arrestee might use to harm the officer and attempt an escape. This rationale, of course, is identical to the rationale of the search permitted in *Terry.* ... Since the underlying rationale of a *Terry* search and the search of a traffic violator are identical, the Court of Appeals held that the scope of the searches must be the same. And in view of its conclusion that the removal of the object from respondent's coat pocket exceeded the scope of a lawful *Terry* frisk, a conclusion not disputed by the Government nor challenged by the majority here, the plurality of the Court of Appeals held that the removal of the package exceeded the scope of a lawful search incident to arrest of a traffic violator.

The problem with this approach, however, is that it ignores several significant differences between the context in which a search incident to arrest for a traffic violation is made, and the situation presented in *Terry.* Some of these differences would appear to suggest permitting a more thorough search in this case than was permitted in *Terry;* other differences suggest a narrower, more limited right to search than was there recognized.

The most obvious difference between the two contexts relates to whether the officer has cause to believe that the individual he is dealing with possesses weapons which might be used against him. *Terry,* did not permit an officer to conduct a weapons frisk of anyone he lawfully stopped on the street, but rather, only where "he has reason to believe that he is dealing with an armed and dangerous individual ...." 392 U.S., at 27. While the policeman who arrests a suspected rapist or robber may well have reason to believe he is dealing with an armed and dangerous person, certainly this does not hold true with equal force with respect to persons arrested for motor vehicle violations of the sort involved in this case.

Nor was there any particular reason in this case to believe that respondent was dangerous. He had not attempted to evade arrest, but had quickly complied with the police both in bringing his car to a stop after being signalled to do so and in producing the documents Officer Jenks requested. In fact, Jenks admitted that he searched respondent face-to-face rather than in spread-eagle fashion because he had no reason to believe respondent would be violent.

While this difference between the situation presented in *Terry* and the context presented in this case would tend to suggest a lesser authority to search here than was permitted in *Terry,* other distinctions between the two contexts suggest just the opposite. As the Court of Appeals noted, a crucial feature distinguishing the in-custody arrest from the *Terry* context "is not the greater likelihood that a person taken into custody is armed, but rather the increased likelihood of danger to the officer *if* in fact the person is armed." 153 U.S.App.D.C., at 130, 471 F.2d, at 1098, quoting People v. Superior Court of Los Angeles County 7 Cal.3d [186 (1972)], at 214, 496 P.2d [1205] at 1225 (Wright, C.J., concurring) (emphasis in original). A *Terry* stop involves a momentary encounter between officer and suspect, while an in-custody arrest places the two in close proximity for a much longer period of time. If the individual happens to have a weapon on his person, he will certainly have much more opportunity to use it against the officer in the in-custody situation. The prolonged proximity also makes it more likely that the individual will be able to extricate any small hidden weapon which might go undetected in a weapons frisk, such as a safety pin or razor blade. In addition, a suspect taken into custody may feel more threatened by the serious restraint on his liberty than a person who is simply stopped by an officer for questioning, and may therefore be more likely to resort to force.

Thus, in some senses there is less need for a weapons search in the in-custody traffic arrest situation than in a *Terry* context; while in other ways, there is a greater need. Balancing these competing considerations in order to determine what is a reasonable warrant-less search in the traffic arrest context is a difficult process, one for which there may be no easy analytical guideposts. We are dealing in factors not easily quantified and, therefore, not easily weighed one against the other. And the competing interests we are protecting—the individual's interest in remaining free from unnecessarily intrusive invasions of privacy and society's interest that police officers not take unnecessary risks in the performance of their duties—are each deserving of our most serious attention and do not themselves tip the balance in any particular direction.

As will be explained more fully below, I do not think it necessary to solve this balancing equation in this particular case. It is important to note, however, in view of the reasoning adopted by the majority, that available empirical evidence supports the result reached by the plurality of the Court of Appeals, rather than the result reached by the Court today.

The majority relies on statistics indicating that a significant percentage of police officer murders occur when the officers are making traffic stops. But these statistics only confirm what we recognized in *Terry*—that "American criminals have a long tradition of armed violence, and every year in this country many law enforcement officers are killed in the line of duty, and thousands more are wounded." Terry v. Ohio, supra, at 23. As the very next sentence in *Terry* recognized, however, "Virtually all of these deaths and a substantial portion of the injuries are inflicted with guns and knives." Id., at 24. The statistics relied on by the Government in this case support this observation. Virtually all of the killings are caused by guns and knives, the very type of weapons which will not go undetected in a properly conducted weapons frisk. It requires more than citation to these statistics, then, to support the proposition that it is reasonable for police officers to conduct more than a *Terry*-type frisk for weapons when seeking to disarm a traffic offender who is taken into custody.

C

The majority opinion fails to recognize that the search conducted by Officer Jenks did not merely involve a search of respondent's person. It also included a separate search of effects found on his person. And even were we to assume, *arguendo,* that it was reasonable for Jenks to remove the object he felt in respondent's pocket, clearly there was no justification consistent with the Fourth Amendment which would authorize his opening the package and looking inside.

To begin with, after Jenks had the cigarette package in his hands, there is no indication that he had reason to believe or did in fact believe that the package contained a weapon. More importantly, even if the crumpled up cigarette package had in fact contained some sort of small weapon, it would have been impossible for respondent to have used it once the package was in the officer's hands. Opening the package therefore did not further the protective purpose of the search. ...

It is suggested, however, that since the custodial arrest itself represents a significant intrusion into the privacy of the person, any additional intrusion by way of opening or examining effects found on the person is not worthy of constitutional protection. But such an approach was expressly rejected by the Court in *Chimel.* There it was suggested that since the police had lawfully entered petitioner's house to effect an arrest, the additional invasion of privacy stemming from an accompanying search of the entire house was inconsequential. The Court answered: "[W]e see no reason why, simply because some interference with an individual's privacy and freedom of movement has lawfully taken place, further intrusions should automatically be allowed despite the absence of a warrant that the Fourth Amendment would otherwise require." 395 U.S., at 766 n. 12.

The Fourth Amendment preserves the right of "the people to be secure in their persons, houses, papers, and effects, against unreasonable searches and seizures ...." *Chimel* established the principle that the lawful right of the police to interfere with the security of the person did not, standing alone, automatically confer the right to interfere with the security and privacy of his house. Hence, the mere fact of an arrest should be no justification, in and of itself, for invading the privacy of the individual's personal effects.

The Government argues that it is difficult to see what constitutionally protected "expectation of privacy" a prisoner has in the interior of a cigarette pack. One wonders if the result in this case would have been the same were respondent a businessman who was lawfully taken into custody for driving without a license and whose wallet was taken from him by the police. Would it be reasonable for the police officer, because of the possibility that a razor blade was hidden somewhere in the wallet, to open it, remove all the contents, and examine each item carefully? Or suppose a lawyer lawfully arrested for a traffic offense is found to have a sealed envelope on his person. Would it be permissible for the arresting officer to tear open the envelope in order to make sure that it did not contain a clandestine weapon—perhaps a pin or a razor blade? ... Would it not be more consonant with the purpose of the Fourth Amendment and the legitimate needs of the police to require the officer, if he has any question whatsoever about what the wallet or letter contains, to hold onto it until the arrestee is brought to the precinct station?

I, for one, cannot characterize any of these intrusions into the privacy of an individual's papers and effects as being negligible incidents to the more serious intrusion into the individual's privacy stemming from the arrest itself. Nor can any principled distinction be drawn between the hypothetical searches I have posed and the search of the cigarette package in this case. The only reasoned distinction is between warrantless searches which serve legitimate protective and evidentiary functions and those that do not. ...

The search conducted by Officer Jenks in this case went far beyond what was reasonably necessary to protect him from harm or to ensure that respondent would not effect an escape from custody. In my view, it therefore fell outside the scope of a properly drawn "search incident to arrest" exception to the Fourth Amendment's warrant requirement. I would affirm the judgment of the Court of Appeals holding that the fruits of the search should have been suppressed at respondent's trial.[*]

[*] The Supreme Court has held that "except in those situations in which there is at least articulable and reasonable suspicion that a motorist is unlicensed or that an automobile is not registered, or that either the vehicle or an occupant is otherwise subject to seizure for violation of law, stopping an automobile and detaining the driver in order to check his driver's license and the registration of the automobile are unreasonable under the Fourth Amendment." Delaware v. Prouse, 440 U.S. 648, 663 (1979) (8–1). Other kinds of stops "that involve less intrusion or that do not involve the unconstrained exercise of discretion," including road-block-type stops of all traffic, were distinguished. Id.

UNITED STATES v. CHADWICK

433 U.S. 1, 97 S.Ct. 2476, 53 L.Ed.2d 538 (1977).

MR. CHIEF JUSTICE BURGER delivered the opinion of the Court.

We granted certiorari in this case to decide whether a search warrant is required before federal agents may open a locked footlocker which they have lawfully seized at the time of the arrest of its owners, when there is probable cause to believe the footlocker contains contraband.

(1)

On May 8, 1973, Amtrak railroad officials in San Diego observed respondents Gregory Machado and Bridget Leary load a brown footlocker onto a train bound for Boston. Their suspicions were aroused when they noticed that the trunk was unusually heavy for its size, and that it was leaking talcum powder, a substance often used to mask the odor of marihuana or hashish. Because Machado matched a profile used to spot drug traffickers, the railroad officials reported these circumstances to federal agents in San Diego, who in turn relayed the information, together with detailed descriptions of Machado and the footlocker, to their counterparts in Boston.

When the train arrived in Boston two days later, federal narcotics agents were on hand. Though the officers had not obtained an arrest or search warrant, they had with them a police dog trained to detect marihuana. The agents identified Machado and Leary and kept them under surveillance as they claimed their suitcases and the footlocker, which had been transported by baggage cart from the train to the departure area. Machado and Leary lifted the footlocker from the baggage cart, placed it on the floor and sat down on it.

The agents then released the dog near the footlocker. Without alerting respondents, the dog signaled the presence of a controlled substance inside. Respondent Chadwick then joined Machado and Leary, and they engaged an attendant to move the footlocker outside to Chadwick's waiting automobile. Machado, Chadwick, and the attendant together lifted the 200-pound footlocker into the trunk of the car, while Leary waited in the front seat. At that point, while the trunk of the car was still open and before the car engine had been started, the officers arrested all three. A search disclosed no weapons, but the keys to the footlocker were apparently taken from Machado.

Respondents were taken to the Federal Building in Boston; the agents followed with Chadwick's car and the footlocker. As the

Government concedes, from the moment of respondents' arrests at about 9 p.m., the footlocker remained under the exclusive control of law enforcement officers at all times. The footlocker and luggage were placed in the Federal Building, where, as one of the agents later testified, "there was no risk that whatever was contained in the footlocker trunk would be removed by the defendants or their associates." App. 44. The agents had no reason to believe that the footlocker contained explosives or other inherently dangerous items, or that it contained evidence which would lose its value unless the footlocker were opened at once. Facilities were readily available in which the footlocker could have been stored securely; it is not contended that there was any exigency calling for an immediate search.

At the Federal Building an hour and a half after the arrests, the agents opened the footlocker and luggage. They did not obtain respondents' consent; they did not secure a search warrant. The footlocker was locked with a padlock and a regular trunk lock. It is unclear whether it was opened with the keys taken from respondent Machado, or by other means. Large amounts of marihuana were found in the footlocker.

Respondents were indicted for possession of marihuana with intent to distribute it, in violation of 21 U.S.C. § 841(a)(1), and for conspiracy, in violation of 21 U.S.C. § 846. Before trial, they moved to suppress the marihuana obtained from the footlocker. In the District Court, the Government sought to justify its failure to secure a search warrant under the "automobile exception" of Chambers v. Maroney, 399 U.S. 42 (1970), and as a search incident to the arrests. Holding that "[w]arrantless searches are *per se* unreasonable, subject to a few carefully delineated and limited exceptions," the District Court rejected both justifications. 393 F.Supp. 763, 771 (Mass.1975). The court saw the relationship between the footlocker and Chadwick's automobile as merely coincidental, and held that the double-locked, 200-pound footlocker was not part of "the area from within which [respondents] might gain possession of a weapon or destructible evidence." Chimel v. California, 395 U.S. 752, 763 (1969).

A divided Court of Appeals for the First Circuit affirmed the suppression of the seized marihuana. ...

... We granted certiorari, 429 U.S. 814 (1976). We affirm.

(2)

In this Court the Government again contends that the Fourth Amendment Warrant Clause protects only interests traditionally identified with the home. Recalling the colonial writs of assistance, which were often executed in searches of private dwellings, the Government claims that the Warrant Clause was adopted primarily, if not exclusively, in response to unjustified intrusions into private homes on the authority of general warrants. The Government argues there is no evidence that the Framers of the Fourth Amendment intended to disturb the established practice of permitting warrantless searches outside the home, or to modify the initial clause of the Fourth Amendment by making warrantless searches supported by probable cause *per se* unreasonable.

Drawing on its reading of history, the Government argues that only homes, offices, and private communications implicate interests which lie at the core of the Fourth Amendment. Accordingly, it is only in these contexts that the determination whether a search or seizure is reasonable should turn on whether a warrant has been obtained. In all other situations, the Government contends, less significant privacy values are at stake, and the reasonableness of a government intrusion should depend solely on whether there is probable cause to believe evidence of criminal conduct is present. Where personal effects are lawfully seized outside the home on probable cause, the Government would thus regard searches without a warrant as not "unreasonable."

We do not agree that the Warrant Clause protects only dwellings and other specifically designated locales. As we have noted before, the Fourth Amendment "protects people, not places," Katz v. United States, 389 U.S. 347, 351 (1967); more particularly, it protects people from unreasonable government intrusions into their legitimate expectations of privacy. In this case, the Warrant Clause makes a significant contribution to that protection. The question, then, is whether a warrantless search in these circumstances was unreasonable.

(3)

It cannot be doubted that the Fourth Amendment's commands grew in large measure out of the colonists' experience with the writs of assistance and their memories of the general warrants formerly in use in England. . . .

Although the searches and seizures which deeply concerned the colonists, and which were foremost in the minds of the Framers, were those involving invasions of the home, it would be a mistake to conclude, as the Government contends, that the Warrant Clause was therefore intended to guard only against intrusions into the home. First, the Warrant Clause does not in terms distinguish between searches conducted in private homes and other searches. There is also a strong historical connection between the Warrant Clause and the initial clause of the Fourth Amendment, which draws no distinctions among "persons, houses, papers, and effects" in safeguarding against unreasonable searches and seizures. . . .

Moreover, if there is little evidence that the Framers intended the Warrant Clause to operate outside the home, there is no evidence at all that they intended to exclude from protection of the

Clause all searches occurring outside the home. The absence of a contemporary outcry against warrantless searches in public places was because, aside from searches incident to arrest, such warrantless searches were not a large issue in colonial America. Thus, silence in the historical record tells us little about the Framers' attitude toward application of the Warrant Clause to the search of respondents' footlocker. What we do know is that the Framers were men who focused on the wrongs of that day but who intended the Fourth Amendment to safeguard fundamental values which would far outlast the specific abuses which gave it birth.

Moreover, in this area we do not write on a clean slate. Our fundamental inquiry in considering Fourth Amendment issues is whether or not a search or seizure is reasonable under all the circumstances. ... The judicial warrant has a significant role to play in that it provides the detached scrutiny of a neutral magistrate, which is a more reliable safeguard against improper searches than the hurried judgment of a law enforcement officer "engaged in the often competitive enterprise of ferreting out crime." Johnson v. United States, 333 U.S. 10, 14 (1948). Once a lawful search has begun, it is also far more likely that it will not exceed proper bounds when it is done pursuant to a judicial authorization "particularly describing the place to be searched and the persons or things to be seized." Further, a warrant assures the individual whose property is searched or seized of the lawful authority of the executing officer, his need to search, and the limits of his power to search. ...

Just as the Fourth Amendment "protects people, not places," the protections a judicial warrant offers against erroneous governmental intrusions are effective whether applied in or out of the home. Accordingly, we have held warrantless searches unreasonable, and therefore unconstitutional, in a variety of settings. ... These cases illustrate the applicability of the Warrant Clause beyond the narrow limits suggested by the Government. They also reflect the settled constitutional principle, discussed earlier, that a fundamental purpose of the Fourth Amendment is to safeguard individuals from unreasonable government invasions of legitimate privacy interests, and not simply those interests found inside the four walls of the home. ...

In this case, important Fourth Amendment privacy interests were at stake. By placing personal effects inside a double-locked footlocker, respondents manifested an expectation that the contents would remain free from public examination. No less than one who locks the doors of his home against intruders, one who safeguards his personal possessions in this manner is due the protection of the Fourth Amendment Warrant Clause. There being no exigency, it was unreasonable for the Government to conduct this search without the safeguards a judicial warrant provides.

(4)

The Government does not contend that the footlocker's brief contact with Chadwick's car makes this an automobile search, but it is argued that the rationale of our automobile search cases demonstrates the reasonableness of permitting warrantless searches of luggage; the Government views such luggage as analogous to motor vehicles for Fourth Amendment purposes. It is true that, like the footlocker in issue here, automobiles are "effects" under the Fourth Amendment, and searches and seizures of automobiles are therefore subject to the constitutional standard of reasonableness. But this Court has recognized significant differences between motor vehicles and other property which permit warrantless searches of automobiles in circumstances in which warrantless searches would not be reasonable in other contexts. . . .

Our treatment of automobiles has been based in part on their inherent mobility, which often makes obtaining a judicial warrant impracticable. Nevertheless, we have also sustained "warrantless searches of vehicles . . . in cases in which the possibilities of the vehicle's being removed or evidence in it destroyed were remote, if not nonexistent." Cady v. Dombrowski, 413 U.S. 433, 441–442 (1973) . . . .

The answer lies in the diminished expectation of privacy which surrounds the automobile . . . . Other factors reduce automobile privacy. "All States require vehicles to be registered and operators to be licensed. States and localities have enacted extensive and detailed codes regulating the condition and manner in which motor vehicles may be operated on public streets and highways." Cady v. Dombrowski, supra, at 441. Automobiles periodically undergo official inspection, and they are often taken into police custody in the interests of public safety. . . .

The factors which diminish the privacy aspects of an automobile do not apply to respondents' footlocker. Luggage contents are not open to public view, except as a condition to a border entry or common carrier travel; nor is luggage subject to regular inspections and official scrutiny on a continuing basis. Unlike an automobile, whose primary function is transportation, luggage is intended as a repository of personal effects. In sum, a person's expectations of privacy in personal luggage are substantially greater than in an automobile.

Nor does the footlocker's mobility justify dispensing with the added protections of the Warrant Clause. Once the federal agents had seized it at the railroad station and had safely transferred it to the Boston Federal Building under their exclusive control, there was not the slightest danger that the footlocker or its contents could have been removed before a valid search warrant could be obtained. The initial seizure and detention of the footlocker, the validity of which respondents do not contest, were sufficient to guard against any risk that evidence might be lost. With the footlocker safely immobilized, it was unreasonable to undertake the additional and greater intrusion of a search without a warrant.[8]

Finally, the Government urges that the Constitution permits the warrantless search of any property in the possession of a person arrested in public, so long as there is probable cause to believe that the property contains contraband or evidence of crime. Although recognizing that the footlocker was not within respondents' immediate control, the Government insists that the search was reasonable because the footlocker was seized contemporaneously with respondents' arrests and was searched as soon thereafter as was practicable. The reasons justifying search in a custodial arrest are quite different. When a custodial arrest is made, there is always some danger that the person arrested may seek to use a weapon, or that evidence may be concealed or destroyed. To safeguard himself and others, and to prevent the loss of evidence, it has been held reasonable for the arresting officer to conduct a prompt, warrantless "search of the arrestee's person and the area 'within his immediate control'—construing that phrase to mean the area from within which he might gain possession of a weapon or destructible evidence." Chimel v. California, 395 U.S., at 763. . . .

Such searches may be conducted without a warrant, and they may also be made whether or not there is probable cause to believe that the person arrested may have a weapon or is about to destroy evidence. The potential dangers lurking in all custodial arrests make warrantless searches of items within the "immediate control" area reasonable without requiring the arresting officer to calculate the probability that weapons or destructible evidence may be involved. . . . However, warrantless searches of luggage or other property seized at the time of an arrest cannot be justified as incident to that arrest either if the "search is remote in time or place from the arrest," Preston v. United States, 376 U.S., at 367, or no exigency exists. Once law enforcement officers have reduced luggage or other personal property not immediately associated with the person of the arrestee to their exclusive control, and there is no longer any danger that the arrestee might gain access to the property to seize a weapon or destroy evidence, a search of that

---

8. Respondents' principal privacy interest in the footlocker was, of course, not in the container itself, which was exposed to public view, but in its contents. A search of the interior was therefore a far greater intrusion into Fourth Amendment values than the impoundment of the footlocker. Though surely a substantial infringement of respondents' use and possession, the seizure did not diminish respondents' legitimate expectation that the footlocker's contents would remain private.

It was the greatly reduced expectation of privacy in the automobile, coupled with the transportation function of the vehicle, which made the Court in *Chambers* unwilling to decide whether an immediate search of an automobile, or its seizure and indefinite immobilization, constituted a greater interfer-

property is no longer an incident of the arrest.[9]

Here the search was conducted more than an hour after federal agents had gained exclusive control of the footlocker and long after respondents were securely in custody; the search therefore cannot be viewed as incidental to the arrest or as justified by any other exigency. Even though on this record the issuance of a warrant by a judicial officer was reasonably predictable, a line must be drawn. In our view, when no exigency is shown to support the need for an immediate search, the Warrant Clause places the line at the point where the property to be searched comes under the exclusive dominion of police authority. Respondents were therefore entitled to the protection of the Warrant Clause with the evaluation of a neutral magistrate, before their privacy interests in the contents of the footlocker were invaded.[10]

Accordingly, the judgment is

Affirmed.[*]

ence with the rights of the owner. This is clearly not the case with locked luggage.

9. Of course, there may be other justifications for a warrantless search of luggage taken from a suspect at the time of his arrest; for example, if officers have reason to believe that luggage contains some immediately dangerous instrumentality, such as explosives, it would be foolhardy to transport it to the station house without opening the luggage and disarming the weapon. . . .

10. Unlike searches of the person . . . searches of possessions within an arrestee's immediate control cannot be justified by any reduced expectations of privacy caused by the arrest. Respondents' privacy interest in the contents of the footlocker was not eliminated simply because they were under arrest.

[*] Justice Brennan wrote a concurring opinion. Justice Blackmun wrote a dissenting opinion, which Justice Rehnquist joined.

CALIFORNIA v. ACEVEDO

500 U.S. 565, 111 S.Ct. 1982, 114 L.Ed.2d 619 (1991).

JUSTICE BLACKMUN delivered the opinion of the Court.

This case requires us once again to consider the so-called "automobile exception" to the warrant requirement of the Fourth Amendment and its application to the search of a closed container in the trunk of a car.

I

On October 28, 1987, Officer Coleman of the Santa Ana, Cal., Police Department received a telephone call from a federal drug enforcement agent in Hawaii. The agent informed Coleman that he had seized a package containing marijuana which was to have been delivered to the Federal Express Office in Santa Ana and which was addressed to J.R. Daza at 805 West Stevens Avenue in that city. The agent arranged to send the package to Coleman instead. Coleman then was to take the package to the Federal Express office and arrest the person who arrived to claim it.

Coleman received the package on October 29, verified its contents, and took it to the Senior Operations Manager at the Federal Express office. At about 10:30 a.m. on October 30, a man, who identified himself as Jamie Daza, arrived to claim the package. He accepted it and drove to his apartment on West Stevens. He carried the package into the apartment.

At 11:45 a.m., officers observed Daza leave the apartment and drop the box and paper that had contained the marijuana into a trash bin. Coleman at that point left the scene to get a search warrant. About 12:05 p.m., the officers saw Richard St. George leave the apartment carrying a blue knapsack which appeared to be half full. The officers stopped him as he was driving off, searched the knapsack, and found 1½ pounds of marijuana.

At 12:30 p.m., respondent Charles Steven Acevedo arrived. He entered Daza's apartment, stayed for about 10 minutes, and reappeared carrying a brown paper bag that looked full. The officers noticed that the bag was the size of one of the wrapped marijuana packages sent from Hawaii. Acevedo walked to a silver Honda in the parking lot. He placed the bag in the trunk of the car and started to drive away. Fearing the loss of evidence, officers in a marked police car stopped him. They opened the trunk and the bag, and found marijuana.

Respondent was charged in state court with possession of marijuana for sale, in violation of Cal. Health & Safety Code Ann.

§ 11359 (West Supp.1991). App. 2. He moved to suppress the marijuana found in the car. The motion was denied. He then pleaded guilty but appealed the denial of the suppression motion.

The California Court of Appeal, Fourth District, concluded that the marijuana found in the paper bag in the car's trunk should have been suppressed. 216 Cal.App.3d 586, 265 Cal.Rptr. 23 (1990). The court concluded that the officers had probable cause to believe that the paper bag contained drugs but lacked probable cause to suspect that Acevedo's car, itself, otherwise contained contraband. Because the officers' probable cause was directed specifically at the bag, the court held that the case was controlled by United States v. Chadwick, 433 U.S. 1 (1977), rather than by United States v. Ross, 456 U.S. 798 (1982). Although the court agreed that the officers could seize the paper bag, it held that, under *Chadwick,* they could not open the bag without first obtaining a warrant for that purpose. The court then recognized "the anomalous nature" of the dichotomy between the rule in *Chadwick* and the rule in *Ross.* 216 Cal.App.3d, at 592, 265 Cal.Rptr., at 27. That dichotomy dictates that if there is probable cause to search a car, then the entire car—including any closed container found therein—may be searched without a warrant, but if there is probable cause only as to a container in the car, the container may be held but not searched until a warrant is obtained.

The Supreme Court of California denied the State's petition for review. . . .

We granted certiorari, 498 U.S. 807 (1990), to reexamine the law applicable to a closed container in an automobile, a subject that has troubled courts and law enforcement officers since it was first considered in *Chadwick.*

II

The Fourth Amendment protects the "right of the people to be secure in their persons, houses, papers, and effects, against unreasonable searches and seizures." Contemporaneously with the adoption of the Fourth Amendment, the First Congress, and, later, the Second and Fourth Congresses, distinguished between the need for a warrant to search for contraband concealed in "a dwelling house or similar place" and the need for a warrant to search for contraband concealed in a movable vessel. See *Carroll v. United States,* 267 U.S. 132, 151 (1925). . . . In *Carroll,* this Court established an exception to the warrant requirement for moving vehicles, for it recognized

"a necessary difference between a search of a store, dwelling house or other structure in respect of which a proper official warrant readily may be obtained, and a search of a ship, motor boat, wagon or automobile, for contraband goods, where it is not practicable to secure a warrant because the vehicle can be quickly moved out of the locality or jurisdiction in which the warrant must be sought." 267 U.S., at 153.

It therefore held that a warrantless search of an automobile, based upon probable cause to believe that the vehicle contained evidence of crime in the light of an exigency arising out of the likely disappearance of the vehicle, did not contravene the Warrant Clause of the Fourth Amendment. . . .

The Court refined the exigency requirement in Chambers v. Maroney, 399 U.S. 42 (1970), when it held that the existence of exigent circumstances was to be determined at the time the automobile is seized. The car search at issue in *Chambers* took place at the police station, where the vehicle was immobilized, some time after the driver had been arrested. Given probable cause and exigent circumstances at the time the vehicle was first stopped, the Court held that the later warrantless search at the station passed constitutional muster. The validity of the later search derived from the ruling in *Carroll* that an immediate search without a warrant at the moment of seizure would have been permissible. . . . The Court reasoned in *Chambers* that the police could search later whenever they could have searched earlier, had they so chosen. . . . Following *Chambers*, if the police have probable cause to justify a warrantless seizure of an automobile on a public roadway, they may conduct either an immediate or a delayed search of the vehicle.

In United States v. Ross, 456 U.S. 798, decided in 1982, we held that a warrantless search of an automobile under the *Carroll* doctrine could include a search of a container or package found inside the car when such a search was supported by probable cause. The warrantless search of Ross' car occurred after an informant told the police that he had seen Ross complete a drug transaction using drugs stored in the trunk of his car. The police stopped the car, searched it, and discovered in the trunk a brown paper bag containing drugs. We decided that the search of Ross' car was not unreasonable under the Fourth Amendment: "The scope of a warrantless search based on probable cause is no narrower—and no broader—than the scope of a search authorized by a warrant supported by probable cause." Id., at 823. Thus, "[i]f probable cause justifies the search of a lawfully stopped vehicle, it justifies the search of every part of the vehicle and its contents that may conceal the object of the search." Id., at 825. In *Ross,* therefore, we clarified the scope of the *Carroll* doctrine as properly including a "probing search" of compartments and containers within the automobile so long as the search is supported by probable cause. Id., at 800.

In addition to this clarification, *Ross* distinguished the *Carroll* doctrine from the separate rule that governed the search of closed containers. See 456 U.S., at 817. The Court had announced this separate rule, unique to luggage and other closed packages, bags, and containers, in United States v. Chadwick, 433 U.S. 1 (1977). In *Chadwick,* federal narcotics agents had probable cause to believe that a 200-pound double-locked footlocker contained marijuana. The agents tracked the locker as the defendants removed it from a train and carried it through the station to a waiting car. As soon as the defendants lifted the locker into the trunk of the car, the agents arrested them, seized the locker, and searched it. In this Court, the United States did not contend that the locker's brief contact with the automobile's trunk sufficed to make the *Carroll* doctrine applicable. Rather, the United States urged that the search of movable luggage could be considered analogous to the search of an automobile. . . .

The Court rejected this argument because, it reasoned, a person expects more privacy in his luggage and personal effects than he does in his automobile. . . . Moreover, it concluded that as "may often not be the case when automobiles are seized," secure storage facilities are usually available when the police seize luggage. [433 U.S.] at 13, n. 7.

In Arkansas v. Sanders, 442 U.S. 753 (1979), the Court extended *Chadwick's* rule to apply to a suitcase actually being transported in the trunk of a car. In *Sanders,* the police had probable cause to believe a suitcase contained marijuana. They watched as the defendant placed the suitcase in the trunk of a taxi and was driven away. The police pursued the taxi for several blocks, stopped it, found the suitcase in the trunk, and searched it. Although the Court had applied the *Carroll* doctrine to searches of integral parts of the automobile itself, (indeed, in *Carroll,* contraband whiskey was in the upholstery of the seats, see 267 U.S., at 136), it did not extend the doctrine to the warrantless search of personal luggage "merely because it was located in an automobile lawfully stopped by the police." 442 U.S., at 765. Again, the *Sanders* majority stressed the heightened privacy expectation in personal luggage and concluded that the presence of luggage in an automobile did not diminish the owner's expectation of privacy in his personal items.

In *Ross,* the Court endeavored to distinguish between *Carroll,* which governed the *Ross* automobile search, and *Chadwick,* which governed the *Sanders* automobile search. It held that the *Carroll* doctrine covered searches of automobiles when the police had probable cause to search an entire vehicle but that the *Chadwick* doctrine governed searches of luggage when the officers had probable cause to search only a container within the vehicle. Thus, in a *Ross* situation, the police could conduct a reasonable search under the Fourth Amendment without obtaining a warrant, whereas in a *Sanders* situation, the police had to obtain a warrant before they searched.

Justice Stevens is correct, of course, that *Ross* involved the scope of an automobile search. . . . *Ross* held that closed containers encountered by the police during a warrantless search of a car pursuant to the automobile exception could also be searched. Thus, this Court in *Ross* took the critical step of saying that closed containers in cars could be searched without a warrant because of their presence within the automobile. Despite the protection that *Sanders* purported to extend to closed containers, the privacy interest in those closed containers yielded to the broad scope of an automobile search.

III

The facts in this case closely resemble the facts in *Ross.* In *Ross,* the police had probable cause to believe that drugs were stored in the trunk of a particular car. . . . Here, the California Court of Appeal concluded that the police had probable cause to believe that respondent was carrying marijuana in a bag in his car's trunk. . . .

This Court in *Ross* rejected *Chadwick*'s distinction between containers and cars. It concluded that the expectation of privacy in one's vehicle is equal to one's expectation of privacy in the container, and noted that "the privacy interests in a car's trunk or glove compartment may be no less than those in a movable container." 456 U.S., at 823. It also recognized that it was arguable that the same exigent circumstances that permit a warrantless search of an automobile would justify the warrantless search of a movable container. . . . In deference to the rule of *Chadwick* and *Sanders,* however, the Court put that question to one side. . . . It concluded that the time and expense of the warrant process would be misdirected if the police could search every cubic inch of an automobile until they discovered a paper sack, at which point the Fourth Amendment required them to take the sack to a magistrate for permission to look inside. We now must decide the question deferred in *Ross:* whether the Fourth Amendment requires the police to obtain a warrant to open the sack in a movable vehicle simply because they lack probable cause to search the entire car. We conclude that it does not.

IV

Dissenters in *Ross* asked why the suitcase in *Sanders* was "more private, less difficult for police to seize and store, or in any other relevant respect more properly subject to the warrant requirement, then a container that police discover in a probable-cause search of an entire automobile?" Id., at 839–840. We now agree that a container found after a general search of the automobile and a container found in a car after a limited search for the container are equally easy for the police to store and for the suspect to hide or destroy. In fact, we see no principled distinction in terms of either the privacy expectation or the exigent circumstances between the paper bag found by the police in *Ross* and the paper bag found by

the police here. Furthermore, by attempting to distinguish between a container for which the police are specifically searching and
a container which they come across in a car, we have provided only
minimal protection for privacy and have impeded effective law
enforcement.

The line between probable cause to search a vehicle and
probable cause to search a package in that vehicle is not always
clear, and separate rules that govern the two objects to be searched
may enable the police to broaden their power to make warrantless
searches and disserve privacy interests. We noted this in *Ross* in
the context of a search of an entire vehicle. Recognizing that under
Carroll, the "entire vehicle itself . . . could be searched without a
warrant," we concluded that "prohibiting police from opening
immediately a container in which the object of the search is most
likely to be found and instead forcing them first to comb the entire
vehicle would actually exacerbate the intrusion on privacy interests." 456 U.S., at 821, n. 28. At the moment when officers stop
an automobile, it may be less than clear whether they suspect with a
high degree of certainty that the vehicle contains drugs in a bag or
simply contains drugs. If the police know that they may open a bag
only if they are actually searching the entire car, they may search
more extensively than they otherwise would in order to establish
the general probable cause required by *Ross.*

Such a situation is not far fetched. In United States v. Johns,
469 U.S. 478 (1985), customs agents saw two trucks drive to a
private airstrip and approach two small planes. The agents drew
near the trucks, smelled marijuana, and then saw in the backs of the
trucks packages wrapped in a manner that marijuana smugglers
customarily employed. The agents took the trucks to headquarters
and searched the packages without a warrant. Id., at 481. Relying
on *Chadwick,* the defendants argued that the search was unlawful.
Id., at 482. The defendants contended that *Ross* was inapplicable
because the agents lacked probable cause to search anything but the
packages themselves and supported this contention by noting that a
search of the entire vehicle never occurred. Id., at 483. We
rejected that argument and found *Chadwick* and *Sanders* inapposite because the agents had probable cause to search the entire
body of each truck, although they had chosen not to do so. Id., at
482–483. We cannot see the benefit of a rule that requires law
enforcement officers to conduct a more intrusive search in order to
justify a less intrusive one.

To the extent that the *Chadwick-Sanders* rule protects privacy,
its protection is minimal. Law enforcement officers may seize a
container and hold it until they obtain a search warrant. *Chadwick,*
433 U.S., at 13. "Since the police, by hypothesis, have probable
cause to seize the property, we can assume that a warrant will be
routinely forthcoming in the overwhelming majority of cases."
Sanders, 442 U.S., at 770 (dissenting opinion). And the police

often will be able to search containers without a warrant, despite the *Chadwick-Sanders* rule, as a search incident to a lawful arrest. In New York v. Belton, 453 U.S. 454 (1981), the Court said:

"[W]e hold that when a policeman has made a lawful custodial arrest of the occupant of an automobile, he may, as a contemporaneous incident of that arrest, search the passenger compartment of that automobile.

"It follows from this conclusion that the police may also examine the contents of any containers found within the passenger compartment." Id., at 460 (footnote omitted).

Under *Belton,* the same probable cause to believe that a container holds drugs will allow the police to arrest the person transporting the container and search it.

Finally, the search of a paper bag intrudes far less on individual privacy than does the incursion sanctioned long ago in *Carroll.* In that case, prohibition agents slashed the upholstery of the automobile. This Court nonetheless found their search to be reasonable under the Fourth Amendment. If destroying the interior of an automobile is not unreasonable, we cannot conclude that looking inside a closed container is. In light of the minimal protection to privacy afforded by the *Chadwick-Sanders* rule, and our serious doubt whether that rule substantially serves privacy interests, we now hold that the Fourth Amendment does not compel separate treatment for an automobile search that extends only to a container within the vehicle.

V

The *Chadwick-Sanders* rule not only has failed to protect privacy but it has also confused courts and police officers and impeded effective law enforcement. The conflict between the *Carroll* doctrine cases and the *Chadwick-Sanders* line has been criticized in academic commentary. . . .

The discrepancy between the two rules has led to confusion for law enforcement officers. For example, when an officer, who has developed probable cause to believe that a vehicle contains drugs, begins to search the vehicle and immediately discovers a closed container, which rule applies? The defendant will argue that the fact that the officer first chose to search the container indicates that his probable cause extended only to the container and that *Chadwick* and *Sanders* therefore require a warrant. On the other hand, the fact that the officer first chose to search in the most obvious location should not restrict the propriety of the search. The *Chadwick* rule, as applied in *Sanders,* has devolved into an anomaly such that the more likely the police are to discover drugs in a container, the less authority they have to search it. We have noted the virtue of providing " ' "clear and unequivocal" guidelines to the law enforcement profession.' " Minnick v. Mississippi, 498 U.S.

146, 151 (1990), quoting Arizona v. Roberson, 486 U.S. 675, 682 (1988). The *Chadwick-Sanders* rule is the antithesis of a " 'clear and unequivocal' guideline."

. . .

Although we have recognized firmly that the doctrine of *stare decisis* serves profoundly important purposes in our legal system, this Court has overruled a prior case on the comparatively rare occasion when it has bred confusion or been a derelict or led to anomalous results. . . . *Sanders* was explicitly undermined in *Ross,* 456 U.S., at 824, and the existence of the dual regimes for automobile searches that uncover containers has proved as confusing as the *Chadwick* and *Sanders* dissenters predicted. We conclude that it is better to adopt one clear-cut rule to govern automobile searches and eliminate the warrant requirement for closed containers set forth in *Sanders.*

VI

The interpretation of the *Carroll* doctrine set forth in *Ross* now applies to all searches of containers found in an automobile. In other words, the police may search without a warrant if their search is supported by probable cause. The Court in *Ross* put it this way:

> "The scope of a warrantless search of an automobile . . . is not defined by the nature of the container in which the contraband is secreted. Rather, it is defined by the object of the search and the places in which there is probable cause to believe that it may be found." 456 U.S., at 824.

It went on to note: "Probable cause to believe that a container placed in the trunk of a taxi contains contraband or evidence does not justify a search of the entire cab." Ibid. We reaffirm that principle. In the case before us, the police had probable cause to believe that the paper bag in the automobile's trunk contained marijuana. That probable cause now allows a warrantless search of the paper bag. The facts in the record reveal that the police did not have probable cause to believe that contraband was hidden in any other part of the automobile and a search of the entire vehicle would have been without probable cause and unreasonable under the Fourth Amendment.

Our holding today neither extends the *Carroll* doctrine nor broadens the scope of the permissible automobile search delineated in *Carroll, Chambers,* and *Ross.* It remains a "cardinal principle that 'searches conducted outside the judicial process, without prior approval by judge or magistrate, are *per se* unreasonable under the Fourth Amendment—subject only to a few specifically established and well-delineated exceptions.' " Mincey v. Arizona, 437 U.S. 385, 390 (1978), quoting Katz v. United States, 389 U.S. 347, 357 (1967) (footnote omitted). We held in *Ross:* "The exception recognized in

Carroll is unquestionably one that is 'specifically established and well delineated.' " 456 U.S., at 825.

Until today, this Court has drawn a curious line between the search of an automobile that coincidentally turns up a container and the search of a container that coincidentally turns up in an automobile. The protections of the Fourth Amendment must not turn on such coincidences. We therefore interpret *Carroll* as providing one rule to govern all automobile searches. The police may search an automobile and the containers within it where they have probable cause to believe contraband or evidence is contained.

The judgment of the California Court of Appeals is reversed and the case is remanded to that court for further proceedings not inconsistent with this opinion.

It is so ordered.[*]

[*] Justice Scalia wrote an opinion concurring in the judgment. Justice Stevens wrote a dissenting opinion, which Justice Marshall joined. Justice White noted his dissent and agreement with most of Justice Stevens' opinion.

UNITED STATES v. EDWARDS

415 U.S. 800, 94 S.Ct. 1234, 39 L.Ed.2d 771 (1974).

MR. JUSTICE WHITE delivered the opinion of the Court.

The question here is whether the Fourth Amendment should be extended to exclude from evidence certain clothing taken from respondent Edwards while he was in custody at the city jail approximately 10 hours after his arrest.

Shortly after 11 p.m. on May 31, 1970, respondent Edwards was lawfully arrested on the streets of Lebanon, Ohio, and charged with attempting to break into that city's Post Office. He was taken to the local jail and placed in a cell. Contemporaneously or shortly thereafter, investigation at the scene revealed that the attempted entry had been made through a wooden window which apparently had been pried up with a pry bar, leaving paint chips on the window sill and wire mesh screen. The next morning, trousers and a T-shirt were purchased for Edwards to substitute for the clothing which he had been wearing at the time of and since his arrest. His clothing was then taken from him and held as evidence. Examination of the clothing revealed paint chips matching the samples that had been taken from the window. This evidence and his clothing were received at trial over Edwards' objection that neither the clothing nor the results of its examination were admissible because the warrantless seizure of his clothing was invalid under the Fourth Amendment.

The Court of Appeals reversed. Expressly disagreeing with two other courts of appeals, it held that although the arrest was lawful and probable cause existed to believe that paint chips would be discovered on petitioner's clothing, the warrantless seizure of the clothing carried out "after the administrative process and mechanics of arrest have come to a halt" was nevertheless unconstitutional under the Fourth Amendment. United States v. Edwards, 474 F.2d 1206, 1211 (CA 6 1973). We granted certiorari, 414 U.S. 818, and now conclude that the Fourth Amendment should not be extended to invalidate the search and seizure in the circumstances of this case.

The prevailing rule under the Fourth Amendment that searches and seizures may not be made without a warrant is subject to various exceptions. One of them permits warrantless searches incident to custodial arrests ... and has traditionally been justified by the reasonableness of searching for weapons, instruments of escape and evidence of crime when a person is taken into official custody and lawfully detained. ...

167

It is also plain that searches and seizures that could be made on the spot at the time of arrest may legally be conducted later when the accused arrives at the place of detention.   ...

The Courts of Appeals have followed this same rule, holding that both the person and the property in his immediate possession may be searched at the station house after the arrest has occurred at another place and if evidence of crime is discovered, it may be seized and admitted in evidence.   Nor is there any doubt that clothing or other belongings may be seized upon arrival of the accused at the place of detention and later subjected to laboratory analysis or that the test results are admissible at trial.

Conceding all this, the Court of Appeals in this case nevertheless held that a warrant is required where the search occurs after the administrative mechanics of arrest have been completed and the prisoner is incarcerated.   But even on these terms, it seems to us that the normal processes incident to arrest and custody had not been completed when Edwards was placed in his cell on the night of May 31.   With or without probable cause, the authorities were entitled at that point in time not only to search Edwards' clothing but also to take it from him and keep it in official custody.   There was testimony that this was the standard practice in this city.   The police were also entitled to take from Edwards any evidence of the crime in his immediate possession, including his clothing.   And the Court of Appeals acknowledged that contemporaneously with or shortly after the time Edwards went to his cell, the police had probable cause to believe that the articles of clothing he wore were themselves material evidence of the crime for which he had been arrested.   474 F.2d, at 1210.   But it was late at night; no substitute clothing was then available for Edwards to wear, and it would certainly have been unreasonable for the police to have stripped petitioner of his clothing and left him exposed in his cell throughout the night.   ...   When the substitutes were purchased the next morning, the clothing he had been wearing at the time of arrest was taken from him and subjected to laboratory analysis.   This was no more than taking from petitioner the effects in his immediate possession that constituted evidence of crime.   This was and is a normal incident of a custodial arrest, and reasonable delay in effectuating it does not change the fact that Edwards was no more imposed upon than he could have been at the time and place of the arrest or immediately upon arrival at the place of detention.   The police did no more on June 1 than they were entitled to do incident to the usual custodial arrest and incarceration.

Other closely related considerations sustain the examination of the clothing in this case.   It must be remembered that on both May 31 and June 1 the police had lawful custody of Edwards and necessarily of the clothing he wore.   When it became apparent that the articles of clothing were evidence of the crime for which Edwards was being held, the police were entitled to take, examine, and preserve them for use as evidence, just as they are normally permitted to seize evidence of crime when it is lawfully encountered. . . . Surely, the clothes could have been brushed down and vacuumed while Edwards had them on in the cell, and it was similarly reasonable to take and examine them as the police did, particularly in view of the existence of probable cause linking the clothes to the crime. Indeed, it is difficult to perceive what is unreasonable about the police examining and holding as evidence those personal effects of the accused that they already have in their lawful custody as the result of a lawful arrest.

. . .

. . . [M]ost cases in the courts of appeals . . . have long since concluded that once the defendant is lawfully arrested and is in custody, the effects in his possession at the place of detention that were subject to search at the time and place of his arrest may lawfully be searched and seized without a warrant even though a substantial period of time has elapsed between the arrest and subsequent administrative processing on the one hand and the taking of the property for use as evidence on the other. This is true where the clothing or effects are immediately seized upon arrival at the jail, held under the defendant's name in the "property room" of the jail and at a later time searched and taken for use at the subsequent criminal trial. The result is the same where the property is not physically taken from the defendant until sometime after his incarceration.

In upholding this search and seizure, we do not conclude that the warrant clause of the Fourth Amendment is never applicable to postarrest seizures of the effects of an arrestee.[9] But we do think that the Court of Appeals for the First Circuit captured the essence of situations like these when it said in United States v. DeLeo, 422 F.2d 487 (1970) at 493 (footnote omitted):

> "While the legal arrest of a person should not destroy the privacy of his premises, it does—for at least a reasonable time and to a reasonable extent—take his own privacy out of the realm of protection from police interest in weapons, means of escape and evidence."

The judgment of the Court of Appeals is reversed.

So ordered.

---

9. Holding the Warrant Clause inapplicable in the circumstances present here does not leave law enforcement officials subject to no restraints. This type of police conduct "must [still] be tested by the Fourth Amendment's general proscription against unreasonable searches and seizures." Terry v. Ohio, 392 U.S. 1, 20 (1968). But the Court of Appeals here conceded that probable cause existed for the search and seizure of petitioner's clothing, and petitioner complains only that a warrant should have been secured. We thus have no occasion to express a view concerning those circumstances surrounding custodial searches incident to incarceration which might "violate the dictates of reason either because of their number or their manner of perpetration." Charles v. United States, 278 F.2d 386, 389 (CA9 1960), cert. denied, 364 U.S. 831. Cf. Schmerber v. California, 384 U.S. 757 (1966); Rochin v. California, 342 U.S. 165 (1952).

MR. JUSTICE STEWART, with whom MR. JUSTICE DOUGLAS, MR. JUSTICE BRENNAN, and MR. JUSTICE MARSHALL join, dissenting.

The Court says that the question before us "is whether the Fourth Amendment should be extended" to prohibit the warrantless seizure of Edwards' clothing. I think, on the contrary, that the real question in this case is whether the Fourth Amendment is to be ignored. For in my view the judgment of the Court of Appeals can be reversed only by disregarding established Fourth Amendment principles firmly embodied in many previous decisions of this Court.

As the Court has repeatedly emphasized in the past, "the most basic constitutional rule in this area is that 'searches conducted outside the judicial process, without prior approval by judge or magistrate, are *per se* unreasonable under the Fourth Amendment— subject only to a few specifically established and well-delineated exceptions.' " Coolidge v. New Hampshire, 403 U.S. 443, 454–455; Katz v. United States, 389 U.S. 347, 357. Since it is conceded here that the seizure of Edwards' clothing was not made pursuant to a warrant, the question becomes whether the Government has met its burden of showing that the circumstances of this seizure brought it within one of the "jealously and carefully drawn" [1] exceptions to the warrant requirement.

The Court finds a warrant unnecessary in this case because of the custodial arrest of the respondent. It is of course well-settled that the Fourth Amendment permits a warrantless search or seizure incident to a constitutionally valid custodial arrest. ... But the mere fact of an arrest does not allow the police to engage in warrantless searches of unlimited geographic or temporal scope. Rather, the search must be spatially limited to the person of the arrestee and the area within his reach ... and must, as to time, be "substantially contemporaneous with the arrest." Stoner v. California, 376 U.S. 483, 486 ....

Under the facts of this case, I am unable to agree with the Court's holding that the search was "incident" to Edwards' custodial arrest. The search here occurred fully 10 hours after he was arrested, at a time when the administrative processing and mechanics of arrest had long since come to an end. His clothes were not seized as part of an "inventory" of a prisoner's effects, nor were they taken pursuant to a routine exchange of civilian clothes for jail garb. And the considerations that typically justify a warrantless search incident to a lawful arrest were wholly absent here. ...

Accordingly, I see no justification for dispensing with the warrant requirement here. The police had ample time to seek a warrant, and no exigent circumstances were present to excuse their failure to do so. Unless the exceptions to the warrant requirement

1. Jones v. United States, 357 U.S. 493, 499.

are to be "enthroned into the rule," United States v. Rabinowitz, 339 U.S. 56, 80 (Frankfurter, J., dissenting), this is precisely the sort of situation where the Fourth Amendment requires a magistrate's prior approval for a search.

The Court says that the relevant question is "not whether it was reasonable to procure a search warrant, but whether the search itself was reasonable." Ante, at 807. Precisely such a view, however, was explicitly rejected in Chimel v. California, 395 U.S. [752 (1969)] at 764–765, where the Court characterized the argument as "founded on little more than a subjective view regarding the acceptability of certain sorts of police conduct, and not on considerations relevant to Fourth Amendment interests." . . .

The intrusion here was hardly a shocking one, and it cannot be said that the police acted in bad faith. The Fourth Amendment, however, was not designed to apply only to situations where the intrusion is massive and the violation of privacy shockingly flagrant. . . .

Because I believe that the Court today unjustifiably departs from well-settled constitutional principles, I respectfully dissent.

ILLINOIS v. LAFAYETTE

462 U.S. 640, 103 S.Ct. 2605, 77 L.Ed.2d 65 (1983).

CHIEF JUSTICE BURGER delivered the opinion of the Court.

The question presented is whether, at the time an arrested person arrives at a police station, the police may, without obtaining a warrant, search a shoulder bag carried by that person.

I

On September 1, 1980, at about 10 p.m., Officer Maurice Mietzner of the Kankakee City Police arrived at the Town Cinema in Kankakee, Ill., in response to a call about a disturbance. There he found respondent involved in an altercation with the theater manager. He arrested respondent for disturbing the peace, handcuffed him, and took him to the police station. Respondent carried a purse-type shoulder bag on the trip to the station.

At the police station respondent was taken to the booking room; there, Officer Mietzner removed the handcuffs from respondent and ordered him to empty his pockets and place the contents on the counter. After doing so, respondent took a package of cigarettes from his shoulder bag and placed the bag on the counter. Mietzner then removed the contents of the bag, and found ten amphetamine pills inside the plastic wrap of a cigarette package.

Respondent was subsequently charged with violating § 402(b) of the Illinois Controlled Substances Act, Ill.Rev.Stat. ch. 56½, ¶ 1402(b) (1981), on the basis of the controlled substances found in his shoulder bag. A pretrial suppression hearing was held at which the State argued that the search of the shoulder bag was a valid inventory search under South Dakota v. Opperman, 428 U.S. 364 (1976). Officer Mietzner testified that he examined the bag's contents because it was standard procedure to inventory "everything" in the possession of an arrested person. . . . He testified that he was not seeking and did not expect to find drugs or weapons when he searched the bag and he conceded that the shoulder bag was small enough that it could have been placed and sealed in a bag, container or locker for protective purposes. . . . After the hearing, but before any ruling, the State submitted a brief in which it argued for the first time that the search was valid as a delayed search incident to arrest. Thereafter, the trial court ordered the suppression of the amphetamine pills. . . .

On appeal, the Illinois Appellate Court affirmed. 99 Ill.App.3d 830, 425 N.E.2d 1383 (3d Dist.1981). It first held that the State had waived the argument that the search was incident to a valid arrest by

172

failing to raise that argument at the suppression hearing. . . .
However, the court went on to discuss and reject the State's
argument: "[E]ven assuming, *arguendo,* that the State has not
waived this argument, the stationhouse search of the shoulder bag
did not constitute a valid search incident to a lawful arrest." Id., at
833, 425 N.E.2d, at 1385.

The State court also held that the search was not a valid
inventory of respondent's belongings. It purported to distinguish
South Dakota v. Opperman, supra, on the basis that there is a
greater privacy interest in a purse-type shoulder bag than in an
automobile, and that the State's legitimate interests could have been
met in a less intrusive manner, by "sealing [the shoulder bag]
within a plastic bag or box and placing it in a secured locker." 99
Ill.App.3d, at 834–835, 425 N.E.2d, at 1386. The Illinois court
concluded:

> "Therefore, the postponed warrantless search of the [respon-
> dent's] shoulder bag was neither incident to his lawful arrest
> nor a valid inventory of his belongings, and thus, violated the
> fourth amendment." Id., at 835, 425 N.E.2d, at 1386.

The Illinois Supreme Court denied discretionary review. App.
to Pet. for Cert. 1b. We granted certiorari, 459 U.S. 986 (1982),
because of the frequency with which this question confronts police
and courts, and we reverse.

II

The question here is whether, consistent with the Fourth
Amendment, it is reasonable for police to search the personal effects
of a person under lawful arrest as part of the routine administrative
procedure at a police station house incident to booking and jailing
the suspect. The justification for such searches does not rest on
probable cause, and hence the absence of a warrant is immaterial to
the reasonableness of the search. Indeed, we have previously
established that the inventory search constitutes a well-defined
exception to the warrant requirement. . . .

A so-called inventory search is not an independent legal concept but
rather an incidental administrative step following arrest and preceding incarceration. To determine whether the search of respondent's shoulder bag was unreasonable we must "balanc[e] its
intrusion on the individual's Fourth Amendment interests against its
promotion of legitimate governmental interests." Delaware v.
Prouse, 440 U.S. 648, 654 (1979).

In order to see an inventory search in proper perspective, it is
necessary to study the evolution of interests along the continuum
from arrest to incarceration. We have held that immediately upon
arrest an officer may lawfully search the person of an arrestee, . . . ;
he may also search the area within the arrestee's immediate control.
. . .

An arrested person is not invariably taken to a police station or confined; if an arrestee is taken to the police station, that is no more than a continuation of the custody inherent in the arrest status. Nonetheless, the factors justifying a search of the person and personal effects of an arrestee upon reaching a police station but prior to being placed in confinement are somewhat different from the factors justifying an immediate search at the time and place of arrest.

The governmental interests underlying a station-house search of the arrestee's person and possessions may in some circumstances be even greater than those supporting a search immediately following arrest. Consequently, the scope of a station-house search will often vary from that made at the time of arrest. Police conduct that would be impractical or unreasonable—or embarrassingly intrusive—on the street can more readily—and privately—be performed at the station. For example, the interests supporting a search incident to arrest would hardly justify disrobing an arrestee on the street, but the practical necessities of routine jail administration may even justify taking a prisoner's clothes before confining him, although that step would be rare. This was made clear in United States v. Edwards, 415 U.S. 800, 804 (1974): "With or without probable cause, the authorities were entitled [at the station-house] not only to search [the arrestee's] clothing but also to take it from him and keep it in official custody." [2]

At the station house, it is entirely proper for police to remove and list or inventory property found on the person or in the possession of an arrested person who is to be jailed. A range of governmental interests support an inventory process. It is not unheard of for persons employed in police activities to steal property taken from arrested persons; similarly, arrested persons have been known to make false claims regarding what was taken from their possession at the station-house. A standardized procedure for making a list or inventory as soon as reasonable after reaching the station house not only deters false claims but also inhibits theft or careless handling of articles taken from the arrested person. Arrested persons have also been known to injure themselves—or others—with belts, knives, drugs, or other items on their person while being detained. Dangerous instrumentalities—such as razor blades, bombs, or weapons—can be concealed in innocent-looking articles taken from the arrestee's possession. The bare recital of these mundane realities justifies reasonable measures by police to limit these risks—either while the items are in police possession or at the time they are returned to the arrestee upon his release. Examining all the items removed from the arrestee's person or possession and listing or inventorying them is an entirely reasonable administrative procedure. It is immaterial whether the police actually fear any

2. We were not addressing in *Edwards,* and do not discuss here, the circumstances in which a strip search of an arrestee may or may not be appropriate.

particular package or container; the need to protect against such risks arises independently of a particular officer's subjective concerns. ... Finally, inspection of an arrestee's personal property may assist the police in ascertaining or verifying his identity. ... In short, every consideration of orderly police administration benefiting both police and the public points toward the appropriateness of the examination of respondent's shoulder bag prior to his incarceration.

Our prior cases amply support this conclusion. In South Dakota v. Opperman, 428 U.S. 364 (1976), we upheld a search of the contents of the glove compartment of an abandoned automobile lawfully impounded by the police. We held that the search was reasonable because it served legitimate governmental interests that outweighed the individual's privacy interests in the contents of his car. Those measures protected the owner's property while it was in the custody of the police and protected police against possible false claims of theft. We found no need to consider the existence of less intrusive means of protecting the police and the property in their custody—such as locking the car and impounding it in safe storage under guard. Similarly, standardized inventory procedures are appropriate to serve legitimate governmental interests at stake here.

The Illinois court held that the search of respondent's shoulder bag was unreasonable because "preservation of the defendant's property and protection of police from claims of lost or stolen property, 'could have been achieved in a less intrusive manner.' For example, ... the defendant's shoulder bag could easily have been secured by sealing it within a plastic bag or box and placing it in a secured locker." 99 Ill.App.3d, at 835, 425 N.E.2d, at 1386 (citation omitted). Perhaps so, but the real question is not what "could have been achieved," but whether the Fourth Amendment *requires* such steps; it is not our function to write a manual on administering routine, neutral procedures of the station-house. Our role is to assure against violations of the Constitution.

The reasonableness of any particular governmental activity does not necessarily or invariably turn on the existence of alternative "less intrusive" means. ... We are hardly in a position to second-guess police departments as to what practical administrative method will best deter theft by and false claims against its employees and preserve the security of the station house. It is evident that a station-house search of every item carried on or by a person who has lawfully been taken into custody by the police will amply serve the important and legitimate governmental interests involved.

Even if less intrusive means existed of protecting some particular types of property, it would be unreasonable to expect police officers in the everyday course of business to make fine and subtle distinctions in deciding which containers or items may be searched and which must be sealed as a unit. ...

Applying these principles, we hold that it is not "unreasonable" for police, as part of the routine procedure incident to incarcerating an arrested person, to search any container or article in his possession, in accordance with established inventory procedures.

The judgment of the Illinois Appellate Court is reversed, and the case is remanded for proceedings not inconsistent with this opinion.

It is so ordered.[*]

[*] Justice Marshall wrote an opinion concurring in the judgment, which Justice Brennan joined.

CUPP v. MURPHY

412 U.S. 291, 93 S.Ct. 2000, 36 L.Ed.2d 900 (1973).

MR. JUSTICE STEWART delivered the opinion of the Court.

The respondent, Daniel Murphy, was convicted by a jury in an Oregon court of the second-degree murder of his wife. The victim died by strangulation in her home in the city of Portland, and abrasions and lacerations were found on her throat. There was no sign of a break-in or robbery. Word of the murder was sent to the respondent who was not then living with his wife. Upon receiving the message, Murphy promptly telephoned the Portland police and voluntarily came into Portland for questioning. Shortly after the respondent's arrival at the station house, where he was met by retained counsel, the police noticed a dark spot on the respondent's finger. Suspecting that the spot might be dried blood and knowing that evidence of strangulation is often found under the assailant's fingernails, the police asked Murphy if they could take a sample of scrapings from his fingernails. He refused. Under protest and without a warrant, the police proceeded to take the samples, which turned out to contain traces of skin and blood cells, and fabric from the victim's nightgown. This incriminating evidence was admitted at the trial.

The respondent appealed his conviction, claiming that the fingernail scrapings were the product of an unconstitutional search under the Fourth and Fourteenth Amendments. The Oregon Court of Appeals affirmed the conviction, 2 Ore.App. 251, 465 P.2d 900, and we denied certiorari, 400 U.S. 944. Murphy then commenced the present action for federal habeas corpus relief. The District Court, in an unreported decision, denied the habeas petition, and the Court of Appeals for the Ninth Circuit reversed, 461 F.2d 1006. The Court of Appeals assumed the presence of probable cause to search or arrest, but held that in the absence of an arrest or other exigent circumstances, the search was unconstitutional. Id., at 1007. We granted the State's petition for certiorari, 409 U.S. 1036, to consider the constitutional question presented.

The trial court, the Oregon Court of Appeals, and the Federal District Court all agreed that the police had probable cause to arrest the respondent at the time they detained him and scraped his fingernails. . . .

The Court of Appeals for the Ninth Circuit did not disagree with the conclusion that the police had probable cause to make an arrest, 461 F.2d, at 1007, nor do we.

177

It is also undisputed that the police did not obtain an arrest warrant nor formally "arrest" the respondent, as that term is understood under Oregon law. The respondent was detained only long enough to take the fingernail scrapings, and was not formally "arrested" until approximately one month later. Nevertheless, the detention of the respondent against his will constituted a seizure of his person, and the Fourth Amendment guarantee of freedom from "unreasonable searches and seizures" is clearly implicated, cf. United States v. Dionisio, 410 U.S. 1, Terry v. Ohio, 392 U.S. 1, 19. As the Court said in Davis v. Mississippi, 394 U.S. 721, 726–727, "Nothing is more clear than that the Fourth Amendment was meant to prevent wholesale intrusions upon the personal security of our citizenry, whether these intrusions be termed 'arrests' or 'investigatory detentions.'"

In *Davis,* the Court held that fingerprints obtained during the brief detention of persons seized in a police dragnet procedure, without probable cause, were inadmissible in evidence. . . .

The respondent in this case, like Davis, was briefly detained at the station house. Yet here, there was, as three courts have found, probable cause to believe that the respondent had committed the murder. The vice of the detention in *Davis* is therefore absent in the case before us. Cf. United States v. Dionisio, supra.

The inquiry does not end here, however, because Murphy was subjected to a search as well as a seizure of his person. Unlike the fingerprinting in *Davis,* the voice exemplar obtained in United States v. Dionisio, supra, or the handwriting exemplar obtained in United States v. Mara, 410 U.S. 19, the search of the respondent's fingernails went beyond mere "physical characteristics . . . constantly exposed to the public," United States v. Dionisio, supra, and constituted the type of "severe though brief intrusion upon cherished personal security" that is subject to constitutional scrutiny. Terry v. Ohio, supra, at 24–25.

We believe this search was constitutionally permissible under the principles of Chimel v. California, 395 U.S. 752. *Chimel* stands in a long line of cases recognizing an exception to the warrant requirement when a search is incident to a valid arrest. Id., at 755–762. The basis for this exception is that when an arrest is made, it is reasonable for a police officer to expect the arrestee to use any weapons he may have and to attempt to destroy any incriminating evidence then in his possession. Id., at 762–763. The Court recognized in *Chimel* that the scope of a warrantless search must be commensurate with the rationale that excepts the search from the warrant requirement. Thus a warrantless search incident to arrest, the Court held in *Chimel,* must be limited to the area "into which an arrestee might reach." 395 U.S., at 763.

Where there is no formal arrest, as in the case before us, a person might well be less hostile to the police and less likely to take conspicuous, immediate steps to destroy incriminating evidence on his person. Since he knows he is going to be released, he might be likely instead to be concerned with diverting attention away from himself. Accordingly, we do not hold that a full *Chimel* search would have been justified in this case without a formal arrest and without a warrant. But the respondent was not subjected to such a search.

At the time Murphy was being detained at the station house, he was obviously aware of the detectives' suspicions. Though he did not have the full warning of official suspicion that a formal arrest provides, Murphy was sufficiently apprised of his suspected role in the crime to motivate him to attempt to destroy what evidence he could without attracting further attention. Testimony at trial indicated that after he refused to consent to the taking of fingernail samples, he put his hands behind his back and appeared to rub them together. He then put his hands in his pockets, and a "metallic sound, such as keys or change rattling" was heard. The rationale of *Chimel,* in these circumstances, justified the police in subjecting him to the very limited search necessary to preserve the highly evanescent evidence they found under his fingernails, cf. Schmerber v. California, 384 U.S. 757.

On the facts of this case, considering the existence of probable cause, the very limited intrusion undertaken incident to the station house detention, and the ready destructibility of the evidence, we cannot say that this search violated the Fourth and Fourteenth Amendments. Accordingly, the judgment of the Court of Appeals is

Reversed.[*]

[*] Justice Marshall wrote a concurring opinion. Justice Blackmun wrote a brief concurring opinion, which Chief Justice Burger joined. Justice Powell wrote a brief concurring opinion, which Chief Justice Burger and Justice Rehnquist joined. Justice White noted that he thought the issue of probable cause remained open on remand. Justice Douglas and Justice Brennan wrote opinions dissenting in part.

WARDEN v. HAYDEN

387 U.S. 294, 87 S.Ct. 1642, 18 L.Ed.2d 782 (1967).

MR. JUSTICE BRENNAN delivered the opinion of the Court.

We review in this case the validity of the proposition that there is under the Fourth Amendment a "distinction between merely evidentiary materials, on the one hand, which may not be seized either under the authority of a search warrant or during the course of a search incident to arrest, and on the other hand, those objects which may validly be seized including the instrumentalities and means by which a crime is committed, the fruits of crime such as stolen property, weapons by which escape of the person arrested might be effected, and property the possession of which is a crime." [1]

A Maryland court sitting without a jury convicted respondent of armed robbery. Items of his clothing, a cap, jacket, and trousers, among other things were seized during a search of his home, and were admitted in evidence without objection. After unsuccessful state court proceedings, he sought and was denied federal habeas corpus relief in the District Court for Maryland. A divided panel of the Court of Appeals for the Fourth Circuit reversed. 363 F.2d 647. The Court of Appeals believed that Harris v. United States, 331 U.S. 145, 154, sustained the validity of the search, but held that respondent was correct in his contention that the clothing seized was improperly admitted in evidence because the items had "evidential value only" and therefore were not lawfully subject to seizure. We granted certiorari. 385 U.S. 926. We reverse.

I

About 8 a.m. on March 17, 1962, an armed robber entered the business premises of the Diamond Cab Company in Baltimore, Maryland. He took some $363 and ran. Two cab drivers in the vicinity, attracted by shouts of "Holdup," followed the man to 2111 Cocoa Lane. One driver notified the company dispatcher by radio that the man was a Negro about 5′8″ tall, wearing a light cap and dark jacket, and that he had entered the house on Cocoa Lane. The dispatcher relayed the information to police who were proceeding to the scene of the robbery. Within minutes, police arrived at the house in a number of patrol cars. An officer knocked and announced their presence. Mrs. Hayden answered, and the officers told her they believed that a robber had entered the house, and asked to search the house. She offered no objection.

1. Harris v. United States, 331 U.S. 145, 154 ....

The officers spread out through the first and second floors and the cellar in search of the robber. Hayden was found in an upstairs bedroom feigning sleep. He was arrested when the officers on the first floor and in the cellar reported that no other man was in the house. Meanwhile an officer was attracted to an adjoining bathroom by the noise of running water, and discovered a shotgun and a pistol in a flush tank; another officer who, according to the District Court, "was searching the cellar for a man or the money" found in a washing machine a jacket and trousers of the type the fleeing man was said to have worn. A clip of ammunition for the pistol and a cap were found under the mattress of Hayden's bed, and ammunition for the shotgun was found in a bureau drawer in Hayden's room. All these items of evidence were introduced against respondent at his trial.

II

We agree with the Court of Appeals that neither the entry without warrant to search for the robber, nor the search for him without warrant was invalid. Under the circumstances of this case, "the exigencies of the situation made that course imperative." McDonald v. United States, 335 U.S. 451, 456. The police were informed that an armed robbery had taken place, and that the suspect had entered 2111 Cocoa Lane less than five minutes before they reached it. They acted reasonably when they entered the house and began to search for a man of the description they had been given and for weapons which he had used in the robbery or might use against them. The Fourth Amendment does not require police officers to delay in the course of an investigation if to do so would gravely endanger their lives or the lives of others. Speed here was essential, and only a thorough search of the house for persons and weapons could have insured that Hayden was the only man present and that the police had control of all weapons which could be used against them or to effect an escape.

We do not rely upon Harris v. United States, supra, in sustaining the validity of the search. The principal issue in *Harris* was whether the search there could properly be regarded as incident to the lawful arrest, since Harris was in custody before the search was made and the evidence seized. Here, the seizures occurred prior to or immediately contemporaneous with Hayden's arrest, as part of an effort to find a suspected felon, armed, within the house into which he had run only minutes before the police arrived. The permissible scope of search must, therefore, at the least, be as broad as may reasonably be necessary to prevent the dangers that the suspect at large in the house may resist or escape.

It is argued that, while the weapons, ammunition, and cap may have been seized in the course of a search for weapons, the officer who seized the clothing was searching neither for the suspect nor for weapons when he looked into the washing machine in which he found the clothing. But even if we assume, although we do not decide, that the exigent circumstances in this case made lawful a search without warrant only for the suspect or his weapons, it cannot be said on this record that the officer who found the clothes in the washing machine was not searching for weapons. He testified that he was searching for the man or the money, but his failure to state explicitly that he was searching for weapons, in the absence of a specific question to that effect, can hardly be accorded controlling weight. He knew that the robber was armed and he did not know that some weapons had been found at the time he opened the machine. In these circumstances the inference that he was in fact also looking for weapons is fully justified.

III

We come, then, to the question whether, even though the search was lawful, the Court of Appeals was correct in holding that the seizure and introduction of the items of clothing violated the Fourth Amendment because they are "mere evidence." The distinction made by some of our cases between seizure of items of evidential value only and seizure of instrumentalities, fruits, or contraband has been criticized by courts and commentators. The Court of Appeals, however, felt "obligated to adhere to it." 363 F.2d, at 655. We today reject the distinction as based on premises no longer accepted as rules governing the application of the Fourth Amendment.

. . .

Nothing in the language of the Fourth Amendment supports the distinction between "mere evidence" and instrumentalities, fruits of crime, or contraband. On its face, the provision assures the "right of the people to be secure in their persons, houses, papers, and effects . . .," without regard to the use to which any of these things are applied. This "right of the people" is certainly unrelated to the "mere evidence" limitation. Privacy is disturbed no more by a search directed to a purely evidentiary object than it is by a search directed to an instrumentality, fruit, or contraband. A magistrate can intervene in both situations, and the requirements of probable cause and specificity can be preserved intact. Moreover, nothing in the nature of property seized as evidence renders it more private than property seized, for example, as an instrumentality; quite the opposite may be true. Indeed, the distinction is wholly irrational, since, depending on the circumstances, the same "papers and effects" may be "mere evidence" in one case and "instrumentality" in another. . . .

In Gouled v. United States, 255 U.S. 298, 309, the Court said that search warrants "may not be used as a means of gaining access to a man's house or office and papers solely for the purpose of making search to secure evidence to be used against him in a criminal or penal proceeding . . . ." The Court derived from Boyd

v. United States [116 U.S. 616 (1886)], the proposition that warrants "may be resorted to only when a primary right to such search and seizure may be found in the interest which the public or the complainant may have in the property to be seized, or in the right to the possession of it, or when a valid exercise of the police power renders possession of the property by the accused unlawful and provides that it may be taken," 255 U.S., at 309; that is, when the property is an instrumentality or fruit of crime, or contraband. Since it was "impossible to say, on the record . . . that the Government had any interest" in the papers involved "other than as evidence against the accused . . . ," "to permit them to be used in evidence would be, in effect, as ruled in the *Boyd* case, to compel the defendant to become a witness against himself." Id., at 311.

The items of clothing involved in this case are not "testimonial" or "communicative" in nature, and their introduction therefore did not compel respondent to become a witness against himself in violation of the Fifth Amendment. Schmerber v. California, 384 U.S. 757. This case thus does not require that we consider whether there are items of evidential value whose very nature precludes them from being the object of a reasonable search and seizure.

The Fourth Amendment ruling in *Gouled* was based upon the dual, related premises that historically the right to search for and seize property depended upon the assertion by the Government of a valid claim of superior interest, and that it was not enough that the purpose of the search and seizure was to obtain evidence to use in apprehending and convicting criminals. . . . Thus stolen property—the fruits of crime—was always subject to seizure. And the power to search for stolen property was gradually extended to cover "any property which the private citizen was not permitted to possess," which included instrumentalities of crime (because of the early notion that items used in crime were forfeited to the State) and contraband. Kaplan, Search and Seizure: A No-Man's Land in the Criminal Law, 49 Calif.L.Rev. 474, 475. No separate governmental interest in seizing evidence to apprehend and convict criminals was recognized; it was required that some property interest be asserted. The remedial structure also reflected these dual premises. Trespass, replevin, and the other means of redress for persons aggrieved by searches and seizures, depended upon proof of a superior property interest. And since a lawful seizure presupposed a superior claim, it was inconceivable that a person could recover property lawfully seized. . . .

The premise that property interests control the right of the Government to search and seize has been discredited. Searches and seizures may be "unreasonable" within the Fourth Amendment even though the Government asserts a superior property interest at common law. We have recognized that the principal object of the Fourth Amendment is the protection of privacy rather than property, and have increasingly discarded fictional and procedural barriers rested on property concepts. ...

The development of search and seizure law since *Silverthorne* and *Gouled* is replete with examples of the transformation in substantive law brought about through the interaction of the felt need to protect privacy from unreasonable invasions and the flexibility in rulemaking made possible by the remedy of exclusion. ...

The premise in *Gouled* that government may not seize evidence simply for the purpose of proving crime has likewise been discredited. The requirement that the Government assert in addition some property interest in material it seizes has long been a fiction,[11] obscuring the reality that government has an interest in solving crime. *Schmerber* settled the proposition that it is reasonable, within the terms of the Fourth Amendment, to conduct otherwise permissible searches for the purpose of obtaining evidence which would aid in apprehending and convicting criminals. The requirements of the Fourth Amendment can secure the same protection of privacy whether the search is for "mere evidence" or for fruits, instrumentalities or contraband. There must, of course, be a nexus—automatically provided in the case of fruits, instrumentalities or contraband—between the item to be seized and criminal behavior. Thus in the case of "mere evidence," probable cause must be examined in terms of cause to believe that the evidence sought will aid in a particular apprehension or conviction. In so doing, consideration of police purposes will be required. Cf. Kremen v. United States, 353 U.S. 346. But no such problem is presented in this case. The clothes found in the washing machine matched the description of those worn by the robber and the police therefore could reasonably believe that the items would aid in the identification of the culprit.

The remedy of suppression, moreover, which made possible protection of privacy from unreasonable searches without regard to proof of a superior property interest, likewise provides the procedural device necessary for allowing otherwise permissible searches and seizures conducted solely to obtain evidence of crime. For just as the suppression of evidence does not entail a declaration of

---

11. At common law the Government did assert a superior property interest when it searched lawfully for stolen property, since the procedure then followed made it necessary that the true owner swear that his goods had been taken. But no such procedure need be followed today; the Government may demonstrate probable cause and lawfully search for stolen property even though the true owner is unknown or unavailable to request and authorize the Government to assert his interest. As to instrumentalities, the Court in *Gouled* allowed their seizure, not because the Government had some property interest in them (under the ancient, fictitious forfeiture theory), but because they could be used to perpetrate further crime. 255 U.S., at 309. The same holds true, of course, for "mere evidence"; the prevention of crime is served at least as much by allowing the Government to identify and capture the criminal, as it is by allowing the seizure of his instrumentalities. Finally, contraband is indeed property in which the Government holds a superior interest, but only because the Government decides to vest such an interest in itself. And while there may be limits to what may be declared contraband, the concept is hardly more than a form through which the Government seeks to prevent and deter crime.

superior property interest in the person aggrieved, thereby enabling him to suppress evidence unlawfully seized despite his inability to demonstrate such an interest (as with fruits, instrumentalities, contraband), the refusal to suppress evidence carries no declaration of superior property interest in the State, and should thereby enable the State to introduce evidence lawfully seized despite its inability to demonstrate such an interest. And, unlike the situation at common law, the owner of property would not be rendered remediless if "mere evidence" could lawfully be seized to prove crime. For just as the suppression of evidence does not in itself necessarily entitle the aggrieved person to its return (as, for example, contraband), the introduction of "mere evidence" does not in itself entitle the State to its retention. Where public officials "unlawfully seize *or hold* a citizen's realty or chattels, recoverable by appropriate action at law or in equity . . .," the true owner may "bring his possessory action to reclaim that which is wrongfully withheld." Land v. Dollar, 330 U.S. 731, 738. (Emphasis added.) . . .

The survival of the *Gouled* distinction is attributable more to chance than considered judgment. Legislation has helped perpetuate it. Thus, Congress has never authorized the issuance of search warrants for the seizure of mere evidence of crime. . . . Even in the Espionage Act of 1917, where Congress for the first time granted general authority for the issuance of search warrants, the authority was limited to fruits of crime, instrumentalities, and certain contraband. 40 Stat. 228. *Gouled* concluded, needlessly it appears, that the Constitution virtually limited searches and seizures to these categories. After *Gouled*, pressure to test this conclusion was slow to mount. Rule 41(b) of the Federal Rules of Criminal Procedure incorporated the *Gouled* categories as limitations on federal authorities to issue warrants, and Mapp v. Ohio, 367 U.S. 643, only recently made the "mere evidence" rule a problem in the state courts. Pressure against the rule in the federal courts has taken the form rather of broadening the categories of evidence subject to seizure, thereby creating considerable confusion in the law. . . .

The rationale most frequently suggested for the rule preventing the seizure of evidence is that "limitations upon the fruit to be gathered tend to limit the quest itself." United States v. Poller, 43 F.2d 911, 914 (C.A.2d Cir.1930). But privacy "would be just as well served by a restriction on search to the even-numbered days of the month. . . . And it would have the extra advantage of avoiding hair-splitting questions . . . ." Kaplan, op. cit. supra, at 479. The "mere evidence" limitation has spawned exceptions so numerous and confusion so great, in fact, that it is questionable whether it affords meaningful protection. But if its rejection does enlarge the area of permissible searches, the intrusions are nevertheless made after fulfilling the probable cause and particularity requirements of the Fourth Amendment and after the intervention of "a neutral and detached magistrate . . . ." Johnson v. United States, 333 U.S. 10,

14. The Fourth Amendment allows intrusions upon privacy under these circumstances, and there is no viable reason to distinguish intrusions to secure "mere evidence" from intrusions to secure fruits, instrumentalities, or contraband.

The judgment of the Court of Appeals is

Reversed.

. . .

MR. JUSTICE DOUGLAS, dissenting.

We start with the Fourth Amendment . . . .

This constitutional guarantee, now as applicable to the States (Mapp v. Ohio, 367 U.S. 643) as to the Federal Government, has been thought, until today, to have two faces of privacy:

> (1) One creates a zone of privacy that may not be invaded by the police through raids, by the legislators through laws, or by magistrates through the issuance of warrants.

> (2) A second creates a zone of privacy that may be invaded either by the police in hot pursuit or by a search incident to arrest or by a warrant issued by a magistrate on a showing of probable cause.

. . .

. . . Our question is whether the Government, though armed with a proper search warrant or though making a search incident to an arrest, may seize, and use at the trial, testimonial evidence, whether it would otherwise be barred by the Fifth Amendment or would be free from such strictures. The teaching of *Boyd* [v. United States, 116 U.S. 616 (1886)], is that such evidence, though seized pursuant to a lawful search, is inadmissible.

That doctrine had its full flowering in Gouled v. United States, 255 U.S. 298, where an opinion was written by Mr. Justice Clarke for a unanimous Court that included both Mr. Justice Holmes and Mr. Justice Brandeis. The prosecution was for defrauding the Government under procurement contracts. Documents were taken from defendant's business office under a search warrant and used at the trial as evidence against him. Stolen or forged papers could be so seized, the Court said; so could lottery tickets; so could contraband; so could property in which the public had an interest, for reasons tracing back to warrants allowing the seizure of stolen property. But the papers or documents fell in none of those categories and the Court therefore held that even though they had been taken under a warrant, they were inadmissible at the trial as not even a warrant, though otherwise proper and regular, could be used "for the purpose of making search to secure evidence" of a crime. Id., at 309. The use of those documents against the accused might, of course, violate the Fifth Amendment. Id., at 311. But whatever may be the intrinsic nature of the evidence, the owner is then "the unwilling source of the evidence" (id., at 306), there being no difference so far as the Fifth Amendment is concerned "whether he be obliged to supply evidence against himself or whether such evidence be obtained by an illegal search of his premises and seizure of his private papers." Id.

We have, to be sure, breached that barrier, Schmerber v. California, 384 U.S. 757, being a conspicuous example. But I dissented then and renew my opposing view at this time. That which is taken from a person without his consent and used as testimonial evidence violates the Fifth Amendment.

.   .   .

Judge Learned Hand stated a part of the philosophy of the Fourth Amendment in United States v. Poller, 43 F.2d 911, 914:

> "[I]t is only fair to observe that the real evil aimed at by the Fourth Amendment is the search itself, that invasion of a man's privacy which consists in rummaging about among his effects to secure evidence against him. If the search is permitted at all, perhaps, it does not make so much difference what is taken away, since the officers will ordinarily not be interested in what does not incriminate, and there can be no sound policy in protecting what does. Nevertheless, limitations upon the fruit to be gathered tend to limit the quest itself ...."

The right of privacy protected by the Fourth Amendment relates in part of course to the precincts of the home or the office. But it does not make them sanctuaries where the law can never reach. There are such places in the world. A mosque in Fez, Morocco, that I have visited, is by custom a sanctuary where any refugee may hide, safe from police intrusion. We have no such sanctuaries here. A policeman in "hot pursuit" or an officer with a search warrant can enter any house, any room, any building, any office. The privacy of those *places* is of course protected against invasion except in limited situations. The full privacy protected by the Fourth Amendment is, however, reached when we come to books, pamphlets, papers, letters, documents, and other personal effects. Unless they are contraband or instruments of the crime, they may not be reached by any warrant nor may they be lawfully seized by the police who are in "hot pursuit." By reason of the Fourth Amendment the police may not rummage around among these personal effects, no matter how formally perfect their authority may appear to be. They may not seize them. If they do, those articles may not be used in evidence. Any invasion whatsoever of those personal effects is "unreasonable" within the meaning of the Fourth Amendment. That is the teaching of Entick v. Carrington [19 How.St.Tr. 1029 (1765)], Boyd v. United States, and Gouled v. United States.

.   .   .

The constitutional philosophy is, I think, clear. The personal effects and possessions of the individual (all contraband and the like excepted) are sacrosanct from prying eyes, from the long arm of the law, from any rummaging by police. Privacy involves the choice of the individual to disclose or to reveal what he believes, what he thinks, what he possesses. The article may be a nondescript work of art, a manuscript of a book, a personal account book, a diary, invoices, personal clothing, jewelry, or whatnot. Those who wrote the Bill of Rights believed that every individual needs both to communicate with others and to keep his affairs to himself. That dual aspect of privacy means that the individual should have the freedom to select for himself the time and circumstances when he will share his secrets with others and decide the extent of that sharing. This is his prerogative not the States'. The Framers, who were as knowledgeable as we, knew what police surveillance meant and how the practice of rummaging through one's personal effects could destroy freedom.

It was in that tradition that we held in Griswold v. Connecticut, 381 U.S. 479, that lawmakers could not, as respects husband and wife at least, make the use of contraceptives a crime. . . .

This right of privacy, sustained in *Griswold* is kin to the right of privacy created by the Fourth Amendment. That there is a zone that no police can enter—whether in "hot pursuit" or armed with a meticulously proper warrant—has been emphasized by *Boyd* and by *Gouled*. They have been consistently and continuously approved. I would adhere to them and leave with the individual the choice of opening his private effects (apart from contraband and the like) to the police or keeping their contents a secret and their integrity inviolate. The existence of that choice is the very essence of the right of privacy. Without it the Fourth Amendment and the Fifth are ready instruments for the police state that the Framers sought to avoid.[*]

[*] Justice Fortas wrote a concurring opinion, which Chief Justice Warren joined. Justice Black concurred in the result.

STONER v. CALIFORNIA

376 U.S. 483, 84 S.Ct. 889, 11 L.Ed.2d 856 (1964).

MR. JUSTICE STEWART delivered the opinion of the Court.

The petitioner was convicted of armed robbery after a jury trial in the Superior Court of Los Angeles County, California. At the trial several articles which had been found by police officers in a search of the petitioner's hotel room during his absence were admitted into evidence over his objection. A District Court of Appeal of California affirmed the conviction, and the Supreme Court of California denied further review. We granted certiorari, limiting review "to the question of whether evidence was admitted which had been obtained by an unlawful search and seizure." 374 U.S. 826. For the reasons which follow, we conclude that the petitioner's conviction must be set aside.

The essential facts are not in dispute. On the night of October 25, 1960, the Budget Town Food Market in Monrovia, California, was robbed by two men, one of whom was described by eyewitnesses as carrying a gun and wearing horn-rimmed glasses and a grey jacket. Soon after the robbery a checkbook belonging to the petitioner was found in an adjacent parking lot and turned over to the police. Two of the stubs in the checkbook indicated that checks had been drawn to the order of the Mayfair Hotel in Pomona, California. Pursuing this lead, the officers learned from the Police Department of Pomona that the petitioner had a previous criminal record, and they obtained from the Pomona police a photograph of the petitioner. They showed the photograph to the two eyewitnesses to the robbery, who both stated that the picture looked like the man who had carried the gun. On the basis of this information the officers went to the Mayfair Hotel in Pomona at about 10 o'clock on the night of October 27. They had neither search nor arrest warrants. There then transpired the following events, as later recounted by one of the officers:

> "We approached the desk, the night clerk, and asked him if there was a party by the name of Joey L. Stoner living at the hotel. He checked his records and stated 'Yes, there is.' And we asked him what room he was in. He stated he was in Room 404 but he was out at this time.
>
> "We asked him how he knew that he was out. He stated that the hotel regulations required that the key to the room would be placed in the mail box each time they left the hotel. The key was in the mail box, that he therefore knew he was out of the room.

189

"We asked him if he would give us permission to enter the room, explaining our reasons for this.

"Q. What reasons did you explain to the clerk?

"A. We explained that we were there to make an arrest of a man who had possibly committed a robbery in the City of Monrovia, and that we were concerned about the fact that he had a weapon. He stated 'In this case, I will be more than happy to give you permission and I will take you directly to the room.'

"Q. Is that what the clerk told you?

"A. Yes, sir.

"Q. What else happened?

"A. We left one detective in the lobby, and Detective Oliver, Officer Collins, and myself, along with the night clerk, got on the elevator and proceeded to the fourth floor, and went to Room 404. The night clerk placed a key in the lock, unlocked the door, and says, 'Be my guest.' "

The officers entered and made a thorough search of the room and its contents. They found a pair of horn-rimmed glasses and a grey jacket in the room, and a .45-caliber automatic pistol with a clip and several cartridges in the bottom of a bureau drawer. The petitioner was arrested two days later in Las Vegas, Nevada. He waived extradition and was returned to California for trial on the charge of armed robbery. The gun, the cartridges and clip, the horn-rimmed glasses, and the grey jacket were all used as evidence against him at his trial.

The search of the petitioner's room by the police officers was conducted without a warrant of any kind, and it therefore "can survive constitutional inhibition only upon a showing that the surrounding facts brought it within one of the exceptions to the rule that a search must rest upon a search warrant. . . . The District Court of Appeal thought the search was justified as an incident to a lawful arrest. But a search can be incident to an arrest only if it is substantially contemporaneous with the arrest and is confined to the immediate vicinity of the arrest. Agnello v. United States, 269 U.S. 20. Whatever room for leeway there may be in these concepts, it is clear that the search of the petitioner's hotel room in Pomona, California, on October 27 was not incident to his arrest in Las Vegas, Nevada, on October 29. The search was completely unrelated to the arrest, both as to time and as to place. See Preston v. United States, decided this day, ante, p. 364.

In this Court the respondent has recognized that the reasoning of the California District Court of Appeal cannot be reconciled with our decision in *Agnello,* nor, indeed, with the most recent California decisions. Accordingly, the respondent has made no argument that the search can be justified as an incident to the petitioner's arrest.

Instead, the argument is made that the search of the hotel room, although conducted without the petitioner's consent, was lawful because it was conducted with the consent of the hotel clerk. We find this argument unpersuasive.

Even if it be assumed that a state law which gave a hotel proprietor blanket authority to authorize the police to search the rooms of the hotel's guests could survive constitutional challenge, there is no intimation in the California cases cited by the respondent that California has any such law. Nor is there any substance to the claim that the search was reasonable because the police, relying upon the night clerk's expressions of consent, had a reasonable basis for the belief that the clerk had authority to consent to the search. Our decisions make clear that the rights protected by the Fourth Amendment are not to be eroded by strained applications of the law of agency or by unrealistic doctrines of "apparent authority." As this Court has said,

> "it is unnecessary and ill-advised to import into the law surrounding the constitutional right to be free from unreasonable searches and seizures subtle distinctions, developed and refined by the common law in evolving the body of private property law which, more than almost any other branch of law, has been shaped by distinctions whose validity is largely historical. ... [W]e ought not to bow to them in the fair administration of the criminal law. To do so would not comport with our justly proud claim of the procedural protections accorded to those charged with crime." Jones v. United States, 362 U.S. 257, 266–267.

It is important to bear in mind that it was the petitioner's constitutional right which was at stake here, and not the night clerk's nor the hotel's. It was a right, therefore, which only the petitioner could waive by word or deed, either directly or through an agent. It is true that the night clerk clearly and unambiguously consented to the search. But there is nothing in the record to indicate that the police had any basis whatsoever to believe that the night clerk had been authorized by the petitioner to permit the police to search the petitioner's room.

At least twice this Court has explicitly refused to permit an otherwise unlawful police search of a hotel room to rest upon consent of the hotel proprietor. Lustig v. United States, 338 U.S. 74; United States v. Jeffers, 342 U.S. 48. In *Lustig* the manager of a hotel allowed police to enter and search a room without a warrant in the occupant's absence, and the search was held unconstitutional. In *Jeffers* the assistant manager allowed a similar search, and that search was likewise held unconstitutional.

It is true, as was said in *Jeffers,* that when a person engages a hotel room he undoubtedly gives "implied or express permission" to "such persons as maids, janitors or repairmen" to enter his room "in the performance of their duties." 342 U.S., at 51. But the conduct of the night clerk and the police in the present case was of an entirely different order. In a closely analogous situation the Court has held that a search by police officers of a house occupied by a tenant invaded the tenant's constitutional right, even though the search was authorized by the owner of the house, who presumably had not only apparent but actual authority to enter the house for some purposes, such as to "view waste." Chapman v. United States, 365 U.S. 610. The Court pointed out that the officers' purpose in entering was not to view waste but to search for distilling equipment, and concluded that to uphold such a search without a warrant would leave tenants' homes secure only in the discretion of their landlords.

No less than a tenant of a house, or the occupant of a room in a boarding house, McDonald v. United States, 335 U.S. 451, a guest in a hotel room is entitled to constitutional protection against unreasonable searches and seizures. Johnson v. United States, 333 U.S. 10. That protection would disappear if it were left to depend upon the unfettered discretion of an employee of the hotel. It follows that this search without a warrant was unlawful. Since evidence obtained through the search was admitted at the trial, the judgment must be reversed. Mapp v. Ohio, 367 U.S. 643.

It is so ordered.[*]

---

[*] Justice Harlan wrote an opinion concurring in part and dissenting in part.

BUMPER v. NORTH CAROLINA

391 U.S. 543, 88 S.Ct. 1788, 20 L.Ed.2d 797 (1968).

MR. JUSTICE STEWART delivered the opinion of the Court.

The petitioner was brought to trial in a North Carolina court upon a charge of rape, an offense punishable in that State by death unless the jury recommends life imprisonment. Among the items of evidence introduced by the prosecution at the trial was a .22-caliber rifle allegedly used in the commission of the crime. The jury found the petitioner guilty, but recommended a sentence of life imprisonment. The trial court imposed that sentence, and the Supreme Court of North Carolina affirmed the judgment. We granted certiorari .... [T]he petitioner contends that the .22-caliber rifle introduced in evidence against him was obtained by the State in a search and seizure violative of the Fourth and Fourteenth Amendments.

. . .

The petitioner lived with his grandmother, Mrs. Hattie Leath, a 66-year-old Negro widow, in a house located in a rural area at the end of an isolated mile-long dirt road. Two days after the alleged offense but prior to the petitioner's arrest, four white law enforcement officers—the county sheriff, two of his deputies, and a state investigator—went to this house and found Mrs. Leath there with some young children. She met the officers at the front door. One of them announced, "I have a search warrant to search your house." Mrs. Leath responded, "Go ahead," and opened the door. In the kitchen the officers found the rifle that was later introduced in evidence at the petitioner's trial after a motion to suppress had been denied.

At the hearing on this motion, the prosecutor informed the court that he did not rely upon a warrant to justify the search, but upon the consent of Mrs. Leath. She testified at the hearing, stating, among other things:

"Four of them came. I was busy about my work, and they walked into the house and one of them walked up and said, 'I have a search warrant to search your house,' and I walked out and told them to come on in. ... He just come on in and said he had a warrant to search the house, and he didn't read it to me or nothing. So, I just told him to come on in and go ahead and search, and I went on about my work. I wasn't concerned what he was about. I was just satisfied. He just told me he had a search warrant, but he didn't read it to me. He did tell me he had a search warrant.

193

"... He said he was the law and had a search warrant to search the house, why I thought he could go ahead. I believed he had a search warrant. I took him at his word. ... I just seen them out there in the yard. They got through the door when I opened it. At that time, I did not know my grandson had been charged with crime. Nobody told me anything. They didn't tell me anything, just picked it up like that. They didn't tell me nothing about my grandson."

Upon the basis of Mrs. Leath's testimony, the trial court found that she had given her consent to the search, and denied the motion to suppress. The Supreme Court of North Carolina approved the admission of the evidence on the same basis.

The issue thus presented is whether a search can be justified as lawful on the basis of consent when that "consent" has been given only after the official conducting the search has asserted that he possesses a warrant.[11] We hold that there can be no consent under such circumstances.

When a prosecutor seeks to rely upon consent to justify the lawfulness of a search, he has the burden of proving that the consent was, in fact, freely and voluntarily given. This burden cannot be discharged by showing no more than acquiescence to a claim of lawful authority. A search conducted in reliance upon a warrant cannot later be justified on the basis of consent if it turns out that the warrant was invalid. The result can be no different when it turns out that the State does not even attempt to rely upon the validity of the warrant, or fails to show that there was, in fact, any warrant at all.

When a law enforcement officer claims authority to search a home under a warrant, he announces in effect that the occupant has no right to resist the search. The situation is instinct with coercion—albeit colorably lawful coercion. Where there is coercion there cannot be consent.

We hold that Mrs. Leath did not consent to the search, and that it was constitutional error to admit the rifle in evidence against the petitioner. Mapp v. Ohio, 367 U.S. 643. Because the rifle was plainly damaging evidence against the petitioner with respect to all three of the charges against him, its admission at the trial was not harmless error. Chapman v. California, 386 U.S. 18.

The judgment of the Supreme Court of North Carolina is, accordingly, reversed, and the case is remanded for further proceedings not inconsistent with this opinion.

---

11. Mrs. Leath owned both the house and the rifle. The petitioner concedes that her voluntary consent to the search would have been binding upon him. Conversely, there can be no question of the petitioner's standing to challenge the lawfulness of the search. He was the "one against whom the search was directed," Jones v. United States, 362 U.S. 257, 261, and the house searched was his home. The rifle was used by all members of the household and was found in the common part of the house.

It is so ordered.[*]

[*] Justice Harlan wrote a concurring opinion. Justice Black and Justice White wrote dissenting opinions. Justice Douglas joined the portion of the opinion quoted above and noted an additional reason for reversal.

SCHNECKLOTH v. BUSTAMONTE

412 U.S. 218, 93 S.Ct. 2041, 36 L.Ed.2d 854 (1973).

MR. JUSTICE STEWART delivered the opinion of the Court.

It is well settled under the Fourth and Fourteenth Amendments that a search conducted without a warrant issued upon probable cause is "per se unreasonable ... subject only to a few specifically established and well-delineated exceptions." Katz v. United States, 389 U.S. 347, 357 .... It is equally well settled that one of the specifically established exceptions to the requirements of both a warrant and probable cause is a search that is conducted pursuant to consent. ... The constitutional question in the present case concerns the definition of "consent" in this Fourth and Fourteenth Amendment context.

I

The respondent was brought to trial in a California court upon a charge of possessing a check with intent to defraud. He moved to suppress the introduction of certain material as evidence against him on the ground that the material had been acquired through an unconstitutional search and seizure. In response to the motion, the trial judge conducted an evidentiary hearing where it was established that the material in question had been acquired by the State under the following circumstances:

While on routine patrol in Sunnyvale, California, at approximately 2:40 in the morning, Police Officer James Rand stopped an automobile when he observed that one headlight and its license plate light were burned out. Six men were in the vehicle. Joe Alcala and the respondent, Robert Bustamonte, were in the front seat with Joe Gonzales, the driver. Three older men were seated in the rear. When, in response to the policeman's question, Gonzales could not produce a driver's license, Officer Rand asked if any of the other five had any evidence of identification. Only Alcala produced a license, and he explained that the car was his brother's. After the six occupants had stepped out of the car at the officer's request and after two additional policemen had arrived, Officer Rand asked Alcala if he could search the car. Alcala replied, "Sure, go ahead." Prior to the search no one was threatened with arrest and, according to Officer Rand's uncontradicted testimony, it "was all very congenial at this time." Gonzales testified that Alcala actually helped in the search of the car, by opening the trunk and glove compartment. In Gonzales' words: "[T]he police officer asked Joe [Alcala], he goes, 'Does the trunk open?' And Joe said, 'Yes.' He went to the car and got the keys and opened up the trunk."

196

Wadded up under the left rear seat, the police officers found three checks that had previously been stolen from a car wash.

The trial judge denied the motion to suppress, and the checks in question were admitted in evidence at Bustamonte's trial. On the basis of this and other evidence he was convicted, and the California Court of Appeal for the First Appellate District affirmed the conviction. 270 Cal.App.2d 648, 76 Cal.Rptr. 17. In agreeing that the search and seizure were constitutionally valid, the appellate court applied the standard earlier formulated by the Supreme Court of California in an opinion by then Justice Traynor: "Whether in a particular case an apparent consent was in fact voluntarily given or was in submission to an express or implied assertion of authority, is a question of fact to be determined in the light of all the circumstances." People v. Michael, 45 Cal.2d 751, 753, 290 P.2d 852, 854. The appellate court found that "[i]n the instant case the prosecution met the necessary burden of showing consent . . . since there were clearly circumstances from which the trial court could ascertain that consent had been freely given without coercion or submission to authority. Not only Officer Rand, but Gonzales, the driver of the automobile, testified that Alcala's assent to the search of his brother's automobile was freely given. At the time of the request to search the automobile, the atmosphere, according to Rand, was 'congenial' and there had been no discussion of any crime. As noted, Gonzales said Alcala even attempted to aid in the search." 270 Cal.App.2d, at 652, 76 Cal.Rptr., at 20. The California Supreme Court denied review.

Thereafter, the respondent sought a writ of habeas corpus in a federal district court. It was denied. On appeal, the Court of Appeals for the Ninth Circuit . . . set aside the District Court's order. 448 F.2d 699. The appellate court reasoned that a consent was a waiver of a person's Fourth and Fourteenth Amendment rights, and that the State was under an obligation to demonstrate not only that the consent had been uncoerced, but that it had been given with an understanding that it could be freely and effectively withheld. Consent could not be found, the court held, solely from the absence of coercion and a verbal expression of assent. Since the District Court had not determined that Alcala had *known* that his consent could have been withheld and that he could have refused to have his vehicle searched, the Court of Appeals vacated the order denying the writ and remanded the case for further proceedings. We granted the State's petition for certiorari to determine whether the Fourth and Fourteenth Amendments require the showing thought necessary by the Court of Appeals. 405 U.S. 953.

II

It is important to make it clear at the outset what is not involved in this case. The respondent concedes that a search conducted pursuant to a valid consent is constitutionally permissible. . . . And similarly the State concedes that "[w]hen a prosecutor seeks to rely upon consent to justify the lawfulness of a search, he has the burden of proving that the consent was, in fact, freely and voluntarily given." Bumper v. North Carolina, 391 U.S. 543, 548. . . .

The precise question in this case, then, is what must the state prove to demonstrate that a consent was "voluntarily" given. . . .

A

The most extensive judicial exposition of the meaning of "voluntariness" has been developed in those cases in which the Court has had to determine the "voluntariness" of a defendant's confession for purposes of the Fourteenth Amendment. Almost 40 years ago, in Brown v. Mississippi, 297 U.S. 278, the Court held that a criminal conviction based upon a confession obtained by brutality and violence was constitutionally invalid under the Due Process Clause of the Fourteenth Amendment. In some 30 different cases decided during the era that intervened between *Brown* and Escobedo v. Illinois, 378 U.S. 478, the Court was faced with the necessity of determining whether in fact the confessions in issue had been "voluntarily" given. It is to that body of case law to which we turn for initial guidance on the meaning of "voluntariness" in the present context.

Those cases yield no talismanic definition of "voluntariness," mechanically applicable to the host of situations where the question has arisen. "The notion of 'voluntariness,' " Mr. Justice Frankfurter once wrote, "is itself an amphibian." Culombe v. Connecticut, 367 U.S. 568, 604–605. It cannot be taken literally to mean a "knowing" choice. "Except where a person is unconscious or drugged or otherwise lacks capacity for conscious choice, all incriminating statements—even those made under brutal treatment—are 'voluntary' in the sense of representing a choice of alternatives. On the other hand, if 'voluntariness' incorporates notions of 'but-for' cause, the question should be whether the statement would have been made even absent inquiry or other official action. Under such a test, virtually no statement would be voluntary because very few people give incriminating statements in the absence of official action of some kind." [7] It is thus evident that neither linguistics nor epistemology will provide a ready definition of the meaning of "voluntariness."

Rather, "voluntariness" has reflected an accommodation of the complex of values implicated in police questioning of a suspect. At one end of the spectrum, is the acknowledged need for police questioning as a tool for the effective enforcement of criminal laws. . . . Without such investigation, those who were innocent might be

---

7. Bator & Vorenberg, Arrest, Detention, Interrogation and the Right to Counsel: Basic Problems and Possible Legislative Solutions, 66 Colum.L.Rev. 62, 72–73. . . .

falsely accused, those who were guilty might wholly escape prosecution, and many crimes would go unsolved. In short, the security of all would be diminished. ... At the other end of the spectrum, is the set of values reflecting society's deeply felt belief that the criminal law cannot be used as an instrument of unfairness, and that the possibility of unfair and even brutal police tactics poses a real and serious threat to civilized notions of justice. "[I]n cases involving involuntary confessions, this Court enforces the strongly felt attitude of our society that important human values are sacrificed where an agency of the government, in the course of securing a conviction, wrings a confession out of an accused against his will." Blackburn v. Alabama, 361 U.S. 199, 206–207. ...

This Court's decisions reflect a frank recognition that the Constitution requires the sacrifice of neither security nor liberty. The Due Process Clause does not mandate that the police forego all questioning, or that they be given carte blanche to extract what they can from a suspect. "The ultimate test remains that which has been the only clearly established test in Anglo-American Courts for two hundred years: the test of voluntariness. Is the confession the product of an essentially free and unconstrained choice by its maker? If it is, if he has willed to confess, it may be used against him. If it is not, if his will has been overborne and his capacity for self-determination critically impaired, the use of his confession offends due process." Culombe v. Connecticut, supra, at 602.

In determining whether a defendant's will was overborne in a particular case, the Court has assessed the totality of all the surrounding circumstances—both the characteristics of the accused and the details of the interrogation. Some of the factors taken into account have included the youth of the accused ... his lack of education ... or his low intelligence ... the lack of any advice to the accused of his constitutional rights ... the length of detention ...the repeated and prolonged nature of the questioning ... and the use of physical punishment such as the deprivation of food or sleep .... In all of these cases, the Court determined the factual circumstances surrounding the confession, assessed the psychological impact on the accused, and evaluated the legal significance of how the accused reacted. ...

The significant fact about all of these decisions is that none of them turned on the presence or absence of a single controlling criterion; each reflected a careful scrutiny of all the surrounding circumstances. ... In none of them did the Court rule that the Due Process Clause required the prosecution to prove as part of its initial burden that the defendant knew he had a right to refuse to answer the questions that were put. While the state of the accused's mind, and the failure of the police to advise the accused of his rights, were certainly factors to be evaluated in assessing the "voluntariness" of an accused's responses, they were not in and of themselves determinative. ...

B

Similar considerations lead us to agree with the courts of California that the question whether a consent to a search was in fact "voluntary" or was the product of duress or coercion, express or implied, is a question of fact to be determined from the totality of all the circumstances. While knowledge of the right to refuse consent is one factor to be taken into account, the government need not establish such knowledge as the *sine qua non* of an effective consent. As with police questioning, two competing concerns must be accommodated in determining the meaning of a "voluntary" consent—the legitimate need for such searches and the equally important requirement of assuring the absence of coercion.

In situations where the police have some evidence of illicit activity, but lack probable cause to arrest or search, a search authorized by a valid consent may be the only means of obtaining important and reliable evidence. In the present case for example, while the police had reason to stop the car for traffic violations, the State does not contend that there was probable cause to search the vehicle or that the search was incident to a valid arrest of any of the occupants. Yet, the search yielded tangible evidence that served as a basis for a prosecution, and provided some assurance that others, wholly innocent of the crime, were not mistakenly brought to trial. And in those cases where there is probable cause to arrest or search, but where the police lack a warrant, a consent search may still be valuable. If the search is conducted and proves fruitless, that in itself may convince the police that an arrest with its possible stigma and embarrassment is unnecessary, or that a far more extensive search pursuant to a warrant is not justified. In short a search pursuant to consent may result in considerably less inconvenience for the subject of the search, and, properly conducted, is a constitutionally permissible and wholly legitimate aspect of effective police activity.

But the Fourth and Fourteenth Amendments require that a consent not be coerced, by explicit or implicit means, by implied threat or covert force. For, no matter how subtly the coercion were applied, the resulting "consent" would be no more than a pretext for the unjustified police intrusion against which the Fourth Amendment is directed. ...

The problem of reconciling the recognized legitimacy of consent searches with the requirement that they be free from any aspect of official coercion cannot be resolved by any infallible touchstone. To approve such searches without the most careful scrutiny would sanction the possibility of official coercion; to place artificial restrictions upon such searches would jeopardize their basic validity. Just as was true with confessions, the requirement of a "voluntary" consent reflects a fair accommodation of the constitutional requirements involved. In examining all the surrounding circumstances to determine if in fact the consent to search was coerced, account must be taken of subtly coercive police questions as well as the possibly vulnerable subjective state of the person who consents. Those searches that are the product of police coercion can thus be filtered out without undermining the continuing validity of consent searches. In sum, there is no reason for us to depart in the area of consent searches, from the traditional definition of "voluntariness."

The approach of the Court of Appeals for the Ninth Circuit finds no support in any of our decisions that have attempted to define the meaning of "voluntariness." Its ruling, that the State must affirmatively prove that the subject of the search knew that he had a right to refuse consent, would, in practice, create serious doubt whether consent searches could continue to be conducted. There might be rare cases where it could be proved from the record that a person in fact affirmatively knew of his right to refuse—such as a case where he announced to the police that if he didn't sign the consent form, "you [police] are going to get a search warrant;" [11] or a case where by prior experience and training a person had clearly and convincingly demonstrated such knowledge. But more commonly where there was no evidence of any coercion, explicit or implicit, the prosecution would nevertheless be unable to demonstrate that the subject of the search in fact had known of his right to refuse consent.

The very object of the inquiry—the nature of a person's subjective understanding—underlines the difficulty of the prosecution's burden under the rule applied by the Court of Appeals in this case. Any defendant who was the subject of a search authorized solely by his consent could effectively frustrate the introduction into evidence of the fruits of that search by simply failing to testify that he in fact knew he could refuse to consent. And the near impossibility of meeting this prosecutorial burden suggests why this Court has never accepted any such litmus-paper test of voluntariness. . . .

One alternative that would go far towards proving that the subject of a search did know he had a right to refuse consent would be to advise him of that right before eliciting his consent. That, however, is a suggestion that has been almost universally repudiated by both federal and state courts, and, we think, rightly so. For it would be thoroughly impractical to impose on the normal consent search the detailed requirements of an effective warning. Consent searches are part of the standard investigatory techniques of law enforcement agencies. They normally occur on the highway, or in a person's home or office, and under informal and unstructured conditions. The circumstances that prompt the initial request to search may develop quickly or be a logical extension of investigative police questioning. The police may seek to investigate further suspicious circumstances or to follow up leads developed in ques-

---

11. United States v. Curiale, 414 F.2d 744, 747.

tioning persons at the scene of a crime. These situations are a far cry from the structured atmosphere of a trial where, assisted by counsel if he chooses, a defendant is informed of his trial rights. ... And, while surely a closer question, these situations are still immeasurably far removed from "custodial interrogation" where, in Miranda v. Arizona [384 U.S. 436 (1966)], we found that the Constitution required certain now familiar warnings as a prerequisite to police interrogation. ...

Consequently, we cannot accept the position of the Court of Appeals in this case that proof of knowledge of the right to refuse consent is a necessary prerequisite to demonstrating a "voluntary" consent. Rather, it is only by analyzing all the circumstances of an individual consent that it can be ascertained whether in fact it was voluntary or coerced. It is this careful sifting of the unique facts and circumstances of each case that is evidenced in our prior decisions involving consent searches.

. . .

... [I]f under all the circumstances it has appeared that the consent was not given voluntarily—that it was coerced by threats or force, or granted only in submission to a claim of lawful authority—then we have found the consent invalid and the search unreasonable. ...

Implicit in all of these cases is the recognition that knowledge of a right to refuse is not a prerequisite of a voluntary consent. ...

In short, neither this Court's prior cases, nor the traditional definition of "voluntariness" requires proof of knowledge of a right to refuse as the *sine qua non* of an effective consent to a search.

C

It is said, however, that a "consent" is a "waiver" of a person's rights under the Fourth and Fourteenth Amendments. The argument is that by allowing the police to conduct a search, a person "waives" whatever right he had to prevent the police from searching. It is argued that under the doctrine of Johnson v. Zerbst, 304 U.S. 458, 464, to establish such a "waiver" the state must demonstrate "an intentional relinquishment or abandonment of a known right or privilege."

But these standards were enunciated in *Johnson* in the context of the safeguards of a fair criminal trial. Our cases do not reflect an uncritical demand for a knowing and intelligent waiver in every situation where a person has failed to invoke a constitutional protection. As Mr. Justice Black once observed for the Court: "'Waiver' is a vague term used for a great variety of purposes, good and bad, in the law." Green v. United States, 355 U.S. 184, 191.

. . .

. . .

There is a vast difference between those rights that protect a fair criminal trial and the rights guaranteed under the Fourth Amendment. Nothing, either in the purposes behind requiring a "knowing" and "intelligent" waiver of trial rights, or in the practical application of such a requirement suggests that it ought to be extended to the constitutional guarantee against unreasonable searches and seizures.

A strict standard of waiver has been applied to those rights guaranteed to a criminal defendant to insure that he will be accorded the greatest possible opportunity to utilize every facet of the constitutional model of a fair criminal trial. Any trial conducted in derogation of that model leaves open the possibility that the trial reached an unfair result precisely because all the protections specified in the Constitution were not provided. A prime example is the right to counsel. For without that right, a wholly innocent accused faces the real and substantial danger that simply because of his lack of legal expertise he may be convicted. As Justice Harlan once wrote: "The sound reason why [the right to counsel] is so freely extended for a criminal trial is the severe injustice risked by confronting an untrained defendant with a range of technical points of law, evidence, and tactics familiar to the prosecutor but not to himself." Miranda v. Arizona, supra, at 514 (dissenting opinion). The Constitution requires that every effort be made to see to it that a defendant in a criminal case has not unknowingly relinquished the basic protections that the Framers thought indispensible to a fair trial.

The protections of the Fourth Amendment are of a wholly different order, and have nothing whatever to do with promoting the fair ascertainment of truth at a criminal trial. Rather, as Mr. Justice Frankfurter's opinion for the Court put it in Wolf v. Colorado, 338 U.S. 25, 27, the Fourth Amendment protects the "security of one's privacy against arbitrary intrusion by the police. . . ." . . . The Fourth Amendment "is not an adjunct to the ascertainment of truth." The guarantees of the Fourth Amendment stand "as a protection of quite different constitutional values—values reflecting the concern of our society for the right of each individual to be let alone. To recognize this is no more than to accord those values undiluted respect." Tehan v. United States ex rel. Schott, 382 U.S. 406, 416.

Nor can it even be said that a search, as opposed to an eventual trial, is somehow "unfair" if a person consents to a search. While the Fourth and Fourteenth Amendments limit the circumstances under which the police can conduct a search, there is nothing constitutionally suspect in a person voluntarily allowing a search. The actual conduct of the search may be precisely the same as if the police had obtained a warrant. And, unlike those constitutional guarantees that protect a defendant at trial, it cannot be said every reasonable presumption ought to be indulged against voluntary relinquishment. We have only recently stated: "[I]t is no part of the policy underlying the Fourth and Fourteenth Amendments to discourage citizens from aiding to the utmost of their ability in the apprehension of criminals." Coolidge v. New Hampshire, [403 U.S. 443 (1971)], at 488. Rather the community has a real interest in encouraging consent, for the resulting search may yield necessary evidence for the solution and prosecution of crime, evidence that may insure that a wholly innocent person is not wrongly charged with a criminal offense.

Those cases that have dealt with the application of the Johnson v. Zerbst rule make clear that it would be next to impossible to apply to a consent search the standard of "an intentional relinquishment or abandonment of a known right or privilege." To be true to *Johnson* and its progeny, there must be examination into the knowing and understanding nature of the waiver, an examination that was designed for a trial judge in the structured atmosphere of a courtroom. . . .

It would be unrealistic to expect that in the informal, unstructured context of a consent search, a policeman, upon pain of tainting the evidence obtained, could make the detailed type of examination demanded by *Johnson*. And, if for this reason a diluted form of "waiver" were found acceptable, that would itself be ample recognition of the fact that there is no universal standard that must be applied in every situation where a person forgoes a constitutional right.[33]

Similarly, a "waiver" approach to consent searches would be thoroughly inconsistent with our decisions that have approved "third party consents." In Coolidge v. New Hampshire, supra, at 487–490, where a wife surrendered to the police guns and clothing belonging to her husband, we found nothing constitutionally impermissible in the admission of that evidence at trial since the wife had not been coerced. Frazier v. Cupp, 394 U.S. 731, 740, held that evidence seized from the defendant's duffel bag in a search authorized by his cousin's consent was admissible at trial. We found that the defendant had assumed the risk that his cousin with whom he shared the bag would allow the police to search it. See also Abel v. United States, 362 U.S. 217. And in Hill v. California, 401 U.S. 797, 802–805, we held that the police had validly seized evidence from the petitioner's apartment incident to the arrest of a third party, since the police had probable cause to arrest the petitioner and reasonably though mistakenly believed the man they had arrested was he. Yet it is inconceivable that the Constitution could countenance the waiver of a defendant's right to counsel by a third party, or that a waiver could be found because a trial judge reasonably

---

33. It seems clear that even a limited view of the demands of "an intentional relinquishment or abandonment of a known right or privilege" standard would inevitably lead to a requirement of detailed warnings before any consent search—a requirement all but universally rejected to date. . . .

though mistakenly believed a defendant had waived his right to plead not guilty.

In short, there is nothing in the purposes or application of the waiver requirements of Johnson v. Zerbst that justifies, much less compels, the easy equation of a knowing waiver with a consent search. To make such an equation is to generalize from the broad rhetoric of some of our decisions, and to ignore the substance of the differing constitutional guarantees. We decline to follow what one judicial scholar has termed "the domino method of constitutional adjudication ... wherein every explanatory statement in a previous opinion is made the basis for extension to a wholly different situation." [35]

D

Much of what has already been said disposes of the argument that the Court's decision in the *Miranda* case requires the conclusion that knowledge of a right to refuse is an indispensable element of a valid consent. The considerations that informed the Court's holding in *Miranda* are simply inapplicable in the present case. In *Miranda* the Court found that the techniques of police questioning and the nature of custodial surroundings produce an inherently coercive situation. ...

In this case there is no evidence of any inherently coercive tactics—either from the nature of the police questioning or the environment in which it took place. Indeed, since consent searches will normally occur on a person's own familiar territory, the spectre of incommunicado police interrogation in some remote station house is simply inapposite. There is no reason to believe, under circumstances such as are present here, that the response to a policeman's question is presumptively coerced; and there is, therefore, no reason to reject the traditional test for determining the voluntariness of a person's response. *Miranda*, of course, did not reach investigative questioning of a person not in custody, which is most directly analogous to the situation of a consent search, and it assuredly did not indicate that such questioning ought to be deemed inherently coercive. See p. 406, supra.

It is also argued that the failure to require the Government to establish knowledge as a prerequisite to a valid consent, will relegate the Fourth Amendment to the special province of "the sophisticated, the knowledgeable, and the privileged." We cannot agree. The traditional definition of voluntariness we accept today has always taken into account evidence of minimal schooling, low intelligence, and the lack of any effective warnings to a person of his rights; and the voluntariness of any statement taken under those

35. Friendly, ["The Bill of Rights as a   929 (1925)], at 950.
Code of Criminal Procedure," 53 Calif.L.Rev.

conditions has been carefully scrutinized to determine whether it was in fact voluntarily given.

E

Our decision today is a narrow one. We hold only that when the subject of a search is not in custody and the State attempts to justify a search on the basis of his consent, the Fourth and Fourteenth Amendments require that it demonstrate that the consent was in fact voluntarily given, and not the result of duress or coercion, express or implied. Voluntariness is a question of fact to be determined from all the circumstances, and while the subject's knowledge of a right to refuse is a factor to be taken into account, the prosecution is not required to demonstrate such knowledge as a prerequisite to establishing a voluntary consent. Because the California courts followed these principles in affirming the respondent's conviction, and because the Court of Appeals for the Ninth Circuit in remanding for an evidentiary hearing required more, its judgment must be reversed.

It is so ordered.

MR. JUSTICE MARSHALL, dissenting.

. . .

I

I believe that the Court misstates the true issue in this case. That issue is not, as the Court suggests, whether the police overbore Alcala's will in eliciting his consent, but rather, whether a simple statement of assent to search, without more, should be sufficient to permit the police to search and thus act as a relinquishment of Alcala's constitutional right to exclude the police. This Court has always scrutinized with great care claims that a person has foregone the opportunity to assert constitutional rights. . . . I see no reason to give the claim that a person consented to a search any less rigorous scrutiny. Every case in this Court involving this kind of search has therefore spoken of consent as a waiver. . . . Perhaps one skilled in linguistics or epistemology can disregard those comments, but I find them hard to ignore.

To begin, it is important to understand that the opinion of the Court is misleading in its treatment of the issue here in three ways. First, it derives its criterion for determining when a verbal statement of assent to search operates as a relinquishment of a person's right to preclude entry from a justification of consent searches that is inconsistent with our treatment in earlier cases of exceptions to the requirements of the Fourth Amendment, and that is not responsive to the unique nature of the consent search exception. Second, it applies a standard of voluntariness that was developed in a very different context, where the standard was based on policies different from those involved in this case. Third, it mischaracterizes our prior cases involving consent searches.

A

The Court assumes that the issue in this case is, what are the standards by which courts are to determine that consent is voluntarily given? It then imports into the law of search and seizure standards developed to decide entirely different questions about coerced confessions.

The Fifth Amendment, in terms, provides that no person "shall be compelled in any criminal case to be a witness against himself." Nor is the interest protected by the Due Process Clause of the Fourteenth Amendment any different. The inquiry in a case where a confession is challenged as having been elicited in an unconstitutional manner is, therefore, whether the behavior of the police amounted to compulsion of the defendant. Because of the nature of the right to be free of compulsion, it would be pointless to ask whether a defendant knew of it before he made a statement; no sane person would knowingly relinquish a right to be free of compulsion. Thus, the question of compulsion and of violation of the right itself are inextricably intertwined. The cases involving coerced confessions therefore pass over the question of knowledge of that right as irrelevant, and turn directly to the question of compulsion.

. . .

B

In contrast, this case deals not with "coercion," but with "consent," a subtly different concept to which different standards have been applied in the past. Freedom from coercion is a substantive right, guaranteed by the Fifth and Fourteenth Amendments. Consent, however, is a mechanism by which substantive requirements, otherwise applicable, are avoided. In the context of the Fourth Amendment, the relevant substantive requirements are that searches be conducted only after evidence justifying them has been submitted to an impartial magistrate for a determination of probable cause. There are, of course, exceptions to these requirements based on a variety of exigent circumstances that make it impractical to invalidate a search simply because the police failed to get a warrant. But none of the exceptions relating to the overriding needs of law enforcement are applicable when a search is justified solely by consent. On the contrary, the needs of law enforcement are significantly more attenuated, for probable cause to search may be lacking but a search permitted if the subject's consent has been obtained. Thus, consent searches are permitted not because such an exception to the requirements of probable cause and warrant is essential to proper law enforcement, but because we permit our citizens to choose whether or not they wish to exercise their constitutional rights. Our prior decisions simply do not support the view that a meaningful choice has been made solely because no coercion was brought to bear on the subject.

. . .

II

My approach to the case is straightforward and, to me, obviously required by the notion of consent as a relinquishment of Fourth Amendment rights. I am at a loss to understand why consent "cannot be taken literally to mean a 'knowing' choice." *Ante,* at 224. In fact, I have difficulty in comprehending how a decision made without knowledge of available alternatives can be treated as a choice at all.

If consent to search means that a person has chosen to forego his right to exclude the police from the place they seek to search, it follows that his consent cannot be considered a meaningful choice unless he knew that he could in fact exclude the police. The Court appears, however, to reject even the modest proposition that, if the subject of a search convinces the trier of fact that he did not know of his right to refuse assent to a police request for permission to search, the search must be held unconstitutional. For it says only that "knowledge of the right to refuse consent is one factor to be taken into account." *Ante,* at 227. I find this incomprehensible. I can think of no other situation in which we would say that a person agreed to some course of action if he convinced us that he did not know that there was some other course he might have pursued. I would therefore hold, at a minimum, that the prosecution may not rely on a purported consent to search if the subject of the search did not know that he could refuse to give consent. That, I think, is the import of Bumper v. North Carolina, *supra.* Where the police claim authority to search yet in fact lack such authority, the subject does not know that he may permissibly refuse them entry, and it is this lack of knowledge that invalidates the consent.

If one accepts this view, the question then is a simple one: must the Government show that the subject knew of his rights, or must the subject show that he lacked such knowledge?

I think that any fair allocation of the burden would require that it be placed on the prosecution. On this question, the Court indulges in what might be called the "straw man" method of adjudication. The Court responds to this suggestion by overinflating the burden. And, when it is suggested that the *prosecution's* burden of proof could be easily satisfied if the police informed the subject of his rights, the Court responds by refusing to require the *police* to make a "detailed" inquiry. *Ante,* at 245. If the Court candidly faced the real question of allocating the burden of proof, neither of these maneuvers would be available to it.

If the burden is placed on the defendant, all the subject can do is to testify that he did not know of his rights. And I doubt that many trial judges will find for the defendant simply on the basis of that testimony. Precisely because the evidence is very hard to come by, courts have traditionally been reluctant to require a party to prove negatives such as the lack of knowledge. ....

In contrast, there are several ways by which the subject's knowledge of his rights may be shown. The subject may affirmatively demonstrate such knowledge by his responses at the time the search took place .... Where, as in this case, the person giving consent is someone other than the defendant, the prosecution may require him to testify under oath. Denials of knowledge may be disproved by establishing that the subject had, in the recent past, demonstrated his knowledge of his rights, for example, by refusing entry when it was requested by the police. The prior experience or training of the subject might in some cases support an inference that he knew of his right to exclude the police.

The burden on the prosecutor would disappear, of course, if the police, at the time they requested consent to search, also told the subject that he had a right to refuse consent and thus his decision to refuse would be respected. The Court's assertions to the contrary notwithstanding, there is nothing impractical about this method of satisfying the prosecution's burden of proof. It must be emphasized that the decision about informing the subject of his rights would lie with the officers seeking consent. If they believed that providing such information would impede their investigation, they might simply ask for consent, taking the risk that at some later date the prosecutor would be unable to prove that the subject knew of his rights or that some other basis for the search existed.

The Court contends that if an officer paused to inform the subject of his rights, the informality of the exchange would be destroyed. I doubt that a simple statement by an officer of an individual's right to refuse consent would do much to alter the informality of the exchange, except to alert the subject to a fact that he surely is entitled to know. It is not without significance that for many years the agents of the Federal Bureau of Investigation have routinely informed subjects of their right to refuse consent, when they request consent to search. ... The reported cases in which the police have informed subjects of their right to refuse consent show, also, that the information can be given without disrupting the casual flow of events. ... What evidence there is, then, rather strongly suggests that nothing disastrous would happen if the police, before requesting consent, informed the subject that he had a right to refuse consent and that his refusal would be respected.

I must conclude, with some reluctance, that when the Court speaks of practicality, what it really is talking of is the continued ability of the police to capitalize on the ignorance of citizens so as to accomplish by subterfuge what they could not achieve by relying only on the knowing relinquishment of constitutional rights. Of course it would be "practical" for the police to ignore the commands of the Fourth Amendment, if by practicality we mean that more criminals will be apprehended, even though the constitutional rights of innocent people also go by the boards. But such a practical advantage is achieved only at the cost of permitting the police to disregard the limitations that the Constitution places on their behavior, a cost that a constitutional democracy cannot long absorb.

I find nothing in the opinion of the Court to dispel my belief that, in such a case, as the Court of Appeals for the Ninth Circuit said, "[u]nder many circumstances a reasonable person might read an officer's 'May I' as the courteous expression of a demand backed by force of law." Bustamonte v. Schneckloth, 448 F.2d 699, 701. Most cases, in my view, are akin to Bumper v. North Carolina, 391 U.S. 543 (1968): consent is ordinarily given as acquiescence in an implicit claim of authority to search. Permitting searches in such circumstances, without any assurance at all that the subject of the search knew that, by his consent, he was relinquishing his constitutional rights, is something that I cannot believe is sanctioned by the Constitution.

III

The proper resolution of this case turns, I believe, on a realistic assessment of the nature of the interchange between citizens and the police, and of the practical import of allocating the burden of proof in one way rather than another. The Court seeks to escape such assessments by escalating its rhetoric to unwarranted heights, but no matter how forceful the adjectives the Court uses, it cannot avoid being judged by how well its image of these interchanges accords with reality. Although the Court says without real elaboration that it "cannot agree," ante, p. 163 the holding today confines the protection of the Fourth Amendment against searches conducted without probable cause to the sophisticated, the knowledgeable, and, I might add, the few. In the final analysis, the Court now sanctions a game of blindman's buff, in which the police always have the upper hand, for the sake of nothing more than the convenience of the police. But the guarantees of the Fourth Amendment were never intended to shrink before such an ephemeral and changeable interest. The Framers of the Fourth Amendment struck the balance against this sort of convenience and in favor of certain basic civil rights. It is not for this Court to restrike that balance because of its own views of the needs of law enforcement officers. I fear that that is the effect of the Court's decision today.

It is regrettable that the obsession with validating searches like that conducted in this case, so evident in the Court's hyperbole, has obscured the Court's vision of how the Fourth Amendment was designed to govern the relationship between police and citizen in our society. I believe that experience and careful reflection show how narrow and inaccurate that vision is, and I respectfully dissent.[*]

[*] Justice Blackmun wrote a concurring opinion. Justice Powell also wrote a concurring opinion, which Chief Justice Burger and Justice Rehnquist joined. Justice Douglas and Justice Brennan wrote dissenting opinions.

FLORIDA v. BOSTICK

501 U.S. 429, 111 S.Ct. 2382, 115 L.Ed.2d 389 (1991).

JUSTICE O'CONNOR delivered the opinion of the Court.

We have held that the Fourth Amendment permits police officers to approach individuals at random in airport lobbies and other public places to ask them questions and to request consent to search their luggage, so long as a reasonable person would understand that he or she could refuse to cooperate. This case requires us to determine whether the same rule applies to police encounters that take place on a bus.

I

Drug interdiction efforts have led to the use of police surveillance at airports, train stations, and bus depots. Law enforcement officers stationed at such locations routinely approach individuals, either randomly or because they suspect in some vague way that the individuals may be engaged in criminal activity, and ask them potentially incriminating questions. Broward County has adopted such a program. County Sheriff's Department officers routinely board buses at scheduled stops and ask passengers for permission to search their luggage.

In this case, two officers discovered cocaine when they searched a suitcase belonging to Terrance Bostick. The underlying facts of the search are in dispute, but the Florida Supreme Court, whose decision we review here, stated explicitly the factual premise for its decision:

" 'Two officers, complete with badges, insignia and one of them holding a recognizable zipper pouch, containing a pistol, boarded a bus bound from Miami to Atlanta during a stopover in Fort Lauderdale. Eyeing the passengers, the officers, admittedly without articulable suspicion, picked out the defendant passenger and asked to inspect his ticket and identification. The ticket, from Miami to Atlanta, matched the defendant's identification and both were immediately returned to him as unremarkable. However, the two police officers persisted and explained their presence as narcotics agents on the lookout for illegal drugs. In pursuit of that aim, they then requested the defendant's consent to search his luggage. Needless to say, there is a conflict in the evidence about whether the defendant consented to the search of the second bag in which the contraband was found and as to whether he was informed of his right to refuse consent. However, any conflict must be resolved in favor of the state, it being a question of fact decided

212

by the trial judge.' " 554 So.2d 1153, 1154–1155 (1989), quoting 510 So.2d 321, 322 (Fla.App.1987) (Letts, J., dissenting in part).

Two facts are particularly worth noting. First, the police specifically advised Bostick that he had the right to refuse consent. Bostick appears to have disputed the point, but, as the Florida Supreme Court noted explicitly, the trial court resolved this evidentiary conflict in the State's favor. Second, at no time did the officers threaten Bostick with a gun. The Florida Supreme Court indicated that one officer carried a zipper pouch containing a pistol—the equivalent of carrying a gun in a holster—but the court did not suggest that the gun was ever removed from its pouch, pointed at Bostick, or otherwise used in a threatening manner. The dissent's characterization of the officers as "gun-wielding inquisitor[s]," post, at 448, is colorful, but lacks any basis in fact.

Bostick was arrested and charged with trafficking in cocaine. He moved to suppress the cocaine on the grounds that it had been seized in violation of his Fourth Amendment rights. The trial court denied the motion but made no factual findings. Bostick subsequently entered a plea of guilty, but reserved the right to appeal the denial of the motion to suppress.

The Florida District Court of Appeal affirmed, but considered the issue sufficiently important that it certified a question to the Florida Supreme Court. 510 So.2d, at 322. The Supreme Court reasoned that Bostick had been seized because a reasonable passenger in his situation would not have felt free to leave the bus to avoid questioning by the police. 554 So.2d, at 1154. It rephrased and answered the certified question so as to make the bus setting dispositive in every case. It ruled categorically that " 'an impermissible seizure result[s] when police mount a drug search on buses during scheduled stops and question boarded passengers without articulable reasons for doing so, thereby obtaining consent to search the passengers' luggage.' " Ibid. The Florida Supreme Court thus adopted a *per se* rule that the Broward County Sheriff's practice of "working the buses" is unconstitutional. The result of this decision is that police in Florida, as elsewhere, may approach persons at random in most public places, ask them questions and seek consent to a search, see id., at 1156; but they may not engage in the same behavior on a bus. Id., at 1157. We granted certiorari, 498 U.S. 894 (1990), to determine whether the Florida Supreme Court's *per se* rule is consistent with our Fourth Amendment jurisprudence.

II

The sole issue presented for our review is whether a police encounter on a bus of the type described above necessarily constitutes a "seizure" within the meaning of the Fourth Amendment. The State concedes, and we accept for purposes of this decision, that the officers lacked the reasonable suspicion required to justify a seizure and that, if a seizure took place, the drugs found in Bostick's suitcase must be suppressed as tainted fruit.

Our cases make it clear that a seizure does not occur simply because a police officer approaches an individual and asks a few questions. So long as a reasonable person would feel free "to disregard the police and go about his business," California v. Hodari D., 499 U.S. 621, 628 (1991), the encounter is consensual and no reasonable suspicion is required. The encounter will not trigger Fourth Amendment scrutiny unless it loses its consensual nature. . . .

. . . [W]e have held repeatedly that mere police questioning does not constitute a seizure. . . .

There is no doubt that if this same encounter had taken place before Bostick boarded the bus or in the lobby of the bus terminal, it would not rise to the level of a seizure. The Court has dealt with similar encounters in airports and has found them to be "the sort of consensual encounter[s] that implicat[e] no Fourth Amendment interest." Florida v. Rodriguez, 469 U.S. 1, 5–6 (1984). We have stated that even when officers have no basis for suspecting a particular individual, they may generally ask questions of that individual . . . ask to examine the individual's identification . . . and request consent to search his or her luggage . . . as long as the police do not convey a message that compliance with their requests is required.

Bostick insists that this case is different because it took place in the cramped confines of a bus. A police encounter is much more intimidating in this setting, he argues, because police tower over a seated passenger and there is little room to move around. Bostick claims to find support in language from Michigan v. Chesternut, 486 U.S. 567, 573 (1988), and other cases, indicating that a seizure occurs when a reasonable person would believe that he or she is not "free to leave." Bostick maintains that a reasonable bus passenger would not have felt free to leave under the circumstances of this case because there is nowhere to go on a bus. Also, the bus was about to depart. Had Bostick disembarked, he would have risked being stranded and losing whatever baggage he had locked away in the luggage compartment.

The Florida Supreme Court found this argument persuasive, so much so that it adopted a *per se* rule prohibiting the police from randomly boarding buses as a means of drug interdiction. The state court erred, however, in focusing on whether Bostick was "free to leave" rather than on the principle that those words were intended to capture. When police attempt to question a person who is walking down the street or through an airport lobby, it makes sense to inquire whether a reasonable person would feel free to continue walking. But when the person is seated on a bus and has no desire to leave, the degree to which a reasonable person would feel that he or she could leave is not an accurate measure of the coercive effect of the encounter.

Here, for example, the mere fact that Bostick did not feel free to leave the bus does not mean that the police seized him. Bostick was a passenger on a bus that was scheduled to depart. He would not have felt free to leave the bus even if the police had not been present. Bostick's movements were "confined" in a sense, but this was the natural result of his decision to take the bus; it says nothing about whether or not the police conduct at issue was coercive.

In this respect, the Court's decision in INS v. Delgado, [466 U.S. 210 (1984)], is dispositive. At issue there was the INS' practice of visiting factories at random and questioning employees to determine whether any were illegal aliens. Several INS agents would stand near the building's exits, while other agents walked through the factory questioning workers. The Court acknowledged that the workers may not have been free to leave their worksite, but explained that this was not the result of police activity: "Ordinarily, when people are at work their freedom to move about has been meaningfully restricted, not by the actions of law enforcement officials, but by the workers' voluntary obligations to their employers." Id., at 218. We concluded that there was no seizure because, even though the workers were not free to leave the building without being questioned, the agents' conduct should have given employees "no reason to believe that they would be detained if they gave truthful answers to the questions put to them or if they simply refused to answer." Ibid.

The present case is analytically indistinguishable from *Delgado.* Like the workers in that case, Bostick's freedom of movement was restricted by a factor independent of police conduct—*i.e.,* by his being a passenger on a bus. Accordingly, the "free to leave" analysis on which Bostick relies is inapplicable. In such a situation, the appropriate inquiry is whether a reasonable person would feel free to decline the officers' requests or otherwise terminate the encounter. This formulation follows logically from prior cases and breaks no new ground. We have said before that the crucial test is whether, taking into account all of the circumstances surrounding the encounter, the police conduct would "have communicated to a reasonable person that he was not at liberty to ignore the police presence and go about his business." *Chesternut,* supra, at 569. . . . Where the encounter takes place is one factor, but it is not the only one. And, as the Solicitor General correctly observes, an individual may decline an officer's request without fearing prosecution. . . . We have consistently held that a refusal to cooperate, without more, does not furnish the minimal level of objective justification needed for a detention or seizure. . . .

The facts of this case, as described by the Florida Supreme Court, leave some doubt whether a seizure occurred. Two officers walked up to Bostick on the bus, asked him a few questions, and asked if they could search his bags. As we have explained, no seizure occurs when police ask questions of an individual, ask to examine the individual's identification, and request consent to search his or her luggage—so long as the officers do not convey a message that compliance with their requests is required. Here, the facts recited by the Florida Supreme Court indicate that the officers did not point guns at Bostick or otherwise threaten him and that they specifically advised Bostick that he could refuse consent.

Nevertheless, we refrain from deciding whether or not a seizure occurred in this case. The trial court made no express findings of fact, and the Florida Supreme Court rested its decision on a single fact—that the encounter took place on a bus—rather than on the totality of the circumstances. We remand so that the Florida courts may evaluate the seizure question under the correct legal standard. We do reject, however, Bostick's argument that he must have been seized because no reasonable person would freely consent to a search of luggage that he or she knows contains drugs. This argument cannot prevail because the "reasonable person" test presupposes an *innocent* person. . . .

The dissent characterizes our decision as holding that police may board buses and by an "*intimidating* show of authority," post, at 447 (emphasis added), demand of passengers their "voluntary" cooperation. That characterization is incorrect. Clearly, a bus passenger's decision to cooperate with law enforcement officers authorizes the police to conduct a search without first obtaining a warrant *only* if the cooperation is voluntary. "Consent" that is the product of official intimidation or harassment is not consent at all. Citizens do not forfeit their constitutional rights when they are coerced to comply with a request that they would prefer to refuse. The question to be decided by the Florida courts on remand is whether Bostick chose to permit the search of his luggage.

The dissent also attempts to characterize our decision as applying a lesser degree of constitutional protection to those individuals who travel by bus, rather than by other forms of transportation. This, too, is an erroneous characterization. Our Fourth Amendment inquiry in this case—whether a reasonable person would have felt free to decline the officers' requests or otherwise terminate the encounter—applies equally to police encounters that take place on trains, planes, and city streets. It is the dissent that would single out this particular mode of travel for differential treatment by adopting a *per se* rule that random bus searches are unconstitutional.

The dissent reserves its strongest criticism for the proposition that police officers can approach individuals as to whom they have no reasonable suspicion and ask them potentially incriminating questions. But this proposition is by no means novel; it has been endorsed by the Court any number of times....

This Court, as the dissent correctly observes, is not empowered to suspend constitutional guarantees so that the Government may more effectively wage a "war on drugs." See post, at 440, 450–451. If that war is to be fought, those who fight it must respect the rights of individuals, whether or not those individuals are suspected of having committed a crime. By the same token, this Court is not empowered to forbid law enforcement practices simply because it considers them distasteful. The Fourth Amendment proscribes unreasonable searches and seizures; it does not proscribe voluntary cooperation. The cramped confines of a bus are one relevant factor that should be considered in evaluating whether a passenger's consent is voluntary. We cannot agree, however, with the Florida Supreme Court that this single factor will be dispositive in every case.

We adhere to the rule that, in order to determine whether a particular encounter constitutes a seizure, a court must consider all the circumstances surrounding the encounter to determine whether the police conduct would have communicated to a reasonable person that the person was not free to decline the officers' requests or otherwise terminate the encounter. That rule applies to encounters that take place on a city street or in an airport lobby, and it applies equally to encounters on a bus. The Florida Supreme Court erred in adopting a *per se* rule.

The judgment of the Florida Supreme Court is reversed, and the case remanded for further proceedings not inconsistent with this opinion.

It is so ordered.

JUSTICE MARSHALL, with whom JUSTICE BLACKMUN and JUSTICE STEVENS join, dissenting.

Our Nation, we are told, is engaged in a "war on drugs." No one disputes that it is the job of law-enforcement officials to devise effective weapons for fighting this war. But the effectiveness of a law-enforcement technique is not proof of its constitutionality. The general warrant, for example, was certainly an effective means of law enforcement. Yet it was one of the primary aims of the Fourth Amendment to protect citizens from the tyranny of being singled out for search and seizure without particularized suspicion *notwithstanding* the effectiveness of this method.... In my view, the law-enforcement technique with which we are confronted in this case—the suspicionless police sweep of buses in intrastate or interstate travel—bears all of the indicia of coercion and unjustified intrusion associated with the general warrant. Because I believe that the bus sweep at issue in this case violates the core values of the Fourth Amendment, I dissent.

I

At issue in this case is a "new and increasingly common tactic in the war on drugs": the suspicionless police sweep of buses in interstate or intrastate travel. . . .   Typically under this technique, a group of state or federal officers will board a bus while it is stopped at an intermediate point on its route.   Often displaying badges, weapons or other indicia of authority, the officers identify themselves and announce their purpose to intercept drug traffickers. They proceed to approach individual passengers, requesting them to show identification, produce their tickets, and explain the purpose of their travels.   Never do the officers advise the passengers that they are free not to speak with the officers.   An "interview" of this type ordinarily culminates in a request for consent to search the passenger's luggage. . . .

These sweeps are conducted in "dragnet" style.   The police admittedly act without an "articulable suspicion" in deciding which buses to board and which passengers to approach for interviewing. By proceeding systematically in this fashion, the police are able to engage in a tremendously high volume of searches. . . .   The percentage of successful drug interdictions is low. . . .

To put it mildly, these sweeps "are inconvenient, intrusive, and intimidating."   United States v. Chandler, 744 F.Supp. [333 (D.D.C. 1990)], at 335.   They occur within cramped confines, with officers typically placing themselves in between the passenger selected for an interview and the exit of the bus. . . .   Because the bus is only temporarily stationed at a point short of its destination, the passengers are in no position to leave as a means of evading the officers' questioning.   Undoubtedly, such a sweep holds up the progress of the bus. . . .   Thus, this "new and increasingly common tactic," United States v. Lewis, [287 U.S.App.D.C. 306 (1990)], at 307 . . . burdens the experience of traveling by bus with a degree of governmental interference to which, until now, our society has been proudly unaccustomed. . . .

        . . .

The question for this Court, then, is whether the suspicionless, dragnet-style sweep of buses in intrastate and interstate travel is consistent with the Fourth Amendment.   The majority suggests that this latest tactic in the drug war is perfectly compatible with the Constitution.   I disagree.

II

I have no objection to the manner in which the majority frames the test for determining whether a suspicionless bus sweep amounts to a Fourth Amendment "seizure."   I agree that the appropriate question is whether a passenger who is approached during such a sweep "would feel free to decline the officers' requests or otherwise terminate the encounter."   Ante, at 436.   What I cannot understand is how the majority can possibly suggest an affirmative answer to this question.

. . .

[The facts in this case] exhibit all of the elements of coercion associated with a typical bus sweep. Two officers boarded the Greyhound bus on which respondent was a passenger while the bus, en route from Miami to Atlanta, was on a brief stop to pick up passengers in Fort Lauderdale. The officers made a visible display of their badges and wore bright green "raid" jackets bearing the insignia of the Broward County Sheriff's Department; one held a gun in a recognizable weapons pouch. See 554 So.2d, at 1154, 1157. These facts alone constitute an intimidating "show of authority." See Michigan v. Chesternut, 486 U.S. 567, 575 (1988). . . . Once on board, the officers approached respondent, who was sitting in the back of the bus, identified themselves as narcotics officers and began to question him. . . . One officer stood in front of respondent's seat, partially blocking the narrow aisle through which respondent would have been required to pass to reach the exit of the bus. . . .

As far as is revealed by facts on which the Florida Supreme Court premised its decision, the officers did not advise respondent that he was free to break off this "interview." Inexplicably, the majority repeatedly stresses the trial court's implicit finding that the police officers advised respondent that he was free to refuse permission to search his travel bag. . . . This aspect of the exchange between respondent and the police is completely irrelevant to the issue before us. For as the State concedes, and as the majority purports to "accept," id., at 433–434, *if* respondent was unlawfully seized when the officers approached him and initiated questioning, the resulting search was likewise unlawful no matter how well advised respondent was of his right to refuse it. . . . Consequently, the issue is not whether a passenger in respondent's position would have felt free to deny consent to the search of his bag, but whether such a passenger—without being apprised of his rights—would have felt free to terminate the antecedent encounter with the police.

Unlike the majority, I have no doubt that the answer to this question is no. Apart from trying to accommodate the officers, respondent had only two options. First, he could have remained seated while obstinately refusing to respond to the officers' questioning. But in light of the intimidating show of authority that the officers made upon boarding the bus, respondent reasonably could have believed that such behavior would only arouse the officers' suspicions and intensify their interrogation. Indeed, officers who carry out bus sweeps like the one at issue here frequently admit that this is the effect of a passenger's refusal to cooperate. . . . The majority's observation that a mere refusal to answer questions, "without more," does not give rise to a reasonable basis for seizing a passenger, ante, at 437, is utterly beside the point, because a passenger unadvised of his rights and otherwise unversed in constitutional law *has no reason to know* that the police cannot hold his refusal to cooperate against him.

Second, respondent could have tried to escape the officers' presence by leaving the bus altogether. But because doing so would have required respondent to squeeze past the gun-wielding inquisitor who was blocking the aisle of the bus, this hardly seems like a course that respondent reasonably would have viewed as available to him. The majority lamely protests that nothing in the stipulated facts shows that the questioning officer "*point[ed]* [his] gu[n] at [respondent] or otherwise *threaten[ed]* him" with the weapon. Ante, at 437 (emphasis added). Our decisions recognize the obvious point, however, that the choice of the police to "display" their weapons during an encounter exerts significant coercive pressure on the confronted citizen.... We have never suggested that the police must go so far as to put a citizen in immediate apprehension of *being shot* before a court can take account of the intimidating effect of being questioned by an officer with weapon in hand.

Even if respondent had perceived that the officers would *let* him leave the bus, moreover, he could not reasonably have been expected to resort to this means of evading their intrusive questioning. For so far as respondent knew, the bus' departure from the terminal was imminent. Unlike a person approached by the police on the street ... or at a bus or airport terminal after reaching his destination ... a passenger approached by the police at a intermediate point in a long bus journey cannot simply leave the scene and repair to a safe haven to avoid unwanted probing by law-enforcement officials. The vulnerability that an intrastate or interstate traveler experiences when confronted by the police outside of his "own familiar territory" surely aggravates the coercive quality of such an encounter....

The case on which the majority primarily relies, INS v. Delgado, 466 U.S. 210 (1984), is distinguishable in every relevant respect. In *Delgado,* this Court held that workers approached by law-enforcement officials inside of a factory were not "seized" for purposes of the Fourth Amendment. The Court was careful to point out, however, that the presence of the agents did not furnish the workers with a reasonable basis for believing that they were not free to leave the factory, as at least some of them did.... Unlike passengers confronted by law-enforcement officials on a bus stopped temporarily at an intermediate point in its journey, workers approached by law-enforcement officials at their workplace need not abandon personal belongings and venture into unfamiliar environs in order to avoid unwanted questioning. Moreover, the workers who did not leave the building in *Delgado* remained free to move about the entire factory ... a considerably less confining environment than a bus. Finally, contrary to the officer who confronted respondent, the law-enforcement officials in *Delgado* did not conduct their interviews with guns in hand....

Rather than requiring the police to justify the coercive tactics employed here, the majority blames respondent for his own sensation of constraint. The majority concedes that respondent "did not feel free to leave the bus" as a means of breaking off the interrogation by the Broward County officers. Ante, at 436. But this experience of confinement, the majority explains, "was the natural result of *his* decision to take the bus." Ibid. (emphasis added). Thus, in the majority's view, because respondent's "freedom of movement was restricted by a factor independent of police conduct—i.e., by his being a passenger on a bus," ante, at 437, respondent was not seized for purposes of the Fourth Amendment.

This reasoning borders on sophism and trivializes the values that underlie the Fourth Amendment. Obviously, a person's "voluntary decision" to place himself in a room with only one exit does not authorize the police to force an encounter upon him by placing themselves in front of the exit. It is no more acceptable for the police to force an encounter on a person by exploiting his "voluntary decision" to expose himself to perfectly legitimate personal or social constraints. By consciously deciding to single out persons who have undertaken interstate or intrastate travel, officers who conduct suspicionless, dragnet-style sweeps put passengers to the choice of cooperating or of exiting their buses and possibly being stranded in unfamiliar locations. It is exactly because this "choice" is no "choice" at all that police engage this technique.

In my view, the Fourth Amendment clearly condemns the suspicionless, dragnet-style sweep of intrastate or interstate buses. Withdrawing this particular weapon from the government's drug-war arsenal would hardly leave the police without any means of combating the use of buses as instrumentalities of the drug trade. The police would remain free, for example, to approach passengers whom they have a reasonable, articulable basis to suspect of criminal wrongdoing. Alternatively, they could continue to confront passengers without suspicion so long as they took simple steps, like advising the passengers confronted of their right to decline to be questioned, to dispel the aura of coercion and intimidation that pervades such encounters. There is no reason to expect that such requirements would render the Nation's buses law-enforcement-free zones.

III

The majority attempts to gloss over the violence that today's decision does to the Fourth Amendment with empty admonitions. "If th[e] [war on drugs] is to be fought," the majority intones, "those who fight it must respect the rights of individuals, whether or not those individuals are suspected of having committed a crime." Ante, at 439. The majority's actions, however, speak louder than its words.

I dissent.

UNITED STATES v. MATLOCK

415 U.S. 164, 94 S.Ct. 988, 39 L.Ed.2d 242 (1974).

MR. JUSTICE WHITE delivered the opinion of the Court.

In Schneckloth v. Bustamonte, 412 U.S. 218 (1973), the Court reaffirmed the principle that the search of property, without warrant and without probable cause, but with proper consent voluntarily given, is valid under the Fourth Amendment. The question now before us is whether the evidence presented by the United States with respect to the voluntary consent of a third party to search the living quarters of the respondent was legally sufficient to render the seized materials admissible in evidence at the respondent's criminal trial.

I

Respondent Matlock was indicted in February 1971 for the robbery of a federally insured bank in Wisconsin, in violation of 18 U.S.C. § 2113. A week later, he filed a motion to suppress evidence seized by law enforcement officers from a home in the town of Pardeeville, Wisconsin, in which he had been living. Suppression hearings followed. As found by the District Court, the facts were that respondent was arrested in the yard in front of the Pardeeville home on November 12, 1970. The home was leased from the owner by Mr. and Mrs. Marshall. Living in the home were Mrs. Marshall, several of her children, including her daughter Mrs. Gayle Graff, Gayle's three-year-old son, and respondent. Although the officers were aware at the time of the arrest that respondent lived in the house, they did not ask him which room he occupied or whether he would consent to a search. Three of the arresting officers went to the door of the house and were admitted by Mrs. Graff, who was dressed in a robe and was holding her son in her arms. The officers told her they were looking for money and a gun and asked if they could search the house. Although denied by Mrs. Graff at the suppression hearing, it was found that she consented voluntarily to the search of the house, including the east bedroom on the second floor which she said was jointly occupied by Matlock and herself. The east bedroom was searched and the evidence at issue here, $4,995 in cash, was found in a diaper bag in the only closet in the room. The issue came to be whether Mrs. Graff's relationship to the east bedroom was sufficient to make her consent to search valid against respondent Matlock.

The District Court ruled that before the seized evidence could be admitted in evidence, the Government must prove first, that it reasonably appeared to the searching officers "just prior to the search, that facts exist which will render the consenter's consent binding on the putative defendant," and second, that "just prior to the search, facts do exist which render the consenter's consent binding on the putative defendant." There was no requirement that express permission from respondent to Mrs. Graff to allow the officers to search be shown; it was sufficient to show her authority to consent in her own right, by reason of her relationship to the premises. The first requirement was held satisfied because of respondent's presence in the yard of the house at the time of his arrest, because of Gayle Graff's residence in the house for some time and her presence in the house just prior to the search, and because of her statement to the officers that she and the respondent occupied the east bedroom.

The District Court concluded, however, that the Government had failed to satisfy the second requirement and had not satisfactorily proved Mrs. Graff's actual authority to consent to the search. ... The District Court also rejected the Government's claim that it was required to prove only that at the time of the search the officers could reasonably have concluded that Gayle Graff's relationship to the east bedroom was sufficient to make her consent binding on respondent.

The Court of Appeals affirmed the judgment of the District Court in all respects. 476 F.2d 1083. We granted certiorari, 412 U.S. 917, and now reverse the Court of Appeals.

II

It has been assumed by the parties and the courts below that the voluntary consent of any joint occupant of a residence to search the premises jointly occupied is valid against the co-occupant, permitting evidence discovered in the search to be used against him at a criminal trial. ... This Court left open, in Amos v. United States, 255 U.S. 313, 317 (1921), the question whether a wife's permission to search the residence in which she lived with her husband could "waive his constitutional rights," but more recent authority here clearly indicates that the consent of one who possesses common authority over premises or effects is valid as against the absent, nonconsenting person with whom that authority is shared. In Frazier v. Cupp, 394 U.S. 731, 740 (1969), the Court "dismissed rather quickly" the contention that the consent of the petitioner's cousin to the search of a duffel bag, which was being used jointly by both men and had been left in the cousin's home, would not justify the seizure of petitioner's clothing found inside; joint use of the bag rendered the cousin's authority to consent to its search clear. Indeed, the Court was unwilling to engage in the "metaphysical subtleties" raised by Frazier's claim that his cousin only had permission to use one compartment within the bag. By allowing the cousin the use of the bag, and by leaving it in his house, Frazier was held to have assumed the risk that his cousin would allow someone else to look inside. Ibid. More generally, in Schneckloth v. Busta-monte, supra, 412 U.S., at 245–246, we noted that our prior recognition of the constitutional validity of "third party consent searches" in cases like *Frazier* and Coolidge v. New Hampshire, 403 U.S. 443, 487–490 (1971), supported the view that a consent search is fundamentally different in nature from the waiver of a trial right. These cases at least make clear that when the prosecution seeks to justify a warrantless search by proof of voluntary consent, it is not limited to proof that consent was given by the defendant, but may show that permission to search was obtained from a third party who possessed common authority over or other sufficient relationship to the premises or effect sought to be inspected.[7] The issue now before us is whether the Government made the requisite showing in this case.

III

The District Court excluded from evidence at the suppression hearing, as inadmissible hearsay, the out-of-court statements of Mrs. Graff with respect to her and respondent's joint occupancy and use of the east bedroom, as well as the evidence that both respondent and Mrs. Graff at various times and to various persons had represented themselves as husband and wife. The Court of Appeals affirmed the ruling. Both courts were in error.

. . .

IV

It appears to us, given the admissibility of Mrs. Graff's and respondent's out-of-court statements, that the Government sustained its burden of proving by the preponderance of the evidence that Mrs. Graff's voluntary consent to search the east bedroom was legally sufficient to warrant admitting into evidence the $4,995 found in the diaper bag.[14] But we prefer that the District Court first reconsider the sufficiency of the evidence in the light of this decision and opinion. The judgment of the Court of Appeals is reversed and the case is remanded to the Court of Appeals with

7. Common authority is, of course, not to be implied from the mere property interest a third party has in the property. The authority which justifies the third-party consent does not rest upon the law of property, with its attendant historical and legal refinements . . . but rests rather on mutual use of the property by persons generally having joint access or control for most purposes, so that it is reasonable to recognize that any of the co-inhabitants has the right to permit the inspection in his own right and that the others have assumed the risk that one of their number might permit the common area to be searched.

14. Accordingly, we do not reach another major contention of the United States in bringing this case here: that the Government in any event had only to satisfy the District Court that the searching officers reasonably believed that Mrs. Graff had sufficient authority over the premises to consent to the search.

. . .

directions to remand the case to the District Court for further proceedings consistent with this opinion.

So ordered.[*]

[*] Justice Douglas wrote a dissenting opinion. Justice Brennan wrote a dissenting opinion, which Justice Marshall joined.

ILLINOIS v. RODRIGUEZ

497 U.S. 177, 110 S.Ct. 2793, 111 L.Ed.2d 148 (1990).

JUSTICE SCALIA delivered the opinion of the Court.

In United States v. Matlock, 415 U.S. 164 (1974), this Court reaffirmed that a warrantless entry and search by law enforcement officers does not violate the Fourth Amendment's proscription of "unreasonable searches and seizures" if the officers have obtained the consent of a third party who possesses common authority over the premises. The present case presents an issue we expressly reserved in *Matlock,* see id., at 177, n. 14: whether a warrantless entry is valid when based upon the consent of a third party whom the police, at the time of the entry, reasonably believe to possess common authority over the premises, but who in fact does not do so.

I

Respondent Edward Rodriguez was arrested in his apartment by law enforcement officers and charged with possession of illegal drugs. The police gained entry to the apartment with the consent and assistance of Gail Fischer, who had lived there with respondent for several months. The relevant facts leading to the arrest are as follows.

On July 26, 1985, police were summoned to the residence of Dorothy Jackson on South Wolcott in Chicago. They were met by Ms. Jackson's daughter, Gail Fischer, who showed signs of a severe beating. She told the officers that she had been assaulted by respondent Edward Rodriguez earlier that day in an apartment on South California Avenue. Fischer stated that Rodriguez was then asleep in the apartment, and she consented to travel there with the police in order to unlock the door with her key so that the officers could enter and arrest him. During this conversation, Fischer several times referred to the apartment on South California as "our" apartment, and said that she had clothes and furniture there. It is unclear whether she indicated that she currently lived at the apartment, or only that she used to live there.

The police officers drove to the apartment on South California, accompanied by Fischer. They did not obtain an arrest warrant for Rodriguez, nor did they seek a search warrant for the apartment. At the apartment, Fischer unlocked the door with her key and gave the officers permission to enter. They moved through the door into the living room, where they observed in plain view drug paraphernalia and containers filled with white powder that they believed (correctly, as later analysis showed) to be cocaine. They proceeded to the bedroom, where they found Rodriguez asleep and discovered additional containers of white powder in two open attaché cases. The officers arrested Rodriguez and seized the drugs and related paraphernalia.

Rodriguez was charged with possession of a controlled substance with intent to deliver. He moved to suppress all evidence seized at the time of his arrest, claiming that Fischer had vacated the apartment several weeks earlier and had no authority to consent to the entry. The Cook County Circuit Court granted the motion, holding that at the time she consented to the entry Fischer did not have common authority over the apartment. The Court concluded that Fischer was not a "usual resident" but rather an "infrequent visitor" at the apartment on South California, based upon its findings that Fischer's name was not on the lease, that she did not contribute to the rent, that she was not allowed to invite others to the apartment on her own, that she did not have access to the apartment when respondent was away, and that she had moved some of her possessions from the apartment. The Circuit Court also rejected the State's contention that, even if Fischer did not possess common authority over the premises, there was no Fourth Amendment violation if the police *reasonably believed* at the time of their entry that Fischer possessed the authority to consent.

The Appellate Court of Illinois affirmed the Circuit Court in all respects. The Illinois Supreme Court denied the State's Petition for Leave to Appeal, 125 Ill.2d 572, 537 N.E.2d 816 (1989), and we granted certiorari. 493 U.S. 932 (1989).

II

The Fourth Amendment generally prohibits the warrantless entry of a person's home, whether to make an arrest or to search for specific objects. . . . The prohibition does not apply, however, to situations in which voluntary consent has been obtained, either from the individual whose property is searched . . . or from a third party who possesses common authority over the premises . . . . The State of Illinois contends that that exception applies in the present case.

As we stated in *Matlock,* 415 U.S., at 171, n. 7, "[c]ommon authority" rests "on mutual use of the property by persons generally having joint access or control for most purposes . . . ." The burden of establishing that common authority rests upon the State. On the basis of this record, it is clear that burden was not sustained. . . . To the contrary, the Appellate Court's determination of no common authority over the apartment was obviously correct.

III

A

The State contends that, even if Fischer did not in fact have authority to give consent, it suffices to validate the entry that the law enforcement officers reasonably believed she did. . . .

. . .

B

On the merits of the issue, respondent asserts that permitting a reasonable belief of common authority to validate an entry would cause a defendant's Fourth Amendment rights to be "vicariously waived." Brief for Respondent 32. We disagree.

We have been unyielding in our insistence that a defendant's waiver of his trial rights cannot be given effect unless it is "knowing" and "intelligent." Colorado v. Spring, 479 U.S. 564, 574–575 (1987) . . . . We would assuredly not permit, therefore, evidence seized in violation of the Fourth Amendment to be introduced on the basis of a trial court's mere "reasonable belief"—derived from statements by unauthorized persons—that the defendant has waived his objection. But one must make a distinction between, on the one hand, trial rights that *derive* from the violation of constitutional guarantees and, on the other hand, the nature of those constitutional guarantees themselves . . . .

What Rodriguez is assured by the trial right of the exclusionary rule, where it applies, is that no evidence seized in violation of the Fourth Amendment will be introduced at his trial unless he consents. What he is assured by the Fourth Amendment itself, however, is not that no government search of his house will occur unless he consents; but that no such search will occur that is "unreasonable." U.S. Const., Amdt. 4. There are various elements, of course, that can make a search of a person's house "reasonable"—one of which is the consent of the person or his cotenant. The essence of respondent's argument is that we should impose upon this element a requirement that we have not imposed upon other elements that regularly compel government officers to exercise judgment regarding the facts: namely, the requirement that their judgment be not only responsible but correct.

The fundamental objective that alone validates all unconsented government searches is, of course, the seizure of persons who have committed or are about to commit crimes, or of evidence related to crimes. But "reasonableness," with respect to this necessary element, does not demand that the government be factually correct in its assessment that that is what a search will produce. Warrants need only be supported by "probable cause," which demands no more than a proper "assessment of probabilities in particular factual contexts . . . ." Illinois v. Gates, 462 U.S. 213, 232 (1983) . . . .

Another element often, though not invariably, required in order to render an unconsented search "reasonable" is, of course, that the officer be authorized by a valid warrant. Here also we have not held that "reasonableness" precludes error with respect to those factual judgments that law enforcement officials are expected to make . . . .

. . .

... It is apparent that in order to satisfy the "reasonableness" requirement of the Fourth Amendment, what is generally demanded of the many factual determinations that must regularly be made by agents of the government—whether the magistrate issuing a warrant, the police officer executing a warrant, or the police officer conducting a search or seizure under one of the exceptions to the warrant requirement—is not that they always be correct, but that they always be reasonable....

We see no reason to depart from this general rule with respect to facts bearing upon the authority to consent to a search. Whether the basis for such authority exists is the sort of recurring factual question to which law enforcement officials must be expected to apply their judgment; and all the Fourth Amendment requires is that they answer it reasonably. The Constitution is no more violated when officers enter without a warrant because they reasonably (though erroneously) believe that the person who has consented to their entry is a resident of the premises, than it is violated when they enter without a warrant because they reasonably (though erroneously) believe they are in pursuit of a violent felon who is about to escape.... *

. . .

... [W]hat we hold today does not suggest that law enforcement officers may always accept a person's invitation to enter premises. Even when the invitation is accompanied by an explicit assertion that the person lives there, the surrounding circumstances could conceivably be such that a reasonable person would doubt its truth and not act upon it without further inquiry. As with other factual determinations bearing upon search and seizure, determination of consent to enter must "be judged against an objective standard: would the facts available to the officer at the moment ... 'warrant a man of reasonable caution in the belief'" that the consenting party had authority over the premises? Terry v. Ohio, 392 U.S. 1, 21–22 (1968). If not, then warrantless entry without further inquiry is unlawful unless authority actually exists. But if so, the search is valid.

. . .

---

* Justice Marshall's dissent rests upon a rejection of the proposition that searches pursuant to valid third-party consent are "generally reasonable." Post, at 196. Only a warrant or exigent circumstances, he contends, can produce "reasonableness"; consent validates the search only because the object of the search thereby "limit[s] his expectation of privacy," post, at 198, so that the search becomes not really a search at all. We see no basis for making such an artificial distinction. To describe a consented search as a noninvasion of privacy and thus a nonsearch is strange in the extreme. And while it must be admitted that this ingenious device can explain why consented searches are lawful, it cannot explain why seemingly consented searches are "unreasonable," which is all that the Constitution forbids.... The only basis for contending that the constitutional standard could not possibly have been met here is the argument that reasonableness must be judged by the facts as they were, rather than by the facts as they were known. As we have discussed in text, that argument has long since been rejected.

In the present case, the Appellate Court found it unnecessary to determine whether the officers reasonably believed that Fischer had the authority to consent, because it ruled as a matter of law that a reasonable belief could not validate the entry. Since we find that ruling to be in error, we remand for consideration of that question. The judgment of the Illinois Appellate Court is reversed, and the case is remanded for further proceedings not inconsistent with this opinion.

So ordered.

JUSTICE MARSHALL, with whom JUSTICE BRENNAN and JUSTICE STEVENS join, dissenting.

. . .

The majority agrees with the Illinois Appellate Court's determination that Fischer did not have authority to consent to the officers' entry of Rodriguez's apartment.... The Court holds that the warrantless entry into Rodriguez's home was nonetheless valid if the officers reasonably believed that Fischer had authority to consent.... The majority's defense of this position rests on a misconception of the basis for third-party consent searches. That such searches do not give rise to claims of constitutional violations rests not on the premise that they are "reasonable" under the Fourth Amendment ... but on the premise that a person may voluntarily limit his expectation of privacy by allowing others to exercise authority over his possessions.... Thus, an individual's decision to permit another "joint access [to] or control [over the property] for most purposes," United States v. Matlock, 415 U.S. 164, 171, n. 7 (1974), limits that individual's reasonable expectation of privacy and to that extent limits his Fourth Amendment protections.... If an individual has not so limited his expectation of privacy, the police may not dispense with the safeguards established by the Fourth Amendment.

The baseline for the reasonableness of a search or seizure in the home is the presence of a warrant.... Indeed, "searches and seizures inside a home without a warrant are presumptively unreasonable." Payton v. New York, 445 U.S. 573, 586 (1980). Exceptions to the warrant requirement must therefore serve "compelling" law enforcement goals. Mincey v. Arizona, 437 U.S. 385, 394 (1978). Because the sole law enforcement purpose underlying third-party consent searches is avoiding the inconvenience of securing a warrant, a departure from the warrant requirement is not justified simply because an officer reasonably believes a third party has consented to a search of the defendant's home. In holding otherwise, the majority ignores our longstanding view that "the informed and deliberate determinations of magistrates ... as to what searches and seizures are permissible under the Constitution are to be preferred over the hurried action of officers and others who may happen to make arrests." United States v. Lefkowitz, 285 U.S. 452, 464 (1932).

I

. . .

The Court has tolerated departures from the warrant requirement only when an exigency makes a warrantless search imperative to the safety of the police and of the community. . . . The Court has often heard, and steadfastly rejected, the invitation to carve out further exceptions to the warrant requirement for searches of the home because of the burdens on police investigation and prosecution of crime. Our rejection of such claims is not due to a lack of appreciation of the difficulty and importance of effective law enforcement, but rather to our firm commitment to "the view of those who wrote the Bill of Rights that the privacy of a person's home and property may not be totally sacrificed in the name of maximum simplicity in enforcement of the criminal law." *Mincey,* supra, at 393 (citing United States v. Chadwick, 433 U.S. 1, 6–11 (1977)).

In the absence of an exigency, then, warrantless home searches and seizures are unreasonable under the Fourth Amendment. The weighty constitutional interest in preventing unauthorized intrusions into the home overrides any law enforcement interest in relying on the reasonable but potentially mistaken belief that a third party has authority to consent to such a search or seizure. Indeed, as the present case illustrates, only the minimal interest in avoiding the inconvenience of obtaining a warrant weighs in on the law enforcement side.

Against this law enforcement interest in expediting arrests is "the right of a man to retreat into his own home and there be free from unreasonable governmental intrusion." Silverman v. United States, 365 U.S. 505, 511 (1961). To be sure, in some cases, in which police officers reasonably rely on a third party's consent, the consent will prove valid, no intrusion will result, and the police will have been spared the inconvenience of securing a warrant. But in other cases, such as this one, the authority claimed by the third party will be false. The reasonableness of police conduct must be measured in light of the possibility that the target has not consented. . . .

Unlike searches conducted pursuant to the recognized exceptions to the warrant requirement . . . third-party consent searches are not based on an exigency and therefore serve no compelling social goal. Police officers, when faced with the choice of relying on consent by a third party or securing a warrant, should secure a warrant, and must therefore accept the risk of error should they instead choose to rely on consent.

II

. . .

A search conducted pursuant to an officer's reasonable but mistaken belief that a third party had authority to consent is . . . on an entirely different constitutional footing from one based on the consent of a third party who in fact has such authority. Even if the officers reasonably believed that Fischer had authority to consent, she did not, and Rodriguez's expectation of privacy was therefore undiminished. Rodriguez accordingly can challenge the warrantless intrusion into his home as a violation of the Fourth Amendment. . . .

III

Acknowledging that the third party in this case lacked authority to consent, the majority seeks to rely on cases suggesting that reasonable but mistaken factual judgments by police will not invalidate otherwise reasonable searches. The majority reads these cases as establishing a "general rule" that "what is generally demanded of the many factual determinations that must regularly be made by agents of the government—whether the magistrate issuing a warrant, the police officer executing a warrant, or the police officer conducting a search or seizure under one of the exceptions to the warrant requirement—is not that they always be correct, but that they always be reasonable." Ante, at 185–186.

The majority's assertion, however, is premised on the erroneous assumption that third-party consent searches are generally reasonable. The cases the majority cites thus provide no support for its holding. . . . [T]he possibility of factual error is built into the probable cause standard, and such a standard, by its very definition, will in some cases result in the arrest of a suspect who has not actually committed a crime. Because probable cause defines the reasonableness of searches and seizures outside of the home, a search is reasonable under the Fourth Amendment whenever that standard is met, notwithstanding the possibility of "mistakes" on the part of police. . . . In contrast, our cases have already struck the balance against warrantless home intrusions in the absence of an exigency. . . . Because reasonable factual errors by law enforcement officers will not validate unreasonable searches, the reasonableness of the officer's mistaken belief that the third party had authority to consent is irrelevant.

. . .

IV

Our cases demonstrate that third-party consent searches are free from constitutional challenge only to the extent that they rest on consent by a party empowered to do so. The majority's conclusion to the contrary ignores the legitimate expectations of privacy on which individuals are entitled to rely. That a person who allows another joint access to his property thereby limits his expectation of privacy does not justify trampling the rights of a person who has not similarly relinquished any of his privacy expectation.

Instead of judging the validity of consent searches, as we have in the past, based on whether a defendant has in fact limited his expectation of privacy, the Court today carves out an additional exception to the warrant requirement for third-party consent searches without pausing to consider whether " 'the exigencies of the situation' make the needs of law enforcement so compelling that the warrantless search is objectively reasonable under the Fourth Amendment," *Mincey,* 437 U.S., at 394 (citations omitted). Where this free-floating creation of "reasonable" exceptions to the warrant requirement will end, now that the Court has departed from the balancing approach that has long been part of our Fourth Amendment jurisprudence, is unclear. But by allowing a person to be subjected to a warrantless search in his home without his consent and without exigency, the majority has taken away some of the liberty that the Fourth Amendment was designed to protect.

ARIZONA v. HICKS

480 U.S. 321, 107 S.Ct. 1149, 94 L.Ed.2d 347 (1987).

JUSTICE SCALIA delivered the opinion of the Court.

In Coolidge v. New Hampshire, 403 U.S. 443 (1971), we said that in certain circumstances a warrantless seizure by police of an item that comes within plain view during their lawful search of a private area may be reasonable under the Fourth Amendment. . . . We granted certiorari, 475 U.S. 1107 (1986), in the present case to decide whether this "plain view" doctrine may be invoked when the police have less than probable cause to believe that the item in question is evidence of a crime or is contraband.

I

On April 18, 1984, a bullet was fired through the floor of respondent's apartment, striking and injuring a man in the apartment below. Police officers arrived and entered respondent's apartment to search for the shooter, for other victims, and for weapons. They found and seized three weapons, including a sawed-off rifle, and in the course of their search also discovered a stocking-cap mask.

One of the policemen, Officer Nelson, noticed two sets of expensive stereo components, which seemed out of place in the squalid and otherwise ill-appointed four-room apartment. Suspecting that they were stolen, he read and recorded their serial numbers—moving some of the components, including a Bang and Olufsen turntable, in order to do so—which he then reported by phone to his headquarters. On being advised that the turntable had been taken in an armed robbery, he seized it immediately. It was later determined that some of the other serial numbers matched those on other stereo equipment taken in the same armed robbery, and a warrant was obtained and executed to seize that equipment as well. Respondent was subsequently indicted for the robbery.

The state trial court granted respondent's motion to suppress the evidence that had been seized. The Court of Appeals of Arizona affirmed. . . . The Arizona Supreme Court denied review, and the State filed this petition.

II

As an initial matter, the State argues that Officer Nelson's actions constituted neither a "search" nor a "seizure" within the meaning of the Fourth Amendment. We agree that the mere recording of the serial numbers did not constitute a seizure. To be sure, that was the first step in a process by which respondent was eventually deprived of the stereo equipment. In and of itself, however, it did not "meaningfully interfere" with respondent's possessory interest in either the serial numbers or the equipment, and therefore did not amount to a seizure. See Maryland v. Macon, 472 U.S. 463, 469 (1985).

Officer Nelson's moving of the equipment, however, did constitute a "search" separate and apart from the search for the shooter, victims, and weapons that was the lawful objective of his entry into the apartment. Merely inspecting those parts of the turntable that came into view during the latter search would not have constituted an independent search, because it would have produced no additional invasion of respondent's privacy interest. ... But taking action, unrelated to the objectives of the authorized intrusion, which exposed to view concealed portions of the apartment or its contents, did produce a new invasion of respondent's privacy unjustified by the exigent circumstance that validated the entry. This is why, contrary to Justice Powell's suggestion, *post,* at 333, the "distinction between 'looking' at a suspicious object in plain view and 'moving' it even a few inches" is much more than trivial for purposes of the Fourth Amendment. It matters not that the search uncovered nothing of any great personal value to the respondent—serial numbers rather than (what might conceivably have been hidden behind or under the equipment) letters or photographs. A search is a search, even if it happens to disclose nothing but the bottom of a turntable.

III

The remaining question is whether the search was "reasonable" under the Fourth Amendment.

On this aspect of the case we reject, at the outset, the apparent position of the Arizona Court of Appeals that because the officers' action directed to the stereo equipment was unrelated to the justification for their entry into respondent's apartment, it was *ipso facto* unreasonable. That lack of relationship *always* exists with regard to action validated under the "plain view" doctrine; where action is taken for the purpose justifying the entry, invocation of the doctrine is superfluous. Mincey v. Arizona, supra, in saying that a warrantless search must be "strictly circumscribed by the exigencies which justify its initiation," 437 U.S., at 393 (citation omitted), was addressing only the scope of the primary search itself, and was not overruling by implication the many cases acknowledging that the "plain view" doctrine can legitimate action beyond that scope.

We turn, then, to application of the doctrine to the facts of this case. "It is well established that under certain circumstances the police may *seize* evidence in plain view without a warrant," Coolidge v. New Hampshire, 403 U.S., at 465 (plurality opinion) (empha-

sis added).   Those circumstances include situations "[w]here the
initial intrusion that brings the police within plain view of such
[evidence] is supported . . . by one of the recognized exceptions to
the warrant requirement," ibid., such as the exigent-circumstances
intrusion here.   It would be absurd to say that an object could
lawfully be seized and taken from the premises but could not be
moved for closer examination.   It is clear, therefore, that the search
here was valid if the "plain view" doctrine would have sustained a
seizure of the equipment.

There is no doubt it would have done so if Officer Nelson had
probable cause to believe that the equipment was stolen.   The State
has conceded, however, that he had only a "reasonable suspicion,"
by which it means something less than probable cause.   . . . We
have not ruled on the question whether probable cause is required
in order to invoke the "plain view" doctrine. . . .

We now hold that probable cause is required.   To say otherwise would be to cut the "plain view" doctrine loose from its
theoretical and practical moorings.   The theory of that doctrine
consists of extending to nonpublic places such as the home, where
searches and seizures without a warrant are presumptively unreasonable, the police's longstanding authority to make warrantless
seizures in public places of such objects as weapons and contraband.   . . . And the practical justification for that extension is the
desirability of sparing police, whose viewing of the object in the
course of a lawful search is as legitimate as it would have been in a
public place, the inconvenience and the risk—to themselves or to
preservation of the evidence—of going to obtain a warrant.   . . .
Dispensing with the need for a warrant is worlds apart from
permitting a lesser standard of *cause* for the seizure than a warrant
would require, i. e., the standard of probable cause.   No reason is
apparent why an object should routinely be seizable on lesser
grounds, during an unrelated search and seizure, than would have
been needed to obtain a warrant for that same object if it has been
known to be on the premises.

We do not say, of course, that a seizure can never be justified
on less than probable cause.   We have held that it can—where, for
example, the seizure is minimally intrusive and operational necessities render it the only practicable means of detecting certain types
of crime.   . . . No special operational necessities are relied on here,
however—but rather the mere fact that the items in question came
lawfully within the officer's plain view.   That alone cannot supplant
the requirement of probable cause.

The same considerations preclude us from holding that, even
though probable cause would have been necessary for a *seizure*, the
search of objects in plain view that occurred here could be sustained on lesser grounds.   A dwelling-place search, no less than a
dwelling-place seizure, requires probable cause, and there is no

reason in theory or practicality why application of the plain-view doctrine would supplant that requirement. Although the interest protected by the Fourth Amendment injunction against unreasonable searches is quite different from that protected by its injunction against unreasonable seizures . . . neither the one nor the other is of inferior worth or necessarily requires only lesser protection. We have not elsewhere drawn a categorical distinction between the two insofar as concerns the degree of justification needed to establish the reasonableness of police action, and we see no reason for a distinction in the particular circumstances before us here. Indeed, to treat searches more liberally would especially erode the plurality's warning in *Coolidge* that 'plain view' doctrine may not be used to extend a general exploratory search from one object to another until something incriminating at last emerges." 403 U.S., at 466. In short, whether legal authority to move the equipment could be found only as an inevitable concomitant of the authority to seize it, or also as a consequence of some independent power to search certain objects in plain view, probable cause to believe the equipment was stolen was required.

Justice O'Connor's dissent suggests that we uphold the action here on the ground that it was a "cursory inspection" rather than a "full-blown search," and could therefore be justified by reasonable suspicion instead of probable cause. As already noted, a truly cursory inspection—one that involves merely looking at what is already exposed to view, without disturbing it—is not a "search" for Fourth Amendment purposes, and therefore does not even require reasonable suspicion. We are unwilling to send police and judges into a new thicket of Fourth Amendment law, to seek a creature of uncertain description that is neither a plain-view inspection nor yet a "full-blown search." Nothing in the prior opinions of this Court supports such a distinction. . . .

Justice Powell's dissent reasonably asks what it is we would have had Officer Nelson do in these circumstances. . . . The answer depends, of course, upon whether he had probable cause to conduct a search, a question that was not preserved in this case. If he had, then he should have done precisely what he did. If not, then he should have followed up his suspicions, if possible, by means other than a search—just as he would have had to do if, while walking along the street, he had noticed the same suspicious stereo equipment sitting inside a house a few feet away from him, beneath an open window. It may well be that, in such circumstances, no effective means short of a search exist. But there is nothing new in the realization that the Constitution sometimes insulated the criminality of a few in order to protect the privacy of us all. Our disagreement with the dissenters pertain to where the proper balance should be struck; we choose to adhere to the textual and traditional standard of probable cause.

The State contends that, even if Officer Nelson's search violated the Fourth Amendment, the court below should have admitted the evidence thus obtained under the "good faith" exception to the exclusionary rule. That was not the question on which certiorari was granted, and we decline to consider it.

For the reasons stated, the judgment of the Court of Appeals of Arizona is

Affirmed.

JUSTICE POWELL, with whom THE CHIEF JUSTICE and JUSTICE O'CONNOR join, dissenting.

I join Justice O'Connor's dissenting opinion, and write briefly to highlight what seem to me the unfortunate consequences of the Court's decision.

Today the Court holds for the first time that the requirement of probable cause operates as a separate limitation on the application of the plain-view doctrine. ... The Court ... holds that "merely looking at" an object in plain view is lawful, ante, at 328, but "moving" or "disturbing" the object to investigate a reasonable suspicion is not, ante, at 324, 328. The facts of this case well illustrate the unreasonableness of this distinction.

The officers' suspicion that the stereo components at issue were stolen was both reasonable and based on specific, articulable facts. Indeed, the State was unwise to concede the absence of probable cause. The police lawfully entered respondent's apartment under exigent circumstances that arose when a bullet fired through the floor of the apartment struck a man in the apartment below. What they saw in the apartment hardly suggested that it was occupied by law-abiding citizens. A .25-caliber automatic pistol lay in plain view on the living room floor. During a concededly lawful search, the officers found a .45-caliber automatic, a .22-caliber sawed-off rifle, and a stocking-cap mask. The apartment was littered with drug paraphernalia. ... The officers also observed two sets of expensive stereo components of a type that frequently were stolen.

It is fair to ask what Officer Nelson should have done in these circumstances. Accepting the State's concession that he lacked probable cause, he could not have obtained a warrant to seize the stereo components. Neither could he have remained on the premises and forcibly prevented their removal. Officer Nelson's testimony indicates that he was able to read some of the serial numbers without moving the components. To read the serial number on a Bang and Olufsen turntable, however, he had to "turn it around or turn it upside down." Id., at 19. Officer Nelson noted the serial numbers on the stereo components and telephoned the National Crime Information Center to check them against the Center's computerized listing of stolen property. The computer confirmed his suspicion that at least the Bang and Olufsen turntable had been stolen. On the basis of this information, the officers obtained a warrant to seize the turntable and other stereo components that also proved to be stolen.

The Court holds that there was an unlawful search of the turntable. It agrees that the the "mere recording of the serial numbers did not constitute a seizure." Ante, at 324. Thus, if the computer had identified as stolen property a component with a visible serial number, the evidence would have been admissible. But the Court further holds that "Officer Nelson's moving of the equipment ... did constitute a 'search' ...." Ante, at 324. It perceives a constitutional distinction between reading a serial number on an object and moving or picking up an identical object to see its serial number. To make its position unmistakably clear, the Court concludes that a "search is a search, even if it happens to disclose nothing but the bottom of a turntable." Ante, at 325. With all respect, this distinction between "looking" at a suspicious object in plain view and "moving" it even a few inches trivializes the Fourth Amendment. The Court's new rule will cause uncertainty, and could deter conscientious police officers from lawfully obtaining evidence necessary to convict guilty persons. Apart from the importance of rationality in the interpretation of the Fourth Amendment, today's decision may handicap law enforcement without enhancing privacy interests. Accordingly I dissent.

JUSTICE O'CONNOR, with whom THE CHIEF JUSTICE and JUSTICE POWELL join, dissenting.

The Court today gives the right answer to the wrong question. The Court asks whether the police must have probable cause before either seizing an object in plain view or conducting a full-blown search of that object, and concludes that they must. I agree. In my view, however, this case presents a different question: whether police must have probable cause before conducting a cursory inspection of an item in plain view. Because I conclude that such an inspection is reasonable if the police are aware of facts or circumstances that justify a reasonable suspicion that the item is evidence of a crime, I would reverse the judgment of the Arizona Court of Appeals, and therefore dissent.

In Coolidge v. New Hampshire, 403 U.S. 443 (1971), Justice Stewart summarized three requirements that the plurality thought must be satisfied for a plain view search or seizure. First, the police must lawfully make an initial intrusion or otherwise be in a position from which they can view a particular area. Second, the officer must discover incriminating evidence "inadvertently." Third, it must be "immediately apparent" to the police that the items they observe may be evidence of a crime, contraband, or otherwise subject to seizure. As another plurality observed in Texas v. Brown, 460 U.S. 730, 737 (1983), these three requirements have never been expressly adopted by a majority of this Court, but "as the considered opinion of four Members of this Court [the *Coolidge* plurality] should obviously be the point of reference for further discussion of the issue." There is no dispute in this case that the first two requirements have been satisfied. The officers were lawfully in the apartment pursuant to exigent circumstances, and the discovery of the stereo was inadvertent—the officers did not "know in advance the location of [certain] evidence and intend to seize it,' relying on the plain-view doctrine only as a pretext." Ibid. (quoting Coolidge v. New Hampshire, supra, at 470). Instead, the dispute in this case focuses on the application of the "immediately apparent" requirement; at issue is whether a police officer's reasonable suspicion is adequate to justify a cursory examination of an item in plain view.

The purpose of the "immediately apparent" requirement is to prevent "general, exploratory rummaging in a person's belongings." Coolidge v. New Hampshire, 403 U.S., at 467. If an officer could indiscriminately search every item in plain view, a search justified by a limited purpose—such as exigent circumstances—could be used to eviscerate the protections of the Fourth Amendment. In order to prevent such a general search, therefore, we require that the relevance of the item be "immediately apparent." . . .

Thus, I agree with the Court that even under the plain-view doctrine, probable cause is required before the police seize an item, or conduct a full-blown search of evidence in plain view. . . . Such a requirement of probable cause will prevent the plain-view doctrine from authorizing general searches. This is not to say, however, that even a mere inspection of a suspicious item must be supported by probable cause. When a police officer makes a cursory inspection of a suspicious item in plain view in order to determine whether it is indeed evidence of a crime, there is no "exploratory rummaging." Only those items that the police officer "reasonably suspects" as evidence of a crime may be inspected, and perhaps more importantly, the scope of such an inspection is quite limited. In short, if police officers have a reasonable, articulable suspicion that an object they come across during the course of a lawful search is evidence of crime, in my view they may make a cursory examination of the object to verify their suspicion. If the officers wish to go beyond such a cursory examination of the object, however, they must have probable cause.

. . .

. . . [T]he overwhelming majority of both state and federal courts have held that probable cause is not required for a minimal inspection of an item in plain view. . . . Thus, while courts require probable cause for more extensive examination, cursory inspections—including picking up or moving objects for a better view—require only a reasonable suspicion. . . .

. . .

This distinction between search based on their relative intrusiveness—and its subsequent adoption by a consensus of American courts—is entirely consistent with our Fourth Amendment jurisprudence. We have long recognized that searches can vary in intrusiveness, and that some brief searches "may be so minimally intrusive of Fourth Amendment interests that strong countervailing governmental interests will justify a [search] based only on specific articulable facts" that the item in question is contraband or evidence of a crime. United States v. Place, 462 U.S. 696, 706 (1983). ... The test is whether these law enforcement interests are sufficiently "substantial," not, as the Court would have it, whether "operational necessities render [a standard less than probable cause] the only practicable means of detecting certain types of crimes." Ante, at 327....

In my view, the balance of the governmental and privacy interests strongly supports a reasonable-suspicion standard for the cursory examination of items in plain view. The additional intrusion caused by an inspection of an item in plain view for its serial number is minuscule. Indeed, the intrusion in this case was even more transitory and less intrusive than the seizure of luggage from a suspected drug dealer in United States v. Place, supra, and the "severe, though brief, intrusion upon cherished personal security" in Terry v. Ohio, at 24–25.

Weighed against this minimal additional invasion of privacy are rather major gains in law enforcement. The use of identification numbers in tracing stolen property is a powerful law enforcement tool. Serial numbers are far more helpful and accurate in detecting stolen property than simple police recollection of the evidence. ... Given the prevalence of mass produced goods in our national economy, a serial number is often the only sure method of detecting stolen property. The balance of governmental and private interests strongly supports the view accepted by a majority of courts that a standard of reasonable suspicion meets the requirements of the Fourth Amendment.

Unfortunately, in its desire to establish a "bright-line" test, the Court has taken a step that ignores a substantial body of precedent and that places serious roadblocks to reasonable law enforcement practices. Indeed, in this case no warrant to search the stereo equipment for its serial number could have been obtained by the officers based on reasonable suspicion alone, and in the Court's view the officers may not even move the stereo turntable to examine its serial number. The theoretical advantages of the "search is a search" approach adopted by the Court today are simply too remote to justify the tangible and severe damage it inflicts on legitimate and effective law enforcement.

Even if probable cause were the appropriate standard, I have little doubt that it was satisfied here. When police officers, during the course of a search inquiring into grievously unlawful activity, discover the tools of a thief (a sawed-off rifle and a stocking mask) and observe in a small apartment *two* sets of stereo equipment that are both inordinately expensive in relation to their surroundings and known to be favored targets of larcenous activity, the "flexible, commonsense standard" of probable cause has been satisfied. Texas v. Brown, 460 U.S., at 742 (plurality opinion).

Because the Court today ignores the existence of probable cause, and in doing so upsets a widely accepted body of precedent on the standard of reasonableness for the cursory examination of evidence in plain view, I respectfully dissent.[*]

[*] Justice White wrote a concurring opinion.

HORTON v. CALIFORNIA

496 U.S. 128, 110 S.Ct. 2301, 110 L.Ed.2d 112 (1990).

JUSTICE STEVENS delivered the opinion of the Court.

In this case we revisit an issue that was considered, but not conclusively resolved, in Coolidge v. New Hampshire, 403 U.S. 443 (1971): Whether the warrantless seizure of evidence of crime in plain view is prohibited by the Fourth Amendment if the discovery of the evidence was not inadvertent. We conclude that even though inadvertence is a characteristic of most legitimate "plain view" seizures, it is not a necessary condition.

I

Petitioner was convicted of the armed robbery of Erwin Wallaker, the treasurer of the San Jose Coin Club. When Wallaker returned to his home after the Club's annual show, he entered his garage and was accosted by two masked men, one armed with a machine gun and the other with an electrical shocking device, sometimes referred to as a "stun gun." The two men shocked Wallaker, bound and handcuffed him, and robbed him of jewelry and cash. During the encounter sufficient conversation took place to enable Wallaker subsequently to identify petitioner's distinctive voice. His identification was partially corroborated by a witness who saw the robbers leaving the scene and by evidence that petitioner had attended the coin show.

Sergeant LaRault, an experienced police officer, investigated the crime and determined that there was probable cause to search petitioner's home for the proceeds of the robbery and for the weapons used by the robbers. His affidavit for a search warrant referred to police reports that described the weapons as well as the proceeds, but the warrant issued by the Magistrate only authorized a search for the proceeds, including three specifically described rings.

Pursuant to the warrant, LaRault searched petitioner's residence, but he did not find the stolen property. During the course of the search, however, he discovered the weapons in plain view and seized them. Specifically, he seized an Uzi machine gun, a .38 caliber revolver, two stun guns, a handcuff key, a San Jose Coin Club advertising brochure, and a few items of clothing identified by the victim. LaRault testified that while he was searching for the rings, he also was interested in finding other evidence connecting petitioner to the robbery. Thus, the seized evidence was not discovered "inadvertently."

The trial court refused to suppress the evidence found in petitioner's home and, after a jury trial, petitioner was found guilty and sentenced to prison. The California Court of Appeal affirmed.... It rejected petitioner's argument that our decision in *Coolidge* required suppression of the seized evidence that had not been listed in the warrant because its discovery was not inadvertent.... The California Supreme Court denied petitioner's request for review....

Because the California courts' interpretation of the "plain view" doctrine conflicts with the view of other courts, and because the unresolved issue is important, we granted certiorari, 493 U.S. 889 (1989).

II

The Fourth Amendment provides:

"The right of the people to be secure in their persons, houses, papers, and effects, against unreasonable searches and seizures, shall not be violated, and no Warrants shall issue, but upon probable cause, supported by Oath or affirmation, and particularly describing the place to be searched, and the persons or things to be seized."

The right to security in person and property protected by the Fourth Amendment may be invaded in quite different ways by searches and seizures. A search compromises the individual interest in privacy; a seizure deprives the individual of dominion over his or her person or property.... The "plain view" doctrine is often considered an exception to the general rule that warrantless searches are presumptively unreasonable, but this characterization overlooks the important difference between searches and seizures. If an article is already in plain view, neither its observation nor its seizure would involve any invasion of privacy.... A seizure of the article, however, would obviously invade the owner's possessory interest.... If "plain view" justifies an exception from an otherwise applicable warrant requirement, therefore, it must be an exception that is addressed to the concerns that are implicated by seizures rather than by searches.

The criteria that generally guide "plain view" seizures were set forth in Coolidge v. New Hampshire, 403 U.S. 443 (1971). The Court held that the police, in seizing two automobiles parked in plain view on the defendant's driveway in the course of arresting the defendant, violated the Fourth Amendment. Accordingly, particles of gun powder that had been subsequently found in vacuum sweepings from one of the cars could not be introduced in evidence against the defendant. The State endeavored to justify the seizure of the automobiles, and their subsequent search at the police station, on four different grounds, including the "plain–view" doctrine. The scope of that doctrine as it had developed in earlier cases was fairly summarized in these three paragraphs from Justice Stewart's opinion:

"It is well established that under certain circumstances the police may seize evidence in plain view without a warrant. But it is important to keep in mind that, in the vast majority of cases, *any* evidence seized by the police will be in plain view, at least at the moment of seizure. The problem with the 'plain–view' doctrine has been to identify the circumstances in which plain view has legal significance rather than being simply the normal concomitant of any search, legal or illegal.

"An example of the applicability of the 'plain–view' doctrine is the situation in which the police have a warrant to search a given area for specified objects, and in the course of the search come across some other article of incriminating character. [. . .] Where the initial intrusion that brings the police within plain view of such an article is supported, not by a warrant, but by one of the recognized exceptions to the warrant requirement, the seizure is also legitimate. Thus the police may inadvertently come across evidence while in 'hot pursuit' of a fleeing suspect. [. . .] And an object that comes into view during a search incident to arrest that is appropriately limited in scope under existing law may be seized without a warrant. [. . .] Finally, the 'plain–view' doctrine has been applied where a police officer is not searching for evidence against the accused, but nonetheless inadvertently comes across an incriminating object. [. . .]

"What the 'plain–view' cases have in common is that the police officer in each of them had a prior justification for an intrusion in the course of which he came inadvertently across a piece of evidence incriminating the accused. The doctrine serves to supplement the prior justification—whether it be a warrant for another object, hot pursuit, search incident to lawful arrest, or some other legitimate reason for being present unconnected with a search directed against the accused—and permits the warrantless seizure. Of course, the extension of the original justification is legitimate only where it is immediately apparent to the police that they have evidence before them; the 'plain view' doctrine may not be used to extend a general exploratory search from one object to another until something incriminating at last emerges." Id., at 465–466 (footnote omitted).

Justice Stewart then described the two limitations on the doctrine that he found implicit in its rationale: First, "that plain view *alone* is never enough to justify the warrantless seizure of evidence," id., at 468; and second, that "the discovery of evidence in plain view must be inadvertent." Id., at 469.

Justice Stewart's analysis of the "plain view" doctrine did not command a majority, and a plurality of the Court has since made clear that the discussion is "not a binding precedent." Texas v. Brown, 460 U.S. [730, 737 (1983)], at 737 (opinion of Rehnquist, J.) . . . .

. . .

III

Justice Stewart concluded that the inadvertence requirement was necessary to avoid a violation of the express constitutional requirement that a valid warrant must particularly describe the things to be seized. He explained:

> "The rationale of the exception to the warrant requirement, as just stated, is that a plain-view seizure will not turn an initially valid (and therefore limited) search into a 'general' one, while the inconvenience of procuring a warrant to cover an inadvertent discovery is great. But where the discovery is anticipated, where the police know in advance the location of the evidence and intend to seize it, the situation is altogether different. The requirement of a warrant to seize imposes no inconvenience whatever, or at least none which is constitutionally cognizable in a legal system that regards warrantless searches as *'per se* unreasonable' in the absence of 'exigent circumstances.'

> "If the initial intrusion is bottomed upon a warrant that fails to mention a particular object, though the police know its location and intend to seize it, then there is a violation of the express constitutional requirement of 'Warrants . . . particularly describing . . . [the] things to be seized.' " 403 U.S., at 469–471.

We find two flaws in this reasoning. First, evenhanded law enforcement is best achieved by the application of objective standards of conduct, rather than standards that depend upon the subjective state of mind of the officer. The fact that an officer is interested in an item of evidence and fully expects to find it in the course of a search should not invalidate its seizure if the search is confined in area and duration by the terms of a warrant or a valid exception to the warrant requirement. If the officer has knowledge approaching certainty that the item will be found, we see no reason why he or she would deliberately omit a particular description of the item to be seized from the application for a search warrant. Specification of the additional item could only permit the officer to expand the scope of the search. On the other hand, if he or she has a valid warrant to search for one item and merely a suspicion concerning the second, whether or not it amounts to probable cause, we fail to see why that suspicion should immunize the second item from seizure if it is found during a lawful search for the first.   The hypothetical case put by Justice White in his dissenting opinion in *Coolidge* is instructive:

> "Let us suppose officers secure a warrant to search a house for a rifle.   While staying well within the range of a rifle search, they discover two photographs of the murder victim, both in plain sight in the bedroom.   Assume also that the discovery of the one photograph was inadvertent but finding the other was anticipated.   The Court would permit the seizure of only one of the photographs.   But in terms of the 'minor' peril to Fourth Amendment values there is surely no difference between these two photographs: the interference with possession is the same in each case and the officers' appraisal of the photograph they expected to see is no less reliable than their judgment about the other.   And in both situations the actual inconvenience and danger to evidence remain identical if the officers must depart and secure a warrant."   Id., at 516.

Second, the suggestion that the inadvertence requirement is necessary to prevent the police from conducting general searches, or from converting specific warrants into general warrants, is not persuasive because that interest is already served by the requirements that no warrant issue unless it "particularly describ[es] the place to be searched and the persons or things to be seized," . . . and that a warrantless search be circumscribed by the exigencies which justify its initiation. . . .   Scrupulous adherence to these requirements serves the interests in limiting the area and duration of the search that the inadvertence requirement inadequately protects.   Once those commands have been satisfied and the officer has a lawful right of access, however, no additional Fourth Amendment interest is furthered by requiring that the discovery of evidence be inadvertent.   If the scope of the search exceeds that permitted by the terms of a validly issued warrant or the character of the relevant exception from the warrant requirement, the subsequent seizure is unconstitutional without more.   Thus, in the case of a search incident to a lawful arrest, "[i]f the police stray outside the scope of an authorized *Chimel* search they are already in violation of the Fourth Amendment, and evidence so seized will be excluded; adding a second reason for excluding evidence hardly seems worth the candle."   *Coolidge,* 403 U.S., at 517 (White, J., concurring and dissenting).   Similarly, the object of a warrantless search of an automobile also defines its scope:

> "The scope of a warrantless search of an automobile thus is not defined by the nature of the container in which the contraband is secreted.   Rather, it is defined by the object of the search and the places in which there is probable cause to believe that it may be found.   Just as probable cause to believe that a stolen lawnmower may be found in a garage will not support a warrant to search an upstairs bedroom, probable cause to believe that undocumented aliens are being transport-

ed in a van will not justify a warrantless search of a suitcase. Probable cause to believe that a container placed in the trunk of a taxi contains contraband or evidence does not justify a search of the entire cab." United States v. Ross, 456 U.S. 798, 824 (1982).

In this case, the scope of the search was not enlarged in the slightest by the omission of any reference to the weapons in the warrant. Indeed, if the three rings and other items named in the warrant had been found at the outset—or if petitioner had them in his possession and had responded to the warrant by producing them immediately—no search for weapons could have taken place. Again, Justice White's dissenting opinion in *Coolidge* is instructive:

> "Police with a warrant for a rifle may search only places where rifles might be and must terminate the search once the rifle is found; the inadvertence rule will in no way reduce the number of places into which they may lawfully look." 403 U.S., at 517.

As we have already suggested, by hypothesis the seizure of an object in plain view does not involve an intrusion on privacy. If the interest in privacy has been invaded, the violation must have occurred before the object came into plain view and there is no need for an inadvertence limitation on seizures to condemn it. The prohibition against general searches and general warrants serves primarily as a protection against unjustified intrusions on privacy. But reliance on privacy concerns that support that prohibition is misplaced when the inquiry concerns the scope of an exception that merely authorizes an officer with a lawful right of access to an item to seize it without a warrant.

In this case the items seized from petitioner's home were discovered during a lawful search authorized by a valid warrant. When they were discovered, it was immediately apparent to the officer that they constituted incriminating evidence. He had probable cause, not only to obtain a warrant to search for the stolen property, but also to believe that the weapons and handguns had been used in the crime he was investigating. The search was authorized by the warrant, the seizure was authorized by the "plain view" doctrine. The judgment is affirmed.

It is so ordered.

JUSTICE BRENNAN, with whom JUSTICE MARSHALL joins, dissenting.

I remain convinced that Justice Stewart correctly articulated the plain view doctrine in Coolidge v. New Hampshire, 403 U.S. 443 (1971). The Fourth Amendment permits law enforcement officers to seize items for which they do not have a warrant when those items are found in plain view and (1) the officers are lawfully in a position to observe the items, (2) the discovery of the items is "inadvertent," and (3) it is immediately apparent to the officers that the items are evidence of a crime, contraband, or otherwise subject to seizure. In eschewing the inadvertent discovery requirement, the majority ignores the Fourth Amendment's express command that warrants particularly describe not only the *places* to be searched, but also the *things* to be seized. I respectfully dissent from this rewriting of the Fourth Amendment.

I

... The [Fourth] Amendment protects two distinct interests. The prohibition against unreasonable searches and the requirement that a warrant "particularly describ[e] the place to be searched" protect an interest in privacy. The prohibition against unreasonable seizures and the requirement that a warrant "particularly describ[e] ... the ... things to be seized" protect a possessory interest in property.[1] ... The Fourth Amendment, by its terms, declares the privacy and possessory interests to be equally important. As this Court recently stated: "Although the interest protected by the Fourth Amendment injunction against unreasonable searches is quite different from that protected by its injunction against unreasonable seizures, neither the one nor the other is of inferior worth or necessarily requires only lesser protection." Arizona v. Hicks, 480 U.S. 321, 328 (1987) (citation omitted).

The Amendment protects these equally important interests in precisely the same manner: by requiring a neutral and detached magistrate to evaluate, before the search or seizure, the government's showing of probable cause and its particular description of the place to be searched and the items to be seized. Accordingly, just as a warrantless search is *per se* unreasonable absent exigent circumstances, so too a seizure of personal property is *"per se* unreasonable within the meaning of the Fourth Amendment unless it is accomplished pursuant to a judicial warrant issued upon probable cause and particularly describing the items to be seized." United States v. Place, 462 U.S. 696, 701 (1983) (footnote omitted) (citing Marron v. United States, 275 U.S. 192, 196 (1927))....

The plain–view doctrine is an exception to the general rule that a seizure of personal property must be authorized by a warrant. As Justice Stewart explained in *Coolidge,* 403 U.S., at 470, we accept a warrantless seizure when an officer is lawfully in a location and inadvertently sees evidence of a crime because of "the inconvenience of procuring a warrant" to seize this newly discovered piece of evidence. But "where the discovery is anticipated, where the police know in advance the location of the evidence and intend to

---

1. As the majority recognizes, the requirement that warrants particularly describe the things to be seized also protects privacy interests by preventing general searches.... The scope of a search is limited to those places in which there is probable cause to believe an item particularly described in the warrant might be found. A police officer cannot search for a lawnmower in a bedroom, or for an undocumented alien in a suitcase.... Similarly, once all of the items particularly described in a warrant have been found, the search must cease and no further invasion of privacy is permitted....

seize it," the argument that procuring a warrant would be "inconvenient" loses much, if not all, of its force. Ibid. Barring an
exigency, there is no reason why the police officers could not have
obtained a warrant to seize this evidence before entering the
premises. The rationale behind the inadvertent discovery requirement is simply that we will not excuse officers from the general
requirement of a warrant to seize if the officers know the location of
evidence, have probable cause to seize it, intend to seize it, and yet
do not bother to obtain a warrant particularly describing that
evidence. To do so would violate "the express constitutional
requirement of 'Warrants . . . particularly describing . . . [the] things
to be seized,' " and would "fly in the face of the basic rule that no
amount of probable cause can justify a warrantless seizure." Id., at
471.

             . . .

The Court posits two "flaws" in Justice Stewart's reasoning that
it believes demonstrate the inappropriateness of the inadvertent
discovery requirement. But these flaws are illusory. First, the
majority explains that it can see no reason why an officer who "has
knowledge approaching certainty" that an item will be found in a
particular location "would deliberately omit a particular description
of the item to be seized from the application for a search warrant."
Ante, at 138. But to the individual whose possessory interest has
been invaded, it matters not *why* the police officer decided to omit
a particular item from his application for a search warrant. When
an officer with probable cause to seize an item fails to mention that
item in his application for a search warrant—for whatever reason—
and then seizes the item anyway, his conduct is *per se* unreasonable.
Suppression of the evidence so seized will encourage officers to be
more precise and complete in future warrant applications.

Furthermore, there are a number of instances in which a law
enforcement officer might deliberately choose to omit certain items
from a warrant application even though he has probable cause to
seize them, knows they are on the premises, and intends to seize
them when they are discovered in plain view. For example, the
warrant application process can often be time consuming, especially
when the police attempt to seize a large number of items. An
officer interested in conducting a search as soon as possible might
decide to save time by listing only one or two hard-to-find items,
such as the stolen rings in this case, confident that he will find in
plain view all of the other evidence he is looking for before he
discovers the listed items. Because rings could be located almost
anywhere inside or outside a house, it is unlikely that a warrant to
search for and seize the rings would restrict the scope of the search.
An officer might rationally find the risk of immediately discovering
the items listed in the warrant—thereby forcing him to conclude the
search immediately—outweighed by the time saved in the application process.

The majority also contends that, once an officer is lawfully in a house and the scope of his search is adequately circumscribed by a warrant, "no additional Fourth Amendment interest is furthered by requiring that the discovery of evidence be inadvertent." Ante, at 140. Put another way, " 'the inadvertence rule will in no way reduce the number of places into which [law enforcement officers] may lawfully look.' " Ante, at 140 (quoting *Coolidge,* 403 U.S., at 517 (White, J., concurring in part and dissenting)). The majority is correct, but it has asked the wrong question. It is true that the inadvertent discovery requirement furthers no privacy interests. The requirement in no way reduces the scope of a search or the number of places into which officers may look. But it does protect possessory interests.... The inadvertent discovery requirement is essential if we are to take seriously the Fourth Amendment's protection of possessory interests as well as privacy interests.... The Court today eliminates a rule designed to further possessory interests on the ground that it fails to further privacy interests. I cannot countenance such constitutional legerdemain.

. . . .

III

The Fourth Amendment demands that an individual's possessory interest in property be protected from unreasonable governmental seizures, not just by requiring a showing of probable cause, but also by requiring a neutral and detached magistrate to authorize the seizure in advance. The Court today ignores the explicit language of the Fourth Amendment, which protects possessory interests in the same manner as it protects privacy interests, in order to eliminate a generally accepted element of the plain–view doctrine that has caused no apparent difficulties for law enforcement officers. I am confident, however, that when confronted with more egregious police conduct than that found in this case ... such as pretextual searches, the Court's interpretation of the Constitution will be less parsimonious than it is today. I respectfully dissent.

[Appendix omitted.]

CALIFORNIA v. GREENWOOD

486 U.S. 35, 108 S.Ct. 1625, 100 L.Ed.2d 30 (1988).

JUSTICE WHITE delivered the opinion of the Court.

The issue here is whether the Fourth Amendment prohibits the warrantless search and seizure of garbage left for collection outside the curtilage of a home. We conclude, in accordance with the vast majority of lower courts that have addressed the issue, that it does not.

I

In early 1984, Investigator Jenny Stracner of the Laguna Beach Police Department received information indicating that respondent Greenwood might be engaged in narcotics trafficking. Stracner learned that a criminal suspect had informed a federal drug-enforcement agent in February 1984 that a truck filled with illegal drugs was en route to the Laguna Beach address at which Greenwood resided. In addition, a neighbor complained of heavy vehicular traffic late at night in front of Greenwood's single-family home. The neighbor reported that the vehicles remained at Greenwood's house for only a few minutes.

Stracner sought to investigate this information by conducting a surveillance of Greenwood's home. She observed several vehicles make brief stops at the house during the late-night and early-morning hours, and she followed a truck from the house to a residence that had previously been under investigation as a narcotics trafficking location.

On April 6, 1984, Stracner asked the neighborhood's regular trash collector to pick up the plastic garbage bags that Greenwood had left on the curb in front of his house and to turn the bags over to her without mixing their contents with garbage from other houses. The trash collector cleaned his truck bin of other refuse, collected the garbage bags from the street in front of Greenwood's house, and turned the bags over to Stracner. The officer searched through the rubbish and found items indicative of narcotics use. She recited the information that she had gleaned from the trash search in an affidavit in support of a warrant to search Greenwood's home.

Police officers encountered both respondents at the house later that day when they arrived to execute the warrant. The police discovered quantities of cocaine and hashish during their search of the house. Respondents were arrested on felony narcotics charges. They subsequently posted bail.

The police continued to receive reports of many late-night visitors to the Greenwood house. On May 4, Investigator Robert Rahaeuser obtained Greenwood's garbage from the regular trash collector in the same manner as had Stracner. The garbage again contained evidence of narcotics use.

Rahaeuser secured another search warrant for Greenwood's home based on the information from the second trash search. The police found more narcotics and evidence of narcotics trafficking when they executed the warrant. Greenwood was again arrested.

The Superior Court dismissed the charges against respondents on the authority of People v. Krivda, 5 Cal.3d 357, 486 P.2d 1262 (1971), which held that warrantless trash searches violate the Fourth Amendment and the California Constitution. The court found that the police would not have had probable cause to search the Greenwood home without the evidence obtained from the trash searches.

The Court of Appeal affirmed. 182 Cal.App.3d 729, 227 Cal. Rptr. 539 (1986). . . .

The California Supreme Court denied the State's petition for review of the Court of Appeal's decision. We granted certiorari, 483 U.S. 1019, and now reverse.

II

The warrantless search and seizure of the garbage bags left at the curb outside the Greenwood house would violate the Fourth Amendment only if respondents manifested a subjective expectation of privacy in their garbage that society accepts as objectively reasonable. . . . Respondents do not disagree with this standard.

They assert, however, that they had, and exhibited, an expectation of privacy with respect to the trash that was searched by the police: The trash, which was placed on the street for collection at a fixed time, was contained in opaque plastic bags, which the garbage collector was expected to pick up, mingle with the trash of others, and deposit at the garbage dump. The trash was only temporarily on the street, and there was little likelihood that it would be inspected by anyone.

It may well be that respondents did not expect that the contents of their garbage bags would become known to the police or other members of the public. An expectation of privacy does not give rise to Fourth Amendment protection, however, unless society is prepared to accept that expectation as objectively reasonable.

Here, we conclude that respondents exposed their garbage to the public sufficiently to defeat their claim to Fourth Amendment protection. It is common knowledge that plastic garbage bags left on or at the side of a public street are readily accessible to animals, children, scavengers, snoops, and other members of the public.

... Moreover, respondents placed their refuse at the curb for the express purpose of conveying it to a third party, the trash collector, who might himself have sorted through respondents' trash or permitted others, such as the police, to do so. Accordingly, having deposited their garbage "in an area particularly suited for public inspection and, in a manner of speaking, public consumption, for the express purpose of having strangers take it," United States v. Reicherter, 647 F.2d 397, 399 (CA3 1981), respondents could have had no reasonable expectation of privacy in the inculpatory items that they discarded.

Furthermore, as we have held, the police cannot reasonably be expected to avert their eyes from evidence of criminal activity that could have been observed by any member of the public. Hence, "[w]hat a person knowingly exposes to the public, even in his own home or office, is not a subject of Fourth Amendment protection." Katz v. United States, [389 U.S. 347 (1967)], at 351. We held in Smith v. Maryland, 442 U.S. 735 (1979), for example, that the police did not violate the Fourth Amendment by causing a pen register to be installed at the telephone company's offices to record the telephone numbers dialed by a criminal suspect. An individual has no legitimate expectation of privacy in the numbers dialed on his telephone, we reasoned, because he voluntarily conveys those numbers to the telephone company when he uses the telephone. Again, we observed that "a person has no legitimate expectation of privacy in information he voluntarily turns over to third parties." Id., at 743–744.

Similarly, we held in California v. Ciraolo, [476 U.S. 207 (1986)], that the police were not required by the Fourth Amendment to obtain a warrant before conducting surveillance of the respondent's fenced backyard from a private plane flying at an altitude of 1,000 feet. We concluded that the respondent's expectation that his yard was protected from such surveillance was unreasonable because "[a]ny member of the public flying in this airspace who glanced down could have seen everything that these officers observed." 476 U.S., at 213–214.

Our conclusion that society would not accept as reasonable respondents' claim to an expectation of privacy in trash left for collection in an area accessible to the public is reinforced by the unanimous rejection of similar claims by the Federal Courts of Appeals. ... In addition, of those state appellate courts that have considered the issue, the vast majority have held that the police may conduct warrantless searches and seizures of garbage discarded in public areas. ...[5]

5. Given that the dissenters are among the tiny minority of judges whose views are contrary to ours, we are distinctly unimpressed with the dissent's prediction that "society will be shocked to learn" of today's decision. Post, at 46.

... [The Court rejected the respondents' further arguments that their expectation of privacy in the trash should be deemed reasonable because a search of the trash was illegal under state law and that the Due Process Clause required California to apply the exclusionary rule to a search in violation of state law.]

The judgment of the California Court of Appeal is therefore reversed, and this case is remanded for further proceedings not inconsistent with this opinion.

It is so ordered.

JUSTICE BRENNAN, with whom JUSTICE MARSHALL joins, dissenting.

Every week for two months, and at least once more a month later, the Laguna Beach police clawed through the trash that respondent Greenwood left in opaque, sealed bags on the curb outside his home. Record 113. Complete strangers minutely scrutinized their bounty, undoubtedly dredging up intimate details of Greenwood's private life and habits. The intrusions proceeded without a warrant, and no court before or since has concluded that the police acted on probable cause to believe Greenwood was engaged in any criminal activity.

Scrutiny of another's trash is contrary to commonly accepted notions of civilized behavior. I suspect, therefore, that members of our society will be shocked to learn that the Court, the ultimate guarantor of liberty, deems unreasonable our expectation that the aspects of our private lives that are concealed safely in a trash bag will not become public.

I

"A container which can support a reasonable expectation of privacy may not be searched, even on probable cause, without a warrant." United States v. Jacobsen, 466 U.S. 109, 120, n. 17 (1984) (citations omitted). Thus, as the Court observes, if Greenwood had a reasonable expectation that the contents of the bags that he placed on the curb would remain private, the warrantless search of those bags violated the Fourth Amendment. Ante, at 39.

. . .

II

Respondents deserve no less protection just because Greenwood used the bags to discard rather than to transport his personal effects. Their contents are not inherently any less private, and Greenwood's decision to discard them, at least in the manner in which he did, does not diminish his expectation of privacy.

A trash bag, like any of the above-mentioned containers, "is a common repository for one's personal effects" and, even more than many of them, is "therefore ... inevitably associated with the expectation of privacy." [Arkansas v.] Sanders, [442 U.S. 753 (1979)], at 762 (citing [United States v.] Chadwick, [433 U.S. 1 (1977)] at 13). "[A]lmost every human activity ultimately manifests itself in waste products. ..." Smith v. State, 510 P.2d 793, 798 (Alaska), cert. denied, 414 U.S. 1086 (1973). ... A single bag of trash testifies eloquently to the eating, reading, and recreational habits of the person who produced it. A search of trash, like a search of the bedroom, can relate intimate details about sexual practices, health, and personal hygiene. Like rifling through desk drawers or intercepting phone calls, rummaging through trash can divulge the target's financial and professional status, political affiliations and inclinations, private thoughts, personal relationships, and romantic interests. It cannot be doubted that a sealed trash bag harbors telling evidence of the "intimate activity associated with the 'sanctity of a man's home and the privacies of life,' " which the Fourth Amendment is designed to protect. Oliver v. United States, 466 U.S. 170, 180 (1984) (quoting Boyd v. United States, 116 U.S. 616, 630 (1886)). ...

The Court properly rejects the State's attempt to distinguish trash searches from other searches on the theory that trash is abandoned and therefore not entitled to an expectation of privacy. As the author of the Court's opinion observed last Term, a defendant's "property interest [in trash] does not settle the matter for Fourth Amendment purposes, for the reach of the Fourth Amendment is not determined by state property law." [California v.] Rooney, supra, at 320 (White, J., dissenting). In evaluating the reasonableness of Greenwood's expectation that his sealed trash bags would not be invaded, the Court has held that we must look to "understandings that are recognized and permitted by society."[3] Most of us, I believe, would be incensed to discover a meddler— whether a neighbor, a reporter, or a detective—scrutinizing our sealed trash containers to discover some detail of our personal lives. . . .

Beyond a generalized expectation of privacy, many municipalities, whether for reasons of privacy, sanitation, or both, reinforce confidence in the integrity of sealed trash containers by "prohibit[ing] anyone, except authorized employees of the Town ..., to rummage into, pick up, collect, move or otherwise interfere with articles or materials placed on ... any public street for collection." United States v. Dzialak, 441 F.2d 212, 215 (CA2 1971) (paraphrasing ordinance for town of Cheektowaga, New York). ... In fact, the California Constitution, as interpreted by the State's highest court, guarantees a right of privacy in trash vis-à-vis government officials. . . .

That is not to deny that isolated intrusions into opaque, sealed trash containers occur. When, acting on their own, "animals,

3. Rakas v. Illinois, 439 U.S. 128, 143–144, n. 12 (1978). ...

children, scavengers, snoops, [or] other members of the general public," ante, at 40 (footnotes omitted), *actually* rummage through a bag of trash and expose its contents to plain view, "police cannot reasonably be expected to avert their eyes from evidence of criminal activity that could have been observed by any member of the public," ante, at 41. . . .

Had Greenwood flaunted his intimate activity by strewing his trash all over the curb for all to see, or had some nongovernmental intruder invaded his privacy and done the same, I could accept the Court's conclusion that an expectation of privacy would have been unreasonable. Similarly, had police searching the city dump run across incriminating evidence that, despite commingling with the trash of others, still retained its identity as Greenwood's, we would have a different case. But all that Greenwood "exposed . . . to the public," ante, at 40, were the exteriors of several opaque, sealed containers. Until the bags were opened by police, they hid their contents from the public's view every bit as much as did Chadwick's double-locked footlocker and Robbins' green, plastic wrapping [Robbins v. California, 453 U.S. 420 (1981)]. Faithful application of the warrant requirement does not require police to "avert their eyes from evidence of criminal activity that could have been observed by any member of the public." Rather, it only requires them to adhere to norms of privacy that members of the public plainly acknowledge.

The mere *possibility* that unwelcome meddlers *might* open and rummage through the containers does not negate the expectation of privacy in its contents any more than the possibility of a burglary negates an expectation of privacy in the home; or the possibility of a private intrusion negates an expectation of privacy in an unopened package; or the possibility that an operator will listen in on a telephone conversation negates an expectation of privacy in the words spoken on the telephone. "What a person . . . seeks to preserve as private, *even in an area accessible to the public*, may be constitutionally protected." *Katz*, 389 U.S., at 351–352. We have therefore repeatedly rejected attempts to justify a State's invasion of privacy on the ground that the privacy is not absolute. . . .

Nor is it dispositive that "respondents placed their refuse at the curb for the express purpose of conveying it to a third party, . . . who might himself have sorted through respondents' trash or permitted others, such as police, to do so." Ante, at 40. In the first place, Greenwood can hardly be faulted for leaving trash on his curb when a county ordinance commanded him to do so, Orange County Code § 4–3–45(a) (1986) (must "remov[e] from the premises at least once each week" all "solid waste created, produced or accumulated in or about [his] dwelling house"), and prohibited him from disposing of it in any other way, see Orange County Code § 3–3–85 (1988) (burning trash is unlawful). Unlike in other circumstances where privacy is compromised, Greenwood could not "avoid exposing personal belongings ... by simply leaving them at home." O'Connor [v. Ortega, 480 U.S. 709 (1987)], at 725. More importantly, even the voluntary relinquishment of possession or control over an effect does not necessarily amount to a relinquishment of a privacy expectation in it. Were it otherwise, a letter or package would lose all Fourth Amendment protection when placed in a mail box or other depository with the "express purpose" of entrusting it to the postal officer or a private carrier; those bailees are just as likely as trash collectors (and certainly have greater incentive) to "sor[t] through" the personal effects entrusted to them, "or permi[t] others, such as police to do so." Yet, it has been clear for at least 110 years that the possibility of such an intrusion does not justify a warrantless search by police in the first instance. ...

III

In holding that the warrantless search of Greenwood's trash was consistent with the Fourth Amendment, the Court paints a grim picture of our society. It depicts a society in which local authorities may command their citizens to dispose of their personal effects in the manner least protective of the "sanctity of [the] home and the privacies of life," Boyd v. United States, 116 U.S., at 630, and then monitor them arbitrarily and without judicial oversight—a society that is not prepared to recognize as reasonable an individual's expectation of privacy in the most private of personal effects sealed in an opaque container and disposed of in a manner designed to commingle it imminently and inextricably with the trash of others. Ante, at 39. The American society with which I am familiar "chooses to dwell in reasonable security and freedom from surveillance," Johnson v. United States, 333 U.S. 10, 14 (1948), and is more dedicated to individual liberty and more sensitive to intrusions on the sanctity of the home than the Court is willing to acknowledge.

I dissent.

OLIVER v. UNITED STATES

466 U.S. 170, 104 S.Ct. 1735, 80 L.Ed.2d 214 (1984).

JUSTICE POWELL delivered the opinion of the Court.

The "open fields" doctrine, first enunciated by this Court in Hester v. United States, 265 U.S. 57 (1924), permits police officers to enter and search a field without a warrant. We granted certiorari in these cases to clarify confusion that has arisen as to the continued vitality of the doctrine.

I

No. 82–15. Acting on reports that marihuana was being raised on the farm of petitioner Oliver, two narcotics agents of the Kentucky State Police went to the farm to investigate.[1] Arriving at the farm, they drove past petitioner's house to a locked gate with a "No Trespassing" sign. A footpath led around one side of the gate. The agents walked around the gate and along the road for several hundred yards, passing a barn and a parked camper. At that point, someone standing in front of the camper shouted: "No hunting is allowed, come back up here." The officers shouted back that they were Kentucky State Police officers, but found no one when they returned to the camper. The officers resumed their investigation of the farm and found a field of marihuana over a mile from petitioner's home.

Petitioner was arrested and indicted for "manufactur[ing]" a "controlled substance." 21 U.S.C. § 841(a)(1). After a pretrial hearing, the District Court suppressed evidence of the discovery of the marihuana field. Applying Katz v. United States, 389 U.S. 347, 357 (1967), the court found that petitioner had a reasonable expectation that the fields would remain private because petitioner "had done all that could be expected of him to assert his privacy in the area of farm that was searched." He had posted "No Trespassing" signs at regular intervals and had locked the gate at the entrance to the center of the farm. App. to Pet. for Cert. in No. 82–15, pp. 23–24. Further, the court noted that the fields themselves are highly secluded: it is bounded on all sides by woods, fences and embankments and cannot be seen from any point of public access. The court concluded that this was not an "open" field that invited casual intrusion.

---

1. It is conceded that the police did not have a warrant authorizing the search, that there was no probable cause for the search, and that no exception to the warrant requirement is applicable.

259

The Court of Appeals for the Sixth Circuit, sitting *en banc,* reversed the District Court.   686 F.2d 356 (1982). . . . We granted certiorari.   459 U.S. 1168 (1983).

No. 82–1273. After receiving an anonymous tip that marihuana was being grown in the woods behind respondent Thornton's residence, two police officers entered the woods by a path between this residence and a neighboring house.   They followed a footpath through the woods until they reached two marihuana patches fenced with chicken wire.   Later, the officers determined that the patches were on the property of respondent, obtained a warrant to search the property and seized the marihuana.   On the basis of this evidence, respondent was arrested and indicted.

The trial court granted respondent's motion to suppress the fruits of the second search.   The warrant for this search was premised on information that the police had obtained during their previous warrantless search, that the court found to be unreasonable.   "No Trespassing" signs and the secluded location of the marihuana patches evinced a reasonable expectation of privacy. Therefore, the court held, the "open fields" doctrine did not apply.

The Maine Supreme Judicial Court affirmed.   453 A.2d 489 (1982). . . . We granted certiorari.   460 U.S. 1068 (1983).

II

The rule announced in Hester v. United States was founded upon the explicit language of the Fourth Amendment.   That Amendment indicates with some precision the places and things encompassed by its protections.   As Justice Holmes explained for the Court in his characteristically laconic style: "[T]he special protection accorded by the Fourth Amendment to the people in their 'persons, houses, papers, and effects,' is not extended to the open fields.   The distinction between the latter and the house is as old as the common law."   Hester v. United States, 265 U.S., at 59.[6]

Nor are the open fields "effects" within the meaning of the Fourth Amendment.   In this respect, it is suggestive that James Madison's proposed draft of what became the Fourth Amendment preserves "[t]he rights of the people to be secured in their persons, their houses, their papers, and their other property, from all unreasonable searches and seizures. . . ." See N. Lasson, The History and Development of the Fourth Amendment to the United States Consti-

---

6. . . . *Katz'* "reasonable expectation of privacy" standard did not sever Fourth Amendment doctrine from the Amendment's language. *Katz* itself construed the Amendment's protection of the person against unreasonable searches to encompass electronic eavesdropping of telephone conversations sought to be kept private; and *Katz'* fundamental recognition that "the Fourth Amendment protects people—and not simply 'areas'—against unreasonable searches and seizures," see 389 U.S., at 353, is faithful to the Amendment's language. As *Katz* demonstrates, the Court fairly may respect the constraints of the Constitution's language without wedding itself to an unreasoning literalism. In contrast, the dissent's approach would ignore the language of the Constitution itself as well as overturn this Court's governing precedent.

tution 100, n. 77 (1937). Although Congress' revisions of Madison's proposal broadened the scope of the Amendment in some respects, id., at 100–103, the term "effects" is less inclusive than "property" and cannot be said to encompass open fields. We conclude, as did the Court in deciding Hester v. United States, that the government's intrusion upon the open fields is not one of those "unreasonable searches" proscribed by the text of the Fourth Amendment.

III

This interpretation of the Fourth Amendment's language is consistent with the understanding of the right to privacy expressed in our Fourth Amendment jurisprudence. Since Katz v. United States, 389 U.S. 347 (1967), the touchstone of Amendment analysis has been the question whether a person has a "constitutionally protected reasonable expectation of privacy." Id., at 360 (Harlan, J., concurring). The Amendment does not protect the merely subjective expectation of privacy, but only those "expectation[s] that society is prepared to recognize as 'reasonable.' " Id., at 361. See also Smith v. Maryland, 442 U.S. 735, 740–741 (1979).

A

No single factor determines whether an individual legitimately may claim under the Fourth Amendment that a place should be free of government intrusion not authorized by warrant. ... In assessing the degree to which a search infringes upon individual privacy, the Court has given weight to such factors as the intention of the Framers of the Fourth Amendment ... the uses to which the individual has put a location ... and our societal understanding that certain areas deserve the most scrupulous protection from government invasion .... These factors are equally relevant to determining whether the government's intrusion upon open fields without a warrant or probable cause violates reasonable expectations of privacy and is therefore a search proscribed by the Amendment.

In this light, the rule of Hester v. United States, supra, that we reaffirm today, may be understood as providing that an individual may not legitimately demand privacy for activities conducted out of doors in fields, except in the area immediately surrounding the home. ... This rule is true to the conception of the right to privacy embodied in the Fourth Amendment. The Amendment reflects the recognition of the Founders that certain enclaves should be free from arbitrary government interference. For example, the Court since the enactment of the Fourth Amendment has stressed "the overriding respect for the sanctity of the home that has been embedded in our traditions since the origins of the Republic." Payton v. New York [445 U.S. 573 (1980)], at 601....

In contrast, open fields do not provide the setting for those intimate activities that the Amendment is intended to shelter from government interference or surveillance. There is no social interest in protecting the privacy of those activities, such as the cultivation of crops, that occur in open fields. Moreover, as a practical matter these lands usually are accessible to the public and the police in ways that a home, an office or commercial structure would not be. It is not generally true that fences or "No Trespassing" signs effectively bar the public from viewing open fields in rural areas. And both petitioner Oliver and respondent Thornton concede that the public and police lawfully may survey lands from the air. For these reasons, the asserted expectation of privacy in open fields is not an expectation that "society recognizes as reasonable." [10]

The historical underpinnings of the open fields doctrine also demonstrate that the doctrine is consistent with respect for "reasonable expectations of privacy." As Justice Holmes, writing for the Court, observed in Hester, 265 U.S., at 59, the common law distinguished "open fields" from the "curtilage," the land immediately surrounding and associated with the home. See 4 W. Blackstone, Commentaries *225. The distinction implies that only the curtilage, not the neighboring open fields, warrants the Fourth Amendment protections that attach to the home. At common law, the curtilage is the area to which extends the intimate activity associated with the "sanctity of a man's home and the privacies of life," Boyd v. United States, 116 U.S. 616, 630 (1886), and therefore has been considered part of the home itself for Fourth Amendment purposes. Thus, courts have extended Fourth Amendment protection to the curtilage; and they have defined the curtilage, as did the common law, by reference to the factors that determine whether an individual reasonably may expect that an area immediately adjacent to the home will remain private. ... Conversely, the common law implies, as we reaffirm today, that no expectation of privacy legitimately attaches to open fields.[11]

---

10. The dissent conceives of open fields as bustling with private activity as diverse as lovers' trysts and worship services. Post, at 191–193. But in most instances police will disturb no one when they enter upon open fields. These fields, by their very character as open and unoccupied, are unlikely to provide the setting for activities whose privacy is sought to be protected by the Fourth Amendment. One need think only of the vast expanse of some western ranches or of the undeveloped woods of the Northwest to see the unreality of the dissent's conception. Further, the Fourth Amendment provides ample protection to activities in the open fields that might implicate an individual's privacy. An individual who enters a place defined to be "public" for Fourth Amendment analysis does not lose all claims to privacy or personal security. ... For example, the Fourth Amendment's protections against unreasonable arrest or unreasonable seizure of effects upon the person remain fully applicable. ...

11. Neither petitioner Oliver nor respondent Thornton has contended that the property searched was within the curtilage. Nor is it necessary in this case to consider the scope of the curtilage exception to the open fields doctrine or the degree of Fourth Amendment protection afforded the curtilage, as opposed to the home itself. It is clear, however, that the term "open fields" may include any unoccupied or undeveloped area outside of the curtilage. An open field need be neither "open" nor a "field" as those terms are used in common speech. ...

We conclude, from the text of the Fourth Amendment and from the historical and contemporary understanding of its purposes, that an individual has no legitimate expectation that open fields will remain free from warrantless intrusion by government officers.

B

Petitioner Oliver and respondent Thornton contend, to the contrary, that the circumstances of a search sometimes may indicate that reasonable expectations of privacy were violated; and that courts therefore should analyze these circumstances on a case-by-case basis. The language of the Fourth Amendment itself answers their contention.

Nor would a case-by-case approach provide a workable accommodation between the needs of law enforcement and the interests protected by the Fourth Amendment. Under this approach, police officers would have to guess before every search whether landowners had erected fences sufficiently high, posted a sufficient number of warning signs, or located contraband in an area sufficiently secluded to establish a right of privacy. The lawfulness of a search would turn on "[a] highly sophisticated set of rules, qualified by all sorts of ifs, ands, and buts and requiring the drawing of subtle nuances and hairline distinctions. ..." New York v. Belton, 453 U.S. 454, 458 (1981) (quoting LaFave, "Case-By-Case Adjudication" versus "Standardized Procedures": The Robinson Dilemma, 1974 S.Ct.Rev. 127, 142). This Court repeatedly has acknowledged the difficulties created for courts, police and citizens by an *ad hoc,* case-by-case definition of Fourth Amendment standards to be applied in differing factual circumstances. ... The *ad hoc* approach not only makes it difficult for the policeman to discern the scope of his authority ...; it also creates a danger that constitutional rights will be arbitrarily and inequitably enforced. ...[12]

IV

In any event, while the factors that petitioner Oliver and respondent Thornton urge the courts to consider may be relevant to Fourth Amendment analysis in some contexts, these factors cannot be decisive on the question whether the search of an open field is subject to the Amendment. Initially, we reject the suggestion that steps taken to protect privacy establish that expectations of privacy in an open field are legitimate. It is true, of course, that petitioner Oliver and respondent Thornton, in order to conceal their criminal

---

12. The clarity of the open fields doctrine that we reaffirm today is not sacrificed, as the dissent suggests by our recognition that the curtilage remains within the protections of the Fourth Amendment. Most of the many millions of acres that are "open fields" are not close to any structure and so not arguably within the curtilage. And, for most homes, the boundaries of the curtilage will be clearly marked; and the conception defining the curtilage—as the area around the home to which the activity of home life extends—is a familiar one easily understood from our daily experience. The occasional difficulties that courts might have in applying this, like other, legal concepts, do not argue for the unprecedented expansion of the Fourth Amendment advocated by the dissent.

activities, planted the marihuana upon secluded land and erected fences and "No Trespassing" signs around the property. And it may be that because of such precautions, few members of the public stumbled upon the marihuana crops seized by the police. Neither of these suppositions demonstrates, however, that the expectation of privacy was *legitimate* in the sense required by the Fourth Amendment. The test of legitimacy is not whether the individual chooses to conceal assertedly "private" activity.[13] Rather, the correct inquiry is whether the government's intrusion infringes upon the personal and societal values protected by the Fourth Amendment. As we have explained, we find no basis for concluding that a police inspection of open fields accomplishes such an infringement.

Nor is the government's intrusion upon an open field a "search" in the constitutional sense because that intrusion is a trespass at common law. The existence of a property right is but one element in determining whether expectations of privacy are legitimate. " 'The premise that property interests control the right of the Government to search and seize has been discredited.' " *Katz,* 389 U.S., at 353 (quoting Warden v. Hayden, 387 U.S. 294, 304 (1967)). "[E]ven a property interest in premises may not be sufficient to establish a legitimate expectation of privacy with respect to particular items located on the premises or activity conducted thereon." Rakas v. Illinois, 439 U.S., at 144, n. 12.

The common law may guide consideration of what areas are protected by the Fourth Amendment search by defining areas whose invasion by others is wrongful. . . . The law of trespass, however, forbids intrusions upon land that the Fourth Amendment would not proscribe. For trespass law extends to instances where the exercise of the right to exclude vindicates no legitimate privacy interest. Thus, in the case of open fields, the general rights of property protected by the common law of trespass have little or no relevance to the applicability of the Fourth Amendment.

V

We conclude that the open fields doctrine, as enunciated in *Hester,* is consistent with the plain language of the Fourth Amendment and its historical purposes. Moreover, Justice Holmes' interpretation of the Amendment in *Hester* accords with the "reasonable expectation of privacy" analysis developed in subsequent decisions of this Court. We therefore affirm Oliver v. United States; Maine v. Thornton is reversed and remanded for further proceedings not inconsistent with this opinion.

It is so ordered.

---

13. Certainly the Framers did not intend that the Fourth Amendment should shelter criminal activity wherever persons with criminal intent choose to erect barriers and post "No Trespassing" signs.

JUSTICE MARSHALL, with whom JUSTICE BRENNAN and JUS-
TICE STEVENS join, dissenting.

In each of these consolidated cases, police officers, ignoring
clearly visible "No Trespassing" signs, entered upon private land in
search of evidence of a crime. At a spot that could not be seen
from any vantage point accessible to the public, the police discovered contraband, which was subsequently used to incriminate the
owner of the land. In neither case did the police have a warrant
authorizing their activities.

The Court holds that police conduct of this sort does not
constitute an "unreasonable search" within the meaning of the
Fourth Amendment. The Court reaches that startling conclusion by
two independent analytical routes. First, the Court argues that,
because the Fourth Amendment by its terms renders people secure
in their "persons, houses, papers, and effects," it is inapplicable to
trespasses upon land not lying within the curtilage of a dwelling.
Ante, at 176–177. Second, the Court contends that "an individual
may not legitimately demand privacy for activities conducted out of
doors in fields, except in the area immediately surrounding the
home." Ante, at 178. Because I cannot agree with either of these
propositions, I dissent.

I

The first ground on which the Court rests its decision is that
the Fourth Amendment "indicates with some precision the places
and things encompassed by its protections," and that real property
is not included in the list of protected spaces and possessions.
Ante, at 176. This line of argument has several flaws. Most
obviously, it is inconsistent with the results of many of our previous
decisions, none of which the Court purports to overrule. For
example, neither a public telephone booth nor a conversation
conducted therein can fairly be described as a person, house, paper,
or effect; yet we have held that the Fourth Amendment forbids the
police without a warrant to eavesdrop on such a conversation. . . .
Nor can it plausibly be argued that an office or commercial establishment is covered by the plain language of the Amendment; yet
we have held that such premises are entitled to constitutional
protection if they are marked in a fashion that alerts the public to
the fact that they are private. . . .

Indeed, the Court's reading of the plain language of the Fourth
Amendment is incapable of explaining even its own holding in this
case. The Court rules that the curtilage, a zone of real property
surrounding a dwelling, is entitled to constitutional protection.
Ante, at 180. We are not told, however, whether the curtilage is a
"house" or an "effect"—or why, if the curtilage can be incorporated
into the list of things and spaces shielded by the Amendment, a field
cannot.

The Court's inability to reconcile its parsimonious reading of the phrase "persons, houses, papers, and effects" with our prior decisions or even its own holding is a symptom of a more fundamental infirmity in the Court's reasoning. The Fourth Amendment, like the other central provisions of the Bill of Rights that loom large in our modern jurisprudence, was designed, not to prescribe with "precision" permissible and impermissible activities, but to identify a fundamental human liberty that should be shielded forever from government intrusion. We do not construe constitutional provisions of this sort the way we do statutes, whose drafters can be expected to indicate with some comprehensiveness and exactitude the conduct they wish to forbid or control and to change those prescriptions when they become obsolete. Rather, we strive, when interpreting these seminal constitutional provisions, to effectuate their purposes—to lend them meanings that ensure that the liberties the Framers sought to protect are not undermined by the changing activities of government officials.

The liberty shielded by the Fourth Amendment, as we have often acknowledged, is freedom "from unreasonable government intrusions into . . . legitimate expectations of privacy." United States v. Chadwick, 433 U.S. 1, 7 (1977). That freedom would be incompletely protected if only government conduct that impinged upon a person, house, paper, or effect were subject to constitutional scrutiny. Accordingly, we have repudiated the proposition that the Fourth Amendment applies only to a limited set of locales or kinds of property. In Katz v. United States, we expressly rejected a proffered locational theory of the coverage of the Amendment, holding that it "protects people, not places." 389 U.S. [347 (1967)], at 351. Since that time we have consistently adhered to the view that the applicability of the provision depends solely upon "whether the person invoking its protection can claim a 'justifiable,' a 'reasonable,' or a 'legitimate expectation of privacy' that has been invaded by government action." Smith v. Maryland, 442 U.S. 735, 740 (1979). The Court's contention that, because a field is not a house or effect, it is not covered by the Fourth Amendment is inconsistent with this line of cases and with the understanding of the nature of constitutional adjudication from which it derives.

II

The second ground for the Court's decision is its contention that any interest a landowner might have in the privacy of his woods and fields is not one that "society is prepared to recognize as 'reasonable.'" Ante, at 177, (quoting Katz v. United States, 389 U.S., at 361 (Harlan, J., concurring)). The mode of analysis that underlies this assertion is certainly more consistent with our prior decisions than that discussed above. But the Court's conclusion cannot withstand scrutiny.

As the Court acknowledges, we have traditionally looked to a variety of factors in determining whether an expectation of privacy asserted in a physical space is "reasonable." Ante, at 177–178. Though those factors do not lend themselves to precise taxonomy, they may be roughly grouped into three categories. First, we consider whether the expectation at issue is rooted in entitlements defined by positive law. Second, we consider the nature of the uses to which spaces of the sort in question can be put. Third, we consider whether the person claiming a privacy interest manifested that interest to the public in a way that most people would understand and respect. When the expectations of privacy asserted by petitioner Oliver and respondent Thornton are examined through these lenses, it becomes clear that those expectations are entitled to constitutional protection.

A

We have frequently acknowledged that privacy interests are not coterminous with property rights. . . . However, because "property rights reflect society's explicit recognition of a person's authority to act as he wishes in certain areas, [they] should be considered in determining whether an individual's expectations of privacy are reasonable." Rakas v. Illinois, 439 U.S. [128 (1978)], at 153 (Powell, J., concurring). Indeed, the Court has suggested that, insofar as "[o]ne of the main rights attaching to property is the right to exclude others, . . . one who owns or lawfully possesses or controls property will in all likelihood have a legitimate expectation of privacy by virtue of this right to exclude." Id., at 144, n. 12 (opinion of the Court).

It is undisputed that Oliver and Thornton each owned the land into which the police intruded. That fact alone provides considerable support for their assertion of legitimate privacy interests in their woods and fields. But even more telling is the nature of the sanctions that Oliver and Thornton could invoke, under local law, for violation of their property rights. In Kentucky, a knowing entry upon fenced or otherwise enclosed land, or upon unenclosed land conspicuously posted with signs excluding the public, constitutes criminal trespass. Ky.Rev.Stat. §§ 511.070(1), 511.080, 511.090(4) (1975). The law in Maine is similar. An intrusion into "any place from which [the intruder] may lawfully be excluded and which is posted in a manner prescribed by law or in a manner reasonably likely to come to the attention of intruders or which is fenced or otherwise enclosed" is a crime. Me.Rev.Stat.Ann., Tit. 17A, § 402(1)(C) (1964). Thus, positive law not only recognizes the legitimacy of Oliver's and Thornton's insistence that strangers keep off their land, but subjects those who refuse to respect their wishes to the most severe of penalties—criminal liability. Under these circumstances, it is hard to credit the Court's assertion that Oliver's and Thornton's expectations of privacy were not of a sort that society is prepared to recognize as reasonable.

B

The uses to which a place is put are highly relevant to the assessment of a privacy interest asserted therein. ... If, in light of our shared sensibilities, those activities are of a kind in which people should be able to engage without fear of intrusion by private persons or government officials, we extend the protection of the Fourth Amendment to the space in question, even in the absence of any entitlement derived from positive law. ... [13]

Privately-owned woods and fields that are not exposed to public view regularly are employed in a variety of ways that society acknowledges deserve privacy. Many landowners like to take solitary walks on their property, confident that they will not be confronted in their rambles by strangers or policemen. Others conduct agricultural businesses on their property. Some landowners use their secluded spaces to meet lovers, others to gather together with fellow worshippers, still others to engage in sustained creative endeavor. Private land is sometimes used as a refuge for wildlife, where flora and fauna are protected from human intervention of any kind. Our respect for the freedom of landowners to use their posted "open fields" in ways such as these partially explains the seriousness with which the positive law regards deliberate invasions of such spaces, see supra, at 190–191, and substantially reinforces the landowners contention that their expectations of privacy are "reasonable."

C

Whether a person "took normal precautions to maintain his privacy" in a given space affects whether his interest is one protected by the Fourth Amendment. ... The reason why such precautions are relevant is that we do not insist that a person who has a right to exclude others exercise that right. A claim to privacy is therefore strengthened by the fact that the claimant somehow manifested to other people his desire that they keep their distance.

---

13. In most circumstances, this inquiry requires analysis of the sorts of uses to which a given space is susceptible, not the manner in which the person asserting an expectation of privacy in the space was in fact employing it. ... We make exceptions to this principle and evaluate uses on a case-by-case basis in only two contexts: when called upon to assess (what formerly was called) the "standing" of a particular person to challenge an intrusion by government officials into an area over which that person lacked primary control ... and when it is possible to ascertain how a person is using a particular space without violating the very privacy interest he is asserting. ... (In cases of the latter sort, the inquiries described in this Part and in Part II–C, infra, are coextensive). Neither of these exceptions is applicable here. Thus, the majority's contention that, because the cultivation of marihuana is not an activity that society wishes to protect, Oliver and Thornton had no legitimate privacy interest in their fields, ante, at 182–183 and n. 13, reflects a misunderstanding of the level of generality on which the constitutional analysis must proceed.

Certain spaces are so presumptively private that signals of this sort are unnecessary; a homeowner need not post a "Do Not Enter" sign on his door in order to deny entrance to uninvited guests. Privacy interests in other spaces are more ambiguous, and the taking of precautions is consequently more important; placing a lock on one's footlocker strengthens one's claim that an examination of its contents is impermissible. ... Still other spaces are, by positive law and social convention, presumed accessible to members of the public *unless* the owner manifests his intention to exclude them.

Undeveloped land falls into the last-mentioned category. If a person has not marked the boundaries of his fields or woods in a way that informs passersby that they are not welcome, he cannot object if members of the public enter onto the property. There is no reason why he should have any greater rights as against government officials. Accordingly, we have held that an official may, without a warrant, enter private land from which the public is not excluded and make observations from that vantage point. ... Fairly read, the case on which the majority so heavily relies, Hester v. United States, 265 U.S. 57 (1924), affirms little more than the foregoing unremarkable proposition. From aught that appears in the opinion in that case, the defendants, fleeing from revenue agents who had observed them committing a crime, abandoned incriminating evidence on private land from which the public had not been excluded. Under such circumstances, it is not surprising that the Court was unpersuaded by the defendants' argument that the entry onto their fields by the agents violated the Fourth Amendment.

A very different case is presented when the owner of undeveloped land has taken precautions to exclude the public. As indicated above, a deliberate entry by a private citizen onto private property marked with "No Trespassing" signs will expose him to criminal liability. I see no reason why a government official should not be obliged to respect such unequivocal and universally understood manifestations of a landowner's desire for privacy.

In sum, examination of the three principal criteria we have traditionally used for assessing the reasonableness of a person's expectation that a given space would remain private indicates that interests of the sort asserted by Oliver and Thornton are entitled to constitutional protection. An owner's right to insist that others stay off his posted land is firmly grounded in positive law. Many of the uses to which such land may be put deserve privacy. And, by marking the boundaries of the land with warnings that the public should not intrude, the owner has dispelled any ambiguity as to his desires.

The police in these cases proffered no justification for their invasions of Oliver's and Thornton's privacy interests; in neither case was the entry legitimated by a warrant or by one of the established exceptions to the warrant requirement. I conclude, therefore, that the searches of their land violated the Fourth Amendment, and the evidence obtained in the course of those searches should have been suppressed.

III

A clear, easily administrable rule emerges from the analysis set forth above: Private land marked in a fashion sufficient to render entry thereon a criminal trespass under the law of the state in which the land lies is protected by the Fourth Amendment's proscription of unreasonable searches and seizures. One of the advantages of the foregoing rule is that it draws upon a doctrine already familiar to both citizens and government officials. In each jurisdiction, a substantial body of statutory and case law defines the precautions a landowner must take in order to avail himself of the sanctions of the criminal law. The police know that body of law, because they are entrusted with responsibility for enforcing it against the public; it therefore would not be difficult for the police to abide by it themselves.

By contrast, the doctrine announced by the Court today is incapable of determinate application. Police officers, making warrantless entries upon private land, will be obliged in the future to make on-the-spot judgments as to how far the curtilage extends, and to stay outside that zone. In addition, we may expect to see a spate of litigation over the question of how much improvement is necessary to remove private land from the category of "unoccupied or undeveloped area" to which the "open fields exception" is now deemed applicable. See ante, at 180, n. 11.

The Court's holding not only ill serves the need to make constitutional doctrine "workable for application by rank and file, trained police officers," Illinois v. Andreas, 463 U.S. 765, 772 (1983), it withdraws the shield of the Fourth Amendment from privacy interests that clearly deserve protection. By exempting from the coverage of the Amendment large areas of private land, the Court opens the way to investigative activities we would all find repugnant. . . .

The Fourth Amendment, properly construed, embodies and gives effect to our collective sense of the degree to which men and women, in civilized society, are entitled "to be let alone" by their governments. Olmstead v. United States, 277 U.S. 438, 478 (1928) (Brandeis, J., dissenting) . . . . The Court's opinion bespeaks and will help to promote an impoverished vision of that fundamental right.

I dissent.[*]

[*] Justice White wrote a brief concurring opinion.

NEW JERSEY v. T.L.O.

469 U.S. 325, 105 S.Ct. 733, 83 L.Ed.2d 720 (1985).

JUSTICE WHITE delivered the opinion of the Court.

We granted certiorari in this case to examine the appropriateness of the exclusionary rule as a remedy for searches carried out in violation of the Fourth Amendment by public school authorities. Our consideration of the proper application of the Fourth Amendment to the public schools, however, has led us to conclude that the search that gave rise to the case now before us did not violate the Fourth Amendment. Accordingly, we here address only the questions of the proper standard for assessing the legality of searches conducted by public school officials and the application of that standard to the facts of this case.

I

On March 7, 1980, a teacher at Piscataway High School in Middlesex County, N. J., discovered two girls smoking in a lavatory. One of the two girls was the respondent T. L. O., who at that time was a 14-year-old high school freshman. Because smoking in the lavatory was a violation of a school rule, the teacher took the two girls to the Principal's office, where they met with Assistant Vice Principal Theodore Choplick. In response to questioning by Mr. Choplick, T. L. O.'s companion admitted that she had violated the rule. T. L. O., however, denied that she had been smoking in the lavatory and claimed that she did not smoke at all.

Mr. Choplick asked T. L. O. to come into his private office and demanded to see her purse. Opening the purse, he found a pack of cigarettes, which he removed from the purse and held before T. L. O. as he accused her of having lied to him. As he reached into the purse for the cigarettes, Mr. Choplick also noticed a package of cigarette rolling papers. In his experience, possession of rolling papers by high school students was closely associated with the use of marihuana. Suspecting that a closer examination of the purse might yield further evidence of drug use, Mr. Choplick proceeded to search the purse thoroughly. The search revealed a small amount of marihuana, a pipe, a number of empty plastic bags, a substantial quantity of money in one-dollar bills, an index card that appeared to be a list of students who owed T. L. O. money, and two letters that implicated T. L. O. in marihuana dealing.

Mr. Choplick notified T. L. O.'s mother and the police, and turned the evidence of drug dealing over to the police. At the request of the police, T. L. O.'s mother took her daughter to police headquarters, where T. L. O. confessed that she had been selling

marihuana at the high school.   On the basis of the confession and
the evidence seized by Mr. Choplick, the State brought delinquency
charges against T. L. O. in the Juvenile and Domestic Relations
Court of Middlesex County.   Contending that Mr. Choplick's search
of her purse violated the Fourth Amendment, T. L. O. moved to
suppress the evidence found in her purse as well as her confession,
which, she argued, was tainted by the allegedly unlawful search.
The Juvenile Court denied the motion to suppress.   State ex rel. T.
L. O., 178 N.J.Super. 329, 428 A.2d 1327 (1980)....

... Having denied the motion to suppress, the court on March
23, 1981, found T. L. O. to be a delinquent and on January 8, 1982,
sentenced her to a year's probation.

On appeal from the final judgment of the Juvenile Court, a
divided Appellate Division affirmed the trial court's finding that
there had been no Fourth Amendment violation....   State ex rel.
T. L. O., 185 N.J.Super. 279, 448 A.2d 493 (1982).   T. L. O.
appealed the Fourth Amendment ruling, and the Supreme Court of
New Jersey reversed the judgment of the Appellate Division and
ordered the suppression of the evidence found in T. L. O.'s purse.
State ex rel. T. L. O., 94 N.J. 331, 463 A.2d 934 (1983).

... We granted the State of New Jersey's petition for certiorari.
464 U.S. 991 (1983)....

Although we originally granted certiorari to decide the issue of
the appropriate remedy in juvenile court proceedings for unlawful
school searches, our doubts regarding the wisdom of deciding that
question in isolation from the broader question of what limits, if
any, the Fourth Amendment places on the activities of school
authorities prompted us to order reargument on that question.
Having heard argument on the legality of the search of T. L. O.'s
purse, we are satisfied that the search did not violate the Fourth
Amendment.

II

In determining whether the search at issue in this case violated
the Fourth Amendment, we are faced initially with the question
whether that Amendment's prohibition on unreasonable searches
and seizures applies to searches conducted by public school officials. We hold that it does.

It is now beyond dispute that "the Federal Constitution, by
virtue of the Fourteenth Amendment, prohibits unreasonable
searches and seizures by state officers."   Elkins v. United States, 364
U.S. 206, 213 (1960)....   Equally indisputable is the proposition
that the Fourteenth Amendment protects the rights of students
against encroachment by public school officials....

These two propositions—that the Fourth Amendment applies
to the States through the Fourteenth Amendment, and that the
actions of public school officials are subject to the limits placed on

state action by the Fourteenth Amendment—might appear sufficient to answer the suggestion that the Fourth Amendment does not proscribe unreasonable searches by school officials. On reargument, however, the State of New Jersey has argued that the history of the Fourth Amendment indicates that the Amendment was intended to regulate only searches and seizures carried out by law enforcement officers; accordingly, although public school officials are concededly state agents for purposes of the Fourteenth Amendment, the Fourth Amendment creates no rights enforceable against them.

It may well be true that the evil toward which the Fourth Amendment was primarily directed was the resurrection of the pre-Revolutionary practice of using general warrants or "writs of assistance" to authorize searches for contraband by officers of the Crown. ... But this Court has never limited the Amendment's prohibition on unreasonable searches and seizures to operations conducted by the police. Rather, the Court has long spoken of the Fourth Amendment's strictures as restraints imposed upon "governmental action"—that is, "upon the activities of sovereign authority." Burdeau v. McDowell, 256 U.S. 465, 475 (1921). Accordingly, we have held the Fourth Amendment applicable to the activities of civil as well as criminal authorities: building inspectors ... and even firemen entering privately owned premises to battle a fire ... are all subject to the restraints imposed by the Fourth Amendment. As we observed in Camara v. Municipal Court [387 U.S. 523 (1967)], "[t]he basic purpose of this Amendment, as recognized in countless decisions of this Court, is to safeguard the privacy and security of individuals against arbitrary invasions by governmental officials." 387 U.S., at 528. Because the individual's interest in privacy and personal security "suffers whether the government's motivation is to investigate violations of criminal laws or breaches of other statutory or regulatory standards," Marshall v. Barlow's, Inc. [436 U.S. 307 (1978)], at 312–313, it would be "anomalous to say that the individual and his private property are fully protected by the Fourth Amendment only when the individual is suspected of criminal behavior." Camara v. Municipal Court, supra, at 530.

Notwithstanding the general applicability of the Fourth Amendment to the activities of civil authorities, a few courts have concluded that school officials are exempt from the dictates of the Fourth Amendment by virtue of the special nature of their authority over schoolchildren. ... Teachers and school administrators, it is said, act *in loco parentis* in their dealings with students: their authority is that of the parent, not the State, and is therefore not subject to the limits of the Fourth Amendment. ...

Such reasoning is in tension with contemporary reality and the teachings of this Court. We have held school officials subject to the commands of the First Amendment ... and the Due Process Clause of the Fourteenth Amendment. ... If school authorities are state actors for purposes of the constitutional guarantees of freedom of expression and due process, it is difficult to understand why they should be deemed to be exercising parental rather than public authority when conducting searches of their students. More generally, the Court has recognized that "the concept of parental delegation" as a source of school authority is not entirely "consonant with compulsory education laws." Ingraham v. Wright, 430 U.S. 651, 662 (1977). Today's public school officials do not merely exercise authority voluntarily conferred on them by individual parents; rather, they act in furtherance of publicly mandated educational and disciplinary policies.... In carrying out searches and other disciplinary functions pursuant to such policies, school officials act as representatives of the State, not merely as surrogates for the parents, and they cannot claim the parents' immunity from the strictures of the Fourth Amendment.

III

To hold that the Fourth Amendment applies to searches conducted by school authorities is only to begin the inquiry into the standards governing such searches. Although the underlying command of the Fourth Amendment is always that searches and seizures be reasonable, what is reasonable depends on the context within which a search takes place. The determination of the standard of reasonableness governing any specific class of searches requires "balancing the need to search against the invasion which the search entails." Camara v. Municipal Court, supra, at 536–537. On one side of the balance are arrayed the individual's legitimate expectations of privacy and personal security; on the other, the government's need for effective methods to deal with breaches of public order.

We have recognized that even a limited search of the person is a substantial invasion of privacy. ... We have also recognized that searches of closed items of personal luggage are intrusions on protected privacy interests, for "the Fourth Amendment provides protection to the owner of every container that conceals its contents from plain view." United States v. Ross, 456 U.S. 798, 822–823 (1982). A search of a child's person or of a closed purse or other bag carried on her person,[5] no less than a similar search carried out on an adult, is undoubtedly a severe violation of subjective expectations of privacy.

Of course, the Fourth Amendment does not protect subjective expectations of privacy that are unreasonable or otherwise "illegitimate." See, e.g., Hudson v. Palmer, 468 U.S. 517 (1984) .... To

5. We do not address the question, not presented by this case, whether a schoolchild has a legitimate expectation of privacy in lockers, desks, or other school property provided for the storage of school supplies. Nor do we express any opinion on the standards (if any) governing searches of such areas by school officials or by other public authorities acting at the request of school officials....

receive the protection of the Fourth Amendment, an expectation of privacy must be one that society is "prepared to recognize as legitimate." Hudson v. Palmer, supra, at 526. The State of New Jersey has argued that because of the pervasive supervision to which children in the schools are necessarily subject, a child has virtually no legitimate expectation of privacy in articles of personal property "unnecessarily" carried into a school. This argument has two factual premises: (1) the fundamental incompatibility of expectations of privacy with the maintenance of a sound educational environment; and (2) the minimal interest of the child in bringing any items of personal property into the school. Both premises are severely flawed.

Although this Court may take notice of the difficulty of maintaining discipline in the public schools today, the situation is not so dire that students in the schools may claim no legitimate expectations of privacy. We have recently recognized that the need to maintain order in a prison is such that prisoners retain no legitimate expectations of privacy in their cells, but it goes almost without saying that "[t]he prisoner and the schoolchild stand in wholly different circumstances, separated by the harsh facts of criminal conviction and incarceration." Ingraham v. Wright [430 U.S. 651 (1977)], at 669. We are not yet ready to hold that the schools and the prisons need be equated for purposes of the Fourth Amendment.

Nor does the State's suggestion that children have no legitimate need to bring personal property into the schools seem well anchored in reality. Students at a minimum must bring to school not only the supplies needed for their studies, but also keys, money, and the necessaries of personal hygiene and grooming. In addition, students may carry on their persons or in purses or wallets such nondisruptive yet highly personal items as photographs, letters, and diaries. Finally, students may have perfectly legitimate reasons to carry with them articles of property needed in connection with extracurricular or recreational activities. In short, schoolchildren may find it necessary to carry with them a variety of legitimate, noncontraband items, and there is no reason to conclude that they have necessarily waived all rights to privacy in such items merely by bringing them onto school grounds.

Against the child's interest in privacy must be set the substantial interest of teachers and administrators in maintaining discipline in the classroom and on school grounds. Maintaining order in the classroom has never been easy, but in recent years, school disorder has often taken particularly ugly forms: drug use and violent crime in the schools have become major social problems.... Even in schools that have been spared the most severe disciplinary problems, the preservation of order and a proper educational environment requires close supervision of schoolchildren, as well as the enforcement of rules against conduct that would be perfectly permissible if undertaken by an adult.... Accordingly, we have recognized that maintaining security and order in the schools requires a certain degree of flexibility in school disciplinary procedures, and we have respected the value of preserving the informality of the student-teacher relationship....

How, then, should we strike the balance between the schoolchild's legitimate expectations of privacy and the school's equally legitimate need to maintain an environment in which learning can take place? It is evident that the school setting requires some easing of the restrictions to which searches by public authorities are ordinarily subject. The warrant requirement, in particular, is unsuited to the school environment: requiring a teacher to obtain a warrant before searching a child suspected of an infraction of school rules (or of the criminal law) would unduly interfere with the maintenance of the swift and informal disciplinary procedures needed in the schools. Just as we have in other cases dispensed with the warrant requirement when "the burden of obtaining a warrant is likely to frustrate the governmental purpose behind the search," Camara v. Municipal Court, 387 U.S., at 532–533, we hold today that school officials need not obtain a warrant before searching a student who is under their authority.

The school setting also requires some modification of the level of suspicion of illicit activity needed to justify a search. Ordinarily, a search—even one that may permissibly be carried out without a warrant—must be based upon "probable cause" to believe that a violation of the law has occurred.... However, "probable cause" is not an irreducible requirement of a valid search. The fundamental command of the Fourth Amendment is that searches and seizures be reasonable, and although "both the concept of probable cause and the requirement of a warrant bear on the reasonableness of a search, ... in certain limited circumstances neither is required." Almeida-Sanchez v. United States [413 U.S. 266 (1973)], at 277 (Powell, J., concurring). Thus, we have in a number of cases recognized the legality of searches and seizures based on suspicions that, although "reasonable," do not rise to the level of probable cause.... Where a careful balancing of governmental and private interests suggests that the public interest is best served by a Fourth Amendment standard of reasonableness that stops short of probable cause, we have not hesitated to adopt such a standard.

We join the majority of courts that have examined this issue in concluding that the accommodation of the privacy interests of schoolchildren with the substantial need of teachers and administrators for freedom to maintain order in the schools does not require strict adherence to the requirement that searches be based on probable cause to believe that the subject of the search has violated or is violating the law. Rather, the legality of a search of a student should depend simply on the reasonableness, under all the circumstances, of the search. Determining the reasonableness of any search involves a twofold inquiry: first, one must consider "whether the ... action was justified at its inception," Terry v. Ohio, 392 U.S. [1 (1968)], at 20; second, one must determine whether the search as actually conducted "was reasonably related in scope to the circumstances which justified the interference in the first place," ibid. Under ordinary circumstances, a search of a student by a teacher or other school official[7] will be "justified at its inception" when there are reasonable grounds for suspecting that the search will turn up evidence that the student has violated or is violating either the law or the rules of the school.[8] Such a search will be permissible in its scope when the measures adopted are reasonably related to the objectives of the search and not excessively intrusive in light of the age and sex of the student and the nature of the infraction.

This standard will, we trust, neither unduly burden the efforts of school authorities to maintain order in their schools nor authorize unrestrained intrusions upon the privacy of schoolchildren. By focusing attention on the question of reasonableness, the standard will spare teachers and school administrators the necessity of schooling themselves in the niceties of probable cause and permit them to regulate their conduct according to the dictates of reason and common sense. At the same time, the reasonableness standard should ensure that the interests of students will be invaded no more than is necessary to achieve the legitimate end of preserving order in the schools.

IV

There remains the question of the legality of the search in this case. We recognize that the "reasonable grounds" standard applied by the New Jersey Supreme Court in its consideration of this question is not substantially different from the standard that we have adopted today. Nonetheless, we believe that the New Jersey court's application of that standard to strike down the search of T. L. O.'s purse reflects a somewhat crabbed notion of reasonableness. Our review of the facts surrounding the search leads us to conclude that the search was in no sense unreasonable for Fourth Amendment purposes.

The incident that gave rise to this case actually involved two separate searches, with the first—the search for cigarettes—providing the suspicion that gave rise to the second—the search for marihuana. Although it is the fruits of the second search that are at issue here, the validity of the search for marihuana must depend on

7. We here consider only searches carried out by school authorities acting alone and on their own authority. This case does not present the question of the appropriate standard for assessing the legality of searches conducted by school officials in conjunction with or at the behest of law enforcement agencies, and we express no opinion on that question. ...

8. We do not decide whether individualized suspicion is an essential element of the reasonableness standard we adopt for searches by school authorities. ...

the reasonableness of the initial search for cigarettes, as there would have been no reason to suspect that T. L. O. possessed marihuana had the first search not taken place. Accordingly, it is to the search for cigarettes that we first turn our attention.

The New Jersey Supreme Court pointed to two grounds for its holding that the search for cigarettes was unreasonable. First, the court observed that possession of cigarettes was not in itself illegal or a violation of school rules. Because the contents of T. L. O.'s purse would therefore have "no direct bearing on the infraction" of which she was accused (smoking in a lavatory where smoking was prohibited), there was no reason to search her purse. Second, even assuming that a search of T. L. O.'s purse might under some circumstances be reasonable in light of the accusation made against T. L. O., the New Jersey court concluded that Mr. Choplick in this particular case had no reasonable grounds to suspect that T. L. O. had cigarettes in her purse. At best, according to the court, Mr. Choplick had "a good hunch." 94 N.J., at 347, 463 A.2d, at 942.

Both these conclusions are implausible. T. L. O. had been accused of smoking, and had denied the accusation in the strongest possible terms when she stated that she did not smoke at all. Surely it cannot be said that under these circumstances, T. L. O.'s possession of cigarettes would be irrelevant to the charges against her or to her response to those charges. T. L. O.'s possession of cigarettes, once it was discovered, would both corroborate the report that she had been smoking and undermine the credibility of her defense to the charge of smoking. To be sure, the discovery of the cigarettes would not prove that T. L. O. had been smoking in the lavatory; nor would it, strictly speaking, necessarily be inconsistent with her claim that she did not smoke at all. But it is universally recognized that evidence, to be relevant to an inquiry, need not conclusively prove the ultimate fact in issue, but only have "any tendency to make the existence of any fact that is of consequence to the determination of the action more probable or less probable than it would be without the evidence." Fed. Rule Evid. 401. The relevance of T. L. O.'s possession of cigarettes to the question whether she had been smoking and to the credibility of her denial that she smoked supplied the necessary "nexus" between the item searched for and the infraction under investigation. . . . Thus, if Mr. Choplick in fact had a reasonable suspicion that T. L. O. had cigarettes in her purse, the search was justified despite the fact that the cigarettes, if found, would constitute "mere evidence" of a violation. . . .

Of course, the New Jersey Supreme Court also held that Mr. Choplick had no reasonable suspicion that the purse would contain cigarettes. This conclusion is puzzling. A teacher had reported that T. L. O. was smoking in the lavatory. Certainly this report gave Mr. Choplick reason to suspect that T. L. O. was carrying cigarettes with her; and if she did have cigarettes, her purse was the obvious place in which to find them. Mr. Choplick's suspicion that there were cigarettes in the purse was not an "inchoate and unparticularized suspicion or 'hunch,' " Terry v. Ohio, 392 U.S., at 27; rather, it was the sort of "common-sense conclusio[n] about human behavior" upon which "practical people"—including government officials—are entitled to rely. United States v. Cortez, 449 U.S. 411, 418 (1981). Of course, even if the teacher's report were true, T. L. O. *might* not have had a pack of cigarettes with her; she might have borrowed a cigarette from someone else or have been sharing a cigarette with another student. But the requirement of reasonable suspicion is not a requirement of absolute certainty: "sufficient probability, not certainty, is the touchstone of reasonableness under the Fourth Amendment. . . ." Hill v. California, 401 U.S. 797, 804 (1971). Because the hypothesis that T. L. O. was carrying cigarettes in her purse was itself not unreasonable, it is irrelevant that other hypotheses were also consistent with the teacher's accusation. Accordingly, it cannot be said that Mr. Choplick acted unreasonably when he examined T. L. O.'s purse to see if it contained cigarettes.

Our conclusion that Mr. Choplick's decision to open T. L. O.'s purse was reasonable brings us to the question of the further search for marihuana once the pack of cigarettes was located. The suspicion upon which the search for marihuana was founded was provided when Mr. Choplick observed a package of rolling papers in the purse as he removed the pack of cigarettes. Although T. L. O. does not dispute the reasonableness of Mr. Choplick's belief that the rolling papers indicated the presence of marihuana, she does contend that the scope of the search Mr. Choplick conducted exceeded permissible bounds when he seized and read certain letters that implicated T. L. O. in drug dealing. This argument, too, is unpersuasive. The discovery of the rolling papers concededly gave rise to a reasonable suspicion that T. L. O. was carrying marihuana as well as cigarettes in her purse. This suspicion justified further exploration of T. L. O.'s purse, which turned up more evidence of drug-related activities: a pipe, a number of plastic bags of the type commonly used to store marihuana, a small quantity of marihuana, and a fairly substantial amount of money. Under these circumstances, it was not unreasonable to extend the search to a separate zippered compartment of the purse; and when a search of that compartment revealed an index card containing a list of "people who owe me money" as well as two letters, the inference that T. L. O. was involved in marihuana trafficking was substantial enough to justify Mr. Choplick in examining the letters to determine whether they contained any further evidence. In short, we cannot conclude that the search for marihuana was unreasonable in any respect.

Because the search resulting in the discovery of the evidence of marihuana dealing by T. L. O. was reasonable, the New Jersey Supreme Court's decision to exclude that evidence from T. L. O.'s juvenile delinquency proceedings on Fourth Amendment grounds was erroneous. Accordingly, the judgment of the Supreme Court of New Jersey is

Reversed.

JUSTICE BRENNAN, with whom JUSTICE MARSHALL joins, concurring in part and dissenting in part.

I fully agree with Part II of the Court's opinion. Teachers, like all other government officials, must conform their conduct to the Fourth Amendment's protections of personal privacy and personal security. ... [T]his principle is of particular importance when applied to schoolteachers, for children learn as much by example as by exposition. It would be incongruous and futile to charge teachers with the task of embuing their students with an understanding of our system of constitutional democracy, while at the same time immunizing those same teachers from the need to respect constitutional protections. ...

I do not, however, otherwise join the Court's opinion. Today's decision sanctions school officials to conduct full-scale searches on a "reasonableness" standard whose only definite content is that it is *not* the same test as the "probable cause" standard found in the text of the Fourth Amendment. In adopting this unclear, unprecedented, and unnecessary departure from generally applicable Fourth Amendment standards, the Court carves out a broad exception to standards that this Court has developed over years of considering Fourth Amendment problems. Its decision is supported neither by precedent nor even by a fair application of the "balancing test" it proclaims in this very opinion.

I

Three basic principles underly this Court's Fourth Amendment jurisprudence. First, warrantless searches are *per se* unreasonable, subject only to a few specifically delineated and well-recognized exceptions. ... Second, full-scale searches—whether conducted in accordance with the warrant requirement or pursuant to one of its exceptions—are "reasonable" in Fourth Amendment terms only on a showing of probable cause to believe that a crime has been committed and that evidence of the crime will be found in the place to be searched. ... Third, categories of intrusions that are substantially less intrusive than full-scale searches or seizures may be justifiable in accordance with a balancing test even absent a warrant or probable cause, provided that the balancing test used gives sufficient weight to the privacy interests that will be infringed. ...

Assistant Vice Principal Choplick's thorough excavation of T. L. O.'s purse was undoubtedly a serious intrusion on her privacy. Unlike the searches in Terry v. Ohio [392 U.S. 1 (1968)], or Adams v. Williams, 407 U.S. 143 (1972), the search at issue here encompassed a detailed and minute examination of respondent's pocketbook, in which the contents of private papers and letters were thoroughly scrutinized. Wisely, neither petitioner nor the Court today attempts to justify the search of T. L. O.'s pocketbook as a minimally intrusive search in the *Terry* line. To be faithful to the Court's settled doctrine, the inquiry therefore must focus on the warrant and probable-cause requirements.

A

I agree that schoolteachers or principals, when not acting as agents of law enforcement authorities, generally may conduct a search of their students' belongings without first obtaining a warrant. To agree with the Court on this point is to say that school searches may justifiably be held to that extent to constitute an exception to the Fourth Amendment's warrant requirement. Such an exception, however, is not to be justified, as the Court apparently holds, by assessing net social value through application of an unguided "balancing test" in which "the individual's legitimate expectations of privacy and personal security" are weighed against "the government's need for effective methods to deal with breaches of public order." Ante, at 337. The Warrant Clause is something more than an exhortation to this Court to maximize social welfare as *we* see fit. It requires that the authorities must obtain a warrant before conducting a full-scale search. The undifferentiated governmental interest in law enforcement is insufficient to justify an exception to the warrant requirement. Rather, some *special* governmental interest beyond the need merely to apprehend lawbreakers is necessary to justify a categorical exception to the warrant requirement. For the most part, special governmental needs sufficient to override the warrant requirement flow from "exigency"— that is, from the press of time that makes obtaining a warrant either impossible or hopelessly infeasible. ... Only after finding an extraordinary governmental interest of this kind do we—or ought we—engage in a balancing test to determine if a warrant should nonetheless be required.

To require a showing of some extraordinary governmental interest before dispensing with the warrant requirement is not to undervalue society's need to apprehend violators of the criminal law. To be sure, forcing law enforcement personnel to obtain a warrant before engaging in a search will predictably deter the police from conducting some searches that they would otherwise like to conduct. But this is not an unintended *result* of the Fourth Amendment's protection of privacy; rather, it is the very *purpose* for which the Amendment was thought necessary. Only where the governmental interests at stake exceed those implicated in any ordinary law enforcement context—that is, only where there is some extraordinary governmental interest involved—is it legitimate to engage in a balancing test to determine whether a warrant is indeed necessary.

In this case, such extraordinary governmental interests do exist and are sufficient to justify an exception to the warrant requirement. Students are necessarily confined for most of the school day in close proximity to each other and to the school staff. I agree with the Court that we can take judicial notice of the serious problems of drugs and violence that plague our schools. As Justice Blackmun notes, teachers must not merely "maintain an environment conducive to learning" among children who "are inclined to test the outer boundaries of acceptable conduct," but must also "protect the very safety of students and school personnel." Ante, at 352–353.[*] A teacher or principal could neither carry out essential teaching functions nor adequately protect students' safety if required to wait for a warrant before conducting a necessary search.

B

I emphatically disagree with the Court's decision to cast aside the constitutional probable-cause standard when assessing the constitutional validity of a schoolhouse search. The Court's decision jettisons the probable-cause standard—the only standard that finds support in the text of the Fourth Amendment—on the basis of its Rohrschach-like "balancing test." Use of such a "balancing test" to determine the standard for evaluating the validity of a full-scale search represents a sizable innovation in Fourth Amendment analysis. This innovation finds support neither in precedent nor policy and portends a dangerous weakening of the purpose of the Fourth Amendment to protect the privacy and security of our citizens. Moreover, even if this Court's historic understanding of the Fourth Amendment were mistaken and a balancing test of some kind were appropriate, any such test that gave adequate weight to the privacy and security interests protected by the Fourth Amendment would not reach the preordained result the Court's conclusory analysis reaches today. Therefore, because I believe that the balancing test used by the Court today is flawed both in its inception and in its execution, I respectfully dissent.

. . .

2

I ... do not accept the majority's premise that "[t]o hold that the Fourth Amendment applies to searches conducted by school authorities is only to begin the inquiry into the standards governing such searches." Ante, at 337. For me, the finding that the Fourth Amendment applies, coupled with the observation that what is at issue is a full-scale search, is the end of the inquiry. But even if I believed that a "balancing test" appropriately replaces the judgment of the Framers of the Fourth Amendment, I would nonetheless object to the cursory and shortsighted "test" that the Court employs

[*] Opinion concurring in the judgment.

to justify its predictable weakening of Fourth Amendment protections. In particular, the test employed by the Court vastly overstates the social costs that a probable-cause standard entails and, though it plausibly articulates the serious privacy interests at stake, inexplicably fails to accord them adequate weight in striking the balance.

. . .

A legitimate balancing test whose function was something more substantial than reaching a predetermined conclusion acceptable to this Court's impressions of what authority teachers need would therefore reach rather a different result than that reached by the Court today. On one side of the balance would be the costs of applying traditional Fourth Amendment standards—the "practical" and "flexible" probable-cause standard where a full-scale intrusion is sought, a lesser standard in situations where the intrusion is much less severe and the need for greater authority compelling. Whatever costs were toted up on this side would have to be discounted by the costs of applying an unprecedented and ill-defined "reasonableness under all the circumstances" test that will leave teachers and administrators uncertain as to their authority and will encourage excessive fact-based litigation.

On the other side of the balance would be the serious privacy interests of the student, interests that the Court admirably articulates in its opinion ... but which the Court's new ambiguous standard places in serious jeopardy. I have no doubt that a fair assessment of the two sides of the balance would necessarily reach the same conclusion that, as I have argued above, the Fourth Amendment's language compels—that school searches like that conducted in this case are valid only if supported by probable cause.

II

Applying the constitutional probable-cause standard to the facts of this case, I would find that Mr. Choplick's search violated T. L. O.'s Fourth Amendment rights. After escorting T. L. O. into his private office, Mr. Choplick demanded to see her purse. He then opened the purse to find evidence of whether she had been smoking in the bathroom. When he opened the purse, he discovered the pack of cigarettes. At this point, his search for evidence of the smoking violation was complete.

Mr. Choplick then noticed, below the cigarettes, a pack of cigarette rolling papers. Believing that such papers were "associated," see ante, at 328, with the use of marihuana, he proceeded to conduct a detailed examination of the contents of her purse, in which he found some marihuana, a pipe, some money, an index card, and some private letters indicating that T. L. O. had sold marihuana to other students. The State sought to introduce this latter material in evidence at a criminal proceeding, and the issue before the Court is whether it should have been suppressed.

On my view of the case, we need not decide whether the initial search conducted by Mr. Choplick—the search for evidence of the smoking violation that was completed when Mr. Choplick found the pack of cigarettes—was valid. For Mr. Choplick at that point did not have probable cause to continue to rummage through T.L.O.'s purse. Mr. Choplick's suspicion of marihuana possession at this time was based *solely* on the presence of the package of cigarette papers. The mere presence without more of such a staple item of commerce is insufficient to warrant a person of reasonable caution in inferring both that T.L.O. had violated the law by possessing marihuana and that evidence of that violation would be found in her purse. Just as a police officer could not obtain a warrant to search a home based solely on his claim that he had seen a package of cigarette papers in that home. Mr. Choplick was not entitled to search possibly the most private possessions of T.L.O. based on the mere presence of a package of cigarette papers. Therefore, the fruits of this illegal search must be excluded and the judgment of the New Jersey Supreme Court affirmed.

III

In the past several Terms, this Court has produced a succession of Fourth Amendment opinions in which "balancing tests" have been applied to resolve various questions concerning the proper scope of official searches. . . .

All of these "balancing tests" amount to brief nods by the Court in the direction of a neutral utilitarian calculus while the Court in fact engages in an unanalyzed exercise of judicial will. Perhaps this doctrinally destructive nihilism is merely a convenient umbrella under which a majority that cannot agree on a genuine rationale can conceal its differences. . . . And it may be that the real force underlying today's decision is the belief that the Court purports to reject—the belief that the unique role served by the schools justifies an exception to the Fourth Amendment on their behalf. If so, the methodology of today's decision may turn out to have as little influence in future cases as will its result, and the Court's departure from traditional Fourth Amendment doctrine will be confined to the schools.

On my view, the presence of the word "unreasonable" in the text of the Fourth Amendment does not grant a shifting majority of this Court the authority to answer *all* Fourth Amendment questions by consulting its momentary vision of the social good. Full-scale searches unaccompanied by probable cause violate the Fourth Amendment. I do not pretend that our traditional Fourth Amendment doctrine automatically answers all of the difficult legal questions that occasionally arise. I do contend, however, that this Court has an obligation to provide some coherent framework to resolve such questions on the basis of more than a conclusory recitation of the results of a "balancing test." The Fourth Amendment itself supplies that framework and, because the Court today fails to heed its message, I must respectfully dissent.[*]

[*] Justice Powell wrote a concurring opinion, which Justice O'Connor joined. Justice Blackmun wrote an opinion concurring in the judgment. Justice Stevens wrote an opinion concurring in part and dissenting in part, which Justice Marshall joined and in part of which Justice Brennan joined.

SKINNER v. RAILWAY LABOR EXECUTIVES' ASSOCIATION

489 U.S. 602, 109 S.Ct. 1402, 103 L.Ed.2d 639 (1989).

JUSTICE KENNEDY delivered the opinion of the Court.

The Federal Railroad Safety Act of 1970 authorizes the Secretary of Transportation to "prescribe, as necessary, appropriate rules, regulations, orders, and standards for all areas of railroad safety." 84 Stat. 971, 45 U.S.C. § 431(a). Finding that alcohol and drug abuse by railroad employees poses a serious threat to safety, the Federal Railroad Administration (FRA) has promulgated regulations that mandate blood and urine tests of employees who are involved in certain train accidents. The FRA also has adopted regulations that do not require, but do authorize, railroads to administer breath and urine tests to employees who violate certain safety rules. The question presented by this case is whether these regulations violate the Fourth Amendment.

I

A

The problem of alcohol use on American railroads is as old as the industry itself, and efforts to deter it by carrier rules began at least a century ago. For many years, railroads have prohibited operating employees from possessing alcohol or being intoxicated while on duty and from consuming alcoholic beverages while subject to being called for duty. More recently, these proscriptions have been expanded to forbid possession or use of certain drugs. These restrictions are embodied in "Rule G," an industry-wide operating rule promulgated by the Association of American Railroads, and are enforced, in various formulations, by virtually every railroad in the country. The customary sanction for Rule G violations is dismissal.

In July 1983, the FRA expressed concern that these industry efforts were not adequate to curb alcohol and drug abuse by railroad employees. The FRA pointed to evidence indicating that on-the-job intoxication was a significant problem in the railroad industry. The FRA also found, after a review of accident investigation reports, that from 1972 to 1983 "the nation's railroads experienced at least 21 significant train accidents involving alcohol or drug use as a probable cause or contributing factor," and that these accidents "resulted in 25 fatalities, 61 non-fatal injuries, and property damage estimated at $19 million (approximately $27 million in 1982 dollars)." 48 Fed.Reg. 30726 (1983). The FRA further identified "an additional 17 fatalities to operating employees working on or around rail rolling stock that involved alcohol or drugs as a

286

contributing factor." Ibid. In light of these problems, the FRA solicited comments from interested parties on various regulatory approaches to the problems of alcohol and drug abuse throughout the Nation's railroad system.

Comments submitted in response to this request indicated that railroads were able to detect a relatively small number of Rule G violations, owing, primarily, to their practice of relying on observation by supervisors and co-workers to enforce the rule. 49 Fed.Reg. 24266–24267 (1984). At the same time, "industry participants . . . confirmed that alcohol and drug use [did] occur on the railroads with unacceptable frequency," and available information from all sources "suggest[ed] that the problem includ[ed] 'pockets' of drinking and drug use involving multiple crew members (before and during work), sporadic cases of individuals reporting to work impaired, and repeated drinking and drug use by individual employees who are chemically or psychologically dependent on those substances." Id., at 24253–24254. "Even without the benefit of regular post-accident testing," the Agency "identified 34 fatalities, 66 injuries and over $28 million in property damage (in 1983 dollars) that resulted from the errors of alcohol and drug-impaired employees in 45 train accidents and train incidents during the period 1975 through 1983." Id., at 24254. Some of these accidents resulted in the release of hazardous materials and, in one case, the ensuing pollution required the evacuation of an entire Louisiana community. Id., at 24254, 24259. In view of the obvious safety hazards of drug and alcohol use by railroad employees, the FRA announced in June 1984 its intention to promulgate federal regulations on the subject.

B

After reviewing further comments from representatives of the railroad industry, labor groups, and the general public, the FRA, in 1985, promulgated regulations addressing the problem of alcohol and drugs on the railroads. The final regulations apply to employees assigned to perform service subject to the Hours of Service Act, ch. 2939, 34 Stat. 1415, as amended, 45 U.S.C. § 61 et seq. The regulations prohibit covered employees from using or possessing alcohol or any controlled substance. 49 CFR § 219.101(a)(1) (1987). The regulations further prohibit those employees from reporting for covered service while under the influence of, or impaired by, alcohol, while having a blood alcohol concentration of .04 or more, or while under the influence of, or impaired by any controlled substance. § 219.101(a)(2). The regulations do not restrict, however, a railroad's authority to impose an absolute prohibition on the presence of alcohol or any drug in the body fluids of persons in its employ, § 219.101(c), and, accordingly, they do not "replace Rule G or render it unenforceable." 50 Fed.Reg. 31538 (1985).

To the extent pertinent here, two subparts of the regulations relate to testing. Subpart C, which is entitled "Post-Accident Toxicological Testing," is mandatory. It provides that railroads "shall take all practicable steps to assure that all covered employees of the railroad directly involved . . . provide blood and urine samples for toxicological testing by FRA," § 219.203(a), upon the occurrence of certain specified events. Toxicological testing is required following a "major train accident," which is defined as any train accident that involves (i) a fatality, (ii) the release of hazardous material accompanied by an evacuation or a reportable injury, or (iii) damage to railroad property of $500,000 or more. § 219.201(a)(1). The railroad has the further duty of collecting blood and urine samples for testing after an "impact accident," which is defined as a collision that results in a reportable injury, or in damage to railroad property of $50,000 or more. § 219.201(a)(2). Finally, the railroad is also obligated to test after "[a]ny train incident that involves a fatality to any on-duty railroad employee." § 219.201(a)(3).

After occurrence of an event which activates its duty to test, the railroad must transport all crew members and other covered employees directly involved in the accident or incident to an independent medical facility, where both blood and urine samples must be obtained from each employee. After the samples have been collected, the railroad is required to ship them by prepaid air freight to the FRA laboratory for analysis. § 219.205(d). There, the samples are analyzed using "state-of-the-art equipment and techniques" to detect and measure alcohol and drugs. The FRA proposes to place primary reliance on analysis of blood samples, as blood is "the only available body fluid . . . that can provide a clear indication not only of the presence of alcohol and drugs but also their current impairment effects." 49 Fed.Reg. 24291 (1984). Urine samples are also necessary, however, because drug traces remain in the urine longer than in blood, and in some cases it will not be possible to transport employees to a medical facility before the time it takes for certain drugs to be eliminated from the bloodstream. In those instances, a "positive urine test, taken with specific information on the pattern of elimination for the particular drug and other information on the behavior of the employee and the circumstances of the accident, may be crucial to the determination of" the cause of an accident. Ibid.

The regulations require that the FRA notify employees of the results of the tests and afford them an opportunity to respond in writing before preparation of any final investigative report. See § 219.211(a)(2). Employees who refuse to provide required blood or urine samples may not perform covered service for nine months, but they are entitled to a hearing concerning their refusal to take the test. § 219.213.

Subpart D of the regulations, which is entitled "Authorization to Test for Cause," is permissive. It authorizes railroads to require covered employees to submit to breath or urine tests in certain circumstances not addressed by Subpart C. Breath or urine tests, or both, may be ordered (1) after a reportable accident or incident, where a supervisor has a "reasonable suspicion" that an employee's acts or omissions contributed to the occurrence or severity of the accident or incident, § 219.301(b)(2); or (2) in the event of certain specific rule violations, including noncompliance with a signal and excessive speeding, § 219.301(b)(3). A railroad also may require breath tests where a supervisor has a "reasonable suspicion" that an employee is under the influence of alcohol, based upon specific, personal observations concerning the appearance, behavior, speech, or body odors of the employee. § 219.301(b)(1). Where impairment is suspected, a railroad, in addition, may require urine tests, but only if two supervisors make the appropriate determination, § 219.301(c)(2)(i), and, where the supervisors suspect impairment due to a substance other than alcohol, at least one of those supervisors must have received specialized training in detecting the signs of drug intoxication. § 219.301(c)(2)(ii).

Subpart D further provides that whenever the results of either breath or urine tests are intended for use in a disciplinary proceeding, the employee must be given the opportunity to provide a blood sample for analysis at an independent medical facility. § 219.303(c). If an employee declines to give a blood sample, the railroad may presume impairment, absent persuasive evidence to the contrary, from a positive showing of controlled substance residues in the urine. The railroad must, however, provide detailed notice of this presumption to its employees, and advise them of their right to provide a contemporaneous blood sample. As in the case of samples procured under Subpart C, the regulations set forth procedures for the collection of samples, and require that samples "be analyzed by a method that is reliable within known tolerances." § 219.307(b).

C

Respondents, the Railway Labor Executives' Association and various of its member labor organizations, brought the instant suit in the United States District Court for the Northern District of California, seeking to enjoin the FRA's regulations on various statutory and constitutional grounds. In a ruling from the bench, the District Court granted summary judgment in petitioners' favor. The court concluded that railroad employees "have a valid interest in the integrity of their own bodies" that deserved protection under the Fourth Amendment. App. to Pet. for Cert. 53a. The court held, however, that this interest was outweighed by the competing "public and governmental interest in the ... promotion of ... railway safety, safety for employees, and safety for the general public that is involved with the transportation." Id., at 52a. The District Court found respondents' other constitutional and statutory arguments meritless.

A divided panel of the Court of Appeals for the Ninth Circuit reversed. Railway Labor Executives' Assn. v. Burnley, 839 F.2d 575 (1988)....

....

We granted the federal parties' petition for a writ of certiorari, 486 U.S. 1042 (1988), to consider whether the regulations invalidated by the Court of Appeals violate the Fourth Amendment. We now reverse.

II

The Fourth Amendment provides that "[t]he right of the people to be secure in their persons, houses, papers, and effects, against unreasonable searches and seizures, shall not be violated...." The Amendment guarantees the privacy, dignity, and security of persons against certain arbitrary and invasive acts by officers of the Government or those acting at their direction.... Before we consider whether the tests in question are reasonable under the Fourth Amendment, we must inquire whether the tests are attributable to the Government or its agents, and whether they amount to searches or seizures. We turn to those matters.

....

[The Court concluded that the testing program is sufficiently attributable to the government to implicate the Fourth Amendment and that the tests are searches under the Fourth Amendment.]

III

A

To hold that the Fourth Amendment is applicable to the drug and alcohol testing prescribed by the FRA regulations is only to begin the inquiry into the standards governing such intrusions.... For the Fourth Amendment does not proscribe all searches and seizures, but only those that are unreasonable.... What is reasonable, of course, "depends on all the circumstances surrounding the search or seizure and the nature of the search or seizure itself." United States v. Montoya de Hernandez, 473 U.S. 531, 537 (1985). Thus, the permissibility of a particular practice "is judged by balancing its intrusion on the individual's Fourth Amendment interests against its promotion of legitimate governmental interests." Delaware v. Prouse, 440 U.S. [648 (1979)], at 654....

In most criminal cases, we strike this balance in favor of the procedures described by the Warrant Clause of the Fourth Amendment.... Except in certain well-defined circumstances, a search or seizure in such a case is not reasonable unless it is accomplished pursuant to a judicial warrant issued upon probable cause.... We have recognized exceptions to this rule, however, "when 'special needs, beyond the normal need for law enforcement, make the warrant and probable-cause requirement impracticable.' " Griffin v. Wisconsin, 483 U.S. 868, 873 (1987), quoting New Jersey v. T.L.O., 469 U.S. [325 (1985)] at 351 (Blackmun, J., concurring in judgment). When faced with such special needs, we have not hesitated to balance the governmental and privacy interests to assess the practicality of the warrant and probable cause requirements in the particular context. . . .

The Government's interest in regulating the conduct of railroad employees to ensure safety, like its supervision of probationers or regulated industries, or its operation of a government office, school, or prison, "likewise presents 'special needs' beyond normal law enforcement that may justify departures from the usual warrant and probable-cause requirements." Griffin v. Wisconsin, 483 U.S., at 873–874. The hours of service employees covered by the FRA regulations include persons engaged in handling orders concerning train movements, operating crews, and those engaged in the maintenance and repair of signal systems. . . . It is undisputed that these and other covered employees are engaged in safety-sensitive tasks. The FRA so found, and respondents conceded the point at oral argument. . . . As we have recognized, the whole premise of the Hours of Service Act is that "[t]he length of hours of service has direct relation to the efficiency of the human agencies upon which protection [of] life and property necessarily depends." Baltimore & Ohio R. Co. v. ICC, 221 U.S. 612, 619 (1911). . . .

The FRA has prescribed toxicological tests, not to assist in the prosecution of employees, but rather "to prevent accidents and casualties in railroad operations that result from impairment of employees by alcohol or drugs." 49 CFR § 219.1(a) (1987). This governmental interest in ensuring the safety of the traveling public and of the employees themselves plainly justifies prohibiting covered employees from using alcohol or drugs on duty, or while subject to being called for duty. This interest also "require[s] and justif[ies] the exercise of supervision to assure that the restrictions are in fact observed." Griffin v. Wisconsin, 483 U.S., at 875. The question that remains, then, is whether the Government's need to monitor compliance with these restrictions justifies the privacy intrusions at issue absent a warrant or individualized suspicion.

B

An essential purpose of a warrant requirement is to protect privacy interests by assuring citizens subject to a search or seizure that such intrusions are not the random or arbitrary acts of government agents. A warrant assures the citizen that the intrusion is authorized by law, and that it is narrowly limited in its objectives and scope. . . . A warrant also provides the detached scrutiny of a neutral magistrate, and thus ensures an objective determination whether an intrusion is justified in any given case.... In the present context, however, a warrant would do little to further these aims. Both the circumstances justifying toxicological testing and the permissible limits of such intrusions are defined narrowly and specifically in the regulations that authorize them, and doubtless are well known to covered employees.... Indeed, in light of the standardized nature of the tests and the minimal discretion vested in those charged with administering the program, there are virtually no facts for a neutral magistrate to evaluate....

We have recognized, moreover, that the Government's interest in dispensing with the warrant requirement is at its strongest when, as here, "the burden of obtaining a warrant is likely to frustrate the governmental purpose behind the search." Camara v. Municipal Court of San Francisco, [387 U.S. 522 (1967)], at 533.... As the FRA recognized, alcohol and other drugs are eliminated from the bloodstream at a constant rate ... and blood and breath samples taken to measure whether these substances were in the bloodstream when a triggering event occurred must be obtained as soon as possible.... Although the metabolites of some drugs remain in the urine for longer periods of time and may enable the FRA to estimate whether the employee was impaired by those drugs at the time of a covered accident, incident, or rule violation ... the delay necessary to procure a warrant nevertheless may result in the destruction of valuable evidence.

The Government's need to rely on private railroads to set the testing process in motion also indicates that insistence on a warrant requirement would impede the achievement of the Government's objective. Railroad supervisors, like school officials ... and hospital administrators ... are not in the business of investigating violations of the criminal laws or enforcing administrative codes, and otherwise have little occasion to become familiar with the intricacies of this Court's Fourth Amendment jurisprudence. "Imposing unwieldy warrant procedures ... upon supervisors, who would otherwise have no reason to be familiar with such procedures, is simply unreasonable." [O'Connor v. Ortega, 480 U.S. 709, 722 (1987)].

In sum, imposing a warrant requirement in the present context would add little to the assurances of certainty and regularity already afforded by the regulations, while significantly hindering, and in many cases frustrating, the objectives of the Government's testing program. We do not believe that a warrant is essential to render the intrusions here at issue reasonable under the Fourth Amendment.

C

Our cases indicate that even a search that may be performed without a warrant must be based, as a general matter, on probable cause to believe that the person to be searched has violated the

law. . . .   When the balance of interests precludes insistence on a
showing of probable cause, we have usually required "some quantum of individualized suspicion" before concluding that a search is
reasonable.   See, e.g., United States v. Martinez-Fuerte, 428 U.S.
[549 (1976)], at 560.   We made it clear, however, that a showing of
individualized suspicion is not a constitutional floor, below which a
search must be presumed unreasonable. . . .   In limited circumstances, where the privacy interests implicated by the search are
minimal, and where an important governmental interest furthered
by the intrusion would be placed in jeopardy by a requirement of
individualized suspicion, a search may be reasonable despite the
absence of such suspicion.   We believe this is true of the intrusions
in question here.

By and large, intrusions on privacy under the FRA regulations
are limited.   To the extent transportation and like restrictions are
necessary to procure the requisite blood, breath, and urine samples
for testing, this interference alone is minimal given the employment
context in which it takes place.   Ordinarily, an employee consents
to significant restrictions in his freedom of movement where necessary for his employment, and few are free to come and go as they
please during working hours. . . .   Any additional interference with
a railroad employee's freedom of movement that occurs in the time
it takes to procure a blood, breath, or urine sample for testing
cannot, by itself, be said to infringe significant privacy interests.

Our decision in Schmerber v. California, 384 U.S. 757 (1966),
indicates that the same is true of the blood tests required by the FRA
regulations.   In that case, we held that a State could direct that a
blood sample be withdrawn from a motorist suspected of driving
while intoxicated, despite his refusal to consent to the intrusion.
We noted that the test was performed in a reasonable manner, as
the motorist's "blood was taken by a physician in a hospital
environment according to accepted medical practices."   Id., at 771.
We said also that the intrusion occasioned by a blood test is not
significant, since such "tests are a commonplace in these days of
periodic physical examinations and experience with them teaches
that the quantity of blood extracted is minimal, and that for most
people the procedure involves virtually no risk, trauma, or pain."
Ibid.   *Schmerber* thus confirmed "society's judgment that blood
tests do not constitute an unduly extensive imposition on an
individual's privacy and bodily integrity."   Winston v. Lee, 470 U.S.
[753 (1985)], at 762. . . .

The breath tests authorized by Subpart D of the regulations are
even less intrusive than the blood tests prescribed by Subpart C.
Unlike blood tests, breath tests do not require piercing the skin and
may be conducted safely outside a hospital environment and with a
minimum of inconvenience or embarrassment.   Further, breath
tests reveal the level of alcohol in the employee's bloodstream and
nothing more.   Like the blood-testing procedures mandated by

Subpart C, which can be used only to ascertain the presence of alcohol or controlled substances in the bloodstream, breath tests reveal no other facts in which the employee has a substantial privacy interest. . . . In all the circumstances, we cannot conclude that the administration of a breath test implicates significant privacy concerns.

A more difficult question is presented by urine tests. Like breath tests, urine tests are not invasive of the body and, under the regulations, may not be used as an occasion for inquiring into private facts unrelated to alcohol or drug use. We recognize, however, that the procedures for collecting the necessary samples, which require employees to perform an excretory function traditionally shielded by great privacy, raise concerns not implicated by blood or breath tests. While we would not characterize these additional privacy concerns as minimal in most contexts, we note that the regulations endeavor to reduce the intrusiveness of the collection process. The regulations do not require that samples be furnished under the direct observation of a monitor, despite the desirability of such a procedure to ensure the integrity of the sample. . . . The sample is also collected in a medical environment, by personnel unrelated to the railroad employer, and is thus not unlike similar procedures encountered often in the context of a regular physical examination.

More importantly, the expectations of privacy of covered employees are diminished by reason of their participation in an industry that is regulated pervasively to ensure safety, a goal dependent, in substantial part, on the health and fitness of covered employees. This relation between safety and employee fitness was recognized by Congress when it enacted the Hours of Service Act in 1907 . . . and also when it authorized the Secretary to "test . . . railroad facilities, equipment, rolling stock, operations, *or persons*, as he deems necessary to carry out the provisions" of the Federal Railroad Safety Act of 1970. 45 U.S.C. § 437(a) (emphasis added). It has also been recognized by state governments, and has long been reflected in industry practice, as evidenced by the industry's promulgation and enforcement of Rule G. Indeed, the FRA found, and the Court of Appeals acknowledged, see 839 F.2d, at 585, that "most railroads require periodic physical examinations for train and engine employees and certain other employees." 49 Fed.Reg. 24278 (1984). . . .

We do not suggest, of course, that the interest in bodily security enjoyed by those employed in a regulated industry must always be considered minimal. Here, however, the covered employees have long been a principal focus of regulatory concern. As the dissenting judge below noted: "[t]he reason is obvious. An idle locomotive, sitting in the roundhouse, is harmless. It becomes lethal when operated negligently by persons who are under the influence of alcohol or drugs." 839 F.2d, at 593. Though some of the privacy interests implicated by the toxicological testing at issue reasonably might be viewed as significant in other contexts, logic and history show that a diminished expectation of privacy attaches to information relating to the physical condition of covered employees and to this reasonable means of procuring such information. We conclude, therefore, that the testing procedures contemplated by Subparts C and D pose only limited threats to the justifiable expectations of privacy of covered employees.

By contrast, the Government interest in testing without a showing of individualized suspicion is compelling. Employees subject to the tests discharge duties fraught with such risks of injury to others that even a momentary lapse of attention can have disastrous consequences. Much like persons who have routine access to dangerous nuclear power facilities ... employees who are subject to testing under the FRA regulations can cause great human loss before any signs of impairment become noticeable to supervisors or others. An impaired employee, the FRA found, will seldom display any outward "signs detectable by the lay person or, in many cases, even the physician." 50 Fed.Reg. 31526 (1985). This view finds ample support in the railroad industry's experience with Rule G, and in the judgment of the courts that have examined analogous testing schemes.... Indeed, while respondents posit that impaired employees might be detected without alcohol or drug testing, the premise of respondents' lawsuit is that even the occurrence of a major calamity will not give rise to a suspicion of impairment with respect to any particular employee.

While no procedure can identify all impaired employees with ease and perfect accuracy, the FRA regulations supply an effective means of deterring employees engaged in safety-sensitive tasks from using controlled substances or alcohol in the first place.... The railroad industry's experience with Rule G persuasively shows, and common sense confirms, that the customary dismissal sanction that threatens employees who use drugs or alcohol while on duty cannot serve as an effective deterrent unless violators know that they are likely to be discovered. By ensuring that employees in safety-sensitive positions know they will be tested upon the occurrence of a triggering event, the timing of which no employee can predict with certainty, the regulations significantly increase the deterrent effect of the administrative penalties associated with the prohibited conduct ... concomitantly increasing the likelihood that employees will forgo using drugs or alcohol while subject to being called for duty.

The testing procedures contemplated by Subpart C also help railroads obtain invaluable information about the causes of major accidents, see 50 Fed.Reg. 31541 (1985), and to take appropriate measures to safeguard the general public.... Positive test results would point toward drug or alcohol impairment on the part of members of the crew as a possible cause of an accident, and may help to establish whether a particular accident, otherwise not drug related, was made worse by the inability of impaired employees to respond appropriately. Negative test results would likewise furnish invaluable clues, for eliminating drug impairment as a potential cause or contributing factor would help establish the significance of equipment failure, inadequate training, or other potential causes, and suggest a more thorough examination of these alternatives. Tests performed following the rule violations specified in Subpart D likewise can provide valuable information respecting the causes of those transgressions, which the FRA found to involve "the potential for a serious train accident or grave personal injury, or both." 50 Fed.Reg. 31553 (1985).

A requirement of particularized suspicion of drug or alcohol use would seriously impede an employer's ability to obtain this information, despite its obvious importance. Experience confirms the FRA's judgment that the scene of a serious rail accident is chaotic. Investigators who arrive at the scene shortly after a major accident has occurred may find it difficult to determine which members of a train crew contributed to its occurrence. Obtaining evidence that might give rise to the suspicion that a particular employee is impaired, a difficult endeavor in the best of circumstances, is most impracticable in the aftermath of a serious accident. While events following the rule violations that activate the testing authority of Subpart D may be less chaotic, objective indicia of impairment are absent in these instances as well. Indeed, any attempt to gather evidence relating to the possible impairment of particular employees likely would result in the loss or deterioration of the evidence furnished by the tests. ... It would be unrealistic, and inimical to the Government's goal of ensuring safety in rail transportation, to require a showing of individualized suspicion in these circumstances.

Without quarreling with the importance of these governmental interests, the Court of Appeals concluded that the postaccident testing regulations were unreasonable because "[b]lood and urine tests intended to establish drug use other than alcohol ... cannot measure current drug intoxication or degree of impairment." 839 F.2d, at 588. The court based its conclusion on its reading of certain academic journals that indicate that the testing of urine can disclose only drug metabolites, which "may remain in the body for days or weeks after the ingestion of the drug." Id., at 589. We find this analysis flawed for several reasons.

As we emphasized in New Jersey v. T.L.O., "it is universally recognized that evidence, to be relevant to an inquiry, need not conclusively prove the ultimate fact in issue, but only have 'any tendency to make the existence of any fact that is of consequence to the determination [of the point in issue] more probable or less probable than it would be without the evidence.'" 469 U.S., at 345, quoting Fed.Rule Evid. 401. Even if urine test results disclosed nothing more specific than the recent use of controlled substances by a covered employee, this information would provide the basis for further investigative work designed to determine whether the employee used drugs at the relevant times. See Field Manual B–4. The record makes clear, for example, that a positive test result, coupled with known information concerning the pattern of elimination for the particular drug and information that may be gathered from other sources about the employee's activities, may allow the FRA to reach an informed judgment as to how a particular accident occurred.

More importantly, the Court of Appeals overlooked the FRA's policy of placing principal reliance on the results of blood tests, which unquestionably can identify very recent drug use, see, *e.g.*, 49 Fed.Reg. 24291 (1984), while relying on urine tests as a secondary source of information designed to guard against the possibility that certain drugs will be eliminated from the bloodstream before a blood sample can be obtained. The court also failed to recognize that the FRA regulations are designed not only to discern impairment but also to deter it. Because the record indicates that blood and urine tests, taken together, are highly effective means of ascertaining on-the-job impairment and of deterring the use of drugs by railroad employees, we believe the Court of Appeals erred in concluding that the post-accident testing regulations are not reasonably related to the Government objectives that support them.

We conclude that the compelling Government interests served by the FRA's regulations would be significantly hindered if railroads were required to point to specific facts giving rise to a reasonable suspicion of impairment before testing a given employee. In view of our conclusion that, on the present record, the toxicological testing contemplated by the regulations is not an undue infringement on the justifiable expectations of privacy of covered employees, the Government's compelling interests outweigh privacy concerns.

IV

The possession of unlawful drugs is a criminal offense that the Government may punish, but it is a separate and far more dangerous wrong to perform certain sensitive tasks while under the influence of those substances. Performing those tasks while impaired by alcohol is, of course, equally dangerous, though consumption of alcohol is legal in most other contexts. The Government may take all necessary and reasonable regulatory steps to prevent or deter that hazardous conduct, and since the gravamen of the evil is performing certain functions while concealing the substance in the body, it may be necessary, as in the case before us, to examine the body or its fluids to accomplish the regulatory purpose. The necessity to perform that regulatory function with respect to railroad employees engaged in safety-sensitive tasks, and the reasonableness of the system for doing so, have been established in this case.

Alcohol and drug tests conducted in reliance on the authority of Subpart D cannot be viewed as private action outside the reach of the Fourth Amendment. Because the testing procedures mandated or authorized by Subparts C and D effect searches of the person, they must meet the Fourth Amendment's reasonableness requirement. In light of the limited discretion exercised by the railroad employers under the regulations, the surpassing safety interests served by toxicological tests in this context, and the diminished expectation of privacy that attaches to information pertaining to the fitness of covered employees, we believe that it is reasonable to conduct such tests in the absence of a warrant or reasonable suspicion that any particular employee may be impaired. We hold that the alcohol and drug tests contemplated by Subparts C and D of the FRA's regulations are reasonable within the meaning of the Fourth Amendment. The judgment of the Court of Appeals is accordingly reversed.

It is so ordered.[*] [**]

[*] Justice Stevens wrote an opinion concurring in part and concurring in the judgment. Justice Marshall wrote a dissenting opinion, which Justice Brennan joined.

[**] In a companion case, National Treasury Employees Union v. Von Raab, 489 U.S. 656 (5–4), the Court upheld the U.S. Customs Service's program requiring drug tests by urinalysis of employees seeking assignment to positions involving the interdiction of drugs or the carrying of firearms. The Court remanded the case for determination whether, as applied to employees seeking assignment to positions involving the handling of classified information, the program identified the category of employees covered to include only employees likely to gain access to sensitive material.

CAMARA v. MUNICIPAL COURT OF THE CITY
AND COUNTY OF SAN FRANCISCO

387 U.S. 523, 87 S.Ct. 1727, 18 L.Ed.2d 930 (1967).

MR. JUSTICE WHITE delivered the opinion of the Court.

In Frank v. Maryland, 359 U.S. 360, this Court upheld, by a five-to-four vote, a state court conviction of a homeowner who refused to permit a municipal health inspector to enter and inspect his premises without a search warrant. In Easton v. Price, 364 U.S. 263, a similar conviction was affirmed by an equally divided Court. Since those closely divided decisions, more intensive efforts at all levels of government to contain and eliminate urban blight have led to increasing use of such inspection techniques, while numerous decisions of this Court have more fully defined the Fourth Amendment's effect on state and municipal action.... In view of the growing nationwide importance of the problem, we noted probable jurisdiction in this case ... to re-examine whether administrative inspection programs, as presently authorized and conducted, violate Fourth Amendment rights as those rights are enforced against the States through the Fourteenth Amendment. 385 U.S. 808.

Appellant brought this action in a California Superior Court alleging that he was awaiting trial on a criminal charge of violating the San Francisco Housing Code by refusing to permit a warrantless inspection of his residence, and that a writ of prohibition should issue to the criminal court because the ordinance authorizing such inspections is unconstitutional on its face. The Superior Court denied the writ, the District Court of Appeal affirmed, and the Supreme Court of California denied a petition for hearing. Appellant properly raised and had considered by the California courts the federal constitutional questions he now presents to this Court.

Though there were no judicial findings of fact in this prohibition proceeding, we shall set forth the parties' factual allegations. On November 6, 1963, an inspector of the Division of Housing Inspection of the San Francisco Department of Public Health entered an apartment building to make a routine annual inspection for possible violations of the city's Housing Code.[1] The building's manager informed the inspector that appellant, lessee of the ground floor, was using the rear of his leasehold as a personal residence.

---

1. The inspection was conducted pursuant to § 86(3) of the San Francisco Municipal Code, which provides that apartment house operators shall pay an annual license fee in part to defray the cost of periodic inspections of their buildings. The inspections are to be made by the Bureau of Housing Inspection "at least once a year and as often thereafter as may be deemed necessary." The permit of occupancy, which prescribes the apartment units which a building may contain, is not issued until the license is obtained.

Claiming that the building's occupancy permit did not allow residential use of the ground floor, the inspector confronted appellant and demanded that he permit an inspection of the premises. Appellant refused to allow the inspection because the inspector lacked a search warrant.

The inspector returned on November 8, again without a warrant, and appellant again refused to allow an inspection. A citation was then mailed ordering appellant to appear at the district attorney's office. When appellant failed to appear, two inspectors returned to his apartment on November 22. They informed appellant that he was required by law to permit an inspection under § 503 of the Housing Code:

> "Sec. 503 RIGHT TO ENTER BUILDING. Authorized employees of the City departments or City agencies, so far as may be necessary for the performance of their duties, shall, upon presentation of proper credentials, have the right to enter, at reasonable times, any building, structure, or premises in the City to perform any duty imposed upon them by the Municipal Code."

Appellant nevertheless refused the inspectors access to his apartment without a search warrant. Thereafter, a complaint was filed charging him with refusing to permit a lawful inspection in violation of § 507 of the Code. Appellant was arrested on December 2 and released on bail. When his demurrer to the criminal complaint was denied, appellant filed this petition for a writ of prohibition.

Appellant has argued throughout this litigation that § 503 is contrary to the Fourth and Fourteenth Amendments in that it authorizes municipal officials to enter a private dwelling without a search warrant and without probable cause to believe that a violation of the Housing Code exists therein. Consequently, appellant contends, he may not be prosecuted under § 507 for refusing to permit an inspection unconstitutionally authorized by § 503. Relying on Frank v. Maryland, Eaton v. Price, and decisions in other States, the District Court of Appeal held that § 503 does not violate Fourth Amendment rights because it "is part of a regulatory scheme which is essentially civil rather than criminal in nature, inasmuch as that section creates a right of inspection which is limited in scope and may not be exercised under unreasonable conditions." Having concluded that Frank v. Maryland, to the extent that it sanctioned such warrantless inspections, must be overruled, we reverse.

I.

The Fourth Amendment provides that, "The right of the people to be secure in their persons, houses, papers, and effects, against unreasonable searches and seizures, shall not be violated, and no Warrants shall issue, but upon probable cause, supported by Oath or affirmation, and particularly describing the place to be searched, and the persons or things to be seized." The basic purpose of this

Amendment, as recognized in countless decisions of this Court, is to safeguard the privacy and security of individuals against arbitrary invasions by governmental officials. The Fourth Amendment thus gives concrete expression to a right of the people which "is basic to a free society." Wolf v. Colorado, 338 U.S. 25, 27. As such, the Fourth Amendment is enforceable against the States through the Fourteenth Amendment. . . .

Though there has been general agreement as to the fundamental purpose of the Fourth Amendment, translation of the abstract prohibition against "unreasonable searches and seizures" into workable guidelines for the decision of particular cases is a difficult task which has for many years divided the members of this Court. Nevertheless, one governing principle, justified by history and by current experience, has consistently been followed: except in certain carefully defined classes of cases, a search of private property without proper consent is "unreasonable" unless it has been authorized by a valid search warrant. . . . As the Court explained in Johnson v. United States, 333 U.S. 10, 14:

> "The right of officers to thrust themselves into a home is also a grave concern, not only to the individual but to a society which chooses to dwell in reasonable security and freedom from surveillance. When the right of privacy must reasonably yield to the right of search is, as a rule, to be decided by a judicial officer, not by a policeman or government enforcement agent."

In Frank v. Maryland, this Court upheld the conviction of one who refused to permit a warrantless inspection of private premises for the purposes of locating and abating a suspected public nuisance. Although *Frank* can arguably be distinguished from this case on its facts, the *Frank* opinion has generally been interpreted as carving out an additional exception to the rule that warrantless searches are unreasonable under the Fourth Amendment. . . . The District Court of Appeal so interpreted *Frank* in this case, and that ruling is the core of appellant's challenge here. We proceed to a re-examination of the factors which persuaded the *Frank* majority to adopt this construction of the Fourth Amendment's prohibition against unreasonable searches.

To the *Frank* majority, municipal fire, health, and housing inspection programs "touch at most upon the periphery of the important interests safeguarded by the Fourteenth Amendment's protection against official intrusion," 359 U.S., at 367, because the inspections are merely to determine whether physical conditions exist which do not comply with minimum standards prescribed in local regulatory ordinances. Since the inspector does not ask that the property owner open his doors to a search for "evidence of criminal action" which may be used to secure the owner's criminal conviction, historic interests of "self-protection" jointly protected by the Fourth and Fifth Amendments are said not to be involved, but only the less intense "right to be secure from intrusion into personal privacy." Id., at 365.

We may agree that a routine inspection of the physical condition of private property is a less hostile intrusion than the typical policeman's search for the fruits and instrumentalities of crime. For this reason alone, *Frank* differed from the great bulk of Fourth Amendment cases which have been considered by this Court. But we cannot agree that the Fourth Amendment interests at stake in these inspection cases are merely "peripheral." It is surely anomalous to say that the individual and his private property are fully protected by the Fourth Amendment only when the individual is suspected of criminal behavior. For instance, even the most law-abiding citizen has a very tangible interest in limiting the circumstances under which the sanctity of his home may be broken by official authority, for the possibility of criminal entry under the guise of official sanction is a serious threat to personal and family security. And even accepting *Frank*'s rather remarkable premise, inspections of the kind we are here considering do in fact jeopardize "self-protection" interests of the property owner. Like most regulatory laws, fire, health, and housing codes are enforced by criminal processes. In some cities, discovery of a violation by the inspector leads to a criminal complaint. Even in cities where discovery of a violation produces only an administrative compliance order, refusal to comply is a criminal offense, and the fact of compliance is verified by a second inspection, again without a warrant. Finally, as this case demonstrates, refusal to permit an inspection is itself a crime, punishable by fine or even by jail sentence.

The *Frank* majority suggested, and appellee reasserts, two other justifications for permitting administrative health and safety inspections without a warrant. First, it is argued that these inspections are "designed to make the least possible demand on the individual occupant." 359 U.S., at 367. The ordinances authorizing inspections are hedged with safeguards, and at any rate the inspector's particular decision to enter must comply with the constitutional standard of reasonableness even if he may enter without a warrant. In addition, the argument proceeds, the warrant process could not function effectively in this field. The decision to inspect an entire municipal area is based upon legislative or administrative assessment of broad factors such as the area's age and condition. Unless the magistrate is to review such policy matters, he must issue a "rubber stamp" warrant which provides no protection at all to the property owner.

In our opinion, these arguments unduly discount the purposes behind the warrant machinery contemplated by the Fourth Amendment. Under the present system, when the inspector demands entry, the occupant has no way of knowing whether enforcement of the municipal code involved requires inspection of his premises, no way of knowing the lawful limits of the inspector's power to search, and no way of knowing whether the inspector himself is acting under proper authorization. These are questions which may be reviewed by a neutral magistrate without any reassessment of the basic agency decision to canvass an area. Yet, only by refusing entry and risking a criminal conviction can the occupant at present challenge the inspector's decision to search. And even if the occupant possesses sufficient fortitude to take this risk, as appellant did here, he may never learn any more about the reason for the inspection than that the law generally allows housing inspectors to gain entry. The practical effect of this system is to leave the occupant subject to the discretion of the official in the field. This is precisely the discretion to invade private property which we have consistently circumscribed by a requirement that a disinterested party warrant the need to search.... We simply cannot say that the protections provided by the warrant procedure are not needed in this context; broad statutory safeguards are no substitute for individualized review, particularly when those safeguards may only be invoked at the risk of a criminal penalty.

The final justification suggested for warrantless administrative searches is that the public interest demands such a rule: it is vigorously argued that the health and safety of entire urban populations is dependent upon enforcement of minimum fire, housing, and sanitation standards, and that the only effective means of enforcing such codes is by routine systematized inspection of all physical structures. Of course, in applying any reasonableness standard, including one of constitutional dimension, an argument that the public interest demands a particular rule must receive careful consideration. But we think this argument misses the mark. The question is not, at this stage at least, whether these inspections may be made, but whether they may be made without a warrant. For example, to say that gambling raids may not be made at the discretion of the police without a warrant is not necessarily to say that gambling raids may never be made. In assessing whether the public interest demands creation of a general exception to the Fourth Amendment's warrant requirement, the question is not whether the public interest justifies the type of search in question, but whether the authority to search should be evidenced by a warrant, which in turn depends in part upon whether the burden of obtaining a warrant is likely to frustrate the governmental purpose behind the search.... It has nowhere been urged that fire, health, and housing code inspection programs could not achieve their goals within the confines of a reasonable search warrant requirement. Thus, we do not find the public need argument dispositive.

In summary, we hold that administrative searches of the kind at issue here are significant intrusions upon the interests protected by the Fourth Amendment, that such searches when authorized and conducted without a warrant procedure lack the traditional safeguards which the Fourth Amendment guarantees to the individual, and that the reasons put forth in Frank v. Maryland and in other cases for upholding these warrantless searches are insufficient to justify so substantial a weakening of the Fourth Amendment's protections. Because of the nature of the municipal programs under consideration, however, these conclusions must be the beginning, not the end, of our inquiry. The *Frank* majority gave recognition to the unique character of these inspection programs by refusing to require search warrants; to reject that disposition does not justify ignoring the question whether some other accommodation between public need and individual rights is essential.

II.

The Fourth Amendment provides that, "no Warrants shall issue, but upon probable cause." Borrowing from more typical Fourth Amendment cases, appellant argues not only that code enforcement inspection programs must be circumscribed by a warrant procedure, but also that warrants should issue only when the inspector possesses probable cause to believe that a particular dwelling contains violations of the minimum standards prescribed by the code being enforced. We disagree.

In cases in which the Fourth Amendment requires that a warrant to search be obtained, "probable cause" is the standard by which a particular decision to search is tested against the constitutional mandate of reasonableness. To apply this standard, it is obviously necessary first to focus upon the governmental interest which allegedly justifies official intrusion upon the constitutionally protected interests of the private citizen. For example, in a criminal investigation, the police may undertake to recover specific stolen or contraband goods. But that public interest would hardly justify a sweeping search of an entire city conducted in the hope that these goods might be found. Consequently, a search for these goods, even with a warrant, is "reasonable" only when there is "probable cause" to believe that they will be uncovered in a particular dwelling.

Unlike the search pursuant to a criminal investigation, the inspection programs at issue here are aimed at securing city-wide compliance with minimum physical standards for private property. The primary governmental interest at stake is to prevent even the unintentional development of conditions which are hazardous to public health and safety. Because fires and epidemics may ravage large urban areas, because unsightly conditions adversely affect the economic values of neighboring structures, numerous courts have upheld the police power of municipalities to impose and enforce such minimum standards even upon existing structures. In determining whether a particular inspection is reasonable—and thus in determining whether there is probable cause to issue a warrant for that inspection—the need for the inspection must be weighed in terms of these reasonable goals of code enforcement.

There is unanimous agreement among those most familiar with this field that the only effective way to seek universal compliance with the minimum standards required by municipal codes is through routine periodic inspections of all structures. It is here that the probable cause debate is focused, for the agency's decision to conduct an area inspection is unavoidably based on its appraisal of conditions in the area as a whole, not on its knowledge of conditions in each particular building. Appellee contends that, if the probable cause standard urged by appellant is adopted, the area inspection will be eliminated as a means of seeking compliance with code standards and the reasonable goals of code enforcement will be dealt a crushing blow.

In meeting this contention, appellant argues first, that his probable cause standard would not jeopardize area inspection programs because only a minute portion of the population will refuse to consent to such inspections, and second, that individual privacy in any event should be given preference to the public interest in conducting such inspections. The first argument, even if true, is irrelevant to the question whether the area inspection is reasonable within the meaning of the Fourth Amendment. The second argument is in effect an assertion that the area inspection is an unreasonable search. Unfortunately, there can be no ready test for determining reasonableness other than by balancing the need to search against the invasion which the search entails. But we think that a number of persuasive factors combine to support the reasonableness of area code-enforcement inspections. First, such programs have a long history of judicial and public acceptance.... Second, the public interest demands that all dangerous conditions be prevented or abated, yet it is doubtful that any other canvassing technique would achieve acceptable results. Many such conditions—faulty wiring is an obvious example—are not observable from outside the building and indeed may not be apparent to the inexpert occupant himself. Finally, because the inspections are neither personal in nature nor aimed at the discovery of evidence of crime, they involve a relatively limited invasion of the urban citizen's privacy....

Having concluded that the area inspection is a "reasonable" search of private property within the meaning of the Fourth Amendment, it is obvious that "probable cause" to issue a warrant to inspect must exist if reasonable legislative or administrative standards for conducting an area inspection are satisfied with respect to a particular dwelling. Such standards, which will vary with the municipal program being enforced, may be based upon the passage of time, the nature of the building (e.g., a multi-family apartment house), or the condition of the entire area, but they will not necessarily depend upon specific knowledge of the condition of the particular dwelling. It has been suggested that so to vary the probable cause test from the standard applied in criminal cases would be to authorize a "synthetic search warrant" and thereby to lessen the overall protections of the Fourth Amendment. Frank v. Maryland, 359 U.S. at 373. But we do not agree. The warrant procedure is designed to guarantee that a decision to search private property is justified by a reasonable governmental interest. But reasonableness is still the ultimate standard. If a valid public interest justifies the intrusion contemplated, then there is probable cause to issue a suitably restricted search warrant.... Such an approach neither endangers time-honored doctrines applicable to criminal investigations nor makes a nullity of the probable cause requirement in this area. It merely gives full recognition to the competing public and private interests here at stake and, in so doing, best fulfills the historic purpose behind the constitutional right to be free from unreasonable government invasions of privacy....

III.

Since our holding emphasizes the controlling standard of reasonableness, nothing we say today is intended to foreclose prompt inspections, even without a warrant, that the law has traditionally upheld in emergency situations.... On the other hand, in the case of most routine area inspections, there is no compelling urgency to inspect at a particular time or on a particular day. Moreover, most citizens allow inspections of their property without a warrant. Thus, as a practical matter and in light of the Fourth Amendment's requirement that a warrant specify the property to be searched, it seems likely that warrants should normally be sought only after entry is refused unless there has been a citizen complaint or there is other satisfactory reason for securing immediate entry. Similarly, the requirement of a warrant procedure does not suggest any change in what seems to be the prevailing local policy, in most situations, of authorizing entry, but not entry by force, to inspect.

IV.

In this case, appellant has been charged with a crime for his refusal to permit housing inspectors to enter his leasehold without a warrant. There was no emergency demanding immediate access; in fact, the inspectors made three trips to the building in an attempt to obtain appellant's consent to search. Yet no warrant was obtained and thus appellant was unable to verify either the need for or the appropriate limits of the inspection. No doubt, the inspectors entered the public portion of the building with the consent of the landlord, through the building's manager, but appellee does not contend that such consent was sufficient to authorize inspection of appellant's premises.... Assuming the facts to be as the parties have alleged, we therefore conclude that appellant had a constitutional right to insist that the inspectors obtain a warrant to search and that appellant may not constitutionally be convicted for refusing to consent to the inspection. It appears from the opinion of the District Court of Appeal that under these circumstances a writ of prohibition will issue to the criminal court under California law.

The judgment is vacated and the case is remanded for further proceedings not inconsistent with this opinion.

It is so ordered.[*] [**]

[*] Justice Clark wrote a dissenting opinion, which Justice Harlan and Justice Stewart joined.

[**] In a companion case, See v. City of Seattle, 387 U.S. 541 (1967) (6–3), the Court held that *Camara* applies to commercial structures that are not used as private residences.

NEW YORK v. BURGER

482 U.S. 691, 107 S.Ct. 2636, 96 L.Ed.2d 601 (1987).

JUSTICE BLACKMUN delivered the opinion of the Court.

This case presents the question whether the warrantless search of an automobile junkyard, conducted pursuant to a statute authorizing such a search, falls within the exception to the warrant requirement for administrative inspections of pervasively regulated industries. The case also presents the question whether an otherwise proper administrative inspection is unconstitutional because the ultimate purpose of the regulatory statute pursuant to which the search is done—the deterrence of criminal behavior—is the same as that of penal laws, with the result that the inspection may disclose violations not only of the regulatory statute but also of the penal statutes.

I

Respondent Joseph Burger is the owner of a junkyard in Brooklyn, N.Y. His business consists, in part, of the dismantling of automobiles and the selling of their parts. His junkyard is an open lot with no buildings. A high metal fence surrounds it, wherein are located, among other things, vehicles and parts of vehicles. At approximately noon on November 17, 1982, Officer Joseph Vega and four other plainclothes officers, all members of the Auto Crimes Division of the New York City Police Department, entered respondent's junkyard to conduct an inspection pursuant to N.Y.Veh. & Traf.Law § 415–a5 (McKinney 1986). ... On any given day, the Division conducts from 5 to 10 inspections of vehicle dismantlers, automobile junkyards, and related businesses. ...

Upon entering the junkyard, the officers asked to see Burger's license and his "police book"—the record of the automobiles and vehicle parts in his possession. Burger replied that he had neither a license nor a police book. The officers then announced their intention to conduct a § 415–a5 inspection. Burger did not object. ... In accordance with their practice, the officers copied down the Vehicle Identification Numbers (VINs) of several vehicles and parts of vehicles that were in the junkyard. ... After checking these numbers against a police computer, the officers determined that respondent was in possession of stolen vehicles and parts. Accordingly, Burger was arrested and charged with five counts of possession of stolen property and one count of unregistered operation as a vehicle dismantler, in violation of § 415–a1.

In the Kings County Supreme Court, Burger moved to suppress the evidence obtained as a result of the inspection, primarily on the ground that § 415–a5 was unconstitutional. After a hearing, the court denied the motion. It reasoned that the junkyard business was a "pervasively regulated" industry in which warrantless administrative inspections were appropriate, that the statute was properly limited in "time, place and scope," and that, once the officers had reasonable cause to believe that certain vehicles and parts were stolen, they could arrest Burger and seize the property without a warrant. . . . [T]he Appellate Division affirmed. . . .

The New York Court of Appeals, however, reversed. 67 N.Y.2d 338, 493 N.E.2d 926 (1986). In its view, § 415–a5 violated the Fourth Amendment's prohibition of unreasonable searches and seizures. According to the Court of Appeals, "[t]he fundamental defect [of § 415–a5] . . . is that [it] authorize[s] searches undertaken solely to uncover evidence of criminality and not to enforce a comprehensive regulatory scheme. The asserted 'administrative schem[e]' here [is], in reality, designed simply to give the police an expedient means of enforcing penal sanctions for possession of stolen property." Id., at 344, 493 N.E.2d, at 929. . . .

Because of the important state interest in administrative schemes designed to regulate the vehicle-dismantling or automobile-junkyard industry, we granted certiorari. 479 U.S. 812 (1986).

II

A

The Court long has recognized that the Fourth Amendment's prohibition on unreasonable searches and seizures is applicable to commercial premises, as well as to private homes. . . . An owner or operator of a business thus has an expectation of privacy in commercial property, which society is prepared to consider to be reasonable . . . . This expectation exists not only with respect to traditional police searches conducted for the gathering of criminal evidence but also with respect to administrative inspections designed to enforce regulatory statutes. See Marshall v. Barlow's, Inc., 436 U.S. 307, 312–313 (1978). An expectation of privacy in commercial premises, however, is different from, and indeed less than, a similar expectation in an individual's home. . . . This expectation is particularly attenuated in commercial property employed in "closely regulated" industries. The Court observed in Marshall v. Barlow's, Inc.: "Certain industries have such a history of government oversight that no reasonable expectation of privacy . . . could exist for a proprietor over the stock of such an enterprise." 436 U.S., at 313.

The Court first examined the "unique" problem of inspections of "closely regulated" businesses in two enterprises that had "a long tradition of close government supervision." Ibid. In Colonnade Corp. v. United States, 397 U.S. 72 (1970), it considered a warrantless search of a catering business pursuant to several federal revenue statutes authorizing the inspection of the premises of liquor dealers. Although the Court disapproved the search because the statute provided that a sanction be imposed when entry was refused, and because it did not authorize entry without a warrant as an alternative in this situation, it recognized that "the liquor industry [was] long subject to close supervision and inspection." Id., at 77. We returned to this issue in United States v. Biswell, 406 U.S. 311 (1972), which involved a warrantless inspection of the premises of a pawnshop operator, who was federally licensed to sell sporting weapons pursuant to the Gun Control Act of 1968, 18 U.S.C. § 921 et seq. While noting that "[f]ederal regulation of the interstate traffic in firearms is not as deeply rooted in history as is governmental control of the liquor industry," 406 U.S., at 315, we nonetheless concluded that the warrantless inspections authorized by the Gun Control Act would "pose only limited threats to the dealer's justifiable expectations of privacy." Id., at 316. We observed: "When a dealer chooses to engage in this pervasively regulated business and to accept a federal license, he does so with the knowledge that his business records, firearms, and ammunition will be subject to effective inspection." Ibid.

The *"Colonnade–Biswell"* doctrine, stating the reduced expectation of privacy by an owner of commercial premises in a "closely regulated" industry, has received renewed emphasis in more recent decisions. In Marshall v. Barlow's, Inc., we noted its continued vitality but declined to find that warrantless inspections, made pursuant to the Occupational Safety and Health Act of 1970, 84 Stat. 1598, 29 U.S.C. § 657(a), of *all* businesses engaged in interstate commerce fell within the narrow focus of this doctrine. 436 U.S., at 313–314. However, we found warrantless inspections made pursuant to the Federal Mine Safety and Health Act of 1977, 91 Stat. 1290, 30 U.S.C. § 801 *et seq.,* proper because they were of a "closely regulated" industry. Donovan v. Dewey, [452 U.S. 594 (1981)].

Indeed, in Donovan v. Dewey, we declined to limit our consideration to the length of time during which the business in question—stone quarries—had been subject to federal regulation. . . . We pointed out that the doctrine is essentially defined by "the pervasiveness and regularity of the federal regulation" and the effect of such regulation upon an owner's expectation of privacy. See id., at 600, 606. We observed, however, that "the duration of a particular regulatory scheme" would remain an "important factor" in deciding whether a warrantless inspection pursuant to the scheme is permissible. Id., at 606.

B

Because the owner or operator of commercial premises in a "closely regulated" industry has a reduced expectation of privacy, the warrant and probable-cause requirements, which fulfill the traditional Fourth Amendment standard of reasonableness for a government search ... have lessened application in this context. Rather, we conclude that, as in other situations of "special need," see New Jersey v. T.L.O., 469 U.S. 325, 353 (1985) (opinion concurring in judgment), where the privacy interests of the owner are weakened and the government interests in regulating particular businesses are concomitantly heightened, a warrantless inspection of commercial premises may well be reasonable within the meaning of the Fourth Amendment.

This warrantless inspection, however, even in the context of a pervasively regulated business, will be deemed to be reasonable only so long as three criteria are met. First, there must be a "substantial" government interest that informs the regulatory scheme pursuant to which the inspection is made. See Donovan v. Dewey, 452 U.S., at 602 ("substantial federal interest in improving the health and safety conditions in the Nation's underground and surface mines"); United States v. Biswell, 406 U.S., at 315 (regulation of firearms is "of central importance to federal efforts to prevent violent crime and to assist the States in regulating the firearms traffic within their borders"); Colonnade Corp. v. United States, 397 U.S., at 75 (federal interest "in protecting the revenue against various types of fraud").

Second, the warrantless inspections must be "necessary to further [the] regulatory scheme." Donovan v. Dewey, 452 U.S., at 600. For example, in *Dewey* we recognized that forcing mine inspectors to obtain a warrant before every inspection might alert mine owners or operators to the impending inspection, thereby frustrating the purposes of the Mine Safety and Health Act—to detect and thus to deter safety and health violations. Id., at 603.

Finally, "the statute's inspection program, in terms of the certainty and regularity of its application, [must] provid[e] a constitutionally adequate substitute for a warrant." Ibid. In other words, the regulatory statute must perform the two basic functions of a warrant: it must advise the owner of the commercial premises that the search is being made pursuant to the law and has a properly defined scope, and it must limit the discretion of the inspecting officers. ... To perform this first function, the statute must be "sufficiently comprehensive and defined that the owner of commercial property cannot help but be aware that his property will be subject to periodic inspections undertaken for specific purposes." Donovan v. Dewey, 452 U.S., at 600. In addition, in defining how a statute limits the discretion of the inspectors, we have observed that it must be "carefully limited in time, place, and scope." United States v. Biswell, 406 U.S., at 315.

III

A

Searches made pursuant to § 415–a5, in our view, clearly fall within this established exception to the warrant requirement for administrative inspections in "closely regulated" businesses. First, the nature of the regulatory statute reveals that the operation of a junkyard, part of which is devoted to vehicle dismantling, is a "closely regulated" business in the State of New York. The provisions regulating the activity of vehicle dismantling are extensive. An operator cannot engage in this industry without first obtaining a license, which means that he must meet the registration requirements and must pay a fee. Under § 415–a5(a), the operator must maintain a police book recording the acquisition and disposition of motor vehicles and vehicle parts, and make such records and inventory available for inspection by the police or any agent of the Department of Motor Vehicles. The operator also must display his registration number prominently at his place of business, on business documentation, and on vehicles and parts that pass through his business. § 415–a5(b). Moreover, the person engaged in this activity is subject to criminal penalties, as well as to loss of license or civil fines, for failure to comply with these provisions. See §§ 415–a1, 5, and 6. That other States besides New York have imposed similarly extensive regulations on automobile junkyards further supports the "closely regulated" status of this industry. . . .

In determining whether vehicle dismantlers constitute a "closely regulated" industry, the "duration of [this] particular regulatory scheme," Donovan v. Dewey, 452 U.S., at 606, has some relevancy. Section 415–a could be said to be of fairly recent vintage, see 1973 N.Y.Laws, ch. 225, § 1 (McKinney), and the inspection provision of § 415–a5 was added only in 1979, see 1979 N.Y.Laws, ch. 691, § 2 (McKinney). But because the automobile is a relatively new phenomenon in our society and because its widespread use is even newer, automobile junkyards and vehicle dismantlers have not been in existence very long and thus do not have an ancient history of government oversight. Indeed, the industry did not attract government attention until the 1950's, when all used automobiles were no longer easily reabsorbed into the steel industry and attention then focused on the environmental and aesthetic problems associated with abandoned vehicles. . . .

The automobile-junkyard business, however, is simply a new branch of an industry that has existed, and has been closely regulated, for many years. The automobile junkyard is closely akin to the secondhand shop or the general junkyard. Both share the purpose of recycling salvageable articles and components of items no longer usable in their original form. As such, vehicle dismantlers represent a modern, specialized version of a traditional activity. In New York, general junkyards and secondhand shops long have been subject to regulation. . . . The history of government regulation of junk-related activities argues strongly in favor of the "closely regulated" status of the automobile junkyard.

Accordingly, in light of the regulatory framework governing his business and the history of regulation of related industries, an operator of a junkyard engaging in vehicle dismantling has a reduced expectation of privacy in this "closely regulated" business.

The New York regulatory scheme satisfies the three criteria necessary to make reasonable warrantless inspections pursuant to § 415–a5. First, the State has a substantial interest in regulating the vehicle-dismantling and automobile-junkyard industry because motor vehicle theft has increased in the State and because the problem of theft is associated with this industry. In this day, automobile theft has become a significant social problem, placing enormous economic and personal burdens upon the citizens of different States. . . . Because contemporary automobiles are made from standardized parts, the nation-wide extent of vehicle theft and concern about it are understandable.

Second, regulation of the vehicle-dismantling industry reasonably serves the State's substantial interest in eradicating automobile theft. It is well established that the theft problem can be addressed effectively by controlling the receiver of, or market in, stolen property. . . . Thus, the State rationally may believe that it will reduce car theft by regulations that prevent automobile junkyards from becoming markets for stolen vehicles and that help trace the origin and destination of vehicle parts.

Moreover, the warrantless administrative inspections pursuant to § 415–a5 "are necessary to further [the] regulatory scheme." Donovan v. Dewey, 452 U.S., at 600. In this respect, we see no difference between these inspections and those approved by the Court in United States v. Biswell and Donovan v. Dewey. We explained in *Biswell:*

> "[I]f inspection is to be effective and serve as a credible deterrent, unannounced, even frequent, inspections are essential. In this context, the prerequisite of a warrant could easily frustrate inspection; and if the necessary flexibility as to time, scope, and frequency is to be preserved, the protections afforded by a warrant would be negligible." 406 U.S., at 316.

. . . Similarly, in the present case, a warrant requirement would interfere with the statute's purpose of deterring automobile theft accomplished by identifying vehicles and parts as stolen and shutting down the market in such items. Because stolen cars and parts often pass quickly through an automobile junkyard, "frequent" and "unannounced" inspections are necessary in order to detect them. In sum, surprise is crucial if the regulatory scheme aimed at remedying this major social problem is to function at all.

Third, § 415–a5 provides a "constitutionally adequate substitute for a warrant." Donovan v. Dewey, 452 U.S., at 603. The statute informs the operator of a vehicle dismantling business that inspections will be made on a regular basis. . . . Thus, the vehicle dismantler knows that the inspections to which he is subject do not constitute discretionary acts by a government official but are conducted pursuant to statute. . . . Section 415–a5 also sets forth the scope of the inspection and, accordingly, places the operator on notice as to how to comply with the statute. In addition, it notifies the operator as to who is authorized to conduct an inspection.

Finally, the "time, place, and scope" of the inspection is limited, United States v. Biswell, 406 U.S., at 315, to place appropriate restraints upon the discretion of the inspecting officers. . . . The officers are allowed to conduct an inspection only "during [the] regular and usual business hours." § 415–a5. The inspections can be made only of vehicle-dismantling and related industries. And the permissible scope of these searches is narrowly defined: the inspectors may examine the records, as well as "any vehicles or parts of vehicles which are subject to the record keeping requirements of this section and which are on the premises." Ibid.

IV

A search conducted pursuant to § 415–a5, therefore, clearly falls within the well-established exception to the warrant requirement for administrative inspections of "closely regulated" businesses. The Court of Appeals, nevertheless, struck down the statute as violative of the Fourth Amendment because, in its view, the statute had no truly administrative purpose but was "designed simply to give the police an expedient means of enforcing penal sanctions for possession of stolen property." 67 N.Y.2d, at 344, 493 N.E.2d, at 929. The court rested its conclusion that the administrative goal of the statute was pretextual and that § 415–a5 really "authorize[d] searches undertaken solely to uncover evidence of criminality" particularly on the fact that, even if an operator failed to produce his police book, the inspecting officers could continue their inspection for stolen vehicles and parts. Id., at 344, 345, 493 N.E.2d, at 929, 930. The court also suggested that the identity of the inspectors—police officers—was significant in revealing the true nature of the statutory scheme. . . .

In arriving at this conclusion, the Court of Appeals failed to recognize that a State can address a major social problem *both* by way of an administrative scheme *and* through penal sanctions. Administrative statutes and penal laws may have the same *ultimate* purpose of remedying the social problem, but they have different subsidiary purposes and prescribe different methods of addressing the problem. An administrative statute establishes how a particular business in a "closely regulated" industry should be operated, setting forth rules to guide an operator's conduct of the business and allowing government officials to ensure that those rules are followed. Such a regulatory approach contrasts with that of the penal laws, a major emphasis of which is the punishment of individuals for specific acts of behavior.

In United States v. Biswell, we recognized this fact that both administrative and penal schemes can serve the same purposes by observing that the ultimate purposes of the Gun Control Act were "to prevent violent crime and to assist the States in regulating the firearms traffic within their borders." 406 U.S., at 315. It is beyond dispute that certain state penal laws had these same purposes. Yet the regulatory goals of the Gun Control Act were narrower: the Act ensured that "weapons [were] distributed through regular channels and in a traceable manner and [made] possible the prevention of sales to undesirable customers and the detection of the origin of particular firearms." Id., at 315–316. The provisions of the Act, including those authorizing the warrantless inspections, served these immediate goals and also contributed to achieving the same ultimate purposes that the penal laws were intended to achieve.

This case, too, reveals that an administrative scheme may have the same ultimate purpose as penal laws, even if its regulatory goals are narrower. As we have explained above, New York, like many States, faces a serious social problem in automobile theft and has a substantial interest in regulating the vehicle-dismantling industry because of this problem. The New York penal laws address automobile theft by punishing it or the possession of stolen property, including possession by individuals in the business of buying and selling property. ... In accordance with its interest in regulating the automobile-junkyard industry, the State also has devised a regulatory manner of dealing with this problem. Section 415–a, as a whole, serves the regulatory goals of seeking to ensure that vehicle dismantlers are legitimate businesspersons and that stolen vehicles and vehicle parts passing through automobile junkyards can be identified. In particular, § 415–a5 was designed to contribute to these goals .... Accordingly, to state that § 415–a5 is "really" designed to gather evidence to enable convictions under the penal laws is to ignore the plain administrative purposes of § 415–a, in general, and § 415–a5, in particular.

If the administrative goals of § 415–a5 are recognized, the difficulty the Court of Appeals perceives in allowing inspecting officers to examine vehicles and vehicle parts even in the absence of records evaporates. The regulatory purposes of § 415–a5 certainly are served by having the inspecting officers compare the records of a particular vehicle dismantler with vehicles and vehicle parts in the junkyard. The purposes of maintaining junkyards in the hands of legitimate businesspersons and of tracing vehicles that pass through these businesses, however, *also* are served by having the officers examine the operator's inventory even when the operator, for whatever reason, fails to produce the police book. Forbidding inspecting officers to examine the inventory in this situation would permit an illegitimate vehicle dismantler to thwart the purposes of the administrative scheme and would have the absurd result of subjecting his counterpart who maintained records to a more extensive search.

Nor do we think that this administrative scheme is unconstitutional simply because, in the course of enforcing it, an inspecting officer may discover evidence of crimes, besides violations of the scheme itself. . . .   The discovery of evidence of crimes in the course of an otherwise proper administrative inspection does not render that search illegal or the administrative scheme suspect. . . .

Finally, we fail to see any constitutional significance in the fact that police officers, rather than "administrative" agents, are permitted to conduct the § 415–a5 inspection. The significance respondent alleges lies in the role of police officers as enforcers of the penal laws and in the officers' power to arrest for offenses other than violations of the administrative scheme. It is, however, important to note that state police officers, like those in New York, have numerous duties in addition to those associated with traditional police work. . . .   As a practical matter, many States do not have the resources to assign the enforcement of a particular administrative scheme to a specialized agency. So long as a regulatory scheme is properly administrative, it is not rendered illegal by the fact that the inspecting officer has the power to arrest individuals for violations other than those created by the scheme itself. In sum, we decline to impose upon the States the burden of requiring the enforcement of their regulatory statutes to be carried out by specialized agents.

V

Accordingly, the judgment of the New York Court of Appeals is reversed, and the case is remanded to that court for further proceedings not inconsistent with this opinion.

It is so ordered.[*]

[*] Justice Brennan wrote a dissenting opinion, which Justice Marshall and Justice O'Connor joined.

WOLF v. COLORADO

338 U.S. 25, 69 S.Ct. 1359, 93 L.Ed. 1782 (1949).

MR. JUSTICE FRANKFURTER delivered the opinion of the Court.

The precise question for consideration is this: Does a conviction by a State court for a State offense deny the "due process of law" required by the Fourteenth Amendment, solely because evidence that was admitted at the trial was obtained under circumstances which would have rendered it inadmissible in a prosecution for violation of a federal law in a court of the United States because there deemed to be an infraction of the Fourth Amendment as applied in Weeks v. United States, 232 U.S. 383? The Supreme Court of Colorado has sustained convictions in which such evidence was admitted, 117 Col. 279, 187 P.2d 926; 117 Col. 321, 187 P.2d 928, and we brought the cases here. 333 U.S. 879.

Unlike the specific requirements and restrictions placed by the Bill of Rights (Amendments I to VIII) upon the administration of criminal justice by federal authority, the Fourteenth Amendment did not subject criminal justice in the States to specific limitations. The notion that the "due process of law" guaranteed by the Fourteenth Amendment is shorthand for the first eight amendments of the Constitution and thereby incorporates them has been rejected by this Court again and again, after impressive consideration.... Only the other day the Court reaffirmed this rejection after thorough reexamination of the scope and function of the Due Process Clause of the Fourteenth Amendment. Adamson v. California, 332 U.S. 46. The issue is closed.

For purposes of ascertaining the restrictions which the Due Process Clause imposed upon the States in the enforcement of their criminal law, we adhere to the views expressed in Palko v. Connecticut, supra, 302 U.S. 319. That decision speaks to us with the great weight of the authority, particularly in matters of civil liberty, of a court that included Mr. Chief Justice Hughes, Mr. Justice Brandeis, Mr. Justice Stone and Mr. Justice Cardozo, to name only the dead. In rejecting the suggestion that the Due Process Clause incorporated the original Bill of Rights, Mr. Justice Cardozo reaffirmed on behalf of that Court a different but deeper and more pervasive conception of the Due Process Clause. This Clause exacts from the States for the lowliest and the most outcast all that is "implicit in the concept of ordered liberty." 302 U.S. at 325.

Due process of law thus conveys neither formal nor fixed nor narrow requirements. It is the compendious expression for all those rights which the courts must enforce because they are basic to our free society. But basic rights do not become petrified as of any one time, even though, as a matter of human experience, some may not too rhetorically be called eternal verities. It is of the very nature of a free society to advance in its standards of what is deemed reasonable and right. Representing as it does a living principle, due process is not confined within a permanent catalogue of what may at a given time be deemed the limits or the essentials of fundamental rights.

To rely on a tidy formula for the easy determination of what is a fundamental right for purposes of legal enforcement may satisfy a longing for certainty but ignores the movements of a free society. It belittles the scale of the conception of due process. The real clue to the problem confronting the judiciary in the application of the Due Process Clause is not to ask where the line is once and for all to be drawn but to recognize that it is for the Court to draw it by the gradual and empiric process of "inclusion and exclusion." Davidson v. New Orleans, 96 U.S. 97, 104. This was the Court's insight when first called upon to consider the problem; to this insight the Court has on the whole been faithful as case after case has come before it since Davidson v. New Orleans was decided.

The security of one's privacy against arbitrary intrusion by the police—which is at the core of the Fourth Amendment—is basic to a free society. It is therefore implicit in "the concept of ordered liberty" and as such enforceable against the States through the Due Process Clause. The knock at the door, whether by day or by night, as a prelude to a search, without authority of law but solely on the authority of the police, did not need the commentary of recent history to be condemned as inconsistent with the conception of human rights enshrined in the history and the basic constitutional documents of English-speaking peoples.

Accordingly, we have no hesitation in saying that were a State affirmatively to sanction such police incursion into privacy it would run counter to the guaranty of the Fourteenth Amendment. But the ways of enforcing such a basic right raise questions of a different order. How such arbitrary conduct should be checked, what remedies against it should be afforded, the means by which the right should be made effective, are all questions that are not to be so dogmatically answered as to preclude the varying solutions which spring from an allowable range of judgment on issues not susceptible of quantitative solution.

In Weeks v. United States, supra, this Court held that in a federal prosecution the Fourth Amendment barred the use of evidence secured through an illegal search and seizure. This ruling was made for the first time in 1914. It was not derived from the explicit requirements of the Fourth Amendment; it was not based on legislation expressing Congressional policy in the enforcement of the Constitution. The decision was a matter of judicial implication. Since then it has been frequently applied and we stoutly adhere to it. But the immediate question is whether the basic right to protection against arbitrary intrusion by the police demands the exclusion of logically relevant evidence obtained by an unreasonable search and seizure because, in a federal prosecution for a federal crime, it would be excluded. As a matter of inherent reason, one would suppose this to be an issue as to which men with complete devotion to the protection of the right of privacy might give different answers. When we find that in fact most of the English-speaking world does not regard as vital to such protection the exclusion of evidence thus obtained, we must hesitate to treat this remedy as an essential ingredient of the right. The contrariety of views of the States is particularly impressive in view of the careful reconsideration which they have given the problem in the light of the *Weeks* decision.

I. Before the *Weeks* decision 27 States had passed on the admissibility of evidence obtained by unlawful search and seizure.

   (a) Of these, 26 States opposed the *Weeks* doctrine. (See Appendix, Table A.)

   (b) Of these, 1 State anticipated the *Weeks* doctrine. (Table B.)

II. Since the *Weeks* decision 47 States all told have passed on the *Weeks* doctrine. (Table C.)

   (a) Of these, 20 passed on it for the first time.

      (1) Of the foregoing States, 6 followed the *Weeks* doctrine. (Table D.)

      (2) Of the foregoing States, 14 rejected the *Weeks* doctrine. (Table E.)

   (b) Of these, 26 States reviewed prior decisions contrary to the *Weeks* doctrine.

      (1) Of these, 10 States have followed *Weeks*, overruling or distinguishing their prior decisions. (Table F.)

      (2) Of these, 16 States adhered to their prior decisions against *Weeks*. (Table G.)

   (c) Of these, 1 State repudiated its prior formulation of the *Weeks* doctrine. (Table H.)

III. As of today 31 States reject the *Weeks* doctrine, 16 States are in agreement with it. (Table I.)

IV. Of 10 jurisdictions within the United Kingdom and the British Commonwealth of Nations which have passed on the question, none has held evidence obtained by illegal search and seizure inadmissible. (Table J.)

The jurisdictions which have rejected the *Weeks* doctrine have not left the right to privacy without other means of protection.

Indeed, the exclusion of evidence is a remedy which directly serves only to protect those upon whose person or premises something incriminating has been found. We cannot, therefore, regard it as a departure from basic standards to remand such persons, together with those who emerge scatheless from a search, to the remedies of private action and such protection as the internal discipline of the police, under the eyes of an alert public opinion, may afford. Granting that in practice the exclusion of evidence may be an effective way of deterring unreasonable searches, it is not for this Court to condemn as falling below the minimal standards assured by the Due Process Clause a State's reliance upon other methods which, if consistently enforced, would be equally effective. Weighty testimony against such an insistence on our own view is furnished by the opinion of Mr. Justice (then Judge) Cardozo in People v. Defore, 242 N.Y. 13, 150 N.E. 585. We cannot brush aside the experience of States which deem the incidence of such conduct by the police too slight to call for a deterrent remedy not by way of disciplinary measures but by overriding the relevant rules of evidence. There are, moreover, reasons for excluding evidence unreasonably obtained by the federal police which are less compelling in the case of police under State or local authority. The public opinion of a community can far more effectively be exerted against oppressive conduct on the part of police directly responsible to the community itself than can local opinion, sporadically aroused, be brought to bear upon remote authority pervasively exerted throughout the country.

We hold, therefore, that in a prosecution in a State court for a State crime the Fourteenth Amendment does not forbid the admission of evidence obtained by an unreasonable search and seizure. And though we have interpreted the Fourth Amendment to forbid the admission of such evidence, a different question would be presented if Congress under its legislative powers were to pass a statute purporting to negate the *Weeks* doctrine. We would then be faced with the problem of the respect to be accorded the legislative judgment on an issue as to which, in default of that judgment, we have been forced to depend upon our own. Problems of a converse character, also not before us, would be presented should Congress under § 5 of the Fourteenth Amendment undertake to enforce the rights there guaranteed by attempting to make the *Weeks* doctrine binding upon the States.

Affirmed.

. . . [Appendix omitted.]

MR. JUSTICE MURPHY, with whom MR. JUSTICE RUTLEDGE joins, dissenting.

It is disheartening to find so much that is right in an opinion which seems to me so fundamentally wrong. Of course I agree with the Court that the Fourteenth Amendment prohibits activities which are proscribed by the search and seizure clause of the Fourth Amendment. . . . Quite apart from the blanket application of the Bill of Rights to the States, a devotee of democracy would ill suit his name were he to suggest that his home's protection against unlicensed governmental invasion was not "of the very essence of a scheme of ordered liberty." Palko v. Connecticut, 302 U.S. 319, 325. It is difficult for me to understand how the Court can go this far and yet be unwilling to make the step which can give some meaning to the pronouncements it utters.

Imagination and zeal may invent a dozen methods to give content to the commands of the Fourth Amendment. But this Court is limited to the remedies currently available. It cannot legislate the ideal system. If we would attempt the enforcement of the search and seizure clause in the ordinary case today, we are limited to three devices: judicial exclusion of the illegally obtained evidence; criminal prosecution of violators; and civil action against violators in the action of trespass.

Alternatives are deceptive. Their very statement conveys the impression that one possibility is as effective as the next. In this case their statement is blinding. For there is but one alternative to the rule of exclusion. That is no sanction at all.

This has been perfectly clear since 1914, when a unanimous Court decided Weeks v. United States, 232 U.S. 383, 393. "If letters and private documents can thus be seized and held and used in evidence against a citizen accused of an offense," we said, "the protection of the Fourth Amendment declaring his right to be secure against such searches and seizures is of no value, and, so far as those thus placed are concerned, might as well be stricken from the Constitution." "It reduces the Fourth Amendment to a form of words." Holmes, J., for the Court, in Silverthorne Lumber Co. v. United States, 251 U.S. 385, 392.

Today the Court wipes those statements from the books with its bland citation of "other remedies." Little need be said concerning the possibilities of criminal prosecution. Self-scrutiny is a lofty ideal, but its exaltation reaches new heights if we expect a District Attorney to prosecute himself or his associates for well-meaning violations of the search and seizure clause during a raid the District Attorney or his associates have ordered. But there is an appealing ring in another alternative. A trespass action for damages is a venerable means of securing reparation for unauthorized invasion of the home. Why not put the old writ to a new use? When the Court cites cases permitting the action, the remedy seems complete.

But what an illusory remedy this is, if by "remedy" we mean a positive deterrent to police and prosecutors tempted to violate the Fourth Amendment. The appealing ring softens when we recall that in a trespass action the measure of damages is simply the extent of the injury to physical property. If the officer searches with care, he can avoid all but nominal damages—a penny, or a dollar. Are punitive damages possible? Perhaps. But a few states permit none, whatever the circumstances. In those that do, the plaintiff must show the real ill will or malice of the defendant and surely it is not unreasonable to assume that one in honest pursuit of crime bears no malice toward the search victim. If that burden is carried, recovery may yet be defeated by the rule that there must be physical damages before punitive damages may be awarded. In addition, some states limit punitive damages to the actual expenses of litigation.... Others demand some arbitrary ratio between actual and punitive damages before a verdict may stand.... Even assuming the ill will of the officer, his reasonable grounds for belief that the home he searched harbored evidence of crime is admissible in mitigation of punitive damages.... The bad reputation of the plaintiff is likewise admissible.... If the evidence seized was actually used at a trial, that fact has been held a complete justification of the search, and a defense against the trespass action.... And even if the plaintiff hurdles all these obstacles, and gains a substantial verdict, the individual officer's finances may well make the judgment useless—for the municipality, of course, is not liable without its consent. Is it surprising that there is so little in the books concerning trespass actions for violation of the search and seizure clause?

The conclusion is inescapable that but one remedy exists to deter violations of the search and seizure clause. That is the rule which excludes illegally obtained evidence. Only by exclusion can we impress upon the zealous prosecutor that violation of the Constitution will do him no good. And only when that point is driven home can the prosecutor be expected to emphasize the importance of observing constitutional demands in his instructions to the police.

.   .   .

I cannot believe that we should decide due process questions by simply taking a poll of the rules in various jurisdictions, even if we follow the *Palko* "test." Today's decision will do inestimable harm to the cause of fair police methods in our cities and states. Even more important, perhaps, it must have tragic effect upon public respect for our judiciary. For the Court now allows what is indeed shabby business: lawlessness by officers of the law.

Since the evidence admitted was secured in violation of the Fourth Amendment, the judgment should be reversed.[*]

[*] Justice Black wrote a concurring opinion. Justice Douglas and Justice Rutledge wrote dissenting opinions.

MAPP v. OHIO

367 U.S. 643, 81 S.Ct. 1684, 6 L.Ed.2d 1081 (1961).

MR. JUSTICE CLARK delivered the opinion of the Court.

Appellant stands convicted of knowingly having had in her possession and under her control certain lewd and lascivious books, pictures, and photographs in violation of § 2905.34 of Ohio's Revised Code. As officially stated in the syllabus to its opinion, the Supreme Court of Ohio found that her conviction was valid though "based primarily upon the introduction in evidence of lewd and lascivious books and pictures unlawfully seized during an unlawful search of defendant's home ...." 170 Ohio St. 427–428, 166 N.E.2d 387, 388.

On May 23, 1957, three Cleveland police officers arrived at appellant's residence in that city pursuant to information that "a person [was] hiding out in the home, who was wanted for questioning in connection with a recent bombing, and that there was a large amount of policy paraphernalia being hidden in the home." Miss Mapp and her daughter by a former marriage lived on the top floor of the two-family dwelling. Upon their arrival at that house, the officers knocked on the door and demanded entrance but appellant, after telephoning her attorney, refused to admit them without a search warrant. They advised their headquarters of the situation and undertook a surveillance of the house.

The officers again sought entrance some three hours later when four or more additional officers arrived on the scene. When Miss Mapp did not come to the door immediately, at least one of the several doors to the house was forcibly opened [2] and the policemen gained admittance. Meanwhile Miss Mapp's attorney arrived, but the officers, having secured their own entry, and continuing in their defiance of the law, would permit him neither to see Miss Mapp nor to enter the house. It appears that Miss Mapp was halfway down the stairs from the upper floor to the front door when the officers, in this highhanded manner, broke into the hall. She demanded to see the search warrant. A paper, claimed to be a warrant, was held up by one of the officers. She grabbed the "warrant" and placed it in her bosom. A struggle ensued in which the officers recovered the piece of paper and as a result of which they handcuffed appellant because she had been "belligerent" in resisting their official rescue of the "warrant" from her person. Running rough-

---

2. A police officer testified that "we did pry the screen door to gain entrance"; the attorney on the scene testified that a policeman "tried ... to kick in the door" and then "broke the glass in the door and somebody reached in and opened the door and let them in"; the appellant testified that "The back door was broken."

323

shod over appellant, a policeman "grabbed" her, "twisted [her] hand," and she "yelled [and] pleaded with him" because "it was hurting." Appellant, in handcuffs, was then forcibly taken upstairs to her bedroom where the officers searched a dresser, a chest of drawers, a closet and some suitcases. They also looked into a photo album and through personal papers belonging to the appellant. The search spread to the rest of the second floor including the child's bedroom, the living room, the kitchen and a dinette. The basement of the building and a trunk found therein were also searched. The obscene materials for possession of which she was ultimately convicted were discovered in the course of that widespread search.

At the trial no search warrant was produced by the prosecution, nor was the failure to produce one explained or accounted for. At best, "There is, in the record, considerable doubt as to whether there ever was any warrant for the search of defendant's home." 170 Ohio St., at 430, 166 N.E.2d, at 389. The Ohio Supreme Court believed a "reasonable argument" could be made that the conviction should be reversed "because the 'methods' employed to obtain the [evidence] . . . were such as to 'offend "a sense of justice," ' " but the court found determinative the fact that the evidence had not been taken "from defendant's person by the use of brutal or offensive physical force against defendant." 170 Ohio St., at 431, 166 N.E.2d, at 389–390.

The State says that even if the search were made without authority, or otherwise unreasonably, it is not prevented from using the unconstitutionally seized evidence at trial, citing Wolf v. Colorado, 338 U.S. 25 (1949), in which this Court did indeed hold "that in a prosecution in a State court for a State crime the Fourteenth Amendment does not forbid the admission of evidence obtained by an unreasonable search and seizure." At p. 33. On this appeal, of which we have noted probable jurisdiction, 364 U.S. 868, it is urged once again that we review that holding.

I

Seventy-five years ago, in Boyd v. United States, 116 U.S. 616, 630 (1886), considering the Fourth and Fifth Amendments as running "almost into each other" on the facts before it, this Court held that the doctrines of those Amendments

> "apply to all invasions on the part of the government and its employés of the sanctity of a man's home and the privacies of life. It is not the breaking of his doors, and the rummaging of his drawers, that constitutes the essence of the offence; but it is the invasion of his indefeasible right of personal security, personal liberty and private property . . . Breaking into a house and opening boxes and drawers are circumstances of aggravation; but any forcible and compulsory extortion of a man's own testimony or of his private papers to be used as evidence to

convict him of crime or to forfeit his goods, is within the condemnation ... [of those Amendments]."

The Court noted that

"constitutional provisions for the security of person and property should be liberally construed. .... It is the duty of courts to be watchful for the constitutional rights of the citizen, and against any stealthy encroachments thereon." At p. 635.

In this jealous regard for maintaining the integrity of individual rights, the Court gave life to Madison's prediction that "independent tribunals of justice ... will be naturally led to resist every encroachment upon rights expressly stipulated for in the Constitution by the declaration of rights." I Annals of Cong. 439 (1789). Concluding, the Court specifically referred to the use of the evidence there seized as "unconstitutional." At p. 638.

Less than 30 years after *Boyd,* this Court, in Weeks v. United States, 232 U.S. 383 (1914), stated that

"the Fourth Amendment ... put the courts of the United States and Federal officials, in the exercise of their power and authority, under limitations and restraints [and] ... forever secure[d] the people, their persons, houses, papers and effects against all unreasonable searches and seizures under the guise of law ... and the duty of giving to it force and effect is obligatory upon all entrusted under our Federal system with the enforcement of the laws." At pp. 391–392.

Specifically dealing with the use of the evidence unconstitutionally seized, the Court concluded:

"If letters and private documents can thus be seized and held and used in evidence against a citizen accused of an offense, the protection of the Fourth Amendment declaring his right to be secure against such searches and seizures is of no value, and, so far as those thus placed are concerned, might as well be stricken from the Constitution. The efforts of the courts and their officials to bring the guilty to punishment, praiseworthy as they are, are not to be aided by the sacrifice of those great principles established by years of endeavor and suffering which have resulted in their embodiment in the fundamental law of the land." At p. 393.

Finally, the Court in that case clearly stated that use of the seized evidence involved "a denial of the constitutional rights of the accused." At p. 398. Thus, in the year 1914, in the *Weeks* case, this Court "for the first time" held that "in a federal prosecution the Fourth Amendment barred the use of evidence secured through an illegal search and seizure." Wolf v. Colorado, supra, at 28. This Court has ever since required of federal law officers a strict adherence to that command which this Court has held to be a clear, specific, and constitutionally required—even if judicially implied—

deterrent safeguard without insistence upon which the Fourth Amendment would have been reduced to "a form of words." Holmes, J., Silverthorne Lumber Co. v. United States, 251 U.S. 385, 392 (1920). It meant, quite simply, that "conviction by means of unlawful seizures and enforced confessions ... should find no sanction in the judgments of the courts ...," Weeks v. United States, supra, at 392, and that such evidence "shall not be used at all." Silverthorne Lumber Co. v. United States, supra, at 392.

There are in the cases of this Court some passing references to the *Weeks* rule as being one of evidence. But the plain and unequivocal language of *Weeks* —and its later paraphrase in *Wolf* — to the effect that the *Weeks* rule is of constitutional origin, remains entirely undisturbed. ...

II

In 1949, 35 years after *Weeks* was announced, this Court, in Wolf v. Colorado, supra, again for the first time, discussed the effect of the Fourth Amendment upon the States through the operation of the Due Process Clause of the Fourteenth Amendment. It said:

> "[W]e have no hesitation in saying that were a State affirmative-ly to sanction such police incursion into privacy it would run counter to the guaranty of the Fourteenth Amendment." At p. 28.

Nevertheless, after declaring that the "security of one's privacy against arbitrary intrusion by the police" is "implicit in 'the concept of ordered liberty' and as such enforceable against the States through the Due Process Clause," cf. Palko v. Connecticut, 302 U.S. 319 (1937), and announcing that it "stoutly adhere[d]" to the *Weeks* decision, the Court decided that the *Weeks* exclusionary rule would not then be imposed upon the States as "an essential ingredient of the right." 338 U.S., at 27–29. The Court's reasons for not considering essential to the right to privacy, as a curb imposed upon the States by the Due Process Clause, that which decades before had been posited as part and parcel of the Fourth Amendment's limitation upon federal encroachment of individual privacy, were bottomed on factual considerations.

While they are not basically relevant to a decision that the exclusionary rule is an essential ingredient of the Fourth Amend-ment as the right it embodies is vouchsafed against the States by the Due Process Clause, we will consider the current validity of the factual grounds upon which *Wolf* was based.

The Court in *Wolf* first stated that "[t]he contrariety of views of the States" on the adoption of the exclusionary rule of *Weeks* was "particularly impressive" (at p. 29); and, in this connection, that it could not "brush aside the experience of States which deem the incidence of such conduct by the police too slight to call for a deterrent remedy ... by overriding the [States'] relevant rules of evidence." At pp. 31–32. While in 1949, prior to the *Wolf* case, almost two-thirds of the States were opposed to the use of the exclusionary rule, now, despite the *Wolf* case, more than half of those since passing upon it, by their own legislative or judicial decision, have wholly or partly adopted or adhered to the *Weeks* rule.... Significantly, among those now following the rule is California, which, according to its highest court, was "compelled to reach that conclusion because other remedies have completely failed to secure compliance with the constitutional provisions ...." People v. Cahan, 44 Cal.2d 434, 445, 282 P.2d 905, 911 (1955). In connection with this California case, we note that the second basis elaborated in *Wolf* in support of its failure to enforce the exclusionary doctrine against the States was that "other means of protection" have been afforded "the right to privacy." 338 U.S., at 30. The experience of California that such other remedies have been worthless and futile is buttressed by the experience of other States. The obvious futility of relegating the Fourth Amendment to the protection of other remedies has, moreover, been recognized by this Court since *Wolf*....

Likewise, time has set its face against what *Wolf* called the "weighty testimony" of People v. Defore, 242 N.Y. 13, 150 N.E. 585 (1926). There Justice (then Judge) Cardozo, rejecting adoption of the *Weeks* exclusionary rule in New York, had said that "[t]he Federal rule as it stands is either too strict or too lax." 242 N.Y., at 22, 150 N.E., at 588. However, the force of that reasoning has been largely vitiated by later decisions of this Court. These include the recent discarding of the "silver platter" doctrine which allowed federal judicial use of evidence seized in violation of the Constitution by state agents ... the relaxation of the formerly strict requirements as to standing to challenge the use of evidence thus seized, so that now the procedure of exclusion, "ultimately referable to constitutional safeguards," is available to anyone even "legitimately on [the] premises" unlawfully searched, Jones v. United States, 362 U.S. 257, 266–267 (1960); and, finally, the formulation of a method to prevent state use of evidence unconstitutionally seized by federal agents.... Because there can be no fixed formula, we are admittedly met with "recurring questions of the reasonableness of searches," but less is not to be expected when dealing with a Constitution, and, at any rate, "[r]easonableness is in the first instance for the [trial court] ... to determine." United States v. Rabinowitz, 339 U.S. 56, 63 (1950).

It, therefore, plainly appears that the factual considerations supporting the failure of the *Wolf* Court to include the *Weeks* exclusionary rule when it recognized the enforceability of the right to privacy against the States in 1949, while not basically relevant to the constitutional consideration, could not, in any analysis, now be deemed controlling.

III

Some five years after *Wolf,* in answer to a plea made here Term after Term that we overturn its doctrine on applicability of the *Weeks* exclusionary rule, this Court indicated that such should not be done until the States had "adequate opportunity to adopt or reject the [*Weeks*] rule." Irvine v. California, [347 U.S. 128 (1954)], at 134. There again it was said:

> "Never until June of 1949 did this Court hold the basic search-and-seizure prohibition in any way applicable to the states under the Fourteenth Amendment." Id.

And only last Term, after again carefully re-examining the *Wolf* doctrine in Elkins v. United States, [364 U.S. 206 (1960)], the Court pointed out that "the controlling principles" as to search and seizure and the problem of admissibility "seemed clear" (at p. 212) until the announcement in *Wolf* "that the Due Process Clause of the Fourteenth Amendment does not itself require state courts to adopt the exclusionary rule" of the *Weeks* case. At p. 213. At the same time, the Court pointed out, "the underlying constitutional doctrine which *Wolf* established . . . that the Federal Constitution . . . prohibits unreasonable searches and seizures by state officers" had undermined the "foundation upon which the admissibility of state-seized evidence in a federal trial originally rested . . . ." Ibid. The Court concluded that it was therefore obliged to hold, although it chose the narrower ground on which to do so, that all evidence obtained by an unconstitutional search and seizure was inadmissible in a federal court regardless of its source. Today we once again examine *Wolf's* constitutional documentation of the right to privacy free from unreasonable state intrusion, and, after its dozen years on our books, are led by it to close the only courtroom door remaining open to evidence secured by official lawlessness in flagrant abuse of that basic right, reserved to all persons as a specific guarantee against that very same unlawful conduct. We hold that all evidence obtained by searches and seizures in violation of the Constitution is, by that same authority, inadmissible in a state court.

IV

Since the Fourth Amendment's right of privacy has been declared enforceable against the States through the Due Process Clause of the Fourteenth, it is enforceable against them by the same sanction of exclusion as is used against the Federal Government. Were it otherwise, then just as without the *Weeks* rule the assurance against unreasonable federal searches and seizures would be "a form of words," valueless and undeserving of mention in a perpetual charter of inestimable human liberties, so too, without that rule the freedom from state invasions of privacy would be so ephemeral and so neatly severed from its conceptual nexus with the freedom from all brutish means of coercing evidence as not to merit this Court's high regard as a freedom "implicit in the concept of ordered liberty." At the time that the Court held in *Wolf* that the Amendment was applicable to the States through the Due Process Clause, the cases of this Court, as we have seen, had steadfastly held that as to federal officers the Fourth Amendment included the exclusion of the evidence seized in violation of its provisions. Even *Wolf* "stoutly adhered" to that proposition. The right to privacy, when conceded operatively enforceable against the States, was not susceptible of destruction by avulsion of the sanction upon which its protection and enjoyment had always been deemed dependent under the *Boyd, Weeks* and *Silverthorne* cases. Therefore, in extending the substantive protections of due process to all constitutionally unreasonable searches—state or federal—it was logically and constitutionally necessary that the exclusion doctrine—an essential part of the right to privacy—be also insisted upon as an essential ingredient of the right newly recognized by the *Wolf* case. In short, the admission of the new constitutional right by *Wolf* could not consistently tolerate denial of its most important constitutional privilege, namely, the exclusion of the evidence which an accused had been forced to give by reason of the unlawful seizure. To hold otherwise is to grant the right but in reality to withhold its privilege and enjoyment. Only last year the Court itself recognized that the purpose of the exclusionary rule "is to deter—to compel respect for the constitutional guaranty in the only effectively available way—by removing the incentive to disregard it." Elkins v. United States, supra, at 217.

Indeed, we are aware of no restraint, similar to that rejected today, conditioning the enforcement of any other basic constitutional right. The right to privacy, no less important than any other right carefully and particularly reserved to the people, would stand in marked contrast to all other rights declared as "basic to a free society." Wolf v. Colorado, supra, at 27. This Court has not hesitated to enforce as strictly against the States as it does against the Federal Government the rights of free speech and of a free press, the rights to notice and to a fair, public trial, including, as it does, the right not to be convicted by use of a coerced confession, however logically relevant it be, and without regard to its reliability.... And nothing could be more certain than that when a coerced confession is involved, "the relevant rules of evidence" are overridden without regard to "the incidence of such conduct by the police," slight or frequent. Why should not the same rule apply to what is tantamount to coerced testimony by way of unconstitutional seizure of goods, papers, effects, documents, etc.? We find that, as to the Federal Government, the Fourth and Fifth Amendments and, as to the States, the freedom from unconscionable invasions of privacy and the freedom from convictions based upon coerced confessions do enjoy an "intimate relation" in their perpetuation of "principles of humanity and civil liberty [secured] ... only after years of struggle," Bram v. United States, 168 U.S. 532, 543–544

(1897).   They express "supplementing phases of the same constitutional purpose—to maintain inviolate large areas of personal privacy."   Feldman v. United States, 322 U.S. 487, 489–490 (1944).   The philosophy of each Amendment and of each freedom is complementary to, although not dependent upon, that of the other in its sphere of influence—the very least that together they assure in either sphere is that no man is to be convicted on unconstitutional evidence. . . .

V

Moreover, our holding that the exclusionary rule is an essential part of both the Fourth and Fourteenth Amendments is not only the logical dictate of prior cases, but it also makes very good sense. There is no war between the Constitution and common sense. Presently, a federal prosecutor may make no use of evidence illegally seized, but a State's attorney across the street may, although he supposedly is operating under the enforceable prohibitions of the same Amendment.   Thus the State, by admitting evidence unlawfully seized, serves to encourage disobedience to the Federal Constitution which it is bound to uphold. Moreover, as was said in *Elkins,* "[t]he very essence of a healthy federalism depends upon the avoidance of needless conflict between state and federal courts."   364 U.S., at 221.   Such a conflict, hereafter needless, arose this very Term, in Wilson v. Schnettler, 365 U.S. 381 (1961), in which, and in spite of the promise made by *Rea,* we gave full recognition to our practice in this regard by refusing to restrain a federal officer from testifying in a state court as to evidence unconstitutionally seized by him in the performance of his duties.   Yet the double standard recognized until today hardly put such a thesis into practice.   In non-exclusionary States, federal officers, being human, were by it invited to and did, as our cases indicate, step across the street to the State's attorney with their unconstitutionally seized evidence.   Prosecution on the basis of that evidence was then had in a state court in utter disregard of the enforceable Fourth Amendment.   If the fruits of an unconstitutional search had been inadmissible in both state and federal courts, this inducement to evasion would have been sooner eliminated.   There would be no need to reconcile such cases as *Rea* and *Schnettler,* each pointing up the hazardous uncertainties of our heretofore ambivalent approach.

Federal-state cooperation in the solution of crime under constitutional standards will be promoted, if only by recognition of their now mutual obligation to respect the same fundamental criteria in their approaches.   "However much in a particular case insistence upon such rules may appear as a technicality that inures to the benefit of a guilty person, the history of the criminal law proves that tolerance of shortcut methods in law enforcement impairs its enduring effectiveness."   Miller v. United States, 357 U.S. 301, 313 (1958).   Denying shortcuts to only one of two cooperating law enforcement agencies tends naturally to breed legitimate suspicion of "working arrangements" whose results are equally tainted. Byars v. United States, 273 U.S. 28 (1927); Lustig v. United States, 338 U.S. 74 (1949).

There are those who say, as did Justice (then Judge) Cardozo, that under our constitutional exclusionary doctrine "[t]he criminal is to go free because the constable has blundered." People v. Defore, 242 N.Y., at 21, 150 N.E., at 587. In some cases this will undoubtedly be the result. But, as was said in *Elkins*, "there is another consideration—the imperative of judicial integrity." 364 U.S., at 222. The criminal goes free, if he must, but it is the law that sets him free. Nothing can destroy a government more quickly than its failure to observe its own laws, or worse, its disregard of the charter of its own existence. As Mr. Justice Brandeis, dissenting, said in Olmstead v. United States, 277 U.S. 438, 485 (1928): "Our Government is the potent, the omnipresent teacher. For good or for ill, it teaches the whole people by its example. ... If the Government becomes a lawbreaker, it breeds contempt for law; it invites every man to become a law unto himself; it invites anarchy." Nor can it lightly be assumed that, as a practical matter, adoption of the exclusionary rule fetters law enforcement. Only last year this Court expressly considered that contention and found that "pragmatic evidence of a sort" to the contrary was not wanting. Elkins v. United States, supra, at 218. The Court noted that

> "The federal courts themselves have operated under the exclusionary rule of *Weeks* for almost half a century; yet it has not been suggested either that the Federal Bureau of Investigation has thereby been rendered ineffective, or that the administration of criminal justice in the federal courts has thereby been disrupted. Moreover, the experience of the states is impressive. ... The movement towards the rule of exclusion has been halting but seemingly inexorable." Id., at 218–219.

The ignoble shortcut to conviction left open to the State tends to destroy the entire system of constitutional restraints on which the liberties of the people rest. Having once recognized that the right to privacy embodied in the Fourth Amendment is enforceable against the States, and that the right to be secure against rude invasions of privacy by state officers is, therefore, constitutional in origin, we can no longer permit that right to remain an empty promise. Because it is enforceable in the same manner and to like effect as other basic rights secured by the Due Process Clause, we can no longer permit it to be revocable at the whim of any police officer who, in the name of law enforcement itself, chooses to suspend its enjoyment. Our decision, founded on reason and truth, gives to the individual no more than that which the Constitution guarantees him, to the police officer no less than that to which honest law enforcement is entitled, and, to the courts, that judicial integrity so necessary in the true administration of justice.

The judgment of the Supreme Court of Ohio is reversed and the cause remanded for further proceedings not inconsistent with this opinion.

Reversed and remanded.

MR. JUSTICE BLACK, concurring.

. . .

I am still not persuaded that the Fourth Amendment, standing alone, would be enough to bar the introduction into evidence against an accused of papers and effects seized from him in violation of its commands. For the Fourth Amendment does not itself contain any provision expressly precluding the use of such evidence, and I am extremely doubtful that such a provision could properly be inferred from nothing more than the basic command against unreasonable searches and seizures. Reflection on the problem, however, in the light of cases coming before the Court since *Wolf,* has led me to conclude that when the Fourth Amendment's ban against unreasonable searches and seizures is considered together with the Fifth Amendment's ban against compelled self-incrimination, a constitutional basis emerges which not only justifies but actually requires the exclusionary rule.

. . .

MR. JUSTICE HARLAN, whom MR. JUSTICE FRANKFURTER and MR. JUSTICE WHITTAKER join, dissenting.

. . .

Essential to the majority's argument against *Wolf* is the proposition that the rule of Weeks v. United States, 232 U.S. 383, excluding in federal criminal trials the use of evidence obtained in violation of the Fourth Amendment, derives not from the "supervisory power" of this Court over the federal judicial system, but from Constitutional requirement. This is so because no one, I suppose, would suggest that this Court possesses any general supervisory power over the state courts. Although I entertain considerable doubt as to the soundness of this foundational proposition of the majority, cf. Wolf v. Colorado, 338 U.S., at 39–40 (concurring opinion), I shall assume, for present purposes, that the *Weeks* rule "is of constitutional origin."

At the heart of the majority's opinion in this case is the following syllogism: (1) the rule excluding in federal criminal trials evidence which is the product of an illegal search and seizure is "part and parcel" of the Fourth Amendment; (2) *Wolf* held that the "privacy" assured against federal action by the Fourth Amendment is also protected against state action by the Fourteenth Amendment; and (3) it is therefore "logically and constitutionally necessary" that the *Weeks* exclusionary rule should also be enforced against the States.

This reasoning ultimately rests on the unsound premise that because *Wolf* carried into the States, as part of "the concept of ordered liberty" embodied in the Fourteenth Amendment, the principle of "privacy" underlying the Fourth Amendment (338 U.S., at 27), it must follow that whatever configurations of the Fourth Amendment have been developed in the particularizing federal precedents are likewise to be deemed a part of "ordered liberty," and as such are enforceable against the States. For me, this does not follow at all.

It cannot be too much emphasized that what was recognized in *Wolf* was not that the Fourth Amendment *as such* is enforceable against the States as a facet of due process, a view of the Fourteenth Amendment which, as *Wolf* itself pointed out (338 U.S., at 26), has long since been discredited, but the principle of privacy "which is at the core of the Fourth Amendment." (Id., at 27.) It would not be proper to expect or impose any precise equivalence, either as regards the scope of the right or the means of its implementation, between the requirements of the Fourth and Fourteenth Amendments. For the Fourth, unlike what was said in *Wolf* of the Fourteenth, does not state a general principle only; it is a particular command, having its setting in a pre-existing legal context on which both interpreting decisions and enabling statutes must at least build.

Thus, even in a case which presented simply the question of whether a particular search and seizure was constitutionally "unreasonable"—say in a tort action against state officers—we would not be true to the Fourteenth Amendment were we merely to stretch the general principle of individual privacy on a Procrustean bed of federal precedents under the Fourth Amendment. But in this instance more than that is involved, for here we are reviewing not a determination that what the state police did was Constitutionally permissible (since the state court quite evidently assumed that it was not), but a determination that appellant was properly found guilty of conduct which, for present purposes, it is to be assumed the State could Constitutionally punish. Since there is not the slightest suggestion that Ohio's policy is "affirmatively to sanction . . . police incursion into privacy" (338 U.S., at 28), compare Marcus v. Search Warrants, post, p. 717, what the Court is now doing is to impose upon the States not only federal substantive standards of "search and seizure" but also the basic federal remedy for violation of those standards. For I think it entirely clear that the *Weeks* exclusionary rule is but a remedy which, by penalizing past official misconduct, is aimed at deterring such conduct in the future.

I would not impose upon the States this federal exclusionary remedy. The reasons given by the majority for now suddenly turning its back on *Wolf* seem to me notably unconvincing.

First, it is said that "the factual grounds upon which *Wolf* was based" have since changed, in that more States now follow the *Weeks* exclusionary rule than was so at the time *Wolf* was decided. While that is true, a recent survey indicates that at present one-half of the States still adhere to the common-law non-exclusionary rule, and one, Maryland, retains the rule as to felonies.... But in any case surely all this is beside the point, as the majority itself indeed seems to recognize. Our concern here, as it was in *Wolf*, is not with the desirability of that rule but only with the question whether the States are Constitutionally free to follow it or not as they may themselves determine, and the relevance of the disparity of views among the States on this point lies simply in the fact that the judgment involved is a debatable one. Moreover, the very fact on which the majority relies, instead of lending support to what is now being done, points away from the need of replacing voluntary state action with federal compulsion.

The preservation of a proper balance between state and federal responsibility in the administration of criminal justice demands patience on the part of those who might like to see things move faster among the States in this respect. Problems of criminal law enforcement vary widely from State to State. One State, in considering the totality of its legal picture, may conclude that the need for embracing the *Weeks* rule is pressing because other remedies are unavailable or inadequate to secure compliance with the substantive Constitutional principle involved. Another, though equally solicitous of Constitutional rights, may choose to pursue one purpose at a time, allowing all evidence relevant to guilt to be brought into a criminal trial, and dealing with Constitutional infractions by other means. Still another may consider the exclusionary rule too rough-and-ready a remedy, in that it reaches only unconstitutional intrusions which eventuate in criminal prosecution of the victims. Further, a State after experimenting with the *Weeks* rule for a time may, because of unsatisfactory experience with it, decide to revert to a non-exclusionary rule. And so on. From the standpoint of Constitutional permissibility in pointing a State in one direction or another, I do not see at all why "time has set its face against" the considerations which led Mr. Justice Cardozo, then chief judge of the New York Court of Appeals, to reject for New York in People v. Defore, 242 N.Y. 13, 150 N.E. 585, the *Weeks* exclusionary rule. For us the question remains, as it has always been, one of state power, not one of passing judgment on the wisdom of one state course or another. In my view this Court should continue to forbear from fettering the States with an adamant rule which may embarrass them in coping with their own peculiar problems in criminal law enforcement.

Further, we are told that imposition of the *Weeks* rule on the States makes "very good sense," in that it will promote recognition by state and federal officials of their "mutual obligation to respect the same fundamental criteria" in their approach to law enforcement, and will avoid " 'needless conflict between state and federal courts.' " Indeed the majority now finds an incongruity in *Wolf's* discriminating perception between the demands of "ordered liberty" as respects the basic right of "privacy" and the means of securing it among the States. That perception, resting both on a sensitive regard for our federal system and a sound recognition of this Court's remoteness from particular state problems, is for me the strength of that decision.

An approach which regards the issue as one of achieving procedural symmetry or of serving administrative convenience surely disfigures the boundaries of this Court's functions in relation to the state and federal courts. Our role in promulgating the *Weeks* rule and its extensions in such cases as *Rea, Elkins,* and *Rios* [11] was quite a different one than it is here. There, in implementing the Fourth Amendment, we occupied the position of a tribunal having the ultimate responsibility for developing the standards and procedures of judicial administration within the judicial system over which it presides. Here we review state procedures whose measure is to be taken not against the specific substantive commands of the Fourth Amendment but under the flexible contours of the Due Process Clause. I do not believe that the Fourteenth Amendment empowers this Court to mould state remedies effectuating the right to freedom from "arbitrary intrusion by the police" to suit its own notions of how things should be done, as, for instance, the California Supreme Court did in People v. Cahan, 44 Cal.2d 434, 282 P.2d 905, with reference to procedures in the California courts or as this Court did in *Weeks* for the lower federal courts.

A state conviction comes to us as the complete product of a sovereign judicial system. Typically a case will have been tried in a trial court, tested in some final appellate court, and will go no further. In the comparatively rare instance when a conviction is reviewed by us on due process grounds we deal then with a finished product in the creation of which we are allowed no hand, and our task, far from being one of over-all supervision, is, speaking generally, restricted to a determination of whether the prosecution was Constitutionally fair. The specifics of trial procedure, which in every mature legal system will vary greatly in detail, are within the sole competence of the States. I do not see how it can be said that a trial becomes unfair simply because a State determines that evidence may be considered by the trier of fact, regardless of how it was obtained, if it is relevant to the one issue with which the trial is concerned, the guilt or innocence of the accused. Of course, a court may use its procedures as an incidental means of pursuing other ends than the correct resolution of the controversies before it.

11. Rea v. United States, 350 U.S. 214;   United States, 364 U.S. 253.
Elkins v. United States, 364 U.S. 206; Rios v.

Such indeed is the *Weeks* rule, but if a State does not choose to use its courts in this way, I do not believe that this Court is empowered to impose this much-debated procedure on local courts, however efficacious we may consider the *Weeks* rule to be as a means of securing Constitutional rights.

Finally, it is said that the overruling of *Wolf* is supported by the established doctrine that the admission in evidence of an involuntary confession renders a state conviction Constitutionally invalid. Since such a confession may often be entirely reliable, and therefore of the greatest relevance to the issue of the trial, the argument continues, this doctrine is ample warrant in precedent that the way evidence was obtained, and not just its relevance, is Constitutionally significant to the fairness of a trial. I believe this analogy is not a true one. The "coerced confession" rule is certainly not a rule that any illegally obtained statements may not be used in evidence. I would suppose that a statement which is procured during a period of illegal detention, McNabb v. United States, 318 U.S. 332, is, as much as unlawfully seized evidence, illegally obtained, but this Court has consistently refused to reverse state convictions resting on the use of such statements. Indeed it would seem the Court laid at rest the very argument now made by the majority when in Lisenba v. California, 314 U.S. 219, a state-coerced confession case, it said (at 235):

> "It may be assumed [that the] treatment of the petitioner [by the police] ... deprived him of his liberty without due process and that the petitioner would have been afforded preventive relief if he could have gained access to a court to seek it.

> "But illegal acts, as such, committed in the course of obtaining a confession ... do not furnish an answer to the constitutional question we must decide. ... The gravamen of his complaint is the unfairness of the *use* of his confessions, and what occurred in their procurement is relevant only as it bears on that issue." (Emphasis supplied.)

The point, then, must be that in requiring exclusion of an involuntary statement of an accused, we are concerned not with an appropriate remedy for what the police have done, but with something which is regarded as going to the heart of our concepts of fairness in judicial procedure. The operative assumption of our procedural system is that "Ours is the accusatorial as opposed to the inquisitorial system. Such has been the characteristic of Anglo-American criminal justice since it freed itself from practices borrowed by the Star Chamber from the Continent whereby the accused was interrogated in secret for hours on end." Watts v. Indiana, 338 U.S. 49, 54. See Rogers v. Richmond, 365 U.S. 534, 541. The pressures brought to bear against an accused leading to a confession, unlike an unconstitutional violation of privacy, do not, apart from the use of the confession at trial, necessarily involve independent Constitutional violations. What is crucial is that the trial defense to which an accused is entitled should not be rendered an empty formality by reason of statements wrung from him, for then "a prisoner . . . [has been] made the deluded instrument of his own conviction." 2 Hawkins, Pleas of the Crown (8th ed., 1824), c. 46, § 34. That this is a *procedural right,* and that its violation occurs at the time his improperly obtained statement is admitted at trial, is manifest. For without this right all the careful safeguards erected around the giving of testimony, whether by an accused or any other witness, would become empty formalities in a procedure where the most compelling possible evidence of guilt, a confession, would have already been obtained at the unsupervised pleasure of the police.

This, and not the disciplining of the police, as with illegally seized evidence, is surely the true basis for excluding a statement of the accused which was unconstitutionally obtained. In sum, I think the coerced confession analogy works strongly *against* what the Court does today.

. . .

I regret that I find so unwise in principle and so inexpedient in policy a decision motivated by the high purpose of increasing respect for Constitutional rights. But in the last analysis I think this Court can increase respect for the Constitution only if it rigidly respects the limitations which the Constitution places upon it, and respects as well the principles inherent in its own processes. In the present case I think we exceed both, and that our voice becomes only a voice of power, not of reason.[*] [**]

[*] Justice Douglas wrote a concurring opinion. Justice Stewart wrote a brief memorandum declining to state a view on the merits of the Fourth Amendment issue.

[**] In Walder v. United States, 347 U.S. 62 (1954), the Supreme Court held that illegally obtained evidence could be used by the prosecution to impeach the credibility of the defendant's own testimony. In *Walder,* the defendant had testified that he had never possessed narcotics. The prosecution was permitted to introduce into evidence narcotics obtained by an illegal search. *Walder* was applied to statements obtained in violation of the *Miranda* requirements, in Harris v. New York, 401 U.S. 222 (1971), below. In James v. Illinois, 493 U.S. 307 (1990) (5–4), the Court held that the *Walder* exception to the exclusionary rule does not extend to the use of illegally obtained evidence to impeach testimony of a defense witness other than the defendant. In *James,* the evidence in question was statements of the defendant made while he was unlawfully arrested.

UNITED STATES v. LEON

468 U.S. 897, 104 S.Ct. 3405, 82 L.Ed.2d 677 (1984).

JUSTICE WHITE delivered the opinion of the Court.

This case presents the question whether the Fourth Amendment exclusionary rule should be modified so as not to bar the use in the prosecution's case-in-chief of evidence obtained by officers acting in reasonable reliance on a search warrant issued by a detached and neutral magistrate but ultimately found to be unsupported by probable cause. To resolve this question, we must consider once again the tension between the sometimes competing goals of, on the one hand, deterring official misconduct and removing inducements to unreasonable invasions of privacy and, on the other, establishing procedures under which criminal defendants are "acquitted or convicted on the basis of all the evidence which exposes the truth." Alderman v. United States, 394 U.S. 165, 175 (1969).

I

In August 1981, a confidential informant of unproven reliability informed an officer of the Burbank Police Department that two persons known to him as "Armando" and "Patsy" were selling large quantities of cocaine and methaqualone from their residence at 620 Price Drive in Burbank, Cal. The informant also indicated that he had witnessed a sale of methaqualone by "Patsy" at the residence approximately five months earlier and had observed at that time a shoebox containing a large amount of cash that belonged to "Patsy." He further declared that "Armando" and "Patsy" generally kept only small quantities of drugs at their residence and stored the remainder at another location in Burbank.

On the basis of this information, the Burbank police initiated an extensive investigation focusing first on the Price Drive residence and later on two other residences as well. Cars parked at the Price Drive residence were determined to belong to respondents Armando Sanchez, who had previously been arrested for possession of marihuana, and Patsy Stewart, who had no criminal record. During the course of the investigation, officers observed an automobile belonging to respondent Ricardo Del Castillo, who had previously been arrested for possession of 50 pounds of marihuana, arrive at the Price Drive residence. The driver of that car entered the house, exited shortly thereafter carrying a small paper sack, and drove away. A check of Del Castillo's probation records led the officers to respondent Alberto Leon, whose telephone number Del Castillo had listed as his employer's. Leon had been arrested in 1980 on drug

338

charges, and a companion had informed the police at that time that Leon was heavily involved in the importation of drugs into this country. Before the current investigation began, the Burbank officers had learned that an informant had told a Glendale police officer that Leon stored a large quantity of methaqualone at his residence in Glendale. During the course of this investigation, the Burbank officers learned that Leon was living at 716 South Sunset Canyon in Burbank.

Subsequently, the officers observed several persons, at least one of whom had prior drug involvement, arriving at the Price Drive residence and leaving with small packages; observed a variety of other material activity at the two residences as well as at a condominium at 7902 Via Magdalena; and witnessed a variety of relevant activity involving respondents' automobiles. The officers also observed respondents Sanchez and Stewart board separate flights for Miami. The pair later returned to Los Angeles together, consented to a search of their luggage that revealed only a small amount of marihuana, and left the airport. Based on these and other observations summarized in the affidavit. . . . Officer Cyril Rombach of the Burbank Police Department, an experienced and well-trained narcotics investigator, prepared an application for a warrant to search 620 Price Drive, 716 South Sunset Canyon, 7902 Via Magdalena, and automobiles registered to each of the respondents for an extensive list of items believed to be related to respondents' drug-trafficking activities. Officer Rombach's extensive application was reviewed by several Deputy District Attorneys.

A facially valid search warrant was issued in September 1981 by a State Superior Court Judge. The ensuing searches produced large quantities of drugs at the Via Magdalena and Sunset Canyon addresses and a small quantity at the Price Drive residence. Other evidence was discovered at each of the residences and in Stewart's and Del Castillo's automobiles. Respondents were indicted by a grand jury in the District Court for the Central District of California and charged with conspiracy to possess and distribute cocaine and a variety of substantive counts.

The respondents then filed motions to suppress the evidence seized pursuant to the warrant. The District Court held an evidentiary hearing and, while recognizing that the case was a close one . . . granted the motions to suppress in part. It concluded that the affidavit was insufficient to establish probable cause, but did not suppress all of the evidence as to all of the respondents because none of the respondents had standing to challenge all of the searches. In response to a request from the Government, the court made clear that Officer Rombach had acted in good faith, but it rejected the Government's suggestion that the Fourth Amendment exclusionary rule should not apply where evidence is seized in reasonable, good-faith reliance on a search warrant.

The District Court denied the Government's motion for reconsideration, ... and a divided panel of the Court of Appeals for the Ninth Circuit affirmed, judgment order reported at 701 F.2d 187 (1983). . . . The Court of Appeals refused the Government's invitation to recognize a good-faith exception to the Fourth Amendment exclusionary rule. . . .

The Government's petition for certiorari expressly declined to seek review of the lower courts' determinations that the search warrant was unsupported by probable cause and presented only the question "[w]hether the Fourth Amendment exclusionary rule should be modified so as not to bar the admission of evidence seized in reasonable, good-faith reliance on a search warrant that is subsequently held to be defective." We granted certiorari to consider the propriety of such a modification. 463 U.S. 1206 (1983). . . .

We have concluded that, in the Fourth Amendment context, the exclusionary rule can be modified somewhat without jeopardizing its ability to perform its intended functions. Accordingly, we reverse the judgment of the Court of Appeals.

II

Language in opinions of this Court and of individual Justices has sometimes implied that the exclusionary rule is a necessary corollary of the Fourth Amendment ... or that the rule is required by the conjunction of the Fourth and Fifth Amendments. ... These implications need not detain us long. The Fifth Amendment theory has not withstood critical analysis or the test of time ... and the Fourth Amendment "has never been interpreted to proscribe the introduction of illegally seized evidence in all proceedings or against all persons." Stone v. Powell, 428 U.S. 465, 486 (1976).

A

The Fourth Amendment contains no provision expressly precluding the use of evidence obtained in violation of its commands, and an examination of its origin and purposes makes clear that the use of fruits of a past unlawful search or seizure "work[s] no new Fourth Amendment wrong." United States v. Calandra, 414 U.S. 338, 354 (1974). The wrong condemned by the Amendment is "fully accomplished" by the unlawful search or seizure itself, ibid., and the exclusionary rule is neither intended nor able to "cure the invasion of the defendant's rights which he has already suffered." Stone v. Powell, supra, at 540 (White J., dissenting). The rule thus operates as "a judicially created remedy designed to safeguard Fourth Amendment rights generally through its deterrent effect, rather than a personal constitutional right of the party aggrieved." United States v. Calandra, supra, at 348.

Whether the exclusionary sanction is appropriately imposed in a particular case, our decisions make clear, is "an issue separate from the question whether the Fourth Amendment rights of the party seeking to invoke the rule were violated by police conduct." Illinois v. Gates, [462 U.S. 213 (1983)], at 223. Only the former question is currently before us, and it must be resolved by weighing the costs and benefits of preventing the use in the prosecution's case-in-chief of inherently trustworthy tangible evidence obtained in reliance on a search warrant issued by a detached and neutral magistrate that ultimately is found to be defective.

The substantial social costs exacted by the exclusionary rule for the vindication of Fourth Amendment rights have long been a source of concern. "Our cases have consistently recognized that unbending application of the exclusionary sanction to enforce ideals of governmental rectitude would impede unacceptably the truth-finding functions of judge and jury." United States v. Payner, 447 U.S. 727, 734 (1980). An objectionable collateral consequence of this interference with the criminal justice system's truth-finding function is that some guilty defendants may go free or receive reduced sentences as a result of favorable plea bargains. Particularly when law enforcement officers have acted in objective good faith or their transgressions have been minor, the magnitude of the benefit conferred on such guilty defendants offends basic concepts of the criminal justice system. ... Indiscriminate application of the exclusionary rule, therefore, may well "generat[e] disrespect for the law and the administration of justice." [Stone v. Powell, supra], at 491. Accordingly, "[a]s with any remedial device, the application of the rule has been restricted to those areas where its remedial objectives are thought most efficaciously served." United States v. Calandra, supra, at 348 ....

B

Close attention to those remedial objectives has characterized our recent decisions concerning the scope of the Fourth Amendment exclusionary rule. The Court has, to be sure, not seriously questioned, "in the absence of a more efficacious sanction, the continued application of the rule to suppress evidence from the [prosecution's] case where a Fourth Amendment violation has been substantial and deliberate ...." Franks v. Delaware, 438 U.S. 154, 171 (1978) .... Nevertheless, the balancing approach that has evolved in various contexts—including criminal trials—"forcefully suggest[s] that the exclusionary rule be more generally modified to permit the introduction of evidence obtained in the reasonable good-faith belief that a search or seizure was in accord with the Fourth Amendment." Illinois v. Gates, 462 U.S., at 225 (White J., concurring in the judgment).

In Stone v. Powell, supra, the Court emphasized the costs of the exclusionary rule, expressed its view that limiting the circum-

stances under which Fourth Amendment claims could be raised in
federal habeas corpus proceedings would not reduce the rule's
deterrent effect, id., at 489–495, and held that a state prisoner who
has been afforded a full and fair opportunity to litigate a Fourth
Amendment claim may not obtain federal habeas relief on the
ground that unlawfully obtained evidence had been introduced at
his trial. ... Proposed extensions of the exclusionary rule to
proceedings other than the criminal trial itself have been evaluated
and rejected under the same analytic approach. In United States v.
Calandra, for example, we declined to allow grand jury witnesses to
refuse to answer questions based on evidence obtained from an
unlawful search or seizure since "[a]ny incremental deterrent effect
which might be achieved by extending the rule to grand jury
proceedings is uncertain at best." 414 U.S., at 348. Similarly, in
United States v. Janis, [428 U.S. 433 (1976)], we permitted the use
in federal civil proceedings of evidence illegally seized by state
officials since the likelihood of deterring police misconduct through
such an extension of the exclusionary rule was insufficient to
outweigh its substantial social costs. In so doing, we declared that,
"[i]f ... the exclusionary rule does not result in appreciable deterrence, then, clearly, its use in the instant situation is unwarranted."
Id., at 454.

As cases considering the use of unlawfully obtained evidence in
criminal trials themselves make clear, it does not follow from the
emphasis on the exclusionary rule's deterrent value that "anything
which deters illegal searches is thereby commanded by the Fourth
Amendment." Alderman v. United States, 394 U.S., at 174. In
determining whether persons aggrieved solely by the introduction
of damaging evidence unlawfully obtained from their co-conspirators or codefendants could seek suppression, for example, we
found that the additional benefits of such an extension of the
exclusionary rule would not outweigh its costs. Id., at 174–175.
Standing to invoke the rule has thus been limited to cases in which
the prosecution seeks to use the fruits of an illegal search or seizure
against the victim of police misconduct. ...

Even defendants with standing to challenge the introduction in
their criminal trials of unlawfully obtained evidence cannot prevent
every conceivable use of such evidence. Evidence obtained in
violation of the Fourth Amendment and inadmissible in the prosecution's case in chief may be used to impeach a defendant's direct
testimony. ... A similar assessment of the "incremental further-
ing" of the ends of the exclusionary rule led us to conclude in
United States v. Havens, 446 U.S. 620, 627 (1980), that evidence
inadmissible in the prosecution's case in chief or otherwise as
substantive evidence of guilt may be used to impeach statements
made by a defendant in response to "proper cross-examination
reasonably suggested by the defendant's direct examination." Id.,
at 627–628.

When considering the use of evidence obtained in violation of the Fourth Amendment in the prosecution's case in chief, moreover, we have declined to adopt a *per se* or "but for" rule that would render inadmissible any evidence that came to light through a chain of causation that began with an illegal arrest. ... We also have held that a witness' testimony may be admitted even when his identity was discovered in an unconstitutional search. ... The perception underlying these decisions—that the connection between police misconduct and evidence of crime may be sufficiently attenuated to permit the use of that evidence at trial—is a product of considerations relating to the exclusionary rule and the constitutional principles it is designed to protect. ... In short, the "dissipation of the taint" concept that the Court has applied in deciding whether exclusion is appropriate in a particular case "attempts to mark the point at which the detrimental consequences of illegal police action becomes so attenuated that the deterrent effect of the exclusionary rule no longer justifies its cost." Brown v. Illinois, [422 U.S. 590 (1975)], at 609 (Powell, J., concurring in part.) Not surprisingly in view of this purpose, an assessment of the flagrancy of the police misconduct constitutes an important step in the calculus. ...

The same attention to the purposes underlying the exclusionary rule also has characterized decisions not involving the scope of the rule itself. We have not required suppression of the fruits of a search incident to an arrest made in good-faith reliance on a substantive criminal statute that subsequently is declared unconstitutional. ... Similarly, although the Court has been unwilling to conclude that new Fourth Amendment principles are always to have only prospective effect ... no Fourth Amendment decision marking a "clear break with the past" has been applied retroactively. ... The propriety of retroactive application of a newly announced Fourth Amendment principle, moreover, has been assessed largely in terms of the contribution retroactivity might make to the deterrence of police misconduct. ...

As yet, we have not recognized any form of good-faith exception to the Fourth Amendment exclusionary rule. But the balancing approach that has evolved during the years of experience with the rule provides strong support for the modification currently urged upon us. As we discuss below, our evaluation of the costs and benefits of suppressing reliable physical evidence seized by officers reasonably relying on a warrant issued by a detached and neutral magistrate leads to the conclusion that such evidence should be admissible in the prosecution's case in chief.

III

A

Because a search warrant "provides the detached scrutiny of a neutral magistrate, which is a more reliable safeguard against improper searches than the hurried judgment of a law enforcement officer 'engaged in the often competitive enterprise of ferreting out crime,' " United States v. Chadwick, 433 U.S. 1, 9 (1971) (quoting Johnson v. United States, 333 U.S. 10, 14 (1948)), we have expressed a strong preference for warrants and declared that "in a doubtful or marginal case a search under a warrant may be sustainable where without one it would fail." United States v. Ventresca, 380 U.S. 102, 106 (1965). . . . Reasonable minds frequently may differ on the question whether a particular affidavit establishes probable cause, and we have thus concluded that the preference for warrants is most appropriately effectuated by according "great deference" to a magistrate's determination. Spinelli v. United States, 393 U.S., at 419. . . .

Deference to the magistrate, however, is not boundless. It is clear, first, that the deference accorded to a magistrate's finding of probable cause does not preclude inquiry into the knowing or reckless falsity of the affidavit on which that determination was based. . . . Second, the courts must also insist that the magistrate purport to "perform his 'neutral and detached' function and not serve merely as a rubber stamp for the police." Aguilar v. Texas, supra, at 111. . . . A magistrate failing to "manifest that neutrality and detachment demanded of a judicial officer when presented with a warrant application" and who acts instead as "an adjunct law enforcement officer" cannot provide valid authorization for an otherwise unconstitutional search. Lo-Ji Sales, Inc. v. New York, 442 U.S. 319, 326–327 (1979).

Third, reviewing courts will not defer to a warrant based on an affidavit that does not "provide the magistrate with a substantial basis for determining the existence of probable cause." Illinois v. Gates, 462 U.S., at 239. "Sufficient information must be presented to the magistrate to allow that official to determine probable cause; his action cannot be a mere ratification of the bare conclusions of others." Ibid. . . . Even if the warrant application was supported by more than a "bare bones" affidavit, a reviewing court may properly conclude that, notwithstanding the deference that magistrates deserve, the warrant was invalid because the magistrate's probable-cause determination reflected an improper analysis of the totality of the circumstances, Illinois v. Gates, supra, at 238–239, or because the form of the warrant was improper in some respect.

Only in the first of these three situations, however, has the Court set forth a rationale for suppressing evidence obtained pursuant to a search warrant; in the other areas, it has simply excluded such evidence without considering whether Fourth Amendment interests will be advanced. To the extent that proponents of exclusion rely on its behavioral effects on judges and magistrates in these areas, their reliance is misplaced. First, the exclusionary rule is designed to deter police misconduct rather than to punish the errors of judges and magistrates. Second, there exists no evidence suggesting that judges and magistrates are inclined to ignore or subvert the Fourth Amendment or that lawlessness among these actors requires application of the extreme sanction of exclusion.

Third, and most important, we discern no basis, and are offered none, for believing that exclusion of evidence seized pursuant to a warrant will have a significant deterrent effect on the issuing judge or magistrate. Many of the factors that indicate that the exclusionary rule cannot provide an effective "special" or "general" deterrent for individual offending law enforcement officers apply as well to judges or magistrates. And, to the extent that the rule is thought to operate as a "systemic" deterrent on a wider audience, it clearly can have no such effect on individuals empowered to issue search warrants. Judges and magistrates are not adjuncts to the law enforcement team; as neutral judicial officers, they have no stake in the outcome of particular criminal prosecutions. The threat of exclusion thus cannot be expected significantly to deter them. Imposition of the exclusionary sanction is not necessary meaningfully to inform judicial officers of their errors, and we cannot conclude that admitting evidence obtained pursuant to a warrant while at the same time declaring that the warrant was somehow defective will in any way reduce judicial officers' professional incentives to comply with the Fourth Amendment, encourage them to repeat their mistakes, or lead to the granting of all colorable warrant requests.[18]

B

If exclusion of evidence obtained pursuant to a subsequently invalidated warrant is to have any deterrent effect, therefore, it must alter the behavior of individual law enforcement officers or the policies of their departments. One could argue that applying the exclusionary rule in cases where the police failed to demonstrate probable cause in the warrant application deters future inadequate presentations or "magistrate shopping" and thus promotes the ends of the Fourth Amendment. Suppressing evidence obtained pursuant to a technically defective warrant supported by probable cause also might encourage officers to scrutinize more closely the form of the warrant and to point out suspected judicial errors. We find such arguments speculative and conclude that suppression of evidence obtained pursuant to a warrant should be ordered only on a case-by-case basis and only in those unusual cases in which exclusion will further the purposes of the exclusionary rule.

---

18. Limiting the application of the exclusionary sanction may well increase the care with which magistrates scrutinize warrant applications. We doubt that magistrates are more desirous of avoiding the exclusion of evidence obtained pursuant to warrants they have issued than of avoiding invasions of privacy.

Federal magistrates, moreover, are subject to the direct supervision of district courts.

They may be removed for "incompetency, misconduct, neglect of duty, or physical or mental disability." 28 U.S.C. § 631(i). If a magistrate serves merely as a "rubber stamp" for the police or is unable to exercise mature judgment, closer supervision or removal provides a more effective remedy than the exclusionary rule.

We have frequently questioned whether the exclusionary rule can have any deterrent effect when the offending officers acted in the objectively reasonable belief that their conduct did not violate the Fourth Amendment. "No empirical researcher, proponent or opponent of the rule, has yet been able to establish with any assurance whether the rule has a deterrent effect . . . ." United States v. Janis, 428 U.S., at 452, n. 22. But even assuming that the rule effectively deters some police misconduct and provides incentives for the law enforcement profession as a whole to conduct itself in accord with the Fourth Amendment, it cannot be expected, and should not be applied, to deter objectively reasonable law enforcement activity.[20]

. . .

This is particularly true, we believe, when an officer acting with objective good faith has obtained a search warrant from a judge or magistrate and acted within its scope. In most such cases, there is no police illegality and thus nothing to deter. It is the magistrate's responsibility to determine whether the officer's allegations establish probable cause and, if so, to issue a warrant comporting in form with the requirements of the Fourth Amendment. In the ordinary case, an officer cannot be expected to question the magistrate's probable-cause determination or his judgment that the form of the warrant is technically sufficient. "[O]nce the warrant issues, there is literally nothing more the policeman can do in seeking to comply with the law." Id., at 498 (Burger, C.J., concurring). Penalizing the officer for the magistrate's error, rather than his own, cannot logically contribute to the deterrence of Fourth Amendment violations.

C

We conclude that the marginal or nonexistent benefits produced by suppressing evidence obtained in objectively reasonable reliance on a subsequently invalidated search warrant cannot justify the substantial costs of exclusion. We do not suggest, however, that exclusion is always inappropriate in cases where an officer has obtained a warrant and abided by its terms. "[S]earches pursuant to a warrant will rarely require any deep inquiry into reasonableness," Illinois v. Gates, 462 U.S., at 267 (White, J., concurring in judgment), for "a warrant issued by a magistrate normally suffices to establish" that a law enforcement officer has "acted in good faith in conducting the search." United States v. Ross, 456 U.S. 798, 823, n.

20. We emphasize that the standard of reasonableness we adopt is an objective one. Many objections to a good-faith exception assume that the exception will turn on the subjective good faith of individual officers. "Grounding the modification in objective reasonableness, however, retains the value of the exclusionary rule as an incentive for the law enforcement profession as a whole to conduct themselves in accord with the Fourth Amendment." Illinois v. Gates, 462 U.S., at 261, n. 15 (White, J., concurring in judgment) . . . . The objective standard we adopt, moreover, requires officers to have a reasonable knowledge of what the law prohibits. . . .

32 (1982). Nevertheless, the officer's reliance on the magistrate's probable-cause determination and on the technical sufficiency of the warrant he issues must be objectively reasonable . . . and it is clear that in some circumstances the officer [24] will have no reasonable grounds for believing that the warrant was properly issued.

Suppression therefore remains an appropriate remedy if the magistrate or judge in issuing a warrant was misled by information in an affidavit that the affiant knew was false or would have known was false except for his reckless disregard of the truth. . . . The exception we recognize today will also not apply in cases where the issuing magistrate wholly abandoned his judicial role in the manner condemned in Lo-Ji Sales, Inc. v. New York, 442 U.S. 319 (1979); in such circumstances, no reasonably well-trained officer should rely on the warrant. Nor would an officer manifest objective good faith in relying on a warrant based on an affidavit "so lacking in indicia of probable cause as to render official belief in its existence entirely unreasonable." Brown v. Illinois, 422 U.S., at 610–611 (Powell, J., concurring in part) . . . . Finally, depending on the circumstances of the particular case, a warrant may be so facially deficient—i.e., in failing to particularize the place to be searched or the things to be seized—that the executing officers cannot reasonably presume it to be valid. . . .

In so limiting the suppression remedy, we leave untouched the probable-cause standard and the various requirements for a valid warrant. Other objections to the modification of the Fourth Amendment exclusionary rule we consider to be insubstantial. The good-faith exception for searches conducted pursuant to warrants is not intended to signal our unwillingness strictly to enforce the requirements of the Fourth Amendment, and we do not believe that it will have this effect. As we have already suggested, the good-faith exception, turning as it does on objective reasonableness, should not be difficult to apply in practice. When officers have acted pursuant to a warrant, the prosecution should ordinarily be able to establish objective good faith without a substantial expenditure of judicial time.

Nor are we persuaded that application of a good-faith exception to searches conducted pursuant to warrants will preclude review of the constitutionality of the search or seizure, deny needed guidance from the courts, or freeze Fourth Amendment law in its present state. There is no need for courts to adopt the inflexible practice of always deciding whether the officers' conduct manifested objective good faith before turning to the question whether the Fourth

---

24. References to "officer" throughout this opinion should not be read too narrowly. It is necessary to consider the objective reasonableness, not only of the officers who eventually executed a warrant, but also of the officers who originally obtained it or who provided information material to the proba-ble-cause determination. Nothing in our opinion suggests, for example, that an officer could obtain a warrant on the basis of a "bare bones" affidavit and then rely on colleagues who are ignorant of the circumstances under which the warrant was obtained to conduct the search. . . .

Amendment has been violated. Defendants seeking suppression of the fruits of allegedly unconstitutional searches or seizures undoubtedly raise live controversies which Art. III empowers federal courts to adjudicate. As cases addressing questions of good-faith immunity under 42 U.S.C. § 1983, ... and cases involving the harmless-error doctrine ... make clear, courts have considerable discretion in conforming their decisionmaking processes to the exigencies of particular cases.

If the resolution of a particular Fourth Amendment question is necessary to guide future action by law enforcement officers and magistrates, nothing will prevent reviewing courts from deciding that question before turning to the good-faith issue. Indeed, it frequently will be difficult to determine whether the officers acted reasonably without resolving the Fourth Amendment issue. Even if the Fourth Amendment question is not one of broad import, reviewing courts could decide in particular cases that magistrates under their supervision need to be informed of their errors and so evaluate the officers' good faith only after finding a violation. In other circumstances, those courts could reject suppression motions posing no important Fourth Amendment questions by turning immediately to a consideration of the officers' good faith. We have no reason to believe that our Fourth Amendment jurisprudence would suffer by allowing reviewing courts to exercise an informed discretion in making this choice.

IV

When the principles we have enunciated today are applied to the facts of this case, it is apparent that the judgment of the Court of Appeals cannot stand. The Court of Appeals applied the prevailing legal standards to Officer Rombach's warrant application and concluded that the application could not support the magistrate's probable-cause determination. In so doing, the court clearly informed the magistrate that he had erred in issuing the challenged warrant. This aspect of the court's judgment is not under attack in this proceeding.

Having determined that the warrant should not have issued, the Court of Appeals understandably declined to adopt a modification of the Fourth Amendment exclusionary rule that this Court had not previously sanctioned. Although the modification finds strong support in our previous cases, the Court of Appeals' commendable self-restraint is not to be criticized. We have now reexamined the purposes of the exclusionary rule and the propriety of its application in cases where officers have relied on a subsequently invalidated search warrant. Our conclusion is that the rule's purposes will only rarely be served by applying it in such circumstances.

In the absence of an allegation that the magistrate abandoned his detached and neutral role, suppression is appropriate only if the officers were dishonest or reckless in preparing their affidavit or could not have harbored an objectively reasonable belief in the existence of probable cause. Only respondent Leon has contended that no reasonably well-trained police officer could have believed that there existed probable cause to search his house; significantly, the other respondents advance no comparable argument. Officer Rombach's application for a warrant clearly was supported by much more than a "bare bones" affidavit. The affidavit related the results of an extensive investigation and, as the opinions of the divided panel of the Court of Appeals make clear, provided evidence sufficient to create disagreement among thoughtful and competent judges as to the existence of probable cause. Under these circumstances, the officers' reliance on the magistrate's determination of probable cause was objectively reasonable, and application of the extreme sanction of exclusion is inappropriate.

Accordingly, the judgment of the Court of Appeals is

Reversed.

JUSTICE BRENNAN, with whom JUSTICE MARSHALL joins, dissenting.

Ten years ago in United States v. Calandra, 414 U.S. 338 (1974), I expressed the fear that the Court's decision "may signal that a majority of my colleagues have positioned themselves to reopen the door [to evidence secured by official lawlessness] still further and abandon altogether the exclusionary rule in search-and-seizure cases." Id., at 365 (dissenting opinion). Since then, in case after case, I have witnessed the Court's gradual but determined strangulation of the rule. It now appears that the Court's victory over the Fourth Amendment is complete. That today's decision represents the *pièce de résistance* of the Court's past efforts cannot be doubted, for today the Court sanctions the use in the prosecution's case-in-chief of illegally obtained evidence against the individual whose rights have been violated—a result that had previously been thought to be foreclosed.

The Court seeks to justify this result on the ground that the "costs" of adhering to the exclusionary rule in cases like those before us exceed the "benefits." But the language of deterrence and of cost/benefit analysis, if used indiscriminately, can have a narcotic effect. It creates an illusion of technical precision and ineluctability. It suggests that not only constitutional principle but also empirical data support the majority's result. When the Court's analysis is examined carefully, however, it is clear that we have not been treated to an honest assessment of the merits of the exclusionary rule, but have instead been drawn into a curious world where the "costs" of excluding illegally obtained evidence loom to exaggerated heights and where the "benefits" of such exclusion are made to disappear with a mere wave of the hand.

The majority ignores the fundamental constitutional importance of what is at stake here. While the machinery of law enforce-

ment and indeed the nature of crime itself have changed dramatically since the Fourth Amendment became part of the Nation's fundamental law in 1791, what the Framers understood then remains true
today—that the task of combatting crime and convicting the guilty
will in every era seem of such critical and pressing concern that we
may be lured by the temptations of expediency into forsaking our
commitment to protecting individual liberty and privacy. It was for
that very reason that the Framers of the Bill of Rights insisted that
law enforcement efforts be permanently and unambiguously restricted in order to preserve personal freedoms. In the constitutional
scheme they ordained, the sometimes unpopular task of ensuring
that the government's enforcement efforts remain within the strict
boundaries fixed by the Fourth Amendment was entrusted to the
courts. As James Madison predicted in his address to the First
Congress on June 8, 1789:

> "If [these rights] are incorporated into the Constitution, inde-
> pendent tribunals of justice will consider themselves in a
> peculiar manner the guardians of those rights; they will be an
> impenetrable bulwark against every assumption of power in the
> Legislative or Executive; they will naturally be led to resist
> every encroachment upon rights expressly stipulated for in the
> Constitution by the declaration of rights." 1 Annals of Cong.
> 439.

If those independent tribunals lose their resolve, however, as the
Court has done today, and give way to the seductive call of
expediency, the vital guarantees of the Fourth Amendment are
reduced to nothing more than a "form of words." Silverthorne
Lumber Co. v. United States, 251 U.S. 385, 392 (1920).

A proper understanding of the broad purposes sought to be
served by the Fourth Amendment demonstrates that the principles
embodied in the exclusionary rule rest upon a far firmer constitutional foundation than the shifting sands of the Court's deterrence
rationale. But even if I were to accept the Court's chosen method
of analyzing the question posed by these cases, I would still
conclude that the Court's decision cannot be justified.

I

The Court holds that physical evidence seized by police officers
reasonably relying upon a warrant issued by a detached and neutral
magistrate is admissible in the prosecution's case-in-chief, even
though a reviewing court has subsequently determined either that
the warrant was defective, No. 82–963, or that those officers failed
to demonstrate when applying for the warrant that there was
probable cause to conduct the search, No. 82–1771. I have no
doubt that these decisions will prove in time to have been a grave
mistake. But, as troubling and important as today's new doctrine
may be for the administration of criminal justice in this country, the
mode of analysis used to generate that doctrine also requires critical

examination, for it may prove in the long run to pose the greater threat to our civil liberties.

A

At bottom, the Court's decision turns on the proposition that the exclusionary rule is merely a " 'judicially created remedy designed to safeguard Fourth Amendment rights generally through its deterrent effect, rather than a personal constitutional right.' " Ante, at 906, quoting United States v. Calandra, 414 U.S., at 348. . . . The essence of this view, as expressed initially in the *Calandra* opinion and as reiterated today, is that the sole "purpose of the Fourth Amendment is to prevent unreasonable governmental intrusions into the privacy of one's person, house, papers, or effects. The wrong condemned is the unjustified governmental invasion of these areas of an individual's life. That wrong . . . is *fully accomplished* by the original search without probable cause." 414 U.S., at 354 (emphasis added); see also ante, at 906. This reading of the Amendment implies that its proscriptions are directed solely at those government agents who may actually invade an individual's constitutionally protected privacy. The courts are not subject to any direct constitutional duty to exclude illegally obtained evidence, because the question of the admissibility of such evidence is not addressed by the Amendment. This view of the scope of the Amendment relegates the judiciary to the periphery. Because the only constitutionally cognizable injury has already been "fully accomplished" by the police by the time a case comes before the courts, the Constitution is not itself violated if the judge decides to admit the tainted evidence. Indeed, the most the judge *can* do is wring his hands and hope that perhaps by excluding such evidence he can deter future transgressions by the police.

Such a reading appears plausible, because, as critics of the exclusionary rule never tire of repeating, the Fourth Amendment makes no express provision for the exclusion of evidence secured in violation of its commands. A short answer to this claim, of course, is that many of the Constitution's most vital imperatives are stated in general terms and the task of giving meaning to these precepts is therefore left to subsequent judicial decisionmaking in the context of concrete cases. . . .

A more direct answer may be supplied by recognizing that the Amendment, like other provisions of the Bill of Rights, restrains the power of the government as a whole; it does not specify only a particular agency and exempt all others. The judiciary is responsible, no less than the executive, for ensuring that constitutional rights are respected.

When that fact is kept in mind, the role of the courts and their possible involvement in the concerns of the Fourth Amendment comes into sharper focus. Because seizures are executed principally to secure evidence, and because such evidence generally has utility in our legal system only in the context of a trial supervised by a judge, it is apparent that the admission of illegally obtained evidence implicates the same constitutional concerns as the initial seizure of that evidence. Indeed, by admitting unlawfully seized evidence, the judiciary becomes a part of what is in fact a single governmental action prohibited by the terms of the Amendment. Once that connection between the evidence-gathering role of the police and the evidence-admitting function of the courts is acknowledged, the plausibility of the Court's interpretation becomes more suspect. Certainly nothing in the language or history of the Fourth Amendment suggests that a recognition of this evidentiary link between the police and the courts was meant to be foreclosed. It is difficult to give any meaning at all to the limitations imposed by the Amendment if they are read to proscribe only certain conduct by the police but to allow other agents of the same government to take advantage of evidence secured by the police in violation of its requirements. The Amendment therefore must be read to condemn not only the initial unconstitutional invasion of privacy—which is done after all, for the purpose of securing evidence—but also the subsequent use of any evidence so obtained.

The Court evades this principle by drawing an artificial line between the constitutional rights and responsibilities that are engaged by actions of the police and those that are engaged when a defendant appears before the courts. According to the Court, the substantive protections of the Fourth Amendment are wholly exhausted at the moment when police unlawfully invade an individual's privacy and thus no substantive force remains to those protections at the time of trial when the government seeks to use evidence obtained by the police.

I submit that such a crabbed reading of the Fourth Amendment casts aside the teaching of those Justices who first formulated the exclusionary rule, and rests ultimately on an impoverished understanding of judicial responsibility in our constitutional scheme. For my part, "[t]he right of the people to be secure in their persons, houses, papers and effects, against unreasonable searches and seizures" comprises a personal right to exclude all evidence secured by means of unreasonable searches and seizures. The right to be free from the initial invasion of privacy and the right of exclusion are coordinate components of the central embracing right to be free from unreasonable searches and seizures.

. . .

That conception of the rule, in my view, is more faithful to the meaning and purpose of the Fourth Amendment and to the judiciary's role as the guardian of the people's constitutional liberties. In contrast to the present Court's restrictive reading, the Court in *Weeks* [v. United States, 232 U.S. 383 (1914)], recognized that, if the Amendment is to have any meaning, police and the courts cannot be regarded as constitutional strangers to each other; because the evidence-gathering role of the police is directly linked to the evidence-admitting function of the courts, an individual's Fourth Amendment rights may be undermined as completely by one as by the other.

B

From the foregoing, it is clear why the question whether the exclusion of evidence would deter future police misconduct was never considered a relevant concern in the early cases from *Weeks* to *Olmstead* [v. United States, 277 U.S. 438 (1928)]. In those formative decisions, the Court plainly understood that the exclusion of illegally obtained evidence was compelled not by judicially fashioned remedial purposes, but rather by a direct constitutional command. . . .

. . .

. . . [T]he Court since *Calandra* has gradually pressed the deterrence rationale for the rule back to center stage. . . . The various arguments advanced by the Court in this campaign have only strengthened my conviction that the deterrence theory is both misguided and unworkable. First, the Court has frequently bewailed the "cost" of excluding reliable evidence. In large part, this criticism rests upon a refusal to acknowledge the function of the Fourth Amendment itself. If nothing else, the Amendment plainly operates to disable the government from gathering information and securing evidence in certain ways. In practical terms, of course, this restriction of official power means that some incriminating evidence inevitably will go undetected if the government obeys these constitutional restraints. It is the loss of that evidence that is the "price" our society pays for enjoying the freedom and privacy safeguarded by the Fourth Amendment. Thus, some criminals will go free *not*, in Justice (then Judge) Cardozo's misleading epigram, "because the constable has blundered," People v. Defore, 242 N.Y. 13, 21, 150 N.E. 585, 587 (1926), but rather because official compliance with Fourth Amendment requirements makes it more difficult to catch criminals. Understood in this way, the Amendment directly contemplates that some reliable and incriminating evidence will be lost to the government; therefore, it is not the exclusionary rule, but the Amendment itself that has imposed this cost.

In addition, the Court's decisions over the past decade have made plain that the entire enterprise of attempting to assess the benefits and costs of the exclusionary rule in various contexts is a virtually impossible task for the judiciary to perform honestly or accurately. Although the Court's language in those cases suggests that some specific empirical basis may support its analyses, the reality is that the Court's opinions represent inherently unstable compounds of intuition, hunches, and occasional pieces of partial and often inconclusive data. In *Calandra*, for example, the Court, in considering whether the exclusionary rule should apply in grand jury proceedings, had before it no concrete evidence whatever concerning the impact that application of the rule in such proceedings would have either in terms of the long-term costs or the expected benefits. To the extent empirical data is available regarding the general costs and benefits of the exclusionary rule, it has shown, on the one hand, as the Court acknowledges today, that the costs are not as substantial as critics have asserted in the past, see ante, at 707–708, n. 6, and, on the other hand, that while the exclusionary rule may well have certain deterrent effects, it is extremely difficult to determine with any degree of precision whether the incidence of unlawful conduct by police is now lower than it was prior to *Mapp.* . . . The Court has sought to turn this uncertainty to its advantage by casting the burden of proof upon proponents of the rule . . . . "Obviously," however, "the assignment of the burden of proof on an issue where evidence does not exist and cannot be obtained is outcome determinative. [The] assignment of the burden is merely a way of announcing a predetermined conclusion." [10]

By remaining within its redoubt of empiricism and by basing the rule solely on the deterrence rationale, the Court has robbed the rule of legitimacy. A doctrine that is explained as if it were an empirical proposition but for which there is only limited empirical support is both inherently unstable and an easy mark for critics. The extent of this Court's fidelity to Fourth Amendment requirements, however, should not turn on such statistical uncertainties. I share the view, expressed by Justice Stewart for the Court in Faretta v. California, 422 U.S. 806 (1975), that "[p]ersonal liberties are not based on the law of averages." Id., at 834. Rather than seeking to give effect to the liberties secured by the Fourth Amendment through guesswork about deterrence, the Court should restore to its proper place the principle framed 70 years ago in *Weeks* that an individual whose privacy has been invaded in violation of the Fourth Amendment has a right grounded in that Amendment to prevent the government from subsequently making use of any evidence so obtained.

II

Application of that principle clearly requires affirmance in the two cases decided today. . . .

. . .

III

Even if I were to accept the Court's general approach to the exclusionary rule, I could not agree with today's result. There is no

---

10. Dworkin, Fact Style Adjudication and the Fourth Amendment: The Limits of Law-   yering, 48 Ind.L.J. 329, 332–333 (1973). . . .

question that in the hands of the present Court the deterrence rationale has proved to be a powerful tool for confining the scope of the rule....

... [I]n this bit of judicial stagecraft, while the sets sometimes change, the actors always have the same lines. Given this well-rehearsed pattern, one might have predicted with some assurance how the present case would unfold. First there is the ritual incantation of the "substantial social costs" exacted by the exclusionary rule, followed by the virtually foreordained conclusion that, given the marginal benefits, application of the rule in the circumstances of these cases is not warranted. Upon analysis, however, such a result cannot be justified even on the Court's own terms.

At the outset, the Court suggests that society has been asked to pay a high price—in terms either of setting guilty persons free or of impeding the proper functioning of trials—as a result of excluding relevant physical evidence in cases where the police, in conducting searches and seizing evidence, have made only an "objectively reasonable" mistake concerning the constitutionality of their actions. See ante, at 907–908. But what evidence is there to support such a claim?

Significantly, the Court points to none, and, indeed, as the Court acknowledges ... recent studies have demonstrated that the "costs" of the exclusionary rule—calculated in terms of dropped prosecutions and lost convictions—are quite low. Contrary to the claims of the rule's critics that exclusion leads to "the release of countless guilty criminals," Bivens v. Six Unknown Federal Narcotics Agents, 403 U.S. 388, 416 (Burger, C.J., dissenting), these studies have demonstrated that federal and state prosecutors very rarely drop cases because of potential search and seizure problems. For example, a 1979 study prepared at the request of Congress by the General Accounting Office reported that only 0.4% of all cases actually declined for prosecution by federal prosecutors were declined primarily because of illegal search problems. Report of the Comptroller General of the United States, Impact of the Exclusionary Rule on Federal Criminal Prosecutions 14 (1979). If the GAO data are restated as a percentage of *all* arrests, the study shows that only 0.2% of all felony arrests are declined for prosecution because of potential exclusionary rule problems. ... Of course, these data describe only the costs attributable to the exclusion of evidence in all cases; the costs due to the exclusion of evidence in the narrower category of cases where police have made objectively reasonable mistakes must necessarily be even smaller....

What then supports the Court's insistence that this evidence be admitted? Apparently, the Court's only answer is that even though the costs of exclusion are not very substantial, the potential deterrent effect in these circumstances is so marginal that exclusion cannot be justified. The key to the Court's conclusion in this respect is its belief that the prospective deterrent effect of the exclusionary rule operates only in those situations in which police officers, when deciding whether to go forward with some particular search, have reason to know that their planned conduct will violate the requirements of the Fourth Amendment. . . .

At first blush, there is some logic to this position. Undoubtedly, in the situation hypothesized by the Court, the existence of the exclusionary rule cannot be expected to have any deterrent effect on the particular officers at the moment they are deciding whether to go forward with the search. Indeed, the subsequent exclusion of any evidence seized under such circumstances appears somehow "unfair" to the particular officers involved. As the Court suggests, these officers have acted in what they thought was an appropriate and constitutionally authorized manner, but then the fruit of their efforts is nullified by the application of the exclusionary rule. . . .

The flaw in the Court's argument, however, is that its logic captures only one comparatively minor element of the generally acknowledged deterrent purposes of the exclusionary rule. To be sure, the rule operates to some extent to deter future misconduct by individual officers who have had evidence suppressed in their own cases. But what the Court overlooks is that the deterrence rationale for the rule is not designed to be, nor should it be thought of as, a form of "punishment" of individual police officers for their failures to obey the restraints imposed by the Fourth Amendment. . . . Instead, the chief deterrent function of the rule is its tendency to promote institutional compliance with Fourth Amendment requirements on the part of law enforcement agencies generally. . . . It is only through such an institutionwide mechanism that information concerning Fourth Amendment standards can be effectively communicated to rank and file officers.

If the overall educational effect of the exclusionary rule is considered, application of the rule to even those situations in which individual police officers have acted on the basis of a reasonable but mistaken belief that their conduct was authorized can still be expected to have a considerable long-term deterrent effect. If evidence is consistently excluded in these circumstances, police departments will surely be prompted to instruct their officers to devote greater care and attention to providing sufficient information to establish probable cause when applying for a warrant, and to review with some attention the form of the warrant that they have been issued, rather than automatically assuming that whatever document the magistrate has signed will necessarily comport with Fourth Amendment requirements.

After today's decision, however, that institutional incentive will be lost. Indeed, the Court's "reasonable mistake" exception to the exclusionary rule will tend to put a premium on police ignorance of the law. Armed with the assurance provided by today's decision that evidence will always be admissible whenever an officer has "reasonably" relied upon a warrant, police departments will be encouraged to train officers that if a warrant has simply been signed, it is reasonable, without more, to rely on it. Since in close cases there will no longer be any incentive to err on the side of constitutional behavior, police would have every reason to adopt a "let's-wait-until-its-decided" approach in situations in which there is a question about a warrant's validity or the basis for its issuance. ...

Although the Court brushes these concerns aside, a host of grave consequences can be expected to result from its decision to carve this new exception out of the exclusionary rule. A chief consequence of today's decision will be to convey a clear and unambiguous message to magistrates that their decisions to issue warrants are now insulated from subsequent judicial review. Creation of this new exception for good faith reliance upon a warrant implicitly tells magistrates that they need not take much care in reviewing warrant applications, since their mistakes will from now on have virtually no consequence: If their decision to issue a warrant was correct, the evidence will be admitted; if their decision was incorrect but the police relied in good faith on the warrant, the evidence will also be admitted. Inevitably, the care and attention devoted to such an inconsequential chore will dwindle. Although the Court is correct to note that magistrates do not share the same stake in the outcome of a criminal case as the police, they nevertheless need to appreciate that their role is of some moment in order to continue performing the important task of carefully reviewing warrant applications. Today's decision effectively removes that incentive.

Moreover, the good faith exception will encourage police to provide only the bare minimum of information in future warrant applications. The police will now know that if they can secure a warrant, so long as the circumstances of its issuance are not "entirely unreasonable," ante, at 923, all police conduct pursuant to that warrant will be protected from further judicial review. The clear incentive that operated in the past to establish probable cause adequately because reviewing courts would examine the magistrate's judgment carefully ... has now been so completely vitiated that the police need only show that it was not "entirely unreasonable" under the circumstances of a particular case for them to believe that the warrant they were issued was valid. See ante, at 923. The long-run effect unquestionably will be to undermine the integrity of the warrant process.

Finally, even if one were to believe, as the Court apparently does, that police are hobbled by inflexible and hyper-technical warrant procedures, today's decision cannot be justified. This is because, given the relaxed standard for assessing probable cause established just last Term in Illinois v. Gates, 462 U.S. 213 (1983), the Court's newly fashioned good-faith exception, when applied in the warrant context, will rarely, if ever, offer any greater flexibility for police than the *Gates* standard already supplies. In *Gates,* the Court held that "[t]he task of an issuing magistrate is simply to make a practical, commonsense decision whether, given all the circumstances set forth in the affidavit before him, . . . there is a fair probability that contraband or evidence of a crime will be found in a particular place." Id., at 238. The task of a reviewing court is confined to determining whether "the magistrate had a 'substantial basis' for . . . concluding that probable cause existed." Ibid. Given such a relaxed standard, it is virtually inconceivable that a reviewing court, when faced with a defendant's motion to suppress, could first find that a warrant was invalid under the new *Gates* standard, but then, at the same time, find that a police officer's reliance on such an invalid warrant was nevertheless "objectively reasonable" under the test announced today. Because the two standards overlap so completely, it is unlikely that a warrant could be found invalid under *Gates* and yet the police reliance upon it could be seen as objectively reasonable; otherwise, we would have to entertain the mind-boggling concept of objectively reasonable reliance upon an objectively unreasonable warrant.

. . .

IV

When the public, as it quite properly has done in the past as well as in the present, demands that those in government increase their efforts to combat crime, it is all too easy for those government officials to seek expedient solutions. In contrast to such costly and difficult measures as building more prisons, improving law enforcement methods, or hiring more prosecutors and judges to relieve the overburdened court systems in the country's metropolitan areas, the relaxation of Fourth Amendment standards seems a tempting, costless means of meeting the public's demand for better law enforcement. In the long run, however, we as a society pay a heavy price for such expediency, because as Justice Jackson observed, the rights guaranteed in the Fourth Amendment "are not mere second-class rights but belong in the catalog of indispensable freedoms." Brinegar v. United States, 338 U.S. 160, 180 (1949) (dissenting opinion). Once lost, such rights are difficult to recover. There is hope, however, that in time this or some later Court will restore these precious freedoms to their rightful place as a primary protection for our citizens against overreaching officialdom.

I dissent.[*] [**]

---

[*] Justice Blackmun wrote a concurring opinion. Justice Stevens wrote a dissenting opinion.

[**] In a companion case, Massachusetts v. Sheppard, 468 U.S. 981 (1984) (7–2), the Court applied the good-faith exception to the exclusionary rule to uphold the admission of evidence obtained pursuant to a search warrant that was "technically" defective because

of an inadvertent failure particularly to describe the items to be seized. The items in question were identified in an affidavit accompanying the warrant.

NIX v. WILLIAMS

467 U.S. 431, 104 S.Ct. 2501, 81 L.Ed.2d 377 (1984).

CHIEF JUSTICE BURGER delivered the opinion of the Court.

We granted certiorari to consider whether, at respondent Williams' second murder trial in state court, evidence pertaining to the discovery and condition of the victim's body was properly admitted on the ground that it would ultimately or inevitably have been discovered even if no violation of any constitutional or statutory provision had taken place.

I

A

On December 24, 1968, 10-year-old Pamela Powers disappeared from a YMCA building in Des Moines, Iowa, where she had accompanied her parents to watch an athletic contest. Shortly after she disappeared, Williams was seen leaving the YMCA carrying a large bundle wrapped in a blanket; a 14-year-old-boy who had helped Williams open his car door reported that he had seen "two legs in it and they were skinny and white."

Williams' car was found the next day 160 miles east of Des Moines in Davenport, Iowa. Later several items of clothing belonging to the child, some of Williams' clothing, and an army blanket like the one used to wrap the bundle that Williams carried out of the YMCA were found at a rest stop on Interstate 80 near Grinnell, between Des Moines and Davenport. A warrant was issued for Williams' arrest.

Police surmised that Williams had left Pamela Powers or her body somewhere between Des Moines and the Grinnell rest stop where some of the young girl's clothing had been found. On December 26, the Iowa Bureau of Criminal Investigation initiated a large-scale search. Two hundred volunteers divided into teams began the search 21 miles east of Grinnell, covering an area several miles to the north and south of Interstate 80. They moved westward from Poweshiek County, in which Grinnell was located, into Jasper County. Searchers were instructed to check all roads, abandoned farm buildings, ditches, culverts, and any other place in which the body of a small child could be hidden.

Meanwhile, Williams surrendered to local police in Davenport, where he was promptly arraigned. Williams contacted a Des Moines attorney who arranged for an attorney in Davenport to meet Williams at the Davenport police station. Des Moines police informed counsel they would pick Williams up in Davenport and return him to Des Moines without questioning him. Two Des Moines detectives then drove to Davenport, took Williams into custody, and proceeded to drive him back to Des Moines.

During the return trip, one of the policemen, Detective Leaming, began a conversation with Williams, saying:

> "I want to give you something to think about while we're traveling down the road. . . . They are predicting several inches of snow for tonight, and I feel that you yourself are the only person that knows where this little girl's body is . . . and if you get a snow on top of it you yourself may be unable to find it. And since we will be going right past the area [where the body is] on the way into Des Moines, I feel that we could stop and locate the body, that the parents of this little girl should be entitled to a Christian burial for the little girl who was snatched away from them on Christmas [E]ve and murdered. . . . [A]fter a snow storm [we may not be] able to find it at all."

Leaming told Williams he knew the body was in the area of Mitchellville—a town they would be passing on the way to Des Moines. He concluded the conversation by saying, "I do not want you to answer me. . . . Just think about it . . . ."

Later, as the police car approached Grinnell, Williams asked Leaming whether the police had found the young girl's shoes. After Leaming replied that he was unsure, Williams directed the police to a point near a service station where he said he had left the shoes; they were not found. As they continued the drive to Des Moines, Williams asked whether the blanket had been found and then directed the officers to a rest area in Grinnell where he said he had disposed of the blanket; they did not find the blanket. At this point Leaming and his party were joined by the officers in charge of the search. As they approached Mitchellville, Williams, without any further conversation, agreed to direct the officers to the child's body.

The officers directing the search had called off the search at 3 p.m., when they left the Grinnell Police Department to join Leaming at the rest area. At that time, one search team near the Jasper County-Polk County line was only two and one-half miles from where Williams soon guided Leaming and his party to the body. The child's body was found next to a culvert in a ditch beside a gravel road in Polk County, about two miles south of Interstate 80, and essentially within the area to be searched.

B

First Trial

In February 1969 Williams was indicted for first-degree murder. Before trial in the Iowa court, his counsel moved to suppress evidence of the body and all related evidence including the condition of the body as shown by the autopsy. The ground for the motion was that such evidence was the "fruit" or product of Williams' statements made during the automobile ride from Davenport to Des Moines and prompted by Leaming's statements. The motion to suppress was denied.

The jury found Williams guilty of first-degree murder; the judgment of conviction was affirmed by the Iowa Supreme Court. State v. Williams, 182 N.W.2d 396 (1970). Williams then sought release on habeas corpus in the United States District Court for the Southern District of Iowa. That court concluded that the evidence in question had been wrongly admitted at Williams' trial, Williams v. Brewer, 375 F.Supp. 170 (1974); a divided panel of the Court of Appeals for the Eighth Circuit agreed. 509 F.2d 227 (1974).

We granted certiorari, 432 U.S. 1031 (1975), and a divided Court affirmed, holding that Detective Leaming had obtained incriminating statements from Williams by what was viewed as interrogation in violation of his right to counsel. Brewer v. Williams, 430 U.S. 387 (1977). This Court's opinion noted, however, that although Williams' incriminating statements could not be introduced into evidence at a second trial, evidence of the body's location and condition "might well be admissible on the theory that the body would have been discovered in any event, even had incriminating statements not been elicited from Williams." Id., at 407, n. 12.

C

Second Trial

At Williams' second trial in 1977 in the Iowa court, the prosecution did not offer Williams' statements into evidence, nor did it seek to show that Williams had directed the police to the child's body. However, evidence of the condition of her body as it was found, articles and photographs of her clothing, and the results of post mortem medical and chemical tests on the body were admitted. The trial court concluded that the State had proved by a preponderance of the evidence that, if the search had not been suspended and Williams had not led the police to the victim, her body would have been discovered *"within a short time"* in essentially the same condition as it was actually found. The trial court also ruled that if the police had not located the body, "the search would clearly have been taken up again where it left off, given the extreme circumstances of this case and the body would [have] been found *in short order*." App. 86 (emphasis added).

In finding that the body would have been discovered in essentially the same condition as it was actually found, the court noted that freezing temperatures had prevailed and tissue deterioration would have been suspended. Id., at 87. The challenged evidence was admitted and the jury again found Williams guilty of first-degree murder; he was sentenced to life in prison.

On appeal, the Supreme Court of Iowa again affirmed. 285 N.W.2d 248 (1979). That court held that there was in fact a "hypothetical independent source" exception to the exclusionary rule:

> "After the defendant has shown unlawful conduct on the part of the police, the State has the burden to show by a preponderance of the evidence that (1) the police did not act in bad faith for the purpose of hastening discovery of the evidence in question, and (2) that the evidence in question would have been discovered by lawful means." Id., at 260.

As to the first element, the Iowa Supreme Court, having reviewed the relevant cases, stated:

> "The issue of the propriety of the police conduct in this case, as noted earlier in this opinion, has caused the closest possible division of views in every appellate court which has considered the question. In light of the legitimate disagreement among individuals well versed in the law of criminal procedure who were given the opportunity for calm deliberation, it cannot be said that the actions of the police were taken in bad faith." Id., at 260–261.

The Iowa court then reviewed the evidence *de novo* and concluded that the State had shown by a preponderance of the evidence that, even if Williams had not guided police to the child's body, it would inevitably have been found by lawful activity of the search party before its condition had materially changed.

In 1980 Williams renewed his attack on the state-court conviction by seeking a writ of habeas corpus in the United States District Court for the Southern District of Iowa. The District Court conducted its own independent review of the evidence and concluded, as had the state courts, that the body would inevitably have been found by the searchers in essentially the same condition it was in when Williams led police to its discovery. The District Court denied Williams' petition. 528 F.Supp. 664 (1981).

The Court of Appeals for the Eighth Circuit reversed. 700 F.2d 1164 (1983); an equally divided court denied rehearing en banc. 700 F.2d 1175 (1983). That court assumed, without deciding, that there is an inevitable discovery exception to the exclusionary rule and that the Iowa Supreme Court correctly stated that exception to require proof that the police did not act in bad faith and that the evidence would have been discovered absent any constitutional violation. . . .

We granted the State's petition for certiorari, 461 U.S. 956 (1983), and we reverse.

II

A

The Iowa Supreme Court correctly stated that the "vast majority" of all courts, both state and federal, recognize an inevitable discovery exception to the exclusionary rule. We are now urged to adopt and apply the so-called ultimate or inevitable discovery exception to the exclusionary rule.

Williams contends that evidence of the body's location and condition is "fruit of the poisonous tree," i.e., the "fruit" or product of Detective Leaming's plea to help the child's parents give her "a Christian burial," which this Court had already held equated to interrogation. He contends that admitting the challenged evidence violated the Sixth Amendment whether it would have been inevitably discovered or not. Williams also contends that, if the inevitable discovery doctrine is constitutionally permissible, it must include a threshold showing of police good faith.

B

The doctrine requiring courts to suppress evidence as the tainted "fruit" of unlawful governmental conduct had its genesis in Silverthorne Lumber Co. v. United States, 251 U.S. 385 (1920); there, the Court held that the exclusionary rule applies not only to the illegally obtained evidence itself, but also to other incriminating evidence derived from the primary evidence. The holding of *Silverthorne* was carefully limited, however, for the Court emphasized that such information does not automatically become "sacred and inaccessible." Id., at 392.

> "If knowledge of [such facts] is gained from an *independent source*, they may be proved like any others ... ." Ibid. (emphasis added).

Wong Sun v. United States, 371 U.S. 471 (1963), extended the exclusionary rule to evidence that was the indirect product or "fruit" of unlawful police conduct, but there again the Court emphasized that evidence that has been illegally obtained need not always be suppressed, stating:

> "We need not hold that all evidence is 'fruit of the poisonous tree' simply because it would not have come to light *but for the illegal actions* of the police. Rather, the more apt question in such a case is 'whether, granting establishment of the primary illegality, the evidence to which instant objection is made has been come at by exploitation of that illegality or instead by means sufficiently distinguishable to be purged of the primary taint.'" Id., at 487–488 (emphasis added) (quoting J. Maguire, Evidence of Guilt 221 (1959)).

The Court thus pointedly negated the kind of good-faith requirement advanced by the Court of Appeals in reversing the District Court.

Although *Silverthorne* and *Wong Sun* involved violations of the Fourth Amendment, the "fruit of the poisonous tree" doctrine has not been limited to cases in which there has been a Fourth Amendment violation. The Court has applied the doctrine where the violations were of the Sixth Amendment, see United States v. Wade, 388 U.S. 218 (1967), as well as of the Fifth Amendment.

The core rationale consistently advanced by this Court for extending the exclusionary rule to evidence that is the fruit of unlawful police conduct has been that this admittedly drastic and socially costly course is needed to deter police from violations of constitutional and statutory protections. This Court has accepted the argument that the way to ensure such protections is to exclude evidence seized as a result of such violations notwithstanding the high social cost of letting persons obviously guilty go unpunished for their crimes. On this rationale, the prosecution is not to be put in a better position than it would have been in if no illegality had transpired.

By contrast, the derivative evidence analysis ensures that the prosecution is not put in a *worse* position simply because of some earlier police error or misconduct. The independent source doctrine allows admission of evidence that has been discovered by means wholly independent of any constitutional violation. That doctrine, although closely related to the inevitable discovery doctrine, does not apply here; Williams' statements to Leaming indeed led police to the child's body, but that is not the whole story. The independent source doctrine teaches us that the interest of society in deterring unlawful police conduct and the public interest in having juries receive all probative evidence of a crime are properly balanced by putting the police in the same, not a *worse*, position than they would have been in if no police error or misconduct had occurred. ... When the challenged evidence has an independent source, exclusion of such evidence would put the police in a worse position than they would have been in absent any error or violation. There is a functional similarity between these two doctrines in that exclusion of evidence that would inevitably have been discovered would also put the government in a worse position, because the police would have obtained that evidence if no misconduct had taken place. Thus, while the independent source exception would not justify admission of evidence in this case, its rationale is wholly consistent with and justifies our adoption of the ultimate or inevitable discovery exception to the exclusionary rule.

It is clear that the cases implementing the exclusionary rule "begin with the premise that the challenged evidence is *in some sense* the product of illegal governmental activity." United States v. Crews, 445 U.S. 463, 471 (1980) (emphasis added). Of course, this does not end the inquiry. If the prosecution can establish by a preponderance of the evidence that the information ultimately or inevitably would have been discovered by lawful means—here the volunteers' search—then the deterrence rationale has so little basis that the evidence should be received. Anything less would reject logic, experience and common sense.

The requirement that the prosecution must prove the absence of bad faith, imposed here by the Court of Appeals, would place courts in the position of withholding from juries relevant and undoubted truth that would have been available to police absent any unlawful police activity. Of course, that view would put the police in a *worse* position than they would have been in if no unlawful conduct had transpired. And, of equal importance, it wholly fails to take into account the enormous societal cost of excluding truth in the search for truth in the administration of justice. Nothing in this Court's prior holdings supports any such formalistic, pointless, and punitive approach.

The Court of Appeals concluded, without analysis, that if an absence-of-bad-faith requirement were not imposed, "the temptation to risk deliberate violations of the Sixth Amendment would be too great, and the deterrent effect of the Exclusionary Rule reduced too far." 700 F.2d, at 1169, n. 5. We reject that view. A police officer who is faced with the opportunity to obtain evidence illegally will rarely, if ever, be in a position to calculate whether the evidence sought would inevitably be discovered. ... On the other hand, when an officer is aware that the evidence will inevitably be discovered, he will try to avoid engaging in any questionable practice. In that situation, there will be little to gain from taking any dubious "shortcuts" to obtain the evidence. Significant disincentives to obtaining evidence illegally—including the possibility of departmental discipline and civil liability—also lessen the likelihood that the ultimate or inevitable discovery exception will promote police misconduct. ... In these circumstances, the societal costs of the exclusionary rule far outweigh any possible benefits to deterrence that a good-faith requirement might produce.

Williams contends that because he did not waive his right to the assistance of counsel, the Court may not balance competing values in deciding whether the challenged evidence was properly admitted. He argues that, unlike the exclusionary rule in the Fourth Amendment context, the essential purpose of which is to deter police misconduct, the Sixth Amendment exclusionary rule is designed to protect the right to a fair trial and the integrity of the factfinding process. Williams contends that, when those interests are at stake, the societal costs of excluding evidence obtained from responses presumed involuntary are irrelevant in determining whether such evidence should be excluded. We disagree.

Exclusion of physical evidence that would inevitably have been discovered adds nothing to either the integrity or fairness of a criminal trial. The Sixth Amendment right to counsel protects against unfairness by preserving the adversary process in which the reliability of proffered evidence may be tested in cross-examination. ... Here, however, Detective Leaming's conduct did nothing to impugn the reliability of the evidence in question—the body of the child and its condition as it was found, articles of clothing found on the body, and the autopsy. No one would seriously contend that the presence of counsel in the police car when Leaming appealed to Williams' decent human instincts would have had any bearing on the reliability of the body as evidence. Suppression, in these circumstances, would do nothing whatever to promote the integrity of the trial process, but would inflict a wholly unacceptable burden on the administration of criminal justice.

Nor would suppression ensure fairness on the theory that it tends to safeguard the adversary system of justice. ... Fairness can be assured by placing the State and the accused in the same positions they would have been in had the impermissible conduct not taken place. However, if the government can prove that the evidence would have been obtained inevitably and, therefore, would have been admitted regardless of any overreaching by the police, there is no rational basis to keep that evidence from the jury in order to ensure the fairness of the trial proceedings. In that situation, the State has gained no advantage at trial and the defendant has suffered no prejudice. Indeed, suppression of the evidence would operate to undermine the adversary system by putting the State in a *worse* position than it would have occupied without any police misconduct. Williams' argument that inevitable discovery constitutes impermissible balancing of values is without merit.

. . .

C

The Court of Appeals did not find it necessary to consider whether the record fairly supported the finding that the volunteer search party would ultimately or inevitably have discovered the victim's body. However, three courts independently reviewing the evidence have found that the body of the child inevitably would have been found by the searchers. ...

. . .

On this record it is clear that the search parties were approaching the actual location of the body and we are satisfied, along with three courts earlier, that the volunteer search teams would have resumed the search had Williams not earlier led the police to the body and the body inevitably would have been found. The evidence asserted by Williams as newly discovered, i.e., certain photographs of the body and deposition testimony of Agent Ruxlow made in connection with the federal habeas proceeding, does not demonstrate that the material facts were inadequately developed in the suppression hearing in state court or that Williams was denied a full, fair, and adequate opportunity to present all relevant facts at the suppression hearing.

The judgment of the Court of Appeals is reversed, and the case is remanded for further proceedings consistent with this opinion.

It is so ordered.[*]

[*] Justice White wrote a concurring opinion. Justice Stevens wrote an opinion concurring in the judgment. Justice Brennan wrote a dissenting opinion, which Justice Marshall joined.

RAKAS v. ILLINOIS

439 U.S. 128, 99 S.Ct. 421, 58 L.Ed.2d 387 (1978).

MR. JUSTICE REHNQUIST delivered the opinion of the Court.

Petitioners were convicted of armed robbery in the Circuit Court of Kankakee County, Ill., and their convictions were affirmed on appeal. At their trial, the prosecution offered into evidence a sawed-off rifle and rifle shells that had been seized by police during a search of an automobile in which petitioners had been passengers. Neither petitioner is the owner of the automobile and neither has ever asserted that he owned the rifle or shells seized. The Illinois Appellate Court held that petitioners lacked standing to object to the allegedly unlawful search and seizure and denied their motion to suppress the evidence. We granted certiorari in light of the obvious importance of the issues raised to the administration of criminal justice, 435 U.S. 922 (1978), and now affirm.

I

Because we are not here concerned with the issue of probable cause, a brief description of the events leading to the search of the automobile will suffice. A police officer on a routine patrol received a radio call notifying him of a robbery of a clothing store in Bourbonnais, Ill., and describing the getaway car. Shortly thereafter, the officer spotted an automobile which he thought might be the getaway car. After following the car for some time and after the arrival of assistance, he and several other officers stopped the vehicle. The occupants of the automobile, petitioners and two female companions, were ordered out of the car and after the occupants had left the car, two officers searched the interior of the vehicle. They discovered a box of rifle shells in the glove compartment, which had been locked, and a sawed-off rifle under the front passenger seat. App. 10–11. After discovering the rifle and the shells, the officers took petitioners to the station and placed them under arrest.

Before trial petitioners moved to suppress the rifle and shells seized from the car on the ground that the search violated the Fourth and Fourteenth Amendments. They conceded that they did not own the automobile and were simply passengers; the owner of the car had been the driver of the vehicle at the time of the search. Nor did they assert that they owned the rifle or the shells seized. The prosecutor challenged petitioners' standing to object to the lawfulness of the search of the car because neither the car, the shells nor the rifle belonged to them. The trial court agreed that petitioners lacked standing and denied the motion to suppress the evi-

369

dence. App. 23–24. In view of this holding, the court did not determine whether there was probable cause for the search and seizure. On appeal after petitioners' conviction, the Appellate Court of Illinois, Third Judicial District, affirmed the trial court's denial of petitioners' motion to suppress because it held that "without a proprietary or other similar interest in an automobile, a mere passenger therein lacks standing to challenge the legality of the search of the vehicle." 46 Ill.App.3d 569, 571, 360 N.E.2d 1252, 1253 (1977). ... The Illinois Supreme Court denied petitioners leave to appeal.

II

Petitioners first urge us to relax or broaden the rule of standing enunciated in Jones v. United States, 362 U.S. 257 (1960), so that any criminal defendant at whom a search was "directed" would have standing to contest the legality of that search and object to the admission at trial of evidence obtained as a result of the search. Alternatively, petitioners argue that they have standing to object to the search under *Jones* because they were "legitimately on [the] premises" at the time of the search.

The concept of standing discussed in *Jones* focuses on whether the person seeking to challenge the legality of a search as a basis for suppressing evidence was himself the "victim" of the search or seizure. Id., at 261. Adoption of the so-called "target" theory advanced by petitioners would in effect permit a defendant to assert that a violation of the Fourth Amendment rights of a third party entitled him to have evidence suppressed at his trial. If we reject petitioners' request for a broadened rule of standing such as this, and reaffirm the holding of *Jones* and other cases that Fourth Amendment rights are personal rights that may not be asserted vicariously, we will have occasion to re-examine the "standing" terminology emphasized in *Jones*. For we are not at all sure that the determination of a motion to suppress is materially aided by labeling the inquiry identified in *Jones* as one of standing, rather than simply recognizing it as one involving the substantive question of whether or not the proponent of the motion to suppress has had his own Fourth Amendment rights infringed by the search and seizure which he seeks to challenge. We shall therefore consider in turn petitioners' target theory, the necessity for continued adherence to the notion of standing discussed in *Jones* as a concept that is theoretically distinct from the merits of a defendant's Fourth Amendment claim, and finally, the proper disposition of petitioners' ultimate claim in this case.

A

We decline to extend the rule of standing in Fourth Amendment cases in the manner suggested by petitioners. As we stated in Alderman v. United States, 394 U.S. 165, 174 (1969), "Fourth

Amendment rights are personal rights which, like some other constitutional rights, may not be vicariously asserted." . . . A person who
is aggrieved by an illegal search and seizure only through the
introduction of damaging evidence secured by a search of a third
person's premises or property has not had any of his Fourth
Amendment rights infringed. . . . And since the exclusionary rule is
an attempt to effectuate the guaranties of the Fourth Amendment
. . . it is proper to permit only defendants whose Fourth Amendment rights have been violated to benefit from the rule's protections. . . . There is no reason to think that a party whose rights
have been infringed will not, if evidence is used against him, have
ample motivation to move to suppress it. . . . Even if such a person
is not a defendant in the action, he may be able to recover damages
for the violation of his Fourth Amendment rights . . . or seek redress
under state law for invasion of privacy or trespass.

   . . .

Conferring standing to raise vicarious Fourth Amendment
claims would necessarily mean a more widespread invocation of the
exclusionary rule during criminal trials. . . . Each time the exclusionary rule is applied it exacts a substantial social cost for the
vindication of Fourth Amendment rights. Relevant and reliable
evidence is kept from the trier of fact and the search for truth at trial
is deflected. . . . Since our cases generally have held that one
whose Fourth Amendment rights are violated may successfully suppress evidence obtained in the course of an illegal search and
seizure, misgivings as to the benefit of enlarging the class of persons
who may invoke that rule are properly considered when deciding
whether to expand standing to assert Fourth Amendment violations.

B

Had we accepted petitioners' request to allow persons other
than those whose own Fourth Amendment rights were violated by a
challenged search and seizure to suppress evidence obtained in the
course of such police activity, it would be appropriate to retain
Jones' use of standing in Fourth Amendment analysis. Under
petitioners' target theory, a court could determine that a defendant
had standing to invoke the exclusionary rule without having to
inquire into the substantive question of whether the challenged
search or seizure violated the Fourth Amendment rights of that
particular defendant. However, having rejected petitioners' target
theory and reaffirmed the principle that the "rights assured by the
Fourth Amendment are personal rights, [which] . . . may be enforced by exclusion of evidence only at the instance of one whose
own protection was infringed by the search and seizure," Simmons
v. United States, 390 U.S., at 389, the question necessarily arises
whether it serves any useful analytical purpose to consider this
principle a matter of standing, distinct from the merits of a defendant's Fourth Amendment claim. We can think of no decided cases

from this Court that would have come out differently had we concluded, as we do now, that the type of standing requirement discussed in *Jones* and reaffirmed today is more properly subsumed under substantive Fourth Amendment doctrine. Rigorous application of the principle that the rights secured by this Amendment are personal, in place of a notion of "standing," will produce no additional situations in which evidence must be excluded. The inquiry under either approach is the same. But we think the better analysis forthrightly focuses on the extent of a particular defendant's rights under the Fourth Amendment, rather than on any theoretically separate, but invariably intertwined concept of standing. The Court in *Jones* also may have been aware that there was a certain artificiality to analyzing this question in terms of standing because in at least three separate places in its opinion the Court placed that term within quotation marks. 362 U.S., at 261, 263, 265.

It should be emphasized that nothing we say here casts the least doubt on cases which recognize that, as a general proposition, the issue of standing involves two inquiries: first, whether the proponent of a particular legal right has alleged "injury in fact," and, second, whether the proponent is asserting his own legal rights and interests rather than basing his claim for relief upon the rights of third parties. ... But this Court's long history of insistence that Fourth Amendment rights are personal in nature has already answered many of these traditional standing inquiries, and we think that definition of those rights is more properly placed within the purview of substantive Fourth Amendment law than within that of standing. ...

Analyzed in these terms, the question is whether the challenged search or seizure violated the Fourth Amendment rights of a criminal defendant who seeks to exclude the evidence obtained during it. That inquiry in turn requires a determination of whether the disputed search and seizure has infringed an interest of the defendant which the Fourth Amendment was designed to protect. We are under no illusion that by dispensing with the rubric of standing used in *Jones* we have rendered any simpler the determination of whether the proponent of a motion to suppress is entitled to contest the legality of a search and seizure. But by frankly recognizing that this aspect of the analysis belongs more properly under the heading of substantive Fourth Amendment doctrine than under the heading of standing, we think the decision of this issue will rest on sounder logical footing.

C

Here petitioners, who were passengers occupying a car which they neither owned nor leased, seek to analogize their position to that of the defendant in Jones v. United States. In *Jones*, petitioner was present at the time of the search of an apartment which was owned by a friend. The friend had given Jones permission to use the apartment and a key to it, with which Jones had admitted himself on the day of the search. He had a suit and shirt at the apartment and had slept there "maybe a night," but his home was elsewhere. At the time of the search, Jones was the only occupant of the apartment because the lessee was away for a period of several days. 362 U.S., at 259. Under these circumstances, this Court stated that while one wrongfully on the premises could not move to suppress evidence obtained as a result of searching them, "anyone legitimately on premises where a search occurs may challenge its legality." Id., at 267. Petitioners argue that their occupancy of the automobile in question was comparable to that of Jones in the apartment and that they therefore have standing to contest the legality of the search—or as we have rephrased the inquiry, that they, like Jones, had their Fourth Amendment rights violated by the search.

We do not question the conclusion in *Jones* that the defendant in that case suffered a violation of his personal Fourth Amendment rights if the search in question were unlawful. Nonetheless, we believe that the phrase "legitimately on premises" coined in *Jones* creates too broad a gauge for measurement of Fourth Amendment rights. For example, applied literally, this statement would permit a casual visitor who has never seen, or been permitted to visit the basement of another's house to object to a search of the basement if the visitor happened to be in the kitchen of the house at the time of the search. Likewise, a casual visitor who walks into a house one minute before a search of the house commences and leaves one minute after the search ends would be able to contest the legality of the search. The first visitor would have absolutely no interest or legitimate expectation of privacy in the basement, the second would have none in the house, and it advances no purpose served by the Fourth Amendment to permit either of them to object to the lawfulness of the search.[11]

We think that *Jones* on its facts merely stands for the unremarkable proposition that a person can have a legally sufficient interest in a place other than his own home so that the Fourth Amendment protects him from unreasonable governmental intrusion into that place. . . . In defining the scope of that interest, we adhere to the view expressed in *Jones* and echoed in later cases that arcane distinctions developed in property and tort law between guests, licensees, invitees, and the like, ought not to control. . . . But the *Jones* statement that a person need only be "legitimately on premises" in order to challenge the validity of the search of a dwelling place cannot be taken in its full sweep beyond the facts of that case.

Katz v. United States, 389 U.S. 347 (1967), provides guidance in defining the scope of the interest protected by the Fourth Amend-

---

11. This is not to say that such visitors could not contest the lawfulness of the seizure of evidence or the search if their own property were seized during the search.

ment. In the course of repudiating the doctrine . . . that if police officers had not been guilty of a common-law trespass they were not prohibited by the Fourth Amendment from eavesdropping, the Court in *Katz* held that capacity to claim the protection of the Fourth Amendment depends not upon a property right in the invaded place but upon whether the person who claims the protection of the Amendment has a legitimate expectation of privacy in the invaded place. . . . Viewed in this manner, the holding in *Jones* can best be explained by the fact that Jones had a legitimate expectation of privacy in the premises he was using and therefore could claim the protection of the Fourth Amendment with respect to a governmental invasion of those premises, even though his "interest" in those premises might not have been a recognized property interest at common law.[12] . . .

Our Brother White in dissent expresses the view that by rejecting the phrase "legitimately on [the] premises" as the appropriate measure of Fourth Amendment rights, we are abandoning a thoroughly workable, "bright line" test in favor of a less certain analysis of whether the facts of a particular case give rise to a legitimate expectation of privacy. Post, at 168. If "legitimately on premises" were the successful litmus test of Fourth Amendment rights that he assumes it is, his approach would have at least the merit of easy application, whatever it lacked in fidelity to the history and purposes of the Fourth Amendment. But a reading of lower court cases that have applied the phrase "legitimately on premises," and of the dissent itself, reveals that this expression is not a shorthand

---

12. Obviously, however, a "legitimate" expectation of privacy by definition means more than a subjective expectation of not being discovered. A burglar plying his trade in a summer cabin during the off season may have a thoroughly justified subjective expectation of privacy, but it is not one which the law recognizes as "legitimate." His presence, in the words of *Jones*, 362 U.S., at 267, is "wrongful"; his expectation is not "one that society is prepared to recognize as 'reasonable.'" Katz v. United States, 389 U.S. 347, 361 (1967) (Harlan, J., concurring). And it would, of course, be merely tautological to fall back on the notion that those expectations of privacy which are legitimate depend primarily on cases deciding exclusionary rule issues in criminal cases. Legitimation of expectations of privacy by law must have a source outside of the Fourth Amendment, either by reference to concepts of real or personal property law or to understandings that are recognized and permitted by society. One of the main rights attaching to property is the right to exclude others, see W. Blackstone, Commentaries, Book II, Ch. I, and one who owns or lawfully possesses or controls property will in all likelihood have a legitimate expectation of privacy by virtue of this right to exclude. Expectations of privacy protected by the Fourth Amendment, of course, need not be based on a common-law interest in real or personal property, or on the invasion of such an interest. These ideas were rejected both in *Jones*, supra, and *Katz*, supra. But by focusing on legitimate expectations of privacy in Fourth Amendment jurisprudence, the Court has not altogether abandoned use of property concepts in determining the presence or absence of the privacy interests protected by that Amendment. No better demonstration of this proposition exists than the decision in Alderman v. United States, 394 U.S. 165 (1969), where the Court held that an individual's property interest in his own home was so great as to allow him to object to electronic surveillance of conversations emanating from his home, even though he himself was not a party to the conversations. On the other hand, even a property interest in premises may not be sufficient to establish a legitimate expectation of privacy with respect to particular items located on the premises or activity conducted thereon. See *Katz*, supra, at 351; Lewis v. United States, 385 U.S. 206, 210 (1966) . . . .

summary for a bright line rule which somehow encapsulates the "core" of the Fourth Amendment's protections.

The dissent itself shows that the facile consistency it is striving for is illusory. The dissenters concede that "there comes a point when use of an area is shared with so many that one simply cannot reasonably expect seclusion." Post, at 164. But surely the "point" referred to is not one demarcating a line which is black on one side and white on another; it is inevitably a point which separates one shade of gray from another. We are likewise told by the dissent that a person "legitimately on *private* premises ..., though his privacy is *not absolute,* is entitled to expect that he is sharing it only with those persons and that governmental officials will intrude only with *consent* or by complying with the Fourth Amendment." Ibid. (emphasis added). This single sentence describing the contours of the supposedly easily applied rule virtually abounds with unanswered questions: What are "private" premises? Indeed, what are the "premises?" It may be easy to describe the "premises" when one is confronted with a one-room apartment, but what of the case of a 10-room house, or of a house with an attached garage that is searched? Also, if one's privacy is not absolute, how is it bounded? If he risks governmental intrusion "with consent," who may give that consent?

Again, we are told by the dissent that the Fourth Amendment assures that "*some* expectations of privacy are justified and will be protected from official intrusion." Post, at 166. (emphasis added). But we are not told which of many possible expectations of privacy are embraced within this sentence. And our dissenting Brethren concede that "perhaps the Constitution provides some degree less protection for the personal freedom from unreasonable governmental intrusion when one does not have a possessory interest in the invaded private place." Ibid. But how much "less" protection is available when one does not have such a possessory interest?

Our disagreement with the dissent is not that it leaves these questions unanswered, or that the questions are necessarily irrelevant in the context of the analysis contained in this opinion. Our disagreement is rather with the dissent's bland and self-refuting assumption that there will not be fine lines to be drawn in Fourth Amendment cases as in other areas of the law, and that its rubric, rather than a meaningful exegesis of Fourth Amendment doctrine, is more desirable or more easily resolves Fourth Amendment cases. In abandoning "legitimately on premises" for the doctrine that we announce today, we are not forsaking a time-tested and workable rule, which has produced consistent results when applied, solely for the sake of fidelity to the values underlying the Fourth Amendment. We also are rejecting blind adherence to a phrase which at most has superficial clarity and which conceals underneath that thin veneer all of the problems of line drawing which must be faced in any conscientious effort to apply the Fourth Amendment. Where the factual premises for a rule are so generally prevalent that little would be lost and much would be gained by abandoning case-by-case analysis, we have not hesitated to do so. ... But the phrase "legitimately on premises" has not shown to be an easily applicable measure of Fourth Amendment rights so much as it has proved to be simply a label placed by the courts on results which have not been subjected to careful analysis. We would not wish to be understood as saying that legitimate presence on the premises is irrelevant to one's expectation of privacy, but it cannot be deemed controlling.

D

Judged by the foregoing analysis, petitioners' claims must fail. They asserted neither a property nor a possessory interest in the automobile, nor an interest in the property seized. And as we have previously indicated, the fact that they were "legitimately on [the] premises" in the sense that they were in the car with the permission of its owner is not determinative of whether they had a legitimate expectation of privacy in the particular areas of the automobile searched. It is unnecessary for us to decide here whether the same expectations of privacy are warranted in a car as would be justified in a dwelling place in analogous circumstances. We have on numerous occasions pointed out that cars are not to be treated identically with houses or apartments for Fourth Amendment purposes. ... But here petitioners' claim is one which would fail even in an analogous situation in a dwelling place since they made no showing that they had any legitimate expectation of privacy in the glove compartment or area under the seat of the car in which they were merely passengers. Like the trunk of an automobile, these are areas in which a passenger *qua* passenger simply would not normally have a legitimate expectation of privacy. Supra, at 142.

Jones v. United States, 362 U.S. 257 (1960) and Katz v. United States, 389 U.S. 347 (1967), involved significantly different factual circumstances. Jones not only had permission to use the apartment of his friend, but had a key to the apartment with which he admitted himself on the day of the search and kept possessions in the apartment. Except with respect to his friend, Jones had complete dominion and control over the apartment and could exclude others from it. Likewise in *Katz,* the defendant occupied the telephone booth, shut the door behind him to exclude all others and paid the toll, which "entitled [him] to assume that the words he utter[ed] into the mouthpiece would not be broadcast to the world." 389 U.S., at 352.[16] Katz and Jones could legitimately

---

16. The dissent states that Katz v. United States expressly recognized protection for passengers of taxicabs and asks why that protection should not also extend to these petitioners. *Katz* relied on Rios v. United States, 364 U.S. 253 (1960), as support for that proposition. The question of Rios' right to contest the search was not presented to or addressed by the Court and the property seized appears to have belonged to Rios. ...

expect privacy in the areas which were the subject of the search and seizure they sought to contest. No such showing was made by these petitioners with respect to those portions of the automobile which were searched and from which incriminating evidence was seized.[17]

III

The Illinois courts were therefore correct in concluding that it was unnecessary to decide whether the search of the car might have violated the rights secured to someone else by the Fourth and Fourteenth Amendments to the United States Constitution. Since it did not violate any rights of these petitioners, their judgment of conviction is

Affirmed.

MR. JUSTICE WHITE, with whom MR. JUSTICE BRENNAN, MR. JUSTICE MARSHALL, and MR. JUSTICE STEVENS join, dissenting.

The Court today holds that the Fourth Amendment protects property, not people, and specifically that a legitimate occupant of an automobile may not invoke the exclusionary rule and challenge a search of that vehicle unless he happens to own or have a possessory interest in it. Though professing to acknowledge that the primary purpose of the Fourth Amendment's prohibition of unreasonable searches is the protection of privacy—not property—the Court nonetheless effectively ties the application of the Fourth Amendment and the exclusionary rule in this situation to property law concepts. Insofar as passengers are concerned, the Court's opinion today declares an "open season" on automobiles. However unlawful stopping and searching a car may be, absent a possessory or ownership interest, no "mere" passenger may object, regardless of his relationship to the owner. Because the majority's conclusion has no support in the Court's controlling decisions, in

Additionally, the facts of that case are quite different from those of the present case. Rios had hired the cab and occupied the rear passenger section. When police stopped the car, he placed a package he had been holding on the floor of the rear section. The police saw the package and seized it after defendant was removed from the cab.

17. For reasons which they do not explain, our dissenting Brethren repeatedly criticize our "holding" that unless one has a common-law property interest in the premises searched, one cannot object to the search. We have rendered no such "holding," however. To the contrary, we have taken pains to reaffirm the statements in *Jones* and *Katz* that "arcane distinctions developed in property ... law ... ought not to control." *Supra,* at 143, and n. 12. In a similar vein, the dissenters repeatedly state or imply that we

now "hold" that a passenger lawfully in an automobile "may not invoke the exclusionary rule and challenge a search of that vehicle unless he happens to own or have a possessory interest in it." *Post,* at 156 .... It is not without significance that these statements of today's "holding" come from the dissenting opinion, and not from the Court's opinion. The case before us involves the search of and seizure of property from the glove compartment and area under the seat of a car in which petitioners were riding as passengers. Petitioners claimed only that they were "legitimately on [the] premises" and did not claim that they had any legitimate expectation of privacy in the areas of the car which were searched. We cannot, therefore, agree with the dissenters' insistence that our decision will encourage the police to violate the Fourth Amendment. ...

the logic of the Fourth Amendment, or in common sense, I must respectfully dissent. If the Court is troubled by the practical impact of the exclusionary rule, it should face the issue of that rule's continued validity squarely instead of distorting other doctrines in an attempt to reach what are perceived as the correct results in specific cases. . . .

I

Two intersecting doctrines long established in this Court's opinions control here. The first is the recognition of some cognizable level of privacy in the interior of an automobile. Though the reasonableness of the expectation of privacy in a vehicle may be somewhat weaker than that in a home . . . "[a] search, even of an automobile, is a substantial invasion of privacy. To protect that privacy from official arbitrariness, the Court has always regarded probable cause as the minimum requirement for a lawful search." United States v. Ortiz, 422 U.S. 891, 896 (1975) (footnote omitted). So far, the Court has not strayed from this application of the Fourth Amendment.

The second tenet is that when a person is legitimately present in a private place, his right to privacy is protected from unreasonable governmental interference even if he does not own the premises. . . .

These two fundamental aspects of Fourth Amendment law demand that petitioners be permitted to challenge the search and seizure of the automobile in this case. It is of no significance that a car is different for Fourth Amendment purposes from a house, for if there is some protection for the privacy of an automobile then the only relevant analogy is between a person legitimately in someone else's vehicle and a person legitimately in someone else's home. If both strands of the Fourth Amendment doctrine adumbrated above are valid, the Court must reach a different result. Instead, it chooses to eviscerate the *Jones* [v. United States, 362 U.S. 257 (1960)], principle, an action in which I am unwilling to participate.

II

Though we had reserved the very issue over 50 years ago . . . and never expressly dealt with it again until today, many of our opinions have assumed that a mere passenger in an automobile is entitled to protection against unreasonable searches occurring in his presence. In decisions upholding the validity of automobile searches, we have gone directly to the merits even though some of the petitioners did not own or possess the vehicles in question. . . . The Court's silence on this issue in light of its actions can only mean that, until now, we, like most lower courts, had assumed that *Jones* foreclosed the answer now supplied by the majority. That assumption was perfectly understandable, since all private premises would seem to be the same for the purposes of the analysis set out in *Jones.*

III

The logic of Fourth Amendment jurisprudence compels the result reached by the above decisions. Our starting point is "[t]he established principle that suppression of the product of a Fourth Amendment violation can be successfully urged only by those whose rights were violated by the search itself ..." Alderman v. United States, 394 U.S. 165, 171–172 (1969). Though the Amendment protects one's liberty and property interests against unreasonable seizures of self and effects, "the primary object of the Fourth Amendment [is] ... the protection of privacy." Cardwell v. Lewis, 417 U.S. 583, 589 (1974) (plurality opinion). And privacy is the interest asserted here, so the first step is to ascertain whether the premises searched "fall within a protected zone of privacy." United States v. Miller, 425 U.S. 435, 440 (1976). My Brethren in the majority assertedly do not deny that automobiles warrant at least some protection from official interference with privacy. Thus, the next step is to decide who is entitled, vis-à-vis the State, to enjoy that privacy. The answer to that question must be found by determining "whether petitioner had an interest in connection with the searched premises that gave rise to 'a reasonable expectation [on his part] of freedom from governmental intrusion' upon those premises." Combs v. United States, 408 U.S., at 227, quoting Mancusi v. DeForte, 392 U.S., at 368 (bracketed material in original).

Not only does *Combs* supply the relevant inquiry, it also directs us to the proper answer. We recognized there that *Jones* had held that one of those protected interests is created by legitimate presence on the searched premises, even absent any possessory interest. 408 U.S., at 227 n. 4. This makes unquestionable sense. We have concluded on numerous occasions that the entitlement to an expectation of privacy does not hinge on ownership .... The proposition today overruled was stated most directly in Mancusi v. DeForte, supra, at 368: "the protection of the Amendment depends not upon a property right in the invaded place but upon whether the area was one in which there was a reasonable expectation of freedom from governmental intrusion."

... Indeed, the decision today is contrary to Mr. Justice Brandeis' dissent in Olmstead v. United States, 277 U.S. 438, 478 (1928), expressing a view of the Fourth Amendment thought to have been vindicated by Katz [v. United States, 389 U.S. 347 (1967)]. The majority in *Olmstead* found the Fourth Amendment inapplicable absent a trespass on property rights. 227 U.S., at 466. That is exactly what the Court holds in this case; but Justice Brandeis asserted 50 years ago that more than mere property rights are involved, and the Court's opinion in *Katz* reemphasized that " '[t]he premise that property interests control the right of the Government to search and seize has been discredited.'" 389 U.S., at 353, quoting Warden v. Hayden, 387 U.S. 294, 304 (1967). That logic led us inescapably to the conclusion that "[n]o less than an individual in a business office, in a friend's apartment, or in a taxicab, a person in a telephone booth may rely upon the protection of the Fourth Amendment." 389 U.S., at 352 (footnotes omitted). And if all of those situations are protected, surely a person riding in an automobile next to his friend the owner, or a child or wife with the father or spouse, must have some protection as well.

The same result is reached by tracing other lines of our Fourth Amendment decisions. If a nonowner may consent to a search merely because he is a joint user or occupant of a "premises," Frazier v. Cupp, 394 U.S. 731, 740 (1969), then that same nonowner must have a protected privacy interest. The scope of the authority sufficient to grant a valid consent can hardly be broader than the contours of protected privacy. And why should the owner of a vehicle be entitled to challenge the seizure from it of evidence even if he is absent at the time of the search, see Coolidge v. New Hampshire, 403 U.S. 443 (1971), while a nonowner enjoying in person, and with the owner's permission, the privacy of an automobile is not so entitled?

In sum, one consistent theme in our decisions under the Fourth Amendment has been, until now, that "the Amendment does not shield only those who have title to the searched premises." Mancusi v. DeForte, 392 U.S., at 367. Though there comes a point when use of an area is shared with so many that one simply cannot reasonably expect seclusion, see id., at 377 (White, J., dissenting) ... short of that limit a person legitimately on private premises knows the others allowed there and, though his privacy is not absolute, is entitled to expect that he is sharing it only with those persons and that governmental officials will intrude only with consent or by complying with the Fourth Amendment. ...

It is true that the Court asserts that it is not limiting the Fourth Amendment bar against unreasonable searches to the protection of property rights, but in reality it is doing exactly that. Petitioners were in a private place with the permission of the owner, but the Court states that that is not sufficient to establish entitlement to a legitimate expectation of privacy. ... But if that is not sufficient, what would be? We are not told, and it is hard to imagine anything short of a property interest that would satisfy the majority. Insofar as the Court's rationale is concerned, no passenger in an automobile, without an ownership or possessory interest and regardless of his relationship to the owner, may claim Fourth Amendment protection against illegal stops and searches of the automobile in which he is rightfully present. The Court approves the result in *Jones,* but it fails to give any explanation why the facts in *Jones* differ, in a fashion material to the Fourth Amendment, from the facts here.

More importantly, how is the Court able to avoid answering the question why presence in a private place with the owner's permission is insufficient? If it is "tautological to fall back on the notion that those expectations of privacy which are legitimate depend primarily on cases deciding exclusionary rule issues in criminal cases," ante, at 144 n. 12, then it surely must be tautological to decide that issue simply by unadorned fiat.

As a control on governmental power, the Fourth Amendment assures that some expectations of privacy are justified and will be protected from official intrusion. That should be true in this instance, for if protected zones of privacy can only be purchased or obtained by possession of property, then much of our daily lives will be unshielded from unreasonable governmental prying, and the reach of the Fourth Amendment will have been narrowed to protect chiefly those with possessory interests in real or personal property. I had thought that *Katz* firmly established that the Fourth Amendment was intended as more than simply a trespass law applicable to the government. Katz had no possessory interest in the public telephone booth, at least no more than petitioners had in their friend's car; Katz was simply legitimately present. And the decision in *Katz* was based not on property rights but on the theory that it was essential to securing "conditions favorable to the pursuit of happiness" [16] that the expectation of privacy in question be recognized.

At most, one could say that perhaps the Constitution provides some degree less protection for the personal freedom from unreasonable governmental intrusion when one does not have a possessory interest in the invaded private place. But that would only change the extent of the protection; it would not free police to do the unreasonable, as does the decision today. And since the accused should be entitled to litigate the application of the Fourth Amendment where his privacy interest is merely arguable, the failure to allow such litigation here is the more incomprehensible.

IV

The Court's holding is contrary not only to our past decisions and the logic of the Fourth Amendment, but also to the everyday expectations of privacy that we all share. Because of that, it is unworkable in all the various situations that arise in real life. If the owner of the car had not only invited petitioners to join her but had said to them, "I give you a temporary possessory interest in my vehicle so that you will share the right to privacy that the Supreme Court says that I own," then apparently the majority would reverse. But people seldom say such things, though they may mean their invitation to encompass them if only they had thought of the problem. If the nonowner were the spouse or child of the owner,

16. Olmstead v. United States, 277 U.S. 438, 478 (1928) (Brandeis, J., dissenting).

would the Court recognize a sufficient interest? If so, would distant relatives somehow have more of an expectation of privacy than close friends? What if the nonowner were driving with the owner's permission? Would nonowning drivers have more of an expectation of privacy than mere passengers? What about a passenger in a taxicab? *Katz* expressly recognized protection for such passengers. Why should Fourth Amendment rights be present when one pays a cabdriver for a ride but be absent when one is given a ride by a friend?

The distinctions the Court would draw are based on relationships between private parties, but the Fourth Amendment is concerned with the relationship of one of those parties to the government. Divorced as it is from the purpose of the Fourth Amendment, the Court's essentially property-based rationale can satisfactorily answer none of the questions posed above. That is reason enough to reject it. The *Jones'* rule is relatively easily applied by police and courts; the rule announced today will not provide law enforcement officials with a bright line between the protected and the unprotected. Only rarely will police know whether one private party has or has not been granted a sufficient possessory or other interest by another private party. Surely in this case the officers had no such knowledge. The Court's rule will ensnare defendants and police in needless litigation over factors that should not be determinative of Fourth Amendment rights.

More importantly, the ruling today undercuts the force of the exclusionary rule in the one area in which its use is most certainly justified—the deterrence of bad-faith violations of the Fourth Amendment. . . . This decision invites police to engage in patently unreasonable searches every time an automobile contains more than one occupant. Should something be found, only the owner of the vehicle, or of the item, will have standing to seek suppression, and the evidence will presumably be usable against the other occupants. The danger of such bad faith is especially high in cases such as this one where the officers are only after the passengers and can usually infer accurately that the driver is the owner. The suppression remedy for those owners in whose vehicles something is found and who are charged with crime is small consolation for all those owners *and* occupants whose privacy will be needlessly invaded by officers following mistaken hunches not rising to the level of probable cause but operated on in the knowledge that someone in a crowded car will probably be unprotected if contraband or incriminating evidence happens to be found. After this decision, police will have little to lose by unreasonably searching vehicles occupied by more than one person.

Of course, most police officers will decline the Court's invitation and will continue to do their jobs as best they can in accord with the Fourth Amendment. But the very purpose of the Bill of Rights was to answer the justified fear that governmental agents cannot be left totally to their own devices, and the Bill of Rights is enforceable in the courts because human experience teaches that not all such officials will otherwise adhere to the stated precepts. Some policemen simply do act in bad faith, even if for understandable ends, and some deterrent is needed. In the rush to limit the applicability of the exclusionary rule somewhere, anywhere, the Court ignores precedent, logic, and common sense to exclude the rule's operation from situations in which, paradoxically, it is justified and needed.[*] [**]

[*] Justice Powell wrote a concurring opinion, which Chief Justice Burger joined.

[**] In Rawlings v. Kentucky, 448 U.S. 98 (1980) (5–2–2), the Court held that the defendant did not have a sufficient legitimate expectation of privacy to contest the legality of a search of his friend's purse, in which police found narcotics owned by him. Both the defendant and his friend were present when the purse was found and searched. The defendant had known his friend for only a few days and had not previously had access to the purse; the circumstances of the transaction did not suggest that the defendant was taking precautions to maintain his privacy. His ownership of the seized items, while relevant, was insufficient by itself to create the necessary interest under the Fourth Amendment.

MINNESOTA v. OLSON

495 U.S. 91, 110 S.Ct. 1684, 109 L.Ed.2d 85 (1990).

JUSTICE WHITE delivered the opinion of the Court.

The police in this case made a warrantless, nonconsensual entry into a house where respondent Robert Olson was an overnight guest and arrested him. The issue is whether the arrest violated Olson's Fourth Amendment rights. We hold that it did.

I

Shortly before 6 a.m. on Saturday, July 18, 1987, a lone gunman robbed an Amoco gasoline station in Minneapolis, Minnesota, and fatally shot the station manager. A police officer heard the police dispatcher report and suspected Joseph Ecker. The officer and his partner drove immediately to Ecker's home, arriving at about the same time that an Oldsmobile arrived. The driver of the Oldsmobile took evasive action, and the car spun out of control and came to a stop. Two men fled the car on foot. Ecker, who was later identified as the gunman, was captured shortly thereafter inside his home. The second man escaped.

Inside the abandoned Oldsmobile, police found a sack of money and the murder weapon. They also found a title certificate with the name Rob Olson crossed out as a secured party, a letter addressed to a Roger R. Olson of 3151 Johnson Street, and a videotape rental receipt made out to Rob Olson and dated two days earlier. The police verified that a Robert Olson lived at 3151 Johnson Street.

The next morning, Sunday, July 19, a woman identifying herself as Dianna Murphy, called the police and said that a man by the name of Rob drove the car in which the gas-station killer left the scene and that Rob was planning to leave town by bus. About noon, the same woman called again, gave her address and phone number, and said that a man named Rob had told a Maria and two other women, Louanne and Julie, that he was the driver in the Amoco robbery. The caller stated that Louanne was Julie's mother and that the two women lived at 2406 Fillmore Northeast. The detective-in-charge who took the second phone call sent police officers to 2406 Fillmore to check out Louanne and Julie. When police arrived they determined that the dwelling was a duplex and that Louanne Bergstrom and her daughter Julie lived in the upper unit but were not home. Police spoke to Louanne's mother, Helen Niederhoffer, who lived in the lower unit. She confirmed that a Rob Olson had been staying upstairs but was not then in the unit. She promised to call the police when Olson returned. At 2 p.m., a

384

pickup order, or "probable cause arrest bulletin," was issued for Olson's arrest. The police were instructed to stay away from the duplex.

At approximately 2:45 p.m., Niederhoffer called police and said Olson had returned. The detective-in-charge instructed police officers to go to the house and surround it. He then telephoned Julie from headquarters and told her Rob should come out of the house. The detective heard a male voice say "tell them I left." Julie stated that Rob had left, whereupon at 3 p.m. the detective ordered the police to enter the house. Without seeking permission and with weapons drawn, the police entered the upper unit and found respondent hiding in a closet. Less than an hour after his arrest, respondent made an inculpatory statement at police headquarters.

The Hennepin County trial court held a hearing and denied respondent's motion to suppress his statement. App. 3–13. The statement was admitted into evidence at Olson's trial, and he was convicted on one count of first-degree murder, three counts of armed robbery, and three counts of second-degree assault. On appeal, the Minnesota Supreme Court reversed. 436 N.W.2d 92 (1989). The court ruled that respondent had a sufficient interest in the Bergstrom home to challenge the legality of his warrantless arrest there, that the arrest was illegal because there were no exigent circumstances to justify a warrantless entry,[1] and that respondent's statement was tainted by that illegality and should have been suppressed.[2] Because the admission of the statement was not harmless beyond reasonable doubt, the court reversed Olson's conviction and remanded for a new trial.

We granted the State's petition for certiorari, 493 U.S. 806 (1989), and now affirm.

II

It was held in Payton v. New York, 445 U.S. 573 (1980), that a suspect should not be arrested in his house without an arrest warrant, even though there is probable cause to arrest him. The purpose of the decision was not to protect the person of the suspect but to protect his home from entry in the absence of a magistrate's finding of probable cause. In this case, the court below held that Olson's warrantless arrest was illegal because he had a sufficient connection with the premises to be treated like a householder. The State challenges that conclusion.

---

1. Because the absence of a warrant made respondent's arrest illegal, the court did not review the trial court's determination that the police had probable cause for the arrest. 436 N.W.2d, at 95. Hence, we judge the case on the assumption that there was probable cause.

2. The State had not argued that, if the arrest was illegal, respondent's statement was nevertheless not tainted by the illegality. Id., at 98. Likewise, at oral argument before this Court, counsel for the State expressly disavowed any claim that the statement was not a fruit of the arrest. Tr. of Oral Arg. 4–5. We will therefore not raise *sua sponte* the applicability of New York v. Harris, 495 U.S. 14 (1990), to the facts of this case.

Since the decision in Katz v. United States, 389 U.S. 347 (1967), it has been the law that "capacity to claim the protection of the Fourth Amendment depends ... upon whether the person who claims the protection of the Amendment has a legitimate expectation of privacy in the invaded place." Rakas v. Illinois, 439 U.S. 128, 143 (1978). A subjective expectation of privacy is legitimate if it is " 'one that society is prepared to recognize as "reasonable," ' " id., at 143–144, n. 12, quoting Katz, supra, at 361 (Harlan, J., concurring).

The State argues that Olson's relationship to the premises does not satisfy the 12 factors which in its view determine whether a dwelling is a "home."[4] Aside from the fact that it is based on the mistaken premise that a place must be one's "home" in order for one to have a legitimate expectation of privacy there, the State's proposed test is needlessly complex. We need go no further than to conclude, as we do, that Olson's status as an overnight guest is alone enough to show that he had an expectation of privacy in the home that society is prepared to recognize as reasonable.

As recognized by the Minnesota Supreme Court, the facts of this case are similar to those in Jones v. United States, 362 U.S. 257 (1960). In Jones, the defendant was arrested in a friend's apartment during the execution of a search warrant and sought to challenge the warrant as not supported by probable cause.

> "[Jones] testified that the apartment belonged to a friend, Evans, who had given him the use of it, and a key, with which [Jones] had admitted himself on the day of the arrest. On cross-examination [Jones] testified that he had a suit and shirt at the apartment, that his home was elsewhere, that he paid nothing for the use of the apartment, that Evans had let him use it 'as a friend,' that he had slept there 'maybe a night,' and that at the time of the search Evans had been away in Philadelphia for about five days." Id., at 259.[6]

---

4.   The 12 factors are:

(1) the visitor has some property rights in the dwelling;

(2) the visitor is related by blood or marriage to the owner or lessor of the dwelling;

(3) the visitor receives mail at the dwelling or has his name on the door;

(4) the visitor has a key to the dwelling;

(5) the visitor maintains regular or continuous presence in the dwelling, especially sleeping there regularly;

(6) the visitor contributes to the upkeep of the dwelling, either monetarily or otherwise;

(7) the visitor has been present at the dwelling for a substantial length of time prior to the arrest;

(8) the visitor stores his clothes or other possessions in the dwelling;

(9) the visitor has been granted by the owner exclusive use of a particular area of the dwelling;

(10) the visitor has the right to exclude other persons from the dwelling;

(11) the visitor is allowed to remain in the dwelling when the owner is absent;

(12) the visitor has taken precautions to develop and maintain his privacy in the dwelling. Brief for Petitioner 21.

6.   Olson, who had been staying at Ecker's home for several days before the robbery, spent the night of the robbery on the floor of the Bergstroms' home, with their permission. He had a change of clothes with him at the duplex.

The Court ruled that Jones could challenge the search of the apartment because he was "legitimately on [the] premises," id., at 267. Although the "legitimately on [the] premises" standard was rejected in *Rakas* as too broad, 439 U.S., at 142–148, the *Rakas* Court explicitly reaffirmed the factual holding in *Jones:*

> "We do not question the conclusion in *Jones* that the defendant in that case suffered a violation of his personal Fourth Amendment rights if the search in question was unlawful. . . .

> "We think that *Jones* on its facts merely stands for the unremarkable proposition that a person can have a legally sufficient interest in a place other than his own home so that the Fourth Amendment protects him from unreasonable governmental intrusion into that place." 439 U.S., at 141–142.

Rakas thus recognized that, as an overnight guest, Jones was much more than just legitimately on the premises.

The distinctions relied on by the State between this case and *Jones* are not legally determinative. The State emphasizes that in this case Olson was never left alone in the duplex or given a key, whereas in *Jones* the owner of the apartment was away and Jones had a key with which he could come and go and admit and exclude others. These differences are crucial, it is argued, because in not disturbing the holding in *Jones,* the Court pointed out that while his host was away, Jones had complete dominion and control over the apartment and could exclude others from it. *Rakas,* 439 U.S., at 149. We do not understand *Rakas,* however, to hold that an overnight guest can never have a legitimate expectation of privacy except when his host is away and he has a key, or that only when those facts are present may an overnight guest assert the "unremarkable proposition," id., at 142, that a person may have a sufficient interest in a place other than his home to enable him to be free in that place from unreasonable searches and seizures.

To hold that an overnight guest has a legitimate expectation of privacy in his host's home merely recognizes the everyday expectations of privacy that we all share. Staying overnight in another's home is a longstanding social custom that serves functions recognized as valuable by society. We stay in others' homes when we travel to a strange city for business or pleasure, when we visit our parents, children, or more distant relatives out of town, when we are in between jobs or homes, or when we house-sit for a friend. We will all be hosts and we will all be guests many times in our lives. From either perspective, we think that society recognizes that a houseguest has a legitimate expectation of privacy in his host's home.

From the overnight guest's perspective, he seeks shelter in another's home precisely because it provides him with privacy, a place where he and his possessions will not be disturbed by anyone but his host and those his host allows inside. We are at our most vulnerable when we are asleep because we cannot monitor our own safety or the security of our belongings. It is for this reason that, although we may spend all day in public places, when we cannot sleep in our own home we seek out another private place to sleep, whether it be a hotel room, or the home of a friend. Society expects at least as much privacy in these places as in a telephone booth—"a temporarily private place whose momentary occupants' expectations of freedom from intrusion are recognized as reasonable," *Katz*, 389 U.S., at 361 (Harlan, J., concurring).

That the guest has a host who has ultimate control of the house is not inconsistent with the guest having a legitimate expectation of privacy. The houseguest is there with the permission of his host, who is willing to share his house and his privacy with his guest. It is unlikely that the guest will be confined to a restricted area of the house; and when the host is away or asleep, the guest will have a measure of control over the premises. The host may admit or exclude from the house as he prefers, but it is unlikely that he will admit someone who wants to see or meet with the guest over the objection of the guest. On the other hand, few houseguests will invite others to visit them while they are guests without consulting their hosts; but the latter, who have the authority to exclude despite the wishes of the guest, will often be accommodating. The point is that hosts will more likely than not respect the privacy interests of their guests, who are entitled to a legitimate expectation of privacy despite the fact that they have no legal interest in the premises and do not have the legal authority to determine who may or may not enter the household. If the untrammeled power to admit and exclude were essential to Fourth Amendment protection, an adult daughter temporarily living in the home of her parents would have no legitimate expectation of privacy because her right to admit or exclude would be subject to her parents' veto.

Because respondent's expectation of privacy in the Bergstrom home was rooted in "understandings that are recognized and permitted by society," *Rakas,* supra, at 144, n. 12, it was legitimate, and respondent can claim the protection of the Fourth Amendment.

III

In Payton v. New York, the Court had no occasion to "consider the sort of emergency or dangerous situation, described in our cases as 'exigent circumstances,' that would justify a warrantless entry into a home for the purpose of either arrest or search," 445 U.S., at 583. This case requires us to determine whether the Minnesota Supreme Court was correct in holding that there were no exigent circumstances that justified the warrantless entry into the house to make the arrest.

The Minnesota Supreme Court applied essentially the correct standard in determining whether exigent circumstances existed.

The court observed that "a warrantless intrusion may be justified by hot pursuit of a fleeing felon, or imminent destruction of evidence, Welsh [v. Wisconsin], 466 U.S. 740 [(1984)], or the need to prevent a suspect's escape, or the risk of danger to the police or to other persons inside or outside the dwelling." 436 N.W.2d, at 97. The court also apparently thought that in the absence of hot pursuit there must be at least probable cause to believe that one or more of the other factors justifying the entry were present and that in assessing the risk of danger, the gravity of the crime and likelihood that the suspect is armed should be considered. Applying this standard, the state court determined that exigent circumstances did not exist.

We are not inclined to disagree with this fact-specific application of the proper legal standard. The court pointed out that although a grave crime was involved, respondent "was known not to be the murderer but thought to be the driver of the getaway car," ibid., and that the police had already recovered the murder weapon, ibid. "The police knew that Louanne and Julie were with the suspect in the upstairs duplex with no suggestion of danger to them. Three or four Minneapolis police squads surrounded the house. The time was 3 p.m., Sunday.... It was evident the suspect was going nowhere. If he came out of the house he would have been promptly apprehended." Ibid. We do not disturb the state court's judgment that these facts do not add up to exigent circumstances.

IV

We therefore affirm the judgment of the Minnesota Supreme Court.

It is so ordered. [*]

---

[*] Justice Stevens wrote a concurring opinion. Justice Kennedy wrote a brief concurring opinion. Chief Justice Rehnquist and Justice Blackmun dissented.

WONG SUN v. UNITED STATES

371 U.S. 471, 83 S.Ct. 407, 9 L.Ed.2d 441 (1963).

MR. JUSTICE BRENNAN delivered the opinion of the Court.

The petitioners were tried without a jury in the District Court for the Northern District of California under a two-count indictment for violation of the Federal Narcotics Laws, 21 U.S.C. § 174. They were acquitted under the first count which charged a conspiracy, but convicted under the second count which charged the substantive offense of fraudulent and knowing transportation and concealment of illegally imported heroin. The Court of Appeals for the Ninth Circuit, one judge dissenting, affirmed the convictions. 288 F.2d 366. We granted certiorari. 368 U.S. 817. We heard argument in the 1961 Term and reargument this Term. 370 U.S. 908.

About 2 a.m. on the morning of June 4, 1959, federal narcotics agents in San Francisco, after having had one Hom Way under surveillance for six weeks, arrested him and found heroin in his possession. Hom Way, who had not before been an informant, stated after his arrest that he had bought an ounce of heroin the night before from one known to him only as "Blackie Toy," proprietor of a laundry on Leavenworth Street.

About 6 a.m. that morning six or seven federal agents went to a laundry at 1733 Leavenworth Street. The sign above the door of this establishment said "Oye's Laundry." It was operated by the petitioner James Wah Toy. There is, however, nothing in the record which identifies James Wah Toy and "Blackie Toy" as the same person. The other federal officers remained nearby out of sight while Agent Alton Wong, who was of Chinese ancestry, rang the bell. When petitioner Toy appeared and opened the door, Agent Wong told him that he was calling for laundry and dry cleaning. Toy replied that he didn't open until 8 o'clock and told the agent to come back at that time. Toy started to close the door. Agent Wong thereupon took his badge from his pocket and said, "I am a federal narcotics agent." Toy immediately "slammed the door and started running" down the hallway through the laundry to his living quarters at the back where his wife and child were sleeping in a bedroom. Agent Wong and the other federal officers broke open the door and followed Toy down the hallway to the living quarters and into the bedroom. Toy reached into a nightstand drawer. Agent Wong thereupon drew his pistol, pulled Toy's hand out of the drawer, placed him under arrest and handcuffed him. There was nothing in the drawer and a search of the premises uncovered no narcotics.

One of the agents said to Toy "... [Hom Way] says he got narcotics from you." Toy responded, "No, I haven't been selling any narcotics at all. However, I do know somebody who has." When asked who that was, Toy said, "I only know him as Johnny. I don't know his last name." However, Toy described a house on Eleventh Avenue where he said Johnny lived; he also described a bedroom in the house where he said "Johnny kept about a piece" of heroin, and where he and Johnny had smoked some of the drug the night before. The agents left immediately for Eleventh Avenue and located the house. They entered and found one Johnny Yee in the bedroom. After a discussion with the agents, Yee took from a bureau drawer several tubes containing in all just less than one ounce of heroin, and surrendered them. Within the hour Yee and Toy were taken to the Office of the Bureau of Narcotics. Yee there stated that the heroin had been brought to him some four days earlier by petitioner Toy and another Chinese known to him only as "Sea Dog."

Toy was questioned as to the identity of "Sea Dog" and said that "Sea Dog" was Wong Sun. Some agents, including Agent Alton Wong, took Toy to Wong Sun's neighborhood where Toy pointed out a multifamily dwelling where he said Wong Sun lived. Agent Wong rang a downstairs door bell and a buzzer sounded, opening the door. The officer identified himself as a narcotics agent to a woman on the landing and asked "for Mr. Wong." The woman was the wife of petitioner Wong Sun. She said that Wong Sun was "in the back room sleeping." Alton Wong and some six other officers climbed the stairs and entered the apartment. One of the officers went into the back room and brought petitioner Wong Sun from the bedroom in handcuffs. A thorough search of the apartment followed, but no narcotics were discovered.

Petitioner Toy and Johnny Yee were arraigned before a United States Commissioner on June 4 on a complaint charging a violation of 21 U.S.C. § 174. Later that day, each was released on his own recognizance. Petitioner Wong Sun was arraigned on a similar complaint filed the next day and was also released on his own recognizance. Within a few days, both petitioners and Yee were interrogated at the office of the Narcotics Bureau by Agent William Wong, also of Chinese ancestry. The agent advised each of the three of his right to withhold information which might be used against him, and stated to each that he was entitled to the advice of counsel, though it does not appear that any attorney was present during the questioning of any of the three. The officer also explained to each that no promises or offers of immunity or leniency were being or could be made.

The agent interrogated each of the three separately. After each had been interrogated the agent prepared a statement in English from rough notes. The agent read petitioner Toy's statement to him in English and interpreted certain portions of it for him in

Chinese. Toy also read the statement in English aloud to the agent, said there were corrections to be made, and made the corrections in his own hand. Toy would not sign the statement, however; in the agent's words "he wanted to know first if the other persons involved in the case had signed theirs." Wong Sun had considerable difficulty understanding the statement in English and the agent restated its substance in Chinese. Wong Sun refused to sign the statement although he admitted the accuracy of its contents.

Hom Way did not testify at petitioners' trial. The Government offered Johnny Yee as its principal witness but excused him after he invoked the privilege against self-incrimination and flatly repudiated the statement he had given to Agent William Wong. That statement was not offered in evidence nor was any testimony elicited from him identifying either petitioner as the source of the heroin in his possession, or otherwise tending to support the charges against the petitioners.

The statute expressly provides that proof of the accused's possession of the drug will support a conviction under the statute unless the accused satisfactorily explains the possession. The Government's evidence tending to prove the petitioners' possession (the petitioners offered no exculpatory testimony) consisted of four items which the trial court admitted over timely objections that they were inadmissible as "fruits" of unlawful arrests or of attendant searches: (1) the statements made orally by petitioner Toy in his bedroom at the time of his arrest; (2) the heroin surrendered to the agents by Johnny Yee; (3) petitioner Toy's pretrial unsigned statement; and (4) petitioner Wong Sun's similar statement. The dispute below and here has centered around the correctness of the rulings of the trial judge allowing these items in evidence.

The Court of Appeals held that the arrests of both petitioners were illegal because not based on " 'probable cause' within the meaning of the Fourth Amendment" nor "reasonable grounds" within the meaning of the Narcotic Control Act of 1956. The court said as to Toy's arrest, "There is no showing in this case that the agent knew Hom Way to be reliable," and, furthermore, found "nothing in the circumstances occurring at Toy's premises that would provide sufficient justification for his arrest without a warrant." 288 F.2d, at 369, 370. As to Wong Sun's arrest, the Court said "there is no showing that Johnnie Yee was a reliable informer." The Court of Appeals nevertheless held that the four items of proof were not the "fruits" of the illegal arrests and that they were therefore properly admitted in evidence.

. . .

We believe that significant differences between the cases of the two petitioners require separate discussion of each. We shall first consider the case of petitioner Toy.

I

The Court of Appeals found there was neither reasonable grounds nor probable cause for Toy's arrest. Giving due weight to that finding, we think it is amply justified by the facts clearly shown on this record. ...

Whether or not the requirements of reliability and particularity of the information on which an officer may act are more stringent where an arrest warrant is absent, they surely cannot be less stringent than where an arrest warrant is obtained. Otherwise, a principal incentive now existing for the procurement of arrest warrants would be destroyed. The threshold question in this case, therefore, is whether the officers could, on the information which impelled them to act, have procured a warrant for the arrest of Toy. We think that no warrant would have issued on evidence then available.

. . .

... Thus we conclude that the Court of Appeals' finding that the officers' uninvited entry into Toy's living quarters was unlawful and that the bedroom arrest which followed was likewise unlawful, was fully justified on the evidence. It remains to be seen what consequences flow from this conclusion.

II

It is conceded that Toy's declarations in his bedroom are to be excluded if they are held to be "fruits" of the agents' unlawful action.

In order to make effective the fundamental constitutional guarantees of sanctity of the home and inviolability of the person ... this Court held nearly half a century ago that evidence seized during an unlawful search could not constitute proof against the victim of the search. ... The exclusionary prohibition extends as well to the indirect as the direct products of such invasions. ...

The exclusionary rule has traditionally barred from trial physical, tangible materials obtained either during or as a direct result of an unlawful invasion. It follows from our holding in Silverman v. United States, 365 U.S. 505, that the Fourth Amendment may protect against the overhearing of verbal statements as well as against the more traditional seizure of "papers and effects." Similarly, testimony as to matters observed during an unlawful invasion has been excluded in order to enforce the basic constitutional policies. ... Thus, verbal evidence which derives so immediately from an unlawful entry and an unauthorized arrest as the officers' action in the present case is no less the "fruit" of official illegality than the more common tangible fruits of the unwarranted intrusion. ... Nor do the policies underlying the exclusionary rule invite any logical distinction between physical and verbal evidence. Either in terms of deterring lawless conduct by federal officers ... or of closing the doors of the federal courts to any use of evidence unconstitutionally obtained ... the danger in relaxing the exclusionary rules in the case of verbal evidence would seem too great to warrant introducing such a distinction.

The Government argues that Toy's statements to the officers in his bedroom, although closely consequent upon the invasion which we hold unlawful, were nevertheless admissible because they resulted from "an intervening independent act of a free will." This contention, however, takes insufficient account of the circumstances. Six or seven officers had broken the door and followed on Toy's heels into the bedroom where his wife and child were sleeping. He had been almost immediately handcuffed and arrested. Under such circumstances it is unreasonable to infer that Toy's response was sufficiently an act of free will to purge the primary taint of the unlawful invasion.

The Government also contends that Toy's declarations should be admissible because they were ostensibly exculpatory rather than incriminating. There are two answers to this argument. First, the statements soon turned out to be incriminating, for they led directly to the evidence which implicated Toy. Second, when circumstances are shown such as those which induced these declarations, it is immaterial whether the declarations be termed "exculpatory." Thus we find no substantial reason to omit Toy's declarations from the protection of the exclusionary rule.

III

We now consider whether the exclusion of Toy's declarations requires also the exclusion of the narcotics taken from Yee, to which those declarations led the police. The prosecutor candidly told the trial court that "we wouldn't have found those drugs except that Mr. Toy helped us to." Hence this is not the case envisioned by this Court where the exclusionary rule has no application because the Government learned of the evidence "from an independent source," Silverthorne Lumber Co. v. United States, 251 U.S. 385, 392; nor is this a case in which the connection between the lawless conduct of the police and the discovery of the challenged evidence has "become so attenuated as to dissipate the taint." Nardone v. United States, 308 U.S. 338, 341. We need not hold that all evidence is "fruit of the poisonous tree" simply because it would not have come to light but for the illegal actions of the police. Rather, the more apt question in such a case is "whether, granting establishment of the primary illegality, the evidence to which instant objection is made has been come at by exploitation of that illegality or instead by means sufficiently distinguishable to be purged of the primary taint." Maguire, Evidence of Guilt, 221 (1959). We think it clear that the narcotics were "come at by the exploitation of that illegality" and hence that they may not be used against Toy.

IV

. . .

[The Court concluded that Toy's conviction should be set aside without deciding whether, "in light of the fact that Toy was free on his own recognizance when he made the statement [to the agent], that statement was a fruit of the illegal arrest."]

V

We turn now to the case of the other petitioner, Wong Sun. We have no occasion to disagree with the finding of the Court of Appeals that his arrest, also, was without probable cause or reasonable grounds. At all events no evidentiary consequences turn upon that question. For Wong Sun's unsigned confession was not the fruit of that arrest, and was therefore properly admitted at trial. On the evidence that Wong Sun had been released on his own recognizance after a lawful arraignment, and had returned voluntarily several days later to make the statement, we hold that the connection between the arrest and the statement had "become so attenuated as to dissipate the taint." Nardone v. United States, 308 U.S. 338, 341. ...

We must then consider the admissibility of the narcotics surrendered by Yee. Our holding, supra, that this ounce of heroin was inadmissible against Toy does not compel a like result with respect to Wong Sun. The exclusion of the narcotics as to Toy was required solely by their tainted relationship to information unlawfully obtained from Toy, and not by any official impropriety connected with their surrender by Yee. The seizure of this heroin invaded no right of privacy of person or premises which would entitle Wong Sun to object to its use at his trial. ...

. . .

[The Court set aside Wong Sun's conviction on other grounds.] [*]

[*] Justice Douglas wrote a brief concurring opinion. Justice Clark wrote a dissenting opinion, which Justice Harlan, Justice Stewart, and Justice White joined.

FRISBIE v. COLLINS

342 U.S. 519, 72 S.Ct. 509, 96 L.Ed. 541 (1952).

MR. JUSTICE BLACK delivered the opinion of the Court.

Acting as his own lawyer, the respondent Shirley Collins brought this habeas corpus case in a United States District Court seeking release from a Michigan state prison where he is serving a life sentence for murder. His petition alleges that while he was living in Chicago, Michigan officers forcibly seized, handcuffed, blackjacked and took him to Michigan. He claims that trial and conviction under such circumstances is in violation of the Due Process Clause of the Fourteenth Amendment and the Federal Kidnaping Act, and that therefore his conviction is a nullity.

The District Court denied the writ without a hearing on the ground that the state court had power to try respondent "regardless of how presence was procured." The Court of Appeals, one judge dissenting, reversed and remanded the cause for hearing. 189 F.2d 464. It held that the Federal Kidnaping Act had changed the rule declared in prior holdings of this Court, that a state could constitutionally try and convict a defendant after acquiring jurisdiction by force. To review this important question we granted certiorari. 342 U.S. 865.

. . .

This Court has never departed from the rule announced in Ker v. Illinois, 119 U.S. 436, 444, that the power of a court to try a person for crime is not impaired by the fact that he had been brought within the court's jurisdiction by reason of a "forcible abduction." No persuasive reasons are now presented to justify overruling this line of cases. They rest on the sound basis that due process of law is satisfied when one present in court is convicted of crime after having been fairly apprized of the charges against him and after a fair trial in accordance with constitutional procedural safeguards. There is nothing in the Constitution that requires a court to permit a guilty person rightfully convicted to escape justice because he was brought to trial against his will.

Despite our prior decisions, the Court of Appeals, relying on the Federal Kidnaping Act, held that respondent was entitled to the writ if he could prove the facts he alleged. The Court thought that to hold otherwise after the passage of the Kidnaping Act "would in practical effect lend encouragement to the commission of criminal acts by those sworn to enforce the law." In considering whether the law of our prior cases has been changed by the Federal Kidnaping Act, we assume, without intimating that it is so, that the

Michigan officers would have violated it if the facts are as alleged. This Act prescribes in some detail the severe sanctions Congress wanted it to have. Persons who have violated it can be imprisoned for a term of years or for life; under some circumstances violators can be given the death sentence. We think the Act cannot fairly be construed so as to add to the list of sanctions detailed a sanction barring a state from prosecuting persons wrongfully brought to it by its officers. It may be that Congress could add such a sanction. We cannot.

The judgment of the Court of Appeals is reversed and that of the District Court is affirmed.

It is so ordered.

UNITED STATES v. ALVAREZ–MACHAIN

504 U.S. 655, 112 S.Ct. 2188, 119 L.Ed.2d 441 (1992).

CHIEF JUSTICE REHNQUIST delivered the opinion of the Court.

The issue in this case is whether a criminal defendant, abducted to the United States from a nation with which it has an extradition treaty, thereby acquires a defense to the jurisdiction of this country's courts. We hold that he does not, and that he may be tried in federal district court for violations of the criminal law of the United States.

Respondent, Humberto Alvarez–Machain, is a citizen and resident of Mexico. He was indicted for participating in the kidnap and murder of United States Drug Enforcement Administration (DEA) special agent Enrique Camarena–Salazar and a Mexican pilot working with Camarena, Alfredo Zavala–Avelar. The DEA believes that respondent, a medical doctor, participated in the murder by prolonging Agent Camarena's life so that others could further torture and interrogate him. On April 2, 1990, respondent was forcibly kidnaped from his medical office in Guadalajara, Mexico, to be flown by private plane to El Paso, Texas, where he was arrested by DEA officials. The District Court concluded that DEA agents were responsible for respondent's abduction, although they were not personally involved in it. United States v. Caro–Quintero, 745 F.Supp. 599, 602–604, 609 (CD Cal.1990).[2]

Respondent moved to dismiss the indictment, claiming that his abduction constituted outrageous governmental conduct, and that the District Court lacked jurisdiction to try him because he was abducted in violation of the extradition treaty between the United States and Mexico.... The District Court rejected the outrageous governmental conduct claim, but held that it lacked jurisdiction to try respondent because his abduction violated the Extradition Treaty. The District Court discharged respondent and ordered that he be repatriated to Mexico....

The Court of Appeals affirmed the dismissal of the indictment and the repatriation of respondent, relying on its decision in United States v. Verdugo–Urquidez, 939 F.2d 1341 (CA9 1991), cert. pending, No. 91–670, 946 F.2d 1466 (1991). In *Verdugo,* the Court of Appeals held that the forcible abduction of a Mexican national with the authorization or participation of the United States violated the

---

2. Apparently, DEA officials had attempted to gain respondent's presence in the United States through informal negotiations with Mexican officials, but were unsuccessful. DEA officials then, through a contact in Mexico, offered to pay a reward and expenses in return for the delivery of respondent to the United States....

398

Extradition Treaty between the United States and Mexico. Although the Treaty does not expressly prohibit such abductions, the Court of Appeals held that the "purpose" of the Treaty was violated by a forcible abduction, 939 F.2d, at 1350, which, along with a formal protest by the offended nation, would give a defendant the right to invoke the Treaty violation to defeat jurisdiction of the district court to try him. The Court of Appeals further held that the proper remedy for such a violation would be dismissal of the indictment and repatriation of the defendant to Mexico.

In the instant case, the Court of Appeals affirmed the District Court's finding that the United States had authorized the abduction of respondent, and that letters from the Mexican government to the United States Government served as an official protest of the Treaty violation. Therefore, the Court of Appeals ordered that the indictment against respondent be dismissed and that respondent be repatriated to Mexico. 946 F.2d, at 1467. We granted certiorari, 502 U.S. 1024 (1992), and now reverse.

Although we have never before addressed the precise issue raised in the present case, we have previously considered proceedings in claimed violation of an extradition treaty and proceedings against a defendant brought before a court by means of a forcible abduction. We addressed the former issue in United States v. Rauscher, 119 U.S. 407 (1886); more precisely, the issue whether the Webster–Ashburton Treaty of 1842, 8 Stat. 576, which governed extraditions between England and the United States, prohibited the prosecution of defendant Rauscher for a crime other than the crime for which he had been extradited. Whether this prohibition, known as the doctrine of specialty, was an intended part of the treaty had been disputed between the two nations for some time. *Rauscher,* 119 U.S., at 411. Justice Miller delivered the opinion of the Court, which carefully examined the terms and history of the treaty; the practice of nations in regards to extradition treaties; the case law from the States; and the writings of commentators, and reached the following conclusion:

> "[A] person who has been brought within the jurisdiction of the court *by virtue of proceedings under an extradition treaty,* can only be tried for one of the offences described in that treaty, and for the offence with which he is charged in the proceedings for his extradition, until a reasonable time and opportunity have been given him, after his release or trial upon such charge, to return to the country from whose asylum he had been forcibly taken under those proceedings." Id., at 430 (emphasis added).

In addition, Justice Miller's opinion noted that any doubt as to this interpretation was put to rest by two federal statutes which imposed the doctrine of specialty upon extradition treaties to which the United States was a party. Id., at 423. Unlike the case before us today, the defendant in *Rauscher* had been brought to the United States by way of an extradition treaty; there was no issue of a forcible abduction.

In Ker v. Illinois, 119 U.S. 436 (1886), also written by Justice Miller and decided the same day as *Rauscher,* we addressed the issue of a defendant brought before the court by way of a forcible abduction. Frederick Ker had been tried and convicted in an Illinois court for larceny; his presence before the court was procured by means of forcible abduction from Peru. A messenger was sent to Lima with the proper warrant to demand Ker by virtue of the extradition treaty between Peru and the United States. The messenger, however, disdained reliance on the treaty processes, and instead forcibly kidnaped Ker and brought him to the United States. We distinguished Ker's case from *Rauscher,* on the basis that Ker was not brought into the United States by virtue of the extradition treaty between the United States and Peru, and rejected Ker's argument that he had a right under the extradition treaty to be returned to this country only in accordance with its terms. We rejected Ker's due process argument more broadly, holding in line with "the highest authorities" that "such forcible abduction is no sufficient reason why the party should not answer when brought within the jurisdiction of the court which has the right to try him for such an offence, and presents no valid objection to his trial in such court." *Ker*, supra, at 444.

In Frisbie v. Collins, 342 U.S. 519, rehearing denied, 343 U.S. 937 (1952), we applied the rule in *Ker* to a case in which the defendant had been kidnapped in Chicago by Michigan officers and brought to trial in Michigan. We upheld the conviction over objections based on the Due Process Clause and the federal Kidnaping Act and stated:

> "This Court has never departed from the rule announced in [*Ker*] that the power of a court to try a person for crime is not impaired by the fact that he had been brought within the court's jurisdiction by reason of a 'forcible abduction.' No persuasive reasons are now presented to justify overruling this line of cases. They rest on the sound basis that due process of law is satisfied when one present in court is convicted of crime after having been fairly apprized of the charges against him and after a fair trial in accordance with constitutional procedural safeguards. There is nothing in the Constitution that requires a court to permit a guilty person rightfully convicted to escape justice because he was brought to trial against his will." *Frisbie,* supra, at 522 (citation and footnote omitted).

The only differences between *Ker* and the present case are that *Ker* was decided on the premise that there was no governmental involvement in the abduction, 119 U.S., at 443; and Peru, from which Ker was abducted, did not object to his prosecution. Respondent finds these differences to be dispositive, as did the Court of Appeals in *Verdugo,* 939 F.2d, at 1346, contending that they show that respondent's prosecution, like the prosecution of Rauscher, violates the implied terms of a valid extradition treaty. The Government, on the other hand, argues that *Rauscher* stands as an "exception" to the rule in *Ker* only when an extradition treaty is invoked, and the terms of the treaty provide that its breach will limit the jurisdiction of a court. Brief for United States 17. Therefore, our first inquiry must be whether the abduction of respondent from Mexico violated the Extradition Treaty between the United States and Mexico. If we conclude that the Treaty does not prohibit respondent's abduction, the rule in *Ker* applies, and the court need not inquire as to how respondent came before it.

. . .

. . . [R]espondent reasons, as did the Court of Appeals, that all the processes and restrictions on the obligation to extradite established by the Treaty would make no sense if either nation were free to resort to forcible kidnaping to gain the presence of an individual for prosecution in a manner not contemplated by the Treaty. . . .

We do not read the Treaty in such a fashion. . . . [The Treaty] does not purport to specify the only way in which one country may gain custody of a national of the other country for the purposes of prosecution. In the absence of an extradition treaty, nations are under no obligation to surrender those in their country to foreign authorities for prosecution. . . . Extradition treaties exist so as to impose mutual obligations to surrender individuals in certain defined sets of circumstances, following established procedures. . . . The Treaty thus provides a mechanism which would not otherwise exist, requiring, under certain circumstances, the United States and Mexico to extradite individuals to the other country, and establishing the procedures to be followed when the Treaty is invoked.

The history of negotiation and practice under the Treaty also fails to show that abductions outside of the Treaty constitute a violation of the Treaty. . . .

Thus, the language of the Treaty, in the context of its history, does not support the proposition that the Treaty prohibits abductions outside of its terms. The remaining question, therefore, is whether the Treaty should be interpreted so as to include an implied term prohibiting prosecution where the defendant's presence is obtained by means other than those established by the Treaty. . . .

Respondent contends that the Treaty must be interpreted against the backdrop of customary international law, and that international abductions are "so clearly prohibited in international law" that there was no reason to include such a clause in the Treaty itself. Brief for Respondent 11. The international censure of international abductions is further evidenced, according to respondent, by the United Nations Charter and the Charter of the Organization of American States. Id., at 17. Respondent does not argue that these sources of international law provide an independent basis for the right respondent asserts not to be tried in the United States, but rather that they should inform the interpretation of the Treaty terms.

The Court of Appeals deemed it essential, in order for the individual defendant to assert a right under the Treaty, that the affected foreign government had registered a protest.... Respondent agrees that the right exercised by the individual is derivative of the nation's right under the treaty, since nations are authorized, notwithstanding the terms of an extradition treaty, to voluntarily render an individual to the other country on terms completely outside of those provided in the Treaty. The formal protest, therefore, ensures that the "offended" nation actually objects to the abduction and has not in some way voluntarily rendered the individual for prosecution. Thus the Extradition Treaty only prohibits gaining the defendant's presence by means other than those set forth in the Treaty when the nation from which the defendant was abducted objects.

This argument seems to us inconsistent with the remainder of respondent's argument. The Extradition Treaty has the force of law, and if, as respondent asserts, it is self-executing, it would appear that a court must enforce it on behalf of an individual regardless of the offensiveness of the practice of one nation to the other nation. In *Rauscher,* the Court noted that Great Britain had taken the position in other cases that the Webster–Ashburton Treaty included the doctrine of specialty, but no importance was attached to whether or not Great Britain had protested the prosecution of Rauscher for the crime of cruel and unusual punishment as opposed to murder.

More fundamentally, the difficulty with the support respondent garners from international law is that none of it relates to the practice of nations in relation to extradition treaties. In *Rauscher,* we implied a term in the Webster–Ashburton Treaty because of the practice of nations with regard to extradition treaties. In the instant case, respondent would imply terms in the extradition treaty from the practice of nations with regards to international law more generally. Respondent would have us find that the Treaty acts as a prohibition against a violation of the general principle of international law that one government may not "exercise its police power in the territory of another state." Brief for Respondent 16. There are many actions which could be taken by a nation that would violate this principle, including waging war, but it cannot seriously be contended an invasion of the United States by Mexico would violate the terms of the extradition treaty between the two nations.

In sum, to infer from this Treaty and its terms that it prohibits all means of gaining the presence of an individual outside of its terms goes beyond established precedent and practice. In *Rauscher,* the implication of a doctrine of specialty into the terms of the Webster–Ashburton Treaty which, by its terms, required the presentation of evidence establishing probable cause of the crime of extradition before extradition was required, was a small step to take. By contrast, to imply from the terms of this Treaty that it prohibits obtaining the presence of an individual by means outside of the procedures the Treaty establishes requires a much larger inferential leap, with only the most general of international law principles to support it. The general principles cited by respondent simply fail to persuade us that we should imply in the United States–Mexico Extradition Treaty a term prohibiting international abductions.

Respondent and his *amici* may be correct that respondent's abduction was "shocking," Tr. of Oral Arg. 40, and that it may be in violation of general international law principles. Mexico has protested the abduction of respondent through diplomatic notes, App. 33–38, and the decision of whether respondent should be returned to Mexico, as a matter outside of the Treaty, is a matter for the Executive Branch. We conclude, however, that respondent's abduction was not in violation of the Extradition Treaty between the United States and Mexico, and therefore the rule of *Ker v. Illinois* is fully applicable to this case. The fact of respondent's forcible abduction does not therefore prohibit his trial in a court in the United States for violations of the criminal laws of the United States.

The judgment of the Court of Appeals is therefore reversed, and the case is remanded for further proceedings consistent with this opinion.

So ordered.

JUSTICE STEVENS, with whom JUSTICE BLACKMUN and JUSTICE O'CONNOR join, dissenting.

The Court correctly observes that this case raises a question of first impression.... The case is unique for several reasons. It does not involve an ordinary abduction by a private kidnaper, or bounty hunter, as in Ker v. Illinois, 119 U.S. 436 (1886); nor does it involve the apprehension of an American fugitive who committed a crime in one State and sought asylum in another, as in Frisbie v. Collins, 342 U.S. 519 (1952). Rather, it involves this country's abduction of another country's citizen; it also involves a violation of the territorial integrity of that other country, with which this country has signed an extradition treaty.

A Mexican citizen was kidnaped in Mexico and charged with a crime committed in Mexico; his offense allegedly violated both Mexican and American law. Mexico has formally demanded on at least two separate occasions that he be returned to Mexico and has represented that he will be prosecuted and, if convicted, punished for his offense. It is clear that Mexico's demand must be honored if this official abduction violated the 1978 Extradition Treaty between the United States and Mexico. In my opinion, a fair reading of the treaty in light of our decision in United States v. Rauscher, 119 U.S. 407 (1886), and applicable principles of international law, leads inexorably to the conclusion that the District Court, United States v. Caro–Quintero, 745 F.Supp. 599 (CD Cal.1990), and the Court of Appeals for the Ninth Circuit, 946 F.2d 1466 (1991) (per curiam), correctly construed that instrument.

I

The Extradition Treaty with Mexico is a comprehensive document containing 23 articles and an appendix listing the extraditable offenses covered by the agreement. The parties announced their purpose in the preamble: The two Governments desire "to cooperate more closely in the fight against crime and, to this end, to mutually render better assistance in matters of extradition." From the preamble, through the description of the parties' obligations with respect to offenses committed within as well as beyond the territory of a requesting party, the delineation of the procedures and evidentiary requirements for extradition, the special provisions for political offenses and capital punishment, and other details, the Treaty appears to have been designed to cover the entire subject of extradition. . . .

Petitioner's claim that the Treaty is not exclusive, but permits forcible governmental kidnaping, would transform these, and other provisions into little more than verbiage. . . . As the Court of Appeals for the Ninth Circuit recognized in a related case, "[e]ach of these provisions would be utterly frustrated if a kidnapping were held to be a permissible course of governmental conduct." United States v. Verdugo–Urquidez, 939 F.2d 1341, 1349 (1991). In addition, all of these provisions "only make sense if they are understood as *requiring* each treaty signatory to comply with those procedures whenever it wishes to obtain jurisdiction over an individual who is located in another treaty nation." Id., at 1351.

It is true, as the Court notes, that there is no express promise by either party to refrain from forcible abductions in the territory of the other Nation. . . . Relying on that omission, the Court, in effect, concludes that the Treaty merely creates an optional method of obtaining jurisdiction over alleged offenders, and that the parties silently reserved the right to resort to self help whenever they deem force more expeditious than legal process. If the United States, for example, thought it more expedient to torture or simply to execute a person rather than to attempt extradition, these options would be equally available because they, too, were not explicitly prohibited by the Treaty. That, however, is a highly improbable interpretation of a consensual agreement, which on its face appears to have been intended to set forth comprehensive and exclusive rules concerning the subject of extradition. In my opinion, "the manifest scope and object of the treaty itself," *Rauscher,* 119 U.S., at 422, plainly imply a mutual undertaking to respect the territorial integrity of the other contracting party. That opinion is confirmed by a consideration of the "legal context" in which the Treaty was negotiated. Cannon v. University of Chicago, 441 U.S. 677, 699 (1979).

. . .

III

A critical flaw pervades the Court's entire opinion. It fails to differentiate between the conduct of private citizens, which does not violate any treaty obligation, and conduct expressly authorized by the Executive Branch of the Government, which unquestionably constitutes a flagrant violation of international law, and in my opinion, also constitutes a breach of our Treaty obligations. Thus, at the outset of its opinion, the Court states the issue as "whether a criminal defendant, abducted to the United States from a nation with which it has an extradition treaty, thereby acquires a defense to the jurisdiction of this country's courts." Ante, at 657. That, of course, is the question decided in Ker v. Illinois, 119 U.S. 436 (1886); it is not, however, the question presented for decision today.

. . .

IV

As the Court observes at the outset of its opinion, there is reason to believe that respondent participated in an especially brutal murder of an American law enforcement agent. That fact, if true, may explain the Executive's intense interest in punishing respondent in our courts. Such an explanation, however, provides no justification for disregarding the Rule of Law that this Court has a duty to uphold. That the Executive may wish to reinterpret the Treaty to allow for an action that the Treaty in no way authorizes should not influence this Court's interpretation. Indeed, the desire for revenge exerts "a kind of hydraulic pressure . . . before which even well settled principles of law will bend," Northern Securities Co. v. United States, 193 U.S. 197, 401 (1904) (Holmes, J., dissenting), but it is precisely at such moments that we should remember and be guided by our duty "to render judgment evenly and dispassionately according to law, as each is given understanding to ascertain and apply it." United States v. Mine Workers, 330 U.S. 258, 342 (1947) (Rutledge, J., dissenting). The way that we perform that duty in a case of this kind sets an example that other tribunals in other countries are sure to emulate.

. . .

I respectfully dissent.

TERRY v. OHIO

392 U.S. 1, 88 S.Ct. 1868, 20 L.Ed.2d 889 (1968).

MR. CHIEF JUSTICE WARREN delivered the opinion of the Court.

This case presents serious questions concerning the role of the Fourth Amendment in the confrontation on the street between the citizen and the policeman investigating suspicious circumstances.

Petitioner Terry was convicted of carrying a concealed weapon and sentenced to the statutorily prescribed term of one to three years in the penitentiary. Following the denial of a pretrial motion to suppress, the prosecution introduced in evidence two revolvers and a number of bullets seized from Terry and a codefendant, Richard Chilton, by Cleveland Police Detective Martin McFadden. At the hearing on the motion to suppress this evidence, Officer McFadden testified that while he was patrolling in plain clothes in downtown Cleveland at approximately 2:30 in the afternoon of October 31, 1963, his attention was attracted by two men, Chilton and Terry, standing on the corner of Huron Road and Euclid Avenue. He had never seen the two men before, and he was unable to say precisely what first drew his eye to them. However, he testified that he had been a policeman for 39 years and a detective for 35 and that he had been assigned to patrol this vicinity of downtown Cleveland for shoplifters and pickpockets for 30 years. He explained that he had developed routine habits of observation over the years and that he would "stand and watch people or walk and watch people at many intervals of the day." He added: "Now, in this case when I looked over they didn't look right to me at the time."

His interest aroused, Officer McFadden took up a post of observation in the entrance to a store 300 to 400 feet away from the two men. "I get more purpose to watch them when I seen their movements," he testified. He saw one of the men leave the other one and walk southwest on Huron Road, past some stores. The man paused for a moment and looked in a store window, then walked on a short distance, turned around and walked back toward the corner, pausing once again to look in the same store window. He rejoined his companion at the corner, and the two conferred briefly. Then the second man went through the same series of motions, strolling down Huron Road, looking in the same window, walking on a short distance, turning back, peering in the store window again, and returning to confer with the first man at the corner. The two men repeated this ritual alternately between five and six times apiece—in all, roughly a dozen trips. At one point, while the two were standing together on the corner, a third man approached them and engaged them briefly in conversation. This man then left the two others and walked west on Euclid Avenue. Chilton and Terry resumed their measured pacing, peering, and conferring. After this had gone on for 10 to 12 minutes, the two men walked off together, heading west on Euclid Avenue, following the path taken earlier by the third man.

By this time Officer McFadden had become thoroughly suspicious. He testified that after observing their elaborately casual and oft-repeated reconnaissance of the store window on Huron Road, he suspected the two men of "casing a job, a stick-up," and that he considered it his duty as a police officer to investigate further. He added that he feared "they may have a gun." Thus, Officer McFadden followed Chilton and Terry and saw them stop in front of Zucker's store to talk to the same man who had conferred with them earlier on the street corner. Deciding that the situation was ripe for direct action, Officer McFadden approached the three men, identified himself as a police officer and asked for their names. At this point his knowledge was confined to what he had observed. He was not acquainted with any of the three men by name or by sight, and he had received no information concerning them from any other source. When the men "mumbled something" in response to his inquiries, Officer McFadden grabbed petitioner Terry, spun him around so that they were facing the other two, with Terry between McFadden and the others, and patted down the outside of his clothing. In the left breast pocket of Terry's overcoat Officer McFadden felt a pistol. He reached inside the overcoat pocket, but was unable to remove the gun. At this point, keeping Terry between himself and the others, the officer ordered all three men to enter Zucker's store. As they went in, he removed Terry's overcoat completely, removed a .38-caliber revolver from the pocket and ordered all three men to face the wall with their hands raised. Officer McFadden proceeded to pat down the outer clothing of Chilton and the third man, Katz. He discovered another revolver in the outer pocket of Chilton's overcoat, but no weapons were found on Katz. The officer testified that he only patted the men down to see whether they had weapons, and that he did not put his hands beneath the outer garments of either Terry or Chilton until he felt their guns. So far as appears from the record, he never placed his hands beneath Katz' outer garments. Officer McFadden seized Chilton's gun, asked the proprietor of the store to call a police wagon, and took all three men to the station, where Chilton and Terry were formally charged with carrying concealed weapons.

On the motion to suppress the guns the prosecution took the position that they had been seized following a search incident to a lawful arrest. The trial court rejected this theory, stating that it "would be stretching the facts beyond reasonable comprehension" to find that Officer McFadden had had probable cause to arrest the men before he patted them down for weapons. However, the court denied the defendants' motion on the ground that Officer McFadden, on the basis of his experience, "had reasonable cause to believe ... that the defendants were conducting themselves suspiciously, and some interrogation should be made of their action." Purely for his own protection, the court held, the officer had the right to pat down the outer clothing of these men, who he had reasonable cause to believe might be armed. The court distinguished between an investigatory "stop" and an arrest, and between a "frisk" of the outer clothing for weapons and a full-blown search for evidence of crime. The frisk, it held, was essential to the proper performance of the officer's investigatory duties, for without it "the answer to the police officer may be a bullet, and a loaded pistol discovered during the frisk is admissible."

After the court denied their motion to suppress, Chilton and Terry waived jury trial and pleaded not guilty. The court adjudged them guilty, and the Court of Appeals for the Eighth Judicial District, Cuyahoga County, affirmed. State v. Terry, 5 Ohio App.2d 122, 214 N.E.2d 114 (1966). The Supreme Court of Ohio dismissed their appeal on the ground that no "substantial constitutional question" was involved. We granted certiorari, 387 U.S. 929 (1967), to determine whether the admission of the revolvers in evidence violated petitioner's rights under the Fourth Amendment, made applicable to the States by the Fourteenth. Mapp v. Ohio, 367 U.S. 643 (1961). We affirm the conviction.

I

The Fourth Amendment provides that "the right of the people to be secure in their persons, houses, papers, and effects, against unreasonable searches and seizures, shall not be violated ...." This inestimable right of personal security belongs as much to the citizen on the streets of our cities as to the homeowner closeted in his study to dispose of his secret affairs. ... We have recently held that "the Fourth Amendment protects people, not places," Katz v. United States, 389 U.S. 347, 351 (1967), and wherever an individual may harbor a reasonable "expectation of privacy," id., at 361 (Mr. Justice Harlan, concurring), he is entitled to be free from unreasonable governmental intrusion. Of course, the specific content and incidents of this right must be shaped by the context in which it is asserted. For "what the Constitution forbids is not all searches and seizures, but unreasonable searches and seizures." Elkins v. United States, 364 U.S. 206, 222 (1960). Unquestionably petitioner was entitled to the protection of the Fourth Amendment as he walked down the street in Cleveland. ... The question is whether in all the circumstances of this on-the-street encounter, his right to personal security was violated by an unreasonable search and seizure.

We would be less than candid if we did not acknowledge that this question thrusts to the fore difficult and troublesome issues regarding a sensitive area of police activity—issues which have never before been squarely presented to this Court. Reflective of the tensions involved are the practical and constitutional arguments pressed with great vigor on both sides of the public debate over the power of the police to "stop and frisk"—as it is sometimes euphemistically termed—suspicious persons.

On the one hand, it is frequently argued that in dealing with the rapidly unfolding and often dangerous situations on city streets the police are in need of an escalating set of flexible responses, graduated in relation to the amount of information they possess. For this purpose it is urged that distinctions should be made between a "stop" and an "arrest" (or a "seizure" of a person), and between a "frisk" and a "search". Thus, it is argued, the police should be allowed to "stop" a person and detain him briefly for questioning upon suspicion that he may be connected with criminal activity. Upon suspicion that the person may be armed, the police should have the power to "frisk" him for weapons. If the "stop" and the "frisk" give rise to probable cause to believe that the suspect has committed a crime, then the police should be empowered to make a formal "arrest," and a full incident "search" of the person. This scheme is justified in part upon the notion that a "stop" and a "frisk" amount to a mere "minor inconvenience and petty indignity," which can properly be imposed upon the citizen in the interest of effective law enforcement on the basis of a police officer's suspicion.

On the other side the argument is made that the authority of the police must be strictly circumscribed by the law of arrest and search as it has developed to date in the traditional jurisprudence of the Fourth Amendment. It is contended with some force that there is not—and cannot be—a variety of police activity which does not depend solely upon the voluntary cooperation of the citizen and yet which stops short of an arrest based upon probable cause to make such an arrest. The heart of the Fourth Amendment, the argument runs, is a severe requirement of specific justification for any intrusion upon protected personal security, coupled with a highly developed system of judicial controls to enforce upon the agents of the State the commands of the Constitution. Acquiescence by the courts in the compulsion inherent in the field interrogation practices at issue here, it is urged, would constitute an abdication of judicial control over, and indeed an encouragement of, substantial interference with liberty and personal security by police officers whose judgment is necessarily colored by their primary involvement in "the often competitive enterprise of ferreting out crime." Johnson v. United States, 333 U.S. 10, 14 (1948). This, it is argued, can only serve to exacerbate police-community tensions in the crowded centers of our Nation's cities.

In this context we approach the issues in this case mindful of the limitations of the judicial function in controlling the myriad

daily situations in which policemen and citizens confront each other
on the street.   The State has characterized the issue here as "the
right of a police officer . . . to make an on-the-street stop, interrogate and pat down for weapons (known in street vernacular as 'stop
and frisk')." [8]   But this is only partly accurate.   For the issue is not
the abstract propriety of the police conduct, but the admissibility
against petitioner of the evidence uncovered by the search and
seizure.   Ever since its inception, the rule excluding evidence seized
in violation of the Fourth Amendment has been recognized as a
principal mode of discouraging lawless police conduct.   . . . Thus
its major thrust is a deterrent one . . . and experience has taught
that it is the only effective deterrent to police misconduct in the
criminal context, and that without it the constitutional guarantee
against unreasonable searches and seizures would be a mere "form
of words."   Mapp v. Ohio, 367 U.S. 643, 655 (1961).   The rule also
serves another vital function—"the imperative of judicial integrity."
Elkins v. United States, 364 U.S. 206, 222 (1960).   Courts which sit
under our Constitution cannot and will not be made party to
lawless invasions of the constitutional rights of citizens by permitting unhindered governmental use of the fruits of such invasions.
Thus in our system evidentiary rulings provide the context in which
the judicial process of inclusion and exclusion approves some
conduct as comporting with constitutional guarantees and disapproves other actions by state agents.   A ruling admitting evidence in
a criminal trial, we recognize, has the necessary effect of legitimizing
the conduct which produced the evidence, while an application of
the exclusionary rule withholds the constitutional imprimatur.

The exclusionary rule has its limitations, however, as a tool of
judicial control.   It cannot properly be invoked to exclude the
products of legitimate police investigative techniques on the ground
that much conduct which is closely similar involves unwarranted
intrusions upon constitutional protections.   Moreover, in some
contexts the rule is ineffective as a deterrent.   Street encounters
between citizens and police officers are incredibly rich in diversity.
They range from wholly friendly exchanges of pleasantries or mutually useful information to hostile confrontations of armed men
involving arrests, or injuries, or loss of life.   Moreover, hostile
confrontations are not all of a piece.   Some of them begin in a
friendly enough manner, only to take a different turn upon the
injection of some unexpected element into the conversation.   Encounters are initiated by the police for a wide variety of purposes,
some of which are wholly unrelated to a desire to prosecute for
crime.   Doubtless some police "field interrogation" conduct violates the Fourth Amendment.   But a stern refusal by this Court to
condone such activity does not necessarily render it responsive to
the exclusionary rule.   Regardless of how effective the rule may be
where obtaining convictions is an important objective of the police,

8. Brief for Respondent 2.

it is powerless to deter invasions of constitutionally guaranteed rights where the police either have no interest in prosecuting or are willing to forgo successful prosecution in the interest of serving some other goal.

Proper adjudication of cases in which the exclusionary rule is invoked demands a constant awareness of these limitations. The wholesale harassment by certain elements of the police community, of which minority groups, particularly Negroes, frequently complain, will not be stopped by the exclusion of any evidence from any criminal trial. Yet a rigid and unthinking application of the exclusionary rule, in futile protest against practices which it can never be used effectively to control, may exact a high toll in human injury and frustration of efforts to prevent crime. No judicial opinion can comprehend the protean variety of the street encounter, and we can only judge the facts of the case before us. Nothing we say today is to be taken as indicating approval of police conduct outside the legitimate investigative sphere. Under our decision, courts still retain their traditional responsibility to guard against police conduct which is overbearing or harassing, or which trenches upon personal security without the objective evidentiary justification which the Constitution requires. When such conduct is identified, it must be condemned by the judiciary and its fruits must be excluded from evidence in criminal trials. And, of course, our approval of legitimate and restrained investigative conduct undertaken on the basis of ample factual justification should in no way discourage the employment of other remedies than the exclusionary rule to curtail abuses for which that sanction may prove inappropriate.

Having thus roughly sketched the perimeters of the constitutional debate over the limits on police investigative conduct in general and the background against which this case presents itself, we turn our attention to the quite narrow question posed by the facts before us: whether it is always unreasonable for a policeman to seize a person and subject him to a limited search for weapons unless there is probable cause for an arrest. Given the narrowness of this question, we have no occasion to canvass in detail the constitutional limitations upon the scope of a policeman's power when he confronts a citizen without probable cause to arrest him.

II

Our first task is to establish at what point in this encounter the Fourth Amendment becomes relevant. That is, we must decide whether and when Officer McFadden "seized" Terry and whether and when he conducted a "search." There is some suggestion in the use of such terms as "stop" and "frisk" that such police conduct is outside the purview of the Fourth Amendment because neither action rises to the level of a "search" or "seizure" within the meaning of the Constitution. We emphatically reject this notion. It is quite plain that the Fourth Amendment governs "seizures" of the person which do not eventuate in a trip to the station house and prosecution for crime—"arrests" in traditional terminology. It must be recognized that whenever a police officer accosts an individual and restrains his freedom to walk away, he has "seized" that person. And it is nothing less than sheer torture of the English language to suggest that a careful exploration of the outer surfaces of a person's clothing all over his or her body in an attempt to find weapons is not a "search." Moreover, it is simply fantastic to urge that such a procedure performed in public by a policeman while the citizen stands helpless, perhaps facing a wall with his hands raised, is a "petty indignity." It is a serious intrusion upon the sanctity of the person, which may inflict great indignity and arouse strong resentment, and it is not to be undertaken lightly.

The danger in the logic which proceeds upon distinctions between a "stop" and an "arrest," or "seizure" of the person, and between a "frisk" and a "search" is two-fold. It seeks to isolate from constitutional scrutiny the initial stages of the contact between the policeman and the citizen. And by suggesting a rigid all-or-nothing model of justification and regulation under the Amendment, it obscures the utility of limitations upon the scope, as well as the initiation, of police action as a means of constitutional regulation. This Court has held in the past that a search which is reasonable at its inception may violate the Fourth Amendment by virtue of its intolerable intensity and scope. ... The scope of the search must be "strictly tied to and justified by" the circumstances which rendered its initiation permissible. Warden v. Hayden, 387 U.S. 294, 310 (1967) (Mr. Justice Fortas, concurring) ....

The distinctions of classical "stop-and-frisk" theory thus serve to divert attention from the central inquiry under the Fourth Amendment—the reasonableness in all the circumstances of the particular governmental invasion of a citizen's personal security. "Search" and "seizure" are not talismans. We therefore reject the notions that the Fourth Amendment does not come into play at all as a limitation upon police conduct if the officers stop short of something called a "technical arrest" or a "full-blown search."

In this case there can be no question, then, that Officer McFadden "seized" petitioner and subjected him to a "search" when he took hold of him and patted down the outer surfaces of his clothing. We must decide whether at that point it was reasonable for Officer McFadden to have interfered with petitioner's personal security as he did.[16] And in determining whether the

---

16. We thus decide nothing today concerning the constitutional propriety of an investigative "seizure" upon less than probable cause for purposes of "detention" and/or interrogation. Obviously, not all personal intercourse between policemen and citizens involves "seizures" of persons. Only when the officer, by means of physical force or show of authority, has in some way restrained the liberty of a citizen may we conclude that a "seizure" has occurred. We cannot tell with any certainty upon this record whether any such "seizure" took place here prior to Officer McFadden's initiation of physical contact for

seizure and search were "unreasonable" our inquiry is a dual one—whether the officer's action was justified at its inception, and whether it was reasonably related in scope to the circumstances which justified the interference in the first place.

III

If this case involved police conduct subject to the Warrant Clause of the Fourth Amendment, we would have to ascertain whether "probable cause" existed to justify the search and seizure which took place. However, that is not the case. We do not retreat from our holdings that the police must, whenever practicable, obtain advance judicial approval of searches and seizures through the warrant procedure ... or that in most instances failure to comply with the warrant requirement can only be excused by exigent circumstances .... But we deal here with an entire rubric of police conduct—necessarily swift action predicated upon the on-the-spot observations of the officer on the beat—which historically has not been, and as a practical matter could not be, subjected to the warrant procedure. Instead, the conduct involved in this case must be tested by the Fourth Amendment's general proscription against unreasonable searches and seizures.

Nonetheless, the notions which underlie both the warrant procedure and the requirement of probable cause remain fully relevant in this context. In order to assess the reasonableness of Officer McFadden's conduct as a general proposition, it is necessary "first to focus upon the governmental interest which allegedly justifies official intrusion upon the constitutionally protected interests of the private citizen," for there is "no ready test for determining reasonableness other than by balancing the need to search [or seize] against the invasion which the search [or seizure] entails." Camara v. Municipal Court, 387 U.S. 523, 534–535, 536–537 (1967). And in justifying the particular intrusion the police officer must be able to point to specific and articulable facts which, taken together with rational inferences from those facts, reasonably warrant that intrusion. The scheme of the Fourth Amendment becomes meaningful only when it is assured that at some point the conduct of those charged with enforcing the laws can be subjected to the more detached, neutral scrutiny of a judge who must evaluate the reasonableness of a particular search or seizure in light of the particular circumstances. And in making that assessment it is imperative that the facts be judged against an objective standard: would the facts available to the officer at the moment of the seizure or the search "warrant a man of reasonable caution in the belief" that the action taken was appropriate? Cf. Carroll v. United States, 267 U.S. 132 (1925); Beck v. Ohio, 379 U.S. 89, 96–97 (1964). Anything less would invite intrusions upon constitutionally guaranteed rights

purposes of searching Terry for weapons, and we thus may assume that up to that point no intrusion upon constitutionally protected rights had occurred.

based on nothing more substantial than inarticulate hunches, a result this Court has consistently refused to sanction. . . . And simple " 'good faith on the part of the arresting officer is not enough.' . . . If subjective good faith alone were the test, the protections of the Fourth Amendment would evaporate, and the people would be 'secure in their persons, houses, papers, and effects,' only in the discretion of the police." Beck v. Ohio, supra, at 97.

Applying these principles to this case, we consider first the nature and extent of the governmental interests involved. One general interest is of course that of effective crime prevention and detection; it is this interest which underlies the recognition that a police officer may in appropriate circumstances and in an appropriate manner approach a person for purposes of investigating possibly criminal behavior even though there is no probable cause to make an arrest. It was this legitimate investigative function Officer McFadden was discharging when he decided to approach petitioner and his companions. He had observed Terry, Chilton, and Katz go through a series of acts, each of them perhaps innocent in itself, but which taken together warranted further investigation. There is nothing unusual in two men standing together on a street corner, perhaps waiting for someone. Nor is there anything suspicious about people in such circumstances strolling up and down the street, singly or in pairs. Store windows, moreover, are made to be looked in. But the story is quite different where, as here, two men hover about a street corner for an extended period of time, at the end of which it becomes apparent that they are not waiting for anyone or anything; where these men pace alternately along an identical route, pausing to stare in the same store window roughly 24 times; where each completion of this route is followed immediately by a conference between the two men on the corner; where they are joined in one of these conferences by a third man who leaves swiftly; and where the two men finally follow the third and rejoin him a couple of blocks away. It would have been poor police work indeed for an officer of 30 years' experience in the detection of thievery from stores in this same neighborhood to have failed to investigate this behavior further.

The crux of this case, however, is not the propriety of Officer McFadden's taking steps to investigate petitioner's suspicious behavior, but rather, whether there was justification for McFadden's invasion of Terry's personal security by searching him for weapons in the course of that investigation. We are now concerned with more than the governmental interest in investigating crime; in addition, there is the more immediate interest of the police officer in taking steps to assure himself that the person with whom he is dealing is not armed with a weapon that could unexpectedly and fatally be used against him. Certainly it would be unreasonable to require that police officers take unnecessary risks in the performance of their duties. American criminals have a long tradition of armed violence, and every year in this country many law enforcement officers are killed in the line of duty, and thousands more are wounded. Virtually all of these deaths and a substantial portion of the injuries are inflicted with guns and knives.

In view of these facts, we cannot blind ourselves to the need for law enforcement officers to protect themselves and other prospective victims of violence in situations where they may lack probable cause for an arrest. When an officer is justified in believing that the individual whose suspicious behavior he is investigating at close range is armed and presently dangerous to the officer or to others, it would appear to be clearly unreasonable to deny the officer the power to take necessary measures to determine whether the person is in fact carrying a weapon and to neutralize the threat of physical harm.

We must still consider, however, the nature and quality of the intrusion on individual rights which must be accepted if police officers are to be conceded the right to search for weapons in situations where probable cause to arrest for crime is lacking. Even a limited search of the outer clothing for weapons constitutes a severe, though brief, intrusion upon cherished personal security, and it must surely be an annoying, frightening, and perhaps humiliating experience. Petitioner contends that such an intrusion is permissible only incident to a lawful arrest, either for a crime involving the possession of weapons or for a crime the commission of which led the officer to investigate in the first place. However, this argument must be closely examined.

Petitioner does not argue that a police officer should refrain from making any investigation of suspicious circumstances until such time as he has probable cause to make an arrest; nor does he deny that police officers in properly discharging their investigative function may find themselves confronting persons who might well be armed and dangerous. Moreover, he does not say that an officer is always unjustified in searching a suspect to discover weapons. Rather, he says it is unreasonable for the policeman to take that step until such time as the situation evolves to a point where there is probable cause to make an arrest. When that point has been reached, petitioner would concede the officer's right to conduct a search of the suspect for weapons, fruits or instrumentalities of the crime, or "mere" evidence, incident to the arrest.

There are two weaknesses in this line of reasoning, however. First, it fails to take account of traditional limitations upon the scope of searches, and thus recognizes no distinction in purpose, character, and extent between a search incident to an arrest and a limited search for weapons. The former, although justified in part by the acknowledged necessity to protect the arresting officer from assault with a concealed weapon ... is also justified on other grounds, id., and can therefore involve a relatively extensive exploration of the person. A search for weapons in the absence of probable cause to arrest, however, must, like any other search, be strictly circumscribed by the exigencies which justify its initiation. ... Thus it must be limited to that which is necessary for the discovery of weapons which might be used to harm the officer or others nearby, and may realistically be characterized as something less than a "full" search, even though it remains a serious intrusion.

A second, and related, objection to petitioner's argument is that it assumes that the law of arrest has already worked out the balance between the particular interests involved here—the neutralization of danger to the policeman in the investigative circumstance and the sanctity of the individual. But this is not so. An arrest is a wholly different kind of intrusion upon individual freedom from a limited search for weapons, and the interests each is designed to serve are likewise quite different. An arrest is the initial stage of a criminal prosecution. It is intended to vindicate society's interest in having its laws obeyed, and it is inevitably accompanied by future interference with the individual's freedom of movement, whether or not trial or conviction ultimately follows. The protective search for weapons, on the other hand, constitutes a brief, though far from inconsiderable, intrusion upon the sanctity of the person. It does not follow that because an officer may lawfully arrest a person only when he is apprised of facts sufficient to warrant a belief that the person has committed or is committing a crime, the officer is equally unjustified, absent that kind of evidence, in making any intrusions short of an arrest. Moreover, a perfectly reasonable apprehension of danger may arise long before the officer is possessed of adequate information to justify taking a person into custody for the purpose of prosecuting him for a crime. Petitioner's reliance on cases which have worked out standards of reasonableness with regard to "seizures" constituting arrests and searches incident thereto is thus misplaced. It assumes that the interests sought to be vindicated and the invasions of personal security may be equated in the two cases, and thereby ignores a vital aspect of the analysis of the reasonableness of particular types of conduct under the Fourth Amendment. ...

Our evaluation of the proper balance that has to be struck in this type of case leads us to conclude that there must be a narrowly drawn authority to permit a reasonable search for weapons for the protection of the police officer, where he has reason to believe that he is dealing with an armed and dangerous individual, regardless of whether he has probable cause to arrest the individual for a crime. The officer need not be absolutely certain that the individual is armed; the issue is whether a reasonably prudent man in the circumstances would be warranted in the belief that his safety or that of others was in danger. ... And in determining whether the officer acted reasonably in such circumstances, due weight must be given, not to his inchoate and unparticularized suspicion or "hunch," but to the specific reasonable inferences which he is entitled to draw from the facts in light of his experience.   . . .

IV

We must now examine the conduct of Officer McFadden in this case to determine whether his search and seizure of petitioner were reasonable, both at their inception and as conducted. He had observed Terry, together with Chilton and another man, acting in a manner he took to be preface to a "stick-up." We think on the facts and circumstances Officer McFadden detailed before the trial judge a reasonably prudent man would have been warranted in believing petitioner was armed and thus presented a threat to the officer's safety while he was investigating his suspicious behavior. The actions of Terry and Chilton were consistent with McFadden's hypothesis that these men were contemplating a daylight robbery— which, it is reasonable to assume would be likely to involve the use of weapons—and nothing in their conduct from the time he first noticed them until the time he confronted them and identified himself as a police officer gave him sufficient reason to negate that hypothesis. Although the trio had departed the original scene, there was nothing to indicate abandonment of an intent to commit a robbery at some point. Thus, when Officer McFadden approached the three men gathered before the display window at Zucker's store he had observed enough to make it quite reasonable to fear that they were armed; and nothing in their response to his hailing them, identifying himself as a police officer, and asking their names served to dispel that reasonable belief. We cannot say his decision at that point to seize Terry and pat his clothing for weapons was the product of a volatile or inventive imagination, or was undertaken simply as an act of harassment; the record evidences the tempered act of a policeman who in the course of an investigation had to make a quick decision as to how to protect himself and others from possible danger, and took limited steps to do so.

The manner in which the seizure and search were conducted is, of course, as vital a part of the inquiry as whether they were warranted at all. The Fourth Amendment proceeds as much by limitations upon the scope of governmental action as by imposing preconditions upon its initiation.   . . . The entire deterrent purpose of the rule excluding evidence seized in violation of the Fourth Amendment rests on the assumption that "limitations upon the fruit to be gathered tend to limit the quest itself." United States v. Poller, 43 F.2d 911, 914 (C.A. 2d Cir.1930) . . . . Thus, evidence may not be introduced if it was discovered by means of a seizure and search which were not reasonably related in scope to the justification for their initiation.   . . .

We need not develop at length in this case, however, the limitations which the Fourth Amendment places upon a protective seizure and search for weapons. These limitations will have to be developed in the concrete factual circumstances of individual cases. ...] Suffice it to note that such a search, unlike a search without a warrant incident to a lawful arrest, is not justified by any need to prevent the disappearance or destruction of evidence of crime. ... The sole justification of the search in the present situation is the protection of the police officer and others nearby, and it must therefore be confined in scope to an intrusion reasonably designed to discover guns, knives, clubs, or other hidden instruments for the assault of the police officer.

The scope of the search in this case presents no serious problem in light of these standards. Officer McFadden patted down the outer clothing of petitioner and his two companions. He did not place his hands in their pockets or under the outer surface of their garments until he had felt weapons, and then he merely reached for and removed the guns. He never did invade Katz' person beyond the outer surfaces of his clothes, since he discovered nothing in his pat-down which might have been a weapon. Officer McFadden confined his search strictly to what was minimally necessary to learn whether the men were armed and to disarm them once he discovered the weapons. He did not conduct a general exploratory search for whatever evidence of criminal activity he might find.

V

We conclude that the revolver seized from Terry was properly admitted in evidence against him. At the time he seized petitioner and searched him for weapons, Officer McFadden had reasonable grounds to believe that petitioner was armed and dangerous, and it was necessary for the protection of himself and others to take swift measures to discover the true facts and neutralize the threat of harm if it materialized. The policeman carefully restricted his search to what was appropriate to the discovery of the particular items which he sought. Each case of this sort will, of course, have to be decided on its own facts. We merely hold today that where a police officer observes unusual conduct which leads him reasonably to conclude in light of his experience that criminal activity may be afoot and that the persons with whom he is dealing may be armed and presently dangerous, where in the course of investigating this behavior he identifies himself as a policeman and makes reasonable inquiries, and where nothing in the initial stages of the encounter serves to dispel his reasonable fear for his own or others' safety, he is entitled for the protection of himself and others in the area to conduct a carefully limited search of the outer clothing of such persons in an attempt to discover weapons which might be used to assault him. Such a search is a reasonable search under the Fourth Amendment, and any weapons seized may properly be introduced in evidence against the person from whom they were taken.

Affirmed.

MR. JUSTICE HARLAN, concurring.

While I unreservedly agree with the Court's ultimate holding in this case, I am constrained to fill in a few gaps, as I see them, in its opinion. I do this because what is said by this Court today will serve as initial guidelines for law enforcement authorities and courts throughout the land as this important new field of law develops.

A police officer's right to make an on-the-street "stop" and an accompanying "frisk" for weapons is of course bounded by the protections afforded by the Fourth and Fourteenth Amendments. The Court holds, and I agree, that while the right does not depend upon possession by the officer of a valid warrant, nor upon the existence of probable cause, such activities must be reasonable under the circumstances as the officer credibly relates them in court. Since the question in this and most cases is whether evidence produced by a frisk is admissible, the problem is to determine what makes a frisk reasonable.

If the State of Ohio were to provide that police officers could, on articulable suspicion less than probable cause, forcibly frisk and disarm persons thought to be carrying concealed weapons, I would have little doubt that action taken pursuant to such authority could be constitutionally reasonable. Concealed weapons create an immediate and severe danger to the public, and though that danger might not warrant routine general weapons checks, it could well warrant action on less than a "probability." I mention this line of analysis because I think it vital to point out that it cannot be applied in this case. On the record before us Ohio has not clothed its policemen with routine authority to frisk and disarm on suspicion; in the absence of state authority, policemen have no more right to "pat down" the outer clothing of passers-by, or of persons to whom they address casual questions, than does any other citizen. Consequently, the Ohio courts did not rest the constitutionality of this frisk upon any general authority in Officer McFadden to take reasonable steps to protect the citizenry, including himself, from dangerous weapons.

The state courts held, instead, that when an officer is lawfully confronting a possibly hostile person in the line of duty he has a right, springing only from the necessity of the situation and not from any broader right to disarm, to frisk for his own protection. This holding, with which I agree and with which I think the Court agrees, offers the only satisfactory basis I can think of for affirming this conviction. The holding has, however, two logical corollaries that I do not think the Court has fully expressed.

In the first place, if the frisk is justified in order to protect the officer during an encounter with a citizen, the officer must first have constitutional grounds to insist on an encounter, to make a *forcible* stop. Any person, including a policeman, is at liberty to avoid a person he considers dangerous. If and when a policeman has a right instead to disarm such a person for his own protection, he must first have a right not to avoid him but to be in his presence. That right must be more than the liberty (again, possessed by every citizen) to address questions to other persons, for ordinarily the person addressed has an equal right to ignore his interrogator and walk away; he certainly need not submit to a frisk for the questioner's protection. I would make it perfectly clear that the right to frisk in this case depends upon the reasonableness of a forcible stop to investigate a suspected crime.

Where such a stop is reasonable, however, the right to frisk must be immediate and automatic if the reason for the stop is, as here, an articulable suspicion of a crime of violence. Just as a full search incident to a lawful arrest requires no additional justification, a limited frisk incident to a lawful stop must often be rapid and routine. There is no reason why an officer, rightfully but forcibly confronting a person suspected of a serious crime, should have to ask one question and take the risk that the answer might be a bullet.

The facts of this case are illustrative of a proper stop and an incident frisk. Officer McFadden had no probable cause to arrest Terry for anything, but he had observed circumstances that would reasonably lead an experienced, prudent policeman to suspect that Terry was about to engage in burglary or robbery. His justifiable suspicion afforded a proper constitutional basis for accosting Terry, restraining his liberty of movement briefly, and addressing questions to him, and Officer McFadden did so. When he did, he had no reason whatever to suppose that Terry might be armed, apart from the fact that he suspected him of planning a violent crime. McFadden asked Terry his name, to which Terry "mumbled something." Whereupon McFadden, without asking Terry to speak louder and without giving him any chance to explain his presence or his actions, forcibly frisked him.

I would affirm this conviction for what I believe to be the same reasons the Court relies on. I would, however, make explicit what I think is implicit in affirmance on the present facts. Officer McFadden's right to interrupt Terry's freedom of movement and invade his privacy arose only because circumstances warranted forcing an encounter with Terry in an effort to prevent or investigate a crime. Once that forced encounter was justified, however, the officer's right to take suitable measures for his own safety followed automatically.

Upon the foregoing premises, I join the opinion of the Court.[*]

[*] Justice White wrote a concurring opinion. Justice Black noted his concurrence in the opinion of the Court with specific reservations. Justice Douglas wrote a dissenting opinion.

ADAMS v. WILLIAMS

407 U.S. 143, 92 S.Ct. 1921, 32 L.Ed.2d 612 (1972).

MR. JUSTICE REHNQUIST delivered the opinion of the Court.

Respondent Robert Williams was convicted in a Connecticut state court of illegal possession of a handgun found during a "stop and frisk," as well as of possession of heroin that was found during a full search incident to his weapons arrest. After respondent's conviction was affirmed by the Supreme Court of Connecticut, 157 Conn. 114, 249 A.2d 245 (1968), this Court denied certiorari. 395 U.S. 927 (1969). Williams' petition for federal habeas corpus relief was denied by the District Court and by a divided panel of the Second Circuit, 436 F.2d 30 (1970), but on rehearing *en banc* the Court of Appeals granted relief. 441 F.2d 394 (1971). That court held that evidence introduced at Williams' trial had been obtained by an unlawful search of his person and car, and thus the state court judgments of conviction should be set aside. Since we conclude that the policeman's actions here conformed to the standards this Court laid down in Terry v. Ohio, 392 U.S. 1 (1968), we reverse.

Police Sgt. John Connolly was alone early in the morning on car patrol duty in a high-crime area of Bridgeport, Connecticut. At approximately 2:15 a.m. a person known to Sgt. Connolly approached his cruiser and informed him that an individual seated in a nearby vehicle was carrying narcotics and had a gun at his waist.

After calling for assistance on his car radio, Sgt. Connolly approached the vehicle to investigate the informant's report. Connolly tapped on the car window and asked the occupant, Robert Williams, to open the door. When Williams rolled down the window instead, the sergeant reached into the car and removed a fully loaded revolver from Williams' waistband. The gun had not been visible to Connolly from outside the car, but it was in precisely the place indicated by the informant. Williams was then arrested by Connolly for unlawful possession of the pistol. A search incident to that arrest was conducted after other officers arrived. They found substantial quantities of heroin on Williams' person and in the car, and they found a machete and a second revolver hidden in the automobile.

Respondent contends that the initial seizure of his pistol, upon which rested the later search and seizure of other weapons and narcotics, was not justified by the informant's tip to Sgt. Connolly. He claims that absent a more reliable informant, or some corroboration of the tip, the policeman's actions were unreasonable under the standards set forth in Terry v. Ohio, supra.

422

In *Terry* this Court recognized that "a police officer may in appropriate circumstances and in an appropriate manner approach a person for purposes of investigating possibly criminal behavior even though there is no probable cause to make an arrest." Id., at 22. The Fourth Amendment does not require a policeman who lacks the precise level of information necessary for probable cause to arrest to simply shrug his shoulders and allow a crime to occur or a criminal to escape. On the contrary, *Terry* recognizes that it may be the essence of good police work to adopt an intermediate response. See id., at 23. A brief stop of a suspicious individual, in order to determine his identity or to maintain the status quo momentarily while obtaining more information, may be most reasonable in light of the facts known to the officer at the time. Id., at 21–22 . . . .

The Court recognized in *Terry* that the policeman making a reasonable investigatory stop should not be denied the opportunity to protect himself from attack by a hostile suspect. "When an officer is justified in believing that the individual whose suspicious behavior he is investigating at close range is armed and presently dangerous to the officer or to others," he may conduct a limited protective search for concealed weapons. 392 U.S., at 24. The purpose of this limited search is not to discover evidence of crime, but to allow the officer to pursue his investigation without fear of violence, and thus the frisk for weapons might be equally necessary and reasonable, whether or not carrying a concealed weapon violated any applicable state law. So long as the officer is entitled to make a forcible stop,[1] and has reason to believe that the suspect is armed and dangerous, he may conduct a weapons search limited in scope to this protective purpose. Id., at 30.

Applying these principles to the present case, we believe that Sgt. Connolly acted justifiably in responding to his informant's tip. The informant was known to him personally and had provided him with information in the past. This is a stronger case than obtains in the case of an anonymous telephone tip. The informant here came forward personally to give information that was immediately verifiable at the scene. Indeed, under Connecticut law, the informant might have been subject to immediate arrest for making a false complaint had Sgt. Connolly's investigation proved the tip incorrect. Thus, while the Court's decisions indicate that this informant's unverified tip may have been insufficient for a narcotics arrest or search warrant . . . the information carried enough indicia of reliability to justify the officer's forcible stop of Williams.

In reaching this conclusion, we reject respondent's argument that reasonable cause for a stop and frisk can only be based on the officer's personal observation, rather than on information supplied

---

1. Petitioner does not contend that Williams acted voluntarily in rolling down the window of his car.

by another person. Informants' tips, like all other clues and evidence coming to a policeman on the scene, may vary greatly in their value and reliability. One simple rule will not cover every situation. Some tips, completely lacking in indicia of reliability, would either warrant no police response or require further investigation before a forcible stop of a suspect would be authorized. But in some situations—for example, when the victim of a street crime seeks immediate police aid and gives a description of his assailant, or when a credible informant warns of a specific impending crime— the subtleties of the hearsay rule should not thwart an appropriate police response.

While properly investigating the activity of a person who was reported to be carrying narcotics and a concealed weapon and who was sitting alone in a car in a high-crime area at 2:15 in the morning, Sgt. Connolly had ample reason to fear for his safety. When Williams rolled down his window, rather than complying with the policeman's request to step out of the car so that his movements could more easily be seen, the revolver allegedly at Williams' waist became an even greater threat. Under these circumstances the policeman's action in reaching to the spot where the gun was thought to be hidden constituted a limited intrusion designed to insure his safety, and we conclude that it was reasonable. The loaded gun seized as a result of this intrusion was therefore admissible at Williams' trial. Terry v. Ohio, 392 U.S., at 30.

Once Sgt. Connolly had found the gun precisely where the informant had predicted, probable cause existed to arrest Williams for unlawful possession of the weapon. ... Under the circumstances surrounding Williams' possession of the gun seized by Sgt. Connolly, the arrest on the weapons charge was supported by probable cause, and the search of his person and of the car incident to that arrest was lawful. ... The fruits of the search were therefore properly admitted at Williams' trial, and the Court of Appeals erred in reaching a contrary conclusion.

Reversed.

MR. JUSTICE BRENNAN, dissenting.

The crucial question on which this case turns, as the Court concedes, is whether, there being no contention that Williams acted voluntarily in rolling down the window of his car, the State had shown sufficient cause to justify Sgt. Connolly's "forcible" stop. I would affirm, believing, for the following reasons stated by Judge, now Chief Judge, Friendly, dissenting, 436 F.2d, at 38–39, that the State did not make that showing:

> "To begin, I have the gravest hesitancy in extending [Terry v. Ohio, 392 U.S. 1 (1968)] to crimes like the possession of narcotics .... There is too much danger that, instead of the stop being the object and the protective frisk an incident thereto, the reverse will be true. Against that we have here the

added fact of the report that Williams had a gun on his person.
... [But] Connecticut allows its citizens to carry weapons,
concealed or otherwise, at will, provided only they have a
permit, Conn.Gen.Stat. §§ 29–35 and 29–38, and gives its police officers no special authority to stop for the purpose of
determining whether the citizen has one. ...

"If I am wrong in thinking that *Terry* should not be applied
at all to mere possessory offenses, ... I would not find the
combination of Officer Connolly's almost meaningless observation and the tip in this case to be sufficient justification for the
intrusion. The tip suffered from a threefold defect, with each
fold compounding the others. The informer was unnamed, he
was not shown to have been reliable with respect to guns or
narcotics, and he gave no information which demonstrated
personal knowledge or—what is worse—could not readily have
been manufactured by the officer after the event. To my mind,
it has not been sufficiently recognized that the difference between this sort of tip and the accurate prediction of an unusual
event is as important on the latter score as on the former. [In
Draper v. United States, 358 U.S. 307 (1959),] Narcotics Agent
Marsh would hardly have been at the Denver Station at the
exact moment of the arrival of the train Draper had taken from
Chicago unless *someone* had told him *something* important,
although the agent might later have embroidered the details to
fit the observed facts. ... There is no such guarantee of a
patrolling officer's veracity when he testifies to a 'tip' from an
unnamed informer saying no more than that the officer will
find a gun and narcotics on a man across the street, as he later
does. If the state wishes to rely on a tip of that nature to
validate a stop and frisk, revelation of the name of the informer
or demonstration that his name is unknown and could not
reasonably have been ascertained should be the price.

"Terry v. Ohio was intended to free a police officer from
the rigidity of a rule that would prevent his doing anything to a
man reasonably suspected of being about to commit or having
just committed a crime of violence, no matter how grave the
problem or impelling the need for swift action, unless the
officer had what a court would later determine to be probable
cause for arrest. It was meant for the serious cases of imminent danger or of harm recently perpetrated to persons or
property, not the conventional ones of possessory offenses. If
it is to be extended to the latter at all, this should be only
where observation by the officer himself or well authenticated
information shows 'that criminal activity may be afoot.' 392
U.S., at 30. ... I greatly fear that if the [contrary view] should
be followed, *Terry* will have opened the sluicegates for serious
and unintended erosion of the protection of the Fourth Amendment."

MR. JUSTICE MARSHALL, with whom MR. JUSTICE DOUGLAS joins, dissenting.

Four years have passed since we decided Terry v. Ohio, 392 U.S. 1 (1968), and its companion cases, Sibron v. New York and Peters v. New York, 392 U.S. 40 (1968). They were the first cases in which this Court explicitly recognized the concept of "stop and frisk" and squarely held that police officers may, under appropriate circumstances, stop and frisk persons suspected of criminal activity even though there is less than probable cause for an arrest. This case marks our first opportunity to give some flesh to the bones of *Terry et al.* Unfortunately, the flesh provided by today's decision cannot possibly be made to fit on *Terry's* skeletal framework.

. . .

In today's decision the Court ignores the fact that *Terry* begrudgingly accepted the necessity for creating an exception from the warrant requirement of the Fourth Amendment and treats this case as if warrantless searches were the rule rather than the "narrowly drawn" exception. This decision betrays the careful balance that *Terry* sought to strike between a citizen's right to privacy and his government's responsibility for effective law enforcement and expands the concept of warrantless searches far beyond anything heretofore recognized as legitimate. I dissent.

I

. . .

B. The Court erroneously attempts to describe the search for the gun as a protective search incident to a reasonable investigatory stop. But, as in *Terry, Sibron* and *Peters*, supra, there is no occasion in this case to determine whether or not police officers have a right to seize and to restrain a citizen in order to interrogate him. The facts are clear that the officer intended to make the search as soon as he approached the respondent. He asked no questions; he made no investigation; he simply searched. There was nothing apart from the information supplied by the informant to cause the officer to search. Our inquiry must focus, therefore, as it did in *Terry* on whether the officer had sufficient facts from which he could reasonably infer that respondent was not only engaging in illegal activity, but also that he was armed and dangerous. The focus falls on the informant.

The only information that the informant had previously given the officer involved homosexual conduct in the local railroad station. The following colloquy took place between respondent's counsel and the officer at the hearing on respondent's motion to suppress the evidence that had been seized from him.

"Q. Now, with respect to the information that was given you about homosexuals in the Bridgeport Police Station [*sic*], did that lead to an arrest? A. No.

"Q. An arrest was not made. A. No. There was no substantiating evidence.

.   .   .   .

"Q. There was no substantiating evidence? A. No.

"Q. And what do you mean by that? A. I didn't have occasion to witness these individuals committing any crime of any nature.

"Q. In other words, after this person gave you the information, you checked for corroboration before you made an arrest. Is that right? A. Well, I checked to determine the possibility of homosexual activity.

"Q. And since an arrest was made, I take it you didn't find any substantiating information. A. I'm sorry counselor, you say since an arrest was made.

"Q. Was not made. Since an arrest was not made, I presume you didn't find any substantiating information. A. No.

"Q. So that, you don't recall any other specific information given you about the commission of crimes by this informant. A. No.

"Q. And you still thought this person was reliable. A. Yes." [1]

Were we asked to determine whether the information supplied by the informant was sufficient to provide probable cause for an arrest and search, rather than a stop and frisk, there can be no doubt that we would hold that it was insufficient. This Court has squarely held that a search and seizure cannot be justified on the basis of conclusory allegations of an unnamed informant who is allegedly credible. ... In the recent case of Spinelli v. United States, 393 U.S. 410 (1969), Mr. Justice Harlan made it plain beyond any doubt that where police rely on an informant to make a search and seizure, they must know that the informant is generally trustworthy and that he has obtained his information in a reliable way. Id., at 417. Since the testimony of the arresting officer in the instant case patently fails to demonstrate that the informant was known to be trustworthy and since it is also clear that the officer had no idea of the source of the informant's "knowledge," a search and seizure would have been illegal.

Assuming *arguendo,* that this case truly involves, not an arrest and a search incident thereto, but a stop and frisk, we must decide whether or not the information possessed by the officer justified this interference with respondent's liberty. *Terry,* our only case to actually uphold a stop and frisk, is not directly in point, because the

---

1. App. 96–97.

police officer in that case acted on the basis of his own personal observations. No informant was involved. But the rationale of *Terry* is still controlling, and it requires that we condemn the conduct of the police officer in encountering the respondent.

Terry did not hold that whenever a policeman has a hunch that a citizen is engaging in criminal activity, he may engage in a stop and frisk. It held that if police officers want to stop and frisk, they must have specific facts from which they can reasonably infer that an individual is engaged in criminal activity and is armed and dangerous. It was central to our decision in *Terry* that the police officer acted on the basis of his own personal observations and that he carefully scrutinized the conduct of his suspects before interfering with them in any way. When we legitimated the conduct of the officer in *Terry* we did so because of the substantial *reliability* of the information on which the officer based his decision to act.

If the Court does not ignore the care with which we examined the knowledge possessed by the officer in *Terry* when he acted, then I cannot see how the actions of the officer in this case can be upheld. The Court explains what the officer knew about respondent before accosting him. But what is more significant is what he did not know. With respect to the scene generally, the officer had no idea how long respondent had been in the car, how long the car had been parked, or to whom the car belonged. With respect to the gun, the officer did not know if or when the informant had ever seen the gun, or whether the gun was carried legally, as Connecticut law permitted or illegally. And with respect to the narcotics, the officer did not know what kind of narcotics respondent allegedly had, whether they were legally or illegally possessed, what the basis of the informant's knowledge was, or even whether the informant was capable of distinguishing narcotics from other substances.

Unable to answer any of these questions, the officer nevertheless determined that it was necessary to intrude on respondent's liberty. I believe that his determination was totally unreasonable. As I read *Terry,* an officer may act on the basis of *reliable* information short of probable cause to make a stop, and ultimately a frisk, if necessary; but, the officer may not use unreliable, unsubstantiated conclusory hearsay to justify an invasion of liberty. *Terry* never meant to approve the kind of knee-jerk police reaction that we have before us in this case.

Even assuming that the officer had some legitimate reason for relying on the informant, *Terry* requires, before any stop and frisk is made, that the reliable information in the officer's possession demonstrate that the suspect is both armed and *dangerous.* The fact remains that Connecticut specifically authorizes persons to carry guns so long as they have a permit. Thus, there was no reason for the officer to infer from anything that the informant said that the respondent was dangerous. His frisk was, therefore, illegal under *Terry*.

II

Even if I could agree with the Court that the stop and frisk in this case was proper, I could not go further and sustain the arrest and the subsequent searches. ...

Once the officer seized the gun from respondent, it is uncontradicted that he did not ask whether respondent had a license to carry it, or whether respondent carried it for any other legal reason under Connecticut law. Rather, the officer placed him under arrest immediately and hastened to search his person. Since Connecticut has not made it illegal for private citizens to carry guns, there is nothing in the facts of this case to warrant a man "of prudence and caution" to believe that any offense had been committed merely because respondent had a gun on his person. Any implication that respondent's silence was some sort of a tacit admission of guilt would be utterly absurd.

It is simply not reasonable to expect someone to protest that he is not acting illegally before he is told that he is suspected of criminal activity. It would have been a simple matter for the officer to ask whether respondent had a permit, but he chose not to do so. In making this choice, he clearly violated the Fourth Amendment.

. . .

III

Mr. Justice Douglas was the sole dissenter in *Terry*. He warned of the "powerful hydraulic pressures throughout our history that bear heavily on the Court to water down constitutional guarantees ...." 392 U.S., at 39. While I took the position then that we were not watering down rights, but were hesitantly and cautiously striking a necessary balance between the rights of American citizens to be free from government intrusion into their privacy and their government's urgent need for a narrow exception to the warrant requirement of the Fourth Amendment, today's decision demonstrates just how prescient Mr. Justice Douglas was.

It seems that the delicate balance that *Terry* struck was simply too delicate, too susceptible to the "hydraulic pressures" of the day. As a result of today's decision, the balance struck in *Terry* is now heavily weighted in favor of the government. And the Fourth Amendment, which was included in the Bill of Rights to prevent the kind of arbitrary and oppressive police action involved herein, is dealt a serious blow. Today's decision invokes the specter of a society in which innocent citizens may be stopped, searched, and arrested at the whim of police officers who have only the slightest suspicion of improper conduct.[*]

[*] Justice Douglas wrote a dissenting opinion, which Justice Marshall joined.

UNITED STATES v. HENSLEY

469 U.S. 221, 105 S.Ct. 675, 83 L.Ed.2d 604 (1985).

JUSTICE O'CONNOR delivered the opinion of the Court.

We granted certiorari in this case, 467 U.S. 1203 (1984), to determine whether police officers may stop and briefly detain a person who is the subject of a "wanted flyer" while they attempt to find out whether an arrest warrant has been issued. We conclude that such stops are consistent with the Fourth Amendment under appropriate circumstances.

I

On December 4, 1981, two armed men robbed a tavern in the Cincinnati suburb of St. Bernard, Ohio. Six days later, a St. Bernard police officer, Kenneth Davis, interviewed an informant who passed along information that respondent Thomas Hensley had driven the getaway car during the armed robbery. Officer Davis obtained a written statement from the informant and immediately issued a "wanted flyer" to other police departments in the Cincinnati metropolitan area.

The flyer twice stated that Hensley was wanted for investigation of an aggravated robbery. It described both Hensley and the date and location of the alleged robbery, and asked other departments to pick up and hold Hensley for the St. Bernard police in the event he were located. The flyer also warned other departments to use caution and to consider Hensley armed and dangerous.

The St. Bernard Police Department's "wanted flyer" was received by teletype in the headquarters of the Covington Police Department on December 10, 1981. Covington is a Kentucky suburb of Cincinnati that is approximately five miles from St. Bernard. The flyer was read aloud at each change of shift in the Covington Police Department between December 10 and December 16, 1981. Some of the Covington officers were acquainted with Hensley, and after December 10 they periodically looked for him at places in Covington he was known to frequent.

On December 16, 1981, Covington Officer Terence Eger saw a white Cadillac convertible stopped in the middle of a Covington street. Officer Eger saw Hensley in the driver's seat and asked him to move on. As Hensley drove away, Eger inquired by radio whether there was a warrant outstanding for Hensley's arrest. Before the dispatcher could answer, two other Covington officers who were in separate cars on patrol interrupted to say that there might be an Ohio robbery warrant outstanding on Hensley. The officers, Daniel Cope and David Rassache, subsequently testified that they had heard or read the St. Bernard flyer on several occasions, that they recalled that the flyer sought a stop for investigation only, and that in their experience the issuance of such a flyer was usually followed by the issuance of an arrest warrant. While the dispatcher checked to see whether a warrant had been issued, Officer Cope drove to a Holman Strcct address where Hensley occasionally stayed, and Officer Rassache went to check a second location.

The dispatcher had difficulty in confirming whether a warrant had been issued. Unable to locate the flyer, she called the Cincinnati Police Department on the mistaken belief that the flyer had originated in Cincinnati. The Cincinnati Police Department transferred the call to its records department, which placed the dispatcher on hold. In the meantime, Officer Cope reported that he had sighted a white Cadillac approaching him on Holman Street. Cope turned on his flashing lights and Hensley pulled over to the curb. Before Cope left his patrol car, the dispatcher advised him that she had "Cincinnati hunting for the warrant," App. 49, but that she had not yet confirmed it. Cope approached Hensley's car with his service revolver drawn and pointed into the air. He had Hensley and a passenger seated next to him step out of the car.

Moments later, Officer Rassache arrived in his separate car. He recognized the passenger, Albert Green, a convicted felon. Rassache stepped up to the open passenger door of Hensley's car and observed the butt of a revolver protruding from underneath the passenger's seat. Green was then arrested. A search of the car uncovered a second handgun wrapped in a jacket in the middle of the front seat and a third handgun in a bag in the back seat. After the discovery of these weapons, Hensley was also arrested.

After state handgun possession charges against Hensley were dismissed, Hensley was indicted by a federal grand jury in the Eastern District of Kentucky for being a convicted felon in possession of firearms in violation of 18 U.S.C.App. § 1202(a)(1). Hensley moved to suppress the handguns from evidence on the grounds that the Covington police had impermissibly stopped him in violation of the Fourth Amendment and the principles announced in Terry v. Ohio, 392 U.S. 1 (1968). The District Judge held the stop to be proper and denied the motion. Respondent was convicted after a bench trial and sentenced to two years in federal prison.

The United States Court of Appeals for the Sixth Circuit reversed the conviction. 713 F.2d 220 (1983). The panel noted that the Covington police could not justifiably conclude from the St. Bernard flyer that a warrant had been issued for Hensley's arrest; nor could the Covington police stop the respondent while they attempted to find out whether a warrant had in fact been issued. Reviewing this Court's decisions applying *Terry,* the Sixth Circuit concluded that investigative stops remain a narrow exception to the probable-cause requirement, and that this Court has manifested a "clear intention to restrict investigative stops to settings involving the investigation of ongoing crimes." 713 F.2d, at 225. Since Covington police encountered Hensley almost two weeks after the armed robbery in St. Bernard, they had no reason to believe they were investigating an ongoing crime. Because the Covington police were familiar only with the St. Bernard flyer, and not with the specific information which led the St. Bernard police to issue the flyer, the Court of Appeals held they lacked a reasonable suspicion sufficient to justify an investigative stop. The Court of Appeals concluded that Hensley's conviction rested on evidence obtained through an illegal arrest, and therefore had to be reversed. We disagree, and now reverse.

II

The Fourth Amendment protects the right of the people to be secure in their persons, houses, papers, and effects against unreasonable searches and seizures. In *Terry,* supra, and subsequent cases, this Court has held that, consistent with the Fourth Amendment, police may stop persons in the absence of probable cause under limited circumstances. . . . In particular, the Court has noted that law enforcement agents may briefly stop a moving automobile to investigate a reasonable suspicion that its occupants are involved in criminal activity. . . . Although stopping a car and detaining its occupants constitute a seizure within the meaning of the Fourth Amendment, the governmental interest in investigating an officer's reasonable suspicion, based on specific and articulable facts, may outweigh the Fourth Amendment interest of the driver and passengers in remaining secure from the intrusion. . . .

In this case, the Sixth Circuit announced two prerequisites to such an investigatory stop and held that they were lacking: first, the crime being investigated was not imminent or ongoing, but rather was already completed; second, the "wanted flyer" was insufficient to create a reasonable suspicion that respondent had engaged in criminal activity. If either part of this analysis is correct, then it was indeed improper to stop respondent, and his conviction cannot stand. We accordingly turn to the separate but related issues of *Terry* stops to investigate completed crimes and *Terry* stops in reliance on another police department's "wanted flyer."

A

This is the first case we have addressed in which police stopped a person because they suspected he was involved in a completed crime. In our previous decisions involving investigatory stops on less than probable cause, police stopped or seized a person because they suspected he was about to commit a crime . . . or was committing a crime at the moment of the stop. . . . Noting that Florida v. Royer, 460 U.S. 491 (1983), struck down a particularly intrusive detention of a person suspected of committing an ongoing crime, the Court of Appeals in this case concluded that we clearly intended to restrict investigative stops to the context of ongoing crimes.

We do not agree with the Court of Appeals that our prior opinions contemplate an inflexible rule that precludes police from stopping persons they suspect of past criminal activity unless they have probable cause for arrest. To the extent previous opinions have addressed the issue at all, they have suggested that some investigative stops based on a reasonable suspicion of past criminal activity could withstand Fourth Amendment scrutiny. ... Indeed, Florida v. Royer itself suggests that certain seizures are justifiable under the Fourth Amendment even in the absence of probable cause "if there is articulable suspicion that a person *has committed* or is about to commit a crime." 460 U.S., at 498 (plurality opinion) (emphasis added).

At the least, these dicta suggest that the police are not automatically shorn of authority to stop a suspect in the absence of probable cause merely because the criminal has completed his crime and escaped from the scene. The precise limits on investigatory stops to investigate past criminal activity are more difficult to define. The proper way to identify the limits is to apply the same test already used to identify the proper bounds of intrusions that further investigations of imminent or ongoing crimes. That test, which is grounded in the standard of reasonableness embodied in the Fourth Amendment, balances the nature and quality of the intrusion on personal security against the importance of the governmental interests alleged to justify the intrusion. ... When this balancing test is applied to stops to investigate past crimes, we think that probable cause to arrest need not always be required.

The factors in the balance may be somewhat different when a stop to investigate past criminal activity is involved rather than a stop to investigate ongoing criminal conduct. This is because the governmental interests and the nature of the intrusions involved in the two situations may differ. As we noted in *Terry*, one general interest present in the context of ongoing or imminent criminal activity is "that of effective crime prevention and detection." *Terry*, 392 U.S., at 22. A stop to investigate an already completed crime does not necessarily promote the interest of crime prevention as directly as a stop to investigate suspected ongoing criminal activity. Similarly, the exigent circumstances which require a police officer to step in before a crime is committed or completed are not necessarily as pressing long afterwards. Public safety may be less threatened by a suspect in a past crime who now appears to be going about his lawful business than it is by a suspect who is currently in the process of violating the law. Finally, officers making a stop to investigate past crimes may have a wider range of opportunity to choose the time and circumstances of the stop. ...

Despite these differences, where police have been unable to locate a person suspected of involvement in a past crime, the ability to briefly stop that person, ask questions, or check identification in the absence of probable cause promotes the strong government interest in solving crimes and bringing offenders to justice. Restraining police action until after probable cause is obtained would not only hinder the investigation, but might also enable the suspect to flee in the interim and to remain at large. Particularly in the context of felonies or crimes involving a threat to public safety, it is in the public interest that the crime be solved and the suspect detained as promptly as possible. The law enforcement interests at stake in these circumstances outweigh the individual's interest to be free of a stop and detention that is no more extensive than permissible in the investigation of imminent or ongoing crimes.

We need not and do not decide today whether *Terry* stops to investigate all past crimes, however serious, are permitted. It is enough to say that, if police have a reasonable suspicion, grounded in specific and articulable facts, that a person they encounter was involved in or is wanted in connection with a completed felony, then a *Terry* stop may be made to investigate that suspicion. The automatic barrier to such stops erected by the Court of Appeals accordingly cannot stand.

B

At issue in this case is a stop of a person by officers of one police department in reliance on a flyer issued by another department indicating that the person is wanted for investigation of a felony. The Court of Appeals concluded that "the Fourth Amendment does not permit police officers in one department to seize a person simply because a neighboring police department has circulated a flyer reflecting the desire to question that individual about some criminal investigation that does not involve the arresting officers or their department." 713 F.2d, at 225. This holding apparently rests on the omission from the flyer of the specific and articulable facts which led the first department to suspect respondent's involvement in a completed crime. Ibid.

This Court discussed a related issue in Whiteley v. Warden, 401 U.S. 560 (1971). In *Whiteley,* a county sheriff in Wyoming obtained an arrest warrant for a person suspected of burglary. The sheriff then issued a message through a statewide law enforcement radio network describing the suspect, his car, and the property taken. At least one version of the message also indicated that a warrant had been issued. Id., at 564, and n. 5. The message did not specify the evidence that gave the sheriff probable cause to believe the suspect had committed the breaking and entering. In reliance on the radio message, police in Laramie stopped the suspect and searched his car. The Supreme Court, in an opinion by Justice Harlan, ultimately concluded that the sheriff had lacked probable cause to obtain the warrant and that the evidence obtained during the search by the police in Laramie had to be excluded. In so ruling, however, the Court noted:

> "We do not, of course, question that the Laramie police were entitled to act on the strength of the radio bulletin. Certainly police officers called upon to aid other officers in executing arrest warrants are entitled to assume that the officers requesting aid offered the magistrate the information requisite to support an independent judicial assessment of probable cause. Where, however, the contrary turns out to be true, an otherwise illegal arrest cannot be insulated from challenge by the decision of the instigating officer to rely on fellow officers to make the arrest." Id., at 568.

This language in *Whiteley* suggests that, had the sheriff who issued the radio bulletin possessed probable cause for arrest, then the Laramie police could have properly arrested the defendant even though they were unaware of the specific facts that established probable cause. ... Thus *Whiteley* supports the proposition that, when evidence is uncovered during a search incident to an arrest in reliance merely on a flyer or bulletin, its admissibility turns on whether the officers who *issued* the flyer possessed probable cause to make the arrest. It does not turn on whether those relying on the flyer were themselves aware of the specific facts which led their colleagues to seek their assistance. In an era when criminal suspects are increasingly mobile and increasingly likely to flee across jurisdictional boundaries, this rule is a matter of common sense: it minimizes the volume of information concerning suspects that must be transmitted to other jurisdictions and enables police in one jurisdiction to act promptly in reliance on information from another jurisdiction.

Neither respondent nor the Court of Appeals suggests any reason why a police department should be able to act on the basis of a flyer indicating that another department has a warrant, but should not be able to act on the basis of a flyer indicating that another department has a reasonable suspicion of involvement with a crime. ...

It could be argued that police can more justifiably rely on a report that a magistrate has issued a warrant than on a report that another law enforcement agency has simply concluded that it has a reasonable suspicion sufficient to authorize an investigatory stop. We do not find this distinction significant. The law enforcement interests promoted by allowing one department to make investigatory stops based upon another department's bulletins or flyers are considerable, while the intrusion on personal security is minimal. The same interests that weigh in favor of permitting police to make a *Terry* stop to investigate a past crime ... support permitting police in other jurisdictions to rely on flyers or bulletins in making stops to investigate past crimes.

We conclude that, if a flyer or bulletin has been issued on the basis of articulable facts supporting a reasonable suspicion that the wanted person has committed an offense, then reliance on that flyer or bulletin justifies a stop to check identification ... to pose questions to the person, or to detain the person briefly while attempting to obtain further information. ... If the flyer has been issued in the absence of a reasonable suspicion, then a stop in the objective reliance upon it violates the Fourth Amendment. In such a situation, of course, the officers making the stop may have a good-faith defense to any civil suit. ... It is the objective reading of the flyer or bulletin that determines whether other police officers can defensibly act in reliance on it. ... Assuming the police make a *Terry* stop in objective reliance on a flyer or bulletin, we hold that the evidence uncovered in the course of the stop is admissible if the police who *issued* the flyer or bulletin possessed a reasonable suspicion justifying a stop ... and if the stop that in fact occurred was not significantly more intrusive than would have been permitted the issuing department.

III

It remains to apply the two sets of principles described above to the stop and subsequent arrest of respondent Hensley.

At the outset, we assume, *arguendo,* that the St. Bernard police who issued the "wanted flyer" on Hensley lacked probable cause for his arrest. ...

We agree with the District Court that the St. Bernard police possessed a reasonable suspicion, based on specific and articulable facts, that Hensley was involved in an armed robbery. The District Judge heard testimony from the St. Bernard officer who interviewed the informant. On the strength of the evidence, the District Court concluded that the wealth of detail concerning the robbery revealed by the informant, coupled with her admission of tangential participation in the robbery, established that the informant was sufficiently reliable and credible "to arouse a reasonable suspicion of criminal activity by [Hensley] and to constitute the specific and articulable facts needed to underly a stop." App. to Pet. for Cert. 14a. Under the circumstances, "the information carried enough indicia of reliability," Adams v. Williams, [407 U.S. 143 (1972)], at 147, to justify an investigatory stop of Hensley.

The justification for a stop did not evaporate when the armed robbery was completed. Hensley was reasonably suspected of involvement in a felony and was at large from the time the suspicion arose until the stop by the Covington police. A brief stop and detention at the earliest opportunity after the suspicion arose is fully consistent with the principles of the Fourth Amendment.

Turning to the flyer issued by the St. Bernard police, we believe it satisfies the objective test announced today. An objective reading of the entire flyer would lead an experienced officer to conclude that Thomas Hensley was at least wanted for questioning and investigation in St. Bernard. Since the flyer was issued on the basis of articulable facts supporting a reasonable suspicion, this objective reading would justify a brief stop to check Hensley's identification, pose questions, and inform the suspect that the St. Bernard police wished to question him. As an experienced officer could well assume that a warrant might have been obtained in the period after the flyer was issued, we think the flyer would further justify a brief detention at the scene of the stop while officers checked whether a warrant had in fact been issued. It is irrelevant whether the Covington officers intended to detain Hensley only long enough to confirm the existence of a warrant, or for some longer period; what matters is that the stop and detention that occurred were in fact no more intrusive than would have been permitted an experienced officer on an objective reading of the flyer.

To be sure, the St. Bernard flyer at issue did not request that other police departments briefly detain Hensley merely to check his identification or confirm the existence of a warrant. Instead, it asked other departments to pick up and hold Hensley for St. Bernard. Our decision today does not suggest that such a detention, whether at the scene or at the Covington police headquarters, would have been justified. Given the distance involved and the time required to identify and communicate with the department that issued the flyer, such a detention might well be so lengthy or intrusive as to exceed the permissible limits of a *Terry* stop. . . . Nor do we mean to endorse St. Bernard's request in its flyer for actions that could foreseeably violate the Fourth Amendment. We hold only that this flyer, objectively read and supported by a reasonable suspicion on the part of the issuing department, justified the length and intrusiveness of the stop and detention that actually occurred.

When the Covington officers stopped Hensley, they were authorized to take such steps as were reasonably necessary to protect their personal safety and to maintain the status quo during the course of the stop. The Covington officers' conduct was well within the permissible range in the context of suspects who are reported to be armed and dangerous. . . . Having stopped Hensley, the Covington police were entitled to seize evidence revealed in plain view in the course of the lawful stop, to arrest Hensley's passenger when evidence discovered in plain view gave probable cause to believe the passenger had committed a crime . . . and subsequently to search the passenger compartment of the car because it was within the passenger's immediate control. . . . Finally, having discovered additional weapons in Hensley's car during the course of a lawful search, the Covington officers had probable cause to arrest Hensley himself for possession of firearms.

The length of Hensley's detention from his stop to his arrest on probable cause was brief. A reasonable suspicion on the part of the St. Bernard police underlies and supports their issuance of the flyer. Finally, the stop that occurred was reasonable in objective reliance on the flyer and was not significantly more intrusive than would have been permitted the St. Bernard police. Under these circumstances, the investigatory stop was reasonable under the Fourth Amendment, and the evidence discovered during the stop was admissible.

The judgment of the Court of Appeals is reversed, and the case is remanded for proceedings consistent with this opinion.

It is so ordered.[*]

[*] Justice Brennan wrote a concurring opinion.

MINNESOTA v. DICKERSON

___ U.S. ___, 113 S.Ct. 2130, 124 L.Ed.2d 334 (1993).

JUSTICE WHITE delivered the opinion of the Court.

In this case, we consider whether the Fourth Amendment permits the seizure of contraband detected through a police officer's sense of touch during a protective patdown search.

I

On the evening of November 9, 1989, two Minneapolis police officers were patrolling an area on the city's north side in a marked squad car. At about 8:15 p.m., one of the officers observed respondent leaving a 12–unit apartment building on Morgan Avenue North. The officer, having previously responded to complaints of drug sales in the building's hallways and having executed several search warrants on the premises, considered the building to be a notorious "crack house." According to testimony credited by the trial court, respondent began walking toward the police but, upon spotting the squad car and making eye contact with one of the officers, abruptly halted and began walking in the opposite direction. His suspicion aroused, this officer watched as respondent turned and entered an alley on the other side of the apartment building. Based upon respondent's seemingly evasive actions and the fact that he had just left a building known for cocaine traffic, the officers decided to stop respondent and investigate further.

The officers pulled their squad car into the alley and ordered respondent to stop and submit to a patdown search. The search revealed no weapons, but the officer conducting the search did take an interest in a small lump in respondent's nylon jacket. The officer later testified:

> "[A]s I pat-searched the front of his body, I felt a lump, a small lump, in the front pocket. I examined it with my fingers and it slid and it felt to be a lump of crack cocaine in cellophane." Tr. 9 (Feb. 20, 1990).

The officer then reached into respondent's pocket and retrieved a small plastic bag containing one fifth of one gram of crack cocaine. Respondent was arrested and charged in Hennepin County District Court with possession of a controlled substance.

Before trial, respondent moved to suppress the cocaine. The trial court first concluded that the officers were justified under Terry v. Ohio, 392 U.S. 1 (1968), in stopping respondent to investigate whether he might be engaged in criminal activity. The court further found that the officers were justified in frisking respondent to ensure that he was not carrying a weapon. Finally, analogizing to the "plain-view" doctrine, under which officers may make a warrantless seizure of contraband found in plain view during a lawful search for other items, the trial court ruled that the officers' seizure of the cocaine did not violate the Fourth Amendment . . . .

His suppression motion having failed, respondent proceeded to trial and was found guilty.

On appeal, the Minnesota Court of Appeals reversed. The court agreed with the trial court that the investigative stop and protective patdown search of respondent were lawful under *Terry* because the officers had a reasonable belief based on specific and articulable facts that respondent was engaged in criminal behavior and that he might be armed and dangerous. The court concluded, however, that the officers had overstepped the bounds allowed by *Terry* in seizing the cocaine. In doing so, the Court of Appeals "decline[d] to adopt the plain feel exception" to the warrant requirement. 469 N.W.2d 462, 466 (1991).

The Minnesota Supreme Court affirmed. Like the Court of Appeals, the State Supreme Court held that both the stop and the frisk of respondent were valid under *Terry,* but found the seizure of the cocaine to be unconstitutional. The court expressly refused "to extend the plain view doctrine to the sense of touch" on the grounds that "the sense of touch is inherently less immediate and less reliable than the sense of sight" and that "the sense of touch is far more intrusive into the personal privacy that is at the core of the [F]ourth [A]mendment." 481 N.W.2d 840, 845 (1992). The court thus appeared to adopt a categorical rule barring the seizure of any contraband detected by an officer through the sense of touch during a patdown search for weapons. The court further noted that "[e]ven if we recognized a 'plain feel' exception, the search in this case would not qualify" because "[t]he pat search of the defendant went far beyond what is permissible under *Terry."* Id., at 843 and 844, n. 1. As the State Supreme Court read the record, the officer conducting the search ascertained that the lump in respondent's jacket was contraband only after probing and investigating what he certainly knew was not a weapon. See id., at 844.

We granted certiorari, 506 U.S. ___ (1992), to resolve a conflict among the state and federal courts over whether contraband detected through the sense of touch during a patdown search may be admitted into evidence. We now affirm.

II

A

The Fourth Amendment, made applicable to the States by way of the Fourteenth Amendment, Mapp v. Ohio, 367 U.S. 643 (1961), guarantees "[t]he right of the people to be secure in their persons, houses, papers, and effects, against unreasonable searches and

seizures." Time and again, this Court has observed that searches
and seizures " 'conducted outside the judicial process, without
prior approval by judge or magistrate, are *per se* unreasonable
under the Fourth Amendment—subject only to a few specifically
established and well delineated exceptions.' " Thompson v. Louisiana, 469 U.S. 17, 19–20 (1984) (per curiam) (quoting Katz v. United
States, 389 U.S. 347, 357 (1967) (footnotes omitted)), ... One
such exception was recognized in Terry v. Ohio, 392 U.S. 1 (1968),
which held that "where a police officer observes unusual conduct
which leads him reasonably to conclude in light of his experience
that criminal activity may be afoot" the officer may briefly stop the
suspicious person and make "reasonable inquiries" aimed at confirming or dispelling his suspicions. Id. at 30 ....

Terry further held that "[w]hen an officer is justified in believing that the individual whose suspicious behavior he is investigating
at close range is armed and presently dangerous to the officer or to
others," the officer may conduct a patdown search "to determine
whether the person is in fact carrying a weapon." 392 U.S., at 24.
"The purpose of this limited search is not to discover evidence of
crime, but to allow the officer to pursue his investigation without
fear of violence...." Adams [v. Williams, 407 U.S. 143 (1972)], at
146. Rather, a protective search—permitted without a warrant and
on the basis of reasonable suspicion less than probable cause—must
be strictly "limited to that which is necessary for the discovery of
weapons which might be used to harm the officer or others nearby." *Terry,* supra, at 26.... If the protective search goes beyond
what is necessary to determine if the suspect is armed, it is no
longer valid under *Terry* and its fruits will be suppressed....

These principles were settled 25 years ago .... The question
presented today is whether police officers may seize nonthreatening
contraband detected during a protective patdown search of the sort
permitted by *Terry.* We think the answer is clearly that they may, so
long as the officer's search stays within the bounds marked by *Terry.*

B

We have already held that police officers, at least under certain
circumstances, may seize contraband detected during the lawful
execution of a *Terry* search. In Michigan v. Long, [463 U.S. 1032
(1983)], for example, police approached a man who had driven his
car into a ditch and who appeared to be under the influence of
some intoxicant. As the man moved to reenter the car from the
roadside, police spotted a knife on the floorboard. The officers
stopped the man, subjected him to a patdown search, and then
inspected the interior of the vehicle for other weapons. During the
search of the passenger compartment, the police discovered an
open pouch containing marijuana and seized it. This Court upheld
the validity of the search and seizure under *Terry.* The Court held
first that, in the context of a roadside encounter, where police have

reasonable suspicion based on specific and articulable facts to believe that a driver may be armed and dangerous, they may conduct a protective search for weapons not only of the driver's person but also of the passenger compartment of the automobile. 463 U.S., at 1049. Of course, the protective search of the vehicle, being justified solely by the danger that weapons stored there could be used against the officers or bystanders, must be "limited to those areas in which a weapon may be placed or hidden." Ibid. The Court then held: "If, while conducting a legitimate *Terry* search of the interior of the automobile, the officer should, as here, discover contraband other than weapons, he clearly cannot be required to ignore the contraband, and the Fourth Amendment does not require its suppression in such circumstances." Id., at 1050 . . . .

The Court in *Long* justified this latter holding by reference to our cases under the "plain-view" doctrine. . . . Under that doctrine, if police are lawfully in a position from which they view an object, if its incriminating character is immediately apparent, and if the officers have a lawful right of access to the object, they may seize it without a warrant. . . . If, however, the police lack probable cause to believe that an object in plain view is contraband without conducting some further search of the object—i.e., if "its incriminating character [is not] 'immediately apparent,' " *Horton* [v. California, 496 U.S. 128 (1990)], at 136—the plain-view doctrine cannot justify its seizure. Arizona v. Hicks, 480 U.S. 321 (1987).

We think that this doctrine has an obvious application by analogy to cases in which an officer discovers contraband through the sense of touch during an otherwise lawful search. The rationale of the plain view doctrine is that if contraband is left in open view and is observed by a police officer from a lawful vantage point, there has been no invasion of a legitimate expectation of privacy and thus no "search" within the meaning of the Fourth Amendment—or at least no search independent of the initial intrusion that gave the officers their vantage point. . . . The warrantless seizure of contraband that presents itself in this manner is deemed justified by the realization that resort to a neutral magistrate under such circumstances would often be impracticable and would do little to promote the objectives of the Fourth Amendment. . . . The same can be said of tactile discoveries of contraband. If a police officer lawfully pats down a suspect's outer clothing and feels an object whose contour or mass makes its identity immediately apparent, there has been no invasion of the suspect's privacy beyond that already authorized by the officer's search for weapons; if the object is contraband, its warrantless seizure would be justified by the same practical considerations that inhere in the plain view context.

The Minnesota Supreme Court rejected an analogy to the plain-view doctrine on two grounds: first, its belief that "the sense of touch is inherently less immediate and less reliable than the sense of sight," and second, that "the sense of touch is far more intrusive into the personal privacy that is at the core of the [F]ourth [A]mendment." 481 N.W.2d, at 845. We have a somewhat different view. First, *Terry* itself demonstrates that the sense of touch is capable of revealing the nature of an object with sufficient reliability to support a seizure. The very premise of *Terry,* after all, is that officers will be able to detect the presence of weapons through the sense of touch and *Terry* upheld precisely such a seizure. Even if it were true that the sense of touch is generally less reliable than the sense of sight, that only suggests that officers will less often be able to justify seizures of unseen contraband. Regardless of whether the officer detects the contraband by sight or by touch, however, the Fourth Amendment's requirement that the officer have probable cause to believe that the item is contraband before seizing it ensures against excessively speculative seizures. The court's second concern—that touch is more intrusive into privacy than is sight—is inapposite in light of the fact that the intrusion the court fears has already been authorized by the lawful search for weapons. The seizure of an item whose identity is already known occasions no further invasion of privacy.... Accordingly, the suspect's privacy interests are not advanced by a categorical rule barring the seizure of contraband plainly detected through the sense of touch.

III

It remains to apply these principles to the facts of this case. Respondent has not challenged the finding made by the trial court and affirmed by both the Court of Appeals and the State Supreme Court that the police were justified under *Terry* in stopping him and frisking him for weapons. Thus, the dispositive question before this Court is whether the officer who conducted the search was acting within the lawful bounds marked by *Terry* at the time he gained probable cause to believe that the lump in respondent's jacket was contraband. The State District Court did not make precise findings on this point, instead finding simply that the officer, after feeling "a small, hard object wrapped in plastic" in respondent's pocket, "formed the opinion that the object ... was crack ... cocaine." App. to Pet. for Cert. C-2. The District Court also noted that the officer made "no claim that he suspected this object to be a weapon," id., at C-5, a finding affirmed on appeal, see 469 N.W.2d, at 464 (the officer "never thought the lump was a weapon"). The Minnesota Supreme Court, after "a close examination of the record," held that the officer's own testimony "belies any notion that he 'immediately' " recognized the lump as crack cocaine. See 481 N.W.2d, at 844. Rather, the court concluded, the officer determined that the lump was contraband only after "squeezing, sliding and otherwise manipulating the contents of the defendant's pocket"—a pocket which the officer already knew contained no weapon. Ibid.

Under the State Supreme Court's interpretation of the record before it, it is clear that the court was correct in holding that the police officer in this case overstepped the bounds of the "strictly circumscribed" search for weapons allowed under *Terry.* See *Terry*, 392 U.S., at 26. Where, as here, "an officer who is executing a valid search for one item seizes a different item," this Court rightly "has been sensitive to the danger . . . that officers will enlarge a specific authorization, furnished by a warrant or an exigency, into the equivalent of a general warrant to rummage and seize at will." Texas v. Brown, 460 U.S. [730 (1983)], at 748 (Stevens, J., concurring in judgment). Here, the officer's continued exploration of respondent's pocket after having concluded that it contained no weapon was unrelated to "[t]he sole justification of the search [under *Terry:*] . . . the protection of the police officer and others nearby." 392 U.S., at 29. It therefore amounted to the sort of evidentiary search that *Terry* expressly refused to authorize . . . and that we have condemned in subsequent cases. . . .

Once again, the analogy to the plain-view doctrine is apt. In Arizona v. Hicks, 480 U.S. 321 (1987), this Court held invalid the seizure of stolen stereo equipment found by police while executing a valid search warrant for other evidence. Although the police were lawfully on the premises pursuant to the search warrant, they obtained probable cause to believe that the stereo equipment was contraband only after moving the equipment to permit officers to read its serial numbers. The subsequent seizure of the equipment could not be justified by the plain-view doctrine, this Court explained, because the incriminating character of the stereo equipment was not immediately apparent; rather, probable cause to believe that the equipment was stolen arose only as a result of a further search—the moving of the equipment—that was not authorized by the search warrant or by any exception to the warrant requirement. The facts of this case are very similar. Although the officer was lawfully in a position to feel the lump in respondent's pocket, because *Terry* entitled him to place his hands upon respondent's jacket, the court below determined that the incriminating character of the object was not immediately apparent to him. Rather, the officer determined that the item was contraband only after conducting a further search, one not authorized by *Terry* or by any other exception to the warrant requirement. Because this further search of respondent's pocket was constitutionally invalid, the seizure of the cocaine that followed is likewise unconstitutional. . . .

IV

For these reasons, the judgment of the Minnesota Supreme Court is

Affirmed.[*]

---

[*] Justice Scalia wrote a concurring opinion. Chief Justice Rehnquist wrote an opinion concurring in part and dissenting in part, which Justice Blackmun and Justice Thomas joined.

UNITED STATES v. SHARPE

470 U.S. 675, 105 S.Ct. 1568, 84 L.Ed.2d 605 (1985).

CHIEF JUSTICE BURGER delivered the opinion of the Court.

We granted certiorari to decide whether an individual reasonably suspected of engaging in criminal activity may be detained for a period of 20 minutes, when the detention is necessary for law enforcement officers to conduct a limited investigation of the suspected criminal activity.

I

A

On the morning of June 9, 1978, Agent Cooke of the Drug Enforcement Administration (DEA) was on patrol in an unmarked vehicle on a coastal road near Sunset Beach, North Carolina, an area under surveillance for suspected drug trafficking. At approximately 6:30 a.m., Cooke noticed a blue pickup truck with an attached camper shell traveling on the highway in tandem with a blue Pontiac Bonneville. Respondent Savage was driving the pickup, and respondent Sharpe was driving the Pontiac. The Pontiac also carried a passenger, Davis, the charges against whom were later dropped. Observing that the truck was riding low in the rear and that the camper did not bounce or sway appreciably when the truck drove over bumps or around curves, Agent Cooke concluded that it was heavily loaded. A quilted material covered the rear and side windows of the camper.

Cooke's suspicions were sufficiently aroused to follow the two vehicles for approximately 20 miles as they proceeded south into South Carolina. He then decided to make an "investigative stop" and radioed the State Highway Patrol for assistance. Officer Thrasher, driving a marked patrol car, responded to the call. Almost immediately after Thrasher caught up with the procession, the Pontiac and the pickup turned off the highway and onto a campground road. Cooke and Thrasher followed the two vehicles as the latter drove along the road at 55 to 60 miles an hour, exceeding the speed limit of 35 miles an hour. The road eventually looped back to the highway, onto which Savage and Sharpe turned and continued to drive south.

At this point, all four vehicles were in the middle lane of the three right-hand lanes of the highway. Agent Cooke asked Officer Thrasher to signal both vehicles to stop. Thrasher pulled alongside the Pontiac, which was in the lead, turned on his flashing light, and motioned for the driver of the Pontiac to stop. As Sharpe moved

447

the Pontiac into the right lane, the pickup truck cut between the Pontiac and Thrasher's patrol car, nearly hitting the patrol car, and continued down the highway. Thrasher pursued the truck while Cooke pulled up behind the Pontiac.

Cooke approached the Pontiac and identified himself. He requested identification, and Sharpe produced a Georgia driver's license bearing the name of Raymond J. Pavlovich. Cooke then attempted to radio Thrasher to determine whether he had been successful in stopping the pickup truck, but he was unable to make contact for several minutes, apparently because Thrasher was not in his patrol car. Cooke radioed the local police for assistance, and two officers from the Myrtle Beach Police Department arrived about 10 minutes later. Asking the two officers to "maintain the situation," Cooke left to join Thrasher.

In the meantime, Thrasher had stopped the pickup truck about one-half mile down the road. After stopping the truck, Thrasher had approached it with his revolver drawn, ordered the driver, Savage, to get out and assume a "spread eagled" position against the side of the truck, and patted him down. Thrasher then holstered his gun and asked Savage for his driver's license and the truck's vehicle registration. Savage produced his own Florida driver's license and a bill of sale for the truck bearing the name of Pavlovich. In response to questions from Thrasher concerning the ownership of the truck, Savage said that the truck belonged to a friend and that he was taking it to have its shock absorbers repaired. When Thrasher told Savage that he would be held until the arrival of Cooke, whom Thrasher identified as a DEA agent, Savage became nervous, said that he wanted to leave, and requested the return of his driver's license. Thrasher replied that Savage was not free to leave at that time.

Agent Cooke arrived at the scene approximately 15 minutes after the truck had been stopped. Thrasher handed Cooke Savage's license and the bill of sale for the truck; Cooke noted that the bill of sale bore the same name as Sharpe's license. Cooke identified himself to Savage as a DEA agent and said that he thought the truck was loaded with marihuana. Cooke twice sought permission to search the camper, but Savage declined to give it, explaining that he was not the owner of the truck. Cooke then stepped on the rear of the truck and, observing that it did not sink any lower, confirmed his suspicion that it was probably overloaded. He put his nose against the rear window, which was covered from the inside, and reported that he could smell marihuana. Without seeking Savage's permission, Cooke removed the keys from the ignition, opened the rear of the camper, and observed a large number of burlap-wrapped bales resembling bales of marihuana that Cooke had seen in previous investigations. Agent Cooke then placed Savage under arrest and left him with Thrasher.

Cooke returned to the Pontiac and arrested Sharpe and Davis. Approximately 30 to 40 minutes had elapsed between the time Cooke stopped the Pontiac and the time he returned to arrest Sharpe and Davis. Cooke assembled the various parties and vehicles and led them to the Myrtle Beach police station. That evening, DEA agents took the truck to the Federal Building in Charleston, South Carolina. Several days later, Cooke supervised the unloading of the truck, which contained 43 bales weighing a total of 2,629 pounds. Acting without a search warrant, Cooke had eight randomly selected bales opened and sampled. Chemical tests showed that the samples were marihuana.

B

Sharpe and Savage were charged with possession of a controlled substance with intent to distribute it in violation of 21 U.S.C. § 841(a)(1) and 18 U.S.C. § 2. The United States District Court for the District of South Carolina denied respondents' motion to suppress the contraband, and respondents were convicted.

A divided panel of the Court of Appeals for the Fourth Circuit reversed the convictions. Sharpe v. United States, 660 F.2d 967 (1981). . . . .

The Government petitioned for certiorari . . . . We granted the petition, vacated the judgment of the Court of Appeals, and remanded the case for further consideration in the light of the intervening decision in United States v. Ross, 456 U.S. 798 (1982). United States v. Sharpe, 457 U.S. 1127 (1982).

On remand, a divided panel of the Court of Appeals again reversed the convictions. 712 F.2d 65 (1983). . . .

We granted certiorari, 467 U.S. 1250 (1984), and we reverse.

II

A

The Fourth Amendment is not, of course, a guarantee against *all* searches and seizures, but only against *unreasonable* searches and seizures. The authority and limits of the Amendment apply to investigative stops of vehicles such as occurred here. . . . In Terry v. Ohio, 392 U.S. 1 (1968), we adopted a dual inquiry for evaluating the reasonableness of an investigative stop. Under this approach, we examine

"whether the officer's action was justified at its inception, and whether it was reasonably related in scope to the circumstances which justified the interference in the first place." Id., at 20.

As to the first part of this inquiry, the Court of Appeals assumed that the police had an articulable and reasonable suspicion that Sharpe and Savage were engaged in marihuana trafficking, given the setting and all the circumstances when the police attempted to stop the Pontiac and the pickup. 660 F.2d, at 970. That assumption is abundantly supported by the record. As to the second part of the inquiry, however, the court concluded that the 30- to 40-minute detention of Sharpe and the 20-minute detention of Savage "failed to meet the [Fourth Amendment's] requirement of brevity." Ibid.

It is not necessary for us to decide whether the length of Sharpe's detention was unreasonable, because that detention bears no causal relation to Agent Cooke's discovery of the marihuana. The marihuana was in Savage's pickup, not in Sharpe's Pontiac; the contraband introduced at respondents' trial cannot logically be considered the "fruit" of Sharpe's detention. The only issue in this case, then, is whether it was reasonable under the circumstances facing Agent Cooke and Officer Thrasher to detain Savage, whose vehicle contained the challenged evidence, for approximately 20 minutes. We conclude that the detention of Savage clearly meets the Fourth Amendment's standard of reasonableness.

The Court of Appeals did not question the reasonableness of Officer Thrasher's or Agent Cooke's conduct during their detention of Savage. Rather, the court concluded that the length of the detention alone transformed it from a *Terry* stop into a *de facto* arrest. Counsel for respondents, as *amicus curiae,* assert that conclusion as their principal argument before this Court, relying particularly upon our decisions in Dunaway v. New York, 442 U.S. 200 (1979); Florida v. Royer, 460 U.S. 491 (1983); and United States v. Place, 462 U.S. 696 (1983). That reliance is misplaced.

In *Dunaway,* the police picked up a murder suspect from a neighbor's home and brought him to the police station, where, after being interrogated for an hour, he confessed. The state conceded that the police lacked probable cause when they picked up the suspect, but sought to justify the warrantless detention and interrogation as an investigative stop. The Court rejected this argument, concluding that the defendant's detention was "in important respects indistinguishable from a traditional arrest." 442 U.S., at 212. *Dunaway* is simply inapposite here: the Court was not concerned with the length of the defendant's detention, but with events occurring during the detention.

In *Royer,* government agents stopped the defendant in an airport, seized his luggage, and took him to a small room used for questioning, where a search of the luggage revealed narcotics. The Court held that the defendant's detention constituted an arrest. See 460 U.S., at 503 (plurality opinion); id., at 509 (Powell, J., concurring); ibid. (Brennan, J., concurring in the result). As in *Dunaway,* though, the focus was primarily on facts other than the duration of the defendant's detention—particularly the fact that the police confined the defendant in a small airport room for questioning.

The plurality in *Royer* did note that "an investigative detention must be temporary and last no longer than is necessary to effectuate the purpose of the stop." 460 U.S., at 500. The Court followed a similar approach in *Place*. In that case, law enforcement agents stopped the defendant after his arrival in an airport and seized his luggage for 90 minutes to take it to a narcotics detection dog for a "sniff test." We decided that an investigative seizure of personal property could be justified under the *Terry* doctrine, but that "[t]he length of the detention of respondent's luggage alone precludes the conclusion that the seizure was reasonable in the absence of probable cause." 462 U.S., at 709. However, the rationale underlying that conclusion was premised on the fact that the police knew of respondent's arrival time for several hours beforehand, and the Court assumed that the police could have arranged for a trained narcotics dog in advance and thus avoided the necessity of holding respondent's luggage for 90 minutes. "[I]n assessing the effect of the length of the detention, we take into account whether the police diligently pursue their investigation." Ibid.; see also *Royer*, supra, at 500.

Here, the Court of Appeals did not conclude that the police acted less than diligently, or that they *unnecessarily* prolonged Savage's detention. *Place* and *Royer* thus provide no support for the Court of Appeals' analysis.

Admittedly, *Terry*, *Dunaway*, *Royer*, and *Place*, considered together, may in some instances create difficult line-drawing problems in distinguishing an investigative stop from a *de facto* arrest. Obviously, if an investigative stop continues indefinitely, at some point it can no longer be justified as an investigative stop. But our cases impose no rigid time limitation on *Terry* stops. While it is clear that "the brevity of the invasion of the individual's Fourth Amendment interests is an important factor in determining whether the seizure is so minimally intrusive as to be justifiable on reasonable suspicion," United States v. Place, supra, at 709, we have emphasized the need to consider the law enforcement purposes to be served by the stop as well as the time reasonably needed to effectuate those purposes. ... Much as a "bright line" rule would be desirable, in evaluating whether an investigative detention is unreasonable, common sense and ordinary human experience must govern over rigid criteria.

... The Court of Appeals' decision would effectively establish a *per se* rule that a 20-minute detention is too long to be justified under the *Terry* doctrine. Such a result is clearly and fundamentally at odds with our approach in this area.

B

In assessing whether a detention is too long in duration to be justified as an investigative stop, we consider it appropriate to examine whether the police diligently pursued a means of investigation that was likely to confirm or dispel their suspicions quickly, during which time it was necessary to detain the defendant. ... A court making this assessment should take care to consider whether the police are acting in a swiftly developing situation, and in such cases the court should not indulge in unrealistic second-guessing. ... A creative judge engaged in *post hoc* evaluation of police conduct can almost always imagine some alternative means by which the objectives of the police might have been accomplished. But "[t]he fact that the protection of the public might, in the abstract, have been accomplished by 'less intrusive' means does not, in itself, render the search unreasonable." Cady v. Dombrowski, 413 U.S. 433, 447 (1973) .... The question is not simply whether some other alternative was available, but whether the police acted unreasonably in failing to recognize or to pursue it.

We readily conclude that, given the circumstances facing him, Agent Cooke pursued his investigation in a diligent and reasonable manner. During most of Savage's 20-minute detention, Cooke was attempting to contact Thrasher and enlisting the help of the local police who remained with Sharpe while Cooke left to pursue Officer Thrasher and the pickup. Once Cooke reached Officer Thrasher and Savage,[5] he proceeded expeditiously: within the space of a few minutes, he examined Savage's driver's license and the truck's bill of sale, requested (and was denied) permission to search the truck, stepped on the rear bumper and noted that the truck did not move, confirming his suspicion that it was probably overloaded. He then detected the odor of marihuana.

Clearly this case does not involve any delay unnecessary to the legitimate investigation of the law enforcement officers. Respondents presented no evidence that the officers were dilatory in their investigation. The delay in this case was attributable almost entirely to the evasive actions of Savage, who sought to elude the police as Sharpe moved his Pontiac to the side of the road. Except for Savage's maneuvers, only a short and certainly permissible pre-arrest detention would likely have taken place. The somewhat longer detention was simply the result of a "graduate[d] ... respons[e] to the demands of [the] particular situation," *Place,* supra, at 709, n. 10.

We reject the contention that a 20-minute stop is unreasonable when the police have acted diligently and a suspect's actions contribute to the added delay about which he complains. The judgment of the Court of Appeals is reversed, and the case is remanded for further proceedings consistent with this opinion.

5. It was appropriate for Officer Thrasher to hold Savage for the brief period pending Cooke's arrival. Thrasher could not be certain that he was aware of all of the facts that had aroused Cooke's suspicions; and, as a highway patrolman, he lacked Cooke's training and experience in dealing with narcotics investigations. In this situation, it cannot realistically be said that Thrasher, a state patrolman called in to assist a federal agent in making a stop, acted unreasonably because he did not release Savage based solely on his own limited investigation of the situation and without the consent of Agent Cooke.

Reversed and remanded.[*]

[*] Justice Blackmun wrote a concurring opinion. Justice Marshall wrote an opinion concurring in the judgment. Justice Brennan and Justice Stevens wrote dissenting opinions.

BROWN v. TEXAS

443 U.S. 47, 99 S.Ct. 2637, 61 L.Ed.2d 357 (1979).

MR. CHIEF JUSTICE BURGER delivered the opinion of the Court.

This appeal presents the question whether appellant was validly convicted for refusing to comply with a policeman's demand that he identify himself pursuant to a provision of the Texas Penal Code which makes it a crime to refuse such identification on request.

I

At 12:45 on the afternoon of December 9, 1977, officers Venegas and Sotelo of the El Paso Police Department were cruising in a patrol car. They observed appellant and another man walking in opposite directions away from one another in an alley. Although the two men were a few feet apart when they first were seen, officer Venegas later testified that both officers believed the two had been together or were about to meet until the patrol car appeared.

The car entered the alley, and officer Venegas got out and asked appellant to identify himself and explain what he was doing there. The other man was not questioned or detained. The officer testified that he stopped appellant because the situation "looked suspicious and we had never seen that subject in that area before." The area of El Paso where appellant was stopped has a high incidence of drug traffic. However, the officers did not claim to suspect appellant of any specific misconduct, nor did they have any reason to believe that he was armed.

Appellant refused to identify himself and angrily asserted that the officers had no right to stop him. Officer Venegas replied that he was in a "high drug problem area"; officer Sotelo then "frisked" appellant, but found nothing.

When appellant continued to refuse to identify himself, he was arrested for violation of Texas Penal Code Ann., Tit. 8, § 38.02(a) (1974), which makes it a criminal act for a person to refuse to give his name and address to an officer "who has lawfully stopped him and requested the information." Following the arrest the officers searched appellant; nothing untoward was found.

While being taken to the El Paso County Jail appellant identified himself. Nonetheless, he was held in custody and charged with violating § 38.02(a). When he was booked he was routinely searched a third time. Appellant was convicted in the El Paso Municipal Court and fined $20 plus court costs for violation of § 38.02. He then exercised his right under Texas law to a trial *de*

454

novo in the El Paso County Court. There, he moved to set aside the information on the ground that § 38.02(a) of the Texas Penal Code violated the First, Fourth, and Fifth Amendments and was unconstitutionally vague in violation of the Fourteenth Amendment. The motion was denied. Appellant waived jury, and the court convicted him and imposed a fine of $45 plus court costs.

Under Texas law an appeal from an inferior court to a county court is subject to further review only if a fine exceeding $100 is imposed. Texas Code Crim.Proc.Ann., Art. 4.03 (Vernon 1977). Accordingly, the County Court's rejection of appellant's constitutional claims was a decision "by the highest court of a State in which a decision could be had." 28 U.S.C. § 1257(2). On appeal here we noted probable jurisdiction. 439 U.S. 909 (1978). We reverse.

II

When the officers detained appellant for the purpose of requiring him to identify himself, they performed a seizure of his person subject to the requirements of the Fourth Amendment. In convicting appellant, the County Court necessarily found as a matter of fact that the officers "lawfully stopped" appellant. ... The Fourth Amendment, of course, "applies to all seizures of the person, including seizures that involve only a brief detention short of traditional arrest. Davis v. Mississippi, 394 U.S. 721 (1969); Terry v. Ohio, 392 U.S. 1, 16–19 (1968). '[W]henever a police officer accosts an individual and restrains his freedom to walk away, he has "seized" that person,' id., at 16, and the Fourth Amendment requires that the seizure be 'reasonable.'" United States v. Brignoni-Ponce, 422 U.S. 873, 878 (1975).

The reasonableness of seizures that are less intrusive than a traditional arrest ... depends "on a balance between the public interest and the individual's right to personal security free from arbitrary interference by law officers." Pennsylvania v. Mimms, 434 U.S. 106, 109 (1977) .... Consideration of the constitutionality of such seizures involves a weighing of the gravity of the public concerns served by the seizure, the degree to which the seizure advances the public interest, and the severity of the interference with individual liberty. See, e.g., 422 U.S., at 878–883.

A central concern in balancing these competing considerations in a variety of settings has been to assure that an individual's reasonable expectation of privacy is not subject to arbitrary invasions solely at the unfettered discretion of officers in the field. ... To this end, the Fourth Amendment requires that a seizure must be based on specific, objective facts indicating that society's legitimate interests require the seizure of the particular individual, or that the seizure must be carried out pursuant to a plan embodying explicit, neutral limitations on the conduct of individual officers. ...

The State does not contend that appellant was stopped pursuant to a practice embodying neutral criteria, but rather maintains that the officers were justified in stopping appellant because they had a "reasonable, articulable suspicion that a crime had just been, was being, or was about to be committed." We have recognized that in some circumstances an officer may detain a suspect briefly for questioning although he does not have "probable cause" to believe that the suspect is involved in criminal activity, as is required for a traditional arrest. ... However, we have required the officers to have a reasonable suspicion, based on objective facts, that the individual is involved in criminal activity. ....

The flaw in the State's case is that none of the circumstances preceding the officers' detention of appellant justified a reasonable suspicion that he was involved in criminal conduct. Officer Venegas testified at appellant's trial that the situation in the alley "looked suspicious," but he was unable to point to any facts supporting that conclusion.[2] There is no indication in the record that it was unusual for people to be in the alley. The fact that appellant was in a neighborhood frequented by drug users, standing alone, is not a basis for concluding that appellant himself was engaged in criminal conduct. In short, the appellant's activity was no different from the activity of other pedestrians in that neighborhood. When pressed, officer Venegas acknowledged that the only reason he stopped appellant was to ascertain his identity. The record suggests an understandable desire to assert a police presence; however that purpose does not negate Fourth Amendment guarantees.

In the absence of any basis for suspecting appellant of misconduct, the balance between the public interest and appellant's right to personal security and privacy tilts in favor of freedom from police interference. The Texas statute under which appellant was stopped and required to identify himself is designed to advance a weighty social objective in large metropolitan centers: prevention of crime. But even assuming that purpose is served to some degree by stopping and demanding identification from an individual without any specific basis for believing he is involved in criminal activity, the guarantees of the Fourth Amendment do not allow it. When such a stop is not based on objective criteria, the risk of arbitrary and abusive police practices exceeds tolerable limits. ...

The application of Texas Penal Code Ann., Tit. 8, § 38.02 (1974), to detain appellant and require him to identify himself violated the Fourth Amendment because the officers lacked any reasonable suspicion to believe appellant was engaged or had engaged in criminal conduct. Accordingly, appellant may not be punished for refusing to identify himself, and the conviction is

Reversed.

[Appendix omitted.]

---

2. This situation is to be distinguished from the observations of a trained, experienced police officer who is able to perceive and articulate meaning in given conduct which would be wholly innocent to the untrained observer. ...

MICHIGAN DEPARTMENT OF STATE POLICE v. SITZ

496 U.S. 444, 110 S.Ct. 2481, 110 L.Ed.2d 412 (1990).

CHIEF JUSTICE REHNQUIST delivered the opinion of the Court.

This case poses the question whether a State's use of highway sobriety checkpoints violates the Fourth and Fourteenth Amendments to the United States Constitution. We hold that it does not and therefore reverse the contrary holding of the Court of Appeals of Michigan.

Petitioners, the Michigan Department of State Police and its director, established a sobriety checkpoint pilot program in early 1986. The director appointed a Sobriety Checkpoint Advisory Committee comprising representatives of the State Police force, local police forces, state prosecutors, and the University of Michigan Transportation Research Institute. Pursuant to its charge, the advisory committee created guidelines setting forth procedures governing checkpoint operations, site selection, and publicity.

Under the guidelines, checkpoints would be set up at selected sites along state roads. All vehicles passing through a checkpoint would be stopped and their drivers briefly examined for signs of intoxication. In cases where a checkpoint officer detected signs of intoxication, the motorist would be directed to a location out of the traffic flow where an officer would check the motorist's driver's license and car registration and, if warranted, conduct further sobriety tests. Should the field tests and the officer's observations suggest that the driver was intoxicated, an arrest would be made. All other drivers would be permitted to resume their journey immediately.

The first—and to date the only—sobriety checkpoint operated under the program was conducted in Saginaw County with the assistance of the Saginaw County Sheriff's Department. During the 75-minute duration of the checkpoint's operation, 126 vehicles passed through the checkpoint. The average delay for each vehicle was approximately 25 seconds. Two drivers were detained for field sobriety testing, and one of the two was arrested for driving under the influence of alcohol. A third driver who drove through without stopping was pulled over by an officer in an observation vehicle and arrested for driving under the influence.

On the day before the operation of the Saginaw County checkpoint, respondents filed a complaint in the Circuit Court of Wayne County seeking declaratory and injunctive relief from potential subjection to the checkpoints. Each of the respondents "is a

457

licensed driver in the State of Michigan ... who regularly travels throughout the State in his automobile." See Complaint, App. 3a–4a. During pretrial proceedings, petitioners agreed to delay further implementation of the checkpoint program pending the outcome of this litigation.

After the trial, at which the court heard extensive testimony concerning, *inter alia,* the "effectiveness" of highway sobriety checkpoint programs, the court ruled that the Michigan program violated the Fourth Amendment and Art. 1, § 11, of the Michigan Constitution.... On appeal, the Michigan Court of Appeals affirmed the holding that the program violated the Fourth Amendment and, for that reason, did not consider whether the program violated the Michigan Constitution. 170 Mich.App. 433, 445, 429 N.W.2d 180, 185 (1988). After the Michigan Supreme Court denied petitioners' application for leave to appeal, we granted certiorari. 493 U.S. 806 (1989).

To decide this case the trial court performed a balancing test derived from our opinion in Brown v. Texas, 443 U.S. 47 (1979). As described by the Court of Appeals, the test involved "balancing the state's interest in preventing accidents caused by drunk drivers, the effectiveness of sobriety checkpoints in achieving that goal, and the level of intrusion on an individual's privacy caused by the checkpoints." 170 Mich.App., at 439, 429 N.W.2d, at 182 (citing *Brown,* supra, at 50–51). The Court of Appeals agreed that "the *Brown* three-prong balancing test was the correct test to be used to determine the constitutionality of the sobriety checkpoint plan." 170 Mich.App., at 439, 429 N.W.2d, at 182.

As characterized by the Court of Appeals, the trial court's findings with respect to the balancing factors were that the State has "a grave and legitimate" interest in curbing drunken driving; that sobriety checkpoint programs are generally "ineffective" and, therefore, do not significantly further that interest; and that the checkpoints' "subjective intrusion" on individual liberties is substantial. Id., at 439, 440, 429 N.W.2d, at 183, 184. According to the court, the record disclosed no basis for disturbing the trial court's findings, which were made within the context of an analytical framework prescribed by this Court for determining the constitutionality of seizures less intrusive than traditional arrests....

In this Court respondents seek to defend the judgment in their favor by insisting that the balancing test derived from Brown v. Texas, supra, was not the proper method of analysis. Respondents maintain that the analysis must proceed from a basis of probable cause or reasonable suspicion and rely for support on language from our decision last Term in Treasury Employees v. Von Raab, 489 U.S. 656 (1989). We said in *Von Raab:*

"[W]here a Fourth Amendment intrusion serves special governmental needs, beyond the normal need for law enforcement, it is necessary to balance the individual's privacy expectations against the Government's interests to determine whether it is impractical to require a warrant or some level of individualized suspicion in the particular context." Id., at 665–666.

Respondents argue that there must be a showing of some special governmental need "beyond the normal need" for criminal law enforcement before a balancing analysis is appropriate, and that petitioners have demonstrated no such special need.

But it is perfectly plain from a reading of *Von Raab,* which cited and discussed with approval our earlier decision in United States v. Martinez–Fuerte, 428 U.S. 543 (1976), that it was in no way designed to repudiate our prior cases dealing with police stops of motorists on public highways. *Martinez–Fuerte,* supra, which utilized a balancing analysis in approving highway checkpoints for detecting illegal aliens, and Brown v. Texas, supra, are the relevant authorities here.

Petitioners concede, correctly in our view, that a Fourth Amendment "seizure" occurs when a vehicle is stopped at a checkpoint.... The question thus becomes whether such seizures are "reasonable" under the Fourth Amendment.

It is important to recognize what our inquiry is *not* about. No allegations are before us of unreasonable treatment of any person after an actual detention at a particular checkpoint.... As pursued in the lower courts, the instant action challenges only the use of sobriety checkpoints generally. We address only the initial stop of each motorist passing through a checkpoint and the associated preliminary questioning and observation by checkpoint officers. Detention of particular motorists for more extensive field sobriety testing may require satisfaction of an individualized suspicion standard....

No one can seriously dispute the magnitude of the drunken driving problem or the States' interest in eradicating it. Media reports of alcohol-related death and mutilation on the Nation's roads are legion. The anecdotal is confirmed by the statistical....

Conversely, the weight bearing on the other scale—the measure of the intrusion on motorists stopped briefly at sobriety checkpoints—is slight. We reached a similar conclusion as to the intrusion on motorists subjected to a brief stop at a highway checkpoint for detecting illegal aliens.... We see virtually no difference between the levels of intrusion on law-abiding motorists from the brief stops necessary to the effectuation of these two types of checkpoints, which to the average motorist would seem identical save for the nature of the questions the checkpoint officers might ask. The trial court and the Court of Appeals, thus, accurately gauged the "objective" intrusion, measured by the duration of the seizure and the intensity of the investigation, as minimal....

With respect to what it perceived to be the "subjective" intrusion on motorists, however, the Court of Appeals found such intrusion substantial.... The court first affirmed the trial court's finding that the guidelines governing checkpoint operation minimize the discretion of the officers on the scene. But the court also agreed with the trial court's conclusion that the checkpoints have the potential to generate fear and surprise in motorists. This was so because the record failed to demonstrate that approaching motorists would be aware of their option to make U-turns or turnoffs to avoid the checkpoints. On that basis, the court deemed the subjective intrusion from the checkpoints unreasonable....

We believe the Michigan courts misread our cases concerning the degree of "subjective intrusion" and the potential for generating fear and surprise. The "fear and surprise" to be considered are not the natural fear of one who has been drinking over the prospect of being stopped at a sobriety checkpoint but, rather, the fear and surprise engendered in law abiding motorists by the nature of the stop. This was made clear in *Martinez–Fuerte*. Comparing checkpoint stops to roving patrol stops considered in prior cases, we said,

> "we view checkpoint stops in a different light because the subjective intrusion—the generating of concern or even fright on the part of lawful travelers—is appreciably less in the case of a checkpoint stop. In [United States v.] Ortiz, [422 U.S. 891 (1975),] we noted:

> " '[T]he circumstances surrounding a checkpoint stop and search are far less intrusive than those attending a roving-patrol stop. Roving patrols often operate at night on seldom-traveled roads, and their approach may frighten motorists. At traffic checkpoints the motorist can see that other vehicles are being stopped, he can see visible signs of the officers' authority, and he is much less likely to be frightened or annoyed by the intrusion. 422 U.S., at 894–895.' " Martinez–Fuerte, 428 U.S., at 558.

... Here, checkpoints are selected pursuant to the guidelines, and uniformed police officers stop every approaching vehicle. The intrusion resulting from the brief stop at the sobriety checkpoint is for constitutional purposes indistinguishable from the checkpoint stops we upheld in *Martinez–Fuerte*.

The Court of Appeals went on to consider as part of the balancing analysis the "effectiveness" of the proposed checkpoint program. Based on extensive testimony in the trial record, the court concluded that the checkpoint program failed the "effectiveness" part of the test, and that this failure materially discounted petitioners' strong interest in implementing the program. We think the Court of Appeals was wrong on this point as well.

The actual language from Brown v. Texas, upon which the Michigan courts based their evaluation of "effectiveness," describes the balancing factor as "the degree to which the seizure advances the public interest." 443 U.S., at 51. This passage from *Brown* was not meant to transfer from politically accountable officials to the courts the decision as to which among reasonable alternative law enforcement techniques should be employed to deal with a serious public danger. Experts in police science might disagree over which of several methods of apprehending drunken drivers is preferable as an ideal. But for purposes of Fourth Amendment analysis, the choice among such reasonable alternatives remains with the governmental officials who have a unique understanding of, and a responsibility for, limited public resources, including a finite number of police officers. *Brown*'s rather general reference to "the degree to which the seizure advances the public interest" was derived, as the opinion makes clear, from the line of cases culminating in *Martinez–Fuerte,* supra. Neither *Martinez–Fuerte* nor Delaware v. Prouse, 440 U.S. 648 (1979), however, the two cases cited by the Court of Appeals as providing the basis for its "effectiveness" review, see 170 Mich.App., at 442, 429 N.W.2d, at 183, supports the searching examination of "effectiveness" undertaken by the Michigan court.

In Delaware v. Prouse, supra, we disapproved random stops made by Delaware Highway Patrol officers in an effort to apprehend unlicensed drivers and unsafe vehicles. We observed that *no* empirical evidence indicated that such stops would be an effective means of promoting roadway safety and said that "[i]t seems common sense that the percentage of all drivers on the road who are driving without a license is very small and that the number of licensed drivers who will be stopped in order to find one unlicensed operator will be large indeed." Id., at 659–660. We observed that the random stops involved the "kind of standardless and unconstrained discretion [which] is the evil the Court has discerned when in previous cases it has insisted that the discretion of the official in the field be circumscribed, at least to some extent." Id., at 661. We went on to state that our holding did not "cast doubt on the permissibility of roadside truck weigh-stations and inspection checkpoints, at which some vehicles may be subject to further detention for safety and regulatory inspection than are others." Id., at 663, n. 26.

Unlike *Prouse,* this case involves neither a complete absence of empirical data nor a challenge to random highway stops. During the operation of the Saginaw County checkpoint, the detention of the 126 vehicles that entered the checkpoint resulted in the arrest of two drunken drivers. Stated as a percentage, approximately 1.6 percent of the drivers passing through the checkpoint were arrested for alcohol impairment. In addition, an expert witness testified at the trial that experience in other States demonstrated that, on the whole, sobriety checkpoints resulted in drunken driving arrests of around 1 percent of all motorists stopped. . . . By way of comparison, the record from one of the consolidated cases in *Martinez–Fuerte* showed that in the associated checkpoint, illegal aliens were found in only 0.12 percent of the vehicles passing through the checkpoint.... The ratio of illegal aliens detected to vehicles stopped (considering that on occasion two or more illegal aliens were found in a single vehicle) was approximately 0.5 percent.... We concluded that this "record ... provides a rather complete picture of the effectiveness of the San Clemente checkpoint", [428 U.S. at 554], and we sustained its constitutionality. We see no justification for a different conclusion here.

In sum, the balance of the State's interest in preventing drunken driving, the extent to which this system can reasonably be said to advance that interest, and the degree of intrusion upon individual motorists who are briefly stopped, weighs in favor of the state program. We therefore hold that it is consistent with the Fourth Amendment. The judgment of the Michigan Court of Appeals is accordingly reversed, and the case is remanded for further proceedings not inconsistent with this opinion.

It is so ordered.

JUSTICE STEVENS, with whom JUSTICE BRENNAN and JUSTICE MARSHALL join as to Parts I and II, dissenting.

A sobriety checkpoint is usually operated at night at an unannounced location. Surprise is crucial to its method. The test operation conducted by the Michigan State Police and the Saginaw County Sheriff's Department began shortly after midnight and lasted until about 1 a.m. During that period, the 19 officers participating in the operation made two arrests and stopped and questioned 125 other unsuspecting and innocent drivers. It is, of course, not known how many arrests would have been made during that period if those officers had been engaged in normal patrol activities. However, the findings of the trial court, based on an extensive record and affirmed by the Michigan Court of Appeals, indicate that the net effect of sobriety checkpoints on traffic safety is infinitesimal and possibly negative.

Indeed, the record in this case makes clear that a decision holding these suspicionless seizures unconstitutional would not impede the law enforcement community's remarkable progress in reducing the death toll on our highways. Because the Michigan program was patterned after an older program in Maryland, the trial judge gave special attention to that State's experience. Over a period of several years, Maryland operated 125 checkpoints; of the 41,000 motorists passing through those checkpoints, only 143 persons (0.3%) were arrested. The number of man-hours devoted to these operations is not in the record, but it seems inconceivable that a higher arrest rate could not have been achieved by more conventional means. Yet, even if the 143 checkpoint arrests were assumed to involve a net increase in the number of drunken driving arrests per year, the figure would still be insignificant by comparison to the 71,000 such arrests made by Michigan State Police without checkpoints in 1984 alone. . . .

Any relationship between sobriety checkpoints and an actual reduction in highway fatalities is even less substantial than the minimal impact on arrest rates. . . .

In light of these considerations, it seems evident that the Court today misapplies the balancing test announced in Brown v. Texas, 443 U.S. 47, 50–51 (1979). The Court overvalues the law enforcement interest in using sobriety checkpoints, undervalues the citizen's interest in freedom from random, unannounced investigatory seizures, and mistakenly assumes that there is "virtually no difference" between a routine stop at a permanent, fixed checkpoint and a surprise stop at a sobriety checkpoint. I believe this case is controlled by our several precedents condemning suspicionless random stops of motorists for investigatory purposes. Delaware v. Prouse, 440 U.S. 648 (1979); United States v. Brignoni–Ponce, 422 U.S. 873 (1975); United States v. Ortiz, 422 U.S. 891 (1975); Almeida–Sanchez v. United States, 413 U.S. 266 (1973) . . . .

I

There is a critical difference between a seizure that is preceded by fair notice and one that is effected by surprise. . . . That is one reason why a border search, or indeed any search at a permanent and fixed checkpoint, is much less intrusive than a random stop. A motorist with advance notice of the location of a permanent checkpoint has an opportunity to avoid the search entirely, or at least to prepare for, and limit, the intrusion on her privacy.

No such opportunity is available in the case of a random stop or a temporary checkpoint, which both depend for their effectiveness on the element of surprise. A driver who discovers an unexpected checkpoint on a familiar local road will be startled and distressed. She may infer, correctly, that the checkpoint is not simply "business as usual," and may likewise infer, again correctly, that the police have made a discretionary decision to focus their law enforcement efforts upon her and others who pass the chosen point.

This element of surprise is the most obvious distinction between the sobriety checkpoints permitted by today's majority and the interior border checkpoints approved by this Court in [United States v.] Martinez–Fuerte [428 U.S. 543 (1976)]. The distinction casts immediate doubt upon the majority's argument, for *Martinez–Fuerte* is the only case in which we have upheld suspicionless seizures of motorists. But the difference between notice and surprise is only one of the important reasons for distinguishing between permanent and mobile checkpoints. With respect to the former, there is no room for discretion in either the timing or the location of the stop—it is a permanent part of the landscape. In the latter case, however, although the checkpoint is most frequently employed during the hours of darkness on weekends (because that is when drivers with alcohol in their blood are most apt to be found on the road), the police have extremely broad discretion in determining the exact timing and placement of the roadblock.

There is also a significant difference between the kind of discretion that the officer exercises after the stop is made. A check for a driver's license, or for identification papers at an immigration checkpoint, is far more easily standardized than is a search for evidence of intoxication. A Michigan officer who questions a motorist at a sobriety checkpoint has virtually unlimited discretion to detain the driver on the basis of the slightest suspicion. A ruddy complexion, an unbuttoned shirt, bloodshot eyes or a speech impediment may suffice to prolong the detention. Any driver who had just consumed a glass of beer, or even a sip of wine, would almost certainly have the burden of demonstrating to the officer that her driving ability was not impaired.

Finally, it is significant that many of the stops at permanent checkpoints occur during daylight hours, whereas the sobriety checkpoints are almost invariably operated at night. A seizure followed by interrogation and even a cursory search at night is surely more offensive than a daytime stop that is almost as routine as going through a toll gate....

These fears are not, as the Court would have it, solely the lot of the guilty.... To be law abiding is not necessarily to be spotless, and even the most virtuous can be unlucky. Unwanted attention from the local police need not be less discomforting simply because one's secrets are not the stuff of criminal prosecutions. Moreover, those who have found—by reason of prejudice or misfortune—that encounters with the police may become adversarial or unpleasant without good cause will have grounds for worrying at any stop designed to elicit signs of suspicious behavior. Being stopped by the police is distressing even when it should not be terrifying, and what begins mildly may by happenstance turn severe.

For all these reasons, I do not believe that this case is analogous to *Martinez–Fuerte*. In my opinion, the sobriety checkpoints are instead similar to—and in some respects more intrusive than—the random investigative stops that the Court held unconstitutional in *Brignoni–Ponce* and *Prouse*....

II

The Court, unable to draw any persuasive analogy to *Martinez–Fuerte*, rests its decision today on application of a more general balancing test taken from Brown v. Texas, 443 U.S. 47 (1979).... In our opinion, we stated:

"Consideration of the constitutionality of such seizures involves a weighing of the gravity of the public concerns served by the seizure, the degree to which the seizure advances the public interest, and the severity of the interference with individual liberty." Id., at 50–51.

The gravity of the public concern with highway safety that is implicated by this case is, of course, undisputed. Yet, that same grave concern was implicated in Delaware v. Prouse. Moreover, I do not understand the Court to have placed any lesser value on the importance of the drug problem implicated in Texas v. Brown [sic] or on the need to control the illegal border crossings that were at stake in *Almeida–Sanchez* and its progeny. A different result in this case must be justified by the other two factors in the *Brown* formulation.

As I have already explained, I believe the Court is quite wrong in blithely asserting that a sobriety checkpoint is no more intrusive than a permanent checkpoint. In my opinion, unannounced investigatory seizures are, particularly when they take place at night, the hallmark of regimes far different from ours; the surprise intrusion upon individual liberty is not minimal. On that issue, my difference with the Court may amount to nothing less than a difference in our respective evaluations of the importance of individual liberty, a serious, albeit inevitable, source of constitutional disagreement. On the degree to which the sobriety checkpoint seizures advance the public interest, however, the Court's position is wholly indefensible.

The Court's analysis of this issue resembles a business decision that measures profits by counting gross receipts and ignoring expenses. The evidence in this case indicates that sobriety checkpoints result in the arrest of a fraction of one percent of the drivers who are stopped, but there is absolutely no evidence that this figure represents an increase over the number of arrests that would have been made by using the same law enforcement resources in conventional patrols. Thus, although the *gross* number of arrests is more than zero, there is a complete failure of proof on the question whether the wholesale seizures have produced any *net* advance in the public interest in arresting intoxicated drivers.

. . .

III

The most disturbing aspect of the Court's decision today is that it appears to give no weight to the citizen's interest in freedom from suspicionless unannounced investigatory seizures.... On the other hand, the Court places a heavy thumb on the law enforcement interest by looking only at gross receipts instead of net benefits. Perhaps this tampering with the scales of justice can be explained by the Court's obvious concern about the slaughter on our highways and a resultant tolerance for policies designed to alleviate the problem by "setting an example" of a few motorists. . . .

. . .

This is a case that is driven by nothing more than symbolic state action—an insufficient justification for an otherwise unreasonable program of random seizures. Unfortunately, the Court is transfixed by the wrong symbol—the illusory prospect of punishing countless intoxicated motorists—when it should keep its eyes on the road plainly marked by the Constitution.

I respectfully dissent. [*]

[*] Justice Blackmun wrote an opinion concurring in the judgment. Justice Brennan wrote a dissenting opinion, which Justice Marshall joined.

470 U.S. 811, 105 S.Ct. 1643, 84 L.Ed.2d 705 (1985).

JUSTICE WHITE delivered the opinion of the Court.

The issue before us in this case is whether the Fourth Amendment to the Constitution of the United States, applicable to the States by virtue of the Fourteenth Amendment, was properly applied by the District Court of Appeal of Florida, Second District, to allow police to transport a suspect to the station house for fingerprinting, without his consent and without probable cause or prior judicial authorization.

A series of burglary-rapes occurred in Punta Gorda, Florida, in 1980. Police found latent fingerprints on the doorknob of the bedroom of one of the victims, fingerprints they believed belonged to the assailant. The police also found a herringbone pattern tennis shoe print near the victim's front porch. Although they had little specific information to tie petitioner Hayes to the crime, after police interviewed him along with 30 to 40 other men who generally fit the description of the assailant, the investigators came to consider petitioner a principal suspect. They decided to visit petitioner's home to obtain his fingerprints or, if he was uncooperative, to arrest him. They did not seek a warrant authorizing this procedure.

Arriving at petitioner's house, the officers spoke to petitioner on his front porch. When he expressed reluctance voluntarily to accompany them to the station for fingerprinting, one of the investigators explained that they would therefore arrest him. Petitioner, in the words of the investigator, then "blurted out" that he would rather go with the officers to the station than be arrested. App. 20. While the officers were on the front porch, they also seized a pair of herringbone pattern tennis shoes in plain view.

Petitioner was then taken to the station house, where he was fingerprinted. When police determined that his prints matched those left at the scene of the crime, petitioner was placed under formal arrest. Before trial, petitioner moved to suppress the fingerprint evidence, claiming it was the fruit of an illegal detention. The trial court denied the motion and admitted the evidence without expressing a reason. Petitioner was convicted of the burglary and sexual battery committed at the scene where the latent fingerprints were found.

The District Court of Appeal of Florida, Second District, affirmed the conviction. 439 So.2d 896 (1983). The court declined to find consent, reasoning that in view of the threatened arrest it was, "at best, highly questionable" that Hayes voluntarily accompa-

467

nied the officers to the station. Id., at 898. The court also expressly found that the officers did not have probable cause to arrest petitioner until after they obtained his fingerprints. Id., at 899. Nevertheless, although finding neither consent nor probable cause, the court held, analogizing to the stop and frisk rule of Terry v. Ohio, 392 U.S. 1 (1968), that the officers could transport petitioner to the station house and take his fingerprints on the basis of their reasonable suspicion that he was involved in the crime. 439 So.2d, at 899, 904.

The Florida Supreme Court denied review by a four-to-three decision, 447 So.2d 886 (1983). We granted certiorari to review this application of *Terry*, 469 U.S. 816 (1984), and we now reverse.

We agree with petitioner that Davis v. Mississippi, 394 U.S. 721 (1969), requires reversal of the judgment below. In *Davis*, in the course of investigating a rape, police officers brought petitioner Davis to police headquarters on December 3, 1965. He was fingerprinted and briefly questioned before being released. He was later charged and convicted of the rape. An issue there was whether the fingerprints taken on December 3 were the inadmissible fruits of an illegal detention. Concededly, the police at that time were without probable cause for an arrest, there was no warrant, and Davis had not consented to being taken to the station house. The State nevertheless contended that the Fourth Amendment did not forbid an investigative detention for the purpose of fingerprinting, even in the absence of probable cause or a warrant. We rejected that submission, holding that Davis' detention for the purpose of fingerprinting was subject to the constraints of the Fourth Amendment and exceeded the permissible limits of those temporary seizures authorized by Terry v. Ohio, supra. This was so even though fingerprinting, because it involves neither repeated harassment nor any of the probing into private life and thoughts that often marks interrogation and search, represents a much less serious intrusion upon personal security than other types of searches and detentions. 394 U.S., at 727. Nor was it a sufficient answer to the Fourth Amendment issue to recognize that fingerprinting is an inherently more reliable and effective crime-solving mechanism than other types of evidence such as lineups and confessions. Ibid. The Court indicated that perhaps under narrowly confined circumstances, a detention for fingerprinting on less than probable cause might comply with the Fourth Amendment, but found it unnecessary to decide that question since no effort was made to employ the procedures necessary to satisfy the Fourth Amendment. Id., at 728. Rather, Davis had been detained at police headquarters without probable cause to arrest and without authorization by a judicial officer.

Here, as in *Davis*, there was no probable cause to arrest, no consent to the journey to the police station, and no judicial authorization for such a detention for fingerprinting purposes. Unless later cases have undermined *Davis* or we now disavow that decision, the judgment below must be reversed.

None of our later cases have undercut the holding in *Davis* that transportation to and investigative detention at the station house without probable cause or judicial authorization together violate the Fourth Amendment. Indeed, some 10 years later, in Dunaway v. New York, 442 U.S. 200 (1979), we refused to extend Terry v. Ohio, supra, to authorize investigative interrogations at police stations on less than probable cause, even though proper warnings under Miranda v. Arizona, 384 U.S. 436 (1966), had been given. We relied on and reaffirmed the holding in *Davis* that in the absence of probable cause or a warrant investigative detentions at the police station for fingerprinting purposes could not be squared with the Fourth Amendment, 442 U.S., at 213–216, while at the same time repeating the possibility that the Amendment might permit a narrowly circumscribed procedure for fingerprinting detentions on less than probable cause. Since that time, we have several times revisited and explored the reach of Terry v. Ohio. . . . But none of these cases has sustained against Fourth Amendment challenge the involuntary removal of a suspect from his home to a police station and his detention there for investigative purposes, whether for interrogation or fingerprinting, absent probable cause or judicial authorization.

Nor are we inclined to forswear *Davis*. There is no doubt that at some point in the investigative process, police procedures can qualitatively and quantitatively be so intrusive with respect to a suspect's freedom of movement and privacy interests as to trigger the full protection of the Fourth and Fourteenth Amendments. . . . And our view continues to be that the line is crossed when the police, without probable cause or a warrant, forcibly remove a person from his home or other place in which he is entitled to be and transport him to the police station, where he is detained, although briefly, for investigative purposes. We adhere to the view that such seizures, at least where not under judicial supervision, are sufficiently like arrests to invoke the traditional rule that arrests may constitutionally be made only on probable cause.

None of the foregoing implies that a brief detention in the field for the purpose of fingerprinting, where there is only reasonable suspicion not amounting to probable cause, is necessarily impermissible under the Fourth Amendment. In addressing the reach of a *Terry* stop in Adams v. Williams, 407 U.S. 143, 146 (1972), we observed that "[a] brief stop of a suspicious individual, in order to determine his identity or to maintain the status quo momentarily while obtaining more information, may be most reasonable in light of the facts known to the officer at the time." Also, just this Term, we concluded that if there are articulable facts supporting a reasonable suspicion that a person has committed a criminal offense, that person may be stopped in order to identify him, to question him briefly, or to detain him briefly while attempting to obtain additional information. United States v. Hensley, [469 U.S. 221 (1985)], at 229, 232, 234. ... There is thus support in our cases for the view that the Fourth Amendment would permit seizures for the purpose of fingerprinting, if there is reasonable suspicion that the suspect has committed a criminal act, if there is a reasonable basis for believing that fingerprinting will establish or negate the suspect's connection with that crime, and if the procedure is carried out with dispatch. ... Of course, neither reasonable suspicion nor probable cause would suffice to permit the officers to make a warrantless entry into a person's house for the purpose of obtaining fingerprint identification. ...

We also do not abandon the suggestion in *Davis* and *Dunaway* that under circumscribed procedures, the Fourth Amendment might permit the judiciary to authorize the seizure of a person on less than probable cause and his removal to the police station for the purpose of fingerprinting. We do not, of course, have such a case before us. We do note, however, that some States, in reliance on the suggestion in *Davis,* have enacted procedures for judicially authorized seizures for the purpose of fingerprinting. The state courts are not in accord on the validity of these efforts to insulate investigative seizures from Fourth Amendment invalidation. ...

As we have said, absent probable cause and a warrant, Davis v. Mississippi, 394 U.S. 721 (1969), requires the reversal of the judgment of the Florida District Court of Appeal.

It is so ordered.[*]

[*] Justice Brennan wrote an opinion concurring in the judgment, which Justice Marshall joined. Justice Blackmun concurred in the judgment.

DUNAWAY v. NEW YORK

442 U.S. 200, 99 S.Ct. 2248, 60 L.Ed.2d 824 (1979).

MR. JUSTICE BRENNAN delivered the opinion of the Court.

We decide in this case the question reserved 10 years ago in Morales v. New York, 396 U.S. 102 (1969), namely, "the question of the legality of custodial questioning on less than probable cause for a full-fledged arrest." Id., at 106.

I

On March 26, 1971, the proprietor of a pizza parlor in Rochester, N.Y. was killed during an attempted robbery. On August 10, 1971, Detective Anthony Fantigrossi of the Rochester Police was told by another officer that an informant had supplied a possible lead implicating petitioner in the crime. Fantigrossi questioned the supposed source of the lead—a jail inmate awaiting trial for burglary—but learned nothing that supplied "enough information to get a warrant" for petitioner's arrest. App. 60. Nevertheless, Fantigrossi ordered other detectives to "pick up" petitioner and "bring him in." Id., at 54. Three detectives located petitioner at a neighbor's house on the morning of August 11. Petitioner was taken into custody; although he was not told he was under arrest, he would have been physically restrained if he had attempted to leave. Opinion in People v. Dunaway (Monroe County Ct., Mar. 11, 1977). He was driven to police headquarters in a police car and placed in an interrogation room, where he was questioned by officers after being given the warnings required by Miranda v. Arizona, 384 U.S. 436 (1966). Petitioner waived counsel and eventually made statements and drew sketches that incriminated him in the crime.[2]

At petitioner's jury trial for attempted robbery and felony murder his motions to suppress the statements and sketches were denied, and he was convicted. On appeal, both the Appellate Division of the Fourth Department and the New York Court of Appeals initially affirmed the conviction without opinion. People v. Dunaway, 42 App.Div.2d 689, 346 N.Y.S.2d 779 (1973), aff'd 35 N.Y.2d 741, 320 N.E.2d 646 (1974). However, this Court granted certiorari, vacated the judgment, and remanded the case for further consideration in light of the Court's supervening decision in Brown v. Illinois, 422 U.S. 590 (1975). 422 U.S. 1053 (1975). The petitioner in *Brown*, like petitioner Dunaway, made inculpatory statements after receiving *Miranda* warnings during custodial inter-

2. See 61 App.Div.2d 299, 301, 402 N.Y.S.2d 490, 491 (1978). The first statement was made within an hour after Dunaway reached the police station; the following day he made a second, more complete statement.

471

rogation following his seizure—in that case a formal arrest—on less than probable cause. Brown's motion to suppress the statements was also denied and the statements were used to convict him. Although the Illinois Supreme Court recognized that Brown's arrest was unlawful, it affirmed the admission of the statements on the ground that the giving of *Miranda* warnings served to break the causal connection between the illegal arrest and the giving of the statements. This Court reversed, holding that the Illinois courts erred in adopting a *per se* rule that *Miranda* warnings in and of themselves sufficed to cure the Fourth Amendment violation; rather the Court held that in order to use such statements, the prosecution must show not only that the statements meet the Fifth Amendment voluntariness standard, but also that the causal connection between the statements and the illegal arrest is broken sufficiently to purge the primary taint of the illegal arrest in light of the distinct policies and interests of the Fourth Amendment.

In compliance with the remand, the New York Court of Appeals directed the Monroe County Court to make further factual findings as to whether there was a detention of petitioner, whether the police had probable cause, "and, in the event there was a detention and probable cause is not found for such detention, to determine the further question as to whether the making of the confessions was rendered infirm by the illegal arrest (see Brown v. Illinois, 422 U.S. 590, supra)." People v. Dunaway, 38 N.Y.2d 812, 813–814, 345 N.E.2d 583, 584 (1975).

The County Court determined after a supplementary suppression hearing that Dunaway's motion to suppress should have been granted. . . .

A divided Appellate Division reversed. . . . The Court of Appeals dismissed petitioner's application for leave to appeal. App. 134.

We granted certiorari, 439 U.S. 979 (1978), to clarify the Fourth Amendment's requirements as to the permissible grounds for custodial interrogation and to review the New York court's application of Brown v. Illinois. We reverse.

II

We first consider whether the Rochester police violated the Fourth and Fourteenth Amendments when, without probable cause to arrest, they took petitioner into custody, transported him to the police station, and detained him there for interrogation.

The Fourth Amendment, applicable to the States through the Fourteenth Amendment, Mapp v. Ohio, 367 U.S. 643 (1961), provides: "The right of the people to be secure in their persons . . . against unreasonable searches and seizures, shall not be violated, and no Warrants shall issue, but upon probable cause . . . ." There can be little doubt that petitioner was "seized" in the Fourth

Amendment sense when he was taken involuntarily to the police station. And respondent State concedes that the police lacked probable cause to arrest petitioner before his incriminating statement during interrogation. Nevertheless respondent contends that the seizure of petitioner did not amount to an arrest and was therefore permissible under the Fourth Amendment because the police had a "reasonable suspicion" that petitioner possessed "intimate knowledge about a serious and unsolved crime." Brief for Respondent 10. We disagree.

Before Terry v. Ohio, 392 U.S. 1 (1968), the Fourth Amendment's guarantee against unreasonable seizures of persons was analyzed in terms of arrest, probable cause for arrest, and warrants based on such probable cause. The basic principles were relatively simple and straightforward: The term "arrest" was synonymous with those seizures governed by the Fourth Amendment. While warrants were not required in all circumstances, the requirement of probable cause, as elaborated in numerous precedents, was treated as absolute. The "long prevailing standards" of probable cause embodied "the best compromise that has been found for accommodating the [] often opposing interests" in "safeguard[ing] citizens from rash and unreasonable interferences with privacy" and in "seek[ing] to give fair leeway for enforcing the law in the community's protection." Brinegar v. United States, 338 U.S. 160, 176 (1949). The standard of probable cause thus represented the accumulated wisdom of precedent and experience as to the minimum justification necessary to make the kind of intrusion involved in an arrest "reasonable" under the Fourth Amendment. The standard applied to all arrests, without the need to "balance" the interests and circumstances involved in particular situations. . . .

Terry for the first time recognized an exception to the requirement that Fourth Amendment seizures of persons must be based on probable cause. That case involved a brief, on-the-spot stop on the street and a frisk for weapons, a situation that did not fit comfortably within the traditional concept of an "arrest." Nevertheless, the Court held that even this type of "necessarily swift action predicated upon the on-the-spot observations of the officer on the beat" constituted a "serious intrusion upon the sanctity of the person, which may inflict great indignity and arouse strong resentment," 392 U.S., at 20, 17, and therefore "must be tested by the Fourth Amendment's general proscription against unreasonable searches and seizures." Id., at 20. However, since the intrusion involved in a "stop and frisk" was so much less severe than that involved in traditional "arrests," the Court declined to stretch the concept of "arrest"—and the general rule requiring probable cause to make arrests "reasonable" under the Fourth Amendment—to cover such intrusions. Instead, the Court treated the stop and frisk intrusion as a *sui generis* "rubric of police conduct," ibid. And to determine the justification necessary to make this specially limited intrusion "reasonable" under the Fourth Amendment, the Court balanced the limited violation of individual privacy involved against the opposing interests in crime prevention and detection and in the police officer's safety. Id., at 22–27. As a consequence, the Court established "a narrowly drawn authority to permit a reasonable search for weapons for the protection of the police officer, where he has reason to believe that he is dealing with an armed and dangerous individual, regardless of whether he has probable cause to arrest the individual for a crime." Id., at 27.[11] Thus, *Terry* departed from traditional Fourth Amendment analysis in two respects. First, it defined a special category of Fourth Amendment "seizures" so substantially less intrusive than arrests that the general rule requiring probable cause to make Fourth Amendment "seizures" reasonable could be replaced by a balancing test. Second, the application of this balancing test led the Court to approve this narrowly defined less intrusive seizure on grounds less rigorous than probable cause, but only for the purpose of a pat-down for weapons.

Because *Terry* involved an exception to the general rule requiring probable cause, this Court has been careful to maintain its narrow scope. *Terry* itself involved a limited, on-the-street frisk for weapons.[12] Two subsequent cases which applied *Terry* also involved limited weapons frisks. See Adams v. Williams, 407 U.S. 143 (1972) (frisk for weapons on basis of reasonable suspicion); Pennsylvania v. Mimms, 434 U.S. 106 (1977) (order to get out of car is permissible "de minimis" intrusion after car is lawfully detained for traffic violations; frisk for weapons justified after "bulge" observed in jacket). United States v. Brignoni-Ponce, 422 U.S. 873 (1975), applied *Terry* in the special context of roving border patrols stopping automobiles to check for illegal immigrants. The investigative stops usually consumed less than a minute and involved "a brief question or two." 422 U.S., at 880. The Court stated that "[b]ecause of the limited nature of the intrusion, stops of this sort may be justified on facts that do not amount to the probable cause required for an arrest." Ibid. See also United States v. Martinez-Fuerte, 428 U.S. 543 (1976) (fixed checkpoint to stop and check vehicles for aliens); Delaware v. Prouse, 440 U.S. 648 (1979) (random checks for drivers' licenses and proper vehicle registration not permitted on less than articulable reasonable suspicion).

Respondent State now urges the Court to apply a balancing test, rather than the general rule, to custodial interrogations, and to hold that "seizures" such as that in this case may be justified by

---

11. The Court stressed the limits of its holding: the police officer's belief that his safety or that of others is in danger must be objectively reasonable—based on reasonable inferences from known facts—so that it can be tested at the appropriate time by "the more detached, neutral scrutiny of a judge," 392 U.S., at 21, 27; and the extent of the intrusion must be carefully tailored to the rationale justifying it.

12. *Terry* specifically declined to address "the constitutional propriety of an investigative 'seizure' upon less than probable cause for purposes of 'detention' and/or interrogation." Id. at 19 n. 16. . . .

mere "reasonable suspicion." *Terry* and its progeny clearly do not support such a result. The narrow intrusions involved in those cases were judged by a balancing test rather than by the general principle that Fourth Amendment seizures must be supported by the "long prevailing standards" of probable cause, Brinegar v. United States, 338 U.S., at 176, only because these intrusions fell far short of the kind of intrusion associated with an arrest. Indeed, Brignoni-Ponce expressly refused to extend *Terry* in the manner respondent now urges. The Court there stated: "The officer may question the driver and passengers about their citizenship and immigration status, and he may ask them to explain suspicious circumstances, *but any further detention or search must be based on consent or probable-cause.*" 422 U.S., at 881–882 (emphasis added).

. . .

In contrast to the brief and narrowly circumscribed intrusions involved in those cases, the detention of petitioner was in important respects indistinguishable from a traditional arrest. Petitioner was not questioned briefly where he was found. Instead, he was taken from a neighbor's home to a police car, transported to a police station, and placed in an interrogation room. He was never informed that he was "free to go"; indeed, he would have been physically restrained if he had refused to accompany the officers or had tried to escape their custody. The application of the Fourth Amendment's requirement of probable cause does not depend on whether an intrusion of this magnitude is termed an "arrest" under state law. The mere facts that petitioner was not told he was under arrest, was not "booked," and would not have had an arrest record if the interrogation had proved fruitless, while not insignificant for all purposes ... obviously do not make petitioner's seizure even roughly analogous to the narrowly defined intrusions involved in *Terry* and its progeny. Indeed, any "exception" that could cover a seizure as intrusive as that in this case would threaten to swallow the general rule that Fourth Amendment seizures are "reasonable" only if based on probable cause.

The central importance of the probable cause requirement to the protection of a citizen's privacy afforded by the Fourth Amendment's guarantees cannot be compromised in this fashion. "The requirement of probable cause has roots that are deep in our history." Henry v. United States, 361 U.S. 98, 100 (1959). Hostility to seizures based on mere suspicion was a prime motivation for the adoption of the Fourth Amendment, and decisions immediately after its adoption affirmed that "common rumor or report, suspicion, or even 'strong reason to suspect' was not adequate to support a warrant for arrest." Id., at 101 (footnotes omitted). The familiar threshold standard of probable cause for Fourth Amendment seizures reflects the benefit of extensive experience accommodating the factors relevant to the "reasonableness" requirement of the Fourth Amendment, and provides the relative simplicity and clarity necessary to the implementation of a workable rule.   . . .

In effect, respondents urge us to adopt a multifactor balancing test of "reasonable police conduct under the circumstances" to cover all seizures that do not amount to technical arrests. But the protections intended by the Framers could all too easily disappear in the consideration and balancing of the multifarious circumstances presented by different cases, especially when that balancing may be done in the first instance by police officers engaged in the "often competitive enterprise of ferreting out crime." Johnson v. United States, 333 U.S. 10, 14 (1948). A single, familiar standard is essential to guide police officers, who have only limited time and expertise to reflect on and balance the social and individual interests involved in the specific circumstances they confront. Indeed, our recognition of these dangers, and our consequent reluctance to depart from the proven protections afforded by the general rule, is reflected in the narrow limitations emphasized in the cases employing the balancing test. For all but those narrowly defined intrusions, the requisite "balancing" has been performed in centuries of precedent and is embodied in the principle that seizures are "reasonable" only if supported by probable cause.

Moreover, two important decisions since *Terry* confirm the conclusion that the treatment of petitioner, whether or not it is technically characterized as an arrest, must be supported by probable cause. Davis v. Mississippi, 394 U.S. 721 (1969), decided the term after *Terry,* considered whether fingerprints taken from a suspect detained without probable cause must be excluded from evidence. The State argued that the detention "was of a type which does not require probable cause," 394 U.S., at 726, because it occurred during an investigative, rather than accusatory stage, and because it was for the sole purpose of taking fingerprints. Rejecting the State's first argument, the Court warned:

> "[T]o argue that the Fourth Amendment does not apply to the investigatory stage is fundamentally to misconceive the purposes of the Fourth Amendment. Investigatory seizures would subject unlimited numbers of innocent persons to the harassment and ignominy incident to involuntary detention. Nothing is more clear than that the Fourth Amendment was meant to prevent wholesale intrusions upon the personal security of our citizenry, whether these intrusions be termed 'arrests' or 'investigatory detentions.' " Id., at 726–727.

The State's second argument in *Davis* was more substantial, largely because of the *distinctions* between taking fingerprints and interrogation:

> "Fingerprinting involves none of the probing into an individual's private life and thoughts that marks an interrogation or search. Nor can fingerprint detention be employed repeatedly

to harass any individual, since the police need only one set of each person's prints. Furthermore, fingerprinting is an inherently more reliable and effective crime-solving tool than eyewitness identifications or confessions and is not subject to such abuses as the improper line-up and the 'third degree.' Finally, because there is no danger of destruction of fingerprints, the limited detention need not come unexpectedly or at an inconvenient time." Id., at 727.

In *Davis,* however, the Court found it unnecessary to decide the validity of a "narrowly circumscribed procedure for obtaining" the fingerprints of suspects without probable cause—in part because, as the Court emphasized, "petitioner was not merely fingerprinted during the . . . detention but *also subjected to interrogation.*" Id., at 728 (emphasis added). The detention therefore violated the Fourth Amendment.

Brown v. Illinois, 422 U.S. 590 (1975), similarly disapproved arrests made for "investigatory" purposes on less than probable cause. Although Brown's arrest had more of the trappings of a technical formal arrest than petitioner's, such differences in form must not be exalted over substance. Once in the police station, Brown was taken to an interrogation room, and his experience was indistinguishable from petitioner's. Our condemnation of the police conduct in *Brown* fits equally the police conduct in this case:

"The impropriety of the arrest was obvious; awareness of the fact was virtually conceded by the two detectives when they repeatedly acknowledged, in their testimony, that the purpose of their action was 'for investigation' or for 'questioning.' . . . The arrest, both in design and in execution, was investigatory. The detectives embarked upon this expedition for evidence in the hope that something might turn up." Id., at 605. See also id., at 602.

These passages from *Davis* and *Brown* reflect the conclusion that detention for custodial interrogation—regardless of its label—intrudes so severely on interests protected by the Fourth Amendment as necessarily to trigger the traditional safeguards against illegal arrest. We accordingly hold that the Rochester police violated the Fourth and Fourteenth Amendments when, without probable cause, they seized petitioner and transported him to the police station for interrogation.

III

There remains the question whether the connection between this unconstitutional police conduct and the incriminating statements and sketches obtained during petitioner's illegal detention was nevertheless sufficiently attenuated to permit the use at trial of the statements and sketches. . . .

The New York courts have consistently held, and petitioner does not contest, that proper *Miranda* warnings were given and that his statements were "voluntary" for purposes of the Fifth Amendment. But Brown v. Illinois, supra, settled that "[t]he exclusionary rule, . . . when utilized to effectuate the Fourth Amendment, serves interests and policies that are distinct from those it serves under the Fifth." 422 U.S., at 601, and held therefore that "*Miranda* warnings, and the exclusion of a confession made without them, do not alone sufficiently deter a Fourth Amendment violation." Ibid. . . .

Consequently, although a confession after proper *Miranda* warnings may be found "voluntary" for purposes of the Fifth Amendment, this type of "voluntariness" is merely a "threshold requirement" for Fourth Amendment analysis, 422 U.S. at 604. Indeed, if the Fifth Amendment has been violated, the Fourth Amendment issue would not have to be reached.

Beyond this threshold requirement, *Brown* articulated a test designed to vindicate the "distinct policies and interests of the Fourth Amendment." Id., at 602. Following *Wong Sun,* the Court eschewed any *per se* or "but for" rule, and identified the relevant inquiry as "whether Brown's statements were obtained by exploitation of the illegality of his arrest," 422 U.S., at 600; see Wong Sun v. United States, supra, at 488. *Brown's* focus on "the causal connection between the illegality and the confession," 422 U.S., at 603, reflected the two policies behind the use of the exclusionary rule to effectuate the Fourth Amendment. When there is a close causal connection between the illegal seizure and the confession, not only is exclusion of the evidence more likely to deter similar police misconduct in the future, but use of the evidence is more likely to compromise the integrity of the courts.

Brown identified several factors to be considered "in determining whether the confession is obtained by exploitation of an illegal arrest[:] [t]he temporal proximity of the arrest and the confession, the presence of intervening circumstances, . . . and, particularly, the purpose and flagrancy of the official misconduct . . . . And the burden of showing admissibility rests, of course, on the prosecution." Id., at 603–604. Examining the case before it, the Court readily concluded that the State had failed to sustain its burden of showing the confession was admissible. In the "less than two hours" that elapsed between the arrest and the confession "there was no intervening event of significance whatsoever." Ibid. Furthermore, the arrest without probable cause had a "quality of purposefulness" in that it was an "expedition for evidence" admittedly undertaken "in the hope that something might turn up." Id., at 605.

The situation in this case is virtually a replica of the situation in *Brown.* Petitioner was also admittedly seized without probable cause in the hope that something might turn up, and confessed without any intervening event of significance. Nevertheless, three members of the Appellate Division purported to distinguish *Brown* on the ground that the police did not threaten or abuse petitioner (presumably putting aside his illegal seizure and detention) and that the police conduct was "highly protective of defendant's Fifth and Sixth Amendment rights." 61 App.Div.2d, at 303, 402 N.Y.S.2d, at 493. This betrays a lingering confusion between "voluntariness" for purposes of the Fifth Amendment and the "causal connection" test established in *Brown*. Satisfying the Fifth Amendment is only the "threshold" condition of the Fourth Amendment analysis required by *Brown*. No intervening events broke the connection between petitioner's illegal detention and his confession. To admit petitioner's confession in such a case would allow "law enforcement officers to violate the Fourth Amendment with impunity, safe in the knowledge that they could wash their hands in the 'procedural safeguards' of the Fifth." [21]

Reversed.[*]

21. Comment, 25 Emory L.J. 227, 238 (1976).

[*] Justice White and Justice Stevens wrote concurring opinions. Justice Rehnquist wrote a dissenting opinion, which Chief Justice Burger joined.

NEW YORK v. HARRIS

495 U.S. 14, 110 S.Ct. 1640, 109 L.Ed.2d 13 (1990).

JUSTICE WHITE delivered the opinion of the Court.

On January 11, 1984, New York City police found the body of Ms. Thelma Staton murdered in her apartment. Various facts gave the officers probable cause to believe that the respondent in this case, Bernard Harris, had killed Ms. Staton. As a result, on January 16, 1984, three police officers went to Harris's apartment to take him into custody. They did not first obtain an arrest warrant.

When the police arrived, they knocked on the door, displaying their guns and badges. Harris let them enter. Once inside, the officers read Harris his rights under Miranda v. Arizona, 384 U.S. 436 (1966). Harris acknowledged that he understood the warnings, and agreed to answer the officers' questions. At that point, he reportedly admitted that he had killed Ms. Staton.

Harris was arrested, taken to the station house, and again informed of his *Miranda* rights. He then signed a written inculpatory statement. The police subsequently read Harris the *Miranda* warnings a third time and videotaped an incriminating interview between Harris and a district attorney, even though Harris had indicated that he wanted to end the interrogation.

The trial court suppressed Harris' first and third statements; the State does not challenge those rulings. The sole issue in this case is whether Harris' second statement—the written statement made at the station house—should have been suppressed because the police, by entering Harris' home without a warrant and without his consent, violated Payton v. New York, 445 U.S. 573 (1980), which held that the Fourth Amendment prohibits the police from effecting a warrantless and nonconsensual entry into a suspect's home in order to make a routine felony arrest. The New York trial court concluded that the statement was admissible. Following a bench trial, Harris was convicted of second-degree murder. The Appellate Division affirmed, 124 A.D.2d 472, 507 N.Y.S.2d 823 (1986).

A divided New York Court of Appeals reversed, 72 N.Y.2d 614, 532 N.E.2d 1229 (1988). That court first accepted the trial court's finding that Harris did not consent to the police officers' entry into his home and that the warrantless arrest therefore violated *Payton* even though there was probable cause. Applying Brown v. Illinois, 422 U.S. 590 (1975), and its progeny, the court then determined that the station house statement must be deemed to be the inadmissible fruit of the illegal arrest because the connection between the

480

statement and the arrest was not sufficiently attenuated. The court noted that some courts had reasoned that the "wrong in *Payton* cases ... lies not in the arrest, 'but in the unlawful *entry* into a dwelling without proper judicial authorization' " and had therefore declined to suppress confessions that were made following *Payton* violations. 72 N.Y.2d, at 623, 532 N.E.2d, at 1234. The New York court disagreed with this analysis, finding it contrary to *Payton* and its own decisions interpreting *Payton*'s scope. We granted certiorari to resolve the admissibility of the station house statement. 490 U.S. 1018 (1989).

For present purposes, we accept the finding below that Harris did not consent to the police officers' entry into his home and the conclusion that the police had probable cause to arrest him. It is also evident, in light of *Payton,* that arresting Harris in his home without an arrest warrant violated the Fourth Amendment. But, as emphasized in earlier cases, "we have declined to adopt a '*per se* or "but for" rule' that would make inadmissible any evidence, whether tangible or live-witness testimony, which somehow came to light through a chain of causation that began with an illegal arrest." United States v. Ceccolini, 435 U.S. 268, 276 (1978). Rather, in this context, we have stated that "[t]he penalties visited upon the Government, and in turn upon the public, because its officers have violated the law must bear some relation to the purposes which the law is to serve." Id., at 279. In light of these principles, we decline to apply the exclusionary rule in this context because the rule in *Payton* was designed to protect the physical integrity of the home; it was not intended to grant criminal suspects, like Harris, protection for statements made outside their premises where the police have probable cause to arrest the suspect for committing a crime.

Payton itself emphasized that our holding in that case stemmed from the "overriding respect for the sanctity of the home that has been embedded in our traditions since the origins of the Republic." 445 U.S., at 601. Although it had long been settled that a warrantless arrest in a public place was permissible as long as the arresting officer had probable cause ... *Payton* nevertheless drew a line at the entrance to the home. This special solicitude was necessary because " 'physical entry of the home is the chief evil against which the wording of the Fourth Amendment is directed.' " 445 U.S., at 585 (citation omitted). The arrest warrant was required to "interpose the magistrate's determination of probable cause" to arrest before the officers could enter a house to effect an arrest. Id., at 602–603.

Nothing in the reasoning of that case suggests that an arrest in a home without a warrant but with probable cause somehow renders unlawful continued custody of the suspect once he is removed from the house. There could be no valid claim here that Harris was immune from prosecution because his person was the fruit of an illegal arrest. ... Nor is there any claim that the warrantless arrest required the police to release Harris or that Harris could not be immediately rearrested if momentarily released. Because the officers had probable cause to arrest Harris for a crime, Harris was not unlawfully in custody when he was removed to the station house, given *Miranda* warnings, and allowed to talk. For Fourth Amendment purposes, the legal issue is the same as it would be had the police arrested Harris on his door step, illegally entered his home to search for evidence, and later interrogated Harris at the station house. Similarly, if the police had made a warrantless entry into Harris' home, not found him there, but arrested him on the street when he returned, a later statement made by him after proper warnings would no doubt be admissible.

This case is therefore different from Brown v. Illinois, 422 U.S. 590 (1975), Dunaway v. New York, 442 U.S. 200 (1979), and Taylor v. Alabama, 457 U.S. 687 (1982). In each of those cases, evidence obtained from a criminal defendant following arrest was suppressed because the police lacked probable cause. The three cases stand for the familiar proposition that the indirect fruits of an illegal search or arrest should be suppressed when they bear a sufficiently close relationship to the underlying illegality.... We have emphasized, however, that attenuation analysis is only appropriate where, as a threshold matter, courts determine that "the challenged evidence is in some sense the product of illegal governmental activity." United States v. Crews, [445 U.S. 463 (1980)], at 471....

Harris' statement taken at the police station was not the product of being in unlawful custody. Neither was it the fruit of having been arrested in the home rather than someplace else. The case is analogous to United States v. Crews, supra. In that case, we refused to suppress a victim's in-court identification despite the defendant's illegal arrest. The Court found that the evidence was not " 'come at by exploitation' of ... the defendant's Fourth Amendment rights," and that it was not necessary to inquire whether the "taint" of the Fourth Amendment violation was sufficiently attenuated to permit the introduction of the evidence. 445 U.S., at 471. Here, likewise, the police had a justification to question Harris prior to his arrest; therefore, his subsequent statement was not an exploitation of the illegal entry into Harris' home.

We do not hold, as the dissent suggests, that a statement taken by the police while a suspect is in custody is always admissible as long as the suspect is in legal custody. Statements taken during legal custody would of course be inadmissible, for example, if they were the product of coercion, if *Miranda* warnings were not given, or if there was a violation of the rule of Edwards v. Arizona, 451 U.S. 477 (1981). We do hold that the station house statement in this case was admissible because Harris was in legal custody, as the dissent concedes, and because the statement, while the product of an arrest and being in custody, was not the fruit of the fact that the arrest was made in the house rather than someplace else.

To put the matter another way, suppressing the statement taken outside the house would not serve the purpose of the rule that made Harris' in-house arrest illegal. The warrant requirement for an arrest in the home is imposed to protect the home, and anything incriminating the police gathered from arresting Harris in his home, rather than elsewhere, has been excluded, as it should have been; the purpose of the rule has thereby been vindicated. We are not required by the Constitution to go further and suppress statements later made by Harris in order to deter police from violating *Payton.* ... Even though we decline to suppress statements made outside the home following a *Payton* violation, the principal incentive to obey *Payton* still obtains: the police know that a warrantless entry will lead to the suppression of any evidence found, or statements taken, inside the home. If we did suppress statements like Harris', moreover, the incremental deterrent value would be minimal. Given that the police have probable cause to arrest a suspect in Harris' position, they need not violate *Payton* in order to interrogate the suspect. It is doubtful therefore that the desire to secure a statement from a criminal suspect would motivate the police to violate *Payton.* As a result, suppressing a station house statement obtained after a *Payton* violation will have little effect on the officers' actions, one way or another.

We hold that, where the police have probable cause to arrest a suspect, the exclusionary rule does not bar the State's use of a statement made by the defendant outside of his home, even though the statement is taken after an arrest made in the home in violation of *Payton.* The judgment of the court below is accordingly

Reversed. [*]

[*] Justice Marshall wrote a dissenting opinion, which Justice Brennan, Justice Blackmun, and Justice Stevens joined.

UNITED STATES v. DIONISIO

410 U.S. 1, 93 S.Ct. 764, 35 L.Ed.2d 67 (1973).

MR. JUSTICE STEWART delivered the opinion of the Court.

A special grand jury was convened in the Northern District of Illinois in February 1971, to investigate possible violations of federal criminal statutes relating to gambling. In the course of its investigation the grand jury received in evidence certain voice recordings that had been obtained pursuant to court orders.

The grand jury subpoenaed approximately 20 persons, including the respondent Dionisio, seeking to obtain from them voice exemplars for comparison with the recorded conversations that had been received in evidence. Each witness was advised that he was a potential defendant in a criminal prosecution. Each was asked to examine a transcript of an intercepted conversation, and to go to a nearby office of the United States Attorney to read the transcript into a recording device. The witnesses were advised that they would be allowed to have their attorneys present when they read the transcripts. Dionisio and other witnesses refused to furnish the voice exemplars, asserting that these disclosures would violate their rights under the Fourth and Fifth Amendments.

The Government then filed separate petitions in the United States District Court to compel Dionisio and the other witnesses to furnish the voice exemplars to the grand jury. The petitions stated that the exemplars were "essential and necessary" to the grand jury investigation, and that they would "be used solely as a standard of comparison in order to determine whether or not the witness is the person whose voice was intercepted . . . ."

Following a hearing, the district judge rejected the witnesses' constitutional arguments and ordered them to comply with the grand jury's request. He reasoned that voice exemplars, like handwriting exemplars or fingerprints, were not testimonial or communicative evidence, and that consequently the order to produce them would not compel any witness to testify against himself. The district judge also found that there would be no Fourth Amendment violation, because the grand jury subpoena did not itself violate the Fourth Amendment, and the order to produce the voice exemplars would involve no unreasonable search and seizure within the proscription of that Amendment . . . . When Dionisio persisted in his refusal to respond to the grand jury's directive, the District Court adjudged him in civil contempt and ordered him committed to custody until he obeyed the court order, or until the expiration of 18 months.

484

The Court of Appeals for the Seventh Circuit reversed. 442 F.2d 276. It agreed with the District Court in rejecting the Fifth Amendment claims, but concluded that to compel the voice recordings would violate the Fourth Amendment. In the Court's view, the grand jury was "seeking to obtain the voice exemplars of the witnesses by the use of its subpoena powers because probable cause did not exist for their arrest or for some other, less unusual, method of compelling the production of the exemplars." Id., at 280. The Court found that the Fourth Amendment applied to grand jury process, and that "under the fourth amendment law enforcement officials may not compel the production of physical evidence absent a showing of the reasonableness of the seizure. Davis v. Mississippi, 394 U.S. 721 ...." Id.

In *Davis* this Court held that it was error to admit the petitioner's fingerprints into evidence at his trial for rape, because they had been obtained during a police detention following a lawless wholesale roundup of the petitioner and more than 20 other youths. Equating the procedures followed by the grand jury in the present case to the fingerprint detentions in *Davis*, the Court of Appeals reasoned that "[t]he dragnet effect here, where approximately 20 persons were subpoenaed for purposes of identification, has the same invidious effect on fourth amendment rights as the practice condemned in *Davis*." Id., at 281.

In view of a clear conflict between this decision and one in the Court of Appeals for the Second Circuit,[5] we granted the Government's petition for certiorari. 406 U.S. 956.

I

The Court of Appeals correctly rejected the contention that the compelled production of the voice exemplars would violate the Fifth Amendment. It has long been held that the compelled display of identifiable physical characteristics infringes no interest protected by the privilege against compulsory self-incrimination.

. . .

... The voice recordings were to be used solely to measure the physical properties of the witnesses' voices, not for the testimonial or communicative content of what was to be said.

II

The Court of Appeals held that the Fourth Amendment required a preliminary showing of reasonableness before a grand jury witness could be compelled to furnish a voice exemplar, and that in this case the proposed "seizures" of the voice exemplars would be unreasonable because of the large number of witnesses summoned

---

5. United States v. Doe (Schwartz), 457 F.2d 895 (affirming civil contempt judgment against grand jury witness for refusal to furnish handwriting exemplars).

by the grand jury and directed to produce such exemplars. We disagree.

The Fourth Amendment guarantees that all people shall be "secure in their persons, houses, papers, and effects, against unreasonable searches and seizures ...." Any Fourth Amendment violation in the present setting must rest on a lawless governmental intrusion upon the privacy of "persons" rather than on interference with "property relationships or private papers." Schmerber v. California, 384 U.S. 757, 767 .... In Terry v. Ohio, 392 U.S. 1, the Court explained the protection afforded to "persons" in terms of the statement in Katz v. United States, 389 U.S. 347, that "the Fourth Amendment protects people, not places," id., at 351, and concluded that "wherever an individual may harbor a reasonable 'expectation of privacy,' ... he is entitled to be free from unreasonable governmental intrusion." Terry v. Ohio, supra, at 9.

As the Court made clear in *Schmerber,* supra, the obtaining of physical evidence from a person involves a potential Fourth Amendment violation at two different levels—the "seizure" of the "person" necessary to bring him into contact with government agents, see, Davis v. Mississippi, 394 U.S. 721, and the subsequent search for and seizure of the evidence. In *Schmerber* we found the initial seizure of the accused justified as a lawful arrest, and the subsequent seizure of the blood sample from his body reasonable in light of the exigent circumstances. And in *Terry,* we concluded that neither the initial seizure of the person, an investigatory "stop" by a policeman, nor the subsequent search, a pat down of his outer clothing for weapons, constituted a violation of the Fourth and Fourteenth Amendments. The constitutionality of the compulsory production of exemplars from a grand jury witness necessarily turns on the same dual inquiry—whether either the initial compulsion of the person to appear before the grand jury, or the subsequent directive to make a voice recording is an unreasonable "seizure" within the meaning of the Fourth Amendment.

It is clear that a subpoena to appear before a grand jury is not a "seizure" in the Fourth Amendment sense, even though that summons may be inconvenient or burdensome. Last Term we again acknowledged what has long been recognized, that "[c]itizens generally are not constitutionally immune from grand jury subpoenas ...." Branzburg v. Hayes, 408 U.S. 665, 682. We concluded that:

> "Although the powers of the grand jury are not unlimited and are subject to the supervision of a judge, the longstanding principle that 'the public ... has a right to every man's evidence,' except for those persons protected by a constitutional common-law, or statutory privilege, United States v. Bryan, 339 U.S., at 331; Blackmer v. United States, 284 U.S. 421, 438 (1932); 8 J. Wigmore, Evidence § 2192 (McNaughton rev.

1961), is particularly applicable to grand jury proceedings." Id., at 688.

These are recent reaffirmations of the historically grounded obligation of every person to appear and give his evidence before the grand jury. ... And while the duty may be "onerous" at times, it is "necessary to the administration of justice." Blair v. United States, supra, at 281.[8]

The compulsion exerted by a grand jury subpoena differs from the seizure effected by an arrest or even an investigative "stop" in more than civic obligation. For, as Judge Friendly wrote for the Court of Appeals for the Second Circuit:

> "The latter is abrupt, is effected with force or the threat of it and often in demeaning circumstances, and, in the case of arrest, results in a record involving social stigma. A subpoena is served in the same manner as other legal process; it involves no stigma whatever; if the time for appearance is inconvenient, this can generally be altered; and it remains at all times under the control and supervision of a court." United States v. Doe (Schwartz) 457 F.2d 895, 898.

Thus the Court of Appeals for the Seventh Circuit correctly recognized in a case subsequent to the one now before us, that a "grand jury subpoena to testify is not that kind of governmental intrusion on privacy against which the Fourth Amendment affords protection, once the Fifth Amendment is satisfied." Fraser v. United States, 452 F.2d 616, 620 ....

This case is thus quite different from Davis v. Mississippi, supra, on which the Court of Appeals primarily relied. For in *Davis* it was the initial seizure—the lawless dragnet detention—that violated the Fourth and Fourteenth Amendments—not the taking of the fingerprints. We noted that "[i]nvestigatory seizures would subject unlimited numbers of innocent persons to the harassment and ignominy incident to involuntary detention," 394 U.S., at 726, and we left open the question whether, consistently with the Fourth and Fourteenth Amendments, narrowly circumscribed procedures might be developed for obtaining fingerprints from people when there was no probable cause to arrest them. Id., at 728. *Davis* is plainly inapposite to a case where the initial restraint does not itself infringe the Fourth Amendment.

This is not to say that a grand jury subpoena is some talisman that dissolves all constitutional protections. The grand jury cannot require a witness to testify against himself. It cannot require the production by a person of private books and records that would incriminate him. ... The Fourth Amendment provides protection against a grand jury subpoena *duces tecum* too sweeping in its

---

8. The obligation to appear is no different for a person who may himself be the subject of the grand jury inquiry. See United States v. Doe (Schwartz), 457 F.2d 895, 898; United States v. Winter, 348 F.2d 204, 207–208.

terms "to be regarded as reasonable." Hale v. Henkel, 201 U.S. 43, 76 .... And last Term, in the context of a First Amendment claim, we indicated that the Constitution could not tolerate the transformation of the grand jury into an instrument of oppression: "Official harassment of the press undertaken not for purposes of law enforcement but to disrupt a reporter's relationship with his news sources would have no justification. Grand juries are subject to judicial control and subpoenas to motions to quash. We do not expect courts will forget that grand juries must operate within the limits of the First Amendment as well as the Fifth." Branzburg v. Hayes, 408 U.S. 665, 707–708. See also, id., at 710 (Powell, J., concurring).

But we are here faced with no such constitutional infirmities in the subpoena to appear before the grand jury or in the order to make the voice recordings. There is, as we have said, no valid Fifth Amendment claim. There was no order to produce private books and papers, and no sweeping subpoena *duces tecum.* And even if *Branzburg* be extended beyond its First Amendment moorings and tied to a more generalized due process concept, there is still no indication in this case of the kind of harassment that was of concern there.

The Court of Appeals found critical significance in the fact that the grand jury had summoned approximately 20 witnesses to furnish voice exemplars. We think that fact is basically irrelevant to the constitutional issues here. The grand jury may have been attempting to identify a number of voices on the tapes in evidence, or it might have summoned the 20 witnesses in an effort to identify one voice. But whatever the case, "[a] grand jury's investigation is not fully carried out until every available clue has been run down and all witnesses examined in every proper way to find if a crime has been committed ...." United States v. Stone, 429 F.2d 138, 140. ... As the Court recalled last Term, "Because its task is to inquire into the existence of possible criminal conduct and to return only well-founded indictments, its investigative powers are necessarily broad." Branzburg v. Hayes, 408 U.S. at 688. The grand jury may well find it desirable to call numerous witnesses in the course of an investigation. It does not follow that each witness may resist a subpoena on the ground that too many witnesses have been called. Neither the order to Dionisio to appear, nor the order to make a voice recording was rendered unreasonable by the fact that many others were subjected to the same compulsion.

But the conclusion that Dionisio's compulsory appearance before the grand jury was not an unreasonable "seizure" is the answer to only the first part of the Fourth Amendment inquiry here. Dionisio argues that the grand jury's subsequent directive to make the voice recording was itself an infringement of his rights under the Fourth Amendment. We cannot accept that argument.

In Katz v. United States, supra, we said that the Fourth Amendment provides no protection for what "a person knowingly exposes to the public, even in his home or office . . . ." 389 U.S. 347, 351. The physical characteristics of a person's voice, its tone and manner, as opposed to the content of a specific conversation, are constantly exposed to the public. Like a man's facial characteristics, or handwriting, his voice is repeatedly produced for others to hear. No person can have a reasonable expectation that others will not know the sound of his voice, any more than he can reasonably expect that his face will be a mystery to the world. . . .

The required disclosure of a person's voice is thus immeasurably further removed from the Fourth Amendment protection than was the intrusion into the body effected by the blood extraction in *Schmerber*. "The interests in human dignity and privacy which the Fourth Amendment protects forbid any such intrusions on the mere chance that desired evidence might be obtained." Schmerber v. California, 384 U.S. 757, 769–770. Similarly, a seizure of voice exemplars does not involve the "severe, though brief, intrusion upon cherished personal security," effected by the "patdown" in *Terry*—"surely . . . an annoying, frightening, and perhaps humiliating experience." Terry v. Ohio, 392 U.S. 1, 24–25. Rather, this is like the fingerprinting in *Davis*, where, though the initial dragnet detentions were constitutionally impermissible, we noted that the fingerprinting itself, "involves none of the probing into an individual's private life and thoughts that marks an interrogation or search." Davis v. Mississippi, 394 U.S. 721, 727 . . . .

Since neither the summons to appear before the grand jury, nor its directive to make a voice recording infringed upon any interest protected by the Fourth Amendment, there was no justification for requiring the grand jury to satisfy even the minimal requirement of "reasonableness" imposed by the Court of Appeals. . . . A grand jury has broad investigative powers to determine whether a crime has been committed and who has committed it. The jurors may act on tips, rumors, evidence offered by the prosecutor, or their own personal knowledge. Branzburg v. Hayes, 408 U.S. 665, 701. No grand jury witness is "entitled to set limits to the investigation that the grand jury may conduct." Blair v. United States, 250 U.S. 273, 282. And a sufficient basis for an indictment may only emerge at the end of the investigation when all the evidence has been received. . . .

Since Dionisio raised no valid Fourth Amendment claim, there is no more reason to require a preliminary showing of reasonableness here than there would be in the case of any witness who, despite the lack of any constitutional or statutory privilege, declined to answer a question or comply with a grand jury request. Neither the Constitution nor our prior cases justify any such interference with grand jury proceedings.

The Fifth Amendment guarantees that no civilian may be brought to trial for an infamous crime "unless on a presentment or indictment of a Grand Jury." This constitutional guarantee presupposes an investigative body "acting independently of either prosecuting attorney or judge," Stirone v. United States, 361 U.S. 212, 218, whose mission is to clear the innocent, no less than to bring to trial those who may be guilty. Any holding that would saddle a grand jury with mini-trials and preliminary showings would assuredly impede its investigation and frustrate the public's interest in the fair and expeditious administration of the criminal laws. ... The grand jury may not always serve its historic role as a protective bulwark standing solidly between the ordinary citizen and an overzealous prosecutor, but if it is even to approach the proper performance of its constitutional mission, it must be free to pursue its investigations unhindered by external influence or supervision so long as it does not trench upon the legitimate rights of any witness called before it.

Since the Court of Appeals found an unreasonable search and seizure where none existed, and imposed a preliminary showing of reasonableness where none was required, its judgment is reversed and this case is remanded to that Court for further proceedings consistent with this opinion.

It is so ordered.[*]

[*] Justice Douglas and Justice Marshall wrote dissenting opinions. Justice Brennan wrote a brief opinion concurring in part and dissenting in part.

4. ELECTRONIC SURVEILLANCE, AGENTS AND INFORMERS, AND ENTRAPMENT

OLMSTEAD v. UNITED STATES

277 U.S. 438, 48 S.Ct. 564, 72 L.Ed. 944 (1928).

MR. CHIEF JUSTICE TAFT delivered the opinion of the Court.

These cases are here by certiorari from the Circuit Court of Appeals for the Ninth Circuit. 19 F.(2d) 842 and 850. The petition in No. 493 was filed August 30, 1927; in Nos. 532 and 533, September 9, 1927. They were granted with the distinct limitation that the hearing should be confined to the single question whether the use of evidence of private telephone conversations between the defendants and others, intercepted by means of wire tapping, amounted to a violation of the Fourth and Fifth Amendments.

The petitioners were convicted in the District Court for the Western District of Washington of a conspiracy to violate the National Prohibition Act by unlawfully possessing, transporting and importing intoxicating liquors and maintaining nuisances, and by selling intoxicating liquors. Seventy-two others in addition to the petitioners were indicted. Some were not apprehended, some were acquitted and others pleaded guilty.

The evidence in the records discloses a conspiracy of amazing magnitude to import, possess and sell liquor unlawfully. It involved the employment of not less than fifty persons, of two seagoing vessels for the transportation of liquor to British Columbia, of smaller vessels for coastwise transportation to the State of Washington, the purchase and use of a ranch beyond the suburban limits of Seattle, with a large underground cache for storage and a number of smaller caches in that city, the maintenance of a central office manned with operators, the employment of executives, salesmen, deliverymen, dispatchers, scouts, bookkeepers, collectors and an attorney. In a bad month sales amounted to $176,000; the aggregate for a year must have exceeded two millions of dollars.

Olmstead was the leading conspirator and the general manager of the business. He made a contribution of $10,000 to the capital; eleven others contributed $1,000 each. The profits were divided one-half to Olmstead and the remainder to the other eleven. Of the several offices in Seattle the chief one was in a large office building. In this there were three telephones on three different lines. There were telephones in an office of the manager in his own home, at the homes of his associates, and at other places in the city. Communication was had frequently with Vancouver, British Columbia. Times

491

were fixed for the deliveries of the "stuff," to places along Puget Sound near Seattle and from there the liquor was removed and deposited in the caches already referred to. One of the chief men was always on duty at the main office to receive orders by telephones and to direct their filling by a corps of men stationed in another room—the "bull pen." The call numbers of the telephones were given to those known to be likely customers. At times the sales amounted to 200 cases of liquor per day.

The information which led to the discovery of the conspiracy and its nature and extent was largely obtained by intercepting messages on the telephones of the conspirators by four federal prohibition officers. Small wires were inserted along the ordinary telephone wires from the residences of four of the petitioners and those leading from the chief office. The insertions were made without trespass upon any property of the defendants. They were made in the basement of the large office building. The taps from house lines were made in the streets near the houses.

The gathering of evidence continued for many months. Conversations of the conspirators of which refreshing stenographic notes were currently made, were testified to by the government witnesses. They revealed the large business transactions of the partners and their subordinates. Men at the wires heard the orders given for liquor by customers and the acceptances; they became auditors of the conversations between the partners. All this disclosed the conspiracy charged in the indictment. Many of the intercepted conversations were not merely reports but parts of the criminal acts. The evidence also disclosed the difficulties to which the conspirators were subjected, the reported news of the capture of vessels, the arrest of their men and the seizure of cases of liquor in garages and other places. It showed the dealing by Olmstead, the chief conspirator, with members of the Seattle police, the messages to them which secured the release of arrested members of the conspiracy, and also direct promises to officers of payments as soon as opportunity offered.

The Fourth Amendment provides—"The right of the people to be secure in their persons, houses, papers, and effects against unreasonable searches and seizures shall not be violated; and no warrants shall issue but upon probable cause, supported by oath or affirmation and particularly describing the place to be searched and the persons or things to be seized." And the Fifth: "No person . . . shall be compelled, in any criminal case, to be a witness against himself."

. . .

There is no room in the present case for applying the Fifth Amendment unless the Fourth Amendment was first violated. There was no evidence of compulsion to induce the defendants to talk over their many telephones. They were continually and voluntarily transacting business without knowledge of the interception. Our consideration must be confined to the Fourth Amendment.

. . .

The well known historical purpose of the Fourth Amendment, directed against general warrants and writs of assistance, was to prevent the use of governmental force to search a man's house, his person, his papers and his effects; and to prevent their seizure against his will. . . .

. . .

The Amendment itself shows that the search is to be of material things—the person, the house, his papers or his effects. The description of the warrant necessary to make the proceeding lawful, is that it must specify the place to be searched and the person or *things* to be seized.

. . .

. . . The Amendment does not forbid what was done here. There was no searching. There was no seizure. The evidence was secured by the use of the sense of hearing and that only. There was no entry of the houses or offices of the defendants.

By the invention of the telephone, fifty years ago, and its application for the purpose of extending communications, one can talk with another at a far distant place. The language of the Amendment can not be extended and expanded to include telephone wires reaching to the whole world from the defendant's house or office. The intervening wires are not part of his house or office any more than are the highways along which they are stretched.

. . .

Congress may of course protect the secrecy of telephone messages by making them, when intercepted, inadmissible in evidence in federal criminal trials, by direct legislation, and thus depart from the common law of evidence. But the courts may not adopt such a policy by attributing an enlarged and unusual meaning to the Fourth Amendment. The reasonable view is that one who installs in his house a telephone instrument with connecting wires intends to project his voice to those quite outside, and that the wires beyond his house and messages while passing over them are not within the protection of the Fourth Amendment. Here those who intercepted the projected voices were not in the house of either party to the conversation.

Neither the cases we have cited nor any of the many federal decisions brought to our attention hold the Fourth Amendment to have been violated as against a defendant unless there has been an official search and seizure of his person, or such a seizure of his papers or his tangible material effects, or an actual physical invasion of his house "or curtilage" for the purpose of making a seizure.

We think, therefore, that the wire tapping here disclosed did not amount to a search or seizure within the meaning of the Fourth Amendment.

What has been said disposes of the only question that comes within the terms of our order granting certiorari in these cases. But some of our number, departing from that order, have concluded that there is merit in the two-fold objection overruled in both courts below that evidence obtained through intercepting of telephone messages by government agents was inadmissible because the mode of obtaining it was unethical and a misdemeanor under the law of Washington. To avoid any misapprehension of our views of that objection we shall deal with it in both of its phases.

While a Territory, the English common law prevailed in Washington and thus continued after her admission in 1889. The rules of evidence in criminal cases in courts of the United States sitting there, consequently are those of the common law. ...

The common law rule is that the admissibility of evidence is not affected by the illegality of the means by which it was obtained. ...

. . .

Nor can we, without the sanction of congressional enactment, subscribe to the suggestion that the courts have a discretion to exclude evidence, the admission of which is not unconstitutional, because unethically secured. This would be at variance with the common law doctrine generally supported by authority. There is no case that sustains, nor any recognized text book that gives color to such a view. Our general experience shows that much evidence has always been receivable although not obtained by conformity to the highest ethics. The history of criminal trials shows numerous cases of prosecutions of oath-bound conspiracies for murder, robbery, and other crimes, where officers of the law have disguised themselves and joined the organizations, taken the oaths and given themselves every appearance of active members engaged in the promotion of crime, for the purpose of securing evidence. Evidence secured by such means has always been received.

A standard which would forbid the reception of evidence if obtained by other than nice ethical conduct by government officials would make society suffer and give criminals greater immunity than has been known heretofore. In the absence of controlling legislation by Congress, those who realize the difficulties in bringing offenders to justice may well deem it wise that the exclusion of evidence should be confined to cases where rights under the Constitution would be violated by admitting it.

. . .

Affirmed.

MR. JUSTICE HOLMES:

My brother Brandeis has given this case so exhaustive an examination that I desire to add but a few words. While I do not deny it, I am not prepared to say that the penumbra of the Fourth and Fifth Amendments covers the defendant, although I fully agree that Courts are apt to err by sticking too closely to the words of a law where those words import a policy that goes beyond them. Gooch v. Oregon Short Line R.R. Co., 258 U.S. 22, 24. But I think, as Mr. Justice Brandeis says, that apart from the Constitution the Government ought not to use evidence obtained and only obtainable by a criminal act. There is no body of precedents by which we are bound, and which confines us to logical deduction from established rules. Therefore we must consider the two objects of desire, both of which we cannot have, and make up our minds which to choose. It is desirable that criminals should be detected, and to that end that all available evidence should be used. It also is desirable that the Government should not itself foster and pay for other crimes, when they are the means by which the evidence is to be obtained. If it pays its officers for having got evidence by crime I do not see why it may not as well pay them for getting it in the same way, and I can attach no importance to protestations of disapproval if it knowingly accepts and pays and announces that in future it will pay for the fruits. We have to choose, and for my part I think it a less evil that some criminals should escape than that the Government should play an ignoble part.

For those who agree with me, no distinction can be taken between the Government as prosecutor and the Government as judge. If the existing code does not permit district attorneys to have a hand in such dirty business it does not permit the judge to allow such iniquities to succeed. See Silverthorne Lumber Co. v. United States, 251 U.S. 385. And if all that I have said so far be accepted it makes no difference that in this case wire tapping is made a crime by the law of the State, not by the law of the United States. It is true that a State cannot make rules of evidence for Courts of the United States, but the State has authority over the conduct in question, and I hardly think that the United States would appear to greater advantage when paying for an odious crime against State law than when inciting to the disregard of its own. I am aware of the often repeated statement that in a criminal proceeding the Court will not take notice of the manner in which papers offered in evidence have been obtained. But that somewhat rudimentary mode of disposing of the question has been overthrown by Weeks v. United States, 232 U.S. 383 and the cases that have followed it. I have said that we are free to choose between two principles of policy. But if we are to confine ourselves to precedent and logic the reason for excluding evidence obtained by violating the Constitution seems to me logically to lead to excluding evidence obtained by a crime of the officers of the law.

MR. JUSTICE BRANDEIS, dissenting.

The defendants were convicted of conspiring to violate the National Prohibition Act. Before any of the persons now charged had been arrested or indicted, the telephones by means of which they habitually communicated with one another and with others had been tapped by federal officers. To this end, a lineman of long experience in wire-tapping was employed, on behalf of the Government and at its expense. He tapped eight telephones, some in the homes of the persons charged, some in their offices. Acting on behalf of the Government and in their official capacity, at least six other prohibition agents listened over the tapped wires and reported the messages taken. Their operations extended over a period of nearly five months. The type-written record of the notes of conversations overheard occupies 775 typewritten pages. By objections seasonably made and persistently renewed, the defendants objected to the admission of the evidence obtained by wire-tapping, on the ground that the Government's wire-tapping constituted an unreasonable search and seizure, in violation of the Fourth Amendment; and that the use as evidence of the conversations overheard compelled the defendants to be witnesses against themselves, in violation of the Fifth Amendment.

The Government makes no attempt to defend the methods employed by its officers. Indeed, it concedes that if wire-tapping can be deemed a search and seizure within the Fourth Amendment, such wire-tapping as was practiced in the case at bar was an unreasonable search and seizure, and that the evidence thus obtained was inadmissible. But it relies on the language of the Amendment; and it claims that the protection given thereby cannot properly be held to include a telephone conversation.

"We must never forget," said Mr. Chief Justice Marshall in McCulloch v. Maryland, 4 Wheat. 316, 407, "that it is a constitution we are expounding." Since then, this Court has repeatedly sustained the exercise of power by Congress, under various clauses of that instrument, over objects of which the Fathers could not have dreamed. ... We have likewise held that general limitations on the powers of Government, like those embodied in the due process clauses of the Fifth and Fourteenth Amendments, do not forbid the United States or the States from meeting modern conditions by regulations which "a century ago, or even half a century ago, probably would have been rejected as arbitrary and oppressive." Village of Euclid v. Ambler Realty Co., 272 U.S. 365, 387; Buck v. Bell, 274 U.S. 200. Clauses guaranteeing to the individual protection against specific abuses of power, must have a similar capacity of adaptation to a changing world. It was with reference to such a clause that this Court said in Weems v. United States, 217 U.S. 349, 373: "Legislation, both statutory and constitutional, is enacted, it is true, from an experience of evils, but its general language should not, therefore, be necessarily confined to the form that evil had theretofore taken. Time works changes, brings into existence new conditions and purposes. Therefore a principle to be vital must be capable of wider application than the mischief which gave it birth. This is peculiarly true of constitutions. They are not ephemeral enactments, designed to meet passing occasions. They are, to use the words of Chief Justice Marshall 'designed to approach immortality as nearly as human institutions can approach it.' The future is their care and provision for events of good and bad tendencies of which no prophecy can be made. In the application of a constitution, therefore, our contemplation cannot be only of what has been but of what may be. Under any other rule a constitution would indeed be as easy of application as it would be deficient in efficacy and power. Its general principles would have little value and be converted by precedent into impotent and lifeless formulas. Rights declared in words might be lost in reality.''

When the Fourth and Fifth Amendments were adopted, "the form that evil had theretofore taken," had been necessarily simple. Force and violence were then the only means known to man by which a Government could directly effect self-incrimination. It could compel the individual to testify—a compulsion effected, if need be, by torture. It could secure possession of his papers and other articles incident to his private life—a seizure effected, if need be, by breaking and entry. Protection against such invasion of "the sanctities of a man's home and the privacies of life" was provided in the Fourth and Fifth Amendments by specific language. Boyd v. United States, 116 U.S. 616, 630. But "time works changes, brings into existence new conditions and purposes." Subtler and more far-reaching means of invading privacy have become available to the Government. Discovery and invention have made it possible for the Government, by means far more effective than stretching upon the rack, to obtain disclosure in court of what is whispered in the closet.

Moreover, "in the application of a constitution, our contemplation cannot be only of what has been but of what may be." The progress of science in furnishing the Government with means of espionage is not likely to stop with wire-tapping. Ways may some day be developed by which the Government, without removing papers from secret drawers, can reproduce them in court, and by which it will be enabled to expose to a jury the most intimate occurrences of the home. Advances in the psychic and related sciences may bring means of exploring unexpressed beliefs, thoughts and emotions. "That places the liberty of every man in the hands of every petty officer" was said by James Otis of much lesser intrusions than these.[1] To Lord Camden, a far slighter intrusion seemed "subversive of all the comforts of society."[2] Can

---

1. Otis' Argument against Writs of Assistance. . . .   **2.** Entick v. Carrington, 19 Howell's State Trials, 1030, 1066.

it be that the Constitution affords no protection against such invasions of individual security?

A sufficient answer is found in Boyd v. United States, 116 U.S. 616, 627–630, a case that will be remembered as long as civil liberty lives in the United States. This Court there reviewed the history that lay behind the Fourth and Fifth Amendments. We said with reference to Lord Camden's judgment in Entick v. Carrington, 19 Howell's State Trials, 1030: "The principles laid down in this opinion affect the very essence of constitutional liberty and security. They reach farther than the concrete form of the case there before the court, with its adventitious circumstances; they apply to all invasions on the part of the Government and its employés of the sanctities of a man's home and the privacies of life. It is not the breaking of his doors, and the rummaging of his drawers, that constitutes the essence of the offence; but it is the invasion of his indefeasible right of personal security, personal liberty and private property, where that right has never been forfeited by his conviction of some public offence,—it is the invasion of this sacred right which underlies and constitutes the essence of Lord Camden's judgment. Breaking into a house and opening boxes and drawers are circum-stances of aggravation; but any forcible and compulsory extortion of a man's own testimony or of his private papers to be used as evidence of a crime or to forfeit his goods, is within the condemna-tion of that judgment. In this regard the Fourth and Fifth Amend-ments run almost into each other."

. . .

Time and again, this Court in giving effect to the principle underlying the Fourth Amendment, has refused to place an unduly literal construction upon it. . . . The provision against self-incrimi-nation in the Fifth Amendment has been given an equally broad construction. . . .

. . . The makers of our Constitution undertook to secure condi-tions favorable to the pursuit of happiness. They recognized the significance of man's spiritual nature, of his feelings and of his intellect. They knew that only a part of the pain, pleasure and satisfactions of life are to be found in material things. They sought to protect Americans in their beliefs, their thoughts, their emotions and their sensations. They conferred, as against the Government, the right to be let alone—the most comprehensive of rights and the right most valued by civilized men. To protect that right, every unjustifiable intrusion by the Government upon the privacy of the individual, whatever the means employed, must be deemed a viola-tion of the Fourth Amendment. And the use, as evidence in a criminal proceeding, of facts ascertained by such intrusion must be deemed a violation of the Fifth.

Applying to the Fourth and Fifth Amendments the established rule of construction, the defendants' objections to the evidence obtained by wire-tapping must, in my opinion, be sustained.   It is, of course, immaterial where the physical connection with the tele- phone wires leading into the defendants' premises was made.   And it is also immaterial that the intrusion was in aid of law enforce- ment.   Experience should teach us to be most on our guard to protect liberty when the Government's purposes are beneficent. Men born to freedom are naturally alert to repel invasion of their liberty by evil-minded rulers.   The greatest dangers to liberty lurk in insidious encroachment by men of zeal, well-meaning but without understanding.

Independently of the constitutional question, I am of opinion that the judgment should be reversed.   By the laws of Washington, wire-tapping is a crime.   Pierce's Code, 1921, § 8976(18).   To prove its case, the Government was obliged to lay bare the crimes committed by its officers on its behalf.   A federal court should not permit such a prosecution to continue.   Compare Harkin v. Brund- age, 276 U.S. 36, id. 604.

The situation in the case at bar differs widely from that present- ed in Burdeau v. McDowell, 256 U.S. 465.   There, only a single lot of papers was involved.   They had been obtained by a private detective while acting on behalf of a private party; without the knowledge of any federal official; long before anyone had thought of instituting a federal prosecution.   Here, the evidence obtained by crime was obtained at the Government's expense, by its officers, while acting on its behalf; the officers who committed these crimes are the same officers who were charged with the enforcement of the Prohibition Act; the crimes of these officers were committed for the purpose of securing evidence with which to obtain an indictment and to secure a conviction.   The evidence so obtained constitutes the warp and woof of the Government's case.   The aggregate of the Government evidence occupies 306 pages of the printed record. More than 210 of them are filled by recitals of the details of the wire-tapping and of facts ascertained thereby.   There is literally no other evidence of guilt on the part of some of the defendants except that illegally obtained by these officers.   As to nearly all the defen- dants (except those who admitted guilt), the evidence relied upon to secure a conviction consisted mainly of that which these officers had so obtained by violating the state law.

. . .

When these unlawful acts were committed, they were crimes only of the officers individually.   The Government was innocent, in legal contemplation; for no federal official is authorized to commit a crime on its behalf.   When the Government, having full knowl- edge, sought, through the Department of Justice, to avail itself of the fruits of these acts in order to accomplish its own ends, it assumed moral responsibility for the officers' crimes.   ... And if this Court should permit the Government, by means of its officers' crimes, to effect its purpose of punishing the defendants, there would seem to be present all the elements of a ratification. If so, the Government itself would become a lawbreaker.

. . .

Decency, security and liberty alike demand that government officials shall be subjected to the same rules of conduct that are commands to the citizen. In a government of laws, existence of the government will be imperilled if it fails to observe the law scrupulously. Our Government is the potent, the omnipresent teacher. For good or for ill, it teaches the whole people by its example. Crime is contagious. If the Government becomes a lawbreaker, it breeds contempt for law; it invites every man to become a law unto himself; it invites anarchy. To declare that in the administration of the criminal law the end justifies the means—to declare that the Government may commit crimes in order to secure the conviction of a private criminal—would bring terrible retribution. Against that pernicious doctrine this Court should resolutely set its face.[*]

[*] Justice Butler and Justice Stone wrote dissenting opinions.

LEWIS v. UNITED STATES

385 U.S. 206, 87 S.Ct. 424, 17 L.Ed.2d 312 (1966).

MR. CHIEF JUSTICE WARREN delivered the opinion of the Court.

The question for resolution here is whether the Fourth Amendment was violated when a federal narcotics agent, by misrepresenting his identity and stating his willingness to purchase narcotics, was invited into petitioner's home where an unlawful narcotics transaction was consummated and the narcotics were thereafter introduced at petitioner's criminal trial over his objection. We hold that under the facts of this case it was not. Those facts are not disputed and may be briefly stated as follows:

On December 3, 1964, Edward Cass, an undercover federal narcotics agent, telephoned petitioner's home to inquire about the possibility of purchasing marihuana. Cass, who previously had not met or dealt with petitioner, falsely identified himself as one "Jimmy the Pollack [sic]" and stated that a mutual friend had told him petitioner might be able to supply marihuana. In response, petitioner said, "Yes. I believe, Jimmy, I can take care of you," and then directed Cass to his home where, it was indicated, a sale of marihuana would occur. Cass drove to petitioner's home, knocked on the door, identified himself as "Jim," and was admitted. After discussing the possibility of regular future dealings at a discounted price, petitioner led Cass to a package located on the front porch of his home. Cass gave petitioner $50, took the package, and left the premises. The package contained five bags of marihuana. On December 17, 1964, a similar transaction took place, beginning with a phone conversation in which Cass identified himself as "Jimmy the Pollack" and ending with an invited visit by Cass to petitioner's home where a second sale of marihuana occurred. Once again, Cass paid petitioner $50, but this time he received in return a package containing six bags of marihuana.

Petitioner was arrested on April 27, 1965, and charged by a two-count indictment with violations of the narcotics laws relating to transfers of marihuana. 26 U.S.C. § 4742(a). A pretrial motion to suppress as evidence the marihuana and the conversations between petitioner and the agent was denied, and they were introduced at the trial. The District Court, sitting without a jury, convicted petitioner on both counts and imposed concurrent five-year penitentiary sentences. The Court of Appeals for the First Circuit affirmed, 352 F.2d 799, and we granted certiorari, 382 U.S. 1024.

Petitioner does not argue that he was entrapped, as he could not on the facts of this case; nor does he contend that a search of his home was made or that anything other than the purchased narcotics was taken away. His only contentions are that, in the absence of a warrant, any official intrusion upon the privacy of a home constitutes a Fourth Amendment violation and that the fact the suspect invited the intrusion cannot be held a waiver when the invitation was induced by fraud and deception.

Both petitioner and the Government recognize the necessity for some undercover police activity and both concede that the particular circumstances of each case govern the admissibility of evidence obtained by stratagem or deception. Indeed, it has long been acknowledged by the decisions of this Court ... that, in the detection of many types of crime, the Government is entitled to use decoys and to conceal the identity of its agents. The various protections of the Bill of Rights, of course, provide checks upon such official deception for the protection of the individual. ...

Petitioner argues that the Government overstepped the constitutional bounds in this case and places principal reliance on Gouled v. United States, 255 U.S. 298 (1921). But a short statement of that case will demonstrate how misplaced his reliance is. There, a business acquaintance of the petitioner, acting under orders of federal officers, obtained entry into the petitioner's office by falsely representing that he intended only to pay a social visit. In the petitioner's absence, however, the intruder secretly ransacked the office and seized certain private papers of an incriminating nature. This Court had no difficulty concluding that the Fourth Amendment had been violated by the secret and general ransacking, notwithstanding that the initial intrusion was occasioned by a fraudulently obtained invitation rather than by force or stealth.

In the instant case, on the other hand, the petitioner invited the undercover agent to his home for the specific purpose of executing a felonious sale of narcotics. Petitioner's only concern was whether the agent was a willing purchaser who could pay the agreed price. Indeed, in order to convince the agent that his patronage at petitioner's home was desired, petitioner told him that, if he became a regular customer there, he would in the future receive an extra bag of marihuana at no additional cost; and in fact petitioner did hand over an extra bag at a second sale which was consummated at the same place and in precisely the same manner. During neither of his visits to petitioner's home did the agent, see, hear, or take anything that was not contemplated, and in fact intended, by petitioner as a necessary part of his illegal business. Were we to hold the deceptions of the agent in this case constitutionally prohibited, we would come near to a rule that the use of undercover agents in any manner is virtually unconstitutional *per se*. Such a rule would, for example, severely hamper the Government in ferreting out those organized criminal activities that are characterized by

covert dealings with victims who either cannot or do not protest.[6]
A prime example is provided by the narcotics traffic.

The fact that the undercover agent entered petitioner's home
does not compel a different conclusion. Without question, the
home is accorded the full range of Fourth Amendment protections.
. . . But when, as here, the home is converted into a commercial
center to which outsiders are invited for purposes of transacting
unlawful business, that business is entitled to no greater sanctity
than if it were carried on in a store, a garage, a car, or on the street.
A government agent, in the same manner as a private person, may
accept an invitation to do business and may enter upon the premises for the very purposes contemplated by the occupant. Of course,
this does not mean that, whenever entry is obtained by invitation
and the locus is characterized as a place of business, an agent is
authorized to conduct a general search for incriminating materials;
a citation to the *Gouled* case, supra, is sufficient to dispose of that
contention.

Finally, petitioner also relies on Rios v. United States, 364 U.S.
253 (1960); Jones v. United States, 362 U.S. 257 (1960); McDonald
v. United States, 335 U.S. 451 (1948); and Johnson v. United States,
332 U.S. 10 (1948). But those cases all dealt with the exclusion of
evidence that had been forcibly seized against the suspects' desires
and without the authorization conferred by search warrants. A
reading of them will readily demonstrate that they are inapposite to
the facts of this case; and, in this area, each case must be judged on
its own particular facts. Nor is Silverman v. United States, 365 U.S.
505 (1961), in point; for there, the conduct proscribed was that of
eavesdroppers, unknown and unwanted intruders who furtively
listened to conversations occurring in the privacy of a house. The
instant case involves no such problem; it has been well summarized
by the Government at the conclusion of its brief as follows:

> "In short, this case involves the exercise of no governmen-
> tal power to intrude upon protected premises; the visitor was
> invited and willingly admitted by the suspect. It concerns no
> design on the part of a government agent to observe or hear
> what was happening in the privacy of a home; the suspect
> chose the location where the transaction took place. It pres-
> ents no question of the invasion of the privacy of a dwelling;
> the only statements repeated were those that were willingly
> made to the agent and the only things taken were the packets
> of marihuana voluntarily transferred to him. The pretense
> resulted in no breach of privacy; it merely encouraged the

6. "Particularly, in the enforcement of
vice, liquor or narcotics laws, it is all but
impossible to obtain evidence for prosecution
save by the use of decoys. There are rarely
complaining witnesses. The participants in
the crime enjoy themselves. Misrepresentation by a police officer or agent concerning
the identity of the purchaser of illegal narcotics is a practical necessity. . . . Therefore,
the law must attempt to distinguish between
those deceits and persuasions which are permissible and those which are not." Model
Penal Code § 2.10, comment, p. 16 (Tent.
Draft No. 9, 1959). . . .

suspect to say things which he was willing and anxious to say to anyone who would be interested in purchasing marihuana.''

Further elaboration is not necessary. The judgment is

Affirmed.[*]

[*] Justice Brennan wrote a concurring opinion, which Justice Fortas joined. Justice Douglas wrote a dissenting opinion, applicable also to Hoffa v. United States, 385 U.S. 293 (1966), below.

HOFFA v. UNITED STATES

385 U.S. 293, 87 S.Ct. 408, 17 L.Ed.2d 374 (1966).

MR. JUSTICE STEWART delivered the opinion of the Court.

Over a period of several weeks in the late autumn of 1962 there took place in a federal court in Nashville, Tennessee, a trial by jury in which James Hoffa was charged with violating a provision of the Taft-Hartley Act. That trial, known in the present record as the Test Fleet trial, ended with a hung jury. The petitioners now before us—James Hoffa, Thomas Parks, Larry Campbell, and Ewing King— were tried and convicted in 1964 for endeavoring to bribe members of that jury. The convictions were affirmed by the Court of Appeals. A substantial element in the Government's proof that led to the convictions of these four petitioners was contributed by a witness named Edward Partin, who testified to several incriminating statements which he said petitioners Hoffa and King had made in his presence during the course of the Test Fleet trial. Our grant of certiorari was limited to the single issue of whether the Government's use in this case of evidence supplied by Partin operated to invalidate these convictions. 382 U.S. 1024.

The specific question before us, as framed by counsel for the petitioners, is this:

> "Whether evidence obtained by the Government by means of deceptively placing a secret informer in the quarters and councils of a defendant during one criminal trial so violates the defendant's Fourth, Fifth and Sixth Amendment rights that suppression of such evidence is required in a subsequent trial of the same defendant on a different charge."

At the threshold the Government takes issue with the way this question is worded, refusing to concede that it " 'placed' the informer anywhere, much less that it did so 'deceptively.' " In the view we take of the matter, however, a resolution of this verbal controversy is unnecessary to a decision of the constitutional issues before us. The basic facts are clear enough, and a lengthy discussion of the detailed minutiae to which a large portion of the briefs and oral arguments was addressed would serve only to divert attention from the real issues before us.

The controlling facts can be briefly stated. The Test Fleet trial, in which James Hoffa was the sole individual defendant, was in progress between October 22 and December 23, 1962, in Nashville, Tennessee. James Hoffa was president of the International Brotherhood of Teamsters. During the course of the trial he occupied a three-room suite in the Andrew Jackson Hotel in Nashville. One of

505

his constant companions throughout the trial was the petitioner King, president of the Nashville local of the Teamsters Union. Edward Partin, a resident of Baton Rouge, Louisiana, and a local Teamsters Union official there, made repeated visits to Nashville during the period of the trial. On these visits he frequented the Hoffa hotel suite, and was continually in the company of Hoffa and his associates, including King, in and around the hotel suite, the hotel lobby, the courthouse, and elsewhere in Nashville. During this period Partin made frequent reports to a federal agent named Sheridan concerning conversations he said Hoffa and King had had with him and with each other, disclosing endeavors to bribe members of the Test Fleet jury. Partin's reports and his subsequent testimony at the petitioners' trial unquestionably contributed, directly or indirectly, to the convictions of all four of the petitioners.

The chain of circumstances which led Partin to be in Nashville during the Test Fleet trial extended back at least to September of 1962. At that time Partin was in jail in Baton Rouge on a state criminal charge. He was also under a federal indictment for embezzling union funds, and other indictments for state offenses were pending against him. Between that time and Partin's initial visit to Nashville on October 22 he was released on bail on the state criminal charge, and proceedings under the federal indictment were postponed. On October 8, Partin telephoned Hoffa in Washington, D.C., to discuss local union matters and Partin's difficulties with the authorities. In the course of this conversation Partin asked if he could see Hoffa to confer about these problems, and Hoffa acquiesced. Partin again called Hoffa on October 18 and arranged to meet him in Nashville. During this period Partin also consulted on several occasions with federal law enforcement agents, who told him that Hoffa might attempt to tamper with the Test Fleet jury, and asked him to be on the lookout in Nashville for such attempts and to report to the federal authorities any evidence of wrongdoing that he discovered. Partin agreed to do so.

After the Test Fleet trial was completed, Partin's wife received four monthly installment payments of $300 from government funds, and the state and federal charges against Partin were either dropped or not actively pursued.

Reviewing these circumstances in detail, the Government insists the fair inference is that Partin went to Nashville on his own initiative to discuss union business and his own problems with Hoffa, that Partin ultimately cooperated closely with federal authorities only after he discovered evidence of jury tampering in the Test Fleet trial, that the payments to Partin's wife were simply in partial reimbursement of Partin's subsequent out-of-pocket expenses, and that the failure to prosecute Partin on the state and federal charges had no necessary connection with his services as an informer. The findings of the trial court support this version of the facts, and these findings were accepted by the Court of Appeals as "supported by substantial evidence." 349 F.2d, at 36. But whether or not the Government "placed" Partin with Hoffa in Nashville during the Test Fleet trial, we proceed upon the premise that Partin was a government informer from the time he first arrived in Nashville on October 22, and that the Government compensated him for his services as such. It is upon that premise that we consider the constitutional issues presented.

Before turning to those issues we mention an additional preliminary contention of the Government. The petitioner Hoffa was the only individual defendant in the Test Fleet case, and Partin had conversations during the Test Fleet trial only with him and with the petitioner King. So far as appears, Partin never saw either of the other two petitioners during that period. Consequently, the Government argues that, of the four petitioners, only Hoffa has standing to raise a claim that his Sixth Amendment right to counsel in the Test Fleet trial was impaired, and only he and King have standing with respect to the other constitutional claims. . . . It is clear, on the other hand, that Partin's reports to the agent Sheridan uncovered leads that made possible the development of evidence against petitioners Parks and Campbell. But we need not pursue the nuances of these "standing" questions, because it is evident in any event that none of the petitioners can prevail unless the petitioner Hoffa prevails. For that reason, the ensuing discussion is confined to the claims of the petitioner Hoffa (hereinafter petitioner), all of which he clearly has standing to invoke.

I

It is contended that only by violating the petitioner's rights under the Fourth Amendment was Partin able to hear the petitioner's incriminating statements in the hotel suite, and that Partin's testimony was therefore inadmissible under the exclusionary rule of Weeks v. United States, 232 U.S. 383. The argument is that Partin's failure to disclose his role as a government informer vitiated the consent that the petitioner gave to Partin's repeated entries into the suite, and that by listening to the petitioner's statements Partin conducted an illegal "search" for verbal evidence.

The preliminary steps of this argument are on solid ground. A hotel room can clearly be the object of Fourth Amendment protection as much as a home or an office. United States v. Jeffers, 342 U.S. 48. The Fourth Amendment can certainly be violated by guileful as well as by forcible intrusions into a constitutionally protected area. Gouled v. United States, 255 U.S. 298. And the protections of the Fourth Amendment are surely not limited to tangibles, but can extend as well to oral statements. Silverman v. United States, 365 U.S. 505.

Where the argument falls is in its misapprehension of the fundamental nature and scope of Fourth Amendment protection. What the Fourth Amendment protects is the security a man relies

upon when he places himself or his property within a constitutionally protected area, be it his home or his office, his hotel room or
his automobile. There he is protected from unwarranted governmental intrusion. And when he puts something in his filing cabinet, in his desk drawer, or in his pocket, he has the right to know it
will be secure from an unreasonable search or an unreasonable
seizure. So it was that the Fourth Amendment could not tolerate
the warrantless search of the hotel room in *Jeffers,* the purloining of
the petitioner's private papers in *Gouled,* or the surreptitious electronic surveillance in *Silverman.* Countless other cases which have
come to this Court over the years have involved a myriad of
differing factual contexts in which the protections of the Fourth
Amendment have been appropriately invoked. No doubt the future
will bring countless others. By nothing we say here do we either
foresee or foreclose factual situations to which the Fourth Amendment may be applicable.

   In the present case, however, it is evident that no interest
legitimately protected by the Fourth Amendment is involved. It is
obvious that the petitioner was not relying on the security of his
hotel suite when he made the incriminating statements to Partin or
in Partin's presence. Partin did not enter the suite by force or by
stealth. He was not a surreptitious eavesdropper. Partin was in
the suite by invitation, and every conversation which he heard was
either directed to him or knowingly carried on in his presence. The
petitioner, in a word, was not relying on the security of the hotel
room; he was relying upon his misplaced confidence that Partin
would not reveal his wrongdoing.[6] As counsel for the petitioner
himself points out, some of the communications with Partin did not
take place in the suite at all, but in the "hall of the hotel," in the
"Andrew Jackson Hotel lobby," and "at the courthouse."

   Neither this Court nor any member of it has ever expressed the
view that the Fourth Amendment protects a wrongdoer's misplaced
belief that a person to whom he voluntarily confides his wrongdoing will not reveal it. . . .

         . . .

   Adhering to these views, we hold that no right protected by the
Fourth Amendment was violated in the present case.

II

   The petitioner argues that his right under the Fifth Amendment
not to "be compelled in any criminal case to be a witness against
himself" was violated by the admission of Partin's testimony. The
claim is without merit.

   There have been sharply differing views within the Court as to
the ultimate reach of the Fifth Amendment right against compulsory

---

   6. The applicability of the Fourth Amendment if Partin had been a stranger to the
petitioner is a question we do not decide. Cf.
Lewis v. United States, ante, p. 206.

self-incrimination. Some of those differences were aired last Term in Miranda v. Arizona, 384 U.S. 436, 499, 504, 526. But since at least as long ago as 1807, when Chief Justice Marshall first gave attention to the matter in the trial of Aaron Burr, all have agreed that a necessary element of compulsory self-incrimination is some kind of compulsion. ...

In the present case no claim has been or could be made that the petitioner's incriminating statements were the product of any sort of coercion, legal or factual. The petitioner's conversations with Partin and in Partin's presence were wholly voluntary. For that reason, if for no other, it is clear that no right protected by the Fifth Amendment privilege against compulsory self-incrimination was violated in this case.

III

The petitioner makes two separate claims under the Sixth Amendment, and we give them separate consideration.

A

During the course of the Test Fleet trial the petitioner's lawyers used his suite as a place to confer with him and with each other, to interview witnesses, and to plan the following day's trial strategy. Therefore, argues the petitioner, Partin's presence in and around the suite violated the petitioner's Sixth Amendment right to counsel, because an essential ingredient thereof is the right of a defendant and his counsel to prepare for trial without intrusion upon their confidential relationship by an agent of the Government, the defendant's trial adversary. Since Partin's presence in the suite thus violated the Sixth Amendment, the argument continues, any evidence acquired by reason of his presence there was constitutionally tainted and therefore inadmissible against the petitioner in this case. We reject this argument.

In the first place, it is far from clear to what extent Partin was present at conversations or conferences of the petitioner's counsel. Several of the petitioner's Test Fleet lawyers testified at the hearing on the motion to suppress Partin's testimony in the present case. Most of them said that Partin had heard or had been in a position to hear at least some of the lawyers' discussions during the Test Fleet trial. On the other hand, Partin himself testified that the lawyers "would move you out" when they wanted to discuss the case, and denied that he made any effort to "get into or be present at any conversations between lawyers or anything of that sort," other than engaging in such banalities as "how things looked," or "how does it look?" He said he might have heard some of the lawyers' conversations, but he didn't know what they were talking about, "because I wasn't interested in what they had to say about the case." He testified that he did not report any of the lawyers' conversations to Sheridan, because the latter "wasn't interested in what the attorneys said." Partin's testimony was largely confirmed by Sheridan. Sheridan did testify, however, to one occasion when Partin told him about a group of prospective character witnesses being interviewed in the suite by one of the petitioner's lawyers, who "was going over" some written "questions and answers" with them. This information was evidently relayed by Sheridan to the chief government attorney at the Test Fleet trial.

The District Court in the present case apparently credited Partin's testimony, finding "there has been no interference by the government with any attorney-client relationship of any defendant in this case." The Court of Appeals accepted this finding. 349 F.2d, at 36. In view of Sheridan's testimony about Partin's report of the interviews with the prospective character witnesses, however, we proceed here on the hypothesis that Partin did observe and report to Sheridan at least some of the activities of defense counsel in the Test Fleet trial.

The proposition that a surreptitious invasion by a government agent into the legal camp of the defense may violate the protection of the Sixth Amendment has found expression in two cases decided by the Court of Appeals for the District of Columbia Circuit, Caldwell v. United States, 92 U.S.App.D.C. 355, 205 F.2d 879, and Coplon v. United States, 89 U.S.App.D.C. 103, 191 F.2d 749. Both of those cases dealt with government intrusion of the grossest kind upon the confidential relationship between the defendant and his counsel. In *Coplon,* the defendant alleged that government agents deliberately intercepted telephone consultations between the defendant and her lawyer before and during trial. In *Caldwell,* the agent, "[i]n his dual capacity as defense assistant and Government agent . . . gained free access to the planning of the defense. . . . Neither his dealings with the defense nor his reports to the prosecution were limited to the proposed unlawful acts of the defense: they covered many matters connected with the impending trial." 92 U.S.App.D.C., at 356, 205 F.2d, at 880.

We may assume that the *Coplon* and *Caldwell* cases were rightly decided, and further assume, without deciding, that the Government's activities during the Test Fleet trial were sufficiently similar to what went on in *Coplon* and *Caldwell* to invoke the rule of those decisions. Consequently, if the Test Fleet trial had resulted in a conviction instead of a hung jury, the conviction would presumptively have been set aside as constitutionally defective. Cf. Black v. United States, ante, p. 26.

But a holding that it follows from this presumption that the petitioner's conviction in the present case should be set aside would be both unprecedented and irrational. In *Coplon* and in *Caldwell,* the Court of Appeals held that the Government's intrusion upon the defendant's relationship with his lawyer "invalidates the trial at which it occurred." 89 U.S.App.D.C., at 114, 191 F.2d, at 759; 92

U.S.App.D.C., at 357, 205 F.2d, at 881.   In both of those cases the court directed a new trial, and the second trial in *Caldwell* resulted in a conviction which this Court declined to review.   95 U.S.App. D.C. 35, 218 F.2d 370, 349 U.S. 930.   The argument here, therefore, goes far beyond anything decided in *Caldwell* or in *Coplon*.   For if the petitioner's argument were accepted, not only could there have been no new conviction on the existing charges in *Caldwell,* but not even a conviction on other and different charges against the same defendant.

It is possible to imagine a case in which the prosecution might so pervasively insinuate itself into the councils of the defense as to make a new trial on the same charges impermissible under the Sixth Amendment.   But even if it were further arguable that a situation could be hypothesized in which the Government's previous activities in undermining a defendant's Sixth Amendment rights at one trial would make evidence obtained thereby inadmissible in a different trial on other charges, the case now before us does not remotely approach such a situation.

This is so because of the clinching basic fact in the present case that none of the petitioner's incriminating statements which Partin heard were made in the presence of counsel, in the hearing of counsel, or in connection in any way with the legitimate defense of the Test Fleet prosecution.   The petitioner's statements related to the commission of a quite separate offense—attempted bribery of jurors—and the statements were made to Partin out of the presence of any lawyers.

Even assuming, therefore, as we have, that there might have been a Sixth Amendment violation which might have made invalid a conviction, if there had been one, in the Test Fleet case, the evidence supplied by Partin in the present case was in no sense the "fruit" of any such violation.   In Wong Sun v. United States, 371 U.S. 471, a case involving exclusion of evidence under the Fourth Amendment, the Court stated that "the more apt question in such a case is 'whether, granting establishment of the primary illegality, the evidence to which instant objection is made has been come at by exploitation of that illegality or instead by means sufficiently distinguishable to be purged of the primary taint.'   Maguire, Evidence of Guilt, 221 (1959)."   371 U.S., at 488.

Even upon the premise that this same strict standard of excludability should apply under the Sixth Amendment—a question we need not decide—it is clear that Partin's evidence in this case was not the consequence of any "exploitation" of a Sixth Amendment violation.   The petitioner's incriminating statements to which Partin testified in this case were totally unrelated in both time and subject matter to any assumed intrusion by Partin into the conferences of the petitioner's counsel in the Test Fleet trial.   These incriminating statements, all of them made out of the presence or hearing of any of the petitioner's counsel, embodied the very antithesis of any legitimate defense in the Test Fleet trial.

B

The petitioner's second argument under the Sixth Amendment needs no extended discussion. That argument goes as follows: Not later than October 25, 1962, the Government had sufficient ground for taking the petitioner into custody and charging him with endeavors to tamper with the Test Fleet jury. Had the Government done so, it could not have continued to question the petitioner without observance of his Sixth Amendment right to counsel. Massiah v. United States, 377 U.S. 201; Escobedo v. Illinois, 378 U.S. 478. Therefore, the argument concludes, evidence of statements made by the petitioner subsequent to October 25 was inadmissible, because the Government acquired that evidence only by flouting the petitioner's Sixth Amendment right to counsel.

Nothing in *Massiah,* in *Escobedo,* or in any other case that has come to our attention, even remotely suggests this novel and paradoxical constitutional doctrine, and we decline to adopt it now. There is no constitutional right to be arrested. The police are not required to guess at their peril the precise moment at which they have probable cause to arrest a suspect, risking a violation of the Fourth Amendment if they act too soon, and a violation of the Sixth Amendment if they wait too long. Law enforcement officers are under no constitutional duty to call a halt to a criminal investigation the moment they have the minimum evidence to establish probable cause, a quantum of evidence which may fall far short of the amount necessary to support a criminal conviction.

IV

Finally, the petitioner claims that even if there was no violation—"as separately measured by each such Amendment"—of the Fourth Amendment, the compulsory self-incrimination clause of the Fifth Amendment, or of the Sixth Amendment in this case, the judgment of conviction must nonetheless be reversed. The argument is based upon the Due Process Clause of the Fifth Amendment. The "totality" of the Government's conduct during the Test Fleet trial operated, it is said, to " 'offend those canons of decency and fairness which express the notions of justice of English-speaking peoples even toward those charged with the most heinous offenses' (Rochin v. California, 342 U.S. 165, 169)."

The argument boils down to a general attack upon the use of a government informer as "a shabby thing in any case," and to the claim that in the circumstances of this particular case the risk that Partin's testimony might be perjurious was very high. Insofar as the general attack upon the use of informers is based upon historic "notions" of "English-speaking peoples," it is without historical foundation. In the words of Judge Learned Hand, "Courts have

countenanced the use of informers from time immemorial; in cases of conspiracy, or in other cases when the crime consists of preparing for another crime, it is usually necessary to rely upon them or upon accomplices because the criminals will almost certainly proceed covertly. ..." United States v. Dennis, 183 F.2d 201, at 224.

This is not to say that a secret government informer is to the slightest degree more free from all relevant constitutional restrictions than is any other government agent. ... It *is* to say that the use of secret informers is not *per se* unconstitutional.

The petitioner is quite correct in the contention that Partin, perhaps even more than most informers, may have had motives to lie. But it does not follow that his testimony was untrue, nor does it follow that his testimony was constitutionally inadmissible. The established safeguards of the Anglo-American legal system leave the veracity of a witness to be tested by cross-examination, and the credibility of his testimony to be determined by a properly instructed jury. At the trial of this case, Partin was subjected to rigorous cross-examination, and the extent and nature of his dealings with federal and state authorities were insistently explored. The trial judge instructed the jury, both specifically and generally, with regard to assessing Partin's credibility. The Constitution does not require us to upset the jury's verdict.

Affirmed.

MR. CHIEF JUSTICE WARREN, dissenting.

. . .

At this late date in the annals of law enforcement, it seems to me that we cannot say either that every use of informers and undercover agents is proper or, on the other hand, that no uses are. There are some situations where the law could not adequately be enforced without the employment of some guile or misrepresentation of identity. A law enforcement officer performing his official duties cannot be required always to be in uniform or to wear his badge of authority on the lapel of his civilian clothing. Nor need he be required in all situations to proclaim himself an arm of the law. It blinks the realities of sophisticated, modern-day criminal activity and legitimate law enforcement practices to argue the contrary. However, one of the important duties of this Court is to give careful scrutiny to practices of government agents when they are challenged in cases before us, in order to insure that the protections of the Constitution are respected and to maintain the integrity of federal law enforcement.

. . .

... Here, Edward Partin, a jailbird languishing in a Louisiana jail under indictments for such state and federal crimes as embezzlement, kidnapping, and manslaughter (and soon to be charged with perjury and assault), contacted federal authorities and told them he was willing to become, and would be useful as, an informer against Hoffa who was then about to be tried in the Test Fleet case. A motive for his doing this is immediately apparent—namely, his strong desire to work his way out of jail and out of his various legal entanglements with the State and Federal Governments. And it is interesting to note that, if this was his motive, he has been uniquely successful in satisfying it. In the four years since he first volunteered to be an informer against Hoffa he has not been prosecuted on any of the serious federal charges for which he was at that time jailed, and the state charges have apparently vanished into thin air.

. . .

This type of informer and the uses to which he was put in this case evidence a serious potential for undermining the integrity of the truth-finding process in the federal courts. Given the incentives and background of Partin, no conviction should be allowed to stand when based heavily on his testimony. And that is exactly the quicksand upon which these convictions rest, because without Partin, who was the principal government witness, there would probably have been no convictions here. Thus, although petitioners make their main arguments on constitutional grounds and raise serious Fourth and Sixth Amendment questions, it should not even be necessary for the Court to reach those questions. For the affront to the quality and fairness of federal law enforcement which this case presents is sufficient to require an exercise of our supervisory powers. . . .

I do not say that the Government may never use as a witness a person of dubious or even bad character. In performing its duty to prosecute crime the Government must take the witnesses as it finds them. They may be persons of good, bad, or doubtful credibility, but their testimony may be the only way to establish the facts, leaving it to the jury to determine their credibility. In this case, however, we have a totally different situation. Here the Government reaches into the jailhouse to employ a man who was himself facing indictments far more serious (and later including one for perjury) than the one confronting the man against whom he offered to inform. It employed him not for the purpose of testifying to something that had already happened, but rather for the purpose of infiltration to see if crimes would in the future be committed. The Government in its zeal even assisted him in gaining a position from which he could be a witness to the confidential relationship of attorney and client engaged in the preparation of a criminal defense. And, for the dubious evidence thus obtained, the Government paid an enormous price. Certainly if a criminal defendant insinuated his informer into the prosecution's camp in this manner he would be guilty of obstructing justice. I cannot agree that what happened in this case is in keeping with the standards of justice in our federal system and I must, therefore, dissent.[*]

[*] Justice Clark wrote an opinion, which Justice Douglas joined, stating that the writs of certiorari should be dismissed as improvidently granted.

KATZ v. UNITED STATES

389 U.S. 347, 88 S.Ct. 507, 19 L.Ed.2d 576 (1967).

MR. JUSTICE STEWART delivered the opinion of the Court.

The petitioner was convicted in the District Court for the Southern District of California under an eight-count indictment charging him with transmitting wagering information by telephone from Los Angeles to Miami and Boston, in violation of a federal statute. At trial the Government was permitted, over the petitioner's objection, to introduce evidence of the petitioner's end of telephone conversations, overheard by FBI agents who had attached an electronic listening and recording device to the outside of the public telephone booth from which he had placed his calls. In affirming his conviction, the Court of Appeals rejected the contention that the recordings had been obtained in violation of the Fourth Amendment, because "[t]here was no physical entrance into the area occupied by [the petitioner]." [2] We granted certiorari in order to consider the constitutional questions thus presented.

The petitioner has phrased those questions as follows:

"A. Whether a public telephone booth is a constitutionally protected area so that evidence obtained by attaching an electronic listening recording device to the top of such a booth is obtained in violation of the right to privacy of the user of the booth.

"B. Whether physical penetration of a constitutionally protected area is necessary before a search and seizure can be said to be violative of the Fourth Amendment to the United States Constitution."

We decline to adopt this formulation of the issues. In the first place, the correct solution of Fourth Amendment problems is not necessarily promoted by incantation of the phrase "constitutionally protected area." Secondly, the Fourth Amendment cannot be translated into a general constitutional "right to privacy." That Amendment protects individual privacy against certain kinds of governmental intrusion, but its protections go further, and often have nothing to do with privacy at all. Other provisions of the Constitution protect personal privacy from other forms of governmental invasion. But the protection of a person's *general* right to privacy—his right to be let alone by other people—is, like the protection of his property and of his very life, left largely to the law of the individual States.

2. 369 F.2d 130, 134.

Because of the misleading way the issues have been formulated, the parties have attached great significance to the characterization of the telephone booth from which the petitioner placed his calls. The petitioner has strenuously argued that the booth was a "constitutionally protected area." The Government has maintained with equal vigor that it was not. But this effort to decide whether or not a given "area," viewed in the abstract, is "constitutionally protected" deflects attention from the problem presented by this case. For the Fourth Amendment protects people, not places. What a person knowingly exposes to the public, even in his own home or office, is not a subject of Fourth Amendment protection. ... But what he seeks to preserve as private, even in an area accessible to the public, may be constitutionally protected. ...

The Government stresses the fact that the telephone booth from which the petitioner made his calls was constructed partly of glass, so that he was as visible after he entered it as he would have been if he had remained outside. But what he sought to exclude when he entered the booth was not the intruding eye—it was the uninvited ear. He did not shed his right to do so simply because he made his calls from a place where he might be seen. No less than an individual in a business office, in a friend's apartment, or in a taxicab, a person in a telephone booth may rely upon the protection of the Fourth Amendment. One who occupies it, shuts the door behind him, and pays the toll that permits him to place a call is surely entitled to assume that the words he utters into the mouthpiece will not be broadcast to the world. To read the Constitution more narrowly is to ignore the vital role that the public telephone has come to play in private communication.

The Government contends, however, that the activities of its agents in this case should not be tested by Fourth Amendment requirements, for the surveillance technique they employed involved no physical penetration of the telephone booth from which the petitioner placed his calls. It is true that the absence of such penetration was at one time thought to foreclose further Fourth Amendment inquiry. Olmstead v. United States, 277 U.S. 438, 457, 464, 466; Goldman v. United States, 316 U.S. 129, 134–136, for that Amendment was thought to limit only searches and seizures of tangible property. But "[t]he premise that property interests control the right of the Government to search and seize has been discredited." Warden v. Hayden, 387 U.S. 294, 304. Thus, although a closely divided Court supposed in *Olmstead* that surveillance without any trespass and without the seizure of any material object fell outside the ambit of the Constitution, we have since departed from the narrow view on which that decision rested. Indeed, we have expressly held that the Fourth Amendment governs not only the seizure of tangible items, but extends as well to the recording of oral statements, overheard without any "technical trespass under . . . local property law." Silverman v. United States, 365 U.S. 505, 511. Once this much is acknowledged, and once it is recognized that the Fourth Amendment protects people—and not simply "areas"—against unreasonable searches and seizures, it becomes clear that the reach of that Amendment cannot turn upon the presence or absence of a physical intrusion into any given enclosure.

We conclude that the underpinnings of *Olmstead* and *Goldman* have been so eroded by our subsequent decisions that the "trespass" doctrine there enunciated can no longer be regarded as controlling. The Government's activities in electronically listening to and recording the petitioner's words violated the privacy upon which he justifiably relied while using the telephone booth and thus constituted a "search and seizure" within the meaning of the Fourth Amendment. The fact that the electronic device employed to achieve that end did not happen to penetrate the wall of the booth can have no constitutional significance.

The question remaining for decision, then, is whether the search and seizure conducted in this case complied with constitutional standards. In that regard, the Government's position is that its agents acted in an entirely defensible manner: They did not begin their electronic surveillance until investigation of the petitioner's activities had established a strong probability that he was using the telephone in question to transmit gambling information to persons in other States, in violation of federal law. Moreover, the surveillance was limited, both in scope and in duration, to the specific purpose of establishing the contents of the petitioner's unlawful telephonic communications. The agents confined their surveillance to the brief periods during which he used the telephone booth,[14] and they took great care to overhear only the conversations of the petitioner himself.[15]

Accepting this account of the Government's actions as accurate, it is clear that this surveillance was so narrowly circumscribed that a duly authorized magistrate, properly notified of the need for such investigation, specifically informed of the basis on which it was to proceed, and clearly apprised of the precise intrusion it would entail, could constitutionally have authorized, with appropriate safeguards, the very limited search and seizure that the Government asserts in fact took place. . . . [A] . . . judicial order could have

---

14. Based upon their previous visual observations of the petitioner, the agents correctly predicted that he would use the telephone booth for several minutes at approximately the same time each morning. The petitioner was subjected to electronic surveillance only during this predetermined period. Six recordings, averaging some three minutes each, were obtained and admitted in evidence. They preserved the petitioner's end of conversations concerning the placing of bets and the receipt of wagering information.

15. On the single occasion when the statements of another person were inadvertently intercepted, the agents refrained from listening to them.

accommodated "the legitimate needs of law enforcement" [17] by authorizing the carefully limited use of electronic surveillance.

The Government urges that, because its agents relied upon the decisions in *Olmstead* and *Goldman,* and because they did no more here than they might properly have done with prior judicial sanction, we should retroactively validate their conduct. That we cannot do. It is apparent that the agents in this case acted with restraint. Yet the inescapable fact is that this restraint was imposed by the agents themselves, not by a judicial officer. They were not required, before commencing the search, to present their estimate of probable cause for detached scrutiny by a neutral magistrate. They were not compelled, during the conduct of the search itself, to observe precise limits established in advance by a specific court order. Nor were they directed, after the search had been completed, to notify the authorizing magistrate in detail of all that had been seized. In the absence of such safeguards, this Court has never sustained a search upon the sole ground that officers reasonably expected to find evidence of a particular crime and voluntarily confined their activities to the least intrusive means consistent with that end. Searches conducted without warrants have been held unlawful "notwithstanding facts unquestionably showing probable cause," Agnello v. United States, 269 U.S. 20, 33, for the Constitution requires "that the deliberate, impartial judgment of a judicial officer ... be interposed between the citizen and the police ...." Wong Sun v. United States, 371 U.S. 471, 481–482. "Over and again this Court has emphasized that the mandate of the [Fourth] Amendment requires adherence to judicial processes," United States v. Jeffers, 342 U.S. 48, 51, and that searches conducted outside the judicial process, without prior approval by judge or magistrate, are *per se* unreasonable under the Fourth Amendment—subject only to a few specifically established and well-delineated exceptions.

It is difficult to imagine how any of those exceptions could ever apply to the sort of search and seizure involved in this case. Even electronic surveillance substantially contemporaneous with an individual's arrest could hardly be deemed an "incident" of that arrest. Nor could the use of electronic surveillance without prior authorization be justified on grounds of "hot pursuit." And, of course, the very nature of electronic surveillance precludes its use pursuant to the suspect's consent.

The Government does not question these basic principles. Rather, it urges the creation of a new exception to cover this case. It argues that surveillance of a telephone booth should be exempted from the usual requirement of advance authorization by a magistrate upon a showing of probable cause. We cannot agree. Omission of such authorization

---

17. Lopez v. United States, 373 U.S. 427, 464 (dissenting opinion of Mr. Justice Brennan).

"bypasses the safeguards provided by an objective predetermination of probable cause, and substitutes instead the far less reliable procedure of an after-the-event justification for the . . . search, too likely to be subtly influenced by the familiar shortcomings of hindsight judgment." Beck v. Ohio, 379 U.S. 89, 96.

And bypassing a neutral predetermination of the *scope* of a search leaves individuals secure from Fourth Amendment violations "only in the discretion of the police." Id., at 97.

These considerations do not vanish when the search in question is transferred from the setting of a home, an office, or a hotel room to that of a telephone booth. Wherever a man may be, he is entitled to know that he will remain free from unreasonable searches and seizures. The government agents here ignored "the procedure of antecedent justification . . . that is central to the Fourth Amendment,"[24] a procedure that we hold to be a constitutional precondition of the kind of electronic surveillance involved in this case. Because the surveillance here failed to meet that condition, and because it led to the petitioner's conviction, the judgment must be reversed.

It is so ordered.

MR. JUSTICE HARLAN, concurring.

I join the opinion of the Court, which I read to hold only (a) that an enclosed telephone booth is an area where, like a home, Weeks v. United States, 232 U.S. 383, and unlike a field, Hester v. United States, 265 U.S. 57, a person has a constitutionally protected reasonable expectation of privacy; (b) that electronic as well as physical intrusion into a place that is in this sense private may constitute a violation of the Fourth Amendment; and (c) that the invasion of a constitutionally protected area by federal authorities is, as the Court has long held, presumptively unreasonable in the absence of a search warrant.

As the Court's opinion states, "the Fourth Amendment protects people, not places." The question, however, is what protection it affords to those people. Generally, as here, the answer to that question requires reference to a "place." My understanding of the rule that has emerged from prior decisions is that there is a twofold requirement, first that a person have exhibited an actual (subjective) expectation of privacy and, second, that the expectation be one that society is prepared to recognize as "reasonable." Thus a man's home is, for most purposes, a place where he expects privacy, but objects, activities, or statements that he exposes to the "plain view" of outsiders are not "protected" because no intention to keep them to himself has been exhibited. On the other hand, conversations in the open would not be protected against being overheard, for the

24. See Osborn v. United States, 385 U.S. 323, 330.

expectation of privacy under the circumstances would be unreasonable. . . .

The critical fact in this case is that "[o]ne who occupies it, [a telephone booth] shuts the door behind him, and pays the toll that permits him to place a call is surely entitled to assume" that his conversation is not being intercepted. Ante, at 352. The point is not that the booth is "accessible to the public" at other times, ante, at 351, but that it is a temporarily private place whose momentary occupants' expectations of freedom from intrusion are recognized as reasonable. . . .[*]

. . .

[*] Justice Douglas wrote a concurring opinion, which Justice Brennan joined. Justice White also wrote a concurring opinion. Justice Black wrote a dissenting opinion.

UNITED STATES v. WHITE

401 U.S. 745, 91 S.Ct. 1122, 28 L.Ed.2d 453 (1971).

MR. JUSTICE WHITE announced the judgment of the Court and an opinion in which THE CHIEF JUSTICE, MR. JUSTICE STEWART, and MR. JUSTICE BLACKMUN join.

In 1966, respondent James A. White was tried and convicted under two consolidated indictments charging various illegal transactions in narcotics violative of 26 U.S.C. § 4705(a) and 21 U.S.C. § 174. He was fined and sentenced as a second offender to 25-year concurrent sentences. The issue before us is whether the Fourth Amendment bars from evidence the testimony of governmental agents who related certain conversations which had occurred between defendant White and a government informant, Harvey Jackson, and which the agents overheard by monitoring the frequency of a radio transmitter carried by Jackson and concealed on his person. On four occasions the conversations took place in Jackson's home; each of these conversations was overheard by an agent concealed in a kitchen closet with Jackson's consent and by a second agent outside the house using a radio receiver. Four other conversations—one in respondent's home, one in a restaurant, and two in Jackson's car—were overheard by the use of radio equipment. The prosecution was unable to locate and produce Jackson at the trial and the trial court overruled objections to the testimony of the agents who conducted the electronic surveillance. The jury returned a guilty verdict and defendant appealed.

The Court of Appeals read Katz v. United States, 389 U.S. 347 (1967), as overruling On Lee v. United States, 343 U.S. 747 (1952), and interpreting the Fourth Amendment to forbid the introduction of the agents' testimony in the circumstances of this case. Accordingly, the court reversed .... In our view, the Court of Appeals misinterpreted both the *Katz* case and the Fourth Amendment ....

I

Until Katz v. United States, neither wiretapping nor electronic eavesdropping violated a defendant's Fourth Amendment rights "unless there has been an official search and seizure of his person, or such a seizure of his papers or his tangible material effects, or an actual physical invasion of his house 'or curtilage' for the purpose of making a seizure." Olmstead v. United States, 277 U.S. 438, 466 (1928); Goldman v. United States, 316 U.S. 129, 135–136 (1942). But where "eavesdropping was accomplished by means of an unauthorized physical penetration into the premises occupied" by the defendant, although falling short of a "technical trespass under the

522

local property law," the Fourth Amendment was violated and any evidence of what was seen and heard, as well as tangible objects seized, was considered the inadmissible fruit of an unlawful invasion. . . .

Katz v. United States, however, finally swept away doctrines that electronic eavesdropping is permissible under the Fourth Amendment unless physical invasion of a constitutionally protected area produced the challenged evidence. In that case government agents, without petitioner's consent or knowledge, attached a listening device to the outside of a public telephone booth and recorded the defendant's end of his telephone conversations. In declaring the recordings inadmissible in evidence in the absence of a warrant authorizing the surveillance, the Court overruled *Olmstead* and *Goldman* and held that the absence of physical intrusion into the telephone booth did not justify using electronic devices in listening to and recording Katz' words, thereby violating the privacy on which he justifiably relied while using the telephone in those circumstances.

The Court of Appeals understood *Katz* to render inadmissible against White the agents' testimony concerning conversations that Jackson broadcast to them. We cannot agree. *Katz* involved no revelation to the Government by a party to conversations with the defendant nor did the Court indicate in any way that a defendant has a justifiable and constitutionally protected expectation that a person with whom he is conversing will not then or later reveal the conversation to the police.

Hoffa v. United States, 385 U.S. 293 (1966), which was left undisturbed by *Katz*, held that however strongly a defendant may trust an apparent colleague, his expectations in this respect are not protected by the Fourth Amendment when it turns out that the colleague is a government agent regularly communicating with the authorities. In these circumstances, "no interest legitimately protected by the Fourth Amendment is involved," for that amendment affords no protection to "a wrongdoer's misplaced belief that a person to whom he voluntarily confides his wrongdoing will not reveal it." Hoffa v. United States, at 302. No warrant to "search and seize" is required in such circumstances, nor is it when the Government sends to defendant's home a secret agent who conceals his identity and makes a purchase of narcotics from the accused, Lewis v. United States, 385 U.S. 206 (1966), or when the same agent, unbeknown to the defendant, carries electronic equipment to record the defendant's words and the evidence so gathered is later offered in evidence. Lopez v. United States, 373 U.S. 427 (1963).

Conceding that *Hoffa, Lewis,* and *Lopez* remained unaffected by *Katz*, the Court of Appeals nevertheless read both *Katz* and the Fourth Amendment to require a different result if the agent not only records his conversations with the defendant but instantaneously transmits them electronically to other agents equipped with radio receivers. Where this occurs, the Court of Appeals held, the Fourth Amendment is violated and the testimony of the listening agents must be excluded from evidence.

To reach this result it was necessary for the Court of Appeals to hold that On Lee v. United States was no longer good law. In that case, which involved facts very similar to the case before us, the Court first rejected claims of a Fourth Amendment violation because the informer had not trespassed when he entered the defendant's premises and conversed with him. To this extent the Court's rationale cannot survive *Katz*. See 389 U.S., at 352–353. But the Court announced a second and independent ground for its decision; for it went on to say that overruling *Olmstead* and *Goldman* would be of no aid to On Lee since he "was talking confidentially and indiscreetly with one he trusted, and he was overheard. . . . It would be a dubious service to the genuine liberties protected by the Fourth Amendment to make them bedfellows with spurious liberties improvised by farfetched analogies which would liken eaves-dropping on a conversation, with the connivance of one of the parties, to an unreasonable search or seizure. We find no violation of the Fourth Amendment here." 343 U.S., at 753–754. We see no indication in *Katz* that the Court meant to disturb that understanding of the Fourth Amendment or to disturb the result reached in the *On Lee* case, nor are we now inclined to overturn this view of the Fourth Amendment.

Concededly a police agent who conceals his police connections may write down for official use his conversations with a defendant and testify concerning them, without a warrant authorizing his encounters with the defendant and without otherwise violating the latter's Fourth Amendment rights. Hoffa v. United States, 385 U.S. 293, 300–303. For constitutional purposes, no different result is required if the agent instead of immediately reporting and transcrib-ing his conversations with defendant, either (1) simultaneously records them with electronic equipment which he is carrying on his person, Lopez v. United States, supra; (2) or carries radio equip-ment which simultaneously transmits the conversations either to recording equipment located elsewhere or to other agents monitor-ing the transmitting frequency. On Lee v. United States, supra. If the conduct and revelations of an agent operating without electron-ic equipment do not invade the defendant's constitutionally justifi-able expectations of privacy, neither does a simultaneous recording of the same conversations made by the agent or by others from transmissions received from the agent to whom the defendant is talking and whose trustworthiness the defendant necessarily risks.

Our problem is not what the privacy expectations of particular defendants in particular situations may be or the extent to which they may in fact have relied on the discretion of their companions. Very probably, individual defendants neither know nor suspect that their colleagues have gone or will go to the police or are carrying recorders or transmitters. Otherwise, conversation would cease and our problem with these encounters would be nonexistent or far different from those now before us. Our problem, in terms of the principles announced in *Katz,* is what expectations of privacy are constitutionally "justifiable"—what expectations the Fourth Amendment will protect in the absence of a warrant. So far, the law permits the frustration of actual expectations of privacy by permitting authorities to use the testimony of those associates who for one reason or another have determined to turn to the police, as well as by authorizing the use of informants in the manner exemplified by *Hoffa* and *Lewis.* If the law gives no protection to the wrongdoer whose trusted accomplice is or becomes a police agent, neither should it protect him when that same agent has recorded or transmitted the conversations which are later offered in evidence to prove the State's case. See Lopez v. United States, 373 U.S. 427 (1963).

Inescapably, one contemplating illegal activities must realize and risk that his companions may be reporting to the police. If he sufficiently doubts their trustworthiness, the association will very probably end or never materialize. But if he has no doubts, or allays them, or risks what doubt he has, the risk is his. In terms of what his course will be, what he will or will not do or say, we are unpersuaded that he would distinguish between probable informers on the one hand and probable informers with transmitters on the other. Given the possibility or probability that one of his colleagues is cooperating with the police, it is only speculation to assert that the defendant's utterances would be substantially different or his sense of security any less if he also thought it possible that the suspected colleague is wired for sound. At least there is no persuasive evidence that the difference in this respect between the electronically equipped and the unequipped agent is substantial enough to require discrete constitutional recognition, particularly under the Fourth Amendment which is ruled by fluid concepts of "reasonableness."

Nor should we be too ready to erect constitutional barriers to relevant and probative evidence which is also accurate and reliable. An electronic recording will many times produce a more reliable rendition of what a defendant has said than will the unaided memory of a police agent. It may also be that with the recording in existence it is less likely that the informant will change his mind, less chance that threat or injury will suppress unfavorable evidence and less chance that cross-examination will confound the testimony. Considerations like these obviously do not favor the defendant, but we are not prepared to hold that a defendant who has no constitutional right to exclude the informer's unaided testimony nevertheless has a Fourth Amendment privilege against a more accurate version of the events in question.

It is thus untenable to consider the activities and reports of the police agent himself, though acting without a warrant, to be a "reasonable" investigative effort and lawful under the Fourth Amendment but to view the same agent with a recorder or transmitter as conducting an "unreasonable" and unconstitutional search and seizure. Our opinion is currently shared by Congress and the Executive Branch ... and the American Bar Association. ... It is also the result reached by prior cases in this Court. On Lee, supra; Lopez v. United States, supra.

No different result should obtain where, as in *On Lee* and the instant case, the informer disappears and is unavailable at trial; for the issue of whether specified events on a certain day violate the Fourth Amendment should not be determined by what later happens to the informer. His unavailability at trial and proffering the testimony of other agents may raise evidentiary problems or pose issues of prosecutorial misconduct with respect to the informer's disappearance, but they do not appear critical to deciding whether prior events invaded the defendant's Fourth Amendment rights.

. . .

The judgment of the Court of Appeals is reversed.

It is so ordered.

MR. JUSTICE HARLAN, dissenting.

The uncontested facts of this case squarely challenge the continuing viability of On Lee v. United States, 343 U.S. 747 (1952). As the plurality opinion of Mr. Justice White itself makes clear, important constitutional developments since *On Lee* mandate that we reassess that case, which has continued to govern official behavior of this sort in spite of the subsequent erosion of its doctrinal foundations. With all respect, my agreement with the majority ends at that point.

I think that a perception of the scope and role of the Fourth Amendment, as elucidated by this Court since *On Lee* was decided, and full comprehension of the precise issue at stake leads to the conclusion that *On Lee* can no longer be regarded as sound law.
. . .

I

Before turning to matters of precedent and policy, several preliminary observations should be made. We deal here with the constitutional validity of instantaneous third-party electronic eavesdropping, conducted by federal law enforcement officers, without any prior judicial approval of the technique utilized, but with the consent and cooperation of a participant in the conversation, and where the substance of the matter electronically overheard is related in a federal criminal trial by those who eavesdropped as direct, not merely corroborative, evidence of the guilt of the nonconsenting party. The magnitude of the issue at hand is evidenced not simply by the obvious doctrinal difficulty of weighing such activity in the Fourth Amendment balance, but also, and more importantly, by the prevalence of police utilization of this technique. Professor Westin has documented in careful detail the numerous devices that make technologically feasible the Orwellian Big Brother. Of immediate relevance is his observation that " 'participant recording,' in which one participant in a conversation or meeting, either a police officer or a cooperating party, wears a concealed device that records the conversation or broadcasts it to others nearby . . . is used tens of thousands of times each year throughout the country, particularly in cases involving extortion, conspiracy, narcotics, gambling, prostitution, corruption by police officials . . . and similar crimes." [3]

Moreover, as I shall undertake to show later in this opinion, the factors that must be reckoned with in reaching constitutional conclusions respecting the use of electronic eavesdropping as a tool of law enforcement are exceedingly subtle and complex. They have provoked sharp differences of opinion both within and without the judiciary, and the entire problem has been the subject of continuing study by various governmental and nongovernmental bodies.

Finally, given the importance of electronic eavesdropping as a technique for coping with the more deep-seated kinds of criminal activity, and the complexities that are encountered in striking a workable constitutional balance between the public and private interests at stake, I believe that the courts should proceed with specially measured steps in this field. More particularly, I think this Court should not foreclose itself from reconsidering doctrines that would prevent the States from seeking, independently of the niceties of federal restrictions as they may develop, solutions to such vexing problems . . . . I also think that in the adjudication of federal cases, the Court should leave ample room for congressional developments.

. . .

III

A

That the foundations of *On Lee* have been destroyed does not, of course, mean that its result can no longer stand. Indeed, the plurality opinion today fastens upon our decisions in *Lopez* [373 U.S. 427 (1963)], Lewis v. United States, 385 U.S. 206 (1966), and Hoffa v. United States, 385 U.S. 293 (1966), to resist the undercurrents of more recent cases emphasizing the warrant procedure as a safeguard to privacy. But this category provides insufficient support. In each of these cases the risk the general populace faced was different from that surfaced by the instant case. No surreptitious

3. A. Westin, Privacy and Freedom 131 (1967). . . .

third ear was present, and in each opinion that fact was carefully noted.

In *Lewis,* a federal agent posing as a potential purchaser of narcotics gained access to petitioner's home and there consummated an illegal sale, the fruits of which were admitted at trial along with the testimony of the agent. Chief Justice Warren, writing for the majority, expressly distinguished the third-party overhearing involved, by way of example, in a case like Silverman v. United States, [365 U.S. 505 (1961)], noting that "there, the conduct proscribed was that of eavesdroppers, unknown and unwanted intruders who furtively listened to conversations occurring in the privacy of a house." 385 U.S., at 212. Similarly in *Hoffa,* Mr. Justice Stewart took care to mention that "surreptitious" monitoring was not there before the Court, and so too in *Lopez,* supra.

The plurality opinion seeks to erase the crucial distinction between the facts before us and these holdings by the following reasoning: if A can relay verbally what is revealed to him by B (as in *Lewis* and *Hoffa*), or record and later divulge it (as in *Lopez*), what difference does it make if A conspires with another to betray B by contemporaneously transmitting to the other all that is said? The contention is, in essence, an argument that the distinction between third-party monitoring and *other* undercover techniques is one of form and not substance. The force of the contention depends on the evaluation of two separable but intertwined assumptions: first, that there is no greater invasion of privacy in the third-party situation, and, second, that uncontrolled consensual surveillance in an electronic age is a tolerable technique of law enforcement, given the values and goals of our political system.

The first of these assumptions takes as a point of departure the so-called "risk analysis" approach of *Lewis,* and *Lopez*, and to a lesser extent *On Lee,* or the expectations approach of *Katz.* . . . While these formulations represent an advance over the unsophisticated trespass analysis of the common law, they too have their limitations and can, ultimately, lead to the substitution of words for analysis. The analysis must, in my view, transcend the search for subjective expectations or legal attribution of assumptions of risk. Our expectations, and the risks we assume, are in large part reflections of laws that translate into rules the customs and values of the past and present.

Since it is the task of the law to form and project, as well as mirror and reflect, we should not, as judges, merely recite the expectations and risks without examining the desirability of saddling them upon society. The critical question, therefore, is whether under our system of government, as reflected in the Constitution, we should impose on our citizens the risks of the electronic listener or observer without at least the protection of a warrant requirement.

This question must, in my view, be answered by assessing the nature of a particular practice and the likely extent of its impact on the individual's sense of security balanced against the utility of the conduct as a technique of law enforcement. For those more extensive intrusions that significantly jeopardize the sense of security which is the paramount concern of Fourth Amendment liberties, I am of the view that more than self-restraint by law enforcement officials is required and at the least warrants should be necessary . . .

B

The impact of the practice of third-party bugging, must, I think, be considered such as to undermine that confidence and sense of security in dealing with one another that is characteristic of individual relationships between citizens in a free society. It goes beyond the impact on privacy occasioned by the ordinary type of "informer" investigation upheld in *Lewis* and *Hoffa*. The argument of the plurality opinion, to the effect that it is irrelevant whether secrets are revealed by the mere tattletale or the transistor, ignores the differences occasioned by third-party monitoring and recording which insures full and accurate disclosure of all that is said, free of the possibility of error and oversight that inheres in human reporting.

Authority is hardly required to support the proposition that words would be measured a good deal more carefully and communication inhibited if one expected his conversations were being transmitted and transcribed. Were third-party bugging a prevalent practice, it might well smother that spontaneity—reflected in frivolous, impetuous, sacrilegious, and defiant discourse—that liberates daily life. Much off-hand exchange is easily forgotten and one may count on the obscurity of his remarks, protected by the very fact of a limited audience, and the likelihood that the listener will either overlook or forget what is said, as well as the listener's inability to reformulate a conversation without having to contend with a documented record.[24] All these values are sacrificed by a rule of law that

24. From the same standpoint it may also be thought that electronic recording by an informer of a face-to-face conversation with a criminal suspect, as in *Lopez*, should be differentiated from third-party monitoring, as in *On Lee* and the case before us, in that the latter assures revelation to the Government by obviating the possibility that the informer may be tempted to renege in his undertaking to pass on to the Government all that he has learned. While the continuing vitality of *Lopez* is not drawn directly into question by this case, candor compels me to acknowledge that the views expressed in this opinion may impinge upon that part of the reasoning in *Lopez* which suggested that a suspect has no right to anticipate unreliable testimony. I am now persuaded that such an approach misconceives the basic issue, focusing, as it does, on the interests of a particular individual rather than evaluating the impact of a practice on the sense of security that is the true concern of the Fourth Amendment's protection of privacy. Distinctions do, however, exist between *Lopez*, where a known government agent uses a recording device, and this case which involves third-party overhearing. However unlikely that the participant recorder will not play his tapes, the fact of the matter is that in a third-party situation the intrusion is instantaneous. Moreover, differences in the prior relationship between the investigator and the

permits official monitoring of private discourse limited only by the need to locate a willing assistant.

It matters little that consensual transmittals are less obnoxious than wholly clandestine eavesdrops. This was put forward as justification for the conduct in Boyd v. United States, 116 U.S. 616 (1886), where the Government relied on mitigating aspects of the conduct in question. The Court, speaking through Mr. Justice Bradley, declined to countenance literalism.

> "Though the proceeding in question is divested of many of the aggravating incidents of actual search and seizure, yet, as before said, it contains their substance and essence, and effects their substantial purpose. It may be that it is the obnoxious thing in its mildest and least repulsive form; but illegitimate and unconstitutional practices get their first footing in that way, namely, by silent approaches and slight deviations from legal modes of procedure." 116 U.S., at 635.

Finally, it is too easy to forget—and, hence, too often forgotten—that the issue here is whether to interpose a search warrant procedure between law enforcement agencies engaging in electronic eavesdropping and the public generally. By casting its "risk analysis" solely in terms of the expectations and risks that "wrongdoers" or "one contemplating illegal activities" ought to bear, the plurality opinion, I think, misses the mark entirely. *On Lee* does not simply mandate that criminals must daily run the risk of unknown eavesdroppers prying on their private affairs; it subjects each and every law-abiding member of society to that risk. The very purpose of interposing the Fourth Amendment warrant requirement is to redistribute the privacy risks throughout society in a way that produces the results the plurality opinion ascribes to the *On Lee* rule. Abolition of *On Lee* would not end electronic eavesdropping. It would prevent public officials from engaging in that practice unless they first had probable cause to suspect an individual of involvement in illegal activities and had tested their version of the facts before a detached judicial officer. The interest *On Lee* fails to protect is the expectation of the ordinary citizen, who has never engaged in illegal conduct in his life, that he may carry on his private discourse freely, openly, and spontaneously without measuring his every word against the connotations it might carry when instantaneously heard by others unknown to him and unfamiliar with his situation or analyzed in a cold, formal record played days, months, or years after the conversation. Interposition of a warrant requirement is designed not to shield "wrongdoers," but to secure a measure of privacy and a sense of personal security throughout our society.

The Fourth Amendment does, of course, leave room for the employment of modern technology in criminal law enforcement,

suspect may provide a focus for future distinctions. . . .

but in the stream of current developments in Fourth Amendment law I think it must be held that third-party electronic monitoring, subject only to the self-restraint of law enforcement officials, has no place in our society.[*]

.   .   .

[*] Justice Brennan wrote an opinion concurring in the result. Justice Black noted his concurrence in the result. Justice Douglas and Justice Marshall wrote dissenting opinions.

UNITED STATES v. RUSSELL

411 U.S. 423, 93 S.Ct. 1637, 36 L.Ed.2d 366 (1973).

MR. JUSTICE REHNQUIST delivered the opinion of the Court.

Respondent Richard Russell was charged in three counts of a five count indictment returned against him and codefendants John and Patrick Connolly. After a jury trial in the District Court, in which his sole defense was entrapment, respondent was convicted on all three counts of having unlawfully manufactured and processed methamphetamine ("speed") and of having unlawfully sold and delivered that drug in violation of 21 U.S.C. §§ 331(q)(1), (2), 360a(a), (b) (Supp. V, 1964). He was sentenced to concurrent terms of two years in prison for each offense, the terms to be suspended on the condition that he spend six months in prison and be placed on probation for the following three years. On appeal the United States Court of Appeals for the Ninth Circuit, one judge dissenting, reversed the conviction solely for the reason that an undercover agent supplied an essential chemical for manufacturing the methamphetamine which formed the basis of respondent's conviction. The court concluded that as a matter of law "a defense to a criminal charge may be founded upon an intolerable degree of governmental participation in the criminal enterprise." United States v. Russell, 459 F.2d 671, 673 (C.A.9 1972). We granted certiorari, 409 U.S. 911 (1972), and now reverse that judgment.

There is little dispute concerning the essential facts in this case. On December 7, 1969, Joe Shapiro, an undercover agent for the Federal Bureau of Narcotics and Dangerous Drugs, went to respondent's home on Whidbey Island in the State of Washington where he met with respondent and his two codefendants, John and Patrick Connolly. Shapiro's assignment was to locate a laboratory where it was believed that methamphetamine was being manufactured illicitly. He told the respondent and the Connollys that he represented an organization in the Pacific Northwest that was interested in controlling the manufacture and distribution of methamphetamine. He then made an offer to supply the defendants with the chemical phenyl-2-propanone, an essential ingredient in the manufacture of methamphetamine, in return for one-half of the drug produced. This offer was made on the condition that Agent Shapiro be shown a sample of the drug which they were making and the laboratory where it was being produced.

During the conversation Patrick Connolly revealed that he had been making the drug since May 1969 and since then had produced three pounds of it. John Connolly gave the agent a bag containing a quantity of methamphetamine that he represented as being from "the last batch that we made." Shortly thereafter Shapiro and Patrick Connolly left respondent's house to view the laboratory which was located in the Connolly house on Whidbey Island. At the house Shapiro observed an empty bottle bearing the chemical label phenyl-2-propanone.

By prearrangement Shapiro returned to the Connolly house on December 9, 1969, to supply 100 grams of propanone and observe the manufacturing process. When he arrived he observed Patrick Connolly and the respondent cutting up pieces of aluminum foil and placing them in a large flask. There was testimony that some of the foil pieces accidentally fell on the floor and were picked up by the respondent and Shapiro and put into the flask. Thereafter Patrick Connolly added all of the necessary chemicals, including the propanone brought by Shapiro, to make two batches of methamphetamine. The manufacturing process having been completed the following morning, Shapiro was given one-half of the drug and respondent kept the remainder. Shapiro offered to buy, and the respondent agreed to sell, part of the remainder for $60.

About a month later Shapiro returned to the Connolly house and met with Patrick Connolly to ask if he was still interested in their "business arrangement." Connolly replied that he was interested but that he had recently obtained two additional bottles of phenyl-2-propanone and would not be finished with them for a couple of days. He provided some additional methamphetamine to Shapiro at that time. Three days later Shapiro returned to the Connolly house with a search warrant and, among other items, seized an empty 500-gram bottle of propanone and a 100-gram bottle, not the one he had provided, that was partially filled with the chemical.

There was testimony at the trial of respondent and Patrick Connolly that phenyl-2-propanone was generally difficult to obtain. At the request of the Bureau of Narcotics and Dangerous Drugs, some chemical supply firms had voluntarily ceased selling the chemical.

At the close of the evidence, and after receiving the District Judge's standard entrapment instruction,[4] the jury found the respondent guilty on all counts charged. On appeal the respondent conceded that the jury could have found him predisposed to commit the offenses, 459 F.2d at 672, but argued that on the facts presented there was entrapment as a matter of law. The Court of Appeals agreed, although it did not find the District Court had

4. The District Judge stated the governing law on entrapment as follows: "Where a person has the willingness and the readiness to break the law, the mere fact that the government agent provides what appears to be a favorable opportunity is not entrapment." He then instructed the jury to acquit respondent if it had a "reasonable doubt whether the defendant had the previous intent or purpose to commit the offense . . . and did so only because he was induced or persuaded by some officer or agent of the government." No exception was taken by respondent to this instruction.

misconstrued or misapplied the traditional standards governing the entrapment defense. Rather, the court in effect expanded the traditional notion of entrapment, which focuses on the predisposition of the defendant, to mandate dismissal of a criminal prosecution whenever the court determines that there has been "an intolerable degree of governmental participation in the criminal enterprise." In this case the court decided that the conduct of the agent in supplying a scarce ingredient essential for the manufacture of a controlled substance established that defense.

. . .

This Court first recognized and applied the entrapment defense in Sorrells v. United States, 287 U.S. 435 (1932). In *Sorrells* a federal prohibition agent visited the defendant while posing as a tourist and engaged him in conversation about their common war experiences. After gaining the defendant's confidence the agent asked for some liquor, was twice refused, but upon asking a third time the defendant finally capitulated, and was subsequently prosecuted for violating the National Prohibition Act.

Chief Justice Hughes, speaking for the Court, held that as a matter of statutory construction the defense of entrapment should have been available to the defendant. Under the theory propounded by the Chief Justice, the entrapment defense prohibits law enforcement officers from instigating criminal acts by persons "otherwise innocent in order to lure them to its commission and to punish them." 287 U.S., at 448. Thus, the thrust of the entrapment defense was held to focus on the intent or predisposition of the defendant to commit the crime. "[I]f the defendant seeks acquittal by reason of entrapment he cannot complain of an appropriate and searching inquiry into his own conduct and predisposition as bearing upon that issue." 287 U.S., at 451.

Mr. Justice Roberts concurred but was of the view "that courts must be closed to the trial of a crime instigated by the government's own agents." 287 U.S., at 459. The difference in the view of the majority and the concurring opinions is that in the former the inquiry focuses on the predisposition of the defendant, whereas in the latter the inquiry focuses on whether the government "instigated the crime."

In 1958 the Court again considered the theory underlying the entrapment defense and expressly reaffirmed the view expressed by the *Sorrells* majority. Sherman v. United States, 356 U.S. 369 (1958). In *Sherman* the defendant was convicted of selling narcotics to a government informer. As in *Sorrells* it appears that the government agent gained the confidence of the defendant and, despite initial reluctance, the defendant finally acceded to the repeated importunings of the agent to commit the criminal act. On the basis of *Sorrells,* this Court reversed the affirmance of the defendant's conviction.

In affirming the theory underlying *Sorrells,* Mr. Chief Justice Warren for the Court, held that "[t]o determine whether entrapment has been established, a line must be drawn between the trap for the unwary innocent and the trap for the unwary criminal." 356 U.S., at 372. Mr. Justice Frankfurter stated in an opinion concurring in the result that he believed Mr. Justice Roberts had the better view in *Sorrells* and would have framed the question to be asked in an entrapment defense in terms of "whether the police conduct revealed in the particular case falls below standards ... for the proper use of governmental power." 356 U.S., at 382.

In the instant case respondent asks us to reconsider the theory of the entrapment defense as it is set forth in the majority opinions in *Sorrells* and *Sherman.* His principal contention is that the defense should rest on constitutional grounds. He argues that the level of Shapiro's involvement in the manufacture of the methamphetamine was so high that a criminal prosecution for the drug's manufacture violates the fundamental principles of due process. The respondent contends that the same factors that led this Court to apply the exclusionary rule to illegal searches and seizures, Weeks v. United States, 232 U.S. 383 (1914); Mapp v. Ohio, 367 U.S. 643 (1961), and confessions, Miranda v. Arizona, 384 U.S. 436 (1966), should be considered here. But he would have the Court go further in deterring undesirable official conduct by requiring that any prosecution be barred absolutely because of the police involvement in criminal activity. The analogy is imperfect in any event, for the principal reason behind the adoption of the exclusionary rule was the government's "failure to observe its own laws." Mapp v. Ohio, supra, 367 U.S., at 659. Unlike the situations giving rise to the holdings in *Mapp* and *Miranda,* the government's conduct here violated no independent constitutional right of the respondent. Nor did Shapiro violate any federal statute or rule or commit any crime in infiltrating the respondent's drug enterprise.

Respondent would overcome this basic weakness in his analogy to the exclusionary rule cases by having the Court adopt a rigid constitutional rule that would preclude any prosecution when it is shown that the criminal conduct would not have been possible had not an undercover agent "supplied an indispensable means to the commission of the crime that could not have been obtained otherwise, through legal or illegal channels." Even if we were to surmount the difficulties attending the notion that due process of law can be embodied in fixed rules, and those attending respondent's particular formulation, the rule he proposes would not appear to be of significant benefit to him. For on the record presented it appears that he cannot fit within the terms of the very rule he proposes.

The record discloses that although the propanone was difficult to obtain it was by no means impossible. The defendants admitted making the drug both before and after those batches made with the propanone supplied by Shapiro. Shapiro testified that he saw an empty bottle labeled phenyl-2-propanone on his first visit to the laboratory on December 7, 1969. And when the laboratory was searched pursuant to a search warrant on January 10, 1970, two additional bottles labeled phenyl-2-propanone were seized. Thus, the facts in the record amply demonstrate that the propanone used in the illicit manufacture of methamphetamine not only *could* have been obtained without the intervention of Shapiro but was in fact obtained by these defendants.

While we may some day be presented with a situation in which the conduct of law enforcement agents is so outrageous that due process principles would absolutely bar the government from invoking judicial processes to obtain a conviction, cf. Rochin v. California, 342 U.S. 165 (1952), the instant case is distinctly not of that breed. Shapiro's contribution of propanone to the criminal enterprise already in process was scarcely objectionable. The chemical is by itself a harmless substance and its possession is legal. While the government may have been seeking to make it more difficult for drug rings, such as that of which respondent was a member, to obtain the chemical, the evidence described above shows that it nonetheless was obtainable. The law enforcement conduct here stops far short of violating that "fundamental fairness, shocking to the universal sense of justice," mandated by the Due Process Clause of the Fifth Amendment. Kinsella v. United States ex rel. Singleton, 361 U.S. 234, 246 (1960).

The illicit manufacture of drugs is not a sporadic, isolated criminal incident, but a continuing, though illegal, business enterprise. In order to obtain convictions for illegally manufacturing drugs, the gathering of evidence of past unlawful conduct frequently proves to be an all but impossible task. Thus in drug-related offenses law enforcement personnel have turned to one of the only practicable means of detection: the infiltration of drug rings and a limited participation in their unlawful present practices. Such infiltration is a recognized and permissible means of apprehension; if that be so, then the supply of some item of value that the drug ring requires must, as a general rule, also be permissible. For an agent will not be taken into the confidence of the illegal entrepreneurs unless he has something of value to offer them. Law enforcement tactics such as this can hardly be said to violate "fundamental fairness" or "shocking to the universal sense of justice," *Kinsella,* supra.

Respondent also urges as an alternative to his constitutional argument, that we broaden the nonconstitutional defense of entrapment in order to sustain the judgment of the Court of Appeals. This Court's opinions in Sorrells v. United States, supra, and Sherman v. United States, supra, held that the principal element in the defense of entrapment was the defendant's predisposition to commit the crime. Respondent conceded in the Court of Appeals, as well he might, "that he may have harbored a predisposition to commit the charged offenses." 459 F.2d, at 672. Yet he argues that the jury's refusal to find entrapment under the charge submitted to it by the trial court should be overturned and the views of Justices Roberts and Frankfurter, concurring in *Sorrells* and *Sherman*, respectively, which make the essential element of the defense turn on the type and degree of governmental conduct, be adopted as the law.

We decline to overrule these cases. *Sorrells* is a precedent of long standing that has already been once reexamined in *Sherman* and implicitly there reaffirmed. Since the defense is not of a constitutional dimension, Congress may address itself to the question and adopt any substantive definition of the defense that it may find desirable.

Critics of the rule laid down in *Sorrells* and *Sherman* have suggested that its basis in the implied intent of Congress is largely fictitious, and have pointed to what they conceive to be the anomalous difference between the treatment of a defendant who is solicited by a private individual and one who is entrapped by a government agent. Questions have been likewise raised as to whether "predisposition" can be factually established with the requisite degree of certainty. Arguments such as these, while not devoid of appeal, have been twice previously made to this Court, and twice rejected by it, first in *Sorrells* and then in *Sherman*.

We believe that at least equally cogent criticism has been made of the concurring views in these cases. Commenting in *Sherman* on Mr. Justice Roberts' position in *Sorrells* that "although the defendant could claim that the government had induced him to commit the crime, the government could not reply by showing the defendant's criminal conduct was due to his own readiness and not to the persuasion of government agents." Sherman v. United States, supra, 356 U.S., at 376–377, Mr. Chief Justice Warren quoted the observation of Judge Learned Hand in an earlier stage of that proceeding:

> " 'Indeed, it would seem probable that, if there were no reply [to the claim of inducement], it would be impossible ever to secure convictions of any offenses which consist of transactions that are carried on in secret.' United States v. Sherman, 200 F.2d 880, 882." Sherman v. United States, supra, 356 U.S., at 377 n. 7.

Nor does it seem particularly desirable for the law to grant complete immunity from prosecution to one who himself planned to commit a crime, and then committed it, simply because government undercover agents subjected him to inducements which might have seduced a hypothetical individual who was not so predisposed. We are content to leave the matter where it was left by the Court in *Sherman*:

"The function of law enforcement is the prevention of crime
and the apprehension of criminals. Manifestly, that function
does not include the manufacturing of crime. Criminal activity
is such that stealth and strategy are necessary weapons in the
arsenal of the police officer. However, 'A different question is
presented when the criminal design originates with the officials
of the government, and they implant in the mind of an innocent person the disposition to commit the alleged offense and
induce its commission in order that they may prosecute.'"
356 U.S., at 372, quoting Sorrells v. United States, supra, 287
U.S., at 442.

Several decisions of the United States district courts and courts
of appeals have undoubtedly gone beyond this Court's opinions in
Sorrells and *Sherman* in order to bar prosecutions because of what
they thought to be for want of a better term "overzealous law
enforcement." But the defense of entrapment enunciated in those
opinions was not intended to give the federal judiciary a "chancel-
lor's foot" veto over law enforcement practices of which it did not
approve. The execution of the federal laws under our Constitution
is confided primarily to the Executive Branch of the Government,
subject to applicable constitutional and statutory limitations and to
judicially fashioned rules to enforce those limitations. We think
that the decision of the Court of Appeals in this case quite unnecessarily introduces an unmanageably subjective standard which is
contrary to the holdings of this Court in *Sorrells* and *Sherman*.

Those cases establish that entrapment is a relatively limited
defense. It is rooted not in any authority of the Judicial Branch to
dismiss prosecutions for what it feels to have been "overzealous law
enforcement," but instead in the notion that Congress could not
have intended criminal punishment for a defendant who has committed all the elements of a prescribed offense, but who was
induced to commit them by the government.

Sorrells and *Sherman* both recognize "that the fact that officers
or employees of the government merely afford opportunities or
facilities for the commission of the offense does not defeat the
prosecution." 287 U.S., at 441; 356 U.S., at 372. Nor will the
mere fact of deceit defeat a prosecution, see, e.g., Lewis v. United
States, 385 U.S. 206, 208–209 (1966), for there are circumstances
when the use of deceit is the only practicable law enforcement
technique available. It is only when the government's deception
actually implants the criminal design in the mind of the defendant
that the defense of entrapment comes into play.

Respondent's concession in the Court of Appeals that the jury
finding as to predisposition was supported by the evidence is,
therefore, fatal to his claim of entrapment. He was an active
participant in an illegal drug manufacturing enterprise which began
before the government agent appeared on the scene, and continued

after the government agent had left the scene. He was, in the words of *Sherman,* supra, not an "unwary innocent" but an "unwary criminal." The Court of Appeals was wrong, we believe, when it sought to broaden the principle laid down in *Sorrells* and *Sherman.* Its judgment is therefore

Reversed.

MR. JUSTICE STEWART, with whom MR. JUSTICE BRENNAN and MR. JUSTICE MARSHALL join, dissenting.

It is common ground that "[t]he conduct with which the defense of entrapment is concerned is the manufacturing of crime by law enforcement officials and their agents." Lopez v. United States, 373 U.S. 427, 434 (1963). For the Government cannot be permitted to instigate the commission of a criminal offense in order to prosecute someone for committing it. Sherman v. United States, 356 U.S. 369, 372 (1958). As Mr. Justice Brandeis put it, the Government "may not provoke or create a crime and then punish the criminal, its creature." Casey v. United States, 276 U.S. 413, 423 (1928) (dissenting opinion). It is to prevent this situation from occurring in the administration of federal criminal justice that the defense of entrapment exists. Sorrells v. United States, 287 U.S. 435 (1932) .... But the Court has been sharply divided as to the proper basis, scope, and focus of the entrapment defense, and as to whether, in the absence of a conclusive showing the issue of entrapment is for the judge or the jury to determine.

I

In Sorrells v. United States, supra, and Sherman v. United States, supra, the Court took what might be called a "subjective" approach to the defense of entrapment. In that view, the defense is predicated on an unexpressed intent of Congress to exclude from its criminal statutes the prosecution and conviction of persons, "otherwise innocent," who have been lured to the commission of the prohibited act through the Government's instigation. Sorrells v. United States, supra, at 448. The key phrase in this formulation is "otherwise innocent," for the entrapment defense is available under this approach only to those who would not have committed the crime but for the Government's inducements. Thus, the subjective approach focuses on the conduct and propensities of the particular defendant in each individual case: if he is "otherwise innocent," he may avail himself of the defense; but if he had the "predisposition" to commit the crime, or if the "criminal design" originated with him, then—regardless of the nature and extent of the Government's participation—there has been no entrapment. Id., at 451. And, in the absence of a conclusive showing one way or the other, the question of the defendant's "predisposition" to the crime is a question of fact for the jury. The Court today adheres to this approach.

The concurring opinion of Mr. Justice Roberts, joined by Justices Brandeis and Stone, in the *Sorrells* case, and that of Mr. Justice Frankfurter, joined by Justices Douglas, Harlan, and Brennan, in the *Sherman* case, took a different view of the entrapment defense. In their concept, the defense is not grounded on some unexpressed intent of Congress to exclude from punishment under its statutes those otherwise innocent persons tempted into crime by the Government, but rather on the belief that "the methods employed on behalf of the Government to bring about conviction cannot be countenanced." Sherman v. United States, supra, at 380. Thus, the focus of this approach is not on the propensities and predisposition of a specific defendant, but on "whether the police conduct revealed in the particular case falls below the standards, to which common feelings respond, for the proper use of governmental power." Id., at 382. Phrased another way, the question is whether—regardless of the predisposition to crime of the particular defendant involved—the governmental agents have acted in such a way as is likely to instigate or create a criminal offense. Under this approach, the determination of the lawfulness of the Government's conduct must be made—as it is on all questions involving the legality of law enforcement methods—by the trial judge, not the jury.

In my view, this objective approach to entrapment advanced by the concurring opinions in *Sorrells* and *Sherman* is the only one truly consistent with the underlying rationale of the defense. Indeed, the very basis of the entrapment defense itself demands adherence to an approach that focuses on the conduct of the governmental agents, rather than on whether the defendant was "predisposed" or "otherwise innocent." I find it impossible to believe that the purpose of the defense is to effectuate some unexpressed congressional intent to exclude from its criminal statutes persons who committed a prohibited act, but would not have done so except for the Government's inducements. ... Since, by definition, the entrapment defense cannot arise unless the defendant actually committed the proscribed act, that defendant is manifestly covered by the terms of the criminal statute involved.

Furthermore, to say that such a defendant is "otherwise innocent" or not "predisposed" to commit the crime is misleading, at best. The very fact that he has committed an act that Congress has determined to be illegal demonstrates conclusively that he is not innocent of the offense. He may not have originated the precise plan or the precise details, but he was "predisposed" in the sense that he has proved to be quite capable of committing the crime. That he was induced, provoked, or tempted to do so by government agents does not make him any more innocent or any less predisposed than he would be if he had been induced, provoked, or tempted by a private person—which, of course, would not entitle him to cry "entrapment." Since the only difference between these situations is the identity of the temptor, it follows that the significant focus must be on the conduct of the government agents, and not on the predisposition of the defendant.

The purpose of the entrapment defense, then, cannot be to protect persons who are "otherwise innocent." Rather, it must be to prohibit unlawful governmental activity in instigating crime. . . . If that is so, then whether the particular defendant was "predisposed" or "otherwise innocent" is irrelevant; and the important question becomes whether the Government's conduct in inducing the crime was beyond judicial toleration.

Moreover, a test that makes the entrapment defense depend on whether the defendant had the requisite predisposition permits the introduction into evidence of all kinds of hearsay, suspicion, and rumor—all of which would be inadmissible in any other context—in order to prove the defendant's predisposition. It allows the prosecution, in offering such proof, to rely on the defendant's bad reputation or past criminal activities, including even rumored activities of which the prosecution may have insufficient evidence to obtain an indictment, and to present the agent's suspicions as to why they chose to tempt this defendant. This sort of evidence is not only unreliable, as the hearsay rule recognizes; but it is also highly prejudicial, especially if the matter is submitted to the jury, for, despite instructions to the contrary, the jury may well consider such evidence as probative not simply of the defendant's predisposition, but of his guilt of the offense with which he stands charged.

More fundamentally, focusing on the defendant's innocence or predisposition has the direct effect of making what is permissible or impermissible police conduct depend upon the past record and propensities of the particular defendant involved. Stated another way, this subjective test means that the Government is permitted to entrap a person with a criminal record or bad reputation, and then to prosecute him for the manufactured crime, confident that his record or reputation itself will be enough to show that he was predisposed to commit the offense anyway. . . .

In my view, a person's alleged "predisposition" to crime should not open him to government participation in the criminal transaction that would be otherwise unlawful.

This does not mean, of course, that the Government's use of undercover activity, strategy, or deception is necessarily unlawful. . . . Indeed, many crimes, especially so-called victimless crimes, could not otherwise be detected. Thus, government agents may engage in conduct that is likely, when objectively considered, to afford a person ready and willing to commit the crime an opportunity to do so. . . .

But when the agents' involvement in criminal activities goes beyond the mere offering of such an opportunity, and when their conduct is of a kind that could induce or instigate the commission of a crime by one not ready and willing to commit it, then—regardless of the character or propensities of the particular person induced—I think entrapment has occurred. For in that situation, the Government has engaged in the impermissible manufacturing of crime, and the federal courts should bar the prosecution in order to preserve the institutional integrity of the system of federal criminal justice.

II

In the case before us, I think that the District Court erred in submitting the issue of entrapment to the jury, with instructions to acquit only if it had a reasonable doubt as to the respondent's predisposition to committing the crime. Since, under the objective test of entrapment, predisposition is irrelevant and the issue is to be decided by the trial judge, the Court of Appeals, I believe, would have been justified in reversing the conviction on this basis alone. But since the appellate court did not remand for consideration of the issue by the District Judge under an objective standard, but rather found entrapment as a matter of law and directed that the indictment be dismissed, we must reach the merits of the respondent's entrapment defense.

Since, in my view, it does not matter whether the respondent was predisposed to commit the offense of which he was convicted, the focus must be, rather, on the conduct of the undercover government agent. What the agent did here was to meet with a group of suspected producers of methamphetamine, including the respondent; to request the drug; to offer to supply the chemical phenyl-2-propanone in exchange for one-half of the methamphetamine to be manufactured therewith; and, when that offer was accepted, to provide the needed chemical ingredient, and to purchase some of the drug from the respondent.

It is undisputed that phenyl-2-propanone is an essential ingredient in the manufacture of methamphetamine; that it is not used for any other purpose; and that, while its sale is not illegal, it is difficult to obtain, because a manufacturer's license is needed to purchase it, and because many suppliers, at the request of the Federal Bureau of Narcotics and Dangerous Drugs, do not sell it at all. It is also undisputed that the methamphetamine which the respondent was prosecuted for manufacturing and selling was all produced on December 10, 1969, and that all the phenyl-2-propanone used in the manufacture of that batch of the drug was provided by the government agent. In these circumstances, the agent's undertaking to supply this ingredient to the respondent, thus making it possible for the Government to prosecute him for manufacturing an illicit drug with it, was, I think, precisely the type of governmental conduct that the entrapment defense is meant to prevent.

Although the Court of Appeals found that the phenyl-2-propanone could not have been obtained without the agent's intervention—that "there could not have been the manufacture, delivery, or sale of the illicit drug had it not been for the Government's supply of one of the essential ingredients," 459 F.2d 671, 672—the Court today rejects this finding as contradicted by the facts revealed at trial. The record, as the Court states, discloses that one of the respondent's accomplices, though not the respondent himself, had obtained phenyl-2-propanone from independent sources both before and after receiving the agent's supply, and had used it in the production of methamphetamine. This demonstrates, it is said, that the chemical was obtainable other than through the government agent; and hence the agent's furnishing it for the production of the methamphetamine involved in this prosecution did no more than afford an opportunity for its production to one ready and willing to produce it. ... Thus, the argument seems to be, there was no entrapment here, any more than there would have been if the agent had furnished common table salt, had that been necessary to the drug's production.

It cannot be doubted that if phenyl-2-propanone had been wholly unobtainable from other sources, the agent's undercover offer to supply it to the respondent in return for part of the illicit methamphetamine produced therewith—an offer initiated and carried out by the agent for the purpose of prosecuting the respondent for producing methamphetamine—would be precisely the type of governmental conduct that constitutes entrapment under any definition. For the agent's conduct in that situation would make possible the commission of an otherwise totally impossible crime, and, I should suppose, would thus be a textbook example of instigating the commission of a criminal offense in order to prosecute someone for committing it.

But assuming in this case that the phenyl-2-propanone was obtainable through independent sources, the fact remains that that used for the particular batch of methamphetamine involved in all three counts of the indictment with which the respondent was charged—i.e., that produced on December 10, 1969—was supplied by the Government. This essential ingredient was indisputably difficult to obtain, and yet what was used in committing the offenses of which the respondent was convicted was offered to the respondent by the government agent, on the agent's own initiative, and was readily supplied to the respondent in needed amounts. If the chemical was so easily available elsewhere, then why did not the agent simply wait until the respondent had himself obtained the ingredients and produced the drug, and then buy it from him? The very fact that the agent felt it incumbent upon him to offer to supply phenyl-2-propanone in return for the drug casts considerable doubt on the theory that the chemical could easily have been procured without the agent's intervention, and that therefore the agent merely afforded an opportunity for the commission of a criminal offense.

In this case, the chemical ingredient was available only to licensed persons, and the Government itself had requested suppliers not to sell that ingredient even to people with a license. Yet the government agent readily offered and supplied that ingredient to an unlicensed person and asked him to make a certain illegal drug with it. The Government then prosecuted that person for making the drug produced *with the very ingredient* which its agent had so helpfully supplied. This strikes me as the very pattern of conduct that should be held to constitute entrapment as a matter of law.

It is the Government's duty to prevent crime, not to promote it. Here, the Government's agent asked that the illegal drug be produced for him, solved his quarry's practical problems with the assurance that he could provide the one essential ingredient that was difficult to obtain, furnished that element as he had promised, and bought the finished product from the respondent—all so that the respondent could be prosecuted for producing and selling the very drug for which the agent had asked and for which he had provided the necessary component. Under the objective approach that I would follow, this respondent was entrapped, regardless of his predisposition or "innocence."

In the words of Mr. Justice Roberts:

"The applicable principle is that courts must be closed to the trial of a crime instigated by the government's own agents. No other issue, no comparison of equities as between the guilty official and the guilty defendant, has any place in the enforcement of this overruling principle of public policy." Sorrells v. United States, supra, at 459.

I would affirm the judgment of the Court of Appeals.[*]

[*] Justice Douglas wrote a dissenting opinion, which Justice Brennan joined.

5. THE RIGHT TO COUNSEL

POWELL v. ALABAMA

287 U.S. 45, 53 S.Ct. 55, 77 L.Ed. 158 (1932).

MR. JUSTICE SUTHERLAND delivered the opinion of the Court.

These cases were argued together and submitted for decision as one case.

The petitioners, hereinafter referred to as defendants, are negroes charged with the crime of rape, committed upon the persons of two white girls. The crime is said to have been committed on March 25, 1931. The indictment was returned in a state court of first instance on March 31, and the record recites that on the same day the defendants were arraigned and entered pleas of not guilty. There is a further recital to the effect that upon the arraignment they were represented by counsel. But no counsel had been employed, and aside from a statement made by the trial judge several days later during a colloquy immediately preceding the trial, the record does not disclose when, or under what circumstances, an appointment of counsel was made, or who was appointed. During the colloquy referred to, the trial judge, in response to a question, said that he had appointed all the members of the bar for the purpose of arraigning the defendants and then of course anticipated that the members of the bar would continue to help the defendants if no counsel appeared. Upon the argument here both sides accepted that as a correct statement of the facts concerning the matter.

There was a severance upon the request of the state, and the defendants were tried in three several groups, as indicated above. As each of the three cases was called for trial, each defendant was arraigned, and, having the indictment read to him, entered a plea of not guilty. Whether the original arraignment and pleas were regarded as ineffective is not shown. Each of the three trials was completed within a single day. Under the Alabama statute the punishment for rape is to be fixed by the jury, and in its discretion may be from ten years imprisonment to death. The juries found defendants guilty and imposed the death penalty upon all. The trial court overruled motions for new trials and sentenced the defendants in accordance with the verdicts. The judgments were affirmed by the state supreme court. Chief Justice Anderson thought the defendants had not been accorded a fair trial and strongly dissented. 224 Ala. 524; id. 531; id. 540; 141 So. 215, 195, 201.

In this court the judgments are assailed upon the grounds that the defendants, and each of them, were denied due process of law and the equal protection of the laws, in contravention of the Fourteenth Amendment, specifically as follows: (1) they were not given a fair, impartial and deliberate trial; (2) they were denied the right of counsel, with the accustomed incidents of consultation and opportunity of preparation for trial; and (3) they were tried before juries from which qualified members of their own race were systematically excluded. These questions were properly raised and saved in the courts below.

The only one of the assignments which we shall consider is the second, in respect of the denial of counsel; and it becomes unnecessary to discuss the facts of the case or the circumstances surrounding the prosecution except in so far as they reflect light upon that question.

The record shows that on the day when the offense is said to have been committed, these defendants, together with a number of other negroes, were upon a freight train on its way through Alabama. On the same train were seven white boys and the two white girls. A fight took place between the negroes and the white boys, in the course of which the white boys, with the exception of one named Gilley, were thrown off the train. A message was sent ahead, reporting the fight and asking that every negro be gotten off the train. The participants in the fight, and the two girls, were in an open gondola car. The two girls testified that each of them was assaulted by six different negroes in turn, and they identified the seven defendants as having been among the number. None of the white boys was called to testify, with the exception of Gilley, who was called in rebuttal.

Before the train reached Scottsboro, Alabama, a sheriff's posse seized the defendants and two other negroes. Both girls and the negroes then were taken to Scottsboro, the county seat. Word of their coming and of the alleged assault had preceded them, and they were met at Scottsboro by a large crowd. It does not sufficiently appear that the defendants were seriously threatened with, or that they were actually in danger of, mob violence; but it does appear that the attitude of the community was one of great hostility. The sheriff thought it necessary to call for the militia to assist in safeguarding the prisoners. Chief Justice Anderson pointed out in his opinion that every step taken from the arrest and arraignment to the sentence was accompanied by the military. Soldiers took the defendants to Gadsden for safekeeping, brought them back to Scottsboro for arraignment, returned them to Gadsden for safekeeping while awaiting trial, escorted them to Scottsboro for trial a few days later, and guarded the court house and grounds at every stage of the proceedings. It is perfectly apparent that the proceedings, from beginning to end, took place in an atmosphere of tense, hostile and excited public sentiment. During the entire time, the defendants were closely confined or were under military guard. The record does not disclose their ages, except that one of them was nineteen; but the record clearly indicates that most, if not all, of them were youthful, and they are constantly referred to as "the boys." They were ignorant and illiterate. All of them were residents of other states, where alone members of their families or friends resided.

However guilty defendants, upon due inquiry, might prove to have been, they were, until convicted, presumed to be innocent. It was the duty of the court having their cases in charge to see that they were denied no necessary incident of a fair trial. With any error of the state court involving alleged contravention of the state statutes or constitution we, of course, have nothing to do. The sole inquiry which we are permitted to make is whether the federal Constitution was contravened ... ; and as to that, we confine ourselves, as already suggested, to the inquiry whether the defendants were in substance denied the right of counsel, and if so, whether such denial infringes the due process clause of the Fourteenth Amendment.

First. The record shows that immediately upon the return of the indictment defendants were arraigned and pleaded not guilty. Apparently they were not asked whether they had, or were able to employ, counsel, or wished to have counsel appointed; or whether they had friends or relatives who might assist in that regard if communicated with. That it would not have been an idle ceremony to have given the defendants reasonable opportunity to communicate with their families and endeavor to obtain counsel is demonstrated by the fact that, very soon after conviction, able counsel appeared in their behalf. This was pointed out by Chief Justice Anderson in the course of his dissenting opinion. "They were nonresidents," he said, "and had little time or opportunity to get in touch with their families and friends who were scattered throughout two other states, and time has demonstrated that they could or would have been represented by able counsel had a better opportunity been given by a reasonable delay in the trial of the cases, judging from the number and activity of counsel that appeared immediately or shortly after their conviction." 224 Ala., at pp. 554–555; 141 So. 201.

It is hardly necessary to say that, the right to counsel being conceded, a defendant should be afforded a fair opportunity to secure counsel of his own choice. Not only was that not done here, but such designation of counsel as was attempted was either so indefinite or so close upon the trial as to amount to a denial of effective and substantial aid in that regard. This will be amply demonstrated by a brief review of the record.

April 6, six days after indictment, the trials began. When the first case was called, the court inquired whether the parties were ready for trial. The state's attorney replied that he was ready to proceed. No one answered for the defendants or appeared to represent or defend them. Mr. Roddy, a Tennessee lawyer not a member of the local bar, addressed the court, saying that he had not been employed, but that people who were interested had spoken to him about the case. He was asked by the court whether he intended to appear for the defendants, and answered that he would like to appear along with counsel that the court might appoint. The record then proceeds:

"The Court: If you appear for these defendants, then I will not appoint counsel; if local counsel are willing to appear and assist you under the circumstances all right, but I will not appoint them.

"Mr. Roddy: Your Honor has appointed counsel, is that correct?

"The Court: I appointed all the members of the bar for the purpose of arraigning the defendants and then of course I anticipated them to continue to help them if no counsel appears.

"Mr. Roddy: Then I don't appear then as counsel but I do want to stay in and not be ruled out in this case.

"The Court: Of course I would not do that—

"Mr. Roddy: I just appear here through the courtesy of Your Honor.

"The Court: Of course I give you that right; . . ."

And then, apparently addressing all the lawyers present, the court inquired:

". . . well are you all willing to assist?

"Mr. Moody: Your Honor appointed us all and we have been proceeding along every line we know about it under Your Honor's appointment.

"The Court: The only thing I am trying to do is, if counsel appears for these defendants I don't want to impose on you all, but if you feel like counsel from Chattanooga—

"Mr. Moody: I see his situation of course and I have not run out of anything yet. Of course, if Your Honor purposes to appoint us, Mr. Parks, I am willing to go on with it. Most of the bar have been down and conferred with these defendants in this case; they did not know what else to do.

"The Court: The thing, I did not want to impose on the members of the bar if counsel unqualifiedly appears; if you all feel like Mr. Roddy is only interested in a limited way to assist, then I don't care to appoint—

"Mr. Parks: Your Honor, I don't feel like you ought to impose on any member of the local bar if the defendants are represented by counsel.

"The Court: That is what I was trying to ascertain, Mr. Parks.

"Mr. Parks: Of course if they have counsel, I don't see the necessity of the Court appointing anybody; if they haven't counsel, of course I think it is up to the Court to appoint counsel to represent them.

"The Court: I think you are right about it Mr. Parks and that is the reason I was trying to get an expression from Mr. Roddy.

"Mr. Roddy: I think Mr. Parks is entirely right about it, if I was paid down here and employed, it would be a different thing, but I have not prepared this case for trial and have only been called into it by people who are interested in these boys from Chattanooga. Now, they have not given me an opportunity to prepare the case and I am not familiar with the procedure in Alabama, but I merely came down here as a friend of the people who are interested and not as paid counsel, and certainly I haven't any money to pay them and nobody I am interested in had me to come down here has put up any fund of money to come down here and pay counsel. If they should do it I would be glad to turn it over—a counsel but I am merely here at the solicitation of people who have become interested in this case without any payment of fee and without any preparation for trial and I think the boys would be better off if I step entirely out of the case according to my way of looking at it and according to my lack of preparation of it and not being familiar with the procedure in Alabama, . . ."

Mr. Roddy later observed:

"If there is anything I can do to be of help to them, I will be glad to do it; I am interested to that extent.

"The Court: Well gentlemen, if Mr. Roddy only appears as assistant that way, I think it is proper that I appoint members of this bar to represent them, I expect that is right. If Mr. Roddy will appear, I wouldn't of course, I would not appoint anybody. I don't see, Mr. Roddy, how I can make a qualified appointment or a limited appointment. Of course, I don't mean to cut off your assistance in any way—Well gentlemen, I think you understand it.

"Mr. Moody: I am willing to go ahead and help Mr. Roddy in anything I can do about it, under the circumstances.

"The Court: All right, all the lawyers that will; of course I would not require a lawyer to appear if—

"Mr. Moody: I am willing to do that for him as a member of the bar; I will go ahead and help do anything I can do.

"The Court: All right."

And in this casual fashion the matter of counsel in a capital case was disposed of.

It thus will be seen that until the very morning of the trial no lawyer had been named or definitely designated to represent the defendants. Prior to that time, the trial judge had "appointed all the members of the bar" for the limited "purpose of arraigning the defendants." Whether they would represent the defendants thereafter if no counsel appeared in their behalf, was a matter of speculation only, or, as the judge indicated, of mere anticipation on the part of the court. Such a designation, even if made for all purposes, would, in our opinion, have fallen far short of meeting, in any proper sense, a requirement for the appointment of counsel. How many lawyers were members of the bar does not appear; but, in the very nature of things, whether many or few, they would not, thus collectively named, have been given that clear appreciation of responsibility or impressed with that individual sense of duty which should and naturally would accompany the appointment of a selected member of the bar, specifically named and assigned.

That this action of the trial judge in respect of appointment of counsel was little more than an expansive gesture, imposing no substantial or definite obligation upon any one, is borne out by the fact that prior to the calling of the case for trial on April 6, a leading member of the local bar accepted employment on the side of the prosecution and actively participated in the trial. It is true that he said that before doing so he had understood Mr. Roddy would be employed as counsel for the defendants. This the lawyer in question, of his own accord, frankly stated to the court; and no doubt he acted with the utmost good faith. Probably other members of the bar had a like understanding. In any event, the circumstance lends emphasis to the conclusion that during perhaps the most critical period of the proceedings against these defendants, that is to say, from the time of their arraignment until the beginning of their trial, when consultation, thoroughgoing investigation and preparation were vitally important, the defendants did not have the aid of counsel in any real sense, although they were as much entitled to such aid during that period as at the trial itself. . . .

Nor do we think the situation was helped by what occurred on the morning of the trial. At that time, as appears from the colloquy printed above, Mr. Roddy stated to the court that he did not appear as counsel, but that he would like to appear along with counsel that the court might appoint; that he had not been given an opportunity to prepare the case; that he was not familiar with the procedure in Alabama, but merely came down as a friend of the people who were interested; that he thought the boys would be better off if he should step entirely out of the case. Mr. Moody, a member of the local bar, expressed a willingness to help Mr. Roddy in anything he could do under the circumstances. To this the court responded, "All right, all the lawyers that will; of course I would not require a lawyer to appear if—." And Mr. Moody continued, "I am willing to do that for him as a member of the bar; I will go ahead and help do anything I can do." With this dubious understanding, the trials immediately proceeded. The defendants, young, ignorant, illiterate, surrounded by hostile sentiment, haled back and forth under guard of soldiers, charged with an atrocious crime regarded with especial horror in the community where they were to be tried, were thus put in peril of their lives within a few moments after counsel for the first time charged with any degree of responsibility began to represent them.

It is not enough to assume that counsel thus precipitated into the case thought there was no defense, and exercised their best judgment in proceeding to trial without preparation. Neither they nor the court could say what a prompt and thoroughgoing investigation might disclose as to the facts. No attempt was made to investigate. No opportunity to do so was given. Defendants were immediately hurried to trial. Chief Justice Anderson, after disclaiming any intention to criticize harshly counsel who attempted to represent defendants at the trials, said: " . . . the record indicates that the appearance was rather *pro forma* than zealous and active . . ." Under the circumstances disclosed, we hold that defendants were not accorded the right of counsel in any substantial sense. To decide otherwise, would simply be to ignore actualities. This conclusion finds ample support in the reasoning of an overwhelming array of state decisions . . . .

It is true that great and inexcusable delay in the enforcement of our criminal law is one of the grave evils of our time. Continuances are frequently granted for unnecessarily long periods of time, and delays incident to the disposition of motions for new trial and hearings upon appeal have come in many cases to be a distinct reproach to the administration of justice. The prompt disposition of criminal cases is to be commended and encouraged. But in reaching that result a defendant, charged with a serious crime, must not be stripped of his right to have sufficient time to advise with counsel and prepare his defense. To do that is not to proceed promptly in the calm spirit of regulated justice but to go forward with the haste of the mob.

. . .

Second. The Constitution of Alabama provides that in all criminal prosecutions the accused shall enjoy the right to have the assistance of counsel; and a state statute requires the court in a capital case, where the defendant is unable to employ counsel, to appoint counsel for him. The state supreme court held that these provisions had not been infringed, and with that holding we are powerless to interfere. The question, however, which it is our duty, and within our power, to decide, is whether the denial of the assistance of counsel contravenes the due process clause of the Fourteenth Amendment to the federal Constitution.

. . .

One test which has been applied to determine whether due process of law has been accorded in given instances is to ascertain what were the settled usages and modes of proceeding under the common and statute law of England before the Declaration of Independence, subject, however, to the qualification that they be shown not to have been unsuited to the civil and political conditions of our ancestors by having been followed in this country after it became a nation. . . . Plainly, . . . this test, as thus qualified, has not been met in the present case.

. . .

It never has been doubted by this court, or any other so far as we know, that notice and hearing are preliminary steps essential to the passing of an enforceable judgment, and that they, together with a legally competent tribunal having jurisdiction of the case, constitute basic elements of the constitutional requirement of due process of law. The words of Webster, so often quoted, that by "the law of the land" is intended "a law which hears before it condemns," have been repeated in varying forms of expression in a multitude of decisions. In Holden v. Hardy, 169 U.S. 366, 389, the necessity of due notice and an opportunity of being heard is described as among the "immutable principles of justice which inhere in the very idea of free government which no member of the Union may disregard." And Mr. Justice Field, in an earlier case, Galpin v. Page, 18 Wall. 350, 368–369, said that the rule that no one shall be personally bound until he has had his day in court was as old as the law, and it meant that he must be cited to appear and afforded an opportunity to be heard. "Judgment without such citation and opportunity wants all the attributes of a judicial determination; it is judicial usurpation and oppression, and never can be upheld where justice is justly administered." Citations to the same effect might be indefinitely multiplied, but there is no occasion for doing so.

What, then, does a hearing include? Historically and in practice, in our own country at least, it has always included the right to the aid of counsel when desired and provided by the party asserting the right. The right to be heard would be, in many cases, of little avail if it did not comprehend the right to be heard by counsel. Even the intelligent and educated layman has small and sometimes no skill in the science of law. If charged with crime, he is incapable, generally, of determining for himself whether the indictment is good or bad. He is unfamiliar with the rules of evidence. Left without the aid of counsel he may be put on trial without a proper charge, and convicted upon incompetent evidence, or evidence irrelevant to the issue or otherwise inadmissible. He lacks both the skill and knowledge adequately to prepare his defense, even though he have a perfect one. He requires the guiding hand of counsel at every step in the proceedings against him. Without it, though he be not guilty, he faces the danger of conviction because he does not know how to establish his innocence. If that be true of men of intelligence, how much more true is it of the ignorant and illiterate, or those of feeble intellect. If in any case, civil or criminal, a state or federal court were arbitrarily to refuse to hear a party by counsel, employed by and appearing for him, it reasonably may not be doubted that such a refusal would be a denial of a hearing, and, therefore, of due process in the constitutional sense.

. . .

In the light of the facts outlined in the forepart of this opinion—the ignorance and illiteracy of the defendants, their youth, the circumstances of public hostility, the imprisonment and the close surveillance of the defendants by the military forces, the fact that their friends and families were all in other states and communication with them necessarily difficult, and above all that they stood in deadly peril of their lives—we think the failure of the trial court to give them reasonable time and opportunity to secure counsel was a clear denial of due process.

But passing that, and assuming their inability, even if opportunity had been given, to employ counsel, as the trial court evidently did assume, we are of opinion that, under the circumstances just stated, the necessity of counsel was so vital and imperative that the failure of the trial court to make an effective appointment of counsel was likewise a denial of due process within the meaning of the Fourteenth Amendment. Whether this would be so in other criminal prosecutions, or under other circumstances, we need not determine. All that it is necessary now to decide, as we do decide, is that in a capital case, where the defendant is unable to employ counsel, and is incapable adequately of making his own defense because of ignorance, feeble mindedness, illiteracy, or the like, it is the duty of the court, whether requested or not, to assign counsel for him as a necessary requisite of due process of law; and that duty is not discharged by an assignment at such a time or under such circumstances as to preclude the giving of effective aid in the preparation and trial of the case. To hold otherwise would be to ignore the fundamental postulate, already adverted to, "that there are certain immutable principles of justice which inhere in the very idea of free government which no member of the Union may disregard." Holden v. Hardy, supra. . . .

. . .

The United States by statute and every state in the Union by express provision of law, or by the determination of its courts, make it the duty of the trial judge, where the accused is unable to employ counsel, to appoint counsel for him. In most states the rule applies broadly to all criminal prosecutions, in others it is limited to the more serious crimes, and in a very limited number, to capital cases. A rule adopted with such unanimous accord reflects, if it does not establish, the inherent right to have counsel appointed, at least in cases like the present, and lends convincing support to the conclusion we have reached as to the fundamental nature of that right.

The judgments must be reversed and the causes remanded for further proceedings not inconsistent with this opinion.

Judgments reversed.[*]

[*] Justice Butler wrote a dissenting opinion, which Justice McReynolds joined.

BETTS v. BRADY

316 U.S. 455, 62 S.Ct. 1252, 86 L.Ed. 1595 (1942).

MR. JUSTICE ROBERTS delivered the opinion of the Court.

The petitioner was indicted for robbery in the Circuit Court of Carroll County, Maryland. Due to lack of funds, he was unable to employ counsel, and so informed the judge at his arraignment. He requested that counsel be appointed for him. The judge advised him that this would not be done, as it was not the practice in Carroll County to appoint counsel for indigent defendants, save in prosecutions for murder and rape.

Without waiving his asserted right to counsel, the petitioner pleaded not guilty and elected to be tried without a jury. At his request witnesses were summoned in his behalf. He cross-examined the State's witnesses and examined his own. The latter gave testimony tending to establish an alibi. Although afforded the opportunity, he did not take the witness stand. The judge found him guilty and imposed a sentence of eight years.

While serving his sentence, the petitioner filed with a judge of the Circuit Court for Washington County, Maryland, a petition for a writ of *habeas corpus* alleging that he had been deprived of the right to assistance of counsel guaranteed by the Fourteenth Amendment of the Federal Constitution. The writ issued, the cause was heard, his contention was rejected, and he was remanded to the custody of the prison warden.

Some months later, a petition for a writ of *habeas corpus* was presented to Hon. Carroll T. Bond, Chief Judge of the Court of Appeals of Maryland, setting up the same grounds for the prisoner's release as the former petition. The respondent answered, a hearing was afforded, at which an agreed statement of facts was offered by counsel for the parties, the evidence taken at the petitioner's trial was incorporated in the record, and the cause was argued. Judge Bond granted the writ but, for reasons set forth in an opinion, denied the relief prayed and remanded the petitioner to the respondent's custody.

The petitioner applied to this court for certiorari directed to Judge Bond. The writ was issued on account of the importance of the jurisdictional questions involved and conflicting decisions upon the constitutional question presented. ...

. . .

Since Judge Bond's order was a final disposition by the highest court of Maryland in which a judgment could be had of the issue joined on the instant petition we have jurisdiction to review it.

3.   Was the petitioner's conviction and sentence a deprivation of his liberty without due process of law, in violation of the Fourteenth Amendment, because of the court's refusal to appoint counsel at his request?

. . .

The petitioner, in this instance, asks us, in effect, to apply a rule in the enforcement of the due process clause.   He says the rule to be deduced from our former decisions is that, in every case, whatever the circumstances, one charged with crime, who is unable to obtain counsel, must be furnished counsel by the State.   Expressions in the opinions of this court lend color to the argument, but, as the petitioner admits, none of our decisions squarely adjudicates the question now presented.

. . .

. . .   The question we are now to decide is whether due process of law demands that in every criminal case, whatever the circumstances, a State must furnish counsel to an indigent defendant.   Is the furnishing of counsel in all cases whatever dictated by natural, inherent, and fundamental principles of fairness?   The answer to the question may be found in the common understanding of those who have lived under the Anglo-American system of law. By the Sixth Amendment the people ordained that, in all criminal prosecutions, the accused should "enjoy the right . . . to have the assistance of counsel for his defence."   We have construed the provision to require appointment of counsel in all cases where a defendant is unable to procure the services of an attorney, and where the right has not been intentionally and competently waived. Though, as we have noted, the Amendment lays down no rule for the conduct of the States, the question recurs whether the constraint laid by the Amendment upon the national courts expresses a rule so fundamental and essential to a fair trial, and so, to due process of law, that it is made obligatory upon the States by the Fourteenth Amendment.   Relevant data on the subject are afforded by constitutional and statutory provisions subsisting in the colonies and the States prior to the inclusion of the Bill of Rights in the national Constitution, and in the constitutional, legislative, and judicial history of the States to the present date.   These constitute the most authoritative sources for ascertaining the considered judgment of the citizens of the States upon the question.

. . .

This material demonstrates that, in the great majority of the States, it has been the considered judgment of the people, their representatives and their courts that appointment of counsel is not a fundamental right, essential to a fair trial.   On the contrary, the matter has generally been deemed one of legislative policy.   In the light of this evidence, we are unable to say that the concept of due process incorporated in the Fourteenth Amendment obligates the

States, whatever may be their own views, to furnish counsel in every such case. Every court has power, if it deems proper, to appoint counsel where that course seems to be required in the interest of fairness.

The practice of the courts of Maryland gives point to the principle that the States should not be straight-jacketed in this respect, by a construction of the Fourteenth Amendment. Judge Bond's opinion states, and counsel at the bar confirmed the fact, that in Maryland the usual practice is for the defendant to waive a trial by jury. This the petitioner did in the present case. Such trials, as Judge Bond remarks, are much more informal than jury trials and it is obvious that the judge can much better control the course of the trial and is in a better position to see impartial justice done than when the formalities of a jury trial are involved.

In this case there was no question of the commission of a robbery. The State's case consisted of evidence identifying the petitioner as the perpetrator. The defense was an alibi. Petitioner called and examined witnesses to prove that he was at another place at the time of the commission of the offense. The simple issue was the veracity of the testimony for the State and that for the defendant. As Judge Bond says, the accused was not helpless, but was a man forty-three years old, of ordinary intelligence, and ability to take care of his own interests on the trial of that narrow issue. He had once before been in a criminal court, pleaded guilty to larceny and served a sentence and was not wholly unfamiliar with criminal procedure. It is quite clear that in Maryland, if the situation had been otherwise and it had appeared that the petitioner was, for any reason, at a serious disadvantage by reason of the lack of counsel, a refusal to appoint would have resulted in the reversal of a judgment of conviction. Only recently the Court of Appeals has reversed a conviction because it was convinced on the whole record that an accused, tried without counsel, had been handicapped by the lack of representation.

To deduce from the due process clause a rule binding upon the States in this matter would be to impose upon them, as Judge Bond points out, a requirement without distinction between criminal charges of different magnitude or in respect of courts of varying jurisdiction. As he says: "Charges of small crimes tried before justices of the peace and capital charges tried in the higher courts would equally require the appointment of counsel. Presumably it would be argued that trials in the Traffic Court would require it." And, indeed, it was said by petitioner's counsel both below and in this court, that as the Fourteenth Amendment extends the protection of due process to property as well as to life and liberty, if we hold with the petitioner, logic would require the furnishing of counsel in civil cases involving property.

As we have said, the Fourteenth Amendment prohibits the conviction and incarceration of one whose trial is offensive to the common and fundamental ideas of fairness and right, and while want of counsel in a particular case may result in a conviction lacking in such fundamental fairness, we cannot say that the Amendment embodies an inexorable command that no trial for any offense, or in any court, can be fairly conducted and justice accorded a defendant who is not represented by counsel.

The judgment is

Affirmed.[*]

[*] Justice Black wrote a dissenting opinion,   joined. which Justice Douglas and Justice Murphy

GIDEON v. WAINWRIGHT

372 U.S. 335, 83 S.Ct. 792, 9 L.Ed.2d 799 (1963).

MR. JUSTICE BLACK delivered the opinion of the Court.

Petitioner was charged in a Florida state court with having broken and entered a poolroom with intent to commit a misdemeanor. This offense is a felony under Florida law. Appearing in court without funds and without a lawyer, petitioner asked the court to appoint counsel for him, whereupon the following colloquy took place:

> "The COURT: Mr. Gideon, I am sorry, but I cannot appoint Counsel to represent you in this case. Under the laws of the State of Florida, the only time the Court can appoint Counsel to represent a Defendant is when that person is charged with a capital offense. I am sorry, but I will have to deny your request to appoint Counsel to defend you in this case.

> "The DEFENDANT: The United States Supreme Court says I am entitled to be represented by Counsel."

Put to trial before a jury, Gideon conducted his defense about as well as could be expected from a layman. He made an opening statement to the jury, cross-examined the State's witnesses, presented witnesses in his own defense, declined to testify himself, and made a short argument "emphasizing his innocence to the charge contained in the Information filed in this case." The jury returned a verdict of guilty, and petitioner was sentenced to serve five years in the state prison. Later, petitioner filed in the Florida Supreme Court this habeas corpus petition attacking his conviction and sentence on the ground that the trial court's refusal to appoint counsel for him denied him rights "guaranteed by the Constitution and the Bill of Rights by the United States Government." Treating the petition for habeas corpus as properly before it, the State Supreme Court, "upon consideration thereof" but without an opinion, denied all relief. Since 1942, when Betts v. Brady, 316 U.S. 455, was decided by a divided Court, the problem of a defendant's federal constitutional right to counsel in a state court has been a continuing source of controversy and litigation in both state and federal courts. To give this problem another review here, we granted certiorari. 370 U.S. 908. Since Gideon was proceeding *in forma pauperis,* we appointed counsel to represent him and requested both sides to discuss in their briefs and oral arguments the following: "Should this Court's holding in Betts v. Brady, 316 U.S. 455, be reconsidered?"

559

I

The facts upon which Betts claimed that he had been unconstitutionally denied the right to have counsel appointed to assist him are strikingly like the facts upon which Gideon here bases his federal constitutional claim. Betts was indicted for robbery in a Maryland state court. On arraignment, he told the trial judge of his lack of funds to hire a lawyer and asked the court to appoint one for him. Betts was advised that it was not the practice in that county to appoint counsel for indigent defendants except in murder and rape cases. He then pleaded not guilty, had witnesses summoned, cross-examined the State's witnesses, examined his own, and chose not to testify himself. He was found guilty by the judge, sitting without a jury, and sentenced to eight years in prison. Like Gideon, Betts sought release by habeas corpus, alleging that he had been denied the right to assistance of counsel in violation of the Fourteenth Amendment. Betts was denied any relief, and on review this Court affirmed. It was held that a refusal to appoint counsel for an indigent defendant charged with a felony did not necessarily violate the Due Process Clause of the Fourteenth Amendment, which for reasons given the Court deemed to be the only applicable federal constitutional provision. The Court said:

> "Asserted denial [of due process] is to be tested by an appraisal of the totality of facts in a given case. That which may, in one setting, constitute a denial of fundamental fairness, shocking to the universal sense of justice, may, in other circumstances, and in the light of other considerations, fall short of such denial." 316 U.S., at 462.

Treating due process as "a concept less rigid and more fluid than those envisaged in other specific and particular provisions of the Bill of Rights," the Court held that refusal to appoint counsel under the particular facts and circumstances in the *Betts* case was not so "offensive to the common and fundamental ideas of fairness" as to amount to a denial of due process. Since the facts and circumstances of the two cases are so nearly indistinguishable, we think the Betts v. Brady holding if left standing would require us to reject Gideon's claim that the Constitution guarantees him the assistance of counsel. Upon full reconsideration we conclude that Betts v. Brady should be overruled.

II

The Sixth Amendment provides, "In all criminal prosecutions, the accused shall enjoy the right ... to have the Assistance of Counsel for his defence." We have construed this to mean that in federal courts counsel must be provided for defendants unable to employ counsel unless the right is competently and intelligently waived. Betts argued that this right is extended to indigent defendants in state courts by the Fourteenth Amendment. In response the Court stated that, while the Sixth Amendment laid down "no rule for the conduct of the States, the question recurs whether the constraint laid by the Amendment upon the national courts expresses a rule so fundamental and essential to a fair trial, and so, to due process of law, that it is made obligatory upon the States by the Fourteenth Amendment." 316 U.S., at 465. In order to decide whether the Sixth Amendment's guarantee of counsel is of this fundamental nature, the Court in *Betts* set out and considered "[r]elevant data on the subject ... afforded by constitutional and statutory provisions subsisting in the colonies and the States prior to the inclusion of the Bill of Rights in the national Constitution, and in the constitutional, legislative, and judicial history of the States to the present date." 316 U.S., at 465. On the basis of this historical data the Court concluded that "appointment of counsel is not a fundamental right, essential to a fair trial." 316 U.S., at 471. It was for this reason the *Betts* Court refused to accept the contention that the Sixth Amendment's guarantee of counsel for indigent federal defendants was extended to or, in the words of that Court, "made obligatory upon the States by the Fourteenth Amendment." Plainly, had the Court concluded that appointment of counsel for an indigent criminal defendant was "a fundamental right, essential to a fair trial," it would have held that the Fourteenth Amendment requires appointment of counsel in a state court, just as the Sixth Amendment requires in a federal court.

. . .

We accept Betts v. Brady's assumption, based as it was on our prior cases, that a provision of the Bill of Rights which is "fundamental and essential to a fair trial" is made obligatory upon the States by the Fourteenth Amendment. We think the Court in *Betts* was wrong, however, in concluding that the Sixth Amendment's guarantee of counsel is not one of these fundamental rights. Ten years before Betts v. Brady, this Court, after full consideration of all the historical data examined in *Betts,* had unequivocally declared that "the right to the aid of counsel is of this fundamental character." Powell v. Alabama, 287 U.S. 45, 68 (1932). While the Court at the close of its *Powell* opinion did by its language, as this Court frequently does, limit its holding to the particular facts and circumstances of that case, its conclusions about the fundamental nature of the right to counsel are unmistakable. Several years later, in 1936, the Court reemphasized what it had said about the fundamental nature of the right to counsel in this language:

> "We concluded that certain fundamental rights, safeguarded by the first eight amendments against federal action, were also safeguarded against state action by the due process of law clause of the Fourteenth Amendment, and among them the fundamental right of the accused to the aid of counsel in a criminal prosecution." Grosjean v. American Press Co., 297 U.S. 233, 243–244 (1936).

And again in 1938 this Court said:

> "[The assistance of counsel] is one of the safeguards of the Sixth Amendment deemed necessary to insure fundamental human rights of life and liberty. . . . The Sixth Amendment stands as a constant admonition that if the constitutional safeguards it provides be lost, justice will not 'still be done.' " Johnson v. Zerbst, 304 U.S. 458, 462 (1938). To the same effect, see Avery v. Alabama, 308 U.S. 444 (1940), and Smith v. O'Grady, 312 U.S. 329 (1941).

In light of these and many other prior decisions of this Court, it is not surprising that the *Betts* Court, when faced with the contention that "one charged with crime, who is unable to obtain counsel, must be furnished counsel by the State," conceded that "[e]xpressions in the opinions of this court lend color to the argument . . . ." 316 U.S., at 462–463. The fact is that in deciding as it did—that "appointment of counsel is not a fundamental right, essential to a fair trial"—the Court in Betts v. Brady made an abrupt break with its own well-considered precedents. In returning to these old precedents, sounder we believe than the new, we but restore constitutional principles established to achieve a fair system of justice. Not only these precedents but also reason and reflection require us to recognize that in our adversary system of criminal justice, any person haled into court, who is too poor to hire a lawyer, cannot be assured a fair trial unless counsel is provided for him. This seems to us to be an obvious truth. Governments, both state and federal, quite properly spend vast sums of money to establish machinery to try defendants accused of crime. Lawyers to prosecute are everywhere deemed essential to protect the public's interest in an orderly society. Similarly, there are few defendants charged with crime, few indeed, who fail to hire the best lawyers they can get to prepare and present their defenses. That government hires lawyers to prosecute and defendants who have the money hire lawyers to defend are the strongest indications of the widespread belief that lawyers in criminal courts are necessities, not luxuries. The right of one charged with crime to counsel may not be deemed fundamental and essential to fair trials in some countries, but it is in ours. From the very beginning, our state and national constitutions and laws have laid great emphasis on procedural and substantive safeguards designed to assure fair trials before impartial tribunals in which every defendant stands equal before the law. This noble ideal cannot be realized if the poor man charged with crime has to face his accusers without a lawyer to assist him. . . .

The Court in Betts v. Brady departed from the sound wisdom upon which the Court's holding in Powell v. Alabama rested. Florida, supported by two other States, has asked that Betts v. Brady be left intact. Twenty-two States, as friends of the Court, argue that *Betts* was "an anachronism when handed down" and that it should now be overruled. We agree.

The judgment is reversed and the cause is remanded to the Supreme Court of Florida for further action not inconsistent with this opinion.

Reversed.[*] [**]

[*] Justice Douglas wrote a brief opinion. Justice Clark wrote an opinion concurring in the result. Justice Harlan wrote a concurring opinion.

[**] "... [W]hen a defendant has made a preliminary showing that his sanity at the time of the offense is likely to be a significant factor at trial, the Constitution requires that a State provide access to a psychiatrist's assistance on this issue, if the defendant cannot otherwise afford one." Ake v. Oklahoma, 470 U.S. 68, 74 (1985) (8–1).

DOUGLAS v. CALIFORNIA

372 U.S. 353, 83 S.Ct. 814, 9 L.Ed.2d 811 (1963).

MR. JUSTICE DOUGLAS delivered the opinion of the Court.

Petitioners, Bennie Will Meyes and William Douglas, were jointly tried and convicted in a California court on an information charging them with 13 felonies. A single public defender was appointed to represent them. At the commencement of the trial, the defender moved for a continuance, stating that the case was very complicated, that he was not as prepared as he felt he should be because he was handling a different defense every day, and that there was a conflict of interest between the petitioners requiring the appointment of separate counsel for each of them. This motion was denied. Thereafter, petitioners dismissed the defender, claiming he was unprepared, and again renewed motions for separate counsel and for a continuance. These motions also were denied, and petitioners were ultimately convicted by a jury of all 13 felonies, which included robbery, assault with a deadly weapon, and assault with intent to commit murder. Both were given prison terms. Both appealed as of right to the California District Court of Appeal. That court affirmed their convictions. 187 Cal.App.2d 802, 10 Cal.Rptr. 188. Both Meyes and Douglas then petitioned for further discretionary review in the California Supreme Court, but their petitions were denied without a hearing. 187 Cal.App.2d, at 813, 10 Cal.Rptr., at 195. We granted certiorari. 368 U.S. 815.

Although several questions are presented in the petition for certiorari, we address ourselves to only one of them. The record shows that petitioners requested, and were denied, the assistance of counsel on appeal, even though it plainly appeared they were indigents. In denying petitioners' requests, the California District Court of Appeal stated that it had "gone through" the record and had come to the conclusion that "no good whatever could be served by appointment of counsel." 187 Cal.App.2d 802, 812, 10 Cal.Rptr. 188, 195. The District Court of Appeal was acting in accordance with a California rule of criminal procedure which provides that state appellate courts, upon the request of an indigent for counsel, may make "an independent investigation of the record and determine whether it would be of advantage to the defendant or helpful to the appellate court to have counsel appointed. . . . After such investigation, appellate courts should appoint counsel if in their opinion it would be helpful to the defendant or the court, and should deny the appointment of counsel only if in their judgment such appointment would be of no value to either the defendant or the court." People v. Hyde, 51 Cal.2d 152, 154, 331 P.2d 42, 43.

We agree, however, with Justice Traynor of the California Supreme Court, who said that the "[d]enial of counsel on appeal [to an indigent] would seem to be a discrimination at least as invidious as that condemned in Griffin v. Illinois ...." People v. Brown, 55 Cal.2d 64, 71, 357 P.2d 1072, 1076 (concurring opinion). In Griffin v. Illinois, 351 U.S. 12, we held that a State may not grant appellate review in such a way as to discriminate against some convicted defendants on account of their poverty. There ... the right to a free transcript on appeal was in issue. Here the issue is whether or not an indigent shall be denied the assistance of counsel on appeal. In either case the evil is the same: discrimination against the indigent. For there can be no equal justice where the kind of an appeal a man enjoys "depends on the amount of money he has." Griffin v. Illinois, supra, at p. 19.

In spite of California's forward treatment of indigents, under its present practice the type of an appeal a person is afforded in the District Court of Appeal hinges upon whether or not he can pay for the assistance of counsel. If he can the appellate court passes on the merits of his case only after having the full benefit of written briefs and oral argument by counsel. If he cannot the appellate court is forced to prejudge the merits before it can even determine whether counsel should be provided. At this stage in the proceedings only the barren record speaks for the indigent, and, unless the printed pages show that an injustice has been committed, he is forced to go without a champion on appeal. Any real chance he may have had of showing that his appeal has hidden merit is deprived him when the court decides on an *ex parte* examination of the record that the assistance of counsel is not required.

We are not here concerned with problems that might arise from the denial of counsel for the preparation of a petition for discretionary or mandatory review beyond the stage in the appellate process at which the claims have once been presented by a lawyer and passed upon by an appellate court. We are dealing only with the *first appeal,* granted as a matter of right to rich and poor alike (Cal.Penal Code §§ 1235, 1237), from a criminal conviction. We need not now decide whether California would have to provide counsel for an indigent seeking a discretionary hearing from the California Supreme Court after the District Court of Appeal had sustained his conviction (see Cal.Const., Art. VI, § 4c; Cal.Rules on Appeal, Rules 28, 29), or whether counsel must be appointed for an indigent seeking review of an appellate affirmance of his conviction in this Court by appeal as of right or by petition for a writ of certiorari which lies within the Court's discretion. But it is appropriate to observe that a State can, consistently with the Fourteenth Amendment, provide for differences so long as the result does not amount to a denial of due process or an "invidious discrimination."

Williamson v. Lee Optical Co., 348 U.S. 483, 489; Griffin v. Illinois, supra, p. 18. Absolute equality is not required; lines can be and are drawn and we often sustain them. . . . But where the merits of *the one and only appeal* an indigent has as of right are decided without benefit of counsel, we think an unconstitutional line has been drawn between rich and poor.

When an indigent is forced to run this gantlet of a preliminary showing of merit, the right to appeal does not comport with fair procedure. In the federal courts, on the other hand, an indigent must be afforded counsel on appeal whenever he challenges a certification that the appeal is not taken in good faith. . . . The federal courts must honor his request for counsel regardless of what they think the merits of the case may be; and "representation in the role of an advocate is required." Ellis v. United States, 356 U.S. 674, 675. In California, however, once the court has "gone through" the record and denied counsel, the indigent has no recourse but to prosecute his appeal on his own, as best he can, no matter how meritorious his case may turn out to be. The present case, where counsel was denied petitioners on appeal, shows that the discrimination is not between "possibly good and obviously bad cases," but between cases where the rich man can require the court to listen to argument of counsel before deciding on the merits, but a poor man cannot. There is lacking that equality demanded by the Fourteenth Amendment where the rich man, who appeals as of right, enjoys the benefit of counsel's examination into the record, research of the law, and marshalling of arguments on his behalf, while the indigent, already burdened by a preliminary determination that his case is without merit, is forced to shift for himself. The indigent, where the record is unclear or the errors are hidden, has only the right to a meaningless ritual, while the rich man has a meaningful appeal.

We vacate the judgment of the District Court of Appeal and remand the case to that court for further proceedings not inconsistent with this opinion.

It is so ordered.

MR. JUSTICE HARLAN, whom MR. JUSTICE STEWART joins, dissenting.

In holding that an indigent has an absolute right to appointed counsel on appeal of a state criminal conviction, the Court appears to rely both on the Equal Protection Clause and on the guarantees of fair procedure inherent in the Due Process Clause of the Fourteenth Amendment, with obvious emphasis on "equal protection." In my view the Equal Protection Clause is not apposite, and its application to cases like the present one can lead only to mischievous results. This case should be judged solely under the Due Process Clause, and I do not believe that the California procedure violates that provision.

EQUAL PROTECTION

To approach the present problem in terms of the Equal Protection Clause is, I submit, but to substitute resounding phrases for analysis. I dissented from this approach in Griffin v. Illinois, 351 U.S. 12, 29, 34–36, and I am constrained to dissent from the implicit extension of the equal protection approach here—to a case in which the State denies no one an appeal, but seeks only to keep within reasonable bounds the instances in which appellate counsel will be assigned to indigents.

The States, of course, are prohibited by the Equal Protection Clause from discriminating between "rich" and "poor" *as such* in the formulation and application of their laws. But it is a far different thing to suggest that this provision prevents the State from adopting a law of general applicability that may affect the poor more harshly than it does the rich, or, on the other hand, from making some effort to redress economic imbalances while not eliminating them entirely.

Every financial exaction which the State imposes on a uniform basis is more easily satisfied by the well-to-do than by the indigent. Yet I take it that no one would dispute the constitutional power of the State to levy a uniform sales tax, to charge tuition at a state university, to fix rates for the purchase of water from a municipal corporation, to impose a standard fine for criminal violations, or to establish minimum bail for various categories of offenses. Nor could it be contended that the State may not classify as crimes acts which the poor are more likely to commit than are the rich. And surely, there would be no basis for attacking a state law which provided benefits for the needy simply because those benefits fell short of the goods or services that others could purchase for themselves.

Laws such as these do not deny equal protection to the less fortunate for one essential reason: the Equal Protection Clause does not impose on the States "an affirmative duty to lift the handicaps flowing from differences in economic circumstances."[2] To so construe it would be to read into the Constitution a philosophy of leveling that would be foreign to many of our basic concepts of the proper relations between government and society. The State may have a moral obligation to eliminate the evils of poverty, but it is not required by the Equal Protection Clause to give to some whatever others can afford.

Thus it should be apparent that the present case . . . is not one properly regarded as arising under this clause. California does not discriminate between rich and poor in having a uniform policy permitting everyone to appeal and to retain counsel, and in having a separate rule dealing *only* with the standards for the appointment of counsel for those unable to retain their own attorneys. The sole

---

2. Griffin v. Illinois, supra, at 34 (dissenting opinion of this writer).

classification established by this rule is between those cases that are believed to have merit and those regarded as frivolous. And, of course, no matter how far the state rule might go in providing counsel for indigents, it could never be expected to satisfy an affirmative duty—if one existed—to place the poor on the same level as those who can afford the best legal talent available.

Parenthetically, it should be noted that if the present problem may be viewed as one of equal protection, so may the question of the right to appointed counsel at trial, and the Court's analysis of that right in Gideon v. Wainwright, ante, p. 335, decided today, is wholly unnecessary. The short way to dispose of Gideon v. Wainwright, in other words, would be simply to say that the State deprives the indigent of equal protection whenever it fails to furnish him with legal services, and perhaps with other services as well, equivalent to those that the affluent defendant can obtain.

The real question in this case, I submit, and the only one that permits of satisfactory analysis, is whether or not the state rule, as applied in this case, is consistent with the requirements of fair procedure guaranteed by the Due Process Clause. Of course, in considering this question, it must not be lost sight of that the State's responsibility under the Due Process Clause is to provide justice for all. Refusal to furnish criminal indigents with some things that others can afford may fall short of constitutional standards of fairness. The problem before us is whether this is such a case.

DUE PROCESS

It bears reiteration that California's procedure of screening its criminal appeals to determine whether or not counsel ought to be appointed denies to no one the right to appeal. This is not a case, like Burns v. Ohio, 360 U.S. 252, in which a court rule or statute bars all consideration of the merits of an appeal unless docketing fees are prepaid. Nor is it like Griffin v. Illinois, supra, in which the State conceded that "petitioners needed a transcript in order to get adequate appellate review of their alleged trial errors." 351 U.S., at 16. Here it is *this* Court which finds, notwithstanding California's assertions to the contrary, that as a matter of constitutional law "adequate appellate review" is impossible unless counsel has been appointed. And while *Griffin* left it open to the States to devise "other means of affording adequate and effective appellate review to indigent defendants," 351 U.S., at 20, the present decision establishes what is seemingly an absolute rule under which the State may be left without any means of protecting itself against the employment of counsel in frivolous appeals.

It was precisely towards providing adequate appellate review— as part of what the Court concedes to be "California's forward treatment of indigents"—that the State formulated the system which the Court today strikes down. That system requires the state appellate courts to appoint counsel on appeal for any indigent defendant except "if in their judgment such appointment would be of no value to either the defendant or the court." People v. Hyde, 51 Cal.2d 152, 154, 331 P.2d 42, 43. This judgment can be reached only after an independent investigation of the trial record by the reviewing court. And even if counsel is denied, a full appeal on the merits is accorded to the indigent appellant, together with a statement of the reasons why counsel was not assigned. There is nothing in the present case, or in any other case that has been cited to us, to indicate that the system has resulted in injustice. Quite the contrary, there is every reason to believe that California appellate courts have made a painstaking effort to apply the rule fairly and to live up to the State Supreme Court's mandate. ...

We have today held that in a case such as the one before us, there is an absolute right to the services of counsel at trial. ... But the appellate procedures involved here stand on an entirely different constitutional footing. *First,* appellate review is in itself not required by the Fourteenth Amendment ... and thus the question presented is the narrow one whether the State's rules with respect to the appointment of counsel are so arbitrary or unreasonable, *in the context of the particular appellate procedure that it has established,* as to require their invalidation. *Second,* the kinds of questions that may arise on appeal are circumscribed by the record of the proceedings that led to the conviction; they do not encompass the large variety of tactical and strategic problems that must be resolved at the trial. *Third,* as California applies its rule, the indigent appellant receives the benefit of expert and conscientious legal appraisal of the merits of his case on the basis of the trial record, and whether or not he is assigned counsel, is guaranteed full consideration of his appeal. It would be painting with too broad a brush to conclude that under these circumstances an appeal is just like a trial.

What the Court finds constitutionally offensive in California's procedure bears a striking resemblance to the rules of this Court and many state courts of last resort on petitions for certiorari or for leave to appeal filed by indigent defendants *pro se.* Under the practice of this Court, only if it appears from the petition for certiorari that a case merits review is leave to proceed *in forma pauperis* granted, the case transferred to the Appellate Docket, and counsel appointed. Since our review is generally discretionary, and since we are often not even given the benefit of a record in the proceedings below, the disadvantages to the indigent petitioner might be regarded as more substantial than in California. But as conscientiously committed as this Court is to the great principle of "Equal Justice Under Law," it has never deemed itself constitutionally required to appoint counsel to assist in the preparation of each of the more than 1,000 *pro se* petitions for certiorari currently being filed each Term. We should know from our own experience that appellate courts generally go out of their way to give fair consideration to those who are unrepresented.

The Court distinguishes our review from the present case on the grounds that the California rule relates to "the *first appeal,* granted as a matter of right." Ante, p. 356. But I fail to see the significance of this difference. Surely, it cannot be contended that the requirements of fair procedure are exhausted once an indigent has been given one appellate review. . . . Nor can it well be suggested that having appointed counsel is more necessary to the fair administration of justice in an initial appeal taken as a matter of right, which the reviewing court on the full record has already determined to be frivolous, than in a petition asking a higher appellate court to exercise its discretion to consider what may be a substantial constitutional claim.

Further, there is no indication in this record, or in the state cases cited to us, that the California procedure differs in any material respect from the screening of appeals in federal criminal cases that is prescribed by 28 U.S.C. § 1915. As recently as last Term, in Coppedge v. United States, 369 U.S. 438, we had occasion to pass upon the application of this statute. Although that decision established stringent restrictions on the power of federal courts to reject an application for leave to appeal *in forma pauperis,* it nonetheless recognized that the federal courts could prevent the needless expenditure of public funds by summarily disposing of frivolous appeals. Indeed in some respects, California has outdone the federal system, since it provides a transcript and an appeal on the merits in *all* cases, no matter how frivolous.

I cannot agree that the Constitution prohibits a State, in seeking to redress economic imbalances at its bar of justice and to provide indigents with full review, from taking reasonable steps to guard against needless expense. This is all that California has done. Accordingly, I would affirm the state judgment.[*]

[*] Justice Clark wrote a dissenting opinion.

ARGERSINGER v. HAMLIN

407 U.S. 25, 92 S.Ct. 2006, 32 L.Ed.2d 530 (1972).

MR. JUSTICE DOUGLAS delivered the opinion of the Court.

Petitioner, an indigent, was charged in Florida with carrying a concealed weapon, an offense punishable by imprisonment up to six months, a $1,000 fine, or both. The trial was to a judge, and petitioner was unrepresented by counsel. He was sentenced to serve 90 days in jail, and brought this habeas corpus action in the Florida Supreme Court, alleging that, being deprived of his right to counsel, he was unable as an indigent layman properly to raise and present to the trial court good and sufficient defenses to the charges for which he stands convicted. The Florida Supreme Court by a four-to-three decision, in ruling on the right to counsel, followed the line we marked out in Duncan v. Louisiana, 391 U.S. 145, 159, as respects the right to trial by jury and held that the right to court-appointed counsel extends only to trials "for non-petty offenses punishable by more than six months imprisonment." 236 So.2d 442, 443.

The case is here on a petition for certiorari, which we granted. 401 U.S. 908. We reverse.

The Sixth Amendment, which in enumerated situations has been made applicable to the States by reason of the Fourteenth Amendment (see Duncan v. Louisiana, supra; Washington v. Texas, 388 U.S. 14; Klopfer v. North Carolina, 386 U.S. 213; Pointer v. Texas, 380 U.S. 400; Gideon v. Wainwright, 372 U.S. 335; and In re Oliver, 333 U.S. 257), provides specified standards for "all criminal prosecutions."

One is the requirement of a "public trial." In re Oliver, supra, held that the right to a "public trial" was applicable to a state proceeding even though only a 60-day sentence was involved. 333 U.S., at 272.

Another guarantee is the right to be informed of the nature and cause of the accusation. Still another, the right of confrontation. Pointer v. Texas, supra. And another, compulsory process for obtaining witnesses in one's favor. Washington v. Texas, supra. We have never limited these rights to felonies or to lesser but serious offenses.

In Washington v. Texas, supra, we said, "We have held that due process requires that the accused have the assistance of counsel for his defense, that he be confronted with the witnesses against him, and that he have the right to a speedy and public trial." 388 U.S., at 18. Respecting the right to a speedy and public trial, the right to

571

be informed of the nature and cause of the accusation, the right to confront and cross-examine witnesses, the right to compulsory process for obtaining witnesses, it was recently stated, "It is simply not arguable, nor has any court ever held, that the trial of a petty offense may be held in secret, or without notice to the accused of the charges, or that in such cases the defendant has no right to confront his accusers or to compel the attendance of witnesses in his own behalf." Junker, The Right to Counsel in Misdemeanor Cases, 43 Wash.L.Rev. 685, 705 (1968).

District of Columbia v. Clawans, 300 U.S. 617, illustrates the point. There, the offense was engaging without a license in the business of dealing in second-hand property, an offense punishable by a fine of $300 or imprisonment for not more than 90 days. The Court held that the offense was a "petty" one and could be tried without a jury. But the conviction was reversed and a new trial ordered, because the trial court had prejudicially restricted the right of cross-examination, a right guaranteed by the Sixth Amendment.

The right to trial by jury, also guaranteed by the Sixth Amendment by reason of the Fourteenth, was limited by Duncan v. Louisiana, supra, to trials where the potential punishment was imprisonment of six months or more. But, as the various opinions in Baldwin v. New York, 399 U.S. 66, make plain, the right to trial by jury has a different genealogy and is brigaded with a system of trial to a judge alone. ...

While there is historical support for limiting the "deep commitment" to trial by jury to "serious criminal cases," [*] there is no such support for a similar limitation on the right to assistance of counsel ....

The Sixth Amendment thus extended the right to counsel beyond its common-law dimensions. But there is nothing in the language of the Amendment, its history, or in the decisions of this Court, to indicate that it was intended to embody a retraction of the right in petty offenses wherein the common law previously did require that counsel be provided. ...

We reject, therefore, the premise that since prosecutions for crimes punishable by imprisonment for less than six months may be tried without a jury, they may also be tried without a lawyer.

The assistance of counsel is often a requisite to the very existence of a fair trial. ...

In Gideon v. Wainwright, supra (overruling Betts v. Brady, 316 U.S. 455), we dealt with a felony trial. But we did not so limit the need of the accused for a lawyer. ...

Both *Powell* and *Gideon* involved felonies. But their rationale has relevance to any criminal trial, where an accused is deprived of his liberty. *Powell* and *Gideon* suggest that there are certain

[*] Duncan v. Louisiana, 391 U.S. 145, 156 (1968).

fundamental rights applicable to all such criminal prosecutions, even those, such as In re Oliver, supra, where the penalty is 60 days' imprisonment . . . .

The requirement of counsel may well be necessary for a fair trial even in a petty-offense prosecution. We are by no means convinced that legal and constitutional questions involved in a case that actually leads to imprisonment even for a brief period are any less complex than when a person can be sent off for six months or more. . . .

The trial of vagrancy cases is illustrative. While only brief sentences of imprisonment may be imposed, the cases often bristle with thorny constitutional questions. . . .

In re Gault, 387 U.S. 1, dealt with juvenile delinquency and an offense which, if committed by an adult, would have carried a fine of $5 to $50 or imprisonment in jail for not more than two months (id., at 29), but which when committed by a juvenile might lead to his detention in a state institution until he reached the age of 21. Id., at 36–37. We said (id., at 36) that "[t]he juvenile needs the assistance of counsel to cope with problems of law, to make skilled inquiry into the facts, to insist upon regularity of the proceedings, and to ascertain whether he has a defense and to prepare and submit it. The child 'requires the guiding hand of counsel at every step in the proceedings against him,' " citing Powell v. Alabama, 287 U.S., at 69. The premise of *Gault* is that even in prosecutions for offenses less serious than felonies, a fair trial may require the presence of a lawyer.

Beyond the problem of trials and appeals is that of the guilty plea, a problem which looms large in misdemeanor as well as in felony cases. Counsel is needed so that the accused may know precisely what he is doing, so that he is fully aware of the prospect of going to jail or prison, and so that he is treated fairly by the prosecution.

In addition, the volume of misdemeanor cases,[4] far greater in number than felony prosecutions, may create an obsession for speedy dispositions, regardless of the fairness of the result. . . .

. . .

There is evidence of the prejudice which results to misdemeanor defendants from this "assembly-line justice." One study concluded that "[m]isdemeanants represented by attorneys are five times as likely to emerge from police court with all charges dis-

---

4. In 1965, 314,000 defendants were charged with felonies in state courts, and 24,000 were charged with felonies in federal courts. President's Commission on Law Enforcement and Administration of Justice, Task Force Report: The Courts 55 (1967). Exclusive of traffic offenses, however, it is estimated that there are annually between four and five million court cases involving misdemeanors. Id. And, while there are no authoritative figures, extrapolations indicate that there are probably between 40.8 and 50 million traffic offenses each year. Note, Dollars and Sense of an Expanded Right to Counsel, 55 Iowa L.Rev. 1249, 1261 (1970).

missed as are defendants who face similar charges without counsel."
American Civil Liberties Union, Legal Counsel for Misdemeanants,
Preliminary Report 1 (1970).

We must conclude, therefore, that the problems associated with
misdemeanor and petty offenses often require the presence of
counsel to insure the accused a fair trial. Mr. Justice Powell
suggests that these problems are raised even in situations where
there is no prospect of imprisonment. Post, at 48. We need not
consider the requirements of the Sixth Amendment as regards the
right to counsel where loss of liberty is not involved, however, for
here petitioner was in fact sentenced to jail. And, as we said in
Baldwin v. New York, 399 U.S., at 73, "the prospect of imprisonment for however short a time will seldom be viewed by the
accused as a trivial or 'petty' matter and may well result in quite
serious repercussions affecting his career and his reputation."

We hold, therefore, that absent a knowing and intelligent
waiver, no person may be imprisoned for any offense, whether
classified as petty, misdemeanor, or felony, unless he was represented by counsel at his trial.[7]

. . .

We do not sit as an ombudsman to direct state courts how to
manage their affairs but only to make clear the federal constitutional
requirement. How crimes should be classified is largely a state
matter. The fact that traffic charges technically fall within the
category of "criminal prosecutions" does not necessarily mean that
many of them will be brought into the class where imprisonment
actually occurs.

. . .

Under the rule we announce today, every judge will know
when the trial of a misdemeanor starts that no imprisonment may
be imposed, even though local law permits it, unless the accused is
represented by counsel. He will have a measure of the seriousness
and gravity of the offense and therefore know when to name a
lawyer to represent the accused before the trial starts.

The run of misdemeanors will not be affected by today's ruling.
But in those that end up in the actual deprivation of a person's
liberty, the accused will receive the benefit of "the guiding hand of
counsel" so necessary when one's liberty is in jeopardy.

7. We do not share Mr. Justice Powell's doubt that the Nation's legal resources are insufficient to implement the rule we announce today. It has been estimated that between 1,575 and 2,300 full-time counsel would be required to represent *all* indigent misdemeanants, excluding traffic offenders. Note, Dollars and Sense of an Expanded Right to Counsel, 55 Iowa L.Rev. 1249, 1260–1261 (1970). These figures are relative- ly insignificant when compared to the esti- mated 355,200 attorneys in the United States (Statistical Abstract of the United States 153 (1971)), a number which is projected to double by the year 1985. See Ruud, That Burgeon- ing Law School Enrollment, 58 A.B.A.J. 146, 147. Indeed, there are 18,000 new admis- sions to the bar each year—3,500 more law- yers than are required to fill the "estimated 14,500 average annual openings." Id., at 148.

Reversed.

MR. JUSTICE BRENNAN, with whom MR. JUSTICE DOUGLAS and MR. JUSTICE STEWART join, concurring.

I join the opinion of the Court and add only an observation upon its discussion of legal resources, ante, at 12, n. 7. Law students as well as practicing attorneys may provide an important source of legal representation for the indigent. The Council on Legal Education for Professional Responsibility (CLEPR) informs us that more than 125 of the country's 147 accredited law schools have established clinical programs in which faculty-supervised students aid clients in a variety of civil and criminal matters. ... These programs supplement practice rules enacted in 38 States authorizing students to practice law under prescribed conditions. ... Like the American Bar Association's Model Student Practice Rule (1969), most of these regulations permit students to make supervised court appearances as defense counsel in criminal cases. ... Given the huge increase in law school enrollments over the past few years, ... I think it plain that law students can be expected to make a significant contribution, quantitatively and qualitatively, to the representation of the poor in many areas, including cases reached by today's decision.

MR. JUSTICE POWELL, with whom MR. JUSTICE REHNQUIST joins, concurring in the result.

Gideon v. Wainwright, 372 U.S. 335 (1963), held that the States were required by the Due Process Clause of the Fourteenth Amendment to furnish counsel to all indigent defendants charged with felonies. The question before us today is whether an indigent defendant convicted of an offense carrying a maximum punishment of six months' imprisonment, a fine of $1,000, or both, and sentenced to 90 days in jail, is entitled as a matter of constitutional right to the assistance of appointed counsel. The broader question is whether the Due Process Clause requires that an indigent charged with a state petty offense be afforded the right to appointed counsel.

. . .

I am unable to agree with the Supreme Court of Florida that an indigent defendant, charged with a petty offense, may in every case be afforded a fair trial without the assistance of counsel. Nor can I agree with the new rule of due process, today enunciated by the Court, that "absent a knowing and intelligent waiver, no person may be imprisoned ... unless he was represented by counsel at his trial." Ante, at 25. It seems to me that the line should not be drawn with such rigidity.

There is a middle course, between the extremes of Florida's six-month rule and the Court's rule, which comports with the requirements of the Fourteenth Amendment. I would adhere to the principle of due process that requires fundamental fairness in criminal trials, a principle which I believe encompasses the right to counsel in petty cases whenever the assistance of counsel is necessary to assure a fair trial.

I

I am in accord with the Court that an indigent accused's need for the assistance of counsel does not mysteriously evaporate when he is charged with an offense punishable by six months or less. . . .

This is not to say that due process requires the appointment of counsel in all petty cases, or that assessment of the possible consequences of conviction is the sole test for the need for assistance of counsel. The flat six-month rule of the Florida court and the equally inflexible rule of the majority opinion apply to *all* cases within their defined areas regardless of circumstances. It is precisely because of this mechanistic application that I find these alternatives unsatisfactory. Due process, perhaps the most fundamental concept in our law, embodies principles of fairness rather than immutable line drawing as to every aspect of a criminal trial. While counsel is often essential to a fair trial, this is by no means a universal fact. Some petty offense cases are complex; others are exceedingly simple. As a justification for furnishing counsel to indigents accused of felonies, this Court noted, "That government hires lawyers to prosecute and defendants who have the money hire lawyers to defend are the strongest indications of the widespread belief that lawyers in criminal courts are necessities, not luxuries." [12] Yet government often does not hire lawyers to prosecute petty offenses; instead the arresting police officer presents the case. Nor does every defendant who can afford to do so hire lawyers to defend petty charges. Where the possibility of a jail sentence is remote and the probable fine seems small, or where the evidence of guilt is overwhelming, the costs of assistance of counsel may exceed the benefits. It is anomalous that the Court's opinion today will extend the right of appointed counsel to indigent defendants in cases where the right to counsel would rarely be exercised by nonindigent defendants.

Indeed, one of the effects of this ruling will be to favor defendants classified as indigents over those not so classified, yet who are in low-income groups where engaging counsel in a minor petty-offense case would be a luxury the family could not afford. The line between indigency and assumed capacity to pay for counsel is necessarily somewhat arbitrary, drawn differently from State to State and often resulting in serious inequities to accused persons. The Court's new rule will accent the disadvantage of being barely self-sufficient economically.

12. Gideon v. Wainwright, 372 U.S., at 344.

A survey of state courts in which misdemeanors are tried showed that procedures were often informal, presided over by lay judges. Jury trials were rare, and the prosecution was not vigorous. It is as inaccurate to say that no defendant can obtain a fair trial without the assistance of counsel in such courts as it is to say that no defendant needs the assistance of counsel if the offense charged is only a petty one.

Despite its overbreadth, the easiest solution would be a prophylactic rule that would require the appointment of counsel to indigents in all criminal cases. The simplicity of such a rule is appealing because it could be applied automatically in every case, but the price of pursuing this easy course could be high indeed in terms of its adverse impact on the administration of the criminal justice systems of 50 States. This is apparent when one reflects on the wide variety of petty or misdemeanor offenses, the varying definitions thereof, and the diversity of penalties prescribed. The potential impact on state court systems is also apparent in view of the variations in types of courts and their jurisdictions, ranging from justices of the peace and part-time judges in the small communities to the elaborately staffed police courts which operate 24 hours a day in the great metropolitan centers.

The rule adopted today does not go all the way. It is limited to petty offense cases in which the sentence is some imprisonment. The thrust of the Court's position indicates, however, that when the decision must be made, the rule will be extended to all petty offense cases except perhaps the most minor traffic violations. If the Court rejects on constitutional grounds, as it has today, the exercise of any judicial discretion as to need for counsel if a jail sentence is imposed, one must assume a similar rejection of discretion in other petty-offense cases. It would be illogical—and without discernible support in the Constitution—to hold that no discretion may ever be exercised where a nominal jail sentence is contemplated and at the same time endorse the legitimacy of discretion in "non-jail" petty offense cases which may result in far more serious consequences than a few hours or days of incarceration.

The Fifth and Fourteenth Amendments guarantee that property, as well as life and liberty, may not be taken from a person without affording him due process of law. The majority opinion suggests no constitutional basis for distinguishing between deprivations of liberty and property. In fact, the majority suggests no reason at all for drawing this distinction. The logic it advances for extending the right to counsel to all cases in which the penalty of any imprisonment is imposed applies equally well to cases in which other penalties may be imposed. Nor does the majority deny that some "non-jail" penalties are more serious than brief jail sentences.

Thus, although the new rule is extended today only to the imprisonment category of cases, the Court's opinion foreshadows the adoption of a broad prophylactic rule applicable to all petty offenses. No one can foresee the consequences of such a drastic enlargement of the constitutional right to free counsel. But even today's decision could have a seriously adverse impact upon the day-to-day functioning of the criminal justice system. We should be slow to fashion a new constitutional rule with consequences of such unknown dimensions, especially since it is supported neither by history nor precedent.

II

The majority opinion concludes that, absent a valid waiver, a person may not be imprisoned even for lesser offenses unless he was represented by counsel at the trial. In simplest terms this means that under no circumstances, in any court in the land, may anyone be imprisoned—however briefly—unless he was represented by or waived his right to counsel. The opinion is disquietingly barren of details as to how this rule will be implemented.

There are thousands of statutes and ordinances which authorize imprisonment for six months or less, usually as an alternative to a fine. These offenses include some of the most trivial of misdemeanors, ranging from spitting on the sidewalk to certain traffic offenses. They also include a variety of more serious misdemeanors. This broad spectrum of petty offense cases daily floods the lower criminal courts. The rule laid down today will confront the judges of each of these courts with an awkward dilemma. If counsel is not appointed or knowingly waived, no sentence of imprisonment for any duration may be imposed. The judge will therefore be forced to decide in advance of trial—and without hearing the evidence— whether he will forgo entirely his judicial discretion to impose some sentence of imprisonment and abandon his responsibility to consider the full range of punishments established by the legislature. His alternatives, assuming the availability of counsel, will be to appoint counsel and retain the discretion vested in him by law, or to abandon this discretion in advance and proceed without counsel.

If the latter course is followed, the first victim of the new rule is likely to be the concept that justice requires a personalized decision both as to guilt and the sentence. The notion that sentencing should be tailored to fit the crime and the individual would have to be abandoned in many categories of offenses. In resolving the dilemma as to how to administer the new rule, judges will be tempted arbitrarily to divide petty offenses into two categories— those for which sentences of imprisonment may be imposed and those in which no such sentence will be given regardless of the statutory authorization. In creating categories of offenses which by law are imprisonable but for which he would not impose jail sentences, a judge will be overruling *de facto* the legislative determination as to the appropriate range of punishment for the particular offense. It is true, as the majority notes, that there are some classes of imprisonable offenses for which imprisonment is rarely imposed. But even in these, the occasional imposition of such a sentence may serve a valuable deterrent purpose. At least the legislatures, and until today the courts, have viewed the threat of imprisonment—even when rarely carried out—as serving a legitimate social function.

In the brief for the United States as *amicus curiae,* the Solicitor General suggested that some flexibility could be preserved through the technique of trial *de novo* if the evidence—contrary to pretrial assumptions—justified a jail sentence. Presumably a mistrial would be declared, counsel appointed, and a new trial ordered. But the Solicitor General also recognized that a second trial, even with counsel, might be unfair if the prosecutor could make use of evidence which came out at the first trial when the accused was uncounseled. If the second trial were held before the same judge, he might no longer be open-minded. Finally, a second trial held for no other reason than to afford the judge an opportunity to impose a harsher sentence might run afoul of the guarantee against being twice placed in jeopardy for the same offense. In all likelihood, there will be no second trial and certain offenses classified by legislatures as imprisonable, will be treated by judges as unimprisonable.

The new rule announced today also could result in equal protection problems. There may well be an unfair and unequal treatment of individual defendants, depending on whether the individual judge has determined in advance to leave open the option of imprisonment. Thus, an accused indigent would be entitled in some courts to counsel while in other courts in the same jurisdiction an indigent accused of the same offense would have no counsel. Since the services of counsel may be essential to a fair trial even in cases in which no jail sentence is imposed, the results of this type of pretrial judgment could be arbitrary and discriminatory.

A different type of discrimination could result in the typical petty-offense case where judgment in the alternative is prescribed: for example, "five days in jail or $100 fine." If a judge has predetermined that no imprisonment will be imposed with respect to a particular category of cases, the indigent who is convicted will often receive no meaningful sentence. The defendant who can pay a $100 fine, and does so, will have responded to the sentence in accordance with law, whereas the indigent who commits the identical offense may pay no penalty. Nor would there be any deterrent against the repetition of similar offenses by indigents.[17]

---

17. The type of penalty discussed above (involving the discretionary alternative of "jail or fine") presents serious problems of fairness—both to indigents and nonindigents and to the administration of justice. ... No adequate resolution of these inherently difficult problems has yet been found. The rule adopted by the Court today, depriving the lower courts of all discretion in such cases unless counsel is available and is appointed, could aggravate the problem.

To avoid these equal protection problems and to preserve a range of sentencing options as prescribed by law, most judges are likely to appoint counsel for indigents in all but the most minor offenses where jail sentences are extremely rare. It is doubtful that the States possess the necessary resources to meet this sudden expansion of the right to counsel. The Solicitor General, who suggested on behalf of the United States the rule the Court today adopts, recognized that the consequences could be far reaching. In addition to the expense of compensating counsel, he noted that the mandatory requirement of defense counsel will "require more pre-trial time of prosecutors, more courtroom time, and this will lead to bigger backlogs with present personnel. Court reporters will be needed as well as counsel, and they are one of our worst bottle-necks." [18]

After emphasizing that the new constitutional rule should not be made retroactive, the Solicitor General commented on the "chaos" which could result from any mandatory requirement of counsel in misdemeanor cases:

> "[I]f ... this Court's decision should become fully applicable on the day it is announced, there could be a massive pileup in the state courts which do not now meet this standard. This would involve delays and frustrations which would not be a real contribution to the administration of justice." [19]

The degree of the Solicitor General's concern is reflected by his admittedly unique suggestion regarding the extraordinary demand for counsel which would result from the new rule. Recognizing implicitly that, in many sections of the country, there simply will not be enough lawyers available to meet this demand either in the short or long term, the Solicitor General speculated whether "clergymen, social workers, probation officers, and other persons of that type" could be used "as counsel in certain types of cases involving relatively small sentences." [20] Quite apart from the practical and political problem of amending the laws of each of the 50 States which require a license to practice law, it is difficult to square this suggestion with the meaning of the term "assistance of counsel" long recognized in our law.

The majority's treatment of the consequences of the new rule which so concerned the Solicitor General is not reassuring. In a footnote, it is said that there are presently 355,200 attorneys and that the number will increase rapidly, doubling by 1985. This is asserted to be sufficient to provide the number of full-time counsel, estimated by one source at between 1,575 and 2,300, to represent all indigent misdemeanants, excluding traffic offenders. It is totally unrealistic to imply that 355,200 lawyers are potentially available. Thousands of these are not in practice, and many of those who do

---

18. Tr. of Oral Arg. 34–35.   **20.** Id., at 39.
19. Id., at 36–37.

practice work for governments, corporate legal departments, or the Armed Services and are unavailable for criminal representation. Of those in general practice, we have no indication how many are qualified to defend criminal cases or willing to accept assignments which may prove less than lucrative for most.

It is similarly unrealistic to suggest that implementation of the Court's new rule will require no more than 1,575 to 2,300 "full-time" lawyers. In few communities are there full-time public defenders available for or private lawyers specializing in petty cases. Thus, if it were possible at all, it would be necessary to coordinate the schedules of those lawyers who are willing to take an occasional misdemeanor appointment with the crowded calendars of lower courts in which cases are not scheduled weeks in advance but instead are frequently tried the day after arrest. Finally, the majority's focus on aggregate figures ignores the heart of the problem, which is the distribution and availability of lawyers, especially in the hundreds of small localities across the country.

Perhaps the most serious potential impact of today's holding will be on our already overburdened local courts. The primary cause of "assembly line" justice is a volume of cases far in excess of the capacity of the system to handle efficiently and fairly. The Court's rule may well exacerbate delay and congestion in these courts. We are familiar with the common tactic of counsel of exhausting every possible legal avenue, often without due regard to its probable payoff. In some cases this may be the lawyer's duty; in other cases it will be done for purposes of delay. The absence of direct economic impact on the client, plus the omnipresent ineffective-assistance-of-counsel claim, frequently produces a decision to litigate every issue. It is likely that young lawyers, fresh out of law school, will receive most of the appointments in petty offense cases. The admirable zeal of these lawyers; their eagerness to make a reputation; the time their not yet crowded schedules permit them to devote to relatively minor legal problems; their desire for courtroom exposure; the availability in some cases of hourly fees, lucrative to the novice; and the recent constitutional explosion in procedural rights for the accused—all these factors are likely to result in the stretching out of the process with consequent increased costs to the public and added delay and congestion in the courts.

There is an additional problem. The ability of various States and localities to furnish counsel varies widely. Even if there were adequate resources on a national basis, the uneven distribution of these resources—of lawyers, of facilities, and available funding—presents the most acute problem. A number of state courts have considered the question before the Court in this case, and have been compelled to confront these realities. Many have concluded that the indigent's right to appointed counsel does not extend to all misdemeanor cases. In reaching this conclusion, the state courts have drawn the right-to-counsel line in different places, and most have acknowledged that they were moved to do so, at least in part, by the impracticality of going further. In other States, legislatures and courts through the enactment of laws or rules have drawn the line short of that adopted by the majority. These cases and statutes reflect the judgment of the courts and legislatures of many States, which understand the problems of local judicial systems better than this Court, that the rule announced by the Court today may seriously overtax capabilities.

The papers filed in a recent petition to this Court for a writ of certiorari serve as an example of what today's ruling will mean in some localities. In November 1971 the petition in Wright v. Town of Wood, No. 71–5722, was filed with this Court. The case, arising out of a South Dakota police magistrate court conviction for the municipal offense of public intoxication, raises the same issues before us in this case. The Court requested that the town of Wood file a response. On March 8, 1972, a lawyer occasionally employed by the town filed with the clerk an affidavit explaining why the town had not responded. He explained that Wood, South Dakota, has a population of 132, that it has no sewer or water system and is quite poor, that the office of the nearest lawyer is in a town 40 miles away, and that the town had decided that contesting this case would be an unwise allocation of its limited resources.

Though undoubtedly smaller than most, Wood is not dissimilar to hundreds of communities in the United States with no or very few lawyers, with meager financial resources, but with the need to have some sort of local court system to deal with minor offenses. It is quite common for the more numerous petty offenses in such towns to be tried by local courts or magistrates while the more serious offenses are tried in a county-wide court located in the county seat. It is undoubtedly true that some injustices result from the informal procedures of these local courts when counsel is not furnished; certainly counsel should be furnished to some indigents in some cases. But to require that counsel be furnished virtually every indigent charged with an imprisonable offense would be a practical impossibility for many small town courts. The community could simply not enforce its own laws.

Perhaps it will be said that I give undue weight both to the likelihood of short-term "chaos" and to the possibility of long-term adverse effects on the system. The answer may be given that if the Constitution requires the rule announced by the majority, the consequences are immaterial. If I were satisfied that the guarantee of due process required the assistance of counsel in every case in which a jail sentence is imposed or that the only workable method of insuring justice is to adopt the majority's rule, I would not hesitate to join the Court's opinion despite my misgivings as to its effect upon the administration of justice. But in addition to the resulting problems of availability of counsel, of costs, and especially of intolerable delay in an already overburdened system, the majority's drawing of a new inflexible rule may raise more Fourteenth Amendment problems than it resolves. Although the Court's opinion does not deal explicitly with any sentence other than deprivation of liberty however brief, the according of special constitutional status to cases where such a sentence is imposed may derogate from the need for counsel in other types of cases, unless the Court embraces an even broader prophylactic rule. Due process requires a fair trial in all cases. Neither the six-month rule approved below nor the rule today enunciated by the Court is likely to achieve this result.

III

I would hold that the right to counsel in petty offense cases is not absolute but is one to be determined by the trial courts exercising a judicial discretion on a case-by-case basis. The determination should be made before the accused formally pleads; many petty cases are resolved by guilty pleas in which the assistance of counsel may be required. If the trial court should conclude that the assistance of counsel is not required in any case, it should state its reasons so that the issue could be preserved for review. The trial court would then become obligated to scrutinize carefully the subsequent proceedings for the protection of the defendant. If an unrepresented defendant sought to enter a plea of guilty, the Court should examine the case against him to insure that there is admissible evidence tending to support the elements of the offense. If a case went to trial without defense counsel, the court should intervene, when necessary, to insure that the defendant adequately brings out the facts in his favor and to prevent legal issues from being overlooked. Formal trial rules should not be applied strictly against unrepresented defendants. Finally, appellate courts should carefully scrutinize all decisions not to appoint counsel and the proceedings which follow.

It is impossible, as well as unwise, to create a precise and detailed set of guidelines for judges to follow in determining whether the appointment of counsel is necessary to assure a fair trial. Certainly three general factors should be weighed. First, the court should consider the complexity of the offense charged. For example, charges of traffic law infractions would rarely present complex legal or factual questions, but charges that contain difficult intent elements or which raise collateral legal questions, such as search-and-seizure problems, would usually be too complex for an unassisted layman. If the offense were one where the State is represented by counsel and where most defendants who can afford to do so obtain counsel, there would be a strong indication that the indigent also needs the assistance of counsel.

Second, the court should consider the probable sentence that will follow if a conviction is obtained. The more serious the likely consequences, the greater is the probability that a lawyer should be appointed. As noted in Part I above, imprisonment is not the only serious consequence the court should consider.

Third, the court should consider the individual factors peculiar to each case. These, of course, would be the most difficult to anticipate. One relevant factor would be the competency of the individual defendant to present his own case. The attitude of the community toward a particular defendant or particular incident would be another consideration. But there might be other reasons why a defendant would have a peculiar need for a lawyer which would compel the appointment of counsel in a case where the court would normally think this unnecessary. Obviously, the sensitivity and diligence of individual judges would be crucial to the operation of a rule of fundamental fairness requiring the consideration of the varying factors in each case.

Such a rule is similar in certain respects to the special-circumstances rule applied to felony cases in Betts v. Brady, 316 U.S. 455 (1942) ... which this Court overruled in *Gideon.* One of the reasons for seeking a more definitive standard in felony cases was the failure of many state courts to live up to their responsibilities in determining on a case-by-case basis whether counsel should be appointed. ... But this Court should not assume that the past insensitivity of some state courts to the rights of defendants will continue. Certainly if the Court follows the course of reading rigid rules into the Constitution, so that the state courts will be unable to exercise judicial discretion within the limits of fundamental fairness, there is little reason to think that insensitivity will abate.

In concluding, I emphasize my long-held conviction that the adversary system functions best and most fairly only when all parties are represented by competent counsel. Before becoming a member of this Court, I participated in efforts to enlarge and extend the availability of counsel. The correct disposition of this case, therefore, has been a matter of considerable concern to me—as it has to the other members of the Court. We are all strongly drawn to the ideal of extending the right to counsel, but I differ as to two fundamentals: (i) what the Constitution *requires,* and (ii) the effect upon the criminal justice system, especially in the smaller cities and the thousands of police, municipal, and justice of the peace courts across the country.

The view I have expressed in this opinion would accord considerable discretion to the courts, and would allow the flexibility and opportunity for adjustment which seems so necessary when we are imposing new doctrine on the lowest level of courts of 50 States. Although this view would not precipitate the "chaos" predicted by the Solicitor General as the probable result of the Court's absolutist rule, there would still remain serious practical problems resulting from the expansion of indigents' rights to counsel in petty-offense cases. But the according of reviewable discretion to the courts in determining when counsel is necessary for a fair trial, rather than mandating a completely inflexible rule, would facilitate an orderly transition to a far wider availability and use of defense counsel.

In this process, the courts of first instance which decide these cases would have to recognize a duty to consider the need for counsel in every case where the defendant faces a significant penalty. The factors mentioned above, and such standards or guidelines to assure fairness as might be prescribed in each jurisdiction by legislation or rule of court, should be considered where relevant. The goal should be, in accord with the essence of the adversary system, to expand as rapidly as practicable the availability of counsel so that no person accused of crime must stand alone if counsel is needed.

As the proceedings in the courts below were not in accord with the views expressed above, I concur in the result of the decision in this case.[*] [**]

[*] Chief Justice Burger also wrote an opinion concurring in the result.

[**] In Scott v. Illinois, 440 U.S. 367 (1979) (5–4), the Court applied the rule of *Argersinger* to nonpetty offenses. The defendant in *Scott* was tried without counsel for theft (shoplifting), convicted, and sentenced to pay a fine of $50. The maximum statutory penalty for the offense was a fine of $500 or a year in prison or both. Affirming the conviction, the Court held that counsel need not be appointed in those circumstances.

ROSS v. MOFFITT

417 U.S. 600, 94 S.Ct. 2437, 41 L.Ed.2d 341 (1974).

MR. JUSTICE REHNQUIST delivered the opinion of the Court.

We are asked in this case to decide whether Douglas v. California, 372 U.S. 353 (1963), which requires appointment of counsel for indigent state defendants on their first appeal as of right, should be extended to require counsel for discretionary state appeals and for applications for review in this Court. The Court of Appeals for the Fourth Circuit held that such appointment was required by the Due Process and Equal Protection Clauses of the Fourteenth Amendment.[1]

I

The case now before us has resulted from consolidation of two separate cases, North Carolina criminal prosecutions brought in the respective circuit courts for the counties of Mecklenburg and Guilford. In both cases respondent pleaded not guilty to charges of forgery and uttering a forged instrument, and because of his indigency was represented at trial by court-appointed counsel. He then took separate appeals to the North Carolina Court of Appeals, where he was again represented by court-appointed counsel, and his convictions were affirmed. At this point the procedural histories of the two cases diverge.

Following affirmance of his Mecklenburg County conviction, respondent sought to invoke the discretionary review procedures of the North Carolina Supreme Court. His court-appointed counsel approached the Mecklenburg County Superior Court about possible appointment to represent respondent on this appeal, but counsel was informed that the State was not required to furnish counsel for that petition. Respondent sought collateral relief in both the state and federal courts, first raising his right to counsel contention in a habeas corpus petition filed in the United States District Court for the Western District of North Carolina in February 1971. Relief was denied at that time, and respondent's appeal to the Court of Appeals for the Fourth Circuit was dismissed by stipulation in order to allow respondent to first exhaust state remedies on this issue. After exhausting state remedies, he reapplied for habeas relief, which was again denied. Respondent appealed that denial to the Court of Appeals for the Fourth Circuit.

Following his conviction on the Guilford County charges, respondent also sought discretionary review in the North Carolina

1. Moffitt v. Ross, 483 F.2d 650 (1973).

Supreme Court. On this appeal, however, respondent was not denied counsel but rather was represented by the public defender who had been appointed for the trial and respondent's first appeal. The North Carolina Supreme Court denied certiorari. Respondent then unsuccessfully petitioned the Superior Court for Guilford County for court-appointed counsel to prepare a writ of certiorari to this Court, and also sought post-conviction relief throughout the state courts. After these motions were denied, respondent again sought federal habeas relief, this time in the United States District Court for the Middle District of North Carolina. That court denied relief, and respondent took an appeal to the Court of Appeals for the Fourth Circuit.

The Court of Appeals reversed the two District Court judgments, holding that respondent was entitled to the assistance of counsel at state expense both on his petition for review in the North Carolina Supreme Court and on his petition for certiorari in this Court. Reviewing the procedures of the North Carolina appellate system and the possible benefits that counsel would provide for indigents seeking review in that system, the court stated:

> "As long as the state provides such procedures and allows other convicted felons to seek access to the higher court with the help of retained counsel, there is a marked absence of fairness in denying an indigent the assistance of counsel as he seeks access to the same court." [4]

This principle was held equally applicable to petitions for certiorari in this Court. For, said the Court of Appeals, "[t]he same concepts of fairness and equality, which require counsel in a first appeal of right, require counsel in other and subsequent discretionary appeals." [5]

We granted certiorari, 414 U.S. 1128, to consider the Court of Appeals' decision in light of Douglas v. California, supra, and apparently conflicting decisions of the Courts of Appeals for the Seventh and Tenth Circuits. For the reasons hereafter stated we reverse the Court of Appeals.

II

This Court, in the past 20 years, has given extensive consideration to the rights of indigent persons on appeal. In Griffin v. Illinois, 351 U.S. 12 (1956), the first of the pertinent cases, the Court had before it an Illinois rule allowing a convicted criminal defendant to present claims of trial error to the Supreme Court of Illinois only if he procured a transcript of the testimony adduced at his trial. No exception was made for the indigent defendant, and thus one who was unable to pay the cost of obtaining such a

4. 483 F.2d, at 654.   5. 483 F.2d, at 655. ...

transcript was precluded from obtaining appellate review of asserted trial error. ...

The Court in *Griffin* held that this discrimination violated the Fourteenth Amendment.

Succeeding cases invalidated similar financial barriers to the appellate process, at the same time reaffirming the traditional principle that a State is not obliged to provide any appeal at all for criminal defendants. ... The cases encompassed a variety of circumstances but all had a common theme. For example, Lane v. Brown, 372 U.S. 477 (1963), involved an Indiana provision declaring that only a public defender could obtain a free transcript of a hearing on a *coram nobis* application. If the public defender declined to request one, the indigent prisoner seeking to appeal had no recourse. In Draper v. Washington, 372 U.S. 487 (1963), the State permitted an indigent to obtain a free transcript of the trial at which he was convicted only if he satisfied the trial judge that his contentions on appeal would not be frivolous. The appealing defendant was in effect bound by the trial court's conclusions in seeking to review the determination of frivolousness, since no transcript or its equivalent was made available to him. In Smith v. Bennett, 365 U.S. 708 (1961), Iowa had required a filing fee in order to process a state habeas corpus application by a convicted defendant, and in Burns v. Ohio, 360 U.S. 252 (1959), the State of Ohio required a $20 filing fee in order to move the Supreme Court of Ohio for leave to appeal from a judgment of the Ohio Court of Appeals affirming a criminal conviction. Each of these state-imposed financial barriers to the adjudication of a criminal defendant's appeal was held to violate the Fourteenth Amendment.

These decisions discussed above stand for the proposition that a State cannot arbitrarily cut off appeal rights for indigents while leaving open avenues of appeal for more affluent persons. In Douglas v. California, 372 U.S. 353 (1963), however, a case decided the same day as *Lane* and *Draper,* supra, the Court departed somewhat from the limited doctrine of the transcript and fee cases and undertook an examination of whether an indigent's access to the appellate system was adequate. The Court in *Douglas* concluded that a State does not fulfill its responsibility towards indigent defendants merely by waiving its own requirements that a convicted defendant procure a transcript or pay a fee in order to appeal, and held that the State must go further and provide counsel for the indigent on his first appeal as of right. It is this decision we are asked to extend today.

. . .

This Court held unconstitutional California's requirement that counsel on appeal would be appointed for an indigent only if the appellate court determined that such appointment would be helpful to the defendant or to the court itself. The Court noted that under this system an indigent's case was initially reviewed on the merits without the benefit of any organization or argument by counsel. By contrast, persons of greater means were not faced with the preliminary "*ex parte* examination of the record," 372 U.S., at 356, but had their arguments presented to the Court in fully briefed form. The Court noted, however, that its decision extended only to initial appeals as of right . . . .

The precise rationale for the *Griffin* and *Douglas* lines of cases has never been explicitly stated, some support being derived from the Equal Protection Clause of the Fourteenth Amendment, and some from the Due Process Clause of that Amendment. Neither clause by itself provides an entirely satisfactory basis for the result reached, each depending on a different inquiry which emphasizes different factors. "Due process" emphasizes fairness between the State and the individual dealing with the State, regardless of how other individuals in the same situation may be treated. "Equal protection," on the other hand, emphasizes disparity in treatment by a State between classes of individuals whose situations are arguably indistinguishable. We will address these issues separately in the succeeding sections.

III

Recognition of the due process rationale in *Douglas* is found both in the Court's opinion and in the dissenting opinion of Mr. Justice Harlan. . . .

We do not believe that the Due Process Clause requires North Carolina to provide respondent with counsel on his discretionary appeal to the State Supreme Court. At the trial stage of a criminal proceeding, the right of an indigent defendant to counsel at his trial is fundamental and binding upon the States by virtue of the Sixth and Fourteenth Amendments. Gideon v. Wainwright, 372 U.S. 335 (1963). But there are significant differences between the trial and appellate stages of a criminal proceeding. The purpose of the trial stage from the State's point of view is to convert a criminal defendant from a person presumed innocent to one found guilty beyond a reasonable doubt. To accomplish this purpose, the State employs a prosecuting attorney who presents evidence to the court, challenges any witnesses offered by the defendant, argues rulings of the court, and makes direct arguments to the court or jury seeking to persuade them of the defendant's guilt. Under these circumstances ". . . reason and reflection require us to recognize that in our adversary system of criminal justice, any person haled into court, who is too poor to hire a lawyer, cannot be assured a fair trial unless counsel is provided for him." Gideon v. Wainwright, 372 U.S., at 344.

By contrast, it is ordinarily the defendant, rather than the State, who initiates the appellate process, seeking not to fend off the efforts of the State's prosecutor but rather to overturn a finding of guilt made by a judge or jury below. The defendant needs an attorney on appeal not as a shield to protect him against being "haled into court" by the State and stripped of his presumption of innocence, but rather as a sword to upset the prior determination of guilt. This difference is significant for, while no one would agree that the State may simply dispense with the trial stage of proceedings without a criminal defendant's consent, it is clear that the State need not provide any appeal at all. . . . The fact that an appeal *has* been provided does not automatically mean that a State then acts unfairly by refusing to provide counsel to indigent defendants at every stage of the way. . . . Unfairness results only if indigents are singled out by the State and denied meaningful access to that system because of their poverty. That question is more profitably considered under an equal protection analysis.

IV

Language invoking equal protection notions is prominent both in *Douglas* and in other cases treating the rights of indigents on appeal. . . .

Despite the tendency of all rights "to declare themselves absolute to their logical extreme," [9] there are obviously limits beyond which the equal protection analysis may not be pressed without doing violence to principles recognized in other decisions of this Court. The Fourteenth Amendment "does not require absolute equality or precisely equal advantages," San Antonio Independent School District v. Rodriquez, 411 U.S. 1, 24 (1973), nor does it require the State to "equalize economic conditions." Griffin v. Illinois, supra, at 23 (Frankfurter, J., concurring). It does require that the state appellate system be "free of unreasoned distinctions," Rinaldi v. Yaeger, 384 U.S. 305, 310 (1966), and that indigents have an adequate opportunity to present their claims fairly within the adversarial system. . . . The State cannot adopt procedures which leave an indigent defendant "entirely cut off from any appeal at all," by virtue of his indigency, Lane v. Brown, supra, at 481, or extend to such indigent defendants merely a "meaningless ritual" while others in better economic circumstances have a "meaningful appeal." Douglas v. California, supra, at 358. The question is not one of absolutes, but one of degrees. In this case we do not believe that the Equal Protection Clause, when interpreted in the context of these cases, requires North Carolina to provide free counsel for indigent defendants seeking to take discretionary appeals to the North Carolina Supreme Court, or to file petitions for certiorari in this Court.

A. The North Carolina appellate system, as are the appellate systems of almost half the States, is multi-tiered, providing for both an intermediate Court of Appeals and a Supreme Court. The Court

9. Hudson Water Co. v. McCarter, 209 U.S. 349, 355 (1908).

of Appeals was created effective January 1, 1967, and, like other state courts of appeals, was intended to absorb a substantial share of the case load previously burdening the Supreme Court. In criminal cases, an appeal as of right lies directly to the Supreme Court in all cases which involve a sentence of death or life imprisonment, while an appeal of right in all other criminal cases lies to the Court of Appeals. N.C.Gen.Stat. § 7A–27. A second appeal of right lies to the Supreme Court in any criminal case "(1) [w]hich directly involves a substantial question arising under the Constitution of the United States or of this State, or (2) [i]n which there is a dissent. . . ." N.C.Rev.Stat. § 7A–30. All other decisions of the Court of Appeals on direct review of criminal cases may be further reviewed in the Supreme Court on a discretionary basis.

The statute governing discretionary appeals to the Supreme Court is N.C.Rev.Stat. § 7A–31. This statute provides, in relevant part, that "[i]n any cause in which appeal has been taken to the Court of Appeals . . . the Supreme Court may in its discretion, on motion of any party to the cause or on its own motion, certify the cause for review by the Supreme Court, either before or after it has been determined by the Court of Appeals." The statute further provides that "[i]f the cause is certified for transfer to the Supreme Court after its determination by the Court of Appeals, the Supreme Court reviews the decision of the Court of Appeals." The choice of cases to be reviewed is not left entirely within the discretion of the Supreme Court but is regulated by statutory standards. Subsection (c) of this provision states:

> "In causes subject to certification under subsection (a) of this section, certification may be made by the Supreme Court after determination of the cause by the Court of Appeals when in the opinion of the Supreme Court (1) The subject matter of the appeal has significant public interest, or (2) The cause involves legal principles of major significance to the jurisprudence of the State, or (3) The decision of the Court of Appeals appears likely to be in conflict with a decision of the Supreme Court."

Appointment of counsel for indigents in North Carolina is governed by N.C.Rev.Stat. § 7A–450 et seq. These provisions, although perhaps on their face broad enough to cover appointments such as those respondent sought here, have generally been construed to limit the right to appointed counsel in criminal cases to direct appeals taken as of right. Thus North Carolina has followed the mandate of Douglas v. California, supra, and authorized appointment of counsel for a convicted defendant appealing to the intermediate court of appeals, but has not gone beyond *Douglas* to provide for appointment of counsel for a defendant who seeks either discretionary review in the Supreme Court of North Carolina or a writ of certiorari here.

B. The facts show that respondent, in connection with his
Mecklenburg County conviction, received the benefit of counsel in
examining the record of his trial and in preparing an appellate brief
on his behalf for the state Court of Appeals.   Thus, prior to his
seeking discretionary review in the State Supreme Court, his claims
"had once been presented by a lawyer and passed upon by an
appellate court."   Douglas v. California, supra, 372 U.S., at 356.
We do not believe that it can be said, therefore, that a defendant in
respondent's circumstances is denied meaningful access to the
North Carolina Supreme Court simply because the State does not
appoint counsel to aid him in seeking review in that court.   At that
stage he will have, at the very least, a transcript or other record of
trial proceedings, a brief on his behalf in the Court of Appeals
setting forth his claims of error, and in many cases an opinion by
the Court of Appeals disposing of his case.   These materials, supplemented by whatever submission respondent may make *pro se,*
would appear to provide the Supreme Court of North Carolina with
an adequate basis on which to base its decision to grant or deny
review.

We are fortified in this conclusion by our understanding of the
function served by discretionary review in the North Carolina Supreme Court.   The critical issue in that court, as we perceive it, is
not whether there has been "a correct adjudication of guilt" in
every individual case, see Griffin v. Illinois, supra, 351 U.S., at 18,
but rather whether "the subject matter of the appeal has significant
public interest," whether "the cause involves legal principles of
major significance to the jurisprudence of the state," or whether the
decision below is in probable conflict with a decision of the
Supreme Court.   The Supreme Court may deny certiorari even
though it believes that the decision of the Court of Appeals was
incorrect . . . since a decision which appears incorrect may nevertheless fail to satisfy any of the criteria discussed above.   Once a
defendant's claims of error are organized and presented in a lawyer-
like fashion to the Court of Appeals, the justices of the Supreme
Court of North Carolina who make the decision to grant or deny
discretionary review should be able to ascertain whether his case
satisfies the standards established by the legislature for such review.

This is not to say, of course, that a skilled lawyer, particularly
one trained in the somewhat arcane art of preparing petitions for
discretionary review, would not prove helpful to any litigant able to
employ him.   An indigent defendant seeking review in the Supreme
Court of North Carolina is therefore somewhat handicapped in
comparison with a wealthy defendant who has counsel assisting him
in every conceivable manner at every stage in the proceeding.   But
both the opportunity to have counsel prepare an initial brief in the
Court of Appeals and the nature of discretionary review in the
Supreme Court of North Carolina make this relative handicap far
less than the handicap borne by the indigent defendant denied

counsel on his initial appeal as of right in *Douglas*. And the fact that a particular service might be of benefit to an indigent defendant does not mean that the service is constitutionally required. The duty of the State under our cases is not to duplicate the legal arsenal that may be privately retained by a criminal defendant in a continuing effort to reverse his conviction, but only to assure the indigent defendant an adequate opportunity to present his claims fairly in the context of the State's appellate process. We think respondent was given that opportunity under the existing North Carolina system.

V

Much of the discussion in the preceding section is equally relevant to the question of whether a State must provide counsel for a defendant seeking review of his conviction in this Court. North Carolina will have provided counsel for a convicted defendant's only appeal as of right, and the brief prepared by that counsel together with one and perhaps two North Carolina appellate opinions will be available to this Court in order that it may decide whether or not to grant certiorari. This Court's review, much like that of the Supreme Court of North Carolina, is discretionary and depends on numerous factors other than the perceived correctness of the judgment we are asked to review.

There is also a significant difference between the source of the right to seek discretionary review in the Supreme Court of North Carolina and the source of the right to seek discretionary review in this Court. The former is conferred by the statutes of the State of North Carolina, but the latter is granted by statutes enacted by Congress. Thus the argument relied upon in the *Griffin* and *Douglas* cases, that the State having once created a right of appeal must give all persons an equal opportunity to enjoy the right, is by its terms inapplicable. The right to seek certiorari in this Court is not granted by any State, and exists by virtue of federal statute with or without the consent of the State whose judgment is sought to be reviewed.

The suggestion that a State is responsible for providing counsel to one petitioning this Court simply because it initiated the prosecution which led to the judgment sought to be reviewed is unsupported by either reason or authority. It would be quite as logical under the rationale of *Douglas* and *Griffin*, and indeed perhaps more so, to require that the Federal Government or this Court furnish and compensate counsel for petitioners who seek certiorari here to review state judgments of conviction. Yet this Court has followed a consistent policy of denying applications for appointment of counsel by persons seeking to file jurisdictional statements or petitions for certiorari in this Court. ... In the light of these authorities, it would be odd, indeed, to read the Fourteenth Amendment to impose such a requirement on the States, and we decline to do so.

VI

We do not mean by this opinion to in any way discourage those States which have, as a matter of legislative choice, made counsel available to convicted defendants at all stages of judicial review. Some States which might well choose to do so as a matter of legislative policy may conceivably find that other claims for public funds within or without the criminal justice system preclude the implementation of such a policy at the present time. North Carolina, for example, while it does not provide counsel to indigent defendants seeking discretionary review on appeal, does provide counsel for indigent prisoners in several situations where such appointments are not required by any constitutional decision of this Court. Our reading of the Fourteenth Amendment leaves these choices to the State, and respondent was denied no right secured by the Federal Constitution when North Carolina refused to provide counsel to aid him in obtaining discretionary appellate review.

The judgment of the Court of Appeals' holding to the contrary is

Reversed.

MR. JUSTICE DOUGLAS, with whom MR. JUSTICE BRENNAN and MR. JUSTICE MARSHALL concur, dissenting.

I would affirm the judgment below because I am in agreement with the opinion of Chief Judge Haynsworth for a unanimous panel in the Court of Appeals. *Moffit v. Ross,* 483 F.2d 650.

. . .

Judge Haynsworth could find "no logical basis for differentiation between appeals of right and permissive review procedures in the context of the Constitution and the right to counsel." 483 F.2d, at 653. More familiar with the functioning of the North Carolina criminal justice system than are we, he concluded that "in the context of constitutional questions arising in criminal prosecutions, permissive review in the state's highest court may be predictably the most meaningful review the conviction will receive." Ibid. The North Carolina Court of Appeals, for example, will be constrained in diverging from an earlier opinion of the State Supreme Court, even if subsequent developments have rendered the earlier Supreme Court decision suspect. "[T]he state's highest court remains the ultimate arbiter of the rights of its citizens." Ibid.

Judge Haynsworth also correctly observed that the indigent defendant, proceeding without counsel, is at a substantial disadvantage relative to wealthy defendants represented by counsel when he is forced to fend for himself in seeking discretionary review from the State Supreme Court or from this Court. It may well not be enough to allege error in the courts below in layman's terms; a more sophisticated approach may be demanded:

"An indigent defendant is as much in need of the assistance of a lawyer in preparing and filing a petition for certiorari as he is in the handling of an appeal as of right. In many appeals, an articulate defendant could file an effective brief by telling his story in simple language without legalisms, but the technical requirement for applications for writs of certiorari are hazards which one untrained in the law could hardly be expected to negotiate.

"'Certiorari proceedings constitute a highly specialized aspect of appellate work. The factors which [a court] deems important in connection with deciding whether to grant certiorari are certainly not within the normal knowledge of an indigent appellant. Boskey, The Right to Counsel in Appellate Proceedings, 45 Minn.L.Rev. 783, 797 (1961) (footnote omitted).'" 483 F.2d, at 653.

Furthermore, the lawyer who handled the first appeal in a case would be familiar with the facts and legal issues involved in the case. It would be a relatively easy matter for the attorney to apply his expertise in filing a petition for discretionary review to a higher court, or to advise his client that such a petition would have no chance of succeeding.

Douglas v. California [372 U.S. 353 (1963)], was grounded on concepts of fairness and equality. The right to discretionary review is a substantial one, and one where a lawyer can be of significant assistance to an indigent defendant. It was correctly perceived below that the "same concepts of fairness and equality which require counsel in a first appeal of right, require counsel in other and subsequent discretionary appeals." Id., at 655.

UNITED STATES v. CRONIC

466 U.S. 648, 104 S.Ct. 2039, 80 L.Ed.2d 657 (1984).

JUSTICE STEVENS delivered the opinion of the Court.

Respondent and two associates were indicted on mail fraud charges involving the transfer of over $9,400,000 in checks between banks in Tampa, Fla., and Norman, Okla., during a 4-month period in 1975. Shortly before the scheduled trial date, respondent's retained counsel withdrew. The court appointed a young lawyer with a real estate practice to represent respondent, but allowed him only 25 days for pretrial preparation, even though it had taken the Government over four and one-half years to investigate the case and it had reviewed thousands of documents during that investigation. The two codefendants agreed to testify for the Government; respondent was convicted on 11 of the 13 counts in the indictment and received a 25-year sentence.

The Court of Appeals reversed the conviction because it concluded that respondent did not "have the Assistance of Counsel for his defence" that is guaranteed by the Sixth Amendment to the Constitution. This conclusion was not supported by a determination that respondent's trial counsel had made any specified errors, that his actual performance had prejudiced the defense, or that he failed to exercise "the skill, judgment, and diligence of a reasonably competent defense attorney"; instead the conclusion rested on the premise that no such showing is necessary "when circumstances hamper a given lawyer's preparation of a defendant's case." [2] The question presented by the Government's petition for certiorari is whether the Court of Appeals has correctly interpreted the Sixth Amendment.

I

The indictment alleged a "check kiting" scheme. At the direction of respondent, his codefendant Cummings opened a bank account in the name of Skyproof Manufacturing, Inc. (Skyproof), at a bank in Tampa, Fla., and codefendant Merritt opened two accounts, one in his own name and one in the name of Skyproof, at banks in Norman, Okla. Knowing that there were insufficient funds in either account, the defendants allegedly drew a series of checks and wire transfers on the Tampa account aggregating $4,841,073.95, all of which were deposited in Skyproof's Norman bank account during the period between June 23, 1975, and October 16, 1975; during approximately the same period they drew checks on Sky-

2. 675 F.2d 1126, 1128 (CA10 1982).

596

proof's Norman account for deposits in Tampa aggregating $4,600,881.39. The process of clearing the checks involved the use of the mails. By "kiting" insufficient funds checks between the banks in those two cities, defendants allegedly created false or inflated balances in the accounts. After outlining the overall scheme, Count I of the indictment alleged the mailing of two checks each for less than $1,000 early in May. Each of the additional 12 counts realleged the allegations in Count I except its reference to the two specific checks, and then added an allegation identifying other checks issued and mailed at later dates.

At trial the Government proved that Skyproof's checks were issued and deposited at the times and places, and in the amounts, described in the indictment. Having made plea bargains with defendants Cummings and Merritt, who had actually handled the issuance and delivery of the relevant written instruments, the Government proved through their testimony that respondent had conceived and directed the entire scheme, and that he had deliberately concealed his connection with Skyproof because of prior financial and tax problems.

After the District Court ruled that a prior conviction could be used to impeach his testimony, respondent decided not to testify. Counsel put on no defense. By cross-examination of Government witnesses, however, he established that Skyproof was not merely a sham, but actually was an operating company with a significant cash flow, though its revenues were not sufficient to justify as large a "float" as the record disclosed. Cross-examination also established the absence of written evidence that respondent had any control over Skyproof, or personally participated in the withdrawals or deposits.

The 4-day jury trial ended on July 17, 1980, and respondent was sentenced on August 28, 1980. His counsel perfected a timely appeal, which was docketed on September 11, 1980. Two months later respondent filed a motion to substitute a new attorney in the Court of Appeals, and also filed a motion in the District Court seeking to vacate his conviction on the ground that he had newly discovered evidence of perjury by officers of the Norman bank, and that the Government knew or should have known of that perjury. In that motion he also challenged the competence of his trial counsel. The District Court refused to entertain the motion while the appeal was pending. The Court of Appeals denied the motion to substitute the attorney designated by respondent, but did appoint still another attorney to handle the appeal. Later it allowed respondent's motion to supplement the record with material critical of trial counsel's performance.

The Court of Appeals reversed the conviction because it inferred that respondent's constitutional right to the effective assistance of counsel had been violated. That inference was based on its use of five criteria: " '(1) [T]he time afforded for investigation and preparation; (2) the experience of counsel; (3) the gravity of the charge; (4) the complexity of possible defenses; and (5) the accessibility of witnesses to counsel.' " 675 F.2d 1126, 1129 (CA10 1982) (quoting United States v. Golub, 638 F.2d 185, 189 (CA10 1980)). Under the test employed by the Court of Appeals, reversal is required even if the lawyer's actual performance was flawless. By utilizing this inferential approach, the Court of Appeals erred.

II

An accused's right to be represented by counsel is a fundamental component of our criminal justice system. Lawyers in criminal cases "are necessities, not luxuries." [7] Their presence is essential because they are the means through which the other rights of the person on trial are secured. Without counsel, the right to a trial itself would be "of little avail," [8] as this Court has recognized repeatedly. "Of all the rights that an accused person has, the right to be represented by counsel is by far the most pervasive, for it affects his ability to assert any other right he may have." [10]

The special value of the right to the assistance of counsel explains why "[i]t has long been recognized that the right to counsel is the right to the effective assistance of counsel." McMann v. Richardson, 397 U.S. 759, 771, n. 14 (1970). The text of the Sixth Amendment itself suggests as much. The Amendment requires not merely the provision of counsel to the accused, but "Assistance," which is to be "for his defence." Thus, "the core purpose of the counsel guarantee was to assure 'Assistance' at trial, when the accused was confronted with both the intricacies of the law and the advocacy of the public prosecutor." United States v. Ash, 413 U.S. 300, 309 (1973). If no actual "Assistance" "for" the accused's "defence" is provided, then the constitutional guarantee has been violated. To hold otherwise

> "could convert the appointment of counsel into a sham and nothing more than a formal compliance with the Constitution's requirement that an accused be given the assistance of counsel. The Constitution's guarantee of assistance of counsel cannot be satisfied by mere formal appointment." Avery v. Alabama, 308 U.S. 444, 446 (1940) (footnote omitted).

Thus, in *McMann* the Court indicated that the accused is entitled to "a reasonably competent attorney," 397 U.S., at 770, whose advice is "within the range of competence demanded of attorneys in criminal cases." Id., at 771. In Cuyler v. Sullivan, 446 U.S. 335 (1980), we held that the Constitution guarantees an

---

7. ... Gideon v. Wainwright, 372 U.S. 335, 344 (1963).

8. ... Powell v. Alabama, 287 U.S. 45 (1932) ....

10. Schaefer, Federalism and State Criminal Procedure, 70 Harv.L.Rev. 1, 8 (1956).

accused "adequate legal assistance." Id., at 344. And in Engle v. Isaac, 456 U.S. 107 (1982), the Court referred to the criminal defendant's constitutional guarantee of "a fair trial and a competent attorney." Id., at 134.

The substance of the Constitution's guarantee of the effective assistance of counsel is illuminated by reference to its underlying purpose. "[T]ruth," Lord Eldon said, "is best discovered by powerful statements on both sides of the question."[13] This dictim describes the unique strength of our system of criminal justice. "The very premise of our adversary system of criminal justice is that partisan advocacy on both sides of a case will best promote the ultimate objective that the guilty be convicted and the innocent go free." Herring v. New York, 422 U.S. 853, 862 (1975). It is that "very premise" that underlies and gives meaning to the Sixth Amendment. It "is meant to assure fairness in the adversary criminal process." United States v. Morrison, 449 U.S. 361, 364 (1981). Unless the accused receives the effective assistance of counsel, "a serious risk of injustice infects the trial itself." Culyer v. Sullivan, 446 U.S., at 343.

Thus, the adversarial process protected by the Sixth Amendment requires that the accused have "counsel acting in the role of an advocate." Anders v. California, 386 U.S. 738, 743 (1967). The right to the effective assistance of counsel is thus the right of the accused to require the prosecution's case to survive the crucible of meaningful adversarial testing. When a true adversarial criminal trial has been conducted—even if defense counsel may have made demonstrable errors—the kind of testing envisioned by the Sixth Amendment has occurred.[19] But if the process loses its character as a confrontation between adversaries, the constitutional guarantee is violated. As Judge Wyzanski has written: "While a criminal trial is not a game in which the participants are expected to enter the ring with a near match in skills, neither is it a sacrifice of unarmed prisoners to gladiators." United States ex rel. Williams v. Twomey, 510 F.2d 634, 640 (CA7), cert. denied sub nom. Sielaff v. Williams, 423 U.S. 876 (1975).[21]

13. Quoted in Kaufman, Does the Judge Have a Right to Qualified Counsel?, 61 A.B.A.J. 569, 569 (1975).

19. Of course, the Sixth Amendment does not require that counsel do what is impossible or unethical. If there is no *bona fide* defense to the charge, counsel cannot create one and may disserve the interests of his client by attempting a useless charade. ... At the same time, even when no theory of defense is available, if the decision to stand trial has been made, counsel must hold the prosecution to its heavy burden of proof beyond reasonable doubt. And, of course, even when there is a *bona fide* defense, counsel may still advise his client to plead guilty if that advice falls within the range of reasonable competence under the circumstances. ...

21. Thus, the appropriate inquiry focuses on the adversarial process, not on the accused's relationship with his lawyer as such. If counsel is a reasonably effective advocate, he meets constitutional standards irrespective of his client's evaluation of his performance. ... It is for this reason that we attach no weight to either respondent's expression of satisfaction with counsel's performance at the time of his trial, or to his later expression of dissatisfaction. ...

III

While the Court of Appeals purported to apply a standard of reasonable competence, it did not indicate that there had been an actual breakdown of the adversarial process during the trial of this case. Instead it concluded that the circumstances surrounding the representation of respondent mandated an inference that counsel was unable to discharge his duties.

In our evaluation of that conclusion, we begin by recognizing that the right to the effective assistance of counsel is recognized not for its own sake, but because of the effect it has on the ability of the accused to receive a fair trial. Absent some effect of challenged conduct on the reliability of the trial process, the Sixth Amendment guarantee is generally not implicated. ... Moreover, because we presume that the lawyer is competent to provide the guiding hand that the defendant needs ... the burden rests on the accused to demonstrate a constitutional violation. There are, however, circumstances that are so likely to prejudice the accused that the cost of litigating their effect in a particular case is unjustified.

Most obvious, of course, is the complete denial of counsel. The presumption that counsel's assistance is essential requires us to conclude that a trial is unfair if the accused is denied counsel at a critical stage of his trial. Similarly, if counsel entirely fails to subject the prosecution's case to meaningful adversarial testing, then there has been a denial of Sixth Amendment rights that makes the adversary process itself presumptively unreliable. No specific showing of prejudice was required in Davis v. Alaska, 415 U.S. 308 (1974), because the petitioner had been "denied the right of effective cross-examination" which " 'would be constitutional error of the first magnitude and no amount of showing of want of prejudice would cure it.' " Id., at 318 (citing Smith v. Illinois, 390 U.S. 129, 131 (1968), and Brookhart v. Janis, 384 U.S. 1, 3 (1966)).

Circumstances of that magnitude may be present on some occasions when although counsel is available to assist the accused during trial, the likelihood that any lawyer, even a fully competent one, could provide effective assistance is so small that a presumption of prejudice is appropriate without inquiry into the actual conduct of the trial. Powell v. Alabama, 287 U.S. 45 (1932), was such a case.

The defendants had been indicted for a highly publicized capital offense. Six days before trial, the trial judge appointed "all the members of the bar" for purposes of arraignment. "Whether they would represent the defendants thereafter if no counsel appeared in their behalf, was a matter of speculation only, or, as the judge indicated, of mere anticipation on the part of the court." Id., at 56. On the day of trial, a lawyer from Tennessee appeared on behalf of persons "interested" in the defendants, but stated that he had not had an opportunity to prepare the case or to familiarize himself with local procedure, and therefore was unwilling to represent the defendants on such short notice. The problem was resolved when the court decided that the Tennessee lawyer would represent the defendants, with whatever help the local bar could provide. ...

This Court held that "such designation of counsel as was attempted was either so indefinite or so close upon the trial as to amount to a denial of effective and substantial aid in that regard." Id., at 53. The Court did not examine the actual performance of counsel at trial, but instead concluded that under these circumstances the likelihood that counsel could have performed as an effective adversary was so remote as to have made the trial inherently unfair. *Powell* was thus a case in which the surrounding circumstances made it so unlikely that any lawyer could provide effective assistance that ineffectiveness was properly presumed without inquiry into actual performance at trial.

But every refusal to postpone a criminal trial will not give rise to such a presumption. In Avery v. Alabama, 308 U.S. 444 (1940), counsel was appointed in a capital case only three days before trial, and the trial court denied counsel's request for additional time to prepare. Nevertheless, the Court held that since evidence and witnesses were easily accessible to defense counsel, the circumstances did not make it unreasonable to expect that counsel could adequately prepare for trial during that period of time, id., at 450–453. Similarly, in Chambers v. Maroney, 399 U.S. 42 (1970), the Court refused "to fashion a *per se* rule requiring reversal of every conviction following tardy appointment of counsel." Id., at 54. Thus, only when surrounding circumstances justify a presumption of ineffectiveness can a Sixth Amendment claim be sufficient without inquiry into counsel's actual performance at trial.

The Court of Appeals did not find that respondent was denied the presence of counsel at a critical stage of the prosecution. Nor did it find, based on the actual conduct of the trial, that there was a breakdown in the adversarial process that would justify a presumption that respondent's conviction was insufficiently reliable to satisfy the Constitution. The dispositive question in this case therefore is whether the circumstances surrounding respondent's representation—and in particular the five criteria identified by the Court of Appeals—justified such a presumption.

IV

The five factors listed in the Court of Appeals' opinion are relevant to an evaluation of a lawyer's effectiveness in a particular case, but neither separately nor in combination do they provide a basis for concluding that competent counsel was not able to provide this respondent with the guiding hand that the Constitution guarantees.

Respondent places special stress on the disparity between the duration of the Government's investigation and the period the District Court allowed to newly appointed counsel for trial preparation. The lawyer was appointed to represent respondent on June 12, 1980, and on June 19, filed a written motion for a continuance of the trial that was then scheduled to begin on June 30. Although counsel contended that he needed at least 30 days for preparation, the District Court reset the trial for July 14—thus allowing 25 additional days for preparation.

Neither the period of time that the Government spent investigating the case, nor the number of documents that its agents reviewed during that investigation, is necessarily relevant to the question whether a competent lawyer could prepare to defend the case in 25 days. The Government's task of finding and assembling admissible evidence that will carry its burden of proving guilt beyond a reasonable doubt is entirely different from the defendant's task in preparing to deny or rebut a criminal charge. Of course, in some cases the rebuttal may be equally burdensome and time consuming, but there is no necessary correlation between the two. In this case, the time devoted by the Government to the assembly, organization, and summarization of the thousands of written records evidencing the two streams of checks flowing between the banks in Florida and Oklahoma unquestionably simplified the work of defense counsel in identifying and understanding the basic character of the defendants' scheme. When a series of repetitious transactions fit into a single mold, the number of written exhibits that are needed to define the pattern may be unrelated to the time that is needed to understand it.

The significance of counsel's preparation time is further reduced by the nature of the charges against respondent. Most of the Government's case consisted merely of establishing the transactions between the two banks. A competent attorney would have no reason to question the authenticity, accuracy, or relevance of this evidence—there could be no dispute that these transactions actually occurred. As respondent appears to recognize, the only *bona fide* jury issue open to competent defense counsel on these facts was whether respondent acted with intent to defraud. When there is no reason to dispute the underlying historical facts, the period of 25 days to consider the question whether those facts justify an inference of criminal intent is not so short that it even arguably justifies a presumption that no lawyer could provide the respondent with the effective assistance of counsel required by the Constitution.

That conclusion is not undermined by the fact that respondent's lawyer was young, that his principal practice was in real estate, or that this was his first jury trial. Every experienced criminal defense attorney once tried his first criminal case. Moreover, a lawyer's experience with real estate transactions might be more useful in preparing to try a criminal case involving financial transactions than would prior experience in handling, for example, armed robbery prosecutions. The character of a particular lawyer's experience may shed light in an evaluation of his actual performance, but it does not justify a presumption of ineffectiveness in the absence of such an evaluation.

The three other criteria—the gravity of the charge, the complexity of the case, and the accessibility of witnesses—are all matters that may affect what a reasonably competent attorney could be expected to have done under the circumstances, but none identifies circumstances that in themselves make it unlikely that respondent received the effective assistance of counsel.

V

This case is not one in which the surrounding circumstances make it unlikely that the defendant could have received the effective assistance of counsel. The criteria used by the Court of Appeals do not demonstrate that counsel failed to function in any meaningful sense as the Government's adversary. Respondent can therefore make out a claim of ineffective assistance only by pointing to specific errors made by trial counsel. In this Court, respondent's present counsel argues that the record would support such an attack, but we leave that claim—as well as the other alleged trial errors raised by respondent which were not passed upon by the Court of Appeals—for the consideration of the Court of Appeals on remand.

The judgment is reversed and the case is remanded for further proceedings consistent with this opinion.

It is so ordered.[*]

[*] Justice Marshall concurred in the judgment.

STRICKLAND v. WASHINGTON

466 U.S. 668, 104 S.Ct. 2052, 80 L.Ed.2d 674 (1984).

JUSTICE O'CONNOR delivered the opinion of the Court.

This case requires us to consider the proper standards for judging a criminal defendant's contention that the Constitution requires a conviction or death sentence to be set aside because counsel's assistance at the trial or sentencing was ineffective.

I

A

During a 10-day period in September 1976, respondent planned and committed three groups of crimes, which included three brutal stabbing murders, torture, kidnapping, severe assaults, attempted murders, attempted extortion, and theft. After his two accomplices were arrested, respondent surrendered to police and voluntarily gave a lengthy statement confessing to the third of the criminal episodes. The State of Florida indicted respondent for kidnapping and murder and appointed an experienced criminal lawyer to represent him.

Counsel actively pursued pretrial motions and discovery. He cut his efforts short, however, and he experienced a sense of hopelessness about the case, when he learned that, against his specific advice, respondent had also confessed to the first two murders. By the date set for trial, respondent was subject to indictment for three counts of first degree murder and multiple counts of robbery, kidnapping for ransom, breaking and entering and assault, attempted murder, and conspiracy to commit robbery. Respondent waived his right to a jury trial, again acting against counsel's advice, and pleaded guilty to all charges, including the three capital murder charges.

In the plea colloquy, respondent told the trial judge that, although he had committed a string of burglaries, he had no significant prior criminal record and that at the time of his criminal spree he was under extreme stress caused by his inability to support his family. ... He also stated, however, that he accepted responsibility for the crimes. ... The trial judge told respondent that he had "a great deal of respect for people who are willing to step forward and admit their responsibility" but that he was making no statement at all about his likely sentencing decision. [App.], at 62.

Counsel advised respondent to invoke his right under Florida law to an advisory jury at his capital sentencing hearing. Respondent rejected the advice and waived the right. He chose instead to be sentenced by the trial judge without a jury recommendation.

In preparing for the sentencing hearing, counsel spoke with respondent about his background. He also spoke on the telephone with respondent's wife and mother, though he did not follow up on the one unsuccessful effort to meet with them. He did not otherwise seek out character witnesses for respondent. ... Nor did he request a psychiatric examination, since his conversations with his client gave no indication that respondent had psychological problems. ...

Counsel decided not to present and hence not to look further for evidence concerning respondent's character and emotional state. That decision reflected trial counsel's sense of hopelessness about overcoming the evidentiary effect of respondent's confessions to the gruesome crimes. ... It also reflected the judgment that it was advisable to rely on the plea colloquy for evidence about respondent's background and about his claim of emotional stress: the plea colloquy communicated sufficient information about these subjects, and by foregoing the opportunity to present new evidence on these subjects, counsel prevented the State from cross-examining respondent on his claim and from putting on psychiatric evidence of its own. ...

Counsel also excluded from the sentencing hearing other evidence he thought was potentially damaging. He successfully moved to exclude respondent's "rap sheet." ... Because he judged that a presentence report might prove more detrimental than helpful, as it would have included respondent's criminal history and thereby undermined the claim of no significant history of criminal activity, he did not request that one be prepared. ...

At the sentencing hearing, counsel's strategy was based primarily on the trial judge's remarks at the plea colloquy as well as on his reputation as a sentencing judge who thought it important for a convicted defendant to own up to his crime. Counsel argued that respondent's remorse and acceptance of responsibility justified sparing him from the death penalty. ... Counsel also argued that respondent had no history of criminal activity and that respondent committed the crimes under extreme mental or emotional disturbance, thus coming within the statutory list of mitigating circumstances. He further argued that respondent should be spared death because he had surrendered, confessed, and offered to testify against a codefendant and because respondent was fundamentally a good person who had briefly gone badly wrong in extremely stressful circumstances. The State put on evidence and witnesses largely for the purpose of describing the details of the crimes. Counsel did not cross-examine the medical experts who testified about the manner of death of respondent's victims.

The trial judge found several aggravating circumstances with respect to each of the three murders. He found that all three murders were especially heinous, atrocious, and cruel, all involving repeated stabbings. All three murders were committed in the course of at least one other dangerous and violent felony, and since all involved robbery, the murders were for pecuniary gain. All three murders were committed to avoid arrest for the accompanying crimes and to hinder law enforcement. In the course of one of the murders, respondent knowingly subjected numerous persons to a grave risk of death by deliberately stabbing and shooting the murder victim's sisters-in-law, who sustained severe—in one case, ultimately fatal—injuries.

With respect to mitigating circumstances, the trial judge made the same findings for all three capital murders. First, although there was no admitted evidence of prior convictions, respondent had stated that he had engaged in a course of stealing. In any case, even if respondent had no significant history of criminal activity, the aggravating circumstances "would still clearly far outweigh" that mitigating factor. Second, the judge found that, during all three crimes, respondent was not suffering from extreme mental or emotional disturbance and could appreciate the criminality of his acts. Third, none of the victims was a participant in, or consented to, respondent's conduct. Fourth, respondent's participation in the crimes was neither minor nor the result of duress or domination by an accomplice. Finally, respondent's age (26) could not be considered a factor in mitigation, especially when viewed in light of respondent's planning of the crimes and disposition of the proceeds of the various accompanying thefts.

In short, the trial judge found numerous aggravating circumstances and no (or a single comparatively insignificant) mitigating circumstance. With respect to each of the three convictions for capital murder, the trial judge concluded: "A careful consideration of all matters presented to the court impels the conclusion that there are insufficient mitigating circumstances ... to outweigh the aggravating circumstances." See Washington v. State, 362 So.2d 658, 663–664 (Fla.1978) (quoting trial court findings), cert. denied, 441 U.S. 937 (1979). He therefore sentenced respondent to death on each of the three counts of murder and to prison terms for the other crimes. The Florida Supreme Court upheld the convictions and sentences on direct appeal.

B

Respondent subsequently sought collateral relief in state court on numerous grounds, among them that counsel had rendered ineffective assistance at the sentencing proceeding. Respondent challenged counsel's assistance in six respects. He asserted that counsel was ineffective because he failed to move for a continuance to prepare for sentencing, to request a psychiatric report, to investi-

gate and present character witnesses, to seek a presentence investigation report, to present meaningful arguments to the sentencing
judge, and to investigate the medical examiner's reports or cross-
examine the medical experts. In support of the claim, respondent
submitted 14 affidavits from friends, neighbors, and relatives stating
that they would have testified if asked to do so. He also submitted
one psychiatric report and one psychological report stating that
respondent, though not under the influence of extreme mental or
emotional disturbance, was "chronically frustrated and depressed
because of his economic dilemma" at the time of his crimes. App.
7 . . . .

The trial court denied relief without an evidentiary hearing,
finding that the record evidence conclusively showed that the
ineffectiveness claim was meritless. . . . Four of the assertedly
prejudicial errors required little discussion. First, there were no
grounds to request a continuance, so there was no error in not
requesting one when respondent pleaded guilty. . . . Second,
failure to request a presentence investigation was not a serious
error because the trial judge had discretion not to grant such a
request and because any presentence investigation would have
resulted in admission of respondent's "rap sheet" and thus undermined his assertion of no significant history of criminal activity. . . .
Third, the argument and memorandum given to the sentencing
judge were "admirable" in light of the overwhelming aggravating
circumstances and absence of mitigating circumstances. . . .
Fourth, there was no error in failure to examine the medical
examiner's reports or to cross-examine the medical witnesses testifying on the manner of death of respondent's victims, since respondent admitted that the victims died in the ways shown by the
unchallenged medical evidence. . . .

The trial court dealt at greater length with the two other bases
for the ineffectiveness claim. The court pointed out that a psychiatric examination of respondent was conducted by state order soon
after respondent's initial arraignment. That report states that there
was no indication of major mental illness at the time of the crimes.
Moreover, both the reports submitted in the collateral proceeding
state that, although respondent was "chronically frustrated and
depressed because of his economic dilemma," he was not under the
influence of extreme mental or emotional disturbance. All three
reports thus directly undermine the contention made at the sentencing hearing that respondent was suffering from extreme mental
or emotional disturbance during his crime spree. Accordingly,
counsel could reasonably decide not to seek psychiatric reports;
indeed, by relying solely on the plea colloquy to support the
emotional disturbance contention, counsel denied the State an
opportunity to rebut his claim with psychiatric testimony. In any
event, the aggravating circumstances were so overwhelming that no

substantial prejudice resulted from the absence at sentencing of the psychiatric evidence offered in the collateral attack.

The court rejected the challenge to counsel's failure to develop and to present character evidence for much the same reasons. The affidavits submitted in the collateral proceeding showed nothing more than that certain persons would have testified that respondent was basically a good person who was worried about his family's financial problems. Respondent himself had already testified along those lines at the plea colloquy. Moreover, respondent's admission of a course of stealing rebutted many of the factual allegations in the affidavits. For those reasons, and because the sentencing judge had stated that the death sentence would be appropriate even if respondent had no significant prior criminal history, no substantial prejudice resulted from the absence at sentencing of the character evidence offered in the collateral attack.

Applying the standard for ineffectiveness claims articulated by the Florida Supreme Court in Knight v. State, 394 So.2d 997 (1981), the trial court concluded that respondent had not shown that counsel's assistance reflected any substantial and serious deficiency measurably below that of competent counsel that was likely to have affected the outcome of the sentencing proceeding. The court specifically found: "[A]s a matter of law, the record affirmatively demonstrates beyond any doubt that even if [counsel] had done each of the ... things [that respondent alleged counsel had failed to do] at the time of sentencing, there is not even the remotest chance that the outcome would have been any different. The plain fact is that the aggravating circumstances proved in this case were completely *overwhelming.* ...." App. to Pet. for Cert. A230.

The Florida Supreme Court affirmed the denial of relief. Washington v. State, 397 So.2d 285 (1981). For essentially the reasons given by the trial court, the State Supreme Court concluded that respondent had failed to make out a prima facie case of either "substantial deficiency or possible prejudice" and, indeed, had "failed to such a degree that we believe, to the point of a moral certainty, that he is entitled to no relief. ...." Id., at 287. Respondent's claims were "shown conclusively to be without merit so as to obviate the need for an evidentiary hearing." Id., at 286.

[The Court's recital of subsequent proceedings for habeas corpus in the federal courts is omitted.]

II

In a long line of cases ... this Court has recognized that the Sixth Amendment right to counsel exists, and is needed, in order to protect the fundamental right to a fair trial. The Constitution guarantees a fair trial through the Due Process Clauses, but it defines the basic elements of a fair trial largely through the several

provisions of the Sixth Amendment, including the Counsel Clause
. . . .

Thus, a fair trial is one in which evidence subject to adversarial testing is presented to an impartial tribunal for resolution of issues defined in advance of the proceeding. The right to counsel plays a crucial role in the adversarial system embodied in the Sixth Amendment, since access to counsel's skill and knowledge is necessary to accord defendants the "ample opportunity to meet the case of the prosecution" to which they are entitled. Adams v. United States ex rel. McCann, 317 U.S. 269, 275, 276 (1942) . . . .

Because of the vital importance of counsel's assistance, this Court has held that, with certain exceptions, a person accused of a federal or state crime has the right to have counsel appointed if retained counsel cannot be obtained. . . . That a person who happens to be a lawyer is present at trial alongside the accused, however, is not enough to satisfy the constitutional command. The Sixth Amendment recognizes the right to the assistance of counsel because it envisions counsel's playing a role that is critical to the ability of the adversarial system to produce just results. An accused is entitled to be assisted by an attorney, whether retained or appointed, who plays the role necessary to ensure that the trial is fair.

For that reason, the Court has recognized that "the right to counsel is the right to the effective assistance of counsel." McMann v. Richardson, 397 U.S. 759, 771, n. 14 (1970). Government violates the right to effective assistance when it interferes in certain ways with the ability of counsel to make independent decisions about how to conduct the defense. . . . Counsel, however, can also deprive a defendant of the right to effective assistance, simply by failing to render "adequate legal assistance," Cuyler v. Sullivan, 446 U.S. [335 (1980)], at 344. Id., at 345–350 (actual conflict of interest adversely affecting lawyer's performance renders assistance ineffective).

The Court has not elaborated on the meaning of the constitutional requirement of effective assistance in the latter class of cases—that is, those presenting claims of "actual ineffectiveness." In giving meaning to the requirement, however, we must take its purpose—to ensure a fair trial—as the guide. The benchmark for judging any claim of ineffectiveness must be whether counsel's conduct so undermined the proper functioning of the adversarial process that the trial cannot be relied on as having produced a just result.

The same principle applies to a capital sentencing proceeding such as that provided by Florida law. We need not consider the role of counsel in an ordinary sentencing, which may involve informal proceedings and standardless discretion in the sentencer, and hence may require a different approach to the definition of constitutionally effective assistance. A capital sentencing proceeding like the one involved in this case, however, is sufficiently like a trial in its adversarial format and in the existence of standards for decision ... that counsel's role in the proceeding is comparable to counsel's role at trial—to ensure that the adversarial testing process works to produce a just result under the standards governing decision. For purposes of describing counsel's duties, therefore, Florida's capital sentencing proceeding need not be distinguished from an ordinary trial.

III

A convicted defendant's claim that counsel's assistance was so defective as to require reversal of a conviction or death sentence has two components. First, the defendant must show that counsel's performance was deficient. This requires showing that counsel made errors so serious that counsel was not functioning as the "counsel" guaranteed the defendant by the Sixth Amendment. Second, the defendant must show that the deficient performance prejudiced the defense. This requires showing that counsel's errors were so serious as to deprive the defendant of a fair trial, a trial whose result is reliable. Unless a defendant makes both showings, it cannot be said that the conviction or death sentence resulted from a breakdown in the adversary process that renders the result unreliable.

A

As all the Federal Courts of Appeals have now held, the proper standard for attorney performance is that of reasonably effective assistance. ... When a convicted defendant complains of the ineffectiveness of counsel's assistance, the defendant must show that counsel's representation fell below an objective standard of reasonableness.

More specific guidelines are not appropriate. The Sixth Amendment refers simply to "counsel," not specifying particular requirements of effective assistance. It relies instead on the legal profession's maintenance of standards sufficient to justify the law's presumption that counsel will fulfill the role in the adversary process that the Amendment envisions. ... The proper measure of attorney performance remains simply reasonableness under prevailing professional norms.

Representation of a criminal defendant entails certain basic duties. Counsel's function is to assist the defendant, and hence counsel owes the client a duty of loyalty, a duty to avoid conflicts of interest. ... From counsel's function as assistant to the defendant derive the overarching duty to advocate the defendant's cause and the more particular duties to consult with the defendant on important decisions and to keep the defendant informed of important developments in the course of the prosecution. Counsel also has a duty to bring to bear such skill and knowledge as will render the trial a reliable adversarial testing process. . . .

These basic duties neither exhaustively define the obligations of counsel nor form a checklist for judicial evaluation of attorney performance. In any case presenting an ineffectiveness claim, the performance inquiry must be whether counsel's assistance was reasonable considering all the circumstances. Prevailing norms of practice as reflected in American Bar Association standards and the like . . . are guides to determining what is reasonable, but they are only guides. No particular set of detailed rules for counsel's conduct can satisfactorily take account of the variety of circumstances faced by defense counsel or the range of legitimate decisions regarding how best to represent a criminal defendant. Any such set of rules would interfere with the constitutionally protected independence of counsel and restrict the wide latitude counsel must have in making tactical decisions. . . . Indeed, the existence of detailed guidelines for representation could distract counsel from the overriding mission of vigorous advocacy of the defendant's cause. Moreover, the purpose of the effective assistance guarantee of the Sixth Amendment is not to improve the quality of legal representation, although that is a goal of considerable importance to the legal system. The purpose is simply to ensure that criminal defendants receive a fair trial.

Judicial scrutiny of counsel's performance must be highly deferential. It is all too tempting for a defendant to second-guess counsel's assistance after conviction or adverse sentence, and it is all too easy for a court, examining counsel's defense after it has proved unsuccessful, to conclude that a particular act or omission of counsel was unreasonable. . . . A fair assessment of attorney performance requires that every effort be made to eliminate the distorting effects of hindsight, to reconstruct the circumstances of counsel's challenged conduct, and to evaluate the conduct from counsel's perspective at the time. Because of the difficulties inherent in making the evaluation, a court must indulge a strong presumption that counsel's conduct falls within the wide range of reasonable professional assistance; that is, the defendant must overcome the presumption that, under the circumstances, the challenged action "might be considered sound trial strategy." See Michel v. Louisiana [350 U.S. 91 (1955)], at 101. There are countless ways to provide effective assistance in any given case. Even the best criminal defense attorneys would not defend a particular client in the same way. . . .

The availability of intrusive post-trial inquiry into attorney performance or of detailed guidelines for its evaluation would encourage the proliferation of ineffectiveness challenges. Criminal trials resolved unfavorably to the defendant would increasingly come to be followed by a second trial, this one of counsel's unsuccessful defense. Counsel's performance and even willingness to serve could be adversely affected. Intensive scrutiny of counsel and rigid requirements for acceptable assistance could dampen the ardor and impair the independence of defense counsel, discourage the acceptance of assigned cases, and undermine the trust between attorney and client.

Thus, a court deciding an actual ineffectiveness claim must judge the reasonableness of counsel's challenged conduct on the facts of the particular case, viewed as of the time of counsel's conduct. A convicted defendant making a claim of ineffective assistance must identify the acts or omissions of counsel that are alleged not to have been the result of reasonable professional judgment. The court must then determine whether, in light of all the circumstances, the identified acts or omissions were outside the wide range of professionally competent assistance. In making that determination, the court should keep in mind that counsel's function, as elaborated in prevailing professional norms, is to make the adversarial testing process work in the particular case. At the same time, the court should recognize that counsel is strongly presumed to have rendered adequate assistance and made all significant decisions in the exercise of reasonable professional judgment.

These standards require no special amplification in order to define counsel's duty to investigate, the duty at issue in this case. ... [S]trategic choices made after thorough investigation of law and facts relevant to plausible options are virtually unchallengeable; and strategic choices made after less than complete investigation are reasonable precisely to the extent that reasonable professional judgments support the limitations on investigation. In other words, counsel has a duty to make reasonable investigations or to make a reasonable decision that makes particular investigations unnecessary. In any ineffectiveness case, a particular decision not to investigate must be directly assessed for reasonableness in all the circumstances, applying a heavy measure of deference to counsel's judgments.

The reasonableness of counsel's actions may be determined or substantially influenced by the defendant's own statements or actions. Counsel's actions are usually based, quite properly, on informed strategic choices made by the defendant and on information supplied by the defendant. In particular, what investigation decisions are reasonable depends critically on such information. For example, when the facts that support a certain potential line of defense are generally known to counsel because of what the defendant has said, the need for further investigation may be considerably diminished or eliminated altogether. And when a defendant has given counsel reason to believe that pursuing certain investigations would be fruitless or even harmful, counsel's failure to pursue those investigations may not later be challenged as unreasonable. In short, inquiry into counsel's conversations with the defendant may be critical to a proper assessment of counsel's investigation decisions, just as it may be critical to a proper assessment of counsel's other litigation decisions. ...

B

An error by counsel, even if professionally unreasonable, does not warrant setting aside the judgment of a criminal proceeding if the error had no effect on the judgment. ... The purpose of the Sixth Amendment guarantee of counsel is to ensure that a defendant has the assistance necessary to justify reliance on the outcome of the proceeding. Accordingly, any deficiencies in counsel's performance must be prejudicial to the defense in order to constitute ineffective assistance under the Constitution.

In certain Sixth Amendment contexts, prejudice is presumed. Actual or constructive denial of the assistance of counsel altogether is legally presumed to result in prejudice. So are various kinds of state interference with counsel's assistance. ... Prejudice in these circumstances is so likely that case by case inquiry into prejudice is not worth the cost. ... Moreover, such circumstances involve impairments of the Sixth Amendment right that are easy to identify and, for that reason and because the prosecution is directly responsible, easy for the government to prevent.

One type of actual ineffectiveness claim warrants a similar, though more limited, presumption of prejudice. In Cuyler v. Sullivan, 446 U.S., at 345–350, the Court held that prejudice is presumed when counsel is burdened by an actual conflict of interest. In those circumstances, counsel breaches the duty of loyalty, perhaps the most basic of counsel's duties. Moreover, it is difficult to measure the precise effect on the defense of representation corrupted by conflicting interests. Given the obligation of counsel to avoid conflicts of interest and the ability of trial courts to make early inquiry in certain situations likely to give rise to conflicts, ... it is reasonable for the criminal justice system to maintain a fairly rigid rule of presumed prejudice for conflicts of interest. Even so, the rule is not quite the *per se* rule of prejudice that exists for the Sixth Amendment claims mentioned above. Prejudice is presumed only if the defendant demonstrates that counsel "actively represented conflicting interests" and that "an actual conflict of interest adversely affected his lawyer's performance." Cuyler v. Sullivan, supra, at 350, 348 (footnote omitted).

Conflict of interest claims aside, actual ineffectiveness claims alleging a deficiency in attorney performance are subject to a general requirement that the defendant affirmatively prove prejudice. The government is not responsible for, and hence not able to prevent, attorney errors that will result in reversal of a conviction or sentence. Attorney errors come in an infinite variety and are as likely to be utterly harmless in a particular case as they are to be prejudicial. They cannot be classified according to likelihood of causing prejudice. Nor can they be defined with sufficient precision to inform defense attorneys correctly just what conduct to avoid. Representation is an art, and an act or omission that is unprofessional in one case may be sound or even brilliant in another. Even if a defendant shows that particular errors of counsel were unreasonable, therefore, the defendant must show that they actually had an adverse effect on the defense.

It is not enough for the defendant to show that the errors had some conceivable effect on the outcome of the proceeding. Virtually every act or omission of counsel would meet that test ... and not every error that conceivably could have influenced the outcome undermines the reliability of the result of the proceeding. Respondent suggests requiring a showing that the errors "impaired the presentation of the defense." Brief for Respondent 58. That standard, however, provides no workable principle. Since any error, if it is indeed an error, "impairs" the presentation of the defense, the proposed standard is inadequate because it provides no way of deciding what impairments are sufficiently serious to warrant setting aside the outcome of the proceeding.

On the other hand, we believe that a defendant need not show that counsel's deficient conduct more likely than not altered the outcome in the case. This outcome-determinative standard has several strengths. It defines the relevant inquiry in a way familiar to courts, though the inquiry, as is inevitable, is anything but precise. The standard also reflects the profound importance of finality in criminal proceedings. Moreover, it comports with the widely used standard for assessing motions for new trial based on newly discovered evidence. ... Nevertheless, the standard is not quite appropriate.

Even when the specified attorney error results in the omission of certain evidence, the newly discovered evidence standard is not an apt source from which to draw a prejudice standard for ineffectiveness claims. The high standard for newly discovered evidence claims presupposes that all the essential elements of a presumptively accurate and fair proceeding were present in the proceeding whose result is challenged. ... An ineffective assistance claim asserts the absence of one of the crucial assurances that the result of the proceeding is reliable, so finality concerns are somewhat weaker and the appropriate standard of prejudice should be somewhat lower. The result of a proceeding can be rendered unreliable, and hence the proceeding itself unfair, even if the errors of counsel cannot be shown by a preponderance of the evidence to have determined the outcome.

Accordingly, the appropriate test for prejudice finds its roots in the test for materiality of exculpatory information not disclosed to the defense by the prosecution ... and in the test for materiality of testimony made unavailable to the defense by Government deportation of a witness .... The defendant must show that there is a reasonable probability that, but for counsel's unprofessional errors, the result of the proceeding would have been different. A reasonable probability is a probability sufficient to undermine confidence in the outcome.

In making the determination whether the specified errors resulted in the required prejudice, a court should presume, absent challenge to the judgment on grounds of evidentiary insufficiency, that the judge or jury acted according to law. An assessment of the likelihood of a result more favorable to the defendant must exclude the possibility of arbitrariness, whimsy, caprice, "nullification," and the like. A defendant has no entitlement to the luck of a lawless decisionmaker, even if a lawless decision cannot be reviewed. The assessment of prejudice should proceed on the assumption that the decisionmaker is reasonably, conscientiously, and impartially applying the standards that govern the decision. It should not depend on the idiosyncracies of the particular decisionmaker, such as unusual propensities toward harshness or leniency. Although these factors may actually have entered into counsel's selection of strategies and, to that limited extent, may thus affect the performance inquiry, they are irrelevant to the prejudice inquiry. Thus, evidence about the actual process of decision, if not part of the record of the proceeding under review, and evidence about, for example, a particular judge's sentencing practices, should not be considered in the prejudice determination.

The governing legal standard plays a critical role in defining the question to be asked in assessing the prejudice from counsel's errors. When a defendant challenges a conviction, the question is whether there is a reasonable probability that, absent the errors, the fact-finder would have had a reasonable doubt respecting guilt. When a defendant challenges a death sentence such as the one at issue in this case, the question is whether there is a reasonable probability that, absent the errors, the sentencer—including an appellate court, to the extent it independently reweighs the evidence—would have concluded that the balance of aggravating and mitigating circumstances did not warrant death.

In making this determination, a court hearing an ineffectiveness claim must consider the totality of the evidence before the judge or jury. Some of the factual findings will have been unaffected by the errors, and factual findings that were affected will have been affected in different ways. Some errors will have had a pervasive effect on the inferences to be drawn from the evidence, altering the entire evidentiary picture, and some will have had an isolated, trivial effect. Moreover, a verdict or conclusion only weakly supported by the record is more likely to have been affected by errors than one with overwhelming record support. Taking the unaffected findings as a given, and taking due account of the effect of the errors on the remaining findings, a court making the prejudice inquiry must ask if the defendant has met the burden of showing that the decision reached would reasonably likely have been different absent the errors.

IV

A number of practical considerations are important for the application of the standards we have outlined. Most important, in adjudicating a claim of actual ineffectiveness of counsel, a court should keep in mind that the principles we have stated do not establish mechanical rules. Although those principles should guide the process of decision, the ultimate focus of inquiry must be on the fundamental fairness of the proceeding whose result is being challenged. In every case the court should be concerned with whether, despite the strong presumption of reliability, the result of the particular proceeding is unreliable because of a breakdown in the adversarial process that our system counts on to produce just results.

To the extent that this has already been the guiding inquiry in the lower courts, the standards articulated today do not require reconsideration of ineffectiveness claims rejected under different standards. . . . In particular, the minor differences in the lower courts' precise formulations of the performance standard are insignificant: the different formulations are mere variations of the overarching reasonableness standard. With regard to the prejudice inquiry, only the strict outcome-determinative test, among the standards articulated in the lower courts, imposes a heavier burden on defendants than the tests laid down today. The difference, however, should alter the merit of an ineffectiveness claim only in the rarest case.

Although we have discussed the performance component of an ineffectiveness claim prior to the prejudice component, there is no reason for a court deciding an ineffective assistant claim to approach the inquiry in the same order or even to address both components of the inquiry if the defendant makes an insufficient showing on one. In particular, a court need not determine whether counsel's performance was deficient before examining the prejudice suffered by the defendant as a result of the alleged deficiencies. The object of an ineffectiveness claim is not to grade counsel's performance. If it is easier to dispose of an ineffectiveness claim on the ground of lack of sufficient prejudice, which we expect will often be so, that course should be followed. Courts should strive to ensure that ineffectiveness claims not become so burdensome to defense counsel that the entire criminal justice system suffers as a result.

The principles governing ineffectiveness claims should apply in federal collateral proceedings as they do on direct appeal or in motions for a new trial. As indicated by the "cause and prejudice" test for overcoming procedural waivers of claims of error, the presumption that a criminal judgment is final is at its strongest in collateral attacks on that judgment. . . . An ineffectiveness claim, however, as our articulation of the standards that govern decision of such claims makes clear, is an attack on the fundamental fairness of the proceeding whose result is challenged. Since fundamental fairness is the central concern of the writ of habeas corpus ... no special standards ought to apply to ineffectiveness claims made in habeas proceedings.

Finally, in a federal habeas challenge to a state criminal judgment, a state court conclusion that counsel rendered effective assistance is not a finding of fact binding on the federal court to the extent stated by 28 U.S.C. § 2254(d). Ineffectiveness is not a question of "basic, primary, or historical fact[]," Townsend v. Sain, 372 U.S. 293, 309, n. 6 (1963). Rather, like the question whether multiple representation in a particular case gave rise to a conflict of interest, it is a mixed question of law and fact. ... Although state court findings of fact made in the course of deciding an ineffectiveness claim are subject to the deference requirement of § 2254(d), and although district court findings are subject to the clearly erroneous standard of Federal Rule of Civil Procedure 52(a), both the performance and prejudice components of the ineffectiveness inquiry are mixed questions of law and fact.

V

Having articulated general standards for judging ineffectiveness claims, we think it useful to apply those standards to the facts of this case in order to illustrate the meaning of the general principles. . . .

. . . .

With respect to the performance component, the record shows that respondent's counsel made a strategic choice to argue for the extreme emotional distress mitigating circumstance and to rely as fully as possible on respondent's acceptance of responsibility for his crimes. Although counsel understandably felt hopeless about respondent's prospects ... nothing in the record indicates ... that counsel's sense of hopelessness distorted his professional judgment. Counsel's strategy choice was well within the range of professionally reasonable judgments, and the decision not to seek more character or psychological evidence than was already in hand was likewise reasonable.

The trial judge's views on the importance of owning up to one's crimes were well known to counsel. The aggravating circumstances were utterly overwhelming. Trial counsel could reasonably surmise from his conversations with respondent that character and psychological evidence would be of little help. Respondent had already been able to mention at the plea colloquy the substance of what there was to know about his financial and emotional troubles. Restricting testimony on respondent's character to what had come in at the plea colloquy ensured that contrary character and psychological evidence and respondent's criminal history, which counsel had successfully moved to exclude, would not come in. On these facts there can be little question, even without application of the presumption of adequate performance, that trial counsel's defense, though unsuccessful, was the result of reasonable professional judgment.

With respect to the prejudice component, the lack of merit of respondent's claim is even more stark. The evidence that respondent says his trial counsel should have offered at the sentencing hearing would barely have altered the sentencing profile presented to the sentencing judge. ... [A]t most this evidence shows that numerous people who knew respondent thought he was generally a good person and that a psychiatrist and a psychologist believed he was under considerable emotional stress that did not rise to the level of extreme disturbance. Given the overwhelming aggravating factors, there is no reasonable probability that the omitted evidence would have changed the conclusion that the aggravating circumstances outweighed the mitigating circumstances and, hence, the sentence imposed. Indeed, admission of the evidence respondent now offers might even have been harmful to his case: his "rap sheet" would probably have been admitted into evidence, and the psychological reports would have directly contradicted respondent's claim that the mitigating circumstance of extreme emotional disturbance applied to his case.

. . .

Failure to make the required showing of either deficient performance or sufficient prejudice defeats the ineffectiveness claim. Here there is a double failure. More generally, respondent has made no showing that the justice of his sentence was rendered unreliable by a breakdown in the adversary process caused by deficiencies in counsel's assistance. Respondent's sentencing proceeding was not fundamentally unfair.

We conclude, therefore, that the District Court properly declined to issue a writ of habeas corpus. The judgment of the Court of Appeals is accordingly

Reversed.[*]

[*] Justice Brennan wrote an opinion concurring in part and dissenting in part. Justice Marshall wrote a dissenting opinion.

NIX v. WHITESIDE

475 U.S. 157, 106 S.Ct. 988, 89 L.Ed.2d 123 (1986).

CHIEF JUSTICE BURGER delivered the opinion of the Court.

We granted certiorari to decide whether the Sixth Amendment right of a criminal defendant to assistance of counsel is violated when an attorney refuses to cooperate with the defendant in presenting perjured testimony at his trial.

I

A

Whiteside was convicted of second-degree murder by a jury verdict which was affirmed by the Iowa courts. The killing took place on February 8, 1977, in Cedar Rapids, Iowa. Whiteside and two others went to one Calvin Love's apartment late that night, seeking marihuana. Love was in bed when Whiteside and his companions arrived; an argument between Whiteside and Love over the marihuana ensued. At one point, Love directed his girlfriend to get his "piece," and at another point got up, then returned to his bed. According to Whiteside's testimony, Love then started to reach under his pillow and moved toward Whiteside. Whiteside stabbed Love in the chest, inflicting a fatal wound.

Whiteside was charged with murder, and when counsel was appointed he objected to the lawyer initially appointed, claiming that he felt uncomfortable with a lawyer who had formerly been a prosecutor. Gary L. Robinson was then appointed and immediately began an investigation. Whiteside gave him a statement that he had stabbed Love as the latter "was pulling a pistol from underneath the pillow on the bed." Upon questioning by Robinson, however, Whiteside indicated that he had not actually seen a gun, but that he was convinced that Love had a gun. No pistol was found on the premises; shortly after the police search following the stabbing, which had revealed no weapon, the victim's family had removed all of the victim's possessions from the apartment. Robinson interviewed Whiteside's companions who were present during the stabbing, and none had seen a gun during the incident. Robinson advised Whiteside that the existence of a gun was not necessary to establish the claim of self-defense, and that only a reasonable belief that the victim had a gun nearby was necessary even though no gun was actually present.

Until shortly before trial, Whiteside consistently stated to Robinson that he had not actually seen a gun, but that he was convinced that Love had a gun in his hand. About a week before trial, during preparation for direct examination, Whiteside for the first time told Robinson and his associate Donna Paulsen that he had seen something "metallic" in Love's hand. When asked about this, Whiteside responded:

> "[I]n Howard Cook's case there was a gun. If I don't say I saw a gun, I'm dead."

Robinson told Whiteside that such testimony would be perjury and repeated that it was not necessary to prove that a gun was available but only that Whiteside reasonably believed that he was in danger. On Whiteside's insisting that he would testify that he saw "something metallic" Robinson told him, according to Robinson's testimony:

> "[W]e could not allow him to [testify falsely] because that would be perjury, and as officers of the court we would be suborning perjury if we allowed him to do it; ... I advised him that if he did do that it would be my duty to advise the Court of what he was doing and that I felt he was committing perjury; also, that I probably would be allowed to attempt to impeach that particular testimony." App. to Pet. for Cert. A–85.

Robinson also indicated he would seek to withdraw from the representation if Whiteside insisted on committing perjury.

Whiteside testified in his own defense at trial and stated that he "knew" that Love had a gun and that he believed Love was reaching for a gun and he had acted swiftly in self-defense. On cross-examination, he admitted that he had not actually seen a gun in Love's hand. Robinson presented evidence that Love had been seen with a sawed-off shotgun on other occasions, that the police search of the apartment may have been careless, and that the victim's family had removed everything from the apartment shortly after the crime. Robinson presented this evidence to show a basis for Whiteside's asserted fear that Love had a gun.

The jury returned a verdict of second-degree murder, and Whiteside moved for a new trial, claiming that he had been deprived of a fair trial by Robinson's admonitions not to state that he saw a gun or "something metallic." The trial court held a hearing, heard testimony by Whiteside and Robinson, and denied the motion. The trial court made specific findings that the facts were as related by Robinson.

The Supreme Court of Iowa affirmed respondent's conviction. State v. Whiteside, 272 N.W.2d 468 (1978). That court held that the right to have counsel present all appropriate defenses does not extend to using perjury, and that an attorney's duty to a client does not extend to assisting a client in committing perjury. Relying on DR 7–102(A)(4) of the Iowa Code of Professional Responsibility for Lawyers, which expressly prohibits an attorney from using perjured testimony, and Iowa Code § 721.2 (now Iowa Code § 720.3

(1985)), which criminalizes subornation of perjury, the Iowa court concluded that not only were Robinson's actions permissible, but were required. The court commended "both Mr. Robinson and Ms. Paulsen for the high ethical manner in which this matter was handled."

B

Whiteside then petitioned for a writ of habeas corpus in the United States District Court for the Southern District of Iowa. In that petition Whiteside alleged that he had been denied effective assistance of counsel and of his right to present a defense by Robinson's refusal to allow him to testify as he had proposed. The District Court denied the writ. Accepting the state trial court's factual finding that Whiteside's intended testimony would have been perjurious, it concluded that there could be no grounds for habeas relief since there is no constitutional right to present a perjured defense.

The United States Court of Appeals for the Eighth Circuit reversed and directed that the writ of habeas corpus be granted. Whiteside v. Scurr, 744 F.2d 1323 (1984). The Court of Appeals accepted the findings of the trial judge, affirmed by the Iowa Supreme Court, that trial counsel believed with good cause that Whiteside would testify falsely and acknowledged that under Harris v. New York, 401 U.S. 222 (1971), a criminal defendant's privilege to testify in his own behalf does not include a right to commit perjury. Nevertheless, the court reasoned that an intent to commit perjury, communicated to counsel, does not alter a defendant's right to effective assistance of counsel and that Robinson's admonition to Whiteside that he would inform the court of Whiteside's perjury constituted a threat to violate the attorney's duty to preserve client confidences. According to the Court of Appeals, this threatened violation of client confidences breached the standards of effective representation set down in Strickland v. Washington, 466 U.S. 668 (1984). The court also concluded that *Strickland*'s prejudice requirement was satisfied by an implication of prejudice from the conflict between Robinson's duty of loyalty to his client and his ethical duties. A petition for rehearing en banc was denied, with Judges Gibson, Ross, Fagg, and Bowman dissenting. Whiteside v. Scurr, 750 F.2d 713 (1984). We granted certiorari, 471 U.S. 1014 (1985), and we reverse.

II

A

The right of an accused to testify in his defense is of relatively recent origin. Until the latter part of the preceding century, criminal defendants in this country, as at common law, were considered to be disqualified from giving sworn testimony at their own trial by

reason of their interest as a party to the case.... Iowa was among
the states that adhered to this rule of disqualification....

By the end of the 19th century, however, the disqualification
was finally abolished by statute in most states and in the federal
courts.... Although this Court has never explicitly held that a
criminal defendant has a due process right to testify in his own
behalf, cases in several Circuits have so held, and the right has long
been assumed.... We have also suggested that such a right exists
as a corollary to the Fifth Amendment privilege against compelled
testimony....

B

In Strickland v. Washington, we held that to obtain relief by way
of federal habeas corpus on a claim of a deprivation of effective
assistance of counsel under the Sixth Amendment, the movant must
establish both serious attorney error and prejudice. To show such
error, it must be established that the assistance rendered by counsel
was constitutionally deficient in that "counsel made errors so
serious that counsel was not functioning as 'counsel' guaranteed the
defendant by the Sixth Amendment." *Strickland,* 466 U.S., at 687.
To show prejudice, it must be established that the claimed lapses in
counsel's performance rendered the trial unfair so as to "undermine confidence in the outcome" of the trial. Id., at 694.

In *Strickland,* we acknowledged that the Sixth Amendment
does not require any particular response by counsel to a problem
that may arise. Rather, the Sixth Amendment inquiry is into whether the attorney's conduct was "reasonably effective." To counteract
the natural tendency to fault an unsuccessful defense, a court
reviewing a claim of ineffective assistance must "indulge a strong
presumption that counsel's conduct falls within the wide range of
reasonable professional assistance." Id., at 689. In giving shape to
the perimeters of this range of reasonable professional assistance,
Strickland mandates that

> "[p]revailing norms of practice as reflected in American Bar
> Association Standards and the like, ... are guides to determin-
> ing what is reasonable, but they are only guides." Id., at 688.

Under the *Strickland* standard, breach of an ethical standard
does not necessarily make out a denial of the Sixth Amendment
guarantee of assistance of counsel. When examining attorney conduct, a court must be careful not to narrow the wide range of
conduct acceptable under the Sixth Amendment so restrictively as to
constitutionalize particular standards of professional conduct and
thereby intrude into the state's proper authority to define and apply
the standards of professional conduct applicable to those it admits
to practice in its courts. In some future case challenging attorney
conduct in the course of a state-court trial, we may need to define
with greater precision the weight to be given to recognized canons

of ethics, the standards established by the state in statutes or professional codes, and the Sixth Amendment, in defining the proper scope and limits on that conduct. Here we need not face that question, since virtually all of the sources speak with one voice.

C

We turn next to the question presented: the definition of the range of "reasonable professional" responses to a criminal defendant client who informs counsel that he will perjure himself on the stand. We must determine whether, in this setting, Robinson's conduct fell within the wide range of professional responses to threatened client perjury acceptable under the Sixth Amendment.

In *Strickland,* we recognized counsel's duty of loyalty and his "overarching duty to advocate the defendant's cause." Ibid. Plainly, that duty is limited to legitimate, lawful conduct compatible with the very nature of a trial as a search for truth. Although counsel must take all reasonable lawful means to attain the objectives of the client, counsel is precluded from taking steps or in any way assisting the client in presenting false evidence or otherwise violating the law. This principle has consistently been recognized in most unequivocal terms by expositors of the norms of professional conduct since the first Canons of Professional Ethics were adopted by the American Bar Association in 1908. . . .

. . . Disciplinary Rule 7–102 of the Model Code of Professional Responsibility (1980), entitled "Representing a Client Within the Bounds of the Law," provides:

"(A) In his representation of a client, a lawyer shall not:

.   .   .   .   .

"(4) Knowingly use perjured testimony or false evidence.

.   .   .   .   .

"(7) Counsel or assist his client in conduct that the lawyer knows to be illegal or fraudulent."

This provision has been adopted by Iowa, and is binding on all lawyers who appear in its courts. . . . The more recent Model Rules of Professional Conduct (1983) similarly admonish attorneys to obey all laws in the course of representing a client:

"*RULE 1.2* Scope of Representation

.   .   .   .   .

"(d) A lawyer shall not counsel a client to engage, or assist a client, in conduct that the lawyer knows is criminal or fraudulent. . . ."

Both the Model Code of Professional Responsibility and the Model Rules of Professional Conduct also adopt the specific exception from the attorney-client privilege for disclosure of perjury that his client intends to commit or has committed. DR 4–101(C)(3) (intention of client to commit a crime); Rule 3.3 (lawyer has duty to disclose falsity of evidence even if disclosure compromises client confidences). Indeed, both the Model Code and the Model Rules do not merely *authorize* disclosure by counsel of client perjury; they *require* such disclosure. . . .

These standards confirm that the legal profession has accepted that an attorney's ethical duty to advance the interests of his client is limited by an equally solemn duty to comply with the law and standards of professional conduct; it specifically ensures that the client may not use false evidence. This special duty of an attorney to prevent and disclose frauds upon the court derives from the recognition that perjury is as much a crime as tampering with witnesses or jurors by way of promises and threats, and undermines the administration of justice. . . .

The offense of perjury was a crime recognized at common law . . . and has been made a felony in most states by statute, including Iowa. Iowa Code § 720.2 (1985). . . . An attorney who aids false testimony by questioning a witness when perjurious responses can be anticipated risks prosecution for subornation of perjury under Iowa Code § 720.3 (1985).

It is universally agreed that at a minimum the attorney's first duty when confronted with a proposal for perjurious testimony is to attempt to dissuade the client from the unlawful course of conduct. . . . A statement directly in point is found in the commentary to the Model Rules of Professional Conduct under the heading "False Evidence":

> "When false evidence is offered by the client, however, a conflict may arise between the lawyer's duty to keep the client's revelations confidential and the duty of candor to the court. Upon ascertaining that material evidence is false, the lawyer *should seek to persuade the client that the evidence should not be offered* or, if it has been offered, that its false character should immediately be disclosed." Model Rules of Professional Conduct, Rule 3.3, Comment (1983) (emphasis added).

The commentary thus also suggests that an attorney's revelation of his client's perjury to the court is a professionally responsible and acceptable response to the conduct of a client who has actually given perjured testimony. Similarly, the Model Rules and the commentary, as well as the Code of Professional Responsibility adopted in Iowa, expressly permit withdrawal from representation as an appropriate response of an attorney when the client threatens to commit perjury. . . . Withdrawal of counsel when this situation arises at trial gives rise to many difficult questions including possible mistrial and claims of double jeopardy.

The essence of the brief *amicus* of the American Bar Association reviewing practices long accepted by ethical lawyers is that under no circumstance may a lawyer either advocate or passively tolerate a client's giving false testimony. This, of course, is consistent with the governance of trial conduct in what we have long called "a search for truth." The suggestion sometimes made that "a lawyer must believe his client, not judge him" in no sense means a lawyer can honorably be a party to or in any way give aid to presenting known perjury.

D

Considering Robinson's representation of respondent in light of these accepted norms of professional conduct, we discern no failure to adhere to reasonable professional standards that would in any sense make out a deprivation of the Sixth Amendment right to counsel. Whether Robinson's conduct is seen as a successful attempt to dissuade his client from committing the crime of perjury, or whether seen as a "threat" to withdraw from representation and disclose the illegal scheme, Robinson's representation of Whiteside falls well within accepted standards of professional conduct and the range of reasonable professional conduct acceptable under *Strickland*.

The Court of Appeals assumed for the purpose of the decision that Whiteside would have given false testimony had counsel not intervened . . . .

The Court of Appeals' holding that Robinson's "action deprived [Whiteside] of due process and effective assistance of counsel" is not supported by the record since Robinson's action, at most, deprived Whiteside of his contemplated perjury. Nothing counsel did in any way undermined Whiteside's claim that he believed the victim was reaching for a gun. Similarly, the record gives no support for holding that Robinson's action "also impermissibly compromised [Whiteside's] right to testify in his own defense by conditioning continued representation . . . and confidentiality upon [Whiteside's] *restricted* testimony." The record in fact shows the contrary: (a) that Whiteside did testify, and (b) he was "restricted" or restrained only from testifying falsely and was aided by Robinson in developing the basis for the fear that Love was reaching for a gun. Robinson divulged no client communications until he was compelled to do so in response to Whiteside's post-trial challenge to the quality of his performance. We see this as a case in which the attorney successfully dissuaded the client from committing the crime of perjury.

Paradoxically, even while accepting the conclusion of the Iowa trial court that Whiteside's proposed testimony would have been a criminal act, the Court of Appeals held that Robinson's efforts to persuade Whiteside not to commit that crime were improper, *first,* as forcing an impermissible choice between the right to counsel and the right to testify; and, *second,* as compromising client confidences because of Robinson's threat to disclose the contemplated perjury.

Whatever the scope of a constitutional right to testify, it is elementary that such a right does not extend to testifying *falsely....* *Harris* and other cases make it crystal clear that there is no right whatever—constitutional or otherwise—for a defendant to use false evidence....

The paucity of authority on the subject of any such "right" may be explained by the fact that such a notion has never been responsibly advanced; the right to counsel includes no right to have a lawyer who will cooperate with planned perjury. A lawyer who would so cooperate would be at risk of prosecution for suborning perjury, and disciplinary proceedings, including suspension or disbarment.

Robinson's admonitions to his client can in no sense be said to have forced respondent into an *impermissible* choice between his right to counsel and his right to testify as he proposed for there was no *permissible* choice to testify falsely. For defense counsel to take steps to persuade a criminal defendant to testify truthfully, or to withdraw, deprives the defendant of neither his right to counsel nor the right to testify truthfully.... When an accused proposes to resort to perjury or to produce false evidence, one consequence is the risk of withdrawal of counsel.

On this record, the accused enjoyed continued representation within the bounds of reasonable professional conduct and did in fact exercise his right to testify; at most he was denied the right to have the assistance of counsel in the presentation of false testimony. Similarly, we can discern no breach of professional duty in Robinson's admonition to respondent that he would disclose respondent's perjury to the court. The crime of perjury in this setting is indistinguishable in substance from the crime of threatening or tampering with a witness or a juror. A defendant who informed his counsel that he was arranging to bribe or threaten witnesses or members of the jury would have no "right" to insist on counsel's assistance or silence. Counsel would not be limited to advising against that conduct. An attorney's duty of confidentiality, which totally covers the client's admission of guilt, does not extend to a client's announced plans to engage in future criminal conduct.... In short, the responsibility of an ethical lawyer, as an officer of the court and a key component of a system of justice, dedicated to a search for truth, is essentially the same whether the client announces an intention to bribe or threaten witnesses or jurors or to commit or procure perjury. No system of justice worthy of the name can tolerate a lesser standard.

The rule adopted by the Court of Appeals, which seemingly would require an attorney to remain silent while his client committed perjury, is wholly incompatible with the established standards of ethical conduct and the laws of Iowa and contrary to professional standards promulgated by that State. The position advocated by petitioner, on the contrary, is wholly consistent with the Iowa standards of professional conduct and law, with the overwhelming majority of courts, and with codes of professional ethics. Since there has been no breach of any recognized professional duty, it follows that there can be no deprivation of the right to assistance of counsel under the *Strickland* standard.

E

We hold that, as a matter of law, counsel's conduct complained of here cannot establish the prejudice required for relief under the second strand of the *Strickland* inquiry. Although a defendant need not establish that the attorney's deficient performance more likely than not altered the outcome in order to establish prejudice under *Strickland*, a defendant must show that "there is a reasonable probability that, but for counsel's unprofessional errors, the result of the proceeding would have been different." 466 U.S., at 694. According to *Strickland*, "[a] reasonable probability is a probability sufficient to undermine confidence in the outcome." Ibid. The *Strickland* Court noted that the "benchmark" of an ineffective-assistance claim is the fairness of the adversary proceeding, and that in judging prejudice and the likelihood of a different outcome, "[a] defendant has no entitlement to the luck of a lawless decisionmaker." Id., at 695.

Whether he was persuaded or compelled to desist from perjury, Whiteside has no valid claim that confidence in the result of his trial has been diminished by his desisting from the contemplated perjury. Even if we were to assume that the jury might have believed his perjury, it does not follow that Whiteside was prejudiced.

In his attempt to evade the prejudice requirement of *Strickland*, Whiteside relies on cases involving conflicting loyalties of counsel. In Cuyler v. Sullivan, 446 U.S. 335 (1980), we held that a defendant could obtain relief without pointing to a specific prejudicial default on the part of his counsel, provided it is established that the attorney was "actively represent[ing] conflicting interests." Id., at 350.

Here, there was indeed a "conflict," but of a quite different kind; it was one imposed on the attorney by the client's proposal to commit the crime of fabricating testimony without which, as he put it, "I'm dead." This is not remotely the kind of conflict of interests dealt with in Cuyler v. Sullivan. Even in that case we did not suggest that all multiple representations necessarily resulted in an active conflict rendering the representation constitutionally infirm. If a "conflict" between a client's proposal and counsel's ethical obligation gives rise to a presumption that counsel's assistance was prejudicially ineffective, every guilty criminal's conviction would be suspect if the defendant had sought to obtain an acquittal by illegal means. Can anyone doubt what practices and problems would be spawned by such a rule and what volumes of litigation it would generate?

Whiteside's attorney treated Whiteside's proposed perjury in accord with professional standards, and since Whiteside's truthful testimony could not have prejudiced the result of his trial, the Court of Appeals was in error to direct the issuance of a writ of habeas corpus and must be reversed.

Reversed.

. . .

JUSTICE BLACKMUN, with whom JUSTICE BRENNAN, JUSTICE MARSHALL, and JUSTICE STEVENS join, concurring in the judgment.

How a defense attorney ought to act when faced with a client who intends to commit perjury at trial has long been a controversial issue. But I do not believe that a federal habeas corpus case challenging a state criminal conviction is an appropriate vehicle for attempting to resolve this thorny problem. When a defendant argues that he was denied effective assistance of counsel because his lawyer dissuaded him from committing perjury, the only question properly presented to this Court is whether the lawyer's actions deprived the defendant of the fair trial which the Sixth Amendment is meant to guarantee. Since I believe that the respondent in this case suffered no injury justifying federal habeas relief, I concur in the Court's judgement.

. . .

The touchstone of a claim of prejudice is an allegation that counsel's behavior did something "to deprive the defendant of a fair trial, a trial whose result is reliable." Strickland v. Washington, 466 U.S. [668 (1984)], at 687. The only effect Robinson's threat had on Whiteside's trial is that Whiteside did not testify, falsely, that he saw a gun in Love's hand. Thus, this Court must ask whether its confidence in the outcome of Whiteside's trial is in any way undermined by the knowledge that he refrained from presenting false testimony. . . .

. . . [T]he Court has viewed a defendant's use of such testimony as so antithetical to our system of justice that it has permitted the prosecution to introduce otherwise inadmissible evidence to combat it. . . . The proposition that presenting false evidence could contribute to (or that withholding such evidence could detract from) the reliability of a criminal trial is simply untenable.

. . . To the extent that Whiteside's claim rests on the assertion that he would have been acquitted had he been able to testify falsely, Whiteside claims a right the law simply does not recognize. "A defendant has no entitlement to the luck of a lawless decision-maker, even if a lawless decision cannot be reviewed." Strickland v. Washington, 466 U.S., at 695. Since Whiteside was deprived of neither a fair trial nor any of the specific constitutional rights designed to guarantee a fair trial, he has suffered no prejudice.

. . .

Whether an attorney's response to what he sees as a client's plan to commit perjury violates a defendant's Sixth Amendment rights may depend on many factors: how certain the attorney is that the proposed testimony is false, the stage of the proceedings at which the attorney discovers the plan, or the ways in which the attorney may be able to dissuade his client, to name just three. The complex interaction of factors, which is likely to vary from case to case, makes inappropriate a blanket rule that defense attorneys must reveal, or threaten to reveal, a client's anticipated perjury to the court.

. . . [T]his Court's responsibility extends only to ensuring that the restrictions a State enacts do not infringe a defendant's federal constitutional rights. Thus, I would follow the suggestion made in the joint brief *amici curiae* filed by 37 States at the certiorari stage that we allow the States to maintain their "differing approaches" to a complex ethical question. Brief for State of Indiana et al. as *Amici Curiae* 5. The signal merit of asking first whether a defendant has shown any adverse prejudicial effect before inquiring into his attorney's performance is that it avoids unnecessary federal interference in a State's regulation of its bar. Because I conclude that the respondent in this case failed to show such an effect, I join the Court's judgment that he is not entitled to federal habeas relief.

JUSTICE STEVENS, concurring in the judgment.

. . .

As we view this case, it appears perfectly clear that respondent intended to commit perjury, that his lawyer knew it, and that the lawyer had a duty—both to the court and to his client, for perjured testimony can ruin an otherwise meritorious case—to take extreme measures to prevent the perjury from occurring. The lawyer was successful and, from our unanimous and remote perspective, it is now pellucidly clear that the client suffered no "legally cognizable prejudice."

Nevertheless, beneath the surface of this case there are areas of uncertainty that cannot be resolved today. A lawyer's certainty that a change in his client's recollection is a harbinger of intended perjury—as well as judicial review of such apparent certainty—should be tempered by the realization that, after reflection, the most honest witness may recall (or sincerely believe he recalls) details that he previously overlooked. Similarly, the post-trial review of a lawyer's pretrial threat to expose perjury that had not yet been committed—and, indeed, may have been prevented by the threat— is by no means the same as review of the way in which such a threat may actually have been carried out.   Thus, one can be convinced— as I am—that this lawyer's actions were a proper way to provide his client with effective representation without confronting the much more difficult questions of what a lawyer must, should, or may do after his client has given testimony that the lawyer does not believe. The answer to such questions may well be colored by the particular circumstances attending the actual event and its aftermath.[*]

[*] Justice Brennan wrote an opinion concurring in the judgment.

FARETTA v. CALIFORNIA

422 U.S. 806, 95 S.Ct. 2525, 45 L.Ed.2d 562 (1975).

MR. JUSTICE STEWART delivered the opinion of the Court.

The Sixth and Fourteenth Amendments of our Constitution guarantee that a person brought to trial in any state or federal court must be afforded the right to the assistance of counsel before he can be validly convicted and punished by imprisonment. This clear constitutional rule has emerged from a series of cases decided here over the last 50 years. The question before us now is whether a defendant in a state criminal trial has a constitutional right to proceed *without* counsel when he voluntarily and intelligently elects to do so. Stated another way, the question is whether a State may constitutionally hail a person into its criminal courts and there force a lawyer upon him, even when he insists that he wants to conduct his own defense. It is not an easy question, but we have concluded that a State may not constitutionally do so.

I

Anthony Faretta was charged with grand theft in an information filed in the Superior Court of Los Angeles County, Cal. At the arraignment, the Superior Court Judge assigned to preside at the trial appointed the public defender to represent Faretta. Well before the date of trial, however, Faretta requested that he be permitted to represent himself. Questioning by the judge revealed that Faretta had once represented himself in a criminal prosecution, that he had a high school education, and that he did not want to be represented by the public defender because he believed that that office was "very loaded down with . . . a heavy case load." The judge responded that he believed Faretta was "making a mistake" and emphasized that in further proceedings Faretta would receive no special favors. Nevertheless, after establishing that Faretta wanted to represent himself and did not want a lawyer, the judge, in a "preliminary ruling," accepted Faretta's waiver of the assistance of counsel. The judge indicated, however, that he might reverse this ruling if it later appeared that Faretta was unable adequately to represent himself.

Several weeks thereafter, but still prior to trial, the judge *sua sponte* held a hearing to inquire into Faretta's ability to conduct his own defense, and questioned him specifically about both the hearsay rule and the state law governing the challenge of potential jurors. After consideration of Faretta's answers, and observation of his demeanor, the judge ruled that Faretta had not made an intelligent and knowing waiver of his right to the assistance of counsel, and also ruled that Faretta had no constitutional right to conduct his own defense. The judge, accordingly, reversed his earlier ruling permitting self-representation and again appointed the public defender to represent Faretta. Faretta's subsequent request for leave to act as cocounsel was rejected, as were his efforts to make certain motions on his own behalf. Throughout the subsequent trial, the judge required that Faretta's defense be conducted only through the appointed lawyer from the public defender's office. At the conclusion of the trial, the jury found Faretta guilty as charged, and the judge sentenced him to prison.

The California Court of Appeal ... affirmed the trial judge's ruling that Faretta had no federal or state constitutional right to represent himself. Accordingly, the appellate court affirmed Faretta's conviction. A petition for rehearing was denied without opinion, and the California Supreme Court denied review. We granted certiorari. 415 U.S. 975.

II

In the federal courts, the right of self-representation has been protected by statute since the beginnings of our Nation. Section 35 of the Judiciary Act of 1789, 1 Stat. 73, 92, enacted by the First Congress and signed by President Washington one day before the Sixth Amendment was proposed, provided that "in all the courts of the United States, the parties may plead and manage their own causes personally or by the assistance ... of counsel ..." The right is currently codified in 28 U.S.C. § 1654.

With few exceptions, each of the several States also accords a defendant the right to represent himself in any criminal case. The Constitutions of 36 States explicitly confer that right. Moreover, many state courts have expressed the view that the right is also supported by the Constitution of the United States.

This Court has more than once indicated the same view. In Adams v. United States ex rel. McCann, 317 U.S. 269, 279, the Court recognized that the Sixth Amendment right to the assistance of counsel implicitly embodies a "correlative right to dispense with a lawyer's help." ...

The *Adams* case does not, of course, necessarily resolve the issue before us. It held only that "the Constitution does not force a lawyer upon a defendant." Id., at 279. Whether the Constitution forbids a State from forcing a lawyer upon a defendant is a different question. But the Court in *Adams* did recognize, albeit in dictum, an affirmative right of self-representation:

> "The right to assistance of counsel and the *correlative right to dispense with a lawyer's help* are not legal formalisms. They rest on considerations that go to the substance of an accused's position before the law. ...

"... What were contrived as protections for the accused should not be turned into fetters. ... To deny an accused a choice of procedure in circumstances in which he, though a layman, is as capable as any lawyer of making an intelligent choice, is to impair the worth of great Constitutional safeguards by treating them as empty verbalisms.

"... When the administration of the criminal law ... is hedged about as it is by the Constitutional safeguards for the protection of an accused, to deny him in the exercise of his free choice the right to dispense with some of these safeguards ... is to imprison a man in his privileges and call it the Constitution." Id., at 279–280 (emphasis added).

In other settings as well, the Court has indicated that a defendant has a constitutionally protected right to represent himself in a criminal trial....

The United States Courts of Appeals have repeatedly held that the right of self-representation is protected by the Bill of Rights. ...

This Court's past recognition of the right of self-representation, the federal court authority holding the right to be of constitutional dimension, and the state constitutions pointing to the right's fundamental nature form a consensus not easily ignored. "[T]he mere fact that a path is a beaten one," Mr. Justice Jackson once observed, "is a persuasive reason for following it."[13] We confront here a nearly universal conviction, on the part of our people as well as our courts, that forcing a lawyer upon an unwilling defendant is contrary to his basic right to defend himself if he truly wants to do so.

III

This consensus is soundly premised. The right of self-representation finds support in the structure of the Sixth Amendment, as well as in the English and colonial jurisprudence from which the Amendment emerged.

A

The Sixth Amendment includes a compact statement of the rights necessary to a full defense:

"In all criminal prosecutions, the accused shall enjoy the right ... to be informed of the nature and cause of the accusation; to be confronted with the witnesses against him; to have compulsory process for obtaining witnesses in his favor, and to have the Assistance of Counsel for his defence."

Because these rights are basic to our adversary system of criminal justice, they are part of the "due process of law" that is guaranteed

---

13. Jackson, Full Faith and Credit—The Lawyer's Clause of the Constitution, 45 Col. L.Rev. 1, 26 (1945).

by the Fourteenth Amendment to defendants in the criminal courts of the States. The rights to notice, confrontation, and compulsory process, when taken together, guarantee that a criminal charge may be answered in a manner now considered fundamental to the fair administration of American justice—through the calling and interrogation of favorable witnesses, the cross-examination of adverse witnesses, and the orderly introduction of evidence. In short, the Amendment constitutionalizes the right in an adversary criminal trial to make a defense as we know it. . . .

The Sixth Amendment does not provide merely that a defense shall be made for the accused; it grants to the accused personally the right to make his defense. It is the accused, not counsel, who must be "informed of the nature and cause of the accusation," who must be "confronted with the witnesses against him," and who must be accorded "compulsory process for obtaining witnesses in his favor." Although not stated in the Amendment in so many words, the right to self-representation—to make one's own defense personally—is thus necessarily implied by the structure of the Amendment. The right to defend is given directly to the accused; for it is he who suffers the consequences if the defense fails.

The counsel provision supplements this design. It speaks of the "assistance" of counsel, and an assistant, however expert, is still an assistant. The language and spirit of the Sixth Amendment contemplate that counsel, like the other defense tools guaranteed by the Amendment, shall be an aid to a willing defendant—not an organ of the State interposed between an unwilling defendant and his right to defend himself personally. To thrust counsel upon the accused, against his considered wish, thus violates the logic of the Amendment. In such a case, counsel is not an assistant, but a master; and the right to make a defense is stripped of the personal character upon which the Amendment insists. It is true that when a defendant chooses to have a lawyer manage and present his case, law and tradition may allocate to the counsel the power to make binding decisions of trial strategy in many areas. . . . This allocation can only be justified, however, by the defendant's consent, at the outset, to accept counsel as his representative. An unwanted counsel "represents" the defendant only through a tenuous and unacceptable legal fiction. Unless the accused has acquiesced in such representation, the defense presented is not the defense guaranteed him by the Constitution, for, in a very real sense, it is not *his* defense.

B

The Sixth Amendment, when naturally read, thus implies a right of self-representation. This reading is reinforced by the Amendment's roots in English legal history.

. . .

... The common-law rule, succinctly stated in R. v. Woodward [1944] K.B. 118, 119, [1944] 1 All E.R. 159, 160, has evidently always been that "no person charged with a criminal offense can have counsel forced upon him against his will." ...

C

In the American colonies the insistence upon a right of self-representation was, if anything, more fervent than in England.

. . .

In sum, there is no evidence that the colonists and the Framers ever doubted the right of self-representation, or imagined that this right might be considered inferior to the right of assistance of counsel. To the contrary, the colonists and the Framers, as well as their English ancestors, always conceived of the right to counsel as an "assistance" for the accused, to be used at his option, in defending himself. The Framers selected in the Sixth Amendment a form of words that necessarily implies the right of self-representation. That conclusion is supported by centuries of consistent history.

IV

There can be no blinking the fact that the right of an accused to conduct his own defense seems to cut against the grain of this Court's decisions holding that the Constitution requires that no accused can be convicted and imprisoned unless he has been accorded the right to the assistance of counsel. ... For it is surely true that the basic thesis of those decisions is that the help of a lawyer is essential to assure the defendant a fair trial. And a strong argument can surely be made that the whole thrust of those decisions must inevitably lead to the conclusion that a State may constitutionally impose a lawyer upon even an unwilling defendant.

But it is one thing to hold that every defendant, rich or poor, has the right to the assistance of counsel, and quite another to say that a State may compel a defendant to accept a lawyer he does not want. The value of state-appointed counsel was not unappreciated by the Founders, yet the notion of compulsory counsel was utterly foreign to them. And whatever else may be said of those who wrote the Bill of Rights, surely there can be no doubt that they understood the inestimable worth of free choice.

It is undeniable that in most criminal prosecutions defendants could better defend with counsel's guidance than by their own unskilled efforts. But where the defendant will not voluntarily accept representation by counsel, the potential advantage of a lawyer's training and experience can be realized, if at all, only imperfectly. To force a lawyer on a defendant can only lead him to believe that the law contrives against him. Moreover, it is not inconceivable that in some rare instances, the defendant might in fact present his case more effectively by conducting his own defense. Personal liberties are not rooted in the law of averages. The right to defend is personal. The defendant, and not his lawyer or the State, will bear the personal consequences of a conviction. It is the defendant, therefore, who must be free personally to decide whether in his particular case counsel is to his advantage. And although he may conduct his own defense ultimately to his own detriment, his choice must be honored out of "that respect for the individual which is the lifeblood of the law." Illinois v. Allen, 397 U.S. 337, 350–351 (Brennan, J., concurring).[46]

V

When an accused manages his own defense, he relinquishes, as a purely factual matter, many of the traditional benefits associated with the right to counsel. For this reason, in order to represent himself, the accused must "knowingly and intelligently" forego those relinquished benefits. Johnson v. Zerbst, 304 U.S., at 464–465. ... Although a defendant need not himself have the skill and experience of a lawyer in order competently and intelligently to choose self-representation, he should be made aware of the dangers and disadvantages of self-representation, so that the record will establish that "he knows what he is doing and his choice is made with eyes open." Adams v. United States ex rel. McCann, 317 U.S., at 279.

Here, weeks before trial, Faretta clearly and unequivocally declared to the trial judge that he wanted to represent himself and did not want counsel. The record affirmatively shows that Faretta was literate, competent, and understanding, and that he was voluntarily exercising his informed free will. The trial judge had warned Faretta that he thought it was a mistake not to accept the assistance of counsel, and that Faretta would be required to follow all the "ground rules" of trial procedure. We need make no assessment of how well or poorly Faretta had mastered the intricacies of the hearsay rule and the California code provisions that govern challenges of potential jurors on *voir dire*. For his technical legal knowledge, as such, was not relevant to an assessment of his knowing exercise of the right to defend himself.

In forcing Faretta, under these circumstances, to accept against his will a state-appointed public defender, the California courts deprived him of his constitutional right to conduct his own defense. Accordingly, the judgment before us is vacated, and the case is

---

46. ...

The right of self-representation is not a license to abuse the dignity of the courtroom. Neither is it a license not to comply with relevant rules of procedural and substantive law. Thus, whatever else may or may not be open to him on appeal, a defendant who elects to represent himself cannot thereafter complain that the quality of his own defense amounted to a denial of "effective assistance of counsel."

remanded for further proceedings not inconsistent with this opinion.

It is so ordered.

MR. JUSTICE BLACKMUN, with whom THE CHIEF JUSTICE and MR. JUSTICE REHNQUIST join, dissenting.

Today the Court holds that the Sixth Amendment guarantees to every defendant in a state criminal trial the right to proceed without counsel whenever he elects to do so. I find no textual support for this conclusion in the language of the Sixth Amendment. I find the historical evidence relied upon by the Court to be unpersuasive, especially in light of the recent history of criminal procedure. Finally, I fear that the right to self-representation constitutionalized today frequently will cause procedural confusion without advancing any significant strategic interest of the defendant. I therefore dissent.

I

. . .

. . . The Court . . . concludes that because the specific rights in the Sixth Amendment are personal to the accused, the accused must have a right to exercise those rights personally. Stated somewhat more succinctly, the Court reasons that because the accused has a personal right to "a defense as we know it," he necessarily has a right to make that defense personally. I disagree. Although I believe the specific guarantees of the Sixth Amendment are personal to the accused, I do not agree that the Sixth Amendment guarantees any particular procedural method of asserting those rights. If an accused has enjoyed a speedy trial by an impartial jury in which he was informed of the nature of the accusation, confronted with the witnesses against him, afforded the power of compulsory process, and represented effectively by competent counsel, I do not see that the Sixth Amendment requires more.

The Court suggests that thrusting counsel upon the accused against his considered wish violates the logic of the Sixth Amendment because counsel is to be an assistant, not a master. The Court seeks to support its conclusion by historical analogy to the notorious procedures of the Star Chamber. The potential for exaggerated analogy, however, is markedly diminished when one recalls that petitioner is seeking an absolute right to self-representation. This is not a case where defense counsel, against the wishes of the defendant or with inadequate consultation, has adopted a trial strategy that significantly affects one of the accused's constitutional rights. For such overbearing conduct by counsel, there is a remedy. . . . Nor is this a case where distrust, animosity, or other personal differences between the accused and his would-be counsel have rendered effective representation unlikely or impossible. . . . Nor is this even a case where a defendant has been forced, against his wishes to expend his personal resources to pay for counsel for his defense.   ...   Instead, the Court holds that any defendant in any criminal proceeding may insist on representing himself regardless of how complex the trial is likely to be and regardless of how frivolous the defendant's motivations may be.   I cannot agree that there is anything in the Due Process Clause or the Sixth Amendment that requires the States to subordinate the solemn business of conducting a criminal prosecution to the whimsical—albeit voluntary—caprice of every accused who wishes to use his trial as a vehicle for personal or political self-gratification.

The Court seems to suggest that so long as the accused is willing to pay the consequences of his folly, there is no reason for not allowing a defendant the right to self-representation. . . .   That view ignores the established principle that the interest of the State in a criminal prosecution "is not that it shall win a case, but that justice shall be done."   Berger v. United States, 295 U.S. 78, 88 (1935).   . . . For my part, I do not believe that any amount of *pro se* pleading can cure the injury to society of an unjust result, but I do believe that a just result should prove to be an effective balm for almost any frustrated *pro se* defendant.

II

The Court argues that its conclusion is supported by the historical evidence on self-representation.   It is true that self-representation was common, if not required, in 18th Century English and American prosecutions.   The Court points with special emphasis to the guarantees of self-representation in colonial charters, early state constitutions, and § 35 of the first Judiciary Act as evidence contemporaneous with the Bill of Rights of widespread recognition of a right to self-representation.

I do not participate in the Court's reliance on the historical evidence.   To begin with, the historical evidence seems to me to be inconclusive in revealing the original understanding of the language of the Sixth Amendment.   At the time the Amendment was first proposed, both the right to self-representation and the right to assistance of counsel in federal prosecutions were guaranteed by statute.   The Sixth Amendment expressly constitutionalized the right to assistance of counsel but remained conspicuously silent on any right of self-representation.   The Court believes that this silence of the Sixth Amendment as to the latter right is evidence of the Framers' belief that the right was so obvious and fundamental that it did not need to be included "in so many words" in order to be protected by the Amendment.   I believe it is at least equally plausible to conclude that the Amendment's silence as to the right of self-representation indicates that the Framers simply did not have the subject in mind when they drafted the language.

The paucity of historical support for the Court's position becomes far more profound when one examines it against the background of two developments in the more recent history of criminal procedure. First, until the middle of the 19th Century, the defendant in a criminal proceeding in this country was almost always disqualified from testifying as a witness because of his "interest" in the outcome. ... Thus, the ability to defend "in person" was frequently the defendant's only chance to present his side of the case to the judge or jury. ... Such Draconian rules of evidence, of course, are now a relic of the past because virtually every State has passed a statute abrogating the common-law rule of disqualification. ... With the abolition of the common-law disqualification, the right to appear "in person" as well as by counsel lost most, if not all, of its original importance. ...

The second historical development is this Court's elaboration of the right to counsel. The road the Court has traveled from Powell v. Alabama, 287 U.S. 45 (1932), to Argersinger v. Hamlin, 407 U.S. 25 (1972), need not be recounted here. For our purposes, it is sufficient to recall that from start to finish the development of the right to counsel has been based on the premise that representation by counsel is essential to ensure a fair trial. The Court concedes this and acknowledges that "a strong argument can surely be made that the whole thrust of those decisions must inevitably lead to the conclusion that a State may constitutionally impose a lawyer upon even an unwilling defendant." Ante, at 833. Nevertheless, the Court concludes that self-representation must be allowed despite the obvious dangers of unjust convictions in order to protect the individual defendant's right of free choice. As I have already indicated, I cannot agree to such a drastic curtailment of the interest of the State in seeing that justice is done in a real and objective sense.

III

In conclusion, I note briefly the procedural problems that, I suspect, today's decision will visit upon trial courts in the future. Although the Court indicates that a *pro se* defendant necessarily waives any claim he might otherwise make of ineffective assistance of counsel ... the opinion leaves open a host of other procedural questions. Must every defendant be advised of his right to proceed *pro se?* If so, when must that notice be given? Since the right to assistance of counsel and the right to self-representation are mutually exclusive, how is the waiver of each right to be measured? If a defendant has elected to exercise his right to proceed *pro se,* does he still have a constitutional right to assistance of standby counsel? How soon in the criminal proceeding must a defendant decide between proceeding by counsel or *pro se?* Must he be allowed to switch in midtrial? May a violation of the right to self-representation ever be harmless error? Must the trial court treat the *pro se* defendant differently than it would professional counsel? I assume that many of these questions will be answered with finality in due

course. Many of them, however, such as the standards of waiver
and the treatment of the *pro se* defendant, will haunt the trial of
every defendant who elects to exercise his right to self-representation. The procedural problems spawned by an absolute right to
self-representation will far outweigh whatever tactical advantage the
defendant may feel he has gained by electing to represent himself.

If there is any truth to the old proverb that "[o]ne who is his
own lawyer has a fool for a client," the Court by its opinion today
now bestows a *constitutional* right on one to make a fool of
himself.[*]

[*] Chief Justice Burger wrote a dissenting   Rehnquist joined.
opinion, which Justice Blackmun and Justice

6. THE PRIVILEGE AGAINST SELF-INCRIMINATION

BROWN v. MISSISSIPPI

297 U.S. 278, 56 S.Ct. 461, 80 L.Ed. 682 (1936).

MR. CHIEF JUSTICE HUGHES delivered the opinion of the Court.

The question in this case is whether convictions, which rest solely upon confessions shown to have been extorted by officers of the State by brutality and violence, are consistent with the due process of law required by the Fourteenth Amendment of the Constitution of the United States.

Petitioners were indicted for the murder of one Raymond Stewart, whose death occurred on March 30, 1934. They were indicted on April 4, 1934, and were then arraigned and pleaded not guilty. Counsel were appointed by the court to defend them. Trial was begun the next morning and was concluded on the following day, when they were found guilty and sentenced to death.

Aside from the confessions, there was no evidence sufficient to warrant the submission of the case to the jury. After a preliminary inquiry, testimony as to the confessions was received over the objection of defendants' counsel. Defendants then testified that the confessions were false and had been procured by physical torture. The case went to the jury with instructions, upon the request of defendants' counsel, that if the jury had reasonable doubt as to the confessions having resulted from coercion, and that they were not true, they were not to be considered as evidence. On their appeal to the Supreme Court of the State, defendants assigned as error the inadmissibility of the confessions. The judgment was affirmed. 158 So. 339.

Defendants then moved in the Supreme Court of the State to arrest the judgment and for a new trial on the ground that all the evidence against them was obtained by coercion and brutality known to the court and to the district attorney, and that defendants had been denied the benefit of counsel or opportunity to confer with counsel in a reasonable manner. The motion was supported by affidavits. At about the same time, defendants filed in the Supreme Court a "suggestion of error" explicitly challenging the proceedings of the trial, in the use of the confessions and with respect to the alleged denial of representation by counsel, as violating the due process clause of the Fourteenth Amendment of the Constitution of the United States. The state court entertained the suggestion of error, considered the federal question, and decid-

ed it against defendants' contentions.   161 So. 465.   Two judges
dissented. . . .   We granted a writ of certiorari.

The grounds of the decision were (1) that immunity from self-
incrimination is not essential to due process of law, and (2) that the
failure of the trial court to exclude the confessions after the introduction of evidence showing their incompetency, in the absence of
a request for such exclusion, did not deprive the defendants of life
or liberty without due process of law; and that even if the trial
court had erroneously overruled a motion to exclude the confessions, the ruling would have been mere error reversible on appeal,
but not a violation of constitutional right. . . .

The opinion of the state court did not set forth the evidence as
to the circumstances in which the confessions were procured.   That
the evidence established that they were procured by coercion was
not questioned.   The state court said: "After the state closed its
case on the merits, the appellants, for the first time, introduced
evidence from which it appears that the confessions were not made
voluntarily but were coerced." Id., p. 466.   There is no dispute as
to the facts upon this point and as they are clearly and adequately
stated in the dissenting opinion of Judge Griffith (with whom Judge
Anderson concurred)—showing both the extreme brutality of the
measures to extort the confessions and the participation of the state
authorities—we quote this part of his opinion in full, as follows (Id.,
pp. 470, 471):

"The crime with which these defendants, all ignorant negroes,
are charged, was discovered about one o'clock p.m. on Friday,
March 30, 1934.   On that night one Dial, a deputy sheriff, accompanied by others, came to the home of Ellington, one of the defendants, and requested him to accompany them to the house of the
deceased, and there a number of white men were gathered, who
began to accuse the defendant of the crime.   Upon his denial they
seized him, and with the participation of the deputy they hanged
him by a rope to the limb of a tree, and having let him down, they
hung him again, and when he was let down the second time, and he
still protested his innocence, he was tied to a tree and whipped, and
still declining to accede to the demands that he confess, he was
finally released and he returned with some difficulty to his home,
suffering intense pain and agony.   The record of the testimony
shows that the signs of the rope on his neck were plainly visible
during the so-called trial.   A day or two thereafter the said deputy,
accompanied by another, returned to the home of the said defendant and arrested him, and departed with the prisoner towards the
jail in an adjoining county, but went by a route which led into the
State of Alabama;   and while on the way, in that State, the deputy
stopped and again severely whipped the defendant, declaring that
he would continue the whipping until he confessed, and the
defendant then agreed to confess to such a statement as the deputy
would dictate, and he did so, after which he was delivered to jail.

"The other two defendants, Ed Brown and Henry Shields, were also arrested and taken to the same jail. On Sunday night, April 1, 1934, the same deputy, accompanied by a number of white men, one of whom was also an officer, and by the jailer, came to the jail, and the two last named defendants were made to strip and they were laid over chairs and their backs were cut to pieces with a leather strap with buckles on it, and they were likewise made by the said deputy definitely to understand that the whipping would be continued unless and until they confessed, and not only confessed, but confessed in every matter of detail as demanded by those present; and in this manner the defendants confessed the crime, and as the whippings progressed and were repeated, they changed or adjusted their confession in all particulars of detail so as to conform to the demands of their torturers. When the confessions had been obtained in the exact form and contents as desired by the mob, they left with the parting admonition and warning that, if the defendants changed their story at any time in any respect from that last stated, the perpetrators of the outrage would administer the same or equally effective treatment.

"Further details of the brutal treatment to which these helpless prisoners were subjected need not be pursued. It is sufficient to say that in pertinent respects the transcript reads more like pages torn from some medieval account, than a record made within the confines of a modern civilization which aspires to an enlightened constitutional government.

"All this having been accomplished, on the next day, that is, on Monday, April 2, when the defendants had been given time to recuperate somewhat from the tortures to which they had been subjected, the two sheriffs, one of the county where the crime was committed, and the other of the county of the jail in which the prisoners were confined, came to the jail, accompanied by eight other persons, some of them deputies, there to hear the free and voluntary confession of these miserable and abject defendants. The sheriff of the county of the crime admitted that he had heard of the whipping, but averred that he had no personal knowledge of it. He admitted that one of the defendants, when brought before him to confess, was limping and did not sit down, and that this particular defendant then and there stated that he had been strapped so severely that he could not sit down, and as already stated, the signs of the rope on the neck of another of the defendants were plainly visible to all. Nevertheless the solemn farce of hearing the free and voluntary confessions was gone through with, and these two sheriffs and one other person then present were the three witnesses used in court to establish the so-called confessions, which were received by the court and admitted in evidence over the objections of the defendants duly entered of record as each of the said three witnesses delivered their alleged testimony. There was thus enough before the court when these confessions were first offered to make known to the court that they were not, beyond all reasonable doubt, free and voluntary; and the failure of the court then to exclude the confessions is sufficient to reverse the judgment, under every rule of procedure that has heretofore been prescribed, and hence it was not necessary subsequently to renew the objections by motion or otherwise.

"The spurious confessions having been obtained—and the farce last mentioned having been gone through with on Monday, April 2d—the court, then in session, on the following day, Tuesday, April 3, 1934, ordered the grand jury to reassemble on the succeeding day, April 4, 1934, at nine o'clock, and on the morning of the day last mentioned the grand jury returned an indictment against the defendants for murder. Late that afternoon the defendants were brought from the jail in the adjoining county and arraigned, when one or more of them offered to plead guilty, which the court declined to accept, and, upon inquiry whether they had or desired counsel, they stated that they had none, and did not suppose that counsel could be of any assistance to them. The court thereupon appointed counsel, and set the case for trial for the following morning at nine o'clock, and the defendants were returned to the jail in the adjoining county about thirty miles away.

"The defendants were brought to the courthouse of the county on the following morning, April 5th, and the so-called trial was opened, and was concluded on the next day, April 6, 1934, and resulted in a pretended conviction with death sentences. The evidence upon which the conviction was obtained was the so-called confessions. Without this evidence a peremptory instruction to find for the defendants would have been inescapable. The defendants were put on the stand, and by their testimony the facts and the details thereof as to the manner by which the confessions were extorted from them were fully developed, and it is further disclosed by the record that the same deputy, Dial, under whose guiding hand and active participation the tortures to coerce the confessions were administered, was actively in the performance of the supposed duties of a court deputy in the courthouse and in the presence of the prisoners during what is denominated, in complimentary terms, the trial of these defendants. This deputy was put on the stand by the state in rebuttal, and admitted the whippings. It is interesting to note that in his testimony with reference to the whipping of the defendant Ellington, and in response to the inquiry as to how severely he was whipped, the deputy stated, 'Not too much for a negro; not as much as I would have done if it were left to me.' Two others who had participated in these whippings were introduced and admitted it—not a single witness was introduced who denied it. The facts are not only undisputed, they are admitted, and admitted to have been done by officers of the state, in conjunction with other participants, and all this was definitely well known to everybody connected with the trial, and during the trial, including the state's prosecuting attorney and the trial judge presiding."

1. The State stresses the statement in Twining v. New Jersey, 211 U.S. 78, 114, that "exemption from compulsory self-incrimination in the courts of the States is not secured by any part of the Federal Constitution," and the statement in Snyder v. Massachusetts, 291 U.S. 97, 105, that "the privilege against self-incrimination may be withdrawn and the accused put upon the stand as a witness for the State." But the question of the right of the State to withdraw the privilege against self-incrimination is not here involved. The compulsion to which the quoted statements refer is that of the processes of justice by which the accused may be called as a witness and required to testify. Compulsion by torture to extort a confession is a different matter.

The State is free to regulate the procedure of its courts in accordance with its own conceptions of policy, unless in so doing it "offends some principle of justice so rooted in the traditions and conscience of our people as to be ranked as fundamental." Snyder v. Massachusetts, supra; Rogers v. Peck, 199 U.S. 425, 434. The State may abolish trial by jury. It may dispense with indictment by a grand jury and substitute complaint or information.... But the freedom of the State in establishing its policy is the freedom of constitutional government and is limited by the requirement of due process of law. Because a State may dispense with a jury trial, it does not follow that it may substitute trial by ordeal. The rack and torture chamber may not be substituted for the witness stand. The State may not permit an accused to be hurried to conviction under mob domination—where the whole proceeding is but a mask—without supplying corrective process.... The State may not deny to the accused the aid of counsel.... Nor may a State, through the action of its officers, contrive a conviction through the pretense of a trial which in truth is "but used as a means of depriving a defendant of liberty through a deliberate deception of court and jury by the presentation of testimony known to be perjured." Mooney v. Holohan, 294 U.S. 103, 112. And the trial equally is a mere pretense where the state authorities have contrived a conviction resting solely upon confessions obtained by violence. The due process clause requires "that state action, whether through one agency or another, shall be consistent with the fundamental principles of liberty and justice which lie at the base of all our civil and political institutions." Hebert v. Louisiana, 272 U.S. 312, 316. It would be difficult to conceive of methods more revolting to the sense of justice than those taken to procure the confessions of these petitioners, and the use of the confessions thus obtained as the basis for conviction and sentence was a clear denial of due process.

2. It is in the view that the further contention of the State must be considered. That contention rests upon the failure of counsel for the accused, who had objected to the admissibility of

the confessions, to move for their exclusion after they had been introduced and the fact of coercion had been proved. It is a contention which proceeds upon a misconception of the nature of petitioners' complaint. That complaint is not of the commission of mere error, but of a wrong so fundamental that it made the whole proceeding a mere pretense of a trial and rendered the conviction and sentence wholly void. . . . We are not concerned with a mere question of state practice, or whether counsel assigned to petitioners were competent or mistakenly assumed that their first objections were sufficient. In an earlier case the Supreme Court of the State had recognized the duty of the court to supply corrective process where due process of law had been denied. In Fisher v. State, 145 Miss. 116, 134; 110 So. 361, 365, the court said: "Coercing the supposed state's criminals into confessions and using such confessions so coerced from them against them in trials has been the curse of all countries. It was the chief inequity, the crowning infamy of the Star Chamber, and the Inquisition, and other similar institutions. The constitution recognized the evils that lay behind these practices and prohibited them in this country. . . . The duty of maintaining constitutional rights of a person on trial for his life rises above mere rules of procedure and wherever the court is clearly satisfied that such violations exist, it will refuse to sanction such violations and will apply the corrective."

In the instant case, the trial court was fully advised by the undisputed evidence of the way in which the confessions had been procured. The trial court knew that there was no other evidence upon which conviction and sentence could be based. Yet it proceeded to permit conviction and to pronounce sentence. The conviction and sentence were void for want of the essential elements of due process, and the proceeding thus vitiated could be challenged in any appropriate manner. Mooney v. Holohan, supra. It was challenged before the Supreme Court of the State by the express invocation of the Fourteenth Amendment. That court entertained the challenge, considered the federal question thus presented, but declined to enforce petitioners' constitutional right. The court thus denied a federal right fully established and specially set up and claimed and the judgment must be

Reversed.

SPANO v. NEW YORK

360 U.S. 315, 79 S.Ct. 1202, 3 L.Ed.2d 1265 (1959).

MR. CHIEF JUSTICE WARREN delivered the opinion of the Court.

This is another in the long line of cases presenting the question whether a confession was properly admitted into evidence under the Fourteenth Amendment. As in all such cases, we are forced to resolve a conflict between two fundamental interests of society; its interest in prompt and efficient law enforcement, and its interest in preventing the rights of its individual members from being abridged by unconstitutional methods of law enforcement. Because of the delicate nature of the constitutional determination which we must make, we cannot escape the responsibility of making our own examination of the record. . . .

The State's evidence reveals the following: Petitioner Vincent Joseph Spano is a derivative citizen of this country, having been born in Messina, Italy. He was 25 years old at the time of the shooting in question and had graduated from junior high school. He had a record of regular employment. The shooting took place on January 22, 1957.

On that day, petitioner was drinking in a bar. The decedent, a former professional boxer weighing almost 200 pounds who had fought in Madison Square Garden, took some of petitioner's money from the bar. Petitioner followed him out of the bar to recover it. A fight ensued, with the decedent knocking petitioner down and then kicking him in the head three or four times. Shock from the force of these blows caused petitioner to vomit. After the bartender applied some ice to his head, petitioner left the bar, walked to his apartment, secured a gun, and walked eight or nine blocks to a candy store where the decedent was frequently to be found. He entered the store in which decedent, three friends of decedent, at least two of whom were exconvicts, and a boy who was supervising the store were present. He fired five shots, two of which entered the decedent's body, causing his death. The boy was the only eyewitness; the three friends of decedent did not see the person who fired the shot. Petitioner then disappeared for the next week or so.

On February 1, 1957, the Bronx County Grand Jury returned an indictment for first-degree murder against petitioner. Accordingly, a bench warrant was issued for his arrest, commanding that he be forthwith brought before the court to answer the indictment, or, if the court had adjourned for the term, that he be delivered into the custody of the Sheriff of Bronx County. . . .

On February 3, 1957, petitioner called one Gaspar Bruno, a close friend of 8 or 10 years' standing who had attended school with him. Bruno was a fledgling police officer, having at that time not yet finished attending police academy. According to Bruno's testimony, petitioner told him "that he took a terrific beating, that the deceased hurt him real bad and he dropped him a couple of times and he was dazed; he didn't know what he was doing and that he went and shot at him." Petitioner told Bruno that he intended to get a lawyer and give himself up. Bruno relayed this information to his superiors.

The following day, February 4, at 7:10 p.m., petitioner, accompanied by counsel, surrendered himself to the authorities in front of the Bronx County Building, where both the office of the Assistant District Attorney who ultimately prosecuted his case and the courtroom in which he was ultimately tried were located. His attorney had cautioned him to answer no questions, and left him in the custody of the officers. He was promptly taken to the office of the Assistant District Attorney and at 7:15 p.m. the questioning began, being conducted by Assistant District Attorney Goldsmith, Lt. Gannon, Detectives Farrell, Lehrer and Motta, and Sgt. Clarke. The record reveals that the questioning was both persistent and continuous. Petitioner, in accordance with his attorney's instructions, steadfastly refused to answer. Detective Motta testified: "He refused to talk to me." "He just looked up to the ceiling and refused to talk to me." Detective Farrell testified:

"Q. And you started to interrogate him?

"A. That is right.

.   .   .   .

"Q. What did he say?

"A. He said 'you would have to see my attorney. I tell you nothing but my name.'

.   .   .   .

"Q. Did you continue to examine him?

"A. Verbally, yes, sir."

He asked one officer, Detective Ciccone, if he could speak to his attorney, but that request was denied. Detective Ciccone testified that he could not find the attorney's name in the telephone book. He was given two sandwiches, coffee and cake at 11 p.m.

At 12:15 a.m. on the morning of February 5, after five hours of questioning in which it became evident that petitioner was following his attorney's instructions, on the Assistant District Attorney's orders petitioner was transferred to the 46th Squad, Ryer Avenue Police Station. The Assistant District Attorney also went to the police station and to some extent continued to participate in the interrogation. Petitioner arrived at 12:30 and questioning was resumed at 12:40. The character of the questioning is revealed by the testimony of Detective Farrell:

"Q. Who did you leave him in the room with?

"A. With Detective Lehrer and Sergeant Clarke came in and Mr. Goldsmith came in or Inspector Halk came in. It was back and forth. People just came in, spoke a few words to the defendant or they listened a few minutes and they left."

But petitioner persisted in his refusal to answer, and again requested permission to see his attorney, this time from Detective Lehrer. His request was again denied.

It was then that those in charge of the investigation decided that petitioner's close friend, Bruno, could be of use. He had been called out on the case around 10 or 11 p.m., although he was not connected with the 46th Squad or Precinct in any way. Although, in fact, his job was in no way threatened, Bruno was told to tell petitioner that petitioner's telephone call had gotten him "in a lot of trouble," and that he should seek to extract sympathy from petitioner for Bruno's pregnant wife and three children. Bruno developed this theme with petitioner without success, and petitioner, also without success, again sought to see his attorney, a request which Bruno relayed unavailingly to his superiors. After this first session with petitioner, Bruno was again directed by Lt. Gannon to play on petitioner's sympathies, but again no confession was forthcoming. But the Lieutenant a third time ordered Bruno falsely to importune his friend to confess, but again petitioner clung to his attorney's advice. Inevitably, in the fourth such session directed by the Lieutenant, lasting a full hour, petitioner succumbed to his friend's prevarications and agreed to make a statement. Accordingly, at 3:25 a.m. the Assistant District Attorney, a stenographer, and several other law enforcement officials entered the room where petitioner was being questioned, and took his statement in question and answer form with the Assistant District Attorney asking the questions. The statement was completed at 4:05 a.m.

But this was not the end. At 4:30 a.m. three detectives took petitioner to Police Headquarters in Manhattan. On the way they attempted to find the bridge from which petitioner said he had thrown the murder weapon. They crossed the Triborough Bridge into Manhattan, arriving at Police Headquarters at 5 a.m., and left Manhattan for the Bronx at 5:40 a.m. via the Willis Avenue Bridge. When petitioner recognized neither bridge as the one from which he had thrown the weapon, they re-entered Manhattan via the Third Avenue Bridge, which petitioner stated was the right one, and then returned to the Bronx well after 6 a.m. During that trip the officers also elicited a statement from petitioner that the deceased was always "on [his] back," "always pushing" him and that he was "not sorry" he had shot the deceased. All three detectives testified to that statement at the trial.

Court opened at 10 a.m. that morning, and petitioner was arraigned at 10:15.

At the trial, the confession was introduced in evidence over appropriate objections. The jury was instructed that it could rely on it only if it was found to be voluntary. The jury returned a guilty verdict and petitioner was sentenced to death. The New York Court of Appeals affirmed the conviction over three dissents, 4 N.Y.2d 256, 173 N.Y.S.2d 793, 150 N.E.2d 226, and we granted certiorari to resolve the serious problem presented under the Fourteenth Amendment. 358 U.S. 919.

Petitioner's first contention is that his absolute right to counsel in a capital case, Powell v. Alabama, 287 U.S. 45, became operative on the return of an indictment against him, for at that time he was in every sense a defendant in a criminal case, the grand jury having found sufficient cause to believe that he had committed the crime. He argues accordingly that following indictment no confession obtained in the absence of counsel can be used without violating the Fourteenth Amendment. He seeks to distinguish Crooker v. California, 357 U.S. 433, and Cicenia v. Lagay, 357 U.S. 504, on the ground that in those cases no indictment had been returned. We find it unnecessary to reach that contention, for we find use of the confession obtained here inconsistent with the Fourteenth Amendment under traditional principles.

The abhorrence of society to the use of involuntary confessions does not turn alone on their inherent untrustworthiness. It also turns on the deep-rooted feeling that the police must obey the law while enforcing the law; that in the end life and liberty can be as much endangered from illegal methods used to convict those thought to be criminals as from the actual criminals themselves. Accordingly, the actions of police in obtaining confessions have come under scrutiny in a long series of cases. Those cases suggest that in recent years law enforcement officials have become increasingly aware of the burden which they share, along with our courts, in protecting fundamental rights of our citizenry, including that portion of our citizenry suspected of crime. The facts of no case recently in this Court have quite approached the brutal beatings in Brown v. Mississippi, 297 U.S. 278 (1936), or the 36 consecutive hours of questioning present in Ashcraft v. Tennessee, 322 U.S. 143 (1944). But as law enforcement officers become more responsible, and the methods used to extract confessions more sophisticated, our duty to enforce federal constitutional protections does not cease. It only becomes more difficult because of the more delicate judgments to be made. Our judgment here is that, on all the facts, this conviction cannot stand.

Petitioner was a foreign-born young man of 25 with no past history of law violation or of subjection to official interrogation, at least insofar as the record shows. He had progressed only one-half year into high school and the record indicates that he had a history of emotional instability. He did not make a narrative statement, but was subject to the leading questions of a skillful prosecutor in a question and answer confession. He was subjected to questioning not by a few men, but by many. They included Assistant District Attorney Goldsmith, one Hyland of the District Attorney's Office, Deputy Inspector Halks, Lieutenant Gannon, Detective Ciccone, Detective Motta, Detective Lehrer, Detective Marshal, Detective Farrell, Detective Leira, Detective Murphy, Detective Murtha, Sergeant Clarke, Patrolman Bruno and Stenographer Baldwin. All played some part, and the effect of such massive official interrogation must have been felt. Petitioner was questioned for virtually eight straight hours before he confessed, with his only respite being a transfer to an arena presumably considered more appropriate by the police for the task at hand. Nor was the questioning conducted during normal business hours, but began in early evening, continued into the night, and did not bear fruition until the not-too-early morning. The drama was not played out, with the final admissions obtained, until almost sunrise. In such circumstances slowly mounting fatigue does, and is calculated to, play its part. The questioners persisted in the face of his repeated refusals to answer on the advice of his attorney, and they ignored his reasonable requests to contact the local attorney whom he had already retained and who had personally delivered him into the custody of these officers in obedience to the bench warrant.

The use of Bruno, characterized in this Court by counsel for the State as a "childhood friend" of petitioner's, is another factor which deserves mention in the totality of the situation. Bruno's was the one face visible to petitioner in which he could put some trust. There was a bond of friendship between them going back a decade into adolescence. It was with this material that the officers felt that they could overcome petitioner's will. They instructed Bruno falsely to state that petitioner's telephone call had gotten him into trouble, that his job was in jeopardy, and that loss of his job would be disastrous to his three children, his wife and his unborn child. And Bruno played this part of a worried father, harried by his superiors, in not one, but four different acts, the final one lasting an hour. Cf. Leyra v. Denno, 347 U.S. 556. Petitioner was apparently unaware of John Gay's famous couplet:

> "An open foe may prove a curse,
>
> But a pretended friend is worse,"

and he yielded to his false friend's entreaties.

We conclude that petitioner's will was overborne by official pressure, fatigue and sympathy falsely aroused, after considering all the facts in their post-indictment setting. Here a grand jury had already found sufficient cause to require petitioner to face trial on a charge of first-degree murder, and the police had an eyewitness to the shooting. The police were not therefore merely trying to solve a crime, or even to absolve a suspect.... They were rather concerned primarily with securing a statement from defendant on which they could convict him. The undeviating intent of the officers to extract a confession from petitioner is therefore patent. When such an intent is shown, this Court has held that the confession obtained must be examined with the most careful scrutiny, and has reversed a conviction on facts less compelling than these.... Accordingly, we hold that petitioner's conviction cannot stand under the Fourteenth Amendment.

. . .

Reversed.

MR. JUSTICE DOUGLAS, with whom MR. JUSTICE BLACK and MR. JUSTICE BRENNAN join, concurring.

While I join the opinion of the Court, I add what for me is an even more important ground of decision.

We have often divided on whether state authorities may question a suspect for hours on end when he has no lawyer present and when he has demanded that he have the benefit of legal advice.... But here we deal not with a suspect but with a man who has been formally charged with a crime. The question is whether after the indictment and before the trial the Government can interrogate the accused *in secret* when he asked for his lawyer and when his request was denied. This is a capital case; and under the rule of Powell v. Alabama, 287 U.S. 45, the defendant was entitled to be represented by counsel. This representation by counsel is not restricted to the trial. ...

Depriving a person, formally charged with a crime, of counsel during the period prior to trial may be more damaging than denial of counsel during the trial itself.

... This is a case of an accused, who is scheduled to be tried by a judge and jury, being tried in a preliminary way by the police. This is a kangaroo court procedure whereby the police produce the vital evidence in the form of a confession which is useful or necessary to obtain a conviction. They in effect deny him effective representation by counsel. This seems to me to be a flagrant violation of the principle announced in Powell v. Alabama, supra, that the right of counsel extends to the preparation for trial, as well as to the trial itself. As Professor Chafee once said, "A person accused of crime needs a lawyer right after his arrest probably more than at any other time." Chafee, Documents on Fundamental

Human Rights, Pamphlet 2 (1951–1952), p. 541. When he is deprived of that right after indictment and before trial, he may indeed be denied effective representation by counsel at the only stage when legal aid and advice would help him. ...

MR. JUSTICE STEWART, whom MR. JUSTICE DOUGLAS and MR. JUSTICE BRENNAN join, concurring.

While I concur in the opinion of the Court, it is my view that the absence of counsel when this confession was elicited was alone enough to render it inadmissible under the Fourteenth Amendment.

Let it be emphasized at the outset that this is not a case where the police were questioning a suspect in the course of investigating an unsolved crime. ... When the petitioner surrendered to the New York authorities he was under indictment for first degree murder.

Under our system of justice an indictment is supposed to be followed by an arraignment and a trial. At every stage in those proceedings the accused has an absolute right to a lawyer's help if the case is one in which a death sentence may be imposed. ... Indeed the right to the assistance of counsel whom the accused has himself retained is absolute, whatever the offense for which he is on trial. ...

What followed the petitioner's surrender in this case was not arraignment in a court of law, but an all-night inquisition in a prosecutor's office, a police station, and an automobile. Throughout the night the petitioner repeatedly asked to be allowed to send for his lawyer, and his requests were repeatedly denied. He finally was induced to make a confession. That confession was used to secure a verdict sending him to the electric chair.

Our Constitution guarantees the assistance of counsel to a man on trial for his life in an orderly courtroom, presided over by a judge, open to the public, and protected by all the procedural safeguards of the law. Surely a Constitution which promises that much can vouchsafe no less to the same man under midnight inquisition in the squad room of a police station.

COLORADO v. CONNELLY

479 U.S. 157, 107 S.Ct. 515, 93 L.Ed.2d 473 (1986).

CHIEF JUSTICE REHNQUIST delivered the opinion of the Court.

In this case, the Supreme Court of Colorado held that the United States Constitution requires a court to suppress a confession when the mental state of the defendant, at the time he made the confession, interfered with his "rational intellect" and his "free will." Because this decision seemed to conflict with prior holdings of this Court, we granted certiorari. 474 U.S. 1050 (1986). We conclude that the admissibility of this kind of statement is governed by state rules of evidence, rather than by our previous decisions regarding coerced confessions and *Miranda* waivers. We therefore reverse.

I

On August 18, 1983, Officer Patrick Anderson of the Denver Police Department was in uniform, working in an off-duty capacity in downtown Denver. Respondent Francis Connelly approached Officer Anderson and, without any prompting, stated that he had murdered someone and wanted to talk about it. Anderson immediately advised respondent that he had the right to remain silent, that anything he said could be used against him in court, and that he had the right to an attorney prior to any police questioning. See Miranda v. Arizona, 384 U.S. 436 (1966). Respondent stated that he understood these rights but he still wanted to talk about the murder. Understandably bewildered by this confession, Officer Anderson asked respondent several questions. Connelly denied that he had been drinking, denied that he had been taking any drugs, and stated that, in the past, he had been a patient in several mental hospitals. Officer Anderson again told Connelly that he was under no obligation to say anything. Connelly replied that it was "all right," and that he would talk to Officer Anderson because his conscience had been bothering him. To Officer Anderson, respondent appeared to understand fully the nature of his acts. Tr. 19.

Shortly thereafter, Homicide Detective Stephen Antuna arrived. Respondent was again advised of his rights, and Detective Antuna asked him "what he had on his mind." Id., at 24. Respondent answered that he had come all the way from Boston to confess to the murder of Mary Ann Junta, a young girl whom he had killed in Denver sometime during November 1982. Respondent was taken to police headquarters, and a search of police records revealed that the body of an unidentified female had been found in April 1983.

654

Respondent openly detailed his story to Detective Antuna and Sergeant Thomas Haney, and readily agreed to take the officers to the scene of the killing. Under Connelly's sole direction, the two officers and respondent proceeded in a police vehicle to the location of the crime. Respondent pointed out the exact location of the murder. Throughout this episode, Detective Antuna perceived no indication whatsoever that respondent was suffering from any kind of mental illness. . . .

Respondent was held overnight. During an interview with the public defender's office the following morning, he became visibly disoriented. He began giving confused answers to questions, and for the first time, stated that "voices" had told him to come to Denver and that he had followed the directions of these voices in confessing. . . . Respondent was sent to a state hospital for evaluation. He was initially found incompetent to assist in his own defense. By March 1984, however, the doctors evaluating respondent determined that he was competent to proceed to trial.

At a preliminary hearing, respondent moved to suppress all of his statements. Doctor Jeffrey Metzner, a psychiatrist employed by the state hospital, testified that respondent was suffering from chronic schizophrenia and was in a psychotic state at least as of August 17, 1983, the day before he confessed. Metzner's interviews with respondent revealed that respondent was following the "voice of God." This voice instructed respondent to withdraw money from the bank, to buy an airplane ticket, and to fly from Boston to Denver. When respondent arrived from Boston, God's voice became stronger and told respondent either to confess to the killing or to commit suicide. Reluctantly following the command of the voices, respondent approached Officer Anderson and confessed.

Dr. Metzner testified that, in his expert opinion, respondent was experiencing "command hallucinations." Id., at 56. This condition interfered with respondent's "volitional abilities; that is, his ability to make free and rational choices." Ibid. Dr. Metzner further testified that Connelly's illness did not significantly impair his cognitive abilities. Thus, respondent understood the rights he had when Officer Anderson and Detective Antuna advised him that he need not speak. . . . Dr. Metzner admitted that the "voices" could in reality be Connelly's interpretation of his own guilt, but explained that in his opinion, Connelly's psychosis motivated his confession.

On the basis of this evidence the Colorado trial court decided that respondent's statements must be suppressed because they were "involuntary." Relying on our decisions in Townsend v. Sain, 372 U.S. 293 (1963), and Culombe v. Connecticut, 367 U.S. 568 (1961), the court ruled that a confession is admissible only if it is a product of the defendant's rational intellect and "free will." . . . Although the court found that the police had done nothing wrong or coercive in securing respondent's confession, Connelly's illness destroyed his volition and compelled him to confess. ... The trial court also found that Connelly's mental state vitiated his attempted waiver of the right to counsel and the privilege against compulsory self-incrimination. Accordingly, respondent's initial statements and his custodial confession were suppressed....

The Colorado Supreme Court affirmed. 702 P.2d 722 (1985). In that court's view, the proper test for admissibility is whether the statements are "the product of a rational intellect and a free will." Id., at 728. Indeed, "the absence of police coercion or duress does not foreclose a finding of involuntariness. One's capacity for rational judgment and free choice may be overborne as much by certain forms of severe mental illness as by external pressure." Ibid. The court found that the very admission of the evidence in a court of law was sufficient state action to implicate the Due Process Clause of the Fourteenth Amendment to the United States Constitution. The evidence fully supported the conclusion that respondent's initial statement was not the product of a rational intellect and a free will. The court then considered respondent's attempted waiver of his constitutional rights and found that respondent's mental condition precluded his ability to make a valid waiver.... The Colorado Supreme Court thus affirmed the trial court's decision to suppress all of Connelly's statements.

II

The Due Process Clause of the Fourteenth Amendment provides that no State shall "deprive any person of life, liberty, or property, without due process of law." Just last Term, in Miller v. Fenton, 474 U.S. 104, 109 (1985), we held that by virtue of the Due Process Clause "certain interrogation techniques, either in isolation or as applied to the unique characteristics of a particular suspect, are so offensive to a civilized system of justice that they must be condemned." ...

Indeed, coercive government misconduct was the catalyst for this Court's seminal confession case, Brown v. Mississippi, 297 U.S. 278 (1936). In that case, police officers extracted confessions from the accused through brutal torture. The Court had little difficulty concluding that even though the Fifth Amendment did not at that time apply to the States, the actions of the police were "revolting to the sense of justice." Id., at 286. The Court has retained this due process focus, even after holding, in Malloy v. Hogan, 378 U.S. 1 (1964), that the Fifth Amendment privilege against compulsory self-incrimination applies to the States....

Thus the cases considered by this Court over the 50 years since Brown v. Mississippi have focused upon the crucial element of police overreaching. While each confession case has turned on its own set of factors justifying the conclusion that police conduct was oppressive, all have contained a substantial element of coercive police conduct. Absent police conduct causally related to the confession, there is simply no basis for concluding that any state actor has deprived a criminal defendant of due process of law. Respondent correctly notes that as interrogators have turned to more subtle forms of psychological persuasion, courts have found the mental condition of the defendant a more significant factor in the "voluntariness" calculus. See Spano v. New York, 360 U.S. 315 (1959). But this fact does not justify a conclusion that a defendant's mental condition, by itself and apart from its relation to official coercion, should ever dispose of the inquiry into constitutional "voluntariness."

Respondent relies on Blackburn v. Alabama, 361 U.S. 199 (1960), and Townsend v. Sain, 372 U.S. 293 (1963), for the proposition that the "deficient mental condition of the defendants in those cases was sufficient to render their confessions involuntary." Brief for Respondent 20. But respondent's reading of *Blackburn* and *Townsend* ignores the integral element of police overreaching present in both cases. In *Blackburn,* the Court found that the petitioner was probably insane at the time of his confession and the police learned during the interrogation that Blackburn had a history of mental problems. The police exploited this weakness with coercive tactics: "the eight- to nine-hour sustained interrogation in a tiny room which was upon occasion literally filled with police officers; the absence of Blackburn's friends, relatives, or legal counsel; [and] the composition of the confession by the Deputy Sheriff rather than by Blackburn." 361 U.S., at 207–208. These tactics supported a finding that the confession was involuntary. Indeed, the Court specifically condemned police activity that "wrings a confession out of an accused against his will." Id., at 206–207. *Townsend* presented a similar instance of police wrongdoing. In that case, a police physician had given Townsend a drug with truth-serum properties.... The subsequent confession, obtained by officers who knew that Townsend had been given drugs, was held involuntary. These two cases demonstrate that while mental condition is surely relevant to an individual's susceptibility to police coercion, mere examination of the confessant's state of mind can never conclude the due process inquiry.

Our "involuntary confession" jurisprudence is entirely consistent with the settled law requiring some sort of "state action" to support a claim of violation of the Due Process Clause of the Fourteenth Amendment. The Colorado trial court, of course, found that the police committed no wrongful acts, and that finding has been neither challenged by the respondent nor disturbed by the Supreme Court of Colorado. The latter court, however, concluded that sufficient state action was present by virtue of the admission of the confession into evidence in a court of the State....

The difficulty with the approach of the Supreme Court of Colorado is that it fails to recognize the essential link between coercive activity of the State, on the one hand, and a resulting confession by a defendant, on the other. The flaw in respondent's constitutional argument is that it would expand our previous line of "voluntariness" cases into a far-ranging requirement that courts must divine a defendant's motivation for speaking or acting as he did even though there be no claim that governmental conduct coerced his decision.

The most outrageous behavior by a private party seeking to secure evidence against a defendant does not make that evidence inadmissible under the Due Process Clause.... We have also observed that "[j]urists and scholars have recognized that the exclusionary rule imposes a substantial cost on the societal interest in law enforcement by its proscription of what concededly is relevant evidence." United States v. Janis, 428 U.S. 433, 448–449 (1976). ... Moreover, suppressing respondent's statements would serve absolutely no purpose in enforcing constitutional guarantees. The purpose of excluding evidence seized in violation of the Constitution is to substantially deter future violations of the Constitution.... Only if we were to establish a brand new constitutional right—the right of a criminal defendant to confess to his crime only when totally rational and properly motivated—could respondent's present claim be sustained.

We have previously cautioned against expanding "currently applicable exclusionary rules by erecting additional barriers to placing truthful and probative evidence before state juries...." Lego v. Twomey, 404 U.S. 477, 488–489 (1972). We abide by that counsel now. "[T]he central purpose of a criminal trial is to decide the factual question of the defendant's guilt or innocence," Delaware v. Van Arsdall, 475 U.S. 673, 681 (1986), and while we have previously held that exclusion of evidence may be necessary to protect constitutional guarantees, both the necessity for the collateral inquiry and the exclusion of evidence deflect a criminal trial from its basic purpose. Respondent would now have us require sweeping inquiries into the state of mind of a criminal defendant who has confessed, inquiries quite divorced from any coercion brought to bear on the defendant by the State. We think the Constitution rightly leaves this sort of inquiry to be resolved by state laws governing the admission of evidence and erects no standard of its own in this area. A statement rendered by one in the condition of respondent might be proved to be quite unreliable, but this is a matter to be governed by the evidentiary laws of the forum ... and not by the Due Process Clause of the Fourteenth Amendment. "The aim of the requirement of due process is not to exclude presumptively false evidence, but to prevent fundamental unfairness in the use of evidence, whether true or false." Lisenba v. California, 314 U.S. 219, 236 (1941).

We hold that coercive police activity is a necessary predicate to the finding that a confession is not "voluntary" within the meaning of the Due Process Clause of the Fourteenth Amendment. We also conclude that the taking of respondent's statements, and their admission into evidence, constitute no violation of that Clause.

III

A

The Supreme Court of Colorado went on to affirm the trial court's ruling that respondent's later statements made while in custody should be suppressed because respondent had not waived his right to consult an attorney and his right to remain silent. That court held that the State must bear its burden of proving waiver of these *Miranda* rights by "clear and convincing evidence." 702 P.2d, at 729. Although we have stated in passing that the State bears a "heavy" burden in proving waiver ... we have never held that the "clear and convincing evidence" standard is the appropriate one.

In *Lego v. Twomey,* supra, this Court upheld a procedure in which the State established the voluntariness of a confession by no more than a preponderance of the evidence. We upheld it for two reasons. First, the voluntariness determination has nothing to do with the reliability of jury verdicts; rather, it is designed to determine the presence of police coercion. Thus, voluntariness is irrelevant to the presence or absence of the elements of a crime, which must be proved beyond a reasonable doubt.... Second, we rejected Lego's assertion that a high burden of proof was required to serve the values protected by the exclusionary rule. We surveyed the various reasons for excluding evidence, including a violation of the requirements of *Miranda v. Arizona,* supra, and we stated that "[i]n each instance, and without regard to its probative value, evidence is kept from the trier of guilt or innocence for reasons wholly apart from enhancing the reliability of verdicts." Lego v. Twomey, 404 U.S., at 488. Moreover, we rejected the argument that "the importance of the values served by exclusionary rules is itself sufficient demonstration that the Constitution also requires admissibility to be proved beyond a reasonable doubt." Ibid. Indeed, the Court found that "no substantial evidence has accumulated that federal rights have suffered from determining admissibility by a preponderance of the evidence." Ibid.

We now reaffirm our holding in *Lego:* Whenever the State bears the burden of proof in a motion to suppress a statement that the defendant claims was obtained in violation of our *Miranda* doctrine, the State need prove waiver only by a preponderance of the evidence.... If, as we held in *Lego v. Twomey,* supra, the voluntariness of a confession need be established only by a preponderance of the evidence, then a waiver of the auxiliary protections established in *Miranda* should require no higher burden of proof. "[E]xclusionary rules are very much aimed at deterring lawless conduct by police and prosecution and it is very doubtful that escalating the prosecution's burden of proof in ... suppression hearings would be sufficiently productive in this respect to outweigh the public interest in placing probative evidence before juries for the purpose of arriving at truthful decisions about guilt or innocence." *Lego v. Twomey,* supra, at 489.

B

We also think that the Supreme Court of Colorado was mistaken in its analysis of the question of whether respondent had waived his *Miranda* rights in this case. Of course, a waiver must at a minimum be "voluntary" to be effective against an accused.... The Supreme Court of Colorado in addressing this question relied on the testimony of the court-appointed psychiatrist to the effect that respondent was not capable of making a "free decision with respect to his constitutional right of silence ... and his constitutional right to confer with a lawyer before talking to the police." 702 P.2d, at 729.

We think that the Supreme Court of Colorado erred in importing into this area of constitutional law notions of "free will" that have no place there. There is obviously no reason to require more in the way of a "voluntariness" inquiry in the *Miranda* waiver context than in the Fourteenth Amendment confession context. The sole concern of the Fifth Amendment, on which *Miranda* was based, is governmental coercion.... Indeed, the Fifth Amendment privilege is not concerned "with moral and psychological pressures to confess emanating from sources other than official coercion." Oregon v. Elstad, 470 U.S. 298, 305 (1985). The voluntariness of a waiver of this privilege has always depended on the absence of police overreaching, not on "free choice" in any broader sense of the word....

Respondent urges this Court to adopt his "free will" rationale, and to find an attempted waiver invalid whenever the defendant feels compelled to waive his rights by reason of any compulsion, even if the compulsion does not flow from the police. But such a treatment of the waiver issue would "cut this Court's holding in *[Miranda]* completely loose from its own explicitly stated rationale." Beckwith v. United States, 425 U.S. 341, 345 (1976). *Miranda* protects defendants against government coercion leading them to surrender rights protected by the Fifth Amendment; it goes no further than that. Respondent's perception of coercion flowing from the "voice of God," however important or significant such a perception may be in other disciplines, is a matter to which the United States Constitution does not speak.

IV

The judgment of the Supreme Court of Colorado is accordingly reversed, and the cause remanded for further proceedings not inconsistent with this opinion.

. . .

JUSTICE BRENNAN, with whom JUSTICE MARSHALL joins, dissenting.

Today the Court denies Mr. Connelly his fundamental right to make a vital choice with a sane mind, involving a determination that could allow the State to deprive him of liberty or even life. This holding is unprecedented: "Surely in the present stage of our civilization a most basic sense of justice is affronted by the spectacle of incarcerating a human being upon the basis of a statement he made while insane...." Blackburn v. Alabama, 361 U.S. 199, 207 (1960). Because I believe that the use of a mentally ill person's involuntary confession is antithetical to the notion of fundamental fairness embodied in the Due Process Clause, I dissent.

. . .

II

The absence of police wrongdoing should not, by itself, determine the voluntariness of a confession by a mentally ill person. The requirement that a confession be voluntary reflects a recognition of the importance of free will and of reliability in determining the admissibility of a confession, and thus demands an inquiry into the totality of the circumstances surrounding the confession.

A

Today's decision restricts the application of the term "involuntary" to those confessions obtained by police coercion. Confessions by mentally ill individuals or by persons coerced by parties other than police officers are now considered "voluntary." The Court's failure to recognize all forms of involuntariness or coercion as antithetical to due process reflects a refusal to acknowledge free will as a value of constitutional consequence. But due process derives much of its meaning from a conception of fundamental fairness that emphasizes the right to make vital choices voluntarily: "The Fourteenth Amendment secures against state invasion ... the right of a person to remain silent unless he chooses to speak in the unfettered exercise of his own will...." Malloy v. Hogan, 378 U.S. 1, 8 (1964). This right requires vigilant protection if we are to safeguard the values of private conscience and human dignity.

This Court's assertion that we would be required "to establish a brand new constitutional right" to recognize the respondent's claim, ante, at 166, ignores 200 years of constitutional jurisprudence. As we stated in Culombe v. Connecticut, 367 U.S. 568 (1961):

"The ultimate test remains that which has been the only clearly established test in Anglo–American courts for two hundred years: the test of voluntariness. Is the confession the product of an essentially free and unconstrained choice by its maker?

... The line of distinction is that at which governing self-direction is lost *and compulsion, of whatever nature or however infused,* propels or helps to propel the confession." Id., at 602 (emphasis added).

A true commitment to fundamental fairness requires that the inquiry be "not whether the conduct of state officers in obtaining the confession is shocking, but whether the confession was 'free and voluntary'...." *Malloy v. Hogan,* supra, at 7.

We have never confined our focus to police coercion, because the value of freedom of will has demanded a broader inquiry.... The confession cases decided by this Court over the 50 years since Brown v. Mississippi, 297 U.S. 278 (1936), have focused upon both police overreaching and free will. While it is true that police overreaching has been an element of every confession case to date ... it is also true that in every case the Court has made clear that ensuring that a confession is a product of free will is an independent concern. The fact that involuntary confessions have always been excluded in part because of police overreaching, signifies only that this is a case of first impression. Until today, we have never upheld the admission of a confession that does not reflect the exercise of free will.

. . .

B

Since the Court redefines voluntary confessions to include confessions by mentally ill individuals, the reliability of these confessions becomes a central concern....

Our distrust for reliance on confessions is due, in part, to their decisive impact upon the adversarial process. Triers of fact accord confessions such heavy weight in their determinations that "the introduction of a confession makes the other aspects of a trial in court superfluous, and the real trial, for all practical purposes, occurs when the confession is obtained." E. Cleary, McCormick on Evidence 316 (2d ed. 1972) .... No other class of evidence is so profoundly prejudicial....

Because the admission of a confession so strongly tips the balance against the defendant in the adversarial process, we must be especially careful about a confession's reliability. We have to date not required a finding of reliability for involuntary confessions only because *all* such confessions have been excluded upon a finding of involuntariness, regardless of reliability.... The Court's adoption today of a restrictive definition of an "involuntary" confession will require heightened scrutiny of a confession's reliability.

The instant case starkly highlights the danger of admitting a confession by a person with a severe mental illness. The trial court made no findings concerning the reliability of Mr. Connelly's involuntary confession, since it believed that the confession was excludable on the basis of involuntariness. However, the overwhelming evidence in the record points to the unreliability of Mr. Connelly's delusional mind. Mr. Connelly was found incompetent to stand trial because he was unable to relate accurate information, and the court-appointed psychiatrist indicated that Mr. Connelly was actively hallucinating and exhibited delusional thinking at the time of his confession. . . . The Court, in fact, concedes that "[a] statement rendered by one in the condition of respondent might be proved to be quite unreliable. . . ." Ante, at 167.

Moreover, the record is barren of any corroboration of the mentally ill defendant's confession. No physical evidence links the defendant to the alleged crime. Police did not identify the alleged victim's body as the woman named by the defendant. Mr. Connelly identified the alleged scene of the crime, but it has not been verified that the unidentified body was found there or that a crime actually occurred there. There is not a shred of competent evidence in this record linking the defendant to the charged homicide. There is only Mr. Connelly's confession.

Minimum standards of due process should require that the trial court find substantial indicia of reliability, on the basis of evidence extrinsic to the confession itself, before admitting the confession of a mentally ill person into evidence. I would require the trial court to make such a finding on remand. To hold otherwise allows the State to imprison and possibly to execute a mentally ill defendant based solely upon an inherently unreliable confession.

III

This Court inappropriately reaches out to address two *Miranda* issues not raised by the prosecutor in his petition for certiorari: (1) the burden of proof upon the government in establishing the voluntariness of *Miranda* rights, and (2) the effect of mental illness on the waiver of those rights in the absence of police misconduct. I emphatically dissent from the Court's holding that the government need prove waiver by only a preponderance of the evidence, and from its conclusion that a waiver is automatically voluntary in the absence of police coercion.

A

In holding that the government need only prove the voluntariness of the waiver of *Miranda* rights by a preponderance of the evidence, the Court ignores the explicit command of *Miranda:*

"If the interrogation continues without the presence of an attorney and a statement is taken, a *heavy* burden rests on the government to demonstrate that the defendant knowingly and intelligently waived his privilege against self-incrimination and his right to retained or appointed counsel. This Court has always set *high* standards of proof for the waiver of constitutional rights, and we re-assert these standards as applied to in-custody interrogation." Miranda v. Arizona, 384 U.S. at 475 (emphasis added; citations omitted).

. . .

B

The Court imports its voluntariness analysis, which makes police coercion a requirement for a finding of involuntariness, into its evaluation of the waiver of *Miranda* rights. My reasoning in Part II . . . applies *a fortiori* to involuntary confessions made in custody involving the waiver of constitutional rights. . . . I will not repeat here what I said there.

I turn then to the second requirement, apart from the voluntariness requirement, that the State must satisfy to establish a waiver of *Miranda* rights. Besides being voluntary, the waiver must be knowing and intelligent. See Moran v. Burbine, 475 U.S. 412, 421 (1986). We recently noted that "the waiver must have been made with a full awareness both of the nature of the right being abandoned and the consequences of the decision to abandon it." Id., at 421. The two requirements are independent: "Only if the 'totality of the circumstances surrounding the interrogation' reveal *both* an uncoerced choice *and* the requisite level of comprehension may a court properly conclude that the *Miranda* rights have been waived." Ibid. (emphasis added).

Since the Colorado Supreme Court found that Mr. Connelly was "clearly" unable to make an "intelligent" decision, clearly its judgment should be affirmed. The Court reverses the entire judgment, however, without explaining how a "mistaken view of voluntariness" could "taint" this independent justification for suppressing the custodial confession, but leaving the Supreme Court of Colorado free on remand to reconsider other issues, not inconsistent with the Court's opinion. Such would include, in my view, whether the requirement of a knowing and intelligent waiver was satisfied. . . . Moreover, on the remand, today's holding does not, of course, preclude a contrary resolution of this case based upon the State's separate interpretation of its own constitution. . . .

I dissent.[*]

---

[*] Justice Blackmun wrote a brief concurring opinion. Justice Stevens wrote an opinion concurring in the judgment in part and dissenting in part.

MASSIAH v. UNITED STATES

377 U.S. 201, 84 S.Ct. 1199, 12 L.Ed.2d 246 (1964).

MR. JUSTICE STEWART delivered the opinion of the Court.

The petitioner was indicted for violating the federal narcotics laws. He retained a lawyer, pleaded not guilty, and was released on bail. While he was free on bail a federal agent succeeded by surreptitious means in listening to incriminating statements made by him. Evidence of these statements was introduced against the petitioner at his trial over his objection. He was convicted, and the Court of Appeals affirmed. We granted certiorari to consider whether, under the circumstances here presented, the prosecution's use at the trial of evidence of the petitioner's own incriminating statements deprived him of any right secured to him under the Federal Constitution. 374 U.S. 805.

The petitioner, a merchant seaman, was in 1958 a member of the crew of the S.S. Santa Maria. In April of that year federal customs officials in New York received information that he was going to transport a quantity of narcotics aboard that ship from South America to the United States. As a result of this and other information, the agents searched the *Santa Maria* upon its arrival in New York and found in the afterpeak of the vessel five packages containing about three and a half pounds of cocaine. They also learned of circumstances, not here relevant, tending to connect the petitioner with the cocaine. He was arrested, promptly arraigned, and subsequently indicted for possession of narcotics aboard a United States vessel. In July a superseding indictment was returned, charging the petitioner and a man named Colson with the same substantive offense, and in separate counts charging the petitioner, Colson, and others with having conspired to possess narcotics aboard a United States vessel, and to import, conceal, and facilitate the sale of narcotics. The petitioner, who had retained a lawyer, pleaded not guilty and was released on bail, along with Colson.

A few days later, and quite without the petitioner's knowledge, Colson decided to cooperate with the government agents in their continuing investigation of the narcotics activities in which the petitioner, Colson, and others had allegedly been engaged. Colson permitted an agent named Murphy to install a Schmidt radio transmitter under the front seat of Colson's automobile, by means of which Murphy, equipped with an appropriate receiving device, could overhear from some distance away conversations carried on in Colson's car.

On the evening of November 19, 1959, Colson and the petition-er held a lengthy conversation while sitting in Colson's automobile, parked on a New York street. By prearrangement with Colson, and totally unbeknown to the petitioner, the agent Murphy sat in a car parked out of sight down the street and listened over the radio to the entire conversation. The petitioner made several incriminating statements during the course of this conversation. At the petition-er's trial these incriminating statements were brought before the jury through Murphy's testimony, despite the insistent objection of defense counsel. The jury convicted the petitioner of several related narcotics offenses, and the convictions were affirmed by the Court of Appeals.

The petitioner argues that it was an error of constitutional dimensions to permit the agent Murphy at the trial to testify to the petitioner's incriminating statements which Murphy had overheard under the circumstances disclosed by this record. This argument is based upon two distinct and independent grounds. First, we are told that Murphy's use of the radio equipment violated the petition-er's rights under the Fourth Amendment, and, consequently, that all evidence which Murphy thereby obtained was, under the rule of Weeks v. United States, 232 U.S. 383, inadmissible against the petitioner at the trial. Secondly, it is said that the petitioner's Fifth and Sixth Amendment rights were violated by the use in evidence against him of incriminating statements which government agents had deliberately elicited from him after he had been indicted and in the absence of his retained counsel. Because of the way we dispose of the case, we do not reach the Fourth Amendment issue.

In Spano v. New York, 360 U.S. 315, this Court reversed a state criminal conviction because a confession had been wrongly admit-ted into evidence against the defendant at his trial. In that case the defendant had already been indicted for first-degree murder at the time he confessed. The Court held that the defendant's conviction could not stand under the Fourteenth Amendment. While the Court's opinion relied upon the totality of the circumstances under which the confession had been obtained, four concurring Justices pointed out that the Constitution required reversal of the conviction upon the sole and specific ground that the confession had been deliberately elicited by the police after the defendant had been indicted, and therefore at a time when he was clearly entitled to a lawyer's help. It was pointed out that under our system of justice the most elemental concepts of due process of law contemplate that an indictment be followed by a trial, "in an orderly courtroom, presided over by a judge, open to the public, and protected by all the procedural safeguards of the law." 360 U.S., at 327 (Stewart, J., concurring). It was said that a Constitution which guarantees a defendant the aid of counsel at such a trial could surely vouchsafe no less to an indicted defendant under interrogation by the police in a completely extrajudicial proceeding. Anything less, it was said, might deny a defendant "effective representation by counsel at the only stage when legal aid and advice would help him." 360 U.S., at 326 (Douglas, J., concurring).

. . .

This view no more than reflects a constitutional principle established as long ago as Powell v. Alabama, 287 U.S. 45, where the Court noted that ". . . during perhaps the most critical period of the proceedings . . . that is to say, from the time of their arraignment until the beginning of their trial, when consultation, thoroughgoing investigation and preparation [are] vitally important, the defendants . . . [are] as much entitled to such aid [of counsel] during that period as at the trial itself." Id., at 57. And since the *Spano* decision the same basic constitutional principle has been broadly reaffirmed by this Court. . . .

Here we deal not with a state court conviction, but with a federal case, where the specific guarantee of the Sixth Amendment directly applies. . . . We hold that the petitioner was denied the basic protections of that guarantee when there was used against him at his trial evidence of his own incriminating words, which federal agents had deliberately elicited from him after he had been indicted and in the absence of his counsel. It is true that in the *Spano* case the defendant was interrogated in a police station, while here the damaging testimony was elicited from the defendant without his knowledge while he was free on bail. But, as Judge Hays pointed out in his dissent in the Court of Appeals, "if such a rule is to have any efficacy it must apply to indirect and surreptitious interrogations as well as those conducted in the jailhouse. In this case, Massiah was more seriously imposed upon . . . because he did not even know that he was under interrogation by a government agent." 307 F.2d, at 72–73.

The Solicitor General, in his brief and oral argument, has strenuously contended that the federal law enforcement agents had the right, if not indeed the duty, to continue their investigation of the petitioner and his alleged criminal associates even though the petitioner had been indicted. He points out that the Government was continuing its investigation in order to uncover not only the source of narcotics found on the S.S. Santa Maria, but also their intended buyer. He says that the quantity of narcotics involved was such as to suggest that the petitioner was part of a large and well-organized ring, and indeed that the continuing investigation confirmed this suspicion, since it resulted in criminal charges against many defendants. Under these circumstances the Solicitor General concludes that the government agents were completely "justified in making use of Colson's cooperation by having Colson continue his normal associations and by surveilling them."

We may accept and, at least for present purposes, completely approve all that this argument implies, Fourth Amendment prob-

lems to one side. We do not question that in this case, as in many
cases, it was entirely proper to continue an investigation of the
suspected criminal activities of the defendant and his alleged confederates, even though the defendant had already been indicted.
All that we hold is that the defendant's own incriminating statements, obtained by federal agents under the circumstances here
disclosed, could not constitutionally be used by the prosecution as
evidence against *him* at his trial.

 Reversed.[*]

[*] Justice White wrote a dissenting opinion,   joined.
which Justice Clark and Justice Harlan

BREWER v. WILLIAMS

430 U.S. 387, 97 S.Ct. 1232, 51 L.Ed.2d 424 (1977).

MR. JUSTICE STEWART delivered the opinion of the Court.

An Iowa trial jury found the respondent, Robert Williams, guilty of murder. The judgment of conviction was affirmed in the Iowa Supreme Court by a closely divided vote. In a subsequent habeas corpus proceeding a Federal District Court ruled that under the United States Constitution Williams is entitled to a new trial, and a divided Court of Appeals for the Eighth Circuit agreed. The question before us is whether the District Court and the Court of Appeals were wrong.

I

On the afternoon of December 24, 1968, a 10-year-old girl named Pamela Powers went with her family to the YMCA in Des Moines, Iowa, to watch a wrestling tournament in which her brother was participating. When she failed to return from a trip to the washroom, a search for her began. The search was unsuccessful.

Robert Williams, who had recently escaped from a mental hospital, was a resident of the YMCA. Soon after the girl's disappearance Williams was seen in the YMCA lobby carrying some clothing and a large bundle wrapped in a blanket. He obtained help from a 14-year-old boy in opening the street door of the YMCA and the door to his automobile parked outside. When Williams placed the bundle in the front seat of his car the boy "saw two legs in it and they were skinny and white." Before anyone could see what was in the bundle Williams drove away. His abandoned car was found the following day in Davenport, Iowa, roughly 160 miles east of Des Moines. A warrant was then issued in Des Moines for his arrest on a charge of abduction.

On the morning of December 26, a Des Moines lawyer named Henry McKnight went to the Des Moines police station and informed the officers present that he had just received a long distance call from Williams, and that he had advised Williams to turn himself in to the Davenport police. Williams did surrender that morning to the police in Davenport, and they booked him on the charge specified in the arrest warrant and gave him the warnings required by Miranda v. Arizona, 384 U.S. 436. The Davenport police then telephoned their counterparts in Des Moines to inform them that Williams had surrendered. McKnight, the lawyer was still at the Des Moines police headquarters, and Williams conversed with McKnight on the telephone. In the presence of the Des Moines chief of police and a police detective named Leaming, McKnight advised

Williams that Des Moines police officers would be driving to Davenport to pick him up, that the officers would not interrogate him or mistreat him, and that Williams was not to talk to the officers about Pamela Powers until after consulting with McKnight upon his return to Des Moines. As a result of these conversations, it was agreed between McKnight and the Des Moines police officials that Detective Leaming and a fellow officer would drive to Davenport to pick up Williams, that they would bring him directly back to Des Moines, and that they would not question him during the trip.

In the meantime Williams was arraigned before a judge in Davenport on the outstanding arrest warrant. The judge advised him of his *Miranda* rights and committed him to jail. Before leaving the courtroom, Williams conferred with a lawyer named Kelly, who advised him not to make any statements until consulting with McKnight back in Des Moines.

Detective Leaming and his fellow officer arrived in Davenport about noon to pick up Williams and return him to Des Moines. Soon after their arrival they met with Williams and Kelly, who, they understood, was acting as Williams' lawyer. Detective Leaming repeated the *Miranda* warnings, and told Williams:

> "[W]e both know that you're being represented here by Mr. Kelly and you're being represented by Mr. McKnight in Des Moines, and . . . I want you to remember this because we'll be visiting between here and Des Moines."

Williams then conferred again with Kelly alone, and after this conference Kelly reiterated to Detective Leaming that Williams was not to be questioned about the disappearance of Pamela Powers until after he had consulted with McKnight back in Des Moines. When Leaming expressed some reservations, Kelly firmly stated that the agreement with McKnight was to be carried out—that there was to be no interrogation of Williams during the automobile journey to Des Moines. Kelly was denied permission to ride in the police car back to Des Moines with Williams and the two officers.

The two detectives, with Williams in their charge, then set out on the 160-mile drive. At no time during the trip did Williams express a willingness to be interrogated in the absence of an attorney. Instead, he stated several times that "[w]hen I get to Des Moines and see Mr. McKnight, I am going to tell you the whole story." Detective Leaming knew that Williams was a former mental patient, and knew also that he was deeply religious.

The detective and his prisoner soon embarked on a wide-ranging conversation covering a variety of topics, including the subject of religion. Then, not long after leaving Davenport and reaching the interstate highway, Detective Leaming delivered what has been referred to in the briefs and oral arguments as the "Christian burial speech." Addressing Williams as "Reverend," the detective said:

"I want to give you something to think about while we're traveling down the road. ... Number one, I want you to observe the weather conditions, it's raining, it's sleeting, it's freezing, driving is very treacherous, visibility is poor, it's going to be dark early this evening. They are predicting several inches of snow for tonight, and I feel that you yourself are the only person that knows where this little girl's body is, that you yourself have only been there once, and if you get a snow on top of it you yourself may be unable to find it. And, since we will be going right past the area on the way into Des Moines, I feel that we could stop and locate the body, that the parents of this little girl should be entitled to a Christian burial for the little girl who was snatched away from them on Christmas [E]ve and murdered. And I feel we should stop and locate it on the way in rather than waiting until morning and trying to come back out after a snow storm and possibly not being able to find it at all."

Williams asked Detective Leaming why he thought their route to Des Moines would be taking them past the girl's body, and Leaming responded that he knew the body was in the area of Mitchellville—a town they would be passing on the way to Des Moines. Leaming then stated: "I do not want you to answer me. I don't want to discuss it any further. Just think about it as we're riding down the road."

As the car approached Grinnell, a town approximately 100 miles west of Davenport, Williams asked whether the police had found the victim's shoes. When Detective Leaming replied that he was unsure, Williams directed the officers to a service station where he said he had left the shoes; a search for them proved unsuccessful. As they continued towards Des Moines, Williams asked whether the police had found the blanket, and directed the officers to a rest area where he said he had disposed of the blanket. Nothing was found. The car continued towards Des Moines, and as it approached Mitchellville, Williams said that he would show the officers where the body was. He then directed the police to the body of Pamela Powers.

Williams was indicted for first-degree murder. Before trial, his counsel moved to suppress all evidence relating to or resulting from any statements Williams had made during the automobile ride from Davenport to Des Moines. After an evidentiary hearing the trial judge denied the motion. He found that "an agreement was made between defense counsel and the police officials to the effect that the Defendant was not to be questioned on the return trip to Des Moines," and that the evidence in question had been elicited from Williams during "a critical stage in the proceedings requiring the presence of counsel on his request." The judge ruled, however, that Williams had "waived his right to have an attorney present during the giving of such information."

The evidence in question was introduced over counsel's continuing objection at the subsequent trial. The jury found Williams guilty of murder, and the judgment of conviction was affirmed by the Iowa Supreme Court, a bare majority of whose members agreed with the trial court that Williams had "waived his right to the presence of his counsel" on the automobile ride from Davenport to Des Moines. State v. Williams, 182 N.W.2d 396, 402. The four dissenting justices expressed the view that "when counsel and police have agreed defendant is not to be questioned until counsel is present and defendant has been advised not to talk and repeatedly has stated he will tell the whole story after he talks with counsel, the state should be required to make a stronger showing of intentional voluntary waiver than was made here." Id., at 408.

Williams then petitioned for a writ of habeas corpus in the United States District Court for the Southern District of Iowa. Counsel for the State and for Williams stipulated that "the case would be submitted on the record of facts and proceedings in the trial court, without taking of further testimony." The District Court made findings of fact as summarized above, and concluded as a matter of law that the evidence in question had been wrongly admitted at Williams' trial. This conclusion was based on three alternative and independent grounds: (1) that Williams had been denied his constitutional right to the assistance of counsel; (2) that he had been denied the constitutional protections defined by this Court's decisions in Escobedo v. Illinois, 378 U.S. 478, and Miranda v. Arizona, 384 U.S. 436; and (3) that in any event, his self-incriminatory statements on the automobile trip from Davenport to Des Moines had been involuntarily made. Further, the District Court ruled that there had been no waiver by Williams of the constitutional protections in question. 375 F.Supp. 170.

The Court of Appeals for the Eighth Circuit, with one judge dissenting, affirmed this judgment, 509 F.2d 227, and denied a petition for rehearing en banc. We granted certiorari to consider the constitutional issues presented. 423 U.S. 1031.

II

· · ·

B

As stated above, the District Court based its judgment in this case on three independent grounds. The Court of Appeals appears to have affirmed the judgment on two of those grounds. We have concluded that only one of them need be considered here.

Specifically, there is no need to review in this case the doctrine of Miranda v. Arizona, a doctrine designed to secure the constitutional privilege against compulsory self-incrimination .... It is equally unnecessary to evaluate the ruling of the District Court that

Williams' self-incriminating statements were, indeed, involuntarily made. . . . For it is clear that the judgment before us must in any event be affirmed upon the ground that Williams was deprived of a different constitutional right—the right to the assistance of counsel.

This right, guaranteed by the Sixth and Fourteenth Amendments, is indispensable to the fair administration of our adversary system of criminal justice. Its vital need at the pretrial stage has perhaps nowhere been more succinctly explained than in Mr. Justice Sutherland's memorable words for the Court 44 years ago in Powell v. Alabama, 287 U.S. 45, 57:

> "[D]uring perhaps the most critical period of the proceedings against these defendants, that is to say, from the time of their arraignment until the beginning of their trial, when consultation, thoroughgoing investigation and preparation were vitally important, the defendants did not have the aid of counsel in any real sense, although they were as much entitled to such aid during that period as at the trial itself."

There has occasionally been a difference of opinion within the Court as to the peripheral scope of this constitutional right. . . . But its basic contours, which are identical in state and federal contexts . . . are too well established to require extensive elaboration here. Whatever else it may mean, the right to counsel granted by the Sixth and Fourteenth Amendments means at least that a person is entitled to the help of a lawyer at or after the time that judicial proceedings have been initiated against him—"whether by way of formal charge, preliminary hearing, indictment, information, or arraignment." Kirby v. Illinois, [406 U.S. 682 (1972)], at 689.
. . .

There can be no doubt in the present case that judicial proceedings had been initiated against Williams before the start of the automobile ride from Davenport to Des Moines. A warrant had been issued for his arrest, he had been arraigned on that warrant before a judge in a Davenport courtroom, and he had been committed by the court to confinement in jail. The State does not contend otherwise.

There can be no serious doubt, either, that Detective Leaming deliberately and designedly set out to elicit information from Williams just as surely as—and perhaps more effectively than—if he had formally interrogated him. Detective Leaming was fully aware before departing for Des Moines that Williams was being represented in Davenport by Kelly and in Des Moines by McKnight. Yet he purposely sought during Williams' isolation from his lawyers to obtain as much incriminating information as possible. Indeed, Detective Leaming conceded as much when he testified at Williams' trial . . . .

The state courts clearly proceeded upon the hypothesis that Detective Leaming's "Christian burial speech" had been tantamount to interrogation. Both courts recognized that Williams had been entitled to the assistance of counsel at the time he made the incriminating statements. Yet no such constitutional protection would have come into play if there had been no interrogation.

The circumstances of this case are thus constitutionally indistinguishable from those presented in Massiah v. United States, [377 U.S. 201 (1964)]. The petitioner in that case was indicted for violating the federal narcotics law. He retained a lawyer, pleaded not guilty, and was released on bail. While he was free on bail a federal agent succeeded by surreptitious means in listening to incriminating statements made by him. Evidence of these statements was introduced against the petitioner at his trial, and he was convicted. This Court reversed the conviction, holding "that the petitioner was denied the basic protections of that guarantee [the right to counsel] when there was used against him at his trial evidence of his own incriminating words, which federal agents had deliberately elicited from him after he had been indicted and in the absence of his counsel." 377 U.S., at 206.

That the incriminating statements were elicited surreptitiously in the *Massiah* case, and otherwise here, is constitutionally irrelevant. . . . Rather, the clear rule of *Massiah* is that once adversary proceedings have commenced against an individual, he has a right to legal representation when the government interrogates him. It thus requires no wooden or technical application of the *Massiah* doctrine to conclude that Williams was entitled to the assistance of counsel guaranteed to him by the Sixth and Fourteenth Amendments.

III

The Iowa courts recognized that Williams had been denied the constitutional right to the assistance of counsel. They held, however, that he had waived that right during the course of the automobile trip from Davenport to Des Moines. . . .

. . .

The District Court and the Court of Appeals were correct in the view that the question of waiver was not a question of historical fact, but one which, in the words of Mr. Justice Frankfurter, requires "application of constitutional principles to the facts as found . . . ." Brown v. Allen, 344 U.S. 443, 507 (separate opinion). . . .

The District Court and the Court of Appeals were also correct in their understanding of the proper standard to be applied in determining the question of waiver as a matter of federal constitutional law—that it was incumbent upon the State to prove "an intentional relinquishment or abandonment of a known right or privilege." Johnson v. Zerbst, 304 U.S. [458 (1938)], at 464. That standard has been reiterated in many cases. We have said that the right to counsel does not depend upon a request by the defendant

... and that courts indulge in every reasonable presumption against waiver .... This strict standard applies equally to an alleged waiver of the right to counsel whether at trial or at a critical stage of pretrial proceedings. ...

We conclude, finally, that the Court of Appeals was correct in holding that, judged by these standards, the record in this case falls far short of sustaining petitioner's burden. It is true that Williams had been informed of and appeared to understand his right to counsel. But waiver requires not merely comprehension but relinquishment, and Williams' consistent reliance upon the advice of counsel in dealing with the authorities refutes any suggestion that he waived that right. He consulted McKnight by long distance telephone before turning himself in. He spoke with McKnight by telephone again shortly after being booked. After he was arraigned, Williams sought out and obtained legal advice from Kelly. Williams again consulted with Kelly after Detective Leaming and his fellow officer arrived in Davenport. Throughout, Williams was advised not to make any statements before seeing McKnight in Des Moines, and was assured that the police had agreed not to question him. His statements while in the car that he would tell the whole story *after* seeing McKnight in Des Moines were the clearest expressions by Williams himself that he desired the presence of an attorney before any interrogation took place. But even before making these statements, Williams had effectively asserted his right to counsel by having secured attorneys at both ends of the automobile trip, both of whom, acting as his agents, had made clear to the police that no interrogation was to occur during the journey. Williams knew of that agreement and, particularly in view of his consistent reliance on counsel, there is no basis for concluding that he disavowed it.

Despite Williams' express and implicit assertions of his right to counsel, Detective Leaming proceeded to elicit incriminating statements from Williams. Leaming did not preface this effort by telling Williams that he had a right to the presence of a lawyer, and made no effort at all to ascertain whether Williams wished to relinquish that right. The circumstances of record in this case thus provide no reasonable basis for finding that Williams waived his right to the assistance of counsel.

The Court of Appeals did not hold, nor do we, that under the circumstances of this case Williams *could not*, without notice to counsel, have waived his rights under the Sixth and Fourteenth Amendments. It only held, as do we, that he did not.

IV

The crime of which Williams was convicted was senseless and brutal, calling for swift and energetic action by the police to apprehend the perpetrator and gather evidence with which he could be convicted. No mission of law enforcement officials is more important. Yet "[d]isinterested zeal for the public good does

not assure either wisdom or right in the methods it pursues."
Haley v. Ohio, 332 U.S. 596, 605 (Frankfurter, J., concurring in
judgment). Although we do not lightly affirm the issuance of a writ
of habeas corpus in this case, so clear a violation of the Sixth and
Fourteenth Amendments as here occurred cannot be condoned.
The pressures on state executive and judicial officers charged with
the administration of the criminal law are great, especially when the
crime is murder and the victim a small child. But it is precisely the
predictability of those pressures that makes imperative a resolute
loyalty to the guarantees that the Constitution extends to us all.

The judgment of the Court of Appeals is affirmed.

It is so ordered.[*]

---

[*] Justice Marshall, Justice Powell, and Justice Stevens wrote concurring opinions. Chief Justice Burger wrote a dissenting opinion. Justice White wrote a dissenting opinion, which Justice Blackmun and Justice Rehnquist joined. Justice Blackmun wrote a dissenting opinion, which Justice White and Justice Rehnquist joined.

ESCOBEDO v. ILLINOIS

378 U.S. 478, 84 S.Ct. 1758, 12 L.Ed.2d 977 (1964).

MR. JUSTICE GOLDBERG delivered the opinion of the Court.

The critical question in this case is whether, under the circumstances, the refusal by the police to honor petitioner's request to consult with his lawyer during the course of an interrogation constitutes a denial of "the Assistance of Counsel" in violation of the Sixth Amendment to the Constitution as "made obligatory upon the States by the Fourteenth Amendment," Gideon v. Wainwright, 372 U.S. 335, 342, and thereby renders inadmissible in a state criminal trial any incriminating statement elicited by the police during the interrogation.

On the night of January 19, 1960, petitioner's brother-in-law was fatally shot. In the early hours of the next morning, at 2:30 a.m., petitioner was arrested without a warrant and interrogated. Petitioner made no statement to the police and was released at 5 that afternoon pursuant to a state court writ of habeas corpus obtained by Mr. Warren Wolfson, a lawyer who had been retained by petitioner.

On January 30, Benedict DiGerlando, who was then in police custody and who was later indicted for the murder along with petitioner, told the police that petitioner had fired the fatal shots. Between 8 and 9 that evening, petitioner and his sister, the widow of the deceased, were arrested and taken to police headquarters. En route to the police station, the police "had handcuffed the defendant behind his back," and "one of the arresting officers told defendant that DiGerlando had named him as the one who shot" the deceased. Petitioner testified, without contradiction, that the "detectives said they had us pretty well, up pretty tight, and we might as well admit to this crime," and that he replied, "I am sorry but I would like to have advice from my lawyer." A police officer testified that although petitioner was not formally charged "he was in custody" and "couldn't walk out the door."

Shortly after petitioner reached police headquarters, his retained lawyer arrived. The lawyer described the ensuing events in the following terms:

"On that day I received a phone call [from "the mother of another defendant"] and pursuant to that phone call I went to the Detective Bureau at 11th and State. The first person I talked to was the Sergeant on duty at the Bureau Desk. Sergeant Pidgeon. I asked Sergeant Pidgeon for permission to speak to my client, Danny Escobedo. ... Sergeant Pidgeon

made a call to the Bureau lockup and informed me that the boy
had been taken from the lockup to the Homicide Bureau. This
was between 9:30 and 10:00 in the evening. Before I went
anywhere, he called the Homicide Bureau and told them there
was an attorney waiting to see Escobedo. He told me I could
not see him. Then I went upstairs to the Homicide Bureau.
There were several Homicide Detectives around and I talked to
them. I identified myself as Escobedo's attorney and asked
permission to see him. They said I could not. . . . The police
officer told me to see Chief Flynn who was on duty. I
identified myself to Chief Flynn and asked permission to see my
client. He said I could not. . . . I think it was approximately
11:00 o'clock. He said I couldn't see him because they hadn't
completed questioning. . . . [F]or a second or two I spotted
him in an office in the Homicide Bureau. The door was open
and I could see through the office. . . . I waved to him and he
waved back and then the door was closed, by one of the
officers at Homicide.[1] There were four or five officers milling
around the Homicide Detail that night. As to whether I talked
to Captain Flynn any later that day, I waited around for another
hour or two and went back again and renewed by [*sic*] request
to see my client. He again told me I could not. . . . I filed an
official complaint with Commissioner Phelan of the Chicago
Police Department. I had a conversation with every police
officer I could find. I was told at Homicide that I couldn't see
him and I would have to get a writ of habeas corpus. I left the
Homicide Bureau and from the Detective Bureau at 11th and
State at approximately 1:00 A.M. [Sunday morning] I had no
opportunity to talk to my client that night. I quoted to Captain
Flynn the Section of the Criminal Code which allows an attorney the right to see his client."

Petitioner testified that during the course of the interrogation
he repeatedly asked to speak to his lawyer and that the police said
that his lawyer "didn't want to see" him. The testimony of the
police officers confirmed these accounts in substantial detail.

Notwithstanding repeated requests by each, petitioner and his
retained lawyer were afforded no opportunity to consult during the
course of the entire interrogation. At one point, as previously
noted, petitioner and his attorney came into each other's view for a
few moments but the attorney was quickly ushered away. Petitioner testified "that he heard a detective telling the attorney the latter
would not be allowed to talk to [him] 'until they were done' " and
that he heard the attorney being refused permission to remain in
the adjoining room. A police officer testified that he had told the

---

1. Petitioner testified that this ambiguous
gesture "could have meant most anything,"
but that he "took it upon [his] own to think
that [the lawyer was telling him] not to say
anything," and that the lawyer "wanted to
talk" to him.

lawyer that he could not see petitioner until "we were through interrogating" him.

There is testimony by the police that during the interrogation, petitioner, a 22-year-old of Mexican extraction with no record of previous experience with the police, "was handcuffed" in a standing position and that he "was nervous, he had circles under his eyes and he was upset" and was "agitated" because "he had not slept well in over a week."

It is undisputed that during the course of the interrogation Officer Montejano, who "grew up" in petitioner's neighborhood, who knew his family, and who uses "Spanish language in [his] police work," conferred alone with petitioner "for about a quarter of an hour. . . ." Petitioner testified that the officer said to him "in Spanish that my sister and I could go home if I pinned it on Benedict DiGerlando," that "he would see to it that we would go home and be held only as witnesses, if anything, if we had made a statement against DiGerlando . . ., that we would be able to go home that night." Petitioner testified that he made the statement in issue because of this assurance. Officer Montejano denied offering any such assurance.

A police officer testified that during the interrogation the following occurred:

> "I informed him of what DiGerlando told me and when I did, he told me that DiGerlando was [lying] and I said, 'Would you care to tell DiGerlando that?' and he said, 'Yes, I will.' So, I brought . . . Escobedo in and he confronted DiGerlando and he told him that he was lying and said, 'I didn't shoot Manuel, you did it.'"

In this way, petitioner, for the first time, admitted to some knowledge of the crime. After that he made additional statements further implicating himself in the murder plot. At this point an Assistant State's Attorney, Theodore J. Cooper, was summoned "to take" a statement. Mr. Cooper, an experienced lawyer who was assigned to the Homicide Division to take "statements from some defendants and some prisoners that they had in custody," "took" petitioner's statement by asking carefully framed questions apparently designed to assure the admissibility into evidence of the resulting answers. Mr. Cooper testified that he did not advise petitioner of his constitutional rights, and it is undisputed that no one during the course of the interrogation so advised him.

Petitioner moved both before and during trial to suppress the incriminating statement, but the motions were denied. Petitioner was convicted of murder and he appealed the conviction.

The Supreme Court of Illinois, in its original opinion of February 1, 1963, held the statement inadmissible and reversed the conviction. The court said:

"[I]t seems manifest to us, from the undisputed evidence and the circumstances surrounding defendant at the time of his statement and shortly prior thereto, that the defendant understood he would be permitted to go home if he gave the statement and would be granted an immunity from prosecution."

. . .

The State petitioned for, and the court granted, rehearing. The court then affirmed the conviction. It said: "[T]he officer denied making the promise and the trier of fact believed him. We find no reason for disturbing the trial court's finding that the confession was voluntary." 28 Ill.2d 41, 45–46, 190 N.E.2d 825, 827. The court also held, on the authority of this Court's decisions in Crooker v. California, 357 U.S. 433, and Cicenia v. Lagay, 357 U.S. 504, that the confession was admissible even though "it was obtained after he had requested the assistance of counsel, which request was denied." 28 Ill.2d, at 46, 190 N.E.2d, at 827. We granted a writ of certiorari to consider whether the petitioner's statement was constitutionally admissible at his trial. 375 U.S. 902. We conclude, for the reasons stated below, that it was not and, accordingly, we reverse the judgment of conviction.

In Massiah v. United States, 377 U.S. 201, this Court observed that "a Constitution which guarantees a defendant the aid of counsel at . . . trial could surely vouchsafe no less to an indicted defendant under interrogation by the police in a completely extrajudicial proceeding. Anything less . . . might deny a defendant 'effective representation by counsel at the only stage when legal aid and advice would help him.'" Id., at 204, quoting Douglas, J., concurring in Spano v. New York, 360 U.S. 315, 326.

The interrogation here was conducted before petitioner was formally indicted. But in the context of this case, that fact should make no difference. When petitioner requested, and was denied, an opportunity to consult with his lawyer, the investigation had ceased to be a general investigation of "an unsolved crime." Spano v. New York, 360 U.S. 315, 327 (Stewart, J., concurring). Petitioner had become the accused, and the purpose of the interrogation was to "get him" to confess his guilt despite his constitutional right not to do so. At the time of his arrest and throughout the course of the interrogation, the police told petitioner that they had convincing evidence that he had fired the fatal shots. Without informing him of his absolute right to remain silent in the face of this accusation, the police urged him to make a statement. As this Court observed many years ago:

"It cannot be doubted that, placed in the position in which the accused was when the statement was made to him that the other suspected person had charged him with crime, the result was to produce upon his mind the fear that if he remained silent it would be considered an admission of guilt, and therefore render certain his being committed for trial as the guilty person, and it cannot be conceived that the converse impression would not also have naturally arisen, that by denying there was hope of removing the suspicion from himself." Bram v. United States, 168 U.S. 532, 562.

Petitioner, a layman, was undoubtedly unaware that under Illinois law an admission of "mere" complicity in the murder plot was legally as damaging as an admission of firing of the fatal shots. . . . The "guiding hand of counsel" was essential to advise petitioner of his rights in this delicate situation. Powell v. Alabama, 287 U.S. 45, 69. This was the "stage when legal aid and advice" were most critical to petitioner. Massiah v. United States, supra, at 204. It was a stage surely as critical as was the arraignment in Hamilton v. Alabama, 368 U.S. 52, and the preliminary hearing in White v. Maryland, 373 U.S. 59. What happened at this interrogation could certainly "affect the whole trial," Hamilton v. Alabama, supra, at 54, since rights "may be as irretrievably lost, if not then and there asserted, as they are when an accused represented by counsel waives a right for strategic purposes." Ibid. It would exalt form over substance to make the right to counsel, under these circumstances, depend on whether at the time of the interrogation, the authorities had secured a formal indictment. Petitioner had, for all practical purposes, already been charged with murder.

. . .

In Gideon v. Wainwright, 372 U.S. 335, we held that every person accused of a crime, whether state or federal, is entitled to a lawyer at trial. The rule sought by the State here, however, would make the trial no more than an appeal from the interrogation; and the "right to use counsel at the formal trial [would be] a very hollow thing [if], for all practical purposes, the conviction is already assured by pretrial examination." In re Groban, 352 U.S. 330, 344 (Black, J., dissenting). "One can imagine a cynical prosecutor saying: 'Let them have the most illustrious counsel, now. They can't escape the noose. There is nothing that counsel can do for them at the trial.'" Ex parte Sullivan, 107 F.Supp. 514, 517–518.

It is argued that if the right to counsel is afforded prior to indictment, the number of confessions obtained by the police will diminish significantly, because most confessions are obtained during the period between arrest and indictment, and "any lawyer worth his salt will tell the suspect in no uncertain terms to make no statement to police under any circumstances." Watts v. Indiana, 338 U.S. 49, 59 (Jackson, J., concurring in part and dissenting in part). This argument, of course, cuts two ways. The fact that many confessions are obtained during this period points up its critical nature as a "stage when legal aid and advice" are surely needed. . . . The right to counsel would indeed be hollow if it began at a period when few confessions were obtained. There is necessarily a direct relationship between the importance of a stage to the police in their quest for a confession and the criticalness of that stage to the accused in his need for legal advice. Our Constitution, unlike some others, strikes the balance in favor of the right of the accused to be advised by his lawyer of his privilege against self-incrimination....

We have learned the lesson of history, ancient and modern, that a system of criminal law enforcement which comes to depend on the "confession" will, in the long run, be less reliable and more subject to abuses than a system which depends on extrinsic evidence independently secured through skillful investigation. As Dean Wigmore so wisely said:

> "*[A]ny system of administration which permits the prosecution to trust habitually to compulsory self-disclosure as a source of proof must itself suffer morally thereby.* The inclination develops to rely mainly upon such evidence, and to be satisfied with an incomplete investigation of the other sources. The exercise of the power to extract answers begets a forgetfulness of the just limitations of that power. The simple and peaceful process of questioning breeds a readiness to resort to bullying and to physical force and torture. If there is a right to an answer, there soon seems to be a right to the expected answer,—that is, to a confession of guilt. Thus the legitimate use grows into the unjust abuse; ultimately, the innocent are jeopardized by the encroachments of a bad system. Such seems to have been the course of experience in those legal systems where the privilege was not recognized." 8 Wigmore, Evidence (3d ed. 1940), 309. (Emphasis in original.)

This Court also has recognized that "history amply shows that confessions have often been extorted to save law enforcement officials the trouble and effort of obtaining valid and independent evidence ...." Haynes v. Washington, 373 U.S. 503, 519.

We have also learned the companion lesson of history that no system of criminal justice can, or should, survive if it comes to depend for its continued effectiveness on the citizens' abdication through unawareness of their constitutional rights. No system worth preserving should have to *fear* that if an accused is permitted to consult with a lawyer, he will become aware of, and exercise, these rights. If the exercise of constitutional rights will thwart the effectiveness of a system of law enforcement, then there is something very wrong with that system.

We hold, therefore, that where, as here, the investigation is no longer a general inquiry into an unsolved crime but has begun to focus on a particular suspect, the suspect has been taken into police custody, the police carry out a process of interrogations that lends itself to eliciting incriminating statements, the suspect has requested and been denied an opportunity to consult with his lawyer, and the police have not effectively warned him of his absolute constitutional right to remain silent, the accused has been denied "the Assistance of Counsel" in violation of the Sixth Amendment to the Constitution as "made obligatory upon the States by the Fourteenth Amendment," Gideon v. Wainwright, 372 U.S., at 342, and that no statement elicited by the police during the interrogation may be used against him at a criminal trial.

. . .

Nothing we have said today affects the powers of the police to investigate "an unsolved crime," Spano v. New York, 360 U.S. 315, 327 (Stewart, J., concurring), by gathering information from witnesses and by other "proper investigative efforts." Haynes v. Washington, 373 U.S. 503, 519. We hold only that when the process shifts from investigatory to accusatory—when its focus is on the accused and its purpose is to elicit a confession—our adversary system begins to operate, and, under the circumstances here, the accused must be permitted to consult with his lawyer.

The judgment of the Illinois Supreme Court is reversed and the case remanded for proceedings not inconsistent with this opinion.

Reversed and remanded.

MR. JUSTICE STEWART, dissenting.

. . .

Massiah v. United States, 377 U.S. 201, is not in point here. In that case a federal grand jury had indicted Massiah. He had retained a lawyer and entered a formal plea of not guilty. Under our system of federal justice an indictment and arraignment are followed by a trial, at which the Sixth Amendment guarantees the defendant the assistance of counsel. But Massiah was released on bail, and thereafter agents of the Federal Government deliberately elicited incriminating statements from him in the absence of his lawyer. We held that the use of these statements against him at his trial denied him the basic protections of the Sixth Amendment guarantee. Putting to one side the fact that the case now before us is not a federal case, the vital fact remains that this case does not involve the deliberate interrogation of a defendant after the initiation of judicial proceedings against him. The Court disregards this basic difference between the present case and Massiah's, with the bland assertion that "that fact should make no difference." Ante, p. 485.

It is "that fact," I submit, which makes all the difference. Under our system of criminal justice the institution of formal, meaningful judicial proceedings, by way of indictment, information, or arraignment, marks the point at which a criminal investigation has ended and adversary proceedings have commenced. It is at this point that the constitutional guarantees attach which pertain to a criminal trial. Among those guarantees are the right to a speedy trial, the right of confrontation, and the right to trial by jury. Another is the guarantee of the assistance of counsel. ...

The confession which the Court today holds inadmissible was a voluntary one. It was given during the course of a perfectly legitimate police investigation of an unsolved murder. The Court says that what happened during this investigation "affected" the trial. I had always supposed that the whole purpose of a police investigation of a murder was to "affect" the trial of the murderer, and that it would be only an incompetent, unsuccessful, or corrupt investigation which would not do so. The Court further says that the Illinois police officers did not advise the petitioner of his "constitutional rights" before he confessed to the murder. This Court has never held that the Constitution requires the police to give any "advice" under circumstances such as these.

Supported by no stronger authority than its own rhetoric, the Court today converts a routine police investigation of an unsolved murder into a distorted analogue of a judicial trial. It imports into this investigation constitutional concepts historically applicable only after the onset of formal prosecutorial proceedings. By doing so, I think the Court perverts those precious constitutional guarantees, and frustrates the vital interests of society in preserving the legitimate and proper function of honest and purposeful police investigation.

. . .

MR. JUSTICE WHITE, with whom MR. JUSTICE CLARK and MR. JUSTICE STEWART join, dissenting.

In Massiah v. United States, 377 U.S. 201, the Court held that as of the date of the indictment the prosecution is disentitled to secure admissions from the accused. The Court now moves that date back to the time when the prosecution begins to "focus" on the accused. Although the opinion purports to be limited to the facts of this case, it would be naive to think that the new constitutional right announced will depend upon whether the accused has retained his own counsel ... or has asked to consult with counsel in the course of interrogation....   At the very least the Court holds that once the accused becomes a suspect and, presumably, is arrested, any admission made to the police thereafter is inadmissible in evidence unless the accused has waived his right to counsel. The decision is thus another major step in the direction of the goal which the Court seemingly has in mind—to bar from evidence all admissions obtained from an individual suspected of crime, whether involuntarily made or not. It does of course put us one step "ahead" of the English judges who have had the good sense to leave the matter a discretionary one with the trial court. I reject this step and the invitation to go farther which the Court has now issued.

By abandoning the voluntary-involuntary test for admissibility of confessions, the Court seems driven by the notion that it is uncivilized law enforcement to use an accused's own admissions against him at his trial. It attempts to find a home for this new and nebulous rule of due process by attaching it to the right to counsel guaranteed in the federal system by the Sixth Amendment and binding upon the States by virtue of the due process guarantee of the Fourteenth Amendment.... The right to counsel now not only entitles the accused to counsel's advice and aid in preparing for trial but stands as an impenetrable barrier to any interrogation once the accused has become a suspect. From that very moment apparently his right to counsel attaches, a rule wholly unworkable and impossible to administer unless police cars are equipped with public defenders and undercover agents and police informants have defense counsel at their side. I would not abandon the Court's prior cases defining with some care and analysis the circumstances requiring the presence or aid of counsel and substitute the amorphous and wholly unworkable principle that counsel is constitutionally required whenever he would or could be helpful.... These cases dealt with the requirement of counsel at proceedings in which definable rights could be won or lost, not with stages where probative evidence might be obtained. Under this new approach one might just as well argue that a potential defendant is constitutionally entitled to a lawyer before, not after, he commits a crime, since it is then that crucial incriminating evidence is put within the reach of the Government by the would-be accused. Until now there simply has been no right guaranteed by the Federal Constitution to be free from the use at trial of a voluntary admission made prior to indictment.

It is incongruous to assume that the provision for counsel in the Sixth Amendment was meant to amend or supersede the self-incrimination provision of the Fifth Amendment, which is now applicable to the States.... That amendment addresses itself to the very issue of incriminating admissions of an accused and resolves it by proscribing only compelled statements. Neither the Framers, the constitutional language, a century of decisions of this Court nor Professor Wigmore provides an iota of support for the idea that an accused has an absolute constitutional right not to answer even in the absence of compulsion—the constitutional right not to incriminate himself by making voluntary disclosures.

Today's decision cannot be squared with other provisions of the Constitution which, in my view, define the system of criminal justice this Court is empowered to administer. The Fourth Amendment permits upon probable cause even compulsory searches of the suspect and his possessions and the use of the fruits of the search at trial, all in the absence of counsel. The Fifth Amendment and state constitutional provisions authorize, indeed require, inquisitorial grand jury proceedings at which a potential defendant, in the absence of counsel, is shielded against no more than compulsory incrimination. ... A grand jury witness, who may be a suspect, is

interrogated and his answers, at least until today, are admissible in
evidence at trial. And these provisions have been thought of as
constitutional safeguards to persons suspected of an offense. Furthermore, until now, the Constitution has permitted the accused to
be fingerprinted and to be identified in a line-up or in the courtroom itself.

The Court chooses to ignore these matters and to rely on the
virtues and morality of a system of criminal law enforcement which
does not depend on the "confession." No such judgment is to be
found in the Constitution. It might be appropriate for a legislature
to provide that a suspect should not be consulted during a criminal
investigation; that an accused should never be called before a grand
jury to answer, even if he wants to, what may well be incriminating
questions; and that no person, whether he be a suspect, guilty
criminal or innocent bystander, should be put to the ordeal of
responding to orderly noncompulsory inquiry by the State. But this
is not the system our Constitution requires. The only "inquisitions" the Constitution forbids are those which compel incrimination. Escobedo's statements were not compelled and the Court
does not hold that they were.

This new American judges' rule, which is to be applied in both
federal and state courts, is perhaps thought to be a necessary
safeguard against the possibility of extorted confessions. To this
extent it reflects a deep-seated distrust of law enforcement officers
everywhere, unsupported by relevant data or current material based
upon our own experience. Obviously law enforcement officers can
make mistakes and exceed their authority, as today's decision shows
that even judges can do, but I have somewhat more faith than the
Court evidently has in the ability and desire of prosecutors and of
the power of the appellate courts to discern and correct such
violations of the law.

The Court may be concerned with a narrower matter: the
unknowing defendant who responds to police questioning because
he mistakenly believes that he must and that his admissions will not
be used against him. But this worry hardly calls for the broadside
the Court has now fired. The failure to inform an accused that he
need not answer and that his answers may be used against him is
very relevant indeed to whether the disclosures are compelled.
Cases in this Court, to say the least, have never placed a premium
on ignorance of constitutional rights. If an accused is told he must
answer and does not know better, it would be very doubtful that
the resulting admissions could be used against him. When the
accused has not been informed of his rights at all the Court
characteristically and properly looks very closely at the surrounding
circumstances.... I would continue to do so. But in this case
Danny Escobedo knew full well that he did not have to answer and
knew full well that his lawyer had advised him not to answer.

I do not suggest for a moment that law enforcement will be destroyed by the rule announced today. The need for peace and order is too insistent for that. But it will be crippled and its task made a great deal more difficult, all in my opinion, for unsound, unstated reasons, which can find no home in any of the provisions of the Constitution.[*]

[*] Justice Harlan wrote a brief dissenting opinion.

MIRANDA v. ARIZONA

384 U.S. 436, 86 S.Ct. 1602, 16 L.Ed.2d 694 (1966).

MR. CHIEF JUSTICE WARREN delivered the opinion of the Court.

The cases before us raise questions which go to the roots of our concepts of American criminal jurisprudence: the restraints society must observe consistent with the Federal Constitution in prosecuting individuals for crime. More specifically, we deal with the admissibility of statements obtained from an individual who is subjected to custodial police interrogation and the necessity for procedures which assure that the individual is accorded his privilege under the Fifth Amendment to the Constitution not to be compelled to incriminate himself.

We dealt with certain phases of this problem recently in Escobedo v. Illinois, 378 U.S. 478 (1964). There, as in the four cases before us, law enforcement officials took the defendant into custody and interrogated him in a police station for the purpose of obtaining a confession. The police did not effectively advise him of his right to remain silent or of his right to consult with his attorney. Rather, they confronted him with an alleged accomplice who accused him of having perpetrated a murder. When the defendant denied the accusation and said "I didn't shoot Manuel, you did it," they handcuffed him and took him to an interrogation room. There, while handcuffed and standing, he was questioned for four hours until he confessed. During this interrogation, the police denied his request to speak to his attorney, and they prevented his retained attorney, who had come to the police station, from consulting with him. At his trial, the State, over his objection, introduced the confession against him. We held that the statements thus made were constitutionally inadmissible.

This case has been the subject of judicial interpretation and spirited legal debate since it was decided two years ago. Both state and federal courts, in assessing its implications, have arrived at varying conclusions. A wealth of scholarly material has been written tracing its ramifications and underpinnings. Police and prosecutor have speculated on its range and desirability. We granted certiorari in these cases, 382 U.S. 924, 925, 937, in order further to explore some facets of the problems, thus exposed, of applying the privilege against self-incrimination to in-custody interrogation, and to give concrete constitutional guidelines for law enforcement agencies and courts to follow.

We start here, as we did in *Escobedo,* with the premise that our holding is not an innovation in our jurisprudence, but is an application of principles long recognized and applied in other settings. We have undertaken a thorough re-examination of the *Escobedo* decision and the principles it announced, and we reaffirm it. That case was but an explication of basic rights that are enshrined in our Constitution—that "No person . . . shall be compelled in any criminal case to be a witness against himself," and that "the accused shall . . . have the Assistance of Counsel"—rights which were put in jeopardy in that case through official overbearing. These precious rights were fixed in our Constitution only after centuries of persecution and struggle. And in the words of Chief Justice Marshall, they were secured "for ages to come, and . . . designed to approach immortality as nearly as human institutions can approach it," Cohens v. Virginia, 6 Wheat. 264, 387 (1821).

. . .

Our holding will be spelled out with some specificity in the pages which follow but briefly stated it is this: the prosecution may not use statements, whether exculpatory or inculpatory, stemming from custodial interrogation of the defendant unless it demonstrates the use of procedural safeguards effective to secure the privilege against self-incrimination. By custodial interrogation, we mean questioning initiated by law enforcement officers after a person has been taken into custody or otherwise deprived of his freedom of action in any significant way.[4] As for the procedural safeguards to be employed, unless other fully effective means are devised to inform accused persons of their right of silence and to assure a continuous opportunity to exercise it, the following measures are required. Prior to any questioning, the person must be warned that he has a right to remain silent, that any statement he does make may be used as evidence against him, and that he has a right to the presence of an attorney, either retained or appointed. The defendant may waive effectuation of these rights, provided the waiver is made voluntarily, knowingly and intelligently. If, however, he indicates in any manner and at any stage of the process that he wishes to consult with an attorney before speaking there can be no questioning. Likewise, if the individual is alone and indicates in any manner that he does not wish to be interrogated, the police may not question him. The mere fact that he may have answered some questions or volunteered some statements on his own does not deprive him of the right to refrain from answering any further inquiries until he has consulted with an attorney and thereafter consents to be questioned.

---

4. This is what we meant in *Escobedo* when we spoke of an investigation which had focused on an accused.

I

The constitutional issue we decide in each of these cases is the admissibility of statements obtained from a defendant questioned while in custody or otherwise deprived of his freedom of action in any significant way. In each, the defendant was questioned by police officers, detectives, or a prosecuting attorney in a room in which he was cut off from the outside world. In none of these cases was the defendant given a full and effective warning of his rights at the outset of the interrogation process. In all the cases, the questioning elicited oral admissions, and in three of them, signed statements as well which were admitted at their trials. They all thus share salient features—incommunicado interrogation of individuals in a police-dominated atmosphere, resulting in self-incriminating statements without full warnings of constitutional rights.

An understanding of the nature and setting of this in-custody interrogation is essential to our decisions today. The difficulty in depicting what transpires at such interrogations stems from the fact that in this country they have largely taken place incommunicado. From extensive factual studies undertaken in the early 1930's, including the famous Wickersham Report to Congress by a Presidential Commission, it is clear that police violence and the "third degree" flourished at that time. In a series of cases decided by this Court long after these studies, the police resorted to physical brutality—beating, hanging, whipping—and to sustained and protracted questioning incommunicado in order to extort confessions. The Commission on Civil Rights in 1961 found much evidence to indicate that "some policemen still resort to physical force to obtain confessions," 1961 Comm'n on Civil Rights Rep., Justice, pt. 5, 17. The use of physical brutality and violence is not, unfortunately, relegated to the past or to any part of the country. Only recently in Kings County, New York, the police brutally beat, kicked and placed lighted cigarette butts on the back of a potential witness under interrogation for the purpose of securing a statement incriminating a third party. People v. Portelli, 15 N.Y.2d 235, 205 N.E.2d 857, 257 N.Y.S.2d 931 (1965).

The examples given above are undoubtedly the exception now, but they are sufficiently widespread to be the object of concern. Unless a proper limitation upon custodial interrogation is achieved—such as these decisions will advance—there can be no assurance that practices of this nature will be eradicated in the foreseeable future. . . .

Again we stress that the modern practice of in-custody interrogation is psychologically rather than physically oriented. As we have stated before, "Since Chambers v. Florida, 309 U.S. 227, this Court has recognized that coercion can be mental as well as physical, and that the blood of the accused is not the only hallmark of an unconstitutional inquisition." Blackburn v. Alabama, 361 U.S. 199, 206 (1960). Interrogation still takes place in privacy. Privacy results in secrecy and this in turn results in a gap in our knowledge as to what in fact goes on in the interrogation rooms. A valuable source of information about present police practices, however, may be found in various police manuals and texts, which document procedures employed with success in the past, and which recommend various other effective tactics.[8] These texts are used by law enforcement agencies themselves as guides. It should be noted that these texts professedly present the most enlightened and effective means presently used to obtain statements through custodial interrogation. By considering these texts and other data, it is possible to describe procedures observed and noted around the country.

The officers are told by the manuals that the "principal psychological factor contributing to a successful interrogation is *privacy*— being alone with the person under interrogation."[10] The efficacy of this tactic has been explained as follows:

> "If at all practicable, the interrogation should take place in the investigator's office or at least in a room of his own choice. The subject should be deprived of every psychological advantage. In his own home he may be confident, indignant, or recalcitrant. He is more keenly aware of his rights and more reluctant to tell of his indiscretions or criminal behavior within the walls of his home. Moreover his family and other friends are nearby, their presence lending moral support. In his own office, the investigator possesses all the advantages. The atmosphere suggests the invincibility of the forces of the law."[11]

To highlight the isolation and unfamiliar surroundings, the manuals instruct the police to display an air of confidence in the suspect's guilt and from outward appearance to maintain only an interest in confirming certain details. The guilt of the subject is to be posited as a fact. The interrogator should direct his comments toward the reasons why the subject committed the act, rather than court failure by asking the subject whether he did it. Like other men, perhaps the subject has had a bad family life, had an unhappy childhood, had too much to drink, had an unrequited desire for women. The officers are instructed to minimize the moral seriousness of the offense,[12] to cast blame on the victim or on society.[13] These tactics are designed to put the subject in a psychological state where his story is but an elaboration of what the police purport to know already—that he is guilty. Explanations to the contrary are dismissed and discouraged.

---

8. The manuals quoted in the text following are the most recent and representative of the texts currently available. ...

10. Inbau & Reid, Criminal Interrogation and Confessions (1962), at 1.

11. O'Hara, [Fundamentals of Criminal Investigation (1956)], at 99.

12. Inbau & Reid, supra, at 34–43, 87.

· · ·

13. Inbau & Reid, supra, at 43–55.

The texts thus stress that the major qualities an interrogator should possess are patience and perseverance....

The manuals suggest that the suspect be offered legal excuses for his actions in order to obtain an initial admission of guilt....

Having then obtained the admission of shooting, the interrogator is advised to refer to circumstantial evidence which negates the self-defense explanation. This should enable him to secure the entire story. One text notes that "Even if he fails to do so, the inconsistency between the subject's original denial of the shooting and his present admission of at least doing the shooting will serve to deprive him of a self-defense 'out' at the time of trial."[16]

When the techniques described above prove unavailing, the texts recommend they be alternated with a show of some hostility....

The interrogators sometimes are instructed to induce a confession out of trickery....

The manuals also contain instructions for police on how to handle the individual who refuses to discuss the matter entirely, or who asks for an attorney or relatives. The examiner is to concede him the right to remain silent. "This usually has a very undermining effect. First of all, he is disappointed in his expectation of an unfavorable reaction on the part of the interrogator. Secondly, a concession of this right to remain silent impresses the subject with the apparent fairness of his interrogator."[20] After this psychological conditioning, however, the officer is told to point out the incriminating significance of the suspect's refusal to talk....

Few will persist in their initial refusal to talk, it is said, if this monologue is employed correctly.

In the event that the subject wishes to speak to a relative or an attorney, the following advice is tendered:

"[T]he interrogator should respond by suggesting that the subject first tell the truth to the interrogator himself rather than get anyone else involved in the matter. If the request is for an attorney, the interrogator may suggest that the subject save himself or his family the expense of any such professional service, particularly if he is innocent of the offense under investigation. The interrogator may also add, 'Joe, I'm only looking for the truth, and if you're telling the truth, that's it. You can handle this by yourself.' "[22]

From these representative samples of interrogation techniques, the setting prescribed by the manuals and observed in practice becomes clear. In essence, it is this: To be alone with the subject is essential to prevent distraction and to deprive him of any outside

16. Ibid.

20. Inbau & Reid, supra, at 111.

22. Inbau & Reid, supra, at 112.

support. The aura of confidence in his guilt undermines his will to resist. He merely confirms the preconceived story the police seek to have him describe. Patience and persistence, at times relentless questioning, are employed. To obtain a confession, the interrogator must "patiently maneuver himself or his quarry into a position from which the desired objective may be attained."[23] When normal procedures fail to produce the needed result, the police may resort to deceptive stratagems such as giving false legal advice. It is important to keep the subject off balance, for example, by trading on his insecurity about himself or his surroundings. The police then persuade, trick, or cajole him out of exercising his constitutional rights.

Even without employing brutality, the "third degree" or the specific stratagems described above, the very fact of custodial interrogation exacts a heavy toll on individual liberty and trades on the weakness of individuals.[24] This fact may be illustrated simply by referring to three confession cases decided by this Court in the Term immediately preceding our *Escobedo* decision. In Townsend v. Sain, 372 U.S. 293 (1963), the defendant was a 19-year-old heroin addict, described as a "near mental defective," id., at 307–310. The defendant in Lynumn v. Illinois, 372 U.S. 528 (1963), was a woman who confessed to the arresting officer after being importuned to "cooperate" in order to prevent her children from being taken by relief authorities. This Court as in those cases reversed the conviction of a defendant in Haynes v. Washington, 373 U.S. 503 (1963), whose persistent request during his interrogation was to phone his wife or attorney. In other settings, these individuals might have exercised their constitutional rights. In the incommunicado police-dominated atmosphere, they succumbed.

In the cases before us today, given this background, we concern ourselves primarily with this interrogation atmosphere and the evils it can bring. In No. 759, Miranda v. Arizona, the police arrested the defendant and took him to a special interrogation room where they secured a confession. In No. 760, Vignera v. New York, the defendant made oral admissions to the police after interrogation in the afternoon, and then signed an inculpatory statement upon being questioned by an assistant district attorney later the same evening. In No. 761, Westover v. United States, the defendant was handed over to the Federal Bureau of Investigation by local authorities after they had detained and interrogated him for a lengthy period, both at night and the following morning. After some two hours of questioning, the federal officers had obtained signed statements from the defendant. Lastly, in No. 584, California v. Stewart, the local police held the defendant five days in the station and interrogated him on nine separate occasions before they secured his inculpatory statement.

---

23. Inbau & Reid, Lie Detection and Criminal Interrogation 185 (3d ed. 1953).

24. Interrogation procedures may even give rise to a false confession. . . .

In these cases, we might not find the defendants' statements to have been involuntary in traditional terms. Our concern for adequate safeguards to protect precious Fifth Amendment rights is, of course, not lessened in the slightest. In each of the cases, the defendant was thrust into an unfamiliar atmosphere and run through menacing police interrogation procedures. The potentiality for compulsion is forcefully apparent, for example, in *Miranda,* where the indigent Mexican defendant was a seriously disturbed individual with pronounced sexual fantasies, and in *Stewart,* in which the defendant was an indigent Los Angeles Negro who had dropped out of school in the sixth grade. To be sure, the records do not evince overt physical coercion or patent psychological ploys. The fact remains that in none of these cases did the officers undertake to afford appropriate safeguards at the outset of the interrogation to insure that the statements were truly the product of free choice.

It is obvious that such an interrogation environment is created for no purpose other than to subjugate the individual to the will of his examiner. This atmosphere carries its own badge of intimidation. To be sure, this is not physical intimidation, but it is equally destructive of human dignity. The current practice of incommunicado interrogation is at odds with one of our Nation's most cherished principles—that the individual may not be compelled to incriminate himself. Unless adequate protective devices are employed to dispel the compulsion inherent in custodial surroundings, no statement obtained from the defendant can truly be the product of his free choice.

From the foregoing, we can readily perceive an intimate connection between the privilege against self-incrimination and police custodial questioning. It is fitting to turn to history and precedent underlying the Self-Incrimination Clause to determine its applicability in this situation.

II

We sometimes forget how long it has taken to establish the privilege against self-incrimination, the sources from which it came and the fervor with which it was defended. Its roots go back into ancient times.   ...

. . .

Thus we may view the historical development of the privilege as one which groped for the proper scope of governmental power over the citizen. As a "noble principle often transcends its origins," the privilege has come rightfully to be recognized in part as an individual's substantive right, a "right to a private enclave where he may lead a private life. That right is the hallmark of our democracy." United States v. Grunewald, 233 F.2d 556, 579, 581–582 (Frank, J., dissenting), rev'd, 353 U.S. 391 (1957). We have recently noted that the privilege against self-incrimination—the essential mainstay of our adversary system—is founded on a complex of values .... All these policies point to one overriding thought: the constitutional foundation underlying the privilege is the respect a government—state or federal—must accord to the dignity and integrity of its citizens. To maintain a "fair state-individual balance," to require the government "to shoulder the entire load," 8 Wigmore, Evidence 317 (McNaughton rev. 1961), to respect the inviolability of the human personality, our accusatory system of criminal justice demands that the government seeking to punish an individual produce the evidence against him by its own independent labors, rather than by the cruel, simple expedient of compelling it from his own mouth.... In sum, the privilege is fulfilled only when the person is guaranteed the right "to remain silent unless he chooses to speak in the unfettered exercise of his own will." Malloy v. Hogan, 378 U.S. 1, 8 (1964).

The question in these cases is whether the privilege is fully applicable during a period of custodial interrogation. In this Court, the privilege has consistently been accorded a liberal construction. ... We are satisfied that all the principles embodied in the privilege apply to informal compulsion exerted by law-enforcement officers during in-custody questioning. An individual swept from familiar surroundings into police custody, surrounded by antagonistic forces, and subjected to the techniques of persuasion described above cannot be otherwise than under compulsion to speak. As a practical matter, the compulsion to speak in the isolated setting of the police station may well be greater than in courts or other official investigations, where there are often impartial observers to guard against intimidation or trickery.

. . .

Our holding ... [in Escobedo v. Illinois, 378 U.S. 478 (1964)] stressed the fact that the police had not advised the defendant of his constitutional privilege to remain silent at the outset of the interrogation, and we drew attention to that fact at several points in the decision.... This was no isolated factor, but an essential ingredient in our decision. The entire thrust of police interrogation there, as in all the cases today, was to put the defendant in such an emotional state as to impair his capacity for rational judgment. The abdication of the constitutional privilege—the choice on his part to speak to the police—was not made knowingly or competently because of the failure to apprise him of his rights; the compelling atmosphere of the in-custody interrogation, and not an independent decision on his part, caused the defendant to speak.

A different phase of the *Escobedo* decision was significant in its attention to the absence of counsel during the questioning. There, as in the cases today, we sought a protective device to dispel the compelling atmosphere of the interrogation. In *Escobedo,* however, the police did not relieve the defendant of the anxieties which they had created in the interrogation rooms. Rather, they denied his request for the assistance of counsel.... This heightened his dilemma, and made his later statements the product of this compulsion.... The denial of the defendant's request for his attorney thus undermined his ability to exercise the privilege—to remain silent if he chose or to speak without any intimidation, blatant or subtle. The presence of counsel, in all the cases before us today, would be the adequate protective device necessary to make the process of police interrogation conform to the dictates of the privilege. His presence would insure that statements made in the government-established atmosphere are not the product of compulsion.

It was in this manner that *Escobedo* explicated another facet of the pretrial privilege, noted in many of the Court's prior decisions: the protection of rights at trial. That counsel is present when statements are taken from an individual during interrogation obviously enhances the integrity of the fact-finding processes in court. The presence of an attorney, and the warnings delivered to the individual, enable the defendant under otherwise compelling circumstances to tell his story without fear, effectively, and in a way that eliminates the evils in the interrogation process. Without the protections flowing from adequate warnings and the rights of counsel, "all the careful safeguards erected around the giving of testimony, whether by an accused or any other witness, would become empty formalities in a procedure where the most compelling possible evidence of guilt, a confession, would have already been obtained at the unsupervised pleasure of the police." Mapp v. Ohio, 367 U.S. 643, 685 (1961) (Harlan, J., dissenting)....

III

Today, then, there can be no doubt that the Fifth Amendment privilege is available outside of criminal court proceedings and serves to protect persons in all settings in which their freedom of action is curtailed in any significant way from being compelled to incriminate themselves. We have concluded that without proper safeguards the process of in-custody interrogation of persons suspected or accused of crime contains inherently compelling pressures which work to undermine the individual's will to resist and to compel him to speak where he would not otherwise do so freely. In order to combat these pressures and to permit a full opportunity to exercise the privilege against self-incrimination, the accused must be adequately and effectively apprised of his rights and the exercise of those rights must be fully honored.

It is impossible for us to foresee the potential alternatives for protecting the privilege which might be devised by Congress or the States in the exercise of their creative rule-making capacities. Therefore we cannot say that the Constitution necessarily requires adherence to any particular solution for the inherent compulsions of the interrogation process as it is presently conducted. Our decision in no way creates a constitutional straitjacket which will handicap sound efforts at reform, nor is it intended to have this effect. We encourage Congress and the States to continue their laudable search for increasingly effective ways of protecting the rights of the individual while promoting efficient enforcement of our criminal laws. However, unless we are shown other procedures which are at least as effective in apprising accused persons of their right of silence and in assuring a continuous opportunity to exercise it, the following safeguards must be observed.

At the outset, if a person in custody is to be subjected to interrogation, he must first be informed in clear and unequivocal terms that he has the right to remain silent. For those unaware of the privilege, the warning is needed simply to make them aware of it—the threshold requirement for an intelligent decision as to its exercise. More important, such a warning is an absolute prerequisite in overcoming the inherent pressures of the interrogation atmosphere. It is not just the subnormal or woefully ignorant who succumb to an interrogator's imprecations, whether implied or expressly stated, that the interrogation will continue until a confession is obtained or that silence in the face of accusation is itself damning and will bode ill when presented to a jury. Further, the warning will show the individual that his interrogators are prepared to recognize his privilege should he choose to exercise it.

The Fifth Amendment privilege is so fundamental to our system of constitutional rule and the expedient of giving an adequate warning as to the availability of the privilege so simple, we will not pause to inquire in individual cases whether the defendant was aware of his rights without a warning being given. Assessments of the knowledge the defendant possessed, based on information as to his age, education, intelligence, or prior contact with authorities, can never be more than speculation; a warning is a clearcut fact. More important, whatever the background of the person interrogated, a warning at the time of the interrogation is indispensable to overcome its pressures and to insure that the individual knows he is free to exercise the privilege at that point in time.

The warning of the right to remain silent must be accompanied by the explanation that anything said can and will be used against the individual in court. This warning is needed in order to make him aware not only of the privilege, but also of the consequences of forgoing it. It is only through an awareness of these consequences that there can be any assurance of real understanding and intelligent exercise of the privilege. Moreover, this warning may serve to make the individual more acutely aware that he is faced with a phase of the adversary system—that he is not in the presence of persons acting solely in his interest.

The circumstances surrounding in-custody interrogation can operate very quickly to overbear the will of one merely made aware of his privilege by his interrogators. Therefore, the right to have counsel present at the interrogation is indispensable to the protection of the Fifth Amendment privilege under the system we delineate today. Our aim is to assure that the individual's right to choose between silence and speech remains unfettered throughout the interrogation process. A once-stated warning, delivered by those who will conduct the interrogation, cannot itself suffice to that end among those who most require knowledge of their rights. A mere warning given by the interrogators is not alone sufficient to accomplish that end. Prosecutors themselves claim that the admonishment of the right to remain silent without more "will benefit only the recidivist and the professional." Brief for the National District Attorneys Association as *amicus curiae,* p. 14. Even preliminary advice given to the accused by his own attorney can be swiftly overcome by the secret interrogation process.... Thus, the need for counsel to protect the Fifth Amendment privilege comprehends not merely a right to consult with counsel prior to questioning, but also to have counsel present during any questioning if the defendant so desires.

The presence of counsel at the interrogation may serve several significant subsidiary functions as well. If the accused decides to talk to his interrogators, the assistance of counsel can mitigate the dangers of untrustworthiness. With a lawyer present the likelihood that the police will practice coercion is reduced, and if coercion is nevertheless exercised the lawyer can testify to it in court. The presence of a lawyer can also help to guarantee that the accused gives a fully accurate statement to the police and that the statement is rightly reported by the prosecution at trial....

An individual need not make a pre-interrogation request for a lawyer. While such request affirmatively secures his right to have one, his failure to ask for a lawyer does not constitute a waiver. No effective waiver of the right to counsel during interrogation can be recognized unless specifically made after the warnings we here delineate have been given. The accused who does not know his rights and therefore does not make a request may be the person who most needs counsel....

In Carnley v. Cochran, 369 U.S. 506, 513 (1962), we stated: "[I]t is settled that where the assistance of counsel is a constitutional requisite, the right to be furnished counsel does not depend on a request." This proposition applies with equal force in the context of providing counsel to protect an accused's Fifth Amendment privilege in the face of interrogation. Although the role of counsel at trial differs from the role during interrogation, the differences are not relevant to the question whether a request is a prerequisite.

Accordingly we hold that an individual held for interrogation must be clearly informed that he has the right to consult with a lawyer and to have the lawyer with him during interrogation under the system for protecting the privilege we delineate today. As with the warnings of the right to remain silent and that anything stated can be used in evidence against him, this warning is an absolute prerequisite to interrogation. No amount of circumstantial evidence that the person may have been aware of this right will suffice to stand in its stead. Only through such a warning is there ascertainable assurance that the accused was aware of this right.

If an individual indicates that he wishes the assistance of counsel before any interrogation occurs, the authorities cannot rationally ignore or deny his request on the basis that the individual does not have or cannot afford a retained attorney. The financial ability of the individual has no relationship to the scope of the rights involved here. The privilege against self-incrimination secured by the Constitution applies to all individuals. The need for counsel in order to protect the privilege exists for the indigent as well as the affluent. In fact, were we to limit these constitutional rights to those who can retain an attorney, our decisions today would be of little significance. The cases before us as well as the vast majority of confession cases with which we have dealt in the past involve those unable to retain counsel. While authorities are not required to relieve the accused of his poverty, they have the obligation not to take advantage of indigence in the administration of justice. Denial of counsel to the indigent at the time of interrogation while allowing an attorney to those who can afford one would be no more supportable by reason or logic than the similar situation at trial and on appeal struck down in Gideon v. Wainwright, 372 U.S. 335 (1963), and Douglas v. California, 372 U.S. 353 (1963).

In order fully to apprise a person interrogated of the extent of his rights under this system then, it is necessary to warn him not only that he has the right to consult with an attorney, but also that if he is indigent a lawyer will be appointed to represent him. Without this additional warning, the admonition of the right to consult with counsel would often be understood as meaning only that he can consult with a lawyer if he has one or has the funds to obtain one. The warning of a right to counsel would be hollow if not couched in terms that would convey to the indigent—the person most often subjected to interrogation—the knowledge that he too has a right to have counsel present. As with the warnings of the right to remain silent and of the general right to counsel, only by effective and express explanation to the indigent of this right can there be assurance that he was truly in a position to exercise it.[43]

43. While a warning that the indigent may have counsel appointed need not be given to the person who is known to have an attorney or is known to have ample funds to

Once warnings have been given, the subsequent procedure is clear. If the individual indicates in any manner, at any time prior to or during questioning, that he wishes to remain silent, the interrogation must cease.[44] At this point he has shown that he intends to exercise his Fifth Amendment privilege; any statement taken after the person invokes his privilege cannot be other than the product of compulsion, subtle or otherwise. Without the right to cut off questioning, the setting of in-custody interrogation operates on the individual to overcome free choice in producing a statement after the privilege has been once invoked. If the individual states that he wants an attorney, the interrogation must cease until an attorney is present. At that time, the individual must have an opportunity to confer with the attorney and to have him present during any subsequent questioning. If the individual cannot obtain an attorney and he indicates that he wants one before speaking to police, they must respect his decision to remain silent.

This does not mean, as some have suggested, that each police station must have a "station house lawyer" present at all times to advise prisoners. It does mean, however, that if police propose to interrogate a person they must make known to him that he is entitled to a lawyer and that if he cannot afford one, a lawyer will be provided for him prior to any interrogation. If authorities conclude that they will not provide counsel during a reasonable period of time in which investigation in the field is carried out, they may refrain from doing so without violating the person's Fifth Amendment privilege so long as they do not question him during that time.

If the interrogation continues without the presence of an attorney and a statement is taken, a heavy burden rests on the government to demonstrate that the defendant knowingly and intelligently waived his privilege against self-incrimination and his right to retained or appointed counsel.... This Court has always set high standards of proof for the waiver of constitutional rights ... and we re-assert these standards as applied to in-custody interrogation. Since the State is responsible for establishing the isolated circumstances under which the interrogation takes place and has the only means of making available corroborated evidence of warnings given during incommunicado interrogation, the burden is rightly on its shoulders.

An express statement that the individual is willing to make a statement and does not want an attorney followed closely by a

secure one, the expedient of giving a warning is too simple and the rights involved too important to engage in *ex post facto* inquiries into financial ability when there is any doubt at all on that score.

44. If an individual indicates his desire to remain silent, but has an attorney present, there may be some circumstances in which

further questioning would be permissible. In the absence of evidence of overbearing, statements then made in the presence of counsel might be free of the compelling influence of the interrogation process and might fairly be construed as a waiver of the privilege for purposes of these statements.

statement could constitute a waiver. But a valid waiver will not be presumed simply from the silence of the accused after warnings are given or simply from the fact that a confession was in fact eventually obtained. ... Moreover, where in-custody interrogation is involved, there is no room for the contention that the privilege is waived if the individual answers some questions or gives some information on his own prior to invoking his right to remain silent when interrogated.

Whatever the testimony of the authorities as to waiver of rights by an accused, the fact of lengthy interrogation or incommunicado incarceration before a statement is made is strong evidence that the accused did not validly waive his rights. In these circumstances the fact that the individual eventually made a statement is consistent with the conclusion that the compelling influence of the interrogation finally forced him to do so. It is inconsistent with any notion of a voluntary relinquishment of the privilege. Moreover, any evidence that the accused was threatened, tricked, or cajoled into a waiver will, of course, show that the defendant did not voluntarily waive his privilege. The requirement of warnings and waiver of rights is a fundamental with respect to the Fifth Amendment privilege and not simply a preliminary ritual to existing methods of interrogation.

The warnings required and the waiver necessary in accordance with our opinion today are, in the absence of a fully effective equivalent, prerequisites to the admissibility of any statement made by a defendant. No distinction can be drawn between statements which are direct confessions and statements which amount to "admissions" of part or all of an offense. The privilege against self-incrimination protects the individual from being compelled to incriminate himself in any manner; it does not distinguish degrees of incrimination. Similarly, for precisely the same reason, no distinction may be drawn between inculpatory statements and statements alleged to be merely "exculpatory." If a statement made were in fact truly exculpatory it would, of course, never be used by the prosecution. In fact, statements merely intended to be exculpatory by the defendant are often used to impeach his testimony at trial or to demonstrate untruths in the statement given under interrogation and thus to prove guilt by implication. These statements are incriminating in any meaningful sense of the word and may not be used without the full warnings and effective waiver required for any other statement. In *Escobedo* itself, the defendant fully intended his accusation of another as the slayer to be exculpatory as to himself.

The principles announced today deal with the protection which must be given to the privilege against self-incrimination when the individual is first subjected to police interrogation while in custody at the station or otherwise deprived of his freedom of action in any significant way. It is at this point that our adversary system of criminal proceedings commences, distinguishing itself at the outset from the inquisitorial system recognized in some countries. Under the system of warnings we delineate today or under any other system which may be devised and found effective, the safeguards to be erected about the privilege must come into play at this point.

Our decision is not intended to hamper the traditional function of police officers in investigating crime.... When an individual is in custody on probable cause, the police may, of course, seek out evidence in the field to be used at trial against him. Such investigation may include inquiry of persons not under restraint. General on-the-scene questioning as to facts surrounding a crime or other general questioning of citizens in the fact-finding process is not affected by our holding. It is an act of responsible citizenship for individuals to give whatever information they may have to aid in law enforcement. In such situations the compelling atmosphere inherent in the process of in-custody interrogation is not necessarily present.

In dealing with statements obtained through interrogation, we do not purport to find all confessions inadmissible. Confessions remain a proper element in law enforcement. Any statement given freely and voluntarily without any compelling influences is, of course, admissible in evidence. The fundamental import of the privilege while an individual is in custody is not whether he is allowed to talk to the police without the benefit of warnings and counsel, but whether he can be interrogated. There is no requirement that police stop a person who enters a police station and states that he wishes to confess to a crime, or a person who calls the police to offer a confession or any other statement he desires to make. Volunteered statements of any kind are not barred by the Fifth Amendment and their admissibility is not affected by our holding today.

To summarize, we hold that when an individual is taken into custody or otherwise deprived of his freedom by the authorities in any significant way and is subjected to questioning, the privilege against self-incrimination is jeopardized. Procedural safeguards must be employed to protect the privilege, and unless other fully effective means are adopted to notify the person of his right of silence and to assure that the exercise of the right will be scrupulously honored, the following measures are required. He must be warned prior to any questioning that he has the right to remain silent, that anything he says can be used against him in a court of law, that he has the right to the presence of an attorney, and that if he cannot afford an attorney one will be appointed for him prior to any questioning if he so desires. Opportunity to exercise these rights must be afforded to him throughout the interrogation. After such warnings have been given, and such opportunity afforded him, the individual may knowingly and intelligently waive these rights and agree to answer questions or make a statement. But unless and until such warnings and waiver are demonstrated by the prosecution at trial, no evidence obtained as a result of interrogation can be used against him.

IV

A recurrent argument made in these cases is that society's need for interrogation outweighs the privilege. This argument is not unfamiliar to this Court.... The whole thrust of our foregoing discussion demonstrates that the Constitution has prescribed the rights of the individual when confronted with the power of government when it provided in the Fifth Amendment that an individual cannot be compelled to be a witness against himself. That right cannot be abridged. ...

If the individual desires to exercise his privilege, he has the right to do so. This is not for the authorities to decide. An attorney may advise his client not to talk to police until he has had an opportunity to investigate the case, or he may wish to be present with his client during any police questioning. In doing so an attorney is merely exercising the good professional judgment he has been taught. This is not cause for considering the attorney a menace to law enforcement. He is merely carrying out what he is sworn to do under his oath—to protect to the extent of his ability the rights of his client. In fulfilling this responsibility the attorney plays a vital role in the administration of criminal justice under our Constitution.

In announcing these principles, we are not unmindful of the burdens which law enforcement officials must bear, often under trying circumstances. We also fully recognize the obligation of all citizens to aid in enforcing the criminal laws. This Court, while protecting individual rights, has always given ample latitude to law enforcement agencies in the legitimate exercise of their duties. The limits we have placed on the interrogation process should not constitute an undue interference with a proper system of law enforcement. As we have noted, our decision does not in any way preclude police from carrying out their traditional investigatory functions. Although confessions may play an important role in some convictions, the cases before us present graphic examples of the overstatement of the "need" for confessions. In each case authorities conducted interrogations ranging up to five days in duration despite the presence, through standard investigating practices, of considerable evidence against each defendant. Further examples are chronicled in our prior cases. ...

It is also urged that an unfettered right to detention for interrogation should be allowed because it will often redound to the benefit of the person questioned. When police inquiry determines that there is no reason to believe that the person has committed any crime, it is said, he will be released without need for further formal procedures. The person who has committed no offense, however, will be better able to clear himself after warnings with counsel present than without. It can be assumed that in such circumstances a lawyer would advise his client to talk freely to police in order to clear himself.

Custodial interrogation, by contrast, does not necessarily afford the innocent an opportunity to clear themselves. A serious consequence of the present practice of the interrogation alleged to be beneficial for the innocent is that many arrests "for investigation" subject large numbers of innocent persons to detention and interrogation. In one of the cases before us, No. 584, California v. Stewart, police held four persons, who were in the defendant's house at the time of the arrest, in jail for five days until defendant confessed. At that time they were finally released. Police stated that there was "no evidence to connect them with any crime." Available statistics on the extent of this practice where it is condoned indicate that these four are far from alone in being subjected to arrest, prolonged detention, and interrogation without the requisite probable cause.

Over the years the Federal Bureau of Investigation has compiled an exemplary record of effective law enforcement while advising any suspect or arrested person, at the outset of an interview, that he is not required to make a statement, that any statement may be used against him in court, that the individual may obtain the services of an attorney of his own choice and, more recently, that he has a right to free counsel if he is unable to pay. . . .

The practice of the FBI can readily be emulated by state and local enforcement agencies. The argument that the FBI deals with different crimes than are dealt with by state authorities does not mitigate the significance of the FBI experience.

The experience in some other countries also suggests that the danger to law enforcement in curbs on interrogation is overplayed. . . .

. . .

It is also urged upon us that we withhold decision on this issue until state legislative bodies and advisory groups have had an opportunity to deal with these problems by rule making. We have already pointed out that the Constitution does not require any specific code of procedures for protecting the privilege against self-incrimination during custodial interrogation. Congress and the States are free to develop their own safeguards for the privilege, so long as they are fully as effective as those described above in informing accused persons of their right of silence and in affording a continuous opportunity to exercise it. In any event, however, the issues presented are of constitutional dimensions and must be determined by the courts. The admissibility of a statement in the face of a claim that it was obtained in violation of the defendant's constitutional rights is an issue the resolution of which has long since been undertaken by this Court. . . . Judicial solutions to

problems of constitutional dimension have evolved decade by decade. As courts have been presented with the need to enforce
constitutional rights, they have found means of doing so. That was
our responsibility when *Escobedo* was before us and it is our
responsibility today. Where rights secured by the Constitution are
involved, there can be no rule making or legislation which would
abrogate them.

V

Because of the nature of the problem and because of its
recurrent significance in numerous cases, we have to this point
discussed the relationship of the Fifth Amendment privilege to
police interrogation without specific concentration on the facts of
the cases before us. We turn now to these facts to consider the
application to these cases of the constitutional principles discussed
above. In each instance, we have concluded that statements were
obtained from the defendant under circumstances that did not meet
constitutional standards for protection of the privilege.

. . .

Therefore, in accordance with the foregoing, the judgments of
the Supreme Court of Arizona in No. 759, of the New York Court of
Appeals in No. 760, and of the Court of Appeals for the Ninth
Circuit in No. 761 are reversed. The judgment of the Supreme
Court of California in No. 584 is affirmed.

It is so ordered.

MR. JUSTICE WHITE, with whom MR. JUSTICE HARLAN and
MR. JUSTICE STEWART join, dissenting.

I

The proposition that the privilege against self-incrimination
forbids in-custody interrogation without the warnings specified in
the majority opinion and without a clear waiver of counsel has no
significant support in the history of the privilege or in the language
of the Fifth Amendment. As for the English authorities and the
common-law history, the privilege, firmly established in the second
half of the seventeenth century, was never applied except to prohibit compelled judicial interrogations. The rule excluding coerced
confessions matured about 100 years later, "[b]ut there is nothing
in the reports to suggest that the theory has its roots in the privilege
against self-incrimination. And so far as the cases reveal, the
privilege, as such, seems to have been given effect only in judicial
proceedings, including the preliminary examinations by authorized
magistrates." Morgan, The Privilege Against Self-Incrimination, 34
Minn.L.Rev. 1, 18 (1949).

Our own constitutional provision provides that no person
"shall be compelled in any criminal case to be a witness against
himself." These words, when "[c]onsidered in the light to be shed

by grammar and the dictionary ... appear to signify simply that nobody shall be compelled to give oral testimony against himself in a criminal proceeding under way in which he is defendant." Corwin, The Supreme Court's Construction of the Self-Incrimination Clause, 29 Mich.L.Rev. 1, 2. And there is very little in the surrounding circumstances of the adoption of the Fifth Amendment or in the provisions of the then existing state constitutions or in state practice which would give the constitutional provision any broader meaning.... Such a construction, however, was considerably narrower than the privilege at common law, and when eventually faced with the issues, the Court extended the constitutional privilege to the compulsory production of books and papers, to the ordinary witness before the grand jury and to witnesses generally.... Both rules had solid support in common-law history, if not in the history of our own constitutional provision.

A few years later the Fifth Amendment privilege was similarly extended to encompass the then well-established rule against coerced confessions: "In criminal trials, in the courts of the United States, wherever a question arises whether a confession is incompetent because not voluntary, the issue is controlled by that portion of the Fifth Amendment to the Constitution of the United States, commanding that no person 'shall be compelled in any criminal case to be a witness against himself.'" Bram v. United States, 168 U.S. 532, 542. Although this view has found approval in other cases, ... it has also been questioned, ... and finds scant support in either the English or American authorities .... Whatever the source of the rule excluding coerced confessions, it is clear that prior to the application of the privilege itself to state courts ... the admissibility of a confession in a state criminal prosecution was tested by the same standards as were applied in federal prosecutions....

Bram, however, itself rejected the proposition which the Court now espouses. The question in *Bram* was whether a confession, obtained during custodial interrogation, had been compelled, and if such interrogation was to be deemed inherently vulnerable the Court's inquiry could have ended there. After examining the English and American authorities, however, the Court declared that:

> "In this court also it has been settled that the mere fact that the confession is made to a police officer, while the accused was under arrest in or out of prison, or was drawn out by his questions, does not necessarily render the confession involuntary, but, as one of the circumstances, such imprisonment or interrogation may be taken into account in determining whether or not the statements of the prisoner were voluntary." 168 U.S., at 558.

In this respect the Court was wholly consistent with prior and subsequent pronouncements in this Court.

Thus prior to *Bram* the Court, in Hopt v. Utah, 110 U.S. 574, 583–587, had upheld the admissibility of a confession made to police officers following arrest, the record being silent concerning what conversation had occurred between the officers and the defendant in the short period preceding the confession. Relying on *Hopt*, the Court ruled squarely on the issue in Sparf and Hansen v. United States, 156 U.S. 51, 55:

> "Counsel for the accused insist that there cannot be a voluntary statement, a free open confession, while a defendant is confined and in irons under an accusation of having committed a capital offence. We have not been referred to any authority in support of that position. It is true that the fact of a prisoner being in custody at the time he makes a confession is a circumstance not to be overlooked, because it bears upon the inquiry whether the confession was voluntarily made or was extorted by threats or violence or made under the influence of fear. But confinement or imprisonment is not in itself sufficient to justify the exclusion of a confession, if it appears to have been voluntary, and was not obtained by putting the prisoner in fear or by promises. Wharton's Cr.Ev. 9th ed. §§ 661, 663, and authorities cited."

. . .

And in Wilson v. United States, 162 U.S. 613, 623, the Court had considered the significance of custodial interrogation without any antecedent warnings regarding the right to remain silent or the right to counsel. There the defendant had answered questions posed by a Commissioner, who had failed to advise him of his rights, and his answers were held admissible over his claim of involuntariness. "The fact that [a defendant] is in custody and manacled does not necessarily render his statement involuntary, nor is that necessarily the effect of popular excitement shortly preceding. . . . And it is laid down that it is not essential to the admissibility of a confession that it should appear that the person was warned that what he said would be used against him, but on the contrary, if the confession was voluntary, it is sufficient though it appear that he was not so warned."

Since *Bram*, the admissibility of statements made during custodial interrogation has been frequently reiterated. . . .

Only a tiny minority of our judges who have dealt with the question, including today's majority, have considered in-custody interrogation, without more, to be a violation of the Fifth Amendment. And this Court, as every member knows, has left standing literally thousands of criminal convictions that rested at least in part on confessions taken in the course of interrogation by the police after arrest.

II

That the Court's holding today is neither compelled nor even strongly suggested by the language of the Fifth Amendment, is at odds with American and English legal history, and involves a departure from a long line of precedent does not prove either that the Court has exceeded its powers or that the Court is wrong or unwise in its present reinterpretation of the Fifth Amendment. It does, however, underscore the obvious—that the Court has not discovered or found the law in making today's decision, nor has it derived it from some irrefutable sources; what it has done is to make new law and new public policy in much the same way that it has in the course of interpreting other great clauses of the Constitution. This is what the Court historically has done. Indeed, it is what it must do and will continue to do until and unless there is some fundamental change in the constitutional distribution of governmental powers.

But if the Court is here and now to announce new and fundamental policy to govern certain aspects of our affairs, it is wholly legitimate to examine the mode of this or any other constitutional decision in this Court and to inquire into the advisability of its end product in terms of the long-range interest of the country. At the very least the Court's text and reasoning should withstand analysis and be a fair exposition of the constitutional provision which its opinion interprets. Decisions like these cannot rest alone on syllogism, metaphysics or some ill-defined notions of natural justice, although each will perhaps play its part. In proceeding to such constructions as it now announces, the Court should also duly consider all the factors and interests bearing upon the cases, at least insofar as the relevant materials are available; and if the necessary considerations are not treated in the record or obtainable from some other reliable source, the Court should not proceed to formulate fundamental policies based on speculation alone.

III

First, we may inquire what are the textual and factual bases of this new fundamental rule. To reach the result announced on the grounds it does, the Court must stay within the confines of the Fifth Amendment, which forbids self-incrimination only if *compelled.* Hence the core of the Court's opinion is that because of the "compulsion inherent in custodial surroundings, no statement obtained from [a] defendant [in custody] can truly be the product of his free choice," ante, at 458, absent the use of adequate protective devices as described by the Court. However, the Court does not point to any sudden inrush of new knowledge requiring the rejection of 70 years' experience. Nor does it assert that its novel conclusion reflects a changing consensus among state courts . . . or that a succession of cases had steadily eroded the old rule and proved it unworkable. . . . Rather than asserting new knowledge, the Court concedes that it cannot truly know what occurs during custodial questioning, because of the innate secrecy of such proceedings. It extrapolates a picture of what it conceives to be the norm from police investigatorial manuals, published in 1959 and 1962 or earlier, without any attempt to allow for adjustments in police practices that may have occurred in the wake of more recent decisions of state appellate tribunals or this Court. But even if the relentless application of the described procedures could lead to involuntary confessions, it most assuredly does not follow that each and every case will disclose this kind of interrogation or this kind of consequence. Insofar as appears from the Court's opinion, it has not examined a single transcript of any police interrogation, let alone the interrogation that took place in any one of these cases which it decides today. Judged by any of the standards for empirical investigation utilized in the social sciences the factual basis for the Court's premise is patently inadequate.

Although in the Court's view in-custody interrogation is inherently coercive, the Court says that the spontaneous product of the coercion of arrest and detention is still to be deemed voluntary. An accused, arrested on probable cause, may blurt out a confession which will be admissible despite the fact that he is alone and in custody, without any showing that he had any notion of his right to remain silent or of the consequences of his admission. Yet, under the Court's rule, if the police ask him a single question such as "Do you have anything to say?" or "Did you kill your wife?" his response, if there is one, has somehow been compelled, even if the accused has been clearly warned of his right to remain silent. Common sense informs us to the contrary. While one may say that the response was "involuntary" in the sense the question provoked or was the occasion for the response and thus the defendant was induced to speak out when he might have remained silent if not arrested and not questioned, it is patently unsound to say the response is compelled.

Today's result would not follow even if it were agreed that to some extent custodial interrogation is inherently coercive.... The test has been whether the totality of circumstances deprived the defendant of a "free choice to admit, to deny, or to refuse to answer," Lisenba v. California, 314 U.S. 219, 241, and whether physical or psychological coercion was of such a degree that "the defendant's will was overborne at the time he confessed," Haynes v. Washington, 373 U.S. 503, 513; Lynum v. Illinois, 372 U.S. 528, 534. The duration and nature of incommunicado custody, the presence or absence of advice concerning the defendant's constitutional rights, and the granting or refusal of requests to communicate with lawyers, relatives or friends have all been rightly regarded as important data bearing on the basic inquiry.... But it has never been suggested, until today, that such questioning was so coercive and accused persons so lacking in hardihood that the very first response to the very first question following the commencement of custody must be conclusively presumed to be the product of an overborne will.

If the rule announced today were truly based on a conclusion that all confessions resulting from custodial interrogation are coerced, then it would simply have no rational foundation.... A *fortiori* that would be true of the extension of the rule to exculpatory statements, which the Court effects after a brief discussion of why, in the Court's view, they must be deemed incriminatory but without any discussion of why they must be deemed coerced.... Even if one were to postulate that the Court's concern is not that all confessions induced by police interrogation are coerced but rather that some such confessions are coerced and present judicial procedures are believed to be inadequate to identify the confessions that are coerced and those that are not, it would still not be essential to impose the rule that the Court has now fashioned. Transcripts or observers could be required, specific time limits, tailored to fit the cause, could be imposed, or other devices could be utilized to reduce the chances that otherwise indiscernible coercion will produce an inadmissible confession.

On the other hand, even if one assumed that there was an adequate factual basis for the conclusion that all confessions obtained during in-custody interrogation are the product of compulsion, the rule propounded by the Court would still be irrational, for, apparently, it is only if the accused is also warned of his right to counsel and waives both that right and the right against self-incrimination that the inherent compulsiveness of interrogation disappears. But if the defendant may not answer without a warning a question such as "Where were you last night?" without having his answer be a compelled one, how can the Court ever accept his negative answer to the question of whether he wants to consult his retained counsel or counsel whom the court will appoint? And why if counsel is present and the accused nevertheless confesses, or counsel tells the accused to tell the truth, and that is what the accused does, is the situation any less coercive insofar as the accused is concerned? The Court apparently realizes its dilemma of foreclosing questioning without the necessary warnings but at the same time permitting the accused, sitting in the same chair in front of the same policemen, to waive his right to consult an attorney. It expects, however, that the accused will not often waive the right; and if it is claimed that he has, the State faces a severe, if not impossible burden of proof.

All of this makes very little sense in terms of the compulsion which the Fifth Amendment proscribes. That amendment deals with compelling the accused himself. It is his free will that is involved. Confessions and incriminating admissions, as such, are not forbidden evidence; only those which are compelled are banned. I doubt that the Court observes these distinctions today.

By considering any answers to any interrogation to be compelled regardless of the content and course of examination and by escalating the requirements to prove waiver, the Court not only prevents the use of compelled confessions but for all practical purposes forbids interrogation except in the presence of counsel. That is, instead of confining itself to protection of the right against compelled self-incrimination the Court has created a limited Fifth Amendment right to counsel—or, as the Court expresses it, a "need for counsel to protect the Fifth Amendment privilege . . . ." Ante, at 470. The focus then is not on the will of the accused but on the will of counsel and how much influence he can have on the accused. Obviously there is no warrant in the Fifth Amendment for thus installing counsel as the arbiter of the privilege.

In sum, for all the Court's expounding on the menacing atmosphere of police interrogation procedures, it has failed to supply any foundation for the conclusions it draws or the measures it adopts.

IV

Criticism of the Court's opinion, however, cannot stop with a demonstration that the factual and textual bases for the rule it propounds are, at best, less than compelling. Equally relevant is an assessment of the rule's consequences measured against community values. The Court's duty to assess the consequences of its action is not satisfied by the utterance of the truth that a value of our system of criminal justice is "to respect the inviolability of the human personality" and to require government to produce the evidence against the accused by its own independent labors. Ante, at 460. More than the human dignity of the accused is involved; the human personality of others in the society must also be preserved. Thus the values reflected by the privilege are not the sole desideratum; society's interest in the general security is of equal weight.

The obvious underpinning of the Court's decision is a deep-seated distrust of all confessions. As the Court declares that the accused may not be interrogated without counsel present, absent a waiver of the right to counsel, and as the Court all but admonishes the lawyer to advise the accused to remain silent, the result adds up to a judicial judgment that evidence from the accused should not be used against him in any way, whether compelled or not. This is the not so subtle overtone of the opinion—that it is inherently wrong for the police to gather evidence from the accused himself. And this is precisely the nub of this dissent. I see nothing wrong or immoral, and certainly nothing unconstitutional, in the police's asking a suspect whom they have reasonable cause to arrest whether or not he killed his wife or in confronting him with the evidence on which the arrest was based, at least where he has been plainly advised that he may remain completely silent. . . . Until today, "the admissions or confessions of the prisoner, when voluntarily and freely made, have always ranked high in the scale of incriminating evidence." Brown v. Walker, 161 U.S. 591, 596.... Particularly when corroborated, as where the police have confirmed the accused's disclosure of the hiding place of implements or fruits of the crime, such confessions have the highest reliability and significantly contribute to the certitude with which we may believe the accused is guilty. Moreover, it is by no means certain that the process of confessing is injurious to the accused. To the contrary it may provide psychological relief and enhance the prospects for rehabilitation.

This is not to say that the value of respect for the inviolability of the accused's individual personality should be accorded no weight or that all confessions should be indiscriminately admitted. This Court has long read the Constitution to proscribe compelled confessions, a salutary rule from which there should be no retreat. But I see no sound basis, factual or otherwise, and the Court gives none, for concluding that the present rule against the receipt of coerced confessions is inadequate for the task of sorting out inadmissible evidence and must be replaced by the *per se* rule which is now imposed. Even if the new concept can be said to have advantages of some sort over the present law, they are far outweighed by its likely undesirable impact on other very relevant and important interests.

The most basic function of any government is to provide for the security of the individual and of his property.... These ends of society are served by the criminal laws which for the most part are aimed at the prevention of crime. Without the reasonably effective performance of the task of preventing private violence and retaliation, it is idle to talk about human dignity and civilized values.

The modes by which the criminal laws serve the interest in general security are many. First the murderer who has taken the life of another is removed from the streets, deprived of his liberty and thereby prevented from repeating his offense. In view of the statistics on recidivism in this country and of the number of instances in which apprehension occurs only after repeated offenses, no one can sensibly claim that this aspect of the criminal law does not prevent crime or contribute significantly to the personal security of the ordinary citizen.

Secondly, the swift and sure apprehension of those who refuse to respect the personal security and dignity of their neighbor unquestionably has its impact on others who might be similarly tempted. That the criminal law is wholly or partly ineffective with a segment of the population or with many of those who have been apprehended and convicted is a very faulty basis for concluding that it is not effective with respect to the great bulk of our citizens or for thinking that without the criminal laws, or in the absence of their enforcement, there would be no increase in crime. Arguments of this nature are not borne out by any kind of reliable evidence that I have seen to this date.

Thirdly, the law concerns itself with those whom it has confined. The hope and aim of modern penology, fortunately, is as soon as possible to return the convict to society a better and more law-abiding man than when he left. Sometimes there is success, sometimes failure. But at least the effort is made, and it should be made to the very maximum extent of our present and future capabilities.

The rule announced today will measurably weaken the ability of the criminal law to perform these tasks. It is a deliberate calculus to prevent interrogations, to reduce the incidence of confessions and pleas of guilty and to increase the number of trials. Criminal trials, no matter how efficient the police are, are not sure bets for the prosecution, nor should they be if the evidence is not forthcoming. Under the present law, the prosecution fails to prove its case in about 30% of the criminal cases actually tried in the federal courts. ... But it is something else again to remove from the ordinary criminal case all those confessions which heretofore have been held to be free and voluntary acts of the accused and to thus establish a new constitutional barrier to the ascertainment of truth by the judicial process. There is, in my view, every reason to believe that a good many criminal defendants who otherwise would have been convicted on what this Court has previously thought to be the most satisfactory kind of evidence will now, under this new version of the Fifth Amendment, either not be tried at all or will be acquitted if the State's evidence, minus the confession, is put to the test of litigation.

I have no desire whatsoever to share the responsibility for any such impact on the present criminal process.

In some unknown number of cases the Court's rule will return a killer, a rapist or other criminal to the streets and to the environment which produced him, to repeat his crime whenever it pleases him. As a consequence, there will not be a gain, but a loss, in human dignity. The real concern is not the unfortunate consequences of this new decision on the criminal law as an abstract, disembodied series of authoritative proscriptions, but the impact on those who rely on the public authority for protection and who without it can only engage in violent self-help with guns, knives and the help of their neighbors similarly inclined. There is, of course, a saving factor: the next victims are uncertain, unnamed and unrepresented in this case.

Nor can this decision do other than have a corrosive effect on the criminal law as an effective device to prevent crime. A major component in its effectiveness in this regard is its swift and sure enforcement. The easier it is to get away with rape and murder, the less the deterrent effect on those who are inclined to attempt it.

This is still good common sense. If it were not, we should posthaste liquidate the whole law enforcement establishment as a useless, misguided effort to control human conduct.

And what about the accused who has confessed or would confess in response to simple, noncoercive questioning and whose guilt could not otherwise be proved? Is it so clear that release is the best thing for him in every case? Has it so unquestionably been resolved that in each and every case it would be better for him not to confess and to return to his environment with no attempt whatsoever to help him? I think not. It may well be that in many cases it will be no less than a callous disregard for his own welfare as well as for the interests of his next victim.

There is another aspect to the effect of the Court's rule on the person whom the police have arrested on probable cause. The fact is that he may not be guilty at all and may be able to extricate himself quickly and simply if he were told the circumstances of his arrest and were asked to explain. This effort, and his release, must now await the hiring of a lawyer or his appointment by the court, consultation with counsel and then a session with the police or the prosecutor. Similarly, where probable cause exists to arrest several suspects, as where the body of the victim is discovered in a house having several residents ... it will often be true that a suspect may be cleared only through the results of interrogation of other suspects. Here too the release of the innocent may be delayed by the Court's rule.

Much of the trouble with the Court's new rule is that it will operate indiscriminately in all criminal cases, regardless of the severity of the crime or the circumstances involved. It applies to every defendant, whether the professional criminal or one committing a crime of momentary passion who is not part and parcel of organized crime. It will slow down the investigation and the apprehension of confederates in those cases where time is of the essence, such as kidnapping ... those involving the national security ... and some of those involving organized crime. In the latter context the lawyer who arrives may also be the lawyer for the defendant's colleagues and can be relied upon to insure that no breach of the organization's security takes place even though the accused may feel that the best thing he can do is to cooperate.

At the same time, the Court's *per se* approach may not be justified on the ground that it provides a "bright line" permitting the authorities to judge in advance whether interrogation may safely be pursued without jeopardizing the admissibility of any information obtained as a consequence. Nor can it be claimed that judicial time and effort, assuming that is a relevant consideration, will be conserved because of the ease of application of the new rule. Today's decision leaves open such questions as whether the accused was in custody, whether his statements were spontaneous or the product of interrogation, whether the accused has effectively waived his rights, and whether nontestimonial evidence introduced at trial is the fruit of statements made during a prohibited interrogation, all of which are certain to prove productive of uncertainty during investigation and litigation during prosecution. For all these reasons, if further restrictions on police interrogation are desirable at this time, a more flexible approach makes much more sense than the Court's constitutional straitjacket which forecloses more discriminating treatment by legislative or rule-making pronouncements.

Applying the traditional standards to the cases before the Court, I would hold these confessions voluntary. I would therefore affirm in Nos. 759, 760, and 761, and reverse in No. 584.[*] [**]

[*] Justice Clark wrote an opinion dissenting in three of the cases before the court and concurring in the result in one. Justice Harlan wrote a dissenting opinion, which Justice Stewart and Justice White joined.

[**] In New York v. Quarles, 467 U.S. 649 (1984) (6–3), the Court held that there is a "public safety" exception to the requirement that *Miranda* warnings be given. In *Quarles*, police officers who arrested a man believed to have just committed a rape asked him where he had discarded a gun; the arrest took place in a supermarket, and he was thought to have concealed the gun somewhere inside. In such circumstances, the Court said, "the need for answers to questions in a situation posing a threat to the public safety outweighs the need for the prophylactic rule protecting the Fifth Amendment's privilege against self-incrimination." 467 U.S. at 657.

In Berkemer v. McCarty, 468 U.S. 420, 435, 437 (1984), the Court held that the *Miranda* warnings need not be given before "roadside questioning of a motorist detained pursuant to a routine traffic stop" such stops, the Court said, do not exert on a detained person "pressures that sufficiently impair his free exercise of his privilege against self-incrimination to require that he be warned of his constitutional rights."

MORAN v. BURBINE

475 U.S. 412, 106 S.Ct. 1135, 89 L.Ed.2d 410 (1986).

JUSTICE O'CONNOR delivered the opinion of the Court.

After being informed of his rights pursuant to Miranda v. Arizona, 384 U.S. 436 (1966), and after executing a series of written waivers, respondent confessed to the murder of a young woman. At no point during the course of the interrogation, which occurred prior to arraignment, did he request an attorney. While he was in police custody, his sister attempted to retain a lawyer to represent him. The attorney telephoned the police station and received assurances that respondent would not be questioned further until the next day. In fact, the interrogation session that yielded the inculpatory statements began later that evening. The question presented is whether either the conduct of the police or respondent's ignorance of the attorney's efforts to reach him taints the validity of the waivers and therefore requires exclusion of the confessions.

I

On the morning of March 3, 1977, Mary Jo Hickey was found unconscious in a factory parking lot in Providence, Rhode Island. Suffering from injuries to her skull apparently inflicted by a metal pipe found at the scene, she was rushed to a nearby hospital. Three weeks later she died from her wounds.

Several months after her death, the Cranston, Rhode Island police arrested respondent and two others in connection with a local burglary. Shortly before the arrest, Detective Ferranti of the Cranston police force had learned from a confidential informant that the man responsible for Ms. Hickey's death lived at a certain address and went by the name of "Butch." Upon discovering that respondent lived at that address and was known by that name, Detective Ferranti informed respondent of his *Miranda* rights. When respondent refused to execute a written waiver, Detective Ferranti spoke separately with the two other suspects arrested on the breaking and entering charge and obtained statements further implicating respondent in Ms. Hickey's murder. At approximately 6 p.m., Detective Ferranti telephoned the police in Providence to convey the information he had uncovered. An hour later, three officers from that department arrived at the Cranston headquarters for the purpose of questioning respondent about the murder.

That same evening, at about 7:45 p.m., respondent's sister telephoned the Public Defender's Office to obtain legal assistance for her brother. Her sole concern was the breaking and entering charge, as she was unaware that respondent was then under suspicion for murder. She asked for Richard Casparian who had been scheduled to meet with respondent earlier that afternoon to discuss another charge unrelated to either the break-in or the murder. As soon as the conversation ended, the attorney who took the call attempted to reach Mr. Casparian. When those efforts were unsuccessful, she telephoned Allegra Munson, another Assistant Public Defender, and told her about respondent's arrest and his sister's subsequent request that the office represent him.

At 8:15 p.m., Ms. Munson telephoned the Cranston police station and asked that her call be transferred to the detective division. In the words of the Supreme Court of Rhode Island, whose factual findings we treat as presumptively correct, 28 U.S.C. § 2254(d), the conversation proceeded as follows:

> "A male voice responded with the word 'Detectives.' Ms. Munson identified herself and asked if Brian Burbine was being held; the person responded affirmatively. Ms. Munson explained to the person that Burbine was represented by attorney Casparian who was not available; she further stated that she would act as Burbine's legal counsel in the event that the police intended to place him in a lineup or question him. The unidentified person told Ms. Munson that the police would not be questioning Burbine or putting him in a lineup and that they were through with him for the night. Ms. Munson was not informed that the Providence Police were at the Cranston police station or that Burbine was a suspect in Mary's murder."
> State v. Burbine, 451 A.2d 22, 23–24 (1982).

At all relevant times, respondent was unaware of his sister's efforts to retain counsel and of the fact and contents of Ms. Munson's telephone conversation.

Less than an hour later, the police brought respondent to an interrogation room and conducted the first of a series of interviews concerning the murder. Prior to each session, respondent was informed of his *Miranda* rights, and on three separate occasions he signed a written form acknowledging that he understood his right to the presence of an attorney and explicitly indicating that he "[did] not want an attorney called or appointed for [him]" before he gave a statement. App. to Pet. for Cert. 94, 103, 107. Uncontradicted evidence at the suppression hearing indicated that at least twice during the course of the evening, respondent was left in a room where he had access to a telephone, which he apparently declined to use.... Eventually, respondent signed three written statements fully admitting to the murder.

Prior to trial, respondent moved to suppress the statements. The court denied the motion, finding that respondent had received the *Miranda* warnings and had "knowingly, intelligently, and voluntarily waived his privilege against self-incrimination [and] his right to counsel." App. to Pet. for Cert. 116. Rejecting the contrary testimony of the police, the court found that Ms. Munson did telephone the detective bureau on the evening in question, but concluded that "there was no ... conspiracy or collusion on the part of the Cranston Police Department to secrete this defendant from his attorney." Id., at 114. In any event, the court held, the constitutional right to request the presence of an attorney belongs solely to the defendant and may not be asserted by his lawyer. Because the evidence was clear that respondent never asked for the services of an attorney, the telephone call had no relevance to the validity of the waiver or the admissibility of the statements.

The jury found respondent guilty of murder in the first degree, and he appealed to the Supreme Court of Rhode Island. A divided court rejected his contention that the Fifth and Fourteenth Amendments to the Constitution required the suppression of the inculpatory statements and affirmed the conviction. . . .

After unsuccessfully petitioning the United States District Court for the District of Rhode Island for a writ of habeas corpus, 589 F.Supp. 1245 (1984), respondent appealed to the Court of Appeals for the First Circuit. That court reversed. 753 F.2d 178 (1985). Finding it unnecessary to reach any arguments under the Sixth and Fourteenth Amendments, the court held that the police's conduct had fatally tainted respondent's "otherwise valid" waiver of his Fifth Amendment privilege against self-incrimination and right to counsel. Id., at 184. . . .

We granted certiorari to decide whether a prearraignment confession preceded by an otherwise valid waiver must be suppressed either because the police misinformed an inquiring attorney about their plans concerning the suspect or because they failed to inform the suspect of the attorney's efforts to reach him. 471 U.S. 1098 (1985). We now reverse.

II

In *Miranda v. Arizona*, the Court recognized that custodial interrogations, by their very nature, generate "compelling pressures which work to undermine the individual's will to resist and to compel him to speak where he would not otherwise do so freely." 384 U.S., at 467. To combat this inherent compulsion, and thereby protect the Fifth Amendment privilege against self-incrimination, *Miranda* imposed on the police an obligation to follow certain procedures in their dealings with the accused. . . .

Respondent does not dispute that the Providence police followed these procedures with precision. The record amply supports the state-court findings that the police administered the required warnings, sought to assure that respondent understood his rights, and obtained an express written waiver prior to eliciting each of the three statements. Nor does respondent contest the Rhode Island courts' determination that he at no point requested the presence of a lawyer. He contends instead that the confessions must be suppressed because the police's failure to inform him of the attorney's telephone call deprived him of information essential to his ability to knowingly waive his Fifth Amendment rights. In the alternative, he suggests that to fully protect the Fifth Amendment values served by *Miranda*, we should extend that decision to condemn the conduct of the Providence police. We address each contention in turn.

A

Echoing the standard first articulated in Johnson v. Zerbst, 304 U.S. 458, 464 (1938), *Miranda* holds that "[t]he defendant may waive effectuation" of the rights conveyed in the warnings "provided the waiver is made voluntarily, knowingly and intelligently." 384 U.S., at 444, 475. The inquiry has two distinct dimensions. . . . First the relinquishment of the right must have been voluntary in the sense that it was the product of a free and deliberate choice rather than intimidation, coercion or deception. Second, the waiver must have been made with a full awareness both of the nature of the right being abandoned and the consequences of the decision to abandon it. Only if the "totality of the circumstances surrounding the interrogation" reveals both an uncoerced choice and the requisite level of comprehension may a court properly conclude that the *Miranda* rights have been waived. Fare v. Michael C., 442 U.S. 707, 725 (1979). . . .

Under this standard, we have no doubt that respondent validly waived his right to remain silent and to the presence of counsel. The voluntariness of the waiver is not at issue. As the Court of Appeals correctly acknowledged, the record is devoid of any suggestion that police resorted to physical or psychological pressure to elicit the statements. . . . Indeed it appears that it was respondent, and not the police, who spontaneously initiated the conversation that led to the first and most damaging confession. . . . Nor is there any question about respondent's comprehension of the full panoply of rights set out in the *Miranda* warnings and of the potential consequences of a decision to relinquish them. Nonetheless, the Court of Appeals believed that the "[d]eliberate or reckless" conduct of the police, in particular their failure to inform respondent of the telephone call, fatally undermined the validity of the otherwise proper waiver. We find this conclusion untenable as a matter of both logic and precedent.

Events occurring outside of the presence of the suspect and entirely unknown to him surely can have no bearing on the capacity to comprehend and knowingly relinquish a constitutional right. Under the analysis of the Court of Appeals, the same defendant, armed with the same information and confronted with precisely the same police conduct, would have knowingly waived his *Miranda* rights had a lawyer not telephoned the police station to inquire about his status. Nothing in any of our waiver decisions or in our understanding of the essential components of a valid waiver requires so incongruous a result. No doubt the additional information would have been useful to respondent; perhaps even it might have affected his decision to confess. But we have never read the Constitution to require that the police supply a suspect with a flow of information to help him calibrate his self-interest in deciding whether to speak or stand by his rights. ... Once it is determined that a suspect's decision not to rely on his rights was uncoerced, that he at all times knew he could stand mute and request a lawyer, and that he was aware of the State's intention to use his statements to secure a conviction, the analysis is complete and the waiver is valid as a matter of law.[1] The Court of Appeals' conclusion to the contrary was in error.

Nor do we believe that the level of the police's culpability in failing to inform respondent of the telephone call has any bearing on the validity of the waivers.... [W]hether intentional or inadvertent, the state of mind of the police is irrelevant to the question of the intelligence and voluntariness of respondent's election to abandon his rights. Although highly inappropriate, even deliberate deception of an attorney could not possibly affect a suspect's decision to waive his *Miranda* rights unless he were at least aware of the incident. ... Nor was the failure to inform respondent of the telephone call the kind of "trick[ery]" that can vitiate the validity of a waiver. Miranda, 384 U.S., at 476. Granting that the "deliberate or reckless" withholding of information is objectionable as a matter of ethics, such conduct is only relevant to the constitutional validity of a waiver if it deprives a defendant of knowledge essential to his ability to understand the nature of his rights and the consequences of abandoning them. Because respondent's voluntary decision to speak was made with full awareness and comprehension of all the information *Miranda* requires the police to convey, the waivers were valid.

B

At oral argument respondent acknowledged that a constitutional rule requiring the police to inform a suspect of an attorney's efforts to reach him would represent a significant extension of our

---

1. The dissent incorrectly reads our analysis of the components of a valid waiver to be inconsistent with the Court's holding in Edwards v. Arizona, 451 U.S. 477 (1981). Post, at 452. When a suspect *has* requested counsel, the interrogation must cease, regardless of any question of waiver, unless the suspect himself initiates the conversation. In the course of its lengthy exposition, however, the dissent never comes to grips with the crucial distinguishing feature of this case—that Burbine at no point requested the presence of counsel, as was his right under *Miranda* to do. We do not quarrel with the dissent's characterization of police interrogation as a "privilege terminable at the will of the suspect." Post, at 458. We reject, however, the dissent's entirely undefended suggestion that the Fifth Amendment "right to counsel" requires anything more than that the police inform the suspect of his right to representation and honor his request that the interrogation cease until his attorney is present. ...

precedents. ... He contends, however, that the conduct of the Providence police was so inimical to the Fifth Amendment values *Miranda* seeks to protect that we should read that decision to condemn their behavior. Regardless of any issue of waiver, he urges, the Fifth Amendment requires the reversal of a conviction if the police are less than forthright in their dealings with an attorney or if they fail to tell a suspect of a lawyer's unilateral efforts to contact him. Because the proposed modification ignores the underlying purposes of the *Miranda* rules and because we think that the decision as written strikes the proper balance between society's legitimate law enforcement interests and the protection of the defendant's Fifth Amendment rights, we decline the invitation to further extend *Miranda*'s reach.

At the outset, while we share respondent's distaste for the deliberate misleading of an officer of the court, reading *Miranda* to forbid police deception of an *attorney* "would cut [the decision] completely loose from its own explicitly stated rationale." Beckwith v. United States, 425 U.S. 341, 345 (1976). As is now well established, "[t]he ... *Miranda* warnings are 'not themselves rights protected by the Constitution but [are] instead measures to insure that the [suspect's] right against compulsory self-incrimination [is] protected.'" New York v. Quarles, 467 U.S. 649, 654 (1984), quoting Michigan v. Tucker, 417 U.S. 433, 444 (1974). Their objective is not to mold police conduct for its own sake. Nothing in the Constitution vests in us the authority to mandate a code of behavior for state officials wholly unconnected to any federal right or privilege. The purpose of the *Miranda* warnings instead is to dissipate the compulsion inherent in custodial interrogation and, in so doing, guard against abridgement of the suspect's Fifth Amendment rights. Clearly, a rule that focuses on how the police treat an attorney—conduct that has no relevance at all to the degree of compulsion experienced by the defendant during interrogation— would ignore both *Miranda*'s mission and its only source of legitimacy.

Nor are we prepared to adopt a rule requiring that the police inform a suspect of an attorney's efforts to reach him. While such a rule might add marginally to *Miranda*'s goal of dispelling the compulsion inherent in custodial interrogation, overriding practical considerations counsel against its adoption. As we have stressed on numerous occasions, "[o]ne of the principal advantages" of *Miranda* is the ease and clarity of its application. Berkemer v. McCarty, 468 U.S. 420, 430 (1984) .... We have little doubt that the approach urged by respondent and endorsed by the Court of Appeals would have the inevitable consequence of muddying *Miranda*'s otherwise relatively clear waters. The legal questions it would spawn are legion: To what extent should the police be held accountable for knowing that the accused has counsel? Is it enough that someone in the station house knows, or must the interrogating officer himself know of counsel's efforts to contact the suspect? Do counsel's efforts to talk to the suspect concerning one criminal investigation trigger the obligation to inform the defendant before interrogation may proceed on a wholly separate matter? We are unwilling to modify *Miranda* in a manner that would so clearly undermine the decision's central "virtue of informing police and prosecutors with specificity ... what they may do in conducting [a] custodial interrogation, and of informing courts under what circumstances statements obtained during such interrogation are not admissible." Fare v. Michael C., [442 U.S. 707 (1979)], at 718.

Moreover, problems of clarity to one side, reading *Miranda* to require the police in each instance to inform a suspect of an attorney's efforts to reach him would work a substantial and, we think, inappropriate shift in the subtle balance struck in that decision. Custodial interrogations implicate two competing concerns. On the one hand, "the need for police questioning as a tool for effective enforcement of criminal laws" cannot be doubted. Schneckloth v. Bustamonte, 412 U.S. 218, 225 (1973). Admissions of guilt are more than merely "desirable," United States v. Washington, 431 U.S. [181 (1977)], at 186; they are essential to society's compelling interest in finding, convicting and punishing those who violate the law. On the other hand, the Court has recognized that the interrogation process is "inherently coercive" and that, as a consequence, there exists a substantial risk that the police will inadvertently traverse the fine line between legitimate efforts to elicit admissions and constitutionally impermissible compulsion.... *Miranda* attempted to reconcile these opposing concerns by giving the *defendant* the power to exert some control over the course of the interrogation. Declining to adopt the more extreme position that the actual presence of a lawyer was necessary to dispel the coercion inherent in custodial interrogation ... the Court found that the suspect's Fifth Amendment rights could be adequately protected by less intrusive means. Police questioning, often an essential part of the investigatory process, could continue in its traditional form, the Court held, but only if the suspect clearly understood that, at any time, he could bring the proceeding to a halt or, short of that, call in an attorney to give advice and monitor the conduct of his interrogators.

The position urged by respondent would upset this carefully drawn approach in a manner that is both unnecessary for the protection of the Fifth Amendment privilege and injurious to legitimate law enforcement. Because, as *Miranda* holds, full comprehension of the rights to remain silent and request an attorney are sufficient to dispel whatever coercion is inherent in the interrogation process, a rule requiring the police to inform the suspect of an attorney's efforts to contact him would contribute to the protection of the Fifth Amendment privilege only incidentally, if at all. This minimal benefit, however, would come at a substantial cost to society's legitimate and substantial interest in securing admissions of guilt. Indeed, the very premise of the Court of Appeals was not that awareness of Ms. Munson's phone call would have dissipated the coercion of the interrogation room, but that it might have convinced respondent not to speak at all. . . . Because neither the letter nor purposes of *Miranda* require this additional handicap on otherwise permissible investigatory efforts, we are unwilling to expand the *Miranda* rules to require the police to keep the suspect abreast of the status of his legal representation.

We acknowledge that a number of state courts have reached a contrary conclusion. . . . We recognize also that our interpretation of the Federal Constitution, if given the dissent's expansive gloss, is at odds with the policy recommendations embodied in the American Bar Association Standards of Criminal Justice. . . . Notwithstanding the dissent's protestations, however, our interpretive duties go well beyond deferring to the numerical preponderance of lower court decisions or to the subconstitutional recommendations of even so esteemed a body as the American Bar Association. . . . Nothing we say today disables the States from adopting different requirements for the conduct of its employees and officials as a matter of state law. We hold only that the Court of Appeals erred in construing the Fifth Amendment to the Federal Constitution to require the exclusion of respondent's three confessions.

III

Respondent also contends that the Sixth Amendment requires exclusion of his three confessions. It is clear, of course, that, absent a valid waiver, the defendant has the right to the presence of an attorney during any interrogation occurring after the first formal charging proceeding, the point at which the Sixth Amendment right to counsel initially attaches. . . . And we readily agree that once the right *has* attached, it follows that the police may not interfere with the efforts of a defendant's attorney to act as a " 'medium' between [the suspect] and the State" during the interrogation. Maine v. Moulton, 474 U.S. 159, 176 (1985) . . . . The difficulty for respondent is that the interrogation sessions that yielded the inculpatory statements took place *before* the initiation of "adversary judicial proceedings." United States v. Gouveia, [467 U.S. 180 (1984)], at 192. He contends, however, that this circumstance is not fatal to his Sixth Amendment claim. At least in some situations, he argues, the Sixth Amendment protects the integrity of the attorney-client relationship regardless of whether the prosecution has in fact commenced "by way of formal charge, preliminary hearing, indictment, information or arraignment." 467 U.S., at 188. Placing principal reliance on a footnote in Miranda, 384 U.S., at 465, n. 35, and on Escobedo v. Illinois, 378 U.S. 478 (1964), he maintains that *Gouveia*, Kirby [v. Illinois, 406 U.S. 682 (1972)] and our other "critical stage" cases, concern only the narrow question of when the right *to* counsel—that is, to the appointment or presence of counsel—attaches. The right to non-interference with an attorney's dealings with a criminal suspect, he asserts, arises the moment that the relationship is formed, or, at the very least, once the defendant is placed in custodial interrogation.

We are not persuaded. At the outset, subsequent decisions foreclose any reliance on *Escobedo* and *Miranda* for the proposition that the Sixth Amendment right, in any of its manifestations, applies prior to the initiation of adversary judicial proceedings. Although *Escobedo* was originally decided as a Sixth Amendment case, "the Court in retrospect perceived that the 'prime purpose' of *Escobedo* was not to vindicate the constitutional right to counsel as such, but, like *Miranda*, 'to guarantee full effectuation of the privilege against self-incrimination . . . .' " Kirby v. Illinois, supra, at 689, quoting Johnson v. New Jersey, 384 U.S. 719, 729 (1966). Clearly then, *Escobedo* provides no support for respondent's argument. Nor, of course, does *Miranda*, the holding of which rested exclusively on the Fifth Amendment. Thus, the decision's brief observation about the reach of *Escobedo*'s Sixth Amendment analysis is not only dictum, but reflects an understanding of the case that the Court has expressly disavowed. . . .

Questions of precedent to one side, we find respondent's understanding of the Sixth Amendment both practically and theoretically unsound. As a practical matter, it makes little sense to say that the Sixth Amendment right to counsel attaches at different times depending on the fortuity of whether the suspect or his family happens to have retained counsel prior to interrogation. . . . More importantly, the suggestion that the existence of an attorney-client relationship itself triggers the protections of the Sixth Amendment misconceives the underlying purposes of the right to counsel. The Sixth Amendment's intended function is not to wrap a protective cloak around the attorney-client relationship for its own sake any more than it is to protect a suspect from the consequences of his own candor. Its purpose, rather, is to assure that in any "criminal prosecutio[n]," U.S. Const., Amdt. 6, the accused shall not be left to his own devices in facing the " 'prosecutorial forces of organized society.' " Maine v. Moulton, supra, at 170 (quoting Kirby v. Illinois, 406 U.S., at 689). By its very terms, it becomes applicable only when the government's role shifts from investigation to accusation. For it is only then that the assistance of one versed in the "intricacies . . . of law," ibid., is needed to assure that the prosecution's case encounters "the crucible of meaningful adversarial testing." United States v. Cronic, 466 U.S. 648, 656 (1984).

Indeed, in *Maine v. Moulton,* decided this Term, the Court again confirmed that looking to the initiation of adversary judicial proceedings, far from being mere formalism, is fundamental to the proper application of the Sixth Amendment right to counsel. There, we considered the constitutional implications of a surreptitious investigation that yielded evidence pertaining to two crimes. For one, the defendant had been indicted; for the other, he had not. Concerning the former, the Court reaffirmed that after the first charging proceeding the government may not deliberately elicit incriminating statements from an accused out of the presence of counsel. . . . The Court made clear, however, that the evidence concerning the crime for which the defendant had not been indicted—evidence obtained in precisely the same manner from the identical suspect—would be admissible at a trial limited to those charges. Maine v. Moulton, 474 U.S., at 180, and n. 16. The clear implication of the holding, and one that confirms the teaching of *Gouveia,* is that the Sixth Amendment right to counsel does not attach until after the initiation of formal charges. Moreover, because Moulton already had legal representation, the decision all but forecloses respondent's argument that the attorney-client relationship itself triggers the Sixth Amendment right.

Respondent contends, however, the custodial interrogations require a different rule. Because confessions elicited during the course of police questioning often seal a suspect's fate, he argues, the need for an advocate—and the concomitant right to noninterference with the attorney-client relationship—is at its zenith, regardless of whether the state has initiated the first adversary judicial proceeding. We do not doubt that a lawyer's presence could be of value to the suspect; and we readily agree that if a suspect confesses, his attorney's case at trial will be that much more difficult. But these concerns are no more decisive in this context than they were for the equally damaging pre-indictment lineup at issue in *Kirby,* or the statements pertaining to the unindicted crime elicited from the defendant in *Maine v. Moulton.* . . . For an interrogation, no more or less than for any other "critical" pretrial event, the possibility that the encounter may have important consequences at trial, standing alone, is insufficient to trigger the Sixth Amendment right to counsel. As *Gouveia* made clear, until such time as the " 'government has committed itself to prosecute, and . . . the adverse positions of government and defendant have solidified' " the Sixth Amendment right to counsel does not attach. 467 U.S., at 189 (quoting Kirby v. Illinois, 406 U.S., at 689.).

Because, as respondent acknowledges, the events that led to the inculpatory statements preceded the formal initiation of adversary judicial proceedings, we reject the contention that the conduct of the police violated his rights under the Sixth Amendment.

IV

Finally, respondent contends that the conduct of the police was so offensive as to deprive him of the fundamental fairness guaranteed by the Due Process Clause of the Fourteenth Amendment. Focusing primarily on the impropriety of conveying false information to an attorney, he invites us to declare that such behavior should be condemned as violative of canons fundamental to the " 'traditions and conscience of our people.' " Rochin v. California, 342 U.S. 165, 169 (1952), quoting Snyder v. Massachusetts, 291 U.S. 97, 105 (1934). We do not question that on facts more egregious than those presented here police deception might rise to a level of a due process violation. . . . We hold only that, on these facts, the challenged conduct falls short of the kind of misbehavior that so shocks the sensibilities of civilized society as to warrant a federal intrusion into the criminal processes of the States.

We hold therefore that the Court of Appeals erred in finding that the Federal Constitution required the exclusion of the three inculpatory statements. Accordingly, we reverse and remand for proceedings consistent with this opinion.

So ordered.

JUSTICE STEVENS, with whom JUSTICE BRENNAN and JUSTICE MARSHALL join, dissenting.

This case poses fundamental questions about our system of justice. As this Court has long recognized, and reaffirmed only weeks ago, "ours is an accusatorial and not an inquisitorial system." Miller v. Fenton, 474 U.S. 104, 110 (1985). The Court's opinion today represents a startling departure from that basic insight.

. . .

The Court's holding focuses on the period after a suspect has been taken into custody and before he has been charged with an offense. The core of the Court's holding is that police interference with an attorney's access to her client during that period is not unconstitutional. The Court reasons that a State has a compelling interest, not simply in custodial interrogation, but in lawyer-free, incommunicado custodial interrogation. Such incommunicado interrogation is so important that a lawyer may be given false information that prevents her presence and representation; it is so important that police may refuse to inform a suspect of his attorney's communications and immediate availability. This conclusion flies in the face of this Court's repeated expressions of deep concern about incommunicado questioning. Until today, incommunicado questioning has been viewed with the strictest scrutiny by this Court; today, incommunicado questioning is embraced as a societal goal of the highest order that justifies police deception of the shabbiest kind.

It is not only the Court's ultimate conclusion that is deeply disturbing; it is also its manner of reaching that conclusion. The Court completely rejects an entire body of law on the subject—the many carefully reasoned state decisions that have come to precisely the opposite conclusion. The Court similarly dismisses the fact that the police deception which it sanctions quite clearly violates the American Bar Association's Standards for Criminal Justice—Standards which the Chief Justice has described as "the single most comprehensive and probably the most monumental undertaking in the field of criminal justice ever attempted by the American legal profession in our national history,"[12] and which this Court frequently finds helpful. And, of course, the Court dismisses the fact that the American Bar Association has emphatically endorsed the prevailing state-court position and expressed its serious concern about the effect that a contrary view—a view, such as the Court's, that exalts incommunicado interrogation, sanctions police deception, and demeans the right to consult with an attorney—will have in police stations and courtrooms throughout this Nation. Of greatest importance, the Court misapprehends or rejects the central principles that have, for several decades, animated this Court's decisions concerning incommunicado interrogation.

Police interference with communications between an attorney and his client is a recurrent problem. The factual variations in the many state-court opinions condemning this interference as a violation of the Federal Constitution suggest the variety of contexts in which the problem emerges. In Oklahoma, police led a lawyer to several different locations while they interrogated the suspect;[16] in Oregon, police moved a suspect to a new location when they learned that his lawyer was on his way;[17] in Illinois, authorities failed to tell a suspect that his lawyer had arrived at the jail and asked to see him;[18] in Massachusetts, police did not tell suspects that their lawyers were at or near the police station.[19] In all these cases, the police not only failed to inform the suspect, but also misled the attorneys. The scenarios vary, but the core problem of police interference remains. "Its recurrence suggests that it has roots in some condition fundamental and general to our criminal system." Watts v. Indiana, 338 U.S. 49, 57 (1949) (Jackson, J., concurring in result).

The near-consensus of state courts and the legal profession's Standards about this recurrent problem lends powerful support to the conclusion that police may not interfere with communications between an attorney and the client whom they are questioning. Indeed, at least two opinions from this Court seemed to express precisely that view.[20] The Court today flatly rejects that widely held

---

12. Burger, Introduction: The ABA Standards for Criminal Justice, 12 Am.Crim. L.Rev. 251 (1974). ...

16. Lewis v. State, 695 P.2d 528 (Okl. Crim.App.1984).

17. State v. Haynes, 288 Ore. 59, 602 P.2d 272 (1979) ....

18. People v. Smith, 93 Ill.2d 179, 442 N.E.2d 1325 (1982).

19. Commonwealth v. McKenna, 355 Mass. 313, 244 N.E.2d 560 (1969).

20. See Miranda v. Arizona, 384 U.S., at 465 n. 35 (in Escobedo, "[t]he police also prevented the attorney from consulting with his client. Independent of any other constitutional proscription, this action constitutes a violation of the Sixth Amendment right to the assistance of counsel and excludes any statement obtained in its wake"); Escobedo v. Illinois, 378 U.S. 478, 487 (1964) ("[I]t 'would be highly incongruous if our system of justice permitted the district attorney, the lawyer representing the State, to extract a confession from the accused while his own lawyer, seek-

view and responds to this recurrent problem by adopting the most restrictive interpretation of the federal constitutional restraints on police deception, misinformation, and interference in attorney-client communications.

The exact reach of the Court's opinion is not entirely clear because, on the one hand, it indicates that more egregious forms of police deception might violate the Constitution ... while on the other hand it endeavors to make its disposition of this case palatable by making findings of fact concerning the voluntariness of Burbine's confessions that the trial judge who heard the evidence declined to make. Before addressing the legal issues, it therefore seems appropriate to make certain additional comments about what the record discloses concerning the incriminating statements made by Burbine during the 21-hour period that he was detained by the Cranston and Providence police on June 29 and June 30, 1977.

I

. . .

... [A]lthough there are a number of ambiguities in the record, the state-court findings established (1) that attorney Munson made her call at about 8:15 p.m.; (2) that she was given false information; (3) that Burbine was not told of her call; and (4) that he was thereafter given the *Miranda* warnings, waived his rights, and signed three incriminating statements without receiving any advice from an attorney. The remainder of the record underscores two points. The first is the context of the call—a context in which two Police Departments were on the verge of resolving a highly publicized, hauntingly brutal homicide and in which, as Lieutenant Gannon testified, the police were aware that counsel's advice to remain silent might be an obstacle to obtaining a confession. The second is the extent of the uncertainty about the events that motivated Burbine's decision to waive his rights. The lawyer-free privacy of the interrogation room, so exalted by the majority, provides great difficulties in determining what actually transpired. It is not simply the ambiguity that is troublesome; if so, the problem would be not unlike other difficult evidentiary problems. Rather, the particularly troublesome aspect is that the ambiguity arises in the very situation—incommunicado interrogation—for which this Court has developed strict presumptions and for which this Court has, in the past, imposed the heaviest burden of justification on the government. It is in this context, and the larger context of our accusatorial system, that the deceptive conduct of the police must be evaluated.

ing to speak with him, was kept from him by the police'"), quoting People v. Donovan, 13 N.Y.2d 148, 152, 193 N.E.2d 628, 629 (1963).

II

Well-settled principles of law lead inexorably to the conclusion that the failure to inform Burbine of the call from his attorney makes the subsequent waiver of his constitutional rights invalid. Analysis should begin with an acknowledgment that the burden of proving the validity of a waiver of constitutional rights is always on the *government*. When such a waiver occurs in a custodial setting, that burden is an especially heavy one because custodial interrogation is inherently coercive, because disinterested witnesses are seldom available to describe what actually happened, and because history has taught us that the danger of overreaching during incommunicado interrogation is so real.

In applying this heavy presumption against the validity of waivers, this Court has sometimes relied on a case-by-case totality of the circumstances analysis. We have found, however, that some custodial interrogation situations require strict presumptions against the validity of a waiver. *Miranda* established that a waiver is not valid in the absence of certain warnings. Edwards v. Arizona, 451 U.S. 477 (1981), similarly established that a waiver is not valid if police initiate questioning after the defendant has invoked his right to counsel. In these circumstances, the waiver is invalid as a matter of law even if the evidence overwhelmingly establishes, as a matter of fact, that "a suspect's decision not to rely on his rights was uncoerced, that he at all times knew that he could stand mute and request a lawyer, and that he was aware of the State's intention to use his statements to secure a conviction," see ante at 422. In light of our decision in *Edwards*, the Court is simply wrong in stating that "the analysis is complete and the waiver is valid as a matter of law" when these facts have been established. Ante, at 422–423. Like the failure to give warnings and like police initiation of interrogation after a request for counsel, police deception of a suspect through omission of information regarding attorney communications greatly exacerbates the inherent problems of incommunicado interrogation and requires a clear principle to safeguard the presumption against the waiver of constitutional rights. As in those situations, the police deception should render a subsequent waiver invalid.

Indeed, as *Miranda* itself makes clear, proof that the required warnings have been given is a necessary, but by no means sufficient, condition for establishing a valid waiver. As the Court plainly stated in *Miranda*, "any evidence that the accused was threatened, tricked, or cajoled into a waiver will, of course, show that the defendant did not voluntarily waive his privilege. The requirement of warnings and waiver of rights is fundamental with respect to the Fifth Amendment privilege and not simply a preliminary ritual to existing methods of interrogation." 384 U.S., at 476.

In this case it would be perfectly clear that Burbine's waiver was invalid if, for example, Detective Ferranti had "threatened, tricked, or cajoled" Burbine in their private pre-confession meeting—perhaps by misdescribing the statements obtained from DiOrio and Sparks—even though, under the Court's truncated analysis of the issue, Burbine fully understood his rights. For *Miranda* clearly condemns threats or trickery that cause a suspect to make an unwise waiver of his rights even though he fully understands those rights. In my opinion there can be no constitutional distinction—as the Court appears to draw . . . —between a deceptive misstatement and the concealment by the police of the critical fact that an attorney retained by the accused or his family has offered assistance, either by telephone or in person.

Thus, the Court's truncated analysis, which relies in part on a distinction between deception accomplished by means of an omission of a critically important fact and deception by means of a misleading statement, is simply untenable. If, as the Court asserts, "the analysis is at an end" as soon as the suspect is provided with enough information to have the *capacity* to understand and exercise his rights, I see no reason why the police should not be permitted to make the same kind of misstatements to the suspect that they are apparently allowed to make to his lawyer. *Miranda,* however, clearly establishes that both kinds of deception vitiate the suspect's waiver of his right to counsel.

As the Court notes, the question is whether the deceptive police conduct "deprives a defendant of knowledge essential to his ability to understand the nature of his rights and the consequences of abandoning them." Ante, at 424. This question has been resoundingly answered time and time again by the state courts that, with rare exceptions, have correctly understood the meaning of the *Miranda* opinion. . . . As the Oregon Supreme Court has explained: "To pass up an abstract offer to call some unknown lawyer is very different from refusing to talk with an identified attorney actually available to provide at least initial assistance and advice, whatever might be arranged in the long run. A suspect indifferent to the first offer may well react quite differently to the second." State v. Haynes, 288 Ore. 59, 72, 602 P.2d 272, 278 (1979), cert. denied, 446 U.S. 945 (1980).

In short, settled principles about construing waivers of constitutional rights and about the need for strict presumptions in custodial interrogations, as well as a plain reading of the *Miranda* opinion itself, overwhelmingly support the conclusion reached by almost every state court that has considered the matter—a suspect's waiver of his right to counsel is invalid if police refuse to inform the suspect of his counsel's communications.

III

The Court makes the alternative argument that requiring police to inform a suspect of his attorney's communications to and about him is not required because it would upset the careful "balance" of *Miranda.* Despite its earlier notion that the attorney's call is an "outside event" that has "no bearing" on a knowing and intelligent waiver, the majority does acknowledge that information of attorney Munson's call "would have been useful to respondent" and "might have affected his decision to confess." Ante, at 422. Thus, a rule requiring the police to inform a suspect of an attorney's call would have two predictable effects. It would serve *"Miranda*'s goal of dispelling the compulsion inherent in custodial interrogation" ante, at 425, and it would disserve the goal of custodial interrogation because it would result in fewer confessions. By a process of balancing these two concerns, the Court finds the benefit to the individual outweighed by the "substantial cost of society's legitimate and substantial interest in securing admissions of guilt." Ante, at 427.

The Court's balancing approach is profoundly misguided. The cost of suppressing evidence of guilt will always make the value of a procedural safeguard appear "minimal," "marginal," or "incremental." Indeed, the value of any trial at all seems like a "procedural technicality" when balanced against the interest in administering prompt justice to a murderer or a rapist caught redhanded. The individual interest in procedural safeguards that minimize the risk of error is easily discounted when the fact of guilt appears certain beyond doubt.

What is the cost of requiring the police to inform a suspect of his attorney's call? It would decrease the likelihood that custodial interrogation will enable the police to obtain a confession. This is certainly a real cost, but it is the same cost that this Court has repeatedly found necessary to preserve the character of our free society and our rejection of an inquisitorial system. . . .

    . . .

Just as the "cost" does not justify taking a suspect into custody or interrogating him without giving him warnings simply because police desire to question him, so too the "cost" does not justify permitting police to withhold from a suspect knowledge of an attorney's communication, even though that communication would have an unquestionable effect on the suspect's exercise of his rights. The "cost" that concerns the Court amounts to nothing more than an acknowledgment that the law enforcement interest in obtaining convictions suffers whenever a suspect exercises the rights that are afforded by our system of criminal justice. In other words, it is the fear that an individual may exercise his rights that tips the scales of justice for the Court today. The principle that ours is an accusatorial, not an inquisitorial, system, however, has repeatedly led the Court to reject that fear as a valid reason for inhibiting the invocation of rights.

If the Court's cost-benefit analysis were sound, it would justify a repudiation of the right to a warning about counsel itself. There is only a difference in degree between a presumption that advice about the immediate availability of a lawyer would not affect the voluntariness of a decision to confess, and a presumption that every citizen knows that he has a right to remain silent and therefore no warnings of any kind are needed. In either case, the withholding of information serves precisely the same law enforcement interests. And in both cases, the cost can be described as nothing more than an incremental increase in the risk that an individual will make an unintelligent waiver of his rights.

In cases like *Escobedo, Miranda,* and *Dunaway* [v. New York, 442 U.S. 200 (1979)], the Court has viewed the balance from a much broader prospective. In all these cases—indeed, whenever the distinction between an inquisitorial and an accusatorial system of justice is implicated—the law enforcement interest served by incommunicado interrogation has been weighed against the interest in individual liberty that is threatened by such practices. The balance has never been struck by an evaluation of empirical data of the kind submitted to legislative decisionmakers—indeed, the Court relies on no such data today. Rather, the Court has evaluated the quality of the conflicting rights and interests. In the past, that kind of balancing process has led to the conclusion that the police have *no right* to compel an individual to respond to custodial interrogation, and that the interest in liberty that is threatened by incommunicado interrogation is so precious that special procedures must be followed to protect it. The Court's contrary conclusion today can only be explained by its failure to appreciate the value of the liberty that an accusatorial system seeks to protect.

IV

The Court also argues that a rule requiring the police to inform a suspect of an attorney's efforts to reach him would have an additional cost: it would undermine the "clarity" of the rule of the *Miranda* case.... This argument is not supported by any reference to the experience in the States that have adopted such a rule. The Court merely professes concern about its ability to answer three quite simple questions.[46]

---

46. Thus, the Court asks itself:

(1) "To what extent should the police be held accountable for knowing that the accused has counsel?" Ante, at 425. The simple answer is that police should be held accountable to the extent that the attorney or the suspect informs the police of the representation.

(2) "Is it enough that someone in the station house knows, or must the interrogating officer himself know of counsel's efforts to contact the suspect?" Ibid. Obviously, police should be held responsible for getting a message of this importance from one officer to another.

(3) "Do counsel's efforts to talk to the suspect concerning one criminal investigation trigger the obligation to inform the defendant before interrogation may proceed on a wholly separate matter?" Ibid. As the facts of this case forcefully demonstrate, the answer is "yes."

Moreover, the Court's evaluation of the interest in "clarity" is rather one-sided. For a police officer with a printed card containing the exact text he is supposed to recite, perhaps the rule is clear. But the interest in clarity that the *Miranda* decision was intended to serve is not merely for the benefit of the police. Rather, the decision was also, and primarily, intended to provide adequate guidance to the person in custody who is being asked to waive the protections afforded by the Constitution. Inevitably, the *Miranda* decision also serves the judicial interest in clarifying the inquiry into what actually transpired during a custodial interrogation. Under the Court's conception of the interest in clarity, however, the police would presumably prevail whenever they could convince the trier of fact that a required ritual was performed before the confession was obtained.

V

At the time attorney Munson made her call to the Cranston police station, she was acting as Burbine's attorney. Under ordinary principles of agency law the deliberate deception of Munson was tantamount to deliberate deception of her client. If an attorney makes a mistake in the course of her representation of her client, the client must accept the consequences of that mistake. It is equally clear that when an attorney makes an inquiry on behalf of her client, the client is entitled to a truthful answer. Surely the client must have the same remedy for a false representation to his lawyer that he would have if he were acting *pro se* and had propounded the question himself.

The majority brushes aside the police deception involved in the misinformation of attorney Munson. It is irrelevant to the Fifth Amendment analysis, concludes the majority, because that right is personal; it is irrelevant to the Sixth Amendment analysis, continues the majority, because the Sixth Amendment does not apply until formal adversary proceedings have begun.

In my view, as a matter of law, the police deception of Munson was tantamount to deception of Burbine himself. It constituted a violation of Burbine's right to have an attorney present during the questioning that began shortly thereafter. The existence of that right is undisputed. Whether the source of that right is the Sixth Amendment, the Fifth Amendment, or a combination of the two is of no special importance, for I do not understand the Court to deny the existence of the right.

The pertinent question is whether police deception of the attorney is utterly irrelevant to that right. In my judgment, it blinks at reality to suggest that misinformation which prevented the presence of an attorney has no bearing on the protection and effectuation of the right to counsel in custodial interrogation. The majority parses the role of attorney and suspect so narrowly that the deception of the attorney is of no constitutional significance. In other contexts, however, the Court does not hesitate to recognize an identity between the interest of attorney and accused. The character of the attorney-client relationship requires rejection of the Court's notion that the attorney is some entirely distinct, completely severable entity and that deception of the attorney is irrelevant to the right of counsel in custodial interrogation.

The possible reach of the Court's opinion is stunning. For the majority seems to suggest that police may deny counsel all access to a client who is being held. At least since *Escobedo v. Illinois,* it has been widely accepted that police may not simply deny attorneys access to their clients who are in custody. This view has survived the recasting of *Escobedo* from a Sixth Amendment to a Fifth Amendment case that the majority finds so critically important. That this prevailing view is shared *by the police* can be seen in the state-court opinions detailing various forms of police deception of attorneys. For, if there were no obligation to give attorneys access, there would be no need to take elaborate steps to avoid access, such as shuttling the suspect to a different location, or taking the lawyer to different locations; police could simply refuse to allow the attorneys to see the suspects. But the law enforcement profession has apparently believed, quite rightly in my view, that denying lawyers access to their clients is impermissible. The Court today seems to assume that this view was error—that, from the federal constitutional perspective, the lawyer's access is, as a question from the Court put it in oral argument, merely "a matter of prosecutorial grace." Tr. of Oral Arg. 32. Certainly, nothing in the Court's Fifth and Sixth Amendment analysis acknowledges that there is *any* federal constitutional bar to an absolute denial of lawyer access to a suspect who is in police custody.

In sharp contrast to the majority, I firmly believe that the right to counsel at custodial interrogation is infringed by police treatment of an attorney that prevents or impedes the attorney's representation of the suspect at that interrogation.

VI

The Court devotes precisely five sentences to its conclusion that the police interference in the attorney's representation of Burbine did not violate the Due Process Clause. In the majority's view, the due process analysis is a simple "shock the conscience" test. Finding its conscience troubled, but not shocked, the majority rejects the due process challenge.

In a variety of circumstances, however, the Court has given a more thoughtful consideration to the requirements of due process. For instance, we have concluded that use of a suspect's post-*Miranda* warnings silence against him violates the due process requirement of fundamental fairness because such use breaches an implicit promise that "silence will carry no penalty."[58] Similarly, we have concluded that "the suppression by the prosecution of evidence favorable to an accused upon request violates due process where the evidence is material either to guilt or to punishment."[59] We have also concluded that vindictive prosecution violates due process; so too does vindictive sentencing. Indeed, we have emphasized that analysis of the "voluntariness" of a confession is frequently a "convenient shorthand" for reviewing objectionable police methods under the rubric of the due process requirement of fundamental fairness. What emerges from these cases is not the majority's simple "shock the conscience" test, but the principle that due process requires fairness, integrity, and honor in the operation of the criminal justice system, and in its treatment of the citizen's cardinal constitutional protections.

In my judgment, police interference in the attorney-client relationship is the type of governmental misconduct on a matter of central importance to the administration of justice that the Due Process Clause prohibits. Just as the police cannot impliedly promise a suspect that his silence will not be used against him and then proceed to break that promise, so too police cannot tell a suspect's attorney that they will not question the suspect and then proceed to question him. Just as the government cannot conceal from a suspect material and exculpatory evidence, so too the government cannot conceal from a suspect the material fact of his attorney's communication.

Police interference with communications between an attorney and his client violates the due process requirement of fundamental fairness. Burbine's attorney was given completely false information about the lack of questioning; moreover, she was not told that her client would be questioned regarding a murder charge about which she was unaware. Burbine, in turn, was not told that his attorney had phoned and that she had been informed that he would not be questioned. Quite simply, the Rhode Island police effectively drove a wedge between an attorney and a suspect through misinformation and omissions.

The majority does not "question that on facts more egregious than those presented here police deception might rise to the level of a due process violation." Ante, at 432. In my view, the police deception disclosed by this record plainly does rise to that level.

VII

This case turns on a proper appraisal of the role of the lawyer in our society. If a lawyer is seen as a nettlesome obstacle to the pursuit of wrongdoers—as in an inquisitorial society—then the

---

58. See Wainwright v. Greenfield, 474 U.S. [284 (1986)], at 295; Doyle v. Ohio, 426 U.S. [610 (1976)], at 618.

59. Brady v. Maryland, 373 U.S. 83, 87 (1963)....

Court's decision today makes a good deal of sense. If a lawyer is seen as an aid to the understanding and protection of constitutional rights—as in an accusatorial society—then today's decision makes no sense at all.

Like the conduct of the police in the Cranston station on the evening of June 29, 1977, the Court's opinion today serves the goal of insuring that the perpetrator of a vile crime is punished. Like the police on that June night as well, however, the Court has trampled on well-established legal principles and flouted the spirit of our accusatorial system of justice.

I respectfully dissent.

RHODE ISLAND v. INNIS

446 U.S. 291, 100 S.Ct. 1682, 64 L.Ed.2d 297 (1980).

MR. JUSTICE STEWART delivered the opinion of the Court.

In Miranda v. Arizona, 384 U.S. 436, 474, the Court held that, once a defendant in custody asks to speak with a lawyer, all interrogation must cease until a lawyer is present. The issue in this case is whether the respondent was "interrogated" in violation of the standards promulgated in the *Miranda* opinion.

I

On the night of January 12, 1975, John Mulvaney, a Providence, R.I., taxicab driver, disappeared after being dispatched to pick up a customer. His body was discovered four days later buried in a shallow grave in Coventry, R.I. He had died from a shotgun blast aimed at the back of his head.

On January 17, 1975, shortly after midnight, the Providence police received a telephone call from Gerald Aubin, also a taxicab driver, who reported that he had just been robbed by a man wielding a sawed-off shotgun. Aubin further reported that he had dropped off his assailant near Rhode Island College in a section of Providence known as Mount Pleasant. While at the Providence police station waiting to give a statement, Aubin noticed a picture of his assailant on a bulletin board. Aubin so informed one of the police officers present. The officer prepared a photo array, and again Aubin identified a picture of the same person. That person was the respondent. Shortly thereafter, the Providence police began a search of the Mount Pleasant area.

At approximately 4:30 a.m. on the same date, Patrolman Lovell, while cruising the streets of Mount Pleasant in a patrol car, spotted the respondent standing in the street facing him. When Patrolman Lovell stopped his car, the respondent walked towards it. Patrolman Lovell then arrested the respondent, who was unarmed, and advised him of his so-called *Miranda* rights. While the two men waited in the patrol car for other police officers to arrive, Patrolman Lovell did not converse with the respondent other than to respond to the latter's request for a cigarette.

Within minutes, Sergeant Sears arrived at the scene of the arrest, and he also gave the respondent the *Miranda* warnings. Immediately thereafter, Captain Leyden and other police officers arrived. Captain Leyden advised the respondent of his *Miranda* rights. The respondent stated that he understood those rights and wanted to speak with a lawyer. Captain Leyden then directed that the respondent be placed in a "caged wagon," a four-door police car with a wire screen mesh between the front and rear seats, and be driven to the central police station. Three officers, Patrolmen Gleckman, Williams, and McKenna, were assigned to accompany the respondent to the central station. They placed the respondent in the vehicle and shut the doors. Captain Leyden then instructed the officers not to question the respondent or intimidate or coerce him in any way. The three officers then entered the vehicle, and it departed.

While en route to the central station, Patrolman Gleckman initiated a conversation with Patrolman McKenna concerning the missing shotgun. As Patrolman Gleckman later testified:

> "A. At this point, I was talking back and forth with Patrolman McKenna stating that I frequent this area while on patrol and [that because a school for handicapped children is located nearby,] there's a lot of handicapped children running around in this area, and God forbid one of them might find a weapon with shells and they might hurt themselves." App. 43–44.

Patrolman McKenna apparently shared his fellow officer's concern:

> "A. I more or less concurred with him [Gleckman] that it was a safety factor and that we should, you know, continue to search for the weapon and try to find it." Id., at 53.

While Patrolman Williams said nothing, he overheard the conversation between the two officers:

> "A. He [Gleckman] said it would be too bad if the little—I believe he said a girl—would pick up the gun, maybe kill herself." Id., at 59.

The respondent then interrupted the conversation, stating that the officers should turn the car around so he could show them where the gun was located. At this point, Patrolman McKenna radioed back to Captain Leyden that they were returning to the scene of the arrest, and that the respondent would inform them of the location of the gun. At the time the respondent indicated that the officers should turn back, they had traveled no more than a mile, a trip encompassing only a few minutes.

The police vehicle then returned to the scene of the arrest where a search for the shotgun was in progress. There, Captain Leyden again advised the respondent of his *Miranda* rights. The respondent replied that he understood those rights but that he "wanted to get the gun out of the way because of the kids in the area in the school." The respondent then led the police to a nearby field, where he pointed out the shotgun under some rocks by the side of the road.

On March 20, 1975, a grand jury returned an indictment charging the respondent with the kidnaping, robbery, and murder of John Mulvaney. Before trial, the respondent moved to suppress the shotgun and the statements he had made to the police regarding it. After an evidentiary hearing at which the respondent elected not to testify, the trial judge found that the respondent had been "repeatedly and completely advised of his *Miranda* rights." He further found that it was "entirely understandable that [the officers in the police vehicle] would voice their concern [for the safety of the handicapped children] to each other." The judge then concluded that the respondent's decision to inform the police of the location of the shotgun was "a waiver, clearly, and on the basis of the evidence that I have heard, and [*sic*] intelligent waiver, of his [*Miranda*] right to remain silent." Thus, without passing on whether the police officers had in fact "interrogated" the respondent, the trial court sustained the admissibility of the shotgun and testimony related to its discovery. That evidence was later introduced at the respondent's trial, and the jury returned a verdict of guilty on all counts.

On appeal, the Rhode Island Supreme Court, in a 3–2 decision, set aside the respondent's conviction. 120 R.I. 641, 391 A.2d 1158. Relying at least in part on this Court's decision in Brewer v. Williams, 430 U.S. 387, the court concluded that the respondent had invoked his *Miranda* right to counsel and that, contrary to *Miranda*'s mandate that, in the absence of counsel all custodial interrogation then cease, the police officers in the vehicle had "interrogated" the respondent without a valid waiver of his right to counsel. . . .

We granted certiorari to address for the first time the meaning of "interrogation" under Miranda v. Arizona. 440 U.S. 934.

II

In its *Miranda* opinion, the Court concluded that in the context of "custodial interrogation" certain procedural safeguards are necessary to protect a defendant's Fifth and Fourteenth Amendment privilege against compulsory self-incrimination. More specifically, the Court held that "the prosecution may not use statements, whether exculpatory or inculpatory, stemming from custodial interrogation of the defendant unless it demonstrates the use of procedural safeguards effective to secure the privilege against self-incrimination." 384 U.S., at 444. Those safeguards included the now familiar *Miranda* warnings—namely, that the defendant be informed "that he has the right to remain silent, that anything he says can be used against him in a court of law, that he has the right to the presence of an attorney, and that if he cannot afford an attorney one will be appointed for him prior to any questioning if he so desires"—or their equivalent. Id., at 479.

The Court in the *Miranda* opinion also outlined in some detail the consequences that would result if a defendant sought to invoke those procedural safeguards. With regard to the right to the presence of counsel, the Court noted:

> "Once warnings have been given, the subsequent procedure is clear. ... If the individual states that he wants an attorney, the interrogation must cease until an attorney is present. At that time, the individual must have an opportunity to confer with the attorney and to have him present during any subsequent questioning. If the individual cannot obtain an attorney and he indicates that he wants one before speaking to police, they must respect his decision to remain silent." Id., at 473–474.

In the present case, the parties are in agreement that the respondent was fully informed of his *Miranda* rights and that he invoked his *Miranda* right to counsel when he told Captain Leyden that he wished to consult with a lawyer. It is also uncontested that the respondent was "in custody" while being transported to the police station.

The issue, therefore, is whether the respondent was "interrogated" by the police officers in violation of the respondent's undisputed right under *Miranda* to remain silent until he had consulted with a lawyer. In resolving this issue, we first define the term "interrogation" under *Miranda* before turning to a consideration of the facts of this case.

A

The starting point for defining "interrogation" in this context is, of course, the Court's *Miranda* opinion. There the Court observed that "[b]y custodial interrogation, we mean *questioning* initiated by law enforcement officers after a person has been taken into custody or otherwise deprived of his freedom of action in any significant way." Id., at 444 (emphasis added). This passage and other references throughout the opinion to "questioning" might suggest that the *Miranda* rules were to apply only to those police interrogation practices that involve express questioning of a defendant while in custody.

We do not, however, construe the *Miranda* opinion so narrowly. The concern of the Court in *Miranda* was that the "interrogation environment" created by the interplay of interrogation and custody would "subjugate the individual to the will of his examiner" and thereby undermine the privilege against compulsory self-incrimination. Id., at 457–458. The police practices that evoked this concern included several that did not involve express questioning.... The Court in *Miranda* also included in its survey of interrogation practices the use of psychological ploys, such as to "posi[t]" "the guilt of the subject," to "minimize the moral seriousness of the offense," and "to cast blame on the victim or on society." Id., at 450. It is clear that these techniques of persuasion, no less than express questioning, were thought, in a custodial setting, to amount to interrogation.

This is not to say, however, that all statements obtained by the police after a person has been taken into custody are to be considered the product of interrogation. As the Court in *Miranda* noted:

> "Confessions remain a proper element in law enforcement. Any statement given freely and voluntarily without any compelling influences is, of course, admissible in evidence. *The fundamental import of the privilege while an individual is in custody is not whether he is allowed to talk to the police without the benefit of warnings and counsel, but whether he can be interrogated.* ... Volunteered statements of any kind are not barred by the Fifth Amendment and their admissibility is not affected by our holding today." *Id.,* at 478 (emphasis added).

It is clear therefore that the special procedural safeguards outlined in *Miranda* are required not where a suspect is simply taken into custody, but rather where a suspect in custody is subjected to interrogation. "Interrogation," as conceptualized in the *Miranda* opinion, must reflect a measure of compulsion above and beyond that inherent in custody itself.[4]

We conclude that the *Miranda* safeguards come into play whenever a person in custody is subjected to either express questioning or its functional equivalent. That is to say, the term "interrogation" under *Miranda* refers not only to express questioning, but also to any words or actions on the part of the police (other than those normally attendant to arrest and custody) that the police should know are reasonably likely to elicit an incriminating response from the suspect. The latter portion of this definition focuses primarily upon the perceptions of the suspect, rather than the intent of the police. This focus reflects the fact that the *Miranda* safeguards were designed to vest a suspect in custody with an added measure of protection against coercive police practices, without regard to objective proof of the underlying intent of the

---

4. There is language in the opinion of the Rhode Island Supreme Court in this case suggesting that the definition of "interrogation" under *Miranda* is informed by this Court's decision in Brewer v. Williams, 430 U.S. 387. 120 R.I. 641, ___ 391 A.2d 1158, 1161–1162. This suggestion is erroneous. Our decision in *Brewer* rested solely on the Sixth and Fourteenth Amendment right to counsel. 430 U.S., at 397–399. That right, as we held in Massiah v. United States, 377 U.S. 201, 206, prohibits law enforcement officers from "deliberately elicit[ing]" incriminating information from a defendant in the absence of counsel after a formal charge against the defendant has been filed. Custody in such a case is not controlling; indeed, the petitioner in *Massiah* was not in custody. By contrast, the right to counsel at issue in the present case is based not on the Sixth and Fourteenth Amendments, but rather on the Fifth and Fourteenth Amendments as interpreted in the *Miranda* opinion. The definitions of "interrogation" under the Fifth and Sixth Amendments, if indeed the term "interrogation" is even apt in the Sixth Amendment context, are not necessarily interchangeable, since the policies underlying the two constitutional protections are quite distinct. ...

police. A practice that the police should know is reasonably likely to evoke an incriminating response from a suspect thus amounts to interrogation.[7] But, since the police surely cannot be held accountable for the unforeseeable results of their words or actions, the definition of interrogation can extend only to words or actions on the part of police officers that they *should have known* were reasonably likely to elicit an incriminating response.

B

Turning to the facts of the present case, we conclude that the respondent was not "interrogated" within the meaning of *Miranda*. It is undisputed that the first prong of the definition of "interrogation" was not satisfied, for the conversation between Patrolmen Gleckman and McKenna included no express questioning of the respondent. Rather, that conversation was, at least in form, nothing more than a dialogue between the two officers to which no response from the respondent was invited.

Moreover, it cannot be fairly concluded that the respondent was subjected to the "functional equivalent" of questioning. It cannot be said, in short, that Patrolmen Gleckman and McKenna should have known that their conversation was reasonably likely to elicit an incriminating response from the respondent. There is nothing in the record to suggest that the officers were aware that the respondent was peculiarly susceptible to an appeal to his conscience concerning the safety of handicapped children. Nor is there anything in the record to suggest that the police knew that the respondent was unusually disoriented or upset at the time of his arrest.

The case thus boils down to whether, in the context of a brief conversation, the officers should have known that the respondent would suddenly be moved to make a self-incriminating response. Given the fact that the entire conversation appears to have consisted of no more than a few offhand remarks, we cannot say that the officers should have known that it was reasonably likely that Innis would so respond. This is not a case where the police carried on a lengthy harangue in the presence of the suspect. Nor does the record support the respondent's contention that, under the circumstances, the officers' comments were particularly "evocative." It is our view, therefore, that the respondent was not subjected by the police to words or actions that the police should have known were reasonably likely to elicit an incriminating response from him.

---

7. This is not to say that the intent of the police is irrelevant, for it may well have a bearing on whether the police should have known that their words or actions were reasonably likely to evoke an incriminating response. In particular, where a police practice is designed to elicit an incriminating response from the accused, it is unlikely that the practice will not also be one which the police should have known was reasonably likely to have that effect.

The Rhode Island Supreme Court erred, in short, in equating "subtle compulsion" with interrogation. That the officers' comments struck a responsive chord is readily apparent. Thus, it may be said, as the Rhode Island Supreme Court did say, that the respondent was subjected to "subtle compulsion." But that is not the end of the inquiry. It must also be established that a suspect's incriminating response was the product of words or actions on the part of the police that they should have known were reasonably likely to elicit an incriminating response. This was not established in the present case.

For the reasons stated, the judgment of the Supreme Court of Rhode Island is vacated, and the case is remanded to that court for further proceedings not inconsistent with this opinion.

It is so ordered.[*]

[*] Justice White wrote a brief note, indicating his concurrence. Chief Justice Burger wrote an opinion concurring in the judgment. Justice Marshall wrote a dissenting opinion, which Justice Brennan joined. Justice Stevens also wrote a dissenting opinion.

ILLINOIS v. PERKINS

496 U.S. 292, 110 S.Ct. 2394, 110 L.Ed.2d 243 (1990).

JUSTICE KENNEDY delivered the opinion of the Court.

An undercover government agent was placed in the cell of respondent Perkins, who was incarcerated on charges unrelated to the subject of the agent's investigation. Respondent made statements that implicated him in the crime that the agent sought to solve. Respondent claims that the statements should be inadmissible because he had not been given *Miranda* warnings by the agent. We hold that the statements are admissible. *Miranda* warnings are not required when the suspect is unaware that he is speaking to a law enforcement officer and gives a voluntary statement.

I

In November 1984, Richard Stephenson was murdered in a suburb of East St. Louis, Illinois. The murder remained unsolved until March 1986, when one Donald Charlton told police that he had learned about a homicide from a fellow inmate at the Graham Correctional Facility, where Charlton had been serving a sentence for burglary. The fellow inmate was Lloyd Perkins, who is the respondent here. Charlton told police that, while at Graham, he had befriended respondent, who told him in detail about a murder that respondent had committed in East St. Louis. On hearing Charlton's account, the police recognized details of the Stephenson murder that were not well known, and so they treated Charlton's story as a credible one.

By the time the police heard Charlton's account, respondent had been released from Graham, but police traced him to a jail in Montgomery County, Illinois, where he was being held pending trial on a charge of aggravated battery, unrelated to the Stephenson murder. The police wanted to investigate further respondent's connection to the Stephenson murder, but feared that the use of an eavesdropping device would prove impracticable and unsafe. They decided instead to place an undercover agent in the cellblock with respondent and Charlton. The plan was for Charlton and undercover agent John Parisi to pose as escapees from a work release program who had been arrested in the course of a burglary. Parisi and Charlton were instructed to engage respondent in casual conversation and report anything he said about the Stephenson murder.

Parisi, using the alias "Vito Bianco," and Charlton, both clothed in jail garb, were placed in the cellblock with respondent at the Montgomery County jail. The cellblock consisted of 12 separate cells that opened onto a common room. Respondent greeted Charlton who, after a brief conversation with respondent, introduced Parisi by his alias. Parisi told respondent that he "wasn't going to do any more time," and suggested that the three of them escape. Respondent replied that the Montgomery County jail was "rinky-dink" and that they could "break out." The trio met in respondent's cell later that evening, after the other inmates were asleep, to refine their plan. Respondent said that his girlfriend could smuggle in a pistol. Charlton said: "Hey, I'm not a murderer, I'm a burglar. That's your guys' profession." After telling Charlton that he would be responsible for any murder that occurred, Parisi asked respondent if he had ever "done" anybody. Respondent said that he had and proceeded to describe at length the events of the Stephenson murder. Parisi and respondent then engaged in some casual conversation before respondent went to sleep. Parisi did not give respondent *Miranda* warnings before the conversations.

Respondent was charged with the Stephenson murder. Before trial, he moved to suppress the statements made to Parisi in the jail. The trial court granted the motion to suppress, and the State appealed. The Appellate Court of Illinois affirmed, 176 Ill.App.3d 443, 531 N.E.2d 141 (1988), holding that Miranda v. Arizona, 384 U.S. 436 (1966), prohibits all undercover contacts with incarcerated suspects that are reasonably likely to elicit an incriminating response.

We granted certiorari, 493 U.S. 808 (1989), to decide whether an undercover law enforcement officer must give *Miranda* warnings to an incarcerated suspect before asking him questions that may elicit an incriminating response. We now reverse.

II

In Miranda v. Arizona, supra, the Court held that the Fifth Amendment privilege against self-incrimination prohibits admitting statements given by a suspect during "custodial interrogation" without a prior warning. Custodial interrogation means "questioning initiated by law enforcement officers after a person has been taken into custody...." Id., at 444. The warning mandated by *Miranda* was meant to preserve the privilege during "incommunicado interrogation of individuals in a police-dominated atmosphere." Id., at 445. That atmosphere is said to generate "inherently compelling pressures which work to undermine the individual's will to resist and to compel him to speak where he would not otherwise do so freely." Id., at 467. "Fidelity to the doctrine announced in *Miranda* requires that it be enforced strictly, but only in those types of situations in which the concerns that powered the decision are implicated." Berkemer v. McCarty, 468 U.S. 420, 437 (1984).

Conversations between suspects and undercover agents do not implicate the concerns underlying *Miranda*. The essential ingredients of a "police-dominated atmosphere" and compulsion are not present when an incarcerated person speaks freely to someone whom he believes to be a fellow inmate. Coercion is determined from the perspective of the suspect.... When a suspect considers himself in the company of cellmates and not officers, the coercive atmosphere is lacking.... There is no empirical basis for the assumption that a suspect speaking to those whom he assumes are not officers will feel compelled to speak by the fear of reprisal for remaining silent or in the hope of more lenient treatment should he confess.

It is the premise of *Miranda* that the danger of coercion results from the interaction of custody and official interrogation. We reject the argument that *Miranda* warnings are required whenever a suspect is in custody in a technical sense and converses with someone who happens to be a government agent. Questioning by captors, who appear to control the suspect's fate, may create mutually reinforcing pressures that the Court has assumed will weaken the suspect's will, but where a suspect does not know that he is conversing with a government agent, these pressures do not exist. The state court here mistakenly assumed that because the suspect was in custody, no undercover questioning could take place. When the suspect has no reason to think that the listeners have official power over him, it should not be assumed that his words are motivated by the reaction he expects from his listeners. "[W]hen the agent carries neither badge nor gun and wears not 'police blue,' but the same prison gray" as the suspect, there is no "*interplay* between police interrogation and police custody." Kamisar, *Brewer v. Williams, Massiah* and *Miranda:* What is "Interrogation"? When Does it Matter?, 67 Geo.L.J. 1, 67, 63 (1978).

Miranda forbids coercion, not mere strategic deception by taking advantage of a suspect's misplaced trust in one he supposes to be a fellow prisoner. As we recognized in *Miranda,* "[c]onfessions remain a proper element in law enforcement. Any statement given freely and voluntarily without any compelling influences is, of course, admissible in evidence." 384 U.S., at 478. Ploys to mislead a suspect or lull him into a false sense of security that do not rise to the level of compulsion or coercion to speak are not within *Miranda's* concerns....

Miranda was not meant to protect suspects from boasting about their criminal activities in front of persons whom they believe to be their cellmates. This case is illustrative. Respondent had no reason to feel that undercover agent Parisi had any legal authority to force him to answer questions or that Parisi could affect respondent's future treatment. Respondent viewed the cellmate-agent as an equal and showed no hint of being intimidated by the atmosphere of the jail. In recounting the details of the Stephenson murder, respondent was motivated solely by the desire to impress his fellow inmates. He spoke at his own peril.

The tactic employed here to elicit a voluntary confession from a suspect does not violate the Self-Incrimination Clause. We held in Hoffa v. United States, 385 U.S. 293 (1966), that placing an undercover agent near a suspect in order to gather incriminating information was permissible under the Fifth Amendment. In *Hoffa,* while petitioner Hoffa was on trial, he met often with one Partin, who, unbeknownst to Hoffa, was cooperating with law enforcement officials. Partin reported to officials that Hoffa had divulged his attempts to bribe jury members. We approved using Hoffa's statements at his subsequent trial for jury tampering, on the rationale that "no claim ha[d] been or could [have been] made that [Hoffa's] incriminating statements were the product of any sort of coercion, legal or factual." Id., at 304. In addition, we found that the fact that Partin had fooled Hoffa into thinking that Partin was a sympathetic colleague did not affect the voluntariness of the statements. . . . The only difference between this case and *Hoffa* is that the suspect here was incarcerated, but detention, whether or not for the crime in question, does not warrant a presumption that the use of an undercover agent to speak with an incarcerated suspect makes any confession thus obtained involuntary.

Our decision in Mathis v. United States, 391 U.S. 1 (1968), is distinguishable. In *Mathis,* an inmate in a state prison was interviewed by an Internal Revenue Service agent about possible tax violations. No *Miranda* warning was given before questioning. The Court held that the suspect's incriminating statements were not admissible at his subsequent trial on tax fraud charges. The suspect in *Mathis* was aware that the agent was a Government official, investigating the possibility of non-compliance with the tax laws. The case before us now is different. Where the suspect does not know that he is speaking to a government agent there is no reason to assume the possibility that the suspect might feel coerced. (The bare fact of custody may not in every instance require a warning even when the suspect is aware that he is speaking to an official, but we do not have occasion to explore that issue here.)

This Court's Sixth Amendment decisions in Massiah v. United States, 377 U.S. 201 (1964) . . . also do not avail respondent. We held in those cases that the government may not use an undercover agent to circumvent the Sixth Amendment right to counsel once a suspect has been charged with the crime. After charges have been filed, the Sixth Amendment prevents the government from interfering with the accused's right to counsel. . . . In the instant case no charges had been filed on the subject of the interrogation, and our Sixth Amendment precedents are not applicable.

Respondent can seek no help from his argument that a bright-line rule for the application of *Miranda* is desirable. Law enforcement officers will have little difficulty putting into practice our holding that undercover agents need not give *Miranda* warnings to incarcerated suspects. The use of undercover agents is a recognized law enforcement technique, often employed in the prison context to detect violence against correctional officials or inmates, as well as for the purposes served here. The interests protected by *Miranda* are not implicated in these cases, and the warnings are not required to safeguard the constitutional rights of inmates who make voluntary statements to undercover agents.

We hold that an undercover law enforcement officer posing as a fellow inmate need not give *Miranda* warnings to an incarcerated suspect before asking questions that may elicit an incriminating response. The statements at issue in this case were voluntary, and there is no federal obstacle to their admissibility at trial. We now reverse and remand for proceedings not inconsistent with our opinion.

It is so ordered.[*]

---

[*] Justice Brennan wrote an opinion concurring in the judgment. Justice Marshall wrote a dissenting opinion.

OREGON v. MATHIASON

429 U.S. 492, 97 S.Ct. 711, 50 L.Ed.2d 714 (1977).

PER CURIAM.

Respondent Carl Mathiason was convicted of first-degree burglary after a bench trial in which his confession was critical to the State's case. At trial he moved to suppress the confession as the fruit of questioning by the police not preceded by the warnings required in Miranda v. Arizona, 384 U.S. 436 (1966). The trial court refused to exclude the confession because it found that Mathiason was not in custody at the time of the confession.

The Oregon Court of Appeals affirmed respondent's conviction, but on his petition for review in the Supreme Court of Oregon that court by a divided vote reversed the conviction. It found that although Mathiason had not been arrested or otherwise formally detained, "the interrogation took place in a 'coercive environment' " of the sort to which *Miranda* was intended to apply. . . . The State of Oregon has petitioned for certiorari to review the judgment of the Supreme Court of Oregon. We think that court has read *Miranda* too broadly, and we therefore reverse its judgment.

The Supreme Court of Oregon described the factual situation surrounding the confession as follows:

"An officer of the State Police investigated a theft at a residence near Pendleton. He asked the lady of the house which had been burglarized if she suspected anyone. She replied that the defendant was the only one she could think of. The defendant was a parolee and a 'close associate' of her son. The officer tried to contact defendant on three or four occasions with no success. Finally, about 25 days after the burglary, the officer left his card at defendant's apartment with a note asking him to call because 'I'd like to discuss something with you.' The next afternoon the defendant did call. The officer asked where it would be convenient to meet. The defendant had no preference; so the officer asked if the defendant could meet him at the state patrol office in about an hour and a half, about 5:00 p.m. The patrol office was about two blocks from defendant's apartment. The building housed several state agencies.

"The officer met defendant in the hallway, shook hands and took him into an office. The defendant was told he was not under arrest. The door was closed. The two sat across a desk. The police radio in another room could be heard. The officer told defendant he wanted to talk to him about a burglary and that his truthfulness would possibly be considered by the district attorney or judge. The officer further advised that the police believed defendant was involved in the burglary and [falsely stated that] defendant's fingerprints were found at the scene. The defendant sat for a few minutes and then said he had taken the property. This occurred within five minutes after defendant had come to the office. The officer then advised defendant of his *Miranda* rights and took a taped confession.

"At the end of the taped conversation the officer told defendant he was not arresting him at this time; he was released to go about his job and return to his family. The officer said he was referring the case to the district attorney for him to determine whether criminal charges would be brought. It was 5:30 p.m. when the defendant left the office.

"The officer gave all the testimony relevant to this issue. The defendant did not take the stand either at the hearing on the motion to suppress or at the trial." 275 Ore. 1, 3–4, 549 P.2d 673, 674 (1976).

The Supreme Court of Oregon reasoned from these facts that:

"We hold the interrogation took place in a 'coercive environment.' The parties were in the offices of the State Police; they were alone behind closed doors; the officer informed the defendant he was a suspect in a theft and the authorities had evidence incriminating him in the crime; and the defendant was a parolee under supervision. We are of the opinion that this evidence is not overcome by the evidence that the defendant came to the office in response to a request and was told he was not under arrest." Id., at 5, 549 P.2d, at 675.

Our decision in *Miranda* set forth rules of police procedure applicable to "custodial interrogation." "By custodial interrogation, we mean questioning initiated by law enforcement officers after a person has been taken into custody or otherwise deprived of his freedom of action in any significant way." 384 U.S., at 444. Subsequently we have found the *Miranda* principle applicable to questioning which takes place in a prison setting during a suspect's term of imprisonment on a separate offense, Mathis v. United States, 391 U.S. 1 (1968), and to questioning taking place in a suspect's home, after he has been arrested and is no longer free to go where he pleases, Orozco v. Texas, 394 U.S. 324 (1969).

In the present case, however, there is no indication that the questioning took place in a context where respondent's freedom to depart was restricted in any way. He came voluntarily to the police station, where he was immediately informed that he was not under arrest. At the close of a ½-hour interview respondent did in fact leave the police station without hindrance. It is clear from these facts that Mathiason was not in custody "or otherwise deprived of his freedom of action in any significant way."

Such a noncustodial situation is not converted to one in which *Miranda* applies simply because a reviewing court concludes that, even in the absence of any formal arrest or restraint on freedom of movement, the questioning took place in a "coercive environment." Any interview of one suspected of a crime by a police officer will have coercive aspects to it, simply by virtue of the fact that the police officer is part of a law enforcement system which may ultimately cause the suspect to be charged with a crime. But police officers are not required to administer *Miranda* warnings to everyone whom they question. Nor is the requirement of warnings to be imposed simply because the questioning takes place in the station house, or because the questioned person is one whom the police suspect. *Miranda* warnings are required only where there has been such a restriction on a person's freedom as to render him "in custody." It was *that* sort of coercive environment to which *Miranda* by its terms was made applicable, and to which it is limited.

The officer's false statement about having discovered Mathiason's fingerprints at the scene was found by the Supreme Court of Oregon to be another circumstance contributing to the coercive environment which makes the *Miranda* rationale applicable. Whatever relevance this fact may have to other issues in the case, it has nothing to do with whether respondent was in custody for purposes of the *Miranda* rule.

The petition for certiorari is granted, the judgment of the Oregon Supreme Court is reversed, and the case is remanded for proceedings not inconsistent with this opinion.

So ordered.[*]

---

[*] Justice Marshall and Justice Stevens wrote dissenting opinions. Justice Brennan also dissented.

HARRIS v. NEW YORK

401 U.S. 222, 91 S.Ct. 644, 28 L.Ed.2d 1 (1971).

MR. CHIEF JUSTICE BURGER delivered the opinion of the Court.

We granted the writ in this case to consider petitioner's claim that a statement made by him to police under circumstances rendering it inadmissible to establish the prosecution's case in chief under Miranda v. Arizona, 384 U.S. 436 (1966), may not be used to impeach his credibility.

The State of New York charged petitioner in a two-count indictment with twice selling heroin to an undercover police officer. At a subsequent jury trial the officer was the State's chief witness, and he testified as to details of the two sales. A second officer verified collateral details of the sales, and a third offered testimony about the chemical analysis of the heroin.

Petitioner took the stand in his own defense. He admitted knowing the undercover police officer but denied a sale on January 4, 1966. He admitted making a sale of contents of a glassine bag to the officer on January 6 but claimed it was baking powder and part of a scheme to defraud the purchaser.

On cross-examination petitioner was asked seriatim whether he had made specified statements to the police immediately following his arrest on January 7—statements that partially contradicted petitioner's direct testimony at trial. In response to the cross-examination, petitioner testified that he could not remember virtually any of the questions or answers recited by the prosecutor. At the request of petitioner's counsel the written statement from which the prosecutor had read questions and answers in his impeaching process was placed in the record for possible use on appeal; the statement was not shown to the jury.

The trial judge instructed the jury that the statements attributed to petitioner by the prosecution could be considered only in passing on petitioner's credibility and not as evidence of guilt. In closing summations both counsel argued the substance of the impeaching statements. The jury then found petitioner guilty on the second count of the indictment. The New York Court of Appeals affirmed in a per curiam opinion, 25 N.Y.2d 175, 250 N.E.2d 349 (1969).

At trial the prosecution made no effort in its case in chief to use the statements allegedly made by petitioner, conceding that they were inadmissible under Miranda v. Arizona, 384 U.S. 436 (1966). The transcript of the interrogation used in the impeachment, but

752

not given to the jury, shows that no warning of a right to appointed counsel was given before questions were put to petitioner when he was taken into custody. Petitioner makes no claim that the statements made to the police were coerced or involuntary.

Some comments in the *Miranda* opinion can indeed be read as indicating a bar to use of an uncounseled statement for any purpose, but discussion of that issue was not at all necessary to the Court's holding and cannot be regarded as controlling. *Miranda* barred the prosecution from making its case with statements of an accused made while in custody prior to having or effectively waiving counsel. It does not follow from *Miranda* that evidence inadmissible against an accused in the prosecution's case in chief is barred for all purposes, provided of course that the trustworthiness of the evidence satisfies legal standards.

In Walder v. United States, 347 U.S. 62 (1954), the Court permitted physical evidence, inadmissible in the case in chief, to be used for impeachment purposes.

"It is one thing to say that the Government cannot make an affirmative use of evidence unlawfully obtained. It is quite another to say that the defendant can turn the illegal method by which evidence in the Government's possession was obtained to his own advantage, and provide himself with a shield against contradiction of his untruths. Such an extension of the *Weeks* doctrine would be a perversion of the Fourth Amendment.

"[T]here is hardly justification for letting the defendant affirmatively resort to perjurious testimony in reliance on the Government's disability to challenge his credibility." 347 U.S., at 65.

It is true that Walder was impeached as to collateral matters included in his direct examination, whereas petitioner here was impeached as to testimony bearing more directly on the crimes charged. We are not persuaded that there is a difference in principle that warrants a result different from that reached by the Court in *Walder*. Petitioner's testimony in his own behalf concerning the events of January 7 contrasted sharply with what he told the police shortly after his arrest. The impeachment process here undoubtedly provided valuable aid to the jury in assessing petitioner's credibility, and the benefits of this process should not be lost, in our view, because of the speculative possibility that impermissible police conduct will be encouraged thereby. Assuming that the exclusionary rule has a deterrent effect on proscribed police conduct, sufficient deterrence flows when the evidence in question is made unavailable to the prosecution in its case in chief.

Every criminal defendant is privileged to testify in his own defense, or to refuse to do so. But that privilege cannot be construed to include the right to commit perjury.... Having voluntarily taken the stand, petitioner was under an obligation to speak truthfully and accurately, and the prosecution here did no more than utilize the traditional truth-testing devices of the adversary process. Had inconsistent statements been made by the accused to some third person, it could hardly be contended that the conflict could not be laid before the jury by way of cross-examination and impeachment.

The shield provided by *Miranda* cannot be perverted into a license to use perjury by way of a defense, free from the risk of confrontation with prior inconsistent utterances. We hold, therefore, that petitioner's credibility was appropriately impeached by use of his earlier conflicting statements.

Affirmed.

MR. JUSTICE BRENNAN, with whom MR. JUSTICE DOUGLAS and MR. JUSTICE MARSHALL join, dissenting.

It is conceded that the question-and-answer statement used to impeach petitioner's direct testimony was, under Miranda v. Arizona, 384 U.S. 436 (1966), constitutionally inadmissible as part of the State's direct case against petitioner. I think that the Constitution also denied the State the use of the statement on cross-examination to impeach the credibility of petitioner's testimony given in his own defense. The decision in Walder v. United States, 347 U.S. 62 (1954), is not, as the Court today holds, dispositive to the contrary. Rather, that case supports my conclusion.

. . .

Walder v. United States was not a case where tainted evidence was used to impeach an accused's direct testimony on matters directly related to the case against him. In *Walder* the evidence was used to impeach the accused's testimony on matters *collateral* to the crime charged.... The evidence tended solely to impeach the credibility of the defendant's direct testimony that he had never in his life possessed heroin. But that evidence was completely unrelated to the indictment on trial and did not in any way interfere with his freedom to deny all elements of that case against him. In contrast, here, the evidence used for impeachment, a statement concerning the details of the very sales alleged in the indictment, was directly related to the case against petitioner.

While *Walder* did not identify the constitutional specifics that guarantee "a defendant the fullest opportunity to meet the accusation against him ... [and permit him to] be free to deny all the elements of the case against him," in my view Miranda v. Arizona, 384 U.S. 436 (1966), identified the Fifth Amendment's privilege against self-incrimination as one of those specifics. That privilege has been extended against the States. Malloy v. Hogan, 378 U.S. 1 (1964). It is fulfilled only when an accused is guaranteed the right "to remain silent unless he chooses to speak in the *unfettered* exercise of his own will," id., at 8 (emphasis added). The choice of whether to testify in one's own defense must therefore be "unfettered," since that choice is an exercise of the constitutional privilege, Griffin v. California, 380 U.S. 609 (1965). *Griffin* held that comment by the prosecution upon the accused's failure to take the stand or a court instruction that such silence is evidence of guilt is impermissible because it "fetters" that choice—"[i]t cuts down on the privilege by making its assertion costly." Id., at 614. For precisely the same reason the constitutional guarantee forbids the prosecution from using a tainted statement to impeach the accused who takes the stand: The prosecution's use of the tainted statement "cuts down on the privilege by making its assertion costly." Id. Thus, the accused is denied an "unfettered" choice when the decision whether to take the stand is burdened by the risk that an illegally obtained prior statement may be introduced to impeach his direct testimony denying complicity in the crime charged against him. We settled this proposition in *Miranda*....

The objective of deterring improper police conduct is only part of the larger objective of safeguarding the integrity of our adversary system. The "essential mainstay" of that system, Miranda v. Arizona, 384 U.S., at 460, is the privilege against self-incrimination, which for that reason has occupied a central place in our jurisprudence since before the Nation's birth. Moreover, "we may view the historical development of the privilege as one which groped for the proper scope of governmental power over the citizen. ... All these policies point to one overriding thought: the constitutional foundation underlying the privilege is the respect a government ... must accord to the dignity and integrity of its citizens." Id. These values are plainly jeopardized if an exception against admission of tainted statements is made for those used for impeachment purposes. Moreover, it is monstrous that courts should aid or abet the lawbreaking police officer. It is abiding truth that "[n]othing can destroy a government more quickly than its failure to observe its own laws, or worse, its disregard of the charter of its own existence." Mapp v. Ohio, 367 U.S. 643, 659 (1961). Thus, even to the extent that *Miranda* was aimed at deterring police practices in disregard of the Constitution, I fear that today's holding will seriously undermine the achievement of that objective. The Court today tells the police that they may freely interrogate an accused incommunicado and without counsel and know that although any statement they obtain in violation of *Miranda* cannot be used on the State's direct case, it may be introduced if the defendant has the temerity to testify in his own defense. This goes far toward undoing much of the progress made in conforming police methods to the Constitution. I dissent.[*] [**]

---

[*] Justice Black noted his dissent.

[**] *Harris* was applied in Oregon v. Hass, 420 U.S. 714 (1975), in which a state police officer gave the defendant full *Miranda* warnings at the time of his arrest. In the patrol car, the defendant said that he would like to talk to an attorney, which the officer said he could do when they got to the police

station. Before they got to the station, the defendant made incriminating statements. The officer was allowed to testify about those statements for the limited purpose of impeaching the credibility of the defendant as a witness on the stand.

The Supreme Court said that it saw no valid distinction between this case and *Harris*. Here, as there, "the shield provided by *Miranda* is not to be perverted to a license to testify inconsistently, or even perjuriously, free from the risk of confrontation with prior inconsistent utterances." 420 U.S. at 722. (Justice Brennan and Justice Marshall wrote dissenting opinions.)

In James v. Illinois, 493 U.S. 307 (1990) (5–4), the Supreme Court held that statements of the defendant that were suppressed because they were fruit of an unlawful arrest could *not* be used by the prosecution to impeach the testimony of a defense witness other than the defendant.

DOYLE v. OHIO

426 U.S. 610, 96 S.Ct. 2240, 49 L.Ed.2d 91 (1976).

MR. JUSTICE POWELL delivered the opinion of the Court.

The question in these consolidated cases is whether a state prosecutor may seek to impeach a defendant's exculpatory story, told for the first time at trial, by cross-examining the defendant about his failure to have told the story after receiving *Miranda* warnings [1] at the time of his arrest. We conclude that use of the defendant's post-arrest silence in this manner violates due process, and therefore reverse the convictions of both petitioners.

I

Petitioners Doyle and Wood were arrested together and charged with selling 10 pounds of marihuana to a local narcotics bureau informant. They were convicted in the Common Pleas Court of Tuscarawas County, Ohio, in separate trials held about one week apart. The evidence at their trials was identical in all material respects.

The State's witnesses sketched a picture of a routine marihuana transaction. William Bonnell, a well-known "street person" with a long criminal record, offered to assist the local narcotics investigation unit in setting up drug "pushers" in return for support in his efforts to receive lenient treatment in his latest legal problems. The narcotics agents agreed. A short time later, Bonnell advised the unit that he had arranged a "buy" of 10 pounds of marihuana and needed $1,750 to pay for it. Since the banks were closed and time was short, the agents were able to collect only $1,320. Bonnell took this money and left for the rendezvous, under surveillance by four narcotics agents in two cars. As planned, he met petitioners in a bar in Dover, Ohio. From there, he and petitioner Wood drove in Bonnell's pickup truck to the nearby town of New Philadelphia, Ohio, while petitioner Doyle drove off to obtain the marihuana and then meet them at a prearranged location in New Philadelphia. The narcotics agents followed the Bonnell truck. When Doyle arrived at Bonnell's waiting truck in New Philadelphia, the two vehicles proceeded to a parking lot where the transaction took place. Bonnell left in his truck, and Doyle and Wood departed in Doyle's car. They quickly discovered that they had been paid some $430 less than the agreed-upon price, and began circling the neighborhood looking for Bonnell. They were stopped within minutes by New Philadelphia police acting on radioed instructions from the narcotics

---

1. Miranda v. Arizona, 384 U.S. 436, 467–473 (1966).

agents. One of those agents, Kenneth Beamer, arrived on the scene promptly, arrested petitioners, and gave them *Miranda* warnings. A search of the car, authorized by warrant, uncovered the $1,320.

At both trials, defense counsel's cross-examination of the participating narcotics agents was aimed primarily at establishing that, due to a limited view of the parking lot, none of them had seen the actual transaction but had seen only Bonnell standing next to Doyle's car with a package under his arm, presumably after the transaction. Each petitioner took the stand at his trial and admitted practically everything about the State's case except the most crucial point: who was selling marihuana to whom. According to petitioners, Bonnell had framed them. The arrangement had been for Bonnell to sell Doyle 10 pounds of marihuana. Doyle had left the Dover bar for the purpose of borrowing the necessary money, but while driving by himself had decided that he only wanted one or two pounds instead of the agreed-upon 10 pounds. When Bonnell reached Doyle's car in the New Philadelphia parking lot, with the marihuana under his arm, Doyle tried to explain his change of mind. Bonnell grew angry, threw the $1,320 into Doyle's car, and took all 10 pounds of marihuana back to his truck. The ensuing chase was the effort of Wood and Doyle to catch Bonnell to find out what the $1,320 was all about.

Petitioners' explanation of the events presented some difficulty for the prosecution, as it was not entirely implausible and there was little if any direct evidence to contradict it. As part of a wide-ranging cross-examination for impeachment purposes, and in an effort to undercut the explanation, the prosecutor asked each petitioner at his respective trial why he had not told the frameup story to agent Beamer when he arrested petitioners. In the first trial, that of petitioner Wood, the following colloquy occurred: [4]

> "Q: [By the prosecutor] Mr. Beamer did arrive on the scene?
>
> "A: [By Wood] Yes, he did.
>
> "Q: And I assume you told him all about what happened to you?
>
> .   .   .   .
>
> "A: No.
>
> "Q: You didn't tell Mr. Beamer?
>
> .   .   .   .
>
> "A: No.

4. Trial transcript in Ohio v. Wood, No. 10657, Common Pleas Court, Tuscarawas County, Ohio ..., 465–470.

"Q: You didn't tell Mr. Beamer this guy put $1,300 in your car?

.   .   .   .

"A: No, sir.

"Q: And we can't understand any reason why anyone would put money in your car and you were chasing him around town and trying to give it back?

.   .   .   .

"A: I didn't understand that.

"Q: You mean you didn't tell him that?

.   .   .   .

"A: Tell him what?

.   .   .   .

"Q: Mr. Wood, if that is all you had to do with this and you are innocent, when Mr. Beamer arrived on the scene why didn't you tell him?

.   .   .   .

"Q: But in any event you didn't bother to tell Mr. Beamer anything about this?

"A: No, sir."

Defense counsel's timely objections to each of the prosecutor's questions were overruled. The cross-examination of petitioner Doyle at his trial contained a similar exchange, and again defense counsel's timely objections were overruled.

Each petitioner appealed to the Court of Appeals, Fifth District, Tuscarawas County, alleging, *inter alia*, that the trial court erred in allowing the prosecutor to cross-examine the petitioner at his trial about his post-arrest silence. The Court of Appeals affirmed the convictions, stating as to the contentions about the post-arrest silence:

"This was not evidence offered by the state in its case in chief as confession by silence or as substantive evidence of guilt but rather cross examination of a witness as to why he had not told the same story earlier at his first opportunity.

"We find no error in this. It goes to credibility of the witness."

The Supreme Court of Ohio denied further review. We granted certiorari to decide whether impeachment use of a defendant's post-arrest silence violates any provision of the Constitution....

II

The State pleads necessity as justification for the prosecutor's action in these cases. It argues that the discrepancy between an exculpatory story at trial and silence at time of arrest gives rise to an inference that the story was fabricated somewhere along the way, perhaps to fit within the seams of the State's case as it was developed at pretrial hearings. Noting that the prosecution usually has little else with which to counter such an exculpatory story, the State seeks only the right to cross-examine a defendant as to post-arrest silence for the limited purpose of impeachment. In support of its position the State emphasizes the importance of cross-examination in general ... and relies upon those cases in which this Court has permitted use for impeachment purposes of post-arrest statements that were inadmissible as evidence of guilt because of an officer's failure to follow *Miranda's* dictates.... Thus, although the State does not suggest petitioners' silence could be used as evidence of guilt, it contends that the need to present to the jury all information relevant to the truth of petitioners' exculpatory story fully justifies the cross-examination that is at issue.

Despite the importance of cross-examination, we have concluded that the *Miranda* decision compels rejection of the State's position. The warnings mandated by that case, as a prophylactic means of safeguarding Fifth Amendment rights ... require that a person taken into custody be advised immediately that he has the right to remain silent, that anything he says may be used against him, and that he has a right to retained or appointed counsel before submitting to interrogation. Silence in the wake of these warnings may be nothing more than the arrestee's exercise of these *Miranda* rights. Thus, every post-arrest silence is insolubly ambiguous because of what the State is required to advise the person arrested. ... Moreover, while it is true that the *Miranda* warnings contain no express assurance that silence will carry no penalty, such assurance is implicit to any person who receives the warnings. In such circumstances, it would be fundamentally unfair and a deprivation of due process to allow the arrested person's silence to be used to impeach an explanation subsequently offered at trial. ...

We hold that the use for impeachment purposes of petitioners' silence, at the time of arrest and after receiving *Miranda* warnings, violated the Due Process Clause of the Fourteenth Amendment.[11]

---

11. It goes almost without saying that the fact of post-arrest silence could be used by the prosecution to contradict a defendant who testifies to an exculpatory version of events and claims to have told the police the same version upon arrest. In that situation the fact of earlier silence would not be used to impeach the exculpatory story, but rather to challenge the defendant's testimony as to his behavior following arrest. ...

The State has not claimed that such use in the circumstances of this case might have been harmless error. Accordingly, petitioners' convictions are reversed and their causes remanded to the state courts for further proceedings not inconsistent with this opinion.

So ordered.[*]

[*] Justice Stevens wrote a dissenting opinion, which Justice Blackmun and Justice Rehnquist joined.

OREGON v. ELSTAD

470 U.S. 298, 105 S.Ct. 1285, 84 L.Ed.2d 222 (1985).

JUSTICE O'CONNOR delivered the opinion of the Court.

This case requires us to decide whether an initial failure of law enforcement officers to administer the warnings required by Miranda v. Arizona, 384 U.S. 436 (1966), without more, "taints" subsequent admissions made after a suspect has been fully advised of and has waived his *Miranda* rights. Respondent, Michael James Elstad, was convicted of burglary by an Oregon trial court. The Oregon Court of Appeals reversed, holding that respondent's signed confession, although voluntary, was rendered inadmissible by a prior remark made in response to questioning without benefit of *Miranda* warnings. We granted certiorari, 465 U.S. 1078 (1984), and we now reverse.

I

In December, 1981, the home of Mr. and Mrs. Gilbert Gross, in the town of Salem, Polk County, Ore., was burglarized. Missing were art objects and furnishings valued at $150,000. A witness to the burglary contacted the Polk County Sheriff's office, implicating respondent Michael Elstad, an 18-year-old neighbor and friend of the Grosses' teenage son. Thereupon, Officers Burke and McAllister went to the home of respondent Elstad, with a warrant for his arrest. Elstad's mother answered the door. She led the officers to her son's room where he lay on his bed, clad in shorts and listening to his stereo. The officers asked him to get dressed and to accompany them into the living room. Officer McAllister asked respondent's mother to step into the kitchen, where he explained that they had a warrant for her son's arrest for the burglary of a neighbor's residence. Officer Burke remained with Elstad in the living room. He later testified:

> "I sat down with Mr. Elstad and I asked him if he was aware of why Detective McAllister and myself were there to talk with him. He stated no, he had no idea why we were there. I then asked him if he knew a person by the name of Gross, and he said yes, he did, and also added that he heard that there was a robbery at the Gross house. And at that point I told Mr. Elstad that I felt he was involved in that, and he looked at me and stated, 'Yes, I was there.'" App. 19–20.

The officers then escorted Elstad to the back of the patrol car. As they were about to leave for the Polk County Sheriff's office, Elstad's father arrived home and came to the rear of the patrol car. The officers advised him that his son was a suspect in the burglary.

Officer Burke testified that Mr. Elstad became quite agitated, opened the rear door of the car and admonished his son: "I told you that you were going to get into trouble. You wouldn't listen to me. You never learn." Id., at 21.

Elstad was transported to the Sheriff's headquarters and approximately one hour later, Officers Burke and McAllister joined him in McAllister's office. McAllister then advised respondent for the first time of his *Miranda* rights, reading from a standard card. Respondent indicated he understood his rights, and, having these rights in mind, wished to speak with the officers. Elstad gave a full statement, explaining that he had known that the Gross family was out of town and had been paid to lead several acquaintances to the Gross residence and show them how to gain entry through a defective sliding glass door. The statement was typed, reviewed by respondent, read back to him for correction, initialed and signed by Elstad and both officers. As an afterthought, Elstad added and initialed the sentence, "After leaving the house Robby & I went back to [the] van & Robby handed me a small bag of grass." App. 42. Respondent concedes that the officers made no threats or promises either at his residence or at the Sheriff's office.

Respondent was charged with first-degree burglary. He was represented at trial by retained counsel. Elstad waived his right to a jury and his case was tried by a Circuit Court Judge. Respondent moved at once to suppress his oral statement and signed confession. He contended that the statement he made in response to questioning at his house "let the cat out of the bag," citing United States v. Bayer, 331 U.S. 532 (1947), and tainted the subsequent confession as "fruit of the poisonous tree," citing Wong Sun v. United States, 371 U.S. 471 (1963). The judge ruled that the statement, "I was there," had to be excluded because the defendant had not been advised of his *Miranda* rights. The written confession taken after Elstad's arrival at the Sheriff's office, however, was admitted in evidence. The court found:

> "[H]is written statement was given freely, voluntarily and knowingly by the defendant after he had waived his right to remain silent and have counsel present which waiver was evidenced by the card which the defendant had signed. [It] was not tainted in any way by the previous brief statement between the defendant and the Sheriff's Deputies that had arrested him." App. 45.

Elstad was found guilty of burglary in the first degree. He received a 5-year sentence and was ordered to pay $18,000 in restitution.

Following his conviction, respondent appealed to the Oregon Court of Appeals, relying on *Wong Sun* and *Bayer.* The State conceded that Elstad had been in custody when he made his statement, "I was there," and accordingly agreed that this statement was inadmissible as having been given without the prescribed

Miranda warnings. But the State maintained that any conceivable "taint" had been dissipated prior to the respondent's written confession by McAllister's careful administration of the requisite warnings. The Court of Appeals reversed respondent's conviction, identifying the crucial constitutional inquiry as "whether there was a sufficient break in the stream of events between [the] inadmissible statement and the written confession to insulate the latter statement from the effect of what went before." 61 Ore.App. 673, 676, 658 P.2d 552, 554 (1983). The Oregon court concluded:

> "Regardless of the absence of actual compulsion, the coercive impact of the unconstitutionally obtained statement remains, because in a defendant's mind it has sealed his fate. It is this impact that must be dissipated in order to make a subsequent confession admissible. In determining whether it has been dissipated, lapse of time, and change of place from the original surroundings are the most important considerations." Id., at 677, 658 P.2d, at 554.

Because of the brief period separating the two incidents, the "cat was sufficiently out of the bag to exert a coercive impact on [respondent's] later admissions." Id., at 678, 658 P.2d, at 555.

The State of Oregon petitioned the Oregon Supreme Court for review, and review was declined. This Court granted certiorari to consider the question whether the Self-Incrimination Clause of the Fifth Amendment requires the suppression of a confession, made after proper *Miranda* warnings and a valid waiver of rights, solely because the police had obtained an earlier voluntary but unwarned admission from the defendant.

II

The arguments advanced in favor of suppression of respondent's written confession rely heavily on metaphor. One metaphor, familiar from the Fourth Amendment context, would require that respondent's confession, regardless of its integrity, voluntariness, and probative value, be suppressed as the "tainted fruit of the poisonous tree" of the *Miranda* violation. A second metaphor questions whether a confession can be truly voluntary once the "cat is out of the bag." Taken out of context, each of these metaphors can be misleading. They should not be used to obscure fundamental differences between the role of the Fourth Amendment exclusionary rule and the function of *Miranda* in guarding against the prosecutorial use of compelled statements as prohibited by the Fifth Amendment. The Oregon court assumed and respondent here contends that a failure to administer *Miranda* warnings necessarily breeds the same consequences as police infringement of a constitutional right, so that evidence uncovered following an unwarned statement must be suppressed as "fruit of the poisonous tree." We believe this view misconstrues the nature of the protections afforded by *Miranda* warnings and therefore misreads the consequences of police failure to supply them.

A

Prior to *Miranda,* the admissibility of an accused's in custody statements was judged solely by whether they were "voluntary" within the meaning of the Due Process Clause. . . . If a suspect's statements had been obtained by "techniques and methods offensive to due process," Haynes v. Washington, 373 U.S. [503 (1963)], at 515, or under circumstances in which the suspect clearly had no opportunity to exercise "a free and unconstrained will," id., at 514, the statements would not be admitted. The Court in *Miranda* required suppression of many statements that would have been admissible under traditional due process analysis by presuming that statements made while in custody and without adequate warnings were protected by the Fifth Amendment. The Fifth Amendment, of course, is not concerned with nontestimonial evidence. . . . Nor is it concerned with moral and psychological pressures to confess emanating from sources other than official coercion. . . . Voluntary statements "remain a proper element in law enforcement." Miranda v. Arizona, 384 U.S., at 478. "Indeed, far from being prohibited by the Constitution, admissions of guilt by wrongdoers, if not coerced, are inherently desirable. . . . Absent some officially coerced self-accusation, the Fifth Amendment privilege is not violated by even the most damning admissions." United States v. Washington, 431 U.S. 181, 187 (1977). As the Court noted last Term in New York v. Quarles, 467 U.S. 649, 654 (1984) (footnote omitted):

> "The *Miranda* Court, however, presumed that interrogation in certain custodial circumstances is inherently coercive and . . . that statements made under those circumstances are inadmissible unless the suspect is specifically informed of his *Miranda* rights and freely decides to forgo those rights. The prophylactic *Miranda* warnings therefore are 'not themselves rights protected by the Constitution but [are] instead measures to insure that the right against compulsory self-incrimination [is] protected.' Michigan v. Tucker, 417 U.S. 433, 444 (1974); see Edwards v. Arizona, 451 U.S. 477, 492 (1981) (Powell, J., concurring). Requiring *Miranda* warnings before custodial interrogation provides 'practical reinforcement' for the Fifth Amendment right."

Respondent's contention that his confession was tainted by the earlier failure of the police to provide *Miranda* warnings and must be excluded as "fruit of the poisonous tree" assumes the existence of a constitutional violation. This figure of speech is drawn from Wong Sun v. United States, 371 U.S. 471 (1963), in which the Court held that evidence and witnesses discovered as a result of a search in violation of the Fourth Amendment must be excluded from evidence. The *Wong Sun* doctrine applies as well when the fruit of the Fourth Amendment violation is a confession. It is settled law that "a confession obtained through custodial interrogation after an illegal arrest should be excluded unless intervening events break the causal connection between the illegal arrest and the confession so that the confession is 'sufficiently an act of free will to purge the primary taint.' " Taylor v. Alabama, 457 U.S. 687, 690 (1982) (quoting Brown v. Illinois, 422 U.S. 590, 602 (1975)).

But as we explained in *Quarles* and *Tucker,* a procedural *Miranda* violation differs in significant respects from violations of the Fourth Amendment, which have traditionally mandated a broad application of the "fruits" doctrine. The purpose of the Fourth Amendment exclusionary rule is to deter unreasonable searches, no matter how probative their fruits. ... "The exclusionary rule, ... when utilized to effectuate the Fourth Amendment, serves interests and policies that are distinct from those it serves under the Fifth." [Brown v. Illinois, 422 U.S.], at 601. Where a Fourth Amendment violation "taints" the confession, a finding of voluntariness for the purposes of the Fifth Amendment is merely a threshold requirement in determining whether the confession may be admitted in evidence. ... Beyond this, the prosecution must show a sufficient break in events to undermine the inference that the confession was caused by the Fourth Amendment violation.

The *Miranda* exclusionary rule, however, serves the Fifth Amendment and sweeps more broadly than the Fifth Amendment itself. It may be triggered even in the absence of a Fifth Amendment violation. The Fifth Amendment prohibits use by the prosecution in its case in chief only of *compelled* testimony. Failure to administer *Miranda* warnings creates a presumption of compulsion. Consequently, unwarned statements that are otherwise voluntary within the meaning of the Fifth Amendment must nevertheless be excluded from evidence under *Miranda.* Thus, in the individual case, *Miranda's* preventive medicine provides a remedy even to the defendant who has suffered no identifiable constitutional harm.
. . .

But the *Miranda* presumption, though irrebuttable for purposes of the prosecution's case in chief, does not require that the statements and their fruits be discarded as inherently tainted. Despite the fact that patently *voluntary* statements taken in violation of *Miranda* must be excluded from the prosecution's case, the presumption of coercion does not bar their use for impeachment purposes on cross-examination. Harris v. New York, 401 U.S. 222 (1971). The Court in *Harris* rejected as an "extravagant extension of the Constitution," the theory that a defendant who had confessed under circumstances that made the confession inadmissible, could thereby enjoy the freedom to "deny every fact disclosed or discovered as a 'fruit' of his confession, free from confrontation with his prior statements" and that the voluntariness of his confession would be totally irrelevant. Id., at 225, and n. 2. Where an unwarned statement is preserved for use in situations that fall outside the sweep of the *Miranda* presumption, "the primary criterion of admissibility [remains] the 'old' due process voluntariness test." Schulhofer, Confessions and the Court, 79 Mich.L.Rev. 865, 877 (1981).

In Michigan v. Tucker, 417 U.S. 433 (1974), the Court was asked to extend the *Wong Sun* fruits doctrine to suppress the testimony of a witness for the prosecution whose identity was discovered as the result of a statement taken from the accused without benefit of full *Miranda* warnings. As in respondent's case, the breach of the *Miranda* procedures in *Tucker* involved no actual compulsion. The Court concluded that the unwarned questioning "did not abridge respondent's constitutional privilege ... but departed only from the prophylactic standards later laid down by this Court in *Miranda* to safeguard that privilege." 417 U.S., at 446. Since there was no actual infringement of the suspect's constitutional rights, the case was not controlled by the doctrine expressed in *Wong Sun* that fruits of a constitutional violation must be suppressed. In deciding "how sweeping the judicially imposed consequences" of a failure to administer *Miranda* warnings should be, 417 U.S., at 445, the *Tucker* Court noted that neither the general goal of deterring improper police conduct nor the Fifth Amendment goal of assuring trustworthy evidence would be served by suppression of the witness' testimony. The unwarned confession must, of course, be suppressed, but the Court ruled that introduction of the third-party witness' testimony did not violate Tucker's Fifth Amendment rights.

We believe that this reasoning applies with equal force when the alleged "fruit" of a noncoercive *Miranda* violation is neither a witness nor an article of evidence but the accused's own voluntary testimony. As in *Tucker,* the absence of any coercion or improper tactics undercuts the twin rationales—trustworthiness and deterrence—for a broader rule. Once warned, the suspect is free to exercise his own volition in deciding whether or not to make a statement to the authorities. The Court has often noted: " '[A] living witness is not to be mechanically equated with the proffer of inanimate evidentiary objects illegally seized. ... [T]he living witness is an individual human personality whose attributes of will, perception, memory and *volition* interact to determine what testimony he will give.' " United States v. Ceccolini, 435 U.S. 268, 277 (1978) (emphasis added) (quoting from Smith v. United States, 117 U.S.App.D.C. 1, 3–4, 324 F.2d 879, 881–882 (1963) (Burger, J.) (footnotes omitted), cert. denied, 377 U.S. 954 (1964)).

Because *Miranda* warnings may inhibit persons from giving information, this Court has determined that they need be administered only after the person is taken into "custody" or his freedom has otherwise been significantly restrained. Miranda v. Arizona, 384 U.S., at 478. Unfortunately, the task of defining "custody" is a slippery one, and "policemen investigating serious crimes [cannot realistically be expected to] make no errors whatsoever." Michigan v. Tucker, supra, at 446. If errors are made by law enforcement officers in administering the prophylactic *Miranda* procedures, they should not breed the same irremediable consequences as police infringement of the Fifth Amendment itself. It is an unwarranted extension of *Miranda* to hold that a simple failure to administer the warnings, unaccompanied by any actual coercion or other circumstances calculated to undermine the suspect's ability to exercise his free will so taints the investigatory process that a subsequent voluntary and informed waiver is ineffective for some indeterminate period. Though *Miranda* requires that the unwarned admission must be suppressed, the admissibility of any subsequent statement should turn in these circumstances solely on whether it is knowingly and voluntarily made.

B

The Oregon court, however, believed that the unwarned remark compromised the voluntariness of respondent's later confession. It was the court's view that the prior *answer* and not the unwarned questioning impaired respondent's ability to give a valid waiver and that only lapse of time and change of place could dissipate what it termed the "coercive impact" of the inadmissible statement. When a prior statement is actually coerced, the time that passes between confessions, the change in place of interrogations, and the change in identity of the interrogators all bear on whether that coercion has carried over into the second confession. . . . The failure of police to administer *Miranda* warnings does not mean that the statements received have actually been coerced, but only that courts will presume the privilege against compulsory self-incrimination has not been intelligently exercised. . . . Of the courts that have considered whether a properly warned confession must be suppressed because it was preceded by an unwarned but clearly voluntary admission, the majority have explicitly or implicitly recognized that . . . [the] requirement of a break in the stream of events is inapposite. In these circumstances, a careful and thorough administration of *Miranda* warnings serves to cure the condition that rendered the unwarned statement inadmissible. The warning conveys the relevant information and thereafter the suspect's choice whether to exercise his privilege to remain silent should ordinarily be viewed as an "act of free will." Wong Sun v. United States, 371 U.S., at 486.

The Oregon court nevertheless identified a subtle form of lingering compulsion, the psychological impact of the suspect's conviction that he has let the cat out of the bag and, in so doing, has sealed his own fate. But endowing the psychological effects of *voluntary* unwarned admissions with constitutional implications would, practically speaking, disable the police from obtaining the suspect's informed cooperation even when the official coercion proscribed by the Fifth Amendment played no part in either his warned or unwarned confessions. As the Court remarked in *Bayer:*

"[A]fter an accused has once let the cat out of the bag by confessing, no matter what the inducement, he is never thereafter free of the psychological and practical disadvantages of having confessed. He can never get the cat back in the bag. The secret is out for good. In such a sense, a later confession may always be looked upon as fruit of the first. But this Court has never gone so far as to hold that making a confession under circumstances which preclude its use, perpetually disables the confessor from making a usable one after those conditions have been removed." 331 U.S., at 540–541.

Even in such extreme cases as Lyons v. Oklahoma, 322 U.S. 596 (1944), in which police forced a full confession from the accused through unconscionable methods of interrogation, the Court has assumed that the coercive effect of the confession could, with time, be dissipated. ...

This Court has never held that the psychological impact of voluntary disclosure of a guilty secret qualifies as state compulsion or compromises the voluntariness of a subsequent informed waiver. The Oregon court, by adopting this expansive view of Fifth Amendment compulsion, effectively immunizes a suspect who responds to pre-*Miranda* warning questions from the consequences of his subsequent informed waiver of the privilege of remaining silent. See 61 Ore.App., at 679, 658 P.2d, at 555 (Gillette, P.J., concurring). This immunity comes at a high cost to legitimate law enforcement activity, while adding little desirable protection to the individual's interest in not being *compelled* to testify against himself. ... When neither the initial nor the subsequent admission is coerced, little justification exists for permitting the highly probative evidence of a voluntary confession to be irretrievably lost to the factfinder.

There is a vast difference between the direct consequences flowing from coercion of a confession by physical violence or other deliberate means calculated to break the suspect's will and the uncertain consequences of disclosure of a "guilty secret" freely given in response to an unwarned but noncoercive question, as in this case. Justice Brennan's contention,[*] that it is impossible to perceive any causal distinction between this case and one involving a confession that is coerced by torture is wholly unpersuasive. Certainly, in respondent's case, the causal connection between any psychological disadvantage created by his admission and his ultimate decision to cooperate is speculative and attenuated at best. It is difficult to tell with certainty what motivates a suspect to speak. A suspect's confession may be traced to factors as disparate as "a prearrest event such as a visit with a minister," Dunaway v. New

_____

[*] In a dissenting opinion.

York, 442 U.S. [200 (1979)], at 220 (Stevens, J., concurring), or an intervening event such as the exchange of words respondent had with his father. We must conclude that, absent deliberately coercive or improper tactics in obtaining the initial statement, the mere fact that a suspect has made an unwarned admission does not warrant a presumption of compulsion. A subsequent administration of *Miranda* warnings to a suspect who has given a voluntary but unwarned statement ordinarily should suffice to remove the conditions that precluded admission of the earlier statement. In such circumstances, the finder of fact may reasonably conclude that the suspect made a rational and intelligent choice whether to waive or invoke his rights.

III

Though belated, the reading of respondent's rights was undeniably complete. McAllister testified that he read the *Miranda* warnings aloud from a printed card and recorded Elstad's responses. There is no question that respondent knowingly and voluntarily waived his right to remain silent before he described his participation in the burglary. It is also beyond dispute that respondent's earlier remark was voluntary, within the meaning of the Fifth Amendment. Neither the environment nor the manner of either "interrogation" was coercive. The initial conversation took place at midday, in the living room area of respondent's own home, with his mother in the kitchen area, a few steps away. Although in retrospect the officers testified that respondent was then in custody, at the time he made his statement he had not been informed that he was under arrest. The arresting officers' testimony indicates that the brief stop in the living room before proceeding to the station house was not to interrogate the suspect but to notify his mother of the reason for his arrest. . . .

The state has conceded the issue of custody and thus we must assume that Burke breached *Miranda* procedures in failing to administer *Miranda* warnings before initiating the discussion in the living room. This breach may have been the result of confusion as to whether the brief exchange qualified as "custodial interrogation" or it may simply have reflected Burke's reluctance to initiate an alarming police procedure before McAllister had spoken with respondent's mother. Whatever the reason for Burke's oversight, the incident had none of the earmarks of coercion. . . . Nor did the officers exploit the unwarned admission to pressure respondent into waiving his right to remain silent.

Respondent, however, has argued that he was unable to give a fully *informed* waiver of his rights because he was unaware that his prior statement could not be used against him. Respondent suggests that Deputy McAllister, to cure this deficiency, should have added an additional warning to those given him at the Sheriff's office. Such a requirement is neither practicable nor constitutionally necessary. In many cases, a breach of *Miranda* procedures may not be identified as such until long after full *Miranda* warnings are administered and a valid confession obtained. ... The standard *Miranda* warnings explicitly inform the suspect of his right to consult a lawyer before speaking. Police officers are ill equipped to pinch-hit for counsel, construing the murky and difficult questions of when "custody" begins or whether a given unwarned statement will ultimately be held admissible. ...

This Court has never embraced the theory that a defendant's ignorance of the full consequences of his decisions vitiates their voluntariness. ... [W]e have not held that the *sine qua non* for a knowing and voluntary waiver of the right to remain silent is a full and complete appreciation of all of the consequences flowing from the nature and the quality of the evidence in the case.

IV

When police ask questions of a suspect in custody without administering the required warnings, *Miranda* dictates that the answers received be presumed compelled and that they be excluded from evidence at trial in the State's case in chief. The Court has carefully adhered to this principle, permitting a narrow exception only where pressing public safety concerns demanded. ... The Court today in no way retreats from the bright line rule of *Miranda*. We do not imply that good faith excuses a failure to administer *Miranda* warnings; nor do we condone inherently coercive police tactics or methods offensive to due process that render the initial admission involuntary and undermine the suspect's will to invoke his rights once they are read to him. A handful of courts has, however, applied our precedents relating to confessions obtained under coercive circumstances to situations involving wholly voluntary admissions, requiring a passage of time or break in events before a second, fully warned statement can be deemed voluntary. Far from establishing a rigid rule, we direct courts to avoid one; there is no warrant for presuming coercive effect where the suspect's initial inculpatory statement, though technically in violation of *Miranda*, was voluntary. The relevant inquiry is whether, in fact, the second statement was also voluntarily made. As in any such inquiry, the finder of fact must examine the surrounding circumstances and the entire course of police conduct with respect to the suspect in evaluating the voluntariness of his statements. The fact that a suspect chooses to speak after being informed of his rights is, of course, highly probative. We find that the dictates of *Miranda* and the goals of the Fifth Amendment proscription against use of compelled testimony are fully satisfied in the circumstances of this case by barring use of the unwarned statement in the case in chief. No further purpose is served by imputing "taint" to subsequent statements obtained pursuant to a voluntary and knowing waiver. We hold today that a suspect who has once responded to unwarned yet uncoercive questioning is not thereby disabled from waiving his rights and confessing after he has been given the requisite *Miranda* warnings.

The judgment of the Court of Appeals of Oregon is reversed, and the case is remanded for further proceedings not inconsistent with this opinion.

It is so ordered.[*]

---

[*] Justice Brennan wrote a dissenting opinion, which Justice Marshall joined. Justice Stevens also wrote a dissenting opinion.

SCHMERBER v. CALIFORNIA

384 U.S. 757, 86 S.Ct. 1826, 16 L.Ed.2d 908 (1966).

MR. JUSTICE BRENNAN delivered the opinion of the Court.

Petitioner was convicted in Los Angeles Municipal Court of the criminal offense of driving an automobile while under the influence of intoxicating liquor. He had been arrested at a hospital while receiving treatment for injuries suffered in an accident involving the automobile that he had apparently been driving. At the direction of a police officer, a blood sample was then withdrawn from petitioner's body by a physician at the hospital. The chemical analysis of this sample revealed a percent by weight of alcohol in his blood at the time of the offense which indicated intoxication, and the report of this analysis was admitted in evidence at the trial. Petitioner objected to receipt of this evidence of the analysis on the ground that the blood had been withdrawn despite his refusal, on the advice of his counsel, to consent to the test. He contended that in that circumstance the withdrawal of the blood and the admission of the analysis in evidence denied him due process of law under the Fourteenth Amendment, as well as specific guarantees of the Bill of Rights secured against the States by that Amendment: his privilege against self-incrimination under the Fifth Amendment; his right to counsel under the Sixth Amendment; and his right not to be subjected to unreasonable searches and seizures in violation of the Fourth Amendment. The Appellate Department of the California Superior Court rejected these contentions and affirmed the conviction. In view of constitutional decisions since we last considered these issues in Breithaupt v. Abram, 352 U.S. 432 ... we granted certiorari. We affirm.

I

THE DUE PROCESS CLAUSE CLAIM

Breithaupt was also a case in which police officers caused blood to be withdrawn from the driver of an automobile involved in an accident, and in which there was ample justification for the officer's conclusion that the driver was under the influence of alcohol. There, as here, the extraction was made by a physician in a simple, medically acceptable manner in a hospital environment. There, however, the driver was unconscious at the time the blood was withdrawn and hence had no opportunity to object to the procedure. We affirmed the conviction there resulting from the use of the test in evidence, holding that under such circumstances the withdrawal did not offend "that 'sense of justice' of which we spoke in Rochin v. California, 342 U.S. 165." 352 U.S., at 435. *Brei-*

773

thaupt thus requires the rejection of petitioner's due process argument, and nothing in the circumstances of this case [4] or in supervening events persuades us that this aspect of *Breithaupt* should be overruled.

II

THE PRIVILEGE AGAINST SELF-INCRIMINATION CLAIM

Breithaupt summarily rejected an argument that the withdrawal of blood and the admission of the analysis report involved in that state case violated the Fifth Amendment privilege of any person not to "be compelled in any criminal case to be a witness against himself," citing Twining v. New Jersey, 211 U.S. 78. But that case, holding that the protections of the Fourteenth Amendment do not embrace this Fifth Amendment privilege, has been succeeded by Malloy v. Hogan, 378 U.S. 1, 8. We there held that "[t]he Fourteenth Amendment secures against state invasion the same privilege that the Fifth Amendment guarantees against federal infringement—the right of a person to remain silent unless he chooses to speak in the unfettered exercise of his own will, and to suffer no penalty . . . for such silence." We therefore must now decide whether the withdrawal of the blood and admission in evidence of the analysis involved in this case violated petitioner's privilege. We hold that the privilege protects an accused only from being compelled to testify against himself, or otherwise provide the State with evidence of a testimonial or communicative nature,[5] and that the withdrawal of blood and use of the analysis in question in this case did not involve compulsion to these ends.

It could not be denied that in requiring petitioner to submit to the withdrawal and chemical analysis of his blood the State compelled him to submit to an attempt to discover evidence that might be used to prosecute him for a criminal offense. He submitted only after the police officer rejected his objection and directed the physician to proceed. The officer's direction to the physician to administer the test over petitioner's objection constituted compul-

---

4. We "cannot see that it should make any difference whether one states unequivocally that he objects or resorts to physical violence in protest or is in such condition that he is unable to protest." Breithaupt v. Abram, 352 U.S., at 441 (Warren, C.J., dissenting). It would be a different case if the police initiated the violence, refused to respect a reasonable request to undergo a different form of testing, or responded to resistance with inappropriate force. Compare the discussion at Part IV, infra.

5. A dissent suggests that the report of the blood test was "testimonial" or "communicative," because the test was performed in order to obtain the testimony of others, com-

municating to the jury facts about petitioner's condition. Of course, all evidence received in court is "testimonial" or "communicative" if these words are thus used. But the Fifth Amendment relates only to acts on the part of the person to whom the privilege applies, and we use these words subject to the same limitations. A nod or head-shake is as much a "testimonial" or "communicative" act in this sense as are spoken words. But the terms as we use them do not apply to evidence of acts noncommunicative in nature as to the person asserting the privilege, even though, as here, such acts are compelled to obtain the testimony of others.

sion for the purposes of the privilege. The critical question, then, is whether petitioner was thus compelled "to be a witness against himself."

If the scope of the privilege coincided with the complex of values it helps to protect, we might be obliged to conclude that the privilege was violated. In Miranda v. Arizona, ante, at 460, the Court said of the interests protected by the privilege: "All these policies point to one overriding thought: the constitutional foundation underlying the privilege is the respect a government—state or federal—must accord to the dignity and integrity of its citizens. To maintain a 'fair state-individual balance,' to require the government 'to shoulder the entire load' . . . to respect the inviolability of the human personality, our accusatory system of criminal justice demands that the government seeking to punish an individual produce the evidence against him by its own independent labors, rather than by the cruel, simple expedient of compelling it from his own mouth." The withdrawal of blood necessarily involves puncturing the skin for extraction, and the percent by weight of alcohol in that blood, as established by chemical analysis, is evidence of criminal guilt. Compelled submission fails on one view to respect the "inviolability of the human personality." Moreover, since it enables the State to rely on evidence forced from the accused, the compulsion violates at least one meaning of the requirement that the State procure the evidence against an accused "by its own independent labors."

As the passage in *Miranda* implicitly recognizes, however, the privilege has never been given the full scope which the values it helps to protect suggest. History and a long line of authorities in lower courts have consistently limited its protection to situations in which the State seeks to submerge those values by obtaining the evidence against an accused through "the cruel, simple expedient of compelling it from his own mouth. . . . In sum, the privilege is fulfilled only when the person is guaranteed the right 'to remain silent unless he chooses to speak in the unfettered exercise of his own will.' " Id. The leading case in this Court is Holt v. United States, 218 U.S. 245. There the question was whether evidence was admissible that the accused, prior to trial and over his protest, put on a blouse that fitted him. It was contended that compelling the accused to submit to the demand that he model the blouse violated the privilege. Mr. Justice Holmes, speaking for the Court, rejected the argument as "based upon an extravagant extension of the Fifth Amendment," and went on to say: "[T]he prohibition of compelling a man in a criminal court to be witness against himself is a prohibition of the use of physical or moral compulsion to extort communications from him, not an exclusion of his body as evidence when it may be material. The objection in principle would forbid a jury to look at a prisoner and compare his features with a photograph in proof." 218 U.S., at 252–253.

It is clear that the protection of the privilege reaches an accused's communications, whatever form they might take, and the compulsion of responses which are also communications, for example, compliance with a subpoena to produce one's papers. Boyd v. United States, 116 U.S. 616. On the other hand, both federal and state courts have usually held that it offers no protection against compulsion to submit to fingerprinting, photographing, or measurements, to write or speak for identification, to appear in court, to stand, to assume a stance, to walk, or to make a particular gesture. The distinction which has emerged, often expressed in different ways, is that the privilege is a bar against compelling "communications" or "testimony," but that compulsion which makes a suspect or accused the source of "real or physical evidence" does not violate it.

Although we agree that this distinction is a helpful framework for analysis, we are not to be understood to agree with past applications in all instances. There will be many cases in which such a distinction is not readily drawn. Some tests seemingly directed to obtain "physical evidence," for example, lie detector tests measuring changes in body function during interrogation, may actually be directed to eliciting responses which are essentially testimonial. To compel a person to submit to testing in which an effort will be made to determine his guilt or innocence on the basis of physiological responses, whether willed or not, is to evoke the spirit and history of the Fifth Amendment. Such situations call to mind the principle that the protection of the privilege "is as broad as the mischief against which it seeks to guard," Counselman v. Hitchcock, 142 U.S. 547, 562.

In the present case, however, no such problem of application is presented. Not even a shadow of testimonial compulsion upon or enforced communication by the accused was involved either in the extraction or in the chemical analysis. Petitioner's testimonial capacities were in no way implicated; indeed, his participation, except as a donor, was irrelevant to the results of the test, which depend on chemical analysis and on that alone.[9] Since the blood

---

9. This conclusion would not necessarily govern had the State tried to show that the accused had incriminated himself when told that he would have to be tested. Such incriminating evidence may be an unavoidable by-product of the compulsion to take the test, especially for an individual who fears the extraction or opposes it on religious grounds. If it wishes to compel persons to submit to such attempts to discover evidence, the State may have to forgo the advantage of any *testimonial* products of administering the test— products which would fall within the privilege. Indeed, there may be circumstances in which the pain, danger, or severity of an operation would almost inevitably cause a person to prefer confession to undergoing the "search," and nothing we say today should be taken as establishing the permissibility of compulsion in that case. But no such situation is presented in this case. . . .

Petitioner has raised a similar issue in this case, in connection with a police request that he submit to a "breathalyzer" test of air expelled from his lungs for alcohol content. He refused the request, and evidence of his refusal was admitted in evidence without objection. He argues that the introduction of this evidence and a comment by the prosecutor in closing argument upon his refusal is ground for reversal under Griffin v. California, 380 U.S. 609. We think general Fifth

test evidence, although an incriminating product of compulsion, was neither petitioner's testimony nor evidence relating to some communicative act or writing by the petitioner, it was not inadmissible on privilege grounds.

III

THE RIGHT TO COUNSEL CLAIM

This conclusion also answers petitioner's claim that, in compelling him to submit to the test in face of the fact that his objection was made on the advice of counsel, he was denied his Sixth Amendment right to the assistance of counsel. Since petitioner was not entitled to assert the privilege, he has no greater right because counsel erroneously advised him that he could assert it. His claim is strictly limited to the failure of the police to respect his wish, reinforced by counsel's advice, to be left inviolate. No issue of counsel's ability to assist petitioner in respect of any rights he did possess is presented. The limited claim thus made must be rejected.

IV

THE SEARCH AND SEIZURE CLAIM

In *Breithaupt*, as here, it was also contended that the chemical analysis should be excluded from evidence as the product of an unlawful search and seizure in violation of the Fourth and Fourteenth Amendments. The Court did not decide whether the extraction of blood in that case was unlawful, but rejected the claim on the basis of Wolf v. Colorado, 338 U.S. 25. That case had held that the Constitution did not require, in state prosecutions for state crimes, the exclusion of evidence obtained in violation of the Fourth Amendment's provisions. We have since overruled *Wolf* in that respect, holding in Mapp v. Ohio, 367 U.S. 643, that the exclusionary rule adopted for federal prosecutions in Weeks v. United States, 232 U.S. 383, must also be applied in criminal prosecutions in state courts. The question is squarely presented therefore, whether the chemical analysis introduced in evidence in this case should have been excluded as the product of an unconstitutional search and seizure.

The overriding function of the Fourth Amendment is to protect personal privacy and dignity against unwarranted intrusion by the State. In *Wolf* we recognized "[t]he security of one's privacy against arbitrary intrusion by the police" as being "at the core of the Fourth Amendment" and "basic to a free society." 338 U.S., at 27.

Amendment principles, rather than the particular holding of *Griffin*, would be applicable in these circumstances, see Miranda v. Arizona, ante, at 468, n. 37. Since trial here was conducted after our decision in Malloy v. Ho-

gan, supra, making those principles applicable to the States, we think petitioner's contention is foreclosed by his failure to object on this ground to the prosecutor's question and statements.

We reaffirmed that broad view of the Amendment's purpose in applying the federal exclusionary rule to the States in *Mapp*.

The values protected by the Fourth Amendment thus substantially overlap those the Fifth Amendment helps to protect. History and precedent have required that we today reject the claim that the Self-Incrimination Clause of the Fifth Amendment requires the human body in all circumstances to be held inviolate against state expeditions seeking evidence of crime. But if compulsory administration of a blood test does not implicate the Fifth Amendment, it plainly involves the broadly conceived reach of a search and seizure under the Fourth Amendment. That Amendment expressly provides that "[t]he right of the people to be secure in their *persons,* houses, papers, and effects, against unreasonable searches and seizures, shall not be violated . . . ." (Emphasis added.) It could not reasonably be argued, and indeed respondent does not argue, that the administration of the blood test in this case was free of the constraints of the Fourth Amendment. Such testing procedures plainly constitute searches of "persons," and depend antecedently upon seizures of "persons," within the meaning of that Amendment.

Because we are dealing with intrusions into the human body rather than with state interferences with property relationships or private papers—"houses, papers, and effects"—we write on a clean slate. Limitations on the kinds of property which may be seized under warrant, as distinct from the procedures for search and the permissible scope of search, are not instructive in this context. We begin with the assumption that once the privilege against self-incrimination has been found not to bar compelled intrusions into the body for blood to be analyzed for alcohol content, the Fourth Amendment's proper function is to constrain, not against all intrusions as such, but against intrusions which are not justified in the circumstances, or which are made in an improper manner. In other words, the questions we must decide in this case are whether the police were justified in requiring petitioner to submit to the blood test, and whether the means and procedures employed in taking his blood respected relevant Fourth Amendment standards of reasonableness.

In this case, as will often be true when charges of driving under the influence of alcohol are pressed, these questions arise in the context of an arrest made by an officer without a warrant. Here, there was plainly probable cause for the officer to arrest petitioner and charge him with driving an automobile while under the influence of intoxicating liquor. The police officer who arrived at the scene shortly after the accident smelled liquor on petitioner's breach, and testified that petitioner's eyes were "bloodshot, watery, sort of a glassy appearance." The officer saw petitioner again at the hospital, within two hours of the accident. There he noticed similar symptoms of drunkenness. He thereupon informed petitioner "that he was under arrest and that he was entitled to the services of an attorney, and that he could remain silent, and that anything that he told me would be used against him in evidence."

While early cases suggest that there is an unrestricted "right on the part of the Government, always recognized under English and American law, to search the person of the accused when legally arrested to discover and seize the fruits or evidences of crime," Weeks v. United States, 232 U.S. 383, 392 ... the mere fact of a lawful arrest does not end our inquiry. The suggestion of these cases apparently rests on two factors—first, there may be more immediate danger of concealed weapons or of destruction of evidence under the direct control of the accused ... ; second, once a search of the arrested person for weapons is permitted, it would be both impractical and unnecessary to enforcement of the Fourth Amendment's purpose to attempt to confine the search to those objects alone.... Whatever the validity of these considerations in general, they have little applicability with respect to searches involving intrusions beyond the body's surface. The interests in human dignity and privacy which the Fourth Amendment protects forbid any such intrusions on the mere chance that desired evidence might be obtained. In the absence of a clear indication that in fact such evidence will be found, these fundamental human interests require law officers to suffer the risk that such evidence may disappear unless there is an immediate search.

Although the facts which established probable cause to arrest in this case also suggested the required relevance and likely success of a test of petitioner's blood for alcohol, the question remains whether the arresting officer was permitted to draw these inferences himself, or was required instead to procure a warrant before proceeding with the test. Search warrants are ordinarily required for searches of dwellings, and, absent an emergency, no less could be required where intrusions into the human body are concerned. The requirement that a warrant be obtained is a requirement that the inferences to support the search "be drawn by a neutral and detached magistrate instead of being judged by the officer engaged in the often competitive enterprise of ferreting out crime." Johnson v. United States, 333 U.S. 10, 13–14.... The importance of informed, detached and deliberate determinations of the issue whether or not to invade another's body in search of evidence of guilt is indisputable and great.

The officer in the present case, however, might reasonably have believed that he was confronted with an emergency, in which the delay necessary to obtain a warrant, under the circumstances, threatened "the destruction of evidence," Preston v. United States, 376 U.S. 364, 367. We are told that the percentage of alcohol in the blood begins to diminish shortly after drinking stops, as the body functions to eliminate it from the system. Particularly in a case such as this, where time had to be taken to bring the accused to a hospital and to investigate the scene of the accident, there was no time to seek out a magistrate and secure a warrant. Given these special facts, we conclude that the attempt to secure evidence of blood-alcohol content in this case was an appropriate incident to petitioner's arrest.

Similarly, we are satisfied that the test chosen to measure petitioner's blood-alcohol level was a reasonable one. Extraction of blood samples for testing is a highly effective means of determining the degree to which a person is under the influence of alcohol. . . . Such tests are a commonplace in these days of periodic physical examinations and experience with them teaches that the quantity of blood extracted is minimal, and that for most people the procedure involves virtually no risk, trauma, or pain. Petitioner is not one of the few who on grounds of fear, concern for health, or religious scruple might prefer some other means of testing, such as the "breathalyzer" test petitioner refused, see n. 9, supra. We need not decide whether such wishes would have to be respected.

Finally, the record shows that the test was performed in a reasonable manner. Petitioner's blood was taken by a physician in a hospital environment according to accepted medical practices. We are thus not presented with the serious questions which would arise if a search involving use of a medical technique, even of the most rudimentary sort, were made by other than medical personnel or in other than a medical environment—for example, if it were administered by police in the privacy of the stationhouse. To tolerate searches under these conditions might be to invite an unjustified element of personal risk of infection and pain.

We thus conclude that the present record shows no violation of petitioner's right under the Fourth and Fourteenth Amendments to be free of unreasonable searches and seizures. It bears repeating, however, that we reach this judgment only on the facts of the present record. The integrity of an individual's person is a cherished value of our society. That we today hold that the Constitution does not forbid the States minor intrusions into an individual's body under stringently limited conditions in no way indicates that it permits more substantial intrusions, or intrusions under other conditions.

Affirmed.

MR. JUSTICE BLACK with whom MR. JUSTICE DOUGLAS joins, dissenting.

I would reverse petitioner's conviction. I agree with the Court that the Fourteenth Amendment made applicable to the States the Fifth Amendment's provision that "No person . . . shall be compelled in any criminal case to be a witness against himself . . . ." But I disagree with the Court's holding that California did not violate petitioner's constitutional right against self-incrimination when it compelled him, against his will, to allow a doctor to puncture his blood vessels in order to extract a sample of blood and analyze it for alcoholic content, and then used that analysis as evidence to convict petitioner of a crime.

The Court admits that "the State compelled [petitioner] to submit to an attempt to discover evidence [in his blood] that might be [and was] used to prosecute him for a criminal offense." To reach the conclusion that compelling a person to give his blood to help the State convict him is not equivalent to compelling him to be a witness against himself strikes me as quite an extraordinary feat. The Court, however, overcomes what had seemed to me to be an insuperable obstacle to its conclusion by holding that

> ". . . the privilege protects an accused only from being compelled to testify against himself, or otherwise provide the State with evidence of a testimonial or communicative nature, and that the withdrawal of blood and use of the analysis in question in this case did not involve compulsion to these ends." (Footnote omitted.)

I cannot agree that this distinction and reasoning of the Court justify denying petitioner his Bill of Rights' guarantee that he must not be compelled to be a witness against himself.

In the first place it seems to me that the compulsory extraction of petitioner's blood for analysis so that the person who analyzed it could give evidence to convict him had both a "testimonial" and a "communicative nature." The sole purpose of this project which proved to be successful was to obtain "testimony" from some person to prove that petitioner had alcohol in his blood at the time he was arrested. And the purpose of the project was certainly "communicative" in that the analysis of the blood was to supply information to enable a witness to communicate to the court and jury that petitioner was more or less drunk.

I think it unfortunate that the Court rests so heavily for its very restrictive reading of the Fifth Amendment's privilege against self-incrimination on the words "testimonial" and "communicative." These words are not models of clarity and precision as the Court's rather labored explication shows. Nor can the Court, so far as I know, find precedent in the former opinions of this Court for using these particular words to limit the scope of the Fifth Amendment's protection. There is a scholarly precedent, however, in the late Professor Wigmore's learned treatise on evidence. He used "testimonial" which, according to the latest edition of his treatise revised by McNaughton, means "communicative" (8 Wigmore, Evidence § 2263 (McNaughton rev. 1961), p. 378), as a key word in his vigorous and extensive campaign designed to keep the privilege against self-incrimination "within limits the strictest possible." 8 Wigmore, Evidence § 2251 (3d ed. 1940), p. 318. Though my admiration for Professor Wigmore's scholarship is great, I regret to see the word he used to narrow the Fifth Amendment's protection play such a major part in any of this Court's opinions.

I am happy that the Court itself refuses to follow Professor Wigmore's implication that the Fifth Amendment goes no further than to bar the use of forced self-incriminating statements coming from a "person's own lips." It concedes, as it must so long as Boyd v. United States, 116 U.S. 616, stands, that the Fifth Amendment bars a State from compelling a person to produce papers he has that might tend to incriminate him. It is a strange hierarchy of values that allows the State to extract a human being's blood to convict him of a crime because of the blood's content but proscribes compelled production of his lifeless papers. Certainly there could be few papers that would have any more "testimonial" value to convict a man of drunken driving than would an analysis of the alcoholic content of a human being's blood introduced in evidence at a trial for driving while under the influence of alcohol. In such a situation blood, of course, is not oral testimony given by an accused but it can certainly "communicate" to a court and jury the fact of guilt.

The Court itself, at page 764, expresses its own doubts, if not fears, of its own shadowy distinction between compelling "physical evidence" like blood which it holds does not amount to compelled self-incrimination, and "eliciting responses which are essentially testimonial." ...

. . .

... Petitioner Schmerber has undoubtedly been compelled to give his blood "to furnish evidence against himself," yet the Court holds that this is not forbidden by the Fifth Amendment. With all deference I must say that the Court here gives the Bill of Rights' safeguard against compulsory self-incrimination a construction that would generally be considered too narrow and technical even in the interpretation of an ordinary commercial contract.

. . .

MR. JUSTICE FORTAS, dissenting.

I would reverse. In my view, petitioner's privilege against self-incrimination applies. I would add that, under the Due Process Clause, the State, in its role as prosecutor, has no right to extract blood from an accused or anyone else, over his protest. As prosecutor, the State has no right to commit any kind of violence upon the person, or to utilize the results of such a tort, and the extraction of blood, over protest, is an act of violence. Cf. Chief Justice Warren's dissenting opinion in Breithaupt v. Abram, 352 U.S. 432, 440.[*]

---

[*] Justice Harlan wrote a brief concurring opinion, which Justice Stewart joined. Chief Justice Warren and Justice Douglas wrote dissenting opinions.

496 U.S. 582, 110 S.Ct. 2638, 110 L.Ed.2d 528 (1990).

JUSTICE BRENNAN delivered the opinion of the Court, except as to Part III–C.

We must decide in this case whether various incriminating utterances of a drunk-driving suspect, made while performing a series of sobriety tests, constitute testimonial responses to custodial interrogation for purposes of the Self-Incrimination Clause of the Fifth Amendment.

I

During the early morning hours of November 30, 1986, a patrol officer spotted respondent Inocencio Muniz and a passenger parked in a car on the shoulder of a highway. When the officer inquired whether Muniz needed assistance, Muniz replied that he had stopped the car so he could urinate. The officer smelled alcohol on Muniz's breath and observed that Muniz's eyes were glazed and bloodshot and his face was flushed. The officer then directed Muniz to remain parked until his condition improved, and Muniz gave assurances that he would do so. But as the officer returned to his vehicle, Muniz drove off. After the officer pursued Muniz down the highway and pulled him over, the officer asked Muniz to perform three standard field sobriety tests: a "horizontal gaze nystagmus" test, a "walk and turn" test, and a "one leg stand" test.[1] Muniz performed these tests poorly, and he informed the officer that he had failed the tests because he had been drinking.

The patrol officer arrested Muniz and transported him to the West Shore facility of the Cumberland County Central Booking Center. Following its routine practice for receiving persons suspected of driving while intoxicated, the Booking Center videotaped the ensuing proceedings. Muniz was informed that his actions and voice were being recorded, but he was not at this time (nor had he been previously) advised of his rights under Miranda v. Arizona, 384 U.S. 436 (1966). Officer Hosterman first asked Muniz his name,

---

1. The "horizontal gaze nystagmus" test measures the extent to which a person's eyes jerk as they follow an object moving from one side of the person's field of vision to the other. The test is premised on the understanding that, whereas everyone's eyes exhibit some jerking while turning to the side, when the subject is intoxicated "the onset of the jerking occurs after fewer degrees of turning, and the jerking at more extreme angles becomes more distinct." 1 R. Erwin et al., Defense of Drunk Driving Cases § 8A.99, pp. 8A–43, 8A–45 (1989). The "walk and turn" test requires the subject to walk heel to toe along a straight line for nine paces, pivot, and then walk back heel to toe along the line for another nine paces. The subject is required to count each pace aloud from one to nine. The "one leg stand" test requires the subject to stand on one leg with the other leg extended in the air for 30 seconds, while counting aloud from 1 to 30.

address, height, weight, eye color, date of birth, and current age. He responded to each of these questions, stumbling over his address and age. The officer then asked Muniz, "Do you know what the date was of your sixth birthday?" After Muniz offered an inaudible reply, the officer repeated, "When you turned six years old, do you remember what the date was?" Muniz responded, "No, I don't."

Officer Hosterman next requested Muniz to perform each of the three sobriety tests that Muniz had been asked to perform earlier during the initial roadside stop. The videotape reveals that his eyes jerked noticeably during the gaze test, that he did not walk a very straight line, and that he could not balance himself on one leg for more than several seconds. During the latter two tests, he did not complete the requested verbal counts from 1 to 9 and from 1 to 30. Moreover, while performing these tests, Muniz "attempted to explain his difficulties in performing the various tasks, and often requested further clarification of the tasks he was to perform." 377 Pa.Super. 382, 390, 547 A.2d 419, 423 (1988).

Finally, Officer Deyo asked Muniz to submit to a breathalyzer test designed to measure the alcohol content of his expelled breath. Officer Deyo read to Muniz the Commonwealth's Implied Consent Law, 75 Pa.Cons.Stat. § 1547 (1987), and explained that under the law his refusal to take the test would result in automatic suspension of his driver's license for one year. Muniz asked a number of questions about the law, commenting in the process about his state of inebriation. Muniz ultimately refused to take the breath test. At this point, Muniz was for the first time advised of his *Miranda* rights. Muniz then signed a statement waiving his rights and admitted in response to further questioning that he had been driving while intoxicated.

Both the video and audio portions of the videotape were admitted into evidence at Muniz's bench trial, along with the arresting officer's testimony that Muniz failed the roadside sobriety tests and made incriminating remarks at that time. Muniz was convicted of driving under the influence of alcohol in violation of 75 Pa.Cons.Stat. § 3731(a)(1) (1987). Muniz filed a motion for a new trial, contending that the court should have excluded the testimony relating to the field sobriety tests and the videotape taken at the booking center "because they were incriminating and completed prior to [Muniz's] receiving his Miranda warnings." App. to Pet. for Cert. C–5–C–6. The trial court denied the motion, holding that " 'requesting a driver, suspected of driving under the influence of alcohol, to perform physical tests or take a breath analysis does not violate [his] privilege against self-incrimination because [the] evidence procured is of a physical nature rather than testimonial, and therefore no *Miranda* warnings are required.' " Id., at C–6, quoting Commonwealth v. Benson, 280 Pa.Super. 20, 29, 421 A.2d 383, 387 (1980).

On appeal, the Superior Court of Pennsylvania reversed. . . . Concluding that the audio portion of the videotape should have been suppressed in its entirety, the court reversed Muniz's conviction and remanded the case for a new trial. After the Pennsylvania Supreme Court denied the Commonwealth's application for review, 522 Pa. 575, 559 A.2d 36 (1989), we granted certiorari. 493 U.S. 916 (1989).

II

The Self-Incrimination Clause of the Fifth Amendment provides that no "person . . . shall be compelled in any criminal case to be a witness against himself." Although the text does not delineate the ways in which a person might be made a "witness against himself," cf. Schmerber v. California, 384 U.S. 757, 761–762, n. 6 (1966), we have long held that the privilege does not protect a suspect from being compelled by the State to produce "real or physical evidence." Id., at 764. Rather, the privilege "protects an accused only from being compelled to testify against himself, or otherwise provide the State with evidence of a testimonial or communicative nature." Id., at 761. "[I]n order to be testimonial, an accused's communication must itself, explicitly or implicitly, relate a factual assertion or disclose information. Only then is a person compelled to be a 'witness' against himself." Doe v. United States, 487 U.S. 201, 210 (1988).

In Miranda v. Arizona, 384 U.S. 436 (1966), we reaffirmed our previous understanding that the privilege against self-incrimination protects individuals not only from legal compulsion to testify in a criminal courtroom but also from "informal compulsion exerted by law-enforcement officers during in-custody questioning." Id., at 461. Of course, voluntary statements offered to police officers "remain a proper element in law enforcement." Id., at 478. . . .

This case implicates both the "testimonial" and "compulsion" components of the privilege against self-incrimination in the context of pretrial questioning. Because Muniz was not advised of his *Miranda* rights until after the videotaped proceedings at the booking center were completed, any verbal statements that were both testimonial in nature and elicited during custodial interrogation should have been suppressed. We focus first on Muniz's responses to the initial informational questions, then on his questions and utterances while performing the physical dexterity and balancing tests, and finally on his questions and utterances surrounding the breathalyzer test.

III

In the initial phase of the recorded proceedings, Officer Hosterman asked Muniz his name, address, height, weight, eye color, date of birth, current age, and the date of his sixth birthday. Both the delivery and content of Muniz's answers were incriminating. As the state court found, "Muniz's videotaped responses ... certainly led the finder of fact to infer that his confusion and failure to speak clearly indicated a state of drunkenness that prohibited him from safely operating his vehicle." 377 Pa.Super., at 390, 547 A.2d, at 423. The Commonwealth argues, however, that admission of Muniz's answers to these questions does not contravene Fifth Amendment principles because Muniz's statement regarding his sixth birthday was not "testimonial" and his answers to the prior questions were not elicited by custodial interrogation. We consider these arguments in turn.

A

We agree with the Commonwealth's contention that Muniz's answers are not rendered inadmissible by *Miranda* merely because the slurred nature of his speech was incriminating. The physical inability to articulate words in a clear manner due to "the lack of muscular coordination of his tongue and mouth," Brief for Petitioner 16, is not itself a testimonial component of Muniz's responses to Officer Hosterman's introductory questions. In Schmerber v. California, supra, we drew a distinction between "testimonial" and "real or physical evidence" for purposes of the privilege against self-incrimination. We noted that in Holt v. United States, 218 U.S. 245, 252–253 (1910), Justice Holmes had written for the Court that " '[t]he prohibition of compelling a man in a criminal court to be witness against himself is a prohibition of the use of physical or moral compulsion to extort communications from him, not an exclusion of his body as evidence when it may be material.' " 384 U.S., at 763. We also acknowledged that "both federal and state courts have usually held that it offers no protection against compulsion to submit to fingerprinting, photographing, or measurements, to write or speak for identification, to appear in court, to stand, to assume a stance, to walk, or to make a particular gesture." Id., at 764. Embracing this view of the privilege's contours, we held that "the privilege is a bar against compelling 'communications' or 'testimony,' but that compulsion which makes a suspect or accused the source of 'real or physical evidence' does not violate it." Ibid. Using this "helpful framework for analysis," ibid., we held that a person suspected of driving while intoxicated could be forced to provide a blood sample, because that sample was "real or physical evidence" outside the scope of the privilege and the sample was obtained in manner by which "[p]etitioner's testimonial capacities were in no way implicated." Id., at 765.

We have since applied the distinction between "real or physical" and "testimonial" evidence in other contexts where the evidence could be produced only through some volitional act on the part of the suspect. In United States v. Wade, 388 U.S. 218 (1967), we held that a suspect could be compelled to participate in a lineup and to repeat a phrase provided by the police so that witnesses could view him and listen to his voice. We explained that requiring his presence and speech at a lineup reflected "compulsion of the accused to exhibit his physical characteristics, not compulsion to disclose any knowledge he might have." Id., at 222 . . . . In Gilbert v. California, 388 U.S. 263 (1967), we held that a suspect could be compelled to provide a handwriting exemplar, explaining that such an exemplar, "in contrast to the content of what is written, like the voice or body itself, is an identifying physical characteristic outside [the privilege's] protection." Id., at 266–267. And in United States v. Dionisio, 410 U.S. 1 (1973), we held that suspects could be compelled to read a transcript in order to provide a voice exemplar, explaining that the "voice recordings were to be used solely to measure the physical properties of the witnesses' voices, not for the testimonial or communicative content of what was to be said." Id., at 7.

Under *Schmerber* and its progeny, we agree with the Commonwealth that any slurring of speech and other evidence of lack of muscular coordination revealed by Muniz's responses to Officer Hosterman's direct questions constitute nontestimonial components of those responses. Requiring a suspect to reveal the physical manner in which he articulates words, like requiring him to reveal the physical properties of the sound produced by his voice, see *Dionisio,* supra, does not, without more, compel him to provide a "testimonial" response for purposes of the privilege.

B

This does not end our inquiry, for Muniz's answer to the sixth birthday question was incriminating, not just because of his delivery, but also because of his answer's *content;* the trier of fact could infer from Muniz's answer (that he did not *know* the proper date) that his mental state was confused. The Commonwealth and United States as *amicus curiae* argue that this incriminating inference does not trigger the protections of the Fifth Amendment privilege because the inference concerns "the physiological functioning of [Muniz's] brain," Brief for Petitioner 21, which is asserted to be every bit as "real or physical" as the physiological makeup of his blood and the timbre of his voice.

But this characterization addresses the wrong question; that the "fact" to be inferred might be said to concern the physical status of Muniz's brain merely describes the way in which the inference is incriminating. The correct question for present purposes is whether the incriminating inference of mental confusion is drawn from a testimonial act or from physical evidence. In *Schmerber,* for example, we held that the police could compel a suspect to provide a blood sample in order to determine the physical makeup of his blood and thereby draw an inference about whether he was intoxicated. This compulsion was outside of the Fifth Amendment's protection, not simply because the evidence concerned the suspect's physical body, but rather because the evidence was obtained in a manner that did not entail any testimonial act on the part of the suspect: "Not even a shadow of testimonial compulsion upon or enforced communication by the accused was involved either in the extraction or in the chemical analysis." 384 U.S., at 765. In contrast, had the police instead asked the suspect directly whether his blood contained a high concentration of alcohol, his affirmative response would have been testimonial even though it would have been used to draw the same inference concerning his physiology. See ibid. ("[T]he blood test evidence . . . was neither [the suspect's] testimony nor evidence relating to some communicative act"). In this case, the question is not whether a suspect's "impaired mental faculties" can fairly be characterized as an aspect of his physiology, but rather whether Muniz's response to the sixth birthday question that gave rise to the inference of such an impairment was testimonial in nature.

We recently explained in Doe v. United States, 487 U.S. 201 (1988), that "in order to be testimonial, an accused's communication must itself, explicitly or implicitly, relate a factual assertion or disclose information." Id., at 210. . . . After canvassing the purposes of the privilege recognized in prior cases, we concluded that "[t]hese policies are served when the privilege is asserted to spare the accused from having to reveal, directly or indirectly, his knowledge of facts relating him to the offense or from having to share his thoughts and beliefs with the Government." Id., at 213.

This definition of testimonial evidence reflects an awareness of the historical abuses against which the privilege against self-incrimination was aimed. "Historically, the privilege was intended to prevent the use of legal compulsion to extract from the accused a sworn communication of facts which would incriminate him. Such was the process of the ecclesiastical courts and the Star Chamber— the inquisitorial method of putting the accused upon his oath and compelling him to answer questions designed to uncover uncharged offenses, without evidence from another source. The major thrust of the policies undergirding the privilege is to prevent such compulsion." Id., at 212 (citations omitted) . . . . At its core, the privilege reflects our fierce " 'unwillingness to subject those suspected of crime to the cruel trilemma of self-accusation, perjury or contempt,' " Doe, supra, at 212 (citation omitted), that defined the operation of the Star Chamber, wherein suspects were forced to choose between revealing incriminating private thoughts and forsaking their oath by committing perjury. . . .

We need not explore the outer boundaries of what is "testimonial" today, for our decision flows from the concept's core meaning. Because the privilege was designed primarily to prevent "a recurrence of the Inquisition and the Star Chamber, even if not in their stark brutality," Ullmann v. United States, 350 U.S. 422, 428 (1956), it is evident that a suspect is "compelled . . . to be a witness against himself'' at least whenever he must face the modern-day analog of the historic trilemma—either during a criminal trial where a sworn witness faces the identical three choices, or during custodial interrogation where, as we explained in *Miranda,* the choices are analogous and hence raise similar concerns.[10] Whatever else it may include, therefore, the definition of "testimonial" evidence articulated in *Doe* must encompass all responses to questions that, if asked of a sworn suspect during a criminal trial, could place the suspect in the "cruel trilemma." This conclusion is consistent with our recognition in *Doe* that "[t]he vast majority of verbal statements thus will be testimonial" because "[t]here are very few instances in which a verbal statement, either oral or written, will not convey information or assert facts." 487 U.S., at 213. Whenever a suspect is asked for a response requiring him to communicate an express or implied assertion of fact or belief, the suspect confronts the "trilemma" of truth, falsity, or silence and hence the response (whether based on truth or falsity) contains a testimonial component.

This approach accords with each of our post-*Schmerber* cases finding that a particular oral or written response to express or implied questioning was nontestimonial; the questions presented in these cases did not confront the suspects with this trilemma. As we noted in *Doe,* supra, at 210–211, the cases upholding compelled writing and voice exemplars did not involve situations in which suspects were asked to communicate any personal beliefs or knowledge of facts, and therefore the suspects were not forced to choose between truthfully or falsely revealing their thoughts. We carefully noted in Gilbert v. California, 388 U.S. 263 (1967), for example, that a "mere handwriting exemplar, *in contrast to the content of what is written,* like the voice or body itself, is an identifying physical characteristic outside [the privilege's] protection." Id., at 266–267 (emphasis added). Had the suspect been asked to provide a writing sample of his own composition, the content of the writing would have reflected his assertion of facts or beliefs and hence would have been testimonial; but in *Gilbert* "[n]o claim [was] made that the content of the exemplars was testimonial or communicative matter." Id., at 267. And in *Doe,* the suspect was asked merely to sign a consent form waiving a privacy interest in foreign bank records. Because the consent form spoke in the hypothetical

---

10. During custodial interrogation, the pressure on the suspect to respond flows not from the threat of contempt sanctions, but rather from the "inherently compelling pressures which work to undermine the individual's will to resist and to compel him to speak where he would not otherwise do so freely." Miranda v. Arizona, 384 U.S. 436, 467 (1966). Moreover, false testimony does not give rise directly to sanctions (either religious sanctions for lying under oath or prosecutions for perjury), but only indirectly (false testimony might itself prove incriminating, either be- cause it links (albeit falsely) the suspect to the crime or because the prosecution might later prove at trial that the suspect lied to the police, giving rise to an inference of guilty conscience). Despite these differences, however, "[w]e are satisfied that all the principles embodied in the privilege apply to informal compulsion exerted by law-enforcement officers during in-custody questioning." Id., at 461; see id., at 458 (noting "intimate connection between the privilege against self-incrimination and police custodial questioning").

and did not identify any particular banks, accounts, or private records, the form neither "communicate[d] any factual assertions, implicit or explicit, [n]or convey[ed] any information to the Government." 487 U.S., at 215. We concluded, therefore, that compelled execution of the consent directive did not "forc[e] [the suspect] to express the contents of his mind," id., at 210, n. 9, but rather forced the suspect only to make a "nonfactual statement." Id., at 213, n. 11.

In contrast, the sixth birthday question in this case required a testimonial response. When Officer Hosterman asked Muniz if he knew the date of his sixth birthday and Muniz, for whatever reason, could not remember or calculate that date, he was confronted with the trilemma. By hypothesis, the inherently coercive environment created by the custodial interrogation precluded the option of remaining silent, see n. 10, supra. Muniz was left with the choice of incriminating himself by admitting that he did not then know the date of his sixth birthday, or answering untruthfully by reporting a date that he did not then believe to be accurate (an incorrect guess would be incriminating as well as untruthful). The content of his truthful answer supported an inference that his mental faculties were impaired, because his assertion (he did not know the date of his sixth birthday) was different from the assertion (he knew the date was [correct date]) that the trier of fact might reasonably have expected a lucid person to provide. Hence, the incriminating inference of impaired mental faculties stemmed, not just from the fact that Muniz slurred his response, but also from a testimonial aspect of that response.[13]

The state court held that the sixth birthday question constituted an unwarned interrogation for purposes of the privilege against self-incrimination ... and that Muniz's answer was incriminating.... The Commonwealth does not question either conclusion. Therefore, because we conclude that Muniz's response to the sixth birthday question was testimonial, the response should have been suppressed.

C

The Commonwealth argues that the seven questions asked by Officer Hosterman just *prior* to the sixth birthday question—regarding Muniz's name, address, height, weight, eye color, date of birth, and current age—did not constitute custodial interrogation as we have defined the term in *Miranda* and subsequent cases. In *Miranda,* the Court referred to "interrogation" as actual "question-

---

13. The Commonwealth's protest that it had no investigatory interest in the actual date of Muniz's sixth birthday ... is inapposite. The critical point is that the Commonwealth had an investigatory interest in Muniz's assertion of belief that was communicated by his answer to the question. Putting it another way, the Commonwealth may not have cared about the *correct* answer, but it cared about *Muniz's* answer. The incriminating inference stems from the then-existing contents of Muniz's mind as evidenced by his assertion of his knowledge at that time.

. . .

ing initiated by law enforcement officers." 384 U.S., at 444. We have since clarified that definition, finding that the "goals of the *Miranda* safeguards could be effectuated if those safeguards extended not only to express questioning, but also to 'its functional equivalent.'" Arizona v. Mauro, 481 U.S. 520, 526 (1987). In Rhode Island v. Innis, 446 U.S. 291 (1980), the Court defined the phrase "functional equivalent" of express questioning to include "any words or actions on the part of the police (other than those normally attendant to arrest and custody) that the police should know are reasonably likely to elicit an incriminating response from the suspect. The latter portion of this definition focuses primarily upon the perceptions of the suspect, rather than the intent of the police." Id., at 301 (footnotes omitted)....

We disagree with the Commonwealth's contention that Officer Hosterman's first seven questions regarding Muniz's name, address, height, weight, eye color, date of birth, and current age do not qualify as custodial interrogation as we defined the term in *Innis,* supra, merely because the questions were not intended to elicit information for investigatory purposes. ...We agree with *amicus* United States, however, that Muniz's answers to these first seven questions are nonetheless admissible because the questions fall within a "routine booking question" exception which exempts from *Miranda's* coverage questions to secure the "'biographical data necessary to complete booking or pretrial services.'" Brief for the United States as *Amicus Curiae* 12, quoting United States v. Horton, 873 F.2d 180, 181, n. 2 (CA8 1989). The state court found that the first seven questions were "requested for record-keeping purposes only," App. B16, and therefore the questions appear reasonably related to the police's administrative concerns. In this context, therefore, the first seven questions asked at the Booking Center fall outside the protections of *Miranda* and the answers thereto need not be suppressed.

IV

During the second phase of the videotaped proceedings, Officer Hosterman asked Muniz to perform the same three sobriety tests that he had earlier performed at roadside prior to his arrest: the "horizontal gaze nystagmus" test, the "walk and turn" test, and the "one leg stand" test. While Muniz was attempting to comprehend Officer Hosterman's instructions and then perform the requested sobriety tests, Muniz made several audible and incriminating statements. Muniz argued to the state court that both the videotaped performance of the physical tests themselves and the audiorecorded verbal statements were introduced in violation of *Miranda.*

The court refused to suppress the videotaped evidence of Muniz's paltry performance on the physical sobriety tests, reasoning that "[r]equiring a driver to perform physical [sobriety] tests ... does not violate the privilege against self-incrimination because the evidence procured is of a physical nature rather than testimonial." 377 Pa.Super., at 387, 547 A.2d, at 422 (quoting Commonwealth v. Benson, 280 Pa.Super., at 29, 421 A.2d, at 387). With respect to Muniz's verbal statements, however, the court concluded that "none of Muniz's utterances were spontaneous, voluntary verbalizations," 377 Pa.Super., at 390, 547 A.2d, at 423, and because they were "elicited before Muniz received his *Miranda* warnings, they should have been excluded as evidence." Ibid.

We disagree. Officer Hosterman's dialogue with Muniz concerning the physical sobriety tests consisted primarily of carefully scripted instructions as to how the tests were to be performed. These instructions were not likely to be perceived as calling for any verbal response and therefore were not "words or actions" constituting custodial interrogation, with two narrow exceptions not relevant here. The dialogue also contained limited and carefully worded inquiries as to whether Muniz understood those instructions, but these focused inquiries were necessarily "attendant to" the police procedure held by the court to be legitimate. Hence, Muniz's incriminating utterances during this phase of the videotaped proceedings were "voluntary" in the sense that they were not elicited in response to custodial interrogation. . . .

Similarly, we conclude that *Miranda* does not require suppression of the statements Muniz made when asked to submit to a breathalyzer examination. Officer Deyo read Muniz a prepared script explaining how the test worked, the nature of Pennsylvania's Implied Consent Law, and the legal consequences that would ensue should he refuse. Officer Deyo then asked Muniz whether he understood the nature of the test and the law and whether he would like to submit to the test. Muniz asked Officer Deyo several questions concerning the legal consequences of refusal, which Deyo answered directly, and Muniz then commented upon his state of inebriation. 377 Pa.Super., at 387, 547 A.2d, at 422. After offering to take the test only after waiting a couple of hours or drinking some water, Muniz ultimately refused.

We believe that Muniz's statements were not prompted by an interrogation within the meaning of *Miranda,* and therefore the absence of *Miranda* warnings does not require suppression of these statements at trial. As did Officer Hosterman when administering the three physical sobriety tests, see supra, at 19–20, Officer Deyo carefully limited her role to providing Muniz with relevant information about the breathalyzer test and the Implied Consent Law. She questioned Muniz only as to whether he understood her instructions and wished to submit to the test. These limited and focused inquiries were necessarily "attendant to" the legitimate police procedure, see *Neville,* supra, at 564, n. 15, and were not likely to be perceived as calling for any incriminating response.

V

We agree with the state court's conclusion that *Miranda* requires suppression of Muniz's response to the question regarding the date of his sixth birthday, but we do not agree that the entire audio portion of the videotape must be suppressed. Accordingly, the court's judgment reversing Muniz's conviction is vacated, and the case is remanded for further proceedings not inconsistent with this opinion.

It is so ordered.

CHIEF JUSTICE REHNQUIST, with whom JUSTICE WHITE, JUSTICE BLACKMUN and JUSTICE STEVENS join, concurring in part, concurring in the result in part, and dissenting in part.

I join Parts I, II, III–A, and IV of the Court's opinion. In addition, although I agree with the conclusion in Part III–C that the seven "booking" questions should not be suppressed. I do so for a reason different from that of Justice Brennan. I dissent from the Court's conclusion that Muniz's response to the "sixth birthday question" should have been suppressed.

The Court holds that the sixth birthday question Muniz was asked required a testimonial response, and that its admission at trial therefore violated Muniz's privilege against compulsory self-incrimination. The Court says that

> "[w]hen Officer Hosterman asked Muniz if he knew the date of his sixth birthday and Muniz, for whatever reason, could not remember or calculate that date, he was confronted with the trilemma [i.e. the ' "trilemma" of truth, falsity, or silence,' see ante, at 597] . . . . Muniz was left with the choice of incriminating himself by admitting that he did not then know the date of his sixth birthday, or answering untruthfully by reporting a date that he did not then believe to be accurate (an incorrect guess would be incriminating as well as untruthful)." Ante, at 598–599.

As an assumption about human behavior, this statement is wrong. Muniz would no more have felt compelled to fabricate a false date than one who cannot read the letters on an eye chart feels compelled to fabricate false letters; nor does a wrong guess call into question a speaker's veracity. The Court's statement is also a flawed predicate on which to base its conclusion that Muniz' answer to this question was "testimonial" for purposes of the Fifth Amendment.

The need for the use of the human voice does not automatically make an answer testimonial . . . any more than does the fact that a question calls for the exhibition of one's handwriting in written characters. . . .

The sixth birthday question here was an effort on the part of the police to check how well Muniz was able to do a simple mathematical exercise.... If the police may require Muniz to use his body in order to demonstrate the level of his physical coordination, there is no reason why they should not be able to require him to speak or write in order to determine his mental coordination. That was all that was sought here. Since it was permissible for the police to extract and examine a sample of Schmerber's blood to determine how much that part of his system had been affected by alcohol, I see no reason why they may not examine the functioning of Muniz's mental processes for the same purpose.

Surely if it were relevant, a suspect might be asked to take an eye examination in the course of which he might have to admit that he could not read the letters on the third line of the chart. At worst, he might utter a mistaken guess. Muniz likewise might have attempted to guess the correct response to the sixth birthday question instead of attempting to calculate the date or answer "I don't know." But the potential for giving a bad guess does not subject the suspect to the truth-falsity-silence predicament that renders a response testimonial and, therefore, within the scope of the Fifth Amendment privilege.

For substantially the same reasons, Muniz's responses to the videotaped "booking" questions were not testimonial and do not warrant application of the privilege. Thus, it is unnecessary to determine whether the questions fall within the "routine booking question" exception to *Miranda* Justice Brennan recognizes.

I would reverse in its entirety the judgment of the Superior Court of Pennsylvania. But given the fact that five members of the Court agree that Muniz's response to the sixth birthday question should have been suppressed, I agree that the judgment of the Superior Court should be vacated so that on remand, the court may consider whether admission of the response at trial was harmless error.[*]

[*] Justice Marshall wrote an opinion concurring in part and dissenting in part.

WINSTON v. LEE

470 U.S. 753, 105 S.Ct. 1611, 84 L.Ed.2d 662 (1985).

JUSTICE BRENNAN delivered the opinion of the Court.

Schmerber v. California, 384 U.S. 757 (1966), held *inter alia,* that a State may, over the suspect's protest, have a physician extract blood from a person suspected of drunken driving without violation of the suspect's right secured by the Fourth Amendment not to be subjected to unreasonable searches and seizures. However, *Schmerber* cautioned: "That we today hold that the Constitution does not forbid the States' minor intrusions into an individual's body under stringently limited conditions in no way indicates that it permits more substantial intrusions, or intrusions under other conditions." Id., at 772. In this case, the Commonwealth of Virginia seeks to compel the respondent Rudolph Lee, who is suspected of attempting to commit armed robbery, to undergo a surgical procedure under a general anesthetic for removal of a bullet lodged in his chest. Petitioners allege that the bullet will provide evidence of respondent's guilt or innocence. We conclude that the procedure sought here is an example of the "more substantial intrusion" cautioned against in *Schmerber,* and hold that to permit the procedure would violate respondent's right to be secure in his person guaranteed by the Fourth Amendment.

I

A

At approximately 1 a.m. on July 18, 1982, Ralph E. Watkinson was closing his shop for the night. As he was locking the door, he observed someone armed with a gun coming toward him from across the street. Watkinson was also armed and when he drew his gun, the other person told him to freeze. Watkinson then fired at the other person, who returned his fire. Watkinson was hit in the legs, while the other individual, who appeared to be wounded in his left side, ran from the scene. The police arrived on the scene shortly thereafter, and Watkinson was taken by ambulance to the emergency room of the Medical College of Virginia (MCV) Hospital.

Approximately 20 minutes later, police officers responding to another call found respondent eight blocks from where the earlier shooting occurred. Respondent was suffering from a gunshot wound to his left chest area and told the police that he had been shot when two individuals attempted to rob him. An ambulance took respondent to the MCV Hospital. Watkinson was still in the MCV emergency room and, when respondent entered that room, said "[t]hat's the man that shot me." App. 14. After an investigation, the police decided that respondent's story of having been himself the victim of a robbery was untrue and charged respondent with attempted robbery, malicious wounding, and two counts of using a firearm in the commission of a felony.

B

The Commonwealth shortly thereafter moved in state court for an order directing respondent to undergo surgery to remove an object thought to be a bullet lodged under his left collarbone. The court conducted several evidentiary hearings on the motion. At the first hearing, the Commonwealth's expert testified that the surgical procedure would take 45 minutes and would involve a three to four percent chance of temporary nerve damage, a one percent chance of permanent nerve damage, and a one-tenth of one percent chance of death. At the second hearing, the expert testified that on reexamination of respondent, he discovered that the bullet was not "back inside close to the nerves and arteries," id., at 52, as he originally had thought. Instead, he now believed the bullet to be located "just beneath the skin." Id., at 57. He testified that the surgery would require an incision of only one and one-half centimeters (slightly more than one-half inch), could be performed under local anesthesia, and would result in "no danger on the basis that there's no general anesthesia employed." Id., at 51.

The state trial judge granted the motion to compel surgery. Respondent petitioned the Virginia Supreme Court for a writ of prohibition and/or a writ of habeas corpus, both of which were denied. Respondent then brought an action in the United States District Court for the Eastern District of Virginia to enjoin the pending operation on Fourth Amendment grounds. The court refused to issue a preliminary injunction, holding that respondent's cause had little likelihood of success on the merits. 551 F.Supp. 247, 247–253 (1982).

On October 18, 1982, just before the surgery was scheduled, the surgeon ordered that X rays be taken of respondent's chest. The X rays revealed that the bullet was in fact lodged two and one-half to three centimeters (approximately one inch) deep in muscular tissue in respondent's chest, substantially deeper than had been thought when the state court granted the motion to compel surgery. The surgeon now believed that a general anesthetic would be desirable for medical reasons.

Respondent moved the state trial court for a rehearing based on the new evidence. After holding an evidentiary hearing, the state trial court denied the rehearing and the Virginia Supreme Court affirmed. Respondent then returned to federal court, where he moved to alter or amend the judgment previously entered against him. After an evidentiary hearing, the District Court enjoined the threatened surgery. 551 F.Supp., at 253–261 (supplemental opinion). A divided panel of the Court of Appeals for the Fourth Circuit affirmed. 717 F.2d 888 (1983). We granted certiorari, 466 U.S. 935 (1984), to consider whether a State may consistently with the Fourth Amendment compel a suspect to undergo surgery of this kind in a search for evidence of a crime.

II

The Fourth Amendment protects "expectations of privacy," see Katz v. United States, 389 U.S. 347 (1967)—the individual's legitimate expectations that in certain places and at certain times he has "the right to be let alone—the most comprehensive of rights and the right most valued by civilized men." Olmstead v. United States, 277 U.S. 438, 478 (1928) (Brandeis, J., dissenting). Putting to one side the procedural protections of the warrant requirement, the Fourth Amendment generally protects the "security" of "persons, houses, papers, and effects" against official intrusions up to the point where the community's need for evidence surmounts a specified standard, ordinarily "probable cause." Beyond this point, it is ordinarily justifiable for the community to demand that the individual give up some part of his interest in privacy and security to advance the community's vital interests in law enforcement; such a search is generally "reasonable" in the Amendment's terms.

A compelled surgical intrusion into an individual's body for evidence, however, implicates expectations of privacy and security of such magnitude that the intrusion may be "unreasonable" even if likely to produce evidence of a crime. In Schmerber v. California, 384 U.S. 757 (1966), we addressed a claim that the State had breached the Fourth Amendment's protection of the "right of the people to be secure in their *persons* ... against unreasonable searches and seizures" (emphasis added) when it compelled an individual suspected of drunken driving to undergo a blood test....

. . .

The reasonableness of surgical intrusions beneath the skin depends on a case-by-case approach, in which the individual's interests in privacy and security are weighed against society's interests in conducting the procedure. In a given case, the question whether the community's need for evidence outweighs the substantial privacy interests at stake is a delicate one admitting of few categorical answers. We believe that *Schmerber*, however, provides the appropriate framework of analysis for such cases.

Schmerber recognized that the ordinary requirements of the Fourth Amendment would be the threshold requirements for conducting this kind of surgical search and seizure. We noted the importance of probable cause.... And we pointed out: "Search warrants are ordinarily required for searches of dwellings, and, absent an emergency, no less could be required where intrusions into the human body are concerned. ... The importance of informed, detached and deliberate determinations of the issue whether or not to invade another's body in search of evidence of guilt is indisputable and great." Id., at 770.

Beyond these standards, *Schmerber's* inquiry considered a number of other factors in determining the "reasonableness" of the blood test. A crucial factor in analyzing the magnitude of the intrusion in *Schmerber* is the extent to which the procedure may threaten the safety or health of the individual. "[F]or most people [a blood test] involves virtually no risk, trauma, or pain." Id., at 771. Moreover, all reasonable medical precautions were taken and no unusual or untested procedures were employed in *Schmerber*; the procedure was performed "by a physician in a hospital environment according to accepted medical practices." Ibid. Notwithstanding the existence of probable cause, a search for evidence of a crime may be unjustifiable if it endangers the life or health of the suspect.

Another factor is the extent of intrusion upon the individual's dignitary interests in personal privacy and bodily integrity. Intruding into an individual's living room ... eavesdropping upon an individual's telephone conversations ... or forcing an individual to accompany police officers to the police station ... typically do not injure the physical person of the individual. Such intrusions do, however, damage the individual's sense of personal privacy and security and are thus subject to the Fourth Amendment's dictates. In noting that a blood test was "a commonplace in these days of periodic physical examinations," 384 U.S., at 771, *Schmerber* recognized society's judgment that blood tests do not constitute an unduly extensive imposition on an individual's personal privacy and bodily integrity.

Weighed against these individual interests is the community's interest in fairly and accurately determining guilt or innocence. This interest is of course of great importance. We noted in *Schmerber* that a blood test is "a highly effective means of determining the degree to which a person is under the influence of alcohol." Id., at 771. Moreover, there was "a clear indication that in fact [desired] evidence [would] be found" if the blood test were undertaken. Id., at 770. Especially given the difficulty of proving drunkenness by other means, these considerations showed that results of the blood test were of vital importance if the State were to enforce its drunken driving laws. In *Schmerber*, we concluded that this state interest was sufficient to justify the intrusion, and the compelled blood test was thus "reasonable" for Fourth Amendment purposes.

III

Applying the *Schmerber* balancing test in this case, we believe that the Court of Appeals reached the correct result. The Commonwealth plainly had probable cause to conduct the search. In addition, all parties apparently agree that respondent has had a full measure of procedural protections and has been able fully to litigate the difficult medical and legal questions necessarily involved in analyzing the reasonableness of a surgical incision of this magnitude. Our inquiry therefore must focus on the extent of the intrusion on respondent's privacy interests and on the State's need for the evidence.

The threats to the health or safety of respondent posed by the surgery are the subject of sharp dispute between the parties. Before the new revelations of October 18, the District Court found that the procedure could be carried out "with virtually no risk to [respondent]." 551 F.Supp., at 252. On rehearing, however, with new evidence before it, the District Court held that "the risks previously involved have increased in magnitude even as new risks are being added." Id., at 260.

The Court of Appeals examined the medical evidence in the record and found that respondent would suffer some risks associated with the surgical procedure. One surgeon had testified that the difficulty of discovering the exact location of the bullet "could require extensive probing and retracting of the muscle tissue," carrying with it "the concomitant risks of injury to the muscle as well as injury to the nerves, blood vessels and other tissue in the chest and pleural cavity." 717 F.2d, at 900. The court further noted that "the greater intrusion and the larger incisions increase the risks of infection." Ibid. Moreover, there was conflict in the testimony concerning the nature and the scope of the operation. One surgeon stated that it would take 15–20 minutes, while another predicted the procedure could take up to two and one-half hours. Ibid. The court properly took the resulting uncertainty about the medical risks into account.

Both lower courts in this case believed that the proposed surgery, which for purely medical reasons required the use of a general anesthetic, would be an "extensive" intrusion on respondent's personal privacy and bodily integrity. Ibid. When conducted with the consent of the patient, surgery requiring general anesthesia is not necessarily demeaning or intrusive. In such a case, the surgeon is carrying out the patient's own will concerning the patient's body and the patient's right to privacy is therefore preserved. In this case, however, the Court of Appeals noted that the Commonwealth proposes to take control of respondent's body, to "drug this citizen—not yet convicted of a criminal offense—with narcotics and barbiturates into a state of unconsciousness," id., at 901, and then to search beneath his skin for evidence of a crime. This kind of surgery involves a virtually total divestment of respondent's ordinary control over surgical probing beneath his skin.

The other part of the balance concerns the Commonwealth's need to intrude into respondent's body to retrieve the bullet. The Commonwealth claims to need the bullet to demonstrate that it was fired from Watkinson's gun, which in turn would show that respondent was the robber who confronted Watkinson. However, although we recognize the difficulty of making determinations in advance as to the strength of the case against respondent, petitioners' assertions of a compelling need for the bullet are hardly persuasive. The very circumstances relied on in this case to demonstrate probable cause to believe that evidence will be found tend to vitiate the Commonwealth's need to compel respondent to undergo surgery. The Commonwealth has available substantial additional evidence that respondent was the individual who accosted Watkinson on the night of the robbery. No party in this case suggests that Watkinson's entirely spontaneous identification of respondent at the hospital would be inadmissible. In addition, petitioners can no doubt prove that Watkinson [sic-Lee?] was found a few blocks from Watkinson's store shortly after the incident took place. And petitioners can certainly show that the location of the bullet (under respondent's left collarbone) seems to correlate with Watkinson's report that the robber "jerked" to the left. App. 13. The fact that the Commonwealth has available such substantial evidence of the origin of the bullet restricts the need for the Commonwealth to compel respondent to undergo the contemplated surgery.

In weighing the various factors in this case, we therefore reach the same conclusion as the courts below. The operation sought will intrude substantially on respondent's protected interests. The medical risks of the operation, although apparently not extremely severe, are a subject of considerable dispute; the very uncertainty militates against finding the operation to be "reasonable." In addition, the intrusion on respondent's privacy interests entailed by the operation can only be characterized as severe. On the other hand, although the bullet may turn out to be useful to the Commonwealth in prosecuting respondent, the Commonwealth has failed to demonstrate a compelling need for it. We believe that in these circumstances the Commonwealth has failed to demonstrate that it would be "reasonable" under the terms of the Fourth Amendment to search for evidence of this crime by means of the contemplated surgery.

IV

The Fourth Amendment is a vital safeguard of the right of the citizen to be free from unreasonable governmental intrusions into any area in which he has a reasonable expectation of privacy. Where the Court has found a lesser expectation of privacy ... or where the search involves a minimal intrusion on privacy interests ... the Court has held that the Fourth Amendment's protections are correspondingly less stringent. Conversely, however, the Fourth Amendment's command that searches be "reasonable" requires that when the State seeks to intrude upon an area in which our society recognizes a significantly heightened privacy interest, a more sub-

stantial justification is required to make the search "reasonable."
Applying these principles, we hold that the proposed search in this
case would be "unreasonable" under the Fourth Amendment.

    Affirmed.[*]

[*] Chief Justice Burger wrote a brief concurring opinion. Justice Blackmun and Justice Rehnquist concurred in the judgment.

ANDRESEN v. MARYLAND

427 U.S. 463, 96 S.Ct. 2737, 49 L.Ed.2d 627 (1976).

MR. JUSTICE BLACKMUN delivered the opinion of the Court.

This case presents the issue whether the introduction into evidence of a person's business records, seized during a search of his offices, violates the Fifth Amendment's command that "[n]o person . . . shall be compelled in any criminal case to be a witness against himself." We also must determine whether the particular searches and seizures here were "unreasonable" and thus violated the prohibition of the Fourth Amendment.

I

In early 1972, a Bi-County Fraud Unit, acting under the joint auspices of the State's Attorneys' Offices of Montgomery and Prince George's Counties, Md., began an investigation of real estate settlement activities in the Washington, D.C., area. At the time, petitioner Andresen was an attorney who, as a sole practitioner, specialized in real estate settlements in Montgomery County. During the Fraud Unit's investigation, his activities came under scrutiny, particularly in connection with a transaction involving Lot 13T in the Potomac Woods subdivision of Montgomery County. The investigation, which included interviews with the purchaser, the mortgage holder, and other lienholders of Lot 13T, as well as an examination of county land records, disclosed that petitioner, acting as settlement attorney, had defrauded Standard-Young Associates, the purchaser of Lot 13T. Petitioner had represented that the property was free of liens and that, accordingly, no title insurance was necessary, when in fact, he knew that there were two outstanding liens on the property. In addition, investigators learned that the lienholders, by threatening to foreclose their liens, had forced a halt to the purchaser's construction on the property. When Standard-Young had confronted petitioner with this information, he responded by issuing, as an agent of a title insurance company, a title policy guaranteeing clear title to the property. By this action, petitioner also defrauded that insurance company by requiring it to pay the outstanding liens.

The investigators, concluding that there was probable cause to believe that petitioner had committed the state crime of false pretenses, see Md.Ann.Code, Art. 27, § 140 (1976), against Standard-Young, applied for warrants to search petitioner's law office and the separate office of Mount Vernon Development Corporation, of which petitioner was incorporator, sole shareholder, resident agent, and director. The application sought permission to search for specified documents pertaining to the sale and conveyance of Lot 13T. A judge of the Sixth Judicial Circuit of Montgomery County concluded that there was probable cause and issued the warrants.

The searches of the two offices were conducted simultaneously during daylight hours on October 13, 1972. Petitioner was present during the search of his law office and was free to move about. Counsel for him was present during the latter half of the search. Between 2% and 3% of the files in the office were seized. A single investigator, in the presence of a police officer, conducted the search of Mount Vernon Development Corporation. This search, taking about four hours, resulted in the seizure of less than 5% of the corporation's files.

Petitioner eventually was charged, partly by information and partly by indictment, with the crime of false pretenses, based on his misrepresentation to Standard-Young concerning Lot 13T, and with fraudulent misappropriation by a fiduciary, based on similar false claims made to three home purchasers. Before trial began, petitioner moved to suppress the seized documents. The trial court held a full suppression hearing. At the hearing, the State returned to petitioner 45 of the 52 items taken from the offices of the corporation. The trial court suppressed six other corporation items on the ground that there was no connection between them and the crimes charged. The net result was that the only item seized from the corporation's offices that was not returned by the State or suppressed was a single file labelled "Potomac Woods General." In addition, the State returned to petitioner seven of the 28 items seized from his law office, and the trial court suppressed four other law office items based on its determination that there was no connection between them and the crime charged.

With respect to all the items not suppressed or returned, the trial court ruled that admitting them into evidence would not violate the Fifth and Fourth Amendments. It reasoned that the searches and seizures did not force petitioner to be a witness against himself because he had not been required to produce the seized documents, nor would he be compelled to authenticate them. Moreover, the search warrants were based on probable cause, and the documents not returned or suppressed were either directly related to Lot 13T, and therefore within the express language of the warrants, or properly seized and otherwise admissible to show a pattern of criminal conduct relevant to the charge concerning Lot 13T.

At trial, the State proved its case primarily by public land records and by records provided by the complaining purchasers, lienholders, and the title insurance company. It did introduce into evidence, however, a number of the seized items. Three documents from the "Potomac Woods General" file, seized during the search of petitioner's corporation, were admitted. These were notes in the handwriting of an employee who used them to prepare abstracts in the course of his duties as a title searcher and law clerk. The notes concerned deeds of trust affecting the Potomac Woods subdivision and related to the transaction involving Lot 13T.[2] Five items seized from petitioner's law office were also admitted. One contained information relating to the transactions with one of the defrauded home buyers. The second was a file partially devoted to the Lot 13T transaction; among the documents were settlement statements, the deed conveying the property to Standard-Young Associates, and the original and a copy of a notice to the buyer about releases of liens. The third item was a file devoted exclusively to Lot 13T. The fourth item consisted of a copy of a deed of trust, dated March 27, 1972, from the seller of certain lots in the Potomac Woods subdivision to a lienholder. The fifth item contained drafts of documents and memoranda written in petitioner's handwriting.

After a trial by jury, petitioner was found guilty upon five counts of false pretenses and three counts of fraudulent misappropriation by a fiduciary. He was sentenced to eight concurrent two-year prison terms.

On appeal to the Court of Special Appeals of Maryland, four of the five false pretenses counts were reversed because the indictment had failed to allege intent to defraud, a necessary element of the state offense. Only the count pertaining to Standard-Young's purchase of Lot 13T remained. With respect to this count of false pretenses and the three counts of misappropriation by a fiduciary, the Court of Special Appeals rejected petitioner's Fourth and Fifth Amendment Claims. Specifically, it held that the warrants were supported by probable cause, that they did not authorize a general search in violation of the Fourth Amendment, and that the items admitted into evidence against petitioner at trial were within the scope of the warrants or were otherwise properly seized. It agreed with the trial court that the search had not violated petitioner's Fifth Amendment rights because petitioner had not been compelled to do anything. 24 Md.App. 128, 331 A.2d 78 (1975).

We granted certiorari limited to the Fourth and Fifth Amendment issues. 423 U.S. 822 (1975).

II

The Fifth Amendment, made applicable to the States by the Fourteenth Amendment, Malloy v. Hogan, 378 U.S. 1, 8 (1964), provides that "[n]o person ... shall be compelled in any criminal case to be a witness against himself." As the Court often has noted,

---

2. It is established that the privilege against self-incrimination may not be invoked with respect to corporate records. ... It appears, however, that the records seized at the corporation's office were really not corporate records, but were records generated by petitioner's practice as a real estate lawyer. ...

the development of this protection was in part a response to certain historical practices, such as ecclesiastical inquisitions and the proceedings of the Star Chamber, "which placed a premium on compelling subjects of the investigation to admit guilt from their own lips." Michigan v. Tucker, 417 U.S. 433, 440 (1974). ... The "historic function" of the privilege has been to protect a " 'natural individual from compulsory incrimination through his own testimony or personal records.' " Bellis v. United States, 417 U.S. 85, 89–90 (1974), quoting from United States v. White, 322 U.S. 694, 701 (1944).

There is no question that the records seized from petitioner's offices and introduced against him were incriminating. Moreover, it is undisputed that some of these business records contain statements made by petitioner. ... The question, therefore, is whether the seizure of these business records, and their admission into evidence at his trial, compelled petitioner to testify against himself in violation of the Fifth Amendment. This question may be said to have been reserved in Warden v. Hayden, 387 U.S. 294, 302–303 (1967), and it was adverted to in United States v. Miller, 425 U.S. 435, 441 n. 3 (1976).

Petitioner contends that "the Fifth Amendment prohibition against compulsory self-incrimination applies as well to personal business papers seized from his offices as it does to the same papers being required to be produced under a subpoena." Brief for Petitioner 9. He bases his argument, naturally, on dicta in a number of cases which imply, or state, that the search for and seizure of a person's private papers violate the privilege against self-incrimination. Thus, in Boyd v. United States, 116 U.S. 616, 633 (1886), the Court said: "[W]e have been unable to perceive that the seizure of a man's private books and papers to be used in evidence against him is substantially different from compelling him to be a witness against himself." And in Hale v. Henkel, 201 U.S. 43, 76 (1906), it was observed that "the substance of the offense is the compulsory production of private papers, whether under a search warrant or a *subpoena duces tecum,* against which the person ... is entitled to protection."

We do not agree, however, that these broad statements compel suppression of this petitioner's business records as a violation of the Fifth Amendment. In the very recent case of Fisher v. United States, 425 U.S. 391 (1976), the Court held that an attorney's production, pursuant to a lawful summons, of his client's tax records in his hands did not violate the Fifth Amendment privilege of the taxpayer "because enforcement against a taxpayer's lawyer would not 'compel' the taxpayer to do anything—and certainly would not compel him to be a 'witness' against himself." Id., at 397. We recognized that the continued validity of the broad statements contained in some of the Court's earlier cases had been discredited by later opinions.... In those earlier cases, the legal predicate for the inadmissibility of the evidence seized was a violation of the Fourth Amendment; the unlawfulness of the search and seizure was thought to supply the compulsion of the accused necessary to invoke the Fifth Amendment. . . .

Similarly, in this case, petitioner was not asked to say or to do anything. The records seized contained statements that petitioner had voluntarily committed to writing. The search for and seizure of these records were conducted by law enforcement personnel. Finally, when these records were introduced at trial, they were authenticated by a handwriting expert, not by petitioner. Any compulsion of petitioner to speak, other than the inherent psychological pressure to respond at trial to unfavorable evidence, was not present.

This case thus falls within the principle stated by Mr. Justice Holmes: "A party is privileged from producing the evidence but not from its production." Johnson v. United States, 228 U.S. 457, 458 (1913). This principle recognizes that the protection afforded by the self-incrimination clause of the Fifth Amendment "adheres basically to the person, not to information that may incriminate him." Couch v. United States, 409 U.S., at 328. Thus, although the Fifth Amendment may protect an individual from complying with a subpoena for the production of his personal records in his possession because the very act of production may constitute a compulsory authentication of incriminating information, see Fisher v. United States, supra, a seizure of the same materials by law enforcement officers differs in a crucial respect—the individual against whom the search is directed is not required to aid in the discovery, production, or authentication of incriminating evidence.

A contrary determination that the seizure of a person's business records and their introduction into evidence at a criminal trial violates the Fifth Amendment, would undermine the principles announced in earlier cases. Nearly a half century ago, in Marron v. United States, 275 U.S. 192 (1927), the Court upheld, against both Fourth and Fifth Amendment claims, the admission into evidence of business records seized during a search of the accused's illegal liquor business. And in Abel v. United States, 362 U.S. 217 (1960), the Court again upheld, against both Fourth and Fifth Amendment claims, the introduction into evidence at an espionage trial of false identity papers and a coded message seized during a search of the accused's hotel room. These cases recognize a general rule: "There is no special sanctity in papers, as distinguished from other forms of property, to render them immune from search and seizure, if only they fall within the scope of the principles of the cases in which other property may be seized, and if they be adequately described in the affidavit and warrant." Gouled v. United States, 255 U.S. 298, 309 (1921).

Moreover, a contrary determination would prohibit the admission of evidence traditionally used in criminal cases and traditionally admissible despite the Fifth Amendment. For example, it would bar the admission of an accused's gambling records in a prosecution for gambling; a note given temporarily to a bank teller during a robbery and subsequently seized in the accused's automobile or home in a prosecution for bank robbery; and incriminating notes prepared, but not sent, by an accused in a kidnapping or blackmail prosecution.

We find a useful analogy to the Fifth Amendment question in those cases that deal with the "seizure" of oral communications. As the Court has explained, " '[t]he constitutional privilege against self-incrimination . . . is designed to prevent the use of legal process to force from the lips of the accused individual the evidence necessary to convict him or to force him to produce and authenticate any personal documents or effects that might incriminate him.' " Bellis v. United States, 417 U.S., at 88, quoting United States v. White, 322 U.S., at 698. The significant aspect of this principle was apparent and applied in Hoffa v. United States, 385 U.S. 293 (1966), where the Court rejected the contention that an informant's "seizure" of the accused's conversation with him, and his subsequent testimony at trial concerning that conversation, violated the Fifth Amendment. The rationale was that, although the accused's statements may have been elicited by the informant for the purpose of gathering evidence against him, they were made voluntarily. We see no reasoned distinction to be made between the compulsion upon the accused in that case and the compulsion in this one. In each, the communication, whether oral or written, was made voluntarily. The fact that seizure was contemporaneous with the communication in *Hoffa* but subsequent to the communication here does not affect the question whether the accused was compelled to speak.

Finally, we do not believe that permitting the introduction into evidence of a person's business records seized during an otherwise lawful search would offend or undermine any of the policies undergirding the privilege. . . .

In this case, petitioner, at the time he recorded his communication, at the time of the search, and at the time the records were admitted at trial, was not subjected to "the cruel trilemma of self-accusation, perjury or contempt." Ibid. Indeed, he was never required to say or to do anything under penalty of sanction. Similarly, permitting the admission of the records in question does not convert our accusatorial system of justice into an inquisitorial system. "The requirement of specific charges, their proof beyond a reasonable doubt, the protection of the accused from confessions extorted through whatever form of police pressures, the right to a prompt hearing before a magistrate, the right to assistance of counsel, to be supplied by government when circumstances make it necessary, the duty to advise an accused of his constitutional rights—these are all characteristics of the accusatorial system and manifestations of its demands." Watts v. Indiana, 338 U.S. 49, 54 (1949). None of these attributes is endangered by the introduction of business records "independently secured through skillful investigation." Ibid. Further, the search for and seizure of business records pose no danger greater than that inherent in every search that evidence will be "elicited by inhumane treatment and abuses." 378 U.S., at 55. In this case, the statements seized were voluntarily committed to paper before the police arrived to search for them, and petitioner was not treated discourteously during the search. Also, the "good cause" to "disturb," ibid., petitioner was independently determined by the judge who issued the warrants; and the State bore the burden of executing them. Finally, there is no chance, in this case, of petitioner's statements being self-deprecatory and untrustworthy because they were extracted from him—they were already in existence and had been made voluntarily.

We recognize, of course, that the Fifth Amendment protects privacy to some extent. However, "the Court has never suggested that every invasion of privacy violates the privilege." Fisher v. United States, 425 U.S., at 399. Indeed, we recently held that unless incriminating testimony is "compelled," any invasion of privacy is outside the scope of the Fifth Amendment's protection, saying that "the Fifth Amendment protects against 'compelled self-incrimination, not [the disclosure of] private information.' " Fisher v. United States. Id., at 401. Here, as we have already noted, petitioner was not compelled to testify in any manner.

Accordingly, we hold that the search of an individual's office for business records, their seizure, and subsequent introduction into evidence does not offend the Fifth Amendment's prescription that "[n]o person ... shall be compelled in any criminal case to be a witness against himself."

    . . .

[The Court rejected also the defendant's claims under the Fourth Amendment.]

The judgment of the Court of Special Appeals of Maryland is affirmed.

It is so ordered.

MR. JUSTICE BRENNAN, dissenting.

In a concurring opinion earlier this Term in Fisher v. United States, 425 U.S. 391, 414 (1976), I stated my view that the Fifth Amendment protects an individual citizen against the compelled production of testimonial matter that might tend to incriminate him, provided it is matter that comes within the zone of privacy recognized by the Amendment to secure to the individual "a private inner sanctum of individual feeling and thought." Couch v. United States, 409 U.S. 322, 327 (1973). Accordingly, the production of testimonial material falling within this zone of privacy may not be compelled by subpoena. The Court holds today that the search and seizure, pursuant to a valid warrant, of business records in petitioner's possession and containing statements made by the petitioner does not violate the Fifth Amendment. I can perceive no distinction of meaningful substance between compelling the production of such records through subpoena and seizing such records against the will of the petitioner. Moreover, I believe that the warrants under which petitioner's papers were seized were impermissibly general. I therefore dissent.

I

"There is no question that the records seized from petitioner's offices and introduced against him were incriminating. Moreover, it is undisputed that some of these business records contain statements made by petitioner." Ante, at 471. It also cannot be questioned that these records fall within the zone of privacy protected by the Fifth Amendment. Bellis v. United States, 417 U.S. 85, 87–88 (1974), squarely recognized that "[t]he privilege applies to the business records of the sole proprietor or sole practitioner as well as to personal documents containing more intimate information about the individual's private life." The Court today retreats from this view. Though recognizing the value of privacy protected by the Fifth Amendment . . . and the " 'right of each individual "to a private enclave where he may lead a private life," ' " ante, at 476 n. 8, the Court declines, without adequate explanation, to include business records within that private zone comprising the mere physical extensions of an individual's thoughts and knowledge. As I noted in *Fisher,* the failure to give effect to such a zone ignores the essential spirit of the Fifth Amendment: "[Business] records are at least an extension of an aspect of a person's activities, though concededly not the more intimate aspects of one's life. Where the privilege would have protected one's mental notes of his business affairs in a less complicated day and age, it would seem that the protection should not fall away because the complexities of another time compel one to keep business records. Cf. Olmstead v. United States, 277 U.S. 438, 474 (1928) (Brandeis, J., dissenting)." 425 U.S., at 426–427 (Brennan, J., concurring in judgment).

As indicated at the outset, today's assault on the Fifth Amendment is not limited to narrowing this view of the scope of privacy respected by it. The Court also sanctions circumvention of the Amendment by indulging an unjustified distinction between production compelled by subpoena and production secured against the will of the petitioner through warrant. But a privilege protecting against the compelled production of testimonial material is a hollow guarantee where production of that material may be secured through the expedient of search and seizure.

The matter cannot be resolved on any simplistic notion of compulsion. Search and seizure is as rife with elements of compulsion as subpoena. The intrusion occurs under the lawful process of the State. The individual is not free to resist that authority. To be sure, as the Court observes, "[p]etitioner was present during the search of his law office and was free to move about," ante, at 466, but I do not believe the Court means to suggest that petitioner was free to obstruct the investigators' search through his files.

And compulsion does not disappear merely because the individual is absent at the time of search and seizure. The door to one's house, for example, is as much the individual's resistance to the intrusion of outsiders as his personal physical efforts to prevent the same. To refuse recognition to the sanctity of that door and, more generally, to confine the dominion of privacy to the mind, compels an unconstitutional disclosure by denying to the individual a zone of physical freedom necessary for conducting one's affairs. . . .

. . .

. . . As early as Boyd v. United States, 116 U.S. 616, 633 (1886), the Court was "unable to perceive that the seizure of a man's private books and papers to be used in evidence against him is substantially different from compelling him to be a witness against himself." Though the Court in *Boyd* held that compelling a person to be a witness against himself was tantamount to an unreasonable search and seizure, it never required a search and seizure to be independently unreasonable in order that it violate the Fifth Amendment. And though the several decisions which have found a Fifth Amendment violation stemming from a search and seizure all involved unreasonable search and seizures, it has never been established, contrary to the Court's assertion . . . that the unlawfulness of the search and seizure is necessary to invoke the Fifth Amendment. Gouled v. United States, 255 U.S. 298 (1921), though also involving a Fourth Amendment violation, makes it clear that the illegality of the search and seizure is not a prerequisite for a Fifth Amendment violation. Under *Gouled*, a Fifth Amendment violation exists because the "[accused] is the unwilling source of the evidence," id., at 306, a matter which does not depend on the illegality *vel non* of the search and seizure.

Until today, no decision by this Court had held that the seizure of testimonial evidence by legal process did not violate the Fifth Amendment. Indeed, with few exceptions, the indications were strongly to the contrary. . . . These cases all reflect the root understanding of Boyd v. United States, 116 U.S., at 630: "It is not the breaking of his doors, and the rummaging of his drawers, that constitutes the essence of the offence [to the Fifth Amendment]; but it is the invasion of his indefeasible right of personal security, personal liberty and private property . . . . [A]ny forcible and compulsory extortion of a man's own testimony or his private papers to be used as evidence to convict him of crime ..., is within the condemnation of [the Amendment]. In this regard the Fourth and Fifth Amendments run almost into each other."

[*] [**]
. . .

[*] Justice Marshall wrote a brief dissenting opinion, indicating his agreement with Justice Brennan on the Fourth Amendment issue and expressing no view on the Fifth Amendment issue.

[**] In Fisher v. United States, 425 U.S. 391 (1976), discussed in *Andresen*, above, the Court concluded that the attorney-client privilege barred enforcement of a summons directing an attorney to produce documents which a client has transferred to him for the purpose of obtaining legal advice, if the privilege against self-incrimination was a barrier to compelled production by the client. It held, however, that in that case the taxpayers' privilege would not have been violated by enforcement of a summons directing the taxpayers themselves to produce the documents in question, which were their accountants' work papers prepared in connection with the taxpayers' income tax returns. The Court stated that its decision did not answer the question whether the privilege would protect a taxpayer against compelled production of his own retained tax records.

GARRITY v. NEW JERSEY

385 U.S. 493, 87 S.Ct. 616, 17 L.Ed.2d 562 (1967).

MR. JUSTICE DOUGLAS delivered the opinion of the Court.

Appellants were police officers in certain New Jersey boroughs. The Supreme Court of New Jersey ordered that alleged irregularities in handling cases in the municipal courts of those boroughs be investigated by the Attorney General, invested him with broad powers of inquiry and investigation, and directed him to make a report to the court. The matters investigated concerned alleged fixing of traffic tickets.

Before being questioned, each appellant was warned (1) that anything he said might be used against him in any state criminal proceeding; (2) that he had the privilege to refuse to answer if the disclosure would tend to incriminate him; but (3) that if he refused to answer he would be subject to removal from office.

Appellants answered the questions. No immunity was granted, as there is no immunity statute applicable in these circumstances. Over their objections, some of the answers given were used in subsequent prosecutions for conspiracy to obstruct the administration of the traffic laws. Appellants were convicted and their convictions were sustained over their protests that their statements were coerced, by reason of the fact that, if they refused to answer, they could lose their positions with the police department. See 44 N.J. 209, 207 A.2d 689, 44 N.J. 259, 208 A.2d 146.

. . .

The choice imposed on petitioners was one between self-incrimination or job forfeiture. Coercion that vitiates a confession under Chambers v. Florida, 309 U.S. 227, and related cases can be "mental as well as physical"; "the blood of the accused is not the only hallmark of an unconstitutional inquisition." Blackburn v. Alabama, 361 U.S. 199, 206. Subtle pressures . . . may be as telling as coarse and vulgar ones. The question is whether the accused was deprived of his "free choice to admit, to deny, or to refuse to answer." Lisenba v. California, 314 U.S. 219, 241.

We adhere to Boyd v. United States, 116 U.S. 616, a civil forfeiture action against property. A statute offered the owner an election between producing a document or forfeiture of the goods at issue in the proceeding. This was held to be a form of compulsion in violation of both the Fifth Amendment and the Fourth Amendment. . . .

812

The choice given petitioners was either to forfeit their jobs or to incriminate themselves. The option to lose their means of livelihood or to pay the penalty of self-incrimination is the antithesis of free choice to speak out or to remain silent. That practice, like interrogation practices we reviewed in Miranda v. Arizona, 384 U.S. 436, 464–465, is "likely to exert such pressure upon an individual as to disable him from making a free and rational choice." We think the statements were infected by the coercion inherent in this scheme of questioning and cannot be sustained as voluntary under our prior decisions.

It is said that there was a "waiver." That, however, is a federal question for us to decide. . . .

Where the choice is "between the rock and the whirlpool," duress is inherent in deciding to "waive" one or the other. . . .

. . . In these cases . . . though petitioners succumbed to compulsion, they preserved their objections, raising them at the earliest possible point. . . . The cases are therefore quite different from the situation where one who is anxious to make a clean breast of the whole affair volunteers the information.

Mr. Justice Holmes in McAuliffe v. New Bedford, 155 Mass. 216, 29 N.E. 517, stated a dictum on which New Jersey heavily relies:

> "The petitioner may have a constitutional right to talk politics, but he has no constitutional right to be a policeman. There are few employments for hire in which the servant does not agree to suspend his constitutional right of free speech, as well as of idleness, by the implied terms of his contract. The servant cannot complain, as he takes the employment on the terms which are offered him. On the same principle, the city may impose any reasonable condition upon holding offices within its control." Id., at 220, 29 N.E., at 517–518.

The question in this case, however, is not cognizable in those terms. Our question is whether a State, contrary to the requirement of the Fourteenth Amendment, can use the threat of discharge to secure incriminatory evidence against an employee.

We held in Slochower v. Board of Education, 350 U.S. 551, that a public school teacher could not be discharged merely because he had invoked the Fifth Amendment privilege against self-incrimination when questioned by a congressional committee:

> "The privilege against self-incrimination would be reduced to a hollow mockery if its exercise could be taken as equivalent either to a confession of guilt or a conclusive presumption of perjury. . . . The privilege serves to protect the innocent who otherwise might be ensnared by ambiguous circumstances." Id., at 557–558.

We conclude that policemen, like teachers and lawyers, are not relegated to a watered-down version of constitutional rights.

There are rights of constitutional stature whose exercise a State may not condition by the exaction of a price. Engaging in interstate commerce is one. ... Resort to the federal courts in diversity of citizenship cases is another. ... Assertion of a First Amendment right is still another. ... The imposition of a burden on the exercise of a Twenty-fourth Amendment right is also banned. ... We now hold the protection of the individual under the Fourteenth Amendment against coerced statements prohibits use in subsequent criminal proceedings of statements obtained under threat of removal from office, and that it extends to all, whether they are policemen or other members of our body politic.

Reversed.

MR. JUSTICE HARLAN, whom MR. JUSTICE CLARK and MR. JUSTICE STEWART join, dissenting.

. . .

The majority employs a curious mixture of doctrines to invalidate these convictions, and I confess to difficulty in perceiving the intended relationships among the various segments of its opinion. I gather that the majority believes that the possibility that these policemen might have been discharged had they refused to provide information pertinent to their public responsibilities is an impermissible "condition" imposed by New Jersey upon petitioners' privilege against self-incrimination. From this premise the majority draws the conclusion that the statements obtained from petitioners after a warning that discharge was possible were inadmissible. Evidently recognizing the weakness of its conclusion, the majority attempts to bring to its support illustrations from the lengthy series of cases in which this Court, in light of all the relevant circumstances, has adjudged the voluntariness *in fact* of statements obtained from accused persons.

The majority is apparently engaged in the delicate task of riding two unruly horses at once: it is presumably arguing simultaneously that the statements were involuntary as a matter of fact ... and that the statements were inadmissible as a matter of law, on the premise that they were products of an impermissible condition imposed on the constitutional privilege. These are very different contentions and require separate replies, but in my opinion both contentions are plainly mistaken, for reasons that follow.

I

I turn first to the suggestion that these statements were involuntary in fact. An assessment of the voluntariness of the various statements in issue here requires a more comprehensive examination of the pertinent circumstances than the majority has undertaken.

. . .

It would be difficult to imagine interrogations to which these criteria of duress were more completely inapplicable, or in which the requirements which have subsequently been imposed by this Court on police questioning were more thoroughly satisfied. Each of the petitioners received a complete and explicit reminder of his constitutional privilege. Three of the petitioners had counsel present; at least a fourth had consulted counsel but freely determined that his presence was unnecessary. These petitioners were not in any fashion "swept from familiar surroundings into police custody, surrounded by antagonistic forces, and subjected to the techniques of persuasion . . . ." Miranda v. Arizona, 384 U.S. 436, 461. I think it manifest that, under the standards developed by this Court to assess voluntariness, there is no basis for saying that any of these statements were made involuntarily.

II

The issue remaining is whether the statements were inadmissible because they were "involuntary as a matter of law," in that they were given after a warning that New Jersey policemen may be discharged for failure to provide information pertinent to their public responsibilities. What is really involved on this score, however, is not in truth a question of "voluntariness" at all, but rather whether the condition imposed by the State on the exercise of the privilege against self-incrimination, namely dismissal from office, in this instance serves in itself to render the statements inadmissible. Absent evidence of involuntariness in fact, the admissibility of these statements thus hinges on the validity of the consequence which the State acknowledged might have resulted if the statements had not been given. If the consequence is constitutionally permissible, there can surely be no objection if the State cautions the witness that it may follow if he remains silent. If both the consequence and the warning are constitutionally permissible, a witness is obliged, in order to prevent the use of his statements against him in a criminal prosecution, to prove under the standards established since Brown v. Mississippi, 297 U.S. 278, that as a matter of fact the statements were involuntarily made. The central issues here are therefore . . . whether consequences may properly be permitted to result to a claimant after his invocation of the constitutional privilege, and if so, whether the consequence in question is permissible. . . . [I]n my view nothing in the logic or purposes of the privilege demands that all consequences which may result from a witness' silence be forbidden merely because that silence is privileged. The validity of a consequence depends both upon the hazards, if any, it presents to the integrity of the privilege and upon the urgency of the public interests it is designed to protect.

It can hardly be denied that New Jersey is permitted by the Constitution to establish reasonable qualifications and standards of conduct for its public employees. Nor can it be said that it is arbitrary or unreasonable for New Jersey to insist that its employees furnish the appropriate authorities with information pertinent to their employment.... Finally, it is surely plain that New Jersey may in particular require its employees to assist in the prevention and detection of unlawful activities by officers of the state government. The urgency of these requirements is the more obvious here, where the conduct in question is that of officials directly entrusted with the administration of justice. The importance for our systems of justice of the integrity of local police forces can scarcely be exaggerated. Thus, it need only be recalled that this Court itself has often intervened in state criminal prosecutions precisely on the ground that this might encourage high standards of police behavior.... It must be concluded, therefore, that the sanction at issue here is reasonably calculated to serve the most basic interests of the citizens of New Jersey.

The final question is the hazard, if any, which this sanction presents to the constitutional privilege. The purposes for which, and the circumstances in which, an officer's discharge might be ordered under New Jersey law plainly may vary. It is of course possible that discharge might in a given case be predicated on an imputation of guilt drawn from the use of the privilege, as was thought by this Court to have occurred in Slochower v. Board of Education, [350 U.S. 551 (1956)]. But from our vantage point, it would be quite improper to assume that New Jersey will employ these procedures for purposes other than to assess in good faith an employee's continued fitness for public employment. This Court, when a state procedure for investigating the loyalty and fitness of public employees might result either in the *Slochower* situation or in an assessment in good faith of an employee, has until today consistently paused to examine the actual circumstances of each case.... I am unable to see any justification for the majority's abandonment of that process; it is well calculated both to protect the essential purposes of the privilege and to guarantee the most generous opportunities for the pursuit of other public values. The majority's broad prohibition, on the other hand, extends the scope of the privilege beyond its essential purposes, and seriously hampers the protection of other important values. Despite the majority's disclaimer, it is quite plain that the logic of its prohibitory rule would in this situation prevent the discharge of these policemen. It would therefore entirely forbid a sanction which presents, at least on its face, no hazard to the purposes of the constitutional privilege, and which may reasonably be expected to serve important public interests. We are not entitled to assume that discharges will be used either to vindicate impermissible inferences of guilt or to penalize privileged silence, but must instead presume that this procedure is only intended and will only be used to establish and enforce standards of conduct for public employees. As such, it does not minimize or endanger the petitioners' constitutional privilege against self-incrimination.

I would therefore conclude that the sanction provided by the State is constitutionally permissible. From this, it surely follows that the warning given of the possibility of discharge is constitutionally unobjectionable. Given the constitutionality both of the sanction and of the warning of its application, the petitioners would be constitutionally entitled to exclude the use of their statements as evidence in a criminal prosecution against them only if it is found that the statements were, when given, involuntary in fact. For the reasons stated above, I cannot agree that these statements were involuntary in fact.

I would affirm the judgments of the Supreme Court of New Jersey.[*]

[*] Justice White wrote a dissenting opinion.

GARDNER v. BRODERICK

392 U.S. 273, 88 S.Ct. 1913, 20 L.Ed.2d 1082 (1968).

MR. JUSTICE FORTAS delivered the opinion of the Court.

Appellant brought this action in the Supreme Court of the State of New York seeking reinstatement as a New York City patrolman and back pay. He claimed he was unlawfully dismissed because he refused to waive his privilege against self-incrimination. In August 1965, pursuant to subpoena, appellant appeared before a New York County grand jury which was investigating alleged bribery and corruption of police officers in connection with unlawful gambling operations. He was advised that the grand jury proposed to examine him concerning the performance of his official duties. He was advised of his privilege against self-incrimination, but he was asked to sign a "waiver of immunity" after being told that he would be fired if he did not sign. Following his refusal, he was given an administrative hearing and was discharged solely for this refusal, pursuant to § 1123 of the New York City Charter.

The New York Supreme Court dismissed his petition for reinstatement, 27 App.Div.2d 800, 279 N.Y.S.2d 150 (1967), and the New York Court of Appeals affirmed. 20 N.Y.2d 227, 229 N.E.2d 184 (1967). We noted probable jurisdiction. 390 U.S. 918 (1968).

Our decisions establish beyond dispute the breadth of the privilege to refuse to respond to questions when the result may be self-incriminatory, and the need fully to implement its guaranty.... The privilege is applicable to state as well as federal proceedings. ... The privilege may be waived in appropriate circumstances if the waiver is knowingly and voluntarily made. Answers may be compelled regardless of the privilege if there is immunity from federal and state use of the compelled testimony or its fruits in connection with a criminal prosecution against the person testifying. ...

The question presented in the present case is whether a policeman who refuses to waive the protections which the privilege gives him may be dismissed from office because of that refusal.

About a year and a half after New York City discharged petitioner for his refusal to waive this immunity, we decided Garrity v. New Jersey, 385 U.S. 493 (1967). In that case, we held that when a policeman had been compelled to testify by the threat that otherwise he would be removed from office, the testimony that he gave could not be used against him in a subsequent prosecution. Garrity had not signed a waiver of immunity and no immunity statute was applicable in the circumstances. ...

818

The New York Court of Appeals considered that *Garrity* did not control the present case. It is true that *Garrity* related to the attempted use of compelled testimony. It did not involve the precise question which is presented here: namely, whether a State may discharge an officer for refusing to waive a right which the Constitution guarantees to him. The New York Court of Appeals also distinguished our post-*Garrity* decision in Spevack v. Klein, [385 U.S. 511 (1967)]. In *Spevack*, we ruled that a lawyer could not be disbarred solely because he refused to testify at a disciplinary proceeding on the ground that his testimony would tend to incriminate him. The Court of Appeals concluded that *Spevack* does not control the present case because different considerations apply in the case of a public official such as a policeman. A lawyer, it stated, although licensed by the state is not an employee. This distinction is now urged upon us. It is argued that although a lawyer could not constitutionally be confronted with Hobson's choice between self-incrimination and forfeiting his means of livelihood, the same principle should not protect a policeman. Unlike the lawyer, he is directly, immediately, and entirely responsible to the city or State which is his employer. He owes his entire loyalty to it. He has no other "client" or principal. He is a trustee of the public interest, bearing the burden of great and total responsibility to his public employer. Unlike the lawyer who is directly responsible to his client, the policeman is either responsible to the State or to no one.

We agree that these factors differentiate the situations. If appellant, a policeman, had refused to answer questions specifically, directly, and narrowly relating to the performance of his official duties, without being required to waive his immunity with respect to the use of his answers or the fruits thereof in a criminal prosecution of himself, Garrity v. New Jersey, supra, the privilege against self-incrimination would not have been a bar to his dismissal.

The facts of this case, however, do not present this issue. Here, petitioner was summoned to testify before a grand jury in an investigation of alleged criminal conduct. He was discharged from office, not for failure to answer relevant questions about his official duties, but for refusal to waive a constitutional right. He was dismissed for failure to relinquish the protections of the privilege against self-incrimination. The Constitution of New York State and the City Charter both expressly provided that his failure to do so, as well as his failure to testify, would result in dismissal from his job. He was dismissed solely for his refusal to waive the immunity to which he is entitled if he is required to testify despite his constitutional privilege. Garrity v. New Jersey, supra.

We need not speculate whether, if appellant had executed the waiver of immunity in the circumstances, the effect of our subsequent decision in Garrity v. New Jersey, supra, would have been to nullify the effect of the waiver. New York City discharged him for refusal to execute a document purporting to waive his constitutional rights and to permit prosecution of himself on the basis of his compelled testimony. Petitioner could not have assumed—and certainly he was not required to assume—that he was being asked to do an idle act of no legal effect. In any event, the mandate of the great privilege against self-incrimination does not tolerate the attempt, regardless of its ultimate effectiveness, to coerce a waiver of the immunity it confers on penalty of the loss of employment. It is clear that petitioner's testimony was demanded before the grand jury in part so that it might be used to prosecute him, and not solely for the purpose of securing an accounting of his performance of his public trust. If the latter had been the only purpose, there would have been no reason to seek to compel petitioner to waive his immunity.

Proper regard for the history and meaning of the privilege against self-incrimination, applicable to the States under our decision in Malloy v. Hogan, 378 U.S. 1 (1964), and for the decisions of this Court, dictate the conclusion that the provision of the New York City Charter pursuant to which petitioner was dismissed cannot stand. Accordingly, the judgment is

Reversed.[*]

[*] Justice Black concurred in the result.

KASTIGAR v. UNITED STATES

406 U.S. 441, 92 S.Ct. 1653, 32 L.Ed.2d 212 (1972).

MR. JUSTICE POWELL delivered the opinion of the Court.

This case presents the question whether the United States Government may compel testimony from an unwilling witness, who invokes the Fifth Amendment privilege against compulsory self-incrimination, by conferring on the witness immunity from use of the compelled testimony in subsequent criminal proceedings, as well as immunity from use of evidence derived from the testimony.

Petitioners were subpoenaed to appear before a United States grand jury in the Central District of California on February 4, 1971. The Government believed that petitioners were likely to assert their Fifth Amendment privilege. Prior to the scheduled appearances, the Government applied to the District Court for an order directing petitioners to answer questions and produce evidence before the grand jury under a grant of immunity conferred pursuant to 18 U.S.C. §§ 6002–6003. Petitioners opposed issuance of the order, contending primarily that the scope of the immunity provided by the statute was not coextensive with the scope of the privilege against self-incrimination, and therefore was not sufficient to supplant the privilege and compel their testimony. The District Court rejected this contention, and ordered petitioners to appear before the grand jury and answer its questions under the grant of immunity.

Petitioners appeared but refused to answer questions, asserting their privilege against compulsory self-incrimination. They were brought before the District Court, and each persisted in his refusal to answer the grand jury's questions, notwithstanding the grant of immunity. The court found both in contempt, and committed them to the custody of the Attorney General until either they answered the grand jury's questions or the term of the grand jury expired. The Court of Appeals for the Ninth Circuit affirmed. Stewart v. United States, 440 F.2d 954 (CA9 1971). This Court granted certiorari to resolve the important question whether testimony may be compelled by granting immunity from the use of compelled testimony and evidence derived therefrom ("use and derivative use" immunity), or whether it is necessary to grant immunity from prosecution for offenses to which compelled testimony relates ("transactional" immunity). 402 U.S. 971 (1971).

I

The power of government to compel persons to testify in court or before grand juries and other governmental agencies is firmly established in Anglo-American jurisprudence. . . .

821

But the power to compel testimony is not absolute. There are a number of exemptions from the testimonial duty, the most important of which is the Fifth Amendment privilege against compulsory self-incrimination. The privilege reflects a complex of our fundamental values and aspirations, and marks an important advance in the development of our liberty. It can be asserted in any proceeding, civil or criminal, administrative or judicial, investigatory or adjudicatory; and it protects against any disclosures that the witness reasonably believes could be used in a criminal prosecution or could lead to other evidence that might be so used. This Court has been zealous to safeguard the values that underlie the privilege.

Immunity statutes, which have historical roots deep in Anglo-American jurisprudence, are not incompatible with these values. Rather, they seek a rational accommodation between the imperatives of the privilege and the legitimate demands of government to compel citizens to testify. The existence of these statutes reflects the importance of testimony, and the fact that many offenses are of such a character that the only persons capable of giving useful testimony are those implicated in the crime. Indeed, their origins were in the context of such offenses, and their primary use has been to investigate such offenses. Congress included immunity statutes in many of the regulatory measures adopted in the first half of this century. Indeed, prior to the enactment of the statute under consideration in this case, there were in force over 50 federal immunity statutes. In addition, every State in the Union, as well as the District of Columbia and Puerto Rico, has one or more such statutes. The commentators, and this Court on several occasions, have characterized immunity statutes as essential to the effective enforcement of various criminal statutes. As Mr. Justice Frankfurter observed, speaking for the Court in Ullmann v. United States, 350 U.S. 422 (1956), such statutes have "become part of our constitutional fabric." Id., at 438.

II

Petitioners contend, first, that the Fifth Amendment's privilege against compulsory self-incrimination, which is that "[n]o person . . . shall be compelled in any criminal case to be a witness against himself," deprives Congress of power to enact laws that compel self-incrimination, even if complete immunity from prosecution is granted prior to the compulsion of the incriminatory testimony. In other words, petitioners assert that no immunity statute, however drawn, can afford a lawful basis for compelling incriminatory testimony. They ask us to reconsider and overrule Brown v. Walker, 161 U.S. 591 (1896), and Ullmann v. United States, supra, decisions that uphold the constitutionality of immunity statutes. We find no merit to this contention and reaffirm the decisions in *Brown* and *Ullmann*.

III

Petitioners' second contention is that the scope of immunity provided by the federal witness immunity statute, 18 U.S.C. § 6002, is not coextensive with the scope of the Fifth Amendment privilege against compulsory self-incrimination, and therefore is not sufficient to supplant the privilege and compel testimony over a claim of the privilege. The statute provides that when a witness is compelled by district court order to testify over a claim of the privilege:

> "the witness may not refuse to comply with the order on the basis of his privilege against self-incrimination; but no testimony or other information compelled under the order (or any information directly or indirectly derived from such testimony or other information) may be used against the witness in any criminal case, except a prosecution for perjury, giving a false statement, or otherwise failing to comply with the order." 18 U.S.C. § 6002.

The constitutional inquiry, rooted in logic and history, as well as in the decisions of this Court, is whether the immunity granted under this statute is coextensive with the scope of the privilege. If so, petitioners' refusals to answer based on the privilege were unjustified, and the judgments of contempt were proper, for the grant of immunity has removed the dangers against which the privilege protects. Brown v. Walker, supra. If, on the other hand, the immunity granted is not as comprehensive as the protection afforded by the privilege, petitioners were justified in refusing to answer, and the judgments of contempt must be vacated. . . .

Petitioners draw a distinction between statutes that provide transactional immunity and those that provide, as does the statute before us, immunity from use and derivative use. They contend that a statute must at a minimum grant full transactional immunity in order to be coextensive with the scope of the privilege. In support of this contention, they rely on Counselman v. Hitchcock, 142 U.S. 547 (1892), the first case in which this Court considered a constitutional challenge to an immunity statute. The statute, a re-enactment of the Immunity Act of 1868,[26] provided that no "evidence obtained from a party or witness by means of a judicial proceeding . . . shall be given in evidence, or in any manner used against him . . . in any court of the United States . . . ."[27] Notwithstanding a grant of immunity and order to testify under the revised 1868 Act, the witness, asserting his privilege against compulsory self-incrimination, refused to testify before a federal grand jury. He was consequently adjudged in contempt of court. On appeal, this Court construed the statute as affording a witness protection only against the use of the specific testimony compelled from him under the grant of immunity. This construction meant that the statute

---

26. 15 Stat. 37.

27. See Counselman v. Hitchcock, supra, at 560.

"could not, and would not, prevent the use of his testimony to search out other testimony to be used in evidence against him." [29] Since the revised 1868 Act, as construed by the Court, would permit the use against the immunized witness of evidence derived from his compelled testimony, it did not protect the witness to the same extent that a claim of the privilege would protect him. Accordingly, under the principle that a grant of immunity cannot supplant the privilege, and is not sufficient to compel testimony over a claim of the privilege, unless the scope of the grant of immunity is coextensive with the scope of the privilege, the witness' refusal to testify was held proper. In the course of its opinion, the Court made the following statement, on which petitioners heavily rely:

> "We are clearly of opinion that no statute which leaves the party or witness subject to prosecution after he answers the criminating question put to him, can have the effect of supplanting the privilege conferred by the Constitution of the United States. [The immunity statute under consideration] does not supply a complete protection from all the perils against which the constitutional prohibition was designed to guard, and is not a full substitute for that prohibition. In view of the constitutional provision, a statutory enactment, to be valid, must afford absolute immunity against future prosecution for the offence to which the question relates." 142 U.S., at 585–586.

Sixteen days after the *Counselman* decision, a new immunity bill was introduced by Senator Cullom, who urged that enforcement of the Interstate Commerce Act would be impossible in the absence of an effective immunity statute. The bill, which became the Compulsory Testimony Act of 1893, was drafted specifically to meet the broad language in *Counselman* set forth above. The new Act removed the privilege against self-incrimination in hearings before the Interstate Commerce Commission and provided that:

> "no person shall be prosecuted or subjected to any penalty or forfeiture for or on account of any transaction, matter or thing, concerning which he may testify, or produce evidence, documentary or otherwise . . . ." Act of Feb. 11, 1893, 27 Stat. 444.

This transactional immunity statute became the basic form for the numerous federal immunity statutes until 1970, when, after re-examining applicable constitutional principles and the adequacy of existing law, Congress enacted the statute here under consideration. The new statute, which does not "afford [the] absolute immunity against future prosecution" referred to in *Counselman,* was drafted to meet what Congress judged to be the conceptual basis of *Counselman,* as elaborated in subsequent decisions of the Court, namely, that immunity from the use of compelled testimony and

---

29. Counselman v. Hitchcock, supra, at 564.

evidence derived therefrom is coextensive with the scope of the privilege.

The statute's explicit proscription of the use in any criminal case of "testimony or other information compelled under the order (or any information directly or indirectly derived from such testimony or other information)" is consonant with Fifth Amendment standards. We hold that such immunity from use and derivative use is coextensive with the scope of the privilege against self-incrimination, and therefore is sufficient to compel testimony over a claim of the privilege. While a grant of immunity must afford protection commensurate with that afforded by the privilege, it need not be broader. Transactional immunity, which accords full immunity from prosecution for the offense to which the compelled testimony relates, affords the witness considerably broader protection than does the Fifth Amendment privilege. The privilege has never been construed to mean that one who invokes it cannot subsequently be prosecuted. Its sole concern is to afford protection against being "forced to give testimony leading to the infliction of 'penalties affixed to ... criminal acts.' "[38] Immunity from the use of compelled testimony, as well as evidence derived directly and indirectly therefrom, affords this protection. It prohibits the prosecutorial authorities from using the compelled testimony in *any* respect, and it therefore insures that the testimony cannot lead to the infliction of criminal penalties on the witness.

Our holding is consistent with the conceptual basis of *Counselman*. The *Counselman* statute, as construed by the Court, was plainly deficient in its failure to prohibit the use against the immunized witness of evidence derived from his compelled testimony. The Court repeatedly emphasized this deficiency .... The broad language in *Counselman* relied upon by petitioners was unnecessary to the Court's decision, and cannot be considered binding authority.

IV

Although an analysis of prior decisions and the purpose of the Fifth Amendment privilege indicates that use and derivative-use immunity is coextensive with the privilege, we must consider additional arguments advanced by petitioners against the sufficiency of such immunity. We start from the premise, repeatedly affirmed by this Court, that an appropriately broad immunity grant is compatible with the Constitution.

Petitioners argue that use and derivative-use immunity will not adequately protect a witness from various possible incriminating uses of the compelled testimony: for example, the prosecutor or

38. Ullmann v. United States, 350 U.S., at U.S., at 634. ...
438–439, quoting Boyd v. United States, 116

other law enforcement officials may obtain leads, names of witnesses, or other information not otherwise available that might result in a prosecution. It will be difficult and perhaps impossible, the argument goes, to identify, by testimony or cross-examination, the subtle ways in which the compelled testimony may disadvantage a witness, especially in the jurisdiction granting the immunity.

This argument presupposes that the statute's prohibition will prove impossible to enforce. The statute provides a sweeping proscription of any use, direct or indirect, of the compelled testimony and any information derived therefrom:

> "no testimony or other information compelled under the order (or any information directly or indirectly derived from such testimony or other information) may be used against the witness in any criminal case ...." 18 U.S.C. § 6002.

This total prohibition on use provides a comprehensive safeguard, barring the use of compelled testimony as an "investigatory lead," and also barring the use of any evidence obtained by focusing investigation on a witness as a result of his compelled disclosures.

A person accorded this immunity under 18 U.S.C. § 6002, and subsequently prosecuted, is not dependent for the preservation of his rights upon the integrity and good faith of the prosecuting authorities. As stated in Murphy [v. Waterfront Commission, 378 U.S. 52 (1964)]:

> "Once a defendant demonstrates that he has testified, under a state grant of immunity, to matters related to the federal prosecution, the federal authorities have the burden of showing that their evidence is not tainted by establishing that they had an independent, legitimate source for the disputed evidence." 378 U.S., at 79 n. 18.

This burden of proof, which we reaffirm as appropriate, is not limited to a negation of taint; rather, it imposes on the prosecution the affirmative duty to prove that the evidence it proposes to use is derived from a legitimate source wholly independent of the compelled testimony.

This is very substantial protection, commensurate with that resulting from invoking the privilege itself. The privilege assures that a citizen is not compelled to incriminate himself by his own testimony. It usually operates to allow a citizen to remain silent when asked a question requiring an incriminatory answer. This statute, which operates after a witness has given incriminatory testimony, affords the same protection by assuring that the compelled testimony can in no way lead to the infliction of criminal penalties. The statute, like the Fifth Amendment, grants neither pardon nor amnesty. Both the statute and the Fifth Amendment allow the government to prosecute using evidence from legitimate independent sources.

The statutory proscription is analogous to the Fifth Amendment requirement in cases of coerced confessions. A coerced confession, as revealing of leads as testimony given in exchange for immunity, is inadmissible in a criminal trial, but it does not bar prosecution. Moreover, a defendant against whom incriminating evidence has been obtained through a grant of immunity may be in a stronger position at trial than a defendant who asserts a Fifth Amendment coerced-confession claim. One raising a claim under this statute need only show that he testified under a grant of immunity in order to shift to the government the heavy burden of proving that all of the evidence it proposes to use was derived from legitimate independent sources. On the other hand, a defendant raising a coerced-confession claim under the Fifth Amendment must first prevail in a voluntariness hearing before his confession and evidence derived from it become inadmissible.

There can be no justification in reason or policy for holding that the Constitution requires an amnesty grant where, acting pursuant to statute and accompanying safeguards, testimony is compelled in exchange for immunity from use and derivative use when no such amnesty is required where the government, acting without colorable right, coerces a defendant into incriminating himself.

We conclude that the immunity provided by 18 U.S.C. § 6002 leaves the witness and the prosecutorial authorities in substantially the same position as if the witness had claimed the Fifth Amendment privilege. The immunity therefore is coextensive with the privilege and suffices to supplant it. The judgment of the Court of Appeals for the Ninth Circuit accordingly is

Affirmed.[*]

[*] Justice Douglas and Justice Marshall wrote dissenting opinions.

7. LINEUPS

UNITED STATES v. WADE

388 U.S. 218, 87 S.Ct. 1926, 18 L.Ed.2d 1149 (1967).

MR. JUSTICE BRENNAN delivered the opinion of the Court.

The question here is whether courtroom identifications of an accused at trial are to be excluded from evidence because the accused was exhibited to the witnesses before trial at a post-indictment lineup conducted for identification purposes without notice to and in the absence of the accused's appointed counsel.

The federally insured bank in Eustace, Texas, was robbed on September 21, 1964. A man with a small strip of tape on each side of his face entered the bank, pointed a pistol at the female cashier and the vice president, the only persons in the bank at the time, and forced them to fill a pillowcase with the bank's money. The man then drove away with an accomplice who had been waiting in a stolen car outside the bank. On March 23, 1965, an indictment was returned against respondent, Wade, and two others for conspiring to rob the bank, and against Wade and the accomplice for the robbery itself. Wade was arrested on April 2, and counsel was appointed to represent him on April 26. Fifteen days later an FBI agent, without notice to Wade's lawyer, arranged to have the two bank employees observe a lineup made up of Wade and five or six other prisoners and conducted in a courtroom of the local county courthouse. Each person in the line wore strips of tape such as allegedly worn by the robber and upon direction each said something like "put the money in the bag," the words allegedly uttered by the robber. Both bank employees identified Wade in the lineup as the bank robber.

At trial, the two employees, when asked on direct examination if the robber was in the courtroom, pointed to Wade. The prior lineup identification was then elicited from both employees on cross-examination. At the close of testimony, Wade's counsel moved for a judgment of acquittal or, alternatively, to strike the bank officials' courtroom identifications on the ground that conduct of the lineup, without notice to and in the absence of his appointed counsel, violated his Fifth Amendment privilege against self-incrimination and his Sixth Amendment right to the assistance of counsel. The motion was denied, and Wade was convicted. The Court of Appeals for the Fifth Circuit reversed the conviction and ordered a new trial at which the in-court identification evidence was to be excluded, holding that, though the lineup did not violate Wade's Fifth Amendment rights, "the lineup, held as it was, in the absence of counsel, already chosen to represent appellant, was a violation of his Sixth Amendment rights .…" 358 F.2d 557, 560. We granted certiorari, 385 U.S. 811, and set the case for oral argument with No. 223, Gilbert v. California, post, p. 263, and No. 254, Stovall v. Denno, post, p. 293, which present similar questions. We reverse the judgment of the Court of Appeals and remand to that court with direction to enter a new judgment vacating the conviction and remanding the case to the District Court for further proceedings consistent with this opinion.

I

Neither the lineup itself nor anything shown by this record that Wade was required to do in the lineup violated his privilege against self-incrimination. We have only recently reaffirmed that the privilege "protects an accused only from being compelled to testify against himself, or otherwise provide the State with evidence of a testimonial or communicative nature .…" Schmerber v. California, 384 U.S. 757, 761.…

We have no doubt that compelling the accused merely to exhibit his person for observation by a prosecution witness prior to trial involves no compulsion of the accused to give evidence having testimonial significance. It is compulsion of the accused to exhibit his physical characteristics, not compulsion to disclose any knowledge he might have.… [C]ompelling Wade to speak within hearing distance of the witnesses, even to utter words purportedly uttered by the robber, was not compulsion to utter statements of a "testimonial" nature; he was required to use his voice as an identifying physical characteristic, not to speak his guilt. …

Moreover, it deserves emphasis that this case presents no question of the admissibility in evidence of anything Wade said or did at the lineup which implicates his privilege. The Government offered no such evidence as part of its case, and what came out about the lineup proceedings on Wade's cross-examination of the bank employees involved no violation of Wade's privilege.

II

The fact that the lineup involved no violation of Wade's privilege against self-incrimination does not, however, dispose of his contention that the courtroom identifications should have been excluded because the lineup was conducted without notice to and in the absence of his counsel. Our rejection of the right to counsel claim in *Schmerber* rested on our conclusion in that case that "[n]o issue of counsel's ability to assist petitioner in respect of any rights he did possess is presented." 384 U.S., at 766. In contrast, in this case it is urged that the assistance of counsel at the lineup was indispensable to protect Wade's most basic right as a criminal defendant—his right to a fair trial at which the witnesses against him might be meaningfully cross-examined.

... [T]oday's law enforcement machinery involves critical confrontations of the accused by the prosecution at pretrial proceedings
where the results might well settle the accused's fate and reduce the
trial itself to a mere formality. In recognition of these realities of
modern criminal prosecution, our cases have construed the Sixth
Amendment guarantee to apply to "critical" stages of the proceedings. The guarantee reads: "In all criminal prosecutions, the
accused shall enjoy the right ... to have the Assistance of Counsel
for his defence." (Emphasis supplied.) The plain wording of this
guarantee thus encompasses counsel's assistance whenever necessary to assure a meaningful "defence."

        . . .

... [I]n addition to counsel's presence at trial, the accused is
guaranteed that he need not stand alone against the State at any
stage of the prosecution, formal or informal, in court or out, where
counsel's absence might derogate from the accused's right to a fair
trial. The security of that right is as much the aim of the right to
counsel as it is of the other guarantees of the Sixth Amendment—
the right of the accused to a speedy and public trial by an impartial
jury, his right to be informed of the nature and cause of the
accusation, and his right to be confronted with the witnesses against
him and to have compulsory process for obtaining witnesses in his
favor. The presence of counsel at such critical confrontations, as at
the trial itself, operates to assure that the accused's interests will be
protected consistently with our adversary theory of criminal prosecution....

In sum, the principle of Powell v. Alabama [287 U.S. 45 (1932)]
and succeeding cases requires that we scrutinize *any* pretrial confrontation of the accused to determine whether the presence of his
counsel is necessary to preserve the defendant's basic right to a fair
trial as affected by his right meaningfully to cross-examine the
witnesses against him and to have effective assistance of counsel at
the trial itself. It calls upon us to analyze whether potential
substantial prejudice to defendant's rights inheres in the particular
confrontation and the ability of counsel to help avoid that prejudice.

III

The Government characterizes the lineup as a mere preparatory
step in the gathering of the prosecution's evidence, not different—
for Sixth Amendment purposes—from various other preparatory
steps, such as systematized or scientific analyzing of the accused's
fingerprints, blood sample, clothing, hair, and the like. We think
there are differences which preclude such stages being characterized
as critical stages at which the accused has the right to the presence
of his counsel. Knowledge of the techniques of science and technology is sufficiently available, and the variables in techniques few
enough, that the accused has the opportunity for a meaningful
confrontation of the Government's case at trial through the ordinary

processes of cross-examination of the Government's expert witnesses and the presentation of the evidence of his own experts. The denial of a right to have his counsel present at such analyses does not therefore violate the Sixth Amendment; they are not critical stages since there is minimal risk that his counsel's absence at such stages might derogate from his right to a fair trial.

IV

But the confrontation compelled by the State between the accused and the victim or witnesses to a crime to elicit identification evidence is peculiarly riddled with innumerable dangers and variable factors which might seriously, even crucially, derogate from a fair trial. The vagaries of eyewitness identification are well-known; the annals of criminal law are rife with instances of mistaken identification. Mr. Justice Frankfurter once said: "What is the worth of identification testimony even when uncontradicted? The identification of strangers is proverbially untrustworthy. The hazards of such testimony are established by a formidable number of instances in the records of English and American trials. These instances are recent—not due to the brutalities of ancient criminal procedure." The Case of Sacco and Vanzetti 30 (1927). A major factor contributing to the high incidence of miscarriage of justice from mistaken identification has been the degree of suggestion inherent in the manner in which the prosecution presents the suspect to witnesses for pretrial identification. A commentator has observed that "[t]he influence of improper suggestion upon identifying witnesses probably accounts for more miscarriages of justice than any other single factor—perhaps it is responsible for more such errors than all other factors combined." Wall, Eye-Witness Identification in Criminal Cases 26. Suggestion can be created intentionally or unintentionally in many subtle ways. And the dangers for the suspect are particularly grave when the witness' opportunity for observation was insubstantial, and thus his susceptibility to suggestion the greatest.

Moreover, "[i]t is a matter of common experience that, once a witness has picked out the accused at the line-up, he is not likely to go back on his word later on, so that in practice the issue of identity may (in the absence of other relevant evidence) for all practical purposes be determined there and then, before the trial."[8]

The pretrial confrontation for purpose of identification may take the form of a lineup, also known as an "identification parade" or "showup," as in the present case, or presentation of the suspect alone to the witness, as in Stovall v. Denno, supra. It is obvious that risks of suggestion attend either form of confrontation and increase the dangers inhering in eyewitness identification. But as is

---

8. Williams & Hammelmann, Identification Parades, Part I, [1963] Crim.L.Rev. 479, 482.

the case with secret interrogations, there is serious difficulty in depicting what transpires at lineups and other forms of identification confrontations. "Privacy results in secrecy and this in turn results in a gap in our knowledge as to what in fact goes on . . . ." Miranda v. Arizona, [384 U.S. 436 (1966)] at 448. For the same reasons, the defense can seldom reconstruct the manner and mode of lineup identification for judge or jury at trial. Those participating in a lineup with the accused may often be police officers; in any event, the participants' names are rarely recorded or divulged at trial. The impediments to an objective observation are increased when the victim is the witness. Lineups are prevalent in rape and robbery prosecutions and present a particular hazard that a victim's understandable outrage may excite vengeful or spiteful motives. In any event, neither witnesses nor lineup participants are apt to be alert for conditions prejudicial to the suspect. And if they were, it would likely be of scant benefit to the suspect since neither witnesses nor lineup participants are likely to be schooled in the detection of suggestive influences. Improper influences may go undetected by a suspect, guilty or not, who experiences the emotional tension which we might expect in one being confronted with potential accusers. Even when he does observe abuse, if he has a criminal record he may be reluctant to take the stand and open up the admission of prior convictions. Moreover, any protestations by the suspect of the fairness of the lineup made at trial are likely to be in vain; the jury's choice is between the accused's unsupported version and that of the police officers present. In short, the accused's inability effectively to reconstruct at trial any unfairness that occurred at the lineup may deprive him of his only opportunity meaningfully to attack the credibility of the witness' courtroom identification.

What facts have been disclosed in specific cases about the conduct of pretrial confrontations for identification illustrate both the potential for substantial prejudice to the accused at that stage and the need for its revelation at trial.

. . . [S]tate reports, in the course of describing prior identifications admitted as evidence of guilt, reveal numerous instances of suggestive procedures, for example, that all in the lineup but the suspect were known to the identifying witness, that the other participants in a lineup were grossly dissimilar in appearance to the suspect, that only the suspect was required to wear distinctive clothing which the culprit allegedly wore, that the witness is told by the police that they have caught the culprit after which the defendant is brought before the witness alone or is viewed in jail, that the suspect is pointed out before or during a lineup, and that the participants in the lineup are asked to try on an article of clothing which fits only the suspect.

The potential for improper influence is illustrated by the circumstances, insofar as they appear, surrounding the prior identifications in the three cases we decide today. In the present case, the testimony of the identifying witnesses elicited on cross-examination revealed that those witnesses were taken to the courthouse and seated in the courtroom to await assembly of the lineup. The courtroom faced on a hallway observable to the witnesses through an open door. The cashier testified that she saw Wade "standing in the hall" within sight of an FBI agent. Five or six other prisoners later appeared in the hall. The vice president testified that he saw a person in the hall in the custody of the agent who "resembled the person that we identified as the one that had entered the bank."

The lineup in *Gilbert,* supra, was conducted in an auditorium in which some 100 witnesses to several alleged state and federal robberies charged to Gilbert made wholesale identifications of Gilbert as the robber in each other's presence, a procedure said to be fraught with dangers of suggestion. And the vice of suggestion created by the identification in *Stovall,* supra, was the presentation to the witness of the suspect alone handcuffed to police officers. It is hard to imagine a situation more clearly conveying the suggestion to the witness that the one presented is believed guilty by the police. . . .

The few cases that have surfaced therefore reveal the existence of a process attended with hazards of serious unfairness to the criminal accused and strongly suggest the plight of the more numerous defendants who are unable to ferret out suggestive influences in the secrecy of the confrontation. We do not assume that these risks are the result of police procedures intentionally designed to prejudice an accused. Rather we assume they derive from the dangers inherent in eyewitness identification and the suggestibility inherent in the context of the pretrial identification. Willams & Hammelmann, in one of the most comprehensive studies of such forms of identification, said, "[T]he fact that the police themselves have, in a given case, little or no doubt that the man put up for identification has committed the offense, and that their chief pre-occupation is with the problem of getting sufficient proof, because he has not 'come clean,' involves a danger that this persuasion may communicate itself even in a doubtful case to the witness in some way . . . ." Identification Parades, Part I, [1963] Crim.L.Rev. 479, 483.

Insofar as the accused's conviction may rest on a courtroom identification in fact the fruit of a suspect pretrial identification which the accused is helpless to subject to effective scrutiny at trial, the accused is deprived of that right of cross-examination which is an essential safeguard to his right to confront the witnesses against him. . . . And even though cross-examination is a precious safeguard to a fair trial, it cannot be viewed as an absolute assurance of accuracy and reliability. Thus in the present context, where so many variables and pitfalls exist, the first line of defense must be the prevention of unfairness and the lessening of the hazards of eyewitness identification at the lineup itself. The trial which might determine the accused's fate may well not be that in the courtroom but that at the pretrial confrontation, with the State aligned against the accused, the witness the sole jury, and the accused unprotected against the overreaching, intentional or unintentional, and with little or no effective appeal from the judgment there rendered by the witness—"that's the man."

Since it appears that there is grave potential for prejudice, intentional or not, in the pretrial lineup, which may not be capable of reconstruction at trial, and since presence of counsel itself can often avert prejudice and assure a meaningful confrontation at trial, there can be little doubt that for Wade the post-indictment lineup was a critical stage of the prosecution at which he was "as much entitled to such aid [of counsel] . . . as at the trial itself." Powell v. Alabama, 287 U.S. 45, 57. Thus both Wade and his counsel should have been notified of the impending lineup, and counsel's presence should have been a requisite to conduct of the lineup, absent an "intelligent waiver." See Carnley v. Cochran, 369 U.S. 506. No substantial countervailing policy considerations have been advanced against the requirement of the presence of counsel. Concern is expressed that the requirement will forestall prompt identifications and result in obstruction of the confrontations. As for the first, we note that in the two cases in which the right to counsel is today held to apply, counsel had already been appointed and no argument is made in either case that notice to counsel would have prejudicially delayed the confrontations. Moreover, we leave open the question whether the presence of substitute counsel might not suffice where notification and presence of the suspect's own counsel would result in prejudicial delay. And to refuse to recognize the right to counsel for fear that counsel will obstruct the course of justice is contrary to the basic assumptions upon which this Court has operated in Sixth Amendment cases. . . . In our view counsel can hardly impede legitimate law enforcement; on the contrary, for the reasons expressed, law enforcement may be assisted by preventing the infiltration of taint in the prosecution's identification evidence. That result cannot help the guilty avoid conviction but can only help assure that the right man has been brought to justice.

Legislative or other regulations, such as those of local police departments, which eliminate the risks of abuse and unintentional suggestion at lineup proceedings and the impediments to meaningful confrontation at trial may also remove the basis for regarding the stage as "critical." But neither Congress nor the federal authorities have seen fit to provide a solution. What we hold today "in no way creates a constitutional straitjacket which will handicap sound efforts at reform, nor is it intended to have this effect." Miranda v. Arizona, supra, at 467.

V

We come now to the question whether the denial of Wade's motion to strike the courtroom identification by the bank witnesses

at trial because of the absence of his counsel at the lineup required, as the Court of Appeals held, the grant of a new trial at which such evidence is to be excluded. We do not think this disposition can be justified without first giving the Government the opportunity to establish by clear and convincing evidence that the in-court identifications were based upon observations of the suspect other than the lineup identification.... Where, as here, the admissibility of evidence of the lineup identification itself is not involved, a *per se* rule of exclusion of courtroom identification would be unjustified.[32] ...
A rule limited solely to the exclusion of testimony concerning identification at the lineup itself, without regard to admissibility of the courtroom identification, would render the right to counsel an empty one. The lineup is most often used, as in the present case, to crystallize the witnesses' identification of the defendant for future reference. We have already noted that the lineup identification will have that effect. The State may then rest upon the witnesses' unequivocal courtroom identification, and not mention the pretrial identification as part of the State's case at trial. Counsel is then in the predicament in which Wade's counsel found himself—realizing that possible unfairness at the lineup may be the sole means of attack upon the unequivocal courtroom identification, and having to probe in the dark in an attempt to discover and reveal unfairness, while bolstering the government witness' courtroom identification by bringing out and dwelling upon his prior identification. Since counsel's presence at the lineup would equip him to attack not only the lineup identification but the courtroom identification as well, limiting the impact of violation of the right to counsel to exclusion of evidence only of identification at the lineup itself disregards a critical element of that right.

We think it follows that the proper test to be applied in these situations is that quoted in Wong Sun v. United States, 371 U.S. 471, 488, " '[W]hether, granting establishment of the primary illegality, the evidence to which instant objection is made has been come at by exploitation of that illegality or instead by means sufficiently distinguishable to be purged of the primary taint.' Maguire, Evidence of Guilt 221 (1959)." ... Application of this test in the present context requires consideration of various factors; for example, the prior opportunity to observe the alleged criminal act, the existence of any discrepancy between any pre-lineup description and the defendant's actual description, any identification prior to lineup of another person, the identification by picture of the defendant prior to the lineup, failure to identify the defendant on a prior occasion, and the lapse of time between the alleged act and the lineup identification. It is also relevant to consider those facts which, despite the absence of counsel, are disclosed concerning the conduct of the lineup.

---

32. We reach a contrary conclusion in Gilbert v. California, supra, as to the admissibility of the witness' testimony that he also identified the accused at the lineup.

. . .

The judgment of the Court of Appeals is vacated and the case is remanded to that court with direction to enter a new judgment vacating the conviction and remanding the case to the District Court for further proceedings consistent with this opinion.

It is so ordered.

MR. JUSTICE WHITE, whom MR. JUSTICE HARLAN and MR. JUSTICE STEWART join, dissenting in part and concurring in part.

The Court has again propounded a broad constitutional rule barring use of a wide spectrum of relevant and probative evidence, solely because a step in its ascertainment or discovery occurs outside the presence of defense counsel. This was the approach of the Court in Miranda v. Arizona, 384 U.S. 436. I objected then to what I thought was an uncritical and doctrinaire approach without satisfactory factual foundation. I have much the same view of the present ruling and therefore dissent from the judgment and from Parts II, IV, and V of the Court's opinion.

The Court's opinion is far-reaching. It proceeds first by creating a new *per se* rule of constitutional law: a criminal suspect cannot be subjected to a pretrial identification process in the absence of his counsel without violating the Sixth Amendment. If he is, the State may not buttress a later courtroom identification of the witness by any reference to the previous identification. Furthermore, the courtroom identification is not admissible at all unless the State can establish by clear and convincing proof that the testimony is not the fruit of the earlier identification made in the absence of defendant's counsel—admittedly a heavy burden for the State and probably an impossible one. To all intents and purposes, courtroom identifications are barred if pretrial identifications have occurred without counsel being present.

The rule applies to any lineup, to any other techniques employed to produce an identification and *a fortiori* to a face-to-face encounter between the witness and the suspect alone, regardless of when the identification occurs, in time or place, and whether before or after indictment or information. It matters not how well the witness knows the suspect, whether the witness is the suspect's mother, brother, or long-time associate, and no matter how long or well the witness observed the perpetrator at the scene of the crime. The kidnap victim who has lived for days with his abductor is in the same category as the witness who has had only a fleeting glimpse of the criminal. Neither may identify the suspect without defendant's counsel being present. The same strictures apply regardless of the number of other witnesses who positively identify the defendant and regardless of the corroborative evidence showing that it was the defendant who had committed the crime.

The premise for the Court's rule is not the general unreliability of eyewitness identifications nor the difficulties inherent in observation, recall, and recognition. The Court assumes a narrower evil as the basis for its rule—improper police suggestion which contributes to erroneous identifications. The Court apparently believes that improper police procedures are so widespread that a broad prophylactic rule must be laid down, requiring the presence of counsel at all pretrial identifications, in order to detect recurring instances of police misconduct. I do not share this pervasive distrust of all official investigations. None of the materials the Court relies upon supports it. Certainly, I would bow to solid fact, but the Court quite obviously does not have before it any reliable, comprehensive survey of current police practices on which to base its new rule. Until it does, the Court should avoid excluding relevant evidence from state criminal trials. . . .

The Court goes beyond assuming that a great majority of the country's police departments are following improper practices at pretrial identifications. To find the lineup a "critical" stage of the proceeding and to exclude identifications made in the absence of counsel, the Court must also assume that police "suggestion," if it occurs at all, leads to erroneous rather than accurate identifications and that reprehensible police conduct will have an unavoidable and largely undiscoverable impact on the trial. This in turn assumes that there is now no adequate source from which defense counsel can learn about the circumstances of the pretrial identification in order to place before the jury all of the considerations which should enter into an appraisal of courtroom identification evidence. But these are treacherous and unsupported assumptions,[3] resting as they do on the notion that the defendant will not be aware, that the police and the witnesses will forget or prevaricate, that defense counsel will be unable to bring out the truth and that neither jury, judge, nor appellate court is a sufficient safeguard against unacceptable police conduct occurring at a pretrial identification procedure. I am unable to share the Court's view of the willingness of the police and the ordinary citizen-witness to dissemble, either with respect to the identification of the defendant or with respect to the circumstances surrounding a pretrial identification.

3. The instant case and its companions, Gilbert v. California, post, p. 279, and Stovall v. Denno, post, p. 309, certainly lend no support to the Court's assumptions. The police conduct deemed improper by the Court in the three cases seems to have come to light at trial in the ordinary course of events. One can ask what more counsel would have learned at the pretrial identifications that would have been relevant for truth determination at trial. When the Court premises its constitutional rule on police conduct so subtle as to defy description and subsequent disclosure it deals in pure speculation. If police conduct is intentionally veiled, the police will know about it, and I am unwilling to speculate that defense counsel at trial will be unable to reconstruct the known circumstances of the pretrial identification. And if the "unknown" influence on identifications is "innocent," the Court's general premise evaporates and the problem is simply that of the inherent shortcomings of eyewitness testimony.

There are several striking aspects to the Court's holding. First, the rule does not bar courtroom identifications where there have been no previous identifications in the presence of the police, although when identified in the courtroom, the defendant is known to be in custody and charged with the commission of a crime. Second, the Court seems to say that if suitable legislative standards were adopted for the conduct of pretrial identifications, thereby lessening the hazards in such confrontations, it would not insist on the presence of counsel. But if this is true, why does not the Court simply fashion what it deems to be constitutionally acceptable procedures for the authorities to follow? Certainly the Court is correct in suggesting that the new rule will be wholly inapplicable where police departments themselves have established suitable safeguards.

Third, courtroom identification may be barred, absent counsel at a prior identification, regardless of the extent of counsel's information concerning the circumstances of the previous confrontation between witness and defendant—apparently even if there were recordings or sound-movies of the events as they occurred. But if the rule is premised on the defendant's right to have his counsel know, there seems little basis for not accepting other means to inform. A disinterested observer, recordings, photographs—any one of them would seem adequate to furnish the basis for a meaningful cross-examination of the eyewitness who identifies the defendant in the courtroom.

I share the Court's view that the criminal trial, at the very least, should aim at truthful factfinding, including accurate eyewitness identifications. I doubt, however, on the basis of our present information, that the tragic mistakes which have occurred in criminal trials are as much the product of improper police conduct as they are the consequence of the difficulties inherent in eyewitness testimony and in resolving evidentiary conflicts by court or jury. I doubt that the Court's new rule will obviate these difficulties, or that the situation will be measurably improved by inserting defense counsel into the investigative processes of police departments everywhere.

But, it may be asked, what possible state interest militates against requiring the presence of defense counsel at lineups? After all, the argument goes, he *may* do some good, he *may* upgrade the quality of identification evidence in state courts and he can scarcely do any harm. Even if true, this is a feeble foundation for fastening an ironclad constitutional rule upon state criminal procedures. Absent some reliably established constitutional violation, the processes by which the States enforce their criminal laws are their own prerogative. The States *do* have an interest in conducting their own affairs, an interest which cannot be displaced simply by saying that there are no valid arguments with respect to the merits of a federal rule emanating from this Court.

Beyond this, however, requiring counsel at pretrial identifications as an invariable rule trenches on other valid state interests. One of them is its concern with the prompt and efficient enforcement of its criminal laws. Identifications frequently take place after arrest but before an indictment is returned or an information is filed. The police may have arrested a suspect on probable cause but may still have the wrong man. Both the suspect and the State have every interest in a prompt identification at that stage, the suspect in order to secure his immediate release and the State because prompt and early identification enhances *accurate* identification and because it must know whether it is on the right investigative track. Unavoidably, however, the absolute rule requiring the presence of counsel will cause significant delay and it may very well result in no pretrial identification at all. Counsel must be appointed and a time arranged convenient for him and the witnesses. Meanwhile, it may be necessary to file charges against the suspect who may then be released on bail, in the federal system very often on his own recognizance, with neither the State nor the defendant having the benefit of a properly conducted identification procedure.

Nor do I think the witnesses themselves can be ignored. They will now be required to be present at the convenience of counsel rather than their own. Many may be much less willing to participate if the identification stage is transformed into an adversary proceeding not under the control of a judge. Others may fear for their own safety if their identity is known at an early date, especially when there is no way of knowing until the lineup occurs whether or not the police really have the right man.

Finally, I think the Court's new rule is vulnerable in terms of its own unimpeachable purpose of increasing the reliability of identification testimony.

Law enforcement officers have the obligation to convict the guilty and to make sure they do not convict the innocent. They must be dedicated to making the criminal trial a procedure for the ascertainment of the true facts surrounding the commission of the crime. To this extent, our so-called adversary system is not adversary at all; nor should it be. But defense counsel has no comparable obligation to ascertain or present the truth. Our system assigns him a different mission. He must be and is interested in preventing the conviction of the innocent, but, absent a voluntary plea of guilty, we also insist that he defend his client whether he is innocent or guilty. The State has the obligation to present the evidence. Defense counsel need present nothing, even if he knows what the truth is. He need not furnish any witnesses to the police, or reveal any confidences of his client, or furnish any other information to help the prosecution's case. If he can confuse a witness, even a truthful one, or make him appear at a disadvantage, unsure or indecisive, that will be his normal course. Our interest in not convicting the innocent permits counsel to put the State to its proof, to put the State's case in the worst possible light, regardless of what he thinks or knows to be the truth. Undoubtedly there are some limits which defense counsel must observe but more often than not, defense counsel will cross-examine a prosecution witness, and impeach him if he can, even if he thinks the witness is telling the truth, just as he will attempt to destroy a witness who he thinks is lying. In this respect, as part of our modified adversary system and as part of the duty imposed on the most honorable defense counsel, we countenance or require conduct which in many instances has little, if any, relation to the search for truth.

I would not extend this system, at least as it presently operates, to police investigations and would not require counsel's presence at pretrial identification procedures. Counsel's interest is in not having his client placed at the scene of the crime, regardless of his whereabouts. Some counsel may advise their clients to refuse to make any movements or to speak any words in a lineup or even to appear in one. To that extent the impact on truthful factfinding is quite obvious. Others will not only observe what occurs and develop possibilities for later cross-examination but will hover over witnesses and begin their cross-examination then, menacing truthful factfinding as thoroughly as the Court fears the police now do. Certainly there is an implicit invitation to counsel to suggest rules for the lineup and to manage and produce it as best he can. I therefore doubt that the Court's new rule, at least absent some clearly defined limits on counsel's role, will measurably contribute to more reliable pretrial identifications. My fears are that it will have precisely the opposite result. It may well produce fewer convictions, but that is hardly a proper measure of its long-run acceptability. In my view, the State is entitled to investigate and develop its case outside the presence of defense counsel. This includes the right to have private conversations with identification witnesses, just as defense counsel may have his own consultations with these and other witnesses without having the prosecutor present.

Whether today's judgment would be an acceptable exercise of supervisory power over federal courts is another question. But as a constitutional matter, the judgment in this case is erroneous and although I concur in Parts I and III of the Court's opinion I respectfully register this dissent.[*]

[*] Chief Justice Warren and Justice Douglas noted that they joined the opinion of the Court except for Part I. Justice Clark wrote a brief concurring opinion. Justice Black wrote an opinion dissenting in part and concurring in part. Justice Fortas wrote an opinion concurring in part and dissenting in part, which Chief Justice Warren and Justice Douglas joined.

KIRBY v. ILLINOIS

406 U.S. 682, 92 S.Ct. 1877, 32 L.Ed.2d 411 (1972).

MR. JUSTICE STEWART announced the judgment of the Court and an opinion in which THE CHIEF JUSTICE, MR. JUSTICE BLACK-MUN, and MR. JUSTICE REHNQUIST join.

In United States v. Wade, 388 U.S. 218, and Gilbert v. California, 388 U.S. 263, this Court held "that a post-indictment pretrial lineup at which the accused is exhibited to identifying witnesses is a critical stage of the criminal prosecution; that police conduct of such a lineup without notice to and in the absence of his counsel denies the accused his Sixth [and Fourteenth] Amendment right to counsel and calls in question the admissibility at trial of the in-court identifications of the accused by witnesses who attended the line-up." Gilbert v. California, supra, at 272. Those cases further held that no "in-court identifications" are admissible in evidence if their "source" is a lineup conducted in violation of this constitutional standard. "Only a *per se* exclusionary rule as to such testimony can be an effective sanction," the Court said, "to assure that law enforcement authorities will respect the accused's constitutional right to the presence of his counsel at the critical lineup." Id., at 273. In the present case we are asked to extend the *Wade-Gilbert per se* exclusionary rule to identification testimony based upon a police station showup that took place *before* the defendant had been indicted or otherwise formally charged with any criminal offense.

On February 21, 1968, a man named Willie Shard reported to the Chicago police that the previous day two men had robbed him on a Chicago street of a wallet containing, among other things, traveler's checks and a Social Security card. On February 22, two police officers stopped the petitioner and a companion, Ralph Bean, on West Madison Street in Chicago.[1] When asked for identification, the petitioner produced a wallet that contained three traveler's checks and a Social Security card, all bearing the name of Willie Shard. Papers with Shard's name on them were also found in Bean's possession. When asked to explain his possession of Shard's property, the petitioner first said that the traveler's checks were "play money," and then told the officers that he had won them in a crap game. The officers then arrested the petitioner and Bean and took them to a police station.

---

1. The officers stopped the petitioner and his companion because they thought the petitioner was a man named Hampton, who was "wanted" in connection with an unrelated criminal offense. The legitimacy of this stop and the subsequent arrest is not before us.

Only after arriving at the police station, and checking the records there, did the arresting officers learn of the Shard robbery. A police car was then dispatched to Shard's place of employment, where it picked up Shard and brought him to the police station. Immediately upon entering the room in the police station where the petitioner and Bean were seated at a table, Shard positively identified them as the men who had robbed him two days earlier. No lawyer was present in the room, and neither the petitioner nor Bean had asked for legal assistance, or been advised of any right to the presence of counsel.

More than six weeks later, the petitioner and Bean were indicted for the robbery of Willie Shard. Upon arraignment, counsel was appointed to represent them, and they pleaded not guilty. A pretrial motion to suppress Shard's identification testimony was denied, and at the trial Shard testified as a witness for the prosecution. In his testimony he described his identification of the two men at the police station on February 22, and identified them again in the courtroom as the men who had robbed him on February 20. He was cross-examined at length regarding the circumstances of his identification of the two defendants.... The jury found both defendants guilty, and the petitioner's conviction was affirmed on appeal. People v. Kirby, 121 Ill.App.2d 323, 257 N.E.2d 589. The Illinois appellate court held that the admission of Shard's testimony was not error, relying upon an earlier decision of the Illinois Supreme Court ... holding that the *Wade-Gilbert per se* exclusionary rule is not applicable to pre-indictment confrontations. We granted certiorari, limited to this question. 402 U.S. 995.

I

We note at the outset that the constitutional privilege against compulsory self-incrimination is in no way implicated here. The Court emphatically rejected the claimed applicability of that constitutional guarantee in *Wade* itself ....

It follows that the doctrine of Miranda v. Arizona, 384 U.S. 436, has no applicability whatever to the issue before us; for the *Miranda* decision was based exclusively upon the Fifth and Fourteenth Amendment privilege against compulsory self-incrimination, upon the theory that custodial *interrogation* is inherently coercive.

The *Wade-Gilbert* exclusionary rule, by contrast, stems from a quite different constitutional guarantee—the guarantee of the right to counsel contained in the Sixth and Fourteenth Amendments. Unless all semblance of principled constitutional adjudication is to be abandoned, therefore, it is to the decisions construing that guarantee that we must look in determining the present controversy.

In a line of constitutional cases in this Court stemming back to the Court's landmark opinion in Powell v. Alabama, 287 U.S. 45, it has been firmly established that a person's Sixth and Fourteenth Amendment right to counsel attaches only at or after the time that adversary judicial proceedings have been initiated against him. ...

This is not to say that a defendant in a criminal case has a constitutional right to counsel only at the trial itself. The *Powell* case makes clear that the right attaches at the time of arraignment, and the Court has recently held that it exists also at the time of a preliminary hearing. Coleman v. Alabama, [399 U.S. 1 (1970)]. But the point is that, while members of the Court have differed as to existence of the right to counsel in the contexts of some of the above cases, *all* of those cases have involved points of time at or after the initiation of adversary judicial criminal proceedings— whether by way of formal charge, preliminary hearing, indictment, information, or arraignment.

The only seeming deviation from this long line of constitutional decisions was Escobedo v. Illinois, 378 U.S. 478. But *Escobedo* is not apposite here for two distinct reasons. First, the Court in retrospect perceived that the "prime purpose" of *Escobedo* was not to vindicate the constitutional right to counsel as such, but, like *Miranda,* "to guarantee full effectuation of the privilege against self-incrimination ...." Johnson v. New Jersey, 384 U.S. 719, 729. Secondly, and perhaps even more important for purely practical purposes, the Court has limited the holding of *Escobedo* to its own facts, Johnson v. New Jersey, supra, at 733–734, and those facts are not remotely akin to the facts of the case before us.

The initiation of judicial criminal proceedings is far from a mere formalism. It is the starting point of our whole system of adversary criminal justice. For it is only then that the government has committed itself to prosecute, and only then that the adverse positions of government and defendant have solidified. It is then that a defendant finds himself faced with the prosecutorial forces of organized society, and immersed in the intricacies of substantive and procedural criminal law. It is this point, therefore, that marks the commencement of the "criminal prosecutions" to which alone the explicit guarantees of the Sixth Amendment are applicable. ...

In this case we are asked to import into a routine police investigation an absolute constitutional guarantee historically and rationally applicable only after the onset of formal prosecutorial proceedings. We decline to do so. Less than a year after *Wade* and *Gilbert* were decided, the Court explained the rule of those decisions as follows: "The rationale of those cases was that an accused is entitled to counsel at any 'critical stage of the *prosecution*,' and that a post-indictment lineup is such a 'critical stage.' " (Emphasis supplied.) Simmons v. United States, 390 U.S. 377, 382–383. We decline to depart from that rationale today by imposing a *per se* exclusionary rule upon testimony concerning an identification that took place long before the commencement of any prosecution whatever.

II

What has been said is not to suggest that there may not be occasions during the course of a criminal investigation when the police do abuse identification procedures. Such abuses are not beyond the reach of the Constitution. As the Court pointed out in *Wade* itself, it is always necessary to "scrutinize *any* pretrial confrontation . . . ." 388 U.S., at 227. The Due Process Clause of the Fifth and Fourteenth Amendments forbids a lineup that is unnecessarily suggestive and conducive to irreparable mistaken identification. Stovall v. Denno, 388 U.S. 293; Foster v. California, 394 U.S. 440. When a person has not been formally charged with a criminal offense, *Stovall* strikes the appropriate constitutional balance between the right of a suspect to be protected from prejudicial procedures and the interest of society in the prompt and purposeful investigation of an unsolved crime.

The judgment is affirmed.

MR. JUSTICE BRENNAN, with whom MR. JUSTICE DOUGLAS and MR. JUSTICE MARSHALL join, dissenting.

. . .

While it should go without saying, it appears necessary, in view of the plurality opinion today, to re-emphasize that [United States v.] *Wade* [388 U.S. 218 (1967)] did not require the presence of counsel at pretrial confrontations for identification purposes simply on the basis of an abstract consideration of the words "criminal prosecutions" in the Sixth Amendment. Counsel is required at those confrontations because "the dangers inherent in eyewitness identification and the suggestibility inherent in the context of the pretrial identification," id., at 235, mean that protection must be afforded to the "most basic right [of] a criminal defendant—his right to a fair trial at which the witnesses against him might be meaningfully cross-examined," id., at 224. Indeed, the Court expressly stated that "[l]egislative or other regulations, such as those of local police departments, which eliminate the risks of abuse and unintentional suggestion at lineup proceedings and the impediments to meaningful confrontation at trial may also remove the basis for regarding the stage as 'critical.'" Id., at 239; see id., at 239 n. 30; Gilbert v. California, 388 U.S., at 273. Hence, "the initiation of adversary judicial criminal proceedings," ante, at 689, is completely irrelevant to whether counsel is necessary at a pretrial confrontation for identification in order to safeguard the accused's constitutional rights to confrontation and the effective assistance of counsel at his trial.

In view of *Wade*, it is plain, and the plurality today does not attempt to dispute it, that there inhere in a confrontation for identification conducted after arrest the identical hazards to a fair trial that inhere in such a confrontation conducted "after the onset of formal prosecutorial proceedings." Id., at 690. The plurality apparently considers an arrest, which for present purposes we must assume to be based upon probable cause, to be nothing more than part of "a routine police investigation." ibid., and thus not "the starting point of our whole system of adversary criminal justice," id., at 689. An arrest, according to the plurality, does not face the accused "with the prosecutorial forces of organized society," nor immerse him "in the intricacies of substantive and procedural criminal law." Those consequences ensue, says the plurality, only with "[t]he initiation of judicial criminal proceedings," "[f]or it is only then that the government has committed itself to prosecute, and only then that the adverse positions of government and defendant have solidified." Id. If these propositions do not amount to "mere formalism," id., it is difficult to know how to characterize them. An arrest evidences the belief of the police that the perpetrator of a crime has been caught. A post-arrest confrontation for identification is not "a mere preparatory step in the gathering of the prosecution's evidence." *Wade,* supra, at 227. A primary, and frequently sole, purpose of the confrontation for identification at that stage is to accumulate proof to buttress the conclusion of the police that they have the offender in hand. The plurality offers no reason, and I can think of none, for concluding that a post-arrest confrontation for identification, unlike a post-charge confrontation, is not among those "critical confrontations of the accused by the prosecution at pretrial proceedings where the results might well settle the accused's fate and reduce the trial itself to a mere formality." Id., at 224.

The highly suggestive form of confrontation employed in this case underscores the point. This showup was particularly fraught with the peril of mistaken identification. In the setting of a police station squad room where all present except petitioner and Bean were police officers, the danger was quite real that Shard's understandable resentment might lead him too readily to agree with the police that the pair under arrest, and the only persons exhibited to him, were indeed the robbers. "It is hard to imagine a situation more clearly conveying the suggestion to the witness that the one presented is believed guilty by the police." Id., at 234. The State had no case without Shard's identification testimony, and safeguards against that consequence were therefore of critical importance. Shard's testimony itself demonstrates the necessity for such safeguards. On direct examination, Shard identified petitioner and Bean not as the alleged robbers on trial in the courtroom, but as the pair he saw at the police station. His testimony thus lends strong support to the observation, quoted by the Court in *Wade,* 388 U.S., at 229, that "[i]t is a matter of common experience that, once a witness has picked out the accused at the line-up, he is not likely to go back on his word later on, so that in practice the issue of identity may (in the absence of other relevant evidence) for all practical purposes be determined there and then, before the trial." Williams & Hammelmann, Identification Parades, Part I, [1963] Crim.L.Rev. 479, 482.

[*]

. . .

---

[*] Chief Justice Burger wrote a brief concurring opinion. Justice Powell wrote a brief opinion concurring in the result. Justice White wrote a brief dissenting opinion.

SIMMONS v. UNITED STATES

390 U.S. 377, 88 S.Ct. 967, 19 L.Ed.2d 1247 (1968).

MR. JUSTICE HARLAN delivered the opinion of the Court.

This case presents issues arising out of the petitioners' trial and conviction in the United States District Court for the Northern District of Illinois for the armed robbery of a federally insured savings and loan association.

The evidence at trial showed that at about 1:45 p.m. on February 27, 1964, two men entered a Chicago savings and loan association. One of them pointed a gun at a teller and ordered her to put money into a sack which the gunman supplied. The men remained in the bank about five minutes. After they left, a bank employee rushed to the street and saw one of the men sitting on the passenger side of a departing white 1960 Thunderbird automobile with a large scrape on the right door. Within an hour police located in the vicinity a car matching this description. They discovered that it belonged to a Mrs. Rey, sister-in-law of petitioner Simmons. She told the police that she had loaned the car for the afternoon to her brother, William Andrews.

At about 5:15 p.m. the same day, two FBI agents came to the house of Mrs. Mahon, Andrews' mother, about half a block from the place where the car was then parked. The agents had no warrant, and at trial it was disputed whether Mrs. Mahon gave them permission to search the house. They did search, and in the basement they found two suitcases, of which Mrs. Mahon disclaimed any knowledge. One suitcase contained, among other items, a gun holster, a sack similar to the one used in the robbery, and several coin cards and bill wrappers from the bank which had been robbed.

The following morning the FBI obtained from another of Andrews' sisters some snapshots of Andrews and of petitioner Simmons, who was said by the sister to have been with Andrews the previous afternoon. These snapshots were shown to the five bank employees who had witnessed the robbery. Each witness identified pictures of Simmons as representing one of the robbers. A week or two later, three of these employees identified photographs of petitioner Garrett as depicting the other robber, the other two witnesses stating that they did not have a clear view of the second robber.

The petitioners, together with William Andrews, subsequently were indicted and tried for the robbery, as indicated. Just prior to the trial, Garrett moved to suppress the Government's exhibit consisting of the suitcase containing the incriminating items. In order to establish his standing so to move, Garrett testified that, although he could not identify the suitcase with certainty, it was similar to one he had owned, and that he was the owner of clothing found inside the suitcase. The District Court denied the motion to suppress. Garrett's testimony at the "suppression" hearing was admitted against him at trial.

During the trial, all five bank employee witnesses identified Simmons as one of the robbers. Three of them identified Garrett as the second robber, the other two testifying that they did not get a good look at the second robber.   . . .

The jury found Simmons and Garrett, as well as Andrews, guilty as charged. On appeal, the Court of Appeals for the Seventh Circuit affirmed as to Simmons and Garrett, but reversed the conviction of Andrews on the ground that there was insufficient evidence to connect him with the robbery. 371 F.2d 296.

We granted certiorari as to Simmons and Garrett, 388 U.S. 906, to consider the following claims. First, Simmons asserts that his pretrial identification by means of photographs was in the circumstances so unnecessarily suggestive and conducive to misidentification as to deny him due process of law, or at least to require reversal of his conviction in the exercise of our supervisory power over the lower federal courts. . . . Garrett urges that his constitutional rights were violated when testimony given by him in support of his "suppression" motion was admitted against him at trial. For reasons which follow, we affirm the judgment of the Court of Appeals as to Simmons, but reverse as to Garrett.

I

The facts as to the identification claim are these. As has been noted previously, FBI agents on the day following the robbery obtained from Andrews' sister a number of snapshots of Andrews and Simmons. There seem to have been at least six of these pictures, consisting mostly of group photographs of Andrews, Simmons, and others. Later the same day, these were shown to the five bank employees who had witnessed the robbery at their place of work, the photographs being exhibited to each employee separately. Each of the five employees identified Simmons from the photographs. At later dates, some of these witnesses were again interviewed by the FBI and shown indeterminate numbers of pictures. Again, all identified Simmons. At trial, the Government did not introduce any of the photographs, but relied upon in-court identification by the five eyewitnesses, each of whom swore that Simmons was one of the robbers.

In support of his argument, Simmons looks to last Term's "lineup" decisions—United States v. Wade, 388 U.S. 218, and Gilbert v. California, 388 U.S. 263—in which this Court first departed from the rule that the manner of an extra-judicial identification affects only the weight, not the admissibility, of identification testimony at trial. The rationale of those cases was that an accused is entitled to counsel at any "critical stage of the prosecution," and that a post-indictment lineup is such a "critical stage." See 388 U.S., at 236–237. Simmons, however, does not contend that he was entitled to counsel at the time the pictures were shown to the witnesses. Rather, he asserts simply that in the circumstances the identification procedure was so unduly prejudicial as fatally to taint his conviction. This is a claim which must be evaluated in light of the totality of surrounding circumstances.... Viewed in that context, we find the claim untenable.

It must be recognized that improper employment of photographs by police may sometimes cause witnesses to err in identifying criminals. A witness may have obtained only a brief glimpse of a criminal, or may have seen him under poor conditions. Even if the police subsequently follow the most correct photographic identification procedures and show him the pictures of a number of individuals without indicating whom they suspect, there is some danger that the witness may make an incorrect identification. This danger will be increased if the police display to the witness only the picture of a single individual who generally resembles the person he saw, or if they show him the pictures of several persons among which the photograph of a single such individual recurs or is in some way emphasized. The chance of misidentification is also heightened if the police indicate to the witness that they have other evidence that one of the persons pictured committed the crime. Regardless of how the initial misidentification comes about, the witness thereafter is apt to retain in his memory the image of the photograph rather than of the person actually seen, reducing the trustworthiness of subsequent lineup or courtroom identification.

Despite the hazards of initial identification by photograph, this procedure has been used widely and effectively in criminal law enforcement, from the standpoint both of apprehending offenders and of sparing innocent suspects the ignominy of arrest by allowing eyewitnesses to exonerate them through scrutiny of photographs. The danger that use of the technique may result in convictions based on misidentification may be substantially lessened by a course of cross-examination at trial which exposes to the jury the method's potential for error. We are unwilling to prohibit its employment, either in the exercise of our supervisory power or, still less, as a matter of constitutional requirement. Instead, we hold that each case must be considered on its own facts, and that convictions based on eyewitness identification at trial following a pretrial identification by photograph will be set aside on that ground only if the photographic identification procedure was so impermissibly suggestive as to give rise to a very substantial likelihood of irreparable misidentification. This standard accords with our resolution of a similar issue in Stovall v. Denno, 388 U.S. 293, 301–302, and with decisions of other courts on the question of identification by photograph.

Applying the standard to this case, we conclude that petitioner Simmons' claim on this score must fail. In the first place, it is not suggested that it was unnecessary for the FBI to resort to photographic identification in this instance. A serious felony had been committed. The perpetrators were still at large. The inconclusive clues which law enforcement officials possessed led to Andrews and Simmons. It was essential for the FBI agents swiftly to determine whether they were on the right track, so that they could properly deploy their forces in Chicago and, if necessary, alert officials in other cities. The justification for this method of procedure was hardly less compelling than that which we found to justify the "one-man lineup" in Stovall v. Denno, supra.

In the second place, there was in the circumstances of this case little chance that the procedure utilized led to misidentification of Simmons. The robbery took place in the afternoon in a well-lighted bank. The robbers wore no masks. Five bank employees had been able to see the robber later identified as Simmons for periods ranging up to five minutes. Those witnesses were shown the photographs only a day later, while their memories were still fresh. At least six photographs were displayed to each witness. Apparently, these consisted primarily of group photographs, with Simmons and Andrews each appearing several times in the series. Each witness was alone when he or she saw the photographs. There is no evidence to indicate that the witnesses were told anything about the progress of the investigation, or that the FBI agents in any other way suggested which persons in the pictures were under suspicion.

Under these conditions, all five eyewitnesses identified Simmons as one of the robbers. None identified Andrews, who apparently was as prominent in the photographs as Simmons. These initial identifications were confirmed by all five witnesses in subsequent viewings of photographs and at trial, where each witness identified Simmons in person. Notwithstanding cross-examination, none of the witnesses displayed any doubt about their respective identifications of Simmons. Taken together, these circumstances leave little room for doubt that the identification of Simmons was correct, even though the identification procedure employed may have in some respects fallen short of the ideal. We hold that in the factual surroundings of this case the identification procedure used was not such as to deny Simmons due process of law or to call for reversal under our supervisory authority.[*]

.   .   .

---

[*] In United States v. Ash, 413 U.S. 300 (1973), the Supreme Court held that the Sixth Amendment (see United States v. Wade, 388 U.S. 218 (1967), above) does not require the presence of counsel at a post-indictment photographic identification.

III

Finally, it is contended that it was reversible error to allow the Government to use against Garrett on the issue of guilt the testimony given by him upon his unsuccessful motion to suppress as evidence the suitcase seized from Mrs. Mahon's basement and its contents. That testimony established that Garrett was the owner of the suitcase.

In order to effectuate the Fourth Amendment's guarantee of freedom from unreasonable searches and seizures, this Court long ago conferred upon defendants in federal prosecutions the right, upon motion and proof, to have excluded from trial evidence which had been secured by means of an unlawful search and seizure. Weeks v. United States, 232 U.S. 383. More recently, this Court has held that "the exclusionary rule is an essential part of both the Fourth and Fourteenth Amendments . . . ." Mapp v. Ohio, 367 U.S. 643, 657.

However, we have also held that rights assured by the Fourth Amendment are personal rights, and that they may be enforced by exclusion of evidence only at the instance of one whose own protection was infringed by the search and seizure. . . . Throughout this case, petitioner Garrett has justifiably, and without challenge from the Government, proceeded on the assumption that the standing requirements must be satisfied. On that premise, he contends that testimony given by a defendant to meet such requirements should not be admissible against him at trial on the question of guilt or innocence. We agree.

. . . Garrett evidently was not in Mrs. Mahon's house at the time his suitcase was seized from her basement. The only, or at least the most natural, way in which he could found standing to object to the admission of the suitcase was to testify that he was its owner. Thus, his testimony is to be regarded as an integral part of his Fourth Amendment exclusion claim. Under the rule laid down by the courts below, he could give that testimony only by assuming the risk that the testimony would later be admitted against him at trial. Testimony of this kind, which links a defendant to evidence which the Government considers important enough to seize and to seek to have admitted at trial, must often be highly prejudicial to a defendant. This case again serves as an example, for Garrett's admitted ownership of a suitcase which only a few hours after the robbery was found to contain money wrappers taken from the victimized bank was undoubtedly a strong piece of evidence against him. Without his testimony, the Government might have found it hard to prove that he was the owner of the suitcase.

. . . The lower courts which have considered the matter . . . have with two exceptions agreed with the holdings of the courts below that the defendant's testimony may be admitted when, as here, the motion to suppress has failed. The reasoning of some of these courts would seem to suggest that the testimony would be admissible even if the motion to suppress had succeeded, but the only court which has actually decided that question held that when the motion to suppress succeeds the testimony given in support of it is excludable as a "fruit" of the unlawful search. The rationale for admitting the testimony when the motion fails has been that the testimony is voluntarily given and relevant, and that it is therefore entitled to admission on the same basis as any other prior testimony or admission of a party.

It seems obvious that a defendant who knows that his testimony may be admissible against him at trial will sometimes be deterred from presenting the testimonial proof of standing necessary to assert a Fourth Amendment claim. The likelihood of inhibition is greatest when the testimony is known to be admissible regardless of the outcome of the motion to suppress. But even in jurisdictions where the admissibility of the testimony depends upon the outcome of the motion, there will be a deterrent effect in those marginal cases in which it cannot be estimated with confidence whether the motion will succeed. Since search-and-seizure claims depend heavily upon their individual facts, and since the law of search and seizure is in a state of flux, the incidence of such marginal cases cannot be said to be negligible. In such circumstances, a defendant with a substantial claim for the exclusion of evidence may conclude that the admission of the evidence, together with the Government's proof linking it to him, is preferable to risking the admission of his own testimony connecting himself with the seized evidence.

The rule adopted by the courts below does not merely impose upon a defendant a condition which may deter him from asserting a Fourth Amendment objection—it imposes a condition of a kind to which this Court has always been peculiarly sensitive. For a defendant who wishes to establish standing must do so at the risk that the words which he utters may later be used to incriminate him. Those courts which have allowed the admission of testimony given to establish standing have reasoned that there is no violation of the Fifth Amendment's Self-Incrimination Clause because the testimony was voluntary. As an abstract matter, this may well be true. A defendant is "compelled" to testify in support of a motion to suppress only in the sense that if he refrains from testifying he will have to forgo a benefit, and testimony is not always involuntary as a matter of law simply because it is given to obtain a benefit. However, the assumption which underlies this reasoning is that the defendant has a choice: he may refuse to testify and give up the benefit. When this assumption is applied to a situation in which the "benefit" to be gained is that afforded by another provision of the Bill of Rights, an undeniable tension is created. Thus, in this case Garrett was obliged either to give up what he believed, with advice of counsel, to be a valid Fourth Amendment claim or, in legal effect, to waive his Fifth Amendment privilege against self-incrimination. In these circumstances, we find it intolerable that one constitutional right should have to be surrendered in order to assert another. We therefore hold that when a defendant testifies in support of a motion to suppress evidence on Fourth Amendment grounds, his testimony may not thereafter be admitted against him at trial on the issue of guilt unless he makes no objection.

For the foregoing reasons, we affirm the judgment of the Court of Appeals so far as it relates to petitioner Simmons. We reverse the judgment with respect to petitioner Garrett, and as to him remand the case to the Court of Appeals for further proceedings consistent with this opinion.

It is so ordered.[*]

---

[*] Justice Black wrote an opinion concurring in part and dissenting in part. Justice White also wrote a brief opinion concurring in part and dissenting in part.

NEIL v. BIGGERS

409 U.S. 188, 93 S.Ct. 375, 34 L.Ed.2d 401 (1972).

MR. JUSTICE POWELL delivered the opinion of the Court.

In 1965, after a jury trial in a Tennessee court, respondent was convicted of rape and was sentenced to 20 years' imprisonment. The State's evidence consisted in part of testimony concerning a station house identification of respondent by the victim. The Tennessee Supreme Court affirmed. Biggers v. State, 219 Tenn. 553, 411 S.W.2d 696 (1967). On certiorari, the judgment of the Tennessee Supreme Court was "affirmed by an equally divided Court." Biggers v. Tennessee, 390 U.S. 404 (1968) (Mr. Justice Marshall not participating). Respondent then brought a federal habeas corpus action raising several claims. . . .

The District Court held that the claims were not barred and, after a hearing, held in an unreported opinion that the station house identification procedure was so suggestive as to violate due process. The Court of Appeals affirmed. Biggers v. Neil, 448 F.2d 91 (1971). We granted certiorari . . . .

. . .

We proceed, then, to consider respondent's due process claim. As the claim turns upon the facts, we must first review the relevant testimony at the jury trial and at the habeas corpus hearing regarding the rape and the identification. The victim testified at trial that on the evening of January 22, 1965, a youth with a butcher knife grabbed her in the doorway to her kitchen:

"A. [H]e grabbed me from behind, and grappled—twisted me on the floor. Threw me down on the floor.

"Q. And there was no light in that kitchen?

"A. Not in the kitchen.

"Q. So you couldn't have seen him then?

"A. Yes, I could see him, when I looked up in his face.

"Q. In the dark?

"A. He was right in the doorway—it was enough light from the bedroom shining through. Yes, I could see who he was.

"Q. You could see? No light? And you could see him and know him then?

"A. Yes." Tr. of Rec., pp. 33–34.

When the victim screamed, her 12-year-old daughter came out of her bedroom and also began to scream. The assailant directed the victim to "tell her [the daughter] to shut up, or I'll kill you both." She did so, and was then walked at knifepoint about two blocks along a railroad track, taken into a woods, and raped there. She testified that "the moon was shining brightly, full moon." After the rape, the assailant ran off, and she returned home, the whole incident having taken between 15 minutes and half an hour.

She then gave the police what the Federal District Court characterized as "only a very general description," describing him as "being fat and flabby with smooth skin, bushy hair and a youthful voice." Additionally, though not mentioned by the District Court, she testified at the habeas corpus hearing that she had described her assailant as being between 16 and 18 years old and between five feet ten inches and six feet tall, as weighing between 180 and 200 pounds, and as having a dark brown complexion. This testimony was substantially corroborated by that of a police officer who was testifying from his notes.

On several occasions over the course of the next seven months, she viewed suspects in her home or at the police station, some in lineups and others in showups, and was shown between 30 and 40 photographs. She told the police that a man pictured in one of the photographs had features similar to those of her assailant, but identified none of the suspects. On August 17, the police called her to the station to view petitioner, who was being detained on another charge. In an effort to construct a suitable lineup, the police checked the city jail and the city juvenile home. Finding no one at either place fitting petitioner's unusual physical description, they conducted a showup instead.

The showup itself consisted of two detectives walking respondent past the victim. At the victim's request, the police directed petitioner to say "shut up or I'll kill you." The testimony at trial was not altogether clear as to whether the victim first identified him and then asked that he repeat the words or made her identification after he had spoken. In any event, the victim testified that she had "no doubt" about her identification. At the habeas corpus hearing, she elaborated in response to questioning.

"A. That I have no doubt, I mean that I am sure that when—see, when I first laid eyes on him, I knew that it was the individual, because his face—well, there was just something that I don't think I could ever forget. I believe—

"Q. You say when you first laid eyes on him, which time are you referring to?

"A. When I identified him in the courthouse when I was took up to view the suspect." Pet. App., p. 127.

We must decide whether, as the courts below held, this identification and the circumstances surrounding it failed to comport with due process requirements.

III

We have considered on four occasions the scope of due process protection against the admission of evidence deriving from suggestive identification procedures. . . .

. . .

Some general guidelines emerge from these cases as to the relationship between suggestiveness and misidentification. It is, first of all, apparent that the primary evil to be avoided is "a very substantial likelihood of irreparable misidentification." Simmons v. United States, 390 U.S. [377 (1968)] at 384. While the phrase was coined as a standard for determining whether an in-court identification would be admissible in the wake of a suggestive out-of-court identification, with the deletion of "irreparable" it serves equally well as a standard for the admissibility of testimony concerning the out-of-court identification itself. It is the likelihood of misidentification which violates a defendant's right to due process. . . . Suggestive confrontations are disapproved because they increase the likelihood of misidentification, and unnecessarily suggestive ones are condemned for the further reason that the increased chance of misidentification is gratuitous. But as Stovall [v. Denno, 388 U.S. 293 (1967)] makes clear, the admission of evidence of a showup without more does not violate due process.

What is less clear from our cases is whether, as intimated by the District Court, unnecessary suggestiveness alone requires the exclusion of evidence. While we are inclined to agree with the courts below that the police did not exhaust all possibilities in seeking persons physically comparable to petitioner, we do not think that the evidence must therefore be excluded. The purpose of a strict rule barring evidence of unnecessarily suggestive confrontations would be to deter the police from using a less reliable procedure where a more reliable one may be available, not because in every instance the admission of evidence of such a confrontation offends due process. . . . Such a rule would have no place in the present case, since both the confrontation and the trial preceded Stovall v. Denno, supra, when we first gave notice that the suggestiveness of confrontation procedures was anything other than a matter to be argued to the jury.

We turn, then, to the central question, whether under the "totality of the circumstances" the identification was reliable even though the confrontation procedure was suggestive. As indicated by our cases, the factors to be considered in evaluating the likelihood of misidentification include the opportunity of the witness to view the criminal at the time of the crime, the witness' degree of attention, the accuracy of the witness' prior description of the criminal, the level of certainty demonstrated by the witness at the confrontation, and the length of time between the crime and the confrontation. Applying these factors, we disagree with the District Court's conclusion.

In part, as discussed above, we think the District Court focused unduly on the relative reliability of a lineup as opposed to a showup, the issue on which expert testimony was taken at the evidentiary hearing. It must be kept in mind also that the trial was conducted before *Stovall* and that therefore the incentive was lacking for the parties to make a record at trial of facts corroborating or undermining the identification. The testimony was addressed to the jury, and the jury apparently found the identification reliable. Some of the State's testimony at the federal evidentiary hearing may well have been self-serving in that it too neatly fit the case law, but it surely does nothing to undermine the state record, which itself fully corroborated the identification.

We find that the District Court's conclusions on the critical facts are unsupported by the record and clearly erroneous. The victim spent a considerable period of time with her assailant, up to half an hour. She was with him under adequate artificial light in her house and under a full moon outdoors, and at least twice, once in the house and later in the woods, faced him directly and intimately. She was no casual observer, but rather the victim of one of the most personally humiliating of all crimes. Her description to the police, which included the assailant's approximate age, height, weight, complexion, skin texture, build, and voice, might not have satisfied Proust but was more than ordinarily thorough. She had "no doubt" that respondent was the person who raped her. In the nature of the crime, there are rarely witnesses to a rape other than the victim, who often has a limited opportunity of observation. The victim here, a practical nurse by profession, had an unusual opportunity to observe and identify her assailant. She testified at the habeas corpus hearing that there was something about his face "I don't think I could ever forget." Pet. App., p. 128.

There was, to be sure, a lapse of seven months between the rape and the confrontation. This would be a seriously negative factor in most cases. Here, however, the testimony is undisputed that the victim made no previous identification at any of the showups, lineups, or photographic showings. Her record for reliability was thus a good one, as she had previously resisted whatever suggestiveness inheres in a showup. Weighing all the factors, we find no substantial likelihood of misidentification. The evidence was properly allowed to go to the jury.

Affirmed in part, reversed in part, and remanded.[*]

[*] Justice Brennan wrote an opinion concurring in part and dissenting in part, which Justice Douglas and Justice Stewart joined.

8. PRELIMINARY EXAMINATION

COLEMAN v. ALABAMA

399 U.S. 1, 90 S.Ct. 1999, 26 L.Ed.2d 387 (1970).

MR. JUSTICE BRENNAN announced the judgment of the Court and delivered the following opinion.

Petitioners were convicted in an Alabama Circuit Court of assault with intent to murder in the shooting of one Reynolds after he and his wife parked their car on an Alabama highway to change a flat tire. The Alabama Court of Appeals affirmed, 44 Ala.App. 429, 211 So.2d 917 (1968), and the Alabama Supreme Court denied review, 282 Ala. 725, 211 So.2d 927 (1968). We granted certiorari, 394 U.S. 916 (1969). We vacate and remand.

Petitioners . . . argue that the preliminary hearing prior to their indictment was a "critical stage" of the prosecution and that Alabama's failure to provide them with appointed counsel at the hearing therefore unconstitutionally denied them the assistance of counsel.

II [2]

This Court has held that a person accused of crime "requires the guiding hand of counsel at every step in the proceedings against him," Powell v. Alabama, 287 U.S. 45, 69 (1932), and that that constitutional principle is not limited to the presence of counsel at trial. "It is central to that principle that in addition to counsel's presence at trial, the accused is guaranteed that he need not stand alone against the State at any stage of the prosecution, formal or informal, in court or out, where counsel's absence might derogate from the accused's right to a fair trial." United States v. Wade, [388 U.S. 218 (1967)], at 226. Accordingly, "the principle of Powell v. Alabama and succeeding cases requires that we scrutinize *any* pretrial confrontation of the accused to determine whether the presence of his counsel is necessary to preserve the defendant's basic right to a fair trial as affected by his right meaningfully to cross-examine the witnesses against him and to have effective assistance of counsel at the trial itself. It calls upon us to analyze whether potential substantial prejudice to defendant's rights inheres in the particular confrontation and the ability of counsel to help avoid that prejudice." Id., at 227. Applying this test, the Court has held that "critical stages" include the pretrial type of arraignment

2. Mr. Justice Douglas, Mr. Justice White, and Mr. Justice Marshall join this Part II. [Mr. Justice Black and Mr. Justice Harlan concurred in the conclusion of this Part in separate opinions.]

where certain rights may be sacrificed or lost ... and the pretrial lineup ... where the Court held that the privilege against compulsory self-incrimination includes a right to counsel at a pretrial custodial interrogation. . . .

The preliminary hearing is not a required step in an Alabama prosecution. The prosecutor may seek an indictment directly from the grand jury without a preliminary hearing. . . . The opinion of the Alabama Court of Appeals in this case instructs us that under Alabama law the sole purposes of a preliminary hearing are to determine whether there is sufficient evidence against the accused to warrant presenting his case to the grand jury, and, if so, to fix bail if the offense is bailable. . . . The court continued:

> "At the preliminary hearing ... the accused is not required to advance any defenses, and failure to do so does not preclude him from availing himself of every defense he may have upon the trial of the case. Also Pointer v. State of Texas [380 U.S. 400 (1965)] bars the admission of testimony given at a pre-trial proceeding where the accused did not have the benefit of cross-examination by and through counsel. Thus, nothing occurring at the preliminary hearing in absence of counsel can substantially prejudice the rights of the accused on trial." 44 Ala.App., at 433, 211 So.2d, at 921.

This Court is of course bound by this construction of the governing Alabama law. . . . However, from the fact that in cases where the accused has no lawyer at the hearing the Alabama courts prohibit the State's use at trial of anything that occurred at the hearing, it does not follow that the Alabama preliminary hearing is not a "critical stage" of the State's criminal process. The determination whether the hearing is a "critical stage" requiring the provision of counsel depends, as noted, upon an analysis "whether potential substantial prejudice to defendant's rights inheres in the ... confrontation and the ability of counsel to help avoid that prejudice." United States v. Wade, supra, at 227. Plainly the guiding hand of counsel at the preliminary hearing is essential to protect the indigent accused against an erroneous or improper prosecution. First, the lawyer's skilled examination and cross-examination of witnesses may expose fatal weaknesses in the State's case that may lead the magistrate to refuse to bind the accused over. Second, in any event, the skilled interrogation of witnesses by an experienced lawyer can fashion a vital impeachment tool for use in cross-examination of the State's witnesses at the trial, or preserve testimony favorable to the accused of a witness who does not appear at the trial. Third, trained counsel can more effectively discover the case the State has against his client and make possible the preparation of a proper defense to meet that case at the trial. Fourth, counsel can also be influential at the preliminary hearing in making effective arguments for the accused on such matters as the necessity for an early psychiatric examination or bail.

The inability of the indigent accused on his own to realize these advantages of a lawyer's assistance compels the conclusion that the Alabama preliminary hearing is a "critical stage" of the State's criminal process at which the accused is "as much entitled to such aid [of counsel] . . . as at the trial itself." Powell v. Alabama, supra, at 57.

III [4]

There remains, then, the question of the relief to which petitioners are entitled. The trial transcript indicates that the prohibition against use by the State at trial of anything that occurred at the preliminary hearing was scrupulously observed. Cf. White v. Maryland, supra. But on the record it cannot be said whether or not petitioners were otherwise prejudiced by the absence of counsel at the preliminary hearing. That inquiry in the first instance should more properly be made by the Alabama courts. The test to be applied is whether the denial of counsel at the preliminary hearing was harmless error. . . .

We accordingly vacate the petitioners' convictions and remand the case to the Alabama courts for such proceedings not inconsistent with this opinion as they may deem appropriate to determine whether such denial of counsel was harmless error . . . and therefore whether the convictions should be reinstated or a new trial ordered.

It is so ordered.

MR. JUSTICE STEWART, with whom THE CHIEF JUSTICE joins, dissenting.

On a July night in 1966 Casey Reynolds and his wife stopped their car on Green Springs Highway in Birmingham, Alabama, in order to change a flat tire. They were soon accosted by three men whose evident purpose was armed robbery and rape. The assailants shot Reynolds twice before they were frightened away by the lights of a passing automobile. Some two months later the petitioners were arrested, and later identified by Reynolds as two of the three men who had assaulted him and his wife.

A few days later the petitioners were granted a preliminary hearing before a county judge. At this hearing the petitioners were neither required nor permitted to enter any plea. The sole purpose of such a hearing in Alabama is to determine whether there is sufficient evidence against the accused to warrant presenting the case to a grand jury, and, if so, to fix bail if the offense is bailable. At the conclusion of the hearing the petitioners were bound over to the grand jury, and their bond was set at $10,000. No record or transcript of any kind was made of the hearing.

---

4. Mr. Justice Black, Mr. Justice Douglas, join this Part III.
Mr. Justice White, and Mr. Justice Marshall

Less than a month later the grand jury returned an indictment against the petitioners, charging them with assault to commit murder. Promptly after their indictment, a lawyer was appointed to represent them. At their arraignment two weeks later, where they were represented by their appointed counsel, they entered a plea of not guilty.... Some months later they were brought to trial, again represented by appointed counsel.... The jury found them guilty as charged, and they were sentenced to the penitentiary.

If at the trial the prosecution had used any incriminating statements made by the petitioners at the preliminary hearing, the convictions before us would quite properly have to be set aside.... But that did not happen in this case. Or if the prosecution had used the statement of any other witness at the preliminary hearing against the petitioners at their trial, we would likewise quite properly have to set aside these convictions.... But that did not happen in this case either. For, as the prevailing opinion today perforce concedes, "the prohibition against use by the State at trial of anything that occurred at the preliminary hearing was scrupulously observed."

Nevertheless, the Court sets aside the convictions because, it says, counsel should have been provided for the petitioners at the preliminary hearing. None of the cases relied upon in that opinion points to any such result. Even the *Miranda* decision does not require counsel to be present at "pretrial custodial interrogation." That case simply held that the constitutional guarantee against compulsory self-incrimination prohibits the introduction at the *trial* of statements made by the defendant during custodial interrogation if the *Miranda* "guidelines" were not followed.... And I repeat that in this case no evidence of anything said or done at the preliminary hearing was introduced at the petitioners' trial.

But the prevailing opinion holds today that the Constitution required Alabama to provide a lawyer for the petitioners at their preliminary hearing, not so much, it seems, to assure a fair trial as to assure a fair preliminary hearing. A lawyer at the preliminary hearing, the opinion says, might have led the magistrate to "refuse to bind the accused over." Or a lawyer might have made "effective arguments for the accused on such matters as the necessity for an early psychiatric examination or bail."

If *those* are the reasons a lawyer must be provided, then the most elementary logic requires that a new preliminary hearing must now be held, with counsel made available to the petitioners. In order to provide such relief, it would, of course, be necessary not only to set aside these convictions, but also to set aside the grand jury indictments, and the magistrate's orders fixing bail and binding over the petitioners. Since the petitioners have now been found by a jury in a constitutional trial to be guilty beyond a reasonable doubt, the prevailing opinion understandably boggles at these logical consequences of the reasoning therein. It refrains, in short, from now turning back the clock by ordering a new preliminary hearing to determine all over again whether there is sufficient evidence against the accused to present their case to a grand jury. Instead, the Court sets aside these convictions and remands the case for determination "whether the convictions should be reinstated or a new trial ordered," and this action seems to me even more quixotic.

The petitioners have simply not alleged that anything that happened at the preliminary hearing turned out in this case to be critical to the fairness of their *trial*. They have not alleged that they were affirmatively prejudiced at the trial by anything that occurred at the preliminary hearing. They have not pointed to any affirmative advantage they would have enjoyed at the trial if they had had a lawyer at their preliminary hearing.

No record or transcript of any kind was made of the preliminary hearing. Therefore, if the burden on remand is on the petitioners to show that they were prejudiced, it is clear that that burden cannot be met, and the remand is a futile gesture. If, on the other hand, the burden is on the State to disprove beyond a reasonable doubt any and all speculative advantages that the petitioners might conceivably have enjoyed if counsel had been present at their preliminary hearing, then obviously that burden cannot be met either, and the Court should simply reverse these convictions. All I can say is that if the Alabama courts can figure out what they are supposed to do with this case now that it has been remanded to them, their perceptiveness will far exceed mine.

The record before us makes clear that no evidence of what occurred at the preliminary hearing was used against the petitioners at their now completed trial. I would hold, therefore, that the absence of counsel at the preliminary hearing deprived the petitioners of no constitutional rights. Accordingly, I would affirm these convictions.[*]

---

[*] Justice Black and Justice White wrote concurring opinions. Justice Douglas wrote an opinion. Justice Harlan wrote an opinion concurring in part and dissenting in part. Chief Justice Burger wrote a dissenting opinion. Justice Stewart wrote a dissenting opinion, which Chief Justice Burger joined.

GERSTEIN v. PUGH

420 U.S. 103, 95 S.Ct. 854, 43 L.Ed.2d 54 (1975).

MR. JUSTICE POWELL delivered the opinion of the Court.

The issue in this case is whether a person arrested and held for trial under a prosecutor's information is constitutionally entitled to a judicial determination of probable cause for pretrial restraint of liberty.

I

In March 1971 respondents Pugh and Henderson were arrested in Dade County, Florida. Each was charged with several offenses under a prosecutor's information.[1] Pugh was denied bail because one of the charges against him carried a potential life sentence, and Henderson remained in custody because he was unable to post a $4,500 bond.

In Florida, indictments are required only for prosecution of capital offenses. Prosecutors may charge all other crimes by information, without a prior preliminary hearing and without obtaining leave of court. ... At the time respondents were arrested, a Florida rule seemed to authorize adversary preliminary hearings to test probable cause for detention in all cases. ... But the Florida courts had held that the filing of an information foreclosed the suspect's right to a preliminary hearing. ...[2] They had also held that habeas corpus could not be used, except perhaps in exceptional circumstances, to test the probable cause for detention under an information. ... The only possible methods for obtaining a judicial determination of probable cause were a special statute allowing a preliminary hearing after 30 days ... and arraignment, which the District Court found was often delayed a month or more after arrest. ... As a result, a person charged by information could be detained for a substantial period solely on the decision of a prosecutor.

Respondents Pugh and Henderson filed a class action against Dade County officials in the Federal District Court, claiming a constitutional right to a judicial hearing on the issue of probable cause and requesting declaratory and injunctive relief. Respondents Turner and Faulk, also in custody under informations, subse-

1. Respondent Pugh was arrested on March 3, 1971. On March 16 an information was filed charging him with robbery, carrying a concealed weapon, and possession of a firearm during commission of a felony. Respondent Henderson was arrested on March 2, and charged by information on March 19 with the offenses of breaking and entering and assault and battery. The record does not indicate whether there was an arrest warrant in either case.

2. Florida law also denies preliminary hearings to persons confined under indictment ....

quently intervened.[7] Petitioner Gerstein, the State Attorney for Dade County, was one of several defendants.[8]

After an initial delay while the Florida Legislature considered a bill that would have afforded preliminary hearings to persons charged by information, the District Court granted the relief sought. Pugh v. Rainwater, [332 F.Supp. 1107 (S.D.Fla.1971)]. The court certified the case as a class action under Fed.Rule Civ.Proc. 23(b)(2), and held that the Fourth and Fourteenth Amendments give all arrested persons charged by information a right to a judicial hearing on the question of probable cause. The District Court ordered the Dade County defendants to give the named plaintiffs an immediate preliminary hearing to determine probable cause for further detention. It also ordered them to submit a plan providing preliminary hearings in all cases instituted by information.

The defendants submitted a plan prepared by Sheriff E. Wilson Purdy, and the District Court adopted it with modifications. The final order prescribed a detailed post-arrest procedure. 336 F.Supp. 490 (S.D.Fla.1972). Upon arrest the accused would be taken before a magistrate for a "first appearance hearing." The magistrate would explain the charges, advise the accused of his rights, appoint counsel if he was indigent, and proceed with a probable cause determination unless either the prosecutor or the accused was unprepared. If either requested more time, the magistrate would set the date for a "preliminary hearing," to be held within four days if the accused was in custody and within 10 days if he had been released pending trial. The order provided sanctions for failure to hold the hearing at prescribed times. At the "preliminary hearing" the accused would be entitled to counsel, and he would be allowed to confront and cross-examine adverse witnesses, to summon favorable witnesses, and to have a transcript made on request. If the magistrate found no probable cause, the accused would be discharged. He then could not be charged with the same offense by complaint or information, but only by indictment returned within 30 days.

The Court of Appeals for the Fifth Circuit stayed the District Court's order pending appeal, but while the case was awaiting decision, the Dade County judiciary voluntarily adopted a similar procedure of its own. Upon learning of this development, the Court of Appeals remanded the case for specific findings on the constitutionality of the new Dade County system. Before the District Court issued its findings, however, the Florida Supreme Court amended the procedural rules governing preliminary hearings

---

7. Turner was being held on a charge of auto theft, following arrest on March 11, 1971. Faulk was arrested on March 19 on charges of soliciting a ride and possession of marihuana.

8. The named defendants included justices of the peace and judges of small-claims courts, who were authorized to hold preliminary hearings in criminal cases, and a group of law enforcement officers with power to make arrests in Dade County. Gerstein was the only one who petitioned for certiorari.

statewide, and the parties agreed that the District Court should direct its inquiry to the new rules rather than the Dade County procedures.

Under the amended rules every arrested person must be taken before a judicial officer within 24 hours.... This "first appearance" is similar to the "first appearance hearing" ordered by the District Court in all respects but the crucial one: the magistrate does not make a determination of probable cause. The rule amendments also changed the procedure for preliminary hearings, restricting them to felony charges and codifying the rule that no hearings are available to persons charged by information or indictment....

In a supplemental opinion the District Court held that the amended rules had not answered the basic constitutional objection, since a defendant charged by information still could be detained pending trial without a judicial determination of probable cause. 355 F.Supp. 1286 (SD Fla.1973). Reaffirming its original ruling, the District Court declared that the continuation of this practice was unconstitutional. The Court of Appeals affirmed, 483 F.2d 778 ([5th Cir.] 1973), modifying the District Court's decree in minor particulars and suggesting that the form of preliminary hearing provided by the amended Florida rules would be acceptable, as long as it was provided to all defendants in custody pending trial. Id., at 788–789.

State Attorney Gerstein petitioned for review, and we granted certiorari because of the importance of the issue.[11] 414 U.S. 1062 (1973). We affirm in part and reverse in part.

II

As framed by the proceedings below, this case presents two issues: whether a person arrested and held for trial on an information is entitled to a judicial determination of probable cause for detention, and if so, whether the adversary hearing ordered by the District Court and approved by the Court of Appeals is required by the Constitution.

A

Both the standards and procedures for arrest and detention have been derived from the Fourth Amendment and its common-law antecedents. ... The standard for arrest is probable cause, defined in terms of facts and circumstances "sufficient to warrant a prudent man in believing that the [suspect] had committed or was committing an offense." Beck v. Ohio, 379 U.S. 89, 91 (1964). ...

---

11. At oral argument counsel informed us that the named respondents have been convicted. Their pretrial detention therefore has ended. This case belongs, however, to that narrow class of cases in which the termination of a class representative's claim does not moot the claims of the unnamed members of the class....

. . .

This standard, like those for searches and seizures, represents a necessary accommodation between the individual's right to liberty and the State's duty to control crime.

. . .

To implement the Fourth Amendment's protection against unfounded invasions of liberty and privacy, the Court has required that the existence of probable cause be decided by a neutral and detached magistrate whenever possible. . . .

. . .

Maximum protection of individual rights could be assured by requiring a magistrate's review of the factual justification prior to any arrest, but such a requirement would constitute an intolerable handicap for legitimate law enforcement. Thus, while the Court has expressed a preference for the use of arrest warrants when feasible, . . . it has never invalidated an arrest supported by probable cause solely because the officers failed to secure a warrant. . . .

Under this practical compromise, a policeman's on-the-scene assessment of probable cause provides legal justification for arresting a person suspected of crime, and for a brief period of detention to take the administrative steps incident to arrest. Once the suspect is in custody, however, the reasons that justify dispensing with the magistrate's neutral judgment evaporate. There no longer is any danger that the suspect will escape or commit further crimes while the police submit their evidence to a magistrate. And, while the State's reasons for taking summary action subside, the suspect's need for a neutral determination of probable cause increases significantly. The consequences of prolonged detention may be more serious than the interference occasioned by arrest. Pretrial confinement may imperil the suspect's job, interrupt his source of income, and impair his family relationships. . . . Even pretrial release may be accompanied by burdensome conditions that effect a significant restraint of liberty. . . . When the stakes are this high, the detached judgment of a neutral magistrate is essential if the Fourth Amendment is to furnish meaningful protection from unfounded interference with liberty. Accordingly, we hold that the Fourth Amendment requires a judicial determination of probable cause as a prerequisite to extended restraint of liberty following arrest.

This result has historical support in the common law that has guided interpretation of the Fourth Amendment. . . . At common law it was customary, if not obligatory, for an arrested person to be brought before a justice of the peace shortly after arrest. . . . The justice of the peace would "examine" the prisoner and the witnesses to determine whether there was reason to believe the prisoner had committed a crime. If there was, the suspect would be committed to jail or bailed pending trial. If not, he would be discharged from custody. . . . The initial determination of probable cause also could be reviewed by higher courts on a writ of habeas

corpus. ... This practice furnished the model for criminal proce-
dure in America immediately following the adoption of the Fourth
Amendment ... and there are indications that the Framers of the
Bill of Rights regarded it as a model for a "reasonable" seizure. ...

B

Under the Florida procedures challenged here, a person arrested without a warrant and charged by information may be jailed or
subjected to other restraints pending trial without any opportunity
for a probable cause determination.[18] Petitioner defends this practice on the ground that the prosecutor's decision to file an information is itself a determination of probable cause that furnishes
sufficient reason to detain a defendant pending trial. Although a
conscientious decision that the evidence warrants prosecution affords a measure of protection against unfounded detention, we do
not think prosecutorial judgment standing alone meets the requirements of the Fourth Amendment. Indeed, we think the Court's
previous decisions compel disapproval of the Florida procedure. In
Albrecht v. United States, 273 U.S. 1, 5 (1927), the Court held that
an arrest warrant issued solely upon a United States Attorney's
information was invalid because the accompanying affidavits were
defective. Although the Court's opinion did not explicitly state that
the prosecutor's official oath could not furnish probable cause, that
conclusion was implicit in the judgment that the arrest was illegal
under the Fourth Amendment.[19] More recently, in Coolidge v. New
Hampshire, 403 U.S. 443, 449–453 (1971), the Court held that a
prosecutor's responsibility to law enforcement is inconsistent with
the constitutional role of a neutral and detached magistrate. We
reaffirmed that principle in Shadwick v. City of Tampa, 407 U.S. 345
(1972), and held that probable cause for the issuance of an arrest
warrant must be determined by someone independent of police and
prosecution. ... The reason for this separation of functions was
expressed by Justice Frankfurter in a similar context:

> "A democratic society, in which respect for the dignity of all
> men is central, naturally guards against the misuse of the law
> enforcement process. Zeal in tracking down crime is not in
> itself an assurance of soberness of judgment. Disinterestedness
> in law enforcement does not alone prevent disregard of cher-

---

18. A person arrested under a warrant
would have received a prior judicial determination of probable cause. Under Fla.Rule
Crim.Proc. 3.120, a warrant may be issued
upon a sworn complaint that states facts
showing that the suspect has committed a
crime. The magistrate may also take testimony under oath to determine if there is
reasonable ground to believe the complaint is
true.

19. By contrast, the Court has held that
an indictment, "fair upon its face," and returned by a "properly constituted grand
jury," conclusively determines the existence
of probable cause and requires issuance of an
arrest warrant without further inquiry....
The willingness to let a grand jury's judgment substitute for that of a neutral and
detached magistrate is attributable to the
grand jury's relationship to the courts and its
historical role of protecting individuals from
unjust prosecution. ...

ished liberties. Experience has therefore counseled that safe-guards must be provided against the dangers of the overzealous as well as the despotic. The awful instruments of the criminal law cannot be entrusted to a single functionary. The compli-cated process of criminal justice is therefore divided into differ-ent parts, responsibility for which is separately vested in the various participants upon whom the criminal law relies for its vindication." McNabb v. United States, 318 U.S. 332, 343 (1943).

In holding that the prosecutor's assessment of probable cause is not sufficient alone to justify restraint of liberty pending trial, we do not imply that the accused is entitled to judicial oversight or review of the decision to prosecute. Instead, we adhere to the Court's prior holding that a judicial hearing is not prerequisite to prosecution by information. . . . Nor do we retreat from the estab-lished rule that illegal arrest or detention does not void a subse-quent conviction. . . . Thus, as the Court of Appeals noted below, although a suspect who is presently detained may challenge the probable cause for that confinement, a conviction will not be vacated on the ground that the defendant was detained pending trial without a determination of probable cause. . . .

III

Both the District Court and the Court of Appeals held that the determination of probable cause must be accompanied by the full panoply of adversary safeguards—counsel, confrontation, cross-ex-amination, and compulsory process for witnesses. A full prelimi-nary hearing of this sort is modeled after the procedure used in many States to determine whether the evidence justifies going to trial under an information or presenting the case to a grand jury. . . . The standard of proof required of the prosecution is usually referred to as "probable cause," but in some jurisdictions it may approach a prima facie case of guilt. . . . When the hearing takes this form, adversary procedures are customarily employed. The importance of the issue to both the State and the accused justifies the presentation of witnesses and full exploration of their testimony on cross-examination. This kind of hearing also requires appoint-ment of counsel for indigent defendants. . . . And, as the hearing assumes increased importance and the procedures become more complex, the likelihood that it can be held promptly after arrest diminishes. . . .

These adversary safeguards are not essential for the probable cause determination required by the Fourth Amendment. The sole issue is whether there is probable cause for detaining the arrested person pending further proceedings. This issue can be determined reliably without an adversary hearing. The standard is the same as that for arrest. That standard—probable cause to believe the sus-pect has committed a crime—traditionally has been decided by a magistrate in a nonadversary proceeding on hearsay and written testimony, and the Court has approved these informal modes of proof.

. . .

The use of an informal procedure is justified not only by the lesser consequences of a probable cause determination but also by the nature of the determination itself. It does not require the fine resolution of conflicting evidence that a reasonable-doubt or even a preponderance standard demands, and credibility determinations are seldom crucial in deciding whether the evidence supports a reasonable belief in guilt. . . . This is not to say that confrontation and cross-examination might not enhance the reliability of probable cause determinations in some cases. In most cases, however, their value would be too slight to justify holding, as a matter of constitutional principle, that these formalities and safeguards designed for trial must also be employed in making the Fourth Amendment determination of probable cause.[23]

Because of its limited function and its nonadversary character, the probable cause determination is not a "critical stage" in the prosecution that would require appointed counsel. The Court has identified as "critical stages" those pretrial procedures that would impair defense on the merits if the accused is required to proceed without counsel. . . . In Coleman v. Alabama, [399 U.S. 1 (1970)], where the Court held that a preliminary hearing was a critical stage of an Alabama prosecution, the majority and concurring opinions identified two critical factors that distinguish the Alabama preliminary hearing from the probable cause determination required by the Fourth Amendment. First, under Alabama law the function of the preliminary hearing was to determine whether the evidence justified charging the suspect with an offense. A finding of no probable cause could mean that he would not be tried at all. The Fourth Amendment probable cause determination is addressed only to pretrial custody. To be sure, pretrial custody may affect to some extent the defendant's ability to assist in preparation of his defense, but this does not present the high probability of substantial harm identified as controlling in [United States v.] *Wade* [388 U.S. 218 (1967)] and *Coleman*. Second, Alabama allowed the suspect to confront and cross-examine prosecution witnesses at the preliminary hearing. The Court noted that the suspect's defense on the merits could be compromised if he had no legal assistance for exploring or preserving the witnesses' testimony. This consideration does not apply when the prosecution is not required to produce witnesses for cross-examination.

---

23. Criminal justice is already overburdened by the volume of cases and the complexities of our system. The processing of misdemeanors, in particular, and the early stages of prosecution generally are marked by delays that can seriously affect the quality of justice. A constitutional doctrine requiring adversary hearings for all persons detained pending trial could exacerbate the problem of pretrial delay.

Although we conclude that the Constitution does not require an adversary determination of probable cause, we recognize that state systems of criminal procedure vary widely. There is no single preferred pretrial procedure, and the nature of the probable cause determination usually will be shaped to accord with a State's pretrial procedure viewed as a whole. While we limit our holding to the precise requirement of the Fourth Amendment, we recognize the desirability of flexibility and experimentation by the States. It may be found desirable, for example, to make the probable cause determination at the suspect's first appearance before a judicial officer . . . or the determination may be incorporated into the procedure for setting bail or fixing other conditions of pretrial release. In some States, existing procedures may satisfy the requirement of the Fourth Amendment. Others may require only minor adjustment, such as acceleration of existing preliminary hearings. Current proposals for criminal procedure reform suggest other ways of testing probable cause for detention. Whatever procedure a State may adopt, it must provide a fair and reliable determination of probable cause as a condition for any significant pretrial restraint of liberty,[26] and this determination must be made by a judicial officer either before or promptly after arrest.[27]

IV

We agree with the Court of Appeals that the Fourth Amendment requires a timely judicial determination of probable cause as a prerequisite to detention, and we accordingly affirm that much of

26. Because the probable cause determination is not a constitutional prerequisite to the charging decision, it is required only for those suspects who suffer restraints on liberty other than the condition that they appear for trial. There are many kinds of pretrial release and many degrees of conditional liberty. . . . We cannot define specifically those that would require a prior probable cause determination, but the key factor is significant restraint on liberty.

27. In his concurring opinion, Mr. Justice Stewart objects to the Court's choice of the Fourth Amendment as the rationale for decision and suggests that the Court offers less procedural protection to a person in jail than it requires in certain civil cases. Here we deal with the complex procedures of a criminal case and a threshold right guaranteed by the Fourth Amendment. The historical basis of the probable cause requirement is quite different from the relatively recent application of variable procedural due process in debtor-creditor disputes and termination of government-created benefits. The Fourth Amendment was tailored explicitly for the criminal justice system, and its balance between individual and public interests always has been thought to define the "process that is due" for seizures of person or property in criminal cases, including the detention of suspects pending trial. Part II-A, supra. Moreover, the Fourth Amendment probable cause determination is in fact only the *first* stage of an elaborate system, unique in jurisprudence, designed to safeguard the rights of those accused of criminal conduct. The relatively simple civil procedures (e.g., prior interview with school principal before suspension) presented in the cases cited in the concurring opinion are inapposite and irrelevant in the wholly different context of the criminal justice system.

It would not be practicable to follow the further suggestion implicit in Mr. Justice Stewart's concurring opinion that we leave for another day determination of the procedural safeguards that are required in making a probable cause determination under the Fourth Amendment. The judgment under review both declares the right not to be detained without a probable cause determination and affirms the District Court's order prescribing an adversary hearing for the implementation of that right. The circumstances of the case thus require a decision on both issues.

the judgment. As we do not agree that the Fourth Amendment requires the adversary hearing outlined in the District Court's decree, we reverse in part and remand to the Court of Appeals for further proceedings consistent with this opinion.

It is so ordered.

MR. JUSTICE STEWART, with whom MR. JUSTICE DOUGLAS, MR. JUSTICE BRENNAN, and MR. JUSTICE MARSHALL join, concurring.

I concur in Parts I and II of the Court's opinion, since the Constitution clearly requires at least a timely judicial determination of probable cause as a prerequisite to pretrial detention. Because Florida does not provide all defendants in custody pending trial with a fair and reliable determination of probable cause for their detention, the respondents and the members of the class they represent are entitled to declaratory and injunctive relief.

Having determined that Florida's current pretrial detention procedures are constitutionally inadequate, I think it is unnecessary to go further by way of dicta. In particular, I would not, in the abstract, attempt to specify those procedural protections that constitutionally need *not* be accorded incarcerated suspects awaiting trial.

Specifically, I see no need in this case for the Court to say that the Constitution extends less procedural protection to an imprisoned human being than is required to test the propriety of garnishing a commercial bank account ... the custody of a refrigerator ... the temporary suspension of a public school student ... or the suspension of a driver's license.... Although it may be true that the Fourth Amendment's "balance between individual and public interests always has been thought to define the 'process that is due' for seizures of person or property in criminal cases," ante, p. 125, n. 27, this case does not involve an initial arrest, but rather the continuing incarceration of a presumptively innocent person. Accordingly, I cannot join the Court's effort to foreclose any claim that the traditional requirements of constitutional due process are applicable in the context of pretrial detention.

It is the prerogative of each State in the first instance to develop pretrial procedures that provide defendants in pretrial custody with the fair and reliable determination of probable cause for detention required by the Constitution. ... The constitutionality of any particular method for determining probable cause can be properly decided only by evaluating a State's pretrial procedures as a whole, not by isolating a particular part of its total system. As the Court recognizes, great diversity exists among the procedures employed by the States in this aspect of their criminal justice systems. ...

There will be adequate opportunity to evaluate in an appropriate future case the constitutionality of any new procedures that may be adopted by Florida in response to the Court's judgment today holding that Florida's present procedures are constitutionally inadequate.

COUNTY OF RIVERSIDE v. McLAUGHLIN

500 U.S. 44, 111 S.Ct. 1661, 114 L.Ed.2d 49 (1991).

JUSTICE O'CONNOR delivered the opinion of the Court.

In Gerstein v. Pugh, 420 U.S. 103 (1975), this Court held that the Fourth Amendment requires a prompt judicial determination of probable cause as a prerequisite to an extended pretrial detention following a warrantless arrest. This case requires us to define what is "prompt" under *Gerstein*.

I

This is a class action brought under 42 U.S.C. § 1983 challenging the manner in which the County of Riverside, California (County), provides probable cause determinations to persons arrested without a warrant. At issue is the County's policy of combining probable cause determinations with its arraignment procedures. Under County policy, which tracks closely the provisions of Cal.Penal Code Ann. § 825 (West 1985), arraignments must be conducted without unnecessary delay and, in any event, within two days of arrest. This two-day requirement excludes from computation weekends and holidays. Thus, an individual arrested without a warrant late in the week may in some cases be held for as long as five days before receiving a probable cause determination. Over the Thanksgiving holiday, a 7-day delay is possible.

The parties dispute whether the combined probable cause/arraignment procedure is available to *all* warrantless arrestees. Testimony by Riverside County District Attorney Grover Trask suggests that individuals arrested without warrants for felonies do not receive a probable cause determination until the preliminary hearing, which may not occur until 10 days after arraignment. ... Before this Court, however, the County represents that its policy is to provide probable cause determinations at arraignment for all persons arrested without a warrant, regardless of the nature of the charges against them. ... We need not resolve the factual inconsistency here. For present purposes, we accept the County's representation.

In August 1987, Donald Lee McLaughlin filed a complaint in the United States District Court for the Central District of California, seeking injunctive and declaratory relief on behalf of himself and "'all others similarly situated.'" The complaint alleged that McLaughlin was then currently incarcerated in the Riverside County Jail and had not received a probable cause determination. He requested "'an order and judgment requiring that the defendants and the County of Riverside provide in-custody arrestees, arrested without warrants, prompt probable cause, bail and arraignment hearings.' " Pet. for Cert. 6. . . .

. . .

The second amended complaint named three additional plaintiffs—Johnny E. James, Diana Ray Simon, and Michael Scott Hyde—individually and as class representatives. The amended complaint alleged that each of the named plaintiffs had been arrested without a warrant, had received neither a prompt probable cause nor a bail hearing, and was still in custody. . . . In November 1988, the District Court certified a class comprising "all present and future prisoners in the Riverside County Jail including those pretrial detainees arrested without warrants and held in the Riverside County Jail from August 1, 1987 to the present, and all such future detainees who have been or may be denied prompt probable cause, bail or arraignment hearings." 1 App. 7.

In March 1989, plaintiffs asked the District Court to issue a preliminary injunction requiring the County to provide all persons arrested without a warrant a judicial determination of probable cause within 36 hours of arrest. . . . The District Court issued the injunction, holding that the County's existing practice violated this Court's decision in *Gerstein*. Without discussion, the District Court adopted a rule that the County provide probable cause determinations within 36 hours of arrest, except in exigent circumstances. The court "retained jurisdiction indefinitely" to ensure that the County established new procedures that complied with the injunction. 2 App. 333–334.

. . .

On November 8, 1989, the Court of Appeals affirmed the order granting the preliminary injunction against Riverside County. . . .

The Court of Appeals . . . determined that the County's policy of providing probable cause determinations at arraignment within 48 hours was "not in accord with *Gerstein's* requirement of a determination 'promptly after arrest' " because no more than 36 hours were needed "to complete the administrative steps incident to arrest." [888 F.2d], at 1278.

The Ninth Circuit thus joined the Fourth and Seventh Circuits in interpreting *Gerstein* as requiring a probable cause determination immediately following completion of the administrative procedures incident to arrest. . . . By contrast, the Second Circuit understands *Gerstein* to "stres[s] the need for flexibility" and to permit States to combine probable cause determinations with other pretrial proceedings. Williams v. Ward, 845 F.2d 374, 386 (1988), cert. denied, 488 U.S. 1020 (1989). We granted certiorari to resolve this conflict among the Circuits as to what constitutes a "prompt" probable cause determination under *Gerstein*.

. . .

III

A

In *Gerstein,* this Court held unconstitutional Florida procedures under which persons arrested without a warrant could remain in police custody for 30 days or more without a judicial determination of probable cause. In reaching this conclusion we attempted to reconcile important competing interests. On the one hand, States have a strong interest in protecting public safety by taking into custody those persons who are reasonably suspected of having engaged in criminal activity, even where there has been no opportunity for a prior judicial determination of probable cause. ... On the other hand, prolonged detention based on incorrect or unfounded suspicion may unjustly "imperil [a] suspect's job, interrupt his source of income, and impair his family relationships." Id., at 114. We sought to balance these competing concerns by holding that States "must provide a fair and reliable determination of probable cause as a condition for any significant pretrial restraint of liberty, and this determination must be made by a judicial officer either before *or promptly after* arrest." Id., at 125 (emphasis added).

The Court thus established a "practical compromise" between the rights of individuals and the realities of law enforcement. Id., at 113. Under *Gerstein,* warrantless arrests are permitted but persons arrested without a warrant must promptly be brought before a neutral magistrate for a judicial determination of probable cause. ... Significantly, the Court stopped short of holding that jurisdictions were constitutionally compelled to provide a probable cause hearing immediately upon taking a suspect into custody and completing booking procedures. We acknowledged the burden that proliferation of pretrial proceedings places on the criminal justice system and recognized that the interests of everyone involved, including those persons who are arrested, might be disserved by introducing further procedural complexity into an already intricate system. ... Accordingly, we left it to the individual States to integrate prompt probable cause determinations into their differing systems of pretrial procedures. ...

In so doing, we gave proper deference to the demands of federalism. We recognized that "state systems of criminal procedure vary widely" in the nature and number of pretrial procedures they provide, and we noted that there is no single "preferred" approach. Id., at 123. We explained further that "flexibility and experimentation by the States" with respect to integrating probable cause determinations was desirable and that each State should settle upon an approach "to accord with [the] State's pretrial procedure viewed as a whole." Ibid. Our purpose in *Gerstein* was to make clear that the Fourth Amendment requires every State to provide prompt determinations of probable cause, but that the Constitution does not impose on the States a rigid procedural framework. Rather, individual States may choose to comply in different ways.

Inherent in *Gerstein*'s invitation to the States to experiment and adapt was the recognition that the Fourth Amendment does not compel an immediate determination of probable cause upon completing the administrative steps incident to arrest. Plainly, if a probable cause hearing is constitutionally compelled the moment a suspect is finished being "booked," there is no room whatsoever for "flexibility and experimentation by the States." Ibid. Incorporating probable cause determinations "into the procedure for setting bail or fixing other conditions of pretrial release"—which *Gerstein* explicitly contemplated, id., at 124—would be impossible. Waiting even a few hours so that a bail hearing or arraignment could take place at the same time as the probable cause determination would amount to a constitutional violation. Clearly, *Gerstein* is not that inflexible.

Notwithstanding *Gerstein*'s discussion of flexibility, the Court of Appeals for the Ninth Circuit held that no flexibility was permitted. It construed *Gerstein* as "requir[ing] a probable cause determination to be made *as soon as the administrative steps incident to arrest were completed,* and that such steps should require only a brief period." 888 F.2d, at 1278 (emphasis added) (internal quotations omitted). This same reading is advanced by the dissents. The foregoing discussion readily demonstrates the error of this approach. *Gerstein* held that probable cause determinations must be prompt—not immediate. The Court explained that "flexibility and experimentation" were "desirab[le]"; that "[t]here is no single preferred pretrial procedure"; and that "the nature of the probable cause determination usually will be shaped to accord with a State's pretrial procedure viewed as a whole." 420 U.S., at 123. The Court of Appeals and Justice Scalia disregard these statements, relying instead on selective quotations from the Court's opinion. As we have explained, *Gerstein* struck a balance between competing interests; a proper understanding of the decision is possible only if one takes into account both sides of the equation.

Justice Scalia claims to find support for his approach in the common law. It points to several statements from the early 1800's to the effect that an arresting officer must bring a person arrested without a warrant before a judicial officer " 'as soon as he *reasonably* can.' " Post, at 61 (emphasis in original). This vague admonition offers no more support for the dissent's inflexible standard than does *Gerstein*'s statement that a hearing follow "promptly after arrest." 420 U.S., at 125. As mentioned at the outset, the question before us today is what is "prompt" under *Gerstein*. We answer that question by recognizing that *Gerstein* struck a balance between competing interests.

B

Given that *Gerstein* permits jurisdictions to incorporate probable cause determinations into other pretrial procedures, some delays are inevitable. For example, where, as in Riverside County, the probable cause determination is combined with arraignment, there will be delays caused by paperwork and logistical problems. Records will have to be reviewed, charging documents drafted, appearance of counsel arranged, and appropriate bail determined. On weekends, when the number of arrests is often higher and available resources tend to be limited, arraignments may get pushed back even further. In our view, the Fourth Amendment permits a reasonable postponement of a probable cause determination while the police cope with the everyday problems of processing suspects through an overly burdened criminal justice system.

But flexibility has its limits; *Gerstein* is not a blank check. A State has no legitimate interest in detaining for extended periods individuals who have been arrested without probable cause. The Court recognized in *Gerstein* that a person arrested without a warrant is entitled to a fair and reliable determination of probable cause and that this determination must be made promptly.

Unfortunately, as lower court decisions applying *Gerstein* have demonstrated, it is not enough to say that probable cause determinations must be "prompt." This vague standard simply has not provided sufficient guidance. Instead, it has led to a flurry of systemic challenges to city and county practices, putting federal judges in the role of making legislative judgments and overseeing local jailhouse operations. . . .

Our task in this case is to articulate more clearly the boundaries of what is permissible under the Fourth Amendment. Although we hesitate to announce that the Constitution compels a specific time limit, it is important to provide some degree of certainty so that States and counties may establish procedures with confidence that they fall within constitutional bounds. Taking into account the competing interests articulated in *Gerstein*, we believe that a jurisdiction that provides judicial determinations of probable cause within 48 hours of arrest will, as a general matter, comply with the promptness requirement of *Gerstein*. For this reason, such jurisdictions will be immune from systemic challenges.

This is not to say that the probable cause determination in a particular case passes constitutional muster simply because it is provided within 48 hours. Such a hearing may nonetheless violate *Gerstein* if the arrested individual can prove that his or her probable cause determination was delayed unreasonably. Examples of unreasonable delay are delays for the purpose of gathering additional evidence to justify the arrest, a delay motivated by ill will against the arrested individual, or delay for delay's sake. In evaluating whether the delay in a particular case is unreasonable, however, courts must allow a substantial degree of flexibility. Courts cannot ignore the often unavoidable delays in transporting arrested persons from one facility to another, handling late-night bookings where no magistrate is readily available, obtaining the presence of an arresting officer who may be busy processing other suspects or securing the premises of an arrest, and other practical realities.

Where an arrested individual does not receive a probable cause determination within 48 hours, the calculus changes. In such a case, the arrested individual does not bear the burden of proving an unreasonable delay. Rather, the burden shifts to the government to demonstrate the existence of a bona fide emergency or other extraordinary circumstance. The fact that in a particular case it may take longer than 48 hours to consolidate pretrial proceedings does not qualify as an extraordinary circumstance. Nor, for that matter, do intervening weekends. A jurisdiction that chooses to offer combined proceedings must do so as soon as is reasonably feasible, but in no event later than 48 hours after arrest.

Justice Scalia urges that 24 hours is a more appropriate outer boundary for providing probable cause determinations. ... In arguing that any delay in probable cause hearings beyond completing the administrative steps incident to arrest and arranging for a magistrate is unconstitutional, Justice Scalia, in effect, adopts the view of the Court of Appeals. Yet he ignores entirely the Court of Appeals' determination of the time required to complete those procedures. That court, better situated than this one, concluded that it takes 36 hours to process arrested persons in Riverside County. ... In advocating a 24-hour rule, Justice Scalia would compel Riverside County—and countless others across the Nation—to speed up its criminal justice mechanisms substantially, presumably by allotting local tax dollars to hire additional police officers and magistrates. There may be times when the Constitution compels such direct interference with local control, but this is not one. As we have explained, *Gerstein* clearly contemplated a reasonable accommodation between legitimate competing concerns. We do no more than recognize that such accommodation can take place without running afoul of the Fourth Amendment.

Everyone agrees that the police should make every attempt to minimize the time a presumptively innocent individual spends in jail. One way to do so is to provide a judicial determination of probable cause immediately upon completing the administrative steps incident to arrest—i.e., as soon as the suspect has been booked, photographed, and fingerprinted. As Justice Scalia explains, several States, laudably, have adopted this approach. The Constitution does not compel so rigid a schedule, however. Under *Gerstein*, jurisdictions may choose to combine probable cause determinations with other pretrial proceedings, so long as they do so promptly. This necessarily means that only certain proceedings are candidates for combination. Only those proceedings that arise very

early in the pretrial process—such as bail hearings and arraignments—may be chosen. Even then, every effort must be made to
expedite the combined proceedings. . . .

IV

For the reasons we have articulated, we conclude that Riverside
County is entitled to combine probable cause determinations with
arraignments. The record indicates, however, that the County's
current policy and practice do not comport fully with the principles
we have outlined. The County's current policy is to offer combined
proceedings within two days, exclusive of Saturdays, Sundays, or
holidays. As a result, persons arrested on Thursdays may have to
wait until the following Monday before they receive a probable
cause determination. The delay is even longer if there is an
intervening holiday. Thus, the County's regular practice exceeds
the 48-hour period we deem constitutionally permissible, meaning
that the County is not immune from systemic challenges, such as
this class action.

As to arrests that occur early in the week, the County's practice
is that "arraignment[s] usually tak[e] place on the last day" possible. 1 App. 82. There may well be legitimate reasons for this
practice; alternatively, this may constitute delay for delay's sake.
We leave it to the Court of Appeals and the District Court, on
remand, to make this determination.

The judgment of the Court of Appeals is vacated and the case is
remanded for further proceedings consistent with this opinion.

It is so ordered.

JUSTICE SCALIA, dissenting.

. . .

I

The Court views the task before it as one of "balanc[ing] [the]
competing concerns" of "protecting public safety," on the one
hand, and avoiding "prolonged detention based on incorrect or
unfounded suspicion," on the other hand, ante, at 52. It purports
to reaffirm the "practical compromise" between these concerns
struck in Gerstein v. Pugh, 420 U.S. 103 (1975), ante, at 53. There
is assuredly room for such an approach in resolving novel questions
of search and seizure under the "reasonableness" standard that the
Fourth Amendment sets forth. But not, I think, in resolving those
questions on which a clear answer already existed in 1791 and has
been generally adhered to by the traditions of our society ever
since. As to those matters, the "balance" has already been struck,
the "practical compromise" reached—and it is the function of the
Bill of Rights to *preserve* that judgment, not only against the
changing views of Presidents and Members of Congress, but also

against the changing views of Justices whom Presidents appoint and Members of Congress confirm to this Court.

The issue before us today is of precisely that sort. As we have recently had occasion to explain, the Fourth Amendment's prohibition of "unreasonable seizures," insofar as it applies to seizure of the person, preserves for our citizens the traditional protections against unlawful arrest afforded by the common law. ... One of those—one of the most important of those—was that a person arresting a suspect without a warrant must deliver the arrestee to a magistrate "as soon as he reasonably can." 2 M. Hale, Pleas of the Crown 95, n. 13 (1st Am. ed. 1847). ... The practice in the United States was the same. ... It was clear, moreover, that the only element bearing upon the reasonableness of delay was, not such circumstances as the pressing need to conduct further investigation, but the arresting officer's ability, once the prisoner had been secured, to reach a magistrate who could issue the needed warrant for further detention. ... Any detention beyond the period within which a warrant could have been obtained rendered the officer liable for false imprisonment. ...

We discussed and relied upon this common-law understanding in *Gerstein*, see 420 U.S., at 114–116, holding that the period of warrantless detention must be limited to the time necessary to complete the arrest and obtain the magistrate's review. ... We said that "the Fourth Amendment requires a judicial determination of probable cause as a prerequisite to extended restraint of liberty," id., at 114, "either before or promptly after arrest," id., at 125. Though *how* "promptly" we did not say, it was plain enough that the requirement left no room for intentional delay unrelated to the completion of "the administrative steps incident to arrest." Plain enough, at least, that all but one federal court considering the question understood *Gerstein* that way. ...

Today, however, the Court discerns something quite different in *Gerstein*. It finds that the plain statements set forth above (not to mention the common-law tradition of liberty upon which they were based) were trumped by the *implication* of a later dictum in the case which, according to the Court, manifests a "recognition that the Fourth Amendment does *not* compel an immediate determination of probable cause upon completing the administrative steps incident to arrest." Ante, at 8 (emphasis added). Of course *Gerstein* did not say, nor do *I* contend, that an "immediate" determination is required. But what the Court today means by "not immediate" is that the delay can be attributable to something other than completing the administrative steps incident to arrest and arranging for the magistrate—namely, to the administrative convenience of combining the probable-cause determination with other state proceedings. The result, we learn later in the opinion, is that what *Gerstein* meant by "a brief period of detention to take the administrative steps incident to arrest" is two full days. I think it is clear that the case neither said nor meant any such thing.

. . .

Of course even if the implication of the dictum in *Gerstein* were what the Court says, that would be poor reason for keeping a wrongfully arrested citizen in jail contrary to the clear dictates of the Fourth Amendment. What is most revealing of the frailty of today's opinion is that it relies upon *nothing* but that implication from a dictum, plus its own (quite irrefutable because entirely value laden) "balancing" of the competing demands of the individual and the State. With respect to the point at issue here, different times and different places—even highly liberal times and places—have struck that balance in different ways. Some Western democracies currently permit the executive a period of detention without impartially adjudicated cause. ... It was the purpose of the Fourth Amendment to put this matter beyond time, place and judicial predilection, incorporating the traditional common-law guarantees against unlawful arrest. The Court says not a word about these guarantees, and they are determinative. *Gerstein*'s approval of a "brief period" of delay to accomplish "administrative steps incident to an arrest" is already a questionable extension of the traditional formulation, though it probably has little practical effect and can perhaps be justified on *de minimis* grounds. To expand *Gerstein*, however, into an authorization for 48-hour detention related neither to the obtaining of a magistrate nor the administrative "completion" of the arrest seems to me utterly unjustified. Mr. McLaughlin was entitled to have a *prompt* impartial determination that there was reason to deprive him of his liberty—not according to a schedule that suits the State's convenience in piggybacking various proceedings, but as soon as his arrest was completed and the magistrate could be procured.

II

I have finished discussing what I consider the principal question in this case, which is what factors determine whether the postarrest determination of probable cause has been (as the Fourth Amendment requires) "reasonably prompt." The Court and I both accept two of those factors, completion of the administrative steps incident to arrest and arranging for a magistrate's probable-cause determination. Since we disagree, however, upon a third factor— the Court believing, as I do not, that "combining" the determination with other proceedings justifies a delay—we necessarily disagree as well on the subsequent question, which can be described as the question of the absolute time limit. Any determinant of "reasonable promptness" that is within the control of the State (as the availability of the magistrate, the personnel and facilities for completing administrative procedures incident to arrest, and the timing of "combined procedures" all are) must be restricted by some outer time limit, or else the promptness guarantee would be worthless. If, for example, it took a full year to obtain a probable-cause determination in California because only a single magistrate had been authorized to perform that function throughout the State, the hearing would assuredly not qualify as "reasonably prompt." At some point, legitimate reasons for delay become illegitimate.

. . .

With one exception, no federal court considering the question has regarded 24 hours as an inadequate amount of time to complete arrest procedures, and with the same exception every court actually setting a limit for probable-cause determination based on those procedures has selected 24 hours. (The exception would not count Sunday within the 24-hour limit.) . . . Federal courts have reached a similar conclusion in applying Federal Rule of Criminal Procedure 5(a), which requires presentment before a federal magistrate "without unnecessary delay." . . . And state courts have similarly applied a 24-hour limit under state statutes requiring presentment without "unreasonable delay." New York, for example, has concluded that no more than 24 hours is necessary from arrest to *arraignment* . . . . Twenty-nine States have statutes similar to New York's, which require either presentment or arraignment "without unnecessary delay" or "forthwith"; eight States explicitly require presentment or arraignment within 24 hours; and only seven States have statutes explicitly permitting a period longer than 24 hours. . . . Since the States requiring a probable-cause hearing within 24 hours include both New York and Alaska, it is unlikely that circumstances of population or geography demand a longer period. Twenty-four hours is consistent with the American Law Institute's Model Code. ALI, Model Code of Pre-Arraignment Procedure § 310.1 (1975). And while the American Bar Association in its proposed rules of criminal procedure initially required that presentment simply be made "without unnecessary delay," it has recently concluded that no more than six hours should be required, except at night. Uniform Rules of Criminal Procedure, 10 U.L.A. App., Criminal Justice Standard 10–4.1 (Spec. Pamph. 1987). Finally, the conclusions of these commissions and judges, both state and federal, are supported by commentators who have examined the question. . . .

In my view, absent extraordinary circumstances, it is an "unreasonable seizure" within the meaning of the Fourth Amendment for the police, having arrested a suspect without a warrant, to delay a determination of probable cause for the arrest either (1) for reasons unrelated to arrangement of the probable-cause determination or completion of the steps incident to arrest, or (2) beyond 24 hours after the arrest. Like the Court, I would treat the time limit as a presumption; when the 24 hours are exceeded the burden shifts to the police to adduce unforeseeable circumstances justifying the additional delay.

. . .

    . . . The common-law rule of *prompt* hearing had as its primary
beneficiaries the innocent—not those whose fully justified convictions must be overturned to scold the police; nor those who avoid
conviction because the evidence, while convincing, does not establish guilt beyond a reasonable doubt; but those so blameless that
there was not even good reason to arrest them. While in recent
years we have invented novel applications of the Fourth Amendment to release the unquestionably guilty, we today repudiate one
of its core applications so that the presumptively innocent may be
left in jail. Hereafter a law-abiding citizen wrongfully arrested may
be compelled to await the grace of a Dickensian bureaucratic
machine, as it churns its cycle for up to two days—never once given
the opportunity to show a judge that there is absolutely no reason
to hold him, that a mistake has been made. In my view, this is the
image of a system of justice that has lost its ancient sense of priority,
a system that few Americans would recognize as our own.

    I respectfully dissent.[*]

---

[*] Justice Marshall wrote a dissenting opin-   vens joined.
ion, which Justice Blackmun and Justice Ste-

9. BAIL

STACK v. BOYLE

342 U.S. 1, 72 S.Ct. 1, 96 L.Ed. 3 (1951).

MR. CHIEF JUSTICE VINSON delivered the opinion of the Court.

Indictments have been returned in the Southern District of California charging the twelve petitioners with conspiring to violate the Smith Act, 18 U.S.C. (Supp. IV) §§ 371, 2385. Upon their arrest, bail was fixed for each petitioner in the widely varying amounts of $2,500, $7,500, $75,000 and $100,000. On motion of petitioner Schneiderman following arrest in the Southern District of New York, his bail was reduced to $50,000 before his removal to California. On motion of the Government to increase bail in the case of other petitioners, and after several intermediate procedural steps not material to the issues presented here, bail was fixed in the District Court for the Southern District of California in the uniform amount of $50,000 for each petitioner.

Petitioners moved to reduce bail on the ground that bail as fixed was excessive under the Eighth Amendment. In support of their motion, petitioners submitted statements as to their financial resources, family relationships, health, prior criminal records, and other information. The only evidence offered by the Government was a certified record showing that four persons previously convicted under the Smith Act in the Southern District of New York had forfeited bail. No evidence was produced relating those four persons to the petitioners in this case. At a hearing on the motion, petitioners were examined by the District Judge and cross-examined by an attorney for the Government. Petitioners' factual statements stand uncontroverted.

After their motion to reduce bail was denied, petitioners filed applications for habeas corpus in the same District Court. Upon consideration of the record on the motion to reduce bail, the writs were denied. The Court of Appeals for the Ninth Circuit affirmed. 192 F.2d 56. Prior to filing their petition for certiorari in this Court, petitioners filed with Mr. Justice Douglas an application for bail and an alternative application for habeas corpus seeking interim relief. Both applications were referred to the Court and the matter was set down for argument on specific questions covering the issues raised by this case.

Relief in this type of case must be speedy if it is to be effective. The petition for certiorari and the full record are now before the

Court and, since the questions presented by the petition have been fully briefed and argued, we consider it appropriate to dispose of the petition for certiorari at this time. Accordingly, the petition for certiorari is granted for review of questions important to the administration of criminal justice.

First. From the passage of the Judiciary Act of 1789, 1 Stat. 73, 91, to the present Federal Rules of Criminal Procedure, Rule 46(a)(1), federal law has unequivocally provided that a person arrested for a non-capital offense *shall* be admitted to bail. This traditional right to freedom before conviction permits the unhampered preparation of a defense, and serves to prevent the infliction of punishment prior to conviction.... Unless this right to bail before trial is preserved, the presumption of innocence, secured only after centuries of struggle, would lose its meaning.

The right to release before trial is conditioned upon the accused's giving adequate assurance that he will stand trial and submit to sentence if found guilty.... Like the ancient practice of securing the oaths of responsible persons to stand as sureties for the accused, the modern practice of requiring a bail bond or the deposit of a sum of money subject to forfeiture serves as additional assurance of the presence of an accused. Bail set at a figure higher than an amount reasonably calculated to fulfill this purpose is "excessive" under the Eighth Amendment....

Since the function of bail is limited, the fixing of bail for any individual defendant must be based upon standards relevant to the purpose of assuring the presence of that defendant. The traditional standards as expressed in the Federal Rules of Criminal Procedure are to be applied in each case to each defendant. In this case petitioners are charged with offenses under the Smith Act and, if found guilty, their convictions are subject to review with the scrupulous care demanded by our Constitution.... Upon final judgment of conviction, petitioners face imprisonment of not more than five years and a fine of not more than $10,000. It is not denied that bail for each petitioner has been fixed in a sum much higher than that usually imposed for offenses with like penalties and yet there has been no factual showing to justify such action in this case. The Government asks the courts to depart from the norm by assuming, without the introduction of evidence, that each petitioner is a pawn in a conspiracy and will, in obedience to a superior, flee the jurisdiction. To infer from the fact of indictment alone a need for bail in an unusually high amount is an arbitrary act. Such conduct would inject into our own system of government the very principles of totalitarianism which Congress was seeking to guard against in passing the statute under which petitioners have been indicted.

If bail in an amount greater than that usually fixed for serious charges of crimes is required in the case of any of the petitioners, that is a matter to which evidence should be directed in a hearing so that the constitutional rights of each petitioner may be preserved. In the absence of such a showing, we are of the opinion that the fixing of bail before trial in these cases cannot be squared with the statutory and constitutional standards for admission to bail.

. . .

The Court concludes that bail has not been fixed by proper methods in this case and that petitioners' remedy is by motion to reduce bail, with right of appeal to the Court of Appeals. Accordingly, the judgment of the Court of Appeals is vacated and the case is remanded to the District Court with directions to vacate its order denying petitioners' applications for writs of habeas corpus and to dismiss the applications without prejudice. Petitioners may move for reduction of bail in the criminal proceeding so that a hearing may be held for the purpose of fixing reasonable bail for each petitioner.

It is so ordered.[*]

[*] Justice Jackson wrote an opinion, which Justice Frankfurter joined.

UNITED STATES v. SALERNO

481 U.S. 739, 107 S.Ct. 2095, 95 L.Ed.2d 697 (1987).

CHIEF JUSTICE REHNQUIST delivered the opinion of the Court.

The Bail Reform Act of 1984 allows a federal court to detain an arrestee pending trial if the Government demonstrates by clear and convincing evidence after an adversary hearing that no release conditions "will reasonably assure . . . the safety of any other person and the community." The United States Court of Appeals for the Second Circuit struck down this provision of the Act as facially unconstitutional, because, in that court's words, this type of pretrial detention violates "substantive due process." We granted certiorari because of a conflict among the Courts of Appeals regarding the validity of the Act.[1] 479 U.S. 929 (1986). We hold that, as against the facial attack mounted by these respondents, the Act fully comports with constitutional requirements. We therefore reverse.

I

Responding to "the alarming problem of crimes committed by persons on release," S. Rep. No. 98–225, p. 3 (1983), Congress formulated the Bail Reform Act of 1984, 18 U.S.C. § 3141 et seq. (1982 ed., Supp. III), as the solution to a bail crisis in the federal courts. The Act represents the National Legislature's considered response to numerous perceived deficiencies in the federal bail process. By providing for sweeping changes in both the way federal courts consider bail applications and the circumstances under which bail is granted, Congress hoped "give the courts adequate authority to make release decisions that give appropriate recognition to the danger a person may pose to others if released." S.Rep. No. 98–225, at 3.

To this end, § 3141(a) of the Act requires a judicial officer to determine whether an arrestee shall be detained. Section 3142(e) provides that "[i]f, after a hearing pursuant to the provisions of subsection (f), the judicial officer finds that no condition or combination of conditions will reasonably assure the appearance of the person as required and the safety of any other person and the community, he shall order the detention of the person prior to trial." Section 3142(f) provides the arrestee with a number of procedural safeguards. He may request the presence of counsel at the detention hearing, he may testify and present witnesses in his behalf, as well as proffer evidence, and he may cross-examine other

---

1. Every other Court of Appeals to have considered the validity of the Bail Reform Act of 1984 has rejected the facial constitutional challenge. . . .

886

witnesses appearing at the hearing. If the judicial officer finds that no conditions of pretrial release can reasonably assure the safety of other persons and the community, he must state his findings of fact in writing, § 3142(i), and support his conclusion with "clear and convincing evidence," § 3142(f).

The judicial officer is not given unbridled discretion in making the detention determination. Congress has specified the considerations relevant to that decision. These factors include the nature and seriousness of the charges, the substantiality of the Government's evidence against the arrestee, the arrestee's background and characteristics, and the nature and seriousness of the danger posed by the suspect's release. § 3142(g). Should a judicial officer order detention, the detainee is entitled to expedited appellate review of the detention order. §§ 3145(b), (c).

Respondents Anthony Salerno and Vincent Cafaro were arrested on March 21, 1986, after being charged in a 29-count indictment alleging various Racketeer Influenced and Corrupt Organizations Act (RICO) violations, mail and wire fraud offenses, extortion, and various criminal gambling violations. The RICO counts alleged 35 acts of racketeering activity, including fraud, extortion, gambling, and conspiracy to commit murder. At respondents' arraignment, the Government moved to have Salerno and Cafaro detained pursuant to § 3142(e), on the ground that no condition of release would assure the safety of the community or any person. The District Court held a hearing at which the Government made a detailed proffer of evidence. The Government's case showed that Salerno was the "boss" of the Genovese Crime Family of La Cosa Nostra and that Cafaro was a "captain" in the Genovese Family. According to the Government's proffer, based in large part on conversations intercepted by a court-ordered wiretap, the two respondents had participated in wide-ranging conspiracies to aid their illegitimate enterprises through violent means. The Government also offered the testimony of two of its trial witnesses, who would assert that Salerno personally participated in two murder conspiracies. Salerno opposed the motion for detention, challenging the credibility of the Government's witnesses. He offered the testimony of several character witnesses as well as a letter from his doctor stating that he was suffering from a serious medical condition. Cafaro presented no evidence at the hearing, but instead characterized the wiretap conversations as merely "tough talk."

The District Court granted the Government's detention motion, concluding that the Government had established by clear and convincing evidence that no condition or combination of conditions of release would ensure the safety of the community or any person:

> "The activities of a criminal organization such as the Genovese Family do not cease with the arrest of its principals and their release on even the most stringent of bail conditions.

The illegal businesses, in place for many years, require constant attention and protection, or they will fail. Under these circumstances, this court recognizes a strong incentive on the part of its leadership to continue business as usual. When business as usual involves threats, beatings, and murder, the present danger such people pose in the community is self-evident." 631 F.Supp. 1364, 1375 (SDNY 1986).

Respondents appealed, contending that to the extent that the Bail Reform Act permits pretrial detention on the ground that the arrestee is likely to commit future crimes, it is unconstitutional on its face. Over a dissent, the United States Court of Appeals for the Second Circuit agreed. 794 F.2d 64 (1986). Although the court agreed that pretrial detention could be imposed if the defendants were likely to intimidate witnesses or otherwise jeopardize the trial process, it found "§ 3142(e)'s authorization of pretrial detention [on the ground of future dangerousness] repugnant to the concept of substantive due process, which we believe prohibits the total deprivation of liberty simply as a means of preventing future crimes." Id., at 71–72. The court concluded that the Government could not, consistent with due process, detain persons who had not been accused of any crime merely because they were thought to present a danger to the community. ... It reasoned that our criminal law system holds persons accountable for past actions, not anticipated future actions. Although a court could detain an arrestee who threatened to flee before trial, such detention would be permissible because it would serve the basic objective of a criminal system—bringing the accused to trial. The court distinguished our decision in Gerstein v. Pugh, 420 U.S. 103 (1975), in which we upheld police detention pursuant to arrest. The court construed *Gerstein* as limiting such detention to the "'administrative steps incident to arrest.'" 794 F.2d, at 74, quoting Gerstein, 420 U.S., at 114. The Court of Appeals also found our decision in Schall v. Martin, 467 U.S. 253 (1984), upholding postarrest pretrial detention of juveniles, inapposite because juveniles have a lesser interest in liberty than do adults. The dissenting judge concluded that on its face, the Bail Reform Act adequately balanced the Federal Government's compelling interests in public safety against the detainee's liberty interests.

II

A facial challenge to a legislative Act is, of course, the most difficult challenge to mount successfully, since the challenger must establish that no set of circumstances exists under which the Act would be valid. The fact that the Bail Reform Act might operate unconstitutionally under some conceivable set of circumstances is insufficient to render it wholly invalid, since we have not recognized an "overbreadth" doctrine outside the limited context of the First Amendment. Schall v. Martin, supra, at 269, n. 18. We think respondents have failed to shoulder their heavy burden to demonstrate that the Act is "facially" unconstitutional.

Respondents present two grounds for invalidating the Bail Reform Act's provisions permitting pretrial detention on the basis of future dangerousness. First, they rely upon the Court of Appeals' conclusion that the Act exceeds the limitations placed upon the Federal Government by the Due Process Clause of the Fifth Amendment. Second, they contend that the Act contravenes the Eighth Amendment's proscription against excessive bail. We treat these contentions in turn.

A

The Due Process Clause of the Fifth Amendment provides that "No person shall . . . be deprived of life, liberty, or property, without due process of law . . . ." This Court has held that the Due Process Clause protects individuals against two types of government action. So-called "substantive due process" prevents the government from engaging in conduct that "shocks the conscience," Rochin v. California, 342 U.S. 165, 172 (1952), or interferes with rights "implicit in the concept of ordered liberty," Palko v. Connecticut, 302 U.S. 319, 325–326 (1937). When government action depriving a person of life, liberty, or property survives substantive due process scrutiny, it must still be implemented in a fair manner. . . . This requirement has traditionally been referred to as "procedural" due process.

Respondents first argue that the Act violates substantive due process because the pretrial detention it authorizes constitutes impermissible punishment before trial. . . . The Government, however, has never argued that pretrial detention could be upheld if it were "punishment." The Court of Appeals assumed that pretrial detention under the Bail Reform Act is regulatory, not penal, and we agree that it is.

As an initial matter, the mere fact that a person is detained does not inexorably lead to the conclusion that the government has imposed punishment. . . . To determine whether a restriction on liberty constitutes impermissible punishment or permissible regulation, we first look to legislative intent. . . . Unless Congress expressly intended to impose punitive restrictions, the punitive/regulatory distinction turns on " 'whether an alternative purpose to which [the restriction] may rationally be connected is assignable for it, and whether it appears excessive in relation to the alternative purpose assigned [to it].' " [Schall v. Martin, supra, 467 U.S., at 269], quoting Kennedy v. Mendoza-Martinez, 372 U.S. 144, 168–169 (1963).

We conclude that the detention imposed by the Act falls on the regulatory side of the dichotomy. The legislative history of the Bail Reform Act clearly indicates that Congress did not formulate the pretrial detention provisions as punishment for dangerous individuals. ... Congress instead perceived pretrial detention as a potential solution to a pressing societal problem.... There is no doubt that preventing danger to the community is a legitimate regulatory goal....

Nor are the incidents of pretrial detention excessive in relation to the regulatory goal Congress sought to achieve. The Bail Reform Act carefully limits the circumstances under which detention may be sought to the most serious of crimes. ... The arrestee is entitled to a prompt detention hearing ... and the maximum length of pretrial detention is limited by the stringent time limitations of the Speedy Trial Act.[4] ... Moreover, as in Schall v. Martin, the conditions of confinement envisioned by the Act "appear to reflect the regulatory purposes relied upon by the" Government. 467 U.S., at 270. As in *Schall*, the statute at issue here requires that detainees be housed in a "facility separate, to the extent practicable, from persons awaiting or serving sentences or being held in custody pending appeal." 18 U.S.C. § 3142(i)(2). We conclude, therefore, that the pretrial detention contemplated by the Bail Reform Act is regulatory in nature, and does not constitute punishment before trial in violation of the Due Process Clause.

The Court of Appeals nevertheless concluded that "the Due Process Clause prohibits pretrial detention on the ground of danger to the community as a regulatory measure, without regard to the duration of the detention." 794 F.2d, at 71. Respondents characterize the Due Process Clause as erecting an impenetrable "wall" in this area that "no governmental interest—rational, important, compelling or otherwise—may surmount." Brief for Respondents 16.

We do not think the Clause lays down any such categorical imperative. We have repeatedly held that the Government's regulatory interest in community safety can, in appropriate circumstances, outweigh an individual's liberty interest. For example, in times of war or insurrection, when society's interest is at its peak, the Government may detain individuals whom the Government believes to be dangerous. ... Even outside the exigencies of war, we have found that sufficiently compelling governmental interests can justify detention of dangerous persons. Thus, we have found no absolute constitutional barrier to detention of potentially dangerous resident aliens pending deportation proceedings. ... We have also held that the government may detain mentally unstable individuals who present a danger to the public ... and dangerous defendants who become incompetent to stand trial .... We have approved of postarrest regulatory detention of juveniles when they present a continuing danger to the community. ... Even competent adults may face substantial liberty restrictions as a result of the operation

---

4. We intimate no view as to the point at which detention in a particular case might become excessively prolonged, and therefore punitive, in relation to Congress' regulatory goal.

of our criminal justice system. If the police suspect an individual of a crime, they may arrest and hold him until a neutral magistrate determines whether probable cause exists. ... Finally, respondents concede and the Court of Appeals noted that an arrestee may be incarcerated until trial if he presents a risk of flight ... or a danger to witnesses.

Respondents characterize all of these cases as exceptions to the "general rule" of substantive due process that the government may not detain a person prior to a judgment of guilt in a criminal trial. Such a "general rule" may freely be conceded, but we think that these cases show a sufficient number of exceptions to the rule that the congressional action challenged here can hardly be characterized as totally novel. Given the well-established authority of the government, in special circumstances, to restrain individuals' liberty prior to or even without criminal trial and conviction, we think that the present statute providing for pretrial detention on the basis of dangerousness must be evaluated in precisely the same manner that we evaluated the laws in the cases discussed above.

The government's interest in preventing crime by arrestees is both legitimate and compelling. ... In *Schall*, supra, we recognized the strength of the State's interest in preventing juvenile crime. This general concern with crime prevention is no less compelling when the suspects are adults. Indeed, "[t]he harm suffered by the victim of a crime is not dependent upon the age of the perpetrator." Schall v. Martin, 467 U.S., at 264–265. The Bail Reform Act of 1984 responds to an even more particularized governmental interest than the interest we sustained in *Schall*. The statute we upheld in *Schall* permitted pretrial detention of any juvenile arrested on any charge after a showing that the individual might commit some undefined further crimes. The Bail Reform Act, in contrast, narrowly focuses on a particularly acute problem in which the Government interests are overwhelming. The Act operates only on individuals who have been arrested for a specific category of extremely serious offenses. ... Congress specifically found that these individuals are far more likely to be responsible for dangerous acts in the community after arrest. ... Nor is the Act by any means a scattershot attempt to incapacitate those who are merely suspected of these serious crimes. The Government must first of all demonstrate probable cause to believe that the charged crime has been committed by the arrestee, but that is not enough. In a fullblown adversary hearing, the Government must convince a neutral decisionmaker by clear and convincing evidence that no conditions of release can reasonably assure the safety of the community or any person. ... While the Government's general interest in preventing crime is compelling, even this interest is heightened when the Government musters convincing proof that the arrestee, already indicted or held to answer for a serious crime, presents a demonstrable danger to the community. Under these narrow circumstances, society's interest in crime prevention is at its greatest.

On the other side of the scale, of course, is the individual's strong interest in liberty. We do not minimize the importance and fundamental nature of this right. But, as our cases hold, this right may, in circumstances where the government's interest is sufficiently weighty, be subordinated to the greater needs of society. We think that Congress' careful delineation of the circumstances under which detention will be permitted satisfies this standard. When the Government proves by clear and convincing evidence that an arrestee presents an identified and articulable threat to an individual or the community, we believe that, consistent with the Due Process Clause, a court may disable the arrestee from executing that threat. Under these circumstances, we cannot categorically state that pretrial detention "offends some principle of justice so rooted in the traditions and conscience of our people as to be ranked as fundamental." Snyder v. Massachusetts, 291 U.S. 97, 105 (1934).

Finally, we may dispose briefly of respondents' facial challenge to the procedures of the Bail Reform Act. To sustain them against such a challenge, we need only find them "adequate to authorize the pretrial detention of at least some [persons] charged with crimes," *Schall*, supra, at 264, whether or not they might be insufficient in some particular circumstances. We think they pass that test. As we stated in *Schall*, "there is nothing inherently unattainable about a prediction of future criminal conduct." 467 U.S., at 278 . . . .

Under the Bail Reform Act, the procedures by which a judicial officer evaluates the likelihood of future dangerousness are specifically designed to further the accuracy of that determination. Detainees have a right to counsel at the detention hearing. . . . They may testify in their own behalf, present information by proffer or otherwise, and cross-examine witnesses who appear at the hearing. . . . The judicial officer charged with the responsibility of determining the appropriateness of detention is guided by statutorily enumerated factors, which include the nature and the circumstances of the charges, the weight of the evidence, the history and characteristics of the putative offender, and the danger to the community. . . . The Government must prove its case by clear and convincing evidence. . . . Finally, the judicial officer must include written findings of fact and a written statement of reasons for a decision to detain. . . . The Act's review provisions . . . provide for immediate appellate review of the detention decision.

We think these extensive safeguards suffice to repel a facial challenge. The protections are more exacting than those we found sufficient in the juvenile context . . . and they far exceed what we found necessary to effect limited postarrest detention in Gerstein v. Pugh, 420 U.S. 103 (1975). Given the legitimate and compelling regulatory purpose of the Act and the procedural protections it offers, we conclude that the Act is not facially invalid under the Due Process Clause of the Fifth Amendment.

B

Respondents also contend that the Bail Reform Act violates the Excessive Bail Clause of the Eighth Amendment. The Court of Appeals did not address this issue because it found that the Act violates the Due Process Clause. We think that the Act survives a challenge founded upon the Eighth Amendment.

The Eighth Amendment addresses pretrial release by providing merely that "[e]xcessive bail shall not be required." This Clause, of course, says nothing about whether bail shall be available at all. Respondents nevertheless contend that this Clause grants them a right to bail calculated solely upon considerations of flight. They rely on Stack v. Boyle, 342 U.S. 1, 5 (1951), in which the Court stated that "[b]ail set at a figure higher than an amount reasonably calculated [to ensure the defendant's presence at trial] is 'excessive' under the Eighth Amendment." In respondents' view, since the Bail Reform Act allows a court essentially to set bail at an infinite amount for reasons not related to the risk of flight, it violates the Excessive Bail Clause. Respondents concede that the right to bail they have discovered in the Eighth Amendment is not absolute. A court may, for example, refuse bail in capital cases. And, as the Court of Appeals noted and respondents admit, a court may refuse bail when the defendant presents a threat to the judicial process by intimidating witnesses. . . . Respondents characterize these exceptions as consistent with what they claim to be the sole purpose of bail—to ensure integrity of the judicial process.

While we agree that a primary function of bail is to safeguard the courts' role in adjudicating the guilt or innocence of defendants, we reject the proposition that the Eighth Amendment categorically prohibits the government from pursuing other admittedly compelling interests through regulation of pretrial release. The above-quoted dictum in Stack v. Boyle is far too slender a reed on which to rest this argument. The Court in *Stack* had no occasion to consider whether the Excessive Bail Clause requires courts to admit all defendants to bail, because the statute before the Court in that case in fact allowed the defendants to be bailed. Thus, the Court had to determine only whether bail, admittedly available in that case, was excessive if set at a sum greater than that necessary to ensure the arrestees' presence at trial.

The holding of *Stack* is illuminated by the Court's holding just four months later in Carlson v. Landon, 342 U.S. 524 (1952). In that case, remarkably similar to the present action, the detainees had been arrested and held without bail pending a determination of deportability. The Attorney General refused to release the individuals, "on the ground that there was reasonable cause to believe that [their] release would be prejudicial to the public interest and *would endanger the welfare and safety of the United States.*" Id., at 529 (emphasis added). The detainees brought the same challenge that respondents bring to us today: the Eighth Amendment required them to be admitted to bail. The Court squarely rejected this proposition:

> "The bail clause was lifted with slight changes from the English Bill of Rights Act. In England that clause has never been thought to accord a right to bail in all cases, but merely to provide that bail shall not be excessive in those cases where it is proper to grant bail. When this clause was carried over into our Bill of Rights, nothing was said that indicated any different concept. The Eighth Amendment has not prevented Congress from defining the classes of cases in which bail shall be allowed in this country. Thus, in criminal cases bail is not compulsory where the punishment may be death. Indeed, the very language of the Amendment fails to say all arrests must be bailable." Id., at 545–546 (footnotes omitted).

Carlson v. Landon was a civil case, and we need not decide today whether the Excessive Bail Clause speaks at all to Congress' power to define the classes of criminal arrestees who shall be admitted to bail. For even if we were to conclude that the Eighth Amendment imposes some substantive limitations on the National Legislature's powers in this area, we would still hold that the Bail Reform Act is valid. Nothing in the text of the Bail Clause limits permissible government considerations solely to questions of flight. The only arguable substantive limitation of the Bail Clause is that the government's proposed conditions of release or detention not be "excessive" in light of the perceived evil. Of course, to determine whether the government's response is excessive, we must compare that response against the interest the government seeks to protect by means of that response. Thus, when the government has admitted that its only interest is in preventing flight, bail must be set by a court at a sum designed to ensure that goal, and no more. . . . We believe that when Congress has mandated detention on the basis of a compelling interest other than prevention of flight, as it has here, the Eighth Amendment does not require release on bail.

III

In our society liberty is the norm, and detention prior to trial or without trial is the carefully limited exception. We hold that the provisions for pretrial detention in the Bail Reform Act of 1984 fall within that carefully limited exception. The Act authorizes the detention prior to trial of arrestees charged with serious felonies who are found after an adversary hearing to pose a threat to the safety of individuals or to the community which no condition of release can dispel. The numerous procedural safeguards detailed above must attend this adversary hearing. We are unwilling to say that this congressional determination, based as it is upon that primary concern of every government—a concern for the safety and indeed the lives of its citizens—on its face violates either the Due Process Clause of the Fifth Amendment or the Excessive Bail Clause of the Eighth Amendment.

The judgment of the Court of Appeals is therefore

Reversed.

JUSTICE MARSHALL, with whom JUSTICE BRENNAN joins, dissenting.

This case brings before the Court for the first time a statute in which Congress declares that a person innocent of any crime may be jailed indefinitely, pending the trial of allegations which are legally presumed to be untrue, if the Government shows to the satisfaction of a judge that the accused is likely to commit crimes, unrelated to the pending charges, at any time in the future. Such statutes, consistent with the usages of tyranny and the excesses of what bitter experience teaches us to call the police state, have long been thought incompatible with the fundamental human rights protected by our Constitution. Today a majority of this Court holds otherwise. Its decision disregards basic principles of justice established centuries ago and enshrined beyond the reach of governmental interference in the Bill of Rights.

. . .

II

The majority approaches respondents' challenge to the Act by dividing the discussion into two sections, one concerned with the substantive guarantees implicit in the Due Process Clause, and the other concerned with the protection afforded by the Excessive Bail Clause of the Eighth Amendment. This is a sterile formalism, which divides a unitary argument into two independent parts and then professes to demonstrate that the parts are individually inadequate.

On the due process side of this false dichotomy appears an argument concerning the distinction between regulatory and punitive legislation. The majority concludes that the Act is a regulatory rather than a punitive measure. The ease with which the conclusion is reached suggests the worthlessness of the achievement. The major premise is that "[u]nless Congress expressly intended to impose punitive restrictions, the punitive/regulatory distinction turns on ' "whether an alternative purpose to which [the restriction] may rationally be connected is assignable for it, and whether it appears excessive in relation to the alternative purpose assigned [to it]." ' " Ante, at 747 (citations omitted). The majority finds that "Congress did not formulate the pretrial detention provisions as punishment for dangerous individuals," but instead was pursuing the "legitimate regulatory goal" of "preventing danger to the community." Ante, at 747. Concluding that pretrial detention is not an excessive solution to the problem of preventing danger to the community, the majority thus finds that no substantive element of the guarantee of due process invalidates the statute.

This argument does not demonstrate the conclusion it purports to justify. Let us apply the majority's reasoning to a similar, hypothetical case. After investigation, Congress determines (not unrealistically) that a large proportion of violent crime is perpetrated by persons who are unemployed. It also determines, equally reasonably, that much violent crime is committed at night. From amongst the panoply of "potential solutions," Congress chooses a statute which permits, after judicial proceedings, the imposition of a dusk-to-dawn curfew on anyone who is unemployed. Since this is not a measure enacted for the purpose of punishing the unemployed, and since the majority finds that preventing danger to the community is a legitimate regulatory goal, the curfew statute would, according to the majority's analysis, be a mere "regulatory" detention statute, entirely compatible with the substantive components of the Due Process Clause.

The absurdity of this conclusion arises, of course, from the majority's cramped concept of substantive due process. The majority proceeds as though the only substantive right protected by the Due Process Clause is a right to be free from punishment before conviction. The majority's technique for infringing this right is simple: merely redefine any measure which is claimed to be punishment as "regulation," and, magically, the Constitution no longer prohibits its imposition. Because, as I discuss in Part III, infra, the Due Process Clause protects other substantive rights which are infringed by this legislation, the majority's argument is merely an exercise in obfuscation.

The logic of the majority's Eighth Amendment analysis is equally unsatisfactory. The Eighth Amendment, as the majority notes, states that "[e]xcessive bail shall not be required." The majority then declares, as if it were undeniable, that: "[t]his Clause, of course, says nothing about whether bail shall be available at all." Ante, at 752. If excessive bail is imposed the defendant stays in jail. The same result is achieved if bail is denied altogether. Whether the magistrate sets bail at $1 billion or refuses to set bail at all, the consequences are indistinguishable. It would be mere sophistry to suggest that the Eighth Amendment protects against the former decision, and not the latter. Indeed, such a result would lead to the conclusion that there was no need for Congress to pass a preventive detention measure of any kind; every federal magistrate and district judge could simply refuse, despite the absence of any evidence of risk of flight or danger to the community, to set bail. This would be entirely constitutional, since, according to the majority, the Eighth Amendment "says nothing about whether bail shall be available at all."

But perhaps, the majority says, this manifest absurdity can be avoided. Perhaps the Bail Clause is addressed only to the judiciary. "[W]e need not decide today," the majority says, "whether the Excessive Bail Clause speaks at all to Congress' power to define the classes of criminal arrestees who shall be admitted to bail." Ante, at 754. The majority is correct that this question need not be decided today; it was decided long ago. Federal and state statutes which purport to accomplish what the Eighth Amendment forbids, such as imposing cruel and unusual punishments, may not stand. ... The text of the Amendment, which provides simply that "[e]xcessive bail shall not be required, nor excessive fines imposed, nor cruel and unusual punishments inflicted," provides absolutely no support for the majority's speculation that both courts and Congress are forbidden to inflict cruel and unusual punishments, while only the courts are forbidden to require excessive bail.

The majority's attempts to deny the relevance of the Bail Clause to this case are unavailing, but the majority is nonetheless correct that the prohibition of excessive bail means that in order "to determine whether the government's response is excessive, we must compare that response against the interest the government seeks to protect by means of that response." Ante, at 754. The majority concedes, as it must, that "when the government has admitted that its only interest is in preventing flight, bail must be set by a court at a sum designed to ensure that goal, and no more." Ibid. But, the majority says, "when Congress has mandated detention on the basis of a compelling interest other than prevention of flight, as it has here, the Eighth Amendment does not require release on bail." Ante, at 754–755. This conclusion follows only if the "compelling" interest upon which Congress acted is an interest which the Constitution permits Congress to further through the denial of bail. The majority does not ask, as a result of its disingenuous division of the analysis, if there are any substantive limits contained in both the Eighth Amendment and the Due Process Clause which render this system of preventive detention unconstitutional. The majority does not ask because the answer is apparent and, to the majority, inconvenient.

III

The essence of this case may be found, ironically enough, in a provision of the Act to which the majority does not refer. Title 18 U.S.C. § 3142(j) (1982 ed., Supp. III) provides that "[n]othing in this section shall be construed as modifying or limiting the presumption of innocence." But the very pith and purpose of this statute is an abhorrent limitation of the presumption of innocence. The majority's untenable conclusion that the present Act is constitutional arises from a specious denial of the role of the Bail Clause and the Due Process Clause in protecting the invaluable guarantee afforded by the presumption of innocence.

"The principle that there is a presumption of innocence in favor of the accused is the undoubted law, axiomatic and elementary, and its enforcement lies at the foundation of the administration of our criminal law." Coffin v. United States, 156 U.S. 432, 453 (1895). Our society's belief, reinforced over the centuries, that all are innocent until the state has proved them to be guilty, like the companion principle that guilt must be proved beyond a reasonable doubt, is "implicit in the concept of ordered liberty," Palko v. Connecticut, 302 U.S. 319, 325 (1937), and is established beyond legislative contravention in the Due Process Clause. . . .

The statute now before us declares that persons who have been indicted may be detained if a judicial officer finds clear and convincing evidence that they pose a danger to individuals or to the community. The statute does not authorize the Government to imprison anyone it has evidence is dangerous; indictment is necessary. But let us suppose that a defendant is indicted and the Government shows by clear and convincing evidence that he is dangerous and should be detained pending a trial, at which trial the defendant is acquitted. May the Government continue to hold the defendant in detention based upon its showing that he is dangerous? The answer cannot be yes, for that would allow the Government to imprison someone for uncommitted crimes based upon "proof" not beyond a reasonable doubt. The result must therefore be that once the indictment has failed, detention cannot continue. But our fundamental principles of justice declare that the defendant is as innocent on the day before his trial as he is on the morning after his acquittal. Under this statute an untried indictment somehow acts to permit a detention, based on other charges, which after an acquittal would be unconstitutional. The conclusion is inescapable that the indictment has been turned into evidence, if not that the defendant is guilty of the crime charged, then that left to his own devices he will soon be guilty of something else. " 'If it suffices to accuse, what will become of the innocent?' " Coffin v. United States, supra, at 455 (quoting Ammianus Marcellinus, Rerum Gestarum Libri Qui Supersunt, L. XVIII, c. 1, A.D. 359.).

To be sure, an indictment is not without legal consequences. It establishes that there is probable cause to believe that an offense was committed, and that the defendant committed it. Upon probable cause a warrant for the defendant's arrest may issue; a period of administrative detention may occur before the evidence of probable cause is presented to a neutral magistrate. . . . Once a defendant has been committed for trial he may be detained in custody if the magistrate finds that no conditions of release will prevent him from becoming a fugitive. But in this connection the charging instrument is evidence of nothing more than the fact that there will be a trial, and

> "release before trial is conditioned upon the accused's giving adequate assurance that he will stand trial and submit to

sentence if found guilty. Like the ancient practice of securing the oaths of responsible persons to stand as sureties for the accused, the modern practice of requiring a bail bond or the deposit of a sum of money subject to forfeiture serves as additional assurance of the presence of an accused." Stack v. Boyle, 342 U.S. 1, 4–5 (1951) (citation omitted).[6]

The finding of probable cause conveys power to try, and the power to try imports of necessity the power to assure that the processes of justice will not be evaded or obstructed.[7] "Pretrial detention to prevent future crimes against society at large, however, is not justified by any concern for holding a trial on the charges for which a defendant has been arrested." 794 F.2d 64, 73 (CA2 1986) (quoting United States v. Melendez-Carrion, 790 F.2d 984, 1002 (CA2 1986) (opinion of Newman, J.)). The detention purportedly authorized by this statute bears no relation to the Government's power to try charges supported by a finding of probable cause, and thus the interests it serves are outside the scope of interests which may be considered in weighing the excessiveness of bail under the Eighth Amendment.

It is not a novel proposition that the Bail Clause plays a vital role in protecting the presumption of innocence. Reviewing the application for bail pending appeal by members of the American Communist Party convicted under the Smith Act, 18 U.S.C. § 2385, Justice Jackson wrote:

> "Grave public danger is said to result from what [the defendants] may be expected to do, in addition to what they have done since their conviction. If I assume that defendants are disposed to commit every opportune disloyal act helpful to Communist countries, it is still difficult to reconcile with traditional American law the jailing of persons by the courts because of anticipated but as yet uncommitted crimes. Imprisonment to protect society from predicted but unconsummated offenses is ... unprecedented in this country and ... fraught with danger of excesses and injustice...." Williamson v. United States, 95 L.Ed. 1379, 1382 (1950) (Jackson, J., in chambers) (footnote omitted).

---

6. The majority states that denial of bail in capital cases has traditionally been the rule rather than the exception. And this of course is so, for it has been the considered presumption of generations of judges that a defendant in danger of execution has an extremely strong incentive to flee. If in any particular case the presumed likelihood of flight should be made irrebuttable, it would in all probability violate the Due Process Clause. Thus what the majority perceives as an exception is nothing more than an example of the traditional operation of our system of bail.

7. It is also true, as the majority observes, that the Government is entitled to assurance, by incarceration if necessary, that a defendant will not obstruct justice through destruction of evidence, procuring the absence or intimidation of witnesses, or subornation of perjury. But in such cases the Government benefits from no presumption that any particular defendant is likely to engage in activities inimical to the administration of justice, and the majority offers no authority for the proposition that bail has traditionally been denied *prospectively,* upon speculation that witnesses would be tampered with....

As Chief Justice Vinson wrote for the Court in Stack v. Boyle, supra: "Unless th[e] right to bail before trial is preserved, the presumption of innocence, secured only after centuries of struggle, would lose its meaning." 342 U.S. at 4.

IV

There is a connection between the peculiar facts of this case and the evident constitutional defects in the statute which the Court upholds today. Respondent Cafaro was originally incarcerated for an indeterminate period at the request of the Government, which believed (or professed to believe) that his release imminently threatened the safety of the community. That threat apparently vanished, from the Government's point of view, when Cafaro agreed to act as a covert agent of the Government. There could be no more eloquent demonstration of the coercive power of authority to imprison upon prediction, or of the dangers which the almost inevitable abuses pose to the cherished liberties of a free society.

"It is a fair summary of history to say that the safeguards of liberty have frequently been forged in controversies involving not very nice people." United States v. Rabinowitz, 339 U.S. 56, 69 (1950) (Frankfurter, J., dissenting). Honoring the presumption of innocence is often difficult; sometimes we must pay substantial social costs as a result of our commitment to the values we espouse. But at the end of the day the presumption of innocence protects the innocent; the shortcuts we take with those whom we believe to be guilty injure only those wrongfully accused and, ultimately, ourselves.

Throughout the world today there are men, women, and children interned indefinitely, awaiting trials which may never come or which may be a mockery of the word, because their governments believe them to be "dangerous." Our Constitution, whose construction began two centuries ago, can shelter us forever from the evils of such unchecked power. Over 200 years it has slowly, through our efforts, grown more durable, more expansive, and more just. But it cannot protect us if we lack the courage, and the self-restraint, to protect ourselves. Today a majority of the Court applies itself to an ominous exercise in demolition. Theirs is truly a decision which will go forth without authority, and come back without respect.

I dissent.[*]

---

[*] Justice Stevens wrote a dissenting opinion.

10. INDICTMENT

UNITED STATES v. WILLIAMS

504 U.S. 36, 112 S.Ct. 1735, 118 L.Ed.2d 352 (1992).

JUSTICE SCALIA delivered the opinion of the Court.

The question presented in this case is whether a district court may dismiss an otherwise valid indictment because the Government failed to disclose to the grand jury "substantial exculpatory evidence" in its possession.

I

On May 4, 1988, respondent John H. Williams, Jr., a Tulsa, Oklahoma investor, was indicted by a federal grand jury on seven counts of "knowingly mak[ing] [a] false statement or report . . . for the purpose of influencing . . . the action [of a federally insured financial institution]," in violation of 18 U.S.C. § 1014 (1988 ed., Supp. II). According to the indictment, between September 1984 and November 1985 Williams supplied four Oklahoma banks with "materially false" statements that variously overstated the value of his current assets and interest income in order to influence the banks' actions on his loan requests.

Williams' misrepresentation was allegedly effected through two financial statements provided to the banks, a "Market Value Balance Sheet" and a "Statement of Projected Income and Expense." The former included as "current assets" approximately $6 million in notes receivable from three venture capital companies. Though it contained a disclaimer that these assets were carried at cost rather than at market value, the Government asserted that listing them as "current assets"—i.e., assets quickly reducible to cash—was misleading, since Williams knew that none of the venture capital companies could afford to satisfy the notes in the short term. The second document—the Statement of Projected Income and Expense—allegedly misrepresented Williams' interest income, since it failed to reflect that the interest payments received on the notes of the venture capital companies were funded entirely by Williams' own loans to those companies. The Statement thus falsely implied, according to the Government, that Williams was deriving interest income from "an independent outside source." Brief for United States 3.

Shortly after arraignment, the District Court granted Williams' motion for disclosure of all exculpatory portions of the grand jury transcripts, see Brady v. Maryland, 373 U.S. 83 (1963). Upon reviewing this material, Williams demanded that the District Court dismiss the indictment, alleging that the Government had failed to fulfill its obligation under the Tenth Circuit's prior decision in United States v. Page, 808 F.2d 723, 728 (1987), to present "substantial exculpatory evidence" to the grand jury (emphasis omitted). His contention was that evidence which the Government had chosen not to present to the grand jury—in particular, Williams' general ledgers and tax returns, and Williams' testimony in his contemporaneous Chapter 11 bankruptcy proceeding—disclosed that, for tax purposes and otherwise, he had regularly accounted for the "notes receivable" (and the interest on them) in a manner consistent with the Balance Sheet and the Income Statement. This, he contended, belied an intent to mislead the banks, and thus directly negated an essential element of the charged offense.

The District Court initially denied Williams' motion, but upon reconsideration ordered the indictment dismissed without prejudice. It found, after a hearing, that the withheld evidence was "relevant to an essential element of the crime charged," created " 'a reasonable doubt about [respondent's] guilt,' " App. to Pet. for Cert. 23a–24a (quoting United States v. Gray, 502 F.Supp. 150, 152 (DC1980)), and thus "render[ed] the grand jury's decision to indict gravely suspect." App. to Pet. for Cert. 26a. Upon the Government's appeal, the Court of Appeals affirmed the District Court's order, following its earlier decision in *Page*, supra. It first sustained as not "clearly erroneous" the District Court's determination that the Government had withheld "substantial exculpatory evidence" from the grand jury, see 899 F.2d 898, 900–903 (CA10 1990). It then found that the Government's behavior " 'substantially influence[d]' " the grand jury's decision to indict, or at the very least raised a " 'grave doubt that the decision to indict was free from such substantial influence.' " Id., at 903 (quoting Bank of Nova Scotia v. United States, 487 U.S. 250, 263 (1988)); see 899 F.2d, at 903–904. Under these circumstances, the Tenth Circuit concluded, it was not an abuse of discretion for the District Court to require the Government to begin anew before the grand jury. We granted certiorari, 502 U.S. 905 (1991).

. . .

III

Respondent does not contend that the Fifth Amendment itself obliges the prosecutor to disclose substantial exculpatory evidence in his possession to the grand jury. Instead, building on our statement that the federal courts "may, within limits, formulate procedural rules not specifically required by the Constitution or the Congress," United States v. Hasting, 461 U.S. 499, 505 (1983), he argues that imposition of the Tenth Circuit's disclosure rule is supported by the courts' "supervisory power." We think not. *Hasting,* and the cases that rely upon the principle it expresses, deal

strictly with the courts' power to control their *own* procedures. . . .
That power has been applied not only to improve the truth-finding
process of the trial, . . . but also to prevent parties from reaping
benefit or incurring harm from violations of substantive or procedural rules (imposed by the Constitution or laws) governing matters
apart from the trial itself . . . Thus, Bank of Nova Scotia v. United
States, 487 U.S. 250 (1988), makes clear that the supervisory power
can be used to dismiss an indictment because of misconduct before
the grand jury, at least where that misconduct amounts to a
violation of one of those "few, clear rules which were carefully
drafted and approved by this Court and by Congress to ensure the
integrity of the grand jury's functions," United States v. Mechanik,
475 U.S. 66, 74 (1986) (O'Connor, J., concurring in judgment).

We did not hold in *Bank of Nova Scotia*, however, that the
courts' supervisory power could be used, not merely as a means of
enforcing or vindicating legally compelled standards of prosecutorial conduct before the grand jury, but as a means of *prescribing*
those standards of prosecutorial conduct in the first instance—just
as it may be used as a means of establishing standards of prosecutorial conduct before the courts themselves. It is this latter exercise
that respondent demands. Because the grand jury is an institution
separate from the courts, over whose functioning the courts do not
preside, we think it clear that, as a general matter at least, no such
"supervisory" judicial authority exists, and that the disclosure rule
applied here exceeded the Tenth Circuit's authority.

A

"[R]ooted in long centuries of Anglo–American history," Han-
nah v. Larche, 363 U.S. 420, 490 (1960) (Frankfurter, J., concurring
in result), the grand jury is mentioned in the Bill of Rights, but not
in the body of the Constitution. It has not been textually assigned,
therefore, to any of the branches described in the first three Articles.
It " 'is a constitutional fixture in its own right.' " United States v.
Chanen, 549 F.2d 1306, 1312 (CA9 1977) (quoting Nixon v. Sirica,
159 U.S.App.D.C. 58, 70, n. 54, 487 F.2d 700, 712, n. 54 (1973)),
cert. denied, 434 U.S. 825 (1977). In fact the whole theory of its
function is that it belongs to no branch of the institutional Government, serving as a kind of buffer or referee between the Government and the people. . . . Although the grand jury normally operates, of course, in the courthouse and under judicial auspices, its
institutional relationship with the Judicial Branch has traditionally
been, so to speak, at arm's length. Judges' direct involvement in
the functioning of the grand jury has generally been confined to the
constitutive one of calling the grand jurors together and administering their oaths of office. . . .

The grand jury's functional independence from the Judicial
Branch is evident both in the scope of its power to investigate
criminal wrongdoing, and in the manner in which that power is

exercised. "Unlike [a] [c]ourt, whose jurisdiction is predicated upon a specific case or controversy, the grand jury 'can investigate merely on suspicion that the law is being violated, or even because it wants assurance that it is not.'" United States v. R. Enterprises, 498 U.S. 292, 297 (1991) (slip op. 4) (quoting United States v. Morton Salt Co., 338 U.S. 632, 642–643 (1950)). It need not identify the offender it suspects, or even "the precise nature of the offense" it is investigating. Blair v. United States, 250 U.S. 273, 282 (1919). The grand jury requires no authorization from its constituting court to initiate an investigation ... nor does the prosecutor require leave of court to seek a grand jury indictment. And in its day-to-day functioning, the grand jury generally operates without the interference of a presiding judge.... It swears in its own witnesses, Fed. Rule Crim. Proc. 6(c), and deliberates in total secrecy ....

True, the grand jury cannot compel the appearance of witnesses and the production of evidence, and must appeal to the court when such compulsion is required.... And the court will refuse to lend its assistance when the compulsion the grand jury seeks would override rights accorded by the Constitution ... or even testimonial privileges recognized by the common law .... Even in this setting, however, we have insisted that the grand jury remain "free to pursue its investigations unhindered by external influence or supervision so long as it does not trench upon the legitimate rights of any witness called before it." United States v. Dionisio, 410 U.S. 1, 17–18 (1973). Recognizing this tradition of independence, we have said that the Fifth Amendment's "constitutional guarantee *presupposes* an investigative body 'acting independently of either prosecuting attorney or *judge* '...." Id., at 16 (emphasis added) (quoting *Stirone* [v. United States, 361 U.S. 212 (1960)], at 218).

No doubt in view of the grand jury proceeding's status as other than a constituent element of a "criminal prosecutio[n]," U.S. Const., Amdt. VI, we have said that certain constitutional protections afforded defendants in criminal proceedings have no application before that body. The Double Jeopardy Clause of the Fifth Amendment does not bar a grand jury from returning an indictment when a prior grand jury has refused to do so.... We have twice suggested, though not held, that the Sixth Amendment right to counsel does not attach when an individual is summoned to appear before a grand jury, even if he is the subject of the investigation.... And although "the grand jury may not force a witness to answer questions in violation of [the Fifth Amendment's] constitutional guarantee" against self-incrimination, [United States v.] Calandra, [414 U.S. 338 (1974)], at 346 (citing Kastigar v. United States, 406 U.S. 441 (1972)), our cases suggest that an indictment obtained through the use of evidence previously obtained in violation of the privilege against self-incrimination "is nevertheless valid." *Calandra,* supra, at 346 . . . .

Given the grand jury's operational separateness from its constituting court, it should come as no surprise that we have been reluctant to invoke the judicial supervisory power as a basis for prescribing modes of grand jury procedure. Over the years, we have received many requests to exercise supervision over the grand jury's evidence-taking process, but we have refused them all, including some more appealing than the one presented today. In United States v. Calandra, supra, a grand jury witness faced questions that were allegedly based upon physical evidence the Government had obtained through a violation of the Fourth Amendment; we rejected the proposal that the exclusionary rule be extended to grand jury proceedings, because of "the potential injury to the historic role and functions of the grand jury." 414 U.S., at 349. In Costello v. United States, 350 U.S. 359 (1956), we declined to enforce the hearsay rule in grand jury proceedings, since that "would run counter to the whole history of the grand jury institution, in which laymen conduct their inquiries unfettered by technical rules." Id., at 364.

These authorities suggest that any power federal courts may have to fashion, on their own initiative, rules of grand jury procedure is a very limited one, not remotely comparable to the power they maintain over their own proceedings. . . . It certainly would not permit judicial reshaping of the grand jury institution, substantially altering the traditional relationships between the prosecutor, the constituting court, and the grand jury itself. . . . As we proceed to discuss, that would be the consequence of the proposed rule here.

B

Respondent argues that the Court of Appeals' rule can be justified as a sort of Fifth Amendment "common law," a necessary means of assuring the constitutional right to the judgment "of an independent and informed grand jury," Wood v. Georgia, 370 U.S. 375, 390 (1962). Brief for Respondent 27. Respondent makes a generalized appeal to functional notions: Judicial supervision of the quantity and quality of the evidence relied upon by the grand jury plainly facilitates, he says, the grand jury's performance of its twin historical responsibilities, i.e., bringing to trial those who may be justly accused and shielding the innocent from unfounded accusation and prosecution. . . . We do not agree. The rule would neither preserve nor enhance the traditional functioning of the institution that the Fifth Amendment demands. To the contrary, requiring the prosecutor to present exculpatory as well as inculpatory evidence would alter the grand jury's historical role, transforming it from an accusatory to an adjudicatory body.

It is axiomatic that the grand jury sits not to determine guilt or innocence, but to assess whether there is adequate basis for bringing a criminal charge.... That has always been so; and to make the assessment it has always been thought sufficient to hear only the prosecutor's side. As Blackstone described the prevailing practice in 18th–century England, the grand jury was "only to hear evidence on behalf of the prosecution[,] for the finding of an indictment is only in the nature of an enquiry or accusation, which is afterwards to be tried and determined." 4 W. Blackstone, Commentaries 300 (1769); see also 2 M. Hale, Pleas of the Crown 157 (1st Am. ed. 1847). So also in the United States. According to the description of an early American court, three years before the Fifth Amendment was ratified, it is the grand jury's function not "to enquire ... upon what foundation [the charge may be] denied," or otherwise to try the suspect's defenses, but only to examine "upon what foundation [the charge] is made" by the prosecutor. Respublica v. Shaffer, 1 Dall. 236 (O.T. Phila. 1788) .... As a consequence, neither in this country nor in England has the suspect under investigation by the grand jury ever been thought to have a right to testify, or to have exculpatory evidence presented....

Imposing upon the prosecutor a legal obligation to present exculpatory evidence in his possession would be incompatible with this system. If a "balanced" assessment of the entire matter is the objective, surely the first thing to be done—rather than requiring the prosecutor to say what he knows in defense of the target of the investigation—is to entitle the target to tender his own defense. To require the former while denying (as we do) the latter would be quite absurd. It would also be quite pointless, since it would merely invite the target to circumnavigate the system by delivering his exculpatory evidence to the prosecutor, whereupon it would *have* to be passed on to the grand jury—unless the prosecutor is willing to take the chance that a court will not deem the evidence important enough to qualify for mandatory disclosure....

Respondent acknowledges (as he must) that the "common law" of the grand jury is not violated if the *grand jury itself* chooses to hear no more evidence than that which suffices to convince it an indictment is proper.... Thus, had the Government offered to familiarize the grand jury in this case with the five boxes of financial statements and deposition testimony alleged to contain exculpatory information, and had the grand jury rejected the offer as pointless, respondent would presumably agree that the resulting indictment would have been valid. Respondent insists, however, that courts must require the modern prosecutor to alert the grand jury to the nature and extent of the available exculpatory evidence, because otherwise the grand jury "merely functions as an arm of the prosecution." Brief for Respondent 27. We reject the attempt to convert a nonexistent duty of the grand jury itself into an obligation of the prosecutor. The authority of the prosecutor to seek an indictment has long been understood to be "coterminous with the authority of the grand jury to entertain [the prosecutor's] charges." United States v. Thompson, 251 U.S., at 414. If the grand jury has no obligation to consider all "substantial exculpatory" evidence, we do not understand how the prosecutor can be said to have a binding obligation to present it.

There is yet another respect in which respondent's proposal not only fails to comport with, but positively contradicts, the "common law" of the Fifth Amendment grand jury. Motions to quash indictments based upon the sufficiency of the evidence relied upon by the grand jury were unheard of at common law in England .... And the traditional American practice was described by Justice Nelson, riding circuit in 1852, as follows:

> "No case has been cited, nor have we been able to find any, furnishing an authority for looking into and revising the judgment of the grand jury upon the evidence, for the purpose of determining whether or not the finding was founded upon sufficient proof, or whether there was a deficiency in respect to any part of the complaint...." United States v. Reed, 27 Fed.Cas. 727, 738 (No. 16, 134) (CC NDNY 1852).

We accepted Justice Nelson's description in Costello v. United States, where we held that "it would run counter to the whole history of the grand jury institution" to permit an indictment to be challenged "on the ground that there was inadequate or incompetent evidence before the grand jury." 350 U.S., at 363–364. And we reaffirmed this principle recently in *Bank of Nova Scotia*, where we held that "the mere fact that evidence itself is unreliable is not sufficient to require a dismissal of the indictment," and that "a challenge to the reliability or competence of the evidence presented to the grand jury" will not be heard. 487 U.S., at 261. It would make little sense, we think, to abstain from reviewing the evidentiary support for the grand jury's judgment while scrutinizing the sufficiency of the prosecutor's presentation. A complaint about the quality or adequacy of the evidence can always be recast as a complaint that the prosecutor's presentation was "incomplete" or "misleading." Our words in *Costello* bear repeating: Review of facially valid indictments on such grounds "would run counter to the whole history of the grand jury institution[,] [and] [n]either justice nor the concept of a fair trial requires [it]." 350 U.S., at 364.

. . .

Echoing the reasoning of the Tenth Circuit in United States v. Page, 808 F.2d, at 728, respondent argues that a rule requiring the prosecutor to disclose exculpatory evidence to the grand jury would, by removing from the docket unjustified prosecutions, save valuable judicial time. That depends, we suppose, upon what the ratio would turn out to be between unjustified prosecutions eliminated and grand jury indictments challenged—for the latter as well as the former consume "valuable judicial time." We need not pursue the matter; if there is an advantage to the proposal, Congress is free to prescribe it. For the reasons set forth above, however, we conclude that courts have no authority to prescribe such a duty pursuant to their inherent supervisory authority over their own proceedings. The judgment of the Court of Appeals is accordingly reversed and the cause remanded for further proceedings consistent with this opinion.

So ordered.

JUSTICE STEVENS, with whom JUSTICE BLACKMUN and JUSTICE O'CONNOR join, and with whom JUSTICE THOMAS joins as to Parts II and III, dissenting.

. . .

II

Like the Hydra slain by Hercules, prosecutorial misconduct has many heads. Some are cataloged in Justice Sutherland's classic opinion for the Court in Berger v. United States, 295 U.S. 78 (1935):

> "That the United States prosecuting attorney overstepped the bounds of that propriety and fairness which should characterize the conduct of such an officer in the prosecution of a criminal offense is clearly shown by the record. He was guilty of misstating the facts in his cross-examination of witnesses; of putting into the mouths of such witnesses things which they had not said; of suggesting by his questions that statements had been made to him personally out of court, in respect of which no proof was offered; of pretending to understand that a witness had said something which he had not said and persistently cross-examining the witness upon that basis; of assuming prejudicial facts not in evidence; of bullying and arguing with witnesses; and in general, of conducting himself in a thoroughly indecorous and improper manner....

> "The prosecuting attorney's argument to the jury was undignified and intemperate, containing improper insinuations and assertions calculated to mislead the jury." Id., at 84–85.

This, of course, is not an exhaustive list of the kinds of improper tactics that overzealous or misguided prosecutors have adopted in judicial proceedings. The reported cases of this Court alone contain examples of the knowing use of perjured testimony ... the suppression of evidence favorable to an accused person ... and misstatements of the law in argument to the jury ... to name just a few.

Nor has prosecutorial misconduct been limited to judicial proceedings: the reported cases indicate that it has sometimes infected grand jury proceedings as well. The cases contain examples of prosecutors presenting perjured testimony ... questioning a witness outside the presence of the grand jury and then failing to inform the grand jury that the testimony was exculpatory ... failing to inform the grand jury of its authority to subpoena witnesses ... operating under a conflict of interest ... misstating the law ... and misstating the facts on cross-examination of a witness ....

Justice Sutherland's identification of the basic reason why that sort of misconduct is intolerable merits repetition:

> "The United States Attorney is the representative not of an ordinary party to a controversy, but of a sovereignty whose obligation to govern impartially is as compelling as its obligation to govern at all; and whose interest, therefore, in a criminal prosecution is not that it shall win a case, but that justice shall be done. As such, he is in a peculiar and very definite sense the servant of the law, the twofold aim of which is that guilt shall not escape or innocence suffer. He may prosecute with earnestness and vigor—indeed, he should do so. But, while he may strike hard blows, he is not at liberty to strike foul ones. It is as much his duty to refrain from improper methods calculated to produce a wrongful conviction as it is to use every legitimate means to bring about a just one." Berger v. United States, 295 U.S., at 88.

It is equally clear that the prosecutor has the same duty to refrain from improper methods calculated to produce a wrongful indictment. Indeed, the prosecutor's duty to protect the fundamental fairness of judicial proceedings assumes special importance when he is presenting evidence to a grand jury. As the Court of Appeals for the Third Circuit recognized, "the costs of continued unchecked prosecutorial misconduct" before the grand jury are particularly substantial because there

> "the prosecutor operates without the check of a judge or a trained legal adversary, and virtually immune from public scrutiny. The prosecutor's abuse of his special relationship to the grand jury poses an enormous risk to defendants as well. For while in theory a trial provides the defendant with a full opportunity to contest and disprove the charges against him, in practice, the handing up of an indictment will often have a devastating personal and professional impact that a later dismissal or acquittal can never undo. Where the potential for abuse is so great, and the consequences of a mistaken indictment so serious, the ethical responsibilities of the prosecutor, and the obligation of the judiciary to protect against even the appearance of unfairness, are correspondingly heightened." United States v. Serubo, 604 F.2d 807, 817 (CA3 1979).

In his dissent in United States v. Ciambrone, 601 F.2d 616 (CA2 1979), Judge Friendly also recognized the prosecutor's special role in grand jury proceedings:

"As the Supreme Court has noted, 'the Founders thought the grand jury so essential to basic liberties that they provided in the Fifth Amendment that federal prosecution for serious crimes can only be instituted by "a presentment or indictment of a Grand Jury."' United States v. Calandra, 414 U.S. 338, 343, ... (1974). Before the grand jury the prosecutor has the dual role of pressing for an indictment and of being the grand jury adviser. In case of conflict, the latter duty must take precedence. United States v. Remington, 208 F.2d 567, 573–74 (2d Cir.1953) (L. Hand, J., dissenting), cert. denied, 347 U.S. 913 ... (1954).

"The *ex parte* character of grand jury proceedings makes it peculiarly important for a federal prosecutor to remember that, in the familiar phrase, the interest of the United States 'in a criminal prosecution is not that it shall win a case, but that justice shall be done.' Berger v. United States, 295 U.S. 78, 88 ... (1935)." Id., at 628–629.

The standard for judging the consequences of prosecutorial misconduct during grand jury proceedings is essentially the same as the standard applicable to trials. In United States v. Mechanik, 475 U.S. 66 (1986), we held that there was "no reason not to apply [the harmless error rule] to 'errors, defects, irregularities, or variances' occurring before a grand jury just as we have applied it to such error occurring in the criminal trial itself," id., at 71–72. We repeated that holding in Bank of Nova Scotia v. United States, 487 U.S. 250 (1988), when we rejected a defendant's argument that an indictment should be dismissed because of prosecutorial misconduct and irregularities in proceedings before the grand jury. Referring to the prosecutor's misconduct before the grand jury, we "concluded that our customary harmless-error inquiry is applicable where, as in the cases before us, a court is asked to dismiss an indictment prior to the conclusion of the trial." Id., at 256. Moreover, in reviewing the instances of misconduct in that case, we applied precisely the same standard to the prosecutor's violations of Rule 6 of the Federal Rules of Criminal Procedure and to his violations of the general duty of fairness that applies to all judicial proceedings. ...

In an opinion that I find difficult to comprehend, the Court today repudiates the assumptions underlying these cases and seems to suggest that the Court has no authority to supervise the conduct of the prosecutor in grand jury proceedings so long as he follows the dictates of the Constitution, applicable statutes, and Rule 6 of the Federal Rules of Criminal Procedure. The Court purports to support this conclusion by invoking the doctrine of separation of powers and citing a string of cases in which we have declined to impose categorical restraints on the grand jury. Needless to say, the Court's reasoning is unpersuasive.

Although the grand jury has not been "textually assigned" to "any of the branches described in the first three Articles" of the Constitution, ante, at 9, it is not an autonomous body completely beyond the reach of the other branches. Throughout its life, from the moment it is convened until it is discharged, the grand jury is subject to the control of the court. ...

This Court has, of course, long recognized that the grand jury has wide latitude to investigate violations of federal law as it deems appropriate and need not obtain permission from either the court or the prosecutor. ... Correspondingly, we have acknowledged that "its operation generally is unrestrained by the technical procedural and evidentiary rules governing the conduct of criminal trials." Calandra, 414 U.S., at 343. But this is because Congress and the Court have generally thought it best not to impose procedural restraints on the grand jury; it is not because they lack all power to do so.

To the contrary, the Court has recognized that it has the authority to create and enforce limited rules applicable in grand jury proceedings. Thus, for example, the Court has said that the grand jury "may not itself violate a valid privilege, whether established by the Constitution, statutes, or the common law." Id., at 346. And the Court may prevent a grand jury from violating such a privilege by quashing or modifying a subpoena ... or issuing a protective order forbidding questions in violation of the privilege .... Moreover, there are, as the Court notes ... a series of cases in which we declined to impose categorical restraints on the grand jury. In none of those cases, however, did we question our power to reach a contrary result.

Although the Court recognizes that it may invoke its supervisory authority to fashion and enforce privilege rules applicable in grand jury proceedings ... and suggests that it may also invoke its supervisory authority to fashion other limited rules of grand jury procedure ... it concludes that it has no authority to "*prescribe* standards of prosecutorial conduct before the grand jury," ante, at 46–47, because that would alter the grand jury's historic role as an independent, inquisitorial institution. I disagree.

We do not protect the integrity and independence of the grand jury by closing our eyes to the countless forms of prosecutorial misconduct that may occur inside the secrecy of the grand jury room. After all, the grand jury is not merely an investigatory body; it also serves as a "protector of citizens against arbitrary and oppressive governmental action." United States v. Calandra, 414 U.S., at 343. Explaining why the grand jury must be both "independent" and "informed," the Court wrote in Wood v. Georgia, 370 U.S. 375 (1962):

"Historically, this body has been regarded as a primary security to the innocent against hasty, malicious and oppressive persecution; it serves the invaluable function in our society of standing between the accuser and the accused, whether the latter be an individual, minority group, or other, to determine whether a charge is founded upon reason or was dictated by an intimidating power or by malice and personal ill will." Id., at 390.

It blinks reality to say that the grand jury can adequately perform this important historic role if it is intentionally misled by the prosecutor—on whose knowledge of the law and facts of the underlying criminal investigation the jurors will, of necessity, rely.

Unlike the Court, I am unwilling to hold that countless forms of prosecutorial misconduct must be tolerated—no matter how prejudicial they may be, or how seriously they may distort the legitimate function of the grand jury—simply because they are not proscribed by Rule 6 of the Federal Rules of Criminal Procedure or a statute that is applicable in grand jury proceedings. Such a sharp break with the traditional role of the federal judiciary is unprecedented, unwarranted, and unwise. Unrestrained prosecutorial misconduct in grand jury proceedings is inconsistent with the administration of justice in the federal courts and should be redressed in appropriate cases by the dismissal of indictments obtained by improper methods.

.   .   .

III

.   .   .

Although I question whether the evidence withheld in this case directly negates respondent's guilt, I need not resolve my doubts because the Solicitor General did not ask the Court to review the nature of the evidence withheld. Instead, he asked us to decide the legal question whether an indictment may be dismissed because the prosecutor failed to present exculpatory evidence. Unlike the Court and the Solicitor General, I believe the answer to that question is yes, if the withheld evidence would plainly preclude a finding of probable cause. I therefore cannot endorse the Court's opinion.

.   .   .

11. THE RIGHT TO A SPEEDY TRIAL

UNITED STATES v. MARION

404 U.S. 307, 92 S.Ct. 455, 30 L.Ed.2d 468 (1971).

MR. JUSTICE WHITE delivered the opinion of the Court.

This appeal requires us to decide whether dismissal of a federal indictment was constitutionally required by reason of a period of three years between the occurrence of the alleged criminal acts and the filing of the indictment.

On April 21, 1970, the two appellees were indicted and charged in 19 counts with operating a business known as Allied Enterprises, Inc., which was engaged in the business of selling and installing home improvements such as intercom sets, fire control devices, and burglary detection systems. Allegedly, the business was fraudulently conducted and involved misrepresentations, alterations of documents, and deliberate nonperformance of contracts. The period covered by the indictment was March 15, 1965, to February 6, 1967; the earliest specific act alleged occurred on September 3, 1965, the latest on January 19, 1966.

On May 5, 1970, appellees filed a motion to dismiss the indictment "for failure to commence prosecution of the alleged offenses charged therein within such time as to afford [them their] rights to due process of law and to a speedy trial under the Fifth and Sixth Amendments to the Constitution of the United States." No evidence was submitted, but from the motion itself and the arguments of counsel at the hearing on the motion, it appears that Allied Enterprises had been subject to a Federal Trade Commission cease-and-desist order on February 6, 1967, and that a series of articles appeared in the Washington Post in October 1967, reporting the results of that newspaper's investigation of practices employed by home improvement firms such as Allied. The articles also contained purported statements of the then United States Attorney for the District of Columbia describing his office's investigation of these firms and predicting that indictments would soon be forthcoming. Although the statements attributed to the United States Attorney did not mention Allied specifically, that company was mentioned in the course of the newspaper stories. In the summer of 1968, at the request of the United States Attorney's office, Allied delivered certain of its records to that office, and in an interview there appellee Marion discussed his conduct as an officer of Allied Enterprises. The grand jury that indicted appellees was not impaneled until September 1969, appellees were not informed of the

913

grand jury's concern with them until March 1970, and the indictment was finally handed down in April.

Appellees moved to dismiss because the indictment was returned "an unreasonably oppressive and unjustifiable time after the alleged offenses." They argued that the indictment required memory of many specific acts and conversations occurring several years before, and they contended that the delay was due to the negligence or indifference of the United States Attorney in investigating the case and presenting it to a grand jury. No specific prejudice was claimed or demonstrated. The District Court judge dismissed the indictment for "lack of speedy prosecution" at the conclusion of the hearing and remarked that since the Government must have become aware of the relevant facts in 1967, the defense of the case "is bound to have been seriously prejudiced by the delay of at least some three years in bringing the prosecution that should have been brought in 1967, or at the very latest early 1968."

The United States appeals directly to this Court pursuant to 18 U.S.C. § 3731 (1964 ed., Supp. V). We postponed consideration of the question of jurisdiction until the hearing on the merits of the case. We now hold that the Court has jurisdiction, and on the merits we reverse the judgment of the District Court.

. . .

II

Appellees do not claim that the Sixth Amendment was violated by the two-month delay between the return of the indictment and its dismissal. Instead, they claim that their rights to a speedy trial were violated by the period of approximately three years between the end of the criminal scheme charged and the return of the indictment; it is argued that this delay is so substantial and inherently prejudicial that the Sixth Amendment required the dismissal of the indictment. In our view, however, the Sixth Amendment speedy trial provision has no application until the putative defendant in some way becomes an "accused," an event that occurred in this case only when the appellees were indicted on April 21, 1970.

The Sixth Amendment provides that "[i]n all criminal prosecutions, the accused shall enjoy the right to a speedy and public trial . . . ." On its face, the protection of the Amendment is activated only when a criminal prosecution has begun and extends only to those persons who have been "accused" in the course of that prosecution. These provisions would seem to afford no protection to those not yet accused, nor would they seem to require the Government to discover, investigate, and accuse any person within any particular period of time. The Amendment would appear to guarantee to a criminal defendant that the Government will move with the dispatch which is appropriate to assure him an early and proper disposition of the charges against him. "[T]he essential ingredient is orderly expedition and not mere speed." Smith v. United States, 360 U.S. 1, 10 (1959).

Our attention is called to nothing in the circumstances surrounding the adoption of the Amendment indicating that it does not mean what it appears to say, nor is there more than marginal support for the proposition that, at the time of the adoption of the Amendment, the prevailing rule was that prosecutions would not be permitted if there had been long delay in presenting a charge. The framers could hardly have selected less appropriate language if they had intended the speedy trial provision to protect against pre-accusation delay. No opinions of this Court intimate support for appellees' thesis, and the Courts of Appeals that have considered the question in constitutional terms have never reversed a conviction or dismissed an indictment solely on the basis of the Sixth Amendment's speedy trial provision where only pre-indictment delay was involved.

Legislative efforts to implement federal and state speedy trial provisions also plainly reveal the view that these guarantees are applicable only after a person has been accused of a crime. The Court has pointed out that "[a]t the common law and in the absence of special statutes of limitations the mere failure to find an indictment will not operate to discharge the accused from the offense nor will a *nolle prosequi* entered by the Government or the failure of the grand jury to indict." United States v. Cadarr, 197 U.S. 475, 478 (1905). Since it is "doubtless true that in some cases the power of the Government has been abused and charges have been kept hanging over the heads of citizens, and they have been committed for unreasonable periods, resulting in hardship," the Court noted that many States "[w]ith a view to preventing such wrong to the citizen ... [and] in aid of the constitutional provisions, National and state, intended to secure to the accused a speedy trial" had passed statutes limiting the time within which such trial must occur after charge or indictment. Characteristically, these statutes to which the Court referred are triggered only when a citizen is charged or accused. The statutes vary greatly in substance, structure, and interpretation, but a common denominator is that "[i]n no event ... [does] the right to speedy trial arise before there is some charge or arrest, even though the prosecuting authorities had knowledge of the offense long before this." Note, The Right to a Speedy Trial, 57 Col.L.Rev. 846, 848 (1957).

No federal statute of general applicability has been enacted by Congress to enforce the speedy trial provision of the Sixth Amendment, but Rule 48(b) of the Federal Rules of Criminal Procedure, which has the force of law, authorizes dismissal of an indictment, information, or complaint "[i]f there is unnecessary delay in presenting the charge to a grand jury or in filing an information against a defendant who has been held to answer to the district court, or if

there is unnecessary delay in bringing a defendant to trial ...."
The rule clearly is limited to post-arrest situations.

Appellees' position is, therefore, at odds with longstanding
legislative and judicial constructions of the speedy trial provisions in
both national and state constitutions.

III

It is apparent also that very little support for appellees' position
emerges from a consideration of the purposes of the Sixth Amendment's speedy trial provision, a guarantee that this Court has
termed "an important safeguard to prevent undue and oppressive
incarceration prior to trial, to minimize anxiety and concern accompanying public accusation and to limit the possibilities that long
delay will impair the ability of an accused to defend himself."
United States v. Ewell, 383 U.S. 116, 120 (1966). ... Inordinate
delay between arrest, indictment, and trial may impair a defendant's
ability to present an effective defense. But the major evils protected against by the speedy trial guarantee exist quite apart from actual
or possible prejudice to an accused's defense. To legally arrest and
detain, the Government must assert probable cause to believe the
arrestee has committed a crime. Arrest is a public act that may
seriously interfere with the defendant's liberty, whether he is free
on bail or not, and that may disrupt his employment, drain his
financial resources, curtail his associations, subject him to public
obloquy, and create anxiety in him, his family and his friends. ...
So viewed, it is readily understandable that it is either a formal
indictment or information or else the actual restraints imposed by
arrest and holding to answer a criminal charge that engage the
particular protections of the speedy trial provision of the Sixth
Amendment.

Invocation of the speedy trial provision thus need not await
indictment, information, or other formal charge. But we decline to
extend the reach of the amendment to the period prior to arrest.
Until this event occurs, a citizen suffers no restraints on his liberty
and is not the subject of public accusation: his situation does not
compare with that of a defendant who has been arrested and held
to answer. Passage of time, whether before or after arrest, may
impair memories, cause evidence to be lost, deprive the defendant
of witnesses, and otherwise interfere with his ability to defend
himself. But this possibility of prejudice at trial is not itself sufficient reason to wrench the Sixth Amendment from its proper
context. Possible prejudice is inherent in any delay, however short;
it may also weaken the Government's case.

The law has provided other mechanisms to guard against
possible as distinguished from actual prejudice resulting from the
passage of time between crime and arrest or charge. As we said in
United States v. Ewell, supra, at 122, "the applicable statute of
limitations ... is ... the primary guarantee against bringing overly

stale criminal charges." Such statutes represent legislative assessments of relative interests of the State and the defendant in administering and receiving justice; they "are made for the repose of society and the protection of those who may [during the limitation] . . . have lost their means of defence." Public Schools v. Walker, 9 Wall. 282, 288 (1870). These statutes provide predictability by specifying a limit beyond which there is an irrebuttable presumption that a defendant's right to a fair trial would be prejudiced. . . .

Since appellees rely only on potential prejudice and the passage of time between the alleged crime and the indictment, see Part IV, infra, we perhaps need go no further to dispose of this case, for the indictment was the first official act designating appellees as accused individuals and that event occurred within the statute of limitations. Nevertheless, since a criminal trial is the likely consequence of our judgment and since appellees may claim actual prejudice to their defense, it is appropriate to note here that the statute of limitations does not fully define the appellees' rights with respect to the events occurring prior to indictment. Thus, the Government concedes that the Due Process Clause of the Fifth Amendment would require dismissal of the indictment if it were shown at trial that the pre-indictment delay in this case caused substantial prejudice to appellees' rights to a fair trial and that the delay was an intentional device to gain tactical advantage over the accused. . . . However, we need not, and could not now, determine when and in what circumstances actual prejudice resulting from preaccusation delays requires the dismissal of the prosecution. Actual prejudice to the defense of a criminal case may result from the shortest and most necessary delay; and no one suggests that every delay-caused detriment to a defendant's case should abort a criminal prosecution. To accommodate the sound administration of justice to the rights of the defendant to a fair trial will necessarily involve a delicate judgment based on the circumstances of each case. It would be unwise at this juncture to attempt to forecast our decision in such cases.

IV

In the case before us, neither appellee was arrested, charged, or otherwise subjected to formal restraint prior to indictment. It was this event, therefore, which transformed the appellees into "accused" defendants who are subject to the speedy trial protections of the Sixth Amendment.

The 38-month delay between the end of the scheme charged in the indictment and the date the defendants were indicted did not extend beyond the period of the applicable statute of limitations here. Appellees have not, of course, been able to claim undue delay pending trial, since the indictment was brought on April 21, 1970, and dismissed on June 8, 1970. Nor have appellees adequately demonstrated that the pre-indictment delay by the Government violated the Due Process Clause. No actual prejudice to the conduct of the defense is alleged or proved, and there is no showing that the Government intentionally delayed to gain some tactical advantage over appellees or to harass them. Appellees rely solely on the real possibility of prejudice inherent in any extended delay: that memories will dim, witnesses become inaccessible, and evidence lost. In light of the applicable statute of limitations, however, these possibilities are not in themselves enough to demonstrate that appellees cannot receive a fair trial and to therefore justify the dismissal of the indictment. Events of the trial may demonstrate actual prejudice, but at the present time appellees' due process claims are speculative and premature.

Reversed.[*]

[*] Justice Douglas wrote an opinion concurring in the result, which Justice Brennan and Justice Marshall joined.

BARKER v. WINGO

407 U.S. 514, 92 S.Ct. 2182, 33 L.Ed.2d 101 (1972).

MR. JUSTICE POWELL delivered the opinion of the Court.

Although a speedy trial is guaranteed the accused by the Sixth Amendment to the Constitution, this Court has dealt with that right on infrequent occasions. ... The Court's opinion in Klopfer v. North Carolina, 386 U.S. 213 (1967), established that the right to a speedy trial is "fundamental" and is imposed by the Due Process Clause of the Fourteenth Amendment on the States. ... As Mr. Justice Brennan pointed out in his concurring opinion in *Dickey* [v. Florida, 398 U.S. 30 (1970)], in none of these cases have we attempted to set out the criteria by which the speedy trial right is to be judged. 398 U.S., at 40–41. This case compels us to make such an attempt.

I

On July 20, 1958, in Christian County, Kentucky, an elderly couple was beaten to death by intruders wielding an iron tire tool. Two suspects, Silas Manning and Willie Barker, the petitioner, were arrested shortly thereafter. The grand jury indicted them on September 15. Counsel was appointed on September 17, and Barker's trial was set for October 21. The Commonwealth had a stronger case against Manning, and it believed that Barker could not be convicted unless Manning testified against him. Manning was naturally unwilling to incriminate himself. Accordingly, on October 23, the day Silas Manning was brought to trial, the Commonwealth sought and obtained the first of what was to be a series of 16 continuances of Barker's trial.[3] Barker made no objection. By first convicting Manning, the Commonwealth would remove possible problems of self-incrimination and would be able to assure his testimony against Barker.

The Commonwealth encountered more than a few difficulties in its prosecution of Manning. The first trial ended in a hung jury. A second trial resulted in a conviction, but the Kentucky Court of Appeals reversed because of the admission of evidence obtained by an illegal search.... At his third trial, Manning was again convicted, and the Court of Appeals again reversed because the trial court had not granted a change of venue.... A fourth trial resulted in a hung jury. Finally, after five trials, Manning was convicted, in

---

3. There is no explanation in the record why although Barker's initial trial was set for October 21, no continuance was sought until October 23, two days after the trial should have begun.

March 1962, of murdering one victim, and after a sixth trial, in December 1962, he was convicted of murdering the other.[4]

The Christian County Circuit Court holds three terms each year—in February, June, and September. Barker's initial trial was to take place in the September term of 1958. The first continuance postponed it until the February 1959 term. The second continuance was granted for one month only. Every term thereafter for as long as the Manning prosecutions were in process, the Commonwealth routinely moved to continue Barker's case to the next term. When the case was continued from the June 1959 term until the following September, Barker, having spent 10 months in jail, obtained his release by posting a $5,000 bond. He thereafter remained free in the community until his trial. Barker made no objection, through his counsel, to the first 11 continuances.

When on February 12, 1962, the Commonwealth moved for the twelfth time to continue the case until the following term, Barker's counsel filed a motion to dismiss the indictment. The motion to dismiss was denied two weeks later, and the Commonwealth's motion for a continuance was granted. The Commonwealth was granted further continuances in June 1962 and September 1962, to which Barker did not object.

In February 1963, the first term of court following Manning's final conviction, the Commonwealth moved to set Barker's trial for March 19. But on the day scheduled for trial, it again moved for a continuance until the June term. It gave as its reason the illness of the ex-sheriff who was the chief investigating officer in the case. To this continuance, Barker objected unsuccessfully.

The witness was still unable to testify in June, and the trial, which had been set for June 19, was continued again until the September term over Barker's objection. This time the court announced that the case would be dismissed for lack of prosecution if it were not tried during the next term. The final trial date was set for October 9, 1963. On that date, Barker again moved to dismiss the indictment, and this time specified that his right to a speedy trial had been violated.[5] The motion was denied; the trial commenced with Manning as the chief prosecution witness; Barker was convicted and given a life sentence.

. . .

II

The right to a speedy trial is generically different from any of the other rights enshrined in the Constitution for the protection of

4. Apparently Manning chose not to appeal these final two convictions.

5. The written motion Barker filed alleged that he had objected to every continuance since February 1959. The record does not reflect any objections until the motion to dismiss, filed in February 1962, and the objections to the continuances sought by the Commonwealth in March 1963 and June 1963.

the accused. In addition to the general concern that all accused persons be treated according to decent and fair procedures, there is a societal interest in providing a speedy trial which exists separate from, and at times in opposition to, the interests of the accused. The inability of courts to provide a prompt trial has contributed to a large backlog of cases in urban courts which, among other things, enables defendants to negotiate more effectively for pleas of guilty to lesser offenses and otherwise manipulate the system. In addition, persons released on bond for lengthy periods awaiting trial have an opportunity to commit other crimes. It must be of little comfort to the residents of Christian County, Kentucky, to know that Barker was at large on bail for over four years while accused of a vicious and brutal murder of which he was ultimately convicted. Moreover, the longer an accused is free awaiting trial, the more tempting becomes his opportunity to jump bail and escape. Finally, delay between arrest and punishment may have a detrimental effect on rehabilitation.

If an accused cannot make bail, he is generally confined, as was Barker for 10 months, in a local jail. This contributes to the overcrowding and generally deplorable state of those institutions. Lengthy exposure to these conditions "has a destructive effect on human character and makes the rehabilitation of the individual offender much more difficult." [12] At times the result may even be violent rioting. Finally, lengthy pretrial detention is costly. The cost of maintaining a prisoner in jail varies from $3 to $9 per day, and this amounts to millions across the Nation. In addition, society loses wages which might have been earned, and it must often support families of incarcerated breadwinners.

A second difference between the right to speedy trial and the accused's other constitutional rights is that deprivation of the right may work to the accused's advantage. Delay is not an uncommon defense tactic. As the time between the commission of the crime and trial lengthens, witnesses may become unavailable or their memories may fade. If the witnesses support the prosecution, its case will be weakened, sometimes seriously so. And it is the prosecution which carries the burden of proof. Thus, unlike the right to counsel or the right to be free from compelled self-incrimination, deprivation of the right to speedy trial does not *per se* prejudice the accused's ability to defend himself.

Finally, and perhaps most importantly, the right to speedy trial is a more vague concept than other procedural rights. It is, for example, impossible to determine with precision when the right has been denied. We cannot definitely say how long is too long in a system where justice is supposed to be swift but deliberate. As a

---

12. Testimony of James V. Bennett, Director, Bureau of Prisons, Hearings on Federal Bail Procedures before the Subcommittee on Constitutional Rights and the Subcommittee on Improvements in Judicial Machinery of the Senate Committee on the Judiciary, 88th Cong., 2d Sess., 46 (1964).

consequence, there is no fixed point in the criminal process when the State can put the defendant to the choice of either exercising or waiving the right to a speedy trial. If, for example, the State moves for a 60-day continuance, granting that continuance is not a violation of the right to speedy trial unless the circumstances of the case are such that further delay would endanger the values the right protects. It is impossible to do more than generalize about when those circumstances exist. There is nothing comparable to the point in the process when a defendant exercises or waives his right to counsel or his right to a jury trial. Thus, as we recognized in Beavers v. Haubert, supra, any inquiry into a speedy trial claim necessitates a functional analysis of the right in the particular context of the case:

> "The right of a speedy trial is necessarily relative. It is consistent with delays and depends upon circumstances. It secures rights to a defendant. It does not preclude the rights of public justice." 198 U.S., at 87.

The amorphous quality of the right also leads to the unsatisfactorily severe remedy of dismissal of the indictment when the right has been deprived. This is indeed a serious consequence because it means that a defendant who may be guilty of a serious crime will go free, without having been tried. Such a remedy is more serious than an exclusionary rule or a reversal for a new trial, but it is the only possible remedy.

III

Perhaps because the speedy trial right is so slippery, two rigid approaches are urged upon us as ways of eliminating some of the uncertainty which courts experience in protecting the right. The first suggestion is that we hold that the Constitution requires a criminal defendant to be offered a trial within a specified time period. The result of such a ruling would have the virtue of clarifying when the right is infringed and of simplifying courts' application of it. Recognizing this, some legislatures have enacted laws, and some courts have adopted procedural rules which more narrowly define the right.[17] The United States Court of Appeals for the Second Circuit has promulgated rules for the district courts in that Circuit establishing that the government must be ready for trial within six months of the date of arrest, except in unusual circumstances, or the charge will be dismissed.[18] This type of rule is also recommended by the American Bar Association.[19]

But such a result would require this Court to engage in legislative or rulemaking activity, rather than in the adjudicative

---

17. For examples, see American Bar Association Project on Standards for Criminal Justice, Speedy Trial 14–16 (Approved Draft 1968); Note, The Right to a Speedy Criminal Trial, 57 Col.L.Rev. 846, 863 (1957).

18. Second Circuit Rules Regarding Prompt Disposition of Criminal Cases (1971).

19. ABA Project, supra, n. 17, at 14. ...

process to which we should confine our efforts. We do not establish procedural rules for the States, except when mandated by the Constitution. We find no constitutional basis for holding that the speedy trial right can be quantified into a specified number of days or months. The States, of course, are free to prescribe a reasonable period consistent with constitutional standards, but our approach must be less precise.

The second suggested alternative would restrict consideration of the right to those cases in which the accused has demanded a speedy trial. Most States have recognized what is loosely referred to as the "demand rule," although eight States reject it. It is not clear, however, precisely what is meant by that term. Although every federal court of appeals that has considered the question has endorsed some kind of demand rule, some have regarded the rule within the concept of waiver, whereas others have viewed it as a factor to be weighed in assessing whether there has been a deprivation of the speedy trial right. We shall refer to the former approach as the demand-waiver doctrine. The demand-waiver doctrine provides that a defendant waives any consideration of his right to speedy trial for any period prior to which he has not demanded a trial. Under this rigid approach, a prior demand is a necessary condition to the consideration of the speedy trial right. This essentially was the approach the Sixth Circuit took below.

Such an approach, by presuming waiver of a fundamental right from inaction, is inconsistent with this Court's pronouncements on waiver of constitutional rights. The Court has defined waiver as "an intentional relinquishment or abandonment of a known right or privilege." Johnson v. Zerbst, 304 U.S. 458, 464 (1938). Courts should "indulge every reasonable presumption against waiver," Aetna Ins. Co. v. Kennedy, 301 U.S. 389, 393 (1937), and they should "not presume acquiescence in the loss of fundamental rights," Ohio Bell Tel. Co. v. Public Utilities Comm'n, 301 U.S. 292, 307 (1937). In Carnley v. Cochran, 369 U.S. 506 (1962), we held:

> "Presuming waiver from a silent record is impermissible. The record must show, or there must be an allegation and evidence which show, that an accused was offered counsel but intelligently and understandably rejected the offer. Anything less is not waiver." Id., at 516.

The Court has ruled similarly with respect to waiver of other rights designed to protect the accused. See, e.g., Miranda v. Arizona, 384 U.S. 436, 475–476 (1966); Boykin v. Alabama, 395 U.S. 238 (1969).

In excepting the right to speedy trial from the rule of waiver we have applied to other fundamental rights, courts that have applied the demand-waiver rule have relied on the assumption that delay usually works for the benefit of the accused and on the absence of any readily ascertainable time in the criminal process for a defendant to be given the choice of exercising or waiving his right. But it is not necessarily true that delay benefits the defendant. There are cases in which delay appreciably harms the defendant's ability to defend himself. Moreover, a defendant confined to jail prior to trial is obviously disadvantaged by delay as is a defendant released on bail but unable to lead a normal life because of community suspicion and his own anxiety.

The nature of the speedy trial right does make it impossible to pinpoint a precise time in the process when the right must be asserted or waived, but that fact does not argue for placing the burden of protecting the right solely on defendants. A defendant has no duty to bring himself to trial; the State has that duty as well as the duty of insuring that the trial is consistent with due process. Moreover, for the reasons earlier expressed, society has a particular interest in bringing swift prosecutions, and society's representatives are the ones who should protect that interest.

It is also noteworthy that such a rigid view of the demand-waiver rule places defense counsel in an awkward position. Unless he demands a trial early and often, he is in danger of frustrating his client's right. If counsel is willing to tolerate some delay because he finds it reasonable and helpful in preparing his own case, he may be unable to obtain a speedy trial for his client at the end of that time. Since under the demand-waiver rule no time runs until the demand is made, the government will have whatever time is otherwise reasonable to bring the defendant to trial after a demand has been made. Thus, if the first demand is made three months after arrest in a jurisdiction which prescribes a six-month rule, the prosecution will have a total of nine months—which may be wholly unreasonable under the circumstances. The result in practice is likely to be either an automatic, *pro forma* demand made immediately after appointment of counsel or delays which, but for the demand-waiver rule, would not be tolerated. Such a result is not consistent with the interests of defendants, society, or the Constitution.

We reject, therefore, the rule that a defendant who fails to demand a speedy trial forever waives his right. This does not mean, however, that the defendant has no responsibility to assert his right. We think the better rule is that the defendant's assertion of or failure to assert his right to a speedy trial is one of the factors to be considered in an inquiry into the deprivation of the right. Such a formulation avoids the rigidities of the demand-waiver rule and the resulting possible unfairness in its application. It allows the trial court to exercise a judicial discretion based on the circumstances, including due consideration of any applicable formal procedural rule. It would permit, for example, a court to attach a different weight to a situation in which the defendant knowingly fails to object from a situation in which his attorney acquiesces in long delay without adequately informing his client, or from a situation in which no counsel is appointed. It would also allow a court to weigh the frequency and force of the objections as opposed to attaching significant weight to a purely *pro forma* objection.

In ruling that a defendant has some responsibility to assert a speedy trial claim, we do not depart from our holdings in other cases concerning the waiver of fundamental rights, in which we have placed the entire responsibility on the prosecution to show that the claimed waiver was knowingly and voluntarily made. Such cases have involved rights which must be exercised or waived at a specific time or under clearly identifiable circumstances, such as the rights to plead not guilty, to demand a jury trial, to exercise the privilege against self incrimination, and to have the assistance of counsel. We have shown above that the right to a speedy trial is unique in its uncertainty as to when and under what circumstances it must be asserted or may be deemed waived. But the rule we announce today, which comports with constitutional principles, places the primary burden on the courts and the prosecutors to assure that cases are brought to trial. We hardly need add that if delay is attributable to the defendant, then his waiver may be given effect under standard waiver doctrine, the demand rule aside.

We, therefore, reject both of the inflexible approaches—the fixed-time period because it goes further than the Constitution requires; the demand-waiver rule because it is insensitive to a right which we have deemed fundamental. The approach we accept is a balancing test, in which the conduct of both the prosecution and the defendant are weighed.[29]

IV

A balancing test necessarily compels courts to approach speedy trial cases on an *ad hoc* basis. We can do little more than identify some of the factors which courts should assess in determining whether a particular defendant has been deprived of his right. Though some might express them in different ways, we identify four such factors: Length of delay, the reason for the delay, the defendant's assertion of his right, and prejudice to the defendant.

The length of the delay is to some extent a triggering mechanism. Until there is some delay which is presumptively prejudicial, there is no necessity for inquiry into the other factors that go into the balance. Nevertheless, because of the imprecision of the right to speedy trial, the length of delay that will provoke such an inquiry is necessarily dependent upon the peculiar circumstances of the case. To take but one example, the delay that can be tolerated for an ordinary street crime is considerably less than for a serious, complex conspiracy charge.

29. Nothing we have said should be interpreted as disapproving a presumptive rule adopted by a court in the exercise of its supervisory powers which establishes a fixed time period within which cases must normally be brought....

Closely related to length of delay is the reason the government assigns to justify the delay. Here, too, different weights should be assigned to different reasons. A deliberate attempt to delay the trial in order to hamper the defense should be weighed heavily against the government. A more neutral reason such as negligence or overcrowded courts should be weighed less heavily but nevertheless should be considered since the ultimate responsibility for such circumstances must rest with the government rather than with the defendant. Finally, a valid reason, such as a missing witness, should serve to justify appropriate delay.

We have already discussed the third factor, the defendant's responsibility to assert his right. Whether and how a defendant asserts his right is closely related to the other factors we have mentioned. The strength of his efforts will be affected by the length of the delay, to some extent by the reason for the delay, and most particularly by the personal prejudice, which is not always readily identifiable, that he experiences. The more serious the deprivation, the more likely a defendant is to complain. The defendant's assertion of his speedy trial right, then, is entitled to strong evidentiary weight in determining whether the defendant is being deprived of the right. We emphasize that failure to assert the right will make it difficult for a defendant to prove that he was denied a speedy trial.

A fourth factor is prejudice to the defendant. Prejudice, of course, should be assessed in the light of the interests of defendants which the speedy trial right was designed to protect. This Court has identified three such interests: (i) to prevent oppressive pretrial incarceration; (ii) to minimize anxiety and concern of the accused; and (iii) to limit the possibility that the defense will be impaired. Of these, the most serious is the last, because the inability of a defendant adequately to prepare his case skews the fairness of the entire system. If witnesses dic or disappear during a delay, the prejudice is obvious. There is also prejudice if defense witnesses are unable to recall accurately events of the distant past. Loss of memory, however, is not always reflected in the record because what has been forgotten can rarely be shown.

We have discussed previously the societal disadvantages of lengthy pretrial incarceration, but obviously the disadvantages for the accused who cannot obtain his release are even more serious. The time spent in jail awaiting trial has a detrimental impact on the individual. It often means loss of a job; it disrupts family life; and it enforces idleness. Most jails offer little or no recreational or rehabilitative programs. The time spent in jail is simply dead time. Moreover, if a defendant is locked up, he is hindered in his ability to gather evidence, contact witnesses, or otherwise prepare his defense. Imposing those consequences on anyone who has not yet been convicted is serious. It is especially unfortunate to impose them on those persons who are ultimately found to be innocent.

Finally, even if an accused is not incarcerated prior to trial, he is still disadvantaged by restraints on his liberty and by living under a cloud of anxiety, suspicion, and often hostility. . . .

We regard none of the four factors identified above as either a necessary or sufficient condition to the finding of a deprivation of the right of speedy trial. Rather, they are related factors and must be considered together with such other circumstances as may be relevant. In sum, these factors have no talismanic qualities; courts must still engage in a difficult and sensitive balancing process. But, because we are dealing with a fundamental right of the accused, this process must be carried out with full recognition that the accused's interest in a speedy trial is specifically affirmed in the Constitution.

V

The difficulty of the task of balancing these factors is illustrated by this case, which we consider to be close. It is clear that the length of delay between arrest and trial—well over five years—was extraordinary. Only seven months of that period can be attributed to a strong excuse, the illness of the ex-sheriff who was in charge of the investigation. Perhaps some delay would have been permissible under ordinary circumstances, so that Manning could be utilized as a witness in Barker's trial, but more than four years was too long a period, particularly since a good part of that period was attributable to the Commonwealth's failure or inability to try Manning under circumstances that comported with due process.

Two counterbalancing factors, however, outweigh these deficiencies. The first is that prejudice was minimal. Of course, Barker was prejudiced to some extent by living for over four years under a cloud of suspicion and anxiety. Moreover, although he was released on bond for most of the period, he did spend 10 months in jail before trial. But there is no claim that any of Barker's witnesses died or otherwise became unavailable owing to the delay. The trial transcript indicates only two very minor lapses of memory—one on the part of a prosecution witness—which were in no way significant to the outcome.

More important than the absence of serious prejudice, is the fact that Barker did not want a speedy trial. Counsel was appointed for Barker immediately after his indictment and represented him throughout the period. No question is raised as to the competency of such counsel. Despite the fact that counsel had notice of the motions for continuances, the record shows no action whatever taken between October 21, 1958, and February 12, 1962, that could be construed as the assertion of the speedy trial right. On the latter date, in response to another motion for continuance, Barker moved to dismiss the indictment. The record does not show on what ground this motion was based, although it is clear that no alternative motion was made for an immediate trial. Instead the record strongly suggests that while he hoped to take advantage of the delay in which he had acquiesced, and thereby obtain a dismissal of the charges, he definitely did not want to be tried.   Counsel conceded as much at oral argument . . . .   The probable reason for Barker's attitude was that he was gambling on Manning's acquittal.   The evidence was not very strong against Manning, as the reversals and hung juries suggest, and Barker undoubtedly thought that if Manning were acquitted, he would never be tried.   Counsel also conceded this . . . .

That Barker was gambling on Manning's acquittal is also suggested by his failure, following the *pro forma* motion to dismiss filed in February 1962, to object to the Commonwealth's next two motions for continuances.   Indeed, it was not until March 1963, after Manning's convictions were final, that Barker, having lost his gamble, began to object to further continuances.   At that time, the Commonwealth's excuse was the illness of the ex-sheriff, which Barker has conceded justified the further delay.

We do not hold that there may never be a situation in which an indictment may be dismissed on speedy trial grounds where the defendant has failed to object to continuances.   There may be a situation in which the defendant was represented by incompetent counsel, was severely prejudiced, or even cases in which the continuances were granted *ex parte*.   But barring extraordinary circumstances, we would be reluctant indeed to rule that a defendant was denied this constitutional right on a record that strongly indicates, as does this one, that the defendant did not want a speedy trial. We hold, therefore, that Barker was not deprived of his due process right to a speedy trial.

The judgment of the Court of Appeals is

Affirmed.[*]

[*] Justice White wrote a concurring opinion, which Justice Brennan joined.

12. PLEA–BARGAINING

BRADY v. UNITED STATES

397 U.S. 742, 90 S.Ct. 1463, 25 L.Ed.2d 747 (1970).

MR. JUSTICE WHITE delivered the opinion of the Court.

In 1959, petitioner was charged with kidnaping in violation of 18 U.S.C. § 1201(a). Since the indictment charged that the victim of the kidnaping was not liberated unharmed, petitioner faced a maximum penalty of death if the verdict of the jury should so recommend. Petitioner, represented by competent counsel throughout, first elected to plead not guilty. Apparently because the trial judge was unwilling to try the case without a jury, petitioner made no serious attempt to reduce the possibility of a death penalty by waiving a jury trial. Upon learning that his codefendant, who had confessed to the authorities, would plead guilty and be available to testify against him, petitioner changed his plea to guilty. His plea was accepted after the trial judge twice questioned him as to the voluntariness of his plea. Petitioner was sentenced to 50 years' imprisonment, later reduced to 30.

In 1967, petitioner sought relief under 28 U.S.C. § 2255, claiming that his plea of guilty was not voluntarily given because § 1201(a) operated to coerce his plea, because his counsel exerted impermissible pressure upon him, and because his plea was induced by representations with respect to reduction of sentence and clemency. . . .

After a hearing, the District Court for the District of New Mexico denied relief. According to the District Court's findings, petitioner's counsel did not put impermissible pressure on petitioner to plead guilty and no representations were made with respect to a reduced sentence or clemency. The court held that § 1201(a) was constitutional and found that petitioner decided to plead guilty when he learned that his codefendant was going to plead guilty: petitioner pleaded guilty "by reason of other matters and not by reason of the statute" or because of any acts of the trial judge. The court concluded that "the plea was voluntarily and knowingly made."

The Court of Appeals for the Tenth Circuit affirmed, determining that the District Court's findings were supported by substantial evidence and specifically approving the finding that petitioner's plea of guilty was voluntary. 404 F.2d 601 (1968). We granted certiorari, 395 U.S. 976 (1969), to consider the claim that the Court of Appeals was in error in not reaching a contrary result on the

authority of this Court's decision in United States v. Jackson, 390
U.S. 570 (1968). We affirm.

I

In United States v. Jackson, supra, the defendants were indicted
under § 1201(a). The District Court dismissed the § 1201(a) count
of the indictment, holding the statute unconstitutional because it
permitted imposition of the death sentence only upon a jury's
recommendation and thereby made the risk of death the price of a
jury trial. This Court held the statute valid, except for the death
penalty provision; with respect to the latter, the Court agreed with
the trial court "that the death penalty provision ... imposes an
impermissible burden upon the exercise of a constitutional right
...." 390 U.S., at 572. The problem was to determine "whether
the Constitution permits the establishment of such a death penalty,
applicable only to those defendants who assert the right to contest
their guilt before a jury." 390 U.S., at 581. The inevitable effect of
the provision was said to be to discourage assertion of the Fifth
Amendment right not to plead guilty and to deter exercise of the
Sixth Amendment right to demand a jury trial. Because the legitimate goal of limiting the death penalty to cases in which a jury
recommends it could be achieved without penalizing those defendants who plead not guilty and elect a jury trial, the death penalty
provision "needlessly penalize[d] the assertion of a constitutional
right," 390 U.S., at 583, and was therefore unconstitutional.

Since the "inevitable effect" of the death penalty provision of
§ 1201(a) was said by the Court to be the needless encouragement
of pleas of guilty and waivers of jury trial, Brady contends that
Jackson requires the invalidation of every plea of guilty entered
under that section, at least when the fear of death is shown to have
been a factor in the plea. Petitioner, however, has read far too
much into the *Jackson* opinion.

. . .

Plainly, it seems to us, *Jackson* ruled neither that all pleas of
guilty encouraged by the fear of a possible death sentence are
involuntary pleas nor that such encouraged pleas are invalid whether involuntary or not. *Jackson* prohibits the imposition of the
death penalty under § 1201(a), but that decision neither fashioned
a new standard for judging the validity of guilty pleas nor mandated
a new application of the test theretofore fashioned by courts and
since reiterated that guilty pleas are valid if both "voluntary" and
"intelligent." . . .

That a guilty plea is a grave and solemn act to be accepted only
with care and discernment has long been recognized. Central to
the plea and the foundation for entering judgment against the
defendant is the defendant's admission in open court that he
committed the acts charged in the indictment. He thus stands as a

witness against himself and he is shielded by the Fifth Amendment from being compelled to do so—hence the minimum requirement that his plea be the voluntary expression of his own choice. But the plea is more than an admission of past conduct; it is the defendant's consent that judgment of conviction may be entered without a trial—a waiver of his right to trial before a jury or a judge. Waivers of constitutional rights not only must be voluntary but must be knowing, intelligent acts done with sufficient awareness of the relevant circumstances and likely consequences. On neither score was Brady's plea of guilty invalid.

II

The trial judge in 1959 found the plea voluntary before accepting it; the District Court in 1968, after an evidentiary hearing, found that the plea was voluntarily made; the Court of Appeals specifically approved the finding of voluntariness. We see no reason on this record to disturb the judgment of those courts. Petitioner, advised by competent counsel, tendered his plea after his codefendant, who had already given a confession, determined to plead guilty and became available to testify against petitioner. It was this development that the District Court found to have triggered Brady's guilty plea.

The voluntariness of Brady's plea can be determined only by considering all of the relevant circumstances surrounding it. . . . One of these circumstances was the possibility of a heavier sentence following a guilty verdict after a trial. It may be that Brady, faced with a strong case against him and recognizing that his chances for acquittal were slight, preferred to plead guilty and thus limit the penalty to life imprisonment rather than to elect a jury trial which could result in a death penalty. But even if we assume that Brady would not have pleaded guilty except for the death penalty provision of § 1201(a), this assumption merely identifies the penalty provision as a "but for" cause of his plea. That the statute caused the plea in this sense does not necessarily prove that the plea was coerced and invalid as an involuntary act.

The State to some degree encourages pleas of guilty at every important step in the criminal process. For some people, their breach of a State's law is alone sufficient reason for surrendering themselves and accepting punishment. For others, apprehension and charge, both threatening acts by the Government, jar them into admitting their guilt. In still other cases, the post-indictment accumulation of evidence may convince the defendant and his counsel that a trial is not worth the agony and expense to the defendant and his family. All these pleas of guilty are valid in spite of the State's responsibility for some of the factors motivating the pleas; the pleas are no more improperly compelled than is the decision by a defendant at the close of the State's evidence at trial that he must take the stand or face certain conviction.

Of course, the agents of the State may not produce a plea by actual or threatened physical harm or by mental coercion overbearing the will of the defendant. But nothing of the sort is claimed in this case; nor is there evidence that Brady was so gripped by fear of the death penalty or hope of leniency that he did not or could not, with the help of counsel, rationally weigh the advantages of going to trial against the advantages of pleading guilty. Brady's claim is of a different sort: that it violates the Fifth Amendment to influence or encourage a guilty plea by opportunity or promise of leniency and that a guilty plea is coerced and invalid if influenced by the fear of a possibly higher penalty for the crime charged if a conviction is obtained after the State is put to its proof.

Insofar as the voluntariness of his plea is concerned, there is little to differentiate Brady from (1) the defendant, in a jurisdiction where the judge and jury have the same range of sentencing power, who pleads guilty because his lawyer advises him that the judge will very probably be more lenient than the jury; (2) the defendant, in a jurisdiction where the judge alone has sentencing power, who is advised by counsel that the judge is normally more lenient with defendants who plead guilty than with those who go to trial; (3) the defendant who is permitted by prosecutor and judge to plead guilty to a lesser offense included in the offense charged; and (4) the defendant who pleads guilty to certain counts with the understanding that other charges will be dropped. In each of these situations,[8] as in Brady's case, the defendant might never plead guilty absent the possibility or certainty that the plea will result in a lesser penalty than the sentence that could be imposed after a trial and a verdict of guilty. We decline to hold, however, that a guilty plea is compelled and invalid under the Fifth Amendment whenever motivated by the defendant's desire to accept the certainty or probability of a lesser penalty rather than face a wider range of possibilities extending from acquittal to conviction and a higher penalty authorized by law for the crime charged.

The issue we deal with is inherent in the criminal law and its administration because guilty pleas are not constitutionally forbidden, because the criminal law characteristically extends to judge or jury a range of choice in setting the sentence in individual cases, and because both the State and the defendant often find it advantageous to preclude the possibility of the maximum penalty authorized by law. For a defendant who sees slight possibility of acquittal, the advantages of pleading guilty and limiting the probable penalty are obvious—his exposure is reduced, the correctional processes can begin immediately, and the practical burdens of a trial

---

8. We here make no reference to the situation where the prosecutor or judge, or both, deliberately employ their charging and sentencing powers to induce a particular defendant to tender a plea of guilty. In Brady's case there is no claim that the prosecutor threatened prosecution on a charge not justified by the evidence or that the trial judge threatened Brady with a harsher sentence if convicted after trial in order to induce him to plead guilty.

are eliminated. For the State there are also advantages—the more promptly imposed punishment after an admission of guilt may more effectively attain the objectives of punishment; and with the avoidance of trial, scarce judicial and prosecutorial resources are conserved for those cases in which there is a substantial issue of the defendant's guilt or in which there is substantial doubt that the State can sustain its burden of proof. It is this mutuality of advantage that perhaps explains the fact that at present well over three-fourths of the criminal convictions in this country rest on pleas of guilty, a great many of them no doubt motivated at least in part by the hope or assurance of a lesser penalty than might be imposed if there were a guilty verdict after a trial to judge or jury.

Of course, that the prevalence of guilty pleas is explainable does not necessarily validate those pleas or the system which produces them. But we cannot hold that it is unconstitutional for the State to extend a benefit to a defendant who in turn extends a substantial benefit to the State and who demonstrates by his plea that he is ready and willing to admit his crime and to enter the correctional system in a frame of mind that affords hope for success in rehabilitation over a shorter period of time than might otherwise be necessary.

A contrary holding would require the States and Federal Government to forbid guilty pleas altogether, to provide a single invariable penalty for each crime defined by the statutes, or to place the sentencing function in a separate authority having no knowledge of the manner in which the conviction in each case was obtained. In any event, it would be necessary to forbid prosecutors and judges to accept guilty pleas to selected counts, to lesser included offenses or to reduced charges. The Fifth Amendment does not reach so far.

Bram v. United States, 168 U.S. 532 (1897), held that the admissibility of a confession depended upon whether it was compelled within the meaning of the Fifth Amendment. To be admissible, a confession must be " 'free and voluntary: that is, must not be extracted by any sort of threats or violence, nor obtained by any direct or implied promises, however slight, nor by the exertion of any improper influence.' " 168 U.S., at 542–543. More recently, Malloy v. Hogan, 378 U.S. 1 (1964), carried forward the *Bram* definition of compulsion in the course of holding applicable to the States the Fifth Amendment privilege against compelled self-incrimination.

Bram is not inconsistent with our holding that Brady's plea was not compelled even though the law promised him a lesser maximum penalty if he did not go to trial. *Bram* dealt with a confession given by a defendant in custody, alone and unrepresented by counsel. In such circumstances, even a mild promise of leniency was deemed sufficient to bar the confession, not because the promise was an illegal act as such, but because defendants at such times are too sensitive to inducement and the possible impact on them too great to ignore and too difficult to assess. But *Bram* and its progeny did not hold that the possibly coercive impact of a promise of leniency could not be dissipated by the presence and advice of counsel, any more than Miranda v. Arizona, 384 U.S. 436 (1966), held that the possibly coercive atmosphere of the police station could not be counteracted by the presence of counsel or other safeguards.

Brady's situation bears no resemblance to Bram's. Brady first pleaded not guilty; prior to changing his plea to guilty he was subjected to no threats or promises in face-to-face encounters with the authorities. He had competent counsel and full opportunity to assess the advantages and disadvantages of a trial as compared with those attending a plea of guilty; there was no hazard of an impulsive and improvident response to a seeming but unreal advantage. His plea of guilty was entered in open court and before a judge obviously sensitive to the requirements of the law with respect to guilty pleas. Brady's plea, unlike Bram's confession, was voluntary.

The standard as to the voluntariness of guilty pleas must be essentially that defined by Judge Tuttle of the Court of Appeals for the Fifth Circuit:

> " '[A] plea of guilty entered by one fully aware of the direct consequences, including the actual value of any commitments made to him by the court, prosecutor, or his own counsel, must stand unless induced by threats (or promises to discontinue improper harassment), misrepresentation (including unfulfilled or unfulfillable promises), or perhaps by promises that are by their nature improper as having no proper relationship to the prosecutor's business (e.g. bribes).' 242 F.2d at page 115." [13]

Under this standard, a plea of guilty is not invalid merely because entered to avoid the possibility of a death penalty.

III

The record before us also supports the conclusion that Brady's plea was intelligently made. He was advised by competent counsel, he was made aware of the nature of the charge against him, and there was nothing to indicate that he was incompetent or otherwise not in control of his mental faculties; once his confederate had pleaded guilty and became available to testify, he chose to plead guilty, perhaps to ensure that he would face no more than life imprisonment or a term of years. Brady was aware of precisely what he was doing when he admitted that he had kidnaped the victim and had not released her unharmed.

13. Shelton v. United States, 246 F.2d 571, 572 n. 2 (C.A.5th Cir.1957) (en banc), rev'd on confession of error on other grounds, 356 U.S. 26 (1958).

It is true that Brady's counsel advised him that § 1201(a) empowered the jury to impose the death penalty and that nine years later in United States v. Jackson, supra, the Court held that the jury had no such power as long as the judge could impose only a lesser penalty if trial was to the court or there was a plea of guilty. But these facts do not require us to set aside Brady's conviction.

Often the decision to plead guilty is heavily influenced by the defendant's appraisal of the prosecution's case against him and by the apparent likelihood of securing leniency should a guilty plea be offered and accepted. Considerations like these frequently present imponderable questions for which there are no certain answers; judgments may be made that in the light of later events seem improvident, although they were perfectly sensible at the time. The rule that a plea must be intelligently made to be valid does not require that a plea be vulnerable to later attack if the defendant did not correctly assess every relevant factor entering into his decision. A defendant is not entitled to withdraw his plea merely because he discovered long after the plea has been accepted that his calculus misapprehended the quality of the State's case or the likely penalties attached to alternative courses of action. More particularly, absent misrepresentation or other impermissible conduct by state agents . . . a voluntary plea of guilty intelligently made in the light of the then applicable law does not become vulnerable because later judicial decisions indicate that the plea rested on a faulty premise. A plea of guilty triggered by the expectations of a competently counseled defendant that the State will have a strong case against him is not subject to later attack because the defendant's lawyer correctly advised him with respect to the then existing law as to possible penalties but later pronouncements of the courts, as in this case, hold that the maximum penalty for the crime in question was less than was reasonably assumed at the time the plea was entered.

The fact that Brady did not anticipate United States v. Jackson, supra, does not impugn the truth or reliability of his plea. We find no requirement in the Constitution that a defendant must be permitted to disown his solemn admissions in open court that he committed the act with which he is charged simply because it later develops that the State would have had a weaker case than the defendant had thought or that the maximum penalty then assumed applicable has been held inapplicable in subsequent judicial decisions.

This is not to say that guilty plea convictions hold no hazards for the innocent or that the methods of taking guilty pleas presently employed in this country are necessarily valid in all respects. This mode of conviction is no more foolproof than full trials to the court or to the jury. Accordingly, we take great precautions against unsound results, and we should continue to do so, whether conviction is by plea or by trial. We would have serious doubts about this case if the encouragement of guilty pleas by offers of leniency substantially increased the likelihood that defendants, advised by competent counsel, would falsely condemn themselves. But our view is to the contrary and is based on our expectations that courts will satisfy themselves that pleas of guilty are voluntarily and intelligently made by competent defendants with adequate advice of counsel and that there is nothing to question the accuracy and reliability of the defendants' admissions that they committed the crimes with which they are charged. In the case before us, nothing in the record impeaches Brady's plea or suggests that his admissions in open court were anything but the truth.

Although Brady's plea of guilty may well have been motivated in part by a desire to avoid a possible death penalty, we are convinced that his plea was voluntarily and intelligently made and we have no reason to doubt that his solemn admission of guilt was truthful.

Affirmed.[*]

[*] Justice Black noted his concurrence in the judgment and "substantially all" of the Court's opinion. Justice Brennan wrote an opinion concurring in the result, which Justice Douglas and Justice Marshall joined.

In McMann v. Richardson, 397 U.S. 759 (1970), decided with Brady v. United States, above, the Supreme Court considered the question "whether and to what extent an otherwise valid guilty plea may be impeached in collateral proceedings by assertions or proof that the plea was motivated by a prior coerced confession." 397 U.S. at 760. The Court concluded: "In our view a defendant's plea of guilty based on reasonably competent advice is an intelligent plea not open to attack on the ground that counsel may have misjudged the admissibility of the defendant's confession. Whether a plea of guilty is unintelligent and therefore vulnerable when motivated by a confession erroneously thought admissible in evidence depends as an initial matter, not on whether a court would retrospectively consider counsel's advice to be right or wrong, but on whether that advice was within the range of competence demanded of attorneys in criminal cases. On the one hand, uncertainty is inherent in predicting court decisions; but on the other hand defendants facing felony charges are entitled to the effective assistance of competent counsel. Beyond this we think the matter, for the most part, should be left to the good sense and discretion of the trial courts with the admonition that if the right to counsel guaranteed by the Constitution is to serve its purpose, defendants cannot be left to the mercies of incompetent counsel, and that judges should strive to maintain proper standards of performance by attorneys who are representing defendants in criminal cases in their courts." 397 U.S. at 770–771.

NORTH CAROLINA v. ALFORD

400 U.S. 25, 91 S.Ct. 160, 27 L.Ed.2d 162 (1970).

MR. JUSTICE WHITE delivered the opinion of the Court.

On December 2, 1963, Alford was indicted for first-degree murder, a capital offense under North Carolina law. The court appointed an attorney to represent him, and this attorney questioned all but one of the various witnesses who appellee said would substantiate his claim of innocence. The witnesses, however, did not support Alford's story but gave statements that strongly indicated his guilt. Faced with strong evidence of guilt and no substantial evidentiary support for the claim of innocence, Alford's attorney recommended that he plead guilty, but left the ultimate decision to Alford himself. The prosecutor agreed to accept a plea of guilty to a charge of second-degree murder, and on December 10, 1963, Alford pleaded guilty to the reduced charge.

Before the plea was finally accepted by the trial court, the court heard the sworn testimony of a police officer who summarized the State's case. Two other witnesses besides Alford were also heard. Although there was no eyewitness to the crime, the testimony indicated that shortly before the killing Alford took his gun from his house, stated his intention to kill the victim, and returned home with the declaration that he had carried out the killing. After the summary presentation of the State's case, Alford took the stand and testified that he had not committed the murder but that he was pleading guilty because he faced the threat of the death penalty if he did not do so. In response to the questions of his counsel, he acknowledged that his counsel had informed him of the difference between second- and first-degree murder and of his rights in case he chose to go to trial. The trial court then asked appellee if, in light of his denial of guilt, he still desired to plead guilty to second-degree murder and appellee answered, "Yes, sir. I plead guilty on—from the circumstances that he [Alford's attorney] told me." After eliciting information about Alford's prior criminal record, which was a long one, the trial court sentenced him to 30 years' imprisonment, the maximum penalty for second-degree murder.

Alford sought post-conviction relief in the state court. Among the claims raised was the claim that his plea of guilty was invalid because it was the product of fear and coercion. After a hearing, the state court in 1965 found that the plea was "willingly, knowingly, and understandingly" made on the advice of competent counsel and in the face of a strong prosecution case. Subsequently, Alford petitioned for a writ of habeas corpus, first in the United States District Court for the Middle District of North Carolina, and then in

937

the Court of Appeals for the Fourth Circuit. Both courts denied the writ on the basis of the state court's findings that Alford voluntarily and knowingly agreed to plead guilty. In 1967, Alford again petitioned for a writ of habeas corpus in the District Court for the Middle District of North Carolina. That court, without an evidentiary hearing, again denied relief on the grounds that the guilty plea was voluntary and waived all defenses and nonjurisdictional defects in any prior stage of the proceedings, and that the findings of the state court in 1965 clearly required rejection of Alford's claim that he was denied effective assistance of counsel prior to pleading guilty. On appeal, a divided panel of the Court of Appeals for the Fourth Circuit reversed on the ground that Alford's guilty plea was made involuntarily. 405 F.2d 340 (1968). In reaching its conclusion, the Court of Appeals relied heavily on United States v. Jackson, 390 U.S. 570 (1968), which the court read to require invalidation of the North Carolina statutory framework for the imposition of the death penalty because North Carolina statutes encouraged defendants to waive constitutional rights by the promise of no more than life imprisonment if a guilty plea was offered and accepted. Conceding that *Jackson* did not require the automatic invalidation of pleas of guilty entered under the North Carolina statutes, the Court of Appeals ruled that Alford's guilty plea was involuntary because its principal motivation was fear of the death penalty. By this standard, even if both the judge and the jury had possessed the power to impose the death penalty for first-degree murder or if guilty pleas to capital charges had not been permitted, Alford's plea of guilty to second-degree murder should still have been rejected because impermissibly induced by his desire to eliminate the possibility of a death sentence. We noted probable jurisdiction. 394 U.S. 956 (1969). We vacate the judgment of the Court of Appeals and remand the case for further proceedings.

We held in Brady v. United States, 397 U.S. 742 (1970), that a plea of guilty which would not have been entered except for the defendant's desire to avoid a possible death penalty and to limit the maximum penalty to life imprisonment or a term of years was not for that reason compelled within the meaning of the Fifth Amendment. *Jackson* established no new test for determining the validity of guilty pleas. The standard was and remains whether the plea represents a voluntary and intelligent choice among the alternative courses of action open to the defendant. . . . That he would not have pleaded except for the opportunity to limit the possible penalty does not necessarily demonstrate that the plea of guilty was not the product of a free and rational choice, especially where the defendant was represented by competent counsel whose advice was that the plea would be to the defendant's advantage. The standard fashioned and applied by the Court of Appeals was therefore erroneous and we would, without more, vacate and remand the case for further proceedings with respect to any other claims of

Alford which are properly before that court, if it were not for other circumstances appearing in the record which might seem to warrant an affirmance of the Court of Appeals.

As previously recounted, after Alford's plea of guilty was offered and the State's case was placed before the judge, Alford denied that he had committed the murder but reaffirmed his desire to plead guilty to avoid a possible death sentence and to limit the penalty to the 30-year maximum provided for second-degree murder. Ordinarily, a judgment of conviction resting on a plea of guilty is justified by the defendant's admission that he committed the crime charged against him and his consent that judgment be entered without a trial of any kind. The plea usually subsumes both elements, and justifiably so, even though there is no separate, express admission by the defendant that he committed the particular acts claimed to constitute the crime charged in the indictment. ... Here Alford entered his plea but accompanied it with the statement that he had not shot the victim.

If Alford's statements were to be credited as sincere assertions of his innocence, there obviously existed a factual and legal dispute between him and the State. Without more, it might be argued that the conviction entered on his guilty plea was invalid, since his assertion of innocence negatived any admission of guilt, which, as we observed last Term in *Brady,* is normally "[c]entral to the plea and the foundation for entering judgment against the defendant ...." 397 U.S., at 748.

In addition to Alford's statement, however, the court had heard an account of the events on the night of the murder, including information from Alford's acquaintances that he had departed from his home with his gun stating his intention to kill and that he had later declared that he had carried out his intention. Nor had Alford wavered in his desire to have the trial court determine his guilt without a jury trial. Although denying the charge against him, he nevertheless preferred the dispute between him and the State to be settled by the judge in the context of a guilty plea proceeding rather than by a formal trial. Thereupon, with the State's telling evidence and Alford's denial before it, the trial court proceeded to convict and sentence Alford for second-degree murder.

State and lower federal courts are divided upon whether a guilty plea can be accepted when it is accompanied by protestations of innocence and hence contains only a waiver of trial but no admission of guilt. Some courts, giving expression to the principle that "[o]ur law only authorizes a conviction where guilt is shown," Harris v. State, 76 Tex.Cr.R. 126, 131, 172 S.W. 975, 977 (1915), require that trial judges reject such pleas. ... But others have concluded that they should not "force any defense on a defendant in a criminal case," particularly when advancement of the defense might "end in disaster ...." Tremblay v. Overholser, 199 F.Supp.

569, 570 (DC 1961). They have argued that, since "guilt, or the degree of guilt, is at times uncertain and elusive," "[a]n accused, though believing in or entertaining doubts respecting his innocence, might reasonably conclude a jury would be convinced of his guilt and that he would fare better in the sentence by pleading guilty ...." McCoy v. United States, 124 U.S.App.D.C. 177, 179, 363 F.2d 306, 308 (1966). As one state court observed nearly a century ago, "[r]easons other than the fact that he is guilty may induce a defendant to so plead, ... [and] [h]e must be permitted to judge for himself in this respect." State v. Kaufman, 51 Iowa 578, 580, 2 N.W. 275, 276 (1879) (dictum). ...[7]

This Court has not confronted this precise issue, but prior decisions do yield relevant principles. In Lynch v. Overholser, 369 U.S. 705 (1962), Lynch, who had been charged in the Municipal Court of the District of Columbia with drawing and negotiating bad checks, a misdemeanor punishable by a maximum of one year in jail, sought to enter a plea of guilty, but the trial judge refused to accept the plea since a psychiatric report in the judge's possession indicated that Lynch had been suffering from "a manic depressive psychosis, at the time of the crime charged," and hence might have been not guilty by reason of insanity. Although at the subsequent trial Lynch did not rely on the insanity defense, he was found not guilty by reason of insanity and committed for an indeterminate period to a mental institution. On habeas corpus, the Court ordered his release, construing the congressional legislation seemingly authorizing the commitment as not reaching a case where the accused preferred a guilty plea to a plea of insanity. The Court expressly refused to rule that Lynch had an absolute right to have his guilty plea accepted, see id., at 719, but implied that there would have been no constitutional error had his plea been accepted even though evidence before the judge indicated that there was a valid defense.

The issue in Hudson v. United States, 272 U.S. 451 (1926), was whether a federal court has power to impose a prison sentence after accepting a plea of *nolo contendere,* a plea by which a defendant does not expressly admit his guilt, but nonetheless waives his right to a trial and authorizes the court for purposes of the case to treat him as if he were guilty. The Court held that a trial court does have such power, and, except for the cases which were rejected in *Hudson,* the federal courts have uniformly followed this rule, even in cases involving moral turpitude. ... Implicit in the *nolo contendere* cases is a recognition that the Constitution does not bar imposition of a prison sentence upon an accused who is unwilling expressly to admit his guilt but who, faced with grim alternatives, is willing to waive his trial and accept the sentence.

7. A third approach has been to decline to rule definitively that a trial judge must either accept or reject an otherwise valid plea containing a protestation of innocence, but to leave that decision to his sound discretion....

These cases would be directly in point if Alford had simply insisted on his plea but refused to admit the crime. The fact that his plea was denominated a plea of guilty rather than a plea of *nolo contendere* is of no constitutional significance with respect to the issue now before us, for the Constitution is concerned with the practical consequences, not the formal categorizations, of state law. ... Thus, while most pleas of guilty consist of both a waiver of trial and an express admission of guilt, the latter element is not a constitutional requisite to the imposition of criminal penalty. An individual accused of crime may voluntarily, knowingly, and understandingly consent to the imposition of a prison sentence even if he is unwilling or unable to admit his participation in the acts constituting the crime.

Nor can we perceive any material difference between a plea that refuses to admit commission of the criminal act and a plea containing a protestation of innocence when, as in the instant case, a defendant intelligently concludes that his interests require entry of a guilty plea and the record before the judge contains strong evidence of actual guilt. Here the State had a strong case of first-degree murder against Alford. Whether he realized or disbelieved his guilt, he insisted on his plea because in his view he had absolutely nothing to gain by a trial and much to gain by pleading. Because of the overwhelming evidence against him, a trial was precisely what neither Alford nor his attorney desired. Confronted with the choice between a trial for first-degree murder, on the one hand, and a plea of guilty to second-degree murder, on the other, Alford quite reasonably chose the latter and thereby limited the maximum penalty to a 30-year term. When his plea is viewed in light of the evidence against him, which substantially negated his claim of innocence and which further provided a means by which the judge could test whether the plea was being intelligently entered ... its validity cannot be seriously questioned. In view of the strong factual basis for the plea demonstrated by the State and Alford's clearly expressed desire to enter it despite his professed belief in his innocence, we hold that the trial judge did not commit constitutional error in accepting it.[11]

Relying on United States v. Jackson, *supra*, Alford now argues in effect that the State should not have allowed him this choice but should have insisted on proving him guilty of murder in the first degree. The States in their wisdom may take this course by statute or otherwise and may prohibit the practice of accepting pleas to

11. Our holding does not mean that a trial judge must accept every constitutionally valid guilty plea merely because a defendant wishes so to plead. A criminal defendant does not have an absolute right under the Constitution to have his guilty plea accepted by the court ... although the States may by statute or otherwise confer such a right. Likewise, the States may bar their courts from accepting guilty pleas from any defendants who assert their innocence. Cf. Fed. Rule Crim.Proc. 11, which gives a trial judge discretion to "refuse to accept a plea of guilty ...." We need not now delineate the scope of that discretion.

lesser included offenses under any circumstances. But this is not the mandate of the Fourteenth Amendment and the Bill of Rights. The prohibitions against involuntary or unintelligent pleas should not be relaxed, but neither should an exercise in arid logic render those constitutional guarantees counterproductive and put in jeopardy the very human values they were meant to preserve.

The Court of Appeals for the Fourth Circuit was in error to find Alford's plea of guilty invalid because it was made to avoid the possibility of the death penalty. That court's judgment directing the issuance of the writ of habeas corpus is vacated and the case is remanded to the Court of Appeals for further proceedings consistent with this opinion.

It is so ordered.[*]

[*] Justice Black noted his concurrence in the judgment and "substantially all" of the Court's opinion. Justice Brennan wrote a dissenting opinion, which Justice Douglas and Justice Marshall joined.

MR. JUSTICE STEWART delivered the opinion of the Court.

The question in this case is whether the Due Process Clause of the Fourteenth Amendment is violated when a state prosecutor carries out a threat made during plea negotiations to reindict the accused on more serious charges if he does not plead guilty to the offense with which he was originally charged.

I

The respondent, Paul Lewis Hayes, was indicted by a Fayette County, Ky., grand jury on a charge of uttering a forged instrument in the amount of $88.30, an offense then punishable by a term of 2 to 10 years in prison. Ky.Rev.Stat. § 434.130 (1973) (repealed 1975). After arraignment, Hayes, his retained counsel, and the Commonwealth's Attorney met in the presence of the Clerk of the Court to discuss a possible plea agreement. During these conferences the prosecutor offered to recommend a sentence of five years in prison if Hayes would plead guilty and "save the court the inconvenience and necessity of a trial," he would return to the grand jury to seek an indictment under the Kentucky Habitual Criminal Act, then Ky.Rev.Stat. § 431.190 (1973) (repealed 1975), which would subject Hayes to a mandatory sentence of life imprisonment by reason of his two prior felony convictions. Hayes chose not to plead guilty, and the prosecutor did obtain an indictment charging him under the Habitual Criminal Act. It is not disputed that the recidivist charge was fully justified by the evidence, that the prosecutor was in possession of this evidence at the time of the original indictment, and that Hayes' refusal to plead guilty to the original charge was what led to his indictment under the habitual criminal statute.

A jury found Hayes guilty on the principal charge of uttering a forged instrument and, in a separate proceeding, further found that he had twice before been convicted of felonies. As required by the habitual offender statute, he was sentenced to a life term in the penitentiary. The Kentucky Court of Appeals rejected Hayes' constitutional objections to the enhanced sentence, holding in an unpublished opinion that imprisonment for life with the possibility of parole was constitutionally permissible in light of the previous felonies of which Hayes had been convicted,[3] and that the prosecu-

---

3. According to his own testimony, Hayes had pleaded guilty in 1961, when he was 17 years old, to a charge of detaining a female, a lesser included offense of rape, and as a

tor's decision to indict him as a habitual offender was a legitimate use of available leverage in the plea-bargaining process.

On Hayes' petition for a federal writ of habeas corpus, the United States District Court for the Eastern District of Kentucky agreed that there had been no constitutional violation in the sentence or the indictment procedure, and denied the writ. The Court of Appeals for the Sixth Circuit reversed the District Court's judgment. Hayes v. Cowan, 547 F.2d 42. While recognizing "that plea bargaining now plays an important role in our criminal justice system," id., at 43, the appellate court thought that the prosecutor's conduct during the bargaining negotiations had violated the principles of Blackledge v. Perry, 417 U.S. 21, which "protect[ed] defendants from the vindictive exercise of a prosecutor's discretion." 547 F.2d, at 44. Accordingly, the court ordered that Hayes be discharged "except for his confinement under a lawful sentence imposed solely for the crime of uttering a forged instrument." Id., at 45. We granted certiorari to consider a constitutional question of importance in the administration of criminal justice. 431 U.S. 953.

II

It may be helpful to clarify at the outset the nature of the issue in this case. While the prosecutor did not actually obtain the recidivist indictment until after the plea conferences had ended, his intention to do so was clearly expressed at the outset of the plea negotiations. Hayes was thus fully informed of the true terms of the offer when he made his decision to plead not guilty. This is not a situation, therefore, where the prosecutor without notice brought an additional and more serious charge after plea negotiations relating only to the original indictment had ended with the defendant's insistence on pleading not guilty. As a practical matter, in short, this case would be no different if the grand jury had indicted Hayes as a recidivist from the outset, and the prosecutor had offered to drop that charge as part of the plea bargain.

The Court of Appeals nonetheless drew a distinction between "concessions relating to prosecution under an existing indictment," and threats to bring more severe charges not contained in the original indictment—a line it thought necessary in order to establish a prophylactic rule to guard against the evil of prosecutorial vindictiveness. Quite apart from this chronological distinction, however, the Court of Appeals found that the prosecutor had acted vindictively in the present case since he had conceded that the indictment was influenced by his desire to induce a guilty plea. The ultimate conclusion of the Court of Appeals thus seems to have been that a prosecutor acts vindictively and in violation of due process of law

result had served five years in the state reformatory. In 1970 he had been convicted of robbery and sentenced to five years' impris-onment, but had been released on probation immediately.

whenever his charging decision is influenced by what he hopes to gain in the course of plea bargaining negotiations.

III

We have recently had occasion to observe: "Whatever might be the situation in an ideal world, the fact is that the guilty plea and the often concomitant plea bargain are important components of this country's criminal justice system. Properly administered, they can benefit all concerned." Blackledge v. Allison, 431 U.S. 63, 71. The open acknowledgment of this previously clandestine practice has led this Court to recognize the importance of counsel during plea negotiations ... the need for a public record indicating that a plea was knowingly and voluntarily made ... and the requirement that a prosecutor's plea-bargaining promise must be kept.... The decision of the Court of Appeals in the present case, however, did not deal with considerations such as these, but held that the substance of the plea offer itself violated the limitations imposed by the Due Process Clause of the Fourteenth Amendment.... For the reasons that follow, we have concluded that the Court of Appeals was mistaken in so ruling.

IV

This Court held in North Carolina v. Pearce, 395 U.S. 711, 725, that the Due Process Clause of the Fourteenth Amendment "requires that vindictiveness against a defendant for having successfully attacked his first conviction must play no part in the sentence he receives after a new trial." The same principle was later applied to prohibit a prosecutor from reindicting a convicted misdemeanant on a felony charge after the defendant had invoked an appellate remedy, since in this situation there was also a "realistic likelihood of 'vindictiveness.' " Blackledge v. Perry, 417 U.S., at 27.

In those cases the Court was dealing with the State's unilateral imposition of a penalty upon a defendant who had chosen to exercise a legal right to attack his original conviction—a situation "very different from the give-and-take negotiation common in plea bargaining between the prosecution and defense, which arguably possess relatively equal bargaining power." Parker v. North Carolina, 397 U.S. 790, 809 (opinion of Brennan, J.). The Court has emphasized that the due process violation in cases such as *Pearce* and *Perry* lay not in the possibility that a defendant might be deterred from the exercise of a legal right ..., but rather in the danger that the State might be retaliating against the accused for lawfully attacking his conviction....

To punish a person because he has done what the law plainly allows him to do is a due process violation of the most basic sort ... and for an agent of the State to pursue a course of action whose objective is to penalize a person's reliance on his legal rights is "patently unconstitutional." Chaffin v. Stynchcombe, [412 U.S. 17] at 32–33, n. 20.... But in the "give-and-take" of plea bargaining, there is no such element of punishment or retaliation so long as the accused is free to accept or reject the prosecution's offer.

Plea bargaining flows from "the mutuality of advantage" to defendants and prosecutors, each with his own reasons for wanting to avoid trial.... Defendants advised by competent counsel and protected by other procedural safeguards are presumptively capable of intelligent choice in response to prosecutorial persuasion, and unlikely to be driven to false self-condemnation.... Indeed, acceptance of the basic legitimacy of plea bargaining necessarily implies rejection of any notion that a guilty plea is involuntary in a constitutional sense simply because it is the end result of the bargaining process. By hypothesis, the plea may have been induced by promises of a recommendation of a lenient sentence or a reduction of charges, and thus by fear of the possibility of a greater penalty upon conviction after a trial....

While confronting a defendant with the risk of more severe punishment clearly may have a "discouraging effect on the defendant's assertion of his trial rights, the imposition of these difficult choices [is] an inevitable"—and permissible—"attribute of any legitimate system which tolerates and encourages the negotiation of pleas." Chaffin v. Stynchcombe, supra, at 31. It follows that, by tolerating and encouraging the negotiation of pleas, this Court has necessarily accepted as constitutionally legitimate the simple reality that the prosecutor's interest at the bargaining table is to persuade the defendant to forgo his right to plead not guilty.

It is not disputed here that Hayes was properly chargeable under the recidivist statute, since he had in fact been convicted of two previous felonies. In our system, so long as the prosecutor has probable cause to believe that the accused committed an offense defined by statute, the decision whether or not to prosecute, and what charge to file or bring before a grand jury, generally rests entirely in his discretion. Within the limits set by the legislature's constitutionally valid definition of chargeable offenses, "the conscious exercise of some selectivity in enforcement is not in itself a federal constitutional violation" so long as "the selection was [not] deliberately based upon an unjustifiable standard such as race, religion, or other arbitrary classification." Oyler v. Boles, 368 U.S. 448, 456. To hold that the prosecutor's desire to induce a guilty plea is an "unjustifiable standard," which, like race or religion, may play no part in his charging decision, would contradict the very premises that underlie the concept of plea bargaining itself. Moreover, a rigid constitutional rule that would prohibit a prosecutor from acting forthrightly in his dealings with the defense could only invite unhealthy subterfuge that would drive the practice of plea bargaining back into the shadows from which it has so recently emerged....

There is no doubt that the breadth of discretion that our country's legal system vests in prosecuting attorneys carries with it the potential for both individual and institutional abuse. And broad though that discretion may be, there are undoubtedly constitutional limits upon its exercise. We hold only that the course of conduct engaged in by the prosecutor in this case, which no more than openly presented the defendant with the unpleasant alternatives of forgoing trial or facing charges on which he was plainly subject to prosecution, did not violate the Due Process Clause of the Fourteenth Amendment.

Accordingly, the judgment of the Court of Appeals is

Reversed.[*]

. . .

---

[*] Justice Blackmun wrote a dissenting opinion, which Justice Brennan and Justice Marshall joined. Justice Powell also wrote a dissenting opinion.

13. TRIAL BY JURY

BATSON v. KENTUCKY

476 U.S. 79, 106 S.Ct. 1712, 90 L.Ed.2d 69 (1986).

JUSTICE POWELL delivered the opinion of the Court.

This case requires us to reexamine that portion of Swain v. Alabama, 380 U.S. 202 (1965), concerning the evidentiary burden placed on a criminal defendant who claims that he has been denied equal protection through the State's use of peremptory challenges to exclude members of his race from the petit jury.

I

Petitioner, a black man, was indicted in Kentucky on charges of second-degree burglary and receipt of stolen goods. On the first day of trial in Jefferson Circuit Court, the judge conducted *voir dire* examination of the venire, excused certain jurors for cause, and permitted the parties to exercise peremptory challenges.[2] The prosecutor used his peremptory challenges to strike all four black persons on the venire, and a jury composed only of white persons was selected. Defense counsel moved to discharge the jury before it was sworn on the ground that the prosecutor's removal of the black veniremen violated petitioner's rights under the Sixth and Fourteenth Amendments to a jury drawn from a cross section of the community, and under the Fourteenth Amendment to equal protection of the laws. Counsel requested a hearing on his motion. Without expressly ruling on the request for a hearing, the trial judge observed that the parties were entitled to use their peremptory challenges to "strike anybody they want to." The judge then denied petitioner's motion, reasoning that the cross section requirement applies only to selection of the venire and not to selection of the petit jury itself.

The jury convicted petitioner on both counts. On appeal to the Supreme Court of Kentucky, petitioner pressed, among other claims, the argument concerning the prosecutor's use of peremptory challenges. Conceding that *Swain v. Alabama,* supra, apparently foreclosed an equal protection claim based solely on the prosecu-

---

2. The Kentucky Rules of Criminal Procedure authorize the trial court to permit counsel to conduct *voir dire* examination or to conduct the examination itself. Ky.Rule Crim.Proc. 9.38. After jurors have been excused for cause, the parties exercise their peremptory challenges simultaneously by striking names from a list of qualified jurors equal to the number to be seated plus the number of allowable peremptory challenges. Rule 9.36. Since the offense charged in this case was a felony, and an alternate juror was called, the prosecutor was entitled to six peremptory challenges, and defense counsel to nine. Rule 9.40.

tor's conduct in this case, petitioner urged the court to follow decisions of other States ... and to hold that such conduct violated his rights under the Sixth Amendment and Section 11 of the Kentucky Constitution to a jury drawn from a cross section of the community. Petitioner also contended that the facts showed that the prosecutor had engaged in a "pattern" of discriminatory challenges in this case and established an equal protection violation under *Swain.*

The Supreme Court of Kentucky affirmed. In a single paragraph, the court declined petitioner's invitation to adopt the reasoning of ... [the other state courts]. The court observed that it recently had reaffirmed its reliance on *Swain,* and had held that a defendant alleging lack of a fair cross section must demonstrate systematic exclusion of a group of jurors from the venire. ... We granted certiorari, 471 U.S. 1052 (1985), and now reverse.

II

In *Swain v. Alabama,* this Court recognized that a "State's purposeful or deliberate denial to Negroes on account of race of participation as jurors in the administration of justice violates the Equal Protection Clause." 380 U.S., at 203–204. This principle has been "consistently and repeatedly" reaffirmed, id., at 204, in numerous decisions of this Court both preceding and following *Swain.* We reaffirm the principle today.

A

More than a century ago, the Court decided that the State denies a black defendant equal protection of the laws when it puts him on trial before a jury from which members of his race have been purposefully excluded. Strauder v. West Virginia, 100 U.S. 303 (1880). That decision laid the foundation for the Court's unceasing efforts to eradicate racial discrimination in the procedures used to select the venire from which individual jurors are drawn. In *Strauder,* the Court explained that the central concern of the recently ratified Fourteenth Amendment was to put an end to governmental discrimination on account of race. ... Exclusion of black citizens from service as jurors constitutes a primary example of the evil the Fourteenth Amendment was designed to cure.

In holding that racial discrimination in jury selection offends the Equal Protection Clause, the Court in *Strauder* recognized, however, that a defendant has no right to a "petit jury composed in whole or in part of persons of his own race." Id., at 305. "The number of our races and nationalities stands in the way of evolution of such a conception" of the demand of equal protection. Akins v. Texas, 325 U.S. 398, 403 (1945). But the defendant does have the right to be tried by a jury whose members are selected pursuant to nondiscriminatory criteria. ... The Equal Protection Clause guarantees the defendant that the State will not exclude members of his race from the jury venire on account of race ... or on the false assumption that members of his race as a group are not qualified to serve as jurors ... .

Purposeful racial discrimination in selection of the venire violates a defendant's right to equal protection because it denies him the protection that a trial by jury is intended to secure. "The very idea of a jury is a body ... composed of the peers or equals of the person whose rights it is selected or summoned to determine; that is, of his neighbors, fellows, associates, persons having the same legal status in society as that which he holds." *Strauder*, supra, at 308 ... The petit jury has occupied a central position in our system of justice by safeguarding a person accused of crime against the arbitrary exercise of power by prosecutor or judge. ... Those on the venire must be "indifferently chosen,"[9] to secure the defendant's right under the Fourteenth Amendment to "protection of life and liberty against race or color prejudice." *Strauder*, supra, at 309.

Racial discrimination in selection of jurors harms not only the accused whose life or liberty they are summoned to try. Competence to serve as a juror ultimately depends on an assessment of individual qualifications and ability impartially to consider evidence presented at a trial. See Thiel v. Southern Pacific Co., 328 U.S. 217, 223–224 (1946). A person's race simply "is unrelated to his fitness as a juror." Id., at 227 (Frankfurter, J., dissenting). As long ago as *Strauder,* therefore, the Court recognized that by denying a person participation in jury service on account of his race, the State unconstitutionally discriminated against the excluded juror. ...

The harm from discriminatory jury selection extends beyond that inflicted on the defendant and the excluded juror to touch the entire community. Selection procedures that purposefully exclude black persons from juries undermine public confidence in the fairness of our system of justice. ... Discrimination within the judicial system is most pernicious because it is "a stimulant to that race prejudice which is an impediment to securing to [black citizens] that equal justice which the law aims to secure to all others." *Strauder*, 100 U.S., at 308.

B

In *Strauder,* the Court invalidated a state statute that provided that only white men could serve as jurors. ... We can be confident that no State now has such a law.... While decisions of this Court have been concerned largely with discrimination during selection of the venire, the principles announced there also forbid discrimination on account of race in selection of the petit jury....

9. 4 W. Blackstone, Commentaries 350 (Cooley ed. 1899) (quoted in Duncan v. Louisiana, 391 U.S., at 152).

Accordingly, the component of the jury selection process at issue here, the State's privilege to strike individual jurors through peremptory challenges, is subject to the commands of the Equal Protection Clause.[12] Although a prosecutor ordinarily is entitled to exercise permitted peremptory challenges "for any reason at all, as long as that reason is related to his view concerning the outcome" of the case to be tried, United States v. Robinson, 421 F.Supp. 467, 473 (Conn.1976), mandamus granted sub nom. United States v. Newman, 549 F.2d 240 (CA2 1977), the Equal Protection Clause forbids the prosecutor to challenge potential jurors solely on account of their race or on the assumption that black jurors as a group will be unable impartially to consider the State's case against a black defendant.

III

The principles announced in *Strauder* never have been questioned in any subsequent decision of this Court. Rather, the Court has been called upon repeatedly to review the application of those principles to particular facts. A recurring question in these cases, as in any case alleging a violation of the Equal Protection Clause, was whether the defendant had met his burden of proving purposeful discrimination on the part of the State. . . . That question also was at the heart of the portion of Swain v. Alabama we reexamine today.

A

Swain required the Court to decide, among other issues, whether a black defendant was denied equal protection by the State's exercise of peremptory challenges to exclude members of his race from the petit jury. . . . The record in *Swain* showed that the prosecutor had used the State's peremptory challenges to strike the six black persons included on the petit jury venire. . . . While rejecting the defendant's claim for failure to prove purposeful discrimination, the Court nonetheless indicated that the Equal Protection Clause placed some limits on the State's exercise of peremptory challenges. . . .

12. We express no views on whether the Constitution imposes any limit on the exercise of peremptory challenges by defense counsel.

Nor do we express any views on the techniques used by lawyers who seek to obtain information about the community in which a case is to be tried, and about members of the venire from which the jury is likely to be drawn. . . . Prior to *voir dire* examination, which serves as the basis for exercise of challenges, lawyers wish to know as much as possible about prospective jurors, including their age, education, employment, and economic status, so that they can ensure selection of jurors who at least have an open mind about the case. In some jurisdictions, where a pool of jurors serves for a substantial period of time . . . counsel also may seek to learn which members of the pool served on juries in other cases and the outcome of those cases. Counsel even may employ professional investigators to interview persons who have served on a particular petit jury. We have had no occasion to consider particularly this practice. Of course, counsel's effort to obtain possibly relevant information about prospective jurors is to be distinguished from the practice at issue here.

The Court sought to accommodate the prosecutor's historical privilege of peremptory challenge free of judicial control ... and the constitutional prohibition on exclusion of persons from jury service on account of race .... While the Constitution does not confer a right to peremptory challenges ... those challenges traditionally have been viewed as one means of assuring the selection of a qualified and unbiased jury .... To preserve the peremptory nature of the prosecutor's challenge, the Court in *Swain* declined to scrutinize his actions in a particular case by relying on a presumption that he properly exercised the State's challenges. ...

The Court went on to observe, however, that a State may not exercise its challenges in contravention of the Equal Protection Clause. It was impermissible for a prosecutor to use his challenges to exclude blacks from the jury "for reasons wholly unrelated to the outcome of the particular case on trial" or to deny to blacks "the same right and opportunity to participate in the administration of justice enjoyed by the white population." [380 U.S.], at 224. Accordingly, a black defendant could make out a prima facie case of purposeful discrimination on proof that the peremptory challenge system was "being perverted" in that manner. Ibid. For example, an inference of purposeful discrimination would be raised on evidence that a prosecutor, "in case after case, whatever the circumstances, whatever the crime and whoever the defendant or the victim may be, is responsible for the removal of Negroes who have been selected as qualified jurors by the jury commissioners and who have survived challenges for cause, with the result that no Negroes ever serve on petit juries." Id., at 223. Evidence offered by the defendant in *Swain* did not meet that standard. While the defendant showed that prosecutors in the jurisdiction had exercised their strikes to exclude blacks from the jury, he offered no proof of the circumstances under which prosecutors were responsible for striking black jurors beyond the facts of his own case. ...

A number of lower courts following the teaching of *Swain* reasoned that proof of repeated striking of blacks over a number of cases was necessary to establish a violation of the Equal Protection Clause. Since this interpretation of *Swain* has placed on defendants a crippling burden of proof, prosecutors' peremptory challenges are now largely immune from constitutional scrutiny. For reasons that follow, we reject this evidentiary formulation as inconsistent with standards that have been developed since *Swain* for assessing a prima facie case under the Equal Protection Clause.

B

Since the decision in *Swain,* we have explained that our cases concerning selection of the venire reflect the general equal protection principle that the "invidious quality" of governmental action claimed to be racially discriminatory "must ultimately be traced to a racially discriminatory purpose." Washington v. Davis, 426 U.S.

229, 240 (1976). As in any equal protection case, the "burden is, of course," on the defendant who alleges discriminatory selection of the venire "to prove the existence of purposeful discrimination." Whitus v. Georgia, 385 U.S. [545 (1967)] at 550 (citing Tarrance v. Florida, 188 U.S. 519 (1903)) . . . .

Moreover, since *Swain,* we have recognized that a black defendant alleging that members of his race have been impermissibly excluded from the venire may make out a prima facie case of purposeful discrimination by showing that the totality of the relevant facts gives rise to an inference of discriminatory purpose. . . . Once the defendant makes the requisite showing, the burden shifts to the State to explain adequately the racial exclusion. . . . The State cannot meet this burden on mere general assertions that its officials did not discriminate or that they properly performed their official duties. . . . Rather, the State must demonstrate that "permissible racially neutral selection criteria and procedures have produced the monochromatic result." Alexander v. Louisiana [405 U.S. 625 (1972)], at 632 . . . .

The showing necessary to establish a prima facie case of purposeful discrimination in selection of the venire may be discerned in this Court's decisions. . . . The defendant initially must show that he is a member of a racial group capable of being singled out for differential treatment. . . . In combination with that evidence, a defendant may then make a prima facie case by proving that in the particular jurisdiction members of his race have not been summoned for jury service over an extended period of time. . . . Proof of systematic exclusion from the venire raises an inference of purposeful discrimination because the "result bespeaks discrimination." Hernandez v. Texas, 347 U.S. [475 (1954)], at 482 . . . .

Since the ultimate issue is whether the State has discriminated in selecting the defendant's venire, however, the defendant may establish a prima facie case "in other ways then by evidence of long-continued unexplained absence" of members in his race "from many panels." Cassell v. Texas, 339 U.S. 282, 290 (1950) (plurality opinion). In cases involving the venire, this Court has found a prima facie case on proof that members of the defendant's race were substantially underrepresented on the venire from which his jury was drawn, and that the venire was selected under a practice providing "the opportunity for discrimination." Whitus v. Georgia, 385 U.S., at 552 . . . . This combination of factors raises the necessary inference of purposeful discrimination because the Court has declined to attribute to chance the absence of black citizens on a particular jury array where the selection mechanism is subject to abuse. When circumstances suggest the need, the trial court must undertake a "factual inquiry" that "takes into account all possible explanatory factors" in the particular case. Alexander v. Louisiana, supra, at 630.

Thus, since the decision in *Swain,* this Court has recognized that a defendant may make a prima facie showing of purposeful racial discrimination in selection of the venire by relying solely on the facts concerning its selection *in his case.*   These decisions are in accordance with the proposition, articulated in Arlington Heights v. Metropolitan Housing Development Corp., that "a consistent pattern of official racial discrimination" is not "a necessary predicate to a violation of the Equal Protection Clause.   A single invidiously discriminatory governmental act" is not "immunized by the absence of such discrimination in the making of other comparable decisions."   429 U.S., at 266, n. 14.   For evidentiary requirements to dictate that "several must suffer discrimination" before one could object, McCray v. New York, 461 U.S. [961 (1983)], at 965 (Marshall, J., dissenting from denial of certiorari), would be inconsistent with the promise of equal protection to all.

C

The standards for assessing a prima facie case in the context of discriminatory selection of the venire have been fully articulated since *Swain.* . . .   These principles support our conclusion that a defendant may establish a prima facie case of purposeful discrimination in selection of the petit jury solely on evidence concerning the prosecutor's exercise of peremptory challenges at the defendant's trial.   To establish such a case, the defendant first must show that he is a member of a cognizable racial group . . . and that the prosecutor has exercised peremptory challenges to remove from the venire members of the defendant's race.   Second, the defendant is entitled to rely on the fact, as to which there can be no dispute, that peremptory challenges constitute a jury selection practice that permits "those to discriminate who are of a mind to discriminate." Avery v. Georgia, 345 U.S., at 562.   Finally, the defendant must show that these facts and any other relevant circumstances raise an inference that the prosecutor used that practice to exclude the veniremen from the petit jury on account of their race.   This combination of factors in the empanelling of the petit jury, as in the selection of the venire, raises the necessary inference of purposeful discrimination.

In deciding whether the defendant has made the requisite showing, the trial court should consider all relevant circumstances. For example, a "pattern" of strikes against black jurors included in the particular venire might give rise to an inference of discrimination.   Similarly, the prosecutor's questions and statements during *voir dire* examination and in exercising his challenges may support or refute an inference of discriminatory purpose.   These examples are merely illustrative.   We have confidence that trial judges, experienced in supervising *voir dire,* will be able to decide if the circumstances concerning the prosecutor's use of peremptory challenges creates a prima facie case of discrimination against black jurors.

Once the defendant makes a prima facie showing, the burden shifts to the State to come forward with a neutral explanation for challenging black jurors. Though this requirement imposes a limitation in some cases on the full peremptory character of the historic challenge, we emphasize that the prosecutor's explanation need not rise to the level justifying exercise of a challenge for cause. ... But the prosecutor may not rebut the defendant's prima facie case of discrimination by stating merely that he challenged jurors of the defendant's race on the assumption—or his intuitive judgment—that they would be partial to the defendant because of their shared race. ... Just as the Equal Protection Clause forbids the States to exclude black persons from the venire on the assumption that blacks as a group are unqualified to serve as jurors ... so it forbids the States to strike black veniremen on the assumption that they will be biased in a particular case simply because the defendant is black. The core guarantee of equal protection, ensuring citizens that their State will not discriminate on account of race, would be meaningless were we to approve the exclusion of jurors on the basis of such assumptions, which arise solely from the jurors' race. Nor may the prosecutor rebut the defendant's case merely by denying that he had a discriminatory motive or "affirm[ing] [his] good faith in individual selections." Alexander v. Louisiana, 405 U.S., at 632. If these general assertions were accepted as rebutting a defendant's prima facie case, the Equal Protection Clause "would be but a vain and illusory requirement." Norris v. Alabama, supra, at 598. The prosecutor therefore must articulate a neutral explanation related to the particular case to be tried. The trial court then will have the duty to determine if the defendant has established purposeful discrimination.

IV

The State contends that our holding will eviscerate the fair trial values served by the peremptory challenge. Conceding that the Constitution does not guarantee a right to peremptory challenges and that *Swain* did state that their use ultimately is subject to the strictures of equal protection, the State argues that the privilege of unfettered exercise of the challenge is of vital importance to the criminal justice system.

While we recognize, of course, that the peremptory challenge occupies an important position in our trial procedures, we do not agree that our decision today will undermine the contribution the challenge generally makes to the administration of justice. The reality of practice, amply reflected in many state and federal court opinions, shows that the challenge may be, and unfortunately at times has been, used to discriminate against black jurors. By requiring trial courts to be sensitive to the racially discriminatory use of peremptory challenges, our decision enforces the mandate of equal protection and furthers the ends of justice. In view of the heterogeneous population of our Nation, public respect for our criminal justice system and the rule of law will be strengthened if we ensure that no citizen is disqualified from jury service because of his race.

Nor are we persuaded by the State's suggestion that our holding will create serious administrative difficulties. In those States applying a version of the evidentiary standard we recognize today, courts have not experienced serious administrative burdens, and the peremptory challenge system has survived. We decline, however, to formulate particular procedures to be followed upon a defendant's timely objection to a prosecutor's challenges.

V

In this case, petitioner made a timely objection to the prosecutor's removal of all black persons on the venire. Because the trial court flatly rejected the objection without requiring the prosecutor to give an explanation for his action, we remand this case for further proceedings. If the trial court decides that the facts establish, prima facie, purposeful discrimination and the prosecutor does not come forward with a neutral explanation for his action, our precedents require that petitioner's conviction be reversed. ... [25]

It is so ordered.

JUSTICE MARSHALL, concurring.

I join Justice Powell's eloquent opinion for the Court, which takes a historic step toward eliminating the shameful practice of racial discrimination in the selection of juries. The Court's opinion cogently explains the pernicious nature of the racially discriminatory use of peremptory challenges, and the repugnancy of such discrimination to the Equal Protection Clause. The Court's opinion also ably demonstrates the inadequacy of any burden of proof for racially discriminatory use of peremptories that requires that "justice ... sit supinely by" and be flouted in case after case before a remedy is available. I nonetheless write separately to express my views. The decision today will not end the racial discrimination that peremptories inject into the jury-selection process. That goal can be accomplished only by eliminating peremptory challenges entirely.

. . .

Misuse of the peremptory challenge to exclude black jurors has become both common and flagrant. Black defendants rarely have been able to compile statistics showing the extent of that practice, but the few cases setting out such figures are instructive. See United States v. Carter, 528 F.2d 844, 848 (CA8 1975) (in 15 criminal cases in 1974 in the Western District of Missouri involving black defendants, prosecutors peremptorily challenged 81% of black

---

25. To the extent that anything in Swain v. Alabama, 380 U.S. 202 (1965), is contrary to the principles we articulate today, that decision is overruled.

jurors) . . .; United States v. McDaniels, 379 F.Supp. 1243 (ED La. 1974) (in 53 criminal cases in 1972–1974 in the Eastern District of Louisiana involving black defendants, federal prosecutors used 68.9% of their peremptory challenges against black jurors, who made up less than one quarter of the venire); McKinney v. Walker, 394 F.Supp. 1015, 1017–1018 (SC 1974) (in 13 criminal trials in 1970–1971 in Spartansburg County, South Carolina, involving black defendants, prosecutors peremptorily challenged 82% of black jurors) . . . . Prosecutors have explained to courts that they routinely strike black jurors, ... An instruction book used by the prosecutor's office in Dallas County, Texas, explicitly advised prosecutors that they conduct jury selection so as to eliminate " 'any member of a minority group.' " In 100 felony trials in Dallas County in 1983–1984, prosecutors peremptorily struck 405 out of 467 eligible black jurors; the chance of a qualified black sitting on a jury was 1 in 10 compared to 1 in 2 for a white.

. . .

II

I wholeheartedly concur in the Court's conclusion that use of the peremptory challenge to remove blacks from juries, on the basis of their race, violates the Equal Protection Clause. I would go further, however, in fashioning a remedy adequate to eliminate that discrimination. Merely allowing defendants the opportunity to challenge the racially discriminatory use of peremptory challenges in individual cases will not end the illegitimate use of the peremptory challenge.

Evidentiary analysis similar to that set out by the Court . . . has been adopted as a matter of state law in States including Massachusetts and California. Cases from those jurisdictions illustrate the limitations of the approach. First, defendants cannot attack the discriminatory use of peremptory challenges at all unless the challenges are so flagrant as to establish a prima facie case. This means, in those States, that where only one or two black jurors survive the challenges for cause, the prosecutor need have no compunction about striking them from the jury because of their race. . . . Prosecutors are left free to discriminate against blacks in jury selection provided that they hold that discrimination to an "acceptable" level.

Second, when a defendant can establish a prima facie case, trial courts face the difficult burden of assessing prosecutors' motives. See King v. County of Nassau, 581 F.Supp. 493, 501–502 (EDNY 1984). Any prosecutor can easily assert facially neutral reasons for striking a juror, and trial courts are ill-equipped to second-guess those reasons. How is the court to treat a prosecutor's statement that he struck a juror because the juror had a son about the same age as defendant, see People v. Hall, 35 Cal.3d 161, 672 P.2d 854 (1983), or seemed "uncommunicative," *King*, supra, at 498, or "never cracked a smile" and, therefore "did not possess the sensitivities necessary to realistically look at the issues and decide the facts in this case," *Hall*, supra, at 165, 672 P.2d, at 856? If such easily generated explanations are sufficient to discharge the prosecutor's obligation to justify his strikes on nonracial grounds, then the protection erected by the Court today may be illusory.

Nor is outright prevarication by prosecutors the only danger here. "[I]t is even possible that an attorney may lie to himself in an effort to convince himself that his motives are legal." *King*, supra, at 502. A prosecutor's own conscious or unconscious racism may lead him easily to the conclusion that a prospective black juror is "sullen," or "distant," a characterization that would not have come to his mind if a white juror had acted identically. A judge's own conscious or unconscious racism may lead him to accept such an explanation as well supported. As Justice Rehnquist concedes, prosecutors' peremptories are based on their "seat-of-the-pants instincts" as to how particular jurors will vote. Post, at 138 . . . . Yet "seat-of-the-pants instincts" may often be just another term for racial prejudice. Even if all parties approach the Court's mandate with the best of conscious intentions, that mandate requires them to confront and overcome their own racism on all levels—a challenge I doubt all of them can meet. It is worth remembering that "114 years after the close of the War Between the States and nearly 100 years after *Strauder*, racial and other forms of discrimination still remain a fact of life, in the administration of justice as in our society as a whole." Rose v. Mitchell, 443 U.S. 545, 558–559 (1979), quoted in Vasquez v. Hillery, 474 U.S. 254, 264 (1986).

III

The inherent potential of peremptory challenges to distort the jury process by permitting the exclusion of jurors on racial grounds should ideally lead the Court to ban them entirely from the criminal justice system. . . . Justice Goldberg, dissenting in *Swain*, emphasized that "[w]ere it necessary to make an absolute choice between the right of a defendant to have a jury chosen in conformity with the requirements of the Fourteenth Amendment and the right to challenge peremptorily, the Constitution compels a choice of the former." 380 U.S., at 244. I believe that this case presents just such a choice, and I would resolve that choice by eliminating peremptory challenges entirely in criminal cases.

Some authors have suggested that the courts should ban prosecutors' peremptories entirely, but should zealously guard the defendant's peremptory as "essential to the fairness of trial by jury," Lewis v. United States, 146 U.S. 370, 376 (1892), and "one of the most important of the rights secured to the accused," Pointer v. United States, 151 U.S. 396, 408 (1894). . . . I would not find that an acceptable solution. Our criminal justice system "requires not only freedom from any bias against the accused, but also from any prejudice against his prosecution. Between him and the state the scales are to be evenly held." Hayes v. Missouri, 120 U.S. 68, 70 (1887). We can maintain that balance, not by permitting both prosecutor and defendant to engage in racial discrimination in jury selection, but by banning the use of peremptory challenges by prosecutors and by allowing the States to eliminate the defendant's peremptory as well.

Much ink has been spilled regarding the historic importance of defendants' peremptory challenges. The approving comments of the *Lewis* and *Pointer* Courts are noted above; the *Swain* Court emphasized the "very old credentials" of the peremptory challenge, 380 U.S., at 212, and cited the "long and widely held belief that peremptory challenge is a necessary part of trial by jury." Id., at 219. But this Court has also repeatedly stated that the right of peremptory challenge is not of constitutional magnitude, and may be withheld altogether without impairing the constitutional guarantee of impartial jury and fair trial. ... The potential for racial prejudice, further, inheres in the defendant's challenge as well. If the prosecutor's peremptory challenge could be eliminated only at the cost of eliminating the defendant's challenge as well, I do not think that would be too great a price to pay.

I applaud the Court's holding that the racially discriminatory use of peremptory challenges violates the Equal Protection Clause, and I join the Court's opinion. However, only by banning peremptories entirely can such discrimination be ended.

JUSTICE REHNQUIST, with whom THE CHIEF JUSTICE joins, dissenting.

The Court states, in the opening line of its opinion, that this case involves only a reexamination of that portion of Swain v. Alabama, 380 U.S. 202 (1965), concerning "the evidentiary burden placed on a criminal defendant who claims that he has been denied equal protection through the State's use of peremptory challenges to exclude members of his race from the petit jury." Ante, at 82 (footnote omitted). But in reality the majority opinion deals with much more than "evidentiary burden[s]." With little discussion and less analysis, the Court also overrules one of the fundamental substantive holdings of *Swain*, namely, that the State may use its peremptory challenges to remove from the jury, on a case-specific basis, prospective jurors of the same race as the defendant. Because I find the Court's rejection of this holding both ill-considered and unjustifiable under established principles of equal protection, I dissent.

. . .

I cannot subscribe to the Court's unprecedented use of the Equal Protection Clause to restrict the historic scope of the peremptory challenge, which has been described as "a necessary part of trial by jury." Swain, 380 U.S., at 219. In my view, there is simply nothing "unequal" about the State's using its peremptory challenges to strike blacks from the jury in cases involving black defendants, so long as such challenges are also used to exclude whites in cases involving white defendants, Hispanics in cases involving Hispanic defendants, Asians in cases involving Asian defendants, and so on. This case-specific use of peremptory challenges by the State does not single out blacks, or members of any other race for that matter, for discriminatory treatment. Such use of peremptories is at best based upon seat-of-the-pants instincts, which are undoubtedly crudely stereotypical and may in many cases be hopelessly mistaken. But as long as they are applied across the board to jurors of all races and nationalities, I do not see—and the Court most certainly has not explained—how their use violates the Equal Protection Clause.

Nor does such use of peremptory challenges by the State infringe upon any other constitutional interests. The Court does not suggest that exclusion of blacks from the jury through the State's use of peremptory challenges results in a violation of either the fair-cross-section or impartiality component of the Sixth Amendment. . . . And because the case-specific use of peremptory challenges by the State does not deny blacks the right to serve as jurors in cases involving nonblack defendants, it harms neither the excluded jurors nor the remainder of the community. See ante, at 87–88.

The use of group affiliations, such as age, race, or occupation, as a "proxy" for potential juror partiality, based on the assumption or belief that members of one group are more likely to favor defendants who belong to the same group, has long been accepted as a legitimate basis for the State's exercise of peremptory challenges. . . . Indeed, given the need for reasonable limitations on the time devoted to *voir dire,* the use of such "proxies" by both the State and the defendant may be extremely useful in eliminating from the jury persons who might be biased in one way or another. The Court today holds that the State may not use its peremptory challenges to strike black prospective jurors on this basis without violating the Constitution. But I do not believe there is anything in the Equal Protection Clause, or any other constitutional provision, that justifies such a departure from the substantive holding contained in Part II of *Swain.* Petitioner in the instant case failed to make a sufficient showing to overcome the presumption announced in *Swain* that the State's use of peremptory challenges was related to the context of the case. I would therefore affirm the judgment of the court below.[*] [**]

[*] Justice White and Justice O'Connor wrote concurring opinions. Justice Stevens wrote a concurring opinion, which Justice Brennan joined. Chief Justice Burger wrote a dissenting opinion, which Justice Rehnquist joined.

[**] "The Equal Protection Clause prohibits a prosecutor from using the State's peremptory challenges to exclude otherwise qualified and unbiased persons from the petit jury solely by reason of their race, a practice that forecloses a significant opportunity to participate in civic life. An individual juror does not have a right to sit on any particular petit jury, but he or she does possess the right not

to be excluded from one on account of race." Powers v. Ohio, 499 U.S. 400, 409 (1991) (7–2).

"Invoking the Equal Protection Clause and federal statutory law, and relying upon well-established principles of standing, we hold that a criminal defendant may object to race-based exclusions of jurors effected through peremptory challenges whether or not the defendant and the excluded juror share the same race." 499 U.S. at 402.

J.E.B. v. ALABAMA EX REL. T.B.

___ U.S. ___, 114 S.Ct. 1419, 128 L.Ed.2d 89 (1994).

JUSTICE BLACKMUN delivered the opinion of the Court.

In Batson v. Kentucky, 476 U.S. 79 (1986), this Court held that the Equal Protection Clause of the Fourteenth Amendment governs the exercise of peremptory challenges by a prosecutor in a criminal trial. The Court explained that although a defendant has "no right to a 'petit jury composed in whole or in part of persons of his own race,'" *id.*, at 85, quoting Strauder v. West Virginia, 100 U.S. 303, 305 (1880), the "defendant does have the right to be tried by a jury whose members are selected pursuant to nondiscriminatory criteria." Id., at 85–86. Since *Batson,* we have reaffirmed repeatedly our commitment to jury selection procedures that are fair and nondiscriminatory. We have recognized that whether the trial is criminal or civil, potential jurors, as well as litigants, have an equal protection right to jury selection procedures that are free from state-sponsored group stereotypes rooted in, and reflective of, historical prejudice. . . .

Although premised on equal protection principles that apply equally to gender discrimination, all our recent cases defining the scope of *Batson* involved alleged racial discrimination in the exercise of peremptory challenges. Today we are faced with the question whether the Equal Protection Clause forbids intentional discrimination on the basis of gender, just as it prohibits discrimination on the basis of race. We hold that gender, like race, is an unconstitutional proxy for juror competence and impartiality.

I

On behalf of relator T.B., the mother of a minor child, respondent State of Alabama filed a complaint for paternity and child support against petitioner J.E.B. in the District Court of Jackson County, Alabama. On October 21, 1991, the matter was called for trial and jury selection began. The trial court assembled a panel of 36 potential jurors, 12 males and 24 females. After the court excused three jurors for cause, only 10 of the remaining 33 jurors were male. The State then used 9 of its 10 peremptory strikes to remove male jurors; petitioner used all but one of his strikes to remove female jurors. As a result, all the selected jurors were female.

Before the jury was empaneled, petitioner objected to the State's peremptory challenges on the ground that they were exercised against male jurors solely on the basis of gender, in violation of the Equal Protection Clause of the Fourteenth Amendment. . . .

Petitioner argued that the logic and reasoning of Batson v. Kentucky, which prohibits peremptory strikes solely on the basis of race, similarly forbids intentional discrimination on the basis of gender. The court rejected petitioner's claim and empaneled the all-female jury. ... The jury found petitioner to be the father of the child and the court entered an order directing him to pay child support. On post-judgment motion, the court reaffirmed its ruling that *Batson* does not extend to gender-based peremptory challenges. ... The Alabama Court of Civil Appeals affirmed ... relying on Alabama precedent .... The Supreme Court of Alabama denied certiorari ....

We granted certiorari, ___ U.S. ___ (1993), to resolve a question that has created a conflict of authority—whether the Equal Protection Clause forbids peremptory challenges on the basis of gender as well as on the basis of race. Today we reaffirm what, by now, should be axiomatic: Intentional discrimination on the basis of gender by state actors violates the Equal Protection Clause, particularly where, as here, the discrimination serves to ratify and perpetuate invidious, archaic, and overbroad stereotypes about the relative abilities of men and women.

II

Discrimination on the basis of gender in the exercise of peremptory challenges is a relatively recent phenomenon. Gender-based peremptory strikes were hardly practicable for most of our country's existence, since, until the 19th century, women were completely excluded from jury service. So well-entrenched was this exclusion of women that in 1880 this Court, while finding that the exclusion of African–American men from juries violated the Fourteenth Amendment, expressed no doubt that a State "may confine the selection [of jurors] to males." Strauder v. West Virginia, 100 U.S. 303, 310 ....

Many States continued to exclude women from jury service well into the present century, despite the fact that women attained suffrage upon ratification of the Nineteenth Amendment in 1920. States that did permit women to serve on juries often erected other barriers, such as registration requirements and automatic exemptions, designed to deter women from exercising their right to jury service. ...

The prohibition of women on juries was derived from the English common law which, according to Blackstone, rightfully excluded women from juries under "the doctrine of *propter defectum sexus,* literally, the 'defect of sex.' " United States v. DeGross, 960 F.2d 1433, 1438 (CA9 1992) (en banc), quoting 2 W. Blackstone, Commentaries *362. In this country, supporters of the exclusion of women from juries tended to couch their objections in terms of the ostensible need to protect women from the ugliness and depravity of trials. Women were thought to be too fragile and virginal to withstand the polluted courtroom atmosphere. ...

This Court in Ballard v. United States, 329 U.S. 187 (1946), first questioned the fundamental fairness of denying women the right to serve on juries. Relying on its supervisory powers over the federal courts, it held that women may not be excluded from the venire in federal trials in States where women were eligible for jury service under local law. In response to the argument that women have no superior or unique perspective, such that defendants are denied a fair trial by virtue of their exclusion from jury panels, the Court explained:

> "It is said ... that an all male panel drawn from the various groups within a community will be as truly representative as if women were included. The thought is that the factors which tend to influence the action of women are the same as those which influence the action of men—personality, background, economic status—and not sex. Yet it is not enough to say that women when sitting as jurors neither act nor tend to act as a class. Men likewise do not act like a class.... The truth is that the two sexes are not fungible; a community made up exclusively of one is different from a community composed of both; the subtle interplay of influence one on the other is among the imponderables. To insulate the courtroom from either may not in a given case make an iota of difference. Yet a flavor, a distinct quality is lost if either sex is excluded." Id., at 193–194 (footnotes omitted).

Fifteen years later, however, the Court still was unwilling to translate its appreciation for the value of women's contribution to civic life into an enforceable right to equal treatment under state laws governing jury service. In Hoyt v. Florida, 368 U.S., at 61, the Court found it reasonable, "despite the enlightened emancipation of women," to exempt women from mandatory jury service by statute, allowing women to serve on juries only if they volunteered to serve. The Court justified the differential exemption policy on the ground that women, unlike men, occupied a unique position "as the center of home and family life." Id., at 62.

In 1975, the Court finally repudiated the reasoning of *Hoyt* and struck down, under the Sixth Amendment, an affirmative registration statute nearly identical to the one at issue in *Hoyt*. ... We explained: "Restricting jury service to only special groups or excluding identifiable segments playing major roles in the community cannot be squared with the constitutional concept of jury trial." Id., at 530. The diverse and representative character of the jury must be maintained "partly as assurance of a diffused impartiality and partly because sharing in the administration of justice is a phase of civic responsibility.' " [Taylor v. Louisiana, 419 U.S. 522

(1975)], at 530–531, quoting Thiel v. Southern Pacific Co., 328 U.S. 217, 227 (1946) (Frankfurter, J., dissenting).   . . .

III

Taylor relied on Sixth Amendment principles, but the opinion's approach is consistent with the heightened equal protection scrutiny afforded gender-based classifications.   Since Reed v. Reed, 404 U.S. 71 (1971), this Court consistently has subjected gender-based classifications to heightened scrutiny in recognition of the real danger that government policies that professedly are based on reasonable considerations in fact may be reflective of "archaic and overbroad" generalizations about gender, see Schlesinger v. Ballard, 419 U.S. 498, 506–507 (1975), or based on "outdated misconceptions concerning the role of females in the home rather than in the 'marketplace and world of ideas.'"   Craig v. Boren, 429 U.S. 190, 198–199 (1976).   . . .

Despite the heightened scrutiny afforded distinctions based on gender, respondent argues that gender discrimination in the selection of the petit jury should be permitted, though discrimination on the basis of race is not.   Respondent suggests that "gender discrimination in this country . . . has never reached the level of discrimination" against African–Americans, and therefore gender discrimination, unlike racial discrimination, is tolerable in the courtroom. Brief for Respondent 9.

While the prejudicial attitudes toward women in this country have not been identical to those held toward racial minorities, the similarities between the experiences of racial minorities and women, in some contexts, "overpower those differences."   Note, Beyond *Batson:* Eliminating Gender–Based Peremptory Challenges, 105 Harv.L.Rev. 1920, 1921 (1992).   . . . Certainly, with respect to jury service, African–Americans and women share a history of total exclusion, a history which came to an end for women many years after the embarrassing chapter in our history came to an end for African–Americans.

We need not determine, however, whether women or racial minorities have suffered more at the hands of discriminatory state actors during the decades of our Nation's history.   It is necessary only to acknowledge that "our Nation has had a long and unfortunate history of sex discrimination," [Frontiero v. Richardson, 411 U.S. 677 (1973)], at 684, a history which warrants the heightened scrutiny we afford all gender-based classifications today.   Under our equal protection jurisprudence, gender-based classifications require "an exceedingly persuasive justification" in order to survive constitutional scrutiny.   See Personnel Administrator of Mass. v. Feeney, 442 U.S. 256, 273 (1979).   . . . Thus, the only question is whether discrimination on the basis of gender in jury selection substantially furthers the State's legitimate interest in achieving a fair and impartial trial.   In making this assessment, we do not weigh the value of peremptory challenges as an institution against our asserted commitment to eradicate invidious discrimination from the courtroom. Instead, we consider whether peremptory challenges based on gender stereotypes provide substantial aid to a litigant's effort to secure a fair and impartial jury.

Far from proffering an exceptionally persuasive justification for its gender-based peremptory challenges, respondent maintains that its decision to strike virtually all the males from the jury in this case "may reasonably have been based upon the perception, supported by history, that men otherwise totally qualified to serve upon a jury might be more sympathetic and receptive to the arguments of a man alleged in a paternity action to be the father of an out-of-wedlock child, while women equally qualified to serve upon a jury might be more sympathetic and receptive to the arguments of the complaining witness who bore the child." Brief for Respondent 10.

We shall not accept as a defense to gender-based peremptory challenges "the very stereotype the law condemns." Powers v. Ohio, 499 U.S. 400, 410 (1991). Respondent's rationale, not unlike those regularly expressed for gender-based strikes, is reminiscent of the arguments advanced to justify the total exclusion of women from juries. Respondent offers virtually no support for the conclusion that gender alone is an accurate predictor of juror's attitudes; yet it urges this Court to condone the same stereotypes that justified the wholesale exclusion of women from juries and the ballot box.[11] Respondent seems to assume that gross generalizations that would be deemed impermissible if made on the basis of race are somehow permissible when made on the basis of gender.

Discrimination in jury selection, whether based on race or on gender, causes harm to the litigants, the community, and the individual jurors who are wrongfully excluded from participation in the judicial process. The litigants are harmed by the risk that the prejudice which motivated the discriminatory selection of the jury will infect the entire proceedings. ... The community is harmed by the State's participation in the perpetuation of invidious group stereotypes and the inevitable loss of confidence in our judicial

---

11. Even if a measure of truth can be found in some of the gender stereotypes used to justify gender-based peremptory challenges, that fact alone cannot support discrimination on the basis of gender in jury selection. We have made abundantly clear in past cases that gender classifications that rest on impermissible stereotypes violate the Equal Protection Clause, even when some statistical support can be conjured up for the generalization. ... The generalization advanced by Alabama in support of its asserted right to discriminate on the basis of gender is, at the least, overbroad, and serves only to perpetuate the same "outmoded notions of the relative capabilities of men and women," Cleburne v. Cleburne Living Center, Inc., 473 U.S. 432, 441 (1985), that we have invalidated in other contexts. ... The Equal Protection Clause, as interpreted by decisions of this Court, acknowledges that a shred of truth may be contained in some stereotypes, but requires that state actors look beyond the surface before making judgments about people that are likely to stigmatize as well as to perpetuate historical patterns of discrimination.

system that state-sanctioned discrimination in the courtroom engenders.

When state actors exercise peremptory challenges in reliance on gender stereotypes, they ratify and reinforce prejudicial views of the relative abilities of men and women. Because these stereotypes have wreaked injustice in so many other spheres of our country's public life, active discrimination by litigants on the basis of gender during jury selection "invites cynicism respecting the jury's neutrality and its obligation to adhere to the law." Powers v. Ohio, 499 U.S., at 412. The potential for cynicism is particularly acute in cases where gender-related issues are prominent, such as cases involving rape, sexual harassment, or paternity. Discriminatory use of peremptory challenges may create the impression that the judicial system has acquiesced in suppressing full participation by one gender or that the "deck has been stacked" in favor of one side. See id., at 413 . . . .

In recent cases we have emphasized that individual jurors themselves have a right to nondiscriminatory jury selection procedures. . . . Contrary to respondent's suggestion, this right extends to both men and women. . . . All persons, when granted the opportunity to serve on a jury, have the right not to be excluded summarily because of discriminatory and stereotypical presumptions that reflect and reinforce patterns of historical discrimination. Striking individual jurors on the assumption that they hold particular views simply because of their gender is "practically a brand upon them, affixed by law, an assertion of their inferiority." Strauder v. West Virginia, 100 U.S. 303, 308 (1880). It denigrates the dignity of the excluded juror, and, for a woman, reinvokes a history of exclusion from political participation.[14] The message it sends to all those in the courtroom, and all those who may later learn of the discriminatory act, is that certain individuals, for no reason other than gender, are presumed unqualified by state actors to decide important questions upon which reasonable persons could disagree.

IV

Our conclusion that litigants may not strike potential jurors solely on the basis of gender does not imply the elimination of all peremptory challenges. Neither does it conflict with a State's legitimate interest in using such challenges in its effort to secure a fair and impartial jury. Parties still may remove jurors whom they feel might be less acceptable than others on the panel; gender simply may not serve as a proxy for bias. Parties may also exercise

---

14. The popular refrain is that *all* peremptory challenges are based on stereotypes of some kind, expressing various intuitive and frequently erroneous biases. See post, at 6. But where peremptory challenges are made on the basis of group characteristics other than race or gender (like occupation, for example), they do not reinforce the same stereotypes about the group's competence or predispositions that have been used to prevent them from voting, participating on juries, pursuing their chosen professions, or otherwise contributing to civic life. . . .

their peremptory challenges to remove from the venire any group or class of individuals normally subject to "rational basis" review. See Cleburne v. Cleburne Living Center, Inc., 473 U.S. 432, 439–442 (1985) .... Even strikes based on characteristics that are disproportionately associated with one gender could be appropriate, absent a showing of pretext.[16]

If conducted properly, *voir dire* can inform litigants about potential jurors, making reliance upon stereotypical and pejorative notions about a particular gender or race both unnecessary and unwise. *Voir dire* provides a means of discovering actual or implied bias and a firmer basis upon which the parties may exercise their peremptory challenges intelligently. ...

The experience in the many jurisdictions that have barred gender-based challenges belies the claim that litigants and trial courts are incapable of complying with a rule barring strikes based on gender. ... As with race-based *Batson* claims, a party alleging gender discrimination must make a prima facie showing of intentional discrimination before the party exercising the challenge is required to explain the basis for the strike. ... When an explanation is required, it need not rise to the level of a "for cause" challenge; rather, it merely must be based on a juror characteristic other than gender, and the proffered explanation may not be pretextual. ...

Failing to provide jurors the same protection against gender discrimination as race discrimination could frustrate the purpose of *Batson* itself. Because gender and race are overlapping categories, gender can be used as a pretext for racial discrimination. Allowing parties to remove racial minorities from the jury not because of their race, but because of their gender, contravenes well-established equal protection principles and could insulate effectively racial discrimination from judicial scrutiny.

V

Equal opportunity to participate in the fair administration of justice is fundamental to our democratic system. It not only furthers the goals of the jury system. It reaffirms the promise of equality under the law—that all citizens, regardless of race, ethnicity, or gender, have the chance to take part directly in our democracy. ... When persons are excluded from participation in our democratic processes solely because of race or gender, this promise of equality dims, and the integrity of our judicial system is jeopardized.

16. For example, challenging all persons who have had military experience would disproportionately affect men at this time, while challenging all persons employed as nurses would disproportionately affect women. Without a showing of pretext, however, these challenges may well not be unconstitutional, since they are not gender- or race-based. ...

In view of these concerns, the Equal Protection Clause prohibits discrimination in jury selection on the basis of gender, or on the assumption that an individual will be biased in a particular case for no reason other than the fact that the person happens to be a woman or happens to be a man. As with race, the "core guarantee of equal protection, ensuring citizens that their State will not discriminate ..., would be meaningless were we to approve the exclusion of jurors on the basis of such assumptions, which arise solely from the jurors' [gender]." *Batson,* 476 U.S., at 97–98.

The judgment of the Court of Civil Appeals of Alabama is reversed and the case is remanded to that court for further proceedings not inconsistent with this opinion.

It is so ordered.

JUSTICE O'CONNOR, concurring.

I agree with the Court that the Equal Protection Clause prohibits the government from excluding a person from jury service on account of that person's gender. ... The State's proffered justifications for its gender-based peremptory challenges are far from the "exceedingly persuasive" showing required to sustain a gender-based classification. ... I therefore join the Court's opinion in this case. But today's important blow against gender discrimination is not costless. I write separately to discuss some of these costs, and to express my belief that today's holding should be limited to the *government's* use of gender-based peremptory strikes.

Batson v. Kentucky, 476 U.S. 79 (1986), itself was a significant intrusion into the jury selection process. *Batson* mini-hearings are now routine in state and federal trial courts, and *Batson* appeals have proliferated as well. Demographics indicate that today's holding may have an even greater impact than did *Batson* itself. In further constitutionalizing jury selection procedures, the Court increases the number of cases in which jury selection—once a sideshow—will become part of the main event.

For this same reason, today's decision further erodes the role of the peremptory challenge. The peremptory challenge is "a practice of ancient origin" and is "part of our common law heritage." Edmonson v. Leesville Concrete Co., 500 U.S. 614, 639 (1991) (O'Connor, J., dissenting). The principal value of the peremptory is that it helps produce fair and impartial juries. ... The peremptory's importance is confirmed by its persistence: it was well established at the time of Blackstone and continues to endure in all the States. ...

Moreover, "[t]he essential nature of the peremptory challenge is that it is one exercised without a reason stated, without inquiry and without being subject to the court's control." Swain [v. Alabama] 380 U.S. [202 (1965)], at 220. Indeed, often a reason for it cannot be stated, for a trial lawyer's judgments about a juror's

sympathies are sometimes based on experienced hunches and educated guesses, derived from a juror's responses at voir dire or a
juror's " 'bare looks and gestures.' " Ibid. That a trial lawyer's
instinctive assessment of a juror's predisposition cannot meet the
high standards of a challenge for cause does not mean that the
lawyer's instinct is erroneous. ... Our belief that experienced
lawyers will often correctly intuit which jurors are likely to be the
least sympathetic, and our understanding that the lawyer will often
be unable to explain the intuition, are the very reason we cherish
the peremptory challenge. But, as we add, layer by layer, additional
constitutional restraints on the use of the peremptory, we force
lawyers to articulate what we know is often inarticulable.

In so doing we make the peremptory challenge less discretionary and more like a challenge for cause. We also increase the
possibility that biased jurors will be allowed onto the jury, because
sometimes a lawyer will be unable to provide an acceptable gender-
neutral explanation even though the lawyer is in fact correct that
the juror is unsympathetic. Similarly, in jurisdictions where lawyers
exercise their strikes in open court, lawyers may be deterred from
using their peremptories, out of the fear that if they are unable to
justify the strike the court will seat a juror who knows that the
striking party thought him unfit. Because I believe the peremptory
remains an important litigator's tool and a fundamental part of the
process of selecting impartial juries, our increasing limitation of it
gives me pause.

Nor is the value of the peremptory challenge to the litigant
diminished when the peremptory is exercised in a gender-based
manner. We know that like race, gender matters. A plethora of
studies make clear that in rape cases, for example, female jurors are
somewhat more likely to vote to convict than male jurors. ...
Moreover, though there have been no similarly definitive studies
regarding, for example, sexual harassment, child custody, or spousal
or child abuse, one need not be a sexist to share the intuition that
in certain cases a person's gender and resulting life experience will
be relevant to his or her view of the case. " 'Jurors are not
expected to come into the jury box and leave behind all that their
human experience has taught them.' " Beck v. Alabama, 447 U.S.
625, 642 (1980). Individuals are not expected to ignore as jurors
what they know as men—or women.

Today's decision severely limits a litigant's ability to act on this
intuition, for the import of our holding is that any correlation
between a juror's gender and attitudes is irrelevant as a matter of
constitutional law. But to say that gender makes no difference as a
matter of law is not to say that gender makes no difference as a
matter of fact. ... Today's decision is a statement that, in an effort
to eliminate the potential discriminatory use of the peremptory ...
gender is now governed by the special rule of relevance formerly
reserved for race. Though we gain much from this statement, we

cannot ignore what we lose. In extending *Batson* to gender we have added an additional burden to the state and federal trial process, taken a step closer to eliminating the peremptory challenge, and diminished the ability of litigants to act on sometimes accurate gender-based assumptions about juror attitudes.

These concerns reinforce my conviction that today's decision should be limited to a prohibition on the government's use of gender-based peremptory challenges. The Equal Protection Clause prohibits only discrimination by state actors. ... Our commitment to eliminating discrimination from the legal process should not allow us to forget that not all that occurs in the courtroom is state action. Private civil litigants are just that—*private* litigants. ...

Clearly, criminal defendants are not state actors. ... The peremptory challenge is " 'one of the most important of the rights secured to the *accused.*' " *Swain,* 380 U.S., at 219 (emphasis added) .... Limiting the accused's use of the peremptory is "a serious misordering of our priorities," for it means "we have exalted the right of citizens to sit on juries over the rights of the criminal defendant, even though it is the defendant, not the jurors, who faces imprisonment or even death." [Georgia v.] McCollum, [505 U.S. ___ (1992)], at ___ (Thomas, J., concurring in judgment) (slip op., at 3).

Accordingly, I adhere to my position that the Equal Protection Clause does not limit the exercise of peremptory challenges by private civil litigants and criminal defendants. This case itself presents no state action dilemma, for here the State of Alabama itself filed the paternity suit on behalf of petitioner. But what of the next case? Will we, in the name of fighting gender discrimination, hold that the battered wife—on trial for wounding her abusive husband—is a state actor? Will we preclude her from using her peremptory challenges to ensure that the jury of her peers contains as many women members as possible? I assume we will, but I hope we will not.[*]

[*] Justice Kennedy wrote an opinion concurring in the judgment. Chief Justice Rehnquist wrote a dissenting opinion. Justice Scalia also wrote a dissenting opinion, which Chief Justice Rehnquist and Justice Thomas joined.

GEORGIA v. McCOLLUM

505 U.S. 42, 112 S.Ct. 2348, 120 L.Ed.2d 33 (1992).

JUSTICE BLACKMUN delivered the opinion of the Court.

For more than a century, this Court consistently and repeatedly has reaffirmed that racial discrimination by the State in jury selection offends the Equal Protection Clause. ... Last Term this Court held that racial discrimination in a civil litigant's exercise of peremptory challenges also violates the Equal Protection Clause. See Edmonson v. Leesville Concrete Co., 500 U.S. ___ (1991). Today, we are asked to decide whether the Constitution prohibits a *criminal defendant* from engaging in purposeful racial discrimination in the exercise of peremptory challenges.

I

On August 10, 1990, a grand jury sitting in Dougherty County, Ga., returned a six-count indictment charging respondents with aggravated assault and simple battery. See App. 2. The indictment alleged that respondents beat and assaulted Jerry and Myra Collins. Respondents are white; the alleged victims are African–Americans. Shortly after the events, a leaflet was widely distributed in the local African–American community reporting the assault and urging community residents not to patronize respondents' business.

Before jury selection began, the prosecution moved to prohibit respondents from exercising peremptory challenges in a racially discriminatory manner. The State explained that it expected to show that the victims' race was a factor in the alleged assault. According to the State, counsel for respondents had indicated a clear intention to use peremptory strikes in a racially discriminatory manner, arguing that the circumstances of their case gave them the right to exclude African–American citizens from participating as jurors in the trial. Observing that 43 percent of the county's population is African–American, the State contended that, if a statistically representative panel is assembled for jury selection, 18 of the potential 42 jurors would be African–American. With 20 peremptory challenges, respondents therefore would be able to remove all the African–American potential jurors. Relying on Batson v. Kentucky, 476 U.S. 79 (1986), the Sixth Amendment, and the Georgia Constitution, the State sought an order providing that, if it succeeded in making out a prima facie case of racial discrimination by respondents, the latter would be required to articulate a racially neutral explanation for peremptory challenges.

The trial judge denied the State's motion, holding that "[n]either Georgia nor federal law prohibits criminal defendants from exercising peremptory strikes in a racially discriminatory manner." App. 14. The issue was certified for immediate appeal. Id., at 15 and 18.

The Supreme Court of Georgia, by a 4–3 vote, affirmed the trial court's ruling. State v. McCollum, 261 Ga. 473, 405 S.E.2d 688 (1991). The court acknowledged that in Edmonson v. Leesville Concrete Co., 500 U.S. ___ (1991), this Court had found that the exercise of a peremptory challenge in a racially discriminatory manner "would constitute an impermissible injury" to the excluded juror. 261 Ga., at 473, 405 S.E.2d, at 689. The court noted, however, that *Edmonson* involved private civil litigants, not criminal defendants. "Bearing in mind the long history of jury trials as an essential element of the protection of human rights," the court "decline[d] to diminish the free exercise of peremptory strikes by a criminal defendant." Ibid. Three justices dissented, arguing that *Edmonson* and other decisions of this Court establish that racially based peremptory challenges by a criminal defendant violate the Constitution. 261 Ga., at 473, 405 S.E.2d, at 689 (Hunt, J.); id., at 475, 405 S.E.2d, at 690 (Benham, J.); id., at 479, 405 S.E.2d, at 693 (Fletcher, J.). A motion for reconsideration was denied. App. 60.

We granted certiorari to resolve a question left open by our prior cases—whether the Constitution prohibits a criminal defendant from engaging in purposeful racial discrimination in the exercise of peremptory challenges. ___ U.S. ___ (1991).

II

Over the last century, in an almost unbroken chain of decisions, this Court gradually has abolished race as a consideration for jury service. In Strauder v. West Virginia, 100 U.S. 303 (1880), the Court invalidated a state statute providing that only white men could serve as jurors. While stating that a defendant has no right to a "petit jury composed in whole or in part of persons of his own race," id., at 305, the Court held that a defendant does have the right to be tried by a jury whose members are selected by nondiscriminatory criteria. ...

In Swain v. Alabama, 380 U.S. 202 (1965), the Court was confronted with the question whether an African–American defendant was denied equal protection by the State's exercise of peremptory challenges to exclude members of his race from the petit jury. ... Although the Court rejected the defendant's attempt to establish an equal protection claim premised solely on the pattern of jury strikes in his own case, it acknowledged that proof of systematic exclusion of African–Americans through the use of peremptories over a period of time might establish such a violation. ...

In Batson v. Kentucky, 476 U.S. 79 (1986), the Court discarded *Swain*'s evidentiary formulation. The *Batson* Court held that a defendant may establish a prima facie case of purposeful discrimination in selection of the petit jury based solely on the prosecutor's exercise of peremptory challenges at the defendant's trial. . . . "Once the defendant makes a prima facie showing, the burden shifts to the State to come forward with a neutral explanation for challenging black jurors." Id., at 97.

Last Term this Court applied the *Batson* framework in two other contexts. In Powers v. Ohio, 499 U.S. ___ (1991), it held that in the trial of a white criminal defendant, a prosecutor is prohibited from excluding African–American jurors on the basis of race. In Edmonson v. Leesville Concrete Co., 500 U.S. ___ (1991), the Court decided that in a civil case, private litigants cannot exercise their peremptory strikes in a racially discriminatory manner.

In deciding whether the Constitution prohibits criminal defendants from exercising racially discriminatory peremptory challenges, we must answer four questions. First, whether a criminal defendant's exercise of peremptory challenges in a racially discriminatory manner inflicts the harms addressed by *Batson*. Second, whether the exercise of peremptory challenges by a criminal defendant constitutes state action. Third, whether prosecutors have standing to raise this constitutional challenge. And fourth, whether the constitutional rights of a criminal defendant nonetheless preclude the extension of our precedents to this case.

III

A

The majority in *Powers* recognized that "*Batson* 'was designed "to serve multiple ends," ' only one of which was to protect individual defendants from discrimination in the selection of jurors." 499 U.S., at ___ (slip op. 5). As in *Powers* and *Edmonson*, the extension of *Batson* in this context is designed to remedy the harm done to the "dignity of persons" and to the "integrity of the courts." *Powers,* at ___ (slip op. 1).

As long ago as *Strauder,* this Court recognized that denying a person participation in jury service on account of his race unconstitutionally discriminates against the excluded juror. 100 U.S., at 308. . . . While "[a]n individual juror does not have a right to sit on any particular petit jury, . . . he or she does possess the right not to be excluded from one on account of race." *Powers,* 499 U.S., at ___ (slip op. 9). Regardless of who invokes the discriminatory challenge, there can be no doubt that the harm is the same—in all cases, the juror is subjected to open and public racial discrimination.

But "the harm from discriminatory jury selection extends beyond that inflicted on the defendant and the excluded juror to touch the entire community." *Batson,* 476 U.S., at 87. One of the goals of our jury system is "to impress upon the criminal defendant and the community as a whole that a verdict of conviction or acquittal is given in accordance with the law by persons who are fair." *Powers*, 499 U.S., at ___ (slip op. 12). Selection procedures that purposefully exclude African–Americans from juries undermine that public confidence—as well they should. "The overt wrong, often apparent to the entire jury panel, casts doubt over the obligation of the parties, the jury, and indeed the court to adhere to the law throughout the trial of the case." Id., at ___ (slip op. 11–12). . . .

The need for public confidence is especially high in cases involving race-related crimes. In such cases, emotions in the affected community will inevitably be heated and volatile. Public confidence in the integrity of the criminal justice system is essential for preserving community peace in trials involving race-related crimes. . . .

Be it at the hands of the State or the defense, if a court allows jurors to be excluded because of group bias, it is a willing participant in a scheme that could only undermine the very foundation of our system of justice—our citizens' confidence in it. Just as public confidence in criminal justice is undermined by a conviction in a trial where racial discrimination has occurred in jury selection, so is public confidence undermined where a defendant, assisted by racially discriminatory peremptory strikes, obtains an acquittal.

B

The fact that a defendant's use of discriminatory peremptory challenges harms the jurors and the community does not end our equal protection inquiry. Racial discrimination, although repugnant in all contexts, violates the Constitution only when it is attributable to state action. . . . Thus, the second question that must be answered is whether a criminal defendant's exercise of a peremptory challenge constitutes state action for purposes of the Equal Protection Clause.

Until *Edmonson*, the cases decided by this Court that presented the problem of racially discriminatory peremptory challenges involved assertions of discrimination by a prosecutor, a quintessential state actor. In *Edmonson*, by contrast, the contested peremptory challenges were exercised by a private defendant in a civil action. In order to determine whether state action was present in that setting, the Court in *Edmonson* used the analytical framework summarized in Lugar v. Edmonson Oil Co., 457 U.S. 922 (1982).

The first inquiry is "whether the claimed [constitutional] deprivation has resulted from the exercise of a right or privilege having its source in state authority." Id., at 939. "There can be no question" that peremptory challenges satisfy this first requirement, as they "are permitted only when the government, by statute or decisional law, deems it appropriate to allow parties to exclude a given number of persons who otherwise would satisfy the requirements for service on the petit jury." *Edmonson,* 500 U.S., at ___ (slip op. 5). As in *Edmonson,* a Georgia defendant's right to exercise peremptory challenges and the scope of that right are established by a provision of state law. . . .

The second inquiry is whether the private party charged with the deprivation can be described as a state actor. See *Lugar,* 457 U.S., at 941–942. In resolving that issue, the Court in *Edmonson* found it useful to apply three principles: 1) "the extent to which the actor relies on governmental assistance and benefits"; 2) "whether the actor is performing a traditional governmental function"; and 3) "whether the injury caused is aggravated in a unique way by the incidents of governmental authority." 500 U.S., at ___ (slip op. 6–7).

As to the first principle, the *Edmonson* Court found that the peremptory challenge system, as well as the jury system as a whole, "simply could not exist" without the "overt and significant participation of the government." Id., at ___ (slip op. 7). Georgia provides for the compilation of jury lists by the board of jury commissioners in each county and establishes the general criteria for service and the sources for creating a pool of qualified jurors representing a fair cross section of the community. . . . State law further provides that jurors are to be selected by a specified process . . .; they are to be summoned to court under the authority of the State . . .; and they are to be paid an expense allowance by the State whether or not they serve on a jury. . . . At court, potential jurors are placed in panels in order to facilitate examination by counsel . . .; they are administered an oath . . .; they are questioned on voir dire to determine whether they are impartial . . .; and they are subject to challenge for cause. . . .

In light of these procedures, the defendant in a Georgia criminal case relies on "governmental assistance and benefits" that are equivalent to those found in the civil context in *Edmonson.* "By enforcing a discriminatory peremptory challenge, the Court 'has . . . elected to place its power, property and prestige behind the [alleged] discrimination.' " *Edmonson,* 500 U.S., at ___ (slip op. 9) (citation omitted).

In regard to the second principle, the Court in *Edmonson* found that peremptory challenges perform a traditional function of the government: "Their sole purpose is to permit litigants to assist the government in the selection of an impartial trier of fact." Id., at ___ (slip op. 5). And, as the *Edmonson* Court recognized, the jury system in turn "performs the critical governmental functions of guarding the rights of litigants and 'insur[ing] continued acceptance of the laws by all of the people' " Id., at ___ (slip op. 9) (citation omitted). These same conclusions apply with even greater force in the criminal context because the selection of a jury in a criminal case fulfills a unique and constitutionally compelled governmental function. . . . The State cannot avoid its constitutional responsibilities by delegating a public function to private parties. . . .

Finally, the *Edmonson* Court indicated that the courtroom setting in which the peremptory challenge is exercised intensifies the harmful effects of the private litigant's discriminatory act and contributes to its characterization as state action. These concerns are equally present in the context of a criminal trial. Regardless of who precipitated the jurors' removal, the perception and the reality in a criminal trial will be that the court has excused jurors based on race, an outcome that will be attributed to the State.

Respondents nonetheless contend that the adversarial relationship between the defendant and the prosecution negates the governmental character of the peremptory challenge. Respondents rely on Polk County v. Dodson, 454 U.S. 312 (1981), in which a defendant sued, under 42 U.S.C. § 1983, the public defender who represented him. The defendant claimed that the public defender had violated his constitutional rights in failing to provide adequate representation. This Court determined that a public defender does not qualify as a state actor when engaged in his general representation of a criminal defendant.

Polk County did not hold that the adversarial relationship of a public defender with the State precludes a finding of state action—it held that this adversarial relationship prevented the attorney's public employment from *alone* being sufficient to support a finding of state action. Instead, the determination whether a public defender is a state actor for a particular purpose depends on the nature and context of the function he is performing. . . .

The exercise of a peremptory challenge differs significantly from other actions taken in support of a defendant's defense. In exercising a peremptory challenge, a criminal defendant is wielding the power to choose a quintessential governmental body—indeed, the institution of government on which our judicial system depends. Thus, as we held in *Edmonson,* when "a government confers on a private body the power to choose the government's employees or officials, the private body will be bound by the constitutional mandate of race neutrality." 500 U.S., at ___ (slip op. 10).

Lastly, the fact that a defendant exercises a peremptory challenge to further his interest in acquittal does not conflict with a finding of state action. Whenever a private actor's conduct is deemed "fairly attributable" to the government, it is likely that private motives will have animated the actor's decision. Indeed, in *Edmonson,* the Court recognized that the private party's exercise of peremptory challenges constituted state action, even though the motive underlying the exercise of the peremptory challenge may be to protect a private interest. See 500 U.S., at ___ (slip op. 11).

C

Having held that a defendant's discriminatory exercise of a peremptory challenge is a violation of equal protection, we move to the question whether the State has standing to challenge a defendant's discriminatory use of peremptory challenges. In *Powers,* 499 U.S., at ___, this Court held that a white criminal defendant has standing to raise the equal protection rights of black jurors wrongfully excluded from jury service. While third-party standing is a limited exception, the *Powers* Court recognized that a litigant may raise a claim on behalf of a third party if the litigant can demonstrate that he has suffered a concrete injury, that he has a close relation to the third party, and that there exists some hindrance to the third party's ability to protect its own interests. Id., at ___ (slip op. 10). In *Edmonson,* the Court applied the same analysis in deciding that civil litigants had standing to raise the equal protection rights of jurors excluded on the basis of their race.

In applying the first prong of its standing analysis, the *Powers* Court found that a criminal defendant suffered cognizable injury "because racial discrimination in the selection of jurors 'casts doubt on the integrity of the judicial process,' and places the fairness of a criminal proceeding in doubt." Id., at ___ (slip op. 11) (citation omitted). In *Edmonson,* this Court found that these harms were not limited to the criminal sphere.... Surely, a State suffers a similar injury when the fairness and integrity of its own judicial process is undermined.

In applying the second prong of its standing analysis, the *Powers* Court held that *voir dire* permits a defendant to "establish a relation, if not a bond of trust, with the jurors," a relation that "continues throughout the entire trial." 499 U.S., at ___ (slip op. 13). "Exclusion of a juror on the basis of race severs that relation in an invidious way." *Edmonson,* 500 U.S., at ___ (slip op. 14).

The State's relation to potential jurors in this case is closer than the relationships approved in *Powers* and *Edmonson.* As the representative of all its citizens, the State is the logical and proper party to assert the invasion of the constitutional rights of the excluded jurors in a criminal trial. Indeed, the Fourteenth Amendment forbids the State from denying persons within its jurisdiction the equal protection of the laws.

In applying the final prong of its standing analysis, the *Powers* Court recognized that, although individuals excluded from jury service on the basis of race have a right to bring suit on their own behalf, the "barriers to a suit by an excluded juror are daunting." 499 U.S., at ___ (slip op. 14).... The barriers are no less formidable in this context.... Accordingly, we hold that the State has standing to assert the excluded jurors' rights.

D

The final question is whether the interests served by *Batson* must give way to the rights of a criminal defendant. As a preliminary matter, it is important to recall that peremptory challenges are not constitutionally protected fundamental rights; rather, they are but one state-created means to the constitutional end of an impartial jury and a fair trial. This Court repeatedly has stated that the right to a peremptory challenge may be withheld altogether without impairing the constitutional guarantee of an impartial jury and a fair trial. . . .

Yet in *Swain,* the Court reviewed the "very old credentials," id., at 212, of the peremptory challenge and noted the "long and widely held belief that the peremptory challenge is a necessary part of trial by jury." Id., at 219 . . . . This Court likewise has recognized that "the role of litigants in determining the jury's composition provides one reason for wide acceptance of the jury system and of its verdicts." *Edmonson,* 500 U.S., at ___ (slip op. 15).

We do not believe that this decision will undermine the contribution of the peremptory challenge to the administration of justice. Nonetheless, "if race stereotypes are the price for acceptance of a jury panel as fair," we reaffirm today that such a "price is too high to meet the standard of the Constitution." *Edmonson,* 500 U.S., at ___ (slip op. 15–16). Defense counsel is limited to "legitimate, lawful conduct." Nix v. Whiteside, 475 U.S. 157, 166 (1986) . . . It is an affront to justice to argue that a fair trial includes the right to discriminate against a group of citizens based upon their race.

Nor does a prohibition of the exercise of discriminatory peremptory challenges violate a defendant's Sixth Amendment right to the effective assistance of counsel. Counsel can ordinarily explain the reasons for peremptory challenges without revealing anything about trial strategy or any confidential client communications. In the rare case in which the explanation for a challenge would entail confidential communications or reveal trial strategy, an *in camera* discussion can be arranged. . . . In any event, neither the Sixth Amendment right nor the attorney-client privilege gives a criminal defendant the right to carry out through counsel an unlawful course of conduct. . . .

Lastly, a prohibition of the discriminatory exercise of peremptory challenges does not violate a defendant's Sixth Amendment right to a trial by an impartial jury. The goal of the Sixth Amendment is "jury impartiality with respect to both contestants." Holland v. Illinois, 493 U.S. 474, 483 (1990) . . . .

We recognize, of course, that a defendant has the right to an impartial jury that can view him without racial animus, which so long has distorted our system of criminal justice. We have, accordingly, held that there should be a mechanism for removing those on the venire whom the defendant has specific reason to believe would be incapable of confronting and suppressing their racism. . . .

But there is a distinction between exercising a peremptory challenge to discriminate invidiously against jurors on account of race and exercising a peremptory challenge to remove an individual juror who harbors racial prejudice. This Court firmly has rejected the view that assumptions of partiality based on race provide a legitimate basis for disqualifying a person as an impartial juror. As this Court stated just last Term in *Powers,* "[w]e may not accept as a defense to racial discrimination the very stereotype the law condemns." 499 U.S., at ___ (slip op. 9). "In our heterogeneous society policy as well as constitutional considerations militate against the divisive assumption—as a *per se* rule—that justice in a court of law may turn upon the pigmentation of skin, the accident of birth, or the choice of religion." Ristaino v. Ross, 424 U.S. 589, 596, n. 8 (1976). We therefore reaffirm today that the exercise of a peremptory challenge must not be based on either the race of the juror or the racial stereotypes held by the party.

IV

We hold that the Constitution prohibits a criminal defendant from engaging in purposeful discrimination on the ground of race in the exercise of peremptory challenges. Accordingly, if the State demonstrates a prima facie case of racial discrimination by the defendants, the defendants must articulate a racially neutral explanation for peremptory challenges. The judgment of the Supreme Court of Georgia is reversed and the case is remanded for further proceedings not inconsistent with this opinion.

It is so ordered.[*]

[*] Chief Justice Rehnquist wrote a concurring opinion. Justice Thomas wrote an opinion concurring in the judgment. Justice O'Connor and Justice Scalia wrote dissenting opinions.

SULLIVAN v. LOUISIANA

___ U.S. ___, 113 S.Ct. 2078, 124 L.Ed.2d 182 (1993).

JUSTICE SCALIA delivered the opinion of the Court.

The question presented is whether a constitutionally deficient reasonable-doubt instruction may be harmless error.

I

Petitioner was charged with first-degree murder in the course of committing an armed robbery at a New Orleans bar. His alleged accomplice in the crime, a convicted felon named Michael Hillhouse, testifying at the trial pursuant to a grant of immunity, identified petitioner as the murderer. Although several other people were in the bar at the time of the robbery, only one testified at trial. This witness, who had been unable to identify either Hillhouse or petitioner at a physical lineup, testified that they committed the robbery, and that she saw petitioner hold a gun to the victim's head. There was other circumstantial evidence supporting the conclusion that petitioner was the triggerman. . . . In closing argument, defense counsel argued that there was reasonable doubt as to both the identity of the murderer and his intent.

In his instructions to the jury, the trial judge gave a definition of "reasonable doubt" that was, as the State conceded below, essentially identical to the one held unconstitutional in Cage v. Louisiana, 498 U.S. 39 (1990) (per curiam). . . . The jury found petitioner guilty of first-degree murder and subsequently recommended that he be sentenced to death. The trial court agreed. On direct appeal, the Supreme Court of Louisiana held . . . that the erroneous instruction was harmless beyond a reasonable doubt. 596 So.2d, at 186. It therefore upheld the conviction, though remanding for a new sentencing hearing because of ineffectiveness of counsel in the sentencing phase. We granted certiorari, 506 U.S. ___ (1992).

II

The Sixth Amendment provides that "[i]n all criminal prosecutions, the accused shall enjoy the right to a speedy and public trial, by an impartial jury . . . ." In Duncan v. Louisiana, 391 U.S. 145, 149 (1968), we found this right to trial by jury in serious criminal cases to be "fundamental to the American scheme of justice," and therefore applicable in state proceedings. The right includes, of course, as its most important element, the right to have the jury, rather than the judge, reach the requisite finding of "guilty." . . . Thus, although a judge may direct a verdict for the defendant if the evidence is legally insufficient to establish guilt, he may not direct a verdict for the State, no matter how overwhelming the evidence. . . .

What the factfinder must determine to return a verdict of guilty is prescribed by the Due Process Clause. The prosecution bears the burden of proving all elements of the offense charged . . . and must persuade the factfinder "beyond a reasonable doubt" of the facts necessary to establish each of those elements, see, e.g., In re Winship, 397 U.S. 358, 364 (1970) . . . . This beyond-a-reasonable-doubt requirement, which was adhered to by virtually all common-law jurisdictions, applies in state as well as federal proceedings. . . .

It is self-evident, we think, that the Fifth Amendment requirement of proof beyond a reasonable doubt and the Sixth Amendment requirement of a jury verdict are interrelated. It would not satisfy the Sixth Amendment to have a jury determine that the defendant is *probably* guilty, and then leave it up to the judge to determine (as *Winship* requires) whether he is guilty beyond a reasonable doubt. In other words, the jury verdict required by the Sixth Amendment is a jury verdict of guilty beyond a reasonable doubt. Our *per curiam* opinion in *Cage*, which we accept as controlling, held that an instruction of the sort given here does not produce such a verdict. Petitioner's Sixth Amendment right to jury trial was therefore denied.

III

In Chapman v. California, 386 U.S. 18 (1967), we rejected the view that all federal constitutional errors in the course of a criminal trial require reversal. We held that the Fifth Amendment violation of prosecutorial comment upon the defendant's failure to testify would not require reversal of the conviction if the State could show "beyond a reasonable doubt that the error complained of did not contribute to the verdict obtained." Id., at 24. The *Chapman* standard recognizes that "certain constitutional errors, no less than other errors, may have been 'harmless' in terms of their effect on the factfinding process at trial." Delaware v. Van Arsdall, 475 U.S. 673, 681 (1986). Although most constitutional errors have been held amenable to harmless-error analysis . . . some will always invalidate the conviction. Id., at ___ (slip op., at 8) (citing, *inter alia*, Gideon v. Wainwright, 372 U.S. 335 (1963) (total deprivation of the right to counsel); Tumey v. Ohio, 273 U.S. 510 (1927) (trial by a biased judge); McKaskle v. Wiggins, 465 U.S. 168 (1984) (right to self-representation)). The question in the present case is to which category the present error belongs.

Chapman itself suggests the answer. Consistent with the jury-trial guarantee, the question it instructs the reviewing court to consider is not what effect the constitutional error might generally be expected to have upon a reasonable jury, but rather what effect it had upon the guilty verdict in the case at hand. . . . Harmless-error review looks, we have said, to the basis on which "the jury *actually rested* its verdict." Yates v. Evatt, 500 U.S. ___, ___ (1991) (emphasis added). The inquiry, in other words, is not whether, in a trial that occurred without the error, a guilty verdict would surely have been rendered, but whether the guilty verdict actually rendered in *this* trial was surely unattributable to the error. That must be so, because to hypothesize a guilty verdict that was never in fact rendered—no matter how inescapable the findings to support that verdict might be—would violate the jury-trial guarantee. . . .

Once the proper role of an appellate court engaged in the *Chapman* inquiry is understood, the illogic of harmless-error review in the present case becomes evident. Since, for the reasons described above, there has been no jury verdict within the meaning of the Sixth Amendment, the entire premise of *Chapman* review is simply absent. There being no jury verdict of guilty-beyond-a-reasonable-doubt, the question whether the *same* verdict of guilty-beyond-a-reasonable-doubt would have been rendered absent the constitutional error is utterly meaningless. There is no *object*, so to speak, upon which harmless-error scrutiny can operate. The most an appellate court can conclude is that a jury *would surely have found* petitioner guilty beyond a reasonable doubt—not that the jury's actual finding of guilty beyond a reasonable doubt *would surely not have been different* absent the constitutional error. That is not enough. . . . The Sixth Amendment requires more than appellate speculation about a hypothetical jury's action, or else directed verdicts for the State would be sustainable on appeal; it requires an actual jury finding of guilty. . . .

Insofar as the possibility of harmless-error review is concerned, the jury-instruction error in this case is quite different from the jury-instruction error of erecting a presumption regarding an element of the offense. A mandatory presumption—for example, the presumption that a person intends the ordinary consequences of his voluntary acts—violates the Fourteenth Amendment, because it may relieve the State of its burden of proving all elements of the offense. . . . But "[w]hen a jury is instructed to presume malice from predicate facts, it still must find the existence of those facts beyond a reasonable doubt." Rose v. Clark, 478 U.S. 570, 580 (1986). And when the latter facts "are so closely related to the ultimate fact to be presumed that no rational jury could find those facts without also finding that ultimate fact, making those findings is functionally equivalent to finding the element required to be presumed." Carella v. California, 491 U.S. 263, 271 (1989) (Scalia, J., concurring in judgment). . . . A reviewing court may thus be able to conclude that the presumption played no significant role in the finding of guilt beyond a reasonable doubt. . . . But the essential connection to a "beyond-a-reasonable-doubt" factual finding cannot be made where the instructional error consists of a misdescription of the burden of proof, which vitiates *all* the jury's findings. A reviewing court can only engage in pure speculation—its view of what a reasonable jury would have done. And when it does that, "the wrong entity judge[s] the defendant guilty." *Rose,* supra, at 578.

Another mode of analysis leads to the same conclusion that harmless-error analysis does not apply: In [Arizona v.] *Fulminante,* [499 U.S. ___ (1991)], we distinguished between, on the one hand, "structural defects in the constitution of the trial mechanism, which defy analysis by 'harmless-error' standards," and, on the other hand, trial errors which occur "during the presentation of the case to the jury, and which may therefore be quantitatively assessed in the context of other evidence presented." *Fulminante,* supra, at ___, ___ (slip op., at 6, 8). Denial of the right to a jury verdict of guilt beyond a reasonable doubt is certainly an error of the former sort, the jury guarantee being a "basic protectio[n]" whose precise effects are unmeasurable, but without which a criminal trial cannot reliably serve its function, *Rose,* supra, at 577. The right to trial by jury reflects, we have said, "a profound judgment about the way in which law should be enforced and justice administered." Duncan v. Louisiana, 391 U.S., at 155. The deprivation of that right, with consequences that are necessarily unquantifiable and indeterminate, unquestionably qualifies as "structural error."

The judgment of the Supreme Court of Louisiana is reversed, and the case is remanded for proceedings not inconsistent with this opinion.

It is so ordered.[*]

[*] Chief Justice Rehnquist wrote a concurring opinion.

14. TRIAL

ILLINOIS v. ALLEN

397 U.S. 337, 90 S.Ct. 1057, 25 L.Ed.2d 353 (1970).

MR. JUSTICE BLACK delivered the opinion of the Court.

The Confrontation Clause of the Sixth Amendment to the United States Constitution provides that: "In all criminal prosecutions, the accused shall enjoy the right ... to be confronted with the witnesses against him ...." We have held that the Fourteenth Amendment makes the guarantees of this clause obligatory upon the States.... One of the most basic of the rights guaranteed by the Confrontation Clause is the accused's right to be present in the courtroom at every stage of his trial.... The question presented in this case is whether an accused can claim the benefit of this constitutional right to remain in the courtroom while at the same time he engages in speech and conduct which is so noisy, disorderly, and disruptive that it is exceedingly difficult or wholly impossible to carry on the trial.

The issue arose in the following way. The respondent, Allen, was convicted by an Illinois jury of armed robbery and was sentenced to serve 10 to 30 years in the Illinois State Penitentiary. The evidence against him showed that on August 12, 1956, he entered a tavern in Illinois and, after ordering a drink, took $200 from the bartender at gunpoint. The Supreme Court of Illinois affirmed his conviction, People v. Allen, 37 Ill.2d 167, 226 N.E.2d 1 (1967), and this Court denied certiorari. 389 U.S. 907 (1967). Later Allen filed a petition for a writ of habeas corpus in federal court alleging that he had been wrongfully deprived by the Illinois trial judge of his constitutional right to remain present throughout his trial. Finding no constitutional violation, the District Court declined to issue the writ. The Court of Appeals reversed, 413 F.2d 232 (1969), Judge Hastings dissenting.

The facts surrounding Allen's expulsion from the courtroom are set out in the Court of Appeals' opinion sustaining Allen's contention:

> "After his indictment and during the pretrial stage, the petitioner [Allen] refused court-appointed counsel and indicated to the trial court on several occasions that he wished to conduct his own defense. After considerable argument by the petitioner, the trial judge told him, 'I'll let you be your own lawyer, but I'll ask Mr. Kelly [court-appointed counsel] [to] sit in and protect the record for you, insofar as possible.'

"The trial began on September 9, 1957. After the State's Attorney had accepted the first four jurors following their voir dire examination, the petitioner began examining the first juror and continued at great length. Finally, the trial judge interrupted the petitioner, requesting him to confine his questions solely to matters relating to the prospective juror's qualifications. At that point, the petitioner started to argue with the judge in a most abusive and disrespectful manner. At last, and seemingly in desperation, the judge asked appointed counsel to proceed with the examination of the jurors. The petitioner continued to talk, proclaiming that the appointed attorney was not going to act as his lawyer. He terminated his remarks by saying, 'When I go out for lunchtime, you're [the judge] going to be a corpse here.' At that point he tore the file which his attorney had and threw the papers on the floor. The trial judge thereupon stated to the petitioner, 'One more outbreak of that sort and I'll remove you from the courtroom.' This warning had no effect on the petitioner. He continued to talk back to the judge, saying, 'There's not going to be no trial, either. I'm going to sit here and you're going to talk and you can bring your shackles out and straight jacket and put them on me and tape my mouth, but it will do no good because there's not going to be no trial.' After more abusive remarks by the petitioner, the trial judge ordered the trial to proceed in the petitioner's absence. The petitioner was removed from the courtroom. The voir dire examination then continued and the jury was selected in the absence of the petitioner.

"After a noon recess and before the jury was brought into the courtroom, the petitioner, appearing before the judge, complained about the fairness of the trial and his appointed attorney. He also said he wanted to be present in the court during his trial. In reply, the judge said that the petitioner would be permitted to remain in the courtroom if he 'behaved [himself] and [did] not interfere with the introduction of the case.' The jury was brought in and seated. Counsel for the petitioner then moved to exclude the witnesses from the courtroom. The [petitioner] protested this effort on the part of his attorney, saying: 'There is going to be no proceeding. I'm going to start talking and I'm going to keep on talking all through the trial. There's not going to be no trial like this. I want my sister and my friends here in court to testify for me.' The trial judge thereupon ordered the petitioner removed from the courtroom." 413 F.2d, at 233–234.

After this second removal, Allen remained out of the courtroom during the presentation of the State's case-in-chief, except that he was brought in on several occasions for purposes of identification. During one of these latter appearances, Allen responded to one of the judge's questions with vile and abusive language. After the prosecution's case had been presented, the trial judge reiterated his promise to Allen that he could return to the courtroom whenever he agreed to conduct himself properly. Allen gave some assurances of proper conduct and was permitted to be present through the remainder of the trial, principally his defense, which was conducted by his appointed counsel.

The Court of Appeals went on to hold that the Supreme Court of Illinois was wrong in ruling that Allen had by his conduct relinquished his constitutional right to be present....

The Court of Appeals felt that the defendant's Sixth Amendment right to be present at his own trial was so "absolute" that, no matter how unruly or disruptive the defendant's conduct might be, he could never be held to have lost that right so long as he continued to insist upon it, as Allen clearly did. Therefore the Court of Appeals concluded that a trial judge could never expel a defendant from his own trial and that the judge's ultimate remedy when faced with an obstreperous defendant like Allen who determines to make his trial impossible is to bind and gag him. We cannot agree that the Sixth Amendment, the cases upon which the Court of Appeals relied, or any other cases of this Court so handicap a trial judge in conducting a criminal trial. The broad dicta ... that a trial can never continue in the defendant's absence have been expressly rejected.... We accept instead the statement of Mr. Justice Cardozo who, speaking for the Court in Snyder v. Massachusetts, 291 U.S. 97, 106 (1934), said: "No doubt the privilege [of personally confronting witnesses] may be lost by consent or at times even by misconduct." Although mindful that courts must indulge every reasonable presumption against the loss of constitutional rights ... we explicitly hold today that a defendant can lose his right to be present at trial if, after he has been warned by the judge that he will be removed if he continues his disruptive behavior, he nevertheless insists on conducting himself in a manner so disorderly, disruptive, and disrespectful of the court that his trial cannot be carried on with him in the courtroom. Once lost, the right to be present can, of course, be reclaimed as soon as the defendant is willing to conduct himself consistently with the decorum and respect inherent in the concept of courts and judicial proceedings.

It is essential to the proper administration of criminal justice that dignity, order, and decorum be the hallmarks of all court proceedings in our country. The flagrant disregard in the courtroom of elementary standards of proper conduct should not and cannot be tolerated. We believe trial judges confronted with disruptive, contumacious, stubbornly defiant defendants must be given sufficient discretion to meet the circumstances of each case. No one formula for maintaining the appropriate courtroom atmosphere will be best in all situations. We think there are at least three constitutionally permissible ways for a trial judge to handle an obstreperous defendant like Allen: (1) bind and gag him, thereby keeping him present; (2) cite him for contempt; (3) take him out of the courtroom until he promises to conduct himself properly.

I

Trying a defendant for a crime while he sits bound and gagged before the judge and jury would to an extent comply with that part of the Sixth Amendment's purposes that accords the defendant an opportunity to confront the witnesses at the trial. But even to contemplate such a technique, much less see it, arouses a feeling that no person should be tried while shackled and gagged except as a last resort. Not only is it possible that the sight of shackles and gags might have a significant effect on the jury's feelings about the defendant, but the use of this technique is itself something of an affront to the very dignity and decorum of judicial proceedings that the judge is seeking to uphold. Moreover, one of the defendant's primary advantages of being present at the trial, his ability to communicate with his counsel, is greatly reduced when the defendant is in a condition of total physical restraint. It is in part because of these inherent disadvantages and limitations in this method of dealing with disorderly defendants that we decline to hold with the Court of Appeals that a defendant cannot under any possible circumstances be deprived of his right to be present at trial. However, in some situations which we need not attempt to foresee, binding and gagging might possibly be the fairest and most reasonable way to handle a defendant who acts as Allen did here.

II

In a footnote the Court of Appeals suggested the possible availability of contempt of court as a remedy to make Allen behave in his robbery trial, and it is true that citing or threatening to cite a contumacious defendant for criminal contempt might in itself be sufficient to make a defendant stop interrupting a trial. If so, the problem would be solved easily, and the defendant could remain in the courtroom. Of course, if the defendant is determined to prevent *any* trial, then a court in attempting to try the defendant for contempt is still confronted with the identical dilemma that the Illinois court faced in this case. And criminal contempt has obvious limitations as a sanction when the defendant is charged with a crime so serious that a very severe sentence such as death or life imprisonment is likely to be imposed. In such a case the defendant might not be affected by a mere contempt sentence when he ultimately faces a far more serious sanction. Nevertheless, the contempt remedy should be borne in mind by a judge in the circumstances of this case.

Another aspect of the contempt remedy is the judge's power, when exercised consistently with state and federal law, to imprison an unruly defendant such as Allen for civil contempt and discontinue the trial until such time as the defendant promises to behave

himself. This procedure is consistent with the defendant's right to
be present at trial, and yet it avoids the serious shortcomings of the
use of shackles and gags. It must be recognized, however, that a
defendant might conceivably, as a matter of calculated strategy, elect
to spend a prolonged period in confinement for contempt in the
hope that adverse witnesses might be unavailable after a lapse of
time. A court must guard against allowing a defendant to profit
from his own wrong in this way.

III

The trial court in this case decided under the circumstances to
remove the defendant from the courtroom and to continue his trial
in his absence until and unless he promised to conduct himself in a
manner befitting an American courtroom. As we said earlier, we
find nothing unconstitutional about this procedure. Allen's behavior was clearly of such an extreme and aggravated nature as to
justify either his removal from the courtroom or his total physical
restraint. Prior to his removal he was repeatedly warned by the trial
judge that he would be removed from the courtroom if he persisted
in his unruly conduct, and, as Judge Hastings observed in his
dissenting opinion, the record demonstrates that Allen would not
have been at all dissuaded by the trial judge's use of his criminal
contempt powers. Allen was constantly informed that he could
return to the trial when he would agree to conduct himself in an
orderly manner. Under these circumstances we hold that Allen lost
his right guaranteed by the Sixth and Fourteenth Amendments to be
present throughout his trial.

IV

It is not pleasant to hold that the respondent Allen was
properly banished from the court for a part of his own trial. But
our courts, palladiums of liberty as they are, cannot be treated
disrespectfully with impunity. Nor can the accused be permitted by
his disruptive conduct indefinitely to avoid being tried on the
charges brought against him. It would degrade our country and
our judicial system to permit our courts to be bullied, insulted, and
humiliated and their orderly progress thwarted and obstructed by
defendants brought before them charged with crimes. As guardians
of the public welfare, our state and federal judicial systems strive to
administer equal justice to the rich and the poor, the good and the
bad, the native and foreign born of every race, nationality, and
religion. Being manned by humans, the courts are not perfect and
are bound to make some errors. But, if our courts are to remain
what the Founders intended, the citadels of justice, their proceedings cannot and must not be infected with the sort of scurrilous,
abusive language and conduct paraded before the Illinois trial judge
in this case. The record shows that the Illinois judge at all times
conducted himself with that dignity, decorum, and patience that

befit a judge. Even in holding that the trial judge had erred, the Court of Appeals praised his "commendable patience under severe provocation."

We do not hold that removing this defendant from his own trial was the only way the Illinois judge could have constitutionally solved the problem he had. We do hold, however, that there is nothing whatever in this record to show that the judge did not act completely within his discretion. Deplorable as it is to remove a man from his own trial, even for a short time, we hold that the judge did not commit legal error in doing what he did.

The judgment of the Court of Appeals is

Reversed.[*]

[*] Justice Brennan wrote a concurring opinion. Justice Douglas wrote an opinion, stating that the court should not have reached the merits of the case on a stale record.

ESTELLE v. WILLIAMS

425 U.S. 501, 96 S.Ct. 1691, 48 L.Ed.2d 126 (1976).

MR. CHIEF JUSTICE BURGER delivered the opinion of the Court.

We granted certiorari in this case to determine whether an accused who is compelled to wear identifiable prison clothing at his trial by a jury is denied due process or equal protection of the laws.

In November 1970, respondent Williams was convicted in state court in Harris County, Tex., for assault with intent to commit murder with malice. The crime occurred during an altercation between respondent and his former landlord on the latter's property. The evidence showed that respondent returned to the apartment complex where he had formerly resided to visit a female tenant. While there, respondent and his former landlord became involved in a quarrel. Heated words were exchanged, and a fight ensued. Respondent struck the landlord with a knife in the neck, chest, and abdomen, severely wounding him.

Unable to post bond, respondent was held in custody while awaiting trial. When he learned that he was to go on trial, respondent asked an officer at the jail for his civilian clothes. This request was denied. As a result, respondent appeared at trial in clothes that were distinctly marked as prison issue. Neither respondent nor his counsel raised an objection to the prison attire at any time.

A jury returned a verdict of guilty on the charge of assault with intent to murder with malice. The Texas Court of Criminal Appeals affirmed the conviction. Williams v. State, 477 S.W.2d 24 (1972). Williams then sought release in the United States District Court on a petition for a writ of habeas corpus. Although holding that requiring a defendant to stand trial in prison garb was inherently unfair, the District Court denied relief on the ground that the error was harmless.

The Court of Appeals reversed. . . . The Fifth Circuit disagreed with the District Court solely on the issue of harmless error.

(1)

The right to a fair trial is a fundamental liberty secured by the Fourteenth Amendment. . . . The presumption of innocence, although not articulated in the Constitution, is a basic component of a fair trial under our system of criminal justice. . . .

To implement the presumption, courts must be alert to factors that may undermine the fairness of the fact-finding process. In the administration of criminal justice, courts must carefully guard against dilution of the principle that guilt is to be established by probative evidence and beyond a reasonable doubt. ...

The actual impact of a particular practice on the judgment of jurors cannot always be fully determined. But this Court has left no doubt that the probability of deleterious effects on fundamental rights calls for close judicial scrutiny. ... Courts must do the best they can to evaluate the likely effects of a particular procedure, based on reason, principle, and common human experience.

The potential effects of presenting an accused before the jury in prison attire need not, however, be measured in the abstract. Courts have, with few exceptions, determined that an accused should not be compelled to go to trial in prison or jail clothing because of the possible impairment of the presumption so basic to the adversary system. ... The American Bar Association's Standards for Criminal Justice also disapprove the practice.... This is a recognition that the constant reminder of the accused's condition implicit in such distinctive, identifiable attire may affect a juror's judgment. The defendant's clothing is so likely to be a continuing influence throughout the trial that, not unlike placing a jury in the custody of deputy sheriffs who were also witnesses for the prosecution, an unacceptable risk is presented of impermissible factors coming into play. ...

That such factors cannot always be avoided is manifest in Illinois v. Allen, 397 U.S. 337 (1970), where we expressly recognized that "the sight of shackles and gags might have a significant effect on the jury's feelings about the defendant ...," id., at 344; yet the Court upheld the practice when necessary to control a contumacious defendant. For that reason, the Court authorized removal of a disruptive defendant from the courtroom or, alternatively, binding and gagging of the accused until he agrees to conduct himself properly in the courtroom.

Unlike physical restraints, permitted under *Allen,* supra, compelling an accused to wear jail clothing furthers no essential state policy. That it may be more convenient for jail administrators, a factor quite unlike the substantial need to impose physical restraints upon contumacious defendants, provides no justification for the practice. Indeed, the State of Texas asserts no interest whatever in maintaining this procedure.

Similarly troubling is the fact that compelling the accused to stand trial in jail garb operates usually against only those who cannot post bail prior to trial. Persons who can secure release are not subjected to this condition. To impose the condition on one category of defendants, over objection, would be repugnant to the concept of equal justice embodied in the Fourteenth Amendment.
...

(2)

The Fifth Circuit in this as well as in prior decisions, has not purported to adopt a per se rule invalidating all convictions where a defendant had appeared in identifiable prison clothes. That court has held, for instance, that the harmless-error doctrine is applicable to this line of cases. . . .

In other situations, when, for example, the accused is being tried for an offense committed in confinement, or in an attempted escape, courts have refused to find error in the practice. . . .

Consequently, the courts have refused to embrace a mechanical rule vitiating any conviction, regardless of the circumstances, where the accused appeared before the jury in prison garb. Instead, they have recognized that the particular evil proscribed is compelling a defendant, against his will, to be tried in jail attire. The reason for this judicial focus upon compulsion is simple; instances frequently arise where a defendant prefers to stand trial before his peers in prison garments. The cases show, for example, that it is not an uncommon defense tactic to produce the defendant in jail clothes in the hope of eliciting sympathy from the jury. . . . This is apparently an accepted practice in Texas courts . . . including the court where respondent was tried.

Courts have therefore required an accused to object to being tried in jail garments, just as he must invoke or abandon other rights. . . .

(3)

The record is clear that no objection was made to the trial judge concerning the jail attire either before or at any time during the trial. This omission plainly did not result from any lack of appreciation of the issue, for respondent had raised the question with the jail attendant prior to trial. At trial, defense counsel expressly referred to respondent's attire during *voir dire*. The trial judge was thus informed that respondent's counsel was fully conscious of the situation.

Despite respondent's failure to raise the issue at trial, the Court of Appeals held:

> "Waiver of the objection cannot be inferred merely from failure to object if trial in prison garb is customary in the jurisdiction." 500 F.2d, at 208.

The District Court had concluded that at the time of respondent's trial the majority of nonbailed defendants in Harris County were indeed tried in jail clothes. From this, the Court of Appeals concluded that the practice followed in respondent's case was customary. . . .

However, that analysis ignores essential facts adduced at the evidentiary hearing. Notwithstanding the evidence as to the general practice in Harris County, there was no finding that nonbailed defendants were compelled to stand trial in prison garments if timely objection was made to the trial judge. On the contrary, the District Court concluded that the practice of the particular judge presiding in respondent's case was to permit any accused who so desired to change into civilian clothes. . . .

The state judge's policy was confirmed at the evidentiary hearing by the prosecutor and by a defense attorney who practiced in the judge's court.

Significantly, at the evidentiary hearing respondent's trial counsel did not intimate that he feared any adverse consequences attending an objection to the procedure. There is nothing to suggest that there would have been any prejudicial effect on defense counsel had he made objection, given the decisions on this point in that jurisdiction. . . . Prior Texas cases had made it clear that an objection should be interposed. . . .

Nothing in this record, therefore, warrants a conclusion that respondent was compelled to stand trial in jail garb or that there was sufficient reason to excuse the failure to raise the issue before trial. Nor can the trial judge be faulted for not asking the respondent or his counsel whether he was deliberately going to trial in jail clothes. To impose this requirement suggests that the trial judge operates under the same burden here as he would in the situation in Johnson v. Zerbst, 304 U.S. 458 (1938), where the issue concerned whether the accused willingly stood trial without the benefit of counsel. Under our adversary system, once a defendant has the assistance of counsel the vast array of trial decisions, strategic and tactical, which must be made before and during trial rests with the accused and his attorney. Any other approach would rewrite the duties of trial judges and counsel in our legal system.

Accordingly, although the State cannot, consistently with the Fourteenth Amendment, compel an accused to stand trial before a jury while dressed in identifiable prison clothes, the failure to make an objection to the court as to being tried in such clothes, for whatever reason, is sufficient to negate the presence of compulsion necessary to establish a constitutional violation.

The judgment of the Court of Appeals is therefore reversed, and the cause is remanded for further proceedings consistent with this opinion.

Reversed and remanded.[*]

[*] Justice Powell wrote a concurring opinion, which Justice Stewart joined. Justice Brennan wrote a dissenting opinion, which Justice Marshall joined.

SHEPPARD v. MAXWELL

384 U.S. 333, 86 S.Ct. 1507, 16 L.Ed.2d 600 (1966).

MR. JUSTICE CLARK delivered the opinion of the Court.

This federal habeas corpus application involves the question whether Sheppard was deprived of a fair trial in his state conviction for the second-degree murder of his wife because of the trial judge's failure to protect Sheppard sufficiently from the massive, pervasive and prejudicial publicity that attended his prosecution.[1] The United States District Court held that he was not afforded a fair trial and granted the writ subject to the State's right to put Sheppard to trial again, 231 F.Supp. 37 (D.C.S.D.Ohio 1964). The Court of Appeals for the Sixth Circuit reversed by a divided vote, 346 F.2d 707 (1965). We granted certiorari, 382 U.S. 916 (1965). We have concluded that Sheppard did not receive a fair trial consistent with the Due Process Clause of the Fourteenth Amendment and, therefore, reverse the judgment.

I

Marilyn Sheppard, petitioner's pregnant wife, was bludgeoned to death in the upstairs bedroom of their lake-shore home in Bay Village, Ohio, a suburb of Cleveland. On the day of the tragedy, July 4, 1954, Sheppard pieced together for several local officials the following story: He and his wife had entertained neighborhood friends, the Aherns, on the previous evening at their home. After dinner they watched television in the living room. Sheppard became drowsy and dozed off to sleep on a couch. Later, Marilyn partially awoke him saying that she was going to bed. The next thing he remembered was hearing his wife cry out in the early morning hours. He hurried upstairs and in the dim light from the hall saw a "form" standing next to his wife's bed. As he struggled with the "form" he was struck on the back of the neck and rendered unconscious. On regaining his senses he found himself on the floor next to his wife's bed. He rose, looked at her, took her pulse and "felt that she was gone." He then went to his son's room and found him unmolested. Hearing a noise he hurried downstairs. He saw a "form" running out the door and pursued it to the lake shore. He grappled with it on the beach and again lost consciousness. Upon his recovery he was lying face down with the lower portion of his body in the water. He returned to his home,

---

1. Sheppard was convicted in 1954 in the Court of Common Pleas of Cuyahoga County, Ohio. His conviction was affirmed by the Court of Appeals for Cuyahoga County, 100 Ohio App. 345, 128 N.E.2d 471 (1955), and the Ohio Supreme Court, 165 Ohio St. 293, 135 N.E.2d 340 (1956). We denied certiorari on the original application for review. 352 U.S. 910 (1956).

---

checked the pulse on his wife's neck, and "determined or thought that she was gone." He then went downstairs and called a neighbor, Mayor Houk of Bay Village. The Mayor and his wife came over at once, found Sheppard slumped in an easy chair downstairs and asked, "What happened?" Sheppard replied: "I don't know but somebody ought to try to do something for Marilyn." Mrs. Houk immediately went up to the bedroom. The Mayor told Sheppard, "Get hold of yourself. Can you tell me what happened?" Sheppard then related the above-outlined events. After Mrs. Houk discovered the body, the Mayor called the local police, Dr. Richard Sheppard, petitioner's brother, and the Aherns. The local police were the first to arrive. They in turn notified the Coroner and Cleveland police. Richard Sheppard then arrived, determined that Marilyn was dead, examined his brother's injuries, and removed him to the nearby clinic operated by the Sheppard family. When the Coroner, the Cleveland police and other officials arrived, the house and surrounding area were thoroughly searched, the rooms of the house were photographed, and many persons, including the Houks and the Aherns, were interrogated. The Sheppard home and premises were taken into "protective custody" and remained so until after the trial.[4]

From the outset officials focused suspicion on Sheppard. After a search of the house and premises on the morning of the tragedy, Dr. Gerber, the Coroner, is reported—and it is undenied—to have told his men, "Well, it is evident the doctor did this, so let's go get the confession out of him." He proceeded to interrogate and examine Sheppard while the latter was under sedation in his hospital room. On the same occasion, the Coroner was given the clothes Sheppard wore at the time of the tragedy together with the personal items in them. Later that afternoon Chief Eaton and two Cleveland police officers interrogated Sheppard at some length, confronting him with evidence and demanding explanations. Asked by Officer Shotke to take a lie detector test, Sheppard said he would if it were reliable. Shotke replied that it was "infallible" and "you might as well tell us all about it now." At the end of the interrogation Shotke told Sheppard: "I think you killed your wife." Still later in the same afternoon a physician sent by the Coroner was permitted to make a detailed examination of Sheppard. Until the Coroner's inquest on July 22, at which time he was subpoenaed, Sheppard made himself available for frequent and extended questioning without the presence of an attorney.

On July 7, the day of Marilyn Sheppard's funeral, a newspaper story appeared in which Assistant County Attorney Mahon—later the chief prosecutor of Sheppard—sharply criticized the refusal of the Sheppard family to permit his immediate questioning. From there on headline stories repeatedly stressed Sheppard's lack of coopera-

---

4. But newspaper photographers and reporters were permitted access to Sheppard's home from time to time and took pictures throughout the premises.

tion with the police and other officials. Under the headline "Testify Now In Death, Bay Doctor Is Ordered," one story described a visit by Coroner Gerber and four police officers to the hospital on July 8. When Sheppard insisted that his lawyer be present, the Coroner wrote out a subpoena and served it on him. Sheppard then agreed to submit to questioning without counsel and the subpoena was torn up. The officers questioned him for several hours. On July 9, Sheppard, at the request of the Coroner, re-enacted the tragedy at his home before the Coroner, police officers, and a group of newsmen, who apparently were invited by the Coroner. The home was locked so that Sheppard was obliged to wait outside until the Coroner arrived. Sheppard's performance was reported in detail by the news media along with photographs. The newspapers also played up Sheppard's refusal to take a lie detector test and "the protective ring" thrown up by his family. Front-page newspaper headlines announced on the same day that "Doctor Balks At Lie Test; Retells Story." A column opposite that story contained an "exclusive" interview with Sheppard headlined: " 'Loved My Wife, She Loved Me,' Sheppard Tells News Reporter." The next day, another headline story disclosed that Sheppard had "again late yesterday refused to take a lie detector test" and quoted an Assistant County Attorney as saying that "at the end of a nine-hour questioning of Dr. Sheppard, I felt he was now ruling [a test] out completely." But subsequent newspaper articles reported that the Coroner was still pushing Sheppard for a lie detector test. More stories appeared when Sheppard would not allow authorities to inject him with "truth serum."[5]

On the 20th, the "editorial artillery" opened fire with a front-page charge that somebody is "getting away with murder." The editorial attributed the ineptness of the investigation to "friendships, relationships, hired lawyers, a husband who ought to have been subjected instantly to the same third-degree to which any other person under similar circumstances is subjected . . . ." The following day, July 21, another page-one editorial was headed: "Why No Inquest? Do It Now, Dr. Gerber." The Coroner called an inquest the same day and subpoenaed Sheppard. It was staged the next day in a school gymnasium; the Coroner presided with the County Prosecutor as his advisor and two detectives as bailiffs. In the front of the room was a long table occupied by reporters, television and radio personnel, and broadcasting equipment. The hearing was broadcast with live microphones placed at the Coroner's seat and the witness stand. A swarm of reporters and photographers attended. Sheppard was brought into the room by police who searched him in full view of several hundred spectators. Sheppard's counsel were present during the three-day inquest but

---

5. At the same time, the newspapers reported that other possible suspects had been "cleared" by lie detector tests. One of these persons was quoted as saying that he could not understand why an innocent man would refuse to take such a test.

were not permitted to participate. When Sheppard's chief counsel attempted to place some documents in the record, he was forcibly ejected from the room by the Coroner, who received cheers, hugs, and kisses from ladies in the audience. Sheppard was questioned for five and one-half hours about his actions on the night of the murder, his married life, and a love affair with Susan Hayes.[6] At the end of the hearing the Coroner announced that he "could" order Sheppard held for the grand jury, but did not do so.

Throughout this period the newspapers emphasized evidence that tended to incriminate Sheppard and pointed out discrepancies in his statements to authorities. At the same time, Sheppard made many public statements to the press and wrote feature articles asserting his innocence.[7] During the inquest on July 26, a headline in large type stated: "Kerr [Captain of the Cleveland Police] Urges Sheppard's Arrest." In the story, Detective McArthur "disclosed that scientific tests at the Sheppard home have definitely established that the killer washed off a trail of blood from the murder bedroom to the downstairs section," a circumstance casting doubt on Sheppard's accounts of the murder. No such evidence was produced at trial. The newspapers also delved into Sheppard's personal life. Articles stressed his extramarital love affairs as a motive for the crime. The newspapers portrayed Sheppard as a Lothario, fully explored his relationship with Susan Hayes, and named a number of other women who were allegedly involved with him. The testimony at trial never showed that Sheppard had any illicit relationships besides the one with Susan Hayes.

On July 28, an editorial entitled "Why Don't Police Quiz Top Suspect" demanded that Sheppard be taken to police headquarters. It described him in the following language:

> "Now proved under oath to be a liar, still free to go about his business, shielded by his family, protected by a smart lawyer who has made monkeys of the police and authorities, carrying a gun part of the time, left free to do whatever he pleases . . . ."

A front-page editorial on July 30 asked: "Why Isn't Sam Sheppard in Jail?" It was later titled "Quit Stalling—Bring Him In." After calling Sheppard "the most unusual murder suspect ever seen around these parts" the article said that "[e]xcept for some superficial questioning during Coroner Sam Gerber's inquest he has been scot-free of any official grilling . . ." It asserted that he was "surrounded by an iron curtain of protection [and] concealment."

That night at 10 o'clock Sheppard was arrested at his father's home on a charge of murder. He was taken to the Bay Village City

---

6. The newspapers had heavily emphasized Sheppard's illicit affair with Susan Hayes, and the fact that he had initially lied about it.

7. A number of articles calculated to evoke sympathy for Sheppard were printed,

such as the letters Sheppard wrote to his son while in jail. These stories often appeared together with news coverage which was unfavorable to him.

Hall where hundreds of people, newscasters, photographers and reporters were awaiting his arrival. He was immediately arraigned—having been denied a temporary delay to secure the presence of counsel—and bound over to the grand jury.

The publicity then grew in intensity until his indictment on August 17. Typical of the coverage during this period is a front-page interview entitled: "DR. SAM: 'I Wish There Was Something I Could Get Off My Chest—but There Isn't.'" Unfavorable publicity included items such as a cartoon of the body of a sphinx with Sheppard's head and the legend below: "'I Will Do Everything In My Power to Help Solve This Terrible Murder.'—Dr. Sam Sheppard." Headlines announced, *inter alia,* that: "Doctor Evidence is Ready for Jury," "Corrigan Tactics Stall Quizzing," "Sheppard 'Gay Set' Is Revealed By Houk," "Blood Is Found In Garage," "New Murder Evidence Is Found, Police Claim," "Dr. Sam Faces Quiz At Jail On Marilyn's Fear Of Him." On August 18, an article appeared under the headline "Dr. Sam Writes His Own Story." And reproduced across the entire front page was a portion of the typed statement signed by Sheppard: "I am not guilty of the murder of my wife, Marilyn. How could I, who have been trained to help people and devoted my life to saving life, commit such a terrible and revolting crime?" We do not detail the coverage further. There are five volumes filled with similar clippings from each of the three Cleveland newspapers covering the period from the murder until Sheppard's conviction in December 1954. The record includes no excerpts from newscasts on radio and television but since space was reserved in the courtroom for these media we assume that their coverage was equally large.

II

With this background the case came on for trial two weeks before the November general election at which the chief prosecutor was a candidate for common pleas judge and the trial judge, Judge Blythin, was a candidate to succeed himself. Twenty-five days before the case was set, 75 veniremen were called as prospective jurors. All three Cleveland newspapers published the names and addresses of the veniremen. As a consequence, anonymous letters and telephone calls, as well as calls from friends, regarding the impending prosecution were received by all of the prospective jurors. The selection of the jury began on October 18, 1954.

The courtroom in which the trial was held measured 26 by 48 feet. A long temporary table was set up inside the bar, in back of the single counsel table. It ran the width of the courtroom, parallel to the bar railing, with one end less than three feet from the jury box. Approximately 20 representatives of newspapers and wire services were assigned seats at this table by the court. Behind the bar railing there were four rows of benches. These seats were likewise assigned by the court for the entire trial. The first row was occupied by representatives of television and radio stations, and the second and third rows by reporters from out-of-town newspapers and magazines. One side of the last row, which accommodated 14 people, was assigned to Sheppard's family and the other to Marilyn's. The public was permitted to fill vacancies in this row on special passes only. Representatives of the news media also used all the rooms on the courtroom floor, including the room where cases were ordinarily called and assigned for trial. Private telephone lines and telegraphic equipment were installed in these rooms so that reports from the trial could be speeded to the papers. Station WSRS was permitted to set up broadcasting facilities on the third floor of the courthouse next door to the jury room, where the jury rested during recesses in the trial and deliberated. Newscasts were made from this room throughout the trial, and while the jury reached its verdict.

On the sidewalk and steps in front of the courthouse, television and newsreel cameras were occasionally used to take motion pictures of the participants in the trial, including the jury and the judge. Indeed, one television broadcast carried a staged interview of the judge as he entered the courthouse. In the corridors outside the courtroom there was a host of photographers and television personnel with flash cameras, portable lights and motion picture cameras. This group photographed the prospective jurors during selection of the jury. After the trial opened, the witnesses, counsel, and jurors were photographed and televised whenever they entered or left the courtroom. Sheppard was brought to the courtroom about 10 minutes before each session began; he was surrounded by reporters and extensively photographed for the newspapers and television. A rule of court prohibited picture-taking in the courtroom during the actual sessions of the court, but no restraints were put on photographers during recesses, which were taken once each morning and afternoon, with a longer period for lunch.

All of these arrangements with the news media and their massive coverage of the trial continued during the entire nine weeks of the trial. The courtroom remained crowded to capacity with representatives of news media. Their movement in and out of the courtroom often caused so much confusion that, despite the loudspeaker system installed in the courtroom, it was difficult for the witnesses and counsel to be heard. Furthermore, the reporters clustered within the bar of the small courtroom made confidential talk among Sheppard and his counsel almost impossible during the proceedings. They frequently had to leave the courtroom to obtain privacy. And many times when counsel wished to raise a point with the judge out of the hearing of the jury it was necessary to move to the judge's chambers. Even then, news media representatives so packed the judge's anteroom that counsel could hardly return from the chambers to the courtroom. The reporters vied with each other to find out what counsel and the judge had discussed, and often these matters later appeared in newspapers accessible to the jury.

The daily record of the proceedings was made available to the newspapers and the testimony of each witness was printed verbatim in the local editions, along with objections of counsel, and rulings by the judge. Pictures of Sheppard, the judge, counsel, pertinent witnesses, and the jury often accompanied the daily newspaper and television accounts. At times the newspapers published photographs of exhibits introduced at the trial, and the rooms of Sheppard's house were featured along with relevant testimony.

The jurors themselves were constantly exposed to the news media. Every juror, except one, testified at *voir dire* to reading about the case in the Cleveland papers or to having heard broadcasts about it. Seven of the 12 jurors who rendered the verdict had one or more Cleveland papers delivered in their home; the remaining jurors were not interrogated on the point. Nor were there questions as to radios or television sets in the jurors' homes, but we must assume that most of them owned such conveniences. As the selection of the jury progressed, individual pictures of prospective members appeared daily. During the trial, pictures of the jury appeared over 40 times in the Cleveland papers alone. The court permitted photographers to take pictures of the jury in the box, and individual pictures of the members in the jury room. One newspaper ran pictures of the jurors at the Sheppard home when they went there to view the scene of the murder. Another paper featured the home life of an alternate juror. The day before the verdict was rendered—while the jurors were at lunch and sequestered by two bailiffs—the jury was separated into two groups to pose for photographs which appeared in the newspapers.

III

We now reach the conduct of the trial. While the intense publicity continued unabated, it is sufficient to relate only the more flagrant episodes:

1. On October 9, 1954, nine days before the case went to trial, an editorial in one of the newspapers criticized defense counsel's random poll of people on the streets as to their opinion of Sheppard's guilt or innocence in an effort to use the resulting statistics to show the necessity for change of venue. The article said the survey "smacks of mass jury tampering," called on defense counsel to drop it, and stated that the bar association should do something about it. It characterized the poll as "non-judicial, non-legal, and nonsense." The article was called to the attention of the court but no action was taken.

2. On the second day of *voir dire* examination a debate was staged and broadcast live over WHK radio. The participants, newspaper reporters, accused Sheppard's counsel of throwing road-

blocks in the way of the prosecution and asserted that Sheppard conceded his guilt by hiring a prominent criminal lawyer. Sheppard's counsel objected to this broadcast and requested a continuance, but the judge denied the motion. When counsel asked the court to give some protection from such events, the judge replied that "WHK doesn't have much coverage," and that "[a]fter all, we are not trying this case by radio or in newspapers or any other means. We confine ourselves seriously to it in this courtroom and do the very best we can."

3. While the jury was being selected, a two-inch headline asked: "But Who Will Speak for Marilyn?" The front-page story spoke of the "perfect face" of the accused. "Study that face as long as you want. Never will you get from it a hint of what might be the answer . . . ." The two brothers of the accused were described as "Prosperous, poised. His two sisters-in-law. Smart, chic, well-groomed. His elderly father. Courtly, reserved. A perfect type for the patriarch of a staunch clan." The author then noted Marilyn Sheppard was "still off stage," and that she was an only child whose mother died when she was very young and whose father had no interest in the case. But the author—through quotes from Detective Chief James McArthur—assured readers that the prosecution's exhibits would speak for Marilyn. "Her story," McArthur stated, "will come into this courtroom through our witnesses." The article ends:

> "Then you realize how what and who is missing from the perfect setting will be supplied.
>
> "How in the Big Case justice will be done.
>
> "Justice to Sam Sheppard.
>
> "And to Marilyn Sheppard."

4. As has been mentioned, the jury viewed the scene of the murder on the first day of the trial. Hundreds of reporters, cameramen and onlookers were there, and one representative of the news media was permitted to accompany the jury while it inspected the Sheppard home. The time of the jury's visit was revealed so far in advance that one of the newspapers was able to rent a helicopter and fly over the house taking pictures of the jurors on their tour.

5. On November 19, a Cleveland police officer gave testimony that tended to contradict details in the written statement Sheppard made to the Cleveland police. Two days later, in a broadcast heard over Station WHK in Cleveland, Robert Considine likened Sheppard to a perjurer and compared the episode to Alger Hiss' confrontation with Whittaker Chambers. Though defense counsel asked the judge to question the jury to ascertain how many heard the broadcast, the court refused to do so. The judge also overruled the motion for continuance based on the same ground, saying:

"Well, I don't know, we can't stop people, in any event, listening to it. It is a matter of free speech, and the court can't control everybody. ... We are not going to harass the jury every morning. ... It is getting to the point where if we do it every morning, we are suspecting the jury. I have confidence in this jury ...."

6. On November 24, a story appeared under an eight-column heading: "Sam Called A 'Jekyll-Hyde' By Marilyn, Cousin To Testify." It related that Marilyn had recently told friends that Sheppard was a "Dr. Jekyll and Mr. Hyde" character. No such testimony was ever produced at the trial. The story went on to announce: "The prosecution has a 'bombshell witness' on tap who will testify to Dr. Sam's display of fiery temper—countering the defense claim that the defendant is a gentle physician with an even disposition." Defense counsel made motions for change of venue, continuance and mistrial, but they were denied. No action was taken by the court.

7. When the trial was in its seventh week, Walter Winchell broadcast over WXEL television and WJW radio that Carole Beasley, who was under arrest in New York City for robbery, had stated that, as Sheppard's mistress, she had borne him a child. The defense asked that the jury be queried on the broadcast. Two jurors admitted in open court that they had heard it. The judge asked each: "Would that have any effect upon your judgment?" Both replied, "No." This was accepted by the judge as sufficient; he merely asked the jury to "pay no attention whatever to that type of scavenging. Let's confine ourselves to this courtroom, if you please." In answer to the motion for mistrial, the judge said:

"Well, even, so, Mr. Corrigan, how are you ever going to prevent those things, in any event? I don't justify them at all. I think it is outrageous, but in a sense, it is outrageous even if there were no trial here. The trial has nothing to do with it in the Court's mind, as far as its outrage is concerned, but—

"MR. CORRIGAN: I don't know what effect it had on the mind of any of these jurors, and I can't find out unless inquiry is made.

"THE COURT: How would you ever, in any jury, avoid that kind of a thing?"

8. On December 9, while Sheppard was on the witness stand he testified that he had been mistreated by Cleveland detectives after his arrest. Although he was not at the trial, Captain Kerr of the Homicide Bureau issued a press statement denying Sheppard's allegations which appeared under the headline: " 'Bare-faced Liar,' Kerr Says of Sam." Captain Kerr never appeared as a witness at the trial.

9. After the case was submitted to the jury, it was sequestered for its deliberations, which took five days and four nights. After the

verdict, defense counsel ascertained that the jurors had been allowed to make telephone calls to their homes every day while they were sequestered at the hotel. Although the telephones had been removed from the jurors' rooms, the jurors were permitted to use the phones in the bailiffs' rooms. The calls were placed by the jurors themselves; no record was kept of the jurors who made calls, the telephone numbers or the parties called. The bailiffs sat in the room where they could hear only the jurors' end of the conversation. The court had not instructed the bailiffs to prevent such calls. By a subsequent motion, defense counsel urged that this ground alone warranted a new trial, but the motion was overruled and no evidence was taken on the question.

IV

The principle that justice cannot survive behind walls of silence has long been reflected in the "Anglo-American distrust for secret trials." In re Oliver, 333 U.S. 257, 268 (1948). A responsible press has always been regarded as the handmaiden of effective judicial administration, especially in the criminal field. Its function in this regard is documented by an impressive record of service over several centuries. The press does not simply publish information about trials but guards against the miscarriage of justice by subjecting the police, prosecutors, and judicial processes to extensive public scrutiny and criticism. This Court has, therefore, been unwilling to place any direct limitations on the freedom traditionally exercised by the news media for "[w]hat transpires in the court room is public property." Craig v. Harney, 331 U.S. 367, 374 (1947). The "unqualified prohibitions laid down by the framers were intended to give to liberty of the press . . . the broadest scope that could be countenanced in an orderly society." Bridges v. California, 314 U.S. 252, 265 (1941). And where there was "no threat or menace to the integrity of the trial," Craig v. Harney, supra, at 377, we have consistently required that the press have a free hand, even though we sometimes deplored its sensationalism.

But the Court has also pointed out that "[l]egal trials are not like elections, to be won through the use of the meeting-hall, the radio, and the newspaper." Bridges v. California, supra, at 271. And the Court has insisted that no one be punished for a crime without "a charge fairly made and fairly tried in a public tribunal free of prejudice, passion, excitement, and tyrannical power." Chambers v. Florida, 309 U.S. 227, 236–237 (1940). "Freedom of discussion should be given the widest range compatible with the essential requirement of the fair and orderly administration of justice." Pennekamp v. Florida, 328 U.S. 331, 347 (1946). But it must not be allowed to divert the trial from the "very purpose of a court system . . . to adjudicate controversies, both criminal and civil, in the calmness and solemnity of the courtroom according to legal procedures." Cox v. Louisiana, 379 U.S. 559, 583 (1965) (Black, J., dissenting). Among these "legal procedures" is the requirement that the jury's verdict be based on evidence received in open court, not from outside sources. Thus, in Marshall v. United States, 360 U.S. 310 (1959), we set aside a federal conviction where the jurors were exposed "through news accounts" to information that was not admitted at trial. We held that the prejudice from such material "may indeed be greater" than when it is part of the prosecution's evidence "for it is then not tempered by protective procedures." At 313. At the same time, we did not consider dispositive the statement of each juror "that he would not be influenced by the news articles, that he could decide the case only on the evidence of record, and that he felt no prejudice against petitioner as a result of the articles." At 312. Likewise, in Irvin v. Dowd, 366 U.S. 717 (1961), even though each juror indicated that he could render an impartial verdict despite exposure to prejudicial newspaper articles, we set aside the conviction holding:

> "With his life at stake, it is not requiring too much that petitioner be tried in an atmosphere undisturbed by so huge a wave of public passion ...." At 728.

The undeviating rule of this Court was expressed by Mr. Justice Holmes over half a century ago in Patterson v. Colorado, 205 U.S. 454, 462 (1907):

> "The theory of our system is that the conclusions to be reached in a case will be induced only by evidence and argument in open court, and not by any outside influence, whether of private talk or public print."

Moreover, "the burden of showing essential unfairness ... as a demonstrable reality," Adams v. United States ex rel. McCann, 317 U.S. 269, 281 (1942), need not be undertaken when television has exposed the community "repeatedly and in depth to the spectacle of [the accused] personally confessing in detail to the crimes with which he was later to be charged." Rideau v. Louisiana, 373 U.S. 723, 726 (1963). In Turner v. Louisiana, 379 U.S. 466 (1965), two key witnesses were deputy sheriffs who doubled as jury shepherds during the trial. The deputies swore that they had not talked to the jurors about the case, but the Court nonetheless held that,

> "even if it could be assumed that the deputies never did discuss the case directly with any members of the jury, it would be blinking reality not to recognize the extreme prejudice inherent in this continual association ...." At 473.

Only last Term in Estes v. Texas, 381 U.S. 532 (1965), we set aside a conviction despite the absence of any showing of prejudice. We said there:

> "It is true that in most cases involving claims of due process deprivations we require a showing of identifiable prejudice to the accused. Nevertheless, at times a procedure employed by

the State involves such a probability that prejudice will result that it is deemed inherently lacking in due process." At 542–543.

And we cited with approval the language of Mr. Justice Black for the Court in In re Murchison, 349 U.S. 133, 136 (1955), that "our system of law has always endeavored to prevent even the probability of unfairness."

V

It is clear that the totality of circumstances in this case also warrants such an approach. Unlike Estes, Sheppard was not granted a change of venue to a locale away from where the publicity originated; nor was his jury sequestered. The Estes jury saw none of the television broadcasts from the courtroom. On the contrary, the Sheppard jurors were subjected to newspaper, radio and television coverage of the trial while not taking part in the proceedings. They were allowed to go their separate ways outside of the courtroom, without adequate directions not to read or listen to anything concerning the case. The judge's "admonitions" at the beginning of the trial are representative:

> "I would suggest to you and caution you that you do not read any newspapers during the progress of this trial, that you do not listen to radio comments nor watch or listen to television comments, insofar as this case is concerned. You will feel very much better as the trial proceeds .... I am sure that we shall all feel very much better if we do not indulge in any newspaper reading or listening to any comments whatever about the matter while the case is in progress. After it is all over, you can read it all to your heart's content ...."

At intervals during the trial, the judge simply repeated his "suggestions" and "requests" that the jurors not expose themselves to comment upon the case. Moreover, the jurors were thrust into the role of celebrities by the judge's failure to insulate them from reporters and photographers.... The numerous pictures of the jurors, with their addresses, which appeared in the newspapers before and during the trial itself exposed them to expressions of opinion from both cranks and friends. The fact that anonymous letters had been received by prospective jurors should have made the judge aware that this publicity seriously threatened the jurors' privacy.

The press coverage of the Estes trial was not nearly as massive and pervasive as the attention given by the Cleveland newspapers and broadcasting stations to Sheppard's prosecution. Sheppard stood indicted for the murder of his wife; the State was demanding the death penalty. For months the virulent publicity about Sheppard and the murder had made the case notorious. Charges and countercharges were aired in the news media besides those for which Sheppard was called to trial. In addition, only three months before trial, Sheppard was examined for more than five hours without counsel during a three-day inquest which ended in a public brawl. The inquest was televised live from a high school gymnasium seating hundreds of people. Furthermore, the trial began two weeks before a hotly contested election at which both Chief Prosecutor Mahon and Judge Blythin were candidates for judgeships.[9]

While we cannot say that Sheppard was denied due process by the judge's refusal to take precautions against the influence of pretrial publicity alone, the court's later rulings must be considered against the setting in which the trial was held. In light of this background, we believe that the arrangements made by the judge with the news media caused Sheppard to be deprived of that "judicial serenity and calm to which [he] was entitled." Estes v. Texas, supra, at 536. The fact is that bedlam reigned at the courthouse during the trial and newsmen took over practically the entire courtroom, hounding most of the participants in the trial, especially Sheppard. At a temporary table within a few feet of the jury box and counsel table sat some 20 reporters staring at Sheppard and taking notes. The erection of a press table for reporters inside the bar is unprecedented. The bar of the court is reserved for counsel, providing them a safe place in which to keep papers and exhibits, and to confer privately with client and co-counsel. It is designed to protect the witness and the jury from any distractions, intrusions or influences, and to permit bench discussions of the judge's rulings away from the hearing of the public and the jury. Having assigned almost all of the available seats in the courtroom to the news media the judge lost his ability to supervise that environment. The movement of the reporters in and out of the courtroom caused frequent confusion and disruption of the trial. And the record reveals constant commotion within the bar. Moreover, the judge gave the throng of newsmen gathered in the corridors of the courthouse absolute free rein. Participants in the trial, including the jury, were forced to run a gantlet of reporters and photographers each time they entered or left the courtroom. The total lack of consideration for the privacy of the jury was demonstrated by the assignment to a broadcasting station of space next to the jury room on the floor above the courtroom, as well as the fact that jurors were allowed to make telephone calls during their five-day deliberation.

---

9. At the commencement of trial, defense counsel made motions for continuance and change of venue. The judge postponed ruling on these motions until he determined whether an impartial jury could be impaneled. *Voir dire* examination showed that with one exception all members selected for jury service had read something about the case in the newspapers. Since, however, all of the jurors stated that they would not be influenced by what they had read or seen, the judge overruled both of the motions. Without regard to whether the judge's actions in this respect reach dimensions that would justify issuance of the habeas writ, it should be noted that a short continuance would have alleviated any problem with regard to the judicial elections. . . .

VI

There can be no question about the nature of the publicity which surrounded Sheppard's trial. We agree, as did the Court of Appeals, with the findings in Judge Bell's opinion for the Ohio Supreme Court:

> "Murder and mystery, society, sex and suspense were combined in this case in such a manner as to intrigue and captivate the public fancy to a degree perhaps unparalleled in recent annals. Throughout the preindictment investigation, the subsequent legal skirmishes and the nine-week trial, circulation-conscious editors catered to the insatiable interest of the American public in the bizarre. ... In this atmosphere of a 'Roman holiday' for the news media, Sam Sheppard stood trial for his life." 165 Ohio St., at 294, 135 N.E.2d, at 342.

Indeed, every court that has considered this case, save the court that tried it, has deplored the manner in which the news media inflamed and prejudiced the public.

Much of the material printed or broadcast during the trial was never heard from the witness stand, such as the charges that Sheppard had purposely impeded the murder investigation and must be guilty since he had hired a prominent criminal lawyer; that Sheppard was a perjurer; that he had sexual relations with numerous women; that his slain wife had characterized him as a "Jekyll-Hyde"; that he was "a bare-faced liar" because of his testimony as to police treatment; and, finally, that a woman convict claimed Sheppard to be the father of her illegitimate child. As the trial progressed, the newspapers summarized and interpreted the evidence, devoting particular attention to the material that incriminated Sheppard, and often drew unwarranted inferences from testimony. At one point, a front-page picture of Mrs. Sheppard's bloodstained pillow was published after being "doctored" to show more clearly an alleged imprint of a surgical instrument.

Nor is there doubt that this deluge of publicity reached at least some of the jury. On the only occasion that the jury was queried, two jurors admitted in open court to hearing the highly inflammatory charge that a prison inmate claimed Sheppard as the father of her illegitimate child. Despite the extent and nature of the publicity to which the jury was exposed during trial, the judge refused defense counsel's other requests that the jurors be asked whether they had read or heard specific prejudicial comment about the case, including the incidents we have previously summarized. In these circumstances, we can assume that some of this material reached members of the jury....

VII

The court's fundamental error is compounded by the holding that it lacked power to control the publicity about the trial. From the very inception of the proceedings the judge announced that neither he nor anyone else could restrict prejudicial news accounts. And he reiterated this view on numerous occasions. Since he viewed the news media as his target, the judge never considered other means that are often utilized to reduce the appearance of prejudicial material and to protect the jury from outside influence. We conclude that these procedures would have been sufficient to guarantee Sheppard a fair trial and so do not consider what sanctions might be available against a recalcitrant press nor the charges of bias now made against the state trial judge.

The carnival atmosphere at trial could easily have been avoided since the courtroom and courthouse premises are subject to the control of the court. As we stressed in *Estes,* the presence of the press at judicial proceedings must be limited when it is apparent that the accused might otherwise be prejudiced or disadvantaged. Bearing in mind the massive pretrial publicity, the judge should have adopted stricter rules governing the use of the courtroom by newsmen, as Sheppard's counsel requested. The number of reporters in the courtroom itself could have been limited at the first sign that their presence would disrupt the trial. They certainly should not have been placed inside the bar. Furthermore, the judge should have more closely regulated the conduct of newsmen in the courtroom. For instance, the judge belatedly asked them not to handle and photograph trial exhibits lying on the counsel table during recesses.

Secondly, the court should have insulated the witnesses. All of the newspapers and radio stations apparently interviewed prospective witnesses at will, and in many instances disclosed their testimony. A typical example was the publication of numerous statements by Susan Hayes, before her appearance in court, regarding her love affair with Sheppard. Although the witnesses were barred from the courtroom during the trial the full verbatim testimony was available to them in the press. This completely nullified the judge's imposition of the rule....

Thirdly, the court should have made some effort to control the release of leads, information, and gossip to the press by police officers, witnesses, and the counsel for both sides. Much of the information thus disclosed was inaccurate, leading to groundless rumors and confusion. That the judge was aware of his responsibility in this respect may be seen from his warning to Steve Sheppard, the accused's brother, who had apparently made public statements in an attempt to discredit testimony for the prosecution. The judge made this statement in the presence of the jury:

> "Now, the Court wants to say a word. That he was told— he has not read anything about it at all—but he was informed that Dr. Steve Sheppard, who has been granted the privilege of remaining in the court room during the trial, has been trying

the case in the newspapers and making rather uncomplimentary comments about the testimony of the witnesses for the State.

"Let it be now understood that if Dr. Steve Sheppard wishes to use the newspapers to try his case while we are trying it here, he will be barred from remaining in the court room during the progress of the trial if he is to be a witness in the case.

"The Court appreciates he cannot deny Steve Sheppard the right of free speech, but he can deny him the . . . privilege of being in the court room, if he wants to avail himself of that method during the progress of the trial."

Defense counsel immediately brought to the court's attention the tremendous amount of publicity in the Cleveland press that "misrepresented entirely the testimony" in the case. Under such circumstances, the judge should have at least warned the newspapers to check the accuracy of their accounts. And it is obvious that the judge should have further sought to alleviate this problem by imposing control over the statements made to the news media by counsel, witnesses, and especially the Coroner and police officers. The prosecution repeatedly made evidence available to the news media which was never offered in the trial. Much of the "evidence" disseminated in this fashion was clearly inadmissible. The exclusion of such evidence in court is rendered meaningless when news media make it available to the public. For example, the publicity about Sheppard's refusal to take a lie detector test came directly from police officers and the Coroner. The story that Sheppard had been called a "Jekyll-Hyde" personality by his wife was attributed to a prosecution witness. No such testimony was given. The further report that there was "a 'bombshell witness' on tap" who would testify as to Sheppard's "fiery temper" could only have emanated from the prosecution. Moreover, the newspapers described in detail clues that had been found by the police, but not put into the record.

The fact that many of the prejudicial news items can be traced to the prosecution, as well as the defense, aggravates the judge's failure to take any action. . . . Effective control of these sources—concededly within the court's power—might well have prevented the divulgence of inaccurate information, rumors, and accusations that made up much of the inflammatory publicity, at least after Sheppard's indictment.

More specifically, the trial court might well have proscribed extrajudicial statements by any lawyer, party, witness, or court official which divulged prejudicial matters, such as the refusal of Sheppard to submit to interrogation or take any lie detector tests; any statement made by Sheppard to officials; the identity of prospective witnesses or their probable testimony; any belief in guilt or innocence; or like statements concerning the merits of the case.

See State v. Van Duyne, 43 N.J. 369, 389, 204 A.2d 841, 852 (1964), in which the court interpreted Canon 20 of the American Bar Association's Canons of Professional Ethics to prohibit such statements. Being advised of the great public interest in the case, the mass coverage of the press, and the potential prejudicial impact of publicity, the court could also have requested the appropriate city and county officials to promulgate a regulation with respect to dissemination of information about the case by their employees. In addition, reporters who wrote or broadcast prejudicial stories, could have been warned as to the impropriety of publishing material not introduced in the proceedings. The judge was put on notice of such events by defense counsel's complaint about the WHK broadcast on the second day of trial. See p. 346, supra. In this manner, Sheppard's right to a trial free from outside interference would have been given added protection without corresponding curtailment of the news media. Had the judge, the other officers of the court, and the police placed the interest of justice first, the news media would have soon learned to be content with the task of reporting the case as it unfolded in the courtroom—not pieced together from extrajudicial statements.

From the cases coming here we note that unfair and prejudicial news comment on pending trials has become increasingly prevalent. Due process requires that the accused receive a trial by an impartial jury free from outside influences. Given the pervasiveness of modern communications and the difficulty of effacing prejudicial publicity from the minds of the jurors, the trial courts must take strong measures to ensure that the balance is never weighed against the accused. And appellate tribunals have the duty to make an independent evaluation of the circumstances. Of course, there is nothing that proscribes the press from reporting events that transpire in the courtroom. But where there is a reasonable likelihood that prejudicial news prior to trial will prevent a fair trial, the judge should continue the case until the threat abates, or transfer it to another county not so permeated with publicity. In addition, sequestration of the jury was something the judge should have raised *sua sponte* with counsel. If publicity during the proceedings threatens the fairness of the trial, a new trial should be ordered. But we must remember that reversals are but palliatives; the cure lies in those remedial measures that will prevent the prejudice at its inception. The courts must take such steps by rule and regulation that will protect their processes from prejudicial outside interferences. Neither prosecutors, counsel for defense, the accused, witnesses, court staff nor enforcement officers coming under the jurisdiction of the court should be permitted to frustrate its function. Collaboration between counsel and the press as to information affecting the fairness of a criminal trial is not only subject to regulation, but is highly censurable and worthy of disciplinary measures.

Since the state trial judge did not fulfill his duty to protect Sheppard from the inherently prejudicial publicity which saturated the community and to control disruptive influences in the court-room, we must reverse the denial of the habeas petition. The case is remanded to the District Court with instructions to issue the writ and order that Sheppard be released from custody unless the State puts him to its charges again within a reasonable time.

It is so ordered.[*] [**]

[*] Justice Black dissented.

[**] In Nebraska Press Ass'n v. Stuart, 427 U.S. 539 (1976), the Court held that the First Amendment did not permit a prior restraint on publication of news about the criminal trial in question. The case involved a state trial judge's order restraining news media from disseminating information pertaining to evidence highly incriminatory of the accused, in a sensational murder case in a small Nebraska town. The order was effective only until a jury was impanelled. Considering the nature and extent of the pretrial news coverage, the availability of other means to protect the defendant's right to a fair trial, and the likely efficacy of the restraining order, the Court concluded that the "extraordinary" remedy of a prior restraint had not been warranted. In a concurring opinion which Justice Stewart and Justice Marshall joined, Justice Brennan expressed the view that the First Amendment in all circumstances barred prior restraints as a means to ensure a fair trial.

RICHMOND NEWSPAPERS, INC. v. VIRGINIA

448 U.S. 555, 100 S.Ct. 2814, 65 L.Ed.2d 973 (1980).

MR. CHIEF JUSTICE BURGER announced the judgment of the Court and delivered an opinion in which MR. JUSTICE WHITE and MR. JUSTICE STEVENS joined.

The narrow question presented in this case is whether the right of the public and press to attend criminal trials is guaranteed under the United States Constitution.

I

In March 1976, one Stevenson was indicted for the murder of a hotel manager who had been found stabbed to death on December 2, 1975. Tried promptly in July 1976, Stevenson was convicted of second-degree murder in the Circuit Court of Hanover County, Va. The Virginia Supreme Court reversed the conviction in October 1977, holding that a bloodstained shirt purportedly belonging to Stevenson had been improperly admitted into evidence. Stevenson v. Commonwealth, 218 Va. 462, 237 S.E.2d 779.

Stevenson was retried in the same court. This second trial ended in a mistrial on May 30, 1978 when a juror asked to be excused after trial had begun and no alternate was available.

A third trial, which began in the same court on June 6, 1978, also ended in a mistrial. It appears that the mistrial may have been declared because a prospective juror had read about Stevenson's previous trials in a newspaper and had told other prospective jurors about the case before the retrial began. See App. 35a–36a.

Stevenson was tried in the same court for a fourth time beginning on September 11, 1978. Present in the courtroom when the case was called were appellants Wheeler and McCarthy, reporters for appellant Richmond Newspapers, Inc. Before the trial began, counsel for the defendant moved that it be closed to the public:

"[T]here was this woman that was with the family of the deceased when we were here before. She had sat in the Courtroom. I would like to ask that everybody be excluded from the Courtroom because I don't want any information being shuffled back and forth when we have a recess as to what—who testified to what." Trans. of Sept. 11, 1978 Hearing on Defendant's Motion to Close Trial to the Public 2–3.

The trial judge, who had presided over two of the three previous trials, asked if the prosecution had any objection to clearing the courtroom. The prosecutor stated he had no objection and would leave it to the discretion of the court. Id., at 4. Presumably referring to Virginia Code § 19.2–266 (Supp.1980), the trial judge then announced: "[T]he statute gives me that power specifically and the defendant has made the motion." He then ordered "that the Courtroom be kept clear of all parties except the witnesses when they testify." Tr., supra, at 4–5.[2] The record does not show that any objections to the closure order were made by anyone present at the time, including appellants Wheeler and McCarthy.

Later that same day, however, appellants sought a hearing on a motion to vacate the closure order. The trial judge granted the request and scheduled a hearing to follow the close of the day's proceedings. When the hearing began, the court ruled that the hearing was to be treated as part of the trial; accordingly, he again ordered the reporters to leave the courtroom, and they complied.

At the closed hearing, counsel for appellants observed that no evidentiary findings had been made by the court prior to the entry of its closure order and pointed out that the court had failed to consider any other, less drastic measures within its power to ensure a fair trial. Trans. of Sept. 11, 1978 Hearing on Motion to Vacate 11–12. Counsel for appellants argued that constitutional considerations mandated that before ordering closure, the court should first decide that the rights of the defendant could be protected in no other way.

Counsel for defendant Stevenson pointed out that this was the fourth time he was standing trial. He also referred to "difficulty with information between the jurors," and stated that he "didn't want information to leak out," be published by the media, perhaps inaccurately, and then be seen by the jurors. Defense counsel argued that these things, plus the fact that "this is a small community," made this a proper case for closure. Id., at 16–18.

The trial judge noted that counsel for the defendant had made similar statements at the morning hearing. The court also stated:

> "[O]ne of the other points that we take into consideration in this particular Courtroom is layout of the Courtroom. I think that having people in the Courtroom is distracting to the jury. Now, we have to have certain people in here and maybe that's not a very good reason. When we get into our new Court Building, people can sit in the audience so the jury can't see them. The rule of the Court may be different under those circumstances. ..." Id., at 19.

---

2. Virginia Code § 19.2–266 (Supp.1980) provides in part:

"In the trial of all criminal cases, whether the same be felony or misdemeanor cases, the court may, in its discretion, exclude from the trial any persons whose presence would impair the conduct of a fair trial, provided that the right of the accused to a public trial shall not be violated."

The prosecutor again declined comment, and the court summed up by saying:

> "I'm inclined to agree with [defense counsel] that, if I feel that the rights of the defendant are infringed in any way, [when] he makes the motion to do something and it doesn't completely override all rights of everyone else, then I'm inclined to go along with the defendant's motion." Id., at 20.

The court denied the motion to vacate and ordered the trial to continue the following morning "with the press and public excluded." Id., at 27; App. at 21a.

What transpired when the closed trial resumed the next day was disclosed in the following manner by an order of the court entered September 12, 1978:

> "[I]n the absence of the jury, the defendant by counsel made a Motion that a mis-trial be declared, which motion was taken under advisement.
>
> "At the conclusion of the Commonwealth's evidence, the attorney for the defendant moved the Court to strike the Commonwealth's evidence on grounds stated to the record, which Motion was sustained by the Court.
>
> "And the jury having been excused, the Court doth find the accused NOT GUILTY of Murder, as charged in the Indictment, and he was allowed to depart." Id. at 22a.

On September 27, 1978, the trial court granted appellants' motion to intervene *nunc pro tunc* in the Stevenson case. Appellants then petitioned the Virginia Supreme Court for writs of mandamus and prohibition and filed an appeal from the trial court's closure order. On July 9, 1979, the Virginia Supreme Court dismissed the mandamus and prohibition petitions and, finding no reversible error, denied the petition for appeal. Id., at 23a–28a.

Appellants then sought review in this Court, invoking both our appellate, 28 U.S.C. § 1257(2), and certiorari jurisdiction. § 1257(3). We postponed further consideration of the question of our jurisdiction to the hearing of the case on the merits. 444 U.S. 896 (1979). We conclude that jurisdiction by appeal does not lie; however, treating the filed papers as a petition for a writ of certiorari pursuant to 28 U.S.C. § 2103, we grant the petition.

. . .

II

We begin consideration of this case by noting that the precise issue presented here has not previously been before this Court for decision. In Gannett Co., Inc. v. DePasquale, [443 U.S. 368 (1979)], the Court was not required to decide whether a right of access to *trials,* as distinguished from hearings on *pre*trial motions, was constitutionally guaranteed. The Court held that the Sixth

Amendment's guarantee to the accused of a public trial gave neither the public nor the press an enforceable right of access to a *pretrial* suppression hearing. One concurring opinion specifically emphasized that "a hearing on a motion before trial to suppress evidence is not a *trial.* ..." 443 U.S., at 394 (Burger, C.J., concurring). Moreover, the Court did not decide whether the First and Fourteenth Amendments guarantee a right of the public to attend trials, id., at 392, and n. 24; nor did the dissenting opinion reach this issue. Id., at 447 (opinion of Blackmun, J.).

In prior cases the Court has treated questions involving conflicts between publicity and a defendant's right to a fair trial; as we observed in Nebraska Press Assn. v. Stuart, [427 U.S. 539 (1976)], at 547, "[t]he problems presented by this [conflict] are almost as old as the Republic." ... But here for the first time the Court is asked to decide whether a criminal trial itself may be closed to the public upon the unopposed request of a defendant, without any demonstration that closure is required to protect the defendant's superior right to a fair trial, or that some other overriding consideration requires closure.

A

The origins of the proceeding which has become the modern criminal trial in Anglo-American justice can be traced back beyond reliable historical records. We need not here review all details of its development, but a summary of that history is instructive. What is significant for present purposes is that throughout its evolution, the trial has been open to all who cared to observe.

. . .

We have found nothing to suggest that the presumptive openness of the trial, which English courts were later to call "one of the essential qualities of a court of justice," Daubney v. Cooper, 10 B. & C. 237, 240, 109 Eng.Rep. 438, 440 (K.B.1829), was not also an attribute of the judicial systems of colonial America. . . .

. . .

B

As we have shown, and as was shown in both the Court's opinion and the dissent in *Gannett,* supra, at 384, 386, n. 15; 418–425, the historical evidence demonstrates conclusively that at the time when our organic laws were adopted, criminal trials both here and in England had long been presumptively open. This is no quirk of history; rather, it has long been recognized as an indispensible attribute of an Anglo-American trial. . . .

. . .

... "[t]he publicity of a judicial proceeding is a requirement of much broader bearing than its mere effect on the quality of testimony." 6 J. Wigmore, Evidence § 1834, p. 435 (Chadbourn rev. 1976). The early history of open trials in part reflects the widespread acknowledgement, long before there were behavioral scientists, that public trials had significant community therapeutic value. Even without such experts to frame the concept in words, people sensed from experience and observation that, especially in the administration of criminal justice, the means used to achieve justice must have the support derived from public acceptance of both the process and its results.

When a shocking crime occurs, a community reaction of outrage and public protest often follows. ... Thereafter the open processes of justice serve an important prophylactic purpose, providing an outlet for community concern, hostility, and emotion. Without an awareness that society's responses to criminal conduct are underway, natural human reactions of outrage and protest are frustrated and may manifest themselves in some form of vengeful "self-help," as indeed they did regularly in the activities of vigilante "committees" on our frontiers. "The accusation and conviction or acquittal, as much perhaps as the execution of punishment, operat[e] to restore the imbalance which was created by the offense or public charge, to reaffirm the temporarily lost feeling of security, and, perhaps, to satisfy that latent 'urge to punish.'" Mueller, Problems Posed by Publicity to Crime and Criminal Proceedings, 110 U.Pa.L.Rev. 1, 6 (1961).

Civilized societies withdraw both from the victim and the vigilante the enforcement of criminal laws, but they cannot erase from people's consciousness the fundamental, natural yearning to see justice done—or even the urge for retribution. The crucial prophylactic aspects of the administration of justice cannot function in the dark; no community catharsis can occur if justice is "done in a corner [or] in any covert manner." Supra, at 567. It is not enough to say that results alone will satiate the natural community desire for "satisfaction." A result considered untoward may undermine public confidence, and where the trial has been concealed from public view an unexpected outcome can cause a reaction that the system at best has failed and at worst has been corrupted. To work effectively, it is important that society's criminal process "satisfy the appearance of justice," Offutt v. United States, 348 U.S. 11, 14 (1954), and the appearance of justice can best be provided by allowing people to observe it.

Looking back, we see that when the ancient "town meeting" form of trial became too cumbersome, 12 members of the community were delegated to act as its surrogates, but the community did not surrender its right to observe the conduct of trials. The people retained a "right of visitation" which enabled them to satisfy themselves that justice was in fact being done.

People in an open society do not demand infallibility from their institutions, but it is difficult for them to accept what they are prohibited from observing. When a criminal trial is conducted in the open, there is at least an opportunity both for understanding the system in general and its workings in a particular case:

> "The educative effect of public attendance is a material advantage. Not only is respect for the law increased and intelligent acquaintance acquired with the methods of government, but a strong confidence in judicial remedies is secured which could never be inspired by a system of secrecy." 6 Wigmore, supra, at 438. See also 1 J. Bentham, Rationale of Judicial Evidence at 525.

In earlier times, both in England and America, attendance at court was a common mode of "passing the time." . . . With the press, cinema, and electronic media now supplying the representations or reality of the real life drama once available only in the courtroom, attendance at court is no longer a widespread pastime. Yet "[i]t is not unrealistic even in this day to believe that public inclusion affords citizens a form of legal education and hopefully promotes confidence in the fair administration of justice." State v. Schmit, 273 Minn. 78, 87–88, 139 N.W.2d 800, 807 (1966). Instead of acquiring information about trials by firsthand observation or by word of mouth from those who attended, people now acquire it chiefly through the print and electronic media. In a sense, this validates the media claim of functioning as surrogates for the public. While media representatives enjoy the same right of access as the public, they often are provided special seating and priority of entry so that they may report what people in attendance have seen and heard. This "contribute[s] to public understanding of the rule of law and to comprehension of the functioning of the entire criminal justice system. . . ." Nebraska Press Assn. v. Stuart, 427 U.S., at 587 (Brennan, J., concurring in judgment).

C

From this unbroken, uncontradicted history, supported by reasons as valid today as in centuries past, we are bound to conclude that a presumption of openness inheres in the very nature of a criminal trial under our system of justice. This conclusion is hardly novel; without a direct holding on the issue, the Court has voiced its recognition of it in a variety of contexts over the years. . . .

Despite the history of criminal trials being presumptively open since long before the Constitution, the State presses its contention that neither the Constitution nor the Bill of Rights contains any provision which by its terms guarantees to the public the right to attend criminal trials. Standing alone, this is correct, but there remains the question whether, absent an explicit provision, the Constitution affords protection against exclusion of the public from criminal trials.

III

A

The First Amendment, in conjunction with the Fourteenth, prohibits governments from "abridging the freedom of speech, or of the press; or the right of the people peaceably to assemble, and to petition the Government for a redress of grievances." These expressly guaranteed freedoms share a common core purpose of assuring freedom of communication on matters relating to the functioning of government. Plainly it would be difficult to single out any aspect of government of higher concern and importance to the people than the manner in which criminal trials are conducted; as we have shown, recognition of this pervades the centuries-old history of open trials and the opinions of this Court. . . .

The Bill of Rights was enacted against the backdrop of the long history of trials being presumptively open. Public access to trials was then regarded as an important aspect of the process itself; the conduct of trials "before as many of the people as chuse to attend" was regarded as one of "the inestimable advantages of a free English constitution of government." 1 Journals 106, 107. In guaranteeing freedoms such as those of speech and press, the First Amendment can be read as protecting the right of everyone to attend trials so as to give meaning to those explicit guarantees. "[T]he First Amendment goes beyond protection of the press and the self-expression of individuals to prohibit government from limiting the stock of information from which members of the public may draw." First National Bank of Boston v. Bellotti, 435 U.S. 765, 783 (1978). Free speech carries with it some freedom to listen. "In a variety of contexts this Court has referred to a First Amendment right to 'receive information and ideas.' " Kleindienst v. Mandel, 408 U.S. 753, 762 (1972). What this means in the context of trials is that the First Amendment guarantees of speech and press, standing alone, prohibit government from summarily closing courtroom doors which had long been open to the public at the time that Amendment was adopted. "For the First Amendment does not speak equivocally. . . . It must be taken as a command of the broadest scope that explicit language, read in the context of a liberty-loving society, will allow." Bridges v. California, 314 U.S. 252, 263 (1941) (footnote omitted).

It is not crucial whether we describe this right to attend criminal trials to hear, see, and communicate observations concerning them as a "right of access," cf. *Gannett,* supra, at 397 (Powell, J., concurring) . . . or a "right to gather information," for we have recognized that "without some protection for seeking out the news, freedom of the press could be eviscerated." Branzburg v. Hayes, 408 U.S. 665, 681 (1972). The explicit, guaranteed rights to speak and to publish concerning what takes place at a trial would lose much meaning if access to observe the trial could, as it was here, be foreclosed arbitrarily.

B

The right of access to places traditionally open to the public, as criminal trials have long been, may be seen as assured by the amalgam of the First Amendment guarantees of speech and press; and their affinity to the right of assembly is not without relevance. From the outset, the right of assembly was regarded not only as an independent right but also as a catalyst to augment the free exercise of the other First Amendment rights with which it was deliberately linked by the draftsmen. "The right of peaceable assembly is a right cognate to those of free speech and free press and is equally fundamental." DeJonge v. Oregon, 299 U.S. 353, 364 (1937). People assemble in public places not only to speak or to take action, but also to listen, observe, and learn; indeed, they may "assembl[e] for any lawful purpose," Hague v. C.I.O., 307 U.S. 496, 519 (1939) (opinion of Stone, J.). Subject to the traditional time, place, and manner restrictions ... streets, sidewalks, and parks are places traditionally open, where First Amendment rights may be exercised ...; a trial courtroom also is a public place where the people generally—and representatives of the media—have a right to be present, and where their presence historically has been thought to enhance the integrity and quality of what takes place.

C

The State argues that the Constitution nowhere spells out a guarantee for the right of the public to attend trials, and that accordingly no such right is protected. The possibility that such a contention could be made did not escape the notice of the Constitution's draftsmen; they were concerned that some important rights might be thought disparaged because not specifically guaranteed. It was even argued that because of this danger no Bill of Rights should be adopted....

But arguments such as the State makes have not precluded recognition of important rights not enumerated. Notwithstanding the appropriate caution against reading into the Constitution rights not explicitly defined, the Court has acknowledged that certain unarticulated rights are implicit in enumerated guarantees. For example, the rights of association and of privacy, the right to be presumed innocent and the right to be judged by a standard of proof beyond a reasonable doubt in a criminal trial, as well as the right to travel, appear nowhere in the Constitution or Bill of Rights. Yet these important but unarticulated rights have nonetheless been found to share constitutional protection in common with explicit guarantees. The concerns expressed by Madison and others have thus been resolved; fundamental rights, even though not expressly guaranteed, have been recognized by the Court as indispensable to the enjoyment of rights explicitly defined.

We hold that the right to attend criminal trials [17] is implicit in the guarantees of the First Amendment; without the freedom to attend such trials, which people have exercised for centuries, important aspects of freedom of speech and "of the press could be eviscerated." *Branzburg*, 408 U.S., at 681.

D

Having concluded there was a guaranteed right of the public under the First and Fourteenth Amendments to attend the trial of Stevenson's case, we return to the closure order challenged by appellants. The Court in *Gannett* made clear that although the Sixth Amendment guarantees the accused a right to a public trial, it does not give a right to a private trial.... Despite the fact that this was the fourth trial of the accused, the trial judge made no findings to support closure; no inquiry was made as to whether alternative solutions would have met the need to ensure fairness; there was no recognition of any right under the Constitution for the public or press to attend the trial. In contrast to the pretrial proceeding dealt with in *Gannett*, there exist in the context of the trial itself various tested alternatives to satisfy the constitutional demands of fairness. ... There was no suggestion that any problems with witnesses could not have been dealt with by their exclusion from the courtroom or their sequestration during the trial. ... Nor is there anything to indicate that sequestration of the jurors would not have guarded against their being subjected to any improper information. All of the alternatives admittedly present difficulties for trial courts, but none of the factors relied on here was beyond the realm of the manageable. Absent an overriding interest articulated in findings, the trial of a criminal case must be open to the public.[18] Accordingly, the judgment under review is

17. Whether the public has a right to attend trials of civil cases is a question not raised by this case, but we note that historically both civil and criminal trials have been presumptively open.

18. We have no occasion here to define the circumstances in which all or parts of a criminal trial may be closed to the public ... but our holding today does not mean that the First Amendment rights of the public and representatives of the press are absolute. Just as a government may impose reasonable time, place, and manner restrictions upon the use of its streets in the interest of such objectives as the free flow of traffic ... so may a trial judge, in the interest of the fair administration of justice, impose reasonable limitations on access to a trial. "[T]he question in a particular case is whether that control is exerted so as not to deny or unwarrantedly abridge ... the opportunities for the communication of thought and the discussion of public questions immemorially associated with resort to public places." [Cox v. New Hampshire, 312 U.S. 569 (1941)] at 574. It is far more important that trials be conducted in a quiet and orderly setting than it is to preserve that atmosphere on city streets. ... Moreover, since courtrooms have limited capacity, there may be occasions when not every person who wishes to attend can be accommodated. In such situations, reasonable restrictions on general access are traditionally imposed, including preferential seating for media representatives. ...

Reversed.[*] [**]

[*] Justice White and Justice Stevens wrote concurring opinions. Justice Brennan wrote an opinion concurring in the judgment, which Justice Marshall joined. Justice Stewart and Justice Blackmun also wrote opinions concurring in the judgment. Justice Rehnquist wrote a dissenting opinion.

[**] In Waller v. Georgia, 467 U.S. 39 (1984), the Court held that the Sixth Amendment right to a public trial extends to a pretrial hearing on a motion to suppress evidence.

POINTER v. TEXAS

380 U.S. 400, 85 S.Ct. 1065, 13 L.Ed.2d 923 (1965).

MR. JUSTICE BLACK delivered the opinion of the Court.

The Sixth Amendment provides in part that:

> "In all criminal prosecutions, the accused shall enjoy the right . . . to be confronted with the witnesses against him . . . and to have the Assistance of Counsel for his defence."

Two years ago in Gideon v. Wainwright, 372 U.S. 335, we held that the Fourteenth Amendment makes the Sixth Amendment's guarantee of right to counsel obligatory upon the States. The question we find necessary to decide in this case is whether the Amendment's guarantee of a defendant's right "to be confronted with the witnesses against him," which has been held to include the right to cross-examine those witnesses, is also made applicable to the States by the Fourteenth Amendment.

The petitioner Pointer and one Dillard were arrested in Texas and taken before a state judge for a preliminary hearing (in Texas called the "examining trial") on a charge of having robbed Kenneth W. Phillips of $375 "by assault, or violence, or by putting in fear of life or bodily injury," in violation of Texas Penal Code Art. 1408. At this hearing an Assistant District Attorney conducted the prosecution and examined witnesses, but neither of the defendants, both of whom were laymen, had a lawyer. Phillips as chief witness for the State gave his version of the alleged robbery in detail, identifying petitioner as the man who had robbed him at gunpoint. Apparently Dillard tried to cross-examine Phillips but Pointer did not, although Pointer was said to have tried to cross-examine some other witnesses at the hearing. Petitioner was subsequently indicted on a charge of having committed the robbery. Some time before the trial was held, Phillips moved to California. After putting in evidence to show that Phillips had moved and did not intend to return to Texas, the State at the trial offered the transcript of Phillips' testimony given at the preliminary hearing as evidence against petitioner. Petitioner's counsel immediately objected to introduction of the transcript, stating, "Your Honor, we will object to that, as it is a denial of the confrontment of the witnesses against the Defendant." Similar objections were repeatedly made by petitioner's counsel but were overruled by the trial judge, apparently in part because, as the judge viewed it, petitioner had been present at the preliminary hearing and therefore had been "accorded the opportunity of cross examining the witnesses there against him." The Texas Court of Criminal Appeals, the highest state court to which the case could be taken, affirmed petitioner's conviction, rejecting his contention that use of the transcript to convict him denied him rights guaranteed by the Sixth and Fourteenth Amendments. 375 S.W.2d 293. We granted certiorari to consider the important constitutional question the case involves. 379 U.S. 815.

In this Court we do not find it necessary to decide one aspect of the question petitioner raises, that is, whether failure to appoint counsel to represent him at the preliminary hearing unconstitutionally denied him the assistance of counsel within the meaning of Gideon v. Wainwright, supra. . . . In this case the objections and arguments in the trial court as well as the arguments in the Court of Criminal Appeals and before us make it clear that petitioner's objection is based not so much on the fact that he had no lawyer when Phillips made his statement at the preliminary hearing, as on the fact that use of the transcript of that statement at the trial denied petitioner any opportunity to have the benefit of counsel's cross-examination of the principal witness against him. It is that latter question which we decide here.

I

The Sixth Amendment is a part of what is called our Bill of Rights. . . . We hold today that the Sixth Amendment's right of an accused to confront the witnesses against him is likewise a fundamental right and is made obligatory on the States by the Fourteenth Amendment.

It cannot seriously be doubted at this late date that the right of cross-examination is included in the right of an accused in a criminal case to confront the witnesses against him. And probably no one, certainly no one experienced in the trial of lawsuits, would deny the value of cross-examination in exposing falsehood and bringing out the truth in the trial of a criminal case. . . . The fact that this right appears in the Sixth Amendment of our Bill of Rights reflects the belief of the Framers of those liberties and safeguards that confrontation was a fundamental right essential to a fair trial in a criminal prosecution. Moreover, the decisions of this Court and other courts throughout the years have constantly emphasized the necessity for cross-examination as a protection for defendants in criminal cases. . . . There are few subjects, perhaps, upon which this Court and other courts have been more nearly unanimous than in their expressions of belief that the right of confrontation and cross-examination is an essential and fundamental requirement for the kind of fair trial which is this country's constitutional goal. Indeed, we have expressly declared that to deprive an accused of the right to cross-examine the witnesses against him is a denial of the Fourteenth Amendment's guarantee of due process of law. . . .

We are aware that some cases . . . have stated that the Sixth Amendment's right of confrontation does not apply to trials in state courts, on the ground that the entire Sixth Amendment does not so apply. . . . But of course since Gideon v. Wainwright, supra, it no longer can broadly be said that the Sixth Amendment does not apply to state courts. And as this Court said in Malloy v. Hogan, [378 U.S. 1 (1964)], "The Court has not hesitated to re-examine past decisions according the Fourteenth Amendment a less central role in the preservation of basic liberties than that which was contemplated by its Framers when they added the Amendment to our constitutional scheme." 378 U.S., at 5. In the light of *Gideon, Malloy,* and other cases cited in those opinions holding various provisions of the Bill of Rights applicable to the States by virtue of the Fourteenth Amendment, the statements . . . generally declaring that the Sixth Amendment does not apply to the States can no longer be regarded as the law. We hold that petitioner was entitled to be tried in accordance with the protection of the confrontation guarantee of the Sixth Amendment, and that that guarantee, like the right against compelled self-incrimination, is "to be enforced against the States under the Fourteenth Amendment according to the same standards that protect those personal rights against federal encroachment." Malloy v. Hogan, supra, 378 U.S., at 10.

II

Under this Court's prior decisions, the Sixth Amendment's guarantee of confrontation and cross-examination was unquestionably denied petitioner in this case. As has been pointed out, a major reason underlying the constitutional confrontation rule is to give a defendant charged with crime an opportunity to cross-examine the witnesses against him. . . . This Court has recognized the admissibility against an accused of dying declarations . . . and of testimony of a deceased witness who has testified at a former trial. . . . Nothing we hold here is to the contrary. The case before us would be quite a different one had Phillips' statement been taken at a full-fledged hearing at which petitioner had been represented by counsel who had been given a complete and adequate opportunity to cross-examine. . . . There are other analogous situations which might not fall within the scope of the constitutional rule requiring confrontation of witnesses. The case before us, however, does not present any situation like those mentioned above or others analogous to them. Because the transcript of Phillips' statement offered against petitioner at his trial had not been taken at a time and under circumstances affording petitioner through counsel an adequate opportunity to cross-examine Phillips, its introduction in a federal court in a criminal case against Pointer would have amounted to denial of the privilege of confrontation guaranteed by the Sixth Amendment. Since we hold that the right of an accused to be confronted with the witnesses against him must be determined by the same standards whether the right is denied in a federal or state proceeding, it follows that use of the transcript to convict petitioner denied him a constitutional right, and that his conviction must be reversed.

Reversed and remanded.[*]

[*] Justice Harlan and Justice Stewart wrote opinions concurring in the result. Justice Goldberg wrote a concurring opinion.

410 U.S. 284, 93 S.Ct. 1038, 35 L.Ed.2d 297 (1973).

MR. JUSTICE POWELL delivered the opinion of the Court.

Petitioner, Leon Chambers, was tried by a jury in a Mississippi trial court and convicted of murdering a policeman. The jury assessed punishment at life imprisonment and the Mississippi Supreme Court affirmed, one justice dissenting. Chambers v. Mississippi, 252 So.2d 217 (1971). Pending disposition of his application for certiorari to this Court, petitioner was granted bail by order of the Circuit Justice dated February 1, 1972. Two weeks later, on the State's request for reconsideration, that order was reaffirmed. 405 U.S. 1205 (1972). Subsequently the petition for certiorari was granted, 405 U.S. 987 (1972), to consider whether petitioner's trial was conducted in accord with principles of due process under the Fourteenth Amendment. We conclude that it was not.

I

The events that led to petitioner's prosecution for murder occurred in the small town of Woodville in southern Mississippi. On Saturday evening, June 14, 1969, two Woodville policemen, James Forman and Aaron "Sonny" Liberty, entered a local bar and pool hall to execute a warrant for the arrest of a youth named C. C. Jackson. Jackson resisted and a hostile crowd of some 50 or 60 persons gathered. The officers' first attempt to handcuff Jackson was frustrated when 20 or 25 men in the crowd intervened and wrestled him free. Forman then radioed for assistance and Liberty removed his riot gun, a 12-gauge sawed-off shotgun, from the car. Three deputy sheriffs arrived shortly thereafter and the officers again attempted to make their arrest. Once more the officers were attacked by the onlookers and during the commotion five or six pistol shots were fired. Forman was looking in a different direction when the shooting began, but immediately saw that Liberty had been shot several times in the back. Before Liberty died he turned around and fired both barrels of his riot gun into an alley in the area from which the shots appeared to have come. The first shot was wild and high and scattered the crowd standing at the face of the alley. Liberty appeared, however, to take more deliberate aim before the second shot and hit one of the men in the crowd in the back of the head and neck as he ran down the alley. That man was Leon Chambers.

Officer Forman could not see from his vantage point who shot Liberty or whether Liberty's shots hit anyone. One of the deputy sheriffs testified at trial that he was standing several feet from

1027

Liberty and that he saw Chambers shoot him. Another deputy sheriff stated that, although he could not see whether Chambers had a gun in his hand, he did see Chambers "break his arm down" shortly before the shots were fired. The officers who saw Chambers fall testified that they thought he was dead but they made no effort at that time either to examine him or to search for the murder weapon. Instead they attended to Liberty, who was placed in the police car and taken to the hospital where he was declared dead on arrival. A subsequent autopsy showed that he had been hit with four bullets from a .22-caliber revolver.

Shortly after the shooting, three of Chambers' friends discovered that he was not yet dead. James Williams, Berkley Turner, and Gable McDonald loaded him into a car and transported him to the same hospital. Later that night, when the county sheriff discovered that Chambers was still alive, a guard was placed outside his room. Chambers was subsequently charged with Liberty's murder. He pleaded not guilty and has asserted his innocence throughout.

The story of Leon Chambers is intertwined with the story of another man, Gable McDonald. McDonald, a lifelong resident of Woodville, was in the crowd on the evening of Liberty's death. Sometime shortly after that day he left his wife in Woodville and moved to Louisiana and found a job at a sugar mill. In November of that same year he returned to Woodville when his wife informed him that an acquaintance of his, known as Reverend Stokes, wanted to see him. Stokes owned a gas station in Natchez, Mississippi, several miles north of Woodville, and upon his return McDonald went to see him. After talking to Stokes, McDonald agreed to make a statement to Chambers' attorneys, who maintained offices in Natchez. Two days later he appeared at the attorneys' offices and gave a sworn confession that he shot Officer Liberty. He also stated that he had already told a friend of his, James Williams, that he shot Liberty. He said that he used his own pistol, a nine-shot .22-caliber revolver, which he had discarded shortly after the shooting. In response to questions from Chambers' attorneys, McDonald affirmed that his confession was voluntary and that no one had compelled him to come to them. Once the confession had been transcribed, signed and witnessed, McDonald was turned over to the local police authorities and was placed in jail.

One month later, at a preliminary hearing, McDonald repudiated his prior sworn confession. He testified that Stokes had persuaded him to confess that he shot Liberty. He claimed that Stokes had promised that he would not go to jail and that he would share in the proceeds of a lawsuit that Chambers would bring against the town of Woodville. On examination by his own attorney and on cross-examination by the State, McDonald swore that he had not been on the scene when Liberty was shot but had been down the street drinking beer in a cafe with a friend, Berkley Turner. When he and Turner heard the shooting he testified that they walked up the street and found Chambers lying in the alley. He, Turner and Williams took Chambers to the hospital. McDonald further testified at the preliminary hearing that he did not know what had happened, that there was no discussion about the shooting either going to or coming back from the hospital, and that it was not until the next day that he learned that Chambers had been felled by a blast from Liberty's riot gun. In addition, McDonald stated that while he once owned a .22-caliber pistol he had lost it many months before the shooting and did not own or possess a weapon at that time. The local justice of the peace accepted McDonald's repudiation, released him from custody, and the local authorities undertook no further investigation of his possible involvement.

Chambers' case came on for trial in October of the next year. At trial he endeavored to develop two grounds of defense. He first attempted to show that he did not shoot Liberty. Only one officer testified that he actually saw Chambers fire the shots. Although three officers saw Liberty shoot Chambers and testified that they assumed he was shooting his attacker, none of them examined Chambers to see whether he was still alive or whether he possessed a gun. Indeed, no weapon was ever recovered from the scene and there was no proof that Chambers had ever owned a .22-caliber pistol. One witness testified that he was standing in the street near where Liberty was shot, that he was looking at Chambers when the shooting began, and that he was sure that Chambers did not fire the shots.

Petitioner's second defense was that Gable McDonald had shot Officer Liberty. He was only partially successful, however, in his efforts to bring before the jury the testimony supporting this defense. Sam Hardin, a lifelong friend of McDonald's, testified that he saw McDonald shoot Liberty. A second witness, one of Liberty's cousins, testified that he saw McDonald immediately after the shooting with a pistol in his hand. In addition to the testimony of these two witnesses, Chambers endeavored to show the jury that McDonald had repeatedly confessed to the crime. Chambers attempted to prove that McDonald had admitted responsibility for the murder on four separate occasions, once when he gave the sworn statement to Chambers' counsel and three other times prior to that occasion in private conversations with friends.

In large measure, he was thwarted in his attempt to present this portion of his defense by the strict application of certain Mississippi rules of evidence. Chambers asserts in this Court, as he did unsuccessfully in his motion for new trial and on appeal to the State Supreme Court, that the application of these evidentiary rules rendered his trial fundamentally unfair and deprived him of due process of law. It is necessary, therefore, to examine carefully the rulings made during the trial.

II

Chambers filed a pretrial motion requesting the court to order McDonald to appear. Chambers also sought a ruling at that time that, if the State chose not to call McDonald itself, he be allowed to call him as an adverse witness. Attached to the motion were copies of McDonald's sworn confession and of the transcript of his preliminary hearing at which he repudiated that confession. The trial court granted the motion requiring McDonald to appear but reserved ruling on the adverse witness motion. At trial, after the State failed to put McDonald on the stand, Chambers called McDonald, laid a predicate for the introduction of his sworn out-of-court confession, had it admitted into evidence, and read it to the jury. The State, upon cross-examination, elicited from McDonald the fact that he had rejected his prior confession. McDonald further testified, as he had at the preliminary hearing, that he did not shoot Liberty, and that he confessed to the crime only on the promise of Reverend Stokes that he would not go to jail and would share in a sizable tort recovery from the town. He also retold his own story of his actions on the evening of the shooting, including his visit to the cafe down the street, his absence from the scene during the critical period, and his subsequent trip to the hospital with Chambers.

At the conclusion of the State's cross-examination, Chambers renewed his motion to examine McDonald as an adverse witness. The trial court denied the motion, stating: "He may be hostile, but he is not adverse in the sense of the word, so your request will be overruled." On appeal, the State Supreme Court upheld the trial court's ruling, finding that "McDonald's testimony was not adverse to appellant" because "[n]owhere did he point the finger at Chambers." 252 So.2d., at 220.

Defeated in his attempt to challenge directly McDonald's renunciation of his prior confession, Chambers sought to introduce the testimony of the three witnesses to whom McDonald had admitted that he shot the officer. The first of these, Sam Hardin, would have testified that, on the night of the shooting, he spent the late evening hours with McDonald at a friend's house after their return from the hospital and that, while driving McDonald home later that night, McDonald stated that he shot Liberty. The State objected to the admission of this testimony on the ground that it was hearsay. The trial court sustained the objection.

Berkley Turner, the friend with whom McDonald said he was drinking beer when the shooting occurred, was then called to testify. In the jury's presence, and without objection, he testified that he had not been in the cafe that Saturday and had not had any beers with McDonald. The jury was then excused. In the absence of the jury, Turner recounted his conversations with McDonald while they were riding with James Williams to take Chambers to the hospital. When asked whether McDonald said anything regarding the shooting of Liberty, Turner testified that McDonald told him that he "shot him." Turner further stated that one week later, when he met McDonald at a friend's house, McDonald reminded him of their prior conversation and urged Turner not to "mess him up." Petitioner argued to the court that, especially where there was other proof in the case that was corroborative of these out-of-court statements, Turner's testimony as to McDonald's self-incriminating remarks should have been admitted as an exception to the hearsay rule. Again, the trial court sustained the State's objection.

The third witness, Albert Carter, was McDonald's neighbor. They had been friends for about 25 years. Although Carter had not been in Woodville on the evening of the shooting, he stated that he learned about it the next morning from McDonald. That same day he and McDonald walked out to a well near McDonald's house and there McDonald told him that he was the one who shot Officer Liberty. Carter testified that McDonald also told him that he had disposed of the .22-caliber revolver later that night. He further testified that several weeks after the shooting he accompanied McDonald to Natchez where McDonald purchased another .22 pistol to replace the one he had discarded. The jury was not allowed to hear Carter's testimony. Chambers urged that these statements were admissible, the State objected, and the court sustained the objection. On appeal, the State Supreme Court approved the lower court's exclusion of these witnesses' testimony on hearsay grounds. 252 So.2d, at 220.

In sum, then, this was Chambers' predicament. As a consequence of the combination of Mississippi's "party witness" or "voucher" rule and its hearsay rule, he was unable either to cross-examine McDonald or to present witnesses in his own behalf who would have discredited McDonald's repudiation and demonstrated his complicity. Chambers had, however, chipped away at the fringes of McDonald's story by introducing admissible testimony from other sources indicating that he had not been seen in the cafe where he says he was when the shooting started, that he had not been having beer with Turner, and that he possessed a .22 pistol at the time of the crime. But all that remained from McDonald's own testimony was a single written confession countered by an arguably acceptable renunciation. Chambers' defense was far less persuasive than it might have been had he been given an opportunity to subject McDonald's statements to cross-examination or had the other confessions been admitted.

III

The right of an accused in a criminal trial to due process is, in essence, the right to a fair opportunity to defend against the State's accusations. The rights to confront and cross-examine witnesses and to call witnesses in one's own behalf have long been recognized as essential to due process. Mr. Justice Black, writing for the Court in In re Oliver, 333 U.S. 257, 273 (1948), identified these rights as among the minimum essentials of a fair trial. ... Both of these elements of a fair trial are implicated in the present case.

A

Chambers was denied an opportunity to subject McDonald's damning repudiation and alibi to cross-examination. He was not allowed to test the witness' recollection, to probe into the details of his alibi, or to "sift" his conscience so that the jury might judge for itself whether McDonald's testimony was worthy of belief. Mattox v. United States, 156 U.S. 237, 242–243 (1895). The right of cross-examination is more than a desirable rule of trial procedure. It is implicit in the constitutional right of confrontation, and helps assure the "accuracy of the truth-determining process." Dutton v. Evans, 400 U.S. 74, 89 (1970).... It is, indeed, "an essential and fundamental requirement for the kind of fair trial which is this country's constitutional goal." Pointer v. Texas, 380 U.S. 400, 405 (1965). Of course, the right to confront and to cross-examine is not absolute and may, in appropriate cases, bow to accommodate other legitimate interests in the criminal trial process.... But its denial or significant diminution calls into question the ultimate "integrity of the fact-finding process" and requires that the competing interest be closely examined. Berger v. California, 393 U.S. 314, 315 (1969).

In this case, petitioner's request to cross-examine McDonald was denied on the basis of a Mississippi common law rule that a party may not impeach his own witness. The rule rests on the presumption—without regard to the circumstances of the particular case—that a party who calls a witness "vouches for his credibility." Clark v. Lansford, 191 So.2d 123, 125 (Miss.1966). Although the historical origins of the "voucher" rule are uncertain, it appears to be a remnant of primitive English trial practice in which "oath-takers" or "compurgators" were called to stand behind a particular party's position in any controversy. Their assertions were strictly partisan and, quite unlike witnesses in criminal trials today, their role bore little relation to the impartial ascertainment of the facts.

Whatever validity the "voucher" rule may have once enjoyed, and apart from whatever usefulness it retains today in the civil trial process, it bears little present relationship to the realities of the criminal process. It might have been logical for the early common law to require a party to vouch for the credibility of witnesses he brought before the jury to affirm his veracity. Having selected them especially for that purpose, the party might reasonably be expected to stand firmly behind their testimony. But in modern criminal trials defendants are rarely able to select their witnesses: they must take them where they find them. Moreover, as applied in this case, the "voucher" rule's impact was doubly harmful to Chambers' efforts to develop his defense. Not only was he precluded from cross-examining McDonald, but, as the State conceded at oral argument, he was also restricted in the scope of his direct examination by the rule's corollary requirement that the party calling the witness is bound by anything he might say. He was, therefore, effectively prevented from exploring the circumstances of McDonald's three prior oral confessions and from challenging the renunciation of the written confession.

In this Court Mississippi has not sought to defend the rule or explain its underlying rationale. Nor has it contended that its rule should override the accused's right of confrontation. Instead, it argues that there is no incompatability between the rule and Chambers' rights because no right of confrontation exists unless the testifying witness is "adverse" to the accused. The State's brief asserts that the "right of confrontation is limited to witnesses *against* an accused." [11] Relying on the trial court's determination that McDonald was not "adverse," and on the State Supreme Court's holding that McDonald "did not point the finger at Chambers," [12] the State contends that Chambers' constitutional right was not involved.

The argument that McDonald's testimony was not "adverse" to, or "against," Chambers is not convincing. The State's proof at trial excluded the theory that more than one person participated in the shooting of Liberty. To the extent that McDonald's sworn confession tended to incriminate him, it tended also to exculpate Chambers. And, in the circumstances of this case, McDonald's retraction inculpated Chambers to the same extent that it exculpated McDonald. It can hardly be disputed that McDonald's testimony was in fact seriously adverse to Chambers. The availability of the right to confront and to cross-examine those who give damaging testimony against the accused has never been held to depend on whether the witness was initially put on the stand by the accused or by the State. We reject the notion that a right of such substance in the criminal process may be governed by that technicality or by any narrow and unrealistic definition of the word "against." The "voucher" rule, as applied in this case, plainly interfered with Chambers' right to defend against the State's charges.

B

We need not decide, however, whether this error alone would occasion reversal since Chambers' claimed denial of due process rests on the ultimate impact of that error when viewed in conjunction with the trial court's refusal to permit him to call other witnesses. The trial court refused to allow him to introduce the testimony of Hardin, Turner and Carter. Each would have testified to the statements purportedly made by McDonald, on three separate

---

11. Respondent's Brief, at 9 (emphasis supplied).

12. 252 So.2d, at 220.

occasions shortly after the crime, naming himself as the murderer. The State Supreme Court approved the exclusion of this evidence on the ground that it was hearsay.

The hearsay rule, which has long been recognized and respected by virtually every State, is based on experience and grounded in the notion that untrustworthy evidence should not be presented to the triers of fact. Out-of-court statements are traditionally excluded because they lack the conventional indicia of reliability; they are usually not made under oath or other circumstances that impress the speaker with the solemnity of his statements; the declarant's word is not subject to cross-examination; and he is not available in order that his demeanor and credibility may be assessed by the jury.... A number of exceptions have developed over the years to allow admission of hearsay statements made under circumstances that tend to assure reliability and thereby compensate for the absence of the oath and opportunity for cross-examination. Among the most prevalent of these exceptions is the one applicable to declarations against interest—an exception founded on the assumption that a person is unlikely to fabricate a statement against his own interest at the time it is made. Mississippi recognizes this exception but applies it only to declarations against pecuniary interest. It recognizes no such exception for declarations, like McDonald's in this case, that are against the penal interest of the declarant....

This materialistic limitation on the declaration-against-interest hearsay exception appears to be accepted by most States in their criminal trial processes, although a number of States have discarded it. Declarations against penal interest have also been excluded in federal courts under the authority of Donnelly v. United States, 228 U.S. 243, 272–273 (1913), although exclusion would not be required under the newly proposed Federal Rules of Evidence. Exclusion, where the limitation prevails, is usually premised on the view that admission would lead to the frequent presentation of perjured testimony to the jury. It is believed that confessions of criminal activity are often motivated by extraneous considerations and, therefore, are not as inherently reliable as statements against pecuniary or proprietary interest. While that rationale has been the subject of considerable scholarly criticism, we need not decide in this case whether, under other circumstances, it might serve some valid state purpose by excluding untrustworthy testimony.

The hearsay statements involved in this case were originally made and subsequently offered at trial under circumstances that provided considerable assurance of their reliability. First, each of McDonald's confessions was made spontaneously to a close acquaintance shortly after the murder had occurred. Second, each one was corroborated by some other evidence in the case—McDonald's sworn confession, the testimony of an eyewitness to the shooting, the testimony that McDonald was seen with a gun immediately after the shooting, and proof of his prior ownership of a .22-caliber revolver and subsequent purchase of a new weapon. The sheer number of independent confessions provided additional corroboration for each. Third, whatever may be the parameters of the penal-interest rationale, each confession here was in a very real sense self-incriminatory and unquestionably against interest. . . . McDonald stood to benefit nothing by disclosing his role in the shooting to any of his three friends and he must have been aware of the possibility that disclosure would lead to criminal prosecution. Indeed, after telling Turner of his involvement, he subsequently urged Turner not to "mess him up." Finally, if there was any question about the truthfulness of the extrajudicial statements, McDonald was present in the courtroom and had been under oath. He could have been cross-examined by the State, and his demeanor and responses weighed by the jury. . . . The availability of McDonald significantly distinguishes this case from the prior Mississippi precedent . . . and from the *Donnelly*-type situation, since in both cases the declarant was unavailable at the time of trial.

Few rights are more fundamental than that of an accused to present witnesses in his own defense. . . . In the exercise of this right, the accused, as is required of the State, must comply with established rules of procedure and evidence designed to assure both fairness and reliability in the ascertainment of guilt and innocence. Although perhaps no rule of evidence has been more respected or more frequently applied in jury trials than that applicable to the exclusion of hearsay, exceptions tailored to allow the introduction of evidence which in fact is likely to be trustworthy have long existed. The testimony rejected by the trial court here bore persuasive assurances of trustworthiness and thus was well within the basic rationale of the exception for declarations against interest. That testimony also was critical to Chambers' defense. In these circumstances, where constitutional rights directly affecting the ascertainment of guilt are implicated, the hearsay rule may not be applied mechanistically to defeat the ends of justice.

We conclude that the exclusion of this critical evidence, coupled with the State's refusal to permit Chambers to cross-examine McDonald, denied him a trial in accord with traditional and fundamental standards of due process. In reaching this judgment we establish no new principles of constitutional law. Nor does our holding signal any diminution in the respect traditionally accorded to the States in the establishment and implementation of their own criminal trial rules and procedures. Rather, we hold quite simply that under the facts and circumstances of this case the rulings of the trial court deprived Chambers of a fair trial.

The judgment is reversed and the case is remanded to the Supreme Court of Mississippi for further proceedings not inconsistent with this opinion.

It is so ordered.[*]

[*] Justice White wrote a concurring opin-   opinion.
ion. Justice Rehnquist wrote a dissenting

TAYLOR v. ILLINOIS

484 U.S. 400, 108 S.Ct. 646, 98 L.Ed.2d 798 (1988).

JUSTICE STEVENS delivered the opinion of the Court.

As a sanction for failing to identify a defense witness in response to a pretrial discovery request, an Illinois trial judge refused to allow the undisclosed witness to testify. The question presented is whether that refusal violated the petitioner's constitutional right to obtain the testimony of favorable witnesses. We hold that such a sanction is not absolutely prohibited by the Compulsory Process Clause of the Sixth Amendment and find no constitutional error on the specific facts of this case.

I

A jury convicted petitioner in 1984 of attempting to murder Jack Bridges in a street fight on the south side of Chicago on August 6, 1981. The conviction was supported by the testimony of Bridges, his brother, and three other witnesses. They described a twenty-minute argument between Bridges and a young man named Derrick Travis, and a violent encounter that occurred over an hour later between several friends of Travis, including the petitioner, on the one hand, and Bridges, belatedly aided by his brother, on the other. The incident was witnessed by twenty or thirty bystanders. It is undisputed that at least three members of the group which included Travis and petitioner were carrying pipes and clubs that they used to beat Bridges. Prosecution witnesses also testified that petitioner had a gun, that he shot Bridges in the back as he attempted to flee, and that, after Bridges fell, petitioner pointed the gun at Bridges' head but the weapon misfired.

Two sisters, who are friends of petitioner, testified on his behalf. In many respects their version of the incident was consistent with the prosecution's case, but they testified that it was Bridges' brother, rather than petitioner, who possessed a firearm and that he had fired into the group hitting his brother by mistake. No other witnesses testified for the defense.

Well in advance of trial, the prosecutor filed a discovery motion requesting a list of defense witnesses.[2] In his original response,

---

2. Illinois Sup.Ct. Rule 413(d) provides in pertinent part:

"Subject to constitutional limitations and within a reasonable time after the filing of a written motion by the State, defense counsel shall inform the State of any defenses which he intends to make at a hearing or trial and shall furnish the State with the following material and information within his possession or control:

"(i) *the names and last known addresses of persons he intends to call as witnesses* together with their relevant written or recorded statements, including memoranda reporting

1037

petitioner's attorney identified the two sisters who later testified and two men who did not testify. On the first day of trial, defense counsel was allowed to amend his answer by adding the names of Derrick Travis and a Chicago police officer; neither of them actually testified.

On the second day of trial, after the prosecution's two principal witnesses had completed their testimony, defense counsel made an oral motion to amend his "Answer to Discovery" to include two more witnesses, Alfred Wormley and Pam Berkhalter. In support of the motion, counsel represented that he had just been informed about them and that they had probably seen the "entire incident."

In response to the court's inquiry about the defendant's failure to tell him about the two witnesses earlier, counsel acknowledged that defendant had done so, but then represented that he had been unable to locate Wormley. After noting that the witnesses' names could have been supplied even if their addresses were unknown, the trial judge directed counsel to bring them in the next day, at which time he would decide whether they could testify. The judge indicated that he was concerned about the possibility "that witnesses are being found that really weren't there."

The next morning Wormley appeared in court with defense counsel. After further colloquy about the consequences of a violation of discovery rules, counsel was permitted to make an offer of proof in the form of Wormley's testimony outside the presence of the jury. It developed that Wormley had not been a witness to the incident itself. He testified that prior to the incident he saw Jack Bridges and his brother with two guns in a blanket, that he heard them say "they were after Ray [petitioner] and the other people," and that on his way home he "happened to run into Ray and them" and warned them "to watch out because they got weapons." On cross-examination, Wormley acknowledged that he had first met the defendant "about four months ago" (i.e., over two years after the incident). He also acknowledged that defense counsel had visited him at his home on the Wednesday of the week before the trial began. Thus, his testimony rather dramatically contradicted defense counsel's representations to the trial court.

After hearing Wormley testify, the trial judge concluded that the appropriate sanction for the discovery violation was to exclude his testimony. The judge explained:

> "THE COURT: All right, I am going to deny Wormley an opportunity to testify here. He is not going to testify. I find this is a blatent [*sic*] violation of the discovery rules, willful violation of the rules. I also feel that defense attorneys have been violating discovery in this courtroom in the last three or

or summarizing their oral statements, any record of prior criminal convictions known to   him ..." (emphasis added).

four cases blatantly and I am going to put a stop to it and this is one way to do so.

"Further, for whatever value it is, because this is a jury trial, I have a great deal of doubt in my mind as to the veracity of this young man that testified as to whether he was an eyewitness on the scene, sees guns that are wrapped up. He doesn't know Ray but he stops Ray.

"At any rate, Mr. Wormley is not going to testify, be a witness in this courtroom." App. 28.

The Illinois Appellate Court affirmed petitioner's conviction. 141 Ill.App.3d 839, 491 N.E.2d 3 (1986). It held that when "discovery rules are violated, the trial judge may exclude the evidence which the violating party wishes to introduce" and that "[t]he decision of the severity of the sanction to impose on a party who violates discovery rules rests within the sound discretion of the trial court." The court concluded that in this case "the trial court was within its discretion in refusing to allow the additional witnesses to testify." Id., at 844–845, 491 N.E.2d, at 7. The Illinois Supreme Court denied leave to appeal and we granted the petition for certiorari, 479 U.S. 1063 (1987).

In this Court petitioner makes two arguments. He first contends that the Sixth Amendment bars a court from ever ordering the preclusion of defense evidence as a sanction for violating a discovery rule. Alternatively, he contends that even if the right to present witnesses is not absolute, on the facts of this case the preclusion of Wormley's testimony was constitutional error. Before addressing these contentions, we consider the State's argument that the Compulsory Process Clause of the Sixth Amendment is merely a guarantee that the accused shall have the power to subpoena witnesses and simply does not apply to rulings on the admissibility of evidence.

II

In the State's view, no Compulsory Process Clause concerns are even raised by authorizing preclusion as a discovery sanction, or by the application of the Illinois rule in this case. The State's argument is supported by the plain language of the Clause ... by the historical evidence that it was intended to provide defendants with subpoena power that they lacked at common law, by some scholarly comment, and by a brief excerpt from the legislative history of the Clause. We have, however, consistently given the Clause the broader reading reflected in contemporaneous state constitutional provisions.

As we noted just last Term, "[o]ur cases establish, at a minimum, that criminal defendants have the right to the government's assistance in compelling the attendance of favorable witnesses at trial and the right to put before a jury evidence that might influence the determination of guilt." Pennsylvania v. Ritchie, 480 U.S. 39, 56 (1987). Few rights are more fundamental than that of an accused to present witnesses in his own defense . . . . Indeed, this right is an essential attribute of the adversary system itself.

. . .

The right to compel a witness' presence in the courtroom could not protect the integrity of the adversary process if it did not embrace the right to have the witness' testimony heard by the trier of fact. The right to offer testimony is thus grounded in the Sixth Amendment even though it is not expressly described in so many words . . . .

The right of the defendant to present evidence "stands on no lesser footing than the other Sixth Amendment rights that we have previously held applicable to the States." [Washington v. Texas, 388 U.S. 14 (1967)], at 18. We cannot accept the State's argument that this constitutional right may never be offended by the imposition of a discovery sanction that entirely excludes the testimony of a material defense witness.

III

Petitioner's claim that the Sixth Amendment creates an absolute bar to the preclusion of the testimony of a surprise witness is just as extreme and just as unacceptable as the State's position that the Amendment is simply irrelevant. The accused does not have an unfettered right to offer testimony that is incompetent, privileged, or otherwise inadmissible under standard rules of evidence. The Compulsory Process Clause provides him with an effective weapon, but it is a weapon that cannot be used irresponsibly.

There is a significant difference between the Compulsory Process Clause weapon and other rights that are protected by the Sixth Amendment—its availability is dependent entirely on the defendant's initiative. Most other Sixth Amendment rights arise automatically on the initiation of the adversary process and no action by the defendant is necessary to make them active in his or her case. While those rights shield the defendant from potential prosecutorial abuses, the right to compel the presence and present the testimony of witnesses provides the defendant with a sword that may be employed to rebut the prosecution's case. The decision whether to employ it in a particular case rests solely with the defendant. The very nature of the right requires that its effective use be preceded by deliberate planning and affirmative conduct.

The principle that undergirds the defendant's right to present exculpatory evidence is also the source of essential limitations on the right. The adversary process could not function effectively without adherence to rules of procedure that govern the orderly presentation of facts and arguments to provide each party with a fair opportunity to assemble and submit evidence to contradict or explain the opponent's case. The trial process would be a shambles if either party had an absolute right to control the time and content of his witnesses' testimony. Neither may insist on the right to interrupt the opposing party's case, and obviously there is no absolute right to interrupt the deliberations of the jury to present newly discovered evidence. The State's interest in the orderly conduct of a criminal trial is sufficient to justify the imposition and enforcement of firm, though not always inflexible, rules relating to the identification and presentation of evidence.

The defendant's right to compulsory process is itself designed to vindicate the principle that the "ends of criminal justice would be defeated if judgments were to be founded on a partial or speculative presentation of the facts." United States v. Nixon, 418 U.S. [683 (1974)], at 709. Rules that provide for pretrial discovery of an opponent's witnesses serve the same high purpose. Discovery, like cross-examination, minimizes the risk that a judgment will be predicated on incomplete, misleading, or even deliberately fabricated testimony. The "State's interest in protecting itself against an eleventh hour defense" is merely one component of the broader public interest in a full and truthful disclosure of critical facts.

To vindicate that interest we have held that even the defendant may not testify without being subjected to cross-examination. . . . Moreover, in United States v. Nobles, 422 U.S. 225 (1975), we upheld an order excluding the testimony of an expert witness tendered by the defendant because he had refused to permit discovery of a "highly relevant" report. . . .

Petitioner does not question the legitimacy of a rule requiring pretrial disclosure of defense witnesses, but he argues that the sanction of preclusion of the testimony of a previously undisclosed witness is so drastic that it should never be imposed. He argues, correctly, that a less drastic sanction is always available. Prejudice to the prosecution could be minimized by granting a continuance or a mistrial to provide time for further investigation; moreover, further violations can be deterred by disciplinary sanctions against the defendant or defense counsel.

It may well be true that alternative sanctions are adequate and appropriate in most cases, but it is equally clear that they would be less effective than the preclusion sanction and that there are instances in which they would perpetuate rather than limit the prejudice to the State and the harm to the adversary process. One of the purposes of the discovery rule itself is to minimize the risk that fabricated testimony will be believed. Defendants who are willing to fabricate a defense may also be willing to fabricate excuses for failing to comply with a discovery requirement. The risk of a contempt violation may seem trivial to a defendant facing the threat of imprisonment for a term of years. A dishonest client can mislead an honest attorney, and there are occasions when an attorney assumes that the duty of loyalty to the client outweighs elementary obligations to the court.

We presume that evidence that is not discovered until after the trial is over would not have affected the outcome. It is equally reasonable to presume that there is something suspect about a defense witness who is not identified until after the eleventh hour has passed. If a pattern of discovery violations is explicable only on the assumption that the violations were designed to conceal a plan to present fabricated testimony, it would be entirely appropriate to exclude the tainted evidence regardless of whether other sanctions would also be merited.

In order to reject petitioner's argument that preclusion is *never* a permissible sanction for a discovery violation it is neither necessary nor appropriate for us to attempt to draft a comprehensive set of standards to guide the exercise of discretion in every possible case. It is elementary, of course, that a trial court may not ignore the fundamental character of the defendant's right to offer the testimony of witnesses in his favor. But the mere invocation of that right cannot automatically and invariably outweigh countervailing public interests. The integrity of the adversary process, which depends both on the presentation of reliable evidence and the rejection of unreliable evidence, the interest in the fair and efficient administration of justice, and the potential prejudice to the truth-determining function of the trial process must also weigh in the balance.

A trial judge may certainly insist on an explanation for a party's failure to comply with a request to identify his or her witnesses in advance of trial. If that explanation reveals that the omission was willful and motivated by a desire to obtain a tactical advantage that would minimize the effectiveness of cross-examination and the ability to adduce rebuttal evidence, it would be entirely consistent with the purposes of the Compulsory Process Clause simply to exclude the witness' testimony. . . .

The simplicity of compliance with the discovery rule is also relevant. As we have noted, the Compulsory Process Clause cannot be invoked without the prior planning and affirmative conduct of the defendant. Lawyers are accustomed to meeting deadlines. Routine preparation involves location and interrogation of potential witnesses and the serving of subpoenas on those whose testimony will be offered at trial. The burden of identifying them in advance of trial adds little to these routine demands of trial preparation.

It would demean the high purpose of the Compulsory Process Clause to construe it as encompassing an absolute right to an automatic continuance or mistrial to allow presumptively perjured testimony to be presented to a jury. We reject petitioner's argument that a preclusion sanction is never appropriate no matter how serious the defendant's discovery violation may be.

IV

Petitioner argues that the preclusion sanction was unnecessarily harsh in this case because the *voir dire* examination of Wormley adequately protected the prosecution from any possible prejudice resulting from surprise. Petitioner also contends that it is unfair to visit the sins of the lawyer upon his client. Neither argument has merit.

More is at stake than possible prejudice to the prosecution. We are also concerned with the impact of this kind of conduct on the integrity of the judicial process itself. The trial judge found that the discovery violation in this case was both willful and blatant. In view of the fact that petitioner's counsel had actually interviewed Wormley during the week before the trial began and the further fact that he amended his Answer to Discovery on the first day of trial without identifying Wormley while he did identify two actual eyewitnesses whom he did not place on the stand, the inference that he was deliberately seeking a tactical advantage is inescapable. Regardless of whether prejudice to the prosecution could have been avoided in this particular case, it is plain that the case fits into the category of willful misconduct in which the severest sanction is appropriate. After all, the court, as well as the prosecutor, has a vital interest in protecting the trial process from the pollution of perjured testimony. Evidentiary rules which apply to categories of inadmissible evidence—ranging from hearsay to the fruits of illegal searches—may properly be enforced even though the particular testimony being offered is not prejudicial. The pretrial conduct revealed by the record in this case gives rise to a sufficiently strong inference that "witnesses are being found that really weren't there," to justify the sanction of preclusion.

The argument that the client should not be held responsible for his lawyer's misconduct strikes at the heart of the attorney-client relationship. Although there are basic rights that the attorney cannot waive without the fully informed and publicly acknowledged consent of the client, the lawyer has—and must have—full authority to manage the conduct of the trial. The adversary process could not function effectively if every tactical decision required client approval. Moreover, given the protections afforded by the attorney-client privilege and the fact that extreme cases may involve unscrupulous conduct by both the client and the lawyer, it would be highly impracticable to require an investigation into their relative responsibilities before applying the sanction of preclusion. In responding to discovery, the client has a duty to be candid and forthcoming with the lawyer, and when the lawyer responds, he or she speaks for the client. Putting to one side the exceptional cases in which counsel is ineffective, the client must accept the consequences of the lawyer's decision to forgo cross-examination, to decide not to put certain witnesses on the stand, or to decide not to disclose the identity of certain witnesses in advance of trial. In this case, petitioner has no greater right to disavow his lawyer's decision to conceal Wormley's identity until after the trial had commenced than he has to disavow the decision to refrain from adducing testimony from the eyewitnesses who were identified in the Answer to Discovery. Whenever a lawyer makes use of the sword provided by the Compulsory Process Clause, there is some risk that he may wound his own client.

The judgment of the Illinois Appellate Court is

Affirmed.

JUSTICE BRENNAN, with whom JUSTICE MARSHALL and JUSTICE BLACKMUN join, dissenting.

Criminal discovery is not a game. It is integral to the quest for truth and the fair adjudication of guilt or innocence. Violations of discovery rules thus cannot go uncorrected or undeterred without undermining the truthseeking process. The question in this case, however, is not whether discovery rules should be enforced but whether the need to correct and deter discovery violations requires a sanction that itself distorts the truthseeking process by excluding material evidence of innocence in a criminal case. I conclude that, at least where a criminal defendant is not personally responsible for the discovery violation, alternative sanctions are not only adequate to correct and deter discovery violations but are far superior to the arbitrary and disproportionate penalty imposed by the preclusion sanction. Because of this, and because the Court's balancing test creates a conflict of interest in every case involving a discovery violation, I would hold that, absent evidence of the defendant's personal involvement in a discovery violation, the Compulsory Process Clause *per se* bars discovery sanctions that exclude criminal defense evidence.

[*]

. . .

[*] Justice Blackmun wrote a brief dissenting opinion.

UNITED STATES v. AGURS

427 U.S. 97, 96 S.Ct. 2392, 49 L.Ed.2d 342 (1976).

MR. JUSTICE STEVENS delivered the opinion of the Court.

After a brief interlude in an inexpensive motel room respondent repeatedly stabbed James Sewell, causing his death. She was convicted of second-degree murder. The question before us is whether the prosecutor's failure to provide defense counsel with certain background information about Sewell, which would have tended to support the argument that respondent acted in self-defense, deprived her of a fair trial under the rule of Brady v. Maryland, 373 U.S. 83.

The answer to the question depends on (1) a review of the facts, (2) the significance of the failure of defense counsel to request the material, and (3) the standard by which the prosecution's failure to volunteer exculpatory material should be judged.

I

At about 4:30 p.m. on September 24, 1971, respondent, who had been there before, and Sewell, registered in a motel as man and wife. They were assigned a room without a bath. Sewell was wearing a bowie knife in a sheath, and carried another knife in his pocket. Less than two hours earlier, according to the testimony of his estranged wife, he had had $360 in cash on his person.

About 15 minutes later three motel employees heard respondent screaming for help. A forced entry into their room disclosed Sewell on top of respondent struggling for possession of the bowie knife. She was holding the knife; his bleeding hand grasped the blade; according to one witness he was trying to jam the blade into her chest. The employees separated the two and summoned the authorities. Respondent departed without comment before they arrived. Sewell was dead on arrival at the hospital.

Circumstantial evidence indicated that the parties had completed an act of intercourse, that Sewell had then gone to the bathroom down the hall, and the struggle occurred upon his return. The contents of his pockets were in disarray on the dresser and no money was found; the jury may have inferred that respondent took Sewell's money and that the fight started when Sewell re-entered the room and saw what she was doing.

On the following morning respondent surrendered to the police. She was given a physical examination which revealed no cuts or bruises of any kind except needle marks on her upper arm. An autopsy of Sewell disclosed that he had several deep stab wounds in

1045

his chest and abdomen and a number of slashes on his arms and hands, characterized by the pathologist as "defensive wounds."

Respondent offered no evidence. Her sole defense was the argument made by her attorney that Sewell had initially attacked her with the knife, and that her actions had all been directed toward saving her own life. The support for this self-defense theory was based on the fact that she had screamed for help. Sewell was on top of her when help arrived, and his possession of two knives indicated that he was a violence-prone person. It took the jury about 25 minutes to elect a foreman and return a verdict.

Three months later defense counsel filed a motion for a new trial asserting that he had discovered (1) that Sewell had a prior criminal record that would have further evidenced his violent character; (2) that the prosecutor had failed to disclose this information to the defense; and (3) that a recent opinion of the United States Court of Appeals for the District of Columbia Circuit made it clear that such evidence was admissible even if not known to the defendant. Sewell's prior record included a plea of guilty to a charge of assault and carrying a deadly weapon in 1963, and another guilty plea to a charge of carrying a deadly weapon in 1971. Apparently both weapons were knives.

The Government opposed the motion, arguing that there was no duty to tender Sewell's prior record to the defense in the absence of an appropriate request; that the evidence was readily discoverable in advance of trial and hence was not the kind of "newly discovered" evidence justifying a new trial; and that, in all events, it was not material.

The District Court denied the motion. It rejected the Government's argument that there was no duty to disclose material evidence unless requested to do so, assumed that the evidence was admissible, but held that it was not sufficiently material. The District Court expressed the opinion that the prior conviction shed no light on Sewell's character that was not already apparent from the uncontradicted evidence, particularly the fact that he carried two knives; the court stressed the inconsistency between the claim of self-defense and the fact that Sewell had been stabbed repeatedly while respondent was unscathed.

The Court of Appeals reversed.[5] The Court found no lack of diligence on the part of the defense and no misconduct by the prosecutor in this case. It held, however, that the evidence was material, and that its nondisclosure required a new trial because the jury might have returned a different verdict if the evidence had been received.

The decision of the Court of Appeals represents a significant departure from this Court's prior holding; because we believe that

5. 167 U.S.App.D.C. 28, 510 F.2d 1249 (1975). ...

that Court has incorrectly interpreted the constitutional requirement of due process, we reverse.

II

The rule of Brady v. Maryland, 373 U.S. 83, arguably applies in
three quite different situations. Each involves the discovery, after
trial, of information which had been known to the prosecution but
unknown to the defense.

In the first situation, typified by Mooney v. Holohan, 294 U.S.
103, the undisclosed evidence demonstrates that the prosecution's
case includes perjured testimony and that the prosecution knew, or
should have known, of the perjury. In a series of subsequent cases,
the Court has consistently held that a conviction obtained by the
knowing use of perjured testimony is fundamentally unfair, and
must be set aside if there is any reasonable likelihood that the false
testimony could have affected the judgment of the jury. It is this
line of cases on which the Court of Appeals placed primary reliance.
In those cases the Court has applied a strict standard of materiality,
not just because they involve prosecutorial misconduct, but more
importantly because they involve a corruption of the truth-seeking
function of the trial process. Since this case involves no misconduct, and since there is no reason to question the veracity of any of
the prosecution witnesses, the test of materiality followed in the
Mooney line of cases is not necessarily applicable to this case.

The second situation, illustrated by the *Brady* case itself, is
characterized by a pretrial request for specific evidence. In that
case defense counsel had requested the extrajudicial statements
made by Brady's accomplice, one Boblit. This Court held that the
suppression of one of Boblit's statements deprived Brady of due
process, noting specifically that the statement had been requested
and that it was "material." A fair analysis of the holding in *Brady*
indicates that implicit in the requirement of materiality is a concern
that the suppressed evidence might have affected the outcome of
the trial.

Brady was found guilty of murder in the first degree. Since the
jury did not add the words "without capital punishment" to the
verdict, he was sentenced to death. At his trial Brady did not deny
his involvement in the deliberate killing, but testified that it was his
accomplice, Boblit, rather than he, who had actually strangled the
decedent. This version of the event was corroborated by one of
several confessions made by Boblit but not given to Brady's counsel
despite an admittedly adequate request.

After his conviction and sentence had been affirmed on appeal,
Brady filed a motion to set aside the judgment, and later a post-
conviction proceeding, in which he alleged that the State had
violated his constitutional rights by suppressing the Boblit confession. The trial judge denied relief largely because he felt that

Boblit's confession would have been inadmissible at Brady's trial. The Maryland Court of Appeals disagreed; it ordered a new trial on the issue of punishment. It held that the withholding of material evidence, even "without guile," was a denial of due process and that there were valid theories on which the confession might have been admissible in Brady's defense.

This Court granted certiorari to consider Brady's contention that the violation of his constitutional right to a fair trial vitiated the entire proceeding. The holding that the suppression of exculpatory evidence violated Brady's right to due process was affirmed, as was the separate holding that he should receive a new trial on the issue of punishment but not on the issue of guilt or innocence. The Court interpreted the Maryland Court of Appeals opinion as ruling that the confession was inadmissible on that issue. For that reason, the confession could not have affected the outcome on the issue of guilt but could have affected Brady's punishment. It was material on the latter issue but not the former. And since it was not material on the issue of guilt, the entire trial was not lacking in due process.

The test of materiality in a case like *Brady* in which specific information has been requested by the defense is not necessarily the same as in a case in which no such request has been made. Indeed, this Court has not yet decided whether the prosecutor has any obligation to provide defense counsel with exculpatory information when no request has been made. Before addressing that question, a brief comment on the function of the request is appropriate.

In *Brady* the request was specific. It gave the prosecutor notice of exactly what the defense desired. Although there is, of course, no duty to provide defense counsel with unlimited discovery of everything known by the prosecutor, if the subject matter of such a request is material, or indeed if a substantial basis for claiming materiality exists, it is reasonable to require the prosecutor to respond either by furnishing the information or by submitting the problem to the trial judge. When the prosecutor receives a specific and relevant request, the failure to make any response is seldom, if ever, excusable.

In many cases, however, exculpatory information in the possession of the prosecutor may be unknown to defense counsel. In such a situation he may make no request at all, or possibly ask for "all *Brady* material" or for "anything exculpatory." Such a request really gives the prosecutor no better notice than if no request is made. If there is a duty to respond to a general request of that kind, it must derive from the obviously exculpatory character of certain evidence in the hands of the prosecutor. But if the evidence is so clearly supportive of a claim of innocence that it gives the prosecution notice of a duty to produce, that duty should equally arise even if no request is made. Whether we focus on the desirability of a precise definition of the prosecutor's duty or on the potential harm to the defendant, we conclude that there is no significant difference between cases in which there has been merely a general request for exculpatory matter and cases, like the one we must now decide, in which there has been no request at all. The third situation in which the *Brady* rule arguably applies, typified by this case, therefore embraces the case in which only a general request for "*Brady* material" has been made.

We now consider whether the prosecutor has any constitutional duty to volunteer exculpatory matter to the defense, and if so, what standard of materiality gives rise to that duty.

III

We are not considering the scope of discovery authorized by the Federal Rules of Criminal Procedure, or the wisdom of amending those Rules to enlarge the defendant's discovery rights. We are dealing with the defendant's right to a fair trial mandated by the Due Process Clause of the Fifth Amendment to the Constitution. Our construction of that Clause will apply equally to the comparable clause in the Fourteenth Amendment applicable to trials in state courts.

The problem arises in two principal contexts. First, in advance of trial, and perhaps during the course of a trial as well, the prosecutor must decide what, if anything, he should voluntarily submit to defense counsel. Second, after trial a judge may be required to decide whether a nondisclosure deprived the defendant of his right to due process. Logically the same standard must apply at both times. For unless the omission deprived the defendant of a fair trial, there was no constitutional violation requiring that the verdict be set aside; and absent a constitutional violation, there was no breach of the prosecutor's constitutional duty to disclose.

Nevertheless, there is a significant practical difference between the pretrial decision of the prosecutor and the post-trial decision of the judge. Because we are dealing with an inevitably imprecise standard, and because the significance of an item of evidence can seldom be predicted accurately until the entire record is complete, the prudent prosecutor will resolve doubtful questions in favor of disclosure. But to reiterate a critical point, the prosecutor will not have violated his constitutional duty of disclosure unless his omission is of sufficient significance to result in the denial of the defendant's right to a fair trial.

The Court of Appeals appears to have assumed that the prosecutor has a constitutional obligation to disclose any information that might affect the jury's verdict. That statement of a constitutional standard of materiality approaches the "sporting theory of justice" which the Court expressly rejected in *Brady*. For a jury's appraisal of a case "might" be affected by an improper or trivial consideration as well as by evidence giving rise to a legitimate doubt on the issue of guilt. If everything that might influence a jury must be disclosed, the only way a prosecutor could discharge his constitutional duty would be to allow complete discovery of his files as a matter of routine practice.

Whether or not procedural rules authorizing such broad discovery might be desirable, the Constitution surely does not demand that much. While expressing the opinion that representatives of the State may not "suppress substantial material evidence," former Chief Justice Traynor of the California Supreme Court has pointed out that "they are under no duty to report sua sponte to the defendant all that they learn about the case and about their witnesses." In re Imbler, 60 Cal.2d 554, 569, 387 P.2d 6, 14 (1963). And this Court recently noted that there is "no constitutional requirement that the prosecution make a complete and detailed accounting to the defense of all police investigatory work on a case." Moore v. Illinois, 408 U.S. 786, 795. The mere possibility that an item of undisclosed information might have helped the defense, or might have affected the outcome of the trial, does not establish "materiality" in the constitutional sense.

Nor do we believe the constitutional obligation is measured by the moral culpability, or the willfulness, of the prosecutor. If evidence highly probative of innocence is in his file, he should be presumed to recognize its significance even if he has actually overlooked it. ... Conversely, if evidence actually has no probative significance at all, no purpose would be served by requiring a new trial simply because an inept prosecutor incorrectly believed he was suppressing a fact that would be vital to the defense. If the suppression of evidence results in constitutional error, it is because of the character of the evidence, not the character of the prosecutor.

As the District Court recognized in this case, there are situations in which evidence is obviously of such substantial value to the defense that elementary fairness requires it to be disclosed even without a specific request. For though the attorney for the sovereign must prosecute the accused with earnestness and vigor, he must always be faithful to his client's overriding interest that "justice shall be done." He is the "servant of the law, the twofold aim of which is that guilt shall not escape nor innocence suffer." Berger v. United States, 295 U.S. 78, 88. This description of the prosecutor's duty illuminates the standard of materiality that governs his obligation to disclose exculpatory evidence.

On the one hand, the fact that such evidence was available to the prosecutor and not submitted to the defense places it in a different category than if it had simply been discovered from a neutral source after trial. For that reason the defendant should not have to satisfy the severe burden of demonstrating that newly discovered evidence probably would have resulted in acquittal.[19] If

---

19. This is the standard generally applied by lower courts in evaluating motions for new trial under Fed.Rule Crim.Proc. 33 of the Federal Rules of Criminal Procedure based on newly discovered evidence. ...

the standard applied to the usual motion for a new trial based on newly discovered evidence were the same when the evidence was in the State's possession as when it was found in a neutral source, there would be no special significance to the prosecutor's obligation to serve the cause of justice.

On the other hand, since we have rejected the suggestion that the prosecutor has a constitutional duty routinely to deliver his entire file to defense counsel, we cannot consistently treat every nondisclosure as though it were error. It necessarily follows that the judge should not order a new trial every time he is unable to characterize a nondisclosure as harmless under the customary harmless-error standard. Under that standard when error is present in the record, the reviewing judge must set aside the verdict and judgment unless his "conviction is sure that the error did not influence the jury, or had but very slight effect." Kotteakos v. United States, 328 U.S. 750, 764. Unless every nondisclosure is regarded as automatic error, the constitutional standard of materiality must impose a higher burden on the defendant.

The proper standard of materiality must reflect our overriding concern with the justice of the finding of guilt.[20] Such a finding is permissible only if supported by evidence establishing guilt beyond a reasonable doubt. It necessarily follows that if the omitted evidence creates a reasonable doubt that did not otherwise exist, constitutional error has been committed. This means that the omission must be evaluated in the context of the entire record. If there is no reasonable doubt about guilt whether or not the additional evidence is considered, there is no justification for a new trial. On the other hand, if the verdict is already of questionable validity, additional evidence of relatively minor importance might be sufficient to create a reasonable doubt.

This statement of the standard of materiality describes the test which courts appear to have applied in actual cases although the standard has been phrased in different language. It is also the standard which the trial judge applied in this case. He evaluated the significance of Sewell's prior criminal record in the context of the full trial which he recalled in detail. Stressing in particular the incongruity of a claim that Sewell was the aggressor with the evidence of his multiple wounds and respondent's unscathed condi-

---

20. It has been argued that the standard should focus on the impact of the undisclosed evidence on the defendant's ability to prepare for trial, rather than the materiality of the evidence to the issue of guilt or innocence.... Such a standard would be unacceptable for determining the materiality of what has been generally recognized as "*Brady* material" for two reasons. First, that standard would necessarily encompass incriminating evidence as well as exculpatory evidence, since knowledge of the prosecutor's entire case would always be useful in planning the defense. Second, such an approach would primarily involve an analysis of the adequacy of the notice given to the defendant by the State, and it has always been the Court's view that the notice component of due process refers to the charge rather than the evidentiary support for the charge.

tion, the trial judge indicated his unqualified opinion that respondent was guilty. He noted that Sewell's prior record did not contradict any evidence offered by the prosecutor, and was largely cumulative of the evidence that Sewell was wearing a bowie knife in a sheath and carrying a second knife in his pocket when he registered at the motel.

Since the arrest record was not requested and did not even arguably give rise to any inference of perjury, since after considering it in the context of the entire record the trial judge remained convinced of respondent's guilt beyond a reasonable doubt, and since we are satisfied that his firsthand appraisal of the record was thorough and entirely reasonable, we hold that the prosecutor's failure to tender Sewell's record to the defense did not deprive respondent of a fair trial as guaranteed by the Due Process Clause of the Fifth Amendment. Accordingly, the judgment of the Court of Appeals is

Reversed.[*]

[*] Justice Marshall wrote a dissenting opinion, which Justice Brennan joined.

ARIZONA v. YOUNGBLOOD

488 U.S. 51, 109 S.Ct. 333, 102 L.Ed.2d 281 (1988).

CHIEF JUSTICE REHNQUIST delivered the opinion of the Court.

Respondent Larry Youngblood was convicted by a Pima County, Arizona, jury of child molestation, sexual assault, and kidnaping. The Arizona Court of Appeals reversed his conviction on the ground that the State had failed to preserve semen samples from the victim's body and clothing. 153 Ariz. 50, 734 P.2d 592 (1986). We granted certiorari to consider the extent to which the Due Process Clause of the Federal Constitution requires the State to preserve evidentiary material that might be useful to a criminal defendant.

On October 29, 1983, David L., a 10-year-old boy, attended a church service with his mother. After he left the service at about 9:30 p.m., the boy went to a carnival behind the church, where he was abducted by a middle-aged man of medium height and weight. The assailant drove the boy to a secluded area near a ravine and molested him. He then took the boy to an unidentified, sparsely furnished house where he sodomized the boy four times. Afterwards, the assailant tied the boy up while he went outside to start his car. Once the assailant started the car, albeit with some difficulty, he returned to the house and again sodomized the boy. The assailant then sent the boy to the bathroom to wash up before he returned him to the carnival. He threatened to kill the boy if he told anyone about the attack. The entire ordeal lasted about 1½ hours.

After the boy made his way home, his mother took him to Kino Hospital. At the hospital, a physician treated the boy for rectal injuries. The physician also used a "sexual assault kit" to collect evidence of the attack. The Tuscon Police Department provided such kits to all hospitals in Pima County for use in sexual assault cases. Under standard procedure, the victim of a sexual assault was taken to a hospital, where a physician used the kit to collect evidence. The kit included paper to collect saliva samples, a tube for obtaining a blood sample, microscopic slides for making smears, a set of Q-tip like swabs, and a medical examination report. Here, the physician used the swab to collect samples from the boy's rectum and mouth. He then made a microscopic slide of the samples. The doctor also obtained samples of the boy's saliva, blood, and hair. The physician did not examine the samples at any time. The police placed the kit in a secure refrigerator at the police station. At the hospital, the police also collected the boy's underwear and T-shirt. This clothing was not refrigerated or frozen.

Nine days after the attack, on November 7, 1983, the police asked the boy to pick out his assailant from a photographic lineup. The boy identified respondent as the assailant. Respondent was not located by the police until four weeks later; he was arrested on December 9, 1983.

On November 8, 1983, Edward Heller, a police criminologist, examined the sexual assault kit. He testified that he followed standard department procedure, which was to examine the slides and determine whether sexual contact had occurred. After he determined that such contact had occurred, the criminologist did not perform any other tests, although he placed the assault kit back in the refrigerator. He testified that tests to identify blood group substances were not routinely conducted during the initial examination of an assault kit and in only about half of all cases in any event. He did not test the clothing at this time.

Respondent was indicted on charges of child molestation, sexual assault, and kidnaping. The State moved to compel respondent to provide blood and saliva samples for comparison with the material gathered through the use of the sexual assault kit, but the trial court denied the motion on the ground that the State had not obtained a sufficiently large semen sample to make a valid comparison. The prosecutor then asked the State's criminologist to perform an ABO blood group test on the rectal swab sample in an attempt to ascertain the blood type of the boy's assailant. This test failed to detect any blood group substances in the sample.

In January 1985, the police criminologist examined the boy's clothing for the first time. He found one semen stain on the boy's underwear and another on the rear of his T-shirt. The criminologist tried to obtain blood group substances from both stains using the ABO technique, but was unsuccessful. He also performed a P–30 protein molecule test on the stains, which indicated that only a small quantity of semen was present on the clothing; it was inconclusive as to the assailant's identity. The Tucson Police Department had just begun using this test, which was then used in slightly more than half of the crime laboratories in the country.

Respondent's principal defense at trial was that the boy had erred in identifying him as the perpetrator of the crime. In this connection, both a criminologist for the State and an expert witness for respondent testified as to what might have been shown by tests performed on the samples shortly after they were gathered, or by later tests performed on the samples from the boy's clothing had the clothing been properly refrigerated. The court instructed the jury that if they found the State had destroyed or lost evidence, they might "infer that the true fact is against the State's interest." 10 Tr. 90.

The jury found respondent guilty as charged, but the Arizona Court of Appeals reversed the judgment of conviction. It stated that " 'when identity is an issue at trial and the police permit the destruction of evidence that could eliminate the defendant as the perpetrator, such loss is material to the defense and is a denial of due process.' "   153 Ariz., at 54, 734 P.2d, at 596, quoting State v. Escalante, 153 Ariz. 55, 61, 734 P.2d 597, 603 (App.1986).   The Court of Appeals concluded on the basis of the expert testimony at trial that timely performance of tests with properly preserved semen samples could have produced results that might have completely exonerated respondent.   The Court of Appeals reached this conclusion even though it did "not imply any bad faith on the part of the State."   153 Ariz., at 54, 734 P.2d, at 596.   The Supreme Court of Arizona denied the State's petition for review, and we granted certiorari.   485 U.S. 903 (1988).   We now reverse.

Decision of this case requires us to again consider "what might loosely be called the area of constitutionally guaranteed access to evidence."   United States v. Valenzuela-Bernal, 458 U.S. 858, 867 (1982).   In Brady v. Maryland, 373 U.S. 83 (1963), we held "that the suppression by the prosecution of evidence favorable to the accused upon request violates due process where the evidence is material either to guilt or to punishment, irrespective of the good faith or bad faith of the prosecution."   Id., at 87.   In United States v. Agurs, 427 U.S. 97 (1976), we held that the prosecution had a duty to disclose some evidence of this description even though no requests were made for it, but at the same time we rejected the notion that a "prosecutor has a constitutional duty routinely to deliver his entire file to defense counsel."   Id., at 111 . . . .

There is no question but that the State complied with *Brady* and *Agurs* here.   The State disclosed relevant police reports to respondent, which contained information about the existence of the swab and the clothing, and the boy's examination at the hospital. The State provided respondent's expert with the laboratory reports and notes prepared by the police criminologist, and respondent's expert had access to the swab and to the clothing.

If respondent is to prevail on federal constitutional grounds, then, it must be because of some constitutional duty over and above that imposed by cases such as *Brady* and *Agurs*.   Our most recent decision in this area of the law, California v. Trombetta, 467 U.S. 479 (1984), arose out of a drunk driving prosecution in which the State had introduced test results indicating the concentration of alcohol in the blood of two motorists.   The defendants sought to suppress the test results on the ground that the State had failed to preserve the breath samples used in the test.   We rejected this argument for several reasons: first, "the officers here were acting in 'good faith and in accord with their normal practice,' " id., at 488, quoting Killian v. United States, 368 U.S. 231, 242 (1961); second, in the light of the procedures actually used the chances that preserved samples would have exculpated the defendants were slim, 467 U.S., at 489; and, third, even if the samples might have shown inaccuracy in the tests, the defendants had "alternative means of demonstrating their innocence." Id., at 490. In the present case, the likelihood that the preserved materials would have enabled the defendant to exonerate himself appears to be greater than it was in *Trombetta*, but here, unlike in *Trombetta*, the State did not attempt to make any use of the materials in its own case in chief.

Our decisions in related areas have stressed the importance for constitutional purposes of good or bad faith on the part of the Government when the claim is based on loss of evidence attributable to the Government. In United States v. Marion, 404 U.S. 307 (1971), we said that "[n]o actual prejudice to the conduct of the defense is alleged or proved, and there is no showing that the Government intentionally delayed to gain some tactical advantage over appellees or to harass them." Id., at 325 .... Similarly, in United States v. Valenzuela-Bernal, supra, we considered whether the Government's deportation of two witnesses who were illegal aliens violated due process. We held that the prompt deportation of the witnesses was justified "upon the Executive's good-faith determination that they possess no evidence favorable to the defendant in a criminal prosecution." 458 U.S., at 872.

The Due Process Clause of the Fourteenth Amendment, as interpreted in *Brady*, makes the good or bad faith of the State irrelevant when the State fails to disclose to the defendant material exculpatory evidence. But we think the Due Process Clause requires a different result when we deal with the failure of the State to preserve evidentiary material of which no more can be said than that it could have been subjected to tests, the results of which might have exonerated the defendant. Part of the reason for the difference in treatment is found in the observation made by the Court in *Trombetta*, supra, at 486, that "[w]henever potentially exculpatory evidence is permanently lost, courts face the treacherous task of divining the import of materials whose contents are unknown and, very often, disputed." Part of it stems from our unwillingness to read the "fundamental fairness" requirement of the Due Process Clause ... as imposing on the police an undifferentiated and absolute duty to retain and to preserve all material that might be of conceivable evidentiary significance in a particular prosecution. We think that requiring a defendant to show bad faith on the part of the police both limits the extent of the police's obligation to preserve evidence to reasonable bounds and confines it to that class of cases where the interests of justice most clearly require it, i.e., those cases in which the police themselves by their conduct indicate that the evidence could form a basis for exonerating the defendant. We therefore hold that unless a criminal defendant can show bad faith on the part of the police, failure to preserve potentially useful evidence does not constitute a denial of due process of law.

In this case, the police collected the rectal swab and clothing on the night of the crime; respondent was not taken into custody until six weeks later. The failure of the police to refrigerate the clothing and to perform tests on the semen samples can at worst be described as negligent. None of this information was concealed from respondent at trial, and the evidence—such as it was—was made available to respondent's expert who declined to perform any tests on the samples. The Arizona Court of Appeals noted in its opinion—and we agree—that there was no suggestion of bad faith on the part of the police. It follows, therefore, from what we have said, that there was no violation of the Due Process Clause.

The Arizona Court of Appeals also referred somewhat obliquely to the State's "inability to quantitatively test" certain semen samples with the newer P–30 test. 153 Ariz., at 54, 734 P.2d, at 596. If the court meant by this statement that the Due Process Clause is violated when the police fail to use a particular investigatory tool, we strongly disagree. The situation here is no different than a prosecution for drunk driving that rests on police observation alone; the defendant is free to argue to the finder of fact that a breathalizer test might have been exculpatory, but the police do not have a constitutional duty to perform any particular tests.

The judgment of the Arizona Court of Appeals is reversed and the case remanded for further proceedings not inconsistent with this opinion.

Reversed.[*]

---

[*] Justice Stevens wrote an opinion concurring in the judgment. Justice Blackmun wrote a dissenting opinion, which Justice Brennan and Justice Marshall joined.

VICTOR v. NEBRASKA

___ U.S. ___, 114 S.Ct. 1239, 127 L.Ed.2d 583 (1994).

JUSTICE O'CONNOR delivered the opinion of the Court.

The government must prove beyond a reasonable doubt every element of a charged offense. In re Winship, 397 U.S. 358 (1970). Although this standard is an ancient and honored aspect of our criminal justice system, it defies easy explication. In these cases, we consider the constitutionality of two attempts to define "reasonable doubt."

I

The beyond a reasonable doubt standard is a requirement of due process, but the Constitution neither prohibits trial courts from defining reasonable doubt nor requires them to do so as a matter of course. . . . Indeed, so long as the court instructs the jury on the necessity that the defendant's guilt be proven beyond a reasonable doubt. . . . the Constitution does not require that any particular form of words be used in advising the jury of the government's burden of proof. . . . Rather, "taken as a whole, the instructions [must] correctly conve[y] the concept of reasonable doubt to the jury." Holland v. United States, 348 U.S. 121, 140 (1954).

In only one case have we held that a definition of reasonable doubt violated the Due Process Clause. Cage v. Louisiana, 498 U.S. 39 (1990) *(per curiam)*. There, the jurors were told:

> " '[A reasonable doubt] is one that is founded upon a real tangible substantial basis and not upon mere caprice and conjecture. *It must be such doubt as would give rise to a grave uncertainty,* raised in your mind by reasons of the unsatisfactory character of the evidence or lack thereof. A reasonable doubt is not a mere possible doubt. *It is an actual substantial doubt.* It is a doubt that a reasonable man can seriously entertain. What is required is not an absolute or mathematical certainty, but a *moral certainty.*' " Id., at 40 (emphasis added by this Court in *Cage*).

We held that the highlighted portions of the instruction rendered it unconstitutional:

> "It is plain to us that the words 'substantial' and 'grave,' as they are commonly understood, suggest a higher degree of doubt than is required for acquittal under the reasonable doubt standard. When those statements are then considered with the reference to 'moral certainty,' rather than evidentiary certainty, it becomes clear that a reasonable juror could have interpreted

the instruction to allow a finding of guilt based on a degree of proof below that required by the Due Process Clause." Id., at 41.

In a subsequent case, we made clear that the proper inquiry is not whether the instruction "could have" been applied in an unconstitutional manner, but whether there is a reasonable likelihood that the jury *did* so apply it. Estelle v. McGuire, 502 U.S. ___, ___, and n. 4 (1991) (slip op., at 9, and n. 4). The constitutional question in the present cases, therefore, is whether there is a reasonable likelihood that the jury understood the instructions to allow conviction based on proof insufficient to meet the *Winship* standard. Although other courts have held that instructions similar to those given at petitioners' trials violate the Due Process Clause ... both the Nebraska and the California Supreme Courts held that the instructions were constitutional. We granted certiorari, 509 U.S. ___ (1993), and now affirm both judgments.

II

On October 14, 1984, petitioner Sandoval shot three men, two of them fatally, in a gang-related incident in Los Angeles. About two weeks later, he entered the home of a man who had given information to the police about the murders and shot him dead; Sandoval then killed the man's wife because she had seen him murder her husband. Sandoval was convicted on four counts of first degree murder. The jury found that Sandoval personally used a firearm in the commission of each offense, and found the special circumstance of multiple murder. ... He was sentenced to death for murdering the woman and to life in prison without possibility of parole for the other three murders. The California Supreme Court affirmed the convictions and sentences....

The jury in Sandoval's case was given the following instruction on the government's burden of proof:

"A defendant in a criminal action is presumed to be innocent until the contrary is proved, and in case of a reasonable doubt whether his guilt is satisfactorily shown, he is entitled to a verdict of not guilty. This presumption places upon the State the burden of proving him guilty beyond a reasonable doubt.

"Reasonable doubt is defined as follows: It is *not a mere possible doubt;* because everything relating to human affairs, and *depending on moral evidence,* is open to some possible or imaginary doubt. It is that state of the case which, after the entire comparison and consideration of all the evidence, leaves the minds of the jurors in that condition that they cannot say they feel an abiding conviction, *to a moral certainty,* of the truth of the charge." App. in No. 92–9049, p. 49 (emphasis added) (Sandoval App.).

The California Supreme Court rejected Sandoval's claim that the instruction, particularly the highlighted passages, violated the Due Process Clause. . . .

The instruction given in Sandoval's case has its genesis in a charge given by Chief Justice Shaw of the Massachusetts Supreme Judicial Court more than a century ago:

> "[W]hat is reasonable doubt? It is a term often used, probably pretty well understood, but not easily defined. It is not mere possible doubt; because every thing relating to human affairs, and depending on moral evidence, is open to some possible or imaginary doubt. It is that state of the case, which, after the entire comparison and consideration of all the evidence, leaves the minds of jurors in that condition that they cannot say they feel an abiding conviction, to a moral certainty, of the truth of the charge. The burden of proof is upon the prosecutor. All the presumptions of law independent of evidence are in favor of innocence; and every person is presumed to be innocent until he is proved guilty. If upon such proof there is reasonable doubt remaining, the accused is entitled to the benefit of it by an acquittal. For it is not sufficient to establish a probability, though a strong one arising from the doctrine of chances, that the fact charged is more likely to be true than the contrary; but the evidence must establish the truth of the fact to a reasonable and moral certainty; a certainty that convinces and directs the understanding, and satisfies the reason and judgment, of those who are bound to act conscientiously upon it. This we take to be proof beyond reasonable doubt." Commonwealth v. Webster, 59 Mass. 295, 320 (1850).

The *Webster* charge is representative of the time when "American courts began applying [the beyond a reasonable doubt standard] in its modern form in criminal cases." Apodaca v. Oregon, 406 U.S. 404, 412, n. 6 (1972) (plurality opinion). . . . In People v. Strong, 30 Cal. 151, 155 (1866), the California Supreme Court characterized the *Webster* instruction as "probably the most satisfactory definition ever given to the words 'reasonable doubt' in any case known to criminal jurisprudence." In People v. Paulsell, 115 Cal. 6, 12, 46 P. 734 (1896), the court cautioned state trial judges against departing from that formulation. And in 1927, the state legislature adopted the bulk of the *Webster* instruction as a statutory definition of reasonable doubt. Cal.Penal Code Ann. § 1096 (West 1985); see California Jury Instructions, Criminal, No. 2.90 (4th ed. 1979). Indeed, the California Legislature has directed that "the court may read to the jury section 1096 of this code, and no further instruction on the subject of the presumption of innocence or defining reasonable doubt need be given." § 1096a. The statutory instruction was given in Sandoval's case.

The California instruction was criticized in People v. Brigham, 25 Cal.3d 283, 292–316, 599 P.2d 100, 106–121 (1979) (Mosk, J., concurring). Justice Mosk apparently did not think the instruction was unconstitutional, but he "urge[d] the Legislature to reconsider its codification." Id., at 293, 599 P.2d, at 106. The California Assembly and Senate responded by requesting the committee on jury instructions of the Los Angeles Superior Court "to study alternatives to the definition of 'reasonable doubt' set forth in Section 1096 of the Penal Code, and to report its findings and recommendations to the Legislature." Cal.Assem.Con.Res. No. 148, 1986 Cal.Stats. 5634. The committee recommended that the legislature retain the statutory definition unmodified ... and § 1096 has not been changed.

A

Sandoval's primary objection is to the use of the phrases "moral evidence" and "moral certainty" in the instruction. As noted, this part of the charge was lifted verbatim from Chief Justice Shaw's *Webster* decision; some understanding of the historical context in which that instruction was written is accordingly helpful in evaluating its continuing validity.

By the beginning of the Republic, lawyers had borrowed the concept of "moral evidence" from the philosophers and historians of the 17th and 18th centuries. . . . James Wilson, who was instrumental in framing the Constitution and who served as one of the original Members of this Court, explained in a 1790 lecture on law that "evidence ... is divided into two species—demonstrative and moral." 1 Works of James Wilson 518 (J. Andrews ed. 1896). Wilson went on to explain the distinction thus:

> "Demonstrative evidence has for its subject abstract and necessary truths, or the unchangeable relations of ideas. Moral evidence has for its subject the real but contingent truths and connections, which take place among things actually existing. . . .

> "In moral evidence, there not only may be, but there generally is, contrariety of proofs: in demonstrative evidence, no such contrariety can take place. . . . [T]o suppose that two contrary demonstrations can exist, is to suppose that the same proposition is both true and false: which is manifestly absurd. With regard to moral evidence, there is, for the most part, real evidence on both sides. On both sides, contrary presumptions, contrary testimonies, contrary experiences must be balanced." Id., at 518–519.

A leading 19th century treatise observed that "[m]atters of fact are proved by *moral evidence* alone; ... [i]n the ordinary affairs of life, we do not require demonstrative evidence, . . . and to insist upon it would be unreasonable and absurd." 1 S. Greenleaf, Law of Evidence 3–4 (13th ed. 1876).

The phrase "moral certainty" shares an epistemological pedigree with moral evidence. . . . Moral certainty was the highest degree of certitude based on such evidence. . . . At least one early treatise explicitly equated moral certainty with proof beyond a reasonable doubt . . . .

Thus, when Chief Justice Shaw penned the *Webster* instruction in 1850, moral certainty meant a state of subjective certitude about some event or occurrence. As the Massachusetts Supreme Judicial Court subsequently explained:

> "Proof 'beyond a reasonable doubt' . . . is proof 'to a moral certainty,' as distinguished from an absolute certainty. As applied to a judicial trial for crime, the two phrases are synonymous and equivalent; each has been used by eminent judges to explain the other; and each signifies such proof as satisfies the judgment and consciences of the jury, as reasonable men, and applying their reason to the evidence before them, that the crime charged has been committed by the defendant, and so satisfies them as to leave no other reasonable conclusion possible." Commonwealth v. Costley, 118 Mass. 1, 24 (1875).

Indeed, we have said that "[p]roof to a 'moral certainty' is an equivalent phrase with 'beyond a reasonable doubt.' " Fidelity Mut. Life Assn. v. Mettler, 185 U.S. 308, 317 (1902), citing Commonwealth v. Costley, *supra.* . . .

We recognize that the phrase "moral evidence" is not a mainstay of the modern lexicon, though we do not think it means anything different today than it did in the 19th century. The few contemporary dictionaries that define moral evidence do so consistently with its original meaning. . . .

Moreover, the instruction itself gives a definition of the phrase. The jury was told that "everything relating to human affairs, and depending on moral evidence, is open to some possible or imaginary doubt"—in other words, that absolute certainty is unattainable in matters relating to human affairs. Moral evidence, in this sentence, can only mean empirical evidence offered to prove such matters—the proof introduced at trial.

This conclusion is reinforced by other instructions given in Sandoval's case. The judge informed the jurors that their duty was "to determine the facts of the case from the evidence received in the trial and not from any other source." Sandoval App. 38. The judge continued: "Evidence consists of testimony of witnesses, writings, material objects, or anything presented to the senses and offered to prove the existence or non-existence of a fact." Id., at

40. The judge also told the jurors that "you must not be influenced by pity for a defendant or by prejudice against him," and that "[y]ou must not be swayed by mere sentiment, conjecture, sympathy, passion, prejudice, public opinion or public feeling." Id., at 39. These instructions correctly pointed the jurors' attention to the facts of the case before them, not (as Sandoval contends) the ethics or morality of Sandoval's criminal acts. Accordingly, we find the reference to moral evidence unproblematic.

We are somewhat more concerned with Sandoval's argument that the phrase "moral certainty" has lost its historical meaning, and that a modern jury would understand it to allow conviction on proof that does not meet the beyond a reasonable doubt standard. Words and phrases can change meaning over time: a passage generally understood in 1850 may be incomprehensible or confusing to a modern juror. And although some contemporary dictionaries contain definitions of moral certainty similar to the 19th century understanding of the phrase ... we are willing to accept Sandoval's premise that "moral certainty," standing alone, might not be recognized by modern jurors as a synonym for "proof beyond a reasonable doubt." But it does not necessarily follow that the California instruction is unconstitutional.

Sandoval first argues that moral certainty would be understood by modern jurors to mean a standard of proof lower than beyond a reasonable doubt. In support of this proposition, Sandoval points to contemporary dictionaries that define moral certainty in terms of probability. ... But the beyond a reasonable doubt standard is itself probabilistic. ... The problem is not that moral certainty may be understood in terms of probability, but that a jury might understand the phrase to mean something less than the very high level of probability required by the Constitution in criminal cases.

Although in this respect moral certainty is ambiguous in the abstract, the rest of the instruction given in Sandoval's case lends content to the phrase. The jurors were told that they must have "an abiding conviction, to a moral certainty, of the truth of the charge." Sandoval App. 49. An instruction cast in terms of an abiding conviction as to guilt, without reference to moral certainty, correctly states the government's burden of proof. ... And the judge had already informed the jury that matters relating to human affairs are proven by moral evidence ...; giving the same meaning to the word moral in this part of the instruction, moral certainty can only mean certainty with respect to human affairs. As used in this instruction, therefore, we are satisfied that the reference to moral certainty, in conjunction with the abiding conviction language, "impress[ed] upon the factfinder the need to reach a subjective state of near certitude of the guilt of the accused." Jackson v. Virginia, 443 U.S. [307 (1979)], at 315. Accordingly, we reject Sandoval's contention that the moral certainty element of the California instruction invited the jury to convict him on proof below that required by the Due Process Clause.

Sandoval's second argument is a variant of the first. Accepting that the instruction requires a high level of confidence in the defendant's guilt, Sandoval argues that a juror might be convinced to a moral certainty that the defendant is guilty even though the government has failed to *prove* his guilt beyond a reasonable doubt. A definition of moral certainty in a widely used modern dictionary lends support to this argument . . . and we do not gainsay its force. As we have noted, "[t]he constitutional standard recognized in the *Winship* case was expressly phrased as one that protects an accused against a conviction except on '*proof* beyond a reasonable doubt.' " Jackson v. Virginia, supra, at 315 (emphasis in original). Indeed, in *Cage* we contrasted "moral certainty" with "evidentiary certainty." 498 U.S., at 41.

But the moral certainty language cannot be sequestered from its surroundings. In the *Cage* instruction, the jurors were simply told that they had to be morally certain of the defendant's guilt; there was nothing else in the instruction to lend meaning to the phrase. Not so here. The jury in Sandoval's case was told that a reasonable doubt is "that state of the case which, *after the entire comparison and consideration of all the evidence,* leaves the minds of the jurors in that condition that they cannot say they feel an abiding conviction, to a moral certainty, of the truth of the charge." Sandoval App. 49 (emphasis added). The instruction thus explicitly told the jurors that their conclusion had to be based on the evidence in the case. Other instructions reinforced this message. The jury was told "to determine the facts of the case from the evidence received in the trial and not from any other source." Id., at 38. The judge continued that "you must not be influenced by pity for a defendant or by prejudice against him. . . . You must not be swayed by mere sentiment, conjecture, sympathy, passion, prejudice, public opinion or public feeling." Id., at 39. Accordingly, there is no reasonable likelihood that the jury would have understood moral certainty to be disassociated from the evidence in the case.

We do not think it reasonably likely that the jury understood the words moral certainty either as suggesting a standard of proof lower than due process requires or as allowing conviction on factors other than the government's proof. At the same time, however, we do not condone the use of the phrase. As modern dictionary definitions of moral certainty attest, the common meaning of the phrase has changed since it was used in the *Webster* instruction, and it may continue to do so to the point that it conflicts with the *Winship* standard. Indeed, the definitions of reasonable doubt most widely used in the federal courts do not contain any reference to moral certainty. . . . But we have no supervisory power over the state courts, and in the context of the instructions as a whole we cannot say that the use of the phrase rendered the instruction given in Sandoval's case unconstitutional.

B

Finally, Sandoval objects to the portion of the charge in which the judge instructed the jury that a reasonable doubt is "not a mere possible doubt." The *Cage* instruction included an almost identical reference to "not a mere possible doubt," but we did not intimate that there was anything wrong with that part of the charge. See 498 U.S., at 40. That is because "[a] 'reasonable doubt,' at a minimum, is one based upon 'reason.'" Jackson v. Virginia, supra, at 317. A fanciful doubt is not a reasonable doubt. As Sandoval's defense attorney told the jury: "[A]nything can be possible.... [A] planet could be made out of blue cheese. But that's really not in the realm of what we're talking about." Sandoval App. 79 (excerpt from closing argument). That this is the sense in which the instruction uses "possible" is made clear from the final phrase of the sentence, which notes that everything "is open to some possible or imaginary doubt." We therefore reject Sandoval's challenge to this portion of the instruction as well.

III

On December 26, 1987, petitioner Victor went to the Omaha home of an 82 year-old woman for whom he occasionally did gardening work. Once inside, he beat her with a pipe and cut her throat with a knife, killing her. Victor was convicted of first degree murder. A three-judge panel found the statutory aggravating circumstances that Victor had previously been convicted of murder ... and that the murder in this case was especially heinous, atrocious, and cruel. Finding none of the statutory mitigating circumstances, the panel sentenced Victor to death. The Nebraska Supreme Court affirmed the conviction and sentence. ...

At Victor's trial, the judge instructed the jury that "[t]he burden is always on the State to prove beyond a reasonable doubt all of the material elements of the crime charged, and this burden never shifts." App. in No. 92–8894, p. 8 (Victor App.). The charge continued:

> " 'Reasonable doubt' is such a doubt as would cause a reasonable and prudent person, in one of the graver and more important transactions of life, to pause and hesitate before taking the represented facts as true and relying and acting thereon. It is such a doubt as will not permit you, after full, fair, and impartial consideration of all the evidence, to have an abiding conviction, *to a moral certainty,* of the guilt of the accused. At the same time, absolute or mathematical certainty is not required. You may be convinced of the truth of a fact beyond a reasonable doubt and yet be fully aware that possibly you may be mistaken. You may find an accused guilty upon

the *strong probabilities of the case*, provided such probabilities are strong enough to exclude any doubt of his guilt that is reasonable. A reasonable doubt is an *actual and substantial doubt* arising from the evidence, from the facts or circumstances shown by the evidence, or from the lack of evidence on the part of the state, as distinguished from a doubt arising from mere possibility, from bare imagination, or from fanciful conjecture." Id., at 11 (emphasis added).

On state postconviction review, the Nebraska Supreme Court rejected Victor's contention that the instruction, particularly the emphasized phrases, violated the Due Process Clause. ... Because the last state court in which review could be had considered Victor's constitutional claim on the merits, it is properly presented for our review despite Victor's failure to object to the instruction at trial or raise the issue on direct appeal. ...

The instruction given in Victor's case can be traced to two separate lines of cases. Much of the charge is taken from Chief Justice Shaw's *Webster* instruction. ... The rest derives from a series of decisions approving instructions cast in terms of an "actual doubt" that would cause a reasonable person to hesitate to act. ... In 1968, a committee appointed by the Nebraska Supreme Court developed model jury instructions; a court rule in effect at the time Victor was tried directed that those instructions were to be used where applicable. ... The model instruction on reasonable doubt, is the one given at Victor's trial. (Since Victor was tried, a revised reasonable-doubt instruction ... has been adopted, although the prior version may still be used.)

A

Victor's primary argument is that equating a reasonable doubt with a "substantial doubt" overstated the degree of doubt necessary for acquittal. We agree that this construction is somewhat problematic. On the one hand, "substantial" means "not seeming or imaginary"; on the other, it means "that specified to a large degree." Webster's Third New International Dictionary [unabridged 1981], at 2280. The former is unexceptionable, as it informs the jury only that a reasonable doubt is something more than a speculative one; but the latter could imply a doubt greater than required for acquittal under *Winship*. Any ambiguity, however, is removed by reading the phrase in the context of the sentence in which it appears: "A reasonable doubt is an actual and substantial doubt ... *as distinguished from* a doubt arising from mere possibility, from bare imagination, or from fanciful conjecture." Victor App. 11 (emphasis added).

This explicit distinction between a substantial doubt and a fanciful conjecture was not present in the *Cage* instruction. We did say in that case that "the words 'substantial' and 'grave,' as they are commonly understood, suggest a higher degree of doubt than is required for acquittal under the reasonable doubt standard." 498 U.S., at 41. But we did not hold that the reference to substantial doubt alone was sufficient to render the instruction unconstitutional. ... Rather, we were concerned that the jury would interpret the term "substantial doubt" in parallel with the preceding reference to "grave uncertainty," leading to an overstatement of the doubt necessary to acquit. In the instruction given in Victor's case, the context makes clear that "substantial" is used in the sense of existence rather than magnitude of the doubt, so the same concern is not present.

In any event, the instruction provided an alternative definition of reasonable doubt: a doubt that would cause a reasonable person to hesitate to act. This is a formulation we have repeatedly approved ... and to the extent the word substantial denotes the quantum of doubt necessary for acquittal, the hesitate to act standard gives a common-sense benchmark for just how substantial such a doubt must be. We therefore do not think it reasonably likely that the jury would have interpreted this instruction to indicate that the doubt must be anything other than a reasonable one.

B

Victor also challenges the "moral certainty" portion of the instruction. In another case involving an identical instruction, the Nebraska Supreme Court distinguished *Cage* as follows: "[U]nder the *Cage* instruction a juror is to vote for conviction unless convinced to a moral certainty that there exists a reasonable doubt, whereas under the questioned instruction a juror is to vote for acquittal unless convinced to a moral certainty that no reasonable doubt exists." State v. Morley, 239 Neb. 141, 155, 474 N.W.2d 660, 670 (1991) .... We disagree with this reading of *Cage*. The moral certainty to which the *Cage* instruction referred was clearly related to the defendant's guilt; the problem in *Cage* was that that the rest of the instruction provided insufficient context to lend meaning to the phrase. But the Nebraska instruction is not similarly deficient.

Instructing the jurors that they must have an abiding conviction of the defendant's guilt does much to alleviate any concerns that the phrase moral certainty might be misunderstood in the abstract. ... The instruction also equated a doubt sufficient to preclude moral certainty with a doubt that would cause a reasonable person to hesitate to act. In other words, a juror morally certain of a fact would not hesitate to rely on it; and such a fact can fairly be said to have been proven beyond a reasonable doubt. ... The jurors were told that they must be convinced of Victor's guilt "after full, fair, and impartial consideration of all the evidence." Victor App. 11. The judge also told them: "In determining any issues of fact presented in this case, you should be governed solely by the evidence introduced before you. You should not indulge in speculation, conjectures, or inferences not supported by the evidence." Id., at 2.

There is accordingly no reasonable likelihood that the jurors under-stood the reference to moral certainty to allow conviction on a standard insufficient to satisfy *Winship,* or to allow conviction on factors other than the government's proof. Though we reiterate that we do not countenance its use, the inclusion of the moral certainty phrase did not render the instruction given in Victor's case unconstitutional.

C

Finally, Victor argues that the reference to "strong probabili-ties" in the instruction unconstitutionally understated the govern-ment's burden. But in the same sentence, the instruction informs the jury that the probabilities must be strong enough to prove the defendant's guilt beyond a reasonable doubt. We upheld a nearly identical instruction in Dunbar v. United States, 156 U.S. 185, 199 (1895): "While it is true that [the challenged instruction] used the words 'probabilities' and 'strong probabilities,' yet it emphasized the fact that those probabilities must be so strong as to exclude any reasonable doubt, and that is unquestionably the law".... That conclusion has lost no force in the course of a century, and we therefore consider *Dunbar* controlling on this point.

IV

The Due Process Clause requires the government to prove a criminal defendant's guilt beyond a reasonable doubt, and trial courts must avoid defining reasonable doubt so as to lead the jury to convict on a lesser showing than due process requires. In these cases, however, we conclude that "taken as a whole, the instruc-tions correctly conveyed the concept of reasonable doubt to the jury." Holland v. United States, 348 U.S., at 140. There is no reasonable likelihood that the jurors who determined petitioners' guilt applied the instructions in a way that violated the Constitution. The judgments in both cases are accordingly

Affirmed.[*]

[*] Justice Kennedy wrote a concurring opinion. Justice Ginsburg wrote an opinion concurring in part and concurring in the judg-ment. Justice Blackmun wrote an opinion concurring in part and dissenting in part, which Justice Souter joined.

15. DOUBLE JEOPARDY

ASHE v. SWENSON

397 U.S. 436, 90 S.Ct. 1189, 25 L.Ed.2d 469 (1970).

MR. JUSTICE STEWART delivered the opinion of the Court.

In Benton v. Maryland, 395 U.S. 784, the Court held that the Fifth Amendment guarantee against double jeopardy is enforceable against the States through the Fourteenth Amendment. The question in this case is whether the State of Missouri violated that guarantee when it prosecuted the petitioner a second time for armed robbery in the circumstances here presented.

Sometime in the early hours of the morning of January 10, 1960, six men were engaged in a poker game in the basement of the home of John Gladson at Lee's Summit, Missouri. Suddenly three or four masked men, armed with a shotgun and pistols, broke into the basement and robbed each of the poker players of money and various articles of personal property. The robbers—and it has never been clear whether there were three or four of them—then fled in a car belonging to one of the victims of the robbery. Shortly thereafter the stolen car was discovered in a field, and later that morning three men were arrested by a state trooper while they were walking on a highway not far from where the abandoned car had been found. The petitioner was arrested by another officer some distance away.

The four were subsequently charged with seven separate offenses—the armed robbery of each of the six poker players and the theft of the car. In May 1960 the petitioner went to trial on the charge of robbing Donald Knight, one of the participants in the poker game. At the trial the State called Knight and three of his fellow poker players as prosecution witnesses. Each of them described the circumstances of the holdup and itemized his own individual losses. The proof that an armed robbery had occurred and that personal property had been taken from Knight as well as from each of the others was unassailable. The testimony of the four victims in this regard was consistent both internally and with that of the others. But the State's evidence that the petitioner had been one of the robbers was weak. Two of the witnesses thought that there had been only three robbers altogether, and could not identify the petitioner as one of them. Another of the victims, who was the petitioner's uncle by marriage, said that at the "patrol station" he had positively identified each of the other three men accused of the holdup, but could say only that the petitioner's voice "sounded very much like" that of one of the robbers. The fourth participant in the poker game did identify the petitioner, but only by his "size and height, and his actions."

The cross-examination of these witnesses was brief, and it was aimed primarily at exposing the weakness of their identification testimony. Defense counsel made no attempt to question their testimony regarding the holdup itself or their claims as to their losses. Knight testified without contradiction that the robbers had stolen from him his watch, $250 in cash, and about $500 in checks. His billfold, which had been found by the police in the possession of one of the three other men accused of the robbery, was admitted in evidence. The defense offered no testimony and waived final argument.

The trial judge instructed the jury that if it found that the petitioner was one of the participants in the armed robbery, the theft of "any money" from Knight would sustain a conviction. He also instructed the jury that if the petitioner was one of the robbers, he was guilty under the law even if he had not personally robbed Knight. The jury—though not instructed to elaborate upon its verdict—found the petitioner "not guilty due to insufficient evidence."

Six weeks later the petitioner was brought to trial again, this time for the robbery of another participant in the poker game, a man named Roberts. The petitioner filed a motion to dismiss, based on his previous acquittal. The motion was overruled, and the second trial began. The witnesses were for the most part the same, though this time their testimony was substantially stronger on the issue of the petitioner's identity. For example, two witnesses who at the first trial had been wholly unable to identify the petitioner as one of the robbers, now testified that his features, size, and mannerisms matched those of one of their assailants. Another witness who before had identified the petitioner only by his size and actions now also remembered him by the unusual sound of his voice. The State further refined its case at the second trial by declining to call one of the participants in the poker game whose identification testimony at the first trial had been conspicuously negative. The case went to the jury on instructions virtually identical to those given at the first trial. This time the jury found the petitioner guilty, and he was sentenced to a 35-year term in the state penitentiary.

The Supreme Court of Missouri affirmed the conviction, holding that the "plea of former jeopardy must be denied." State v. Ashe, 350 S.W.2d 768, 771. A collateral attack upon the conviction in the state courts five years later was also unsuccessful. State v. Ashe, 403 S.W.2d 589. The petitioner then brought the present habeas corpus proceeding in the United States District Court for the Western District of Missouri, claiming that the second prosecution had violated his right not to be twice put in jeopardy. Considering itself bound by this court's decision in Hoag v. New Jersey, 356 U.S.

464, the District Court denied the writ, although apparently finding merit in the petitioner's claim. The Court of Appeals for the Eighth Circuit affirmed, also upon the authority of Hoag v. New Jersey, supra. We granted certiorari to consider the important constitutional question this case presents. 393 U.S. 1115.

As the District Court and the Court of Appeals correctly noted, the operative facts here are virtually identical to those of Hoag v. New Jersey, supra. In that case the defendant was tried for the armed robbery of three men who, along with others, had been held up in a tavern. The proof of the robbery was clear, but the evidence identifying the defendant as one of the robbers was weak, and the defendant interposed an alibi defense. The jury brought in a verdict of not guilty. The defendant was then brought to trial again, on an indictment charging the robbery of a fourth victim of the tavern holdup. This time the jury found him guilty. After appeals in the state courts proved unsuccessful, Hoag brought his case here.

Viewing the question presented solely in terms of Fourteenth Amendment due process—whether the course that New Jersey had pursued had "led to fundamental unfairness," 356 U.S., at 467—this Court declined to reverse the judgment of conviction, because "in the circumstances shown by this record, we cannot say that petitioner's later prosecution and conviction violated due process." 356 U.S., at 466. The Court found it unnecessary to decide whether "collateral estoppel"—the principle that bars relitigation between the same parties of issues actually determined at a previous trial—is a due process requirement in a state criminal trial, since it accepted New Jersey's determination that the petitioner's previous acquittal did not in any event give rise to such an estoppel. 356 U.S., at 471. And in the view the Court took of the issues presented, it did not, of course, even approach consideration of whether collateral estoppel is an ingredient of the Fifth Amendment guarantee against double jeopardy.

The doctrine of Benton v. Maryland, 395 U.S. 784, puts the issues in the present case in a perspective quite different from that in which the issues were perceived in Hoag v. New Jersey, supra. The question is no longer whether collateral estoppel is a requirement of due process, but whether it is a part of the Fifth Amendment's guarantee against double jeopardy. And if collateral estoppel is embodied in that guarantee, then its applicability in a particular case is no longer a matter to be left for state court determination within the broad bounds of "fundamental fairness," but a matter of constitutional fact we must decide through an examination of the entire record. . . .

"Collateral estoppel" is an awkward phrase, but it stands for an extremely important principle in our adversary system of justice. It means simply that when an issue of ultimate fact has once been determined by a valid and final judgment, that issue cannot again be litigated between the same parties in any future lawsuit. Although first developed in civil litigation, collateral estoppel has been an established rule of federal criminal law at least since this Court's decision more than 50 years ago in United States v. Oppenheimer, 242 U.S. 85. As Mr. Justice Holmes put the matter in that case, "It cannot be that the safeguards of the person, so often and so rightly mentioned with solemn reverence, are less than those that protect from a liability in debt." 242 U.S., at 87. As a rule of federal law, therefore, "[i]t is much too late to suggest that this principle is not fully applicable to a former judgment in a criminal case, either because of lack of 'mutuality' or because the judgment may reflect only a belief that the Government had not met the higher burden of proof exacted in such cases for the Government's evidence as a whole although not necessarily as to every link in the chain." United States v. Kramer, 289 F.2d 909, 913.

The federal decisions have made clear that the rule of collateral estoppel in criminal cases is not to be applied with the hypertechnical and archaic approach of a 19th century pleading book, but with realism and rationality. Where a previous judgment of acquittal was based upon a general verdict, as is usually the case, this approach requires a court to "examine the record of a prior proceeding, taking into account the pleadings, evidence, charge, and other relevant matter, and conclude whether a rational jury could have grounded its verdict upon an issue other than that which the defendant seeks to foreclose from consideration." The inquiry "must be set in a practical frame and viewed with an eye to all the circumstances of the proceedings." Sealfon v. United States, 332 U.S. 575, 579. Any test more technically restrictive would, of course, simply amount to a rejection of the rule of collateral estoppel in criminal proceedings, at least in every case where the first judgment was based upon a general verdict of acquittal.

Straightforward application of the federal rule to the present case can lead to but one conclusion. For the record is utterly devoid of any indication that the first jury could rationally have found that an armed robbery had not occurred, or that Knight had not been a victim of that robbery. The single rationally conceivable issue in dispute before the jury was whether the petitioner had been one of the robbers. And the jury by its verdict found that he had not. The federal rule of law, therefore, would make a second prosecution for the robbery of Roberts wholly impermissible.

The ultimate question to be determined, then, in the light of Benton v. Maryland, supra, is whether this established rule of federal law is embodied in the Fifth Amendment guarantee against double jeopardy. We do not hesitate to hold that it is. For whatever else that constitutional guarantee may embrace ... it surely protects a man who has been acquitted from having to "run the gantlet" a second time.   Green v. United States, 355 U.S. 184, 190.

The question is not whether Missouri could validly charge the petitioner with six separate offenses for the robbery of the six poker players.   It is not whether he could have received a total of six punishments if he had been convicted in a single trial of robbing the six victims.   It is simply whether, after a jury determined by its verdict that the petitioner was not one of the robbers, the State could constitutionally hale him before a new jury to litigate that issue again.

After the first jury had acquitted the petitioner of robbing Knight, Missouri could certainly not have brought him to trial again upon that charge.   Once a jury had determined upon conflicting testimony that there was at least a reasonable doubt that the petitioner was one of the robbers, the State could not present the same or different identification evidence in a second prosecution for the robbery of Knight in the hope that a different jury might find that evidence more convincing.   The situation is constitutionally no different here, even though the second trial related to another victim of the same robbery.   For the name of the victim, in the circumstances of this case, had no bearing whatever upon the issue of whether the petitioner was one of the robbers.

In this case the State in its brief has frankly conceded that following the petitioner's acquittal, it treated the first trial as no more than a dry run for the second prosecution: "No doubt the prosecutor felt the state had a provable case on the first charge and, when he lost, he did what every good attorney would do—he refined his presentation in light of the turn of events at the first trial."   But this is precisely what the constitutional guarantee forbids.

The judgment is reversed, and the case is remanded to the Court of Appeals for the Eighth Circuit for further proceedings consistent with this opinion.

It is so ordered.[*]

[*] Justice Brennan wrote a concurring opinion, which Justice Douglas and Justice Marshall joined.   Chief Justice Burger wrote a dissenting opinion.

UNITED STATES v. WILSON

420 U.S. 332, 95 S.Ct. 1013, 43 L.Ed.2d 232 (1975).

MR. JUSTICE MARSHALL delivered the opinion of the Court.

Respondent George J. Wilson, Jr., was tried in the Eastern District of Pennsylvania for converting union funds to his own use, in violation of § 501(c) of the Labor-Management Reporting and Disclosure Act of 1959, 73 Stat. 536, 29 U.S.C. § 501(c). The jury entered a guilty verdict, but on a post-verdict motion the District Court dismissed the indictment. The court ruled that the delay between the offense and the indictment had prejudiced the defendant, and that dismissal was called for under this Court's decision in United States v. Marion, 404 U.S. 307 (1971). The Government sought to appeal the dismissal to the Court of Appeals for the Third Circuit, but that court held that the Double Jeopardy Clause barred review of the District Court's ruling. 492 F.2d 1345 (1973). We granted certiorari to consider the applicability of the Double Jeopardy Clause to appeals from postverdict rulings by the trial court. 417 U.S. 908 (1974). We reverse.

I

In April 1968 the FBI began an investigation of respondent Wilson, the business manager of Local 367 of the International Brotherhood of Electrical Workers. The investigation focused on Wilson's suspected conversion in 1966 of $1,233.15 of union funds to pay part of the expenses of his daughter's wedding reception. The payment was apparently made by a check drawn on union funds and endorsed by the treasurer and the president of the local union. Respondent contended at trial that he had not authorized the two union officials to make the payment on his behalf and that he did not know the bill for the reception had been paid out of union funds. In June 1970 the FBI completed its investigation and reported to the Organized Crime Strike Force and the local United States Attorney's Office. There the matter rested for some 16 months until, three days prior to the running of the statute of limitations, respondent was indicted for illegal conversion of union funds.

Wilson made a pretrial motion to dismiss the indictment on the ground that the Government's delay in filing the action had denied him the opportunity for a fair trial. His chance to mount an effective defense was impaired, Wilson argued, because the two union officers who had signed the check for the reception were unavailable to testify. One had died in 1968, and the other was suffering from a terminal illness. After a hearing, the court denied the pretrial motion, and the case proceeded to trial. The jury returned a verdict of guilty, after which the defendant filed various motions including a motion for arrest of judgment, a motion for a judgment of acquittal, and a motion for a new trial.

The District Court reversed its earlier ruling and dismissed the indictment on the ground that the preindictment delay was unreasonable and had substantially prejudiced the defendant's right to a fair trial. The union treasurer had died prior to 1970, the court noted, so the loss of his testimony could not be attributed to the preindictment delay. The union president, however, had become unavailable during the period of delay. The court ruled that since he was the only remaining witness who could explain the circumstances of the payment of the check, the preindictment delay violated the respondent's Fifth Amendment right to a fair trial. This disposition of the *Marion* claim made it unnecessary to rule on the defendant's other post-verdict motions.

The Government sought to appeal the District Court's ruling pursuant to the Criminal Appeals Act, 18 U.S.C. § 3731, but the Court of Appeals dismissed the appeal in a judgment order, citing our decision in United States v. Sisson, 399 U.S. 267 (1970). On the Government's petition for rehearing, the court wrote an opinion in which it reasoned that since the District Court had relied on facts brought out at trial in finding prejudice from the preindictment delay, its ruling was in effect an acquittal. Under the Double Jeopardy Clause, the Court of Appeals held, the Government could not constitutionally appeal the acquittal, even though it was rendered by the judge after the jury had returned a verdict of guilty.

II

The Government argues that the Court of Appeals read the Double Jeopardy Clause too broadly and that it mischaracterized the District Court's ruling in terming it an acquittal. In the Government's view, the constitutional restriction on governmental appeals is intended solely to protect against exposing the defendant to multiple trials, not to shield every determination favorable to the defendant from appellate review. Since a new trial would not be necessary where the trier of fact has returned a verdict of guilty, the Government argues that it should be permitted to appeal from any adverse postverdict ruling. In the alternative, the Government urges that even if the Double Jeopardy Clause is read to bar appeal of any judgment of acquittal, the District Court's order in this case was not an acquittal and it should therefore be appealable. The respondent argues that under our prior cases the Double Jeopardy Clause prohibits appeal of any order discharging the defendant when, as here, that order is based on facts outside the indictment. Because we agree with the Government that the constitutional protection against Government appeals attaches only where there is a danger of subjecting the defendant to a second trial for the same offense, we have no occasion to determine whether the ruling in Wilson's favor was actually an "acquittal" even though the District Court characterized it otherwise.

A

This Court early held that the Government could not take an appeal in a criminal case without express statutory authority. United States v. Sanges, 144 U.S. 310 (1892). Not reaching the underlying constitutional issue, the Court held only that the general appeals provisions of the Judiciary Act of 1891, 26 Stat. 827, 828, were not sufficiently explicit to overcome the common-law rule that the State could not sue out a writ of error in a criminal case unless the legislature had expressly granted it that right. 144 U.S., at 318, 322–323.

Fifteen years later, Congress passed the first Criminal Appeals Act, which conferred jurisdiction on this Court to consider criminal appeals by the Government in limited circumstances. 34 Stat. 1246. The Act permitted the Government to take an appeal from a decision dismissing an indictment or arresting judgment where the decision was based on "the invalidity, or construction of the statute upon which the indictment is founded," and from a decision sustaining a special plea in bar, when the defendant had not been put in jeopardy. The Act was construed in accordance with the common-law meaning of the terms employed, and the rules governing the conditions of appeal became highly technical. This Court had a number of occasions to struggle with the vagaries of the Act; in one of the last of these unhappy efforts, we concluded that the Act was "a failure . . . a most unruly child that has not improved with age." United States v. Sisson, 399 U.S., at 307.

Congress finally disposed of the statute in 1970 and replaced it with a new Criminal Appeals Act intended to broaden the Government's appeal rights.[5] While the language of the new Act is not dispositive, the legislative history makes it clear that Congress intended to remove all statutory barriers to Government appeals and to allow appeals whenever the Constitution would permit.

. . .

. . . The District Court's order in this case is therefore appealable unless the appeal is barred by the Constitution.

B

The statutory restrictions on Government appeals long made it unnecessary for this Court to consider the constitutional limitations on the appeal rights of the prosecution except in unusual circumstances. Even in the few relevant cases, the discussion of the question has been brief. Now that Congress has removed the

---

5. The new statute, 18 U.S.C. § 3731 (1970), was passed as Title III of the Omnibus Crime Control Act of 1970, Pub.L. 91–644, 84 Stat. 1890.

statutory limitations and the Double Jeopardy Clause has been held to apply to the States ... it is necessary to take a closer look at the policies underlying the Clause in order to determine more precisely the boundaries of the Government's appeal rights in criminal cases.

As has been documented elsewhere, the idea of double jeopardy is very old. ... The early development of the principle can be traced through a variety of sources ranging from legal maxims to casual references in contemporary commentary. Although the form and breadth of the prohibition varied widely, the underlying premise was generally that a defendant should not be twice tried or punished for the same offense. ... Writing in the Seventeenth Century, Lord Coke described the protection afforded by the principle of double jeopardy as a function of three related common-law pleas: *autrefois acquit, autrefois convict,* and pardon. With some exceptions, these pleas could be raised to bar the second trial of a defendant if he could prove that he had already been convicted of the same crime.... Blackstone later used the ancient term "jeopardy" in characterizing the principle underlying the two pleas of *autrefois acquit* and *autrefois convict.* That principle, he wrote, was a "universal maxim of the common law of England, that no man is to be brought into jeopardy of his life more than once, for the same offence." 4 W. Blackstone, Commentaries *335–336.

This history of the adoption of the Double Jeopardy Clause sheds some light on what the drafters thought Blackstone's "universal maxim" should mean as applied in this country. ...

In the course of the debates over the Bill of Rights, there was no suggestion that the Double Jeopardy Clause imposed any general ban on appeals by the prosecution. ... Nor does the common-law background of the Clause suggest an implied prohibition against state appeals. ... The development of the Double Jeopardy Clause from its common-law origins thus suggests that it was directed at the threat of multiple prosecutions, not at Government appeals, at least where those appeals would not require a new trial.

C

This Court's cases construing the Double Jeopardy Clause reinforce this view of the constitutional guarantee. In North Carolina v. Pearce, 395 U.S. 711 (1969), we observed that the Double Jeopardy Clause provides three related protections:

> "It protects against a second prosecution for the same offense after acquittal. It protects against a second prosecution for the same offense after conviction. And it protects against multiple punishments for the same offense." Id., at 717.

The interests underlying these three protections are quite similar. When a defendant has been once convicted and punished for a particular crime, principles of fairness and finality require that he not be subjected to the possibility of further punishment by being again tried or sentenced for the same offense. ... When a defendant has been acquitted of an offense, the Clause guarantees that the State shall not be permitted to make repeated attempts to convict him, "thereby subjecting him to embarrassment, expense and ordeal and compelling him to live in a continuing state of anxiety and insecurity, as well as enhancing the possibility that even though innocent he may be found guilty." Green v. United States, 355 U.S. 184, 187–188 (1957).

The policy of avoiding multiple trials has been regarded as so important that exceptions to the principle have been only grudgingly allowed. Initially, a new trial was thought to be unavailable after appeal, whether requested by the prosecution or the defendant. ... It was not until 1896 that it was made clear that a defendant could seek a new trial after conviction, even though the Government enjoyed no similar right.... [11] Following the same policy, the Court has granted the Government the right to retry a defendant after a mistrial only where "there is a manifest necessity for the act, or the ends of public justice would otherwise be defeated." United States v. Perez, 9 Wheat. 579, 580 (1824).

By contrast, where there is no threat of either multiple punishment or successive prosecutions, the Double Jeopardy Clause is not offended. In various situations where appellate review would not subject the defendant to a second trial, this Court has held that an order favoring the defendant could constitutionally be appealed by the Government. Since the 1907 Criminal Appeals Act, for example, the Government has been permitted without serious constitutional challenge to appeal from orders arresting judgment after a verdict has been entered against the defendant. ... Since reversal on appeal would merely reinstate the jury's verdict, review of such an order does not offend the policy against multiple prosecution.

Similarly, it is well settled that an appellate court's order reversing a conviction is subject to further review even when the appellate court has ordered the indictment dismissed and the defendant discharged. Forman v. United States, 361 U.S. 416, 426 (1960). If reversal by a court of appeals operated to deprive the Government of its right to seek further review, disposition in the Court of Appeals would be "tantamount to a verdict of acquittal at the hands of the jury, not subject to review by motion for rehearing, appeal, or certiorari in this Court." Ibid. ...

It is difficult to see why the rule should be any different simply because the defendant has gotten a favorable postverdict ruling of law from the District Judge rather than from the Court of Appeals,

---

11. This exception to the "one trial" rule has been explained on the conclusory theories that the defendant waives his double jeopardy claim by appealing his conviction, or that the first jeopardy continues until he is acquitted or his conviction becomes final.... As Mr. Justice Harlan noted in United States v. Tateo, 377 U.S. 463, 465–466 (1964), however, the practical justification for the exception is simply that it is fairer to both the defendant and the Government.

or because the District Judge has relied to some degree on evidence presented at trial in making his ruling. Although review of any ruling of law discharging a defendant obviously enhances the likelihood of conviction and subjects him to continuing expense and anxiety, a defendant has no legitimate claim to benefit from an error of law when that error could be corrected without subjecting him to a second trial before a second trier of fact.

As we have noted, this Court has had relatively few occasions to comment directly on the constitutional restrictions on Government appeals. The few relevant cases are nonetheless consistent with double jeopardy cases from related areas, in focusing on the prohibition against multiple trials as the controlling constitutional principle.

. . .

D

The Government has not seriously contended in this case that any ruling of law by a judge in the course of a trial is reviewable on the prosecution's motion, although this view has had some support among the commentators since Mr. Justice Holmes adopted it in his dissent to Kepner v. United States [195 U.S. 100 (1905)]. Justice Holmes accepted as common ground that the Double Jeopardy Clause forbids "a trial in a new and independent case where a man already has been tried once." 195 U.S., at 134. But in his view the first jeopardy should be treated as continuing until both sides have exhausted their appeals on claimed errors of law, regardless of the possibility that the defendant may be subjected to retrial after a verdict of acquittal.

A system permitting review of all claimed legal errors would have symmetry to recommend it and would avoid the release of some defendants who have benefited from instructions or evidentiary rulings that are unduly favorable to them. But we have rejected this position in the past, and we continue to be of the view that the policies underlying the Double Jeopardy Clause militate against permitting the Government to appeal after a verdict of acquittal. Granting the Government such broad appeal rights would allow the prosecutor to seek to persuade a second trier of fact of the defendant's guilt after having failed with the first; it would permit him to re-examine the weaknesses in his first presentation in order to strengthen it in the second; and it would disserve the defendant's legitimate interest in the finality of a verdict of acquittal. These interests, however, do not apply in the case of a postverdict ruling of law by a trial judge. Correction of an error of law at that stage would not grant the prosecutor a new trial or subject the defendant to the harassment traditionally associated with multiple prosecutions. We therefore conclude that when a judge rules in favor of the defendant after a verdict of guilty has been entered by the trier of fact, the Government may appeal from that ruling without running afoul of the Double Jeopardy Clause.

III

Applying these principles to the present case is a relatively straightforward task. The jury entered a verdict of guilty against Wilson. The ruling in his favor on the *Marion* motion could be acted on by the Court of Appeals or indeed this Court without subjecting him to a second trial at the Government's behest. If he prevails on appeal, the matter will become final, and the Government will not be permitted to bring a second prosecution against him for the same offense. If he loses, the case must go back to the District Court for disposition of his remaining motions. We therefore reverse the judgment and remand for the Court of Appeals to consider the merits of the Government's appeal.

Reversed and remanded.[*]

___

[*] Justice Douglas wrote a dissenting opinion, which Justice Brennan joined.

ILLINOIS v. SOMERVILLE

410 U.S. 458, 93 S.Ct. 1066, 35 L.Ed.2d 425 (1973).

MR. JUSTICE REHNQUIST delivered the opinion of the Court.

We must here decide whether declaration of a mistrial over the defendant's objection, because the trial court concluded that the indictment was insufficient to charge a crime, necessarily prevents a State from subsequently trying the defendant under a valid indictment. We hold that the mistrial met the "manifest necessity" requirement of our cases, since the trial court could reasonably have concluded that the "ends of public justice" would be defeated by having allowed the trial to continue. Therefore, the Double Jeopardy Clause of the Fifth Amendment, made applicable to the States through the Due Process Clause of the Fourteenth Amendment . . . did not bar retrial under a valid indictment.

I

On March 19, 1964, respondent was indicted by an Illinois grand jury for the crime of theft. The case was called for trial and a jury impaneled and sworn on November 1, 1965. The following day, before any evidence had been presented, the prosecuting attorney realized that the indictment was fatally deficient under Illinois law because it did not allege that respondent intended to permanently deprive the owner of his property. Under the applicable Illinois criminal statute, such intent is a necessary element of the crime of theft, and failure to allege intent renders the indictment insufficient to charge a crime. But under the Illinois Constitution, an indictment is the sole means by which a criminal proceeding such as this may be commenced against a defendant. Illinois further provides that only formal defects, of which this was not one, may be cured by amendment. The combined operation of these rules of Illinois procedure and substantive law meant that the defect in the indictment was "jurisdictional"; it could not be waived by the defendant's failure to object, and could be asserted on appeal or in a postconviction proceeding to overturn a final judgment of conviction.

Faced with this situation, the Illinois trial court concluded that further proceedings under this defective indictment would be useless and granted the State's motion for a mistrial. On November 3, the grand jury handed down a second indictment alleging the requisite intent. Respondent was arraigned two weeks after the first trial was aborted, raised a claim of double jeopardy which was overruled, and the second trial commenced shortly thereafter. The jury returned a verdict of guilty, sentence was imposed, and the

1081

Illinois courts upheld the conviction. Respondent then sought federal habeas corpus, alleging that the conviction constituted double jeopardy contrary to the prohibition of the Fifth and Fourteenth Amendments. The Seventh Circuit affirmed the denial of habeas corpus prior to our decision in United States v. Jorn, 400 U.S. 470 (1971). The respondent's petition for certiorari was granted, and the case remanded for reconsideration in light of *Jorn* and Downum v. United States, 372 U.S. 734 (1963). On remand, the Seventh Circuit held that respondent's petition for habeas corpus should have been granted because, although he had not been tried and *acquitted* as in United States v. Ball, 163 U.S. 662 (1896), and Benton v. Maryland, 395 U.S. 784 (1969), jeopardy had attached when the jury was impaneled and sworn, and a declaration of mistrial over respondent's objection precluded a retrial under a valid indictment. For the reasons stated below, we reverse that judgment.

II

The fountainhead decision construing the Double Jeopardy Clause in the context of a declaration of a mistrial over a defendant's objection is United States v. Perez, 9 Wheat. 579 (1824). Mr. Justice Story, writing for a unanimous Court, set forth the standards for determining whether a retrial, following a declaration of a mistrial over a defendant's objection, constitutes double jeopardy within the meaning of the Fifth Amendment. In holding that the failure of the jury to agree on a verdict of either acquittal or conviction did not bar retrial of the defendant, Mr. Justice Story wrote:

> "We think, that in all cases of this nature, the law has invested Courts of justice with the authority to discharge a jury from giving any verdict, whenever, in their opinion, taking all the circumstances into consideration, there is a manifest necessity for the act, or the ends of public justice would otherwise be defeated. They are to exercise a sound discretion on the subject; and it is impossible to define all the circumstances, which would render it proper to interfere. To be sure, the power ought to be used with the greatest caution, under urgent circumstances, and for very plain and obvious causes; and, in capital cases especially, Courts should be extremely careful how they interfere with any of the chances of life, in favour of the prisoner. But, after all, they have the right to order the discharge; and the security which the public have for the faithful, sound, and conscientious exercise of this discretion, rests, in this, as in other cases, upon the responsibility of the Judges, under their oaths of office." Id., at 580.

This formulation, consistently adhered to by this Court in subsequent decisions, abjures the application of any mechanical formula by which to judge the propriety of declaring a mistrial in the varying and often unique situations arising during the course of a criminal trial. The broad discretion reserved to the trial judge in such circumstances has been consistently reiterated in decisions of this Court. In Wade v. Hunter, 336 U.S. 684 (1949), the Court, in reaffirming this flexible standard, wrote:

> "We are asked to adopt the *Cornero* rule under which petitioner contends the absence of witnesses can never justify discontinuance of a trial. Such a rigid formula is inconsistent with the guiding principles of the *Perez* decision to which we adhere. Those principles command courts in considering whether a trial should be terminated without judgment to take 'all circumstances into account' and thereby forbid the mechanical application of an abstract formula. The value of the *Perez* principles thus lies in their capacity for informed application under widely different circumstances without injury to defendants or to the public interest." Id., at 691.

Similarly, in Gori v. United States, 367 U.S. 364 (1961), the Court again underscored the breadth of a trial judge's discretion, and the reasons therefor, to declare a mistrial.

> "Where, for reasons deemed compelling by the trial judge, who is best situated intelligently to make such a decision, the ends of substantial justice cannot be attained without discontinuing the trial, a mistrial may be declared without the defendant's consent and even over his objection, and he may be retried consistently with the Fifth Amendment." Id., at 368.

In reviewing the propriety of the trial judge's exercise of his discretion, this Court, following the counsel of Mr. Justice Story, has scrutinized the action to determine whether, in the context of that particular trial, the declaration of a mistrial was dictated by "manifest necessity" or the "ends of public justice." The interests of the public in seeing that a criminal prosecution proceed to verdict, either of acquittal or conviction, need not be forsaken by the formulation or application of rigid rules that necessarily preclude the vindication of that interest. This consideration, whether termed the "ends of public justice," United States v. Perez, supra, at 580, or, more precisely, "the public's interest in fair trials designed to end in just judgments," Wade v. Hunter, supra, at 689, has not been disregarded by this Court.

In United States v. Perez, supra, and Logan v. United States, 144 U.S. 263 (1892), this Court held that "manifest necessity" justified the discharge of juries unable to reach verdicts, and, therefore, the Double Jeopardy Clause did not bar retrial. ... In Simmons v. United States, 142 U.S. 148 (1891), a trial judge dismissed the jury, over defendant's objection, because one of the jurors had been acquainted with the defendant, and, therefore, was probably prejudiced against the Government; this Court held that the trial judge properly exercised his power "to prevent the defeat of the ends of public justice." Id., at 154. In Thompson v. United States, 155 U.S. 271 (1894), a mistrial was declared after the trial judge learned that one of the jurors was disqualified, he having been a member of the grand jury that indicted the defendant. Similarly, in Lovato v. New Mexico, 242 U.S. 199 (1916), the defendant demurred to the indictment, his demurrer was overruled, and a jury sworn. The district attorney, realizing that the defendant had not pleaded to the indictment after the demurrer had been overruled, moved for the discharge of the jury and arraignment of the defendant for pleading; the jury was discharged, the defendant pleaded not guilty, the same jury was again impaneled, and a verdict of guilty rendered. In both of those cases this Court held that the Double Jeopardy Clause did not bar reprosecution.

While virtually all of the cases turn on the particular facts and thus escape meaningful categorization, see Gori v. United States, supra, Wade v. Hunter, supra, it is possible to distill from them a general approach, premised on the "public justice" policy enunciated in United States v. Perez, to situations such as that presented by this case. A trial judge properly exercises his discretion to declare a mistrial if an impartial verdict cannot be reached, or if a verdict of conviction could be reached but would have to be reversed on appeal due to an obvious procedural error in the trial. If an error would make reversal on appeal a certainty, it would not serve "the ends of public justice" to require that the Government proceed with its proof when, if it succeeded before the jury, it would automatically be stripped of that success by an appellate court. This was substantially the situation in both Thompson v. United States, supra, and Lovato v. New Mexico, supra. While the declaration of a mistrial on the basis of a rule or a defective procedure that would lend itself to prosecutorial manipulation would involve an entirely different question, cf. Downum v. United States, supra, such was not the situation in the above cases or in the instant case.

In Downum v. United States, supra, the defendant was charged with six counts of mail theft, and forging and uttering stolen checks. A jury was selected and sworn in the morning, and instructed to return that afternoon. When the jury returned, the Government moved for the discharge of the jury on the ground that a key prosecution witness, for two of the six counts against defendant, was not present. The prosecution knew, prior to the selection and swearing of the jury, that this witness could not be found and had not been served with a subpoena. The trial judge discharged the jury over the defendant's motions to dismiss two counts for failure to prosecute and to continue the other four. This Court, in reversing the convictions on the ground of double jeopardy, emphasized that "[e]ach case must turn on its facts," 372 U.S., at 737, and held that the second prosecution constituted double jeopardy, because the absence of the witness and the reason therefor did not there justify, in terms of "manifest necessity," the declaration of a mistrial.

In United States v. Jorn, supra, the Government called a taxpayer witness in a prosecution for willfully assisting in the preparation of fraudulent income tax returns. Prior to his testimony, defense counsel suggested he be warned of his constitutional right against compulsory self-incrimination. The trial judge warned him of his rights, and the witness stated that he was willing to testify and that the Internal Revenue Service agent who first contacted him warned him of his rights. The trial judge, however, did not believe the witness' declaration that the IRS had so warned him, and refused to allow him to testify until after he had consulted with an attorney. After learning from the Government that the remaining four witnesses were "similarly situated," and after surmising that they, too, had not been properly informed of their rights, the trial judge declared a mistrial to give the witnesses the opportunity to consult with attorneys. In sustaining a plea in bar of double jeopardy to an attempted second trial of the defendant, the plurality opinion of the Court, emphasizing the importance to the defendant of proceeding before the first jury sworn, concluded:

> "It is apparent from the record that no consideration was given to the possibility of a trial continuance; indeed, the trial judge acted so abruptly in discharging the jury that, had the prosecutor been disposed to suggest a continuance, or the defendant to object to the discharge of the jury, there would have been no opportunity to do so. When one examines the circumstances surrounding the discharge of this jury, it seems abundantly apparent that the trial judge made no effort to exercise a sound discretion to assure that, taking all the circumstances into account, there was a manifest necessity for the *sua sponte* declaration of this mistrial. United States v. Perez, 9 Wheat., at 580. Therefore, we must conclude that in the circumstances of this case, appellee's reprosecution would violate the double jeopardy provision of the Fifth Amendment." 400 U.S., at 487.

III

Respondent advances two arguments to support the conclusion that the Double Jeopardy Clause precluded the second trial in the instant case. The first is that since United States v. Ball, 163 U.S. 662 (1896), held that jeopardy obtained even though the indictment upon which the defendant was first acquitted had been defective, and since Downum v. United States, supra, held that jeopardy "attaches" when a jury has been selected and sworn, the Double Jeopardy Clause precluded the State from instituting the second proceeding that resulted in respondent's conviction. Alternatively, respondent argues that our decision in United States v. Jorn, supra, which respondent interprets as narrowly limiting the circumstances in which a mistrial is manifestly necessary, requires affirmance.

Emphasizing the " 'valued right to have his trial completed by a particular tribunal,' " United States v. Jorn, supra, at 484, quoting Wade v. Hunter, 336 U.S., at 689, respondent contends that the circumstances did not justify depriving him of that right.

Respondent's first contention is precisely the type of rigid, mechanical rule which the Court had eschewed since the seminal decision in *Perez.* The major premise of the syllogism—that trial on a defective indictment precludes retrial—is not applicable to the instant case because it overlooks a crucial element of the Court's reasoning in United States v. Ball, supra. There, three men were indicted and tried for murder; two were convicted by a jury and one acquitted. This Court reversed the convictions on the ground that the indictment was fatally deficient in failing to allege that the victim died within a year and a day of the assault. Ball v. United States, 140 U.S. 118 (1891). A proper indictment was returned and the Government retried all three of the original defendants; that trial resulted in the conviction of all. This Court reversed the conviction of the one defendant who originally had been acquitted, sustaining his plea of double jeopardy. But the Court was obviously and properly influenced by the fact that the first trial had proceeded to verdict. This focus of the Court is reflected in the opinion:

> "[W]e are unable to resist the conclusion that a general verdict of acquittal upon the issue of not guilty to an indictment undertaking to charge murder, and not objected to before the verdict as insufficient in that respect, is a bar to a second indictment for the same killing.
>
> ". . . [T]he accused, *whether convicted or acquitted,* is equally put in jeopardy at the first trial. . . ." 163 U.S., at 669 (emphasis added).

In *Downum,* the Court held, as respondent argues, that jeopardy "attached" when the first jury was selected and sworn. But in cases in which a mistrial has been declared prior to verdict, the conclusion that jeopardy has attached begins, rather than ends, the inquiry as to whether the Double Jeopardy Clause bars retrial. That, indeed, was precisely the rationale of *Perez* and subsequent cases. Only if jeopardy has attached is a court called upon to determine whether the declaration of a mistrial was required by "manifest necessity" or the "ends of public justice."

We believe that in light of the State's established rules of criminal procedure, the trial judge's declaration of a mistrial was not an abuse of discretion. Since this Court's decision in Benton v. Maryland, supra, federal courts will be confronted with such claims that arise in large measure from the often diverse procedural rules existing in the 50 States. Federal courts should not be quick to conclude that simply because a state procedure does not conform to the corresponding federal statute or rule, it does not serve a legitimate state policy. Last Term, recognizing this fact, we dismissed a writ of certiorari as improvidently granted in a case involving a claim of double jeopardy stemming from the dismissal of an indictment under the "rules of criminal pleading peculiar to" an individual State followed by a retrial under a proper indictment. Duncan v. Tennessee, 405 U.S. 127 (1972).

In the instant case, the trial judge terminated the proceeding because a defect was found to exist in the indictment that was, as a matter of Illinois law, not curable by amendment. The Illinois courts have held that even after a judgment of conviction has become final, the defendant may be released on habeas corpus, because the defect in the indictment deprives the trial court of "jurisdiction." The rule prohibiting the amendment of all but formal defects in indictments is designed to implement the State's policy of preserving the right of each defendant to insist that a criminal prosecution against him be commenced by the action of a grand jury. The trial judge was faced with a situation similar to those in *Simmons, Lovato,* and *Thompson,* in which a procedural defect might or would preclude the public from either obtaining an impartial verdict or keeping a verdict of conviction if its evidence persuaded the jury. If a mistrial were constitutionally unavailable in situations such as this, the State's policy could only be implemented by conducting a second trial after verdict and reversal on appeal, thus wasting time, energy, and money for all concerned. Here, the trial judge's action was a rational determination designed to implement a legitimate state policy, with no suggestion that the implementation of that policy in this manner could be manipulated so as to prejudice the defendant. This situation is thus unlike *Downum,* where the mistrial entailed not only a delay for the defendant, but also operated as a post-jeopardy continuance to allow the prosecution an opportunity to strengthen its case. Here, the delay was minimal, and the mistrial was, under Illinois law, the only way in which a defect in the indictment could be corrected. Given the established standard of discretion set forth in *Perez, Gori,* and *Hunter,* we cannot say that the declaration of a mistrial was not required by "manifest necessity" and the "ends of public justice."

Our decision in *Jorn,* relied upon by the court below and respondent, does not support the opposite conclusion. While it is possible to excise various portions of the plurality opinion to support the result reached below, divorcing the language from the facts of the case serves only to distort its holdings. That opinion dealt with action by a trial judge that can fairly be described as erratic. The Court held that the lack of apparent harm to the defendant from the declaration of a mistrial did not itself justify the mistrial, and concluded that there was no "manifest necessity" for the mistrial, as opposed to less drastic alternatives. The Court emphasized that the absence of any manifest need for the mistrial had deprived the defendant of his right to proceed before the first jury, but it did not hold that that right may never be forced to yield, as in this case, to "the public's interest in fair trials designed to end in just judgments." The Court's opinion in *Jorn* is replete with approving references to Wade v. Hunter, supra, which latter case stated:

> "The double-jeopardy provision of the Fifth Amendment, however, does not mean that every time a defendant is put to trial before a competent tribunal he is entitled to go free if the trial fails to end in a final judgment. Such a rule would create an insuperable obstacle to the administration of justice in many cases in which there is no semblance of the type of oppressive practices at which the double-jeopardy prohibition is aimed. There may be unforeseeable circumstances that arise during a trial making its completion impossible, such as the failure of a jury to agree on a verdict. In such event the purpose of law to protect society from those guilty of crimes frequently would be frustrated by denying courts power to put the defendant to trial again. And there have been instances where a trial judge has discovered facts during a trial which indicated that one or more members of the jury might be biased against the Government or the defendant. It is settled that the duty of the judge in this event is to discharge the jury and direct a retrial. *What has been said is enough to show that a defendant's valued right to have his trial completed by a particular tribunal must in some instances be subordinated to the public's interest in fair trials designed to end in just judgments.*" Wade v. Hunter, 336 U.S., at 688–689 (footnote omitted; emphasis added).

The determination by the trial court to abort a criminal proceeding where jeopardy has attached is not one to be lightly undertaken, since the interest of the defendant in having his fate determined by the jury first impaneled is itself a weighty one. . . . Nor will the lack of demonstrable additional prejudice preclude the defendant's invocation of the double jeopardy bar in the absence of some important countervailing interest of proper judicial administration. . . . But where the declaration of a mistrial implements a reasonable state policy and aborts a proceeding that at best would have produced a verdict that could have been upset at will by one of the parties, the defendant's interest in proceeding to verdict is outweighed by the competing and equally legitimate demand for public justice. . . .

Reversed.

MR. JUSTICE WHITE, with whom MR. JUSTICE DOUGLAS and MR. JUSTICE BRENNAN join, dissenting.

For the purposes of the Double Jeopardy Clause, jeopardy attaches when a criminal trial commences before judge or jury . . . and this point has arrived when a jury has been selected and sworn, even though no evidence has been taken. Clearly, Somerville was placed in jeopardy at his first trial despite the fact that the indictment against him was defective under Illinois law. ... The question remains, however, whether the facts of this case present one of those circumstances where a trial, once begun, may be aborted over the defendant's objection and the defendant retried without twice being placed in jeopardy contrary to the Constitution.

. . .

United States v. Jorn [400 U.S. 470 (1971)] and Downum v. United States [372 U.S. 734 (1963)] for example, make it abundantly clear that trial courts should have constantly in mind the purposes of the Double Jeopardy Clause to protect the defendant from continued exposure to embarrassment, anxiety, expense, and restrictions on his liberty, as well as to preserve his " 'valued right to have his trial completed by a particular tribunal.' " United States v. Jorn, supra, at 484, quoting from Wade v. Hunter, 336 U.S. [684 (1949)] at 689.

. . .

It was in light of this interest that the Court in *Downum* reversed a conviction on double jeopardy grounds where a mistrial was declared to permit further efforts to secure the attendance of a key prosecution witness who should have been, but was not, subpoenaed. Although no prosecutorial misconduct other than mere oversight and mistake was claimed or proved, the policies of the Double Jeopardy Clause, and the interest of the defendant in taking his case to the jury that he had just accepted, were sufficient to raise the double jeopardy barrier to a second trial.

Similarly, in *Jorn,* a trial was terminated when the trial judge, *sua sponte* and mistakenly, declared a mistrial, apparently to protect nonparty witnesses from the possibility of self-incrimination. There was no showing of intent by the prosecutor or the judge to harass the defendant or to enhance chances of conviction at a second trial; the defendant was given a complete preview of the Government's case, and no specific prejudice to the defense at a second trial was shown. Noting that the courts "must bear in mind the potential risks of abuse by the defendant of society's unwillingness to unnecessarily subject him to repeated prosecutions," 400 U.S., at 486, this Court held that the defendant's interest in submitting his case to the initial jury was itself sufficient to invoke the Double Jeopardy Clause and, as in *Downum,* to override the Government's concern with enforcing the criminal laws by having another chance to try the defendant for the crime with which he was charged. In neither case was there "manifest necessity" for a mistrial and a double trial of the defendant.

Very similar considerations govern this case. Somerville asserts a right to but one trial and to a verdict by the initial jury. A mistrial was directed at the instance of the State, over Somerville's objection, and was occasioned by official error in drafting the indictment—error unaccompanied by bad faith, overreaching, or specific prejudice to the defense at a later trial. The State may no more try the defendant a second time in these circumstances than could the United States in *Downum* and *Jorn.* Although the exact extent of the emotional and physical harm suffered by Somerville during the period between his first and second trial is open to debate, it cannot be gainsaid that Somerville lost "his option to go to the first jury and, perhaps, end the dispute then and there with an acquittal." United States v. Jorn, 400 U.S., at 484. *Downum* and *Jorn,* over serious dissent, rejected the view that the Double Jeopardy Clause protects only against those mistrials that lend themselves to prosecutorial manipulation and underwrote the independent right of a defendant in a criminal case to have the verdict of the initial jury. Both cases made it quite clear that the discretion of the trial court to declare mistrials is reviewable and that the defendant's right to a verdict by his first jury is not to be overridden except for "manifest necessity." There was not, in this case any more than in *Downum* and *Jorn,* "manifest necessity" for the loss of that right.

The majority recognizes that "the interest of the defendant in having his fate determined by the jury first impaneled is itself a weighty one," but finds that interest outweighed by the State's desire to avoid "conducting a second trial after verdict and reversal on appeal [on the basis of a defective indictment], thus wasting time, energy, and money for all concerned." The majority finds paramount the interest of the State in "keeping a verdict of conviction if its evidence persuaded the jury." Such analysis, however, completely ignores the possibility that the defendant might be acquitted by the initial jury. It is, after all, that possibility—the chance to "end the dispute then and there with an acquittal," United States v. Jorn, supra, at 484—that makes the right to a trial before a particular tribunal of importance to a defendant. In addition, the majority's balancing gives too little weight to the fundamental place of the Double Jeopardy Clause, and the purposes which it seeks to serve, in "the framework of procedural protections which the Constitution establishes for the conduct of a criminal trial." Id., at 479.

Apparently the majority finds "manifest necessity" for a mistrial and the retrial of the defendant in "the State's policy of preserving the right of each defendant to insist that a criminal prosecution against him be commenced by the action of a grand jury" and the implementation of that policy in the absence from Illinois procedural rules of any procedure for the amendment of indictments. Conceding the reasonableness of such a policy, it must be remembered that the inability to amend an indictment does not come into play, and a mistrial is not necessitated, unless an error on the part of the State in the framing of the indictment is committed. Only when the indictment is defective—only when the State has failed to properly execute its responsibility to frame a proper indictment—does the State's procedural framework necessitate a mistrial.

Although recognizing that "a criminal trial is, even in the best of circumstances, a complicated affair to manage," ibid., the Court has not thought prosecutorial error sufficient excuse for not applying the Double Jeopardy Clause. In *Jorn,* for instance, the Court declared that "unquestionably an important factor to be considered is the need to hold litigants on both sides to standards of responsible professional conduct in the clash of an adversary criminal process," id., at 485–486, and cautioned, "The trial judge must recognize that lack of preparedness by the Government ... directly implicates policies underpinning both the double jeopardy provision and the speedy trial guarantee." Id., at 486.... Here, the prosecutorial error, not the independent operation of a state procedural rule, necessitated the mistrial. Judged by the standards of *Downum* and *Jorn* I cannot find, in the words of the majority, an "important countervailing interest of proper judicial administration" in this case; I cannot find "manifest necessity" for a mistrial to compensate for prosecutorial mistake.

Finally, the majority notes that "the declaration of a mistrial on the basis of a rule or a defective procedure that would lend itself to prosecutorial manipulation would involve an entirely different question." See United States v. Jorn, 400 U.S., at 479 .... Surely there is no evidence of bad faith or overreaching on this record. However, the words of the Court in [United States v.] Ball [163 U.S. 662 (1896)] seem particularly appropriate.

> "This case, in short, presents the novel and unheard of spectacle, of a public officer, whose business it was to frame a correct bill, openly alleging his own inaccuracy or neglect, as a reason for a second trial, when it is not pretended that the merits were not fairly in issue on the first. ... If this practice be tolerated, when are trials of the accused to end? If a conviction take place, whether an indictment be good, or otherwise, it is ten to one that judgment passes; for, if he read the bill, it is not probable he will have penetration enough to discern its defects. His counsel, if any be assigned to him, will be content with hearing the substance of the charge without looking farther; and the court will hardly, of its own accord, think it a duty to examine the indictment to detect errors in it. Many hundreds, perhaps, are now in the state prison on erroneous indictments, who, however, have been fairly tried on the merits." 163 U.S., at 667–668.

I respectfully dissent.[*]

[*] Justice Marshall wrote a dissenting opinion.

WITTE v. UNITED STATES

___ U.S. ___, 115 S.Ct. 2199, ___ L.Ed.2d ___ (1995).

JUSTICE O'CONNOR delivered the opinion of the Court.*

The Double Jeopardy Clause of the Fifth Amendment to the United States Constitution prohibits successive prosecution or multiple punishment for "the same offence." This case, which involves application of the United States Sentencing Guidelines, asks us to consider whether a court violates that proscription by convicting and sentencing a defendant for a crime when the conduct underlying that offense has been considered in determining the defendant's sentence for a previous conviction.

I

In June 1990, petitioner Steven Kurt Witte and several co-conspirators, including Dennis Mason and Tom Pokorny, arranged with Roger Norman, an undercover agent of the Drug Enforcement Administration, to import large amounts of marijuana from Mexico and cocaine from Guatemala. Norman had the task of flying the contraband into the United States, with Witte providing the ground transportation for the drugs once they had been brought into the country. The following month, the Mexican marijuana source advised the conspiracy participants that cocaine might be added to the first shipment if there was room on the plane or if an insufficient quantity of marijuana was available. Norman was informed in August 1990 that the source was prepared to deliver 4,400 pounds of marijuana. Once Norman learned the location of the airstrip from which the narcotics would be transported, federal agents arranged to have the participants in the scheme apprehended in Mexico. Local authorities arrested Mason and four others on August 12 and seized 591 kilograms of cocaine at the landing field. While still undercover, Norman met Witte the following day to explain that the pilots had been unable to land in Mexico because police had raided the airstrip. Witte was not taken into custody at that time, and the activities of the conspiracy lapsed for several months.

Agent Norman next spoke with Witte in January 1991 and asked if Witte would be interested in purchasing 1,000 pounds of marijuana. Witte agreed, promised to obtain a $50,000 down payment, and indicated that he would transport the marijuana in a horse trailer he had purchased for the original 1990 transaction and in a

* The Chief Justice and Justice Kennedy join all but part III of this opinion, and Justice Stevens joins only part III.

motor home owned by an acquaintance, Sam Kelly. On February 7, Witte, Norman, and Kelly met in Houston, Texas. Norman agreed to give the drugs to Witte in exchange for the $25,000 in cash Witte had been able to secure at that time and for a promise to pay the balance of the down payment in three days. Undercover agents took the motor home and trailer away to load the marijuana, and Witte escorted Norman to Witte's hotel room to view the money. The agents returned the vehicles the next morning loaded with approximately 375 pounds of marijuana, and they arrested Witte and Kelly when the two men took possession of the contraband.

In March 1991, a federal grand jury in the Southern District of Texas indicted Witte and Kelly for conspiring and attempting to possess marijuana with intent to distribute it, in violation of 21 U.S.C. §§ 841(a) and 846. The indictment was limited on its face to conduct occurring on or about January 25 through February 8, 1991, thus covering only the later marijuana transaction. On February 21, 1992, Witte pleaded guilty to the attempted possession count and agreed to cooperate "with the Government by providing truthful and complete information concerning this and all other offenses about which [he] might be questioned by agents of law enforcement," and by testifying if requested to do so. App. 14. In exchange, the Government agreed to dismiss the conspiracy count and, if Witte's cooperation amounted to "substantial assistance," to file a motion for a downward departure under the Sentencing Guidelines. See United States Sentencing Commission, Guidelines Manual § 5K1.1 (Nov. 1994).

In calculating Witte's base offense level under the Sentencing Guidelines, the presentence report prepared by the United States Probation Office considered the total quantity of drugs involved in all of the transactions contemplated by the conspirators, including the planned 1990 shipments of both marijuana and cocaine. Under the Sentencing Guidelines, the sentencing range for a particular offense is determined on the basis of all "relevant conduct" in which the defendant was engaged and not just with regard to the conduct underlying the offense of conviction. USSG § 1B1.3. The Sentencing Commission has noted that, "[w]ith respect to offenses involving contraband (including controlled substances), the defendant is accountable for all quantities of contraband with which he was directly involved and, in the case of a jointly undertaken criminal activity, all reasonably foreseeable quantities of contraband that were within the scope of the criminal activity that he jointly undertook." USSG § 1B1.3, comment., n. 2; see also USSG § 2D1.1, comment., nn. 6, 12. The presentence report therefore suggested that Witte was accountable for the 1,000 pounds of marijuana involved in the attempted possession offense to which he pleaded guilty, 15 tons of marijuana that Witte, Mason, and Pokorny had planned to import from Mexico in 1990, 500 kilograms of cocaine that the conspirators originally proposed to import from

Guatemala, and the 591 kilograms of cocaine seized at the Mexican airstrip in August 1990.

At the sentencing hearing, both petitioner and the Government urged the court to hold that the 1990 activities concerning importation of cocaine and marijuana were not part of the same course of conduct as the 1991 marijuana offense to which Witte had pleaded guilty, and therefore should not be considered in sentencing for the 1991 offense. The District Court concluded, however, that because the 1990 importation offenses were part of the same continuing conspiracy, they were "relevant conduct" under § 1B1.3 of the Guidelines and should be taken into account. The court therefore accepted the presentence report's aggregation of the quantities of drugs involved in the 1990 and 1991 episodes, resulting in a base offense level of 40, with a Guideline range of 292 to 365 months' imprisonment.... From that base offense level, Witte received a two-level increase for his aggravating role in the offense, see USSG § 3B1.1, and an offsetting two-level decrease for acceptance of responsibility, see USSG § 3E1.1. Finally, the court granted the Government's § 5K1.1 motion for downward departure based on Witte's substantial assistance. By virtue of that departure, the court sentenced Witte to 144 months in prison, see App. 76, which was 148 months below the minimum sentence of 292 months under the pre-departure Guideline range. Witte appealed, but the Court of Appeals dismissed the case when Witte failed to file a brief.

In September 1992, another grand jury in the same district returned a two-count indictment against Witte and Pokorny for conspiring and attempting to import cocaine, in violation of 21 U.S.C. §§ 952(a) and 963. The indictment alleged that, between August 1989 and August 1990, Witte tried to import about 1,091 kilograms of cocaine from Central America. Witte moved to dismiss, arguing that he had already been punished for the cocaine offenses because the cocaine involved in the 1990 transactions had been considered as "relevant conduct" at sentencing for the 1991 marijuana offense. The District Court dismissed the indictment in February 1993 on grounds that punishment for the indicted offenses would violate the prohibition against multiple punishments contained in the Double Jeopardy Clause of the Fifth Amendment....

The Court of Appeals for the Fifth Circuit reversed. 25 F.3d 250 (1994). Relying on our decision in Williams v. Oklahoma, 358 U.S. 576 (1959), the court held that "the use of relevant conduct to increase the punishment of a charged offense does not punish the offender for the relevant conduct." 25 F.3d, at 258. Thus, although the sentencing court took the quantity of cocaine involved in the 1990 importation scheme into account when determining the sentence for Witte's 1991 marijuana possession offense, the Court of Appeals concluded that Witte had not been punished for the cocaine offenses in the first prosecution—and that the Double

Jeopardy Clause therefore did not bar the later action. In reaching this result, the court expressly disagreed with contrary holdings ... that when a defendant's actions are included in relevant conduct in determining the punishment under the Sentencing Guidelines for one offense, those actions may not form the basis for a later indictment without violating double jeopardy. We granted certiorari to resolve the conflict among the circuits, 513 U.S. ___ (1995), and now affirm.

II

The Double Jeopardy Clause provides: "[N]or shall any person be subject for the same offence to be twice put in jeopardy of life or limb." U.S. Const. Amend. 5. We have explained that "the Clause serves the function of preventing both successive punishment and successive prosecution," United States v. Dixon, 509 U.S. ___, ___ (1993) (slip op., at 15) (citing North Carolina v. Pearce, 395 U.S. 711 (1969)), and that "the Constitution was designed as much to prevent the criminal from being twice punished for the same offence as from being twice tried for it," Ex parte Lange, 18 Wall. 163, 173 (1874).... Significantly, the language of the Double Jeopardy Clause protects against more than the actual imposition of two punishments for the same offense; by its terms, it protects a criminal defendant from being *twice put in jeopardy* for such punishment.... That is, the Double Jeopardy Clause "prohibits merely punishing twice, or *attempting a second time to punish criminally*, for the same offense." Helvering v. Mitchell, 303 U.S. 391, 399 (1938) (emphasis added).

Petitioner clearly was neither prosecuted for nor convicted of the cocaine offenses during the first criminal proceeding. The offense to which petitioner pleaded guilty and for which he was sentenced in 1992 was attempted possession of marijuana with intent to distribute it, whereas the crimes charged in the instant indictment are conspiracy to import cocaine and attempted importation of the same. Under Blockburger v. United States, 284 U.S. 299, 304 (1932), "where the same act or transaction constitutes a violation of two distinct statutory provisions, the test to be applied to determine whether there are two offenses or only one, is whether each provision requires proof of a fact which the other does not." ... Under the *Blockburger* test, the indictment in this case did not charge the same offense to which petitioner formerly had pleaded guilty.

Petitioner nevertheless argues that, because the conduct giving rise to the cocaine charges *was* taken into account during sentencing for the marijuana conviction, he effectively was "punished" for that conduct during the first proceeding. As a result, he contends, the Double Jeopardy Clause bars the instant prosecution.... [I]f petitioner is correct that the present case constitutes a second attempt to punish him criminally for the same cocaine offenses ...

then the prosecution may not proceed. We agree with the Court of Appeals, however, that petitioner's double jeopardy theory—that consideration of uncharged conduct in arriving at a sentence within the statutorily authorized punishment range constitutes "punishment" for that conduct—is not supported by our precedents, which make clear that a defendant in that situation is punished, for double jeopardy purposes, only for the offense of which the defendant is convicted.

Traditionally, "[s]entencing courts have not only taken into consideration a defendant's prior convictions, but have also considered a defendant's past criminal behavior, even if no conviction resulted from that behavior." Nichols v. United States, 511 U.S. ___, ___ (1994) (slip op., at 9). We explained in Williams v. New York, 337 U.S. 241, 246 (1949), that "both before and since the American colonies became a nation, courts in this country and in England practiced a policy under which a sentencing judge could exercise a wide discretion in the sources and types of evidence used to assist him in determining the kind and extent of punishment to be imposed within limits fixed by law." That history, combined with a recognition of the need for individualized sentencing, led us to conclude that the Due Process Clause did not require "that courts throughout the Nation abandon their age-old practice of seeking information from out-of-court sources to guide their judgment toward a more enlightened and just sentence." Id., at 250–251. Thus, "[a]s a general proposition, a sentencing judge 'may appropriately conduct an inquiry broad in scope, largely unlimited either as to the kind of information he may consider, or the source from which it may come.'" Nichols, 511 U.S., at ___ (slip op., at 9) (quoting United States v. Tucker, 404 U.S. 443, 446 (1972)). . . .

Against this background of sentencing history, we specifically have rejected the claim that double jeopardy principles bar a later prosecution or punishment for criminal activity where that activity has been considered at sentencing for a separate crime. Williams v. Oklahoma, 358 U.S., at 576, arose out of a kidnaping and murder committed by the petitioner while attempting to escape from police after a robbery. Following his arrest, Williams pleaded guilty to murder and was given a life sentence. He was later convicted of kidnaping, which was then a capital offense in Oklahoma, and the sentencing court took into account, in assessing the death penalty, the fact that the kidnaping victim had been murdered. We rejected Williams' contention that this use of the conduct that had given rise to the prior conviction violated double jeopardy. Emphasizing that "the exercise of a sound discretion in such a case required consideration of all the circumstances of the crime," we made clear that "one of the aggravating circumstances involved in this kidnaping crime was the fact that petitioner shot and killed the victim in the course of its commission," and rejected the claim "that the sentencing judge was not entitled to consider that circumstance, along with all the other circumstances involved, in determining the proper sentence to be imposed for the kidnaping crime." Id., at 585–586. We then disposed of the petitioner's double jeopardy claim as follows: "[I]n view of the obvious fact that, under the law of Oklahoma, kidnaping is a separate crime, entirely distinct from the crime of murder, the court's consideration of the murder as a circumstance involved in the kidnaping crime cannot be said to have resulted in punishing petitioner a second time for the same offense . . . ." Id., at 586. We thus made clear that use of evidence of related criminal conduct to enhance a defendant's sentence for a separate crime within the authorized statutory limits does not constitute punishment for that conduct within the meaning of the Double Jeopardy Clause.

We find this case to be governed by *Williams*; it makes no difference in this context whether the enhancement occurred in the first or second sentencing proceeding. Here, petitioner pleaded guilty to attempted possession of marijuana with intent to distribute it, in violation of 21 U.S.C. §§ 841(a) and 846. The statute provides that the sentence for such a crime involving 100 kilograms or more of marijuana must be between 5 and 40 years in prison. § 841(b)(1)(B). By including the cocaine from the earlier transaction—and not just the marijuana involved in the offense of conviction—in the drug quantity calculation, the District Court ended up with a higher offense level (40), and a higher sentence range (292 to 365 months), than it would have otherwise under the applicable Guideline, which specifies different base offense levels depending on the quantity of drugs involved. USSG § 2D1.1. This higher guideline range, however, still falls within the scope of the legislatively authorized penalty (5–40 years). As in *Williams*, the uncharged criminal conduct was used to enhance petitioner's sentence within the range authorized by statute. If use of the murder to justify the death sentence for the kidnapping conviction was not "punishment" for the murder in *Williams*, it is impossible to conclude that taking account of petitioner's plans to import cocaine in fixing the sentence for the marijuana conviction constituted "punishment" for the cocaine offenses.

Williams, like this case, concerned the double jeopardy implications of taking the circumstances surrounding a particular course of criminal activity into account in sentencing for a conviction arising therefrom. Similarly, we have made clear in other cases, which involved a defendant's background more generally and not conduct arising out of the same criminal transaction as the offense of which the defendant was convicted, that "[e]nhancement statutes, whether in the nature of criminal history provisions such as those contained in the Sentencing Guidelines, or recidivist statutes which are common place in state criminal laws, do not change the penalty imposed for the earlier conviction." *Nichols*, 511 U.S., at

___ (slip op., at 9) (approving consideration of a defendant's previous uncounseled misdemeanor conviction in sentencing him for a subsequent offense). In repeatedly upholding such recidivism statutes, we have rejected double jeopardy challenges because the enhanced punishment imposed for the later offense "is not to be viewed as either a new jeopardy or additional penalty for the earlier crimes," but instead as "a stiffened penalty for the latest crime, which is considered to be an aggravated offense because a repetitive one." Gryger v. Burke, 334 U.S. 728, 732 (1948)....

In addition, by authorizing the consideration of offender-specific information at sentencing without the procedural protections attendant at a criminal trial, our cases necessarily imply that such consideration does not result in "punishment" for such conduct. In McMillan v. Pennsylvania, 477 U.S. 79 (1986), we upheld against a due process challenge Pennsylvania's Mandatory Minimum Sentencing Act, which imposed a 5-year minimum sentence for certain enumerated felonies if the sentencing judge found, by a preponderance of the evidence, that the defendant "visibly possessed a firearm" during the commission of the offense. Significantly, we emphasized that the statute at issue "neither alters the maximum penalty for the crime committed nor creates a separate offense calling for a separate penalty; it operates solely to limit the sentencing court's discretion in selecting a penalty within the range already available to it without the special finding of visible possession of a firearm." Id., at 87–88. That is, the statute "simply took one factor that has always been considered by sentencing courts to bear on punishment—the instrumentality used in committing a violent felony—and dictated the precise weight to be given that factor if the instrumentality is a firearm." Id., at 89–90. For this reason, we approved the lesser standard of proof provided for in the statute, thereby "reject[ing] the claim that whenever a State links the 'severity of punishment' to 'the presence or absence of an identified fact' the State must prove that fact beyond a reasonable doubt." Id., at 84 (quoting Patterson v. New York, 432 U.S. 197, 214 (1977)). These decisions reinforce our conclusion that consideration of information about the defendant's character and conduct at sentencing does not result in "punishment" for any offense other than the one of which the defendant was convicted.

We are not persuaded by petitioner's suggestion that the Sentencing Guidelines somehow change the constitutional analysis. A defendant has not been "punished" any more for double jeopardy purposes when relevant conduct is included in the calculation of his offense level under the Guidelines than when a pre-Guidelines court, in its discretion, took similar uncharged conduct into account.... As the Government argues, "[t]he fact that the sentencing process has become more transparent under the Guidelines ... does not mean that the defendant is now being 'punished' for uncharged relevant conduct as though it were a distinct criminal 'offense.' " Brief for United States 23. The relevant conduct provisions are designed to channel the sentencing discretion of the district courts and to make mandatory the consideration of factors that previously would have been optional. . . . Regardless of whether particular conduct is taken into account by rule or as an act of discretion, the defendant is still being punished only for the offense of conviction.

Justice Stevens disagrees with our conclusion because, he contends, "[u]nder the Guidelines, an offense that is included as 'relevant conduct' does not relate to the character of the offender (which is reflected instead by criminal history), but rather measures only the character of the offense." Post, at 5. The criminal history section of the Guidelines, however, does not seem to create this bright line distinction; indeed, the difference between "criminal history" and "relevant conduct" is more temporal than qualitative, with the former referring simply to a defendant's *past* criminal conduct (as evidenced by convictions and prison terms), see USSG § 4A1.1, and the latter covering activity arising out of the same course of criminal conduct as the instant offense, see USSG § 1B1.3.

To the extent that the Guidelines aggravate punishment for related conduct outside the elements of the crime on the theory that such conduct bears on the "character of the offense," the offender is still punished only for the fact that the *present* offense was carried out in a manner that warrants increased punishment, not for a *different* offense (which that related conduct may or may not constitute). But, while relevant conduct thus may relate to the severity of the particular crime, the commission of multiple offenses in the same course of conduct also necessarily provides important evidence that the character of the offender requires special punishment. Similarly, as we have said in the recidivism cases, a crime committed by an offender with a prior conviction "is considered to be an aggravated offense because a repetitive one." *Gryger*, 334 U.S., at 732. Nothing about the labels given to these categories controls the use to which such information is put at sentencing. . . .

The relevant conduct provisions of the Sentencing Guidelines, like their criminal history counterparts and the recidivism statutes discussed above, are sentencing enhancement regimes evincing the judgment that a particular offense should receive a more serious sentence within the authorized range if it was either accompanied by or preceded by additional criminal activity. Petitioner does not argue that the range fixed by Congress is so broad, and the enhancing role played by the relevant conduct so significant, that consideration of that conduct in sentencing has become "a tail which wags the dog of the substantive offense." *McMillan*, 477 U.S., at 88; cf. Mullaney v. Wilbur, 421 U.S. 684, 700 (1975). We hold that, where the legislature has authorized such a particular punishment range for a given crime, the resulting sentence within that range constitutes punishment only for the offense of conviction for purposes of the double jeopardy inquiry. Accordingly, the instant prosecution for the cocaine offenses is not barred by the Double Jeopardy Clause as a second attempt to punish petitioner for the same crime.

.   .   .

IV

Because consideration of relevant conduct in determining a defendant's sentence within the legislatively authorized punishment range does not constitute punishment for that conduct, the instant prosecution does not violate the Double Jeopardy Clause's prohibition against the imposition of multiple punishments for the same offense.   Accordingly, the judgment of the Court of Appeals is

Affirmed.[*]

[*] Justice Scalia wrote an opinion concurring in the judgment, which Justice Thomas joined. Justice Stevens wrote an opinion concurring in part and dissenting in part.

16. SENTENCE

UNITED STATES v. GRAYSON

438 U.S. 41, 98 S.Ct. 2610, 57 L.Ed.2d 582 (1978).

MR. CHIEF JUSTICE BURGER delivered the opinion of the Court.

We granted certiorari to review a holding of the Court of Appeals that it was improper for a sentencing judge, in fixing the sentence within the statutory limits, to give consideration to the defendant's false testimony observed by the judge during the trial.

I

In August 1975, respondent Grayson was confined in a federal prison camp under a conviction for distributing a controlled substance. In October, he escaped but was apprehended two days later by FBI agents in New York City. He was indicted for prison escape in violation of 18 U.S.C. § 751(a) [1976 ed.].

During its case in chief, the United States proved the essential elements of the crime, including his lawful confinement and the unlawful escape. In addition, it presented the testimony of the arresting FBI agents that Grayson, upon being apprehended, denied his true identity.

Grayson testified in his own defense. He admitted leaving the camp but asserted that he did so out of fear: "I had just been threatened with a large stick with a nail protruding through it by an inmate that was serving time at Allenwood, and I was scared, and I just ran." He testified that the threat was made in the presence of many inmates by prisoner Barnes who sought to enforce collection of a gambling debt and followed other threats and physical assaults made for the same purpose. Grayson called one inmate, who testified, "I heard [Barnes] talk to Grayson in a loud voice one day, but that's all. I never seen no harm, no hands or no shuffling whatsoever."

Grayson's version of the facts was contradicted by the Government's rebuttal evidence and by cross-examination on crucial aspects of his story. For example, Grayson stated that after crossing the prison fence he left his prison jacket by the side of the road. On recross, he stated that he also left his prison shirt but not his trousers. Government testimony showed that on the morning after the escape, a shirt marked with Grayson's number, a jacket, and a pair of prison trousers were found outside a hole in the prison fence. Grayson also testified on cross-examination: "I do believe that I phrased the rhetorical question to Captain Kurd, who was in charge of [the prison], and I think I said something if an inmate was being threatened by somebody, what would . . . he do? First of all he said he would want to know who it was." On further cross-examination, however, Grayson modified his description of the conversation. Captain Kurd testified that Grayson had never mentioned in any fashion threats from other inmates. Finally, the alleged assailant, Barnes, by then no longer an inmate, testified that Grayson had never owed him any money and that he had never threatened or physically assaulted Grayson.

The jury returned a guilty verdict, whereupon the District Judge ordered the United States Probation Office to prepare a presentence report. At the sentencing hearing, the judge stated:

> "I'm going to give my reasons for sentencing in this case with clarity, because one of the reasons may well be considered by a Court of Appeals to be impermissible; and although I could come into this Court Room and sentence this Defendant to a five-year prison term without any explanation at all, I think it is fair that I give the reasons so that if the Court of Appeals feels that one of the reasons which I am about to enunciate is an improper consideration for a trial judge, then the Court will be in a position to reverse this court and send the case back for resentencing.

> "In my view a prison sentence is indicated, and the sentence that the Court is going to impose is to deter you, Mr. Grayson, and others who are similarly situated. Secondly, *it is my view that your defense was a complete fabrication without the slightest merit whatsoever. I feel it is proper for me to consider that fact in the sentencing, and I will do so."* (Emphasis added.)

He then sentenced Grayson to a term of two years' imprisonment, consecutive to his unexpired sentence.[2]

On appeal, a divided panel of the Court of Appeals for the Third Circuit directed that Grayson's sentence be vacated and that he be resentenced by the District Court without consideration of false testimony. 550 F.2d 103 (1977). . . .

We granted certiorari to resolve conflicts between holdings of the Courts of Appeals. 434 U.S. 816 (1977). We reverse.

II

In New York v. Williams, 337 U.S. 241, 247 (1949), Mr. Justice Black observed that the "prevalent modern philosophy of penology [is] that the punishment should fit the offender and not merely the

---

2. The District Court in this case could have sentenced Grayson for any period up to five years. 18 U.S.C. § 751(a) [1976 ed.].

crime," and that, accordingly, sentences should be determined with an eye toward the "[r]eformation and rehabilitation of offenders." Id., at 248. But it has not always been so. In the early days of the Republic, when imprisonment had only recently emerged as an alternative to the death penalty, confinement in public stocks, or whipping in the town square, the period of incarceration was generally prescribed with specificity by the legislature. Each crime had its defined punishment. ... The "excessive rigidity of the [mandatory or fixed sentence] system" soon gave way in some jurisdictions, however, to a scheme permitting the sentencing judge—or jury—to consider aggravating and mitigating circumstances surrounding an offense, and, on that basis, to select a sentence within a *range* defined by the legislature. Tappan, Sentencing Under the Model Penal Code, 23 Law & Contemp.Prob. 528, 529 (1958). Nevertheless, the focus remained on the crime: Each particular offense was to be punished in proportion to the social harm caused by it and according to the offender's culpability. ... The purpose of incarceration remained, primarily, retribution and punishment.

Approximately a century ago, a reform movement asserting that the purpose of incarceration, and therefore the guiding consideration in sentencing, should be rehabilitation of the offender, dramatically altered the approach to sentencing. A fundamental proposal of this movement was a flexible sentencing system permitting judges and correctional personnel, particularly the latter, to set the release date of prisoners according to informed judgments concerning their potential for, or actual, rehabilitation and their likely recidivism. ... Indeed, the most extreme formulations of the emerging rehabilitation model, with its "reformatory sentence," posited that "convicts [regardless of the nature of their crime] can never be rightfully imprisoned except upon proof that it is unsafe for themselves and for society to leave them free, and when confined can never be rightfully released until they show themselves fit for membership in a free community." Lewis, The Indeterminate Sentence, 9 Yale L.J. 17, 27 (1899).

This extreme formulation, although influential, was not adopted unmodified by any jurisdiction. See Tappan, supra, at 531–533. "The influences of legalism and realism were powerful enough ... to prevent the enactment of this form of indeterminate sentencing. Concern for personal liberty, skepticism concerning administrative decisions about prisoner reformation and readiness for release, insistence upon the preservation of some measure of deterrent emphasis, and other such factors, undoubtedly, led, instead, to a system—indeed, a complex of systems—in which maximum terms were generally employed." Id., at 530. Thus it is that today the extent of a federal prisoner's confinement is initially determined by the sentencing judge, who selects a term within an often broad, congressionally prescribed range; release on parole is then available on review by the United States Parole Commission, which, as a general rule, may conditionally release a prisoner any time after he serves one-third of the judicially fixed term.... To an unspecified degree, the sentencing judge is obligated to make his decision on the basis, among others, of predictions regarding the convicted defendant's potential, or lack of potential, for rehabilitation.

Indeterminate sentencing under the rehabilitation model presented sentencing judges with a serious practical problem: how rationally to make the required predictions so as to avoid capricious and arbitrary sentences, which the newly conferred and broad discretion placed within the realm of possibility. An obvious, although only partial, solution was to provide the judge with as much information as reasonably practical concerning the defendant's "character and propensities[,] ... his present purposes and tendencies." Pennsylvania ex rel. Sullivan v. Ashe, 302 U.S. 51, 55 (1937), and, indeed, "every aspect of [his] life." Williams v. New York, 337 U.S., at 250. Thus, most jurisdictions provided trained probation officers to conduct presentence investigations of the defendant's life and, on that basis, prepare a presentence report for the sentencing judge.

Constitutional challenges were leveled at judicial reliance on such information, however. In Williams v. New York, a jury convicted the defendant of murder but recommended a life sentence. The sentencing judge, partly on the basis of information not known to the jury but contained in a presentence report, imposed the death penalty. The defendant argued that this procedure deprived him of his federal constitutional right to confront and cross-examine those supplying information to the probation officer and, through him, to the sentencing judge. The Court rejected this argument. It noted that traditionally "a sentencing judge could exercise a wide discretion in the sources and types of evidence used to assist him in determining the kind and extent of punishment to be imposed within limits fixed by law." Id., at 246. "And modern concepts of individualizing punishment have made it all the more necessary that a sentencing judge not be denied an opportunity to obtain pertinent information," id., at 247; indeed, "[t]o deprive sentencing judges of this kind of information would undermine modern penological procedural policies that have been cautiously adopted throughout the nation after careful consideration and experimentation." Id., at 249–250. Accordingly, the sentencing judge was held not to have acted unconstitutionally in considering either the defendant's participation in criminal conduct for which he had not been convicted or information secured by the probation investigator that the defendant was a "menace to society." See id., at 244.

Of course, a sentencing judge is not limited to the often far-ranging material compiled in a presentence report. "[B]efore making [the sentencing] determination, a judge may appropriately conduct an inquiry broad in scope, largely unlimited either as to the kind of information he may consider, or the source from which it may come." United States v. Tucker, 404 U.S. 443, 446 (1972). Congress recently reaffirmed this fundamental sentencing principle by enacting 18 U.S.C. § 3577:

> "No limitation shall be placed on the information concerning the background, character, and conduct of a person convicted of an offense which a court of the United States may receive and consider for the purpose of imposing an appropriate sentence."

Thus, we have acknowledged that a sentencing authority may legitimately consider the evidence heard during trial, as well as the demeanor of the accused.... More to the point presented in this case, one serious study has concluded that the trial judge's "opportunity to observe the defendant, particularly if he chose to take the stand in his defense, can often provide useful insights into an appropriate disposition." ABA Project on Standards for Criminal Justice, Sentencing Alternatives and Procedures § 5.1, at 232 [App. Draft 1968].

A defendant's truthfulness or mendacity while testifying on his own behalf, almost without exception, has been deemed probative of his attitudes toward society and prospects for rehabilitation and hence relevant to sentencing. ... Judge Marvin Frankel's analysis for the Second Circuit is persuasive:

> "The effort to appraise 'character' is, to be sure, a parlous one, and not necessarily an enterprise for which judges are notably equipped by prior training. Yet it is in our existing scheme of sentencing one clue to the rational exercise of discretion. If the notion of 'repentence' is out of fashion today, the fact remains that a manipulative defiance of the law is not a cheerful datum for the prognosis a sentencing judge undertakes .... Impressions about an individual being sentenced—the likelihood that he will transgress no more, the hope that he may respond to rehabilitative efforts to assist with a lawful future career, the degree to which he does or does not deem himself at war with his society—are, for better or worse, central factors to be appraised under our theory of 'individualized' sentencing. The theory has its critics. While it lasts, however, a fact like the defendant's readiness to lie under oath before the judge who will sentence him would seem to be among the more precise and concrete of the available indicia." United States v. Hendrix, 505 F.2d 1233, 1236 (1974).

Only one Circuit has directly rejected the probative value of the defendant's false testimony in his own defense. In Scott v. United States, 135 U.S.App.D.C. 377, 382, 419 F.2d 264, 269 (1969), the court argued that "the peculiar pressures placed upon a defendant threatened with jail and the stigma of conviction make his willingness to deny the crime an unpromising test of his prospects for rehabilitation if guilty. It is indeed unlikely that many men who commit serious offenses would balk on principle from lying in their own defense. The guilty man may quite sincerely repent his crime but yet, driven by the urge to remain free, may protest his innocence in a court of law."

... The *Scott* rationale rests not only on the realism of the psychological pressures on a defendant in the dock—which we can grant—but also on a deterministic view of human conduct that is inconsistent with the underlying precepts of our criminal justice system. A "universal and persistent" foundation stone in our system of law, and particularly in our approach to punishment, sentencing and incarceration, is the "belief in freedom of the human will and a consequent ability and duty of the normal individual to choose between good and evil." Morissette v. United States, 342 U.S. 246, 250 (1952). ... Given that long accepted view of the "ability and duty of the normal individual to choose," we must conclude that the defendant's readiness to lie under oath—especially when, as here, the trial court finds the lie to be flagrant—may be deemed probative of his prospects for rehabilitation.

III

Against this background we evaluate Grayson's constitutional argument that the District Court's sentence constitutes punishment for the crime of perjury for which he has not been indicted, tried or convicted by due process. A second argument is that permitting consideration of perjury will "chill" defendants from exercising their right to testify on their own behalf.

A

In his due process argument, Grayson does not contend directly that the District Court had an impermissible purpose in considering his perjury and selecting the sentence. Rather, he argues that this Court, in order to preserve due process rights, not only must prohibit the impermissible sentencing practice of incarcerating for the purpose of saving the Government the burden of bringing a separate and subsequent perjury prosecution but also must prohibit the otherwise *permissible* practice of considering a defendant's untruthfulness for the purpose of illuminating his need for rehabilitation and society's need for protection. He presents two interrelated reasons. The effect of both permissible and impermissible sentencing practices may be the same: additional time in prison. Further, it is virtually impossible, he contends, to identify and establish the impermissible practice. We find these reasons insufficient justification for prohibiting what the Court and the Congress have declared appropriate judicial conduct.

First, the evolutionary history of sentencing, set out in Part II, demonstrates that it is proper—indeed, even necessary for the rational exercise of discretion—to consider the defendant's whole person and personality, as manifested by his conduct at trial and his testimony under oath, for whatever light those may shed on the sentencing decision. The "parlous" effort to appraise "character," United States v. Hendrix, supra, at 1236, degenerates into a game of chance to the extent that a sentencing judge is deprived of relevant information concerning "every aspect of a defendant's life." Williams v. New York, supra, at 250. The Government's interest, as well as the offender's, in avoiding irrationality is of the highest order. That interest more than justifies the risk that Grayson asserts is present when a sentencing judge considers a defendant's untruthfulness under oath.

Second, in our view, *Williams* fully supports consideration of such conduct in sentencing. There the Court permitted the sentencing judge to consider the offender's history of prior antisocial conduct, including burglaries for which he had not been duly convicted. This it did despite the risk that the judge might use his knowledge of the offender's prior crimes for an improper purpose.

Third, the efficacy of Grayson's suggested "exclusionary rule" is open to serious doubt. No rule of law, even one garbed in constitutional terms, can prevent improper use of firsthand observations of perjury. The integrity of the judges, and their fidelity to their oaths of office, necessarily provide the only, and in our view adequate, assurance against that.

B

Grayson's argument that judicial consideration of his conduct at trial impermissibly "chills" a defendant's statutory right, 28 U.S.C. § 3481, and perhaps a constitutional right to testify on his own behalf is without basis. The right guaranteed by law to a defendant is narrowly the right to testify truthfully in accordance with the oath—unless we are to say that the oath is mere ritual without meaning. This view of the right involved is confirmed by the unquestioned constitutionality of perjury statutes, which punish those who willfully give false testimony. ... Further support for this is found in an important limitation on a defendant's right to the assistance of counsel: Counsel ethically cannot assist his client in presenting what the attorney has reason to believe is false testimony. ... Assuming, *arguendo,* that the sentencing judge's consideration of defendants' untruthfulness in testifying has any chilling effect on a defendant's decision to testify falsely, that effect is entirely permissible. There is no protected right to commit perjury.

Grayson's further argument that the sentencing practice challenged here will inhibit exercise of the right to testify truthfully is entirely frivolous. That argument misapprehends the nature and scope of the practice we find permissible. Nothing we say today requires a sentencing judge to enhance, in some wooden or reflex fashion, the sentences of all defendants whose testimony is deemed false. Rather, we are reaffirming the authority of a sentencing judge to evaluate carefully a defendant's testimony on the stand, determine—with a consciousness of the frailty of human judgment—whether that testimony contained willful and material falsehoods, and, if so, assess in light of all the other knowledge gained about the defendant the meaning of that conduct with respect to his prospects for rehabilitation and restoration to a useful place in society. Awareness of such a process realistically cannot be deemed to affect the decision of an accused but unconvicted defendant to testify truthfully in his own behalf.

Accordingly, we reverse the judgment of the Court of Appeals and remand for reinstatement of the sentence of the District Court.

Reversed and remanded.

MR. JUSTICE STEWART, with whom MR. JUSTICE BRENNAN and MR. JUSTICE MARSHALL join, dissenting.

The Court begins its consideration of this case, ante, at 42, with the assumption that the respondent gave false testimony at his trial. But there has been no determination that his testimony was false. This respondent was given a greater sentence than he would otherwise have received—how much greater we have no way of knowing—solely because a single judge *thought* that he had not testified truthfully. In essence, the Court holds today that *whenever* a defendant testifies in his own behalf and is found guilty, he opens himself to the possibility of an enhanced sentence. Such a sentence is nothing more nor less than a penalty imposed on the defendant's exercise of his constitutional and statutory rights to plead not guilty and to testify in his own behalf.

It does not change matters to say that the enhanced sentence merely reflects the defendant's "prospects for rehabilitation" rather than an additional punishment for testifying falsely. The fact remains that all defendants who choose to testify, and only those who do so, face the very real prospect of a greater sentence based upon the trial judge's unreviewable perception that the testimony was untruthful. The Court prescribes no limitations or safeguards to minimize a defendant's rational fear that his truthful testimony will be perceived as false. Indeed, encumbrance of the sentencing process with the collateral inquiries necessary to provide such assurance would be both pragmatically unworkable and theoretically inconsistent with the assumption that the trial judge is merely considering one more piece of information in his overall evaluation of the defendant's prospects for rehabilitation. But without such safeguards I fail to see how the Court can dismiss as "frivolous" the argument that this sentencing practice will "inhibit the right to testify truthfully," ante, at 55.

A defendant's decision to testify may be inhibited by a number of considerations, such as the possibility that damaging evidence not otherwise admissible will be admitted to impeach his credibility. These constraints arise solely from the fact that the defendant is quite properly treated like any other witness who testifies at trial. But the practice that the Court approves today actually places the defendant at a disadvantage, as compared with any other witness at trial, simply because he is the defendant. Other witnesses risk punishment for perjury only upon indictment and conviction in accord with the full protections of the Constitution. Only the defendant himself, whose testimony is likely to be of critical importance to his defense, faces the additional risk that the disbelief of a single listener will itself result in time in prison.

The minimal contribution that the defendant's possibly untruthful testimony might make to an overall assessment of his potential for rehabilitation ... cannot justify imposing this additional burden on his right to testify in his own behalf. I do not believe that a sentencing judge's discretion to consider a wide range of information in arriving at an appropriate sentence, ... allows him to mete out additional punishment to the defendant simply because of his personal belief that the defendant did not testify truthfully at the trial.

Accordingly, I would affirm the judgment of the Court of Appeals.

SOLEM v. HELM

463 U.S. 277, 103 S.Ct. 3001, 77 L.Ed.2d 637 (1983).

JUSTICE POWELL delivered the opinion of the Court.

The issue presented is whether the Eighth Amendment proscribes a life sentence without possibility of parole for a seventh nonviolent felony.

I

By 1975 the State of South Dakota had convicted respondent Jerry Helm of six nonviolent felonies. In 1964, 1966, and 1969 Helm was convicted of third-degree burglary. In 1972 he was convicted of obtaining money under false pretenses. In 1973 he was convicted of grand larceny. And in 1975 he was convicted of third-offense driving while intoxicated. The record contains no details about the circumstances of any of these offenses, except that they were all nonviolent, none was a crime against a person, and alcohol was a contributing factor in each case.

In 1979 Helm was charged with uttering a "no account" check for $100. The only details we have of the crime are those given by Helm to the state trial court:

> " 'I was working in Sioux Falls, and got my check that day, was drinking and I ended up here in Rapid City with more money than I had when I started. I knew I'd done something I didn't know exactly what. If I would have known this, I would have picked the check up. I was drinking and didn't remember, stopped several places.' " State v. Helm, 287 N.W.2d 497, 501 (S.D.1980) (Henderson, J., dissenting) (quoting Helm).

After offering this explanation, Helm pleaded guilty.

Ordinarily the maximum punishment for uttering a "no account" check would have been five years imprisonment in the state penitentiary and a $5,000 fine.... As a result of his criminal record, however, Helm was subject to South Dakota's recidivist statute:

> "When a defendant has been convicted of at least three prior convictions [*sic*] in addition to the principal felony, the sentence for the principal felony shall be enhanced to the sentence for a Class 1 felony." S.D.Codified Laws § 22–7–8 (1979) (amended 1981).

The maximum penalty for a "Class 1 felony" was life imprisonment in the state penitentiary and a $25,000 fine.... Moreover, South Dakota law explicitly provides that parole is unavailable: "A person

1110

sentenced to life imprisonment is not eligible for parole by the board of pardons and paroles." S.D.Codified Laws § 24–15–4 (1979). The Governor is authorized to pardon prisoners, or to commute their sentences ... but no other relief from sentence is available even to a rehabilitated prisoner.

Immediately after accepting Helm's guilty plea, the South Dakota Circuit Court sentenced Helm to life imprisonment under § 22–7–8. The court explained:

> " 'I think you certainly earned this sentence and certainly proven that you're an habitual criminal and the record would indicate that you're beyond rehabilitation and that the only prudent thing to do is to lock you up for the rest of your natural life, so you won't have further victims of your crimes, just be coming back before Courts. You'll have plenty of time to think this one over.' " State v. Helm, 287 N.W.2d, at 500 (Henderson, J., dissenting) (quoting S.D. Circuit Court, Seventh Judicial Circuit, Pennington County (Parker, J.)).

The South Dakota Supreme Court, in a 3–2 decision, affirmed the sentence despite Helm's argument that it violated the Eighth Amendment. State v. Helm, supra.

After Helm had served two years in the state penitentiary, he requested the Governor to commute his sentence to a fixed term of years. Such a commutation would have had the effect of making Helm eligible to be considered for parole when he had served three-fourths of his new sentence.... The Governor denied Helm's request in May 1981....

In November 1981, Helm sought habeas relief in the United States District Court for the District of South Dakota. Helm argued, among other things, that his sentence constituted cruel and unusual punishment under the Eighth and Fourteenth Amendments. Although the District Court recognized that the sentence was harsh, it concluded that this Court's recent decision in Rummel v. Estelle, 445 U.S. 263 (1980), was dispositive. It therefore denied the writ.

The United States Court of Appeals for the Eighth Circuit reversed. 684 F.2d 582 (1982). ...

We granted certiorari to consider the Eighth Amendment question presented by this case. 459 U.S. 986 (1982). We now affirm.

II

The Eighth Amendment declares: "Excessive bail shall not be required, nor excessive fines imposed, nor cruel and unusual punishments inflicted." The final clause prohibits not only barbaric punishments, but also sentences that are disproportionate to the crime committed.

A

The principle that a punishment should be proportionate to the crime is deeply rooted and frequently repeated in common-law jurisprudence. In 1215 three chapters of Magna Carta were devoted to the rule that "amercements" [8] may not be excessive. And the principle was repeated and extended in the First Statute of Westminster, 3 Edw. I, ch. 6 (1275). These were not hollow guarantees, for the royal courts relied on them to invalidate disproportionate punishments. ... When prison sentences became the normal criminal sanctions, the common law recognized that these, too, must be proportional. ...

The English Bill of Rights repeated the principle of proportionality in language that was later adopted in the Eighth Amendment: "excessive Baile ought not to be required nor excessive Fines imposed nor cruell and unusuall Punishments inflicted." 1 W. & M., sess. 2, ch. 2 (1689). Although the precise scope of this provision is uncertain, it at least incorporated "the longstanding principle of English law that the punishment ... should not be, by reason of its excessive length or severity, greatly disproportionate to the offense charged." R. Perry, Sources of Our Liberties 236 (1959). . . . .

When the Framers of the Eighth Amendment adopted the language of the English Bill of Rights, they also adopted the English principle of proportionality. Indeed, one of the consistent themes of the era was that Americans had all the rights of English subjects. ... Thus our Bill of Rights was designed in part to ensure that these rights were preserved. Although the Framers may have intended the Eighth Amendment to go beyond the scope of its English counterpart, their use of the language of the English Bill of Rights is convincing proof that they intended to provide at least the same protection—including the right to be free from excessive punishments.

B

The constitutional principle of proportionality has been recognized explicitly in this Court for almost a century. In the leading case of Weems v. United States, 217 U.S. 349 (1910), the defendant had been convicted of falsifying a public document and sentenced to 15 years of "cadena temporal," a form of imprisonment that included hard labor in chains and permanent civil disabilities. The Court noted "that it is a precept of justice that punishment for crime should be graduated and proportioned to offense," id., at 367, and held that the sentence violated the Eighth Amendment. The Court endorsed the principle of proportionality as a constitu-

---

8. An amercement was similar to a modern-day fine. It was the most common criminal sanction in 13th century England. ...

tional standard, see, e.g., id., at 372–373, and determined that the sentence before it was "cruel in its excess of imprisonment," id., at 377, as well as in its shackles and restrictions.

The Court next applied the principle to invalidate a criminal sentence in Robinson v. California, 370 U.S. 660 (1962). A 90-day sentence was found to be excessive for the crime of being "addicted to the use of narcotics." The Court explained that "imprisonment for ninety days is not, in the abstract, a punishment which is either cruel or unusual." Id., at 667. Thus there was no question of an inherently barbaric punishment. "But the question cannot be considered in the abstract. Even one day in prison would be a cruel and unusual punishment for the 'crime' of having a common cold." Ibid.

Most recently, the Court has applied the principle of proportionality to hold capital punishment excessive in certain circumstances. . . . And the Court has continued to recognize that the Eighth Amendment proscribes grossly disproportionate punishments, even when it has not been necessary to rely on the proscription. . . .

C

There is no basis for the State's assertion that the general principle of proportionality does not apply to felony prison sentences. The constitutional language itself suggests no exception for imprisonment. We have recognized that the Eighth Amendment imposes "parallel limitations" on bail, fines, and other punishments, Ingraham v. Wright, 430 U.S. [651 (1977)] at 664, and the text is explicit that bail and fines may not be excessive. It would be anomalous indeed if the lesser punishment of a fine and the greater punishment of death were both subject to proportionality analysis, but the intermediate punishment of imprisonment were not. There is also no historical support for such an exception. The common-law principle incorporated into the Eighth Amendment clearly applied to prison terms. . . . And our prior cases have recognized explicitly that prison sentences are subject to proportionality analysis. . . .

When we have applied the proportionality principle in capital cases, we have drawn no distinction with cases of imprisonment. . . . It is true that the "penalty of death differs from all other forms of criminal punishment, not in degree but in kind." Furman v. Georgia, 408 U.S. 238, 306 (1972) (Stewart, J., concurring). As a result, "our decisions [in] capital cases are of limited assistance in deciding the constitutionality of the punishment" in a non-capital case. Rummel v. Estelle, 445 U.S., at 272. We agree, therefore, that, "[o]utside the context of capital punishment, *successful* challenges to the proportionality of particular sentences [will be] exceedingly rare," ibid. (emphasis added) . . . . This does not mean, however, that proportionality analysis is entirely inapplicable in noncapital cases.

In sum, we hold as a matter of principle that a criminal sentence must be proportionate to the crime for which the defendant has been convicted. Reviewing courts, of course, should grant substantial deference to the broad authority that legislatures necessarily possess in determining the types and limits of punishments for crimes, as well as to the discretion that trial courts possess in sentencing convicted criminals.[16] But no penalty is *per se* constitutional. As the Court noted in Robinson v. California, 370 U.S., at 667, a single day in prison may be unconstitutional in some circumstances.

III

A

When sentences are reviewed under the Eighth Amendment, courts should be guided by objective factors that our cases have recognized.[17] First, we look to the gravity of the offense and the harshness of the penalty. In *Enmund* [v. Florida, 458 U.S. 782 (1982)], for example, the Court examined the circumstances of the defendant's crime in great detail. 458 U.S., at 797–801. In *Coker* [v. Georgia, 433 U.S. 584 (1977)], the Court considered the seriousness of the crime of rape, and compared it to other crimes, such as murder. 433 U.S., at 597–598 (plurality opinion); id., at 603 (Powell, J., concurring in the judgment in part and dissenting in part). In *Robinson* the emphasis was placed on the nature of the "crime." 370 U.S., at 666–667. And in *Weems,* the Court's opinion commented in two separate places on the pettiness of the offense. 217 U.S., at 363 and 365. Of course, a court must consider the severity of the penalty in deciding whether it is disproportionate. . . .

Second, it may be helpful to compare the sentences imposed on other criminals in the same jurisdiction. If more serious crimes

---

16. Contrary to the dissent's suggestions, post, at 305, 315, we do not adopt or imply approval of a general rule of appellate review of sentences. Absent specific authority, it is not the role of an appellate court to substitute its judgment for that of the sentencing court as to the appropriateness of a particular sentence; rather, in applying the Eighth Amendment the appellate court decides only whether the sentence under review is within constitutional limits. In view of the substantial deference that must be accorded legislatures and sentencing courts, a reviewing court rarely will be required to engage in extended analysis to determine that a sentence is not constitutionally disproportionate.

17. The dissent concedes—as it must—that some sentences of imprisonment are so

disproportionate that they are unconstitutional under the Cruel and Unusual Punishments Clause. . . . It offers no guidance, however, as to how courts are to judge these admittedly rare cases. We reiterate the objective factors that our cases have recognized. . . . As the Court has indicated, no one factor will be dispositive in a given case. . . . The inherent nature of our federal system and the need for individualized sentencing decisions result in a wide range of constitutional sentences. Thus no single criterion can identify when a sentence is so grossly disproportionate that it violates the Eighth Amendment. . . . But a combination of objective factors can make such analysis possible.

are subject to the same penalty, or to less serious penalties, that is some indication that the punishment at issue may be excessive. Thus in *Enmund* the Court noted that all of the other felony murderers on death row in Florida were more culpable than the petitioner there. 458 U.S., at 795–796. The *Weems* Court identified an impressive list of more serious crimes that were subject to less serious penalties. 217 U.S., at 380–381.

Third, courts may find it useful to compare the sentences imposed for commission of the same crime in other jurisdictions. In *Enmund* the Court conducted an extensive review of capital punishment statutes and determined that "only about a third of American jurisdictions would ever permit a defendant [such as Enmund] to be sentenced to die." 458 U.S., at 792. Even in those jurisdictions, however, the death penalty was almost never imposed under similar circumstances.... The Court's review of foreign law also supported its conclusion.... The analysis in *Coker* was essentially the same.... And in *Weems* the Court relied on the fact that, under federal law, a similar crime was punishable by only two year's imprisonment and a fine....

In sum, a court's proportionality analysis under the Eighth Amendment should be guided by objective criteria, including (i) the gravity of the offense and the harshness of the penalty; (ii) the sentences imposed on other criminals in the same jurisdiction; and (iii) the sentences imposed for commission of the same crime in other jurisdictions.

B

Application of these factors assumes that courts are competent to judge the gravity of an offense, at least on a relative scale. In a broad sense this assumption is justified, and courts traditionally have made these judgments—just as legislatures must make them in the first instance. Comparisons can be made in light of the harm caused or threatened to the victim or society, and the culpability of the offender. Thus in *Enmund* the Court determined that the petitioner's conduct was not as serious as his accomplices' conduct. Indeed, there are widely shared views as to the relative seriousness of crimes. ... For example, as the criminal laws make clear, nonviolent crimes are less serious than crimes marked by violence or the threat of violence. ...

There are other accepted principles that courts may apply in measuring the harm caused or threatened to the victim or society. The absolute magnitude of the crime may be relevant. Stealing a million dollars is viewed as more serious than stealing a hundred dollars—a point recognized in statutes distinguishing petty theft from grand theft. ... Few would dispute that a lesser included offense should not be punished more severely than the greater offense. Thus a court is justified in viewing assault with intent to murder as more serious than simple assault. ... It also is generally recognized that attempts are less serious than completed crimes. ... Similarly, an accessory after the fact should not be subject to a higher penalty than the principal. ...

Turning to the culpability of the offender, there are again clear distinctions that courts may recognize and apply. In *Enmund* the Court looked at the petitioner's lack of intent to kill in determining that he was less culpable than his accomplices.... Most would agree that negligent conduct is less serious than intentional conduct. ... A court, of course, is entitled to look at a defendant's motive in committing a crime. Thus a murder may be viewed as more serious when committed pursuant to a contract. ...

This list is by no means exhaustive. It simply illustrates that there are generally accepted criteria for comparing the severity of different crimes on a broad scale, despite the difficulties courts face in attempting to draw distinctions between similar crimes.

C

Application of the factors that we identify also assumes that courts are able to compare different sentences. This assumption, too, is justified. The easiest comparison, of course, is between capital punishment and noncapital punishments, for the death penalty is different from other punishments in kind rather than degree.[18] For sentences of imprisonment, the problem is not so much one of ordering, but one of line-drawing. It is clear that a 25-year sentence generally is more severe than a 15-year sentence, but in most cases it would be difficult to decide that the former violates the Eighth Amendment while the latter does not. Decisions of this kind, although troubling, are not unique to this area. The courts are constantly called upon to draw similar lines in a variety of contexts.

The Sixth Amendment offers two good examples. A State is constitutionally required to provide an accused with a speedy trial ... but the delay that is permissible must be determined on a case-by-case basis. "[A]ny inquiry into a speedy trial claim necessitates a functional analysis of the right in the particular context of the case ...." Barker v. Wingo, 407 U.S. 514, 522 (1972) (unanimous opinion). In *Barker,* we identified some of the objective factors that courts should consider in determining whether a particular delay was excessive.... None of these factors is "either a necessary or sufficient condition to the finding of a deprivation of the right of speedy trial. Rather, they are related factors and must be considered together with such other circumstances as may be relevant." Id., at 533. Thus the type of inquiry that a court should conduct to determine if a given sentence is constitutionally dispro-

---

18. There is also a clear line between sentences of imprisonment and sentences in- volving no deprivation of liberty. See Argersinger v. Hamlin, 407 U.S. 25 (1972).

portionate is similar to the type of inquiry required by the Speedy Trial Clause.

The right to a jury trial is another example. Baldwin v. New York, 399 U.S. 66 (1970), in particular, illustrates the line-drawing function of the judiciary, and offers guidance on the method by which some lines may be drawn. There the Court determined that a defendant has a right to a jury trial "where imprisonment for more than six months is authorized." Id., at 69 (plurality opinion). In choosing the 6-month standard, the plurality relied almost exclusively on the fact that only New York City denied the right to a jury trial for an offense punishable by more than six months. . . .

In short, *Baldwin* clearly demonstrates that a court properly may distinguish one sentence of imprisonment from another. It also supports our holding that courts properly may look to the practices in other jurisdictions in deciding where lines between sentences should be drawn.

IV

It remains to apply the analytical framework established by our prior decisions to the case before us. We first consider the relevant criteria, viewing Helm's sentence as life imprisonment without possibility of parole. We then consider the State's argument that the possibility of commutation is sufficient to save an otherwise unconstitutional sentence.

A

Helm's crime was "one of the most passive felonies a person could commit." State v. Helm, 287 N.W.2d, at 501 (Henderson, J., dissenting). It involved neither violence nor threat of violence to any person. The $100 face value of Helm's "no-account" check was not trivial, but neither was it a large amount. One hundred dollars was less than half the amount South Dakota required for a felonious theft. It is easy to see why such a crime is viewed by society as among the less serious offenses. . . .

Helm, of course, was not charged simply with uttering a "no account" check, but also with being an habitual offender. And a State is justified in punishing a recidivist more severely than it punishes a first offender. Helm's status, however, cannot be considered in the abstract. His prior offenses, although classified as felonies, were all relatively minor.[22] All were nonviolent and none was a crime against a person. Indeed, there was no minimum amount in either the burglary or the false pretenses statutes . . . and

---

22. Helm, who was 36 years old when he was sentenced, is not a professional criminal. The record indicates an addiction to alcohol, and a consequent difficulty in holding a job. His record involves no instance of violence of any kind. Incarcerating him for life without possibility of parole is unlikely to advance the goals of our criminal justice system in any substantial way. Neither Helm nor the State will have an incentive to pursue clearly needed treatment for his alcohol problem, or any other program of rehabilitation.

the minimum amount covered by the grand larceny statute was fairly small . . . .

Helm's present sentence is life imprisonment without possibility of parole. Barring executive clemency, . . . Helm will spend the rest of his life in the state penitentiary. This sentence is far more severe than the life sentence we considered in Rummel v. Estelle. Rummel was likely to have been eligible for parole within 12 years of his initial confinement,[25] a fact on which the Court relied heavily. . . . Helm's sentence is the most severe punishment that the State could have imposed on any criminal for any crime. . . . Only capital punishment, a penalty not authorized in South Dakota when Helm was sentenced, exceeds it.

We next consider the sentences that could be imposed on other criminals in the same jurisdiction. When Helm was sentenced, a South Dakota court was required to impose a life sentence for murder . . . and was authorized to impose a life sentence for treason . . . first degree manslaughter . . . first degree arson . . . and kidnapping. . . . No other crime was punishable so severely on the first offense. Attempted murder . . . placing an explosive device on an aircraft . . . and first degree rape . . . were only Class 2 felonies. Aggravated riot was only a Class 3 felony. . . . Distribution of heroin . . . and aggravated assault . . . were only Class 4 felonies.

Helm's habitual offender status complicates our analysis, but relevant comparisons are still possible. Under § 22–7–7, the penalty for a second or third felony is increased by one class. Thus a life sentence was mandatory when a second or third conviction was for treason, first degree manslaughter, first degree arson, or kidnapping, and a life sentence would have been authorized when a second or third conviction was for such crimes as attempted murder, placing an explosive device on an aircraft, or first degree rape. Finally, § 22–7–8, under which Helm was sentenced, authorized life imprisonment after three prior convictions, regardless of the crimes.

In sum, there were a handful of crimes that were necessarily punished by life imprisonment: murder, and, on a second or third offense, treason, first degree manslaughter, first degree arson, and kidnapping. There was a larger group for which life imprisonment was authorized in the discretion of the sentencing judge, including: treason, first degree manslaughter, first degree arson, and kidnapping; attempted murder, placing an explosive device on an aircraft, and first degree rape on a second or third offense; and any felony after three prior offenses. Finally, there was a large group of very serious offenses for which life imprisonment was not authorized, including a third offense of heroin dealing or aggravated assault.

Criminals committing any of these offenses ordinarily would be thought more deserving of punishment than one uttering a "no

---

25. We note that Rummel was, in fact, released within eight months of the Court's decision in his case. See L.A. Times, Nov. 16, 1980, p. 1, col. 3.

account" check—even when the bad-check writer had already committed six minor felonies. Moreover, there is no indication in the record that any habitual offender other than Helm has ever been given the maximum sentence on the basis of comparable crimes. It is more likely that the possibility of life imprisonment under § 22-7-8 generally is reserved for criminals such as fourth-time heroin dealers, while habitual bad-check writers receive more lenient treatment. In any event, Helm has been treated in the same manner as, or more severely than, criminals who have committed far more serious crimes.

Finally, we compare the sentences imposed for commission of the same crime in other jurisdictions. The Court of Appeals found that "Helm could have received a life sentence without parole for his offense in only one other state, Nevada," 684 F.2d, at 586, and we have no reason to doubt this finding. ... At the very least, therefore, it is clear that Helm could not have received such a severe sentence in 48 of the 50 States. But even under Nevada law, a life sentence without possibility of parole is merely authorized in these circumstances.... We are not advised that any defendant such as Helm, whose prior offenses were so minor, actually has received the maximum penalty in Nevada. It appears that Helm was treated more severely than he would have been in any other State.

B

The State argues that the present case is essentially the same as Rummel v. Estelle, for the possibility of parole in that case is matched by the possibility of executive clemency here. The State reasons that the Governor could commute Helm's sentence to a term of years. We conclude, however, that the South Dakota commutation system is fundamentally different from the parole system that was before us in *Rummel*.

As a matter of law, parole and commutation are different concepts, despite some surface similarities. Parole is a regular part of the rehabilitative process. Assuming good behavior, it is the normal expectation in the vast majority of cases. The law generally specifies when a prisoner will be eligible to be considered for parole, and details the standards and procedures applicable at that time. ... Thus it is possible to predict, at least to some extent, when parole might be granted. Commutation, on the other hand, is an *ad hoc* exercise of executive clemency. A Governor may commute a sentence at any time for any reason without reference to any standards. ...

We explicitly have recognized the distinction between parole and commutation in our prior cases. ...

The Texas and South Dakota systems in particular are very different. In *Rummel*, the Court did not rely simply on the existence of some system of parole. Rather it looked to the provisions of the system presented, including the fact that Texas had "a relatively liberal policy of granting 'good time' credits to its prisoners, a policy that historically has allowed a prisoner serving a life sentence to become eligible for parole in as little as 12 years." 445 U.S., at 280. A Texas prisoner became eligible for parole when his calendar time served plus "good conduct" time equaled one-third of the maximum sentence imposed or 20 years, whichever is less. ... An entering prisoner earned 20 days good-time per 30 days served ... and this could be increased to 30 days good-time per 30 days served .... Thus Rummel could have been eligible for parole in as few as 10 years, and could have expected to become eligible, in the normal course of events, in only 12 years.

In South Dakota commutation is more difficult to obtain than parole. ... In fact, no life sentence has been commuted in over eight years ... while parole—where authorized—has been granted regularly during that period.... Furthermore, even if Helm's sentence were commuted, he merely would be eligible to be considered for parole. Not only is there no guarantee that he would be paroled, but the South Dakota parole system is far more stringent than the one before us in *Rummel.* Helm would have to serve three-fourths of his revised sentence before he would be eligible for parole ... and the provision for good-time credits is less generous....

The possibility of commutation is nothing more than a hope for "an *ad hoc* exercise of clemency." It is little different from the possibility of executive clemency that exists in every case in which a defendant challenges his sentence under the Eighth Amendment. Recognition of such a bare possibility would make judicial review under the Eighth Amendment meaningless.

V

The Constitution requires us to examine Helm's sentence to determine if it is proportionate to his crime. Applying objective criteria, we find that Helm has received the penultimate sentence for relatively minor criminal conduct. He has been treated more harshly than other criminals in the State who have committed more serious crimes. He has been treated more harshly than he would have been in any other jurisdiction, with the possible exception of a single State. We conclude that his sentence is significantly disproportionate to his crime, and is therefore prohibited by the Eighth Amendment. The judgment of the Court of Appeals is accordingly

Affirmed.

CHIEF JUSTICE BURGER, with whom JUSTICE WHITE, JUSTICE REHNQUIST, and JUSTICE O'CONNOR join, dissenting.

The controlling law governing this case is crystal clear, but today the Court blithely discards any concept of *stare decisis*, trespasses gravely on the authority of the states, and distorts the concept of proportionality of punishment by tearing it from its moorings in capital cases. Only two Terms ago, we held in Rummel v. Estelle, 445 U.S. 263 (1980), that a life sentence imposed after only a *third* nonviolent felony conviction did not constitute cruel and unusual punishment under the Eighth Amendment. Today, the Court ignores its recent precedent and holds that a life sentence imposed after a *seventh* felony conviction constitutes cruel and unusual punishment under the Eighth Amendment. Moreover, I reject the fiction that all Helm's crimes were innocuous or nonviolent. Among his felonies were three burglaries and a third conviction for drunk driving. By comparison Rummel was a relatively "model citizen." Although today's holding cannot rationally be reconciled with *Rummel,* the Court does not purport to overrule *Rummel.* I therefore dissent.

I

A

The Court's starting premise is that the Eighth Amendment's Cruel and Unusual Punishments Clause "prohibits not only barbaric punishments, but also sentences that are disproportionate to the crime committed." Ante, at 284. What the Court means is that a sentence is unconstitutional if it is more severe than five justices think appropriate. In short, all sentences of imprisonment are subject to appellate scrutiny to ensure that they are "proportional" to the crime committed.

. . .

B

The facts in *Rummel* bear repeating. Rummel was convicted in 1964 of fraudulent use of a credit card; in 1969, he was convicted of passing a forged check: finally, in 1973 Rummel was charged with obtaining money by false pretenses, which is also a felony under Texas law. These three offenses were indeed nonviolent. Under Texas' recidivist statute, which provides for a mandatory life sentence upon conviction for a third felony, the trial judge imposed a life sentence as he was obliged to do after the jury returned a verdict of guilty of felony theft.

Rummel, in this Court, advanced precisely the same arguments that respondent advances here; we rejected those arguments notwithstanding that his case was stronger than respondent's. The test in *Rummel* which we rejected would have required us to determine on an abstract moral scale whether Rummel had received his "just deserts" for his crimes. We declined that invitation; today the Court accepts it. Will the Court now recall Rummel's case so five justices will not be parties to "disproportionate" criminal justice?

It is true, as we acknowledged in *Rummel,* that the "Court has on occasion stated that the Eighth Amendment prohibits imposition of a sentence that is grossly disproportionate to the severity of a crime." 445 U.S., at 271. But even a cursory review of our cases shows that this type of proportionality review has been carried out only in a very limited category of cases, and never before in a case involving solely a sentence of imprisonment. In *Rummel*, we said that the proportionality concept of the capital punishment cases was inapposite because of the "unique nature of the death penalty. ..." Id., at 272. ...

The *Rummel* Court also rejected the claim that Weems v. United States, 217 U.S. 349 (1910), required it to determine whether Rummel's punishment was "disproportionate" to his crime. ... In *Rummel* the Court carefully noted that "[*Weems'*] finding of disproportionality cannot be wrenched from the facts of that case." 445 U.S., at 273.

The lesson the *Rummel* Court drew from *Weems* and from the capital punishment cases was that the Eighth Amendment did not authorize courts to review sentences of *imprisonment* to determine whether they were "proportional" to the crime. ...

... The *Rummel* Court emphasized, as has every opinion in capital cases in the past decade, that it was possible to draw a "bright line" between "the punishment of death and the various other permutations and commutations of punishment short of that ultimate sanction"; similarly, a line could be drawn between the punishment in *Weems* and "more traditional forms of imprisonment imposed under the Anglo-Saxon system." 445 U.S. at 275. However, the *Rummel* Court emphasized that drawing lines between different sentences of imprisonment would thrust the Court inevitably "into the basic line-drawing process that is pre-eminently the province of the legislature" and produce judgments that were no more than the visceral reactions of individual Justices. Ibid.

The *Rummel* Court categorically rejected the very analysis adopted by the Court today. Rummel had argued that various objective criteria existed by which the Court could determine whether his life sentence was proportional to his crimes. In rejecting Rummel's contentions, the Court explained why each was insufficient to allow it to determine in an *objective* manner whether a given sentence of imprisonment is proportionate to the crime for which it is imposed.

First, it rejected the distinctions Rummel tried to draw between violent and nonviolent offenses, noting that "the absence of violence does not always affect the strength of society's interest in deterring a particular crime or in punishing a particular criminal." Ibid. Similarly, distinctions based on the amount of money stolen are purely "subjective" matters of line drawing. Id., at 275–276.

Second, the Court squarely rejected Rummel's attempt to compare his sentence with the sentence he would have received in other States—an argument that the Court today accepts. The

Rummel Court explained that such comparisons are flawed for several reasons. For one, the recidivist laws of the various states vary widely. "It is one thing for a court to compare those States that impose capital punishment for a specific offense with those States that do not. It is quite another thing for a court to attempt to evaluate the position of any particular recidivist scheme within Rummel's complex matrix." Id. at 280 (citation and footnote omitted). Another reason why comparison between the recidivist statutes of different states is inherently complex is that some states have comprehensive provisions for parole and others do not. Id., at 280–281. Perhaps most important, such comparisons trample on fundamental concepts of federalism. Different states surely may view particular crimes as more or less severe than other States. Stealing a horse in Texas may have different consequences and warrant different punishment than stealing a horse in Rhode Island or Washington, D.C. Thus, even if the punishment accorded Rummel in Texas were to exceed that which he would have received in any other State,

> "that severity would hardly render Rummel's punishment 'grossly disproportionate' to his offenses or to the punishment he would have received in the other States. ... *Absent a constitutionally imposed uniformity inimical to traditional notions of federalism, some State will always bear the distinction of treating particular offenders more severely than any other State.*" Id. at 281–282. (Emphasis added).

Finally, we flatly rejected Rummel's suggestion that we measure his sentence against the sentences imposed by Texas for other crimes:

> "Other crimes, of course, implicate other societal interests, making any such comparison inherently speculative. ...
>
> "Once the death penalty and other punishments different in kind from fine or imprisonment have been put to one side, there remains little in the way of objective standards for judging whether or not a life sentence imposed under a recidivist statute for several separate felony convictions not involving 'violence' violates the cruel-and-unusual-punishment prohibition of the Eighth Amendment." Id. at 282–283, n. 27.

Rather, we held that the severity of punishment to be accorded different crimes was peculiarly a matter of legislative policy. ...

In short, *Rummel* held that the length of a sentence of imprisonment is a matter of legislative discretion; this is so particularly for recidivist statutes. I simply cannot understand how the Court can square *Rummel* with its holding that "a criminal sentence must be proportionate to the crime for which the defendant has been convicted." Ante, at 290.

If there were any doubts as to the meaning of *Rummel*, they were laid to rest last Term in Hutto v. Davis, 454 U.S. 370 (1982) (per curiam). There a United States District Court held that a 40-year sentence for the possession of nine ounces of marihuana violated the Eighth Amendment. The District Court applied almost exactly the same analysis adopted today by the Court. ...

The Court of Appeals sitting en banc affirmed. Davis v. Davis, 646 F.2d 123 (CA 4 1981) (per curiam). We reversed in a brief per curiam opinion, holding that *Rummel* had disapproved each of the "objective" factors on which the District Court and en banc Court of Appeals purported to rely. ...

³
...

II

Although historians and scholars have disagreed about the Framers' original intentions, the more common view seems to be that the Framers viewed the Cruel and Unusual Punishments Clause as prohibiting the kind of torture meted out during the reign of the Stuarts. Moreover, it is clear that until 1892, over 100 years after the ratification of the Bill of Rights, not a single Justice of this Court even asserted the doctrine adopted for the first time by the Court today. The prevailing view up to now has been that the Eighth Amendment reaches only the *mode* of punishment and not the length of a sentence of imprisonment. In light of this history, it is disingenuous for the Court blandly to assert that "[t]he constitutional principle of proportionality has been recognized explicitly in this Court for almost a century." Ante, at 286. That statement seriously distorts history and our cases.

This Court has applied a proportionality test only in extraordinary cases, *Weems* being one example and the line of capital cases another. ... The Court's reading of the Eighth Amendment as restricting legislatures' authority to choose which crimes to punish by death rests on the finality of the death sentence. Such scrutiny is not required where a sentence of imprisonment is imposed after the State has identified a criminal offender whose record shows he will not conform to societal standards.

The Court's traditional abstention from reviewing sentences of imprisonment to ensure that punishment is "proportionate" to the crime is well founded in history, in prudential considerations, and in traditions of comity. Today's conclusion by five Justices that they

---

3. Both *Rummel* and Hutto v. Davis, 454 U.S. 370 (1982) (per curiam), leave open the possibility that in extraordinary cases—such as a life sentence for overtime parking—it might be permissible for a court to decide whether the sentence is grossly disproportionate to the crime. I agree that the Cruel and Unusual Punishments Clause might apply to those rare cases where reasonable men cannot differ as to the inappropriateness of a punishment. In all other cases, we should defer to the legislature's line-drawing. However, the Court does not contend that this is such an extraordinary case that reasonable men could not differ about the appropriateness of this punishment.

are able to say that one offense has less "gravity" than another is nothing other than a bald substitution of individual subjective moral values for those of the legislature. Nor, as this case well illustrates, are we endowed with Solomonic wisdom that permits us to draw principled distinctions between sentences of different length for a chronic "repeater" who has demonstrated that he will not abide by the law.

The simple truth is that "[n]o neutral principle of adjudication permits a federal court to hold that in a given situation individual crimes are too trivial in relation to the punishment imposed." Rummel v. Estelle, 568 F.2d 1193, 1201–1202 (CA5) (Thornberry, J., dissenting), vacated, 587 F.2d 651 (1978) (*en banc*), aff'd, 445 U.S. 263 (1980). The apportionment of punishment entails, in Justice Frankfurter's words, "peculiarly questions of legislative policy." Gore v. United States, 357 U.S. 386, 393 (1958). Legislatures are far better equipped than we are to balance the competing penal and public interests and to draw the essentially arbitrary lines between appropriate sentences for different crimes.

By asserting the power to review sentences of imprisonment for excessiveness the Court launches into uncharted and unchartable waters. Today it holds that a sentence of life imprisonment, without the possibility of parole, is excessive punishment for a seventh allegedly "nonviolent" felony. How about the eighth "nonviolent" felony? The ninth? The twelfth? Suppose one offense was a simple assault? Or selling liquor to a minor? Or statutory rape? Or price-fixing? The permutations are endless and the Court's opinion is bankrupt of realistic guiding principles. Instead, it casually lists several allegedly "objective" factors and arbitrarily asserts that they show respondent's sentence to be "significantly disproportionate" to his crimes. Ante, at 303. Must all these factors be present in order to hold a sentence excessive under the Eighth Amendment? How are they to be weighed against each other? Suppose several States punish severely a crime that the Court views as trivial or petty? I can see no limiting principle in the Court's holding.

There is a real risk that this holding will flood the appellate courts with cases in which equally arbitrary lines must be drawn. It is no answer to say that appellate courts must review criminal convictions in any event; up to now, that review has been on the validity of the judgment, not the sentence. The vast majority of criminal cases are disposed of by pleas of guilty, and ordinarily there is no appellate review in such cases. To require appellate review of all sentences of imprisonment—as the Court's opinion necessarily does—will "administer the *coup de grace* to the courts of appeal as we know them." H. Friendly, Federal Jurisdiction: A General View 36 (1973). This is judicial usurpation with a vengeance; Congress has pondered for decades the concept of appellate review of sentences and has hesitated to act.

III

Even if I agreed that the Eighth Amendment prohibits imprisonment "disproportionate to the crime committed," ante, at 284, I reject the notion that respondent's sentence is disproportionate to his crimes for, if we are to have a system of laws, not men, *Rummel* is controlling.

The differences between this case and *Rummel* are insubstantial. First, Rummel committed three truly nonviolent felonies, while respondent, as noted at the outset, committed seven felonies, four of which cannot fairly be characterized as "nonviolent." At the very least, respondent's burglaries and his third-offense drunk driving posed real risk of serious harm to others. It is sheer fortuity that the places respondent burglarized were unoccupied and that he killed no pedestrians while behind the wheel. What would have happened if a guard had been on duty during the burglaries is a matter of speculation, but the possibilities shatter the notion that respondent's crimes were innocuous, inconsequential, minor, or "nonviolent." Four of respondent's crimes, I repeat, had harsh potentialities for violence. Respondent, far more than Rummel, has demonstrated his inability to bring his conduct into conformity with the minimum standards of civilized society. Clearly, this difference demolishes any semblance of logic in the Court's conclusion that respondent's sentence constitutes cruel and unusual punishment although Rummel's did not.

The Court's opinion necessarily reduces to the proposition that a sentence of life imprisonment with the possibility of commutation, but without possibility of parole, is so much more severe than a life sentence with the possibility of parole that one is excessive while the other is not. This distinction does not withstand scrutiny; a well-behaved "lifer" in respondent's position is most unlikely to serve for life.

It is inaccurate to say, as the Court does ... that the *Rummel* holding relied on the fact that Texas had a relatively liberal parole policy. In context, it is clear that the *Rummel* Court's discussion of parole merely illustrated the difficulty of comparing sentences between different jurisdictions. 445 U.S., at 280–281. However, accepting the Court's characterization of *Rummel* as accurate, the Court today misses the point. Parole was relevant to an evaluation of Rummel's life sentence because in the "real world," he was unlikely to spend his entire life behind bars. Only a fraction of "lifers" are not released within a relatively few years. In Texas, the historical evidence showed that a prisoner serving a life sentence could become eligible for parole in as little as 12 years. In South Dakota, the historical evidence shows that since 1964, 22 life sentences have been commuted to terms of years, while requests for commutation of 25 life sentences were denied. And, of course, those requests for commutation may be renewed.

In short, there is a significant probability that respondent will experience what so many "lifers" experience. Even assuming that at the time of sentencing respondent was likely to spend more time in prison than Rummel,[8] that marginal difference is surely supported by respondent's greater demonstrated propensity for crime—and for more serious crime at that.

IV

It is indeed a curious business for this Court to so far intrude into the administration of criminal justice to say that a state legislature is barred by the Constitution from identifying its habitual criminals and removing them from the streets. Surely seven felony convictions warrant the conclusion that respondent is incorrigible. It is even more curious that the Court should brush aside controlling precedents that are barely in the bound volumes of United States Reports. The Court would do well to heed Justice Black's comments about judges overruling the considered actions of legislatures under the guise of constitutional interpretation:

> "Such unbounded authority in any group of politically appointed or elected judges would unquestionably be sufficient to classify our Nation as a government of men, not the government of laws of which we boast. With a 'shock the conscience' test of constitutionality, citizens must guess what is the law, guess what a majority of nine judges will believe fair and reasonable. Such a test wilfully throws away the certainty and security that lies in a written constitution, one that does not alter with a judge's health, belief, or his politics." Boddie v. Connecticut, 401 U.S. 371, 393 (1971) (Black, J., dissenting).[*]

---

8. No one will ever know if or when Rummel would have been released on parole since he was released in connection with a separate federal habeas corpus proceeding in 1980. On October 3, 1980, a federal District Court granted Rummel's petition for a writ of habeas corpus on the grounds of ineffective assistance of counsel. Rummel v. Estelle, 498 F.Supp. 793 (WD Tex.1980). Rummel then plead guilty to theft by false pretenses and was sentenced to time served under the terms of a plea bargaining agreement. . . .

[*] In Harmelin v. Michigan, 501 U.S. 957 (1991) (5–4), the Court again considered the issue of sentence proportionality. Three Justices (opinion by Justice Kennedy, which Justice O'Connor and Justice Souter joined) adhered to the view that "the Cruel and Unusual Punishments Clause encompasses a narrow proportionality principle," which forbids only "extreme sentences" that are " 'grossly disproportionate.' " 501 U.S. at 997, 1001. Two Justices (opinion by Justice Scalia, which Chief Justice Rehnquist joined) concluded that the Clause does not include any principle of proportionality. On those bases, the Court upheld a mandatory sentence of life imprisonment without possibility of parole for possession of more than 650 grams of cocaine. The four dissenting Justices concluded that under *Solem* the sentence was unconstitutional.

GREGG v. GEORGIA

428 U.S. 153, 96 S.Ct. 2909, 49 L.Ed.2d 859 (1976).

Judgment of the Court, and opinion of MR. JUSTICE STEWART, MR. JUSTICE POWELL, and MR. JUSTICE STEVENS, announced by MR. JUSTICE STEWART.

The issue in this case is whether the imposition of the sentence of death for the crime of murder under the law of Georgia violates the Eighth and Fourteenth Amendments.

I

The petitioner, Troy Gregg, was charged with committing armed robbery and murder. In accordance with Georgia procedure in capital cases, the trial was in two stages, a guilt stage and a sentencing stage. The evidence at the guilt trial established that on November 21, 1973, the petitioner and a traveling companion, Floyd Allen, while hitchhiking north in Florida were picked up by Fred Simmons and Bob Moore. Their car broke down, but they continued north after Simmons purchased another vehicle with some of the cash he was carrying. While still in Florida, they picked up another hitchhiker, Dennis Weaver, who rode with them to Atlanta, where he was let out about 11 p.m. A short time later the four men interrupted their journey for a rest stop along the highway. The next morning the bodies of Simmons and Moore were discovered in a ditch nearby.

On November 23, after reading about the shootings in an Atlanta newspaper, Weaver communicated with the Gwinnett County police and related information concerning the journey with the victims, including a description of the car. The next afternoon, the petitioner and Allen, while in Simmons' car, were arrested in Asheville, N.C. In the search incident to the arrest a .25-caliber pistol, later shown to be that used to kill Simmons and Moore, was found in the petitioner's pocket. After receiving the warnings required by Miranda v. United States, 384 U.S. 436 (1966), and signing a written waiver of his rights, the petitioner signed a statement in which he admitted shooting, then robbing Simmons and Moore. He justified the slayings on grounds of self-defense. The next day, while being transferred to Lawrenceville, Ga., the petitioner and Allen were taken to the scene of the shootings. Upon arriving there, Allen recounted the events leading to the slayings. His version of these events was as follows: After Simmons and Moore left the car, the petitioner stated that he intended to rob them. The petitioner then took his pistol in hand and positioned himself on the car to improve his aim. As Simmons and Moore came up an embankment towards the car, the petitioner fired three shots and the two men fell near a ditch. The petitioner, at close range, then fired a shot into the head of each. He robbed them of valuables and drove away with Allen.

A medical examiner testified that Simmons died from a bullet wound in the eye and that Moore died from bullet wounds in the cheek and in the back of the head. He further testified that both men had several bruises and abrasions about the face and head which probably were sustained either from the fall into the ditch or from being dragged or pushed along the embankment. Although Allen did not testify, a police detective recounted the substance of Allen's statements about the slayings and indicated that directly after Allen had made these statements the petitioner had admitted that Allen's account was accurate. The petitioner testified in his own defense. He confirmed that Allen had made the statements described by the detective, but denied their truth or ever having admitted to their accuracy. He indicated that he had shot Simmons and Moore because of fear and in self-defense, testifying they had attacked Allen and him, one wielding a pipe and the other a knife.

The trial judge submitted the murder charges to the jury on both felony-murder and nonfelony-murder theories. He also instructed on the issue of self-defense but declined to instruct on manslaughter. He submitted the robbery case to the jury on both an armed-robbery theory and on the lesser included offense of robbery by intimidation. The jury found the petitioner guilty of two counts of armed robbery and two counts of murder.

At the penalty stage, which took place before the same jury, neither the prosecutor nor the petitioner's lawyer offered any additional evidence. Both counsel, however, made lengthy arguments dealing generally with the propriety of capital punishment under the circumstances and with the weight of the evidence of guilt. The trial judge instructed the jury that it could recommend either a death sentence or a life prison sentence on each count. The judge further charged the jury that in determining what sentence was appropriate the jury was free to consider the facts and circumstances, if any, presented by the parties, if any, in mitigation or aggravation.

Finally, the judge instructed the jury that it "would not be authorized to consider [imposing] the sentence of death" unless it first found beyond a reasonable doubt one of these aggravating circumstances:

> "One—That the offense of murder was committed while the offender was engaged in the commission of two other capital felonies, to-wit the armed robbery of [Simmons and Moore].

"Two—That the offender committed the offense of murder for the purpose of receiving money and the automobile described in the indictment.

"Three—The offense of murder was outrageously and wantonly vile, horrible and inhuman, in that they [*sic*] involved the depravity of [the] mind of the defendant."   Tr. 476–477.

Finding the first and second of these circumstances, the jury returned verdicts of death on each count.

The Supreme Court of Georgia affirmed the convictions and the imposition of the death sentences for murder.   233 Ga. 117, 210 S.E.2d 659 (1974).   After reviewing the trial transcript and the record, including the evidence, and comparing the evidence and sentence in similar cases in accordance with the requirements of Georgia law, the court concluded that, considering the nature of the crime and the defendant, the sentences of death had not resulted from prejudice or any other arbitrary factor and were not excessive or disproportionate to the penalty applied in similar cases.   The death sentences imposed for armed robbery, however, were vacated on the grounds that the death penalty had rarely been imposed in Georgia for that offense and that the jury improperly considered the murders as aggravating circumstances for the robberies after having considered the armed robberies as aggravating circumstances for the murders.   ...

We granted the petitioner's application for a writ of certiorari limited to his challenge to the imposition of the death sentences in this case as "cruel and unusual" punishment in violation of the Eighth and the Fourteenth Amendments.   423 U.S. 1082 (1976).

II

Before considering the issues presented it is necessary to understand the Georgia statutory scheme for the imposition of the death penalty.   The Georgia statute, as amended after our decision in Furman v. Georgia, 408 U.S. 238 (1972), retains the death penalty for six categories of crime: murder, kidnapping for ransom or where the victim is harmed, armed robbery, rape, treason, and aircraft hijacking.   ... The capital defendant's guilt or innocence is determined in the traditional manner, either by a trial judge or a jury, in the first stage of a bifurcated trial.

If trial is by jury, the trial judge is required to charge lesser included offenses when they are supported by any view of the evidence.   ... After a verdict, finding, or plea of guilty to a capital crime, a presentence hearing is conducted before whoever made the determination of guilt.   The sentencing procedures are essentially the same in both bench and jury trials.   At the hearing:

"[T]he judge [or jury] shall hear additional evidence in extenuation, mitigation, and aggravation of punishment, including the record of any prior criminal convictions and pleas of guilty or pleas of nolo contendere of the defendant, or the absence of any prior conviction and pleas: Provided, however, that only such evidence in aggravation as the State has made known to the defendant prior to his trial shall be admissible. The judge [or jury] shall also hear argument by defendant or his counsel and the prosecuting attorney ... regarding the punishment to be imposed." § 27–2503. (Supp.1975.)

The defendant is accorded substantial latitude as to the types of evidence that he may introduce. ... Evidence considered during the guilt stage may be considered during the sentencing stage without being resubmitted. ...

In the assessment of the appropriate sentence to be imposed the judge is also required to consider or to include in his instructions to the jury "any mitigating circumstances or aggravating circumstances otherwise authorized by law and any of [10] statutory aggravating circumstances which may be supported by the evidence. ..." § 27–2534.1(b) (Supp.1975). The scope of the nonstatutory aggravating or mitigating circumstances is not delineated in the statute. Before a convicted defendant may be sentenced to death, however, except in cases of treason or aircraft hijacking, the jury, or the trial judge in cases tried without a jury, must find beyond a reasonable doubt one of the 10 aggravating circumstances specified in the statute.[9] The sentence of death may be imposed only if the

---

9. The statute provides in part:

"(a) The death penalty may be imposed for the offenses of aircraft hijacking or treason, in any case.

"(b) In all cases of other offenses for which the death penalty may be authorized, the judge shall consider, or he shall include in his instructions to the jury for it to consider, any mitigating circumstances or aggravating circumstances otherwise authorized by law and any of the following statutory aggravating circumstances which may be supported by the evidence:

"(1) The offense of murder, rape, armed robbery, or kidnapping was committed by a person with a prior record of conviction for a capital felony, or the offense of murder was committed by a person who has a substantial history of serious assaultive criminal convictions.

"(2) The offense of murder, rape, armed robbery, or kidnapping was committed while the offender was engaged in the commission of another capital felony, or aggravated battery, or the offense of murder was committed while the offender was engaged in the commission of burglary or arson in the first degree.

"(3) The offender by his act of murder, armed robbery, or kidnapping knowingly created a great risk of death to more than one person in a public place by means of a weapon or device which would normally be hazardous to the lives of more than one person.

"(4) The offender committed the offense of murder for himself or another, for the purpose of receiving money or any other thing of monetary value.

"(5) The murder of a judicial officer, former judicial officer, district attorney or solicitor or former district attorney or solicitor during or because of the exercise of his official duty.

"(6) The offender caused or directed another to commit murder or committed murder as an agent or employee of another person.

"(7) The offense of murder, rape, armed robbery, or kidnapping was outrageously or wantonly vile, horrible or inhuman in that it involved torture, depravity of mind, or an aggravated battery to the victim.

"(8) The offense of murder was committed against any peace officer, corrections employee or fireman while engaged in the performance of his official duties.

"(9) The offense of murder was committed by a person in, or who has escaped from, the lawful custody of a peace officer or place of lawful confinement.

jury (or judge) finds one of the statutory aggravating circumstances and then elects to impose that sentence. ... If the verdict is death the jury or judge must specify the aggravating circumstance(s) found. ... In jury cases, the trial judge is bound by the jury's recommended sentence. ...

In addition to the conventional appellate process available in all criminal cases, provision is made for special expedited direct review by the Supreme Court of Georgia of the appropriateness of imposing the sentence of death in the particular case. The court is directed to consider "the punishment as well as any errors enumerated by way of appeal," and to determine:

> "(1) Whether the sentence of death was imposed under the influence of passion, prejudice, or any other arbitrary factor, and

> "(2) Whether, in cases other than treason or aircraft hijacking, the evidence supports the jury's or judge's finding of a statutory aggravating circumstance as enumerated in section 27–2534.1(b), and

> "(3) Whether the sentence of death is excessive or disproportionate to the penalty imposed in similar cases, considering both the crime and the defendant." § 27–2537 (Supp.1975).

If the court affirms a death sentence, it is required to include in its decision reference to similar cases that it has taken into consideration. ...

A transcript and complete record of the trial, as well as a separate report by the trial judge, are transmitted to the court for its use in reviewing the sentence. ... The report is in the form of a 6½-page questionnaire, designed to elicit information about the defendant, the crime, and the circumstances of the trial. It requires the trial judge to characterize the trial in several ways designed to test for arbitrariness and disproportionality of sentence. Included in the report are responses to detailed questions concerning the quality of the defendant's representation, whether race played a role in the trial, and, whether, in the trial court's judgment, there was

---

"(10) The murder was committed for the purpose of avoiding, interfering with, or preventing a lawful arrest or custody in a place of lawful confinement, of himself or another.

"(c) The statutory instructions as determined by the trial judge to be warranted by the evidence shall be given in charge and in writing to the jury for its deliberation. The jury, if its verdict be a recommendation of death, shall designate in writing, signed by the foreman of the jury, the aggravating circumstance or circumstances which it found beyond a reasonable doubt. In non-jury cases the judge shall make such designation. Except in cases of treason or aircraft hijacking, unless at least one of the statutory aggravating circumstances enumerated in section 27–2534.1(b) is so found, the death penalty shall not be imposed." § 27–2534.1 (Supp.1975).

The Supreme Court of Georgia, in Arnold v. State, 236 Ga. 534, 540, 224 S.E.2d 386, 391 (1976), recently held unconstitutional the portion of the first circumstance encompassing persons who have a "substantial history of serious assaultive criminal convictions" because it did not set "sufficiently 'clear and objective standards.'"

any doubt about the defendant's guilt or the appropriateness of the sentence. A copy of the report is served upon defense counsel. Under its special review authority, the court may either affirm the death sentence or remand the case for resentencing. In cases in which the death sentence is affirmed there remains the possibility of executive clemency.

III

We address initially the basic contention that the punishment of death for the crime of murder is, under all circumstances, "cruel and unusual" in violation of the Eighth and Fourteenth Amendments of the Constitution. In Part IV of this opinion, we will consider the sentence of death imposed under the Georgia statutes at issue in this case.

The Court on a number of occasions has both assumed and asserted the constitutionality of capital punishment. In several cases that assumption provided a necessary foundation for the decision, as the Court was asked to decide whether a particular method of carrying out a capital sentence would be allowed to stand under the Eighth Amendment. But until Furman v. Georgia, 408 U.S. 238 (1972), the Court never confronted squarely the fundamental claim that the punishment of death always, regardless of the enormity of the offense or the procedure followed in imposing the sentence, is cruel and unusual punishment in violation of the Constitution. Although this issue was presented and addressed in *Furman*, it was not resolved by the Court. Four Justices would have held that capital punishment is not unconstitutional *per se;* [13] two Justices would have reached the opposite conclusion; [14] and three Justices, while agreeing that the statutes then before the Court were invalid as applied, left open the question whether such punishment may ever be imposed.[15] We now hold that the punishment of death does not invariably violate the Constitution.

A

The history of the prohibition of "cruel and unusual" punishment already has been reviewed by this Court at length. . . .

In the earliest cases raising Eighth Amendment claims, the Court focused on particular methods of execution to determine whether they were too cruel to pass constitutional muster. The constitutionality of the sentence of death itself was not at issue, and

13. 408 U.S., at 375 (Burger, C.J., dissenting), 405 (Blackmun, J., dissenting), 414 (Powell, J., dissenting), 465 (Rehnquist, J., dissenting).

14. Id., at 257 (Brennan, J., concurring), 314 (Marshall, J., concurring).

15. Id., at 240 (Douglas, J., concurring), 306 (Stewart, J., concurring), 310 (White, J., concurring).

Since five Justices wrote separately in support of the judgments in *Furman*, the holding of the Court may be viewed as that position taken by those Members who concurred in the judgments on the narrowest grounds— Mr. Justice Stewart and Mr. Justice White. See n. 35, infra.

the criterion used to evaluate the mode of execution was its similarity to "torture" and other "barbarous" methods. . . .

But the Court has not confined the prohibition embodied in the Eighth Amendment to "barbarous" methods that were generally outlawed in the 18th century. Instead, the Amendment has been interpreted in a flexible and dynamic manner. The Court early recognized that "a principle to be vital must be capable of wider application than the mischief which gave it birth." Weems v. United States, 217 U.S. 349, 373 (1910). Thus the clause forbidding "cruel and unusual" punishments "is not fastened to the obsolete but may acquire meaning as public opinion becomes enlightened by a humane justice." Id., at 378. . . .

In *Weems* the Court addressed the constitutionality of the Philippine punishment of *cadena temporal* for the crime of falsifying an official document. That punishment included imprisonment for at least 12 years and one day, in chains, at hard and painful labor; the loss of many basic civil rights; and subjection to lifetime surveillance. Although the Court acknowledged the possibility that "the cruelty of pain" may be present in the challenged punishment, 217 U.S., at 366, it did not rely on that factor, for it rejected the proposition that the Eighth Amendment reaches only punishments that are "inhuman and barbarous, torture and the like." Id., at 368. Rather, the Court focused on the lack of proportion between the crime and the offense . . . .

Later, in Trop v. Dulles, [356 U.S. 86 (1958)], the Court reviewed the constitutionality of the punishment of denationalization imposed upon a soldier who escaped from an Army stockade and became a deserter for one day. Although the concept of proportionality was not the basis of the holding, the plurality observed in dicta that "[f]ines, imprisonment and even execution may be imposed depending upon the enormity of the crime." 356 U.S., at 100.

The substantive limits imposed by the Eighth Amendment on what can be made criminal and punished were discussed in Robinson v. California, 370 U.S. 660 (1962). The Court found unconstitutional a state statute that made the status of being addicted to a narcotic drug a criminal offense. It held, in effect, that it is "cruel and unusual" to impose any punishment at all for the mere status of addiction. The cruelty in the abstract of the actual sentence imposed was irrelevant: "Even one day in prison would be cruel and unusual punishment for the 'crime' of having a common cold." Id., at 667. Most recently, in Furman v. Georgia, supra, three Justices in separate concurring opinions found the Eighth Amendment applicable to procedures employed to select convicted defendants for the sentence of death.

It is clear from the foregoing precedents that the Eighth Amendment has not been regarded as a static concept. As Mr. Chief

Justice Warren said, in an oft-quoted phrase, "[t]he Amendment must draw its meaning from the evolving standards of decency that mark the progress of a maturing society." Trop v. Dulles, supra, at 101. ... Thus, an assessment of contemporary values concerning the infliction of a challenged sanction is relevant to the application of the Eighth Amendment. As we develop below more fully ... this assessment does not call for a subjective judgment. It requires, rather, that we look to objective indicia that reflect the public attitude toward a given sanction.

But our cases also make clear that public perceptions of standards of decency with respect to criminal sanctions are not conclusive. A penalty also must accord with "the dignity of man," which is the "basic concept underlying the Eighth Amendment." Trop v. Dulles, supra, at 100 (plurality opinion). This means, at least, that the punishment not be "excessive." When a form of punishment in the abstract (in this case, whether capital punishment may ever be imposed as a sanction for murder) rather than in the particular (the propriety of death as a penalty to be applied to a specific defendant for a specific crime) is under consideration, the inquiry into "excessiveness" has two aspects. First, the punishment must not involve the unnecessary and wanton infliction of pain. ... Second, the punishment must not be grossly out of proportion to the severity of the crime. ...

B

Of course, the requirements of the Eighth Amendment must be applied with an awareness of the limited role to be played by the courts. This does not mean that judges have no role to play, for the Eighth Amendment is a restraint upon the exercise of legislative power. ...

But, while we have an obligation to insure that constitutional bounds are not overreached, we may not act as judges as we might as legislators. ...

Therefore, in assessing a punishment selected by a democratically elected legislature against the constitutional measure, we presume its validity. We may not require the legislature to select the least severe penalty possible so long as the penalty selected is not cruelly inhumane or disproportionate to the crime involved. And a heavy burden rests on those who would attack the judgment of the representatives of the people.

This is true in part because the constitutional test is intertwined with an assessment of contemporary standards and the legislative judgment weighs heavily in ascertaining such standards. ... Caution is necessary lest this Court become, "under the aegis of the Cruel and Unusual Punishment Clause, the ultimate arbiter of the standards of criminal responsibility ... throughout the country." Powell v. Texas, 392 U.S. 514, 533 (1968). A decision that a given punishment is impermissible under the Eighth Amendment cannot be reversed short of a constitutional amendment. The ability of the people to express their preference through the normal democratic processes, as well as through ballot referenda, is shut off. Revisions cannot be made in the light of further experience.   ...

C

In the discussion to this point we have sought to identify the principles and considerations that guide a court in addressing an Eighth Amendment claim. We now consider specifically whether the sentence of death for the crime of murder is a *per se* violation of the Eighth and Fourteenth Amendments to the Constitution. We note first that history and precedent strongly support a negative answer to this question.

The imposition of the death penalty for the crime of murder has a long history of acceptance both in the United States and in England. The common-law rule imposed a mandatory death sentence on all convicted murderers.   ... And the penalty continued to be used into the 20th century by most American States, although the breadth of the common-law rule was diminished, initially by narrowing the class of murders to be punished by death and subsequently by widespread adoption of laws expressly granting juries the discretion to recommend mercy.   ...

It is apparent from the text of the Constitution itself that the existence of capital punishment was accepted by the Framers. At the time the Eighth Amendment was ratified, capital punishment was a common sanction in every State. Indeed, the First Congress of the United States enacted legislation providing death as the penalty for specified crimes. C. 9, 1 Stat. 112 (1790). The Fifth Amendment, adopted at the same time as the Eighth, contemplated the continued existence of the capital sanction by imposing certain limits on the prosecution of capital cases:

> "No person shall be held to answer for a capital, or otherwise infamous crime, unless on a presentment or indictment of a Grand Jury ...; nor shall any person be subject for the same offense to be twice put in jeopardy of life or limb; ... nor be deprived of life, liberty, or property, without due process of law. ..."

And the Fourteenth Amendment, adopted over three-quarters of a century later, similarly contemplates the existence of the capital sanction in providing that no State shall deprive any person of "life, liberty, or property" without due process of law.

For nearly two centuries, this Court, repeatedly and often expressly, has recognized that capital punishment is not invalid *per se*.   ...

Four years ago, the petitioners in *Furman* and its companion cases predicated their argument primarily upon the asserted proposition that standards of decency had evolved to the point where capital punishment no longer could be tolerated. The petitioners in those cases said, in effect, that the evolutionary process had come to an end, and that standards of decency required that the Eighth Amendment be construed finally as prohibiting capital punishment for any crime regardless of its depravity and impact on society. This view was accepted by two Justices. Three other Justices were unwilling to go so far; focusing on the procedures by which convicted defendants were selected for the death penalty rather than on the actual punishment inflicted, they joined in the conclusion that the statutes before the Court were constitutionally invalid.

The petitioners in the capital cases before the Court today renew the "standards of decency" argument, but developments during the four years since *Furman* have undercut substantially the assumptions upon which their argument rested. Despite the continuing debate, dating back to the 19th century, over the morality and utility of capital punishment, it is now evident that a large proportion of American society continues to regard it as an appropriate and necessary criminal sanction.

The most marked indication of society's endorsement of the death penalty for murder is the legislative response to *Furman.* The legislatures of at least 35 States have enacted new statutes that provide for the death penalty for at least some crimes that result in the death of another person. And the Congress of the United States, in 1974, enacted a statute providing the death penalty for aircraft piracy that results in death. These recently adopted statutes have attempted to address the concerns expressed by the Court in *Furman* primarily (i) by specifying the factors to be weighed and the procedures to be followed in deciding when to impose a capital sentence, or (ii) by making the death penalty mandatory for specified crimes. But all of the post-*Furman* statutes make clear that capital punishment itself has not been rejected by the elected representatives of the people.

In the only statewide referendum occurring since *Furman* and brought to our attention, the people of California adopted a constitutional amendment that authorized capital punishment, in effect negating a prior ruling by the Supreme Court of California in People v. Anderson, 6 Cal.3d 628, 493 P.2d 880, cert. denied, 406 U.S. 958 (1972), that the death penalty violated the California Constitution.

The jury also is a significant and reliable objective index of contemporary values because it is so directly involved. ... The Court has said that "one of the most important functions any jury can perform in making ... a selection [between life imprisonment and death for a defendant convicted in a capital case] is to maintain a link between contemporary community values and the penal system." Witherspoon v. Illinois, 391 U.S. 510, 519 n. 15 (1968). It may be true that evolving standards have influenced juries in

recent decades to be more discriminating in imposing the sentence
of death.   But the relative infrequency of jury verdicts imposing the
death sentence does not indicate rejection of capital punishment
per se.   Rather, the reluctance of juries in many cases to impose the
sentence may well reflect the humane feeling that this most irrevo-
cable of sanctions should be reserved for a small number of extreme
cases.   ...   Indeed, the actions of juries in many States since
Furman is fully compatible with the legislative judgments, reflected
in the new statutes, as to the continued utility and necessity of
capital punishment in appropriate cases.   At the close of 1974 at
least 254 persons had been sentenced to death since *Furman,* and
by the end of March 1976, more than 460 persons were subject to
death sentences.

As we have seen, however, the Eighth Amendment demands
more than that a challenged punishment be acceptable to contemporary society.   The Court also must ask whether it comports with
the basic concept of human dignity at the core of the Amendment.
... Although we cannot "invalidate a category of penalties because
we deem less severe penalties adequate to serve the ends of
penology," Furman v. Georgia, supra, at 451 (Powell, J., dissenting),
the sanction imposed cannot be so totally without penological
justification that it results in the gratuitous infliction of suffering.
. . .

The death penalty is said to serve two principal social purposes:
retribution and deterrence of capital crimes by prospective offenders.

In part, capital punishment is an expression of society's moral
outrage at particularly offensive conduct.   This function may be
unappealing to many, but it is essential in an ordered society that
asks its citizens to rely on legal processes rather than self-help to
vindicate their wrongs.   ...

"Retribution is no longer the dominant objective of the criminal
law," Williams v. New York, 337 U.S. 241, 248 (1949), but neither is
it a forbidden objective nor one inconsistent with our respect for
the dignity of men.   ...   Indeed, the decision that capital punishment may be the appropriate sanction in extreme cases is an
expression of the community's belief that certain crimes are themselves so grievous an affront to humanity that the only adequate
response may be the penalty of death.

Statistical attempts to evaluate the worth of the death penalty as
a deterrent to crimes by potential offenders have occasioned a great
deal of debate.   The results simply have been inconclusive.   ...

Although some of the studies suggest that the death penalty
may not function as a significantly greater deterrent than lesser
penalties, there is no convincing empirical evidence either supporting or refuting this view.   We may nevertheless assume safely that
there are murderers, such as those who act in passion, for whom

the threat of death has little or no deterrent effect. But for many others, the death penalty undoubtedly is a significant deterrent. There are carefully contemplated murders, such as murder for hire, where the possible penalty of death may well enter into the cold calculus that precedes the decision to act. And there are some categories of murder, such as murder by a life prisoner, where other sanctions may not be adequate.

The value of capital punishment as a deterrent of crime is a complex factual issue the resolution of which properly rests with the legislatures, which can evaluate the results of statistical studies in terms of their own local conditions and with a flexibility of approach that is not available to the courts. ... Indeed, many of the post-*Furman* statutes reflect just such a responsible effort to define those crimes and those criminals for which capital punishment is most probably an effective deterrent.

In sum, we cannot say that the judgment of the Georgia legislature that capital punishment may be necessary in some cases is clearly wrong. Considerations of federalism, as well as respect for the ability of a legislature to evaluate, in terms of its particular State, the moral consensus concerning the death penalty and its social utility as a sanction, require us to conclude, in the absence of more convincing evidence, that the infliction of death as a punishment for murder is not without justification and thus is not unconstitutionally severe.

Finally, we must consider whether the punishment of death is disproportionate in relation to the crime for which it is imposed. There is no question that death as a punishment is unique in its severity and irrevocability. ... When a defendant's life is at stake, the Court has been particularly sensitive to insure that every safeguard is observed. ... But we are concerned here only with the imposition of capital punishment for the crime of murder, and when a life has been taken deliberately by the offender,[35] we cannot say that the punishment is invariably disproportionate to the crime. It is an extreme sanction, suitable to the most extreme of crimes.

We hold that the death penalty is not a form of punishment that may never be imposed, regardless of the circumstances of the offense, regardless of the character of the offender, and regardless of the procedure followed in reaching the decision to impose it.

IV

We now consider whether Georgia may impose the death penalty on the petitioner in this case.

---

35. We do not address here the question whether the taking of the criminal's life is a proportionate sanction where no victim has been deprived of life—for example, when cap- ital punishment is imposed for rape, kidnapping, or armed robbery that does not result in the death of any human being.

A

While *Furman* did not hold that the infliction of the death penalty *per se* violates the Constitution's ban on cruel and unusual punishments, it did recognize that the penalty of death is different in kind from any other punishment imposed under our system of criminal justice. Because of the uniqueness of the death penalty, *Furman* held that it could not be imposed under sentencing procedures that created a substantial risk that it would be inflicted in an arbitrary and capricious manner. ...

Furman mandates that where discretion is afforded a sentencing body on a matter so grave as the determination of whether a human life should be taken or spared, that discretion must be suitably directed and limited so as to minimize the risk of wholly arbitrary and capricious action.

It is certainly not a novel proposition that discretion in the area of sentencing be exercised in an informed manner. ...

... If an experienced trial judge, who daily faces the difficult task of imposing sentences, has a vital need for accurate information about a defendant and the crime he committed in order to be able to impose a rational sentence in the typical criminal case, then accurate sentencing information is an indispensable prerequisite to a reasoned determination of whether a defendant shall live or die by a jury of people who may never before have made a sentencing decision.

Jury sentencing has been considered desirable in capital cases in order "to maintain a link between contemporary community values and the penal system—a link without which the determination of punishment could hardly reflect 'the evolving standards of decency that mark the progress of a maturing society.' "[39] But it creates special problems. Much of the information that is relevant to the sentencing decision may have no relevance to the question of guilt, or may even be extremely prejudicial to a fair determination of that question. This problem, however, is scarcely insurmountable. Those who have studied the question suggest that a bifurcated procedure—one in which the question of sentence is not considered until the determination of guilt has been made—is the best answer. ... When a human life is at stake and when the jury must have information prejudicial to the question of guilt but relevant to the question of penalty in order to impose a rational sentence, a bifurcated system is more likely to ensure elimination of the constitutional deficiencies identified in *Furman*.

But the provision of relevant information under fair procedural rules is not alone sufficient to guarantee that the information will be properly used in the imposition of punishment, especially if sen-

---

39. Witherspoon v. Illinois, 391 U.S. at   101 (plurality opinion). ...
519 n. 15, quoting Trop v. Dulles, 356 U.S., at

tencing is performed by a jury. Since the members of a jury will have had little, if any, previous experience in sentencing, they are unlikely to be skilled in dealing with the information they are given. ... To the extent that this problem is inherent in jury sentencing, it may not be totally correctable. It seems clear, however, that the problem will be alleviated if the jury is given guidance regarding the factors about the crime and the defendant that the State, representing organized society, deems particularly relevant to the sentencing decision.

The idea that a jury should be given guidance in its decision-making is also hardly a novel proposition. Juries are invariably given careful instructions on the law and how to apply it before they are authorized to decide the merits of a lawsuit. It would be virtually unthinkable to follow any other course in a legal system that has traditionally operated by following prior precedents and fixed rules of law. ... When erroneous instructions are given, retrial is often required. It is quite simply a hallmark of our legal system that juries be carefully and adequately guided in their deliberations.

While some have suggested that standards to guide a capital jury's sentencing deliberations are impossible to formulate, the fact is that such standards have been developed. ... While such standards are by necessity somewhat general, they do provide guidance to the sentencing authority and thereby reduce the likelihood that it will impose a sentence that fairly can be called capricious or arbitrary. Where the sentencing authority is required to specify the factors it relied upon in reaching its decision, the further safeguard of meaningful appellate review is available to ensure that death sentences are not imposed capriciously or in a freakish manner.

In summary, the concerns expressed in *Furman* that the penalty of death not be imposed in an arbitrary or capricious manner can be met by a carefully drafted statute that ensures that the sentencing authority is given adequate information and guidance. As a general proposition these concerns are best met by a system that provides for a bifurcated proceeding at which the sentencing authority is apprised of the information relevant to the imposition of sentence and provided with standards to guide its use of the information.

We do not intend to suggest that only the above-described procedures would be permissible under *Furman* or that any sentencing system constructed along these general lines would inevitably satisfy the concerns of *Furman,* for each distinct system must be examined on an individual basis. Rather, we have embarked upon this general exposition to make clear that it is possible to construct capital-sentencing systems capable of meeting *Furman's* constitutional concerns.[47]

47. In McGautha v. California, 402 U.S. 183 (1971), this Court held that the Due Pro-

cess Clause of the Fourteenth Amendment did not require that a jury be provided with

B

We now turn to consideration of the constitutionality of Georgia's capital-sentencing procedures. In the wake of *Furman,* Georgia amended its capital punishment statute, but chose not to narrow the scope of its murder provisions. See Part II, supra. Thus, now as before *Furman,* in Georgia "[a] person commits murder when he unlawfully and with malice aforethought, either express or implied, causes the death of another human being." Ga.Code Ann., § 26–1101(a) (1972). All persons convicted of murder "shall be punished by death or by imprisonment for life." § 26–1101(c) (1972).

Georgia did act, however, to narrow the class of murderers subject to capital punishment by specifying 10 statutory aggravating circumstances, one of which must be found by the jury to exist beyond a reasonable doubt before a death sentence can ever be imposed. In addition, the jury is authorized to consider any other appropriate aggravating or mitigating circumstances. ... The jury is not required to find any mitigating circumstance in order to make a recommendation of mercy that is binding on the trial court, ... but it must find a *statutory* aggravating circumstance before recommending a sentence of death.

These procedures require the jury to consider the circumstances of the crime and the criminal before it recommends sentence. No longer can a Georgia jury do as Furman's jury did: reach a finding of the defendant's guilt and then, without guidance or direction, decide whether he should live or die. Instead, the jury's attention is directed to the specific circumstances of the crime: Was it committed in the course of another capital felony? Was it committed for money? Was it committed upon a peace officer or judicial officer? Was it committed in a particularly heinous way or in a manner that endangered the lives of many persons? In addition, the jury's attention is focused on the characteristics of the person who committed the crime: Does he have a record of prior convictions for capital offenses? Are there any special facts about

standards to guide its decision whether to recommend a sentence of life imprisonment or death or that the capital-sentencing proceeding be separated from the guilt determination process. *McGautha* was not an Eighth Amendment decision, and to the extent it purported to deal with Eighth Amendment concerns, it must be read in light of the opinions in Furman v. Georgia. There the Court ruled that death sentences imposed under statutes that left juries with untrammeled discretion to impose or withhold the death penalty violated the Eighth and Fourteenth Amendments. While *Furman* did not overrule *McGautha,* it is clearly in substantial tension with a broad reading of *McGautha's* holding. In view of *Furman, McGautha* can be viewed rationally as a precedent only for the proposition that standardless jury sentencing procedures were not employed in the cases there before the Court so as to violate the Due Process Clause. We note that *McGautha's* assumption that it is not possible to devise standards to guide and regularize jury sentencing in capital cases has been undermined by subsequent experience. In view of that experience and the considerations set forth in the text, we adhere to *Furman's* determination that where the ultimate punishment of death is at issue a system of standardless jury discretion violates the Eighth and Fourteenth Amendments.

this defendant that mitigate against imposing capital punishment (e.g., his youth, the extent of his cooperation with the police, his emotional state at the time of the crime). As a result, while some jury discretion still exists, "the discretion to be exercised is controlled by clear and objective standards so as to produce non-discriminatory application." Coley v. State, 231 Ga. 829, 204 S.E.2d 612, 615 (1974).

As an important additional safeguard against arbitrariness and caprice, the Georgia statutory scheme provides for automatic appeal of all death sentences to the State's Supreme Court. That court is required by statute to review each sentence of death and determine whether it was imposed under the influence of passion or prejudice, whether the evidence supports the jury's finding of a statutory aggravating circumstance, and whether the sentence is disproportionate compared to those sentences imposed in similar cases. . . .

In short, Georgia's new sentencing procedures require as a prerequisite to the imposition of the death penalty, specific jury findings as to the circumstances of the crime or the character of the defendant. Moreover to guard further against a situation comparable to that presented in *Furman*, the Supreme Court of Georgia compares each death sentence with the sentences imposed on similarly situated defendants to ensure that the sentence of death in a particular case is not disproportionate. On their face these procedures seem to satisfy the concerns of *Furman*. No longer should there be "no meaningful basis for distinguishing the few cases in which [the death penalty] is imposed from the many cases in which it is not." 408 U.S., at 313 (White, J., concurring).

The petitioner contends, however, that the changes in the Georgia sentencing procedures are only cosmetic, that the arbitrariness and capriciousness condemned by *Furman* continue to exist in Georgia—both in traditional practices that still remain and in the new sentencing procedures adopted in response to *Furman*.

1

First, the petitioner focuses on the opportunities for discretionary action that are inherent in the processing of any murder case under Georgia law. He notes that the state prosecutor has unfettered authority to select those persons whom he wishes to prosecute for a capital offense and to plea bargain with them. Further, at the trial the jury may choose to convict a defendant of a lesser included offense rather than find him guilty of a crime punishable by death, even if the evidence would support a capital verdict. And finally, a defendant who is convicted and sentenced to die may have his sentence commuted by the Governor of the State and the Georgia Board of Pardons and Paroles.

The existence of these discretionary stages is not determinative of the issues before us. At each of these stages an actor in the criminal justice system makes a decision which may remove a defendant from consideration as a candidate for the death penalty. *Furman,* in contrast, dealt with the decision to impose the death sentence on a specific individual who had been convicted of a capital offense. Nothing in any of our cases suggests that the decision to afford an individual defendant mercy violates the Constitution. *Furman* held only that, in order to minimize the risk that the death penalty would be imposed on a capriciously selected group of offenders, the decision to impose it had to be guided by standards so that the sentencing authority would focus on the particularized circumstances of the crime and the defendant.

2

The petitioner further contends that the capital-sentencing procedures adopted by Georgia in response to *Furman* do not eliminate the dangers of arbitrariness and caprice in jury sentencing that were held in *Furman* to be violative of the Eighth and Fourteenth Amendments. He claims that the statute is so broad and vague as to leave juries free to act as arbitrarily and capriciously as they wish in deciding whether to impose the death penalty. While there is no claim that the jury in this case relied upon a vague or overbroad provision to establish the existence of a statutory aggravating circumstance, the petitioner looks to the sentencing system as a whole (as the Court did in *Furman* and we do today) and argues that it fails to reduce sufficiently the risk of arbitrary infliction of death sentences. Specifically, Gregg urges that the statutory aggravating circumstances are too broad and too vague, that the sentencing procedure allows for arbitrary grants of mercy, and that the scope of the evidence and argument that can be considered at the presentence hearing is too wide.

The petitioner attacks the seventh statutory aggravating circumstance, which authorizes imposition of the death penalty if the murder was "outrageously or wantonly vile, horrible or inhuman in that it involved torture, depravity of mind, or an aggravated battery to the victim," contending that it is so broad that capital punishment could be imposed in any murder case. It is, of course, arguable that any murder involves depravity of mind or an aggravated battery. But this language need not be construed in this way, and there is no reason to assume that the Supreme Court of Georgia will adopt such an open-ended construction. In only one case has it upheld a jury's decision to sentence a defendant to death when the only statutory aggravating circumstance found was that of the seventh . . . and that homicide was a horrifying torture-murder.

The petitioner also argues that two of the statutory aggravating circumstances are vague and therefore susceptible of widely differing interpretations, thus creating a substantial risk that the death penalty will be arbitrarily inflicted by Georgia juries. In light of the decisions of the Supreme Court of Georgia we must disagree. First, the petitioner attacks that part of § 27–2534.1(b)(1) that authorizes a jury to consider whether a defendant has a "substantial history of serious assaultive criminal convictions." The Supreme Court of Georgia, however, has demonstrated a concern that the new sentencing procedures provide guidance to juries. It held this provision to be impermissibly vague in Arnold v. State, 236 Ga. 534, 540, 224 S.E.2d 386, 391 (1976), because it did not provide the jury with "sufficiently 'clear and objective standards.'" Second, the petitioner points to § 27–2534.1(b)(3) which speaks of creating a "great risk of death to more than one person." While such a phrase might be susceptible to an overly broad interpretation, the Supreme Court of Georgia has not so construed it. The only case in which the court upheld a conviction in reliance on this aggravating circumstance involved a man who stood up in a church and fired a gun indiscriminately into the audience. . . . On the other hand, the court expressly reversed a finding of great risk when the victim was simply kidnapped in a parking lot. . . .

The petitioner next argues that the requirements of *Furman* are not met here because the jury has the power to decline to impose the death penalty even if it finds that one or more statutory aggravating circumstances is present in the case. This contention misinterprets *Furman*. . . . Moreover, it ignores the role of the Supreme Court of Georgia which reviews each death sentence to determine whether it is proportional to other sentences imposed for similar crimes. Since the proportionality requirement on review is intended to prevent caprice in the decision to inflict the penalty, the isolated decision of a jury to afford mercy does not render unconstitutional death sentences imposed on defendants who were sentenced under a system that does not create a substantial risk of arbitrariness or caprice.

The petitioner objects, finally, to the wide scope of evidence and argument allowed at presentence hearings. We think that the Georgia court wisely has chosen not to impose unnecessary restrictions on the evidence that can be offered at such a hearing and to approve open and far-ranging argument. . . . So long as the evidence introduced and the arguments made at the presentence hearing do not prejudice a defendant, it is preferable not to impose restrictions. We think it desirable for the jury to have as much information before it as possible when it makes the sentencing decision. . . .

3

Finally, the Georgia statute has an additional provision designed to assure that the death penalty will not be imposed on a capriciously selected group of convicted defendants. The new sentencing procedures require that the State Supreme Court review every death sentence to determine whether it was imposed under the influence of passion, prejudice, or any other arbitrary factor,

whether the evidence supports the findings of a statutory aggravating circumstance, and "[w]hether the sentence of death is excessive
or disproportionate to the penalty imposed in similar cases, considering both the crime and the defendant." § 27–2537(c)(3) (Supp.
1975). In performing its sentence-review function, the Georgia
court has held that "if the death penalty is only rarely imposed for
an act or it is substantially out of line with sentences imposed for
other acts it will be set aside as excessive." Coley v. State, 231 Ga.,
at 834, 204 S.E.2d, at 616 (1974). The court on another occasion
stated that "we view it to be our duty under the similarity standard
to assure that no death sentence is affirmed unless in similar cases
throughout the state the death penalty has been imposed generally
. . . ." Moore v. State, 233 Ga. 861, 864, 213 S.E.2d 829, 832
(1975). . . .

It is apparent that the Supreme Court of Georgia has taken its
review responsibilities seriously. In *Coley,* it held that "[t]he prior
cases indicate that the past practice among juries faced with similar
factual situations and like aggravating circumstances has been to
impose only the sentence of life imprisonment for the offense of
rape, rather than death." 231 Ga., at 835, 204 S.E.2d, at 617. It
thereupon reduced Coley's sentence from death to life imprisonment. Similarly, although armed robbery is a capital offense under
Georgia law . . . the Georgia court concluded that the death sentences imposed in this case for that crime were "unusual in that
they are rarely imposed for [armed robbery]. Thus, under the test
provided by statute, . . . they must be considered to be excessive or
disproportionate to the penalties imposed in similar cases." 233
Ga., at 127, 210 S.E.2d, at 667 (1974). The court therefore vacated
Gregg's death sentences for armed robbery and has followed a
similar course in every other armed robbery death penalty case to
come before it. . . .

The provision for appellate review in the Georgia capital-
sentencing system serves as a check against the random or arbitrary
imposition of the death penalty. In particular, the proportionality
review substantially eliminates the possibility that a person will be
sentenced to die by the action of an aberrant jury. If a time comes
when juries generally do not impose the death sentence in a certain
kind of murder case, the appellate review procedures assure that no
defendant convicted under such circumstances will suffer a sentence
of death.

V

The basic concern of *Furman* centered on those defendants
who were being condemned to death capriciously and arbitrarily.
Under the procedures before the Court in that case, sentencing
authorities were not directed to give attention to the nature or
circumstances of the crime committed or to the character or record
of the defendant. Left unguided, juries imposed the death sentence

in a way that could only be called freakish. The new Georgia sentencing procedures, by contrast, focus the jury's attention on the particularized nature of the crime and the particularized characteristics of the individual defendant. While the jury is permitted to consider any aggravating or mitigating circumstances, it must find and identify at least one statutory aggravating factor before it may impose a penalty of death. In this way the jury's discretion is channeled. No longer can a jury wantonly and freakishly impose the death sentence; it is always circumscribed by the legislative guidelines. In addition, the review function of the Supreme Court of Georgia affords additional assurance that the concerns that prompted our decision in *Furman* are not present to any significant degree in the Georgia procedure applied here.

For the reasons expressed in this opinion, we hold that the statutory system under which Gregg was sentenced to death does not violate the Constitution. Accordingly, the judgment of the Georgia Supreme Court is affirmed.

It is so ordered.

MR. JUSTICE WHITE, with whom THE CHIEF JUSTICE and MR. JUSTICE REHNQUIST join, concurring in the judgment.

. . .

Petitioner's argument that there is an unconstitutional amount of discretion in the system which separates those suspects who receive the death penalty from those who receive life imprisonment, a lesser penalty, or are acquitted or never charged, seems to be in final analysis an indictment of our entire system of justice. Petitioner has argued, in effect, that no matter how effective the death penalty may be as a punishment, government, created and run as it must be by humans, is inevitably incompetent to administer it. This cannot be accepted as a proposition of constitutional law. Imposition of the death penalty is surely an awesome responsibility for any system of justice and those who participate in it. Mistakes will be made and discriminations will occur which will be difficult to explain. However, one of society's most basic tasks is that of protecting the lives of its citizens and one of the most basic ways in which it achieves the task is through criminal laws against murder. I decline to interfere with the manner in which Georgia has chosen to enforce such laws on what is simply an assertion of lack of faith in the ability of the system of justice to operate in a fundamentally fair manner.

. . .

MR. JUSTICE BRENNAN, dissenting.

. . .

In Furman v. Georgia, 408 U.S. 238, 257 (1972) (concurring), I read "evolving standards of decency" as requiring focus upon the essence of the death penalty itself and not primarily or solely upon the procedures under which the determination to inflict the penalty upon a particular person was made. I there said:

> "From the beginning of our Nation, the punishment of death has stirred acute public controversy. Although pragmatic arguments for and against the punishment have been frequently advanced, this longstanding and heated controversy cannot be explained solely as the result of differences over the practical wisdom of a particular government policy. At bottom, the battle has been waged on moral grounds. The country has debated whether a society for which the dignity of the individual is the supreme value can, without a fundamental inconsistency, follow the practice of deliberately putting some of its members to death. In the United States, as in other nations of the western world, 'the struggle about this punishment has been one between ancient and deeply rooted beliefs in retribution, atonement or vengeance on the one hand, and, on the other, beliefs in the personal value and dignity of the common man that were born of the democratic movement of the eighteenth century, as well as beliefs in the scientific approach to an understanding of the motive forces of human conduct, which are the result of the growth of the sciences of behavior during the nineteenth and twentieth centuries.' It is this essentially moral conflict that forms the backdrop for the past changes in and the present operation of our system of imposing death as a punishment for crime." Id., at 296.[2]

That continues to be my view. For the Clause forbidding cruel and unusual punishments under our constitutional system of government embodies in unique degree moral principles restraining the punishments that our civilized society may impose on those persons who transgress its laws. Thus, I too say: "For myself, I do not hesitate to assert the proposition that the only way the law has progressed from the days of the rack, the screw and the wheel is the development of moral concepts, or as stated by the Supreme Court ... the application of 'evolving standards of decency' ...."[3]

This Court inescapably has the duty, as the ultimate arbiter of the meaning of our Constitution, to say whether, when individuals condemned to death stand before our Bar, "moral concepts" require us to hold that the law has progressed to the point where we should declare that the punishment of death, like punishments on the rack, the screw and the wheel, is no longer morally tolerable in our civilized society. My opinion in Furman v. Georgia concluded that our civilization and the law had progressed to this point and that therefore the punishment of death, for whatever crime and under all circumstances, is "cruel and unusual" in violation of the

---

2. Quoting T. Sellin, The Death Penalty, A Report for the Model Penal Code Project of the American Law Institute 15 (1959).

3. Novak v. Beto, 453 F.2d 661, 672 (CA5 1971) (Tuttle, J., concurring in part and dissenting in part).

Eighth and Fourteenth Amendments of the Constitution. I shall not again canvass the reasons that led to that conclusion. I emphasize only that foremost among the "moral concepts" recognized in our cases and inherent in the Clause is the primary moral principle that the State, even as it punishes, must treat its citizens in a manner consistent with their intrinsic worth as human beings—a punishment must not be so severe as to be degrading to human dignity. A judicial determination whether the punishment of death comports with human dignity is therefore not only permitted but compelled by the Clause. ...

I do not understand that the Court disagrees that "[i]n comparison to all other punishments today ... the deliberate extinguishment of human life by the State is uniquely degrading to human dignity." [*Furman*, 408 U.S.] at 291. For three of my Brethren hold today that mandatory infliction of the death penalty constitutes the penalty cruel and unusual punishment. I perceive no principled basis for this limitation. Death for whatever crime and under all circumstances "is truly an awesome punishment. The calculated killing of a human being by the State involves, by its very nature, a denial of the executed person's humanity. ... An executed person has indeed 'lost the right to have rights.' " Id., at 290. Death is not only an unusually severe punishment, unusual in its pain, in its finality, and in its enormity, but it serves no penal purpose more effectively than a less severe punishment; therefore the principle inherent in the Clause that prohibits pointless infliction of excessive punishment when less severe punishment can adequately achieve the same purposes invalidates the punishment. ...

The fatal constitutional infirmity in the punishment of death is that it treats "members of the human race as nonhumans, as objects to be toyed with and discarded. [It is] thus inconsistent with the fundamental premise of the Clause that even the vilest criminal remains a human being possessed of common human dignity." Id., at 273. As such it is a penalty that "subjects the individual to a fate forbidden by the principle of civilized treatment guaranteed by the [Clause]."[5] I therefore would hold, on that ground alone, that death is today a cruel and unusual punishment prohibited by the Clause. "Justice of this kind is obviously no less shocking than the crime itself, and the new 'official' murder, far from offering redress for the offense committed against society, adds instead a second defilement to the first."[6]

. . .

MR. JUSTICE MARSHALL, dissenting.

In Furman v. Georgia, 408 U.S. 238, 314 (1972) (concurring), I set forth at some length my views on the basic issue presented to the Court in these cases. The death penalty, I concluded, is a cruel

---

5. Trop v. Dulles, 356 U.S. at 99 (plurality opinion of Warren, C.J.).

6. A. Camus, Reflections on the Guillotine 5–6 (Fridtjof-Karla Pub.1960).

and unusual punishment prohibited by the Eighth and Fourteenth Amendments. That continues to be my view.

I have no intention of retracing the "long and tedious journey," id., at 370, that led to my conclusion in *Furman*. My sole purposes here are to consider the suggestion that my conclusion in *Furman* has been undercut by developments since then, and briefly to evaluate the basis for my Brethren's holding that the extinction of life is a permissible form of punishment under the Cruel and Unusual Punishments Clause.

In *Furman* I concluded that the death penalty is constitutionally invalid for two reasons. First, the death penalty is excessive. ... And second, the American people, fully informed as to the purposes of the death penalty and its liabilities, would in my view reject it as morally unacceptable. ...

Since the decision in *Furman*, the legislatures of 35 States have enacted new statutes authorizing the imposition of the death sentence for certain crimes, and Congress has enacted a law providing the death penalty for air piracy resulting in death. ... I would be less than candid if I did not acknowledge that these developments have a significant bearing on a realistic assessment of the moral acceptability of the death penalty to the American people. But if the constitutionality of the death penalty turns, as I have urged, on the opinion of an *informed* citizenry, then even the enactment of new death statutes cannot be viewed as conclusive. In *Furman*, I observed that the American people are largely unaware of the information critical to a judgment on the morality of the death penalty, and concluded that if they were better informed they would consider it shocking, unjust, and unacceptable. ... A recent study conducted after the enactment of the post-*Furman* statutes, has confirmed that the American people know little about the death penalty, and that the opinions of an informed public would differ significantly from those of a public unaware of the consequences and effects of the death penalty.

Even assuming, however, that the post-*Furman* enactment of statutes authorizing the death penalty renders the prediction of the views of an informed citizenry an uncertain basis for a constitutional decision, the enactment of those statutes has no bearing whatsoever on the conclusion that the death penalty is unconstitutional because it is excessive. An excessive penalty is invalid under the Cruel and Unusual Punishments Clause "even though popular sentiment may favor" it. Id., at 331 ... The inquiry here, then, is simply whether the death penalty is necessary to accomplish the legitimate legislative purposes in punishment, or whether a less severe penalty—life imprisonment—would do as well. ...

The two purposes that sustain the death penalty as nonexcessive in the Court's view are general deterrence and retribution. In *Furman*, I canvassed the relevant data on the deterrent effect of capital punishment. . . . The state of knowledge at that point, after literally centuries of debate, was summarized as follows by a United Nations Committee:

> "It is generally agreed between the retentionists and abolitionists, whatever their opinions about the validity of comparative studies of deterrence, that the data which now exist show no correlation between the existence of capital punishment and lower rates of capital crime." [3]

The available evidence, I concluded in *Furman,* was convincing that "capital punishment is not necessary as a deterrent to crime in our society." Id., at 353.

. . .

. . . The evidence I reviewed in *Furman* remains convincing, in my view, that "capital punishment is not necessary as a deterrent to crime in our society." 408 U.S., at 353. The justification for the death penalty must be found elsewhere.

The other principal purpose said to be served by the death penalty is retribution. The notion that retribution can serve as a moral justification for the sanction of death finds credence in the opinion of my Brothers Stewart, Powell, and Stevens, and that of my Brother White in Roberts v. Louisiana, post, p. 337. See also Furman v. Georgia, 408 U.S., at 394–395 (1972) (Burger, C.J., dissenting). It is this notion that I find to be the most disturbing aspect of today's unfortunate decisions.

The concept of retribution is a multifaceted one, and any discussion of its role in the criminal law must be undertaken with caution. On one level, it can be said that the notion of retribution or reprobation is the basis of our insistence that only those who have broken the law be punished, and in this sense the notion is quite obviously central to a just system of criminal sanctions. But our recognition that retribution plays a crucial role in determining who may be punished by no means requires approval of retribution as a general justification for punishment. It is the question whether retribution can provide a moral justification for punishment—in particular, capital punishment—that we must consider.

. . . As my Brother Brennan stated in *Furman,* "[t]here is no evidence whatever that utilization of imprisonment rather than death encourages private blood feuds and other disorders." 408 U.S., at 303 (concurring). It simply defies belief to suggest that the death penalty is necessary to prevent the American people from taking the law into their own hands.

In a related vein, it may be suggested that the expression of moral outrage through the imposition of the death penalty serves to

---

3. United Nations, Department of Economic and Social Affairs, Capital Punishment, Pt. II, ¶ 159, p. 123 (1968).

reinforce basic moral values—that it marks some crimes as particularly offensive and therefore to be avoided. The argument is akin to a deterrence argument, but differs in that it contemplates the individual's shrinking from anti-social conduct not because he fears punishment, but because he has been told in the strongest possible way that the conduct is wrong. This contention, like the previous one, provides no support for the death penalty. It is inconceivable that any individual concerned about conforming his conduct to what society says is "right" would fail to realize that murder is "wrong" if the penalty were simply life imprisonment.

The foregoing contentions—that society's expression of moral outrage through the imposition of the death penalty pre-empts the citizenry from taking the law into its own hands and reinforces moral values—are not retributive in the purest sense. They are essentially utilitarian in that they portray the death penalty as valuable because of its beneficial results. These justifications for the death penalty are inadequate because the penalty is, quite clearly I think, not necessary to the accomplishment of those results.

There remains for consideration, however, what might be termed the purely retributive justification for the death penalty—that the death penalty is appropriate, not because of its beneficial effect on society, but because the taking of the murderer's life is itself morally good. Some of the language of the opinion of my Brothers Stewart, Powell, and Stevens in No. 74–6257 appears positively to embrace this notion of retribution for its own sake as a justification for capital punishment. ...

Of course, it may be that these statements are intended as no more than observations as to the popular demands that it is thought must be responded to in order to prevent anarchy. But the implication of the statements appears to me to be quite different—namely, that society's judgment that the murderer "deserves" death must be respected not simply because the preservation of order requires it, but because it is appropriate that society make the judgment and carry it out. It is this latter notion, in particular, that I consider to be fundamentally at odds with the Eighth Amendment. ... The mere fact that the community demands the murderer's life in return for the evil he has done cannot sustain the death penalty, for as the plurality reminds us, "the Eighth Amendment demands more than that a challenged punishment be acceptable to contemporary society." Ante, at 182. To be sustained under the Eighth Amendment, the death penalty must "[comport] with the basic concept of human dignity at the core of the Amendment," ibid.; the objective in imposing it must be "[consistent] with our respect for the dignity of [other] men." Ante, at 183. ... Under these standards, the taking of life "because the wrong-doer deserves it" surely must fall, for such a punishment has as its very basis the total denial of the wrong-doer's dignity and worth.

The death penalty, unnecessary to promote the goal of deterrence or to further any legitimate notion of retribution, is an excessive penalty forbidden by the Eighth and Fourteenth Amendments. I respectfully dissent from the Court's judgment upholding the sentences of death imposed upon the petitioners in these cases.[*] [**]

[*] Chief Justice Burger and Justice Rehnquist issued a brief statement that they joined the opinion of Justice White. Justice Blackmun wrote a brief concurring opinion.

[**] In two companion cases, the Court upheld imposition of the death penalty under statutory schemes differing in some respects from that of Georgia, Proffitt v. Florida, 428 U.S. 242 (1976) (sentence imposed by judge rather than jury); Jurek v. Texas, 428 U.S. 262 (1976). Justice Brennan and Justice Marshall dissented in both cases.

In two other companion cases, the Court declared unconstitutional under the Eighth and Fourteenth Amendments imposition of the death sentence for first-degree murder under statutory schemes that made imposition of that sentence for that crime mandatory. Woodson v. North Carolina, 428 U.S. 280 (1976); Roberts v. Louisiana, 428 U.S. 325 (1976). Chief Justice Burger, Justice White, Justice Blackmun, and Justice Rehnquist dissented in both cases.

Subsequently, in Lockett v. Ohio, 438 U.S. 586, 604–605 (1978), Chief Justice Burger in an opinion joined by Justice Stewart, Justice Powell, and Justice Stevens, wrote:

"... [T]he Eighth and Fourteenth Amendments require that the sentencer, in all but the rarest kind of capital case [no view being expressed 'as to whether the need to deter certain kinds of homicide would justify a mandatory death sentence as, for example, when a prisoner—or escapee—under a life sentence is found guilty of murder'], not be precluded from considering *as a mitigating factor,* any aspect of a defendant's character or record and any of the circumstances of the offense that the defendant proffers as a basis for a sentence less than death. We recognize that, in noncapital cases, the established practice of individualized sentences rests not on constitutional commands but on public policy enacted into statutes. The considerations that account for the wide acceptance of individualization of sentences in noncapital cases surely cannot be thought less important in capital cases. Given that the imposition of death by public authority is so profoundly different from all other penalties, we cannot avoid the conclusion that an individualized decision is essential in capital cases. The need for treating each defen-

dant in a capital case with that degree of respect due the uniqueness of the individual is far more important than in noncapital cases. A variety of flexible techniques— probation, parole, work furloughs, to name a few—and various post conviction remedies, may be available to modify an initial sentence of confinement in noncapital cases. The nonavailability of corrective or modifying mechanisms with respect to an executed capital sentence underscores the need for individualized consideration as a constitutional requirement in imposing the death sentence.

"There is no perfect procedure for deciding in which cases governmental authority should be used to impose death. But a statute that prevents the sentencer in all capital cases from giving independent mitigating weight to aspects of the defendant's character and record and to circumstances of the offense proffered in mitigation creates the risk that the death penalty will be imposed in spite of factors which may call for a less severe penalty. When the choice is between life and death, that risk is unacceptable and incompatible with the commands of the Eighth and Fourteenth Amendments."

In Coker v. Georgia, 433 U.S. 584, 592 (1977), Justice White, in an opinion joined by Justice Stewart, Justice Blackmun, and Justice Stevens, wrote: "We have concluded that a sentence of death is grossly disproportionate and excessive punishment for the crime of rape and is therefore forbidden by the Eighth Amendment as cruel and unusual punishment."

A majority of the Supreme Court has held that imposition of the death penalty for felony murder is inconsistent with the Cruel and Unusual Punishment Clause if the person sentenced did not himself "kill, attempt to kill, or intend that a killing take place or that lethal force will be employed." Enmund v. Florida, 458 U.S. 782, 797 (1982) (5–4). Chief Justice Burger, Justice Powell, Justice Rehnquist, and Justice O'Connor dissented. Distinguishing *Enmund,* the Court held that the Eighth Amendment does not prohibit capital punishment for a defendant convicted of felony murder, who does not himself kill or intend to kill but whose participation in the felony "is major and whose mental state is one of reckless indifference to the value of human life." Tison v. Arizona, 481 U.S. 137, 152 (1987) (5–4). *Enmund*, the majority said, barred capital punishment for someone like Enmund himself: "the minor actor in an armed robbery, not on the scene, who neither intended to kill nor was found to have had any culpable mental state." Id. at 149.

The Constitution does not require that a sentence of death be imposed by a jury. "In light of the facts that the Sixth Amendment does not require jury sentencing, that the demands of fairness and reliability in capital cases do not require it, and that neither the nature of, nor the purpose behind, the death penalty requires jury sentencing, we cannot conclude that placing responsibility on the trial judge to impose the sentence in a capital case is unconstitutional." Spaziano v. Florida, 468 U.S. 447, 464 (1984) (6–3). Accordingly, it is permissible for a state to authorize a judge to override a jury recommendation against imposition of capital punishment. Id.

In McCleskey v. Kemp, 481 U.S. 279 (1987) (5–4), the Court rejected a claim that the imposition of capital punishment was constitutionally invalid because racial considerations had entered into the decision whether it would be imposed. The defendant was black and was convicted of killing a white person during the course of a robbery. Under Georgia law, a jury recommended that he be sentenced to death following a sentencing hearing, and the judge accepted the jury's recommendation. The claim of racial discrimination was supported by extensive statistical studies of Georgia murder cases, which showed, *inter alia*, that black defendants who kill white victims have the greatest likelihood of being sentenced to death. According to one statistical model, defendants charged with killing white victims were 4.3 times as likely to be sentenced to death as defendants charged with killing black victims. The Court emphasized that there was no evidence other than the statistical studies that racial discrimination was a factor in this case. It observed that discretion is intended to and does play a large role in capital sentencing proceedings and that were the statistical evidence accepted as proof of racial discrimination in this case, comparable proof of statistical disparities related to any impermissible factor might likewise invalidate a death sentence. "At most," the Court said, "the . . . [statistical] study indicates a discrepancy that appears to correlate with race," but it "does not demonstrate a constitutionally significant risk of racial bias affecting the Georgia capital-sentencing process." 481 U.S. at 312, 313.

17. COLLATERAL ATTACK

WAINWRIGHT v. SYKES

433 U.S. 72, 97 S.Ct. 2497, 53 L.Ed.2d 594 (1977).

MR. JUSTICE REHNQUIST delivered the opinion of the Court.

We granted certiorari to consider the availability of federal habeas corpus to review a state convict's claim that testimony was admitted at his trial in violation of his rights under Miranda v. Arizona, 384 U.S. 436 (1966), a claim which the Florida courts have previously refused to consider on the merits because of noncompliance with a state contemporaneous-objection rule. Petitioner Wainwright, on behalf of the State of Florida, here challenges a decision of the Court of Appeals for the Fifth Circuit ordering a hearing in state court on the merits of respondent's contention.

Respondent Sykes was convicted of third-degree murder after a jury trial in the Circuit Court of DeSoto County. He testified at trial that on the evening of January 8, 1972, he told his wife to summon the police because he had just shot Willie Gilbert. Other evidence indicated that when the police arrived at respondent's trailer home, they found Gilbert dead of a shotgun wound, lying a few feet from the front porch. Shortly after their arrival, respondent came from across the road and volunteered that he had shot Gilbert, and a few minutes later respondent's wife approached the police and told them the same thing. Sykes was immediately arrested and taken to the police station.

Once there, it is conceded that he was read his *Miranda* rights, and that he declined to seek the aid of counsel and indicated a desire to talk. He then made a statement, which was admitted into evidence at trial through the testimony of the two officers who heard it, to the effect that he had shot Gilbert from the front porch of his trailer home. There were several references during the trial to respondent's consumption of alcohol during the preceding day and to his apparent state of intoxication, facts which were acknowledged by the officers who arrived at the scene. At no time during the trial, however, was the admissibility of any of respondent's statements challenged by his counsel on the ground that respondent had not understood the *Miranda* warnings. Nor did the trial judge question their admissibility on his own motion or hold a fact finding hearing bearing on that issue.

Respondent appealed his conviction, but apparently did not challenge the admissibility of the inculpatory statements. He later filed in the trial court a motion to vacate the conviction and, in the

State District Court of Appeals and Supreme Court, petitions for habeas corpus. These filings, apparently for the first time, challenged the statements made to police on grounds of involuntariness. In all of these efforts respondent was unsuccessful.

Having failed in the Florida courts, respondent initiated the present action under 28 U.S.C. § 2254, asserting the inadmissibility of his statement by reason of his lack of understanding of the *Miranda* warnings.[4] The United States District Court for the Middle District of Florida ruled that Jackson v. Denno, 378 U.S. 368 (1964), requires a hearing in a state criminal trial prior to the admission of an inculpatory out-of-court statement by the defendant. It held further that respondent had not lost his right to assert such a claim by failing to object at trial or on direct appeal, since only "exceptional circumstances" of "strategic decisions at trial" can create such a bar to raising federal constitutional claims in a federal habeas action. The court stayed issuance of the writ to allow the state court to hold a hearing on the "voluntariness" of the statements.

Petitioner warden appealed this decision to the United States Court of Appeals for the Fifth Circuit. That court first considered the nature of the right to exclusion of statements made without a knowing waiver of the right to counsel and the right not to incriminate oneself. It noted that Jackson v. Denno, supra, guarantees a right to a hearing on whether a defendant has knowingly waived his rights as described to him in the *Miranda* warning, and stated that under Florida law "the burden is on the State to secure [a] prima facie determination of voluntariness, not upon the defendant to demand it." 528 F.2d 522, 525 (1976).

The court then directed its attention to the effect on respondent's right of Florida Rule of Criminal Procedure 3.190(i),[5] which it described as "a contemporaneous objection rule" applying to motions to suppress a defendant's inculpatory statements. It ... concluded that the failure to comply with the rule requiring objection at the trial would only bar review of the suppression claim where the right to object was deliberately by-passed for reasons relating to trial tactics. ... Concluding that "[t]he failure to object in this case cannot be dismissed as a trial tactic, and thus a deliberate by-pass," the court affirmed the District Court order that

---

4. Respondent expressly waived "any contention or allegation as regards ineffective assistance of counsel" at his trial. (App., at 47.) ...

5. Rule 3.190(i):

"Motion to Suppress a Confession or Admissions Illegally Obtained.

"(1) *Grounds.* Upon motion of the defendant or upon its own motion, the court shall suppress any confession or admission obtained illegally from the defendant.

"(2) *Time for Filing.* The motion to suppress shall be made prior to trial unless opportunity therefor did not exist or the defendant was not aware of the grounds for the motion, but the court in its discretion may entertain the motion or an appropriate objection at trial.

"(3) *Hearing.* The court shall receive evidence on any issue of fact necessary to be decided in order to rule on the motion."

the State hold a hearing on whether respondent knowingly waived his *Miranda* rights at the time he made the statements.

The simple legal question before the Court calls for a construction of the language of 28 U.S.C. § 2254(a), which provides that the federal courts shall entertain an application for a writ of habeas corpus "in behalf of a person in custody pursuant to the judgment of state court only on the ground that he is in custody in violation of the Constitution or laws or treaties of the United States." But, to put it mildly, we do not write on a clean slate in construing this statutory provision. Its earliest counterpart, applicable only to prisoners detained by federal authority, is found in the Judiciary Act of 1789. Construing that statute for the Court in Ex parte Watkins, 3 Pet. 193, 202 (1830), Mr. Chief Justice Marshall said:

> "An imprisonment under a judgment cannot be unlawful, unless that judgment be an absolute nullity; and it is not a nullity if the Court has general jurisdiction of the subject, although it should be erroneous."

. . .

In 1867, Congress expanded the statutory language so as to make the writ available to one held in state as well as federal custody. For more than a century since the 1867 amendment, this Court has grappled with the relationship between the classical common-law writ of habeas corpus and the remedy provided in 28 U.S.C. § 2254. Sharp division within the Court has been manifested on more than one aspect of the perplexing problems which have been litigated in this connection. Where the habeas petitioner challenges a final judgment of conviction rendered by a state court, this Court has been called upon to decide no fewer than four different questions, all to a degree interrelated with one another: (1) What types of federal claims may a federal habeas court properly consider? (2) Where a federal claim is cognizable by a federal habeas court, to what extent must that court defer to a resolution of the claim in prior state proceedings? (3) To what extent must the petitioner who seeks federal habeas exhaust state remedies before resorting to the federal court? (4) In what instances will an adequate and independent state ground bar consideration of otherwise cognizable federal issues on federal habeas review?

Each of these four issues have spawned its share of litigation.

. . .

. . .

There is no need to consider here in greater detail these first three areas of controversy attendant to federal habeas review of state convictions. Only the fourth area—the adequacy of state grounds to bar federal habeas review—is presented in this case. The foregoing discussion of the other three is pertinent here only as it illustrates this Court's historic willingness to overturn or modify its earlier views of the scope of the writ, even where the statutory language authorizing judicial action has remained unchanged.

As to the role of adequate and independent state grounds, it is a well-established principle of federalism that a state decision resting on an adequate foundation of state substantive law is immune from review in the federal courts. ... The application of this principle in the context of a federal habeas proceeding has therefore excluded from consideration any questions of state *substantive* law, and thus effectively barred federal habeas review where questions of that sort are either the only ones raised by a petitioner or are in themselves dispositive of his case. The area of controversy which has developed has concerned the reviewability of federal claims which the state court has declined to pass on because not presented in the manner prescribed by its *procedural* rules. The adequacy of such an independent state procedural ground to prevent federal habeas review of the underlying federal issue has been treated very differently than where the state-law ground is substantive. ...

. . .

Respondent first contends that any discussion as to the effect that noncompliance with a state procedural rule should have on the availability of federal habeas is quite unnecessary because in his view Florida did not actually have a contemporaneous objection rule. He would have us interpret Florida Rule of Crim.Proc. 3.190(i), which petitioner asserts is a traditional "contemporaneous objection rule," to place the burden on the trial judge to raise on his own motion the question of the admissibility of any inculpatory statement. Respondent's approach is, to say the least, difficult to square with the language of the rule, which in unmistakable terms and with specified exceptions requires that the motion to suppress be raised before trial. Since all of the Florida appellate courts refused to review petitioner's federal claim on the merits after his trial, and since their action in so doing is quite consistent with a line of Florida authorities interpreting the rule in question as requiring a contemporaneous objection, we accept the State's position on this point. ...

Respondent also urges that a defendant has a right under *Jackson v. Denno*, 378 U.S. 368 (1964), to a hearing as to the voluntariness of a confession, even though the defendant does not object to its admission. But we do not read *Jackson* as creating any such requirement. In that case the defendant's objection to the use of his confession was brought to the attention of the trial court ... and nothing in the Court's opinion suggests that a hearing would have been required even if it had not been. To the contrary, the Court prefaced its entire discussion of the merits of the case with a statement of the constitutional rule that was to prove dispositive— that a defendant has a "right at some stage in the proceedings *to object* to the use of the confession and to have a fair hearing and a reliable determination on the issue of voluntariness. . . ." Id., at 376–377 (emphasis added). Language in subsequent decisions of this Court has reaffirmed the view that the Constitution does not require a voluntariness hearing absent some contemporaneous challenge to the use of the confession.

We therefore conclude that Florida procedure did, consistently with the United States Constitution, require that petitioner's confession be challenged at trial or not at all, and thus his failure to timely object to its admission amounted to an independent and adequate state procedural ground which would have prevented direct review here. . . . We thus come to the crux of this case. Shall the rule of Francis v. Henderson, [425 U.S. 536 (1976)], barring federal habeas review absent a showing of "cause" and "prejudice" attendant to a state procedural waiver, be applied to a waived objection to the admission of a confession at trial? We answer that question in the affirmative.

As earlier noted in the opinion, since Brown v. Allen, 344 U.S. 443 (1953), it has been the rule that the federal habeas petitioner who claims he is detained pursuant to a final judgment of a state court in violation of the United States Constitution is entitled to have the federal habeas court make its own independent determination of his federal claim, without being bound by the determination on the merits of that claim reached in the state proceedings. This rule of Brown v. Allen is in no way changed by our holding today. Rather, we deal only with contentions of federal law which were *not* resolved on the merits in the state proceeding due to respondent's failure to raise them there as required by state procedure. We leave open for resolution in future decisions the precise definition of the "cause"-and-"prejudice" standard, and note here only that it is narrower than the standard set forth in dicta in Fay v. Noia, 372 U.S. 391 (1963), which would make federal habeas review generally available to state convicts absent a knowing and deliberate waiver of the federal constitutional contention. It is the sweeping language of Fay v. Noia, going far beyond the facts of the case eliciting it, which we today reject.[12]

The reasons for our rejection of it are several. The contemporaneous-objection rule itself is by no means peculiar to Florida, and deserves greater respect than *Fay* gives it, both for the fact that it is employed by a coordinate jurisdiction within the federal system and for the many interests which it serves in its own right. A contemporaneous objection enables the record to be made with respect to the constitutional claim when the recollections of witnesses are freshest,

12. We have no occasion today to consider the *Fay* rule as applied to the facts there confronting the Court. Whether the *Francis* rule should preclude federal habeas review of claims not made in accordance with state procedure where the criminal defendant has surrendered, other than for reasons of tactical advantage, the right to have all his claims of trial error considered by a state appellate court, we leave for another day.

. . .

not years later in a federal habeas proceeding. It enables the judge who observed the demeanor of those witnesses to make the factual determinations necessary for properly deciding the federal constitutional question. While the 1966 amendment to § 2254 requires deference to be given to such determinations made by state courts, the determinations themselves are less apt to be made in the first instance if there is no contemporaneous objection to the admission of the evidence on federal constitutional grounds.

A contemporaneous-objection rule may lead to the exclusion of the evidence objected to, thereby making a major contribution to finality in criminal litigation. Without the evidence claimed to be vulnerable on federal constitutional grounds, the jury may acquit the defendant, and that will be the end of the case; or it may nonetheless convict the defendant, and he will have one less federal constitutional claim to assert in his federal habeas petition. If the state trial judge admits the evidence in question after a full hearing, the federal habeas court pursuant to the 1966 amendment to § 2254 will gain significant guidance from the state ruling in this regard. Subtler considerations as well militate in favor of honoring a state contemporaneous-objection rule. An objection on the spot may force the prosecution to take a hard look at its hole card, and even if the prosecutor thinks that the state trial judge will admit the evidence he must contemplate the possibility of reversal by the state appellate courts or the ultimate issuance of a writ of federal habeas corpus based on the impropriety of the state court's rejection of the federal constitutional claim.

We think that the rule of Fay v. Noia, broadly stated, may encourage "sand bagging" on the part of defense lawyers, who may take their chances on a verdict of not guilty in a state trial court and intend to raise their constitutional claims in a federal habeas court if their initial gamble does not pay off. The refusal of federal habeas courts to honor contemporaneous objection rules may also make state courts themselves less stringent in their enforcement. Under the rule of Fay v. Noia, state appellate courts know that a federal constitutional issue raised for the first time in the proceeding before them may well be decided in any event by a federal *habeas* tribunal. Thus their choice is between addressing the issue notwithstanding the petitioner's failure to timely object, or else face the prospect that the federal habeas court will decide the question without the benefit of their views.

The failure of the federal habeas courts generally to require compliance with a contemporaneous-objection rule tends to detract from the perception of the trial of a criminal case in state court as a decisive and portentous event. A defendant has been accused of a serious crime, and this is the time and place set for him to be tried by a jury of his peers and found either guilty or not guilty by that jury. To the greatest extent possible all issues which bear on this charge should be determined in this proceeding: the accused is in the court room, the jury is in the box, the judge is on the bench, and the witnesses, having been subpoenaed and duly sworn, await their turn to testify. Society's resources have been concentrated at that time and place in order to decide, within the limits of human fallibility, the question of guilt or innocence of one of its citizens. Any procedural rule which encourages the result that those proceedings be as free of error as possible is thoroughly desirable, and the contemporaneous objection rule surely falls within this classification.

We believe the adoption of the *Francis* rule in this situation will have the salutary effect of making the state trial on the merits the "main event," so to speak, rather than a tryout on the road for what will later be the determinative federal habeas hearing. There is nothing in the Constitution or in the language of § 2254 which requires that the state trial on the issue of guilt or innocence be devoted largely to the testimony of fact witnesses directed to the elements of the state crime, while only later will there occur in a federal habeas hearing a full airing of the federal constitutional claims which were not raised in the state proceedings. If a criminal defendant thinks that an action of the state trial court is about to deprive him of a federal constitutional right there is every reason for his following state procedure in making known his objection.

The "cause"-and-"prejudice" exception of the *Francis* rule will afford an adequate guarantee, we think, that the rule will not prevent a federal habeas court from adjudicating for the first time the federal constitutional claim of a defendant who in the absence of such an adjudication will be the victim of a miscarriage of justice. Whatever precise content may be given those terms by later cases, we feel confident in holding without further elaboration that they do not exist here. Respondent has advanced no explanation whatever for his failure to object at trial, and, as the proceeding unfolded, the trial judge is certainly not to be faulted for failing to question the admission of the confession himself. The other evidence of guilt presented at trial, moreover, was substantial to a degree that would negate any possibility of actual prejudice resulting to the respondent from the admission of his inculpatory statement.

We accordingly conclude that the judgment of the Court of Appeals for the Fifth Circuit must be reversed, and the cause remanded to the United States District Court for the Middle District of Florida with instructions to dismiss respondent's petition for a writ of habeas corpus.

It is so ordered.

MR. CHIEF JUSTICE BURGER, concurring.

I concur fully in the judgment and in the Court's opinion. I write separately to emphasize one point which, to me, seems of critical importance to this case. In my view, the "deliberate bypass" standard enunciated in Fay v. Noia, 372 U.S. 391 (1963), was never designed for, and is inapplicable to, errors—even of constitutional dimension—alleged to have been committed during trial.

In Fay v. Noia, the Court applied the "deliberate bypass" standard to a case where the critical procedural decision—whether to take a criminal appeal—was entrusted to a convicted defendant. Although Noia, the habeas petitioner, was represented by counsel, he himself had to make the decision whether to appeal or not; the role of the attorney was limited to giving advice and counsel. In giving content to the new deliberate bypass standard, *Fay* looked to the Court's decision in Johnson v. Zerbst, 304 U.S. 458 (1938), a case where the defendant had been called upon to make the decision whether to request representation by counsel in his federal criminal trial. Because in both *Fay* and *Zerbst*, important rights hung in the balance of the *defendant's own decision*, the Court required that a waiver impairing such rights be a knowing and intelligent decision by the defendant himself. . . .

The touchstone of *Fay* and *Zerbst*, then, is the exercise of volition by the defendant himself with respect to his own federal constitutional rights. In contrast, the claim in the case before us relates to events during the trial itself. Typically, habeas petitioners claim that unlawfully secured evidence was admitted . . . or that improper testimony was adduced, or that an improper jury charge was given . . . or that a particular line of examination or argument by the prosecutor was improper or prejudicial. But unlike *Fay* and *Zerbst*, preservation of this type of claim under state procedural rules does not generally involve an assertion by the defendant himself; rather, the decision to assert or not to assert constitutional rights or constitutionally based objections at trial is necessarily entrusted to the defendant's attorney, who must make on-the-spot decisions at virtually all stages of a criminal trial. As a practical matter, a criminal defendant is rarely, if ever, in a position to decide, for example, whether certain testimony is hearsay and, if so, whether it implicates interests protected by the Confrontation Clause; indeed, it is because " '[e]ven the intelligent and educated layman has small and sometimes no skill in the science of law' " that we held it constitutionally required that every defendant who faces the possibility of incarceration be afforded counsel. Argersinger v. Hamlin, 407 U.S. 25 (1972); Gideon v. Wainwright, 372 U.S. 335, 345 (1963).

Once counsel is appointed, the day-to-day conduct of the defense rests with the attorney. He, not the client, has the immediate—and ultimate—responsibility of deciding if and when to object, which witnesses, if any, to call, and what defenses to develop. Not only do these decisions rest with the attorney, but such decisions must, as a practical matter, be made without consulting the client. The trial process simply does not permit the type of frequent and protracted interruptions which would be necessary if it were required that clients give knowing and intelligent approval to each of the myriad tactical decisions as a trial proceeds.

Since trial decisions are of necessity entrusted to the accused's attorney, the *Fay-Zerbst* standard of "knowing and intelligent waiver" is simply inapplicable. The dissent in this case, written by the author of Fay v. Noia, implicitly recognizes as much. According to the dissent, *Fay* imposes the knowing-and-intelligent-waiver standard "where possible" during the course of the trial. In an extraordinary modification of *Fay*, Mr. Justice Brennan would now require "that the lawyer actually exercis[e] his expertise and judgment in his client's service and with his client's knowing and intelligent participation *where possible*"; he does not intimate what guidelines would be used to decide when or under what circumstances this would actually be "possible." Post, at 116. (Emphasis supplied.) What had always been thought the standard governing the *accused's* waiver of his own constitutional rights the dissent would change, in the trial setting, into a standard of conduct imposed upon the defendant's *attorney*. This vague "standard" would be unmanageable to the point of impossibility.

The effort to read this expanded concept into *Fay* is to no avail; that case simply did not address a situation where the defendant had to look to his lawyer for vindication of constitutionally based interests. I would leave the core holding of *Fay* where it began, and reject this illogical uprooting of an otherwise defensible doctrine.

MR. JUSTICE BRENNAN, with whom MR. JUSTICE MARSHALL joins, dissenting.

Over the course of the last decade, the deliberate-bypass standard announced in Fay v. Noia, 372 U.S. 391, 438–439 (1963), has played a central role in efforts by the federal judiciary to accommodate the constitutional rights of the individual with the States' interests in the integrity of their judicial procedural regimes. The Court today decides that this standard should no longer apply with respect to procedural defaults occurring during the trial of a criminal defendant. In its place, the Court adopts the two-part "cause"-and-"prejudice" test originally developed in Davis v. United States, 411 U.S. 233 (1973), and Francis v. Henderson, 425 U.S. 536 (1976). As was true with these earlier cases, however, today's decision makes no effort to provide concrete guidance as to the content of those terms. More particularly, left unanswered is the thorny question that must be recognized to be central to a realistic rationalization of this area of law: How should the federal habeas court treat a procedural default in a state court that is attributable purely and simply to the error or negligence of a defendant's trial counsel? Because this key issue remains unresolved, I shall attempt in this opinion a re-examination of the policies that should inform— and in *Fay* did inform—the selection of the standard governing the availability of federal habeas corpus jurisdiction in the face of an intervening procedural default in the state court.

I

I begin with the threshold question: What is the meaning and import of a procedural default? If it could be assumed that a procedural default more often than not is the product of a defendant's conscious refusal to abide by the duly constituted, legitimate processes of the state courts, then I might agree that a regime of collateral review weighted in favor of a State's procedural rules would be warranted. *Fay,* however, recognized that such rarely is the case; and therein lies *Fay's* basic unwillingness to embrace a view of habeas jurisdiction that results in "an airtight system of [procedural] forfeitures." 372 U.S., at 432.

This, of course, is not to deny that there are times when the failure to heed a state procedural requirement stems from an intentional decision to avoid the presentation of constitutional claims to the state forum. *Fay* was not insensitive to this possibility. Indeed, the very purpose of its bypass test is to detect and enforce such intentional procedural forfeitures of outstanding constitutionally based claims. *Fay* does so through application of the long-standing rule used to test whether action or inaction on the part of a criminal defendant should be construed as a decision to surrender the assertion of rights secured by the Constitution: To be an effective waiver, there must be "an intentional relinquishment or abandonment of a known right or privilege." Johnson v. Zerbst, 304 U.S. 458, 464 (1938). Incorporating this standard, *Fay* recognized that if one "understandingly and knowingly forewent the privilege of seeking to vindicate his federal claims in the state courts, whether for strategic, tactical or any other reasons that can fairly be described as the deliberate by-passing of state procedures, then it is open to the federal court on habeas to deny him all relief. . . ." 372 U.S., at 439. For this reason, the Court's assertion that it "think[s]" that the *Fay* rule encourages intentional "sandbagging" on the part of the defense lawyers is without basis, ante, at 89; certainly the Court points to no cases or commentary arising during the past 15 years of actual use of the *Fay* test to support this criticism. Rather, a consistent reading of case law demonstrates that the bypass formula has provided a workable vehicle for protecting the integrity of state rules in those instances when such protection would be both meaningful and just.

But having created the bypass exception to the availability of collateral review, *Fay* recognized that intentional, tactical forfeitures are not the norm upon which to build a rational system of federal habeas jurisdiction. In the ordinary case, litigants simply have no incentive to slight the state tribunal, since constitutional adjudication on the state and federal levels are not mutually exclusive. . . . Under the regime of collateral review recognized since the days of

Brown v. Allen [344 U.S. 443 (1953)], and enforced by the *Fay* bypass test, no rational lawyer would risk the "sandbagging" feared by the Court. If a constitutional challenge is not properly raised on the state level, the explanation generally will be found elsewhere than in an intentional tactical decision.

In brief then, any realistic system of federal habeas corpus jurisdiction must be premised on the reality that the ordinary procedural default is born of the inadvertence, negligence, inexperience, or incompetence of trial counsel. . . . The case under consideration today is typical. The Court makes no effort to identify a tactical motive for the failure of Sykes' attorney to challenge the admissibility or reliability of a highly inculpatory statement. . . . Indeed, there is no basis for inferring that Sykes or his state trial lawyer were even aware of the existence of his claim under the Fifth Amendment; for this is not a case where the trial judge expressly drew the attention of the defense to a possible constitutional contention or procedural requirement . . ., or where the defense signals its knowledge of a constitutional claim by abandoning a challenge previously raised . . . Rather, any realistic reading of the record demonstrates that we are faced here with a lawyer's simple error.

Fay's answer thus is plain: the bypass test simply refuses to credit what is essentially a lawyer's mistake as a forfeiture of constitutional rights. I persist in the belief that the interests of Sykes and the State of Florida are best rationalized by adherence to this test, and by declining to react to inadvertent defaults through the creation of an "airtight system of forfeitures."

II

What are the interests that Sykes can assert in preserving the availability of federal collateral relief in the face of his inadvertent state procedural default? Two are paramount.

As is true with any federal habeas applicant, Sykes seeks access to the federal court for the determination of the validity of his federal constitutional claim. . . .

With respect to federal habeas corpus jurisdiction, Congress explicitly chose to effectuate the federal court's primary responsibility for preserving federal rights and privileges by authorizing the litigation of constitutional claims and defenses in a district court after the State vindicates its own interest through trial of the substantive criminal offense in the state courts. . . . Certainly, we can all agree that once a state court has assumed jurisdiction of a criminal case, the integrity of its own process is a matter of legitimate concern. The *Fay* bypass test, by seeking to discover intentional abuses of the rules of the state forum, is, I believe, compatible with this state institutional interest. See Part III, infra. But whether *Fay* was correct in penalizing a litigant solely for his intentional forfeitures properly must be read in light of Congress' desired norm of widened post-trial access to the federal courts. If the standard adopted today is later construed to require that the simple mistakes of attorneys are to be treated as binding forfeitures, it would serve to subordinate the fundamental rights contained in our constitutional charter to inadvertent defaults of rules promulgated by state agencies, and would essentially leave it to the States, through the enactment of procedure and the certification of the competence of local attorneys, to determine whether a habeas applicant will be permitted the access to the federal forum that is guaranteed him by Congress.

Thus, I remain concerned that undue deference to local procedure can only serve to undermine the ready access to a federal court to which a state defendant otherwise is entitled. But federal review is not the full measure of Sykes' interest, for there is another of even greater immediacy: assuring that his constitutional claims can be addressed to *some* court. For the obvious consequence of barring Sykes from the federal courthouse is to insulate Florida's alleged constitutional violation from any and all judicial review because of a lawyer's mistake. From the standpoint of the habeas petitioner, it is a harsh rule indeed that denies him "any review at all where the state has granted none," Brown v. Allen, 334 U.S., at 552 (Black, J., dissenting)—particularly when he would have enjoyed both state and federal consideration had his attorney not erred.

Fay's answer to Sykes' predicament, measuring the existence and extent of his procedural waiver by the *Zerbst* standard is, I submit, a realistic one. ...

. . .

In sum, I believe that *Fay's* commitment to enforcing intentional but not inadvertent procedural defaults offers a realistic measure of protection for the habeas corpus petitioner seeking federal review of federal claims that were not litigated before the State. The threatened creation of a more "airtight system of forfeitures" would effectively deprive habeas petitioners of the opportunity for litigating their constitutional claims before any forum and would disparage the paramount importance of constitutional rights in our system of government. Such a restriction of habeas corpus jurisdiction should be countenanced, I submit, only if it fairly can be concluded that *Fay's* focus on knowing and voluntary forfeitures unduly interferes with the legitimate interests of state courts or institutions. The majority offers no suggestion that actual experience has shown that *Fay's* bypass test can be criticized on this score. And, as I now hope to demonstrate, any such criticism would be unfounded.

III

A regime of federal habeas corpus jurisdiction that permits the reopening of state procedural defaults does not invalidate any state procedural rule as such; Florida's courts remain entirely free to enforce their own rules as they choose, and to deny any and all state rights and remedies to a defendant who fails to comply with applicable state procedure. The relevant inquiry is whether more is required—specifically, whether the fulfillment of important interests of the State necessitates that federal courts be called upon to impose additional sanctions for inadvertent noncompliance with state procedural requirements such as the contemporaneous-objection rule involved here.

Florida, of course, can point to a variety of legitimate interests in seeking allegiance to its reasonable procedural requirements, the contemporaneous-objection rule included. . . . As *Fay* recognized, a trial, like any organized activity, must conform to coherent process, and "there must be sanctions for the flouting of such procedure." 372 U.S., at 431. The strict enforcement of procedural defaults, therefore, may be seen as a means of deterring any tendency on the part of the defense to slight the state forum, to deny state judges their due opportunity for playing a meaningful role in the evolving task of constitutional adjudication, or to mock the needed finality of criminal trials. All of these interests are referred to by the Court in various forms.[11]

The question remains, however, whether any of these policies or interests are efficiently and fairly served by enforcing both intentional and inadvertent defaults pursuant to the identical stringent standard. I remain convinced that when one pierces the surface justifications for a harsher rule posited by the Court, no standard stricter than *Fay's* deliberate-bypass test is realistically defensible.

Punishing a lawyer's unintentional errors by closing the federal courthouse door to his client is both a senseless and misdirected method of deterring the slighting of state rules. It is senseless because unplanned and unintentional action of any kind generally is not subject to deterrence; and, to the extent that it is hoped that a threatened sanction addressed to the defense will induce greater care and caution on the part of trial lawyers, thereby forestalling negligent conduct or error, the potential loss of all valuable state remedies would be sufficient to this end. And it is a misdirected sanction because even if the penalization of incompetence or carelessness will encourage more thorough legal training and trial preparation, the habeas applicant, as opposed to his lawyer, hardly is the proper recipient of such a penalty. Especially with fundamental constitutional rights at stake, no fictional relationship of

---

11. In my view, the strongest plausible argument for strict enforcement of a contemporary objection rule is one that the Court barely relies on at all: the possibility that the failure of timely objection to the admissibility of evidence may foreclose the making of a fresh record and thereby prejudice the prosecution in later litigation involving that evidence. There may be force to this contention, but it rests on the premise that the State in fact has suffered actual prejudice because of a procedural lapse. Florida demonstrates no such injury here. . . .

principal-agent or the like can justify holding the criminal defendant accountable for the naked errors of his attorney. This is especially true when so many indigent defendants are without any realistic choice in selecting who ultimately represents them at trial. Indeed, if responsibility for error must be apportioned between the parties, it is the State, through its attorney's admissions and certification policies, that is more fairly held to blame for the fact that practicing lawyers too often are ill-prepared or ill-equipped to act carefully and knowledgeably when faced with decisions governed by state procedural requirements.

Hence, while I can well agree that the proper functioning of our system of criminal justice, both federal and state, necessarily places heavy reliance on the professionalism and judgment of trial attorneys, I cannot accept a system that ascribes the absolute forfeiture of an individual's constitutional claims to situations where his lawyer manifestly exercises *no* professional judgment at all—where carelessness, mistake, or ignorance is the explanation for a procedural default. Of course, it is regrettable that certain errors that might have been cured earlier had trial counsel acted expeditiously must be corrected collaterally and belatedly. I can understand the Court's wistfully wishing for the day when the trial was the sole, binding and final "event" of the adversarial process— although I hesitate to agree that in the eyes of the criminal defendant it has ever ceased being the "main" one, ante, at 17. But it should be plain that in the real world, the interest in finality is repeatedly compromised in numerous ways that arise with far greater frequency than do procedural defaults. The federal criminal system, to take one example, expressly disapproves of interlocutory review in the generality of cases even though such a policy would foster finality by permitting the authoritative resolution of all legal and constitutional issues prior to the convening of the "main event." ... Instead, it relies on the belated correction of error, through appeal and collateral review, to ensure the fairness and legitimacy of the criminal sanction. Indeed, the very existence of the well-established right collaterally to reopen issues previously litigated before the state courts ... represents a congressional policy choice that is inconsistent with notions of strict finality—and probably more so than authorizing the litigation of issues that, due to inadvertence, were never addressed to any court. Ultimately, all of these limitations on the finality of criminal convictions emerge from the tension between justice and efficiency in a judicial system that hopes to remain true to its principles and ideals. Reasonable people may disagree on how best to resolve these tensions. But the solution that today's decision risks embracing seems to me the most unfair of all: the denial of any judicial consideration to the constitutional claims of a criminal defendant because of errors made by his attorney which lie outside the power of the habeas petitioner to prevent or deter and for which, under no view of morality or ethics, can be held responsible.

In short, I believe that the demands of our criminal justice system warrant visiting the mistakes of a trial attorney on the head of a habeas corpus applicant only when we are convinced that the lawyer actually exercised his expertise and judgment in his client's service, and with his client's knowing and intelligent participation where possible. This, of course, is the precise system of habeas review established by Fay v. Noia.

IV

Perhaps the primary virtue of *Fay* is that the bypass test at least yields a coherent yardstick for federal district courts in rationalizing their power of collateral review. . . . In contrast, although some four years have passed since its introduction in Davis v. United States, 411 U.S. 233 (1973), the only thing clear about the Court's "cause-and-prejudice" standard is that it exhibits the notable tendency of keeping prisoners in jail without addressing their constitutional complaints. Hence, as of today, all we know of the "cause" standard is its requirement that habeas applicants bear an undefined burden of explanation for the failure to obey the state rule . . . . Left unresolved is whether a habeas petitioner like Sykes can adequately discharge this burden by offering the commonplace and truthful explanation for his default: attorney ignorance or error beyond the client's control. The "prejudice" inquiry, meanwhile, appears to bear a strong resemblance to harmless-error doctrine. . . . I disagree with the Court's appraisal of the harmlessness of the admission of respondent's confession, but if this is what is meant by prejudice, respondent's constitutional contentions could be as quickly and easily disposed of in this regard by permitting federal courts to reach the merits of his complaint. In the absence of a persuasive alternative formulation to the by-pass test, I would simply affirm the judgment of the Court of Appeals and allow Sykes his day in court on the ground that the failure of timely objection in this instance was not a tactical or deliberate decision but stemmed from a lawyer's error that should not be permitted to bind his client.

One final consideration deserves mention. Although the standards recently have been relaxed in various jurisdictions, it is accurate to assert that most courts, this one included, traditionally have resisted any realistic inquiry into the competency of trial counsel. There is nothing unreasonable, however, in adhering to the proposition that it is the responsibility of a trial lawyer who takes on the defense of another to be aware of his client's basic legal rights and of the legitimate rules of the forum in which he practices his profession. If he should unreasonably permit such rules to bar the assertion of the colorable constitutional claims of his client, then his conduct may well fall below the level of competence that can fairly be expected of him. For almost 40 years it has been established that inadequacy of counsel undercuts the very competence and jurisdiction of the trial court and is always open to collateral review. ... Obviously, as a practical matter, a trial counsel cannot procedurally waive his own inadequacy. If the scope of habeas jurisdiction previously governed by Fay v. Noia is to be redefined so as to enforce the errors and neglect of lawyers with unnecessary and unjust rigor, the time may come when conscientious and fairminded federal and state courts, in adhering to the teaching of Johnson v. Zerbst, will have to reconsider whether they can continue to indulge the comfortable fiction that all lawyers are skilled or even competent craftsmen in representing the fundamental rights of their clients.[*]

[*] Justice Stevens wrote a concurring opinion. Justice White wrote an opinion concurring in the judgment.

REED v. ROSS

468 U.S. 1, 104 S.Ct. 2901, 82 L.Ed.2d 1 (1984).

JUSTICE BRENNAN delivered the opinion of the Court.

In March 1969, respondent Daniel Ross was convicted of first-degree murder in North Carolina and sentenced to life imprisonment. At trial, Ross had claimed lack of malice and self-defense. In accordance with well-settled North Carolina law, the trial judge instructed the jury that Ross, the defendant, had the burden of proving each of these defenses. Six years later, this Court decided Mullaney v. Wilbur, 421 U.S. 684 (1975), which struck down, as violative of due process, the requirement that the defendant bear the burden of proving the element of malice. Id., at 704. Two years later, Hankerson v. North Carolina, 432 U.S. 233 (1977), held that *Mullaney* was to have retroactive application. The question presented in this case is whether Ross' attorney forfeited Ross' right to relief under *Mullaney* and *Hankerson* by failing, several years before those cases were decided, to raise on appeal the unconstitutionality of the jury instruction on the burden of proof.

I

A

In 1970, this Court decided In re Winship, 397 U.S. 358, the first case in which we directly addressed the constitutional foundation of the requirement that criminal guilt be established beyond a reasonable doubt. That case held that "[l]est there remain any doubt about the constitutional stature of the reasonable-doubt standard, ... the Due Process Clause protects the accused against conviction except upon proof beyond a reasonable doubt of every fact necessary to constitute the crime with which he is charged." Id., at 364.

Five years after *Winship,* the Court applied the principle to the related question of allocating burdens of proof in a criminal case. Mullaney v. Wilbur, supra. ... *Mullaney* held that due process requires the prosecution to bear the burden of persuasion with respect to each element of a crime.

Finally, Hankerson v. North Carolina, supra, held that *Mullaney* was to have retroactive application. ... In this case, we are called upon again, in effect, to revisit our decision in *Hankerson* with respect to a particular set of administrative costs—namely, the costs imposed on state courts by the federal courts' exercise of their habeas corpus jurisdiction under 28 U.S.C. § 2254.

B

Ross was tried for murder under the same North Carolina burden-of-proof law that gave rise to Hankerson's claim in Hankerson v. North Carolina. That law ... [had been] followed in North Carolina for over 100 years ....

In accordance with this well-settled state law, the jury at Ross' trial was instructed .... On the basis of these instructions, Ross was convicted of first-degree murder. Although Ross appealed his conviction to the North Carolina Supreme Court on a number of grounds, 275 N.C. 517, 169 S.E.2d 879 (1969), he did not challenge the constitutionality of these instructions—we may confidently assume this was because they were sanctioned by a century of North Carolina law and because *Mullaney* was yet six years away.

Ross challenged the jury instructions for the first time in 1977, shortly after this Court decided *Hankerson*. He initially did so in a petition filed in state court for postconviction relief, where his challenge was summarily rejected at both the trial and appellate levels. ... After exhausting his state remedies, Ross brought the instant federal habeas proceeding in the United States District Court for the Eastern District of North Carolina under 28 U.S.C. § 2254. The District Court, however, held that habeas relief was barred because Ross had failed to raise the issue on appeal as required by North Carolina law ... and the Court of Appeals for the Fourth Circuit dismissed Ross' appeal summarily. 660 F.2d 492 (1982). On Ross' first petition for certiorari, however, this Court vacated the judgment of the Court of Appeals and remanded the case for further consideration .... On remand, the Court of Appeals reversed, holding that Ross' claim met the "cause and prejudice" requirements and that the District Court had therefore erred in denying his petition for a writ of habeas corpus. 704 F.2d 705 (1983). The Court of Appeals found the "cause" requirement satisfied because the *Mullaney* issue was so novel at the time of Ross' appeal that Ross' attorney could not reasonably be expected to have raised it. ... And the State had conceded the existence of "prejudice" in light of evidence that had been introduced to indicate that Ross might have acted reflexively in self-defense. The Court of Appeals went on to hold that the jury instruction concerning the burden of proof for both malice and self-defense violated *Mullaney*. ... We granted certiorari, 464 U.S. 1007 (1983), to determine whether the Court of Appeals erred in concluding that Ross had "cause" for failing to raise the *Mullaney* question on appeal. We now affirm.

II

A

Our decisions have uniformly acknowledged that federal courts are empowered under 28 U.S.C. § 2254 to look beyond a state procedural forfeiture and entertain a state prisoner's contention that his constitutional rights have been violated. ... The more difficult question, and the one that lies at the heart of this case is: What standards should govern the exercise of the habeas court's equitable discretion in the use of this power?

A habeas court's decision whether to review the merits of a state prisoner's constitutional claim, when the prisoner has failed to follow applicable state procedural rules in raising the claim, implicates two sets of competing concerns. On the one hand, there is Congress' expressed interest in providing a federal forum for the vindication of the constitutional rights of state prisoners. There can be no doubt that in enacting § 2254, Congress sought to "interpose the federal courts between the States and the people, as guardians of the people's federal rights—to protect the people from unconstitutional action." Mitchum v. Foster, 407 U.S. 225, 242 (1972).

On the other hand, there is the State's interest in the integrity of its rules and proceedings and the finality of its judgments, an interest that would be undermined if the federal courts were too free to ignore procedural forfeitures in state court. The criminal justice system in each of the 50 States is structured both to determine the guilt or innocence of defendants and to resolve all questions incident to that determination, including the constitutionality of the procedures leading up to the verdict. Each State's complement of procedural rules facilitates this complex process, channeling, to the extent possible, the resolution of various types of questions to the stage of the judicial process at which they can be resolved most fairly and efficiently.

North Carolina's rule requiring a defendant initially to raise a legal issue on appeal, rather than on postconviction review, performs such a function. It affords the state courts the opportunity to resolve the issue shortly after trial, while evidence is still available both to assess the defendant's claim and to retry the defendant effectively if he prevails in his appeal. ... This type of rule promotes not only the accuracy and efficiency of judicial decisions, but also the finality of those decisions, by forcing the defendant to litigate all of his claims together, as quickly after trial as the docket will allow, and while the attention of the appellate court is focused on his case. To the extent that federal courts exercise their § 2254 power to review constitutional claims that were not properly raised before the state court, these legitimate state interests may be frustrated: evidence may no longer be available to evaluate the defendant's constitutional claim if it is brought to federal court long after his trial; and it may be too late to retry the defendant effectively if he prevails in his collateral challenge. Thus, we have long recognized that "in some circumstances considerations of comity and concerns for the orderly administration of criminal justice require a federal court to forgo the exercise of its habeas corpus power." Francis v. Henderson, [425 U.S. 536 (1976)] at 539. ...

Where, as in this case, a defendant has failed to abide by a State's procedural rule requiring the exercise of legal expertise and judgment, the competing concerns implicated by the exercise of the federal court's habeas corpus power have come to be embodied in the "cause and prejudice" requirement: When a procedural default bars litigation of a constitutional claim in state court, a state prisoner may not obtain federal habeas corpus relief absent a showing of "cause and actual prejudice." Engle v. Isaac, 456 U.S. [107 (1982)], at 129 .... We therefore turn to the question whether the cause-and-prejudice test was met in this case.

B

As stated above, petitioners have conceded that Ross suffered "actual prejudice" as a result of the trial court's instruction imposing on him the burden of proving self-defense or lack of malice. ... Thus the only question for decision is whether there was "cause" for Ross' failure to raise the *Mullaney* issue on appeal.

The Court of Appeals held that there was cause for Ross' failure to raise the *Mullaney* issue on appeal because of the "novelty" of the issue at the time. As the Court of Appeals characterized the legal basis for raising the *Mullaney* issue at the time of Ross' appeal, there was merely "[a] hint here and there voiced in other contexts," which did not "offe[r] a reasonable basis for a challenge to frequently approved jury instructions which had been used in North Carolina, and many other states, for over a century." 704 F.2d, at 708.

Engle v. Isaac, supra, left open the question whether the novelty of a constitutional issue at the time of a state-court proceeding could, as a general matter, give rise to cause for defense counsel's failure to raise the issue in accordance with applicable state procedures. ... Today, we answer that question in the affirmative.

Because of the broad range of potential reasons for an attorney's failure to comply with a procedural rule, and the virtually limitless array of contexts in which a procedural default can occur, this Court has not given the term "cause" precise content. ... Nor do we attempt to do so here. Underlying the concept of cause, however, is at least the dual notion that, absence exceptional circumstances, a defendant is bound by the tactical decisions of competent counsel ... and that defense counsel may not flout state procedures and then turn around and seek refuge in federal court from the consequences of such conduct .... A defense attorney, therefore, may not ignore a State's procedural rules in the expectation that his client's constitutional claims can be raised at a later date in federal court. ... Similarly, he may not use the prospect of federal habeas corpus relief as a hedge against the strategic risks he takes in his client's defense in state court. ... In general, therefore, defense counsel may not make a tactical decision to forgo a procedural opportunity—for instance, an opportunity to object at trial or to raise an issue on appeal—and then, when he discovers that the tactic has been unsuccessful, pursue an alternative strategy in federal court. The encouragement of such conduct by a federal court on habeas corpus review would not only offend generally accepted principles of comity, but would also undermine the accuracy and efficiency of the state judicial systems to the detriment of all concerned. Procedural defaults of this nature are, therefore, "inexcusable," . . . and cannot qualify as "cause" for purposes of federal habeas corpus review.

On the other hand, the cause requirement may be satisfied under certain circumstances when a procedural failure is not attributable to an intentional decision by counsel made in pursuit of his client's interests. And the failure of counsel to raise a constitutional issue reasonably unknown to him is one situation in which the requirement is met. If counsel has no reasonable basis upon which to formulate a constitutional question, setting aside for the moment exactly what is meant by "reasonable basis," see infra, at 16–18, it is safe to assume that he is sufficiently unaware of the question's latent existence that we cannot attribute to him strategic motives of any sort.

Counsel's failure to raise a claim for which there was no reasonable basis in existing law does not seriously implicate any of the concerns that might otherwise require deference to a State's procedural bar. Just as it is reasonable to assume that a competent lawyer will fail to perceive the possibility of raising such a claim, it is also reasonable to assume that a court will similarly fail to appreciate the claim. It is in the nature of our legal system that legal concepts, including constitutional concepts, develop slowly, finding partial acceptance in some courts while meeting rejection in others. Despite the fact that a constitutional concept may ultimately enjoy general acceptance, as the *Mullaney* issue currently does, when the concept is in its embryonic stage, it will, by hypothesis, be rejected by most courts. Consequently, a rule requiring a defendant to raise a truly novel issue is not likely to serve any functional purpose. Although there is a remote possibility that a given state court will be the first to discover a latent constitutional issue and to order redress if the issue is properly raised, it is far more likely that the court will fail to appreciate the claim and reject it out of hand. Raising such a claim in state court, therefore, would not promote either the fairness or the efficiency of the state criminal justice system. It is true that finality will be disserved if the federal courts reopen a state prisoner's case, even to review claims that were so novel when the cases were in state court that no one would have recognized them. This Court has never held, however, that finality, standing alone, provides a sufficient reason for federal courts to compromise their protection of constitutional rights under § 2254.

In addition, if we were to hold that the novelty of a constitutional question does not give rise to cause for counsel's failure to raise it, we might actually disrupt state-court proceedings by encouraging defense counsel to include any and all remotely plausible constitutional claims that could, some day, gain recognition.　...

Accordingly, we hold that where a constitutional claim is so novel that its legal basis is not reasonably available to counsel, a defendant has cause for his failure to raise the claim in accordance with applicable state procedures.　We therefore turn to the question whether the *Mullaney* issue, which respondent Ross has raised in this action, was sufficiently novel at the time of the appeal from his conviction to excuse his attorney's failure to raise it at that time.

C

As stated above, the Court of Appeals found that the state of the law at the time of Ross' appeal did not offer a "reasonable basis" upon which to challenge the jury instructions on the burden of proof.　704 F.2d, at 708.　We agree and therefore conclude that Ross had cause for failing to raise the issue at that time.　Although the question whether an attorney has a "reasonable basis" upon which to develop a legal theory may arise in a variety of contexts, we confine our attention to the specific situation presented here: one in which this Court has articulated a constitutional principle that had not been previously recognized but which is held to have retroactive application.　In United States v. Jackson, 457 U.S. 537 (1982), we identified three situations in which a "new" constitutional rule, representing "a clear break with the past," might emerge from this Court.　Id., at 549 (quoting Desist v. United States, 394 U.S. 244, 258–259 (1969)).　First, a decision of this Court may explicitly overrule one of our precedents.　United States v. Johnson, 457 U.S., at 551.　Second a decision may "overtur[n] a longstanding and wide-spread practice to which this Court has not spoken, but which a near-unanimous body of lower court authority has expressly approved."　Ibid.　And, finally, a decision may "disapprov[e] a practice this Court arguably has sanctioned in prior cases."　Ibid.　By definition, when a case falling into one of the first two categories is given retroactive application, there will almost certainly have been no reasonable basis upon which an attorney previously could have urged a state court to adopt the position that this Court has ultimately adopted.　Consequently, the failure of a defendant's attorney to have pressed such a claim before a state court is sufficiently excusable to satisfy the cause requirement. Cases falling into the third category, however, present a more difficult question.　Whether an attorney had a reasonable basis for pressing a claim challenging a practice that this Court has arguably sanctioned depends on how direct this Court's sanction of the prevailing practice had been, how well entrenched the practice was in the relevant jurisdiction at the time of defense counsel's failure to challenge it, and how strong the available support is from sources opposing the prevailing practice.

This case is covered by the third category. At the time of Ross' appeal, Leland v. Oregon, 343 U.S. 790 (1952), was the primary authority addressing the due process constraints upon the imposition of the burden of proof on a defendant in a criminal trial. In that case, the Court held that a State may require a defendant on trial for first-degree murder to bear the burden of proving insanity beyond a reasonable doubt, despite the fact that the presence of insanity might tend to imply the absence of the mental state required to support a conviction. ... *Leland* thus confirmed "the long-accepted rule ... that it was constitutionally permissible to provide that various affirmative defenses were to be proved by the defendant," Patterson v. New York, 432 U.S. 197, 211 (1977), and arguably sanctioned the practice by which a State crafts an affirmative defense to shift to the defendant the burden of disproving an essential element of a crime. As stated above, North Carolina had consistently engaged in this practice with respect to the defenses of lack of malice and self-defense for over a century. ... Indeed, it was not until five years after Ross' appeal that the issue first surfaced in the North Carolina courts, and even then it was rejected out of hand. ...

Moreover, prior to Ross' appeal, only one Federal Court of Appeals had held that it was unconstitutional to require a defendant to disprove an essential element of a crime for which he is charged. Stump v. Bennett, 398 F.2d 111 (CA8 1968). Even that case, however, involved the burden of proving an alibi, which the Court of Appeals described as the "den[ial of] the possibility of [the defendant's] having committed the crime by reason of being elsewhere." Id., at 116. The court thus contrasted the alibi defense with "an affirmative defense [which] generally applies to justification for his admitted participation in the act itself," ibid, and distinguished *Leland* on that basis, 398 F.2d, at 119. In addition, at the time of Ross' appeal, the Superior Court of Connecticut had struck down, as violative of due process, a statute making it unlawful for an individual to possess burglary tools "without lawful excuse, the proof of which excuse shall be upon him." State v. Nales, 28 Conn.Sup. 28, 29, 248 A.2d 242 (1968). Because these cases provided only indirect support for Ross' claim, and because they were the only cases that would have supported Ross' claim at all, we cannot conclude that they provided a reasonable basis upon which Ross could have realistically appealed his conviction.

In Engle v. Isaac, 456 U.S. 107 (1982), this Court reached the opposite conclusion with respect to the failure of a group of defendants to raise the *Mullaney* issue in 1975. That case differs from this one, however, in two crucial respects. First, the procedural defaults at issue there occurred five years after we decided *Winship,* which held that "the Due Process Clause protects the accused against conviction except upon proof beyond a reasonable doubt of every fact necessary to constitute the crime with which he is charged." *Winship,* 397 U.S., at 364. As the Court in Engle v. Isaac stated, *Winship* "laid the basis for [the habeas petitioners'] constitutional claim." 456 U.S., at 131. Second, during those five years, "numerous courts agreed that the Due Process Clause requires the prosecution to bear the burden of disproving certain affirmative defenses" (footnotes omitted). See id., at 132, n. 40 (citing cases). Moreover, as evidence of the reasonableness of the legal basis for raising the *Mullaney* issue in 1975, Engle v. Isaac emphasized that "dozens of defendants relied upon [*Winship*] to challenge the constitutionality of rules requiring them to bear a burden of proof." 456 U.S., at 131–132. None of these bases of decision relied upon in Engle v. Isaac is present in this case.

III

We therefore conclude that Ross' claim was sufficiently novel in 1969 to excuse his attorney's failure to raise the *Mullaney* issue at that time. Accordingly, we affirm the decision of the Court of Appeals with respect to the question of "cause."

It is so ordered.[*] [**]

[*] Justice Powell wrote a concurring opinion. Justice Rehnquist wrote a dissenting opinion, which Chief Justice Burger, Justice Blackmun, and Justice O'Connor joined.

[**] In United States v. Frady, 456 U.S. 152 (1982) (6–1), the Court considered the meaning of "prejudice" as part of the standard for allowing collateral relief under Wainwright v. Sykes, 433 U.S. 72 (1977), above. It said: "... [T]he degree of prejudice we have required a prisoner to show before obtaining collateral relief for errors in the jury charge [has been characterized] as ' "whether the ailing instruction by itself so infected the entire trial that the resulting conviction violates due process," not merely whether "the instruction is undesirable, erroneous, or even universally condemned." ' [Henderson v. Kibbe], 431 U.S. [145 (1977)], at 154 .... We reaffirm this formulation, which requires that the degree of prejudice resulting from instruction error be evaluated in the total context of the events at trial.

. . .

... [Frady] must shoulder the burden of showing, not merely that the errors at his trial created a *possibility* of prejudice, but that they worked to his *actual* and substantial disadvantage, infecting his entire trial with error of constitutional dimensions." 456 U.S. at 169–170.

Frady had been convicted of murder. The allegedly erroneous instruction to the jury concerned the element of malice. The Court said: "We conclude that the strong uncontradicted evidence of malice in the record, coupled with Frady's utter failure to come forward with a colorable claim that he acted without malice, disposes of his contention that he suffered such actual prejudice that reversal of his conviction 19 years later could be justified. We perceive no risk of a fundamental miscarriage of justice in this case." 456 U.S. at 172.

†

P9-DTT-138

Promoting
Health
in Families

RT 120 .F34 P766 200
Promoting health in
family re

OKANAGAN UNIVERSITY COLLEGE
LIBRARY
BRITISH COLUMBIA

Third Edition

Promoting Health in Families

*Applying Family Research and
Theory to Nursing Practice*

Perri J. Bomar, PhD, RN

Professor
Associate Dean, Research and Community Partnerships
School of Nursing
University of North Carolina at Wilmington
Wilmington, North Carolina

SAUNDERS

An Imprint of Elsevier

SAUNDERS
An Imprint of Elsevier

The Curtis Center
Independence Square West
Philadelphia, Pennsylvania 19106-3399

PROMOTING HEALTH IN FAMILIES: APPLYING FAMILY RESEARCH AND
THEORY TO NURSING PRACTICE, THIRD EDITION   ISBN 0-7216-0115-4

Copyright © 2004, 1996, 1989 Elsevier Inc. All rights reserved.

No part of this publication may be reproduced or transmitted in any form or by any means, electronic or
mechanical, including photocopying, recording, or any information storage and retrieval system, without
permission in writing from the publisher. Permissions may be sought directly from Elsevier's Health Sciences
Rights Department in Philadelphia, PA, USA: phone: (+1) 215 238 7869, fax: (+1) 215 238 2239, e-mail:
healthpermissions@elsevier.com. You may also complete your request on-line via the Elsevier Science
homepage (http://www.elsevier.com), by selecting 'Customer Support' and then 'Obtaining Permissions.'

NOTICE

Nursing is an ever-changing field. Standard safety precautions must be followed, but as new research
and clinical experience broaden our knowledge, changes in treatment and drug therapy may become
necessary or appropriate. Readers are advised to check the most current product information provided
by the manufacturer of each drug to be administered to verify the recommended dose, the method and
duration of administration, and contraindications. It is the responsibility of the licensed prescriber,
relying on experience and knowledge of the patient, to determine dosages and the best treatment for
each individual patient. Neither the publisher nor the author assumes any liability for any injury
and/or damage to persons or property arising from this publication.

Library of Congress Cataloging in Publication Data
Promoting health in families: applying family research and theory to nursing practice/
   [edited by] Perri J. Bomar.—3rd ed.
     p.; cm.
   Rev. ed. of: Nurses and family health promotion. 2nd ed. c1996.
   Includes bibliographical references and index.
   ISBN 0-7216-0115-4
      1. Family nursing. 2. Health promotion. 3. Family—Health and hygiene. I. Bomar, Perri
   J. II. Nurses and family health promotion.
      [DNLM: 1. Family Nursing. 2. Family Health. 3. Health Promotion. WY 159.5 P965 2004]
   RT120.F34P766 2004
   613—dc21

                                                                              2003054410

Executive Editor: Loren Wilson
Managing Editor: Linda Thomas
Production Services Manager: Deborah L. Vogel
Design Coordinator: Teresa Breckwoldt
Design: Studio Montage

Printed in the United States

Last digit is the print number: 9   8   7   6   5   4   3   2   1

To my beloved husband, Guy,
who exemplifies a love of family and has been my avid supporter
throughout my nursing career.

To my grandchildren, Derek and Dustin,
and their love of family celebrations and family rituals that inspired
the chapter on family rituals.

To my sons, Maurice and Brian, and Brian's wife, Pamela,
and my extended family who were loving and supportive during my
nursing career and sometime absences due to writing.

To my loving God who created the first family
and who is my strength and refuge.

Perri Jane Bomar

Foreword

Few would disagree that a profound, reciprocal relationship exists between families and health. The most recent integrative reviews of nursing research with families (Gilliss & Knafl, 1999; Knafl & Gilliss, 2002; McCubbin, 1999) have documented the many ways that nursing research has creatively and substantively extended the conversation about the reciprocal impact of normative and nonnormative transitions on families. That families play an important role in the promotion, protection, and maintenance of health (including recovery from illness) has been even more strongly supported in a major integrative review by Weihs, Fisher, and Baird (2002). Family factors affecting the management and outcomes of a variety of chronic illnesses were identified from the research literature. The authors summarized their findings using the epidemiological language of family "protective and risk factors" (p. 15) that have been documented in recent studies. It is noteworthy that while intrafamilial conflict and criticism were among several family processes identified as risk factors, family communication, clear family organization, congruent beliefs within the family, and even family time for recreation were among several significant family processes that serve as protective factors (Weihs et al., 2002). In this third edition of *Promoting Health in Families,* Dr. Bomar has invited a group of distinguished contributors who argue persuasively and intentionally that families *do* conserve wellness in a variety of ways across the life span, across cultures, and across the health/illness continuum.

The nursing profession consistently distinguishes "individual," "family," and "community" as distinct systems levels for both assessment and intervention. Bomar's third edition joins an increasing number of textbooks written by nurses for nurses that focus on the family (Denham, 2003; Friedman, Bowden, & Jones, 2003; Hanson, 2001; Wright & Leahey, 2000; Wright, Watson, & Bell, 1996). Despite definitions of family that increasingly account for varied family forms and structures, I believe "family" is a misnomer. What intrigues many of us about "family" is the influence that *significant relationships* have on the experience of health and illness. We say family, when what we really mean is relationships.

Our understanding of the bidirectional influence between relationships and health and well-being is growing. However, we are still at only a beginning stage in our efforts to develop a body of knowledge about how the nurse might assess and intervene at the level of relationships in ways that will promote health and make demonstrable differences in the lives of individuals, families, and communities. Promoting health at the level of relationships, I believe, exists across a continuum of nursing care both in community-based prevention efforts and in contexts where nurses encounter suffering and, more specifically, relationship suffering in the experience of illness. Families, undoubtedly, are at the center of nursing efforts that acknowledge, strengthen, sustain, and alter relationships with the goal of promoting health.

This third edition challenges and extends our thinking about the linkages between relationships and health and honors the bidirectional influence that exists. Descriptions of nursing practice for promoting health are included. I am thrilled that

Dr. Bomar chose to include Canadian content in this third edition of *Promoting Health in Families*. In doing so, she convincingly acknowledges that the world of family nursing is without borders and that international relationships promote health within the discipline!

Janice M. Bell, RN, PhD
Associate Professor, University of Calgary
Director, Family Nursing Unit
Editor, *Journal of Family Nursing*
Calgary, Alberta, Canada

REFERENCES

Denham, S. (2003). *Family health: A framework for nursing.* Philadelphia: F.A. Davis.

Friedman, M.M., Bowden, V.R., & Jones, E.G. (2003). *Family nursing: Research, theory, and practice* (5th ed.). Upper Saddle River, NJ: Prentice Hall.

Gilliss, C.L., & Knafl, K.A. (1999). Nursing care of families in non-normative transitions. The state of science and practice. In A.S. Hinshaw, S.L. Feetham, & J.L.F. Shaver (Eds.), *Handbook of clinical nursing research* (pp. 231-249). Thousand Oaks, CA: Sage.

Hanson, S.M.H. (2001). *Family health care nursing: Theory, practice, and research* (2nd ed.). Philadelphia: F.A. Davis.

Knafl, K.A., & Gilliss, C.L. (2002). Families and chronic illness: A synthesis of current research. *Journal of Family Nursing, 8*(3), 178-198.

McCubbin, M. (1999). Normative family transitions and health outcomes. In A.S. Hinshaw, S.L. Feetham, & J.L.F. Shaver (Eds.), *Handbook of clinical nursing research* (pp. 201-230). Thousand Oaks, CA: Sage.

Weihs, K., Fisher, L., & Baird, M. (2002). Families, health, and behavior. A section of the Commissioned Report by the Committee on Health and Behavior: Research, Practice, and Policy, Division of Neuroscience and Behavioral Health and Division of Health Promotion and Disease Prevention, Institute of Medicine, National Academy of Sciences. *Families, Systems & Health, 20*(1), 7-46.

Wright, L.M., & Leahey, M. (2000). *Nurses and families: A guide to family assessment and intervention* (3rd ed.). Philadelphia: F.A. Davis.

Wright, L.M., Watson, W.L., & Bell, J.M. (1996). *Beliefs: The heart of healing in families and illness.* New York: Basic Books.

Preface

The environment for families and health care has changed dramatically since the second edition published in 1996. There is a heightened awareness of diversity in ethnicity and in family structures and of the interrelatedness of the social, economic, environmental, and political determinants of health. Globally the importance of health promotion is supported by the World Health Organization and nationally with documents such as *Healthy People 2010* in the United States and *Health Canada* for Canadians. One soon realizes that for individuals, the family unit is where heath promotion is supported, taught, or undermined. Therefore families, more than ever in the twenty-first century, will need advocacy, respect for their self-determination, and uniqueness to maintain or regain resilience in a dynamic and complex society. Health promotion by and for families as a unit is more crucial as families are expected to assume more responsibility for the quality of their health, for preventing disease, and for caring for ill family members.

This third edition updates the research, theory, practice, and policy for family health promotion from the last edition. National and international colleagues, students, and reviewers continue to articulate that this text (1) serves as a useful source for selected family assessment tools and references for family health promotion and health protection and (2) supplies a compact reference for undergraduate and graduate students, as well as clinicians practicing in the area of family health promotion.

Some contributors from previous editions have continued with this edition, but others have moved on to other interests or retired. The con-

tributors represent diversity similar to that of families. Examples of the specialties of the nurse contributors include community health nurses, family nurse scholars, family nurses, educators, researchers, family therapists, psychiatric mental health nurses, a nurse-minister, family nurse practitioners, and pediatric and women's health advanced practice nurses. A special feature is the *Canadian Perspective* boxes, edited by Dr. Michel Tarko from Douglas College in Vancouver, British Columbia, Canada. In addition, new to the third edition are interdisciplinary colleagues: Drs. Robert Blundo, Karen Bullock, and Jeanne Denny, social work scholars; Dr. Clyde McDaniel, sociologist and professor; and Dr. Caroline Clements, psychologist and professor.

Purpose of the Book

When the first edition was initiated in 1989, we were in virgin territory introducing family health promotion as a concept. Minimal research has been done specifically to test the family health promotion model. The scholarship of family nurse scholars Dr. Kathryn Anderson; the McGill University Faculty of Nursing guided by the work of Dr. Moyra Allen's Developmental Model of Health and Nursing; Dr. Gayle Hartrick and colleagues and the Family Nursing Assessment framework; Dr. Marie Louise-Friedemann and the Framework for Systemic Organization; and the seminal work of Sharon Denham's research that resulted in the "Family Health Framework" continues to develop the concept of family health and family health promotion as a viable framework for family nursing and family health promotion in the twenty-first century.

Intended Readers and Use

Colleagues and faculty throughout the United States, Canada, and the rest of the world tell me that they use this text for senior-level baccalaureate programs, RN to BSN programs, graduate nursing programs (particularly family nurse practitioner programs), and doctoral programs. Also, others who inform me that they find this book useful are nurses in practice, social worker and health education faculty, community health faculty, family scientists, and psychology faculty.

The sequence to read this book is optional. However, I suggest reading Units I and II initially, followed by any sequence that fits a course design or family health issue. It can be used alone in a family nursing course or to supplement other courses. Faculty and students who evaluated the second edition particularly like the assessment tools and models and the up-to-date references, and they recommended the addition of websites.

New Features in the Third Edition

Based on the recommendations of reviewers and readers, the following new features and content have been added:
- Six new chapters with content on rural families, family rituals and routines, theoretical foundations for family nursing practice, life-threatening illnesses and end of life, and the new millennium
- Brief discussion of family nursing and family issues by Canadian contributors in each chapter
- Research Synopsis boxes that provide a research abstract on family, individuals in the context of the family, or family-related research
- More discussion of diverse family types and structures
- More tables, information boxes, and figures to highlight key points
- Critical Thinking Activities for every chapter
- Case Scenarios that illustrate selected concepts in family life
- A focus on nursing diagnosis, assessment, and intervention with the latest NANDA (North American Nursing Diagnosis Association) descriptions
- Updated references and statistics

- Website Resources boxes in each chapter with URLs for numerous agencies and organizations that are resources for families and family professionals

Intent and Structure of the Third Edition

The standard features in each chapter are *Objectives,* the nursing process, assessment tools, updated references, integration of family or family-relevant research, a *Canadian Perspectives* box, a family *Research Synopsis,* a family *Case Scenario, Chapter Highlights, Critical Thinking Activities,* and a *Website Resources* box. Starting with Chapter 5, each chapter introduces a concept or theory, discusses the family nursing process and collaborating with families, and provides a sample assessment tool or model.

The book is organized into four units. *Unit I, "Foundations of Nursing Care of Families and Family Health Promotion,"* has three chapters. Chapter 1 provides a historical overview of family nursing and family health promotion and introduces the concept of family health promotion and family health. Social work colleagues in Chapter 2 challenge the reader to view the twenty-first century through different lenses because the nuclear family of the twentieth century is no longer representative of the majority of families in the United States. In Chapter 3, family health and family health promotion definitions, models, frameworks, and assessment are presented.

Unit II, "Conceptual Frameworks for Nursing Practice to Promote and Protect Family Health," includes chapters about family roles, social support, family communication, family spirituality, and sociocultural influences on family health promotion. Each chapter includes a discussion of the theories and frameworks specific to the concept or theory, recent research, and practice issues with diverse families. Also included is a new chapter, "Theoretical Foundations for Family Health Nursing Practice," which synthesizes and compares family theories, family science theories, and family nursing frameworks.

Unit III, "Family Nursing Practice," has 11 chapters and starts with Chapter 10, "Using the Nursing Process with Families" and Chapter 11, "Family Assessment and Intervention." Family assessment measures are reviewed and resources for assessing and co-creating interventions with healthy families are listed. Chapters 12 and 19 address family health protections and issues of family violence, family safety, environmental health, and family preparation for natural and human-initiated disasters. New or dramatically revised chapters in this unit are

- Chapter 10, "Using the Nursing Process with Families," based on the Neuman systems model (new)
- Chapter 11, "Family Assessment and Intervention," based on the Neuman systems model (revised)
- Chapter 16, "Family Routines, Rituals, Recreation, and Rules (new)
- Chapter 17, "Family Health Promotion During Transitions" (revised)
- Chapter 18, "Family Heath Promotion During Life-Threatening Illness and End of Life" (new)
- Chapter 19, "Family Environmental Health" (new)
- Chapter 20, "Health Promotion of Families in Rural Settings" (new)

Lastly, *Unit IV, "Social and Family Policy and the Future of Family Health"* has two chapters. Chapter 21 synthesizes family policy issues for the twenty-first century, delineates the role of family professionals, and has a companion Canadian Perspectives box. Chapter 22, "Family Health Promotion and Family Nursing in the New Millennium" is the final chapter and provides perspectives on paramount national and global family issues and implications for the next 10 years and beyond.

Reflections on Twenty-First Century Family Nursing

Since the resurgence in family nursing in the early 1980s, the field has developed exponentially. There are more family nursing and family health textbooks and textbook chapters, the *Journal of Family Nursing* is devoted solely to this topic, there is increased family-focused nursing research, and there is a national and global recognition of the family as crucial to the health of the individual, as well as an emphasis on family resilience and the quality of family life. Many schools of nursing integrate family nursing concepts into the curricula at all levels; however, the consistency in the use of these concepts and frameworks in reality in day-to-day practice is not documented in the literature. During contemporary societal time, with its accompanying fast-paced lifestyles, complex societal chances, and uncertainty, families need advocates in all health care delivery settings. Attention to quality of family life in all realms and health promotion of the family as a unit is paramount.

This text will assist you to view the family and individuals within families as partners in promoting health for their family units through careful assessment, implementation, and evaluation of co-created strategies to promote family health and resilience. Readers often tell me that after reading selected chapters, they sometimes reflect on the quality of their own family life and thereby make changes. My hope is that in the complex social, cultural, economical, and political environment of the twenty-first century, you will sense the necessity to be a caring advocate for diverse families in all arenas. It is an exciting time to study family health promotion. I hope that after reading this text you will understand the saliency of the family health promotion and also catch this excitement.

Perri J. Bomar

Acknowledgments

The creation of this book would not have been possible without the support and assistance of a variety of people. I am indebted to students and practitioners who believe in family health promotion and who incorporate it in today's practice with diverse families in a variety of contexts. The impetus to create a new edition was the result of the continual requests from faculty in the United States and Canada who used the second edition. Their support of *Nurses and Family Health Promotion* is greatly appreciated.

I would like to thank the contributors who wrote and revised chapters or research abstracts and the Canadian contributors who provided the *Canadian Perspectives* boxes for each chapter. Without their commitment and cooperation, the third edition would not be a reality. It was a pleasure to collaborate with Dr. Michel Tarko from Douglas College in Vancouver, British Columbia, Canada, who is a keen supporter for the text and who also served as editor for the *Canadian Perspectives* boxes. He efficiently and diligently recruited, coordinated, and edited the new Canadian feature. Also, a very special thank you goes to each reviewer for their in-depth critiques of and suggestions for the third edition and for each chapter's manuscript. I particularly appreciate the new contributors who started new chapters from scratch: Michel Tarko and Karen Reed, who co-authored Chapter 10, "Using the Nursing Process with Families," and Chapter 11, "Family Assessment and Intervention"; Betty Fomby, who wrote Chapter 16, "Family Routines, Rituals, Recreation, and Rules"; Andrew Weaver, author of Chapter 18, who shared his expertise in "Family Health Promotion in Life-Threatening Illness and at the End of Life"; and Janice Wiegmann, who wrote Chapter 20, "Health Promotion of Families in Rural Settings." Also, my colleagues from social work (Robert Blundo, Clyde McDaniel, Karen Bullock, and Jeanne Denny) and psychology (Caroline Clements) are acknowledged for their interdisciplinary perspectives.

I am also very grateful and indebted to my editor, Linda Thomas, and production manager, Claire Kramer, and other staff from Elsevier for their encouragement, advocacy, "nudging," foresight, and editing during this arduous project. Thank you also to Loren Wilson, Deborah Vogel, and Teresa Breckwoldt of Elsevier and to Studio Montage. My colleague and Dean, Virginia Adams, also made this edition possible by encouraging me to "go for it" and to create a flexible schedule to meet deadlines. I am indebted to Donna Rusch, my administrative assistant, who capably handled calls, took care of a myriad of details during my absence, and assisted with last-minute details.

My greatest sources of strength and encouragement were God and my husband, Guy. I thank Guy for his steadfast love and also his prayers before starting my early morning writing, for picking up the void created by my long hours of writing and editing, and for doing the indoor and outdoor chores. He sacrificed our "couple time" and disruption in our "routines" so that I might write about family health promotion. Lastly, I express deep appreciation to him for critiquing and reading drafts, and contributing content on family environmental violence.

Perri J. Bomar

Contributors

Robert G. Blundo, PhD
Associate Professor
University of North Carolina at Wilmington
Department of Social Work
Wilmington, North Carolina
Chapter 2, The Twenty-First Century Family

Perri J. Bomar, PhD, RN
Professor
Associate Dean, Research and Community
    Partnerships
School of Nursing
University of North Carolina at Wilmington
Wilmington, North Carolina
*Chapter 1, Introduction to Family Health Nursing
    and Promoting Family Health*
*Chapter 3, Family Health Promotion and Health
    Protection*
Chapter 8, Family Spirituality and Religion
*Chapter 9, Sociocultural Influences on Family
    Health Promotion and Health Protection*
Chapter 14, Family Stress Management
Chapter 19, Family Environmental Health
*Chapter 22, Family Health Promotion and Family
    Nursing in the New Millennium*

Karen Bullock, PhD
Assistant Professor
University of Connecticut
School of Social Work
West Hartford, Connecticut
Chapter 6, Family Social Support

Caroline M. Clements, PhD
Assistant Professor
Department of Psychology
University of North Carolina at Wilmington
Wilmington, North Carolina
Chapter 15, Family Sexuality

John A. Crawford, RPN, MA, PhDc
Instructor
Department of Psychiatric Nursing
Department of Nursing
Douglas College
New Westminster, British Columbia, Canada
Chapter 7, Family Communication

Jeanne F. Denny, MSW
Lecturer, Director of Field Education
Department of Social Work
University of North Carolina at Wilmington
Wilmington, North Carolina
Chapter 14, Family Stress Management

Eleanor A. Flores, RN, BSN, MSN, OCN
Clinical Nurse III
University of California, San Diego
San Diego, California
Chapter 13, Family Nutrition

Betty Williams Fomby, PhD, RN
Associate Professor
School of Nursing
Southern University A & M College
Wellness Consultant
Baton Rouge, Louisiana
*Chapter 16, Family Routines, Rituals, Recreation,
    and Rules*

Bettie J. Glenn, EdD, RN
Associate Dean for Academic Affairs
School of Nursing
University of North Carolina at Wilmington
Wilmington, North Carolina
*Chapter 9, Sociocultural Influences on Family
    Health Promotion and Health Protection*

Shirley May Harmon Hanson, RN, PhD, FAAN
Professor
School of Nursing
Oregon Health Sciences University
Portland, Oregon
*Chapter 4, Theoretical Foundations for Family
    Health Nursing Practice*

Shelton M. Hisley, PhD, RNC, WHNP
Assistant Professor
School of Nursing
University of North Carolina at Wilmington
Wilmington, North Carolina
Chapter 15, Family Sexuality

Kathy Shadle James, DNSc, NP
Assistant Professor
Hahn School of Nursing and Health Science
University of San Diego
San Diego, California
Chapter 13, Family Nutrition

Joanna Rowe Kaakinen, PhD, RN
Associate Professor
School of Nursing
University of Portland
Portland, Oregon
*Chapter 4, Theoretical Foundations for Family
    Health Nursing Practice*

Yeoun Soo Kim-Godwin, PhD, RN
Assistant Professor
School of Nursing
University of North Carolina at Wilmington
Wilmington, North Carolina
Chapter 5, Family Roles

David R. Langford, PhD, RN
Associate Professor
College of Nursing
University of North Carolina at Charlotte
Charlotte, North Carolina
Chapter 12, Family Health Protection

Carol J. Loveland-Cherry, PhD, RN, FAAN
Professor and Executive Associate Dean
Office for Academic Affairs
School of Nursing
University of Michigan
Ann Arbor, Michigan
*Chapter 3, Family Health Promotion and Health
    Protection*

Clyde McDaniel, PhD
Associate Professor
Department of Social Work
University of North Carolina at Wilmington
Wilmington, North Carolina
Chapter 2, The Twenty-First Century Family

Karen Reed, PhD, RN
Associate Professor
Coordinator for Educational Progression
    Programs
College of Nursing
University of Akron
Akron, Ohio
*Chapter 10, Using the Nursing Process with
    Families*
Chapter 11, Family Assessment and Intervention

Patricia Roth, EdD, MSN, RN
Professor
Hahn School of Nursing and Health Science
University of San Diego
San Diego, California
*Chapter 17, Family Health Promotion During
    Transitions*

Susan E. Scheuring, RN, PhD, FNPc
Associate Professor
School of Nursing
University of North Carolina at Wilmington
Wilmington, North Carolina
*Chapter 21, Influences of Social and Health
    Policies on Family Health*

Mary Ann Simanello, MSN, RN
Doctoral Student
Hahn School of Nursing and Health Science
University of San Diego
San Diego, California
Chapter 17, Family Health Promotion During Transitions

Joann E. Smith RN, MSN, DNSc, c
Assistant Professor
Western Carolina University
Department of Nursing
University of North Carolina at Asheville
Asheville, North Carolina
Chapter 14, Family Stress Management

Michel A. Tarko, RPN, PhD
Instructor
Department of Psychiatric Nursing
Douglas College
New Westminster, British Columbia, Canada
Chapter 7, Family Communication
Chapter 10, Using the Nursing Process with Families
Chapter 11, Family Assessment and Intervention

Carmen Germaine Warner-Robbins, MSN, RN, MDiv, FAAN
Publishing Consultant
Founder and Executive Director, Welcome Home Ministries
Jail and Prison Chaplain, San Diego County
San Diego, California
Chapter 8, Family Spirituality and Religion

Andrew W. Weaver, FNP-C
Family Nurse Practitioner
Wilmington, North Carolina
Chapter 18, Family Health Promotion During Life-Threatening Illness and at the End of Life

Janice M. Wiegmann, PhD, RN
Associate Professor
Division of Nursing
McKendree College
Lebanon, Illinois
Chapter 20, Health Promotion of Families in Rural Settings

Canadian Perspectives **Contributors**

Michel A. Tarko, RPN, PhD
Instructor
Department of Psychiatric Nursing
Faculty of Health Sciences
Douglas College
New Westminster, British Columbia, Canada
Canadian Perspectives Editor

Megan Aston, PhD, RN
Assistant Professor
School of Nursing
Dalhousie University
Halifax, Nova Scotia, Canada
Canadian Families in the 21st Century (Chapter 22)

Christine Ateah, RN, PhD
Assistant Professor
Helen Glass Centre for Nursing
University of Manitoba
Winnipeg, Manitoba, Canada
*The Parenting Role: Corporal Punishment and Its Negative
    Developmental Outcomes for Children (Chapter 6)*

Suzan Banoub-Baddour, RN, DNSc
Associate Professor
School of Nursing
Memorial University of Newfoundland
St John's, Newfoundland, Canada
*Family Nutrition as Health Promotion: Canadian
    Guidelines (Chapter 13)*

Deborah Beck, BN, MSc(Med), PhD
Associate Professor
School of Nursing
Memorial University of Newfoundland
St John's, Newfoundland, Canada
Family Coping and Stress Management (Chapter 14)

Line Beaudet, MScN
Clinical Nurse Specialist
Montreal University Health Center
Montreal, Quebec, Canada
*Describing Twenty-First Century Canadian Family
    Types and Issues (Chapter 2)*

Ursula Bohn, RN, MN, CNS
Palliative Care Clinical Nurse Specialist
Calgary Health Region
Calgary, Alberta, Canada
Palliative Care (Chapter 18)

Jane Drummond, PhD, RN
Professor, Faculty of Nursing
Child and Family Resiliency Research Program
Edmonton, Alberta, Canada
Milestones of Family Nursing in Canada (Chapter 1)

P. Gaye Hanson, RN, SCM, BScN, MPA
Aboriginal Nurses Association of Canada
President, Hanson and Associates
Whitehorse, Yukon, Canada
*Aboriginal Perspectives in Rural Health Promotion
    Practice (Chapter 20)*

Virginia E. Hayes, RN, PhD
Associate Professor
School of Nursing
University of Victoria
Vancouver, British Columbia, Canada
*Family Health-Promoting Policy and Policy Making in
    Canada (Chapter 21)*

Carl Lacharité, PhD
Professor
Department of Psychology
Director of the Child and Family Development
    Research Group
University of Québec in Trois-Rivières
Trois-Rivières, Québec, Canada
*Family Health Promotion during Transitions: Nurses and
    the Birth of a First Child (Chapter 17)*

Nicole Letourneau, PhD, MN, RN
Assistant Professor
Faculty of Nursing and CIHR/AHFMR Post-Doctoral
    Fellow
University of Alberta
Edmonton, Alberta, Canada
Milestones of Family Nursing in Canada (Chapter 1)
*Canadian Social Support Agencies and Family Issues
    (Chapter 6)*

Michelle Lobchuk, PhD, RN
Assistant Professor
Faculty of Nursing
University of Manitoba
Winnipeg, Manitoba, Canada
*Perspective-Taking as a Real-World Heuristic Device
    (Chapter 7)*

Francine de Montigny, PhD, MSc, Inf
Nursing Director
University of Quebec in Outaouais
Outaouais, Quebec, Canada
Describing Twenty-First Century Canadian Family
Types and Issues (Chapter 2)
Family Health Promotion during Transitions: Nurses and
the Birth of a First Child (Chapter 17)

Verna C. Pangman, RN, MEd, MN
Lecturer
Faculty of Nursing
University of Manitoba
Winnipeg, Manitoba, Canada
A Canadian Context of Spirituality (Chapter 8)

Karen Pielak, MSN, RN
Adjunct Professor
School of Nursing
University of British Columbia
Provincial Nurse Epidemiologist
British Columbia Centre for Disease Control Society
Vancouver, British Columbia, Canada
Family Health Protection Through Immunization
(Chapter 12)

Debbie Sheppard-Lemoine, MN, RN
Lecturer
School of Nursing
Dalhousie University
Halifax, Nova Scotia, Canada
Canada's National Emphasis on Health Promotion
(Chapter 3)
Canadian Families in the Twenty-First Century
(Chapter 22)

Miriam Stewart, PhD
Professor
Faculties of Nursing and Public Health Science
Social Support Research Program
University of Alberta
Edmonton, Alberta, Canada
Canadian Social Support Agencies and Family Issues
(Chapter 6)

Lynne Young, PhD, RN
Associate Professor
School of Nursing
University of Victoria
Vancouver, British Columbia, Canada
Social Determinants of Health: Family Structure as a
Cardiovascular Health Determinant (Chapter 9)
Family Environment and Individual Health: Lessons
from Heart Health Research (Chapter 19)

Reviewers

Kathryn Hoehn Anderson, PhD, RN
Professor
Department of Family Health Nursing
School of Nursing
University of Wisconsin-Eau Claire
Eau Claire, Wisconsin

Ruth M. Carroll, PhD, APRN, PMH
Associate Professor
Department of Nursing
Hensen School of Science and Technology
Salisbury University
Salisbury, Maryland

Virginia E. Hayes, RN, PhD
Associate Professor
School of Nursing
University of Victoria
Vancouver, British Columbia, Canada

Michelle Liken, PhD, RN, CS
Assistant Professor
Department of Family and Community Health
  Nursing
University of South Carolina
Columbia, South Carolina

Marguerite Warner, RN, BN, MScN, PhD
Health Promotion Specialist
Winnipeg, Manitoba, Canada

Contents

UNIT I

Foundations of
Nursing Care of
Families and
Family Health
Promotion

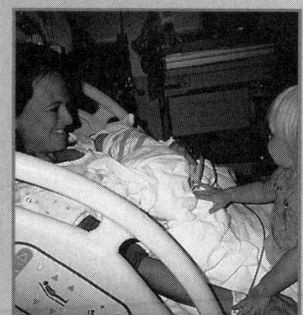

Introduction to Family Health Nursing and Promoting Family Health

Perri J. Bomar

Nursing's goal is to facilitate the health of the family . . . facilitating the development of an increased range of responses of family members to each other and to the world outside the family.

— Margaret A. Newman

OBJECTIVES

On completion of this chapter, the reader will be able to do the following:
1. *Explain the significance of nurses' conceptualizing families as a focal point for care.*
2. *Define family health nursing, family, and family health promotion.*
3. *Trace the historical development of family health nursing as a specialty.*
4. *Discuss factors that have influenced the evolution of family health nursing.*
5. *List several settings for family health nursing practice that focus on health promotion and health protection.*
6. *Identify characteristics of family health nursing practice.*

The process of increasing the capacity of families to promote health is a salient responsibility of family nurses and health care professionals. Although families have been the concern of nurses for centuries, family health nursing as it is known today emerged in the 1970s when, in addition to illness care, nurses began to consider health promotion and families as a unit of care as legitimate concerns for the nursing profession. At the beginning of the twenty-first century, significant advances flourish in the field of family nursing including the following:
1) An increase in the number of comprehensive family nursing texts focusing on theory, research, and practice
2) Publications by family nurses in a variety of scientific journals, including the *Journal of Family Nursing*, on the topics of family health

and family health promotion concepts, theories, and research
3) The inclusion of family content in baccalaureate and graduate nursing curricula
4) Recognition of the contributions of family nurses by colleagues in other disciplines
5) Presentations by family nurses at national and global interdisciplinary, nursing, and family nursing conferences

Health promotion of individuals, families, and communities is a major concern globally (World Health Organization [WHO], WHO, 1997 1998), nationally in North America (Health Canada,

The author wants to express appreciation to Gretchen McNeeley, RN, PhD, and Irene S. Palmer, RN, PhD, FAAN, for their contributions in writing previous editions of this chapter.

2001; U.S. Department of Health and Human Services [USDHHS], 2000), and locally (e.g., statewide). In addition, health promotion for individuals, families, and communities is a priority for the majority of professional health care organizations. Therefore because the family is the environment in which health promotion is taught, provided, carried out, and supported or undermined, it is crucial for nurses and other health care professionals to understand their capacity to empower families, both as individuals and as units, if they are to reach their highest potential in health promotion.

This chapter acquaints the reader with definitions of family, family health, and family nursing; the historical evolution of family health nursing; factors that influenced its evolution; characteristics of family health nursing practice; and nursing education and research.

Defining Family Health Nursing

From the beginning of nursing as a profession, the concept of family nursing has existed (Ford, 1979). Initially, nurses who focused on families as the unit of care used a variety of titles that included *family* or *health*, but only in the 1970s did the title *family health nurse* emerge. Historically, nursing care involving families was called *family-centered care* (Cunningham, 1978), *family-focused care* (Janosik & Miller, 1980), *family interviewing* (Wright & Leahey, 1984); *family health promotion* (Bomar, 1989), *family health care* (Hanson & Boyd, 1996), *family nursing* (Bell, Watson, & Wright, 1990; Gilliss, Higley, Roberts, & Martinson, 1989; Friedman, 1992), *family systems nursing* (Wright & Leahey, 1990), and the *nursing of families* (Feetham, Meister, Bell, & Gillis, 1993).

The specialty has its roots in the specialties of community nursing, maternal-child nursing, nurse midwifery, public health nursing, and psychiatric or mental health nursing and in the role of the nurse practitioner. Controversy and ambiguity exist regarding the focus, education, and clients of the family health nurse. Questions often asked include, "Is family health nursing synonymous with community health nursing or mental health nursing?" and "Is it a distinct specialty?"

Although it does overlap other specialties, family health nursing is decidedly a distinct specialty. In other words, the specialty of family health nursing is both old and new and incorporates theories, concepts, and interventions from other nursing specialties. Simultaneously, family health nursing builds on theories and research from disciplines such as family science and health promotion. This text defines family health nursing as nursing actions directed toward improving the quality of family existence by strengthening and collaborating with families.

This relatively new specialty has spawned a cadre of North American and global nursing scholars who author textbooks, organize national and international family nursing conferences, conduct research on issues of families in sickness and wellness across the life span, develop family nursing theories. and publish articles on family nursing and research. A clear indicator of its status as an established specialty is the February 1995 inaugural issue of the *Journal of Family Nursing* (Bell, 1995), a journal that serves as the chief vehicle for dissemination of family nursing research, theory, education, practice outcomes, and issues. Other examples of the globalization of family nursing are the six international family nursing conferences held since 1988. The first was sponsored by the University of Calgary Faculty of Nursing in May 1988, and a conference has followed every 3 years thereafter in Portland, Oregon; Montreal, Canada; Valdivia, Chile; Chicago, Illinois; and Gaborone, Botswana, Africa, in 2003. The first conference held outside of North America was in Chile. In addition, five major textbooks on family nursing, cited throughout this text, are now in their second to fifth editions.

In the past two decades, family nursing has extended globally to curricula, research, and practice in countries such as Africa, Australia, Chile, Brazil, Denmark, Finland, Japan, Mexico, United Kingdom, Sweden, Taiwan, and Thailand (Hanson, 2001; Sugishita, 1999; Wright & Leahey, 2000). The most prominent international center for family nursing is the Family Nursing Unit at the University of Calgary, where theorists Lorraine Wright and Maureen Wright developed the Calgary Family Assessment Model (Wright & Leahey, 2000). Also, in Japan, faculty have extensively used the concept of family nursing in curricula, have family nursing texts translated into Japanese, and also are involved in family research (Sugishita, 1999).

Although family nursing is not widely adopted in the United Kingdom, scholars suggest the efficacy of family nursing for health visitors (Baggaley & Kean, 1999).

Family nursing is a transformative process that increases the capacity of families to attain higher levels of well-being (Anderson, 2000; Ford-Gilboe, 2002). Figure 1-1 shows an example of a framework for implementing this process (Anderson, 2000; Anderson & Tomlinson, 1992; Friedemann, 1995). As shown in Figure 1-1, a collaborative family nursing process includes systematic appraisal of family processes of development, interaction, coping, integrity, and health aspects of life. Other family nursing models are described in Chapter 4.

In family nursing, some disagreement continues about who the client is and how the specialty differs from community health nursing and family therapy. The literature suggests four approaches to family nursing practice: (1) the individual client in the family context, (2) the family as the client, (3) the family interactional system, and (4) family groups in society (Friedman, Bowen, & Jones, 2003; Wright & Leahey, 2000). These four approaches are prominent in guiding family health nursing practice, education, research, and theory development (Friedman et al., 2003; Hanson, 2001); and specialists in family nursing tend to conceptualize the family unit as the client (Wright & Leahey, 2000; Hanson, 2001).

Individual as Client (Family as Context)

In family nursing care in which the individual is considered the client, as depicted in Figure 1-2, the primary focus or foreground is the health status of the individual family member, and the background is the family system or other members in their context as caregivers, resources, or barriers (Wright & Leahey, 1990; Wright & Leahey, 2000). However, to provide competent care to the individual, the nurse needs to assess family realms (interaction, integrity, health, coping, and developmental processes) that may affect the individual's health status and the outcome of interventions (Anderson, 2000). For example, if the goal is to lower one family member's intake of dietary fat, attaining and maintaining this goal will be diffi-

cult without considering the family environment, nutrition, resources, family's rules about food, and internal social support. Family members in continual interaction with each other subtly influence self-care decisions. To help their dieting member make a permanent lifestyle change, they need to coordinate grocery shopping and meal preparation and possibly obtain outside social support.

The Family as Client

As depicted in Figure 1-3, family nursing assessment and capacity building center on strengthening the family as a unit, placing the family in the foreground and the individual in the background. Each family member is assessed, and the family unit as a whole is viewed as greater than the the sum of the individual members (Friedman et al., 2003). One example is when a family nurse practitioner assists the entire family in sleeping better when they have a newborn in the household. Therefore the focus is on the family as client, rather than solely on the newborn who cries at night. When the problem is a family systems issue, the entire family unit is the focus of holistic assessment, empowerment, interaction, and intervention.

Family Systems Nursing

The third approach to family nursing is *family systems nursing* as described by Wright and Leahey (2000) (Figure 1-4). The focus of family systems nursing is on assessment and intervening with the family unit, subsystems, and individuals concurrently when the family members are sick and when they are healthy. For example, when continuing spousal conflict affects other aspects of family life, nursing intervention focuses on the marital dyad for resolution of the conflict while recognizing the importance of family data and processes that influence the outcome. If the issue is lack of time as a couple and sexual intimacy, contributing factors may be household upkeep and childcare responsibilities that cause fatigue and take time. In this example, although the problem is dyadic and interactive in nature, a healthy resolution involves changes in the family system, and the nurse's role is to facilitate functional family interaction or to serve as

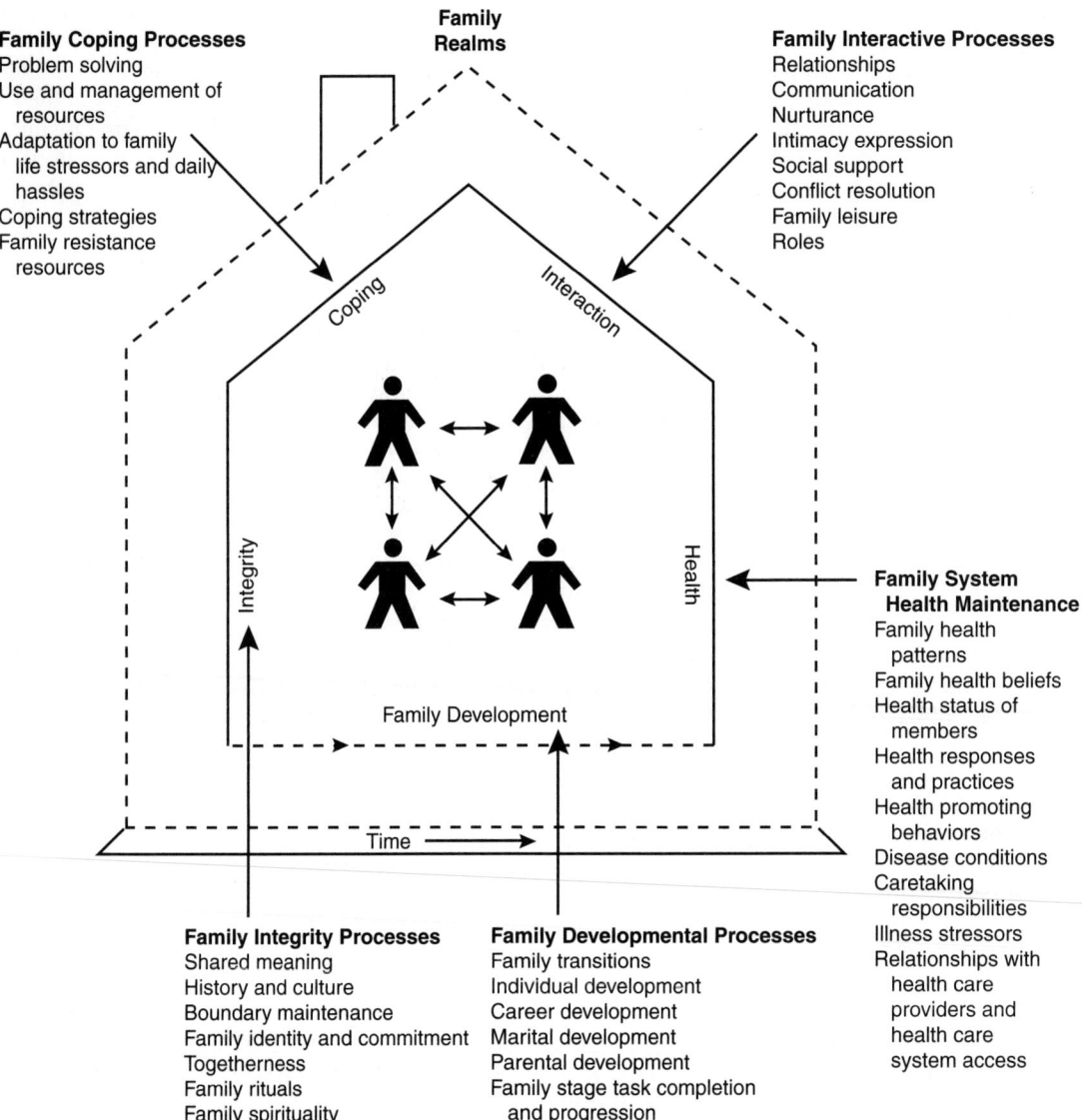

Family Coping Processes
Problem solving
Use and management of
  resources
Adaptation to family
  life stressors and daily
  hassles
Coping strategies
Family resistance
  resources

Family Realms

Family Interactive Processes
Relationships
Communication
Nurturance
Intimacy expression
Social support
Conflict resolution
Family leisure
Roles

Coping

Interaction

Integrity

Health

Family Development

Time →

**Family System
  Health Maintenance**
Family health
  patterns
Family health beliefs
Health status of
  members
Health responses
  and practices
Health promoting
  behaviors
Disease conditions
Caretaking
  responsibilities
Illness stressors
Relationships with
  health care
  providers and
  health care
  system access

Family Integrity Processes
Shared meaning
History and culture
Boundary maintenance
Family identity and commitment
Togetherness
Family rituals
Family spirituality

Family Developmental Processes
Family transitions
Individual development
Career development
Marital development
Parental development
Family stage task completion
  and progression

Figure 1-1 Realms of family life: A focus of family health nursing practice. (Based on data from Anderson, K. H., & Tomlinson, P. [1992]. The family health system as an emerging paradigmatic view for nursing. *Image 24,* 57-63; Anderson, K. H. [2000]. The family health system approach to family systems nursing. *Journal of Family Nursing, 6,* 103-119; Friedemann, M. L. [1995]. *The framework of systemic organization: A conceptual approach to families and nursing.* Thousand Oaks, CA: Sage.)

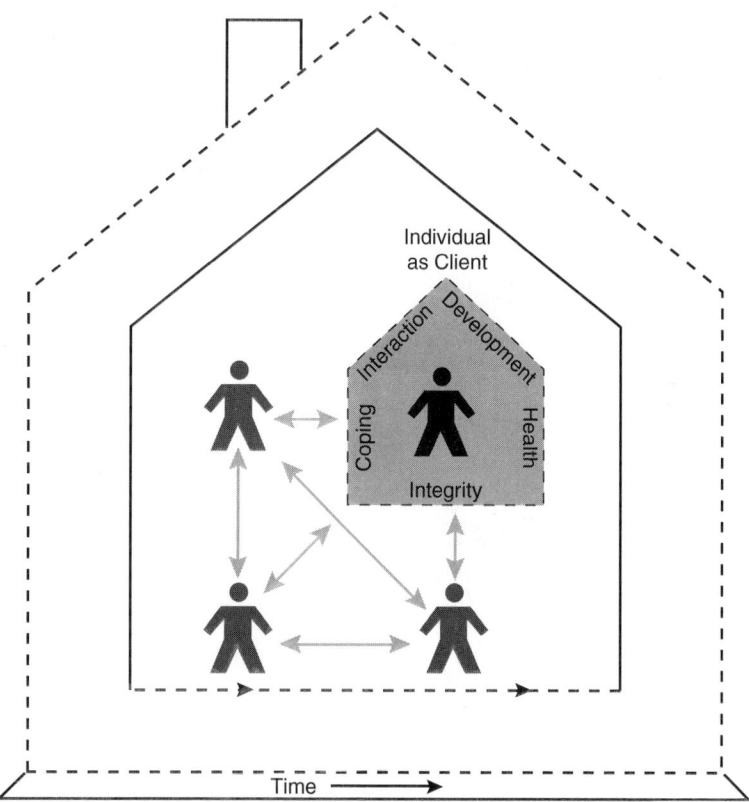

Figure 1-2   Individual as client in the family context.

the moderator as family members explore issues and solve the problem as a unit. The nurse assesses each of the five family processes and assumes a collaborative partnership with the family in decision making about strategies. For example, a change in the family system (e.g., adolescence, a chronic disease, a birth, or a death) creates a need for solutions through adjustments or adaptations in family patterns. In a family whose problem is lack of parenting time as a unit because it is a dual-earner family, the nurse assists the family to negotiate and implement a plan to increase routine couple and family time and shared recreation. Other examples of family-nurse collaboration to promote interaction include providing information on parenting and assistance with communication, decision making, limit setting,

managing illness/health concerns, and negotiation of family roles (Anderson & Tomlinson, 1992; Anderson, 2000; Wright & Leahey, 2000). Some scholars consider this third approach to represent what is specific to family nursing (Friedman et al., 2003; Hanson, 2001).

Family as a Component of Society

Often families share common health or social issues that can be dealt with at the community (aggregate) level (Stanhope & Lancaster, 2000). In this type of family nursing, the family unit is in the background, and the aggregate issue(s) is in the foreground (Figure 1-5). When collaborating with families on community issues, the health practitioner enhances the well-being of multiple-

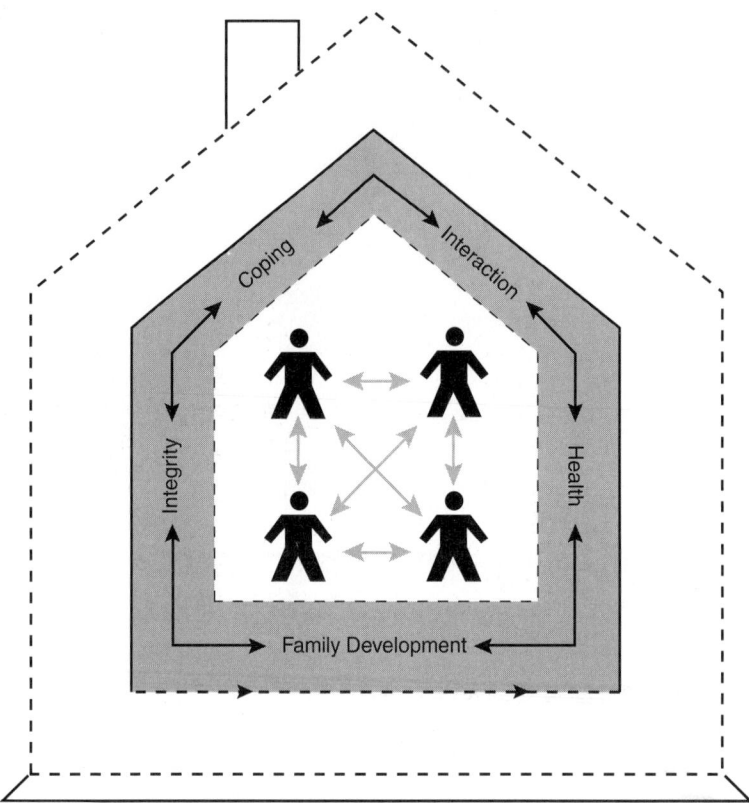

Figure 1-3   Family unit as client.

family units. At the community level, the variables to consider include the social, financial, economic, religious, legal, political, cultural, environmental, and health systems that influence family health.

Examples of family nursing with family aggregates include facilitating parent mutual support groups, empowering teenagers in single-parent families to continue their education, teaching parenting skills to couples, and providing health teaching to families that have members with chronic diseases such as Alzheimer's disease, AIDS, diabetes, or cancer. Family clinical specialist and community health nursing graduate programs focus on family aggregates and community health.

The concept that family nursing is feasible wherever families are encountered prompts the family nurse to decide whether the client is an individual with the family in the background or vice versa. Thus knowing who the client is assists the clinician in illuminating family patterns, collaborating with the family for transformation and healing, and enhancing the family's capacity to promote health (Hartrick, 1997). The use of theories, knowledge, and strategies specific to families and health promotion in guiding transactions with families is crucial.

Defining the Family

The family is central to society and provides the core ingredients that determine the quality of life for its members at all ages. Families of the twenty-first century differ dramatically from families 30 years ago. For example, twenty-first

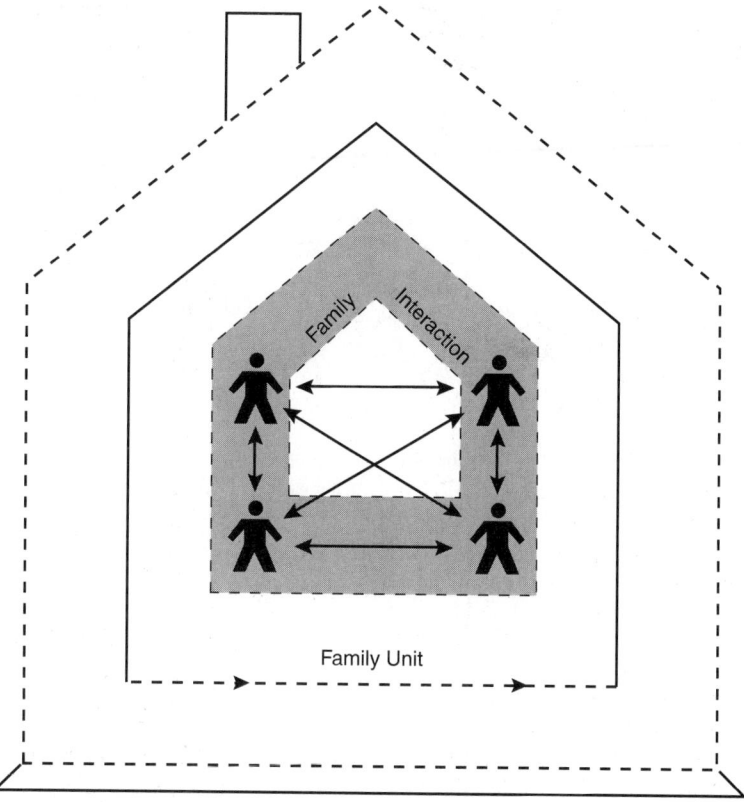

Figure 1-4   Family systems nursing (interpersonal family nursing).

century families are more likely to live separately from extended families, compared with 50 years ago. However, families in some cultures provide different definitions that more broadly reflect an extended family or kin system as family.

In the literature, *family* is defined differently by scholars, organizations, and government agencies. Chapter 2 provides further discussion of family definitions. Basically, a family should be defined as whoever they say they are (Friedman, 2003; Hanson, 2001; Wright & Leahey, 1984; Whall, 1986). For the purposes of this book, *a family is defined as two or more persons who are linked together by intimate association, resources, and values and consider themselves to be a family.*

Because every family is unique, the definition should be broad enough to incorporate familial diversity in structures, functions, values, and ethnicity (Olson & DeFrain, 1994). The definition in current practice often depends on the reason that the clinician, researcher, or theorist wishes to define the family. Therefore clinicians collaborating with families to assess and promote their health should always begin by deriving a definition with the individual or family unit. Chapter 2 discusses this view in more depth, Chapter 10 provides strategies for holistic assessment of the family, and other chapters address how to assess the family in particular realms.

The Function of a Family

The core functions of a family are the exchange of love, affection, and companionship; and provision

Figure 1-5   Family groups in society.

of day-to-day nurturing and care, health care (health promotion, disease prevention, and illness management), economic security, a sense of identity and belonging, raising children, and guidance on commonly held social values. Other functions include serving as a buffer from society and as a bargaining agent between the individual and society.

Defining Family Health

The terms *family health* and *family health promotion* are not interchangeable. Multiple definitions of family health have evolved from anthropological, biological, cultural, developmental, family science, sociological, psychological, religious, and nursing paradigms. *Family health* is a holistic state referring to the complex process of solving, negotiating day-to-day family life events and crises, and providing for quality of life for its members (Bomar, 1989; Demarco, Ford-Gilboe, Friedemann, McCubbin, & McCubbin, 2000). The process encompasses the biological, physical, psychological, sociological, spiritual, cultural, and international aspects of

family life. Chapter 3 examines selected models of family health and family health promotion.

Because of the lack of consensus and conceptual clarity in defining family health, definitions vary depending on their origin (Anderson & Tomlinson, 1992; Bomar & McNeeley, 1996; Denham, 1999; Doherty & Campbell, 1988). Family scientists define healthy families as resilient (McCubbin, 1993) and possessing a balance of cohesion and adaptability facilitated by good communication (Olson, McCubbin, Barnes, Larsen, Muxen, & Wilson, 1983). Family therapists' definitions often emphasize optimal family functioning and freedom from psychopathology (Bradshaw, 1988). From the developmental perspective, healthy families complete developmental tasks at appropriate times (Duval & Miller, 1985). Taking a sociological view, Pratt (1976) describes a healthy family as an *energized family*—a family that responds to the needs and interests of all its members, copes effectively with life transitions and problems, is flexible and egalitarian in distribution of power, experiences regular interaction among members and with the community, and collectively expresses a health-promoting lifestyle.

Other holistic definitions include the totality or *gestalt* that encompasses the family's internal and external environment. Anderson (2000) states that "family health promotion, maintenance, and restoration must necessarily focus on the interactions in the family unit and the enhancement of interactive, developmental, coping, integrity, and health and lifestyle components that compose a healthy family life" (p. 106). A holistic definition of family health encompasses all aspects of family life including interaction and the health care function. The family health care function (Bomar & McNeely, 1996; Friedman et al., 2003; Friedemann, 1995) involves nutrition, the environment, recreation, communication, sleep and rest patterns, problem solving, sexuality, time, space, coping with stress, hygiene and safety, spirituality, illness, health promotion/protection, and emotional health.

Despite the lack of conceptual clarity and consensus on definition among disciplines, family health is a dynamic and complex process that is interactive functionally, contextually, and structurally (Denham, 1999). It is more than the absence of disease in a family member or an absence of dysfunction in family dynamics; it is rather a state of family well-being. For the purposes of this book, *family health is defined as encompassing a family's quality of life, the health of each family member, family interactions, spirituality, nutrition, coping, environment, recreation and routines, sleep, and sexuality*. The scant research on promoting health in families necessitates research to create a theoretical model for studying family health (Denham, 1999).

Defining Family Health Promotion

Family health promotion is the process of achieving family well-being in the biological, emotional, physical, and spiritual realms for individual members and the family unit. Canadian nurse theorist F. Moyra Allen has used the term *health work* to label the process a family uses to maintain or attain well-being (Allen & Warner, 2002; Ford-Gilboe, 2002). The promotion of family health is discussed in more depth in Chapter 3 and throughout this text.

Historical Factors Influencing the Development of Family Health Nursing

It is crucial for family health nurses to understand the historical legacy of this evolving specialty. Family health nursing has its roots in prehistoric times, and the role of women has always been central in family health, for it was their responsibility to care for family members who fell ill, to concoct herbal medications, to prepare food, to make clothing, to provide shelter, to devise remedies, and in their housekeeping to promote health and wellness with a clean environment. Ham and Chamings (1983) noted that "in the pre-industrial era, the home and family were basic units of society, and . . . informal nursing was the work of women in general and encompassed the care of whole families" (p. 34). According to Ford (1979), "The concept of family nursing has always been with us" (p. 88). The following discussion and Table 1-1 trace the historical events that have affected the development of current family nursing practice.

The Nightingale Era

Florence Nightingale advanced both district nursing of the sick and poor and the work of "health missioners" through "health-at-home" teaching. The exorbitant mortality and morbidity rates of British troops during the Crimean War illustrated to Nightingale that British soldiers were subject more "to death in the barracks" than to death by bullets and bayonets, confirming for her the vital importance of improving the health of British citizenry. Realizing the obligation of the mother, she writes: "Upon womanhood the national health, as far as the household goes, depends. . . . I know of no systematic teaching for the ordinary mother, how to keep the baby in health, certainly the most important function to make a healthy nation" (1949, p. 24). From this philosophical and practical perspective, she also promoted the concept that people should be taught the laws of health and how to use them to improve their own conditions.

In her book *Notes on Nursing: What It Is, and What It Is Not*, Nightingale (1946) admonishes mothers not to say, "I am not a doctor. I must

TABLE 1-1   Historical Factors Contributing to the Development of Family Health as a Focus for Nursing

Pre-Nightingale era	Revolutionary War "camp followers": example of family health focus before Nightingale
Mid 1800s	Nightingale influences district nurses and health missioners to maintain clean environment for patients' home and family
	Family members provide for soldiers' needs during Civil War through Ladies' Aid Societies and Women's Central Association for Relief
Late 1800s	Industrial Revolution and immigration influence focus of public health nursing on prevention of illness, health education, and care of the sick for both families and communities
	Lillian Wald establishes Henry Street Visiting Nurse Service (1893)
	Focus on family during childbearing by maternal-child nurses and midwives
Early 1900s	School of nursing established in New York City (1903)
	First White House Conference on Children (1909)
	Red Cross Town and Country Nursing Service (1912)
	Margaret Sanger opens first birth control clinic (1916)
	Family planning and quality care available for families
	Mary Breckinridge forms Frontier Nursing Service (1925)
	Nurses assigned to families
	Red Cross Public Health Nursing Service meets rural health needs after stock market crash (1929)
	Federal Emergency Relief Act passed (1933)
	Social Security Act passed (1935)
	Psychiatric/mental health nursing begins family therapy focus (late 1930s)
1960s	Concept of family as a unit of care introduced into basic nursing curriculum
	National League for Nursing (NLN) requires emphasis on families and communities in nursing curriculum
	Family-centered approach in maternal-child nursing and midwifery programs
	Nurse practitioner movement—programs to provide primary care to children (1965)
	Shift from public health nursing to community health nursing
	Family studies and research produce family theories
1970s	Changing health care system with focus on maintaining health and returning emphasis on family health
	Development and refinement of nursing conceptual models that consider the family as a unit of analysis or care (i.e., King, Newman, Orem, Rogers, and Roy)
	Many specialties focus on the family (e.g., hospice, oncology, geriatrics, school health, psychiatric/mental health, occupational health, and home health)
	Master's and doctoral programs focus on the family (e.g., family health nursing, community health nursing, psychiatric/mental health, and family counseling and therapy)
	American Nurses Association (ANA) Standards of Nursing Practice (1973)
	Surgeon General's Report (1979)
1980s	ANA Social Policy Statement (1980)
	White House Conference on Families
	Greater emphasis on health from very young to very old
	Increasing emphasis on obesity, stress, chemical dependency, and parenting skills
	Graduate level specialization with emphasis on primary care outside of acute-care settings, health teaching, and client self-care
	Increased use of wellness and nursing models in providing care
	Promoting Health/Preventing Disease: Objectives for The Nation (1980) by U.S. Department of Health and Human Services
	Development of family science as a discipline
	Increased family nursing research

TABLE 1-1	Historical Factors Contributing to the Development of Family Health as a Focus for Nursing—cont'd
	National Center for Nursing Research founded with a health promotion and disease prevention research section
	Healthy Cities Initiative (World Health Organization, 1986)
	First International Family Nursing Conference (1988)
1990s	*Healthy People 2000: National Health Promotion and Disease Prevention Objectives* (1990) published by U.S. Department of Health and Human Services
	Nursing's Agenda for Health Care Reform (ANA, 1991)
	Family Leave legislation (1991)
	National Institute for Nursing Research established (1993)
	Journal of Family Nursing (1995)
	Personal Responsibility and Work Opportunity Reconciliation Act (1996)
	The Child Health Insurance Program (CHIP) 1997
	WHO *Health for All for the 21st Century* (1998)
Twenty-First Century	*Healthy People 2010* by U.S. Department of Health and Human Services
	NINR *Strategic Plans on Reducing Health Disparities* (2000)
	National Center of Minority Health and Health Disparities (2000)
	WHO *Family Health for Nursing*. Context, conceptual framework, and curriculum (2000)

leave this to doctors" (p. 6). She notes that girls in her society were being taught such things as astronomy but not "those laws which God has assigned to the relations of our bodies with the world in which He has put them" (p. 7). She further complained that mothers did not consider those "laws of life" worthy of study in order "to give their children healthy existences. . . . They call it medical . . . knowledge, fit only for doctors" (p. 7). Nightingale knew that the high infant mortality rate in London related to mothers' lack of knowledge regarding sanitation and believed that improved hygiene in the home would contribute greatly to diminishing the problem. The use of district nurses and health missioners was part of her plan to teach women how to keep their homes healthy and care for ill relatives (Ham & Chamings, 1983).

Nurses in Colonial America

Women in Colonial America continued the centuries-old tradition of the female householder in nurturing and sustaining family wellness. "Nursing care" during the Revolutionary War was provided by women "camp followers," who often included untrained "nurses" among the wives of soldiers; these women performed a number of functions such as providing comfort, cheer, and encouragement; mending uniforms; darning socks; preparing meals; cleaning; doing the laundry; and providing comfort and physical care for the sick and wounded. Mary Ludwig Hays McCauley, a camp follower, gained national recognition as "Molly Pitcher" for carrying water to thirsty soldiers in her husband John Hays' regiment (Selavan, 1975).

The Civil War (1861-1865)

With rumors of an imminent civil war, American women prepared to care for ill and wounded soldiers. They organized ladies' aid societies, known by various names and led by various women. These ladies met regularly to wrap bandages, sew, prepare food, gather clothing, collect books, prepare medicines, and provide other items that might be needed by the soldiers (Kalisch & Kalisch, 1986; Matejski, 1986).

Among their leaders was Dr. Elizabeth Blackwell, a contributor to the New York Women's Central Association for Relief, and Dorothea Dix, the Superintendent of Women Nurses of the Army. According to Matejski (1986), "Thousands of women whose husbands, sons, and brothers had volunteered for the Army reported for nursing duty" (p. 45). One hundred women received a month's training at either Bellevue Hospital or New York Hospital to prepare them for nursing work before assignment to hospitals and nursing duties in the army. Others served without formal training. All fed and bathed sick and injured men and dressed their wounds. Their other hospital duties entailed housekeeping, cleaning, and cooking.

The Industrial Revolution and Immigration

During the industrial revolution of the late nineteenth century, family members increasingly worked outside the home rather than on a family farm or in a family business. Men especially began to work in factories, leaving the running of the home and the care of children to women. During the last decades of the century, the increase in immigration produced a population of families who needed the income of children for economic survival, resulting in increases in child labor, the difficulties of keeping children in school, and the spread of contagious diseases.

The beginning of public health nursing in the United States along with contributions of Lillian Wald, Linda Rogers, and others in the establishment of the Henry Street Visiting Nurse Service (1893) and its school of nursing (1903) were responses to the postindustrial environment, altered by the massive influx of immigrants, particularly on New York City's Lower East Side. Wald established the Henry Street Settlement House in the immigrant slums in 1893 (Christy, 1970). "The public health nurses of the 19th century were involved in the beginning of the labor movement, concerned with the health of industrial workers, immigrants and their families, and the exploitation of women and children" (Heinrich, 1983, p. 318). Although the family and the community were the intended focus of public health nursing, in practice, the individual continued to receive primary attention. Maternal-child nursing courses and the concepts of family care with specialized clinical treatment were incorporated into the basic nursing curricula of

training schools as an outgrowth of public health nursing and school nursing (Ford, 1979).

Maternity Nursing and Midwifery

Early in the twentieth century, maternity nursing, nurse midwifery, and community nursing also focused on the quality of family health. For example, Margaret Higgins Sanger Slee fought for family planning information to be made available to American women, particularly in the state of New York. She became aware of the contraceptive needs of poor women during her training at White Plains Hospital when many women who could not afford additional children asked the young nurse for contraceptive advice, which she felt inadequate to provide. Later, in the immigrant tenements on the Lower East Side of Manhattan, Margaret Sanger dealt with the horrors of botched illegal abortions and witnessed desperate families receiving insufficient family planning information from physicians and clergy. To correct this social injustice, Sanger opened the first birth control clinic in the United States in 1916 (Forster, 1984; Ham & Chamings, 1983; Kalisch & Kalisch, 1986) and was pilloried for her efforts. Undaunted, she continued a lifelong fight for the rights of women.

Mary Breckinridge, another nurse, made major contributions to family health nursing. Her interest in the care of sick children developed when she was a volunteer nurse in France after World War I. In 1925, after she received midwifery training in London, she returned to Wendover, Kentucky, where she formed the Frontier Nursing Service to train nurses to meet the health needs of the mountain families of Leslie County. There, with two other nurses, she practiced midwifery until her death in 1965 (Ham & Chamings, 1983; Kalisch & Kalisch, 1986; Pletsch, 1981). Her focus on maternity care contributed markedly to the family-centered approach to nursing care.

Expansion of Public Health Nursing Services during the Depression

After the stock market crash of 1929, the health care needs of families in rural America were met primarily by the Red Cross Public Health Nursing

Service, begun by Lillian Wald in 1912 as the Red Cross Town and Country Nursing Service. More nurses were needed in rural areas for public health work during the Depression; however, those who had lost their jobs in the urban areas were not educationally prepared to be rural nurses. This situation forced the nursing profession to re-evaluate nursing education and to assist those who were willing to be reeducated for this new area of practice (Fitzpatrick, 1975).

Many federal programs that provided help for families, women, and children were established during the 1930s as a result of the Depression. The Federal Emergency Relief Act (FERA) of 1933 subsidized voluntary nursing agencies. In 1935, the Social Security Act provided for adequate public health services, and its Title V provided child health services and aid to disabled children. Fitzpatrick (1975) summarizes the period in stating that the "precedents set by government during the Great Depression and through the programs of the 'New Deal' changed the complexion of all that was to follow in health care and nursing services" (p. 2190).

The Nurse Practitioner Movement

The expansion of the nurse's role in well-child care and maternal-child nursing during the early 1960s paved the way for the establishment of pediatric and family nurse practitioner programs later in the decade. Initially, nurse practitioners concentrated on providing primary care for family members across the life span (individuals in the family context). Nurse practitioners with a definitive family focus include the family nurse practitioner and the psychiatric mental health nurse practitioner with a subspecialty in family care. At the beginning of the twenty-first century, there are two types of nurse practitioners: one acts as a physician extender in a medical model practice; the other uses a nursing model practice and focuses on individuals in the family context rather than solely on disease. Education for nurse practitioners has progressed from continuing education programs to graduate preparation, with course work specifically focused on family theory and family nursing. National certification requiring a master's degree is recommended to maintain quality and standardization of care. The American Nurses Credentialing Center and the American Academy of Nurse Practitioners provide certification. Currently, many practitioners orient their practices toward health promotion, maintaining an independent nursing role while collaborating with other health care professionals in ambulatory care settings such as physicians' offices and nurse-managed centers. In the past, the definition of family nurse was often considered to be synonymous with the definition of nurse practitioner; however, this is no longer the case.

Psychiatric or Mental Health Nursing

Although family therapy had its roots in the work of Ackerman in the late 1930s, it was not until the 1970s that the mental health nursing role with families began to emerge (Ham & Chamings, 1983). Ford (1979) noted that "early hospital discharge of the mentally ill forced public health nurses to examine their abilities to cope with family problems in this relocation effort and seek consultation from psychiatric nurse clinicians and others in the mental health field" (p. 91). The evolution of concepts such as family systems and family stress influenced the incorporation of the family as a unit of care into psychiatric nursing. As a result, educational programs in the 1960s and 1970s began to integrate psychiatric/mental health nursing concepts into all aspects of the baccalaureate curriculum and included the family as a major area of study in graduate psychiatric mental health nursing curricula. Today, national certification as a psychiatric or mental health nurse practitioner with a focus on family is available from the American Nurses Credentialing Center. Additional information is available on the American Nurses Association (ANA) (Nursing World) website; its uniform resource locator (URL) is listed in the Website Resources box at the end of the chapter.

Public Health Nursing and Community Health Nursing

The early 1960s witnessed disagreement on the terms *public* health nursing and *community* health nursing, and to some authorities, it was more than just a matter of semantics (Logan & Dawkins, 1986). The major difference was the increased focus on community and family health. In fact, by the mid 1960s, a number of factors had emerged that would contribute to the creation of community health nursing as a specialty. These factors included recognition of the importance of community health nursing in nursing education, resolution of confusion about the role and responsibilities of the community health nurse, and changes in society and health care delivery (Spradley, 1985). Archer (1982) described community health nursing as a "synthesis of public health science and nursing science" (p. 442). According to Spradley (1985), "The purpose of this synthesis is to improve the health of the entire community" (p. 59). Other characteristics of community health nursing seen as salient to the development of family health nursing are its focus on the family and community as the unit of concern and its emphasis on health promotion and disease prevention, interdisciplinary collaboration, and client participation. Stanhope and Lancaster (2000) conceptualize the specialty as "community-oriented nursing practice," which is a philosophy of service delivery. In the new millennium there is agreement that the specialties in community-oriented nursing practice are delineated as public health nursing practice, community health nursing practice, and community-based nursing practice. Each is unique with some overlapping client bases, settings, interventions, and services (Stanhope & Lancaster, 2000, p. 15). The focus for public health nurses is the community (population aggregate) as a whole, and the focus for community health nurses is the health of individuals, families, and groups (Clark, 2003; Nies & McEwen; 2001; Stanhope & Lancaster, 2000). Using this framework, family nurses collaborating with families outside health care institutions have a community-based practice.

Impact of Family Studies and Family Research

Since the 1950s, researchers in more than 20 disciplines have studied the family, and through investigation, have produced family assessment inventories and theoretical frameworks. These disciplines include behavioral health, educational

and family psychology, family ecology, family social science, home economics, sociology, psychology, health education, preventive medicine, public health, social work, theology, and law. Nursing has not only used theories from these related fields but has also developed some of its own and carried out its own research on the family as the unit of measurement. In the 1980s and 1990s, this interdisciplinary work became known as *family science*, and it is now considered by some to be a distinct discipline with its own body of knowledge (Burr & Leigh, 1983). Building on the developments in family studies and family research, many schools have established graduate programs in family science, family and community health nursing, and family health nursing (Hanson & Heims, 1992).

The 1990s

With the escalating costs of health care in the United States, a decreasing number of Americans can obtain appropriate care at a price they can afford. Among the many proposals to reform the health care system, two noteworthy examples are *Nursing's Agenda for Health Care Reform* (ANA, 1992) and *Achieving Access for All Americans* (ANA, 2000). The goal of each is to achieve "access, quality, and service at affordable costs" for all Americans. The proposals call for a restructured health care system that focuses on a national health care access policy and the facilitation of consumer access to competently provided health care in familiar and convenient sites such as the home, nurse-managed centers, schools, and workplaces. Also, the plans call for a shift in focus from a primary emphasis on acute care or illness care and cure to wellness and preventive care. Vulnerable populations such as women, children, senior citizens, the poor, and low-income minorities receive priority as an investment in the future health and prosperity of the United States in this approach.

Modern-Day Factors Shaping the Development of Family Health Nursing

Multiple changes continue to shape family health nursing. As shown in Figure 1-6, numerous phenomena affect this dynamic and revived specialty. An in-depth discussion of each of these

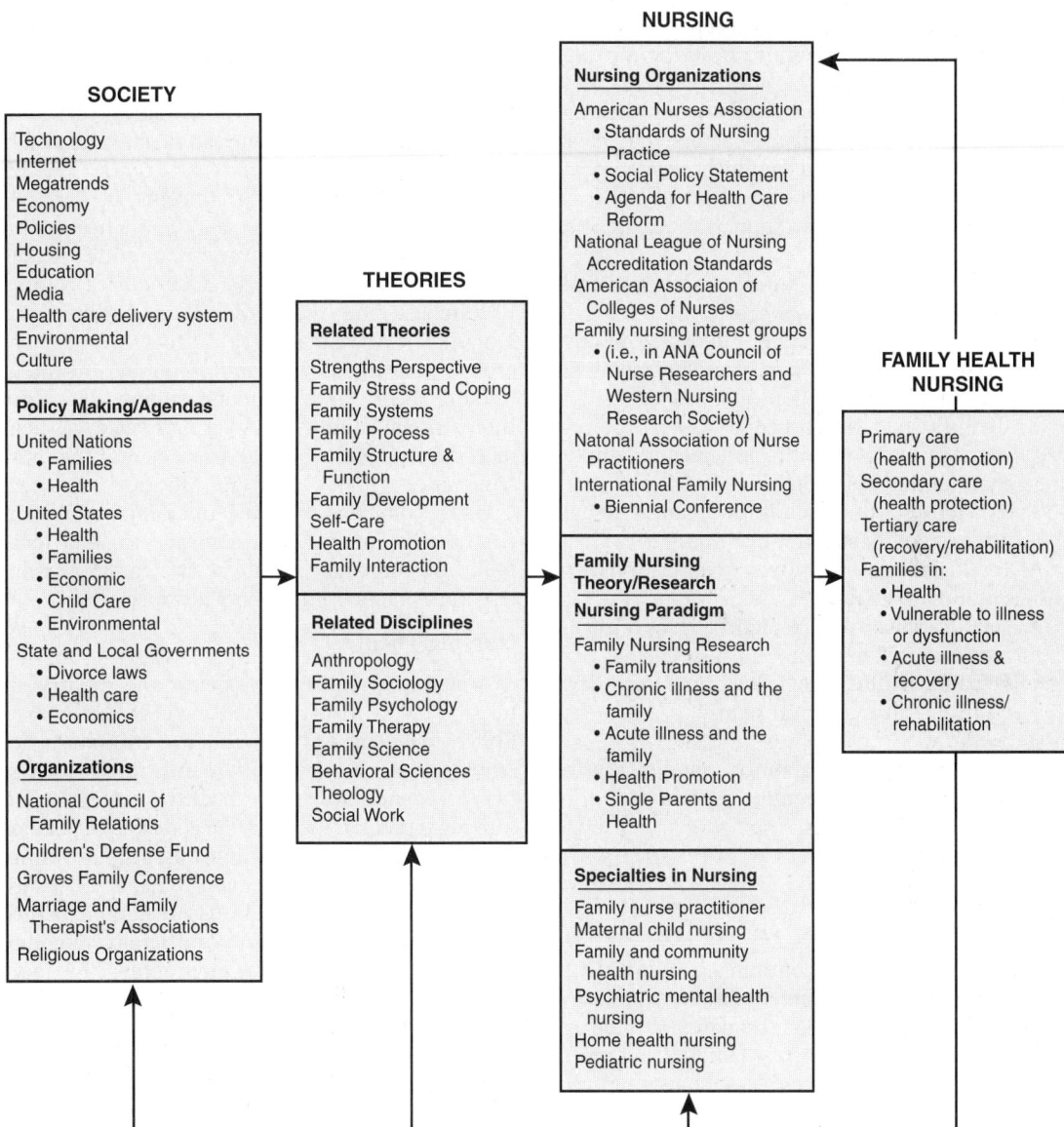

SOCIETY

Technology
Internet
Megatrends
Economy
Policies
Housing
Education
Media
Health care delivery system
Environmental
Culture

Policy Making/Agendas

United Nations
  • Families
  • Health
United States
  • Health
  • Families
  • Economic
  • Child Care
  • Environmental
State and Local Governments
  • Divorce laws
  • Health care
  • Economics

Organizations

National Council of
  Family Relations
Children's Defense Fund
Groves Family Conference
Marriage and Family
  Therapist's Associations
Religious Organizations

THEORIES

Related Theories

Strengths Perspective
Family Stress and Coping
Family Systems
Family Process
Family Structure &
  Function
Family Development
Self-Care
Health Promotion
Family Interaction

Related Disciplines

Anthropology
Family Sociology
Family Psychology
Family Therapy
Family Science
Behavioral Sciences
Theology
Social Work

NURSING

Nursing Organizations

American Nurses Association
  • Standards of Nursing
    Practice
  • Social Policy Statement
  • Agenda for Health Care
    Reform
National League of Nursing
  Accreditation Standards
American Associaion of
  Colleges of Nurses
Family nursing interest groups
  • (i.e., in ANA Council of
    Nurse Researchers and
    Western Nursing
    Research Society)
Natonal Association of Nurse
  Practitioners
International Family Nursing
  • Biennial Conference

**Family Nursing
Theory/Research
Nursing Paradigm**

Family Nursing Research
  • Family transitions
  • Chronic illness and the
    family
  • Acute illness and the
    family
  • Health Promotion
  • Single Parents and
    Health

Specialties in Nursing

Family nurse practitioner
Maternal child nursing
Family and community
  health nursing
Psychiatric mental health
  nursing
Home health nursing
Pediatric nursing

**FAMILY HEALTH
NURSING**

Primary care
  (health promotion)
Secondary care
  (health protection)
Tertiary care
  (recovery/rehabilitation)
Families in:
  • Health
  • Vulnerable to illness
    or dysfunction
  • Acute illness &
    recovery
  • Chronic illness/
    rehabilitation

Figure 1-6   Variables influencing the evolution of contemporary family health nursing.

factors is beyond the scope of this chapter; therefore, only selected contributions from the nursing profession, related disciplines, service and professional organizations, and policy-making organizations are highlighted. Factors that have most significantly affected family health nursing are in the following list. However, currently there is little political administrative support to implement these agenda.

- Professionalization of nursing practice and nursing education
- Development of nursing theories, family nursing frameworks, family nursing research, and family interventions and outcomes
- Evolution of the concept of health promotion, family health, and related family theories and concepts
- Evolution of the disciplines of family social science and behavioral health
- Emphasis of professional organizations on families and health
- Health objectives of national and international organizations
- Dynamic nature of society and public policy
- Family research and family assessment measures
- National and international family health promotion and prevention agenda

Contemporary Nursing

The Nursing Profession

The nursing profession continues to emphasize family health care in a number of documents. For example, many of the ANA's standards of nursing include family issues across the family life course. Standards for clinical specialties such as gerontological nursing (ANA, 2001a), public health nursing (ANA, 1999), pediatric clinical practice nursing (ANA, 1996), and psychiatric/mental health nursing practice (ANA, 2001b) emphasize the family as a focus for nursing practice. Other examples of the linkage between family and nursing practice are noted in the ANA's *Nursing's Social Policy Statement* (1980, 1995), *Nursing's Agenda for Health Care Reform* (ANA, 1992), and *Nursing's Agenda for the Future* (2002); *Healthy People 2000*; and *Healthy People 2010*. Although specific standards for family health nursing have not been developed, many standards mention families or suggest that families are integral to implementing nursing care.

In the past decade, as the attention of health care professionals has turned to promoting health and preventing dysfunction in families, nursing began to incorporate such concepts as wellness, health promotion, self-care, and family health into family nursing. Within many nursing organizations (e.g., the ANA's Council of Nurse Researchers and the Western and Midwestern Nursing Research Society), there are interest groups that focus on family nursing research, nursing theory, and health promotion. The First International Family Nursing Conference was held in 1988 in Calgary, Alberta, Canada; and the third conference (1994), held in Montreal, Quebec, Canada, coincided with the International Year of the Family. Families will continue to be a focal point of nursing's attention as family nursing research, practice, and theory advance.

Nursing Theories

The evolution of nursing science and theories of nursing by theorists such as King (1981), Neuman (1982), Newman (1994), Orem (1980), Rogers (1980), and Roy (1984) contributed to the development of family health nursing. The nursing paradigm includes the concepts of person, nursing, health, and environment. Questions regarding this paradigm remain: What is the family health nursing paradigm? Is it family, family health, family environment, and family nursing? Or is the family simply the environment for individual health? Is the family unit the sole client, or is the individual the client?

Loveland-Cherry in Chapter 3 and Kaakinen and Hanson in Chapter 4 of this text discuss the contributions of nurse theorists to family health promotion and family nursing. The writings of nursing theorists and scholars (Friedman, 1992; Friedemann, 1995; Newman, 1994; Pender, 1987, 1996; Pender, Murdaugh, & Parsons, 2002; Schlotfeldt, 1987) clearly indicate that the goal of family health nursing is to enhance the well-being of the family unit.

Nursing Education

A number of crucial factors influence the shaping of the curricula of schools of nursing. These variables include the use of the nursing paradigm as the basis for curricular planning; recommendations given in the accreditation standards for schools of nursing; the ANA's *Nursing's Social Policy Statement* (1995), and the ANA's 24 standards of nursing practice; consumer demands and changing societal norms; and the global and national policy agenda for health promotion and prevention. As a consequence of these factors and essential documents, numerous family nursing graduate programs have emerged to prepare specialists to care for families through the various types of family nursing practice, and undergraduate curricula have been strengthened to prepare family nurse generalists (Hanson & Heims, 1992; Hanson, 2001). Table 1-2 describes the levels of preparation for family nursing. However, a lack of consistency in curricular design, content, theory, organization of curricula, titles of graduates, and conceptual frameworks used has been noted (Hanson & Heims, 1992).

Family Nursing Research

Although complex and sometimes flawed, family-focused research in nursing has evolved as the result of a nursing and interdisciplinary interest in families (Gilliss & Davis, 1993). Family nursing research has progressed in the past 20 years from a focus on family dyads of mother and infant or husband and wife to also include the family as the unit of analysis. Other research subjects involve the impact of chronic illness and the effects of transitions across the life span on families and individual members (Hymovich & Hoagopian, 1992; McCubbin, 1993; Knafl & Gilliss, 2002). Commitment to family nursing research has been demonstrated by the planning and initiation of the *Journal of Family Nursing* in 1995 by a group of family nurse scholars (Bell, 1995). Further, the National Institute of Nursing Research (NINR) annually awards grants for master's, doctoral, and postdoctoral students in nursing research.

TABLE 1-2   Levels of Family Nursing Practice

Level of Practice	Generalist/Specialist	Education	Client
Expert	Advanced Specialist	Doctorate	All Levels Family Nursing Theory Development Family Nursing Research
Proficient	Advanced Specialist	Master's Degree with Added Experience	All Levels Beginning Family Nursing Research
Competent	Beginning Specialist	Master's Degree	Individual in the Family Context Interpersonal Family Nursing Family Unit as Client Family Aggregates
Advanced Beginner	Generalist	Bachelor's Degree with Experience	Individual in the Family Context Interpersonal Family Nursing (Family Systems Nursing) Family Unit as Client
Novice	Generalist	Bachelor's Degree	Individual in the Family Context

Data compiled from Friedemann, M. L. (1989). The concept of family nursing. *Journal of Advanced Nursing 14*, 211-221; and Benner, P. (2001). *Novice to expert: Excellence and power in clinical nursing practice*. Menlo Park, CA: Prentice Hall.

Family-focused research conducted before the 1970s is often described as sparse and fraught with methodological inconsistencies. In the 1990s the quantity increased and quality improved (Houck & Kodadek, 2001). Scholars urge the conduct of family research topics related to family issues across the life span. An example is the need for research on the health promotion of family caregivers (Acton, 2002). Evidence of the growing emphasis on family related research is noted in NINR's *Research Themes for the Future* (NINR, 2003). The document delineates five nursing research priorities: changing lifestyle behaviors for better health, managing the effects of chronic illness to improve the quality of life, health care practice, self-management of chronic illness symptoms, informal family caregiving, effective strategies to reduce health disparities, harnessing advanced technologies to serve human need, and enhancing the end-of-life experiences for patients and families (NINR, 2003). Readers are encouraged to consult the NINR website for updates, research priorities, and grant opportunities. See the Website Resources box at the end of the chapter for the website's URL.

Related Disciplines

Theoretical advances in related disciplines such as anthropology, family life education, family ecology, psychology, sociology, social work, health promotion, and family counseling/therapy have contributed to family nursing science. In addition, research by family scientists (Doherty & Campbell, 1988; Olson, 2002; McCubbin, 1993; McAdoo, 1999; Pasley & Ihinger-Tallman, 1995) has provided frameworks, theories, and assessment measures for understanding and assessing the health and functioning of families. Family social scientists continue to provide rich resources and a network of colleagues for family nurses. One example is the Life Innovations website for the Marital Communication and Empowering Families and Couples Programs, which is the result of hundreds of research studies on family cohesion and adaptability under the leadership of family scientist David Olson (Olson, 2002). This website's URL is also listed in the Website Resources box.

Family Organizations

Many organizations have contributed to the evolution of family nursing. Interdisciplinary organizations provide publications on the status of families and children, disseminate research on family issues across the life span and the health-illness cycle, and serve as a vehicle to facilitate networking and collaboration. Readers will find several of these organizations and their website URLs listed in the Website Resources box at the end of the chapter. Although there is no formal family nursing organization, family nurses have formal interest groups within a number of interdisciplinary organizations such as the National Council on Family Relations (NCFR), the American Public Health Association, and national groups of marriage and family counselors and therapists. From 1983 until recently, a family nursing focus group within the NCFR met at the annual meeting. More than 100 family nurses from the United States, Canada, and the international community were members of this focus group. Other sections in NCFR to which nurses currently belong include those on family and health single-parent families, remarriage and step-parenting, farm families, ethnic minority families, theory construction, research methodology, family life education and enrichment, family therapy, and family action sections. For more information on NCFR, consult the website listed at the end of this chapter.

National and International Agendas for Family Health

In North America and throughout the world, the concern for health and the quality of life in families has heightened. In the past 30 years nations and communities have joined efforts to understand health promotion and the determinants of health. Many international and national conferences were held with the agendum of health promotion. The World Health Organization set the global health promotion agenda. Consequently WHO, nations, and local communities followed up with their initiatives, which are discussed briefly in the following sections. Examples of initiatives include the WHO's *Health Cities,* Canada's *Health Canada,* and the United States' *Healthy People.*

International Agenda for Healthy Families

The United Nations, the Pan American Health Organization, and WHO maintain concern about the health of individuals, families, communities, and the nations of the globe (Zöllner & Lessor, 1998). For example, WHO initiated the *Healthy Cities* program in 1986. Support for the *Healthy Cities* projects was provided for by the Canadian and U.S. federal governments and private foundations such as the W. K. Kellogg Foundation. The major goals of *Healthy Cities* projects are to

- Reduce inequities in health care and improve access to services
- Develop local policies for healthy citizens
- Strengthen community, social, and physical environments that support family development of healthy lifestyles
- Emphasize health promotion
- Increase primary care provided by local health services (Flynn & Ivanov, 2000)

Barriers to the successful implementation of the WHO *Healthy Cities* projects include lack of political support, lack of broad community representation, and cities with large populations.

Activities of these projects involve city officials, individuals, and families in designing health-promoting and disease prevention activities. For example, the Canadian government (Health Canada, 2001) places a major emphasis on improving family health. This is discussed in the Canadian Perspectives box. The United Kingdom employs "health visitors," and more recently, family nurses who have a goal of improving the quality of individual and family health. Similarly, numerous cities around the world have implemented participative *Healthy Cities* projects that include families.

The United Nations (1991) designated 1994 as "The International Year of the Family" (IYF). The key goals of the IYF were to (1) provide information at national, state, and local levels; (2) communicate and encourage dialogue with and between local governments and people at the grass-roots level; (3) support active partnerships among governments, volunteer organizations, businesses, and labor organizations; (4) review legislation relevant to the health of families; and (5) encourage research on family issues.

Further, the IYF agenda included goals for governments, voluntary organizations, national governmental organizations, the media, opinion leaders, social services, family organizations, education, research, and families. Selected educational goals included (1) the use of educational networks to discuss family needs; (2) the encouragement of family-centered activities in health and education, taking into account the variety of family types; (3) the provision of special education sessions for families with special needs; and (4) further encouragement of research on the role of families in various cultural and social contexts.

The IYF agenda for families aimed to (1) develop family councils to make decisions and respect the capabilities, dignity, and needs of all family members; (2) stress the responsibilities of all with regard to children and disadvantaged members; (3) enhance the feeling of family togetherness through gatherings, shared meals, and leisure activities; and (4) motivate all family members to effectively share all household and other responsibilities.

The current global health promotion agenda was set forth by the 1997 *Jakarta Declaration on Leading Health Promotion into the 21st Century* (WHO, 1997) and created at the Fourth International Conference on Health Promotion. The major tenets of this document are (1) health promotion is an investment in the development of health, which is a human right; (2) the determinants of health (peace shelter, education, social security, food, income, empowerment of women, social justice, a stable environment, respect for human rights, and equity) are global challenges to health; and (3) research demonstrates that health promotion makes a difference in achieving equity in health. The declaration challenges global, national, and local decision makers and policy makers to "unlock the potential for health promotion" in societies, communities, and families. This document provided the basis for the WHO (1998) document *Health for All in the 21st Century* that is used around the globe as support for the need for policies for health promotion among nations, communities, workplaces, schools, and families.

The North American focus on health promotion and the rhetoric of public leaders about the concern

CANADIAN PERSPECTIVES
MILESTONES OF FAMILY NURSING IN CANADA

Nicole Letourneau, PhD, MN, RN
University of Alberta
Jane Drummond, PhD, RN
University of Alberta

Many events have shaped the course of family nursing in Canada. Several events stand out. First, in the 1970s, Moyra Allen of McGill University in Montreal, Quebec, posed a model of nursing in which the unit of central concern is the family (Kravitz & Frey, 1989). This was a departure from other nursing models of the day and derived from Allen's personal perspective in relation to health and nursing and the concurrent movement toward health promotion and primary health care in Canada. Allen defined the family as the social group in which learning takes place. Family is viewed from a systems perspective and is defined broadly to include any natural living group. Health is viewed as a phenomenon of the family. Interactions between the nurse and client recognize the family as the focus of attention. Clients, viewed in the context of the family, are active participants in decision making and the learning process. This approach is consistent with Social Learning Theory. The model has served as the curriculum model of McGill University School of Nursing since its early inception. The model has been tested in a variety of hospital and community settings across Canada through demonstration projects. Ideas central to the model have been adopted in Great Britain and in the World Health Organization (Allen, 1977; Allen, 1983; Stillwell, 1985).

Second, in 1984, Lorraine Wright and Maureen Leahey of the University of Calgary, Alberta, published *Nurses and Families: A Guide to Family Assessment and Intervention* (now in its third edition [2000]). In this work, they describe the Calgary Family Assessment Model (CFAM) and the Calgary Family Intervention Model (CFIM) (Wright & Leahey, 1984). The CFAM is a practical and thorough guide to family assessment through interviewing and has received widespread approval and adoption across Canada. The CFIM was the first family intervention model for nurses and offers interventions to assist with cognitive, affective, and behavioural family functioning. Wright and Leahey have been successful in providing guidance and renewed confidence for nurses who are committed to working with families.

Third, the 1990s saw an emphasis on family resiliency, where protective processes are promoted and vulnerability processes are dampened. The key family protective and risk factors in child and family resiliency were outlined in an influential document prepared for Health Canada by Mangham, McGrath, Reid, and Stewart (1994) titled *Resiliency: Relevance to Health Promotion: Detailed Analysis.* Concurrently, a multidisciplinary group of researchers working at the University of Alberta, Edmonton, developed the Family Adaptation Model (FAM) based on the underlying principles of resiliency theory (McDonald et al., 1997; Drummond, Kysela,

McDonald, & Query, 2002; Drummond, Kysela, McDonald, Alexander, & Fleming, 1996/7). Parsimony, practical utility for family interventionists, and empirical support through research are the principles that guided the researchers during the evolution of this model. The model envisions that families adapt to demands placed on them through the mediating influences of parental appraisals, personal and social supports, and family coping strategies. Modest support for the dimensions of the model has been shown. The model has also been successfully used in research and practice to develop family approaches for assessment and planning that enhance communication and parenting capacity within families (Drummond et al., 2002).

References

Allen, M. (1977). Evaluation of educational programmes in nursing. Geneva: World Health Organization.

Allen, M. (1983). Primary health care nursing: Research in action. In L. Hockey (Ed.), *Recent advances in nursing: Primary care nursing* (pp. 32-77). Edinburgh: Churchill-Livingstone.

Drummond, J., Kysela, G. M., McDonald, L., Alexander, J., & Fleming, D. (1996/7). Risk and resiliency in two samples of Canadian families. *Health and Canadian Society, 4,* 117-152.

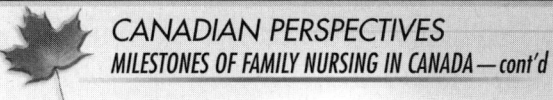

CANADIAN PERSPECTIVES
MILESTONES OF FAMILY NURSING IN CANADA—cont'd

Drummond, J., Kysela, G. M., McDonald, L., & Query, B. (2002). The Family Adaptation Model: Examination of dimensions and relations. *Canadian Journal of Nursing Research, 34*(1), 29-46.

Kravitz, M., & Frey, M. (1989). The Allen Nursing Model. In J. Fitzpatrick & A. Whall (Eds.), *Conceptual models of nursing: Analysis and application* (pp. 313-329). Norwalk, CT: Appleton & Lange.

Mangham, C., McGrath, P., Reid, G., & Stewart, M. (1994). *Resiliency: Relevance to health promotion: Detailed analysis.* Halifax, Nova Scotia: Atlantic Health Promotion Research Centre, Dalhousie University.

McDonald, L., Kysela, G. M., Drummond, J., Martin, C., Wiles, W., & Alexander, J. (1997). Assessment of clinical utility of The Family Adaptation Model. *Journal of Family Studies, 3,* 47-65.

Stillwell, E. (1985). The nurse practitioner: Setting the scene. *Nursing Mirror, 160,* 15-16.

Wright, L. M., & Leahey, M. (1984). *Nurses and families: A guide to family assessment and intervention.* Philadelphia: F. A. Davis.

Wright, L. M., & Leahey, M. (2000). *Nurses and families: A guide to family assessment and intervention* (3rd ed.). Philadelphia: F. A. Davis.

Canadian spelling is used.

for "family values" substantiate the need for family nurses to work in partnership with other professionals and with families in the transformation of the quality of family life with a goal of health promotion (Young & Hayes, 2002). These agendas will significantly affect family nursing practice, research, theory development, and education. Flynn and Ivanov (2000) discuss in more detail the implications for nursing in the twenty-first century.

National Objectives for Health

A crucial factor that energizes many health care professionals involved in health promotion is the existence of national agendas for health promotion in the United States and Canada. The Canadian Perspectives box describes the Canadian emphasis on health promotion and elucidates the social determinants of health as a guide for understanding the dimensions of health. The reader may consult the website for more in-depth review of the Health Canada initiatives and policy state-

ments. See the Website Resources box for this website's URL.

Since 1979, the U.S. federal government has set 10-year goals for the nation's health. The first documents published in the United States were the Surgeon General's landmark report, *Healthy People* (U.S. Public Health Service, 1979), and a companion report, *Promoting Health/Preventing Disease: Objectives for the Nation* (U.S. Public Health Service, 1980). The goal was supported by 226 health objectives to reduce premature deaths and preserve the independence of older adults. Building on achievements from the previous decade, the 1990 document, *Healthy People 2000: National Health Promotion and Disease Prevention Objectives* (USDHHS, 1990), set forth new objectives for the year 2000. Although some improvements were noted during the 1980s and in 1990, most areas of health inadequacies still existed, particularly among minorities and low-income families. For example, issues such as diabetes, chronic diseases, obesity, and physical activity remained priorities. Other issues, such as violence, abusive behaviors, and HIV and AIDS continued to increase and were designated as priorities. During the late 1990s, the U.S. Department of Health and Human Services sought feedback on a nationwide scale from thousands of professionals in a wide range of disciplines, organizations, and citizens about the health status of the nation. This feedback provided data for creation of the goals for the nation's health in a new document titled *Healthy People 2010*. The two overarching goals of the *Healthy People 2010* program are the following:

• Increase the quality and years of healthy life
• Eliminate health disparities among Americans

Undergirded by the nation's policy imperative, family and health care professionals from all disciplines and in many settings use these objectives as models for designing programs to strengthen families and as a rationale for family intervention research. Although many of the priorities are individually focused, it would be nearly impossible to succeed in making significant individual changes unless health promotion and disease prevention approaches are family- and community-centered. The saliency of this document is best stated by David Olson, a past president of the NCFR, in the *NCFR Presidential Report 2001: Preparing Families for the Future*. Olson states that "The family must be a national priority if we are to effectively deal with the multitude of problems in our society today. Most of the problems with individuals and society either begin or end up in the family" (1990, p.1). With an emphasis on the relationship between individual and community health, *Healthy People 2010* will be the basis for many health promotion, health maintenance, and restorative programs for family-centered research, practice, and education with individuals, families, and aggregates in the twenty-first century.

Societal Changes

Twenty-first century families live in a rapidly changing society. As the reader will note in Chapter 3, the structure and norms of families have changed. In addition, a number of societal trends are significantly influencing family life and family nursing. As shown in Box 1-1 these trends are economic, demographic, sociocultural, and family changes. Other trends include expectations for high-touch care (more personal-type care), increasing emphasis on self-help and self-care, consumer demand for participation in decision

---

BOX 1-1 Societal Changes Affecting Twenty-first Century Families

ECONOMIC TRENDS

• Rising cost of living
• Increasing disparities between the affluent and indigent
• Families in the Unites States with children younger than 18 years below the poverty rate in 1999 and 2000, 13.9%; with children younger than 5 years, 17%
• Increasing health care costs

DEMOGRAPHIC TRENDS

• Accelerated population growth
• Aging of the population

SOCIOCULTURAL TRENDS

• Changing racial and ethnic compositions
• Changing gender norms
• Technological advances
• Increases in global terrorism

CHANGES IN THE FAMILY

• Decline in household size
• Delayed marriage and decline in marriage rate
• Higher divorce rate and lower remarriage rate
• Increased configuration of the living arrangements of children
• Increased in single parent families
• Growth in the employment of women
• A shift from the "typical family" to diverse family structures

Adapted from Friedman, M .M., Bowden, V. R., & Jones, E. G. (2003). *Family nursing: Research, theory, and practice* (5th ed.). Upper Saddle River, NJ: Prentice Hall.

making, increased reliance on advanced technology, and changes in the types and age configuration of families (Naisbitt, 2001). Further, dynamic societal changes such as increases in the cost of living and health care costs, global terrorism, change in family structure, the increasing number of poor and homeless families, increasing population of diversity ethnic in families, and the decreasing value placed on family life are dynamic forces affecting family nursing practice, education, research, and theory.

The Changing Family

The family continues to experience dramatic shifts, and families are becoming more diverse and complex in structure and lifestyle than those of the past (Skolnick & Skolnick, 1997). Examples of the diversity in family structure and lifestyle include more divorce and blended families, more cohabitation (heterosexual and same-sex couples), more single-parent and dual-earner families, more elderly family members, decreasing fertility rates, increased urbanization, and increased immigration (McKenry & Price, 2000). In addition, families of the late 1990s and the twenty-first century will be coping with increasing upheavals such as poverty, increasing chronic illness, HIV infections of family members across the life span, and a myriad of other health problems. These conditions necessitate changes in the health care system to provide relevant and adequate health care to all citizens. Chapter 3 includes a discussion of changing family demographics. As families realize that they must assume more responsibility for their health, an increasing number are forming partnerships with professionals to improve the health status of individual family members and the family unit.

In response to numerous developments in theory and research and changes in the ecosystem of families, a new specialty called *family science* has emerged (Burr & Leigh, 1983). Phenomena of interest include such topics as family interaction, family patterns, family health, value placed on the family, diverse family types and issues, culture and ethnicity, family preservation, and strategies useful in assisting families to lead healthier lives.

Family Health Nursing Practice

Family health nursing has many of the characteristics of family-centered community nursing as described by Barkauskas (1986) and family nursing (Clements & Roberts, 1983; Friedman, 1992; Gilliss et al., 1989; Hymovich & Barnard, 1979). It is based on many of the theories and skills from nursing specialties, primary health care, family science, family therapy, and behavioral health. The terms *family nursing, family health nursing,* and *family and community health nursing* and the terms *family nurse practitioner* and *family clinical nurse specialist* are often used interchangeably. This contributes to the confusion about whether there is an actual difference in the roles.

In some instances, it seems that the term chosen is merely a matter of preference of the faculty in graduate programs. For example, some schools that have graduate family health nursing programs deliberately use the term *health* to denote the focus on the care of well or "worried well" family units. However, according to the ANA the term *specialist* does indicate graduate preparation. Hanson (2001) states that "family health care nursing is emerging as a science and an art" (p. 4). In addition, it has always been an integral part of American nursing. It is simultaneously innovative and conservative. The differences in the titles *family nurse, family health nurse,* and *family health care nurse* are merely semantic. In this text the terms will be used interchangeably.

If a clinician defines health as encompassing illness and wellness, as Brubaker (1983) suggests, then all nurses who provide care to families as a unit are family health nurses. Family health nurses may want to direct their practice toward a specific area on the health continuum such as illness care, disease prevention, or health promotion. In addition, some may collaborate with families in specific settings, such as the community, or with families at particular stages in family development, such as childbearing families, families with a member who has an acute or chronic illness, families experiencing transitions, and families seeking approaches to improve their well-being as a unit. However, the ultimate goal with all clients (individual or family units) is to empower them to achieve optimal levels of health.

As shown in Figure 1-1 through Figure 1-5, family processes are multifaceted, and nurses collaborating with families must be cognizant of the five realms of family life. Anderson (2000) suggests this framework to guide systematic assessment and capacity building with families to promote a healthy lifestyle. Chapter 11 in particular and many other chapters in this book provide the reader with examples of measures that can be used to assess family health.

Family nursing, like community health nursing, provides its practitioners with "challenges to apply multiple skills in especially creative and independent ways . . . with clients to maintain health and promote wellness in the client's natural environment" (Barkauskas, 1986, p. 5). Family health nurses also collaborate with other professionals from a variety of disciplines in the promotion of family health and well-being.

Roles of the Family Health Nurse

To be effective in helping families to achieve their goals of promoting, maintaining, or restoring health, family nurse scholars recommend that clinicians reframe their philosophy of practice from a service model to a capacity-building model (Hartrick, 1997). Another philosophy describes health promotion as a transforming process (Young & Hayes, 2002). Family practitioners choose a selected family phenomenon of interest such as (1) a particular developmental stage of the family, (2) developmental transitions such as retirement or parenting (Allen & Warner, 2002), (3) families with acute-care needs or a member with a chronic illness, (4) stress management, (5) fitness, (6) nutrition, and so forth. It is beyond the scope of this text to include the endless possibilities of current and future innovative roles of family health nurses. The area of practice is limited only by the creativity of the nurse. Hartrick (1997) emphasizes that in family health promotion, the role of the nurse is strengthening and "capacity building" rather than providing service. Table 1-3 presents a comparison of these two models. Rather than focusing solely on pathology, the clinician's goal is to emphasize and build on a client's strengths and support. Family nurses have a myriad of resources and journals to support their practice. Box 1-2 lists journals relevant to family health nursing, and each chapter provides a list of selected websites relevant to the chapter topic.

Chapter 3 addresses the role of the family nurse in family health promotion, and Chapter 19 focuses on the nurse's role in preventing disease in family members. Chapters 10 and 11 apply Neuman's Systems Model to family nursing process and family assessment. Unit 3 discusses the role of family nurses in the assessment of family health, nutrition, recreation and exercise, environmental health, coping, and family transitions.

Settings for Family Health Nursing Practice

Family health nurses may practice in any setting where there are families. These include but are not limited to hospital units, home health care settings, schools, physicians' offices, clinics, health education centers, occupational health centers, marriage and family counseling clinics, private practice offices, maternal and child health care settings, wellness centers, and hospices. Family health nurses may also be independent entrepreneurs and may practice in settings such as the following:

- Anticipatory guidance groups, addressing major life events such as pregnancy, menopause, grief, and divorce
- Church health ministries as parish nurses
- Community health centers
- Day care centers for children and older adults
- Diabetes education groups
- Family and marital counseling clinics
- Family life education groups, focusing on areas such as parenting, communication, and sexuality
- Lactation counseling groups
- Nurse-managed centers
- Support groups for families with a member who has a chronic illness (such as AIDS, Alzheimer's disease, or cancer)
- University health centers

Although the focus of this book is on family health promotion, this does not mean that acute-care and rehabilitative nursing are not also legitimate concerns of family nursing. Providing nursing

TABLE 1-3   Comparison of Service Provision and Health-Promoting Practice

Service Model	Capacity Enhancement Model
Language: pathology, problems, function, outcomes, pathology and deficiency, intervention resolution, informing	Language: capacity, health, experience, empowerment, transformation, power with challenges
Emphasizes problems	Emphasizes health/capacity
Service provision	Fostering family capacity
Family as participant	Family as authority
Nurse as expert	Nurse as collaborator
Problem identification	Discovery of health and healing
	Listening
Assumes the health professional has the knowledge to heal the family	Assumes the family has the best knowledge to achieve health and resolve their issues
Assessment and diagnosis	Illumination of meaningful patterns and resources within the family's lived experience of health and healing
Intervention to restore family function	Collaboration to re-image and transform family's health and healing experiences
Doing for the family	
	Give control, facilitate, and listen
Problem resolution	Health promotion
Evaluation	Transformation

Based on data from Hartrick, G. (1997). Beyond the service model of care: Health promotion and the enhancement of family capacity. *Journal of Family Nursing, 3,* 57-70; and Hartrick, G. (2000). Developing health-promoting practice with families: One pedagogical experience. *Journal of Advanced Nursing, 31,* 27–36.

BOX 1-2   Selected Family-Related Journals and Periodicals for Family Health Nursing

American Journal of Health Promotion
American Journal of Public Health
American Journal of Family Therapy
Family and Child Mental Health Journal
Journal of Jewish Board of Family and Children's Service
Family Behavior
Family and Community Health
Family and Community Behavior
Family Health
Family Planning Perspectives
Family Process
Family Medicine
Family Relations
Family Science Review
Family Systems Medicine
Family Systems and Health Care
Family Therapy Collections
Family Therapy Networker

Family Therapy News
Families in Society: The Journal for Contemporary Human Services Health and Social Work
Health Care for Women International
Journal of Comparative Family Studies
Journal of Community Health Nursing
Journal of Consulting Psychology
Journal of Cultural Diversity
Journal of Family Nursing
Journal of Family History
Journal of Families in Society
Journal of Family Issues
Journal of Marriage and Family
Journal of Marital and Family Therapy
Journal of Multicultural Nursing and Health
Journal Family Practice
Journal Family Psychology
Journal of Rural Health
Journal of Transcultural Nursing

BOX 1-2   Selected Family-Related Journals and Periodicals for Family Health Nursing—cont'd

Journal of Family Psychology
Juvenile Justice Bulletin
Marriage and Family Review
Maternal-Child Health
Merrill-Palmer Quarterly of Behavior and Development
Social Forces
Social Work

Social Work and Health Care
Sociology of Health and Illness
The Family Journal: Counseling and Therapy for Couples and Families
Women and Health
Women and Health Care
Youth and Society

---

care to individuals and families with the goal of enhancing well-being in all states of their health, whether illness or wellness, is within the realm of family nursing practice because family health encompasses both illness/dysfunction and wellness/function (Edelman & Mandle, 2002; Danielson, Hamel-Bissel, & Winstead-Fry, 1993).

However, if nurses do not respond to changes in clients' needs for health promotion and disease prevention, other professionals with skills in health teaching and anticipatory guidance will assume nursing's role in family health promotion and health protection. For example, on one occasion, the author visited a clinic where family nurse practitioners were providing physical assessment, diagnosing illness, and prescribing treatment. At the same time, health educators were delegated major responsibility for anticipatory guidance and health teaching such as appropriate use of family planning methods, explanation of the birth process, and directions for taking prescribed medication. In the past both of these activities (health teaching and primary care) were considered the responsibility of the nurse. The framework that family nurses should use as a guide for collaborating with families should be one that focuses on the realms that enhance family well-being rather than on illness or dysfunction (Anderson, 2000; Hartrick, 1998). A framework for assessing family realms is suggested by Anderson, 2000 (Box 1-3). Components for facilitating families in health

promotion are depicted in Figure 1-7 (Allen & Warner, 2002; Bomar, 1996). Rather than being a linear process with the nurse making the decisions, the decision unfolds as the nurse helps the family to identify their strengths and illuminate alternatives.

Assumptions and Beliefs about Families

Assumptions and beliefs about families influence a family nurse's practice. Each nurse must therefore examine his or her own assumptions and beliefs about families. Young and Hayes (2002) suggest that the process of health promotion should be a transformation process. In transformation the nurse does not "do to" the family or intervene but rather co-creates the next phase of their health. A philosophy of family-centered nursing practice encompasses the assumptions noted in Box 1-4. The family nurse's role is to emphasize family health capacity, empower the family to identify options, foster family capacity in health promotion, facilitate the family's discovery of health and healing, and transform family health and family experiences (Hartrick, 1997; Young & Hayes, 2002). To facilitate success with families in promoting health and achieving healthy lifestyles, clinicians will need to use new practice models that encompass strength building, empowerment, and transformation rather than a service perspective. See Table 1-3 for a comparison of the service provision

BOX 1-3   Realms of Family Life: A Focus of Family Health Nursing Practice

FAMILY INTERACTIVE PROCESSES

Relationships
Nurturance
Intimacy expression
Social support
Acceptance of uniqueness of members' opinions and personalities
Conflict resolution
Family leisure
Roles (instrumental and expressive)

FAMILY INTEGRITY PROCESSES

Shared meaning
Family history
Boundary maintenance
Family identity and commitment
Family togetherness
Family values
Family rituals
Family spirituality
Family culture and practices
Individual time and space

FAMILY SYSTEM HEALTH MAINTENANCE

Family health patterns (e.g., eating, exercising, disease prevention, sleeping, dental care, self-care actions)
Family health beliefs
Health status of members
Health responses and practices
Health-promoting behaviors
Disease conditions, treatments, and consequences for the family
Family caretaking responsibilities
Family illness stressors
Relationships with health care providers and health care system access

FAMILY DEVELOPMENTAL PROCESSES

Family transitions
Individual development
Career development
Marital development
Parental development
Family stage task completion and progression

FAMILY COPING PROCESSES

Problem solving
Use and management of resources
Adaptation to family life stressors and daily hassles
Coping strategies
Family resistance resources

Based on data from Anderson, K. H., & Tomlinson, P. (1992). The family health system as an emerging paradigmatic view for nursing. *Image, 24,* 57-63; Anderson, K. H. (2000). The family health system approach to family systems nursing. *Journal of Family Nursing, 6,* 103-119; and Friedemann, M. L. (1995). *The framework of systemic organization: A conceptual approach to families and nursing.* Thousand Oaks, CA: Sage.

Collaboration for Health Promotion	Assessment	Analysis	Implementation	Evaluation
Client Tasks (Individual, Family, or Community)	Clarify concerns and goals Display strengths Gathering information	Analyzing situation Identifying resources and preferences Culling options	Describing alternatives Testing new behaviors	Noting outcomes Valuing outcomes
Family Nurse's Clinical Role	Focuser Stimulator Resource Producer	Integrator Awareness Raiser Identify additional resources	Role Model Teacher Coach, Guide Encourager Mobilizer Empowering Agent	Pacer Reinforcer Reviewer Make Linkages
Other Roles	Author Consultant Educator Theory Developer Researcher	Leader in family health matters Clarifier-Interpreter	Family Advocate Case/Care Manager Environmental Modifier Political Activist	Change Agent Research User

Figure 1-7 Family health nursing roles in collaborating with families for health promotion. Adapted from Allen, F. M. & Warner, M. (2002). A developmental model of health and nursing. *Journal of Family Nursing, 8,* 96-135.

model and the capacity enhancement model (Hartrick, 1997).

Obstacles to Family Health Promotion in Nursing Practice

There are numerous barriers to nurses facilitating family health promotion, which are beyond the scope of this chapter. According to Young and Hayes (2002), who summarize a comprehensive review of health promotion literature, the major barrier is the multiple health promotion theories and frameworks created by several disciplines. Comprehensive assessment measures and strategies for family health promotion are limited. Often, in curricula for nursing, health professions, and family science, health promotion of the family unit is not viewed as the purview of clinical practice. Unfortunately, family health promotion is not reimbursable by insurance carriers because there is no diagnostic code for it. Lastly, the family as a unit is usually not available during established business hours, and many health services are not routinely provided during evenings and on weekends (Hanson, 2001).

Family Health Nursing Education

Although education about family health is believed to be essential content for professional curricula, family nursing curricula are diverse and range from undergraduate to doctoral programs. Many have a limited family focus. Some emphasize the family and community health aspect or the individual in the family context, whereas others focus on family therapy (Hanson & Heims, 1992; Wright & Leahey, 1984). Hanson (1987) states that family content in graduate education is inconsistent. Other curricula focus on individual family members or families at different points in the family life cycle; nurse practitioner skills; well families; and primary, secondary, or tertiary care. Some specifically provide experiences that empower families in health promotion (Hartrick, 1998). The level of sophistication of family health nursing practice depends on the academic preparation a nurse receives. See Table 1-2 for the levels of family health nursing practice.

Graduates of baccalaureate programs are prepared as generalists to assume positions as staff nurses in hospitals and community health agencies. Their area of expertise is the individual in the family context. Graduates of master's degree programs are specialists who may practice more independently and collaboratively. Graduate nurses intervene with individuals and also with the family as a unit and, depending on their preparation, with family interactions. A number of graduate schools

---

BOX 1-4   Assumptions about Families

- Individuals and families are unique.
- Family decisions about their health are influenced by many biological, social, economic, cultural, psychological, orientation to life, and spiritual variables.
- Family decisions about health are made independently of the nurse.
- Transformation of family health is achieved when the family has the authority.
- Family health is a dynamic, multidimensional concept, and what is correct today may be incorrect tomorrow.
- Families will engage in health behaviors that are relevant and pertinent to their family life career and social context.
- Family health is systematic and processed-based.
- Family health is more than the health of the individual members.
- All families have the capacity for illuminating and transforming their quality of life and family health.
- The nurse's role is to listen, facilitate change, and empower the family.

Based on data from Anderson, K. H. (2000). The family health system approach to family systems nursing. *Journal of Family Nursing, 6,* 103-119; Bomar, P. (Ed.). (1996). *Nurses and family health promotion* (2nd ed.). Philadelphia: W. B. Saunders; Hartrick G. (1997). Beyond the service model of care: Health promotion and the enhancement of family capacity. *Family Nursing, 3,* 57-70; and Young, L. E., & Hayes, V. W. (2002). *Transforming health promotion practice.* Philadelphia: F. A. Davis.

have doctoral programs in family nursing, and a few provide opportunities for postdoctoral study in family nursing.

Internationally, there is considerable interest in the development of family nursing education. For example, family health nursing is a relatively new concept of interest in Western Europe. A mounting interest in family health nursing is noted to have begun in the twenty-first century. For example, for the initiation of strategies to improve health and reduce health disparities addressed in WHO's *Health21* (WHO, 1999), a pilot family nursing curriculum was devised by a WHO Europe nursing and midwifery unit expert group and was launched in Scotland and other European countries (WHO, 2000). The purpose of the pilots was to evaluate the efficacy of Family Health Nursing in WHO European region (WHO Regional Office for Europe, 2001).

Research and Theory Development in Family Health Promotion

Previous research on family health tended to lack conceptual clarity and to focus on single parents, women and caregiving, family crises, and the issue of dysfunctional families. In addition, studies of family health promotion are scant, primarily because of inadequate conceptualization of the phenomenon of family health promotion (Ford-Gilboe, 1997). Canadian scholars suggest Allen's *Developmental Model of Health and Nursing* for studying the phenomenon of family health promotion (Ford-Gilboe, 2002; Allen & Warner, 2002). Future research on promoting health in families should test this theoretical model for studying family health promotion and also create new models (Denham, 1999). Projections for family nursing and family health promotion for the first decade of the twenty-first century are discussed in Chapter 22.

Summary

A synopsis of family nursing is provided in this chapter. Family nursing as an evolving specialty is highlighted. Definitions of family, family health, and health promotion, and family nursing are discussed. The historical development of family nursing is traced from the beginning of families to the beginning of the new millennium. The social, political, economic, professional, and family factors influencing family nursing are discussed, as well as family nursing education, practice, and research.

WEBSITE RESOURCES

ORGANIZATION	WEBSITE ADDRESS
American Nurses Association Publications	http://www.nursingworld.org/anp/phome.cfm
	http://www.hc-sc.gc.ca/hppb/phdd/determinants/index.html
Health Canada	http://www.hc-sc.gc.ca/
Healthy People 2010	http://www.health.gov/healthypeople/
National Council on Family Relations (NCFR)	http://www.ncfr.org
National Institute of Nursing Research (NINR)	http://www.nih.gov/ninr
PREPARE-ENRICH	http://www.lifeinnovations.com
Alliance for Children and Families	http://www.alliance1.org/
Healthy Families America (HFA)	http://www.healthyfamiliesamerica.org/
healthfinder	http://www.healthfinder.gov/aboutus/
National Partnership for Women and Families	http://www.nationalpartnership.org/
Health Gap	http://www.healthgap.omhrc.gov/
National Mental Health Association (NMHA)	http://www.nmha.org/
National Resource and Policy Center on Rural Long-Term Care	http://www.kumc.edu/instruction/medicine/NRPC
Institute for Urban Family Health	http://www.institute2000.org/
American Academy of Nurse Practitioners	http://www.aanp.org/default.asp
American Nurses Association	http://www.nursingworld.org
American Association for Marriage and Family	http://www.aamft.org/index_nm.asp
American Public Health Association	http://www.apha.org/
Administration for Children and Families	http://www.acf.hhs.gov/acf_about.html
Agency of Healthcare Research and Quality	http://www.ahcpr.gov/about/
American Association of Retired Persons	http:www.aarp.org
American Cancer Society	http:www.cancer.org
Determination of Health (Canada)	http://www.hc.-sc.gc.ca/hppb/phdd/determinants/index/html
Centers for Disease Control and Disease Prevention	http://www.cdc.goc
Council on Family Health	http://www.cfhinfo.org/
Closing the Health Gap	http://www.healthgap.omhrc.gov/
Family Support and Parenting–Canada	http://www.hc-sc.gc.ca/dca-dea/family_familie/index_e.html
Institute for Family-Centered Care	http://www.familycenteredcare.org/
Office of Minority Health	http://www.omhrc.gov/
National Center for Health Statistics	http:ww.cdc.gov/nchs/fastats/default.htm
National Institute on Aging	http://www.nia.nih.gov/
National Council on Aging	http://www.ncoa.org/index.cfm

WEBSITE RESOURCES—cont'd

National Women's Health Information Center   http://www.4woman.gov/owh/aboutowh.htm
National Parenting Center   http://www.tnpc/com/
Life Innovations   http://www.lifeinnovation.com/
World Health Organization   http://www.who.int

■ CHAPTER HIGHLIGHTS

- The family has been idealized as the client of the nursing profession since the pre-Nightingale era; however, in reality the client is the individual within the family context and not the family unit.

- In the 1970s, the family unit as the client became a realm of concern for assessment and intervention for an emerging nursing specialty, family health or family nursing.

- Many social, political, professional, behavioral, and interdisciplinary variables influenced the development of contemporary family health nursing practice.

- Family nursing assessment and enhancement occurs at four levels of practice: individual within the family as context, the family as client, family as client with family interactions as focus, and family aggregates.

- The family health nurse's practice occurs in any setting where there are families or individuals within a family context.

- The future of family health nursing will be influenced by health policy, health promotion agendas, economics, changes in the nursing profession, family demands, health promotion lifestyle changes, and the growing emphasis by family and health care professionals on capacity building with families to transform their health.

CRITICAL THINKING ACTIVITIES

1. Explain to a colleague why family nursing is considered an evolving nursing specialty.

2. Distinguish between individual health and family health promotion.

3. Clarify what is meant by the concept that the client or family is in the foreground of nurse-client transactions.

4. Explain the ties that family nursing specialties have with other specialties.

5. Identify and explain four different roles of the family health nurse in enhancing family health.

6. Interview a family and ask them how they define "family health promotion." Also ask the family who is the professional that should collaborate with them in increasing their family capacity for health promotion. Share the summary with colleagues.

7. Interview a nurse and ask how he or she defines family health promotion. Share the summary with colleagues.

REFERENCES

Acton, Gayle J. (2002). Health-promotion self-care in family caregivers. *Western Journal of Nursing Research, 24,* 73-86.

Allen, F. M., & Warner, M. (2002). A developmental model of health and nursing. *Journal of Family Nursing, 8,* 96-135.

American Nurses Association. (1980). *Nursing: A social policy statement.* (ANA Publication No. NP6335-M). Kansas City, MO: Author.

American Nurses Association. (1992). *Nursing's agenda for health care reform.* (ANA Publication No. PR-12-91). Washington, DC: Author.

American Nurses Association. (1995). *Nursing's social policy statement.* Kansas City, MO: Author.

American Nurses Association. (1996). *Statement on the scope and standards of pediatric clinical nursing practice.* Kansas City, MO: Author.

American Nurses Association. (1999). *Scope and standards of public health nursing practice.* Kansas City, MO: Author.

American Nurses Association. (2000). *Achieving access for all Americans.* ANA Reading Room. Retrieved October, 1, 2002, from http://nursingworld.org/readroom/ rwjpaper.html

American Nurses Association. (2001a). *Scope and standards of gerontological nursing practice.* Kansas City, MO: Author.

American Nurses Association. (2001b). *Scope and standards of psychiatric-mental health nursing practice.* Kansas City, MO: Author.

American Nurses Association. (2002). *Nursing's agenda for the future.* Washington, DC: Author.

Anderson, K. H. (2000). The family health system approach to family systems nursing. *Journal of Family Nursing, 6,* 103-119.

Anderson, K. H., & Tomlinson, P. S. (1992). The family health system as an emerging paradigmatic view for nursing. *Image, 24,* 57-63.

Archer, S. E. (1982). Synthesis of public health science and nursing science. *Nursing Outlook, 30,* 442–446.

Baggaley, S., & Kean, S. (1999). Health visitors as family nurses: A discussion of research, policy and practice in the United Kingdom. *Journal of Family Nursing, 5,* 388-403.

Barkauskas, V. H. (1986). Community health nursing. In B. B. Logan & C. E. Dawkins (Eds.), *Family-centered nursing in the community* (pp. 4-30). Reading, MA: Addison-Wesley.

Bell, J. M. (1995). Avoiding isomorphism. A call for a different view. *Journal of Family Nursing, 1,* 5–7.

Bell, J. M., Watson, W. L., & Wright, L. M. (1990). *The cutting edge of family nursing.* Calgary, Alberta, Canada: Family Nursing Unit Publications.

Benner, P. E., & Benner, P. D. (2001). *Novice to expert: Excellence and power in clinical nursing practice.* Menlo Park, CA: Prentice Hall.

Bomar, P. (1989). *Nurses and family health promotion: Concepts, assessments and interventions.* Baltimore: Williams & Wilkins.

Bomar, P. (Ed.). (1996). *Nurses and family health promotion* (2nd ed.). Philadelphia: W.B. Saunders.

Bomar, P., & McNeeley G. (1996). Family health nursing role: Past, present and future. In P. Bomar (Ed.). *Nurses and family health promotion* (2nd ed., pp. 3-21). Philadelphia: WB Saunders.

Bradshaw, J. (1988). *Bradshaw on the family.* Deerfield Beach, FL: Heath Communications.

Brubaker, B. H. (1983). Health promotion: A linguistic analysis. *Advances in Nursing Science, 5,* 1-14.

Burr, W. R., & Leigh, G. K. (1983). A new discipline. *Journal of Marriage and the Family, 45,* 467-480.

Christy, T. E. (1970). Portrait of a leader: Lillian D. Wald. *Nursing Outlook, 18,* 50-54.

Clark M. J. (2003). *Community health nursing: Caring for populations* (4th ed.). Upper Saddle River, NJ: Prentice Hall.

Clements, I. W., & Roberts, F. B. (Eds.). (1983). *Family health: A theoretical approach to nursing care.* New York: Wiley & Sons.

Cunningham, R. (1978). Family-centered care. *Canadian Nurse, 2,* 34-37.

Danielson, C. B., Hamel-Bissel, B., & Winstead-Fry, P. (1993). *Families, health and illness.* St. Louis, MO: Mosby.

DeMarco, R., Ford-Gilboe, M., Friedemann, M. L., McCubbin, H. I., & McCubbin, M. A. (2000). Stress, coping and family health. In V. H. Rice (Ed.), *Handbook of stress, coping and health: Implications for nursing research, theory, and practice* (pp. 295-332). Thousand Oaks, CA: Sage.

Denham, S. A. (1999). Part 1: The definition and practice of family health. *Journal of Family Nursing, 9,* 133-159.

Doherty, W. & Campbell, T. (1988). *Families and health.* Newbury Park, CA: Sage.

Duval, E. M., & Miller, B. (1985). *Marriage and family development* (6th ed.). New York: Harper & Row.

Edelman, C. L., & Mandle, C. L. (2002). *Health promotion throughout the lifespan* (5th ed.). St. Louis, MO: Mosby.

Feetham, S. L., Meister, S. B., Bell, J. M., & Gilliss, C. L. (1993). *The nursing of families: Theory, research, education and practice.* Newbury Park, CA: Sage Publications.

Fitzpatrick, M. L. (1975). Nursing and the Great Depression. *American Journal of Nursing, 75,* 2188-2190.

Flynn, B. C., & Ivanov, L. (2000). Health promotion through Healthy Cities. In M. Stanhope & J. Lancaster (Eds.). *Community and public health nursing* (5th ed., pp. 349-359). St. Louis, MO: Mosby.

Ford, L. C. (1979). The development of family nursing. In D. P. Hymovich & M. W. Barnard, (Eds.). *Family health care: General perspectives* (Vol. 1). (2nd ed.). (pp. 88-105). New York: McGraw-Hill.

Ford-Gilboe, M. (1997). Family strengths, motivation, resources as predictors of health promotion in single-parent and two-parent families. *Research in Nursing and Health, 20,* 205-217.

Ford-Gilboe, M. (2002). Developing knowledge about family health promotion by testing the developmental model of health and nursing. *Journal of Family Nursing, 8,* 140-156.

Forster, M. (1984). *Significant sisters.* New York: Knopf.

Friedemann, M. L. (1995). *The framework of systemic organization: A conceptual approach to families and nursing.* Thousand Oaks, CA: Sage.

Friedman, M. M. (1992). *Family nursing: Theory and assessment* (2nd ed.). Norwalk, CT: Appleton-Lange.

Friedman, M. M., Bowen, V. R., & Jones, E. G. (2003). *Family nursing: Theory and assessment* (5th ed.). Upper Saddle River, NJ: Prentice Hall.

Gilliss, C. L., & Davis, L. (1993). Does family interventions make a difference? An integrative review and meta-analysis. In S. L. Feetham, S. B. Meiser, J. M. Bell, & C. L. Gilliss (Eds.), *The nursing of families* (pp. 259-265). Newbury Park, CA: Sage.

Gilliss, C. L., Higley, B. L., Roberts, B. M., & Martinson, I. M. (1989). *Toward a science of family nursing.* Reading, MA: Addison-Wesley.

Ham, L. M., & Chamings, P. A. (1983). Family nursing: Historical perspectives. In I. W. Clements & F. B. Roberts (Eds.), *Family health: A theoretical approach to nursing care* (pp. 33-43). New York: Wiley.

Hanson, S. M. (1987). Family nursing and chronic illness. In L. M. Wright & M. L. Leahey (Eds.), *Families and chronic illness* (pp. 1-31). Springhouse, PA: Springhouse.

Hanson, S. M. H. (2001). *Family health care nursing: Theory, practice, and research* (2nd ed.). Philadelphia: F.A. Davis.

Hanson, S. M. H., & Boyd, S. T. (1996). *Family health care nursing: Theory, practice and research.* Philadelphia: Davis.

Hanson, S. M. H., & Heims, M. L. (1992). Family nursing curricula in U.S. schools of nursing. *Journal of Nursing Education, 31,* 303-308.

Hartrick, G. (1997). Beyond the service model of care: Health promotion and the enhancement of family capacity. *Family Nursing, 3,* 57-70.

Hartrick, G. (1998). Living the question of family nursing. *Journal of Family Nursing, 4,* 8-22.

Hartrick, G. (2000). Developing health-promotion practice with families: one pedagogical experience. *Journal of Advanced Nursing, 31,* 27-36.

Health Canada. (2001). *The population health template: Key elements and actions that define a population health approach.* Retrieved February 7, 2003 from http://www.hc.sc.gc.ca/hppb/pdf/discussion_papers

Heinrich, J. (1983). Historical perspectives on public health nursing. *Nursing Outlook, 31,* 317-320.

Houck, G. M., & Kodadek, S. (2001). Research in families and family nursing. In S. M. Hanson (Ed.), *Family health care nursing: Theory, practice, and research* (2nd ed., pp. 61-71). Philadelphia: F. A. Davis.

Hymovich, D. P., & Barnard, M. U. (Eds.). (1979). *Family health care: General perspectives.* (2nd ed.). New York: McGraw-Hill.

Hymovich, D. P., & Hoagopian, G. A. (1992). *Chronic illness in children and adults. A psychosocial approach.* Philadelphia: Saunders.

Janosik, E. H., & Miller, J. R. (1980). *Family focused care.* New York: McGraw-Hill.

Kalisch, P. A., & Kalisch, B. J. (1986). *The advance of American nursing* (2nd ed.). Boston: Little, Brown.

King, I. (1981). *A theory of nursing.* New York: Wiley.

Knafl, K. A., & Gillis, C. L. (2002). Families and chronic illness: A synthesis of current research. *Journal of Family Nursing, 8,* 178-198.

Logan, B. B., & Dawkins, C. E. (Eds.). (1986). *Family centered nursing in the community.* Menlo Park, CA: Addison-Wesley.

Matejski, M. P. (1986). Ladies' aid societies and the nurses of Lincoln's army. *Journal of Nursing History, 1,* 35–51.

McAdoo, H. P. (1999). Families of color: Strengths that come from diversity. In H. P. McAdoo (Ed.), *Family ethnicity* (2nd ed., pp. 3-14). Thousand Oaks: Sage.

McCubbin, M. A. (1993). Family stress theory and development of nursing knowledge about family adaptation. In S. B. Feetham, S. B. Meister, J. M. Bell, & C. L. Gilliss (Eds.), *The nursing of families* (pp. 46-58). Newbury Park, CA: Sage.

McKenry, P. C. & Price, S. J. (Eds.). (2000). *Families and change.* Thousand Oaks, CA: Sage.

Naisbitt, J. (2001). *High tech/high touch.* London: Nicholas Braely.

National Institute of Nursing Research, National Institutes of Health. (2000). *Strategic plans on reducing health disparities.* [Online]. Retrieved October 10, 2002, from http://www.nih.gov/ninr/research/diversitymission.html.

National Institute of Nursing Research (2003). *Research themes for the future.* Retrieved August 11, 2003, from http://www.nih.gov/ninr/research/themes.doc

Neuman, B. (1982). The *Neuman Systems Model: Application to nursing education and practice.* Norwalk, CT: Appleton-Century-Crofts.

Newman, M. A. (1994). *Health as expanding consciousness* (2nd ed.). New York: National League for Nursing.

Nies, M. A., & McEwen, M. (2001) *Community health nursing: Promoting the health of populations.* Philadelphia: Saunders.

Nightingale, F. (1946). *Notes on nursing: What it is and what it is not.* Philadelphia: Lippincott. (Original work published in 1859.)

Nightingale, F. (1949). Sick nursing and health nursing. In I. A. Hampton (Ed.), *Nursing of the Sick—1893* (pp. 24-43). New York: McGraw-Hill. (Original paper presented in 1893).

Olson, D. H. (1990). *NCFR presidential report: 2001: Preparing families for the future.* Minneapolis, MN: National Council on Family Relations.

Olson, D. H. (2002). *Circumplex model of marital & family systems.* Retrieved October 11, 2002, from http://www.prepare-enrich.com/studies/fpres.html

Olson. D. H. & DeFrain, J. (1994). *Marriage and the family: Diversity and strengths.* Mountain View, CA: Mayfield.

Olson, D. H., McCubbin, H., Barnes, H., Larsen, A, Muxen, M., & Wilson, M. (1983). *Families: What makes them work.* Beverly Hills, CA: Sage.

Orem, D. E. (1980). *Nursing: Concepts of practice.* New York: McGraw-Hill.

Pasley, K. & Ihinger-Tallman, M. (1995). *Stepparenting: Issues in theory, research, and practice.* Westport, CT: Praeger.

Pender, N. J. (1987). *Health promotion in nursing practice* (2nd ed.). Norwalk, CT: Appleton & Lange.

Pender, N. J. (1996). *Health promotion in nursing practice* (3rd ed.). Stamford, CT: Appleton & Lange.

Pender, N. J., Murdaugh, C. L., & Parsons, M. A. (2002). *Health promotion in nursing practice* (4th ed.). Upper Saddle River, NJ: Prentice Hall.

Pletsch, P. K. (1981). Mary Breckinridge: A pioneer who made her mark. *American Journal of Nursing, 81,* 2188-2190.

Pratt, L. (1976). *Family structure and effective health behavior: The energized family.* Boston: Houghton Mifflin.

Rogers, M. E. (1980). Nursing: A science of unitary man. In J. P. Riehl & C. Roy (Eds.), *Conceptual models for nursing practice* (2nd ed., pp. 329-337). New York: Appleton-Century-Crofts.

Roy, C. (1984). *Introduction to nursing: An adaptation model* (2nd ed.). Englewood Cliffs, NJ: Prentice-Hall.

Schlotfeldt, R. M. (1987). Defining nursing: A historic controversy. *Nursing Research, 36,* 64-67.

Selavan, I. C. (1975). Nurses in American history: The Revolution. *American Journal of Nursing, 75,* 592-594.

Skolnick, A. S., & Skolnick, J. H. (1997). *Family transitions* (9th ed.). New York: Longman.

Spradley, B. W. (1985). *Community health nursing: Concepts and practice* (2nd ed.). Boston: Little, Brown.

Stanhope, M., & Lancaster, J. (2000). *Community and public health nursing* (5th ed.). St. Louis, MO: Mosby.

Sugishita, C. (1999). Development of family nursing in Japan: Present and future perspectives. *Journal of Family Nursing, 5,* 239-244.

United Nations. (1991). *1994 International Year of the Family.* Vienna: United Nations.

U.S. Department of Health and Human Services. (1979). *Healthy people: the Surgeon General's report on health promotion and disease prevention* (U.S. Public Health Service, Pub. No. PHS 79-55071). U.S. Department of Health, Education and Welfare. Washington, DC: U.S. Government Printing Office.

U.S. Department of Health and Human Services. (1980). *Promoting health/preventing disease: Objectives for the nation.* Washington, DC: U.S. Government Printing Office.

U.S. Department of Health and Human Services. (1990). *Healthy People 2000: National health promotion and disease prevention objectives* (Pub. No. PHS 915213). Washington, DC: U.S. Government Printing Office.

U.S. Department of Health and Human Services. (2000). *Healthy People 2010* (Vol. 1). Washington, DC: U.S. Government Printing Office. Retrieved October 1, 2002, from http://www.health.gov/healthypeople/Document/tableofcontents.html

U.S. Public Health Service. (1980). *Healthy People: The Surgeon General's report on health promotion and disease prevention* (DHEW Pub. No. PHS 79-55071). Washington, DC: U.S. Government Printing Office.

Whall, A. L. (1986). The family as the unit of care in nursing: A historical review. *Public Health Nursing, 3,* 240-249.

World Health Organization. (1997). *The Jakarta Declaration on leading health promotion into the 21st century.* Fourth International Conference on Health Promotion. Jakarta, Indonesia. Geneva: World Health Organization. Retrieved online October 1, 2002, from http://www.who.int/hpr/archive/docs/jakarta/english.html

World Health Organization. (1998). *Health for all in the 21st century.* Geneva: World Health Organization.

World Health Organization Regional Office for Europe. (1999). *Health21: the health for all policy for the WHO European region.* (European Health for All Series, No. 6). Copenhagen: Author.

World Health Organization (2000). *Family health nursing. Context, conceptual framework and definitive curriculum.* Copenhagen: The WHO Regional Office for Europe.

World Health Organization (2001). Introduction to the European Family Health Nursing Project. Retrieved online February 9, 2003 from http://www.show.scot.nhs.uk/sehd/familyhealthnurseproject/website%20family%health@20nurse%02project.doc

Wright, L., & Leahey, M. (1984). *Nurses and families: A guide to family assessment and intervention.* Philadelphia: F. A. Davis.

Wright, L., & Leahey, M. (1990). Trends in nursing of families. In J. M. Bell, W. L. Watson, & L. M. Wright (Eds.), *The cutting edge of family nursing* (pp. 5-15). Calgary, Alberta, Canada: The University of Calgary.

Wright, L., & Leahey, M. (2000). *Nurses and families: A guide to family assessment and intervention* (2nd ed.). Philadelphia: F. A. Davis.

Young. L. E., & Hayes, V. W. (2002). *Transforming health promotion practice.* Philadelphia: F. A. Davis.

Zöllner, H., & Lessor, S. (1998). *Population health-putting concepts into action.* Copenhagen: WHO Regional Office Europe.

The Twenty-First Century Family

Robert G. Blundo
Clyde McDaniel

Come to the edge, life said.
They said: We are afraid.
Come to the edge, life said.
They came. It pushed them . . . and they flew.

— Guillaume Apollinaire

OBJECTIVES

On completion of this chapter, the reader will be able to do the following:

1. Describe, in general, the shifting conceptualizations of the notion of family.

2. Describe, in general, the shifting demographic descriptions of the United States and Canada from 1900 to the mid twenty-first century.

3. Discuss the metaphorical nature of the knowledge base and what is significant about this in terms of defining families.

4. Describe the family in terms of process and personal constructions in contrast to historical and structural classifications.

5. Describe what is meant by the "strengths perspective" and "thinking locally" and explain what part each plays in terms of practice in the face of metaphorical and changing notions about family.

The family system is where health promotion and illness care is taught and supported or undermined (Pratt, 1976; Bomar, 1989). Therefore it is crucial that nurses and other health care professionals understand and reflect on the reality of diverse family forms rather than on traditional perceptions.

The structure and function of the family were the subjects of much debate in the twentieth century (Skolnick & Skolnick, 1997). At the beginning of the new millennium, it seems that the contextual approach is ideal for examining the family (see, for example, Sprey, 2001). Such an approach allows one to discuss the family nonpejoratively and as a function of the dynamic nature of its temporal, economic, political, and demographic environments. It also allows one to narrow down the concept of family so that it includes only those elements that are specifically oriented to the achievement of emotional, physical, and social tasks and goals that are essential for good health and social survival.

Discussions of the twenty-first century family call for reflections on *the* family rather than on delineating reductionistic developmental stages, prescriptive models, and forms of the *family*. The issue is not *the family* as known in the past, but how to construct one's professional perspective in terms of recognizing and utilizing the relationships that clients label *family* or live out as family.

Personal and professional perspectives that predetermine what a family is or is not should be challenged. Thinking about the family should be done in terms of interactional processes among human beings and how they construct a notion of family within the multiple contexts of race, age, gender, sexual preference, socio-economic status (SES), ethnicity, locality, and history, as well as the changing values and expectations of a modern economy and increasing mobility.

This shift calls for creating greater tolerance. Monica McGoldrick (1998) believes that "our survival as human beings depends on whether we can remove the blinders or denial that prevents our seeking our human connectedness to each other" (p. 7). She says that a perspective on the family must encompass both connectedness and uniqueness and proposes three levels of understanding to be enacted in any practice:

- Uniqueness as individuals
- Various group identities that give a sense of "home"—that define who individuals are in relation to others
- Common partnership with every other human being, without which individuals will surely perish

The development of family practice competency in the twenty-first century will "require us to go beyond the *dominant* values (theories, and models) and explore the complexity of cultures" (McGoldrick, 1998, p. 8) and the voices of those who have not had a voice in the dominant culture of societies from which professional knowledge has been constructed.

As a start, this chapter addresses the metaphorical nature of professional assumptions as they relate to understanding, and ultimately, practice with families. The shifting demographics of the United States and Canada in terms of the consequences for understanding the very notion of family are described. The need to address the societal context in which families reside as an aspect of health is considered. Finally, the strengths perspective is described as one possible means by which the health care profession can begin to adjust its practice in light of this shift in understanding and perspective.

Professional Perspectives: How Health Care Professionals View the Family

The mental constructs or sociological models of what a family is or is not are ultimately reified by our attempts to hold the world still to understand it and make sense of our actions. Personal and professional knowledge so often is viewed as if an actual reality rather than a metaphor. Ernst von Glasersfeld (1984) comments that understanding or "knowledge does not reflect an 'objective' ontological reality, but is exclusively an ordering and organization of a world constituted by our experience" (p. 24). As human beings we are compelled to organize the world by categorizing and creating mental templates and prototypes to guide us in organizing what we see and what we then respond to through action. It makes the world much simpler. When we see the word *family* in the title of an article or a treatment plan, we quickly make many assumptions about its possible content based on our own ideas of what family means through personal experiences and professional training. This immediate response appears as part of nature's plan. That is, the ideas we carry with us about family lose their abstract and descriptive purpose and appear to be predetermined by nature itself. Therefore any deviation becomes suspect of being abnormal, unnatural, or bureaucratically nonexistent. This is the danger. The ease with which this simple cognitive process helps us to organize our world also *prescribes* a world to be seen, usually without immediate reflection. The family represents a socially constructed category that does or does not include a range of possible connections among people who are then seen as representative or not representative of family. Even though categorization helps to control information and gives us comfort by making easy sense of the world, these very classifications and generalizations can lead to *not* recognizing a familial relationship that is significant to a patient or client. This relationship might be the source of support and assistance that the patient needs if caring is to take place. At an organizational level, these constructs are reinforced by being established in a legalistic way through rules and regulations for conducting practice.

Paul Rosenblatt (1994) has helped focus attention on the metaphorical nature of professional language and its impact on what one actually "sees" and "hears" when thinking about families with whom one works. He notes that metaphors hide theoretical assumptions and make reification of ideas about families a natural and easy occurrence. He gives as an example the notion of "family boundaries" becoming a fixed idea and some "thing" that is taken for granted and then looked for and evaluated. The initial idea was to describe families *as if* they had boundaries. It was used to conceptualize the idea of differentiating family functions and has become laden with values, as well as pathological dimensions. It is as if it were some "thing" that actually exists and therefore can be measured and standardized, when, in fact, it is a descriptor only, most often reflecting the cultural values of the dominant population groups. Rosenblatt (1994) states, "the theoretical metaphors used by (professionals) contextualize, reflect, and create their (professional) realities and limit the ways in which they understand client words and actions and come to terms with client problems" (p. 14). As the broader health care system has incorporated and continues to incorporate metaphorical social science language into its models for understanding the concept of family, it has embarked on a road that can hide from view processes and functions that are of significance in working with any set of families and, in particular, culturally diverse family patterns. These reified metaphors become bureaucratized into rules and regulations that then determine the nature of family-centered practice at the levels of social policy, organizational rules and regulations, and professional practice.

The family in the twenty-first century is a mosaic of contemporary perceptions and tailor-made ("designer") units rather than a traditional framework that is inferred by the laity and often guides professional family practitioners. No discussion of twenty-first century families should deal with *the* family as an ideal one-size-fits-all construct. This prescriptive approach can be demonstrated by looking at the varied metaphorical attempts to prescribe the nature of family by means of definitions that take many forms (e.g., legal, social, financial, and political). Box 2-1 provides examples of definitions from various disciplines and organizations. The alternative conceptualization concerns itself with interactional processes

BOX 2-1   Sample of Definitions of Families

- *Dictionary.* 1) Family is a fundamental social group in a society consisting especially of a man and women and their offspring. 2) A group of persons sharing a common ancestry. 3) Lineage, especially distinguished lineage. 4) All of the members of a household under one roof *(American Heritage Dictionary* [2nd ed.], 1982).
- *Legal.* A family is a group of two or more persons residing in the same household who are related by blood, marriage, or adoption (U. S. Census Bureau, 2002).
- *Family Science.* A family is two or more persons who are committed to each other and who share intimacy, resources, decisions, and values (Olson & DeFrain, 1994, p. 9).
- *Sociology.* Family is an intimate association of persons who are related to one another by blood, a marriage, formal or informal adoption, or appropriation; often sharing a common residence (Billingsley, 1992).
- *Family Therapy.* Family is a "natural social system" with rules, ascribed roles, power structures, intricate communication, and a reciprocal emotional attachment that varies across the family life course (Goldberg & Goldberg, 1996).
- *Family Nursing.* A family is two or more persons who are joined together by bonds or sharing and emotional closeness and who identify themselves as being a part of the family (Friedman et al., 2003).
- *Family Systems Nursing.* Family is a group of individuals who are bound by emotional ties, a sense of belonging, and a passion for being involved in one another's lives (Wright, Watson, & Bell, 1996, p. 45).
- *Family Health Care Nursing.* Family refers to two or more individuals who depend on one another for emotional, physical, and economical support. The members are self-defined (Hanson, 2001, p. 6).

among human beings and how they put together and operate on the basis of different notions of family within different contexts (based, for example, on history and demographics—race, ethnicity, age, gender, sexual preference, socio-economic status, and/or locality—as they reflect different values and expectations). As American society enters the twenty-first century, the issue is not what is *the* family but what are the different relationships that individuals label *family*.

Historical Contexts of Families

According to John Naisbitt (1990; 2001), Alvin Toffler (1990), and other futurists, as America moves into the current century, many new social trends are apparent. Principal among them are globalization, an expansion of women's public roles, and a triumph of the individual over the group. These new social trends have affected the way society has come to understand the notion of family. According to futurists, the trends are the end products of a long process of social evolution, the stages of which are well known:

- *Agricultural Era:* Manual labor was valued; people were defined as property; society was rural, static, and provincial; in-group cooperation and ethnocentrism were cohesive forces.
- *Industrial Era:* Machinery was valued; social groups were modeled, and expected to perform, mechanistically; society was urban and mobile; antagonistic economic collaboration through wages was a cohesive force.
- *Technology Era* (a subset of the Industrial Era): Automation was valued; manual labor was no longer highly valued; people were considered less valuable than property.
- *(Contemporary) High-Tech Era:* Information is valued; the economy is service based; orientation to the world is for selfish (egocentric) problem-solving purposes; in effect, America is now an information, high-tech, long-term, self-help, networking, multi-option society.

In these contexts, family relationships developed and thrived, with the driving force for shifting from one stage to another being technological and, by implication, socio-politico-economic. From a historical point of view, the notion of family has evolved; and use of the notions of nuclear, extended, and augmented family types can provide insights regarding change over the previously mentioned eras. The *nuclear* family is thought of

as a married pair and their dependent children living together and is considered a close-knit unit. The *extended* family is thought of as the nuclear family plus relatives and is considered to have several advantages over the nuclear family. The *augmented* family is thought of as consisting of both nuclear and extended family members, as well as nonrelatives. Of course, these basic types may consist of a single-parent environment or not be bound by blood or law (as in cohabitation). These metaphorical frameworks have reflected traditional time-centered ways of constructing the concept of family.

Agricultural Era Families

When the country was mostly rural and non-industrial, although all three types of families could be found, the extended and augmented family models served as guideposts and were clearly evident in most cases. Also, for most families, unions were the result of economic conditions and tradition. Numerous exchanges and mutually supportive relations with other kin existed in extended and augmented family relationships.

Because the early settlers in America were fairly isolated from their extended families in Europe, their families were, for the most part, large nuclear units initially, with each one serving fundamental economic purposes, wherein the home was also the workplace. However, the "extended and augmented family" model was operationalized on a rural community-wide or village-wide basis by families combining their nuclear units cooperatively to perform large-scale tasks, such as barn raising and thrashing wheat, and to provide mutual support. With the westward movement, migration affected family structure and function (contributing, in some cases, to separation, with the wife assuming a larger parental role); but even when they moved to the most remote areas, familial values connoted extended kinship ties (until they established actual on-site extended families of their own).

Industrial Era Families

By the late 1800s, the industrial era was in full swing along with urbanization. During this time, the cities of America were being flooded with European immigrants and indigenous rural dwellers. Again, although all three types of families could be found, most of those in urban areas were nuclear and/or nuclear/augmented families. (In Buffalo, New York, for example, about 20% of families had live-in boarders and/or other relatives [Glasco, 1977].)

With hard-earned affluence in the early and middle parts of the twentieth century came upward social mobility and suburbanization. As the urban dwellers moved toward the periphery of the city, their family patterns changed in the direction of smaller family size and egalitarianism. The husband in particular was not regarded as having more privileges than the wife (Allan, 1986). This was precipitated by America's participation in World Wars I and II and the Korean War (with surges of women in the domestic workforce making family decisions while their husbands were at war), war economies, the expansion of transportation and communication capabilities, the invention of modern conveniences, the movement of industry away from the central city, and a shift in the moral code of the country (e.g., divorce became easier to obtain and more acceptable, and sexual standards became more flexible).

On the surface, modern urban and suburban families were neatly packaged and presented to the public in a fashion similar to the way food service is packaged in the fast food industry (Ritzer, 2000). These "formulaic families" prided themselves on their adherence to standards of social conformity such that they all looked alike. Thus society was the reference source, not the neighborhood community.

High-Tech Era Families

With the shift from the industrial to the present-day service-oriented, high-tech economy, families have adapted in many unique ways. The American middle class culture has tended to shift toward individual gratification and personal achievement, with the whole world becoming a resource pool. With socially prescribed formulaic family structures and functions having been jettisoned, personal preferences and decision making now serve as guideposts for optimum family relationships and interactions, and temporary families and "temporarily committed relationships" can be the result. For instance, some people get together with others to maximize their chances of a personally gratifying relationship. *Complementary desires theory* suggests that people select others for relationships to make up for, balance, or supply features that they do not themselves have. The information era has liberated intimate associations from local residential space; people now associate on the basis of ad hoc interests rather than proximity. Since modern technologies allow interaction outside neighborhood boundaries, spatial agglomeration is only one of the ways family members gain access to one another. All types of virtual families are possible. For example, an individual can exchange ideas on the Web with new partners at any distance. At the same time, new support systems can become an important extension of the family or an important "family" to a single individual. Health-related Web-based and e-mail–based mailing lists that give individuals a chance to learn and support each other through stressful times have resulted in the creation of new high-tech "families."

Family Organization

Traditionally, health care practitioners are trained to think of family organization in terms of linear systems–based theory. The fundamental concept is that a system or family organization is understood to be stable, orderly, and based on rational choice by a specified set of persons as defined by professional convention. For example, the nuclear family is often considered the exemplar or ideal model. A husband, wife, and their biological children who live together in a particular place represent the typical nuclear family. Recognition of how health care practitioners have come to reify this construction occurs only when a different script is encountered. For example, a gay/lesbian family attempts to apply for medical insurance coverage for the non–blood-related child of one member of the family and is turned down. Only when health care practitioners are confronted with scripts that do not meet their expectations do their assumptions become evident. The actual percentage of married couples living together in a home with their children is down to 24.1% of households from 40.3% in 1970 (Smith, 2002, p. 108). Most people would be surprised at this very low number because it does not follow the script for families to which they are accustomed. With the changing demographics and changing arrangements of individuals into families, health care practitioners and health care organizations are and will continue to be challenged to recognize fixed assumptions and learn to be creative and supportive of human constellations, whatever they may be. These forms are varied and in themselves always changing because of changing membership, age, economic conditions, nature of work, culture, locality, and racial and ethnic concerns. This complexity can create considerable variety in terms of shifting forms. For example, in the traditional adults-with-children model of the family, couples of various ages may be rearing children of various ages including infants, young children, adolescent children, and college-age children who have left home. Grandparents may act as the primary parents of their grandchildren. The family might be a newly married heterosexual couple or a newly committed gay/lesbian couple. The ways in which new members are added to these families vary: children may be conceived through sexual union or artificial insemination; children may be adopted; children from previous unions of one or both partners may be brought into the new family; or foster children may be brought into the home. Box 2-2 lists only some of the possible forms that families can take. Even these forms are always in flux in terms of meaning and function as a result of changing ages of the members, socioeconomic shifts, race, ethnicity, religion, geography, and culture. This shifting of the family form requires flexibilities and knowledge to address existing family constellations to provide meaningful family care.

This list is only the beginning of new possibilities for classifying and categorizing members as a family. Within these few forms of family are changes that must be addressed because of a multitude of variables such as aging, demographics, culture, economic conditions, and many others. Box 2-3 presents examples of diverse types of families.

The manner in which all elements of society construct the idea of family is a powerful political issue that has implications for nursing and health care practice. The idea that there is a "family crisis" in that "the family" is being destroyed as a result of changing values and mores has con-

---

BOX 2-2   Examples of Possible Family Forms

Legally married cohabiting adults with or without children

Legally married commuter relationship with or without children

Cohabiting–unmarried (contractual and noncontractual) adult-centered family with or without children

Single parent by choice with child (from relationship, artificial insemination, or adoption)

Single parent not by choice with biological or adopted child

Single parent through death of partner

Divorced parent with or without custody or with joint custody of children

Blended (step) families including children from previous relationships

Grandparents or grandparent and grandchildren

Fictive kin-based families

Foster families

Gay and lesbian families with or without children

Communities that think of their members as family

Extended family of aunts, uncles, cousins

Homeless group trying to work together

A youth gang

---

sequences for legislation and public policy that intimately affect how the health care professions serve families. Demographic data demonstrating increased divorce rates, more single-parent families, increasing numbers of women working outside the home, greater numbers of individuals living alone, and the greater visibility of gay and lesbian families have resulted in the political movement to reassert the heterosexual, middle-class, paternalistic—and for the most part—white suburban nuclear family structure as the only true, natural family of value. The fact is that the very idea of family is and has always been in the process of change. However, to members of a society wanting stability and continuity, this changing relationship is threatening and thus viewed as a crisis. Change does represent an

BOX 2-3 Examples of Diverse Families

A young man is returning home after completing a drug treatment program in a nearby city. Everyone in his small community knows where he has been and why. They know more about him than most friends know about each other. Everyone in his community is in a sense a part of his family and he is a part of theirs. The small community to which he is returning consists of about 1500 American Indians in a rural area surrounded by swamps and pine forests. Nearly everyone in this community is known by name by the other members. Many are related through kinship, being second and third cousins. This young man grew up expecting that neighbors and any other member of the community could and would discipline him if he were caught doing something he shouldn't be doing. They would also care for and support him if necessary. Now that he has returned, his mother feels confident that with all these "eyes" and the community's desire to help him, he will get a great deal of support and guidance. As it turns out, this has been the case, and he has created a new life back among his people. This community is his family in the most significant ways one can think of family. They have nurtured him and then welcomed him back with caring hearts and a willingness to support and protect him. Treatment of the family in a traditional sense would have failed to connect this young man to what was truly his family.

The mail carrier comes to the door and knocks to see whether Mrs. Hylton is doing okay. She is concerned because Mrs. Hylton is usually on her porch waiting for the mail. When no one answers, she goes around the back of the house and discovers Mrs. Hylton lying on the ground. She is conscious and has not been there for long. Emergency services are called, and a neighbor contacts her daughter who lives nearly 700 miles away. Luck, of course, played a part, but in many ways this rural mail carrier has become an important part of Mrs. Hylton's family. She has been a daily part of her life and has acted to help protect her. The mail carrier's daily connection with her has been a source of support for this elderly woman living alone. Her children have all left to pursue careers and are no longer available. Members of this community have taken on many of the supportive and caring roles that we assume families carry out. In many ways, these nontraditional family members have become her family.

Mrs. Argabright has returned home after a long stay in the oncology department at a large metropolitan hospital. Her neighbor has been a friend for the past 30 years and is a registered nurse. Mrs. Argabright's husband has retired and has been her caretaker for the past year of chemotherapy and hospital stays. Her children are unable to be with the family for any length of time because of work and their own new families in distant cities. Although not an "official" family member permitted to visit her in the hospital when in intensive care, this neighbor has been a significant member of this family for many years now. Both "families," Mrs. Argabright's and her neighbor's, have experienced tragedies, and both have been available to each other in ways that their children could not have been, given that they all live far away and have jobs and other responsibilities. Now in this very difficult time, it is the neighbor who calls the children to their mother's bedside. It is the neighbor who provides support and comfort to the husband-caretaker and the children when Mrs. Argabright finally dies. Her presence and concern have seen this family through to this end. She has been an important member of this family and has assisted this family is some of their most trying moments.

ending to an idea, but it is not an end to human bonds and relationships in whatever form they take over time. Yet this notion of a crisis of the family has resulted and will continue to result in efforts to limit services to those who do not meet these traditional values and structures. The restrictions and limitations produced by such efforts determine the very nature of health care services including visitation regulations, who is permitted to participate in decisions, and who is consulted about future care and support.

This politicized notion of the family extends from the intimacy of the nurse-client relationship to the national policies that determine funding for health care services. For example, at the national level, efforts are underway to spend a considerable amount of federal money in an attempt to have single mothers marry as part of social service efforts. This reflects a particular belief about what a family is and who should constitute that family. Even international issues such as terrorism and illegal immigration can have serious consequences for both health care providers and families if they are associated with an ethnic group that has been singled out as threatening. The suspicions and general demeanor of a society can create tensions and anxieties among these families and health care providers, thus altering their relationships and connectedness to their community and their ability to receive needed health care.

Implicated in this continuing shift in the construct of the notion of family is the rapid demographic change taking place and estimated to continue in this new century. The changing cultural and social values being expressed by increasing numbers of diverse groups will continue to have an important impact on health care, ranging from societal policies to individual and family care plans.

The Shifting Population and the Future

The twenty-first century will be marked by significant and swift changes in relationships and communities—changes that could have only been imagined a few decades ago. The acceleration of a geometric progression in demographic changes will take place very rapidly and challenge ideas about normalcy or having a single referent or standard with which to think about and evaluate families. The very notion of the family will no longer suffice as an explanatory tool. The existence of increasing variations on the theme will make such classifications increasingly less meaningful in day-to-day practice.

Louis Hicks (2002) points to a rapidly shifting world and gives a glimpse into the future in terms of an increasing population and changing family context. The following sketch is based on this work. At the start of the twentieth century, the population of the United States was about 75 million people. At the end of the century, the population stood at about 281 million people. It is projected to reach nearly 400 million by the middle of the twenty-first century. At the start of the century, approximately 13% of adults had at least a high school education, and at its end,

approximately 83% had this minimum level of education.

Unmarried heterosexual cohabitation was nearly nonexistent at the start of the twentieth century and is now quite common. A substantial increase in cohabitation began in the 1960s, with a 100% increase from 523,000 in 1970 to 3.8 million in 2000 (Fields & Casper, 2001). The rate of unmarried cohabitation is higher among young adults, but a significant increase has also been noted among senior citizens, widows and widowers, and divorced persons who live together for companionship and to share finances (Goldberg, & Goldberg, 2002). In 2000, two fifths of unmarried-partner households included children younger than 18 years. Twenty-eight percent of unmarried cohabiting women had more education than their partners; 4% of the partners were of a different race, and 6% were of a different ethnicity (Fields & Casper, 2001).

Over the past decade, there has been a 57% increase in the foreign-born population of the United States. Of this group, 51.7% are from Latin America, 26.4% are from Asia, and 15% are from Europe. The proportion of foreign-born persons in the United States in 1970 was about 4.7%, demonstrating a rapid shift and increased migration to the United States. At present, the foreign-born population of the United States stands at 31.1 million (U. S. Census Bureau, 2000).

As the twentieth century began, about 6% of married women worked outside the home; now, approximately 61% are working outside the home. More and more women of all marital statuses are working outside the home, and their earning capacity has yet to approach parity with that of men. In 1996, for instance, 60% of African American women, 59% of white women, and 53% of Hispanic women were officially in the labor force (U.S. Department of Labor, 1997). Obviously, these numbers radically underestimate the true size of the female labor force, for they do not include women who work sporadically; those whose names do not appear on official work lists; those who work in cottage industries, at home, or on a contractual basis; or those who are working more than a year.

At the start of the twentieth century, nearly all children lived with both parents, but by the 1970s, only 75% of children in the United States

TABLE 2-1   Percentages of Population Distribution for Family Households

	1970	1980	1990	2000
Family households	40.3	30.9	26.3	23.8
Married couples without children	30.3	29.9	29.8	24.1
Married couples with children	40.0	30.9	26.3	24.1
Other families with own children	5.0	7.5	8.3	9.2
Other families without children	5.6	5.4	6.5	16.0
Persons living alone	17.1	22.7	24.6	25.5
Other nonfamily households	1.7	3.6	4.6	5.7

From U. S. Census Bureau. (2000). *Current population survey, March Supplements: 1970 to 2000.*

did. At present, only about half live with both parents. At the same time, parents are spending more time with their children now than at the start of the twentieth century. Divorce is increasing in frequency; recent divorce rates show that the chance of a first marriage ending in divorce is about 1 in 2 (the world's highest rate). People are postponing marriage, with many opting instead for living alone, singlehood, and/or cohabitation (actually, cohabitation rates are increasing phenomenally) even after widowhood. Many couples are deciding not to have children. As the U.S. Census Bureau (2000) percentages show in Table 2-1, from 1970 to 2000, the preference for singlehood (and childlessness) seems to be increasing.

In the past three decades, homosexuality has become more tolerated and visible in American society, and gay and lesbian families or legal domestic partnerships are recognized in one state and several counties and cities across the nation (Eitzen & Baca Zinn, 2000). Gay and lesbian families are quite diverse in their composition and form (and may include lovers, friends, biological and adopted children, blood relatives, or ex-lovers). Although these families are usually headed by same-sex partners, single-parent gay and lesbian families do exist (Friedman, Bowden, & Jones, 2003).

The population is shifting geographically. A state such as Florida, which had about a half million people at the start of the twentieth century, is now the fastest growing state with about 16 million people. Many people moving into the state are elderly, members of minorities, and poor. States in the western part of the country are growing in numbers and diversity, as is the rest of the nation. Within a little more than 50 years, in many areas of the country, white persons will be the numerical minority in the population. At present, California is home to 34 million people, and the non-Hispanic white population is no longer in the majority. At present, Hispanics (persons of Latin American descent, especially Mexico, Puerto Rico, and Cuba) and Latinos (persons of Latin-American origin) have just surpassed African Americans in terms of overall population, and it is estimated that the Hispanic and Latino populations will continue to increase as a result of immigration to the United States and high birth rates (Moore, 2002, p. 31). In addition, multiracial identities were counted, and the count showed that about 7 million people identified themselves as multiracial (Barefoot, 2002, p. 61).

The racial and ethnic composition of the general American population has changed since the last century and is expected to change even more in the future. Some researchers go to great lengths to specify the wide range of family adaptations implemented by some racial and ethnic groups compared with others. (See, for example, Billingsley [1992], for a detailed discussion of the 12 structural types of the African American family that have evolved since the days of slavery.) Table 2-2 lists projections for the

TABLE 2-2   Projections for Percentages of Different Racial/Ethnic Groups for 1990, 2000, 2025, and 2050

	1990	2000	2025	2050
White, non-Hispanic	76	72	62	52
African American	12	13	14	16
American Indian, Eskimo, and Aleut	0.8	0.9	1.0	1.1
Asian and Pacific Islander	3	4	8	10
Hispanic	9	11	17	23

U. S. Census Bureau. (1995). *Population profile of the United States, 1995.* (Current populations reports, Series P23-189). Washington, DC: U.S. Government Printing Office.

percentages of different racial and ethnic groups in the U.S. population for the years 1990, 2000, 2025, and 2050.

The twenty-first century marks the start of a dramatic increase in the aging populations around the world. According to the *New York Times* ("Growing Tide," 2002), at the start of this new century, the population of North Americans who are 60 years or older stands at about 15%. This number will grow to about 27% by the middle of the century. The ratio of persons 15 to 64 years old to persons 65 years or older is presently 5 younger persons for every person 65 years of age or older. By 2050, this ratio will be 3 younger persons for every person 65 years of age or older. By 2050, the world's population of persons older than 65 years will exceed the world's population of children 14 years of age and younger. The makeup of families will be changing along with the needs and demands on members of families and society. This increasing proportion of older adults and their increasing health needs will place more demands on those who care for and work with families of the aging population. Monetary support will be provided by fewer working members of society and will have a serious impact on funding sources and health policies. These are issues that health care professionals must be prepared to address.

An important factor in health care is the increasing aging population worldwide. Related to this aging population is the finding that grandparents are often the primary caretakers of their grandchildren. Efforts are underway to help these grandparents gain custody of many of these children so that they may qualify for subsidized health insurance and day care and to assist them in dealing with medical regulations that prevent them from making critical medical decisions for these children (Cohen & Cohen, 2002). This is another example of a challenge to the definition of family.

Finally, families vary by socioeconomic status (SES), and the income and wealth disparities in the country have widened. In fact, SES confers different connections with the broader social environment and different ways of acquiring the necessities of life. Middle and upper middle class families tend to be nuclear with tight boundaries but with crucial links (principally through occupations) to nonfamily institutions. Recently, however, these families have been able to maintain their economic status only by having both spouses work. Clearly, this has created a hardship in terms of childrearing and other functions of the home. However, these families do survive by virtue of their broad involvement in the public sector.

Working-class families, whose resources depend primarily on their wages, have expanded notions of the family; they may call on friends and sometimes neighbors to help out when there is a need for, for example, baby-sitting, help with moving, or borrowing money. Resources are pooled when connections with outside opportunities are tenuous (e.g., when a job folds). The family boundaries are flexible for purposes of expedience and reflect a network of sharing and support.

Canada's population (Canada.com, 2002) stood at 5.7 million at the start of the twentieth century and now stands at 30 million. Over the past 100 years, the Canadian population has migrated to urban areas that now include about 80% of the population. This is similar to shifts in population in the United States where the rural or nonmetropolitan population has declined to just less than 20%. More than 50% of Canadians are now living in four regions of Canada: the Golden Horseshoe in southern Ontario; Montreal and its environs; British Columbia's Lower Mainland and southern Vancouver Island; and the Calgary-Edmonton corridor. The consequence of this continuing shift of the population to urban areas is complex in that it presents two very different settings for health care. The increasing concentration of populations is and will continue to create increased demands for services in relatively small geographic areas. Centralization of services and sharing of resources may be an increasing likelihood. In addition, there will be an increased need for health care providers. In the increasingly isolated regions, the lack of sustainable facilities and resources will become more pressing. The isolation of families that need health care, particularly in rural regions of Canada, will require innovative uses of resources and technology. Nursing and nurse practitioners, with the use of technology for consultation and support, may fulfill many of the needs now provided by other medical personnel. At the same time, the populations of these regions will include First Nations and aboriginal communities that will require particular sensitivity to, understanding of, and the ability to work with community traditions and values. Likewise, increasing immigration and diversity within larger urban regions will require diverse skills and understanding of the various family constructions.

Using population estimates, the federal department of Indian Affairs has concluded that "Canada's total aboriginal population" stands at nearly 1.4 million (Canada.com, 2002). As a result of the refusal of many aboriginal groups to respond to the census because of unresolved political issues, this is only an estimate (Canada.com,

2002). This refusal itself reflects the multiple issues faced by health care practitioners in reaching out to First Nations members in terms of understanding health care needs and health care approaches that recognize the dynamics of these varied cultural groups. Even within the aboriginal population, there are many diverse communities and variations in ways of constructing health needs and care. More in-depth information about the makeup of the Canadian family in the twenty-first century is presented in the Canadian Perspectives box.

In both Canada and the United States, multicultural values are playing out in health care decisions. In the United States, approximately 20% of the population does not speak English at home (Cohen & Cohen, 2002). Even though Hispanic and Latino groups are among the largest and fastest growing segments of the population, many other diverse groups are increasing in numbers. Numerous Asian subgroups (persons from the Middle East, India, and the Pacific Islands) are increasing in numbers across both the United States and Canada. A wide range of immigrant groups and their first-generation children are in need of health care and must overcome both language and cultural differences to engage the health care system.

Changing Multicultural Family Configurations and Health Practices

To address the shifting populations and locality, as well as changing family configurations, health care practitioners must reconsider the traditional incorporation of social science thinking into practice. The inclusion of multicultural content in a course of training is not sufficient unless this content addresses the very way health practice is carried out. With the rapidly increasing diversity of populations and the range of family constructions, health care practitioners must recognize their own ethnocentrism and theoretical assumptions about people with whom they will be working.

In most courses with multicultural content, students are typically taught about "groups" of culturally, ethnically, and racially diverse peoples. This is helpful only to the extent that it alerts the students to the range of potential differences that

CANADIAN PERSPECTIVES
DESCRIBING TWENTY-FIRST CENTURY CANADIAN FAMILY TYPES AND ISSUES

Francine de Montigny, PhD, MSc, Inf
University of Quebec in Outaouais
Line Beaudet, MScN
Montreal University Health Center

The family, of which there are 7.8 million in Canada, is still the basic unit in Canadian society. Although many different ethnic groups are represented in Canada's population, it consists primarily of individuals whose mother tongue is English (59%) or French (23%). Sixteen percent speak some other language, for example, Chinese (2.5%), Italian (1.7%), or German (1.6%). Less than 0.4% speak an aboriginal language such as Cree or Inuktitut. Canadians are primarily Catholic (46%) or Protestant (36%), while fewer than 2% are followers of Islam or Buddhism.

Nuclear families, consisting of a father, a mother, and their children, account for 45% of all Canadian families while remarriages make up 29% of families (Statistics Canada, 1998a). Fourteen percent of these two-parent families involve people living in a common-law relationships, which is very popular in Quebec where such relationships account for one couple in four. In most two-parent families (64%), both spouses work. In the past, roles in families were determined by gender. The woman was responsible for tasks relating to the education of the children and keeping the house while the man was the provider for the family. Today, men and women tend to divide the family duties in a way that is not determined by gender. The fact remains, however, that women who are members of couples continue to spend almost twice as much time as men on household chores and child care. Thus 64% of women and 39% of men working full time spend 15 hours or more each week caring for children younger than 15 years. The task is even more burdensome for mothers and fathers of children younger than 6 years (Statistics Canada, 1998b).

The Canadian family is less stable than it used to be, as can be seen by the growing number of divorces each year, which now amount to almost one half of marriages. The result is an increase in the number of single-parent families, which now make up 15% of Canadian families. One Canadian child in five lives in a family of this kind. It is very often the mother who raises these children, since women head four out of five of these families. For these women and children, whose average income is approximately one half of total average family income, the economic upshot is poverty for one family in two (Statistics Canada, 1998c).

There are variations on these family patterns, such as families with no children, gay and lesbian families, community families based on religious or philosophical beliefs, and extended families that include close relatives (grandparents, uncles, aunts, and cousins) of the family members (deMontigny & Beaudet, 1997).

A decline in the number of births has been observed in the Canadian family. In 1998, the number of live births recorded declined for the eighth straight year. This development can be explained by the aging of the members of the baby-boom generation and by the decline in fertility rates of women younger than 30 years. Some 80% of Canadian families have only one or two children, and almost one third of women will not have any children if current trends continue.

The drop in the fertility rate, the increases in the divorce rate and the numbers of single-parent and blended families, and more mothers in the work force are only some of the factors that have radically changed the way in which Canadian families function today. These situations require a different distribution of roles within the family and also affect the structure of the labour force. Thus both the family environment and the work environment are affected by these new realities. The fact that families are becoming smaller and less stable has major consequences in psychological and social terms. For example, attention should be paid to the effects of marriage dissolution on the mental health of the spouses and the children.

However, despite these major social upheavals and the extent of the problems caused, certain social aspirations are widely shared by most Canadians. Having children, educating them, and loving them remain some of the fundamental values of Canadian society.

Continued

CANADIAN PERSPECTIVES
DESCRIBING TWENTY-FIRST CENTURY CANADIAN FAMILY TYPES AND ISSUES — cont'd

The fastest population growth in the past decade was among the oldest Canadians, with senior women being the majority. The suburban population is aging more rapidly. The needs of families with elder members will be major health, social, and economic issues in the new millennium.

References

deMontigny, F., & Beaudet, L. (1997). *When life explodes: Impact of a child's death on the family.* Montreal: ERPI.

Statistics Canada (1998a). Canada in statistics. Retrieved from http://www.statcan.ca/english/Pgdb/People/famili.htm

Statistics Canada (1998b). Families: Social and economic characteristics. Government of Canada. Retrieved from http://www.statcan.ca/english/Pgdb/People/famili.htm

Statistics Canada (1998c). Sources of revenue, families' revenues. Government of Canada. Retrieved from http://www.statcan.ca/english/Pgdb/People/famili.htm

Canadian spelling is used.

---

might exist in terms of values, traditions, ways of defining disease and cures, and who is to be consulted and involved in the health care process. The danger is that these are generalizations about large groups that will not be applicable to all members. The federally unrecognized First Nations people residing in small isolated communities in the Eastern United States are hardly known even to their neighbors. These groups have unique cultural values but are unlike the traditional federally recognized First Nations peoples such as the Cheyenne and Navajo living on large Western reservations and in other communities. Neither these large communities on reservations nor the small, unrecognized groups can be assumed to be like all other First Nations peoples. Particular cultural localities and particular ethnic groups do create unique contexts. It is this uniqueness that is expressed by these diverse groups, as well as a particular uniqueness of individual family groupings, to which one must be sensitive. Green (1999) notes that if culture is understood to mean "the ideas, beliefs, responses, conversations, shared wisdom, bodily gestures, invoked emotions, attempted solutions, revised hopes and expectations, and perhaps, even invocations of the supernatural, we are entering into the significance of a place and a people" (p. 51). This is what Geertz (1983) has referred to as *local knowledge,* and it can be used not only with cultural variations but also with basic notions about what constitutes family. The ability to see locally and to use the constructs of those with whom they work will help health care professionals engage the families of this new century.

Seeing locally translates into rethinking health care practice in terms of knowing not only personal meanings but the social or cultural meanings and definitions of what is and what is not disease and how it is to be addressed. For example, McMiller and Weisz (1996) explored "help-seeking" behavior among Latino, African American, and white families for mental health services for their children. They found that there were significant differences in how these families sought help. The white families, for the most part, first sought assistance from the usual health care professionals, whereas the other families were much less likely to do so. The other groups were more likely to turn to persons within their community before seeking any professional services.

This points again to the need for health care professionals to rethink their approaches to the changing construction of family, as well as the diversification of the cultural context of diverse families. James Green (1999) describes cross-cultural practice as consisting of various ways of learning and working, rather than knowing about a specific group in the abstract. If this perspective is expanded to include the growing diversity of the construction of the meaning of the term *family*, the following factors need to be included in any health-related practice perspective:

- Openness to cultural and lived differences
- Awareness of one's own limitations and self-centered definitions
- Appropriate use of cultural and community resources
- Development of a client-centered, strengths-based perspective

The foundation of this approach can start with embracing the strengths-based approach to learning about and collaborating with families. This perspective opens the health care professional to discovering the "constructed family" within that family's cultural context. It is a challenge to both personal and traditional professional perspectives that establishes the practitioner as expert who assumes the misguided notion of being objective. See the Research Synopsis for an example of changing practices by health care practitioners.

RESEARCH SYNOPSIS

MOTHER'S RESILENCE, FAMILY HEALTH WORK, AND MOTHER'S HEALTH-PROMOTING LIFESTYLE PRACTICES IN FAMILIES WITH YOUNG CHILDREN

Understanding family health work and factors contributing to family health promotion is needed for health professionals to empower families to develop a healthy lifestyle. The purpose of this study was to test the *Developmental Model of Health and Nursing* with mothers of young children. In this study the family's strengths of resilience health and health-promoting lifestyle as they relate to health work were tested. The authors define *health work* as the process through which families develop healthy ways of of living by learning how to cope with life events and by promoting healthy development of the family unit and its members. The study was a descriptive correlation survey of 67 mothers of preschool children. Findings indicated that both mother's resilience and family health work were positively related to the mother's health-promoting lifestyle practices. Mother's resilience and health work were found to predict 41% variance in the mother's health-promoting lifestyle practices when income was controlled. Researchers suggest that these findings highlight the importance of the adoption and maintenance of healthy lifestyle in adult family members, particularly mothers. Also noted is that resilience of the mother is a crucial variable in the mother's use of health-promoting lifestyle and the family's health. Implications for further research include the need for a family health-promoting lifestyle profile, studies of family resilience with diverse families, and family issues. The implication for nursing practice suggested included providing individual and family support on health promotion with the concepts of family systems, family development, family health gatekeepers, encouragement of resilience, and advocacy at the policy level for support of family health education and economic support to sustain and promote family health.

In summary, the researchers suggested that the findings continue to support the premise that family and individual health promotions efforts and strengths are intertwined and complex and shaped by multiple internal and external contexts. They advocate that a strength-based approach to family nursing practice should be used and that the Development Model of Health and Nursing is appropriate as a support of family health work and as a guide for further study.

Monteith, B. & Ford-Gilboe, M. (2002). Relationships among mother's resilience, family health work and mother's health promoting lifestyle practices in families with young children. *Journal of Family Nursing, 8*(4), 383-407.

Patricia Furgal, RN, working at the Sanikiluaq Health Center located in the Belcher Islands region of Hudson Bay describes the shifts in perspective that must take place for practice to be successful (personal communication, June 14, 2002). In this Inuit community of about 700 people, there is *one* family that is made up of all the inhabitants. They act and respond as one family. They care for and support each other as one family. Many of the young girls have babies "out of wedlock" as described by the dominant culture. Within this larger family culture, this is acceptable and traditional. All families help to support and care for the children. When a young mother of small children died, Ms. Furgal recalls that she experienced this untimely death as "tragic" for the woman and her children. She was surprised that the members of the community saw it as part of life and knew that the children would be fine. They were not indifferent but looked on this incident as a part of their lives in a way that most outsiders would not.

Collaborating with Families from a Strengths Perspective

The strengths perspective considers the possibilities of peoples' lives. It is a way of seeing the world, a perspective that is profound in its requirements of professional helpers. It asks that we shift our studied view of damage, disease, and pain toward human and social potential. It is an approach that Dennis Saleebey (2002) describes as "honoring the innate wisdom of the human spirit" (p. 1). This is not meant to ignore or make light of the real pain, disease, and trauma experienced by individuals and their families. Instead, it is intended to direct attention toward a balanced understanding to include hope, resilience, creativity, support, and competence as uniquely expressed by families and family members as they face the challenges of life.

Significantly, the strengths perspective is a serious effort to realign the professional perspective with the potentials and possibilities of families and their members. It calls for a collaborative and respectful belief in the complexity of "illnesses and trauma" in terms of the biological, psychological, social, cultural, and spiritual life and the unique personal histories of an individual and his or her family and community. The strengths perspective replaces the cynicism of pathology that more often denies the healing that can take place, as well as the quality of life that is possible. Andrew Weil (1995) reflects on this pessimism fostered by his own medical profession when he states: "I cannot help feeling embarrassed by my own profession when I hear the myriad ways in which doctors convey their pessimism to patients" (p. 64). Lorraine Wright, Wendy Watson, and Janice Bell (1996) point out that "health professionals' beliefs about their ability to influence an illness are also an important factor in how people experience illness" (p. 56). Shifting one's professional perspective from seeing only disease, damage, and distress to one that recognizes the unique possibilities of each individual and family as challenges and possessing unique possibilities for defining "illness" and "health" creates a world of possibilities. Working from a strengths perspective does not mean that some miraculous cure will ensue, but it will have an impact on the part a health care professional plays in how the situation or challenge is met by the individual and his or her family, which can have a profound impact on the course of the challenge or "experience of the illness" (Wright, Watson, & Bell, 1996, p. 55).

The strengths perspective is not a matter of learning some new questions to ask or techniques to use with families. It is personal, as well as professional. It is shifting what Bonnie Bernard (1996) has described as a way of seeing that reflects the heart and mind. Because health care professionals have been trained and socialized into a profession that has advanced on the bases of rationality, objectivity, scientific inquiry, and professional expertise of operationalized models of disease and treatment, it is not an easy task for them to recognize that their subjective beliefs and values have a pivotal part to play in their work. But this is what is required if the strengths perspective is to be more than a faddish addition to the usual practice routine.

Contrasting Belief Systems

Saleebey (1997, 2002) comments about the strengths perspective. He notes that the language

---

TABLE 2-3   Language of the Strengths Perspective

Lexicon of Medical/Pathology	Lexicon of Strengths/Resilience
The family is the problem or pathology named.	The family is much more than a described condition or problem.
Posture of expert constructing objectives case histories, diagnosis, and treatment based on standardized cases and research.	Posture of collaboration and reciprocal relationships. Mutual inquiry and discovery. Significance of family and social context. Personal history and uniqueness central to understanding.
The family is most likely viewed and assessed as an individual without regard to life context.	The family is always seen in the context of membership within a social grouping.
The family is viewed in terms of vulnerability, failures, and weaknesses.	The family is viewed in terms of resilience and possibilities.
Healing is a result of specific intervention protocols.	Healing has many contributors. Healing implies a holistic process that includes relationship with others and spirituality, as well as other beliefs and values.

Based on data from Saleebey, D. (Ed.). (2002). *The strengths perspective in social work practice* (3rd ed.). Boston: Allyn and Bacon; Saleebey, D. (Ed.). (1997). *The strengths perspective in social work practice* (2nd ed.). New York: Longman.

---

of the strengths perspective

> provides us with a vocabulary of appreciation and not aspersion about those with whom we work. In essence, the effort is to move away from defining professional work as the articulation of the power of expert knowledge toward collaboration with the power within the individual (and his or her) community toward a life that is palpably better—and better on the (person's) own terms (p. 12).

Table 2-3 presents a comparison of the language of the strengths perspective with that of traditional medicine.

Recognizing Resiliency, Diversity, and Strengths

Robert Jay Lifton (1993) describes the perspective of seeing the changing and often troubling world as possibilities rather than fraught only with dangers and annihilation. He states that "Rather than collapse under these threats and pulls, the self turns out to be surprisingly resilient. It makes use of bits and pieces here and there and somehow keeps going" (p. 1). This is not to say that a quickly changing society, increased demands, and continued oppression, racism, and poverty experienced by many families should be maintained

as helpful or character-building in any way. It does say that practitioners might start to better understand resilience or how people do "make it" to some degree and learn to assist them in "making it." It also points to the idea of prevention by means of eliminating as many hazards in the way of people and their families from whatever source. The strengths perspective is an overarching construct that includes the work being done on resiliency in families. At the heart of the strengths perspective is the notion that people and their families can, in the face of untold hardship and health crisis, undergo remarkable adaptations and ways of living and dying that maintain quality in their lives.

Strengths as expressed through resilience are complex phenomena, and a simple meaning is hard to pin down. Yet there is growing evidence that given the tribulations of life, many people keep going to create meaningful lives within whatever limitations they have in terms of time or quality. Froma Walsh (1998), a pioneer in bringing the strengths perspective or resilience-based perspective to working with families, describes the work with resilience as an approach aimed at identifying and fortifying "key interactional processes that enable families to withstand and rebound from disruptive life challenges" (p. 3). She describes the strengths or resilience-based professional perspective as "shifting perspective from viewing distressed families as damaged to seeing them as challenged, affirming their potential for repair and growth" (p. 3.).

The Resiliency Model of Family Stress, Adjustment and Adaptation (McCubbin & McCubbin, 1993) was evaluated and developed on the basis of research with ethnic families. It describes elements of the family process of coming to terms with stressful or threatening life events through evaluation and assessment of the stressor, family vulnerabilities, established patterns of family functioning, family capabilities and strengths, family appraisal of the stressor, and problem-solving and coping skills. It looks at the family's responses in terms of outcomes of the previous variables. Important to this discussion are those ideas concerning family resources or strengths and capabilities. Seven categories of individual or personal resources of members within a family are listed in the model (Box 2-4) (McCubbin, McCubbin, Thompson, & Thompson, 1998).

In addition to these personal resources of members, family cohesiveness and ability to support change are noted as strengths that can lead to resilience. Families that have developed a sense of bond or unity among members along with trust, appreciation, and support, as well as a history of adaptability, are noted as being significantly resilient (McCubbin et al., 1998; Olson, Sprenkle, & Russell, 1979).

Health care practitioners can align themselves with these processes if they are willing to recognize this potential and to learn the art of collaboration and thinking locally in terms of possibilities or strengths, that is, recognition of the limitations of prescriptive, as well as legalistic, regulations that define family and a willingness to challenge these in terms of policy and practice. In practice, the health care practitioner would give up the mantel of expert and learn from the patient and his or her family. The strengths-based practitioner would be open to culturally and lived differences in terms of who is available to assist and support this patient. What does this illness mean to this particular patient and family? How do they construct this experience? Jeanna Connors and Ann Donnellan (1998) describe the juncture of traditional scientific knowledge and that of a Navajo tribal member when the member said:

BOX 2-4 Seven Categories of Resources in the Resiliency Model of Family Stress, Adjustment, and Adaptation

1. The innate intelligence (wisdom) of family members, which can enhance awareness and comprehension of demands and facilitate the family's mastery of these
2. Knowledge and skills acquired from education, training, and experience so that individual family members and the family unit can perform tasks with greater efficiency and ease
3. Personality traits (for example, a sense of humor) that facilitate coping
4. Physical, spiritual, and emotional health of members so that intact faculties and personal energy may be available for meeting family demands
5. A sense of mastery, which is the belief that one has some control over the circumstances of one's life
6. Self-esteem that is a positive judgment about one's self-worth
7. The ethnic identity and cultural background of family members and the ethnic orientation or world-view adopted by the family unit to guide the family's functioning

From McCubbin, H. I., McCubbin, M. A., Thompson, A. I., & Thomspon, E. A. (1998). Resiliency in ethnic families: A conceptual model for predicting family adjustment and adaptation. In H. I. McCubbin, E. A. Thompson, A. I. Thompson, & J. E. Fromer (Eds.), *Resiliency in Native American and immigrant families* (pp. 3-48). Thousand Oaks, CA: Sage.

"Before that white man came, we were blind (to disabilities). You brought us the gift of sight. I think we were happier when we couldn't see" (p. 172). They conclude that the "Western practitioners of biomedicine will encounter cultural roadblocks from the very onset, unless the professional is willing and capable of taking into account Navajo definitions and concepts of terms such as health, illness, cure, and progress" (p. 172). The traditional westernized, scientific perspective carries with it not only knowledge but attitudes and values. Health care practitioners view themselves as experts about what they have come to define as deficits, defects, abnormality and disease, which assumes a state of normalcy. They are trained to then discover a cause to which they apply a treatment to address the defective or abnormal condition. Even though this seems so natural and even odd to be considering, as discussed previously, these constructed ideas are not within the cultural and personal framework of many indigenous peoples: they are constructs of a particular Western scientific perspective. It appears so reasonable and true (reification) that most people discount indigenous ideas as "backward" or "unsophisticated" or dangerously ill-informed. The tendency is to challenge these as being primitive ideas and to disregard them as dangerous. Yet, as Connors and Donnellan (1998) have pointed out, the Navajo, for example, do not construct ideas about their autistic children as being abnormal or defective or failing to meet developmental mileposts. Instead, they have constructed a broader understanding of "progress." For many of the Navajo families, progress is not about fixing something but about embracing it into a broader concept of family. For many Navajo families of autistic children, the behavior of these children is understood as "integral parts of who these children were within the family" (Connors & Donnellan, 1998, p. 174). This inclusiveness and acceptance can easily be challenged by the "superior" knowledge and drive toward fixing and treating what the health care profession sees as abnormality. From a strengths perspective, these cultural variations can be viewed as strengths and social supports that can be embraced by the health care practitioner in developing a relationship built on the inherent strengths of a family and a community.

Nancy Feeley and Laurie Gottlieb (2000) believe that "working with strengths is closely integrated with the nature of the nurse-family relationship (i.e., collaboration, situation responsive, and exploratory), the focus and goal of care (i.e., health, coping, and development), and the construct of learning" (pp. 19-20). Using the original conceptualization of the strengths perspective in nursing, the McGill Model of Nursing (Allen, 1977; Allen, 1999), Feeley and Gottlieb (2000) support the beginnings of a shift in nursing practice from the deficit model to a strengths-based model of practice. They point out four categories of strengths that they propose as the basis for nurse-family collaborative relationships:

a) "Traits that reside within an individual or family (e.g., optimism, resilience);
b) Assets that reside within an individual or family (e.g., finances);
c) Capabilities, skills, or competencies that an individual or family has developed (e.g., problem-solving skills); or
d) A quality that is more transient in nature than a trait or asset (e.g., motivation)" (Feeley & Gottlieb, 2000, p. 12)

Given these areas of focus, the nurse-family conversation turns toward what the individual and/or family has done well. How have they managed so far? What has kept things from getting worse? What do they see as helpful? How have they managed past traumas or issues? What helped at those times? These are but a few of the ways that the conversation itself becomes a potent tool in empowerment. These conversations encourage the development of a positive and collaborative relationship. The family starts to think in terms of "making it" and "surviving" in some form that will be unique and reflective of their own culture, beliefs, values, and community. These conversations can be preventative in that, in the long run, they build a history of resiliency that can be called on at later times.

Summary

The twenty-first century is moving the health care practitioner into a world in which families and the idea of "family" are changing. The population is expanding exponentially, as it is growing in complexity and diversity. Simplistic ideas of family structure and process leave practitioners with little understanding of the fluidity and complexity of family life today and in the future. Knowledge must be a process of knowing that will always be changing as each new construct of family emerges in practice. This can only happen if the practitioner is open to local knowledge and to a position of "not knowing" (Anderson & Goolishian, 1992). "Not knowing" is not only starting where the client is but starting without making assumptions or presumptions based on personal and professional knowledge. It is not a state of ignorance but recognition that to know something is also a process of grasping or perceiving the meaning emanating from this "something." In this case, the practitioner "knows" in terms of the client's construction and thus approaches the client from an open place by not imposing prior knowledge or judgment. In this manner, the practitioner can take in the constructed meanings of "family" and the cultural contextual nature of these meanings. The prac-

titioner can align himself or herself with the strengths and context of a particular client's life. In so doing, the practitioner works within the strengths and perspectives of this client and his or her family. This practice recognizes the increasing complexity of people's lives and challenges the tendency to simplify and make efficient our understandings by generalizing, categorizing, and prescribing remedies. It builds on the resiliency and strengths of individuals in the context of their families and culture.

WEBSITE RESOURCES

ORGANIZATION	WEBSITE ADDRESS
Children, Youth and Families Education and Research Network (CYFERNet)	http://www.cyfernet.org/
Statistics Canada	http://www.stat.can.ca/
National Center for Minority Health and Health Disparities	http://www.ncmhd.nih.gov/
Collaborative Family Healthcare Association	http://www.cfhcc.org/
MinorityNurse.Com	http://www.minoritynurse.com
Institute for Urban Family Health	http://www.institute2000.org/
Satir Professional Development Institute of Manitoba	http://www.satir.ca
Family Support America	http://www.familysupportamerica.org
Strengthening America's Families (Office of Juvenile Justice and Delinquency Prevention)	http://www.strengtheningfamilies.org
National Clearinghouse on Families & Youth (NCFY)	http://www.ncfy.com
National Black Nurses Association	http://www.nbna.org
National Alliance for Hispanic Health	http://www.hispanichealth.org
First Nations and Inuit Health Branch (Canada)	http://www.hc-sc.gc.ca/fnihb-dgspni/fnihb/index.htm
Nunavut (Canada) Department of Health and Human Services	http://www.gov.nu.ca/hss.htm
Research and Training Center on Family Support and Children's Mental Health	http://www.rtc.pdx.edu/
Healthy Families (California)	http://www.healthyfamilies.ca.gov/
Families First: Making Families Last	http://www.familiesfirst.org/
Families for Early Autism Treatment	http://www.feat.org/
U.S. Census Bureau	http://www.census.gov

■ CHAPTER HIGHLIGHTS

- Thinking about families should be done in terms of the interactional processes among human beings and the constructs of the meaning of family within the multiple contexts of race, age, gender, sexual preference, socioeconomic status, ethnicity, locality, and history, as well as society's changing values and expectations of the twenty-first century.

- Families in North America are more ethnically diverse than those living in other continents, and because of technological and global factors, they are experiencing dynamic changes in function, structure, and norms.

- The major shifts in the demographics of families in the United States and Canada call for an evaluation of society's mental constructs of family models.

- Definitions of family have many forms, such as legal, social, financial, political, and sociological.

- The preferred definition of the family is the one that the family provides.

- The twenty-first century will be marked by significant and swift societal changes that will have a profound influence on family structures, function, and processes.

- North American countries will experience dramatic increases in the multicultural family configurations that will call for health professionals to provide culturally specific, strength-based health care.

‖ CRITICAL THINKING ACTIVITIES

1. Without analysis or discussion, write down what comes to mind when you think of who makes up your family. Next, suppose that you were critically ill. List the people whom you would want to be able to see you and talk with you. Compare the second list with your list of family members. Now, share and compare these findings with others in the class. What can you say about the concept of family now after sharing this information? What, if any, are the implications for direct practice and policy?

2. Recall an incident or occurrence in your own family. Contact several other members of what you consider your family and ask them to describe what they understand or recall about the incident. Is there any difference in any of the details or outcomes? What does this tell you about how we understand the families we will be working with in our practice?

3. Think in terms of your extended family, that is, in the traditional sense in which we assume that aunts, uncles, grandparents, first and second cousins, and so on make up our family. If you are married or living with someone, which members of your partner's extended family do you consider your family (not technically, but emotionally)? Who are the people you think of, on an emotional level, as a part of your family? If you are not married or with a partner at present, think of past partners and try this exercise or speak with someone whom you could ask to respond to these questions. What have you discovered about the meaning of family and what are the implications for your work with families?

REFERENCES

Allan, G. (1986). *Family life: domestic roles and social organization.* New York: Basal Blackwell, Inc.

Allen, F. M. (1977). Comparative theories of the expanded role in nursing and implications for nursing practice. *Nursing Papers, 9,* 38-45.

Allen, F. M. (1999). Comparative theories of the expanded role of nursing and implications for nursing practice. *Canada Journal of Nursing Research, 30,* 83-90.

Anderson, H., & Goolishian, H. (1992). The client is the expert. In S. McNamee & K. Gergen (Eds.), *Therapy as social construction* (pp. 25-39). Newbury Park, CA: Sage

Barefoot, J. A. S. (2002). Melting pot or salad bowl? In N. Smith (Ed.), *Changing U.S. demographics* (pp. 60-65). New York: H. W. Wilson Co.

Bernard, B. (1996). Roger Mills: A community psychologist discovers health realization [Interview]. *Resiliency in Action, 2,* 15-18.

Billingsley, A. (1992). *Climbing Jacob's ladder.* New York: Simon and Schuster.

Bomar, P. J. (Ed.). (1989). *Nurses and family health promotion: Concepts, assessment, and interventions.* Baltimore: Williams & Wilkins.

Canada.com (2002). *2001 Canada Census.* Retrieved June 14, 2002, from http://www.Canada.com/national/features/special/

Cohen, D. & Cohen, S. (2002). Census sees vast change in language, employment. In N. Smith (Ed.), *Changing U.S. demographics* (pp. 115-118). New York: H. W. Wilson Co.

Connors, J. L., & Donnellan, A. M. (1998). Walk in beauty: Western perspectives on disability and Navajo family/cultural resilience. In H. I. McCubbin, E. A. Thompson, A. I. Thompson, & J. E. Fromer (Eds.), *Resiliency in Native-American and immigrant families* (pp. 159-182). Thousand Oaks, CA: Sage.

Department of Labor, Women's Bureau (1997a). *Non-traditional occupations for employed women in 1997.* Washington, DC: U.S. Government Printing Office.

Eitzen, S., & Baca Zinn L. (2000). *Social problems* (8th ed.). Boston: Allyn and Bacon.

Feeley, N., & Gottlieb, L. N. (2000). Nursing approaches for working with family strengths and resources. *Journal of Family Nursing, 6,* 9-24.

Fields, J., & Casper, L. M. (2001). American families and living arrangements: March 2000. In *Current population reports* (pp. 20-537). Washington, DC: U. S. Census Bureau.

Fitzsimmons , M. (Ed.) (2001). *The emergence of family into the 21st century.* New York: National League for Nursing.

Friedman, M., Bowden, V. R. & Jones, E. (2003). *Family nursing: Research, theory and practice.* Upper Saddle River, NJ: Prentice Hall.

Geertz, C. (1983). *Local knowledge.* New York: Basic Books.

Glasco, L. A. (1977). The life cycles and household structure of American ethnic groups: Irish, German, and native born whites in Buffalo New York, 1855. In T. K. Hareven (Ed.), *Family and kin in urban communities, 1700-1930* (pp. 122-143). New York: New Viewpoints.

Goldberg, I., & Goldberg, J. (2002). *Counseling today's families.* Pacific Grove, CA: Brooks/Cole.

Green, J. W. (1999). *Cultural awareness in the human services: A multi-ethnic approach* (3rd ed.). Boston: Allyn and Bacon.

Growing tide of elderly citizens continues a historical trend that will test social safety nets. (2002, April, 28). *The New York Times,* p. wk16.

Hanson, S. M. H. (2001). *Family health care nursing.* Philadelphia: F. A. Davis.

Hicks, L. (2002). Changing and continuity since 1900. In N. Smith (Ed.), *Changing U.S. demographics* (pp. 5-13). New York: The H. W. Wilson Company.

Lifton, R. J. (1993). *The protean self: Human resilience in an age of fragmentation.* New York: Basic Books.

McCubbin, H. I., McCubbin, M. A., Thompson, A. I., & Thompson, E. A. (1998). Resiliency in ethnic families: A conceptual model for predicting family adjustment and adaptation. In H. I. McCubbin, E. A. Thompson, A. I. Thompson, & J. E. Fromer (Eds.), *Resiliency in Native American and immigrant families* (pp. 3-48). Thousand Oaks, CA: Sage.

McCubbin, M. A., & McCubbin, H. I. (1993). Families coping with illness: The resiliency model of family stress, adjustment and adaptation. In C. Danielson, B. Hamel-Bissell, & P. Winstead-Fry (Eds.), *Families, health and illness: Perspectives on coping and intervention* (pp. 21-63). St. Louis, MO: Mosby.

McDaniel, A. K., & McDaniel, C. O. (2000). *21st century African American social issues: A reader.* Fort Worth, TX: Harcourt.

McGoldrick, M. (1998). Introduction: Re-visioning family therapy through a cultural lens. In M. Goldrick (Ed.), *Re-visioning family therapy: Race, culture, and gender in clinical practice* (pp. 3-19). New York: Guilford Press.

McMiller, W. P. & Weisz, J. R. (1996). Help-seeking preceding mental health clinic intake among African-American, Latino, and Caucasian youths. *Journal of the American Academy of Child and Adolescent Psychiatry, 35,* 1086-1094.

Moore, K. A. (2002). Time to take a closer look at Hispanic children and families. In N. Smith (Ed.), *Changing U.S. demographics* (pp. 31-42). New York: H. W. Wilson Co.

Naisbitt, J., & Aburdene, P. (1990). *Megatrends 2000.* New York: William and Morrow.

Naisbitt, J. (2001). *High tech/high touch.* London: Nicholas Braely Publishing.

Olson, D., Sprenkle, D., & Russell, C. (1979). Circumplex model of marital and family systems 1: Cohesion and adaptability dimensions, family types and clinical applications. *Family Process, 18,* 3-28.

Olson, D. H., & DeFrain, J. (1994). *Marriage and the family.* Mountain View, CA: Mayfield Publishing.

Pratt, L. (1976). *Family structure and effective health behavior: The energized family.* Boston: Houghton, Mifflin.

Ritzer, G. (2000). *The McDonaldization of society.* Thousand Oaks, CA: Pine Forge Press.

Rosenblatt, P. C. (1994). *Metaphors of family systems theory: Toward new constructions.* New York: Guilford Press.

Saleebey, D. (Ed.). (1997). *The strengths perspective in social work practice* (2nd ed.). New York: Longman.

Saleebey, D. (Ed.). (2002). *The strengths perspective in social work practice* (3rd ed.). Boston: Allyn and Bacon.

Skolnick, A. S. & Skolnick, J. H. (1997). *Family transition* (9th ed.). New York: Longman.

Smith, N (Ed.) (2002). *Changing U.S. demographics.* New York: H. W. Wilson Co.

Sprey, J. (2001). Theorizing in family studies: Discovering process. In M. Milardo (Ed.), *Understanding families in the new millennium: A decade in review* (pp. 1-14). Minneapolis, MN: National Council on Family Relations.

Toffler, A. (1991). The third wave. New York: Bantam Books.

U.S. Census Bureau. (1995). *Population profile of the United States, 1995.* (Current populations reports, Series P23-189). Washington, DC: U.S. Government Printing Office.

U.S. Census Bureau. (2000). *Educational attainment in the United States: March 2000.* (Series P20-536). Washington, DC: U.S. Government Printing Office.

U.S. Census Bureau (2002). *Current population survey (CPS)—Definitions and explanations.* Retrieved April 20, 2003, from http://www.census.gov/population/www/cps/cpsdef.html

von Glasersfeld, E. (1984). An introduction to radical constructivism. In P. Waltzlawick (Ed.), *The invented reality: How do we know what we believe we know? Contributions to constructivism* (pp. 17-40). New York: Norton.

Walsh, F. (1998). *Strengthening family resilience.* New York: Guilford Press.

Weil, A. (1995). *Spontaneous healing.* New York: Knopf.

Wright, L. M., Watson, W. L., & Bell, J. M. (1996). *Beliefs: The heart of healing in families and illness.* New York: Basic Books.

Family Health Promotion and Health Protection

3

Carol J. Loveland-Cherry
Perri J. Bomar

Look to your health; and if you have it praise God, and value it next to a good conscience; for health is the second blessing that we mortals are capable of; a blessing that money cannot buy.

— Izaak Walton

OBJECTIVES

On completion of this chapter, the reader will be able to do the following:
1. *Examine the critical dimensions of family health.*
2. *Compare and contrast health promotion, health protection, and health maintenance for American families within the context of levels of prevention.*
3. *Identify the current status of health promotion, health protection, and health maintenance activities in the American family.*
4. *Analyze the current knowledge base regarding health promotion, health protection, and health maintenance in the American family.*
5. *Analyze major factors that influence family health.*
6. *Examine the role of the nurse in family health promotion.*

Although the major emphasis continued to be on illness, a move toward health promotion and health protection was evident throughout the latter part of the twentieth century in both the United States and Canada (Stacctchenko & Jenicek, 1990; Green & Kreuter, 1991). Canada set the stage for the shift to health promotion and health protection in North America with the publication of *A New Perspective on the Health of Canadians* (Lalonde, 1974). In the United States, the Surgeon General's report (U.S. Department of Health, Education, and Welfare, 1979) was a major turning point that emphasized the need to focus on the avoidable aspects of morbidity and mortality. The focus on health promotion is especially evident in the wellness movement (Dunn, 1961, 1975). The import of health promotion in the United States continues in the new millennium with the national agenda published in *Healthy People 2010* (U.S. Department of Health and Human Services [U.S. DHHS], 2000). A discussion of Canada's health promotion efforts is presented in the Canadian Perspectives box.

A concomitant move has been the recognition of the interrelationships of health and the family (Mauksch, 1974; Doherty & McCubbin, 1985; Gilliss, 1989; Bomar, 1990; Rolland, 1994). The need to examine the interplay of family, social, and economic environments related to health promotion is a priority in the effort to improve the health status of the population of the United States (Committee on Health and Behavior, 2001).

CANADIAN PERSPECTIVES
CANADA'S NATIONAL EMPHASIS ON HEALTH PROMOTION

Debbie Sheppard-LeMoine, MN, RN,
Dalhousie University

The Canadian initiative to implement health promotion across the country has been attracting interest from Canadians who are closely associated with the formal structures of health care such as the Population and Public Health Branch of Health Canada, the Canadian Public Health Association, the Canadian Consortium for Health Promotion Research, the Canadian Institutes of Health Research, the Canadian Task Force on Preventative Health Care, and citizens with an interest in the health care system changes. (See the Website Resources box at the end of the chapter for the URL for each of these organizations.)

Academics, politicians, policy makers, and community health professionals have been immersed in the language and work of health promotion for decades, and they are very clear in their interpretation of the concept. Now a universal language is required to facilitate understanding outside the worlds of the experts. Unfortunately, the language used to define health promotion has created confusion and mistrust over the meaning of the concept and how it is implemented.

Urban and rural communities are fearful that health promotion means the end of traditional health care that has been provided in hospitals and the destruction of the communities that have been built around hospitals. One of the earliest Canadian definitions, outlined in the *Ottawa Charter* and supported by the Canadian Public Health Association (1996),

suggests "health promotion is the process of enabling people and communities to take control of and improve their health" (p. 4). Over the last 10 years, the Canadian federal government has recognized the need to develop a plan to foster understanding and has focused on three strategies of health promotion that support the *Ottawa Charter's* definition: (1) encouraging public participation, (2) developing healthy public policy, and (3) strengthening community health services.

Nursing models have been used in academic and practice areas to support the development of a nurse's knowledge and application of health promotion. For example, Dorothy Orem's self-care model and the McGill Model of Health Promotion have been included in nursing curricula (Dallaire, Hagan, & O'Neil, 2000). The primary health care philosophy is a way of thinking about health that emphasizes empowering people to take an active role in their own health and helps to influence the broader health care system. (Canadian Public Health Association, 1996). This philosophy forms the foundation of a nurse's health promotion work (Dallaire, Hagan, & O'Neil, 2000). Wright and Leahey (2000) note that family systems nursing is another philosophy of nursing practice that can guide nurses' health promotion work with families and individuals in all areas of the health care system.

Canadian health promotion themes have included diverse

initiatives such as the following (Health Canada, 2002):

1) Encouraging individual lifestyle changes in the 1970s
2) Focusing on social determinants of health such as poverty, discrimination, and healthy environments in the 1980s
3) Providing evidence to support the identification of nine determinants of health (income and social status; social support; education; employment; environment; biology and genetics; personal health practices; healthy child development; health services; culture and gender) in the 1990s
4) Determining the effectiveness of health promotion interventions to influence new ways of looking at health in the new millennium

Specific Canadian examples of health promotion in action include having First Nation grandmothers direct health activities that are relevant to them; establishing parent resource centers to support families as they begin parenting and are faced with new experiences that can be stressful; and supporting youth through experiences with addictions and challenges with mental and sexual health. A consistent theme throughout the work of health promotion is the concept of "best practices," used as a tool to build processes that support health promotion initiatives as they are

CANADIAN PERSPECTIVES
DESCRIBING TWENTY-FIRST CENTURY CANADIAN FAMILY TYPES AND ISSUES—cont'd

implemented in communities, organizations, and health care institutions (University of Toronto Center for Health Promotion, 2002). Best practices are evidenced-based and provide both guidelines and flexibility for responding to unique situations to ensure the best possible health outcomes for Canadians.

Although the federal government's mandate encourages implementation of health promotion initiatives, the diversity of the province's economic base influences the amount of financial and human resources that are targeted toward the federal plan. Currently, the high costs of health care are forcing Canadian decision makers to closely examine the costs associated with the health care system. Health promotion is now being recognized as an intervention to keep the Canadian population healthier and to avoid the high costs associated with a publicly funded, illness-focused system. Resulting from this trend are government mandates that direct health promotion initiatives across Canada. A current example of a mandate is the institution of antismoking initiatives. Although

there is public resistance to the antismoking laws that are being passed in Canadian legislatures, there is also widespread acceptance of the necessity to prevent the chronic and life-threatening illnesses that are resulting from smoking and exposure to second-hand smoke in public places.

Health promotion is recognized as a legitimate knowledge base that influences perspectives of health and disease, and it is influencing nurses' work with Canadian families (Allemang, 2000). A dominant theme of future health promotion in action will be challenging how traditional health ideas have been constructed and put into practice by health care professionals and decision makers. Creative Canadian approaches based on evidence and outcomes have the potential to support future global initiatives in health promotion with families.

References

Allemang, M. (2000). Development of community health nursing in Canada. In M. J. Stewart (Ed.), *Community nursing: Promoting Canadians' health* (2nd ed., pp. 4-32). Toronto, Ontario, Canada: W. B. Saunders.

Canadian Public Health Association. (1996). *Action statement for health promotion in Canada*. Ottawa, Ontario, Canada: Author.

Dallaire, C., Hagan, L., & O'Neil, M. (2000). Linking health promotion and community health nursing: Conceptual and practical issues. In M. J. Stewart (Ed.), *Community nursing: Promoting Canadians' health* (2nd ed., pp. 317-332). Toronto, Ontario, Canada: W. B. Saunders.

Health Canada. (2002). Health policy research bulletin (No. 1, pp. 1-36). Ottawa, Ontario, Canada: Author.

University of Toronto Center for Health Promotion. (2002). Evaluation and Best Practices Unit. Retrieved July 31, 2002, from http://www.utoronto.ca/chp/bestp.html/

Wright, L. M., & Leahey, M. (2000). *Nurses and families: A guide to family assessment and intervention* (3rd ed.). Philadelphia: F. A. Davis.

Canadian spelling is used.

The knowledge base for understanding both the critical dimensions of health promotion and the factors that contribute to this goal continues to grow and is marked by an increasing emphasis on families rather than individuals. Studies of families and health have focused primarily on childhood and adolescence, with a growing focus on the elderly (Committee on Health and Behavior, 2001). Advances in public health and medical technology provide a physiological base for disease prevention, but psychosocial aspects are not as clearly understood. Thus although there is growing knowledge of the physiological and genetic factors that contribute to health promotion and health protection, this knowledge is incomplete without a similar understanding of the interplay of environmental factors. In the last 15 years, there has been a resurgence of interest in the family as a focus for health, particularly in terms of health promotion and risk reduction. The focus on families and health promotion begins to address Mauksch's (1974) classic assertion that "the most challenging although least studied area in which the family concept could be a significant addition to health care is in the tasks of health maintenance and health maximization" (p. 526).

This chapter focuses on the examination of the current knowledge available to understand health promotion, health protection, and health maintenance in the American family. The family has been viewed from two different perspectives relative to health.

First, the family has been identified as a basic unit within which health behavior, health values, and health risk perceptions are developed, organized, and performed. Thus the family is an important environment for health promotion, health protection, and health maintenance for individual family members.

Second, the health of the family system itself is of concern relative to its ability to fulfill vital functions and tasks. In reality, it is difficult to separate these two perspectives when nurses are working with families. A healthy family system is usually necessary to produce healthy family members and to meet their health-related needs. Conversely, healthy family members are usually a prerequisite for a healthy family system.

Dimensions of Family Health

Family health is a concept that is often mentioned and identified as a goal of intervention in the nursing literature; however, it is seldom defined. Definitions of family health can be derived from theoretical perspectives, from clinical perspectives, and from families themselves. In the first instance, dimensions of family health can be inferred from both family theory and nursing theoretical models.

Walsh (1993) identifies four perspectives for defining "normal" (or healthy) families: (1)

asymptomatic family functioning characterized by an absence of any symptoms of dysfunction or psychopathology in individual members; (2) optimal family functioning as evidenced by an ideal family having the characteristics defined as optimal by a particular model or paradigm; (3) average family functioning determined by a family falling within the range of the usual or prevalent existing mode; and (4) transactional family processes based on the integration, maintenance, and growth of the family system relevant to internal and external demands within societal and temporal contexts. A model for defining family health could be developed within any one of these four views. For example, in the Timberlawn studies a healthy family was originally viewed as one not having an adolescent member in psychiatric treatment, but investigators moved to defining optimal, midrange, and dysfunctional families on the basis of dimensions identified within a systems framework (Beavers & Hampson, 1993; Walsh, 1993). The first three categories define family health as a state; the fourth defines family health as a process.

Additional dimensions of family health can be elaborated from Smith's (1983) models of health. Smith identifies four models of health: *clinical*, *role-performance*, *adaptive*, and *eudaimonistic*. The first is similar to the first perspective described by Walsh (1993); health is viewed as the absence of disease. Within the role-performance model, health is defined as effective performance of roles. Elements of Walsh's second and fourth categories are found in the adaptive and eudaimonistic models. Health in the adaptive model is viewed as effective, productive interaction with the physical and social environment, with the emphasis on flexible adaptation. Within the eudaimonistic model, health is viewed as self-actualization derived from complete development of the potential for general well-being and self-realization. The clinical and role-performance models focus on maintaining stability and thus health protection. The adaptive and eudaimonistic models focus on growth and change and are consistent with health promotion.

Although Smith (1983) discusses the four models primarily in terms of individuals, they could be extended to describe family health (Table 3-1). In the clinical model, family health

TABLE 3-1   Four Models of Family Health

Model	Description
Family health: Clinical model	Lack of evidence of physical, mental, or social disease or deterioration or dysfunction of family system
Family health: Role-performance model	Ability of the family system to carry on family functions effectively and to achieve family developmental tasks
Family health: Adaptive model	Family patterns of interaction with the environment characterized by flexible, effective adaptation or ability to change and grow
Family health: Eudaimonistic model	Ongoing provision of resources, guidance, and support for realization of family's maximum well-being and potential throughout the family life span

would be considered as lack of evidence of physical, mental, or social disease in family members or lack of deterioration or dysfunction of the family system. Family health in the role-performance model could be defined as the ability of the family system to carry on family functions effectively and achieve family developmental tasks. Adaptive family health would be defined as family patterns of interaction with the environment, characterized by flexible, effective adaptation or ability to change and grow. Family health in the eudaimonistic model is characterized as the ongoing provision of resources, guidance, and support for the realization of family members' maximum well-being and potential throughout the family life span. These definitions of family health within the four models are not mutually exclusive. Smith suggests that the four models can be viewed as forming a scale, progressing along an expanding conception of health.

As noted in Chapter 1, Anderson and Tomlinson (1992) identify "conceptual and paradigmatic ambiguity" in current definitions of family health in nursing (p. 61) and conclude that the emerging definitions of family may be more complex than those evident in other disciplines. They suggest that a definition of family health should include five "realms of family experience" that constitute a proposed "family health system." The five realms of family experience include interactive, developmental, coping, integrity, and health processes. The idea that family health is more than the sum of the health of individual family members and is not ascertainable merely through assessment of

individuals is clearly presented in Mauksch's (1974) concept of the "family health estate." The family health estate reflects a pattern characteristic of the family unit, not individual family members, which is developed within the emerging family and involves knowledge, attitudes, values, behaviors, and allocation of tasks and roles. Thus the importance of looking beyond individuals' behaviors, attitudes, beliefs, and values to family system patterns in determining family health is emphasized.

Evaluation of Family Health Status

Determination of family health status in clinical practice is an ongoing effort of family scholars and family nurses. The characteristics of a healthy family have been described by a number of family scholars (Curran, 1983; McCubbin & McCubbin, 1993; Olson & DeFrain, 1994) and are summarized in Box 3-1. Research on the characteristics of a healthy family has been limited, and research is needed to create a theoretical model for studying family health (Denham, 1999).

Clinical measures have been developed to evaluate dimensions of family interaction, strengths, coping with life events, and functioning, which are indirect measures of family clinical health. The Family Function Index (Pless & Satterwhite, 1973), the Family APGAR (Smilkstein, 1978), the Family Hardiness Index (McGubbin & McGubbin, 1987), and the Family Adaptability and Cohesion Evaluation Scale (FACES II) (Olson, Portner, & Lavee, 1985) based on the

---

BOX 3-1   Traits of a Healthy Family

UNITY

Commitment

Develops a sense of trust
Teaches respect for others
Exhibits a sense of shared responsibility
Shares simple and quality time

Time Together

Shares family rituals and traditions
Enjoys each other's company
Shares leisure time

FLEXIBILITY

Ability to Deal with Stress

Displays adaptability
Sees crises as a challenge and opportunity
Shows openness to change
Grows together in crisis
Seeks help with problems

Spiritual Well-Being

Encourages hope
Shares faith
Teaches compassion for others
Teaches ethical values
Respects the privacy of one another

COMMUNICATION

Positive Communication

Communicates and listens effectively
Fosters family table time and conversation
Shares feelings
Displays nonblaming attitudes
Is able to compromise and disagree

Appreciation and Affection

Cares for each other
Exhibits a sense of humor
Maintains friendship
Respects individuality
Has a spirit of playfulness; agrees to disagree

Based on data from Curran, D. (1983). Traits of a healthy family. Minneapolis, MN: Winston; and Olson, D. & DeFrain, J. (1994) Marriage and the family: Diversity and strengths. Mountain View, CA: Mayfield.

Circumplex Model (Olson, 1993) are examples of clinical family assessment measures. Sample nursing models and assessment measures are the following:

1) The *Calgary Family Assessment Model* (CFAM) (Wright & Leahey, 2000)
2) The *Family Systems Strength Inventory* (FS³I) based on the Family Assessment and Intervention Model (Hanson & Mischke, 1996)
3) *The Friedman Family Assessment Model* (Friedman, Bowden, & Jones, 2003)
4) The *Assessment of Strategies in Family-Effectiveness* (ASF-E) based on The Framework of Systemic Organization (Friedemann, 1991; Friedemann, 1995)

In a less frequently used approach, families (both parents and children) were asked to explain what they thought were characteristics of family health (Loveland-Cherry, 1985). Seven major categories of responses were identified. Fifty-five percent of the respondents identified participation in health behaviors (eating healthy foods, getting enough rest, exercising regularly, wearing proper clothing, and avoiding risk behaviors such as smoking or taking drugs); 22% mentioned indicators of absence of illness (very little sickness, no chronic illness, healthy bodies, mental and emotional health); 8% described characteristics of a feeling of well-being (feeling good, having a high energy level, living enthusiastically); 7% described elements that contributed to well-being (happy home, positive atmosphere, supportive and nurturing environment, mutual respect, love, fun together); 4% cited use of health care services (having regular check-ups, seeing a dentist regularly, and receiving good preventive care); 3% mentioned abilities to function in usual roles; and 1% indicated genetic background and luck. These findings indicate that although families have varied perceptions of family health, their perceptions are not that different from those proposed by professionals. Other approaches to assess family health status in selected areas are presented in Units II and III of this text.

In summary, family health has a number of dimensions and can be defined within various contexts and from a number of theoretical and clinical viewpoints. It is essential that the specific understanding of family health be clarified both by the nurse and the family so that goals can be shared and appropriate interventions can be designed.

Family Health Promotion Theories and Frameworks

Theories developed within nursing and in disciplines other than nursing provide direction for understanding families and health promotion and health protection. Chapter 4 and Unit II review such theoretical perspectives. Health promotion frameworks and models are discussed below.

Family Cycle of Health and Illness

Family life is dynamic, and during its life cycle, the family experiences both periods of wellness and illness. Danielson, Hamel-Bissell, and Winsted-Fry (1993) developed a model called the *Family Cycle of Health and Illness* based on the work by Doherty and Campbell (1988). A family's experience of health and illness is described as cyclical and progressing through eight phases, as shown in Figure 3-1.

During the first phase, the members are well and there is no identifiable health problem or family dysfunction. Most of the health problems and chronic disease in North America are the result of unhealthy lifestyle behaviors. These behaviors include smoking, poor nutrition, and sedentary life styles. For example, more than 350,000 deaths that occur annually in the United States are attributed to smoking. The nurse's crucial role in this phase is to provide health education and anticipatory guidance that enhance the ability of individuals,

families, and communities to engage in health-promoting behaviors. To avoid progressing to the next phase, the client must actively participate in activities that promote health and prevent disease. In the second phase, the family is vulnerable to dysfunction, or a member may be vulnerable to illness or display symptoms of an illness. In this phase, family or folk remedies and previous patterns of adjusting and adapting are often used.

During the remaining phases, the family makes adjustments and adaptations to the acute illness and returns to the first phase. If recovery does not occur, the family progresses to the chronic illness phase while coping with the multiple family stressors as a unit and making any necessary family and individual adaptations. Lastly, during the final phase, in which death of a member occurs, the family must make multiple adjustments such as grieving and role changes and family reorganization or dissolution (Danielson et al., 1993; Doherty & Campbell, 1988). After reorganization, the family returns to the first or second phase. The role of the family nurse is to determine the family's strengths and needs in each phase. Assessment and interventions should be carried out with knowledge of the following:

• Family and community resources
• History of illness
• Beliefs
• Family interaction patterns
• The family's perception of their health and vulnerability to illness
• Meaning of the illness
• Family stressors
• The type of family and its problem-solving abilities

Family-focused research in many of the phases is scant and represents a fertile area for future research studies in the next decade.

Levels of Prevention

Prevention has been defined in public health at three levels (Leavell & Clark, 1965): primary, secondary, and tertiary. *Primary prevention* has the goal of increasing resistance to avoid illness or disabling conditions. Actions to achieve this goal include general health behaviors such as healthy nutrition, physical activity, rest, and stress management; development of effective parenting

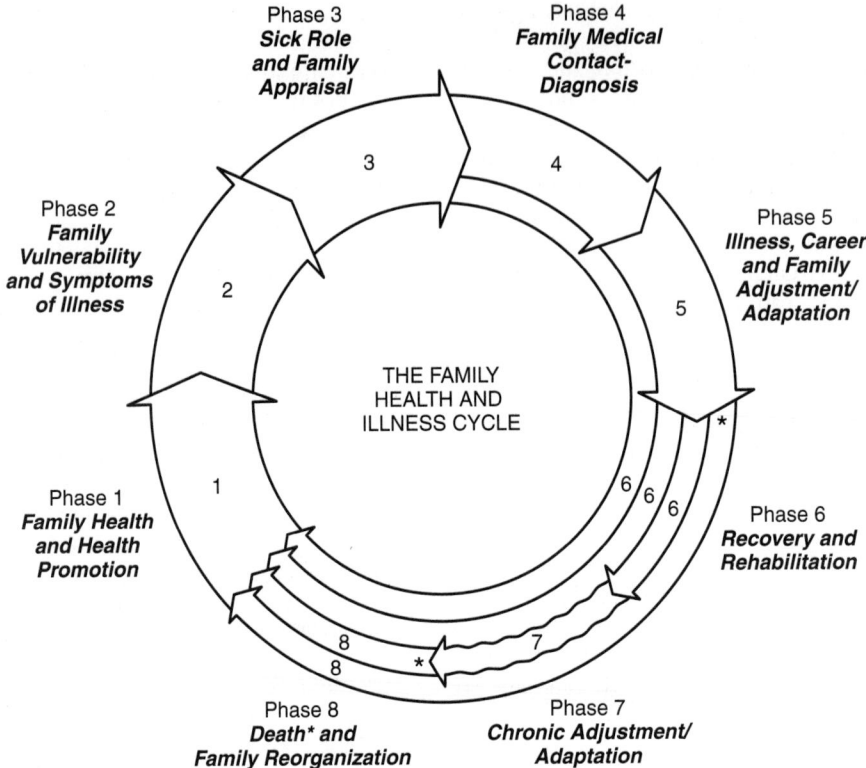

Figure 3-1 Family Cycle of Health and Illness Phases. (From Doherty, W. J. & Campbell [1988]. *Families and Health:* Newbury Park: Sage; Danielson C., Hamel-Bissell, B. & Winstead-Fry P. [1993]. *Families in Health and Illness.* St. Louis: Mosby.)

skills; building self-efficacy; and specific actions such as immunizations. Health risk assessments can also be considered within primary prevention. The emphasis is on identifying factors that may be present that increase the probability of development of illness or conditions rather than on detection of the same. Thus both health promotion and specific prevention foci are inherent in primary prevention. The family unit assists individual family members to be successful with health-promoting behaviors, and women tend to be the health teachers and sentinels for family health (Denham, 2003). For example, if a person is overweight the solution would be changing dietary habits and increasing physical activity. In addition, social support from the family facilitates reaching the weight loss goal and maintaining the weight loss.

Secondary prevention has the goal of early diagnosis and prompt treatment, as well as limitation of disabilities. Actions are focused on early detection and treatment and include health screenings for conditions such as diabetes mellitus, HIV/AIDS, hypertension, hypercholesterolemia, and developmental delays. The second component of secondary prevention is initiation of treatment for identified illnesses or conditions. For example, if hypertension is detected as the result of blood pressure screening, referral for treatment completes the process. The emphasis here is similar to that inherent in health protection. Secondary prevention nursing activities for families with members at risk for obesity include teaching the importance of physical activity and nutrition to the individual and the family "cook" to prevent obesity. Families as a unit could plan joint physical activities and only offer healthy foods.

Tertiary prevention has the goal of rehabilitation or return to the highest level of functioning possible. Actions focus on rebuilding function and developing additional resistance. Health maintenance is most consistent with tertiary prevention. In the case of obesity, the tertiary prevention family intervention would be referral to a professional weight loss program and continued health teaching to the family and the overweight family member on strategies to prevent relapse.

Health Promotion Functions of the Family

Historically, the focus of health professionals' work with families has been in the areas of medical care and disease treatment. Only recently has increased attention been allocated to health promotion. Although health promotion may be the most complex and difficult area in which to intervene, the potential benefits are thought to justify the necessary efforts. The Surgeon General's report (U.S. Department of Health, Education, and Welfare, 1979) delineated three groups of behaviors that would improve the health of the population: (1) preventive health services including family planning, pregnancy and infant care, immunizations, sexually transmissible disease services, and high blood pressure control; (2) health protection actions including toxic agent control, occupational safety and health, accidental injury control, fluoridation of community water supplies, and infectious agent control; and (3) health promotion behaviors including smoking cessation, reduction in misuse of alcohol and drugs, improved nutrition, exercise and fitness, and stress control. The three categories of behaviors served as the basis for the development of health objectives for the nation (U.S. Department of Health and Human Services, 1990). The most recent update of the health objectives for the nation emphasizes two goals, increasing the quality and years of healthy life and eliminating health disparities, and proposes that the physical environment, the social environment, and individual biology and behavior be considered as determinants of health

(U.S. Department of Health and Human Services, 2000).

Environmental and individual factors account for about 70% of all premature deaths in the United States. As the guideline for addressing the nation's health, the two goals will be monitored by using 467 objectives in 28 focus areas, which are listed in Box 3-2. In addition, *Healthy People 2010* delineates 10 "leading health indicators" that are the major health issues in the United States. These indicators of health are shown in Box 3-3. The reader will find a detailed list of the objectives and the indicators on the *Healthy People 2010* website in the Website Resources box at the end of this chapter.

Health promotion is different from disease prevention; the focus is not on avoiding any one specific disease or health problem (Laffrey, Loveland-Cherry, & Winkler, 1986; Pender, Murdaugh, & Parsons, 2002). Rather, the concern is with increasing well-being and quality of life relative to self-identified goals. Brubaker (1983) defines health promotion as

> health care directed toward high-level wellness through processes that encourage alteration of personal habits or the environment in which people live. It occurs after health stability is present and assumes disease prevention and health maintenance as prerequisites or by-products (p. 12).

Similarly, Pender, Murdaugh, and Parsons (2002) state the following:

> Health promotion is directed toward increasing the level of well-being and self-actualization of a given individual or group. Health promotion focuses on efforts to approach or move toward a positively valenced state of high-level health and well-being (p. 34).

Family health promotion is directed toward increasing family unity and quality of life. Families perform a number of functions that contribute directly and indirectly to health promotion. Affection among family members provides a nurturing emotional climate that contributes to healthy growth and development and an increase in personal competence. A sense of cohesiveness and nurturance in families has been found to be related to health promotion behaviors and healthy

BOX 3-2   Healthy People 2010 Objectives

A. GOALS

1. Increase Quality and Years of Health Life
2. Eliminate Health Disparities

B. AIMS AND OBJECTIVES

Promote Healthy Behaviors

1. Physical Activity and Fitness
2. Nutrition
3. Tobacco Use

Promote Healthy and Safe Communities

4. Educational and Community-Based Programs
5. Environmental Health
6. Food Safety
7. Injury/Violence Prevention
   a. Injuries That Cut Across Intent
   b. Unintentional Injuries
   c. Violence and Abuse
8. Occupational Safety and Health
9. Oral Health

Improve Systems for Personal and Public Health

10. Access to Quality Health Services
    a. Preventive Care
    b. Primary Care
    c. Emergency Services
    d. Long-Term Care and Rehabilitative Services
11. Family Planning
12. Maternal, Infant, and Child Health
13. Medical Product Safety
14. Public Health Infrastructure
15. Health Communication

Prevent and Reduce Diseases and Disorders

16. Arthritis, Osteoporosis, and Chronic Back Conditions
17. Cancer
18. Diabetes
19. Disability and Secondary Conditions
20. Heart Disease and Stroke
21. HIV
22. Immunization and Infectious Diseases
23. Mental Health and Mental Disorders
24. Respiratory Diseases
25. Sexually Transmitted Diseases
26. Substance Abuse
27. Tobacco Use
28. Vision and Hearing

From U.S. Department of Health and Human Services. (2000). *Healthy People 2010* (Vol. 1) (2nd ed.): Washington DC: US Government Printing Office. Available at http://www.healthypeople.gov/Document/html/uih/uih_bw/uih_6.htm

outcomes (Ford-Gilboe, 1997; Loveland-Cherry, 1983; Beavers & Hampson, 1993). In a study of 222 diabetic women older than 50 years, researchers found that participants reporting severe family functioning were 75% less likely to undergo an annual screening mammography (Spangler & Kowen, 1996). The importance of the family in maintaining morale and motivation is a related aspect of this function that has obvious implications for health promotion and disease prevention (Adams, Bowden, Humphrey, & McAdams, 2000; Denham, 2003; Niska, Snyder, & Lia-Hoaberg, 1999).

Families also provide for socialization of family members and subsequent placement within the society in which they live. In this way families transmit their cultural heritage, goals, values, attitudes, and patterns of behavior, including those relevant to health. Both the definitions of and the value placed on health and well-being are developed largely within the context of the family, beginning early in childhood. Both the definition of health and the importance, or value, of health are identified as important variables related to participation in health-promoting behaviors (Laffrey, 1985; Pender et al., 1987). The type of

> ## BOX 3-3   Healthy People 2010
> ### Leading Health Indicators
>
> Physical activity
> Overweight and obesity
> Tobacco use
> Substance abuse
> Responsible sexual behavior
> Mental health
> Injury and violence
> Environmental quality
> Immunization
> Access to health care
>
> ---
>
> The 28 focus areas listed in Box 3-2 are broad and are supported by 427 objectives that are to be put into operation by state and local organizations. For additional information, consult the website of Healthy People 2010. (From U. S. Department of Health and Human Services. [2000]. Healthy People 2010. Washington, DC: U. S. Government Printing Office. Retrieved October 1, 2002, from the DHHS Web site: http://www.healthypeople.gov/Document/tableofcontents.htm).

family socialization practices, specifically the type of childrearing methods, has been demonstrated to be related not only to children's health-promoting behaviors but also to those of parents (Loveland-Cherry, 1986). Positive relationships between supportive childrearing methods and health-promoting personal health practices have been found, as well as a negative relationship between mothers' use of aversive control and children's, mothers', and total family health practices (Loveland-Cherry, 1986). Positive relationships exist between health training efforts made by parents and family members' health-promoting personal health practices; parents and siblings act as important role models for children. Purath, Lansinger, and Ragheb (1995) identified mothers as important role models of exercise behavior in school-age children. Families also provide and monitor information that relates to health promotion knowledge from a variety of media and could have an influence on children who smoke (Tilson, McBride, Albright, Sargent, 2001).

The family both provides and regulates economic resources required to meet basic needs and support activities that foster health promotion and health protection. Family decisions about resource allocation are based on both necessity and values. Expenditures on certain activities or purchases that might at first seem frivolous may contribute to the overall well-being of the family by providing for aesthetic needs. However, successful management of families has been shown to promote cohesiveness and satisfaction.

Families function to monitor not only internal interactions but also interactions with social, cultural, political, educational, and other systems. The extent of participation in organizations and activities outside the family, especially for children, has been demonstrated to be positively related to health-promoting behaviors (Loveland-Cherry, 1986). Parents also provide the milieu that promotes the greater physical health, increased self-confidence, better school performance, and healthier social relationships (Goltman, DeClaire, & Goleman, 1998).

Models for Family Health Promotion

Models for health promotion have been developed primarily with the focus on individuals, as have definitions of health. The knowledge base for understanding family health promotion is still in the formative stage. A preliminary model, based on Pender's revised Family Health Promoting Model and family theory and research, is presented in Figure 3-2. It is offered as a starting point for articulating an understanding of family health promotion.

Although the importance of family health promotion has been emphasized, little documentation of intervention strategies or their effectiveness is evident. Pender (1986, 2002) proposes components of family assessment that are consistent with family theory and knowledge regarding healthy families and health promotion. Use of these components offers a point from which to begin implementing and evaluating family health promotion strategies. Such strategies include nutrition, physical activity, stress control and management, health responsibility, family resilience and resources, and family support. Further, a suggested format for a family health promotion-protection plan is provided. As the format in Figure 3-3 illustrates, the family health

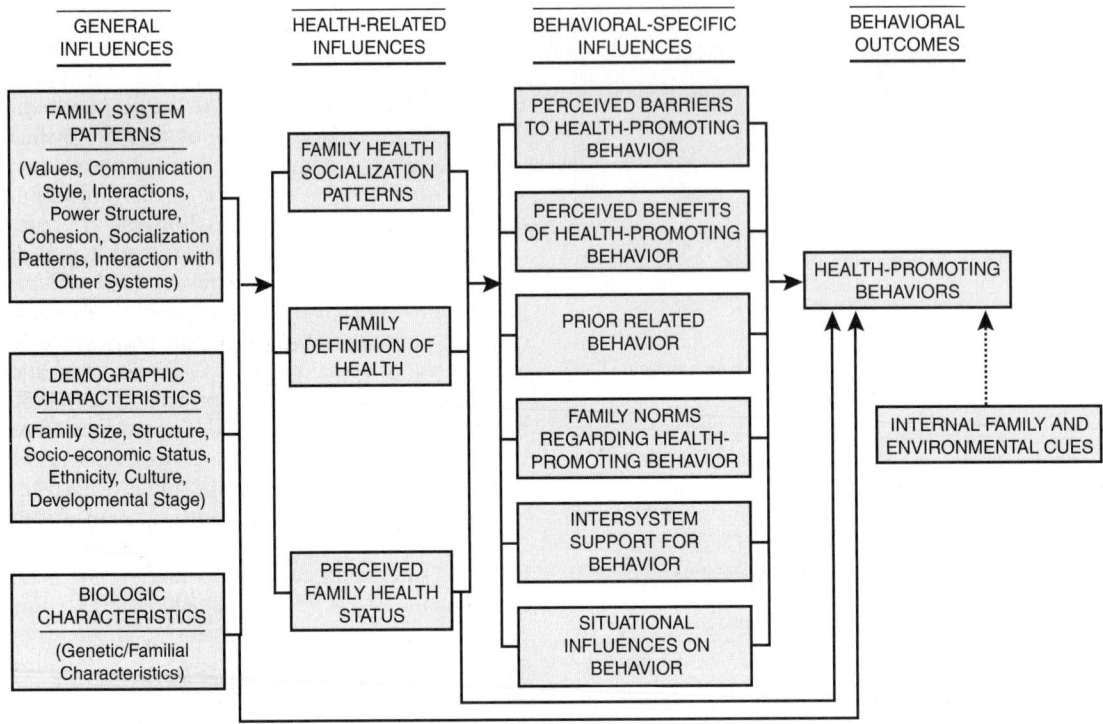

Figure 3-2 Family health promotion model.

promotion-protection plan provides a method for identifying family health goals and monitoring progress toward meeting them. Reports of family interventions to promote diet and exercise behavior indicate some limited success (Nicklas et al., 2001; Madsen et al., 1993). This is an area with tremendous opportunities for the development and testing of nursing interventions. The Research Synopsis presents a study related to developing interventions for family health promotion

Ford-Gilboe (1997, 2002) operationalized the Developmental Model of Health and Nursing developed by Allen to examine health promotion and health protection in families. The model examines the contributions of health potential and style of nursing to health work and the relationships of health work to competence in health behavior and health status. Ford-Gilboe examined the contributions of one component of the model, health potential. The contribution of family strengths (cohesion, pride, mother's nontraditional

sex role orientation), motivation (internal health locus of control, general self-efficacy), and resources (network support, community support, and family income) to families' participation in health work and the extent to which families participated in health promotion behaviors were examined in a Canadian sample of 138 single-parent and two-parent families. Model variables of cohesion, self-efficacy, and mother's sex role orientation significantly predicted 22% to 27% of the variance in health work. Although the components of the model have yet to be operationalized for families, the model has the potential to explicate the correlates of family health promotion.

Health Protection and the Family

In contrast to health promotion, health protection emphasizes maintaining a state of wellness or health by decreasing the risks of specific conditions. Thus activities in this arena are disease specific or

Designed for (Family Name): _____

Family Form: _____

Family Members:

NAME	SEX	POSITION IN FAMILY	BIRTH DATE	OCCUPATION (IF EMPLOYED)
_____	___	_____	_____	_____
_____	___	_____	_____	_____
_____	___	_____	_____	_____
_____	___	_____	_____	_____
_____	___	_____	_____	_____

Home Address: _____

Home Telephone: _____

Work Telephone Number: _____

Cultural Background: _____

Spiritual–Religious Orientation: _____

Type of Housing: _____

Major Formal Roles of Family Members: _____

_____

Community Affiliations of Family: _____

_____

Communication Patterns (Verbal and nonverbal, including expression of caring/affection):

Family Decision-Making Patterns

Family Values with Highest Rank:

1. _____
2. _____
3. _____
4. _____
5. _____

Rank Order of Health as a Value (if not listed above):

_____

Value Conflicts in Family (if any)

Goals Important to Family:

	MUTUAL GOAL OR SPECIFIC TO DYAD (D) OR TRIAD (T)
_____	_____
_____	_____
_____	_____

Family Strengths:

Major Sources of Stress for Family and Perceived Ability to Deal with Stressors:

Current or Recent Family Developmental or Situational Transitions:

Family Concerns or Challenges:

Family Self-Care Patterns

Current Health Protecting or Preventive Behaviors (e.g., immunization, self-examination, periodic screening/examination by health professionals, avoidance of toxic exposure, use of seat belts):

Current Health-Promoting Behaviors (Life Style Review):
Nutritional Practices:

Physical–Recreational Activities:

Sleep–Relaxation Patterns:

Stress Management:

Family Sense of Purpose:

Family Actualization Efforts:

Relationships in Family and with Others:

Environmental Control:

Information-Seeking Patterns of Family in Relation to Health Promotion:

Use of Health-Promotion Facilities or Services by Family:

Other Behaviors:

Consistency Among Family Values, Goals, and Health Actions:

Family Health Goals

GOALS	FAMILY PRIORITY (1 = MOST IMPORTANT)

Areas for Improvement in Family Health

Target Health Goal:

AREA OF CHANGE (SEE CATEGORIES UNDER FAMILY SELF-CARE PATTERNS)	SPECIFIC BEHAVIOR CHANGE	FAMILY PRIORITY (1 = MOST DESIRABLE)	APPROACHES SELECTED TO FACILITATE FAMILY CHANGE

Evaluation of Progress Toward Change in Family Life Style

Two weeks:

One month:

Three months:

Six months:

One year:

Figure 3-3   Format for a family health promotion-protection plan. (Reprinted with permission from Pender N. J., Murdaugh, C. L., & Parsons, M. A. [2002]. *Health promotion in nursing practice* [4th ed.]. Upper Saddle River, NJ: Prentice Hall.)

RESEARCH SYNOPSIS

PREDICTORS OF FAMILY HEALTH PROMOTION BEHAVIOR

Family health promotion is a developing area of nursing intervention. The knowledge needed to develop evidence-based interventions is limited. In a study of 138 female-headed single-parent families and two-parent families, the mother and one child (age 10 to 14 years) each completed mailed self-report surveys to measure family cohesion, family pride, internal health locus of control, general self-efficacy, mother's nonsupport, community support, family income, and health work. The study was framed within Allen's Developmental Health Model. The models predicted 22% to 27% of the variance across family types. Family cohesion predicted health work in both types of families; mother's self-efficacy was an additional significant predictor in single-parent families, and community support was an additional predictor in two-parent families. The author notes the need for additional research to identify additional predictors of family health promotion behavior. The results of this study provide additional support for developing nursing interventions designed to promote and support family cohesion.

Ford-Gilboe, M. (1997). Family strengths, motivation, and resources as predictors of health promotion behavior in single-parent and two-parent families. Research in Nursing and Health, 20, 205-217.

condition specific. Pender, Murdaugh, and Parsons (2002), who prefer the use of "health protecting" behaviors, offer the following definition:

> Health protection is directed toward decreasing the probability of experiencing health problems by active protection against pathologic stressors or detection of health problems in asymptomatic stage. Health protection focuses on efforts to move away from or avoid the negatively valenced states of illness and injury (p. 34).

All of the family functions examined relative to health promotion are also relevant to health protection. Families provide information and resources, make decisions, set goals and priorities, and develop attitudes and behaviors regarding health protection. Families of all socioeconomic and ethnic groups need support from family nurses to adapt a health protective families lifestyle. Information about specific family protective health behaviors is presented in Chapter 12.

Health Maintenance and the Family

The goal of family health maintenance activities is to stabilize health or maintain a current state of health. The function of physical maintenance includes the provision of shelter, food, clothing, and health care. Although the family is largely responsible for the nutritional habits and status of family members, there are social determinants of health as well. Figure 3-4 depicts the relationship of determinants and the quality of health. Adequate shelter influences the comfort, opportunities for privacy and interaction, and rest and relaxation of family members. Having these needs met, in turn, influences the energy levels available for health-promoting behaviors. The role of the family professional is to increase the capacity of families of diverse ethnic groups and socioeconomic status to engage in activities that regularly monitor and maintain a quality family life.

The Family Systems-Illness Model (Rolland, 1994) provides a systems perspective for understanding how components of family functioning interact with health and illness. Although the model was developed to enhance understanding of families and illness, it provides a general context that is useful for understanding families and health maintenance. A basic assumption of the model is that the family is the focus of care. This assumption is consistent with a family approach to health maintenance. Four basic domains of family functioning are identified in this model: (1) family structural/organizational patterns (instrumental and affective style—cohesion, adaptability, communication); (2) communication processes; (3) multigenerational patterns and family life cycle (development—individual and family; multigenerational history—illness/loss/crisis), and (4) family belief systems (paradigm—beliefs and values). Similar to the models proposed by Anderson and Tomlinson (1992), all of these components of family functioning have been demonstrated to be related to family health maintenance.

Determinants of Health

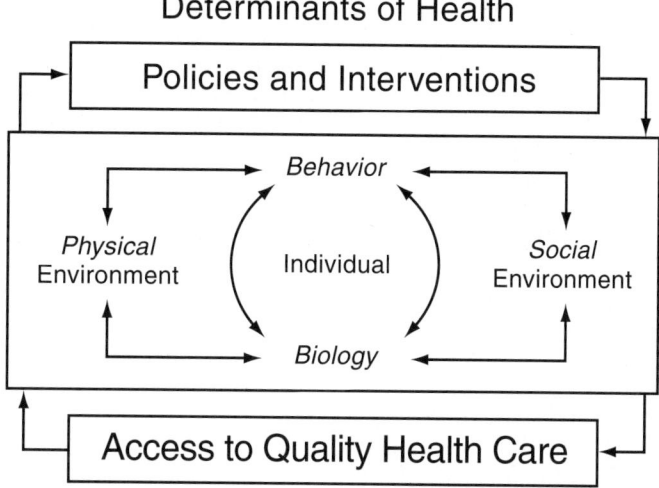

Figure 3-4   Determinants of health. (From U.S. Department of Health and Human Services. [2002]. *Healthy People 2010*. Washington, DC: U.S. Government Printing Office. Retrieved October 1, 2002, from http://www.health.gov/healthypeople/Document/html/ uih/uih_2.htm#deter)

The family functioning elements are proposed to relate to characteristics of the specific illness or condition, that is, *practical and affective demands* (psychosocial typology), *developmental* (time phases), *meaning* (control and stigma), and *historical data* (morbidity and mortality rates). What are termed *spheres of influence* are other important characteristics of the model and direct attention to examination of the type of illness, adversity, or loss within the context of individual, family, and illness life cycles, which are further considered within the context of belief systems of culture and ethnicity. Thus the model provides direction for viewing families as the focal unit within the larger contexts of belief systems of culture and ethnicity.

Use of Health Protective Services

An important aspect of health care for which the family has primary responsibility is the use of professional services aimed at maintaining health and preventing disease or debilitating conditions. These services include family planning, prenatal care, well-child care, immunizations, dental care, routine physical examinations, mammograms and Papanicolaou tests for women, and rehabil-

itative care. The family makes and implements decisions regarding not only the use of economic resources but also time and effort. The role of the family in the use of services has been studied extensively, but study of the family's use of preventive services has been more limited. The most well-developed and widely used model for examining families' use of services was developed by Andersen and his colleagues (Andersen, 1968; Andersen & Aday, 1978).

Andersen (1968) delineated three major categories of variables that contribute to the use of health services. The first category, labeled *predisposing conditions*, includes family composition (age, sex, and marital status of head of the family; family size [and ages of the youngest and oldest members of the family]); family social structure (employment, education, social class, and occupation of wage earner; race; and ethnicity); and family health beliefs. The second category, *enabling factors*, includes family resources (family income, family savings, health insurance, regular source of care, and welfare care) and community resources (availability of services in the community in which the family lives). The final category, *need factors*, includes the amount of illness perceived by the family (health level, symptoms, and disability days) and response (seeking care for symptoms and regular physical examinations).

Results of an early study to test the model (Andersen, 1968) indicated that larger, younger families and families with a well-educated main wage earner employed full-time in a high-prestige occupation tend to use more services. Health beliefs, such as the value of health services, were also related to service use but not as strongly as other variables in the predisposing conditions category. Further, families with higher income, health insurance, a regular source of care, or access to welfare care used more services. However, the need component (the family's perception of symptoms, disability days, and health level) was a major correlate of service use. In an update of the evolution of the model, Andersen (1995) indicates that the unit of analysis has shifted from the family to the individual because of difficulty in developing family level measures. However, family-related variables continue to be included in the category of enabling factors. Ortega and colleagues (2001) emphasize the need to include familial behaviors as a critical variable in understanding disparities in asthma health care for Medicaid and non-Medicaid populations. Use of preventive services has also been linked to family social networks, stage in the family life cycle, the mother's education, parents' health training efforts, parents' health status, and family interaction patterns.

Risk Behaviors

The family plays an important role in the participation or nonparticipation in risk behaviors. There is evidence that both perceived and received support from the family is positively related to pregnant women's abstinence from smoking, alcohol, and caffeine (Aaronson, 1989). Adolescents' participation in the risk behaviors of cigarette, alcohol, and marijuana use has also been examined from the perspective of the family (Loveland-Cherry, Ross, & Kaufman, 1999). Parents may underestimate the percentage of adolescents who smoke cigarettes (Cohen, Felix, & Brownell, 1989). Family problem solving was negatively related to adolescent health risk behaviors, and family stressors and strains were positively related to adolescent health risk

behaviors. Adolescent health risk behaviors have also been related to parents' education, occupation, and religious group; to home climate (maternal affection and control); to parental beliefs, supports, and controls; to parental approval; to family closeness; to parental monitoring and enforcement of rules; to parental involvement in the child's activities; and to parental substance use (Loveland-Cherry et al., 1999).

Family Nursing Diagnoses

Although nursing diagnoses, especially those in the North American Nursing Diagnosis Association (NANDA) system, are increasingly being used in the practice arena, family and health promotion have not been adequately addressed by these systems. Only one NANDA diagnosis is appropriate to family health promotion—Family Coping: Potential for Growth. In the latest revision of the taxonomy, this diagnosis has been renamed *Readiness for Enhanced Family Coping* (NANDA, 2001). It is defined as pertaining to the family's potential to change and grow related to adapting to a family member's health challenge. The diagnosis can be interpreted as encompassing family health promotion, but it does so only in terms of responding to the needs of an individual member. In fact, when interventions for primary care health promotion were linked to NANDA diagnoses for infants, children, and families (Craft-Rosenberg & Denehy, 2001), the client was usually identified as the child or adolescent, rather than the family, and the diagnoses were stated in terms of "deficit" or "risk." Nursing diagnosis continues to be an area that clearly requires additional development if family health promotion is to be adequately addressed.

Nursing Interventions for Family Health Promotion

Family Self-Care

Self-care in health promotion and health protection is a complex mixture of activities directing the family toward being, behaving, and becoming (Gray, 1996). It is defined as "a specific approach to clinical practice that recognizes the uniqueness and strength[s] of the family constellation and places primary emphasis on the family's ability to promote and protect health" (Gray, 1996, p. 85). The clinician's role in self-care involves more than assuming that the individual or family is solely responsible for health. Instead, the clinician's role is to empower families and increase their capacity to reach their highest potential in health (Hartrick, 1997). Another premise of self-care is that people have the potential to use their intellectual and practical skills and the motivation essential for self-care (Orem, 1995). Family professionals, working in concert with families within the capacity-building framework, assist individuals and families in keeping in touch or getting in touch with what promotes health for them. The family nurse facilitates families' appraisal of their health by helping them to define strengths and areas of concern rather than by intervening. The family is the ultimate decision maker in health promotion and health protection.

Factors or variables that may influence family self-care can be derived from two basic approaches: individual characteristics of the family and processes of the suprasystem in which the family is embedded. Family self-care is influenced by factors unique to the family system. The range of self-care behaviors is generally determined by individual factors of age, gender, values, beliefs, life cycle, education, ethnicity, developmental stage, and health of family members (Orem, 1971).

Suprasystem variables include health care access, health insurance, environment, employment status, and educational support. The social determinants of health have been identified and published by the U.S. DHHS (2000) and have also been delineated by the Canadian government's "What Determines Health?" on the Health Canada website. For more in-depth information about the determinants, see Figure 3-4 and refer to the Health Canada website listed at the end of the chapter. Family functioning and characteristics also contribute to self-care through social support, care and socialization of children, provision of healthy physical environments, development of healthy lifestyles including personal health practices and coping skills, access to health care, genetics, and culture.

Families have the role of preparing individual members to care for themselves. Other tasks consist of supporting behaviors that promote the health of the family system and its members. A significant body of research supports the role of the family in promoting responsible sexual behavior (Guthrie et al., 1996; Jemmott & Jemmott, 1992, 1994) and in preventing use of alcohol, tobacco, and other drugs (Loveland-Cherry et al., 1999).

Another area of health protection is the self-care responsibility needed by families to carry out treatment regimens for chronic illness to prevent further disability. Family characteristics influence how individuals view their health, including chronic conditions, and how competent they view themselves to be in caring for their health (Acton, 2002; Denham, 2003). In a study of home treatment for children with cystic fibrosis (Patterson, 1985), family stress was not significantly related to compliance; family expressiveness was positively related to family compliance; and active recreation orientation was negatively related to family compliance. A family emphasis on independence, participation in social and recreational activities, and organization was positively related to perceived competence by children with diabetes (Hauser, Jacobson, Wertlieb, Brink, & Wentworth, 1985). Further, children's adjustment to diabetes was related to a family emphasis on independence, achievement, intellectual or cultural orientation, religious or moral orientation, recreational activities, cohesion, and organization (Hauser et al., 1985). Family interactions have been demonstrated to have long-term effects on self-care for individuals with diabetes (Jacobson, Hauser, Willett, Wolfsdorf, & Herman, 1997). Further, the relationship of family characteristics to management of type 2 diabetes varied for European American and Hispanic adults (Fisher et al., 2000). For European American adults, better general health and better glycosylated hemoglobin levels and less depression were positively related to family coherence. Indicators of poor conflict resolution were related to more depression. Indicators of family structure were related to outcomes for Hispanic patients with diabetes; cohesiveness was related to behavior management; and sex-role traditionalism was related to quality of life in patients with diabetes. Good metabolic control in adults with diabetes was associated with reports of families low in conflict and organization and oriented toward achievement (Edelstein & Linn, 1985). Grey (2000) documents the effects of family interventions in reducing parent-child conflicts about diabetes management and care. The effects of family organization may differ for individuals at different developmental stages. More positive outcomes have been associated with higher levels of organization for adolescents but with lower levels for adults. Thus it appears that families characterized by flexibility, cohesion, support, goal direction, independence, and low levels of conflict are more effective in dealing with the experience of chronic disease.

Lifestyle Changes

Lifestyles are important factors that contribute to health protection. Family influences on eating and exercise patterns are related to the avoidance of specific conditions such as cardiovascular disease, as well as to health promotion. African American women with hypertension report family barriers to maintaining lifestyle changes that control and reduce hypertension including stressors of caring for children, ill parents, and/or spouses; worry about adolescent and adult children; finances; family eating patterns; and lack of social support for lifestyle changes (Bomar, 1995). Positive diet and exercise behaviors have been related to other family members' behaviors in these areas, health training efforts made by parents, promotion of autonomy, cohesiveness, participation in the community, and family interactions (Loveland-Cherry, 1983).

The documented relationship between diet and exercise and cardiovascular health or disease has led to a variety of prevention interventions directed at changing these behaviors through the family unit (Simons-Morton et al., 1986; Perry et al., 1989; Perry, Kelder, Murray, & Klepp, 1992; Madsen et al., 1993). Cullen et al. (2001) demonstrated the relationship between family influence and children's fruit, juice, and vegetable consumption. Baranowski and Nader (1985) found that behaviors can be changed through family communication and support; however, families need assistance in learning these supportive behaviors. Chapters 13 to 16 discuss family lifestyles that influence family health protection, as well as family health promotion.

The importance of families in health protection is well established. Historically, nurses, especially community health nurses, have intervened with families in this arena, using such techniques as anticipatory guidance and health education. Unfortunately, the efficacy of these interventions has not been systematically documented or communicated.

Contracting with Families

The use of written contracts is another approach that has demonstrated effectiveness in increasing confidence and skills to achieve health goals (Haber & Looney, 2000). Contracting incorporates elements that are directed toward building skills and competency through identification of measurable goals, mobilization of support, development of specific strategies, and monitoring progress toward goals. A written contract between the family and the nurse or between members of the family unit specifies expected actions or behavior and the rewards to be gained on completion of specific actions or maintenance of behavior (Koch, Giardina, Ryan, MacQueen, & Hilgartner, 1993).

Development of collaborative partnerships, public commitment to a behavior, reminders of actions to be preformed, and reinforcement of feelings of competency are some of the processes within contracting that promote health behaviors in families. Positive outcomes that have been associated with the use of contracting include improvement of appointment keeping, lower blood pressure, and weight loss (Steckel & Swain, 1977); adherence to treatment regimens (Koch et al., 1993); and achievement of goals related to exercise, weight management, and alcohol abuse (Haber & Looney, 2000). Using calendars as part of the contracting process has been demonstrated to enhance outcomes (Haber & Looney, 2000; Kreuter, Vehige, & McGuire, 1996).

Empowering Families in Health Promotion and Health Protection

A collaborative family-centered approach is one in which professionals, such as nurses, are viewed as working in partnership with families (Dunst, Boyd, Trivette, & Hamby, 2002). Within this approach, the balance of power is shifted from the professional to families, and families are viewed as being "capable of making informed choices and decisions and acting on their choices in ways that support and strengthen family capabilities to improve family functioning" (Dunst et al., 2000, p. 222). Family-centered approaches are consistent with empowerment theory (Rappaport, 1981, 1987; Gutierrez, 1995). An empowerment approach assumes that the family can and will become an agent of change for health promotion and health protection. The end results of an empowerment approach are the development of positive self-esteem, competency, and optimism for the future and the ability to set and reach goals (Rodwell, 1996).

Within an empowerment approach, the nurse works with individuals, families, and communities to identify goals and approaches to meeting those goals, rather than setting goals for them. Once the family has identified health promotion or health protection goals, the nurse works with family members to validate existing skills and to learn new ones that will help them achieve their goals. The emphasis is on capacity building and the mobilization of resources and support by families (Dunst et al., 2002).

The health promotion principles in this approach are as follows (Dunst, et al., 2002; Young & Hayes, 2002).

- Each person lives in a social/historical context that shapes social relations.
- Family members are experts in their own health experiences.
- Diversity is positively valued.
- Professional expertise and skills are used in new ways.
- An expanded view of family history opens the family to new possibilities for wholeness.
- People are the chief actors in making health decisions.

Further research is needed on self-care strategies for families; on behaviors that facilitate empowering families; and on approaches to strengthen individuals, families, and communities in health promotion and health protection.

Influences on Family Health

A number of factors influence family health and the actions families take to promote and maintain health and to prevent disease. As depicted on the social determinants model in Figure 3-4, families do not exist in isolation; they interact with an array of religious, cultural, social, political, and scientific systems. An understanding of the implications of these interactions for family health is critical to strengthening families for health promotion and health protection.

Religious Influences

Religion affects family health by providing an important source of social support, both tangible and intangible; by shaping family values, goals, and socialization practices; and by influencing health-related behaviors (Hummer, Rogers, Nam, & Ellison, 1999). The importance of faith in health outcomes is recognized globally and nationally (McElmurry, Marks, Cianelli, & Mamede, 2002). For example, in 2002 the U.S. DHHS awarded $30 million in grants for "faith- and community-based" health initiatives. These grants represent the first appropriated federal funds in the United States specifically targeted to assist the grass-roots partnerships that are the focus of a faith-based and community initiative. This new federal program officially recognizes that faith-based and community organizations are uniquely situated to partner with the government in serving poor and low-come individuals and families, particularly those with the greatest need such as families in poverty, prisoners reentering the community and their families, children of prisoners, homeless families, and at-risk youth (U.S. DHHS, 2002).

Members of a number of religions, such as Jews, Mormons, Muslims, and Seventh Day Adventists, have dietary restrictions that need to be considered when nurses work with families to plan nutritious and therapeutic diets that will be acceptable. Religious beliefs also influence not only how family planning is viewed but also behavior during pregnancy and childbearing and childrearing practices, including seeking preventive health care. The belief that a higher being is in control may negatively influence a family's participation in a variety of health promotion and health protection practices. For example, some religions discourage the use of medications. It is important to determine the nature and extent of religious involvement with the family and not to assume that identification with a specific faith has the same implications for all families. Chapter 8 in this text explores family religion and the influence on family health in more depth.

Cultural Influences

The American population is a mix of racial and ethnic groups. Major ethnic family subgroups include American Indian and Inuit, African American, Asian American, Mexican American, Hispanic, and Middle Eastern. This is not to discount the numerous ethnic groups that continue to immigrate to the United States. Members of an ethnic group share common beliefs, values, norms, ancestry, language, nationality, and behaviors. Definitions of health, health values, attitudes, and practices vary among cultural groups. Cultural norms and values influence all spheres of family life. An assessment and understanding of the cultural and ethnic backgrounds of families are critical elements of health intervention. However, it is important to be aware that acculturation does occur and that there is diversity within subgroups. Therefore it is important that generalizations from one family to another within any cultural group be made with caution to prevent stereotyping and making inappropriate assumptions. The potential conflict between the formal health care system and folk medicine is well recognized; research on how these two systems can complement each other to provide holistic health care is still in the preliminary stages. The reader is referred to Chapter 9 for a more in-depth discussion of family culture and ethnicity.

Socioeconomic Influences

High socioeconomic status is reported to be conducive to higher levels of health (Wilkinson & Marmot, 1998). A number of social changes have had a significant impact on the family and family health. As noted in Chapter 2, the very structure of families has changed dramatically since the beginning of the twentieth century. The twenty-first century variations in family form include single-parent families, dual-career families, blended families, lesbian and gay domestic partners with and without children, unmarried and married couples with and without children, multigenera-

tional families, and traditional nuclear families. As societal values and norms change, so do the dominant family forms. Increasingly, it is recognized and acknowledged that no one family form is "good" or "bad," "better" or "worse," "functional" or "dysfunctional." Each family is unique. Although the United States is a rich country with a high standard of living, tremendous inequalities continue to exist. A two-tiered health care system is increasingly evident, with one set of resources available to those who can afford them and another to those who cannot. Within the latter group, one subgroup qualifies for subsidized services and a second does not. This last group has increased in numbers, and the need for services is of increasing concern.

Society has grown smaller, in one sense, because of the impact of the media. Now, as never before, families are exposed to a barrage of information on alternative lifestyles, health care practices and products, health care options, and divergent opinions and attitudes. Other social groups, formal and informal, perform functions previously assigned to the family, such as health education, sex education, and socialization. Chapter 6 discusses the various dimensions of internal and external family social support. The increase in the longevity in the population has created both advantages and burdens for families. The increase in multigenerational families has increased social support available to families on the one hand and has increased the burden of caring for elderly family members on the other. The negative effect of some of these social changes is evident in increased levels of substance abuse, adolescent pregnancy, homelessness, family violence, and divorce. Dealing with the stress and frustration of social changes presents challenges to both families and health care professionals in promoting and maintaining family health. Chapter 14 presents information on stress theory and family stress management.

Family income influences the quality of health throughout life. Low-income family members experience a higher incidence of disease and more premature deaths at all ages. Income is one of the major determinants of health (Wilkinson & Marmot, 1998; Health Canada, 2003). For example, in an extensive literature review of research on the health status of black older adults, the barriers to quality health status among this population were low income and inadequate access to health care (Dancy & Ralston, 2002). Because this scenario is repeated with low-income families of all ethnic backgrounds in North America and throughout the world, strategies to improve health promotion are the concern of global organizations such as the World Heath Organization (WHO) and the Pan American Health Organization (Wilkinson & Marmot, 1998).

Political Influences

Although the United States has no national policy related to families, family health is affected by the numerous policy and funding decisions made at local, state, and national levels (see Chapter 21). For example, the shift to increased home health care with increased levels of acuity has placed tremendous burdens on families who provide this care. Part of this shift is accounted for by the institution of a prospective reimbursement system for hospital care based on diagnosis-related groups. Changes in government programs providing support to families, such as nutritional supplements or medical care, in conjunction with the fluctuating economy, result in uncertainty and concern for the health of a growing number of families.

Although increasing recognition has been given to the importance of health promotion and health protection, government programs are primarily reactionary, with the emphasis on illness care. Although attempts at legislative action to bring about national health care reform have failed, major shifts in resources from illness care to primary care are occurring. There are national priorities for the preparation of primary health providers versus specialists. Increasingly, health promotion and risk reduction services and programs are available through managed care systems. Symptom management of chronic illness has become the major activity for monitoring health status. The viability of these changes and their impact on the health of the population have yet to be determined.

Global Influences

The World Health Organization recognizes the importance of families and health promotion and contributes significantly to the family health polices of major nations. Two international documents have shaped global awareness for health promotion. The *Ottawa Charter for Health Promotion* (WHO, 1986) was the outcome of the First International Conference on Health Promotion held in Ottawa, Ontario, Canada. The second document is the *Jakarta Declaration*, the outcome of the WHO Fourth International Conference on Health Promotion, held in Indonesia in 1997 (WHO, 1997).

The *Jakarta Declaration* recommended actions for health promotion in the twenty-first century. Global priorities are as follows (WHO, 1997):

- To promote public and private sector social responsibility for health
- To increase investments in heath (particularly for women, children, and older adults and indigenous, poor, and marginalized populations)
- To consolidate and expand partnerships for health promotion at all levels
- To increase community capacity and empower the individual
- To secure local, national, and global infrastructures for health promotion

Families throughout the world have poor health status because of low socioeconomic status and inadequate access to and public support for health care and safe water and sewers. Documents such as the *Jakarta Declaration* and the *Ottawa Charter* have the goal of persuading nations to not only provide health care systems but also to create socioeconomic policies that address inequity among citizens. Outcomes of the WHO recommendation are projects such as Healthy Cities, Villages, Municipalities; Healthy Islands; Health Promoting Schools; Health Promoting Hospitals; and Health Promoting Workplaces. In addition to national health policies in countries such as Canada and the United States, many nations have imitated health promotion initiatives such as health education on topics such as peace making, self-care behaviors, immunizations, family planning, smoking prevention, and physical activity.

Experts caution that not only is it essential to empower the individual to make personal behavior changes but policy makers must also provide an infrastructure that improves on the socioeconomic and ecological environments of families and individuals (Restrepo, 2000). Although internationally there are inspiring reports of better community participation and improvements in health of powerless groups and families, health care professionals are cautioned that in developing countries such as those in Latin America and Africa, inequities in health care persist (Restrepo, 2000). For global health promotion in the twenty-first century, health care professionals are encouraged to do the following (WHO, 1997):

- Raise the awareness of the changing determinants of health
- Support collaboration and networks for health promotion
- Mobilize resources
- Accumulate and share knowledge on best practices in health promotion
- Promote shared aims in health-related actions
- Foster the accountability of policy makers in health promotion

Globally, nurses and nurse midwives support the role of family health nurse and the collaboration with individuals, families, and communities in the realm of health promotion and prevention. For example, the publication *Nursing and Midwifery Link–a News-Journal of the Global Network of WHO Collaborating Centers for Nursing and Midwifery Development* describes family health issues and illustrates that components of family nursing are prominent internationally in countries such as Africa, Australia, Canada, Japan, Taiwan, Uganda, England, Scotland, and Europe, to name a few. In 1994, the Japanese Family Nursing Society was founded, and the *Japanese Journal of Family Nursing Research* was launched in 1995 (Sugishita, 1999). In the past 10 years there were two "WHO Ministerial Conferences on Nursing and Midwifery in Europe" to address the unique roles of and contributions of Europe's nurses and midwives. A conference outcome specific to families was an appeal to policy makers and nurses to seek ways to establish family-focused community nursing and midwifery programs and the Family Health Nurse role (WHO, 2000) in Europe. Another goal was to advocate that WHO and European policy makers support the creation of family health nursing as a *new role* to partner with families and individuals to create strategies

for health promotion and health maintenance (Billingham, 2000). In 1997, Scottish nurses created the Family Nursing Network in Edinburgh to support the educational preparation of family nurses and the family nursing in practice and research (Claveirole, Mitchell, & Whyte, 2001).

Scientific Influences

Sanitary, medical, and technological advances have decreased the morbidity and mortality rates associated with communicable and infectious diseases. Consequently, the major causes of morbidity and death in this country and throughout the world are chronic diseases and lifestyle-related conditions. Furthermore, infants are now surviving premature birth and its consequences and congenital and birth-related conditions. Coupled with increasing life expectancy, the dependent portion of the population is increasing. Families continue to provide care to these segments of the population. These demands compete with responsibilities for promoting and maintaining family health. However, increasing knowledge regarding health promotion and health protection provides more options to families for promoting and maintaining their health.

The Role of the Nurse in Family Health Promotion

Helping families to achieve or maintain well-being is a goal of family nurses. If families are involved in this process, the goal is more likely to be achieved. Family nursing is not "doing to" or "doing for" the family. Instead, as a transformative process, family health promotion requires a collaborative effort on the part of the family and the nurse (Denham, 2003; Hartrick, 1997; Young & Hayes, 2002). The responsibility is shared, and the competencies of both families and nurses are recognized and used. The nurse may function in a number of roles. First, families often need assistance in illuminating their current health status and appropriate health goals. The assessment should include a review of family lifestyle, identifying both strengths in family patterns and areas for modification.

Second, the nurse can function as a client advocate to enhance the capacity of families to deal with complex systems, to assist families in identifying and using community resources, and to act as a liaison between families and community systems (Hartrick, 1997). Additionally, this advocacy can be expanded to include working for social and policy change that will support and promote family health.

Health education is another important role; however, for it to be effective, it must entail more than "information giving." The beliefs, cultural values, and socioeconomic conditions of families must be respected and considered. Information giving implies a role of facilitation with families; the nurse helps families to identify and evaluate options, as well as helping them use health knowledge effectively. For example, in the twenty-first century, evaluation of the Internet for health information is a crucial need. Health education is a realm in which nurses can join forces with families to understand risk behaviors, develop parenting skills with children of different ages, teach developmental milestones across the life span, develop coping strategies, and facilitate communication to improve marital health and family interaction.

Rankin and Duffy (1983) developed a comprehensive approach to client-family education that emphasizes the importance of including the family in all phases of the educational process. The approach is based on a systems theory framework and assesses four aspects of the "family profile": (1) family education, lifestyles, and beliefs; (2) family understanding of actual or potential health problems; (3) family functioning; and (4) resources available to the family (p. 21).

Other nursing roles include eliciting the family's perception of their strengths and self-care competencies; working with families to establish goals and priorities for change and growth; and helping families to formulate plans for lifestyle modification. Pender's (1986, 2002) Family Health Protection-Promotion Plan in Figure 3-3 provides a format for reviewing family lifestyle, as well as for planning lifestyle modification and monitoring progress toward identified goals. Nurses should use a systematic approach in intervening with families for health promotion, just as they do when they work with individuals. The family nursing process, which is discussed in detail in Chapter 10, provides an organizing framework for assessing family

health and planning and for implementing and evaluating health promotion interventions. Based on the conceptualization of the family health estate described earlier, it is important that the entire family be involved at all stages of the health promotion plan.

Family health promotion both continues and varies over the life span. Much of the interest in family health promotion has focused on the growing family, with considerable attention given to childbearing and parenting skills with children of various ages. The early stages of family development are crucial to the formation of family patterns that affect health attitudes, values, and behaviors. However, recognition of the continuing need for and changing nature of family health promotion has prompted increased interest in families in the child-launching, empty nest, and aging stages. Nursing interventions for family health promotion in the later stages of the family life span are not as well defined as those for earlier stages and warrant increased attention.

In addition to the intervention role, nurses have a role in conducting research in family health promotion, which will contribute to building a sound knowledge base for developing interventions and influencing policy formation. Examples of potential areas for research include delineating specific health promotion tasks and needs for families at various points in the family life span and evaluating the impact of nursing interventions for family health promotion. The nurse who is knowledgeable about family health promotion can also function as a consultant to community groups, other professionals, and legislators. It is also important for nursing to articulate the resulting knowledge and communicate it. Family nurses should be knowledgeable about the human potential for change and how to facilitate health behavior changes by an individual, family, or a group (Pender, Murdaugh & Parsons, 2002). Lastly, the family nurse must be a role model in the area of health promotion and health protection. Nursing has an important role in health promotion across the life span of the family. The remaining chapters in this book offer both the theoretical bases and the nursing processes for effective family health promotion.

CASE SCENARIO

William (age 42) and Jean (age 40) have two sons, Christopher (age 10) and George (age 14), and one daughter, Michelle (age 16). Jean's mother, Mary (age 65), has lived with the family since she was widowed 3 years ago. William is an engineer at an automobile company and commutes approximately 2 hours a day to work and back and often travels out of town on business trips. Jean teaches science at a local middle school. Mary is retired from her job as a librarian and has assumed an active role in meal preparation, supervision of the children, and general housekeeping for the family. The family owns their home, which has four bedrooms and is located in a suburb of a U.S. Midwestern city. The family owns three cars, which are used by each of the adult members of the family.

The family is involved in many activities in addition to work and school commitments. William is finding it difficult to maintain any kind of exercise program because of his travel schedule. Jean is a member of a community advisory board for the local teen center and is completing a graduate degree. Mary is an active member in the community center's activities for senior citizens, takes classes in Spanish, and tries to visit her other children and their families on the East and West Coasts. Christopher enjoys playing video games and watching television but is not active in any organized sports or activities. George loves sports and plays hockey and baseball and enjoys skateboarding. Until last year, Michelle was also active in sports, including swimming and soccer. Now she seems more interested in clothes, dating, and music. She has completed drivers training and wants to get her driver's license. She is also pressuring her parents to let her start dating.

William has a family history of heart disease and was recently given a diagnosis of hypercholesterolemia. His blood pressure is 165/110 mm Hg. The family seldom has the opportunity to eat a meal together. Christopher is overweight. Jean is very concerned about her family's health.

An assessment of the family was completed by using Pender's (2002) framework for family health promotion and health-protection. The results follow.

MAJOR FAMILY STRESSORS

Family stressors include William's health problems, Christopher's sedentary lifestyle, Michelle's potential for risk behaviors related to dating and driving, a busy lifestyle with little time for family togetherness or healthy meals, and the stresses of a three-generation family.

FAMILY STRENGTHS

Family strengths include a stable family structure, adequate financial resources, a high level of education, members' strong positive feelings about their family, and strong support and communications systems.

LIFESTYLE CHANGES INDICATED

Lifestyle changes needed are more regular and healthy family meals and more "family" time. William needs to adopt a low-fat diet and an exercise regimen that fits with his heavy travel schedule. Michelle has a need to develop healthy responsible sexual behavior and avoid early sexual activity. Christopher needs to develop more balanced eating and physical activity patterns. George needs to spend more of his time with the family.

POTENTIAL NURSING INTERVENTIONS

The nurse may contract with the family to develop a plan for healthy family eating patterns and regular family meetings to address family issues and plan family activities.

WEBSITE RESOURCES

ORGANIZATION	WEBSITE ADDRESS
Healthy People	http://www.health.gov/healthypeople/
Public Health Selected Topics, Health Promotion	http://www.ldb.org/vl/top/top-hpr.htm
American Dietetic Association	http://www.eatright.org
International Institute for Health Promotion	http://www.american.edu/academic.depts/cas/health/iihp/
Hispanic Health Council in Connecticut	http://www.hispanichealth.com/
Health Promotion Bookmarks/Hot Links	http://www.web.net/~stirling/
Office of Disease Prevention and Health Promotion	http://www.odphp.osophs.dhhs.gov/
International Union for Health Promotion and Education	http://www.iuhpe.nyu.edu/
Institute of Medicine, Board on Health Promotion and Disease Prevention	http://www.iom.edu/IOM/IOMHome.nsf/Pages/Health+Promotion+and+Disease+Prevention
World Health Organization, Department of Health Promotion, Noncommunicable Disease Prevention and Surveillance	http://www.who.int/hpr/archive/oldhpr/index.html
Health Canada	http://www.hc-sc.gc.ca/english/index.html
Population Health Approach, Health Canada	http://www.hc-sc.gc.ca/hppb/phdd
Canadian Public Health Association	http://www.cpha.ca
Canadian Consortium for Health Promotion Research	http://www.utoronto.ca/chp/chp/consort/
Canadian Institutes of Health Research	http://www.cihr.ca
Canadian Task Force on Preventative Health Care	http://www.ctfphc.org/

■ CHAPTER HIGHLIGHTS

- The health of the family is influenced by the health of its members and influences the health of the members.
- Conceptual definitions of family health are varied (theoretical, clinical, and family).
- Key ideas from definitions indicate that family health is greater than the sum of the health of its members; is a systems process that is dynamic, ranging from functional to dysfunctional; and is influenced by multiple and complex variables.
- Family health is defined as a dynamic process that includes the activities a family uses to promote and protect the well-being of the family as a unit and the individual family members.
- Promoting and protecting the health of the family unit is in the formative stages; therefore health care professionals have challenging opportunities to develop and test interventions in family health promotion.
- The Family Health Promotion Model illustrates that complex multiple factors that influence a family's health-promoting behaviors.
- The role of the nurse in family health promotion includes assessment of and collaboration with families, collaboration with groups and other professionals, capacity building and strengthening families, researching and building a knowledge base for family health promotion, and dissemination of family nursing outcomes and research findings.
- The factors that influence family health promotion are cultural, religious, socioeconomic, political, and global.

CRITICAL THINKING ACTIVITIES

1. What are the major differences between health promotion and health protection? What are the roles of families in each aspect of health?

2. Interview a family about their definition of health, their health goals, and health behaviors. Complete a family health promotion and health protection plan using the format suggested by Pender (see Figure 3-3).

3. How does the role of the family in health promotion and health protection vary across the developmental life span of the family?

4. Identify practice settings in which nurses interact with families. Analyze the opportunities for nursing intervention to enhance family self-care for health promotion and health protection within each of the settings.

REFERENCES

Aaronson, L. S. (1989). Perceived and received support: Effects on health behavior during pregnancy. *Nursing Research, 38*, 4-9.

Adams, M. H., Bowden, A. G., Humphrey, D. S., & McAdams, L. B. (2000). Social support and health promotion lifestyles of rural women. *Online Journal of Rural Nursing and Health Care, 1*(1) [Online]. Retrieved February 24, 2003, from http://www.rno.org/journal/volume1/issue1/adams.html

Acton, G. J. (2002). Health-promotion self-care in family caregivers. *Western Journal of Nursing Research, 24*, 73-86.

Andersen, R. (1968). *A behavioral model of families' use of health services* (Research Series 25). Chicago: Center for Health Administration Studies, Graduate School of Business, The University of Chicago.

Andersen, R. (1995). Revisiting the Behavioral Model and access to medical care: Does it matter? *Journal of Health and Social Behavior, 36*, 1-10.

Andersen, R., & Aday, L. A. (1978). Access to medical care in the U.S.: Realized and potential. *Medical Care, 16*, 533-546.

Anderson, K. H., & Tomlinson, P. S. (1992). The family health system as an emerging paradigmatic view of nursing. *Image, 24*, 57-63.

Baranowski, T. & Nader, P. R. (1985). Family health behavior. In D. C. Turk & R. D. Kerns (Eds.), *Health, illness and families* (pp. 51-77). New York: Wiley

Beavers, W. R., & Hampson, R. B. (1993). Healthy, midrange and severely dysfunctional families. In F. Walsh (Ed.), *Normal family processes* (pp. 73-103). New York: Guilford Press.

Billingham, K. (2000). *Assessing family and community health needs: The contribution of nursing*. Retrieved online February 25, 2003, from http://www.es.euro.who.int/areas_of_work/hrh/nurmid/NursConf/English/PDFe/Microsoft%20Word%20-%2000411rbo.11pdf

Bomar, P. (1990). Perspectives on family health promotion. *Family & Community Health, 12*, 1-11.

Bomar, P. J. (1995). Barriers to health regimens for African-American with hypertension. In J. F. Wang (Ed.), *Proceedings of the Second International and Interdisciplinary Health Research Symposium: Health Care and Culture* (pp. 197-205). Morgantown, WV: Department of Health Systems, School of Nursing, West Virginia University.

Brubaker, B. H. (1983). Health promotion: A linguistic analysis. *Advances in Nursing Science, 5*, 1-14.

Claveirole, A., Mitchell, R., & Whyte, D. (2001). Family Nursing Network: Scottish initiative to support family care. *British Journal of Nursing, 10*(7), 1142-1147.

Cohen, R.Y., Felix, M. R. J., & Brownell, K. D. (1989). The role of parents and older peers in school-based cardiovascular prevention programs: Implications for program development. *Health Education Quarterly, 16*, 245-253.

Committee on Health and Behavior: Research, Practice and Policy, Board on Neuroscience and Behavioral Health, Institute of Medicine (2001). *Health and behavior: The interplay of biological, behavioral, and societal influences*. Washington, DC: National Academies Press. Craft-Rosenberg, M., & Denehy, J. (Eds.). (2001). *Nursing interventions for infants, children, and families*. Thousand Oaks, CA: Sage.

Craft-Rosenberg M., & Denehy, J. (Eds.). (2001). *Nursing interventions for infants, children, and families*. Thousand Oaks, CA: Sage.

Cullen, K. W., Baranowski, T., Rittenberry, L, Cosart, C., Herbert D., & de Moor, C. (2001). Child-reported family and peer influences on fruit juices and vegetable consumption: Reliability and validity of measures. *Health Education Research 16*(2), 187-200.

Curran, D. (1983). *Traits of a healthy family*. Minneapolis, MN: Winston.

Dancy, J., & Ralston, P. (2002). Health promotion and black elders. *Research on Aging, 24*, 218-242.

Danielson, C. B., Hamel-Bissell, B., & Winsted-Fry, P. (Eds.). (1993). *Families, health, and illness: Perspectives on coping and intervention*. St. Louis, MO: Mosby.

Denham, S. A. (1999). Part 1: The definition and practice of family health. *Journal of Family Nursing, 9*, 133-159.

Denham, S. A. (2003). *Family health: A framework for nursing*. Philadelphia: F. A. Davis.

Doherty, W. J., & Campbell, T. J. (1988). *Families and health*. Newbury Park, CA: Sage.

Doherty, W. J., & McCubbin, H. I. (1985). Families and health care: An emerging arena of theory, research, and clinical intervention. *Family Relations, 34*, 5-11.

Dunn, H. L. (1961). *High-level wellness.* Arlington, VA: R. W. Beatty.

Dunn, H. L. (1975). Points of attack for raising the level of wellness. *Journal of the National Medical Association, 49,* 223-235.

Dunst, C. J., Boyd, K., Trivette, C. M., & Hamby, D. W. (2002). Family-oriented program models and professional help giving practices. *Family Relations, 51,* 221-229.

Edelstein, J., & Linn, M. W. (1985). The influence of the family on control of diabetes. *Social Science and Medicine, 21,* 541-544.

Fisher, L., Chesla, C. A., Skaff, M. M., Gilliss, C., Mullan, J. T., Bartz, R.R., et al. (2000). The family and disease management in Hispanic and European-American patients with type 2 diabetes. *Diabetes Care, 23,* 267-272.

Ford-Gilboe, M. (1997). Family strengths, motivation, and resources as predictors of health promotion behavior in single-parent and two-parent families. *Research in Nursing & Health, 20,* 205-217.

Ford-Gilboe, M. (2002). Developing knowledge about family health promotion by testing the Developmental Model of Health and Nursing. *Journal of Family Nursing, 8,* 140-156.

Friedemann, M. L. (1991). An instrument to evaluate effectiveness in family functioning. *Western Journal of Nursing Research, 13*(2), 200-241.

Friedemann, M. L. (1995). *The framework of systemic organization: A conceptual approach to families and nursing.* Thousand Oaks, CA: Sage.

Friedman, M., Bowen, V. R., & Jones, E. G. (2003). *Family nursing research, theory and practice* (5th ed.). Upper Saddle River, NJ: Prentice Hall.

Gilliss, C. L. (1989). Why family health care? In C. L. Gilliss, B. L. Highley, B. M. Roberts, & I. M. Martinson (Eds.), *Toward a science of family nursing* (pp. 3-8), Menlo Park, CA: Addison-Wesley.

Goltman, J. M., DeClaire, J., & Goleman, D. P. (1998). *Raising an emotionally intelligent child: The heart of parenting.* Norfolk, VA: Fireside.

Gray, R. (1996). Family self-care. In P. J. Bomar (Ed.), *Nurses and family health promotion* (2nd ed.). (pp. 83-106). Philadelphia: W.B. Saunders.

Green, L. W., & Kreuter, M. W. (1991). *Health promotion planning: An education and environmental approach* (2nd ed.). Mountain View, CA: Mayfield.

Grey, M. (2000). Interventions for children with diabetes and their families. In J. Fitzpatrick & J. Goeppinger (Eds.), *Annual review of nursing research* (pp. 149-170). New York: Springer.

Guthrie, B. J., Wallace, J., Doerr, K., Janz, N., Schottenfeld, D., & Selig, S. (1996). Girl talk: Development of an intervention for prevention of HIV/AIDS and other sexually transmitted diseases in adolescent females. *Public Health Nursing, 13,* 318-30.

Gutierrez, L. M. (1995). Understanding the empowerment process: Does consciousness make a difference? *Social Work Research, 19,* 229-237.

Haber, D., & Looney, C. (2000). Health contract calendars: A tool for health professionals with older adults. *The Gerontologist, 49,* 235-239.

Hanson, S. M., & Mischke, K. B. (1996). Family nursing assessment and intervention. In P. J. Bomar (Ed.), *Nurses and family health promotion* (2nd ed., pp. 165-202). Philadelphia: Saunders.

Hartrick, G. (1997). Beyond the service model of care: Health promotion and the enhancement of family capacity. *Journal of Family Nursing, 3,* 57-70.

Hauser, S. T., Jacobson, A. M., Wertlieb, D., Brink, S., & Wentworth, S. (1985). The contribution of family environment to perceived competence and illness adjustment in diabetic and acutely ill adolescents. *Family Relations, 34,* 99-108.

Health Canada. (2003). *Determinants of health.* Retrieved February 23, 2003, from http://www.hc-sc.gc.ca/hppb/phdd/determinants/index.html#determinants

Hummer, R., Rogers, R., Nam, C., & Ellision, C. G. (1999). Religious involvement and U.S. adult morality. *Demographics, 36,* 273-285.

Jacobson, A. M., Hauser, S. T., Willett, J., Wolfsdorf, J. I., & Herman, L. (1997). Consequences of irregular versus continuous medical follow-up in children and adolescents with insulin-dependent diabetes mellitus. *Journal of Pediatrics, 131,* 727-733.

Jemmott, J. B., III, & Jemmott, L. S. (1994). Interventions for adolescents in community settings. In R. J. DiClemente & J. L. Peterson (Eds.), *Preventing AIDS: Theories and methods of behavioral interventions* (pp. 141-174). New York: Plenum.

Jemmott, L. S., & Jemmott, J. B., III. (1992). Family structure, parental strictness, and sexual behavior among inner-city black male adolescents. *Journal of Adolescent Research, 7,* 192-207.

Koch, D. A., Giardina, P. J., Ryan, M., MacQueen, M., & Hilgartner, M. W. (1993). Behavioral contracting to improve adherence in patients with thalassemia. *Journal of Pediatric Nursing, 8,* 106-111.

Kreuter, M. W., Vehige, E., & McGuire, A. G. (1996). Using computer-tailored calendars to promote childhood immunization. *Public Health Reports, 111,* 176-178.

Laffrey, S. C. (1985). Health promotion: Relevance for nursing. *Topics in Clinical Nursing, 7,* 29-38.

Laffrey, S. C., Loveland-Cherry, C. J., & Winkler, S. J. (1986). Health behavior: Evolution of two paradigms. *Public Health Nursing, 3,* 92-100.

Lalonde, M. (1974). *A new perspective on the health of Canadians.* Ottawa, Ontario, Canada: Government of Canada.

Leavell, H. R., & Clark, E.G. (1965). *Preventive medicine for the doctor in his community.* New York: McGraw-Hill.

Loveland-Cherry, C. J. (1983). Family system patterns of cohesiveness and autonomy: Relationship to family members' health behavior. (Doctoral dissertation, Wayne State University, 1982). *Dissertation Abstracts International, 43,* 43–11B, 35-37.

Loveland-Cherry, C. J. (1985, April). *Toward a definition of family health.* Paper presented at the meeting of the Midwest Nursing Research Society, Minneapolis, MN.

Loveland-Cherry, C. J. (1986). Personal health practices in single parent and two parent families. *Family Relations, 35,* 133-139.

Loveland-Cherry, C. J., Ross, L., T., Kaufman, S. R. (1999). Effects of a home based family intervention on adolescent alcohol use and misuse. *Journal of Studies on Alcohol. Supplement, 13,* 94-102.

Madsen, J., Sallis, J. F., Rupp, J. W., Senn, K. L., Patterson, T. L., Atkins, C. J., et al. (1993). Process variables as predictors of risk factor changes in a family health behavior change program. *Health Education Research, 8,* 193-204.

Mauksch, H. O. (1974). A social science basis for conceptualizing family health. *Social Science and Medicine, 8,* 521-528.

McCubbin, H. I., & McCubbin, M. A. (1987.) Family Hardiness Index. In H. McCubbin & A. Thompson (Eds.), *Family assessment inventories for research and practice* (pp. 239-306). Madison, WI: University of Wisconsin.

McCubbin, H. I., & McCubbin, M. A. (1993). Families coping with illness: The resiliency model of family stress adjustment and adaptation. In C. B. Danielson, B. Hamel-Bissell, & P. Winsted-Fry (Eds.), *Families, health, and illness. Perspectives on coping and intervention* (pp. 21-63). St. Louis, MO: Mosby.

McElmurry, B. J., Marks, B. A., Cianelli, R., & Mamede, M. (2002). *Primary health care in the Americas: Conceptual frameworks, experiences, challenges and perspectives. Organization and management systems.* Geneva: Pan American Health Organization & World Health Organization. Retrieved October 19, 2002, from the Pan American Organization Web site: http://www.paho.org/English/HSP/HSO/HSO07/primaryhealthcare.doc

Nicklas T. A., Baranowski, T., Baranowski, J. C., Cullen, K., Rittenberry, L., & Olvera, N. (2001). Family and child-care provider influences on preschool children's fruit, juice, and vegetable consumption. *Nutritional Reviews, 59*(7), 224-235.

Niska, K., Snyder, M., & Lia-Hoaberg, B. (1999). The meaning of family health among Mexican American first-time mothers and fathers. *Journal of Family Nursing, 5*(2), 218-233.

North American Nursing Diagnosis Association. (2001). *Nursing diagnosis: Definitions & classification 2001-2002.* Philadelphia: Author.

Olson, D. H. (1993). Circumplex model of marital and family systems: Assessing family functioning. In F. Walsh (Ed.), *Normal family processes* (2nd ed., pp. 104-137). New York: Guilford.

Olson, D. H., & DeFrain, J. (1994). *Marriage and the family: Diversity and strengths.* Mountain View, CA: Mayfield.

Olson, D. H., Portner, J., & Lavee, J. Y. (1985). *FACES III.* St. Paul, MN: Family Social Sciences, University of Minnesota.

Orem, D. E. (1971). *Nursing: Concepts of practice.* New York: McGraw-Hill.

Orem, D. E. (1995). *Nursing: Concepts of practice* (5th ed.). New York: McGraw-Hill.

Ortega, A. N., Belanger, K. D., Paltiel, D. A., Horwitz, S. M., Bracken, M. B, & Leaderer, B. P. (2001). Use of health services by insurance status among children with asthma. *Medical Care, 39*(10), 1065-104.

Patterson, J. (1985). Critical factors affecting family compliance with home treatment for children with cystic fibrosis. *Family Relations, 34,* 79-89.

Pender, N. J., Murdaugh, C. L., & Parsons M. A. (2002). *Health promotion in nursing practice* (4th ed.). Upper Saddle River, NJ: Prentice Hall.

Perry, C. L., Kelder, S. H., Murray, D. M., & Klepp, K. (1992). Community wide smoking prevention long-term outcomes of the Minnesota Heart health program and the Class of 1989 Study. *American Journal of Public Health, 82,* 1210-1216.

Perry, C. L., Luepker, R.V., Murray, D. M., Hearn, M. D., Halper, A., Dudovitz, B., et al. (1989). Parent involvement with children's health promotion: A one-year follow-up of the Minnesota Home Team. *Health Education Quarterly, 16,* 171-180.

Pless, I. B., & Satterwhite, B. (1973). A measure of family functioning and its application. *Social Science and Medicine, 7,* 613-621.

Purath, J., Lansinger, T., & Ragheb, C. (1995). Cardiac risk evaluation for elementary school children. *Public Health Nursing, 12,* 189-195.

Rankin, S. H., & Duffy, K. L. (1983). *Patient education: Issues, principles and guidelines.* Philadelphia: Lippincott.

Rappaport, J. (1981). In praise of paradox: A social policy empowerment over prevention. *American Journal of Community Psychology, 9,* 1-25.

Rappaport, J. (1987). Terms of empowerment/exemplars of prevention: Toward a theory for community psychology. *American Journal of Community Psychology, 15,* 121-148.

Restrepo, H. E. (2000). *Technical report: Increasing community capacity and empowering communities for promoting health.* Fifth Global Conference on Health Promotion, June 5-9, 2000. Retrieved October 18, 2002, from the World Health Organization Web site: http://www.who.int/hpr/conference/products/Techreports/community.pdf

Rodwell, C. M. (1996). An analysis of the concept of empowerment. *Journal of Advanced Nursing, 23,* 305-313.

Rolland, J. S. (1994). *Families, illness, and disability: An integrative treatment model.* New York: Basic Books.

Simons-Morton, B.G., O'Hara, N. M., & Simons-Morton, D. G. (1986). Promoting healthful diet and exercise behaviors in communities, schools, and families. *Family and Community Health, 9,* 1-13.

Smilkstein, G. (1978). The family APGAR: A proposal for a family function test and its use by physicians. *The Journal of Family Practice, 6,* 1231-1239.

Smith, J. A. (1983). *The idea of health: Implications for the nursing professional.* New York: Teachers College Press, Columbia University.

Spangler, J. G, & Kowen, J. C. (1996). Annual screening mammography among diabetic women, demographics, psychological stress, and family functioning. *Issues in Family and Community Health. 18*(4), 1-6.

Stacctchenko, S., & Jenicek, M. (1990). Conceptual differences between prevention and health promotion: Research implications for community health programs. *Canadian Journal of Public Health, 81,* 53-59.

Steckel, S. B., & Swain, M. A. (1977). Contracting with patients to improve noncompliance. *Journal of the American Hospital Association, 51,* 81-84.

Sugishita, C. (1999). Development of family nursing in Japan—Present and future perspectives. *Journal of Family Nursing, 5*(2), 239-244.

Tilson, E. C., McBride, C. M., Albright, J. B., Sargent, J. D. (2001). Attitudes toward smoking and family-based health promotion among rural mothers and other primary care givers who smoke. *Journal of School Health, 71*(10), 489-495.

U.S. Department of Health and Human Services. (1990). *Healthy People 2000: National disease prevention and health promotion objectives.* Washington, DC: U. S. Government Printing Office.

U.S. Department of Health and Human Services. (2000). *Healthy People 2010*. Washington, DC: U. S. Government Printing Office. Retrieved October 1, 2002. from the DHHS Web site: http://www.health.gov/healthypeople/Document/tableofcontents.htm

U.S. Department of Health and Human Services. (2002). *The Compassion Capital Fund and The Faith- and Community-Based Initiative*. Retrieved October 19, 2002, from the Faith and Community-Based Center Web site: http://www.hhs.gov/news/press/2002pres/20020605.html

U.S. Department of Health, Education and Welfare. (1979). *Healthy people: The surgeon general's report on health promotion and disease prevention* (DHEW [PHS] Publication No. 79-55071). Washington, DC: U.S. Government Printing Office.

Walsh, F. (1993). Conceptualizations of normal family functioning. In F. Walsh (Ed.), *Normal family processes*. New York: Guilford Press.

What determines health? Retrieved February 18, 2003, from http://www.hc-sc.gc.ca/hppb/phdd/determinants/index/html

Wilkinson, R., & Marmot, M. (1998). *Social determinants of health: The solid facts*. Geneva: World Health Organization.

World Health Organization. (1986). *Ottawa Charter*. Geneva: Author.

World Health Organization. (1997). *The Jakarta Declaration on Leading Health Promotion into the 21st Century*. Geneva: Author. Retrieved October 1, 2002, from the World Health Organization Web site: http://www.who.int/hpr/archive/docs/jakarta/english.html

World Health Organization. (2000). *Munich Declaration: Nurses and midwives: A force for health, 2000*. Retrieved online February 25, 2003, from http://www.euro.who.int/AboutWHO/Policy/20010828_4

Wright, L. M., & Leahey, M. (2000). *Nurses and families: A guide to family assessment and intervention* (3rd ed.). Philadelphia: F. A. Davis.

Young, L. E., & Hayes, V. E. (2002). *Transforming health promotion practice*. Philadelphia: F. A. Davis.

UNIT II

Conceptual
Frameworks for
Nursing Practice
to Promote
and Protect
Family Health

Theoretical Foundations for Family Health Nursing Practice

4

Joanna Rowe Kaakinen

Shirley May Harmon Hanson

The important thing in science is not so much to obtain new facts as to discover new ways of thinking about them.

— Sir Williams Bragg (1848-1925)

A little experience often upsets a lot of theory.

— Cadman

The important thing is to not stop questioning.

— Albert Einstein

OBJECTIVES

On completion of this chapter, the reader will be able to do the following:
1. *Discuss how theory guides family nursing practice.*
2. *Explain why family nurses need to be knowledgeable and use multiple theoretical frameworks when working with families.*
3. *Describe the meaning of theory.*
4. *Explain the theoretical foundations that inform family nursing practice.*
5. *Examine at least one systems theoretical approach that is used in family nursing.*

Nursing is a profession in which practice is guided by theories, models, and philosophies. Therefore it is said that theory guides practice and practice informs theory. What does this really mean? It means that nurses use knowledge of people, health, environment, and nursing to critically think about clients to determine how to best help them achieve desired outcomes. The way nurses view and think about the whole client picture influences the possible outcomes and interventions that nurses recommend to clients or carry out on their behalf. The way nurses think about people and nursing guides the nature of the questions they ask, the kinds of data they collect, the kinds of relationships they see between different aspects of problems, and the desired outcomes of care and interventions used to achieve the outcomes (Alligood, 1997; Alligood & Tomey, 2002; Meleis, 1997; Mitchell, 1992). Family nursing is based on theory guided by evidence-based knowledge; there is no one overall theory of family nursing.

All families are unique dynamic social structures and have different needs, even when problems appear on the surface to be similar to those of another family. Therefore if nurses view all families through the same theoretical lens, then the number of options possible for family clients may be limited by a single approach or way of thinking. The challenge for nurses is to mentally reflect on various theories or models they have learned to determine which approaches may offer the best outcomes for a particular family. Nurses need to be knowledgeable about multiple theories and have the ability to move among them when using theories or models to assist clients in achieving optimal outcomes.

In this chapter, the basics of theory are presented to assist the reader in understanding the various constructs of theory. The theoretical perspectives that inform family nursing are presented with a specific focus on systems theory. A case study is used to explain and demonstrate Parse's Human Becoming Theory as applied to family nursing. The chapter concludes with a brief description of integrated approaches to working with families and a chapter summary. Appendix 4-1 at the end of the chapter presents a detailed list of references for numerous family theories.

What Are Theories?

Theories are organized systematic ways of explaining or understanding phenomena of interest, specifically the relationships between phenomena, to predict and influence the outcomes. That is, theories are a systematic collection of concepts and relationships (propositions). They are a set of statements about how some part of the world works (Powers & Knapp, 1995; Vogt, 1998). Theories consist of concepts and relationships (propositions) among concepts. Concepts, the building blocks of theories, are words that represent mental images or abstract representations of phenomena. Concepts, or the major ideas expressed by theories, may exist on a continuum from empirical (concrete) to abstract (Powers & Knapp, 1995). *Family* and *health* are examples of highly abstract concepts. *Family vacations, family meetings,* or *family rituals* are far less abstract concepts. The more abstract the concept, the greater is the range of its definitions. For example, there are many ways to define the concept of *family*, and there are even more definitions of the concept *health*.

Propositions are statements about the relationships among two or more concepts (Powers & Knapp, 1995). A proposition might be a statement such as, "The health of the family as a whole interacts with and affects the health of all individual members within that family." The terms *interacts* and *affects* link the two concepts of family and health. A hypothesis is a way of stating an expected relationship among concepts. With the example of families and health, it can be hypothesized that there is an interactive relationship between family functioning and the health of family members. Furthermore, the family's ability to cope with stress affects the health of individual family members, and in turn, the health of these individual members has an impact on family coping and resiliency. This hypothesis may be tested by a study designed to measure family coping mechanisms and family members' health over time in which statistical procedures are used to examine the relationships between the two concepts.

Purpose of Theories

All theories are subject to rules of organization; that is, they are composed of concepts, propositions, relationships between propositions, and connections between propositions and the world of empirical observation (White & Klein, 2002). Thus theories are designed to make sense of the world—to show how one thing is related to another and how together they make a pattern that can predict the consequences of certain clusters of characteristics or events. All theories serve the function of describing, explaining, or making predictions about phenomena (LoBiondo-Wood & Haber, 2002; Polit & Hungler, 1998). Nursing theories ideally represent logical and intelligible patterns that make sense of observations nurses make in practice, which enable nurses to predict what is likely to happen to clients (Fawcett & Downs, 1992). Accordingly, in family nursing, the major function of theories is to provide knowledge and understanding that improve services to the families with whom nurses work.

Specifically, theories help accumulate and organize research findings into coherent patterns. Theories are used to develop and test hypotheses or predictions of what the world will look like. Theories make it possible to articulate ideas more clearly and specifically than is possible in everyday language. Theories are a systematic set of ideas that serve to demonstrate how ideas are connected to each other and to other theories. Finally and most important, theories explain what is happening: they provide answers to *how* and *why* questions, help to interpret and make sense of phenomena, and serve to predict what can happen in the future.

In nursing, the relationship of theories to practice constitutes a dynamic feedback loop rather than a static linear progression. That is, theories grow out of observations made in practice and are then tested by research. Tested theories inform practice, and practice in turn facilitates the further development and refinement of theories. Thus nursing theory, nursing practice, and nursing research related to family nursing are mutually dependent and interact with one another.

In a discussion of nursing theories, Fawcett (2000) writes that theories attempt to account for and/or organize phenomena and are used to describe, explain, or predict specific and concrete phenomena. Theories may be more or less abstract and general, and they vary in the number of phenomena they include and to which they may be may be applied. Depending on their level of abstraction, theories in nursing are generally classified as grand, middle-range, or low-level/single-domain.

Purpose of Conceptual Models

Conceptual models are sets of general propositions that integrate concepts into a meaningful configuration or pattern (Fawcett, 2000). Conceptual models in nursing are based on observations and insights of nursing scholars that combine ideas from multiple fields of inquiry. Conceptual models provide a frame of reference and a coherent way of thinking about nursing phenomena. A conceptual model is more abstract and more comprehensive than a theory. Like a conceptual model, a conceptual framework is a way of integrating concepts into a meaningful pattern, but often conceptual frameworks are less definitive than models. They provide useful conceptual approaches

to or ways of looking at problems or situations, rather than a definite set of propositions. Theories do not stand alone without conceptual frameworks, but frameworks by themselves are not sufficient to explain the relationships between phenomena.

In this chapter the terms *conceptual models/frameworks* and *theoretical theories* and *frameworks* are used interchangeably. In part, this is because there is no single theoretical basis for family nursing; rather, family nurses practice using multiple theoretical approaches. The interchangeable use of these various terms reflects the fact that there is considerable overlap of ideas among the various theories, theoretical frameworks, conceptual models, and conceptual frameworks; therefore all of these "streams of influence" are important for family nursing.

As might be expected, there has been a substantial amount of cross-fertilization among disciplines such as family social science, family therapy, and nursing. Concepts and theories originating in one discipline have been translated into similar concepts for use in another. Many of the concepts in nursing theories were adapted from theories in other disciplines such as sociology, anthropology, and psychology, as well as the more recent fields of family social science and family therapy. For example, concepts such as interaction, stressors, environment, and self-esteem were borrowed from the behavioral and social sciences but have now been integrated into nursing and are used to characterize ideas pertaining to health care. The family social science fields have taken concepts and theories from the general social sciences and applied them to families; examples include developmental theory and general systems theories. Family therapy theorists have adapted concepts and propositions from the family social sciences and applied them specifically to the field of family therapy. For example, general systems theory, which is an idea originally developed in the field of engineering, is one of the foundational theories used to conduct family therapy. As noted previously, no one theoretical or conceptual framework adequately describes the complex relationships of family structure, function, and process. No single theoretical perspective gives nurses a sufficiently broad base of knowledge and understanding to be used as a guide for assessment and interventions with families. Thus no single theory guides nursing care of families. Rather, nurses must draw on multiple theories and frameworks to guide their work with families and take an integrated approach to practice, research, and education in family nursing. Box 4-1 presents criteria for evaluating family theories.

Family Nursing Theoretical or Conceptual Foundations

The conceptual or theoretical frameworks and approaches that provide foundations for family nursing have evolved from three major traditions and disciplines: family social science, family therapy, and nursing (Figure 4-1) (Hanson & Kaakinen, 2001; Hanson & Kaakinen, 2000; Hanson, Kaakinen, & Friedman, 1998). Table 4-1 compares the focus of family across these three disciplines. The *family social science theories* are the most developed and informative about family phenomena such as family function, the environment-family interchange, communications and relationships within the family, changes in the family over time, and the family's reaction to health and illness. Box 4-2 presents selected family social science theories and family therapy theories used in family nursing and provides detailed citations. However, family social science theories are difficult to use in family nursing because the bases of assessment and intervention are too abstract, but recently, some family nursing scholars have made advances in integrating social science theories with family nursing practice (Berkey & Hanson, 1991; Danielson, Hamel-Bissell, & Winstead-Fry, 1993; Friedemann, 1995; Hanson, Kaakinen, & Friedman, 1998; Hanson, 2001; Vaughan-Cole, Johnson, Malone, & Walker, 1998; Wright & Leahey, 2000). The *family therapy theories* are newer and less well developed than family social science theories, but they are more relevant to family nursing because they emanate from a practice discipline (see Box 4-2). Thus today, family nursing theory, practice, research, and education draw heavily on family therapy theories.

Finally, of the three types of theories, *nursing conceptual frameworks* are the least developed for use in family nursing. Nursing models developed in the 1960s and 1970s originated from an

---

BOX 4-1　Criteria for Evaluating Family Theories

1. *Internal consistency:* A theory does not contain logically contradictory assertions.
2. *Clarity or explicitness:* The ideas in a theory are expressed in such a way that they are unambiguous. They are defined and explicated where necessary.
3. *Explanatory power:* A theory explains well what it is intended to explain.
4. *Coherence:* The key ideas in a theory are integrated or interconnected, and loose ends are avoided.
5. *Understanding:* A theory provides a comprehensible sense of the whole phenomenon being examined.
6. *Empirical fit:* A large portion of the results of tests of a theory have been confirmatory or at least have not been interpreted as disconfirming.
7. *Testability:* It is possible for a theory to be empirically supported or refuted.
8. *Heuristic value:* A theory has generated or can generate considerable research and intellectual curiosity (including a large number of empirical studies, as well as much debate or controversy).
9. *Groundedness:* A theory has been built up from detailed information about events and processes observable in the world.
10. *Contextualization:* A theory gives serious consideration to the social and historical contexts affecting or affected by its key ideas.
11. *Interpretive sensitivity:* A theory reflects the experiences practiced and felt by the social units to which it is applied.
12. *Predictive power:* A theory can successfully predict phenomena that have occurred since it was formulated.
13. *Practical utility:* A theory can be readily applied to social problems, policies, and programs of action (i.e., it is useful for teaching, therapy, political action, or some combination of these).

Adapted from White, J. M., & Klein, D. M. (2002). Family theories: An introduction (2nd ed.). Thousand Oaks, CA: Sage.

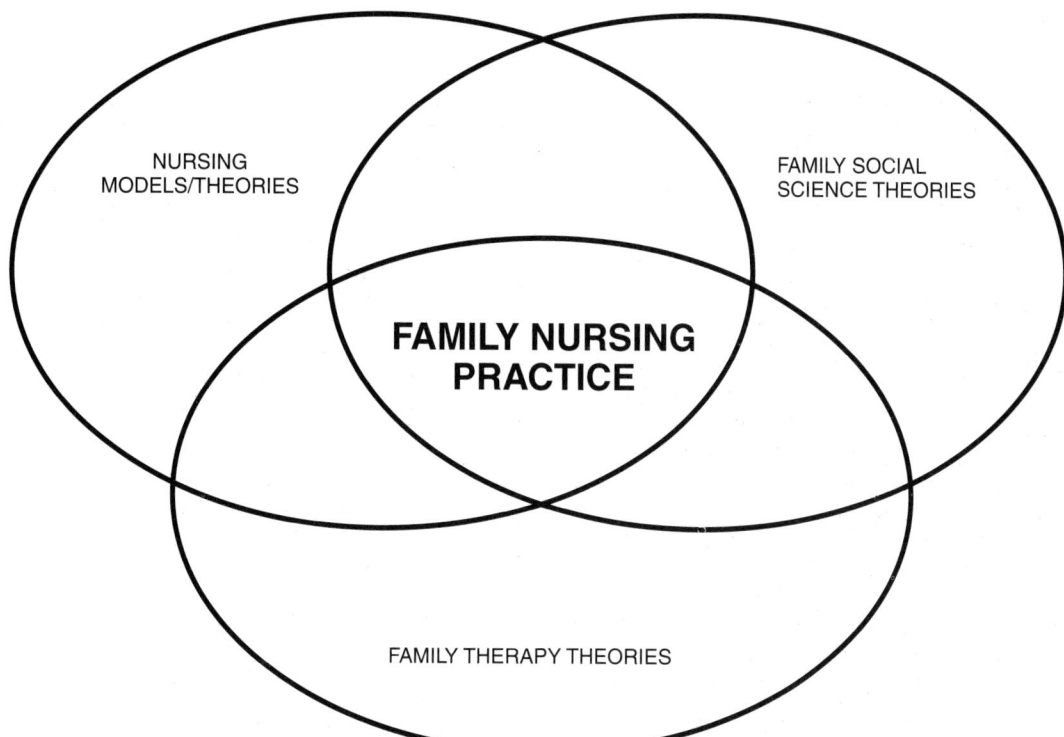

Figure 4-1   Conceptual sources that inform family nursing practice. (Adapted from Hanson, S. M. H., & Kaakinen, J. [2001]. Theoretical foundations for family nursing. In S. M. H. Hanson (Ed.), *Family health care nursing: Theory, practice, and research* (pp. 36-59). Philadelphia: F. A. Davis.)

TABLE 4-1 Differences among Family Social Science Theories, Family Therapy Theories, and Nursing Models and Theories			
Criteria	Family Social Science Theories	Family Therapy Theories	Nursing Theories
Purpose of theory	Descriptive and explanatory (academic models); explain family functioning and dynamics	Descriptive and prescriptive (practice models); explain family dysfunction and guide therapeutic actions.	Descriptive and prescriptive (practice models); guide nursing assessment and intervention efforts.
Discipline focus	Interdisciplinary (although primarily sociological)	Marriage and family therapy and family mental health	Nursing focus
Target population	Primarily "normal" families (normality-oriented)	Primarily "troubled" families (pathology-oriented), although new approaches focus on family strengths	Primarily those families with health and illness problems

Adapted from Hanson, S. M. H. (2001). Family health care nursing theory, practice and research (2nd ed.). Philadelphia: F. A. Davis; Jones, S. L., & Dimond, S. L. (1982). Family theory and family therapy models: Comparative review with implications for nursing practice. Journal of Psychiatric Nursing and Mental Health Services, 20, 12-19.

BOX 4-2   Selected Family Social Science Theories and Family Therapy Theories Used in Family Nursing Practice

FAMILY SOCIAL SCIENCE THEORIES

Systems theory
(von Bertalanffy, 1950, 1966, 1968)
Structural-functional theory
(Artinian, 1994; Nye & Berado, 1981)
Family developmental theory
(Duvall, 1977; Duvall & Miller 1985; Jones & Dimond, 1982)
Family interactional theory
(Blumer, 1969; Burr, Leight, Day, & Constantine, 1979; Crotty, 1998; Hill & Hanson, 1960; Kuhn, 1964; Mead, 1934, Nye, 1976; Rose, 1962; Turner, 1970, 1991)
Family stress theory
(Hill, 1949, 1958; McCubbin & McCubbin, 1996; McCubbin & Patterson, 1983)
Change theory
(Bateson, 1970; Glanz, Lewis, & Rimer, 1997; House, Landis, & Umberson, 1988; Maturana, 1978; Maturana & Varel, 1992; McEwen, 1998; Seeman, 1996; Watzlawick, Weakland, & Fisch, 1974)
Others: Chaos theory
Social exchange theory
Conflict theory
Ecological theory
Anthropological/multicultural theory
Phenomenological theory

FAMILY THERAPY THEORIES

Family systems therapy theory
(Ackerman, 1966; Becvar & Becvar, 1996; Bowen, 1976, 1978; Freeman, 1992; Gladding, 1995; Goldenberg & Goldenberg, 2000; Kerr & Bowen, 1988; Madanes, 1991; Pinsof, 1995; Segrin 2001; Whitaker & Keith, 1981; White & Epston, 1990)
Structural family therapy theory
(Minuchin, 1974; Minuchin & Nichols, 1998; Minuchin, Rosman, & Baker, 1978; Olson, 1993; Toman, 1961)
Interactional family therapy theory
(Broderick, 1993; Jackson, 1965; Kantor & Lehr, 1975; Satir, 1982, 1983; Watzlawick, Weakland, & Jackson, 1967)
Others: Psychodynamic therapy theory
Experiential therapy theory
Humanistic therapy theory
Strategic therapy theory
Behavioral/cognitive therapy theory
Narrative therapy theory
Solution-oriented therapy theory

---

individualized medical-model paradigm, and few have evolved enough to be useful for family nursing. The early nursing models and theories represent a deductive approach to the development of nursing science (i.e., they move from the general to the specific). Theories based on more inductive approaches to nursing theory development (i.e., approaches that move from the specific to the general) have not been well developed. Today, nursing scholars have rediscovered the inductive approach by studying grounded theories (Kim, 2000). "In general, nursing theoretical models are mostly descriptive, with some evidence of development toward explanatory frameworks" (Kim, 2000, p. 240). Table 4-2 outlines nursing models and their family focus.

Much of the recent family nursing studies has been conducted on small, local sample sizes.

Therefore they lack generalizability and systematic approaches, and they do not contribute to the development of family nursing models or frameworks and to a body of evidence for practice (Hallberg, 2003; Knafl & Gilliss, 2002). Gilliss and Knafl (1999) conducted an analysis of the nursing science related to families experiencing nonnormative transitions. They

TABLE 4-2   Nursing Theories and Models That Contribute to Family Nursing

Theorist	Theory or Model	Description of Family Nursing
Florence Nightingale (1859, 1992; Lobo, 1995)	Environmental model	Nightingale encouraged nurses to include families in the care of the ill family member. She addressed concerns of working with families and their environment to maintain and improve the health of the family members.
Martha Rogers (1970, 1986, 1990)	Science of unitary human beings	Rogers primarily addressed the individual as a unitary multidimensional energy field that engages in continuous mutual process with the environment. Nurse researchers have expanded Rogers' theory by looking at family as a unitary entity that interacts with the larger society (Fawcett, 1991; Casey, 1996; Winstead-Fry, 2000).
Dorothea Orem (1971, 1983a, 1983b, 1985, 1991, 2001)	Model of self-care	Orem viewed the family as primarily contributing to the socialization function of its family members with specific emphasis on role development and culture. The role of the family is viewed as caregiver by helping others to achieve self-care or to provide care for family members.
Sister Callista Roy (1976) (Roy & Roberts, 1981)	Adaptation model	In her original work, Roy addressed how the family members influence the health of the individual. Later, Roy and Roberts (1981) expanded the initial view of family as context to family as client by explaining how a family is an adaptive system. They emphasized the functions of the family as it contributes to the development and adaptation of its family members in health promotion and illness.
Imogene King (1981, 1983, 1987)	Theory of goal attainment	King emphasized the communication and socialization function of the family. In her early work, family was viewed as important to the health of the individual (family-in-context perspective). Later, King emphasized that communication is central to the relationship between the nurse and family client. The family was viewed as having a central role in transmitting values of health, health promotion, and maintenance.
Betty Neuman (1982, 1983, 1995)	Neuman systems model	Neuman addressed the family as client since the family provides lines of defense to protect and buffer family members and the whole family as it interacts with other systems to a homeostasis. The family is viewed as an open syste engages in reciprocal exchange with the environme an optimal level of wellness.

TABLE 4-2   Nursing Theories and Models That Contribute to Family Nursing—cont'd

Theorist	Theory or Model	Description of Family Nursing
Moyra Allen (1982; Allen & Warner, 2002)	A developmental model of health and nursing	Allen used a holistic approach to family nursing in describing how health and health practices and beliefs are established in the family and change over time. Her developmental model is a health belief model from a nursing perspective, where health is viewed as more than absence of illness or disease. The family is seen as a dynamic system that adapts over time to situational and maturational developments.
Marie-Louise Friedemann (1995)	Framework of systemic organization	Friedemann viewed the family as a social system that has the express goal of transmitting culture and values to its family members through the socialization function of the family. The family serves as a buffer for its family members because it provides a safe environment for growth and adaptation. The family is seen as having a central role in the health and health promotion of its members through family stability, growth, and spirituality.
Rosemarie Rizzo Parse (1981, 1992, 1998)	Human becoming theory	Parse viewed the family a dynamic being (family as client) that is continually becoming and evolving as the family members interact within the family and the family interacts with other systems. Parse believes that people control their health choices and that the role of the nurse is to help them know what is possible so that people make informed choices. Illness is viewed as a family event.

found that the research was "largely atheoretical, with few empirical findings leading to intervention studies that might ultimately guide nursing practice" (p. 243). Hallberg (2003), in a review of family studies, found that there "was a lack of congruence between the theoretical framework, the intervention, and the outcome measure" (p. 9). The challenge for the twenty-first century is to conduct research on practice issues that are grounded in theory to build a body of knowledge that will have enough power and significance to inform practice.

Boxes 4-1 and 4-2, Tables 4-1 and 4-2, and Figure 4-1 provide a more detailed explanation of the three types of theories—family social science, family therapy, and nursing—that are significant to evolving and integrative family nursing frameworks, and further information can be found in other sources (Friedman, Bowden, & Jones, 2003; Hanson, 2001; Hanson & Kaakinen, 2000). Note that many of the theories listed in Box 4-2 are ⌐ntained in other chapters within this textbook

(e.g., communication theory, role theory, developmental theory, and stress/coping theory).

In the next section of this chapter, family systems theory is selected for focused elaboration. Systems theory from a family social science perspective is described, followed by family therapy's application of systems theory. Then a few of the nursing theories that emanate from systems theory are summarized. This chapter section concludes with a brief discussion of integrating models for nursing care of families.

Systems Theory and Family Social Science

Systems theory and its extrapolation to the family has been the most influential of all the family frameworks. The systems theoretical approach that is used to understand families was originally derived from physics and biology by von Bertalanffy (1950) (Hanson & Kaakinen, 2001). A system is composed of a set of interacting elements; each system is identifiable as distinct from the environment in which it exists. An open system exchanges energy and matter with the environment, whereas a closed system is isolated from its environment. Systems depend on both positive and negative feedback to maintain a steady state (homeostasis). The systems perspective assumes that family systems are greater than and different from the sum of their parts.

The family system is an organized whole, and individuals in the family are interdependent and interactive. However, there are boundaries in the system, which may be open, closed, or random. Further, there are hierarchies within the family system and logical relationships between subsystems (e.g., mother-child and family-community). Every family system has features designed to maintain stability or homeostasis, though these may be adaptive or maladaptive. At the same time, the family is considered to change constantly in response to stresses and strains from within and from the external environment, and change in one part of the family system affects the entire system. Causes and effects are modified by feedback loops. The patterns of the family system are circular rather than linear, and the family system increases in complexity over time, evolving to ensure greater adaptability, tolerance to change, and growth by differentiation. Since patterns are circular, interventions to bring change must be directed toward the cycle of change, not toward isolated events.

The family system perspective encourages nurses to see individual clients as participating members of a family system. For example, nurses using this perspective assess the effects of illness or injury on the entire family and the effects of family functioning on the individual with the illness or injury (Hanson, 2001). Emphasis is on the whole family rather than on individual members. Assessment questions that might be asked from this perspective include, "Who is in the family system?" and "How has a family member's critical illness affected the family and its members?" Interventions by family nurses need to address both subsystem and whole-family processes and functioning.

The strengths of the general systems framework include the fact that this theory covers a large array of phenomena and views the family within the context of its suprasystems (the larger community in which it is embedded) and its subsystems. Further, this is an interactional and holistic theory, which looks at processes within families, rather than at the content and relationships between parts. A family is viewed as a whole, not as merely a sum of its parts. Unfortunately, the strengths of the theory are also its limitations. Because social science theoretical orientation is broad and very general, it can be difficult to apply to practice disciplines such as nursing. Specific concepts and practice guidelines must be developed outside the theory. Further, this approach may not be as helpful as theories oriented toward individuals in dealing with concerns of individual family members.

Family Systems and Family Therapy

Family systems therapy builds on the foundation of family social science and systems theory. Family systems therapy was first developed by Murray Bowen (1978); Bowen was a pioneer in the field of family therapy and is still recognized as the leading theorist in the field. Since his death in 1990, his work has been continued by Michael Kerr (1988), David Freeman (1992), and Peter Titelman (1998).

Murray Bowen's particular version of family systems theory begins with the assumption that anxiety is an inevitable, omnipresent part of life (Gladding, 2001; Goldenberg & Goldenberg, 2000). Chronic anxiety is the basic cause of dysfunction in individuals and in families. The only antidote for chronic anxiety is "resolution through differentiation" (Goldenberg & Goldenberg, 2000, p. 169). Box 4-3 lists the eight interlocking concepts of Bowen's Family Systems Theory.

Thus in Bowen's view, the key to healthy functioning is *differentiation of self,* or the ability of persons to distinguish themselves from their family of origin emotionally and intellectually. According to Bowen, there are two counterbalancing life forces: togetherness and individuality, which exist at two bipolar ends of a continuum. On one end of this continuum is autonomy, which is an ability to see oneself separately from others, think through a situation without confusing self with others, and separate feelings from rational thought. At the other end of the continuum is undifferentiated ego mass, which

---

BOX 4-3   Bowen's Family Systems Theory: Eight Interlocking Concepts

1. Differentiation of self
2. Nuclear family emotional system
3. Multigenerational transmission process
4. Family projection process
5. Triangles
6. Sibling position
7. Emotional cutoff
8. Societal regression

Adapted from Hanson, S. M. H. (2001). Family health care nursing theory, practice, and research (2nd ed.). Philadelphia: F. A. Davis; Goldenberg, I., & Goldenberg, H. (2000). Family therapy: An introduction (5th ed.). Pacific Grove, CA: Brooks/Cole.

---

implies emotional dependence on the family of origin even if one is living away from the family. Individuals can be ranked on a scale of differentiation of self on a continuous scale from low to high. The more differentiated the individual, the more that individual is able to use logical reasoning and adapt to stress and change in the surroundings. Thus well-differentiated persons are less apt to experience emotional difficulties.

In Bowen's family systems theory, the nuclear family is viewed as a *family emotional system*. In this system, the coping strategies and patterns used tend to be passed on from generation to generation, a phenomenon that Bowen calls *the multigenerational transmission process*. Thus families who are dysfunctional have usually carried the problematic behaviors over several generations. Further, families tend to perpetuate their level of differentiation. That is, people usually marry partners at their own level of differentiation, and couples then produce offspring at the same level of differentiation. Parents who are anxious and have poor differentiation of self tend to transfer their anxiety and low level of differentiation to susceptible children. This phenomenon is called the *family projection process*.

According to Bowen, *triangles* are the way that families deal with anxiety. In a triangle, which Bowen says is a basic building block of any emotional system, the tension between two persons is projected onto another object or person in the family; for example, tension between parents may be projected onto children. In particularly stressful situations, anxiety may spread from a triangle within the family to triangles that include persons outside the family. *Sibling position* is another important concept in family systems therapy. From this perspective, people are seen as developing fixed personality characteristics based on their birth order in their family of origin (Toman, 1961). The more closely a marriage replicates the couple's sibling positions in the family of origin, the better chance that couple has of having a successful marriage. For example, it is hypothesized that a marriage of two oldest siblings is likely to have more conflict than a marriage of an oldest sibling and a youngest sibling. *Emotional cutoffs* occur when children have unresolved attachments to parents. Children who are emotionally fused to their parents and family of origin may live near or far from them. They may try to withdraw from parents and stay emotionally distanced from the family, but they are fused regardless of their physical proximity. *Societal regression* occurs on a community level but is similar to failure to differentiate self on an individual level. It occurs when so many toxic forces counter the tendency to achieve differentiation that the society regresses under the stress.

Bowen's family systems therapy focuses on promoting differentiation of self from family and promoting differentiation of intellect from emotion (Becvar & Becvar, 2000). Family members are encouraged to examine the processes described previously to gain insight and understanding into their past and present. They are thus free to choose how they will behave in the future. Using Bowen's approach, a family nurse or therapist would have individuals or couples look at their family tree. The nurse would serve as coach and teacher, asking questions about people's history while helping them to construct a family tree called *a multigenerational genogram*. Using this approach, families are encouraged to ask questions of their own family members to gain an understanding of the past and the ways they currently interact. The goals are to help family members recognize and avoid forming triangles and to develop relationships with individual family members, and end emotional withdrawal.

Because this assessment approach to families is supposedly more objective and neutral, it decreases the likelihood of family members blaming each other. However, this type of therapy emphasizes understanding the past in order to deal with problems in the present and therefore it requires a long commitment. Many people are not inclined to stay with such therapy to completion, and today many health plans are not willing to pay for long-term or family therapy.

Nursing Models and Theories Based on Systems Theory

In recent years, several nursing models and theories that use systems theory as the basis for family nursing interventions have been developed. In this section, Neuman's Systems Model and Friedemann's Framework of Systematic Organization are briefly explained. Parse's Human Becoming Theory is described in more detail because it has not traditionally been applied to the family as client. A case study is also used to demonstrate application of the Parse model to family nursing practice.

The *Neuman Systems Model*, developed by Betty Neuman (1982, 1995), is health-oriented. Health is seen as a continuum of wellness and illness. The client is viewed as an open system. The client can be a person, family, or community. The Neuman Systems Model is based on several family social science theories, including the systems and stress theories (George, 2002).

Neuman defines the family as "a group of two or more persons who create and maintain a common culture; its most central goal is one of continuance" (Neuman, 1982, p. 241). Neuman views the family as an open system that is composed of family member subsystems. Each subsystem is visualized as a whole open system; therefore the sum of the parts is seen as greater than the whole.

In Neuman's Systems Model, the family system strives for equilibrium as it adapts to internal and external stressors that threaten its state of wellness. The family's primary goal is to maintain its stability by preserving the integrity of its structure. Neuman depicts the open system with the core at the center surrounded by concentric rings that represent lines of defense against stressors. The lines of defense are buffers and protect or prevent the core from threatening situations (Alligood & Tomey, 2002). Figure 4-2 shows a system in equilibrium compared with a system in disequilibrium.

To identify the stressors threatening the client system, nurses holistically assess the client from the following five perspectives: physiological, psychological, developmental, sociocultural, and spiritual. Nurses confirm the assessment with clients and seek their input regarding problem identification and interventions. The nursing goal is to assist clients to seek or move toward an optimal state of wellness.

Marie-Louise Friedemann's (1995) *Framework of Systemic Organization* is built on the view of the family as client. The family is viewed as a social system that has the expressed goal of transmitting culture to its members. Consistent with general systems theory, her framework is based on the following assumptions (pp. 16-17):

1) The family, which is embedded in the civil or social system, transmits culture, i.e., the total of human patterns and values.
2) The family and the civil system and environment at large share responsibility for providing physical necessities and safety, teaching social skills to its members, fostering personal growth and development, allowing emotional bonding of family members, and promoting a purpose for life and meaning through spirituality.
3) The family satisfies its members' needs for control over their environment and helps them find their place in the network of systems through spirituality.
4) All family processes include collectively accepted and coordinated behaviors or strategies that aim at regulating space, time, energy and matter in pursuing family stability, growth, control and spirituality.
5) Family processes fall into four dimensions: system maintenance, system change, coherence and individualization. These dimensions are interdependent but also exist independently in that none is emphasized at the expense of another in healthy families.

The elements central to Friedemann's theory are family stability, family growth, family control, and family spirituality. The family offers safety to its members as they learn group values, norms, and acceptable behaviors. As its members grow,

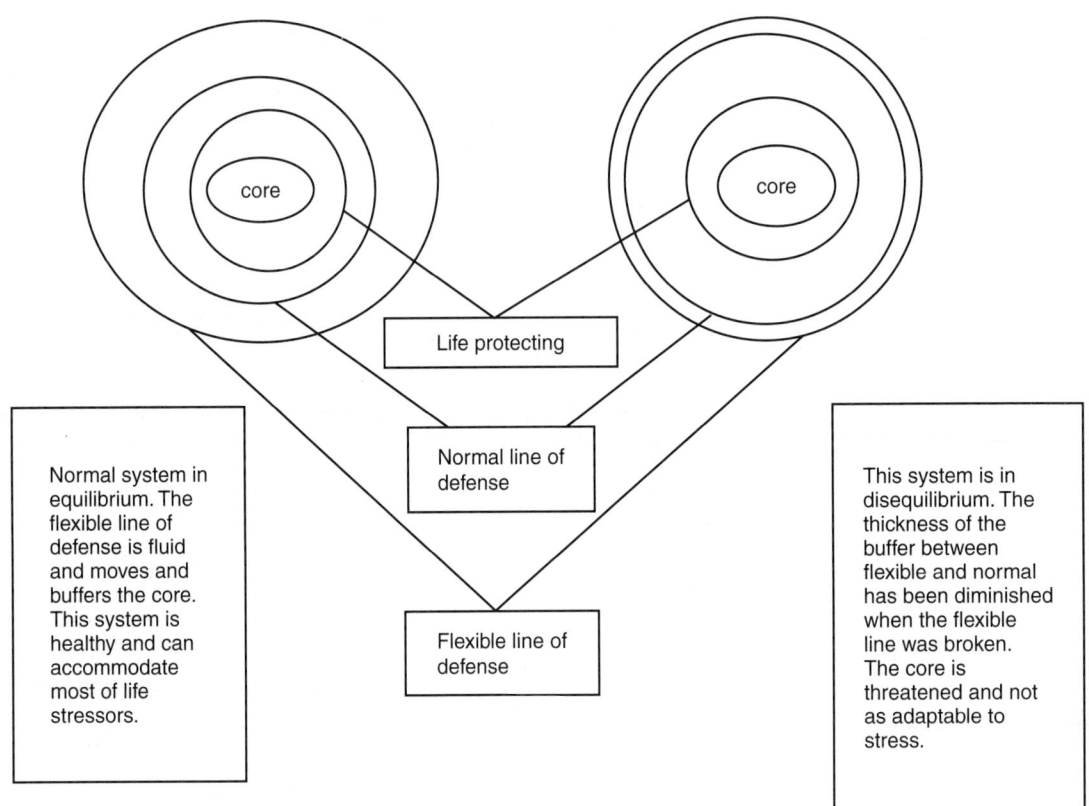

Figure 4-2   Comparison of a system in equilibrium and disequilibrium with the Neuman Systems Model.

the family grows and interacts with other systems such as schools, church, and work. Family growth is facilitated by communication among its members. By selectively opening or closing its boundaries, the family can serve as a buffer between its members and the demands of society. Family control is maintained through the structure of the family. Family spirituality connects family members emotionally and encourages self-growth of individual members (Friedemann, 1995).

Rosemarie Rizzo Parse's theory, originally called *the Man-Living-Health Theory* in 1981, was officially renamed the *Human Becoming Theory* in 1992 (Parse, 1998). The definition of family is dynamic. Who one considers a member of his or her family will likely change over time. Who one places in the category of family is self-defined as persons who depend on one another for emotional, physical, and economic support (Hanson, 2001). Therefore the concept of family can be considered

as continually becoming and evolving. According to this definition of family, it seems logical to consider Parse's Human Becoming School of Thought in the practice of family nursing (1998).

Parse's theory is grounded in existential-phenomenological thought and in the natural sciences perspective. The Human Becoming Theory focuses on the lived experience of people. The central thesis of the theory of human becoming is that "humans in mutual process with the universe structure meaning multi-dimensionally, co-author health, freely choose ways of becoming and move beyond each moment with hopes and dreams" (Parse, 1998, pp. x-xi).

Parse believes that nurses use their body of knowledge in service to people. The goal of the nurse is to be with the family as the family members enhance their quality of life. Nurses use therapeutic communication to invite each member of the family to uncover the meaning of the experience for each individual, learn what the meaning of the experience is for each other, and discuss the meaning of the experience for the family as a whole. Nurses who practice the Human Becoming Theory do not make recommendations or suggestions based on their interpretation of the experience or personal values; rather they are nonjudgmental. Nurses ask the family questions such as the following (Alligood & Tomey, 2002):

• What has this situation been like for you and your family?
• What are you most concerned about?
• How is what you are most concerned about similar to or different from how others in your family see the problem?
• What would you like to know more about?
• How would you like to change your situation?

The role of the nurse is to support the family members while they work through the difficult process of change, but the nurse does not avoid conflict or smooth over the uncomfortableness, pain, and difficult times while the family works through the experience and changing health patterns (Alligood & Tomey, 2002).

Parse focuses primarily on the nurse-client relationship: the role of the nurse is to help the clients tell their illness story, thereby uncovering meaning in the experience. Parse believes that in the telling of their story, people uncover understanding and new insights, verbalize their values, and explore possible choices available to them. A central tenet of Parse's approach is the belief that people control their health choices and the role of the nurse is to help them know what is possible so they can make informed choices. People make health choices based on their unique view of self: "I was," "I am," and "I could possibly be." What is critical about this perspective is that in family nursing the view of self always includes the impact on the family. Individuals do not make health decisions autonomously and in isolation. Illness is a family event.

Parse (1998) describes the Human Becoming Theory School of thought as a "human science system of interrelated concepts describing the unitary human's mutual process with the universe in co-creating becoming. Essential ideas are the human-universe mutual process, the co-constitution of health, the multidimensional meanings the unitary human gives to being and becoming, and the human's freedom in each

situation to choose alternative ways of becoming" (p. 10). According to Hickman, (2002), the following points are distinctive of Parse's theory (p. 433):

1) Humans are more and different than the sum of their parts.
2) Human beings evolve mutually with the environment.
3) Human beings co-create personal health by choosing meaning in situations.
4) Human beings convey meanings that are personal values, which reflect their dreams and hopes.

Three principles constitute the Human Becoming Theory, which are explained and demonstrated in several places in this section. First, people uncover the meaning of the situation. Second, they demonstrate their patterns of relating to others, ideas, and beliefs in making decisions and experiencing conflicts. Lastly, people integrate these changes (transcend) brought about by the current situation into their everyday behaviors and thinking (becoming). The process of change occurs as individuals explore paradoxical views of self in the given situation. A paradoxical view is when a person reflects on both sides of an argument or idea to determine where he or she personally falls on the continuum of opposing ideas or concepts. For example, a person determines how an action will make him or her similar to others or different and unique from others. Another example of a paradoxical view is to determine how much to share (disclose) about a situation with others or how much to conceal from others. The concept of paradox is not "either or" but is seen as a whole, and both ends of the continuum are experienced simultaneously. The paradox gives structure to the person as he or she creates an internal tension by juxtaposing the concepts to determine how to achieve the desired outcome. Table 4-3 lists the three principles of the Human Becoming Theory along with their corresponding paradoxical concepts.

Often students and nurses have difficulty understanding Parse's Theory of Human Becoming because the language used is unfamiliar and they have little experience with the concepts as they are explained in the abstract. Therefore in this chapter, the three principles of Parse's Theory of Human Becoming are explained and followed by Parse's descriptions. The case study of Bob and Nancy is

TABLE 4-3 Principles and Paradoxes in Parse's Human Becoming Theory

Principle	Paradox
1. Structuring meaning multi-dimensionally is co-creating reality through the languaging of valuing and imaging.	A. Explicit–Tacit knowing B. Confirming–Not confirming
2. Co-creating rhythmical patterns of relating is living the paradoxical unity of revealing–concealing and enabling–limiting which connecting and separating.	A. Revealing—Concealing B. Enabling–Limiting C. Connecting–Separating
3. Co-transcending with the possibles is powering unique ways of originating in the process of transforming.	A. Pushing–Resisting B. Conformity–Nonconformity C. Certainty–Uncertainty D. Familiar–Unfamiliar

used after each principle to demonstrate the ideas of Parse's three principles in nursing practice. The term *person* is used instead of *unitary human* to help the reader understand the concepts.

Principle 1: A person assigns significance and meaning to his or her experience. One of the paradoxes explored by the individual in uncovering meaning is imaging self by considering different aspects of the continuum that ranges from explicit knowing to tacit knowing. Explicit knowing consists of ideas, beliefs, and knowledge that one can express logically and reflect on critically. Tacit knowing consists of feelings, concepts, and connections that are intuitive, internal, and vague. A person assigns significance or meaning to an event by juxtaposing and comparing how he or she views the self in relationship to the idea or concept or in that particular context. A person comes to this meaning by comparing it with his or her personal vision of previous self, current self, and the potential future self, given this new situation. Parse's (1998) description of this process is "structuring meaning multi-dimensionally is co-creating reality through the languaging of valuing and imaging" (p. 35).

In determining values, each person engages in the paradox of confirming and not confirming cherished beliefs, principles, and ideas that guide his or her life. The key is that each person is free to choose from different alternatives what is most important to him or her. At one end of the continuum are ideas and principles that guide the

Principle 1: Family Example

Bob and Nancy have been married for 2 years and would like to have children, but Nancy has been unable to conceive. The nurse talks with the couple and encourages them to individually and together *explicitly* express and *critically think* about what this experience of not being able to have children means to each of them, what they believe it means for the other, and what it means for them as a family. At the same time, all members of the family have *tacit* knowing, which is a feeling or unspoken, intuitive way of understanding what this event means for each of them and their individual visions of family. Bob and Nancy *consider the alternatives* of adoption and artificial insemination as a way of expanding their family, which is a paradox of values. The *value they are exploring* is sharing their life with children. The questions they engage in with the nurse are "Do we have children any way we can?" "If the child is adopted, will we be able to love it as 'our own flesh and blood'?" and "What are the odds of becoming pregnant by means of artificial insemination?" In other words, both Bob and Nancy explore their commitment to their family value of having children. Through this discussion with the nurse, both Bob and Nancy articulate and confirm their shared cherished desire to have children. They decide to undergo artificial insemination.

person's life. At the other end of the continuum are principles and beliefs that are not prized or cherished by or affirming to the person. Once the person determines the value(s) that will guide him or her in this situation, the person states them and acts on them.

Principle 2: People demonstrate their patterns of relating to others, to ideas, and to beliefs in making decisions and in experiencing conflicts: in other words, how people typically act or react in given situations can be identified by their patterns of previous behavior. Three paradoxical continuums people experience that affect their health choices are as follows:

1) How much they want to disclose (reveal or conceal) to others
2) How different choices will enable them or limit them in the future
3) How different choices connect them with others or make them unique and separate from others

Parse (1998) describes this principle as "co-creating rhythmical patterns of relating is living the paradoxical unity of revealing—concealing and enabling—limiting while connecting—separating" (p. 42).

In a new situation, people consider actions based on how much a specific action will disclose about themselves to others. They consider how much they want to disclose to others, are comfortable disclosing to others, and what parts they will disclose. This interconnected concept is the concealing and enabling paradox. People protect their core beliefs, values, feelings, and thoughts and choose how much of their interior self they are willing to risk and share with others.

In the process of considering alternatives, people juxtapose how the action will enable them and how that action will limit them. Once a chosen action has been taken, that action is simultaneously enabling and limiting. It is enabling because the action opens avenues for interventions and allows for change and growth. At the same time, the decision limits other possible options as energy is directed toward the chosen action. Another paradoxical situation is considering how an action will simultaneously bring individuals together yet allow them to be separate with their action of choice.

Principle 3: This principle is about change and integrating change into the evolving con-

Principle 2: Family Example

Bob and Nancy decide to undergo artificial insemination. In talking with the nurse, Bob says that he *doesn't want others to know* of their choice until they find out whether Nancy becomes pregnant. Nancy, on the other hand, is so excited she wants to tell everyone but agrees to *reveal* (disclose) their decision to only her mother and sister until she becomes pregnant. Bob remains uncomfortable with this and says that he clearly does not want his mother-in-law to know that it is his sperm count that was the problem. With the help of the nurse, Bob and Nancy are able to discuss and plan what to tell to whom and when to tell. Bob and Nancy's decision to opt for artificial insemination *enables* them to explore their dreams and hopes of having their own biological children. The idea to adopt is no longer actively considered (*limited*); however, the idea is still present but is moved into the background of action and thinking, thus being held in reserve in case artificial insemination does not work for them. The decision to have artificial insemination *connects* Bob and Nancy because they are together in this choice of action. They both value having children, and this is something they are doing together. *At the same time, each of them is alone and separate* with their own thoughts, dreams, and ideas. It is likely that one spouse may not be as committed to the action as the other but has not voiced (disclosed) this concern. It is important for the nurse to encourage Bob and Nancy to openly discuss their feelings during this experience because it is happening to Nancy's body physically and may be difficult for Bob to understand.

cept of self as one experiences the pushing and resisting tension change initiates and the integration of the change in view of self in the present and future. Anytime that change occurs, people experience the paradox of being affirmed or feeling good about how they are changing and the fear, frustration, and uncertainty of the unknown at the same time. Parse (1998) called this *powering*, which is created by the paradox of pushing toward change and simultaneously resisting the change.

People develop ways or patterns of living with and bringing about the desired changes that are unique to them. People strive to be like others (conformity), yet at the same time, they want to be their own unique persons (nonconformity). Parse (1998) called this "originating or ways of distinguishing personal uniqueness" (p. 49) by living everyday with the conformity–nonconformity paradox.

In the process of transforming, each person wrestles with the certainty and uncertainty paradox of the chosen action in imagining possible outcomes while considering the whole picture. When the person makes a choice of action, he or she weighs the familiar with the unfamiliar

---

Principle 3: Family Example

After artificial insemination, Bob and Nancy find out that they are pregnant from a home pregnancy testing kit. They are ecstatic. For the next several months they are sharing (*disclosing*) their news with friends and family. They are planning for their child, *connecting* all the possibilities, and individually thinking (*separateness*) of hopes and dreams that lie ahead. A couple of months after becoming pregnant, Nancy feels some cramping and is worried about miscarriage because she knows the likelihood of miscarriage is high in her age group. Bob and Nancy immediately go to the clinic. While they are waiting for test results and setting up the ultrasound equipment, the nurse explores their fears and concerns with them about a possible miscarriage (*pushing and resisting paradox*). The results of the ultrasound examination are that Nancy is carrying triplets, and bed rest is prescribed for the duration of her pregnancy. The push and pull of their situation is evident. They are both excited about the pregnancy, but three children were *not in their image* of family, or even considered when they were *exploring the unknown*. Both Nancy and Bob were beginning to see themselves in the future as parents (*conformity*), but they did not see themselves as the parents of triplets (*nonconformity*). The nurse discusses with Bob and Nancy this new vision of self as parents of multiple children. The push and pull tension is also felt because now that Nancy cannot work, their family income is compromised. They worry

about the ability to afford three children at one time, the stress on their family life, and how they are going to manage all the details for three children. They worry about the triplets being born prematurely and the medical costs. The role of the nurse is to help Bob and Nancy explore changes they want to make and possible solutions. Seven months into the pregnancy Nancy is in labor. The delivery room nurse talks with Bob and Nancy as they explore the *certainty* and *uncertainty* of actually becoming parents in several hours. It is evident that Bob and Nancy have planned together for their children, are excited about their birth, yet have many concerns about their health and the future. Transforming is about integration of unfamiliar ideas and activities into one's everyday life (Alligood & Tomey, 2002, p. 413).

---

paradox: this is merging the known with the unknown in a deliberative process to shift the patterns of health. Parse (1998) explained this principle as "cotranscending with the possibles is powering unique ways of originating in the process of transforming" (p. 46).

In this section, systems theory was used to demonstrate how theory assists nurses in seeing the whole client. Systems theory offers a framework with which to see interrelationships and patterns of change rather than snapshots or isolated events. In the next section, several models of family assessment that demonstrate integration of multiple approaches in family nursing practice are described.

Integrated Approaches to the Nursing of Families

Some family nursing scholars have used several theories to develop their own integrated approaches to family assessment and intervention. These scholars have acknowledged that families are complex small groups in which multiple processes and dynamics occur simultaneously. Families do not function in one way alone. However, today no one theory or conceptual framework from family social science, family therapy, or nursing fully describes the dynamics of family life. Thus nurses who use only one theoretical approach to working with families are, in essence, limiting the possibilities for families.

Integrating theories allows nurses to view the family from a variety of perspectives, which increases the probability that the interventions selected will be implemented by the family, because they "fit" their structure, processes, and style of functioning. By integrating several theories, nurses acquire different ways to conceptualize problems and this enhances their thinking about interventions. Instead of fragmented knowledge and piecemeal interventions, nursing practice is based on an organized, realistic conceptualization of families. Nurses who use an integrated theoretical approach build on the strengths of families in creative ways.

Hanson and Mischke (1996) merged general systems theory and the Neuman Systems Model (Neuman, 1995) to develop the *Family Assessment Intervention Model and Family Systems Stressor Strength Inventory (FS³I)*. Both the model and the assessment/measurement instrument are microscopic in view and are excellent for assessment of family stressors and strengths leading to family interventions.

Friedman combined general systems theory, developmental theory, and structural-functional theory into assessment guidelines that provide a more macroscopic view of families. The *Friedman Assessment Model* serves as a framework for family assessment and is available in a long form and a short form (Friedman, Bowden, & Jones, 2003).

Another integrated approach to working with families, called the *Calgary Family Model*, was developed by Wright and Leahey (2000). This model integrates general systems theory, communication theory, change theory, and cybernetics in a unique approach to working with families. The model draws on sociological theories and theories such as Maturana and Varela's (1992) theory of the biology of knowing and Bateson's (1979) theory of the mind, as well as constructivist and narrative approaches (Wright, Watson, and Bell, 1996). The Belief Model by Wright, Watson, and Bell (1996) describes strategies that nurses use in working with families to help them uncover beliefs that may be constraining or facilitating their adaptation or reaction to a given life event. Their model demonstrates how beliefs influence peoples' actions and behaviors.

All four of these integrated family nursing assessment models are described in detail elsewhere (Hanson & Kaakinen, 2001; Hanson & Kaakinen, 2000; Hanson, Kaakinen, & Friedman, 1998; Wright, Watson, & Bell, 1996). The following section outlines the work of two other scholars who have contributed to the application of theory to family nursing.

McCubbin and McCubbin (1993) developed the *Resiliency Model of Family Stress, Adjustment and Adaptation* for working with families who are experiencing stress. They were interested in why families react in dramatically different ways when they are faced with similar stressors. Their model is based on Ruben Hill's work on stress and adaptation (1949, 1965) and on the double ABCX Model developed by McCubbin and Patterson (1983). A detailed description of this model can be found elsewhere (Danielson, Hamel-Bissell, & Winstead-Fry, 1993; Vaughn-Cole, Johnson, Malone, & Walker, 1998). The Resiliency Model provides a way for nurses to facilitate family adjustment and adaptation by looking at family strengths and capabilities of responding to stress. Based on the family's response to health stressors, the nurse and family work together to create interventions that are more likely to result in positive family adjustment.

In their book Vaughan-Cole et al. (1998) demonstrate the use of different theories and models to the practice of nursing. They compare nursing practice in multiple situations from the perspectives of the Resiliency Model, an ecological model, and a family systems model. Although each model conceptualizes families differently, there are common themes. They suggest that family nurses need to use a multidimensional definition of family, regardless of family type. They found that nurses use a variety of tools and methods to assess families and individual family members, and many of their interventions are the same, regardless of the conceptual framework used. Regardless of the theoretical approach used to assess problems and develop interventions, family is constant and central to the health care issues of individual members. Health care is not autonomous but is always influenced and carried out by the family. Further, families are extremely knowledgeable about the needs of family members and about the impact that the illness of one member has on the whole family.

Summary

Family nursing requires the use of integrated approaches to guide theory development, practice, research, and education. One theoretical perspective does not give nurses a sufficiently broad knowledge base for use in assessment of and intervention with families. Nurses must draw on multiple theories to be effective in tailoring interventions for specific families with their unique needs. The number of possibilities for effective interventions is increased when nurses use multiple ways of conceptualizing families. There is a need to continue developing integrated approaches that are sensitive to family needs and tested over time. Family nursing today is primarily theory-guided practice, because family nursing has roots in family social science, family therapy, and nursing (Hanson & Kaakinen, 2001). The next generation of family nurses needs to further explore a more evidenced-based research perspective on how these three traditions can be used together to formulate concepts and propositions for nursing care of families. The efforts of some family nursing scholars to develop integrated models for the nursing care of families have been briefly noted in this chapter and are described in more detail elsewhere (Hanson & Kaakinen, 2001). The art and the science of *family nursing* evolved from a rich background and draw on a multitude of disciplines. Just what this broad theoretical and conceptual background means for theory, practice, research, and education in the field of family nursing has yet to be fully explicated for use in the future.

WEBSITE RESOURCES

ORGANIZATION	WEBSITE ADDRESS
National Council on Family Relations	http://www.ncfr.org
American Association of Family and Consumer Sciences	http://www.aafcs.org
American Association for Marriage and Family Therapy	http://www.aamft.org
International Council of Nursing	http://www.icn.ch
Family Nursing	http://www.familynursing.com
Key Theories and Theorists in Psychology	http://www.psy.pdx.edu/PsiCafe/KeyTheorists
Sociological Theories and Perspectives	http://www.pscw.uva.nl/sociosite/TOPICS/Theory.html
Nursing Theory Page	http://www.sandiego.edu/nursing/theory/
Neuman Systems Model	http://www.neumansystemsmodel.com/

■ CHAPTER HIGHLIGHTS

- Nursing is a profession in which practice is guided by theories, models, and philosophies.
- The way nurses view and think about the whole client picture influences the possible outcomes and interventions that nurses recommend to clients or carry out on their behalf.
- The challenge for nurses is to mentally reflect on various theories or models they have learned to determine which approaches may offer the best outcomes for a particular family.
- Theories are organized systematic ways of explaining or understanding phenomena of interest, specifically the relationships between phenomena, to predict and influence the outcomes.
- Theories are designed to make sense of the world—to show how one thing is related to another and how together they make a pattern that can predict the consequences of certain clusters of characteristics or events.
- Nursing theories ideally represent logical and intelligible patterns that make sense of observations nurses make in practice, which enables nurses to predict what is likely to happen to clients.
- Many of the concepts in nursing theories were adapted from theories in the traditional disciplines such as sociology, anthropology, and psychology, as well as the more recent fields of family social science and family therapy.

- No one theoretical or conceptual framework adequately describes the complex relationships of family structure, function, and process. No single theoretical perspective gives nurses a sufficiently broad base of knowledge and understanding for use as a guide to assessment and interventions with families. Thus there is no single theoretical basis that guides nursing care of families. Rather, nurses must draw on multiple theories and frameworks to guide their work with families and take an integrated approach to practice, research, and education in family nursing.
- Systems theory and its extrapolation to the family has been the most influential of all the family frameworks.
- Every family system has features designed to maintain stability or homeostasis, though these may be adaptive or maladaptive.
- The family is considered to change constantly in response to stresses and strains from within, as well as from the external environment, and change in one part of the family system affects the entire system.
- Nursing models are the least well developed of foundations that inform family nursing practice. In this chapter models developed by Neuman, Friedemann, and Parse were used as examples of models based on systems theory.
- Integrated nursing assessment models that illustrate the importance of using multiple theories in family nursing have been developed.

‖ CRITICAL THINKING ACTIVITIES

1. In a small group, discuss how theory guides family nursing practice. In your group, give examples to support your position from your clinical experience. Analyze the theory that was the basis of the interaction.

2. In a small group or class discussion, explore the case study presented in this chapter under the Parse nursing theory and describe it according to the Neuman model. Use Figure 4-2 as a starting point.

3. Discuss why it is important for nurses to integrate conceptual and theoretical frameworks when working with families.

4. Select a research article that investigates a question or describes family function. Review it to determine the conceptual framework or theoretical approaches used to support the study and the findings. Were they from the three disciplines and traditions discussed in the chapter? Did they use an integrated approach to making sense out of the behaviors studied? How did the theoretical concepts on which the study was based contribute to or limit the findings about family? How will this assist nurses in caring for families?

REFERENCES

Alligood, M. R. (1997). Philosophies, models and theories: critical thinking structures. In M. R. Alligood & A. M. Tomey (Eds.), *Nursing theorists and their work* (4th ed., pp. 41-61). St. Louis, MO: Mosby.

Alligood, M. R., & Tomey, A. M. (2002). *Nursing theory: Utilization & application* (2nd ed.). St. Louis, MO: Mosby.

Bateson, G. (1979). Mind and nature. New York: E. P. Dutton.

Becvar, D.S., & Becvar, R. J. (2000). *Family therapy: A systemic integration* (4th ed.). Boston: Allyn and Bacon.

Berkey, K. M., & Hanson, S. M. H. (1991). *Pocket guide to family assessment and intervention.* St. Louis, MO: C. V. Mosby.

Bowen, M. (1978). *Family therapy in clinical practice.* New York: Aronson.

Danielson, C. B., Hamel-Bissell, B., & Winstead-Fry, P. (1993). *Families, health and illness: Perspectives on coping and intervention.* St. Louis, MO: C. V. Mosby.

Fawcett, J. (2000). *Analysis and evaluation of conceptual models of nursing* (4th ed.). Philadelphia: F. A. Davis.

Fawcett, J., & Downs, F. S. (1992). *The relationship of theory and research.* Philadelphia: F. A. Davis.

Freeman, D. S. (1992). *Multigenerational family therapy.* New York: The Haworth Press.

Friedman, M., Bowden, V. R., & Jones, E. G. (2003). *Family nursing: Research, theory, practice* (5th ed.). Upper Saddle River, NJ: Prentice Hall.

Friedman, M. M. (1998). *Family nursing: Research, theory, and practice* (4th ed.). Norwalk, CT: Appleton & Lange.

Friedemann, M. L. (1995). *The framework of systemic organization: A conceptual approach to families and nursing.* Thousand Oaks, CA: Sage Publications.

George, J. B. (2002). *Nursing theories: The base for professional nursing practice* (5th ed.). Upper Saddle River, NJ: Prentice Hall.

Gilliss, C., & Knafl, K. (1999). Nursing care of families in non-normative transitions: The state of science and practice. In A. S. Hinshaw, S. L. Feetham, & J. L. Shaver (Eds.), *Handbook of clinical nursing research* (pp. 231-245). Thousand Oaks, CA: Sage Publications.

Gladding, S. T. (2002). *Family therapy: History, theory, and practice* (3rd ed.). Upper Saddle River, NJ: Prentice Hall.

Goldenberg, I., & Goldenberg, H. (2000). *Family therapy: An overview* (3rd ed.). Pacific Grove, CA: Brooks/Cole Publishing.

Hallberg, I. R. (2003). Evidence-based nursing, interventions, and family nursing: Methodological obstacles and possibility. *Journal of Family Nursing, 9*(1), 3-22.

Hanson, S. M. H. (2001). *Family health care nursing: Theory, practice, and research* (2nd ed.). Philadelphia: F. A. Davis.

Hanson, S. M. H., & Kaakinen, J. (2000). Family development and family nursing assessment. In M. Stanhope & J. Lancaster (Eds.), *Community and public health nursing* (5th ed., pp.476-505). St. Louis, MO: Mosby.

Hanson, S. M. H., & Kaakinen, J. (2001). Theoretical foundations for family nursing. In S. M. H. Hanson (Ed.), *Family health care nursing: Theory, practice and research* (2nd ed., pp. 36-59). Philadelphia: F. A. Davis.

Hanson, S. M. H., Kaakinen, J., & Friedman, M. M. (1998). Theoretical approaches to family nursing. In M. M. Friedman (Ed.), *Family nursing: Research, theory, and practice* (3rd ed., pp. 75-98). Norwalk, CT: Appleton & Lange.

Hanson, S. M. H, & Mischke, K. (1996). Family health assessment and intervention. In P. Bomar (Ed.), *Nurses and family health promotion* (2nd ed., pp. 165-202). Philadelphia: Saunders.

Hickman, J. S. (2002). Theory of human becoming: Rosemarie Rizzo Parse. In J. B. George (Ed.), *Nursing theories: The base for professional nursing practice* (5th ed., pp. 427-461). Upper Saddle River, NJ: Prentice Hall.

Hill, R. (1949). *Families under stress.* New York: Harper and Brothers.

Hill, R. (1965). *Challenges and resources for family development: Family mobility in our dynamic society.* Ames, IA: Iowa State University.

Jones, S. L., & Dimond, S. L. (1982). Family theory and family therapy models: Comparative review with implications for nursing practice. *Journal of Psychiatric Nursing and Mental Health Services, 20,* 12-19.

Kerr, M. E. (1988). *Family evaluation: An approach based on Bowen theory.* New York: Norton.

Kim, H. S. (2000). *The nature of theoretical thinking in nursing* (2nd ed.). New York: Springer.

Knafl, K., & Gilliss, C. (2002). Families and chronic illness: A synthesis of current research. *Journal of Family Nursing, 8*(3), 178-198.

LoBiondo-Wood, G., & Haber, J. (2002). *Nursing research: Methods, critical appraisal, and utilization* (5th ed.). St. Louis, MO: Mosby.

Lobo, M. L. (1995). Florence Nightingale. In J. B. George (Ed.), Nursing theories. Norwalk, CT: Appleton & Lange.

Maturana, H. R., & Varela, F. J. (1992). *The tree of knowledge: The biological roots of human understanding.* Boston: Shambhala (Random House).

McCubbin, H. I., & Patterson, M. (1983). The family stress process: the Double ABCX Model of Adjustment and Adaptation. In H. I. McCubbin, M B., Sussman, & J. M. Patterson (Eds.), *Social stress and the family* [Special issue]. *Marriage and Family Review, 6,* 7-27.

McCubbin, M. A., & McCubbin, H. I. (1993). Family coping with illness: the resiliency model of family stress, adjustment, and adaptation. In C. Danielson, B. Hamel-Bissell, & P. Winstead-Fry (Eds.), *Families, health & illness* (pp. 21-63). St. Louis, MO: Mosby.

Meleis, A. I. (1997). *Theoretical nursing: development and progress* (3rd ed.). Philadelphia: Lippincott.

Mitchell, G. (1992). Specifying the knowledge base of theory in practice. *Nursing Science Quarterly, 5,* 6-7.

Neuman, B. (1982). *The Neuman systems model: Application to nursing education and practice.* Norwalk, CT: Appleton-Century-Crofts.

Neuman, B. (1995). *The Neuman systems model: Application to nursing education and practice* (3rd ed.). Norwalk, CT: Appleton & Lange.

Orem, D., Taylor, S. G., & Repenning, K. M. (2001). *Nursing: concepts of practice.* St. Louis: Mosby.

Parse, R. R. (1981). *Man, living, health: A theory of nursing.* New York: Wiley & Sons.

Parse, R. R. (1992). Human becoming: Parse's theory of nursing. *Nursing Science Quarterly, 5,* 35-42.

Parse, R. R. (1998). *The human becoming school of thought: A perspective for nurses and other health professionals.* Thousand Oaks, CA: Sage.

Polit, D. F., & Hungler, B. P. (1998). *Nursing research: Principles and methods.* (6th ed.). Newbury Park, CA: Sage.

Powers, B., & Knapp, T. (1995). *A dictionary of nursing theory and research* (2nd ed.). Newbury Park, CA: Sage.

Roy, C. (1976). *Introduction to nursing: An adaptation model.* Englewood Cliffs, NJ: Prentice Hall.

Roy, C., & Roberts, S. (1981). *Theory construction in nursing: An adaptation model.* Englewood Cliff, NJ: Prentice Hall.

Titelman, P. (Ed.) (1998). *Clinical applications of Bowen family system theory.* Binghamton, NY: Haworth Press.

Toman, W. (1961). *Family constellation: Its effects on personality and science behavior.* New York: Springer.

Vaughan-Cole, B., Johnson, M. A., Malone, J. A., & Walker, B.L. (1998). *Family nursing practice.* Philadelphia: Saunders.

Vogt, W. P. (1993). *Dictionary of statistics and methodology.* Newbury Park, CA: Sage.

von Bertalanffy, L. V. (1950). The theory of open systems in physics and biology. *Science, 111,* 23-29.

White, J. M., & Klein, D. M. (2002). *Family theories: An introduction* (2nd ed.). Thousand Oaks, CA: Sage.

Winstead-Fry, P. (2000). Rogers' conceptual system and family nursing. *Nursing Science Quarterly, 13*(4), 278-280.

Wright, L. M. & Leahey, M. (2000). *Nurses and families: A guide to family assessment and intervention* (3rd ed.), Philadelphia: F. A. Davis.

Wright, L. M., Watson, W. L. & Bell, J. M. (1996). *Beliefs: The heart of healing in families and illness.* New York: Basic Books.

APPENDIX 4-1   Theoretical References for Family and Family Nursing

FAMILY SOCIAL SCIENCE THEORIES

Systems Theory

von Bertalanffy, L. (1950). The theory of open systems in physics and biology. *Science, 111,* 23-29.

von Bertalanffy, L. (1966). General system theory and psychiatry. In S. Arieti (Ed.), *American handbook of psychiatry Vol. 3.* (pp. 705-721). New York: Basic Books.

von Bertalanffy, L. (1968). *General systems theory.* New York: George Braziller.

Structural Functional Systems Theory

Artinian, N.T. (1994). Selecting a model to guide family assessment. *Dimensions of critical care nursing. 14,* 4-16.

Nye, F.I., & Berardo, F. (Eds.) (1981). *Emerging conceptual frameworks in family analysis.* New York: Praeger.

Family Stress Theory

Hill, R. (1949). *Families under stress.* New York: Harper & Row.

Hill, R. (1958). Social stresses on the family: Generic features of families under stress. *Social Casework, 39,* 139-150.

McCubbin, H.I., & McCubbin, M.A. (1996). Resiliency in families: A conceptual model of family adjustment and adaptation in responses to stress and crisis. In H.I. McCubbin, A. Thompson, & M. McCubbin (Eds.), *Family assessment: Resiliency, coping and adaptation—inventories for research and practice* (pp. 1-64). Madison, WI: University of Wisconsin System.

McCubbin, H.I., & Patterson, J.M. (1983). The family stress process: The double ABCX model of adjustment and adaptation. In H.I. McCubbin, M.B. Sussman, & J. M. Patterson (Eds.), *Stress and the family: Coping with normative transitions* (pp. 5-25). New York: Brunner/Mazel.

Developmental Theory

Duvall, E.M. (1977). *Marriage and family development* (5th ed.). Philadelphia: Lippincott.

Duvall, E.M., & Miller, B.L. (1985). *Marriage and family development* (6th ed.). New York: Harper & Row.

Jones, S.L., & Dimond, M. (1982). Family theory and family therapy models. Comparative review with implications for nursing practice. *Journal of Psychosocial Nursing and Mental Health Services, 20*(10), 12-19.

Change Theory

Bateson, G. (1970). *Mind and nature.* New York: Bantam.

Glanz, K., Lewis, F.M., & Rimer, B.K. (Eds.) (1997). *Health and behavior and health education: Theory, research and practice.* San Francisco: Jossey-Bass.

House, J.S., Landis, K.R., & Umberson, D. (1988). Social relationships and health. *Science, 241,* 540-545.

Maturana, H. (1978). Biology of language: The epistemology of reality. In B. Miller & E. Lenneberg (Eds.), *Psychology and biology of language and thought* (pp. 27-63). New York: Academic Press.

Maturana, H., & Varel, F.J. (1992). *The new knowledge: The biological roots of human understanding* (rev, ed.). Boston: Shambhala.

McEwen, B.S. (1998). Protective and damaging effects of stress mediators. *New England Journal of Medicine, 338,* 171-179.

Seeman, T.E. (1996). Social ties and health: The benefits of social integration. *Annals of Epidemiology, 6,* 442-452.

Watzlawick, P., Weakland, J., & Fisch, R. (1974). *Change: Principles of problem formulation and problem resolution.* New York: Norton.

Interactional Theory

Blumer, H. (1969). Society as symbolic interaction. In A. Rose (Ed.). *Symbolic interactionism.* Englewood Cliffs, NJ: Prentice Hall.

Burr, W. R., Leight, G., Day, R., & Constantine, J. (1979). Symbolic interaction and the family. In W.R. Burr, R. Hill, F.I. Nye, & I. Reiss (Eds.). *Contemporary theories about the family Vol. 2.* (pp. 42-11). New York: Free Press.

Crotty, M. (1998). *The foundations of social research: Meaning and perspective in the research process.* London: Sage.

Hill, R., & Hanson, D. (1960). The identification of conceptual frameworks utilized in family study. *Marriage and family Living, 22,* 299-311.

Kuhn, M. (1964). Major trends in symbolic interaction theory in the past twenty-five years. *Sociological Quarterly, 5,* 61-84.

LaRossa, R., & Reitzes, D. C. (1993). Symbolic interactionism and family studies. In P. G. Boss, W. T. Doherty, R. LaRossa, W. R. Schumm, & S. K. Steinmetz (Eds.), *Sourcebook of family theories and methods: A contextual approach* (pp. 135–166). New York: Plenum Press.

Mead, G. H. (1934). *Mind, self and society.* Chicago: University of Chicago Press.

Nye, F.I. (Ed.). (1979). Choice, exchange, and the family. In W. R. Burr, R. Hill, F. I. Nye, & I. Reisee (Eds.), *Contemporary theories about the family: Vol. 2.* (pp. 42–111). New York: Free Press.

Rose, A.M. (1962). *Human behavior and social processes.* Boston: Houghton Mifflin.

Turner, R.H. (1970). *Family interaction.* New York: Wiley.

Turner, R.H. (1991). *The structure of sociological theory* (5th ed.). Belmont, CA: Wadsworth.

FAMILY THERAPY THEORIES

Family System Therapy Theory

Ackerman, N. (1966). *The psychodynamics of family life.* New York: Basic Books.

Becvar, D.S., & Becvar, R.J. (1996). *Family therapy: A systemic integration.* Boston: Allyn & Bacon.

Bowen, M. (1976). Theory in the practice of psychotherapy. In P.J. Guerin (Ed.) *Family therapy* (pp. 42-90). New York: Gardiner Press.

Bowen, M. (1978). *Family therapy in clinical practice.* New York: Aronson.

Freeman, D.S. (1992). *Multigenerational family therapy.* New York: Haworth Press.

Gladding, S. T. (1998). *Family therapy: History, theory and practice* (2nd ed.). Upper Saddle River, NJ: Prentice-Hall

Goldenberg, I., & Goldenberg, H. (2000). *Family therapy: An overview* (5th ed.). Belmont, CA: Wadsworth.

Kerr, M.E., & Bowen, M. (1988). *Family evaluation: An approach based on Bowen Theory.* New York: Norton.

Madanes, C. (1991). Strategic family therapy. In A.S. Gurman & D.P. Kniskern (Eds.), *Handbook of family therapy Vol. II.* New York: Brunner/Mazel.

Pinsof, W.M. (1995). *Integrative problem-centered therapy: A synthesis of family, individual, and biological therapies.* New York: Basic Books.

Segrin, C.(2001). *Interpersonal processes in psychological problems.* New York: Guilford Press.

Whitaker, C.A., & Keith, D.V. (1981). Symbolic-experiential family therapy. In A.S. Gurman & D.P. Kriskern (Eds.), *Handbook of family therapy.* New York: Brunner/Mazel.

White, M., & Epston, D. (1990). *Narrative means to therapeutic ends.* New York: Norton.

Family Resilience

McCubbin, M. & McCubbin, H. (1996). Resilience in families: A conceptual model of family adjustment and adaptation in response to stress and crisis. In H. McCubbin, A. Thompson, M. McCubbin (Eds.), *Family assessment: resiliency, coping, and adaptation: inventories for research and practice* (pp. 1-64). Madison, WI: University of Wisconsin System.

Walsh, F. (1998). *Strengthening family resilience.* New York: Guilford.

Structural Functional Family Therapy

Minuchin, S. (1974). *Families and family therapy.* Cambridge, MA: Harvard University Press.

Minuchin, S., & Fishman, H.G. (1981). *Family therapy techniques.* Cambridge, MA: Harvard University Press.

Minuchin, S., & Nichols, M.R. (1998). Structural family therapy. In F.M. Dattilio (Ed.), *Case studies in couple family therapy: Systemic and cognitive perspectives.* New York: Guilford Press.

Minuchin, S., Rosman, B.L., & Baker, L. (1978). *Psychosomatic families: Anorexia nervosa in context.* Cambridge, MA: Harvard University Press.

Olson, D. (1993). Circumplex model of marital and family systems: Assessing family functioning. In F. Walsh (Ed.), *Normal family processes.* (pp. 104-1137). New York: Guilford Press.

Toman, W. (1961). *Family constellation: Its effects on personality and social behavior.* New York: Springer.

Interactional Family Therapy

Broderick, C. B. (1993). *Understanding family process: Basics of family systems theory.* Thousand Oaks, CA: Sage.

Jackson, D.D. (1965). Family rules: Martial quid quo. *Archives of General Psychiatry, 12,* 589-594.

Kantor, D., & Lehr, W. (1975). *Inside the family: Toward a theory of family process.* San Francisco: Jossey-Bass.

Satir, V. (1982). The therapist and family therapy: Process model. In A.M. Horne & M.M. Ohlsen (Eds.), *Family counseling and therapy* (pp. 12-42). Itasca, IL: Peacock.

Satir, V. (1983). *Cojoint family therapy* (3rd ed.). Palo Alto, CA: Science and Behavior Books.

Watzlawick, P. Weakland, J., & Jackson, D.D. (1967). *Pragmatics of human communication.* New York: Norton.

Nursing Theories and Models That Inform Family Nursing

Allen, M. (1982). *Shaping health potential: The cutting edge of practice in nursing.* Paper presented at the Rozella M. Scholfeldt Lecture, Case Western Reserve University, Frances Payne Bolton School of Nursing, Cleveland, IL.

Allen, M., & Warner, K. (2002). A developmental model of health and nursing. *Journal of Family Nursing, 8,* 96-135.

Anderson, K. H. (2000). The family health system approach to family systems nursing. *Journal of Family Nursing, 6*(2), 103-119.

Casey, A.H. (1996). The family as a system. In P.J. Bomar (Ed.). *Nurses and family health promotion: Concepts, assessment, and interventions* (2nd ed.). Philadelphia: W. B. Saunders.

Fawcett, J. (1991). Spouses' experiences during pregnancy and the postpartum: a program of research and theory development, In A. Whall & J. Fawcett (Eds.). *Family theory development in nursing: State of the science and art.* Philadelphia: F.A. Davis.

Freidemann, M.I. (1995). *The framework of systemic organization.* Thousand Oaks, CA: Sage.

King, I. (1981). *Family therapy: A comparison of approaches.* Bowie, MD: Brady.

King, I. (1983). King's theory of nursing. In I.W. Clements & J.B. Roberts (Eds.). *Family health: A theoretical approach to nursing* (pp. 177-187). New York: Wiley.

King, I. (1987, May). *King's theory.* [cassette recording]. Paper presented at Nursing Theories Conference, Pittsburgh, PA.

Neuman, B. (1982). *The Neuman systems model: Application to nursing education and practice.* Norwalk, CT: Appleton-Lange.

Neuman, B. (1983). Family intervention using the Betty Neuman health care systems model. In I. W. Clements & F. B. Roberts (Eds.), *Family health: A theoretical approach to nursing care.* New York: Wiley.

Neuman, B. (1995). *The Neuman's systems model: Application to nursing education and practice* (3rd ed.). Norwalk, CT: Appleton-Lange.

Neuman, B., & Fawcett, J. (2002). *The Neuman systems model* (4th ed.). Upper Saddle River, NJ: Prentice Hall.

Nightingale, F. (1992). *Notes on nursing: What it is and what it is not* (Com. Ed.). Philadelphia: Lippincott (Original publication 1859).

Orem, D. E. (1971). *Nursing: Concepts and practice.* New York: McGraw-Hill.

Orem, D. E. (1983a). The family coping with a medical illness. Analysis and application of Orem's theory. In I. W. Clements & F.B. Roberts (Eds.), *Family health: A theoretical approach to nursing care.* New York: Wiley.

Orem, D.E. (1983b). The family experiencing emotional crisis: Analysis and application of Orem's self-care deficit theory. In I. W. Clements & F. B. Roberts (Eds.), *Family health: A theoretical approach to nursing care.* (pp. 385-386). New York: Wiley.

Orem, D.E. (1985). *Nursing: Concepts and practice* (3rd ed.). New York: McGraw-Hill.

Orem, D.E. (1991). *Nursing: Concepts and practice* (4th ed.). St. Louis, MO: Mosby.

Parse, R.R. (1981). *Man, living, health: A theory of nursing.* New York: Wiley & Sons.

Parse, R.R. (1992). Human becoming: Parse's theory of nursing. *Nursing Science Quarterly, 5,* 35-42.

Parse, R.R. (1998). *The human becoming school of thought: A perspective for nurses and other health professionals.* Thousand Oaks, CA: Sage.

Rogers, M. (1970). *Introduction to the theoretical basis of nursing.* Philadelphia: Davis.

Rogers, M. (1986). Science of unitary beings. In V. Malinski (Ed.). *Exploration on Martha Rogers' science of unitary human being* (pp. 3-8). Norwalk,CT: Appleton-Lange.

Rogers, M. (1990). Nursing: Science of unitary irreducible, human beings. Update, 1900. In E. Barret (Ed.). *Visions of Rogers' science-based nursing.* (pp. 5-11). New York: National League for Nursing.

Family Roles

Yeoun Soo Kim-Godwin

5

All the world's a stage,
And all the men and women merely players;
They have their exits and entrances,
And one man in his time plays many parts,

— William Shakespeare

OBJECTIVES

On completion of this chapter, the reader will be able to do the following:

1. *Define role theory–related terms, including role stress, role strain, and role stress typology.*
2. *Describe family roles in relationship to role theory.*
3. *Identify traditional and contemporary family issues regarding gender roles.*
4. *Discuss the contemporary family role issues regarding career-homemaking conflict and parenting.*
5. *Discuss the role of family caregiving and the role of the family in health promotion and disease prevention.*
6. *Synthesize role theory and family concepts with assessment data to develop a meaningful application for family health nursing.*

The study of family health promotion requires an understanding of the family and its roles. The roles and functions assumed and enacted by family members are multiple and complex. Through research and theory development, the nurse gains important information that supports efforts toward promoting family health.

Role theory is the social science concerned with the study of behaviors that are characteristic of persons within contexts and with various processes that presume to produce, explain, or affect those behaviors (Benokraitis, 1999; Hardy & Conway, 1988). Role theory represents a collection of concepts and a variety of hypothetical formulations that predict how actors will perform in a given role or under what circumstances certain types of behaviors can be expected. Family health nurses can offer clients important insight regarding their health status by developing a holistic family assessment that includes

This chapter, originally written by Kathleen O'Grady Winston and revised by Evelyn Anderson (second edition), has been revised by Yeoun Soo Kim-Godwin for the third edition.

evaluation of family roles. As professionals, nurses are aware of the need to understand their role in health promotion and protection. Similar importance should be assigned to understanding the roles of families in their quest for optimal health.

This chapter begins with a review of role theory and a clarification of the associated terms. Concepts critical to understanding role theory are role expectation, stress, strain, conflict, incongruence, ambiguity, overload, sharing, negotiation, reversal, and modeling. The second section examines changing family roles and the characteristics of these roles as they affect the American family today. Discussions of parenting and caregiving roles are included. The third section provides the family role assessment framework, including types of family roles and variables affecting family roles. Finally, implications of family health nursing and health promotion are discussed.

Role Theory

Family roles refer to the established patterns of behavior of family members (Wright & Leahey, 2000). Roles are learned in society by a role-taking process whereby people learn how to play roles correctly by practicing and getting feedback from others (Olson & DeFrain, 2000). According to symbolic interaction theory, each family member has one or more roles, such as husband, father, grandfather, brother, son, and uncle (Benokraitis, 1999). George Herbert Mead (1934), the originator of this theory, pointed out that this role-taking ability is the major difference between humans and primates. His concepts of self, role-taking, and symbolic interaction formed the basis of social psychology. Sarbin (1954) extended the concepts of Mead's interaction theory and explained the dimensions of social role theory, such as role expectation, role perception, and role enactment.

Since Sarbin's early work was published, role theory has evolved from several of the social science disciplines that have related interests in the study of the human condition. Multiple philosophies exist regarding the study of social role theory (Biddle, 1979; Eagly, 1997; Franke, Crown, & Spake, 1997; Hardy & Conway, 1988; Sarbin, 1954). Many social scientists view role theory as simply a subfield of psychology, sociology, or anthropology. Others suggest that rather than a subfield, role theory should be interpreted as a single discipline that combines the core concepts of psychology, sociology, and anthropology. This approach supports a framework that allows the researcher to examine role theory from individualistic, collective, and cultural perspectives.

Another orientation for the discussion of role theory emerges from a concern that other social sciences consider role theory as central to their disciplines' conceptualization. Specifically, the helping professions are well equipped to incorporate role theory into their core concepts. Nursing, with its emphasis on care of the family and its biopsychosocial definition of humankind, applies role theory to its theoretical bases. The role-function mode of Roy's adaptation model includes role concepts in its theory development (Roy & Andrews, 1999). Roy and Andrews describe the development of roles as expected behaviors that a person should perform to maintain a title. Role expectation refers to "beliefs held by society in general, by an individual, or by those in complementary roles, about what is appropriate behavior associated with a role" (Roy & Andrews, 1999, p. 431). Role theorists contend that individuals and groups have shared role expectations regarding their behavior and the behavior of others. For example, family members may expect the father to leave home for work each morning and the mother to get the children off to school. The idea of expectation presumes that individuals are aware of the experiences and the environment. It implies that people will conform their behavior to meet the expectations held for them based on their role (i.e., status, or position). The importance of shared expectations is evidenced by the implication that there are common experiences among those who perform the same roles.

Role Stress and Role Strain

As life in today's society has become more complex, theorists have come to recognize that the field of role analysis is not simply the examination of the performance of expected behaviors. Many people hold a number of roles requiring intense demands.

The intensity of these demands on the expected or prescribed roles of the individual, combined with the playing of several roles at the same time, produces role stress. This condition is generally perceived as external to the role occupant (i.e., the person who holds the role), but it generates a condition of role strain for the individual. *Role strain,* as defined in Goode's (1960) role strain or role scarcity theory, is "the difficulty felt in fulfilling role obligations" (p. 483). Role relations are seen as a sequence of role bargains by which an individual seeks to reduce his or her role strain. In contrast, *role stress,* the potential for subsequent role strain, is primarily external to the individual.

Role Stress Typology

The role stress typology, based on a role stress–role strain framework, includes the following seven role-related problems: (1) role ambiguity, (2) role conflict, (3) role incongruity, (4) role overload, (5) role underload, (6) role overqualification, and (7) role underqualification (Hardy & Conway, 1988). In family settings, conditions that may require interventions are role ambiguity, role conflict, role incongruity, and role overload.

Role Ambiguity

Often the term *role incongruity* is used synonymously with the term *role ambiguity.* Although both terms suggest that the family is at risk for role stress and role strain experiences, their meanings are distinctly different. *Role ambiguity* occurs when the expected role is undefined or incomplete (Reser, 1998). The insufficiency of the expectation leads to vagueness and ambiguity. Role ambiguity produces disharmony as a result of the incompleteness of the role expectation, and role incongruity produces disharmony as a result of the individual's values.

Role Conflict

Role conflict refers to inconsistent expectations held by a person, or by other persons, for a given role in a person's role set (intrarole conflict) or by inconsistent expectations among the roles of the person's role set (interrole conflict) (Roy & Andrews, 1999). Role conflict generally occurs when the demands of two or more roles held by a person are incompatible, and the demands cannot simultaneously be met (Clark, 2001). Role conflict becomes another source of role strain experienced by the individual when multiple roles, with their intense demands, are viewed as competitive with their expectations. The concept of conflict stems from external issues, as does the concept of role stress.

Role Incongruity

Role incongruity emerges when expectations are in disagreement with the individual's self-perception or values (Hardy & Conway, 1988). Role conflict and role incongruity are similar in their production of role strain but differ in their source of stress. The stress and subsequent strain that result from role conflict are due to competition between role behaviors, and the source of role stress and strain caused by incongruity reflects an incompatibility between the role and the role incumbent (actor or person who plays the role).

Role Overload

Role demands are also perceived as difficult to fulfill when the incumbent experiences role overload. *Role overload* produces role strain caused by the incumbent's inability to complete the role obligations or to meet the role expectations within the prescribed amount of time. In studies of families, role overload appears to be a significant source of role stress or role conflict. Many families participate in multiple roles—often while experiencing incongruity, conflict, and stress. These role experiences, combined with the issue of overload, seem to produce the greatest amount of role strain. Previous research data that describe role conflict and role strain generally include examples of women's role overload, often referred to as *the phenomenon of the second shift* or *superwoman syndrome* (Crittenden, 2001; Hochschild, 1989; Maushart, 2001).

Role Strain Theory and Role Enhancement Theory

Role strain and role enhancement are two perspectives central to role theory and predict different outcomes for family members occupying multiple roles. A role strain perspective suggests that multiple roles can make family members feel overburdened, thereby having a detrimental effect on mental and physical well-being (Mui, 1995). The primary assumption is that the energy spent in one role diminishes the amount of energy available for others; therefore the potential negative consequences of stress and competing demands of multiple roles are inevitable. Chronic role strain applicable to family members includes role overload (e.g., when demands exceed capacities), interrole conflict (e.g., when demands of multiple roles are incompatible), role captivity (e.g., when an individual takes on a role unwillingly), and role restructuring (e.g., when adult children assume increasing responsibility for their parents) (Reid & Hardy, 1999).

In contrast, the role enhancement perspective includes the belief that multiple roles improve mental well-being. According to the role enhancement perspective, the accumulation of multiple roles can increase social integration, leading to an increase in "power, prestige, resources, and emotional gratification, including social recognition and a heightened sense of identity" (Moen, Robinson, & Dempster-McClain, 1995, p. 260). In addition, experiences in one role may affect experiences in another through a "role spillover" effect. For example, for an employed woman with a fulfilling job who is involved in a difficult informal caregiving relationship, the positive employment experience may make the caregiving easier, or her negative caregiving experience may interfere with her paid work (Reid & Hardy, 1999).

A third proposed perspective, the role integration model, differs from the role strain and role enhancement models in that it does not predict the direction of the effect of work on health per se but rather considers that the health effects depend on the balance between role satisfaction and role stress within and between key roles (Messias et al., 1997). *Role balance* reflects the tendency to become fully engaged in the performance of every role in the total role system, to approach every typical role and role partner with an attitude of attentiveness and care (Marks & MacDermid, 1996).

Managing Role Stress and Role Strain

It is important to remember that role stress and strain are outcomes of other role experiences. A family's role conflict, incongruence, and overload experiences create the stress, which, when prolonged, is manifested as role strain. Role stress may generate role strain (subjective feelings of frustration, tension, or anxiety) in family members' central role partner or their associated role partners. Role strain may be managed in several ways including (1) role sharing, (2) role negotiation or role bargaining, and (3) role reversals.

Role Sharing

Role sharing is defined as "participation of two or more people in the same roles even though they hold different positions" (Friedman, Bowden, & Jones, 2003, p. 323). A role-sharing family expands the concept to include the children, as well as others considered family members, in family decision making and domestic care responsibilities. However, the stereotypical jobs belonging to a husband or wife have no relevance in the role-sharing marriage (Maushart, 2001).

Although role-sharing marriages and families continue to be in the minority, many modern family functions have characteristics of the role-sharing family. The idea of role sharing extends beyond the division of formal roles and tasks to include new egalitarian values that will also influence the informal roles enacted by the family. Role sharing is not simply the notion of partnership, although partnership is a crucial component. Role sharing strives to reject the traditional role performance that has become comfortable for many American families. Admittedly, efforts toward the achievement of a role-sharing marriage or family often result in a compromise between contemporary and traditional experience.

Role Negotiation and Role Reversals

Role negotiation refers to the agreement among members regarding the appropriate behaviors associated with a role. This term can be interchangeably used with the term *role bargaining*, which is defined as the process of negotiation, involving two or more actors, about acceptable role behaviors to be enacted by the parties involved (Hardy & Conway, 1988). In essence, role negotiation permits mutual acceptance of role expectations. Role taking and role making, described in symbolic interaction theory, may be used in the process of role bargaining. The processes of role taking and role making are influenced by an actor's definition of role. Redefining or cognitive restructuring of the role is a method of resolving conflict.

Related to role negotiation, *role reversal* can be an option for couples trying to cope with full-time employment while balancing home and childcare demands. Although role reversals resulting from sickness can be a source of family stress (Gupton, Heaman, & Ashcroft, 1997), they can provide an opportunity for promoting health and personal growth when the woman deliberately assumes the role of primary breadwinner and the man deliberately assumes the role of primary child and/or home caretaker (Moch, 1988). A detailed discussion on role reversal is presented in the section on parenting roles in this chapter.

Concepts that are critical to understanding family role theory and family health nursing have been discussed. Role theory is still a young field of study with many complex questions waiting to be answered. Currently, it does offer social scientists and helping professionals a framework for understanding human behavior. This field of work is not limited to the use of one social science discipline but affords family nurses the opportunity to examine the human situation from a holistic understanding with significant behavioral perspective. In the next section, an analysis of a family according to role theory will demonstrate the applicability of these concepts to family nursing practice.

Changing Roles in Families

Social behavior is acquired: individuals are not born with knowledge of how to interact with others. Such behavior is developed over time and through the life cycle of social interaction. People adjust their behaviors depending on the prescriptions outlined for them as they interact within their social environment. The individual's first social unit of interaction is the family. Through socialization in the family, the child learns expected and accepted behaviors for his or her prescribed roles (Benokraitis, 1999).

Gender Role Concepts

Gender issues are significant for professionals working with families, and research findings regarding gender roles and gender identity have tremendous social relevance (Cook, 1997). *Gender identity* is a sense of being male or female and occurs as a learned behavior in early childhood. Research has shown that by the age of 2 years, children recognize their own gender and can differentiate between males and females. The development of gender identity occurs through the socialization process. Often this process, which occurs both in the family and in the larger society, is a direct effort toward shaping a child's gender identity, which becomes the basis for gender role development. *Gender role recognition* evolves from the socialization process and extends beyond knowing that one is male or female.

Gender roles (sex roles) are expectations about people's attitudes and behaviors in life based on whether they are male or female (Olson & DeFrain, 2000). Gender roles are established on the basis of sex and on the basis of society's acceptance that men enact instrumental roles and women enact expressive roles. In other words, men perform tasks that represent assertive, controlled behaviors, and women perform tasks that represent nurturing behaviors (Eagly, 1997). Masculinity is the gender-linked constellation of traits traditionally associated with men, and femininity is the constellation of traits associated with women (Olson & DeFrain, 2000).

Gender role development is an important component of the adult role function in a family. Within a family, the social interaction that occurs helps the child develop as a social being and introduces him or her to expected and accepted societal roles. The process begins at birth with sex-appropriate toys, rough versus gentle play, and sex-related behaviors. Assisting the child in developing a sense of maleness or femaleness is a function of the child nurturance/socialization role. Through the discovery of what Mom and Dad do and what boys and girls can do, the child begins to develop an understanding about gender roles (Olson & DeFrain, 2000). Social role theory presumes that people communicate gender-stereotypic expectations in social interactions and can directly induce the targets of these expectations to engage in behaviors that conform to these expectations (Eagly, 1997). The classic work of Komarovsky's *Blue-Collar Marriage,* published 1964, describes a working-class culture that centers on clearly defined gender roles, relatively low interpersonal communication and companionship, a restricted social life, and relatively strong ties with parents and siblings (Voydanoff, 2000).

Traditional and Contemporary Gender Roles

The impact of gender roles on family health is recognized by its potential for producing role strain. Like other role issues mentioned in this chapter, the stress associated with gender roles can precipitate family role conflict. If a woman fails to fit into the accepted expressive dimension traditionally prescribed for women, the potential for conflict within herself and with her significant others increases. Although traditional gender stereotyping is diminishing as the number of women in the labor force continues to increase, as women delay marriage or remain unmarried, and as women choose to bear fewer children, there continues to be a potential for stress associated with the gender role transition. For example in marriage, each spouse may have different perceptions of the roles of husband and wife.

In spite of the persistent notion of traditional gender roles in families, recent literature suggests that gender roles in the modern family are primarily androgynous. *Androgyny* refers to a "blending of traditional masculinity and traditional femininity in the same individual" (Olson & DeFrain, 2000, p. 241). Today, it is more commonly assumed that both sexes are capable of performing and can be successful in a variety of roles at home and at work. Women can be independent, strong, logical, and task-oriented; men can be nurturing, sensitive, cooperative, and detail-oriented. However, the transition from traditional gender stereotyping toward the more androgynous approach to gender identity may also produce stress associated with the transition. Little preparation has been made for these gender role transitions, and limited experience with these new role behaviors can prove stressful.

Stressful gender role transitions are shared by men and children as well. Contemporary male gender roles are enmeshed in parenthood and family. Because children develop attitudes toward gender roles through their observations of adult behaviors, they witness unprecedented diversity. Gender role change is widely documented and

has been caused by factors such as industrialization, mass education, women's participation in the labor force, and the decline of marriage as a social institution (Coltrane, 1996; LaRossa, 1997; Silva & Smart, 1999). Future family roles will be developed in response to such factors as the need for grown children to care for their older parents, the division of household and childcare labor, the effects of remarriage on stepsiblings, and the effects of single parenthood on children.

The family health nurse can intercede with the family and assist it through the stressful adjustments associated with such role transitions. Teaching families about androgyny will help to reduce the stress associated with lack of knowledge. Education will provide the family with the skills to make a sound choice regarding acceptance or rejection of the androgynous approach. Men and women can benefit by learning from each other. However, a tremendous amount of controversy surrounds the subject. Families should be taught about both the concept and its controversies. Heightened awareness regarding actual and potential role stress and strain caused by the transition toward androgyny will strengthen a family's health-promoting behaviors. With increased awareness, self-responsibility for developing healthy attitudes about gender roles will be encouraged. The combined efforts of the family and the family nurse can develop the awareness and self-responsibility into health-promoting behaviors.

Traditional and Contemporary Family Roles

Traditionally in American society, family roles have been relatively clear. Until the age of industrialization, family roles, though clear, more closely resembled nontraditional family roles as they are defined today. Family members collaborated in the home and at work; many of the family roles were shared. Although men and women often had separate and distinct types of work, this occurred because of necessity rather than gender differences or stereotypes. The concept of traditional family roles emerged from the growth of the United States as an industrialized nation. This definition of family includes a mother who serves as primary caretaker of the children and household and who generally does not work outside the home, a father whose primary role is that of economic provider and decision maker for all other family members, and children who clearly are recipients of parental caregiving. A review of the family literature suggests that there are three primary roles within a family: the wage earner role, the domestic care role, and the nurturance/socialization role. In a traditionally structured family, the father is typically the bread-winner, the mother is the domestic caregiver, and both participate in the nurturance/socialization role.

In the twenty-first century, though the family may be traditional in structure (i.e., a nuclear family), it most likely is nontraditional in its enactment of family roles. Role sharing is gaining popularity. For example, men's average contri-butions to household chores (e.g., preparing meals, washing dishes, cleaning, and doing laundry or ironing) have roughly doubled since 1970, whereas women's contributions have decreased by about a third (Coltrane, 1996).

Children also participate in the family today, which was not acceptable in former traditional settings. Children are no longer simply the recip-ients of parental care but serve to nurture siblings and parents in the family system. For example, it is common for children to participate in family decision-making activities. Also, with improved treatment in modern medicine, more people with chronic illness are marrying and becoming parents.

Families today could be compromised by the existence of nontraditional and androgynous family roles. Each family member is involved in multiple roles with intense demands. As noted, the father may no longer concern himself simply with the economic needs of the family but may actively participate in the growth and develop-ment of the children and of his spouse. Although fathers continue to perform the traditional role of provider and to do household maintenance, they must attempt to learn new roles associated with child nurturing and housekeeping. The wife may no longer participate simply as a nurturing mother but may contribute to the financial success of the family. The family also participates in interrole activities that help to link the family to the larger society. Other family roles include social roles such as a commitment to friends, extended family, church, and community.

Moreover, the roles of all family members today are multiple and complex, both in scope and in nature. The increases in single-parent families, stepfamilies, blended families, and dual-career families result in changes in roles for family members. Because each role held by a family member significantly influences the behavior of the entire family, it is essential for family health nurses to recognize that nontraditional roles performed by the modern family can easily be the source of role stress. If the role stress is mani-fested as role strain, the family unit experiences family role strain. The family health nurse should seek to prevent this dysfunction.

Career-Homemaking Conflict

Today both spouses often contribute to the economic success of the family. According to 1998 data, 50% of all American women aged 24 to 54 years were employed full-time year-round (Cohen & Bianchi, 1999). However, despite the fact that more men are participating in childcare and household tasks than in the past, women reported more hours spent in childcare and domestic responsibilities after a full day of work outside the home. For example, according to Hochschild (1989), in *The Second Shift*, American women put in 15 hours more each week than their husbands on all types of work—both paid and unpaid. In her study, 20% of the men she interviewed shared housework equally, 70% did between one third and one half of the housework, and 10% did less than one third of the house-work. Likewise, research conducted throughout the English-speaking world continues to show that wives, whether employed or unemployed, perform 70% to 80% of the unpaid labor within families, and husbands whose wives work full-time for pay do no more domestic labor than husbands of women who are not employed at all (Dempsey, 1997). As evidence, Maushart (2001) cites findings of a long-term study by the University of Michigan's Institute for Social Research: men do about 16 hours of housework per week, compared with 12 hours in 1965, and women do 31 hours per week, compared with 40 hours in 1965.

The family with young children in which both parents are employed is increasingly common.

More than half of mothers with infants younger than 1 years are employed. Killien, Habermann, & Jarrett (2001) explored the work experiences of 149 postpartum mothers who returned to employment during the first year and the relationship of employment characteristics to maternal health. The findings of the study indicated that work-family interference increased significantly between pregnancy and each postpartum occasion, and work-family interference consistently contributed to the variance in health status and functioning of women. These findings imply that learning to balance family needs and responsibilities is a series of adjustments and readjustment throughout the first postpartum year (Killien, Habermann, & Jarrett, 2001).

Although many studies have examined the impact of career women on the family, some studies have focused on spouse role issues such as dual-career couples' multiple roles and parenting role strain and their coping strategies and life or marital satisfaction. Stevens, Kiger, and Riley (2001) examined the effects of domestic labor among 156 dual-earner couples and found that, for women, satisfaction with the division of household tasks and "emotion work" and their contributions to household and status enhancement tasks were the most significant predictors of marital satisfaction. Marks, Huston, Johnson, and MacDermid (2001) examined the role balance among 80 white married couples and found that couples report greater role balance when their level of parental attachment to children is higher and when their marital satisfaction is greater. For example, the more leisure time husbands devote to their children when wives are not present, the higher are the wives' role balance scores. The Research Synopsis details a study examining depression and the multiple roles of women.

Parenting Roles in the Twenty-First Century

Reports have indicated that a growing number of parents have adopted a co-parenting approach and more men are sharing parenting tasks. Even more, in a reversal of traditional roles, some husbands relinquish the role of breadwinner to their wives. In 1992, about 5% of fathers in two-parent families were not in the labor force, and the wives were the breadwinners (Hayghe, 1994).

RESEARCH SYNOPSIS

MULTIPLE ROLES AND WELL-BEING AMONG MIDLIFE WOMEN

Because of the intense demands of women's multiple roles, for decades many studies have focused on the impact of multiple roles on women. Using the nationally represented sample of 12,654 respondents from 7703 households, from the 1992 wave of the Health and Retirement Study, Reid and Hardy examined the association between depressive symptomatology and various dimensions of the roles of wife, mother, paid worker, and informal caregiver to aging parents. The findings indicate that although the number of roles women assume affects their reports of depressive symptoms, once the demand and satisfaction associated with these roles are controlled, number has no effect. The findings suggest that the relationship between role occupancy and well-being is manifested through multiple dimensions of role experiences. The findings demonstrate the importance of women's perceptions of the quality of their roles in relation to their overall well-being. The researchers conclude that although role enhancement and role strain perspectives provide useful points of departure for studying multiple role experiences, neither perspective completely captures the relationship between multiple roles and mental well-being. Women have been targeted by family health nurses for the implementation of health promotion because of their actual or potential health problems resulting from the strain of role overload. Since multiple roles of women are not uniformly beneficial or detrimental, and the quality of the multiple roles affect women's well-being, nurses must assess not only how the roles may constrain or conflict but also how the family members manage their obligations.

Reid, J., & Hardy, M. (1999). Multiple roles and well-being among midlife women: Testing role strain and role enhancement theories, Journal of Gerontology, 54B, S329-S338.

However, it is not clear how many of these men were full-time househusbands. Also, being a househusband is usually a temporary role (Benokraitis, 1999). On the basis of research findings, Radin (1988) suggests the following factors that predict long-term high-level involvement of the father: (1) the mother has an investment in her career growth; (2) the father finds caring for the child gratifying; (3) the mother's salary is sufficiently large to warrant her working outside the home; (4) family members do not pressure the mother to stay home; (5) the father's hours continue to be flexible, or he works on a part-time basis; (6) the family remains small and no catastrophic illness occurs; and (7) the child the father is caring for over a prolonged period is a daughter, or more likely, an independent child.

Researchers have found several advantages to co-parenting including increased marital satisfaction. For example, according to the findings of a national survey of married couples, happy couples are more than three times as likely as unhappy couples to agree on how to share the responsibilities of rearing their children (54% vs. 12%). Also, happy couples tend to be more satisfied than unhappy couples with the amount of attention they focus on their relationship rather than on their children (73% vs. 23%); to agree on how to discipline their children (69% vs. 21%); to agree that having children has brought them closer as a couple (61% vs. 20%); and to feel that the father spends enough time with his children (53% vs. 22%) (Olson, Fye, & Olson, 1999).

However, these reports provide only a partial picture of contemporary parenting. According to Maushart (2001), in the United States, women still do 80% of the childcare—as much as they did in the 1960s. However, the solution may require multidimensional efforts. According to Crittenden (2001) who analyzed the inequality dilemma of women with children, the path to equity requires a greater societal respect for household work, particularly for childrearing. Specifically, employers should redesign work around parental norms.

Other contemporary and future parenting issues include the lack of boundaries in parenting and the absence of one parent. Of the 20.5 million American children younger than 5 years, only about 320,000 (1.5%) have fathers as their primary guardians ("Women's Commutes Often More Complicated," 1999). The 2000 U.S. Census data show that the number of families headed by a women was almost 13 million (12.2% of total families); among these, more than 7.5 million households include children, in-

dicating a 25% increase since 1990 (U.S. Census Bureau, 2002). Another trend is the rapid growth of grandparent-maintained households. The March 1997 Current Population Survey showed 3.9 million or 5.5% of children younger than 18 years living with grandparents and other relatives, up from 3.3 million in 1990 (Burnette, 1999). These trends suggest that parenting roles are multifaceted; therefore nurses should prepare diverse family health promotion and prevention strategies based on different parenting issues in unique families. A Canadian view about parenting roles and discipline is presented in the Canadian Perspectives box.

Family Caregiving Roles

At some time, most families face chronic illness in a family member, often a child or an elderly person. Families are usually the primary caretakers for clients with chronic illness and the major source of emotional and social support. Chronic illness affects all aspects of family life. Old and familiar patterns and shared activities are changed forever, and family roles and responsibilities change. Some families may become too close or enmeshed. By assuming too much responsibility and care for an ill family member, they may inhibit his or her autonomy and independence. However, previous study findings suggest that although providing care to an ill family member temporarily causes distress in family relationships or leads to role strain, most families are able to adapt and find a management style that allows them to overcome the difficulties and does not affect family life (Hulme, 1999; Robinson, 1998). Robinson's study (1998) identified four stages of the adjusting and overcoming process for 14 family members among five families who have a member with chronic illnesses. The final stage addresses each participating woman's new, evolving relationship with self, which was initiated in the therapeutic process and continued as the illness was put in its place.

Using data from the National Study of Families and Households, Eddy and Walker (1999) examined the impact of having a child with a chronic illness or handicapped condition on marital quality and on perceived marital stability and concluded that this situation has no uniform

CANADIAN PERSPECTIVES
THE PARENTING ROLE: CORPORAL PUNISHMENT AND ITS NEGATIVE DEVELOPMENTAL OUTCOMES FOR CHILDREN

Christine A. Ateah, RN, PhD
University of Manitoba

Corporal or physical punishment as a strategy to control or correct the behaviour of children is not uncommon and has a long history in Western culture. A useful definition of corporal punishment identified by Straus (1995) is "the use of physical force with the intention of causing a child to experience pain but not injury for the purposes of correction or control of the child's behavior" (p. 60). Although an increasing number of countries such as Sweden, Austria, and Italy have adopted legal processes banning the use of corporal punishment with children, there are no legal sanctions against its use in the United States and Canada. Durrant and Rose-Krasnor (1995) report that an estimated 70% to 90% of North American families have spanked their preschool children. There is strong evidence of negative developmental outcomes resulting from the use of corporal punishment with children, and therefore health care providers have a responsibility to promote disciplinary strategies that have fewer inherent risks.

Most studies on the implications of corporal punishment use with children have focused on associations between corporal punishment and negative developmental outcomes. Gershoff (2002) reports the following negative outcomes for children from a meta-analysis of research studies on the effects of corporal punishment: lower levels of moral internalization, aggression, delinquent and antisocial behaviour, negative effects on the quality of the parent-child relationship, negative effects on mental health, and physical child abuse.

In particular, the risk of physical abuse resulting from corporal punishment use has been identified by child health and development professionals as being of major concern. By definition, corporal punishment involves the infliction of pain as a disciplinary response and therein lies the risk of possible injury, and thus, abuse. Young children are naturally at greatest risk of injury resulting from the force of corporal punishment. Studies in both Canada and the United States indicate that most cases of child physical abuse result from use of corporal punishment (Health Canada, 2001). The Canadian Incidence Study (CIS) (Health Canada, 2001) on reported child abuse and neglect identified that 69% of substantiated cases of physical abuse consisted of "inappropriate punishment."

Considering the risks and negative developmental outcomes, why do parents continue to use corporal punishment with their children? Numerous studies have examined this issue, and some of the factors associated with corporal punishment use are having a positive attitude toward the use of corporal punishment (Holden, Coleman, & Schmidt, 1995), anger level as a result of the child's misbehaviour (Straus, 1996), parents' experience of receiving corporal punishment when they were children (Rodriquez & Sutherland, 1999), and religious ideology (Flynn, 1996).

Given the risks of corporal punishment with children, it is important that parents be guided and assisted in adopting disciplinary strategies with their children that do not pose such risks. Parents who have experienced physical punishment when they were children may believe that this is the only alternative for effective behaviour management with their own children or may not be aware of alternative behavioural management strategies. Parents may have a positive attitude toward the use of corporal punishment with children because they are unaware of the risks involved and therefore may require education in this area. Parents should be provided with safe, effective, and age-appropriate non-physical disciplinary behaviour management strategies to use with their children. Anger management strategies and programs may also be useful to some parents whose anger levels may dictate their choice and level of response to their child's misbehaviour.

CANADIAN PERSPECTIVES
THE PARENTING ROLE: CORPORAL PUNISHMENT AND ITS NEGATIVE DEVELOPMENTAL OUTCOMES FOR CHILDREN — cont'd

One of the most important responsibilities of parents is to help their children learn appropriate behaviours and practice self-discipline. Disciplinary strategies should include reasonable consequences and explanations for misbehaviour that are appropriate to the developmental stage of the child and should also include a component for teaching the preferred behaviour to the child. Health care professionals, such as nurses, are in an ideal position to help support and educate parents, to provide parents with information such as safe and effective non-physical disciplinary responses to use with their children, and to refer parents to additional resources as appropriate.

References

Durrant, J. E., & Rose-Krasnor, L. (1995). *Corporal punishment: Research review and policy recommendations.* Winnipeg, Manitoba, Canada: Health Canada and Department of Justice Canada.

Flynn, C. P. (1996). Regional differences in spanking experiences and attitudes: A comparison of Northeastern and Southern college students. *Journal of Family Violence, 11,* 59-80.

Gershoff, E. T. (2002). Corporal punishment by parents and associated child behaviors and experiences: A meta-analytic and theoretical review. *Psychological Bulletin, 128,* 539-579.

Health Canada. (2001). *The Canadian incidence study of reported child abuse and neglect.* Ottawa, Ontario, Canada: Author.

Holden, G. W., Coleman, S. M., & Schmidt, K. L. (1995). Why 3-year old children get spanked: Parent and child determinants as reported by college-educated mothers. *Merrill-Palmer Quarterly, 41,* 431-452.

Rodriquez, C. M., & Sutherland, D. (1999). Predictors of parents' physical disciplinary practices. *Child Abuse & Neglect, 23,* 651-657.

Straus, M. A. (1995). Corporal punishment of children and adult depression and suicide ideation. In J. McCord (Ed.), *Coercion and punishment in long-term perspectives* (pp. 59-77). New York: Cambridge University Press.

Straus, M. A. (1996). Spanking and the making of a violent society. *Pediatrics, 98*(Suppl.), 837-842.

Canadian spelling is used.

---

impact on marital quality or perceived marital stability. The findings of qualitative research conducted by Rehm and Catanzaro (1998) also indicated that both parents and children in families in which one parent had multiple sclerosis mostly thought of their families as functioning well, despite the many changes brought about by the chronic illness of one parent.

Regarding the care of frail elderly parents, much research has been focused on the role strain of women, because daughters or daughters-in-law are the major source of help. For example, in research conducted by Dautzenberg, Diederiks, Philipsen, and Tan (1999), cross-sectional comparisons show that daughter-caregivers become more distressed only when heavy caregiving demands interfere with their social and personal lives. However, the caregiver role appeared to have no profound impact on distress levels of middle-aged women with living parents in the longitudinal data within a cohort (n = 934; n = 743). Also, the research showed that multiple roles do not have negative consequences for the caregivers (Dautzenberg et al., 1999). Likewise, according to findings from a population-based probability sample of 581 middle-aged women who have paid jobs, employed women caregivers do not experience more caregiver role strain (Dautzenberg et al., 2000). Consequently, a self-selection process takes place whereby the nearest living daughter with the least competing demands is most likely to accept the caregiver role. Once the caregiver role is accepted, both role strain and the time spent on parent care are determined by factors other than employment status or work hours (Dautzenberg et al., 2000). Similarly, the findings of a study on caregivers' role strain revealed no differences between employed and nonemployed caregivers in terms of role overload, worry, strain, and depression (Edwards, Zarit, Stephens, & Townsend, 2002). The results suggest that caregivers may vary considerably in how they adapt to multiple roles.

Family Roles in Health Promotion and Prevention

Although illness can have a dramatic impact on family roles and functioning, most families seem to adjust along with time or resources (Hulme, 1999; Robinson, 1998). In the discussion of family caregiving, it is assumed that satisfying the health care needs of the ill family member and preservation of family life are the two major challenges faced by families. Most clients and their families effectively cope with stress and the demands of chronic illness and tend to pull together and become closer, as discussed earlier.

Although the belief that the stress associated with having a family member with a chronic condition necessarily leads to family distress may be untrue, role overload usually follows. Therefore nurses need to support family members of the client with a chronic condition to cope with additional caregiver roles. However, it is common for health care providers to focus on the client and overlook the caregiver's or spouse's distress and not attend to his or her physical and emotional needs. The failure of health care professionals to address the needs of family members can lead to negative consequences. The family becomes more distressed and is less able to respond to the needs of the client.

When the family is unable to meet the needs of a family member, linkage with outside resources becomes necessary. Families make decisions regarding their members' health promotion behaviors. If parents value the idea of health prevention activities, such as yearly physical examinations, then children will most likely receive this kind of health care. Children also influence their parents' lifestyle by bringing information from the larger society (e.g., school) that supports health promotion activities. Families have the primary responsibility for meeting the health needs of their members; therefore it is essential that families be provided with wellness opportunities.

The importance of one family member's behavioral influence on the entire family cannot be overstated. Mothers are particularly influential regarding the family's health. In most American homes, the mother has been formally identified with the role of nurse when the family requires health-related interventions. During childhood illnesses, the mother is often the caregiver, and at other times she is the decision maker regarding health checkups. This is a powerful role that must not be overlooked by the family health nurse. Health promotion activities will include the entire family, but the mother's acceptance or rejection of health promotion behaviors will prove decisive.

Although the mother's influence on the family's health appears to be the most distinctive, client behavior is influenced by the entire family's perception of wellness and illness. In nursing, the inhibitors that are often associated with the individual's behavior become manageable when family health nurses acknowledge the family's influence.

Family roles change as members experience acute and chronic illness and varied life transitions. With this information about contemporary family roles, the nurse must begin to examine methods of assessment and intervention that will meet the needs of these modern families.

Assessment of Family Roles

Types of Family Roles

Family roles refer to the established patterns of behavior of family members (Wright & Leahey, 2000). There are numerous family types. Although families are distinct in their structural composition, there is an overlap when attempts are made to include role and function in categorization.

Formal and Informal Family Roles

Friedman, Bowden, and Jones (2003) have described family function through formal and informal roles. *Formal roles* are those roles for which society has broadly agreed on a norm (Wright & Leahey, 2000) and include the behaviors associated with the role positions of mother, father, sister, brother, and grandparent. *Informal roles* refer to the established patterns of behavior that are idiosyncratic to particular individuals in certain settings and include encourager, compromiser, blocker, dominator, blamer, recognition seeker, pal, family scapegoat, placater, pioneer, distractor, family go-between, and bystander (Satir, 1972; Friedman, et al., 2003). Selected examples of other covert roles are presented in Box 5-1. Knowledge about both formal and informal roles enacted by the family will prove essential to the development of effective nursing strategies. For example, it is crucial to know which family member has the role of health teacher and health care provider.

Intraroles and Interroles

The formal and informal roles performed by the family members are referred to as *intrarole activities*. *Interrole activities* represent those role performances that occur outside the family system. Interrole activities include the ability of the family to link its members to the larger society. In the case of the children, this linkage occurs through the nurturance and socialization process. However, all other family members must also be prepared for the movement of the family unit into the greater community life. In the area of health

---

BOX 5-1   Informal Roles

- The *harmonizer* is responsible for mediating among family members. Using all skills available, this individual seeks to smooth over family disagreements.
- The *opposer* or the blocker is described as negative to all family suggestions, ideas, and activities.
- The *martyr* sacrifices everything, including self, for the sake of the family.
- The *blamer* is the fault-finder, a dictator, a bossy "know it all" and is similar to the opposer and the dominator.
- The *follower* goes along with all decisions made by the family and passively accepts the ideas of others in the family.
- The *bystander* is more passive than the follower and observes but does not involve himself or herself and acts like an outsider.
- The *coordinator* serves to bring the family closer together by planning and organizing family activities.
- The *scapegoat* is the identified problem member in the family and serves as a safety valve.
- The *encourager* praises and accepts the contribution of others and makes family members feel their ideas are important.
- The *initiator-contributor* proposes new ideas to the members or changes the ways that problems or goals are viewed.
- The *recognition seeker* tries to call attention to self and his/her deeds, accomplishment, and/or problems in whatever way possible.
- The *distractor* exhibits attention-getting behavior that helps the family avoid or ignore painful or difficult matters.
- The *caretaker* is the member who is called on to help and nurture other members in need.
- The *pioneer* initiates new experiences and moves the family into unknown territory.
- The *family go-between* acts as the family facilitator by bridging and monitoring communication among family members.
- The *great stone face* preaches about the "right" things continually and impassively.
- The *dominator* manipulates the group or certain members in order to claim authority or superiority.

Based on data from Satir, V. (1972). Peoplemaking. Palo Alto, CA: Science and Behavior Books; Hartman, A., & Laird, J. (1983). Family-centered social work practice. New York: Free Press; Kantor, D., & Lehr, W. (1975). Inside the family. San Francisco: Jossey-Bass; and Friedman, M. M., Bowden, V. R., & Jones, E. G. (2003). Family nursing: Research, theory and practice (5th ed.). Upper Saddle River, NJ: Prentice Hall.

care, this becomes an essential part of the family's ability to function.

In addition to the role conflicts that can ensue from interrole activities, the possibility of intra-role conflict exists. Families, though moving toward this contemporary picture of roles, have not quite settled into these behaviors as the societal norm. The overload, conflict, and incongruity associated with multiple roles cause role stress in families today, but the subsequent family role strain experienced by the members themselves poses health risks for the group. The family's role in minimizing role strain for its members is significant, but few families have developed the skills necessary for creating a balance in family roles. The "superwoman syndrome" has tran-scended to include the "super family syndrome," in which all members are perceived to be able to do all things for all people without succumbing to the maladaptive consequences of such physical and psychological strain.

Instrumental and Expressive Roles

The structural-functional family framework divides family roles into an *instrumental role*, such as being in charge of tasks, and an *expressive role*, such as being nurturing. In the family struc-tural framework it is assumed that the family is most functional if the male plays the instrumental role and the female plays the expressive role (Olson & DeFrain, 2000). However, the distinction of these roles has diminished as previously discussed.

Reciprocal or Complementary Roles

A role is interdependent with that of a role partner and is always paired with a reciprocal role of another person (Friedman et al., 2003). The concept of complementary roles is important in social role theory because the existence of these roles supports the function of other roles. For example, the child nurturance/socialization role is enacted most effectively when the mother and father roles are intact. The absence or diminished effectiveness of the mother or father role causes an incompleteness that decreases the function of the child nurturance/socialization role. In complementary roles, one or more roles fit together so that other role activities can be accomplished.

Variables Affecting Family Roles

Cultural Considerations

Expectations regarding the role performance of a mother, even in contemporary America, will look very different in a first-generation Hispanic family than in a white family. Ethnicity has been established as a significant variable in the development of gender role attitudes and behavior in a family (Leininger & McFarland, 2002). Specific examples can be found in trans-cultural nursing literature regarding domestic care, socialization/nurturance, and breadwinner roles (Andrews & Boyle, 1999; Leininger & McFarland, 2002; Purnell, 1998). As discussed in Chapter 9, nurses must explore the cultural background of a family with whom they plan interventions. The insight gained regarding cultural values, beliefs, and experiences will assist in health promotion efforts. For example, if the father in a home is culturally recognized as the decision maker, he becomes an important target for education and intervention, and nurses should include the father in decisions about the family's health. A comparison of family roles among traditional Latino, Asian American, and American Indian family roles is found in Box 5-2. While considering the cultural differences in family roles, nurses also should consider the level of acculturation. For example, traditional Latino family dynamics and gender roles change with increased exposure to the dominant society. Therefore nurses should attempt to avoid stereo-types of family roles when assessing families from different cultural backgrounds.

Socioeconomic Considerations

Socioeconomic variables are also considerations regarding the assignment, expectation, and per-formance of family roles. Often the need for economic survival forces a family with traditional beliefs about the mother's role into a contem-porary role enactment situation. In this example, the mother might be employed outside the home, although the family believes that her roles of domestic care and nurturance/socialization are paramount. Great potential for conflict, stress, and strain exists in such families. Common role issues include role stress or strain, role ambiguity, role conflict, and role induction.

BOX 5-2 Traditional Latino, Asian American, and American Indian Family Roles

LATINO FAMILY ROLES

General characteristics:
Familism; high family cohesion; high family flexibility; supportive kin network system.
Father:
Head of the family who has all family authority and decision-making power, expressed in *machismo;* provider.
Mother:
Primarily the homemaker and cultural guardian of family tradition; submissive to husband; soft, nurturing, and self-sacrificing woman.
Status and roles are usually defined solely by her marriage and children.
Children:
Socialized according to gender role models (e.g., girl should learn how to be a good mother and wife).
Grandparents:
Active roles in taking care of grandchildren.

ASIAN AMERICAN FAMILY ROLES

General characteristics:
Strong family orientation, filial piety; family loyalty; extended family support; multigenerational family.
Father:
Head of the family who has authoritative relationship to the family; decision maker; leader; provider; disciplinarian.
Mother:
Homemaker who takes care of her husband and children; submissive to husband.
Children:
Sons are more valued than daughters. Eldest son is most respected, and family power is passed on from father to eldest son.
Older siblings are expected to be role models for younger siblings.
Grandparents:
Have position of honor by virtue of their older and parental status.

AMERICAN INDIAN FAMILY ROLES

General characteristics:
Extended family system; high family cohesion; respect for elders; tribal support system.
Parents:
Sometimes the father's brothers are called *fathers.*
Spend considerable time and effort in making items for children.
Experience conflict between traditional and modern education system during parenting.
Children:
Are considered important family members.
Spiritual values are taught in special rituals and ceremonies.
Grandparents/Elders:
Have traditionally occupied a central role in a family's decision making.
Play an important role in caring for the young and in passing down family traditions.
Often are the center of family life and hold family together.

Based on data from Benokraitis, N. (1999). Marriages and families: Changes, choices and constraints (3rd ed.). Upper Saddle River, NJ: Prentice-Hall; Friedman, M. M., Bowden, V. R., & Jones, E. G. (2003). Family nursing: Research, theory and practice (5th ed.). Upper Saddle River, NJ: Prentice Hall; and Olson, D. H., & DeFrain, J. (2000). Marriage and the family: Diversity and strengths (3rd ed.). Mountain View, CA: Mayfield.

Another example of socioeconomic impact on roles is the family that expects traditional role behaviors of the mother who seeks a more contemporary performance of her roles. Both cultural and socioeconomic factors will influence formal and informal roles. Informally, a family member may assume the role of martyr because of the financial stress in the home. Under other circumstances, this member might be the family harmonizer. These informal roles are more flexible and mobile than the formal roles discussed in this chapter. A family member may enact a variety of informal roles and quickly change to perform only one. Informal roles are highly subjective. Less conflict and stress are generally associated with these role transitions unless, like changes in formal role performance, the variation creates disequilibrium, conflict, and stress.

Developmental Considerations

In families, role transitions or changes occur regularly and throughout the life cycle. Duvall and Miller (1985) describe the family in terms of life span. Families will enact different roles as they travel through the life span. For a childless couple, the formal roles of domestic care and provider might be easily shared. Once the family enters the developmental phase of childbearing, new role considerations arise. Suddenly nurturance and socialization roles must be performed, and the socioeconomic status of the family may change, causing the breadwinner role to take on new meaning. As families complete the life cycle, even greater changes in their formal roles occur. For older adults, the parenting role is replaced with the role of grandparent. Along the life span, individuals who have been parents will very often become grandparents. Because of the increasing life expectancy and the aging of the baby boomer generation, grandparents will have increased relevance to family health nursing. Several roles within the family have been established. For example, the grandparents are often identified as negotiators between parents and children. They serve as arbitrators, helping to maintain family continuity between the generations. Grandparents are historical links between the past and the future and provide family biography. Currently, grandparents have been identified as a highly diverse group with more differences in their role

enactment as grandparents than in enactment of most other social or family roles. Expectations regarding the roles are unclear because the phenomenon is new. The findings of a qualitative study of 26 grandparents rearing grandchildren revealed that the grandparent-caregivers expressed a lack of role-fit, as well as role ambiguity, and role conflict (Laudry-Meyer, 1999). In particular, these grandparent-caregivers experienced role conflict without being able to enact a traditional grandparent role. Although grandparents differ in age, acceptance of the role, interpretation of the role behaviors, cultural backgrounds, and gender identities, they are a social force whose impact on the family can be positive or negative, but at the very least, significant.

Once children have been launched into society, parents again live together as they did during the childless phase of the life cycle, but those role behaviors no longer apply. The individual maturation that has occurred over the years alters the role of the childless couple as they experience that role in their older years. As mentioned earlier, the subsequent transition into grandparenthood may affect the couple.

In addition to maturational transitions, such as those from singlehood to marriage, to parenthood, and so on, situational role transitions also occur. The multiple and complex roles enacted by all family members today represent these situational role transitions. In both examples, actual and potential stress are evident. The family health nurse's role is to assist the family in identifying role transitions and to facilitate the prevention of role strain. Coping strategies can be introduced, and future role transitions can be anticipated.

Process of Family Role Assessment

The importance of assessing family roles cannot be overemphasized. Appropriate role assessment provides the nurse and the family with insight regarding current and potential health problems and aids in identifying the family's level of wellness. The family health nurse can facilitate achievement of family health by including an assessment of family roles in the holistic family assessment process.

Identifying the family type is the first step in completing a family role assessment. In addition to gaining appropriate data regarding family structure, specific identifying information should be gathered regarding roles of family members. Box 5-3 lists the components of and guidelines for family role assessment. The nurse assesses the family according to its formal interrole behaviors. This simply means that the roles—described in this chapter for mother, father, and other family members—are identified. After the assessment questions regarding these roles have been considered, the nurse explores the informal interrole behaviors unique to the family. The assessment questions are used to search for meanings attached to behaviors as perceived by the family. The interview and observation should also include clarification regarding the family's culture, socioeconomic status, and position in the life cycle. Finally, the nurse examines the intrarole behaviors enacted by the family. Here the impact of school, friends, relatives, church, and other external groups are explored. All the categories combined will provide the nurse with a clear but unique picture of family roles. Health promotion activities, as well as protective strategies, can be used by the family unit to meet the needs of the family. Role theory, family role theory, and the variables of culture, socioeconomic status, and life span development combine to form a salient component of the holistic family health assessment process.

BOX 5-3   Guidelines for Family Role Assessment

FAMILY STRUCTURE

1. How would the family be structurally defined?
   - A. Traditional
   - B. Nontraditional

FAMILY FUNCTION (FORMAL INTERROLE)

1. What are the formal interroles in the family?
   - A. Father
   - B. Mother
   - C. Brother
   - D. Sister
   - E. Spouse
   - F. Child
   - G. Breadwinner
   - H. Domestic caregiver
   - I. Nurturer/socializer
   - J. Health leader
2. Describe how each member enacts his or her formal roles.
3. What are the multiple roles enacted by the family?
4. How does the family support its members in their multiple roles?
5. Which of the following do family members experience regarding their formal roles?
   - A. Role incongruence
   - B. Role overload
   - C. Role conflict
   - D. Role stress
6. Do these experiences further manifest themselves as role strain?
7. How effectively do family members enact their formal interroles?
8. How have the family roles changed from the roles enacted previously?
9. What kind of preparation did the family have for the role changes it has experienced?
10. What are the response patterns of the family to these role changes?

FAMILY FUNCTION (INFORMAL INTERROLE)

1. What are the informal interroles in the family?
2. Describe who enacts these informal roles.
3. Determine whether these informal roles are healthy or dysfunctional to the family unit.
4. How do these informal role enactments facilitate or inhibit the formal role behaviors?

Continued

BOX 5-3   Guidelines for Family Role Assessment—cont'd

5. Do these informal role enactments create role incongruence, role overload, role conflict, and/or role stress in family members?
6. Do these role stresses manifest themselves as role strain in the family?
7. How have these informal roles changed from previous informal roles?
8. What are the family response patterns to these informal roles?
9. What purpose do these informal role behaviors serve for the family?
10. How were these informal role behaviors learned by the family members?

INTRAROLE FUNCTION

1. What are the intrarole functions of the family members?
   A. Friend   C. Community participant
   B. Kinship   D. Church participant
2. Describe how each family member enacts his or her nonhome roles.
3. What are the family's multiple nonhome roles?
4. How do these nonhome roles influence the formal interroles enacted by the family?
5. Does the family support its members in their multiple nonhome roles?
6. Do family members experience role incongruence, conflict, overload, and/or stress regarding these nonhome roles?
7. Do these experiences further manifest themselves as role strain?
8. How do informal interroles affect the intraroles themselves as role strain?
9. How have these roles changed from previously enacted nonhome roles?
10. What kind of preparation did the family have for the role changes it has experienced?

Implications for Family Nursing

An understanding of family roles is essential to the development of effective nursing care for families in need of intervention. Changes in family role structure magnify the potential for family stress. A variety of these role transitions are discussed at length in Chapter 17. With the changing structure of the family, for example, a single-parent family is faced with intense demands for breadwinning, nurturing/socializing, and domestic care—often without adequate support. The potential for role stress and strain leading to physical and psychological health problems is tremendous. Even in the traditionally structured family, significant changes are taking place in the formal role functions of family members. Today the multiple roles held by all members may place the family system in emotional and physical jeopardy. The informal roles acquired by family members also serve to support or suppress a family's wellness. In each family, informal roles will add to or reduce the stress associated with formal family roles.

The scope of family health nursing practice includes understanding the family structure and its family role functions. It is essential that the nurse first examine the interroles and intraroles of the family. Assessment of family roles is best achieved with the use of family assessment tools that facilitate data collection by exploring major areas of family role function and providing clues regarding potential health problems of the family. Information can be obtained through both interview and observation. In this way, the nurse can provide the family with information and resources and can identify strengths to help them achieve family wellness. The synthesized assessment data could be stated as a family nursing diagnosis, and Table 5-1 lists the family role problems in the North American Nursing Diagnosis Association's (NANDA's) standardized format.

TABLE 5-1   Family Role Problems and NANDA Nursing Diagnoses

Family Role Problems	Potential NANDA Nursing Diagnoses
ROLE TRANSITION	
Wellness diagnosis	Opportunity to enhance parenting
Risk diagnosis	Anticipatory grieving related to role loss
	Risk for violence related to role change
	Potential alteration in parenting related to role change or role overload
Actual diagnosis	Dysfunctional grieving related to role strain
	Social isolation related to role change/strain
	Body image disturbance related to role change/strain
ROLE CONFLICT	
Risk diagnosis	Risk for caregiver role strain
Actual diagnosis	Caregiver role strain
	Parental role conflict related to role insufficiency, role ambiguity, or role overload
	Altered family process related to role conflict or role ambiguity
	Altered role performance related to role conflict
	Impaired home maintenance related to role strain
	Ineffective family coping related to role loss, role ambiguity, or role insufficiency
ROLE DISTANCE	
Risk diagnosis	Risk for impaired parent/infant/child attachment related role insufficiency or role ambiguity
Actual diagnosis	Impaired social interaction related to role loss and strain
ROLE FAILURE	
Risk diagnosis	Risk for impaired parenting
Actual diagnosis	Impaired/altered parenting

NANDA, North American Nursing Diagnosis Association.
Based on data from Carpenito, L. J. (2000). Nursing diagnosis: Application to clinical practice (8th ed.). Philadelphia: Lippincott; Friedman, M. M., Bowden, V. R., & Jones, E.G. (2003). Family nursing: Research, theory and practice (5th ed.). Upper Saddle River, NJ: Prentice Hall; and Weber, J., & Kelly, J. (2002). Health assessment in nursing (2nd ed.). Philadelphia: Lippincott.

Family Role Problems and Nursing Interventions

Although NANDA's diagnoses describe the current and potential family role problems, the Nursing Interventions Classification (NIC) provides diverse intervention strategies for family role problems. Box 5-4 presents applicable family nursing intervention strategies according to NIC.

For more in-depth discussion of the classification of NIC related to family roles, see McCloskey and Bulechek (1996).

Managing Role Problems: Role Strain and Role Transition

Role strain and role transition problems are commonly found in family situations. The family health nurse serves as a resource person, providing

---

BOX 5-4 Applicable Family Nursing Intervention Strategies according to the Nursing Interventions Classification System (NIC)

Role Enhancement (5370)
Coping Enhancement (5230)
Developmental Enhancement (7050)
Counseling (5240)
Emotional Support (5270)
Anticipatory Guidance (5210)
Teaching: Infant Care (5608)
Grief Work Facilitation (5290)
Support Group (5430)
Family Involvement (7110)
Emotional Support (5270)
Caregiver Support (7040)
Family Support (7140)
Support System Enhancement (5440)
Home Maintenance Assistance (7180)
Family Mobilization (7120)
Decision-Making Support (5250)
Cognitive Restructuring (4700)
Family Therapy (7150)
Active Listening (4290)
Note: The four-digit number for each intervention indicates the NIC coding system.

From McCloskey, J.C., & Bulechek, G. M. (Eds.). (1996). Iowa Intervention Project: Nursing Interventions Classification (2nd ed.). St. Louis, MO: Mosby.

---

clarification about the formal and informal roles and the meanings attached to these roles and strengthening the problem-solving skills of the family. The nurse assists the family in identifying its current and previous coping strategies and encourages the exploration of feelings and impressions. Family nurses must be able to interpret the meaning of strain by determining the various sources of role strain. Strategies such as role sharing, role negotiation, and role reversals help to reduce stress (see the section about managing role stress and role strain earlier in this chapter).

Role transitions involve adding new roles and dropping others; therefore it is important to help family members clarify expectations about the needed roles and strengthen the family members' abilities to enact new roles (Friedman, Bowden, & Jones, 2003). Role transition may create significant stress for all family members, even though on the surface only one or two family members seem to be affected. Therefore nursing interventions are often directed at the family level. Role enhancement and role modeling are strategies used to develop role clarity and role-taking skills for families.

Role Enhancement

Role enhancement is defined as assisting family members with activities to improve relationships by clarifying and supplementing specific role behaviors (McCloskey & Bulechek, 1996). Examples of these assisting activities include encouraging family members to identify a realistic description of change in role; facilitating role rehearsal by having the family members anticipate others' reactions to enactment; teaching new behaviors needed by a family member to fulfill a role; facilitating reference group interactions as a part of learning new roles; and serving as a role model for learning new behaviors, as appropriate (McCloskey & Bulechek, 1996).

It is helpful to teach the family how to anticipate conflict as new developmental stages are approached, as situational experiences create sudden changes in the family norm, and as individual members experience changes in development. Family nurses are charged with teaching families how to adapt, cope, and grow with role changes that occur. As teachers, family nurses support families in their efforts to find new identities. In addition, families will benefit from instruction about the development of gender identity and techniques that will help children clarify their gender roles.

Role Modeling

Role modeling is a crucial type of teaching and becomes a particularly potent teaching method when family members positively identify with family nurses (Friedman et al., 2003). *Role modeling* is defined as the patterning of behaviors. It provides a standard by which others can measure their progress. Nurses can serve as role models for family members. For example, family nurses working in schools serve as role models for both parents and children (Hanson & Boyd, 1996). A family nurse may serve as a role model for a first-time mother by showing her how to take care of a newborn baby. Through role modeling, the family member begins to imitate the desired behavior, and imitation develops as part of the family member's own behavioral repertoire (Friedman et al., 2003). Role modeling healthy interactions and clearly defined role behaviors for the family will provide a standard for families to follow.

Nursing is offered a unique challenge in working with families today. An important nursing role is teaching the family how to deal with potential and existing family problems. Specifically, the family nurse shares role assessment data with the family as the educational approach develops.

Using teaching strategies, the nurse may offer a historical review of families in American society. This enables the family to discover possible sources of their feelings, beliefs, and family role practices. For example, the nurse will direct her teaching toward role sharing as a method of reducing role strain and will explore family perceptions of such a change. In addition, assisting families in recognizing the impact of values and beliefs on family interaction and family health is another important role for family nurses. Finally, the implications of changing family roles in American culture include the activation of self-care behaviors and family empowerment (Hulme, 1999). Family members must be instructed and encouraged to develop strategies that will support the family unit and its members.

CASE SCENARIO

Mike (age 48) and Jennifer (age 40) have two boys, Josh (age 6) and Noah (age 3). They have been married for 7 years. When Mike lost his job 6 years ago, the couple moved in with Mike's mother (age 78) and lived with her for more than 5 years until Jennifer's income was sufficient to cover a mortgage payment and family expenses. Before Jennifer started her full-time job as an executive director for a nonprofit agency 2 years ago, after she received a graduate degree, the family's income was very minimal. While Mike spent most of his time working on computers and consulting and took part-time teaching jobs, Jennifer worked on a part-time basis while she was in school. Mike started a new consulting business one year ago. Since Mike's new business has not produced any income, Jennifer provides for most of the family expenses. While Mike enjoys working for his business, Jennifer perceives Mike's job as a hobby and a waste of time and hopes that her husband finds a "real" job in the near future. Even though Jennifer has a decent salary, her income barely covers the household expenses. Whenever Jennifer confronts him about the financial situation, Mike usually avoids a discussion.

Because Mike has strong family-centered values, they eat dinner as a family and at least twice a week with Mike's father. Both children are in good health and have pleasant dispositions. However, they often argue over toys and are sometimes cranky and difficult for Jennifer to deal with. Recently, Jennifer has been yelling at the children frequently. Whenever Jennifer is busy at home,

she allows the boys to watch television for significant amounts of time. However, the couple spends at least 1 hour per day in educational activities with the children.

Mike and Jennifer are rather busy. Because Mike works at home from morning to night, there is no clear distinction between the family sphere and Mike's job. Because Mike is overcommitted to his new business, Jennifer is mainly responsible for household activities. Although as a result of numerous heated arguments, Mike has agreed to share some of the parenting responsibility and outdoor chores, Jennifer thinks she is still doing the larger portion of household chores. Jennifer spends weekends doing household chores, grocery shopping, and laundry and attending to the boys.

Mike and Jennifer do not have any close friends and seldom participate in social gatherings as a couple. Jennifer usually takes the children shopping and to church activities and other events, while Mike stays at home. Because Jennifer's family lives far away, she barely sees them and feels isolation and loneliness. Although Jennifer goes to church and attends church-related activities with the children twice a week, she does not have any social life or close friends in the area. Because of frequent family gatherings with her in-laws, Jennifer has not had any time to socialize with her own acquaintances. Over the years, Jennifer has experienced chronic fatigue and stress from caring for the boys and handling family relations and household chores in addition to the demands of her stressful job.

Continued

CASE SCENARIO—cont'd

MAJOR FAMILY STRESSORS

Mike's uncertain new business, insufficient "me" time, insufficient "couple" time and intimacy, lack of shared responsibility, financial insecurity, lack of social activities

FAMILY STRENGTHS

Shared religious observances (Jennifer and the boys), extended family support (Mike's mother)

LIFESTYLE CHANGES INDICATED

Increased and improved individual and couple time for the parents; increased sharing of household responsibilities. For Mike, there is a need to rethink his career change. For Jennifer, there is a need to develop stress management skills. For the boys, there is a need to decrease the amount of time spent watching television.

WEBSITE RESOURCES

ORGANIZATION	WEBSITE ADDRESS
Nurturing Fatherhood:	http://www.fatherhood.hhs.gov/CFSForum/front.htm
Family and Medical Leave Act	http://www.dol.gov/esa/regs/statutes/whd/fmla.htm
Managing Your Dual Career Family	http://www.dr-jane.com/chapters/Jane133.htm
CNN Career Studies: Dual Earners, Double Trouble	http://www.cnn.com/2000/CAREER/trends/11/13/dual.earners/
The National Parenting Center	http://www.tnpc.com/
National Partnership for Women and Families	http://www.nationalpartnership.org/
Administration for Children and Families	http://www.acf.dhhs.gov/
Families and Work Institute	http://www.familiesandwork.org/
Resource Careers	http://www.resourcecareers.com/
Parents without Partners	http://www.parentswithoutpartners.org/
Stepfamily Network Inc.	http://www.stepfamily.net
Alzheimer's Disease Education and Referral Center	http://www.alzheimers.org/
American Society of Aging	http://www.asaging.org

■ CHAPTER HIGHLIGHTS

- The roles and functions of family members are complex and multifaceted.
- The family nurse needs to be cognizant of formal and informal family roles in health promotion, prevention, and illness to assist families in improving, maintaining, or regaining their level of health.
- A holistic assessment of family roles helps the nurse to gain insight about multiple roles and their unique functions in each family.
- An understanding of the definitions of role theory–related terms will assist nurses in comprehending family dynamics and developing effective nursing strategies.

- Formal and informal roles of health teacher and caregiver significantly influence the health behaviors of family members during illness and health promotion and prevention.
- Family roles are influenced by culture, family structure, developmental stage of the family unit and its members, education level, and economic status.
- Assessment of family roles includes observation and interview of multifaceted family overt and covert roles.
- Interventions for family role problems include role enactment, role modeling, role sharing, role negotiation or role bargaining, and role reversal.

‖ CRITICAL THINKING ACTIVITIES

1. Select a television program or movie about a family and analyze the family's roles using role theory–related terms.

2. Discuss factors to be considered in assessment of family roles. Interview a family from a different ethnic background and assess the family roles while considering their level of acculturation.

3. Describe the role theory concepts identified from the case scenario and suggest potential nursing interventions to decrease role strain and mobilize the family strengths.

4. Maushart (2001), in *Wife Work*, predicted increased divorce rates in the future because of unequal distribution of work at home between dual-career spouses. In addition to these feminist and role-strain perspectives, review other views (e.g., role enhancement or role balance perspectives) and apply them to the future working woman's family role issues and dynamics. Finally, based on your belief or theory, discuss the future direction of families in the United States.

5. As noted, multidimensional efforts are required to assist working women with children. Suggest five potential strategies for these women and children using both macro (e.g., development of a new family policy) and micro approaches (e.g., use of role sharing or co-parenting).

REFERENCES

Andrews, M., & Boyle, J. (1999). *Transcultural concepts in nursing care* (3rd ed.). Philadelphia: Lippincott.

Benokraitis, N. (1999). *Marriages and families: Changes, choices and constraints* (3rd ed.) Upper Saddle River, NJ: Prentice-Hall.

Biddle, B. J. (1979). *Role theory: Expectations, identities, and behaviors.* New York: Academic Press.

Burnette, D. (1999). Social relationships of Latino grandparent caregivers: A role theory perspective, *Gerontologist* 39: 49-58.

Carpenito, L. J. (2000). *Nursing diagnosis: Application to clinical practice* (8th ed.). Philadelphia: Lippincott.

Clark, E. (2001). Role conflicts and coping strategies in care-giving: A symbolic interactionist view. *Journal of Psychosocial Nursing, 39,* 28-37, 54-55.

Cohen, P. N., & Bianchi, S. M. (1999, December). Marriage, children, and women's employment: What do we know? *Monthly Labor Review, 122*(12), 22-31.

Coltrane, S. (1996). *Family man: Fatherhood, housework, and gender equity,* Oxford: Oxford University Press.

Cook, E. P. (1997). Gender discrimination in Jessica's career. *Career Development Quarterly 46,* 148-154.

Crittenden, A. (2001). *The price of motherhood: Why the most important job in the world is still the least valued.* New York: Henry Holt.

Dautzenberg, M. G., Diederiks, J. P., Philipsen, H., Stevens, F.

C., Tan, F., & Vernooij-Dassen, E. (2000). The competing demands of paid work and parent care: Middle-aged daughters providing assistance to elderly parents. *Research on Aging, 22*(2), 165-187.

Dautzenberg, M. G., Diederiks, J. P., Philipsen, H., & Tan, F. E. (1999). Multigenerational caregiving and well-being: Distress of middle-aged daughters providing assistance to elderly parents. *Women & Health, 29*(4), 57-74.

Dempsey, K. (1997). Women's perceptions of fairness and the persistence of an unequal division of housework. *Family Matters,* Spring/summer, 15.

Duvall, E. M., & Miller, B. C. (1985). *Family Development* (6th ed.). New York: Harper & Row.

Eagly, A. H. (1997). Sex differences in social behavior: Comparing social role theory and evolutionary psychology. *The American Psychologist, 52,* 1380-1384.

Eddy, L. L., & Walker, A. J. (1999). The impact of children with chronic health problems on marriage. *Journal of Family Nursing, 5,* 10-32.

Edwards, A. B., Zarit, S. H., Stephens, M. A., & Townsend, A. (2002). Employed family caregivers of cognitively impaired elderly: An examination of role strain and depressive symptoms. *Aging & Mental Health, 6,* 55-61.

Franke, G. R., Crown, D. F., & Spake, D. F. (1997). Gender differences in ethical perceptions of business practices: A social role theory perspective. *The Journal of Applied Psychology, 82,* 920-934.

Friedman, M. M., Bowden, V. R., & Jones, E. G. (2003). *Family Nursing: Research, theory and practice* (5th ed.). Upper Saddle River, NJ: Prentice Hall.

Goode, W. J. (1960). A theory of role strain. *American Sociological Review, 25,* 483-496.

Gupton, A., Heaman, M., & Ashcroft, T. (1997). Bed rest from the perspective of the high-risk pregnant woman. *Journal of Obstetric, Gynecologic, and Neonatal Nursing, 26,* 423-430.

Hanson, S. M., & Boyd, S. T. (1996). *Family health nursing: Theory, practice, and research.* Philadelphia: F. A. Davis.

Hardy M. E., & Conway, M.E. (1988). *Role theory perspective for health professionals* (2nd ed.). Norwalk, CT: Appleton & Lange.

Hartman, A., & Laird, J. (1983). *Family-centered social work practice.* New York: Free Press.

Hayghe, H. V. (1994). Are women leaving the labor force? *Monthly Labor Review, 117,* 37-39.

Hochschild, A. (1989). *The second shift: Working parents and the revolution at home.* New York: Viking.

Hulme, P. A. (1999). Family empowerment: A nursing intervention with suggested outcomes for families of children with chronic health condition. *Journal of Family Nursing, 5,* 33-51.

Kantor, D., & Lehr, W. (1975). *Inside the family.* San Francisco: Jossey-Bass.

Killien, M. G., Habermann B., & Jarrett M. (2001). Influence of employment characteristics on postpartum mothers' health. *Women and Health, 33*(1/2), 63-81.

LaRossa, R. (1997). *The modernization of fatherhood: A social and political history.* Chicago: The University of Chicago Press.

Laudry-Meyer, L. (1999). Grandparents raising grandchildren: An investigation of roles and support. *Dissertation Abstracts International, 60*(5), 1783A. (UMI No. DA9931632)

Leininger M., & McFarland, M. (2002). *Transcultural nursing: Concepts, theories, research and practice.* (3rd ed.). New York: McGraw-Hill.

Marks, S. R., Huston, T. L., Johnson, E. M, & MacDermid, S. M. (2001). Role balance among white married couples. *Journal of Marriage and the Family, 63,* 1083-1098.

Marks, S. R., & MacDermid, S. M. (1996). Multiple roles and the self: A theory of role balances. *Journal of Marriage and the Family, 58,* 417-432.

Maushart, S. (2001). *Wife work: What marriage really means for women.* New York: Blomsbury.

McCloskey, J. C., & Bulechek, G. M. (Eds.). (1996). *Iowa Intervention Project: Nursing Interventions Classification* (2nd ed.). St. Louis, MO: Mosby.

Mead, G. H. (1934). *Mind, self and society.* Chicago: University of Chicago Press.

Messias, D. K., Im E., Page A., Regev, H., Spiers, J., Yoder, L., et al.(1997). Defining and redefining women's work: Implications for women's health. *Gender & Society, 11,* 296-323.

Moch, S. D. (1988). Promoting health with role-reversal couples. *Journal of Community Health Nursing, 5,* 195-202.

Moen, P., Robinson, J., & Dempster-McClain, D. (1995). Caregiving and women's well-being: A life course approach. *Journal of Health and Social Behavior, 36,* 259-273.

Mui, A. C. (1995). Caring for frail elderly parents: A comparison of adult sons and daughters. *The Gerontologist, 35,* 86-93.

Olson, D. H., & DeFrain, J. (2000). *Marriage and the family: Diversity and strengths* (3rd ed.). Mountain View, CA: Mayfield.

Olson, D. H., Fye S., & Olson, A. (1999). *National survey of happy and unhappy married couples.* Minneapolis, MN: Life Innovations.

Purnell, L. D. (1998). *Transcultural health care: A culturally competent approach.* Philadelphia: F. A. Davis.

Radin, N. (1988). Primary caregiving fathers of long duration. In P. Bronstein & C. Cowan (Eds.), *Fatherhood today: Men's changing role in the family* (pp. 127-143). New York: John Wiley & Sons.

Rehm, R. S., & Catanzaro, M. L. (1998). "It's just a fact of life": Family members' perceptions of parental chronic illness. *Journal of Family Nursing, 4,* 21-40.

Reid, J., & Hardy, M. (1999). Multiple roles and well-being among midlife women: Testing role strain and role enhancement theories. *Journal of Gerontology, 54B,* S329-S338.

Reser, B. (1998). Role strain among school nurses. *The Journal of School Nursing, 14:* 49-50.

Robinson, C. A. (1998): Women, families, chronic illness, and nursing interventions: From burden to balance. *Journal of Family Nursing, 4,* 271-290.

Roy, C., & Andrews, H. (1999). *Roy adaptation model* (2nd ed.). Stamford, CT: Appleton & Lange.

Sarbin, T. R. (1954). Role theory. In G. Lindzey (Ed.), *Handbook of social psychology* (pp. 488-567). Reading, MA: Addison-Wesley.

Satir, V. (1972). *Peoplemaking.* Palo Alto, CA: Science and Behavior Books.

Silva, E. B., & Smart, C. (1999). *The new family?* Thousand Oaks, CA: Sage.

Stevens, D., Kiger., G., & Riely, P. (2001). Working hard and hardly working: Domestic labor and marital satisfaction among dual-earner couples, *Journal of Marriage and Family, 63,* 514-526.

U.S. Census Bureau. (2002). *American FactFinder.* Retrieved May 23, 2002, from http://www.factsnder.census.gov/servlet/BasicFactsServlet.

Voydanoff, P. (2000). Blue-collar marriage: Book review. *Journal of Marriage and Family, 62*(3), 858.

Weber, J., & Kelly, J. (2002). *Health assessment in nursing* (2nd ed.). Philadelphia: Lippincott.

Women's Commutes Often More Complicated (1999, March 3). *The Washington Post.*

Wright, L. M., & Leahey, M. (2000). *Nurses and families: A guide to family assessment and intervention* (3rd ed.). Philadelphia: F. A. Davis.

6

Family Social Support

Karen Bullock

A kind heart is a fountain of gladness, making everything in its vicinity freshen into smiles.

— Washington Irving

OBJECTIVES

On completion of this chapter, the reader will be able to do the following:

1. *Differentiate between the concepts of social network and social support.*

2. *Analyze the relationship among the variables of social support within ethnically diverse families.*

3. *Describe the influence of contemporary social trends on conventional and progressive family forms.*

4. *Analyze the effectiveness of various types of networks in providing social support to families and individuals.*

5. *Assess family needs for social support with awareness of cultural determinants.*

6. *Evaluate the contribution of social support to the integration of health-promoting behaviors into family lifestyles.*

7. *Develop effective strategies for implementing the concept of social support in nursing education, research, and practice.*

Social networks are generally understood in structural terms, described as linking to and interacting with surrounding social institutions such as family, neighborhood, and religious organizations. Social support, on the other hand, focuses on the interpersonal exchanges among selected network members (Cohen, Underwood, & Gottlieb, 2000). By providing assistance in meeting individuals' emotional and physical needs, as well as buffering the effect of stressful events on quality of life (Chappell, 1991), social support has been viewed as integral to health promotion.

Social support and social networks are beneficial to the health of individuals in a variety of ways; they are associated with a reduction in mortality rates, an improved recovery from serious illness, and an increasing use of preventative health care practices. Social relationships appear

---

This chapter has been updated to provide the reader with knowledge about the relationships among the variables of social support within diverse social systems, as well as recent evidence of the role social relationships play in promoting health and wellness in acknowledgement of the previous author, Patricia Roth.

to be particularly important to families and individuals who are faced with health care decisions. Moreover, health promotion that incorporates social support is a contemporary intervention trend that capitalizes on conventional and progressive family forms. Empirical data on long-term health care use document that family and friends continue to serve as the primary providers of caregiving to the those who are infirm (Blazer, 1982; Bullock, 2002; Williams & Dilworth-Anderson, 2002). Although the idea of family support endures, the structure and role allocation are in a process of transformation. Especially striking are changes in the ways American families are caring for their dependents across the life cycle as more diversity in family lifestyles is experienced.

Shifts in family structure and function are most conspicuous. Many of the burgeoning number of immigrants, for example, develop relational networks that include friends, co-workers, and other community dwellers who provide social support (Bullock, 2002; Oxman & Hull, 2001). The direct effect of these networks is to enhance well-being through support of and help with day-to-day activities and interactions. The indirect, or buffering, effect suggests instead that social support mediates the effect of stressful events on quality of life (Chappell, 1991). Because research has firmly established the extensive involvement of family and friends in health promotion (Cohen, Underwood, & Gottlieb, 2000; Ford-Gilboe, 1997; Hagerty & Williams, 1999; Krause, Ingersol-Dayton, Liang, & Sugisawa, 1999), it becomes apparent that to meet the health care needs of an increasingly older and diverse population, nurse practitioners and other health promotion professionals must understand the influential nature of support systems provided by family, friends, and neighbors, that is, social support networks

Although family social support is not a new phenomenon, public recognition of it has increased as a result of numerous reports of the beneficial effects of informal support networks on the health of poor and culturally diverse populations (Eng & Young, 1992; Suarez, Lloyd, Weiss, Rainbolt, & Pulley, 1994; Williams & Dilworth-Anderson, 2002). In general, research findings continue to suggest that social support can affect mental and physical health through its influence on emotions (Krause, Ellison, & Marcum, 2002; Gale et al., 2001), cognition (Chin, Monroe, & Fiscella, 2000; Ellison, Boardman, Williams, & Jackson, 2001), and behavior (Young, Gittlesohn, Charleston, Felix-Aaron, & Appeal, 2001; Williams & Bond, 2002). Incorporating social support into health promotion and developing interventions to reduce disease and increase wellness among all groups are important roles for nurses. Formal methods of assessing support systems can be achieved through a social network analysis. The purpose of this chapter is to explore the role of social support in health promotion including health status, with particular focus on cultural determinants, and to discuss research on family social support in the health arena.

The Concepts of Social Support and Social Networks

The convincing evidence of the relationship between social support and health status makes evaluation of the social network a necessary tool for intervention. Social support refers to four broad classes of assisting behavior or acts: emotional support (affect, esteem, concern), appraisal support (feedback, affirmation), informational support (suggestion, advice, information), and instrumental support (aid in labor, money, time). Support can be defined as actual provision or receipt of assistance, and the individual perception of the support can be either positive or negative.

For the purposes of understanding how family systems attend to the needs of family members, all these definitions are relevant because each makes an important contribution to what is known about social support specifically and about social relations more generally. Although these definitions and their applications have made significant contributions to the health promotion field, several convincing arguments have been made that the use of a broader social network approach, rather than just an examination of social support, can be advantageous for understanding health behaviors across diverse groups.

As a conceptual tool of analysis the social network provides a framework that enables practitioners to examine numerous network characistics, not just social support. It allows one to investigate the context of interpersonal ties (e.g., the number of ties and the frequency of interactions, which might provide different types of social support with different effects) and to identify and apply network characteristics when developing interventions aimed at improving health status.

Mitchell's (1969) earlier metaphorical use of the term *social networks* referred to "a specific set of linkages among a defined set of persons, with the additional property that the characteristics of these linkages as a whole be used to interpret the social behavior of the person involved" (p. 2). He proposed two categories of criteria to describe the characteristics of a social network: (1) *morphological*, or those referring to the relationship or patterning of the links in the network (e.g., the size and density of the network; the number of people in the network who know one another) and (2) *interactional*, or those referring to the nature of the links (i.e., the dynamics of the network).

The morphological criteria are as follows:
1) Anchor: a specific individual whose behavior an observer is attempting to explain
2) Reachabililty: the extent to which an individual can contact other people who are important to him or her, either directly or through others
3) Density: the extent to which everyone in a set of individual's contacts knows everyone else
4) Range: the number of people with whom an individual might be in direct and regular contact, as well as the social backgrounds of those people

The interactional criteria are the following:
1) Content: the meanings that the persons in the network attribute to the relationship (e.g., kinship, friendship)
2) Reciprocity: the extent to which contact between individuals in the network is unidirectional or mutual
3) Durability: the underlying set of consciously recognized rights and responsibilities regarding other people in the network
4) Intensity: the degree to which individuals in the network are prepared to honor obligations or the emotional closeness between the focal person and network members

5) Frequency: the amount of contact among people in a network

The preceding lists are not necessarily complete, and the significance of these characteristics is quite variable, depending on the needs and situations of a given individual and network. For example, an individual recovering from severe injuries sustained in an automobile accident may benefit from a small, close-knit (high-density), intimate network that provides affective support but may not have enough members who are able to provide instrumental support, such as contacting work associates or providing transportation, household chores, and even assistance with activities of daily living including getting in and out of bed and chairs. Similarly, a recently divorced individual may initially welcome a small, dense network that includes a confidante but later will need a larger network with more weak ties (bridging ties), which can provide new information and access to new social contacts. The empirical evidence regarding the role of social support in buffering stress suggests that different types of support are called for in response to different stressors and in different cultures. Another distinction of a social network is its *functional* characteristics, which refer to the activities or roles performed by network members including affective support (caring, love), instrumental support (tangible aid), development of new social contacts, and maintenance of social identity.

Therefore even though there are some network characteristics that are significantly related to well-being and thus have particular relevance to health promotion, the needs of any individual and network must be assessed before an intervention is carried out.

Social Trends and Support Network

Family

Family plays an important role in individuals' lives and provides a unique set of functions not met by formal organizations. Despite its ever-changing forms and meanings, family is at the center of interpersonal influence; it is a source of mutual exchange, a reference group, and a social context, as well as a health promotion area. Universally, the two most fundamental tasks of the family are to provide care and socialization for a network or an individual. Today, there is no typical American family. It is more accurate to speak of *types* of families with diverse organizational patterns, diverse lifestyles, and diverse living arrangements. There are a variety of family types, ranging from the conventional nuclear family to the contemporary same-sex couple with a child. Such families include the dyadic nuclear family, the single-parent family, the intergenerational family, the middle-aged to elderly couple, the institutional family, the foster family, kin and non-kin networks, the unmarried parent with one or more children, and the unmarried person without children. When a number of family types are conjoined into larger units, they make up the extended or consanguine family (Skolnick & Skolnick, 2000). A critical attribute of the extended family is its morphological characteristic of range or the number of people with whom an individual might be in contact with as a means for meeting certain social needs.

As America has become more urbanized and industrialized and as people have become more mobile, the obsolescence of the extended family may have been anticipated. However, a close look into family life has revealed that the predicted disintegration of the extended family has not come about. Family structure has modified its form, and family ties are maintained by people on the basis of lifestyle rather than biological relationships alone. Ethnic and cultural differences in family social support networks contribute to the variation in patterns and sources of care.

The identification of family support networks requires an examination of gender, socioeconomic, age, and ethnic or minority differences in the structure or makeup of individual networks. Special roles and the importance of various members in the network can determine the extent to which an individual has access to social support. Family helping and intrafamily exchanges are more intense in some ethnic groups than others (Mok & Martinson, 1999; Mui & Burnette, 1994; Delgado & Tennstedt, 1997). Most ethnic minority groups in this country have been shown to have close family ties and a preference for informal support as opposed to formal health care services. Some data, as alluded to previously, suggest that as higher socioeconomic status is

achieved, the norm of family social support sometimes evolves into a norm of linking to formal services when long-term care is imminent. This might be simply based on socioeconomic factors. However, it may also be related to the second factor, which is the changing demographics of ethnic minority groups. Regardless of interethnic group differences, there are tendencies for people to be living longer, for multiple generations to be living at the same time, for fewer children to be born (in most but not all minority groups), and for younger and middle-aged women (the traditional caregivers) to be employed for pay outside the home. Even more ominous are the decrease in socioeconomic status of some groups and the disruptive forces that are devastating some geographical areas and affecting specific minority groups more intensely. These include drug and alcohol dependency, unemployment, and crime, paralleled by more pregnancies, decreases in rates of marriage, and increases in marital disruption. All of these changes serve to decrease the number of people available to provide family social support. Undoubtedly, alternate arrangements will continue to be made in networks that perform these much needed functions. The increase in the number of grandparents raising grandchildren is one such social trend indicative of networks optimizing the interface between conventional and progressive family forms. The Research Synopsis presents a study about grandmothers rearing at least one grandchild.

In the past few years, a growing body of research on family support networks (Anderson & Tomlinson, 1992; Ben-Ari & Pines, 2002; Berkman & Syme, 1979; Oxman & Hull, 2001) has documented the impact of social support on health behaviors, both in prevention and in treatment. Epidemiological data confirm that social support is related to longevity and mortality rates. Berkman and Syme (1979) identified the importance of social ties in a large-scale study, which showed that people with the lowest levels of social contact had mortality rates that were two to four and a half times greater than those with strong social networks. This was constant even when lifestyle factors such as smoking and alcohol consumption, which are known to influence disease, were taken into account. Empirical data have shown that various psychosocial factors are

RESEARCH SYNOPSIS

GRANDPARENTS AS PARENTS

An important aspect of health promotion, nationally and internationally, is family social support, particularly in interventions with poor and ethnic minority populations. Increasingly, grandmothers are the primary caregivers for young children. It behooves health professionals to become knowledgeable about the changing role of family support systems to develop and implement interventions that focus on family strengths and cohesiveness.

In a diverse study of African American, Latina, and white grandmothers who had primary responsibility for providing care to at least one grandchild, researchers concluded that family social support has positive and negative attributes. Some grandmothers reported financial strain, cramped living arrangements, role restrictions, and social isolation. However, there were reported benefits of greater life satisfaction and positive feelings derived from their commitment to maintaining family cohesiveness.

Because family social support can influence health status and behaviors, nurses need to examine the relationship between the variables of social support, stress, and health promotion. Nursing intervention should include the assessment of social support networks to determine effective strategies for promoting health across cultures.

Bullock, K. (2001). Healthy family systems? The changing role of grandparents in rural America. *Education and Ageing, 16,* 163-178.

kin. Family members are willing to make major sacrifices to provide care. Even when the care recipient is impaired, families make great attempts to continue providing care (Bullock, 2000). The structure of support operating in society is "hierarchical-compensatory," with family as the most preferred source of assistance, followed by friends and neighbors, and lastly, formal services or agencies (Cantor, 1983; Jette, Tennstedt, & Branch, 1993). Within this structure, various members provide different functions and support. Either a spouse or an adult child provides the majority of care. Additionally, most family caregivers are women.

The provision of social support has rewards but also includes demands. Health care providers need to be sensitive to the stressors and strains experienced by those who function in such roles. Identification of the demanding aspects of caregiving is an initial step in health promotion intervention plans. The strain can be categorized into three types: financial, physical, and emotional. Financial strain can emerge from the actual expenses of caregiving such as the cost of medications or gas used to take the older person shopping. Financial strain also occurs as a result of the sacrificed opportunities that accompany the role of care provider. For example, a daughter who quits a job to care for her mother gives up money from employment. In this example the daughter is relinquishing her wages to be available for her loved one. This type of stress is particularly difficult for women, who often face difficult decisions about their employment. Compared with men, female care providers are more likely to quit their jobs, cut back on work hours (Bullock, 2000), or decline job promotion or advancement opportunities (Anastas, Gibeau, & Larson, 1990). This situation can cause problems for women in late life because this pattern reduces their ability to save for their own retirement.

Physical exertion is another type of strain in caregiving. The physical demands of caregiving can be great. Someone who requires assistance in toileting or bathing needs to be lifted, moved, and positioned. Continued assistance can result in injuries to the caregiver. Because most family caregivers are spouses or adult children, they may be experiencing some physical limitations themselves (Tennstedt, 1999). The stress of trying to

predictors of health behavior and mental health status. Among these factors are stress and well-being, social support, and social networks. Furthermore, the association between social support and a reduced risk of physical disorders, as well as social support's buffering effect on stress-induced illness, has been documented (Erdwins, 2001).

Although family members continue to be the primary sources of care for those who are dependent, fictive kin are another source of support, either in the absence of or in addition to biological

juggle responsibilities becomes exhausting and physically draining. Many caregivers have full-time jobs, care for children, and assist an older parent. Little time is left for these people to attend to their own health needs, such as exercising and eating balanced meals.

A third type of strain experienced by family caregivers is emotional strain. Having a personal relationship with the care recipient makes the experience of caregiving emotionally charged. Because some people are quite frail, fears of hurting the older person are common. Decision making becomes a source of strain when the caregiver assumes responsibility for health or residential decisions. What happens, for example, when a son thinks his mother should not continue to live alone, but his mother refuses to move? These decisions become even more complicated when other family members choose sides, creating family division. The progression of certain health conditions can evoke strong feelings for a family as well. For example, a grandparent with Alzheimer's disease may not be able to remember the names of the grandchildren or even recognize their faces. This can cause distress within the family support network and greater emotional strain.

Health care professionals helping clients and their families need to be sensitive to the strains of providing informal support. Understanding family issues is an important part of health promotion with any population. Individuals may need to be referred to social service agencies for assistance. Providing family caregivers with information about the normal aging process, medical conditions, possible community linkages, and referrals to professional and medical staff have been found to be useful.

Although these interventions are beneficial for families, financial strain may continue in the absence of an insurance policy that supplements income. Often, poor and minority groups who have low incomes are most likely to rely on social support networks for significant amounts of care and assistance.

Friends and Neighbors

Friends and neighbors are other resources within an informal support network, particularly for an older person. Even when older people have inter-actions with adult children, nearby friends and neighbors may be better suited to perform certain tasks. Frequently, friends live closer to an older person than do family members and are able to respond quickly in case of an emergency. When family members live a long distance away, they rely on information from neighbors about their relative's functioning. A neighbor who notices that newspapers are piling up on a porch or a friend who notices that cigarette butts are being extinguished on living room chairs can provide information about the individual's functioning. Friends and neighbors are the main sources of support for older people with no family. For example, a couple may invite the widow who lives next door to holiday dinners. Friends from church may assist the woman by transporting her to services. Even when family members are involved, friendships allow people to have different types of relationships. Friends provide a sense of intimacy, especially important when an older person loses a significant other, such as a spouse.

Friends and neighbors are important resources in the family social support network and should not be overlooked in health promotion inter-vention. These people are familiar faces for an older person and provide a connection to the larger society. Just looking out a window and knowing the names of people passing on the street can be a source of security and comfort for an older person. Health care providers can foster supportive relationships between an older person and neighbors. Health care professionals must also be sensitive to an older person's desire to remain connected to friends and communities.

Church and Other Religious Affiliates

In addition to family, friends, and neighbors, social support can take the form of organized community involvement. Religious affiliations with churches and synagogues are the most common type of community groups that provide social support. Religious ties continue to be important sources of support, especially for people who grew up during a religious era. Besides providing spiritual and fellowship benefits, many churches and synagogues have outreach programs for members (see Chapter 8 for more information).

These programs include ministries to homebound or hospitalized members, special transportation to worship services, special services for the hearing or visually impaired, meal or grocery supply programs, and social and recreational events (Taylor, Ellison, Chatters, Levin, & Lincoln, 2000).

After decades of neglect, current research is exploring the complex relationships between religious affiliation and health (Derose, Fox, Reigadas, & Hawes-Dawson, 2000; Krause et al., 2002; Krause, Ellison, Shaw, Marcum, & Boardman, 2001; Mirola, 1999). Mounting evidence links church-based social support with a range of health outcomes, including higher levels of psychological well-being among adults living with HIV and AIDS (Ueno & Adams, 2001). In a study of perceived benefits of religious and spiritual support among older adults living with HIV/AIDS, participants reported that religious affiliation helped ease the emotional burden of the illness, facilitate acceptance of it, and relieve associated fears (Siegel & Schrimshaw, 2002).

Healthy lifestyle outcomes including decreased symptoms of depression (Nelson, Rosenfeld, Breitbart, & Galietta, 2002), smoking cessation (Koenig et al., 1998), increased compliance with mammography recommendations (Derose et al., 2000), and weight control (Kumanyika, 2002) have all been linked to social support provided by religious affiliates. Moreover, there is a demonstrable relationship between religious involvement and health for certain segments of the population. The church may be an important and sometimes overlooked resource for health promotion. For African Americans, the church can collaborate with formalized service agencies to provide more comprehensive and accessible services (Taylor et al., 2000). In Japanese culture, religious involvement is associated with the decision to provide social support, and those who are caregivers often rate their own health more favorably than those who are less involved in helping others (Krause, Ingersoll-Dayton, Liang, & Sugisawa, 1999). For people in rural areas where there are few agency support programs, churches are major resources for community and family support services. Informal helpers are also used as referral sources for those who need additional services, such as therapy or financial assistance. Churches provide vital outreach services to link members with needed health and wellness programs and services.

Mutual Self-Help Groups

Social networks include people who care about others and provide guidance and instruction that may come in the forms of emotional, physical, or psychological assistance. Mutual self-help groups are important because they unite individuals with a common goal and because the assistance they provide is thought to supplement individuals' family resources (Roberts et al., 1999). These types of networks have had a positive impact on cancer prevention (Helgeson, Cohen, Schulz, & Yasko, 2000), problem drinking behaviors (Hargerty & Williams, 1999), physical fitness (Young et al., 2001), and even life-threatening diseases such as diabetes (Williams & Bond, 2002). Many participants in these groups indicate that the mutual support provided by the group members is evidenced by cohesiveness, a feeling of belonging, and the sharing of common issues.

Support groups and mutual help systems, although not limited to the elderly, may have special relevance for this age group. "Self-care refers to actions that individuals take to promote their own well-being or that of their families and friends. Mutual help groups are comprised of individuals who share a common condition and meet to give each other support" (Bernadette, Wright, Minkler, & Fullarton, 1981, p. 50). A major advantage of both groups is the emphasis on self-determination of the members, who actively participate and structure the group experiences. Some health care professionals stress the need for more of these kinds of groups because too frequently projects are started and maintained by professionals, rather than by long-term or senior members. Some mutual help networks offer monitoring services for participants with recently diagnosed diabetes; members help each other stay on diets and take medications. Another example is a program in St. Louis that trains informal helpers to provide services such as telephone reassurance, social contact, and shopping assistance to other elderly community members. Additionally, these volunteers maintain regular contact with assigned neighbors and are sources for referrals if other needs arise (Ozawa

& Morrow-Howell, 1988). Furthermore, social support has been associated with exercise self-care, and diet-specific positive family interactions have been associated with better adherence to diet (Williams & Bond, 2002). Self-care and mutual help systems allow participants to be both recipients and providers of service to others.

In a study to test a health promotion intervention, researchers monitored the family social support provided to people older than 65 years with chronic medical conditions who were discharged from the hospital to the home (McWilliam et al., 1999). They concluded that although inherent in self-care and mutual support is the goal of family members helping one another, health care professionals are important components of a successful system. Health care professionals can be instrumental in identifying a need for a support group and in assisting in the facilitation of the group. Thus competencies in family group process and an understanding of behavioral, cultural, and psychological aspects of social network dynamics are essential. Skills in these areas are beneficial in developing and maintaining mutual self-help groups. Health care professionals can also promote group participation and serve as a resource for referral of potential members.

Implications for Social Support

Although networks can be examined from the perspective of the individual and interactions with members of his or her network, the strategies discussed here are examples of entire social systems and the interconnectedness within and among networks. Here, relationships can be identified among sets of individuals and involve multiple networks. Within this perspective, there are two broad categories.

In the first category, networks aim to enhance the entire support system, with the intervention working through the various helpers within the network. The care providers are lay people to whom others naturally turn for advice, emotional support, and tangible aid. These *natural helpers* provide informal, spontaneous assistance, which is so much a part of everyday life that its value is often not recognized. They provide day care for young and old; advice and emotional support on health, personal, family, and financial matters; and referral information to formal agencies when necessary. Natural helpers are most often characterized as persons who are respected and trusted, who listen well, and who are empathic, sufficiently in control of their own life circumstances, and responsive to the needs of others. The identification of such natural helpers for an intervention may be facilitated, for example, through a community center or a church group, given the extent to which these kinds of organizations are accustomed to working with the natural caregiver to strengthen network resources.

In the second category, networks are developed explicitly to bring together interacting and overlapping groups, usually through the identification of key opinion leaders, to engage in community-wide health promotion. The strengthening of supportive network linkages has been shown to affect such health care practices as increased participation in breast and cervical cancer screening tests (McGraw et al., 2000). Social network models depend on the effects from naturally occurring exchanges of social support between individuals or between an individual and a group. Exchanges occur naturally through preexisting ties based on friendship or kinship among a set of people. Support in the form of caring, tangible aid, or information from trusted neighbors can influence perceptions and reactions to medical treatment. These networks may build coalitions to mediate between service agencies and provide effective family support and health promotion intervention. Efforts toward social support in Canada are presented in the Canadian Perspectives box.

Family Social Support Intervention

Research indicates that social support systems influence health behaviors. Family members provide essential psychosocial support and act as a conduit for information necessary for illness prevention and health promotion. In a community of African American and Latina women who reported having breast and cervical cancer screening examinations, family members were most successful in encouraging health behaviors (McGraw et al., 2000). Social support may also be important in recovery from sports-related

CANADIAN PERSPECTIVES
CANADIAN SOCIAL SUPPORT AGENCIES AND FAMILY ISSUES

Nicole Letourneau, PhD, MN, RN
University of Alberta
Miriam Stewart, PhD
University of Alberta

Since the release of the Ottawa Charter for Health Promotion (World Health Organization, 1986) and the more recent report of the National Forum on Health (1997), health system reform in Canada has emphasized health maintenance, health promotion, population health, and primary health care. An important outcome involves the movement of health care from institutions to communities. Consumer involvement in the primary health care movement promotes self-care, mutual aid, and public participation. Canadian governments, both federal and provincial, have been lobbied to emphasize the determinants of health by increasing support for vulnerable people such as low-income families, immigrant and refugee families, aboriginal families, and individuals with chronic health conditions and their family caregivers. In response to this public pressure from health consumers, in 1989 the House of Commons passed a unanimous resolution to eradicate child poverty by 2000 and, in 1991, ratified the United Nations Convention of the Rights of the Child and made commitments to provide special recognition for children and an adequate standard of living for families (National Council of Welfare, 1999). An outcome of this movement has been to provide new parents with up to one year of paid parental leave to care for

their newborns. Canadian provinces have also developed extramural or homecare programs for house-bound acutely or chronically ill clients and for unpaid family caregivers as a result of public demand (Stewart, 2000).

The nursing profession in Canada has embraced the shift toward active participation of clients in their own care and of families in the care of their ill relatives, whether in health promotion or health maintenance. As a result, social support by family, friends, lay helpers, neighbors, volunteers, and mutual aid self-help groups is widely encouraged (Stewart & Reutter, 2001). These shifts are in keeping with the trend toward supporting people with chronic illnesses in their homes. Today, most Canadians living with chronic conditions are cared for and supported by family members. Nevertheless, there is a danger that the health care system will abandon the family caregivers (Neufeld & Harrison, 2000). Family caregivers who stop work to provide care are significantly older and have lower incomes and fewer social supports than their non-caregiving counterparts. Relinquishment of work roles may predispose caregivers to social isolation and social vulnerability (Stewart & Langille, 2000). Homecare services in Canada are still seeking to meet the challenge of providing care to clients and have not provided sufficient

support to unpaid family caregivers. Recent fluctuations in health care funding to provinces compound the challenge of providing adequate homecare support and services (Stewart, 2002a, 2002b).

Canadian demographics are changing, represented by increasing numbers of elderly, immigrants, families in poverty, homeless people, and children with special needs (Statistics Canada, 2001). In spite of the House of Commons' resolution to eradicate child poverty, in 1997 14% of families lived in poverty. The demand for affordable housing for families in poverty is compounded by the movement of new immigrants to cities and the persistent problem of homelessness in cities. Further, medical advances are making it possible for children with special needs (e.g., very low birth weight infants) to live longer and more productive lives with the help of technology. Families face significant burdens (e.g., unpredictability, financial concerns, isolation, and coping with constant demands) in caring for their multiple-needs family members at home, and the community is frequently not equipped to help (Alexander, 2002). The health care demands of the elderly and the technology-dependent may outpace the ability of younger Canadians to fund quality care through their income taxes.

CANADIAN PERSPECTIVES
CANADIAN SOCIAL SUPPORT AGENCIES AND FAMILY ISSUES — cont'd

Funding limitations will continue to challenge nurses to demonstrate that they are uniquely qualified to provide homecare for clients and families rather than their technically trained counterparts, such as personal care attendants and licensed practical nurses. Recent research indicates that the clients of university-educated nurses are better educated about their health needs and practice better self care (O'Brien-Pallas et al., 2002). Nurses will be challenged to demonstrate the effectiveness of support interventions in research and practice to influence government policies that affect families. Interventions tested in the Social Support Research Program include peer visitor support for family caregivers of seniors with chronic conditions, telephone and group support for seniors with disabilities, telephone dyadic support for family caregivers of seniors with strokes or Alzheimer's disease, online support for adolescents with cerebral palsy and spina bifida, telephone support for parents of children with diabetes and cystic fibrosis, and home visiting support for adolescent mothers (Stewart, 2000). Nurses will be challenged to consider these types of transformative and cost-effective models for support services and programs offered to families.

References

Alexander, E. (2002, April). Daily struggles: Living with long-term childhood technology dependence. *9th International Nursing Research Symposium*, Montreal, Quebec, Canada.

National Council of Welfare. (1999). *Preschool children: Promises to keep*. Ottawa, Ontario, Canada: Government of Canada.

National Forum on Health. (1997). *Canada health action: Building on the legacy*. Ottawa, Ontario, Canada: Minister of Public Works and Government Services.

Neufeld, A., & Harrison, M. (2000). Family caregiving: Issues in gaining access to support. In M. Stewart (Ed.), *Chronic conditions and caregiving in Canada: Social support strategies* (pp. 247-273). Toronto, Ontario, Canada: University of Toronto Press.

O'Brien-Pallas, L., et al. (2002). Evaluation of a client care delivery model, part 2: Variability in client outcomes in community home nursing. *Nursing Economics, 20*, 13-21.

Statistics Canada. *2001 Census*. Retrieved from http://www12.statcan.ca/English/census01.

Stewart, M. (2000). *Community nursing: Promoting Canadians' health* (2nd ed.). Toronto, Ontario, Canada: Saunders.

Stewart, M. (2002a, July). *Supporting vulnerable people's health through research*. Invited keynote speaker, 11th International Conference on Personal Relationships, Halifax, Nova Scotia, Canada.

Stewart, M. (2002b, July). *Gender, sex, health, and health care*. Invited presentation to Romanow Commission on Future of Health Care, Calgary, Alberta, Canada.

Stewart, M., & Langille, L. (2000). A framework for social support assessment and intervention in the context of chronic conditions and caregiving. In M. Stewart (Ed.), *Chronic conditions and caregiving in Canada* (pp. 1-28). Toronto, Ontario, Canada: University of Toronto Press.

Stewart, M., & Reutter, L. (2001). Fostering partnerships between peers and professionals. *Canadian Journal of Nursing Research, 33*, 97-116.

World Health Organization (WHO), Health & Welfare Canada (HWC), and Canadian Public Health Association (CPNA). (1986). *Ottawa charter for health promotion*. Ottawa, Ontario, Canada: Canadian Public Health Association.

Canadian spelling is used.

injuries. Research data have revealed that various types of emotional, informational, and tangible support from family networks reduce distress and increase positive outcomes related to injury coping and rehabilitation (Bianco, 2001). Furthermore, social relationships can motivate an individual to adhere to exercise and weight-control regimens. In an examination of influence of spouse participation on the likelihood that individuals would continue attending a 12-month fitness program, it was found that family social support has an effect on mood state and self-motivation to adhere to a program (Raglin, 2001). Social support has been correlated with other healthy lifestyle behaviors including smoking cessation (McMahon & Jason, 2000) and limiting alcohol use (Bonin, McCreary, & Sadava, 2000; West, Sweeting, & Ecob, 1999).

Perhaps the greatest debate concerning intervention with family support networks has to do with assessing family needs for social support with awareness of cultural determinants. In the comparison of minority and majority groups, a major question is whether a substantial proportion of the documented differences in social support is simply artifactual or primarily the result of socioeconomic factors. It is clear that some differences are more resource-based than others. If the focus in question is access to health care and other formal services, it seems likely that economic resources are critical. Nevertheless, the degree to which an individual prefers homogenous, ethnically based experiences in medical or health care services may not be solely a matter of economic resources. There is evidence that ethnic and cultural insensitivity is a barrier to the receipt of services, even in the absence of financial barriers (Gamble, 1993). The question is one that is clearly a complex one because individuals of lower socioeconomic status have networks that are dense, homogeneous, geographically limited, and consist predominantly of family. As an individual moves up the socioeconomic ladder, he or she is more likely to have a less dense, more heterogeneous, geographically dispersed network, which consists of both family and friends, and therefore provides a wider array of potential access to services of other resources.

In ethnic and cultural minority networks, family ties and expectations of family caregiving and filial piety are generally stronger. In certain groups, the church or a specific religion has been shown to play a special role (Williams & Dilworth-Anderson, 2002). This has frequently been noted for African Americans but is also true for other groups in which a unique religion or religious tradition plays an important role (e.g., Catholics, Jews, and American Indians). These differences and others in combination represent a composite difference in values and norms, which affect the individual and his or her family's expectations concerning social support. These other identifying characteristics or forms are not necessarily tied to family. Thus although church members are not family, members of the same church might assume substantial roles as a service providers or facilitators for each other. Approaches to assessment of social support need to clarify how these resources can be optimized and, perhaps, complemented.

Assessment of Social Support

An assessment of individual and family needs for support requires an understanding of the concepts of social support and the extent of the network. It is important to show knowledge and to foster respect, confidence, trust, and hope to gain creditability in clinical practice. This requires a genuinely caring attitude, acknowledgement of the abilities of the individual and family network, an understanding of what is unique and different, and an assessment of how much the uniqueness and differences could promote health practices. Expectations of change should be compatible with the cultural variation of the family lifestyle. The intervention approach should be conceptualized in a manner that is consistent with the cultural value system of the people in the family support network.

Social context is an important component of intervention approach. A helpful tool for assessing potential for support in the social context is the genogram. Members of social networks tend to respond positively when given the opportunity to sketch out a family assemblage that illustrates intergenerational connectedness. An additional tool is the ecomap, which can be quite useful in examining social support networks. This allows for a depiction of family contacts with those outside the nuclear family and extends to formal organizations (Ross & Cobb, 1990).

Genogram

The genogram, a family tree that specifies significant information about each individual for at least three generations, is a useful assessment tool for gaining understanding of support networks (Figure 6-1). By studying a genogram, one can identify the effects of such things as size of family, birth position in the family, naming patterns, and major behavior patterns. This method of exploring the family system can yield much previously unrecognized information and help the interviewer see how the family influences the individual. Discussions with family members about important events in the life of the family can provide deeper understanding about the way the family functions. This search for understanding

can yield fascinating facts but can also open old wounds and thus be painful, yet recognizing and dealing with pain can be effective in the helping process. The genogram as an assessment tool is often central in the management of long-term care for clients because of its utility in identifying and tracking potential social support. However, practitioners should have adequate training and competencies in handling emotional triggers and responses in this process (Wright & Leahey, 1994).

Ecomap

In understanding the functioning of any social system, it is important to know how decisions are made in that network. This includes identifying which decisions are individual ones, which are made in a subgroup, and which belong to the total network. Since the family interacts as a part

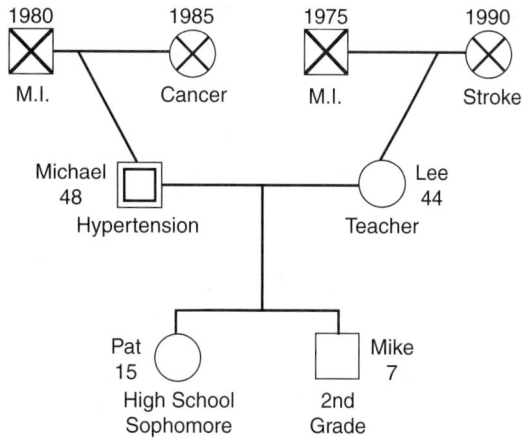

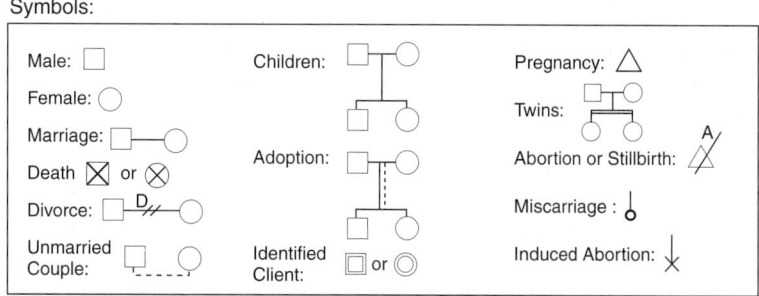

Figure 6-1   Family genogram.

of a larger environment, the ecomap is a helpful tool because it provides an overview of the nature and extent of the influences of systems such as church, school, cultural groups, extended family, and the like on the family (Figure 6-2). At the center is the family or household, and the outer circles denote significant relationships in the network. Lines between the inner and outer circles show the extent of connectedness. Strong connections are illustrated with straight lines, and broken lines signify weak connections. The width of the lines illustrates the strength of the relationship. Directions of arrows demonstrate the flow of resources and energy.

The interactions of the practitioner and the individual are at the center of health promotion.

The practitioner's use of self is a major tool in the helping endeavor. The practitioner's use of self is a major tool in facilitating motivation among clients and members of their social support networks to increase health behaviors and attitudes toward wellness. The genogram and the ecomap can assist in determining how the family network is organized and the extent to which those in the network perform certain tasks and support services.

Indexes of Social Support

The Social Network Index (Berkman & Syme, 1979) has long been a tool for network analysis. It takes into account the number of people con-

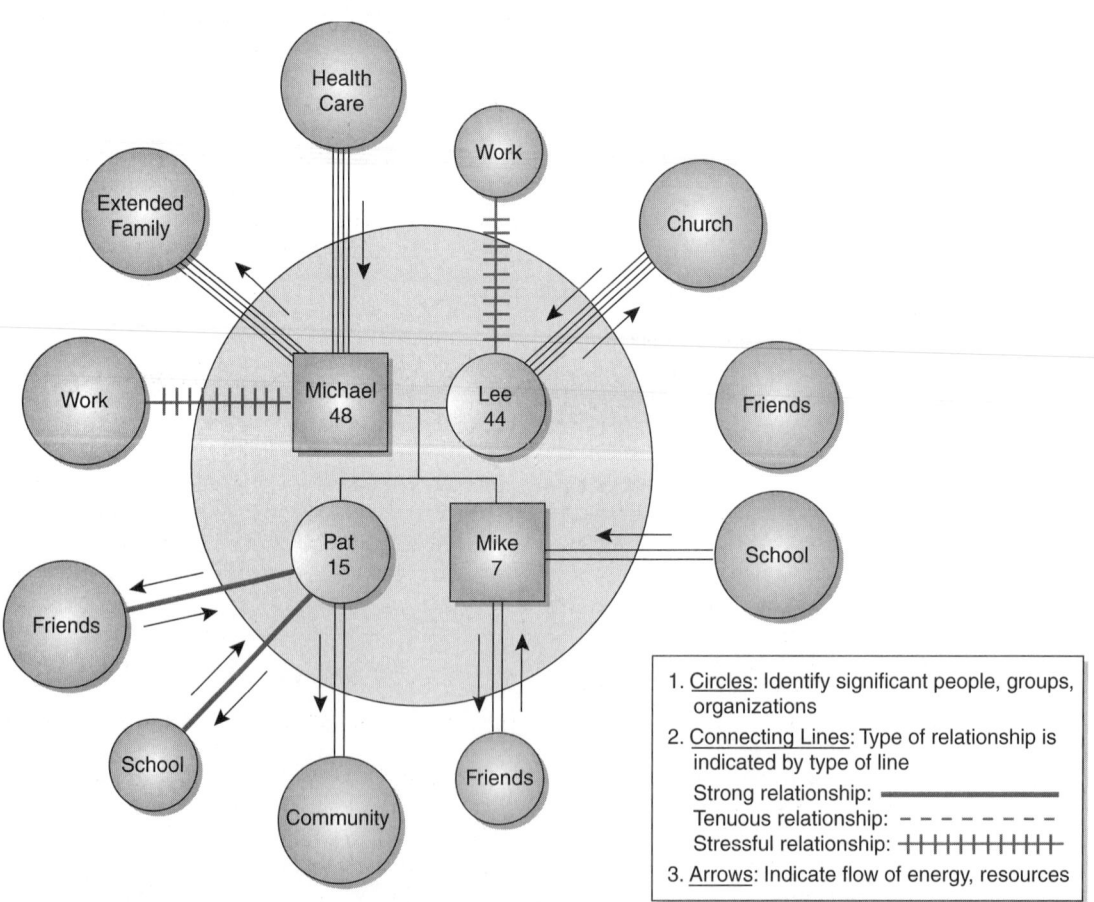

Figure 6-2 Family ecomap.

sidered to be close friends and relatives, frequency of interaction, marital status, and affiliation with formal organizations and social clubs. On the other hand, the Arizona Social Support Interview Schedule includes these measures and more, such as perceived satisfaction with the support that is provided and the assessment of the need for support (Barrera, 1981). These tools are useful in family interviews and can serve as assessment guides. They are also beneficial in the research process of social network analysis. Recently, Brissette, Cohen, and Seeman (2000) provided an update on how to apply social network analysis in measuring social integration for health promotion. This can be done through the assessment of stable patterns that exist among relational ties, which typically correlate with social integration. Network size is the commonly used measure. However, network density, or the extent to which those in the network are acquainted, is a useful point of data collection in assessing family social support. These measures of network structure can be mapped on a sociogram or matrix, simply listing the members in rows and columns, with attributes of the ties (e.g., stressors, strengths) between those involved being given numeric value. This assessment can provide insight into personal networks that may allow for access to social support, and the supportive relations that ensue from these networks can effect healthy lifestyles (Bianco, 2001; Bryan, Fitzpatrick, Crawford, & Fischer, 2001; Raglin, 2001; Ueno & Adams, 2001; Young et al., 2001). The International Network for Social Network Analysis (INSNA) website provides reference sources for analyzing and managing network data. The website address is provided in the Website Resources box at the end of the chapter.

Another dimension of the assessment of social support is the individual's subjective appraisal. This relevant support dimension includes perceived happiness with significant relationships, support satisfaction, and the extent of social attachments. Additionally, the Norbeck Social Questionnaire (Norbeck, Lindsey, & Carrieri, 1983) relies on self-reports of key people in the lives of those receiving support, the availability of the support, and the significance of absent relationships. The Social Support Questionnaire developed by Schaefer, Coyne, and Lazurus (1981) assesses

social support through tangible, emotional, and informational indicators that rate each individual according to actual functions performed. The extent to which social support is adequately provided can be measured by the Personal Resource Questionnaire 85, which also involves identifying the persons in the network (Weinert, 1987; Gibson, Cheavens, & Warren, 1998).

Use of social support indexes makes apparent the transactional nature of the health promotion situation. These assessments can be useful in identifying available strengths and resources. Understanding the relationships among those in the social network involves specific behavioral activities. Social support analysis specifies the nature of the support and complements the maps in the assessment process.

With the goal of identifying and using resources or social supports that are either available or potentially available to individuals, families, and groups, nurses incorporate assessment tools for analysis of family social support networks. This is particularly crucial when nurses are working with disadvantaged or oppressed populations, since locating, developing, and using support networks are avenues to empowerment. It is increasingly important, in a time of managed care and resource constraints, for nurses to develop knowledge in this area.

Social Support in Family Nursing

Meeting family health needs is not simply a matter of meeting the needs of one person at one moment in time. If needs are met at the expense of other people in the social network and if transactions between helping professionals and social systems are not balanced in a way that results in mutual benefit, then the individual will have difficulty in maintaining over time any benefits from the nurse-client relationship. If balance is not achieved, it is likely that the situation will either return to its previous state or perhaps worsen. Using a family social support intervention to assist in health promotion means facilitating interactions of those in the network.

In responding to need, nurses should assist family members in identifying strengths and resources in their social network. The availability or perceived availability of instrumental and emotional support should be viewed as a strength of the network that can be used by the practitioner to create appropriate health promotion strategies. Norbeck (1982) provides a guideline for nurse clinicians in assessing family needs and planning effective intervention. Social support is an imperative in this family health nursing approach. In addition to incorporating assumptions of social support, implementation of this approach should include the following:

1) Identification of the network relationships with the use of a genogram or ecomap
2) Establishment of a partnership with the family network with the use of social support assessment tools
3) Clear articulation of an understanding of the challenges/issues presented by the family network
4) Identification of how the social support network functions with other interacting systems
5) Clarification of the strengths of the social support network
6) Identification of health promotion versus health-hindering forces in the network
7) Use of observation, as well as social support questionnaires, for data collection
8) Engagement of the family support network in the health promotion intervention plan

The focus is on the concerns and health needs of the individual in interaction with the social support network. In responding to need, the nurse develops an understanding of the person in the family social network and then assists the individual in developing and carrying out a health promotion plan for meeting his or her needs. In accomplishing this, the strengths, abilities, assets, and capacities of the entire family support network are included.

Implications for Research

Family health nursing and working with families are complex processes. Each person's health care needs are examined from a systemic point of view, and the various aspects of both the person and the person's situation are seen as interacting. The outcomes of these transactions are unique. The nurse practitioner must develop knowledge of the individual to intervene in an effective manner. The extent to which the nurse needs to understand the factors depends, to a degree, on the client's need for social support and the availability of such support. Anderson & Tomlinson (1992) have proposed a classification of knowledge generation related to a family health system paradigm. Evidence of the benefits of family social support indicates that social support should be included/provided as part of a health promotion plan. The determination of need for social support is not simple process if it is done well. It has been noted that families provide a substantial amount of assistance in many areas of daily life. Further, it has been shown that these helpers are willing to make sizeable sacrifices to provide social support. Research that further explores the functions of social support and specific variables that account for its uses could enhance health promotion. Interventions need to be refined and expanded to include culturally diverse components that meet the needs of our increasingly multiethnic society. Furthermore, research should include network orientation for assessment of the integration of formal and informal support. This research approach would direct attention to the quality and strength of the ties of the family social support network as they relate to functional health care needs. Family health nursing intervention could then be developed and delivered to sustain social support services. Professional nursing roles would compensate for deficits in the social support network's ability to meet the individual's needs rather than compensate for the individual's functional deficits. This approach would give public attention and recognition to the important role of social support networks and further direct intervention efforts toward mobilizing and strengthening families, mutual self-help groups, and church and religious organizations to promote public health.

CASE SCENARIO

Mr. B., an 83-year-old retired railroad worker, had become a source of considerable concern to his wife and family. For 6 months, Mr. B. had been roaming around the neighborhood at night and getting lost. His usually neat appearance had become slovenly; he had marked shifts in mood; his memory for both recent and remote events was poor. When he was seen by a psychiatric nurse, Mr. B. was given a diagnosis of chronic brain syndrome, with dementia, which was moderate and of approximately 7 years' duration. He also had a major affective disorder, which was diagnosed as bipolar disorder, depressive episode.

The psychiatric nurse recommended nursing home care for Mr. B. Mrs. B. concurred because she felt unable to cope with her husband's odd and worrisome behavior. She confided this to her oldest daughter (with whom she was very close), telling her the nature of Mr. B's illness and what the nurse had recommended. The oldest daughter agreed and felt that placing her father in a nursing home was the wisest alternative. However, when the matter was discussed with the two youngest daughters, they were adamantly against nursing home placement. They felt their mother should hire a live-in nurse to care for their father. The family had reached an impasse, and the stress of having to make a decision about Mr. B. that would be in everyone's best interest had caused Mrs. B. to become withdrawn and depressed. In addition, remnants of unresolved anger, hurt feelings, and guilt over these feelings began to surface among the adult children and their elderly parents.

Mrs. B. finally confided in a close friend about her dilemma. The friend suggested that Mrs. B. schedule another meeting with the psychiatric nurse to discuss her role in her husband's care and the influence of other family members in that care. Because the family was experiencing a number of interpersonal stresses, Mrs. B. took the friend's advice and sought mental health care for the family.

An assessment of the family and Mr. & Mrs. B. was completed with the use of Pender's framework for family assessment (Pender, Murdaugh, & Parsons, 2002). The results follow.

MAJOR FAMILY STRESSORS

Family stressors include Mr. B's loss of autonomy (e.g., roaming and getting loss), his memory loss, decision regarding nursing home placement, disagreement among the family members, and unresolved feelings.

FAMILY STRENGTHS

Family strengths include a shared concern about Mr. B's long-term care, value assigned to autonomy, affirmation and support for one another.

LIFESTYLE CHANGES INDICATED

Lifestyle changes needed are increased care for Mr. B., more open expression of feelings, and assistance with mediating the unresolved feelings, as well as assistance with coping with behaviors associated with dementia and other health-related conditions.

WEBSITE RESOURCES

ORGANIZATION	WEBSITE ADDRESS
AARP	http://www.aarp.org
Bright Futures	http://www.brightfutures.org
Office of Minority Health	http://www.omhrc.gov/
Family Social Support Project	http://www.npi.ucla.edu/ssg/
Family Support for Disabled Members	http://www.thearc.org/familysupport.html
Social Support Research Program	http://www.ssrp.ualberta.ca/
Family Support	http://www.familysupportamerica.org
Health Care For All	http://www.hcfama.org/
Pediatric Brain Tumor Foundation of the United States	http://www.pbtfus.org/famsvcs/fam_sprt.htm
The Role of Social Support in Midwifery Practice and Research	http://www.efn.org/~djz/birth/HVMA/socialsupport.html
Substance Abuse and Mental Health Administration	http://www.samhsa.gov/
Center for Mental Health Services	http://www.mentalhealth.org/
The Parenting Place	http://www.parentingplace.org
National Network for Child Care	http://www.nncc.org
National Women's Health Information Center	http://www.hsc.wvu.edu/womens-cvh/
International Network for Social Network Analysis	http://www.sfu.ca/~insna/

■ CHAPTER HIGHLIGHTS

- An informal network includes family, friends, neighbors, and members of social groups. Each of these is an actual or potential resource for health promotion.

- Effective intervention requires an understanding of family dynamics and social relationships.

- It is critical for nurses and other health promotion practitioners to possess knowledge and skills to intervene in a variety of ways within a family social support network. For example, family helpers can be linked to respite services that buffer the strains of caregiving.

- Friends and neighbors can provide essential support to family members and should be included in health promotion initiatives.

- Ethnic and cultural variants may be important in the assessment process. Therefore practitioners need to be knowledgeable about strategies for obtaining critical information from family members of diverse groups.

- Churches and synagogues can be organized to provide important health services and often provide social support to families.

- Effective and appropriate family health nursing care considers the importance of family social support and the role of the network in sustaining health promotion.

- The implementation of effective strategies requires knowledge and awareness of cultural determinants and the dynamics of relationships among those in the family support network.

- Social support and social networks have been found to be beneficial to the health of individuals in a variety of ways including reduction in mortality rates, improving recovery from serious illness, and increasing use of preventative health practices.

- Assessment of social support needs and availability can be facilitated through the mapping of family interconnectedness, as well as through contacts with external systems such as agencies and community organizations. This should be done with an awareness of cultural determinants.

- Providing health care is not simply a matter of meeting the needs of one person at one moment in time. Health promoters must be able to analyze the effectiveness of various types of networks in providing social support to families and individuals.

CRITICAL THINKING ACTIVITIES

1. What are the various social support inventories for assessment of family support? How might they be useful in a health promotion setting?

2. Review the ecomap and all its components (see Figure 6-2). Draw your family's relationships to various people, institutions, or agencies while emphasizing nurturing or stress-laden relationships. Discuss how individuals are linked to significant people and how they engage in social support.

3. What are some of the critical issues in assessing social support for ethnic minority groups? Interview a nurse in a long-term care facility about levels of intervention with family support networks used in the facility. What recommendations would you make to the practitioner based on your reading of this chapter?

4. In what ways to do people vary in their need for family social support?

REFERENCES

Anastas, J. W., Gibeau, J. L., & Larson, P. J. (1990). Working families and eldercare: A national perspective in an aging America. *Social Work, 35,* 405-411.

Anderson, K. H., & Tomlinson, P. S. (1992). The family health system as an emerging paradigmatic view for nursing. *Image: Journal of Nursing Scholarship, 24,* 57-63.

Barrera, M. (1981). Models of social support in the adjustment of pregnant adolescents: Assessment issues. In B. H. Gottlieb (Ed.), *Social networks and social support* (pp. 69-96). Beverly Hills: Sage.

Ben-Ari, A., & Pines, A. M. (2002). The changing role of family in utilization of social support: Views from Israeli Jewish and Arab students. *Families in Society: The Journal of Contemporary Human Services, 83,* 93-101.

Berkman, L. F., & Syme, S. L. (1979). Social networks, host resistance and mortality: A nine year follow-up study of Alameda County residents. *American Journal of Epidemiology, 190,* 186-204.

Bernadette, M., Wright, L. D., Minkler, M., & Fullarton, J. (1981). *Self-care and mutual help. Report of the technical committee on health maintenance and health promotion* (White House Conference on Aging) (Publication No. TR-3). Washington, DC: U.S. Government Printing Office.

Bianco, T. (2001). Social support and recovery from sport injury: Elite skiers share their experiences. *Research Quarterly for Exercise and Sport, 72,* 376-381.

Blazer, D. G. (1982). Social support and mortality in an elderly community population. *American Journal of Epidemiology, 115,* 684-694.

Bonin, M. F., McCreary, D. R., Sadava, S. W. (2000). Problem drinking behavior in two community-based samples of adults: Influence of gender, coping, loneliness, and depression. *Psychology of Addictive Behaviors, 14,* 151-161.

Brissette, I., Cohen, S., & Seeman, T. E. (2000). Measuring social integration and social networks. In S. Cohen, L. G. Underwood, B. H. Gottlieb (Eds.), *Social support measurement and intervention: A guide for health and social scientists* (pp. 53-85). New York: Oxford University Press.

Bryan, L., Fitzpatrick, J., Crawford, D., & Fischer, J. (2001). The role of network support and interference in women's perception of romantic, friend, and parental relationships. *Sex Roles: A Journal of Research, 45,* 481-500.

Bullock, K. (2000). Employment and caregiving: A comparison of three ethnic groups of disabled elders and their informal caregivers (Doctoral dissertation, Boston University, 1999). *Dissertation Abstracts International, 60,* 09A.

Bullock, K. (2001). Healthy family systems? The changing role of grandparents in rural America. *Education and Ageing, 16,* 163-178.

Bullock, K. (2002, May). *Bridging cultures through skills development.* Paper presented at the Ninth Annual Spring Bioethics Conference of the Mountain Area Health Education Center, Asheville, NC.

Cantor, M. (1983). Strain among caregivers: A study of experience in the United States. *The Gerontologist, 23,* 597-604.

Chappell, N. L. (1991). The role of family and friends in quality of life. In J. E. Birren, J. E. Lubben, J. C. Rowe, &

D. E. Deutchman (Eds.), *The concept of measurement of quality of life* (pp. 171-190). New York: Academic Press.

Chin, N. P., Monroe, A., & Fiscella, K. (2000). Social determinants of (Un) healthy behaviors. *Education for Health: Change in Learning, 13,* 317-328.

Cohen, S., Underwood, L. G., & Gottlieb, B. H. (2000). *Social support measurement and intervention: A guide for health and social scientists.* New York: Oxford University Press.

Delgado, M. & Tennstedt, S. L. (1997). Making the case for culturally appropriate community services: Puerto Rican elders and their caregivers. *Health & Social Work, 22,* 246-255.

Derose, K. P., Fox, S. A., Reigadas, E., & Hawes-Dawson, J. (2000). Church-based telephone mammography counseling with peer counselors. *Journal of Health Communication, 5,* 175-188.

Ellison, C. G., Boardman, J. D., Williams, D. R. & Jackson, J. S. (2001). Religious involvement, stress, and mental health: Findings from the 1995 Detroit area study. *Social Forces, 80,* 215-250.

Eng, E. & Young, R. (1992). Lay health advisors as community change agents. *Family Community Health, 15,* 24-40.

Erdwins, C. (2001). The relationship of women's role strain to social support, role satisfaction, and self-efficacy. *Family Relations, 50,* 230-239.

Ford-Gilboe, M. (1997). Family strengths, motivation, and resources as predictors of health promotion behavior in single-parent and two-parent families. *Research in Nursing Health, 20,* 205-217.

Gale, L., Bennett, P. D., Tallon, D., Brooks, E., Munnoch, K., Schreiber-Kounine, C., et al. (2001). Quality of partner relationship and emotional responses to health threat. *Psychology, Health & Medicine, 6,* 373-386.

Gamble, V. N. (1993). A legacy of distrust: African Americans and medical research. *American Journal of Preventive Medicine, 9,* 35-38.

Gibson, P. R., Cheavens, J., & Warren, M. L. (1998). Social support in persons with self-reported sensitivity to chemicals. *Research in Nursing and Health, 21,* 103-115.

Hagerty, B. M., & Williams, R. A. (1999). The effects of sense of belonging, social support, conflict, and loneliness on depression. *Nurse Research, 48,* 215-219.

Helgeson, V. S., Cohen, S., Schulz, R., & Yasko, J. (2000). Group support interventions for women with breast cancer: Who benefits from what? *Health Psychology, 19,* 107-114.

Jette, A. M., Tennstedt, S. L., & Branch, L. G. (1993). Stability of informal long-term care. *Journal of Aging and Health, 4,* 193-211.

Koenig, H. G., George, L. K., Cohen, H. J., Hayes, J. C., Larson, D. B., & Blazer, D. G. (1998). The relationship between religions activities and cigarette smoking in older adults. *Journal of Gerontology: Medical Sciences, 53A,* M426-M434.

Krause, N., Ellison, C. G., & Marcum, P. (2002). The effects of church-based emotional support on health: They vary by gender? *Sociology of Religion, 63,* 21-27.

Krause, N., Ellison, C. G., Shaw, B. A., Marcum, J. P., & Boardman, J. D. (2001). Church-based social support and religious coping. *Journal of the Scientific Study of Religion, 40,* 637-656.

Krause, N., Ingersol-Dayton, B., Liang, J., & Sugisawa, H. (1999). Religion, social support, and health among the Japanese elderly. *The Journal of Health and Social Behavior, 40,* 405-421.

Kumanyika, S. K. (2002). Steps to soulful living (steps): A weight loss program for African-American women. *Ethnicity and Disease, 12,* 363-371.

McGraw, S. A., Gift, H., Costa, L. Smith, K., Cohen, D., Bullock, K. (2000). *Transgenerational recruitment of minority women to a breast and cervical cancer screening trial.* Paper presented at the annual meeting of the Society of General Internal Medicine, Boston.

McMahon, S. D., & Jason, L. A. (2000). Social support in a worksite smoking intervention: A test of theoretical models. *Behavior Modification, 24,* 184-201.

McWilliam, C. L., Stewart, M., Brown, J. B., McNair, S., Allan, D. Desai, K. Coderre, P., & Galajda, J. (1999). Home-based health promotion for chronically ill older persons: Results of a randomized controlled trial of a critical reflection approach. *Health Promotion International, 14,* 27-41.

Mirola, W. A. (1999). A refuge for some: Gender differences in the relationship between religious involvement and depression. *Sociology of Religion, 60,* 419-437.

Mitchell, J. C. (1969). *Social networks in urban situations.* Manchester, England: The University of Manchester Press.

Mok, E., & Martinson, I. (1999). Empowerment of Chinese patients with cancer through self-help groups in Hong Kong. *Cancer Nursing, 23,* 206-279.

Mui, A. C. & Burnette, D. (1994). Long-term care service use by frail elders: Is ethnicity a factor? *The Geronotologist, 34,* 190-198.

Nelson, C. J., Rosenfeld, B. J., Breitbart, W., & Galietta, M. (2002). Spirituality, religion, and depression. *Psychosomatics, 43,* 213-220.

Norbeck, J. S., Lindsey, A. M., & Carrieri, V. L. (1983). Further development of an instrument to measure social support: Normative data and validity testing. *Nursing Research, 32,* 4-9.

Norbeck, J. S. (1982). The clinical use of social support. *Journal of Psychosocial Nursing and Mental Health Services, 20,* 22-29.

Oxman, T. E., & Hull, J. G. (2001). Social support and treatment response in older depressed primary care patients. *The Journal of Gerontology: Psychological Sciences, 56,* 35-45.

Ozawa, M. N. & Morrow-Howell, N. (1988). Services provided by elderly volunteers: An empirical study. *Journal of Gerontological Social Work, 13,* 65-80.

Pender, N. J., Murdaugh, C. L., & Parsons, M. A. (2002). *Health promotion in nursing practice,* (4th ed.). Upper Saddle, NJ: Prentice Hall.

Raglin, J. S. (2001). Factors in exercise adherence: Influence of spouse participation. *Quest, 53,* 356-361.

Roberts, L. J., Salem, D., Rappaport, J. Toro, P. A., Luke, D. A., & Seidman, E. (1999). Giving and receiving help: Interpersonal transactions of members. *American Journal of Community Psychology, 28,* 841-868.,

Ross, B., & Cobb, K. L. (1990). *Family nursing: A nursing process approach.* Redwood City, CA: Addison-Wesley.

Schaefer, C., Coyne, J. C., & Lazarus, R. S. (1981). The health-related functions of social support. *Journal of Behavioral Medicine, 4,* 381-405.

Siegel, K. & Schrimshaw, E. W. (2002). The perceived benefits of religious and spiritual coping among older adults living with HIV/AIDS. *Journal of Scientific Study of Religion, 41,* 91-102.

Skolnick, A. S. & Skolnick, J. H. (2000). *Family in transition* (11th ed.). New York: Longman.

Suarez, L., Lloyd, L., Weiss, N., Rainbolt, T., & Pulley, L. (1994). Effect of social networks on cancer screening behavior of older Mexican-American women. *Journal of National Cancer Institute, 86,* 775-779.

Taylor, R. J., Ellison, C. G., Chatters, L. M., Levin, J. S., & Lincoln, K. D. (2000). Mental health services in faith communities: The role of the clergy in black churches. *Social Work, 45,* 73-87.

Tennstedt, S. (1999). *Family caregiving in an aging society.* Administration on Aging. Retrieved December 2, 2002, from http://www.aoa.gov/caregivers/FamCare.html

Ueno, K. & Adams, R. G. (2001). Perceptions of social support availability and coping behaviors among gay men with HIV. *Sociological Quarterly, 42,* 303-324.

Weinert, C. (1987). A social support measure: PRQ85. *Nursing Research, 36,* 273-277.

West, P., Sweeting, H., & Ecob, R. (1999). Family and friends' influences on the uptake of regular smoking from mid-adolescence to early adulthood. *Addiction, 94,* 1397-1411.

Williams, K. E. & Bond, M. J. (2002). The roles of self-efficacy, outcome expectancies and social support in the self-care behaviours of diabetics. *Psychology, Health & Medicine, 9,* 127-141.

Williams, S. W. & Dilworth-Anderson, P. (2002). Systems of social support in families who care for dependent African American elders. *The Gerontologist, 42,* 224-236.

Wright, L. & Leahey, L. (1994). *Nurses and families.* (2nd ed.). Philadelphia: F. A. Davis.

Young, D. R., Gittlesohn, J., Charleston, J., Felix-Aaron, K., & Appeal, L. J. (2001). Motivation for exercise and weight loss among African-American women: Focus group results and their contributions toward program development. *Ethnicity & Health, 6,* 227-245.

Family Communication

John A. Crawford
Michel A. Tarko

Building communication skills—particularly clear, direct expression of feelings and opinions, negotiations, and problem solving—is considered key to promoting more functional family processes.
— Froma Walsh, 1998

OBJECTIVES

On completion of this chapter, the reader will be able to do the following:

1. *Describe the communication processes that occur in families.*

2. *Differentiate between family communication processes that promote and impede family health and wellness.*

3. *Analyze communication processes used in family development and transitions.*

4. *Identify communication skills and strategies used by nurses that promote facilitation, transition, and termination of nurse-family alliances.*

5. *Apply communication strategies that will promote family health.*

Family communication is viewed as an important dynamic, underpinning the family as a system of care. As a social system, the family interacts continually with its internal and external environment. Nurses need to develop an awareness of family communication patterns. Communicating with families is different from and more complex than communicating with an individual because it involves more individuals with more and different communication patterns. Family nurses are in a unique position to assess communication patterns and provide feedback to families about how these patterns enhance or impede family health and wellness. The functions of family communication are to assist family members in learning about their environment; to provide a means of clarifying family rules regarding behavior; to explicate how conflict is resolved; to nurture and develop self-esteem for all members; to transmit cultural values, beliefs, and mores; and to model expressions of feeling states constructively within the family as a unit (Arnold, 1999b).

Communication is central to the discipline of family nursing and specifically to the work of nurses in developing, maintaining, and terminating therapeutic alliances with individual family members and with the family as a group. Communication theory and processes are important elements of models for family nursing assessments and interventions (Friedman, 1998; Friedman, Bowden, & Jones, 2003; Friedemann,

1995; Neuman, 1983; Reed, 1989, 1993; Wright & Leahey, 2000). Researchers have identified specific communication strategies that address the specific needs of families at different stages of the life cycle in a variety of nursing practice environments (Fox & Jeffrey, 1997; Johnston, 2001; Koegel, 2000; Riesch et al., 1993; Riley, 2000; Tracey & Ceronsky, 2001; Villarruel, Portillo, & Kane, 1999).

Communication patterns may facilitate or hinder the nurse-family therapeutic alliance. It is important for nurses to recognize the stage or phase of the nurse-family alliance of the relationship (pre-orientation, orientation, working, termination) and the emerging group process (Corey, 2000). Both the communication pattern and the phase of the relationship provide the context for application of the family nursing process.

Proficiency with communication skills varies according to the nurse's level of education, clinical practice experience, and expertise. Specific communication skills that may enhance family nursing practice are addressed in more detail later in the chapter (see Boxes 7-2 and 7-3). Communication skills that are addressed include the nurse's use of warmth, respect, empathy, concreteness, genuineness, open and closed questions or probes, paraphrasing, parroting, clarification, self-disclosure, confrontation, immediacy, and interpersonal and situational problem solving (Bradley & Edinberg, 1990; Egan, 2002; Gazda, Childers, & Walters, 1982; Riley, 2000; Schuster, 2000; Tschudin, 1995; Williams, 1997). Conflict resolution and negotiation skills and strategies are important elements of nursing practice (Barsky, 2000; Smith, Tutor, & Phillips, 2001) required by nurses working with diverse family groups across the life span in today's complex and ever-changing health care environment (Smith et al., 2001). Knowledge of group theory and practice (Corey, 2000) applied to families is also an important element in family nursing practice because families comprise diverse groups of individuals.

This chapter examines definitions and models of communication, communication skills, and strategies used to develop and maintain therapeutic alliances with families; discusses factors that affect communication; and explores family communication patterns and communication strategies that may facilitate improved family communication patterns and family health and wellness in the context of family health promotion.

Communication Theory

Communication is described as the exchange of information through verbal, nonverbal, or written means. In *The Concise Oxford Dictionary of Current English* (Sykes, 1989), communication is defined as an act of "imparting, transmitting, or effectively conveying information and achieving understanding" (p. 190). In *Webster's New World Dictionary* (Agnes, 1996), communication is defined as an act of "transmitting or giving/exchanging of information, messages" (p. 119). Kozier, Erb, Berman, and Burke (2000) note that communication is a two-way process involving the sending and receiving of messages.

Pioneers in communication theory include Gregory Bateson, John Weakland, Jay Haley, and Don Jackson (Jackson, 1957) who, in the 1950s, reported on their research toward a theory of schizophrenia (Bateson, Jackson, Haley, & Weakland, 1956). Aims of their research were to explore the nature of face-to-face communication, both verbally and nonverbally, among family and social groups, and as a result their research has had an important impact on influencing human behavior. An example of this is noted in the publication *The Pragmatics of Human Communication* (Watzlawick, Beavin, & Jackson, 1967). According to the communication theorists' perspective, the family is a group of interacting personalities, and communication theorists focus on the interactions of those personalities. These early communication perspectives were rooted in the notion that individuals selectively attend to and assess their interactions through a continual process of interpretation whereby they define the situation and then make choices about how to respond to their interpretations of the situation. This supports the idea of a continual feedback loop of attending, assessing, interpreting, and choosing to act on decisions. Limitations of this perspective include the lack of explicit recognition of the relationships between family and the external environment.

Family communication theorists emerged from strategic/problem-solving therapy or brief family therapy during the mid 1950s. The work of Jay Haley was influenced by Milton Erickson's hypnosis theories and the power elements of "who is in control" (Haley, 1977). Jackson (1957) viewed communication theory from a cognitive perspective, asserting that as individuals think, individuals behave in a certain fashion. The work of Satir (1964) focused on the affective domain, contending that the individual's feelings were of the most importance for the initial exploration of ways to communicate within families.

The scholarly work of John M. Gottman is worthy of noting in relation to his research on marital and couple interactions, emotional strengths and weaknesses of gay and lesbian relationships, and the exploration of the ways family members communicate for more than two decades (Gottman, Notarius, Gonso, & Markman, 1977; Gottman, 1979; Gottman, 1994; Gottman, Katz, & Hooven, 1996; Gottman & Notarius, 2000). The website for the Gottman Institute provides additional information readers can access in relation to resources for marriage and couples, gay and lesbian couples, parenting, and professional training programs.

Family communication not only reveals a message about "who is saying what and when," it also conveys a message about the structure and functions of family relationships in relation to the power base, decision-making processes, affection, trust, and coalitions. Based on these definitions and perspectives of communication, family communication is viewed as a process. In any process of transmitting information, a sender and a receiver are involved. The sender is the individual who attempts to transmit the message to another individual or group of individuals, and the receiver is the target of the sender's message. For communication patterns and processes to be effective, the message intended by the sender needs to be clearly stated. Individual perceptions vary depending on a number of factors such as mood, culture, environment, and context. Being aware of potential factors is important because they may impede or interfere with the transmission and reception of a message from one individual to another. Some of these factors are addressed in the next section in which family communication patterns are explored.

Family Communication Patterns

Family functioning is rooted in the ability of individual family members' ability to communicate their needs openly and freely without fear of reprimand or reprisal. *Family communication* is defined as "the transactional process of sharing information and creating meanings within a family system" (Arnold, 1999b, p. 297). Arnold contends that family communication occurs on a literal meaning level through the use of words and on a relational level through the practice of metacommunication. Family communication experts have noted that family members will discuss the meanings of their communication with each other, and when both verbal and nonverbal messages are discussed, then metacommunication takes place (Hoffer, 1996; Olson et al., 1989). Hoffer defines *metacommunication* as "people discussing the meanings attached to communications, clarifying communications, and discussing ways to improve future communications" (p. 95). Metacommunication may serve to enhance family members' relationships with each other by providing direction to the recipient as to how a message should be interpreted and assistance in identifying relationships between family members.

Satir (1976) claims that clear, open, direct, and congruent communication among family members is functional when family communication patterns and processes support, nurture, and promote family members' self-concepts. Family communication patterns that are unclear and indirect have a negative influence on family members' self-worth and self-esteem (Satir, 1983). An example of indirect communication is the use of sarcasm. When sarcasm is used, the receiver may not clearly interpret the intended message and may feel hurt or uncertain about the true meaning of the message. Satir's communication model for working with families is based on systems theory, with emphasis on the principles of wholeness, systems and subsystems, boundaries, communication processes, feedback, and the evolutionary process of growth. Satir (1976) contends that communicating is to relationships what breathing is to maintaining life. Satir refers to healthy communication as *leveling*, whereby the climate of the interaction is emotionally honest and congruent for all parties involved.

Multiple communication patterns within a family create a risk for alterations in the communication process. When more individuals are involved in communication, especially when health status in the family is altered, there are more possible interpretations of a message and misinterpretations are more likely. Communication patterns within the family are described as *symmetrical* or *complementary* exchanges. Symmetrical relationships are based on interactions in which each individual has "equal power and the exchanges mirror each other" as in the following conversation: "Do you want to go to the movies, Honey?" She replies, "Yes, I'd like that" (Arnold, 1999b, p. 297). Complementary relationships, in contrast, are based on an unequal power base as reflected in the following conversation: "Do you want to go to the movies, Honey?" And she replies, "Okay, I will get ready" (Arnold, p. 297). In the first case, the recipient of the message believes she is being given a choice and indicates her preference in the response. In the second case, the recipient assumes that she is expected to go to the movies and gives the expected answer. The notion of functional family communication is realized when both patterns of exchanges occur; a complementary form of communicating may be warranted between a parent and child; and a symmetrical form, between adult partners (Arnold, 1999b).

Miller, Miller, Nuanally, and Wackerman (1991) describe four patterns of communication that are based on an international couples communication program. The four patterns of communication are (1) small talk, (2) control talk, (3) search talk, and (4) straight talk. *Small talk* is similar to cliché conversation in that it is a shallow, relaxed, and chatty form of communication in which little is accomplished.

Control talk has two levels: light control and heavy control. Light control talk is natural and may alter the status quo by directing, advising, cautioning, praising, instructing, giving expectations, or stating concerns. Heavy control talk is the communication pattern used when a person's primary goal is getting his or her own way through the use of an aggressive or harsh tone. In heavy control talk, the person is often ordering, name-calling, labeling, nagging, accusing, blaming, using sarcasm, and complaining (Miller et al., 1991).

Search talk is the approach used to explore or gather information without accusing. It is used to ascertain the facts without making decisions or judging. An example of search talk is, "You seem down in the dumps. Anything happen to you today?"

The last communication pattern is *straight talk*, which is noted to be the most effective in problem solving, sharing, handling tensions, expressing feelings, discussing anticipated change, and asking forgiveness. This approach attempts to address the behavior rather than attack the person's self-esteem, and blame and sarcasm are not used. The speaker uses "I messages." An example of straight talk is, "I worry when you are late. It would relieve my anxiety if you would call when you are going to be late." Search talk, light talk, control talk, and straight talk are used in various situations, but heavy control talk is discouraged because it causes anger and hurts others.

Functional Family Communication Patterns

Families communicate using a combination of functional and dysfunctional patterns that can be viewed on a continuum from healthy to less healthy ways of relating to each other. Satir (1988) claims that healthy families nurture and promote communication among members based on a number of values including high self-esteem, honesty, flexibility in family rules, openness to change, and social consciousness. As a result, communication is direct, clear, and specific.

Functional communication patterns are realized with the use of direct communication when the message is clearly expressed in a congruent manner, that is, when the receiver is able to comprehend the both the literal meaning of the message and the emotional element attached to it (Arnold, 1999b; Goldenberg & Goldenberg, 2000; Satir, Banmen, Gerber, & Gomori, 1991). Characteristics observed in healthy communicating families include the following: parents share the power base equally; parents listen before they react; members communicate with empathy by responding to the feelings and situation of the other family member; members recognize and pick up on nonverbal cues that foster metacommunication; and parents foster independence and promote ownership of individual feelings, reconciliation, problem solving, and negotiation as tools to be used for growth and development of family closeness and bonding (Curran, 1983; Curran & Renzetti, 2000).

Sending and Receiving Functional Messages

Virginia Satir is one of the dominant communication family therapists, as evidenced by her work over the past four decades. Functional communication skills of the sender and receiver reflect several elements that serve as the underpinnings to functional family communication patterns (Satir, 1964; 1988; Satir et al., 1991). These elements of functional communication patterns are presented in Box 7-1.

Dysfunctional Communication Patterns and Family Outcomes

This section addresses dysfunctional communication patterns of the sender and the receiver and the phenomenon of double-bind communication.

Sending and Receiving Dysfunctional Messages

Dysfunctional patterns of communication usually involve making assumptions about what the sender perceives the receiver is thinking, feeling, or understanding without any verification of the message (Faulkner, 1998). In addition, sending dysfunctional messages is based on indirect expression of ideas, thoughts, and feelings; communicating from a position of being judgmental rather than suspending judgment; and expressing messages in an incongruent manner (the words used do not match the emotional tone) (Arnold, 1999; Faulkner, 1998; Gottman, Notarius, Gonso, & Markman, 1977; Satir, 1983, 1988).

Receiving messages in a dysfunctional manner is based on a number of communication elements. Some of these elements include failure to listen carefully to the message being sent, use of disqualification by responding to parts of the message but ignoring the central idea, use of sarcasm and personal slights that are irrelevant to the intended message, and failure to explore or verify the content of the message as a result of making assumptions or cutting off any efforts to communicate further (Arnold, 1999; Faulkner, 1998; Gottman et al., 1977; Satir, 1983; 1988).

BOX 7-1 Functional Sender and Receiver Communication Skills

FUNCTIONAL SENDER SKILLS

- Clearly stating one's needs and desires with the use of "I" statements
- Clarifying and verifying messages
- Inviting and being open to feedback

FUNCTIONAL RECEIVER SKILLS

- Ability to listen without making judgments or interrupting the sender's efforts to communicate clearly and directly
- Providing feedback to the sender by using clarifying statements
- Checking out perceptions through the use of parroting, reflection, restatement, paraphrasing, or summarizing information back to the sender
- Providing verification or validation that the message was understood or comprehended

---

Sender data based on Satir, V. (1964). Conjoint family therapy. Palo Alto, CA: Science and Behavior Books; Satir, V. (1988). *The new peoplemaking*. Mountain View, CA: Science and Behavior Books; and Satir, V., Baumen, J., Gerber, J., & Gomori, M. (1991). *The Satir model: Family therapy and beyond*. Palo Alto, CA: Science & Behavioral Books. Receiver data based on Arnold, E. (1999). Communicating with families. In E. Arnold & K. U. Boggs (Eds.), *Interpersonal relationships: Professional communication skills for nurses* (3rd ed., pp. 292-321). Philadelphia: W. B. Saunders; Blais, K. K., Hayes, J. S., Kozier, B., & Erb, G. (2002). *Professional nursing practice: Concepts and perspectives* (4th ed.). Upper Saddle River, NJ: Prentice Hall; and Gottman, J., Notarius, C., Gonso, J., & Markman, H. (1977). *A couples' guide to communication*. Champagne, IL: Research Press.

Satir et al. (1991) describe four dysfunctional patterns that individuals use to communicate when experiencing a crisis: placating, blaming, intellectualizing, and being irrelevant. *Placating* refers to agreeing with the message but expressing reservations about the message. *Blaming* is described as attributing responsibility for issues or concerns to others and not assuming personal responsibility for one's own involvement in a given situation. *Intellectualizing* is described as being rational about a problem and leaving out any emotional attachment to the issue at hand, and *being irrelevant* consists of giving responses that do not deal directly with the issue at hand (Satir et al., 1991).

Double-Bind Communication

The notion of double-bind communication was reported by Bateson et al. (1956), and the underpinnings of their theoretical position consist of dysfunctional conflicting communication patterns that are hypothesized as contributing to the development of schizophrenia in some families. Double-bind messages convey contradictions. A double-bind message is a statement accompanied by a nonverbal expression that is inconsistent and incongruent with the verbal message. For example, a father lovingly provides and receives hugs and affection from his 8-year-old son while avoiding eye contact and looking away from his son some of the time, whereas at other times he pushes the boy away. The son receives conflicting messages and is presented with a contradictory dilemma: "To please my father I must not show him that I love him, but if I do not show him that I love him, I am afraid I will lose him." This type of dysfunctional communication tends to inhibit healthy nurturing and reduce individual feelings of self-esteem and self-worth.

Common Family Communication Issues across the Life Span

Each stage or transition in family development embodies new family dynamics and challenges the communication styles, patterns, and processes of each family member. Family development theorists define stages somewhat differently; however, there are more similarities than differences as families progress along a continuum of stages and phases. The next section addresses some common family communication issues across the life span.

Young Adulthood

Single adults strive to separate themselves from their family of origin in an effort to achieve a sense of autonomy and independence and begin to view their lives in the context of starting new families (Carter & McGoldrick, 1989;

McGoldrick & Carter, 1980). Young adults strive for this independence while also maintaining a degree of closeness to the nuclear family (Galvin & Brommel, 1986).

Young adults strive for a balance between achieving autonomy and attachment, and through this process, some may assume lifestyles that may inhibit health promotion. Young adults often do not get adequate sleep, nutrition, and exercise; nor do they have regular medical and dental check-ups. Health choices are often compromised by risk-taking behavior such as experimentation with alcohol, tobacco, and other drugs. Health issues for this population include sexually transmitted diseases, birth control, and mental illness. Family nursing interventions include promoting open, honest communication about health issues and choices made by individuals and the family as a unit and health education related to functional and dysfunctional patterns of communicating with young adults during a time of uncertainty in making choices regarding educational, career, and employment opportunities.

Engagement

In this stage of family development, the communication patterns or styles of the young couple are established. The couple engages in conversations about when and whether to start a family, values and beliefs related to childrearing, financial planning as a couple and in anticipation of starting a family, educational and career goals, and where to live and when to consider purchasing real estate. It is during this stage of development that open, honest, and direct communication can set the stage for a long enduring marital relationship. Navran (as cited in Hoffer, 1996) notes that communication patterns of the couple during the engagement period reflect the nature and duration of the relationship. During this time, the two individuals begin to self-identify themselves in contrast to one another, sometimes perceiving similarities and differences in the context of being a couple.

Beginning Marriage

During this stage any dreams or aspirations expressed during the engagement stage begin to surface and reality begins to set in. The couple's roles and functions are negotiated, and some roles and functions are assumed with the establishment of the power balance in the family. The family communication patterns and processes evolve as the couple openly discusses issues and filters out differences. The couple gains experience in managing conflict over time. Galvin and Brommel (1986) note that couples who ignore any dialogue about conflict or differences are setting themselves up for potential conflicts in relation to their unique ways of communicating and relating to each other as a family unit.

Marital instability is purported to be influenced significantly by the spouses' gender beliefs, expectations, and behaviors that occur through negative marital interaction (Pasley, Kerpelman, & Guilbert, 2001). Negative interaction may result in marital discord, distancing, and, for some, divorce. These researchers also note different couple interaction patterns in same-sex partners. Men tend to communicate for the purpose of information and for status, whereas women tend to communicate for the purpose of interaction to establish emotional ties.

Communication styles will either enhance or detract from the quality of marital satisfaction of couples. In one important study, Hawkins, Weisberg, and Ray (as cited by Hoffer, 1996) point out four different styles of communication patterns among spouses; these are referred to as *conventional*, *controlling*, *speculative*, and *contactful*. When the *conventional* communication pattern is used, discussion of issues is avoided or refused. *Controlling* communication patterns prevent expression of thoughts and feelings by discouraging any dialogue or conversation through the use of closed or rejecting messages. The *speculative* communication pattern reflects an openness to discussions about an issue, and the *contactful* communication pattern reflects a spirit of promoting further dialogue and discussion of issues. Hoffer notes that conventional and controlling communication patterns are perceived as closed and unhealthy, whereas speculative and contactful communication patterns are perceived as open and healthier ways of relating to each other. Healthy communication patterns among family members reflect open, honest, and clear expression of thoughts and feelings, and the messages are congruent in content and tone.

Teaching young adults about gender differences in interaction, and direct communication and conflict resolution skills has the potential to decrease alterations in communication patterns and reduce marital instability or divorce. Providing information about local community workshops in developing communication, negotiation, and conflict resolution skills, as well as couple counseling services, can offer couples ideas to focus on regarding communication styles, patterns, and processes.

Childbearing

In anticipation of the arrival of a newborn, couples discuss their perceptions of how their daily routines will be altered with the addition to their family. Common issues include what name will be given to the child, what type of relationships will be established with extended family members and both sets of grandparents, whether both the mother and father will continue to work outside of the home, whether one spouse will stay home to care for the child, and accessibility of child care services if both parents will continue to work in their chosen careers. During this time, young families may be drawn together or further apart in efforts to gain independence and separate from parents. Communication patterns can be strained during this process of adjustment as new parents develop new ways of relating to each other and to their own parents, who are now grandparents.

Parents have the primary responsibility for teaching the infant to communicate through verbal and nonverbal messages. The infant first learns to communicate primarily through his or her senses in relation to touch, sight, and hearing (Deering & Cody, 2002). Infants are generally calm and quiet when their needs are met, and they will cry when they are hungry, tired, or uncomfortable for any reason. Sieh and Brentin (1997) claim that infants tend to respond well to a calm caregiver with a low, comforting voice, regardless of the words being used. Holding and cuddling with the use of repetitive motions are perceived as comforting by the infant. Deering and Cody suggest that when communicating with infants, the nurse should speak in a soft tone and maintain eye contact without staring or scaring the infant. Communicating through play such as peek-a-boo and the use of a rattle can be effective, providing that the infant is receptive to these strategies (Deering & Cody, 2002; Sieh & Brentin, 1997).

Brazelton (1991) notes that infants are able to distinguish their mother's voice from other female voices as early as 7 days of age and will select their mother's silent face before selecting another woman's face at 10 days. Brazelton reports that the infant will select the father's voice and face rather than a stranger's voice and face at 14 days. This initial recognition is rewarded with increased attention by the parents in the forms of cuddling and ongoing talking with the infant. The infant will respond at 1 month with babbling efforts, and a reciprocal cycle evolves between parents and infant. This process of communicating serves as the beginning stage of developing communication patterns and processes.

Underdown (1998) notes that research has focused on the birth process and the physical health of the mother and baby during the transition to parenthood. Research has shown that some couples cope better than others during this time of transition, often reflecting sensitivity to and understanding of each parent's needs. Underdown identified six domains central to the transition into parenthood: (1) merging of the two selves into "us" (the couple works as a team); (2) gender ideology (differences about the division of labor and roles are resolved); (3) emotionality (each partner recognizes the vulnerability to stress and has ability to handle stress in a way that does not overstress the other partner); (4) conflict management (problems are resolved in a constructive manner, and a pool of common interest is maintained); (5) expectations (the couple realizes that however good a partnership becomes after the baby is born, it will not be as good in the same way as it was before); and (6) communication (the couple has the ability to communicate in a way that sustains the partnership). Underdown contends that it is the role of the nurse to promote communication and conflict resolution skills during this critical transition to parenthood.

Childrearing

During the childrearing stage, communication patterns and processes evolve within the context of the family as a unit through socialization and integration of new children into the family system. Family nursing interventions may include promoting couple relationships internally between the parents, and externally, with extended family members and the community. Health promotion issues continue to focus on parenting skills and strategies, growth and development, family planning, communicable diseases, and the safety of the toddler. Nurses ought to be alert to the potential for sibling rivalry, family violence between partners, or violence directed toward the children in the form of abuse, neglect, and communication difficulties. Initiating conversations about parental lifestyle choices and prevention of any chronic health challenges is always warranted.

Throughout the child development years, parents are modeling ways of communicating with each other, the children, extended family members, school teachers, other parents of their children's friends, neighbors, and church members who become important role models for children. As children grow and become involved in community activities, the parents have a responsibility to know the people with whom their children routinely interact.

When working with preschoolers, the nurse should be aware that their perception is that the world revolves around them and that their communication is direct and literal (Sieh & Brentin, 1997). Play is the work of preschoolers, and through play, small children express their feelings. Using pictures as a communication tool is one strategy for building a therapeutic alliance with this age group. Using pictures to assess the degree of pain or distress a child is in has become a common strategy in pediatric nursing environments.

Communicating with toddlers and preschoolers requires the nurse to teach parents to be consistent in their communication style, allowing children to complete their thoughts without interruption because many children in this age group have conceived language beyond their motor development, which triggers temporary stuttering (Deering & Cody, 2002). In caring for children in the context of the family, Heimann (2000) proposes listening, reflection, and conditions for assessment of family needs: maintaining an open mind to accommodate a variety of perspectives about a given situation, valuing and using assessment methods that create access to the family experience, and sensing and interpreting the family experience in a way that has meaning for the family and for the nurse. An important function of the nurse is to facilitate the use of functional communication skills and strategies among parents in promoting healthy communication patterns with their children.

Sieh and Brentin (1997) note that school-age children are able to comprehend cause and effect and usually want to know what has happened and how things have come to be. They are naturally curious and want information, so they may be observed listening to adult conversation. This becomes problematic when they hear only partial messages or come to incorrect conclusions based on partial information (Deering & Cody, 2002; Sieh & Brentin, 1997). Deering and Cody assert that it is important for parents to understand how school-age children perceive a situation before launching into any teaching about the facts.

In communicating about health care issues, nurses can use anatomical drawings to assist the child in understanding procedures or use simple written materials as communication strategies, thus promoting health teaching among school-age children. Teaching parents about these types of communication strategies may assist them in understanding the school-age child's perceptions and may thus promote better parent-child communication. Sieh and Brentin (1997) suggest asking children to restate their understanding of the procedure using their own words as a strategy to verify the accuracy of the information. During this stage, learning and physical disabilities such as alterations in sensory perception and cognition that may affect the child's hearing, vision, or speech and behavioral difficulties may emerge. In such situations, nurses can assist families in gaining access to appropriate health care resources.

Developing and maintaining trust through open and honest communication is significant when teenagers move away from accepting adult control, protection, and influence as they begin to strive for some sense of autonomy. Sieh and Brentin (1997) note that teenagers can present with a range of behaviors from childlike to adult within the span of a few minutes. Deering and Cody (2002) note that during adolescence, feelings are intense and other persons and events are perceived in extreme terms. Teenagers believe their friends are central to their existence, and the opinions of their friends are valued. In communicating with teenagers, Sieh and Brentin propose talking to them like adults and using their first and last names, as well as their titles "Ms." or "Mr." as a sign of respect. Deering and Cody (2002) note that "one particular important principle is to listen more than you talk, especially at the beginning of a conversation, and to convey an attitude that is not judgmental…, even if you are startled or disturbed by what they are saying" (p. 39). Deering and Cody propose using straightforward talk to explain the purpose of the interaction, talking openly about the limits of confidentiality (e.g., any suicidal thoughts or plans must be reported to a parent or guardian), and ensuring that adolescents always have the opportunity to talk with the nurse in the company of their parents and with the nurse privately.

During any assessment with an adolescent, it is important to ensure privacy and to recognize that the teenager may be too embarrassed to listen and respond to the nurse. Thus offering something in writing for the teenager to take away may assist with clarification of information (Deering & Cody, 2002; Sieh & Brentin, 1997).

Sydnor-Greenberg and Dokken (2001) propose use of the acronym CLEAR (context, listening, empowerment, advice, and reassurance) as a framework for outlining what parents would like in their communication with health care professionals, based on interviews with children ages 4 to 17 years who were living with acute and chronic conditions. The authors emphasize the importance of communication that does the following:

- Explores and provides *context*
- Reflects that the health care professional is *listening*
- Facilitates *empowerment* of the family as a unit
- Gives *advice* about possible actions or next steps
- Offers *reassurance* to the family

Before offering "advice," it is recommended that the nurse have the family explore possible actions or steps. Once the family has attempted problem solving possible actions and solutions, then it is recommended that the nurse propose suggestions for consideration by the family.

Launching

The launching stage of family development begins when the first child leaves the parental home to pursue career, education, or family goals. It is in this stage that adult children aim to become independent from their family of origin. The past decade has seen an extension of the launching period beyond the 6- to 8-year period. This is due in part to adult children remaining in the home during and after completing college education programs or returning to the parental home after a short departure in efforts to gain economic and financial stability before going through a second launching period. Conflicts may arise in relation to adult children remaining in the home longer than their parents had anticipated.

During this period, parents are "letting go" of their 20- to 25-year history of parenting and preparing their children for the launch through teaching and mentoring in areas of self-care, budgeting, household maintenance, and child-rearing. Parents are on the cusp of returning to their original marital dyad before any additions are made to the family (i.e., arrival of grand-children). Facilitating functional communication in the family as a unit is important for health promotion and strengthening of the parental relationship during the pre- and postlaunching stages. Family nursing interventions that target health concerns include promoting communication between parents and young adults; exploring the potential tensions associated with role transitions for both parents; exploring the potential for development of ongoing health issues associated with sedentary lifestyles, such as alcohol use, smoking, and inconsistent dietary practices; family planning for the young adult; and promotion of a wellness lifestyle.

Empty Nest

The emptying of the nest follows the launching period, and during this stage the parents have more time to plan shared activities and continue to build on their relationships with each other and with friends and extended family. Many couples report not having much in common and few things to talk about with each other (Hoffer, 1996). This stage in the parents' marriage is viewed by LeShan (as cited in Friedman, Bowden, & Jones, 2003) as a time of truth during which to explore whether the relationship has enough strength to sustain it in the absence of the excuse of parenthood.

Family communication issues during the empty nest stage include (1) targeting health concerns such as menopause, andropause (male menopause), and chronic health issues; risk factors such as obesity, hypertension, heart disease, and diabetes; and health practices such as sleep, nutrition, and activity patterns; (2) recognizing and building on the strengths of the marital/partner relationship; (3) facilitating communication with children and their partners, grandchildren, and aging parents; and (4) dealing with losses associated with the deaths of family members.

Retirement

The retirement stage is marked by the retirement of one or both partners and continues through to the death of each spouse. Older adults have diverse perceptions about this stage of the life cycle, ranging from feeling unhappy and discontent to believing that these are the best years of their lives. Health status is one of the primary determinants of well-being for older adults; financial resources and the ability to maintain a home are also reported as determinants of well-being for older adults (Quinn, 1993). Adapting to multiple losses is a major issue, with the loss of one's spouse being the most traumatic. Other significant losses include end of employment, failing physical and cognitive wellness, decrease in income, and in many instances, moving out of the family home.

Promotion of family communication among older adults, children, and grandchildren may assist in easing the stress of multiple losses. Communication strategies such as reminiscing are viewed as comforting for older adults in their efforts to derive meaning from their life experiences. Promoting the maintenance and further development of social relationships through recreational and social activities is regarded as a strategy for fostering connections to other older adults and family members.

Sieh and Brentin (1997) propose that older adults be treated like all other groups of individuals. The nurse ought to begin by addressing the older adult by using his or her title and last name. Referring to older adults as *Grandpa*, *Grandma*, *Honey*, or *Sweetie* should be avoided. A nurse should introduce himself or herself as a nurse, speak slowly, and realize that many older adults may not be able to read the name tags that health care professionals routinely wear. Arnold and Boggs (1999) point out that one third of adults older than 65 years have a hearing impairment that negatively affects their social interactions. Talking slowly and clearly and using silence to allow for sufficient response time for the older adult to answer questions is vital to the therapeutic alliance. The use of humor is appreciated when it relates to the older adult's everyday events. Sieh and Brentin contend that focused, detailed conversation is best understood during peak times, such as mid-morning, and that information overload should be avoided. The use of visual aids and a notebook may assist in relaying, as well as retention of, information (Sieh & Brentin, 1997). The nurse promoting family communication needs to emphasize to family members the importance of adopting communication strategies that support and reflect the level of functioning of older adults as individuals and as couples (e.g., recognizing alterations in cognition such as memory deficits).

Family Culture and Communication

Family communication patterns (such as touch, tone of voice, eye contact, and distance) may vary across and within cultures, hence the necessity for intercultural communication awareness among clinicians (Gudykunst, 2001). Similarly, Thomas (2001) asserts that culture is a critical force that shapes human experiences throughout the life span and across generations. Covington (2001) claims that with an increase in minority groups, there is an increasing disparity in health care and health outcomes because many of these client groups enter the health care system at a later stage in their experience with ill health and advanced disease processes. Covington notes that cultural dissonance may be avoided by the family nurse by gaining a broader understanding of the cultural values and beliefs of minority groups whose values may be incongruent with those of

the family nurse (for an additional discussion on culture see Chapter 9).

Culture is believed to affect clients' views of time, environmental space, family structure, illness, and health; therefore family nurses need to tune in to the family's cultural views when engaging in health promotion interventions that are culturally sensitive (Nance, 1995; Wright, Cohen, & Caroselli, 1997). For example, family nurses providing care to children of diverse backgrounds report it to be frustrating and time-consuming as a result of the absence of cultural care theory in their educational programs (Davidhizar, Havens, & Bechtel, 1999). Family nurses who are aware of various cultural perspectives may offer more sensitive cultural care and promote clearer communication, minimizing potential barriers. Gaining a broader perspective of cultural concepts will enable the family nurse to navigate any differences between the family's culture and the culture of the health care system while advocating for clients' health and wellness (Lea, 1994; Wright et al., 1997; Zoucha, 1998). Since research about family communication and culture is limited, scholars are encouraged to conduct studies on how communication varies among, within, and across genders and ethnic groups (Gudykunst, 2001).

Samovar and Porter (as cited in Arnold, 1999a) define intercultural communication "as a communication in which the sender of an intended message is a member of one culture and the receiver of the message is a member of a different culture" (p. 245). Arnold (1999a) notes that in every culture, language has four primary functions: (1) "to direct actions, (2), to interpret the meaning of events and situations, (3) to connect past experiences with the present through imagination, and (4) to establish and maintain relationships with people" (Arnold, 1991, p. 245).

Arnold notes that for individuals who speak English as a second language, intercultural communication goes beyond language translation. For nurses to provide culturally congruent care for any group of clients, such as African Americans, Hispanics, and Native Americans, it is crucial to explore cultural interpretations of illness, behaviors, expression of symptoms, beliefs about treatment traditions, family structure, and decision making.

Effects of Communication on Family Health Status

Communication is the central mechanism used among family members in translating meanings of messages to one another in relation to family roles, functions, and responsibilities. Family structure, roles, functions, and power bases provide a lens through which to view how information is translated in family day-to-day interactions. A number of factors contribute to family communication patterns such as the context or situation, the family's cultural background, the stage of family development, and gender differences between family members.

Healthy family communication is open, honest, clear, and direct. Responding to nonverbal messages is also an indicator of healthy family communication. Minuchin and Nicholis (1998) report that the majority of communications occur in the context of family subsystems such as the parent-parent, parent-child, and sibling-sibling subsystems, thus enabling analysis of subsystem interactions. Satir et al. (1991) claim congruence is key to family communication in healthy families and define congruence as "a state of being and a way of communicating with ourselves and others" (p. 65). Functional family communication is also based on family members' ability to express emotions freely. Wright and Leahey (2000) note that emotional communication encompasses the expression of one's emotions or feeling states.

Wright, Watson, and Bell (1996) offer significant insights into beliefs about families and illness, and they explore the potential for therapeutic change. Based on their clinical work and research, Wright et al. (1996) also offer their insights into creating a context for altering beliefs; delineating illness beliefs; and learning how to challenge, alter, and modify constraining beliefs. The authors illustrate how to explicate change in identifying, affirming, and solidifying facilitative beliefs among families. Wright and Leahey (2000) provided nurses with a framework for conducting family interviews based on four stages: (1) engagement, (2) assessment, (3) intervention, and (4) termination. The authors describe the aims for each stage and the types of family interviewing skills (perceptual/conceptual and executive) required for conducting family interviews.

In assessing the nature of family communication patterns and health outcomes, it is important for the nurse to take time to invite the family to tell their story by sharing their unique perspectives and lived experiences of how they perceive their patterns of communication promoting or inhibiting family health. A few sample questions are presented as exemplars of the types of questions the nurse may consider raising during a family meeting. They include exploring the following:

1) To what extent are family members able to clearly state their individual needs and desires using "I" statements, clarifying and verifying messages, inviting feedback, and being open to receiving feedback from other family members?

2) To what extent are family members able to listen to others without making judgments or interrupting others?

3) How often are clarifying statements made or how often do family members check out perceptions of what was said and what was heard?

4) What degree of openness do family members have in expressing thoughts, ideas, and feelings?

5) In what ways does the family use clarification? Disqualification? Validation?

6) To what degree are assumptions and judgments made without further exploration?

7) In what ways is feedback provided and received by family members?

8) How congruent are the family messages that are expressed to each other?

9) In what ways do family members identify their feelings and the situation leading to their feelings, both surface and underlying feelings?

10) Who in the family has the primary responsibility for communicating important messages to the rest of the family members?

11) How does the family use problem solving (interpersonal and situational) as a method to resolve family issues?

12) How do family communication patterns change during a time of crisis?

Nursing Interventions to Facilitate Family Communication

Communication is a core element in the practice of nursing, yet many undergraduate nursing education programs do not offer courses in advanced communication skills and counseling strategies. Nurses often find themselves in situations in which they are role modeling communication skills in the work they are doing or in facilitating family communication between family subsystems.

Family nursing interventions that facilitate family communication address the teaching and learning of new communication skills and behaviors, counseling, collaborating, contracting, and referral to other services including community centers, outpatient clinics, and day hospital programs.

Wright and Leahey (2000) note that the Calgary Family Intervention Model (CFIM) targets three types of family interventions that focus on cognitive, affective, and behavioral levels of family functioning and involve teaching and counseling. Family nursing interventions focused on the cognitive level aim to provide the family with new ideas about how family members communicate with each other. Such interventions are focused on the family's level of communication and may involve development of self-awareness and examination of problem-solving strategies. The choice of interventions depends on how the family perceives the problem, and interventions should be designed to address the family's perceptions and beliefs in relation to issues of how members communicate. Wright and Leahey (2000) note two interventions as exemplars in addressing the cognitive domain of family functioning: commending family and individual strengths and offering information and opinions.

Family nursing interventions focused on the affective domain address how families express themselves to each other on an emotional level or the level of emotional communication in the family. Such interventions focus on the family as a system and help the family learn new ways to modify expression among members to meet the emotional needs of the family within the cultural context of the family system and to promote clear, congruent communication. For example, the family nurse may encourage family members to share their feelings openly with each other as an indicator of a healthy family unit and address any incongruent messages in the family's emotional communication patterns. Wright and Leahey (2000) note three interventions as exemplars in addressing the affective domain of family functioning: validating or normalizing emotional responses, encouraging the telling of illness narratives, and drawing forth family support.

Family nursing interventions focusing on the behavioral domain are necessary to achieve functional communication patterns among family members. Exploring the impact of family decisions by using open-ended questions in the spirit of inquiry will facilitate exploration of decisions affecting the family as a unit. Wright and Leahey (2000) contend that targeting the behavioral domain will alter perceptions of the family members' reality, and further, that changes in perceptions have the potential to cause changes in behavior. Nurses can focus on behaviors unacceptable to the family as a whole and still emphasize the value of the person as a member of the family. Wright and Leahey note three interventions as exemplars in addressing the behavioral domain of family functioning: encouraging family members to be caregivers, encouraging respite, and devising rituals.

Faulkner (1998) points out that a common barrier to effective interactions by health care professionals is making assumptions about client situations that may result in valuable client data being missed unless open questions are relayed to the family directly. Based on this premise, Faulkner contends that a golden rule in talking to client groups is to make no assumptions at any time during the process of developing, maintaining, or terminating nurse-client alliances. The Research Synopsis presents a study about trust in a client-provider relationship.

Family Communication Assessment Tools and Measurements

A variety of instruments are available to nurses to measure communication patterns in families. The use of these tools enables nurses to construct more accurate assessments. Olson et al. (1989) contend that communication is viewed as a facilitating dimension of the Circumplex Model because it facilitates movement on the cohesion and adaptability dimensions of the Family Adaptability and Cohesion Scales (FACES II).

Parent-adolescence communication patterns can be measured with parent and adolescent

---

RESEARCH SYNOPSIS

TRUST BETWEEN FAMILY AND HEALTH CARE PROVIDER

Lynn-McHale and Deatrick (2000) conducted a concept analysis of trust between the family and health care provider using the literature as data to identify a definition, characteristics, boundaries, preconditions, and outcomes of the concept of trust according to the guidelines put forth by Morris, Mitcham, Hupcey, and Tason (as cited in Lynn-McHale & Deatrick, 2000). Knafl and Deatrick (as cited in Lynn-McHale & Deatrick, 2000) described a concept analysis as "the systematic examination of the attributes or characteristics of a given concept for the purpose of clarifying the meaning of that concept" (p. 211).

The authors report that the findings reveal six characteristics of trust and reflect that trust is defined as a process, consists of varying levels, evolves over time, and is based on mutual intention, reciprocity, and expectations. The authors conclude that trust between the family and health care provider is important because the development and attainment of trust has significant effects on the relationships for both the family and health care provider, family and health care provider communication style, family involvement and support of treatment recommendations, and client and family benefits. Thorne and Robinson (as cited in Lynn-McHale & Deatrick, 2000) contend that being trusted by a health care provider promotes family self-esteem and strengthens the family–health care provider alliance.

Lynn-McHale, D. J., & Deatrick, J. A. (2000). Trust between family and health care provider. *Journal of Family Nursing, 6,* 210–230.

---

instruments constructed by Barnes and Olson (1982). The concepts measured include openness, freedom to exchange ideas, trust, and honesty in both parents and the adolescents. This 20-item self-report scale focuses on assessment of the perceptions of adolescents and their parents in relation to their perceptions and experiences of communicating with one another. The two subscales—Open Family Communication and Problems in Family Communication—are reported as being designed to measure both positive and negative aspects of parent-adolescent communication patterns.

Other instruments are available to couples preparing for marriage. The instruments include the Facilitating Open Couple Communication, Understanding and Study (FOCCUS); Premarital Inventory (PMI); and the Premarital Personal and Relationship Enrichment-Enriching and Nurturing Relationship Issues, Communication and Happiness (PREPARE-ENRICH) scale (Olson et al., 1989; Olson, 2000).

Additional instruments for measuring and assessing family communications include the Marital Communication Scales, which is part of ENRICH (Olson et al., 1989); PREPARE-CC for cohabiting couples (Olson, 2000); the Marital Communication Inventory by Schumm, Anderson, and Griffen (1983); the Affective Sensitivity Scale by Danish and Kagan (1971); the Self-Disclosure Questionnaire by Jourard and Lasakow (1959); the Interpersonal Communication Inventory by Bienvenu and McCain (1970); the McMaster Assessment Device (FAD) by Epstein and Bishop (1993); and the Marital and Family Communication Scale, which is the third dimension of the Circumplex Model of Marital and Family Systems (Olson, 2000).

Olson (2000) notes that the Marital and Family Communication Scale measures couple and family communication by focusing on the family as a group and examining listening skills, speaking skills, self-disclosure skills, clarity, continuity tracking, and respect and regard for others. Olson asserts that listening skills emphasize the use of empathy and attentive listening, and speaking skills reflect speaking for one's self and not speaking for others in the family. The notion of self-disclosure reflects sharing feelings about one's self and the relationship with another family member. Tracking is described by Olson as staying on topic, and respect and regard relate to the affective aspects of the communication and problem solving skills in couples and families. Appendix 7-1 at the end of the chapter presents one family communication rating scale.

Emde (1992a) suggests two ways in which a nurse can assess the quality of family communication: the structured interview and the interactional task. Two sets of questions make up the structured interview. The first set of questions relates to the history of the marital relationship, and the second set focuses on the current marital relationship.

The interactional task selected by the couple must be an important one for them. The task must take about 20 minutes and fit into the time allotted for a home visit by the nurse. An interactional task is described as a task that challenges the couple to work through a given family situation or issue together to arrive at a mutual decision. The task must emphasize concrete, positive behaviors. Emde (1992b) notes that parenting issues are particularly effective interactional tasks. Careful analysis of both the interview and observational data provides confirming or disconfirming communication patterns, which support or deny the identity of the spouses. Confirming is described as being open and respectful, as well as providing validation of the spouse/partner's perspective. Careful linking of the data from both sources should suggest strategies for effective intervention.

Although family health nurses are not therapists, knowledge of communication patterns and use of therapeutic approaches are useful in nursing interventions for well families. Family health nurses should offer appropriate referrals when working with families whose communication problems are beyond the level of their expertise.

Communication Skills and Strategies Aimed at Improving Family Communication

Communication skills and strategies that enhance the nurse's ability to communicate effectively with clients in the context of family nursing are well documented in the nursing literature. Developing, maintaining, and terminating collaborative and flexible nurse-family working alliances are based in part on the nurse's ability to communicate in a

therapeutic manner. The term *working alliance* was first used by Greenson in 1967 (as cited in Egan, 2002). Therapeutic communication skills and strategies are the foundation in positioning the nurse as a role model, teacher, mentor, facilitator, mediator, and negotiator. Boxes 7-2 and 7-3 describe therapeutic communication skills that enhance the nurse's ability to practice family nursing using specific microcommunication skills at different stages of the nurse-family alliance. When a communication framework is used, it is important to be flexible, yet such frameworks provide essential focus and direction. Flexibility in the application of a communication framework is imperative in that the focus is on the

---

BOX 7-2 THERAPEUTIC COMMUNICATION PROCESSES AND SKILLS APPLIED TO CLIENT AS FAMILY

STAGE I

Warmth
Respect
Empathy (basic)

STAGE II

Concreteness
Genuineness
Self-disclosure
Empathy (advanced)

STAGE III

Confrontation
Immediacy
Problem solving (interpersonal and situational)
Conflict resolution

Adapted from Adler, R. B., Rosenfield, L. B., & Proctor, R. F. (2001). *Interplay: The process of interpersonal communication* (8th ed). Orlando, FL: Harcourt, Inc.; Barsky, A. E. (2000). *Conflict resolution for the helping professions.* Belmont, CA: Wadsworth/Thomson Learning; Egan, G. (2002). *The skilled helper: A problem-management and opportunity-development approach to helping* (7th ed.). Pacific, CA: Brooks/Cole; and Gazda, G. M., Childers, W. C., & Walters, R. P. (1982). *Interpersonal communication: A handbook for health professionals.* Rockville, MD: Aspen.

BOX 7-3   Application of Therapeutic Communication Skills to Client as Family

STAGE I: INITIAL STAGE FOR DEVELOPMENT OF NURSE FAMILY ALLIANCE

Goals: Helping the family to tell their story; promoting self-exploration

Warmth

Conveyed by the nurse through the use of attending behaviors such as the use of eye contact, tone of voice, maintaining an open and relaxed posture, use of touch if appropriate, facial expressions such as smiling, and active listening.

Respect

Conveyed by the nurse through behaviors such as calling the family members by their preferred names, not interrupting others, being nonjudgmental, using the same language as the family member, offering undivided attention, use of regular eye contact if this is warranted culturally, and recognizing the care and support family members have offered each other in the family meeting, as well as during other times of stress and crisis.

Basic Empathy

Conveyed by the nurse through accurate reflection of *surface feelings* or emotions associated with the *content* of the situation or context of the individual or family's story. Formula and natural responses are presented as exemplars.

Formula response for basic empathy: *"You feel upset because your mother has taken ill."*
Natural response for basic empathy: *"You're upset because your mother has taken ill."*

The nurse, through each stage of the nurse-family alliance, can use warmth, respect, and empathy. Further, the use of respect and empathy may assist the nurse in obtaining information and in dealing sensitively with families in the context of diversity (i.e., their unique qualities, needs, and behaviors). It is important for the nurse to understand diversity from the worldview of the family; to demonstrate self-awareness of his or her own cultural values, beliefs, attitudes, and biases related to diversity; and to alter communication interventions and strategies based on family culture (e.g., the appropriateness of self-disclosure varies among families and from one culture to another).

STAGE II: TRANSITION STAGE FOR DEVELOPMENT OF NURSE-FAMILY ALLIANCE

Goals: Challenging the family's communication patterns and processes; promoting self-understanding and commitment to change

Concreteness

Conveyed by the nurse by being specific and through the use of descriptive words and phrases, as opposed to use of abstract terms and generalizations.

The use of *open-ended questions* or probes and the use of clarifying, paraphrasing, and summary statements by the nurse facilitate concreteness and the exchange of information about the family.

Examples of open-ended questions or probes include questions such as the following: *"Tell me who...,*
what..., when..., where..., and how...." The use of open-ended questions by the nurse promotes the expression of feelings, thoughts, and ideas.

The use of *closed-ended questions* or probes by the nurse should be avoided because they tend to elicit a "yes" or "no" response, with little or no elaboration. The use of closed-ended questions by the nurse is less effective in facilitating the expression of feelings, thoughts, and ideas.

Examples of closed-ended questions or probes include questions such as the following: *"Are you ..., Can you ..., Do you ..., Did you..., Will you ..., Is it ...."* Closed-ended questions or probes should be avoided *except* during assessment for risk of suicide, homicide, abuse, incest, or family violence, that is, in situations in which the nurse needs a definitive answer in relation to issues of safety of family members, legal requirements, and ethical issues.

Continued

BOX 7-3   Application of Therapeutic Communication Skills to Client as Family—cont'd

The use of *why questions* by the nurse should be avoided because they tend to imply blame, often elicit responses that attempt to justify the family's behavior (rationalization), and have the potential to weaken any gains made in the nurse-family alliance. For example, asking *"Why did the family miss our last meeting?"* is less effective than asking, *"What happened that the family was unable to attend our last meeting?"*

Statements that reflect *clarification* are referred to as paraphrasing and parroting information to the family as client.

> *Parroting*
> Family member: *"I cannot believe this has happened to our mother."*
> Nurse: *"You cannot believe this has happened to your mother."*
> *Paraphrasing*
> Family member: *"I cannot believe this has happened to our mother."*
> Nurse: *"You're finding it hard to believe your mother has had a heart attack."*

Summary statements are intended to capture the content, themes, or essence of what was said by family members. Summarizing can be used at any time during a family assessment or meeting to clarify ideas or messages being conveyed and to enhance the nurse's understanding of the family's situation.

> Nurse: *"What I am hearing from everyone here is that the primary concerns are whether your mother is physically strong enough to cope with open heart surgery and whether she will have a full recovery."*

Genuineness

Conveyed by the nurse through being sincere, honest, and spontaneous and the use of "I" statements. For example, the nurse states, *"I'm concerned...," "I appreciate that each of you feels comfortable in sharing your concerns with me."*

Self-disclosure

Conveyed by the nurse through use of personal information of a similar situation and related feelings currently being experienced by the family. Self-disclosure should be used only when it will benefit the family or family members and should be used with discretion so as not to shift the focus from the family's experience to that of the nurse. When self-disclosure is used, it is important for the nurse to be in the process of resolving the situation or for the situation to have been positively resolved. The use of self-disclosure is intended to validate family members' feelings and let them know they are not alone in their experience and that their situation has the potential to be resolved. It is common for family members to ask the nurse what strategies were used or how the situation was resolved. It is important for the nurse to ask family members what ideas they have for resolving their situation before disclosing what strategies were used to resolve the nurse's situation. In this way the nurse avoids the position of giving advice, and if the family chooses to employ strategies used by the nurse, family members are less likely to blame the nurse if the strategies do not work to resolve the family's unique situation because they were given an opportunity to present their own ideas first.

Advanced empathy

Conveyed when the nurse accurately reflects the underlying feelings or emotions associated with the content, themes, or context of the individual's or family's story. Formula and natural responses are presented as exemplars.

> Formula response for advanced empathy: *"You feel scared/terrified because your mother's cancer has spread, and you feel overwhelmed because she may die if she undergoes surgery."*
> Natural response for advanced empathy: *"I am sensing that you're scared/terrified about your mother's cancer spreading, and you are devastated that she may not be strong enough to survive the surgery."*

BOX 7-3   Application of Therapeutic Communication Skills to Client as Family—cont'd

STAGE III: ACTION STAGE FOR DEVELOPMENT OF FAMILY ALLIANCE

Goals: Focusing on family communication solutions; empowering families to manage communication issues through problem-solving strategies; and developing resources and opportunities

Confrontation

Conveyed by the nurse through the use of empathy: a statement that describes the discrepancies in family member's communication related to feelings, behaviors, and/or actions and communicates the nurse's commitment to continue working with family members.

Discrepancies that the nurse can address through the use of confrontation include (1) discrepancies in family member's feelings and behavior (i.e., differences between what is currently being expressed verbally and what behavior is being observed); (2) what family members have stated previously and what they are saying currently; and (3) how family members behaved previously or what they did previously and how they are behaving currently or what they are doing now.

Prefacing each type of discrepancy statement with a basic empathic response and following the statement of discrepancy with a statement that reflects commitment to further involvement with family members reinforce the therapeutic nature of using such an advanced communication skill.

Basic Empathy: *"You are feeling worried about your mother's illness and her impending surgery."*

Discrepancy 1: *"You say you are not upset, but I notice that some of your feet are tapping, you have tears in your eyes, and some of you are tremulous."*

Commitment: *"I have some time to sit with you. Let's talk about what is bothering each of you right now."*

Discrepancy 2: *"When we met last week, I understood that each member of the family said he or she would take turns spending time with your mother at the hospital, and now I hear you saying that each of you hasn't been able to follow through with your commitment."*

Commitment: *"Let's talk about what is happening for each of you that is interfering with your ability to spend time with your mother."*

Discrepancy 3: *"Last week I noticed that each of you seemed really emotional about your mother, and today I notice that each of you seems more composed and relaxed, and you even have a sense of humor."*

Commitment: *"Let's talk about what has changed for each of you."*

Immediacy

Conveyed by the nurse when calling attention to the relationship between the family and the nurse as to (1) what is happening "here and now" in the nurse-family alliance, that is, in the current interview or meeting and (2) what has been happening in the alliance with the family over time. Conveying how the nurse feels in the context of what is going on requires the nurse to express his or her own feelings or emotions in the context of any barriers to the maintenance and development of the nurse-family alliance.

Nurse:

(1) *"I am concerned that I may have upset some of you with the information I shared about the procedure for open heart surgery. My intent was to share information about what your mother is facing and in no way to make anyone feel more upset. What concerns do you have at this time with regard to your mother's situation?"*

(2) *"I am concerned about what has been happening in our last two meetings. I noticed that some of you are participating less, and I'm wondering if you may be questioning my ability to help you successfully work through your grief associated with your mother's illness. What do you think is happening? I'd appreciate knowing what you are thinking and feeling and how I can help."*

Problem solving

Situational and interpersonal problem solving are two approaches that can be used to work toward resolving two different types of issues or problems.

Continued

| **BOX 7-3** Application of Therapeutic Communication Skills to Client as Family—cont'd |

Situational problem solving aims to explore with families: what events or stressors led to the problem situation; how family members responded to the problem situation; what previous experience the family has had in managing this type of problem situation; what coping strategies the family has used in the past and what has been effective and what has not been effective for the family; what coping strategies are currently effective for the family and what strategies are currently ineffective for the family; and what new or alternative coping strategies the family is aware of or interested in pursuing.

Interpersonal problem solving aims to resolve issues between two or more family members. Two considerations will guide the nurse in deciding whether to attempt to resolve the issue with each of the family members involved. (1) How important is it for the family member to solve the problem? (2) Is the problem solvable? If one or more of the family members are in agreement about attempting to resolve the problem or issue, the nurse has each family member respond to each of the following requests for information in sequence: (1) *"Tell me how the problem looks to you right now."* (2) *"Describe for me how are you involved in the problem."* (3) *"Tell me how you feel about the problem."* (4) *"Tell me how you react to or behave in response to the problem."* and finally, (5) *"Tell me how you think that you contribute to the problem."*

Family members involved are encouraged to work through each step of the process individually and then to share their perceptions with each other. Exploration of options, alternatives, and contracting for change in ways of relating to each other may be outcomes of the process.

Conflict Resolution

The *win-win* problem-solving method of managing conflict is based on seven strategies. The nurse as facilitator and mediator invites the family to work through the series of seven strategies in an effort to promote effective family communication and to reduce family conflict over the course of a few sessions. The strategies are as follows:

(1) Have each family member identify his or her issues and unmet needs.
(2) Establish a time for family members to share their identified issues and needs with the other family members involved.
(3) Have each family member describe his or her issues and needs to the other family members present.
(4) Have each family member listen to the points of views raised by the other family members involved.
(5) Have the family members generate and negotiate possible solutions.
(6) Have the family members implement the solutions.
(7) Follow up with the family by setting a time and date to revisit the effects of the solution (in 1-week or 1-month intervals).

---

family and families may enter the helping process at different points and may proceed through the stages differently. Family members may engage differently within and among the various stages. Further, families and family members may move back and forth among the stages, and in some instances, stages may merge. Although most communication models and frameworks appear rational, linear, and systematic and have limitations, their effectiveness relates to how the nurse understands and uses the framework and integrates the various skills and techniques through the therapeutic use of self in the context of family nursing. It is important that the nurse understand the limitations associated with the helper role, the family as client, and the environment that affect the helping process. Egan (2002) refers to the often jumbled and intermingled steps in real-life problem management situations as "the messiness of helping" (p. 17). The Canadian Perspectives box presents information on perspective-taking as a communication strategy.

Michelle Lobchuk, PhD, RN
University of Manitoba

CANADIAN PERSPECTIVES
PERSPECTIVE-TAKING AS A REAL-WORLD HEURISTIC DEVICE

Perspective-taking is an empathic process that is central to communication competence in interpersonal relationships (Schober, 1998). Researchers in social psychology have explored perspective-taking as an everyday heuristic device that enhances an individual's ability to understand, predict, and adapt to another person's situation. It is defined as the ability, skill, or tendency of an individual to adopt a partner's viewpoint to examine the situation from the partner's perspective (Arriaga & Rusbult, 1998). Perspective-taking is an inference process in which the individual imagines another's viewpoint by temporarily putting aside his or her own perspective and attempting to adopt that of another, asking himself or herself, "What would I feel if I were that individual?" in certain circumstances.

In family relationships, disagreements can flare as a result of misunderstanding the partner's viewpoint. However, conciliatory action is often required to maintain harmony in family partnerships (Arriaga & Rusbult, 1998). As a means of communication competence, perspective-taking is a type of conciliatory action that can promote more accommodative behaviours, such as affirming the other's sense of valued self and unique per-

spective and engaging in reflective responses that portray an attempt at understanding one another.

In nursing literature, perspective-taking and its impact on communication competence have not been extensively explored in the family context, as for example, in family caregiving. Rather, perspective-taking has been explored as a means of communication competence in the context of nurse-patient relationships (Kasch, 1988). Investigators in one Canadian city have begun to explore the impact of perspective-taking on family caregivers' perceptions of the symptom experiences of patients with cancer (Lobchuk & Vorauer, in press). These researchers assumed that first, the patient and the family caregiver perceive the world from different standpoints, and second, perspective-taking is a process that can be induced in family caregivers to help them accurately recognize, interpret, and respond to patients' current needs. Clinical implications arising from this research suggest that simple steps can be taken by nurses to foster enhanced patient-family caregiver agreement and reduce biased reporting by family caregivers on patients' illness experiences. For instance, nurses can encourage the family care-

giver to perspective-take by employing a simple prompt such as, "Putting yourself in the patient's shoes, how do you believe the patient would describe his or her symptom experience?" When this approach is used, the family caregiver is discouraged from responding to the patient's situation from a self-centered stance, thereby producing a more objective patient-oriented response to the situation.

These researchers also found that even though family caregivers appeared to follow this prompt, they also seized the opportunity to share that their own perception of the patient's experience varied from what they believed the patient would say about the experience. It appears that this type of perspective-taking prompt can serve as a trigger for discussion of discrepant perceptions that may arise, based on how the family caregiver perceives the loved one's inner states and how the loved one actually perceives his or her inner experiences. When nurses coach family members to perspective-take, they are actually facilitating a more effective style of communication in the caregiving context, which can ultimately promote enhanced patient and family outcomes (e.g., better quality of life).

Continued

CANADIAN PERSPECTIVES
PERSPECTIVE-TAKING AS A REAL-WORLD HEURISTIC DEVICE—cont'd

References

Arriaga, X. B., & Rusbult, C. E. (1998). Standing in my partner's shoes: Partner perspective-taking and reactions to accommodative dilemmas. *Personality and Social Psychology Bulletin, 24,* 927-948.

Kasch, C. R., & Dine, J. (1988). Person-centered communication and social perspective-taking. *Western Journal of Nursing Research, 10,* 317-326.

Lobchuk, M. M., & Vorauer, J. D. (in press). *Family caregiver perspective-taking and accuracy in estimating cancer patient symptom experiences.*

Schober, M. F. (1998). Different kinds of conversational perspective-taking. In S. R. Fussell & R. J. Kruez (Eds.), *Social and cognitive approaches to interpersonal communication* (pp. 145-174). Mahwah, NJ: Lawrence Erlbaum Associates.

Canadian spelling is used.

WEBSITE RESOURCES

ORGANIZATION	WEBSITE ADDRESS
Life Innovations, Inc.	http://www.prepare-enrich.com/
Couple Communication	http://www.couplecommunication.com/
Journal of Family Communication	http://www.erlbaum.com/Journals/journals/JFC/jfc.htm
National Communication Association	http://www.natcom.org
The Gottman Institute: Researching and Restoring Relationships	http://gottman.com

■ CHAPTER HIGHLIGHTS

- One of the most important activities in the family is the interactional relationship known as communication. Family communications are diverse, complex, dynamic processes that are influenced by family variables such as age, power, cohesion, adaptability, rules, networks, socioeconomic status, political views, developmental stages, and culture.

- Healthy families and relationships are based on functional communication patterns and processes. Communication patterns, rules, and meanings are learned within families and must be negotiated each time a new family is established. Communication is composed of both the verbal and the nonverbal messages that accompany the words called process. The family nurse needs to be aware of both content and process in communicating effectively with families.

■ CHAPTER HIGHLIGHTS—cont'd

- Varied levels of communicating within families reflect the willingness of members to interact. Each family development stage and transition challenges the new family composition to continue developing and maintaining healthy communication patterns and processes for the new family as a system.
- Effective communication may help a family to cope with everyday life stressors, to share and validate feelings, and to continue working together toward family goals.
- Understanding the context is important to the accuracy of the message. The family nurse must

understand all of the details of an event that the family is attempting to communicate.
- Family nursing assessments of communication patterns and processes may be accomplished by observation, interviews, and use of prepared assessment measures.
- Therapeutic nurse-family communication is rooted in the skill set of the nurse in development, maintenance, and termination of the nurse-family working alliance and working toward family goals.

CRITICAL THINKING ACTIVITIES

1. Differentiate between functional and dysfunctional family communication patterns and processes from the perspective of the sender and receiver.

2. Discuss what factors promote or inhibit effective, functional communication in families across the life span.

3. Discuss what nursing interventions family nurses can use to target the previously cited factors that promote or inhibit family communication across the life span.

4. Identify common communication issues experienced by families across the life span and nursing goals and interventions that foster solutions.

5. Differentiate among the stages, goals, and selected communication skills or strategies in fostering a therapeutic nurse-family working alliance.

REFERENCES

Adler, R. B., Rosenfield, L. B., & Proctor, R. F. (2001). Interplay: *The process of interpersonal communication* (8th ed). Orlando, FL: Harcourt, Inc.

Agnes, M. (Ed.). (1996). *Webster's new world dictionary and thesaurus.* New York: Simon & Schuster.

Arnold, E. (1999a). Intercultural communication. In E. Arnold & K. U. Boggs (Eds.), *Interpersonal relationships: Professional communication skills for nurses* (3rd ed., pp. 240-259). Philadelphia: W. B. Saunders.

Arnold, E. (1999b). Communicating with families. In E. Arnold & K. U. Boggs (Eds.), *Interpersonal relationships: Professional communication skills for nurses* (3rd ed., pp. 292-321). Philadelphia: W. B. Saunders.

Arnold, E., & Boggs, K. U. (1999). *Interpersonal relationships: Professional communication skills for nurses* (3rd ed.). Philadelphia: W. B. Saunders.

Barnes, H. L., & Olson, D. H. (1982). Parent-adolescent com-

munication scale. In D. H. Olson (Ed.), *Family inventories: Inventories used in a national survey of families across the family life cycle* (pp. 33-46). St. Paul, MN: Family Social Science, University of Minnesota.

Barsky, A. E. (2000). *Conflict resolution for the helping professions.* Belmont, CA: Wadsworth/Thomson Learning.

Bateson, G., Jackson, D., Haley, J., & Weakland, J. (1956). Toward a theory of schizophrenia. *Behavioral Sciences, 1,* 251-264.

Bienvenu, M. J., & McCain, S. (1970). Parent-adolescent communication and self-concept. *Journal of Home Economics, 62,* 344-345.

Blais, K. K., Hayes, J. S., Kozier, B., & Erb, G. (2002). *Professional nursing practice: Concepts and perspectives* (4th ed.). Upper Saddle River, NJ: Prentice Hall.

Bradley, J. C., & Edinberg, M. A. (1990). *Communication in the nursing context* (3rd ed.). Norwalk, CT: Appleton & Lange.

Brazelton, T. B. (1991). Our changing American values. In V. S. Flowers (Ed.), *Bill Moyers: A world of ideas*. New York: Doubleday.

Carter, B., & McGoldrick, M. (Eds.). (1989). *The changing family life cycle: A framework for family therapy*. New York: Gardner Press.

Corey, G. (2000). *Theory and practice of group counseling* (5th ed.). Belmont, CA: Wadsworth/Thomson Learning.

Covington, L. W. (2001). Cultural competence for critical care nursing practice. *Critical Care Nursing Clinics of North America, 13*, 521-530.

Curran, D. (1983). *Traits of a healthy family*. Minneapolis, MN: Winston Press.

Curran, D. J., & Renzetti, C. M. (2000). *Social problems: Society in crisis* (5th ed.). Boston: Allyn & Bacon.

Danish, S. J., & Kagan, N. (1971). Measurement of affective sensitivity. *Journal of Consulting Psychology, 18*, 51-61.

Davidhizar, R., Havens, R., & Bechtel, G. A. (1999). Assessing culturally diverse pediatric clients. *Pediatric Nursing, 25*, 371-376, 393-394.

Deering, C. G., & Cody, D. J. (2002). Communicating with children and adolescents. *American Journal of Nursing, 102*, 34-42.

Egan, G. (2002). *The skilled helper: A problem-management and opportunity-development approach to helping* (7th ed.). Pacific, CA: Brooks/Cole.

Emde, J. E. (1992a). Marital communication analysis: Strategies for clinicians (part 1). *NCAST National News, 8*(2), 4-6.

Emde, J. E. (1992b). Marital communication analysis: Strategies for clinicians (part 2). *NCAST National News, 8*(3), 1-4.

Epstein, N. B., & Bishop, D. S. (1993). The McMaster assessment device (FAD). In F. Walsh (Ed.), *Normal family processes*. New York: Guilford Press.

Faulkner, A. (1998). *Effective interaction with patients* (2nd ed.). New York: Churchill Livingstone.

Fox, S., & Jeffrey, J. (1997). The role of the nurse with families of patients in ICU: The nurses' perspective. *Canadian Journal of Cardiovascular Nursing, 8*, 17-23.

Friedemann, M. L. (1995). *The framework of systemic organization: A conceptual approach to families and nursing*. Thousand Oaks, CA: Sage.

Friedman, M. M. (1998). *Family nursing: Research, theory and practice* (4th ed.). Norwalk, CT: Appleton & Lange.

Friedman, M. M., Bowden, V. R., & Jones, E. G. (2003). *Family nursing research, theory, and practice* (5th ed.). Upper Saddle River, NJ: Prentice Hall.

Galvin, K. M., & Brommel, B. J. (1986). *Family communication: Cohesion and change* (2nd ed.). Glenview, IL: Scott, Foresman.

Gazda, G. M., Childers, W. C., & Walters, R. P. (1982). *Interpersonal communication: A handbook for health professionals*. Rockville, MD: Aspen.

Goldenberg, I., & Goldenberg, H. (2000). *Family therapy: An overview* (5th ed.). Belmont, CA: Wadsworth.

Gottman, J. M. (1979). *Marital interaction: Experimental investigations*. New York: Academic Press.

Gottman, J. M. (1994). *What predicts divorce? The relationship between marital processes and marital outcomes*. Hillsdale, NJ: Lawrence Erlbaum Associates.

Gottman, J. M., Katz, L. F., & Hooven, C. (1996). Meta-emotion: *How families communicate emotionally*. Mahwah, NJ: Lawrence Erlbaum Associates.

Gottman, J. M., & Notarius C. I. (2000). Decade review: Observing marital interaction. *Journal of Marriage and the Family, 62*, 927-947.

Gottman, J., Notarius C., Gonso, J., & Markman, H. (1977). *A couples' guide to communication*. Champagne, IL: Research Press.

Gudykunst, W.B. (2001). An agenda for studying ethnicity and family communication. *Journal of Family Communication. 1*, 75-85.

Haley, J. (1977). *Problem-solving therapy: New strategies for effective family therapy*. San Francisco, CA: Jossey-Bass.

Heimann, K. (2000). Family needs: How do we know what they want? *Paediatric Nursing, 12*, 31-35.

Hoffer, J. (1996). Family communication. In P. J. Bomar (Ed.), *Nurses and family health promotion: Concepts, assessment, and interventions* (2nd ed., pp. 94-106). Philadelphia: W. B. Saunders.

Jackson, D. (1957). The question of family homeostasis. *Psychiatric Quarterly, Supplement, 30*(Pt. 1), 79-90.

Johnston, J. (2001). Communicating effectively with psychotic patients. *Nursing Times, 97*, 36-37.

Jourard, S. M., & Lasakow, P. (1959). Some factors in self-disclosure. *Journal of Abnormal and Social Psychology, 56*, 91-98.

Koegel, L. K. (2000). Interventions to facilitate communication in autism. *Journal of Autism and Developmental Disorders, 30*, 383-391.

Kozier, B., Erb, G., Berman, A. J., & Burke, K. (2000). *Fundamentals of nursing: Concepts, process, and practice* (6th ed.). Upper Saddle River, NJ: Prentice Hall.

Lea, A. (1994). Nursing in today's multicultural society: A transcultural perspective. *Journal of Advanced Nursing, 20*, 307-313.

Lynn-McHale, D. J., & Deatrick, J. A. (2000). Trust between family and health care provider. *Journal of Family Nursing, 6*, 210-230.

McGoldrick, M., & Carter, E. A. (1980). Forming a remarried family. In E. Carter & M. McGoldrick (Eds.), *The family life cycle: A framework for family therapy* (pp. 265-294). New York: Gardner.

Miller, S., Miller, P., Nuanally, E. W., Wackerman, D.B. (1991). *Talking and listening together*. Littleton, CO: Interpersonal Communication Programs.

Minuchin, S., & Nicholis, M. P. (1998). Structural family therapy. In F. M. Dattilio (Ed.), *Case studies in couple and family therapy: Systemic and cognitive perspectives* (pp. 108-131). New York: Guilford Press.

Nance, T. A. (1995). Intercultural communication: Finding common ground. *Journal of Obstetric, Gynecologic, & Neonatal Nursing, 24*, 249-255.

Neuman, B. (1983). Family intervention using the Betty Neuman health-care systems model. In I. W. Clements & F. B. Roberts (Eds.), *Family health: A theoretical approach to nursing care* (pp. 239-254). New York: Wiley.

Olson, D. H. (2000). Circumplex model of marital and family systems. *Journal of Family Therapy, 22*, 144-167.

Olson, D. H., McCubbin, H. I., Barnes, H., Larsen, A., Muxen, M., & Wilson, M. (1989). *Families: What makes them work* (2nd ed.). Los Angeles: Sage.

Pasley, K. Kerpelman, J., & Guilbert, D. E. (2001). Gender conflict, identity, disruption, and marital instability: Expanding Gottmans's model. *Journal of Social and Personal Relationships, 18*(1), 5-27.

Quinn, W. H. (1993). Personal and family adjustment in later life. *Journal of Marriage and the Family, 51,* 581-591.

Reed, K. S. (1989). Family theory related to the Neuman systems model. In B. Neuman (Ed.), *The Neuman systems model* (2nd ed., pp. 385-394). Norwalk, CT: Appleton & Lange.

Reed, K. S. (1993). Adapting the Neuman systems model for family nursing. *Nursing Science Quarterly, 6,* 93-97.

Riesch, S. K., Tosi, C. B, Thurston, C. A., Forsyth, D. M., Kuenning, T. S., & Kestly, J. (1993). Effects of communication training on parents and young adolescents. *Nursing Research, 42,* 10-16.

Riley, J. B. (2000). *Communications in nursing* (4th ed.). St. Louis, MO: Mosby.

Satir, V. (1964). *Conjoint family therapy.* Palo Alto, CA: Science and Behavior Books.

Satir, V. (1976). *Making contact.* Millbrae, CA: Celestial Arts.

Satir, V. (1983). *Conjoint family therapy* (3rd ed.). Mountain View, CA: Science and Behavior Books.

Satir, V. (1988). *The new peoplemaking.* Mountain View, CA: Science and Behavior Books.

Satir, V., Banmen, J., Gerber, J., & Gomori, M. (1991). *The Satir model: Family therapy and beyond.* Palo Alto, CA: Science & Behavioral Books.

Schumm, W., Anderson, S. A., & Griffen, C. L. (1983). The marital communication inventory. In E. E. Filsinge (Ed.), *Marriage and the family assessment.* Beverly Hills, CA: Sage.

Schuster, P. M. (2000). *Communication: The key to the therapeutic relationship.* Philadelphia: F. A. Davis.

Sieh, A., & Brentin, L. K. (1997). *The nurse communicates... .* Philadelphia: W. B. Saunders.

Smith, S. B., Tutor, B. S., & Phillips, M. N. (2001). Resolving conflict realistically in today's health care environment.

Journal of Psychosocial Nursing and Mental Health Services, 39, 36-45.

Sydnor-Greenberg, N., & Dokken, D. L. (2001). Communicating in healthcare: Thoughts on the child's perspective. *Journal of Child and Family Nursing, 4,* 225-230.

Sykes, J. B. (Ed.). (1989). *The concise Oxford dictionary of current English* (7th ed.). New York: Oxford University Press.

Thomas, N. D. (2001). The importance of culture throughout all of life and beyond. *Holistic Nursing Practice, 15,* 40-46.

Tracey, M. F., & Ceronsky, C. (2001). Creating collaborative environment to care for complex patients and families. *AACN Clinical Issues: Advanced Practice in Acute and Critical Care, 12,* 383-400.

Tschudin, V. (1995). *Counseling skills for nurses* (4th ed.). London: Bailliere Tindal.

Underdown, A. (1998). The transition to parenthood. *British Journal of Midwifery, 6,* 508-511.

Villarruel, A. M., Portillo, C. J., & Kane, P. (1999). Communicating with limited English proficiency persons: Implications for nursing practice. *Nursing Outlook, 47,* 262-270.

Watzlawick, P., Beavin, J., & Jackson, D. (1967). *The pragmatics of human communication.* New York: W. W. Norton.

Williams, D. (1997). *Communication skills in practice: A practical guide for health professionals.* Bristol, PA: Jessica Kingsley.

Wright, F., Cohen, S., & Caroselli, C. (1997). Diverse decisions: How culture affects ethical decision making. *Critical Care Nursing Clinics of North America, 9,* 63-74.

Wright, L. M., & Leahey, M. (2000). *Nurses and families: A guide to family assessment and intervention* (3rd ed.). Philadelphia: F. A. Davis.

Wright, L. M., Watson, W. L., & Bell, J. M. (1996). *Beliefs: The heart of healing in families and illness.* New York: Basic Books.

Zoucha, R. (1998). Understanding the significance of culture in emergency care and treatment. *Topics in Emergency Medicine, 20,* 40-51.

APPENDIX 7-1   Clinical Rating Scale—Family Communication

Couple/Family Score	Low (1-2)	Facilitating (3-4)	High (5-6)
Listener's Skills			
Empathy	Seldom evident	Sometimes evident	Often evident
Attentive listening	Seldom evident	Sometimes evident	Often evident
Speaker's Skills			
Speaking for self	Seldom evident	Sometimes evident	Often evident
Speaking for others*	Often evident	Sometimes evident	Seldom evident
*Note reverse scoring			
Self-disclosure	Infrequent discussion of self, feelings, and relationship	Some discussion of self, feelings, and relationships	Open discussion of self, feelings, and relationships
Clarity	Inconsistent and/or unclear verbal messages	Some degree of clarity but not consistent across time or across all members	Verbal messages very clear
	Frequent incongruence between verbal and nonverbal messages	Some incongruent messages	Generally congruent messages
Continuity/Tracking	Little continuity of content	Some continuity but not consistent across time or across all members	Members consistently tracking
	Irrelevant/distracting nonverbal messages and asides frequently occur	Some irrelevant/distracting nonverbal messages and asides	Few irrelevant/distracting nonverbal messages and asides. Facilitative nonverbal messages
	Frequent/inappropriate topic changes	Topic changes not consistently appropriate	Appropriate topic changes
Respect and regard	Lack respect for feelings or message of others	Somewhat respectful of others but not consistent across time or across all members	Consistently appears respectful of others' feelings and messages
	Possibly overtly disrespectful disrespectful or belittling attitudes	Some incongruent messages	
Global Family Communication Rating (1-6)	The global rating is based on your overall evaluation, not a sum score of the subscale.		

From Olson, D. H., McCubbin, H. I., Barnes, H., Larsen A. Muxen, M. (1989). *Families: What makes them work* (2nd ed.). Newbury Park, CA: Sage.

Family Spirituality and Religion

Carmen Germaine Warner-Robbins
Perri J. Bomar

8

> *I am reminded of your sincere faith, a faith that dwelt first in your grandmother Lois and your mother Eunice and now, I am sure, dwells in you.*
>
> — 2 Timothy 1:5 RSV

OBJECTIVES

On completion of this chapter, the reader will be able to do the following:
1. *Distinguish between religion and spirituality.*
2. *Compare differences in the major religions.*
3. *Discuss the role of religion in family life across the life span.*
4. *Explain the influence of religion on family health across the family life span.*
5. *Examine the role of religion in selected family crises and transitions.*
6. *Discuss the role of the nurse in assisting families in spiritual distress and in the promotion of spiritual health.*
7. *Describe the implications of research for spirituality and family health.*
8. *Explain the role of the nurse in meeting individual and family spiritual needs.*

At the beginning of the twenty-first century, families are facing considerable stresses, crises, and challenges unlike those of previous decades (Boss, 2002). The economy is experiencing the harshest attack since the Great Depression; terrorist attacks are a reality (Farrell & Brill, 2002; Riley, Clark, & Wong, 2002); the incidence of divorce and family breakup has soared to an unbelievable level; and reports of family violence, abuse, and addiction are at an all-time high (Wright, Watson, & Bell, 1996).

Unemployment, abandonment, impending death, workplace stress, total loss and destruction—these are the faces of discouragement and despair that are confronting many families every day. Family nurse clinicians must deal with situations such as the following case examples on a regular basis.

Case Examples

1) *Melissa, age 33, is about to be released from jail; she had been charged with the sale of narcotics. As a single parent and mother of three, she was desperate for money to care for her children. Now, after 6 months in jail, she has lost her children and has no place to go; her family has abandoned her, she is frightened and angry and has a chronic cough, which remains untreated.*

187

2) *For the past 19 years, Tom, father of five, held a position as parts mechanic at a local aircraft plant. Now, at the age of 49, Tom has been laid off, with no alternate positions in sight. After frantically searching for a job, Tom experiences severe abdominal pain, for which the doctor sees no medical cause. "What do I do?" Tom asks as he discusses the future of his family with his wife, now 6 months pregnant. "Where do I turn? Who can help us?"*

3) *Glen, at the age of 15, has suddenly become quiet, withdrawn, and isolated from his mother and younger sister. Although Glen had once led an active life of sports and model car racing with his father, he is now alone, without a father. Glen's father left the home more than 3 years ago. Even his close childhood friends do not come around the house anymore. When Glen's mother inquires about what has happened, he shouts, "Leave me alone! I don't want anything from anybody. I can take care of myself."*

4) *Cindy is 29 years old. She looks back at her life and smiles. She has a wonderful husband and two young children. Even her job offers her more income and professional gratification than she had known before. Now that her twin daughters are in school full-time, Cindy is exploring outside activities and has enrolled in graduate school. During a recent medical examination, a lump was discovered in Cindy's right breast. On surgical exploration, cancer was diagnosed, with metastasis to her liver and kidney. Although she had been active in church all her life, Cindy turns away from her church family and displays her anger toward God. "Why me? What did I do wrong in my life? I hate you, God, for ruining my life and my family's lives."*

5) *It was 3:00 AM, Monday, August 24th. The winds had built up over the past several hours, but protective boards had been placed on the windows, and the family was huddled together in their basement. "We'll make it," Joe said in a comforting voice to his wife and three children. "We've suffered these tropical storms before." At 6:00 AM after the brunt of Hurricane Andrew had passed, Joe and his family began to emerge from the pile of debris and rubble. Their house was completely destroyed; everything was gone. "Oh, my God, my God! What has happened? What do we do now? Where, oh where, do we begin?"*

These are examples for which nursing intervention, listening skills, and resource counseling may not be adequate to address the core of a client's pain, pressure, or problem. As families struggle with real life, textbook references, client care plans, and case study situations may not provide the depth of healing and hope that is crucial and of paramount importance.

According to Dunphy (2001), the import of spirituality as a salient realm for nursing practice dates to Florence Nightingale who perceived her involvement in the Crimean war as a "calling from God." In the twenty-first century, it is still common for health professionals to see families turn to God while facing desperate situations. When everything else fails, prayer, worship, and focus on God become the only foundation on which they can stand. Strength, hope, and a sense of survival grow out of people's religious beliefs as they turn toward God.

The Illness Belief Model

Human beings are assumed to have both a biopsychosocial nature and a spiritual nature. On this grounding was formed The Illness Belief Model (Wright et al., 1996). The religious and spiritual premise of The Illness Belief Model is determined to be at the very core of both the suffering and healing families experience during illness. It is crucial for family health nurses to recognize the suffering and healing components as pivotal aspects of the religious/spiritual focal point. A balance is necessary for wholeness to be achieved, and it is this focal point that occurs in achieving that balance.

Religion and Spirituality: Distinguishing Characteristics

For clarity and uniformity of meaning in this text, the following definitions are used.

Religion

The term *religion* relates to the inward and outward expression of belief, not the content of that belief. Religion is an aspect of the spiritual dimension of life. It is the belief in the reverence for God or some supernatural power that is recognized as the creator and ruler of the universe (Lockyer, 1986). Religion is also defined as a belief in a supernatural or divine force that has power over the universe and commands worship and obedience (Guralnik, 1979). A personal definition may be expressed as an individual and communal commitment to a deity involving a belief system, a value or ethical system, and a worship system. Religion can also be identified as an organized institutionalized system of belief incorporating shared values and beliefs and involvement in a faith community (Fetzer Institute/National Institute on Aging 1999; Wright et al., 1996).

There is hesitancy today to use the word *religion,* in the context of either the Christian faith or its expression in worship and service. The reason is that Christianity reflects an outward expression by believers—not as an attempt to secure salvation, but as a thanks offering for it.

Religiosity

Although it is different from spirituality, the term *religiosity* is often used interchangeably with the term *spirituality.* There are a number of definitions in the literature. *Religiosity* is one's relationship with one's God and things or persons that are sacred. It may also refer to a continual human striving for spiritual growth in and with a community of spiritual people (Fetzer, 1999) Religiosity, noted as intensive excessive or affected religiousness, was proposed by Batson and Ventis (1982) to demonstrate psychodynamically different ways of being religious. The extrinsic religious orientation is one in which religion is used to justify self-centered ends in a strictly utilitarian way for one's safety, social standing, and solace and for endorsing one's chosen way of life. By contrast, the intrinsic religious orientation is one in which religious commitments are carefully thought out and taken seriously as a major goal in life. "The extrinsically motivated individual uses his religion, whereas the intrinsically motivated lives his" (Batson & Ventis, 1982, p. 38).

Spirituality

The broader concept of *spirituality* is a component of health related to the essence of life. It is the vital principle in human beings that gives life to the physical organism in contrast to its purely material aspects and relates to the soul as opposed to the body (Hill & Smith, 1990). It also is clarified as a sensitivity or commitment to religious values and sacred matters (Tenney & Douglas, 1999). Spirituality is associated with transcendence and specific things of the spirit, as distinguished from that which is material (Fetzer Institute/National Institute on Aging, 1999). The etymological roots of *spirit* are the Latin word *spiritus* meaning breath, courage, soul, and vigor, along with the Hebrew word *ruach* and the Greek word *pneuma,* both of which stem from words for breath (Barnhart, 1988).

Support for differences between religion and spirituality is provided in the literature (Shafranske & Maloney, 1990; Underwood & Teresi, 2002). Religion can be described as "adherence to the beliefs and practices of an organized church or religious institution" and spirituality, as "those more personal practices of a religious nature which may or may not emanate from a particular religious institution" (Douglas et al., 1980, p. 74). Capra and Steiendl-Rast (1991) comment that families may have spirituality without religion; however, they could not have authentic religion without spirituality (pp. 12-13). Spirituality also is concerned with the meaning of life and compassion for others (Fetzer Institute/National Institute on Aging, 1999). In essence, spirituality is perceived as experience, and religion represents the intellectual dominion of spirituality.

Family Spirituality

The family as a unit is held together by interwoven threads. These threads represent the various paths and patterns of family life, including areas of security and protection, food and shelter, education and growth, and spiritual cohesiveness and purpose. This important area of spiritual bonding affords the basis for family strength, endurance, and growth.

Family spirituality is the means by which a God-centered focus provides the basis for the harmony, communication, and wholeness among family members from which all other family activities, ties, and beliefs are influenced, guided, and directed.

This God-centered focus provides an opportunity for individual and family growth. Members can challenge and test one another but remain mutually respectful; they grant freedom to one another yet accept the responsibility for both individual and family spiritually focused roles. Family spirituality is vital in discovering the very meaning and purpose in life. In essence, the recognition of the spiritual dimension of the care-giver is necessary for the work of healing to begin. The healing process evolves as harmony develops between caregiver and family, grounded in the recognition and appreciation of family and caregiver spirituality.

Aspects of Spirituality

A review of the literature reveals that scholars define spirituality in different ways (McLeod & Wright, 2001; Elkins, Edstrom, Leaf, & Saunders, 1988). Spirituality is uniquely defined by each professional who incorporates it into his or her nursing practice (Catanzaro & McMullen, 2001). In my personal integration of spirituality, as a minister and a nurse, the following statements depict how I employ spirituality with the families to whom I minister.

1) Strive for the ultimate in seeking inspiration, harmony, reverence, meaning, purpose, and calling in life.
2) Search for the gifts and graces within God's or one's higher power's given blessings.
3) Recognize the human potential for spirituality and spiritual growth.
4) Surrender and be open to God or one's higher power for the ultimate in one's human existence.
5) Identify spirituality as a way of life and a sacred journey.
6) Seek the value of self and integrate that into the ultimate scheme of life.
7) Identify what is most important in one's existence.
8) Seek help and guidance from God.

Common Characteristics of Major Religions

The health and well-being of each family may involve a variety of religions and practices with which the family nurse may not be familiar or comfortable. Depending on the religious prefer-ence of the client, the nurse may be either rela-tively comfortable or uneasy. Despite any existing differences, the ability of practitioners to guide,

direct, and work with members of each religious preference will establish a trusting relationship and an open means of communication.

To facilitate optimum interaction with clients, nurses should have a basic understanding of the common characteristics of religion, which are as follows:

- Basis of authority or source(s) of power
- Portion of scripture or sacred word
- Ethical code that defines right and wrong
- Psychology and identity that fit its adherents into a group and that define the world
- Aspirations or expectations
- Ideas about what follows death

The major world religions are divided into three groups. The first group includes Christianity, Judaism, and Islam. Taoism, Confucianism, and Shintoism are assembled in the second group. The third group includes Buddhism and Hinduism. Table 8-1 lists various religions and their beliefs, practices, and specific relationships to family needs.

Role of Religion in Family Life

The Puritans were the first Anglo-Americans to establish viable families, and this proved crucial to the survival of subsequent revitalization of their religious system. Religion, family, and society intersect, especially at times of develop-mental life transitions, including birth, puberty, marriage, and death. These vital moments in the life cycle were given meaning and significance in the religious ideologies and rituals that social groups used and enacted to interpret them. Even in ancient societies, religion was believed to influence human destiny. Treatment was administered by tribal shamans or medicine men, with later treat-ment being administered in temples by priests.

Over the course of many years, religious and spiritual influences have changed. Today, physi-cians and nurses have become increasingly more specialized, and sophisticated machinery has been deemed essential. As modern health care has evolved, the importance of the religious di-mension has decreased to the extent that it has been deemed least important, which has caused the client to become increasingly dehumanized. Only as a result of the dehumanization process did an eventual upsurge in emphasis on religion and spiritual well-being evolve.

Text continued on p. 196

TABLE 8-1   Beliefs, Practices, and Family Needs of Various Religious Groups

Religion	Belief	Practice	Relation to Family Needs
Adventist	Dead are asleep; to be resurrected when Christ returns Divine healing Literal interpretation of Bible	Anoint with oil in prayer Adult baptism by immersion Children dedicated No alcohol, tobacco, narcotics, or stimulants No special practice regarding death Prohibit eating meat, primarily pork Oppose hypnosis Sabbath is Saturday No immunization or blood transfusions	Healing through prayer Bible provides support Importance of nutrition in religious beliefs
American Indian	300 different tribal groups; each has its own nature-oriented religion Disease has two forms— presence of a material object in the body and the absence of the soul from the body Superhuman powers are used for protection against disease	Practice elements of magic, disease treatment, and herbal medicine Medicine men and shamans perform the symbolic rites against disease	Superhuman powers used to protect from disease Use herbs as treatment Medicine men are to be contacted during illness
Armenian	No conflict between church and medicine	Infants baptized by immersion 8 days after birth Confirmation (called *chrismation*) follows immediately Communion is performed as last rites and also may be given earlier, in infancy and throughout life Laying on of hands Fasting during Lent and before Communion	Child baptized as infant Communion near death Prayer with and for one another
Baptist (more than 27 different groups in the United States)	Bible is supreme authority God works through the physician	Baptize only believers by immersion No infant baptism No alcoholic beverages Laying on of hands Prayer with clergy if near death	Have Bible by bedside If death is imminent, call clergy Prayer very important May delay seeking medical care
Buddhist	No conflict between church and medicine Illness is a trial to aid development of soul	Discourage use of alcohol, tobacco and drugs Last-rite chanting practice at bedside after death Body cremated	Celebrated holy days: Jan.1, 16; Feb. 15; Mar. 21; Apr. 8; May 21; Jul. 15; Sept. 9, 23; Dec. 8, 31

Continued

TABLE 8-1   Beliefs, Practices, and Family Needs of Various Religious Groups—cont'd

Religion	Belief	Practice	Relation to Family Needs
Christian Scientist	Denies reality of illness Sickness and sin are errors of human mind, eliminated by spiritual truth, not drugs	Have own practitioners to offer care No infant baptism No alcohol, coffee, tea, tobacco, or drugs No blood transfusions, biopsies, or autopsies—only by law Creamation and burial acceptable No physical medicine	Secure physicians and nurses of like faith Restrictions to be closely adhered to
Church of Christ	No conflict between church and medicine Recognize human limitations of medicine	Communion Anoint with oil Laying on of hands for healing No alcohol or last rites Baptism by immersion after 8 years of age	Pray with others for healing If child is older than 8 and critically ill, see clergy
Church of God	Divine healing through prayer	No alcohol or tobacco No baptism or last rites or cremation Speak in tongues	Pray with others for healing
Church of Jesus Christ of Latter-Day Saints (Mormons)	Believe in revelations prophecies Blessing of the ill by anointing and laying on of hands by elders	Baptism by immersion after age 8 Baptism by proxy for the dead No alcohol, coffee, tea, caffeine of any kind, or tobacco Use meat sparingly	Observe diet Be aware of dress code Buried with temple garments on
Disciples of Christ (Christian Church)	No conflict between church and medicine	No infant baptism—only a dedication service Adult baptism by immersion Communion important in worship and in hospital	Spiritual support by clergy and elders May desire communion in hospital
Eastern Orthodox	No conflict between church and medicine	Baptism within 40 days after birth Baptism by immersion, followed by immediate confirmation (chrismation) and communion in infancy Last rites obligatory Cremation discouraged Anointing of sick by healing through prayer	Christmas is on Jan. 7 and New Year's on Jan. 14 Observe baptism requirements Prayer very important
Episcopal (Anglican)	No conflict between church and medicine	Infant baptism Baptism urgent if newborn is likely to die Last rites not mandatory Spiritual healing in some cases Some fast before communion and reserve eating meat	Baptism if child's life is in danger May desire prayer for spiritual healing

TABLE 8-1   Beliefs, Practices, and Family Needs of Various Religious Groups—cont'd

Religion	Belief	Practice	Relation to Family Needs
Grace Brethren	No conflict between church and medicine	No infant baptism Dedication for children Baptism only for those old enough to profess faith Anointing of sick for physical and spiritual healing No last rites Clergy needed at time of death Abstinence from alcohol, tobacco, and illicit drugs Cremation permitted Stillborns to be buried	Clergy called for anointing of sick and time of death Stillborns to be buried
Greek Orthodox	No conflict between church and medicine Oppose euthanasia; try to preserve life	Chrismation and communion within 40 days of birth Communion as last rites Autopsies and cremation discouraged Selective fasting on Wednesdays and Fridays and during Lent Holy communion provided by priest on request	Call priest for communion when patient is near death Fasting is important and may need to be coordinated with diet Christmas and Easter observed according to different calendar format
Hindu	Most accept modern medical practices	Prescribed rites follow death Priest ties a thead around the neck or wrist, signifying a blessing Priest pours water into mouth of corpse; family washes the body Bodies cremated Many dietary restrictions; do not eat beef	Be aware of special rituals concerning death Dietary requirements are important to follow
Jehovah's Witnesses	Oppose false teachings of other religions Attempt to convert others	No infant baptism No last rites Alcohol discouraged Cremation acceptable Autopsy by personal decision No abortions or blood transfusions	Be aware of infant and death rites Will not accept blood or abortions
Judaism	No conflict between beliefs and medicine Someone should be with person when soul leaves the body	Male circumcision on 8th day after birth Fetus, organs, and body parts must be buried Abortion only to save life of mother Many special dietary requirements Opposed to euthanasia, autopsy, and cremation Observe Sabbath through rest and worship Burial within 24 hours (not on Sabbath)	In case of impending death, read Psalm 23, 103, or 139 Special dietary needs are important Family present during circumcision

Continued

TABLE 8-1 Beliefs, Practices, and Family Needs of Various Religious Groups—cont'd

Religion	Belief	Practice	Relation to Family Needs
Lutheran (10 different branches)	No conflict between church and medicine	Baptism 6 to 8 weeks after birth by immersion or sprinkling Anointing may be requested	Baptism important Clergy valuable during illness
Mennonite	No conflict between church and medicine Self-determination is important	No infant baptism; but baptism in teens No last rites, communion, or other sacraments No alcohol Prayer very important Women may wear head coverings during hospitalization	No religious rites or sacraments Prayers crucial in time of illness or personal need
Methodist (more than 20 different groups)	Belief in divine judgment (good rewarded and evil punished) Clergy counsels but does not hear confession	Baptism for child and adults Communion, prayer, and scripture important Donation of organs encouraged	Seek prayer, scripture, and communion at time of need
Moravian	Disease is not a form of divine punishment, although breaking from God can lead to physical problems	Infant baptism No last rites Patient to be comfortable, but life not to be extended at all costs Communion and laying on of hands are important	Physical touch and prayer are most important Communion desired
Muslim (Islam)	Conservative groups can have fatalistic view, which can affect compliance with therapy	No baptism Fetus aborted after 130 days must be buried according to custom Abortion forbidden Women can't sign consent forms One must confess sins before death to preserve family Family washes and prepares body after death No autopsies unless required by law Bury as soon as possible after death No cremation No alcohol or pork Koran has many holy requirements to be kept Jewelry may have special meaning	Multiple religious rules and regulations must be observed Diet and death have many special requirements
Nazarene	No conflict between church and medicine Belief in divine healing but not exclusive to medical treatment	Baptism optional No last rites Cremation permitted Stillborns are buried Communion and laying on of hands by pastor No alcohol or tobacco	Special attention to stillborns Prayer and communion important

TABLE 8-1   Beliefs, Practices, and Family Needs of Various Religious Groups—cont'd

Religion	Belief	Practice	Relation to Family Needs
Pentecostal (Assembly of God; Foursquare)	Illness seen as an intrusion of Satan Deliverance from illness is provided in atonement	Baptism by immersion after age of accountability No last rites Divine healing through anointing, prayer, and laying on of hands No alcohol, tobacco, or illicit drugs No eating of strangled animals or anything to which blood has been added No pork products	Prayer, anointing, and laying on of hands for healing
Presbyterian (10 different groups)	Science used for relief of suffering and recognized as gift from God Full forgiveness through repentance for any illness connected with a sin	Infant baptism Last rites not a sacrament; involve prayer and scripture Communion may be required	Communion beneficial to patient Prayer valuable
Quaker (Friends)	No creed, thus a diversity of personal beliefs Pacifists God is in every man and may be approached directly Individual choice and decision making very important	No baptism at birth No rituals related to death Decisions left up to individual Avoid alcohol and drugs	Discuss desires and needs with individual for his/her choice
Roman Catholic	No conflict between church and medicine except for abortion on demand May donate or transplant organs if no harm to donor	Infant baptism mandatory Emergency baptism for neonates with poor prognosis, stillborns, and fetuses (if not clinically dead) Anointing of the sick is mandatory Fasting and abstinence from meat on Ash Wednesday and Good Friday (exceptions okay in hospital)	Baptism mandatory Priest to be called if death is imminent Communion important to patient
Russian Orthodox	No conflict between church and medicine	Baptism by priest only Chrismation and communion in infancy No autopsies, embalming, or cremation After death, arms crossed with fingers in a cross formation Clothing to be of natural fiber to decompose faster Crosses worn; important for them to be left in place No meat or dairy products on Ash Wednesday and during Lent	

Continued

TABLE 8-1 Beliefs, Practices, and Family Needs of Various Religious Groups—cont'd

Religion	Belief	Practice	Relation to Family Needs
Salvation Army	No conflict between church and medicine, except for abortion on demand Bible is the only rule for one's faith	Infant dedication No particular baptism, communion, or death practices	Abortion on demand not accepted Bible is important to one's daily life
Unitarian (Universalist)	Reason and practicality are most important Each person has right to approach values individually Clergy are not always needed if patient is assuming responsibility for self	Baptism by choice, but without formula of the Trinity Dedication of children No sacraments officially Agree to organ donation Prefer cremation Belief in immortality differs	One's own choice and decision are important regarding religious matters

From A. Schroeder (1993). Emotional and spiritual support. In T. C. Kravis, C. G. Warner, & L. Jacobs (Eds.), *Emergency medicine review* (3rd ed.). New York: Raven Press.

In the course of the elevation of religion in family life, people have turned away from organized religion and the notion of one true God. In a misguided attempt to find God inside themselves, people have turned to so-called new age religions. These religions claim to be the new and improved spirituality that can be practiced "individually" through some mixture of metaphysical concepts, workshops and awareness training programs, star charts, crystals, channels, and out-of-body experiences (Pearsall, 1990). "Religion can also be harmful to individuals and families" (Abbott, Berry, & Meredith, 1990, p. 443). Examples of harmful activities include excessive corporal punishment of children, promotion of sexism and racism, rigid doctrines, delay of health care, and disapproval of the use of family planning methods. Regardless of the type of religion practiced, its value and its role in the family are important to family health nurses, because even though religion is seen as a personal belief, a group (family) is involved as well.

Family Spiritual Health Model

The family spiritual health model is important to understand and apply with respect to both personal and family beliefs. The family spiritual health model (Figure 8-1) depicts an inward flow of communication, beginning with the all-encompassing existence of God (supreme being). The presence of God flows through each dimension of life, including community, family, child, and parent. The effects of God's presence culminate in the inner focus of family existence, noted as the core of spirituality.

The model reflects the dynamics of a constant flow of God's presence back and forth, encompassing the totality of family dynamics. As each circle of communication expands, beginning with the core of spirituality, the network broadens, moving from parent to child to family and finally to the community. These concentric circles relate to the expanded communication evident in the ongoing expansive level of family spiritual health.

Between the circles of expanding communication, there is a continuous perforated line representing the focus and ongoing movement toward God, beginning with one's basic spiritual grounding in a relationship with God and expanding to include others. The baseline of the model indicates that this flow occurs throughout time in an unceasing, ever-constant manner over the family's life course.

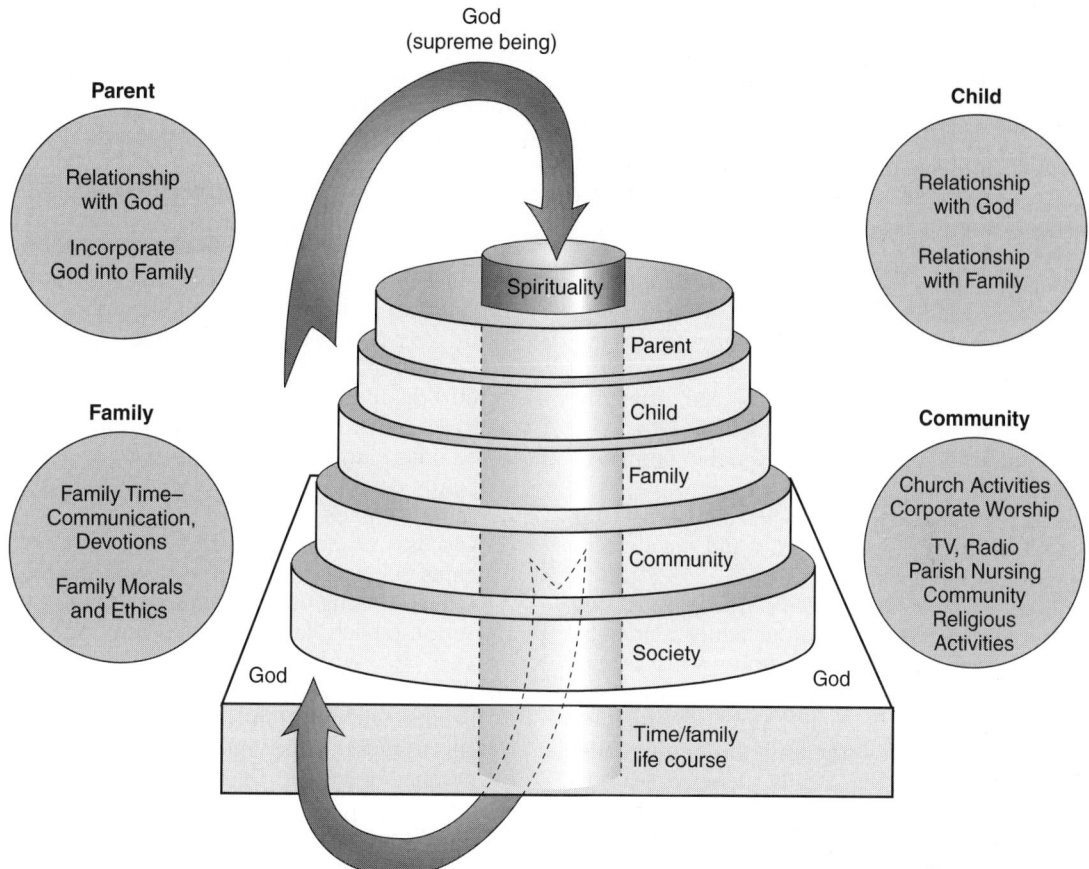

Figure 8-1   Family spiritual health model.

Each ring reflects the characteristics and aspects of family values that are nurtured and expanded through this model. The model also clarifies the means by which religion and spiritual growth can support the total well-being of the family unit.

Religion provides the ultimate means of worship in fellowship with others. Many people seeking guidance for an emotional problem will turn to a religious leader first before seeking any other professional leadership. Through this contact, families are becoming closer to one another and to God and are developing and experiencing valuable family strengths. Research supports the belief that values and religiosity are specific qualities related to family strengths (Olson et al., 1983; Schumm, Hatch, & Schumm, 1990). Researchers have found religiosity to be the most

reliable predictor of family strengths. Religion contributes to family strengths in the following five ways: (1) beliefs or values, (2) beneficial practices or behaviors, (3) social benefits related to organizations with a religious affiliation, (4) family recreation and activities, and (5) assistance in seeking divine intervention with individual and family religious counseling and spiritual direction (Abbott et al., 1990, Brigman & Keating, 1989).

Family Strength through Religion

Family health clinicians can look for growth-producing elements in each family's life and value system that will encourage them to demonstrate flexibility, forgiveness, resilience, patience, love, tolerance, cooperation, and effective communication and to develop a meaningful family way of life (Olson, 1999; Giblin, 1996). As these family strengths grow and mature, the following six specific family characteristics evolve (Brigman, 1992).

- *Faith*: Allows families to discover meaning and purpose in life and enter into fundamental commitment and identifies how families perceive life
- *Hope*: Provides a sense of optimism in times of stress and difficulty
- *Love*: Promotes opportunities for support and nurturing
- *Parenthood of God*: Enhances ego strength, which may strengthen individuals
- *Forgiveness and grace*: Allows the family to resolve conflicts
- *Reverence and commitment:* Fosters respect for and dedication to one's family and the concept and purpose of family

According to Pearsall (1990), if religion is truly to be a source of strength to the family, it must be a religion of closeness and unity with others. Associated with this unity is the opportunity for growth provided through church attendance. Pearsall says that it is primarily through ongoing church attendance that family members learn to nurture, care for, and support one another. This caring association knits families together and provides strength and hope in times of need.

Spiritual Influences on the Family Life Cycle

The importance of a religious influence in the family is a lifelong process—from the cradle to the grave. In fact, this process represents a means of actually bringing aspects of one's life and not just talking about the stages. As Max Jacobs, a Frenchman with a Judeo-Christian background says, "you must live things, not define them" (Anderson, 1999, p. 164).

Childhood

Ideally, an infant's first involvement with feelings and emotions is the development of a sense of trust and the belief in a secure environment. The child feels loved and comforted, which is the initial step in the development of self-esteem and

self-love. Spiritual and religious values are conveyed to the infant in a nonverbal manner throughout these early years, which establishes a basis for future beliefs (Hill & Smith, 1990).

Parents who want to influence the moral and spiritual health of their children by providing a religious foundation, can do the following:

1) Teach children the value of kindness, goodness, patience, faithfulness, gentleness, and self-control.
2) Read books to children, and encourage them to read books that demonstrate the incorporation of these qualities into one's life and into the lives of notable individuals.
3) Read and study selections from the writings of one's faith (scripture) as part of a daily family devotional, discussing personal application to one's situation.
4) Discuss and point out examples of how religious beliefs and principles can be applied.
5) Celebrate religious holidays as a family unit and establish family rituals and practices associated with these holidays.
6) Plan family outings and activities in connection with religious holidays.
7) Discuss the value and importance of the practice of daily prayer as individuals and as a family.
8) Stress that prayer need not be fancy or formal, but an open, natural communication with God (or one's higher power).
9) Pray for one another as a family (for example, before meals, at the beginning and end of each day, and throughout the day) for such things as preparation for school work, guidance at work or in meetings, and strength during times of illness or discouragement.
10) Establish a prayer partner (another parent or church/synagogue member), as done by families in some traditions, who will commit to pray for the family and be present for love and support.
11) Commit to having each child baptized or dedicated in accordance with one's church, synagogue, or other religious institution.
12) Prepare children for their commitment to God through the celebration of the sacraments or rites of passage such as confirmation, first communion, bar mitzvah and bat mitzvah, or the ritual as prescribed by one's faith.

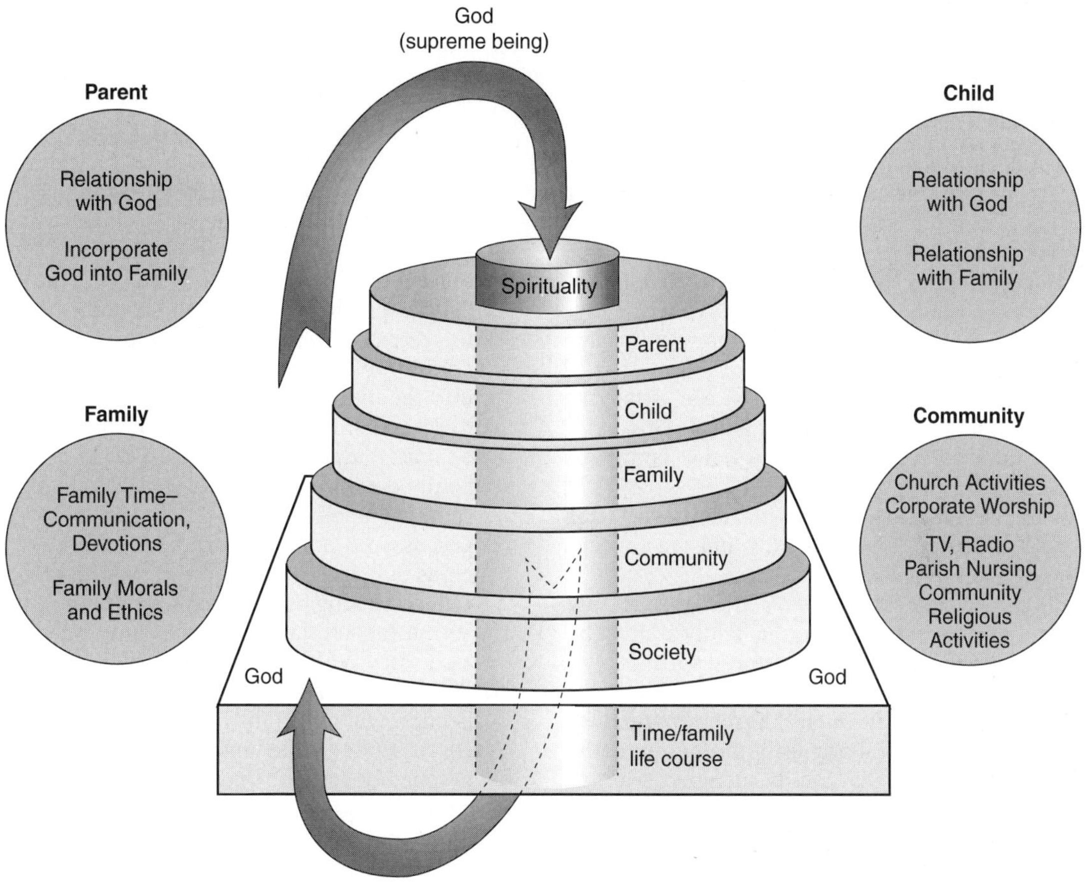

God
(supreme being)

Parent

Relationship
with God

Incorporate
God into Family

Child

Relationship
with God

Relationship
with Family

Family

Family Time–
Communication,
Devotions

Family Morals
and Ethics

Community

Church Activities
Corporate Worship

TV, Radio
Parish Nursing
Community
Religious
Activities

Spirituality

Parent

Child

Family

Community

Society

God   God

Time/family
life course

Figure 8-1   Family spiritual health model.

Each ring reflects the characteristics and aspects of family values that are nurtured and expanded through this model. The model also clarifies the means by which religion and spiritual growth can support the total well-being of the family unit.

Religion provides the ultimate means of worship in fellowship with others. Many people seeking guidance for an emotional problem will turn to a religious leader first before seeking any other professional leadership. Through this contact, families are becoming closer to one another and to God and are developing and experiencing valuable family strengths. Research supports the belief that values and religiosity are specific qualities related to family strengths (Olson et al., 1983; Schumm, Hatch, & Schumm, 1990). Researchers have found religiosity to be the most

reliable predictor of family strengths. Religion contributes to family strengths in the following five ways: (1) beliefs or values, (2) beneficial practices or behaviors, (3) social benefits related to organizations with a religious affiliation, (4) family recreation and activities, and (5) assistance in seeking divine intervention with individual and family religious counseling and spiritual direction (Abbott et al., 1990, Brigman & Keating, 1989).

Family Strength through Religion

Family health clinicians can look for growth-producing elements in each family's life and value system that will encourage them to demonstrate flexibility, forgiveness, resilience, patience, love, tolerance, cooperation, and effective communication and to develop a meaningful family way of life (Olson, 1999; Giblin, 1996). As these family strengths grow and mature, the following six specific family characteristics evolve (Brigman, 1992).

- *Faith*: Allows families to discover meaning and purpose in life and enter into fundamental commitment and identifies how families perceive life
- *Hope*: Provides a sense of optimism in times of stress and difficulty
- *Love*: Promotes opportunities for support and nurturing
- *Parenthood of God*: Enhances ego strength, which may strengthen individuals
- *Forgiveness and grace*: Allows the family to resolve conflicts
- *Reverence and commitment:* Fosters respect for and dedication to one's family and the concept and purpose of family

According to Pearsall (1990), if religion is truly to be a source of strength to the family, it must be a religion of closeness and unity with others. Associated with this unity is the opportunity for growth provided through church attendance. Pearsall says that it is primarily through ongoing church attendance that family members learn to nurture, care for, and support one another. This caring association knits families together and provides strength and hope in times of need.

Spiritual Influences on the Family Life Cycle

The importance of a religious influence in the family is a lifelong process—from the cradle to the grave. In fact, this process represents a means of actually bringing aspects of one's life and not just talking about the stages. As Max Jacobs, a Frenchman with a Judeo-Christian background says, "you must live things, not define them" (Anderson, 1999, p. 164).

Childhood

Ideally, an infant's first involvement with feelings and emotions is the development of a sense of trust and the belief in a secure environment. The child feels loved and comforted, which is the initial step in the development of self-esteem and

self-love. Spiritual and religious values are conveyed to the infant in a nonverbal manner throughout these early years, which establishes a basis for future beliefs (Hill & Smith, 1990).

Parents who want to influence the moral and spiritual health of their children by providing a religious foundation, can do the following:

1) Teach children the value of kindness, goodness, patience, faithfulness, gentleness, and self-control.
2) Read books to children, and encourage them to read books that demonstrate the incorporation of these qualities into one's life and into the lives of notable individuals.
3) Read and study selections from the writings of one's faith (scripture) as part of a daily family devotional, discussing personal application to one's situation.
4) Discuss and point out examples of how religious beliefs and principles can be applied.
5) Celebrate religious holidays as a family unit and establish family rituals and practices associated with these holidays.
6) Plan family outings and activities in connection with religious holidays.
7) Discuss the value and importance of the practice of daily prayer as individuals and as a family.
8) Stress that prayer need not be fancy or formal, but an open, natural communication with God (or one's higher power).
9) Pray for one another as a family (for example, before meals, at the beginning and end of each day, and throughout the day) for such things as preparation for school work, guidance at work or in meetings, and strength during times of illness or discouragement.
10) Establish a prayer partner (another parent or church/synagogue member), as done by families in some traditions, who will commit to pray for the family and be present for love and support.
11) Commit to having each child baptized or dedicated in accordance with one's church, synagogue, or other religious institution.
12) Prepare children for their commitment to God through the celebration of the sacraments or rites of passage such as confirmation, first communion, bar mitzvah and bat mitzvah, or the ritual as prescribed by one's faith.

13) Attend religious services, classes, and fellowship activities as a family unit.

14) Teach the importance of giving of the family's money, talent, prayers, and service to one's place of worship.

Adolescence

Adolescence is a crucial time in the development and formation of an individual's identity (Maslow, 1968). The primary task during this particular stage is to resolve identity versus role diffusion. A significant part of an adolescent's personal identity relates to how he or she views himself or herself with respect to the opposite sex. To be part of the group is very important, and frequently, group pressure might lead to early sexual activity.

An important factor in helping the adolescent deal with the issue of sexuality is the spiritual health and well-being of the family unit. A strong family spiritual foundation, grounded in solid moral beliefs, will afford an adolescent the desire, words, and actions to reject sexual activities and to stand firm on personal beliefs, resisting peer pressure and influence. One way to secure this is through the recognition that sex education and the pertinent values must be broached long before adolescence if the child is to develop psychosexually. One community-oriented approach consists of abstinence education programs that are reported to be successful in creating positive attitudes toward premarital abstinence (Carter-Jessop, Franklin, Heath, Jimenez-Irizarry, & Peace, 2000).

Adolescents need to openly and honestly address the question of "who they are" and "what's their place in the world." Adolescents are adjusting to a new, dramatic awareness of self, causing them to debate and question everything presented to them. They are attempting to determine values, roles, and responsibilities in a world where there is confusion, doubt, and emphasis on personal gain. Individual feelings and emotions are real but frequently unexplainable. Parents can incorporate religion into their communication with adolescents in the following ways:

• Discuss sexual values and religious beliefs.

• Pray with their child concerning specific needs, desires, and wants.

• Join with other parents from their church, synagogues, or school and pray for their children and their classmates. "Moms-in-Touch" (MIT) is a group of mothers from schools throughout the country who meet weekly for this very purpose.

• Involve children in various youth groups and activities to provide spiritual, social, and peer support during these challenging times.

• Encourage the involvement of family in church activities, especially those related to recreation, sports, and meals.

• Initiate a time when an open forum of communication and sharing is possible—a time when a particular event or activity can be related to scripture.

The critical stage of adolescence is identified by Carson (1989) as a time of conflict and rebellion, leading to one's search for self-identity and purpose. During this process, the adolescent seeks faith and purpose from group contact and interaction. Such contact, for example from a church or synagogue, will support, influence, and affirm the adolescent and encourage a commitment to his or her religious beliefs. This affirmation provides a stepping stone to the next stage of young adulthood.

Young Adulthood

Only when adolescents have explored and come to terms with who they are can they commit to an intimate relationship as young adults (Carson, 1989). The personal sacrifices of such a commitment may produce a challenge. During this time, individuals make a conscious decision concerning their commitment to religious symbols, religious beliefs, and a supreme being. Now that the young adult begins the searching part of his or her faith. During this process, a personal conversion experience may occur, usually in a very soft and subtle manner.

Parents can draw on their religion to assist the young adult in the following ways:

• Encourage the young adult to openly share feelings, struggles, and questions.

• Facilitate an opportunity for the young adult to discuss ideas and to ask questions of the family pastor, rabbi, priest, or other religious leader.

• Support and encourage the value of open prayer and communication between young adults and their God.

- Seek printed materials that will support the testing, learning, and decision-making process of the young adult's religious commitment.
- Pray daily for guidance, direction, and peace.

Adulthood

Life's challenges do not end with young adulthood. In fact, the pressures of this time often extend that difficult period of transition into the years of adulthood. Adulthood is a time of planning for the future, reexamining one's focus and purpose in life, and integrating one's religious beliefs into a format for life. Adults must examine and confirm their values, morals, and religious foundations. There is a need to understand and communicate with one's inner self, thus providing solid guidelines for making concrete decisions. It has been stated that during adulthood "there is nowhere you have to go to work on yourself other than where you are at this moment. Everything that is happening to you is part of your work on yourself" (Dass, 1976, p. 12).

Adults can maintain the importance of religion in the family in the following ways:
- Participate in a support group that will provide a forum for shared concerns, challenges, and choices.
- Become involved in learning/growth groups that deal with such issues as finance, parenting struggles, and personal support.
- Join a sacred writings study group or prayer support group for fellowship, spiritual growth, direction, and prayer in one's chosen way.
- Secure a prayer partner for daily prayer, even if not in person. (For example, one person commits to initiating a mutual prayer time. This person, at a previously agreed upon time, calls the prayer partner, lets the telephone ring once, and then hangs up. This one ring calls both parties to prayer.)

Senior Adulthood

At the end of the life cycle, when the pressures of work and raising children have ceased, older adults frequently have more time for, investment in, and devotion to religion and its role in their lives. This trend is consistent with the belief that the first quarter of life relates to growth; the second quarter, to work; the third quarter, to play; and the fourth quarter, to spirituality (Hill & Smith, 1990).

Adults may rely on spirituality, especially during this fourth quarter, to help them deal with issues of chronic illness, pain, suffering, and even death. For example, individuals facing old age might have come to grips with an illness that has no cure but might be seeking emotional and spiritual comfort. For many people, the strength, support, and inner peace they can receive from their religion not only assists them in dealing with physical pain but also provides them with the coping skills needed to relate to the future and the family. During this time, older adults are spending part of their lives preparing for death. Acceptance of death comes with a sense of fulfilled potential.

Fear, resentment, and despair may occur when an individual has not become all that he or she thought was possible. Individuals may need the reassurance of faith, a sense of purpose, and a feeling of well-being about life after death. Such feelings will help the individual develop a positive attitude toward death; a feeling of peace about where the individual is in his or her life cycle; and the humility to love, accept, and forgive himself or herself and others. Wisdom is the gift and virtue to see one's life as a whole and accept past failures and successes with balance. Personal integrity seems to be the foundation of growth in advanced years.

Koenig, McCullough, and Larson (2001) analyzed 100 studies on the relationship of religiousness, well-being, life satisfaction, and morale. In almost 80% of the studies a positive relationship was found between religion and study variables. According to research findings, senior adults can incorporate religion into their family life in the following ways:
- Join a group with mutual interests related to hobbies, recreation, or social gatherings.
- Participate in a grief and loss support group if an individual has lost his or her mate.
- Establish a means by which people check on each other at a prearranged time.
- Seek church activities that encourage and develop personal gifts and talents.
- Welcome church or community groups that incorporate programs such as "adopt-a-grandparent."

The Effect of Religion on Family Health

Family health clinicians are confronted with a responsibility to mobilize, encourage, and reaffirm the internal strengths, goals, and resources of families. Throughout this process, nurses are able to assist individuals in finding the meaning in health, illness, and suffering. The true meaning of life and living unfolds, as family members are able to focus on and openly share a religious base or core in their lives. Faith, strength, and responsibility are instrumental as building blocks for a shared family religious core (Curran, 1983). Faith in God provides the basic foundation for all activities, beliefs, and conversation within a family unit. The strength of the family support system as a whole, built on the existing foundation, evolves from the religious core within the family. Finally, the responsibility for passing on and integrating one's faith into daily life provides the means by which families bond in a positive and meaningful manner.

In a review of the model of family spiritual health, eight benefits can be identified that will influence and support the value of religion in the total health and well-being of the family: goodness, kindness, joy, love, patience, self-control, faithfulness, and peace. These benefits are defined as follows:

• Goodness bridges together the community at large and the structured church.
• Kindness is shared by those who worship in the corporate church or synagogue setting.
• Joy becomes evident when the family-based spiritual values extend and radiate into the community.
• Love knits together all members of the family unit.
• Patience encourages interaction between child and parent.
• Self-control establishes a personal awareness between one's self and God.
• Faithfulness encourages and directs a parent to integrate God into the family structure.
• Peace is experienced as one seeks closeness with God.

Several enablers of one's spiritual perspective can be identified, encouraged, and developed through the direction and guidance of others. These enablers include love and affirmation, understanding or wisdom, and pivotal life events.

Specifically, love and understanding evolve though the involvement and association of significant others, teachers, and role models such as family health nurses. Pivotal life events provide situations that develop a spiritual perspective (Ingersoll-Dayton, Krause, & Morgan, 2002; Newman, 1989).

Love and Affirmation

A basic human need, in addition to one of the primary ingredients of life, is the gift of love. Integrated throughout religious teachings is the principle and call to "love one another" (John 15:12), for it is indeed through the gift of love that people are healed, families are held together, disagreements are resolved, futures are built, and lives are restored.

Examples of love in action become evident in family life through the examples and teachings one secures in a religious environment. In and through a religious community, families experience the fruits of love, including support, affirmation, remembrance, dedication, and fellowship.

Support is important in the face of adversity, as well as the building up and maintenance of one's concept of self. In a religious community, one will experience the shared joys and celebrations, along with the tears and tribulations. Daily life often requires the loving support of a comforting arm, a listening ear, and the quiet presence of someone who is just there for you. The availability of this support is a primary foundation in one's religious surroundings, as evidenced through small groups, prayer, worship, and pastoral care.

The need for and value of personal affirmation builds self-esteem and strengthens personal worth amidst the difficulties, challenges, and trials often experienced in a family. A strong foothold and grounding in one's faith is facilitated by application of the spiritual readings to personal affairs.

Just as an individual is affirmed regarding his or her value and worth in God, it is also important for him or her to experience the value of affirmation by being remembered and recognized as valuable, worthwhile, and wanted. All family members grow and thrive on the knowledge that they are accepted and remembered as unique, special human beings. Even though an individual may have faced and will face joys and sorrows, strengths and weaknesses, health and illness, sin and forgiveness, past heritage and future destiny, there is the assurance that he or she can seek and receive a sense of personal identity in his or her own creation.

Special activities and events within the life of a church are encouraged so that family members of all ages will be received, recognized, and remembered at important times and occasions in their lives.

Understanding

From the time that a small child begins to establish his or her grounding in what is true, there is an understanding of the basic concept of right and wrong and sound moral teachings. These truths are taught and reinforced through learning in class, reading the scripture, and listening to sermons. Not only are children informed of the difference between right and wrong, but they are also taught how to apply these truths and where to seek help and strength when the application may be difficult.

Pivotal Life Events

Pivotal events may occur as a result of peak experiences along life's journey. Some of those experiences, as identified by Olson et al. (1982), are as follows:

- Transitions related to the role or status of family members, the addition of family members, or the relocation of an individual or the family as a unit
- Sexuality focusing on the onset of sexual activity, pregnancy, and childbearing
- Personal losses, such as the death or absence of a family member, relative, or friend or the loss of property or income
- Responsibilities and strains relating to interpersonal tensions, or stressors related to health care and finances
- Substance use, referring to the use of drugs or alcohol, and disagreement over the use of a substance
- Legal conflict involving the arrest or assault of a family member

During such pivotal life events, nurses frequently co-experience with their clients both wellness and suffering. It is believed that during these interactions, both nurse and client become more in agreement with the possibilities of what they can create together (Paterson & Zderad, 1976). Health can be associated with the ability to transcend ordinary living situations to enhance and develop all aspects of the self.

A union between client and nurse can develop as a result of such experiences. In addition to such a union, religious rituals have proven to be very stabilizing forces. Kneeling, fasting, scriptural study, praying, meditating, and chanting are outward and visible expressions of faith.

Family health clinicians should be observant for family life course transitions such as birth, baptism, first communion, confirmation, graduation, marriage, and funerals. These transitions unite and connect the spiritual and social and cultural realms. After experiencing these transitions and being strengthened by their spirituality, families become more resilient for future life course events (Olson et al., 1983; Pearsall, 1990).

Seeking Direction for Families

Each member of the family discovers and applies his or her own source of energy in the family unit. The energy from each member emanates and combines to unify the force of the family as a whole. This is evident when families provide for the physical and emotional needs of the members and share in the spiritual growth and development of the family unit. Family ties are the closest when they are not separated by television, video games, or conflicting outside experiences. In fact, the greatest harmony evolves from talking, sharing, and reflecting on one another's ideas.

An excellent example of this principle in action comes from the practice of making scripture come alive. This can be accomplished at mealtime. A scripture verse is chosen, read aloud, and applied to the activities of everyday life. The situational sharing can be both challenging and rewarding because each member can communicate not only activities but feelings as well. Such building of family reverence can knit members together so that during times of stress, trial, and tribulation, family unity is the stronghold and not the weakest link. Some family health clinicians may believe that inquiries concerning a family's spirituality could be dangerous, intrusive, disrespectful, or not relevant to their practice (McLeod & Wright, 2001). However, if a clinician is to promote complete family healing, spiritual experiences and beliefs are equally as important as the physical and the emotional aspects of care. It will not stand should this dimension be ignored.

Pearsall suggests three distinct paths to be taken in establishing a grounding in family reverence (Pearsall, 1990). These paths are family time saving, finding space for the family, and self as a cell.

Family Time Saving

People often feel that time is "flying" by, but really their lives are flying. With each passing day, there is less time available for family members to spend with loved ones. A person can never make up for lost time once a loved one has a fatal illness. The days in the past are gone forever, yet families can be encouraged to sit down with one another, share with each other, pray for one another, and just be with each other. As shown in Figure 8-1, family time saving is one of the foundations of family health and well-being.

Finding Space for the Family

Continuing into the twenty-first century, people often feel that to accomplish anything, they must always be "doing." The idea of life being worthwhile only if it is filled with constant activity is false. There is greater value and worth in just being with one's family than all the aimless, frantic "doings" society perceives to be so meaningful (Doherty & Carlson, 2002). When family members take the time and effort to meditate on what they have created as a family, they bring the joy of reverence for humanness to each day of their lives. If families practice the art of creating space in their families by gearing down to "slow" and "stay" speeds, the reward will be enormous (Doherty, 2001; Olson & Olson, 2000).

The Self as a Cell

Self really means the "us" of our family. In many ways, this can be portrayed in the phrase, "we are us" (Pearsall, 1990). This is a valuable point to be remembered daily. We need to think each day of what we are actually doing to keep our family close together. Simulations, prearranged quiet times of prayer and reflection (wherever one might

be), family pictures carried by each member, and a concerted effort to join hands in the morning for prayer and scripture reading will keep family ties meaningful and close. This closeness is especially important to implement with children during the infancy and toddler periods. Brief moments of family time can become a way of life if they are initiated when children are young.

The focus and direction of the family unit is a top priority, especially concerning spiritual health and wholeness. The following three elements closely knit the family into a pattern of harmony and purpose:

- The investment of love spent through quality time together
- The gift of joy displayed by just being with each other
- The treasure of patience portrayed in knowing the closeness of one another

Role of Religion in Crises and Transition

Life is a journey of day-to-day uncertainties. Despite all the advances in technology, communication, health care, and research, no human being can predict the future. However, researchers, therapists, and clergy maintain that a religion, faith, or spirituality can often help individuals and families deal with the future and ease stress (Walsh, 1999).

Benefits of Religion to the Quality of Life

For those who are grounded in a sound religion, the fear for tomorrow and the events of the future are minimized. Support, comfort, and direction in times of need and crises are provided through religious belief, a spiritual leader, and the love and support of other faith members, such as those in the local church.

Religion, in fact, helps individuals to make sense of life. People, through religion, are able to bridge life on Earth to life in the hereafter. Through this belief, hope and strength are provided as a guide during difficult times. There are seasons in a person's life, however, when family members are weak, ill, or in pain and unable to deal with life's crises on their own. During these times of doubt, confusion, and grief fellow members of a faith community can provide valuable and necessary support by listening, praying, and giving of their time (Idler & Kasl, 1997; Musgrave, Allen, & Allen, 2002).

The Relationships of Religion and Health

A mounting body of evidence points to positive relationships between spirituality or religion and physical, mental, personal, and family health. In two extensive reviews of well-designed prospective research studies on the relationship of religiousness and health by Koenig and colleagues (Koenig et al., 2001; Koenig, 2002), the benefits of spirituality and religion are summarized as follows:

• Coping is enhanced and depression is lessened in those who depend on religion. In addition, recovery from illness and stressful events is more rapid.

• Suicide and substance abuse are reported to be less common among persons who are more religious.

• Reports of positive emotions and feelings of well-being were significantly greater in 79 of 100 studies when religious practices were more frequent.

• Social support has a significant correlation with religion, as indicated in 19 of 20 studies.

Koenig (2002) reports increasing evidence (particularly in the field of psychoneuroimmunology) that physical health is better among those who are more religious. For example, in an examination of 16 research studies of the relationship between hypertension and religiousness, 90%

RESEARCH SYNOPSIS

BELIEF IN A HIGHER BEING IN HEALING, CHURCH ATTENDANCE AND EXERCISE SELF-EFFICACY IN SOUTHERN AFRICAN AMERICAN AND WHITE WOMEN

Religiosity is often overlooked as a crucial factor in a person's choice of health care practices and adherence to regimens prescribed by health care professionals. Some regions of the United States are called the Bible Belt because of the high concentration of places of worship and the significantly higher number of people who participate in communal worship. African Americans are often described as being more religious; however, there is limited knowledge on how their beliefs in a higher being intervening in healing influence their health-promoting lifestyles and adherence to prescribed health care regimens. The purpose of this secondary analysis of a larger study was to compare the belief in a higher being in healing and religious activities in rural African American and white women with their exercise self-efficacy.

The study was a descriptive correlational study of mothers of seventh, eighth, and ninth graders in a large field of the cardiovascular risk factors of youth from five rural schools in North Carolina. The sample included 77 African American mothers and 113 white mothers with a mean age of 39 years. Religiosity was measured using an 11-item religiosity scale that has two subscales: belief in a higher being and participation in religious activities. The self-efficacy scale was a five-item scale developed by Marcus, 1992. The t test results revealed that African American women had significantly higher beliefs in a higher being intervening in healing ($p = 0.001$) and religious activities ($p = 0.0001$). White women had a significantly higher exercise self-efficacy ($p = 0.006$).

To enhance adherence to prescribed health care regimens by culturally diverse women, nurses must assess clients' self-efficacy (belief in their ability to accomplish a task) and the extent of their belief in the power of a higher being in healing. Low self-efficacy would suggest the potential of not adhering to a prescribed health regimen such as exercise. In addition, for some clients, total reliance on a higher being for healing without a combination of self-care behaviors and medical regimens may impede recovery from an illness or improved level of health.

Bomar, P. J., Harrell, J. S., & Deng, S. (1999, February). *Belief in a higher being in healing, church attendance and exercise self-efficacy in southern African American and white women.* Paper presented at the 1999 Southern Nurse Research Conference, Charleston, S.C.

(14 of 16) reported lower blood pressure among persons with higher religiousness. Lastly, he noted that researchers report the more religious seek health care less often. The Research Synopsis presents a study in which the relationship between religious activities and beliefs and exercise activity was examined.

Religion and Barriers to Health

Although religion has many positive factors, there is evidence that some individuals use their belief in a supreme being in a way that may be detrimental to their health. For example, in a qualitative report on rural African American women with hypertension, Bomar states that some participants believe that "God is in control. If I take pills, then I don't show that I have faith" (Bomar, 1995). Others may believe that their time of death is predestined and they should not interfere. For example, Powe (1995) notes significant fatalism about the outcome of cancer in her study of elderly African Americans. In addition to offering alternatives to delaying or forgoing treatment because of religious beliefs, health professionals may help individuals and families to make informed decisions about their self-care and to continue to practice their religion.

When Spirituality, Religion, and Faith Are Absent from Family Life

Health care professionals at times may be intervening with families who either do not have a religion or have expressed feelings of anger and resentment toward God or a higher being. Researchers note that not all families experience positive outcomes from prayer and church attendance. For example, McAdoo (1995), in a study of African American single mothers, found that those who prayed and attended church less frequently reported lower stress scores. Mothers who prayed more often rated themselves as more depressed. During contact with families, the health care professional should never attempt to force religious beliefs on a family or attempt to talk them out of their feelings toward their God. Instead, it is important to assess the family's spirituality, to focus on the values of religion, and to remain sensitive to the variability in the meaning of God and religion. Rather than confronting any feelings of denial or anger, thus creating possible alienation, the health care professional must be patient and allow individuals an opportunity to explore their emotions, to speak about their feelings, and to receive open and honest feedback from others.

It is essential to ask the family what they want and what their needs might be. Families, if allowed to be themselves, are more likely to be open to an honest response to their feelings, giving the health care professional an opportunity to provide appropriate nurturing and compassionate care.

Stages of Crises and Transitions

Throughout the life cycle, there are multiple occasions for celebrating, rejoicing, grieving, adjusting, and refocusing. In each stage, an individual will experience many events and opportunities for religious support. Some of these events are identified in Table 8-2.

As families deal with issues of stress, trauma, and disruption, it is valuable for members to be laced together in a common bond of unity. It is through the strength of an agreed-upon commitment that families are held together in a steadfast and solid manner that will support them during periods of transition and crisis. An idea the author has developed for the integration of such a bond is noted in Figure 8-2.

As family members face crises together, they are supported through their faith and prayer. Individual members feel supported by the prayers of family members (Curran, 1983). During these times, it is essential for the family to respond to their crisis by being led, focused, and strengthened by their God rather than by their emotions.

Family health nurses can encourage family members to share these ideas (noted in Figure 8-2) with one another, focus on that which is most valuable, and pray about the specifics of what is important. The value and importance of prayer should be addressed in an open, nonthreatening way so family members can feel comfortable in the practice of prayer.

Belief in the Power of Prayer

Not only has the power of prayer deeply touched the lives of those believing in its worth and applying it to their daily lives, its effectiveness

TABLE 8-2   Religion/Spirituality in Family Transitions and Crisis

Event	Ceremony or Ritual	Religious Support
Marriage	Wedding	Rejoicing; celebrating; unifying of family
Birth of child	Baptism	Commitment to God in presence of other believers
Childhood (entering adulthood)	Confirmation (at times)* or Bar mitzvah or Bat mitzvah	Learn laws of the church; assume personal responsibility for religious direction of one's life
Death	Funeral	Celebration of one's life; public affirmation of life after death
Loss, grief, financial concerns, moves	Support groups	Support and/or prayer groups; educational groups; establish connectional networks

*In the Roman Catholic church, first communion is given before confirmation or during the same ceremony. Theologically, confirmation is not perceived as a puberty rite, even though it may be misunderstood as such.

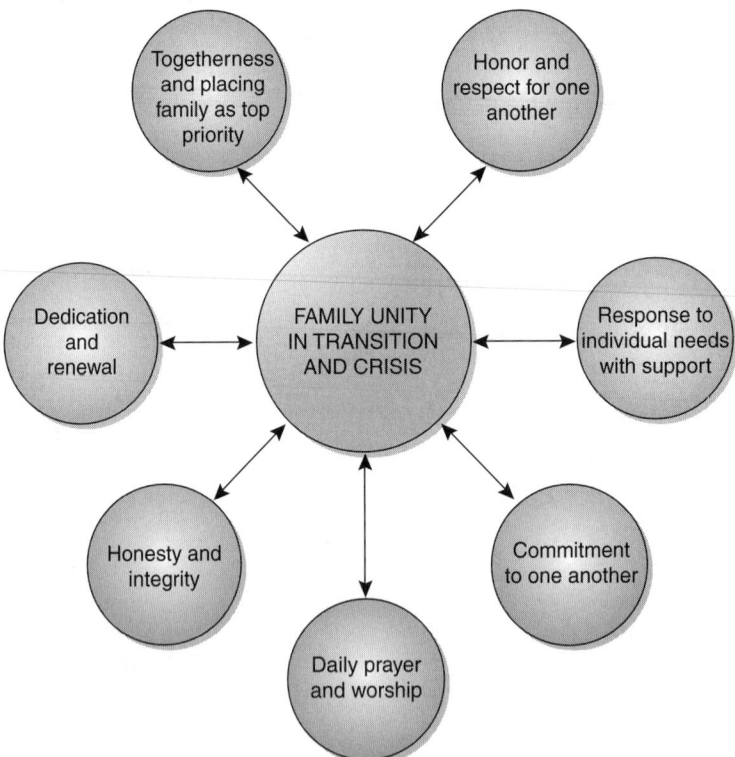

Figure 8-2   Seven integrating beliefs in the family structure.

has become evident through scientific studies (Koenig et al., 2001). Research suggests that prayer, meditation, and Bible study promote well-being and survival over the long term (Helm, Hays, Flint, Koenig, & Blazer, 2000).

In a 10-month study of 393 patients admitted to the coronary care unit at San Francisco General Hospital (Byrd, 1988), a computer randomly assigned patients to two separate groups. Prayer groups prayed for one group of 192 patients, and a second group of 201 patients did not have people praying for them. Strict scientific, double-blind controls were applied in this study. Groups from across the country representing Protestant, Catholic, and Jewish faiths were asked to pray for between five and seven patients. The prayer groups were provided with the name and condition of each patient. However, guidelines on how to pray were not provided.

The results of Byrd's (1986) study were impressive. Those who were prayed for by prayer groups were five times less likely than the unremembered group to require antibiotics (3 patients compared with 16 patients). Those receiving prayer were three times less likely to experience pulmonary edema (6 patients compared with 18 patients). None of the prayed-for group required endotracheal intubation, whereas 12 patients in the unremembered group required mechanical ventilator support. Fewer patients in the prayed-for group died (although this difference was not statistically significant). Similar findings have been noted by researchers at Duke University's Center for the Study of Religion/Spirituality and Health (Koenig, 2002). For sample study abstracts, see the website address listed at the end of the chapter.

Spirituality is important in family and individual health care in all settings. On the basis of his own research and a review of the research on religion and health, Koenig suggests that the reasons for the salience of spiritual care in health care decisions are as follows:

- Many people's religion and religious beliefs help them to cope.
- Religious beliefs influence health care decisions, especially when people are seriously ill.
- Religious beliefs and activities are related to better health and quality of life.
- Many families and clients want health professionals to address their spiritual needs.

- The idea of health care professionals addressing spiritual needs of individuals and families is not new "but, is rooted in the long historical relationship between religion, medicine, [nursing], and health care" (Koenig, 2002, p. 5).

The Nursing Process and Family Spiritual Health

In contrast to application of the nursing process to physical needs, Carson (1989) relates that spiritual needs must be inferred from client behavior, when nurses apply the "tool of themselves" and their gifts of compassion, listening, and kindness.

Although the emphasis on holistic care has been encouraged and advocated throughout nursing's history and modern-day practice, in actuality, the spiritual dimension has not been openly and willingly acknowledged. In addition, health professions schools stress biopsychosocial needs and minimally, if at all, relate to the spiritual aspect of the individual (Carson & Koenig, 2002; Carson, 1989). Religious and spiritual transitions vary across the life span and should be assessed at each stage (Ingersoll-Dayton et al., 2002).

This void in the sensitivity and appreciation of the value of spirituality in nursing stems from several areas of focus. Initially, nurses are more comfortable dealing with facts than with feelings. Throughout the nursing process, it is easier to relate to that which one can see, hear, or touch—that of the physical. The issue of spirituality is often awkward and uncomfortable, almost as if nurses feel it is none of their business. Second, nurses may not wish to "get involved." If one can relate solely to a disease, a symptom, or a causative factor, the process is easier. However, when nurses touch issues that are spiritual in nature, their own spiritual dimensions and issues may surface.

Lastly, the issue of role definition contributes to the lack of sensitivity and true appreciation of the spiritual health of the family. Others, such as pastors, priests, rabbis, and chaplains, are available to assist families with the issue of spiritual matters. However, the crucial factor is the recognition of spiritual distress and the collaborative involvement of the family health practitioner in the initial referral (Treloar, 2000). A Canadian view of spirituality and nursing care is presented in the Canadian Perspectives box.

CANADIAN PERSPECTIVES
A CANADIAN CONTEXT OF SPIRITUALITY

Verna C. Pangman, RN, MEd, MN
University of Manitoba

According to Ameling and Povilonis (2001), an increased interest has evolved concerning the spiritual dimension of nursing. The focus is now being directed toward incorporating spiritual care into nursing practice. Effective spiritual care includes learning how to assess and to respond to the spiritual needs of clients and their families (Myerhoff, Van Hofwegen, Hoe Harwood, Drury, & Emblen, 2002).

As a result of Canada's multicultural diversity, nurses in all settings need to assist not only the client who is experiencing illness but his or her family members as well, to express in a personal and culturally specific manner, their spirituality (Mullin, Lee, Hertwig, & Silverthorn, 2001; Olson, Simington, & Clark, 1998). Such supportive assistance, when provided by a sensitive nurse, helps the client and family to find a deeper meaning in life. In addition, helping the client and family to express their spirituality provides a realistic sense of hope in accordance with their belief systems (Wright, Watson, & Bell, 1996).

Research on the family has confirmed the importance of spirituality in families, particularly in those families that have demonstrated the strength and ability to cope effectively with stress. Wright (1997) states that harmonious family systems can successfully manage the many difficult challenges that occur in life. One such challenge may be the onset of a critical illness in a family member whereby the entire family is confronted by fundamental questions regarding their value systems and spiritual supports.

Many families, after experiencing a significant illness in a family member, find a new meaning in life and an increased depth of spirituality, (Myerhoff et al., 2002). In fact, suffering can present the initial encounter that an individual experiences with his or her own spiritual self. Such an encounter with spirituality can result in a serious examination of one's concept of meaning and purpose in life (Wright, 1997).

Another term that frequently appears in discussions about spirituality is *spiritual well-being* (O'Neill & Kenny, 1998). *Spiritual well-being* may be defined as a sense of inner peace, compassion for others, reverence for life, gratitude, and an appreciation of connectedness and diversity in relationship building. According to Tuck and Baliko (2001), the ability to promote spiritual wellness does not demand that the nurse know specific practices or rituals; nor does the nurse need to share the spiritual philosophy held by the client and his or her family.

The prevalent focus on the holistic care of the client and family has reinforced the importance of the role of nurses in providing spiritual care (O'Connor, 2001). The Canadian Holistic Nurses Association, a recognized interest group of the Canadian Nurses Association, emphasizes the development of holistic nursing practice (Petersen, 1996). The role of the nurse as holistic practitioner must not only recognize, but include, the spiritual dimension (Tuck & Baliko, 2001). In Canada since the mid 1990s, interest in parish nursing has continued to grow (Olson et al., 1998). The role of the parish nurse embraces the concept of holism. According to Wright (1998), nurses who embrace the concept of holism are not only professionally responsible but ethically obliged to provide spiritual care in their nursing practice.

CANADIAN PERSPECTIVES
A CANADIAN CONTEXT OF SPIRITUALITY — cont'd

References

Ameling, A., & Povilonis, M. (2001). Spirituality, meaning, mental health, and nursing. *Journal of Psychosocial Nursing and Mental Health Services, 39(4),* 15-20.

Mullin, J., Lee, L., Hertwig, S., & Silverthorn, G. (2001). A native smudging ceremony. *Canadian Nurse, 97,* 20-22.

Myerhoff, H., Van Hofwegen, L., Hoe Harwood, C., Drury, M., & Emblen, J. (2002). Spiritual nursing interventions. *Canadian Nurse, 98,* 21-24.

O'Connor, C. (2001). Characteristics of spirituality, assessment and prayer in holistic nursing. *Nursing Clinics of North America, 36,* 33-46.

Olson, J., Simington, J., & Clark, M. B. (1998). Educating parish nurses. *The Canadian Nurse, 94,* 40-44.

O'Neill, D., & Kenny, E. (1998). Spirituality and chronic illness. *Image: Journal of Nursing Scholarship, 30,* 275-280.

Petersen, B. (1996). The mind-body connection. *The Canadian Nurse, 92,* 29-31.

Tuck, I., & Baliko, B. (2001). Why deliver health care with spirituality? *Sigma Theta Tau International Honor Society of Nursing Excellence in Clinical Practice, 2,* 1-4.

Wright, K. (1998). Professional, ethical, and legal implications for spiritual care in nursing. *Image: Journal of Nursing Scholarship, 30,* 81-83.

Wright, L. (1997). Suffering and spirituality: The soul of clinical work with families. *Journal of Family Nursing, 3,* 3-14.

Wright, L., Watson, W., & Bell, J. (1996). *Belief: The heart of healing in families and illness.* New York: Basic Books-HarperCollins.

Canadian spelling is used.

Assessment of Family Religious Orientation

Much of this chapter has dealt with the importance of family unity, focus, and direction. For the nurse to relate to and intervene with families, the family as a unit and each member must be first assessed regarding his or her individual spiritual development and growth. For example, prayer, although it is basically talking with God or a higher being, may mean something different to each family member. Some members may feel comfortable with sharing their prayers openly, others may prefer to read prayers that are already written, and others may be uncomfortable with even the idea of prayer. However, the primary focus should be on how the family as a unit relates to and incorporates prayer in daily life.

The spiritual health of the family is commonly assessed by inquiring about the family's involvement or membership in a particular faith community. Surface assessment does not reveal the important feelings and spiritual benefits identified in Table 8-3. Several approaches to assessment of family spirituality are noted in the literature. Initially, the clinician may observe the client's interaction, spiritual artifacts (e.g., jewelry, books, and music), and verbal references to a higher being (Spector, 2000). Spirituality-focused genograms are used to assess the family's spiritual resources and heritage (Frame, 2000, Dunn & Dawes, 1999). Some clinicians use clinical assessment tools such as the Family Spiritual Health Assessent tool presented in Box 8-1. In *Spirituality in Patient Care* (Koenig, 2002), the reader will find a list of short clinical assessment tools that can be used to determine a client's spirituality (see Koenig, 2002, pp. 89-94, for an in-depth discussion of the tools).

Recognizing that a spiritual assessment is not easy to discuss, the clinician may consider the following points:

- Inquiries may be made in response to comments or statements made by family members.
- Questions may be asked based on observations made in the home (obvious religious pictures or literature).

TABLE 8-3   Family Spiritual Health

Benefits	Family Spiritual Health Relationships
Goodness	Expands knowledge and enlightenment and bridges to church
Kindness	Integrates spiritual and social activities into corporate spiritual growth
Joy	Extends family values into the community
Love	Encourages personal/family time
Patience	Facilitates interaction between child and parent
Self-control	Stimulates relationship of child with God
Faithfulness	Integrates spirituality into family process
Peace	Facilitates oneness with God

BOX 8-1   Family Spiritual Health Assessment

1. Is religion or a supreme being important to your family? What do you call your supreme being?
2. Do all your family members believe in the same supreme being?
3. Describe the relationship of each family member to God (supreme being).
4. What is your God like?
5. How do you communicate with your God?
6. How does God (supreme being) relate to your family and to each member?
7. What does faith mean to your family life and to each member?
8. How has your faith influenced your life?
9. Is there anything that has happened in your life or that of your family that has either separated you from or brought you close to God (supreme being)? Explain.
10. Where is the source of your hope?
11. To whom do you talk when in need of spiritual direction?
12. Are there any religious beliefs, practices, or rituals that are important to your family today?
13. Do you read scriptures or religious literature as a family or individually? If so, what do you read? Who reads the most?
14. Do you pray as a family? How often? Do you pray in silence or aloud? Do you pray for each other?
15. What happens when you pray? Does prayer benefit your family?
16. Are there any religious medals, jewelry, or statues that are important to your family?
17. Do you worship as a family or individually? How often do you attend religious services?
18. What are your beliefs about death and life after death?
19. Describe the value of worship to your family and to each member.
20. What relationship have you established at your place of worship?

Based on data from Carson, V. B. (1989). Spirituality and the nursing process. In V. B. Carson (Ed.), *Spiritual dimensions of nursing practice* (pp. 150–179). Philadelphia: Saunders.

- Dialogue may be stimulated through nonverbal communication or in response to the ease or discomfort noted in responses.
- Every question does not need to be asked, and additional questions relative to a particular topic may be added.

For some families, religion may serve as a source of strength, calm, inner peace, and guided direction. Others may be cool toward God, even angry, questioning the nature of suffering, apparent abandonment, and death. No matter what the situation may be, family health practitioners are not to judge, condemn, or criticize a person's religious beliefs. Instead, the nurse's role is to remain sensitive to the family's needs while supporting and affirming them.

Nursing Diagnosis

All the data and information the nurse is able to obtain—whether verbal, nonverbal, visible, or situational or through observation of family relationships—will provide the necessary basis for accurate interpretation. It remains crucial that the nurse continually validate the information to prevent any false assessments, interpretations, or judgments. Open, reflective dialogue will facilitate collection of this information.

Two common nursing diagnoses in the realm of family spiritual health are spiritual well-being and spiritual distress (Johnson, Bulechek, Dochterman, Maas, & Morehead, 2001). *Spiritual well-being* is "personal expressions of connectedness with self, others, higher power, all of life, nature, and the universe that transcend and empower the self" (Johnson, Maas, & Moorhead, 2000, p. 407). *Spiritual distress* is a "disruption in the life principle that pervades a person's entire being and that integrates and transcends one's biological and psychosocial nature" (Johnson et al., 2000, p. 530). The distress may be major or minor and related to pathophysiology, recommended treatment regimens, personal factors, or environmental factors. The North American Nursing Diagnosis Association (NANDA) taxonomy has addressed the following three spiritual needs of an individual: (1) love and relatedness, (2) forgiveness, and (3) meaning and purpose. These identified needs plus observations made from behavior responses, actions or reactions, and direct responses to questions guide nurses in making an appropriate nursing diagnosis. The reader is encouraged to review the spiritual dimensions in NANDA (NANDA, 1999), the *Nursing Interventions Classification* (McCloskey & Bulechek, 2000), and the *Nursing Outcomes Classification* (Johnson et al., 2000).

Intervention

Just as capacity building and strengthening are necessary when a family is confronted with a physical or emotional situation, they are also valuable during times of spiritual distress or conflict or when a spiritual leader is needed. The following are examples of situations in which spiritual support is frequently needed:

- Baptism, confirmation, communion, or marriage of a family member
- Times of illness, long-term caregiving, loss, impending death, or death
- Times of separation, divorce, parent/child problems, financial distress, and other distressing events
- Times of celebration, joy, and reunion when special religious events are in order
- Catastrophes, natural disasters, terrorist attacks, and war

On identification of appropriate nursing diagnoses relating to the overall family's spiritual health care needs, the nurse, along with the family, determines the specific spiritual growth facilitation, type of support, and activities with which to instill hope (Johnson et al., 2000). Use of the Nursing Interventions Classification (NIC) developed by the Iowa Intervention Project at the University of Iowa's College of Nursing (McCloskey & Bulechek, 2000) allows for accuracy at this phase of developing specific family-focused planning.

For example, in the case of Cindy, the 29-year-old woman who received a diagnosis of breast cancer (Case Example 4, presented at the beginning of the chapter), it is imperative to provide significant interventions relating to her and her family's values and beliefs, educational level, and cultural concerns.

Interventions for Cindy and her family require that the nurse individualize a care plan, customizing realistic actions to be performed by the client and family in coping with and managing Cindy's disease process. Box 8-2 lists specific, identified intervention indicators for assisting Cindy and her family in the spiritual coping process, which will balance with the appropriate desired outcomes.

Each family is a unique unit, composed of persons with individual beliefs, spiritual commitments, and ideas for the place of religion in their lives. Many contributing factors constitute the spiritual wholeness of each person. Some factors include personal relationships with others, cultural and ethnic background, life experiences,

> **BOX 8-2 Intervention Indicators Relating to the Spiritual Health Care Needs of Cindy and Her Family**
>
> Shares openly about feelings of illness
> Allows touching of the hand in comforting
> Accepts visits from husband and children
> Expresses emotions or cries when appropriate
> Receives expressed comfort care measures from nurses, such as pain control
> Accepts chaplain referral visit in communicating spiritual and/or religious feelings/concerns
> Discusses openly feelings about death and dying
> Participates in all health care decisions

influences of written materials or worship services, and personal prayer. Consequently, the spiritual profile of each family is quite detailed and unique, as is their personal level and practice of faith.

In fact, this level and practice of faith, although different for each family member, may contribute to the perceived spiritual intervention for the family as a unit. Aden (1976) has identified the spiritual development of a family across the life span in relationship to faith. The author's applied definition of faith progresses from trust, courage, obedience, assent, and identity through adolescence to surrender, unconditional surrender, and unconditional acceptance, concluding in maturity (Aden, 1976).

Concomitant with the assessment process is the means by which family members can set priorities. In essence, establishing priorities is a matter of making choices regarding the importance of religion in daily activities, the commitment to prayer, the practice of worship, the pattern of daily scripture reading, the refocusing of one's lifestyle and example as set forth in religious teachings, and the commitment to live one's religious belief through action and not mere words.

As nurses begin to work with priority identification within the family, a process of goal setting

might prove valuable. Personal goals can be designed by each family member to address his or her religious beliefs and integration of those beliefs into each aspect of daily living.

Regardless of whether a nurse clinician is committed to a particular faith, he or she should be aware of the religious community resources available, including the availability of religious leaders, worship services, support services, and reading materials. Actions to consider with the family's or client's permission might include the following:

• Contacting chaplains within particular health facilities, community agencies, or jails (Parsons & Warner-Robbins, 2002)
• Intervening with the family's pastor, priest, or rabbi
• Locating houses of worship in the neighborhood, if a parish connection has not been established
• Identifying available radio and television religious programming
• Informing family members of local religious bookstores
• Providing information concerning various churches and synagogues, related activities, support groups, or visitation services
• Inquiring about the availability of a parish nurse within a nearby congregation (where a nurse provides referral and resource services within a parish community) (Hemmila, 2002)

Information provided in Table 8-1 can serve as a working tool for referral and reference purposes. It is helpful throughout the implementation process for the family health practitioner to recognize the meaning and value of each religion's sacraments, specific prayers, ceremonies, and specific printed resources. Each religion has its own book of scripture readings and resources relative to specific family needs and issues.

Frequently, a clinician can read from religious works as a means of offering guidance, support, understanding, and peace. Inquiring about an individual's favorite scripture passage or story might afford an opportunity for reading aloud. Some of the most valuable reading comes from the texts such as the Book of Psalms, the Bible, the Torah, the Koran, and the Book of Mormon.

Actions that might benefit the growth and intervention within a family structure, initiated by a nurse, might include the following:

- Select and read passages from books such as the Bible, the Torah, or the Koran.
- Inquire about verses or readings that might have a pertinent family value.
- Encourage family members to join in the religious readings.
- Read specific prayers from a prayer book, relevant to individual or family needs.
- Pray with or for the family or an individual related to particular requests or needs.
- Teach young children right and wrong based on religious tenets.
- Carry specific tapes of either inspirational music or teachings.
- Identify prayer requests to be shared with a prayer support group, prayer chain, a church, or a personal prayer group.
- Encourage families to become involved in scripture studies, home support, or fellowship groups and other spiritually fulfilling relationships.
- Introduce people to the purpose and value of prayer and spiritual journaling.
- Discuss moral and ethical issues with children.

Murray and Zentner (1985, 2000) identified specific practices or ideas that proved helpful for individuals from the Catholic, Protestant, and Jewish religions. The results of their questionnaire noted that for all three religious, reading from the Bible, religious writings, and religious books and magazines was valuable for their spiritual growth, and praying in one's own words, with a religious leader, or aloud with a group was meaningful.

The sample list of prayer books provided in Box 8-3 might be helpful for family use.

Evaluation

It might be helpful to encourage individual and personal journaling as a reflective means by which the family health practitioner could evaluate the effectiveness and value of the spiritual intervention. Much of this awareness will be reflective of an individual's comfort in sharing and identifying personal feelings. It might also be helpful for an individual or family member to respond openly to questions such as the following:

- How are we doing as a family?

- Are we openly and honestly addressing spiritual needs and challenges?
- Are we practicing what we have been taught and have read?
- How can we improve in love, reverence, forgiveness, and in our relationship with God (or a supreme being)?
- Have we been open and honest in our dialogue with our family health nurse?

These questions can be used reflectively as the nurse and the family or individual compare personal questions with previously established goals.

Implications for Practice

The family health nurse fulfills several roles. Each role is a valuable component in the relationship between nurse and family. Fostering a family's religiosity requires playing the role of a supporter and encourager, as well as incorporating listening, empathy, vulnerability, humility, and commitment (Carson & Koenig, 2002)

The Role of the Supporter and Encourager

One of the most valuable tools a nurse can use to meet spiritual needs is simply his or her presence. Personal contact has a physical, emotional, and spiritual effect. The relationship between nurse and client evolves over time as each family member begins to develop a sense of trust and confidence in the nurse. As this relationship of trust matures, both nurse and family have an opportunity to be open and supportive, allowing the uniqueness of the family to be revealed. During this process the nurse can demonstrate support and encouragement while learning about the family's needs, desires, hopes, aspirations, dreams, hurts, joys, and ambitions. At this time, the nurse is able to communicate personal spiritual strength and a sincere willingness to care, to listen, and to just be present with the family. The nurse's unspoken message of acceptance of a client as a unique spiritual being provides a wonderful opportunity for spiritual healing and wholeness.

Travelbee (1966, p. 17) expands on this belief:

The nurse possesses a profound understanding of the human condition. The nurse realizes that personal spiritual values, or philosophical beliefs

---

BOX 8-3   Sample List of Prayer and Meditation Books

Pastoral Care of the Sick and Dying (1984)
Office of Publishing Services
U.S. Catholic Conference
1312 Massachusetts Ave, N.W.
Washington, DC 20005

Praying in the Catholic Tradition (1990)
Author: P. Schineller
Publisher: Liguori Publishing

Prayer Book for Young Catholics
Author: M. Fox
Publisher: Our Sunday Visitor

Prayer Handbook for Today's Catholic
Author: E. Tobin
Publisher: Liguori

Prayers That Avail Much
Publisher: Harrison House

A Diary of Private Prayer
Author: John Baillie
Publisher: Charles Scribner & Sons

PrayerStarters: For Busy People
Author: Daniel Grippo
Publisher: Abbey Press

Prayers for Children
Author: J. Hormen
Publisher: Viking Press

Prayers for the Very Young
Author: D. Roberts
Publisher: Concordia Press

Prayers of Jesus for Children
Author: I. Savary
Publisher: Regina Press

Miracle Hour: A Method of Prayer That Will Change Your Life
Author: Linda Schubert
Publisher: Linda Schubert
P.O. Box 4034
Santa Clara, CA 95056

Jewish Spiritual and Torah Meditations
Author: Rabbi Bernard Raskas
Publisher: Ktav Publishers

The Prayers of Islam
Author: Elijah Mohammod
Publisher: The Nation of Islam

*Prayer**
Author: Spencer W. Kimball et al.
Publisher: Deseret Book Co.

*Hope**
Author: Ezra T. Benson et al.
Publisher: Deseret Book Co.

---

*The Church of the Latter-Day Saints has only a few written prayers. These are primarily read with the sacraments. These two books by Mormon authors are for prayer and meditation.

---

about human beings, illness, and suffering will determine the extent to which he or she will be able to help others find meaning (or no meaning) in these situations.

Travelbee's approach and response calls nurses to continually examine their personal strength, limitations, motivations, and needs. Through this development of self-knowledge, a nurse can become more effective, and his or her ability to support and comfort others can become a living reality.

The art and skill of fostering a family's religiosity requires the following essential elements: listening, empathy, vulnerability, humility, and commitment (Carson & Koenig, 2002).

The Role of the Listener

Good listeners know that listening is both an art and a skill. The family nurse must be attentive with his or her eyes, ears, mind, and heart. Listening is an active skill, requiring both concentration and commitment.

Frequently, family members may hide their true feelings and may not speak openly about either facts or feelings. In this way, they do not have to risk the embarrassment of dealing with their own pain or fears. Neither do they have to take the chance of dealing with a negative or questioning response from the listener.

Frequently, lack of communication may be a result of existing barriers that prohibit the nurse from actively listening. Barriers include the following:

- Outside distractions that prevent the nurse from concentrating completely
- An inability to assess the individual's exact meaning of a word, comment, or gesture
- The interjection of personal feelings or responses into the client's conversation, thus preventing open, honest dialogue
- The formulation of specific responses or solutions while the other person is speaking, which interrupts the level of concentration required to hear exactly what is being said

It is important for the nurse to focus on his or her ability to be rather than to do, to listen rather than speak, to be open rather than judge. These qualities are valuable not only for the nurse but also for each member of the family.

The Role of the Empathizer

A nurse who has the gift of empathy has the ability to experience vicariously the feelings of another individual. A nurse must have the capability of putting specific feelings into words and, at the same time, the ability to remain objective during the process of seeking alternatives.

It is important to be able to distinguish between empathy and sympathy. Carson (1989) clarifies that with sympathy, the listener is allowed to share in the feelings of another person, but in the process of sharing, the listener loses objectivity and is unable to differentiate between his or her feelings and those of the speaker. Empathy, on the other hand, allows the nurse to be present with his or her clients, to be supportive in an attempt to understand the clients' feelings, and to encourage clients as they begin to examine their own alternatives. Thus the nurse would not make the decision or suggest alter-

natives but would work with and stay with the client throughout this process.

If a nurse should find this process difficult, it might be of value to pray, in a manner consistent with his or her own beliefs, before visiting the client. This may provide peace and wisdom.

The Role of Being Vulnerable

As part of the art of caring and the gift of empathy, the ability to be vulnerable allows the nurse to experience the feelings of the family (Watson, 2001). The nurse encourages each family member to deal realistically with his or her inner feelings. A nurse's vulnerability prevents him or her from remaining uninvolved, aloof, or judgmental. This affords the family additional strength, knowing they are not alone in making decisions and choosing alternatives that will help them to move forward. The nurse can share in clients' feelings of pain and abandonment, as well as their feelings of joy and anticipation.

Just as the nurse has received guidance, direction, and strength through prayer, he or she can make his or her personal strength, faith, and hope available to each individual member or the family unit as a whole.

The Role of Humility

Through knowledge and experience of humility a nurse will come face to face with his or her own limitations. In fact, it is through limitations and weaknesses that God can most effectively work through an individual to assist others. In essence, an individual's pride is removed and the door is open for God's strength to prevail. It takes great humility and inner strength for someone to admit that he or she does not have all the answers but that the necessary answers will be sought.

The gift of humility increases the level of faith and trust between nurse and client. Each accepts the other for who he or she is, not what he or she desires to become.

The Role of Commitment

Commitment is based on the availability of the nurse throughout the time the family needs support. To be committed to a nurse-client relationship requires that the nurse be present through all stages of emotional and spiritual growth and not abandon his or her client when the relationship becomes challenging or uncomfortable. This is especially true during times of terminal illness or death. To be truly committed indicates a nurse's inner spiritual strength, which is passed on to the family.

A family health nurse who is involved in maintaining the spiritual well-being of each family may benefit from opportunities for individual spiritual renewal and refreshment. Such opportunities include the following:

- Joining a nurses' spiritual growth and support group, such as Nurses Christian Fellowship
- Organizing or participating in a nurses' prayer support group
- Subscribing to a journal (such as *Journal of Christian Nursing, Journal of Transcultural Nursing,* or *Journal of Multicultural Nursing and Health*)
- Participating in or organizing a "spiritual grand rounds" at his or her facility
- Inquiring about the role and function of a parish or congregational nurse (a health minister for the congregation)
- Conducting and disseminating research on spiritual and religious dimensions of family well-being

Implications for Health Professions Education

The premise of holistic care—that there should be a balance of body, mind, and spirit for the establishment of total health in a person—has been recognized and accepted; however, it has been documented that although health care professionals are aware of the spiritual needs of their clients, such needs are frequently poorly met. There are two issues for health professions education. First, because of the beliefs about separation of church and state, most curricula of health professions schools do not include spirituality because Western health care has focused on tangible and measurable phenomena (Koenig, 2002). Second, spiritual care is seen as the role of hospital chaplains and religious agents (Narayanasomy, 1993).

Therefore health professions faculty are encouraged to incorporate spiritual care into course work and clinical experiences (Koenig, 2002). If family or individual spiritual care is incomplete or inadequate, then members of the family may become distressed or discouraged and may even struggle with their own spirituality. This may lead the family to endure additional suffering, pain, anger, hopelessness, helplessness, and feelings of isolation and self-doubt.

Research suggests that health care professionals are aware that their clients have spiritual needs, but they are unable to provide spiritual care (Koenig, 2002; Narayanasomy, 1993). Curricula for health professionals should include content on spirituality and religion. First, according to Catanzaro & McMullen (2001), the spiritual roots in the history of the nursing profession must be taught, because a profession cannot allow knowledge to remain in the past. Second, faculty members must become comfortable with the language of religion and spirituality if they are to effectively communicate the importance of spirituality to students. Third, opportunities to reflect on the interconnectedness of religion and spirituality can be provided both in the classroom and in the clinical setting. Fourth, students can share their religious journeys and rich religious traditions. Reading and discussion of literature on spirituality are necessary to establish a knowledge base for students. This knowledge would include information about different traditions and cultures, as well as spirituality and health care. Fifth, the election of wide-ranging clinical sites for nursing practice including faith communities, prisons, and gerontology settings is critical. Lastly, educators should consider a renewed understanding of spirituality as a way of life. Spirituality cannot merely be taught; it must be incorporated into one's lifestyle and lead to spiritual growth.

For the most part, caring and the spiritual dimension of nursing continue to represent areas of resistance and reluctance for many nurses, largely because of a lack of awareness, knowledge, assessment, and integration skills and support concepts. A gradual change has been noted as evidenced by the fact that at the beginning of the twenty-first century several graduate schools of nursing offer advanced practice degrees with a specialization in health and nursing ministries. The interdisciplinary curricula include advanced practice nursing theory and practice, as well as theological coursework. For example, the reader may consult the Duke University School of Nursing's web page for information on the Health and Nursing Ministries Program. See the Website Resources box at the end of the chapter for this website address. Recommendations for curricula include the following:

- Include spiritual assessment and its relationship to family healing and wholeness in the curriculum design.
- Establish student discussion and integration forums relating to spirituality in the family.
- Introduce case studies—both written and oral—in laboratory settings in which the challenges and opportunities are presented.
- Provide course content, courses, or advanced nursing practice education in parish or congregational nursing and health ministries (Warner, 1996).

Implications for Research

Twenty-first century scholars recognize the import of religion in individual and family health, stress management, and coping. Koenig (2002) analyzed and summarized more than 12,000 quantitative and qualitative scientific studies on religion and health. Research study topics vary across diverse health issues, cultures, and the family life cycle. For example, Hatch, Burg, Naberhaus, & Hellmich (1998) report the development of a Spiritual Involvement and Beliefs Scale. Picot, Debanne, Namazi, and Wykle (1997) found that the quality of life and coping were rated higher among African American caregivers who reported higher religious support scores than their white counterparts.

Further research is needed on (1) the influence of religion and spirituality on caregiving and health-promoting lifestyles; (2) punitive and negative influences of religion on families and family members; (3) the relationships between religion on marital strengths and family health; (4) the outcomes of religion as an intervention in family-capacity building for marriages and family resilience; and (5) the outcomes of religious interventions on mental health (Exline, Yali & Sanderson, 2000; Weaver, Samford, Morgan, Koenig, & Flannelly, 2000).

Measurement of Spirituality and Religion

Research and clinical tools used to measure religion and spirituality must be culturally sensitive, reliable, and valid. Additionally, the dimensions of religiosity under study need to be carefully delineated. Selected dimensions of religiosity are listed in Box 8-4. Also, the reader who desires an in-depth discussion of measures of religiosity may want to consult the recent book *Measures of Religiosity* (Hill & Hood, 1999).

For the family health nurse to be more productive in the realm of research on family spirituality, the following recommendations are offered.

BOX 8-4   Selected Dimensions of Religion and Spirituality for Research

Religious belief
Belief versus nonbelief
Membership in a faith community
Religious social activity other than attendance
Participation in scripture or prayer groups
Giving financial support to faith community
Receiving the sacraments or other communal religious rituals
Nonorganizational religiosity
Punitiveness and religion
Engaging in private prayer (other than at meals)
Reading religious scriptures or inspirational literature
Watching television or listening to religious radio
Importance of religiosity
Religious quests (searching for religious truths)
Religious well-being (as part of spiritual well-being)
Religious coping (functional)
Religious history and trajectories
Religion and spiritual maturity
Other religious attitudes and practices
Family relationships (parenting, marital satisfaction, caregiving, stress and coping, family health promotion, family life satisfaction, social support, resources from organized faith community)

Adapted from Koenig et al., 2001, pp. 495-496.

- Continue the development of and evaluate reliable and valid instruments for use to measure religiosity and spirituality concepts of diverse faith communities and religions.
- Use both qualitative and quantitative research methods to illuminate spiritual dimensions of culturally and structurally diverse families.
- Examine the relationship of nursing diagnosis indicators to physical health, mental health, and family well-being.
- Identify factors related to the development of spirituality throughout the life span.
- Identify factors that would encourage clinicians to provide spiritual care to families in health, illness, and recovery and at the end of life.
- Assess the effectiveness of clinical intervention in terms of spiritual outcomes for clients.
- Identify the influence of religiosity on health care and outcomes and family well-being.
- Evaluate both the negative and positive influences of religiosity on the health of families and individual members (Warner, 1996).

For a family health nurse to provide and be sensitive to the spiritual strength of families is a demonstration of the clinician's spiritual life. A clinician will demonstrate his or her gifts of kindness, love, gentleness, compassion, understanding, honesty, and patience throughout the assessment, intervention, and evaluation process. As practitioners share these gifts with others, their own qualities are strengthened. When clinicians share themselves, they are fostering spirituality and serving as a bridge between the family and the family's perception of a higher strength and power.

WEBSITE RESOURCES

ORGANIZATION	WEBSITE ADDRESS
The Dovetail Institute for the Interfaith Family	http://www.dovetailinstitute.org/
Duke University Center for the Study of Religion/Spirituality and Health	http://www.geri.duke.edu
International Center for the Integration of Health and Spirituality	http://www.nihr.org
John Templeton Foundation	http://www.tempelton.org
Mind-Body Medical Institute	http://www.mbmi.org
National Abstinence Clearinghouse	http://www.safeinc.org/
Parish Nursing Resources	http://www.parishnursing.umaryland.edu
Health Ministries Association	http://www.healthministriesassociation.org/welcomepage.html
International Parish Nurses Resource Center	http://www.parishnurses.org/
National Center for Faith-Based and Community Initiatives	http://www.hhs.gov/fbci
Faith-based resources	http://www.hhs.gov/faith/features/resources.html
Moms-in-Touch	http://www.momsintouch.org/
Fetzer Institute	http://www.fetzer.org

■ CHAPTER HIGHLIGHTS

- The terms *religion* and *spirituality* are often used interchangeably, yet their meanings are not the same. Religion is the belief in a supernatural or divine force that has power over everything. Spirituality is a philosophical orientation regarding relationships that produce behaviors and feelings of hope, love, trust, and faith, which provide a meaning of life.

- The major religions are divided into three groups: group one (Christianity, Judaism, and Islam), group two (Taoism, Confucianism, Shintoism), and group three (Buddhism and Hinduism).

- Religiosity may enhance family strengths by contributing to the formation of family beliefs and values, encouraging healthy behaviors and practices, providing social interactions with others, providing recreational interaction, and

enhancing family coping during crises and transitions across the life span.

- The effects of religion on the total health and well-being of the family unit include goodness, kindness, joy, love, patience, self-control, faithfulness, peace, affirmation, forgiveness, reverence for family life, support, and understanding.

- The family nurse should assess family religion and spirituality and help families to improve the capacity of the family to strengthen these traits.

- The family nurse's role in family spiritual health includes being humble and vulnerable; acting as a supporter, an encourager, a listener, and an empathizer; and showing commitment to holistic family health promotion.

CRITICAL THINKING ACTIVITIES

1. Interview two people using the Spiritual Health Assessment Tool in this chapter (Box 8-1). Interview one person who describes himself or herself as healthy and one with a chronic illness. Share the different perspectives with a peer.

2. For 1 week, observe the spiritual and religious artifacts or rituals in your clinical practice site. Share your observations with peers. Observe

gender and ethnicity and note the circumstances such as celebration, crisis, or death.

3. Describe the activities of a clinician who would show caring, respect, and deep concern for Melissa in Case Example 1 at the beginning of the chapter.

4. Reflect on how spirituality influenced or did not influence family life in your family of origin.

REFERENCES

Abbott, D. A., Berry, M., & Meredith, W. H. (1990). Religious beliefs and practice. A potential asset in helping families. Family Relations, 39, 443-448.

Aden, L. (1976). Faith and the development cycle. *Pastoral Psychology, 24,* 215-230.

Anderson, H. (1999). Feet planted firmly in midair: Spirituality for family living. In F. Walsh (Ed.), *Spiritual resources for family therapy* (pp. 157-176). New York: Guilford.

Barnhart, R. K. (Ed.). (1988). *The Barnhart dictionary of etymology.* New York: H.W. Wilson.

Batson, C., & Ventis, W. (1982). *The religious experience: A social-psychological perspective.* New York: Oxford University Press.

Bomar, P. (1995, October). *A comparison of rural and urban African-American women: Factors influencing adherence to health promoting lifestyle.* Paper presented at North American Congress on Women's Health Issues, Galveston, TX.

Boss, P. (2002). *Family stress management: A contextual approach.* Thousand Oaks: CA: Sage.

Brigman, K. M. (1992). Religion and family strengths: Implications for mental health professionals. *Topics in Family Psychology and Counseling, 1,* 39-52.

Brigman, K. M., & Keating, B. R. (1989). *Religious attitudes and family strengths: Examining the relationship.* Unpublished manuscript.

Byrd, R. C. (1988). Positive therapeutic effects of intercessory prayer in a coronary care unit population. *Southern Med J, 81,* 826-829.

Capra, F., & Steindl-Rast, D. (1991). *Belonging to the universe: Explorations on the frontiers of science and spirituality*. San Francisco: Harper & Row.

Carson, V. B. (1989). *Spiritual dimension of nursing practice*. Philadelphia: W. B. Saunders.

Carson, V. B., & Koenig, H. G. (2002). *Parish nursing*. Philadelphia: Templeton Foundation Press.

Carter-Jessop, L., Franklin, L.N., Heath, J.W., Jimenez-Irizarry, G., & Peace, M.D., (2000). Abstinence education for urban youth. *Journal of Community Health, 25,* 293-304.

Catanzaro, A., & McMullen, K. (2001). Increasing nursing students' spiritual sensitivity. *Nurse Educator, 5,* 221-226.

Curran, D. (1983). *Traits of a healthy family*. Minneapolis, MN: Winston.

Dass, R. W. (1976). *Grist for the mill*. Santa Cruz, CA: Unity Press.

Doherty, W. J. (2001). *Take back your marriage*. New York: Guildford Press.

Doherty, W. J., & Carlson, B. (2002). *Putting family first*. New York: Owl Books

Dunn, A. B., & Dawes, S. H. (1999). Spirituality-focused genograms: Keys to uncovering spiritual resources in African American families [Electronic version]. *Journal of Multicultural Counseling and Development, 27,* 240-255.

Dunphy, L. H. (2001). Florence Nightingale caring actualized: A legacy for nursing. In Parker, M. (Ed.), *Nursing theories and nursing practice* (pp. 31-53). Philadelphia: F.A. Davis.

Elkins, D. N., Edstrom, L. J., Leaf, J. A., & Saunders, G. C. (1988). Towards a humanistic phenomenological spirituality: Definition, description and measurement. *Journal of Humanistic Psychology, 28,* 5-18.

Exline, J. J., Yali, A. M., & Sanderson, W. C. (2000). Guilt, discord, and alienation: The role of religious strain in depression and suicidality. *Journal of Clinical Psychology, 56(12),* 1481-1496.

Farrell, M. & Brill, M. (2002). United airlines flight 93 crashes in Somerset county. In C. G. Warner & A. Albano (Eds.). Disaster Medicine Part [Special Issue: Disaster Medicine Part II]. *Topic in Emergency Medicine, 24(3),* 64-65.

Fetzer Institute/National Institute on Aging Working Group. (October, 1999). Multidimensional measurement of religiousness/spirituality for use in health research: *A Report of the National Institute on Aging Working Group*. Kalamazoo, MI: Fetzer Institute.

Frame, M. W. (2000). The spiritual genogram in family therapy. *Journal of Marital and Family Therapy, 26,* 211-216.

Giblin, P. (1996). Family strengths. *Family Journal, 4,* 339-248.

Guralnik, D. (Ed.). (1979). *Webster's new world dictionary of the American language* (2nd college ed.). Cleveland: Collins.

Hatch, R. L, Burg, M. A, Naberhaus, D. S., & Hellmich, L. K. (1998). The spiritual involvement and beliefs scale. Development and testing of a new instrument. *Journal of Family Practice, 46(6),* 476-486.

Helm, H., Hays, J. C., Flint, E., Koenig, H. G., & Blazer, D. G. (2000). Effects of private religious activity on mortality of elderly disabled and nondisabled adults. *Journal of Gerontology, 55A,* M400-M405.

Hemmila, D. (2002). You gotta have faith. *Nurse Week, 19,* 16-19.

Hill, P. C., & Hood, R. (1999). *Measures of religiosity*. Birmingham, AL: Religious Education Press.

Hill, L., & Smith, N. (1990). *Self-care nursing: Promoting health*. Englewood Cliffs, NJ: Prentice-Hall.

Idler, E. L., & Kasl, S. V. (1997). Religion among disabled and nondisabled persons II: Attendance at religious services as a predictor of the course of disability. *The Journals of Gerontology. Series B, Psychological Sciences and Social Sciences, 52,* 306-316.

Ingersoll-Dayton, B., Krause, N., & Morgan, D. (2002). Religious trajectories and transitions over the life course. *International Journal of Aging and Human Development, 56(1),* 51-70.

Johnson, M., Bulechek, G., Dochterman, J. M., Maas, M., & Moorhead S. (Eds.). (2001). *Nursing diagnoses, outcomes, and interventions: NANDA, NOC, and NIC linkages*. St. Louis, MO: Mosby.

Johnson, M., Maas, M., & Moorhead, S. (2000). *Nursing outcomes classification* (2nd ed.). St. Louis, MO: Mosby.

Koenig, H. G. (2002). *Spirituality in patient care: Why, how, when, and what*. Philadelphia: Templeton Foundation Press.

Koenig, H. G., McCullough, M. E., & Larson, D. B. (2001). *Handbook on religion and health*. New York: Oxford University.

Lockyer, H. (1986). *Nelson's illustrated Bible dictionary*. New York: Thomas Nelson.

Maslow, A. (1968). *Toward a psychology of being*. New York: Van Nostrand Reinhold.

McAdoo, H. (1995). Stress levels, family help patterns, and religiosity in middle- and working-class African American single mothers. *Journal of Black Psychology, 21,* 424-449.

McCloskey, J. C. & Bulechek, G. M.(Eds.). (2000). *Nursing interventions classifications*. (3rd ed.). St. Louis, MO: Mosby.

McLeod, D. L., & Wright, L. M. (2001). Conversations of spirituality: Spirituality in family systems nursing— making the case with four clinical vignettes. *Journal of Family Nursing, 7,* 391-415.

Murray, R. B. & Zentner, J. P. (1985). Religious influences on the person. In R. B. Murray & J.P. Zentner (Eds.), *Nursing concepts for health promotion* (3rd ed., p. 475). Englewood Cliffs, NJ: Prentice Hall.

Murray, R. B. & Zentner, J. P. (2000). *Nursing concepts for health promotion* (7th ed.). Englewood Cliffs, NJ: Prentice Hall.

Musgrave, C. F., Allen, C. A., & Allen, G. J. (2002). Spirituality and health for women of color. *American Journal of Public Health, 9,* 557-560.

North American Nursing Diagnosis Association. (1999). *Nursing diagnoses: Definitions & classifications (1999-2000)*. Philadelphia: Author.

Narayanasomy, A. R.U. (1993). Nurses' awareness and educational preparation in meeting their patients' spiritual needs. *Nurse Education Today, 13,* 106-201.

Newman, M. (1989). The spirit of nursing. *Holistic Nursing Practice, 3,* 1-6.

Olson, D. H. (1999). Circumplex model of marital and family systems. Retrieved October 5, 2002, from http://www.prepare-enrich.com/studies/fpres/html

Olson, D. H., McCubbin, H. I., Barnes, H. L., Larsen, A. S., Muxen, M. J., & Wilson, M. C. (1982). *Family Interventions*. St. Paul, MN: University of Minnesota.

Olson, D. H., McCubbin, H. I., Barnes, H. L., Larsen, A. S., Muxen, M. J., & Wilson, M. C. (1983). *Families: What makes them work*. Beverly Hills: Sage.

Olson, D. H., & Olson, A., K. (2000). *Empowering couples: Building on your strengths* (2nd ed.). Minneapolis, MN: Life Innovators, Inc.

Parsons, M., & Warner-Robbins, C., (2002). Holistic nursing on the front lines. *American Journal of Nursing, 5,* 73-77.

Paterson, J. G., & Zderad, L. T. (1976). *Humanistic nursing.* New York: John Wiley & Sons.

Pearsall, P. (1990). *Power of the family.* New York: Bantam.

Picot, S. J., Debanne, S. M., Namazi, K. H., and Wykle, M. L. (1997). Religiosity and perceived rewards of black and white caregivers. *The Gerontologist, 37,* 89-101.

Powe, B. D. (1995). Cancer fatalism: A predictor of colorectal cancer screening among elderly African Americans. In J. E. Wang (Ed.), *Proceedings of the Second International Interdisciplinary Health Research Symposium* (pp. 71-78). Morgantown: University of West Virginia, School of Nursing.

Riley, D., Clark, M., & Wong, T. (2002). World trade terror: Explosion trauma. In C. G. Warner & A. Albano (Eds.). [Special Issue: Disaster Medicine Part I], *Topics in Emergency Medicine, 24(2),* 47-59.

Schumm, W. R., Hatch, R. C., & Schumm, K. R. (1990). *Family strengths project: Preliminary data report.* Paper presented at Family Strengths Conference, Washington, DC.

Shafranske, E. P., & Maloney, H. N. (1990). Clinical psychologists' religious and spiritual orientations and their practice of psychotherapy. *Psychotherapy, 27,* 72–78.

Spector, R. E. (2000). *Cultural diversity in health and illness* (5th ed.). Upper Saddle River, NJ: Prentice Hall.

Tenney, M. C., & Douglas, J. D. (1999). The *new international dictionary of the Bible.* Grand Rapids: Zondervan Publishing Co.

Travelbee, J. (1966). *Interpersonal aspects of nursing.* Philadelphia: F. A. Davis.

Treloar, L. L. (2000). Integration of spirituality into health care practice by nurse practitioners. *Journal of the Academy of Nurse Practitioners, 12,* 280-285.

Underwood, L. G., & Teresi, J. A. (2002). The daily spiritual experience scale: Development, theoretical description, reliability, exploratory factor analysis, and preliminary construct validity using health-related data. *Journal of Behavioral Medicine, 24(1),* 22-33.

Walsh, F. (1999). Religion and spirituality: Wellsprings for healing and resilience. In F. Walsh (Ed.), *Spiritual resources in family therapy* (pp. 3-27). New York: Guildford.

Warner, C. G. (1996). Family spirituality. In P. J. Bomar (Ed.), *Nurses and family health promotion* (2nd ed., pp.139-161). Philadelphia: Saunders.

Watson, J. (2001). Jean Watson theory of human caring. In M. E. Parker (Ed.), *Nursing theories and nursing practice.* Philadelphia: Davis.

Weaver, A. J., Samford, J. A., Morgan, V. J., Koenig, H. G., & Flannelly, K. J. (2002). A systemic review of research on religion in six marriage and family journals: 1995-1999. *The American Journal of Family Therapy, 30,* 293-309.

Wright, L. M., Watson, W. L. & Bell, J. M. (1996). *Beliefs: The heart of healing in families and illness.* New York: Basic Books.

9

Sociocultural Influences on Family Health Promotion and Health Protection

Perri J. Bomar
Bettie J. Glenn

The ultimate goal of a professional nurse scientist and humanist is to discover, know, and creatively use culturally based knowledge with its fullest meanings, symbols, and functions for healing, and to promote or maintain well-being (or health) with people of diverse cultures in the world.

— Madeleine M. Leininger

OBJECTIVES

On completion of this chapter, the reader will be able to do the following:

1. *Explain how the influences of increase in population and demographic cultural diversity affect family health.*

2. *Describe the concepts of cultural diversity.*

3. *Examine the impact of family history, customs, beliefs, and values on expectations and behaviors exhibited by individuals.*

4. *Identify standards to help clinicians and staff bridge the complex issues of language and culture.*

5. *Discuss the role and responsibilities of the nurse in meeting the needs of culturally diverse clients.*

6. *Explain policy and advocacy efforts to ensure access to and quality of health care for diverse populations.*

7. *Identify researchable questions that will increase the knowledge base needed to provide culturally proficient care.*

As the twenty-first century begins, health care professionals and family social scientists are called on to care for and collaborate with a deluge of multicultural families who have culturally complex and sensitive issues (Leonard, 2001). During the decade from 1990 to 2000, the United States had the largest increase in population since 1970. Annually, millions of families from around the globe legally and illegally enter the United States, Canada, and other industrialized countries in search of economic security, freedom, and safety.

With current trends, by the year 2080, there will be no single ethnic majority population in North America. In such a pluralistic society, the national system of service and its professions will be challenged to conceptualize the uniqueness that describes the nation as a the whole. The health

The authors express appreciation and acknowledge the work of John Lantz in writing this chapter for the first and second editions.

practitioner working with families needs to be cognizant that cultural forces are powerful determinants of health behaviors in families and groups (Huff & Kline, 1999). Nearly all aspects of family life and health promotion and disease prevention are influenced by culture. This chapter provides an overview of and foundation for a better understanding of cultural elements not reflected in the dominant culture.

Rapid Population Changes Fuel Cultural Diversity

The sources of diversity consist of a number of variables: migration (of immigrants and refugees), ethnic/racial groups, socioeconomic status (SES), social class, sexual orientation, and disability (Lipson, Dibble, & Minarik, 1996). More than 33 million (a 13.2% increase) people migrated to the United States between 1990 and 2000, the largest census-to-census growth ever. Of these, 10% of the U.S. population (1.7 million) was foreign-born, which is a 30% rise since the 1990 census and the largest proportion since 1930 (Perry & Mackun, 2001). The largest increase was among Hispanics, Asians, and Pacific Islanders (U.S. Census Bureau, 2002). Table 9-1 compares the 1990 and 2000 census data to illustrate the dramatic ethnic changes. This increase in cultural, racial, and ethnically diverse families and communities

extends far beyond the nation's cities to virtually every part of America. In fact, 210 nations are represented in the U.S. population, and cultures are continuously blending and merging. The U.S. Census for 2000 included 66 different categories of ethnic and racial combinations (U.S. Census Bureau, 2001). The major nonwhite groups in the United States (sometimes called *people of color*) comprise African Americans, Hispanic Americans, American Indians, and Asian and Pacific Islander Americans. The contention that diversity is found only in large and coastal cities is no longer a reality. Today, cultural diversity is increasing throughout the Midwest and in the suburbs and small towns of the United States and Canada.

Health care professionals and policy makers are increasingly more aware of the influence of culture, SES, and family culture on the health of individuals and families, as illustrated by the U.S. document *Healthy People 2010* (U.S. Department of Health and Human Services [DHHS], 2000), the Canadian Branch on First Nation and Inuit Health Branch (see website), and the American Academy of Nursing (2002) statement on cultural diversity and nursing practice. Some culture-specific national health objectives in the United States for 2010 are presented in Table 9-2. One notes immediately from the baseline and target goal that African Americans, Hispanic Americans, and American Indians have the poorest health

---

TABLE 9-1 United States Population by Race and Hispanic Origin, 1990-2000

Race and Hispanic Origin	Total Populations (in millions)		Population Change 1990-2000		Percent of all residents	
	1990	2000	In Millions	In Percent	1999	2000
Total Population	248.9	281.4	32.7	13.2	100	100
White	199.7	211.5	11.8	5.9	80.3	75.1
Black or African American	30.6	36.5	4.7	15.6	12.1	12.3
American Indian and Alaska Native	2.1	2.5	4.6	0.8	0.9	
Asian and Other Pacific Islander	3.0	10.6	11.9	51.3	3.0	3.7
Hispanic (any race)	22.6	35.3	12.9	57.9	9.0	12.5
Some other race	9.8	15.3	5.5	56.6	3.9	5.5

From U.S. Census Bureau. (2002). *PHC T-1: Population by race or Latino origin for the United States 1999 and 2000.* Washington, DC: Author.

TABLE 9-2 Sample *Healthy People 2010* Objectives by Ethnicity

Objective	Baseline	Target
1-1 Increase the proportion with health insurance.	83%	100%
American Indian or Alaskan Indian	79%	
Asian or Pacific Islander	83%	
Black	84%	
White	87%	
Hispanic	70%	
19-1 Increase the proportion of adults who are at a healthy weight.	30%	60%
American-Indian or Alaskan Indian	DSU	
Asian or Pacific Islander	DSU	
Black	34%	
White	42%	
Mexican American	43%	
9-1 Increase the proportion of intended pregnancies among females 15-44	50%	70%
Black or African American	28%	
White	57%	
Hispanic or Latino	51%	
American Indian or Alaska Native	DSU	
Asian or Pacific Islander	DSU	
22-1 Reduce the proportion of adults who engage in no leisure-time physical activity	40%	20%
Black or African American	52%	
American Indian or Alaskan Native	46%	
Hispanic or Latino	54%	
Asian or Pacific Islander	42%	
White	36%	

From U.S. Department of Health and Human Services. (2000). *Healthy People 2010: Understanding and improving health* (2nd ed.). Washington, DC: U.S. Government Printing Office.
DSU, Data not statistically usable.

status. Families transmit cultural beliefs, values, behaviors, and attitudes about health and illness. Each culture and each family culture have unique ways to stay healthy and to promote the health of the family unit and the individual. Therefore family units from all cultures will need to be engaged in health promotion activities to accomplish the goals of health for all by 2010.

Health promotion is experienced, transformed, and maintained within the context of the family system. Denham's (2003) three qualitative studies of family health with Appalachian families con-tinue to support previous research that women are the primary health caregivers and health teachers in families. To be effective in encouraging families to engage in health-promoting behaviors, the clinician needs to be cognizant of the roles of different family members in health-promoting activities. A key to achieving health promotion goals with families from a culture different than that of the health care professional is the health care professional's knowledge of the clients' culture. In addition, communicating in the clients' language and with respect is essential.

TABLE 9-3   Comparison of 2000 General Population and RN Population Statistics

Race/Ethnicity	Total U.S. Population 281,421,906 Percent by Racial/Ethnic Diversity	Total RN Population 2.7 million Percent by Racial/Ethnic Diversity
African American	12.3	4.9
Hispanic	12.5	2.0
American Indian/Alaska Native	0.9	0.5
Asian	3.6	3.5
Native Hawaiian/Pacific Islander	0.1	0.2
Two or more racial groups	2.4	1.2
White	69.1	86.6
No report	—	1.1

From U.S. Census Bureau. (2000). *Population Statistics.* Washington, DC: Author.

Contributions to world culture are made by people of diverse ethnicity and backgrounds who "migrate" to each country in the world by means of electronics (e.g., the Internet), the mass media, and various forms of communication, as well as people who emigrate (Leininger, 2001). The North American population is becoming increasingly diverse, with projection for even greater increases in racial and ethnic minority groups when compared with birth rates for white persons. According to Leininger (2002a), what people need to grow, maintain health, prevent illness, and survive or face death is human caring. *Caring* is the "heart and soul" of nursing and is the key element for clients seeking nursing and health care services. Therefore development of cultural competencies in the provision of care is the challenge and imperative of the twenty-first century. The focus of nursing in the twentieth century was on identifying, being sensitive to, and addressing clients, with consideration of their diversity in meeting health and illness needs. The challenge in the twenty-first century is for health care professionals, especially registered nurses, to become skilled, adept, and expert in providing care that is culturally competent, if not culturally proficient. For example, in North America, professional nursing is disproportionately mono-racial. Statistics on racial and ethnic diversity

validate a majority of white providers. Table 9-3 presents the results of a comparison of the 2000 general population statistics with the 2000 data reflecting the number of registered nurses in the United States.

Sociocultural Theories and Conceptual Models

Theoretical models and frameworks assist professionals in assessing and planning culturally competent care in collaboration with diverse individuals, families, and groups. Several nursing models are specific to culture.

- Theory of Cultural Diversity and Universality (Leininger, 2001)
- Purnell's Model for Cultural Competence (Purnell & Paulanka, 1998)
- Giger and Davidhizar Transcultural Assessment Model (Giger & Davidhizar, 1999)
- Fong's CONFHER Model (Communication, Orientation, Nutrition Family Health Belief, Education, and Religion, [Fong, 1985]).

Among the earlier models and the most commonly used for understanding and providing culturally competent nursing care is Leininger's Sunrise Model (Leininger, 2001), which is depicted in Figure 9-1. The central concept is

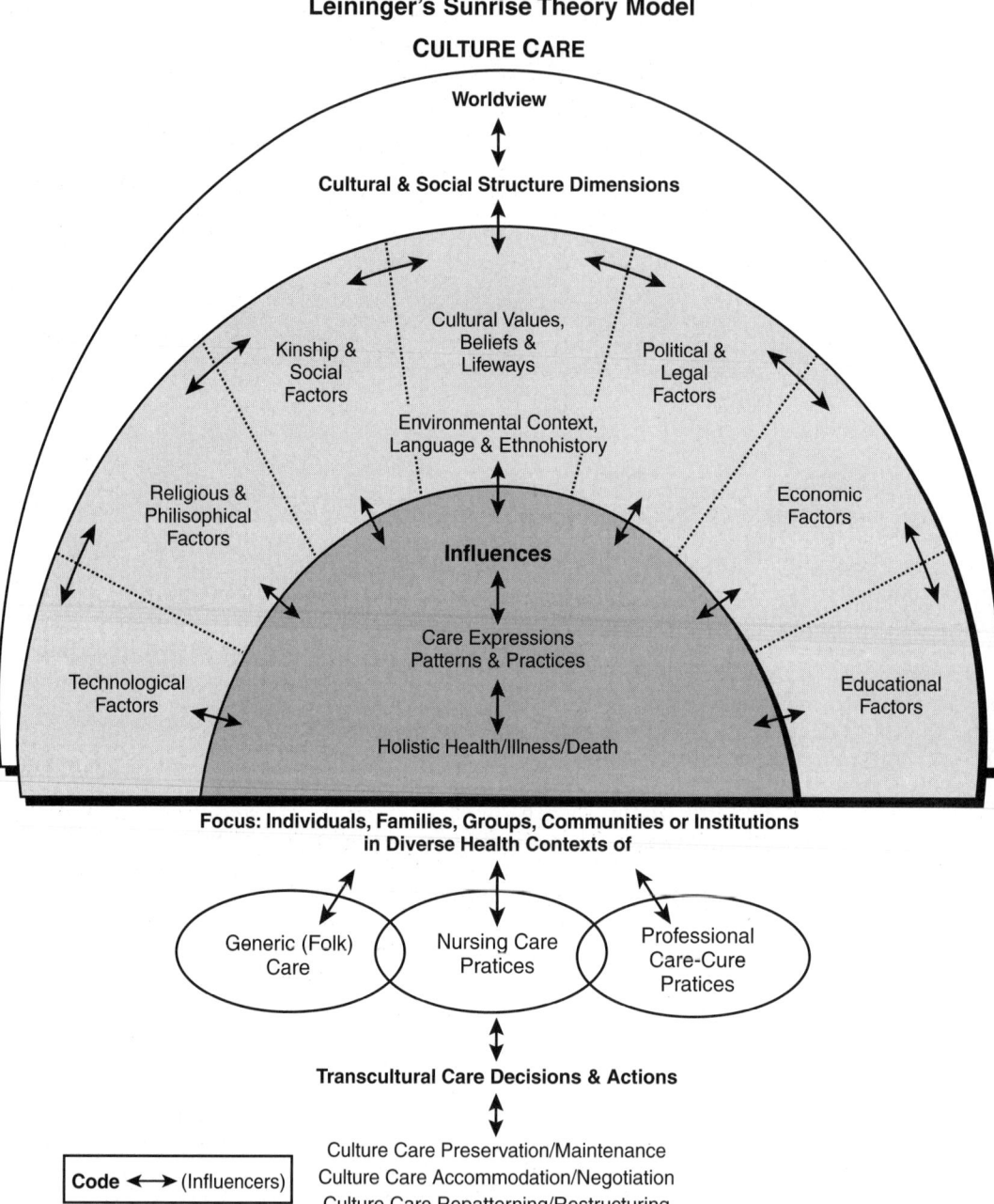

Figure 9-1 Leininger's Sunrise Theory Model. (Used with permission of Madeline Leininger © 2001. From Leininger, M., & McFarland, M. R. [2002]. *Transcultural nursing.* New York: McGraw Hill. p. 80.)

human care and caring. The Sunrise Model has been demonstrated to be useful for clinical practice and research with individuals, families, groups, and communities. The model shows that culturally congruent care includes cultural care patterning, cultural care accommodation, and cultural care preservation. Culturally congruent nursing care occurs in diverse health systems that include the folk system, the professional system, and the nursing care system. Culture occurs within the cultural worldview and social structure dimensions.

Clinicians are encouraged to become familiar with these nursing models and interdisciplinary models and review the assumptions on which each model is based. In addition, health care organizations by necessity must incorporate cultural competence and caring into health care standards. Elements essential to becoming a culturally competent institution or agency are the following:

1) Valuing cultural diversity
2) Having the capacity for cultural self-assessment
3) Being conscious of the dynamics inherent when cultures interact
4) Having institutionalized cultural knowledge
5) Having developed adaptations of service delivery and policies reflecting an understanding of cultural diversity

Nurses remain the health care providers in direct contact with well and ill clients, in some cases 24 hours a day, 7 days a week. Therefore nurses need to examine, discern, verify meanings, demonstrate respect for the client's worldview, and include culture-based factors in assessing, planning, implementing, and evaluating care.

In the past 30 years, significant attention has been given to the notion of culture-based care. The challenges of the future for nursing and health care mandate a renewed interest in and commitment to using both knowledge and practice skills in providing for the many cultures in and among diverse racial and ethnic groups whose members seek health care assistance and services in the United States and the larger global community.

Leininger (2002b) suggests that nurses working within transcultural settings need an understanding of the following five anthropological concepts:

1) *Culture encounter or contact refers to a situation in which a person from another culture meets or briefly meets with another person from another culture* (p. 55).
2) *Enculturation . . .* refers to the *process by which one learns to take on or live by a particular culture with its specific values, beliefs, and practices* (p. 55-56).
3) *Acculturation* refers to *the process by which an individual from group Culture A learns how to take on many (but not all) values, behaviors, norms, and lifestyles of Culture B* (p. 56).
4) *Socialization* [is] the *process whereby an individual or group from a particular culture learns how to function in the larger society (or country), that is to know how to interact appropriately with others and how to survive, work, and live in harmony with in a society* (p. 56).
5) *Assimilation refers to the way an individual or group from one culture very selectively and usually intentionally selects certain features of another culture without necessarily taking on many or all attributes of lifeways that would declare one to be acculturated* (p. 56).

These concepts are useful for assessing, interpreting, understanding, and providing care to families from varied cultures (Leininger, 2002b).

To become part of the central culture, one puts one's heritage aside, and a new culture is assimilated. In this process, individuals gradually conform to the standards of life of the dominant group. The process of assimilation is considered complete when all previous cultural dimensions are fully merged into the dominant cultural group.

The degree to which the *acculturation* process occurs is influenced by age, ability to speak the language of the dominant culture, and amount of contact with the original or dominant culture (Spector, 2000). The political, educational, and health care delivery systems support and endorse this process. Little recognition is given to the fact that acculturation occurs to varying degrees. In addition, the processes of acculturation and assimilation are stressful for families as they learn, make mistakes, reflect, and make modifications to live, work, and play within the prominent culture. As a society, we have consistently failed to accept the reality that different cultures coexist within our national boundaries. However, these differences provide richness and diversity; they are the essence of humankind in the United States and as such can and should be seen as a national strength.

Nursing is concerned with humankind's most valuable asset—health. Nursing is unique among the health professions in that its approach is holistic, and consideration is given to the individuality of the client. These two foundations of nursing practice reflect a transcultural approach to health care, in which the nurse attempts to recognize and transcend barriers and obstacles established by cultural uniqueness. The nurse considers both of these common threads that are held by all cultures and the unique elements that are maintained by a particular group. Only through an approach that combines both can effective, quality, culture-sensitive nursing occur (Leininger, 2002b).

Culturally sensitive nursing is translated into action by respecting people as unique individuals and by exhibiting an understanding that culture is a major force that contributes to this uniqueness. In a culturally sensitive approach to nursing care, a number of elements are included. These elements are especially important in addressing the health promotion and health maintenance needs of the "well" family. Emphasis is placed on family and human values; concern for a total approach to care; achievement of one's maximum level of well-being; and therapeutic partnership with the individual, family, and nurse. A recognition of the indirect and direct impact of the family on health status is essential.

The concept of family exists as an important unit in all cultures. How a culture defines "family" may vary, but the meaning for the individual remains the same. Through this basic unit of society, an individual learns about himself or herself and about his or her culture. Through enculturation, future generations are provided cultural values, beliefs, and attitudes. Included in this process are basic meanings about health and health promotion. The child learns a meaning for health, a meaning for illness, strategies to ensure and maintain health status, and attitudes about health care services. This process is greatly influenced by the family's acculturation status.

Key Concepts and Terms Related to Culture

The people of the world can be seen as a tapestry woven of many different strands.

Lipson et al. (1996)

This section provides a brief discussion of common terms a clinician needs to understand while planning and providing culturally sensitive health care with multicultural families. It is not intended to be a handbook about specific cultures or of cultural terms but is intended to introduce the reader to core cultural concepts for reflection.

Culture

Culture is defined as a specific set of social, shared, educational, religious, and professional behaviors, practices, and values that individuals learn and ascribe to while participating in or outside of groups with whom they typically interact. According to Leininger (2002b) and the Microsoft Encarta Online Encyclopedia (2002) culture has several distinguishing characteristics:

- Culture is based on *symbols*—abstract ways of referring to and understanding ideas, objects, feelings, or behaviors—and the ability to communicate with symbols by using language.
- Culture is *shared*. People in the same society share common behaviors and ways of thinking through culture. In families the beliefs, values, and life ways are passed on to the next generation.
- Culture is *learned*. Although people biologically inherit many physical traits and behavioral instincts, culture is socially inherited. A person must learn culture from other people in a society.
- Culture is *adaptive*. People use culture to flexibly and quickly adjust to changes in the world around them.
- Culture has explicit (readily manifest) and implicit (over and ideal) rules of behavior and expectations (Leininger, 2002b).
- Human cultures have special items, artifacts, objects, dress, and actions that have a special meaning.
- Food, ceremonies, rituals, food feasts, and religious rituals that are passed from one

generations to another are common in all human cultures.

- There are variations between and within cultures.

Culture is the expression of the essence of a people and a learned "design for living" (Murray, 2001, p. 4). Culture is universal, unique, stable, changeable, and variable and is often an unconscious influence. Culture is learned not only through formal education but also through a process of "cultural osmosis." Phenomena that are essential to consider in assessment of the culture of an individual or family are as follows (Giger & Davidhizar, 1999; Purnell & Paulanka, 1998):

- Overview, inhabited localities, and typography
- Artistic expression
- Environmental control
- Family patterns
- Biological variations/race
- A communication system
- Social organization
- Workforce issues
- Pregnancy and childrearing practices
- Form of property
- A means of physical welfare
- Birth and death rituals
- Spatial preferences
- Time orientation
- Spiritual, religious, and magical beliefs
- Food practices
- High-risk health behaviors
- Health care practices
- Health care practitioners
- Family sexual patterns
- Recreation and leisure activities
- Basic human patterns (e.g., competition, conflict, cooperation)

These phenomena provide the basis for an understanding of the universality of culture, and many represent family system patterns basic to health promotion. One can also determine, from examination of these phenomena, how culture structures the development of health beliefs, attitudes, and practices. Guides about specific cultures are available to the reader. For example, based on research and information obtained from representatives of ethnic groups, Lipson et al. (1996) provide a guide that covers more than 24

ethnic groups. A similar guide has been written by Purnell and Paulanka (1998) for more than 25 ethnic groups. It is crucial for nurses to consider ethnicity and cultural variables when providing health care to families across the life course, families experiencing health care issues, and families experiencing crises (e.g., family violence or death [Leininger, 2002a; Leininger & McFarland, 2002]).

Subculture "refers to the subgroups who deviate in certain ways from a dominant culture in values, beliefs, norms, moral codes, and ways of living with distinct features that characterize their unique lifeways" (Leininger, 2002, p. 47).

Race

Race is often viewed interchangeably with the primary characteristic of ethnicity. However, race is an ancient, nonscientific, political classification of human beings and is based on physiological characteristics such as skin color, eye shape, and texture of hair (Melville, 1988). *Race* is a narrower term than *ethnicity* and social construct that denotes a human biological definition. Therefore it should be discarded because of the negative connotation of the words *racism* and *racist* (Boyd-Franklin, 2003).

However, race is used for national statistical analysis. The U.S. Office of Management and Budget issued, in 1977, the "Race and Ethnic Standards for Federal Statistics and Administrative Reporting" contained in *Statistical Policy Directive No. 15*. These categories also implemented the requirements of Public Law 94-311 of June 16, 1976, which called for the collection, analysis, and publication of economic and social statistics on persons of Spanish origin or descent. There are four ethnic categories, four single racial categories, and five racial combinations. For the first time in history, in the 2000 U. S. Census, residents were given the option of recording that they were biracial or multiracial. Race is used to compare and contrast family variables and is a key research demographic item. For example, mean family income is often compared by using the U.S. Office of Management and Budget categories. Box 9-1 provides definitions of each category.

An issue in family research studies of biracial families is the description of the race of the child.

> **BOX 9-1   U.S. Office of Management and Budget Racial and Ethnic Standards for Statistics and Administrative Reporting**
>
> ### RACE
>
> 1. American Indian or Alaska Native. A person having origins in any of the original peoples of North America, and who maintains cultural identification through tribal affiliation or community recognition.
> 2. Asian or Pacific Islander. A person having origins in any of the original peoples of the Far East, Southeast Asia, the Indian subcontinent, or the Pacific Islands. This area includes, for example, China, India, Japan, Korea, the Philippine Islands, and Samoa.
> 3. Black or African American. A person having origins in any of the black racial groups of Africa.
> 4. White. A person having origins in any of the original peoples of Europe, North Africa, or the Middle East.
>
> ### ETHNICITY
>
> Hispanic or Latino Origin. A person of Mexican, Puerto Rican, Cuban, Central or South American or other Spanish culture or origin, regardless of race.
> Not Hispanic Origin. A person not of the above origin.
>
> ### MIXED RACE
>
> American Indian or Alaska Native *and* White
> Asian *and* White
> Black or African American *and* White
> American Indian or Alaska Native and Black or African American
> More than one race
>
> Source: U.S. Office of Management and Budget. (2000). *Guidance on aggregation and allocation of data on race for use in civil rights monitoring and enforcement.* OMB Bulletin No. 00-02. U.S. Office of the President. Retrieved December 16, 2002, from http://www.whitehouse.gov/omb/bulletins/b00-02.html; Recommendations from the Interagency Committee for the Review of the Racial and Ethnic Standards to the Office of Management and Budget Concerning Changes to the Standards for the Classification of Federal Data on Race and Ethnicity. (1997, July 9). *Federal register,* Part II. Retrieved online April 16, 2003, from http://www.whitehouse.gov/omb/fedreg/directive_15.html

In a study of more than 1000 parent-child pairs, researchers noted a 4.5% discrepancy between the self-report of the child's race and the report of race by the parents (Bomar, Harrell, & Webb, 1997). The most frequent disagreement occurred when parents reported the race as white and the child reported race as Hispanic or American Indian.

Racism is a social construct that includes beliefs that assert racial differences in character and in intelligence and suggest a superiority of one race or ethnic group over another. Racism often includes actions of oppressive use of authority, hatred, and bigotry or the denial of resources, rights, or access by one ethnic group toward another. Sample racist practices include withholding adequate services or rights or withholding economic, housing, educational, and health resources from an ethnic group such as African Americans, Native Americans, women, or refugees, immigrants, and religious groups. Health professionals need to be aware of *racism* and *discrimination* against specific cultures, lifestyles, and classes in the health care system (Leininger, 2002b). The outcome of racist beliefs and attitudes or discrimination results in disparities in health care and often causes emotional suffering and poor health status. For example, educational attainment and health care of low-income African American children are among the poorest in the developed nations.

A common outcome of racism, discrimination, cultural insults, and cultural backlash is *cultural pain* (Leininger, 2002b). The concept "cultural pain refers to suffering, discomfort, or being greatly offended by an individual or group who shows a great lack of sensitivity toward another's cultural experience" (Leininger, 2002b, p. 52). Health care professionals may unknowingly cause cultural pain by demeaning remarks or inappropriate touching or interactions. The pain is learned culturally and transmitted throughout the life cycle. African American families that are "trapped in a cycle of poverty" tend to experience increased unemployment, high school drop out rate, drug abuse, domestic and nonfamily violence, and crime. They also are reported to exhibit external and internal anger and rage (Boyd-Franklin, 2003). The rage may be internalized and shown as depression or substance misuse. Also, the results of longer-term poverty can be overt rage and anger directed toward both African American and white health service professionals (Boyd-Franklin, 2003). Clinicians who understand the outcomes of chronic poverty and racism should acknowledge this potential source of rage. It is crucial not to personalize the verbal anger expressed by ethnic clients, but instead the clinician should design strategies to strengthen families in coping with the chronic poverty and serve as an advocate in family, health, and economic policy changes for the poor.

Ethnicity

Ethnicity is the broader social and culturally preferred term that describes a sense of community transmitted over generations by families. It provides an individual the basis by which the "self" can be defined. Ethnicity is part of the essence of humankind "derived from membership, usually through birth in a racial, religious or subgroup with its associated culture" (Hartog & Hartog, 1983, p. 911). It involves a conscious and unconscious association that provides identity and historical continuity. Ethnicity is a major determinant of family patterns and belief systems. Often the terms *ethnic, multicultural,* and *culturally diverse* are used interchangeably to reframe the terms *race* and *minority* (Huff & Kline, 1999). *Race* should not be used interchangeably with *ethnicity.*

Minority

The less preferred term *minority* or *person of color* is used to denote a person or family from a group other than a white ethnic group such as Australian, German, Swedish, or Irish. Unfortunately, this term conjures up a feeling of "less than" and is not preferred by members of ethnic

groups. In addition to the original American Indian and African American minorities, in the past 20 years, a deluge of culturally diverse families immigrated to North American small towns and rural communities, as well as to large metropolitan areas. In addition to the stressors experienced by other American families, ethnic families experience the stress and burden of prejudice, discrimination, and racism. Many are refugees who may have multiple stressors such as obtaining legal documents to remain in the new country, language barriers, financial difficulties, limited access to health care, and conflicts with cultural norms. Therefore clinicians will no longer be able to continue "business as usual" but must accept the demographic mandate to incorporate transcultural caring into their work with twenty-first century families. A number of pocket guides provide snapshot views of common characteristics of selected ethnic groups. One comprehensive guide that presents general guidelines for health care and similarities and differences among ethnic groups is *Culture and Nursing Care Guide* (Lipson et al., 1996).

Beliefs

Although it often appears to individuals that their beliefs are a product of a unique psychic experience, the reality is that beliefs are convictions that certain things are true or real based on life experience. *Belief* implies mental acceptance of truths learned through family and community. As elements of culture, beliefs are the feeling dimensions that are translated into actions. "It includes the beliefs men hold about themselves, and the social, biological, and physical world in which they live, and about their relations to one another, to society and nature, and to such other beings as they discover, accept or conjure up" (Chinoy, 1967, p. 32). Some elements included in the domain of belief are as follows:

- Faith
- Trust
- Confidence
- Credence
- Opinions
- Judgments

Health-focused beliefs may be prescriptive or restrictive, or they may be taboos. Prescriptive beliefs are positively stated, describing accepted behaviors, whereas restrictive beliefs are negatively phrased and limit choices and behaviors. Taboos are restrictive in nature but identify potential supernatural consequences. Two examples of taboos during pregnancy are (1) avoiding moonlight or lunar eclipses so that the baby will not be born with a deformity (Latino) and (2) not having a picture taken during pregnancy because it may cause a stillbirth (African American) (Andrews & Boyle, 1999).

Values

Values are persistent, powerful, and directive standards that people use to make sense of and to direct their lives and interactions. Common areas of difference in values among groups include human nature, privacy, time orientation, family roles and responsibility, and work ethic (Leininger, 2002a, 2002b). Sometimes the values of families and clinicians are incongruent. Health values may cause families to delay treatment, use of resources, or compliance with both preventive and therapeutic regimens. Also, values will determine choice of healers, views of the value of health promotion, and expectations of the health care provider. For example, Leininger (1991) reports that white middle class and upper class families in the United States tend to be individualist and focus on self-reliance, whereas Asian, Latino, Haitian, and African Americans tend to value extended family networks. White ethnic groups also tend to value youth, whereas these minority groups value their elders.

Customs

Customs are usual practices or habits carried out by a defined population. They are orderly, comprehensive, and standardized expectations, specifying ways in which things are and should be done and the rights and obligations of individuals. Customs are sanctioned by tradition and sustained by the pressures of group opinion. A group tends to resist changes in customs both overtly and covertly. The following three evaluative criteria can be considered in identifying a custom (Parsons, 1970):

- Custom establishes the "norm" or "ideal" form of behavior in a given situation.
- Custom compels individuals to conform.
- Custom reveals group judgments about preference through actions and behavior.

Such actions and behaviors include communication, decision making, roles, rituals, etiquette, and routines. Of these actions, communication can be an insurmountable problem in providing family-focused, culturally sensitive care. If a client speaks a different language, it should not be seen as a client problem, but a mutually shared problem. Elements to consider as aspects of communication include dialect, style, volume, use of touch, context of speech, and kinesics (Giger & Davidhizar, 1999).

The major concepts developed as part of the construct of culture are *values, social structure, beliefs,* and *customs.* All elements are socially created, shared, and transmitted as a way of life. A cultural approach to health promotion involves a consideration of these interrelated, interdependent concepts.

Worldview

Worldview is the lens through which individuals, families, or groups view the universe. Generalizations about groups are frequently oversimplifications (Purnell & Paulanka, 1998). The probability that all people within a specific ethnic group will behave exactly the same is highly unlikely. Within all cultures, subcultures and individuals may not adhere to the values of the dominant culture. However, family values reflect both the society and the subculture with which the individual or family identifies. According to Friedman, Bowden, and Jones (2003), most individuals affiliate with a variety of subcultures. Identification with a specific value system is generally based on ethnic background, SES, peer group, religious preference, and gender. Subcultures function within the dominant value system and delineate more specifically the expectations and behaviors of individuals, families, and groups.

Many of the clients for whom nurses are providing and will provide care have distinct health care values, beliefs, and practices that are significantly different from those of the dominant culture in North America. In order for nurses to practice in competent ways, approaches to providing care must be grounded in the knowledge and science of transcultural nursing. For positive outcomes to be achieved, standards must be developed or promulgated as guides not only for teaching and learning but also for practice, research, and the evaluation of both education and practice (Leuning, Swiggum, Wiegert, & McCullough-Zander, 2002).

The 1998 American Nurses Association (ANA) *Standards of Clinical Nursing Practice* state, "The cultural, racial and ethnic diversity of the patient must be taken into account in providing nursing services" (p. 2). The issue raised by the ANA standards is the failure to address care provisions within the context of the client's worldview. According to Leuning et al. (2002), the primary tenet of nursing is caring and "caring is interpreted by the client within the framework of his/her own cultural beliefs, values, and life ways" (pp. 40-41).

Accordingly, the standards undergirding transcultural nursing are the theory of culture care by Leininger (1997) and Josepha Campinha-Bacote's (1998) culturally competent model of care. The cultural desire construct of Campinha-Bacote, "genuine and authentic motivation of the health-care provider to engage in the process of cultural competence" (p. 42), is considered the "core value woven throughout" Leuning and colleagues' proposed transcultural nursing standards (p. 41). The standards address process criteria, outcome criteria, and rationale across eight major areas: theory, cultural information gathering, caring and healing systems, cultural health patterns and caring practices, health care planning, evaluation, research, and professional development. These proposed standards articulate well with the commonly used systematic approach to care delivery of the nursing process. At the same time, the standards address the foundational elements necessary to determine appropriate nursing diagnoses from which plans of care can be determined. The goal of the systematic approach is to assist nurses in providing culturally competent and culturally congruent care (Leuning et al., 2002). Cultural competence is a process rather than a specific end point.

Cultural Competence

Cultural competence is a set of behaviors that promote awareness, respect, and responsiveness toward individuals, families, and groups. In health care cultural competence is a conscious non-linear process of taking into account a person's or family's cultural background, beliefs, and values and co-creating culturally specific health care (Purnell & Paulanka, 1998; Betancourt, Green, & Carrillo, 2002). It includes improving one's ability to control or change one's own false beliefs, assumptions, and stereotypes. Also required are the skills to think flexibly, to find sources of information about those who are different, and to recognize that one's own thinking is not always accurate or appropriate (Williams, 1997). Qualities of a culturally competent person include the following (Purnell & Paulanka, 1992, p. 2):

- Demonstrating an awareness of one's own existence, sensations, thoughts, beliefs, values, and environment without an undue influence on those from another background
- Demonstrating an awareness and knowledge of the client's culture
- Accepting and respecting cultural (regional, ethnic, and class) differences
- Adapting care to be congruent with the client's culture

According to Purnell and Paulanka, the progression of cultural competence is as follows:

- *Unconscious incompetence:* being unaware of one's lack of knowledge about other cultures
- *Conscious incompetence:* being aware that one is lacking knowledge from another culture
- *Conscious competence:* learning about the client's culture, verifying generalizations about the client's culture, and providing culturally congruent care to clients of diverse cultures
- *Unconscious cultural competence:* automatically providing culturally congruent care to clients of diverse cultures

Goldberg and Goldberg (2000) question the notion that one could become "competent" about the culture of another. Instead, Goldberg and Goldberg propose a model in which maintaining an awareness of one's lack of competence is the goal rather than the establishment of competence. With "lack of competence" as the focus, a different view of practicing across cultures emerges. The client is the "expert," and the clinician is in a position of seeking knowledge and trying to understand what life is like for the client. There is no thought of competence: instead, one thinks of gaining understanding of a phenomenon that is evolving and changing, never complete. Barriers to cultural competence include racism and prejudice, stereotyping, ethnocentrism, cultural imposition, cultural conflict, cultural blindness, and cultural shock.

Evans and Severtsen (2001) suggest the Hallmarks of Cultural Competency (Box 9-2) as guidelines for nonjudgmental listening and respecting clients when eliciting information and planning care.

Cultures include different beliefs and practices about the causes of disease, the roles of folk medicines and practitioners, treatment of illness, death and birth, acceptable behaviors, and respect for elders (Clark, 1999). Clinicians should learn what is culturally unacceptable when they are working with multicultural families. Examples of culturally acceptable and unacceptable behaviors are presented in Table 9-4.

Cultural competence is also the concern of health care policy makers at the national and state levels. The key reasons for cultural competence to be salient for health professionals are as follows (National Center for Cultural Competence, 2002):

1) To respond to current and projected demographic changes in the United States
2) To eliminate long-standing disparities in the health status of people of diverse racial, ethnic, and cultural backgrounds
3) To improve the quality of services and health outcomes

4) To meet legislative, regulatory, and accreditation mandates
5) To gain a competitive edge in the marketplace
6) To decrease the likelihood of liability and malpractice claims

As nations become more culturally diverse, health care professionals and organizations are compelled to provide culturally competent care. The U.S. Bureau of Health Professions suggests seven domains of culturally competent care, which are presented in Box 9-3.

BOX 9-2 Hallmarks of Cultural Competency

NONJUDGMENTAL LISTENING

Help the teller articulate the story through open-ended, gentle questioning.

Bear witness to the experience and emotions in the story.

Withhold judgment about the worth or truth of the story.

RESPECTING

Treat the story as a whole that allows the teller to identify meaning.

Focus on meaning rather than diagnostic analysis of the story's components.

Keep the story confidential.

Create a safe place for stories to be told.

From Evans, B. C., & Severtsen, B. (2001). Storytelling as cultural assessment. *Nursing and Health Care Perspectives, 22,* 180.

TABLE 9-4 Sample of Culturally Acceptable and Unacceptable Behaviors

Unacceptable Behavior	Recommended Behavior
Direct eye contact (Arab, Latino, American Indian)	Look at the ground or to the side when speaking to someone
Being late for an appointment (White)	Arrive on time
Putting personal needs before family needs (Asian, Latino, Appalachian, Black)	Try to incorporate personal needs into family goals
Self-disclosure of family information to outsiders (American Indian, Asian, Arab, Black)	Use tact in obtaining family history Establish trust and use trusted interpreters

Adapted from Clark, M. J. (2003). *Nursing in the community: Dimensions of community health nursing.* (4th ed.). Upper Saddle River, NJ: Prentice Hall.

Culture Care

Culture care is a theoretical perspective grounded in anthropology and nursing, highlighting a broad, holistic, yet culture-specific approach to examination of meaningful care with and for diverse cultures. The goal of culture care is to use research findings to promote culturally congruent, safe, relevant care to people of diverse and similar cultures (Leininger, 2002a). Nurses strive to provide holistic care to individuals, families, and groups. In this regard, caring remains the essence of nursing. Accordingly, theorists refine models that support the expansion of research and other evidence-based strategies to ensure culturally congruent nursing practice.

The Sunrise Model is one such approach to systematic integration of the client's worldview, cultural, and social structure dimensions—including kinship, religion/spirituality, political and legal variables, economic factors, educational and technological variables—into the design of care expressions and practices for therapeutic interventions, management of health and illness, and helping the client to survive or face death. Crucial to the success of this approach are the ability and capacity of the nurse to listen with an open mind, to learn from the client, and to refrain from imposing his or her own ideas (Leininger, 2002a, 2002b). See Figure 9-1 for a depiction of the Sunrise Model.

According to Dumas, Rollock, Prinz, Hops, and Blechman (1999), an individual's culture is a principal dimension of his or her identity and behavior. Failure to acknowledge the value of culture will have a negative impact on the effectiveness and appropriateness of the nurse in working with diverse clients, families, and populations. If persons of diverse race and ethnicity are not included in the population from which evidence-based practices are derived, research findings may not be valid.

With the national and global migration of families from diverse ethnic, racial, and cultural backgrounds, nursing educators must strengthen the curricula to incorporate cultural diversity as an essential element, rather than an "add-on" or an elective. Commitment to transcultural and multicultural orientation and education should aim to promote understanding of similarities and differences among families and adaptation of

---

BOX 9-3 Seven Domains of Cultural Competence

1. Values and attitudes
   Promoting mutual respect ... awareness of the varying degrees of acculturation ... a client-centered perspective ... acceptance that beliefs may influence a client's response to health, illness, disease and death ...
2. Communication styles
   Sensitivity ... awareness ... knowledge ... alternatives to written communication...
3. Community/consumer participation
   Continuous, active involvement of community leaders and members ... involved participants are invested participants, health outcomes improve ...
4. Physical environment, materials, resources
   Culturally and linguistically friendly interior design, pictures, posters, and artwork as well as magazines, brochures, audio, videos, films ... literacy sensitive print information ... congruent with the culture and the language ...
5. Policies and procedures
   Written policies, procedures, mission statements, goals, objectives incorporating linguistic and cultural principles ... clinical protocols, orientation, community involvement, outreach ... multicultural and multilingual staff reflecting the community ...
6. Population-based clinical practice
   Culturally skilled clinicians avoid misapplication of scientific knowledge ... avoid stereotyping while appreciating the importance of culture ... know their own world views ... learn about populations ... understand sociopolitical influences ... practice appropriate intervention skills and strategies ...
7. Training and professional development
   Requiring training ... nature of cultural competence training ... duration and frequency of professional development opportunities.

From Bureau of Primary Health Care. (2002) *Cultural competence: A journey.* Retrieved February 12, 2003, from http://www.bphc.hrsa.gov/culturalcompetence/Default.htm#9.

health care and family nursing practice to provide the basis for achieving cultural relevance.

Cultural Proficiency

Although significant attention has been devoted to providing culturally sensitive and culturally competent care, the greatest failure is the apparent lack of movement beyond cultural competence toward *cultural proficiency*. As health care shifts from hospital and institutional settings to community-based settings, the locus of control shifts from the practitioner-driven environment to the client-driven environment. In the client-driven environment, nurses and other health care providers become the "outsiders." Although one third of the U.S. and Canadian population consists of ethnically diverse groups, health care providers, nurses in particular, remain primarily white. Only slightly more than 10% of registered nurses are from other (nonwhite) ethnic and racial groups. According to Wells (2000), "cultural proficiency is the integration of cultural competence into one's repertoire for scholarship (e.g., practice, teaching, and research)" (p. 193). Cultural proficiency encompasses a commitment to individual and institutional change through the unearthing and confronting of potentially disturbing discoveries about one's personal biases and the institutional rhetoric about cultural diversity. Although cosmetic changes may be in place, sustained change requires both time and

patience, complemented by commitment. A cultural audit requiring a thorough examination of assumptions and prejudices communicated by family, society, and the media about people from diverse cultural backgrounds, with a conscious decision to change both personal and organizational culture, is imperative when one is striving for proficiency. The key to a successful transition to cultural proficiency is the development of respect and esteem for a culture different from one's own. The more culturally competent the professional becomes, the more family outcomes will improve. Table 9-5 shows a proposed relationship between the level of cultural proficiency and family outcomes (Leonard, 2001).

The National Institutes of Health (NIH) has an initiative to propel researchers toward cultural proficiency by mandating the inclusion of women, children, and nonwhite subjects in funded research. When such groups are omitted, compelling evidence must be presented to justify conducting the proposed study. It is imperative that researchers from all disciplines take a bold step to demonstrate a commitment to effecting positive change in promoting cultural proficiency. For example, the fastest growing subgroup within the African American population is older adults. The needs of older adults, who are predominately women, are best met by providing informal and formal support systems for health promotion. Crucial to the success of improving the health of this population is community empowerment,

---

TABLE 9-5 Relationship of Levels of Individual and Health Care System Cultural Competence and Family Outcomes

Individual/System Competence	Family Outcomes
Lack of awareness of deficiencies	Fear, lack of trust, failure to use system appropriately, and poor individual and family health outcomes
Awareness of deficiencies and taking steps to improvement	Beginning sense of trust, more appropriate use of providers
Cultural competence becoming normative	Appropriate use of providers, achieving better individual and family health status and increased satisfaction
Cultural proficiency, increased job satisfaction of providers, continuous improvement	Family and individual health outcomes much improved, trust, and satisfaction with care

Adapted from Leonard, B. J. (2001). Quality nursing care celebrates diversity. *Online Journal of Issues in Nursing, 6,* Manuscript 3 Retrieved from http://www.nursingworld.org/ojin/topic15/tpc15_3htm.

responsibility, and self-care (Dancy & Ralston, 2002).

In 2000, the Office of Minority Health (OMH) of the U.S. DHHS released the *National Standards for Culturally and Linguistically Appropriate Services in Health Care* (CLAS). Prior requirements for cultural and linguistic competency in health care service delivery had been developed; however, the previous guidelines were largely defined by individual federal agencies and health care providers. The guidelines also varied widely. Because of the lack of unification across agencies, it was not surprising to find a geographic imbalance with regard to CLAS among health care organizations on either coast, where cultural and linguistic minorities were concentrated.

Clinician Responses to Multicultural Families

Positive responses of health care providers to multicultural families include cultural sensitivity, cultural relativism, cultural accommodation, and cultural brokering (Clark, 1999; Leininger & McFarland, 2002). The provider needs to be cognizant of the relationship of family culture to health promotion (*cultural sensitivity*) and to view health behaviors in the context of the culture in which they are experienced (*cultural relativism*). *Cultural accommodation* is the process of modifying health care to meet the needs of ethnically diverse families. The process of mediating between culturally different individuals, families, or communities is called *cultural brokering*. Negative responses include ethnocentrism, cultural blindness, cultural shock, cultural conflict, stereotyping, racism, prejudice, discrimination, and cultural imposition (Clark, 1999). Avoiding, preventing, and reducing negative responses involves an ongoing process of self-assessment, reflection, and continual learning about diverse ethnic groups and having a philosophy of clinical practice that includes concern for others.

Health Promotion and Culture

Family Culture

Family culture is another concept related to the social structure component of culture. "Family culture consists of ways of living and thinking that constitute the family and sexual aspects of group life" (Murray, 2001, p. 6). Through the family unit, culture is learned, and through culture, the family unit provides individual identity and a sense of responsibility to others. Scholars suggest an ecocultural theory that assumes family beliefs about health are the most powerful influences on health (Bernheimer, Gallimore, & Weisner, 1990; Denham, 2003), with women serving as the health leaders (Denham). Denham and Bernheimer et al. suggest the function of the family household is *production of health*.

Each family culture is unique and provides the following:

- A definition of family
- Roles of family members
- Status of family members
- Family interaction patterns
- Sexual mores
- Status of women and children
- Decision-making processes for health and other factors
- A definition of family health and family health promotion
- Health care practices and beliefs
- Rituals, celebrations, rites, and routines

Other cultural differences in the family include courtship and marital patterns; beliefs about childbirth; discipline and training of children; parent-child relationship; family size; responsibilities of parents; responsibilities for young children, young adults, seniors, and unemployed family members; marital dyad relationships; pace and adjusting to change; status of a person; moral values; and the value of education (Murray, 2001). Cultural heritage is transmitted to children by the family. Through family culture, the unit provides individual and cultural identity and a sense of responsibility toward family members and others.

The elements listed provide both a general framework and a framework for health promotion and health care expectations. Family-focused nurses must consider that although the family is the basic unit of society, its elements are dynamic. For example, an unprecedented change in family structure is the significant increase in the number of female-headed households. In 2000, women comprised 12% of heads of households (U.S. Census Bureau, 2001). Within this group, another related factor that affects health status and health promotion activities has been called the "feminization of poverty." Female heads of households as a group comprise 26% of those below the poverty level (Proctor & Dalaker, 2001). Other significant demographic changes include an increase in interracial unions, the number of young adults living at home, and cohabitation rates (U.S. Census Bureau, 2001). Each family structure includes cultural beliefs, practices, rituals, and routines (Denham, 2003). The Canadian Perspectives box presents information about a research study in which family structure was analyzed as a cardiovascular health determinant.

CANADIAN PERSPECTIVES
SOCIAL DETERMINANTS OF HEALTH: FAMILY STRUCTURE AS A CARDIOVASCULAR HEALTH DETERMINANT

Lynne Young, RN, PhD
University of Victoria

Family, as a social and economic unit, mediates between society and the individual. Family structure and family processes determine how the family unit transforms societal influences on individual members' health. Research designed to explore the risk for cardiovascular disease (CVD) in low-income, lone mothers reveals how family structure influences women's cardiovascular health.

In a U.S./Canadian study (James, Young, DesMeules, & Cunningham, 2001; Wharf-Higgins, Young, Naylor, & Cunningham, in review; Young, Cunningham, & Buist, 2002), secondary analyses of the U.S. National Heath and Nutrition Examination Survey (NHANES III) and the Canadian National Population Health Survey (NPHS) (1998-1999) were augmented by focus-group and individual interviews for the following reasons:

- To compare select CVD lifestyle risk factors (smoking, obesity, physical activity) and relevant socio-demographic, health, and psychosocial variables in partnered versus lone mothers
- To examine the relationship between partner status and CVD risk and having experienced a cardiovascular heart disease (CHD) event (myocardial infarction, stroke, or congestive heart failure)
- To explicate low-income, lone mothers' perceptions of their risk for CVD

NHANES III includes data from 1446 mothers. Weighted logistic regression was used to compare the prevalence of CVD lifestyle risk factors (smoking, obesity, physical activity) in lone (43%) versus partnered (57%) mothers (Young, Cunningham, & Buist, 2002). Multivariate modeling was then used to reveal the relationship between mothers' partner status and having experienced a CHD event. In the NPHS, 2184 mothers were respondents (James, Young, DesMeules, & Cunningham, 2001). Weighted logistic regression was used to compare the prevalence of CVD risk factors in the two groups of mothers, lone (22.9%) versus partnered (78.1%). Focus groups and individual interviews with low-income lone mothers were convened to gather qualitative data that were then analysed to reveal themes and relationships by using constant comparative analysis.

Compared with partnered mothers, lone mothers in both countries were at greater risk for CVD than partnered mothers. In the U.S. sample, obesity was the most prevalent lifestyle risk factor for low-income, lone mothers; whereas in the Canadian sample, smoking was the most prevalent. In both countries, lone mothers were overrepresented in the lowest income and education categories, and lone mothers were more likely to report fair to poor health than partnered mothers. In the analysis of the NHANES III, after adjustments were made for age, poverty income ratio, receipt of Medicaid, education, obesity, and physical activity, mothers who had experienced a CHD event were 3.28 times more likely to be lone mothers than partnered mothers. Further, lone mothers were significantly more likely to have hypercholesterolemia, hypertension, and nongestational diabetes. Analysis of psychosocial variables in the NPHS revealed a possible explanation for the effect of life circumstances and health in that 65% of lone mothers reported low sense of coherence (that life is manageable) in contrast to 46% of partnered mothers.

CANADIAN PERSPECTIVES
SOCIAL DETERMINANTS OF HEALTH: FAMILY STRUCTURE AS A CARDIOVASCULAR HEALTH DETERMINANT—cont'd

In the qualitative study, low-income, lone mothers (n = 44) spoke to the links between their health and the families, communities, and societies in which they live (Young, Naylor, Cunningham, & Wharf-Higgins, 2001). Lone mothers spoke of themselves as strong, self-sacrificing women who are vulnerable, since they bear the burden of child care in a society that does not value their parenting work. Because of their marginalization, they are out of the mainstream, and their lives are shaped by societal policies and practices that elicit emotions ranging from gratitude to despair. The women suggest that their health is particularly vulnerable during times of despair. During these times, women struggle with depression, a key factor that influences their heart health–related choices such as consuming high-fat food, physical inactivity, and smoking.

Family structure emerges from this research as central to mothers' cardiovascular health. Social policies and practices that derive from societal values that honour lone mothers' parenting work have potential to mitigate this health-related phenomena.

References

James, A., Young, L., DesMeules, M., & Cunningham, S. (2001). Heart health behaviours in lone versus partnered mothers: National Population Health Survey (NPHS) 1998-99. *Canadian Journal of Cardiology, 17*(Suppl. C), 240C.

Wharf-Higgins, J., Young, L. E., Naylor, P. J., & Cunningham, S. (in review). Out of the mainstream: Low-income lone mothers' life experiences and perspectives on heart health. *Social Science and Medicine.*

Young, L., Cunningham, S., & Buist, D. (2002). Health disparities in women: Parenting status and risk of cardiovascular disease in women. *Communicating Nursing Research Conference Proceedings: WIN Assembly: Vol. 10. Health Disparities: Meeting the Challenge* (p. 133). Portland, OR: Western Institute of Nursing.

Young, L. E., Naylor, P. J., Cunningham, S., & Wharf-Higgins, J. (2001, June). Low-income, lone mothers' perspectives on their risk for cardiovascular disease: Unraveling the link between health and policy. Institute for Women's Policy Research. *The Status of Women: Facing the facts, forging the future.* June 8, Washington, DC.

Canadian spelling is used.

Social Class Subculture and Health

Subcultures exist in groups of families with similar income, education, and occupation and influence well-being and quality of life. Family socioeconomic levels are categorized by a variety of taxonomies and range from the affluent to the underclass or poor (Murray, 2001). For example, family socioeconomic subcultures categorized by Murray include the following:

- *Upper-upper, affluent,* or *corporate level* includes people whose wealth is derived from owning businesses or property and from investments.
- *Lower-upper level* consists of those whose wealth is recently acquired and who are famous and/or influential.
- *Over class* consists of professionals and managers who have earned their wealth status through hard work.
- *Upper-middle class* is a highly respected community of professionals who are well off and considered pillars of society.
- *Middle-level* includes professionals and business people who have reached the American Dream and live a comfortable lifestyle.

- *Lower-middle* or *working level* includes people who have received degrees from high schools and/or community colleges.
- *Upper-lower level* consists of people who have a difficult time "making ends meet" and are very close to poverty and public assistance.
- *Underclass* comprises those who are poor (short term and long term) and who do not have adequate funds to meet minimum requirements for food, housing, transportation, and health care.

Each class has different values, attitudes, and lifestyle preferences (Murray, 2001; Friedman et al., 2003). Like ethnic groups each SES class differs in role expectations, childrearing practices, marriage, gender responsibilities, dress, housing, reading habits, recreation and leisure activities, spirituality, time orientation, and so forth. For example, the upper class often has a future oriented time, whereas people who live in poverty tend to be present oriented and value that which is visible and tangible. On the other hand, nurses are often from the middle-level class, which values education, high expectations, initiative, and future goal orientation. As a result, nurses will often note difficulty teaching health promotion and prevention to a family who is present oriented because health promotion is focused on the future and is invisible. Cultural conflict occurs when the nurse does not understand that although a client/family may be from the same ethnic background as the nurse, the SES level also influences decision making and lifestyle. Therefore it is helpful for the nurse to understand the subculture of each SES level when working in partnership with diverse families on health-related issues. However, Andrews (2001) cautions that although knowledge of the lifestyle and culture of varied SES levels is useful, nurses are warned to "avoid stereotyping" families based on their knowledge.

Assessing Socioeconomic Status

In addition to family beliefs, a key determinant of health status is income (U.S. DHHS, 2002). Therefore the clinician needs to determine family SES. Assessment of SES is often a private and sensitive issue, particularly among those who are in poverty. Friedman et al. (2003, p. 235) suggest the following questions to determine family SES:

1) What is the level of education attained by members of the family?
2) Who is (are) the wage-earner(s) of the family?
3) Does the family receive any supplemental funds or assistance? If so, what are they and from where do they come (e.g., retirement fund, Social Security, food stamps, other relatives)?
4) What major expenditures does the family have?
5) Does the family consider its income adequate? How does it see itself managing financially?
6) What financial resources does the family or could the family have for [health care]?

Culture of Poverty

One barrier to involvement in health promotion and health protection relates to economics. Since the early 1960s, research and health statistics document that disparities in health are related to race and income (U.S. DHHS, 2000; Health Canada, 1999). In the United States in 2001, it was reported that that more than 32.9 million (11.7%) families were living below the federal poverty level, an increase of 1.3 million (11.3%) from 2000 (U.S. Census Bureau, 2002). Poverty is a major obstacle for families in their efforts to maintain and promote their level of health (U.S. DHHS, 2000). Poverty makes the family less capable of seeking care and accounts for greater susceptibility to illness. Being a member of the underclass cuts across ethnic and racial lines. Like other elements of culture, poverty is usually passed on; it can be cyclic and self-perpetuating and is assumed to be reinforced in the next generation (Spector, 1996).

In the United States, chronic health problems, preventable health problems, and social problems are disproportionately higher among African Americans, American Indians, and Hispanics than among other ethnics (U.S. DHHS, 2000). In response to these differences, the National Center on Minority Health and Health Disparities was created in 2000 by a congressional directive to support research to reduce health disparities among ethnic minorities. Also, nearly all the NIH centers, institutes, and offices and Health Resources and Services Administration (HRSA) departments and bureaus have mission statements related to culture and/or elimination of health disparities. For example, many of the subobjectives of *Healthy People 2010* specifically target health for the poor or ethnic minorities.

The relationship between poverty and poor health status and early death is a direct one. The poor have a higher incidence of disease and death rates twice the rate of people with incomes above the poverty level (U.S. Census Bureau, 2001). A cultural relationship to poverty exists, with the poverty rate higher among people of color. One third of African Americans live below the poverty level, a rate three times greater than the poverty rate of the white population (U.S. Census Bureau, 2002). Also a higher proportion of Latinos and American Indians are reported to earn less than white Americans and Asian Americans. Despite a philosophy that health is a "right of all persons," the poor must prioritize food, adequate shelter, and clothing as more important. Nurses are encouraged to understand the resources of families in poverty such as sources of financial, emotional, mental, and spiritual support; physical health; support systems; role models; and hidden rules (Payne, 2002). For example, one scholar suggests that there are class differences in the value of food. A person who lives in poverty values food for its quantity, a member of the middle class values it for its quality, and a wealthy person values it for its presentation (Payne, 2002). Therefore teaching a low-income family whose members are obese to reduce portion size at meals may be a challenge.

Health promotion is often abstract and a non-reality for the poor. Approximately 40% of children in the United States live in poverty, and the majority of poor children live in single-parent families (U.S. Census Bureau, 2001). The indigent are less likely to make use of available preventive health care because of personal conflicts, economics, culturally incompetent health care systems, and other priorities; whereas the more affluent have their basic needs met and have the resources to participate in health promotion and health protection.

Health promotion efforts by nurses are usually directed toward the white, middle-class, and affluent—the healthiest segments of the population. Strategies for minorities, the "working poor," new immigrants, older individuals, and homeless, migrant, and low-income population segments need to be tailored to their needs. An essential component of collaboration with low-income, diverse families is use of activities that build on family strengths and resources and transform their situations into healthier lifestyles (Tripp-Reimer, 1999). Lastly, clinicians are compelled to seek ways to increase their knowledge and competence in relating to the rainbow of cultures of the twenty-first century. Websites listed in the Website Resources box at the end of the chapter provide links to agencies and organizations that provide information and resources on multiple cultures, poverty, and cultural competence.

> Before asking a group of people to assume new health habits, it is wise to ascertain the existing habits, how these habits are linked to one another, what function they perform, and what they mean to those who practice them.
> Benjamin Paul, 1935

Family Cultural Assessment

A crucial aspect of appraising family strengths and issues is a cultural assessment. Cultural assessments reveal the meaning of patterns of behavior that might otherwise be judged unimportant, inappropriate, or in conflict with the beliefs and values of the provider or the health care delivery system. In fact, failure to complete a family cultural assessment would be considered incompetent care. Family needs cannot be met with inadequate knowledge of their culture, history, beliefs, and practices. For example Kleinman's (1980) *explanatory* model suggests that the cause of disease is explained differently by various ethnic groups. The ethnic family may not hold the Western beliefs about the cause of illness but may explain the cause of disease differently. For example, instead of the germ theory of disease causation, Asian families might believe that disease is caused by an imbalance between cold and heat in the body. Clinicians should learn how each family explains health and the causes of illness. Lastly, the cultural assessment is time-consuming and may need to be completed "over time" (e.g., during several visits) with a client family. For clinicians to understand a multicultural family's lived experience and unique explanatory model, family cultural assessment should be a dynamic process rather than a one-time linear event.

Leininger (1978) defined a cultural assessment as a systematic appraisal of cultural beliefs, values, and practices within the cultural context of the individual being evaluated. Most holistic family assessment tools include a component of culture. A variety of comprehensive, culturally focused assessment tools have been developed by transcultural scholars (Andrews & Boyle, 1999; Friedman, Bowden, & Jones, 2003; Giger & Davidhizar, 1999; Purnell & Paulanka, 1998; Leininger, 1978; Tripp-Reimer, Brink, & Saunders, 1997). Two phases of cultural assessment are delineated by Tripp-Reimer et al. (1997): (1) *data collection,* in which the nurse collects and analyzes cultural data and makes a nursing diagnosis and (2) *data organization,* in which data are used to guide planning culturally appropriate and competent care. Most sociocultural assessment tools include basic cultural information such as the following:

- Ethnic affiliation and country of origin
- Length of time in the current location
- Family cultural patterns
- Spirituality and religion
- Nutrition/food patterns
- Ethnic health care practices and preferences
- Family health-promoting lifestyle
- Space and time preferences
- Communication patterns
- Cultural taboos and myths

A variety of websites, books, and book chapters (Andrews & Boyle, 1999; Leininger & McFarland, 2002; Giger & Davidhizar, 1999; Clark, 2003; Purnell & Paulanka, 1998) that describe numerous cultures are quite useful. Cultural guidebooks provide information on cultural competence, the cultural perspective, strategies of communication, and general guidelines for conducting a cultural assessment. However, clinicians are cautioned to avoid making generalizations about a specific culture and to note that differences exist within cultures and families (Giger & Davidhizar, 1999). An interview with the family allows the clinician to illuminate the ethnic and family culture. Culturally competent health care is based on knowledge, awareness, skill, interaction, and sensitivity to the uniqueness of the culture of *each* client and family.

Before beginning an interview with a family, the nurse should first complete a self-assessment of his or her own culture. Box 9-4 presents questions the nurse should ask himself or herself to assess cultural attitude.

The nurse should begin the cultural assessment of a family by forming a general impression of the individuals and their family unit. Next, the nurse should solicit problem-specific information. Clients are asked to give reasons that they believe health care is needed. A health-focused cultural assessment cannot and does not require information on every element of the client's culture. The assessment must occur openly—without judgments, conclusions, or generalizations. Unlike biological and psychological data that attempt to identify deviations from the norm, cultural assessments are done "to identify deviations in cultural parameters with the goal of modifying the client's system or modifying the health care professional's system in order to increase congruence between them" (Tripp-Reimer, Brink, & Saunders, 1984, p. 81). Response to this assessment allows the nurse an opportunity to categorize and analyze culturally specific directives and interventions.

The following are key questions for the nurse to ask if he or she has a short time with families in settings such as ambulatory care and primary care centers:

- How does the family identify its ethnicity and religion?
- How long have family members been residents in this country and what is their immigration status?
- What language(s) is spoken in the home and what is the preferred language?
- In what language(s) do family members have reading and writing ability?
- What are their perceived issues or problems and beliefs about the causes of illness and treatment?
- What food practices and traditional healing methods are used (Lipson et al., 1996).

Table 9-6 lists key elements of a family cultural assessment tool. Information obtained will assist the nurse in determining whether a more in-depth family cultural assessment is needed. Comprehensive assessments evolve over several visits with the family and information obtained should include ethnic background, degree of acculturation, communication, language, place of birth and immigration history, dietary habits, dress,

BOX 9-4   Self-Assessment of Cultural Attitude

To become more aware of your attitudes toward feelings about people of other racial and ethnic backgrounds, ask yourself the following questions:

1. What are my racial and cultural or subcultural backgrounds?
2. What is my earliest memory of racial, ethnic, class, or gender differences?
3. What are the different messages that I have received in my life about different ethnic and racial groups such as African American/black, Asian, American Indian or Inuit, Arab/West Asian, white, Chinese, Japanese, Korean, Southeast Asian, and Latin American people?
4. If I am from a minority group, what are the different messages that I received from the majority ethnic or racial group when I was growing up?
5. How much experience did I have with any person from a racial or ethnic group different from my own when I was growing up?
6. In what way have these experiences affected my behavior toward people from the group(s)?
7. Describe people from other racial or ethnic minorities with whom you felt comfortable or uncomfortable.
8. What features or characteristics are dominant in people from other racial or ethnic minority groups with whom I have felt comfortable or uncomfortable?
9. What have I observed about the racial composition of my community and how has it changed in the past 5 years?
10. What have I observed about the interactions of people from diverse cultural backgrounds at my school, church, workplace, or an organization to which I belong?
11. Do I consider myself to be a nonracist or a racist? (A member of any race can assume that another race is inferior.)
12. What do I plan to do to increase my understanding of a person different than me?

Adapted from Murray, R. (2001). Sociocultural influences on the person and family. In R. B. Murray & J. P. Zentner (Eds.), *Health promotion strategies through the life span* (7th ed., p. 48). Upper Saddle River, NJ: Prentice Hall.

household appearance, use of folk and alternative health systems, family transitions, acceptance in the community, economics, religion, art, music, gender roles, and education. Assessment of family religion is addressed in Chapter 8. Holistic assessment provides a systems analysis of culture and takes into consideration its relationship to health. A cultural genogram (Hardy & Laszloffy, 1995) and a spiritual genogram (Dunn & Dawes, 1999) are also very useful tools with which to ascertain family culture.

Holistic cultural assessment tools serve as comprehensive useful guides in identifying cultural domains that are important in working with culturally distinct families. A primary concern in cultural assessment is to determine the role of family members with respect to health and illness.

Culturally specific directives that are family focused and aimed at health promotion and disease prevention should include consideration of four domains: values, social structure, beliefs, and customs. Attitudes and responses to health-promoting behaviors are based on the interrelationship of these domains. Any attempts, however sound, are liable to fail unless the nurse takes into consideration his or her own culture and the family's culture, to bridge the cultural gap between the nurse and the family unit. Because culture exists in many different forms, the nurse is advised to acknowledge the diversity of each family's and member's unique health practices. It is impossible to be an expert about all cultures; therefore, the best source of information is the family. Clinicians must also be vigilant in evaluating the impact of culture, race, and immigration status on the health and SES of families. In addition, it is crucial to determine family strengths and resources to increase the family's capacity to relate with the health care system and other cultures and to empower the family in the areas of health promotion and health protection.

TABLE 9-6 Family Cultural Assessment Guidelines

Assessment Criterion	Sample Interview Questions
Ethnicity/racial identity	How does your family identify itself in terms of a racial or ethnic group? Are both parents from the same racial/ethnic background?
Language and communication	What language(s) is spoken in your home? Who speaks the language(s)? What language is preferred when speaking to outsiders? What members of your family read English? What do eye contact and smiles mean in your family?
Place of birth and immigration history	Where were the members of your family born? How long has your family been in the current location? Why did you immigrate?
Geographic mobility	Where has your family lived in this country? How long did your family live at each location?
Family's religious affiliation	Does your family identify with a specific religion? Are all family members from the same religious background? What is the role of religion in family health and illness of members? Does your family use religious healers for illness and disease prevention? What is the involvement of your family in organized communities of faith? Who in your family is most involved in and influenced by religion?
Cultural sanctions and restrictions	What does your family believe about expressions of religious faith and showing of feelings? What are the specific rules for/roles of men, women, and children in your family culture? Are there taboos for children, adolescents, or women?
Ethnic group affiliation	Describe your family relationships with friends and neighbors who are members of your race. Are you involved with your ethnic group in social, educational, political, or recreational or other activities? To what extent does your family use services and shop within your own culture?
Neighborhood connections	Describe the characteristics of the people in your family's neighborhood.
Dietary patterns and use of folk and alternative health systems	What does food mean to your family? What are the preferred and restricted foods in your family? What special herbs, potions, and rituals are used for healing? Does your family use folk healers, practitioners, or alternative health methods?
Dress and jewelry	Do the members of your family wear clothing or jewelry that is specific to your ethnicity? Is there special meaning to the jewelry or clothing?
Household appearance	Is your home decorated with art, furniture, and religious objects from your culture?
Cultural health beliefs	What are your family members' beliefs about the cause, effects, course, and treatment of the health problem(s) of family members?
Family life transitions	What are your family's customs and beliefs about life transitions such as birth, illness, mourning and death, pregnancy and well-child care? What are your rituals for each?
Space, distance, and touch	What do members of your family believe about touching each other? How does your family feel about people outside of the family touching you or members of your family?
Acceptance by community and health professionals	To what extent do you believe your family is treated unjustly in the community or by health/social professionals because of your race?

From Friedman, M. M., Bowden, V. R., & Jones, E. G. (2003). *Family nursing: Research, theory, and practice* (5th ed.). Reprinted by permission of Pearson Education, Inc., Upper Saddle River, NJ.

Interventions with Sociocultural Diverse Families in Health Promotion

Nurses are key advocates and external health teachers for families and individuals in the realms of health promotion and health protection. However, collaborating with families to attain, regain, and maintain health cannot be done effectively without culturally competent care. Unfortunately, because there are hundreds of ethnic groups, there is no one specific intervention for each health issue (Friedman et al., 2003). However, it is useful to understand commonalties among ethnic and SES groups that are explained in detail by a number of authors. Key principles for promoting health with clients from a culture different than one's own include the following:

- Complete a self-cultural assessment to understand one's own beliefs, values, and attitudes (see Box 9-4).
- Conduct a "culturological" assessment (Leininger, 2000a).
- Seek knowledge about local cultures.
- Recognize political issues of culturally diverse groups.
- Recognize culturally based health problems (Andrews, 2001).
- Become familiar with culturally competent organizations in the community to assist families
- Understand that rules governing the communication process differ among cultural groups and that opportunities for miscommunication are significant (Huff & Klein, 1999).
- Use culturally sensitive and linguistically appropriate pamphlets, brochures, and audio-visual materials.

Most of the North American Nursing Diagnosis Association nursing diagnosis and intervention classifications are focused on the individual and tend to be minimally focused on health promotion. However, just as clinicians working with individuals are required to perform holistic physical assessments, clinicians collaborating with families are compelled to complete an analysis of a family's culture and ethnicity-related variables. Friedman et al. (2003) emphasize the importance of clinicians obtaining from families information on their beliefs, views, values, and health practices.

The cultural history is as salient as a thorough physical examination. Collecting the complete cultural history occurs as an integral part of other assessments. For example, assessment of family religion and rituals will include cultural dimensions.

Language and communication processes are often a major issue in providing care for new immigrants and refugees. For example, in some cultures eye contact is not used during conversation, and tone of voice may be softer or louder. Even if the nurse does not speak the clients' language, it is caring and sensitive to learn how to greet clients and to understand their preferences regarding touch and nonverbal language such as smiles. Unless one speaks the language, the use of an interpreter is essential for culturally competent and quality care. Rules for the use of an interpreter include the following (Luckman, 1999):

1) Children or friends should never be used as interpreters unless it is an emergency.
2) The clinician should know the qualifications of the interpreter and employ a qualified interpreter.
3) Interpreters must be trained in their role and ask for clarification if they do not understand a term.
4) The clinician must speak slowly and use low-literacy wording.
5) The clinician should speak directly to the family, not to the interpreter.
6) Interviews between the clinician and interpreter before and after any interpretation are essential.

It is crucial for all health care, research, and health education to be linguistically sensitive. McQuiston, Choi-Hevel, and Clawson (2001) describe an HIV prevention program for Hispanics that was successful because the researchers trained lay health care advisers who spoke Spanish. In addition, they used culturally specific empowerment participatory education strategies.

Policy Implications for Health Care

The twenty-first century began with a noted increase in culturally diverse families in industrialized nations such as Canada, the United

Kingdom, and the United States. The World Health Organization, national policy makers, and private organizations have created programs or agencies to champion the health of diverse families. The Website Resources box at the end of the chapter includes a sample listing of these programs and agencies. For example, the U.S. DHHS created the OMH in 1985 as a result a recommendation in the *Report of the Secretary's Task Force on Black and Minority Health*. The OMH's purpose is to reduce health disparities and address public health issues affecting American Indians and Alaska Natives, Asian Americans, Native Hawaiians and other Pacific Islanders, blacks/African Americans, and Hispanics/Latinos.

Similarly, the Canadian government created the First Nation and Inuit Health Branch to establish a renewed relationship with those ethnic populations. Its purpose is to provide direct health services and a refocused federal role that seeks to improve the health status of First Nations and Inuit people. The mission of each agency emphasizes the need for culturally competent health care providers. Internationally, in the late 1990s the U.S./U.K. Collaborative Initiative on Race and Ethnic Health was created to address common international health care disparities and access to health care for multicultural families (Stinson, 1998).

Nursing Education and Cultural Diversity

Nurses, the largest group of providers in the health care professions, must systematically begin to implement strategies to meet the challenge of fulfilling national standards. To address the political and social mandates for cultural competence in health care, the major nursing organizations—the National League for Nursing (1993) and the American Association of Colleges of Nursing (1998)—recommend that cultural content be incorporated into the basic nursing education curriculum and clinical missions. Many nursing leaders believe that implementing culturally competent care is not only an appropriate response to the changing demographics in America but also a mechanism with which to decrease, and eventually eliminate, racial and ethnic disparities in health care.

Evans and Severtsen (2001) examined the behavior of 222 beginning baccalaureate nursing students related to the concept of culture. They reported that mainstream nursing students tended to view culture as something that only "others" have, especially people of color or individuals from a distant country. Mainstream students experienced significant difficulty verbalizing their own cultural characteristics. Because Caucasians remain the dominant group among registered nurses, these researchers stressed the imperative that Caucasian nurses provide the leadership in listening to the lived experiences of all clients from a framework of beliefs, values, and customs.

By 2050, census projections indicate that all minority groups combined will become the majority, giving birth to the new concept, "the emerging majority." This rapidly emerging "new majority of those originally labeled minorities" promises to challenge schools of nursing and nursing service agencies to strive for greater recruitment and retention of people of diverse ethnic and cultural backgrounds in nursing and health care. A compelling force that will propel nursing education institutions to espouse this challenge is the criteria of two accrediting bodies. The National League for Nursing Accrediting Commission (1999) established new criteria that schools seeking accreditation should provide documentation of commitment to cultural, ethnic, and racial diversity.

Similarly, the American Association of Colleges of Nursing proposed, in their *Baccalaureate Essentials* (1998), that care for the increasingly diverse populations within the United States requires a broad understanding and appreciation of the lived experiences of clients of color, with recognition of the influence of culture on health beliefs and practices. Evans and Severtsen (2001) propose a simple method by which nurses might accomplish this end: listening to their clients. They suggest that nurses need to hear and understand the story each person has to tell. Further, they believe it is essential for caregivers, individually and as members of interdisciplinary care teams, to know these stories because of the impact on assessment, the process central to individualized care. Their research validated that the story can be used to access the details of the client's culture and the client's lived experience of illness within the context of the client's culture, leading to increased effectiveness in the assessment process.

Research Implications

Research with multicultural families and groups describes, predicts, and explains cultural phenomena and is necessary to provide knowledge that assists clinicians in providing culturally sensitive care. For more than 30 years, researchers have consistently reported that for nearly all variables, minorities have inferior health status compared with white persons. Research on the beliefs, customs, health determinants, evidence-based intervention outcomes, and health status of culturally diverse families was very sparse until about 10 years ago. In addition, until the NIH mandate in 1994 that people of color and women must be included in NIH-funded studies, minorities were underrepresented in research studies. Before this, participants active in research were predominately white, male, middle-class, and married. Tripp-Reimer (1999) describes a four-level pyramid model of culturally relevant nursing research. The pyramid base shows four levels of transcultural nursing research as follows:

Level I: *Cultural characteristics*—descriptive research of two types: ethnographic and epidemiological studies

Level II: *Clinical implications*—clinical implications identified through descriptive cultural research

Level III: *Culturally specific interventions*—new or modified clinical interventions for a multicultural population

Level IV: *Effectiveness of cultural interventions*—tests the effectiveness of interventions with ethnic groups

According to Tripp-Reimer, most transcultural research to date is Level I or II and is sparse in Levels III and IV. Major issues identified in recruiting, retaining, and intervening with multicultural families and women for research studies are as follows (Flaskerud & Nyamathi, 2000):

- Access, availability, and affordability vary.
- Burdens and benefits of research differ for culturally diverse groups and women.
- Language, literacy, and instrumentation should be culturally appropriate.
- Cultural values and beliefs differ from the researchers' biomedical middle-class culture.
- Lack of trust and fear of research process impede participation.

- Researchers may be insensitive to human dignity and cultural socioeconomic attributes of participants.

Leininger (1978) states that to provide culturally meaningful health services to clients, nurses must systematically study the client's view concerning health and illness. Four research methods can be used to accomplish this: (1) emic, (2) etic, (3) synchronic, and (4) diachronic. The *emic* method is an in-depth qualitative analysis of the cultural meaning and origins of health promotion behaviors. Through interviewing methods, those behaviors deemed culturally appropriate are identified. With the *etic* method, those beliefs, values, customs, and social structures of culture are examined from the outside. One analyzes such universals by observation (Leininger, 1991). *Synchronic* methods are used to analyze those fixed elements of structure, function, and meaning of culture; and *diachronic* methods are used to examine the historical developments and influences of a changing culture. A combination of these approaches will assist researchers and practitioners in identifying the ideal, *what ought to be;* the real, *what is;* the explicit, *the concrete observable;* and the implicit, *the invisible, silent* dimensions of health promotion.

Two major issues in research with diverse cultures are low participation rates and high dropout rates. Central strategies with which to improve recruitment and retention of diverse families for research studies are caring, working with gatekeepers, reciprocity, and ethnohistory (Hautman & Bomar, 1995). Other approaches to empower an ethnic group to participate in research include the use of a lay board of advisors and health workers, identification of stakeholders (women in leadership positions, faith communities, and individuals from the target populations), and use of ethnically sensitive social marketing and health education materials. The Research Synopsis presents a summary of a research study involving African American mothers with HIV.

Weaver (1999) surveyed American Indian social workers and social work students on their beliefs about culturally competent services with American Indian clients. The research revealed four important areas of knowledge: (1) diversity, (2) history, (3) culture, and (4) contemporary realities. The diversity knowledge component

RESEARCH SYNOPSIS

AFRICAN AMERICAN MOTHERS WITH HIV

Overview: Stigma is a negative social phenomenon that occurs when a person is considered to have an undesirable trait or behavior and is subsequently deemed imperfect in regard to the standards of society. Because stigma is so closely associated with interpersonal relationships, people who have a stigmatizing characteristic may become secretive and isolated and may lose social and emotional support. Few illnesses in modern times have been associated with the high levels of stigma and resulting social isolation that accompanies a diagnosis of HIV. People with HIV experience prejudice and are discounted and discriminated against because transmission of the virus is commonly associated with social and sexual behaviors such as intravenous drug abuse, homosexuality, and prostitution and because HIV is infectious, poses a threat to the health of others, and is fatal.

Stigma involves the family system in a number of ways. Some individuals with HIV struggle to protect their families from experiencing "courtesy stigma," that is, stigma that is experienced by individuals closely associated with a stigmatized individual. Others may experience stigma directly from family members, after the family learns of the diagnosis, through their negative remarks, distancing behaviors, and avoidance strategies. To protect themselves from such stigma, to ensure that family members are not stigmatized, or to ensure that family members do not reveal the diagnosis to others, many individuals with HIV struggle with issues of disclosure and secrecy even within their family. Such issues related to disclosure and stigma are of particular concern to African American women residing in small towns and rural areas of the South.

Purpose: This study was undertaken to increase understanding of the experiences of HIV-positive African American women regarding issues of stigma and disclosure. The purpose was to identify the processes involved in and the patterns of disclosure reported by low-income African American mothers with HIV residing in the southeastern United States.

Design: A qualitative descriptive design was used for this study.

Participants: Fifty HIV-positive African American mothers who were enrolled in a larger study that tested a self-care intervention.

Data Collection Method: Field notes recorded by nurses who provided six in-home interventions with each mother were analyzed by using content analysis. Since issues of stigma and disclosure were salient throughout the intervention, the field notes included detailed information about the issues the women faced and their ways of dealing with them.

Results: Once the women found out they had HIV, they were faced with the issue of determining "what is at stake" in telling others of their diagnosis. This dilemma was characterized by the threat of stigma and feelings of shame and the concurrent need for support. The women used a calculus of disclosure in determining to whom and when to reveal their HIV diagnosis. The women reported making careful disclosure decisions regarding family members, as well as friends and health care professionals. Of particular concern was when and how to disclose the diagnosis to children, including adult children.

The calculus of disclosure involved careful evaluation of the risks and benefits involved in disclosing their illness. Risks of telling were fueled by societal and experienced stigma associated with HIV, whereas the benefits were primarily fueled by personal needs. A major personal factor that pushed disclosure was the need for support from family and friends, such as babysitting for children when they attended the clinic and transportation to the hospital. This calculus of disclosure was a recursive process, with decisions made and remade over time.

Disclosure patterns ranged from secretive, in which only a very few were told and these were usually close family members, to full disclosure in which the diagnosis was made public in dramatic ways. Most subjects, however, described a calculus of disclosure that involved selectivity in determining whom to tell and whom not to tell. Typically, these

RESEARCH SYNOPSIS

AFRICAN AMERICAN MOTHERS WITH HIV—cont'd

women told close family members, such as their partners, mothers, and sisters, and occasionally, all older members of the immediate household, but carefully guarded their diagnosis from their children and were highly selective about whom they told outside of the household.

Conclusions: Issues related to stigma and therefore disclosure of an HIV diagnosis are highly salient to HIV-positive African American women living in rural areas of the Southeast. Nurses have an important role in supporting women with regard to their disclosure decisions.

Written by Margaret Miles, RN, PhD, FAAN, School of Nursing, The University of North Carolina at Chapel Hill. Abstracted from Black, B. P., & Miles, M. S. (2002). Calculating the risks and benefits of disclosure in African American women who have HIV. *Journal of Obstetric, Gynecologic, and Neonatal Nursing, 31*(6), 688-697.

emphasized the need to recognize that variation exists among American Indian nations in factors such as beliefs, customs, and spirituality. One respondent stated, "American Indians are not alike, do not speak the same language, nor have the same tribal system. Each tribe is different." Each client is an individual who may or may not have a strong cultural connection or may experience that cultural connection differently than another native person. Communication and problem-solving skills were frequently identified as important. One respondent commented, "The biggest (most important) skill I can think of is the ability to interact and engage Indian people (collectively and individually) in a problem-solving process that's based on the definition of the problem and arrival of the solution from an Indian perspective."

Much of the research also pointed to instrument flaws, especially in norming for cultural differences. Language barriers and lack of consideration for cultural practices were frequently highlighted as problem areas. The tendency to "lump" people into categories without regard for interethnic variability was noted as problematic, especially with Latinos and Asians. Researchers are encouraged to determine whether their studies incorporate cultural competence in the framework, sample selection, measures specific for the ethnic group, analysis by ethnic group, research team representative of ethnic group, and dissemination of findings for a specific cultural group. The report of findings should be verified and clarified with representatives from the culture.

Also needed is further investigation on the reliability and validity of Likert formats, examination of language or verbal versus written surveys, differentiation of language proficiency, knowledge of customs and practices, and timing elements for administration.

Future multicultural family research should include (1) family health issues and outcomes of programs geared to new immigrant cultural groups such as Middle Eastern immigrants, Latinos, and blacks; (2) interventions for the reduction of low infant birth weight; (3) participatory research for seniors and caregiver health issues; (4) community-based participatory research to reduce substance abuse, the school dropout rate, and school violence; (5) intervention research to improve the quality of life for stepfamilies as a unit and for their members; and (6) implementation of culturally sensitive research focused on the *Health People 2010* and *Health Canada* objectives for health. Other salient topics are the impact of the global economy, catastrophes, war, welfare reform, terrorism, and immigration on family life (McAdoo, 1999; Denham, 2003).

Lastly, researchers are compelled not only to provide culturally sensitive resources to multicultural populations participating in research studies but also to (1) use participative research methods (McQuiston, Choi-Hevel, & Clawson, 2000); (2) empower participants from diverse cultures and poverty with financial support, skills, and knowledge to improve their lives and health

(Flaskerud & Nyamathi, 2000); (3) design and implement Level III and IV research studies (Tripp-Reimer, 1999); (4) use a research advisory group from the ethnic population; and (5) obtain feedback from the advisory group on the research report before dissemination.

Resources and Programs for Multicultural Families

As international, national, state, and local agencies continue to assemble resources to meet the needs of ethnically diverse immigrants and current minorities, policies and resources are developed to create a culturally knowledgeable and competent health care provider workforce. Numerous electronic and printed resources have been created in the past decade to improve the cultural competence of health care providers. The Website Resources box at the end of the chapter includes examples of website resources for health care professionals to empower them to attain and maintain cultural competence in an increasingly diverse society. Also, many professional and civic organizations are valuable resources for information about a culture. Examples of professional organizations include the Asian/Pacific Islander Nursing Association, the Hispanic Nurses Association, the Philippine Nurses Association, and the Black Nurses Association. Specific agencies include the U.S. Indian Health Service and the U.S. DHHS OMH.

Cultural competence is the complex integration of knowledge, skills, and attitudes with consideration of and respect for the client's perspective or viewpoint. The long-range goal of interacting with and providing services for multicultural families is to be culturally conscious and to have knowledge of one's own beliefs, attitudes, and values, as well as those of multicultural clients. According to Maville and Huerta (2002), there are no "ready made answers to real life situations" nor are there books such as "Culture for Dummies, Ten Steps to Cultural Competence or All You Wanted to Know about Culture but Were Afraid to Ask" (p. 111).

> Sometimes the best resource is the client, and clinicians are encouraged to collaborate with families to empower them in culturally appropriate health promotion activities.
>
> Maville and Huerta, 2002

CASE SCENARIO

Older adults of African American origin who live in rural communities are frequently reported to be noncompliant with prescribed dietary management. The case cited is an example of miscommunication that could lead to invalid conclusions and labeling.

An 88-year-old African American woman given a diagnosis of hypertension was informed that she needed to reduce her intake of fats and high-sodium foods. She was also instructed to limit her overall use of salt in cooking. At two subsequent visits, the nurse inquired about the progress achieved in controlling the hypertension. During the second visit, the client happily reported that she no longer used salt in serving foods, used very little salt in cooking, and had definitely limited her fat intake.

The nurse could not understand the lack of positive response to the treatment plan, since the blood pressure remained high even with medication and the reported success with dietary changes. The nurse asked the client to recall the typical menus she had for 1 to 3 days. The client reported having oatmeal and toast without butter for breakfast. She indicated she generally had only vegetables at lunch. She reported eating two to three vegetables and fruit with chicken, fish, or lean ham at dinner. In fact she said, "The ham was so very lean that I ate it three days last week and two days this week. It was a large picnic ham with almost no fat."

When asked about the lean ham, the client indicated that she cut away the fat and baked the ham. When asked if she was aware that cured ham was a high-sodium pork product, the client became visibly upset. The client explained to the nurse that she had been informed that she should eliminate bacon, pork sausage, and chitterlings and concentrate on lean pork, if using pork. Since ham was not one of the foods named for elimination and because she did not buy "country ham with all of that salt," the client thought she was selecting a healthy, lean pork product.

CASE SCENARIO—cont'd

STRESSORS

Ham is a favorite food for many older African Americans for meals and for seasonings. The client was being asked to omit a food that is a traditional comfort food. The communication to the client was not clear when reduction of high-sodium foods was explained.

STRENGTHS

The client has made significant changes in her diet by reducing fat and sodium.

INTERVENTIONS

Initially, praise the client for the changes made. Explore how often the client eats ham and how much. Focus on the strengths; for example, she had reduced the cholesterol by removing the fat. Discuss ways to reduce the frequency and serving size and to gradually decrease how often ham is eaten. Explain how ham is processed with salt. Suggest trying fresh lean pork tenderloin or smoked turkey or using liquid smoke for the smoke flavor. Evaluate the client's physical activity and compliance with her prescribed medication regimen and stressors.

WEBSITE RESOURCES

ORGANIZATION	WEBSITE ADDRESS
The Cross Cultural Health Care Program	http://www.xculture.org
U.S. Office of Minority Health	http://www.omhrc.gov
Office of Research on Minority Health	http://www.nih.gov/ormh
National Center for Cultural Competence	http://www.georgetown.edu/research/gucdc/nccc/index.html
Bridge to Wellness–Cultural Competence	http://www.serve.com/Wellness/culture.html
First Nations and Inuit Health Branch (Canada)	http://www.hc-sc.gc.ca/fnihb
Journal of Multicultural Nursing and Health Care	http://www2.cecomet.net/eestar/jmcnh/index.html
U.S. Department of Health and Human Services Indian Health Service	http://www.ihs.gov/index.asp
Transcultural Nursing	http://www.culturediversity.org/mide.htm
The Transcultural Nursing Society	http://www.tcns.org/
The National Multicultural Institute	http://www.nmci.org/
Diversity Rx	http://www.diversityrx.org/html/divrx.htm
National Health Law Program, Race and Cultural Issues	http://www.healthlaw.org/index.shtml
Center for Cross-Cultural Health	http://www.crosshealth.com/
National Council on Interpreting in Health Care	http://www.ncihc.org
Citizenship and Immigration Canada, Cultural Profiles Project	http://www.cwr.utoronto.ca/cultural/
EthnoMed	http://www.ethnomed.org

■ CHAPTER HIGHLIGHTS

- Cultural competency is based on respect for individuals and cultural differences and the implementation of a trust-promoting method of inquiry.
- The purpose of culture care is to use research findings to promote culturally congruent, safe, relevant care to people of diverse cultures.
- If persons of diverse race and ethnicity are not included in the population from which evidence-based practices are derived, research findings will not be valid.
- As the largest group of providers in the health care professions, nurses, including nurse educators, must systematically begin to implement strategies to meet the challenge in fulfilling national health standards.

- Census projections indicate that by 2050, minority groups combined will become the majority, giving birth to the new concept, "the emerging majority."
- Values are principles or standards that give meaning and worth to an individual, family, group, or community.
- Implementing culturally competent care is not only an appropriate response to the changing multicultural demographics in America but also a mechanism with which to decrease, and eventually eliminate, racial and ethnic disparities in health care.
- Nursing research with multicultural families in the twenty-first century should include more studies that focus on outcomes of culturally specific interventions with diverse families.

CRITICAL THINKING ACTIVITIES

1. Interview an individual of an ethnic group different from your own.
   a. Perform a brief cultural assessment of this individual using the questions provided in this chapter on page 244.
   b. Ask this individual how his or her family defines health and health promotion.
2. Ask two people from an ethnic group different from your own what they do to prevent illness

and to stay healthy. Compare your findings with those of your peers.

3. Attend a festival, read a book, or watch a movie from a culture different than your own. Write your observations on family communication style, distance, touch, folk practices, health beliefs, time orientation, gender roles, rituals, and types of food.

REFERENCES

American Academy of Nursing, Expert Panel on Cultural Competent Nursing Care. (2002). AAN expert panel report: culturally, competent health care. (2002). *Nursing Outlook, 40*(6), 277-283.

American Association of Colleges of Nursing. (1998). *The essentials of baccalaureate education for professional nursing practice.* Washington, DC: Author.

American Nurses Association. (1998). *Standards of clinical nursing practice.* Kansas City, MO: Author.

Andrews, M. M. (2001). Cultural diversity in community health nursing. In M. A. Nies & M. McEwen (Eds.), *Community health nursing: Promoting the health of populations* (pp. 242-285). Philadelphia: Saunders.

Andrews, M. M., & Boyle, J. S. (1999). *Transcultural concepts in nursing care.* (3rd ed.). Philadelphia: Lippincott.

Bernheimer, L. P., Gallimore, R., & Weisner, T. S. (1990). Ecocultural theory as a context for the individual service plan. *Journal of Early Intervention, 14,* 219-233.

Betancourt, J., Green, A. R., & Carillo, J. E. (2002, October). *Cultural competence in health care: Emerging frameworks and practical approaches* (Field Reports). Commonwealth fund. Retrieved February 2, 2003 from http://www.cmwf.org/programs/minority/betancourt_culturalcompetence_576.pdf

Bomar, P., Harrell, J. & Webb, J. (1997). Family member discrepancies in report of a child's race. *Journal of Cultural Diversity, 4,* 104-109.

Boyd-Franklin, N. (2003). Race, class, and poverty. In F. Walsh (Ed.), *Normal family processes: Growing diversity and complexity* (3rd ed., pp. 260-279). New York: The Guildford Press.

Campinha-Bacote, J. (1998). *The process of cultural competence in the delivery of healthcare services: A culturally competent model of care.* (3rd ed.). Cincinnati, OH: Transcultural C.A.R.E. Associates.

Chinoy, E. (1967). *Society: An introduction to sociology.* New York: Random House.

Clark, M. J. (1999). *Nursing in the community: Dimensions of community health nursing.* (3rd ed.). Stamford, CT: Appleton & Lange.

Clark, M. J. (2003). *Community health nursing: Caring for populations* (1st ed.). Upper Saddle River, NJ: Prentice Hall.

Dancy, J. & Ralston, P. A. (2002). Health promotion and black elders. *Research on Aging, 24,* 218-242.

Denham, S. A. (2003). *Family health: A framework for nursing.* Philadelphia: F. A. Davis.

Dumas, J. E., Rollock, D., Prinz, R. J., Hops, H., & Blechman, E. A. (1999). Cultural sensitivity: problems and solutions in applied preventive intervention. *Applied & Preventive Psychology, 8,* 175-196.

Dunn, A. B., & Dawes, S. J. (1999). Spiritually focused genograms: Keys to uncovering spiritual resources in African-American families. *Journal of Multicultural Counseling and Development, 27,* 240-255.

Evans, B., & Severtsen, B. (2001). Storytelling as cultural assessment. *Nursing and Health Care Perspectives, 22,* 180-186.

Flaskerud, J., & Nyamathi, A. (2000). Attaining gender and ethnic diversity in health intervention research: Cultural responsiveness versus resource provision. *Advances in Nursing Science, 22,* 1-15.

Fong, C. M. (1985). Ethnicity and nursing practice. *Topics in Clinical Nursing. 7,* 1-10.

Friedman, M. M., Bowden, V. R., & Jones, E. G. (2003). *Family nursing: Research, theory, and practice* (5th ed.). Upper Saddle River, NJ: Prentice Hall.

Giger, J. N., & Davidhizar, R. E. (1999). *Transcultural nursing: Assessment and intervention* (3rd ed.). St Louis, MO: Mosby.

Goldberg, I, & Goldberg, H. (2000). *Family therapy: An overview* (5th ed.). Belmont, CA: Wadsworth.

Hardy, K. V., & Laszloffy, T. A. (1995). The cultural genogram: Key to training culturally competent family therapists. *Journal of Marital and Family Therapy, 21,* 227-237.

Hartog, J., & Hartog, E. (1983). Cultural aspects of health and illness in hospital. *Western Journal of Medicine, 139,* 910-916.

Hautman, M. A., & Bomar, P. J. (1995). Interactional model for recruiting ethnically diverse research participants. *Journal of Multicultural Nursing and Health, 1,* 8-15.

Health Canada. (1999). *What determines health.* Population Health Homepage. Retrieved online April 2, 2003 from http://www.hc-sc.gc.ca/hppb/phdd/determinants/index.html

Huff, R. M. & Kline M.V. (1999). Health promotion in the context of culture. In R. M. Huff & M. V. Kline (Eds.), *Promoting health in multicultural populations: A handbook for practitioners* (pp. 3-22). Thousand Oaks, CA: Sage.

Kleinman, A. (1980). *Patients and healers in the context of culture.* Berkeley: University of California Press.

Leininger, M. (Ed.). (1991). *Cultural care diversity and universality: A theory of nursing.* New York: National League for Nursing Press. Publication No. 15-2402.

Leininger, M. (1997). Overview and reflection of the theory of culture care and ethnonursing research method. *Journal of Transcultural Nursing, 8,* 32-51.

Leininger, M. (1978). *Transcultural nursing: Concepts, theories and practices.* New York: Wiley and Sons.

Leininger, M. (2001). Madeline M. Leininger: Theory of culture care diversity and universality. In M. Parker (Ed.), *Nursing theories and nursing practice* (pp. 361-376). Philadelphia: F. A. Davis.

Leininger, M. (2002a). Culture care theory: A major contribution to advance transcultural nursing knowledge and practices. *Journal of Transcultural Nursing, 13,* 189-192.

Leininger, M. (2002b). Essentials transcultural nursing care concepts, principles, examples and policy statements. In M. Leininger & M. R. McFarland (Eds.), *Transcultural nursing: Concepts, theories, research and practice* (3rd ed., pp. 45-68). New York: McGraw-Hill.

Leininger, M. & McFarland, M. (2002). *Transcultural nursing: Concepts, theories, research, and practice* (3rd ed.). New York: McGraw-Hill.

Leonard, B. J. (2001). Quality nursing care celebrates diversity. *Online Journal of Issues in Nursing, 6(2).* Manuscript 3. Retrieved November 26, 2002, from http://www.nursingworld.org/ojin/topic15/tpc15_3htm

Leuning, C., Swiggum, P., Wiegert, H., & McCullough-Zander, K. (2002). Proposed standards for transcultural nursing. *Journal of Transcultural Nursing, 13,* 40-46.

Lipson, J. G., Dibble, S. L., & Minarik, P. A. (1996). *Culture & nursing care: A pocket guide.* San Francisco: University of California, San Francisco Nursing Press.

Luckman, J. (1999). *Transcultural communication in nursing.* Albany, NY: Delmar.

Maville, J. A., & Huerta, C. G. (2002). *Health promotion in nursing.* Albany, NY: Delmar.

McAdoo, H. P. (1999). Families of color: Strength that comes from diversity. In H. P. McAdoo (Ed.), *Family ethnicity: Strength in diversity* (2nd ed., pp. 3-14). Thousand Oaks, CA: Sage.

McQuiston, C., Choi-Hevel, S., & Clawson, M. (2001). Protegiendo nuestra coumunidad: Empowerment participatory education for HIV prevention. *Journal of Transcultural Nursing, 12,* 275-284.

Melville, M. B. (1988). Hispanics: Race, class, or ethnicity? *The Journal of Ethnic Studies, 16,* 67-83.

Microsoft Encarta Online Encyclopedia (2002). *Culture.* Retrieved online November 18, 2002, from http://encarta.msn.com/encnet/refpages/srpage.aspx?search=Culture

Murray, R. B. (2001). Sociocultural influences on the person and family. In R. B. Murray & J. P. Zentner (Eds.), *Health promotion strategies through the life span* (7th ed., pp. 3-71). Upper Saddle River, NJ: Prentice Hall.

National Center for Cultural Competence. (2002). *Why is there a compelling need for cultural competence?* Retrieved December 6, 2002, from http://www.georgetown.edu/research/gucdc/nccc/cultural5.html

National League for Nursing. (1993). *A vision for nursing education.* New York: Author.

National League for Nursing Accrediting Commission. (1999). *Interpretive guidelines for standards and criteria 1999: Baccalaureate and higher degree programs.* New York: Author.

Office of Minority Health. (2000). *National standards for cultur-ally and linguistically appropriate services in health care.* Retrieved November 1, 2002, from http://www.omhrc.gov/CLAS/indexfinal.htm

Parsons, T. (1970). *Social structure and personality.* London: Free Press.

Payne, R. K. (2002). Understanding and working with students and adults from poverty. *National Council of Family Relations Report, 47,* 18-20.

Perry, M. J., & Mackun, P. J. (2001). *Population change and distribution 1996 to 2000: Census 2000 brief.* Washington, DC. U.S. Census. Retrieved December 8, 2002, from http://www.census.gov/prod/2001pubs/ c2kbr01-2.pdf

Proctor, B. D., & Dalaker, J. (2001). *Current population reports: Poverty in the United States.* (Publication No. P60-219). Washington, DC: U.S. Government Printing Office.

Purnell, L. D., & Paulanka, B. J. (1998). *Transcultural health care: A culturally competent approach.* Philadelphia: F. A. Davis.

Spector, R. E. (1996). *Cultural diversity in health and Illness* (4th ed.). New York: Appleton-Century Crofts.

Spector, R. E. (2000). *Cultural diversity in health and Illness* (5th ed.). Upper Saddle River, NJ: Prentice Hall.

Stinson, N. (1998). *Second report on the US/UK collaborative meeting on racial and ethnic health.* Collaborative Work Group Meeting. Office of Minority Health. U.S. Department of Health and Human Services. Retrieved December 6, 2002, from http://www.omhrc.gov/us-uk/britishreport.pdf

Tripp-Reimer, T. (1999). Cultural interventions for ethnic groups of color. In A. S. Hinshaw, S. L. Feetham, & J. L. F. Shaver (Eds.), *Handbook of clinical nursing research* (pp. 107-123). Thousand Oaks: Sage.

Tripp-Reimer, T., Brink, P. J. & Saunders, J. M. (1984). Cultural assessment: Content and process. *Nursing Outlook, 2,* 78-82.

Tripp-Reimer, T., Brink, P. J., & Saunders, J. M. (1997). Cultural assessment: Content and process. In B. W. Spradley & J. A. Allender (Eds.), *Readings in community health* (5th ed.). Philadelphia: Lippincott.

U.S. Census Bureau. (2001). *Population profile of the United States: 1999 America at the close of the 21st century.* Current Population Reports Series (Publication No. P23-205). Washington, DC: U.S. Government Printing Office.

U.S. Census Bureau. (2002). *State and county quick facts.* Retrieved November 1, 2002, from http://quickfacts. census.gov/qid/states/00000.htm

U.S. Department of Health and Human Services. (2000). *Healthy People 2010: Understanding and improving health.* (2nd ed.). Washington, DC: U.S. Government Printing Office.

Weaver, H. N. (1999). Indigenous people and the social work profession: Defining culturally competent services. *Social Work, 44,* 217-225. Retrieved January 20, 2003, from http://www.sfsu.edu/~multsowk/

Wells, M. I. (2000). Beyond cultural competence: A model for individual and institutional development. *Journal of Community Health Nursing, 17,* 189-199.

Williams, C. (1997). Personal reflections on permanency planning and cultural competency. *Journal of Multicultural Social Work, 5,* 9-18.

UNIT III

Family Nursing Practice

Using the Nursing Process with Families

Karen Reed
Michel A. Tarko

Understanding is knowing what to do; wisdom is knowing what to do next; virtue is actually doing it.

— Tristan Gylberd

OBJECTIVES

On completion of this chapter, the reader will be able to do the following:
1. *Explain how to use the steps of the nursing process when working with families.*
2. *Use a nursing model to guide the family nursing process.*
3. *Identify key issues surrounding the success of intervening with families.*
4. *List barriers to intervening with families.*

Long before the term *nursing process* meant assessing, planning, implementing, and evaluating, a nurse used it to mean something different. Lydia Hall, an early nursing innovator, describes nursing as a process and "a range of functions, proceeding from simple to complex ones" (1955, p. 213). Hall uses the following four prepositions to describe nursing and the nurse-client relationship in the process:

At the client: The nurse is concerned with showing expertise, and the client is a recipient of some nursing care.

To the client: The nurse tells the client what to do, and the client complies.

For the client: Nursing care is for the "good of the client," and the client participates by asking questions.

With the client: The nurse explores the problem with the client, who is an active participant and resource in solving his or her own health problems.

Although this chapter focuses on the use of the nursing process in the traditional sense, it is pertinent to look at this earlier description because of who, in family nursing, the client is. When the focus of nursing care is the family, the nurse must use different communication skills, different observational skills, and different intervention skills. This brings us back to Lydia Hall's initial idea of nursing as a process. There is no other situation in which it is as imperative to practice nursing *with* the client as it is in family nursing.

Using the nursing process with a family is similar to using the process with an individual in that the steps are the same—establish a nursing diagnosis, define goals and interventions, and evaluate outcomes—but the process is much more complicated. Consider how difficult it is to get accurate information from one person. Then multiply that by two, three, or four more persons. As Ross (2001) points out, "the family nursing process is a very complex undertaking. The nurse is dealing with many individuals rather than a single person and with the multiple relationships that exist among family members. The family nursing process entails the assessment of the family's strength and limitations in meeting its needs and the needs of each of its members" (pp. 156-157).

Because of the very nature of the family, the interaction between nurse and family is complicated. In addition, family nursing often takes place not in the hospital, but at the family's home—outside of the nurse's comfort zone. The nurse's power and authority, accepted within the hospital setting, are not easily transferable to the client's home. Therefore it is important for the nurse to recognize that the nursing relationship will be affected and that if he or she is going to make a difference in the family, he or she must understand that the family-nurse relationship is a cooperative one and on equal footing. In other words, the nurse must work *with* a family to effect change.

The other portion of the equation, the family, must also be viewed differently. Too often, families are seen as additions to the client, often part of the problem but certainly not part of the solution. Only recently have researchers recognized how little is known about the family's process in illness and how best to interact with them (Rennick, 1995). The lack of knowledge about family dynamics is often a detriment to effective interventions.

This chapter focuses on how best to use the nursing process with families. It focuses on the uniqueness of the family-nurse interaction process and the essential elements needed to engage and work with a family unit. The chapter provides guiding principles for developing a relationship with families and the family interview process, as well as a model of how to use the nursing process when the client is a family.

The model chosen as an example for the family nursing process is one developed by Betty Neuman (1974). Neuman specifically acknowledges the family as a system, and her nursing process format emphasizes the collaborative nature of the nurse-client relationship. The Neuman Systems Model nursing process format is composed of three steps: (1) nursing diagnosis,

(2) nursing goals, and (3) nursing outcomes (Neuman, 2002a). These steps are covered in detail later in the chapter. However, principles developed within the chapter can be adapted to any nursing process format. Specific family assessment tools (including those based on Neuman's model) and methods of assessment are addressed in Chapter 11.

Using the Neuman Nursing Process Format with Families

Overview of the Neuman Model

The Neuman Systems Model has four main components describing the interaction among domains of nursing interest—person, environment, health, and nursing. The components and their related terms are as follows:

1) The Client System: made up of the Basic Structure, Lines of Resistance, the Normal Line of Defense, and the Flexible Line of Defense
2) The Environment: internal, external, created, and stressors
3) Nursing: Prevention as Intervention, Reconstitution, Health Promotion
4) Health: Wellness-illness continuum

The Neuman Systems Model is systems-based and provides a framework for nursing. The model is presented in Figure 10-1. The model is dynamic and is centered on the idea that clients continually interact with environmental stress factors. This interaction has the potential to cause a reaction to stress.

The Client System

The client system is made up of a series of concentric circles that surround the Basic Structure. The circles provide protection for the Basic Structure. Each circle has a specific defensive task to perform and is composed of five variables—physiological, psychological, developmental, sociocultural, and spiritual. The Flexible Line of Defense, the outermost circle, is the first defense against stressors, and it buffers the normal state of wellness. The Normal Line of Defense is the base line used by the system to ward off the impact of stressors. It is considered the usual state of wellness. The Lines of Resistance provide protection for the Basic Structure in the event

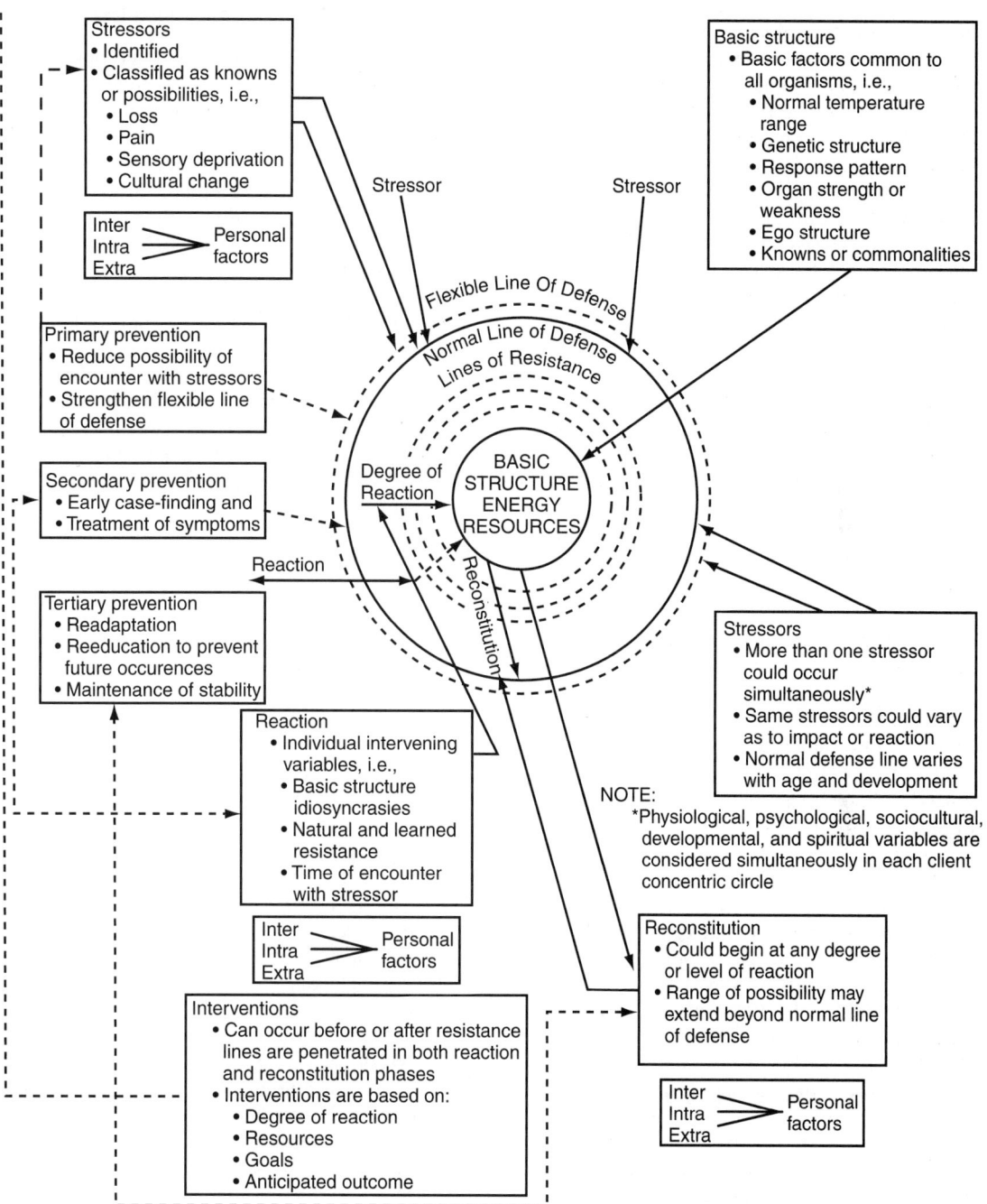

Figure 10-1   The Neuman Systems Model. (Original diagram copyright 1970 by Betty Neuman.)

that a stressor is able to break through the Flexible and Normal Lines of Defense. They are supportive of the Normal Line of Defense, as well as the Basic Structure (Neuman, 2002b).

Variables are the building blocks of the client system. The physiological, psychological, sociocultural, spiritual, and developmental variables are inherent within the client system and are found at all levels from the Flexible Line of Defense to the Basic Structure.

Stressors

The environment is defined in terms of *stressors,* which can be internal or external in nature and positive or negative in effect. There is a feedback loop within the environment so that a stressor affects the family, and the family's response to the stressor may modify or change the stressor. Three things will determine the stressor's impact on the family system: the strength of the stressor, the number of stressors, and the resiliency of the Flexible Line of Defense. Environmental stressors are classified as intrapersonal, interpersonal, and extrapersonal in nature and can be present within, as well as outside of, the client system.

Reconstitution

Reconstitution represents the "feedback from the input and output of secondary intervention. The goal is to maintain an optimal wellness level by supporting existing strengths and conserving client system energy" (Neuman, 2002b, p. 28). In an earlier work, Neuman (1989) describes reconstitution as "a state of adaptation to stressors in the internal and external environment, that can begin at any degree or level of reaction" (p. 35). Thus reconstitution is characterized by phases or clusters of activity in movement toward some goal.

The Nursing Process Format and Families

The nursing process of the Neuman Systems Model (Box 10-1) was designed specifically for nursing implementation of the Neuman Systems Model. The three categories—nursing diagnosis, nursing goals, and nursing outcomes—are believed to "best fit the systematic perspective of the Neuman Systems Model" (Neuman, 2002b, pp. 29-30).

Assessing the Family to Develop a Database

According to Neuman, for a nursing diagnosis to be established, a comprehensive database that focuses on the impact of stressors, the strength of the family system to withstand the stressors, the interaction with the environment, family coping patterns and resources, and perceptual differences among family members must be developed. (See Chapter 11 for an in-depth analysis of nursing diagnosis.) Applying the Neuman Systems Model to client as family involves a conceptual shift in thinking critically about the whole family as client. This is simplified within a holistic perspective by synthesizing individual family member variable data into four major categories: (1) psychosocial relationships, (2) physical status of the family, (3) developmental characteristics of the family, and (4) spiritual influences (Neuman, 1983).

A family stressor is defined as any force that has the potential to produce or produces instability within the family system. The environment of the family system is categorized into three levels of stressors as follows (Neuman, 1983):

• Intrafamily stressors: all things occurring within the family system such as individual interactions among members of the family system
• Interfamily system stressors: all things occurring between the family and the immediate or direct external environment such as individual or family interactions with other families, aggregates, or community groups
• Extrafamily system stressors: all things occurring between the family and the distal or indirect external environment such as forces from society and political issues

Once these data are compiled by using the four major categories, a nursing diagnosis, based on the variance from wellness, is determined by a synthesis of family theory with the family data to identify the condition.

The assessment, or creation of the database, begins with identification and evaluation of potential or actual stressors that pose a threat to the stability of the family system. Validation of each family member's perception is necessary. Next, the assessment continues with an examination of the conditions and strengths of basic structure factors and energy resources. For families, this means assessment of core survival issues such as genetic

BOX 10-1   The Neuman Nursing Process Format*

I. **Nursing Diagnosis**

A. Database—determined by:

1. Identification and evaluation of potential or actual stressors that pose a threat to the stability of the client system.

2. Assessment of condition and strength of basic structure factors and energy resources.

3. Assessment of characteristics of the flexible and normal lines of defense, lines of resistance, degree of potential reaction, reaction, and/or potential for reconstitution following a reaction.

4. Identification, classification, and evaluation of potential and/or actual intrapersonal, interpersonal, and extrapersonal interactions between the client and environment, considering all five variables.

5. Evaluation of influences of past, present, and possible future life process and coping patterns on client system stability.

6. Identification and evaluation of actual and potential internal and external resources for optimal state of wellness.

7. Identification and resolution of perceptual differences between caregivers and the client system.

B. Variances from wellness—determined by:

1. Synthesis of theory with client data to identify condition from which a comprehensive diagnostic statement can be made. Goal prioritization is determined by the client's wellness level, system stability needs, and total available resources to accomplish desired goal outcomes.

2. Hypothetical goals and interventions postulated to reach the desired client

system stability or wellness level, that is to maintain the normal line of defense and retain the flexible line of defense, thus protecting the basic structure.

II. **Nursing Goals**—determined by:

A. Negotiations with the client for desired prescriptive change or goal outcomes to correct variances from wellness, based on classified needs and resources identified in the nursing diagnosis.

B. Appropriate prevention as intervention strategies are negotiated with the client for retention, attainment, and/or maintenance of client system stability as desired outcome goals. Theoretical perspectives used for assessment and client system data synthesis are analogous to those used for intervention.

III. **Nursing Outcomes**—determined by:

A. Nursing intervention accomplished through use of one or more of three prevention modes:

1. Primary prevention (action to retain client system stability)

2. Secondary prevention (action to attain client system stability)

3. Tertiary prevention (action to maintain client system stability), usually following secondary prevention as intervention.

B. Evaluation of outcome goals following intervention either confirms them or serves as a basis for reformulation of subsequent goals based on systemic feedback principles.

C. Intermediate and long-range goals or subsequent nursing actions are structured in relation to short-term goals outcomes.

D. Client system goal outcome validates the nursing process.

---

*Interpret Client System as Family
Copyright 1980 by Betty Neuman. Revised 1987 by Betty Neuman.

components and patterns of interaction, including long-standing patterns that may have multi-generational ramifications. Hanson and Mischke (1996) state that the "basic family structure and energy resources refer to the characteristics, functions, and survival skills common to the family system" (p. 180).

The nurse then assesses characteristics of the Flexible and Normal Lines of Defense, Lines of Resistance, the degree of potential reaction, reaction, and/or potential for reconstitution after a reaction. In a family assessment, this means gathering information on the following:

1) How the family enacts roles, implements rules, makes decisions, and allocates tasks and how members interact with each other (Flexible Line of Defense)

2) How the family communicates, solves problems, shows intimacy and affection, and deals with loss and change (Normal Line of Defense)

3) How family members relate to one another and depend on each other; what they value and what they believe is important in a particular situation (Lines of Resistance)

The nurse then takes this information and determines how much of an impact the stressor has had on the family, the potential for recovery, and whether the family can recover on its own or will need help (Reconstitution).

Next, the nurse begins to identify, classify, and evaluate potential and/or actual intrafamily, interfamily, and extrafamily system stressors and interactions of the family system and environment. During this portion of the assessment, the nurse closely examines the influence of past, present, and possible future life processes and coping patterns on family system stability. Questions to be asked during assessment include the following:

• What is going on in the family now?
• Has this happened in the past?
• How do family members expect this event to influence the future for the family?
• Have coping patterns of the past been successful or unsuccessful?

Identification and evaluation of actual and potential internal and external resources are also important parts of the assessment. Questions to be asked include the following:

• What resources are available for the family, either internally or externally?

• Does the family have support from extended family?
• Will community resources be necessary?

The final step in the development of a database is perhaps one of the more crucial steps. It is imperative that identification and resolution of perceptual differences between the nurse and family system take place. The nurse is often faced with family perceptions that are far different from his or her own. It is important to remember that if there is no agreement on the problem, there will be no agreement on the solution. The Research Synopsis presents a study that indicates

---

RESEARCH SYNOPSIS

PREDICTING FAMILY HEALTH PROMOTION

In order to promote family health, a knowledge of the environment surrounding the family, including barriers to health, is important.

In a study of 63 white families, Riley-Lawless (2000) investigated the impact of psychosocial, behavioral, and physiological risk factors for cardiovascular disease in families with twins. The risk factors included family cohesion and conflict, physical activity, smoking, cholesterol, blood pressure, and body mass index.

Through correlational analysis it was learned that family cohesion was an important predictor of development of cardiovascular disease risk factors. Cohesion was found to be marginally significantly associated with cardiovascular disease fact factors. Higher cohesion was associated with lower smoking, lower blood pressure, lower body mass index, and higher physical activity.

The findings of the study indicate that dimensions of the family environment have an effect on development of cardiovascular disease within families. This has an impact on nursing interventions and points to the need for early intervention/prevention techniques that focus on exploring family decision making, cohesion, and coping as part of the overall plan of care to increase health promotion and primary prevention.

Riley-Lawless, K. (2000). *The relationship among characteristics of the family environment and behavioral and physiologic cardiovascular risk factors in parents and their adolescent twins.* Unpublished doctoral dissertation, University of Pennsylvania.

that family cohesion could be an important predictor of certain disease risk factors.

Developing a Family Nursing Diagnosis

Nontheory-Specific Nursing Diagnoses Developed for Families

According to the North American Nursing Diagnosis Association (NANDA), the purpose of a nursing diagnosis is to "provide the bases for selection of nursing interventions to achieve outcomes for which the nurse is accountable" (Friedman & Levac, 1998, p. 54). However, there are problems with using the predetermined nursing diagnoses developed by NANDA for families, because the diagnoses are primarily oriented toward the individual, with a strong emphasis on illness. Few diagnoses focus specifically on the issues most clinicians see with families, and diagnoses that are developed for families are so broad and unspecific that they cannot be used to guide the selection of nursing interventions (Friedman, Bowden, & Jones, 2003), which is, by definition, their primary purpose. Examples of NANDA diagnoses that are related to family issues are Altered Family Processes and Altered Parenting. These diagnoses must be attached to defining characteristics to be more specific.

The Iowa Intervention Project (McCloskey & Bulechek, 2000) links the nursing diagnoses developed by NANDA to a series of nursing interventions that are applicable to families. Box 10-2 presents an example. This linkage gives the clinician some direction for developing interventions that are specific to family issues. Use of the Iowa classifications along with the NANDA diagnoses modifies the argument that NANDA diagnoses are not specifically geared toward actual family problems.

An alternative classification system, known as the *Omaha System* and developed by the Visiting Nurses Association of Omaha, Nebraska, in 1970 (Martin & Scheet, 1992), has been successfully tested and is used to provide direction for nursing diagnoses in a community setting (see Box 10-2 for an example). Approximately 40 problems encountered by clinicians are categorized into four domains: environmental, psychosocial, physiological, and health-related behavioral. Nurses have the ability to identify the level at which the problem occurs—the individual, family subsystem,

---

BOX 10-2   Examples of Family Nursing Diagnosis Using NANDA or the Omaha System

Example of NANDA Family Nursing Diagnoses with Related Iowa Classification
Altered Family Process related to social isolation and impaired social interactions
Related Nursing Interventions: Family involvement, Family support, Normalization promotion, Socialization enhancement

Example of Nursing Diagnosis Using the Omaha System
Actual Impairment of family social contact as diagnosed by limited social contact and minimal outside stimulation/leisure time activities
Problem: 07
Social Contact: Communication or interactions between individual or family and people outside the immediate household
Choose modifier from each category

Health Promotion

Potential Impairment
Impairment

Family

Individual
List Signs/Symptoms
01. Limited social contact
02. Uses health care provider for social contact
03. Minimal outside stimulation/leisure time activities
04. Other

---

or family system level (Martin & Scheet, 1992). The Omaha System has defined the use of family as one of two modifiers for classifying problems; that is, the nursing problem identified can be seen as either an individual issue or a family one, as well as being a health promotion issue or an issue of potential or actual impairment.

Nursing Diagnoses Used with the Neuman Systems Model

The authors of this chapter believe that family nursing diagnoses should be based on family theory and supported by the data gathered during the assessment phase. The diagnosis is influenced

---

BOX 10-3 Family Nursing Diagnoses Compatible with the Neuman Systems Model

Nursing diagnoses compatible with the Neuman Systems Model and associated with the Flexible Line of Defense (FLD) include the following:
Altered family role enactment (specify the behavior) related to (intrafamily, interfamily, extrafamily stressors)
Altered family rule implementation (specify the behavior) related to (intrafamily, interfamily, extrafamily stressors)
Altered family decision-making mechanisms (specify the behavior) related to (intra, inter, extra-family stressors)
Altered family bonding patterns (specify the behavior) related to (intrafamily, interfamily, extrafamily stressors)
Altered family tasks allocation (specify the behavior) related to (intrafamily, interfamily, extrafamily stressors)

Nursing diagnoses compatible with the Neuman Systems Model and associated with the Normal Line of Defense (NLD) include the following:
Altered family communication patterns (specify the behavior) related to (intrafamily, interfamily, extrafamily stressors)

Altered family problem-solving mechanisms related to (intrafamily, interfamily, extrafamily stressors)
Altered family mechanisms for meeting family members' needs for intimacy/affection related to (intrafamily, interfamily, extrafamily stressors)
Altered family coping (loss or change) related to (intrafamily, interfamily, extrafamily stressors)

Nursing diagnoses compatible with the Neuman Systems Model and associated with the Lines of Resistance (LR) include the following:
Altered family interrelatedness (specify behavior) related to (intrafamily, interfamily, extrafamily stressors)
Altered family interdependence (specify behavior) related to (intrafamily, interfamily, extrafamily stressors)
Altered family values and beliefs (specify behavior) related to (intrafamily, interfamily, extrafamily stressors)

From Tarko, M. A. & Reed, K. (2002). *Taxonomy of family nursing diagnosis based upon the Neuman Systems Model of Nursing.* Unpublished manuscript, New Westminster, British Columbia, Canada: Douglas College.

---

by the theoretical base because the nursing intervention will be influenced by the theoretical base. Thus the theory itself will help define the diagnosis. For example, if a nurse is using the Neuman Systems Model to guide practice, the family diagnosis might be as follows:

> Altered family problem-solving mechanism (specify behavior—uncertainty of paying bills/mortgage) related to (interfamily, extrafamily system stressors—unemployment, lack of resources, and strength of stressor facing the family).

Another theory would define the problem a different way. The underlying rationale for a nursing diagnosis is to provide both the family and practitioner with a focus so that goals can be defined, prioritized, and accomplished (Neuman, 1989, 1995, 2002).

Family Diagnosis Compatible with the Neuman Systems Model

The nursing process and the utility of the Neuman Systems Model provide direction for nursing action as described and reported in the nursing literature related to family nursing assessment and intervention (Crawford & Tarko, 2002; Cross, 1995; Hanson, 2001; Neuman, 2002b; Whall & Fawcett, 1991). A typology of family nursing diagnosis constructed by Tarko and Reed (2002), which is compatible with the Neuman Systems Model, integrates family structure and process concepts delineated by Reed (1982, 1989, 1993). The typology is presented to assist nursing educators, students, and practitioners in constructing nursing diagnoses related to family health concerns when they are using the Neuman Systems Model (Box 10-3).

Planning and Intervening to Promote Health and Protect the Family

Once goals are mutually defined by the nurse and family, planning and implementation to achieve the nursing goals can take place. The goals should focus on prescriptive change or outcomes to benefit the family and should be designed to correct variances from wellness. The goals should be based on the family's needs, priorities, and resources that were identified during the process of data collection and are reflected in the nursing diagnosis.

Prevention as Intervention

One of the key concepts of the Neuman Systems Model is prevention as intervention. Neuman describes this as "an intervention typology"(2002, p. 25) in which the levels of prevention are defined as follows:

- *Primary prevention* is equated with wellness retention, such as developing a plan for helping families with time management skills to increase their family time.
- *Secondary prevention* is equated with wellness attainment, such as exploring what it means to have Grandma moving into the family home and what changes will need to take place in family roles.
- *Tertiary prevention* is equated with wellness maintenance, such as changes necessary in the family's dietary habits when diabetes is discovered in one of its members.

The level of intervention will depend on the degree of disruption in the family from intrafamily, interfamily, or extrafamily system stressors. The goal of nursing intervention in working with the family is to promote family system stability and wellness by way of retaining, attaining, and maintaining family system stability through nursing strategies associated with the notion of prevention as intervention.

The family process concepts aligned with Neuman's Flexible Line of Defense include enactment of roles and rule implementation, decision-making mechanisms, bonding patterns, and task allocation. The family structure concepts aligned with Neuman's Normal Line of Defense include communication patterns, problem-solving mechanisms, mechanisms for meeting family members' needs for intimacy and affection, and ways of dealing with loss and change. The Lines of Resist-ance that protect the Basic Structure or core of the family system are composed of the following concepts: interrelatedness, interdependence, values, and beliefs associated with the family system as a unit. Therefore the level of intervention—primary, secondary, or tertiary—is related to disruption found in these areas. (See the Case Scenario at the end of the chapter for an example.)

A Need for Collaboration

Sometimes in intervention situations with families, multiple support systems must be involved to achieve a good outcome. Often, several agencies are called in to work with the family, particularly if children are involved. For example, child protection agencies, social services, and the mental health system may be involved in a situation in which a family is unable to provide a safe environment for the children. The involvement of multiple organizations emphasizes the need for someone to coordinate that process, so that data are shared and the work of the team can proceed with as little duplication of effort as possible. The nurse is often the best person to provide the leadership in this situation, acting as a liaison between the team and the family. This is particularly applicable if the nurse has been the main contact with the family and has established the necessary trusting relationship. Often, the efforts of the support team are important to help stabilize the system, and energy devoted to a team effort is just as important as energy devoted to dealing with the family directly. The Website Resources box at the end of the chapter is a useful resource.

Legal Issues

It is very important for the nurse to be familiar with the laws governing interventions with families. Family intervention guidelines vary from state to state in the United States. Those given the responsibility of dealing with issues of child endangerment, abuse, incest, and other serious problems will need to know the processes and protocols specific for these situations to ensure that the legal obligations are carried out. If the nurse is unsure about the process, he or she should contact the local authorities to determine the correct procedures.

Evaluating Family Outcomes

The purpose of evaluation of outcome goals after interventions is to verify that they have been met or to provide a basis for reformulation of subsequent goals and interventions. Successful achievement of a family goal validates the nursing process. As with all parts of the nursing process, the family is the ultimate evaluator. If the family does not view the intervention as successful, then is it? Whose opinion is more important? In reality, this is a complicated issue. For example, if children are removed from an unsafe environment, the parents (and perhaps the children) are not going to see this as a successful intervention. However, from the standpoint of the authorities and health care providers, it is considered successful. The reformulation of the family goal is then to help the family understand what must take place for the parent or parents to regain custody of the children (as a long-term goal), while implementing the short-term goal of providing a safe environment for the children.

Terminating Relationships

The issue of termination is most often discussed in psychiatric nursing texts, making it seem as if no other nursing situations have issues surrounding termination. In fact, in any long-term relationship, termination issues can occur. The investment of time and effort needed to promote family health and change can make ending the family-nurse relationship difficult. As in any professional relationship, the termination point should be planned and reinforced as the nurse-family relationship is established and develops over time. As the family is making progress, the nurse should begin introducing the idea of termination. For example, the nurse may say, "You're doing so much better. I think we will only need to have three more meetings. Let's plan what it is we need to accomplish in those sessions." Such comments give the family time to get accustomed to the idea that they are going to be discharged and will be taking over the responsibility of managing issues on their own. Providing referral sources is also a good idea.

May (1990) discusses the disparity of the theoretical nurse-client relationship and the reality of the nurse-client interaction and acknowledges that what is often described in textbooks does not happen in reality. In reality, family-nurse relationships are often sporadic, with contact between the family and nurse occurring in times of crisis, even after the official relationship has ended. However, there has been little research into the benefits or risks of this kind of nurse-client relationship.

For nurses functioning as advanced practice nurses, termination may take on another aspect. If conflicts do arise with the family, such as noncompliance with treatment, a habit of not keeping appointments, or nonpayment of professional fees, it may be necessary to discharge the family to another agency. This may be especially appropriate in court-ordered situations in which the family is mandated to undergo treatment and refuses to comply. In this type of situation, the terms necessary to avoid termination, as well as the consequences of not complying with the conditions, need to be clearly communicated to the family at the beginning of the relationship. Official notices of termination should be sent to the family via certified mail, and these should be worded so that the family understands that it is in their best interest for the relationship to end. The reasons for termination should be specified, the family should be encouraged to seek help, and information regarding other avenues for support should be provided. Above all, the process should be documented (Saxton, 1999).

The Family Interview Process: The Importance of Neutrality, Hypothesizing, and Circularity

How does one go about using the nursing process to help families? Usually, it begins with an interview to obtain information with which to make a diagnosis. Three principles are important to remember in family interviewing: neutrality, hypothesizing, and circularity. These three principles are derived from family therapy theory (Bateson, 1972, 1979) and have been further developed by a group of systemic therapists known as the *Milan Team* to guide interventions with families (Cecchin, 1987). Each principle is helpful in the implementation of the entire nursing process with families, although use of the techniques is most emphasized during the assessment phase.

Neutrality

Neutrality is defined as a state of curiosity about a situation that "leads to exploration and invention of alternate views and moves" (Cecchin, p. 406). Neutrality does not mean that the nurse is uninvolved with what is going on but rather is curious about the situation and comes with an open mind about what might be not only the problem, but also the solution. Neutrality is maintained when the nurse does the following (Nelson, Fleuridas, & Rosenthal, 1986):

1) Avoids taking sides with any one member of the group
2) Acts as an ally for the entire family
3) Accepts everyone in a nonjudgmental way

When a nurse maintains neutrality, he or she is looking for the patterns—not the best description of what is the cause, but the pattern of descriptions and how they fit together (Cecchin, 1987). Neutrality is important in the nursing process with families because it is necessary to hear from more than one person to obtain accurate information. Each person's viewpoint will reveal a different side to the situation. A composite of all persons' viewpoints is perhaps the most accurate one. By maintaining neutrality, the nurse is more likely to keep the family members engaged in the process, thereby allowing important information to be shared.

Hypothesizing

Hypothesizing is defined as asking questions and not taking information at face value. Suppositions or hunches that the nurse might have about what is really going on are important to explore. The purpose of hypothesizing is to connect family behaviors with meaning and to introduce new ideas that will enable family members to develop new ways of viewing the situation (Nelson et al., 1986). Hypothesizing, in conjunction with curiosity, will lead to alternate ideas—about the diagnosis and the intervention.

Circularity

Circularity is an interview technique that permits more information to be shared by the family.

Questions such as, "What brought you here today?" tend to elicit answers such as "Because the school counselor sent us." Although that may be correct, it does little to illuminate the problem. Circular questions elicit information about differences between people, events, relationships, or beliefs (Loos & Bell, 1990). For example, a nurse may ask each member of the family, "In your opinion, what has been going on in your family that made a visit here today necessary?" Circular questions consist of the following four types (Loos & Bell, 1990, p. 47):

1) *Difference-type questions* that explore differences between people, relationships, and times
   Example: "How has Johnny's behavior changed since his mother's absence?"
2) *Behavioral effect–type questions* that explore the effect of one's behavior on another
   Example: "When Susan doesn't do her chores, how does that affect you?"
3) *Hypothetical-type questions* that explore "What if?"
   Example: "What do you think would happen if Sara did her homework every night without being reminded?"
4) *Triadic type–questions* that ask one person to comment on issues facing other family members
   Example: "Ron, what is you perspective on Jim and Jackie's problems?"

Using Neutrality, Hypothesizing, and Circularity in the Nursing Process

As stated previously, the three principles of neutrality, hypothesizing, and circularity are primarily used during the data gathering process. Neutrality allows family members to feel included and not excluded from the interaction. Hypothesizing allows both the nurse and family to ask questions about what has occurred and about the connections between events and behaviors. Circularity allows the nurse to gather information in a manner that is less threatening to the family and allows the family to describe the situation, not just give the facts.

These three principles are also helpful in the other phases of the process. In developing goals and during implementation, neutrality supports the nurse's wish to include all family members in the decision-making process. In evaluation of outcomes, neutrality allows family members to look at their part in the process and not focus on the behavior of one individual. Hypothesizing can be useful during planning and implementation phases: asking "What if?" gives families different scenarios to think about when making decisions. It can also be useful in evaluating what might have been different at the end of the decision-making process. Using circular questions throughout the nursing process is helpful because it keeps the family engaged, allows for continued exchange of information, and helps the family modify decisions and evaluate goals.

The Importance of the Nurse-Family Relationship in the Nursing Process

To begin the nursing process with a family, the nurse must be able to establish a positive relationship with that family. The outcomes of the family-nurse relationship include effective communication, family and nurse satisfaction, and improved client care (Lynn-McHale & Deatrick, 2000). For these outcomes to occur, certain characteristics must be present in the relationship: trust, respect, and motivation.

Trust, Respect, and Motivation

Trust between caregiver and care recipient is essential for a nurse-family relationship to function. According to Lynn-McHale and Deatrick (2000), the development of a trusting relationship between a family and health care provider is characterized by the following:

1) Mutual intention. Each member of the relationship must want the trust to exist.
2) Time. Trust does not develop instantaneously. Particularly in the home setting, trust is developed gradually.
3) Process. Development of trust is a reciprocal process between the health care provider and the family. Phases or stages are common, and characteristic behaviors are seen within each stage.
4) Varying levels. Levels of trust vary from superficial to deep and will affect the relationship and information given by the family.
5) Reciprocity. The family and the health care provider have respect for each other.

6) Expectations. Those involved rely on and expect something of each other. They have faith that their expectations will be met.

Trust cannot exist without competency, respect, reliability, communication, and negotiation. Families evaluate a nurse's competence by technical skills, clinical reasoning, and elements of expert practice, as well as the nurse's capacity to trust the whether the client or family is capable of change. In other words, the nurse must be willing to work with the family, value input from individual family members, and respect their opinions (Thorne, 1993). When nurses and families interact, they bring to the relationship their own values and beliefs. These values and beliefs may be similar or quite different. Despite differences, much can be achieved if (and only if) individual viewpoints are respected by all parties. Nurses may not agree with the family's beliefs but must respect them. In addition to a set of values and beliefs, each family comes with its own system of problem-solving mechanisms and decision-making strategies, which may or may not support good health behaviors. If the decision-making strategies of the family do not support healthy outcomes, the nurse must figure out a way to help the family change them.

Families must be motivated for an outcome of optimal health behavior to be attained. Motivating families to move toward different goals is a challenge faced by all nurses, yet it is a crucial concept in the nursing process with families. Most often, families are seen as entities with problems, who somehow must be convinced to change. However, motivation to change cannot prosper in an atmosphere in which the family's behaviors are viewed as problematic and the nurse's ideas are viewed as the only solution. As Feeley and Gottlieb (2000) point out:

> This orientation toward deficits in clinical practice gives rise to two major problems. First the clinician views the family primarily in terms of their problems or deficits, and fails to see and appreciate the family's strengths and competencies. The second problem with this orientation is that families are perceived as lacking the ability to solve problems and cope or achieve their goals without the help of the professional. The clinician attempts to solve the family's problems rather than work with the family to do so (p. 10).

One way the nurse can motivate families is to emphasize what is right with them, not what is wrong. One of the basic skills in health promotion is to help families develop problem-solving and goal attainment skills. As families become more involved in decision making, thus participating more, they learn to make healthier choices. This is the process Ford-Gilboe (1997) calls "health work" (p. 206).

As can be surmised, issues of trust, motivation, and respect are important throughout the nursing process with families. The establishment of trust is important during the assessment phase of the process, because trust is necessary to obtain accurate information. Trust continues to be an issue during development of plans, implementation of those plans, and evaluation of the plans. Motivation is especially important during the planning and implementation phases of the process, and respect is necessary throughout the process, including the evaluation phase.

Obstacles to Family Nursing

Working with families has many challenges, some more surmountable than others. In the previous portion of the chapter, issues of trust and respect and how these are crucial in developing a nurse-family relationship were discussed. Other barriers to the process have also been discussed. Yet, some problems may inhibit even the development of a family-nurse relationship.

Philosophical Issues

As the authors have pointed out, the work of a nurse with a family requires a different viewpoint than work with an individual. To be successful, the nurse must believe and value the idea that systems such as families can be influenced and changed and that it is not sufficient to "fix" an individual family member without including the entire family in the process. Family nursing requires a different thought process, different interventions, and different communication techniques, which may not be part of the nurse's existing repertoire and will need to be learned. Nurses must be willing to invest the energy to do so.

Theoretical Multiplicity

Even if a nurse is willing to learn a new way of intervening, issues remain because there is no "one way" to do family nursing. Multiple theorists from many disciplines have developed hypotheses about family functioning and the best ways to intervene. This chapter has introduced a specific method of using the nursing process with families, based on the Neuman Systems Model, as an example of how nursing theory may influence process. Other theories can be used to guide family nursing; it is up to the nurse to decide which theory best fits his or her practice and then systematically and thoroughly apply that theory in the clinical setting.

Sociocultural Issues: The Sanctity and Privacy of Family Life

A long-standing debate in the area of family policy concerns the issues of the sanctity of the family and privacy. This debate has played out at the social level around such issues as discipline, home schooling, and interventions by social service agencies when abuse is suspected. It remains a thorny issue. When do health care providers have the right to intervene, and when must they refrain from imposing their values on the family? The bottom line is an issue of safety and legal authority. However, if the issue is not safety related but the family is not amenable to the suggestions, there is little that can be done to further the nurse-family relationship.

Therefore one of the key questions during the assessment phase of the relationship is "What are the family's values and beliefs about accepting/rejecting outside help?" This is particularly important to know if the problem centers on parenting methods but can be just as important in the areas of finance, health behaviors, self-esteem issues, and other sensitive areas. Certainly, the establishment of trust and respect is crucial in helping the family to overcome the innate feeling of invasion by outside "experts."

Economic Issues

As the health care insurance crisis continues in the United States, it must be noted that few insurance companies will cover "family interventions." Often, families must pay out of pocket for such things as family therapy, or family counseling, if this is the treatment recommended. One method of circumventing the issue is to bill for individual services instead of family services.

One other issue around payment is that most insurance companies require that one individual be recognized as the "client." When that client is identified, even for insurance purposes, it tends to reinforce the idea that the problems facing the family are related to one individual. This can be an obstacle, particularly if the family has been reluctant to engage in working with the nurse, because it supports the idea that if the individual is "fixed," then the problem will go away.

The obstacles to family nursing may invite the nurse to ask, "Why do family nursing anyway?" The answer comes in the belief that a systems approach to intervening is more efficacious and long-term than an individual approach. For example, studies in the area of schizophrenia have indicated that family intervention decreases the relapse rate of patients with schizophrenia (Falloon & Pederson, 1985; Goldstein, Rodnick, Evans, May, & Steinberg, 1978; Tarrier et al., 1988). This supports the idea that family intervention can be of great benefit to nursing practice. And it all starts with the process—the nurse working *with* the family to assess, identify, plan, implement, and evaluate care.

CASE SCENARIO

Nancy (age 35) and Jill (age 37) have two daughters, Ashley (age 6) and Melissa (age 8). For the past 10 years, Nancy has been employed as a correctional officer at a local women's correctional institute. Jill has worked as a freelance graphic designer for the past 5 years. Her work is intermittent, with contracts throughout the year. They have a mortgage on their home for which Nancy's monthly salary covers the monthly payments. Jill was recently seen by the public health nurse and referred to the community mental health nurse for follow-up.

Both of the children present with hyperactivity, and there is conflict between Jan and Jill about to how to manage the girls' behavior. Nancy reports stress from work issues at the jail and is under her physician's care for migraine headaches and chronic stomach ailments. Jill notes that she feels stressed out because of intermittent work contracts as a graphic designer and assuming the majority of responsibility for childcare. Meals take place more often with one parent than with both because of Nancy's shift work. On weekends the family tries to catch up with household tasks, spends some time together, and plans schedules for the next week.

Nancy and Jill rarely have shared intimate time together because Jill reports being exhausted from caring for the children at the end of the day and retires early most evenings. Jill states she is experiencing sleep disturbances, decreased appetite, and mood swings and is concerned over Nancy's increased use of alcohol to help cope with the stress she experiences from her work situation.

Family and friends are important people in their lives, and efforts are made to include them in family dinners

on a biweekly basis. The family enjoys hiking as a means of managing stress and increasing family time together. The family attends their community church regularly where Nancy and Jill's domestic relationship was blessed 10 years ago, before they had children.

An assessment of the family was completed by using the Neuman Systems Model (2002) nursing process format for family assessment. An exemplar of family stressors, strengths, family nursing diagnoses, goals, and outcomes is presented as follows:

FAMILY AND NURSE PERCEPTIONS OF STRESSORS

1) Intrafamily stressors: self-esteem issues; insufficient family and couple time; changing sleep, eating, and mood patterns; migraines; stomach problems; and an increase in alcohol consumption

2) Interfamily stressors: hyperactivity associated with both children, disagreement between parents on behavior management, insufficient couple and family time, and dinner hour primarily with one parent

3) Extrafamily stressors: tenuous economic support, alternating shift work

FAMILY STRENGTHS (FAMILY AND NURSE PERCEPTIONS)

1) Commitment to providing a clean and safe home for the family unit

2) One person with full-time employment

3) Regular exercise with the children

4) Ability to maintain the household day-to-day operations

5) Willingness to seek mental health support

6) Strong spiritual beliefs

CASE SCENARIO—cont'd

FAMILY NURSING DIAGNOSIS:

Altered family coping (tension between partners) related to work stress, insufficient couple time, financial strain, and disagreements about managing children's hyperactive behavior

FAMILY/NURSE GOALS

1) The family will explore alternatives to family scheduled time to provide more opportunities for communication, decision making, and intimacy between partners.

2) Parents will achieve consensus on how to manage children's behavior for a trial of 2 weeks.

3) New methods of coping with stress will be introduced and practiced.

PREVENTION AS INTERVENTION

1) Assist the family to distribute household tasks more equitably, including childcare responsibilities.

2) Assist in identification of resources that will support family roles such as the local support group, the Society for Hyperactive Children; Parenting Children Who Can't Sit Still

3) Assist in identifying resources that teach coping strategies for managing stress and anxiety such as seminars at the local gay and lesbian community center.

NURSING OUTCOMES

At 1-month intervals, parents will discuss the impact of the following:

1) Following through with planned distribution of equitable household tasks

2) Utilizing community resources in coping with the children's behavior and stress in the family system

WEBSITE RESOURCES

ORGANIZATION	WEBSITE ADDRESS
American Association for Marriage and Family Therapy	http://www.aamft.org/index_nm.asp
RN Central Care Plan Corner	http://www.rncentral.com/careplans/contents.html
National Institute of Mental Health	http://www.nimh.nih.gov
Children, Youth, and Families Education and Research Network (CYFERNET)	http://www.cyfernet.org
Forum on Child and Family Statistics	http://www.childstats.gov
Farm Family Health, Health Canada	http://www.hc-sc.gc.ca/pphb-dgspsp/publicat/ffh-sfa/
Neuman Systems Model	http://www.Neumansystemsmodel.com
National Alliance for the Mentally Ill	http://www.nami.org
National Family Caregivers Association	www.nfcacares.org

CHAPTER HIGHLIGHTS

- Differences in use of the nursing process with families and individuals are discussed with emphasis on the complexities of working with families.

- An example in which the Neuman nursing process format is used with families is presented to illustrate how the use of a nursing conceptual model can guide the nursing process.

- Concepts important to the development of the nurse-family relationship are discussed and related to the impact on the phases of the nursing process.

- Emphasizing that the family interview process is different from an individual interview, ideas are presented to help the nurse understand the three main concepts of circularity, neutrality, and hypothesizing.

- Obstacles to family assessment and interventions in the real world of family nursing are noted, including socioeconomic, philosophical, and theoretical issues.

CRITICAL THINKING ACTIVITIES

1. Why are respect, trust, and collaboration so important in the nurse-family relationship?

2. Explain how the lack of neutrality can affect the nurse-family relationship.

3. How does a theoretical base affect the nursing process?

4. What obstacles interfere with using a family-focused method of intervention?

5. Describe the interaction between the assessment phase and the establishment of a family nursing diagnosis.

6. Discuss what other family nursing diagnoses are pertinent to the case scenario and alternative primary, secondary, and/or tertiary levels of prevention-as-intervention strategies that may be considered in promoting health for this family.

REFERENCES

Bateson, G. (1972). *Steps to an ecology of mind.* New York: Ballantine.

Bateson, G. (1979). *Mind and nature: A necessary unity.* Toronto, Ontario, Canada: Bantam.

Cecchin, G. (1987). Hypothesizing, circularity, and neutrality revisited: An invitation to curiosity. *Family Process, 26,* 405-413.

Crawford, J. A., & Tarko, M. A. (2002). Using the Neuman Systems Model to guide nursing practice in Canada. In B. Neuman & J. Fawcett (Eds.), *The Neuman Systems Model* (4th ed., pp. 90-110). Upper Saddle River, NJ: Prentice-Hall.

Cross, J. R. (1995). Nursing process of the family: Application of the Neuman Systems Model. In P. J. Christensen & J. W. Kenny (Eds.), *Nursing process: Application of conceptual models* (4th ed., pp. 246-269). St. Louis, MO: Mosby.

Falloon, I. R., & Pederson, J. (1985). Family management in the prevention of morbidity of schizophrenia: The adjustment family unit. *British Journal of Psychiatry, 147,* 156-163.

Feeley, N., & Gottlieb, L. (2000). Nursing approaches for working with family strengths and resources. *Journal of Family Nursing, 6,* 9-24.

Ford-Gilboe, M. (1997). Family strengths, motivation, and resources as predictors of health promotion behavior in single-parent and two-parent families. *Research in Nursing and Health, 20,* 205-217.

Friedman, M., Bowden, V. R., & Jones, E. G. (2003). *Family nursing: Research, theory & practice* (5th ed.). Upper Saddle River, NJ: Prentice-Hall.

Friedman, M., & Levac, A. (1998). The family nursing process. In M. Friedman (Ed.), *Family nursing: Research, theory & practice,* (4th ed., pp. 49-66). Stamford, CT: Appleton & Lange.

Goldstein, M., Rodnick, E., Evans, J., May, P., & Steinberg, M. (1978). Drug and family therapy in the aftercare of acute schizophrenics. *Archives of General Psychiatry, 35,* 1169-1177.

Hall, L. (1955). Quality of nursing care. *Public Health News, 36,* 212-215.

Hanson, M., & Mischke, K. (1996). Family health assessment and intervention. In P. Bomar (Ed.), *Nurses and family health promotion* (2nd ed.). Philadelphia: W. B. Saunders.

Hanson, S. M. H. (2001). Family assessment and intervention. In S. M. H. Hanson (Ed.), *Family health care nursing: Theory practice, and research* (2nd ed., pp. 171-195). Philadelphia: F. A. Davis.

Loos, F., & Bell, J. (1990). Circular questions: A family interviewing strategy. *Dimensions of Critical Care Nursing, 9,* 46-53.

Lynn-McHale, D., & Deatrick, J. (2000). Trust between family and health care provider. *Journal of Family Nursing, 6,* 210-230.

Martin, K., & Scheet, N. (1992). *The Omaha system: Applications for community health nursing*. Philadelphia: Saunders.

May, C. (1990). Research on nurse-patient relationships: Problems of theory, problems of practice. *Journal of Advanced Nursing, 15,* 307-315.

McCloskey, J. C., & Bulechek, G. M. (2000). *Nursing intervention classification (NIC)* (3rd ed.). St. Louis, MO: Mosby.

Nelson, T., Fleuridas, C., & Rosenthal, D. (1986). The evolution of circular questions: Training family therapists. *Journal of Marital and Family Therapy, 12,* 113-127.

Neuman, B. (1974). The Betty Neuman Health-Care Systems Model: A total person approach to patient problems. In J. P. Riehl & C. Roy (Eds.), *Conceptual models for nursing practice* (pp. 99-114). New York: Appleton-Century-Crofts.

Neuman, B. (1983). Family intervention using the Betty Neuman health-care systems model. In I. W. Clements & F. B. Roberts (Eds.), *Family health: A theoretical approach to nursing care* (pp. 239-254). New York: Wiley.

Neuman, B. (1989). The Neuman Systems Model. In B. Neuman (Ed.), *The Neuman Systems Model* (2nd ed., pp. 3-64). Norwalk, CT: Appleton & Lange.

Neuman, B. (1995). The Neuman Systems Model. In B. Neuman (Ed.), *The Neuman Systems Model* (3rd ed., pp. 3-62). Norwalk, CT: Appleton & Lange.

Neuman, B. (2002a). Assessment and intervention based on the Neuman Systems Model. In B. Neuman & J. Fawcett (Eds.), *The Neuman Systems Model* (4th ed., pp. 347-349). Upper Saddle River, NJ: Prentice-Hall.

Neuman, B. (2002b). The Neuman Systems Model. In B. Neuman & J. Fawcett (Eds.), *The Neuman Systems Model* (4th ed., pp. 3-33). Upper Saddle River, NJ: Prentice-Hall.

Reed, K. S. (1982). The Neuman systems model: A basis for family psychosocial assessment and intervention. In B. Neuman (Ed.), *The Neuman systems model: Application to nursing education and practice* (pp. 188-195). Norwalk, CT: Appleton-Century-Crofts.

Reed, K. S. (1989). Family theory related to the Neuman Systems Model: In B. Neuman (Ed.), *The Neuman Systems Model* (2nd ed., pp. 385-96). Norwalk, CT: Appleton & Lange.

Reed, K. S. (1993). Adapting the Neuman systems model for family nursing. *Nursing Science Quarterly, 6,* 93-97.

Rennick, J. (1995). The changing profile of acute childhood illness: A need for the development of family nursing knowledge. *Journal of Advanced Nursing, 22,* 258-266.

Riley-Lawless, K. (2000). *The relationship among characteristics of the family environment and behavioral and physiologic cardiovascular risk factors in parents and their adolescent twins.* Unpublished doctoral dissertation, University of Pennsylvania.

Ross, B. (2001). Nursing process and family health care. In S. M. H. Hanson (Ed.), *Family health care nursing: Theory, practice and research* (2nd ed.). Philadelphia: F. A. Davis.

Saxton, J. (1999, April). Terminating patient relationships appropriately. *Physician's News Digest.* Retrieved from http://www.physicannews.com/law/499saxton.html

Tarko, M. A. & Reed, K. (2002). *Taxonomy of family nursing diagnosis based upon the Neuman Systems Model of Nursing.* Unpublished manuscript, New Westminster, British Columbia, Canada: Douglas College.

Tarrier, N., Barrowclough, C., Vaught, C., Bamrah, J., Porceddu, K., Watts, S., & Freeman, H. (1988). Community management of schizophrenia: A controlled trial of a behavioural intervention with families to reduce relapse. *British Journal of Psychiatry, 153,* 532-542.

Thorne, S. (1993). Trust and confidence. In S. E. Thorne (Ed.), *Negotiating health care: The social context of chronic illness* (pp. 106-125). Newbury Park, CA: Sage.

Whall, A., & Fawcett, J. (Eds.). (1991). *Family theory development in nursing: State of he science and art.* Philadelphia: F. A. Davis.

11

Family Assessment and Intervention

Michel A. Tarko
Karen Reed

Soup is a lot like a family. Each ingredient enhances the others; each batch has its own characteristics; and it needs time to simmer to reach full flavor.

— Marge Kennedy

OBJECTIVES

On completion of this chapter, the reader will be able to do the following:
1. *Describe family nursing tools and models for family health assessment and intervention.*
2. *Describe selected family science assessment models.*
3. *Discuss the Neuman Systems Model as applied to family health promotion.*
4. *Describe the Neuman Systems Model nursing process format applied to family health assessment and intervention (nursing diagnosis, nursing goals, nursing outcomes).*
5. *Discuss family nursing interventions for family health promotion.*
6. *Discuss family nursing outcomes.*

The family unit as client is the primary resource for supporting family members' health and illness care through role modeling, teaching, and learning of self-care strategies and health-promoting behaviors when families experience episodic and ongoing health challenges (Bomar & Baker-Word, 2001). A major focus for family nursing is promoting family health by teaching and learning relevant family health maintenance strategies to enhance optimal family health and wellness.

Nursing education programs, from the associate to the graduate level, vary in focus and amount of time spent on family concepts and frameworks in relation to family health assessment and interventions, as well as in advanced practice roles in caring for families as a whole.

Family nursing assessment tools and frameworks focus on the family as client and also on the family as context. Rooted in general systems theory, developmental theory, family theory, and communication theory, family process and structure concepts are reflected in many family nursing assessment tools and frameworks.

This chapter provides a review of selected family science assessment models and family nursing assessment instruments, tools, and frameworks that have guided family health nursing practice. Specifically, the Friedman Family Assessment Model (FFAM), the Framework of Systemic Organization (FSO), the Calgary Family Assessment Model (CFAM), and the Neuman Systems Model (NSM) are discussed as nursing models that have guided family health assessment and intervention. A case scenario is presented as an exemplar of application of the three-step nursing process format developed by Neuman.

Family Assessment

During the past two decades, the evolution of family nursing assessment in nursing theory, practice, education, and research has been observed and documented in the nursing literature (Friedman, Bowden, & Jones, 2003; Reed, 1993; Wright & Leahey, 2000). The discipline of nursing has witnessed the development of several family nursing health assessment tools and frameworks by nurses.

Family assessment tools created by family scientists examine different elements of the family by means of a quantitative paradigm of research. Bray (1995) points out that it is recognized that many family practitioners do not use formal or standardized family assessment tools in their clinical work. Bray suggests three reasons why practitioners do not use standardized tools: (1) there is a lack of consensus related to theory of family functioning, (2) practitioners perceive that structured assessment methods and tools have little utility for clinical practice, and (3) most instruments for family assessment were developed for research contexts and may not be specifically developed for clinical practice utilization by practitioners. Bray concludes his discussion about the current issues in evaluating families by asserting there are advantages for practitioners in using formal standardized family assessment methods. The advantages include collecting rich data in relation to the initial views held by families and providing direction for therapeutic interventions based on formal standardized assessment findings. Bray argues that combining structured methods with self-report measure and standardized practitioner rating scales has the potential to assist clinicians with observations relating to family dynamics and interactions. The Family Adaptability and Cohesion Scales III (FACES) by Olson, Portner, & Lavee (1985) provide a measure of family satisfaction; the Family Adaptability, Partnership, Growth, Affection, and Resolve (APGAR) scale provides a measure of satisfaction with family functioning; the Family Environment Scale (FES) measures both family interactions

and functioning; and the Family Coping Strategies (F-COPES) scale by Olson et al. (1982) focus on problem solving and strategies used to manage family crises (Neabel, Fothergill-Bourbonnais, & Dunning, 2000). Family nursing frameworks provide an organizing umbrella of family process, structure, function, developmental concepts, and subconcepts associated with each concept to guide the nurse in family assessment (Friedman et al., 2003; Wright & Leahey, 2000).

Family nursing assessment tools and frameworks enable the family nurse to forge into the domain of family health assessment and begin to collaborate with the family as client in planning for family health maintenance and promotion strategies. The selection of a family nursing assessment tool or framework is influenced by the exposure of nurses to various tools and frameworks that fit with their own philosophy of nursing. Some nurses may appreciate an open-ended approach to family assessment as found in the CFAM (Wright & Leahey, 2000), the FFAM (Friedman et al., 2003), or the NSM (Reed, 1993); whereas others may appreciate the structure offered by the FSO (Friedemann, 1995) or the Family Systems Stressor-Strength Inventory (Berkey & Hanson, 1991; Hanson, 2001). Family assessment tools vary in their construction; they may include elements of qualitative assessment of family process, structure, function, and development concepts with open-ended questions (Friedman et al., 2003; Reed, 1993; Wright & Leahey, 2000) or quantitative tools with 5-point Likert scales and additional open-ended questions to be used for collection of data (Friedemann, 1995; Hanson, 2001).

Family nursing assessment tools and frameworks provide a road map for novice nurses in conducting family assessments. Nurse scholars posit that the practice of family nursing interventions at an advanced level of practice requires other requisite knowledge and skills (Friedman et al., 2003; Friedemann, 1995; Reed, 1993; Wright & Leahey, 2000). Nurses at the baccalaureate and graduate levels planning family nursing interventions will integrate their knowledge of interaction and communication theory, systems theory, family structural-functional theory, developmental theory, role theory, social support theory, crisis theory, family stress theory, and change theory reflecting various degrees of synthesis in planning family health promotion strategies.

Conceptual Models of Nursing and Models of Family Nursing Assessment

As discussed in Chapter 4, conceptual models of nursing and their links to family nursing practice over the past two decades are addressed in Table 4-2 and can be found in the nursing literature (King, 1983; Neuman, 1983, Orem, 1983; Rogers, 1983; Roy, 1983). Models of family nursing assessment and intervention derived from conceptual models of nursing have also guided family nursing practice over the past two decades (Friedman et al., 2003; Hanson & Mischke, 1996; Hanson, 2001; Reed, 1982, 1993; Friedemann, 1989a, 1989b, 1995). Moyra Allan

of McGill University in Montreal constructed the Allan Model of nursing, in which the family is the central unit of care (Allan, 1977, 1999; Feeley & Gottlieb, 2000); Marie-Louise Friedemann from Wayne State University constructed the FSO for family nursing (Friedemann, 1989a, 1989b, 1995); and Wright and Leahey (1984, 2000) from the University of Calgary developed the CFAM. Table 11-1 presents the underlying assumptions for several family assessment models developed by nurses.

Friedman Family Assessment Model

The FFAM, developed by Marilyn Friedman in the 1980s, is based on a synthesis of general systems theory, family development theory, and cross-cultural theory that serves as the underpinnings of the model (Friedman et al., 2003).

TABLE 11-1 Assumptions Associated with Selected Family Assessment Models Developed by Nurses

Model	Author	Assumptions
Friedman Family Assessment Model (FFAM)	M. M. Friedman, 1998	"(1) A family is a social system with functional requirements, (2) a family is a small group possessing certain generic features common to all small groups, (3) the family as a social system accomplishes functions that serve both the individual and society, and (4) individuals act in accordance with a set of internalized norms and values that are learned primarily in the family through socialization" (Friedman, 1998, p. 100).
Framework of Systemic Organization (FSO)	M. L. Friedemann, 1995	"(1) The family embedded in the civil system is transmitting culture, the total of human systems patterns and values (2) the family shares with the civil system and the environment at large the responsibility to provide physical necessities and safety, procreate, teach social skills to its members, provide personal growth and development, allow emotional bonding of family members, and promote a purpose for life and meaning through spirituality, (3) the family satisfies its members' needs for control over their environment and guides them in finding their place in the network of systems through spirituality, (4) all family processes include collectively accepted and coordinated behaviors or strategies that aim at regulating the earthly conditions of space, time, energy, and matter in pursuing the four systemic targets, and (5) family strategies fall into the four process dimensions of system maintenance, system change, coherence, and individuation. The dimensions share collinearity but exist independently in that none is emphasized at the expense of another in healthy families" (Friedemann, 1995, pp. 16-17).

TABLE 11-1   Assumptions Associated with Selected Family Assessment Models
Developed by Nurses—cont'd

Model	Author	Assumptions
Calgary Family Assessment Model (CFAM)	L. M. Wright & M. Leahey, 2000	"(1) A family system is part of a larger suprasystem and in turn is composed of many subsystems, (2) the family as a whole is greater than the sum of its parts, (3) a change in one family member affects all family members, (4) the family is able to create a balance between change and stability, and (5) family members' behaviors are best understood from a view of circular rather than linear causality" (Wright & Leahey, 2000, pp. 38-43).
Neuman Systems Model (NSM)	Betty Neuman, 2002	"(1) The family is viewed as a client system, (2) the client is an open system engaging in a dynamic, constant energy exchange between internal and external environments to promote harmony and balance, (3) the client system is a composite of physiologic, psychological, sociocultural, developmental, and spiritual variables that are parts of the whole, (4) the client system has evolved a normal range of responses to the environment (normal lines of defense), or usual wellness/stability state representing change and coping over time, (5) when stressors break through the normal lines of defense, the degree of reaction to the stressor is based upon the interrelationships of the client system variables, (6) client system wellness is viewed on a continuum of available energy to support the system in an optimal state of system stability, (7) the lines of resistance function to stabilize and return the client system to the usual wellness state (normal line of defense) or to a higher level of wellness following an environmental stressor reaction to the client system" (Neuman, 2002, pp. 14-15).
Family Health Promotion-Protection Plan	Nola Pender, 1987	"The family is a logical unit of assessment and intervention for health promotion, because it has the primary responsibility for (1) developing for self-care and dependent care competencies of the family, (2) fostering resilience of family members, (3) providing social and physical resources to the family group, and (4) promoting healthy individuation while maintaining family cohesion" (pp. 136).
Family Assessment and Intervention Model	Berkey & Hanson, 1991	The Model is based on the Neuman Systems Model and assumptions and Curran's model of stressors and strengths. Selected assumptions are as follows: "Many known, unknown, and universal environmental stressors exist. Each differs in its potential for disturbing a family's usual stability level, or normal line of defense. *Primary prevention* relates to general knowledge that is applied in family assessment and intervention in identification and mitigation of risk factors associated with environmental stressors to prevent possible reactions. Secondary prevention is symptomatology following reaction to stressors, appropriate ranking of intervention priorities, and treatment to reduce their noxious effects. *Tertiary prevention* relates to the adjustive process taking place as reconstitution begins and maintenance factors move the client back in a circular manner toward prevention. The family is in dynamic, constant energy exchange with the environment" (pp. 23-24).

The FFAM reflects a structural-functional organization of family data that is intended to assist nurses in their approach to family nursing. The FFAM views the family as an open system with attention directed to the family's structure, functions, and the interplay of relationships with the social systems that provide the context for the family as client. See Table 11-1 for assumptions underlying the FFAM.

Friedemann Framework of Systemic Organization

Marie-Louise Friedemann constructed a nursing framework for families that was derived from nursing science knowledge in the late 1980s and from the work of family specialists and researchers in related disciplines, which evolved into the FSO, having its origins at Wayne State University (Friedemann, 1989a, 1995). The FSO is rooted in general systems theory and is based on the concepts of environment, person, family, health, family health, and nursing with underlying propositions and theoretically deduced processes that explain their relationships to other concepts within the framework (Friedemann, 1995). See Table 11-1 for assumptions associated with the FSO.

The Calgary Family Assessment Model

The CFAM for family nursing, developed by Lorraine Wright and Maureen Leahey, originated during the 1980s at the University of Calgary. Six theoretical foundations that serve as the underpinnings of the CFAM are postmodernism, systems theory, cybernetics, communication theory, change theory, and biology of cognition (Wright & Leahey, 2000). Wright and Leahey point out that the CFAM is a multidimensional model consisting of the three major categories of structure, development, and function. Wright and Leahey note that each category entails several subcategories and it is up to the nurse to decide which subcategories are pertinent when assessing a family during the first family meeting. See Table 11-1 for assumptions associated with the CFAM and rooted in systems theory. Wright and Leahey offer a diagram of the CFAM that illustrates the three categories, eight subcategories, and the areas for assessment targeting the microscopic data within selected subcategories (Figure 11-1).

The Neuman Systems Model

The NSM has its theoretical foundations in general systems theory, gestalt theory, Selye's notion of stress and coping, and Marxist philosophy (Neuman, 2002). The client or client system in the NSM is viewed as "an individual, a family, a group, a community or a social issue" (Neuman, 2000, p. 15). Neuman (1983) defines the family as "a group of two or more persons who create and maintain a common culture; its most central goal is one of continuance" (p. 241). See Table 11-1 for assumptions associated with the NSM and related to the family as a client system. See Figure 10-1 in Chapter 10 for an illustration of the NSM.

The utility of the NSM of nursing for family health promotion is documented in the nursing literature (Amaya, 2002; Crawford & Tarko, 2002; Cross, 1995; Neuman, 1983; Reed, 1993). In the NSM, individuals make up subcomponents of the family system, and the individuals within the family are viewed in the context of the five NSM variables: physiological, psychological, sociocultural, developmental, and spiritual. Further family health assessment is based on four elements: (1) family psychosocial and cultural relationships, (2) physical status of the family as a whole, (3) family developmental characteristics, and (4) spiritual dimensions of the family as a client system (Neuman, 1983).

Analysis of family system data is guided by Neuman's nursing process format, which consists of three steps: (1) nursing diagnosis, (2) nursing goals, and (3) nursing outcomes (Neuman, 2002). Determining the family system's variance from wellness is guided by the integration of the family system assessment database, with appropriate theories such as crisis theory; communication theory; role and systems theories; and developmental, change, and family theories. Holistic and comprehensive nursing diagnostic statements are constructed based on the analysis of specific areas of variance from wellness. Planning family health promotion strategies through the three modes of primary, secondary, and tertiary intervention as prevention is completed collaboratively with the family in efforts to retain, maintain, or attain family system strength and stability.

Identification of stressors and the family system's reaction to the stressors enables the nurse to plan collaborative nursing goals, interventions,

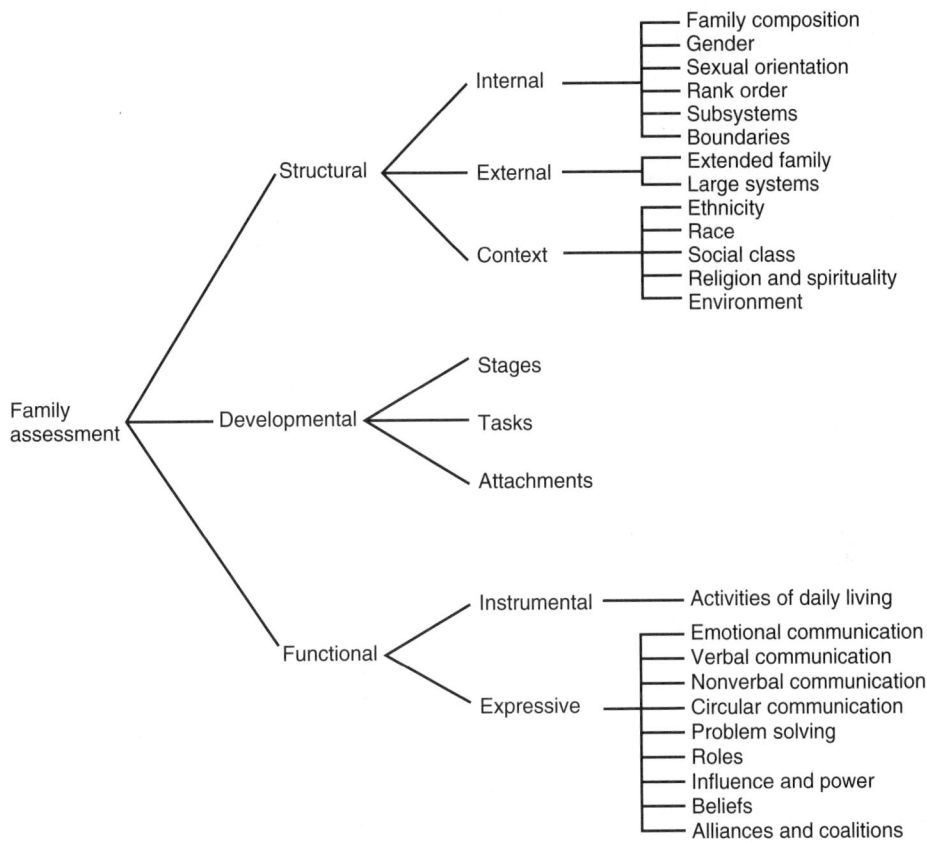

Figure 11-1 Branching diagram of Calgary Family Assessment Model (CFAM). (From Wright, M. L., & Leahey, M. [2000]. *Nurses and families: A guide to family assessment and intervention*, 3rd ed. Philadelphia: F. A. Davis.)

and outcomes with families to assist in retaining, maintaining, and attaining family system stability. Neuman (1983) contends that stressors are "all forces (problems, conditions, situations) that either are or could produce instability within the family system" (p. 246). Neuman (1989) notes that stressors are "tension producing stimuli or forces occurring within the internal and the external environmental boundaries of the client/client system" (p. 9).

According to Neuman (1983, 2002), family stressors are derived from within and outside of the family system and are viewed by way of three clusters derived from the family system's internal and external environments. These are intrafamily, interfamily, and extrafamily system stressors.

Cultural differences, family system perception of stressors, family coping ability, reaction and adaptation to invasion of stressors, changes in family role functions, and adjustment are important factors to consider in assessment of the types of family system stressors (Neuman, 1983).

Neuman (1983) notes that intrafamily system stressors are all forces that take place within the boundary of the family system and have the potential to alter the family system's stability. Interfamily system stressors are all forces that take place between the boundary of the family system and the immediate or direct external environment, whereas extrafamily system stressors entail all forces occurring between the boundary of the family system and the distal or indirect external environment. Curran (1985) and Tarko and Reed (2002) explicates intrafamily, interfamily, and extrafamily system stressors, which are presented in Box 11-1.

Reed (1982, 1993) discusses the NSM structures and concepts in terms of family theory and applies selected family process and structure concepts to the NSM, thus providing direction for family assessment and intervention. Reed delineates elements of family theory as factors influencing the family's Flexible and Normal Lines of Defense and Lines of Resistance (Box 11-2). These factors serve as the basis for holistic family assessment with the NSM. The nurse collaboratively engages with the family in assessing family health and planning health promotion strategies to assist the family in retaining, maintaining, and/or attaining family system stability and wellness through a process of reconstitution by way of prevention as intervention nursing actions.

BOX 11-1   Intrafamily, Interfamily, and Extrafamily System Stressors

Intrafamily System Stressors

Family member(s) feeling unappreciated

Guilt for not accomplishing more

Insufficient "me" time

Self-image/self-esteem/feelings of unattractiveness

Perfectionism

Dieting

Health/illness

Drugs/alcohol

Widowhood

Retirement

Homework/school/grades

Family violence addictions

In-laws

Teen behaviors

New baby

Houseguests

Family vacations

Remarriage/divorce/separation*

Relationship with former spouse

Summer

Weekends

Religious differences

Predinner hours

Older parents

Computer/Internet*

Interfamily System Stressors

Communication with children

Housekeeping standards

Insufficient couple time

Insufficient family playtime

Children's behavior/discipline/sibling fighting

Television

Overscheduled family calendar

Lack of shared responsibility in the family

Moving

Spousal relationship (communication, friendship, sex)

Holidays

Extrafamily System Stressors

Economics/finances/budgets

Unhappiness with work situation

Overvolunteerism

Neighbors

Unemployment

Nuclear and environmental fears

Church/school activities

Unsatisfactory housing

Organized sports activities

Change in work patterns

Two-paycheck family

Terrorist attacks*

From Curran, D. (1985). *Stress and the healthy family.* Minneapolis, MN: Winston Press.
*From Tarko, M. A., & Reed, K. (2002). *Taxonomy of family nursing diagnosis based upon the Neuman systems model of nursing.* Unpublished manuscript, New Westminster, British Columbia, Canada: Douglas College.

BOX 11-2   Exemplars of Family Structure, Process, and Development Concepts Associated with Neuman's Flexible and Normal Lines of Defense and Lines of Resistance

FLEXIBLE LINES OF DEFENSE

Role enactment
Rule implementation
Decision-making mechanisms
Task allocation processes
Bonding patterns

NORMAL LINES OF DEFENSE

Communication patterns
Problem-solving mechanisms
Mechanisms for family intimacy and affection
Mechanisms for managing family loss and change

LINES OF RESISTANCE

Interrelatedness
Interdependence
Values and beliefs

From Reed, K. S. (1993). Adapting the Neuman systems model for family nursing. *Nursing Science Quarterly, 6,* 93-97.

BOX 11-3   Exemplars of Intervention as Prevention Strategies at the Three Modes of Primary, Secondary, and Tertiary Prevention as Intervention

PRIMARY PREVENTION STRATEGIES

Career counseling
Premarital counseling
Parenting classes

SECONDARY PREVENTION STRATEGIES

Family crisis intervention
Grief work
Marital counseling

TERTIARY PREVENTION STRATEGIES

Family therapy
Rehabilitative courses
Support groups

From Reed, K. S. (1993). Adapting the Neuman systems model for family nursing. *Nursing Science Quarterly, 6,* 93-97.

The goals of family health promotion in the context of prevention as intervention are to strengthen the Flexible and Normal Lines of Defense and the Lines of Resistance, thus protecting the basic core of the family system through deliberate nursing actions that facilitate family system stability and wellness. Reed (1993) explicates primary, secondary, and tertiary intervention strategies for family health promotion and maintenance, and these are presented in Box 11-3.

Neuman (1983, 2002) proposes a three-part nursing process format that is derived from the traditional nursing process. The Neuman nursing process, introduced in Chapter 10, includes nursing diagnosis, nursing goals, and nursing outcomes. The case scenario presented at the end of this chapter serves as an exemplar of applying the NSM nursing process format to a family (Neuman, 2002).

Family Nursing Assessment Instrumentation

Choosing a quantitative family assessment tool can be a daunting task. There are multiple assessment tools available, many of which do not come from a nursing perspective. In choosing an instrument, it is important to determine whether the instrument's theoretical base is congruent with the assessment data, the purpose of the instrument, and the availability of information on the reliability and validity of the instrument. As Neabel et al. (2000) point out:

> To date, little attention has been paid to the congruence between the theoretical philosophy of family nursing, the definition of the family unit, and subsequent inferences and conclusions about family function when selecting an

BOX 11-4   Criteria for Selecting Family Assessment Instruments

When selecting family assessment instruments, nurses need to be cognizant of parameters that contribute to the instrument's effectiveness. These are the following:

1. Understandability
2. Administration and scoring
3. Reliability and validity
4. Clinical appropriateness
5. Clinical relevance

The instruments selected for assessment of family health must be clear, uncomplicated, and easily understood. The questions need to be worded at a grade level that family members with poor reading skills and/or limited vocabularies can comprehend. It is suggested that the reading level be set at a sixth grade level.

Families are more likely to complete assessment instruments, and nurses are more apt to use them if they can be administered in a short time period. To be useful in busy clinics, 15 or 20 minutes is probably the maximum amount of time that nurses and families can devote to this process. Another factor worth considering

is the *ease of scoring* and the length of time involved in interpreting results. Reliability and validity is the third area for consideration when selecting a family assessment tool. This involves judgment about the instrument's consistency and whether or not the results honestly reflect what the tool is attempting to measure. It is important that the tool be both valid and reliable.

In order for an assessment instrument to be effective it needs to be constructed in such a way that the questions are *appropriate* for the majority of families. The composition of words, phrases, and concepts should not be geared to a particular social class, age group, or ethnic background. The questions need to be universal in scope. They must also address topics the family deems reasonable and appropriate, or the family may hesitate to participate.

The last area to consider is the clinical relevance of the instrument. Nurses need assessment tools that assist them with gathering relevant clinical material. If the tool is easy to understand, administer, and score but is not relevant, it is ineffectual. Family health measurement tools must focus on those areas of need for which nursing interventions may be planned.

From Speer, J. M., & Sachs, B. (1985). Selecting the appropriate family assessment tool. *Pediatric Nursing, 11*, 349-355. Hanson, S. M. H., & Mischke K. B. (1996). Family assessment interventions. In P. J. Bomar (Ed.). *Nurses and family health promotion* (2nd ed., pp. 165-202). Philadelphia: W. B. Saunders.

assessment tool. Consequently, potential problems may develop, such as family needs being overlooked and interventions being initiated that are not meaningful or beneficial to the family (p. 198).

For example, if the nurse is using a systems-based philosophy in working with families, it is helpful to choose an instrument that is also systems-based. If the nurse is interested in changes over time, then an instrument developed to measure change is warranted. Finally, if possible, the nurse should choose an instrument with known reliability and validity measures. This ensures that the assessment tool is consistently measuring what it is supposed to measure (reliability) and that it collects the data it is supposed to collect (validity). Three measures of reliability are available: homogeneity, stability, and equivalence. Validity measures are content,

criterion-related, and construct. Criteria for selection of a family measure are presented in Box 11-4.

Nursing scholars (Bomar & Baker-Word 2001; Denham, 2003; Pender, Murdaugh, & Parsons, 2002) indicate that the *key components* that are crucial for assessing family health promotion and health protection are the following:

- Nutrition
- Family interaction and nurturance
- Spirituality
- Sleep patterns
- Sexuality
- Environment
- Family physical activity, recreation, and play
- Stress control and management
- Health responsibility
- Family resilience and resources

- Family support
- Family rituals, celebrations, and routines

Assessment measures for many of these components are listed in the varied chapters of this book.

Table 11-2 lists several of the most commonly used quantitative family assessment measures created by nurses and family scientists. Some information on the author, the theoretical back-

ground, and the psychometrics is provided. Full references for the measures can be found in the reference list at the end of the chapter. These sources can be used to find specific information regarding the instrument. Another excellent resource is the article by Neabel et al. (2000) that provides a synopsis of the instruments. Two additional comprehensive interdisciplinary compilations of family assessment measures for research

TABLE 11-2 Selected Family Assessment Measures

Tool	Author	Purpose	Theory	Psychometric Measures Reliability	Validity
Family Adaptability Cohesion Evaluation Scale (FACES III)	Olson, Portner, & Lavee, 1985	Assesses perceptions and provides description of family; assesses changes over time	Circumplex Model (general systems theory)	Homogeneity Stability	Content Construct, by correlation method Criterion
Feetham Family Functioning Survey (FFFS)	Feetham & Humenick, 1982	Assesses the perceptions of parents on family relationships; measures 3 health areas	Ecological Framework (general systems theory)	Homogeneity Stability	Content, Concurrent, Construct, by factor analysis
Family Adaptability, Partnership, Growth, Affection, and Resolve (APGAR)	Smilkstein, 1978	Screens families quickly on general issues of family functioning	Structural/Functional	Homogeneity Stability	Construct, by correlation method Criterion
Family Assessment Device (FAD)	Epstein et al., 1983	Screens families in 7 areas; distinguishes between healthy and unhealthy families	McMaster Model of Family Functioning (structural/ functional)	Homogeneity Stability	Construct, by correlation method Criterion
Family Environment Scale (FES)	Moos & Moos, 1976	Measures perceived family interactions in social environments; useful for measuring change over time	Family Systems theory	Homogeneity Stability	Seldom reported
Family Coping Strategies (F-COPES)	McCubbin, Olson, & Larsen, 1987	Identifies problem-solving strategies used during crisis; normative data available for adolescents and adults	Double ABCX Model of Family Adjustment (family stress theory)	Homogeneity Stability	Construct, by factor analysis
Family Needs Assessment Tool (FNAT)	Rawlins, Rawlins, & Horner, 1990	Identifies needs of families with chronically ill children	King's Theory of Goal Attainment	Homogeneity Stability	Content, Construct, by factor analysis
Family Inventory of Life Events (FILE)	McCubbin & Thompson, 1987	Identifies recent family events, which when accumulated, suggest levels of family stress	Family Stress theory	Homogeneity Stability	Construct, by factor analysis

Continued

TABLE 11-2   Selected Family Assessment Measures—cont'd

Tool	Author	Purpose	Theory	Psychometric Measures	
				Reliability	Validity
Family Function Inventory (FFI)	Pless & Satterwhite, 1973	Assesses the strength of the family relationships and lifestyles; not sensitive to short-term changes	None reported	Homogeneity Stability	Construct by, correlation method Criterion
Critical Care Family Needs Inventory (CCFNI)	Molter & Leske, 1995	Measures the importance of care needs of families of critical care patients. (Adapted also for children and patients with cancer)	Crisis and human needs theories	Homogeneity Stability	Construct, by factor analysis
Family Health Assessment Tool (FAMTOOL)	Weeks & O'Connor, 1997	For rehabilitative nurses to measure family health and strengths; useful in wide variety of primary, secondary, and tertiary settings	Family and health concept analysis	Homogeneity	Not reported
Assessment of Strategies in Families (ASF)	Friedemann, 1991	Screening tool for family functioning effectiveness to determine needs for family therapy	Family Systems Theory	Homogeneity Stability	Construct, by factor analysis
Family Caregiving Factors Inventory (FCFI)	Shyu, 2000	Assesses needs of family caregivers of the frail elderly	Shyu model of family caregiving: "Finding a balance point"	Homogeneity Stability	Construct, by factor analysis

and clinical practice are the *Handbook of Family Measurement Techniques* (Permulter, Toutiatos, & Holden, 2001) and *Family Assessment: Resilience, Coping and Adaptation* (McCubbin, Thompson, & McCubbin, 1996).

Genograms and Ecomaps as Tools for Mapping Family Systems

Genograms

The standardized genogram format (McGoldrick, Gerson, & Shellenberger, 1999) for illustrating family structure through composition, health history, and relationships is documented in the family nursing literature in relation to family health assessment and promotion (Hanson, 2001; Loveland-Cherry, 2000; Murray, Zentner,

Brockhaus, Brockhaus, & Sullivan, 2001; Roth, 1996; Wright & Leahey, 2000). The standard symbols for genogram construction are presented in Figure 11-2. A family genogram may be constructed during the initial family interview on either a white board or pad of paper, with the family serving as a source of information for the family nurse in mapping out who is in the family and the types of relationships and health issues experienced by the family as a system. Genograms have been used in family nursing primarily for documenting family structure across three or more generations, for assessment of family health patterns, and for identification of any health concerns in the context of family health promotion. Beyond this primary purpose of using a genogram in family assessment, the value of involving families in the construction of their own genogram

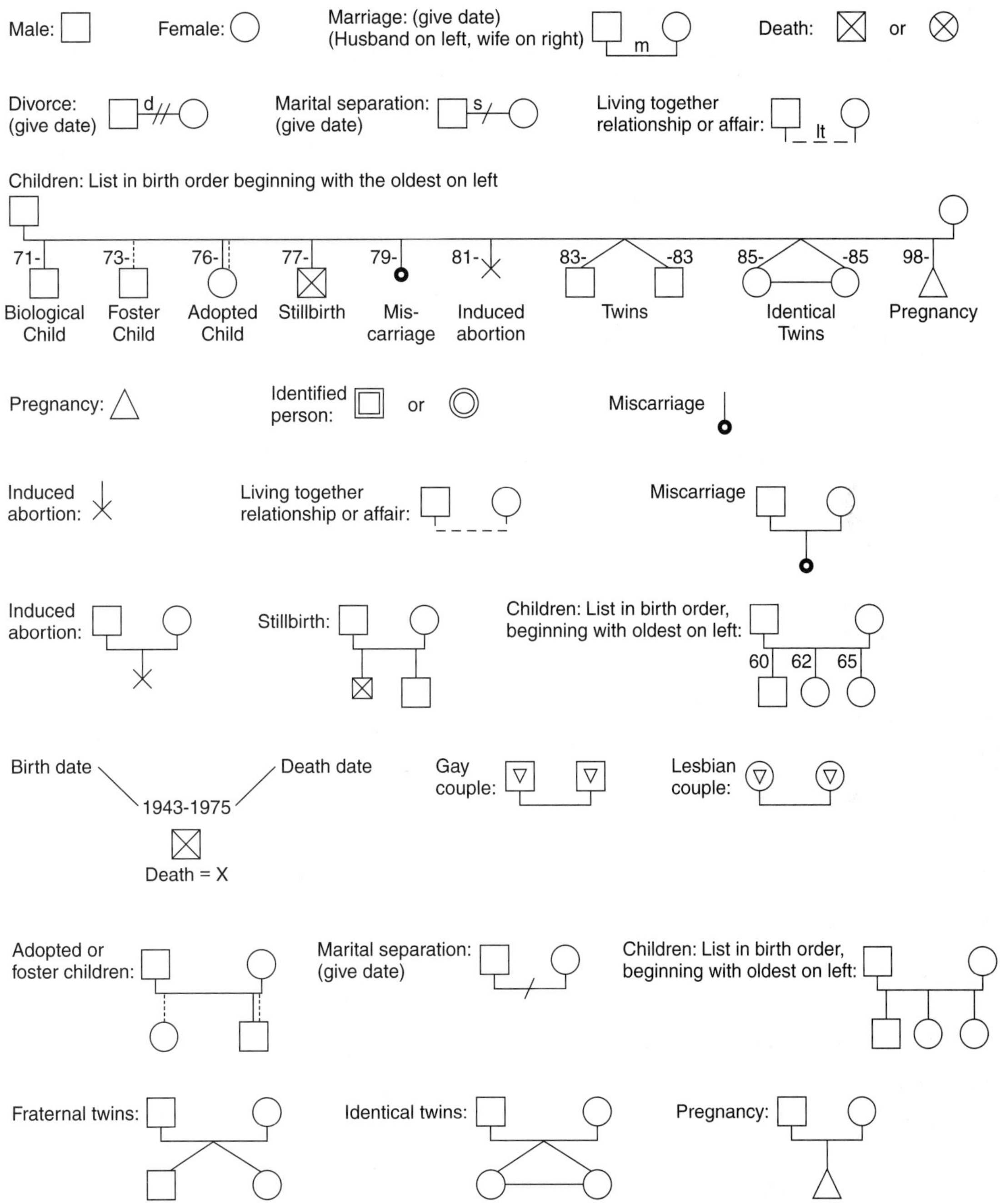

Figure 11-2 Standard symbols for a genogram. From *Genograms: Assessment and Intervention,* 2nd edition, by Monica McGoldrick, Randy Gerson, and Sylvia Shellenberg. Copyright © 1999 by Monica McGoldrick and Sylvia Shellenberg. Copyright © 1985 by Monica McGoldrick and Randy Gerson. Used by permission of W. W. Norton & Company, Inc.

is twofold: (1) the construction of the genogram serves as an activity for family health promotion that can be used as a teaching tool for increasing family awareness of and insights into patterns of family health and wellness, and (2) it empowers the family by enabling family members to teach the nurse about their own health history using a tool that may be perceived as less threatening than a face-to-face conversation with the nurse acting as family health promoter during the first meeting.

Ecomaps

Ecomaps are used in family nursing to broaden the perspective of the family in the context of their community in assessing resources and strengths of family relationships with significant others, organizations, and institutions (Hanson, 2001; Murray et al., 2001; Roth, 1996; Wright & Leahey, 2000). The ecomap, like the genogram, may be used as a teaching tool by the nurse in collaborating with the family and may also be used to empower the family to tell the nurse about relevant family resources, sources of support, and opportunities for maintaining and strengthening family health. The family ecomap may be constructed during the family meeting, with the family serving as a resource for identifying what community resources are currently being used and highlighting which potential community resources may also serve the family's needs for health promotion and wellness. A sample blank ecomap that may be used as a template for family assessment is presented in Figure 11-3.

Nursing Interventions for Family Health Promotion

Although nursing research specifically related to family nursing interventions for promoting family health has been conducted, it remains in the infancy stage (Davis, 1998; Feeley & Gottlieb, 2000; Gilliss, Highley, Roberts, & Martinson, 1989; Wright & Leahey, 2000). Gilliss et al. (1989) suggest that family nursing interventions framed by the levels of prevention as traditionally applied to individuals (primary, secondary, tertiary) ought to be applied to families by family nurses, cautioning them not to slip into patterns of caring for

family members but rather to remain focused on the family as the unit of care. Gilliss et al. note that primary prevention strategies are directed toward identification of families at risk, secondary prevention strategies are used after a family problem has developed, and tertiary prevention is achieved by teaching families new strategies to manage health issues to maximize family strength and resources after the development of a health problem. Gilliss et al. suggest 10 characteristics common to family nursing interventions, which are presented in Box 11-5.

Wright and Leahey (2000) suggest that the "intent of any nursing intervention is to effect change" (p. 20) in the family as a system. Wright and Levac (1992) assert that to effect change with the family, the nurse must offer an intervention that "fits" the structure of the family unit. Family nursing interventions that support family health promotion include the following:

- Family self-care contracting (Gray, 1996)
- Enabling and empowering families (access and control over resources, decision-making and problem-solving skills, and assertive communication for acquisition of resources)
- Mobilizing community resources for families (Loveland-Cherry, 2000; Hanson, 2001)
- Family confluence (promoting family activities that support togetherness and unity) (Bomar & Baker-Word, 2001; Hanson, 2001)

Loveland-Cherry (2000), in the context of primary prevention and family-focused community health nursing interventions, describes the major health risks to families. Risks to family health emerge from several areas: biological risk, social risk, economic risk, lifestyle risk, and life events leading to crisis. A combination of risks from two or more areas is reported as the norm, and acquiring knowledge about each of these areas enables the family nurse to provide a family risk assessment and intervene at the appropriate levels of prevention and promotion of family health.

Pender et al. (2002) note that health promotion interventions encompass four broad areas: (1) physical activity in children, adolescents, and adults; (2) nutrition; (3) stress management; and (4) social support for individual health. All four areas are directed at the individual family member level; however, in viewing individual health from a family nurse perspective, one quickly

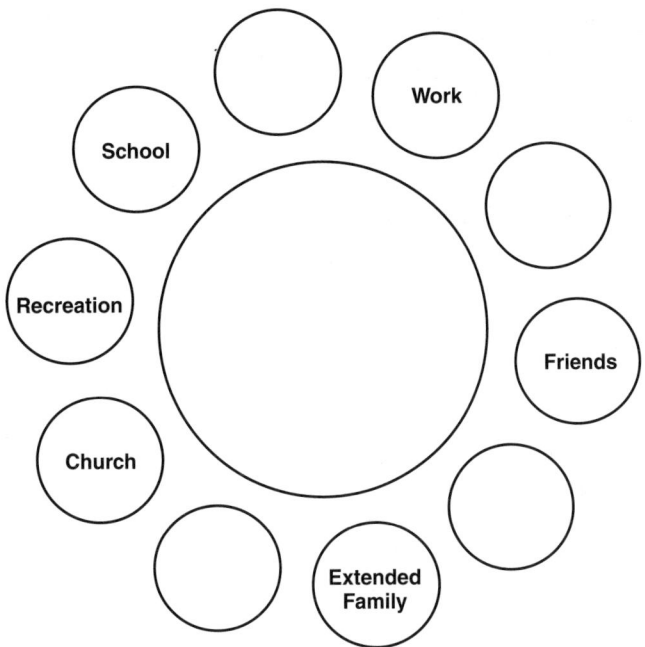

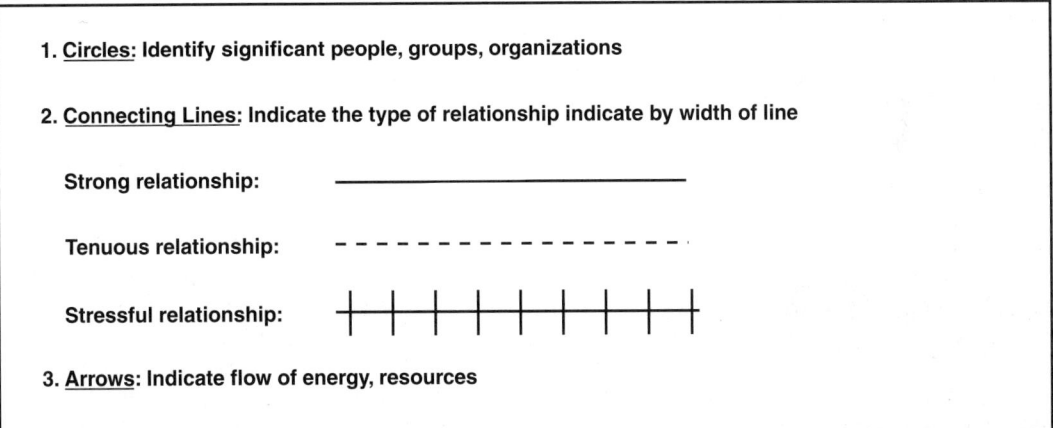

Figure 11-3   Sample ecomap. (Adapted from Roth, P. [1996]. Family social support. In P. J. Bomar [Ed.], *Nurses and family health promotion: Concepts, assessment, and interventions* [2nd ed., pp. 107-138]. Philadelphia: W. B. Saunders.)

BOX 11-5 Ten Characteristics Common to Family Nursing Interventions

1. Family care is concerned with the experience of the family over time.
2. Family nursing is considerate of the community and cultural context of the family group.
3. Family nursing is considerate of the relationships between and among family members and recognizes that in some instances all individuals and the family group will not achieve maximum health simultaneously.
4. Family nursing is directed at families whose members are both healthy and ill.
5. Family nursing is often offered in settings where individuals present problems of physiologic or psychologic stress. However, although family nurses must be competent in the care and treatment of health problems of individual family members, and they must recognize the relationship of these problems to the health of the family group.
6. The family system is influenced by any change in its members; therefore, when caring for individuals in health and illness, the nurse must elect whether or not to attend to the family.
7. Family nursing requires that the nurse manipulate the environment to increase the likelihood of family interaction; however, the absence of family members does not preclude the nurse from offering family care.
8. The family nurse recognizes that the most symptomatic person in a family may change over time. Accordingly, the obvious focus on the nurse's attention may change over time. Despite this, the family nurse assesses the impact of these symptoms on the family, understanding that they are data about the family.
9. Family nursing focuses on the strengths of individual family members and the family group to promote their mutual support and growth where possible.
10. Family nursing requires the nurse to define family. We define family as a group of two or more individuals usually living in close geographic proximity; having close emotional bonds; meeting affectional, socioeconomic, sexual, and socialization needs of the family group and/or the wider social systems.

From Gilliss, C. L., Highley, B. L., Roberts, B. M., Martinson, I. M. (1989). What is family nursing? In C. L. Gilliss, B. L. Highley, B. M. Roberts, & I. M. Martinson (Eds.), *Toward a science of family nursing* (pp. 64-73). Menlo Park, CA: Addison-Wesley.

---

recognizes how individual family member health in turn affects the whole family unit. Nursing interventions offered in the four areas can be integrated into a family health plan, providing that the family also recognizes the health issues and wants change in the family system. More specifically, areas in which the nurse can promote family health, education, and maintenance of its system's strengths include the following (Bomar & Baker-Word, 2001, p. 210):

- Family transitions, such as births, acute and chronic illnesses, separations, launching of children, divorce, death, and retirement
- Family and individual dietary patterns
- Family and individual recreation and exercise
- Family sexuality
- Family sleep and rest patterns
- Family environment practices
- Transitions from illness to wellness
- Socialization and rearing of children
- Risk reduction and socialization in health care practices
- Encouragement of a balance between togetherness and individuation
- Provision for family systems and household maintenance
- Encouragement of family spirituality

Wright and Leahey (2000) suggest that the Calgary Family Intervention Model (CFIM) provides a framework that helps nurses think about the relationship between families and nurses to facilitate change and healing. The CFIM is reported as "a collaborative, nonhierarchical model that recognizes the expertise of family members experiencing illness and the expertise of nurses in managing illness and promoting health" (pp. 26-27). The aims of the interventions used within the CFIM target the family system by developing new ways of interacting within the family unit. Interventions focus on altering cognitive, affective, and behavioral aspects of family dynamics. Wright and Leahey contend that "interventions normally directed at challenging the meanings or beliefs that families give to behavioral events or their experience of illness tend to have the most sustaining changes" (p. 21).

Indications and contraindications for family interventions are reported by Wright and Leahey (2000). Indications for family interventions are as follows:

1) A family experiencing emotional, physical, and/or spiritual suffering or disruption caused by a family crisis (e.g., acute illness, injury, or death).
2) A family is experiencing emotional, physical, and/or spiritual suffering or disruption caused by a developmental milestone (e.g., birth, marriage, or youngest child leaving [home]).
3) A family defines a problem as a family issue and there is a motivation for family assessment (e.g., the impact of chronic illness on the family).
4) A child or adolescent is identified by the family as having difficulties (e.g., school phobia or fear of treatment for cancer).
5) The family is experiencing issues that are serious enough to jeopardize family relationships (e.g., terminal illness or sexual/physical abuse).
6) A family member is about to be admitted to the hospital for psychiatric treatment.
7) A child is about to be admitted to the hospital (p. 17).

Contraindication for family assessment includes the following:

1) Individuation of a family member would be compromised by the family assessment. For example, if a young adult has recently left home for the first time, a family interview many not desirable.
2) The context of a family situation permits little or no leverage. That is, the family might have the fixed belief that the nurse is working as an agent of some other institution (e.g., the court) (Wright & Leahey, 2000, p. 17).

Wright and Leahey point out two additional important contraindications to family intervention: (1) all family members report they are not interested in recommended family treatment, and (2) family members are in agreement with treatment but prefer to see a different health care professional. See Chapter 4 in *Nursing and Families,* which elaborates on specific interventions for sustaining family functioning in the domains of cognition, affect, and behavior at an advanced practice level (Wright & Leahey, 2000).

Feeley and Gottlieb (2000) claim that in recent years, the focus of family nursing practice has shifted from a deficit perspective to a strengths-based view of the family, which is a central element in the McGill Model of Nursing. Feeley and Gottlieb note that one of the goals of nursing, based on the McGill Model, is to "help families use the strengths of the individual family members and of the family as a unit, as well as resources external to the family system" (p. 11). Four different types of strengths are reported that enable family members individually and collectively to manage "life challenges, to change, and to develop: (1) traits that reside within an individual or a family, (2) assets that reside within an individual or a family, (3) capabilities, skills, or competencies that an individual or a family has developed, or (4) a quality that is more transient in nature than a trait or asset" (p. 12).

Three aspects of using strengths in working with families are (1) identifying individual and family strengths through explicit concrete feedback, (2) building on strengths to enhance coping and development, as well as to create a safe climate for change that supports families in their quest to achieve goals or improve problem-solving skills, and (3) calling forth strengths by recognizing and using family strengths and potential as leverage in planning family nursing care (Feeley & Gottlieb, 2000).

In relation to resources, family strengths are viewed as being internal to the family unit, whereas resources as interventions are potential assets external to the family. Examples of external resources are extended family members, neighbors, community agencies, and health care professionals. Feeley and Gottlieb (2000) note three strategies that guide nurses in their work with family resources: (1) identifying resources with the use of an ecomap, (2) mobilizing and using resources available to the family once the family has expressed a need for such services, and (3) regulating the input of resources to ensure that a resource meets the needs of the family and does not add more stress to the family system.

Robinson and Wright (1995) report on which interventions make a difference from the family perspective. In their study of five families living with a member who has a chronic illness, two stages of interventions within the therapeutic change process were named: (1) creating the circumstance for change and (2) moving beyond and overcoming problems. Interventions in stage 1 include "bringing the family together and establishing a therapeutic relationship between nurse and family (achieved by drawing forth comfort and demonstrating trustworthiness)" (p. 335). Interventions in stage 2 include "inviting meaningful conversation, noticing and distinguishing family and individual strengths and resources, careful attention to and exploration of concerns, and putting illness and illness problems in their place (achieved by drawing forth a new family narrative that highlights the family's ability to influence both illness and illness problems)" (p. 335).

A study by Davis (1998) explored the feasibility and effectiveness of telephone-based skill building for reducing caregiving stress and improving coping among family members providing care to individuals with dementia.

Davis describes telephone interventions as being most effective with the use of standardized protocol for content in the form of 15 tip sheets to guide problem solving with the caregivers in relation to caring for family members living with dementia.

Community nurses with graduate degrees in nursing were orientated to using the 15 tip sheets of common problems reported by caregivers of persons living with dementia. The nurse interventionists spoke over the telephone for approximately 45 to 60 minutes with 20 family caregivers weekly for 12 weeks. Nurses educated in this telephone-based intervention focused on facilitating problem solving with family caregivers in relation to common health issues experienced by persons living with dementia.

Exemplars of the common health issues included memory loss and dementia, communication, confusion, restlessness, and agitation. Findings suggest that "telephone-based skill building may increase dementia caregivers' sense of social support, reduce their depressive symptoms, and improve their life satisfaction in the midst of caregiving" (Davis, 1998, p. 265).

Outcomes of the telephone interventions by community nurses revealed that caregivers mentioned six problems more often than others: managing confusion, sudden mood changes, alteration in sleep patterns, and repetitive actions in the elder, coupled with the caregivers' own marital issues and family conflicts regarding caregiving. Community nurses indicated that telephone-based interventions focused on problem-solving issues moved faster when the family caregiver had copies of the tip sheet to refer to as a guide for managing health issues of the family member experiencing dementia. Other outcomes after the 12 weeks of telephone-based support also revealed a significant increase in caregivers' use of social support, a decrease in depressive symptoms, and an increase in life satisfaction (Davis, 1998).

As nurses continue to compete for future research funding to explore evidenced-based family nursing interventions, integration of technology in family-based nursing practice, such as development of websites, has the potential to assist families in accessing family health promotion strategies that support family system maintenance and wellness. The Research Synopsis presents a summary of a research study using the Resiliency Model to empower families who have a member with a severe and persistent mental illness.

Evaluation of Family Health Outcomes

The goal of family nursing in health promotion is to maintain or enhance the family system's health and wellness. This goal can be achieved by evaluating the outcomes of nursing interventions. Nurses working in various clinical practice areas have participated in the implementation of nursing interventions to promote individual and population health; however, little research directly related to family nursing intervention outcomes has been done.

Pender et al. (2002) note that client "outcomes refer to the consequence of a treatment or intervention" (p. 260) directed toward achieving a goal. Outcomes associated with health prevention interventions are reported to vary according to the purpose, complexity, process of implementation, and strength of the nursing intervention. Pender et al. contend that measures for health care quality are based on structure, process, and outcomes.

RESEARCH SYNOPSIS

THE RESILIENCY MODEL FOR FAMILY HEALTH PROMOTION

Rungreangkulkij and Gilliss (2000) note that the current conceptual frameworks commonly used to study family caregivers present significant limitations in relation to the study of the family as a whole. They claim that the Family Resiliency Model developed by McCubbin and McCubbin allows family-level analysis and has promise for the study of families who have a member who has a severe and persistent mental illness.

The model consists of two phases: adjustment and adaptation. The *adjustment* phase is characterized by the family making minor changes in how it usually functions and is determined by the reciprocal interactions of the following features:

- The stressor
- The family's vulnerability
- The family typology
- The family's resistance resources
- The family's appraisal of the stressor
- The family's problem-solving and coping strategies

Rungreangkulkij and Gilliss note that in chronic illness situations hardships are compounded, demanding changes in the family system in relation to new goals, rules, boundaries, and patterns of functioning.

After a period of crisis and disorganization, the family is shifted into the adaptation phase of the Resiliency Model, which is characterized by the following features:

- The pileup of multiple demands on or in the family system created by the illness, family life-cycle change, and unresolved strains
- The family typology
- The family's resources
- Social support from extended family, friends, and the community
- A situational appraisal
- The family's schema appraisal and the family's meaning
- The family's problem-solving and coping strategies

Rungreangkulkij and Gilliss contend that the Family Resiliency Model offers a systems framework to direct research inquiry into the experience of the family who has a member with a severe and persistent mental illness.

Rungreangkulkij, S., & Gilliss, C. L. (2000). Conceptual approaches to studying family caregiving for persons with severe mental illness. *Journal of Family Nursing, 6,* 341-366.

Structure refers to aspects of the environment in which nurses practice nursing. Process refers to what nurses actually do in the practice context, and outcomes refer to the perspectives of the client and health care providers recognizing client choice as being significant when defining outcomes such as balancing preferences for survival versus quality of life. Tools used to measure these areas of health care quality are referred to as *performance measures.* Pender et al. note that health outcomes have historically encompassed the "five 'Ds': death, disease, disability, discomfort, and dissatisfaction" (2002, p. 261). Sidani and Braden (as cited by Pender et al., 2002) group health outcomes into four major areas: clinical end points, functional status, perceptual outcomes, and financial outcomes. Pender et al. (2002) state that nurses must demonstrate the effectiveness of their nursing practice in achieving goals related to health outcomes by client groups. However, individual effectiveness may become blurred when care is provided by an interdisciplinary health care team and outcomes are influenced by other disciplines in addition to nursing.

On a broader scale, Nursing Outcomes Classification (NOC) research began in 1992 at the University of Iowa College of Nursing under the direction of Marion Johnson, principal investigator, and Meridean Mass and Sue Moorhead (co-principal investigators). NOC provides a comprehensive, standardized classification of 260 client outcomes (University of Iowa, 2002). It reflects 247 individual-level, 7 family-level, and 6 community-level outcomes. The 260 outcomes are categorized into 29 classes and 7 domains. The 7 domains are functional health, physiological health, psychosocial health, health knowledge and behavior, perceived health, family health, and community health.

NOC for family health encompasses family coping, family environment, family health status, family integrity, family normalization, and family participation and professional care (University of Iowa, 2002). Further research in this area is required and needs to be performed to offer better health promotion strategies to families.

CASE SCENARIO

Sheila (age 37), a homemaker, is presently on a leave of absence from her position in the accounting department of an oil company. Her husband, Dave (age 38), is employed full-time as a mechanic. They have two daughters, Caroline (age 11) and Beth (age 9). During a family assessment at the community mental health clinic, Sheila discloses that yesterday Dave announced his intention to separate. Because the children do not know of the pending separation, the children are not present at the assessment. Previous marital counseling has not been successful.

Sheila claims to lack energy for routine daily tasks because of a severe depression. She reports decreased concentration, weight gain, sleep difficulties, decreased libido, and lack of interest in physical activities. She does not currently exercise. Sheila notes she has limited friends and social activities; she also reports low self-esteem and experiences discomfort in most social situations. She exhibited cognitive and motor retardation at the beginning of the family meeting. Sheila reports having struggled with depression intermittently since the birth of their first daughter.

Dave highly values physical health and reports that he is never sick. He is active in several different sports. Dave views physical illnesses and frailty as weak and therefore lacks any empathy for others when they are ill. Dave describes himself as "a cold and hard person." He keeps his feelings "bottled up" despite a sense of wanting to explode. Dave refuses to show or express emotions because of a strong belief that this behavior is weak. He reports infidelity a couple of years after their marriage. Dave states he didn't want children and believes that Sheila's pregnancy with their first child occurred as an unspoken solution to marital difficulties at that time. The pregnancy occurred shortly after a miscarriage. Dave reports uncertainty as to what he wants in the marital relationship. He notes he has a strong sense of obligation to his family, claiming "My girls are the most important things in my life."

In the absence of the daughters, the parents provide data on the two girls. Caroline is reported as physically healthy and strong, proficient in anything she attempts, and very popular in school. Beth has asthma, frequent headaches, and common illnesses. She was tested for attention deficit disorder on request by the school because of concentration and social difficulties. Beth has no close friends, and though she has tried several different activities, does not enjoy them and asks to be withdrawn from them.

Sheila and Dave organize daily tasks separately and report remaining apart even when both are in the home. Daily routines are organized such that care and interactions with the children occur on an individual basis, with only rare family activities being planned. Sheila and the girls attend the Lutheran church every Sunday, and Dave occasionally attends. Dave states that he is satisfied with leaving the religious instruction to Sheila. Dave believes in a higher power; however, he professes that he has problems with organized religions.

An assessment of the family was completed by using the Neuman Systems Model nursing process format for family assessment. The results follow. Figure 11-4 presents a genogram of the Smith family, and Figure 11-5 presents an ecomap of the Smith family.

FAMILY STRENGTHS

Strong value of the family unit, strong parental bonding patterns with the children, spiritual beliefs and religious practices, stable financial position, and willingness to open the system to outside help.

FAMILY SYSTEM AND NURSE PERCEPTIONS OF STRESSORS

Intrafamily stressors. Marital discord, Sheila feeling unsupported in parental role, Sheila feeling guilt about the effects of her depression on the family, Dave's ambivalence over his separation decision, Beth's asthma and headaches.

Interfamily stressors. Insufficient couple and family time, Dave's infidelity, differences in parental expressions of spirituality, Beth's isolative behavior.

Extrafamily stressors. Future financial considerations, Sheila's leave of absence from work, potential marital separation and legal involvement, potential effects on peer and school relationships for the daughters.

The following is an exemplar of Neuman's nursing process format based on the case scenario of the Smith family as client.

NURSING DIAGNOSIS

Altered family bonding patterns (between Sheila and Dave) related to Dave's uncertainty about leaving the marriage, unresolved marital discord since Dave's infi-

CASE SCENARIO—cont'd

delity, and Sheila's ongoing health challenges associated with feelings of hopelessness and powerlessness.

NURSING GOALS

Family will participate in couple counseling to resolve altered family bonding patterns and to address factors that weakened the nuclear family unit at the flexible line of defense, lines of resistance, and basic core. Factors to be addressed include bonding patterns, family roles, rule patterning, inadequate coping skills, indirect communication, and tensions within the family in relation to interdependence and interrelatedness.

NURSING OUTCOMES

Prevention as intervention. Primary prevention as intervention aims to retain the strengths within the family system, thereby promoting wellness by strengthening the flexible line of defense and protect-

ing the normal lines of defense from stressor invasion. Interventions available to the Smith family include family crisis counseling, health education, resource materials, and referrals to community support groups. Resources available to assist the family are strong family values, the couple's cooperative intent, and family's commitment to individual members' health.

Evaluation of outcome goals after intervention at 1-week intervals will take place for the first month. Parents will discuss the impact of attending family crisis counseling at the community counseling center, raise questions or clarify understanding of health and treatment issues affecting Sheila, select from resource materials areas they would like to focus attention on in their relationship as a couple and as a family unit, and decide which community support groups are of interest to the family (leisure planning, communication skills, and coping skills).

Written by Christina R. Marcil, Registered Psychiatric Nurse, Primary Therapist, Mental Health Day Program, Rockyview General Hospital, Calgary, Alberta, Canada.

WEBSITE RESOURCES

ORGANIZATION	WEBSITE ADDRESS
National Health Information Center	http://www.health.gov/nhic/
Healthy People 2010	http://www.health.gov/healthypeople
Health Canada	http://www.hc-sc.gc.ca/english/
Centers for Disease Control and Prevention	http://www.cdc.gov/
All Family Resources	http://www.familymanagement.com/
Family Life Resources	http://www.fyd.clemson.edu/famlife.htm/
National Network for Family Resiliency	http://www.nnfr.org/
National Council on Family Relations	http://www.ncfr.com/Default.htm
National Clearing House on Families and Youth	http://www.ncfy.com
Calgary Family Assessment Model	http://www.uic.edu/nursing/genetics/Lecture/Family/Calgary%20Family%20Framework/CFAM/cfam1.htm
Family Risk Assessment Tools	http://www.icyf.msu.edu/publicats/z5dissem/family-r.html
Online Family Assessment Instrument	http://www.home.pacbell.net/frccford/
Alterations in Family Processes Care Plan	http://www.rncentral.com/careplans/plans/fp.html
Neuman Systems Model	http://www.neumansystemsmodel.com
University of Iowa Nursing Outcomes Classification	http://www.uniowa.edu/noc

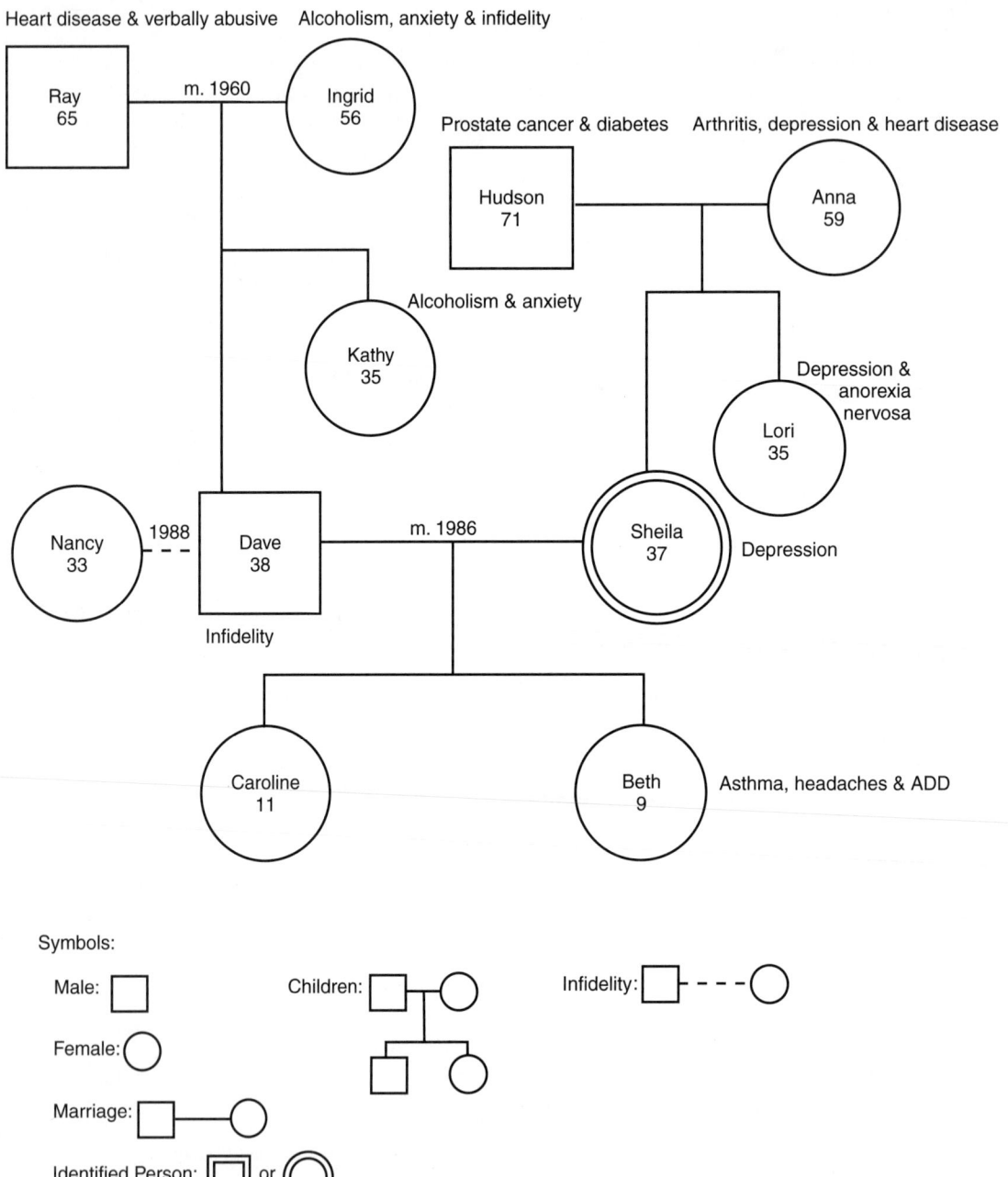

Figure 11-4 Sample genogram for the Smith family. *ADD,* Attention deficit disorder.

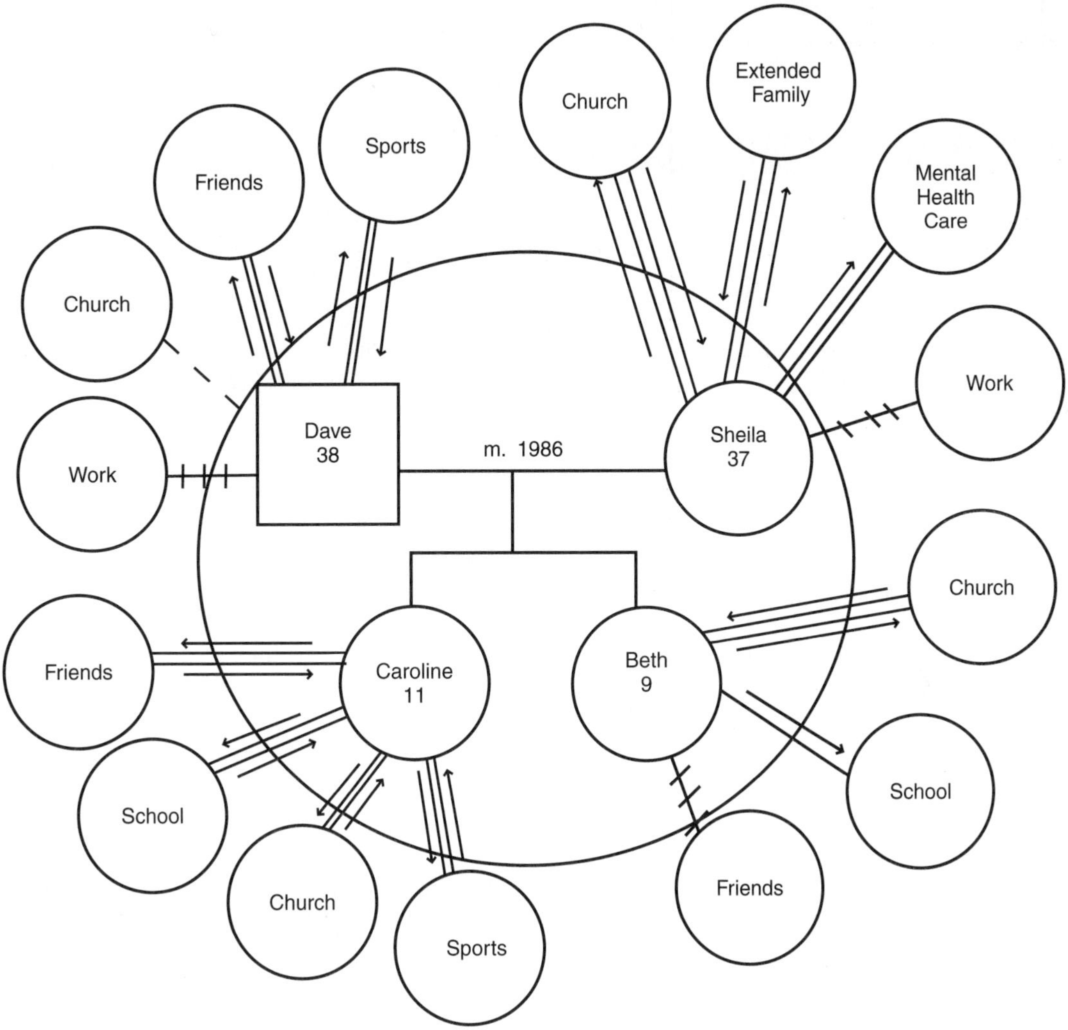

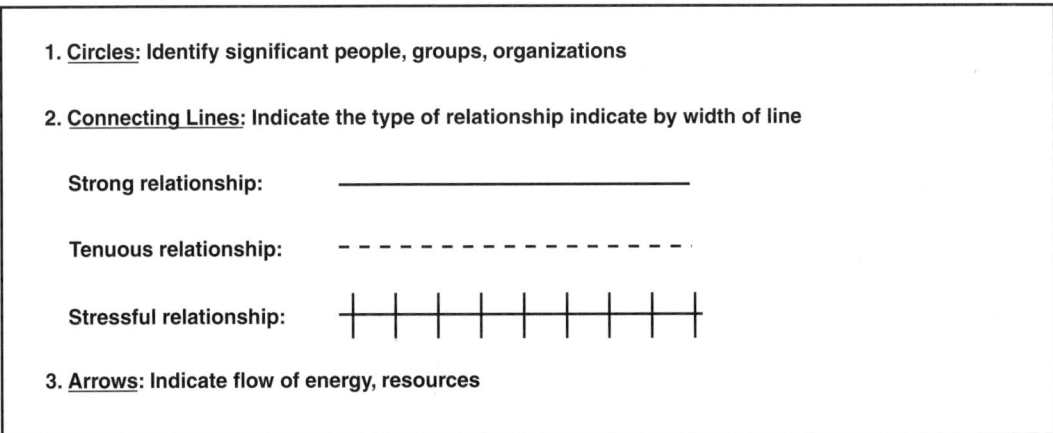

Figure 11-5 Smith family ecomap.

■ CHAPTER HIGHLIGHTS

- Four family nursing models used to guide family assessment and intervention are presented as exemplars of how the discipline of nursing is advancing the profession. The Friedman Family Assessment Model, Framework of Systemic Organization, Calgary Family Assessment Model, and the Neuman Systems Model are intended to offer family nurses guidelines for family nursing practice.

- The Neuman Systems Model applied to the whole family as a client system is a nursing conceptual framework that can be adapted to guide family health promotion through prevention as intervention. Interventions are based on primary, secondary, and tertiary levels of prevention as intervention.

- Family assessment tools offer the family nurse a range of measurement scales that are based on reported reliability and validity measures to consider for use in family nursing practice. The

tools vary in their focus, as do the theories that serve as underpinnings to the family measurement tools.

- The genogram and ecomap are additional tools for family assessment that family nurses may use during initial family meetings or may offer to families as exercises to complete before the next family meeting. Such exercises may empower the family as a system to be involved in exploring family strengths and health patterns across two or more generations and increase family awareness as to potential community resources and opportunities.

- A family case scenario in which the Neuman Systems Model is used to guide the analysis and planning of family health promotion illustrates the utility of the Neuman Systems Model applied to family assessment and intervention at a screening level.

‖ CRITICAL THINKING ACTIVITIES

1. Family nursing models and frameworks guiding family assessment and intervention reflect a number of common family process, structure, function, and development concepts. Discuss which concepts are clear and which concepts need more discussion as you think about how you would approach family assessment.

2. Four models are presented as frameworks to guide family assessment and intervention: the Friedman Family Assessment Model (FFAM), the Framework of Systemic Organization (FSO), the Calgary Family Assessment Model (CFAM), and the Neuman Systems Model (NSM). What are the similarities and differences in the family nursing approach to family assessment and

intervention among the four models and associated assumptions?

3. Genograms and ecomaps are discussed in the chapter. Diagram your own family genogram and ecomap. Share these insights with your family as a springboard for talking about family health issues and strategies to strengthen family coping and wellness.

4. The case scenario illustrates the application of the Neuman Systems Model nursing process format to the Smith family. Discuss what other levels of prevention-as-intervention strategies you would offer the Smith family in an effort to maintain family system stability and optimal wellness.

REFERENCES

Allan, E. M. (1977). Comparative theories of the expanded role in nursing and implications for nursing practice. *Nursing Papers, 9,* 38-45.

Allan, E. M. (1999). Comparative theories of the expanded role in nursing and implications for nursing practice. *Canadian Journal of Nursing Research, 30,* 83-90.

Amaya, M. A. (2002). The Neuman systems model and clinical practice: An integrative review, 1974-2000. In B. Neuman & J. Fawcett (Eds.), *The Neuman systems model* (4th ed., pp. 43-60). Upper Saddle River, NJ: Prentice Hall.

Berkey, K. M., & Hanson, S. M. H. (1991). *Pocket guide to family assessment and intervention.* St. Louis, MO: Mosby–Year Book.

Bomar, P. J., & Baker-Word, P. (2001). Family health promotion. In S. M. H. Hanson (Ed.), *Family health care nursing: theory, practice, and research* (2nd ed., pp. 197-219). Philadelphia: F. A. Davis.

Bray, J. H. (1995). Family assessment: Current issues in evaluating families. *Family Relations, 44,* 469-477.

Crawford, J. A., & Tarko, M. A. (2002). Using the Neuman systems model to guide nursing practice in Canada. In B. Neuman & J. Fawcett (Eds.), *The Neuman systems model* (4th ed., pp. 90-110). Upper Saddle River, NJ: Prentice Hall.

Cross, J. R. (1995). Nursing process of the family client: Application of the Neuman's systems model. In P. J. Christensen & J. W. Kenny (Eds.), *Nursing process: Application of conceptual models* (4th ed., pp. 246-269). St. Louis, MO: Mosby.

Curran, D. (1985). *Stress and the healthy family.* Minneapolis, MN: Winston Press.

Davis, L. L. (1998). Telephone-based interventions with family caregivers: A feasibility study. *Journal of Family Nursing, 4,* 255-270.

Denham, S. (2003). Family health: A framework for nursing. Philadelphia: F. A. Davis.

Epstein, N., Baldwin, L., & Bishop, D. (1983). The McMaster family assessment device. *Journal of Marital and Family Therapy, 9,* 171-180.

Feeley, N., & Gottlieb, L. N. (2000). Nursing approaches for working with family strengths and resources. *Journal of Family Nursing, 6,* 9-24.

Feetham, S., & Humenick, S. S. (1982). The Feetham family functioning survey. In S. S. Humenick (Ed.), *Analysis of current assessment strategies in the health care of young children and childbearing families* (pp. 259-268). Norwalk, CT: Appleton-Century-Crofts.

Friedemann, M. L. (1989a). Closing the gap between grand theory and mental health practice with families: Part 1: The framework of systemic organization for nursing of families and family members. *Archives of Psychiatric Nursing, 3,* 10-19.

Friedemann, M. L. (1989b). Closing the gap between grand theory and mental health practice with families: Part 2: The Control-Congruence Model for mental health nursing of families. *Archives of Psychiatric Nursing, 3,* 20-28.

Friedemann, M. L. (1991). An instrument to evaluate effectiveness in family functioning. *Western Journal of Nursing Research, 13,* 220-241.

Friedemann, M. L. (1995). *The framework of systemic organization: A conceptual approach to families and nursing.* Thousand Oaks, CA: Sage.

Friedman, M. M. (1998). *Family nursing: Research, theory and practice* (4th ed.). Norwalk, CT: Appleton & Lange.

Friedman, M. M., Bowden, V. R., & Jones, E. G. (2003). *Family nursing: Research, theory, and practice* (5th ed.). Upper Saddle River, NJ: Prentice Hall.

Gilliss, C. L., Highley, B. L., Roberts, B. M., Martinson, I. M. (1989). What is family nursing? In C. L. Gilliss, B. L. Highley, B. M. Roberts, & I. M. Martinson (Eds.), *Toward a science of family nursing* (pp. 64-73). Menlo Park, CA: Addison-Wesley.

Gray, V. R. (1996). Family self-care. In P. J. Bomar (Ed.). *Nurses and family health promotion: Concepts, assessment and interventions* (2nd ed., pp. 83-93). Philadelphia: W. B. Saunders.

Hanson, S. M. H. (2001). Family assessment and intervention. In S. M. H. Hanson (Ed.), *Family health care nursing: Theory, practice, and research* (2nd ed., pp. 171-195). Philadelphia: F. A. Davis.

Hanson, S. M. H., & Mischke, K. M. (1996) Family health assessment and intervention. In P. J. Bomar (Ed.), *Nurses and family health promotion: Concepts, assessment and interventions* (2nd ed. pp. 165-202). Philadelphia: W. B. Saunders

King, I. M. (1983). King's theory of nursing. In I. W. Clements & F. B. Roberts (Eds.), *Family health: A theoretical approach to nursing care* (pp. 177-188). New York: Wiley.

Loveland-Cherry, C. (2000). Family health risks. In M. Stanhope & J. Lancaster (Eds.), *Community & public health nursing* (5th ed., pp. 506-525). St. Louis, MO: Mosby.

McCubbin, H., Olson, D., & Larsen, A. (1987). F-COPES family crisis oriented personal evaluation scales. In H. McCubbin & A. Thompson (Eds.), *Family assessment interventions for research and practice* (pp.195-207). Madison: University of Wisconsin-Madison.

McCubbin, H. I., & Thompson, A. I. (1987). *Family assessment inventories for research and practice.* Madison: University of Wisconsin.

McCubbin, H. I., Thompson, A. I., & McCubbin, M. A. (1996). *Family assessment resilience, coping and adaptation: Inventories for research and practice.* Madison: University of Wisconsin.

McGoldrick, M., Gerson, R., & Shellenberger, S. (1999). *Genograms: Assessment and intervention* (2nd ed.). New York: W. W. Norton.

Molter, N. C., & Leske, J. S. (1995). *Critical care family needs inventory.* Jane Leske, Associate Professor, School of Nursing, University of Wisconsin-Milwaukee, WI.

Moos, R. H., & Moos, B. S. (1976). A typology of family social environments. *Family Process, 15,* 357-371.

Mossing, J., & Westwood, A. (1996). *Family assessment in psychiatric nursing.* New Westminster, British Columbia, Canada: Douglas College.

Murray, R. B., Zentner, J. P., Brockhaus, J. P. D., Brockhaus, R., & Sullivan, E. (2001). In R. B. Murray, & J. P. Zentner

(Eds.), *Health promotion strategies through the life span* (7th ed., pp. 157-212). Upper Saddle River, NJ: Prentice Hall.

Neabel, B., Fothergill-Bourbonnais, F., & Dunning, J. (2000). Family assessment tools: A review of the literature from 1978-1997. *Heart and Lung, 29,* 196-209.

Neuman, B. (1983). Family intervention using the Betty Neuman health-care systems model. In I. W. Clements & F. B. Roberts (Eds.), *Family health: A theoretical approach to nursing care* (pp. 239-254). New York: Wiley.

Neuman, B. (1989). *The Neuman systems model* (2nd ed.) Norwalk, CT: Appleton & Lange.

Neuman, B. (2002). The Neuman systems model. In B. Neuman & J. Fawcett (Eds.), *The Neuman systems model* (4th ed., pp. 3-33). Upper Saddle River, NJ: Prentice Hall.

Olson, D., McCubbin, H. I., Barnes, H., Larsen, A., Muxen, M., & Wilson, D. (1982). *Family inventories.* St. Paul: University of Minnesota.

Olson, D. H., Portner, J., & Lavee, Y. (1985). *FACES III.* St. Paul, MN: Family Social Sciences, University of Minnesota.

Orem, D. E. (1983). The family coping with a medical illness. Analysis and application of Orem's theory. In I. W. Clements & F. B. Roberts (Eds.), *Family health: A theoretical approach to nursing care* (pp. 385-386). New York: Wiley.

Pender, N. J. (1987). *Health promotion in nursing practice* (2nd ed.). Norwalk, CT: Appleton & Lange.

Pender, N. J., Murdaugh, C. L., & Parsons, M. A. (2002). *Health promotion in nursing practice* (4th ed.). Upper Saddle River, NJ: Prentice Hall.

Permulter, B. F., Toutiatos, J., & Holden, G. W. (2001). *Handbook of family measurement techniques: Instruments and indexes* (Vol. 3). Thousand Oaks, CA: Sage.

Pless, I. B., & Satterwhite, B. (1973). A measure of family functioning and its application. *Social Science and Medicine, 7,* 613-621.

Rawlins, P., Rawlins, T., & Horner, M. (1990). Development of the family needs assessment tool. *Western Journal of Nursing Research, 12,* 201-214.

Reed, K. S. (1982). The Neuman Systems Model: A basis for family psychosocial assessment and intervention. In B. Neuman (Ed.), *The Neuman Systems Model: Application to nursing education and practice* (pp. 188-195). Norwalk, CT: Appleton-Century-Crofts.

Reed, K. S. (1993). Adapting the Neuman Systems Model for family nursing. *Nursing Science Quarterly, 6,* 93-97.

Robinson, C. A., & Wright, L. M. (1995). Family nursing interventions: What families say makes a difference. *Journal of Family Nursing, 1,* 327-345.

Rogers, M. E. (1983). Science of unitary human beings: A paradigm for nursing. In I. W. Clements & F. B. Roberts (Eds.), *Family health: a theoretical approach to nursing care* (pp. 219-228). New York: Wiley.

Roth, P. (1996). Family social support. In P. J. Bomar (Ed.), *Nurses and family health promotion: Concepts, assessment, and interventions* (2nd ed., pp. 107-120). Philadelphia: W. B. Saunders.

Roy, C. (1983). Roy adaptation model. In I. W. Clements & F. B. Roberts (Eds.), *Family health: A theoretical approach to nursing care* (pp. 255-278). New York: Wiley.

Rungreangkulkij, S., & Gilliss, C. L. (2000). Conceptual approaches to studying family caregiving for persons with severe mental illness. *Journal of Family Nursing, 6,* 341-366.

Shyu, Y. (2000). Development and testing of the Family Care-giving Factors Inventory (FCFI) for home health assessment in Taiwan. *Journal of Advanced Nursing, 32,* 226-234.

Smilkstein, G. (1978). The family APGAR: A proposal for a family function test and its use by physicians. *Journal of Family Practice, 6,* 1231-1239.

Speer, J. M., & Sachs, B. (1985). Selecting the appropriate family assessment tool. *Pediatric Nursing, 11,* 349-355.

Tarko, M. A., & Reed, K. (2002). Taxonomy of family nursing diagnosis based upon the Neuman systems model of nursing. Unpublished manuscript, New Westminster, British Columbia, Canada: Douglas College.

University of Iowa. (2002). *Nursing Outcomes Classification.* Retrieved July 29, 2002, from http://www.uniowa.edu/noc

Weeks, S. K. & O'Connor, P. C. (1997). The FAMTOOL family health assessment tool. *Rehabilitation Nursing, 22,* 188-191.

Wright, L. M., & Leahey, M. (1984). *Nurses and families: A guide to family assessment and intervention.* Philadelphia: F. A. Davis.

Wright, L. M., & Leahey, M. (2000). *Nurses and families: A guide to family assessment and intervention* (3rd ed.). Philadelphia: F. A. Davis.

Wright, L. M., & Levac, A. M. (1992). The non-existence of non-compliant families: The influences of Humberto Maturana. *Journal of Advanced Nursing, 17,* 913-917.

Part A: Biographical Data

General Information

Family Name _____ Date _____

Family Members Involved in the Assessment _____

_____

_____

Ethnic Background _____

Referral Source _____

Interviewer _____

Family members   Relationship in family   Age   Marital status   Education (highest)   Occupation

1. _____

2. _____

3. _____

4. _____

5. _____

Current Reason for Seeking Assistance or for Referral

_____

_____

_____

Attach a Genogram/Ecomap

Part B: Family Members Variable Data

In the following sections, pertinent individual family members' variable assessment data are documented. List each family member's initials with associated data.

Physiological Variable Database : Describe individual family member's physical state and functioning. Note levels of fitness, presence of disease, past/present levels of functioning, genetic factors affecting levels of functioning, presence of predisposing risk factors, lifestyle patterns, level of exposure to substance use/misuse, nutrition, metabolism, and flexibility.

_____

_____

_____

_____

Physiological variables—intrapersonal, interpersonal, and extrapersonal stressors include: _____

_____

_____

Adapted from Mossing, J., & Westwood, A. (1996). *Family assessment in psychiatric nursing.* New Westminster, British Columbia, Canada: Douglas College; and Neuman, B. (1983). Family intervention using the Betty Neuman health-care systems model. In I. W. Clements & F. B. Roberts (Eds.), *Family health: A theoretical approach to nursing care* (pp. 239-254). New York: Wiley.

Psychological Variable Database : Describe individual family member's mental and emotional health. This entails the overall level of functioning with regard to cognitive and affective features. Concepts include self-concept (self-ideal, self-esteem, identity, emotion, roles, sexuality), perceptions of others, adaptability, decision making, and coping.

_____

_____

_____

_____

Psychological variables—intrapersonal, interpersonal, and extrapersonal stressors include:_____

_____

_____

Sociocultural Variable Database: Describe individual family member's social and cultural conditions. Social subconcepts include fam member's ability to interact satisfactorily with people and the environment, ability to experience satisfying interpersonal relationships, the family member's social functioning level, interactional patterns, communication patterns, sibling relationships, role relationships, attachment patterns, ability to view himself or herself as part of the larger social community, and the degree of concern for others. Sociocultural subconcepts include job satisfaction, career advancement, fulfillment of goals related to the greater good, sharing of life experience with others, development of new problem-solving strategies, and broadening professional and personal opportunities.

_____

_____

_____

_____

Sociocultural variables—intrapersonal, interpersonal, and extrapersonal stressors include: _____

_____

_____

Developmental Variable Database: Describe individual family member's developmental life processes from birth to current day. Refer to theoretical developmental tasks and achievement. Address how the developmental stages and tasks support/complement individual and family development. Describe how the family maintains system balance and adapts to changes.

_____

_____

_____

_____

Developmental variables—intrapersonal, interpersonal, and extrapersonal stressors include:_____

_____

_____

Spiritual Variable Database: Describe individual family member's spiritual beliefs and influences. Spiritual influences are derived from individuals, families, and communities. Subconcepts include purpose and meaning, love and belonging, faith, hope, and forgiveness of self and others, belief in God or a higher power, creativity, interrelatedness to others, and nature and all its wonder.

_____

_____

_____

_____

Spiritual variables—intrapersonal, interpersonal, and extrapersonal stressors include: _____

_____

_____

Part C: The Whole Family System

Family Psychosocial Relationships: Based on analysis of the variable data and stressors, describe family behavior patterns: values and family interaction patterns, decision making, coping style, role relationships, communication styles, and interaction patterns, goals, boundaries, socialization processes, sharing, individuation, and differentiation. Comment on the degree to which family member needs are satisfied within the family system.

_____

_____

_____

_____

Family Psychosocial Relationships—intrafamily, interfamily, and extrafamily system stressors include: _____

_____

_____

Physical Status: Based on analysis of the variable data and stressors, describe the physical status of the family system. Focus on family system energy to follow through with family system needs and responsibilities that enable the family system to function at optimal system wellness. Describe the overall physical health status of the family unit, immediate and cumulative effects of individual member variance on the family system, and lifestyle patterns contributing to family system stability and wellness.

_____

_____

_____

_____

Physical Status—intrafamily, interfamily, and extrafamily system stressors include: _____

_____

_____

Developmental Characteristics: Based on analysis of the variable data and stressors, describe the developmental characteristics of the family system. Refer to family developmental theory (stages and tasks). Address what stage the family system is facing and how the family system is managing in relation to the stage and tasks associated with family development. Describe how the family maintains system balance and adapts to changes.

_____

_____

_____

_____

Physical Status—intrafamily, interfamily, and extrafamily system stressors include: _____

_____

_____

Spiritual Influences: Based on analysis of the variable data and stressors, describe the spiritual influences of the family system. Comment on family spiritual support, family beliefs, integrity, ethical principles, feelings of selflessness among members of the family system, ability to love and be loved, and the family's sense of purpose or drive in life.

_____

_____

_____

_____

Spiritual Influences—intrafamily, interfamily, and extrafamily system stressors include: _____

_____

_____

_____

Neuman Nursing Process Format

The database addresses identification and evaluation of potential and actual family system stressors that pose a threat to the stability of the family system. Assessment of the characteristics of the flexible and normal lines of defense, lines of resistance, degree of potential reaction, reaction, and potential for reconstitution after a reaction guides the nursing process format (Neuman, 2002; Reed, 1993).

Sample Family Nursing Diagnoses

•Altered family role enactment (specify the behavior) related to intrafamily, interfamily, extrafamily system stressors.

•Altered family communication patterns (specify between which members) related to intrafamily, interfamily, extrafamily system stressors.

Sample Nursing Goals

•The family will identify specific roles and responsibilities to be carried out equitably in managing childcare and household chores.

•The family will explore alternative communication patterns (open, honest, and direct) with each member.

Sample Nursing Outcomes

•Primary Intervention: Family will attend support group session on stress management in coping with changing roles and responsibilities with the birth of a new child.

•Secondary intervention: Family will role-play scenarios that generate conflict in the family system in the presence of the nurse, explore alternative communication patterns, and apply these new strategies with each other.

•Evaluation of outcome goals after intervention at 2-week intervals: Family will discuss the impact of attending the support group on stress management as related to changing roles and responsibilities in the home and effectiveness of newly learned communication strategies.

Family Health Protection

David R. Langford

The primary goal of health protection is the removal or avoidance of encumbrances throughout the lifecycle that may prevent the emergence of optimum health.

— Nola J. Pender

OBJECTIVES

On completion of this chapter, the reader will be able to do the following:

1. Differentiate between the concepts of health promotion and health protection.
2. Discuss the role of the family in the development and practice of health protective behaviors.
3. Identify threats to health for families as they pass through the family life cycle.
4. Assess the adequacy of health protective behaviors currently practiced by a family.
5. Identify nursing roles that facilitate family health protective behaviors.

The family is critical to development of the values and routines protecting the health of family members. Major threats to health no longer come from disease-producing bacterial or viral agents but rather from chronic conditions produced and fostered by lifestyle-related factors or environmental hazards. Health-related decisions regarding diet, location and quality of residence, health care use, and leisure time activities affect all family members. Health practices of children and adolescents are greatly influenced by the values and examples set by parents and others within the family. Behaviors adopted in childhood will influence health and health-promoting behaviors later in life. Behavior patterns such as overeating; lack of exercise; use of alcohol, tobacco, or drugs; and poor coping are often established in childhood and adolescence and carried into adulthood (Allen & Warner, 2002; Keltner, 1992; Pender, Murdaugh, & Parsons, 2002).

This chapter explores the family processes of protecting members from threats to their health. It describes health protective characteristics in families and identifies some common health threats and the role family nurses play in helping families to protect their health. One of the

This chapter is a revision of the chapter by Karen K. Szafran in the second edition of this book.

The author would also like to acknowledge the contributions of Karen Joyce, RN, and Richelle Kay, RN, in supporting the development of this chapter. Both are graduate students in the School of Nursing at the University of North Carolina at Charlotte.

functions of families is to ensure the health and safety of all family members and to establish these lifelong healthy lifestyle patterns. Specific behaviors that protect family members' health and reduce the threats of illness, disease, or accidents during each developmental stage of the family can be adopted. Nurses play a vital role in helping families to identify risk factors and make the lifestyle changes that will preserve their health. The role of the family nurse is to provide the education and support families need to identify and assess their health risks, to support families' incorporation of heath protective behaviors into their daily routines, and to advocate for adequate resources so that families can achieve their health protection goals.

Defining Family Health Protection

Pender, Murdaugh, and Parsons (2002) define health protection as "behavior motivated by a desire to actively avoid illness, detect it early, or maintain functioning within the constraints of illness" (p. 7). Therefore health protection is specific to actual or perceived health threats and seeks to avoid or minimize insults to health and well-being. Central to this definition of health protection are the family's perceptions of risk and risk factors. Risk factors generally fall into six categories: genetic, age, biological, personal heath habits, lifestyle, and environmental (Pender, Murdaugh, & Parsons, 2002). The quality of family dynamics is an additional risk factor of concern because of the effects that open communication, shared decision making, and family coping processes have on how families fulfill the health function (Friedman, Bowen, & Jones, 2003).

Harris and Guten (1979) introduce the term *health protective behavior* in an exploratory study in which they focused on a wide range of health behaviors that extend beyond those normally defined as preventive or protective by health care professionals. Health protective behaviors are defined as behaviors aimed at protecting, promoting, or maintaining health regardless of health status and whether the behaviors are effective. Harris and Guten conclude that virtually everyone performs at least some routine behaviors related to protecting or maintaining health. They identify five dimensions of health protective

behaviors that are very much a part of most families' daily lives: personal health practices, safety practices, preventive health care, environmental hazard avoidance, and harmful substance avoidance.

The framework of primary, secondary, and tertiary prevention may be useful in determining the appropriate goals and lifestyle changes needed according to the absence or presence of a specific disease. Health protection in families includes identification of risk factors and adoption of lifestyles aimed at promoting health (primary prevention), preventing the occurrence of disease by early screening and detection of disease and through risk reduction (secondary prevention), and preventing exacerbation and complications once the diagnosis of a chronic disease is made (tertiary prevention).

There is considerable disagreement in the meaning and use of the concept of *health protection* (Kulbok, Baldwin, Cox, & Duffy, 1997). In fact, Kulbok and colleagues suggest that health protection is conceptually part of health promotion. They explain that health promotion includes both general wellness-focused behaviors such as maintaining a healthy diet and regular exercise and specific avoidance behaviors such as not smoking or routinely wearing seatbelts. *Healthy People 2010,* an outline of U.S. national health priorities, has also made a fundamental shift from presentation of health protection as a focus for health care providers to a consumer-oriented perspective of 10 health determinants from which families can gain the knowledge, motivation, and opportunities they need to make informed decisions about their health (U.S. Department of Health and Human Services, n.d.). This change in emphasis is consistent with other attempts to locate health protection behaviors under a larger umbrella of health promotion.

The motivation behind health protective behaviors can be vague or confusing when those actions are not related to preventing a specific disease. Although some authors argue that the definitions of health protection and health promotion are conceptually distinct, they are by no means mutually exclusive. Pender, Murdaugh, and Parsons (2002) clearly differentiate health protection from health promotion. Health promotion focuses on well-being and actualizing human health potential, whereas health protection focuses on behaviors in response to perceptions of risk or threat. However, disease-preventive and health protection measures do also promote or maintain health and wellness. Health promotion, defined as health practices aimed at achieving wellness, is an integral part of disease detection and management (Kulbok & Baldwin, 1992). For example, avoiding excessive dietary sodium and maintaining recommended body weight are health-promoting behaviors for most young adults. However, for a young African American adult with a strong family history of hypertension, these behaviors also meet the goals of health protection. Thus many health-promoting behaviors meet functions of both prevention and protection.

Caution must be exercised in shifting the responsibility for family health protection entirely to a consumer-oriented perspective. It is overly simplistic to define family health protection as only self-care and expect families to identify their health risks and implement behaviors to eliminate or reduce threats. Although lifestyle is a major contributor to individual and family health, Liaschenko (2002) is critical of intertwining health protection and self-care. Thinking of health protection as only a self-care issue focuses too much attention on the individual, who often has little control over many social and environmental characteristics related to health status. Families often minimize the responsibility the health care system has for ensuring that basic health promotion is available to all families. Health care providers often have little knowledge about how families learn to identify their health risks. However, when families do not identify or adopt the recommended preventive behaviors, health care providers often have attitudes of contempt and blame families for not changing the unhealthy lifestyle behaviors.

Advances in understanding the genetic contribution to disease and disease risk have complicated family health protection and further confuse definitions of what constitutes health promotion and health protection. The presence of genetic or hereditary risk creates new opportunities for working with families in identifying family history, genetic markers, and the appropriate health protective behaviors. Genetic risk factors have generally been considered unchangeable; however, once families identify a genetic history or risk, they have an opportunity to modify health habits by changing their health-seeking behaviors and altering unhealthy environments in such a way as to potentially delay the onset of some diseases and identify the onset of others at the earliest detectable stage before symptoms appear.

How families interpret genetic risk is complex. The relationship of genetic risk and behavioral risk to specific diseases is often not linear and therefore difficult for many families to understand. For some, knowledge of a significant family history of cardiac disease has led them to smoke less (Hunt, Davison, Emslie, & Ford, 2000); but for others, the relationship of family history and prevention is less clear. Some families are able to see the importance of a family history of heart disease and diabetes but emphasize the importance of protective lifestyle behaviors for only some diseases such as heart disease and cancer (Ponder, Lee, Green, & Richards, 1996). Yet other families determine their risk based on the number and closeness of relatives affected by a disease and their own age in relation to the age of the family members at risk. Even when individuals acknowledge that heart disease runs in their family, perceptions of themselves as different in critical ways from their relatives diminish their perception of personal risk (Hunt, Emslie, & Watt, 2001). Differences in perceptions of risk lead to misunderstandings between families and their health care providers, which delay important screenings and lifestyle changes.

Health protection for aging families in which caregiving is needed is just emerging as an area of study. Messecar, Archbold, Stewart, and Kirschling (2002) examined the use of home modification strategies used by family caregivers of older adults. They found that a number of strategies were used not only to promote safety but also to allow increased efficiency in family caregiving, make the home environment more pleasant and meaningful, supplement the older family member's function and independence, and increase access to professional health care providers and necessary equipment. However, as more family members care for their ill and aging spouses or parents, health protection practices for the caregivers must be stressed.

It is not surprising that family caregivers practice significantly fewer health promotion behaviors than noncaregivers (Acton, 2002). Many family caregivers experience health-threatening conditions resulting from fatigue and increased stress.

Family Characteristics of Health Protection

Many of the same family functions appear to aid families in practicing and maintaining health promotion and health protection behaviors. Family health promotion is presented in detail in Chapter 3 and is only discussed here as it relates to family perceptions of risk and specific health threats. Family pride, family cohesion, mother's nontraditional gender role orientation, internal locus of control, network, and community support are predictive of one- and two-parent families' participation in general health promotion behaviors (Ford-Gilboe, 1997). Family functioning, family connectedness, parental expectations, and parental monitoring are related to fewer unhealthy behaviors and increased help seeking in adolescents (Fallon & Bowles, 2001; Mellin, Neumark-Sztainer, Story, Ireland, & Resnick, 2002).

Parental monitoring and disapproval appear to be effective in preventing high-risk behaviors among teens. DiClemente et al. (2001) found that adolescents who perceived less parental monitoring were more likely to have multiple sex partners, not use contraception, and test positive for sexually transmitted diseases. These same adolescents who had little parental monitoring were also more likely to have a history of alcohol and marijuana use and a history of arrest.

Mothers have emerged as central figures in health protection. They are responsible for addressing daily health-promoting activities, monitoring exposure to disease-causing agents or other health-threatening behaviors, and guiding individual health patterns (Denham, 1999; Denham, 2003). A healthy and open communication pattern is a particularly successfully health protection strategy used by families. Open communication, especially with mothers, is an important family strength responsible for reducing high-risk sexual and drug use behaviors among adolescents (Lehr, DiIorio, Dudley, & Lipana, 2000; McNeely et al., 2002). A mother's relationship with her teen, communication with the

parents of her teen's friends, and her strong disapproval of teen sex have greater significance for teen daughters than for teen sons in regard to delaying sexual intercourse (McNeely et al., 2002).

The presence of a social support network is beneficial, especially as family members age. Among persons in their fifties, married couples living together and married couples living with children report better health status than people living in other types of households (Hughes & Waite, 2002). Household structure has been found to be an important contributor to health for adults in late middle age. Adults living in households with certain structures experience demands that exceed their resources to cope with the stresses. The stress of living in a household in which demands exceed resources leads to poor health behaviors and less time for self-care.

Adults in later life need companionship and social interaction. The frequent company of other people and the companionship of a household pet can provide avenues for expression and add meaning and a sense of purpose to persons in later life (Murray & Huelskoetter, 1991). Older adults living together have a greater survival rate and retain their independence longer than those living alone. The study of families in later life and their health protection needs and practices requires more research. Some parents outlive their children, so to understand families in later life, nurses may be required to re-conceptualize the definition and boundaries of family.

Family routines and rituals also play an important role in family health protective behavior (Fiese, 2000). Families can create routines that support health-protecting or risk-reducing behaviors by linking them to existing family routines. Often, one family member, such as the mother, is responsible for overseeing and sustaining health and family routines. This family member is a key person with whom the family nurse can work to assess a family's health-related routines and to integrate health behaviors into ongoing family routines or create new family health routines. For example, routines can be created around regular well-child health and dental visits, use of sunscreen, or exercise as part of family recreation. In addition, unhealthy routines such as overeating, frequent snacking on high-fat and high-calorie foods, and drinking behaviors related to alcoholism should be changed and replaced with healthier routines. In an interesting study of families of alcoholics, routine practices such as family dinnertime were found to protect children from engaging in problematic drinking behavior (Bennett, Wolin, Reiss, & Teitelbaum, 1987). In families who eat together and celebrate other family rituals, such as birthdays and holidays, together, adolescents have fewer psychological complaints (Compan, Moreno, Ruiz, & Pascual, 2002). See Chapter 16 for more information about family routines.

Health protective behaviors are defensive actions initiated for the purpose of removing or avoiding actual or potential health problems. Unlike health promotion behaviors, they are focused on areas in which the family identifies the risk and are therefore unique to each family. Successful health protection in families is based on characteristics of the family that foster proactive identification of health risks and adoption of protective lifestyle changes and routines. Family nurses and other health care professionals play a vital role in helping individuals or families to identify potential health threats and in developing, in partnership with families, effective strategies for health protection.

Health Protection Throughout the Family Life Cycle

Family lifestyle is a major determinant of individual health. Accidents, heart disease, cancer, cerebrovascular disease, and lung disease are five of the leading causes of death in North America (National Center for Health Statistics, 2001; Health Canada, 2000). These leading causes of death are directly linked to habits or lifestyle factors related to diet, smoking, lack of exercise, alcohol abuse, stress and exposure to environmental hazards and are reflective of values and behaviors learned in the family. Changes in the leading causes of death for individuals as they age reflect the changes in families as they pass through developmental stages. Accidents are the leading cause of death for persons ages 1 to 34 years, and cancer is the leading cause of death for those ages 35 to 74 years. Table 12-1 identifies the five leading causes of death by age group. Much more disturbing is the prevalence of homicide and

suicide among children and young adults ages 10 to 34 years. For families with children, protection of members from accidental and intentional injuries is a primary concern.

Families with children or adolescents or families in which the adults are very young have additional health protection challenges. Three fourths of the deaths among persons ages 10 to 24 years are the result of only four causes: motor vehicle accidents, other accidental injuries, homicide, and suicide (Centers for Disease Control and Prevention, 2002, June 28). Findings from the 2001 national *Youth Risk Behavior Survey* (Centers for Disease Control and Prevention, 2002), which reveal some of the high-risk behaviors of high school students, include the following:

- Fourteen percent had rarely or never worn a seat belt.
- Thirty-one percent had ridden with a driver who had been drinking alcohol.
- Seventeen percent had carried a weapon.
- Forty-seven percent had drunk alcohol.
- Twenty-four percent had used marijuana.
- Two percent had injected an illegal drug.
- Twenty-nine percent had smoked cigarettes during the month preceding the survey.
- Nine percent had attempted suicide during the year preceding the survey.
- Forty-six percent had had sexual intercourse.
- Forty-two percent of those who were sexually active had not used a condom the last time they had sexual intercourse.
- Eleven percent were overweight.
- Sixty-eight percent did not attend daily physical education class.

For many teens and young adults, these behaviors will lead to unplanned pregnancy; early parenting; exposure to sexually transmitted diseases including HIV and human papillomavirus (HPV); addiction; impaired judgment while engaged in other activities; increased risk of illness such as heart or lung disease, cancer, and diabetes; and the potential for accidents and violence.

Chronic diseases such as heart disease, cancer, and diabetes are responsible for 7 of every 10 deaths in the United States (Centers for Disease Control and Prevention, 2002). In addition, disability resulting from chronic diseases affects 1 of every 10 Americans and has an impact on millions of families. These diseases account for 75% of the

---

TABLE 12-1   Five Leading Causes of Death by Age for All Races, Both Sexes

Age	Causes of Death	Age	Causes of Death
1-4 yr	Accidents	25-34 yr	Accidents
	Congenital abnormalities/malformations		Suicide
	Cancer		Assault/homicide
	Assault/homicide		Cancer
	Diseases of heart		Diseases of heart
5-9 yr	Accidents	35-44 yr	Cancer
	Cancer		Accidents
	Congenital abnormalities/malformations		Diseases of heart
	Assault/homicide		Suicide
	Diseases of heart		HIV
10-14 yr	Accidents	45-54 yr	Cancer
	Cancer		Diseases of heart
	Assault/homicide		Accidents
	Suicide		Chronic liver disease and cirrhosis
	Congenital abnormalities/malformations		Cerebrovascular disease
15-19 yrs	Accidents	55-64 yr	Cancer
	Assault/homicide		Diseases of heart
	Suicide		Chronic lower respiratory disease
	Cancer		Cerebrovascular disease
	Diseases of heart		Diabetes mellitus
20-24 yr	Accidents	65 yrs and over	Diseases of heart
	Assault/homicide		Cancer
	Suicide		Cerebrovascular disease
	Cancer		Chronic lower respiratory disease
	Diseases of heart		Influenza and pneumonia

From National Center for Health Statistics (2001). *Deaths: Leading causes for 1999.* Retrieved October 10, 2002, from http://www.cdc.gov/nchs/data/nvsr/nvsr49/nvsr49_11.pdf.

---

nation's total health care costs. Although chronic diseases are among the most prevalent and costly health problems, they are also among the most preventable.

The family plays a critical role in the development of health behavior. Parental influence begins at birth and is the single most important factor affecting the child's physical, emotional, and cognitive development (Keltner, 1992). Many health attitudes and practices are established in early childhood. Lifestyle decisions that are made in childhood or adolescence are often a product of socialization within the context of the family. Thus family values and practices largely determine the future health of individual family members. Lifestyle behaviors adopted by parents both influence the child and establish patterns of health behavior that the child will follow throughout the life span.

Health protective behaviors continue to be important in aging families as they practice behaviors aimed at maintaining their health and delaying or controlling chronic diseases such as arthritis, hypertension, heart disease, and arteriosclerosis. Even slight reductions in an older person's rate of decline can make a significant difference in the quality of life and the degree of independence associated with aging (Ruffing-Rahal, 1991).

The developmental stages in the family life cycle can be useful in understanding a family's health protection needs. For example, accidents are the leading cause of death of individuals in newly formed families and families with children who are active in establishing a career and family identity. Similarly, in families with teenagers, the struggle for independence from parents and feelings of alienation often lead adolescents to engage in high-risk behaviors such as experimentation with sexual activity or alcohol and drug use. Other risks cumulate over a life span and emerge as the family ages. Conditions such as hypertension, heart disease, diabetes, and cancer often show up later in the family life cycle but also reflect health habits and family health practices of the earlier stages of development.

Carter and McGoldrick's (1999) stages of the developing family are used in this chapter to illustrate the relationship of family developmental stages to health protection. The reader is referred to Carter and McGoldrick's text for descriptions of developmental stages for a variety of family types such as families of divorce, gay and lesbian families, and African American families. A family's ability to master the tasks appropriate to each stage of development determines how well that family is able to meet the unique growth and development needs of individual members.

Families have unique health protection needs during the different stages of the family life cycle. For example, risk taking and perceptions of invulnerability by teenagers create very different health protection challenges than those faced by the family with young children or the aging family. Table 12-2 provides an overview of the developmental stages and corresponding health threats to families throughout the family life cycle.

Three areas of family health protection are discussed in the following sections: (1) safety and family behaviors aimed at protecting family members from accidents, (2) domestic violence and its consequences for family health, and (3) risks and family behaviors related to smoking and tobacco use.

Safety and Family Health Protection

Safety may be the leading health protection issue in families. In this section protection of the family from unintentional and intentional injuries is examined. Accidental and intentional injuries are the leading causes of death and disability for young people ages 1 to 30 years (Centers for Disease Control and Prevention, 2001). Safety of family members deserves sustained assessment and intervention efforts by family nurses and other health care providers. Values and beliefs in the family about risk of injury influence individual and family protective strategies. As a result, accidental and intentional injuries differ by sex, ethnicity, and age (Centers for Disease Control and Prevention, n.d.). For example, most accidents in families with infants and toddlers occur at home. As infant and toddler motor skills develop so do mobility and curiosity, which lead to increased risks for burn injury, poisoning, and drowning. Half of the young children killed in automobile accidents were unrestrained. As children age and become more mobile, trauma resulting from falls; participation in sports; use of bicycles, skateboards, and roller blades; and motor vehicle accidents becomes more common. Deaths from suicide, homicide, automobile accidents, and drowning are greater for men than women. However, women are killed or injured in assaults by intimate partners and family members more often than men.

Accident prevention begins in the home. An important element in ensuring family safety is education regarding risk-taking behavior. Parents can promote safety by helping their children to identify and avoid potentially hazardous situations. Family beliefs about safety and active enforcement of protective behaviors such as always using seat belts and car seats for children, wearing bicycle helmets, and supervising and securing swimming pools and firearms are necessary to protect family members from injury.

Because of the vigilance required to prevent many of the accidents in families with children, promoting family safety should be a routine part of nursing care. Gielen et al. (2002) found that many low-income families do not have safety gates for stairs or working smoke detectors and do not store poisons safely. Families receiving safety counseling during well-child visits and

TABLE 12-2   Developmental Stages and Health Threats for Families across the Family Life Cycle

Family Development Stage	Developmental Changes Supporting Health Protection	Health Threats and Issues
Leaving home: single young adults	• Developing supportive intimate and peer relationships • Establishing self-identity in relation to family of origin and work	• Accidents and injury from driving, sports, or other risk behavior • Alcohol and drug experimentation or abuse • Tobacco use • Dating violence • Unplanned pregnancy or exposure to HIV/STD from sexual practices and experimentation
Joining families through marriage: the new couple	• Forming and adapting to marital relationship • Realigning relationships with extended family, friends, and spouse	• Accidents • Tobacco use • Family planning • Planned or unplanned pregnancy and prenatal care • Understanding genetic and family hereditary history • Domestic violence
Families with young children	• Adjusting to addition of new family members • Defining and sharing child rearing, financial, and household tasks • Realigning relationships with extended family, parenting, and grandparenting	• Accidents: burns, drowning, automobile • Immunizations and infectious diseases • Well-child care and screening • Tobacco and drug use • Healthy child-rearing practices • Satisfaction and cohesiveness of family • Communication in marital relationship and with children
Families with adolescents	• Redefining parent and child roles to permit increasing independence of adolescence • Refocusing on midlife marital and career goals • Beginning shift toward caring for older generation	• Accidents and injury from driving, sports, or other risk behavior • Alcohol and drug experimentation or abuse • Tobacco use • Unplanned pregnancy or exposure to HIV/STD from sexual practices and experimentation • Satisfaction and cohesiveness of family • Communication in marital relationship and with children
Launching children and moving on	• Renegotiating marital relationship • Developing adult relationship between grown children and their parents • Realigning relationships to include in-laws and grandchildren • Dealing with disability and deaths of parents and grandparents	• Care and assistance for aging parents • Emergence of chronic illness • Access to primary care for preventive health care

Continued

TABLE 12-2 Developmental Stages and Health Threats for Families across the Family Life Cycle—cont'd

Family Development Stage	Developmental Changes Supporting Health Protection	Health Threats and Issues
Families in later life	• Maintaining individual, couple, and family functioning in face of physiological decline • Supporting an increased role for middle generation • Making room for the wisdom and experience of older generation • Dealing with loss of spouse, siblings, and peers • Preparing for own death	• Declining health and chronic disease • Loss of independence and acceptance of caregiving • Access to health care for health maintenance and preventive care • Immunizations, especially against influenza and pneumococcal pneumonia • Death of spouse or adult children • Safety from falls and other accidents • Alcohol and drug abuse • Depression

Note: Family developmental stages are based on the work of Carter & McGoldrick (1999). *The expanded family life cycle: Individual, family, and social perspectives* (3rd ed.). Boston: Allyn and Bacon. Adapted with permission.

---

those who visited a resource center with low-cost safety supplies had higher rates of safety practices (Gielen et al., 2002).

Prevention of falls again emerges as an important safety concern and a major cause of morbidity and disability among the elderly. Falls are the leading cause of death related to injury in older adults (Centers for Disease Control and Prevention, n.d.). As the population ages and many aging parents are cared for by their adult children, who often have their own younger children living at home, the importance of preventing falls becomes more critical. Falls can be minimized by arranging rooms to provide unobstructed passageways, using night lights, and avoiding area rugs.

Protection from environmental hazards is also important in maintaining family health. For example, the link between exposure to direct sunlight and sunburn as a child and the incidence of skin cancer later in life is well documented. Sunbathing is a popular recreational activity for adolescents and young adults. A deep tan is valued as attractive and a sign of health and vitality. In fact, teens often use sunlamps to enhance and maintain a tan.

For younger children, adequate protection from the sun is dependent on parental beliefs and values. A survey of parents with children ages 1 to 16 years revealed that only 43% regularly used sun protection for their children (Johnson, Davy, Boyett, Weathers, & Roetzheim, 2001). Sunscreen creams and lotions were the most common form of sun protection used, with the goal of preventing sunburn. Many of the parents surveyed believed that sun exposure was healthy, that children looked healthier with a tan, and that long hours of sun exposure were okay if children wore sunscreen. Protective measures related to sun exposure include educating families about the risks of excessive sun exposure and tanning, the proper use of sun-blocking creams and lotions to prevent sunburn, and the signs and symptoms of early skin cancer.

Motor Vehicle Accidents

Motor vehicle accidents are responsible for the deaths of more children and young adults than any other single cause (Centers for Disease Control and Prevention, 2002). Use of safety belts reduces the number of deaths associated with motor vehicle accidents by 45% to 60%. Most states have mandated the use of safety seats for small children and passenger restraints for older

TABLE 12-3   Recommendations for Safely Restraining Children in Cars

Child Age Group	Position	Other
Infants (Birth to 1 yr and up to 20-22 lb)	Ride in back seat Position seat center of car Rear-facing position	Full-harness safety infant or rear-facing convertible seat
Toddlers (Older than 1 yr and >20-40 lb)	Ride in back seat Forward-facing position	Full-harness safety seat
Young and preschool (4-8 yr, >40 lb, unless taller than 4'9")	Ride in back seat Forward-facing position	Keep in full-harness safety seat as long as possible—at least to weight of 40 lb, then use a belt-positioning booster seat, which helps the adult lap and shoulder belt fit better (preferred for children between 40 and 80 lb)
School-age (≥80 lb)	Ride in back seat until age 12 yr Forward-facing booster seat or lap and shoulder belt	Adult lap and shoulder belts normally do not fit a child until he or she is about 4'9" tall and weighs approx. 80 lb Make sure the lap belt fits low and tight across the lap/upper thigh area and the shoulder belt fits snug crossing the chest and shoulder to avoid abdominal injuries

Data based on National Highway and Traffic Safety Administration, Child Passenger Safety. (n.d.). *Proper child safety seat use chart*. Retrieved October 11, 2002, from http://www.nhtsa.dot.gov/people/injury/childps/

children and adults. However, only 6% of parents with small children have correctly installed car safety seats (Lane, Liu, & Newlin, 2000). Few parents have received hands-on instruction on properly installing a child safety seat. This hands-on instruction is credited with reducing the common errors parents make when installing child safety seats. In many communities, police and fire departments offer free programs to check car seats and teach parents how to properly install them. Parents are often confused about or unaware of the guidelines for restraining children in cars. Table 12-3 summarizes recommendations from the Highway Safety Administration.

Driving represents a major step toward independence and maturity for teens. However, parents cognizant of the inherent dangers of driving and risk taking common to adolescence may believe it is necessary to set limits and restrict an adolescent's driving. Age alone does not automatically determine readiness for such independence. Establishing ground rules such as the mandatory use of seat belts and absolute abstinence from drinking when driving should be conditions for use of the family car.

Sports Injuries

Sports activities have an important role in child and adolescent development. They provide exercise and valuable experience in competition and teamwork and help develop a positive self-image. In fact, young women active in sports have better self-esteem and are less sexually active than young women who are not participating in sports (Miller, Sabo, Farrell, Barnes, & Melnick, 1998). However, the rate of sports-related injuries is high among child and adolescent athletes.

Approximately 600,000 injuries related to high school football alone occur each year. Most prevalent are injuries to the head, spine, and extremities. Most sports-related injuries can be prevented by following reasonable safety precautions appropriate to the sport. Participants in potentially dangerous sports should wear proper safety equipment and receive adequate instruction (Mayhew, 1991). Sports-related physical examinations are recommended to ensure that each participant is physically capable of meeting the demands of the sport. A recent report from the Institute of Medicine (2002) recommends that parents and families take a more active role in protecting players from injury. In particular, the report focuses on soccer and on better assessment for concussion in children who have been hit on the head.

Firearms

In one million homes where nearly three million children live, firearms are stored in such a way that they are accessible to children (Schuster, Franke, Bastian, Sor, & Halfon, 2000). Many parents store firearms that are loaded and unlocked in their homes, and they overestimate their children's ability to tell the difference between real and toy guns (Farah, Simon, & Kellermann, 1999). Children often find these firearms and take them to school where they are used to threaten other children, play with friends, or attempt suicide.

A study by Jackman, Farah, Kellerman, and Simon (2001), describing how 8- to 12-year-old boys respond when they find a handgun, produced shocking results. The boys in the study were observed while playing in a room where a handgun had been hidden. While playing, the boys found the gun and handled it. Nearly half of the boys who found the handgun were unsure whether it was a toy or real gun. Most disturbing was the finding that 48% of the boys who discovered the real handgun pulled the trigger. Parental estimates of a child's interest in firearms did not predict whether a child would handle the gun. Boys believed to have a low interest in firearms were as likely to handle the gun or pull the trigger as boys believed to have high or moderate interest in firearms. As a routine part of family health assessment, nurses must ask families about the presence of firearms in the home and storage practices.

For nurses concerned with family safety, assessment is not enough. As demonstrated in the study by Jackman, Farah, Kellerman, and Simon (2001), most 8- to 12-year-old children are curious and unable to refrain from handling firearms that they find. Therefore family nurses must include education as part of well-child care and community outreach. Parents must be given detailed instructions about securely storing firearms, and nurses need to discuss with family members the risks associated with curious children and the presence of firearms in the home.

It is recommended that parents be taught to ask about the presence of guns in the homes where their children play, including relatives' homes (Ahmann, 2001). The ASK (Asking Saves Kids) campaign provides materials for parents and nurses on how to ask neighbors or relatives about firearms. Educational efforts must also be directed toward children. Children must be taught not to handle firearms without adult supervision and to tell adults if they find a firearm or know someone who has brought a gun to school. In a society in which toy guns are plentiful, look realistic, and are often given as gifts to children, it is not surprising that children are not intimidated by them and cannot distinguish real guns from toy guns. Efforts to promote gun safety in families will be very challenging. More information on the ASK campaign is available on the PAX Real Solutions to Gun Violence website, which is listed in the Website Resources box at the end of the chapter.

Family nurses also need to be actively engaged in health policy discussions regarding firearms. Issues such as gun control and requiring firearm manufacturers to use technology to "personalize" or lock firearms so they cannot be discharged should be part of the professional dialogue about promoting and ensuring family safety. The Committee on Injury and Poison Prevention of the American Academy of Pediatrics (2000) makes the following recommendations:

- Firearm regulation and the banning of some firearms are the most effective way to protect against firearm-related injuries to children and adolescents.
- Firearms should be subject to the safety and design regulations of other consumer products.
- Quality violence-free programming should be developed, and the romanticization of guns in media and entertainment should be reduced.
- Injury prevention programs and strategies such as alternatives to violence programs, distribution of trigger locks and other safety devices, and educational programs for children and adolescents should be evaluated.
- Health care providers should receive further education on how to reduce the mortality and morbidity associated with firearm use.

Fear of Violence

Although not traditionally thought of as areas of health protection, safety and the fear of violence and crime are significant concerns for families. Overcrowding and poor-quality housing have a direct relationship to family health status (Bashir, 2002). Overcrowding discourages the interaction among family members that is important for maintaining family health. Overcrowding, unsafe homes, and unsafe communities lead many family members to isolate themselves, stay indoors, increase snacking, spend more time watching television, and reduce their physical activity. These are also often the same families that have difficulties accessing health care because of lack of or inadequate insurance and fear of leaving home. However, children's perceptions of neighborhood hazards do not necessarily lead to reduced levels of physical activity as might be expected (Romero, et al., 2001).

A mother's open communication with her children appears to be a protective strategy. In a study of multiracial fifth and sixth graders from low-income neighborhoods, children who talked to their mothers about neighborhood violence experienced less stress and fewer internalized symptoms (Ceballo, Dahl, Aretakis, & Ramirez, 2001).

Family protection strategies may be different according to neighborhood characteristics. Protective behaviors such as strict parenting or staying at home, often seen in low-income neighborhoods, may be mistakenly credited to race or cultural background when, in fact, differences in parenting may actually reflect differences in neighborhood characteristics (Pinderhughes, Nix, Foster, & Jones, 2001). Family nurses must better assess homes and the conditions in which families live to work with the families toward health-protecting strategies.

School shootings, a number of high-profile child abduction cases, and the terrorist attacks of September 2001 have left families and communities of all socioeconomic groups more concerned with physical safety. Although there is a relatively small risk of experiencing these events, given the much higher risks of death or injury resulting from automobile accidents, drowning, and other accidents, many families and communities have been moved to change how they address safety.

For example, many states such as California, Texas, Maryland, and Virginia are reversing or reconsidering long-standing bans on students having cell phones at school. Likewise, parents are increasingly vigilant of their children and their surroundings while teaching children how to avoid potentially dangerous interactions with strangers.

Health Protection and Domestic Violence

Approximately 20% to 25% of women seeking care from primary health care providers are being battered by an intimate partner (Naumann, Langford, Torres, Campbell, & Glass, 1999). Abuse of female partners has far-reaching and serious health consequences for women. Besides the obvious trauma, battered women have higher rates of substance abuse, suicide, depression, and poor pregnancy outcomes. The rates of headache, back pain, vaginal and urinary tract infections, digestive problems, and pelvic and abdominal pain are 60% higher in battered women than in nonabused women (Campbell et al., 2002).

Domestic violence consists of behaviors that include repeated physical, sexual, and emotional abuse used to control an individual. Use of physical violence is the extreme manifestation of one partner controlling the relationship and is usually accompanied by other controlling behaviors such as threats and intimidation, humiliation, social isolation, and limiting economic resources. Many subtle behaviors, once identified, can serve as warning signs of the potential for abuse. Box 12-1 identifies common early warning signs of power and control imbalances in a relationship. Teaching young men and women to identify the early warning signs of control and abuse holds promise for reducing the incidence of domestic violence. In particular, young men can be targeted for interventions teaching equal and healthy adult relationships.

Violent homes are characterized by sustained, high levels of tension and fear as a result of sporadic and unpredictable violence. The environment in the home created by the use of violence and threats of violence has been described as "social chaos," in which rules governing behavior are constantly changing and being redefined

BOX 12-1   Recognizing the Warning Signs of Abuse

Does your partner or date:

- Put you down in front of other people (belittle, ignore, minimize your ideas, or berate you for not wanting to get high, have sex, or comply with other requirements)?
- Act jealous and possessive toward you?
- Talk negatively about sisters or women in general?
- Have a history of bad relationships, quick temper, and violence toward others?
- Try to control your life and relationship (tells you who you may be friends with, how you should dress, or will not accept your opinion or beliefs)?
- Become easily frustrated and angry?
- Go through extreme highs and lows (for example, is kind one minute and cruel the next)? (Does your partner scare you, or are you afraid of how your partner will react to things you do or say?)
- Blame you for his problems, including those he brought on himself?
- Pressure you into doing things you do not want to do, such as having sex or breaking the law?
- Act in an intimidating way toward you (e.g., sits too close, speaks as if he knows you much better than he does, touches you when you tell him not to)?
- Constantly page, call, or use friends to keep track of you?
- View you as unequal—because of being older, male, or seeing himself as smarter or socially superior?
- Threaten to hurt or kill himself if you leave or break up?

(Langford, 1998). This leaves family members uncertain about how to respond to the changing demands and threats of the person using violence. In addition, many children and adolescents growing up in this environment come to view the chaos and unpredictability as normal.

Exposure of children to violence at home is hypothesized as one of the risk factors for the use of violence in adult relationships. Children are profoundly affected by witnessing abuse and those who do so exhibit a variety of emotional, behavioral, and developmental problems (Martin, 2002). The Research Synopsis presents a study about parental violence and dating violence among adolescent boys.

Family members are not always a good source of support for battered women. Many women have talked to parents about the abuse and receive little support (Rose, Campbell, & Kub, 2000). For many women, friends provide the best source of support. Jealousy, control, and threats of further violence create conditions that make women cautious about disclosing the abuse or forming new relationships. Positive social support can lead women to actively seek help from formal organizations.

Humphreys (2001a) describes stages that daughters of battered women go through as they pass through their own developmental stages. Early childhood vigilance, worry, and fear change to anger and rebellious acting out as they become teenagers. For young women exposed to violence at home, protective behaviors include being involved in school-based activities and spending time with close friends. Although they do not disclose the violence at home, they use these activities to escape their troubled families. Individuals outside the immediate family such as school counselors provide additional support. The adult daughters of battered women identify intelligence, attractiveness, optimism, a belief in self, avoidance of feelings of responsibility for the violence, perseverance, and keeping the violence secret as characteristics that served as protective factors in surviving (Humphreys, 2001b). Adult daughters credit mothers and grandmothers for reinforcing and sustaining their belief in self. These personal characteristics plus the support from friends and school counselors, as well as opportunities to be involved in activities that took them away from home, provided protective mechanisms for women and allowed them to understand and move beyond the violence they had experienced.

Nurses' skill in assessing and talking to women about the experience of violence in their homes is a first step toward protection. Nurses and other health care providers are being urged to universally screen all women for domestic violence. Screening for domestic violence allows nurses

RESEARCH SYNOPSIS

PARENTING BEHAVIORS AND DATING VIOLENCE BY TEEN BOYS

Efforts to understand and prevent violence in dating and intimate relationships have begun focusing on the effects of witnessing violence at home. Children who witness or experience abuse at home are thought to be more likely to use similar violence in their intimate adult relationships. A longitudinal study by Lavoie and colleagues examines the link between parenting behaviors in late childhood and use of violence by adolescent boys in their dating relationships.

Lavoie and colleagues collected data over 8 years. Participants were 717 boys from low socioeconomic backgrounds who were enrolled at age 10. A questionnaire was used to collect data. Boys were asked about their mothers' and fathers' parenting practices, witnessing parental conflict and violence, and harsh parental punishments at ages 10, 11, and 12 years. At age 15 years, the questions focused on delinquency behaviors. At ages 16 and 17 years, the questionnaire asked about dating and dating violence.

Boys living in homes where parents used hitting, insulting, constant quarreling, and rejection were abusive to their dating partners at ages 16 and 17 years. Delinquency at age 15 and lax parental monitoring were also risk factors in boys using violence against their dates. Conflict between parents, family adversity, single parenting, and parental age at birth of child were not associated with dating violence.

Nursing care of families with children should include healthy parenting as part of routine well-child care. Alternatives to harsh or abusive discipline and strategies for monitoring children's and teens' activities while allowing them age-appropriate independence are areas in which nurses could assist many family health protection efforts.

Lavoie, F., Herbert, M., Tremblay, R., Vitaro, F. Vezina, L., & McDuff, P. (2002). History of family dysfunction and perpetration of dating violence by adolescent boys: A longitudinal study. *Journal of Adolescent Health, 30,* 375-383.

to better assess the causes of women's health problems and gives nurses the opportunity to talk to women about the violence. Effective screening identifies survivors so nurses can assist women in assessing their level of danger, identifying resources, and outlining a feasible safety plan for the workplace, school, and home for them and their children. There are many resources to which women and health care providers can be referred for information.

The telephone numbers of local shelters for battered women are inside the front cover of each community's telephone directory so women and health care providers can have rapid access to those resources. The National Domestic Violence Hotline has information for victims of domestic violence, as well as for nurses and other heath care providers, through a toll-free telephone number (1-800-799-7233) and a website. Website URLs for this and other organizations serving domestic violence victims are presented in the Website Resources box at the end of the chapter.

Nearly half of the women in a study by Gielen et al. (2000) supported the idea that health care providers should routinely screen women for domestic violence. However, nearly half of the respondents preferred that women control the information and did not support laws requiring health care providers and others to report suspected abuse to the police. A woman and her family can be placed at greater risk of violence from an abuser when information is shared by health care providers without the woman's knowledge.

Many of the factors that are protective to families involve community-based interventions. Some of these include creating safe places such as shelters and improving how law enforcement and health care personnel identify and respond to domestic violence. Other strategies involve changing social and cultural norms supporting the use of violence and control in families.

Parenting beliefs and practices about disciplining children are such cultural norms. Many health care providers have begun discouraging parents' use of corporal punishment. Physical punishment such as spanking not only harms the mental and physical health of children but also initiates the use of violence in family relationships by becoming part of the family routines. The relationship of spanking or "hitting" children as a form of discipline and the use of physical violence in adult familial relationships has been questioned.

Spanking as a form of discipline is controversial. In a meta-analysis of 88 studies of corporal punishment published over the past 62 years, Gershoff (2002) found that although spanking is effective in achieving compliance, there is substantial evidence that it is associated with a higher prevalence of abuse and other negative long-term consequences on children's health. Children reared in homes where spanking is used as a form of discipline have more delinquent behavior, are more aggressive, have poorer mental health, and have poorer parent-child relationships. The author warns that there are a number of areas needing further study before the outcomes of corporal punishment are understood. First, there is no standard definition or standardized measure of corporal punishment. Second, the relationships between spanking and its effects are not linear. The effects of frequency and severity may be different for children of different ages, ethnicity, and socioeconomic status. There is some evidence that spanking used rarely in anger may be more detrimental for children than spanking used frequently for control.

Substance Abuse Protection

Alcohol and Drug Use

Alcohol and drug use has major implications for adolescent and family health. Approximately one in four children 18 years of age and younger are living in homes in which one or more of the adults abuse alcohol or are alcohol-dependent (Grant, 2000).

Patterns of adolescents' alcohol consumption have recently attracted the attention of health care providers and policy-makers. Four of five college students drink and half engage in heavy episodic drinking known as *binge drinking* (Task Force on

College Drinking, April 2002). Forty percent (2 of every 5 students) reported binge drinking in the 2 weeks preceding the survey. Adolescent drinking, particularly binge drinking, is related to numerous high-risk behaviors with both short-term and long-term health consequences (Maney, Higham-Gardill, & Mahoney, 2002). Underage alcohol use leads to such problems for teens as motor vehicle accidents, unplanned sexual activity, possible pregnancy, risk of HIV and other sexually transmitted diseases, physical and sexual violence, and increased conflict at home and with parents. The report by the Task Force on College Drinking (2002) includes recommendations to parents and families on evaluating the drinking culture of a college and staying engaged and monitoring students during their college experience.

Misuse of alcohol can have many other effects on family health. Alcohol ingestion during pregnancy has detrimental effects on the developing fetus such as congenital defects and on pregnancy outcomes such as low birth weight, premature delivery, and stillbirth. Heavy use of alcohol during pregnancy can result in the characteristic set of abnormalities of fetal alcohol syndrome. Assessment of alcohol misuse and dependence should be part of the standard family assessment, and family patterns and history of alcohol abuse can easily be demonstrated in a genogram.

Family history of problem drinking was identified as a predictor of alcohol abuse for men (Committee on Substance Abuse, 2001). Home is the leading source of alcohol access for adolescents; older siblings often introduce or influence younger siblings' use of alcohol. However, excessive drinking is more likely to occur with peers than with family members.

Some family factors are effective in preventing alcohol and drug abuse in children and teens. Family cohesiveness, support, clear rules for expected behavior, and high levels of parental monitoring have the effect of mediating risk factors and positively influencing teens' alcohol use behaviors (Loveland-Cherry, 2000). Genetic risk of alcoholism or drug abuse can be moderated by family and home environmental controls such as limiting access and use. One of the greatest risk factors is peer relationships. Loveland-Cherry (2000) hypothesizes that peer selection is often based on salient family values and beliefs and that parental involvement in peer selection is protective.

Families need to recognize the early warning signs of drug abuse in children and adolescents. Parents can play a vital role in protection behaviors related to discouraging alcohol use, limiting access at home, and monitoring peer relationships. However, changes in behavior such as gradual and unexplained deterioration in scholastic performance, increasing difficulties with parents or peers, increased frequency of accidents, and unexplained absences from school can be early warning signs that a family member is having problems with drugs or alcohol. Strategies for prevention of alcohol abuse in families should emphasize the proper use of alcohol in family and community life. Limited alcohol use is a part of many important culturally based family traditions and ceremonies.

Smoking

Cigarette smoking is recognized as the single most preventable cause of death in the United States. Smoking during pregnancy is related to risks of low birth weight and sudden infant death syndrome. Infants exposed to maternal smoking have increased morbidity associated with conditions such as sudden infant death syndrome, colic, lower respiratory tract infections, and gastrointestinal reflux (Gaffney, 2001).

Cigarette smoking among adolescents is an even more significant health problem. Most smokers begin smoking in their teen years. The average age smokers first try a cigarette is 14.5 years; the average age at which an individual becomes a daily smoker is 17.7 years (Elders, Perry, Eriksen, & Giorano, 1994). The younger an individual is when he or she begins smoking, the greater is the risk for lung cancer, heart disease, stroke, emphysema, and bronchitis. Twenty-nine percent of high school students currently smoke cigarettes (Centers for Disease Control and Prevention, May 2002). Although this figure is down from 36% in 1997 and 35% in 1999, it is still higher than the 22% of adults who smoke. White and Hispanic students are significantly more likely to smoke than African American students. Also of concern is the recent upsurge in the use of smokeless tobacco, particularly among male adolescents and young adults.

Family environment can have a significant effect on the smoking behavior of children. Only 4% of teenagers from households of nonsmokers will acquire the habit (Winkelstein, 1992). When both parents smoke, there is a greater likelihood that a child will smoke than if only one or neither parent smokes. When an older sibling plus both parents smoke, a child is four times more likely to smoke than if the family includes no smokers. Some research suggests that parental disapproval of smoking reduces teens' smoking behavior even when parents themselves are smokers (Sargent & Dalton, 2001). Messages from family members discouraging adolescents from smoking affect teens differently based on ethnicity (Kegler et al., 2002). Teens who are African American, Asian American, or Pacific Islander American are more concerned that their parents will think less of them if they smoke than are white and Hispanic teens. It is more common for white teens and teens of American Indian descent to feel that their parents believe it is the teen's decision to smoke or not. Kegler and colleagues (2002) conclude that teens receive a variety of "mixed signals" from their families regarding smoking. Nurses working with families need to help parents and other family members reduce the mixed signals they send about smoking during the sensitive developmental stages.

Strategies to prevent smoking must include those focusing on the individual, family, community, and policy arenas. Prevention can start with teaching parents how to clearly communicate to their children that they disapprove of and discourage smoking. Nurses can educate family members about the risks of smoking during routine preventive care visits for children or teens. Promising family-focused interventions might include addressing the extended family's direct and indirect influence on teen smoking, as well as establishing household smoking restrictions, better monitoring of household access to and availability of tobacco supplies, and setting clear expectations about not smoking (Kegler et al., 2002). The nurse can initiate a number of individual smoking cessation therapies for family members who want to quit smoking. Likewise, family nurses need to be involved in community-based education and prevention efforts. Lantz et al. (2000) conducted a comprehensive review of the published literature addressing interventions to reduce teen smoking. They classified tobacco prevention programs as school-based efforts, community-based efforts, public education, advertising restrictions, regulation of youth access, and taxing tobacco. They conclude that although the results have been mixed, efforts must continue and the availability of tobacco settlement money can provide opportunities for innovation and testing of new interventions. Family nurses advocating family heath protection must put pressure on state legislators to fund and support tobacco prevention programs.

Families' Use of Complementary and Alternative Therapies

Families from the many cultural traditions represented in the United States often have culturally oriented practices of health protection based on different understandings of health. Spector (2000) describes three of the most common traditional health protection practices. The first practice consists of wearing, carrying, or hanging in their homes objects believed to have protective value. The second consists of use or ingestion of substances believed to offer health protection. Diet is used by many cultures to protect health; for example, kosher diets are followed by some Jewish persons, the Chinese have dietary customs that balance Yin (positive energy of light and warmth) and Yang (negative energy of dark and cold), and some Hispanic persons believe in a balance of "hot" and "cold" foods. These foods are often eaten in prescribed quantities, at defined times, and in combination with other foods. The third practice consists of religious rites such as prayer, burning candles, and other rituals.

As health care has become increasingly complex, a growing suspicion of pharmaceutical companies and dissatisfaction with approved Western medical treatment outcomes have left many families looking for natural alternatives. It is estimated that 40% of Americans now use some form of alternative therapy, with herbal preparations being most commonly used by families with children (Vessey & Rechkemoner, 2001). These alternatives to traditional Western medicine are known as complementary and alternative medicines (CAMs).

The National Center for Complementary and Alternative Medicine (NCCAM) is one of the newer research centers in the National Institutes of Health and reflects the increasing interest and acceptance of CAMs. The NCCAM (2002) defines complementary and alternative therapies by use and not by treatment. Complementary therapies are defined as those used together with conventional medical practices, whereas alternative therapies are defined as those used in place of conventional medical practices. The NCCAM divides the therapies into five types as follows:

1) Alternative medical systems therapies, which include homeopathy, naturopathy, and traditional Chinese therapies such as acupuncture
2) Mind-body therapies, which include support groups; prayer; meditation; and art, dance, and music therapy
3) Biology-based therapies, which include the use of herbs, foods, vitamins, and dietary supplements
4) Manipulative and body-based therapies, which include massage, chiropractic, and osteopathic manipulation
5) Energy-based therapies, which include therapeutic touch and the unconventional use of bio-magnetic fields

Many of the complementary or alternative therapies have a rich tradition, but until recently, they have been the subject of little formal study. Mantle (2002) has reviewed the research on CAMs for obesity, addiction, anxiety, and depression and concludes that limitations in research design and methodology make it very difficult to interpret the efficacy of CAMs used for health promotion. Nurses working with families using CAMs or nurses recommending any of the therapies need to be knowledgeable about those therapies.

It is important for nurses to be aware that many families are routinely using CAMs. Nonjudgmental questions about a family's use of folk remedies or other CAMs are an important part of assessment. Educating families about the uses of CAMs, and particularly about drug interactions and side effects, is the next step in working with families using CAMs. Families need to be encouraged to discuss with their primary care providers their use of CAMs and any implications it might have for ongoing treatments for hypertension and other chronic health conditions (Kaler & Ravella, 2002). Often, families are hesitant to discuss unconventional therapies with their health care providers because they fear their health care providers will be judgmental or disapprove. Excellent information about current clinical trials and the latest alerts and advisories regarding drug interactions and harmful side effects are available at the NCCAN website, which is provided in the Website Resources box.

Accessing Family Health Protection Information on the Internet

The emergence of the Internet as a primary source of health information for families has changed their access to health-related information. Families are now more knowledgeable than ever before about health issues. They use the Internet to research prescription medicines, explore ways of preventing heart disease or cancer, learn the latest on losing weight, and prepare for visits to their health care providers. As many as 73 million people in the United States (62% of Internet users) have gone online to find health information; more people get health advice online than actually visit health care providers in a given day (PEW Internet Project, 2002). Women and Internet users between the ages of 50 and 64 years comprise the greatest number of persons using the Internet to gather health information.

Greater access to health information is a dramatic advantage for families struggling to introduce health protection activities, but it creates new challenges for nurses in their relationships with families. The Internet allows families to educate themselves, supplement or question their existing heath care, explore alternatives, and participate in support groups or chat with others having similar health concerns; and the relative anonymity provided by the Internet allows family members to explore sensitive questions and topics (Borzekowski & Rickett, 2001). The Internet can be a powerful tool in educating families and assisting them in identifying risk and adopting new health protective behaviors. The Internet has radically altered the relationship of nurses with families. Nurses must learn to interact with families who have a lot of information but do not necessarily know how to organize it. The Internet

has changed families' access to health information in the following ways (Smith, 1999):

1) By shifting the control of information from the health care provider to the consumer
2) By creating a learning environment on the Web where persons get information from multiple sources without any order or sequencing
3) By reinforcing expectations that information is always available and current and that it defies geographical boundaries
4) By producing information overload that often leads to confusion and paralysis
5) By creating new communication communities that include both other professionals and lay persons

The interactive capability of the Internet empowers families and is convenient for families interested in exploring existing digital libraries, asking questions of experts, or communicating with others in a chat, e-mail, or discussion forum (D'Alessandro & Dosa, 2001). In one study 49% of teens reported using the Internet to retrieve health information and scored the value of the information available there as high (Borzekowski & Rickett, 2001).

There are still many who do not have access to the Internet. Because of the so-called digital divide, Internet access is unevenly distributed among families in the United States. Approximately 42% of American households have access to the Internet, and two thirds of the families with Internet access live in households with incomes of $50,000 a year or greater (U.S. Department of Commerce, 2000). The number of families with access to the Internet is slightly lower (39%) in rural areas. African American and Hispanic families and the disabled lag behind: only 24% and 22%, respectively, have household access to the Internet. Two-parent homes are twice as likely to have Internet access as single-parent homes. Only one quarter of the Internet users report following recommended steps for assessing the accuracy, source, and timeliness of the health websites they find (PEW Internet Project, 2002).

The material available is not always accurate, helpful, or easy to understand. The text of most health-related websites exceeds a high school reading level, and nearly half of all Americans read at an eighth grade level or below (D'Alessandro,

Kingsley, & Johnson-West, 2001). Berland and colleagues (2001) also found the text of English- and Spanish-language websites to require a high school reading level or greater.

The vast amount of information available on the Internet makes it difficult to find the information desired. Berland and colleagues (2001) searched the Internet for the topics of depression, obesity, childhood asthma, and breast cancer. They found that users of English-language search engines have only a 1 in 5 chance of finding relevant information on the first page of the search result. For Spanish-language searches, the chance of finding the information requested on the first page of search results was 1 in 9. Fewer than half of the health-related websites were accurate or provided more than minimal coverage on the topic. Much of the information retrieved was superficial, wrong, or outdated.

As a result of the explosion of health information available on the Internet and the increasing use of the Internet as a source of health information, many families need to develop skill in determining the quality of the information they access on the Internet. An emerging role for family nurses is to assist families in organizing the information available, sorting out bias, and evaluating the validity of the information they have found. Assessing the quality of Internet-based information is particularly important as families investigate experimental, complementary, or alternative ways of protecting their health. The NCCAM and the National Cancer Institute have criteria for evaluating health information on the Internet. See the Website Resources box for their website URLs. Box 12-2 outlines criteria for evaluating the validity of websites and information.

There is a dark side for families using the Internet. Nineteen percent of teens who regularly use the Internet received unwanted sexual solicitation in the year preceding a survey by Mitchell, Finkelhor, and Wolak (2001). Sexual solicitation over the Internet was very upsetting for those solicited, especially the younger users. Parental supervision such as limiting the hours spent online, requiring permission before going online, checking teens' computer use while online, and using filtering software appeared to have little effect on solicitation risk. In a survey of adoles-

---

BOX 12-2 Questions to Ask When Evaluating Internet Health Information

Sponsorship and Bias
- Can you tell who operates and sponsors the content or site? Often, the extension of the website URL gives institutional information, for example, "gov" (government), "edu" (educational), "com" (company), "org" (nonprofit organization), and "net" (often personal or community websites). Look beyond the extension. Is it a company promoting a product or an organization promoting a political viewpoint?
- What is the purpose of the site?
- Is there a clear disclaimer posted?
- Does the site provide contact information?

Accuracy
- Is there enough information to determine whether the author is reliable?
- Is the content current?
- Is the content accurate?
- Does the site provide evidence-based references for its content?
- Have the site and its contents been recently updated? Material within the website may be dated. Is there a date when the page was last updated at the bottom of the Web page?
- Is the content opinion or research, and are the sources clearly identified?

Other
- Is the intended audience made clear? Many websites have areas for consumers and for professionals. Are they clearly identified?
- What are the other links? Are they advertising products?
- Do you have confidence that your privacy is protected?
- Does the site ask the user for personal information?

---

cent Internet users, Stahl and Fritz (2002) found that 74% reported contact with a stranger using e-mail or chat rooms and a quarter of those acknowledged sharing personal and identifying information such as a name, address, phone number, and school name. Many of the adolescents reported experiences of feeling unsafe while using the Internet. Only a quarter of the participants had ever discussed Internet safety with an adult or parent.

Role of the Family Health Nurse in Family Health Protection

The family health nurse plays a vital role in developing and fostering health protective behaviors within the family. A family-centered approach is particularly important for health protection because many of the diseases or health conditions to be prevented have a genetic basis or are related to lifestyle. It is vital that the entire family address its potential risks and work together to implement protective behaviors (Bigbee & Jansa, 1991). The family health nurse can assist family members in identifying actual or potential areas of health risk, establishing health goals based on the family's needs and interests, and developing an effective lifelong plan for health protection.

Family members often know little of their family health history (Ponder, Lee, Green, & Richards, 1996). Many stigmatized illnesses and behaviors such as alcoholism and mental illness are kept as family secrets, with only selected family members serving as gatekeepers for the family history. Use of genograms may help family members to identify areas of family health history they do not know and empower them to discover the answers (see Chapter 11).

Health Care Services

Access to health care services and supervision of a family's health care are essential for family health protection efforts. Family protection efforts hinge on early identification of risk so that appropriate prevention strategies can be implemented. Many families will place high priority on areas of health protection if the threat of illness is apparent and easily understood, and yet, families often do not assess risk in the same way as their health care providers do. A good example of this can be seen in a study of mothers assessing the health risk of their obese and overweight children not by the children's weight but by the children's level of activity (Jain et al., 2001). The health care provider's assessment of risk was considerably different because he or she focused more on weight and diet.

Pender, Murdaugh, and Parsons (2002) identify access to screening and risk identification through health education as key protective behaviors. In most cases, screening tests are not available to families except through access to health care providers. Periodic medical evaluations are an established form of preventive health care. Although some disagreement exists regarding the recommended frequency of routine examinations for healthy adults, it is generally acknowledged that regular examinations are needed as family members age. In families with young children, the routine medical examination provides health care providers with the opportunity to monitor infant nutrition and growth, to assess developmental progress, and to administer routine immunizations. It also affords an excellent opportunity to educate parents and other family members about normal development, safety, and risk reduction. As the family moves through the developmental stages, screenings for common health problems such as cervical, breast, prostate, and colorectal cancers and hypertension, diabetes, and glaucoma are recommended. Guidelines for preventive health care indicate that counseling regarding accident prevention, safe sex, and alcoholism and drug use are an integral part of routine preventive care and professional health supervision.

Screening guidelines have been developed by groups such as the U. S. Prevention Taskforce, the American Academy of Pediatrics, and the American Academy of Family Physicians to help family nurses and other health care providers systematically identify health risks in family members and aid families in identifying their health risks so that appropriate protective behaviors can be adopted. The Clinical Prevention Guidelines from the U.S. Preventive Services Task Force for children and adults are presented in Figures 12-1 and 12-2.

Not all families benefit from these prevention guidelines. Swanson and Pearson (2001) found that 40% of physicians are not screening family members for known cardiac risk factors. In addition, a number of the top-ranked prevention recommendations such as tobacco cessation, vision screening, colorectal cancer screening, screening for chlamydia infection in young women, alcohol abuse screening, and pneumococcal vaccinations for adults reach less than half the country (Coffield et al., 2001).

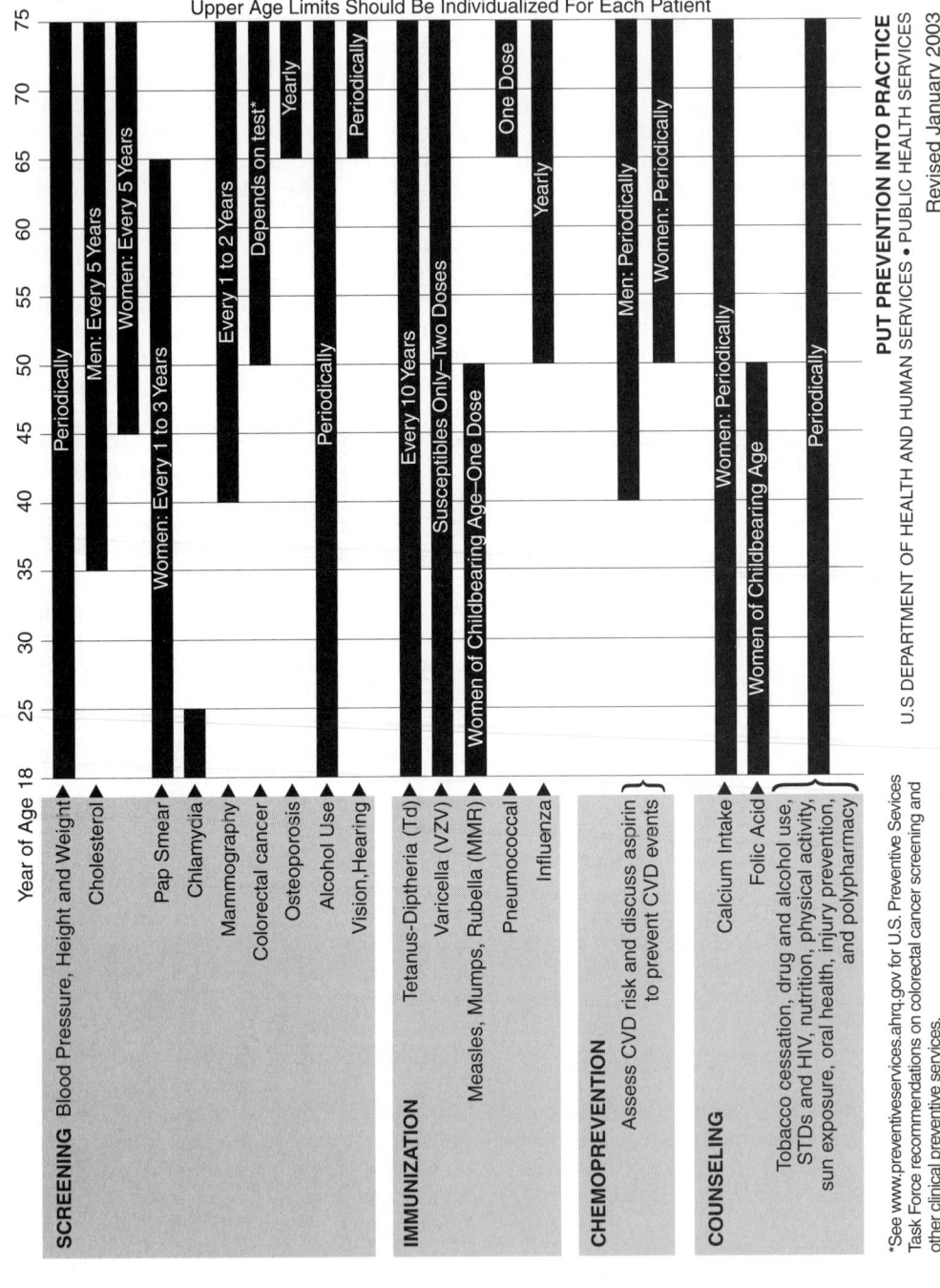

Figure 12-1 Clinical Preventive Services for Normal-Risk Adults Recommended by the U.S. Preventive Services Task Force. (*Put Prevention into Practice*, January 2003. Agency for Healthcare Research and Quality, Rockville, MD, http://www.ahcpr.gov/ppip/adulttm.pdf)

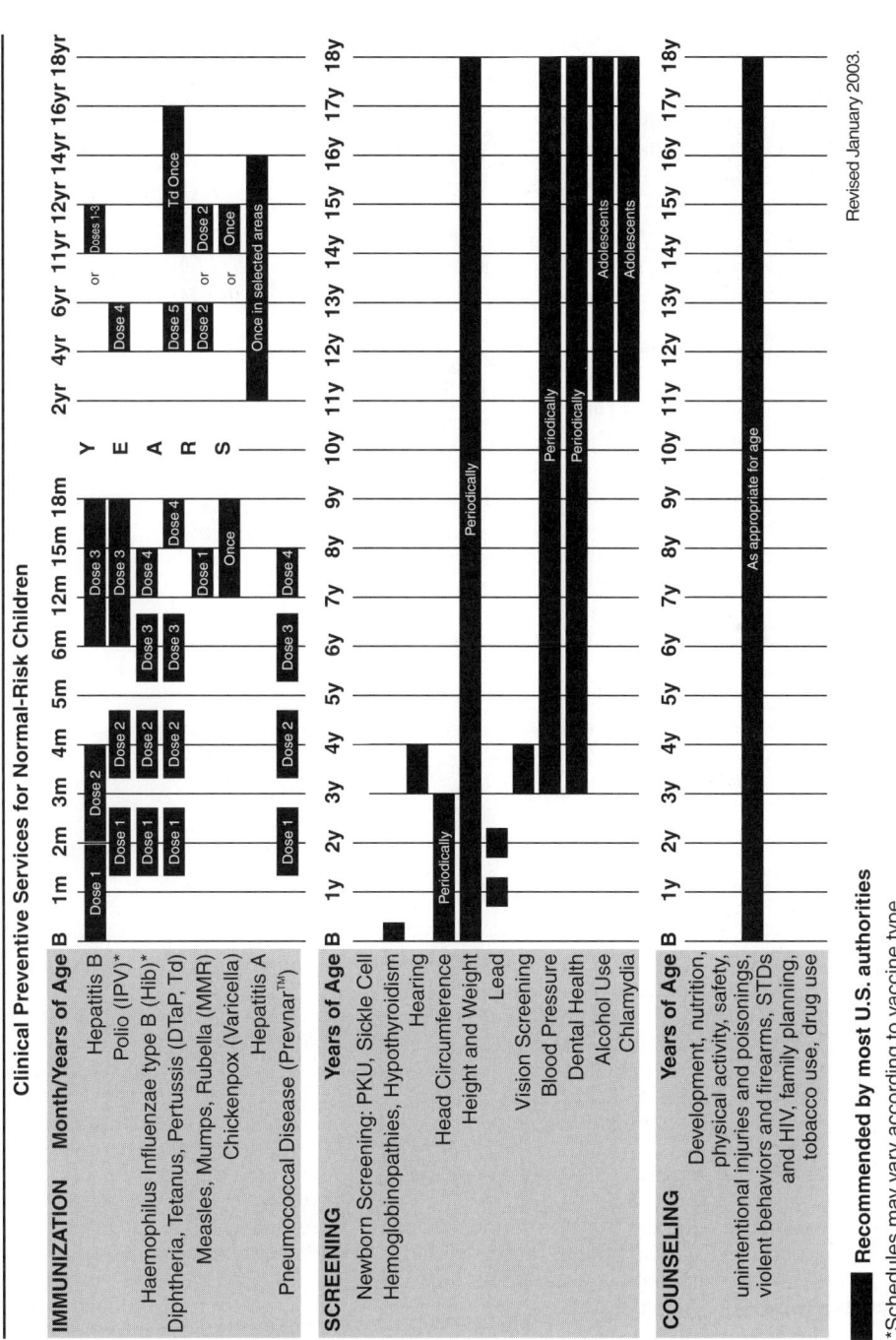

Figure 12-2 Child Preventive Services for Normal-Risk Children Recommended by the U.S. Preventive Services Task Force. (*Put Prevention into Practice*, January 2003. Agency for Healthcare Research and Quality, Rockville, MD, http://www.ahcpr.gov/ppip/childtm.pdf)

Barriers to access such as absence of insurance and lack of qualified health care providers in rural and other underserved areas are important health policy issues that should be addressed by family nurses. Millions of families in the United States have inadequate or no health insurance. Table 12-4 shows who is uninsured. For many families without health insurance, preventive care such as prenatal care or cancer and cholesterol screenings is nearly inaccessible. Williamson and Drummond (2000) found that parents in low-income families often do not know about the availability of preventive services or low-cost and free health care alternatives for their children and themselves. Also, inadequate health care insurance and lack of transportation limit parents' ability to use child and family health services they do know about. Family health protection depends on every effort being made by family nurses to increase the availability and accessibility of health care services for all families, particularly for poor families, racial minorities, and adolescents. The Canadian Perspectives box details Canada's publicly funded immunization programs, which are a significant part of the country's plan for health protection.

TABLE 12-4   Families at Risk: Who Are the Uninsured?

Uninsured 1999-2000	
Type of Family	Percentage of Uninsured
White	11
Black	20
Hispanic	34
Other	21
Younger than 18 yr	12
Age 19 to 64 yr	18
At lease one full-time worker in the family	13

Adapted from Kaiser Family Foundation. (2002). *State health facts online*. Retrieved September 10, 2002, from http://www.statehealthfacts.kff.org

CANADIAN PERSPECTIVES
FAMILY HEALTH PROTECTION THROUGH IMMUNIZATION

Karen Pielak, RN, MSN
British Columbia Centre for Disease Control

Canada's national health insurance plan is considered one of the hallmarks of Canadian society and is highly valued by Canadians. The principles of this plan, as outlined in the Canada Health Act (universality, portability, accessibility, comprehensiveness, and public administration), apply directly to the provision of publicly funded immunization programs (National Forum on Health, 1997). Canadian children in all provinces and territories receive publicly funded vaccinations against nine diseases: diphtheria, pertussis, tetanus,

polio, *Haemophilus influenzae* type b, measles, mumps, rubella, and hepatitis B (Canadian Public Health Association, 2001). Since 1997, all Canadian jurisdictions have had the benefit of using a pentavalent vaccine combination of diphtheria, acellular pertussis, tetanus, polio, and *Haemophilus influenzae* type b. Adults are offered booster immunizations against tetanus and diphtheria. Influenza and pneumococcal vaccine programs are in place for those 65 years of age or older and for the younger high-risk groups.

The immunization of health care workers against influenza and hepatitis B has received increased attention, as has the immunization of post-secondary school students for measles and meningococcal disease. Immunization programs also target populations at increased risk for pneumococcal a meningococcal disease, hepatitis A, and influenza. Immunization is not mandatory in Canada, although some provinces have legislation or requirements for proof of immunization at school entry.

CANADIAN PERSPECTIVES
FAMILY HEALTH PROTECTION THROUGH IMMUNIZATION — cont'd

Vaccines are licensed federally through Health Canada. The National Advisory Committee on Immunization (NACI) provides recommendations on the use of vaccines. This committee is composed of specialists in public health, infectious diseases, and pediatrics from across the country. However, each province and territory decides which vaccine programs will be publicly funded and how they will be operationalized in the area. Immunization programs are implemented through a mixed delivery system of physician and public health administration. Public health tends to deliver immunization programs in the more rural areas of the country. Because the provision of health care is a provincial/territorial jurisdiction in Canada, there is a lack of harmonization of vaccine scheduling and programs. There is an initiative currently underway, the National Immunization Strategy, which is striving to achieve universality and harmonization in the delivery of Canadian immunization programs (Dr. Arlene King, personal communication, October 10, 2001).

Vaccine administration in Canada is regarded as an independent, advanced nursing competency. Almost all provinces and territories have implemented an immunization certification process that includes a written examination and observation of immunization technique. Community health nurses must meet specific criteria

before they are permitted to immunize. This immunization certification process was spearheaded by the Canadian Nursing Coalition for Immunization [CNCI] (2001). The CNCI membership includes one nurse epidemiologist or communicable disease nurse specialist per province and territory. Its primary purpose it to provide a forum in which to share and develop "best practice" concepts and to support standards to optimize delivery of immunization services in the provinces and territories (CNCI, 2001).

Although there is general support for immunization and there are relatively high immunization rates in Canada, immunization of all family members continues to present challenges to Canadian community health nurses. Members of the public increasingly confront Canadian community health with stances of complacency or anti-immunization. Accordingly, a current challenge to Canadian health professionals is to become proficient in vaccine benefit-risk communication. The onus is on clinicians to discuss the most accurate and up-to-date vaccine benefit-risk information with their clients. The goal is not to convince clients to accept immunization but to provide them with the information that enables them to make the most informed, comfortable decision for themselves (Stoto, Evans, & Bostrom, 1998).

Health care professionals also need to continue to advocate for the ongoing success of national immunization programs in promoting the health of the Canadian population. Plotkin and Orenstein (1999) claim that with the exception of safe water, no other modality, not even antibiotics, has had such a major effect on mortality reduction and population growth.

References

Canadian Nursing Coalition for Immunization. (2001). *Terms of reference.* Halifax, Nova Scotia, Canada: Author.

Canadian Public Health Association. (2001). *The value of immunization in the future of Canada's health.* Submission to the Commission on the Future of Health Care in Canada. [online]. Retrieved from http://www.immunize.cpha.ca.

National Forum on Health. (1997). *Canada health action: Building on the legacy.* (Synthesis Reports and Issue Papers, Vol. 2). Ottawa, Ontario, Canada: Author.

Plotkin, S. A., & Orenstein, W. A. (1999). *Vaccines* (3rd ed.). Philadelphia: W. B. Saunders.

Stoto, M. A., Evans, G., & Bostrom A. (1998). Vaccine risk communication. *American Journal of Preventive Medicine, 14,* 237-239.

Family nurses, as well as other health care providers, share much of the responsibility for ensuring that families know their risk factors and are able to provide themselves with adequate health protection. A number of community resources are available to assist families in meeting their health protection needs. For example, local chapters of organizations such as Planned Parenthood, the American Cancer Society, the American Heart Association, and the American Lung Association, worksite health programs, neighborhood health centers, and school-based clinics all provide health and wellness information relevant to families. Families seeking health information can consult a variety of sources: local libraries, hospitals and clinics, self-help groups, health information centers, national health organizations, and U.S. government clearinghouses and information centers. Many of these resources are easily accessible on the Internet. The Website Resources box at the end of the chapter provides the URLs for several of the family health-related websites available to health care professionals and to the public.

Assessment

Assessment of family health protective behaviors involves the collection of data from which family strengths, concerns, and actual or potential problems can be identified. A thorough family assessment and genogram are excellent ways to assess and teach families and are covered in greater detail in other chapters. The first step in family health protection is identification of the family's health risks.

One way to assist families in identifying risk is through the use of a health risk appraisal. Health risk appraisals are commonly used by nurses and other health care professionals as a means of assessing individual and family risk factors and providing families with a realistic estimate of the major health hazards to which they are particularly vulnerable. Family members may be more amenable to recommended lifestyle changes if they are shown specific risk factors and understand that their risk of developing specific health conditions is moderate or high. A number of risk appraisals for specific conditions are available online at the Healthfinder website and other

websites, listed with their URLs in the Website Resources box. Appendix 12-1 at the end of the chapter presents a sample risk appraisal tool that is organized by family developmental stages.

Planning and Implementation

Families must have an active voice in the planning process for a health protection plan to be effective. Family nurses need to consider themselves as partners in the family's health; therefore the steps in developing a family health protection plan involve both the nurse and the family. Pender, Murdaugh, and Parsons (2002) describe the common steps necessary for the nurse and family together to develop a health protection plan. These steps are as follows:

1) Review family assessment data and family health status.
2) Identify and reinforce strengths of the family that provide the basis for health protection actions.
3) Identify family health goals.
4) Identify behavior or health outcomes that will indicate the plan has been successful.
5) Develop a health protection/behavior plan that incorporates the family's readiness to change and assess their knowledge of health protection strategies.
6) Address social, environmental, and interpersonal factors that are barriers to change.
7) Determine the time frame for implementation.
8) Commit to the family's health protection goals and the structure and support needed to accomplish them.

The role of the nurse in health protection and health protection planning varies according to the developmental stage and needs of the family.

The use of "interventive questions" as described by Wright and Leahy (2000) can be very helpful as the family nurse works with a family to identify health risks and behavior changes to reduce the risks. Interventive questions elicit family explanations of cause and effect, but more importantly, also explore the relationships between family members, events, beliefs, and behaviors. Two examples of interventive questions are: "How would your mother feel about you or your sister helping to increase the servings of fruit and vegetables in your meals?" and "What is the best advice you have had on how to approach your son about using alcohol and driving or being with someone who is drinking and driving?" These types of questions can lead the nurse to interventions such as offering education, making referrals to community support agencies, validating emotional responses, and devising rituals and family routines that are specific to the family's needs.

Although the family is ultimately responsible for carrying out the prescribed plan of action, the family nurse continues to play an active role in health protection. Feeley and Gottlieb (2000) advocate an approach building on family strengths such as family capacity, competency, and resources in working with families. Strengths can be identified in one area and applied from one domain or area to another with the aim of successfully reinforcing new health protection behaviors. The expanding family strengths are then nurtured and supported by identifying and mobilizing resources. The family nurse plays a number of important roles in supporting families' health protection function.

Evaluation

Evaluation is the ongoing process between the nurse and the family or its members that measures the progress that has been made toward goal achievement. Because most health protective measures are self-directed, behavior change evaluation is largely based on the family's perception of progress. Periodic revision of goals and the plan of action may be necessary because of the family's

mastery of behavior changes, changes in risk, or changes in family priorities and values; revision may also be needed when new options become available to the family.

The family health nurse can play a vital role in working with families to identify risk and adopt strategies to reduce the family's risk. Much remains to be learned about family health protection practices. More research is needed in understanding how families identify risk and adopt protective behaviors. As families age, there is an increasing need to understand the protective activities of elder family members and family caregivers. Further research on the unique prevention needs and strategies of the many types of families—single-parent families, two- or three-generation families living under one roof, and gay and lesbian families—is needed. Given the aging of the population, there is a significant absence in the literature of research and discussion of the health protection strategies for families in later life. Additional research should focus on the family characteristics and family dynamics that support families' changing old beliefs and behaviors to health conscious and health protective behaviors. In this chapter, the role of the family nurse has been described as working with families to support their risk identification, education, and behavior changes. The role of the family nurse is also being expanded to include strategies for helping families interpret the overwhelming volume of health information available and newly emerging information regarding genetic risk and the implications of genetic screening.

CASE SCENARIO

The Norton family consists of Bruce (48), Cheryl (47), and three daughters—Jesse (10), Penny (13), and Kelly (15). Cheryl's mother, Arlene (81), has just moved into their home because she could no longer live independently. The family is a working-class family. Bruce works as a sales representative and Cheryl was working as a secretary until Arlene moved in. She has quit her job to care for her mother.

The family is generally healthy. Arlene has limited mobility and pain because of rheumatoid arthritis. However, the principal reason Cheryl insisted she move in is that Arlene has become increasingly forgetful

since her husband died almost a year ago. Cheryl has recently begun complaining of joint stiffness. Bruce's parents are both alive and live in a different state. Bruce smokes half a pack of cigarettes a day and has hypertension.

The girls are active in their schools and the community. Their busy schedules create considerable stress in the family. Bruce and Cheryl have a complex schedule of driving the girls to and picking them up from various activities. As a result, the family seldom has meals together. The girls spend several hours a day on the Internet, "chatting." Kelly started smoking,

Continued

CASE SCENARIO—cont'd

mostly because of peer pressure and social inter-actions. Cheryl keeps track of where the girls are and with whom they spend time. She often invites their friends over for dinner and sleepovers as a way of keeping track. Cheryl has become more interested in using the Internet to order things, visit health-related websites, and explore her mother's "forgetfulness."

MAJOR FAMILY STRESSORS

The family has two significant stressors related to its developmental stage. The situation of the family with teenagers is inherently stressful as the family balances the need for autonomy with the need for structure and risk taking of adolescence. In addition, Cheryl's mother has recently moved into the house. The responsibilities of providing care to Cheryl's mother and parenting the teenage girls are not being shared by Cheryl and Bruce. There is little family time, and the girls' activities have been overscheduled.

FAMILY STRENGTHS

The family is generally healthy, and there is open communication in terms of both listening and express-ing needs among family members. Although it creates stress, there is closeness with the older generation as Arlene has been welcomed into the home. The family demonstrates a willingness to take care of themselves and each other, best demonstrated by Cheryl closely monitoring her daughters' activities.

LIFESTYLE CHANGES INDICATED

There are a number of areas in which the nurse can focus on improving the family's health protective behaviors. Because of Arlene's and the girls' ages, safety is the first health protection issue. Home safety measures are essential for Arlene. Removing area rugs is one example. Safety is also an issue for the girls as they enter adolescence. Cheryl's efforts to monitor their activities are positive and need to be supported. Encourage the family to use the open communication they have established to discuss delayed and safe sex, discourage drug and alcohol use, emphasize not riding with friends who have been drinking, and discuss family rules related to using the Internet. Second, Bruce's smoking exposes everyone in the house to second-hand smoke and could imply to the girls parental approval of smoking. The nurse could work with Bruce to quit or form a habit of smoking outside and encourage both parents to express their wishes and concerns about smoking with their daughters. Third, Cheryl needs respite. Start by exploring how existing family roles could be expanded to contribute to better balance. Preventive health care behaviors such as exercise, diet, sleep, and routine preventive health care such as annual physicals, Pap smears, and mammograms are important for protecting Cheryl's health because of the increased risk associated with caregiving. Fourth, Arlene needs pneumonia and influenza vaccinations. Bruce and Cheryl should consider annual influenza vaccinations.

WEBSITE RESOURCES

ORGANIZATION	WEBSITE ADDRESS
Department of Health and Human Services	http://www.hhs.gov
Centers for Disease Control and Prevention	http://www.cdc.gov
Agency for Healthcare Research and Quality (AHRQ)	http://www.ahrq.gov
National Institutes for Health (NIH)	http://www.nih.gov
Healthfinder	http://www.healthfinder.gov
Healthy People 2010	http://www.health.gov/healthypeople
Parenting Resources for the 21st Century	http://www.parentingresources.ncjrs.org/
American Academy of Family Physicians	http://www.familydoctor.org

WEBSITE RESOURCES—cont'd

American Academy of Pediatrics	http://www.aap.org
American Association of Retired Persons	http://www.aarp.org
Kaiser Family Foundation	http://www.kff.org/
Spry Foundation	http://www.spry.org
Children's Defense Fund	www.childrensdefense.org
American Heart Association	http://www.americanheart.org
American Lung Association	http://www.lungusa.org
American Cancer Association	http://www.cancer.org
Family Violence Prevention Fund	http://www.endabuse.org
PAX Real Solutions to Gun Violence	http://www.paxusa.org
National Center for Complementary and Alternative Medicine	http://www.nccam.nih.gov/health/
National Cancer Institute	http://www.nci.nih.gov/cancerinfo/ten-things-to-know
National Domestic Violence Hotline	http://www.ndvh.org
National Women's Health Information Center	www.4woman.gov/violence/index.cfm
Department of Justice Violence Against Women Office	http://www.ojp.usdoj.gov/vawo
Family Violence Prevention Fund	http://www.endabuse.org

■ CHAPTER HIGHLIGHTS

- Health protection behaviors aim to eliminate or minimize threats to health related to risk factors for specific illnesses.

- The family plays a critical role in the development and practice of health protective patterns by members.

- A number of family characteristics such as open communication and parental monitoring support successful adoption of health protective behaviors.

- Families experience specific health risks as they move through family developmental stages.

- Families are using alternative health care as a means of enhancing health protection and are better informed about health as a result of access to a wealth of information through the Internet.

- Family nurses have a vital role in assisting families to identify potential threats to health and to develop effective plans for health protection for individual members and the family unit throughout the family life cycle.

CRITICAL THINKING ACTIVITIES

1. How do cultural beliefs affect a family's perception of risk? For example, what might family health protection behaviors look like if a family believed that respect and treatment of their ancestors was related to good health?

2. It has been argued that the increase in focus on health protection and health promotion by families is a middle and upper socioeconomic class phenomenon because of its relationship to time, money, and access to health care. How can principles of health protection and promotion be made available to families of lower socioeconomic status?

REFERENCES

Acton, G. J. (2002). Health-promoting self-care in family caregivers. *Western Journal of Nursing Research, 24,* 73-86.

Ahmann, E. (2001). Guns in the home: Nurses' role. *Pediatric Nursing, 27,* 587-605.

Allen, F. M., & Warner, M. (2002). A developmental model of health and nursing. *Journal of Family Nursing, 8,* 96-135.

Bashir, S. A. (2002). Home is where the harm is: Inadequate housing as a public health crisis. *American Journal of Public Health, 92,* 733-738.

Bennett, L. A., Wolin, S. J., Reiss, D., & Teitelbaum, M. A. (1987). Couples at risk for transmission of alcoholism: Protective influences. *Family Process, 26,* 111-129.

Berland, G. K., Elliott, M. N., Morales, L. S., Algazy, J. I., Kravitz, R. L., Broder, M. S., et al. (2001). Health information on the Internet: Accessibility, quality, and readability in English and Spanish. *Journal American Medical Association, 285,* 2612-2621.

Bigbee, J., & Jansa, N. (1991). Strategies for promoting health protection. *Nursing Clinics of North America, 26,* 895-913.

Borzekowski, D. L. G., & Rickett, V. I. (2001). Adolescent cybersurfing for health information: A new resource that crosses barriers. *Archives of Pediatric and Adolescent Medicine, 155,* 813-17.

Campaign for Tobacco-Free Kids, American Cancer Society, American Heart Association, & American Lung Association. (2002, January 15). *Show us the money: An update on the states' allocation of the tobacco settlement dollars.* Retrieved October 11, 2002, from http://www.tobaccofreekids.org/reports/settlements/

Campbell, J., Jones, A. S., Dienemann, J., Kub, J., Schollenberger, J. O'Campo, P., et al. (2002). Intimate partner violence and physical health consequences. *Archives of Internal Medicine. 62,* 1157-1164.

Carter, B., & McGoldrick, M. (1999). *The expanded family life cycle: Individual, family and social perspectives* (3rd ed.). Boston: Allyn and Bacon.

Ceballo, R., Dahl, T. A., Aretakis, M. T., & Ramirez, C. (2001). Inner-city children's exposure to community violence: How much do parents know? *Journal of Marriage and Family, 63,* 927-940.

Centers for Disease Control and Prevention. (2002, June 28). Youth risk behavior surveillance—United States, 2001 [Electronic version]. *Morbidity and Mortality Weekly Report, 51*(SS04), 1-64. Retrieved October 11, 2002, from http://www.cdc.gov/mmwr/preview/mmwrhtml/ss5104a1.html

Centers for Disease Control and Prevention. (2002, May). Trends in cigarette smoking among high school students—United States, 1991-2001 [Electronic version]. *Morbidity and Mortality Weekly Report, 51*(19). Retrieved October 11, 2002, from http://www.cdc.gov/tobacco/research_data/youth/mmwr5119.highlights.html

Centers for Disease Control and Prevention. (2002). *The burden of chronic disease and their risk factors: National and state perspectives.* Retrieved October 11, 2002, from http://www.cdc.gov/nccdphp/burdenbook2002/index.html

Centers for Disease Control and Prevention. (n.d.). *Injury fact book, 2001-2002.* Retrieved October 11, 2002, from http://cdc.gov/ncipa/fact_book/factbook.html

Coffield, A. B., Maciosek, M. V., McGinnis, J. M., Harris, J. R., Caldwell, M. B., Teutsch, S. M., et al. (2001). Priorities among recommended clinical preventive services. *American Journal of Preventive Medicine, 21,* 1-9.

Committee on Injury and Poison Prevention, American Academy of Pediatrics. (2000). Firearm-related injuries affecting the pediatric population. *Pediatrics, 105,* 888-895.

Committee on Substance Abuse, American Academy of Pediatrics. (2001). Alcohol use and abuse. A pediatric concern. *Pediatrics, 108,* 185-189.

Compan, E., Moreno, J., Ruiz, M. T., & Pascual, E. (2002). Doing things together: Adolescent health and family rituals. *Journal of Epidemiology and Community Health, 56,* 89-95.

D'Alessandro, D. M., & Dosa, N. P. (2001). Empowering children and families with information technology. *Archives of Pediatric and Adolescent Medicine, 155,* 1131-1136.

D'Alessandro, D. M., Kingsley, P., & Johnson-West, J. (2001). The readability of pediatric patient education materials on the World Wide Web. *Archives of Pediatric and Adolescent Medicine, 155,* 807-812.

Denham, S. A. (1999). Part I: The definition and practice of family health. *Journal of Family Nursing, 5,* 133-160.

Denham, S. A. (2003). *Family health: A framework for nursing.* Philadelphia: Davis.

DiClemente R. J., Wingood G. M., Crosby R., Sionean C., Cobb B. K., Harrington K., et al. (2001). Parental monitoring: Association with adolescents' risk behaviors. *Pediatrics, 107,* 1363-1368.

Elders, M. J., Perry, C. L., Eriksen, M. P., & Giorano, G. A. (1994). The report of the Surgeon General: Preventing tobacco use among young people. *American Journal of Public Health, 84,* 543-547.

Fallon, B. J., & Bowles, T. P. V. (2001). Family functioning and adolescent help-seeking behavior. *Family Relations, 50,* 239-245.

Farah, M. M., Simon, H. K., & Kellermann, A. L. (1999). Firearms in the home: Parental perceptions. *Pediatrics, 104,* 1059-1063.

Feeley, N., & Gottlieb, L. N. (2000). Nursing approaches for working with family strengths and resources. *Journal of Family Nursing, 6,* 9-24.

Fiese, B. H. (2000). Family routines, rituals, and asthma management: A proposal for family-based strategies. *Families, Systems, and Health: The Journal of Collaborative Family Healthcare, 18,* 405-418.

Ford-Gilboe, M. (1997). Family strengths, motivation, and resources as predictors of health promotion behavior in single- and two-parent families. *Research in Nursing and Health, 20,* 205-217.

Friedman, M. M, Bowen, V. R., & Jones, E .G. (2003). *Family nursing: Research, theory, and practice* (5th ed.). Upper Saddle River, NJ: Prentice Hall.

Gaffney, K. F. (2001). Infant exposure to environmental tobacco smoke. *Journal of Nursing Scholarship, 33,* 343-347.

Gershoff, E. T. (2002). Corporal punishment by parents and associated child behaviors and experiences: A meta-analytic and theoretical review. *Psychological Bulletin, 128,* 534-579.

Gielen, A. C., McDonald, E. M., Wilson, M. E. H., Hwang, W., Serwint, J. R., Andrews, J. S., et al. (2002). Effects of improved access to safety counseling, products, and home visits on parents' safety practices: Results of a randomized trial. *Archives of Pediatric and Adolescent Medicine, 156,* 33-41.

Gielen, A. C., O'Campo, P. J., Campbell, J. C., Schollenberger, J., Woods, A. B., Jones, et al. (2000). Women's opinions about domestic violence screening and mandatory reporting. *American Journal of Preventive Medicine, 19,* 279-285.

Grant, B. F. (2000). Estimates of US children exposed to alcohol abuse and dependence in the family. *American Journal of Public Health, 90,* 112-115.

Harris, D. M., & Guten S. (1979). Health protective behavior: An exploratory study. *Journal of Health and Social Behavior, 20,* 17-29.

Health Canada. (2000). Leading causes of deaths and hospitalizations, 2000. Population and Public Health Branch. Retrieved October 11, 2002, from http://www.hc-sc.gc.ca/hpb/lcdc/publicat/pcd97/index.html

Hughes, M. E., & Waite, L. J. (2002). Health in household context: Living arrangements and health in late middle age. *Journal of Health and Social Behavior, 43,* 1-21.

Humphreys, J. C. (2001a). Turnings and adaptations in resilient daughters of battered women. *Journal of Nursing Scholarship, 33,* 245-251.

Humphreys, J. C. (2001b). Growing up in a violent home: The lived experience of daughters of battered women. *Journal of Family Nursing, 7,* 244-260.

Hunt, K., Davison, C., Emslie C., & Ford G. (2000). Are perceptions of a family history of heart disease related to health-related attitudes and behavior? *Health Education Research, 15,* 131-143.

Hunt, K., Emslie, C., & Watt, G. (2001). Lay constructions of a family history of heart disease: Potential for misunderstandings in the clinical encounter? *Lancet, 357,* 1168-1171.

Institute of Medicine. (2002). *Is soccer bad for children's heads? Summary of the IOM Workshop on Neuropsychological Consequences of Head Impact in Youth Soccer.* Washington, DC: National Academy Press.

Jackman, G. A., Farah, M. M., Kellermann, A. L., & Simon, H. K. (2001). Seeing is believing: What do boys do when they find a real gun. *Pediatrics, 107,* 1247-1250.

Jain, A., Sherman, S. N., Chamberlin, L. A., Carter, Y., Powers, S. W., & Whitaker, R. (2001). Why don't low-income mothers worry about their preschoolers being overweight? *Pediatrics, 107,* 1138-1146.

Johnson, K., Davy, L., Boyett, T., Weathers, L., & Roetzheim, R. (2001). Sun protection practices for children: Knowledge, attitudes, and parent behaviors. *Archives of Pediatric and Adolescent Medicine, 155,* 891-896.

Kaler, M., & Ravella, P.C. (2002). Staying on the ethical high ground with complementary and alternative medicine. *Nurse Practitioner 27,* 38-42.

Kegler, M. C., McCormick, L., Crawford, M., Allen, P., Spigner, C., & Ureda, J. (2002). An exploration of family influences on smoking among ethnically diverse adolescents. *Health Education and Behavior, 29,* 473-490.

Keltner, B. R. (1992). Family influences on child health status. *Pediatric Nursing, 18,* 128-131.

Kulbok, P., & Baldwin, J. H. (1992). From preventive health behavior to health promotion: Advancing a positive construct of health. *Advances in Nursing Science, 14,* 50-64.

Kulbok, P. A., Baldwin, J. H., Cox, C. L., & Duffy, R. (1997). Advancing discourse on health promotion: Beyond mainstream thinking. *Advances in Nursing Science, 20,* 12-20.

Lane, W. G., Liu, G. C., & Newlin, E. (2000). The association between hands-on instruction and proper child safety seat installation. *Pediatrics, 106,* 924-929.

Langford, D. R. (1998). Social chaos and danger as context of battered women's lives. *Journal of Family Nursing, 4,* 167-182.

Lantz, P. M., Jacobson, P. D., Warner, K. E., Wasserman, J., Pollack, H. A., Berson, J., et al. (2000). Investing in youth tobacco control: A review of smoking prevention and control strategies. *Tobacco Control, 9,* 47-63.

Lavoie, F., Herbert, M., Tremblay, R., Vitaro, F. Vezina, L., & McDuff, P. (2002). History of family dysfunction and perpetration of dating violence by adolescent boys: A longitudinal study. *Journal of Adolescent Health, 30,* 375-383.

Lehr, S. T., DiIorio, C., Dudley, W. N., & Lipana, J. A. (2000). The relationship between parent-adolescent communication and safer sex behaviors in college students. *Journal of Family Nursing, 6,* 180-196.

Liaschenko, J. (2002). Health promotion, moral harm, and the moral aims of nursing. In L. E. Young & V. Hayes (Eds.), *Transforming health promotion practice: Concepts, issues and application* (pp. 136-147). Philadelphia: F. A. Davis.

Loveland-Cherry, C. J. (2000). Family interventions to prevent substance abuse: Children and adolescents. *Annual Review of Nursing Research, 18,* 195-218.

Maney, D. W., Higham-Gardill, D. A., & Mahoney, B. S. (2002). The alcohol-related psychosocial and behavioral risks of a nationally representative sample of adolescents. *Journal of School Health, 72,* 157-163.

Mantle, F. (2002). Complementary therapies and health promotion. *British Journal of Community Nursing, 7,* 102-107.

Martin, S. G. (2002). Children exposed to domestic violence: Psychological considerations for health care practitioners. *Holistic Nursing Practice, 6,* 7-9.

Mayhew, M. (1991). Strategies for promoting safety and preventing injury. *Nursing Clinics of North America, 26,* 885-893.

McNeely, C., Shew, M. L., Beuhring, T., Sieving, R., Miller, B. C., & Blum R. W. (2002). Mothers' influence on the timing of first sex among 14- and 15-year-olds. *Journal of Adolescent Health, 31,* 256-265.

Mellin, A. E., Neumark-Sztainer, D., Story, M., Ireland, M., & Resnick, M. D. (2002). Unhealthy behaviors and psychosocial difficulties among overweight adolescents: The potential impact of familial factors. *Journal of Adolescent Health, 31,* 145-153.

Messecar, D. C., Archbold, P. G., Stewart, B. J., & Kirschling, J. (2002). Home environmental modification strategies used by caregivers of elderly. *Research in Nursing and Health, 25,* 357-370.

Miller, K. E., Sabo, D. F., Farrell, M. P., Barnes, G. M., & Melnick, M. J. (1998). Athletic participation and sexual behavior in adolescents: The different worlds of boys and girls. *Journal Health and Social Behavior, 39,* 108-123.

Mitchell, K. J., Finkelhor, D., & Wolak, J. (2001). Risk factors for and impact of online sexual solicitation of youth. *Journal of the American Medical Association, 285,* 3011-3014.

Murray, R., & Huelskoetter, M. M. (1991). *Psychiatric mental health nursing: Giving emotional care* (3rd ed.). Norwalk, CT: Appleton Lange.

National Center for Complementary and Alternative Medicine (NCCAM), National Institutes of Health. (2002, September 20). *What is complementary and alternate medicine (CAM).* Retrieved October 11, 2002, from http://nccam.nih.gov/health/whatiscam

National Center for Health Statistics. (2001, October 12). Deaths: Leading causes for 1999. Retrieved October 11, 2002, from http://www.cdc.gov/nchs/data/nvsr/nvsr49/nvsr49_11.pdf

Naumann, P. A., Langford, D. R., Torres, S., Campbell, J. C., & Glass, N. (1999). Woman battering in primary care practice. *Family Practice: An International Journal, 16,* 343-352.

Pender, N. J., Murdaugh C. L., & Parsons M. A. (2002). *Health promotion in nursing practice* (4th ed.). Upper Saddle River, NJ: Prentice Hall.

PEW Internet Project. (2002, May 22). *Vital decisions: How Internet users decide what information to trust when they or their loved ones are sick.* Retrieved October 11, 2002, from http://www.pewinternet.org/reports/toc.asp?Report=59

Pinderhughes, E. E., Nix, R., Foster, E. M., & Jones, D. (2001). Parenting in context: Impact of neighborhood poverty, residential stability, public services, social networks, and danger on parental behaviors. *Journal of Marriage and Family, 63,* 941-953.

Ponder, M., Lee J., Green J., & Richards M. (1996). Family history and perceived vulnerability to some common diseases: A study of young people and their parents. *Journal of Medical Genetics, 33,* 485-492.

Romero, A. J., Robinson, T. N., Kraemer, H. C., Erickson, S. J., Haydel, K. F., Mendoza, F., et al. (2001). Are perceived neighborhood hazards a barrier to physical activity in children? *Archives of Pediatric and Adolescent Medicine, 155,* 1143-1148.

Rose, L. E., Campbell, J., & Kub, J. (2000). The role of social support and family relationships in women's responses to battering. *Health Care for Women International, 21,* 27-39.

Ruffing-Rahal, M. A. (1991). Rationale and design for health promotion with older adults. *Public Health Nursing, 8,* 258-263.

Sargent, J. D., & Dalton, M. (2001). Does parental disapproval of smoking prevent adolescents from becoming established smokers? *Pediatrics, 108,* 1256-1262.

Schuster, M. A., Franke, T. M., Bastian, A. M., Sor, S., & Halfon, N. (2000). Firearm storage patterns in U.S. homes with children, *American Journal of Public Health, 90,* 588-594.

Smith, C. A. (1999). Family life pathfinders on the new electronic frontier. *Family Relations, 48,* 31-34.

Spector, R. E. (2000). *Cultural diversity in health and illness* (5th ed.). Upper Saddle River, NJ: Prentice Hall.

Stahl, C., & Fritz, N. (2002). Internet safety: Adolescents' self-report. *Journal of Adolescent Health, 31,* 7-10.

Swanson, J. R., & Pearson, T. A. (2001). Screening family members at high risk for coronary disease: Why isn't it done? *American Journal of Preventive Medicine, 20,* 50-55.

Task Force on College Drinking. (2002, April). *A call to action: Changing the culture of drinking at U.S. colleges.* Retrieved October 11, 2002, from http://www.collegedrinking prevention.gov/Reports/#task

U. S. Department of Commerce. (2000, October). *Falling through the Net: Toward digital inclusion.* Retrieved October 11, 2002, from http://www.ntia.doc.gov/ntiahome/fttn00/contents00.html

U. S. Department of Health and Human Services, Office of Disease Prevention and Health Promotion. (n.d.). *Healthy People 2010.* Retrieved October 11, 2002, from http://www.health.gov/healthypeople/document/

U. S. Preventive Services Task Force. (n.d.). Preventive care guidelines—adult, children. Retrieved September 10, 2002, from the Agency for Healthcare Research and Quality website, http://www.ahrq.gov/clinic/ppipix.htm#tools

Vessey, J. A., & Rechkemoner, A. (2001). Natural approaches to children's health. *Pediatric Nursing, 27,* 61-64.

Williamson, D. L., & Drummond, J. (2000). Enhancing low-income parent' capacities to promote their children's health: Education is not enough. *Public Health Nursing, 17,* 121-131.

Winkelstein, M. (1992). Adolescent smoking: Influential factors, past preventive efforts, and future nursing implications. *Journal of Pediatric Nursing, 7,* 120-127.

Wright, L. M., & Leahy, M. (2000). *Nurses and families: A guide to family assessment and intervention* (3rd ed.). Philadelphia: F. A. Davis.

APPENDIX 12-1   *Family Health Protective Behaviors*

The nurse should indicate for each item whether the family member accomplishes the item according to criteria indicated in the columns. If an item or section does not apply, the points represented by that item should be so indicated by marking the "not applicable" column. In scoring at the end of each section, the category "total points possible" means the total number of points that could be attained if every item applied. The "total not applicable" category shows the total points for items or sections that do not apply to the family at this time; this number should be subtracted from the "total points possible" to obtain the "total applicable" score. When comparing "total applicable" with the "total points attained," the nurse and family can see the numerical difference in what should or could be achieved and what does exist at the present time.

	Yes (2 pts)	No (0 pts)	Not Applicable
I. Family Health Protective Behaviors			
A. The Expectant Family			
1. Expectant mother receives adequate prenatal care	_____	_____	_____
2. Adequate nutritional intake maintained throughout pregnancy	_____	_____	_____
3. Expectant mother abstains from alcohol, drug, or tobacco use throughout pregnancy	_____	_____	_____
4. Expectant mother avoids environmental hazards during pregnancy	_____	_____	_____
Total points possible			___8___
Total not applicable			_____
Total applicable			_____
Total points attained			_____
B. Families with Infants			
1. Infant screened for inherited metabolic disorders	_____	_____	_____
2. Ongoing health supervision arranged for immunizations and growth and developmental assessment	_____	_____	_____
3. Parents actively seek information related to infant care skills, normal growth and development, and parenting	_____	_____	_____
Total points possible			___6___
Total not applicable			_____
Total applicable			_____
Total points attained			_____
C. Families with Preschool Children			
1. Parents are aware of accident hazards	_____	_____	_____
2. Parents are aware of symptoms and management of common childhood illnesses	_____	_____	_____
3. Parents provide for and encourage:			
a. Good nutrition	_____	_____	_____
b. Adequate sleep	_____	_____	_____
c. Adequate exercise	_____	_____	_____
d. Dental health practices	_____	_____	_____

Adapted from Kandzari, J.H., and Howard, H.R. (1981). *The Well Family: A Developmental Approach to Assessment.* Boston: Little, Brown. Adapted with permission.

4. Parents provide for ongoing health supervision

————————   ————————   ————————

5. Immunizations completed prior to school entry

————————   ————————   ————————

6. Vision and hearing screening prior to school entry

————————   ————————   ————————

7. Preschool facility provides healthy environment
    a. Proper light

————————   ————————   ————————

    b. Adequate heating and cooling

————————   ————————   ————————

    c. Free of accident hazards

————————   ————————   ————————

    d. Ample room for vigorous physical activity

————————   ————————   ————————

8. Preschool caregiver has philosophy congruent with that of family

————————   ————————   ————————

9. Preschool program promotes physical health, proper nutrition, and cognitive and social skill development

————————   ————————   ————————

Total points possible		30
Total not applicable		
Total applicable		
Total points attained		

D. Families with School-Age Children
1. Family teaches safety and accident prevention

————————   ————————   ————————

2. Child demonstrates safe behaviors in play and daily activities

————————   ————————   ————————

3. Child demonstrates increasing responsibility for self-care

————————   ————————   ————————

4. Family provides for and encourages preventive dental care

————————   ————————   ————————

5. School has comprehensive health program
    a. Routine vision/hearing screening

————————   ————————   ————————

    b. Health education

————————   ————————   ————————

6. School sports programs promote mental and physical wellness

————————   ————————   ————————

7. Working parents provide appropriate after-school supervision of child

————————   ————————   ————————

8. Parents monitor and limit television viewing by children

————————   ————————   ————————

9. Family effectively deals with everyday stress

————————   ————————   ————————

Total points possible		20
Total not applicable		
Total applicable		
Total points attained		

E. Families with Adolescents
1. Adolescent assumes nearly total responsibility for self-care

————————   ————————   ————————

2. Adolescent is actively involved in physical fitness program

————————   ————————   ————————

3. Dietary patterns adequately meet the nutritional needs of the adolescent

————————   ————————   ————————

4. Adolescent is aware of the health hazards related to drug, alcohol, and tobacco use

————————   ————————   ————————

5. Family members are aware of the early signs of drug abuse among children or adolescents

————————   ————————   ————————

6. Family members discuss aspects of responsible sexual behavior

————————   ————————   ————————

7. Adolescent receives accurate information about contraceptive methods and where to obtain them

————————   ————————   ————————

8. Adolescent demonstrates effective problem-solving skills

————————   ————————   ————————

9. Adolescent completes drivers education course

Total points possible _____ _____ _____20_____
Total not applicable _____ _____ _____
Total applicable _____ _____ _____
Total points attained _____ _____ _____

F. Families with Young Adults
   1. Young adult assumes total responsibility for self-care
   2. Reviews and updates immunization status
   3. If female:
      a. Performs regular BSE
      b. Obtains Pap smear as indicated
   4. If male, performs regular examination of the testes
   5. Engages in responsible, "safe" sexual practices
   6. Refrains from alcohol, drug, and tobacco use
   7. Obtains and records baseline blood pressure
   8. Develops effective decision-making skills for career, marriage, and parenthood

Total points possible _____ _____ _____18_____
Total not applicable _____ _____ _____
Total applicable _____ _____ _____
Total points attained _____ _____ _____

G. Families with Middle-Aged Adults
   1. Performs monthly breast or testicular self-examination
   2. Obtains routine Pap smear
   3. Obtains mammogram as indicated
   4. Obtains screening for occult blood
   5. Performs visual inspections of body monthly for lumps and changes in moles
   6. Refrains from alcohol, drug, or tobacco use
   7. Obtains screening for diabetes
   8. Obtains screening for hypertension
   9. Obtains screening for glaucoma
   10. Modifies nutrition practices as necessary according to caloric needs
   11. Maintains physical exercise program
   12. Identifies normal changes due to aging and adapts accordingly

Total points possible _____ _____ _____24_____
Total not applicable _____ _____ _____
Total applicable _____ _____ _____
Total points attained _____ _____ _____

H. Families with Older Adults
   1. Maintains good oral hygiene practices
   2. Plans for expected stressful situations such as retirement or relocation
   3. Family aware of potential accident hazards due to sensory and mobility changes
   4. Maintains good nutritional practices
   5. Practices safe use of medications
   6. Obtains recommended immunizations
   7. Obtains physical examinations as necessary
   8. Performs self-screening for cancer
   9. Maintains physical exercise program
   10. Obtains screening for diabetes

11. Obtains screening for glaucoma   _____   _____   _____
12. Identifies normal changes due to aging and
     adapts accordingly   _____   _____   _____

Total points possible	__26__
Total not applicable	_____
Total applicable	_____
Total points attained	_____

I. Families Self-Care
1. Family maintains appropriate medical
    equipment and supplies in the home   _____   _____   _____
2. Family members demonstrate knowledge of
    proper use of equipment and supplies   _____   _____   _____
3. Family members state signs and symptoms
    of physical conditions that warrant medical
    attention   _____   _____   _____
4. Family evaluates the credentials of health
    care providers   _____   _____   _____
5. Family considers personal characteristics and
    wellness attitude when choosing health
    professional   _____   _____   _____
6. Family seeks information on health services
    and reasonable costs   _____   _____   _____
7. Family effectively utilizes available self-care
    resources in the community   _____   _____   _____

Total points possible	__14__
Total not applicable	_____
Total applicable	_____
Total points attained	_____

Assessment Tool Summary

	Subtotal points possible	Subtotal not applicable	Subtotal applicable	Subtotal points attained
I. Family Health Protective Behaviors				
A. The Expectant Family	8	_____	_____	_____
B. Families with Infants	6	_____	_____	_____
C. Families with Preschool Children	30	_____	_____	_____
D. Families with School-Age Children	20	_____	_____	_____
E. Families with Adolescents	20	_____	_____	_____
F. Families with Young Adults	18	_____	_____	_____
G. Families with Middle-Aged Adults	24	_____	_____	_____
H. Families with Older Adults	26	_____	_____	_____
I. Family Self-Care	14	_____	_____	_____

Total points possible	__166__
Total not applicable	_____
Total applicable	_____
Total points attained	_____

Family Nutrition

Kathy Shadle James
Eleanor A. Flores

13

The ritual of a family dinner to end the day, a time to eat in peace and quiet and the comforting support of the family, is the one best thing anyone can do for their own health.

— Paul Pearsall (p. 54)

OBJECTIVES

On completion of this chapter, the reader will be able to do the following:

1. *Describe changing dietary patterns in the United States and the effect on a family's nutritional status.*

2. *Explain the relationship between diet and health.*

3. *Identify one nutritional concern associated with each growth and development stage.*

4. *Identify sociocultural and other factors that affect a family's nutritional behaviors.*

5. *Assess a family's application of the U.S. dietary guidelines.*

6. *Explain the relationship between lifestyle and weight control.*

7. *Formulate nursing diagnoses related to a family's nutritional status.*

8. *Identify nursing approaches to improve a family's nutritional health.*

9. *Establish guidelines for a family to evaluate its nutritional and/or weight control plan.*

This chapter discusses dietary issues, as well as weight control, and provides guidelines for the professional whose goal is to guide families in the attainment of optimal weight and nutritional status throughout the life cycle. To achieve this goal, the family health nurse should emphasize to clients that the key for nutritional wellness comes from within the family. The family becomes the provider of health care by teaching healthful behaviors. An individual's learning of health-promoting behaviors begins at birth, with the family providing the stimulus to incorporate health into its members' value system. The degree of family support often determines the extent to which new behaviors will be adopted (James, 2001). Studies suggest that parents who understand the importance of good nutrition can help children in preschool choose healthful foods, but they have less influence on the choices of school-age children.

Many families feel overwhelmed by the deluge of nutrition information. This chapter presents nutritional information pertaining to the needs of family members of all ages. The guidelines are relative to anyone choosing to alter his or her family's diet for health promotion and effective weight control.

The family health nurse is provided with the knowledge and tools to assist families by teaching, guiding, and supporting decision making regarding health-promoting lifestyle changes.

Changing Family Dietary Patterns

As a nation, the United States suffers from more *over-nutrition* than malnutrition. At the beginning of the twenty-first century, obesity among adults and youth is the new epidemic in the United States (Kimm & Obarzanek, 2002). About one half of adults and one fifth of adolescents in the United States are overweight, which suggests that they have higher energy intakes than expenditures. The impact in this country is so prevalent that the Surgeon General has issued a call to action to prevent and decrease overweight and obesity in the United States. The common American lifestyle is to commute long hours and to eat from the refrigerator and at desks, in cars, and in front of the television at all times of the day, which leaves little time for physical activity.

A vast amount of evidence indicates that the intakes of total fat, saturated fatty acids, and cholesterol have decreased, yet they remain above the recommended levels for most of the population reported (U.S. Department of Health and Human Services [DHHS], 2000a, 2000b). The *Healthy People 2010* report indicates that there has been an alarming increase in the prevalence of overweight among all age groups in the U.S. population since the 1970s.

The once prevalent nutrient deficiencies have been replaced by excesses and imbalances of some food components. The proportion of calories from fat averages 34%. This is too high when compared with the 30% recommendation by groups such as the American Heart Association (AHA) (1996). Fat and sugar constitute 60% of the typical American's daily calories. It appears that caloric intakes have either increased or physical activity has decreased. Although obesity affects all ethnic groups, it is a particular problem for poor and minority populations, especially females in those groups. Data collected between 1988 and 1994 indicate that women of lower socioeconomic status are approximately 50% more likely to be obese than those of higher socioeconomic status. Data also show that Mexican American boys and non-Hispanic black girls have a higher prevalence of overweight than their counterparts in other ethnic groups (National Institutes of Health [NIH], 2002).

Dietary patterns have been affected by many factors. Mealtimes are no longer regular. Family members eat at different times and consume different foods. Three of four families have unhealthy breakfasts or skip breakfast altogether. Lunch is often skipped or includes junk food or cafeteria food. Dinner is often the largest meal, consisting of easy-to-prepare foods or fast foods, which constitute 25% of all meals (Tippett & Cleveland, 1999).

The U.S. DHHS has made the following conclusions:

- Markedly higher percentages of Americans are overweight now than in the late 1970s. Fifty-five percent of adults and 11% to 17% of children and adolescents are overweight or obese. Many adults also report sedentary lifestyles. Because overweight is associated with many chronic diseases and adverse health outcomes, the increased prevalence for overweight is a cause for public health concern.

- Although the proportion of adults having desirable serum cholesterol levels is increasing steadily, many people still have high levels. A high serum cholesterol level is a major risk factor for coronary artery disease.

- Hypertension remains a major public health problem in middle-aged and elderly people.

- Non-Hispanic blacks have a higher age-adjusted prevalence of hypertension than non-Hispanic whites and Mexican Americans. Hypertension is the most important risk factor for stroke and a major risk factor for coronary heart disease (CHD).

- Femoral osteoporosis in women 50 years of age and older in the United States occurs in 21% of non-Hispanic whites, 10% of non-Hispanic blacks, and 16% of Mexican Americans. Low calcium intake and lack of weight-bearing exercise, among other factors, contribute to bone loss.

The low intake of calcium among women is a concern because calcium deficiency is implicated as a contributor to osteoporosis among post-menopausal women. In the population as a whole, intakes of calcium from food averaged below the recommended dietary allowance (RDA), with 68% of the population not meeting the RDA.

The prevalence of health conditions related to nutrition is highest among low-income populations. The food components warranting public health monitoring are based on the findings from 3-day dietary intakes. High dietary consumption included food energy (calories), total fat, saturated fat, cholesterol, sodium, and alcohol. Low dietary consumption included vitamin C, calcium, iron, and fluoride. The same nutritional concerns continue to exist and are reflected in the government's health status objectives found in the report *Healthy People 2010* (U.S. DHHS, 2000a, 2000b). Nutritional goals from *Healthy People 2010* include increasing the number of fruits, vegetables, and grains consumed and decreasing fat intake. Goals also include increasing servings of calcium in the diet, decreasing sodium intake, and decreasing the incidence of iron deficiency anemia. Some good sources of iron are ready-to-eat cereals with added iron; enriched and whole-grain breads; lean meats; turkey dark meat; shellfish; spinach; and cooked dry beans, peas, and lentils. The recognized problem areas identified from national reports should be kept in mind and included in a nutritional assessment. A complete listing of the *Healthy People 2010* nutrition objectives is presented in Box 13-1.

U.S. Dietary Recommendations

The main conclusion from the first Surgeon General's report in 1979 on nutrition and health indicated that overconsumption of certain dietary components was a major concern for Americans. With the focus on the relationship between diet and chronic diseases increasing, the U.S. Department of Agriculture (USDA) and the U.S. DHHS developed Dietary Guidelines for Americans. The 2000 guidelines are summarized in Box 13-2. The recommendations are to be used in combination with the RDAs to achieve a highly desirable pattern for the maintenance of good health. Both the United States and Canada have

dietary guidelines that are based on the principles of balance, variety, and moderation. The Canadian Perspectives box details Canada's dietary guidelines and other national nutritional efforts.

Role of Nutrition and Family Health

Although it is customary to think of nutrition as an individual activity, a systems framework illustrates how food consumption depends on many factors (Box 13-3). The issue of family nutrition and food consumption involves complex interactions of social, family, and individual systems. Social, cultural, economic, cognitive, and physiological characteristics influence the family and its members (James, 2001). As shown in Box 13-3, any number of factors can affect nutritional status within a family. For example, dietary patterns tend to vary in families that are run by single parents or when both parents are working. Fast food intake tends to increase because of ease. Family heath nurses need to remember that nutritional choices are not made by hunger alone. Family health nurses who are aware of these factors will be able to direct families to stay well and to work with families to feel good about themselves, to meet their nutrition goals, and to live longer. By identifying potential barriers and setting realistic goals, the family will be successful in making desired changes.

Diet and Health Consequences

Dietary factors are associated with 5 of the 10 leading causes of death in the United States: CHD, cancer, stroke, non–insulin-dependent diabetes mellitus, and atherosclerosis. For two of three Americans who neither drink nor smoke, eating patterns may shape long-term health status more than any other personal choice.

Adequate nutrition and intake of sufficient calories are essential for optimal growth and development, physical activity, reproduction, lactation, recovery from illness and injury, and maintenance of health throughout the life cycle. The role of nutrients in diseases such as heart disease, type 2 diabetes, high blood pressure, dental caries, and some types of cancer (especially cancers of the esophagus, stomach, large bowel,

---

BOX 13-1   Summary of *Healthy People 2010* Nutrition and Overweight Objectives

Weight Status and Growth

1. Increase the proportion of adults who are at a healthy weight.
2. Reduce the proportion of adults who are obese.
3. Reduce the proportion of children and adolescents who are overweight or obese.
4. Reduce growth retardation among low-income children under age 5 years.

Food and Nutrition Consumption

5. Increase the proportion of persons aged 2 years and older who consume at least 2 daily servings of fruit.
6. Increase the proportion of persons aged 2 years and older who consume at least 3 daily servings of vegetables, with at least one third being dark green or orange vegetables.
7. Increase the proportion of persons aged 2 and older who consume at least 6 daily servings of grain products with at least 3 being whole grains.
8. Increase the proportion of persons aged 2 years and older who consume less than 10% of calories from saturated fat.
9. Increase the proportion of persons aged 2 years and older who consume no more than 30% of calories from fat.

10. Increase the proportion of persons aged 2 years and older who consume 2,400 mg or less of sodium daily.
11. Increase the proportion of persons aged 2 years and older who meet dietary recommendations for calcium.

Iron Deficiency Anemia

12. Reduce iron deficiency anemia among young children and females of childbearing age.
13. Reduce anemia among low-income pregnant females in their third trimester.
14. (Developmental) Reduce iron deficiency anemia in pregnant females.

Schools, Worksites, and Nutrition Counseling

15. (Developmental) Increase the proportion of children and adolescents aged 6 to 19 years whose intake of meals and snacks at school contributes to good overall dietary quality.
16. Increase the proportion of worksites that offer nutrition or weight management classes or counseling.
17. Increase the proportion of physician office visits made by patients with a diagnosis of cardiovascular disease, diabetes, or hyperlipidemia, that include counseling or education related to diet and nutrition.

From U.S. Department of Health and Human Services. (2000). *Healthy People 2010* (Vol. 1). Washington, DC: U. S. Government Printing Office.

---

breast, lung, and prostate) is becoming more clear as epidemiological studies offer important insights on possible relationships between diet and health consequences.

Choosing healthy foods begins with understanding the composition and use of food in the body. Although people vary in size, age, race, appearance, genetic makeup, and activity, all need varying amounts of the same nutrients: protein, carbohydrates, fat, vitamins, minerals, and water. Family health nurses collaborate with families to increase awareness of nutrition and of potential risks associated with dietary choices.

Protein Requirements and Use

Protein plays a crucial role in the growth and maintenance of body tissue and is composed of 22 different amino acids. Of these 22, 8 must be provided by the diet, and the other 14 can, with the necessary materials, be made by the body. In the United States, the RDA is the accepted dietary standard for protein. The RDA of protein is based on age, weight, and general physical state (Table 13-1).

Special periods of rapid growth, such as the growth of a fetus and maternal tissue during

CANADIAN PERSPECTIVES
FAMILY NUTRITION AS HEALTH PROMOTION: CANADIAN GUIDELINES

Suzan Banoub-Baddour, RN, PhD
Memorial University of Newfoundland

The Canadian family is changing in the following ways:
- Twelve percent of Canadians older than 65 years are staying longer in their homes.
- Canada's ethnic diversity is accounted for by 16% of immigrants.
- Only 10% of families have stay-at-home spouses.
- About 70% of preschool children are in day-care arrangements.
- Native communities are witnessing erosion in their traditional way of life.
- Unemployment and poverty are increasing among young, single-parent families and lone seniors (National Institute of Nutrition [NIN], 2001).

This results in a number of implications for the nutritional health of Canadians, such as the following:
- Growing nutrition problems, rising health care costs, and decreasing quality of life
- Growing pressures from the media and peer groups
- Increasing reliance on convenience food

Consequently, Canada made a commitment to examine the nature of nutrition problems and factors affecting Canadians' nutritional status. A national plan of action for nutrition was designed. Guidelines for professionals have been developed by scientists that recommend the following for the Canadian diet (Health Canada, 2002):
- Provide sufficient energy from adequate proteins, vitamins, and minerals corresponding to the recommended nutrient intakes and energy needs, as follows:
  19-24 years: Male 3000 kcal/day, Female 2100 kcal/day
  25-49 years: Male 2700 kcal/day, Female 1900 kcal/day
  50-74 years: Male 2300 kcal/day, Female 1800 kcal/day
- Include no more than 30% of energy as fat, and no more than 10% as saturated fat.
- Provide 55% of energy as carbohydrates from varied food sources.
- Have a reduced sodium content.
- Include no more than 5% of total energy as alcohol (about 2 drinks daily).
- Contain no more caffeine than corresponding to 4 cups of coffee daily.
- In communities where water supplies contain less than 1 mg/L, fluoridation should occur to that level.

A committee of experts in communications further adapted these guidelines into simple statements called *Canada's Guidelines for Healthy Eating* (Health Canada, 2002) as follows:
- Eat a variety of food and enjoy it.
- Emphasize cereals, breads, other grain products, vegetables, and fruits.
- Opt for low-fat dairy products, leaner meats, and recipes with little or no fat.
- Limit salt, caffeine, and alcohol.
- Practice regular physical exercise to attain and maintain healthy body weight.

Additionally, *Canada's Food Guide to Healthy Eating (CFG)*, originally issued in 1993 for the general public, is still freely available from local community health departments (Health Canada, 2002). It is designed to do the following:
- Guide consumers 4 years of age and older with varying energy needs in their selection of foods, including snacks, alcohol, and caffeine.
- Show all four food groups and recommended daily servings.
- Provide 1800 to 3200 calories, depending on number and types of servings from four groups and "other foods" category (fats and oils, jams and jellies, and snacks).
- Include foods suitable for consumers from different cultures and ethnic origins.
- Be used by individuals with limited reading ability and young children.
- Provide a booklet for teachers and health professional for children younger than 4 years.

MONITORING THE NUTRITIONAL STATE OF CANADIANS

National data available for the purpose of monitoring the nutritional state of Canadians come from the nutrition surveys organized by the NIN. These *Tracking Nutrition Trends 1989-1994-1997-2001* gauge the attitudes, awareness, and reported behaviours of Canadians toward nutrition (NIN, 2002). Other available data include the *Apparent per Capita Food Consumption*

Continued

CANADIAN PERSPECTIVES
FAMILY NUTRITION AS HEALTH PROMOTION: CANADIAN GUIDELINES—cont'd

and *Family Food Expenditure* collected every 1 to 2 years by Statistics Canada. In addition, a few provincial nutrition surveys have been carried out under the *Canadian Heart Health Initiative* to study food consumption (e.g., in the provinces of Nova Scotia, Quebec, and Ontario) (NIN, 2002).

National data from Tracking Nutrition Trends 2001 revealed that 53% of Canadians believe nutrition is extremely to very important to them when they are choosing food. This indicates a decline from the 1997 NIN surveys (62%). The main reasons given for low ratings include a busy lifestyle (19%) and eating take-out or fast foods (12%). However, 62% made some efforts to improve their eating habits, with 34% and 26% consuming less fat and more vegetables and fruits, respectively (NIN, 2002). Nevertheless, obesity and overweight are a mounting population health issue, with 30% of Canadians between the ages of 20 and 64 years being overweight. While Canadians are knowledgeable about nutrition, they have difficulty improving their food selection. For healthy nutrition to be ensured, it is imperative that barriers to action be broken down (NIN, 2002).

Canadians need information about nutrients available in their food through adequate nutritional labelling. Currently, labelling is not mandatory. Even when available, labels may be difficult to locate and read, incomplete, and selective in listing only few nutrients and are often written in only one of the two official languages, and hence, seldom useful to the typical consumer (NIN, 2001). That is why, according to the Centre for Science in the Public Interest (2002), consumer groups have been calling on official organizations such as the World Health Organization and the Food and Agriculture Organization to improve international food labelling standards. Improved standards would encourage governments to require companies to provide consumers with better information on ingredients, nutritional values, and processing methods.

Health professionals need to develop sound strategies to address barriers to action. One example of essential and urgent undertaking is dealing with the inconsistent information, easily accessible to the family through the Internet. Indeed, in a recent survey of 365 nutrition-related World Wide Web sites, only 167 provided dietary recommendations. When these were compared with the CFG recommendations, only 55% were consistent with the Canadian standards (Davidson, 1997).

References

Centre for Science in the Public Interest (2002). International consumer coalition urges UN committee to call for improved food labelling. (News Release). From http://www.cspinet.org/canada/labellingpr_050202.html

Davidson, K. (1997). The quality of dietary information on the World Wide Web. *Clinical Performance and Quality Health Care, 5,* 64-6.

Health Canada (2002). *Canadian food guide. Using the food guide.* From http:// www.hc-sc.gc.ca/hppb/nutrition/pube/foodguid/eguide9.html

National Institute of Nutrition. (1999). *Nutrition labelling: Perceptions and preferences of Canadians.*

National Institute of Nutrition. From http://www.nin.ca/Publications/

National Institute of Nutrition. (2001). *Enhancing seniors' nutrition: From awareness to action. Executive summary.* National Institute of Nutrition. From http://www.nin.ca/Publications/

National Institute of Nutrition. (2002). Tracking nutrition trends 1989-1994-1997-2001. *RAPPORT, 17,* No. 1.

Canadian spelling is used.

BOX 13-2 Dietary Guidelines for Americans

To reduce risk of diet-related chronic diseases:

Aim For Fitness . . .
Aim for a healthy weight.
Be physically active each day.

Build a Health Base . . .
Let the Pyramid guide your food choices.
Choose a variety of grains daily, especially
   whole grains.
Choose a variety of fruits and vegetables daily.
Keep food safe to eat.

Choose Sensibly . . .
Choose a diet that is low in saturated fat and
   cholesterol and moderate in total fat.
Choose beverages and foods to moderate your
   intake of sugars.
Choose and prepare foods with less salt.
If you drink alcoholic beverages, do so in
   moderation.

From U.S. Department of Agriculture and U.S. Department of Health
and Human Services. (2000). *Nutrition and your health: Dietary
guidelines for Americans* (5th ed.). Retrieved September 21, 2002,
from http://www.health.gov/dietaryguidelines/

BOX 13-3 Factors Influencing Nutritional Health

SOCIETY

Technology
Media
Status
Foods
Fast Food
Availability of Food
Peers
Ecology

FAMILY SYSTEM

Rituals
Mealtime
Environment
Culture
Values
Religion
Communications
Finances
Family Structure

INDIVIDUAL CHARACTERISTICS

Self-Concept
Activity Level
Nutrients
Eating Style
Knowledge
Age
Gender
Physical Requirements

Copyright Kathy Shadle James, 2002.

---

pregnancy, also require added protein, as does any period of illness or disease. Traumatic injury, postsurgical states, and extensive tissue destruction (such as that caused by burns) require a considerable increase in protein intake for the healing process (Insel, Turner, & Ross, 2003).

The RDA protein standard for adults is 0.8 g/kg of body weight. This amounts to about 63 g of protein per day for a man who weighs 174 pounds (79 kg) and 50 g per day for a woman who weighs 138 pounds (63 kg). It is possible to get the recommended amount of protein without eating meat. Other sources of protein include milk and cheese, beans and peas, tofu, rice, and nuts (Dudek, 2001).

Scientific data suggest positive relationships between reduced risks for some chronic diseases and a vegetarian diet. The position of the American Dietetic Association (ADA) (Messina & Burke, 1997) is that vegetarian diets are healthful and nutritionally adequate when they are appropriately planned. Food guide pyramids for vegetarian meal planning are available through the ADA website. The URL for this website is provided in the Website Resources box at the end of the chapter. Protein sources for the vegetarian often come from the dairy group and legumes. Special attention must be given to the adolescent

TABLE 13-1   Protein Requirements

Group	Protein (g/day)*
Infants	
0 to 1 yr	13
Children	
2 to 3 yrs	16
4 to 6 yrs	24
7 to 10 yrs	28
Boys	
11 to 14 yrs	46
15 to 18 yrs	59
19 to 24 yrs	58
Girls	
11 to 14 yrs	46
15 to 18 yrs	44
19 to 24 yrs	46
Women (63 kg)	50
Pregnancy	60
Lactation	65
Men (79 kg)	63

*All requirements listed are approximate.

athlete to ensure that energy, protein, and iron requirements are met (Anderson et al., 2000).

In contrast, too much protein may have negative effects on the body. High-protein diets have been shown to increase the loss of calcium from bones and to increase the production of uric acid in the blood, which may lead to gout. In people with kidney disease, excess protein can further impair kidney functioning as the kidneys work hard to remove the nitrogen part of the protein molecule that is not needed for building or rebuilding tissues. After the body disposes of the unneeded nitrogen supply, the remainder becomes a source of calories that are stored as fat.

Fat Requirements and Use

In the United States, fat intake constitutes about 34% of daily total calories, although dietary guidelines from the AHA and the National Cholesterol Education Program (NCEP) recommend reducing total fat intake to not more than 30% of one's total calories or less and reducing saturated fat to 10%. If a person knows how many calories he or she needs, that person can determine how much fat to include in his or her diet. For example, someone who consumes 1500 calories per day would have a desired fat intake of about 50 g of fat per day. The top five sources of saturated fat are cheese; beef; milk; sweets such as cakes, cookies, quick breads, and doughnuts; and margarine (Dudek, 2001).

Fat is an essential nutrient, which, in addition to supplying the highest density of energy (9 calories per gram compared with 4 calories per gram for carbohydrates and protein) among the energy nutrients, protects vital organs from damage and insulates the body against low temperatures. It also aids in the formation of cell membrane structure, the transport of molecules such as protein and certain fat-soluble vitamins to the cells, the transmission of nerve impulses, and the production of metabolic precursors (Grodner, Anderson, & DeYoung, 2000).

Fats are composed of glycerol and attached fatty acids of varying degrees of saturation and length. Essential fatty acids cannot be manufactured by the body. The major essential fatty acid is linoleic acid, a polyunsaturated fat found primarily in vegetable oils. Its functions include prolonging clotting time, lowering serum cholesterol levels, improving skin integrity, and developing prostaglandins, which are involved in tissue activities including platelet aggregation and maintenance of smooth muscle tone of blood vessels (Grodner et al., 2000). If fat intake makes up only 10% or less of a diet's daily calories, the body cannot obtain adequate amounts of the essential fatty acids.

Dietary factors in individuals and in entire populations have important effects on blood cholesterol levels. High blood cholesterol levels clearly play a role in CHD and stroke. These diseases continue to kill more than 500,000 Americans annually. About 1,250,000 Americans have myocardial infarctions each year. In addition to their impact on the nation's health, CHD and stroke in the United States cost an estimated $298.2 billion in the year 2001 (AHA, 2001).

Implementations of recommendations to reduce dietary fat and cholesterol will help most Americans lower their levels of blood cholesterol.

Therapeutic lifestyle changes to reduce cholesterol include a change in diet, weight management, and physical activity. A diet low in saturated fat diet and a low-cholesterol eating plan with less than 7% of calories from saturated fat and less than 200 mg of dietary cholesterol are recommended. Soluble fiber and food products that contain plant sterols (cholesterol-lowering margarines) can also be added. Losing weight can help a person lower his or her low-density lipoprotein (LDL) cholesterol level, and regular physical activity can help raise the high-density lipoprotein (HDL) cholesterol level and lower the LDL cholesterol level. The risk factors an individual cannot alter include age, sex, and heredity. Additional information on lowering blood cholesterol levels is available on the National Heart, Lung, and Blood Institute website, the URL for which is listed in the chapter's Website Resources box.

Carbohydrate Requirements and Use

Carbohydrates were thought of as "the bad guys" in weight management. Today, carbohydrates are back in favor—especially complex carbohydrates. Complex carbohydrates, which are large chains of glucose molecules, are found in all plant foods. The storage form of carbohydrates in humans is glycogen. Carbohydrates are transformed to glucose—the main sugar in the blood and the body's basic fuel. They should provide 50% to 60% of total calories, mostly in the form of complex carbohydrates (Dudek, 2001). The primary function of carbohydrates is to provide energy, since carbohydrates are digested and absorbed more rapidly than protein or under normal conditions, glucose is the only energy source or the central nervous system. Carbohydrates maintain liver, heart, brain, and nerve tissue function. They also prevent the breakdown of fats and protein for energy, which results in toxic metabolic byproducts (Grodner et al., 2000).

There are two basic types of carbohydrates: simple and complex. *Simple carbohydrates* are easily digested and provide quick energy. Ordinary table sugar is an example of a simple carbohydrate. *Complex carbohydrates* are promoted over simple carbohydrates because a high concentration of

sugar in large amounts, such as in a piece of cake, is more than the body can use at one time. The excess will be stored as fat. Complex carbohydrates promote energy release more slowly and prevent large fluctuations in blood glucose levels. Good sources of complex carbohydrates include foods such as whole grains, beans and peas, potatoes, and fruits.

The food pyramids offer an excellent guide for families on what and how much to eat. They can be found on the website of the National Agricultural Laboratory. This website URL is presented in the chapter's Website Resources box. Suggestions for people all ages, as well as menu plans at various calorie levels, are available. Additionally, one can find hints on reducing fat, saturated fat, cholesterol, sugar, and sodium. These are useful for both clients and health care professionals.

Overview of Nutrition Concerns and Research

There have been numerous research reports on the health effects of polyunsaturated fatty acids, monosaturated fatty acids, dietary cholesterol, fiber, food additives, sodium, and calcium. The following sections offer a brief overview of conclusions from scientific reports.

Polyunsaturated Fatty Acids

Human diets have an abundance of polyunsaturated fatty acids because of the large amounts of margarine and salad dressings eaten. Omega-3 and omega-6 are two categories of polyunsaturated fatty acids that human bodies cannot manufacture. One of the main omega-3 fatty acids in fish—such as tuna, salmon, bluefish, sardines, and lake trout—appears to decrease the risk of heart disease by reducing the blood clotting process. The major sources of polyunsaturated fatty acids are vegetable oils including corn, safflower, wheat germ, canola, sesame, and sunflower oil; fish; and margarine. The AHA (1996) does not recommend the use of omega-3 fatty acid supplements because their long-term benefits have not been demonstrated. Substituting polyunsaturated and monosaturated fatty acids for saturated fatty acids can help reduce health risks.

TABLE 13-2   Risk Values of Total Cholesterol Levels

Ages (yr)	Moderate Risk (mg/dL)	High Risk (mg/dL)
2-19	170	185
20-29	200	220
30-39	200	240
40 and older	240	260

Monosaturated Fatty Acids

Some research studies show that substitution of monosaturated for saturated fatty acids can lower total cholesterol and LDL cholesterol levels without a reduction in the HDL cholesterol level. Examples of oils that contain predominantly monosaturated fatty acids are olive oil, peanut oil (and peanut butter), and canola oil (Grodner et al., 2000).

The AHA recommends a monosaturated fatty acid intake in the range of 10% to 15% of total calories.

Dietary Cholesterol

Dietary cholesterol raises serum total cholesterol and LDL cholesterol levels and increases the risk of CHD and atherosclerosis. There is individual variability in this response. The NCEP (2001) suggests that anyone with a total cholesterol level greater than 200 should take measures to reduce it. The NCEP states that all children, whatever their family history, can benefit from a heart-healthy diet. After the age of 2 years, children should switch to low-fat dairy products and should keep fat intake to about 30% of their daily calories. Only children who have a family history of very high cholesterol levels, heart disease, or both—and particularly those with a parent who had a heart attack before the age of 50—should have their cholesterol levels measured. This includes as much as 25% of this nation's children (NCEP, 2001).

The NCEP recommends measuring the total cholesterol level in all adults 20 years of age and older once every 5 years. A desirable blood cholesterol level is less than 200 mg/dL for adults; an optimal LDL cholesterol level is considered to be less than 100 mg/dL. Table 13-2 lists moderate- and high-risk values of total blood cholesterol.

According to the latest data from the World Health Organization (2002), the rate of coronary disease in men is highest in North Korea and Finland, and lowest in Beijing, China. For women, the highest rate was in the United Kingdom (Glasgow), and the lowest, in Spain and China. In North America, diseases of the heart are the number one killer and stroke is the number three killer.

People vary in their response to altering dietary cholesterol. For most individuals, following a low-fat diet will keep cholesterol within recommended levels. Research shows that consumption of large amounts of saturated fats increases the amount of cholesterol in the general circulation. Fats from animal foods (e.g., lard, butterfat, chicken fat) tend to be highly saturated. Fats from fish are less saturated than other animal fats, and in fact, fish oil seems to protect against heart disease.

Total serum cholesterol may not be the best predictor of CHD risk, although the risk of having a premature heart attack rises as serum cholesterol is elevated. Other risk factors include gender (male), family history of premature CHD, cigarette smoking, hypertension, low LDL cholesterol concentration, diabetes mellitus, history of definite cerebrovascular or occlusive peripheral vascular disease, and severe obesity (greater than 30% overweight).

To date, HDL cholesterol level is claimed to be the strongest predictor of CHD. HDLs appear to retard the atherosclerotic process by removing early cholesterol deposits and transporting them back to the liver for processing. (In patients with diabetes, however, LDLs appear to be better correlated with risk of CHD than HDLs.)

Factors that appear to influence the HDL level are race, gender, body weight, smoking, alcohol intake, physical activity, hormones, and drugs. Blacks have higher HDL levels than whites; females have higher HDL levels than males; obesity is associated with lower HDL levels; cigarette smoking lowers HDL levels; moderate use of alcohol increases HDL levels; exercise increases HDL levels; estrogens increase HDL levels and androgens lower them; and clofibrate, nicotinic acid, and heparin increase HDL levels, whereas zinc supplements lower them.

LDLs are cholesterol-rich particles that transport cholesterol to peripheral tissues and possibly promote entrance of cholesterol into cells. An elevated LDL level (also called *hypercholesterolemia*) is believed to accelerate the atherosclerotic process and to increase the risk of CHD (Grodner et al., 2000).

The ratio of HDL to LDL, indicating the balance between the cholesterol delivery and removal systems, may be more important than serum cholesterol levels. An ideal ratio is lower than 3.5. A ratio lower than about 4.5 suggests that the risk for CHD is below average; with a ratio higher than that, the risk is higher than average.

Fiber and Health

In the early 1970s, several researchers, notably British epidemiologist Dr. Dennis Burkett, linked a high-fiber intake among rural Africans with a low incidence of diseases common in the Western industrialized countries. The various types of fiber may help to prevent or improve disorders such as constipation, irritable bowel syndrome, and diverticulosis, although people with these disorders should consult their physicians before starting a high-fiber diet. Colon cancer is rare among people with a diet low in meat products and rich in high-fiber foods. Fiber may reduce bacteria that interact with fat and bile acids to create carcinogens as stool moves quickly through the digestive track. A high-fiber diet may also benefit obese persons because fibrous foods take longer to chew and provide a feeling of fullness. Patients with diabetes may also benefit because of the effect of fiber on blood sugar levels. There is no conclusive evidence that dietary fiber, rather than the other components of vegetables, fruits, and cereal products, reduces the risk of those diseases (ADA, 1997).

The source of fiber is plants. Fiber is the plant material that is not digested when plants are eaten. There are two basic types of fiber. Type I, or insoluble, fiber includes cellulose, hemicellulose, and lignin. Type I fiber is like a sponge: it absorbs many times its weight in water, swelling up within the intestine. Cellulose, hemicellulose, and lignin are found primarily in whole grains and beans and other plant products, especially bran. Because insoluble fibers are not digestible by humans, they are not useful as fuel (Marlett & Slavin, 1997). Type II, or soluble, fiber includes pectin (found in apples), gums, and mucilages, which are found in fruits, certain vegetables and legumes, oat bran, and most plant foods. Type II fiber does appear to lower blood cholesterol levels by 5% or more. Gum supplements tend to lower LDL cholesterol, whereas oat bran has been shown in some studies to reduce triglyceride levels. The gums also help manage blood sugar. Although results are not conclusive, epidemiological studies are consistent in showing that a high-fiber diet containing vegetables and a relatively low level of meat and fat products is beneficial with respect to reducing the risk of cancer of the colon and possibly atherogenesis.

Fiber is available in a variety of foods, and the recommended amount is 25 to 35 g per day, which is twice what the average American usually eats. Although based on limited clinical data, the recommendation regarding fiber for children older than 2 years is to increase their intake to an amount equal to or greater than their age plus 5 g/day. Clients should not be coerced into thinking that fiber is some type of medicine that ought to be added to an otherwise unrefined diet. Instead, they should be encouraged to eat a variety of foods while incorporating high-fiber foods (ADA, 1997; Marlett & Slavin, 1997).

Food Additives

Foods in their natural state are mixtures of chemicals. Some of these are nutrients (carbohydrates, protein, fat, minerals, vitamins, and water). Others are nonnutritive substances such as colors, flavors, emulsifiers, antioxidants, and chelating agents. Intentional additives are designed to perform a specific function, such as to prevent spoilage or oxidation or to improve nutritional value. Incidental additives serve no functional purpose in the final food product. Examples include pesticides; fertilizers; adjuvants to animal feed; and packaging materials, such as polyvinyl chloride, which migrate from the wrapping to the food. There are safe and unsafe doses of all chemicals, both natural and synthetic. For example, solanine (a toxic alkaloid) is present in potatoes. Common table salt is toxic in doses three to five times normally used amounts. More is known about the relative safety of food additives than about naturally occurring toxicants.

The Food and Drug Administration regulates the use of additives in food by defining criteria and tolerance levels for additives and by continually monitoring their use. In recent years, cyclamates and the colorants red dye numbers 2 and 4 and carbon black were removed from use because of hazardous effects in animals, even though there have been no observable effects in humans.

There are benefits and risks of additives. Without their use, the scope of the food supply would be limited, and many aesthetic and convenience qualities would be lost. For example, baked goods would go stale overnight, canned fruits and vegetables would be mushy and discolored, and table salt would harden. Three fifths of food additives are artificial flavors and colors, emulsifiers, stabilizers, and thickeners—the main purpose of which is to make food more attractive. Other additives are used as preservatives or as leavening or anti-staling or mold-retarding agents.

Practically any varied, well-selected diet that excludes excessive amounts of highly processed foods can be nutritionally adequate. Clients should be informed that natural, organic, and health foods are neither more nor less nutritious than similar foods available at supermarkets (The Institute of Food Science and Technology, 2001).

Additional diet recommendations related to cancer prevention are (1) limit alcohol consumption, which may lead to cancer of the mouth, larynx, esophagus, and liver; and (2) increase dietary sources of vitamins A, E, and C. Follow-ing these recommendations does not guarantee protection against cancer, but these are prudent and reasonable precautions. For additional information on dietary supplements, refer to the NIH website on dietary supplements (see the Website Resources box at the end of the chapter).

Sodium Intake and Hypertension

According to *Healthy People 2010*, studies in diverse populations have shown that salt intake is linked to increased blood pressure. There is also a link between high sodium intake and the amount of calcium excreted in the urine, thus increasing the body's need for calcium.

Studies show that population groups who consume a lot of sodium tend to have a higher incidence of hypertension. For example, in northern Japan, salt consumption is enormous—20 to 25 grams per day—and hypertension prevalence is also high. In Kenya, preliminary findings indicate that members of the Luo tribe, who live in a region where the diet is low in sodium, tend to have a lower incidence of hypertension. When tribe members migrate to other areas, the incidence of hypertension increases. Many are reluctant to draw conclusions from such studies because some rural diets include large amounts of fresh vegetables that are rich in potassium, a mineral that may protect against hypertension. A high-sodium environment may favor the expression of acquired hypertension variables that may be more common in blacks or those predisposed to hypertension (Kumanyika & Adams-Campbell, 1991). A study supported by the National Heart, Lung, and Blood Institute (NHLBI) revealed dramatic results with the Dietary Approaches to Stop Hypertension (DASH) diet in reducing blood pressure (Sacks et al., 2001). DASH is a dietary plan rich in magnesium, potassium, and calcium, as well as protein and fiber. The nutrients in the plan are based on about 2000 calories. The nutrients include about 4700 mg of potassium, 500 mg of magnesium, and 1240 mg of calcium. These nutrients come from seven to eight servings of grains; four to five servings of vegetables; four to five servings of fruit; two to three servings of dairy; two or fewer servings of meat, poultry, and fish; four to five servings of nuts, seeds, and dry beans; two to three servings of fats and oils; and five sweets a week. To learn more about high blood pressure or the DASH diet, the reader may visit the NHLBI website.

The body's daily requirement for sodium varies with each individual but is quite small. The minimal requirement is about 100 to 200 mg per day, the amount in one tenth of a teaspoon of salt. The National Research Council (1989) recommends that intake of salt (sodium chloride) be less than 6 g a day and indicates that less than 4.5 g is even more desirable. The estimated minimum requirement is even less—500 mg per day.

Estimates indicate that 90% to 95% of the population is sodium-resistant; that is, their blood pressure does not show a significant increase with increased sodium in the diet. The prudent approach is to use salt sparingly, if at all, in cooking and at the table and to check labels for the amount of sodium in foods.

Calcium and Osteoporosis

Osteoporosis is a major public health problem affecting 28 million women. Osteoporosis affects half of all women and one in eight men. "Porous bones" are associated with increased risk of fractures of the hip, wrist, and spine (Grodner et al., 2000). Approximately 20% of women in the United States sustain one or more osteoporotic fractures by age 65, and as many as 40% sustain fractures after age 65. Women who sustain a fracture between the ages of 20 and 50 years have a 74% risk of fractures after age 50 (Davidson & DeSimone, 2002).

Osteoporosis is associated with a low intake of calcium and dietary factors that negatively influence its absorption such as alcohol, aluminum-containing antacids, foods high in phosphorus, foods high in oxalic acids, and over-consumption of protein. Persons who have the greatest risk for osteoporosis are white and Asian females. Risk factors include female gender, advancing age, small stature, absence of menstrual periods, menopause, sedentary lifestyle, dietary risks (low intake of calcium and vitamin D), family history of osteoporosis, use of certain medications, smoking, and consumption of more than five cups of coffee or tea per day. The majority of adolescent and adult females in the United States do not meet the average requirements; they often consume less calcium in food and few milk products relative to soft drinks. The recommendations for adequate daily intake of calcium are 500 mg for children ages 1 to 3 years, 800 mg for children ages 4 to 8 years, 1300 mg for adolescents ages 9 to 18 years, 1000 mg for adults ages 19 to 50 years, and 1200 mg for adults age 51 years and older. The National Research Council recommends an additional 400 mg of calcium per day for pregnant and lactating women.

Although milk and cheese are the best dietary sources of calcium, many people do not eat these foods because of personal preferences, lactose intolerance, or allergies. They should be encouraged to use other good sources of calcium, since daily calcium intake is essential (Grodner et al., 2000). Foods high in calcium include milk, yogurt, cottage cheese, ice cream, fortified orange juice, canned red salmon, sardines with bones, kale, collards, turnip greens, mustard greens, dandelion greens, okra, broccoli, and soybeans (cooked). If supplements are warranted, calcium carbonate or calcium citrate is most easily absorbed.

Practitioners should routinely ask questions about risk factors for osteoporosis. One of the easiest assessments, which is often skipped, is monitoring height in men and women as they age. Height loss and a history of fractures should prompt the professional to consider a dual-energy x-ray absorptiometry scan to evaluate for osteoporosis in high-risk clients. Although advancing age is most commonly associated with osteoporosis, individuals at any age may be at risk.

Nutritional Status and Immunity

The study of nutrition and immunity is ongoing. A nourished body is not as easily infected as a malnourished one. A compromised state makes it difficult for the immune system to respond. Grodner et al. (2000) describe ways in which nutrients play a role. Nutrients are important in the anatomical development of lymphoid tissue, skin health, cell proliferation, synthesis of immunologically active proteins, cellular activity and movement, and modulation and regulation of the immune process. Because the immune response is a rapidly acting system, nutrient functions have dramatic effects on the system's responsiveness. The immune system components that are affected by poor nutrition include antibodies, macrophages and granulocytes, T lymphocytes, skin, gastrointestinal tract, and mucus. Each may be compromised by malnutrition (Grodner et al., 2000). A discussion of the many nutrients that influence immune status is beyond the scope of this chapter. Chang and Dhar (1999) provide a good overview of this topic.

Nutritional Needs throughout the Life Cycle

It is well known that nutritional needs change. When assessing the family, the nurse should be alert to specific needs related to development level. Anticipatory guidance should be provided throughout the growth cycle.

Pregnancy and Lactation

Family health nurses often have the opportunity to provide nutritional counseling to pregnant women. It has been estimated that an additional 30 g of protein and 300 calories are needed during pregnancy to meet the increased energy (caloric) demands for tissue building. This amounts to a total intake of about 2500 calories a day. Active, large, or nutritionally deficient women may require more. Appropriate weight gain during pregnancy will indicate whether sufficient calories are being consumed. The addition of two glasses or servings of milk or milk products to the diet to total four servings will contribute to the protein requirements and supply the additional 400 mg of calcium needed daily during pregnancy (Lovelady, 1996).

By including a variety of foods, a patient can meet the RDA for vitamins and minerals, with the possible exception of iron and folic acid. These are traditionally supplemented.

Overweight or underweight clients should be encouraged to attain an ideal weight before conception. Beginning an exercise program before pregnancy may help with weight control and overall well-being during pregnancy.

The minimum recommended weight gain is 28 pounds for underweight women, 25 pounds for normal-weight women, and 15 pounds for overweight women. Data suggest a relationship between maternal weight gain and infant birth weight. Women who gain less than ideal weight during pregnancy have an increased risk of pre-term delivery and delivery of a low birth weight infant. Minority women are less likely to gain the recommended weight and should be carefully evaluated (U. S. DHHS, 1996).

Pregnant adolescents have additional nutritional requirements because of the dual growth demand: that of the fetus and that of the mother (Zemel & Levin, 1996). Because many teenagers already have poor dietary habits, they have an increased risk for poor nutritional status. The StorkNet website (see the Website Resources box at the end of the chapter) has excellent resources for nutritional guidelines for pregnancy and lactation. Food pyramids are offered for different ethnic groups as well.

Nausea, which is a common complaint during the first 16 weeks of pregnancy, may be diminished by avoiding an empty stomach, eating small meals often, separating meals and fluids, and eating before getting out of bed. It is important to monitor the woman's ability to gain weight during the first trimester if nausea is a problem.

Nutritional Needs in Early Years

The first year of life is an important time for good nutrition. The rapid growth and metabolism demand ample nutrition. The tremendous growth is a composite of the various growth patterns of internal organs. Weight gain in the first 3 months of life is about 1 kg/mo (Chumlea & Guo, 1999). By the end of the first year, the growth rate has slowed, with a resultant gain of approximately 5 pounds between 1 and 2 years of age, and calorie requirements have decreased. At about 1 year of age, children need approximately 1000 calories and only 1300 to 1500 calories by age 3. One tablespoon of food per year of age is the average serving size. Parents who are reminded of this normal decreased need for calories will avoid conflict when children refuse food.

Babies spend an average of $2^1/_2$ hours per day eating, which equals about 1000 hours a year—as much time as a college student spends in classes in 2 years of full-time study. While obtaining nutrients for growth, babies are also learning about their world—about food, about themselves, and about behaviors that win approval and those that do not. Eating can make a great contribution to a child's future well-being physically and psychologically.

Nutritional cautions for mothers include avoiding giving babies honey because of the risk of botulism and reducing the risk of cow's milk anemia by adding other foods after the child has had 2 to 3$\frac{1}{2}$ cups of cow's milk per day. Children should be allowed to stop eating when their stomachs are full to prevent excess weight gain.

Family health nurses should encourage parents to give a child food according to developmental readiness and to encourage self-feeding skills. Hand-eye coordination may be developed by offering finger foods and spoons or a cup when the child is ready. For more specific guidelines, Samour, Helm, and Lang's (1999) handbook on pediatric nutrition is a useful resource. A sample food pyramid for children ages 2 to 6 years is available through the USDA website (refer to the Website Resources box).

Nutritional Needs of School-Age Children and Adolescents

Except during pregnancy, nutrient requirements are higher in adolescence than at any other time. The adolescent growth spurt begins at 10 or 11 years of age in girls, reaches its peak at 12 years of age, and is completed by about 15 years of age. In boys, the growth spurt usually begins at 12 or 13 years of age, peaks around 14 years of age, and ends by about 19 years of age (Lifshitz, Finch, & Lifshitz, 1991).

Because there are wide variations in growth and development during any age period, parents should understand that these variations do not necessarily indicate abnormal growth. Normally, from 8 to 12 years of age, a child's body weight approximately doubles, but rarely at a constant rate. Body fat measurements increase temporarily for boys in early puberty. A persistent increase in body fat is seen in girls throughout adolescence. The increase in fatness usually occurs directly after the peak in growth. Thus it is important to differentiate a temporary tendency toward fatness from a serious weight problem (Chumlea & Guo, 1999). Body mass index for age percentile charts may be used for boys and girls, once they have reached age 2 years, to assess growth. Children above the 85th percentile are considered "at risk" for overweight. This is covered in greater detail later. Research suggests an association between sedentary activities of children (e.g., video games, television, and videotapes) and obesity (Robinson, 1999). See the Research Synopsis for a brief discussion of the study.

RESEARCH SYNOPSIS

TELEVISION VIEWING AND OBESITY

There has been an alarming trend in increases in obesity across all ages. A known risk factor is television watching. More than one fourth of children report watching 4 or more hours of television each day. Prevention is considered to hold the best promise, with family support being a key element. This study examined the effects of reducing television, videotape, and video game use on changes in obesity, physical activity, and dietary intake. The study was carried out in an elementary school with 192 children over a 6-month period.

The children in the intervention group had significant decreases in body mass index, triceps skinfold measurements, and waist circumference and decreases in television viewing and meals eaten in front of the television. Although there were no differences in high-fat food intake and in moderate-to-vigorous activity and cardiovascular fitness, this study demonstrated a direct association between television, videotape, and videogame use and increased adiposity. This may be one promising approach to help prevent childhood obesity.

Robinson, T. N. (1999). Reducing children's television viewing to prevent obesity. *JAMA: The Journal of the American Medical Association, 282,* 1561-1567.

Because of the rapid growth during adolescence, energy (calories) and protein needs are high. Boys tend to gain more weight at a more rapid rate, which accounts for their higher energy and protein needs. They are laying down more muscle and less body fat than girls. Boys end up with about 8% body fat, whereas girls average 20%. The higher percentage of body fat and the lower level of physical activity results in girls needing fewer calories than boys, even at the same weight. Individual calorie needs vary. Girls consume fewer calories than boys—from 1800 to 2200 calories per day; boys need 2300 to 3000 calories per day. Many girls eat less than this to have the thin bodies that some cultures and ethnic groups desire. The pressure to restrict food intake for weight control may inhibit their ability to acquire the nutritional reserves needed for later reproduction (Lifshitz et al., 1991). The Food Guide Pyramid for young children may be accessed through the USDA website (see the Website Resources box). Dietary guidelines for school-age children are presented in Table 13-3.

There is little evidence of insufficient protein intake among teenagers in the United States. Calorie needs might fall below the recommended amount in young people for economic reasons or because of attempts to lose weight. When energy is limited, dietary protein will not be available for synthesis of new tissue. The result is a reduction in growth rate, even though protein intake appears to be adequate.

American adolescents tend to be low in their optimal intake of folacin, calcium, iron, and zinc. It is estimated that 5% to 15% of American adolescents have anemia. As a result of the increased muscle mass and blood volume, the body's need for iron is especially high. After menstruation, girls need to replace the iron lost in the menstrual flow. Symptoms of iron deficiency anemia include lack of energy, fatigue, pale complexion, and increased susceptibility to infection (Burns, Brady, Dunn, & Starr, 2000). See Table 13-3 for a nutrition guide for children and teenagers along with estimated calorie needs.

Overweight and Obesity in Adolescents

Because of the adolescent's precarious balance between striving for independence and dependence on the family for basic physical and emotional needs, the family's role in nutrition is variable. Peers should be involved in any plan for change (James, 2001). They may be involved directly, if the client is willing, by inviting them to a counseling session so that specific problems and strategies can be worked out. Peers are involved indirectly in the assessment because the counselor includes information about what friends do and think to determine whether they will be an obstacle to reaching a goal. Box 13-4 offers guidelines for parents of an overweight child.

Because about one fourth of a teen's calories come from snacks, parents should provide snack foods that contain some essential nutrients, such as milk, fresh fruit, low-fat yogurt, whole-grain breads, fresh vegetables, crackers, reduced fat cheese, nuts, and popcorn. Young adults who are well nourished feel better, have more energy, and are better able to withstand psychological and physiological stress than those with inadequate nutrition. If appropriate eating patterns have been established during the adolescent years, there is no need to change the type or quality of food consumed in adulthood.

A common concern of parents and teens is obesity. In 1999, 13% of children ages 6 to 11 years and 14% of adolescents ages 12 to 19 years in the United States were overweight. The prevalence has nearly tripled for adolescents in the past 2 decades. Overweight adolescents have a 70% chance of becoming obese adults. This increases to 80% if one or both parents are overweight or obese. Often, they are caught in a downward spiral of overeating, depression, inactivity, lowered self-esteem, social isolation, and weight gain (U.S. DHHS, 2001).

Some accepted risk factors for childhood overweight cannot be changed. Factors that *can* be changed are as follows:

1) Parenting style can be adapted to be noncontrolling.
2) Physical activity can be increased throughout childhood and adolescence.
3) Television watching can be limited.
4) Skipping meals can be avoided.
5) Eating patterns can be improved (e.g., by avoiding eating in front of television or while doing homework and by not eating when not hungry).

TABLE 13-3   Suggested Dietary Guidelines for School Children and Teenagers

Food	Age 7 to 10 Years	Age 10 to Teen Years
Milk and cheese (whole, dry, skim, re-liquefied evaporated, soy milk, buttermilk, and other daily products)	6-9 years: 2-3 c 9-10 years: 3 or more c	10-12 years: 3-4 c 12-16 years: 4 c Pregnant teens: 5-6 c

Calcium equivalent of 1 c milk
  1 c plain yogurt
  2 c cottage cheese
  $1\frac{1}{2}$ c ice cream
  $1\frac{1}{3}$ oz cheddar cheese or
  Swiss cheese		

Meat-fish-poultry-beans	2 servings ($\frac{1}{2}$-2 oz/serving)	2 servings (2-3 oz/serving)

Substitutes for protein for 1 oz meat:
  1 egg
  $\frac{1}{2}$-$\frac{3}{4}$ c cooked dry beans, dry peas, soybeans, lentils
  $\frac{1}{4}$-$\frac{1}{2}$ c nuts or seeds
  2 tbsp peanut butter		

Vegetables and fruit	4 or more servings ($\frac{1}{3}$ c each)	4 or more servings ($\frac{1}{2}$ c each)
Eat one vitamin C source daily (e.g., citrus fruit, melon, strawberries, broccoli, tomatoes, raw cabbage)		
Eat one vitamin A source at least every other day (e.g., deep yellow-orange or very dark green vegetable or fruit)		
Use unpeeled fruits and vegetables and those with edible seeds frequently		

Bread and cereal (whole-grain or enriched bread, cereal, rice, or pasta). One serving is:
  1 slice bread
  1 roll, muffin, or biscuit
  $\frac{1}{2}$-$\frac{3}{4}$ c cooked cereal, rice, or pasta
  1 oz dry cereal
	4 servings or more (very active children need more for energy)	4 servings or more
		Teenage boys: 6 or more servings (very active teens and athletes need more)

Additional foods Fats and oils, such as butter, margarine, mayonnaise, and vegetable oils; sweets and desserts; a source of Vitamin D	As needed to meet kilocalorie needs; sweets should be consumed in moderation; a source of vitamin D is recommended throughout the growth period (such as vitamin D-fortified milk)	

Kilocalorie needs	2400 (7-10 years)	Girls:
		  11-14 years: 2200
		  15-22 years: 2200
		Boys:
		  11-14 years: 2500
		  15-18 years: 3000
		  19-22 years: 2900

Adapted from National Research Council. (1989). *Recommended dietary allowances. Subcommittee on the Tenth Edition of RDAs, Food Nutrition Board, Commission on Life Sciences* (10th ed.). Washington, DC: National Academy Press.

> **BOX 13-4 How Parents Can Help Overweight Children**
>
> 1. Let children know that they are okay whatever their weight: be accepting.
> 2. Focus on the family: gradually change eating habits and activities.
>   - Be a role model. Are you eating five servings of fruits and vegetables a day?
>   - Plan family activities such as a walk after dinner or biking together.
>   - Focus on reducing the amount of time spent watching TV and playing video games.
> 3. Teach healthy eating patterns early; have regular meals and eat together often.
>   - Don't place the child on a restrictive diet.
>   - Carefully cut down on fat by using low-fat dairy products and poultry without skin and by limiting consumption of fast food.
>   - Pack lunches whenever possible if school lunches are heavy.
>   - Plan for snacks by making them nutritious but not depriving.
> 4. Seek help from a health professional who is trained to work with obese children if you are finding it difficult. The Weight-Control Information Network (WIN) maintains a list of nationwide university-based medical centers.

Risk factors that *cannot* be changed are parental obesity, socioeconomic factors, and genetics. Children from families with a lower socioeconomic status are more likely to be overweight, as are girls without siblings who have older mothers (Crawford, 1998).

For children, age-specific growth charts facilitate a more accurate evaluation of a child's weight, since they are based on age, sex, and channels of growth of many children across the United States. More recently, body mass index (BMI) (weight divided by height in square meters) has been used as a guideline to determine underweight and overweight. The interpretation of BMI depends on the child's age. BMI for age is plotted according to age-specific charts. The tables of BMI calculations are available through the Centers for Disease Control and Prevention (CDC) website (see the Website Resources box). Underweight is BMI for age <5th percentile. At risk for overweight is BMI for age >85th percentile, and overweight is BMI for age >95th percentile. BMI is related to health risks.

According to Freedman, Dietz, Srinivasan, and Berenson (1999), 60% of children and teens with a BMI for age above the 95th percentile have at least one risk factor, and 20% have two or more risk factors for cardiovascular disease. Family health nurses who work in pediatric clinics or schools may identify adolescents who are at risk for future weight problems and refer them to programs or work with the family and teen to establish goals and a weight reduction plan. Consumer information on obesity trends and nutrition and physical activity is also available through the CDC.

Anorexia and Bulimia

Society's preference for plumpness or thinness tends to set the standard for what is considered to be the ideal body shape or image. Often, it also sets the stage for eating disorders. Eating serves different functions physiologically and symbolically. Apart from a person's desire for thinness, eating disorders can have physiological origins or be associated with family dynamics. An estimated 1 in 100 females between the ages of 13 and 19 has anorexia. Up to 10% die of anorexia (NIH, 2002).

Anorexia is a refusal to maintain body weight at or above 85% of the weight that is normal for that person's age and height. Girls and women with anorexia have an intense fear of gaining weight and a disturbance in how they experience their shape. Anorexia in postmenarchal females causes amenorrhea, which is defined as the absence of at least three consecutive menstrual cycles (Mehler, 1996a). Anorexia nervosa is characterized by a relentless pursuit of thinness that results in life-threatening emaciation and an almost delusional preoccupation with food and body image accompanied by withdrawal from family and friends. It is frequently reported to be an outcome of persistent attempts to lose weight and occurs most frequently among adolescent girls and young women in the upper and middle socioeconomic classes.

The term *anorexia* is actually a misnomer, since the appetite is not lost: the client simply refuses to eat. Hyperactivity, exercising to the point of exhaustion with a denial of fatigue, and a drive for intellectual excellence are also typical of the patient with anorexia. Pursuing a thin body becomes an isolated area of control in a world in which the individual feels ineffective; the dieting provides an artificial sense of mastery and control. In any child who does not gain weight or who ceases to grow, an eating disorder and/or an inappropriate health belief that distorts his or her dietary intake must be considered (Hobbs & Johnson, 1996).

The goal of treatment is to assist the client in developing a positive and secure self-image and a change in attitude about food. For clients who have a mild form of the disorder, counseling may be provided on adolescent growth, normal nutrition, and the serious consequences of malnutrition. If the disorder is complicated by stresses such as family problems or depression, the nurse can shift the focus to deal with the particular stress. Long-term data indicate that no more than 50% of patients recover completely, and the mortality rate for patients with anorexia nervosa is 10% to 15%. Since few organ systems are spared from the progressive deterioration of malnutrition associated with anorexia, inpatient programs are often indicated (Society for Adolescent Medicine, 1995).

The American Psychiatric Association (1994) defines *bulimia nervosa* as eating binges followed by purging that occur at least twice a week for 3 months. Purging may consist of self-induced vomiting, strict dieting or fasting, vigorous exercise to prevent weight gain, or use of diuretics or laxatives. Bulimia is a disorder affecting young women usually 18 years of age or older; there is a much lower incidence among males, although they account for 10% of patients with bulimia. The majority of patients with bulimia are in their twenties, and about one fourth are married. Most come from upper socioeconomic groups and are college students, actresses, or models. More than half of patients with bulimia are of normal weight, but they have an exaggerated fear of becoming fat. Symptoms of bulimia sometimes begin at the conclusion of weight reduction diets. Other causes of chronic bulimia may include unresolved grief,

traumatic neurosis, history of sexual abuse leading to feelings of guilt and shame, and repetitive attempts at self-purification.

Bulimia is characterized by the sudden ingestion of large amounts of food in short periods. As much as 4000 to 5000 kcal may be consumed, followed by fasting, vomiting, or purging (particularly with laxatives or enemas). Foods eaten are usually those clients are attempting to exclude from their diet.

Sometimes the binging is precipitated by feelings of depression, anxiety, boredom, or loneliness. Frequently, the binging is done secretly and is planned. Afterward, there is often a period of drowsiness and a feeling of depression, guilt, and self-disgust. The initial stages of the bulimic episode are not necessarily unpleasant because there is a temporary release from the rigors of strict dieting, a distraction from current problems, and a temporary decline in any feeling of depression or anxiety (Brownell & Wadden, 1986; Mehler, 1996b).

Nurses should be aware that binges can lead to obesity and that binges followed by fasting, vomiting, or purging may lead to severe electrolyte imbalance, dehydration, and malnutrition. Esophageal irritation and extensive dental erosion and decay are also common.

Dietary counseling of the client with bulimia may focus on appropriate quantities of food needed for weight maintenance. The nurse can help the client to structure the daily eating schedule and provide guidelines. This will give the client a feeling of control and assurance of adequate nutrition. Assistance with time management and stress management may help the client to avoid the extremes of overactivity and boredom. The nurse should identify stress relievers and strategies that enable the client to cope with emotions without the use of food. Other goals of treatment involve exploring body image, early dieting behaviors, and issues related to separating from the family to establish intimacy and authentic peer relationships. Individual, group, and family therapies are used in treatment.

Eating disorders require attention and should not be ignored with the hope that the adolescent will grow out of it. The psychological and physiological health hazards warrant professional assistance. Optimal management involves combined approaches including nutritional rehabilitation, psychotherapy, behavior modification, family therapy, and at times, psychotropic medications.

Adulthood

The adult years span approximately 40 years (from age 21 to 60), and adults are a heterogeneous group. Resting metabolic rates decrease approximately 2% each decade after age 30, thus decreasing energy requirements. Because of decreased production of estrogen and lowered metabolism, many menopausal and postmenopausal women are reported to have increased weight gain (ADA, 1999). Family nurses may help women and their families to understand the changes that occur during this stage and provide health teaching about modification of dietary patterns and the relationship of exercise, food intake, and weight maintenance.

Exercise and reduced food intake provide a means by which weight gain can be prevented. Energy and nutrition needs differ for younger versus older adults. Nutrient needs for exercising versus less active adults remain virtually the same, with the possible exception of requirements for riboflavin and vitamin B_6.

Nutrition needs of the exercising adult can be met with the use of some basic guidelines, such as the following:
1) Eat a variety of foods to obtain nutrients without relying on supplements.
2) Use vitamin and mineral supplements with caution.
3) Choose foods high in calcium to prevent osteoporosis and possibly to control high blood pressure.
4) Choose iron-rich meats such as red meat, fish, and poultry.
5) Eat vitamin C–rich foods, such as oranges, with nonmeat sources of iron such as nuts, beans, and fortified cereal to help prevent iron deficiency anemia (particularly a concern for menstruating women).
6) Practice moderation in exercise and eating.
7) Read about nutrition research with discretion.

Nutrition and Older Adults

The nutritional status of the older adult is affected by physiological and psychological parameters. The effects of physiological parameters, such as chronic disease, often coexist with psychosocial factors such as inadequate income or social isolation.

Today's population of older adults is a heterogeneous group that varies widely in age (61 to 115 years), income level, educational level, lifestyle, dietary habits, and health status. The only commonality is chronological age, which is a poor indicator of biological age or health status.

The population of older adults has not been studied to any great extent. Major gaps still exist in knowledge about the energy and nutrient requirements of older adults. The present number of elderly people is expected to double by the year 2030; thus nurses need to be cognizant of their nutritional concerns. Food pyramid guides are also available for adults older than 50 years at the USDA website (refer to the Website Resources box at the end of the chapter).

The family health nurse should assess the individual concerns of the older adult and plan a diet *with*, not for, the adult. Difficulty with food ingestion—such as decreased ability to bite, chew, or swallow; decreased taste and smell acuity; and other physical limitations such as vision or mobility limitations—may affect nutritional status (Grodner et al., 2000).

Digestive and absorptive functioning may decrease with age and lead to vitamin B_{12} deficiency, decreased calcium absorption, and gastrointestinal distress. Symptoms such as heartburn, gas, and abdominal distention are common and may be related to poor eating and bowel habits, a preoccupation with food, and emotional tension.

The older adult may be concerned with an increase in weight, which often occurs with decreasing basal metabolism. As muscle cells are reduced, they are replaced by fat and fibrous connective tissue. Encouraging as much activity as can be tolerated may decrease the physiological changes that come with aging. In spite of the large number of changes that occur with aging, most functions are affected to only a moderate degree.

Psychosocial deterrents to good nutritional status include feelings of despair, limited income, substandard housing, inadequate transportation, social isolation, and long-established food habits. Nurses should assess for the effects of these factors on the availability of food.

Family Supports for Weight Control

As many as 40 million Americans may have weight problems, and the numbers are rising. In fact, obesity in the United States has been described as being at epidemic levels (U. S. DHHS, 2001). Excessive weight increases the risk for gout, gallbladder disease, elevated blood pressure, CHD, and some types of cancer and has been associated with the development of osteoarthritis. The prevalence of obesity is high across the life span, especially among women, children, the indigent, and members of some ethnic groups (Modkad, Serdula, & Dietz, 2000).

BMI is a measure of fatness that correlates highly with direct measures of body fat. The BMI is calculated to define and determine a healthy weight that is reasonably independent of height. Box 13-5 presents a sample calculation of BMI. The panel of obesity experts at the NIH recommends that professionals adopt this index for evaluation. A BMI of 25.0 to 29.9 kg/m^2 is defined as overweight; a BMI of 30 kg/m^2 or more is defined as obesity. The website of the CDC provides basic information about obesity, BMI charts, and resources for clients and professionals. See the Website Resources box at the end of the chapter for the website URL.

More than 65 million people are on a diet at any given time. They go on a diet, then off—losing, then regaining. The following three factors work against the dieter:

1) When calories are restricted by lowering food intake, the body adapts by lowering its metabolic rate and thus resists burning the fat stores. Then, when the person becomes tired of the restricted diet and increases food intake, the body treats the intake as excess, and weight is regained, even though food intake is less than before the diet.

2) Weight lost in the early part of a strict diet is mostly water, not fat. The initial rapid loss is a result of a loss of body sodium and water, which is believed to be secondary to the usual carbohydrate restriction.

3) When dieters consume fewer than 1200 calories a day, they lose muscle tissue, as well as fat. Dieters actually become fatter than before the diet because the percentage of muscle has decreased and the fat percentage has increased.

When counseling an overweight family member, the nurse should encourage a combination of reduced calorie intake and exercise. Because exercise builds muscle tissue and burns calories, an improved muscle-to-fat ratio is ensured. Box 13-6 includes some key suggestions for learning to control weight.

Walking 1 hour per day three times a week will burn about 324 calories per session, 972 calories per week, 3888 calories per month, and 46,656 calories per year. This is equivalent to 13 pounds of body fat. If exercise is accompanied by a decrease in intake of 100 calories per day, the individual will lose a total of 23 pounds without dieting. Box 13-7 offers tips for helping a family select a weight reduction program, if a health care professional is unable to provide the service (AHA, 1994).

Additional features in a program may include instruction in stress reduction techniques, cognitive therapy (learning to change self-talk), and assertiveness training. Family members may be referred to the American Society of Bariatric Physicians, which is a group of physicians and nurses who practice prevention, treatment, and study of overweight and related conditions. There are also many online resources that provide

---

BOX 13-5   Body Mass Index

Body mass index (BMI) is the figure obtained by dividing body weight in kilograms by the square of height in meters.

Example: Kevin is 5 ft 10 in tall and weighs 170 lb. To determine his BMI:

1. Convert weight into kilograms.
   a. 170 lb divided by 2.2 lb/kg = 77.2 kg (2.2 kg = 1 lb)
2. Convert height into meters.
   a. 5 ft 10 in = 70 in (5 ft × 12 in = 60 in + 10 in = 70 in)
   b. 70 in × 2.54 cm/in = 177.8 cm
   c. 177.8 cm divided by 100 cm = 1.8 m
   d. 1.8 m^2 = 3.2 m (1.8 × 1.8 = 3.24)
3. Calculate BMI.
   a. 77.2 divided by 3.2 = 24.12

BOX 13-6 Practical Suggestions for Weight Control

1. Identify what contributes to weight gain.
2. Set realistic goals. A healthy weight loss is 1 pound per week. Focus on changing habits by working on one habit change each week.
3. Reduce caloric intake. Find out how many calories are eaten daily. Reduce the *intake* by 500 to 1000 calories. Do not go below 1000 calories without professional supervision. If necessary, increase the exercise level instead of reducing the intake any further.
4. Limit fat intake to 30% or less of the total calories. Pay attention to how much fat is eaten daily.
5. Exercise aerobically regularly for optimal changes in body fat and lean body mass. An ideal time range is to work up to 45 minutes four to five times per week.
6. Find substitutions for "problem foods" or high-fat, high-sugar foods. If there are none, decide on a desirable serving size.
7. Listen to the hunger level. Eat when hungry and stop when just satisfied.
8. Establish a regular eating pattern. Eating three to five times a day provides the body with small amounts of energy throughout the day.
9. Plan ahead for special occasions. If you are going out for dinner, plan to eat less during the day (without skipping a meal).
10. Use "smart talk." Try to avoid labeling food and yourself as good or bad. You are not a good or bad person based on what you eat on one day.
11. Accept sole responsibility for your dietary choices and health practices. Eating healthy and maintaining weight involves personal choices that only you can make.
12. Separate food and emotions by asking yourself what you are feeling when you want to eat. If it isn't hunger, take care of the feeling (e.g., boredom, anger, frustration, sadness).
13. Be patient and keep practicing until your new habits become a part of your routine. Weight management takes daily practice.

BOX 13-7 Guidelines for Selecting a Diet Program

The following questions will help to evaluate if the program is appropriate for a family.
- Does the program provide a comprehensive approach, combining diet, behavior modification, and exercise?
- Is the program individualized or based on a standard program that is given to everyone?
- Is the program medically supervised?
- Will the frequency of the program meet the client's needs?
- Will the meetings be on a one-to-one basis or will there be a group format?
- What is the program's success record?
- Is there a maintenance program?
- Are special meals or products required?
- Are family members included in any meetings?
- What are the credentials of the staff?
- Are several diet options offered and will they interfere with any medications?
- Is there a contract?

From American Heart Association. (1994). American Heart Association guidelines for weight management programs for healthy adults. *Heart Disease and Stroke, 3,* 221-228.

guidance for losing weight. Shape Up America and Nutrition and Your Health: Dietary Guidelines for Americans are two very good ones. See the Website Resources box for their website URLs. Nurse practitioners may want to refer to two articles by James (1997 & 2001) for protocol and partnership guidelines to be used with clients.

Steps to Weight Loss and Control

A safe diet that promotes long-term weight loss will also do the following:
- Satisfy all nutrient needs except energy
- Minimize hunger
- Accommodate (through adaptation) the tastes and habits of the individual
- Include easily obtained foods
- Encourage the establishment of lifelong eating habits

If the minimum recommended number of servings for adults is consumed from the four food groups, the protein, carbohydrate, and fat supply will be less than 1100 calories a day. Diets of less than 1000 calories are not recommended because they restrict the sources of essential nutrients. Diets greater than 1600 calories a day may result in very slow weight loss for women. Men, however, may lose weight rapidly at this level.

Between-meal hunger is often a problem for many weight watchers. Snacks high in simple sugars or small meals are rapidly digested and absorbed into the bloodstream, causing a sharp rise in the blood glucose level, which stimulates insulin production. Insulin removes the glucose from the blood to the cells. If it removes too much, the blood glucose level can drop rapidly to a level even lower than that before a meal or snack, leaving the person feeling tired, dizzy, and hungry. If between-meal hunger is a problem, the nurse can suggest small servings of low-fat cheese, crackers, or fruit for snacking (Grodner et al., 2000).

Previous studies help to explain why people on low-carbohydrate diets often feel tired and listless and have trouble sleeping. Wurtman's (1986) research at the Massachusetts Institute of Technology has indicated that carbohydrate deprivation depletes the brain of serotonin, an important neurotransmitter, which acts as a sleep inducer and has a calming effect. It may be that when brain levels of serotonin drop too low, cravings are likely to occur. People on low-carbohydrate diets crumble at the sight of a cookie or a piece of bread.

The general rule for any weight loss scheme should be "Don't go on anything that you are not willing (or able) to stay on forever." Going on a diet implies that one will someday go off of it. When clients are told that certain foods are forbidden, those foods become "special" and are often used as rewards or treats. By allowing "heavy" or "junk" foods in small quantities, the weight watcher never has to go off the diet.

Overweight clients can be encouraged to eat "heavy" foods, as they would if they were already at their ideal weight. For example, a client who wants to maintain a weight of 120 pounds, but has decided to eat pie, can be encouraged to imagine eating a sliver of pie instead of one fourth of the pie. This principle may be applied to the management of difficult or high-risk situations. The client can be asked to imagine successful behavior adaptations that can be used on occasions that were once disastrous.

A final consideration is that the diet should accommodate the personal tastes of the individual. The nurse should consider the client's age, sex, and ethnic group.

The Impact of Obesity on the Family

The obese condition of a family member affects the family system, and the family situation affects the obese member through family structure and interaction. Bruch's (1973) classic categories of family characteristics are interesting in anticipating how a family will respond to dietary modification by a member. The three classifications include (1) consistent, but not rigid, cooperation within the family; (2) rigid and over-perfectionist family dynamics; and (3) severe family discord.

In the *consistent* classification, the family reaction is characterized as consistent but not rigid in cooperating with the family member making dietary changes. The entire family would probably act as a team in adjusting eating habits to help the obese member. Food is used neither as a reward nor as a form of discipline. No great hardships or feelings of deprivation are experienced. The dieter in this situation has a good chance of being successful.

Families who are *rigid* in their eating and lifestyle patterns will often respond with excessive cooperation but without real communication about the problem. Emotional reactions are often not shared; thus outwardly, communications appear smooth and normal but in reality are often lacking, and family members are inwardly tense.

A child may be treated as a possession, and food or material objects may be provided instead of love and opportunities to develop effective coping skills. Children with perfectionist parents often have a difficult time reacting to stressful situations that require independent and adaptive behavior. They often have not learned to interpret their needs or to define their goals. They often grow up to be dependent and insecure and are unable to assert themselves. They may feel as though they have no control over their lives.

Family histories of families with obese children suggest discrepancies in parental status, with imbalances in who has power, who makes decisions, or who is recognized as important. The child needs help to develop self-awareness, gain insight into food habits and behavior, and develop skills to resolve conflicts. Encouragement from friends may help the child outgrow obesity. Strict adherence to a diet can result in despair and a return to overeating. Intimidation and disciplinary measures are often detrimental and unsatisfactory (James, 2001).

An extension of the rigid, perfectionist family is the family with *severe family discord.* The family usually demonstrates aggression, antagonism, dissatisfaction, marital disharmony, or mutual contempt. As a result, the child learns to respond to all kinds of feelings as hunger and cannot discriminate among fear, anger, anxiety, and hunger. Food has often been used as a substitute for love, security, and satisfaction. In this type of family, common interests, communication, and participation in social life are absent. Parents of these children often experienced a childhood of loneliness and unfulfilled hopes. They were deprived of affection or family support and lacked a parental figure.

Still accepted is the idea that the obese child in the discordant family often loses weight but breaks the diet and has difficulty accepting a reducing diet. The underlying social problem increases the child's feeling of guilt and frustration. Without the chance to develop independence, the child feels ineffective, out of control, depressed, defiant, unable to cope, and rejected. The child may also feel shame, self-hatred, or disgust.

Family living skills and a positive self-image for a child may be needed before a formal program is offered. Living skills include abilities to share thoughts, feelings, and concerns; to be supportive in trying times; to seek outside resources or alternatives; and to make decisions. James (2001) offers a guide to the assessment and treatment of obese children. Epstein, Myers, Raynor, and Saelens (1998) also offer a comprehensive review of treatment approaches to pediatric obesity.

The family health nurse who focuses on family dimensions and personal development will enhance program success for families with or without problem behaviors. Identification of the underlying contributors is important to long-term success. If the family health nurse believes that the family problems are beyond the scope of his or her practice, the family should be referred for additional counseling. Box 13-8 provides the health care professional with tips for designing a plan for weight loss or control with a family.

A comprehensive weight management program includes behavioral modification, exercise, cognitive change, social support, and nutrition (U.S. DHHS, 2000c). Recommendations include the following:

- Longer treatment programs (at least 16-20 weeks)
- Increased use of "practicing at habit changes"

BOX 13-8 Guidelines for Counseling the Family in Weight Control or Loss

1. The family health nurse should first identify the individual's and family's level of motivation and reasons for desiring to make nutritional changes. The nurse may ask clients to identify the "costs" and "benefits" of losing weight. Fear of failure is often combined with lack of motivation.
2. Identify underlying factors that contribute to excess weight and overeating.
3. Clarify supportive roles of each family member (e.g., parent agrees not to bring junk food in house; or mother agrees not to ask about daily food intake).
4. Write long-term and short-term goals.
5. Teach the family how to use positive self-statements and nonfood rewards. Help the family build confidence by assisting in definition of realistic, attainable goals.
6. Provide for psychological and social support, especially for clients with a significant amount of weight to lose. It is possible to suggest professional, commercial, or self-help groups after the initial assessment and program plan have been completed.
7. Encourage continued follow-up for at least 2 years after the weight has been lost.

- Assessment of rate and amount of food eaten (in the clinic instead of working with "reports")
- Examination of thoughts and emotional factors that disrupt weight control measures
- Differentiation of tasks involved in weight loss and weight maintenance
- Examination of social support and relationships between obese person and spouses, co-workers, and friends

Applying the Nursing Process to Family Nutrition

The clinician's role in promoting family nutritional health includes serving as a resource person and identifier, educator, awareness raiser, coach, mobilizer, role model, reinforcer, and reviewer. Promoting individual and family nutritional health begins with assessment of family and individual nutritional practices and behaviors. An assessment tool is provided in Figure 13-1. It is intended as a guideline for data collection and to help the nurse to empower the family to review their dietary habits and thoughts and feelings related to food. Box 13-9 summarizes ways health professionals can increase families' capacity to transform the nutritional health of obese children.

The use of a comprehensive assessment nutrition tool makes important data that increase the family's awareness of health-supportive behaviors available. Detailed assessment and illumination of family strengths and areas of growth provide data to facilitate increasing family capacity for nutritional health. The analysis serves as a basis for empowering the family to transform their nutritional practices to incorporate more health-promoting choices and practices.

Individual assessments are not specifically covered because of the desire to focus on the family as a unit. However, individual nutritional issues or needs are often a concern of the entire family and should be illuminated so that the capacity to meet the challenge is strengthened.

In collaboration with family members, the nurse determines the strategies, behavior changes, and routines. Suggestions have been described in earlier sections for guiding the family in planning for dietary and lifestyle changes that affect their

| BOX 13-9 | Ways Health Professionals Help Families with Obese Children |

- Identifying children who are overweight/at risk for overweight
- Encouraging families to love and accept children no matter what their size
- Encouraging families to plan to provide more physical activity for parents and children
- Encouraging families to provide healthy foods and snacks for everyone
- Encouraging families to practice good eating behaviors
- Evaluating exercise and activity patterns and designing an appropriate program

From Crawford, P. (1998). *Children and weight: What health professionals can do about it* [Concept Paper]. Unpublished manuscript, School of Public Health, University of California, Berkeley.

health. A selected list of nutritional resources for families and individuals can be found in the Website Resources box at the end of the chapter.

The health care professional's role is not complete until a follow-up evaluation of the family's progress or attainment of goals has been made. At that time, goals are adjusted and plans may include additional follow-up meetings with the family health nurse, or care may be discontinued if the nurse and family believe that the goals have been accomplished.

Future Research and Family Nutritional Health Promotion

The family is the environment in which individual nutritional habits, behaviors, and preferences are learned. The direction for research and family nutrition in the first decade of the new millennium is best delineated by U.S. Surgeon General Dr. David Satcher's call to action, *Overweight and Obesity: A Vision for Future* (U.S. DHHS, 2001). The statement recommends a concerted effort to increase research in the following areas: (1) be-

Text continued on p. 367

Family Members	Age	Educational Level	Developmental Level
1.			
2.			
3.			
4.			
5.			
6.			

SUBJECTIVE ASSESSMENT
Family's perception of health status (describe)

Nutritional practices
Who decides on the menu?
Who does the grocery shopping?
Who prepares the meals?
Meal Pattern
Describe mealtime (who is present, when, where, and atmosphere)
Does mealtime serve a particular function? (For example, are the day's activities planned? Are problems discussed?)
Snacks consumed and frequency
Knows food sources from the food pyramid
24-hour food recall
    Include assessment of intake of at least 5 fruits and vegetables daily, intake of dairy/calcium, intake of fat and sugar (junk foods), protein intake, carbohydrate servings (looking for over or under consumption of primary food categories)

Sources of dietary fat
Use of red meat, fish, and poultry (once a week, three times, etc.)
How often do you eat cheese?
What kinds do you purchase?
How often do you use cold cuts?
How often do you use fish/chicken? (Describe preparation.)
How often do you use processed foods such as bakery products, frozen dinners?
How much milk or other dairy products do you consume? What types?

Cholesterol and saturated fat
How many eggs does the family eat per week?
What kind of fat do you use in cooking?
What kind of vegetable oil do you use?

Sources of complex carbohydrates and fiber
How often do you eat fruit? How do you eat it (juices, fresh, canned)?
What kind of vegetables do you eat (canned, frozen, fresh)?
What kind of bread do you eat (whole grain, white)?

Sugar consumption
Do you use sugar in cooking? Do you buy candy, pastries, sweetened cereals?

Sodium
How often do you use processed foods (canned or packaged such as macaroni and cheese)?
Do you add salt to food?

Alcohol consumption
How often do you use alcohol?

Figure 13-1 Family nutrition assessment tool.

How much coffee and tea do you drink per day?

Supplements
Do you take vitamins or mineral supplements? What and how much? Reason.

Cultural influences
"Special" foods
Eating habits unique to culture
Family food preferences or restrictions

Economics
Do you receive any supplementary income to purchase food items?

Eating problems
Do you have problems with indigestion, vomiting, nausea, sore mouth?
Do you have any difficulty swallowing liquids or solids or chewing and feeding yourself?

Medications
Are you on any medications? Do they affect your appetite or weight?

Weight
Has weight changed in the last 6 months? How much? Describe events associated with the change.

Elimination pattern
Describe bowel and urinary patterns.

Activity and exercise patterns
Usual daily/weekly activities of family members

Source of nutrition information
(magazines, family member, schools, health food store)

Family work patterns
Do family members work outside of the home? Type of work and hours

Family stressors

Family strengths

Lifestyle changes family desires to make:

OBJECTIVE ASSESSMENT:
Physical assessment of family members:
Describe appearance of the family
Height/Weight
Blood Pressure
Pulse/Respirations
Body Mass Index is the standard for 2 years +_____

Relative Weight: $\frac{actual\ weight \times 100}{ideal\ weight}$

Example:
160 (actual weight) × 100 = 16000
(16000 divided by ideal weight of 140 = 114%)
The closer relative weight is to 100%, the better
Labs (cholesterol, triglycerides, glucose)

Figure 13-1, cont'd   *Continued*

120-139 mild obesity
140-159 moderate obesity
160 + severe obesity

ASSESSMENT:
Assessment Summary
Check problem area or potential problems
   1. Dietary fat
   2. Cholesterol and saturated fat
   3. Complex carbohydrates and fiber
   4. Sugar
   5. Alcohol
   7. Caffeine
   8. Supplements
   9. Cultural influences
  10. Economics
  11. Eating problems
  12. Medications
  13. Weight changes
  14. Elimination pattern
  15. Activity and exercise
  16. Nutrition resources
  17. Work patterns
  18. Notes of concern

Family stressors

Family strengths/weaknesses

Lifestyle changes indicated:
(Identify nutritional concerns of the family)
Barriers to change? Are there reasons why the family cannot change the problem area?

Nursing diagnosis:

Plan and intervention/Evaluation

Supplementary Assessment for Obesity Problems
Physical assessment (height, weight, body fat composition, BMI, blood pressure, pulse, respirations)
Highest and lowest weight
Why do you want to lose?
What are the contributing factors to weight gain?
Family weight history
         Maternal   Paternal
Eating patterns
Diets attempted
Medical problems associated with obesity
Activity level
Developmental stage, stresses, significant life events

Nursing diagnosis:
Goal:
Plan/Health Teaching:
Evaluation:

Figure 13-1, cont'd

havioral and environmental causes of obesity and overweight, (2) prevention and treatment of overweight and obesity, (3) development of best practices guidelines, and (4) disparities in health as it influences overweight and obesity among ethnic, gender, socioeconomic, and age groups. Lastly, clinicians are encouraged to identify effec-

tive and culturally appropriate interventions that will only be effective if the family system is included at each stage of the research. Therefore family clinicians in the next decade are compelled to incorporate family variables and interventions in research designs and methodology to improve nutritional health.

CASE SCENARIO

Jill (34) and Bob (37) have one son, Casey, age 12. Jill and Bob have been married for 14 years. Bob works nights and Jill works part time during the day. Jill's father (Mr. Smith) lives close by and watches Casey after school when both parents are busy. Bob likes to gamble and tends to spend the family's income versus setting it aside for savings. Jill has a history of an eating disorder and likes sweets. She is rather quiet. Bob doesn't really care about his diet because he is thin regardless of what he eats. Casey's BMI is greater than 95th percentile (32). Although he is overweight, he appears to be a happy child. Bob admits to taking Casey to McDonalds on his way to school, since Casey gets up too late to eat breakfast. Casey gets okay grades but needs a lot of guidance to get his homework done on time. Casey loves to play Nintendo and watches car racing on TV whenever he can. The school has physical education class three times a week during which the children play basketball or soccer. Casey gets what he wants; he is good at speaking up. The family eats dinner together one to two times a week, usually with the television on. Casey doesn't have anyone to play with where he lives; he reports feeling bored, which is why he entertains himself with sedentary activities. There is no significant family history other than Mr. Smith having diabetes as an adult. Mr. Smith has loaned the family money in the past and feels that he needs to "help out" when it comes to raising Casey. Jill and Bob rarely do anything together; they are each busy with their work. Neither parent exercises on a regular basis. Jill feels that she has not resolved her eating issues. She stays thin by "picking" throughout the day.

Casey's grandfather called the nurse practitioner to make an appointment to talk about his grandson's weight.

MAJOR FAMILY STRESSORS

Bob's lack of interest in being a role model for Casey, insufficient income, different work hours for each parent, little quality time with Casey, too much time playing games and watching TV, an overinvolved grandparent, poor boundaries and limit-setting with son, increasing obesity of son.

FAMILY STRENGTHS

Casey is encouraged to speak up; both parents express love and concern for son; support is provided by extended family.

LIFESTYLE CHANGES INDICATED

Lifestyle changes needed include family meals together, family activity, limits on television and Nintendo, clarification of boundaries between parent and extended family and parents and son, provision of light but not depriving meals, decreasing fat in diet by going to McDonalds less often or changing what Casey orders, parental time together without Casey to strengthen their relationship, a commitment by each parent to role-model healthy eating and behaviors, finding after school activities to increase social interaction and physical activity. The parents may want to ask for outside help to set up a positive supportive environment.

WEBSITE RESOURCES

ORGANIZATION	WEBSITE ADDRESS
American Diabetes Association	http://www.diabetes.org
American Dietetic Association	http://www.eatright.org
American Heart Association	http://www.amhrt.org
American Society of Bariatric Physicians	http://www.asbp.org
Anorexia Nervosa and Related Eating Disorders	http://www.anred.com
Child Obesity	http://w ww.childobesity.com
SHAPEDOWN	http://www.shapedown.com
National Office of Disease Prevention and Health Promotion	http://www.odphp.osophs.dhhs.gov
National Institutes of Health Information on Obesity	http://www.ods.od.nih.gov/databases
Centers for Disease Control and Prevention	http://www.cdc.gov/nccdphhp
Center for Science in the Public Interest	http://www.cspi.org
Center for Weight and Health at University of California, Berkeley	http://www.cnr.berkeley.edu/cwh
Cholesterol Information	http://www.lipidhealth.org
Dietary Approaches to Stop Hypertension (DASH)	http://www.dash.bwh.harvard.edu
Eating Disorders Awareness and Prevention, Inc	http://members/aol.com/edapinc
National Institute on Aging Information Center	http://www.nia.nih.gov/health/
U.S. Surgeon General Call to Action on Obesity	http://www.surgeongeneral.gov/topics/obesity/-
National Agricultural Laboratory	http://www.nal.usda.gov
National Council Against Health Fraud	http://www.ncahf.org
National Heart, Lung, and Blood Institute	http://www.nhlbi.nih.gov/
National Institute on Aging	http://www.nih.gov/nia
Office of Dietary Supplements	http://www.ods.od.nih.gov/
National Guideline Clearinghouse	http://www.guideline.gov
National Osteoporosis Foundation	http://www.nos.org
Nutrition and Your Health: Dietary Guidelines for Americans	http://www.health.gov/dietaryguidelines
Shape Up America	http://www.shapeup.org
Tufts Nutrition Navigator	http://www.navigator.tufts.edu
Weight Control Information Network	http://www.niddk.nih/gov/NutritionDoc.html
StorkNet	http://www.storknet.com

■ CHAPTER HIGHLIGHTS

- Although it is customary to think of nutrition as an individual activity, it is best understood from a systems perspective because social, cultural, cognitive, and biological variables influence family and individual nutrition.
- The average family diet in the United States can be described as imbalanced in nutrients and excessive in fat, sugar, and protein.
- Key tasks of families with children include ensuring adequate nutrient intake, teaching children the importance of good nutrition to achieve growth and a normal body weight, and role-modeling by eating a variety of foods that provide adequate nutrients.
- Nursing assessment of family nutrition should include determination of family and individual developmental levels and family nutritional practices and patterns, dietary intake, beliefs, values, culture, economics, preparation, and exercise.
- The family nurse's role is to assist the family by means of anticipatory guidance, teaching, and supporting nutritional lifestyle changes.

CRITICAL THINKING ACTIVITIES

1. Interview a peer to discuss his or her comfort level in providing a nutritional assessment of a family with an obese child. What strengths do you have as a family health nurse that prepare you to assist this family?

2. A mother of a 3-year-old girl is in your office expressing great concern over her child's eating habits. What information would you provide the concerned mother about caloric needs of a 3-year-old? What resources would you use for educational materials?

3. Assess your intake of food for a day and compare it with the Food Guide Pyramid Guidelines.

   a. Example

Food items	Food Group
2 cups cereal	grains
1 cup milk	milk
$1/2$ chicken breast	meat

   Total of servings from   Meat Milk Fruit Vegetables Grains Other

   # of servings recommended_____

   b. List ways to improve your intake to meet the Food Guide Pyramid recommendations.

4. What are nutritional concerns for teenage athletes?

REFERENCES

American Dietetic Association. (1997). Position of the American Dietetic Association: Health implications of dietary fiber. *Journal of the American Dietetic Association, 97,* 1175-1159.

American Dietetic Association. (1999). Position of the American Dietetic Association and Dieticians of Canada: Women's health and nutrition. *Journal of the American Dietetic Association, 99,* 738-751.

American Heart Association. (1994). American Heart Association guidelines for weight management programs for healthy adults. *Heart Disease and Stroke, 3,* 221-228.

American Heart Association. (1996). Dietary guidelines for healthy American adults: A statement for health professionals from the nutrition committee, American Heart Association. *Circulation, 94,* 1795-1800.

American Heart Association. (2001). *Heart and stroke statistical update.* Retrieved October 15, 2001, from http://www.americanheart.org.

American Psychiatric Association. (1994). *Diagnostic and statistical manual of mental disorders* (4th ed.). Washington, DC: Author.

Anderson, S., Griesemer, B., Johnson, M., Martin, T., McLain, L., Rowland, T., et al. (2000). Medical concerns in the female athlete. *Pediatrics, 106(3),* 610-613.

Brownell, K., & Wadden, T. (1986). Behavior therapy for obesity: Modern approaches and better results. In K. Brownell & J. Foreyt (Eds.), *Handbook of eating disorders: Physiology, psychology, and treatment of obesity, anorexia, and bulimia* (pp. 180-197). New York: Basic Books.

Bruch, H. (1973). *Eating disorders: Obesity, anorexia and the person within.* New York: Basic Books.

Burns, C., Brady, M., Dunn, A., & Starr, N. (2000). *Pediatric primary care: A handbook for nurse practitioners* (2nd ed.). Philadelphia: W. B. Saunders Company.

Chang, C., & Dhar, A. (1999). Nutrition and the immune system. In C. Van Way III (Ed.), *Nutrition secrets: Questions you will be asked* (pp.165-169). Philadelphia: Hanley & Belfus.

Chumlea, W., & Guo, S. (1999). Physical growth and development. In P. Samor, K. Helm, & C. Lang (Eds.), *Handbook of pediatric nutrition* (pp. 3-15). Gaithersburg, MD: Aspen.

Crawford, P. (1998). *Children and weight: What health professionals can do about it* [Concept Paper]. Unpublished manuscript, School of Public Health, University of California, Berkeley.

Davidson, M., & DeSimone, M. (2002). Osteoporosis update: Targeting risks, managing wisely. *Clinician Reviews, 12,* 76-82.

Dudek, S. (2001). *Nutrition essentials for nursing practice* (4th ed.). Philadelphia: Lippincott.

Erickson, E. H. (1956). The problem of ego identity. *Journal of the American Psychoanalytic Association, 4,* 6-121.

Epstein, L. H., Myers, M. D., Raynor, H. A., & Saelens, B. E. (1998). Treatment of pediatric obesity. *Pediatrics 101*(Suppl), 554-574.

Freedman, D. S., Dietz, W. H., Srinivasan, S. R., & Berenson, G. S. (1999). The relation of overweight to cardiovascular risk factors among children and adolescents: The Bogalusa Heart Study. *Pediatrics, 103,* 1175-1182.

Grodner, M., Anderson, S., & DeYoung, S. (2000). *Foundations and clinical applications of nutrition: A nursing approach.* St. Louis, MO: Mosby.

Hobbs, W., & Johnson, C. (1996). Anorexia nervosa: An overview. *American Family Physician, 54,* 1273-1278.

Insel, P., Turner, R., & Ross, D. (2003). *Discovering nutrition.* Sudberry, MA: Jones and Bartlett.

Institute of Food Science and Technology. (2001). *IFST information statement on organic food.* Retrieved October 21, 2001, from http://www.ifst.org/hotop24.htm

James, K. (1997). Evaluating and managing obesity: A guide for health professionals. *Contemporary Nurse Practitioner, 2,* 4-13.

James, K. (2001). All in the family: Treating obesity in children and adolescents. *Advance for Nurse Practitioners, 9,* 26-32.

Kimm S. Y., & Obarzanek, E. (2002). Childhood obesity: A new pandemic of the new millennium. *Pediatrics, 110,* 1003-1007.

Kumanyika, S., & Adams-Campbell, L. L. (1991). Obesity, diet, and psychosocial factors contributing to cardiovascular disease in blacks. *Cardiovascular Clinics, 21,* 47-73.

Lifshitz, F., Finch, N. M., & Lifshitz, J. Z. (1991). Obesity. In F. Lifshitz, N. M. Finch, & J. Z. Lifshitz (Eds.), *Children's nutrition* (pp. 295-322). Boston: Jones and Bartlett.

Lovelady, C. A. (1996). Nutritional concerns during pregnancy and lactation. In D. Krummel and P. Kris-Etherton (Eds.), *Nutrition in women's health* (pp. 212-231). Gaithersburg, MD: Aspen.

Marlett, J., & Slavin, J. (1997). Health implications of dietary fiber: Position of American Dietetic Association. *Journal of the American Dietetic Association, 97,* 1157-1159.

Mehler, P. (1996a). Eating disorders: 1. Anorexia nervosa. *Hospital Practice (Office ed.), 31,* 109-113, 117.

Mehler, P. (1996b). Eating disorders: 2. Bulimia nervosa. *Hospital Practice (Office ed.), 31,* 107-114, 120, 123.

Messina, V. K., & Burke, K. I. (1997). Position of the American Dietetic Association: Vegetarian diets. *Journal of the American Dietetic Association, 97,* 1317-1321.

Modkad, A., Serdula, M., & Dietz, W. (2000). The continuing obesity epidemic in the United States. *Journal of the American Medical Association, 284,* 1650-1651.

National Cholesterol Education Program. (2001, May). *Third Report of the National Cholesterol Education Program (NCEP) Expert Panel on Detection, Evaluation, and Treatment of High Blood Cholesterol in adults (Adult Treatment Panel III). Executive summary* (NIH Publication No. 01-3670). Bethesda, MD: National Heart, Lung, and Blood Institute, National Institutes of Health.

National Institutes of Health. (2002). *National Center for Health Statistics.* Retrieved April 4, 2002, from http://www.nih.gov.

National Research Council. (1989). *Recommended dietary allowances* (9th ed.). Washington, DC: National Academy of Sciences.

Robinson, T. N. (1999). Reducing children's television viewing to prevent obesity. *JAMA: The Journal of the American Medical Association, 282,* 1561-1567.

Sacks, F. M., Svetkey, L. P., Vollmer W. M., Appel L. J., Bray G. A., Harsha D., et al. (2001). Effects on blood pressure of reduced dietary sodium and the Dietary Approaches to Stop Hypertension (DASH). *New England Journal of Medicine. 344,* 3-10.

Samour, P., Helm, K., & Lang, C. (1999). *Handbook of pediatric nutrition.* Gaithersburg, MD: Aspen.

Society for Adolescent Medicine. (1995). Eating disorders in adolescents: A position paper of the Society for Adolescent Medicine. *Journal of Adolescent Health, 16,* 476-448.

Tippett, K., & Cleveland, L. (1999). How current diets stack up: Comparison with the dietary guidelines. In E. Frazao, (Ed.), *America's eating patterns: Changes and consequences.* Washington, DC: U.S. Department of Agriculture, ERS, AIB-750.

U.S. Department of Agriculture & U. S. Department of Health and Human Services.(2000). *Dietary guidelines for Americans* (5th ed.). USDA Home and Garden Bulletin No. 232. Washington, DC: USDA.

U.S. Department of Health and Human Services. (1996). *Pregnancy nutrition surveillance.* Atlanta, GA: Centers for Disease Control and Prevention.

U.S. Department of Health and Human Services. (1998). *Report of clinical guidelines on the identification, evaluation, and treatment of overweight and obesity in adults.* Washington, DC: National Heart, Lung, and Blood Institute, Centers for Disease Control and Prevention.

U.S. Department of Health and Human Services. (2000a). *Healthy People 2010* (Vol. 1). Washington, DC: U.S. Government Printing Office.

U.S. Department of Health and Human Services. (2000b). *Healthy People 2010: Understanding and improving health.* Washington, DC: U. S. Government Printing Office.

U.S. Department of Health and Human Services. (2000c). *The practical guide: Identification, evaluation, and treatment of overweight and obesity in adults.* (NIH Publication Number 00-4084). Washington, DC: Author.

U.S. Department of Health and Human Services; Office of Disease Prevention and Health Promotion; Centers for Disease Control and Prevention, National Institutes of Health. (2001). *The Surgeon General's call to action to prevent and decrease overweight and obesity.* Rockville, MD: U. S. Department of Health and Human Services, Public Health Service, Office of the Surgeon General, U. S. Government Printing Office.

World Health Organization. (2002). Global database on obesity and body mass index. Retrieved July 10, 2001, from http://www.who.int/nut/db

Wurtman, J. (1986). *Managing your mind and mood through food.* New York: Rawson.

Zemel, P., & Levin, B. (1996). Adolescent pregnancy: Implications for nutritional care. In D. Krummel & P. Etherton (Eds.), *Nutrition in women's health* (pp. 35-57). Gaithersburg, MD: Aspen.

Family Stress Management

Perri J. Bomar
Jeanne F. Denny
Joann E. Smith

14

Family stress—inevitable but surmountable.
— Dolores Curran, 1985

OBJECTIVES

On completion of this chapter, the reader will be able to do the following:

1. Explain the concepts of family stress, coping, and stress management.
2. Define physiological, psychological, and social stress.
3. Differentiate between stress and crisis, individual and family stress, and coping and stress management.
4. Discuss theoretical models of family stress.
5. Evaluate theories of effective and ineffective coping.
6. Identify symptoms of stress in families.
7. Describe methods of assessing family stress.
8. Explain nursing diagnoses specific to family stress and coping.
9. Describe approaches to empower families in stress management.
10. Discuss specific strategies for adaptation and management of family stress.
11. List future research implications for families experiencing stress and crises.

All families experience stress as a natural part of human existence. In addition, families throughout the world are experiencing unparalleled change in the twenty-first century as they adapt to rapid shifts in their social, economic, and global environments. However, the ways in which a family manages stress are the most significant factors in determining the effects of life stress on the family's health (Boss, 2002). Although there are many types of families, researchers suggest that the types and causes of stress families experience are similar. However, in similar situations, the strengths and degree of resilience vary among families. Each family system is unique

and has its own repertoire of approaches or strategies to manage the situation, which may or may not be adequate to restore the family system to equilibrium (Boss, 2002). Therefore a major role of the family nurse is to empower families to anticipate and adapt to stressors by using healthy strategies.

In this chapter, a comparison of stress and crisis is provided, and theoretical models of family stress and family stress management are highlighted. Also discussed are specific stressors and strategies to assist families in assessing, recognizing, and managing stress. Lastly, presented is a discussion of how to empower a family to regain or maintain functioning in ways that strengths and resources are mobilized to manage stress.

Stress of Individual Family Members

Often, practitioners are not cognizant of family stress and tend to focus attention on the symptoms of stress in individual family members made popular by the work of Hans Selye (1974). However, Boss (2003), in a review of "what is new in family stress theory" (p. 1), notes that a growing body of research suggests stress of the family unit is often exhibited in individual members such as children and caregivers. Three types of individual stress are physiological, emotional, and social stress. The stress of family members as a result of unresolved family system stressors is often exhibited in physical or emotional symptoms. Although the focus of this chapter is family stress and stress management, clinicians should also be aware of the individual responses to stress (Lyon, 2000), the myriad causes and implications of individual stress, and the impact on the family unit. For example, deployment of one parent for military service, leaving the other to provide childcare and manage the household can have serious ramifications for the health of the family unit.

Physiological Stress

The research of Cannon (1929) and Selye (1976) documented the physiological impact of actual or perceived stress on the body. Selye (1976) defines *stress* as "the nonspecific response of the body to any demand, whether it is caused by or results in unpleasant conditions" (p. 51). Agents that cause the conditions of stress are called *stressors*. Stress can be differentiated in terms of negative or positive stimuli or good or bad stress. Negative or harmful stimuli are called *distress* and may result from actual or perceived threats to the body. Some examples of distress are illness and cognitive processes such as worry or fear. Pleasant or desirable stimuli, such as a birthday or a wedding ceremony, are called *eustress,* or good stress (Selye, 1974). Both distress and eustress cause nonspecific responses in the body. However, the effects of eustress cause less damage. Both eustress and distress initiate the "fight or flight" response in the

body. This response includes activation of the sympathetic nervous system (vasoconstriction of blood vessels, elevated blood pressure, increased heart rate, and increased secretion of adrenaline and cortisol) (Wells-Federman et al., 1995). Prolonged stress has been shown to be associated with many illnesses such as asthma, ulcers, high blood pressure, frequent infections (Maier & Watkins, 1998), heart disease (Williams et al., 2000), cancer (Bryla, 1996), and alteration in the immune response (White & Porth, 2000).

In the past decade, family scholars began to note that the health of individual family members may be related to the level of family stress. For example, Miller and Wood (1997) note that children with asthma experience more difficulty breathing during stress-related situations. Often, the physical symptoms in individual family members are related to the level of family system stress or change in the family system. Psychological stress theory explains the relationship of emotion to physiological stress. Research on caregivers of family members with disabilities or chronic or terminal illness suggests that the health of caregivers is often negatively affected by lack of social support and high stress levels (Schulz & Beach, 1999).

Psychological Stress

Lazarus (1966) has explored psychological stress and states that perceptions and cognitive processes are also stressors. The manner in which an individual copes depends on the intensity of the threat, the individual's personality type, specific culture, locus of control, and beliefs about the stressor. Although Lazarus notes differences among physiological, psychological, and social stress, he emphasizes that the physical responses of the body are the same. Both cognitive processes and physical stress initiate the fight or flight response in the body. Therefore family conflict and stressors may influence the psychological health of individual members and result in depression, anger, family violence, or abuse.

Social Stress

Social stress results from actual or perceived threats in the social environment, such as relationships at work, conflicts at school, or interactions within society. Twenty-first century examples are bullying at school, work, or home; racism and prejudice in social and health care settings and in the workplace; economic recessions and "bull markets"; evaluations of performance at work or school; conflict with co-workers or neighbors; heightened security alerts; immigrant and refugee status; environmental noise; and threats of terrorism or war (Lipson & Meleis, 1999). Families of different cultures may experience cultural stress as a result of conflict with values, rituals, beliefs, customs, and lifestyle patterns of the dominant culture. This is particularly evident in families who relocate to another country, state, or neighborhood.

The following definitions will assist the reader in understanding common terms used in this chapter:

- *Family stress* is "pressure or tension in the family system—a disturbance in the steady state of the family" (Boss, 2002, p. 16). It is change in the family equilibrium that ranges from mild to dramatic.
- A *stressor* is any event that causes change within the family. It is a situation with which the family has limited advance experience and is thus perceived as problematic (Hill, 2003).
- A *family crisis* is "a disturbance in the system equilibrium so acute and strong that the family is at least temporarily immobilized. It cannot function" (Boss, 2002, p. 65).
- *Family resilience* consists of the characteristics, dimensions, and properties of families that help families to be resistant to and adapt to crisis and stress. It has protective factors for families at risk and includes the strengths families use in response to difficulties. Resilience includes commitment, communication, cohesion, adaptability, spirituality, connectedness, time together, and ability to problem solve (McCubbin & McCubbin, 1993; National Network for Family Resiliency, 1996).
- *Empowerment* is the process of promoting informed self-care efforts of individuals, families, or communities directed toward taking charge of such realms as health promotion and health protection. The clinician collaborates, teaches, counsels, and intervenes with clients to facilitate their active involvement in making rational and informed choices about health, health care, well-being, and mastery of their environment (Pender, Murdaugh, & Parsons, 2002).

Crisis and Stress

The terms *crisis* and *stress* are not interchangeable. In family life, stress precedes crisis. When stress is unresolved or inadequate coping strategies are used, and when resources are absent or inappropriate, stress progresses to crisis. Hill (2003) notes that researchers categorize family crises in three ways: (1) crises from outside or inside the family, (2) crises of dismemberment-accession and demoralization, and (3) types of impact stressor events. Examples of each category are presented in Table 14-1. Crises often result from events or relationship changes that are abrupt and sudden. However, stress is always present at some level and progresses to crisis when the family does not have the necessary resources to adapt. Events such as an unexpected death, loss of employment, or military deployment may quickly progress to crisis if the family does not have adequate resources for effective coping. In crisis, customary approaches to problem solving or managing the stressor event are not effective. As a result, disorganization and emotional turmoil are experienced. When a family can no longer cope, it exhibits the following characteristics: "(1) nonperformance of prescribed roles, (2) nonmaintenance of structural boundaries, and (3) immobilization of the system" (Boss, 1987, p. 700). The distinct differences between stress and crisis are presented in Table 14-2. When the crisis is resolved, family functioning will return at one of three levels: below the pre-crisis level, at the pre-crisis level, or above the pre-crisis level.

Family Stress and Stress Management Frameworks

There are a number of models that explain the dynamic and complex phenomenon of family stress. Most evolve from Hill's (1958) ABC-X Model of family crisis, which is

TABLE 14-1 Classification of Family Crises

Extrafamily and Intrafamily	Dismemberment-Accession and Demoralization	Types of Impacts of Crises on Families
Extrafamily Economic crises Religious persecutions Political persecutions Racial/ethnic discrimination Natural disasters Acts of terrorism War	*Dismemberment Only* Death of child, spouse, or parent Hospitalization of spouse War separation or deployment	Sudden impoverishment Prolonged unemployment Sudden wealth or fame Refugee migration (for economic, political and religious reasons) Disasters (e.g., tornadoes, floods, explosions) War bombings, acts of terrorism Deprivation Political declassing
Intrafamily Lack of support Infidelity Substance abuse Premature births Suicide Mental collapse	*Accession Only* Unwanted pregnancy Return of deserter Addition of stepparent Some war reunions Some adoptions, aged grandparents, or orphaned kin	
	Demoralization Plus Dismemberment or Accession Runaways Desertion Divorce Imprisonment Suicide or homicide Institutionalization for mental illness	

Adapted from Hill, R. (2003). Generic features of families under stress. In P. Boss (Ed.), *Family stress: Classic and contemporary readings* (pp. 177–190). Thousand Oaks, CA: Sage.

TABLE 14-2 Differences between Crisis and Stress

	Crisis	Stress
Time	Short-term (limited) Categorical (present or not present) Dependent on stress	Long-term Continuous (low or high levels) Independent of crisis
Equilibrium	Extremely disturbed	Moderately disturbed
Coping	Coping not effective	Coping maintains equilibrium
Family Functioning	Immobilized and disorganized	Continues with adjustments

Data from Boss, P. G. (1987). Family stress. In M. Sussman & S. Steinmetz (Eds.), *Handbook on marriage and the family* (pp. 701-702). New York: Plenum.

as follows: **A** (the provoking event or stressor)—interacting with **B** (the family's resources or strengths meeting)—interacting with **C** (the meaning the family gives to the event)—produces **X** (the crisis).

The degree of stress experienced depends on the appraisal of the stressor, the appraisal of internal and external resources or the meaning of the event, and the family's ability to manage the situation (DeMarco, Ford-Gilboe, Friedemann, McCubbin, & McCubbin, 2000). The two major theoretical models of family stress currently developed from programs of research by family scientists are the Contextual Model of Family Stress (Boss, 1987, 2002) and the Resiliency Model of Family Stress, Adjustment, and Adaptation (McCubbin & McCubbin, 1996). Family stress is change that affects the equilibrium of the family as a unit. Changes range from mild to drastic; however, multiple factors determine whether the impact on the family is good or bad. Suggested assumptions about family stress are proposed by Boss (2002, p. 15) as follows:

1) Even strong families can be stressed to the point of crisis and thus be immobilized.
2) There are differing values and beliefs that influence how a particular family defines what is distressing and how they derive meaning from what is happening.
3) The meaning people construct about an event or situation is often influenced by their gender, age, race, ethnicity, and class.
4) Mind and body are connected, psychological stress can make people physically sick, and this process can affect whole family systems.
5) Some family members are constitutionally stronger or more resilient in withstanding stress than are others.
6) It is not always bad for families to fall into crisis because some have to hit bottom to move on to recovery; those who fall apart often become strong again, even stronger than they were originally.

Contextual Model of Family Stress

Boss (2002) contends that the family stress process is best understood by using the Contextual Model of Family Stress. Families are affected by external and internal ecosystems. In addition to the stressor event, the outcome and cause of the stressor are highly related to the internal and external context. Building on Hill's ABC-X model, Boss's model suggests that the family experience of stress is influenced by the interactions of stressor event or situation (A) interacting with the family resources (B), the meaning or family perception of the event (C), and the degree of stress (X) (Boss, 2002). Table 14-3 classifies various family stressor events and situations.

External Context of the Family

Components outside of the family, over which the family has no control, are defined as the *external context*. According to Boss (2002), the external context has profound influences on the family and how family members perceive, experience, and manage stress. Specific external contexts include culture, history, the economy, development, and heredity. *Historical context* is the time in history during which the event or situation that causes a change in the family occurs. *Cultural context* supplies the customs and mores of a particular group of people, such as American Indians or African Americans; new immigrant subculture prescribes what a family believes, health care practices, social stigma and prejudices, and methods of stress management. Often, an incongruity exists between the subculture's mores and the beliefs of the dominant culture. Whether a nation's economy is strong or weak and the effects on family income provide the *economic context* that influences a family's adjustment to stressors. Family members *inherit* genetic traits or personal characteristics that provide more or less resilience and stamina. *The developmental context* refers to the developmental stage in the family life cycle or that of an individual member. The stage of family or individual life definitively affects stress management outcome, whether the family is a young family with children or a family in later life.

Internal Context of the Family

Boss (2002) labels the elements that the family controls and changes to reduce stress *internal contexts*. There are three facets to the internal context of families. First, the *structural context* includes family boundaries, rules, and roles. For

TABLE 14-3 Classification of Family Stressor Events and Situations

Internal	External
Events that begin within the family, such as illness of a family member or major changes in family routine	Events that occur outside the family, such as changes in the economy, natural disasters, acts of terrorism, or downsizing of industries
Normative	**Catastrophic**
Predictable	Unexpected
Developmental changes that most families experience, such as marriage, birth, holidays, graduation, aging, and death	Unexpected events, such as untimely deaths, disasters of nature or war, and loss of a job
Ambiguous	**Clear**
It is difficult to obtain facts about the event. One is unclear about what is happening to the family or the status of a family member.	Clear facts about the event and family member can be obtained.
Volitional	**Nonvolitional**
Events that are wanted and sought out, such as the purchase of a new home, a planned pregnancy, or attending college	Events that are not sought out but just happen, such as an unplanned pregnancy or an unexpected job loss
Chronic	**Acute**
A situation of long duration, such as racial discrimination or a family member with Alzheimer's disease or diabetes	An event that lasts a short time but is severe, such as a family member requiring major surgery or the failure of a major goal
Cumulative	**Isolated**
Events that pile up, one right after another, before the family is able to make adjustments or adaptations	An event that occurs alone when no other events seem apparent

Data from Boss, P. (2002). *Family stress management* (p. 40). Thousands Oaks, CA: Sage.

example, lack of clarity about whether a person is in or out of the family unit causes stress (*boundary ambiguity*) (see Boss, 2002, for more information on this concept). For example, family members who are missing as a result of kidnapping or running away cause stress to the family unit. Second, the family perception or definition of a stressful event refers to the *psychological context*. According to Boss (2002), this context "essentially determines" a family's ability to mobilize defense mechanisms when a stressful event occurs. The perception can be positive or negative (denial). Third, the *philosophical context* is the family's values and beliefs at the microsystem level. The extent of family stress depends on the extent to which family beliefs and rules are congruent or on the family's ability to make adjustments to live with the macrosystem level beliefs and values.

Although the external context is important, Boss (2002) suggests that the clinician will have more immediate outcomes in empowering families in stress management by focusing on the internal family context. The family has more control over this dimension. First, the clinician would assess the three internal realms and follow up by empowering the family to garner resources and to review or change their perceptions, boundaries, values, and beliefs. For example, the need to change family rules as an adolescent matures could be stressful. Boss's (2002) major thesis is

> The outcome of a particular situation or event depends on the family's perception or meaning of the event. A family cannot begin to manage stress or problem-solve until they recognize they have a problem (p. 49).

Also, Boss (2002) contends that the family stressors that are most difficult to resolve are *ambiguous stressor events* for which the facts and status about a family member remain unclear or unknown. An example of this is the uncertainty of the status of a family member who is missing after a terrorist bombing such as the World Trade Center attack in New York on September 11, 2001, or after a major earthquake.

Resiliency Model of Family Stress, Adjustment, and Adaptation

Built on Hill's ABC-X model and the Double ABC-X Model of Family Stress (LaVee, McCubbin, & Patterson, 1985; McCubbin & Patterson, 1983), the Resiliency Model of Family Stress, Adjustment, and Adaptation was derived from more than 20 years of research by family scientists and nurse scientists (McCubbin, Thompson, & McCubbin, 1996) at the University of Wisconsin at Madison. The major assumption of the model is that "families manage stressful situations over time," and this "emphasizes the family's ability to recover from stressful events and crises by drawing on patterns of functioning, strengths, capabilities, appraisal processes, coping, resources, and problem solving to facilitate adaptation" (DeMarco, Ford-Gilboe, Friedemann, McCubbin, & McCubbin, 2000, p. 297). Other significant findings are that *family schema* and *family resilience* are crucial variables in conceptualizing family stress.

Family resilience is defined as

> the property of the family system that enables the family unit to respond constructively to (a) a stressor (in combination with risk factors) and, in so doing maintain its positive functioning and ensure well-being and development of the family unit and its members (i.e., protective) and (b) disorganization (family crisis brought about by a stressor in combination with risk factors) and, in doing so bounce back and restore the positive functioning and endure the well-being and development of the family unit and its members (DeMarco et al., 2000, p. 299).

Change in families is constant, resulting from individual family member experiences, family unit changes, and external changes. According to McCubbin and McCubbin (1993, 1996), families respond to life events and life transitions in two phases (Figure 14-1). The *adjustment phase* involves the minimal transitory changes the family unit makes in its routine patterns and processes in response to an event or transition that does not pose a hardship (such as changing jobs, moving to a new residence, or minor illness of a member). The *adaptation* phase is a much longer phase. It begins when the family's attempts to make minimal adjustments are no longer effective and result in a crisis. Both the adjustment and adaptation phases are discussed in the following section.

Adjustment Phase

According to DeMarco et al. (2000), the *adjustment phase* is a short-term family response to a stressor. During this phase the family makes minor, short-term adjustments in family patterns and processes to accommodate the stressor. The family will manage the stressor with relative ease (*bonadjustment*) or poor adjustment (*maladjustment*) to the stressor. If the stressor results in major changes in the family, such as a significant decrease in finances, the family experiences a crisis (maladjustment) and progresses to the second stage in the model (McCubbin & McCubbin, 1993).

Family Stressor

The family stressor (actual or perceived threat) may come from external or internal sources. External sources may be jobs, school, the neighborhood, extended family relationships, and so forth. Other stressors include family unit or member normative transitions that are common life events such as births, marriage, graduation, and retirement. Non-normative stressors are events that are unique or rarely occur in families. The severity of the stressor interacting with ongoing family demands threatens the family equilibrium and resources.

Family Vulnerability

Family "vulnerability is the fragile interpersonal and organizational conditions of the family system" (McCubbin & McCubbin, 1993, p. 28). This is the simultaneous accumulation or "pile-up" of ongoing family demands such as finances, developmental changes of members, and family lifestyle that occur at the same time as the new event or transition. If the family has too many demands, family members are more vulnerable to stress (McCubbin & McCubbin, 1996).

Family Type

Patterns of responding to stress and crisis often are related to type of family. *Family type* refers to

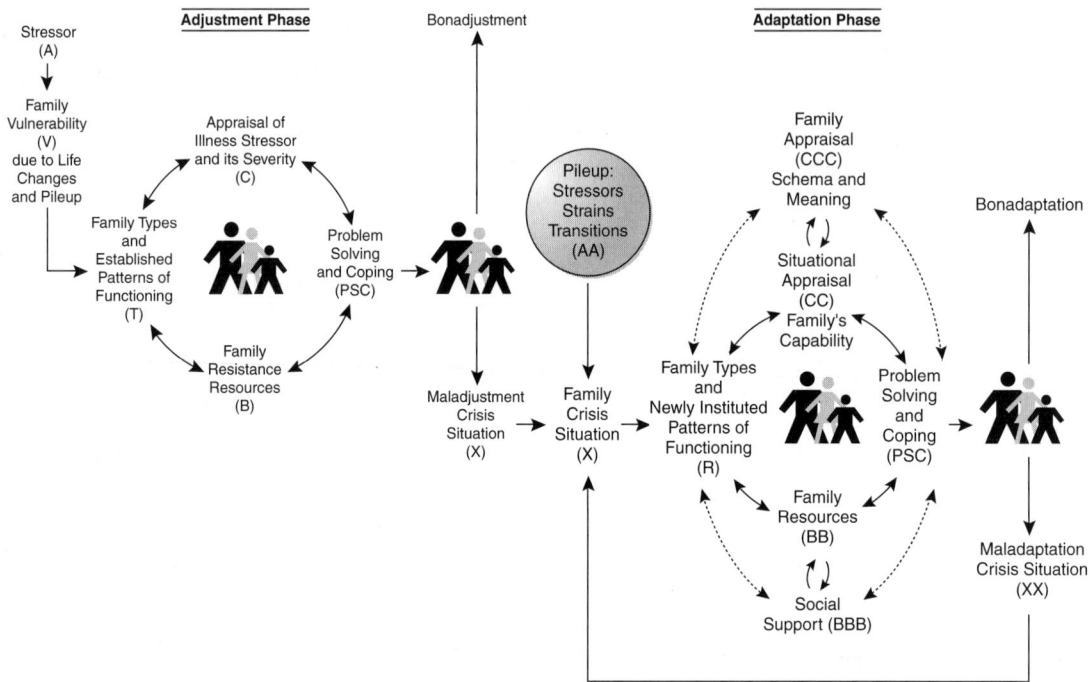

Figure 14-1 The Resiliency Model of Family Stress, Adjustment, and Adaptation. (From Danielson, C.B., Hamel-Bissel, B., and Winstead-Fry, P. (1983). *Family health and illness* (p. 23). St. Louis: Mosby–Year Book.)

a set of attributes of a family system that characterize how it usually operates or functions (McCubbin & McCubbin, 1993). There are various family typologies such as balanced, cohesive, enmeshed (Olson et al., 1983), regenerative, vulnerable, resilient, rhythmic, and traditionalistic (McCubbin & McCubbin, 1993). Although there are numerous family types within the typologies, four typologies are highlighted.

The *regenerative* family typology is characterized by dimension of hardiness (e.g., internal strengths, control, internal meaningfulness of life, being challenged by life) and family coherence (e.g., acceptance, loyalty, pride, trust, caring) that are key factors in a family's ability to adapt to stress. This typology includes four family types ranging from vulnerable families (low coherence and low hardiness) to regenerative families (high coherence and high hardiness). The greater the family's hardiness and coherence, the greater the ease with which a family will adapt to crises

(McCubbin & McCubbin, 1993). The *resilient* model of family system types is characterized by the dimensions of family bonding and family flexibility that range from high to low. The four types of families in this typology are fragile families (low bonding and low flexibility), bonded families, pliant families, and resilient families (high bonding and high flexibility). Bonding includes such attributes as feeling close to each family member, being open to discussing family problems, and doing things as a unit. Flexibility incorporates open communication and ease in changing rules, boundaries, and roles. *Rhythmic* family system types comprise the dimensions of family time and routines and valuing of family time and routines. *Rhythmic* families highly value family times and routines and predictably engage in family togetherness and family routines, whereas unpatterned families have little emphasis on family times and routines and have a low investment in family life. The last typology is the *traditionalistic* model of family systems types. The two dimensions in this typology are family celebrations and family traditions. Family types will vary from those who do not value family traditions or celebrations (situational families) to families who routinely value traditions and celebrations (ritualistic families). Families who value routines, rituals, and family bonding tend to adapt more readily to stress.

The more cohesive, flexible, bonded, and adaptable the family is, the better members are able to cope with stress. In addition, as presented in Chapter 7, good communication is a key factor in all aspects of family functioning and stress management.

Family Resistance Resources

Family resistance resources are the collective strengths a family uses to cope. They reflect the family's abilities to address and make adjustments to meet the demands of stressors without causing a crisis in family functioning (McCubbin & McCubbin, 1996). These resources are found within individual family members or the family unit and include such things as family finances, personality traits, problem-solving skills, reframing, role sharing, religious beliefs, negotiation, flexibility, routines, celebrations, and communication. If a family has resistance resources of sufficient quality and quantity and other variables are appropriate, a crisis can be avoided.

Family Appraisal of the Stressor

Family appraisal, or the meaning the family assigns to an event, significantly determines how the family responds to a stressor. The appraisal influences the strategies the family uses to adjust to that stressor (Boss, 2002; McCubbin & McCubbin, 1996). Some families choose to redefine or reframe the stressor. For example, one family may view an acute illness as temporary and as a challenge to overcome, whereas another family may see it as a catastrophe. Generally, when a family views a stressful situation as a "challenge" or a "growth experience," the family has redefined it. Positive redefining includes (1) clarifying the issues, hardships, and tasks to render them more manageable; (2) decreasing the intensity of the emotional burdens associated with the crisis situation; and (3) encouraging the family unit to carry on with its fundamental tasks of promoting members' social and emotional development (McCubbin & Patterson, 1983). The unique perceptions of individual family members shape the resulting family appraisal.

Family Problem Solving and Coping

Family problem solving and coping (PSC) is the component of adjustment that includes the family's decisions and actions to relieve stress. According to McCubbin and McCubbin (1993), problem solving and coping are the family's efforts to organize their response into manageable steps, such as the realm of interpersonal issues and communication about how to solve the problem. Coping gears the family's cognitive, emotional, and behavioral responses toward restoring balance and relieving the family strain created by a stressor.

Family Bonadjustment, Maladjustment, and Crises

Stressors vary in the strain they put on a family system's balance. The extent of the hardship depends on the family type and strengths, internal and external support, perception and meaning, and coping and problem solving. When a stressor causes minor changes in the family and the adjustment to the stressor occurs with relative ease, the family experiences a positive adjustment (bonadjustment). When the family is not resilient, that is, does not have adequate resources or strengths to make the needed changes, negative coping (maladjustment) and a state of crisis follow.

The experience of family crisis requires changes in the family's established patterns of functioning (McCubbin & McCubbin, 1993, 1996). For example, after the initial diagnosis of AIDS, a family begins to cope with the long-term issues of a chronic disease. A family experiences maladjustment when it is unable to solve the myriad of problems related to incorporating the care of the chronically ill member into the family routine. Crisis occurs when the family system lacks the personal and family resources, skills, and strengths to cope with the chronic illness over time. After the crisis is experienced, the family begins the adaptation process to resolve the crisis.

Adaptation Phase

The second phase in the Resiliency Model is the *adaptation phase* (see Figure 14-1). This phase encompasses the family's long-term actions to recover from a crisis situation (McCubbin & McCubbin, 1996). The family's goal at this time is to restore order and normalcy to family life. Adaptation "is used to describe the *outcome* of family efforts to bring about a new level of balance, harmony, coherence, and functioning to a family-crisis situation" (McCubbin & McCubbin, 1993, p. 35). In this post-crisis phase, the outcome is influenced by a number of interacting components. Family pile-up (the new stressor combined with existing family strains) interacts with family resiliency (determined by the family's ability to recover quickly by such activities as reorganizing roles, routines, and spending). The family's resilience is supported by family and community support resources, which interact with family appraisal (changes in meaning and renegotiating of goals and priorities), problem solving, and coping strategies (McCubbin & McCubbin, 1993). The result of the adaptation phase is the achievement of either positive outcomes (bonadaptation) for individual members and the family unit or inadequate adaptation (maladaptation) within the family unit and possibly within the community. Maladaptation of the family unit results in disintegration of family functioning, and the family experiences crisis again. A brief description of each aspect of the adaptation phase follows.

Pile-up of Demands

Families are seldom dealing with one simple stressor, but rather with numerous stressors that cumulate over time. Contributing to this piling up of stressors are the demands of the new stressor, combined with existing family strains and transitions (both individual family member transitions and family unit transitions), family efforts to cope, and inadequate resources.

Family Types and Patterns of Functioning

The family type and family patterns of functioning determine the strength of the family in adapting to stress over time (McCubbin & McCubbin, 1993). The family that has a shared routine is flexible, yet bonded, and will be more resilient during periods of extreme stress. Over time, families develop new patterns of functioning to incorporate the crisis into their family life. The family's usual pattern of functioning (family type) interacts with new patterns of functioning (resiliency) and significantly influences the manner in which the family will adapt to the crisis or ongoing stressor.

Family Resources, Strengths, and Capabilities

Family resources reflect the family's potential to cope with the demands of the crisis. The strengths and capabilities are the combination of each family member's knowledge and skills, the skills of the family as a unit, and the resources of their external systems (e.g., extended family and social and medical systems). Family resources may be limitless and include such variables as communication, organization, role sharing, problem solving, affirmation of members, sense of family unity, and family hardiness. Other variables may include family routines, rituals, and resilience. The variety, depth, and personal strengths of individual members and the coherence, hardiness, adaptability, skills, and knowledge of the family as a unit are significant factors in enhancing a family's adaptation to crises.

Family Social Support

External social support is provided through resources such as schools, churches, extended family, formal and informal support groups, employers, and social and government agencies. McCubbin & McCubbin (1993) suggest that the greater the family's social support in breadth, depth, and efficacy and the greater the quality of affirming social support the more likely the family will be able to adapt to a crisis situation.

Family Situational Appraisal, Schema, and Meaning

McCubbin and McCubbin's (1993, 1996) research revealed that in addition to the family defining or giving meaning to stressors, there are two other levels of family appraisal: situational appraisal and schema and meaning. The McCubbins' findings are similar to Boss's (2002) contention that a family's meaning and perception of the situation is a key determinant in how the family adapts to a stressful event or situation. *Situational appraisal* is the family's attempt to examine family strengths and potentials in relationship to the demands caused by the crisis or pile-up of stressors. This appraisal determines the family's perception of the manageability of the stressor or crisis and the changes the family will need to make to solve the problem. Crisis precipitates the need for the family to change the rules, organization, and patterns of family functioning. The family is compelled to explore the meaning of the stressor or event and the resultant family changes needed.

Separate from determining the meaning of an event is the consensus on family boundaries. According to Boss (2002), families may experience boundary ambiguity, that is, difficulty in determining who is emotionally and physically present or absent in the family. The family's appraisal and schema are crucial variables in the outcome of the adaptation phase (Boss, 2003; McCubbin & McCubbin, 1996). The greater the congruency in family meaning of the event, the greater the ease with which the family will be able to adapt to the stressor (Boss, 2002).

Family Problem Solving and Coping

Family problem solving and coping is a process that the family uses to cooperatively mobilize its resources. Over time, the problem-solving and coping process interacts with the family resources, family type and patterns, and the meaning of the event. The goal of the coping process is to restore the family unit's balance while removing or reducing the stressor and its accompanying hardships through problem solving.

Family Adaptation Process

The family adaptation process is on a continuum from bonadaptation to maladaptation (see Figure 14-1). This process involves the family's unity and ability to compromise in problem solving to manage the crisis. Interaction with external systems also enhances bonadaptation. The greater the family's strengths in coherence, flexibility, and the previously discussed variables, the greater is the likelihood that the family will be able to adapt to the crisis. When families do not

have adequate resources, family strengths, and the ability to rebound from a crisis event or situation, they will experience maladaptation. Examples of maladaptation are divorce, separation, family violence, alcoholism, and extreme family dysfunction. The outcome of maladaptation is crisis. The process of adaptation begins again with this new crisis combined with ongoing family stress.

Research suggests that many external and internal factors influence the outcomes of family stress events. Key internal factors are family resiliency, perception, and meaning the family assigns to the stressor (Boss, 2002; McCubbin & McCubbin, 1996; DeMarco et al., 2000).

The Coping Process

Since the mid 1970s, the concept of coping has been a component of models related to stress management. Focusing on coping in individuals, Lazarus and Folkman (1989) define coping as "constantly changing cognitive efforts to manage external and/or internal demands that are appraised as taxing or exceeding the resources of the person" (p. 179). This process-oriented definition indicates a difference between coping and automatic behavior: coping represents effort. Thus coping refers to situations of psychological stress that call for mobilization and involve *all* efforts to manage, regardless of outcome. *Managing* may include avoiding, denying, minimizing, tolerating, accepting the stressful situation, or striving for change.

Coping includes both the behaviors and thoughts that help to calm the person and these behaviors and thoughts depend on how the event is cognitively appraised. A *primary appraisal* is used to determine whether a stressful situation has potential for threat, harm or loss, or challenge. If this potential is present, a *secondary appraisal* is done to evaluate what might and can be done. *Reappraisal* is a third component of the coping process and is based on new information. Appraisal processes may or may not be conscious (Lazarus & Folkman, 1989). Effective coping has a number of functions; it is not simply problem solving. Lazarus and Folkman (1989) distinguish between coping that is directed toward managing or altering the problem (problem-focused coping) and emotion-focused coping, which serves the purpose of changing the emotional response to the problem.

A person may decide to meet a stressful situation head-on or to retreat from the stressful environment. For example, a woman experiencing "hot flashes" associated with menopause might manage the stress by learning more about the phenomenon by reading, searching the Internet, or consulting a gynecologist. Other strategies include talking with other women who also are experiencing menopause. If one's environment is stressful, stress-reducing activities include taking short walks outside and listening to nature sounds and soft music. Long-term solutions may include a job change or relocation.

The second form of coping, *emotion-focused*, is used when appraisal indicates that nothing can be done to change the environmental conditions of the harm, threat, or challenge. Many of the management techniques discussed in the latter part of this chapter are emotion-focused because they reduce the affective, visceral, or motor responses to stress. For effective coping, people use a combination of the two modes. Families may continue to live in a stressful environment but may reduce their anxiety level by changing expectations and focusing on assets and strengths rather than difficulties.

Use of a variety of coping strategies provides greater adaptability and flexibility for the family. Boss (2002) suggests that *coping* is a passive behavior and that *managing* is active and more accurately reflects what families ideally do when they are experiencing a stressful situation or event.

Symptoms of Family Stress

Families often exhibit noticeable symptoms of stress and strain: symptoms can be observed in individual members or in the family unit as a whole. Family symptoms might consist of marital discord; changes in the family rules, rituals, and chores; a roller-coaster–like emotional climate; changes in togetherness and cohesion; increased or decreased family communication; changes in family decision making and leadership; or increased contention (Burr et al., 1994). Negative coping behaviors and symptoms of family stress in individual family members include increased smoking; alcohol abuse; abuse of coffee, aspirin, and other medications; overeating; frequent and recurring illnesses such as colds or sore throats; accident and injury proneness; and signs of anxiety and frustration. Infants and children may have recurring illnesses and be extremely irritable or exhibit acting-out behaviors. Older children may have problems with school work, manifest behavior problems in school, or skip school. During stressful phases, family processes and interactions are strained and may include marital conflict, sibling conflict, yelling, shouting, mean talk, sarcasm, swearing, moping, faultfinding, criticism, rigidity, and selfishness—and in extreme cases—abuse, violence, and divorce. Curran (1985) notes that families who are under stress often exhibit the behaviors listed in Box 14-1.

Although many families experience a number of these symptoms at times, distress results when a family lives with all of them continuously. According to Burr et al. (1994), the experience of change and stress in families affects family functioning in five different patterns: a roller-coaster pattern, an increase in the quality and

---

BOX 14-1 Symptoms of Family Stress

- A constant sense of urgency and hurry; no time to release and relax
- A tension that underlies and causes sharp words, sibling or parental conflict or misunderstandings
- A mania to escape—to one's room, car, or garage
- A feeling that time is passing too quickly; children are growing up too quickly
- A nagging desire for a simpler life; constant talk about times that were or will be simpler
- Little "me" or couple time
- A pervasive sense of guilt for not being or doing everything to or for all people in one's life

From Curran, D. (1985). *Stress and the healthy family.* Minneapolis, MN: Winston.

strength of functioning, no change in functioning, a decrease in functioning, and a mixture of these.

Family Stress Management Theories

According to Friedemann (1995), the family as a system seeks congruence that includes harmony, calmness, and well-being. Family stress management is a complex process (Boss, 2003; Day, 2003). It consists of the interactive efforts of family members working as a whole to achieve and maintain balance and harmony over time in response to stressors. Although some stress is growth-producing, most stress requires the family to expend some effort in problem solving to return the family system equilibrium.

Types of Adaptive Behaviors

Pearlin and Schooler (1982) believe that three types of adaptive behaviors are beneficial in the family coping process: (1) changing the stressor event, (2) controlling the family definition of the situation (reframing), and (3) learning more functional coping strategies to control the stressful reaction. Using the first type of adaptive coping strategies, the family may pursue a solution to the problem that eliminates the stressor or that can decrease the pile-up of events that is depleting family resources. Increased understanding of the situation and acquisition of coping skills can bring about constructive change. A resilient family may pull together and coordinate coping efforts, use social support networks as buffering agents to relieve distress, or interact with sources of community support as a way of balancing demands of stress with family resources. Members of a grieving family who have lost a source of financial support will use job services to retrain and search for new employment opportunities while mutually supporting one another to prevent loss of self-esteem and to maintain family morale.

Using the second type of adaptive coping, *reframing*, healthy families control the meaning of the stress by the way they perceive the situation and the relative importance of the threatened loss (Olson, 1989). For example, a religious family may be devastated when an adolescent member rejects the religious practices of the family, whereas another family may think of it as a phase of adolescent development and take it in stride. Families have the potential to neutralize the stressfulness of an event by viewing the meaning relative to the situation at hand. Families may use *positive comparison* to control the meaning of stress by participation in community network or self-help groups. The hardship is reduced by sharing the notion that "we are all in this together" or "compared to others, we have much to be thankful for." *Selective ignoring* is another coping strategy where family members look for the good within a situation. For example, a woman recovering from mastectomy surgery told her nurse how lucky she was that her malignancy was discovered at such an early stage.

The third type of adaptive coping is an attempt to control the reaction to the stress. The family is passive and accepts the stressful situation without being overwhelmed by it. This more passive approach may be based on the belief that good-natured forbearance will have its rewards. Olson et al. (1983) define this type of behavior as *passive appraisal*. This form of adaptive behavior may include controlled reflection, passive forbearance, helpless resignation, optimistic faith, or other strategies that will help to minimize the discomfort caused by the problem. This behavior can be effective for an out-of-work situation but ineffective for dealing with relationship issues such as parenting. Some families who are moderately cohesive and remain flexible during times of stress are hardier than others. Family hardiness is the ability of a family to recover or change in response to major stress or a crisis situation. *Resilient* and hardy families have strengths that include an internal locus of control, having a sense of the meaning of life, and feeling involved with community and committed to the process of growth (McCubbin & McCubbin, 1996).

Healthy families adapt to stressful situations by mobilizing their resources and using a repertoire of many and varied coping strategies. For example, Curran (1985) found that the stress-effective family "(1) views stress as a normal part of family life, (2) shares feelings as well as words, (3) develops conflict-resolution and creative coping skills, (4) makes use of support people and systems, and (5) is adaptable" (p. 61). The effectiveness of coping strategies varies depending on the uniqueness of each family, the developmental stage, and the choices made. Similarly, Day (2003) suggests that the way families manage stress depends on the three different "levels" of abstraction in family life. Level I is the day-to-day observable interactional processes, level II is the "rules or rules about rules" that families create to control the stressor event, and level III occurs when the first two levels are not effective. The family slips into a severe crisis and challenges its basic beliefs such as beliefs in God and life orientation, "and these beliefs may evolve, change, be discarded or reconstructed" (Day, 2003, p. 381).

Healthy families are flexible and capable of changing structure to learn new coping behaviors when the initial problem-solving methods prove ineffective. Table 14-4 compares characteristics of healthy families and the strengths of healthy couples.

External coping strategies are often used by families to ameliorate the effects of stress. These strategies include the use of informal or formal support systems made up of members within the family system, neighbors, extended family, mutual self-help groups, and social institutions such as the health care system. In a study of 21,501 couples, Olson and Olson (2000) found that strong families were identified by the traits of good communication, couple flexibility, couple closeness, personality compatibility, joint and individual leisure, supportive family and friends, financial management, and compatible spiritual beliefs. The family that deals most effectively with stress is often the family that is well integrated in terms of commitment to the group and to collective goals; the members possess inner strengths and they pull together to become cohesive. They can nurture each other and use the resources necessary for maintenance of the family unit and growth of individual members.

Studies of ethnic families suggest that strong family ties and the kin network provide support for African American and Hispanic families; however, the continual support of family members and friends is often a major stressor (McAdoo, 1999; Neighbors, 1997). There is limited research on the specific stressors of ethnic families in the United States.

Family Resources

The manner in which the family manages stress is dependent on the resources available and the constraints present within the context of the

---

TABLE 14-4 Characteristics of Healthy Families and Healthy Marriages

Traits of a Healthy Family	Traits of a Healthy Couple
1. Members tend to listen to each other and communicate well.	1. Partners are satisfied with how they talk to each other.
2. Members support and affirm each other.	2. Creative in handling their differences.
3. Each member shows respect for self and other family members.	3. Feel very close to each other.
4. Have a sense of trust.	4. Partners are seldom controlling.
5. Members interact and share leisure time together.	5. Each partner understands the other's opinion and ideas.
6. Members share family responsibilities.	6. Satisfied with the amount of affection from partner.
7. Have family traditions and rituals.	7. Balanced leisure time spent together and separately
8. Privacy of members is acknowledged.	8. Friends or family rarely interfere with relationship.
9. Humor is present.	9. Partners agree on how to spend money.
10. Opens its boundaries to admit and seek help with problems.	10. Satisfied expression of spiritual values and beliefs

Adapted from Curran, D. (1983). *Traits of a healthy family.* Minneapolis: Winston Press (Harper & Row); Olson, D. H., & Olson, A. K. (2000). *Empowering couples.* Roseville, MN: Life Innovations.

situation. Additional examples of resources are positive beliefs, problem-solving skills, social skills, and social support. Chapter 6 discusses the relationships and types of social support that affect family health. Boss (2002) distinguishes between the coping resources of the family and the process of coping. The *coping resources* are those sociological, economic, psychological, or physical assets of the family that are present at the onset of the stressor event and can be mobilized during coping efforts. Health, family cohesiveness, economic security, open communication, and knowledge are all examples of resources. However, the family may fail to recognize strengths or fail to use them during a stressful situation. In such a case, a family nurse can work with the family to assist members to see their full range of options, to acknowledge their strengths and chances for successful outcome, to acquire new coping skills as necessary, and to follow through with the appropriate actions.

Ineffective Coping

Ineffective coping interferes with vital family functions so that needs of family members are left unfulfilled. For example, if a hospice nurse is helping a family to cope with a dying grandparent in the home, he or she assesses the family's ability to meet the affective needs of its members. During this period of stress, are family coping skills effective, or does the nurse see signs of psychological or physiological stress, such as somatic illness?

Ineffective coping fails to reduce or control the stress and in itself may produce undesirable consequences or risks. Boss (2002) believes that ineffective coping behaviors tend to be automatic rather than rationally planned. Some of these patterns of behavior may be a function of social learning from early family modeling. The phenomenon of child abuse is such a case. An abusive parent may respond to the stress of fatigue and incessant crying with anger, lashing out to strike a crying infant. The rapid move from emotional reaction to behavioral response without the primary appraisal of the consequences is the ineffective aspect of this coping method.

According to Minuchin (1974), ineffective coping occurs when families respond to internal or external stress without acknowledging the need to change. Rather than developing a new level of functioning, the family conveys its rigid structure through stereotyped functioning. Some of the responses to the stressors themselves create greater internal stress for the family. Behaviors that indicate ineffective coping are shown in Box 14-2.

Ineffective Communication Patterns

Ineffective coping is often noted in dysfunctional communication patterns in the family unit. Denial

---

BOX 14-2 Ineffective Family Coping Behaviors

DYSFUNCTIONAL COGNITIVE PROCESSES

- Denial that a problem exists
- Disruption of family routines

DYSFUNCTIONAL COMMUNICATION PATTERNS

- Triangling
- Authoritarianism
- Scapegoating
- Emotional distancing

DYSFUNCTIONAL BEHAVIORS

- Agitation, depression, hostility, guilt
- Addictions (e.g., drugs, alcohol, food)

DISMEMBERMENT

- Abandonment
- Desertion
- Separation or divorce

FAMILY ABUSE OR VIOLENCE

- Neglect of children or ill family member
- Emotional abuse and threats
- Spouse or significant other abuse
- Elder abuse
- Parent abuse

Friedman, M. M., Bowden, V. R., & Jones, E. G. (2003). *Family nursing: Research, theory and practice* (5th ed.). Upper Saddle River, NJ: Prentice-Hall.

that the family has a problem is a common strategy used by the family unit (Friedman, Bowden, & Jones, 2003). Ineffective patterns include emotional outbursts, arguments, scapegoating, name calling, blaming, threatening other family members, and being very controlling or authoritarian with other family members.

Emotional and Physical Abuse

Aggressive quarrels, secondary to stressful life events, may lead to emotionally and/or physically abusive behavior within some families. Family violence is a serious and pervasive health problem; many incidents occur in the home behind closed doors, within family silence, and sometimes under the label of "family matters." Abuse involves the intent by the offender to intimidate the victim either by physical force or threatening the victim's person or property. The word *violence* comes from the Latin *violare,* meaning to violate, injure or to do harm to the person (Agnes, 2001). Family or domestic violence involves action by one family member with the intent to inflict harm on or to control another member (American Psychological Association, 2002). Although it is not clear from research whether violence stems from an innate aggressive drive or is primarily a learned behavior, it is clear that humans have the capacity for violence (American Psychological Association, 2002). Abusive behavior may take various forms such as sexual assault, emotional/psychological abuse, physical assault, homicide, financial abandonment, neglect, property destruction, and mistreatment of pets.

Assessment of Ineffective Coping

A major aspect of prevention of family abuse is assessment. All forms of abusive behavior can cause significant injury and/or death. Physical abuse is the most widely recognized form of family violence because of resulting injuries, whereas other types of ongoing abuse often go unnoticed. As sociologists Gelles and Cornell (1990) and Straus and Gelles (1995) indicate, hitting someone is often explained as a coping mechanism, albeit a dysfunctional one, for example, "I had to hit her because she provoked me." Violent behavior often stems from an inadequate repertoire of behaviors with which to manage stress, which means that the process of

functional coping never begins (Boss, 2002). Families experiencing stress and demonstrating poor coping skills, poor communication patterns, or lack of affection and cohesion are at risk for abusive behaviors. There is also an increased likelihood of abuse occurring when one form of abuse already exists in the family, or it may occur in the future without appropriate intervention. For example, if a child is being abused by the father, there is a high probability that the father is also abusing the child's mother (American Psychological Association, 2002). Family clinicians should be aware of, assess, and create strategies to prevent family violence or abuse. In addition, knowledge of community resources for referral is crucial. Common risk factors associated with various forms of family violence and abuse are listed in Box 14-3.

BOX 14-3 Risk Factors for Family Violence or Abuse

BIOPHYSICAL DIMENSION

- Existing health problems in potential victims
- Physical evidence of past injury caused by abuse
- A current pregnancy in the family
- Long-term debilitating illness

PSYCHOLOGICAL DIMENSION

- Identified psychological stressors
- Unrealistic expectations of family members/children
- Inequitable distribution of power
- Role confusion
- Powerlessness

SOCIAL DIMENSION

- Ineffective interactions among members
- Economic issues
- Social isolation
- Exposure to violence

BEHAVIORAL DIMENSION

- Presence of behaviors that suggest abuse of substances such as alcohol or drugs
- Bullying behaviors

Empowering Families in Family Stress Management

Through the use of the nursing process and self-care concepts, the nurse assists the family in identifying strengths, in enhancing adaptive mechanisms, and in making informed decisions. The major goals of the nurse are to promote wellness; to assist family members in anticipating, recognizing, preventing, reducing, managing, or adapting to stressful high-risk situations (coping); and to help the family to experience a feeling of satisfaction and closeness from working on a problem together. Coping skills can be taught as the nurse helps the family to "re-create" or to move toward wholeness as a unit.

If the network of family support has been disconnected, members may hesitate to call on other members for help. The nurse can encourage the family to reestablish their emotional support system within both the immediate and the extended family.

In times of relative stability, the nurse can use anticipatory guidance to guide the family in developing a plan to prevent stress or to cope effectively. The family, as client, must be an active participant in developing this plan. The nurse's role is to assist with, not control, the process. A strengths-based approach to family stress management includes two phases. First, in collaboration with the family, the clinician identifies family strengths, stressors, and coping skills. Second, the clinician and family together delineate a stress management plan that is ethnically and situationally appropriate for the family.

Family Assessment

Assessment of Family Stress and Coping

Family stress becomes problematic when the degree of stress exceeds the family's resources and coping abilities. Early assessment of family stress and strain is important for the prevention of problems with family function. A structural, functional approach to family assessment is very useful (Friedman, Bowden, & Jones, 2003). The nurse examines roles of family members, power structure within the subsystems of the family, social support and caregiving, boundaries, and communication patterns. As discussed in Chapter 7, because communication is the interaction within the family system that links the members, assessment of communication, including both verbal and nonverbal behaviors, is a vital part of the nurse's role. The use of observation and interview techniques is recommended to help the nurse assess family type communication patterns such as openness, emotional bonding, use of space, active listening, respect, and willingness of members to meet each other's needs. The clinician will observe the family or inquire directly to obtain answers to the following questions:

- Are family communications open and direct, with clear meanings?
- Does the communication system support and affirm family members?
- Does the communication pattern reflect family interactions?
- Does family communication build self-esteem?

Assessment of Family Stress Management

Successful assessment of the strengths and limitations of family functioning requires an awareness of a family system as a dynamic entity, always in some phase of change and transition. The nurse needs to assist families in assessing their responses to stressful events and conditions, while reinforcing family strengths and adaptations that can be achieved; the nurse should also help families assess resources in the external environment that will assist in managing the stressor. Assessment should include the periodic, if not continuous, examination of constructive patterns of communication and interaction, the purpose and effectiveness of coping styles used, and the physical health of the family members. The affect of the family can be used as a thermometer to measure progress and effective functioning. As stress is minimized, or if necessary adapted to, the family should show evidence of improved body image, effective sharing of feelings of happiness, hopefulness, confidence, optimism, and satisfaction with the selected methods of functioning. In the absence of such positive interaction, the practitioner may want to explore possibilities by asking the following questions:

- Has the family unit experienced deaths, unresolved grief, or loss?

- Does anyone have anxiety about exploring new behaviors needed as a result of family changes?
- What does the family fear in the future?
- How does the family feel about the loss of ideal functioning or about the past?

The evaluation of family functioning is essential to the ongoing, dynamic assessment process. The assessment process must also take into account whether the family is coping with stress or has reached a state of crisis, exploring family functioning on a continuum of stress management, to assist in the determination of appropriate interventions. Obviously, the adjustment for a family experiencing the absence of an only child who has gone away to college will differ significantly from the adjustment for a family experiencing the unexpected death of a child in an automobile accident. Depending on the severity of the stressful events and adjustments and the family's interpretation of such events, the practitioner needs to be prepared to respond to family needs with a variety of interventions. These interventions could include the offering of supportive listening through a difficult time (drawing on previous successful coping strategies), medication or hospitalization to protect the family member from harming self or others, or relocation to new living conditions as a result of a devastating flood or other natural disaster. As the family stress escalates to crisis proportions, external resources must be rallied to support the family. Consultation and collaboration with other professionals in the community can mobilize a variety of community services, including crisis intervention counseling, safe housing for victims of domestic violence, and vouchers for temporary housing when a crisis occurs.

Family functioning must be assessed within a social-cultural context determined by family heritage and values. Although an emphasis on cultural competency is emerging in contemporary practice, it is vital that the practitioner gain cultural sensitivity, if unable to achieve cultural competence. Boss (2002) reminds the practitioner that

> Families of color, targeted ethnicities, or same-sex couples are often pressured by a hostile external context and by internalized perceptions of less worth. Prejudice, intolerance, and bigotry

are external stressors that are cumulative with other stressors, thus creating needless vulnerability. The additional and chronic stressor of living in a hostile, stigmatized, and biased environment influences both individual and family perceptions of everything they experience. Regardless of class, this extra layer of stress is still experienced by many today. (Boss, 2002, p. 25)

Keeping in mind the variables in the Resiliency Model of Family Stress, Adjustment, and Adaptation, the nurse assesses both the stressors and the coping processes. The significance of the stressor depends on the values of the family within a cultural and social context, the pile-up of stressors, the previous family life events, and the amount of change demanded by the stressor.

Resilient families are challenged to not become dysfunctional when adversity confronts them (Walsh, 1998). To assess family coping, the nurse determines family strengths that facilitate resilience and community resources, as well as how effectively the family mobilizes them. In addition, the nurse assesses the family's perceptions, adaptations, developmental stage, strengths, social support, finances, education, cultural beliefs, and experiences as a unit (Saleebey, 2002). The Canadian Perspectives Box presents stress and coping issues for Canadian families.

Tools that are used to assess family stress and strengths include the genogram and ecomap discussed in Chapters 10 and 11. Hardy and Laszloffy (1995) suggest that for ethnic families a cultural genogram may provide useful data for strengthening families. Family inventories are valuable tools, in both research and clinical practice, for measuring variables related to family stress and family coping. Initially, the clinician would want to assess the level of individual and family stress. Table 14-5 presents a sample listing of measures.

A commonly used survey is the *Family Inventory of Life Events and Changes* (FILE), presented in Appendix 14-1 (McCubbin, Thompson, & McCubbin, 1996). The FILE is a 71-item survey of the common family stressor/pile-up variables across the family life span. *The Family Crisis Oriented Evaluation Scale* (F-COPES) (McCubbin,

CANADIAN PERSPECTIVES
FAMILY COPING AND STRESS MANAGEMENT

Deborah Beck, BN, MSc (MEd), PhD
Memorial University of Newfoundland

Stress and distress are a part of what Canadian families experience routinely in attempting to cope with internal and external pressures of family living. Canadian families experience stress related to where they live and work and how well they adjust to family issues that confront them routinely in various geographic locations across the country. Canadians, one on one, are generally tolerant and respectful of differences and value diversity. When any differences become group-related, the stress affects the whole family.

Canada has several large metropolitan cities. Family stress experienced in these larger cities is different but not less or more intense than that experienced in towns and rural regions. Perceived stressful family situations include one- and two-parent working families, long commutes to and from work, necessity for child care, driving children to extracurricular activities, and reliance on social services for low-income families. Many parents perceive the need to fill every minute of a child's day, with the idea that these children will be more well-rounded individuals than children who do less. Children complain about lack of free play time and show signs of stress (e.g., stomach pains, headaches, and fatigue). Children, teens, and young adults experience increased peer pressure to engage in substance use and misuse at an early age.

Families often rely on electronic support to aid in coping, but it does not decrease stress. The Internet exposes children to potential child molesters in chat rooms and provides access to pornographic sites and sites with instructions for making a bomb or committing suicide.

In many Canadian schools or neighborhoods, if a child does not have brand-name clothes, he or she is often teased by other children, which creates distress for the child and for the parents, who may not be able to afford such items (Grayson, 1993). Families may have to leave their towns of origin in search of work, or a family may stay in one location while one parent works elsewhere. The working parent returns for brief periods, which may result in a disruption of usual family functioning, since he or she is not a part of the day-to-day family routines.

Young Canadians become discouraged because a university degree no longer promises a secure job. In this world of technology, there are so many possible occupations for young adults that the amount of choice often creates distress. In rural areas, most young adults have to uproot to attend postsecondary institutions located in urban areas. Young adults living alone in larger towns or cities experience stress and distress, depending on what support is found.

Stress is experienced in many ways by different types of families. People living longer, financial problems, lack of support, less sleep, immigration with insufficient help to adjust (Majumdar & Ladak, 1998), blended families, family violence, and lack of time are some of the major factors that cause distress among Canadian families. Researchers discovered that a strong quality relationship between parents and adolescents is a more important factor in helping adolescents better cope than what sort of family they come from (Grossman & Rowat, 1995; Ford-Gilboe, 2000).

In one study, student nurses, more than other health professional students, were found to experience distress as a result of the lack of support and encouragement (Beck, Srivastava, Hackett, McKim, & Rockwell, 1997). Before nurses can effectively deal with the stress in others' lives, they need to come to terms with their own sources of stress, which are similar to those of Canadian families (Perodeau, Paquette, Brisette, St-Pierre, Bernier, & Duquette, 2001). If support and encouragement are important factors to help nurses feel less distress and more able to cope, then the same should be considered important in helping families cope.

Clinicians need to encourage families to be involved in their own health-related decision making. Offering information and alternative possibilities so that parents can make the choice that best meets their family needs, as well as offering support and encouragement to families, has the potential to reduce stress and promote family health coping by providing options and support for resolution (Ford-Gilboe, 2000), a role that is critical in Canada's society today.

Continued

CANADIAN PERSPECTIVES
FAMILY COPING AND STRESS MANAGEMENT—cont'd

References

Beck, D., Strivastava, R., Hackett, M., McKim, E., & Rockwell, B. (1997). Perceived level and sources of stress in university professional schools. *Journal of Nursing Education, 35,* 180-186.

Ford-Gilboe, M. (2000). Dispelling myths and creating opportunity: A comparison of the strengths of single-parent and two-parent families. *Advances in Nursing Science, 23,* 41-58.

Grayson, J. P. (1993). Health, physical activity, and employment status in Canada. *International Journal of Health Services, 23,* 743-761.

Grossman, M., & Rowat, K. M. (1995). Parental relationships, coping strategies, received support, and well-being in adolescents of separated or divorced and married parents. *Research in Nursing and Health, 18,* 249-261.

Majumdar, B., & Ladak, S. (1998). Management of family and workplace stress experienced by women of colour from various cultural backgrounds. *Canadian Journal of Public Health, 89,* 48-52.

Perodeau, G., Paquette, S., Brissette, L., St-Pierre, C., Bernier, D., & Duquette, A. (2001). Health professionals in part-time employment: The challenge of balancing work and family. *Canadian Journal of Community Mental Health, 20,* 53-74.

Canadian spelling is used.

Thompson, & McCubbin, 1996) measures family coping behaviors; this scale is presented in Appendix 14-2. The subscales of the instrument integrate the perception of stressors within the system and use of resources, both internal and external to the family system. The instrument also measures coping that involves direct action and more palliative modes of coping. The internal coping strategies include the confidence of the family in active problem-solving methods, as well as more passive methods such as reframing the family's perspective or passive appraisal. The external strategies used by families include the use of resources such as church or religion; the support of the extended family, friends, and neighbors; and the use of resources available through community organizations.

Scoring the F-COPES instrument is done by summing the numbers circled for items in each subscale, excluding items 17, 26, and 28, which are reversed. The subscales are social support (1, 2, 5, 8, 10, 16, 20, 25, and 29); reframing (3, 7, 11, 13, 15, 19, 22, and 24); spiritual support (14, 23, 27, and 30); mobilizing the family to acquire and accept help (4, 6, 9, and 21); and passive appraisal (12, 17, 26, and 28). A total coping score is the sum of the subscales and has a possible range of 29 to 145. The mean scores reported (McCubbin, Thompson, & McCubbin, 1996) range from 91.24 to 95.64, and standard deviations range from 12.06 to 14.05. For information on permission to use F-COPES, the FILE, and detailed instructions and norms for adults and adolescents, consult *Family Assessment: Resilience, Coping and Adaptation—Inventories for Research and Practice* (McCubbin & Thompson, & McCubbin, 1996). The clinician would use surveys such as these to make a diagnosis of family stress.

Nursing Diagnosis of Family Stress

The next step in the nursing process is the development of a nursing diagnosis of family stress. The North American Nursing Diagnosis Association (NANDA) (1999) has identified

TABLE 14-5 Selected Individual and Family Stress and Coping Assessment Tools

Tool	Dimensions Measured	Source
INDIVIDUAL STRESS ASSESSMENT TOOLS		
Life Change Index	Life events and changes	Holmes & Rahe (1967)
State-Trait Anxiety Inventory	General and current anxiety	Speilberger et al. (1983)
Young Adult Family Inventory of Life Events and Changes (YA-FILES)*	Young adult life events and changes	McCubbin & Gronchowski (1987)
Adolescent Inventory of Family Life Events (A-File)*	Adolescent life events and changes	McCubbin & Patterson (1987)
Coping Health Inventory for Parents (CHIP)*	Family and parental coping; health care, communication	McCubbin, McCubbin, Nevin, & Cauble (1981)
FAMILY STRESS ASSESSMENT TOOLS		
Family Inventory of Life Events (FILE)*	Family life events and changes	McCubbin & Patterson (1983)
Family Stressors (FS)*	Family stressors	McCubbin & Patterson (1987)
Family Strains (FST)*	Family strains	McCubbin & Patterson (1987)
Family Distress Index*	Family distress	McCubbin & Patterson (1987)
Coping and Stress Profile	Family coping and level of stress	Olson (2001), Life Innovations, Inc.

*Found in McCubbin, H. I., Thompson, A. I., & McCubbin, M. (Eds.). (1996). *Family assessment inventories for research and practice.* Madison: University of Wisconsin.

nursing diagnoses relevant to family stress, coping, and adaptation. Family stressors are included in accepted nursing diagnosis categories because stress affects the family structure and ability to function, as well as the health of the individual family members (Gordon, 2002). Stress as an etiologic factor may affect each of the functional health patterns (Gordon, 1994). Interventions and outcomes for family stress and coping are delineated in the book *Nursing Diagnoses, Outcomes, and Interventions: NANDA, NOC, and NIC Linkages* (Johnson, Bulechek, McCloskey-Dochterman, Maas, & Moorhead, 2001). Table 14-6 gives examples of functional health patterns, NANDA diagnoses for family stress, suggested outcomes, and interventions.

Interventions must be co-created with the family and focused on systems level, as well as individual, adaptations to enhance the effectiveness of the outcomes of improved family health status.

Family Stress Management Plan

To enhance the family's successful development of resilience in response to stress, the practitioner should relinquish the role of expert and engage the family in a collaborative problem-solving effort. The traditional role of the practitioner, as emphasized in a diagnostic and prescriptive approach to problem solving, does not facilitate the growth and empowerment of family functioning. Instead, there is a danger that this approach will foster family dependency as the family relies on the professional for expert advice. Just as children need to have a voice in the family decision-making process to gain a sense of empowerment, so too do families need to identify the existing competencies that will help them address concerns and focus on successes to enhance family functioning and resilience. Several authors (Boss, 2002; Metcalf, 1997; Brooks & Goldstein, 2001; Berg, 1994; Selekman, 1997) emphasize the importance of empowerment or

TABLE 14-6 Examples of Functional Health Patterns, Nursing Diagnoses, Outcomes, and Interventions Related to Family Stress

Functional Pattern	Nursing Diagnosis	Family Stressor	Sample Interventions
Health perception/ Health management pattern	Ineffective family health management of therapeutic regimen	Untreated medical condition	Counseling, Health systems guidance, Decision-making support
Nutritional/Merabolic	Alteration in nutrition: Obesity	Unfilled intimacy needs	Health Teaching
Elimination	Alteration in bowel elimination: Diarrhea	Repressed anger— Marital conflict	Counseling, communication skills
Activity/Exercise Pattern	Diversional activity deficit	Excessive overtime at work	Health teaching, decision-making support
Sleep/Rest	Sleep-pattern disturbance	Transition into parenthood	Anticipatory guidance, teach sleep hygiene
Cognitive/Perceptual	Interrupted family processes	Family emotional abuse	Anger control assistance, Anticipatory guidance Spiritual support, communication skills, counseling
Self-perception/Self-concept	Powerlessness	Rigid/Autocratic family structure	Cognitive restructuring, decision-making support
Role/Relationship Pattern	Family coping compromised Risk for other-directed violence	Parental conflict over use of discipline	Teaching communication and parenting skills
Sexuality/Reproductive Pattern	Altered sexuality patterns	Marital relationship problems	Family process maintenance, counseling
Coping/Stress Tolerance Pattern	Compromised family coping	Chronic disease of child	Emotional support, Counseling, Family involvement promotion, respite care
Value/Belief Pattern	Spiritual distress, risk for spiritual distress	Alienation of family from source of spirituality	Spiritual growth and facilitation Hope instillation, Meditation facilitation, Support Group

Adapted from Gordon, M. (2002). *Manual of nursing diagnosis*. St. Louis, MO: Mosby; Johnson, M., Maas, M., Moorhead, S. (2000). *Nursing outcomes classification* (2nd ed.). St. Louis, MO: Mosby; Johnson, M. et al. (2001). *Nursing diagnoses, outcomes, and interventions*. St. Louis, MO: Mosby.

self-efficacy in working with families to develop a stress management plan.

The stress management plan may include some of the following:

1) Identification of willingness of family members to work on the problem, and when possible, a commitment by all family members to participate. For example, if a spouse's belief system is one that views "everything is determined by a higher power (fatalism)" then he or she may not be willing to devote energy to a terminally ill mate. Or, if a child believes he

or she will leave the family soon, that child may not be willing to accept or participate in the family plan.

2) An open and honest family discussion of approaches that have been used in the past to resolve previous stressors. How were these helpful or not helpful? How could these be modified to cope with the current stress?

3) Brainstorming for possible plans. Brainstorming means that all opinions are accepted without judgment until a list of possibilities is created.

4) Discussion of the possible outcomes of each brainstormed plan. What are the positive and negative aspects of each? Can some be combined?

5) Initiation of a plan to manage stress as a group and individually. This may cause increased anxiety for some members who view change as undesirable and frightening. As a result, supportive enactment of the plan by each member should be encouraged by the nurse. Family members might create a contract to work on a particular strategy together.

To support the family in developing and carrying out the stress management plan, the nurse can do the following:

1) *Encourage each family member to participate in the plan.*

2) *Encourage family discussions.*

3) *Provide guided instruction.* Teach the family emotional, intimacy, physical negotiation and communication strategies. Instruction may cover strategies to promote intimacy and how to plan a family meeting; methods may include role playing, role modeling, use of videotapes, and support groups.

4) *Coach the family* through the crisis and make referrals when appropriate. Depending on the extent of the crisis, it may be beyond the skill of the family clinician to work long term with the family in resolving the crisis.

5) *Refer families in crisis* or at risk for crisis to social support resources and/or groups.

6) *Encourage families to seek support* from the extended kin network, spiritual network, and friends.

7) *Promote normalizing activities during stressful times.* Suggest that the family return to, keep, or alter family rituals and routines during stressful times (Boss, 2002; Walsh, 1998).

8) *Assist the family in finding or developing cognitive approaches to stress management.* According to researchers, families who *reframe* the stressful event rather than "awfulize" it have better adaptation to life stressors (Wright, Watson, & Bell, 1996; Walsh, 1999).

9) *Assist in the garnering of spiritual support.* Help the family find meaning, explain the situation, become hopeful, develop purpose, and increase family bonding (see Chapter 8).

The goals of intervention are bonadaptation or adaptation to the stressor and balanced family functioning. The Research Synopsis presents a study conducted for an intervention with families of children who have experienced repeated hospitalization.

Evaluation of Family Coping

The evaluation of nursing care for a family undergoing crisis or stress is an ongoing process. The nurse assesses the response of the family to the stressor event(s), the newly learned coping and adaptation behaviors, and the use of adaptive resources both within the family and in the community.

The evaluation phase includes determining the affective function of the family, the interaction and communication patterns, the function and coping style used, and the physical health of the family members. The affect of the family can be used as a thermometer to measure the progress of recovery. Is the family capable of sharing feelings of happiness, hopefulness, confidence, optimism, and satisfaction with their lives? Are there feelings of unresolved loss or grief in the family? If the recovery is progressing too slowly, there may continue to be evidence of anxiety, tension, fear, depression, despair, or low self-esteem.

Other questions the family clinician might use to evaluate this include the following:

• Is there greater productivity on the part of the family?

• Are the family members resuming their role functions?

• Is the family meeting the needs of the members according to community standards? Is there less dependence on health care services?

• Does the family reflect a desire to recover, and do family members strive to be healthy?

RESEARCH SYNOPSIS

EFFECTS OF STRESS-POINT INTERVENTION WITH FAMILIES OF CHILDREN WHO HAVE BEEN REPEATEDLY HOSPITALIZED

The repeated hospitalization of children with chronic conditions is stressful for both the children and their families. Awareness of family issues, as well as the child's physical, developmental, and emotional needs, is essential to designing a family-specific intervention to assist the family and child in adapting to hospitalization and posthospitalization. The premise of the researchers is that empowering the family will facilitate the child's adaptation, reduce parental stress, and improve family functioning.

Building on previous family and child intervention studies to reduce the stress of families and children during hospitalization, this study tested a "stress-point intervention by nurses" (SPIN). The reported outcome of SPIN used by community health nurses was enhanced parental coping, improved family functioning, and limited hospital-induced developmental regression of children. A new study was designed to test SPIN when it was used by staff nurses working in ambulatory health care centers.

The study was a three-site clinical trial with random assignment of 23 nurses and their respective 115 child-patients and families to experimental SPIN groups or a control group. The SPIN intervention included (a) identification of the family's stressors related to hospitalizations; (b) development with the parents of a plan for their specific stressful issues; and (c) follow-up to reinforce, empower, and evaluate the planned intervention. Assessment included the use of the genogram, assessment of family stressors, and a family interview. Interventions were highly individualized for the family and the child-patient's issues and included inpatient and home visits. Outcomes were measured by using the Feetham Family Functioning Survey and the Coping Health Inventory for Parents.

The stress-point intervention for families and children by ambulatory nurses was shown to be more effective in facilitating families to cope with issues resulting from their child's hospitalizations than for parents that received usual care. Other positive outcomes included improved family functioning.

Burke, S. O., Harrison, M. B., Kauffmann, E., & Wong, C. (2001). Effects of stress-point intervention with families of repeated hospitalized children. *Journal of Family Nursing, 7,* 128-158.

The nurse also assesses the physical health of family members. Are there fewer somatic symptoms, less dependence on medications, fewer alcohol and drug abuse problems, and fewer episodes of infectious disease? Is there an increase in energy and a sense of physical well-being within the family?

The final part of the evaluation of the family is determination of the adaptation and coping activities by means of questions such as the following:

- Has the family learned new coping skills?
- Does the family consistently use problem-solving approaches rather than denial to deal with stressful situations?
- Do family members clearly and realistically identify sources of stress for the family?
- Is the locus of control within the family as a unit, or does the family rely on a member to handle stressful situations?

The progress of the family is evaluated within a specific social-cultural context set by family values. It is important for the nurse to evaluate the success of the plan of care within a developmental framework. The healthy family should evolve to higher levels of function and acquire a rich variety of new skills for future encounters with stressors. The nursing process in stress management with families is a collaborative process. The nurse should remember this because the nurse's goal is to empower the family to garner resources and to promote resilience in managing life's issues.

Family Stress Management Strategies

The following section addresses a number of selected strategies that can be used to increase the family's ability to manage stress. Stress management strategies are useful for both families and individuals of all ethnic groups and cultures and at various developmental stages. Some individuals and families cope effectively with stress, whereas others proceed into crisis and disorganization, often requiring professional assistance to gain equilibrium. Boss (2002) suggests that the family's value orientation in terms of fatalism versus mastery is critical to how (or whether) a family copes. The term *fatalism* refers to the belief that the locus of central events lies with fate or that all wants are predetermined. A family with a mastery orientation may believe that it can control or handle the situation and is more likely to take action. One must use caution in assuming that the active strategy is more effective than the passive approach. A fatalistic belief system may be best when nothing can bring about a change. Families who cope well may be those who select events about which they will be fatalistic and those that they will master or control.

A crucial variable appears to be the *meaning* of the event for the family and for the individuals within it (Patterson & Garwick, 2003). The meaning is related to the perception of the situation and is mediated by the context (Boss, 2002). Human beings have the power to change their perception of an event and to alter its meaning. Thus they can modify their attitudes and responses. An individual can decide to accept a certain situation as a learning opportunity and a challenge or to view it as a disaster or stressor. Curran (1985) suggests that healthy families view stress as normal rather than as a sign of weakness or failure. Such families are adaptable and have developed creative coping skills for conflict resolution.

The experience of "stress" is a personal event; each member of the family can learn to identify his or her own stress warning signals. These are cues to the early symptoms of stress. As stress increases, the symptoms increase in severity, thus adding more stress and beginning a negative feedback loop. The family can be taught to identify warning signs of stress and to choose a preventive strategy. It is often difficult for the person experiencing severe stress to identify the problem; both physical and psychic energy are "bound up" and not available for healthy functioning. A compassionate approach from other family members can often help the person to identify feelings, explore options, and feel less overwhelmed.

Every family has the potential to become more self-actualized and more competent in the promotion and management of health. The family nurse can assist in this move toward wellness by providing information, serving as a role model for desired behavior modification and lifestyle changes, and teaching clients the skills needed for continued growth and maintenance of healthy behaviors.

Stress management approaches for families are presented in Table 14-7. Change is never easy, and barriers can arise from internal and external sources. However, change is often difficult because *one does not know how to behave differently.* Approaches to change involve learning and practicing new habits. The role of the nurse is to facilitate new patterns of family coping and to work with the family in the development of family goals. Once the family is committed to making changes, the nurse uses a systematic approach to plan how those goals can be met over time using a variety of family stress management techniques. Change can occur, but it requires time, effort, and commitment. The process of adopting new patterns to cope with stress can be facilitated by the use of family self-care contracting (Gray, 1996).

The first steps in stress management are prevention of stressors, recognition of stressors, anticipation of stressors, and elimination or avoidance of possible stressors. If families use these first steps, they are less likely to reach crisis in many situations. In addition, individual approaches to stress management affect the family system's quality of health. Some of the many approaches that have been documented to be effective in coping with stress include self-awareness through relaxation (Wells-Federman & Mandle, 2002), innate biofeedback (Ennis, 1992), imagery (Hendricks, 1979), nutrition (Pender, Murdaugh, & Parsons, 2002), and minimal use of drugs and alcohol (Edelman & Mandle, 2002).

Problem Solving

When a problem arises in a family, it is important that the members recognize it and accept the reality of its existence. Denial of the problem is not a healthy alternative. However, the family may decide to avoid the problem or to eliminate the problem when possible. Active problem solving

TABLE 14-7   Family and Individual Stress Management Strategies

Family Stress Management Strategies

Cognitive Strategies (Day 2003)
- Getting the right information
- Visualizing a good outcome
- Focusing on the solution
- Cognitive restructuring
- Reframing

Anticipation of stressors
Prevention of stressors
Elimination or avoidance of stressors
Recognition of stressors
Problem solving
Negotiated housekeeping standards
- Role sharing and flexibility

Effective communication strategies
- Family meetings
- Humor and laughter
- Being open and honest
- Listening to each other genuinely

Time management and control
Family togetherness activities
- Walking or cycling together
- Playing games as a family
- Gardening
- Preparing a meal together
- Building something together

Intimacy
Family centering/meditation
Spiritual strategies
Family recreation and rituals
Realistic family goals

Individual Stress Management Strategies

Biofeedback
Healthy diet
Imagery
Managing emotions
Meditation and prayer
Music
Progressive relaxation
Time alone
   Holistic therapies
   Assertive communication
   Spiritual practices
   Setting realistic goals
   Physical activity
   Good sleep patterns
   Affirmations
   Pets

EXTERNAL SUPPORT

Maintaining active linkages with the community
Social support
- Kin network
- Friends
- Neighbors
- Self-help groups
- Formal support groups
- Spiritual support

Professional family counseling
Pastoral counseling

Based on data from Bomar, P. (1996). *Nurses and family health promotion;* Day, R. (2003). *Introduction to family processes* (4th ed.). Mahwah, NJ: Erlbaum; and Friedman, M. M., Bowden, V. R., & Jones, E. G. (2003). *Family nursing* (5th ed.). Upper Saddle River, NJ: Prentice Hall.

by family members is often an appropriate intervention.

According to Curran (1985), every study related to healthy families suggests that these families are "good problem-solvers." Nurses, taught to use a problem-solving approach in the nursing process, may assume that everyone knows the steps of gathering data, defining the problem, generating alternatives, finding solutions, and evaluating results. In actuality, many persons have not learned this process. Nurses can teach this skill as a coping strategy. The role of the family nurse is to teach clients a general coping strategy so that clients can more effectively control their own lives.

An effective approach may be to write down, in two separate columns, the positive aspects of an approach and the negative aspects. An individual can even "weigh," or rank, the positives and negatives. Often, just the simple act of putting positives and negatives in writing provides data that the family can use to solve problems.

Cognitive Restructuring

Before a family member can focus on more adaptive thoughts or learn new coping skills, negative patterns of thought that sidetrack coping efforts need to be interrupted. Self-defeating thoughts, negative self-talk, and irrational beliefs can evoke emotional and physical arousal that results in stress and has a profound impact on mood, behavior, and health.

The Harvard Negotiation Project (Fisher & Ury, 1992) advocates "four basic steps in inventing options" (p. 70). They are (1) identification of what is wrong, (2) analysis of possible causes and barriers, (3) brainstorming for possible approaches, and (4) generation of specific actions that might be used to solve the problem. Cognitive restructuring is the conscious thought process of redefining or relabeling beliefs or thought patterns (self-talk). Self-talk is a part of every individual's personality, the way that person interprets the world. The thought patterns and beliefs are often illogical or distorted (Ellis, 1988). The interpretation of internal and external conditions may or may not be based on fact. Internal self-evaluation leads to messages of reward or punishment that affect the daily functioning of the individual.

It is possible to change patterns of self-talk, which can lead to reduction of stress. One approach is rational-emotive therapy (RET) (Ellis, 1988). This approach helps the person to critically evaluate the illogical nature of the self-talk and to understand that the way he or she perceives or evaluates a situation determines his or her emotional reaction. All people develop sets of beliefs based on their experiences, and these beliefs mediate or determine their responses in a given situation. However, expectations or beliefs that are irrational or based on false assumptions create problems and increase stress. Cognitive theorists have indicated that people often "awfulize" (intensify) events by irrational self-talk. Breadwinners who have lost their jobs may believe that they are stupid for losing the position or may, in fact, feel that there are better positions waiting for a person with their talents. The process of self-evaluation and self-talk begins in the child at an early age and can aid in the development of self-esteem and healthy growth or can give rise to a harsh internal critic and feelings of inferiority. Parental verbal and nonverbal behaviors have an

important role in this process. If the child hears statements such as "You are bad," "You are lazy," "You are stupid," these may be internalized to "I am bad, lazy, and stupid." Family members might be told to substitute a statement such as "That behavior was not skillful; I can change that to something more useful." This gives the message that growth is possible.

Changing internal messages and replacing negative, illogical self-talk with supportive statements based on realistic beliefs is a coping skill that, in essence, creates a new self-support system. Changing self-talk involves the following:
1) Identification of the self-talk and the situation
2) Evaluation of whether messages are rational or irrational
3) Replacement of the messages with supportive statements
4) Integration of supportive statements into daily life

Imagery, an ancient practice, can be used to empower positive attitudes and change behaviors (Hoblitzelle & Benson, 1992). Imagery can be used to facilitate practice in altering self-talk. The individual or the family can be encouraged to imagine a problematic situation and then use positive self-statements to imagine mastery within the event. Implementing these changes takes time and practice. The nurse is in a position to encourage, to support, and to empower the family to re-label or redefine individual family stressors.

For example, when the family nurse observes that the mother in a family functions with the belief that she must be loved and approved of by all and that any open expression of anger is dangerous, the plan of action might include a family discussion of the effects of this behavior on other family members, as well as on the mother. It could be suggested that no one can be loved and approved of by everyone and that appropriate expression of anger is acceptable. The mother could be encouraged to examine her self-talk when she perceives that no one loves her and to restructure her beliefs about anger. Perhaps reframing an angry situation as "discussing differences" would be a more positive approach.

Conflict Resolution

Fisher and Ury (1992) report that "conflict is a growth industry. Everyone wants to participate in decisions that affect them" (p. xi). Conflict situations related to issues of power, use of resources, relationship needs, and differing value systems arise in families. Whatever the cause, the result is usually increased stress until the conflict is resolved. However, conflict as a concept characterizes a wide range of behaviors from quiet arguing or quarreling to verbal and physical aggression. Most therapists agree that it is healthy to have a degree of conflict in relationships, recognizing that if no disagreements are evident, one person in the relationship may be too submissive and/or may be stockpiling hurts and discomforts. Conflict can be healthy if it promotes open communication. However, conflict resolution is vital to the health of the family. A conflict that is ignored tends to go "underground," where it rises periodically in a new guise or as a new issue, causing increasing dysfunction in the family.

Family life education programs such as Prepare/Enrich (Olson & Olson, 2000), RENEW (Duncan & Brown, 1992), and others offer training to help couples air disagreements and fight therapeutically (Renick, Blumberg, & Harkman, 1992; also see the website for Life Innovations). Conflict resolution demands active listening, effective communication, willingness to address underlying issues, commitment to family relations, and use of negotiation skills. Fisher and Ury (1992) recognize that most conflict falls into one of three categories: perception, emotion, or communication. These authors recommend the following actions: "(1) separate the people from the problem, (2) focus on interests, not positions, (3) invent options for mutual gain, and (4) insist on using objective criteria" (p. 15).

A communication technique that often needs to be taught and that is useful in conflict resolution is the communication skill of *claiming* feelings when upset (e.g., "I feel angry when you overspend our budget"). This approach clearly claims the emotion as a part of the person and allows the other to respond cognitively to the message and to the emotion expressed.

In contrast, a *blaming* message communicates that the other person is responsible for the individual's feelings (e.g., "You make me so angry when you overspend our budget"). The result is usually a defensive reply and little cognitive awareness of the source of the emotion. In addition,

"we statements" may be helpful "when a person wants to turn a problem they 'own' as an individual into a problem that is 'owned' by the relationship" (Burr et al., 1990). When a "we statement" such as "As a family, we don't show much affection" or "We don't seem to have much time for fun" is used, the problem becomes a family group problem. However, it is important to note that a broad statement, such as "The checking account is very low," could be interpreted as a personal attack. It is also important to point out that other people cannot control a person's feelings. Individuals make choices about emotional responses from a diverse set, depending on background, self-esteem, and previous learning. As a result of different perspectives, arguments or quarreling may ensue. Arguments start with a current issue such as the monthly budget, and as sides are taken by each party in the discussion, may focus on old issues such as how each party handled finances in the past. Resolution is usually accomplished through a form of compromise, and the issue is settled. Quarreling and high levels of marital conflict have much more serious ramifications (Bowman, 1990). Quarrels attack the other person's values and usually represent unconscious needs and deprivations of the attacking person. Insults and personal attacks hurled in the anger of a quarrel fan the flame of retribution and cauterize the spirit. The result can only be incineration of the relationship. Family strategies for primary prevention of quarrels include (1) recognition of times when such quarrels are more likely to occur, (2) awareness of the danger signals of impending upsets, and (3) self-awareness of elements that trigger the response.

The nurse is in a key position to assess families for risk factors associated with such abusive behaviors, as well as to assist with developing coping strategies that may prevent conflict. Primary prevention strategies to resolve problems of family violence are (1) establish mutual goals that are put in writing, (2) establish processes that lead to achieving goals, and (3) refrain from imposing solutions on the family. In cases of extreme dysfunction, family therapy by a qualified family nurse therapist or family counselor is recommended. The role of the family nurse is to encourage the use of effective communication, reduce conflicts, and enhance family cohesion.

Role Sharing

Role sharing has evolved in response to societal and family system changes that reflect entry of almost two thirds of the women in the United States into the workforce accompanied by a decrease of nearby extended family (Hochschild, 1989). In role sharing two or more persons participate in the same role while holding different positions (Friedman, 1992). In contrast, role specialization denotes that one person in the family fulfills a particular family function.

Role transitions are not without stress for family members and can affect the homeostasis of the family for varying periods. The knowledge and skills needed to assume new roles are often lacking. In addition, some roles within the family give more or less power to the role taker. When power is related to greater resources (money, possessions), the ability to influence others is increased. However, when a family member determines that a new role is necessary, either developmentally or socially, the result is often confusion on the part of other family members. If a mother decides to go back to school or return to work, her traditional roles of homemaker—including the roles of nurturer, healer, chauffeur, and cook—become available to and must be assumed by other family members to maintain family stability. Or when the wage earner, perhaps the father, becomes ill or unemployed, the family must decide who will assume the role of resource provider.

When the nurse works with a family in which role inadequacy or dissonance is present, it is important for him or her to assess the normative system of what is expected to be done by whom. Assisting the family to evaluate roles enacted in the family system and to negotiate responsibilities and communicate feelings regarding these roles is conducive to stress reduction. For example, a family conference that includes discussion of the rights and responsibilities of each role and each person's feelings can be helpful. If role inadequacy is diagnosed, role playing or contact with persons who have successfully assumed a particular role can provide support. If role dissatisfaction is the problem, negotiation with other members can

often be helpful in the sharing or reassignment of a role. Often, the family system falls into disarray when children or parents have not carried out the tasks assigned to maintain family functioning. At the family conference, discussion of the meaning and impact of the behavior can decrease stress. One successful method of task assignment is the development of a task assignment sheet for the week or month, but coupled with this, an operative description of what each task entails is needed. For example, one child may be assigned the task of taking out the trash every night. The operative description might include the following instructions:

1) Take trash to trash receptacle in garage.
2) Replace cover on can to decrease insects.
3) Reline the kitchen receptacle with plastic liner.
4) Close the cupboard door.

This process reduces argument and stress because it clarifies the totality of the assignment. A clear and effective role assignment coupled with good communication can result in more effective family stress management.

Communication Strategies

Although family communication has been discussed at length in Chapter 7, the following section includes specific approaches suggested to relieve family stress. Communication in families is a powerful force that can foster or destroy relationships, egos, trust, growth, and joy. Satir (1982, p. 30) states that "communication is the largest single factor determining which kinds of relationships he (the person) makes with others and what happens to him in the world about him." In the family unit, communication accomplishes bonding, conflict or harmony, decision making, task allocation, role enactment, and role delineation. Yet clear communication is one of the most difficult processes to accomplish successfully.

Family members occasionally experience interpersonal stress but may feel unable to define a specific cause. A strategy called "sculpting" provides a mechanism for giving nonverbal expression to these feelings. The sculpting process consists of each family member taking his or her turn at the following:

1) Arrangement of all family members, including the sculptor, in "freeze-tag" positions

that symbolize the attitudes and group relationships, as perceived by the sculptor.

2) Discussion of the meaning of the tableau, or arrangement, with all family members. What does each position represent in the emotions of the relationship?

3) Reinforcement that each "sculpting" is neither right nor wrong but is simply the view of the family's emotional relationships by the sculptor.

Papp, Silverstein, and Carter (1973) describe the benefits of family sculpting as "literally worth a thousand words, revealing aspects of the family's inner life that have remained hidden. Vague impressions and confused feelings on the periphery of awareness are given form through physical spatial expression" (p. 197). Because of the nonverbal nature of the process, sculpting cuts through the defense mechanisms of intellectualization, defensiveness, and blame; and each member is enabled to communicate in more depth (Mealey, 1977).

Nursing intervention is directed toward helping family members recognize dysfunctional patterns of communication, practice empathic clarification of messages, and elicit feedback from each other. Supportive encouragement from the nurse is often needed by the family in initiation of change in communication; however, recognition of the value of successful change reinforces the change.

Time Control and Management

Time is not a resource that can be increased, decreased, or borrowed; but control and management of time can structure family activities in a way that decreases the stress of time pressure. According to McKenzie (1997), time control is the strategy of setting aside selected times to attend to specific tasks. Effective time management is tied to the family's values and goals for daily living, as well as long-range plans. Clarification of family values is required to set priorities and manage time well (DeGrote-Sorensen & Sorensen, 2001). Social and cultural expectations play a strong role in influencing family activities and schedules. In the United States today, both adults and children are pressured to "do" many things—physical fitness,

financial planning, relaxation, community service, career planning, and leisure activities—in addition to everyday tasks including work and school. With these pressures and demands, many family members experience a constant, or at least sustained, feeling of being overwhelmed and rushed. Successful coping and achievement of goals can enhance self-efficacy, whereas prolonged feelings of an inability to "keep up" can lead to fatigue and decreased coping. For many persons, the feeling of having too many tasks they must do and not enough time for the things they want to do is a major stressor.

Successful coping with demands on time has evolved over several generations (Covey, 1990). As demands on family time have increased, families have altered behavior to increase management of time. Initially, families turned to checklists; then appointment books and "day timers" emerged, followed by computerized calendars and personal digital assistants. Each of these devices is effective when used routinely, but many family members find that keeping the family schedule updated can be a stressful activity in and of itself. However, Degrote-Sorensen et al. (2001) suggest that families create a family covenant related to family priorities, evaluate what activities are important to the health of the family unit, and take time out for family rituals and the creation of family memories.

To organize time effectively, the family must clarify goals and values, set priorities, and make a commitment to achieving goals according to values and established priorities. This sets expectations in motion, which can cause family stress when some but not all family members are committed to the stated values. Covey (1990) articulates a matrix for identification of family/individual coping to determine whether an individual is crisis-motivated, able to proactively plan, or consumed by unproductive activities (pp. 150-154). Families should be reminded of the importance of focusing beyond planning for daily survival to organize and plan within a context of weekly, monthly, and life goal events (Doherty & Carlson, 2002).

When one member of the family feels overwhelmed and anxious, there is a ripple effect felt by all. Children often have difficulty managing time, and pressure for them may be manifested by emotional, physical, and behavioral disorders.

Behavior changes that will help individuals in the family to use time more effectively and thus enable the entire family to function in a more satisfying manner can be initiated. Techniques to aid in this process have been described in the literature (Doherty & Carlson, 2002; Lakein, 1989; Davis, Eschelman, & McKay, 1995). Lakein (1989), a pioneer in time management, suggests three strategies for time management: (1) the goals statement, (2) the "to-do" list, and (3) the schedule. These strategies can be taught to the family as a group. Approaches summarized by Davis et al. (1995, p. 155) are as follows:

1) Set priorities that list most important goals.
2) Make time by realistic planning, and omit low-priority tasks.
3) Learn to make decisions based on identified goals.

Weekly scheduled meetings can facilitate values clarification and goal attainment, identifying those areas of disagreement that could benefit from negotiation and even mediation to prevent or reduce stress on family relationships. Important matters that are not urgent require more initiative, more proactivity. A family calendar can be created, with input from each member. The calendar can provide information about activities, schedules, needs, and desires. Priorities can be set as each person participates and determines what is to be included on the calendar. Time for play and recreation is as important as time for study or work. A plan may be developed with modifications for each age group. In assisting families with time management, the clinician needs to consider culture time orientation, social class, sense of time, perception of time, and scheduling of time as unique within each family. Implementation of a successful time management plan may open the door to better communication, greater intimacy, and more time to spend with loved ones or in solitude when that is the perceived need.

Intimacy

Intimacy refers to a moment in time or an ongoing relationship in which persons focus on each other. Lerner (1989) identifies the goal as to "have relationships with both men and women that do not operate at the expense of the self, and to have a self that does not operate at the expense of the other" (p. 4).

Issues around intimacy often arise in relation to the increased need for emotional support in times of stress. At these times, each member of the family feels stress and needs support yet has little to give to others. Persons of all ages have a need to relate and a desire to connect with others. Each person can experience another's uniqueness, and often, in a mutual exchange, will feel understood, loved, and wanted. There are many kinds of intimacy: intellectual, recreational, sexual, emotional, and spiritual. People may experience more than one type, which provides other means of nurturing a relationship. Conversely, each form has hazards to be navigated. Some of the barriers to intimacy are fears of conflict, rejection, hurt, control or "engulfment," as well as cultural gender differences and lack of a sense of identity. A person with a strong sense of identity and a feeling of self-worth is able to give in a relationship without fearing loss of self. Intimacy implies the ability of people to share feelings. It is correlated with equality of power and not with a hierarchy of leadership. As a result, each person is more comfortable expressing inadequacies and fears. According to Burns (1989) "Communication is more important to a healthy marriage than sex, money, or a microwave" (p. 41).

Ghoulston (1988) describes men's fear of intimacy and cautions caregivers to help parents stay firmly linked with each other and to view their marital relationship as primary. He provides specific steps to better understanding of the clash between men's need for independence and women's need for intimacy. Intimacy is reciprocal and is manifested as a rhythm. If the rhythm stops or gets stuck, problems can occur. Couples and families can be taught to be aware of the cycle, of the need to refocus on the "other," to renew and maintain the rhythm. They can set aside a special time in which to concentrate on each other, to touch, to listen, to look, and to be present in mutual sharing. A mother could take her teenager to lunch or plan a special one-on-one activity with a younger child. A husband and wife might go out for a night or a weekend without the children. A single parent could create special time for self-care activities. Interventions can be directed toward helping each member to have a stronger sense of self-worth and appreciation of his or her uniqueness.

Several family life education programs for professionals, couples groups, couples, and families provide support and education to promote couple intimacy and family life education. Examples are the international Enrich-Prepare program developed by family scientists David H. Olson, Joan M. Druckman, and David Fournier and the PAIRS (Practical Application of Intimate Relationship Skills) program created by psychotherapist Lori H. Gordon. Programs such as Enrich-Prepare and PAIRS help families, premarital couples, couples with and without children, military families, and cohabitating couples to acquire the skill of creating intimacy to improve family life (see the Website Resources box at the end of the chapter for website addresses for each of these programs).

Family Centering/Meditation

Stressful experiences often bring about feelings of tension and anxiety that evoke a sense of being out of balance, an inability to feel a solid integration of mind and body, a lack of feeling connected ("grounded") in the environment. Thoughts are scattered, making it difficult to focus attention. This lack of harmony can be experienced by the family as a system, as well as by individual members. In contrast, to feel *centered* is to experience a psychological center of gravity, to have a sense of balance and integration, which contributes to feelings of calmness and relaxation.

Centering is the experience of turning within; of stilling the body and the mind; of focusing and maintaining attention on a part of the body, an object, or a thought. This process is passive concentration, "letting it happen" rather than making it happen, and needs to be experienced to be understood. It is possible to develop a feeling of family centeredness, or a feeling of unity within a family group (Hendricks, 1979). The feeling of being centered will be gained and lost and gained again. Hendricks (1979) says that being centered is a process of losing centeredness and getting it back again and that the sense of harmony will improve as the family uses good problem-

solving strategies and improves channels of communication.

A variety of participatory activities may be used to aid in the process of centering. A number of simple techniques suitable for use by the family as a group and for members of all ages are described by Hendricks (1979) and Hendricks and Willis (1975). Meditations and simple visualizations are designed to help children feel secure and cared for. A simple exercise that can be taught to the family group is to pause and focus awareness on an area of the body about 2 inches below the umbilicus (navel). Each person concentrates on this area, sends thoughts and feelings there, and breathes deeply into this center. Another relaxation and centering exercise that enhances a feeling of closeness, love, and caring within the family unit is described in Box 14-4.

Centering is a useful technique for coping with "everyday hassles," as well as in moments of high stress during which it can aid in regaining self-control. The involvement and enthusiasm of the nurse, combined with verbal rewards for the family, can be potent reinforcers for new behaviors. It is helpful to give clients a handout with written instruction for general activities.

Mediation

Mediation is particularly useful for addressing marital and family conflicts, divorce and custodial disputes, blended-family adjustments, and parent-child disputes. The goal is to improve communication and cooperation while also reducing anger and hostility (Gold, 1998). This approach is particularly valuable when power struggles have escalated and the fundamental trust needed to sustain healthy relationships has eroded. Effective mediation is grounded in the ability to engage in active listening, an essential skill that requires each individual participating in the conflict resolution to be willing to set aside his or her own needs. In addition, participants are required to learn skills for effectively defusing emotional reactivity and the development of empathy, which are essential for meaningful conflict resolution and effective mediation of differences (Nichols, 1995).

Prevention of family conflicts can be facilitated by scheduling regular sessions for discussion, as

---

BOX 14-4   Family Closeness Exercise: The Family Tree

Instructions: "Quietly now, gather in a circle, and stand without touching each other. Let your arms hang loosely at your sides as you relax your body— just be loose and limp, like a rag doll. Close your eyes. Take a deep breath through your nose, and feel the air go down to your chest and on down to your stomach—find the place in your body that is *your* center. This is usually right below where *your* navel (belly button) is. Breathe again, and feel the air go to your center and all the way to your fingertips and toes. Feel them tingle. Now, let all the air out. Notice how your body feels more relaxed as your breath flows out. Feel your breath move gently in and out." (Pause) "Now, imagine yourself standing firmly on the ground, like a tree. Send your roots down into the ground. Now, lift your arms up and stretch them high over your head like the branches of a tree. Like a tree, you can bend in the wind and not break. Imagine the wind blowing through your limbs but not breaking them. You are safe, and secure, and strong. Now, gently bring your arms down to your sides. Let your body relax and let go." (Pause 5 seconds) "Now, join hands in the circle. Take another deep breath, and imagine a warm golden light filling your whole body. You feel its energy moving in and through you . . . and going to every person in this room. Feel this wonderful energy . . . and the energy coming to you from those in this circle. Send this energy to the person on your right." (Pause 5 seconds) "You are now connected to every person in the circle. This feels good. Feel the love and the strength being shared now among the members of your family. Gently give a little squeeze to each of the hands you are holding, then let go. Slowly open your eyes, and move forward into the middle of the room for a special group hug."

Source: Haroldyne Richardson.

---

in the use of the family council. This weekly meeting provides a helpful forum that affords families the time to discuss the concerns of each member, as well as to plan family events, before conflicts can escalate. This approach builds a foundation for healthy communication and the development of skills in constructive problem solving. For this approach to be helpful, family members must learn techniques of effective communication. In the absence of such skills, family members can become repetitious in unproductive communication patterns, persevere in avoidance, and use blaming styles that fail to reach any constructive resolution of the conflict. At these times, mediation can be productive because this approach helps family members clearly identify issues of conflict and provides a neutral third party to facilitate discussion and explore options.

Mediation is a collaborative conflict resolution process in which two or more parties in dispute are assisted in their negotiation by a neutral and impartial third party and empowered to voluntarily reach their own mutually acceptable settlement of the issues in dispute. The mediator structures and facilitates the process by which the parties make their own decisions and determine the outcome, in a way that satisfies the interests of all parties in the dispute (Kruk, 1998, p. 4).

Mediation calls families to action and seeks solutions grounded in equitable discussion and debate (Gold, 1998). In addition, "many . . . mediators would argue that the end result of an agreement is less important than exposing the parties to a process of dispute resolution that will serve to prevent future crisis" (Umbreit & Kruk, 1998, p. 97). Such an approach can be particularly successful when there is an imbalance of power between or among disputants, as is the case between parent and child, or among complex family configurations, as is prevalent in blended or stepfamilies (Jacob, 1998).

Spirituality Strategies

The spiritual dimension of stress management integrates and transcends the other dimensions.

"Spirituality may be viewed as the integrating or unifying factor, that which gives meaning and purpose" (Nafai-Jacobsen & Burkhart, 1989, p. 19). In a national study of more than 21,000 couples, 89% reported that spirituality was an aspect that contributed to strengthening their marriage (Olson & Olson, 2000). When family stress levels are high, a period of meditation and prayer may have a calming effect on family members.

Faith communities and groups within faith organizations frequently provide a source of social support, counseling for family and individual problems, and classes on parenting and marriage (Carson, 1989). Mutual support groups such as singles groups, older adult groups, and couples groups are often formed in churches. Spirituality includes more than religious activities such as prayer, faith group activities, and attendance at services. Spirituality also includes such activities as communion with nature, artistic processes, journal writing, songs and chants, self-care of the body, loving relationships with others, reading, social gatherings, and service to others. A holistic approach to facilitating family stress management includes encouraging the family to use a variety of spiritual activities to adapt to life's stresses. Spirituality is not always a useful strategy for families. Particular attention should be given to family preferences and ethnic, developmental, and situational variations in use of spirituality in coping with stress. For example, McAdoo (1995) notes that religiosity is not always a support for working mothers. However, if assessment of the family reveals that members have found spirituality to be a support in the past, the clinician should encourage them to seek spiritual support again. See Chapter 8 for more detail on family spirituality, approaches to assessment of spirituality, and suggestions for facilitating family spirituality.

Humor

Humor is an inexpensive, available, and powerful stress management technique (Bain & Laroach, 1993; Wooten 2000). Often, the family perspective of a situation is the key to successful coping. Being able to laugh at the incongruities of life interrupts the stress-worry cycle. Worry and stress

are antithetical to humor. Research has shown that when a person laughs, levels of catecholamine in the body are increased, endorphin release is stimulated, circulation is stimulated, and ventilation is increased. In the immune system, T lymphocytes are stimulated, blood pressure and muscle tension decrease, and learning and memory are enhanced (Witek-Janusek & Mathews, 2000).

How can a family most effectively bring these benefits to its members? The methods are numerous. Create regular times for enjoying humor, such as joke or funny storytelling at dinner. Cut out favorite cartoons and put them on desks or refrigerators or tuck them in lunch bags. Rent a funny movie and plan a family viewing. Write humorous notes to family members to convey serious messages. Give silly gifts. Dress up in ridiculous outfits for a family dinner. The objective is for the family to take themselves less seriously and take time to enjoy each other.

Negotiated Family Responsibilities

More than 50% of U.S. women work full-time outside of the home and are away from their homes 10 hours a day or more (Hochschild 1997; U.S. Department of Labor, 2000). In a study of family definitions of health, Denham (2003) reports that mothers were responsible for protecting against illness and disease; teaching health promotion, risk reduction, and safety measures; and modeling health behaviors. Mothers reportedly often did not take care of their own health, some were depressed, and stress was prolonged. Women in her study served as orchestrators of family health—health gatekeepers, instructors, and caretakers (Denham, 2003).

In a study of the lived experiences of Fortune 500 company executives, factory and childcare workers, secretaries, and others, Hochschild (1997) notes that women describe their lives as stressful because of the expectations of the corporate culture: doing more with less and spending more time at work. In the twenty-first century, both men and women usually work long hours, which seems to be the corporate norm. Therefore these additional roles for women create "pile-up," leading to lowered housekeeping standards and tasks that are not completed. Often, differences in standards between spouses are points of friction; one is usually extremely neat or tidy, the other less so. Cultural norms are also quickly absorbed from television as advertisers portray the efficient housewife painting in a slinky formal. The disparity between the ideal and the reality is shattering.

Family decision making about equitable sharing of household duties is stress reducing. By weekly assignment of tasks to individuals, the responsibility is shared, as well as the stress. However, increased stress can result if the standard of carrying out the assignments becomes a source of argument. To avoid this trap, families must have operational definitions of the assignments, as discussed earlier in this chapter.

Another element that needs to be addressed is an assessment of the total demands on the family at any specific time. If the mother is working part-time or attending college, the children are in sports, and the father is president of a service club, it may well be that an agreement needs to be reached concerning vital housekeeping chores. Do the beds need to be made daily? Does dust on the table indicate a slovenly family? A conscious family effort to reduce the demands of perfect housekeeping and to share in the tasks that need to be done can reduce stress. In addition, more time can be provided for family and individual recreation and relaxation.

In the past, women attempted to play superwoman to keep dual roles as career woman and homemaker. Hochschild (1989), a sociologist, reports that women who work outside the home have "two shifts," one at home and one at work, which amount to about 15 hours more per week than men's shifts. Hochschild (1989) advocates that men and women negotiate a more equitable division of responsibilities, one that helps prevent the stress and frustration caused by role overload for women. Women also add to their stress by "bringing the second shift to work" (Philipson, 2002). A support group of working women reported making the workplace more "homey" by such activities as baking, organizing parties, and planning celebrations. The result is that they may work longer hours and have higher expectations that are not a part of their job descriptions. In today's world both men and women find themselves involved in conflicts related to time spent at work and with family. The family nurse can assist families and women in learning to manage in a variety of ways: by cutting back on involvement at work, by reducing family commitments, or by establishing good health habits. Women can be assisted in determining whether one of their stressors is role overload in their jobs by making the workplace more "homey." Careful evaluation of role obligations, actual tasks, and the stress associated with each at home and at work will help women to carefully balance their commitments to maintain a healthy family.

Family Life Education

Educating families and individual members about the different family processes such as development of intimacy; parenting; balancing work, home life, and parenthood; communicating with children, co-workers, and intimate partners; teen and childhood issues (e.g. bullying, grades, peer pressure, and sexuality) should help them identify sources of stress and ways to manage it. Multiple credible websites are available to assist families, and the addresses for several of these websites are provided in the Website Resources box at the end of the chapter.

One role of family clinicians is to evaluate programs and to assist families and individuals in the selection of credible websites. In addition, many of the sites provide information that can be printed and given to families. Also, there are a myriad of family life education training programs provided by organizations such as cooperative extensions from universities for professionals to acquire skills in family life education. Cooperative extensions provide information for professional education, as well as for families. For example, Life Innovations, Inc. regularly offers courses on family communication; and other organizations offer group programs on balancing work and family life, parenting, retirement, grief and loss, and other related topics. Family life education focuses on the promotion of resilient families. Activities that build strengths for family resilience include the following:

- *Commitment:* being consistent, involved, and committed to the family as being important.

- *Connectedness:* being connected to each other and to extended family, the community, and other social groups.
- *Cohesion:* a sense of closeness as demonstrated by having family rituals and routine activities that promote closeness.
- *Communication:* honest, open, genuine, affirming conversation between members. The skill of listening is crucial. Constructive problem solving is crucial.
- *Spirituality:* sharing values and beliefs, reading spiritual and inspirational books, and praying for and with each other.
- *Time together:* spending time together daily in daily routines such as meals, reading, and recreation.

Individual Approaches to Manage Stress

Resources that discuss individual approaches to manage stress are numerous and readily available in lay and professional literature. If individual family members cope effectively, they will be more effective in coping with family stress. As discussed previously, as a system the family influences the health of its members and is influenced by the health of individual members. There is strong evidence that when high levels of family stress are present, a person's health can be adversely affected. Associated costs of this may result in severe illnesses and greater use of health care resources (Parkerson, Boardhead, & Tse, 1995). Family members who cope effectively may also act as resources when the family experiences a crisis. Pender et al. (2002) suggest minimizing the frequency of the stress-inducing situation, increasing resistance to stress, and counter conditioning to avoid the physiological effects of stress. Examples of ways to reduce the frequency of stressful situations include changing the environment and avoiding change. The nurse can assist individuals and families in increasing their resistance to stress by promoting exercise, enhancing self-esteem, enhancing self-efficacy and increasing assertiveness, setting realistic goals, and building coping resources. Lastly, the use of counter conditioning, touch, massage, imagery, and relaxation has been reported to reduce physiological arousal and the symptoms of disease (Pender et al., 2002;

Wimbush & Nelson, 2000). Also, a family member with skills in problem solving may help the family resolve a problem. A member with cognitive restructuring skills may encourage the family system to re-label a stressful event as a challenge rather than a problem. The family nurse might use a guide, as shown in Figure 14-2, to encourage family members to evaluate the priorities in their lives in the professional, personal, spiritual, financial, and community realms. Clarification of values and the family's orientation or goals in life may be very useful in reducing stress.

Holistic Family Stress Management

Family stress management includes all aspects of family health promotion that are included in Units II and III of this text. As with individual stress management, family stress management is a dynamic, lifelong process. It is different at each developmental stage; thus there is a need for family life education that addresses each developmental stage and issue. For example, Olson et al. developed a counseling program for unmarried couples to promote better communication (see the Life Innovations website address in the Website Resources box at the end of the chapter). Family nurses can help families to understand their stress by teaching them the developmental tasks of each stage for the family system and individuals. Also, instructions to anticipate a higher level of stress at crucial developmental stages are provided in the case scenario at the end of this chapter. Clinicians should explore strategies that build on families' existing strengths and that increase the capacity of families to adapt to the myriad of family changes and external influences. In addition, families should be taught that stress is ever present and that counseling is a healthy activity. Whether stress influences the quality of family health is directly related to the piling up of stressors, family resilience, strengths, resources, and approaches used by the family to adapt in a healthy manner. Lastly, family clinicians can increase the capacity of families to manage life changes by the use of such interventions as strengths-based empowerment strategies, teaching stress recognition and management skills, contracting, values clarification, counseling, teaching

GOALS: LIST IN EACH CATEGORY	PROFESSIONAL	PERSONAL	SPIRITUAL	FINANCIAL	COMMUNITY
Lifetime					
5 years					
6 months					
If you had only 6 months to live					

Figure 14-2   Put in Motion the Power within You. (Data from Lakein, A. [1973]. *How to get control of your time in life*. New York: Signet.)

how to obtain resources and support, consultation, collaborating, counseling, role modeling, family advocacy, and making referrals when appropriate.

Research Priorities for Family Stress

Additional research studies are needed in the realm of family stress and stress management because families experience a myriad of transitions, stressors, and crises in their life span. Scholars particularly suggest that qualitative studies that illuminate the stories of families as they experience illness, particularly chronic illness, relationship changes, and death in the family context are needed (DeMarco et al., 2000). Because women are usually the health leaders in the family and more than half of North American women work outside the home, continued research is needed to identify the unique stressors experienced by various groups of women (e.g., working women, single mothers, divorced women). As the number of senior adults increases in the next 20 years,

descriptive and intervention research will be needed to provide knowledge of best practices, to aid families and individual family members, and to manage the myriad of stressors associated with aging and later life. Also, as the focus on cost containment and disease processes increases in the twenty-first century, clinicians are urged to create longitudinal studies that examine how families are influenced by the health of family members from the perspectives of oncology, cardiovascular disease, drug abuse cure and prevention, and HIV care (DeMarco et al., 2000). Although most nursing care is directed toward individuals, the quality of family life cannot be ignored because within the context of the family is where "health work" takes place (Allen & Warner, 2002; Denham, 2003). Therefore in the twenty-first century, family-focused stress management and coping research should address diverse cultures and ethnic groups, age and development, socioeconomic status, gender perceptions, motivation, parenting, and caregiving. Lastly, innovative models for intervening to prevent and reduce family stress are needed.

CASE SCENARIO

The Judds are a family of four. The parents, Leigh, age 39, and Ann, also age 39, have been married 18 years. They have two daughters: Jane, age 17, and Palissa, age 14. Leigh owns his own business, with a profit of $100,000 per year, and Ann does part-time book-keeping at home for small businesses.

Their family life pace always has a sense of urgency and rushing from one activity to another. The only meal they usually eat together is dinner. Ann remains in bed when Leigh and the girls get ready for school. Leigh sometimes has breakfast with Palissa. Evening meals are eaten with the TV in front of the table and are generally rushed because a family member has a game, choir practice, a church meeting, or work. Meals are often pizzas, chicken nuggets, fried fish, and fast food. Leigh coaches Little League basketball for the girls, is responsible for the family finances, and does the lawn work, as well as cooking some of the meals. Ann does nearly all of the house cleaning, dishes, meals, and correspondence and has two church com-mittee meetings a month and choir practice. When she is not doing bookkeeping on her home computer, Ann spends her time doing household chores, running errands, and attending the girls' sporting events. Leigh and Ann seldom have intimate time together, and Ann falls asleep as soon as she goes to bed. She often goes to bed at 8:30 pm, and Leigh, at 11:00 pm.

Both of the girls are quite active in sports and after-school social activities. Jane, a high school senior, is very attractive, outgoing, and athletic; she works 20 hours a week and is popular at school. The family telephone rings constantly in the evening, for Jane especially. Palissa is quiet and prefers reading, painting, playing her flute, and writing stories. Palissa is extremely close to her mom, whereas Jane and Ann constantly have arguments and disagreements. Disagreements are about Jane's boyfriend, use of the telephone, uncompleted chores, and learning to drive. Jane has not taken drivers education because her parents believe that she is too young. All her friends have cell phones and she does not. Jane is also preparing to submit applications for college. Ann does not like Jane's boyfriend. Leigh intervenes by taking Jane to the movies and the shopping mall to meet her boyfriend and believes her boyfriend is okay. There is

constant bickering between Jane and Ann. Jane sits sullenly at mandatory family sit-down suppers. Ann insists that Jane look at her directly and "get that look off her face at dinner." Each family meal begins with a prayer, and on Sunday the family has family time when they pray for each other and the family. Another Sunday family ritual is making telephone calls to grandparents and Leigh and Ann's siblings. Each of the family members talks with extended family members. They also communicate by writing letters and by e-mail.

Palissa and Jane also bicker about telephone and television program choices. Palissa and Leigh tell Jane she ought to be nicer and obedient to her mom. Jane, the older daughter, is very close to her grandmother and writes and talks to her at least twice a month. Grandmother encourages her to be future-oriented and to be polite and obedient to her parents. They also discuss career options and college. Palissa and Jane visit their paternal grandparents for 2 weeks in the summer, and the grandparents spend 2 weeks with them at Christmas. Last week, Jane threatened to run away. Ann and Leigh were so fed up with her sullen angry attitude they told her "Go ahead, if that is what you want to do! Go for it!" Then Jane secretly called her grandparents to ask whether she could move in with them. She said "I can't take this any more! I gotta get out of here!" Grandmother suggested that Jane calm down and not run away until she could talk with her son and daughter-in-law.

Ann has been ill for 6 weeks, complains of being very tired, and makes an appointment with the family nurse practitioner. Her chief issues are sinus head-aches, ear aches, always feeling tired, and extreme low back pain. Her blood pressure was 160/105, weight 180 pounds, and temperature normal. She says, "I try everything and the pain just will not go away. I need your help; I cannot stand this pain anymore. I cannot sleep at night. I don't like medicines so I drink Coke or coffee for my headaches and just go to bed for the backaches. Also, my 17-year-daughter is threatening to run away if we don't allow her have her own telephone, talk in her bedroom, and learn to drive. I'm so fed up with her!"

The family nurse practitioner treated Ann's earache,

CASE SCENARIO—cont'd

blood pressure, and back pain. A family assessment was completed by using a genogram, an ecomap (see Chapter 3), or the Anderson (2000) framework for family assessment, and the FS3 by Berkey and Hanson (2000).

MAJOR FAMILY STRESSORS

Family stressors include Leigh's insufficient "me" time, Ann's illness, decreased housekeeping standards, insufficient couple time and intimacy, insufficient family recreation and family togetherness, too much television, inadequate parenting time with Palissa and Jane, overscheduled family calendar, Jane threatening to run away, and lack of shared responsibility.

FAMILY STRENGTHS

Family strengths include a shared religious core, income, support of daughters' recreation, family time on Sunday, and a strong supportive kin network.

LIFESTYLE CHANGES INDICATED

Lifestyle changes needed are increased individual and couple time for the parents, improved family recreation and family time, evaluation of the family calendar, and increased sharing of the household calendar and household chores. Improved communication is needed within the family unit, within in the couple dyad, between parents and children, and between siblings. Ann needs stress management strategies, exercise, and nutritional changes.

WEBSITE RESOURCES

ORGANIZATION	WEBSITE ADDRESS
FAMNET	http://www.nnfr.org/famnet.html
CYFERnet	http://www.cyfernet.org/about.html
Center for the Prevention of Sexual and Domestic Violence	http://www.cpsdv.org/
Parenting and Family	http://home.about.com/parenting/
Life Innovations	http://www.lifeinnovations.com
National Coalition Against Domestic Violence	http://www.ncadv.org/
Single Parent Tips	http://singleparent.lifetips.com/OurGurus.asp
Stress Management	http://stress.about.com/library/weekly/ aa112600a.htm
Forever Families	http://www.foreverfamilies.net
TheFamily.com	http://www.thefamily.com
Center for Working Families	http://workingfamilies.berkeley.edu/welcome.html
Youth and Family Development	http://www.extension.umn.edu/topics.html?topic=3
Ohioline: Family	http://www.ohioline.osu.edu/lines/fami.html
Human Development Publications	http://www.ces.ncsu.edu/depts/fcs/humandev/ hdpub.html#stress
Parent Education Resource Notebook	http://www.ces.ncsu.edu/depts/fcs/smp9/ parent_education/index.htm

■ CHAPTER HIGHLIGHTS

- Stress is inherent in the human experience of all family types across the life cycle.

- Family stressor events are the result of a myriad of phenomena.

- Each family system has its own repertoire of coping and stress management, which may or may not be adequate to restore family equilibrium during times of stress or crises.

- Factors influencing family coping include culture, communication, resources, cohesion, flexibility, variety of coping strategies, social support, family perception, individual and family development, family and individual developmental stages, accumulation of stress, and the family's coping efficacy.

- Family stress management may include changing the exposure to the stressor event, reframing, control of reactions to the stressor, or ineffective coping.

- The role of the family clinician in family stress management includes assessing the family's ability to cope; helping family members to anticipate, recognize, prevent, reduce, manage, or adapt to stress; and helping the family to experience unity as a result of problem solving together.

- A family stress management plan is developed in collaboration with family members.

- Family stress management approaches may include problem solving or emotion-focused coping, cognitive restructuring, conflict resolution, role sharing, functional communication, time control and management, intimacy, family centering or meditation, spirituality, humor, negotiated housekeeping standards, and coping by individual family members.

- When collaborating with families, family professionals should empower families to anticipate, recognize, and prevent stress and/or adapt to stress and to prevent stressors from progressing into crises.

- Further research is needed on family-focused prevention strategies and the relationship between family interactions and stressors on the emotional and physical health of family members at each developmental stage and for both sexes.

- More studies are needed to analyze the myriad of problems faced by increasingly diverse families (Boss, 2003).

║ CRITICAL THINKING ACTIVITIES

1. Please refer to the Case Scenario to answer questions a through c.
   a. Describe the crisis in the Judd family and explain the individual and family pile-ups that are contributing to this crisis.
   b. Discuss with a classmate the FILE score of the Judd family in the Case Scenario.
   c. Explain how you would assist the Judd family in resolving the crisis with Jane.

2. Name four external stressors for twenty-first century families that affect internal family functioning.

3. List several crises that you may encounter in the next 5 years and how you might prepare to manage the crises when they occur.

4. Read a family novel or watch a film about family life.
   a. Describe a family crisis. Explain the incident that precipitated the crisis.
   b. Explain the types of stressors (internal, external, chronic, and short term).
   c. What are the resources that enhance the family's resilience?
   d. What new supports should they seek?
   e. How was the crisis resolved or how did the family adapt to the crisis?
   f. Describe the level of family unit resilience after the crisis was resolved.

REFERENCES

Agnes, M. (2001). *Webster's new world college dictionary* (4th ed.). Foster City, CA: IDG Books Worldwide, Inc.

Allen, F. M., & Warner, M. (2002). A developmental model of health and nursing. *Journal of Family Nursing, 8,* 96-135.

American Psychological Association. (2002). *Violence and the family: Report of the American Psychological Association Presidential Task Force on Violence and the Family.* Washington, DC: Author.

Anderson, K. H. (2000). The family health system approach to family systems nursing. *Journal of Family Nursing, 6,* 103-119.

Bain, M., & Laroche, L. (1993). Jest "n" joy. In H. Benson & E. Stuart (Eds.), *The wellness book: A comprehensive guide to maintaining health and treating stress-related illness* (pp. 266-285). New York: Fireside.

Berg, I. K. (1994). *Family based services, a solution-focused approach.* New York: Norton & Company.

Boss, P. (1987). Family stress: Perception and context. In M. Sussman & S. Steinmetz (Eds.), *Handbook on marriage and the family* (pp. 695-723). New York: Plenum.

Boss, P. (2002). *Family stress management: A contextual approach* (2nd ed.). Thousand Oaks, CA: Sage.

Boss, P. (Ed.). (2003). *Family stress: Classic and contemporary readings.* Thousand Oaks, CA: Sage.

Bowman, M. L. (1990). Coping efforts and mental satisfaction: Measuring mental coping and its correlates. *Journal of Marriage and the Family, 52,* 463-464.

Brooks, R., & Goldstein, S. (2001). *Raising resilient children: Fostering strength, hope, and optimism.* Chicago: Contemporary Books.

Bryla, C. (1996). The relationship between stress and the development of breast cancer: A literature review. *Oncology Nursing Forum, 23,* 441-448.

Burns, M. (1989). *Getting in touch: Intimacy.* Greenville, MI: Empey Enterprises.

Burr, W. R. (1990). Beyond I—statements in family communication. *Family Relations, 39,* 266-273.

Burr, W. R., Klein, S. R., Burr, R. G., Harker, B., Holmn, T. B., Martin, P. H., et al. (1994). *Reexamining family stress: New theory and research.* Thousand Oaks, CA: Sage.

Cannon, W. B. (1929). Bodily changes in pain, hunger, fear and rage. New York: Appleton.

Carson, V. B. (1989). *Spiritual dimensions of nursing practice.* Philadelphia: W. B. Saunders.

Covey, S. (1990). *The 7 habits of highly effective people, powerful lessons in personal change.* New York: Fireside.

Curran, D. (1983). *Traits of a healthy family.* Minneapolis, MN: Winston Press.

Curran, D. (1985). *Stress and the healthy family.* Minneapolis, MN: Winston Press.

Davis, M., Eschelman, E. R., & McKay, M. (1995). *The relaxation and stress reduction workbook* (3rd rev. ed.). Oakland, CA: New Harbinger.

Day, R. D. (2003). *Introduction to family processes* (4th ed.). Mahwah, NJ: Erlbaum.

DeGrote-Sorensen, B., & Sorensen, D. A. (2001). *Escaping the family time trap: A practical guide for over-busy families.* Minneapolis, MN: Augsburg Fortress.

DeMarco, R., Ford-Gilboe, M., Friedemann, M., McCubbin, H. I., & McCubbin, M.A. (2000). Family stress, coping, and family health. In V. H. Rice (Ed.), *Handbook of stress, coping and health: Implications for nursing research, theory, and practice* (pp. 295-332). Thousand Oaks, CA: Sage.

Denham, S. (2003). *Family health.* Philadelphia: F. A. Davis.

Doherty, W. J., & Carlson, B. Z. (2002). *Putting family first.* New York: Owl Books.

Duncan, S. F., & Brown, G. (1992). RENEW: A program for building remarried family strengths. *Families in Society: The Journal of Contemporary Human Services, 73,* 149-158.

Edelman, C. L., & Mandle, C. L. (Eds.). (2002). *Health promotion throughout the lifespan* (5th ed.). St. Louis, MO: Mosby.

Ellis, A., & Grieger, R. (1988). *Handbook of rational-emotive therapy* (Vol. 11). New York: Springer.

Ennis, M. P. (1992). Tuning into your body, tuning up your mind. In E. Benson & E. M. Stuart (Eds.), *The wellness book* (pp. 69-102). New York: Birch Lane Press.

Fisher, R., & Ury, W. (1992). *Getting to yes: Negotiating agreement without giving in.* Harrisburg, VA: R. R. Donnelly & Sons.

Friedemann, M. L. (1995). *The framework of systemic organization: A conceptual approach to families and nursing.* Thousand Oaks, CA: Sage.

Friedman, M. (1992). *Family nursing: Theory and assessment* (3rd ed.). Norfolk: CT: Appleton-Century Crofts.

Friedman, M. M., Bowden, V. R., & Jones, E. G. (2003). *Family nursing: Research, theory and practice* (5th ed.). Upper Saddle River, NJ: Prentice Hall.

Gelles, R. J., & Cornell, C. P. (1990). *Intimate violence in families.* Newbury Park, CA: Sage.

Ghoulston, M. S. (1988). Men's fear of intimacy linked to loneliness of their mothers. *Behavior Today, 19,* 4-6.

Gold, L. (1998). Mediation of couple and family disputes. In E. Kruk (Ed.), *Mediation and conflict resolution in social work and the human services* (pp. 19-35). Chicago: Nelson-Hall.

Gordon, M. (1994). *Manual diagnosis: Process and application.* St. Louis, MO: Mosby

Gordon, M. (2002). *Manual of nursing diagnosis.* St. Louis, MO: Mosby

Gray, V. R. (1996). Family self-care. In P. J. Bomar (Ed.), *Families and health promotion* (2nd ed., pp. 83-93). Philadelphia: Saunders.

Hendricks, G. (1979). *The family centering book.* Englewood Cliffs, NJ: Prentice Hall.

Hendricks, G., & Willis, R. (1975). *The centering book.* Englewood Cliffs, NJ: Prentice Hall.

Hill, R. (1958). Generic features of families under stress. *Social Casework, 49,* 139-150.

Hill, R. (2003). Generic features of families under stress. In P. Boss (Ed.), *Family stress: Classic and contemporary readings* (pp. 117-190). (Originally printed in 1958).

Hoblitzelle, O. J., & Benson, H. (1992). Eliciting the relaxation response. In H. Benson & E. M. Stuart (Eds.), *The wellness book.* New York: Birch Lane Press.

Hochschild, A. (1989). *The second shift.* New York: Avon Books.

Hochschild, A. (1997). *The time bind.* New York: Metropolitan Books.

Jacob, L. C. (1998). Postdivorce mediation with stepfamilies: An overview of issues and process. In E. Kruk (Ed.), *Mediation and conflict resolution in social work and the human services* (pp. 81-95). Chicago: Nelson-Hall.

Johnson, M., Bulechek, G., McCloskey-Dochterman, G., Maas, M., & Moorhead, S. (2001). *Nursing diagnoses, outcomes, and interventions: NANDA, NOC, and NIC linkages.* St. Louis: Mosby.

Johnson, M., Maas, M., & Moorhead, S. (Eds.). (2000). *Nursing outcomes classification* (2nd ed). St. Louis, MO: Mosby.

Jones, L. C., & Heermann, J. A. (1992). Parental division of infant care: Contextual influences and infant characteristics. *Nursing Research, 41,* 228-234.

Kruk, E. (1998). *Mediation and conflict resolution in social work and the human services.* Chicago: Nelson-Hall.

Lakein, A. (1989). *How to get control of your time and life.* New York: Signet.

LaVee, Y., McCubbin, H. I., & Patterson, J.M. (1985). The double ABCX model of family stress and adaptation: An empirical test by analysis of structural equations with latent variables. *Journal of Marriage and the Family, 46,* 811-825.

Lazarus, R. S. (1966). *Psychological stress and coping process.* New York: McGraw-Hill.

Lazarus, R. S., & Folkman, S. (1989). *Stress appraisal and coping.* New York: Springer.

Lipson, J. G., & Meleis, A. I. (1999). Research with immigrants and refugees. In A. S. Hinshaw, S. L. Feetham, & J. L. F. Shaver (Eds.), *Handbook of clinical research* (pp. 87-105). Thousand Oaks, CA: Sage.

Lyon, B. L. (2000). Stress, coping, and health: A conceptual overview. In V. H. Rice (Ed.), *Handbook of stress, coping, and health* (pp. 3-26). Thousand Oaks, CA: Sage.

Maier, S. F., & Watkins, L. R. (1998). Cytokines for psychologists: Implications of biodirectional immune-to-brain communication for understanding, behavior, mood, and cognition. *Psychological Review, 105,* 83-107.

McAdoo, H. P. (1995). Stress levels, family help patterns, and religiosity in middle and working class African American working mothers. *Journal of Black Psychology, 21,* 424-449.

McAdoo, H. P. (Ed.). (1999). *Family ethnicity: Strengths in diversity* (2nd ed.). Thousand Oaks, CA: Sage.

McCubbin, H. I., Larsen, A., & Olson, D. H. (1985). *Family inventories: Inventories used in a national survey of families across the family life cycle* (rev. ed., pp. 120-136). St. Paul: University of Minnesota.

McCubbin, M. A., & McCubbin, H. I. (1993). Families coping with illness: The Resiliency Model of Family Stress, Adjustment and Adaptation. In C. B. Danielson, B. Hamel-Bissell, & P. Winstead-Fry (Eds.), *Families, health, and illness: Perspectives on coping and intervention* (pp. 21-63). St. Louis, MO: C. V. Mosby.

McCubbin, M. A., & McCubbin, H. I. (1996). Resilience and families: A conceptual model of family adjustment and adaptation in response to stress and crises. In H. I. McCubbin., A. I. Thompson, & M. A. McCubbin (Eds.), *Family assessment: Resilience, coping and adaptation—Inventories for research and practice* (pp. 1-64). Madison: University of Wisconsin.

McCubbin, H. I., Olson, D., & Larsen, A. (1996). Family crisis oriented personal scales (F-COPES). In H. I. McCubbin., A. I. Thompson, & M. A. McCubbin (Eds.), *Family assessment: Resilience, coping and adaptation—Inventories for research and practice* (pp. 455-508). Madison: University of Wisconsin. (Original work published in 1981).

McCubbin, H. I., & Patterson, J. M. (1981). Broadening the scope of family: An emphasis on family coping and social support. In N. Stinner, J. DeFrain, K. King, P. Knaub, & G. Rowe (Eds.), *Family strengths: Roots of well-being* (pp. 177-194). Lincoln: University of Nebraska.

McCubbin, H. I., & Patterson, J. M. (1983). Family stress adaptation to crises: A double ABC-X model of family behavior. In D. H. Olson & B. C. Miller (Eds.), *Family studies review year book* (Vol. 1). (pp. 87-106). Beverly Hills, CA: Sage.

McCubbin, H. I., & Patterson, J. M. (1987). FILE: Family inventory of life events and changes. In H. I. McCubbin & A. I. Thompson (Eds.), *Family assessment: Inventories for research and practice* (pp. 79-95). Madison: University of Wisconsin.

McCubbin, H. I., Thompson, A. I., & McCubbin, M. A. (Eds.). (1996). *Family assessment: Resilience, coping and adaptation—Inventories for research and practice.* Madison: University of Wisconsin.

McKenzie, A. (1997). *The time trap* (3rd ed.). New York: AMACOM.

Mealey, A. R. (1977). Sculpting as a group technique for increasing awareness. *Perspectives in Psychiatric Care, 3,* 118-121.

Metcalf, L. (1997). *Parenting toward solutions, how parents can use skills they already have to raise responsible, loving kids.* Englewood Cliffs, NJ: Prentice Hall.

Miller, B. D., & Wood, B. L. (1997). Influence of specific emotional states on autonomic reactivity and pulmonary function in asthmatic children. *Journal of the American Academy of Child and Adolescent Psychiatry, 36,* 669-677.

Minuchin, S. (1974). *Families and family therapy.* Cambridge, MA: Harvard University Press.

Nafai-Jacobson, M. G., & Burkhardt, M. A. (1989). Spirituality: Cornerstone of holistic nursing practice. *Holistic Nursing Practice, 3,* 18-26.

National Network for Family Resilience. (1996). *Family resilience: Building strengths to meet life's challenges.* Retrieved February 20, 2003, from http://www.agnr.umd.edu/nnfr/general/pub_fam.html

Neighbors, H. W. (1997). Husbands, wives, family, friends: Sources of stress, sources of support. In R. J. Taylor, J. S. Jackson, & L. M. Chatters (Eds.), *Family life in Black America* (pp. 277-292). Thousand Oaks, CA: Sage.

Nichols, M. (1995). *The lost art of listening: How learning can improve relationships.* New York: The Guilford Press.

North American Nursing Diagnosis Association. (1999). *Nursing diagnoses: Definitions & classification 1999-2000.* Philadelphia: Author.

Olson, D. H. (1989). Circumplex Model of Family Systems VIII: Family Assessment and Intervention. In D. H. Olson, C. S. Russell, & D. H. Spenkle (Eds.), *Circumplex model: Systematic assessment and treatment of families.* New York: Haworth.

Olson, D. H., McCubbin, H. I., Barnes, H. L., Larsen, A. S., Muxen, M. L., & Wilson, M. A. (1983). *Families: What makes them work?* Beverly Hills, CA: Sage.

Olson, D. H., & Olson, A. K. (2000). *Empowering couples.* Roseville, MN: Life Innovations.

Papp, P., Silverstein, O., & Carter, E. (1973). Family sculpting in preventive work with well families. *Family Process, 2,* 197-204.

Parkerson, G. R., Boardhead, W. E., & Tse, C. J. (1995). Perceived family distress as predictors of health-related outcomes. *Archives of Family Medicine, 4,* 253-260.

Patterson, J. M., & Garwick, A. W. (2003). In P. Boss (Ed.), *Family stress: Classic and contemporary readings* (pp. 105-119). Thousand Oaks, CA: Sage.

Pearlin, L. I., & Schooler, C. (1982). Family stress, coping and social support. In H. I. McCubbin, A. E. Cauble, & J. M. Patterson (Eds.), *The structure of coping.* Springfield, IL: Thomas.

Pender, N. J., Murdaugh, C. L., & Parsons, M. A. (2002). *Health promotion in nursing practice* (4th ed.). Upper Saddle River, NJ: Prentice Hall.

Philipson, I. (2002). Bring the second shift to work. *Working paper 50, May 2002.* Center for Working Families, University of California, Berkeley. Retrieved November 11, 2002, from http://www.working families.berkeley.edu/papers/50.pdf

Renick, M. T., Blumberg, S. H., & Harkman, H. J. (1992). The prevention and relationship enhancement program (PREP): An empirically based prevention program for couples. *Family Relations, 41,* 141-147.

Saleebey, D. (2002). *The strengths perspective in social work practice* (3rd ed.). Boston: Allyn and Bacon.

Satir, V. (1982). *Peoplemaking.* Palo Alto, CA: Science and Behavior Books.

Schulz, F. H., & Beach, S. R. (1999). Caring as a risk factor for mortality: The caregiver health effects study. *Journal of the American Medical Association, 282,* 2215-2219.

Selekman, M. (1997). *Solution-focused therapy with children.* New York: Guilford.

Selye, H. (1974). *Stress without distress.* New York: The New American Library.

Selye, H. (1976). *The stress of life* (rev. ed.). New York: McGraw-Hill.

Strauss, M., & Gelles, R. (1995). *Physical violence in American families.* New Brunswick, NJ: Transaction.

Umbreit, M., & Kruk E. (1998). Parent-child mediation. In E. Kruk (Ed.), *Mediation and conflict resolution in social work and the human services* (pp. 97-115). Chicago: Nelson-Hall.

U.S. Department of Labor, Bureau of Labor Statistics (2000). Women's share of the labor force to edge higher by 2008. *Monthly Labor Review.* Retrieved February 1, 2003, at http://www.bls.gov/opub/ted/2000/ Feb/wk3/art01.htm

Walsh, F. (1998). *Strengthening family resilience.* New York: Guilford.

Walsh, F. (1999). Religion and spirituality: Wellsprings for healing and resilience. In F. Walsh (Ed.), *Spiritual resources in family therapy,* (pp. 3-27). New York: Guilford.

Wells-Federman, C. L., & Mandle, C. L. (2002). Stress management. In C. L. Edelman & C. L. Mandle (Eds.), *Health promotion through the lifespan* (5th ed., pp. 353-374). St. Louis, MO: Mosby.

Wells-Federman C. L., Stuart-Shor, E., Deckro, J., Mandle, C. L., Baim, M., & Medich, C. (1995). The mind/body connection: The psychophysiology of many traditional nursing interventions. *Clinical Nurse Specialist, 9,* 59-66.

White, J. M., & Porth, C. M. (2000). Physiologic measurement of the stress response. In V. H. Rice (Ed.), *Handbook of stress, coping and health* (pp. 69-94). Thousand Oaks, CA: Sage.

Williams, J. E., Paton, C., Siegler, I. C. Eigenbrodt, M. L., Nieto, F. J., & Tyrole, H. A. (2000). Anger proneness predicts coronary heart disease risks: Prospective analysis from the Atherosclerosis Risk in Communities (ARIC) study. *Circulation, 101,* 2034-2039.

Wimbush, F. B., & Nelson, M. L. (2000). *Stress, psychosomatic, illness, and health.* In V. H. Rice (Ed.), *Handbook of stress, coping and health* (pp. 143-171). Thousand Oaks, CA: Sage.

Witek-Janusek, L., & Mathews, H. L. (2000). Stress, immunity, and health outcomes. In V. H. Rice (Ed.), *Handbook of stress, coping and health* (pp. 45-68). Thousand Oaks, CA: Sage.

Wooten, P. (2000). Humor, laugher, and play: Maintaining balance in a serious world. In B. Dossey, C. Guzetta, & L. Keegan (Eds.), *Holistic nursing: A handbook for practice* (3rd ed.). Gaithersburg, MD: Aspen.

Wright, L. M., Watson, W. L., & Bell, J. M. (1996). *Beliefs: The heart of healing in families and illness.* New York: Basic Books.

Appendix 14-1 Family Inventory of Life Events (FILE)

FAMILY STRESS COPING AND HEALTH PROJECT
1300 Linden Drive
University of Wisconsin-Madison
Madison, WI 53706

Family Health Program
FORM C
1983
© H. McCubbin

IID 7	☐ ☐ ☐ ☐
GID	☐ ☐ ☐
FID	☐ ☐ ☐ ☐

FILE

Family Inventory of Life Events and Changes

Hamilton I. McCubbin   Joan M. Patterson   Lance R. Wilson

PURPOSE

Over their life cycle, all families experience many changes as a result of normal growth and development of members and due to external circumstances. The following list of family life changes can happen in a family at any time. Because family members are connected to each other in some way, a life change for any one member affects all the other persons in the family to some degree.

> "FAMILY" means a group of two or more persons living together who are related by blood, marriage or adoption. This includes persons who live with you *and* to whom you have a long term commitment.

DIRECTIONS

"DID THE CHANGE HAPPEN IN YOUR FAMILY?"
Please read each family life change and decide whether it happened to any member of your family—**including you.**

- DURING THE LAST YEAR
  First, decide if it happened any time **during** the last 12 months and check YES or NO.

During Last 12 Months	
Yes	No
☐	☐

FAMILY LIFE CHANGES	During Last 12 Months Yes	No	Score	FAMILY LIFE CHANGES	During Last 12 Months Yes	No	Score
I. INTRA-FAMILY STRAINS				12. Increased difficulty in managing infant(s) (0-1 yr.) **35**	☐	☐	
1. Increase of husband/father's time away from family **46**	☐	☐ 12		13. Increase in the amount of "outside activities" which the child(ren) are involved in **25**	☐	☐	
2. Increase of wife/mother's time away from family **51**	☐	☐		14. Increased disagreement about a member's friends or activities **35**	☐	☐	
3. A member appears to have emotional problems **58**	☐	☐		15. Increase in the number of problems or issues which don't get resolved **45**	☐	☐	
4. A member appears to depend on alcohol or drugs **66**	☐	☐		16. Increase in the number of tasks or chores which don't get done **35**	☐	☐	
5. Increase in conflict between husband and wife **53**	☐	☐		17. Increased conflict with in-laws or relatives **40**	☐	☐ 32	
6. Increase in arguments between parent(s) and child(ren) **45**	☐	☐		**II. MARITAL STRAINS**			
7. Increase in conflict among children in the family **48**	☐	☐		18. Spouse/parent was separated or divorced **79**	☐	☐	
8. Increased difficulty in managing teenage child(ren) **55**	☐	☐		19. Spouse/parent has an "affair" **68**	☐	☐	
9. Increased difficulty in managing school age child(ren) (6-12 yrs.) **39**	☐	☐		20. Increased difficulty in resolving issues with a "former" or separated spouse **47**	☐	☐	
10. Increased difficulty in managing preschool age child(ren) (2½-6 yrs.) **36**	☐	☐		21. Increased difficulty with sexual relationship between husband and wife **58**	☐	☐ 3	
11. Increased difficulty in managing toddler(s) (1-2½ yrs.) **36**	☐	☐					

Subtotal 1 _____

Please turn over and complete ▶
Subtotal 2 _____

From McCubbin, H.I., Thompson, A.I., & McCubbin, M.A. (Eds.) (1996). *Family assessment: Resilience, coping and adaptation—Inventories for research and practice.* Madison: University of Wisconsin. Reprinted with permission.

FAMILY LIFE CHANGES	DID THE CHANGE HAPPEN IN YOUR FAMILY? During Last 12 Months		
	Yes	No	Score
III. PREGNANCY AND CHILDBEARING STRAINS			
22. Spouse had unwanted or difficult pregnancy 45	☐	☐	
23. An unmarried member became pregnant 65	☐	☐	
24. A member had an abortion 50	☐	☐	
25. A member gave birth to or adopted a child 50	☐	☐	
IV. FINANCE AND BUSINESS STRAINS			
26. Took out a loan or refinanced a loan to cover increased expenses 29	☐	☐	
27. Went on welfare 55	☐	☐	
28. Change in conditions (economic, political, weather) which hurts the family business 41	☐	☐	
29. Change in Agriculture Market, Stock Market, or Land Values which hurts family investments and/or income 43	☐	☐	
30. A member started a new business 50	☐	☐	
31. Purchased or built a home 41	☐	☐	
32. A member purchased a car or other major item 19	☐	☐	
33. Increasing financial debts due to over-use of credit cards 31	☐	☐	
34. Increased strain on family "money" for medical/dental expenses 23	☐	☐	
35. Increased strain on family "money" for food, clothing, energy, home care 21	☐	☐	
36. Increased strain on family "money" for child(ren)'s education 22	☐	☐	
37. Delay in receiving child support or alimony payments 41	☐	☐	
V. WORK-FAMILY TRANSITIONS AND STRAINS			
38. A member changed to a new job/career 40	☐	☐	
39. A member lost or quit a job 55	☐	☐	
40. A member retired from work 48	☐	☐	
41. A member started or returned to work 41	☐	☐	
42. A member stopped working for extended period (e.g., laid off, leave of absence, strike) 51	☐	☐	
43. Decrease in satisfaction with job/career 45	☐	☐	
44. A member had increased difficulty with people at work 32	☐	☐	
45. A member was promoted at work or given more responsibilities 40	☐	☐	
46. Family moved to a new home/apartment 43	☐	☐	
47. A child/adolescent member changed to a new school 24	☐	☐	

Subtotal 3 _____

FAMILY LIFE CHANGES	DID THE CHANGE HAPPEN IN YOUR FAMILY? During Last 12 Months		
	Yes	No	Score
VI. ILLNESS AND FAMILY "CARE" STRAINS			
48. Parent/spouse became seriously ill or injured 44	☐	☐	
49. Child became seriously ill or injured 35	☐	☐	
50. Close relative or friend of the family became seriously ill 44	☐	☐	
51. A member became physically disabled or chronically ill 73	☐	☐	
52. Increased difficulty in managing a chronically ill or disabled member 58	☐	☐	
53. Member or close relative was committed to an institution or nursing home 44	☐	☐	
54. Increased responsibility to provide direct care or financial help to husband's and/or wife's parent(s) 47	☐	☐	
55. Experienced difficulty in arranging for satisfactory child care 40	☐	☐	
VII. LOSSES			
56. A parent/spouse died 98	☐	☐	
57. A child member died 99	☐	☐	
58. Death of husband's or wife's parent or close relative 48	☐	☐	
59. Close friend of the family died 47	☐	☐	
60. Married son or daughter was separated or divorced 58	☐	☐	
61. A member "broke up" a relationship with a close friend 35	☐	☐	
VIII. TRANSITIONS "IN AND OUT"			
62. A member was married 42	☐	☐	
63. Young adult member left home 43	☐	☐	
64. A young adult member began college (or post high school training) 28	☐	☐	
65. A member moved back home or a new person moved into the household 42	☐	☐	
66. A parent/spouse started school (or training program) after being away from school for a long time 38	☐	☐	
IX. FAMILY LEGAL VIOLATIONS			
67. A member went to jail or juvenile detention 68	☐	☐	
68. A member was picked up by police or arrested 57	☐	☐	
69. Physical or sexual abuse or violence in the home 75	☐	☐	
70. A member ran away from home 61	☐	☐	
71. A member dropped out of school or was suspended from school 38	☐	☐	

Subtotal 4 _____
Grand Total _____
(1t2t3t4)

When We face Problems or Difficulties in our Family, We respond by:	Strongly Disagree	Moderately Disagree	Neither Agree Nor Disagree	Moderately Agree	Strongly Agree
1. Sharing our difficulties with relatives	1	2	3	4	5
2. Seeking encouragement and support from friends	1	2	3	4	5
3. Knowing we have the power to solve major problems	1	2	3	4	5
4. Seeking information and advice from persons in other families who have faced the same or similar problems	1	2	3	4	5
5. Seeking advice from relatives (grandparents, etc.)	1	2	3	4	5
6. Seeking assistance from community agencies and programs designed to help families in our situation	1	2	3	4	5
7. Knowing that we have the strength within our own family to solve our problems	1	2	3	4	5
8. Receiving gifts and favors from neighbors (e.g. food, taking in mail, etc.)	1	2	3	4	5
9. Seeking information and advice from the family doctor	1	2	3	4	5
10. Asking neighbors for favors and assistance	1	2	3	4	5
11. Facing the problems "head-on" and trying to get solution right away	2	3	4	5	
12. Watching television	1	2	3	4	5
13. Showing that we are strong	1	2	3	4	5
14. Attending church services	1	2	3	4	5
15. Accepting stressful events as a fact of life	1	2	3	4	5

McCubbin, H. I., Olson, D., & Larsen, A. (1996). Family crisis oriented personal scales (F-COPES). In H. I. McCubbin., A. I. Thompson, & M. A. McCubbin (Eds.), *Family assessment: Resilience, coping and adaptation—Inventories for research and practice* (pp. 455-508). Madison: University of Wisconsin. (Original work published in 1981).

When We face Problems or Difficulties in our Family, We respond by:	Strongly Disagree	Moderately Disagree	Neither Agree Nor Disagree	Moderately Agree	Strongly Agree
16. Sharing concerns with close friends	1	2	3	4	5
17. Knowing luck plays a big part in how well we are able to solve family problems	1	2	3	4	5
18. Exercising with friends to stay fit and reduce tension	1	2	3	4	5
19. Accepting that difficulties occur unexpectedly	1	2	3	4	5
20. Doing things with relatives (get-togethers, dinners, etc.)					
21. Seeking professional counseling and help for family difficulties	1	2	3	4	5
22. Believing we can handle our own problems	1	2	3	4	5
23. Participating in church activities	1	2	3	4	5
24. Defining the family problem in a more positive way so that we do not become too discouraged	1	2	3	4	5
25. Asking relatives how they feel about problems we face	1	2	3	4	5
26. Feeling that no matter what we do to prepare, we will have difficulty handling problems	1	2	3	4	5
27. Seeking advice from a minister	1	2	3	4	5
28. Believing if we wait long enough, the problem will go away	1	2	3	4	5
29. Sharing problems with neighbors	1	2	3	4	5
30. Having faith in God	1	2	3	4	5

15

Family Sexuality

Shelton M. Hisley
Caroline M. Clements

Sex lies at the root of life, and we can never learn to reverence life until we know how to understand sex.

— Havelock Ellis

OBJECTIVES

On completion of this chapter, the reader will be able to do the following:

1. *Describe the psychological and sociocultural aspects of sexuality.*

2. *Differentiate between sexual identity and sexual role behavior.*

3. *Identify the role of the family in the development of children's sexuality and sexual identity.*

4. *Describe the role of the family in development of sexuality in infancy, childhood, adolescence, adulthood, and old age.*

5. *Describe relationships in gay and lesbian families.*

6. *Define domestic partnership and discuss its relationship to family life.*

7. *Identify data needed to assess family sexuality.*

8. *Identify nursing diagnoses related to family sexuality.*

9. *Describe interventions to promote healthy family sexuality.*

10. *List criteria to evaluate interventions used to promote healthy family sexuality*

Sexuality encompasses the physical and psychological behaviors that individuals exhibit in attaining affection, sexual response, love, and commitment. All of us can be seen as sexual beings from birth until death (Westheimer & Lopater, 2001). A description of family sexuality requires a broader view of sexuality and its interactional aspects and raises the questions, "How is sexuality lived out in this family? How does the parent's or parents' sexuality influence the children? How does the child's sexuality affect the parent(s)?"

Family life enhances personal and sexual growth and development. A stable family life provides children with security, love, and emotional nourishment that foster healthy sexuality. In fact, parents are the earliest and most important influences on sexuality. Family patterns, especially communication skills and parenting methods, as well as family configuration, strongly affect children's sexual development.

This chapter is a revision of the chapters authored by Rosemary Hogan and Kathleen Heinrich in the first and second editions, respectively.

Sexuality is a complex, multifaceted phenomenon. Because families are systems, sexual issues will affect all members of the family to some degree. This chapter focuses on the biological, psychosocial, and cultural aspects of sexuality as they relate to individuals and to families; on sexuality across the life span; on the effects of social change on families and variations in family sexuality; and finally, on assessment, nursing diagnoses, interventions, and evaluation of family sexuality.

Sexuality and Family Health

Sexual health, like health in general, is relative and includes all aspects of sexuality. Sexuality is intrinsic to one's being. The term *sexuality*, unlike the word *sex*, encompasses biological, psychological, sociocultural, and ethical components of behavior. Family sexual health involves these aspects and the ability of the family to foster positive sexual self-esteem of its members, to validate each member's sexuality, and to maintain a gratifying sexual relationship between the parents. Parents with unresolved issues related to sexuality may have difficulty fostering healthy sexuality in their children.

Family sexuality is more than the sexual interactions of the adults; it is the pattern of same-sex and opposite-sex relationships that includes the quality of parental interactions, parent-child interactions, and sexual learning that occurs in the family (Reiss, 1986). Consequently, the description of sexuality as having biological, psychosocial, and cultural aspects is applicable to the family as a whole because it is through the interactions of all these aspects of sexuality in each of the family members that family sexual health occurs.

Illness and Family Sexuality

Because sexual response involves complex physiological responses, pathological conditions of the nervous system such as stroke, multiple sclerosis, spinal cord injury, or peripheral neuropathies may compromise sexual function. Pathological conditions of the vascular system such as arteriosclerosis that affects pelvic vessels and diseases such as diabetes and kidney failure may be implicated in sexual dysfunction. Surgical procedures such as mastectomy, hysterectomy, or prostatectomy and cancer and its therapy may cause body image disturbance, as well as compromise physiological response. As a result, the sexual relationship may suffer (Bancroft & Guiterrez, 1996; Jackson, 1999).

It is extremely important for the nurse to thoroughly review potential organic causes for sexual dysfunction in the evaluation of the patient experiencing sexual difficulty. Such an evaluation would include asking the patient about licit and illicit substance use. It is also important to consider the psychological impact that organically mediated sexual difficulties may have. Even if disease or injury does not alter function, anxiety and fear that illness will be exacerbated may cause sexual partners to avoid coitus (Rosal, Downing, Littman, & Ahern, 1994). Family roles and relationships may also be strained. Anxiety, depression, or anger that follows may further disrupt the relationship. Families should share their concerns and seek mutually agreed on solutions to problems that arise as a result of sexual concerns. The objective, nonjudgmental presence of a health care provider can be invaluable during these times.

Psychosocial Factors Related to Sexuality

Gender Identity and Sexual Role Behavior

The terms *gender identity* and *gender role behavior* are often confused. Gender identity is the conviction that one belongs to the female or male sex; it is one's sense of oneself as female or male. It is formed in early childhood as a result of biological factors (embryological and central nervous system factors), genital anatomy (which signals the child's sex to parents), sex assignment, and childrearing practices (Money, 1987).

Gender or sexual role behavior has two aspects. It is all that an individual does to disclose himself or herself as male or female to others and the behaviors identified as appropriate for each sex according to social norms. Gender role behavior is developed through learning, imitation, and modeling. The greatest influence is the sexual value system of the family and the community.

Even information that children receive from their peer groups, often the most frequent source of sexual information, is filtered through the parental value system (Mandleco & McCoy, 2002).

The Family and Psychosocial Factors

Parents have important influences on children's sexual behavior (Mandleco & McCoy, 2002). Parents impart information and values to children, and children may challenge adherence to these values. Positive self-concept is formed and nurtured in the family in which loving care by parents and siblings confirms children's worth. Positive body image, the internalized sense that individuals have of their bodies as satisfying and attractive, is developed in the family.

Sexual self-esteem, characterized by acceptance of the value of self as a sexual being, also begins to develop within the family nexus (Mandleco & McCoy, 2002). Family communication transmits attitudes toward sexuality, as well as sexual knowledge, opinions, and beliefs. Adolescents are aware of their parent's sexual attitudes even when parents have not directly verbalized them. Parents' attitudes, even if they are not overtly expressed, can influence their children's sexual behavior (King & Lorusso, 1997).

Parental influence on children and adolescents' gender role socialization is less recognized than parental influence on other aspects of child-rearing. Research indicates that parental attitudes have a central influence on children's gender role formation and their sexual behavior (Lytton & Romney, 1991). Children and adolescents are exposed to less traditional gender role and sexual attitudes now than they were in previous decades. The fact that today's adolescent females grow up in a time when working women are the norm considerably influences their attitudes toward gender roles and sexual behavior. One survey showed that the incidence of premarital intercourse has doubled among adolescent girls in the last 50 years, whereas rates for males have increased only slightly (Laumann, Masi, & Zuckerman, 1994). About one third of high school females reported having engaged in intercourse in 1975. In 2000, more than half of those females surveyed had done so (Kann et al., 2000).

Family Configuration

Type of family unit (e.g., nuclear, blended, one parent) can influence adolescent sexual behavior. Parental divorce or separation has been correlated with adolescents having later first intercourse, as is having a highly educated mother (Brewster, 1994). Flewelling and Bauman (1990) found that increased adolescent sexual activity is associated with greater likelihood of being in a nonintact family. Research suggests that age, alcohol use, lower grade point average, and more time at home without adult supervision are all associated with increased frequency of intercourse among adolescents.

Cultural and Ethnic Variables

The way in which sexuality is expressed is learned through cultural norms, ideals, and ideology. What is considered "normal" sexual behavior varies among ethnic groups and societies.

Religions are important subcultures that may have profound effects on sexuality. Studies show a strong correlation between adolescent sexual behavior and religious participation. Thornton and Camburn (1989) found that young people who attend church frequently and espouse religious values have less permissive attitudes and are less experienced sexually. White and DeBlassie (1992) observed that both the Catholic and Protestant churches in the United States have denounced premarital sex. Although these churches discourage sexual activity, they offer little or no help for those adolescents who wish to use contraception if they are sexually active.

Religion and culture together appear to have an influence on urban African American adolescent girls' level of sexual activity. Keith, McCreary, Collins, Smith, and Bernstein (1991) found that the church and family, including the presence of the father, were associated with not being sexually active during early and middle adolescence. Although Keith et al. suggest that a strong family and participation in church can lead to more responsible sexual behavior, it is also possible that these factors inhibit adolescents from admitting the extent of their sexual activity. More recent data indicate that religion may be a less protective factor than the data of Keith et al. would suggest, playing a role in later first intercourse for Hispanic and white adolescent girls but not for African American adolescents (Norris, Ford, Shyu, & Schork, 1996).

Some cultures permit premarital and extra-marital sexual relationships. Other cultures view sex as a duty, and sexual intercourse is considered weakening or debilitating. In the Hispanic community, women may be protective of their traditional roles in a male-dominated society. In the American Navajo Indian family, however, the mother has the power and runs the family (House, 1997). Mexican American, Arab American, and Asian American men do not usually participate during the birth of a baby. Birth is considered a woman's affair, and women may not want a man's involvement (Reid & Bing, 2000). Because of changing cultural and ethnic values and acculturation into the pluralistic American society, it is difficult to predict with certainty how ethnic background will affect sexual and family relationships. Because of this, it is extremely important for the nurse to carefully assess family attitudes toward sexuality and to avoid making assumptions about behavior based on ethnic or cultural background.

Family Role in Teaching about Sexuality

Although sex education experts agree that parents are ideally the best educators of their own children, many parents are ill-prepared or unable to deal with issues surrounding sexuality. In moving toward independence and identity development, the adolescent must separate from the family. Paradoxically, it is the family that has provided the adolescent with the moral and ethical foundation on which to build his or her ethical code.

Studies indicate that parents are often conflicted or ambivalent about giving adolescents information about sex and sexuality. Although pre-adolescents still receive the majority of the information they have about sex and sexuality from their parents, far less than half of adolescents do so. The most frequently cited sources of information for teenagers are friends and the media (Kaiser Family Foundation, 1998). In one study nearly all the adolescent respondents preferred that parents teach them about sexual issues, but only a minority noted that parents were a major

source of this information. In fact, 60% of adolescents in this study reported that they had *never* had a conversation about sex with either parent (King & Lorusso, 1997).

Parents have a number of barriers to overcome in providing sexual information, including being ill-informed. Chilman (1990) offers additional reasons for parents' difficulty in discussing sexual subjects with their children. He observes that family dissatisfaction tends to reach its peak when children enter adolescence. Stresses at this middle stage of life may include a dwindling sense of marital unity, an adolescent's push for an independent identity, the parents' own unresolved parent-child conflicts, and changing gender role identities. As these stresses intensify, parents' self-esteem may decrease, and they may become either highly impulsive or overly controlling and rigid. Adolescents' sexuality may also be very threatening to parents who are uncomfortable with their own sexuality or who have not resolved their own sexual issues.

Westheimer & Lopater (2001) note that as the prime socializers of their children, parents teach children a range of social skills. These same parents are generally uncomfortable in teaching a child how to be sexual. The authors give the example of the discomfort parents may feel about masturbation, a natural behavior that offers a child bodily enjoyment. Even the youngest child may sense a parent's discomfort about sexual issues and learn to not ask questions. Westheimer & Lopater (2001) encourage parents to teach responsible behaviors in general. The following are their three suggestions for parents about discussing sex with their children:

1) Be proactive. Don't wait for the child to initiate the conversation.
2) Don't worry about nervousness.
3) Realize that children do not do everything they are told.

These authors also suggest that parents need to be educated about sexual issues so they are better informed and feel more comfortable about instructing children and adolescents.

The nature and quality of parental communication are also important. Adolescents want more than proscriptions and admonitions about sexual behavior from their parents. Families who share mutual closeness and a consistent set of values are more likely to encourage adolescents to delay sexual activity. Since schools have a role and a stake in this process, sex education in schools can supplement and augment, rather than diminish, parental influence. Families, schools, and communities need to shift from an avoidant or reluctant stance to a more open, information-focused approach to sex education. Sex education programs stressing information, interpersonal skill development, and personal responsibility are currently being integrated into school systems as one means of decreasing rising rates of early first intercourse (U.S. Department of Health and Human Services, 1999). Also, numerous credible websites for teaching responsible sexual behavior and sexual self-esteem are available (see Website Resource Box at the end of this chapter).

Sexuality across the Family Life Span

With the rapid social changes that have transpired over the last 30 years, parents, children, and professionals in health care are often unsure of what is "normal," healthy sexuality and development. The specter of AIDS has fundamentally changed the consequences of sexual decision making. No longer can risky sexual behavior be cast in terms of inappropriate choices. Today unprotected sexual activity can lead to fatal cases of AIDS and human papillomavirus (HPV). Concern about normality is therefore complicated by real health fears. Simultaneously, issues of right or wrong, good or bad, and healthy or unhealthy arise at all stages of the family life span. What has been accepted by one generation may be condemned by the next.

Sexual Development: Infancy and Childhood

Sexual development begins before birth and is affected by complex biopsychosocial factors (Masters, Johnson, & Kolodny, 1982). Table 15-1 presents the stages and characteristics of normal psychosexual development. Each developmental stage is affected by earlier events in individuals' lives. Some believe that the nature and goals of adult sexual behavior are partially or completely determined by what happens as children move through various psychosexual stages. Sexuality at any age or stage of development encompasses more than sexual behavior in the physical sense, although infants' and children's sexual activity of the most benign types is probably the cause of more anxiety in parents than any other behavior.

Parents' responses to children's sexual behavior may more positively or negatively affect the achievement of healthy sexuality than the behaviors themselves. Childrearing practices and the family environment may have a greater impact than the biological factors of anatomy and physiology. Sexual identity, that is the feeling or belief that one is male or female, is shaped by biological factors and by childrearing practices. Sexual role behavior, what individuals do to distinguish themselves as men or women (dress, for example), is not established at birth but is built up cumulatively through interaction with family, peers, and the social environment.

Birth to Two Years

Biological and social forces interact to shape behavioral sex differences in the growing child, and although neither is solely responsible for the determination of personality and behavior traits, it is likely that postnatal influences have a greater significance in this process. Current research supports the notion that concepts of "the typical male" and the "typical female," or behavior that is stereotypically masculine or feminine, result from socialization and are conditioned by cultural attitudes and expectations (Sloane, 2002).

Acculturation to sex roles is initiated in early infancy when parents' attitudes toward their male and female children differ in accordance with societal perceptions of what is considered appropriate for each sex. Evidence from numerous clinical cases of individuals with ambiguous sex demonstrates that gender identity is firmly imprinted between the ages of 18 months and 3 years. By that time, the child has a strong awareness of his or her gender and the gender-specific behavior that is expected. In fact, the behaviors become firmly rooted into stereotypes of masculine and feminine qualities, personality traits, and activities. Conditioning comes from parents, teachers, textbooks, television, movies, and society in general; children are expected to accept traditional sex roles and value is placed on adherence to the masculine or feminine image (Sloane, 2002).

TABLE 15-1 Normal Psychosexual Development

Stage	Characteristics
Prenatal	Differentiation of fetus into male or female after seventh week
Birth to 2 years	Need for close physical contact
	Touching and exploring genitals
	Establishment of core gender identity
	Learning sexual role behavior
2 years	Neuromuscular coordination and control, bowel and bladder control
	Continued genital manipulation
	Sensual stimulation by hugging, kissing others
	Further sexual role development
3 to 5 years	Further autonomy, independence
	Pride in genitals, exploration, exhibition of own or by others
	Development of relationship with parent of opposite sex
	Genital self-stimulation (masturbation)
6 to 12 years	Final role identification
	Interest in differences between sexes
	Interest in opposite sex
	Beginning preoccupation with bodily changes
	Beginning independence from family emotional ties
13 to 19 years (Adolescence)	Development of secondary sex characteristics
	Focus on body image, appearance
	Interest in sexual activity (petting to coitus) and/or relationship with opposite sex
	Increased ability to love
	Consolidation of sexual identity
20 to 45 years (Early Adulthood)	Independence from family
	Choice of a marital partner or development of a sexual relationship
	Giving and receiving love
	Establishment of family
	Communication of sexual needs, feelings between partners
46 to 65 years (Later Adulthood)	Opportunity for greater sexual freedom
	Menopause in women
	Male climacteric
	Freedom from family responsibilities
66 years and older	Decrease in intensity of sexual response
	Continued fulfilling intimacy if in good health and interested and have interested partner

Regardless of biological factors, life experiences have a tremendous impact on the development of sexuality. The infant needs a warm, physical relationship with the mother (or other caregiver) if sensory and affectional development are to occur (Martinson, 1994). Adults who were not given warm, physical contact in infancy are more likely to have retarded sexual development, exhibit aggressive behavior, and experience social and emotional problems.

There is evidence that male and female infants are capable of sexual arousal, although there is no way of knowing the nature of their subjective experience, since they cannot communicate verbally. Erection has been observed in utero during sonograms and may also be observed right after birth, but it is probably reflexive, mediated through the lumbosacral spinal cord and not dependent on higher brain centers associated with thought and emotion. However, it is not unusual for infants to touch and explore their genitals, and parents should not be concerned about this normal developmental behavior.

Immediately after birth, psychosocial factors influence sexual development. Parental treatment of males and females may differ. Daughters are handled gently and sons are treated more roughly by fathers. Mothers appear to be expressive and open in their affection for their daughters. Although this behavior may be unconscious, it may result in a form of covert imprinting when it is consistently repeated (Lytton & Romney, 1991).

After birth of a male infant, the parents must make a decision about circumcision, the surgical removal of the foreskin that covers the glans penis. Circumcision is sometimes a religious practice, especially in Islam or Judaism. In the United States it may be done primarily for hygienic and health reasons. Inflammation or infection of the glans and cancer of the penis are less likely to occur in circumcised men, and the evidence of cancer of the cervix is lower in spouses of circumcised men (King & Annen-Ricks, 2002).

Those who oppose routine circumcision argue that there is no reason for the procedure, that penile injury may occur, that sexual sensitivity in the area is lessened, and that circumcision is associated with increased risk of premature ejaculation. However, there is no empirical evidence that circumcision affects male sexual function in any way (Masters et al., 1982). In 1999, the American Academy of Pediatrics issued a position statement indicating that there was no medical need for circumcision. Consequently, the decision for circumcision is based primarily on the religious and personal beliefs of the parents.

Two Years

By 2 years of age, children are acquiring neuromuscular coordination and control and language skills and are better able to explore their environment. Bowel and bladder control is a parental goal. Children often avoid accidents to obtain parental approval. However, toilet-training practices that include punitive measures, such as shaming or physically punishing the child for "accidents," may cause further conflicts related to giving and receiving.

Parents may also become anxious about and punish children's growing curiosity about the environment and their genitals. Parental anxiety about the behavior may be communicated to children, who may have difficulty during adulthood accepting sexual activity as normal, good, and right. Two-year-olds may obtain sensual stimulation from hugging and kissing family members, friends, and toys, as well as through rhythmic motor activities such as swinging. Although the "terrible twos" may cause parents to focus on coping with children's negative behaviors, parents must continue to promote children's sense of security, which comes with being held, cuddled, and given other signs of affection.

Three to Five Years

At 3 to 5 years of age, children achieve further autonomy and independence. Physical size increases dramatically but with little change in the genital organs. During this period, children become acutely aware of the differences between boys and girls. They may want to watch as a new brother's or sister's diapers are changed or observe other children using the bathroom at preschool (Pillitteri, 1999).

Children at this age have an increasing sense of privacy but are also proud of their genitals and discover that they can bring pleasure. Children may fondle their genitals, explore those of playmates, or exhibit their own. Masturbation may occur while children are watching television or being read to or before they fall asleep at night. The frequency of this behavior may increase with stress, as does thumb sucking (Pillitteri, 1999).

The quality of the communication between parents and children concerning this behavior may affect sexual development. If parents are too strict and shame the child or if they are too encouraging, that is, if they laugh at the child or show the child how to engage in this behavior, the child may connect feelings of shame or guilt to the pleasure associated with the genitals. If parents threaten children with statements such as "We'll cut off your hand if you don't stop playing with yourself" or "Your penis (or the euphemistic term used) will fall off," children may experience anxiety about losing something that is important, and problems related to sexuality may develop later in life.

Masturbation or genital self-stimulation that results in sexual gratification has no adverse biological or psychological consequences except those caused by guilt, anxiety, and fear. It is believed that most children masturbate by 6 to 8 years of age in sexually permissive societies. (Friedrich, Fisher, Broughton, Houston, & Shafran, 1998). Most genital manipulation is best dealt with by "benign neglect." If parents express concern, the nurse can suggest that they explain to the child that certain things are done in some places but not in others (Pillitteri, 1999).

Excessive masturbation is difficult to define because what is considered excessive is defined by the parent. Masturbation that is compulsive or is used to avoid social interaction, anxiety, or feelings of distress can be considered excessive and a sign of a deeper problem. Compulsive masturbation is not usually accompanied by any real pleasure or satisfaction. When parents call unnecessary attention to the act, anxiety is often increased, resulting in increased, not decreased activity (Pillitteri, 1999).

Parents need to find ways to help children understand parental expectations without threats and misinformation. If parents recognize the normality of the behavior as a part of sexual development, they may be able to respond positively. Parents should give children special attention when the children are *not* masturbating by involving them in other activities and by giving them the love, attention, tenderness, and closeness that fosters feelings of security about the body and healthy sexual development.

During this stage of development, children also begin to form a relationship with the parent of the opposite sex, laying the foundation for future healthy relationships with those of the opposite sex. Although children 3 to 6 years old can be flirtatious, they are not able to understand the nature of sexual activity. To children, adult sex acts seem dangerous and aggressive, especially in the darkness or if the sounds accompanying sex are interpreted as expressions of pain. Closed bedroom doors and/or privacy should be a prerequisite for adult sexual activity. Children should not be exposed to adult sexual activity (Okami, 1995). Even when parents take precautions to maintain privacy, children may be exposed to other aspects of sexuality such as adult nudity and evidence of menstruation. Although casual nudity of the parent of the opposite sex is not usually harmful, it may be detrimental to the young child if it is seductive in nature or presented in a stimulating manner. Children may become frightened when they see menstrual blood on pads, tampons, or clothing. Mothers should explain that they are not hurt or sick but that this is a normal part of being a woman. Children may also be aware of problems in the parents' sexual relationship. When parents are insufficiently sexually satisfied and hostile toward each other, children may develop a negative attitude toward sex that may persist into adulthood. As in the earlier periods of children's lives, warmth, tenderness, and closeness provided by the family foster feelings of security about the body and are needed for children's healthy sexual development. (See Resources for Teaching/Counseling at the end of the chapter.)

An important component of children's sex education during this time is learning how to avoid sexual abuse. For example, children need to be taught that they do not have to allow anyone to touch their bodies unless they agree that it is all right. Children must also be taught what to do if anyone touches them in an inappropriate way. Children should be told, for example, to immediately tell their parents or teachers if a person tries to touch their private parts. Nurses must remember to seek permission when giving children nursing care that involves touching (Pillitteri, 1999).

Five to Twelve Years

During this period, most children are in school where they have increased contact with peers of both sexes. Children from 5 to 7 years of age have increased interest in differences between the sexes; for example, they tend to notice beards on men and breasts on women. There is more interest in having a baby and playing house. Five-year-olds realize that they are to marry someone of the opposite sex who is not a member of the family. Five-year-olds may also begin displaying modesty for the first time.

Around the age of 5 years, about 10% of children have their first sexual experience beyond autoerotic behavior, usually exhibiting the genitals or inspecting those of other children, often under the guise of playing doctor. Boys are more active than girls (Bancroft, Herbenek, & Reynolds, 2002). There may be a great deal of lying on top of one another, but even when children undress, there is usually nothing more than genital opposition. Sexual activities may be more advanced if one partner is older and more experienced. Parents may become concerned about this activity, but it is a reflection of children's natural curiosity about themselves and the world around them rather than any precocious sexual arousal (Mandleco & McCoy, 2002).

Interest in reproduction continues at the ages 8 to 9 years, but sexual exploration is less common. Girls are interested in menstruation, and both sexes want to know about fertility, pregnancy, and birth. Both sexes begin to evaluate their physical attractiveness, but they begin to play separately, in homosocial groupings (Ryan, 2000). Their interest in the opposite sex is evidenced by peeping, sex jokes, and provocative giggling. They are inhibited, self-conscious about their bodies, and concerned with modesty. Kissing games or teasing about boyfriends or girlfriends may take place during mixed play.

By ages 10 to 12, there is increased preoccupation with body changes, especially those connected with puberty, which is occurring increasingly earlier. In a class of 11-year-olds, it is not unusual to discover that more than half of the girls are menstruating (Pillitteri, 1999), and some 9-year-old girls have already experienced menarche (Cunningham et al., 2001). Telling sex jokes may be a favorite pastime of both boys and girls. Although there may be a facade of disinterest in the opposite sex in some, for others, there is the beginning of romantic interest.

Sexual activities of the preadolescent male are generally group-oriented. Activities such as genital exhibition, demonstration of masturbation, or group masturbation usually satisfy social needs rather than relieve sexual tension. At times, sex play may involve homosexual behavior with oral-genital contact and attempts at anal intercourse. Kinsey, Pomeroy, and Martin (1948) found that fewer than half of all males continued homosexual play into puberty. Prepubescent girls confine sexual play to genital exhibition and touching. Sexual activity for the most part is harmless, although there is increasing parental concern about this activity.

The social and cultural impact of the environment is also experienced. Through television, movies, and fiction, children learn about the adult sexual world, at least as portrayed by the mass media. Moral values are learned. It is essential that children gain accurate information, yet information about sexuality is often inadequate and distorted so that it becomes mixed with fantasy life. At times, peers may be the source of myths and misinformation that contribute to the distorted view of sexuality presented by the media, which may be internalized by some children (Mandleco & McCoy, 2002).

Ideally, children should learn accurate information about sexuality primarily from their parents. It is primarily in the family that children learn the importance of male-female relationships. Parents who are loving, tender, and respectful of each other teach children how to use their own sexuality so that it enhances their lives and those of succeeding generations. However, many parents—because of discomfort with the topic, lack of information, or both—are unable to explain sex and sexuality clearly. Thus health care providers often become resource persons for sex education (Swenson, Foster, & Asay, 1995).

Sexual Development: Adolescence

Puberty is marked by accelerated growth and development of secondary sex characteristics. In young women, menstruation is the obvious indication of puberty, although breast enlargement, growth of pubic and axillary hair, and widened hips precede menarche (the onset of menses) by about 2 years. Young women may have ambivalent feelings about their genitalia, negative feelings about menstruation, and various concerns about breast size and general attractiveness. Often, girls have less favorable notions of their bodies than boys do (Mandleco & McCoy, 2002).

In adolescent males, growth of pubic hair and enlargement of the testes herald the beginning of puberty. Penile growth and ejaculation occur later. The first ejaculation may or may not contain viable sperm. A growth spurt is accompanied by increased muscle mass, increased growth of body and facial hair, and a deeper voice. Penile size, body build, and attractiveness cause concerns among adolescent boys, and typically boys tend to be more comfortable with and interested in matters of sex than girls (Pletsch, Johnson, Tosi, Thurston, & Riesch, 1991).

Adolescent females are slower to awaken to sexual activity than are adolescent males. Whether this is culturally determined or related to lower androgen levels is not known. The adolescent girl is usually introduced to erotic feelings by petting, or stimulation by a male partner, rather than by masturbation. If first intercourse takes place within an affectionate relationship and with mutual consent, the girl usually has more satisfaction and enjoyment with few feelings of guilt, shame, or anxiety.

In contrast to adolescent boys, adolescent girls do not experience an increase in sexual activity at puberty. Women show steady increases in responsiveness that peak in their middle twenties to late thirties. Males show a quick upsurge in sexual activity, peaking during adolescence and young adulthood. Masturbation is a fairly common sexual activity, beginning slightly before puberty, peaking during the middle teens, and dropping by the late teens (Oliver & Hyde, 1993). Sex dreams are a very small part of sexual outlet for both sexes. If accompanied by orgasm and ejaculation in young men, "wet dreams" are said to have occurred. Sex dreams, although pleasant, may also frighten the adolescent.

Most adolescents engage in petting (erotic caressing without coitus). Early coital behavior of adolescent boys tends to take place in relatively nonserious relationships and is usually not followed by more than two or three repetitions with the partner. Girls tend to experience first intercourse as disappointing, although the age at first intercourse for girls has decreased over the past 3 decades (Kann et al., 2000).

In piagetian terms, cognitive development in adolescence involves moving from concrete operational thinking to formal operational thinking.

Using formal operational thinking allows adolescents to transform erotic thought into symbolic abstractions. When fantasies are recognized as such, they are not acted on, and potential guilt is averted. If adolescents have not developed formal operational thinking, they are unable to think through a decision-making process based on the understanding of the potential consequences of certain behaviors. Concrete operational thinking or incomplete development of formal operations results in adolescents who see themselves as "omnipotent and infallible," a type of thinking that may result in excessive sexual risk-taking behavior.

In addition to coping with profound bodily changes, adolescents must learn to establish relationships with peers of both sexes; integrate changing body image into self-concept and sexual identity; and deal with new role expectations, responsibilities, and greater autonomy. Erik Erikson refers to this stage as "identity versus role confusion" to highlight the main developmental task of adolescence, that of establishing one's unique place in the world. Adolescents have difficulty relating maturely to others until they establish who they are and for what they stand (Erikson, 1968). Some adolescents have little or no physical sexual contact and still complete healthy sexual development. The nature and quality of adult sexuality is not a function of how much or what kind of sex takes place in adolescence.

One of the "risks" of adolescent sexuality concerns the attempt to use sex to satisfy emotional and interpersonal needs that have little or nothing to do with sex. Sexuality may be used to bolster a faltering self-concept. The Research Synopsis summarizes a research study about the relationship between an adolescent's self-concept and his or her participation in risky behaviors such as sexual intercourse. Adolescent girls may endure promiscuous and joyless encounters to gain or maintain popularity. Others may feel pressured to have sex even though they are unwilling, because they perceive it as a way to have friends (Pillitteri, 1999). Underneath the behavior is a defense against loneliness. Adolescent boys may engage in sexual exploits to protect against self-doubt about their masculinity (Garofalo, Wolf, Kessel, Palfrey, & DuRant, 1998).

RESEARCH SYNOPSIS

ADOLESCENTS, SELF-CONCEPT, AND RISKY BEHAVIORS

How adolescents feel about themselves may affect their likelihood of engaging in various risky behaviors. Researchers conducted a survey to investigate the relationship between several risky behaviors (tobacco use, alcohol use, sexual intercourse, poor school performance) and current and future-oriented self-concept. Self-concept was categorized into three distinct levels: *popular,* defined as well-liked; *deviant,* defined as engaging in problem behaviors; and *conventional,* defined as engaging in culturally sanctioned behavior.

One hundred sixty adolescents from a working-class suburban junior high school completed questionnaires designed to measure their involvement in risky behaviors and their current and future self-concepts. The students participated in the study during the winter of their eighth and ninth grades. Grade point averages were obtained from school records.

The researchers found high correlations between the four risky behaviors, and the prevalence of the risky behaviors increased from the eighth to the ninth grade. Student participation in the risky behaviors during the eighth grade predicted current and future deviant self-concept scores in the ninth grade. Additionally, current popular self-concept scores predicted risky behaviors in the ninth grade.

Investigators concluded that it is important for nurses to recognize that how adolescents feel about themselves (their level of self-concept) may directly affect their decision to engage in risky behaviors such as sexual intercourse. Also, when adolescents engage in risky behaviors early in life, the behaviors have a greater likelihood of becoming enduring components of their later behavior. It was concluded that nurses' intervention efforts should be directed toward not only changing an adolescent's self-concept so that it is more positive but also limiting participation in risky behaviors.

Stein, K., Roeser, R., & Markus, H. (1998). Self-schemas and possible selves as predictors and outcomes of risky behaviors in adolescents. *Nursing Research, 47,* 96-106.

Adolescents of both sexes admit many reasons for engaging in sexual activity, such as peer pressure, the need to love and be loved, experimentation, enhancement of self-esteem, and the desire to "have fun" (Murray & Zentner, 2001; Ryan, 2000). However, encounters with the opposite sex may go beyond the purely sexual and involve feelings of love and tenderness. Establishing an intimate relationship outside the family is a developmental task of adolescence and early adulthood. Sexual intimacy includes a blend of eroticism, emotional closeness, mutual caring, vulnerability, trust, and commitment (Pillitteri, 1999; Sternberg, 1997).

The family has an essential role in the development of adolescent sexuality, because family members, especially parents, hold a new set of expectations for adolescents. Greater autonomy, less supervision, and greater involvement with peer groups are permitted. Yet adolescent sexual

activity is often feared, ignored, or censured by parents. A double standard for male and female adolescents may still exist today. Adolescent boys are usually given more freedom by parents than girls, so their conflict regarding independence and autonomy is not so prevalent. In contrast, girls have more restrictions placed on them. Conflicts may arise because sexual attractiveness, but not sexual activity, is valued.

Further conflict results from parents feeling that they must control adolescents' sexuality. Adolescents want to hear about sex and sexuality but decry preaching or moralizing and may rebel against coercion. Adolescents want facts and information about contraception, sexually transmitted diseases (STDs), pregnancy, and sexual orientation; however, even when they have appropriate information, adolescents engage in sexual behavior that puts them at risk for unintended pregnancy and STDs (Henderson & Yasgur, 2002;

Woodson, 1997). Young people who are sexually active are at risk for STDs and pregnancy because they frequently have multiple partners or do not use condoms or other forms of contraception. Adolescents are particularly vulnerable to common STDs such as chlamydia, papilloma infections, genital herpes, gonorrhea, trichomonas, and AIDS (Murray & Zentner, 2001).

Traditionally, sexual decision making and sexual behavior, dictated by family and societal values, was largely conservative. Teens now have more options than ever before and are faced with societal and family values that are much more liberal than in the past. Today, close to 50% of high school students have engaged in sexual intercourse, and 8.3% experience sexual intercourse before their thirteenth birthday (Kann et al., 2000). Furthermore, 56% of female and 73% of male adolescents report having experienced sexual intercourse before reaching the age of 18. On average, first intercourse occurs at age 17 for females and age 16 for males, and one fourth of adolescents report having engaged in first sexual intercourse by the age of 15. Nineteen percent of sexually active high school students report having had four or more partners (American Academy of Pediatrics Committee on Adolescence, 2000).

In spite of easy access to contraception, more liberal attitudes toward contraceptives, and increased implementation of sex education curricula in schools, teen pregnancy rates continue to rise in epidemic numbers. Most teen pregnancies occur in young women aged 18 to 19 years. Of those, 51% end in a live birth, 35% end in abortion, and 14% end in a miscarriage or stillbirth (American Academy of Pediatrics Committee on Adolescence, 2000). Although birth rates to women younger than 20 have decreased since the 1970s, the United States continues to have one of the highest teenage pregnancy rates among developed countries (Ventura, Curtin, & Matthews, 1998). Teen pregnancy rates among African Americans are higher than rates among white Americans and continue to increase (Murray & Zentner, 2001).

Most teenage mothers are unmarried, and undesired pregnancies result in disrupted education, reduced employment opportunities, low income, unstable marriages, and health and developmental risks to the children of adolescent mothers. Society pays a high price in government financial support, health care, and special education for teenage mothers and their children (White & DeBlassie, 1992). Teenagers become pregnant for various reasons: to have someone to love, to express dislike of school or of the home environment, to trap a man into a relationship or marriage, to prove femininity, or to relieve loneliness and depression (Murray & Zentner, 2001).

Parents' confusion and ambivalence about sexuality results in girls having to interpret mixed messages. Society, which emphasizes adolescents' freedom, makes it difficult for parents to set limits. When pregnancy occurs, parents may feel guilty about their relationship with the daughter, causing further disruption in family relationships. Parents who are able to share sexual information; who exemplify a positive sexual value system and lifestyle; and who show trust, love, and pride in their adolescents provide the best foundation for healthy sexual development (Pillitteri, 1999).

Sexual Development: Adulthood

Choosing a sexual partner or developing a sexual relationship is one of the tasks of adulthood. In Eriksonian terms, the developmental task of this life stage is "intimacy versus isolation." In adulthood, individuals must develop the skills they need to sustain a lasting intimate relationship with another human being (Erikson, 1968). This includes developing a sense of one's own sexual identity, learning sexual preferences, learning how to communicate those preferences, and developing the capacity for sexual and nonsexual intimacy.

There have been rather dramatic changes in young adult sexual behavior over the past 3 decades. Premarital sexual activity has increased. This increase may be related to the fact that age at first menarche is falling in the United States and age at first marriage is increasing (U.S. Bureau of the Census, 2000). Attitudes toward premarital sexual activity have become correspondingly less restrictive. Similarly, cohabitation has become an increasingly common practice. Almost half of young adults cohabit at least once before marriage.

It is usually during the adult years that the family is established. Adults learn to give and receive love in a stable relationship. Marriage combines the responsibilities of a sexual relationship with those of reproduction and socialization. The couple become parents and transmit the sexual values of the culture. Traditionally, childrearing and housekeeping have been the responsibility of women. This traditional view includes the assumption that most women with children do not work or work at jobs that are not essential to financial security. The majority of women with children work. Women now increasingly demand that men assume their fair share of childrearing and housekeeping tasks so that they can continue their careers. Role strain may occur in women who are overwhelmed with career and family responsibilities and in men who have similar ambivalent feelings about dual responsibilities. Loss of self-esteem may occur if either partner perceives assigned tasks as demeaning (Hyde, Delameter, & Hewitt, 1998).

Sexual intimacy may suffer if a couple is fatigued or anxious about their relationship or if work and achievement become more important than family relationships. The addition of children to the family and the responsibilities of childrearing may also negatively affect sexuality. Women may feel they have to choose between love and children and work and accomplishment. Sexual relationships may also suffer as a result of fatigue engendered by overwork or because of job dissatisfaction. Research suggests that couples in satisfying jobs who limit work hours to a reasonable level overall do not report dissatisfaction with their sexual lives after the birth of a child (Hyde et al., 1998).

Perhaps the most important factor in achieving a satisfying family life in relation to sexuality is the partners' ability to communicate to each other their sexual needs, feelings, fears, and love and respect for each other. The most important variable affecting satisfaction with the relationship is the quality of marital communication. Distressed couples tend to communicate through criticism, defensiveness, and withdrawal. Nondistressed couples are much more positive in their communication styles (Gottmann, 1994). Positive communication contributes to stable family relationships and provides the ideal environment for further development of both the parents' and the children's sexuality.

In later adulthood, anxiety about sexual performance and attractiveness may occur in both sexes. In part, this anxiety may reflect negative societal views toward sex among the elderly (Maurer, 1999). Anxiety may also occur as a consequence of physical changes associated with aging. Decreasing estrogen levels may cause lack of lubrication in women, and decreasing testosterone levels can lengthen the refractory period in men (Segraves and Segraves, 1995). Fear of loss of sexual attractiveness may accompany these and other changes. This fear may affect sexual responsiveness of one or both partners. Sexual self-esteem may suffer, and hormonal and emotional changes may reduce or halt sexual activity. Between the ages of 40 and 50, individuals may conclude that they have not reached their potential, and dissatisfaction may lead to depression and decreased sexual activity (Sheehy, 1995).

Sexual Development: Age 65 and Older

Sexual function may be compromised by illness or by the decreased strength and vigor that accompany aging, although with healthy partners, sexual activity may continue into the eighties or nineties. As aging occurs, physical changes do affect sexual behavior. Longer foreplay may be necessary for vaginal lubrication in women. There may be thinning of the vaginal walls and narrowing of the vaginal vault. Exogenous lubricants may alleviate any discomfort accompanying these changes. In men, erections may be less firm, may require increased stimulation to be achieved, and may be lost more readily. The refractory period, during which another erection cannot be achieved, tends to lengthen.

The two most important factors predicting regular sexual activity well into old age are good physical and mental health and regularity of sexual expression (Segraves & Segraves, 1995). Factors such as partner availability and negative expectations regarding aging may be more important determinants of decreases in sexual activity among older adults than physical incapacity. Many older adults report regular sexual activity well into extreme old age. In one sample of adults between the ages of 80 and 102 years, more than half the men and one third of the women were regularly engaging in sexual intercourse

(Bretschneider & McCoy, 1988). In a longstanding relationship, old age may be the golden age of sexuality that has matured through the years, resulting in a close, fulfilling intimacy and concern for one another.

Children do not see their parents as sexually active at any age, and society assumes that the elderly are not interested in sexual activity. If death of one parent occurs, grown children often react with horror if a widowed parent begins to date, and many children discourage remarriage. Paradoxically, just as parents have had concerns about their children's developing sexuality, grown children have concerns about the sexual behavior of their parents. Such concerns may manifest themselves in practices that serve as barriers to adult sexuality. Nursing homes, for example, routinely place even married couples in separate housing. Such routine practices may need to be reassessed in the light of current knowledge about sexual behavior among older adults.

Families with Alternative Lifestyles

Beginning in the new millennium, fewer than 27% of the nation's 91 million households fit the definition of the traditional nuclear family. This means that about 1 in 19 families are composed of a wage-earner father, a mother who stays home, and two or more children. With changing sexual mores, rapidly increasing numbers of single parents, and an economy forcing more people to share households (U.S. Bureau of the Census, 2000), the family must be broadly defined to include a group of people who love and care for each other. Various forms of families who fit this definition include single parents, stepfamilies, and domestic partners. As the divorce rate has increased (one of every two marriages ends in divorce), the incidence of remarriage and stepfamilies has also increased so that stepchildren make up 20% of all children in married-couple families.

Domestic partnership, a term unheard of 20 years ago, refers to cohabitation by gay, lesbian, and heterosexual couples (Allen & Demo, 1995). The U. S. Census Bureau has counted 1.6 million same-sex couples living together (up from 0.6 million in 1970) and 2.6 million heterosexual couples sharing a household (up from a half a million in 1970). Reasons cited for these changes include divorce, delayed marriage, and the growth of the gay liberation movement (Smock, 2000). This section focuses on selected variations in family sexuality patterns, including gay and lesbian partnerships and heterosexual domestic partnerships.

Gay and Lesbian Domestic Partnerships

Homosexuality occurs in all societies, and at present, about 4% of all individuals identify themselves as exclusively gay or lesbian (Laumann et al., 1994). In its broadest definition, homosexuality refers to strong erotic attachment to members of the same sex. The preferred terms are *lesbians* and *gay men* because homosexuality is associated in some cases with negative stereotypes. American society has traditionally discriminated against lesbians and gay men by declaring sexual acts between same-sex partners illegal, not recognizing gay and lesbian marriages as legal, and denying custody or adoption of children to same-sex partners. Gay and lesbian partners may have limited legal rights during illness (e.g. cannot cover one another with health insurance benefits and cannot be listed as next of kin on records). Conservative political and religious groups oppose homosexual marriage and parenthood on the grounds that it is against the natural law, is intrinsically disordered, and is not in harmony with the purposes of male-female psychological and physiological differences. Lesbians and gay men are often perceived as unfit to raise children and a threat to family life. However, a review of the literature by Brooks and Goldberg (2001) suggests that children of same-sex parents are well-adjusted and are not negatively affected by the family experience.

After 25 years of gay and lesbian rights activism, there has been some movement toward mitigating discrimination based on sexual preference. In 1990, Footlick argued that gay men, more than any other group, have benefited from broader social acceptance of alternative lifestyles. Although the gay lifestyle of the 1970s and 1980s often involved multiple liaisons and short-term relationships, lesbians have traditionally developed monogamous relationships with lifelong partners. In the post-AIDS era, many gay men, as well as lesbians, are choosing to live in monogamous relationships. Many of these couples have formed domestic partnerships, participated in marriage ceremonies, and have or are interested in having children as part of their family units (Brooks & Goldberg, 2001).

In the last several years, some corporations and a few local governments have set up domestic partnership programs. These programs provide low-cost or no-cost benefits, such as sick leave or bereavement leave, and some are even beginning to offer more costly benefits such as medical and dental insurance or reimbursement for relocation costs (Ames, 1992). In May 1990, San Francisco's Board of Supervisors passed the "domestic partnership" legislation recognizing homosexual and unmarried heterosexual couples as having the rights of married couples. In the summer of 1990, the New York State Supreme Court expanded the definition to protect a gay survivor of a couple and set four standards for a family: (1) the "exclusivity and longevity of a relationship"; (2) the "level of emotional and financial commitment"; (3) how the couple "conducted their everyday lives and held themselves out to society"; (4) and the "reliance placed on one another for daily services" (Footlick, 1990, p. 18).

If there are children in the case of divorce, the issue of custody arises. Courts have given various reasons for awarding custody to the heterosexual partner, usually stated as "the best interests of the child." The courts' concerns are over short- and long-term consequences of a son or daughter being with a homosexual mother or father. These fears include social stigmatization and confusion over sexual identity (Stein, 1996). However, these fears appear to have little foundation. Research clearly suggests that children of homosexuals are no different in mental health or sexual orientation than children of heterosexuals (Patterson, 1995)

Major health problems that affect gay men and their partners are AIDS and HIV. At the beginning of the AIDS epidemic, most AIDS cases were among young gay males and intravenous drug users. In the United States, the incidence of deaths from AIDS has declined because of advancements in treatment and education. A major issue is that despite the decline of deaths from AIDS, the incidence of HIV/AIDS continues to be a major health problem for gay males and heterosexual males and females in the United States and around the world, particularly in underdeveloped countries. For example, currently in the United States most new HIV/AIDS infections are found in men who have sex with men, followed by men and women who engage in heterosexual sex and intravenous drug use (Centers for Disease Control and Prevention [CDC], 2001). African Americans have the highest rate of new infections, followed by Hispanic and white Americans. Among women, heterosexual women are reported to have 75% of the new HIV/AIDS infections (CDC, 2003). Although in the United States the number of AIDS deaths has decreased, there is a continued need for encouraging persons affected with HIV/AIDS and receiving medication to adhere to the prescribed treatment regimens. There are more people living with AIDS in the United States than ever before (CDC, 2003). Therefore health care providers should continue to teach persons at risk for HIV/AIDS and STDs about the diseases and recommend they take precautions such as avoiding unprotected sex and contact with body fluids of another person.

Heterosexual Domestic Partnerships

Given its prevalence, cohabitation is a "family status" that must be included with marriage if nurses are to understand family life in the new millennium. The number of Americans living together outside of marriage has increased 400% since 1970. Four percent of Americans 19 and older are cohabitating, 25% have cohabitated at some time, and unmarried couples account for 4.5 million of the country's 93 million households (U.S. Bureau of the Census, 2000).

The popularity of cohabitation may be attributed to three factors: Americans postponing marriage, the sexual revolution, and the diminishing social stigma against premarital sex. The large increase in the proportion of people in their early twenties who have never been married does not mean that young people are staying single longer; rather, they are setting up households with heterosexual partners at almost as early an age as they did before the marriage rates declined. Fear of relationships not working out or not being economically viable is often the reason couples choose to cohabit.

Before the 1990s the literature reflected cohabitation among only college students and low-income couples. Since then, in the United

States heterosexual cohabitation among unmarried couples, college students, and divorcees from all socioeconomic backgrounds has risen dramatically (Amato, Johnson, Booth, & Rogers, 2003; Smock, 2000). The literature indicates that cohabitation seems have a negative influence on marriage (Bumpass, Sweet, & Cherlin, 1991). According to Amatao et al. (2003), cohabitation can diminish people's commitment to a lengthy marriage and may undermine marital stability.

Research has called into question a number of common myths about couples who live together. Cohabitation is often viewed as a new stage in the American courtship process and an important step before marriage to assess compatibility (DeMaris & Rao, 1992). In reality, cohabiting relationships tend to be short term and are much less stable than those that begin as marriages (Bumpass et al., 1991). Most couples break up after 18 months. Domestic partnerships tend to last an average of 3 to 5 years and about 50% to 75% lead to marriage and subsequent divorce in an average of 5 years (Hoem & Hoem, 1992; Lowdermilk, Perry, & Bobak, 2000; Thompson & Collela, 1992; U.S. Bureau of the Census, 2000).

Attempting to explain this "cohabitation effect" (DeMaris & Rao, 1992), researchers postulate that cohabitation is a nontraditional lifestyle that attracts people who are more prone to unstable marriages, perceive themselves or their relationship as a poor risk, define marriage in more individual than couple terms and view marital quality as more central to relationships, have a generally weaker commitment to the institution of marriage, and are more likely to accept divorce as a solution (Thompson & Collela, 1992). More research is needed to determine whether cohabitation is more likely among people who are less likely to remain married.

How do cohabiting couples with children differ from married couples with children? Cohabiting couples report lower levels of certainty about their relationship than do married couples. Childrearing is one function that has always defined the family. Individuals with alternatives, such as employed women who do not need marriage to rear children, are likely to delay marriage. Forty percent of cohabiting couples have children in the unit. Webster found that although cohabiting units look like a family, they function differently. For example, cohabiting couples share the housework more equitably than married couples, but they share the childcare less: the children usually belong to and are cared for by the woman. To reduce the possibility of divorce, Olson and Olson (2000) suggest that domestic partners should be empowered to learn how to communicate, resolve conflicts, explore role relationships, discuss sexual issues, manage finances, discuss spiritual beliefs, and establish couple goals.

Nursing Process and Family Sexual Health

Assessment and Diagnosis

Nurses who are comfortable with sexuality either grew up in families who were comfortable with sexual issues or had some life or educational experiences that helped them sort out their feelings, experiences, and values. Few were taught in their nursing programs to include sexuality as a component of routine history taking, and this is especially true of those who completed their education more than 7 years ago. Others have gained "on-the-job training" but explore only those particular aspects of sexuality related to their specialty areas, such as counseling patients who have had myocardial infarction about sexual relations after hospital discharge, and remain uncomfortable with issues beyond their narrow purview (Olds, London, & Ladewig, 2000).

Nurses who assume the role of counselor for clients with sexual and reproductive concerns must first be secure about their own sexuality. It is important that they be aware of their own feelings, values, and attitudes about sexual issues so that they may convey sensitivity and objectivity to others. Accurate, up-to-date information on topics related to sexuality, contraception, sexual practices, and common gynecological problems is essential. It is also necessary to have a working understanding of the structures and functions of the male and female reproductive systems (Olds et al., 2000).

Continuing education courses, in addition to specific courses in undergraduate and graduate nursing education programs, provide basic information about various aspects of sexuality.

Such courses are also helpful in promoting a personal sense of security in sexual matters and can inform nurses about sexual values, attitudes, alternative lifestyles, cultural considerations, and myths and misconceptions about sex and reproduction (Olds et al., 2000).

Before using the nursing process to explore sexual issues with families, the nurse may find it helpful to complete a self-assessment of personal values, experiences, and belief systems related to sexuality. One strategy involves listing topics such as abortion, masturbation, fellatio, and various forms of sexual expression to identify personal feelings about and attitudes toward particular sexual issues. Other methods include completing a "self" sexual history—asking oneself the same questions that a nurse would ask the family when taking a family sexual history (see Box 15-1)—or exploring gender identity by responding to the question, "What has it meant for you to grow up a girl/woman or boy/man in this society?" Nurses may reflect on their lives by considering messages they received and experiences they shared with families, religious groups, classmates, and peers that shaped their femininity or masculinity. Discussing personal sexual history or the experience of gender identity with a colleague fosters insights into and empathy for the vulnerability involved in sharing the intimate details of one's sexual life with another individual and helps to sensitize nurses to the importance of understanding, rather than judging, individuals' and families' views on sexuality.

Any of the preceding exercises can alert nurses to issues that might be uncomfortable or difficult for them to objectively discuss with families. It is important that they be aware of personally sensitive issues so that they may receive guidance in working through their own conflicts or assistance in referring the family to another health care professional.

When taking a sexual history, nurses must realize that this component is not to be taken out of context of the individuals' or families' total being; rather, it is part of the larger health history that provides information about other functional health patterns. Box 15-1 summarizes data that should be collected from all clients and families, with additional information gathered as the situation suggests. Comprehensive outlines of

BOX 15-1 Data to Be Collected for Family Sexual History

- Ages of family members
- Sexes of all family members
- Education, occupation of family members
- Quality of relationships with significant others: parent-children, spouse-spouse (affectionate, punitive, hostile)
- Interests, hobbies of individuals and family as a whole
- Spiritual/religious/philosophical beliefs, congruence among family members
- Attitude of family members about sexual behaviors (e.g., touching, nudity, masturbation, coitus)
- Teaching children about sexuality (knowledge level of parents, responsibility for content given)
- Health problems, medical conditions, surgical procedures in past and anticipated in the future; medication therapy (for parents and children)
- Changes in role relationships and ability to carry out the usual sexual role (of both parents, sexual partners)
- Potential changes in ability to carry out usual sexual role (of both parents, sexual partners)
- Change in perception of self as male or female as a result of illness or life events
- Existing or potential sexual dysfunction of one or both parents, sexual partners
- Presence of family conflict because of difference in values and beliefs about sexuality and sexual behaviors

sexual history information are not suitable for all clients. Instead, questions are chosen selectively as the situation indicates. Box 15-2 also provides information to be considered in assessment of a family for sexuality issues.

Dunn (1990) describes a strategy for obtaining a brief sexual history in about 10 minutes. Specific questions the nurse may ask center on the following four major ideas:

- What is the problem?
- When did it begin?
- Why do you believe this is a problem for you?
- What have been your attempts at a solution?

BOX 15-2   Family Sexuality Assessment

I. Demographic Data
  A. Clients' age, sex, marital status
  B. Parents' age, sex, marital status, religion, education, occupation
  C. Other children, siblings' ages, sexes, assets, problems

II. Biological Factors
  A. Satisfaction with sexual relationship, frequency, pleasure, types of activity, foreplay
  B. Problems: impotence, anorgasmia, painful intercourse, lack of interest (drive)
  C. Illness affecting sexuality: diagnosis, type of problem (body image disturbance, change in physiological response, role change)

III. Psychosocial Data
  A. Parents' relationship: congeniality, demonstration of affection, feelings toward children, communication patterns, mutual decision making, satisfaction with sexual roles, well-defined self-boundaries
  B. Family and child's attitudes toward sexuality: degree of openness or reserve about sex, attitude toward sexual activity, religious beliefs about sexuality
  C. Siblings' relationship: congeniality, affection, communication pattern

  D. Homosexual family: children's acceptance of relationship, fears and concerns

IV. Learning about Sexuality
  A. Parents' knowledge of and attitude toward sexual response, sexual relationships, sexual development (sex play, masturbation, pregnancy, birth, menstruation, nocturnal emission, venereal disease, homosexuality)
  B. Children's knowledge of sexuality (see A, Parent's Knowledge)
  1. Explanations, teaching done by parents
  2. Attitude of children about sexuality

V. Childhood/Adolescent Sex Activity
  A. Incest: nature of activity, person involved, willing or unwilling, form of rewards, feeling about activity
  1. Physiological problems: bedwetting, venereal disease, cystitis, vaginal infection, trauma
  2. Psychosocial problems: runaway behavior, withdrawal
  B. Adolescent pregnancy: age of both parents, attitudes about pregnancy, familial support and attitudes, strengths and weaknesses of adolescents involved, acceptance or rejection of pregnancy, proposed solutions, plans for future, general health and development

---

Hutchinson (1998) suggests that nurses who interview women concerning their sexual behavior include an assessment of personal risk as a component of the discussion.

During assessment for problems related to sexual response, the nurse obtains general demographic data (see the assessment tool at the end of the chapter). Clients' knowledge, values, and attitudes about sexual activity are explored along with the level of satisfaction with sexual practices. It is also important to determine whether conflict exists between the sexual partners because of differing beliefs.

Once the nature of the problem is identified, nurses ascertain (1) whether the client or family has already sought help, (2) the precipitating factors, (3) the sexual partners' knowledge of the problem and points of view, (4) the clients' and family's proposed remedies and needs, (5) effect of the problem on the clients' lifestyles and the

rest of the relationship, and (6) the personality assets and strengths (Alexander, 1981). Data from other health patterns are also analyzed to identify related factors.

The family's attitude toward sexual behavior such as nudity, openness to showing affection, beliefs about masturbation, and premarital sexual relationships is assessed by direct questioning of individual family members. It is important not to communicate personal beliefs and values about sexuality. When a trusting relationship has developed between the nurse and clients, information will be shared and sexual health will be promoted.

Pregnancy and the birth of a child may be a time of sexual distress for the partners as roles and relationships change and the family dyad is expanded. Early in pregnancy, the nurse assesses the couple's knowledge of pregnancy and its effect on sexuality, their attitudes toward the pregnancy and the coming child, and the nature of their sexual relationship.

Common nursing diagnoses and factors related to sexuality and family health include the following (Gordon, 2002; Reeder, Martin, & Koniak-Griffin, 1997):

- Sexual dysfunction, which may be related to physical abuse, harmful relationships, misinformation or lack of knowledge, values conflict, lack of privacy, lack of a significant other, altered body structure or function, or change in roles and relationships
- Ineffective family or individual coping related to sexual dysfunction
- Ineffective sexuality patterns
- Depression related to sexual dysfunction
- Self-esteem disturbances related to sexual dysfunction, loss of sexual role
- Fear, related to possible loss of sexual function and/or knowledge deficit
- Parenting alteration (potential or actual) related to lack of sexual developmental guidelines, support system deficit, physical or psychosocial abuse, family or personal stress
- Lack of information about sexuality
- Negative attitudes about sexuality

Intervention and Evaluation

When intervening to promote sexual health, nurses must be careful not to impose their own beliefs and values on clients, since the amount and kind of information shared can be affected by personal biases. It is crucial to avoid subtle or nonverbal communication of negative attitudes about sexuality when clients ask questions or voice concerns (Pillitteri, 1999; Ross, Channon-Little, & Simon-Rosser, 2000).

To be effective, nurses must be tolerant of human differences in sexual behavior and accepting of clients whose sexual orientation or lifestyle is different from their own. At some point in the interventions, it is appropriate to include the client's sexual partner because relationship factors must be considered. There is no situation in which there is an uninvolved partner (Reeder et al., 1997).

A couple's lack of knowledge about the sexual response cycle and the need for adequate foreplay

can be addressed through counseling of both partners. During counseling, the nurse may provide clients with information about sexual response and suggestions for enhancing sexual response. Arousal techniques may include kissing, oral-genital stimulation (fellatio and cunnilingus), and tactile stimulation to erogenous zones (these usually include the breast, vulva, anus, penis, lips, mouth, and other areas in which individuals experience pleasure). Fondling, caressing, or light scratching of the sexual partner's body and massaging with creams and lotions generally increase sensation. Darkness, soft lights or full illumination, music, pictures or movies of others engaging in sexual activity, and sexual fantasies may also be effective strategies for enhancing foreplay and arousal.

Various positions for coitus besides the male superior (missionary) position include female superior, side-by-side, rear entry, and sitting positions, which may provide variety and increase sexual response. Couples need to communicate what is pleasurable and not pleasurable, and partners must be caring and considerate of each other. The importance of a loving word or glance and an unhurried, private environment should also be addressed.

When couples complain of the fatigue that often accompanies childbearing and childrearing, setting aside different times and/or different places for coitus may be helpful. Getting away from home to spend a weekend together or having a relative take the children for an evening or day gives parents an opportunity for leisurely love-making, sharing of confidences, and keeping in touch with who they are and what they mean to each other. Finally, if there is conflict because of change in sexual roles as a result of illness or other life events, the nurse can serve as a catalyst to increase the partners' communication about the fear, frustration, and anger they may be experiencing.

Interventions during pregnancy also require teaching and counseling both partners. Sexual intimacy and intercourse should be encouraged throughout the pregnancy. For most women, sexual activity can usually continue throughout the gestational period, provided that there is no bleeding, rupture of the membranes (because of the risk for infection), or preterm labor risk, since orgasms cause uterine contractions (Leppert, 1997).

As pregnancy progresses, the female superior, side-by-side, spoon fashion, and rear entry positions are recommended to avoid pressure on the breasts and abdomen. Nurses can counter myths and misconceptions by explaining that the fetus is not harmed by coitus and cannot hear or see in utero. They can also help prospective parents talk about their new roles and the activities and responsibilities that accompany parenthood. Inappropriate parenting can usually be prevented by anticipatory guidance and counseling, and it is important to discuss issues surrounding the resumption of sexual activity after the baby's birth. Group or individual classes with both partners present constitute an essential component of effective postpartum care (Lowdermilk et al., 2000).

After delivery, the woman may experience decreased sexual interest because of fatigue, weakness, and vaginal discomfort. Breast tenderness and other discomforts along with decreased vaginal lubrication may also diminish sexual response, as does postpartum "blues" or depression. When decreased vaginal lubrication caused by depletion of hormones occurs, a water-soluble gel or a contraceptive cream or jelly can be recommended. If vaginal tenderness continues, the partners can be instructed to rotate one or two fingers around inside the vagina to help it relax. Also, the nurse can suggest that assuming a position in which the woman has control of the depth of penile insertion may be helpful. However, if vaginal pain persists for 4 weeks after resumption of sexual activity, the woman should return for evaluation and treatment (Lowdermilk et al., 2000). Kegel exercises can be recommended to strengthen the pubococcygeal muscle that controls not only vaginal response during coitus but also bowel and bladder function. The nurse can also provide the couple with contraception information if they desire it.

The depression that may follow pregnancy is usually self-limiting, especially if the partner gives support and love. Role-relationship problems require mutual discussion and "working out" by the parents. A postpartum support group for mothers and fathers is useful, because it allows them to share concerns and support one another

as they adjust to their parenting roles (Lowdermilk et al., 2000).

Indications that interventions related to family health for couples have been successful include the following:

- Verbal report that partners are satisfied with their sexual relationship
- Resumption of sexual activity that both partners describe as satisfying
- Ability to describe alternative positions for intercourse and different foreplay activities
- Commitment to and satisfaction with parenting as observed by the nurse
- Ability to identify the effects of fatigue and discomfort in the sexual relationship and ability to list ways to relieve these effects
- Identification of the importance of communication and a loving supportive relationship to promote sexual health

Nursing Implications: Sexuality across the Family Life Span

Assessment and Nursing Diagnoses during Infancy, Childhood, and Adolescence

Family nurses are in an ideal position to teach and counsel parents and children about the normality of psychosexual developmental behaviors. It is useful to assess the parents' beliefs and attitudes about these behaviors and their knowledge of normal psychosexual development. The nurse observes infants' and children's relationship with parents, and as appropriate, with peers and siblings. The nurse identifies and addresses any concerns the parents have about children's sexuality, behaviors, and relationships with others. Finally, the nurse may perform a physical examination to identify biological abnormalities.

Adolescents and their parents may be reluctant to seek help, so sexual problems may be identified during legal or medical treatment for other problems. Consequently, nurses must be alert to subtle signs of difficulties. Data collected include the adolescent's level of psychosexual development and knowledge of sexuality, exposure to sexual activity, environmental pressures, family and other support systems, and general physical development and health (Mandleco & McCoy, 2002).

Intervention and Evaluation: Infancy to Adolescence

Although nearly everyone agrees that parents and caregivers should teach children and adolescents about intimacy and sexuality, many do not understand sexuality or have abdicated their responsibility (Raffaelli, Bogenschneider, & Flood, 1998). Parents need anticipatory guidance in teaching children the correct terms for parts of the body and sexual activity. They may also require assistance in providing information appropriate to the child's developmental level and in promoting positive attitudes toward body parts and gender roles. It is helpful to assure parents that masturbation, touching of the genital areas, and genital exhibition constitute normal activities for children. Parents should be encouraged to involve children in family activities; to give children love, attention, and creative stimulation; and to teach children that touching their private parts is an activity to be done in privacy. Families with young children should be given strategies for providing an environment in which sexuality and sexual issues can be discussed in an open and comfortable manner. To protect children from sexual abuse and rape, parents should teach children about inappropriate touching of their genitals by others and how to relate to strangers.

Adolescents should be given an opportunity to discuss their view of self and their feelings about the opposite sex. Developmental and cognitive stages of adolescence must be taken into account during counseling of adolescents and families. Textbooks and articles dedicated to care or treatment of adolescents typically recommend that nurses be nonjudgmental, honor confidentiality, and honestly apprise adolescent clients of the implications of sexual activity (Mandleco & McCoy, 2002).

Nurses who work with families with adolescents need to be aware of and sensitive to adolescents' and families' religious and community attitudes and values. If an individual has been seen by the nurse since childhood, then the nurse-client relationship needs to be redefined at adolescence to accommodate confidentiality. At adolescence, the child replaces the parent as the primary historian and helps establish the agenda for visits. Nurses need to communicate to adolescents that they are approachable, for example, by initiating discussions about sex and sexuality and having sex education materials available in waiting rooms (Mandleco & McCoy, 2002).

Nurses can teach parents how to discuss sexual issues with children and adolescents, suggest ways to clarify values, assist them in decision making, and apprise them of helpful resources in the community and recommended books (Box 15-3). Adolescents are reported to prefer parents as primary sex educators (Raffealli et al., 1998). Parents are often relieved to find out that they do not need to be "sexperts" who have all the answers. It is also important for nurses to identify adolescents who are at risk for sexual acting out. Potential risk factors for this behavior include (1) parental divorce or separation; (2) vague future educational plans—the higher the level of

---

BOX 15-3 SIECUS Guidelines for Parents and Caregivers to Teach Children about Sexuality

1. Parents are the primary sexuality educators of children.
2. Find a teachable moment.
3. It is okay to feel uncomfortable about the topic.
4. Do not wait for the child to ask questions.
5. Be "ask-able."
6. Be aware that there might be a question behind the question.
7. Listen carefully to what a child is saying and not saying.
8. Remember that the facts are not always enough.
9. Talk out about the pleasant aspects of sexuality.
10. Discussing sexuality with a child shows that the parent cares.
11. Be informed about what is taught about the sexuality in the schools, faith community, and youth groups.

Adapted from SIECUS. (2001). *Families are talking, 1(1),* p. 3. Retrieved June 1, 2003, from http://www.siecus.org/pubs/families/Families_Newsletter.pdf

intended education, the less likely it is that the adolescent will engage in early sexual intercourse; (3) no religious affiliation—the more religious the adolescent, the less likely it is that he or she will have sexual intercourse; and (4) negative parental attitudes or teaching—the more affirming the parental messages about sexuality, the less likely it is that the adolescent will be sexually active (Pillitteri, 1999). Adolescents should be taught that coitus should take place in a deep, lasting relationship and that healthy sexuality is based on more than peer approval or ability to "score."

Although adolescents may seem to be sexually sophisticated, they are often ignorant about sexual development and response and are prey to the same myths and misconceptions as adults. Adolescents need information about the physical aspects of sex and sexuality and guidelines about developing and sustaining friendships with those of the opposite sex. They should be provided with facts about date rape and rape prevention in general, since adolescents constitute a high-risk age group for date rape (Pillitteri, 1999).

Adolescents also need reassurance that isolated same-gender experiences do not mean that one is homosexual. Nurses can help young people to recognize that same-gender experimentation is not the same as establishing a same-gender orientation, and few who participate in same-gender behavior during adolescence continue the practice into adulthood (Santrock, 2001).

It is unclear whether routine sex education in schools could alleviate the problems of early sexual activity. Although polls indicate that the majority of Americans favor sex education in the classroom, only half of the states require it, and the remainder officially encourage sex education in the curriculum. Often, such programs are superficial and brief and teachers frequently lack adequate training in the subject. In fact, according to the Sexuality Information and Education Council of the United States (SIECUS) (1999), less than 10% of schools in the United States have a comprehensive sex education program. Even when sex education is included in a classroom curriculum, the focus may be on reproductive physiology, with little content concerning topics such as avoidance of STDs, prevention of pregnancy, and the importance of respect and caring for others in all interpersonal relationships (Sloane, 2002).

Contraceptive information should be given to adolescents who request it, and adolescents who are not sexually active need sources of support for their beliefs that sexual intimacy should be reserved for marriage and that it is all right to say no. The school nurse who initiates teaching programs is in a unique position to foster healthy sexuality. Classes should be held for student groups, as well as for families (Pillitteri, 1999). Box 15-4 summarizes suggested content for classes related to sexuality.

The unmarried adolescent girl who becomes pregnant needs help in making a decision about undergoing an abortion, giving the baby up for adoption, or keeping the baby with or without marriage. Rather than suggesting solutions, the nurse can help the girl identify these alternatives and their advantages and disadvantages, so that she can come to a solution on her own. No matter what the decision, the adolescent may experience guilt and depression and will need support to deal with her feelings. The nurse should also help

---

BOX 15-4 Content of Education about Sexuality

1. Male and female: anatomy and physiology, reproductive system
2. Responses of men and women to sexual stimulation: sexual response cycle
3. Information about growth and development: secondary sex characteristics, menstruation, and wet dreams
4. Fertilization, pregnancy, childbirth, conception control
5. Sexually transmitted diseases: types, prevention
6. Alternative forms of sexual expression: masturbation, homosexuality, bisexuality
7. Married and family love, emphasis on sexuality as part of family life and committed relationships
8. Making a choice about sexual behavior
9. Interpersonal relations: socializing with the opposite sex
10. Factors affecting family life: economic and social mobility, depersonalization, media distortion of sexuality

the father to work through his feelings about the pregnancy and recognize his responsibility to the mother and child. Indications that interventions related to childhood and adolescent sexual health have been successful include the following:

1) Parents describe normal psychosexual development of children and teach children accurate and factual information.
2) Parents state they are satisfied with their child's psychosexual development.
3) Parents show evidence of love and affection for children (e.g., praise them, kiss and hold them appropriately).
4) Adolescents describe biopsychosocial aspects of sexuality and understand conception, STDs, and AIDS.
5) Adolescents make an informed decision to have or not to have sex.
6) Adolescents identify and use contraception measures when needed.
7) Adolescents who become pregnant express reasonable satisfaction with their decision about the pregnancy.
8) Adolescents who become pregnant state they have worked through any guilt and/or depression about their decision.

Nursing Process during Adulthood

In addition to situations discussed earlier in this chapter in the section on the nursing process and family sexual health, the middle years may strain sexual relationships as individuals approach menopause or the "change of life." Nurses can assess women's and their sexual partners' attitudes toward and knowledge of menopause and its effects. Signs and symptoms such as "hot flashes," thinning of the vaginal wall, and decreased lubrication are identified. Myths and misconceptions that sexual activity is not suitable or may be painful after menopause can be dispelled by nurses. If the female client has vaginal atrophy and decreased lubrication, nurses may recommend use of water-soluble jelly, saliva, or insertion of the finger in the vagina to bring out secretions deeper in the vagina. Referral to physicians for estrogen therapy may be indicated (Association of Reproductive Health Professionals, 2000).

Teaching and counseling focuses on the role of hormones and the need for exercise of the pubo-

coccygeal muscle and includes giving the client permission to be sexual. A healthy lifestyle, good nutrition, weight control, and maintaining friendships and activities are all strategies that promote postmenopausal zest (Association of Reproductive Health Professionals, 2000).

It is also important for nurses to teach couples that sexual intimacy encompasses more than penile-vaginal penetration. Unfortunately, many tend to view this type of sexual activity as the "real thing," with the idea that anything else is incomplete. Nurses can work to dispel this myth by helping couples understand that all expressions of sexual behavior—such as hugging, kissing, and oral-genital contact—can be a fulfilling expression of sexuality and the sharing of love (Leppert, 1997). If there is change in sexual interest, causes are determined. If the change in interest is due to illness, the underlying problem can be treated. If the change is due to monotony in the relationship, nurses may suggest that the couple try different times, places, and lovemaking techniques to increase sexual pleasure (Lowdermilk et al., 2000). Olson and Olson (2000) suggest that couples be encouraged to do the following:

1) Always remember that good sex begins while their clothes are still on.
2) Take responsibility for their own sexual pleasure.
3) Talk with their partner about sex.
4) Take time to be together regularly.
5) Do not let sex become routine.
6) Do not carry anger into their bedroom.
7) Nurture the romance in their life.
8) Realize that partners do not have to see eye to eye sexually.
9) Do not be afraid to ask for help.
10) Try to keep their sexual expectations realistic.

Nursing Process during Older Age

Data are collected to help distinguish among illness, disinterest, or relational problems as causes of sexual problems. Information similar to that requested during assessment of adults is obtained by nurses who must be careful not to communicate their own biases and misinformation about older persons' sexuality. Diagnoses similar to those used for adults may be identified.

Interventions include teaching clients about the physiological changes that accompany aging, the need for longer foreplay, supplementation of vaginal lubrication with estrogen creams or water-soluble lubricants, less strenuous positions for coitus such as side-by-side or female superior, and time of day when partners are more rested (early morning or afternoon). Some couples and their families need the reassurance that sexual activity is normal during old age. Nurses may also remind couples that lying together, holding each other, touching, and sharing expressions of love are all forms of sexual intimacy. Coitus is not necessarily the final goal.

Older adults can be encouraged to consult the AARP website for sexual health information. Indications that interventions related to healthy sexuality in older adults have been successful include the following:
1) The aging individual describes biological changes in the sexual response cycle that accompany aging.
2) The aging individual identifies changes in foreplay and coitus that increase their sexual satisfaction.
3) The older individual expresses satisfaction with his or her sexual relationship.
4) The older individual identifies the importance of expressions of love and tenderness to maintain the relationship.

Nursing Implications: Families with Alternative Lifestyles

Assessment and Nursing Diagnosis: Gay and Lesbian Domestic Partners

Assessment data collected from gay and lesbian families are similar to data collected from other families. They have problems and concerns similar to those of heterosexuals: difficulty in finding a partner, vulnerability to STDs (particularly AIDS), interpersonal awkwardness, plus the added pressures that come from an often disapproving and discriminating society.

Children living with a gay or lesbian parent may experience difficulty in dealing with societal attitudes toward the parent's sexual orientation, so nurses need to assess the children's coping ability and self-esteem. These children may have had to deal with ridicule and desertion by friends. Nursing diagnoses similar to those used for heterosexual families may be identified.

Interventions and Evaluation: Gay and Lesbian Domestic Partners

Nurses must be careful not to discriminate against gay and lesbian families or individuals because of ignorance and fear of homosexuality. Regardless of whether the nurse sees this lifestyle as moral or immoral, variant or deviant, gay and lesbian clients and families are entitled to competent and loving care. Parents of gays and lesbians may need support and the opportunity to discuss fears and concerns. In light of the epidemic proportions of AIDS during the past decade among gays and lesbians (particularly gay men), nurses are encouraged to provide sensitive holistic nursing care that includes anticipatory teaching about prevention of STDs and guidelines for safe sex to same-gender domestic partners.

The individual's sex mate should be regarded as a significant other and allowed similar rights and privileges of family care. Many health care problems and family life issues are similar to those of other families, with the additional problem that a legal relationship does not usually exist, and nursing interventions and evaluation are similar. However, gay and lesbian families have unique needs. For the purpose of meeting these needs, recent social and political changes have brought about numerous social support and community resources specifically for gay and lesbian families, in the area of health promotion, disease prevention, and coping with life crises. Nurses should be encouraged to seek out these resources when working with gay and lesbian domestic partners.

Assessment, Nursing Diagnoses, and Interventions: Heterosexual Domestic Partners

Assessment, nursing diagnoses, and interventions are similar to those used with married couples. In nursing intervention for family lifestyle issues, transitions and crises for heterosexual families can be handled by using the nursing process. Since each couple is unique, the nurse can collaborate with the couple to resolve developmental and situational problems.

Resources for Health Care Professionals and Families

Many organizations can serve as good resources for educational information for families and health care professionals who work with them. The American Association of Sex Educators, Counselors, and Therapists; the Sexual Information and Education Council of the United States (SIECUS); the Planned Parenthood Federation of America; and the Association of Reproductive Health Professionals can be contacted for information and resources for any particular area. The website addresses for these and several other organizations are provided in the Website Resources box at the end of the chapter. The public library is also an excellent source of books, audiovisual materials, and pamphlets related to sexuality. Many books about family sexuality are available, and these can supply information that is useful to the nurse, as well as to the client. Some of these books are listed in Box 15-5. Also, the *Journal of School Health* has many excellent articles about sexuality, especially as it relates to children and adolescents.

BOX 15-5   Books on Family Sexuality

Blake, S., & Frances, G. (2001). *Just say no! to abstinence education: Lessons learnt from a sex education study tour to the United States.* London, UK: NCB Books.

Haffner, D. W. (1999). *From diapers to dating: A parent's guide to raising sexually healthy children.* New York: SIECUS.

Gordon, S., & Gordon, J. (2000). *Raising a child responsibly in a sexually permissive world* (2nd ed.). Holbrook, MA: Adams Media Cororation.

Kleven, S., & Bergsma, J. L. (1998). *The right touch: A read aloud book to help prevent child sexual abuse.* New York: Illumination Arts.

Roffman, D. (2001). *Sex and sensibility: The thinking parent's guide to talking sense about sex.* Boulder, CO: Perseus Books.

Schnarch, D. (1998). *Passionate marriage: Love, sex, and intimacy in emotionally committed relationships.* New York: Henry Holt

Wetzel, R. L. (1998). *Sexual wisdom: A guide for parents, young adults, educators, and physicians.* New York: Proctor Publications.

CASE SCENARIO

Belinda, age 25, and Chuck, age 26, have been happily married for 4 years. They arrive at the prenatal clinic for their first visit. A home pregnancy test confirmed what they had hoped—that Belinda was really expecting a baby. They report that Belinda had been pregnant once before, a year ago, but the pregnancy ended in a spontaneous abortion at 8 weeks' gestation. According to Belinda, the couple had not used any contraception in more than 9 months and this pregnancy is "an answer to our prayers." Based on the date of the last normal menstrual period, and confirmed with today's physical examination, Belinda is approximately 11 weeks along in her pregnancy. To date, Belinda has not experienced any problems such as the leakage of fluid or blood from her vagina, vaginal or urinary itching or burning, headaches or abdominal pain, contractions or tenderness. Findings of her initial obstetrical examination are normal, and Belinda appears to be a healthy woman in her first trimester of pregnancy.

However, during the couple's interview, Belinda becomes quite tearful and confides to the nurse that Chuck does not seem to "be interested" in her anymore. She states that they have not had sexual intercourse since they learned of her pregnancy. Chuck responds that he is afraid to touch her for fear that he

CASE SCENARIO—cont'd

will harm the baby. Before the pregnancy, the couple engaged in mutually satisfying coitus approximately three times a week. The couple denied having experienced any sexual problems in the past. Belinda expressed feelings of self-doubt and rejection over Chuck's recent behavior and a sense of confusion concerning her desirability as a sexual partner. Chuck expressed feelings of fear and even guilt as he admitted his concern about potentially harming Belinda or the baby and wondered out loud whether their sexual activity triggered the miscarriage last year.

MAJOR FAMILY STRESSORS

Family stressors include the couple's sexual concerns since confirmation of the pregnancy, Belinda's need for sexual intimacy and feelings of self-doubt as a desirable sexual partner, and Chuck's feelings of guilt and fear concerning the resumption of their sexual relationship.

FAMILY STRENGTHS

Family strengths include Belinda's and Chuck's happy and loving marriage, their previously satisfying sexual relationship, their obvious delight with the pregnancy, and their open willingness to share their present concerns.

LIFESTYLE CHANGES INDICATED

Lifestyle changes needed primarily focus on couple-centered education concerning the safety of sexual

relations during pregnancy. For Belinda, there is a need for reaffirmation that she is a desirable, sexual person who is experiencing a normal, healthy pregnancy. For Chuck, there is a need for reaffirmation that coital activity during the last pregnancy did not cause the miscarriage and that he is a loving, caring person who "has permission" to maintain intimate sexual relations with his pregnant wife.

NURSING INTERVENTIONS

The nurse can encourage the couple to continue to verbalize fears and concerns and dispel Chuck's belief that coitus caused the previous pregnancy loss. Misinformation and misconceptions can be explored as the nurse uses a variety of educational materials, anatomical charts, and other resources to convey the message that because the fetus is well protected in utero, sexual intercourse during pregnancy is permitted until labor begins. The nurse can explain that although contractions may occur with orgasm, they do not harm the fetus and will subside. The couple can be praised for their willingness to express personal feelings and desires and encouraged to explore alternative sexual positions and other means of sharing intimacy, such as fondling, cuddling, stroking, and mutual massage. The nurse can continue to reevaluate the couple's level of satisfaction with their sexual relationship and reinforce the information provided at the initial visit.

WEBSITE RESOURCES

ORGANIZATION	WEBSITE ADDRESS
American Association for Retired Persons	http:www.aarp.org
Association of Reproductive Health Professionals	http://www.arhp.org
National Institutes of Health	http://www.nih.gov
Sexuality Information and Education Council of the United States (SIECUS)	http://www.siecus.org
Kinsey Institute for Research in Sex, Gender, and Reproduction	http://www.indiana.edu/~kinsey/
Sexuality Research Information Service (SRIS)	http://www.indiana.edu/~sris/
Testicular Self-Exam	http://www.mskcc.org/mskcc/html/625.cfm
Men's Health	http://www.menshealth.com/new/guide/index.html
Minnesota Center against Violence and Abuse	http://www.mincava.umn.edu/

Website RESOURCES—cont'd

safersex.org	http://www.safersex.org
CDC Division of Sexually Transmitted Diseases	http://www.cdc.gov/nchstp/dstd/dstdp.html
American Association of Sex Educators, Counselors, and Therapists	http://www.aasect.org/
New York Male Reproductive Center's Sexual Dysfunction Unit	http://cpmcnet.Columbia.edu/dept/urology/impotence.html
National Institute on Aging	http://www.nih.gov/nia
www.iwannaknow.org	http://www.iwannaknow.org/
Sexual Behavior in Children: What's Normal?	http://presidioinc.com/newsletter/2000news/2000aug_normalbehavior.htm
First 9 Months	http://www.parentsplace.com/first9months/main/html
FertilityPlus	http://www.pinelandpress.com/toc.html
Planned Parenthood	http://www.plannedparenthood.org/
National Woman's Health Information Center	http://www.4woman.gov
National Campaign to Prevent Teen Pregnancy	http://www.teenpregnancy.org
Sexual and Reproductive Health Promotion	http://www.hc-sc.gc.ca/hppb/srh/

■ CHAPTER HIGHLIGHTS

- Sexuality includes the physical and psychological energy that individuals expend in attaining warmth, tenderness, sexual response, and love. Therefore each person is a sexual being from birth to death.

- Family sexuality is a complex, multifaceted phenomenon that is more than the sexual interaction of adult family members and includes the unplanned parent-child interactions in everyday family living.

- Family patterns, communication skills, parenting approaches, and family configuration strongly affect children's sexual development. Children learn attitudes toward sexuality within families; therefore parents should be provided with the information and skills to instruct children about sexual issues.

- Sexual behavioral norms and relationships vary by culture, religion, and society. Therefore careful assessment of cultural, religious, and family attitudes and beliefs is important.

- In the past decade, there has been an increase in the number of heterosexual and homosexual domestic partners, and professionals working with these families should provide judgment-free health care to families who choose these lifestyles.

- Sexuality issues vary during the family life course and for members at different developmental levels.

- Nursing assessment of family history is directly affected by how comfortable the nurse feels in discussing and teaching sexuality.

CRITICAL THINKING ACTIVITIES

1. As a nurse, how might you interact effectively with adolescents?

2. What are appropriate health promotion and screening activities nurses need to conduct with adolescents?

3. As a nurse, how would you respond to a child who asks you, "How does a baby get into my mommy's tummy?"

4. What advice would you give to the parents of Tommy, a 3-year-old who masturbates before falling asleep at naps and bedtime?

5. How is it possible to interact effectively and professionally with a client whose sexual values are very different from your own?

6. What sexual stereotypes affect your thinking (e.g., do you find it difficult to think about the elderly having sex?). How might you ensure that these stereotypes do not affect your professionalism?

7. What ethical obligations do you have when a client informs you that he or she has engaged in unsafe sexual practices? Are these obligations different if the client is a minor? What if the actions were criminal?

8. What role do nurses have in screening pregnant women for health practices that may influence fetal development? How might nurses develop rapport so that clients might be more willing to discuss unsafe activities (e.g., smoking during pregnancy)? Should clients be warned beforehand on limits to confidentiality?

9. How might nurses facilitate family communication about sexuality? What should be some limits on the nurse's responsibility in this area?

10. How might biases against gay men and lesbians manifest themselves in a nurse's behavior? What should a nurse do when she detects such biases?

REFERENCES

Alexander, B. (1981). Taking the sexual history. *American Family Physician, 23,* 147-153.

Allen, K. R., & Demo, D. H. (1995). The families of lesbian and gay men: A new frontier in family research. *Journal of Marriage and the Family, 57,* 111-127.

Amato, P. R., Johnson, D. R., Booth, A., & Rogers, S. J. (2003). Continuity and change in marital quality between 1980 and 2000. *Journal of Marriage and Family, 65,* 1-22,

American Academy of Pediatrics Committee on Adolescence. (2000). Adolescent pregnancy—Current trends and issues: 1998. *Pediatrics, 103,* 516-520.

Association of Reproductive Health Professionals. (2000). Mature sexuality: Patient realities and provider challenges. *Clinical Proceedings, 14,* 3-13.

Bancroft, J., & Guiterrez, P. (1996). Erectile dysfunction in men with and without diabetes mellitus. *Diabetic Medicine, 13,* 84-89.

Bancroft, J., Herbeneck, D., & Reynolds, M. (2003). Masturbation as a marker of sexual development. In J. Bancroft (Ed.), *Sexual development in childhood.* Bloomington: Indiana University Press.

Bor, R. (1991). The ABC of AIDS counseling. *Nursing Times, 87,* 32-55.

Bretschneider, J. G., & McCoy, N. L. (1988). Sexual interest and behavior in healthy 80 and 102 year olds. *Archives of Sexual Behavior, 17,* 109-130.

Brewster, K. (1994). Race differences in sexual activity among adolescent women: The role of neighborhood character-istics. *American Sociological Review, 59,* 408-424.

Brooks, D., & Goldberg, S. (2001). Gay and lesbian adoptive and foster care placement: Can they meet the needs of waiting children? *Social Work, 46,* 147-158.

Bumpass, L. L., Sweet, J. A., & Cherlin, A. (1991). The role of cohabitation in declining rates of marriage. *Journal of Marriage and the Family, 53,* 913-927.

Centers for Disease Control and Prevention. (2001). The global HIV and AIDS epidemic. *Morbidity and Mortality Weekly Report, 21,* 434-439.

Centers for Disease Control and Prevention. (2003). *HIV/AIDS update: A glance at the HIV epidemic.* Retrieved May 21, 2003, from http://www.cdc.gov/nchstp/od/news/At-a-Glance.pdf

Chilman, C. S. (1990). Promoting healthy adolescent sexuality. *Family Relations, 39,* 123-130.

Cunningham, F. G., Gant, N. F., Leveno, K. J., Gilstrap, L, C., III, Hauth, J. C., Wenstrom, K. D., et al. (2001). *Williams obstetrics* (21st ed.). Norwalk, CT: McGraw-Hill.

DeMaris, A., & Rao, K. V. (1992). Premarital cohabitation and subsequent marital stability in the United States: A re-assessment. *Journal of Marriage and the Family, 54,* 178-190.

Dickinson, C. (1990). The postpartum period. In R. Lichtman & S. Papera (Eds.), *Gynecology: Well-woman care* (pp. 383-405). Norwalk, CT: Appleton & Lange.

Dunn, M. E. (1990). Sexual health. In R. Lichtman & S. Papera (Eds.), *Gynecology: Well-woman care* (pp. 427-434). Norwalk, CT: Appleton & Lange.

Erikson, E. (1968). *Identity: Youth and crisis.* New York: Norton.

Flewelling, R. L., & Bauman, K. E. (1990). Family structure as a predictor of initial substance abuse and sexual intercourse in early adolescence. *Journal of Marriage and the Family, 52,* 171-180.

Friedrich, W. N., Fisher, J., Broughton, D., Houston, M., & Shafran, M. (1998). Normative sexual behavior in children: A contemporary sample [Electronic version]. *Pediatrics, 101,* e9.

Garofalo, R., Wolf, R. C., Kessel, S., Palfrey, S. J., & DuRant, R. H. (1998). The association between health risk behaviors and sexual orientation among a school-based sample of adolescents. *Pediatrics, 101,* 895-902.

Gordon, M. (2002). *Manual of nursing diagnosis* (10th ed.). St. Louis, MO: Mosby.

Gottmann, J. M. (1994). *Why marriages succeed or fail.* New York: Simon and Schuster.

Henderson, G. S., & Yasgur, B. S. (2002). *Women at risk: The HPV epidemic and your cervical health.* New York: Avery Books.

Hoem, B., & Hoem, J. M. (1992). The disruption of marital and non-marital unions in contemporary Sweden. In J. Trussell, R. Hankinson, & J. Tilton (Eds.), *Demographic applications of event history analysis* (pp. 61-63). Oxford: Clarendon Press.

House, C. (1997). Navajo warrior women: An ancient tradition in a modern world. In S. Jacobs, W. Thomas, & S. Lang, (Eds.), *Two-spirit people* (pp. 223-227). Urbana: University of Illinois Press.

Hutchinson, M. K. (1998). Something to talk about: Sexual communication between young women and their partners. *Journal of Obstetrics, Gynecology, and Neonatal Nursing, 27,* 127-133.

Hyde, J. S., Delamater, J., & Hewitt, E. (1998). Sexuality and the dual career couple: Multiple roles and sexual functioning. *Journal of Family Psychology, 12,* 354-368.

Jackson, G. (1999). Erectile dysfunction and cardiovascular disease. *International Journal of Clinical Practice, 53,* 363-368.

Kaiser Family Foundation. (1998). *Sex in the 90s: Kaiser Family Foundation ABC Television 1998 survey of Americans on sex and sexual health.* Menlo Park, CA: The Henry J. Kaiser Family Foundation.

Kann, L., Kinchen, S. A., Williams, B. I., Ross, J. G., Lowry, R., Grun Baum, J. A., et al. (2000). Youth risk behavior surveillance—United States, 1999. *MMWR. CDC Surveillance Summaries, 49,* 1-32.

Keith, J. B., McCreary, C., Collins, K., Smith, C. P., & Bernstein, I. (1991). Sexual activity and contraceptive use among low-income urban black adolescent females. *Adolescence, 26,* 769-785.

King, B. M., & Lorusso, J. (1997). Discussion in the home about sex: Different recollections by parents and children. *Journal of Sex and Marital Therapy, 23,* 52-60.

King, P., & Annen-Ricks, N. (2002). Growth and development of the newborn. In N. L. Potts & B. L. Mandleco, (Eds.), *Pediatric nursing: Caring for children and their families* (pp. 165-191). New York: Delmar.

Kinsey, A. C., Pomeroy, W. B., & Martin, C. E. (1948). *Sexual behavior in the human male.* Philadelphia: W. B. Saunders.

Laumann, E. O., Masi, C., & Zuckerman, E. W. (1994). The social organization of sexuality: Sexual practices in the United States. Chicago: University of Chicago Press.

Leppert, P. C. (1997). Sexuality. In P. C. Leppert & F. M. Howard (Eds.), *Primary care for women.* Philadelphia: Lippincott-Raven.

Lowdermilk, D. L., Perry, S. E., & Bobak, I. M. (2000). *Maternity & gynecologic care* (7th ed.). St. Louis, MO: Mosby.

Lytton, H., & Romney, D. M. (1991). Parents' differential socialization of boys and girls: A meta-analysis. *Psychological Bulletin, 109,* 267-296.

Mandleco, B., & McCoy, J. K. (2002). Growth and development of the adolescent. In N. L. Potts & B. L. Mandleco (Eds.), *Pediatric nursing: Caring for children and their families.* New York: Delmar.

Martinson, F. M. (1994). *The sexual life of children.* Westport, CT: Bergin & Garvey.

Masters, W. H., Johnson, V. E., & Kolodny, R. C. (1982). *Human sexuality.* Boston: Little, Brown.

Maurer, L. (1999). Transgressing sex and gender: Deconstruction zone ahead? *SIECUS Report, 27,* 14-21.

Money, J. (1987). Sin, sickness or status: Homosexual gender identity and psychoneuroendocrinology. *American Psychologist, 42,* 384-389.

Murray, R., & Zentner, J. (2001). *Health assessment and promotion strategies throughout the lifespan* (7th ed.). Stamford, CT: Appleton & Lange.

Norris, A., Ford, K., Shyu, Y., & Schork, M. (1996). Heterosexual experiences and partnerships of urban, low income African-American and Hispanic youth. *Journal of Acquired Immune Deficiency Syndrome and Human Retrovirology, 11,* 288-300.

Okami, P. (1995). Childhood exposure to parental nudity, parent-child co-sleepings and "primal scene": A review of clinical opinion and empirical evidence. *The Journal of Sex Research, 32,* 51-64.

Olds, S. O., Weiland Ladewig, P. A., & London, M. L. (2000). *Clinical handbook: Maternal newborn nursing: A family and community-based approach* (6th ed.). Upper Saddle River, NJ: Prentice Hall Health.

Oliver, M. B., & Hyde, J. S. (1993). Gender differences in sexuality: A metaanalysis. *Psychological Bulletin, 114,* 29-51.

Olson, D. H., & Olson, A. K. (2000). *Empowering couples: Building on your strengths.* Minneapolis, MN: Life Innovations, Inc.

Patterson, C. (1995). Sexual orientation and human development: An overview. *Developmental Psychology, 31,* 3-11.

Pillitteri, A. (1999). *Maternal & child health nursing* (3rd ed.). Philadelphia: Lippincott Williams & Wilkins.

Pletsch, P. K., Johnson, M. K., Tosi, C. B., Thurston, C. A., & Riesch, S. K. (1991). Self-image among early adolescents: Revisited. *Journal of Community Health Nursing, 8,* 215-231.

Raffaelli, M., Bogenschneider, K., & Flood, M. F. (1998). Parent-teen communication about sexual topics. *Journal of Family Issues, 19,* 315-333.

Reeder, S. J., Martin, L. L., & Koniak-Griffin, D. (1997). *Maternity nursing: Family, newborn, and women's health care* (18th ed.). Philadelphia: Lippincott.

Reid, P. T., & Bing, V. M. (2000). Sexual roles of girls and women: An ethnocultural lifespan perspective. In C. B. Travis & J. W. White (Eds.), *Sexuality, society and feminism* (pp. 141-166). Washington, DC: American Psychological Association.

Reiss, I. L. (1986). *Journey into sexuality: An exploratory voyage*. Englewood Cliffs, NJ: Prentice Hall.

Riche, M. F. (1991, March). The future of the family. *American Demographics, 13,* 43-46.

Rosal, M. C., Downing, J., Littman, A. B., & Ahern, D. K. (1994). Sexual functioning post-myocardial infarction: Effects of beta-blockers, psychological status and safety information. *Journal of Psychosomatic Research, 38,* 655-667.

Ross, M. W., Channon-Little, L. D., & Simon-Rosser, B. R. (2000). *Sexual health concerns: Interviewing and history taking for health practitioners* (2nd ed.). Philadelphia: Davis.

Ryan, G. (2000). Childhood sexuality: A decade of study. Part one: Research and curriculum development. *Child Abuse and Neglect, 24,* 33-48.

Santrock, J. W. (2001). *Adolescence* (8th ed.). Dubuque, IA: Brown & Benchmark.

Segraves, R., & Segraves, K. (1995). Human sexuality and aging. *Journal of Sex Education and Therapy, 21,* 88-102.

Sexuality Information and Education Council of the United States (SIECUS). (1999). *Guidelines for comprehensive sexuality education*. New York: Author.

Sheehy, G. (1995). *New passages: Mapping your life across time*. New York: Random House.

Sloane, E. (2002). *Biology of women*. New York: Delmar.

Smock, P. (2000). Cohabitation in the United States. *Annual Review of Sociology, 26,* 1-20.

Stein, T. J. (1996). Child custody and visitation. The rights of lesbian and gay parents. *Social Service Review, 70,* 435-450.

Sternberg, R. (1997). Construct validation of a triangular love scale. *European Journal of Social Psychology, 27,* 313-335.

Strommen, E. F. (1989). *You're a what: Family member reactions to the disclosure of homosexuality. Homosexuality and the family*. New York: Hayworth Press.

Swenson, I. E., Foster, B., & Asay, M. (1995). Menstruation, menarche, and sexuality in the public school curriculum: School nurses' perceptions. *Adolescence, 30,* 677-683.

Thompson, E., & Collela, U. (1992, May). Cohabitation and marital stability: Quality or commitment? *Journal of Marriage and the Family, 54,* 259-267.

Thornton, A. (1991). Influence of the marital history of parents on the marital and cohabitational experiences of children. *American Journal of Sociology, 96,* 868-894.

Thornton, A., & Camburn, D. (1989). Religious participation and adolescent sexual behavior and attitudes. *Journal of Marriage and the Family, 51,* 641-652.

Trussell, J., Rodriguez, G., & Vaughn, B. (1992). Union dissolution in Sweden. In J. Trussell, R. Hankinson, & J. Tilton (Eds.), *Demographic applications of event history analysis* (pp. 38-60). Oxford: Clarendon Press.

U.S. Bureau of the Census (2000). *Statistical abstract of the United States: 2000*. Washington, DC: U.S. Government Printing Office.

U.S. Department of Health and Human Services. (1999). *A national strategy to prevent teen pregnancy: Annual report 1998-99*. Washington, DC: Author.

Ventura, S., Curtin, S., & Matthews, T. (1998). *Teenage birth rates in the United States: National and state trends, 1990-1996*. Hyattsville, MD: U. S. Department of Health and Human Services.

Westheimer, R., & Lopater, S. (2001). *Human sexuality: A psychosocial perspective*. Philadelphia: Lippincott Williams and Wilkins.

White, S. D., & DeBlassie, R. R. (1992). Adolescent sexual behavior. *Adolescence, 27,* 183-191.

Woodson, S. A. (1997). Sexual health across the lifespan. *Association of Women's Health, Obstetric and Neonatal Nurses Lifelines, 1,* 34.

16

Family Routines, Rituals, Recreation, and Rules

Betty Williams Fomby

Family
Is family a common term
And what does it truly mean?
A family is being there no matter what.
A family is what stands by you
When no one else seems to know you're there.
A family supports you and encourages you
When things go right or wrong.
A family teaches you
What belongingness truly means.
Everyone has a family;
Each one a special kind.

— Betty W. Fomby

OBJECTIVES

On completion of this chapter, the reader will be able to do the following:

1. Explain the importance of building family capacity for improving family health through routines, recreation, rules, and rituals to enhance family strength and unity.

2. Describe how the concepts of family routines, recreation, rules, and rituals can be used to empower families and transform behavior into health-promoting family actions.

3. Analyze the impact of encouraging families to use meaningful patterns and resources, namely family routines, rituals, recreation, and rules that are within the family's lived experience to achieve higher levels of family health.

4. List ways that the family health nurse may use family routines, rituals, recreation, and rules in collaboration with families to re-imagine and transform their health and healing experiences.

Although family routines and rituals are extensively discussed, practicing nurses, nurse educators, and nurse researchers have not used these concepts widely in practice (Denham, 2002). Although the terms *ritual* and *routine* are used in the literature of various disciplines, all too often the meanings are not clearly differentiated. The arbitrary use of these concepts makes application difficult. In many disciplines such as anthropology, sociology, family therapy, and the family life specialty, the concepts of family routines and rituals have been widely discussed, but few studies conducted by nurses have investigated the relationship between family routines and promotion of family health (Denham, 2002).

A lack of attention to the concepts of family routines and family rituals creates a gap in knowledge regarding the potential for assessment of family health, development of therapeutic interventions, and evaluation of family health outcomes. This chapter describes how the family health nurse can use family routines, rituals, recreation, and rules to collaborate with families to empower them to enhance their capacity to transform these family activities into healthier behaviors.

Resources used to create the chapter are from both research and contemporary literature. The use of both types of literature will increase the awareness of the family health nurse on how to use historical and present-day writings to teach families the importance of family routines, family rituals, family recreation, and family rules in promoting family health.

Family Routines for Health Promotion

Maintaining family routines such as family rituals, family recreation, and family rules is essential to promoting healthy families. Box 16-1 presents a comparison of family routines, rituals, recreation, rules, and traditions to distinguish among the five concepts. As shown in the box, routines are regular, repetitive activities; rituals are actions intentionally performed by multiple family members with great consistency, which can be recalled, discussed, and taught; family recreation is engagement in acts selected by families during leisure time; and rules are stated expected behaviors that have consequences.

A *ritual* is any repeated, shared activity that has *significant* meaning for family members. This is different from a *routine,* which is a repeated patterned activity that *may or may not have any special meaning.* Family routines may change as family members continue to interact with other subsystems. Families benefit from both predictable and special routines. Routines usually include regular times for doing homework, doing chores, eating meals together, and going to bed. Having

---

> ### BOX 16-1   Definitions of Family Routines, Family Rituals, Family Recreation, Family Rules, and Family Traditions
>
> *Family routines* are observable, repeated activities practiced by family members that occur with expected regularity (Boyce, Jensen, & Peacock, 1983).
>
> *Family rituals* are actions intentionally performed by multiple family members with great consistency that can be recalled, discussed, and taught (Denham, 1997; Fiese, 1995).
>
> *Family recreation* is the engagement in acts or experiences selected by families during leisure time to promote satisfaction and renewal of family memberships (Bittner, 2000).
>
> *Family rules* are expected behaviors that are clearly stated, have defined consequences, and are discussed as a family until agreement is reached about why rules are important (Lofas, 2002).
>
> *Family traditions* are patterns of behavior passed down from generation to generation or started anew with beginning families. Traditions can remind family members of their ancestors, reinforce family principles, create good family memories, help give family members a sense of belonging, and bond families together (Cole, 2002).

---

regular medical examinations is also an important family routine.

Research Pertaining to Family Routines

Findings from a small number of research studies on the family suggest positive relationships between routines and health status (Denham, 1995, 1996, 1997, & 2002). Research conducted by Denham (1997) indicates that understanding the role that routines play in family health is useful for nursing practice. Three ethnographies were completed over a period of 5 years in two southeastern Appalachian Ohio counties. The purpose of the studies was to determine how families defined and practiced family health. Denham found that identification of family routines provides an organized structure for assessments, interventions, and outcome evaluations.

Denham (1997) reports that families and individuals had different characteristics, but all described health routines associated with dietary practices, sleep and rest patterns, activity, dependent care, avoidance behaviors, medical consultation, and health recovery. Specific domains were identified for each family health routine. For example, in the group of disadvantaged families, one category of family routines was identified as having family fun, especially on vacations, holidays, and special days; other categories were having and sharing humor, participating in individual/group activities, coping with chaos, and creating special family times.

Respondents reported that all family members strived to maintain the family routines but were flexible when changes were needed. As a result of changes in established routines, new patterns often emerged. Unique variations in family routines were found both between and within families. These variations were influenced by individual and family development and by individual traits. Other influences included family-of-origin experiences, family values, resources, culture, religion, tradition, and the overall family context.

It is interesting that respondents identified time as a critical influence on when and how routines were followed. These influences were identified as seasons, clock time, days of the week, scheduled events, and the family's developmental stage. Family routines were usually temporarily changed when family rituals such as holidays, celebrations, and traditional occasions were observed. These changes were acceptable, since family members regarded special events as ways to enjoy emotional and spiritual closeness and enhancement of family identity. An example of this is vacation time when new experiences and memories are shared.

The study by Denham (1997) showed that conflicts often arose when family practices differed from those of the family of origin. Greater harmony was reported when routines were consistent. These findings indicate that family routines have

the potential for organizing families such that family health nurses can determine specific family interventions related to family health needs, which are designed to have an impact on maintenance and promotion of family health. Outcomes of these interventions can be used to evaluate the importance of health policy and social activism.

Denham (1997) concludes that family routines may be useful in validating the capabilities and limitations of family members and in determining family strengths and supports to assess whether information and resources are sufficient for adherence to prescribed medical plans of care. Also, assessing family routines could be a way to identify family stressors, to determine the family's ability to perform health-enhancing behaviors, and to obtain information about characteristics that may influence health outcomes. Finally, findings from this study indicate that examination of family routines may also be a way to address national health objectives related to family health (Denham, 2002).

In a 2-year intervention group study to strengthen families, McDonald (2002) recruited 14 families to participate in the multifamily Family And System Theory (FAST) program. In this program, participants attended eight group sessions and monthly FASTWORKS sessions for 2 years. The activities and instructions for facilitating the multifamily groups were based on family therapy techniques. Positive outcomes of the study were reported. The study revealed that having family routines and rituals brings family members closer and reduces substance abuse risks over time. It was found that those families who eat together, stay together. At FAST research sessions, each family sat at a family-designated table and shared a meal. FAST research shows that the single best predictor of high SAT scores is eating a family meal and spending time together chatting and connecting over the food (McDonald, 2002).

Research conducted by Griswold (2002), a family life educator, shows that predictable routines and meaningful rituals are related to healthier outcomes, regardless of the cause of stress. On the basis of the reported research and a careful literature search, Griswold made the assumption that family recreation, rules, and rituals flow from established routines. Therefore each concept discussed in this chapter is viewed as a process of established family routines.

Maintaining family routines, such as enjoying family recreation and establishing family rules, is essential to promoting family health. For families with children, routines begin during the first days of life and continue to affect the relationship between parents and children throughout the life cycle.

Assessment of Family Routines

Family health nurses can use assessment of family routines to determine the capacity for improving family health behaviors, experience, transformation, and power inherent in a family. On the basis of the assessment data, the nurse can use family routines to emphasize family health and capacity building. In the assessment of family routines, the following basic areas should be considered:

1) Are the routines consistent? Children and other family members are most content when the same thing happens about the same time every day.

2) Are deviations from the routine explained? If plans change, do family members know ahead of time, and if possible, are explanations given?

In assisting families to enhance their capacity for improving family health behaviors, the family health nurse should assess the quality, level, and structure of family routines. Denham (2003) suggests that the core functional processes of caregiving, cathexis, celebration, change, connectedness, and coordination be assessed during completion of a thorough family assessment. Denham's book *Family Health Model: A Framework for Nursing* (2003) contains sample assessment questions and planning and an in-depth family assessment guide. Two shorter measurement tools for assessing family routines are the Family Routine Questionnaire (Venn & Woods-Cripe, 1999) and the Family Times and Routine Scale (FTRS), which is presented in Appendix 16-1 (McCubbin, McCubbin, & Thompson, 1987). Box 16-2 presents a family routine questionnaire adapted from Venn and Woods-Cripe (1997) that can be used to assess a family's routines.

The eight-item questionnaire can be used to open a dialogue about family routines. Each family

---

BOX 16-2 Family Routine Questionnaire

1. What routines or activities does the family enjoy?

2. What do all family members do during the family routine or activity?

3. What makes the routine or activity enjoyable for all family members?

4. How much time is spent in each routine or activity?

5. List the routines or activities the family likes most.

6. List the routines or activities the family likes least.

7. What are the expectations for all family members during the routine or activity?

8. What are the best times or locations that are most comfortable for family routines or activities?

Summation of Family Responses
  Routine:
  Family Member:
  Most Enjoyable Times:
  Least Enjoyable Times:

Adapted from Venn, M., & Woods-Cripe, J. (1997). Using daily routines as learning experiences. In E. S. Szanton (Ed.), *Creating child-centered programs for infants and toddlers* (pp. 105-115). Washington, DC: Children's Resources International, Inc.

---

member should first complete the questionnaire. After each member has completed an individual questionnaire, all the responses should be summarized by using the guide provided in Box 16-2. Once all forms are summarized, all family members should review the responses and make suggestions if changes are needed.

The FTRS is also a tool that can be used to assess family time together and routines that families adopt to indicate family integration and stability. This tool, developed by McCubbin, McCubbin, and Thompson (1987), is a 13-item instrument that measures the workday and leisure time and parental routines. Internal validity of the instrument was 0.88, and concurrent validity was good when correlated with other family scales. When the instrument is used, two scores are generated. One score measures the extent to which each routine is valid for the family, and the other measures the degree to which the family views the routine as important.

Increasing Family Capacity through Family Routines

Informing families about ways routines can be used to increase family health capacity for improving family health behaviors is an important function of the family health nurse. The strength of family routines to increase this family health capacity is validated by Jensen, Boyce, and Hartnett (1983), who state that family routines provide basic behavioral units that impart order and structure to the family's daily activities. Suggestions for creating capacity-enhancing family routines are provided in Box 16-3. Box 16-4 lists some examples of family routines. The family health nurse is encouraged to use the suggestions in these boxes to uncover the meaningful patterns and resources within the family's lived experience

---

BOX 16-4   Examples of Family Routines

1. Washing hands before eating
2. Having regular health check-ups
3. Having regular dental check-ups
4. Making regular time for doing homework
5. Doing household chores together
6. Giving thanks for the prepared family meal
7. Serving healthy, balanced nutritious meals
8. Going to bed at a specified time as a unit
9. Setting daily schedules for outside activities
10. Creating family message centers
11. Placing personal items where they are expected to be stored
12. Selecting clothes the night before work or school

Developed by Betty W. Fomby, PhD.

---

of health and healing, thus assisting families to increase their capacity to transform routines into healthier behaviors.

Family Rituals for Health Promotion

The benefits of family rituals, such as cohesiveness developed among family members, a sense of family pride, continuity, understanding, closeness, and love are evident in strong families and can be used for promoting family health. Family rituals are viewed as one avenue the family can use to help deal with the stresses of daily life.

The family health nurse, in emphasizing family capacity for transformation, should encourage families to negotiate the blending of customs from their own childhoods with new family rituals. However, the nurse should realize that rituals differ from family to family. In many families, rituals begin when children are added to the family. Despite differences in ethnic, religious, and socioeconomic backgrounds, rituals are common to family life.

In the family therapy literature, two basic types of family rituals are identified: secular rituals and

---

BOX 16-3   Suggestions for Creating Capacity-Enhancing Family Routines

1. Establish a consistent bedtime.
2. Make a routine of reading stories at bedtime.
3. Turn off the television 30 minutes before bedtime and have a short family talk.
4. Be consistent in seeing that prayers are said before going to bed.
5. Establish family mealtime.
6. Establish family talk time.
7. Establish daily chores to teach all family members that they are an integral part of the family.
8. Limit outside commitments such that they do not interfere with family time.

Adapted from Wallace (1999).

religious rituals. Secular rituals include relationships between individuals and collective ceremony, whereas in religious rituals a system of principles is used to describe and explain expected behavior (Moore & Myeroff, 1977).

In addition to the two basic types of rituals, Friesen (1990) has identified two other types of family rituals: transition rituals and healing rituals. Transition rituals are used by families to mark changes in the ongoing social structure and those occurring in the individual and family developmental life cycle. These family rituals define such change events as war and peace, the change of seasons, childbirth, transition to adolescence and/or young adulthood, graduation, leaving home, marriage, retirement, and death (Friesen, 1990).

An example of a transition ritual, which is practiced in the developmental stage of a family, is the wedding ceremony. For most families, the wedding ceremony is a particularly important event. In the wedding ceremony the parents give the bride to the groom, indicating their release of the daughter from the family of origin. Through their union, the bride and groom are recognized as having achieved independence, and the wedding marks the beginning of a new nuclear family. As a result of this act, the relationships with the family of origin change. The children now have autonomy and begin a new life together (Friesen, 1990).

Healing rituals are used when personal or relational healing is needed at various stages of human life. These rituals are an important part of the healing process. For example, losses sustained through death or divorce result in a need for healing. The support of a religious or faith community and the conduct of meaningful ceremonies are particularly important during times of loss. Suicides, deaths caused by violence or accidents, and pregnancy losses may especially call for healing rituals (Friesen, 1990).

Typology of Family Rituals

Family health nurses can benefit from the use of a typology of family rituals as they empower families to re-imagine and transform their family rituals to effect healing experiences. Included in the typology are explanations of four categories of families: under-ritualized families, rigidly

ritualized families, families with skewed rituals, and families with hollow rituals (Roberts, 1988).

In *under-ritualized* families, members neither celebrate nor mark transitions. For example, these families do not celebrate holidays and consequently do not experience the family togetherness that accompanies celebrations. For these families, family life often appears empty and distant.

In *rigidly ritualized* families, rituals are conducted in a very rigid manner and are not allowed to be changed regardless of developmental needs. These families tend to be overorganized, do many things together, do things precisely on time, eat out at the same places, and visit the same people. The family norms are rigid and unusually clear, and no deviations are allowed.

In families with *skewed rituals*, one particular ethnic or religious tradition is emphasized at the expense of other aspects of the family. Skewed ritualization is particularly a problem in mixed marriages in which one spouse may not wish to participate in the rituals of the other's cultural or religious tradition. For example, a Jew who marries a Christian may have considerable difficulty accommodating rituals associated with Christmas or Easter. Interpersonal conflict surrounding the practice of rituals often occurs in mixed marriages.

Rituals are *hollow* when people celebrate them out of a sense of obligation with little appreciation for the event or the process. Rituals become hollow when they lose their meaning, when the family does not adequately accommodate change, or when they become a burden and create stress for the family. They also lose their meaning and become hollow when only one person prepares for the rituals, and the other family members do not actively participate (Roberts, 1988).

Assessment of Family Rituals

The quality, level, and structure of family rituals may be assessed by use of measuring instruments (Wolin, Bennett, & Jacobs, 1988) or by observation of family dynamics. Assessments of families experiencing relationship problems can also be made by using the categories of under-ritualized, rigidly ritualized, skewed, and hollow in rituals (Roberts, 1988).

Two surveys to assess family rituals are used by families and family professionals to assess family rituals. The first reliable measure is the FTRS created by McCubbin, McCubbin, and Thompson (1987), which is presented in Appendix 16-1 at the end of the chapter. This easy-to-use survey contains 32 items. The second is the Family Ritual Questionnaire designed by Fiese and Kline (1993). This 56-item measurement tool is based on the Family Ritual Inventory designed by Wolin and Bennett (1984). Within the instrument are seven subscales used to measure dinner time, weekends, vacations, annual celebrations, religious holidays, and cultural and ethnic traditions. The internal consistency for the subscales ranges from 0.56 to 0.88. Over a 4-week period, the test-retest reliability was found to be 0.88 (Fiese and Kline, 1993).

The *Family Assessment Handbook* (Thomlison, 2002) is a useful guide to assessment of family rituals. The handbook uses theory that has been developed from evidence-based research for guiding practice decisions. This practical book presents the interplay of concepts, values, and skill dilemmas with the use of case studies from the author's practice experience. By developing a "family journal," the user can apply family systems thinking, theory, and concepts. This text addresses the need of professionals for an effective applied practice approach to changing social environments that can be used with ethnically and culturally diverse families. The author provides practical suggestions for both assessment and intervention activities within a multisystems framework (Thomlison, 2002).

The Typology of Rituals (Roberts, 1988) can also be used to assess family rituals. After determining the type of rituals practiced by the family, the family health nurse should plan interventions that will help structure family rituals that promote change and strengthen the family.

Research Pertaining to Family Rituals

Educators, clinicians, and researchers can benefit from research conducted to support the role of family rituals in providing structure for family-focused practice as the focus of family health nursing care moves away from provision of care with the service model to provision of care with the capacity enhancement model. Three examples of reported research studies that have been conducted to study the benefits of family rituals are presented.

A research study of 80 preschools that investigated the benefits of the family mealtime ritual demonstrated that regular family meals can sharpen a child's intellect and also revealed that mealtime conversation built vocabulary even more effectively than listening to stories or reading aloud (Beals & Tabor, 1995).

In a recent online poll in which people were asked how they feel about their family dinnertime habits, only 37.8% of the respondents answered that the family dinner is a firm ritual in their family's daily life and that they sit and eat together at the same time and table every night. Although 14.6% of the respondents stated that because of scheduling conflicts they rarely eat together as a family, 4% said that family mealtime is observed once a week with no exceptions. Eight percent of the respondents admitted to not always having family mealtime and cited other family rituals that the family regularly shares. Many families, 33.8%, said that although the family meal is a good idea, they wanted the flexibility to decide where and when they would have the dinner meal. A surprising 2.5% of the respondents felt that sit-down family dinners are not a part of their family's lifestyle and that everyone is expected to fend for himself or herself (Wallace, 1999).

Research on family mealtime reveals that families who take time to eat together are twice as likely to eat five servings of fruits and vegetables and are less likely to consume excessive amounts of fried food and carbonated beverages (Reinhart, 2002). These families also eat a diet higher in fiber, calcium, iron, vitamin C, and B vitamins. Additionally, children who eat with their families have higher grades, better test scores, a more diverse vocabulary, and a greater sense of belonging (Reinhart, 2002).

Research is needed to investigate the relationship between family rituals and chronic disease outcomes. For example, Fiese (2000) examined how family rituals may protect children with asthma from anxiety-related symptoms. In a sample of 86 families, the comparison groups, 43 children with asthma and 43 healthy children, completed measures of anxiety and health. Their parents completed measures of stress, family rituals, and family health. Fiese concluded that family rituals may serve a protective function for children with asthma under conditions of increased family stress.

Earlier, Fiese (1995) had investigated the association between family rituals and adolescent identity across two generations. In this study, a total of 77 families with one adolescent member completed the Family Ritual Questionnaire. In addition to the family questionnaire, the adolescents also completed a measure of self-esteem. Factor analysis yielded shared representation of family rituals across two generations, with one factor loading on the symbolic qualities of family rituals and the second factor loading on the routine aspects of family rituals. A positive relationship between family rituals and adolescent identity was found.

Increasing Family Capacity through Family Rituals

In fostering family capacity, the family health nurse can suggest many activities such as family mealtime; a family reunion; having a weekly family night; always saying "I love you"; and activities related to family unity, learning, culture, nature, physical fitness or sports, and family preparedness. New ritual activities such as instilling a passion for books by reading aloud together, planning a birthday tribute for a favorite famous person, or commemorating a national event can be established.

Family Mealtime

A most important family ritual is family mealtime. A generation ago, many American families sat down to eat with their families every night at a given hour. All family members knew and respected the rule of family mealtime and adjusted their schedules so that nothing interfered with them being at the dinner table promptly at the appointed hour. Mealtime was a valued and pleasant time when family members looked forward to being together as a family. What has happened to family mealtime in the new millennium?

Today, in many families, the phrase *family meal* has become almost synonymous with commitment to family. For a family to get together for a meal, every family member must make it a priority.

Family members cannot allow band practice, a television show, or a late commute interfere. An astonishing 66% of families eat dinner while also watching television or videos (Wallace, 1999), which allows little time for family conversation.

Family mealtime is often the only time during the whole day when family members are in the same room having a conversation, says Doherty, author of *The Intentional Family* (1997). According to Doherty, mealtime becomes a time when the family's culture gets created. A family meal provides a natural environment in which basic courtesies are taught, such as "Please," "Thank you," and "Keep your mouth closed when you chew." At the family meal table, wisdom and tales are passed between family members, and arguments and conflicts are resolved as a unit.

In many television commercials advertising food, the family is sitting together eating as a family unit. Not only are holiday family meals shown, but also breakfast, lunch, and dinner meals. Popular movies often show families eating together. In these media, family members are seen smiling and sharing.

Many families believe that the family dinner is a good idea but not worth the hassle. Fast food restaurants are now the scene for meals, with play stations and other offerings serving as distractions.

Although many families view family mealtime as a hassle and have family schedules that do not allow time for family meals, family mealtime does not have to be elaborate. It is not realistic to envision a happy family eating a three-course, perfectly balanced meal. A family can have a sandwich and a salad or scrambled eggs and cheese, as long as the meal is nutritious. The time together at mealtime is much more important than the table setting.

Unfortunately, some families have gradually moved away from shared dinner rituals altogether. Even for those who rarely or never experienced it, the family dinner endures as a powerful family ritual that functions as a symbol of family unity. Box 16-5 provides a guide to assist families in establishing regular family mealtime.

Family Reunion

Another important ritual, the family reunion, serves to unify and strengthen family ties. The ritual of family reunion serves as a time for family members to validate their membership in the family

BOX 16-5 Ground Rules for Family Mealtime

1. Attendance is not optional. Set aside a special time and encourage family members to adjust outside commitments.
2. Turn off the television and videos.
3. Avoid having distractions that limit conversation.
4. Do not use this time to lecture, scold, or squabble.
5. Make mealtime a happy and memorable time together, so that all family members anticipate the coming together as a family unit.
6. Eat together as often as possible and make the time spent together pleasant
7. Have family members assist with the preparation of the meal.
8. Alternate the family mealtime. Be flexible in scheduling time but persistent that at least one meal is spent together as a family unit. The key is flexibility.

From Wallace (1999).

constellation and to introduce children to members they have not met. In many families the family reunion provides a time for sharing and caring and is so valued a ritual that it is repeated year after year.

A reunion is defined as a gathering of relatives, friends, or associates after a period of separation (Laird, 2002). Most family reunion activities require planning to get them up and running. The focus of the family reunion is to bring family members closer together. Family members should work together to make the reunion a fun time of sharing and valuing family unity. A theme may be included in the planning. T-shirts printed with the family name, the family crest or symbols of the family character, and the date and the year may be a standard feature of a family reunion.

Having a theme and/or items for special family recognition such as T-shirts can act as an ice-breaker for attendees who do not know each other. When the reunion is planned, someone can be assigned to take a lot of pictures or a professional photographer can be hired. Pictures will serve as

mementoes of the reunion and will make sure that memories stay fresh. Photographs can be mailed or scanned into a computer and sent out by e-mail. Helpful tips for planning a family reunion can be found on the website about reunions listed in the Website Resources box at the end of the chapter.

Two rituals often practiced at family reunions are saying a family prayer and playing traditional music. The ritual of all members dressing alike ensures that no distinctions are made among family members who are professionals, laborers, or unemployed.

In the southern region of the United States, the annual family reunion is a greatly anticipated ritual. In many African American families, members travel from long distances at great expense just to attend a family reunion. For these families, family reunions are often synchronized with the ritual of an annual church revival.

Family Night

The value of family night as a health-promoting ritual should be recognized if family health nurses are to facilitate the use of meaningful patterns and resources within the family's lived experience of health and healing. Family night can be an effective family ritual during which all members come together to participate in an activity each week. During the family night activity, each family member should take an active role. If a preteen child is not participating, the rules can be changed and he or she can be allowed to plan the meeting and dictate the activity.

There are many ways to hold a family night, depending on the family's goals and temperament. Many families hold a business meeting first, in which they do the weekly scheduling, make announcements everyone should hear, recognize achievements, and assign chores on a rotating basis. It is also a good time to work out family problems. A family might use the meeting to devise new rules to handle curfew problems or to establish and assign a new chore. Members might work as a family to decide how to cut the budget to afford a family vacation.

After the business meeting, many families take advantage of this opportunity to teach children a brief lesson. This can be a spiritual lesson on topics such as prayer, the value of scriptures, or making moral choices. It can also be a practical lesson, such as teaching children how to plan their own budget or savings activities.

Family nights can seem like a lot of work, but if everyone shares in the responsibility, there is not much for each member to do. Even a 3-year-old, paired with an adult or teenager, can help out. The jobs can be rotated so that no one gets stuck with the dirty work every time and everyone grows a little. To help families get started having productive family night activities, the family health nurse may suggest the following roles:

Director: The director checks with everyone to be sure plans are in progress and makes sure that all family members agree on the activities.

Conductor: The conductor can also be the director. He or she welcomes each person to the meeting and directs the evening, explaining what is happening and who is in charge of each part.

Music Leader: The music leader chooses opening and closing songs, conducts, and maybe teaches a new song. Plans can be made for family members to play instruments or sing a solo.

Teacher: The teacher plans and presents the lesson. Younger children can also teach a lesson if they are assisted by parents or teens.

Activity Chairman: The activity chairman plans the fun part of the night.

Refreshment Chairman: The refreshment chairman selects the food and drink to be served, shops for ingredients, and prepares the food alone or with recruited assistants. The refreshment chairman should have a budget, and this job should be rotated fairly, even among boys and dads (Bittner, 2000).

The family health nurse can assist small families to explore ways to combine some of these jobs. The details can be worked out and a chart can be made to ensure that everyone gets a chance to do every job. It is important to make this activity a sharing time with no preaching or judgment (Bittner, 2000).

During this activity, it is important to listen to each opinion respectfully. When teaching families how to conduct family night, the family health nurse should be sure to use teaching and praise skills liberally. The family can be reminded that a ritual is what helps the family cope with the most harrowing of life's transitions in such a way that they can know that they have lived.

Other Family Rituals that Promote Health

Other family rituals can be used to promote family health. For example, Biziou (1999) suggests the family ritual of saying "I love you," cultural activities, and nature activities. Ovard (1998) suggests family unity activities, learning activities, physical activities, family preparedness, and volunteering as a family. As the family nurse collaborates with families to re-imagine and transform their health and healing experiences, family rituals can be used to help them to achieve this goal.

Saying "I Love You"

Parents should be encouraged to make a habit of telling their children "I love you." Love and affection can be shown by giving children plenty of hugs or just holding their hands. Parents can write poems or letters that express special love feelings to children and save the poems or letters in a special box, or they can make up a silly song of praise. No matter what their age, all children love to be loved. Parents need to say "I love you" often and mean it (Biziou, 1999).

Cultural Activities

Learning about the family and regional culture is an important family activity. Family night can be used to teach the family about different types of music, arts and crafts projects, poems, or ethnic dances. A family may want to write a script for a family play about cultural differences. A family can visit nearby historical sites and learn about the pioneers in their region. A family can learn about how other religions or cultures celebrate holidays around the world and about their own heritage and genealogy by visiting museums, obtaining material from the library, and attending local cultural events (Biziou, 1999).

Nature Activities

During family activities, members can acquire an appreciation for nature by learning about the area's natural resources and planning and engaging in recreational activities at nearby mountains, lakes, or caves. Some excellent nature activities are growing a garden, planting fruit trees, making snow sculptures, gathering seashells, and bird watching. Family members can learn about conservation and plan ways to conserve energy in the home (Biziou, 1999).

Family Unity Activities

Long-lasting effects of family togetherness can be realized by establishing family unity activities while children are young. For example, family night can be used to address home problems in such a way that challenges that threaten the harmony of the home can be addressed without singling out individual family members. The lessons should be kept short and appropriate for age. Young children may need lessons on sharing or understanding individuals who are different, whereas older children may be ready for a family discussion on how to treat classmates or peers from a different culture (Ovard, 1998).

Other family rituals may include attending public events such as festivals and cultural or holiday celebrations. An example of such an event that may promote family unity is the Mardi Gras ("Fat Tuesday") celebration in New Orleans or Cinco de Mayo for Hispanic families. Large family groups take to the streets with food, beverages, strollers, and wheelchairs; businesses and all schools including colleges close to allow families to enjoy this annual ritual. Other examples of public events that can be considered unifying family activities and appeal to people of all ages are military air shows, parades, and county fairs.

Learning Activities

Family learning activities might include cooking, learning magic tricks, going to the library, or doing puzzles together (Doherty & Carlson, 2002). These activities do not always need to include a serious discussion. Important concepts of fair play, sharing, pride of winning, and caring can be taught during these lessons. Family unity can be strengthened when members play board or card games together. Doherty and Carlson (2002) suggest planning a grandparent "play date" if grandparents live nearby. This togetherness can last even when the children become adults. One family started a ritual of playing games while the children were young, and now more than 50 years later, members of this family continue to look forward to and value the time spent playing games together. This ritual has now been carried out by two generations. Families that started attending football games together and enjoying tailgating at sports events are continuing this ritual, which now includes married families, children, and great grandchildren. It is clear that family rituals are the ties that bind generations (Ovard, 1998).

Physical Activities

Families can learn to play a new sport together. Holding a family athletic competition in which prizes are given to the winners can teach important lessons about sportsmanship. Families can teach children about bike safety by going on a family bike ride. Having a family exercise program can teach children about physical fitness and health promotion (Ovard, 1998). Families without children or families in which children no longer live at home can plan special times to walk together.

Family Preparedness Activities

Families can plan activities that prepare them to respond appropriately to a fire, a natural disaster, or human-initiated disaster. Families should ensure that all family members know the fire escape plan and what to do in other types of emergencies. Families can practice responding to an emergency by having drills or creating plans to make contact with each other in an emergency or disaster. Families can also work together to create a survival kit or make a list of emergency telephone numbers. Children can be taught about CPR, choking, bleeding, and water safety (Ovard, 1998).

Volunteering as a Family

In families with children, making a difference as volunteers can be an opportunity for parents to teach children charity and caring for others. Working along with a parent in a meal program for the homeless or elderly can provide children with a warm feeling of having done something for someone other than themselves (Ovard, 1998). Encouraging a young child to help someone—for example, to volunteer to walk a blind person to the store each week—may instill in that child a lifetime habit of providing service to others.

Influence of Family Variations on Family Rituals

Family rituals are greatly influenced by variations in family types, culture, developmental stage, and socioeconomic status. Many families have celebrations in which they observe holidays or occasions that are widely practiced by their culture and are special to them as a family. Occasions such as funerals, weddings, baptisms, bar mitzvahs; religious holidays such as Christmas, Easter and Passover; and secular holidays such as New Year's Day, the Fourth of July, and Halloween are or may include family celebrations. These rituals are observed specifically by the cultural groups and allow family members an opportunity to identify themselves with the larger family group. As family rituals are repeated over time, they contribute to family stability.

Family rituals carry religious and cultural meaning that has been passed down through many generations. In this sense, rituals maintain the traditional forms of culture and religious experience and help people link the events of the past with their experience of the present.

Regardless of family type, developmental stage, culture, or socioeconomic status, rituals provide support during periods of mourning such as those observed after a death (Scheff, 1979). This is an important function of rituals. During periods of mourning, family members join with each other to bear each others' burdens; they may gather for a funeral or memorial service, share food, wear certain clothes, and express certain words of comfort. During periods of loss, the observation of mourning rituals may include sharing meals or visiting each other, which may reduce isolation and loneliness.

In the Jewish tradition, the bar mitzvah is a classic example of a family ritual that is also a religious ritual. During the bar mitzvah, a young man must demonstrate several competencies, such as competency in the sacred language, Hebrew, and ability to lead the congregation in religious services for a short period. The family uses this occasion to express unity with the religious community and to bestow gifts on the young man to acknowledge his new status in that community.

Another example of a family ritual that is also religious ritual is the Thanksgiving holiday. On Thanksgiving, some individuals attend religious services in conjunction with a national celebration. The event is also marked as a special holiday by preparation of special foods. The turkey dinner served on Thanksgiving has traditionally represented gratitude. The Thanksgiving ritual has become a national custom in which religious and personal symbols and practices are interwoven (Friesen, 1990).

Throughout the family cycle, many important events and rituals that take place may not be recognized as rituals. However, even if unrecognized, rituals are important and useful ways of assisting individuals and families in dealing with transitions and losses, bringing about healing, and transmitting values from generation to generation. The effective use of rituals is one avenue for strengthening families and creating a family environment in which personal well-being is enhanced.

To effect empowerment and transformation and to foster family capacity for using recreation, rules, and rituals, the family health nurse needs to be cognizant of the influences of variations in family types, culture, developmental stage, and socioeconomic status on each activity. Each of these factors greatly affects the family's ability to achieve maximum well-being.

Family Recreation for Health Promotion

Understanding the benefits of family recreation time can assist the family health nurse in using recreation activities to foster family capacity building. The benefits of family recreation cannot be minimized. Family recreation can serve as a beneficial force that provides family members with common goals and experiences that strengthen family bonds. However, if family members participate in individual activities that exclude other members, it can separate members for extended periods.

The changing American lifestyle is greatly influenced by an increase in work time, an increase in financial resources, the lure of exciting vacation locations seen on television, and the multiple family fun activities exploding over the Internet. As a result, families are bombarded with opportunities for family recreation. A search of the Internet revealed that opportunities are available for family golfing, family camping, and family instruction in flying an airplane, but when is an ideal time to participate in fun, creative activities with the family? For many family members, an ideal time may depend on the following conditions:

1) When it is not raining and not too hot or cold outside
2) When family members have had plenty of sleep the night before
3) When that big project at the office has finally been completed
4) When all of the phone messages have been answered
5) When no one has a runny nose, a dirty bottom, or an upset stomach
6) When older children are not involved in another activity and are actually home

The family health nurse should help families to identify an ideal time to begin family recreation activities. It should be recognized that parents and other family members do not plan to neglect engaging in family activities, but it can easily happen. Often, families have good intentions but a lack of time to carry them out. The family health nurse can help families to plan for short periods of recreation, as well as large blocks of time to do special things together. For example, a family can plan a pleasant and relaxing 2-day vacation that gives each family member enough memories to last another year. A family can plan one day of just spending time together doing things that children like to do; family members might go to the mall or a park together. Although an adolescent may not appreciate a parent hanging out in the mall, younger children like to spend this time with their parents.

Suggestions for adding a little laughter to that special day or any day include the following:

1) Spend time looking through old scrapbooks and pictures.
2) Go see a funny movie together or read a funny book aloud.
3) Cut out cartoons from the paper and put them on the refrigerator door.
4) Play games that children want to play. Don't be ashamed to play softball even if you can't hit the ball. The game will be even funnier to them.

5) Be vulnerable: talk about the silly things various family members have done. Learn to laugh. Did something funny happen to any family member today? Share the experience and laugh together.

Types of Family Recreation

There are many fun and easy ways to create family memories that last a lifetime, and although building memories does take time, it does not necessarily take large blocks of time. Most memories cherished by a family happen in small bits of time spent together.

Family Vacations

The family vacation is a great form of family recreation that can be used to enhance family capacity to promote health. During this time, there are no other outside-of-the-family activities that require the attention of parents, children, and other family members. Full attention can be given to enjoying the vacation activities and meeting the needs of the family to confirm the feelings of togetherness and unity.

When working with families who are planning vacations, the family health nurse should provide instruction regarding safety, immunizations, identification records, and emergency procedures. Additionally, families should be encouraged to purchase a first aid kit to be used to handle minor emergencies.

The family health nurse can instruct families with children who plan car trips to include activities for the children while traveling, be flexible in the timing of rest stops, and bring along healthy snacks for in between meals. Before beginning a trip that includes driving to the vacation site, the estimated length of time should be explained to all members. Planning plenty of learning activities and games will keep the children entertained and prevent restlessness during long rides. It can be suggested that a family bring along regular school notebooks that can be used by the children as travel journals in which they can make notes and paste pictures.

If a vacation that covers several days or a week is not feasible for a family, shorter but interesting trips can be planned. These vacation destinations might include state parks and historical sites.

Information about such places can be obtained from a tourism website or the local community, county, or state calendar of events. Family vacations should provide family members with memories that last and increase the bond between family members. Taking pictures of family activities during vacation will preserve cherished memories. Family vacation plans should be discussed with all family members, especially the children, before the plans are finalized. All family members should be encouraged to voice their opinions about the vacation plans. The best time to get input from all members is during a family meeting when members listen carefully to each other's comments. Once comments are heard, the family should be flexible in making adjustments so that the vacation is an enjoyable time for all family members.

Movies, Videos, Television, and Computers

As the family health nurse works with families to foster family capacity, how the family uses family movies, videos, television shows, and computers in family recreation should be carefully examined. Families need advice for turning movies, videos, and television into interactive learning opportunities. The family health nurse can advise families that the most appropriate types of family movies, videos, and television shows are ones that are devoid of violence and conflict. Although the activities selected should be entertaining, they should also have some intrinsic value. Children should be guided as to what shows are appropriate for them to watch on television and blocks should be placed on channels that children are not to watch. The Research Synopsis presents a study about families who do not watch television.

RESEARCH SYNOPSIS

TV-FREE FAMILIES

A national survey was conducted from February to March 2000 to investigate families that never watch TV (Brock, 2002). There were four research questions:

1) What portion of the American population does and does not watch television?
2) Of those who do not, who are they?
3) Why do they turn the television off?
4) What makes them tick?
5) Are they recluses or antiestablishment types as many think?

Of the 365 families from 43 states that responded, 280 returned the survey. Most are in their thirties, are married with two children, have college degrees, and earn $60,000 to $80,000 per year (range, less than $20,000 to $130,000 and up); two thirds have religious affiliations; and 41% send their children to public schools. It was found that 98% of American adults and families spend 40% of their leisure time "sitting and watching" television. Among the families that are television-free, many have about an hour of meaningful conversation per day with their children (national average, 38 minutes per week). The majority of parents said their children "never or rarely" complain about the lack of television or pressure them to buy brand names and popular toys. Eighty percent felt their marriages are stronger because of the absence of television, thus allowing for more cuddle time. More than half of children who did not watch TV got all A's in school. It was reported that in most homes the computer does not take over the role of television. Although 98% of respondents own a computer, parents reported that only 1 to 3 hours of recreational time is spent on the computer per week. Seventy percent of parents felt their children got along better without television and had fewer sibling fights. A child with attention-deficit/hyperactivity disorder, whose family was advised by their pediatrician to remove the television from the home, blossomed and took tremendous strides in development.

Brock, B. J. (2002). *TV free families: Are they lola granolas, normal joes or high and holy snots?* Retrieved November 16, 2002, from http://www.tvturnoff.org/brocksumm.htm

The family can be instructed that the age of computers has provided another means of recreation that must be monitored closely for appropriateness. Although the Internet opens up a vista of information, it also provides an opportunity for children to receive messages and information that can be unsafe. Parents should monitor a child's activity on the computer and periodically review e-mail messages received and sites entered by the child. Planning family time on the computer can be fun.

Security software programs are available to filter, block, or monitor computer and Internet activity so that parents can screen their children's activity. Examples of helpful security software programs are Policy Central and Cyber Sentinel Network. Parents using either of these software security programs can reduce unproductive time; limit legal liability; reduce network congestion; and manage risks associated with inappropriate Internet, instant messaging and chat room and e-mail use.

When using Cyber Sentinel Network, children are protected not only from pornography and sexually explicit material but also from predators and pedophiles who seek out potential victims through chat rooms, instant messaging, and e-mail. In addition to using security software programs, families should be guided as to how the computer and the Internet can be used in a safe manner. Box 16-6 presents safety tips for family use of computers and the Internet. While parents are teaching a child these safety tips, they should also set rules for the use of the Internet. Just as there are rules for how children should deal with strangers and which television shows, movies, and videos they are allowed to watch, there should also be rules for children's use of the Internet.

The family health nurse can encourage parents to set limits on the amount of time a child can spend online each day or week. An alarm clock or timer can be used in case the child loses track of time. Parents or guardians should not allow surfing the Internet to take the place of homework, playing outside or with friends, or pursuing other interests. Families should make sure a child knows that people online are not always who they say they are and that online information is not necessarily private.

BOX 16-6 Safety Tips for Family Use of Computers and the Internet

- Keep the computer in a public area of the house.
- Do not allow children to use the computer just to pass or occupy time.
- Know how to use the services that the younger members of the household will be using.
- Focus on the excitement of learning and discovery.
- Together as a family, set Internet and computer rules that will be followed by all users.
- Teach children not to give personal information about themselves (name, address, school name or location, phone number, financial information, or friends' names) on the Internet.
- Monitor children as they use the Internet, even if the computer is being used at a public place such as a library.
- Never use a credit card online without a parent's permission.
- Never share passwords, even with friends.
- Never arrange a face-to-face meeting with someone the child has met online, unless the parent approves of the meeting and the parent goes with the child to a public place. Teenagers in particular need to be aware of the risks.
- Never respond to messages that make the child feel confused or uncomfortable. The child should be taught to ignore the sender, end the communication, and tell a trusted adult right away.
- NEVER use bad language or send mean messages online.

From American Academy of Child and Adolescent Psychiatry. (1997). *Children online: The facts for families.* Publication No. 59. Retrieved October 14, 2002, from http://www.aacap.org/publications/factsfam/online.htm

---

Outdoor Family Activities

Family fun time outdoors can be an opportunity for children and adults to exercise and enjoy the healthy benefits of play. Because play is the business of children, families should capitalize on it. Although family outdoor activities generally involve participation in sports such as football, baseball, soccer, or volleyball, the family health nurse can encourage the family to be creative and plan other activities. Planting a tree or a small garden can also be an enjoyable outdoor family activity.

Celebrate National Family Recreation Week

The American Association for Leisure and Recreation—an organization for recreation professionals, practitioners, educators, and students that serves to advance the profession and enhance quality of life through creative and meaningful leisure and recreation experiences—has designated the first week in June as National Family Recreation Week. During this week all families are encouraged to make a special effort to plan and implement one or more special family recreation activities. For more information regarding National Family Recreation Week, the reader may refer to the organization's website listed in the Website Resources box at the end of the chapter.

Influence of Family Variations on Family Recreation

Variations in family type, culture, developmental stage, and socioeconomic status exert a decisive influence on the way families institute family recreation activities. Awareness of these influences can enhance the family health nurse's ability to use family recreation activities to foster family empowerment, transformation, and capacity building to promote family health. Further, the nurse should use this knowledge to highlight the meaningful patterns and resources within the family's lived experiences of family functioning to achieve healthy family behaviors.

Family Types

Understanding the family type and the relationships that influence with whom and when families get together for family recreation is critical to the success of the outcome. Nuclear families tend to spend more time together and are more involved in recreational activities than other types of families. Single-parent families tend to involve members from the extended family in their

planned vacations. In these families, grandparents are often invited to share in vacation activities. Blended or stepparent families face special challenges in planning vacations as they attempt to incorporate new family vacation traditions with two sets of previous ones.

Culture

Understanding the influence of family culture on planning family recreation is fundamental to how the family health nurse develops interventions for promoting family health. Health promotion interventions should be based on the unique cultural beliefs and practices of each family unit. Recreational activities planned for a family should not conflict with or be perceived as threatening to the family's culture. For example, suggesting playing soccer instead of football may be unfamiliar to some African American families. Pleck (2000) describes the influence of ethnicity, consumer culture, and family rituals in a multicultural, comparative history of American family celebration, which provides insight into the significance of ethnicity and consumer culture in shaping what people regard as the most memorable moments of family life.

Developmental Stage

Duvall and Miller (1985) list nine fluctuating developmental tasks that span the family life cycle. These authors support the idea that family members face individual and family developmental tasks sometimes simultaneously. An understanding of family developmental tasks will be useful to the family health nurse who is helping families plan recreational activities according to their stage of development.

For the childless family, planning recreational activities involves meeting the needs of only two people, but once a couple enters the developmental phase of childbearing, children's needs for recreation must be considered. As the family grows to include adolescents, it is a good idea to include carefully planned activities selected by the teen, and if possible, activities that include the teen's friends. When the oldest child leaves the family home, if possible, periodic get-togethers with all members should be planned to celebrate the family. When all children have left the nuclear family, this time can be used by the couple to plan a fun trip such as a romantic cruise. As the family ages, the older members should be included in annual family reunions, and big celebrations can be planned for their special birthdays. Seeing a 97-year-old aunt out on the dance floor at her special birthday celebration can become a cherished memory.

Socioeconomic Considerations

Economic factors will influence the type of recreation a family will enjoy. Planning an expensive family vacation that puts a financial strain on the family budget may cause a stressful aftermath. To avoid this, the nurse can assist families in searching the Internet for affordable local activities and vacations. Low-cost family-centered activities such as an inexpensive day in the park can be just as much fun as a trip to the movies.

Research Pertaining to Family Recreation

Although some research has indicated that families who participate in well-organized recreational activities report greater satisfaction and feelings of family unity, there is a need for more research into the benefits of family recreation. Also, when parents, especially fathers, are actively involved, the family recreation activity is more likely to be successful (Smith, 1985).

Leisure scholars recognize the importance of recreation in family life (Kelly, 1997). Although a rich heritage of family leisure research has been developed and reviewed (Freysinger, 1997; Hawkes, 1991; Holman & Epperson, 1984, Kelly, 1997; Shaw, 1997), no systematic approach has guided this body of work or necessarily connected the divergent themes (Freeman, Hill, & Huff, 2002).

A Delphi study was conducted by Freeman, Hill, and Huff (2002) to develop family recreation research agenda. To determine the future direction for family recreation research, a panel of 19 academics and professionals was asked the question, "What topics, issues and specific research questions should be addressed and answered to build the body of knowledge in family recreation?" (Abstract section, para. 1).

Initially, a list of 20 general topic areas for future research was identified. The final top five were developing healthy and successful families, increasing family cohesion, improving family functioning, examining demands for family time, and defining family and family structure (Freeman, et al., 2002). Ten research questions were also identified for future studies and include the following (Freeman, et al., 2002, Results section, Table 2):

1) Under what conditions is family leisure most productive for families?
2) What is the value of family recreation to child and adolescent development?
3) How does recreation contribute to family cohesiveness?
4) What is the role and value of family recreation in a work-obsessed, time-starved culture?
5) What is the role of recreation across the life cycle, especially as families experience change?
6) What are the best types of family recreational activities and what are their perceived benefits?
7) What are the differences in joint/individual/parallel leisure activities in developing family cohesion? Does this differ with couples?
8) Can theories be developed specific to family recreation that are more contextual and account for human/social ecology?
9) What is the range of individual, relationship, and family outcomes from participating in family recreation?
10) How can families best balance recreation and work?

The researchers noted a strong focus on the need for programs that emphasize family cohesion and family functioning. The highest priority was for recreation research on experiences and programs that strengthen families. Other recommendations include the need to develop theory that incorporates a systems approach to guide family recreation research and improved research questions that require empirical examination and further theory development (Freeman, Hill, & Huff, 2002).

Assessment of Family Recreation

A survey of the existence of family assessment and measurement instruments that have been developed by nurses and other health care professionals reveals that one appropriate family assessment measurement for family recreation is the Family Systems Strengths of the Family Systems Stressor-Strength Inventory (FS³I), which was developed by Mischke-Berkey and Hanson (1991). In Part III of FS³I, 20 traits or attributes that deal with some aspect of family life and its overall functioning are listed. Traits included in this section that specifically relate to recreation are (1) display of a sense of play and humor, (2) a balance of interaction among family members, and (3) shared leisure time. A full version of the FS³I, along with scoring instructions, is available in Bomar, 1996, Hanson, 2001. Another assessment measure is the Family Time and Routine Scale (Appendix 16-1) developed by McCubbin, McCubbin, and Thompson (1997).

The family health nurse should instruct parents—whether they are couples, single parents, guardians, grandparents, aunts, or uncles—that they should start today and use the little moments available to build memories so that when their children grow up and leave home, they will not leave empty-handed. Planned family recreation empowers families to use family capacity to promote health and create a special feeling of belongingness (Doherty & Carlson, 2002).

Family Rules For Health Promotion

Family rules that determine the general behavior of family members are important in determining the health-promoting behaviors of a family. Rules have existed since prehistoric days when the man hunted and the woman gathered. During this period, rules led to productive and predictable interactions between family members (Lofas, 2002). The role of each family member was clear and well understood. However, today, both partners typically work outside the home. Because of the stress of juggling a job and family, rules for the home seem to have fallen through the cultural cracks (Lofas, 2002). Rules lead to productive and predictable interaction between people.

Family rules set standards for acceptable behaviors. All children need rules to set guidelines for the way they treat family members and others. Children must be taught how to play with others. Children must be taught how to respect

the rights of others and how to appropriately respond to others. For a child to respond to an older person disrespectfully is unacceptable behavior.

Positive rules create emotional order. Emotional order builds character, strength, and a feeling of being loved. All of these are necessary for a child to grow. Establishing understandable rules is the best way to diffuse conflict, resolve problems, and maintain a positive relationship with children. Box 16-7 presents guidelines for making family rules.

Families need to be consistent in enforcing established rules. Frequent changing of the rules can be confusing to a child. It is helpful to write out the rules and post them where the child can

---

BOX 16-7   General Guidelines for Making Family Rules

1. Make reasonable rules and discuss them as a family. Talk about each rule and come to an agreement about why it is important.
2. State rules clearly, including what is the expected behavior. Be clear and concise when stating the rule, for example, "No playing outside until your room is cleaned."
3. Explain the reason for each rule. Understanding the reason for the rule helps children see why it is important to follow.
4. State clearly the consequences for not following the rule. If the child understands the penalty, he or she is more likely to follow the rule.
5. Be consistent in enforcing the rules. Frequent changing of the rules can be confusing to a child.
6. Post rules where the child can see them. Write out the rules and post them visibly on the refrigerator or in some other conspicuous place.
7. Allow for rules to be renegotiated from time to time. If a rule does not work, talk again as a family and change the rule if needed.

From University of Wisconsin Cooperative Extension. (1997). *What are the family rules?* Wisconsin Cooperation Extension Publication, Kensington Publishing Corp., No. 597-2.

TABLE 16-1   Family Rules Sheet

Date: _____ Next Review Time: _____

Rule	Expected Behavior	Consequence
1.		
2.		
3.		
4.		
5.		

see them. After rules have been established, they may need to be renegotiated from time to time. If a rule does not work, a family can discuss it and change the rule if necessary.

Using the guidelines in Box 16-7, the nurse can suggest that the family create a Family Rules Sheet on which rules, expected behaviors, and consequences are written (Table 16-1). The sheet can be posted on the refrigerator or in some other conspicuous place where all family members can see it. The nurse can suggest that the family put a date on each sheet and specify a date to review the list again.

Family rules that are accompanied by appropriate discipline prepare a child to accept restrictions on his or her behavior. Appropriate discipline teaches a child desirable behavior. *Webster's New World Dictionary and Thesaurus* defines *discipline* as "1) instruction; 2) a subject that is taught; 3) training that corrects, molds, or perfects; and 4) orderly or prescribed conduct or pattern of behavior" (Laird, 2002, p. 383). There is a clear distinction between discipline and *punish,* which is defined as "1) to chase, 2) to reprove, 3) to strike, and 4) to chastise" (Laird, 2002, p. 955). Families need to be taught the distinction between the two terms and guided as to how consistent rules with stated consequences can lead to appropriate discipline. Family rules must be adapted to meet the needs of individual families; and family type, culture, developmental stage, and socioeconomic status should also be considered in the creation of these rules.

Family Types and Rules

An example of the influence of family type on the establishment of family rules can be seen in the single-parent family. Making family rules in the single-parent family is especially challenging. A single working parent must often make unilateral rules, and in single-parent families, rules may be stringent because of the parent's multiple responsibilities.

Another family type that faces many challenges in setting and enforcing family rules is the stepfamily. It is reported that one third of all Americans belong to stepfamilies. These families create new challenges to meet novel situations of a new family form (Lofas, 1995).

Adjusting to blended family-type arrangements is hard enough when only one partner brings children to the relationship, but with the added complications of two sets of children, setting rules can be very difficult. Blending children from two (or more) families requires establishing a new form of kinship. Recent research suggests that younger adolescents (ages 10 to 14) may have the most difficult time adjusting to a stepfamily. Older adolescents (age 15 and older) need less parenting and may have less investment in stepfamily life, whereas younger children (age 10 and younger) are usually more accepting of a new adult in the family, particularly when the adult is a positive influence. However, young adolescents, who are dealing with identity formation issues, tend to be more oppositional (McGoldrick & Carter, 1988).

In setting family rules, stepparents should at first establish a relationship with the children similar to that of a friend or "camp counselor," rather than a disciplinarian. Couples in stepparent families should agree that the custodial parent will remain primarily responsible for control and discipline of the children until the stepparent and children form a solid bond. Until stepparents can take on more parenting responsibilities, they can simply monitor the children's behavior and activities and keep their spouses informed. Each spouse should have a list of household rules. These may include, for example, "We agree to respect each family member" or "Every family member agrees to clean up after himself or herself." Next, the spouses should negotiate three to five rules that will be implemented in the family. The rules should be discussed with the children and then posted in a prominent place. When the rules are explicit, the stepparent is not seen as the disciplinarian for the family because the children are simply following the house rules (Lofas, 1995).

Culture and Family Rules

Culture greatly influences family rules. In many Asian American and American Indian families, rules are passed from one generation to the next. Children in these families know the expectations and are required to follow them. Many modern American families use more flexibility in the rules to allow for children to express feelings and concerns. In some African American families, rules for younger children are more flexible, but when a rule is broken and behavior becomes intolerable, loud voice commands and corporal punishment may be used as a form of discipline.

According to McAdoo (1999), factors that influence childrearing approaches in African American families are embedded in the racial, cultural, and economic situations of African Americans. Research on African American families continues to show differences in behaviors and lifestyles between black and white individuals. Survival in a hostile environment and living in a unique economy and cultural and racial circumstances are also factors that affect family rules (McAdoo, 1993). Many African American families teach their children rules that will afford them opportunities to both survive and achieve.

Another example of the influence of culture on family rules is described by a Chinese descendent of Emperor Chou Tai-Wang (Wu, 2002). From this dynasty evolved the Wu Family rules: 4 female rules, 12 meditation rules, 24 endurance rules, and 9 forbidden rules. According to Wu, selected Wu family rules include the following:

1) Obey parents and elders
2) Respect elders and keep their graves clean
3) Always respect your siblings
4) Remember and respect the rank of relatives
5) Be on good terms with relatives and help each other
6) Keep a home that is clean and orderly
7) Control anger and be kind to each other

Developmental Stage

Today, in many families, the roles have changed and so have the rules. Rules for disciplining a child are now much more relaxed. For the younger child, "time out" is called and the child must respond appropriately. Many teens now have cell phones and use them in attempts to make arrangements for changes in the rules. In many families, all too often, grandparents are regarded as buffers rather than disciplinarians, allowing them to bend or even break family rules. Other family members who attempt to discipline a young child may get a response such as "You are not my mother. I do not have to mind you." Generally, teenage parents tend to be much more lenient with family rules than older parents.

Socioeconomic Considerations

A search of the health and sociology literature indicates that a void exists in research pertaining to the role socioeconomic status plays in establishing family rules. In families in which parents are actively involved in encouraging healthy living for all family members, the rules remain the same for all economic levels. Rules and expectations for safety, conduct, deportment, and courtesy remain the same regardless of whether the family is above or below the poverty level. A child from an affluent family should be expected to follow the same safety and courtesy rules as one living in an impoverished family.

However, when nursing students and practicing health professionals were asked whether family rules differ according to socioeconomic status, each respondent said that there are decided differences. The major areas of differences were education, socialization, family expectations, and discipline. The richness, diversity, and intensity of the responses were varied and enlightening.

Research Pertaining to Family Rules

The influence of family rules on the development of healthy families is another area in need of additional research. Two studies of family rules are presented. In the research conducted by Lee, Burr, Beutler, Yorgason, and Harker (1989), a major outcome was the development of a family measurement tool called *The Family Profile: A Tool for Family Life Education*. When the tool is used, each family member responds to statements about family life. The survey reveals how each family member views the family. It is an excellent tool for stimulating family discussions.

In a study on spanking, the University of Minnesota's Extension Service in Goodhue County, in partnership with researchers and a number of other Goodhue County agencies, followed up a group of parents for 18 months and documented changes in their attitudes and practices. This study showed that (1) after participation in the study the use of physical punishment by Goodhue County parents dropped from 36% to 12%; (2) parents who spanked their children reported a considerable increase in their children's aggressiveness; (3) parents who reduced physical punishment reported that their children were less aggressive; (4) parents who attended classes conducted by the researchers reported changes in both their own parenting behavior and their children's behavior; (5) generally, parents were better at setting limits and enforcing consequences, and became calm and less agitated by their children's behavior, more nurturing, better listeners, and more positive about their parenting; and (6) parents who did not spank their children reported that their children were more compliant, communicated more openly, had a better attitude, and were calmer (Olson, 2002). Rules lead to productive and predictable interactions between people.

The Nursing Process and Family Routines, Rituals, Recreation, and Rules

As the family health nurse develops practice skills for the twenty-first century, it is necessary to move away from the use of the service model of delivery of care to the Capacity Enhancement Model (Hartrick, 1997). When this model is used, the nursing process is less like the traditional method and reflects twenty-first century practice. The new language to be used with the Capacity Enhancement Model includes terms such as *collaboration*, *capacity building*, *empowerment*, *transformation*, *listening*, and *giving control*; in this model meaningful patterns and resources within the family's lived experience are identified and used to promote family health. This language replaces the previous language in which terms such as *pathology*, *problem identification and resolution*, *deficiency*, *intervention*, *informing*, *doing for the patient*, and *outcomes* were used (Hartrick, 2000). For more information, see Hartrick (2000).

Implications for Research and Practice in the Twenty-First Century

The research conducted by Denham (2002) indicated a need for the development of models that demonstrate the relationship between family health and family routines. Nurses and health care professionals could benefit from further study of the frequency and implications of family routines in planning, teaching, and implementing health interventions. Examples of areas of study include studying family routines, rituals, recreation, and rules in the early, middle, and late phases of family development. Also, researchers might use Denham's family routines construct as a framework for study and implementation of family-focused care (Denham, 2003). Also, studies of high ritualization, balanced ritualtzation, and low ritualization with families from varied ethnic and cultural backgrounds would be useful.

Considering the gap in knowledge that exists in nursing practice regarding the use of family routines, rituals, recreation, and rules to promote family health, nurses are encouraged to conduct health research involving empowering and fostering family health capacity using these concepts for family health promotion.

CASE SCENARIO

The Miller family was brought to the attention of the family health nurse through a routine health promotion visit to a day care center. The preschool teacher reported that Jerry Miller, age 3, had frequent episodes of otitis media and that the family was concerned. The family requested a visit with the family health nurse. Before beginning to implement the Capacity Enhancement Model of care, the nurse obtained family background information.

The Miller family is a blended family consisting of one child, Jerry, age 3, who is the child of the current marriage, and two other children from previous marriages, both of whom are 11 years old. Both parents work and the youngest child attends day care while the two 11-year-old children are at home unsupervised for 3 hours each day. Mr. Miller works as an auto mechanic with somewhat irregular hours. Mrs. Miller is a secretary at the local high school and is almost always home by 5:30 pm. All family members of both blended families attend the same church.

Mr. and Mrs. Miller state that a major problem for the family is establishing rules for each child and enforcing appropriate discipline when the rules are not followed. This problem is compounded by interference from both parents from the previous marriages and from the three sets of grandparents. Frequently, these family members will allow the rules set by the parents to be relaxed or even broken. Mr. and Mrs. Miller are attempting to appease everyone and the children are becoming unruly because of the lack of consistency in rule setting and enforcement.

MAJOR FAMILY STRESSORS

The major stressors are the frequent otitis media of Jerry, who is 3 years old; the 11-year-old children, who are unattended for 3 hours; and extended family members who do not adhere to family rules for the children. Children are unruly and do not respond to discipline. One parent is strict, and the other is lenient.

FAMILY STRENGTHS

Family strengths include the shared religious core between Mr. and Mrs. Miller and the children, family income and insurance, and extended family support.

LIFESTYLE CHANGES INDICATED

Increase/improve individual and couple time for the parents and increase discussion with extended family and grandparents about the importance of rules for the children's well-being. Plan a family meeting about the importance of rules. Establish family rituals and routines for the new blended family. A strategy is needed to cope with the repeated otitis of the 3 year old. The parents need to agree on discipline and rules and have a family meeting with the children. Write down the rules and consequences for not following them. Because of the family's busy week schedule, plan a family night as a family unit. Plan family mealtime and use as a time to enjoy each other's company.

WEBSITE RESOURCES

ORGANIZATION	WEBSITE ADDRESS
American Association for Leisure and Recreation	http://www.aahperd.org/aalr/template.cfm?template=main.html
California Inventory for Family Assessment (CIFA)	http://www.ourworld.compuserve.com/homepages/pdwerner/cifa1.htm
FACETS	http://www.parsons.lsi.ukans.edu/facets/
Family Connectivity Quiz	http://www.Beliefnet.com/frameset.asp?pagehoc+/stor
Family Reunion Planning	http://www.family-reunion.com/reunion.htm
Online Safety Tips for Parents and Caregivers	http://www.jwf.org/jwf_ols_par_car.html
Rituals and Family Strength	http://www.directionjournal.org/article/?654
Bar/Bat Mitzvah	http://www.jewish.com/askarabbi/askarabbi/askr5003.htm
Family Meals	http://www.askdrbettyonline.com

■ CHAPTER HIGHLIGHTS

- Rituals are activities that help families cope with the most disturbing life transitions in such a way that families can experience all that membership has to offer and let each member know that he or she has lived.

- Rituals and routines give families a sense of belonging and of being committed to a set of traditions and habits that bind families together.

- As families grow and change, their rituals and routines may continue to change over the years as they create new ones that are designed to bring family members closer together.

- Families need to be empowered to learn how to use their resources to enhance some routines and rituals, displace others, and create entirely new ones that improve quality family time.

- The promotion of all aspects of wellness through the creation of healthy family lifestyles is emerging as a major focus in family recreation activities, with increasing benefits for stress reduction and overall family mental health.

- Establishing understandable rules with stated consequences is the best way to diffuse conflict, resolve problems, and maintain a positive relationship with family members.

‖ CRITICAL THINKING ACTIVITIES

Please refer to the Case Scenario to answer questions 1 through 8.

1. What is the first activity the family health nurse should undertake with this family?

2. How should the family health nurse emphasize family health and capacity building?

3. In structuring the family night, what family member would serve as the best director for the family night activity?

4. How should the family health nurse instruct this family to develop more consistency and enforcement of the rules set?

5. How can the family health nurse illuminate meaningful patterns and resources within the family's lived experience of health and healing?

6. How could the nurse determine how the children feel when they are allowed to break the rules?

7. How can rituals be used to assist this blended family develop health-promoting behaviors?

8. How will the nurse evaluate the outcomes of the family's transformation?

The following questions do not pertain to the Case Scenario.

9. How can family health nurses use family rituals to re-imagine and transform families' health and healing experiences?

10. What benefits of family mealtime, as reported in research, can be cited to help families to value this family ritual?

11. What instructions can the family health nurse give to families to foster family health capacity with regard to the appropriate use of movies, videos, television, and the computer?

12. What rituals assist families in dealing with sickness and death?

REFERENCES

American Academy of Child and Adolescent Psychiatry. (1997). *Children online: The facts for families.* Publication No. 59. Retrieved October 14, 2002, from http://www.aacap.org/publications/factsfam/online.htm

American Association for Leisure and Recreation (2002). *National family recreation week.* Retrieved October 7, 2002, from http://www.aahperd.org/aalr/template.cfm?template=main.html

Beals, D., & Tabors, P. (1995, March). *Contextual support for word learning in family mealtime conversation.* Paper presented at the biennial meeting of the Society for Research in Child Development, Indianapolis, IN.

Bittner, T. (2000). *Family night: Not just for games.* Retrieved November 11, 2002, from http://www.suite101.com/article cfm/3111/28867

Biziou, B. (1999). *The power of family rituals.* Retrieved November 25, 2002, from http://www.parents,comarticle/family-time/4002.jsp.page=2

Boyce, W. T., Jensen, E. W., & Peacock, J. L. (1983). Family routines inventory: Theoretical origins. *Social Science Medicine, 17,* 193-200.

Cole, K. (2002). *Family traditions.* Retrieved August 17, 2002, from http://www.Suite.101.com/article.cfm/1223/

Denham, S. A. (1995). Family routines: A construct for considering family health. *Holistic Nursing Practice, 9,* 11-23.

Denham, S. A. (1996). Family health in a rural Appalachian Ohio county. *Journal of Appalachian Studies, 2,* 1-12.

Denham, S. A. (1997). *An ethnographic study of family health in Appalachian microsystems.* Unpublished doctoral dissertation. University of Birmingham, Birmingham, AL.

Denham, S. A. (2002). Family routines: A structural perspective for viewing family health. *Advances in Nursing Science, 24,* 60-74.

Denham, S. A. (2003). *Family health model: A framework for nursing.* Philadelphia: F. A. Davis.

Doherty, W. J. (1997). *The intentional family: Simple rituals to strengthen family ties.* New York: Avon Press.

Doherty, W. J., Carlson, B. Z. (2002). *Putting family first.* New York: Owl Books.

Duvall, E. M., & Miller, B. C. (1985). *Marriage and family development* (6th ed.). Philadelphia: J. B. Lippincott.

Freeman, P. A., Hill, B. J., & Huff, C. (2002, March). Development of family recreation research agenda. *LARNet; The Cyber Journal of Applied Leisure and Recreation Research, 22,* 125-137. Retrieved May 24, 2002, at http://www.nccu.edu/larnet/2002-5.html

Freysinger, V. J. (1997). Redefining family, redefining leisure: Progress made and challenges ahead in research on leisure and families. *Journal of Leisure Research, 29,* 1-4.

Fiese, B. H. (1995). Family rituals. In D. Levinson (Ed.), *Encyclopedia of marriage and the family* (pp. 275-278). New York: Simon & Schuster Macmillan.

Fiese, B. H. (2000). Family rituals as a protective factor for children with asthma. *Journal of Pediatric Psychology, 25,* 471-480.

Fiese, B. H., & Kline, C. A. (1993). Development of the Family Ritual Questionnaire: Initial reliability and validation studies. *Journal of Family Psychology, 6,* 290-299.

Friesen, J. D. (1990). Rituals and family strength. *Canada: Direction Journal, 19,* 39-48.

Griswold, A. (2002) *Reduce stress with family routines and rituals: Parenting again.* Retrieved October 26, 2002, from the University of Illinois Extension, University of Illinois at Urbana Champaign website http://www.web.extension.uiuc/RockfordCenter/

Hanson, S. M. H. (2001). *Family health care nursing: theory, practice, and research* (2nd ed.). Philadelphia: F. A. Davis.

Hartrick, G. (1997). Beyond the service model of care: Health promotion and the enhancement of family capacity. *Journal of Family Nursing, 3,* 57-70.

Hartrick, G. (2000). Developing health-promoting practice with families: One pedagological experience. *Journal of Advanced Nursing, 31,* 27-36.

Hawkes, S. R. (1991). Recreation in the family. In S. J. Bahr (Ed.), *Family research: A sixty-year review, 1930-1990, Vol. 1* (pp. 387-433). New York: Lexington Books.

Holman, T. B., & Epperson, A. (1984). Family and leisure: A review of the literature with research recommendations. *Journal of Leisure Research, 16,* 277-294.

Jensen, E. W., Boyce, W. T., & Hartnett, J. L. (1983). The family routines inventory: Development and validation. *Social Science Medicine, 17,* 201-211.

Kelly, J. R. (1997). Changing issues in leisure-family research—again. *Journal of Leisure Research, 29,* 132-134.

Laird, C. C. (2002). *Webster's new world dictionary and thesaurus.* New York: Book Essential Promotions.

Lee, T., Burr, W., Beutler, I., Yorgason, F., & Harker, B. (1989). *The family profile: A tool for family life.* Retrieved August 8, 2002, from http://www.fww.org/solutions/survey1.htm

Lofas, J. (2002). *Family rules 2000.* Retrieved October 17, 2002, from http://www.longevity.comparenting/parenting advice/

Lofas, J. (1995). *Family rules: Helping stepfamilies and single parents build happy homes.* New York: Kensington.

McAdoo, H. P. (Ed.). (1993). *Family ethnicity: Strength in diversity.* Newbury Park, CA: Sage.

McAdoo, H. P. (1999) *Black families* (2nd ed.). Thousand Oaks, CA: Sage.

McCubbin, H. I., McCubbin, M. A., & Thompson, A. I. (1987). Family time and routines index. In H. I. McCubbin & A. I. Thompson (Eds.), *Family assessment inventories for research and practice* (pp. 133-141). Madison: University of Wisconsin.

McDonald, L. (2002, November). *Applying family system theory to strengthen the family unit protective factor of strong family unit by increasing family strengths: Cohesiveness, family unity, family pride.* Retrieved October 1, 2002, from http:// www.wcer.wisc.edu/fast/research/FamilySystemTheory.htm

McGoldrick, M., & Carter, B. (1988). Forming a remarried family. In M. McGoldrick and B. Carter (Eds.), *The changing family life cycle* (2nd ed). New York: Gardner.

Mischke-Berkey, K., & Hanson, S. (1991). Family Systems Strengths of the Family Systems Stressor-Strength Inventory (FS3I). In B. Mischke-Berkey & S. Hanson (Eds.), *Pocket guide to family assessment and intervention* (pp. 72-83). St. Louis, MO: Mosby–Year Book.

Moore, S. F., & Myeroff, B. G. (1977). Secular ritual: Forms and meaning. In S. Moore & B. Myeroff (Eds.), *Secular ritual* (pp. 3-24). Amsterdam: Van Gorcum.

Olson, K. (2002, January). *Changes in Goodhue County parenting practices 1993-2001*. University of Minnesota Extension Service. Retrieved May 6, 2002, from http://www.Extension.umn.edu/county/goodhue/Fact Sheet.pdf

Ovard, C. (1998, May). *A family that plays together.* Retrieved August 7, 2002, from http://www.suite 101.com/article.cfm/1049/7538

Pleck, E. (2000) *Celebrating the family: Ethnicity, consumer culture and family rituals.* Cambridge, MA: Harvard University Press.

Reinhart, A. (2002). *Make time for family meals: Parenting again.* Retrieved September 20, 2002, from http://www.urbanext.uiuc.edu/grandparents/0209b.html

Roberts, J. (1988). Setting the frame, definition, functions and typology of rituals. In E. Imber-Black, J. Roberts, & R. Whiting (Eds.), *Rituals in families and family therapy* (pp. 3-46). New York: W. W. Norton.

Shaw, S. M. (1997). Controversies and contradictions in family leisure: An analysis of conflicting paradigms. *Journal of Leisure Research, 29,* 98.

Smith, S. L. J. (1985). Effects of family recreation. University of Waterloo. Retrieved July 5, 2002, from http://www.ahs.uwaterloo.ca/rec/bios.html

Thomlison, B. (2002) *The family assessment handbook: An introductory practice guide to family assessment and intervention.* Pacific Grove, CA: Brooks/Cole Thomson Learning.

University of Wisconsin Cooperative Extension. (1997). *What are the family rules?* NCR Publication No. 597-2. Madison: University of Wisconsin Cooperative Extension Publications.

Venn, M., & Woods-Cripe, J. (1997). Using daily routines as learning experiences. In E. S. Szanton (Ed.), *Creating child-centered programs for infants and toddlers* (pp. 105-108). Washington, DC: Children's Resources International, Inc.

Wallace, C. (1999, May). *The new family dinner: Different ways to come together.* Retrieved August 24, 2002, from. http://www.parents.com/articles/family_time/4001.jsp?page=2

Wolin, S. J., & Bennett, L. A. (1984). Family rituals. *Family Process, 23,* 401-420.

Wolin, S. J., Bennett, L. A., & Jacobs, J. S. (1988). Assessing family rituals in alcoholic families. In E. Imber-Black, J. Roberts, & R. Whiting (Eds.), *Rituals in families and family therapy* (pp. 404-416). New York: W. W. Norton.

Wu, J. (2002). Wu family rules. Retrieved October 30, 2002, from http://www.wushuboy.com/newwushu/famrule.htm

Appendix 16-1 Family Time and Routines Scale

| Family Stress, Coping and Health Project
1300 Linden Drive
University of Wisconsin-Madison
Madison, Wisconsin 53706 | **FAMILY TIME and ROUTINES SCALE** ©

Hamilton I. McCubbin   Marilyn A. McCubbin   Anne I. Thompson |

Directions:

First, read the following statements and decide to what extent each of these routines listed below is false or true about your family *Please circle the number (0, 1, 2, 3) which best expresses your family experiences:* (False (0),   Mostly False (1),   Mostly True (2),   True (3)).

Second, determine the importance of each routine to keeping your family together and strong (NI = Not Important,   SI = Somewhat Important,   VI = Very Important). *Please circle the letters (NI, SI, or VI) which best expresses how important the routines are to your family. If you do not have children, relatives, teenagers, etc., please circle NA = Not Applicable.*

ROUTINES	False	Mostly False	Mostly True	True	How Important to Keeping the Family Together and Strong			
					Important to Family			*Not Applicable*
					Not	Somewhat	Very	
Work day and Leisure Time Routines 1. Parent(s) have some time each day for just talking with the children	0	1	2	3	NI	SI	VI	NA
2. Working parent has a regular play time with the children after coming home from work	0	1	2	3	NI	SI	VI	NA
3. Working parent takes care of the children sometime almost every day	0	1	2	3	NI	SI	VI	NA
4. Non-working parent and children do something together outside the home almost every day (e.g., shopping, walking, etc.)	0	1	2	3	NI	SI	VI	NA
5. Family has a quiet time each evening when everyone talks or plays quietly	0	1	2	3	NI	SI	VI	NA
6. Family goes some place special together each week	0	1	2	3	NI	SI	VI	NA
7. Family has a certain family time each week when they do things together at home	0	1	2	3	NI	SI	VI	NA
8. Parent(s) read or tell stories to the children almost every day	0	1	2	3	NI	SI	VI	NA
9. Each child has some time each day for playing alone	0	1	2	3	NI	SI	VI	NA
10. Children/Teens play with friends daily	0	1	2	3	NI	SI	VI	NA
Parent(s)' routines 11. Parents have a certain hobby or sport they do together regularly	0	1	2	3	NI	SI	VI	NA
12. Parents have time with each other quite often	0	1	2	3	NI	SI	VI	NA
13. Parents go out together one or more times a week	0	1	2	3	NI	SI	VI	NA

Reprinted with permission from McCubbin, H. I., McCubbin, M. A., & Thompson, A. I. (1987). FTRI: Family Time and Routine Index. In H. I. McCubbin & A. I. Thompson (Eds.), *Family assessment inventories for research and practice* (pp. 132-141). Family Stress, Coping and Health Project. Madison: University of Wisconsin.

ROUTINES	False	Mostly False	Mostly True	True	How Important to Keeping the Family Together and Strong			
					Important to Family			Not
					Not	Somewhat	Very	Applicable
14. Parents often spend time with teenagers for private talks	0	1	2	3	NI	SI	VI	NA
Family Bedtime Routines 15. Children have special things they do or ask for each night at bedtime (e.g., story, good-night kiss, hug)	0	1	2	3	NI	SI	VI	NA
16. Children go to bed at the same time almost every night	0	1	2	3	NI	SI	VI	NA
Family Meals 17. Family eats at about the same time each night	0	1	2	3	NI	SI	VI	NA
18. Whole family eats one meal together daily	0	1	2	3	NI	SI	VI	NA
Extended Family Routines 19. At least one parent talks to his or her parents regularly	0	1	2	3	NI	SI	VI	NA
20. Family has regular visits with the relatives	0	1	2	3	NI	SI	VI	NA
21. Children/Teens spend time with grandparent(s) quite often	0	1	2	3	NI	SI	VI	NA
22. We talk with/write to relatives usually once a week	0	1	2	3	NI	SI	VI	NA
Leaving and Coming Home 23. Family checks in or out with each other when someone leaves or comes home	0	1	2	3	NI	SI	VI	NA
24. Working parent(s) comes home from work at the same time each day	0	1	2	3	NI	SI	VI	NA
25. Family has certain things they almost always do to greet each other at the end of the day	0	1	2	3	NI	SI	VI	NA
26. We express caring and affection for each other daily	0	1	2	3	NI	SI	VI	NA
Family Disciplinary Routines 27. Parent(s) have certain things they almost always do each time the children get out of line	0	1	2	3	NI	SI	VI	NA
28. Parents discuss new rules for children/ teenagers with them quite often	0	1	2	3	NI	SI	VI	NA
Family Chores 29. Children do regular household chores	0	1	2	3	NI	SI	VI	NA
30. Mothers do regular household chores	0	1	2	3	NI	SI	VI	NA
31. Fathers do regular household chores	0	1	2	3	NI	SI	VI	NA
32. Teenagers do regular household chores	0	1	2	3	NI	SI	VI	NA

©1986 H. McCubbin and M. McCubbin

Family Health Promotion during Transitions

Patricia Roth
Mary Ann Simanello

17

There is a time for everything and a season for every activity under heaven.

— Ecclesiastes 3:1 NIV

OBJECTIVES

On completion of the chapter, the reader will be able to do the following:

1. *Identify the various types of transitions that families experience as they progress from one developmental stage to another.*
2. *Analyze the corresponding changes in the role complex that occur in families experiencing transition.*
3. *Explicate the key concepts and variables associated with the addition of family members.*
4. *Analyze the sources of stress and coping strategies associated with family role changes and life transitions.*
5. *Incorporate variables concerning family adaptation to transitions into a nursing assessment.*
6. *Implement effective health promotion strategies to mitigate the stress families experience during life transitions.*
7. *Delineate researchable problems concerning the effects of transitions on the health of families and individual members.*

Contemporary families are faced with many daily challenges and problems that have the potential to produce stress and crisis. Among them are family developmental transitions, those transitions that are normative and expected as part of the family life cycle. Although considered normal, these events have the potential to change a family's level of stress as a result of changes in the equilibrium of the family system. Crisis occurs only if the family does not adapt to the changes brought about by these events (Boss, 2002). Nonnormative events are the products of some situations that

could not be predicted and are not likely to be repeated. They can be positive events or disastrous, and they also have the potential to change the level of family stress.

Although several key family theories are focused on the experience of families in transition, family developmental theory and family stress theory have played a major role in understanding family stages of development and the process by which families adapt to change and transition from one stage to another. Family developmental stages are identified by using the criteria of major change in

477

family size, the development of the oldest child, and the work status of the primary provider. At each stage, families complete certain developmental tasks or growth responsibilities to meet biological and cultural requirements (Duvall & Miller, 1985). In a later conceptualization, Aldous (1996) addresses the concept of transition. A specific event may signify the move into a new stage, involving role changes and creating a period of disequilibrium for the family unit. Time within a stage is viewed as relatively stable and refers to both event and stage sequencing. Although traditional family development theory has many important applications, it has some limitations in terms of understanding nonnuclear stepfamilies and ethnically diverse families. Societal changes, gender issues, and newer family forms make it difficult to determine what a normal family life cycle is (McGoldrick, Heiman, & Carter, 1993). Another limitation is the inability to provide insight into the processes of developmental change by which families transform their interaction structures.

Merderer and Hill (1983) note that families experience a series of critical transitions over the life span, observing that these transitions necessitate changes in family role complex. The family role complex consists of the interrelated roles assumed by other family members. A major reorganization may be needed if multiple changes in the role complex occur, particularly if they occur within the same period. Three types of structural events were identified, which could be stressful if they occurred within the same period, precipitating a critical transition and demarcating a new state of development. These included changes in the number of family members; changes in age composition caused by individual development status change; and major changes in status such as marriage, parenthood, divorce, widowhood, relocation, changes in network affiliation, and changes in career status. As discussed in Chapter 14, family transitions, associated with both eustress and distress, cause stress in individual members and the family system.

This chapter explores selected normative and nonnormative family transitions, with a major focus on the impact of these events on the family unit and the individual. Adaptation to specific life events is examined, as well as opportunities for family reaffirmation or high-level functioning.

The first section covers the addition of family members and major life status changes.

Forming a Family

Change in the number of family members is identified as one of the structural events that might be expected to be stressful, particularly if it occurs with other events, such as a major status change. The addition of a family member, such as a spouse or child, necessitates change in the predictable patterns of behavior among members in terms of role structure. Decision making, affection, communication, and division of tasks must be renegotiated to meet the changing needs of the family and individual members. Marriage, remarriage, and parenthood are all major status changes that affect the number of family members and require considerable role alteration. Each of the transitions is briefly explored in terms of potential stressors and family role complex.

Marriage

In a major review of trends and attitudes toward marriage in the United States, Thorton and Young-Demarco (2001) explore three major themes permeating changing family and behavior relationships. One theme concerns the continuing commitment of Americans to the institutions of marriage and family life. A second theme focuses on freedom, autonomy, and tolerance for different family forms. A third theme addresses the issue of equality in terms of opportunities, prestige, resources, and decision making. After a careful review of related research, the authors conclude that there is a strong emphasis on and commitment to marriage, children, and family life in the United States today.

Trends toward freedom of choice in personal behavior have found expression in a variety of living arrangements and childbearing practices and in the endorsement of gender equality. There is also a strong current of continued support for a gender-based division of labor, with more men than women believing that men have the primary responsibility outside of the home and that women are in charge of the home. The increasing acceptance of gender equality accompanied by continued support for some gender-based roles in the family suggest that this will be an area of continuing adjustment and potential conflict in marriages. However, as more young people with a high level of commitment to gender equality reach adulthood, they will probably negotiate more egalitarian family arrangements than their parents did (Thorton & Young-DeMarco, 2001). A key question posed by these authors is how individuals can take advantage of the freedom to pursue their own goals and aspirations while maintaining family commitments and responsibilities. One of the major areas of concern in successfully negotiating the transition from single life to married life is adjustment to changes in role and status.

Conflict Management and Intimacy in Marriage

As relationships progress, couples inevitably experience conflicting needs and responses. Marital distress is a function of couple interaction patterns, resulting from ineffective resolution of conflict or aversive responses to conflict (Koerner & Jacobson, 1994). Styles of conflict management differentiate distressed couples from nondistressed couples. In his authoritative work on marital distress, Gottman (1994) identifies two types of marriages, regulated and nonregulated. In regulated marriages, couples are able to manage tensions in a way that promotes closeness or intimacy. In nonregulated marriages, couples manage ordinary difficulties in ways that result in negativity and distress in the relationship. These couples also have difficulty in rebounding from disagreements and complaints. Nonregulated couples use patterns of interaction characterized by defensiveness, criticisms, contempt, and withdrawal. Negativity and distancing begin when complaints are viewed as criticisms. Such critical attacks lead to erosion of mutual respect, which may be replaced by mutual contempt. As contempt increases, hope for the future of the relationship diminishes. Gottman (1994) finds that distressed couples not only lose hope for the future of their relationship but also engage in a process of focusing on selective negative aspects of the history of their relationship.

Regulated couples have complaints and conflict situations in their relationships as well, but Gottman (1994) identifies three styles of conflict management used by these couples that lead to continued intimacy and successful relationships. In the validating couple style, there is a low level of negative expressed emotion: partners listen to one another respectfully and validate each other's feelings. The volatile couple style is characterized by intense emotion, confrontation, and persuasive argument; but in spite of bitter attacks and counterattacks, partners maintain a sense of connection and intimacy. The third style is that of minimizing or avoiding conflict. Couples who minimize or avoid conflict may lack the skills necessary to work through conflict, and they may live with the pain of unsolved problems that may have solutions. In spite of the limitations of this particular style, these couples still maintain a sense of cohesion and are able to create distance between one another. Not all approaches are recommended conflict management strategies. Nonetheless, Gottman (1994) found that these couples are successful in their ability to maintain intimacy because their positive interactions outnumber the negative ones, and they tend to have compatible styles of conflict resolution. The ability to effectively deal with conflict situations before they overwhelm the relationship is a primary means of preventing marital distress and its subsequent destructive effects on the health and well-being of the individuals concerned.

Marriage and Family Health

Research suggests that social interaction with significant others may be a determinant of physical and psychological well-being. In a comprehensive analysis of the literature, Burman and Margolin (1992) found that the psychosocial quality of marriages is linked to mortality and morbidity rates, but the effect is indirect and nonspecific. For men, marriage offers health-buffering effects. Women are more likely to experience health-related problems if the marriage is distressed. Marital distress is associated with suppressed immune function and increases in stress-related hormones such as catecholamine and corticosteroids (Kiecolt-Glaser, Malarky, Cacioppo, & Glaser, 1994). Research in the past decade has established a strong association between marital interaction and a wide range of outcomes for family members. For example, in several studies, the issue of depression was considered. McCabe and Gotlib (1993) found that depressed wives become increasingly negative in their verbal behavior as they perceive that marital interactions are more hostile. In a study of couples in which either the husband or wife was depressed, Johnson and Jacob (1997) found that depressed couples were more negative than nondepressed couples and couples with a depressed wife were more negative than those with a depressed husband. In exploring the interaction behaviors associated with the wives' depression, Schmaling, Whisman, Fruzzetti, and Truax (1991) found that active summarization of issues or problems by the wife was associated with fewer depressive symptoms and the absence of a diagnosis of major depression. Issues of power and control have been the focus of some studies, with increasing attention given to the area of family violence.

One perspective on violence more prominent in the therapy literature is the emphasis on anger management for batterers. Exploration of the power dimension provides a somewhat different perspective. The research of Jacobson and Gottman (1998) indicates that there may be a systematic use of violence to intimidate and control the abused wife, instead of periodic uncontrolled outbursts. In another study of violence and power, Babcock, Waltz, Jacobson, and Gottman (1993) found that couples who experience domestic violence are also more likely to engage in husband-demand and wife-withdraw patterns than are nonviolent, distressed couples or happily married couples. In the domestically violent group, those husbands who had less power were more physically abusive of their wives. Among the batterers in their study, Jacobson, Gottman, Gortner, Berns, and Shortt (1997) found that there was a high (38%) divorce or separation rate, predicted by the husband's dominance and the wife's report of emotional abuse. In a 10-year review of marital interaction reported in the *Journal of Marriage and the Family,* Coleman, Ganong, and Fine (2000) conclude that further exploration of the issues of marital interaction, power, and violence will be an evolving focus of research in coming years. The issues of power and violence are also noteworthy because family nurses, as primary health care providers, may discover violent or abusive relationships through a definitive assessment and may be key sources of referral. In spite of the linkages between marital interaction and the physiological and psychological health of indi-

viduals, McCubbin (1999) notes that there has been little research conducted by nurses on the transition to marriage. Given the potential health risks for family members and the continuing exploration of linkages among morbidity and mortality rates and the quality of marriages, this area merits further investigation by nurse researchers.

Remarriage

When the family life cycle is interrupted by death or divorce, family members must undergo a complex process to stabilize and redefine relationships and roles. They must undergo this process again if a widowed or divorced parent remarries. Remarriage and the formation of stepfamilies as a result of divorce have become more common transitions in the family life cycle in recent years. Terminology associated with families attempting to negotiate new roles brought on by this transition is indicative of the problems and stressors these families encounter. Crosbie-Burnett and McClintic (2000) use the term *recoupling* as opposed to *remarriage* because it is more inclusive and includes heterosexual and gay and lesbian couples, as well as first married parents. A *stepfamily* is described as one in which at least one of the recoupling adults has one or more children from a previous relationship and the children spend time in the household. Mason (1998) classifies stepfamilies as simple and complex. The simple stepfamily is one in which the remarriage is formed by a parent to a person who is not a parent, and the complex stepfamily is formed by the remarriage of two people who are parents.

Stressors Affecting Remarriage

Coleman, Ganong, and Goodwin's (1994) review of 26 textbooks on marriage and family lists 12 categories mentioned most often as sources of stress in remarriage and the formation of stepfamilies. Stressors are classified as step-relationships, general stepfamily stressors, complexity of families and relationships, role ambiguity, financial pressures, former spouse relationships, negative stereotyping, unrealistic expectations, family conflict, incest/sexual tensions, lack of legal status, and kinship terms. In addition, they also note that more is written on the stressors associated with remarriage and stepfamilies than on the benefits and strengths of this particular family structure.

Among the identified problems specific to remarriage are the complexity of the kinship network and the lack of institutionalized social regulations concerning relationships and social roles. Previously divorced parents must interact with additional children while maintaining a parental role with their biological children, and children acquire an additional parent. When two families are joined by remarriage, two previously established family cultures are brought together, creating the potential for conflict in values, habits, and interests. Integration of the two families requires renegotiating and establishing new family traditions and habits, which may cause friction and conflict for all those involved. Besides the addition of new family members, other stressors include the redistribution of resources, boundary ambiguity, conflicting life cycle stages, sexual tension, and stepparent and stepchild role ambiguity. Issues of discipline, loyalty, visitation, and distribution of household tasks are sources of stress related to role ambiguity (Crosbie-Burnett & McClintic, 2000). Boundary ambiguity results from family members' various views on the status of the new family, lack of agreement between the parental subsystems of the two families, and children's continual movement between households to maintain visitation rights of children and noncustodial parents. Issues of loyalty for the children, the new partner, an ex-spouse, or other family members are additional challenges and sources of stress (Berger, 2000).

The economic aspect of remarriage may be complicated by obligations of the noncustodial parent or the custodial parent's dependency on a former spouse for child support. The economic situation is frequently marked by unpredictability, adding another stressor. Sweeney's (1997) analysis of remarriage among the Wisconsin Longitudinal Study of high school graduates of 1957 explores the role between socioeconomic prospects and remarriage after divorce. She identifies two important reasons to study remarriage as an entity separate from first marriage: (1) remarriage generally occurs later in life, and consequently, people are in different situations regarding occupation and are more likely to have children;

and (2) socioeconomic status takes on additional importance in making the decision to remarry. When women's age, occupational status, and socioeconomic status at the time of separation or divorce were examined, socioeconomic prospects were found to be generally more important in making the decision to remarry for women than for men.

Remarriage and Family Health

Clearly, the potential stressors affecting remarried families and the increasing evidence of decreased marital satisfaction suggest that remarriage may have some effect on the health of both men and women. Recognizing the sparseness of research concerning remarried families and the lack of information concerning the effect of remarriage on the health of husband and wife, Ganong and Coleman (1991) conducted a study to explore the health of remarried men and remarried women and examine the correlates of health complaints of remarried adults. They found no major health differences between men and women, although women experienced more changes in health complaints overall after remarriage than men did. In general, these researchers found that the health of both men and women was affected most by their feelings toward one another and by having decision-making power within the family. For women, positive feelings toward their spouses and less decision-making power were associated with health, whereas for men a high level of marital satisfaction and more decision-making power in the family were associated with health. Women also had better health if there were fewer children in the family and if the children were their own. Ganong and Coleman concluded that participants in their study did not perceive a decline in their health after remarriage, in spite of the complex stressors involved. However, a relationship did appear to exist between family dynamics and health for the remarried individuals in their study.

Over the past decade, an enormous amount of literature has been generated from researchers' study of remarriage and stepfamilies (Coleman, Ganong, & Fine, 2000). However, this extensive review of the literature showed that only a few studies on the health effects of remarriage on adults and the family unit have been conducted. The focus of investigation of these few studies was health status associated with depressive symptoms and psychological distress. The topics of primary interest to investigators over the last decade include demographic trends, remarriage relationships, the effects of living with a stepparent on children, stepfamily processes, societal views of stepfamilies, and legal issues. Increased research efforts are needed to identify the positive health aspects of remarriage and to determine successful health-promoting strategies.

Parenthood as a Critical Transition

The transition to parenthood is identified as being a major life stressor for both women and men. The arrival of the first child changes a person into a parent and a couple into a family with children. Few other events have more impact on a family than the birth of a child, both in terms of the general consequences of adding members to a group and the more specific changes in the role and power structure of a marriage. The transition to parenthood usually describes movement from the early married stage to the stage in which the oldest child is younger than 2 years. Whether the addition of a child to a family constitutes a crisis and to what extent has been the subject of many studies for nearly half a century. Among the stressors identified as contributing to the critical transition of first parenthood is the accession of an infant member and the change from dyad to triad, resulting in the activation of the parental roles of mother and father. For some families, the temporary or permanent withdrawal of the wife from the workforce to accommodate childrearing contributes to a major status change. Additionally, residential changes may also occur to accommodate the needs of a family with an infant.

CANADIAN PERSPECTIVES
FAMILY HEALTH PROMOTION DURING TRANSITIONS: NURSES AND THE BIRTH OF A FIRST CHILD

Francine de Montigny, PhD, MSc, Inf
University of Quebec in Outaouais
Carl Lacharité, PhD
University of Québec in Trois-Riviéres

The birth of a first child is a critical moment in the development of a family. Building a sense of efficacy as a parent (perceived self-efficacy) is a pivotal challenge to maintaining the equilibrium of the family. Perceived self-efficacy means that the parents have, over time, come to believe that they can meet the demands of parenting (Bandura, 1995, 1996, 1997). Research has shown that less stressed parents and parents who have support from their spouses see themselves as more efficacious with their children (Reece & Harkless, 1998). It used to be assumed that, through their actions and their words, nurses influenced parents' perceived self-efficacy. However, before a recent Canadian study was done by deMontigny and Lacharité (2002), no figures on the strength and direction of this influence were available.

This study was essential, given the shortening hospital stay after a birth, now lasting only 24 to 48 hours. This early discharge has lowered health care costs, but it has also limited opportunities for mothers to receive support from nurses (Fishbein & Burggraf, 1998) and offers few opportunities to meet the learning needs of fathers (Ménard, 1999).

DeMontigny and Lacharité (2002) began by interviewing 13 first-time fathers and 13 first-time mothers in the 12 days after the birth of their first child. These fathers and mothers shared their experiences of the important moments in the immediate post-

partum period. Five categories of significant events were identified: (1) coming to terms with the physical and emotional changes during the postpartum period, (2) coping with parental demands, (3) maintaining conjugal functioning, (4) coming to terms with environmental demands, and (5) exchanging information with nurses. Both the fathers and the mothers experience a variety of critical moments during the immediate postpartum period in the hospital. Of these, events related to the parenting experience (getting to know the baby, caring for and feeding the baby), interactions with nursing staff, and interactions with spouses emerged as themes.

DeMontigny (2002) then met

with 160 mothers and 160 fathers from the same couples 16 days after the birth of their first child. These parents completed a series of questionnaires relating to events during the postpartum period, the help given to them by nurses, their perception of control, their level of anxiety, their alliance as parents, their perceived self-efficacy, their previous experience with children, their social support, their baby's temperament, and their relationship style. Structural equation modeling (SEM) was used to analyze the data and allowed a common model of parents' postpartum experience to be established. In this model, the nurses' collaboration and help-giving practices contribute directly and indirectly to the perception of control and perceptions of events during the postpartum period. Nurses contribute to a parent's perceived self-efficacy through their alliance with parents.

In the context of health promotion, these results indicate that the help given by nurses to parents after the birth of a child makes a major difference in the parents' experiences. This reinforces the importance of nurses putting specific support strategies in place. A nurse who meets with the parents after the birth of their child creates a context for change. The nurse gives structure to the relationship, speaks with the father and the mother, and is eager to learn about their different experiences. She works with the parents to empower them by recognizing their strengths and skills, as well as their capacity to take charge of the situations that arise. The nurse asks questions, provides information, and offers support to accompany the decisions made by the parents and the actions they take. She encourages interactions with the baby. She listens to the parents' concerns and worries and helps them communicate with each other, thus supporting family health promotion during this life transition.

References

Bandura, A. (1995). *Exercise of personal and collective efficacy in changing societies.* Cambridge: Cambridge University Press.

Bandura, A. (1996). Ontological and epistemological terrains revisited. *Journal of Behavior Therapy and Experimental Psychiatry, 27,* 323-345.

Bandura, A. (1997). *Self-efficacy: The exercise of control.* New York: W. H. Freeman.

DeMontigny, F., & Lacharité, C. (2002). Primiparous fathers and mothers' perceptions of critical moments in the immediate postpartum period. *Quebec Journal of Psychology, 23*(3), 57-78.

DeMontigny, F. (2002). *First time parents' perceptions of significant events in the postpartum period, nurses' help-giving practices and parental self-efficacy.* Unpublished doctoral dissertation, University of Quebec in Trois Rivières, Trois Rivières, Quebec, Canada.

Fishbein, E. G., & Burggraf, E. (1998). Early postpartum discharge: How are mothers managing? *Journal of Obstetric, Gynecologic and Neonatal Nursing, 27,* 142-148.

Ménard, A. M. (1999). *Représentations du rôle paternel chez les infirmières.* Unpublished master's thesis, Université d'Ottawa, Ottawa, Ontario, Canada.

Reece, S. M., & Harkless, G. (1998). Self-efficacy, stress, and parental adaptation: Applications to the care of childbearing families. *Journal of Family Nursing, 4,* 198-215.

Canadian spelling is used.

Cowan and Cowan (1995) note that enough research has been done on the transition to parenthood to reasonably conclude that it is a time of stress with the potential for maladaptive change for a significant number of new parents. Because of this newly acquired stress on the couple, it is reasonable to assume that the tension resulting from this transition may affect other relationships within the family unit, which may in turn affect the best possible development of the child. Cowan and Cowan suggest that preventive intervention programs be designed and implemented for both low-risk and high-risk families to minimize the stress associated with this major lifestyle change.

Vessey and Knauth (2001) assess the transition to parenthood and its influence on marital change using an ecological conceptual framework and conclude that marital change during this transition is influenced by several factors such as individual characteristics of the parents, individual characteristics of the infant, relationships within the nuclear family, relationships with the multigenerational family, and the division of labor inside and outside the home (Box 17-1).

Social networks and supports are especially important during critical transition periods such as the birth of the first child (Bost, 2002). Married couples with larger network sizes and more support before the birth of the first child report having larger and more supportive networks 2 years later. Kinship networks include grandparents, aunts and uncles, and other members of the extended family. Maintaining friendship networks is equally important during the transition to parenthood. Such structural events or changes in the family role complex that occur simultaneously generate major family reorganization.

BOX 17-1 Key Areas of Assessment During Transition to Parenthood

CHARACTERISTICS OF THE PARENTS

How has parenting changed your own life?
How well are you coping with the new responsibilities of parenting?
How has it affected your work outside of the home?
How much time do you spend with your spouse without your infant?

CHARACTERISTICS OF THE INFANT

How well does your infant sleep?
How content does your infant seem with her/his feedings?
Is your infant easily consoled?
What kind of reactions does your infant elicit from you or other family members?

RELATIONSHIPS WITHIN THE NUCLEAR FAMILY

How has your marriage changed since the birth of your infant?
Does your spouse show as much affection for you since the birth of your infant?

Do you confide in each other?
How much time do you and your spouse spend in leisure activities without your infant each week?

RELATIONSHIPS WITH THE MULTIGENERATIONAL FAMILY

How did your parents relate to each other and to you when you were growing up?
Do you plan to parent your child in a similar manner?
How much help do your relatives give you with the care of your infant and with household tasks?
Does your relationship with your parents affect your relationships with your spouse and children?

DIVISION OF LABOR WITHIN AND OUTSIDE OF THE HOME

How much time and responsibility does your spouse assume for the care of your infant?
Is the division of childcare and household tasks a source of conflict in your marriage?
How satisfying is your work?
Does your work conflict with family relationships?

Adapted from Vessey, J., & Knauth, D. G. (2001). Marital change during the transition to parenthood. *Pediatric Nursing, 27*(2), 169-172, 184.

Children and the Effect on Couple Relationships

Marital satisfaction is a major focus of the literature that explores the effect of children on the marital relationship, usually by examination of the attitudes of husbands and wives. Changes in the marriage may occur in division of household tasks, companionship between the couple, and leisure activity time. Direct negative effects on the expression of intimacy of the couple may occur as a result of decreased communication, role strain, interference with a sexual relationship, and a segregation of husbands and wives based on traditional spheres of activity. For example, Dalgas-Pelish (1993) explored the effect children have on marital happiness and found that the level of marital happiness was lower for childbearing families compared with childless couples. Various role conflicts and the total role change that occur as a result of having a child influence marital happiness. Rholes, Simpson, Campbell, and Grich (2001) also examined how the transition to parenthood affects marital satisfaction and functioning among persons with different attachment orientations and established that highly ambivalent women who entered parenthood perceiving lower levels of support from their husbands experienced declines in marital satisfaction. Additionally, wives' ambivalence was a strong predictor of their own and their husbands' marital satisfaction. In Helms-Erikson's (2001) study on the timing of parenthood and the division of housework, marital satisfaction for dual-career couples was ultimately due to similarities in their behaviors, beliefs, and backgrounds—not only during the initial transition to parenthood but throughout their childrearing years.

A positive transition to parenthood can best be achieved if the couple has established a loving relationship and has engaged in open dialogue concerning parenting roles and expectations before the arrival of the first child (Newman, 2000). Children can create a bond that solidifies the marriage. The couple shares many pleasant experiences as they interact with the child as a family throughout the various developmental phases. Freysinger (1994) examined the leisure–parental satisfaction relationship between children and mothers and fathers and found that marital satisfaction was a strong predictor of parental satisfaction. Leisure interaction between fathers and children had a significant effect on the parental role but was not found to be significant for the mothers. The data suggest that mothers are less likely to identify time alone with the children and caring for them as leisure time. However, cross-sectional analyses done with a panel of parents over a 4-year period by Rogers and White (1998) showed parenting satisfaction to be significantly greater for married couples with a high level of marital satisfaction, for parents raising their own biological children, and for mothers. Other factors that contribute to marital satisfaction include the potential for fulfillment of personal needs as individuals and the possibility that satisfaction in the parental role may energize performance in other areas, benefiting the marital relationship (Box 17-2).

BOX 17-2   Key Research Findings on Marital Relationships and Transition to Parenthood

- Most couples show more of a partnership and less of a romance after the birth of their infant, creating less satisfaction in the marriage.
- Imbalances in the division of labor, including infant care and household tasks, are significant sources of marital conflict for new parents.
- Maladaptive marital change is associated with negative developmental outcomes for children.
- When parents do not directly address the conflicts within their own relationship, they often project their anxiety onto their child, which interferes with the child's development.
- When parents create a calm, respectful, engaged environment in which they are attentive to their marital relationship and connected to their children, they are more likely to rear responsible children.

Adapted from Vessey, J., & Knauth, D. G. (2001). Marital change during the transition to parenthood. *Pediatric Nursing, 27*(2), 169-172, 184.

Single-Parent Families

In the United States, the shift in the majority of families away from the nuclear family (consisting of a father, a mother, and their children living in the same household) to varied family structures has been a dramatic societal change. A statistical picture reveals that more than half of all American children will live in a single-parent household during some period of their childhood. One third of children are born to an unmarried parent, and one fourth live with a single parent. For every 24 children born, one child lives with neither parent, but in foster care or with grandparents (World Almanac & Book of Facts, 2002). Single-parent families have diverse forms, sometimes resulting from the death of a spouse, divorce or separation, unplanned pregnancies, or even the choice to have children as a single person. Some single parents have sole custody of their children, others share custody, and some rarely see their children. Some single parents are heterosexual and others are gay or lesbian. The diversity of family forms, issues, and potential stressors is immediately apparent. As a result, becoming a single parent can be perceived as a crisis, a life transition, or a critical transition, depending on changes in the family role complex.

Most single parents are women, with the number increasing from 3 million in 1970 to 10 million in the year 2000 (Fields & Casper, 2001). However, during this same period, the number of single-father families also grew from 393,000 to 2 million. Demographic trends that have affected the shift from two-parent to single-parent families include the increasing number of births to unmarried women and the high rate of divorce in families with children. These changes in the family structure have significant implications for the well-being of the children in relation to the social programs and policies that affect health, welfare, education, and other areas of work and family life. Furthermore, single-parent families headed by women are more likely to include more than one child and have family incomes below the poverty level, and the women are more likely to have never been married. However, children living with divorced single mothers generally have an economic advantage over those living with mothers who have never been married (Fields & Casper, 2001; Muehlenberg, 2002).

The parent who is single as the result of divorce encounters the same life cycle changes and family responsibilities as parents in a two-parent family but carries the load of family duties such as child-rearing, support and companionship, and role modeling for the children almost exclusively alone (Friedman, Connelly, Miller, & Williams, 1998). Fine indicates (as cited in Steil, 2001) that children living in single-parent families are twice as likely to have emotional and behavioral problems, repeat a grade, and drop out of school. They are less likely to attend college and more likely to be involved in the criminal justice system. Also, a girl from a single-parent family is more likely to become a single teenage parent. Biblarz and Gottainer (2000) compared children reared by single mothers because of the death of the father with those reared by single mothers because of divorce. They found that divorced single mothers are not significantly different from widowed mothers in childrearing, gender role, family values, health-related behaviors, and other areas of lifestyle. However, divorced single mothers have significantly lower levels of education, hold lower-level jobs, have more financial stress, participate in the workforce at a higher rate, and are generally less happy in their adult life. They postulate that the structure of different types of single-mother families may indeed account for known differences in child outcomes.

Tsushima and Gecas (2001) examined conditions and consequences of role taking in single-parent families and how they affect child socialization. Role taking occurs when there is a parental commitment to the parent-child relationship and to the child in general. They found that low-income single parents who reported problems with relating to their children and problems with discipline, authority, school, and supervision are those who lack role-taking skills and have difficulties in parenting their children. Single parents have less time and fewer resources and social networks, and in general, they are more stressed as sole providers for the family. In addition to role taking for effective parenting and effective child socialization, commitment to the child as a valued member of the family is essential.

Single-Parent Families and Health

After a divorce, children, as well as parents, may experience emotional stress and a number of health-related problems. These might include feelings of depression and anger; behavior problems in school; and physiological symptoms such as abdominal pain, headaches, eating and sleeping disturbances, and frequent illnesses. Eliciting advice and counseling from a family physician or other health care provider may assist both the parent and child in coping with single-parent family life (American Academy of Pediatrics, 2001; Meurer, Meurer, & Holloway, 1996). In a study of low-income single mothers, Hall, Gurley, Sachs, and Kruyscio (1991) found that more than half of the women interviewed experienced depressive symptoms. More depressive symptoms were associated with everyday stressors, fewer social resources, and greater use of avoidance coping. Neither social resources nor coping strategies buffered the relationship between everyday stressors and depressive symptoms. Depressive symptoms predicted parenting attitudes, which in turn predicted child behavior. These findings suggest that considerable attention should be focused on low-income single mothers to determine more effective ways to assist them and their children in developing effective coping strategies. In a later study done with low-income single mothers, Lutenbacher and Hall (1998) also concluded that depressive symptoms were linked to the effects of childhood physical and sexual abuse, everyday stressors, and self-esteem on at-risk parenting attitudes. As self-esteem decreased, everyday stressors increased, as did depressive symptoms. These findings support the argument that the potential for child abuse among single mothers is great, especially for those who have low incomes, are unemployed, have little education, and/or have many depressive symptoms.

As noted previously, many single mothers have low incomes and limited education and are unskilled and unable to find adequate and affordable care for their children while they work. This means that health care providers are challenged to provide care to families with children who have fewer financial resources. Therefore family health nurses should focus on health promotion and prevention for families early on; stress management during transitional periods; and primary care, especially for pregnant women, young children, and low-income women and families. Because so many single-parent families are at the poverty level, health care professionals must be aware of the dynamic effect this has on the whole family system (Cox, 1997).

Adoption

Although parenting is often thought of as a role assumed in the traditional two-parent biological family, couples and single adults can also become parents though adoption. Just as couples have different reasons for having children, they give a variety of reasons for adopting children. Many adoptions involve stepparents and other relatives, but infertility of one or both partners is another major factor. Choosing to adopt when infertility has been a problem may involve ambivalent feelings, but advances in technology and the increasing availability of in vitro fertilization programs provide infertile couples with an alternative to adoption. Couples may wish to explore this option before considering adoption.

The adoption process is an important but stressful experience for all persons involved: the child, the adoptive parents, and the birth parents. A formal adoption occurs when, through legal recognition, a parental relationship is established between the adoptive parent(s) and the child, giving the adoptive parent(s) the same legal rights as if the child were born to them. At this point the biological parents legally relinquish their parental rights and terminate all contact with the child. Adoption arrangements and placements can be made in a number of ways, such as through public and private agencies or independently through an attorney, physician, or clergy person (Schwartz, 2000). Second-parent adoption allows a person to adopt a child without terminating the parental rights and responsibilities of the biological parent. This form of adoption is common among married couples but is also being used by same-sex couples who are not able to marry (Paik, 2001). Open adoption involves direct contact between the biological and adoptive parents, but with varying degrees of interaction with the child (Sobol, Daly, & Kelloway, 2000). Data reveal that of the 127,000 children in the United States who were waiting to be adopted in the public foster care system on September 30, 1999, 46,000 were adopted in fiscal year 1999 (U. S. Department of Health and Human Services, 2001).

Stress Related to Adoption

Stressors faced by adoptive parents include the shortage of available infants, the unknown timetable involved, and the unpredictable complications the adoption process may create (Bitler & Zavodny, 2002). Adopting couples may find that the experience is unique and their circle of family and friends has not experienced the stressors involved, nor are they necessarily supportive or encouraging. In some cases, family members may be openly negative, expressing concerns about incompatibility and biological deficits. Factors associated with the family adjustment to adoption are the availability of support services to assist in both the preadoption and postadoption periods. Other factors that may affect family adjustment to adoption include characteristics of the child, such as age or special needs; characteristics of the parents, such as high expectations of the child, lack of parental experience, and negative feelings about the adoption process; family socioeconomic and educational levels (McDonald, Propp, & Murphy, 2001); and family structure (Lansford, Ceballo, Abbey, & Stewart, 2001). These factors add to the anxieties of the adoptive parents, who may need to seek support and assistance outside their circle of family and friends.

In general, societal beliefs about adoption tend to create informal social sanctions that make it difficult to obtain support from other sources. The willingness to select adoption as an alternative or to be successful in the process may be influenced by social values dictated by the community in which the adoptive parents live. Additional stress may be experienced by families who decide to adopt a child of a different racial background or a child with special needs, by those who pursue international adoption, or by same-sex couples. In the case of transracial adoption, there are opposing viewpoints. Hollingsworth (1998) argues that transracial adoption is not necessary to ensure that children of color are adopted in a timely manner; but McRoy, Oglesby, and Grape (1997) contend that in the case of African American children, there are not enough homes available for the thousands of needy children waiting to be adopted.

International adoption is an increasingly popular alternative for adoptive parents, especially in the United States, which becomes home for nearly 50% of all children who are adopted internationally (Varnis, 2001). The adoption of Chinese children has grown through the support of Chinese and Western adoptive parents and nonprofit agencies, with approximately 5000 children adopted by American and other Western families in recent years (Lihua, 2001). Before The 1993 Hague Convention on the Protection of Children and Cooperation in Respect to Intercountry Adoption, intercountry adoption was not a well-monitored process because it was generally an autonomous endeavor. The 1993 Hague Convention's goal is to put into practice international legislation that will assign a central authority in each signatory country to monitor all intercountry adoptions, oversee the accreditation of agencies and disciplines allowed to engage in intercountry adoption activities, and ensure compliance with the agreement provisions between the countries that have endorsed the treaty (Masson, 2001; Selinske, Naughton, Flanagan, Fry, & Pickles, 2001).

Special needs adoptees include older children; sets of siblings; and children with a variety of medical, behavioral, or developmental problems. Families who adopt children with special needs may require additional or unique support and advice. Kramer and Houston (1998) found that in addition to the adoption agency with which the parents are working, parents rely on various resources to meet their child's needs such as community-based professionals to assist with medical, educational, and mental health concerns; informal support groups; parents and other extended family members; and friends. Parenting by same-sex parents through the adoption of a child by the second parent or co-parent is also an area that deserves special attention because of the social, emotional, and legal implications of the situation (American Academy of Pediatrics, 2002).

Social trends and technological advances, including management of infertility problems (Van Den Akker, 2001), surrogate motherhood (Van Zyl & Van Niekerk, 2000), and adoption of children by single adults, add many new dimensions to the concept of adoptive families. These trends in themselves may be a further indication that regardless of the stress involved in decision making or the transition to the parental role, the joint venture of the parent-child relationship is a rewarding undertaking. Assistance in exploring adoption and alternatives to adoption is available from health care professionals, adoption agencies, and mutual self-help or support groups.

Maturing Families and Transitions

Because of individual, gender, and social class variations in the nature and timing of role transitions, it is difficult to identify exactly when midlife begins or ends. Moen and Wethington (1999) suggest that midlife is a time when people are enacting a full set of social and personal responsibilities in the early phases and later relinquishing the parenting role and the employment role. Life course analysis emphasizes the interdependency of lives, with changes in family roles influencing relationships and resources in midlife. Experiences for women are more closely linked to stressors or life contingencies of other family members. Options for women may change as children leave or return home, husbands retire or become ill or die, or parents require care or die. The midlife experience for men is more typically associated with their employment roles or role as the family provider. Timing may be an important issue in understanding midlife development. For example, an adult child returning to the parental home in his or her forties with children to manage is a different issue than a single 25-year-old son or daughter coming home to return to school. Another factor is the degree of predictability of transitions during midlife and whether the transitions are expected. Role changes are embedded in social context and are affected by class, education, gender, race, and health. These factors may affect individual motivations to seek other roles or retain familiar ones (Brim, 1992). The following section explores several key transitions in midlife: children leaving home, retirement, and shifting from independent to dependent living.

Children Leaving Home

The family life cycle theory developed by Carter and McGoldrick (1989) provides a more traditional family life cycle theory that includes launching children and then moving on. At this stage, children need to differentiate themselves from their families of origin to develop intimate peer relationships and establish careers and financial independence. Young adults moving successfully through this period develop separate identities and views without severing relationships with their families of origin (Johnson & Wilkinson, 1995). Parents need to develop an ability to tolerate separation and the increasing independence of young adults while remaining connected to them. Parents also need to be tolerant of ambiguity in the work life of adult children and accept a range of lifestyles and emotional attachments outside of the family. When the last child leaves home, a time termed *the empty nest period*, attention is again focused on the couple and the marital relationship. Dennerstein, Dudley, and Guthrie (2002) found that for the majority of women, the departure of the last child leads to positive changes in the mood state and a reduced number of daily hassles. Regardless of the children's characteristics, White and Edwards (1990) found that the empty nest was associated with significant improvement in marital happiness for parents. Most parents experience the transition of children leaving home positively, regardless of the characteristics of parents or children.

A more recent phenomenon that may affect this family developmental phase is the return of young adults to the home and family of origin. There are a number of reasons for adult children returning home, including social and economic events, high divorce rates, and the increasing cost of living. In addition, more people are postponing marriage and more children are being born to unmarried women. The interface of these two experiences may generate some conflict as children return home at a time when their parents may be adjusting to retirement or be assuming caretaking responsibilities for their own aging parents. Studies of the return of children to parental homes have revealed both positive and negative effects. Dennerstein, Dudley, and Guthrie (2002) indicate that the return of adult children may have an adverse effect on the sexual relationship of parents. Supporting grandchildren, as well as children, may be a part of the returning home experience, adding another set of complications. Parents of lower socioeconomic status seem to have fewer negative feelings about adult children residing with them than do middle-class parents. Johnson and Wilkinson (1995) suggest that about

50% of families are comfortable with a living arrangement that includes adult children, whereas others have difficulty because of the resumption of former dependency and caretaking roles.

Families may successfully experience the transition of *re-nesting* by providing additional space for returned children to allow for privacy for both generations. Family health care professionals can facilitate bonadaptation, or positive adjustment, by encouraging regular open family meetings regarding allocation of household tasks, finances, privacy, and use of space. Most importantly, family members need to respect the lifestyle choices of each generation. Parents may need to focus on developing a satisfying marital relationship, and adult children may need to cultivate relationships outside of the family. Johnson and Wilkinson (1995) identify many positive effects that can result from the experience of adult children returning home, including the opportunity to grow and to move beyond former roles and patterns of behavior.

The research related to adult children leaving home and re-nesting has focused primarily on white middle-class families. There is a need to broaden the area of study to include members of various ethnic and racial groups and to shed additional light on the effect of economic status. The role of grandparent to the children of returning adult children is also complex and challenging, and further research is needed to explore both the positive and negative effects of this role on the physical and psychological well-being of involved family members. Family professionals can facilitate harmony in the re-nested family by encouraging family members to plan regular meetings about "what is working" and "what is not working" as they negotiate living arrangements and a different family structure.

Families and Retirement

For many people, their place of employment and the activities involved in their work interact significantly with their identities. Occupation affects leisure time, friendships, hobbies, values, choice of residence, financial well-being, social class, and social status. Although retirement does not represent a major life crisis for some men and women, it undoubtedly changes the individual's financial status, social relationships, and lifestyle. Retirement is usually seen as a transition point, since it marks the end of full-time work and the beginning of a period of relative leisure. Although many persons are content to retire in their sixties or seventies, a substantial number of persons continue to work by choice or because of economic necessity (Thomas, 1992). In any event, the decision to retire has many important ramifications and requires substantial adjustment in individual roles and family relationships. Retired persons need to develop new approaches to active involvement in their communities and social networks and consider ways to fill a time void. Achievements and commitments must be re-evaluated and one's outlook on life needs to be reconsidered in light of role and lifestyle changes.

Family relationships also merit consideration. Dual-career families may need to consider the effect of one spouse retiring while the other continues to work. On the other hand, there may also be adjustments for a retiring individual and the spouse who has managed the home and assumed childrearing responsibilities. Brown (1994) suggests that women may not perceive retirement as a crisis because they have had to remain flexible as a result of constant role modifications in childrearing, home-making, and career responsibilities. Weiss (1997) found that both men and women retiring from professional and managerial positions had less stress but needed to accept themselves as no longer active in the work world. Couples also needed to restructure the marital relationship, since retirement is a turning point in the marriage, as well as the work life.

The decision to retire may occur in a variety of different contexts. It may be a planned, systematic, voluntary decision; the result of ill health or illness of another family member; or the realization that one is no longer able to deal effectively with work requirements. For others, it may result from an involuntary process based on position elimination caused by corporate restructuring. When the decision to retire must be made before the individual is ready, before the family is able to reorient itself, or in the face of serious economic consequences, the stress of the transition may take different forms and be more significant than that associated with an anticipated, desired event.

Pre-retirement programs can help individuals prepare for retirement, particularly when the programs encompass psychosocial and health issues, as well as information on financial and legal issues. LaBauve and Robinson (1999) have identified a formal broad-based intervention model that involves working with clients from 5 years before retirement through the transition and adjustment phases. They suggest that many issues can contribute to retirement adjustment including culture, gender, financial status, leisure activities, social functioning, health, and interests. More effective programs and effective intervention strategies may assist older persons in making the transition in a more personally satisfying manner. Effective informal types of preparation include discussing the retirement experience with friends and family members and increasing knowledge about retirement, health, aging, and a more leisure-oriented lifestyle. Other aspects may include financial planning and decision making about relocation. Lo and Brown (1999) suggest that preparation for retirement that involves relocation or emigration should include counseling for those who are considering leaving behind family and friends. The loss of role through retirement and the loss of support systems through relocation may alter the adjustment period and require different coping strategies.

Relocation may involve transition to a retirement community, a lifestyle that promotes independent living while continuing to provide social interaction and community support systems. Most persons who consider a retirement community do so because of the loss of a spouse, a decline in health, or a desire to be closer to family. Others are seeking a less stressful way of life and warmer climates. Many persons are attracted to the planned activities, social interactions, security, and assistance with home upkeep and maintenance (Arrington, 1997).

Preparation with sound advice and education regarding economic factors and relocation facilitate the transition to retirement and are important issues in family health promotion. The continued pursuit of hobbies, interests, and social contacts is a priority and helps to reduce social isolation and loneliness. Retired persons living with spouses may need to restructure their roles to allow for a redesigned division of labor. Sharpley

(1997) identifies three major sources of retirees' stress in everyday living: missing work, personal health issues, and relationship issues. In Sharpley's study, measures of these issues correlated significantly with measures of anxiety and depression. Increased attention may need to be given to attitudes toward retirement and coping strategies to effectively deal with these sources of stress.

In their study of psychosocial changes after retirement, Rosenkoetter and Garris (1998) found that the majority of participants were adjusting effectively to retirement; however, significant numbers were experiencing difficulty. These respondents expressed concerns about health, the future, marital relationships, self-esteem needs, and changes in life structure. Based on their findings, Rosenkoetter and Garris (1998) recommend that health care providers give greater consideration to retirement issues in individual and family assessments. They maintain that assessing the potential impact of retirement on an individual and significant others could provide considerable insight into existing health problems. They caution against assuming that retirement is a "satisfying" experience and recommend that it be considered as any other life transition with possible positive and negative effects. Further research regarding adjustment factors in retirement is needed to reduce or prevent psychosocial health problems in older, retired populations and to develop effective health promotion strategies.

Independent to Dependent Living

The aging process in later life is a period of transitions that will likely involve losses that affect the person's social status, income, family members, and close friends. As for most people, change is often difficult for older adults. Uncertainties involved with later life transitions include coping with changes in housing, health status, financial insecurity, dependency, and the loss of family relationships and friends (Davey, Murphy, & Price, 2000; Friedman et al., 1998). Nearly 40% of elderly people identify themselves as being in excellent or very good health (National Center for Health Statistics, 1999). However, as more people live to the oldest ages, more will face chronic, limiting illnesses or conditions such as arthritis, diabetes, osteoporosis, and dementia.

These conditions result in becoming dependent on others for assistance with instrumental activities such as meal preparation, shopping, and financial management and help with performing activities of daily living such as grooming, toileting, and getting around inside the home (Davey, 2000).

In the United States in the year 2000, the older population, defined as those people age 65 years and older, numbered 35 million. This represents a 12% increase since 1990. During this time, the percentage of the older population living in nursing home facilities declined from 5.1% to 4.5%. This decline was especially notable in the population of adults age 85 years and older: only 18.2% resided in nursing homes in 2000, compared with 24.5% in 1990 (Hetzel & Smith, 2001). Although many older adults are able to continue to live independently in their own homes, it is not unusual for some to make the transition from independent living to living with adult children or other family members or to supervised living in a residential facility. The successful transition from independent to dependent living is a stressful event not only for the elderly individual but also for family members and others who may be involved in the complex decisions required to accomplish a healthy change in residence (McCubbin, 1993).

Stress Associated with Transitions in Mature and Aging Families

Older persons generally prefer to care for themselves and retain their independence for as long as possible. Use of in-home support services, home health agencies, homemaker aides, and adult day programs allow many older adults to remain in the secure environment of their own home or within a family member's home for a longer period. However, life changes in the later years involve losses and adjustments that may be overwhelming for many people, resulting in stress and other health-related issues.

Relocating to another living environment is a life adjustment that occurs for a number of older adults. Armer (1996) found that factors affecting relocation adjustment were similar for urban institutionalized older adults and rural older adults who relocated to a planned housing unit. Factors identified as affecting the ability to experience a positive adjustment included perceived choice, social interaction and support, predictability, prior

life satisfaction, and recent loss. Suggestions for health care professionals and families that may ease this adjustment process include assisting older adults in exploring alternatives to relocation, preparing them in advance for what may be expected in their new surroundings, encouraging and supporting social interaction with family and friends, and maintaining an awareness of their recent losses and prior life satisfaction experiences.

The loss of a spouse can be especially devastating to the surviving elderly partner. Combined with physical losses that occur naturally with age, such as diminished hearing, eyesight, and functional ability, the grieving process can put the surviving spouse at risk for accidents, depression, and feelings of loneliness and despair. Sadly, usual sources of support may no longer exist if other family and friends have also died or are incapacitated. However, emotional needs can be met through socialization in structured support groups and volunteer work and even through pets (Fischer & Hegge, 2000).

Having an animal for a companion can alleviate feelings of loss and reduce stress during periods of transition. The daily routine of caring for a special pet maintains a sense of order when a person's life has been disrupted by loss and change. An animal can provide companionship, comfort, and the continued opportunity to care for another being when human contact is limited (Suthers-McCabe, 2001). In addition to people and companion animals, objects of attachment such as special material possessions, special places, and ideas and beliefs may provide emotional support that can be cultivated to help sustain the health and well-being of the older person (Cookman, 1996).

Health Implications in Later Life

Health promotion and illness prevention continue to be essential during this final phase of the life cycle. Primary prevention programs specifically designed for aging Americans include education in the areas of nutrition, exercise, the safe use of medications, home and community safety assessment, injury prevention, smoking cessation, and use of preventive resources. Secondary actions include encouraging preventive screening examinations such as mammography, sigmoidoscopy, and annual physical examinations and controlling problems such as diabetes, hypertension, and stress (Davidhizar, Eshleman, & Moody, 2002).

However, uncontrollable events such as falls, wandering, worsening dementia, or declining functional status may suddenly lead to the need for an elderly person to relocate to an assisted living or skilled nursing environment. When family is involved, this decision may result in feelings of guilt, anger, and a sense of failure at not being able to continue to provide for the elderly family member. Baldwin and Shaul's (2001) case study of an elderly woman's transition from independent to supervised living shows how Carter and McGoldrick's (1999) Expanded Family Life Cycle Theory can be used by the nurse and other health care providers in assessment of an older adult who may be experiencing the stress of making such a change. Systematic assessment, individualized planning with the client, and family involvement combined with support and open communication can facilitate the process.

Clearly, family relationships play a key role in the transition from independent to dependent living. Although this discussion provides some insight into the wide variability in the experience of aging and transition, it also illuminates the scarcity of research in many areas. McHenry and Price (2000) identify some areas that need to be explored regarding aging in the family context. Although considerable research on the stress and adaptation to the caregiving role has been done, little is known about the process by which families decide who will be the primary caregiver. In addition, little is known about how past family relationships affect adjustment to caregiving. More importantly, few studies have addressed how older persons adjust to the role of care recipient. The range of ability in dealing with transitions associated with aging within and between ethnocultural groups is another area in need of further exploration. There is a pressing need to examine these areas in light of population trends and increasing recognition of how family development issues influence generations to come.

Families and Relocation

In an increasingly technology-driven society, attention has been focused on understanding the interaction of work and workers and the effect of work on families. In the growing number of studies concerning families and work, the effect of relocation on family life has emerged as a topic of concern. Moving may be considered a transition, since it involves adaptation to a new environment, social structure, and possibly, new roles. Although frequently associated with job transfers, relocation potentially affects individuals of all ages. It may be a factor for adolescents if their parents move or if they decide to attend college in another area. Relocation may figure importantly in retirement planning or may result from the loss of a spouse or the illness of an aging parent. In later years, it may also be significant as individuals and families seek supportive care environments. The decision to relocate may be influenced by many factors including career advancement, higher income, prestige, personal gratification, and the desire to be closer to or more distant from relatives. Each decision involves a balancing of gains and losses in relation to the individual and to the family's continued existence as a unit. Family relationships, children's education and well-being, proximity to aging relatives, lifestyle, economic aspects, and concerns for security all enter the analysis if the decision is voluntary. In some situations, the decision is not voluntary, and additional stressors may be involved as families relocate because of political unrest, unemployment, or loss of significant supportive relationships. The degree of stress involved in relocation can be substantial. For some, it may lead to the fulfillment of a long-desired goal and may not be perceived as stressful. For others, the process of relocation may be perceived as growth-producing and may even signal the end of a very stressful period in life. Given the variety of issues, situations, and developmental stages that could be involved, many opportunities for research into the process of relocation and the effectiveness of interventions to support families through this transition exist. In this section, several types of relocation are considered including work-related changes, migration, and homelessness. Although each of these transitions has unique characteristics, all concern families and the experience of relocation.

Work-Related Changes

Various aspects of family life can be threatened when work-related changes occur. Sudden, unpredictable loss of employment may have serious negative effects on individuals and families, adding a dimension of stress without the opportunity for psychological or financial preparation. Issues may arise in relation to financial hardship, spending behavior, division of labor, parental authority, and marital power. Unemployment also means the loss of a major role that has social value and is sometimes closely linked to the identity of an individual. Families differ in their ability to cope with sudden or imminent unemployment, depending on their perception of the event and their ability to mobilize resources.

Issues of uncertainty, such as threatened job loss, may also have negative effects, particularly in relation to the health of individuals. There are some methodological limitations to examining this issue, since only longitudinal studies that measure employee health before any rumor of change occurs can provide adequate data for examining this type of change. In a major study of employment security conducted over a 5-year period, Ferrie et al. (1998) found that self-reported morbidity and physiological risk factors tended to increase among respondents from a threatened department compared with those from other departments. Both men and women had significant increases in body mass index, altered sleep patterns, cholesterol levels, and ischemia. Women also experienced a significant relative increase in blood pressure. These adverse effects on health status were unexplained by health-related behaviors. This study has significant advantages over other studies of workplace closure that lack a control group or sufficient data from phase 1 (lack of awareness of future changes) through phase 3 (the termination phase). Although there is clearly a need for further research to explore the health-related changes of threats to economic security, this study clearly identifies health-related changes that do not seem to be linked to health-related behaviors. More longitudinal studies are needed to provide additional data and to determine what type of interventions might be successful in decreasing negative effects on health when job security is threatened.

Job relocation refers to situations in which an employee simultaneously changes job and home location. Both moving households and changing jobs are considered highly stressful life events. Some of the literature suggests that individuals learn to cope with moving by moving, and those individuals who have moved more often may feel more confident about moving and adjust to a move more quickly (Fisher & Shaw, 1994). However, Martin (1995) found that current research has failed to substantiate a relationship between prior moves and aspects of psychological well-being or attitudes toward relocation. Martin's study examined the relationships among the number of prior moves, time living in an area, and psychological reactions of employees undergoing job evaluation. Participants responded to measures before and after the move. Sex and age were not predictive of relocation stress after the move, but having a child was. Although Martin (1995) found support for the view that number of prior moves is related to well-being, it is a complex situation. The longer the re-locator had lived in an area before a move, the greater was the change in general stress, job-related anxiety, and depression.

In another study, Martin, Leach, Norman, and Silvester (2000) found that those individuals who were relocating and had many relocation problems, as well as pessimistic attributions, reported the worst mental health relocation-specific stress. In a further analysis in which attributions of perceived control were used, those re-locators who were predicted to be most at risk with many problems and low control reported the most negative changes in mental health during the course of the move.

Relocation related to job loss or transfer is a complex transition experience, compounded by the many adjustments that each family member must make. Coping mechanisms for families include maintaining the quality of family relationships and using other social supports effectively. Re-establishing intimate relationships and building these social supports is a challenge for individuals who are relocating. Strategies that enhance family flexibility and allow members to redefine their roles and restructure their daily patterns may also be helpful during these transitions. Family cohesiveness can be enhanced by open communication, avoidance of blaming, and engaging in family activities that foster unity.

Homelessness

The issue of family homelessness has become one of the most misunderstood and least documented social policy issues of this time. The United States Conference of Mayors (1998) has indicated that homeless families are the fastest growing segment of the homeless population. As many as 400,000 homeless families are living in shelters, representing more than a million homeless children across America (The Institute for Children and Poverty, 1996). The most common method of counting homeless individuals, point-in-time estimation, tends to underestimate the number and does not account for people who are homeless for short periods, those who are living on the street, or those who are living with others (Sherman & Redlener, 1999). The situation is made more complex by the difficulty in obtaining accurate data, by the collective social denial of the existence and importance of the problem, and by the lack of public policy that addresses the myriad of problems related to homelessness (Nunez & Fox, 1999).

In response to the gap between research and public policy, Nunez and Fox (1999) conducted a study of more than 700 homeless parents with more than 2000 homeless children recruited from 58 residential and supportive service facilities located in 10 cities across the country. They concluded that family homelessness is a complex web of issues that varies widely by community. Race, low educational levels, poor employability, and welfare dependence emerged as common themes in their study. The typical homeless family in America today consists of a single mother, about 30 years of age, with two or three children who have an average age of 5 years.

In this study Nunez and Fox (1999) found that 78% of all families surveyed were headed by single mothers, 19% by two parents, and 3% by single fathers. Approximately 95% of the participants in this study were naturalized or native-born U. S. citizens. Nationally, 58% of homeless families are African American (compared with 12% of the population), 22% of homeless families are white (compared with 74% of the general population), and 15% of homeless families are Hispanic or Latino (compared with 10% in the general population). In this study 43% of the homeless parents had never rented or owned their own residence. Among those participants in this study who had previously lived with a spouse or partner, 76% left because of domestic violence, overcrowding, or disagreement reasons; and domestic violence alone was identified by 57% as the reason for leaving. This study presents a significant amount of additional data on undereducation and identifies teen pregnancy as one of the leading explanations for it. The majority of homeless parents have worked at some point in their lives; however, 28% have never worked. Among the many barriers to employment mentioned by homeless families, lack of child care or pregnancy is identified by 41%. This study provides additional data formally quantifying the nature of the problem of homeless families as the first step in providing a national picture of homelessness, identifying regional differences, and serving as a foundation for future research.

Risk and Protective Factors of Homelessness

In attempting to determine the nature of risk and protective factors, Bassuk et al. (1997) noted that the question of why homelessness exists has been confused with the question of which persons are most likely to become homeless. They attempted to identify individual level risk factors that increase the likelihood of a female-headed family becoming homeless. Both housed and homeless low-income mothers had experienced high rates of early family disruption, trauma, and loss. Foster care placement and drug use by the primary female caretaker were the most salient childhood predictors of subsequent family homelessness in adulthood. Finally, in contrast to other studies, Bassuk et al. found that violent victimization, although present in these participants' lives, was not a risk factor for family homelessness in this model.

Factors that increase social or community resources or supports are protective against family homelessness. Living in an area for a longer period increases knowledge of resources. Completion of high school was found to be protective against family homelessness because better employment opportunities may enable a single parent to be self-supporting. Other protective factors included being a primary tenant and receiving cash assistance or a housing subsidy. Bassuk et al. (1997) concluded that factors that compromise an individual's social and economic resources are associated with greater risk of homelessness.

Current research indicates that homeless families are a heterogeneous population, with some experiencing adverse economic circumstances and others experiencing lack of education, mental illness, substance abuse, or victimization. What is less clear is whether the experience of homelessness affects a person's ability to function. Although there have been differences in the psychological and developmental characteristics of homeless children compared with children who have permanent homes, it is not clear whether this is a result of circumstances before homelessness or precipitated by the experience of homelessness. These factors, regardless of origin, may continue to hamper the health and well-being of children as they mature. Homelessness may also affect parental well-being, increasing the possibility of future episodes of homelessness. Some experiences of institutional living may decrease skills needed to function autonomously (Sherman & Redlener, 1999).

Issues of health and well-being in relation to homeless women have become the focus of nursing researchers as the nature of the experience and effect of transitional shelters have received more attention. Hatton (1997) has explored approaches to identifying and managing health problems among women and children living in a transitional shelter. Another dimension is the nature of the intimate relationships homeless women form, particularly those with men who have addictions, and the subsequent effect on their own health and well-being (Nyamathi, Wenzel, Keenan, Leake, & Gelberg, 1999). The types of social support among homeless women and the effect on their health, health behaviors, and use of health services are the focus of another study, which concluded that modifying the social network of homeless women could improve mental health outcomes and decrease risky health behaviors (Nyamathi, Leake, Keenan, & Gelberg, 2000). The Research Synopsis details this study.

Although this brief review of the extent and experience of family homelessness, as well as risk and protective factors, illuminates the magnitude of the problem, the inconsistency in findings suggests a need for further research, particularly in relation to family-centered health-protecting and health-promoting behaviors. However, the existing body of research does provide a significant foundation for further exploration of risk prevention and health promotion among families

at risk for homelessness and those who are already experiencing homelessness.

Migration

In a seminal article on issues of global migration, McGuire (1998) states that global migration is a rising phenomenon, indicating that an unprecedented number of people throughout the world are crossing international borders to live in new locations. She suggests that immigrants are at increased risk for health problems derived from the hardships of escape and travel, anxiety and depression related to loss, and the challenges of unsafe living or working conditions on arrival. Issues of language, access to support systems,

---

RESEARCH SYNOPSIS

HOMELESS WOMEN AND SOCIAL SUPPORT

The purpose of this study was to examine the impact that various levels of support from substance abusers and nonusers have on homeless women's psychosocial profiles, health, health behaviors, and use of health services. A cross-sectional survey was the method of study used.

The most significant findings of the study were as follows:

1) Women whose support included substance nonusers reported better psychosocial profiles and somewhat greater use of health services.
2) Support from substance nonusers only was associated with better health behaviors and somewhat greater use of health services.
3) Support from substance users only was essentially equivalent to not having support.

These findings are relevant to nursing practice because the modification of social networks of homeless women appears to be associated with improved mental outcomes, fewer risky health behaviors, and greater use of health care services.

Nyamathi, A., Leake, B., Keenan, C., & Gelberg, L. (2000). Types of social support among homeless women: Its impact on psychosocial resources, health and health behaviors, and use of health services. *Nursing Research 49*, 318-326.

and lack of familiarity with health systems add to the potential health risks faced by immigrant families. Women and children may be particularly vulnerable to violence, physiological deprivation, and victimization during the process of immigration and assimilation. Thus the issues surrounding relocation of large numbers of people is a worldwide phenomenon, driven by global economic and social forces.

Although immigrant families have come to the United States for centuries, seeking a better way of life, there are changes occurring in the ethnic and racial composition of the population as a result of current immigration patterns. The foreign-born share of the population has doubled since 1970, increasing from 5% to 10% in 1998. Another 10% of the population consists of the children of immigrants (also known as the *second generation*). By the 1990s, 17% of immigrants to the United States came from Canada, 30% from Asia, and almost half from Latin America. The number of ethnic and racial categories has increased, as well as the heterogeneity within these categories (Waters, 2000). Therefore the process of relocation and assimilation is even more challenging and complex. The future composition of the population will be very much determined by how these immigrant families identify themselves and whether and how much they intermarry.

For some people, the decision to migrate is linked to poverty, lack of social mobility, and the tragedies of war and persecution. Balcazar and Qian (2000) suggest that every family has a different story to tell about the reasons for and the circumstances surrounding their departure from their native country. Although stories of migration may be linked to sadness and suffering, arrival in the United States leads to stories of hope, freedom, and opportunity for improvement. However, immigration is often linked to multiple changes and difficult challenges in new environments. Issues of language and acculturation, lack of job skills, and loss of supportive social networks are some of the problems immigrants face. In addition, most immigrants are identified as members of racial minorities and frequently experience discrimination (Benson, 1990). Clearly, the process of immigration and the issues of acculturation have many implications for the health of immigrant families.

As the process of acculturation takes place, some form of social disintegration or psychological stress may occur. Thomas (1995) suggests that this type of stress can result in a wide range of behaviors and experiences including depression, anxiety, deviant behaviors, psychosomatic symptoms, and substance abuse. Positive or negative outcomes may result from this process, depending on such moderating factors as the psychological characteristics of the individual, demographics, social factors, and modes of acculturation (Berry, 1990). Other types of stress experienced by immigrants include culture shock and homesickness.

Although each experience of migration is unique for each individual, a fundamental goal of family health care is to enhance the well-being of the family. Many immigrants come from cultures that value a family orientation as opposed to an individualistic orientation. For example, Balcazar, Castro, and Krull (1995) identify this strong familial orientation as an important value in Hispanic families (particularly of low acculturation) in addition to an emphasis on harmony in interpersonal relationships, a deference to authority figures, strong gender roles, and loyalty to nuclear and extended family members. As families experience the process of acculturation and cultural transitions occur, values begin to change, and family conflicts may arise. Children exposed to the dominant culture may experience intergenerational conflicts with parental values; gender issues concerning role interpretation and behavioral control may develop; and new patterns of family life may emerge around patterns of study and work. Families' ability to cope with these transitions is an important focus for research according to Roer-Strier (1997). Parental experiences, relationships with grandparents, and the experience of maturation of the first generation after migration are all important areas for further research, which may have direct implications for stress, coping, successful adaptation, and health.

To foster health-promoting lifestyles, family health nurses should be particularly cognizant of the heterogeneity of the migration experience and should ascertain the predominant values that shape the beliefs and behaviors of the individuals they encounter in health care settings. For those who prefer a family orientation, the family as a system should be the focus of care. Others who may have lost their nuclear and extended family may have special needs for support and affiliation. Nurses may be first-line providers of care and be uniquely positioned to identify and to promote resolution of family and community issues concerning migratory populations and stress. Balcazar and Qian (2000) suggest that greater attention needs to be focused on the education and development of culturally sensitive health care professionals and the development of culturally attuned mental health support services for those persons experiencing severe stress associated with refugee or migrant status.

Implications of Transitions for Family Health Nursing

Families today are challenged with numerous transitions that have the capacity to produce stress. McKenry and Price (2000) note that there may be nothing inherent in the event per se that is stressful or crisis-producing but that perceptions and resources may have moderating effects. They state that most research is currently focused on the ability of families to cope with and adapt to stressor events. Coping is an ongoing process that promotes the growth of individuals and facilitates family organization. Adaptation is the ability to make needed changes and ultimately recover from stressor events. The authors caution that families are always growing and changing and that serenity and stability, often synonymous with adaptation, are not always functional for family members. McCubbin, Futrell, Thompson, and Thompson (1998) have found that families may benefit from the challenges of adversity, that family members develop resiliency in the face of stressor events. Family professionals must be cognizant of these varying family coping strategies and determine whether transitions are resulting in a cumulative effect that destabilizes family systems and negatively affects health.

Nursing Assessment

Characteristically, nursing assessment of families includes evaluation of individual and family characteristics, the environment, and areas of client concern. In assessment of families who may be experiencing the cumulative stress of transi-

tion, attention is focused on the psychosocial characteristics of each family member, incorporating data concerning life stage, value orientation, ethnic beliefs, unique needs and demands of the family, socioeconomic status, and other social, demographic factors. Patterson (1999) maintains that consideration must also be given to family interconnections within the contexts of community and society (schools, churches, and neighborhoods), advocating an ecological perspective to assessing families and defining interventions.

Areas of client concern may not be specifically related to transition, but these areas should be explored for relevance to the family. Specific topics include whether individuals are engaged in the addition or loss of roles, whether the change is external or internal, and whether the transition is viewed as a positive or negative occurrence. Additional variables are the life cycle timing of the event, the suddenness of onset, and the permanent or transitory nature of the change. Because adaptation to transition may be dependent on individual and family resources or deficits, environmental differences, and involvement of various support systems, nursing assessments should include exploration of these areas as a means of identifying the stability of the system and potential family strengths.

Golan (1986) provides input on the nature of transitional problems that may be helpful to nurses in structuring interventions. First, families may be unable to separate themselves from the past or to distance themselves from relationships with persons, places, or things over which they have little control. Second, they may be unable to make a decision about which direction to take or the consequences inherent in their decision. In addition, some individuals or families have difficulty in implementing a decision, such as locating and mobilizing resources, obtaining information, or coping with the new conditions inherent in their choices. Finally, some families experience problems of adjustment and have difficulty adapting to new roles and changed conditions until the situation stabilizes. Although Golan (1986) identifies these as "stuck points" in the process of transition and adaptation, other problems that are less directly connected with transitions may be present, such as substance abuse, nutritional deficiencies, insomnia, or other physical symptoms that may not be resolved until the underlying issue is explored. When obtaining a family history, nurses need to be cognizant of these transitional elements and their effect on health and incorporate them into the assessment process.

Facilitating Family Coping

Specific nursing interventions for families in transition are tailored to individual family needs, which can vary considerably depending on the setting, the goals of the client and family system, and the availability of resources that can be mobilized to facilitate family adaptation. After assessment, a mutual exploration of concerns may assist family nurses and their clients to narrow the focus and identify specific problems or needs. There may be an initial concern with a current issue that reaches back to the disruption or event that triggered the current response, followed by a return to the present and the development of specific goals. Emphasis is placed on assisting families to resume a forward movement if they are unable to separate themselves from the past or to determine a more appropriate direction if difficulties have occurred. Selected approaches to problem solving are discussed in Chapter 14.

Using a problem-solving approach, Golan (1986) has identified a series of behavior-oriented instrumental and affective coping tasks for families. Instrumental coping tasks involve the recognition of a lack or insufficiency and the need to change; the exploration of possible alternatives, resources, and roles; the implementation of a decision and use of new solutions and resources to function in a new role; and adaptation to the new situation with the development of increasing competence.

Affective coping tasks incorporate both cognitive and emotional components and involve coping with insecurity and dealing with feelings of loss; dealing with the anxiety involved in making decisions and the feelings of pressure and ambivalence; handling the pressure initiated during implementation; and adjusting to the new solution with its attendant shifts in role position and its potential for being initially unsatisfying. Finally, the family may need to develop different standards of daily living until the level of functioning rises to acceptable norms and the family comes to terms with the new reality. Some of these coping tasks may be easily undertaken by family members, whereas others may require considerable support, education, and mustering of individual and family strengths.

In some situations, nurses may be in the unique position of establishing a helping relationship that is sufficient to provide the necessary information, support, and mobilization of resources. Because of the stressful nature of transitions and the implications for changes in health status, nurses may be the first professional contact families have as they attempt to resolve their current concerns. Therefore nurses become important sources for assessment, interventions, and appropriate referral. Nurses must also be able to recognize when and under what circumstances the expertise of another type of health care professional may be needed to facilitate family adaptation, or whether a different type of institutional support may be more useful.

Nursing Roles and Family Transitions

Family health nurses are probably more effective in handling situations when families have histories of adequate, positive coping and there are no entrenched pathologic conditions or intractable social problems that would limit nursing intervention. In addition to providing a supportive relationship directed toward helping families to use their own resources and serving as a resource for referral, nurses may be well qualified to develop and implement educational programs. The ability to combine health promotion with specific information regarding the complexities of life transitions is a unique function of nurses that is sorely needed by families as they experience parenthood for the first time, attempt to blend families with children of other family groups, or move to a new location where they have no extended family or supports. These types of programs can be adapted to hospital, home, school, or office settings as family health nurses expand their scope of practice to meet community needs and become more involved in the public sector. Consultation in development of educational materials and media consultation are other facets of this educational role.

Nursing Research

Finally, it is apparent from this brief review of the literature concerning families in transition that it is a developing field of exploration for a variety of disciplines. A limited use of theoretical frameworks, inherent methodological problems, a heavy reliance on cross-sectional data, lack of appropriate instrumentation, and conflicting findings are criticisms of existing studies. Nursing scholars could contribute significantly to this growing body of knowledge, particularly in relation to the effects of life transitions on the health of the families and the processes involved as families negotiate these transitions. Because family health nurses function in many settings and have access to families experiencing transitions, they can work collaboratively with other disciplines to establish longitudinal approaches to data collection to delineate family strengths and needs more effectively as families move through life transitions.

In their critical review of the state of the science of nursing research of families, Feetham and Meister (1999) note that nursing research on families rarely includes intervention studies. Therefore interventions are rarely understood as strategies that can be converted into service programs or used to influence health policy. They recommend that research should continue to be used to guide practice and also to promote the development of interventions into social strategies for improving family health and well-being. Increased correspondence among practice, research, and policy is vital to achieving this goal.

Currently, nurses continue to support families through normative and nonnormative transitions, basing interventions on strong research findings. McCubbin (1999) suggests that the unique contribution of research from the discipline of nursing is to demonstrate how to optimize health outcomes during normative transitions and how to promote health for the family and its individual members. Greater attention should be focused on those families that stay healthy, negotiate transitions successfully, and function effectively during transitions, particularly transitions that may be accompanied by illness of one of the members. The complexity and challenges inherent in family transitions necessitate an interdisciplinary approach to effectively design and implement research studies to more fully explore phenomena that affect families and to design effective intervention programs.

CASE SCENARIO

Mrs. W, an 88-year-old woman, lives alone in a senior apartment complex in a southwestern city. She and her husband had retired to this area approximately 30 years ago, seeking an escape from the harsh northern winters. Mrs. W. participates in a wide range of social activities, including bridge, volunteer work, and lunches with friends. She continues to drive in the immediate vicinity of her home to do errands and attend church services. Mrs. W. has two children: a daughter, 58 years old, who is an elementary school teacher living in the northeast, and a son, 50 years old, who is a self-employed appliance repairman living in the northwest. He and his wife have four children, two in college and two in high school. Mrs. W. has been in reasonably good health but has some heart disease and increasingly debilitating macular degeneration.

Recently, she fell outside of her apartment and sustained a left hip fracture. After a hip replacement, Mrs. W. entered a rehabilitation center for continued therapy. Her daughter had taken 4 weeks of vacation to be with her at this time. During a team conference, they are informed that Mrs. W. will no longer be able to live independently. Although Mrs. W. has a limited income and a small savings account, she cannot qualify for assistance with custodial care from government sources such as Medicaid. The immediate problem concerns a safe living situation for Mrs. W. for the short term and the long term.

MAJOR FAMILY STRESSORS

Mrs. W. is facing a deteriorating physical condition due to heart disease, vision loss, and some loss of function due to a recent hip fracture. She is unable to live independently and must consider relocation to a more supportive environment. Her adult children are very concerned about her but do not live in the area and have multiple role responsibilities of families and jobs in another area. Their mother's situation has disrupted their lives, created uncertainty, and created concern for her well-being and the financial security of the entire family.

CASE SCENARIO—cont'd

FAMILY STRENGTHS

Mrs. W. is independent, is realistic, and has a positive outlook. There is a close relationship between all of the family members. Mrs. W.'s daughter has taken a month's leave of absence from work to be with her mother during her hospitalization and rehabilitation program. Her son has four children and owns his business. Although he has been unable to visit, he has called and has been involved in future planning. Both children are concerned about the safety and quality of life of their mother. Both would be willing to assume the responsibility of relocating her to their own cities but would not be able to provide care in their own homes.

LIFESTYLE CHANGES INDICATED

Mrs. W. has a limited income and a small savings account. She is unable to qualify for any state assistance for care at this time. She does not wish to leave her own home, her church, and her close circle of friends. Her options are very limited, and she realizes that she needs assistance. If she moves to the same city as her son, she would have his support and be closer to the grandchildren. There are several assisted living facilities in his area, and she may be able to reside in one until her savings account is exhausted. At that time, the family would need to reevaluate the situation.

Her son is visiting various facilities in the area to determine the best living situation for his mother that is financially feasible. He and his family will be assisting with the sale of her home and her relocation. They are willing to include her in their family gatherings and celebrations. The family is excited about having her closer but realizes that this will create additional responsibilities for them. Mrs. W.'s daughter will assist her mother in choosing the possessions she wishes to

retain and in facilitating her move. She is arranging to visit her mother in her new location several times a month. Both children are concerned about their mother's adjustment to this new situation and her deteriorating health. Both recognize that they will need to reorganize their own lives to provide the additional support she will need to facilitate a successful transition.

Based on a systematic assessment and evaluation of family functioning and coping abilities, the health care team identifies a close relationship between the mother and daughter. However, the daughter is unable to move to this area on a permanent basis. She is willing to relocate her mother to the northeast but could not care for her in her home on a long-term basis because of her work situation. The responsibilities of managing his own business and raising a family have made it impossible for Mrs. W.'s son to be of assistance during this illness crisis. He would, however, be willing to oversee his mother's care in his home if she relocated to his community. The cost of care in the home, even on a part-time basis, is prohibitive for any of the family members but could provide a short-term solution. In facilitating family decision making, members of the health care team need to provide this family with some assistance in identifying the level of physical and social needs of Mrs. W., alternative living situations, the advantages and disadvantages of relocation, and the potential disruption to the lives of all concerned members. Attention must be given to the ability of Mrs. W. and her adult children to adapt to this new and challenging situation, which will so dramatically affect each of their lives. Lastly, it is essential to provide information and sources of assistance regarding long-term planning, including financial and legal issues.

WEBSITE RESOURCES

ORGANIZATION	WEBSITE ADDRESS
Adoption Resources	
Infant Adoption Awareness	http://www.infantadopt.org/
National Adoption Information Clearinghouse	http://www.calib.com/naic/index.htm
Aging/Elderly Resources	
Aging Network Services	http://www.agingnets.com
American Association of Homes and Services for the Aging	http://www.aahsa.org

WEBSITE RESOURCES—cont'd

American Association of Retired Persons	http://www.aarp.org
American Federation for Aging Research	http://www.afar.org
American Society on Aging	http://www.asaging.org
FirstGov for Seniors	http://www.seniors.gov
Gerontological Society of America	http://www.geron.org
Medicare Hotline	http://www.medicare.gov
National Association of Area Agencies on Aging	http://www.n4A.org
National Family Caregivers Association	http://www.nfcacares.org
National Council on the Aging	http://www.ncoa.org
Clinical Geriatrics Physician's National Resource Directory for Older Americans	http://www.medprograms.com/directory
The Resource Directory for Older People	http://www.aoa.dhhs.gov/directory
Family and Children Resources	
All Family Resources	http://www.familymanagement.com
Association of Maternal and Child Health Programs	http://www.amchp.org
Bureau of Primary Health Care	http://www.bphc.hrsa.gov
Center for Children with Special Health Care Needs	http://www.cshcn.org
Clearinghouse on Elementary and Early Childhood Education	http://www.ericeece.org/
Family Caregiver Alliance	http://www.caregiver.org
Family Voices	http://www.familyvoices.org
FirstGov for Kids	http://www.kids.gov
Human Development and Family Life Education Resource Center	http://www.hec.ohio-state.edu/famlife/index.htm
Institute for Child Health Policy	http://www.ichp.edu
Institute for Family-Centered Care	http://www.familycenteredcare.org
Maternal and Child Health Policy Research Center	http://www.mchpolicy.org
National Child Care Information Center	http://www.nccic.org
National Partnership for Women and Families	http://www.nationalpartnership.org
Single Parent Central	http://www.singleparentcentral.com
Social Security Administration, Office of Employment Support Programs	http://www.ssa.gov/work
Stepfamily Association of America	http://www.saafamilies.org
Administration for Children and Families	http://www.acf.dhhs.gov
Well Spouse Foundation	http://www.wellspouse.org
U.S. Department of Labor	http://www.dol.gov

■ CHAPTER HIGHLIGHTS

- Forming a family and rearing children are major transitions for families because role adjustments, economics, relationships, and family lifestyle patterns are being established and changes are constant over the family life course.

- Single-parent, adoptive, remarried, and re-nested families each experience unique stressors and transitions that need to be recognized by the family professional to assist families in adapting to life stressors and transitions.

- Families in later life and during retirement experience issues of declining health status, economics, relocation, the transition from independent to dependent living, and caregiving. Family professionals can assist families to adapt by providing health teaching,

anticipatory guidance on resources, and social support at each stage.

- The dynamic global economy has spearheaded immense international and national migration of families. The impact on families can be stressful during migration and assimilation.

- The number of homeless families has grown phenomenally in recent times. Family professionals should be cognizant of the stressors and health needs of homeless families.

- Family transitions have the capacity to produce stress. Therefore family health professionals are compelled to provide support and resources to families and to continue to conduct research on how families adapt to the stressors of both normative and nonnormative transitions throughout the family life cycle.

||| CRITICAL THINKING ACTIVITIES

1. Analyze several theoretical perspectives that may be helpful in understanding family transitions across the life span.

2. Identify the key factors that determine how maturing families will cope with the transitions they experience in their lives.

3. Evaluate key strategies in family health promotion for a selected transition in the lives of maturing families at midlife.

4. Analyze the contribution of nursing research to the care of families in transition.

5. Provide an example of how existing health policy concerning families influences their health or well-being.

6. Discuss the role of ethnicity and culture in determining family response to transitions in members' lives.

REFERENCES

Adoption and Safe Families Act of 1997, Pub. L. No. 105-89, §42 USC 1305, 101# Stat. 2115 (1997).

Aldous, J. (1996). *Family careers: Rethinking the developmental perspective.* Thousand Oaks, CA: Sage.

American Academy of Pediatrics. (2001). The pediatrician's role in family support programs. *Pediatrics, 107,* 195-197.

American Academy of Pediatrics. (2002). Co-parent or second-parent adoption by the same-sex parents. *Pediatrics, 109,* 339-340.

Armer, J. M. (1996). An exploration of factors influencing adjustment among relocating rural elders. *Image: Journal of Nursing Scholarship, 28,* 35-38.

Arrington, D. T. (1997). Retirement communities as creative clinical opportunities. *Nursing and Health Care: Perspectives on Community, 18,* 82-85.

Babcock, J. C., Waltz, J., Jacobson, N. S., & Gottman, J. M. (1993). Power and violence: The relation between communication patterns, power discrepancies and domestic violence. *Journal of Consulting and Clinical Psychology, 61,* 40-50.

Balcazar, H., Castro, F., & Krull, J. (1995). Cancer risk reduction in Mexican-American women: The role of acculturation, education, and health risk factors. *Health Education Quarterly, 22,* 61-84.

Balcazar, H., & Qian, Z. (2000). Immigrant families and sources of stress. In P. C. McHenry & S. J. Price (Eds.), *Families and change: Coping with stressful life events and transitions* (pp. 359-377). Thousand Oaks, CA: Sage.

Baldwin, K., & Shaul, M. (2001). When your patient can no longer live independently: A guide to supporting the patient and family. *Journal of Gerontological Nursing, 27,* 10-18.

Bassuk, E. L., Buckner, J. C., Weinreb, L. F., Browne, A., Bassuk, S. S., Dawson, R., et al. (1997). Homelessness in female-headed families: Childhood and adult risk and protective factors. *American Journal of Public Health, 87,* 241-248.

Benson, J. E. (1990). Households, migration and community context. *Urban Anthropology, 19,* 9-29.

Berger, R. (2000). Remarried families of 2000: Definitions, description, and interventions. In W. C. Nichols, M. A. Pace-Nichols, D. S. Becvar, & A. Y. Napier (Eds.), *Handbook of family development and interventions* (pp. 371-390). New York: John Wiley & Sons, Inc.

Biblarz, T. J., & Gottainer, G. (2000). Family structure and children's success: A comparison of widowed and divorced single-mother families. *Journal of Marriage and the Family, 62,* 533-548.

Bitler, M., & Zavodny, M. (2002). Did abortion legalization reduce the number of unwanted children? Evidence from adoptions. *Perspectives on Sexual and Reproductive Health, 34,* 25-33.

Boss, P. (2002). *Family stress management: A contextual approach* (2nd ed.). Thousand Oaks, CA: Sage.

Bost, K. K. (2002). Structural and supportive changes in couples' family and friendship networks across the transition to parenthood. *Journal of Marriage and the Family, 64,* 517-532.

Brim, G. (1992). *Ambition: How we manage success and failure throughout our lives.* New York: Basic Books.

Brown, P. (1994). *Health care and the aged: A nursing perspective.* Sydney, Australia: MacLennan & Petty.

Burman, B., & Margolin, G. (1992). Analysis of the association between marital relationships and health problems: An interactional perspective. *Psychological Bulletin, 112,* 39-63.

Carter, B., & McGoldrick, M. (1999). Overview: The expanded family life cycle. In B. Carter & M. McGoldrick (Eds.), *The expanded family life cycle: Individual, family, and social perspectives* (3rd ed., pp. 1-24). Boston: Allyn & Bacon.

Coleman, M., Ganong, L. H., & Fine, M. (2000). Reinvestigating remarriage: Another decade of progress. *Journal of Marriage and the Family, 62,* 1288-1307.

Coleman, M., Ganong, L. H., & Goodwin, C. (1994). The presentation of stepfamilies in marriage and family textbooks: A reexamination. *Family Relations, 43,* 289-297.

Cookman, C. A. (1996). Older people and attachment to things, places, pets, and ideas. *Image: Journal of Nursing Scholarship, 28,* 227-231.

Cowan, C. P., & Cowan, P. A. (1995). Interventions to ease the transition to parenthood. *Family Relations, 44,* 412-423.

Cox, R. P. (1997). Family health care delivery for the 21st century. *Journal of Obstetric, Gynecologic, and Neonatal Nursing, 26,* 109-188.

Crosbie-Burnett, M., & McClintic, K. M. (2000). Remarriage and recoupling: A stress perspective. In P. C. McKenry & S. J. Price (Eds.), *Families and change: Coping with stressful events and transitions* (2nd ed., pp. 303-332). Thousand Oaks, CA: Sage.

Dalgas-Pelish, P. L. (1993). The impact of the first child on marital happiness. *Journal of Advanced Nursing, 18,* 437-441.

Davey, A. (2000). Aging and adaptation: How families cope. In P. C. McKenry & S. J. Price (Eds.), *Families and change: Coping with stressful events and transitions* (2nd ed., pp. 94-119). Thousand Oaks, CA: Sage.

Davey, A., Murphy, M. J., & Price, S. J. (2000). Aging and the family: Dynamics and therapeutic interventions. In W. C. Nichols, M. A. Pace-Nichols, D. S. Becvar, & A. Y. Napier (Eds.), *Handbook of family development and interventions* (pp. 235-252). New York: John Wiley & Sons, Inc.

Davidhizar, R., Eshleman, J., & Moody, M. (2002). Health promotion for aging adults. *Geriatric Nursing, 23,* 28-35.

Dennerstein, L., Dudley, E., & Guthrie, J. (2002). Empty nest or revolving door? A prospective study of women's quality of life in midlife during the phase of children leaving and re-entering the home. *Psychological Medicine, 32,* 545-550.

Duvall, E. M., & Miller, B. C. (1985). *Marriage and family development* (6th ed). New York: Harper & Row.

Feetham, S. L., & Meister, S. B. (1999). Nursing research of families: State of the science and correspondence with policy. In A. S. Hinshaw, S. L. Feetham, & J. L Shaver (Eds.), *Handbook of clinical nursing research* (pp. 251-271). Thousand Oaks, CA: Sage.

Ferrie, J., Shipley, M., Martin, J., Marmot, M. Stansfeld, S., & Smith, G. (1998). An uncertain future: The effects of threats to employment security in white-collar men and women. *American Journal of Public Health, 88,* 1030-1036.

Fields, J., & Casper, L. M. (2001). *America's families and living arrangements: March 2000* (Current Population Reports, pp. 20-537). Washington, DC: U. S. Census Bureau.

Fischer, C., & Hegge, M. (2000). The elderly woman at risk. *American Journal of Nursing, 100,* 54-57.

Fisher, C. D., & Shaw, J. B. (1994). Relocation attitude and adjustment: A longitudinal study. *Journal of Organizational Behavior, 15,* 209-224.

Freysinger, V. J. (1994). Leisure with children and parental satisfaction: Further evidence of a sex difference in the experience of adult roles and leisure. *Journal of Leisure Research, 26,* 212-226.

Friedman, M. M., Connelly, C. D., Miller, K., & Williams, R. P. (1998). Family development theory. In M. M. Friedman (Ed.), *Family nursing: Research, theory, & practice* (4th ed., pp. 111-152). Stamford, CT: Appleton & Lange.

Gagnong, L. H., & Coleman, M. (1991). Remarriage and health. *Research in Nursing and Health, 14,* 105-211.

Golan, N. (1986). *The perilous bridge.* New York: Free Press.

Gottman, J. M. (1994). *Why marriages succeed or fail.* New York: Simon and Schuster.

Hall, L., Gurley, D., Sachs, B., Kryscio, R. (1991). Psychosocial predictors of maternal depression symptoms, parenting attitudes, and child behaviors in single-parent families *Nursing Research, 40,* 214-220.

Hatton, D. (1997). Managing health problems among homeless women with children in a transitional shelter. *Image: Journal of Nursing Scholarship, 29,* 33-37.

Helms-Erikson, H. (2001). Marital quality ten years after the transition to parenthood: Implications of the timing of parenthood and the division of housework. *Journal of Marriage and the Family, 63,* 1099-1110.

Hetzel, L., & Smith, A. (2001). The 65 years and over population: 2000. Washington, DC: U. S. Department of Commerce, Economics and Statistics Administration, U. S. Census Bureau.

Hollingsworth, L. D. (1998). Promoting same-race adoption for children of color. *Social Work, 43,* 104-116.

The Institute for Children and Poverty. (1996). *A tale of two nations: The creation of American poverty nomads.* New York: Author.

Jacobson, N. S., & Gottman, J. M. (1998). *When men batter women.* New York: Simon & Schuster.

Jacobson, N. S., Gottman, J. M., Gortner, E., Berns, S., & Shortt, J. W. (1997). The longitudinal course of battering: When do couples split up? When does the abuse decrease? *Violence and Victims, 11,* 371-392.

Johnson, P., & Wilkinson, W. (1995). The "re-nesting effect": Implications for family development. *Family Journal, 3,* 126-136.

Johnson, S. L., & Jacob, T. (1997). Marital interactions of depressed men and women. *Journal of Consulting and Clinical Psychology, 65,* 15-23.

Kiecolt-Glaser, J. K., Malarkey, W. B., Cacioppo, J. T., & Glaser, R. (1994). Stressful personal relationships: Immune and endocrine function. In R. Glaser & J. K. Kiecolt-Glaser (Eds.), *Human stress and immunity* (pp. 321-329). San Diego, CA: Academic Press.

Koerner, K., & Jacobson, N. S. (1994). Emotion and behavioral couple therapy. In S. M. Johnson & L. S. Greenberg (Eds.), *The heart of the matter: Perspectives on emotion in marital therapy* (pp. 207-226). New York: Brunner/Mazel.

Kramer, L., & Houston, D. (1998). Supporting families as they adopt children with special needs. *Family Relations, 47,* 423-432.

LaBauve, B. J. & Robinson, C. R. (1999). Adjusting to retirement: Considerations for counselors. *Adultspan Journal, 1,* 2-12.

Lansford, J. E., Ceballo, R., Abbey, A., & Stewart, A. J. (2001). Does family structure matter? A comparison of adoptive, two-parent biological, single-mother, stepfather, and stepmother households. *Journal of Marriage and the Family, 63,* 840-851.

Lihau, H. (2001). Chinese adoption: Practices and challenges. *Child Welfare, 80,* 529-540.

Lo, R., & Brown, R. (1999). Stress and adaptation: Preparation for successful retirement. *Australian and New Zealand Journal of Mental Health Nursing, 8,* 30-38.

Lutenbacher, M., & Hall, L. A. (1998). The effects of maternal psychosocial factors on parenting attitudes of low-income, single mothers with young children. *Nursing Research, 47,* 25-34.

Martin, R. (1995). The effects of prior moves on job relocation stress. *Journal of Occupational and Organizational Psychology, 68,* 49-56.

Martin, R., Leach, D., Normal, P., & Silvester, J. (2000). The role of attributions in psychological reactions to job relocation. *Work and Stress, 14,* 347-362.

Mason, M. A. (1998). The modern American stepfamily: Problems and possibilities. In M. A. Mason & A. Skolnick (Eds.), *All our families: New policies for a new century* (pp. 95-116). New York: Oxford University Press.

Masson, J. (2001). Intercountry adoption: A global problem or a global solution. *Journal of International Affairs, 55,* 141-166.

McCabe, S. B., & Gotlib, I. H. (1993). Interactions of couples with and without a depressed spouse: Self-report and observations of problem-solving situations. *Journal of Personal and Social Relationships, 10,* 589-599.

McCubbin, J. I., Futrell, J. A., Thompson, E. A., & Thompson, A. I. (1998). Resilient families in an ethnic and cultural context. In H. I. McCubbin, E. A. Thompson, A. I. Thompson, & J. A. Futrell (Eds.), *Resiliency in African-American families* (pp. 329-352). Thousand Oaks, CA: Sage.

McCubbin, M. (1999). Normative family transitions and health outcomes. In A. S. Hinshaw, S. L. Feetham, & J. L. Shayer (Eds.), *Handbook of clinical nursing research* (pp. 201-230). Thousand Oaks, CA: Sage.

McCubbin, M. A. (1993). Family stress theory and the development of nursing knowledge about family adaptation. In S. L. Feetham, S. B. Meister, J. M. Bell, & C. L. Gilliss (Eds.), *The nursing of families* (pp. 46-585). Newbury Park, CA: Sage.

McDonald, T. P., Propp, J. R., & Murphy, K. C. (2001). The post adoption experience: Child, parent, and family predictors of family adjustment to adoption. *Child Welfare, 80,* 71-94.

McGoldrick, M., Heiman, M., & Carter, B. (1993). *The changing family life cycle: A perspective on normalcy.* In F. Walsh (Ed.), *Normal family processes* (pp. 405-443). New York: Guilford.

McGuire, S. (1998). Global migration and health: Ecofeminist perspectives. *Advances in Nursing Science, 21,* 1-16.

McKenry, P. C., & Price, S. J. (2000). Families coping with problems and change. In P. C. McKenry & S. J. Price (Eds.), *Families and change: Coping with stressful events and transitions* (pp. 1-21). Thousand Oaks, CA: Sage.

McRoy, R. G., Oglesby, Z., & Grape, H. (1997). Achieving same-race adoptive placements for African American children: Culturally sensitive practice approaches. *Child Welfare, 76,* 85-104.

Merderer, H., & Hill, R. (1983). Critical transitions over the family life span: Theory and research. *Marriage and Family Review, 6,* 39-60.

Meurer, J. R., Meurer, L. N., & Holloway, R. L. (1996). Clinical problems and counseling for single-parent families medicine and society. *American Family Physician, 54,* 864-867.

Moen, P., & Wethington, E. (1999). Midlife development in a life-course context. In S. L. Willis & D. Reid (Eds.), *Life in the middle psychological and social development in middle age.* San Diego: Academic Press.

Muehlenberg, B. (2002). The case for the two-parent family: Part I. *National Observer, 52,* 44-49.

National Center for Health Statistics. (1999). *Health of the elderly.* FASTATS A to Z, Centers for Disease Control and Prevention. Retrieved January 20, 2003, from http:// www.cdc.gov/nchs/fastats/elderly.htm

Newman, B. M. (2000). The challenges of parenting infants and young children. In P. C. McKenry & S. J. Price (Eds.), *Families and change: Coping with stressful events and transitions* (2nd ed., pp. 45-70). Thousand Oaks, CA: Sage.

Nunez, P., & Fox, C. (1999). A snapshot of family homelessness across America. *Political Science Quarterly 114*, 289-306.

Nyamathi, A., Leake, B., Keenan, C., & Gelberg, L. (2000). Types of social support among homeless women: Its impact on psychosocial resources, health and health behaviors and use of health services. *Nursing Research, 49*, 318-326.

Nyamathi, A., Wenzel, S., Keenan, C., Leake, B., & Gelberg, L. (1999). Associations between homeless women's intimate relationships and their health and well-being. *Research in Nursing and Health, 22*, 486-495.

Paik, S. Z. (2001). Adoption and foster parenting. *Georgetown Journal of Gender and the Law, 2*, 369-379.

Patterson, J. (1999). Healthy American families in a post-modern society: An ecological perspective. In H. M. Wallace, G. Green, K. J. Jaros, L. L. Paine, & M. Story (Eds.), *Health and welfare for families in the 21st century* (pp. 31-51). Boston: Jones and Bartlett.

Rholes, W. S., Simpson, J. A., Campbell, L., & Grich, J. (2001). Adult attachment and the transition to parenthood. *Journal of Personality and Social Psychology, 81*, 421-435.

Roer-Strier, D. (1997). In the mind of the beholder: Evaluation of coping styles of immigrant parents. *International Migration, 35*, 271-286.

Rosenkoetter, M. M., & Garris, J. M. (1998). Psychosocial changes following retirement. *Journal of Advanced Nursing, 27*, 966-996.

Rogers, S. J., & White, L. K. (1998). Satisfaction with parenting: The role of marital happiness, family structure, and parents' gender. *Journal of Marriage and the Family, 60*, 293-308.

Schmaling, K. B., Whisman, M. A., Fruzzetti, A. E., & Truax, P. (1991). Identifying areas of marital conflict: Interactional behaviors associated with depression. *Journal of Family Psychology, 5*, 145-157.

Schwartz, L. L. (2000). Families by choice: Adoptive and foster families. In W. C. Nichols, M. A. Pace-Nichols, D. S. Becvar, & A. Y. Napier (Eds.), *Handbook of family development and intervention* (pp. 255-278). New York: John Wiley & Sons, Inc.

Selinske, J., Naughton, D., Flanagan, K., Fry, P., & Pickles, A. (2001). Ensuring the best interest of the child in inter-country adoption practices: Case studies from the United Kingdom and the United States. *Child Welfare, 80*, 656-667.

Sharpley, C. F. (1997). Psychometric properties of the self-perceived stress in retirement scale. *Psychological Reports, 81*, 319-322.

Sherman, P., & Redlener, I. (1999). Homeless women and their children. In H. M. Wallace, G. Green, K. J. Jaros, L. L. Paine, & M. Story (Eds.), *Health and welfare for families in the 21st century* (pp. 205-218). Boston: Jones and Bartlett.

Sobol, M. P., Daly, K. J., & Kelloway, E. K. (2000). Paths to the facilitation of open adoption. *Family Relations, 49*, 419-424.

Steil, J. M. (2001). Family forms and member well-being: A research agenda for the decade of behavior. *Psychology of Women Quarterly, 25*, 344-363.

Suthers-McCabe, H. M. (2001). Take one pet and call me in the morning. *Generations, 25*, 93-95.

Sweeney, M. M. ('1997). Remarriage of women and men after divorce. *Journal of Family Issues 18*, 479-502.

Thomas, J. (1992). *Adulthood and aging*. Boston: Allyn and Bacon.

Thomas, T. (1995). Accumulative stress in the adjustment of immigrant families. *Journal of Social Distress and the Homeless, 4*, 131-142.

Thorton, A., & Young-DeMarco, L. (2001). Four decades of trends in attitudes toward family issues in the United States: The 1960's through the 1990's. *Journal of Marriage and the Family, 63*, 1009-1037.

Tsushima, T., & Gecas, V. (2001). Role taking and socialization in single-parent families. *Journal of Family Issues, 22*, 267-286.

U.S. Department of Health and Human Services, Administration for Children and Families, Administration on Children, Youth and Families, Children's Bureau. (2001). *Adoption and foster care analysis and reporting system*. Data submitted for the FY 1999, 10/01/98 through 09/30/99. Washington, DC: Author.

The United States Conference of Mayors. (1998). A status report on hunger and homelessness in American cities (1998). Washington, DC: Author.

Van Den Akker, O. B. A. (2001). Adoption in the age of reproductive technology. *Journal of Reproductive and Infant Psychology, 19*, 147-159.

Van Zyl, L., & Van Niekerk, A. (2000). Interpretations, perspectives and intentions in surrogate motherhood. *Journal of Medical Ethics, 26*, 404-409.

Varnis, S. L. (2001). Regulating the global adoption of children. *Society, 38*, 39-46.

Vessey, J., & Knauth, D. G. (2001). Marital change during the transition to parenthood. *Pediatric Nursing, 2*, 169-172, 184.

Waters, M. (2000). Immigration, intermarriage, and the challenges of measuring racial/ethnic identities. *American Journal of Public Health, 90*, 1735-1737.

Weiss, R. S. (1997). Adaptation to retirement. In I. H. Gotlib & B. Wheaton (Eds.), *Stress and adversity over the life course: Trajectories and turning points* (pp. 232-245). New York: Cambridge University Press.

World Almanac & Book of Facts. (2002). *Special feature—children: A statistical portrait—families* (p. 69). New York: World Almanac Education Group, Inc.

White, L., & Edwards, J. (1990). Emptying the nest and parental well-being: An analysis of national panel data. *American Sociological Review, 55*, 235-242.

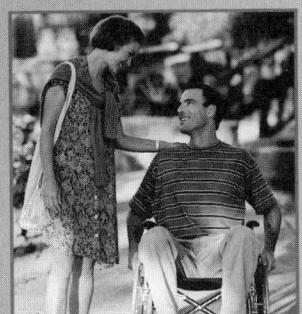

Family Health Promotion during Life-Threatening Illness and at the End of Life

Andrew W. Weaver

18

It is not the strongest of the species that survives, nor the most intelligent; it is the one that is most adaptable to change.

— Charles Darwin

OBJECTIVES

On completion of the chapter, the reader will be able to do the following:

1. *Identify factors that influence family health maintenance and promotion during the life-threatening illness of a family member.*

2. *Discuss family health promotion needs during health care crises in the family.*

3. *Develop care plans that include family health maintenance during a member's life-threatening illness.*

4. *Facilitate family decision making by encouraging dialogue about a dying member's end-of-life care preferences.*

5. *Collaborate more effectively with other clinicians and families regarding their loved one's end-of-life care needs.*

6. *Describe the natural dying process to clients and families and discuss end-of-life care options.*

7. *Formulate, with multidisciplinary teams, holistic end-of-life care plans that meet clients' and families' needs.*

8. *Identify interventions for improving family health by using the Nursing Support with Families Framework and the Theory of Human Caring.*

During a loved one's life-threatening illness or end-of-life experience, family health routines are strained by emotional, financial, and physical demands. Also, health promotion becomes increasingly more challenging, thereby prompting nurses to co-create with families activities to improve the health of individual members and the family unit.

Now families, clients, and care providers are confronted with clinical and ethical dilemmas that hardly existed 50 years ago such as the following:

- Advances in medical technology with a resultant increase in treatment options
- Changes in the structure of American families
- Changes in public health, health care, and social policy
- Changes in attitudes regarding respect for an individual's autonomy

507

Phenomena that were unimaginable in the very recent past include advance directives (ADs), individual autonomy, the right to die, physician-assisted suicide, intubation, artificial hydration and nutrition, HIV infection and AIDS, dialysis, minimally invasive surgical techniques, and implantable devices. Instead of dying at home aided by the family with visits from the doctor and clergy, Americans include hospitals, high-technology treatments, and an ever-increasing number of choices with inherent ethical dilemmas in their end-of-life care. Care for a person with a life-threatening illness and care at the end of life used to be guided by the natural course of events, a paternalistic physician's counsel, and commitment to the medical model from cradle to grave (Nixon & Roscoe, 1999). This is no longer the case. Now individuals and families are presented with new challenges in decision making that strain families' coping abilities and cause feelings of disorganization, anxiety, and doubt that may linger after the crisis is resolved (Goodell & Hanson, 1999). Families of persons with life-threatening illness can be assured that the situation will change because the course will invariably be one of improvement, decline, or death. Nurses are uniquely positioned in the health care system, allowing them to provide care and support to help families navigate a series of traumatic events.

Nurses are intimately involved in developing, implementing, and evaluating care in emergency departments, critical care units, acute care units, rehabilitation centers, skilled nursing facilities, assisted living facilities, the home, or hospice regardless of the setting. Nurses often work with families who have feelings of despair, fear, anger, helplessness, doubt, or confusion, and nurses are challenged to respond therapeutically to maintain and improve the family's health (Twibell, 1998; Goodell & Hanson, 1999). They have many opportunities to optimize family functioning and health promotion during times of family crisis (Bartels & Faber-Langendoen, 2001).

This chapter explores issues that affect family health promotion when life-threatening illness is encountered and covers aspects of end-of-life care that may help nurses meet families' needs when the client's recovery from an illness is not possible. The following topics are examined to better prepare nurses and other care providers to meet the challenge of providing holistic care in these circumstances: family health as affected by life-threatening illness, caring, nursing support, assessment of family stress and well-being, ADs, quality of life, palliative care, the dying process, family resources, and nursing interventions to promote and maintain health.

Life-Threatening Illness

Life-threatening illness challenges families in ways that may be overwhelming and may compromise their ability to maintain family health. Conditions that are potentially fatal may require emergency interventions, surgery, intensive care, lengthy hospital stays, and protracted inpatient rehabilitation courses at different types of facilities. Trauma, myocardial infarction, cerebrovascular accidents, and poisoning are examples of serious, acute medical crises for families. Some disease processes may not have acute or emergent aspects but are life-threatening and produce similar stress levels, possibly for much longer periods. Malignancies, HIV and AIDS, renal failure, coronary artery disease, and dementia are life-threatening diseases and conditions that may have some similarities to chronic illnesses in their longevity or trajectory, but the prognoses are often terminal. Disease states have their own unique courses and trajectories, and some are significantly more stress-producing. Responses vary depending on the family's strengths and vulnerabilities. Issues that affect the ability to maintain and promote family health are family structure and composition, communication styles, individual and collective coping skills, family support system, cultural perspectives, geographical and emotional closeness, cultural and social competence, socioeconomic status, religious beliefs, and expectations of the health care system.

Twenty-first century family health care crises present dilemmas that did not exist in earlier generations. The United State's health care system leaves family members with the added stress of having to navigate a fragmented system that may not meet the needs of their loved ones. An estimated 41 million people in the United States are without health insurance (Patton, 2002), many lack access to preventative care, and others find that a family member's care is not fully covered. This results in financial burden being an additional threat to family well-being. The health care system presents challenges to family coping that require social resourcefulness to resolve. These include insurance coverage that is unaffordable or unavailable; requirements for prior approval of care; denial of coverage by insurance carriers for procedures that are considered inappropriate or cost-prohibitive; restricted access to specialists; and coordination of care among insurance carriers, clinicians, and facilities (Armstrong, 2002; Rowland & Garfield, 2002).

Studies indicate that the major needs of families in the critical care area are assurance of the adequacy of care, proximity to the client, clear and honest information, and comfort and support (Goodell & Hanson, 1999). Nurses are accessible to families who need clarification of information obtained from other care providers. Severity of an illness can be difficult for some people to comprehend, especially in a critical care setting, and nurses can facilitate their understanding. For families that have difficulty grasping the severity of a condition or the individual's potential for rehabilitation and recovery, graphs and number lines can be used to reduce misunderstandings of

descriptive terms. These graphic representations of someone's condition and prognosis can be easily reproduced and shared with other family members. Nurses can be instrumental in helping families interpret all the information they need to enable them to make informed choices and can provide social support to the client.

Nursing Support of Families during a Life-Threatening Illness

Providing nursing support for families with seriously ill members and genuinely caring for the client have been goals of nursing throughout its history. Vandall-Walker (2002) notes that research has confirmed the need to support families during medical crises; but lack of a clear, meaningful, explanatory model has produced a research-practice gap, or the existence of knowledge that is not translated into practice. Vandall-Walker developed the Nursing Support with Families (NSWF) Framework to help reduce this imbalance between knowledge and practice. The NSWF Framework has four dimensions of nursing support focused on holistic family health

TABLE 18-1   Dimensions, Action Categories, and Referents of Nursing Support with Families

Dimension	Action Category	Subjective Referents	Objective Referents
Emotional Nursing Support	Connecting	Demonstrate: Empathy	Provide: Presencing Listening
		Respect	Information
		Concern	Presencing Touch (as appropriate)
		Trustworthiness	Honest reassurance Explain role Explain procedures
		Caring	Social chitchat Touch (as appropriate)
		Valuing	Sharing of information/common bond Requesting a photograph of the client Asking about client's life before

Continued

TABLE 18-1 Dimensions, Action Categories, and Referents of Nursing Support
with Families—cont'd

Dimension	Action Category	Subjective Referents	Objective Referents
Instrumental Nursing Support	Being Instrumental	Promote: Comfort	Provide: Telephone, blankets, food, sleep, and bathing facilities nearby Comfortable chairs at bedside
		Proximity	Open visitation Waiting room nearby Encourage family to engage in care Phone calls about changes
		Understanding	Advice Clarification
		Client/family interests	Atmosphere that invites questions
		Financial security	Advocacy Referral to a social worker
Informational Nursing Support	Promoting Empowerment	Promote: Understanding	Provide: Answers to who, what, where, why, how?
		Learning	Suggest a contact person Technology and treatment information
		Control	How to provide client care Description of staff functions Nurse-family-physician meetings
		Questioning	Opportunities to give care
		Trust	Nurse-family-physician meetings Honest information
		Validation	Information about credentials Honest praise
		Self-confidence	Referral to support group Encourage questions and suggestions for care Praise for care provided Nonthreatening environment
Spiritual Nursing Support	Discovering Meaning	Promote: Hope	Provide: Listening for sources of hope (faith, organ donation, etc.) Hopeful and honest demeanor Realistic appraisal of client condition
		Prayer	Referrals to clergy Time and quiet place for prayer
		Understanding of why	Listening
		Understanding	Discussion of possibility of disability, death

From Vandall-Walker, V. (2002). Nursing support with family members of the critically ill: A framework to guide practice. In L. Young & V. Hayes (Eds.), *Transforming health promotion practice* (pp. 174-189). Philadelphia: F. A. Davis.

promotion: emotional, instrumental, informational, and spiritual nursing support. The four dimensions result from nursing actions related to connecting, empowering, being instrumental, and discovering meaning. These types of nursing support and nursing interventions to provide each type of support are shown in Table 18-1. Holistic nursing support of families experiencing a medical crisis results in improved coping, adjustment, and adaptation of the family. The framework can guide nursing practice and enable nurses to provide social support for the client, regardless of the outcome (Vandall-Walker, 2002). Although developed in an intensive care environment, concepts in the NSWF Framework may be adaptable to other care settings.

Watson (2001) suggests that her Theory of Human Caring can be considered a philosophical and moral/ethical foundation for professional nursing and part of the central focus for nursing at the disciplinary level. Its development has spanned the last 3 decades and has evolved from 10 *carative factors* to a more refined version of *caritas processes*. The term *caritas* is derived from the Greek word meaning "to cherish, to appreciate, to give special attention, if not loving, attention to." The theory now incorporates a more spiritual dimension and an overt evocation of love. The 10 carative factors from which the caritas processes were developed are as follows:

1) Formation of a humanistic, altruistic system of values
2) Instillation of faith and hope
3) Cultivation of sensitivity to one's self and to others
4) Development of a helping-trusting, human caring relationship
5) Promotion and acceptance of the expression of positive and negative feelings
6) Systematic use of a creative problem-solving caring process
7) Promotion of transpersonal teaching and learning
8) Provision of a supportive, protective, and/ or corrective mental, physical, societal, and spiritual environment
9) Assistance with gratification of human needs
10) Allowance of existential-phenomenological spiritual forces

Watson (2001) notes that the future of nursing is dependent on the maturation of the profession as a distinct health, healing, and caring discipline. Her theory can guide nursing practice, education, and research. When incorporated with the NSWF Framework, the Theory of Human Caring can give nurses the foundation they need to optimize the well-being of families experiencing the challenges of a life-threatening illness.

Family Burden and Nursing Assessment of Family Needs

Family health promotion can be compromised by many factors when a member is critically ill. The term *burden* is used frequently when the impact of severe illness and caregiving is described. A burden is a load, duty, or responsibility that can be overwhelming, oppressive, and worrisome. The nursing literature is full of descriptions of family members' responses to their responsibility as caregivers that include the term *burden*. Families are encouraged and often required to take a greater part in the care of the critically ill family member (Titler, Bombei, & Schutte, 1995; Goodell & Hanson, 1999). The burden is sometimes inequitably distributed because of geographical proximity, personal skills, inclination to contribute, career considerations, family responsibilities, and relationship with the client. Acton (2002) notes that increased levels of family stress result in decreased health promotion behaviors, and Sisk (2000) found that family health promotion behaviors increased when levels of burden were decreased. Bowen's family system theory assumes that chronic, unrelieved stress lies at the core of family dysfunction (Goodell & Hanson, 1999).

Providing care to a loved one with a life-threatening illness can stretch family coping to its limit. Families may experience loss of work and income while they are meeting the critically ill member's needs. Time spent with children and spouses can be greatly affected. Many caregivers sacrifice their own health and well-being to meet the needs of a loved one. People who are in denial of their illness and its impact on the family can create high levels of stress for caregivers. Denial may take the form of resistance to adhering to a medication regimen or recommended follow-up visits to care providers, causing frequent exacerbations of an illness; resistance to making lifestyle changes when they can no longer care for themselves; or refusal to accept assistance from caregivers other than family members. Families may have to place a loved one in an institution involuntarily to ensure the loved one's safety and to maintain family health. Studies on caregiver burden show that women and spouses are most often the primary caregivers and therefore have higher levels of stress (Lowenstein & Gilbar, 2000). Respite care alone is often marginally adequate in relieving caregiver burden because the periods of respite are many times too brief or infrequent for the caregiver to derive significant benefit (Strang & Haughey, 1998, 1999). Although caregiver stress and burden are not causes of elder abuse, they indicate a lack of coping ability, support, or social resourcefulness. Four to six percent of older adults report experiencing incidences of domestic elder abuse, neglect, and financial exploitation (Wolf, 2000). The cause of elder abuse lies in the interplay of characteristics of perpetrator and victim within the context of their relationship and interactions (Anetzberger, 2000).

The burden of caring for a loved one at home is borne almost entirely by the family (Asch-Goodkin, 2000). The health care system in the United States provides very limited assistance to families caring for members at home. Programs such as the Program of All-Inclusive Care of the Elderly (PACE), a jointly funded federal and state program, are designed to keep people's care centered in the home. This program significantly increases an individual's ability to live and die at home, but it is not available in many areas. There are currently 30 PACE programs in 13 states serving approximately 6000 clients (Temkin-Greener & Mukamel, 2002). Medicaid provides limited home care assistance for those who qualify, and Medicare offers temporary therapy at home after discharge from a hospital or skilled nursing facility. Hospice services, for those who qualify, can provide basic nursing care for a few hours a week, counseling, spiritual support, required equipment, and financial assistance with medication costs. All these programs are helpful, but the U. S. health care system is primarily designed for care to be institutionalized rather than provided in the home; thus families bear almost

the entire emotional, financial, and physical burden of giving care (Asch-Goodkin, 2000). In the United States it is estimated that 25 million unpaid family caregivers provide an average of 20 hours of care a week, worth between $115 and $288 billion annually (Young, 2001).

Nurses working in advanced practice settings, emergency departments, critical care units, acute care units, rehabilitation centers, long-term care facilities, or home care strive to provide care that encompasses all aspects of the client's needs. Nurses differentiate their care from other practice disciplines by their holistic approach to care management. The holistic approach has been regarded as a model to "put back together again" clients whose care has been fractured by specialization (Jacobs, 2001). Life-threatening illness of a family member may result in the need for early, comprehensive interventions to support families and to promote and maintain family health (Vandall-Walker, 2002; Goodell & Hanson, 1999). Nurses are usually the first health care professionals who assess and attempt to meet the family's needs. They are often responsible for identifying families in need of other interventions to assist them in coping with crises. Nurses are frequently involved in multidisciplinary teams that manage clients' care. Multidisciplinary teams include physicians; occupational, speech, and physical therapists; social workers; clergy; and dieticians—all of whom have their roles in addressing client and family needs.

A number of assessment tools are available to provide clinicians with more objective and reproducible evaluations of family needs, strengths, and areas of concern. The tools listed in Table 18-2 can be used to assess families with physically compromised members and the needs of caregivers.

Impact of Certain Life-Threatening Illnesses on Families

Disease states and medical conditions have great variation in course and trajectory, each bringing distinct obstacles to recovery of the individual and maintenance of family health. The critically ill person's course of treatment may be relatively brief and end abruptly with a rapid recovery or death or may be protracted with multiple exacerbations and complications. Loss of function

---

TABLE 18-2   Family Stress and Well-Being Assessment Tools

Assessment Tool	Purpose
Caregiver Well-Being Scale (Rubio, Berg-Weger, & Tebb, 1999)	Measurement of caregiver burden as subjective level of well-being
Caregiver Strain Index (Rubio et al., 1999)	Measurement of caregiver burden as perceived level of stress
Caregiver Reaction Assessment (CRA) (Given et al., 1992)	Assessment of the reaction of family members caring for elderly persons with physical impairments
Coping Health Inventory for Parents (CHIP) (McCubbin, Thompson, & McCubbin, 1996)	Assessment of parents' appraisal of their coping responses to management of family life when a child is seriously or chronically ill
Demands-of-Illness Scale (Haberman, Woods, & Packard, 1990)	Assessment of impact of disease on entire family's health, coping, and functioning
Family Hardiness Index (FHI) (McCubbin, Thompson, & McCubbin, 1996)	Measurement of the characteristic of hardiness as a stress-resistance and adaptation resource in families
Family Needs Assessment Tool (Rawlins, Rawlins, & Horner, 1990)	Assessment of needs of families of chronically ill children
Family Pressures Scale-Ethnic (FPRES-E) (McCubbin, Thompson, & McCubbin, 1996)	Assessment of pressure related to life experiences of families of color; provides index of severity of these pressures on the family system
Impact-on-Family Scale (Stein & Riessman, 1980)	Measurement of stressors related to childhood illness
Parent/Caretaker Involvement Scale (Comfort & Farran, 1994)	Assessment of dyadic family interactions
Parents of Children with Disabilities Inventory (PCDI) (Noojin & Wallander, 1996)	Measurement of perceived disability-related stress, to be used with mothers of children with physical disabilities

---

and quality of life are sometimes dramatic. Families may not have time to work through their grief or have an opportunity to come to terms with a sudden death until long after the event. Nurses must understand the grieving process as it applies to loss of function and capacity, as well as loss of life, to prevent family dysfunction. Many conditions have a terminal prognosis with long, sometimes *vacillating trajectories* that compromise family health, often for years. For example, most dementias result in death, but families may not recognize this until very late in the course of the disease. This can result in unrealistic expectations for care and a lack of awareness about the disease that manifests itself in an emotional response similar to denial. The following sections include examinations of how some life-threatening illnesses can differ in their impact on families.

Malignant Diagnoses of Cancer

Malignant diagnoses of cancer are possible throughout the life span. Diagnoses of cancer are difficult at any age but can be devastating for families when children are affected (Kazak et al., 1998). Major issues for families experiencing cancer are numerous and include the following (Coscarelli, 2000; Hendricks-Ferguson, 2000; Murray, 2000):

- The courses of cancer are often unpredictable, and prognoses can be difficult to determine.
- The treatments often have side effects that seem as dreadful as the disease for some people.
- The possibilities for cures may be uncertain.
- Pain may be taxing, and the management of pain can be extremely challenging.

- Costs for medications and treatments can be prohibitive and may not be covered by insurance.
- Use of experimental therapies can be disappointing, and the uncertainty of their potential benefit may produce significant anxiety.
- Loss of function from the malignancy or as the result of an associated vascular event, such as a stroke, may require transfer to a long-term care facility.
- Symptom management may exceed the family's capacity for caregiving.

Cerebrovascular Accidents

Cerebrovascular accidents have potentially devastating results, ranging from mild cognitive deficits to sudden death. Many people experience some level of cognitive or functional deficit, which decreases the possibility of living independently because of safety issues and inability to perform activities of daily living. The effects of cerebrovascular accidents are often progressive, so the trajectory is one of general decline, which can rapidly accelerate with subsequent, unpredictable events. Since the atherosclerotic process is rarely limited to one organ system, complications or comorbid conditions such as peripheral vascular disease with neuropathies may be present, which increases the risks for falls and skin breakdown. Vascular dementia with psychosis and/or depression may be a residual deficit with the potential for significant disability. These conditions can be very difficult to stabilize because of waxing and waning cognitive function or mood and may result in the need for institutionalization (Buchalter & Lantz, 2001). Dysphagia with aspiration may predispose the client to recurrent episodes of pneumonia. Impaired judgment, as with a right hemipheric infarct, may require supervision at all times, and the cost may equal that of placement in a skilled nursing facility.

Coronary Artery Disease

Coronary artery disease may result in significant disability, the need for major surgery with an uncertain outcome, and a protracted rehabilitation period that usually incorporates lifestyle changes. The potentially devastating emotional, physical, and financial burden on the family may

be long-lasting. Medication regimens can be complex and require frequent monitoring and diagnostic testing by a number of different specialists. Lifestyle changes, such as changes in diet and nutrition, smoking cessation, and reduced alcohol consumption, can affect the whole family. Frequent angina attacks, oxygen dependence, intolerance of any physical exertion, multiple expensive medications, depression, role strain, and loss of income may decrease the family's capacity for health maintenance (Lukkarinen, 1999; Spertus, McDonell, Woodman, & Fihn, 2000).

Dementias

Most dementias are terminal processes that eventually lead to an inability to maintain basic functions such as swallowing. Treatments for the different types of dementia vary, and there are mixed types that make treatment significantly more difficult. Misdiagnosis and the use of medications that are inappropriate may provide no symptom relief or contribute to a decline in the person's condition (McKeith et al., 2000).

Alzheimer's Dementia

Dementia of the Alzheimer's type is the most widely recognized and most prevalent, affecting almost 4 million people. It has a relatively stable trajectory with a steady, global decline in functional ability that lasts about 4 to 8 years after diagnosis. The average annual cost of care at home or in an institution for a person with Alzheimer's disease is more than $47,000 (National Institutes of Health, 1996). Behavioral manifestations can often be relatively well managed with current medications, but the behaviors may be disconcerting to families, especially if children are involved. Agitation, aggression, hallucinations, paranoia, incontinence, and inappropriate sexual behaviors may prevent care at home. A terminal decline is usually inevitable when decreased cognitive function results in dysphagia with aspiration or anorexia with malnutrition and dehydration (Philippe, 2002).

Vascular or Multi-Infarct Dementia

Vascular or multi-infarct dementia produces widely varied severity of symptoms, ranging from mild to severe. The damage to brain tissue is random and may result in waxing and waning cognitive function, dementia with psychosis, and often depression. This form of dementia can present with behaviors that are very difficult to stabilize, resulting in frustration of caregivers and care providers and in the need for institutionalization. Transient ischemic attacks are relatively common, and the person's functional decline can have a very unpredictable course. Fluctuations in mood may be profound and disconcerting to the family (Buchalter & Lantz, 2001).

Dementia with Lewy Bodies

Dementia with Lewy bodies (DLB), often misdiagnosed as Alzheimer's disease, causes early hallucinations, psychosis, possibly severe insomnia, waxing and waning cognitive function, early parkinsonian-like motor dysfunction, frequent unexplained falls, and often a very poor response to antipsychotic medications, which are usually administered to control hallucinations and behavioral problems. DLB is believed to be the second most common type of dementia, and it affects 15% to 25% of clients with dementia. Inappropriate medications can precipitate a rapid, terminal decline in 30% of clients with DLB. Families usually recognize that their family member has something other than Alzheimer's disease and are frustrated or angry about unexplained responses to treatment. The trajectory for DLB can be as short as 3 years, even when it is diagnosed and treated properly (McKeith et al., 2000).

HIV Infection and AIDS

HIV infection and AIDS produce some of the most devastating effects on family health of any disease or condition. According to the U.S. Centers for Disease Control and Prevention (2001), more than 40,000 people continue to be infected annually. Although the trajectory has changed significantly with pharmacological advances, AIDS remains a terminal condition. Because the majority of victims are young adults, children are often affected and sometimes infected. One or both parents may be infected, which eventually orphans any surviving children. Because HIV infection is most often transmitted sexually or among intravenous drug users, the social stigma adds to family stress. The stigma also makes disclosure of the disease to children and other family members extremely difficult. Children are at risk of being ostracized, discriminated against, and ridiculed. Infected parents may lose employment if the diagnosis is disclosed at the workplace. Caring for children may not be possible for someone in the advanced stages of the disease. A need or desire for secrecy may prevent infected individuals from seeking assistance from support agencies, and they may also fear losing custody of their children (Antle, Wells, Goldie, DeMatteo, & King, 2001). The cost and complexity of the medication regimens can be daunting. It is estimated that approximately 80,000 children and adolescents in the United States are orphaned by HIV infection and AIDS (American Academy of Pediatrics, Committee on Pediatric AIDS, 1999).

Emotional Impact of Life-Threatening Illnesses on Families

The course of events in life-threatening illnesses may leave clients and family members with feelings of helplessness and hopelessness. Persons who experience repeated uncontrollable events may ultimately manifest learned helplessness, or a view that they have no control of their situation. Such feelings place these persons at higher risk for depression and anxiety, which may lead to feelings of hopelessness and despair and a desire to give up. Feelings of guilt may contribute to the family's dilemma because one or more members may believe there was something they could have done to prevent the situation. A feeling of being completely responsible for the situation increases feelings of hopelessness. At a time when decision making becomes critical, persons with feelings of hopelessness may become immobilized by indecisiveness (Miller, 2000). Nurses should alert other members of the multidisciplinary care team to family needs that are beyond the family's capacity to resolve. Clinical social workers, spiritual counselors, and psychotherapists may be of particular assistance. Nursing support and care are crucial to health maintenance and promotion for families who are coping with the stressors life-threatening illnesses impose.

Family's Role in Surrogate Decision Making

Families generally act as surrogate decision makers, or health care proxies, for hospitalized dying and seriously ill patients who are unable to express their treatment preferences (Tilden, Tolle, Nelson, & Fields, 2001). The process of health care decision making is unfamiliar to most families (Roberto, 1999). Family health can be significantly affected by the burden of decision making when a family member experiences a life-threatening condition. Families may be required to make agonizing decisions about limiting care or withdrawal of life support with little guidance from their loved one (Tilden et al., 2001). The burden may be reduced dramatically when persons' wishes about their care are known before they become seriously ill and are unable to communicate.

The family decision-making burden is often related to ignorance of a loved one's wishes for care in the event of life-threatening illness. Families and health care proxies are far more likely to be comfortable with their decisions about care for life-threatening conditions if they know they are honoring the wishes of their loved one. Individuals and families that are reluctant to have frank discussions about end-of-life care preferences must be reminded that these cannot be deduced intuitively. Nurses and care providers empowering clients to make decisions about care preferences must stress to the client that "their family members will know only what they are told" (Weaver, 2000. p. 67). Nursing informational, emotional, and spiritual support may significantly reduce the decision-making burden and promote family health.

Advance Directives

Research on family decision making has shown that the most important decisional factors influencing family members are the persons' prognoses and their own preferences about their care and quality of life. Americans overwhelmingly support informed consent and individual autonomy as the guiding principles of client care (Hallenbeck, 1999). For example, in recent years numerous websites were created for the provision of resources such as reading materials, support groups, newsletters, forms for ADs, living wills, organ donations, and power of attorney. For instance, Last Acts is a multidisciplinary collaboration to serve as a resource for clients, families, and health care professionals. An AD is a person's stated wishes, either written or oral, regarding care in the event of a serious illness that would prevent the person from communicating his or her preferences. An AD is a directive, or set of instructions, given in advance to the family and to the person(s) chosen to make decisions (also known as a *health care proxy* or *health care power of attorney*) if the client is in a state of decisional incompetence. Numerous websites and related links provide resources and information on ADs. Examples of such sites are provided at the end of this chapter in the Website Resources box.

Anyone competent to make decisions can complete an AD. Pediatric patients with cancer (Weir & Peter, 1997) and some persons with mild to moderate dementia (American Geriatrics Society, 1996; Tunzi, 2001) can often assist their families with decisions about end-of-life care, thereby relieving some of the decision-making burden. Many patients with neurological or psychiatric conditions, those younger than 18 years, and those who are very old are able to make decisions about some aspects of their medical care. Decisional competence should be assessed when there are abrupt mental status changes, when treatment is refused without rationale, when rapid consent for controversial care is given without deliberation, or when there is a known risk factor for impaired decision making (Tunzi, 2001).

ADs have almost universal support in the United States, but few families benefit from them for a number of reasons. Clients are usually admitted to institutions with their end-of-life wishes expressed in one of the following four ways:

1) A completed AD
2) Health care proxy or health care power of attorney designation completed, with and without an AD
3) Directions that are unwritten but have been discussed with the family, health care proxy, primary clinician, nurse, or possibly all of these
4) No written or orally expressed wishes to any person involved in care

Ideally, clients would have completed ADs, including designation of a health care proxy, and would have discussed them with their family, physician or care provider, and their health care proxy. Ninety percent of Americans voice support for the use of ADs; however, only about 15% of Americans have completed an AD or done any advance care planning (Haynor, 1998). Although

70% to 90% of Americans indicate a preference to die at home, 74% currently die in institutions (Asch-Goodkin, 2000; Farber, Egnew, & Herman-Bertsch, 2002). Decisions to limit aggressive care were made in about 70% of hospital deaths. ADs and frank discussions with clinicians were two factors that helped family members feel more positive about foregoing life-extending treatments (Tilden et al., 2001). Use of ADs has been disappointing because they are not used widely, and many ADs are too vague to provide families with sufficient guidance to allay fears of making the wrong treatment decisions. Some families expect more direction from ADs than they generally provide. They may perceive that ADs with statements such as a "declaration of desire for a natural death" will provide a definitive direction for the treatment plan (Tilden et al., 2001). This perception is quickly dispelled when they are asked how their family member might interpret the language and feel about specific treatment options. When ADs lack detail or contain terms that require interpretation by the family, they lack value. Some researchers believe that ADs have not consistently improved the dying process because they are reconstructions, by health care proxies, of documents or non-specific oral communications (Sullivan, 2002).

The Study to Understand Prognoses and Preferences for Outcomes and Risks of Treatments (SUPPORT) revealed that when ADs are ambiguous or incomplete, they may be disregarded by caregivers and family members (Prendergast, 2001). In a study at the George Washington University Center to Improve Care for the Dying, only 688 of 4804 terminally ill clients had a written AD, and of these, only 22 were detailed enough to guide medical care (Parsons, 1997; Greene, 1997). The limited use of ADs indicates a deficiency in the informed consent process for persons with life-threatening illnesses (Doukas, 1999). Without knowledge of their family member's wishes about care in life-threatening situations, families are often left with feelings of doubt and guilt about the decisions they have made. It is clear that one of the most loving acts people can perform for their family is to have a candid conversation about their preferences for end-of-life care. Huffman (2001) found that people are more satisfied with their care

when ADs are discussed. The lack of communication about treatment preferences puts nurses in a challenging position of trying to ensure that their clients' end-of-life wishes are respected (Haynor, 1998).

Timing of the discussion of end-of-life care can play an important role in the success of any intervention to increase the use of ADs. Clients are more receptive when ADs are introduced during routine periodic health examinations and in ambulatory, noncrisis situations (Carney & Morrison, 1997). Aitkin (1999) believes the primary care setting is ideal for discussing ADs. Cugliari, Miller, and Sobal (1995) note that people who received information on ADs several days before their hospital admission were 36% more likely to complete one. Making a decision about end-of-life care in a time of crisis is not a good idea. These issues should be addressed when an individual is healthy and able to discuss them with his or her family and care provider. For example, clients and families could be encouraged to complete the *Five Wishes* document that helps families to determine an individual's

---

BOX 18-1   Five Wishes

Five Wishes is a document that lets a person's family and doctors know how he or she wants to be treated when they are seriously ill or unable to speak for himself or herself. To be legal and valid the document must witnessed and notarized. The person writes a response to the following questions:

- Which person do I want to make health care decisions for me when I can't make them?
- What kind of medical treatment do I want and what kind of treatment do I *not* want?
- How comfortable do I want to be?
- How do I want people to treat me?
- What do I want my loved ones to know?

From Aging with Dignity. *Five wishes.* Retrieved April 16, 2002, from http://www.agingwithdignity.org/5wishes.pdf. Five Wishes is available from the Aging with Dignity website (www.agingwithdignity.org).

medical, emotional, spiritual, and personal preferences about death and dying (Box 18-1). The form is legal in 35 states and is easily obtained from hospices or from the website of Aging with Dignity.

Advanced Directives and Cardiopulmonary Resuscitation

Discussions about ADs and end-of-life care must include the topic of cardiopulmonary resuscitation (CPR). There are misconceptions about the efficacy of CPR and what it means to choose that it not be a part of the end-of-life experience. Clients and families must be reassured that foregoing resuscitation in the event of a cardiac or respiratory arrest does not equate to a "do not treat" order. The choice for palliative care can be made at another time when, and if, the person fails to respond to the care plan or aggressive care is no longer desirable because it is not contributing to quality of life. CPR survival statistics must be reviewed with the decision makers so that they can make an informed decision. Consent or refusal cannot be considered informed unless outcome data are included in the instructions given to decision makers (Dunlap, 1997). Survival rates for CPR show that aggressive treatments at the end of life are often futile and may only contribute to a longer period of suffering, decreased quality of life, and increased expense (Carney & Morrison, 1997; Watt, 2001). Studies have shown that public perception of CPR survival is that the technique is successful about 60% to 70% of the time. This correlates with the 77% CPR survival rate for "clients" in popular television shows (Diem, Lantos, & Tulsky, 1996). The distinction between perception of the public and reality must be made to clarify the potential benefit of CPR. The survival rate for people of all ages who have an arrest outside of the hospital ranges from 2% to 30%. In cases of in-hospital cardiopulmonary arrest, 6% to 15% of patients survive to discharge from the hospital. In cases of cardiac arrest that take place in skilled nursing facilities, 1% to 2% of those younger than 85 years survive, and less than 1% of those older than 85 years survive to discharge from a hospital. All CPR survivors have a 30% chance that they will have a significant disability requiring extensive home care or institutionalization. Smaller percentages have severe mental impairment (Carney & Morrison, 1997).

Barriers to the Use of Advance Directives

There are a number of barriers to the use of ADs. Barriers vary with ethnic, economic, and educational backgrounds; age; access to health care; cultural beliefs; gender; race; health status; perceived risk; religious beliefs; choice of health care provider; temporal considerations; knowledge of ADs; and knowledge of end-of-life care (Darr, 1996; Hallenbeck, 1999; Haynor, 1998; Johns, 1996; Morrison, Olson, Mertz, & Meier, 1995). One of the major obstacles to the completion of ADs or a discussion about end-of-life care preferences is physicians' reluctance to discuss these issues with their clients (Crawshaw, 2001). The most common barrier is lack of initiative on the part of the clinician. Seniors who were asked about ADs by their physicians were three times more likely to complete one (Gordon & Shade, 1999) and those with HIV infection were six times more likely (Henderson, 2001). Lack of training in discussion of ADs, discomfort with the subject, lack of desire to invest in the time to discuss ADs, lack of reimbursement for time spent discussing end-of-life care issues (Eliasson et al., 1999; Doukas, 1999), and lack of cultural competence are other barriers to completion of ADs (Hallenbeck, 1999). People expect their physicians to initiate the conversation about end-of-life care (Balaban, 2000). Inadequate and unclear documentation (Johns, 1996), family distress, patriarchal medical counsel, and inconsistent communication can prevent completion of ADs (Basile, 1998).

Gockel and Morrow-Howell (1998) cited procrastination, fear of family upset, and need for assistance with the forms as obstacles to completing ADs. In addition, people with more hospitalizations and chronic illnesses were less likely to have an AD. Orlander (1999) found that health care professionals were not any more likely to have completed an AD than the general public. Gordon and Shade (1999) report that college graduates were significantly less likely to have an AD than those with less education, even after controls for extraneous variables were applied. Affluent, well-educated white persons were found to have more prevalent use of ADs (Hallenbeck, 1999).

Cultural considerations can influence discussions of ADs and their completion. Studies indicate that African Americans' experiences with the health care system are significantly different from those of other Americans. Institutional racism has reduced access to the system for many years (Schulman et al., 1999). Other factors influencing African Americans' health care experiences and attitudes toward ADs include fear of inadequate care, religious beliefs (Haynor, 1998), hopelessness, inability to identify with care providers (Burrs, 1995), fatalism (Powe, 1996), skepticism about the intent of ADs (Galambos, 1998), and folk beliefs (Landrine & Klonoff, 1994). Research suggests that African Americans tend to request more life-sustaining treatments than their white counterparts (Haynor, 1998). Even African American physicians have similar patterns of preference for more aggressive end-of-life care (Hallenbeck, 1999; Mebane, Oman, Kroonen, & Goldstein, 1999). Dupree (2000) found that threats to dignity, family relationships, and spirituality emerged as themes in her study of the attitudes of African Americans toward ADs. She believes that a perceived lack of utility, rather than a lack of information, was the cause of infrequent use of ADs. Other barriers identified are fear that discussion of end-of-life issues may be prophetic, distrust of the medical profession (Krakauer & Truog, 1997), fundamentalist faith and the belief in predestination and the futility of interventions, perceptions of one's level of autonomy, confusion of living wills with estate wills (Palker & Nettles-Carlson, 1995), cultural attributions for illness (Landrine & Klonoff, 1994), difficulty in understanding medical-legal language, and knowledge deficit regarding end-of-life care (Dunlap, 1997).

Cultural Influences on the Use of Advance Directives

The cultural heritage of a family may profoundly affect their decision making regarding the end-of-life care of a loved one. Individual autonomy and respecting a person's end-of-life care preferences are considered ethical obligations in this country, but this is not the case in some other parts of the world. Studies of diagnosis disclosure and end-of-life care for terminally ill clients in Japan indicate that physicians and families have a tendency to withhold disclosure of terminal diagnoses to them. This leads to aggressive end-of-life care because it is considered unethical to limit care to

persons who are unaware of their terminal condition. Thirty-six percent of the physicians in one study would override the explicit request of a competent, moribund patient with cancer to withdraw all life support. CPR was common for clients who had cardiac arrests to enable their families to be at the bedside at the time of death (Asai, Fukuhara, & Lo, 1995; Asai et al., 1997; Asai, Miura, Tanabe, Kurihara, & Fukuhara, 1998; Asai et al., 1999).

Communication with family members and care providers has a significant impact on African Americans' use of ADs. Gordon and Shade (1999) found that lack of client-provider communications contributed to decreased awareness and knowledge of ADs. Cooper-Patrick et al. (1999) found that African Americans rated their physician visits as significantly less participatory than did white Americans. Seventy-one percent of the participants in a pilot study of rural, elderly African Americans in North Carolina saw their physicians every 1 to 6 months, and none had conversations regarding end-of-life care. Only one participant was asked whether she had an AD. She answered "No," and there was no further discussion about ADs. Almost 80% of the participants in this study expressed a strong desire to avoid machines, tubes, and CPR in their end-of-life experience after a brief educational session and believed that ADs were a means of ensuring these wishes were honored. Respondents preferred a "quiet, easy way" to die or said they did not want aggressive care. One of their greatest frustrations was that the younger members of their families were uncomfortable with the subject of end-of-life care and prevented them from letting their wishes be known. They expressed an appreciation for the utility of ADs, such as *Five Wishes* (Commission on Aging with Dignity, 2000), which provides a means of designating a health care proxy, addresses specific end-of-life care issues, clarifies how the individual wishes to be treated, and allows for additions and deletions based on personal preference. Also noted was that not everyone in their communities was as comfortable with the topic of end-of-life care (Weaver, 2000). More nursing research is needed to fully understand cultural influences on the use of ADs. Americans' cultural diversity challenges nurses to be receptive, flexible, and creative when providing support to families in crisis.

Nursing Advocacy for Client Autonomy

The Patient Self-Determination Act became effective in 1991 and was developed to increase the use of ADs, thereby increasing individuals' decision-making autonomy and ensuring that their wishes are respected. Although it specifically addresses the use of ADs at facilities that accept Medicare and Medicaid funding, the Patient Self-Determination Act has had an expanded reach because it strengthens awareness of clients' rights and reinforces the societal belief in individual autonomy. The American Nurses Association (ANA) (1991) believes that nurses should play a primary role in its implementation. The ANA, in its position statement, makes clear its stance on nurses assuming the role of client advocate and ensuring clients' autonomy:

> It is the responsibility of nurses to facilitate informed decision-making for patients making choices about end-of-life care. The nurse's role in education, research, patient care, and advocacy is critical to implementation of the Patient Self-Determination Act within all health care settings. . . . It is imperative that the decision-making that will fall to patients and their families as they make choices about end-of-life care be facilitated by nurses. . . . The nurse is one of several heath care professionals who has a responsibility for ensuring that the advance care directives initiated by the patient are current and reflective of the patient's choices. Facilitating self-determination of patients with respect to end-of-life decisions is a process that includes evaluating changes in the patient's perspective and health state. The nurse has a responsibility to facilitate informed decision-making, including, but not limited to, advance directives (ANA, 1991).

In accepting the responsibility involved in the role of client advocate, nurses can help improve family health and relieve families of significant decision-making burdens by keeping them focused on the person's wishes and decisions about care in life-threatening situations. By reinforcing and supporting the client's decisions, nurses help families gain confidence in the decisions they make, thereby reducing feelings of anxiety, doubt, confusion, and guilt. In the absence of guidance from the individual, as with a pediatric client, nursing advocacy for the person's autonomy may take the form of finding resources the family can enlist to resolve conflict, clarify goals, and maintain a sense of control.

Intervention by a third party may be necessary to resolve differences when families or health care proxies choose a care option that care providers believe is inconsistent with the client's best interest or previously stated wishes, consider it to be futile and therefore unwarranted, or have ethical objections to the decision. The American Medical Association (1999) recommends a process-based approach. First, the parties should try to establish the person's wishes and care preferences before a state of decisional incompetence is reached. Second, the care provider and client should make decisions jointly to clarify treatment goals based on informed consent. Third, participation of consultants should be encouraged to facilitate planning a course of action. Lastly, the parties should enlist the help of an ethics committee if the previous steps fail to resolve the dispute. In the event that all of these efforts fail, the care provider should consider transferring the client to another doctor in the same institution or transferring the client to another facility. Two factors can undermine the best efforts to resolve conflicts of this nature: first, a growing distrust on the part of clients and their families arising from managed care and its emphasis on cost control, and second, the lack of sufficient credible data for most treatment outcomes.

Medical decision making during a medical crisis is stress-producing and may have a significantly negative impact on family health. The NSWF Framework provides interventions nurses can use to reduce stress and promote family health. The dimension of informational nursing support can reduce the burden of decision making and enable clients and families to make informed decisions about medical care. Emotional and spiritual nursing support may help validate their feelings and decisions. "Caritas processes" can be the driving force behind these interventions and provide families with an environment that optimizes their ability to support their loved one and to maintain family health.

End-of-Life Nursing Care

Managing end-of-life experiences is not something that society or the health care system does well for many people. Those who speak no English and those who are African American, Hispanic or Latino, poor, elderly, or female have a greater chance of dying in pain (Pierce, 1999; Asch-Goodkin, 2000). Two of the most difficult questions for care providers to answer are (1) When has someone reached the point in the course of treatment at which additional interventions are futile? and (2) When is the person dying? Without the answers to those basic questions, clients, families, and care providers have difficulty planning effectively for end-of-life care. Determining medical futility involves careful consideration of the risks, benefits, and burdens of treatment based on individual and family-centered goals. At the end of life, when tests and treatments result in fewer benefits and greater risks and burdens, individual and family needs and goals should dictate when there should be a change from cure to care (Farber et al., 2002). As with all client care, end-of-life care must be driven by the informed consent of the client or health care proxy and be based on the person's wishes.

Physicians have historically been trained to view death as an enemy and to keep it at bay as long as possible. With that mindset, death is the physician's failure (Asch-Goodkin, 2000). This likely explains the difficulty that many care providers have in identifying when treatment becomes futile and the care plan should move from one of curing to one of caring, or when the end of someone's life begins. An inability to recognize when someone is dying results in futile care that increases suffering. Nurses, because of their intimate contact with clients regardless of the care setting, can be instrumental in helping other clinicians determine when care becomes futile or is contrary to the client's or family's wishes (Shotton, 2000). Many nurses do not consider themselves to be well prepared to deal with end-of-life care issues, but their clinical expertise positions them to make significant changes in a person's end-of-life care (Tuttas, 2002).

Decisions to withdraw life support systems are traumatic for families. No defined rituals exist for orchestrated deaths in an acute care setting, and the pace of events can be staggering. Ventilator withdrawal is invariably traumatic for families, partly because the family agonizingly decides when their loved one will die. Withdrawal of this type of life support is unique in the following four ways (Bartels & Faber-Langendoen, 2001):

1) Artificial ventilation is initiated as an acute lifesaving measure.
2) Ventilator withdrawal is usually performed in an intensive care unit that is specifically designed to spare lives.
3) The end-of-life care following ventilator withdrawal occurs in an environment that is foreign to the experience of most families.
4) Families are exclusively responsible for making the decisions for their loved one in this setting.

Families experiencing these events need nursing support in all the dimensions of the NSWF Framework to facilitate decision making. It is not unusual for families to need weeks before they can be certain further interventions are futile. They may require a great deal of reinforcement regarding the client's condition and prognosis. Because of their clinical expertise and intimate relationship with the individual, nurses are often asked to validate families' perceptions of the client's suffering. Most family members prefer to have a clear understanding of the expected sequence of events before proceeding. The need for emotional, instrumental, informational, and spiritual nursing support during this type of family experience is self-evident and, when provided, may significantly improve family health.

Twenty-first century practitioners and students can learn state-of-the-science principles of end-of-life nursing care from courses offered through the End-of-Life Nursing Education Consortium developed by nurse researchers at the City of Hope in collaboration with the American Association of Colleges of Nursing (see the website in the Website Resources box at the end of the chapter). The curriculum contains modules on the following topics: (1) nursing care at the end of life; (2) pain management; (3) symptom management; (4) ethical and legal issues; (5) cultural considerations; (6) communications; (7) grief, loss, and bereavement; (8) achieving quality of care; and (9) preparation and care for death.

Palliative Care

The interest in improving palliative care by a number of health care institutions and private organizations has improved the quality of end-of-life care. Numerous organizations have created position statements on care of the dying client and palliative care. Some examples include the following:

- *Position Statement: The Care of Dying Patients* (American Geriatrics Society, 1998)
- *Position Statement on End of Life Care* (American Society of Pain Management Nurses, 1998)
- *Peaceful Death: Recommended Competencies and Curricular Guidelines for End-of-Life Nursing Care* (American Association of Colleges of Nursing, 2002)

Palliative care is the comprehensive management of physical, social, spiritual, and existential needs of clients, in particular those with incurable, progressive illnesses. Also of import is the provision of support for the dying client and the client's family. The goal of palliative care is to achieve the best quality of life through relief of suffering, control of symptoms, and the restoration of functional capacity while remaining sensitive to personal, cultural, and religious values, beliefs, and practices (Nixon & Roscoe, 1999; Douglas, 2001). Education for Physicians on End-of-Life Care and the End-of-Life Nursing Education Consortium, mentioned in the previous section, are two programs designed to educate physicians and nurses on the essential clinical competencies required to provide quality end-of-life care. See the Website Resources box at the end of the chapter for website URLs for each program. Cohen, Boston, Mount, and Porterfield (2001) used the McGill Quality of Life Questionnaire in a study of hospice/palliative care clients and found that existential well-being was improved in addition to psychological and physical symptoms. The five domains of quality end-of-life care from the individuals' perspective identified in one study were (1) receiving adequate pain and symptom management, (2) avoiding inappropriate prolongation of dying, (3) achieving a sense of control, (4) relieving burden on loved ones, and (5) strengthening relationships with loved ones (Singer, Martin, & Kelner, 1999). *Five Wishes* (see Box 18-1) is an example of an AD that addresses these areas of concern about end-of-life care (Commission on Aging with Dignity, 2002).

Quality of life should be determined from the client's perspective when an end-of-life care plan is developed, because objective measures often do not account for cultural influences and a subjective measure is more reflective of the reaction to individual health status and perception of well-being (Muldoon, Barger, Flory, & Manuck, 1998; Miettinen, Alaviuhkola, & Pietila, 2001). One anonymous sixteenth century physician believed we should "cure sometimes, relieve often, but comfort always" (Douglas, 2001). Telling clients you cannot cure them does not mean you cannot help them (Crawshaw, 2001). The Research Synopsis discusses a study in which relatives of dying persons were asked for their perceptions of palliative care. The Canadian Perspectives box presents a discussion of the Illness Beliefs Model regarding palliative care.

RESEARCH SYNOPSIS

QUALITY OF LIFE AND GOOD PALLIATIVE CARE

Improving care for those who are dying has become an area of great interest in many countries. In a study conducted in Finland, nine relatives of dying clients were asked about their perceptions of what good palliative care contributes to an end-of-life experience. Three clients died in their homes, five died in a hospital, and one died in a health center. The families identified beliefs in three categories that contribute to quality of life in the dying process. The first is "way of living," or maintaining as normal a life as possible with spiritual and social well-being and environmental comfort. The second category was dignity, which correlated very closely to maintenance of autonomy. Last was professional palliative care, which included genuine concern and caring; adequate symptom management; and honest,

RESEARCH SYNOPSIS

QUALITY OF LIFE AND GOOD PALLIATIVE CARE—cont'd

supportive communications. Poor care was identified as client or family neglect, lack of care continuity, inadequate symptom management, futile treatments, and lack of joy and hope. Professional palliative care contributes to quality of life by maintaining dignity. It was important for the client to live a near-normal, enjoyable life in a familiar environment, with dignity and autonomy, and to be surrounded by sincere, dedicated professional caregivers. These categories of care that improve quality of life for the dying are consistent with the goals of hospice programs and nurses striving to provide family-focused holistic care during end-of-life experiences.

Miettinen, T., Alaviuhkola, H., & Pietila, A. (2001). The contribution of good palliative care to quality of life in dying patients: Family members' perceptions. *Journal of Family Nursing, 7,* 261-280.

CANADIAN PERSPECTIVES
PALLIATIVE CARE

Ursula Bohn, RN, MN, CNS
Calgary Health Region

The goal of all care in palliative care is to alleviate suffering. How does the nurse understand the suffering of the individual and family living with a life-threatening illness? Which nursing interventions are helpful to the family? Are there ways in which nursing practice might contribute to the family's suffering?

The Illness Beliefs Model (Wright, Watson, & Bell, 1996) proposes that suffering may be related to the beliefs that are held about the illness: beliefs about etiology, diagnosis, healing and treatment, prognosis, the role of family members, the role of health care professionals, religion and spirituality, and the place of illness in lives and relationships. Suffering may reside where the beliefs of the individual intersect with the beliefs of the family; where the beliefs of the family intersect with the beliefs of health professionals. The beliefs that are held about the illness may affect not only the way the individual and family cope with the illness but also the illness itself. A therapeutic conversation that includes the identification of, assessment of, and intervention with constraining beliefs around illness may have a powerful and sustaining influence on an individual's and family's ability to cope with the challenge of integrating illness into their lives (Wright et al., 1996).

One example from practice may be a therapeutic conversation that invites a family to speak about their beliefs about prognosis. Persons living with life-threatening illness have ongoing internal dialogues about the possible progression of their illness. Family members have similar worries and concerns. These conversations are rarely externalized; family members protect the ill person and the ill person reciprocally protects the family (Tapp, 2001). Families stop communicating to protect each other from anxiety (Wright & Nagy, 1993).

The clinician may ask the individual, "What conversations are you having with yourself these days? On good days? On bad days? With whom in the family would you most want to share these worries and concerns? If you were to believe that your spouse and you would feel closer by talking about your concerns, what would you most want him or her to know?" The clinician may ask the family, "In your family, who believes most strongly that talking helps families cope? What is the biggest change you have noticed in your conversations with your spouse since the diagnosis?

Continued

CANADIAN PERSPECTIVES
PALLIATIVE CARE—cont'd

What do you worry will happen if you share your worries with your dad? Is it your belief that sharing your concern about the future may make him even more sick?" Inviting families living with life-threatening illness to speak about their beliefs about prognosis brings forth the families' core beliefs, those beliefs that cause the most suffering, and brings the therapeutic conversation to the "heart of the matter" (Wright et al., 1996).

The health care profession may inadvertently contribute to families' difficulties in speaking to each other about serious illness. Family meetings are often organized without the ill person in attendance. "Bad news" is given to patients without family members in attendance. Individuals and families who internalize their conversations of worry are often labeled "in denial." The clinician may ask the individual and family, "Have you been having conversations about your worries with your doctor or nurse? Do you wish you could have more or less of these conversations? Was there anything else you were hoping we would talk about today? If there was just one question you could have answered, what might that be?" (Wright et al., 1996).

When families are invited to have conversations about their illness beliefs such as their beliefs about prognosis, they may not only be able to decrease their suffering but also increase their intimacy and closeness. Quality of life may be improved, and sense of burden may be lessened. These conversations may help the surviving family members deal with grief and bereavement.

References

Tapp, D. M. (2001). Conserving the vitality of suffering: Addressing family constraints to illness conversations. *Nursing Inquiry, 8*, 97-105.

Wright, L. M., & Nagy, J. (1993). Death: The most troublesome family secret of all. In E. Imber Black, E. (1993). (Ed.), *Secrets in families and family therapy* (pp.121-137). New York: W. W. Norton.

Wright, L. M., Watson, W. L., & Bell, J. M. (1996). *Beliefs: The heart of healing in families and illness.* New York: Basic Books.

Canadian spelling is used.

In 1996 representatives from medical specialty societies created and then released in 1999 the "Core Principles for End of Life Care" (Cassel & Foley, 1999), which are presented in Box 18-2. More than 14 societies have adopted these policies, which should strengthen the quality of care given to families during the end of life.

The role of the nursing professional during the dying process is to assist the family and dying person to transcend the pain and suffering and to remain close to one another. Many books, websites, and community resources such as hospice are available to support the client and family during the dying process. Some of the websites are listed in the Website Resources box at the end of the chapter.

The Dying Process

Determining when someone is in the dying process is sometimes difficult and requires that all other potential causes for the client's decline must be eliminated. For the critically ill in the hospital, diagnostic testing is readily available and can provide much of the objective information needed to assess responses to treatment. Families or clients may wish to limit the number and extent of diagnostic tests because of perceived benefits or burdens. In settings such as the home and skilled nursing or assisted living facilities, diagnostic testing may be seen as undesirable or as a burden. When all other causes for a decline have been eliminated and a person has not responded to the care plan, the family should be

---

BOX 18-2 Core Principles for End-of-Life Care

Clinical policy for care at the end of life, and the professional practice it guides, should do the following:

1. Respect the dignity of clients and caregivers
2. Be respectful of client's/family's wishes
3. Use measures that are consistent with the client's
4. Address alleviation of pain and physical symptoms
5. Coordinate care for psychological, social, and spiritual issues
6. Offer continuity to maximize quality of care.
7. Provide access to any therapy that may improve the patient's quality of life, including alternative or nontraditional treatments
8. Offer/coordinate palliative care and hospice care services
9. Respect the client's right to refuse recommended treatment options
10. Respect the physician's judgment to discontinue treatments, when appropriate, with consideration for both client and family preferences
11. Promote clinical and evidence-based research on end-of-life care

From Cassel, C. K., & Foley, K. M. (1999). *Principles for care at the end of life: An emerging consensus among specialties of medicine.* New York: Milbank Memorial Fund. Retrieved December 21, 2002, from http://www.milbank.org/endoflife/

---

prepared for the likelihood that the client's death is imminent. People are considered to be dying when they are sick with a progressive condition that is expected to end in death and for which there is no treatment that can substantially alter the outcome. Thus "people are dying when they have illnesses such as advanced dementia or severe congestive heart failure, in addition to illnesses more routinely recognized as terminal, such as advanced cancer. Care of dying patients also encompasses patients who have elected to forgo available treatments that might forestall death, such as dialysis for end stage renal disease" (American Geriatrics Society, 1998, p. 1). Some clinicians recognize the start of the dying process as being the point at which all the right things are being done to improve the client's condition, but the client continues to decline. Families often come to terms with the failure of treatment in a loved one when they recognize the person's suffering and realize that ongoing treatment contributes to that suffering (Tilden et al., 2001). Because of their frequent and close contact with critically ill clients, nurses are in a position to acquire useful knowledge about acute dying processes (Dendaas, 2002).

When the decision to change to a palliative care plan is made, one option available in most areas of the country is *hospice*, a system of specialized professional palliative care providers. Professional palliative care contributes to quality of life by maintaining the person's dignity (Miettinen et al., 2001). The concept of a "good death" is often noted to be marked by dignity, tranquility, comfort, being surrounded by family, and taking place in the home. Hospice programs have shown that a good death is possible in all care settings. A Medicare hospice benefit was established in 1983, and now there are more than 3000 hospice programs serving at least 700,000 people. Hospice programs provide family care at a time when loss is expected, and hospice care can be used as a model for nursing care that can meet a variety of family health needs. Family needs include physical, emotional, social, spiritual, and resource supports (Denham, 1999). Hospice services can be obtained in all types of care settings, often including residential facilities that are operated by the hospice. The fundamental elements of hospice care are as follows:

1) Comfort rather than cure as the goal of care
2) A commitment to securing comfort through whatever means of pain relief and symptom control the person needs

3) A holistic perception of the family

4) A belief in empowering the individual and family by encouraging them to set the agenda of daily care

5) The provision of services by an egalitarian, multidisciplinary team that includes nurses, volunteers, chaplains, therapists, social workers, physicians, nurse practitioners, bereavement counselors, and often, compounding pharmacists

6) The inclusion of a spiritual component of care to assist clients in coping with ultimate questions of reconciliation and meaning at the end of life

7) A definition of care that continues beyond the death of a loved one to encompass long-term bereavement support for family and friends

Families can benefit from bereavement counseling for up to 1 year after the death of a hospice client. One difficulty with the hospice movement is the basic qualification of a life expectancy of 6 months or less. This results in many people who would benefit from early hospice intervention not being eligible and in getting very late referrals. Late referrals may be a result of family or client resistance, inability to establish a prognosis earlier, a more rapid trajectory of illness than anticipated, or lack of understanding of the hospice benefit (Asch-Goodkin, 2000).

Natural Death

Families usually need help understanding the natural dying process. The concept of a natural death is unfamiliar to many Americans because it has been many decades since the norm for the dying was to stay at home and be cared for by the family. Treatment options were limited, and interventions were usually basic nursing care. Technological and pharmacological advances now present families with many treatment options for life-threatening illnesses. The availability of options does not make them efficacious in every situation, and families may misunderstand their utility. Many believe that to withdraw or withhold artificial hydration and nutrition constitutes "starving to death" or "dying of thirst." There is no evidence that foregoing artificial nutrition and hydration imposes an additional burden on or causes suffering for the client at the end of life. In fact, cessation of intake has been associated with feelings of euphoria (Carney & Morrison, 1997). It may be helpful to remind families of their own experiences with relatively minor illnesses and how anorexia and dehydration are common, since individuals are usually not hungry or thirsty and may refuse nourishment until they feel better. The distinctions between hunger and anorexia and thirst and dehydration must be made clear to the client and family. A healthy person stranded in a desert will become hungry and thirsty. A dying person is anorexic and becomes dehydrated as a result of the instinctive response to serious illness. People will often refuse their favorite foods and lose any desire for intake at a level that can sustain them. Their level of consciousness decreases, usually to a comatose state from which they may not awaken. Durham and Weiss (1997) discuss many of the physiological changes nurses can anticipate when a person is actively dying. The course of these events varies depending on persons' diagnoses and their hydration and nutritional status at the time intake ceases. Adequate symptom control, if needed, can make the person comfortable and provide the family with the satisfaction of fulfilling their loved one's wishes.

Our bodies instinctively protect us from fluid and nutrients we cannot assimilate during the dying process. Tube feedings and intravenous fluids can cause an increase in discomfort when given to someone who is dying, because the fluids and nutrients are introduced into body systems that are no longer functioning normally and are unable to assimilate them in a normal way. Care providers must stress that the client's desire for food and fluid should guide his or her intake. If not, the result may be constipation or fecal impaction, nausea and vomiting, increased risk for pulmonary edema, congestion, and possibly severe dyspnea (Durham & Weiss, 1997). Families must realize that once food or fluid is in the body, there may be no way to remove it. When organ systems are ceasing to function, diuretics, cathartics, and other treatments for relief of these symptoms may be ineffective. Artificial hydration and nutrition cannot improve the condition of the person who is dying. No data have shown that tube feeding prevents aspiration pneumonia and other infections, nor does it prevent or speed the healing of decubitus ulcers. No studies have shown a survival benefit when clients with dementia are tube fed (Finucane, 2002). When the decision to forgo artificial hydration and nutrition is made, nurses continue to provide high-quality care, minimize discomfort, and promote the person's dignity. Pain management, skin care, personal hygiene including frequent oral care, privacy, compassionate touch, and family support are the focus of end-of-life nursing care (ANA, 1992).

Nursing Care of the Dying

Adequate symptom management of pain, nausea, dyspnea, constipation, anxiety, and delirium for those who are dying can be achieved without great expense or high-technology equipment (Asch-Goodkin, 2000). There are drug delivery systems and techniques that allow administration of medications to those who are incapable of safely taking standard forms by mouth. Examples are rapidly dissolving tablets for relief of anxiety, agitation, and delirium; transdermal patches that deliver analgesics for pain relief; transdermal anticholinergics to decrease secretions and nausea; concentrated oral analgesic solutions that can be readily absorbed through buccal mucous membranes; and suppositories for fever control, constipation, or seizure management. Hospice services consult pharmacists with training in custom compounding to find solutions to medication administration dilemmas. Client-controlled analgesic devices can deliver medications subcutaneously and allow for the individual to manage titration that may decrease pain and increase the person's autonomy. Some medications, such as benzodiazepines, can be administered and absorbed sublingually or buccally to help control anxiety or relieve insomnia. Although the use of oxygen may not provide comfort to those who are dying, it may be viewed as helpful by families and may decrease feelings of helplessness. However, for the actively dying person, oxygen can extend the dying process and can, for that reason, be considered an extraordinary measure that prolongs discomfort and suffering. The use of opioids can provide symptom relief for dyspnea without altering the natural course of dying. Palliative

care specialists are proficient with these and other methods of symptom management that provide comfort to the dying.

Nurses are often the first care providers to recognize the imminence of death in their clients (Shotton, 2000). Programs are available to help nurses develop the skills they need to become proficient in handling end-of-life care issues and help families maintain their health while they experience this normal part of a loved one's life cycle. Hospice programs have provided professional palliative care to many, with nurses administering much of the care. Hospice programs can serve as models for holistic nursing care of clients in the dying process. Nurses have the capacity to make this experience comfortable for their clients and gratifying for their families. Managing the dying process in the health care system leaves much to be desired, which creates an excellent opportunity for nurses to reshape the last act in many people's lives. "To help someone die in comfort, in peace, and with dignity is to give one final gift of life" (Balaban, 2000, p. 200). When the Theory of Human Caring and the NSWF Framework are used to guide nursing practice, a "good death" is an achievable goal for end-of-life care of clients.

Implications for Nursing Practice, Education, and Research

Family health promotion during life-threatening illness presents challenges to nurses seeking to provide holistic care to their clients. The Theory of Human Caring can guide nurses' emotional and spiritual support of the client and family. The NSWF Framework has emotional and spiritual dimensions, as well as components addressing the physical and informational needs of families in the critical care setting. The possibility of adapting this framework to other settings is encouraging and points to the need for more research on nursing support. Watson (2001) asserts that nursing has not fully matured into the distinct health, healing, and caring profession it strives to be. Therefore further research is needed on caring and healing for families experiencing life-threatening illnesses and the end of life of a member. Providing holistic care to clients has become more difficult as the pressures of the rapidly changing and fragmented health care system strain nurses' ability to do so. Regardless of the setting, clients and their families bear an increasing share of the emotional, financial, and physical burden created by widening gaps in the health care system. As the burden of caring for a seriously ill loved one increases, nurses must find ways to adapt to these changes and meet clients' and families' needs.

The dynamic nature of the health care system may divert nurses' attention from incorporating research into practice models to managing change, thereby contributing to the research-practice gap. More research is needed to examine the causal factors of this gap and to determine strategies that promote the health of families during this major life event. The ANA sees nurses playing a primary role in the informed consent process and ensuring client autonomy. Nursing opportunities for increasing the use and effectiveness of ADs abound. Nurses trained in end-of-life care could provide the public education needed to significantly improve comprehension of the issues pertaining to use of ADs. Many nurses believe that they lack proficiency in the provision of competent end-of-life care. This indicates a need for more emphasis on nursing educational opportunities such as the End-of-Life Nursing Education Consortium (ELNEC) project that provides a curriculum for practicing nurses and nursing students. Vandall-Walker (2002) and Watson (2001) have presented guidelines for the provision of holistic care during life-threatening illness that promote family health through nursing support and caring and reduce the dehumanizing effects of the fragmented health care system. The great challenge for nurses is to incorporate these guidelines into practice.

CASE SCENARIO

Mr. K, a 72-year-old African American, had been in and out of the hospital six times in 8 months, all for protracted periods. He was being treated for severe exacerbations of congestive heart failure, type 2 diabetes, end-stage renal failure, multiple unexplained falls, urinary retention from prostate cancer, Alzheimer's type dementia with psychosis, depression, and severe insomnia. He had been married for 45 years, had a large family living locally, and had been active in the church. With each successive hospital admission, his condition declined, and during the last hospital admission, his family was told he had very little time left to live. He refused "to be on any machines or tubes" and requested only palliative care. He had previously spoken frankly about his end-of-life care preferences with all involved. After consulting with his multidisciplinary team, the family decided to have a hospice assume his care. His behavior prevented him from being cared for at home (his preference), so he was transferred to the hospice residential care center. Managing his psychological symptoms along with all the other medical conditions was extremely challenging. After 8 weeks, his condition stabilized but remained poor, but he did not appear to be imminently dying so he was transferred to a skilled nursing facility. His condition improved dramatically when he was diagnosed with dementia with Lewy bodies and began receiving the appropriate medications. He fell and survived a hip replacement soon after admission to the nursing home. He became lucid and was ambulatory without assistance. His medical conditions were unstable, and medication titrations and laboratory work were required at least weekly to maintain his functional status. His family was large and very supportive. He wanted to go home, but his wife had undergone heart surgery and experienced complications that lasted for 8 months. He persevered for almost 18 months before there was another significant decline in his condition. Hospice assumed his care in the nursing home and covered much of the cost of his medications. He was finally taken home to honor his wishes. He had 23 scheduled medications with a complex regimen, and the cost of his care had reached $65,000 a year in the nursing facility. On returning home, his condition progressively declined and he required supervision at all times. Family members and hospice staff had difficulty participating in his care because he refused to cooperate with anyone but his wife as his dementia progressed. The stress on his wife was significant, and she relied on friends for brief respite care. Hospice staff and family were present when he died peacefully 5 months later. His wife and family continued to receive grief counseling for almost a year after his death.

FAMILY STRENGTHS

Family strengths were cultural competence and adherence to his advance directives, thereby decreasing

CASE SCENARIO—cont'd

the decision-making burden; social competence in obtaining services; strong spiritual support; close family ties and proximity; and good communication skills.

FAMILY STRESSORS

Family stressors included the long, vacillating course of his illness with numerous events that appeared terminal, prolonged vigils in the hospital and in hospice, behavioral disturbances, lack of equitable distribution of care burden, caregiver stress experienced by his wife, decreased family time, lack of time for family health promotion rituals, and financial strain.

LIFESTYLE CHANGES INDICATED

The family had made significant changes to accommodate Mr. K's care and needed help focusing on family health maintenance. The protracted nature of his illness resulted in a lengthy recovery process for the family and the need for hospice and spiritual support.

WEBSITE RESOURCES

ORGANIZATION	WEBSITE ADDRESS
Aging with Dignity	http://www.agingwithdignity.org
Center to Advance Palliative Care	http://www.capcmssm.org
City of Hope	http://www.cityofhope.org
End-of-Life Nursing Education Consortium (ELNEC)	http://www.aacn.nche.edu/elnec
Last Acts	http://www.lastacts.org
National Hospice and Palliative Care Organization	http://www.nhpco.org
Education for Physicians on End-of-Life Care	http://www.epec.net
National Institute on Aging	http://www.nia.nih.gov/

■ CHAPTER HIGHLIGHTS

- Family experiences during a loved one's life-threatening illness challenge coping skills and compromise family health promotion and maintenance.
- Rapidly increasing numbers of treatment options, ethical dilemmas, lack of adequate insurance or financial resources, a fragmented health care system, inadequate communications with care providers, and decision-making burden threaten family health promotion when health care crises arise.
- Family health promotion behaviors increase when levels of burden and stress are decreased.
- Vandall-Walker's Nursing Support with Families Framework and Watson's Theory of Human Caring can guide and inform nurses' endeavors to improve the health of families experiencing a health care crisis.
- The burden of caring for a loved one at home is borne almost entirely by the family.
- An estimated 25 million unpaid caregivers provide care valued at approximately $115 to $288 billion annually.
- The average annual cost for a person's long-term care at home or in an institution is $47,000.
- Seventy to ninety percent of Americans would prefer to die at home, but 74% die in institutions.

■ CHAPTER HIGHLIGHTS—cont'd

- Use of advance directives is supported by 90% of Americans, but only 15% complete one.
- Advance directives lack value when they are incomplete, vague, or have not been discussed with surrogate decision makers.
- Families cannot guess the end-of-life care wishes of a loved one; they know only what they are told.
- Public perception of cardiopulmonary resuscitation (CPR) survival correlates with the survival seen in fictional television shows (77%). Actual survival of CPR is, at best, about 30%.
- Quality of life should be determined from the client's perspective.

- Palliative care professionals and hospice programs can provide clients with a "good death" in most care settings.
- Persons dying naturally do not get hungry or thirsty; they become anorexic and dehydrated, which protects them from fluids and nutrients they can not assimilate.
- The variety of medications and alternative administration options provides caregivers of the dying client with the means to successfully provide comfort.
- Hospice programs can serve as a model for holistic nursing care of dying clients.

CRITICAL THINKING ACTIVITIES

1. What aspects of the Nursing Support with Families Framework and Theory of Human Caring are currently part of your nursing practice when you are working with families experiencing a medical crisis?

2. What intervention could nurses initiate in the primary care setting to increase the use of ADs and reduce the family decision-making burden?

3. Can the cultural barriers to the use of ADs in the African American community be overcome with more participative client-provider experiences in the primary care setting?

4. What family health promotion interventions could be established by nurses in the facility and setting where you practice?

5. How can nurses facilitate recognition of the dying process by other clinicians and families?

6. What are the empirical and contextual aspects of acute dying processes and how can nurses incorporate concepts of nursing support and caring to improve family health?

REFERENCES

Acton, G. (2002). Health-promoting self-care in family caregivers. *Western Journal of Nursing Research, 24*, 73-86.

Aitkin, P. (1999). Incorporating advance care planning into family practice. *American Family Physician, 59*, 605-613.

American Academy of Pediatrics, Committee on Pediatric AIDS. (1999). Planning for children whose parents are dying of HIV/AIDS. *Pediatrics, 103*, 509-511.

American Association of Colleges of Nursing. (2002). *Peaceful death: Recommended competencies and curricular guidelines for end-of-life nursing care.* American Association of Colleges of Nursing. Retrieved December 20, 2002, from http://www.aacn.nche.edu/Publications/deathfin.htm

American Geriatrics Society, Ethics Committee. (1996). Making treatment decisions for incapacitated older adults without advance directives. *Journal of American Geriatrics Society, 44*, 986-987.

American Geriatrics Society, Ethics Committee. (1998, January 1). *Position statement: The care of dying patients.* Retrieved April 16, 2002, from http://www.americangeriatrics.org/products/positionpapers/careofd.shtml

American Medical Association, Council on Ethical and Judicial Affairs. (1999). Medical futility in end-of-life care. *Journal of the American Medical Association, 281*, 937-941.

American Nurses Association, Task Force on End of Life Decisions. (1991). *Nursing and the patient self-determination acts.* Retrieved February 20, 2002, from http://nursingworld.org/readroom/position/ethics/etsdet.htm

American Nurses Association, Task Force on the Nurses Role in End of Life Decisions. (1992). *Foregoing nutrition and hydration*. Retrieved February 20, 2002, from http://nursingworld.org/readroom/position/ethics/etnutr.htm

American Society of Pain Management Nurses. (1998). *Position statement on end of life care*. Retrieved December 20, 2002, from http://www.aspmn.org/html/PSeolcare.htm

Anetzberger, G. (2000). Caregiving: Primary cause of elder abuse? *Generations, 24*, 46-54.

Antle, B., Wells, L., Goldie, R., DeMatteo, D., & King, S. (2001). Challenges of parenting for families living with HIV/AIDS. *Social Work, 46*, 159-170.

Armstrong, J. (2002). Physicians cope with rise in uninsured. *Physician's Financial News, 20*, 1, 16.

Asai, A., Fukuhara, S., Inoshita, O., Miura, Y., Tanabe, N., & Kurokawa, K. (1997). Medical decisions concerning the end of life: A discussion with Japanese physicians. *Journal of Medical Ethics, 23*, 323-327.

Asai, A., Fukuhara, S., & Lo, B. (1995). Attitudes of Japanese and Japanese-American physicians towards life-sustaining treatment. *The Lancet, 346*, 356-359.

Asai, A., Maekawa, M., Akiguchi, I., Fukui, T., Miura, Y., Tanabe, N., et al. (1999). Survey of Japanese physicians' attitudes towards the care of adult patients in persistent vegetative state. *Journal of Medical Ethics, 25*, 302-308.

Asai, A., Miura, Y., Tanabe, N., Kurihara, M., & Fukuhara, S. (1998). Advance directives and other medical decisions concerning the end of life in cancer patients in Japan. *European Journal of Cancer Prevention, 34*, 1582-1586.

Asch-Goodkin, J. (2000). The virtues of hospice. *Patient Care for the Nurse Practitioner, 3*, 6-18.

Balaban, R. (2000). A physician's guide to talking about end-of-life care. *Journal of General Internal Medicine, 15*, 195-200.

Bartels, D., & Faber-Langendoen, K. (2001). Caring in progress: Family perspectives on ventilator withdrawal at the end of life. *Families, Systems & Health: The Journal of Collaborative Family Healthcare, 19*, 169-176.

Basile, C. (1998). Advance directives and advocacy in end-of-life decisions. *The Nurse Practitioner, 23*, 44-60.

Buchalter, E., & Lantz, M. (2001). Treatment of impulsivity and aggression in a patient with vascular dementia. *Geriatrics, 56*, 53-54.

Burrs, F. (1995). The African American experience: Breaking the barriers to hospices. *Hospice Care and Cultural Diversity, 10*, 15-18.

Carney, M., & Morrison, R. (1997). Advance directives: When, why, and how to start talking. *Geriatrics, 52*, 65-72.

Cassel, C. K., & Foley, K. M. (1999). *Principles for care at the end of life: An emerging consensus among specialties of medicine*. New York: Milbank Memorial Fund. Retrieved December 21, 2002, from http://www.milbank.org/endoflife/

Centers for Disease Control and Prevention. *HIV/Aids. Fast Stats A to Z*. Retrieved December 15, 2002, from http://www.cdc.gov/nchs/fastats/aids-hiv.htm

Cohen, S., Boston, P., Mount, B., & Porterfield, P. (2001). Changes in quality of life following admission to palliative care units. *Palliative Medicine, 15*, 363-371.

Comfort, M., & Farran, D. (1994). Parent-child interaction assessment in family-centered intervention. *Infants and Young Children, 6*, 33-45.

Commission on Aging with Dignity. (2000). *Five wishes* [Brochure]. Tallahassee, FL: Author.

Cooper-Patrick, L., Gallo, J., Gonzales, J., Bu, H., Powe, N., Nelson, C., et al. (1999). Race, gender, and partnership in the patient-physician relationship. *Journal of the American Medical Association, 282*, 583-589.

Coscarelli, A. (2000). Treating cancer as a family disease. *Western Journal of Medicine, 173*, 389-390.

Crawshaw, J. (2001). End-of-life care still far from satisfactory. *Critical Care Alert, 9*, 57-60.

Cugliari, A., Miller, T., & Sobal, J. (1995). Factors promoting completion of advance directives in the hospital. *Archives of Internal Medicine, 155*, 1893-1898.

Darr, K. (1996). Availability and use of advance directives. *Hospital Topics, 74*, 4-7.

Dendaas, NR. (2002). Prognostication in advance cancer: Nurses' perceptions of the dying process. *Oncology Nursing Forum, 29*, 493-499.

Denham, S. (1999). Family health during and after death of a family member. *Journal of Family Nursing, 5*, 160-183.

Diem S., Lantos, J., & Tulsky, J. (1996). Study finds TV portrayals of CPR are misleading. *The New England Journal of Medicine, 334*, 1578-1582.

Douglas, A. (2001). Managing pain at the end of life. *American Family Physician, 64*, 1154-1157.

Doukas, D. (1999). Advance directives in patient care: If you ask, they will tell you. *American Family Physician, 59*, 530-532.

Dunlap, R. (1997). Teaching advance directives: The why, when, and how. *Journal of Gerontological Nursing, 23*, 11-16.

Dupree, C. (2000). The attitudes of black Americans toward advance directives. *Journal of Transcultural Nursing, 11*, 12-18.

Durham, E., & Weiss, L. (1997). How patients die. *American Journal of Nursing, 97*, 41-47.

Eliasson, A., Parker, J., Shorr, A., Babb, K., Harris, R., Aaronson, B., et al. (1999). Impediments to writing do-not-resuscitate orders. *Archives of Internal Medicine, 159*, 2213-2218.

Farber, S., Egnew, T., & Herman-Bertsch, J. (2002). Defining effective clinician roles in end-of-life care. *Journal of Family Practice, 51*, 153-158.

Finucane, T. E. (2002). *Tube feeding in the demented elderly: A review of the evidence*. Retrieved October 28, 2002, from http://www.medscape.com/viewarticle/420780

Galambos, C. (1998). Preserving end-of-life autonomy: The Patient Self-Determination Act and the Uniform Healthy Care Decisions Act. *Health and Social Work, 23*, 275-282.

Given, C., Given, B., Stommel, M., Collins, C., King, S., & Franklin, S. (1992). The Caregiver Reaction Assessment (CRA) for caregivers to persons with chronic physical and mental impairments. *Research in Nursing and Allied Health Professions, 15*, 271-283.

Gockel, J., & Morrow-Howell, N. (1998). Advance directives: A social work initiative to increase participation. *Research on Social Work Practice, 8*, 5520-5529.

Goodell, T., & Hanson, S. (1999). Nurse-family interactions in adult critical care: A Bowen family systems perspective. *Journal of Family Nursing, 5*, 72-91.

Gordon, N., & Shade, S. (1999). Advance directives are more likely among seniors asked about end-of-life care preferences. *Archives of Internal Medicine, 159*, 701-704.

Greene, J. (1997). Ethics. *Hospitals & Health Networks, 71,* 15-17.

Haberman, M., Woods, N., & Packard, N. (1990). Demands of chronic illness: Reliability and validity assessment of a Demands-of-Illness Inventory. *Holistic Nursing, 5,* 25-35.

Hallenbeck, J. (1999). Decisions at the end of life: Cultural considerations beyond medical ethics. *Generations, 23,* 24-30.

Haynor, P. (1998). Meeting the challenge of advance directives. *American Journal of Nursing, 98,* 27-33.

Henderson, C. (2001, July 2). Study suggests need for advanced care planning interventions in clinical HIV programs. *AIDS Weekly,* 5-7.

Hendricks-Ferguson, V. (2000). Crisis intervention strategies when caring for families of children with cancer. *Journal of Pediatric Oncology Nursing, 17,* 3-11.

Huffman, G. (2001). Benefits of discussing advance directives with patients. *American Family Physician, 64,* 319-320.

Jacobs, B. (2001). Respect for human dignity: A central phenomenon to philosophically unite nursing theory and practice through consilience of knowledge. *Advances in Nursing Science, 24,* 17-35.

Johns, J. (1996). Advance directives and opportunities for nurses. *Image: Journal of Nursing Scholarship, 28,* 149-153.

Kazak, A., Stuber, M., Barakat, L., Meeske, K., Guthrie, D., Meadows, A. (1998). Predicting posttraumatic stress symptoms in mothers and fathers of survivors of childhood cancers. *Journal of the American Academy of Child and Adolescent Psychiatry, 37,* 823-831.

Krakauer, E., & Truog, R. (1997). Mistrust, racism, and end-of-life treatment. *Hastings Center Report, 27,* 23-26.

Landrine, H., & Klonoff, E. (1994). Cultural diversity in causal attributions for illness: The role of the supernatural. *Journal of Behavioral Medicine, 17,* 188-193.

Lowenstein, A., & Gilbar, O. (2000). The perception of caregiving burden on the part of the elderly cancer patients, spouses, and adult children. *Families, Systems & Health: The Journal of Collaborative Family Healthcare, 18,* 337-346.

Lukkarinen, H. (1999). Life course of people with coronary artery disease. *Journal of Clinical Nursing, 8,* 701-711.

McCubbin, H., Thompson, A., & McCubbin, M. (1996). *Family assessment: Resiliency, coping, and adaptation.* Madison: University of Wisconsin.

McKeith, I., Del Ser, T., Spano, P., Emre, M., Wesnes, K., Anand, R., et al. (2000). Efficacy of rivastigmine in dementia with Lewy bodies: A randomized, double-blind, placebo-controlled international study. *The Lancet, 356,* 2031-2036.

Mebane, E., Oman, R., Kroonen, L., & Goldstein, M. (1999). The influence of physician race, age, and gender on physician attitudes toward advance care directives and preferences for end-of-life decision-making. *Journal of American Geriatrics Society, 47,* 579-591.

Miettinen, T., Alaviuhkola, H., & Pietila, A. (2001). The contribution of "good" palliative care to quality of life in dying patients: Family member's perceptions. *Journal of Family Nursing, 7,* 261-280.

Miller, J. (2000). Development of the concept of powerlessness. In J. Miller (Ed.), *Coping with chronic illness: Overcoming powerlessness* (3rd ed., pp. 55-88). Philadelphia: F. A. Davis.

Morrison, R., Olson, E., Mertz, K., & Meier, D. (1995). The inaccessibility of advance directives on transfer from ambulatory to acute care settings. *Journal of the American Medical Association, 274,* 478-482.

Muldoon, M., Barger, S., Flory, J., & Manuck, S. (1998). What are quality of life measurements measuring? *British Medical Journal, 316,* 542-545.

Murray, J. (2000). Attachment theory and adjustment difficulties in siblings of children with cancer. *Issues in Mental Health Nursing, 21,* 149-169.

National Institutes of Health, National Institute on Aging. (1996). *Progress report on Alzheimer's disease, 1996* (NIH Publication No. 96-4137) [pamphlet]. Bethesda, MD: Author.

Nixon, L., & Roscoe, L. (1999). How can you improve end-of-life decision making? *Trustee, 52,* 12-15.

Noojin, A., & Wallander, J. (1996). Development and evaluation of a measure of concerns related to raising a child with a physical disability. *Journal of Pediatric Psychology, 21,* 483-498.

Orlander, J. (1999). Use of advance directives by health care workers and their families. *Southern Medical Journal, 92,* 481-485.

Palker, N., & Nettles-Carlson, B. (1995). The prevalence of advance directives: Lessons from a nursing home. *The Nurse Practitioner, 20,* 7-21.

Parsons, Y. (1997). Will they or won't they? *Contemporary Long-term Care, 20,* 19.

Patton, C. (2002). Coalition forms to tackle the problem of uninsured patients. *Physician's Financial News, 20,* 12.

Philippe, R. (2002). Understanding and managing behavioral symptoms in Alzheimer's disease and related dementias: Focus on rivastigmine. *Current Medical Research and Opinion, 18,* 156-171.

Pierce, S. (1999). Improving end-of-life care: Gathering suggestions from family members. *Nursing Forum, 34,* 5-14.

Powe, B. (1996). Cancer fatalism among African Americans: A review of the literature. *Nursing Outlook, 44,* 18-21.

Prendergast, T. (2001). Advance care planning: Pitfalls, progress, promise. *Critical Care Medicine, 29*(Suppl. 2), N34-N39.

Rawlins, P., Rawlins, R., & Horner, M. (1990). Development of the Family Needs Assessment Tool. *Western Journal of Nursing Research, 12,* 201-214.

Roberto, K. (1999). Making critical health care decisions for older adults: Consensus among family members. *Family Relations, 48,* 167-176.

Rowland, D., & Garfield, R. (2002, February 15). Health insurance for unemployed workers. *Medscape General Medicine, 4,* Article 423660. Retrieved October 2, 2002, from http://www.medscape.com/viewarticle/423660

Rubio, D., Berg-Weger, M., & Tebb, S. (1999). Assessing the validity and reliability of well-being and stress in family caregivers. *Social Work Research, 23,* 54-64.

Schulman, J., Berlin, J., Harless, W., Kerner, J., Sistrunk, S., Gersh, B., et al. (1999). The effect of race and sex on physicians' recommendations for cardiac catheterization. *The New England Journal of Medicine, 340,* 618-626.

Shotton, L. (2000). Can nurses contribute to better end-of-life care? *Nursing Ethics, 7,* 134-140.

Singer, P., Martin, D., & Kelner, M. (1999). Quality end-of-life care: Patients' perspectives. *Journal of the American Medical Association, 281,* 163-168.

Sisk, R. (2000). Caregiver burden and health promotion. *International Journal of Nursing Studies, 37*, 37-43.

Spertus, J., McDonell, M., Woodman, C., & Fihn, S. (2000). Association between depression and worse disease-specific functional status in outpatients with coronary artery disease. *Journal of the American Heart Association, 140*, 105-110.

Stein, R., & Riessman, C. (1980). The development of an Impact-on-Family Scale: Preliminary findings. *Medical Care, 18*, 324-330.

Strang, V., & Haughey, M. (1998). Factors influencing the caregiver's ability to experience respite. *Journal of Family Nursing, 4*, 231-254.

Strang, V., & Haughey, M. (1999). Respite—A coping strategy for family caregivers. *Western Journal of Nursing Research, 21*, 450-470.

Sullivan, M. (2002). The illusion of patient choice in end-of-life decisions. *American Journal of Geriatric Psychiatry, 10*, 365-372.

Temkin-Greener, H., & Mukamel, D. (2002). Predicting the place of death in the Program of All-Inclusive Care for the Elderly (PACE): Participant versus program characteristics. *Journal of the American Geriatrics Society, 50*, 125-135.

Tilden, V., Tolle, S., Nelson, C., & Fields, J. (2001). Family decision-making to withdraw life-sustaining treatments from hospitalized patients. *Nursing Research, 50*, 105-115.

Titler, M., Bombei, C., & Schutte, D. (1995). Developing family-focused care. *Critical Care Nursing Clinics of North America, 7*, 375-386.

Tunzi, M. (2001). Can the patient decide? Evaluating patient capacity in practice. *American Family Physician, 64*, 299-307.

Tuttas, C. (2002). The facts of end-of-life care. *Journal of Nursing Care Quality, 16*, 10-16.

Twibell, R. (1998). Family coping during critical illness. *Dimensions of Critical Care Nursing, 17*, 100-112.

Vandall-Walker, V. (2002). Nursing support with family members of the critically ill: A framework to guide practice. In L. Young & V. Hayes (Eds.), *Transforming health promotion practice* (pp. 174-189). Philadelphia: F. A. Davis.

Watson, J. (2001). Theory of Human Caring. In M. Parker (Ed.), *Nursing theories and nursing practice* (pp. 344-354). Philadelphia: F. A. Davis.

Watt, H. (2001). Decisions relating to cardiopulmonary resuscitation: Commentary 3: Degrading lives? *Journal of Medical Ethics, 27*, 321-324.

Weaver, A. (2000). Advance directives: Increasing use by rural African Americans through community teaching programs. Unpublished manuscript, University of North Carolina at Wilmington.

Weir, R., & Peter, C. (1997). Affirming the decisions adolescents make about life and death. *Hastings Center Report, 27*, 29-41.

Wolf, R. (2000). The nature and scope of elder abuse. *Generations, 24*, 6-12.

Young, M. (2001). Providing care for the caregiver. *Patient Care, 35*, 68-79.

19

Family Environmental Health

Perri J. Bomar

Safe environments: a sustainable basis or human health.
— World Health Organization, 2003

Poor environment means poor health.
— WHO Fact Sheet 170, August 1997

OBJECTIVES

On completion of this chapter, the reader will be able to do the following:

1. *Define multiple elements of environment, as it applies to family health and nursing practice.*

2. *State disease risk factors associated with a family's environment.*

3. *Identify key elements of major environmental risk areas for families and family members.*

4. *Discuss one or more threats to family wellness within the home environment.*

5. *Describe family preparations for threats to safety from the external environment.*

6. *Examine the common social environmental issues impacting family health.*

7. *Use Neuman's Health Care Systems model to plan, intervene, and evaluate the environment for individuals and families.*

8. *Discuss the role of health care professionals in promoting environmental health and environmental justice.*

9. *Describe nursing research and education issues for environmental health.*

Family Health and Environmental Stressors

Environmental issues generate a concern for the effect of the environment on family health. An early U.S. activist for environmental health, Carson, in her book *Silent Spring* (1962), encourages increased awareness and concern for the impact of environment on health. This book was one of the first to advocate that laypeople should assume self-care responsibility for their environmental health. A later crusader for the environment was Vice President Al Gore (1992),

The author wishes to give credit to Dorothy Wiley who authored this chapter for the first two editions of the text. Also, a special appreciation is expressed to my husband, Guy Bomar, for assistance in creating the sections on unexpected disasters and violence.

with his book, *Earth in Balance: Ecology and the Human Spirit*. Environmental advocacy of the early 1990s was supported by President Clinton who, in February 1994, signed Executive Order 12898, Federal Actions to Address Environmental Justice in Minority Populations and Low-Income Populations. The purpose of this order was to focus federal attention on the environmental and human health conditions of minority and low-income populations, with the goal of achieving environmental protection for all communities.

One need only listen to national television news programming, read current books and periodicals, or routinely sample radio newscasts to be aware of the diverse environmental concerns that exist in the United States and the rest of the world (Markowitz & Rosner, 2002). Poor environmental quality is estimated to be directly responsible for approximately 25% to 33% of all preventable ill health in the world, with diarrheal diseases and respiratory tract infections heading the list (Smith, Corvalan, & Kjellstrom, 1999; Department of Health and Human Services [DHHS], 2000).

The most recent environmental concerns are the result of national and international bioterrorism and terrorist acts. In addition, human beings are affected by many pollutants in different occupational, avocational, and home settings. Each setting may impose a variety of physical and psychological stressors on the individual or family unit, and each presents different challenges to families and health care professionals.

Environmental health is a vast topic that is a social, policy, ethical, and health concern at multiple levels, from families and local governments to a myriad of national and international agencies and organizations such as the World Health Organization (WHO). According to WHO, issues of concern at each level are air quality, chemical safety, children's environmental health, climate and health, food safety, environment and disease, noise, occupational health, radiation safety, water, and sanitation. Each of these topics has been the subject of thousands of articles and books. More recently, since the invention of the Internet, these topics have been addressed on numerous websites.

This chapter focuses on the impact of the environment on family health and includes a definition of environment and a brief overview of the multidimensional current problems and issues in environmental health, the environmental hazards that affect the health of individuals and families, and the role of the nurse in family environmental health.

The Environment: A Multidimensional Concept

The topic of environmental health has received little emphasis in nursing literature, and environmental health is not currently part of the curricula in most schools of nursing (Sattler & Lipscomb, 2003). Environment is one of the four concepts in the nursing paradigm of nursing, health, person, and environment. Nursing's concern for the impact of environment on family health status began with Florence Nightingale's concern for the sanitary environment of families and soldiers (Nightingale, 1859/1992). In recent years, nursing models have addressed the influence of environmental variables on the quality of individual and family health in more depth. Johnson's Behavioral Systems Model includes assessment of society relative to the environment that surrounds the individual (Johnson, 1990). Roy's Adaptation Model (Roy & Roberts, 1984) systematically accounts for environmental stimuli as input to the feedback loop. In King's Open Systems Model, the natural environment is considered a variable that needs to be assessed (King, 1981). Neuman (1982) describes the family as always in interaction with the environment, with flexible lines of resistance to stressors. This chapter uses the definition, from the nursing paradigm perspective, that environment is "all the internal and external factors or influences surrounding the identified client or client system" (Neuman, 2002, p. 18).

According to Neuman (2002), there are three relevant environments for families: internal, external, and created. This chapter does not focus on the intrapersonal environment but rather on selected internal and external family environments. A primary concern for the nurse is the burden of disease and social issues that are caused by unsafe environmental factors. Figure 19-1 shows the myriad of environmental hazards and risk factors that make up the ecosystem of families of the twenty-first century. World Health Report 2002 (WHO, 2002) lists the following

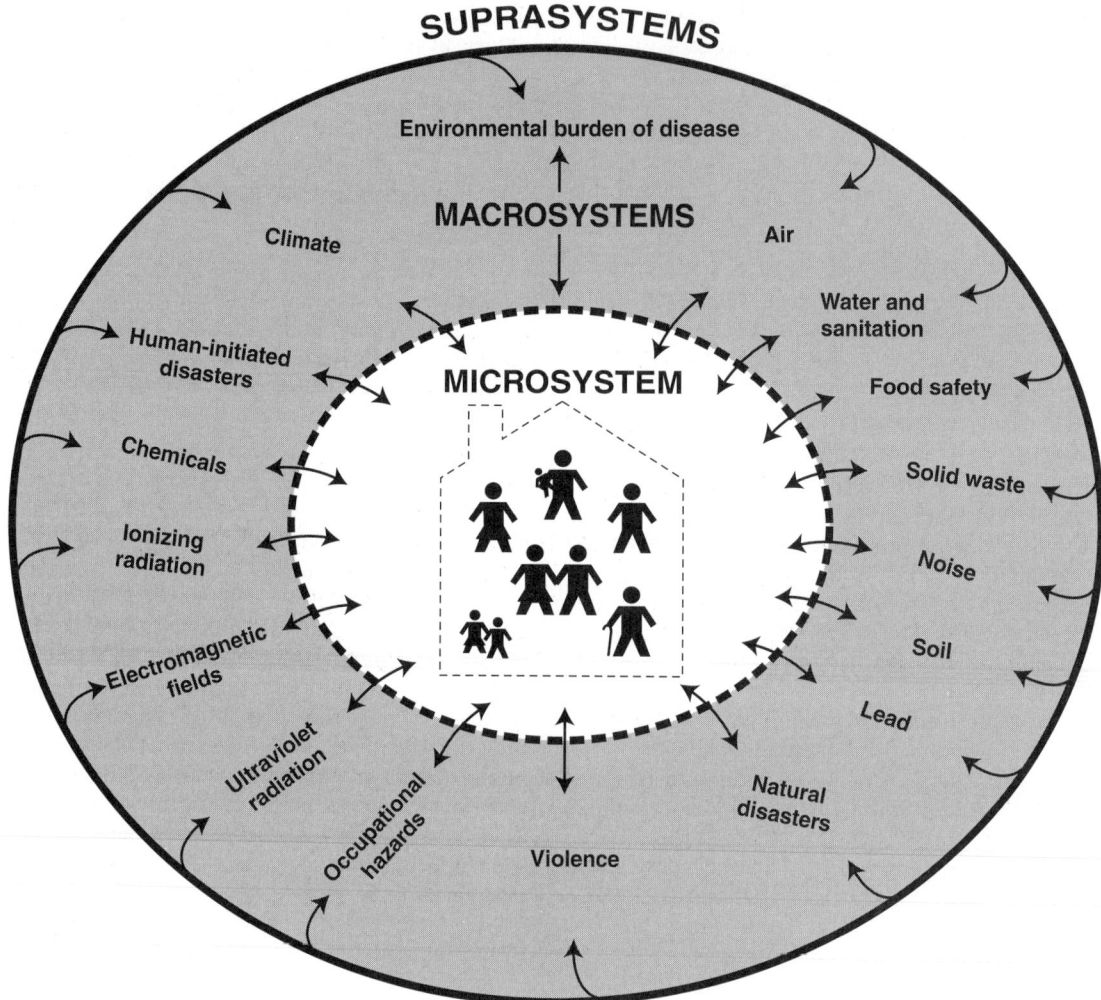

Figure 19-1   Family Environmental Systems.(Adapted from World Health Organization. [2003]. *Global estimates of burden of disease caused by the environment*. Geneva: Author.)

six disease risk factors associated with the environment:

1) Ambient air
2) Indoor air
3) Lead
4) Water, sanitation, and hygiene
5) Climate change
6) Selected occupational risks, including the following:
   - Risk factors for injuries
   - Carcinogens
   - Selected airborne particulates
   - Ergonomic stressors
   - Noise
   - Sharps injuries in health care workers

In addition to the variables listed in this WHO report, disasters classified as natural and human-initiated also influence health. More than 25 million preventable deaths each year are attributed to environmental causes such as unsafe water and air. WHO provides resources to reduce unnecessary health risks and deaths throughout the world.

In the United States, environmental health is monitored and resources are provided by five federal agencies: the Environmental Protection Agency (EPA), the Department of Agriculture, the Food and Drug Administration (FDA), the Centers for Disease Control and Prevention (CDC), and the National Center for Environmental Health (NCEH). U.S. policies for environmental health are guided by the Healthy People 2010 objectives (DHHS, 2000). Table 19-1 provides

specific objectives that family nurses can use in collaboration with families to promote health and prevent disease. Canadian environmental issues are addressed in the Canadian Perspectives box, and additional Canadian resources are provided on the Health Canada website (see the Website Resources box at the end of the chapter).

TABLE 19-1   Selected *Healthy People 2010* Environmental Objectives Specific to Families

Number	Objective Short Title
Outdoor Air Quality	
8-1	Reduce harmful air pollutants
8-2	Increase use of alternative modes of transportation
8-3	Increase the use of cleaner alternative fuels
8-4	Reduce air toxic emissions
Water Quality	
8-5	Increase the number of people receiving safe drinking water
8-6R	Reduce waterborne disease outbreaks
8-7	Increase water conservation
8-8	Increase the quality of surface water to reduce health risks
8-10	Reduce human consumption of contaminated fish
Toxics and Waste	
8-11	Reduce elevated blood lead levels in children
8-12	Minimize risks posed by hazardous sites
8-13	Reduce pesticide exposures
8-14	Reduce toxic pollutants in the environment
Healthy Homes and Healthy Communities	
8-16	Reduce indoor allergens
8-17	Increase the number of office buildings tested for air quality
8-18	Increase the number of homes tested for radon
8-20	Implement school policies to protect against environmental hazards
8-21	Increase disaster preparedness plans and protocols
8-22	Increase lead-based paint testing in homes at risk and employees at risk
8-23	Reduce the number of occupied substandard housing units
Other environmental objectives specific to children and other family members	
20-7	Reduce the number of persons who have elevated blood lead concentrations from work exposures
20-8	Reduce occupational skin diseases or disorders among full-time workers
24-1	Reduce asthma deaths
24-2	Reduce hospitalizations from asthma
24-3	Reduce hospital emergency department visits for asthma

Continued

TABLE 19-1   Selected *Healthy People 2010* Environmental Objectives
Specific to Families—cont'd

24-2a	Reduce asthma-related hospitalizations of children under 5
27-9	Reduce the percentage of children regularly exposed to secondhand smoke
15	**Injury and Violence Prevention**
15-1	Nonfatal head injuries
15-7	Death from poisoning
15-19	Seat belts
15-23	Bicycle helmet use
15-25	Residential fires
15-27	Death from falls
15-29	Drownings
15-38	Fighting among adolescents

From U.S. Department of Health and Human Services. (2000). *Healthy People 2010.* Washington, DC: U.S. Government Printing Office. Retrieved December 10, 2002, from http://www.healthy.gov/healthypeople

---

CANADIAN PERSPECTIVES
FAMILY ENVIRONMENT AND INDIVIDUAL HEALTH: LESSONS FROM HEART HEALTH RESEARCH

Lynne E. Young, RN, PhD
University of Victoria

Cardiovascular disease is currently the leading cause of death in developed countries (Yusuf, Reddy, Ounpuu, & Anand, 2001). Lifestyle risks for cardiovascular disease include high-fat diet, sedentary lifestyle, obesity, and smoking (Heart and Stroke Foundation of Canada, 1999; American Heart Association, 2002). Community-based interventions aimed at reducing these lifestyle risks have been implemented and evaluated in numerous developed countries with a view to reducing the incidence of cardiovascular disease. Research increasingly points to the impact of environment on heart health-related patterns of living (Marmot & Wilkinson, 1999). Three decades of trend analysis

and evaluation of community-based heart health interventions indicate that these interventions have been moderately successful, most notably with more affluent segments of Western societies (Winkleby, 1994). Future success depends on creating supportive environments and policies that make healthful choices possible for all (Raphael, 2000).

Family is the social unit at the heart of health. In families, members share diets, recreational activities, and a smoke-free or smoking environment. Yet, family is one environment not well understood in terms of its influence on individual heart-health choices. Therefore a study was undertaken to explore family

environment and its influence on individual members' heart health-related decision making (Maxwell, 1997). The objective of this study was to explore social processes in families that influence individual members' health-related decisions in response to community-based heart-health initiatives. Grounded theory, informed by critical perspectives, was the methodology of this study. Twenty-eight families participated, representing considerable diversity with regard to family type, socioeconomic status, age, and geographic location. Participants' accounts are rich and, when analysed, generate a theory of family influence on individual members' health-related decisions.

CANADIAN PERSPECTIVES
FAMILY ENVIRONMENT AND INDIVIDUAL HEALTH: LESSONS FROM HEART HEALTH RESEARCH—cont'd

Participants were consistent in their view that health decisions made in response to heart-health initiatives are conceived within a broad definition of health, of which heart health is a part. Family climate of stress or comfort emerged as an important overall environmental influence on individual members' heart health-related decisions.

Family climates of stress and comfort were viewed by participants like the weather, ever-present and changing, rather than as opposing concepts. Further, family climate was perceived differently by family members. Family climate was found to have relational and contextual dimensions. A family climate of comfort is characterised by respectful, caring, and loving relationships (relational dimension); access to financial and community resources; and adequate time and energy for self-care (contextual dimensions). Family stress is characterised by disrespectful, uncaring, and unloving relationships (relational dimension); limited access to financial and community resources; and little or no time or energy for self-care (contextual dimension). Family stress was found to have a unique relational dimension—perpetrated stress that occurs when one family member perpetrates destructive actions on other family members. A family climate of comfort was perceived as an environment that enhances individual members' sense of self-

worth and capacity for action, thereby strengthening the will to be healthy, whereas a family climate of stress was viewed by participants as consuming this will. The will to be healthy, according to participants, is basic to making and acting on heart-health decisions.

Two family processes, talking (productive, unproductive, or dismissive) and modelling, are key family action strategies that inform individuals about what other family members perceive as valued, possible, and/or important about diet, activity levels, and smoking options. Together, family climate and family processes shape individual family members' sense of self-worth and capacity for action with regard to the capacity for making heart health-related decisions. These findings are similar to those evident in a growing body of research linking agency, communion, and mastery (Strage, 1997; Smith, Gallo, Goble, Ngu, & Stark, 1998). Community heart-health interventions should attend to family environment as an essential influence on individual members' capacity for heart-healthy living.

References

American Heart Association. (2002). *Heart and stroke statistical update*. Washington, DC: Author.

Heart and Stroke Foundation of Canada. (1999). *The changing face of heart disease and stroke in Canada*. Ottawa, Ontario, Canada: Author.

Marmot, M. G., & Wilkinson, R.G. (Eds.). (1999). *Social determinants of health*. Oxford: Oxford University Press.

Maxwell, L. (1997). *Family influences on individual health-related decisions in response to heart-health initiatives.* Unpublished doctoral dissertation, University of British Columbia, Vancouver, British Columbia, Canada.

Raphael, D. (2000). Health inequities in the United States: Prospects and solutions. *Journal of Public Health Policy, 21,* 392-425.

Smith, T. W., Gallo, L. C., Goble, L., Ngu, L. Q., & Stark, K. A. (1998). Agency, communion, and cardiovascular reactivity during marital interaction. *Health Psychology, 17,* 537-545.

Strage, A. (1997). Agency, communion, and achievement motivation. *Adolescence, 32,* 299-312.

Winkleby, M. A. (1994). The future of community-based cardiovascular disease prevention. *American Journal of Public Health, 84,* 1369-1372.

Yusuf, S., Reddy, S., Ounpuu, S., & Anand, S. (2001). Global burden of cardiovascular diseases: Part II: Variations in cardiovascular disease by specific ethnic groups and geographic regions and prevention strategies. *Circulation, 104,* 2855-2864.

Canadian spelling is used.

Ethnic and socioeconomic disparities and poorer quality of health result from environmental exposure to toxicants and hazards. For example, inner-city children and young adults and African American, Hispanic, and low-income populations have been found to have hospitalization and death rates from asthma three to five times higher than other residents (Eggleston et al., 1999). Families with low incomes are often at higher risk for exposure to pollutants and chemicals for the following reasons:

- They tend to live in substandard, older housing with crowded conditions.
- Low-income housing is often located near industrial sites, toxic waste dumps, areas of congested traffic, and sources of noise.
- A greater percentage of adults from low socioeconomic backgrounds are employed in occupations in which chemicals and pollutants are manufactured or used.

The environment is made up of all that surrounds human beings—both visible and invisible—and of human beings themselves. Individuals contribute to the environment by their presence, their activities, and the by-products of their actions. From an ecological perspective, environments are categorized into microsystems, macrosystems, and suprasystems. Individuals encounter environmental stressors in the home (microsystem) and at play that may be physical, biological, or chemical in nature. Family members interact with a myriad of substances outside the home (the macrosystem), within social and work systems. The exposure may be primary; an individual may have direct contact with a substance. Exposure may also be relayed to an individual through contact with a family member, or in the case of an unborn child, may be transmitted genetically. The global and national sociopolitical contexts comprise the suprasystem environment.

Technological advances have allowed the monitoring of many individuals and environments, but such advances are frequently fraught with issues of cost, accuracy, and violations of personal privacy (Markowitz & Rosner, 2002). Ignorance may complicate screening and research efforts, because many individuals are unaware of the many substances with which they come in contact during the course of a day. This chapter highlights several major environmental areas of risk for families: air, water, and soil quality; lead; selected occupational and avocational hazards; and unexpected natural and human-initiated environmental disasters.

Air Quality

Air quality is a microsystem, macrosystem, and suprasystem level issue. At the suprasystem level, air quality (indoor and ambient air) continues to be a major health problem in the United States and internationally. Indoor air pollution is the cause of more than 1.9 million deaths in developing countries annually, and more than 500,000 deaths are the result of pollution in ambient air (WHO, 1999). Also, in North America, the major health issues associated with pollutants are premature death, cancer, asthma, and long-term damage to the respiratory and cardiovascular systems (Abelsohn, Stieb, Sanborn, & Weir, 2002; DHHS, 2000). In addition, the estimated annual health costs of human exposure to all outdoor air pollutants from all sources range from $40 billion to $50 billion, with an associated 50,000 premature deaths (DHHS, 2000). Contamination of the ambient environment with particulate matter, gases, and vapors presents difficult challenges to modern society. Humans have grown dependent on automobiles, factories, and power plants but suffer the consequences of dumping enormous amounts of waste into the air. Smog, acid rain, and "dwelling" pollution are but three examples of environmental contamination of current concern.

Scientific consensus indicates that wet and dry deposition of sulfur dioxide and nitrogen dioxide within our air causes acid rain (EPA, 2003a). This phenomenon may be related to natural occurrences such as volcanic eruptions but may also be the result of fossil fuel combustion. Unlike other forms of air pollution, acid rain is caused by substances that are organic and not "foreign" to the environment. The problem varies from region to region, depending on manufacturing practices, natural sources, and the prevalence of emission control devices. Despite recent advances, the timetable and impact of emission control, as well as the long-range transport of acidic substances, are unknown.

At the macrosystems level, common air pollution, "smog," results from an accumulation of combustion by-products. Domestic and industrial heating, incineration, manufacturing, and automobile emissions are thought to be the major contributors to unclean air. The chemicals commonly constituting smog are sulfur oxides, nitrogen oxides, hydrocarbons, lead, cadmium, beryllium, asbestos, and ozone.

Metropolitan area residents are familiar with smog reports and warnings during summer months and periods when weather patterns cause inversion layers to form. Most localities advise that vigorous exercise be curtailed and that individuals with preexisting respiratory and cardiovascular disease limit outdoor activity during high smog periods. Initiated in 1970, the U.S. Clear Air Act created the National Ambient Air Quality Standards (NAAQS), which established the maximal doses of particulate matter, sulfur oxides, carbon monoxide, nitrogen dioxide, photochemical oxidants, and nonmethane hydrocarbons. The maximal dose of carbon dioxide, for example, was determined by plotting the onset of chest pain among patients with coronary artery disease who were exposed to the gas (Higgins, 1986).Outdoor air pollution is the major cause of preventable chronic illness and deaths in young children, the elderly, and people with asthma and other cardiac or respiratory diseases (Abelsohn et al., 2002).

Formaldehyde may be present within public buildings and homes insulated with urea foam, and asbestos has been historically used in building construction as a fireproofing material. Organic vapors may be present in homes where solvents and resin products are used.

The development of superior home insulation materials has brought another "air pollution" problem to contemporary society. Highly insulated dwellings are less costly to heat in frigid areas of the United States. Without compensatory ventilation systems, though, limited fresh air circulation may allow the accumulation of toxic gases. Nitrogen dioxide, carbon monoxide, particulate matter, and formaldehyde may cause health problems for family members.

According to *Healthy People 2010* (DHHS, 2000), everyone should be aware of the possible risk of disease associated with air pollution both within and outside the home. In the home, unhealthy air is usually odorless. The common health problems are asthma, bronchitis, headaches, sinus infections, and eye irritation. Air pollution outside the home also has serious health consequences.

A major preventable health problem is asthma, which is caused by allergens, air pollutants, and smoke (EPA, 2003c). Children are particularly vulnerable to asthma, with low-income African American children four to six times more likely to die of complications (Institute of Medicine [IOM], 1999). In 2000, 4487 people in the United States died of asthma; 223 of these were children 17 years of age or younger (this translates to 0.3 deaths per 100,000 children compared with 2.1 deaths per 100,000 adults aged 18 and older). Non-Hispanic African Americans had an asthma death rate more than 200% higher than non-Hispanic white Americans and 160% higher than Hispanics. Females had an asthma death rate about 40% higher than males (National Center for Health Statistics [NCHS], 2003).

Air quality in the home is a crucial concern because most people spend about 90% of their time indoors. EPA studies of human exposure to air pollutants indicate that indoor levels of pollutants may be two to five times, and occasionally more than 100 times, higher than outdoor levels (EPA, 2003b). Air pollution within homes is related to a variety of activities and substances. Common indoor, inhaled air pollutants in the home are listed in Box 19-1. Families should be made aware of the toxicity of these substances and should be taught to label them appropriately and to store them out of the reach of young children. Nurses collaborating with individuals with asthma and families of children who have asthma should strive to increase their self-care capacity and reduce the number of asthma triggers in the indoor air by suggesting strategies to reduce the level of air toxins.

Radon is an odorless, colorless radioactive gas that comes from rock and soil and is emitted through cracks in basement walls and floors. The result is contamination of water and air. Prolonged exposure to radon is the second leading cause of lung cancer in the United States (EPA, 2002). The reduction of radon is one of the major objectives of *Healthy People 2010* (DHHS, 2000).

BOX 19-1 Common Air Pollutants in the Home

Air fresheners
Asbestos
Animal dander
Biological pollutants
• Carbon monoxide
• Nitrogen oxide
• Radon
• Respirable particles
• Organic gases
Chemicals from dry-cleaned clothes
Combustion substances
Dust mites and mold
Formaldehyde/pressed wood products
Household cleaning products, personal care and hobby products
Lead
Mixtures of solutions
Moth balls
Paints
Pesticides
Secondhand smoke/environmental tobacco smoke
Wastes of rodents and insects

Adapted from Environmental Protection Agency. (1995). *The inside story: A guide to indoor air pollution* (EPA Document No. 402-K-93-007). Washington, DC: Author.

Goal 8-19 is to increase the number of homes constructed to be radon-resistant.

Primary prevention activities for families include an understanding of the impact of ambient and indoor air quality on the health of each member. Box 19-2 provides a list of selected self-care activities for improving and monitoring indoor and ambient air quality. Secondary prevention activities for families include reducing exposure to allergens by cleaning and the use of high-efficiency particulate air (HEPA) filters in heating and cooling systems and portable air cleaners. Tertiary prevention activities include family adherence to prescribed medications and self-care measures and making adjustments in family lifestyle and behaviors to reduce exposure to air pollutants.

Periodic, assessment of housing insulation, ventilation, and sources of combustion and a general awareness of ambient air conditions is a prudent risk reduction and prevention activity. Persons living in high-risk circumstances should be assisted in obtaining risk assessment information, information on location and costs of rehabilitative services, and pertinent information regarding health risks. Examples of these types of interventions include providing descriptive information about industry type and distribution within a community and details about local smog patterns and supplying copies of housing codes and regulations, names of local contractors, and the phone number of the air pollution control district.

Air quality for destitute families is frequently affected by substandard crowded housing, inadequate toilet and water facilities, inadequate heating, and crowded sleeping arrangements, which often lead to disease and accidents. Examples of diseases include the following (Friedeman, Bowman, & Jones, 2003):

1) Respiratory tract infections and skin diseases caused by sharing of towels and utensils, close sleeping quarters, and poor ventilation and heating
2) Intestinal infections caused by unrefrigerated food and inadequate dishwashing facilities
3) Skin infections transmitted by shared towels and inadequate bathing and laundry facilities
4) Respiratory diseases related to asbestos, radon, rodents, mold, and insects

Lead Exposure

Beginning as early as the 1950s in the United States and around the world, lead poisoning was noted to cause disability and death in young children, damage fetuses, and cause severe disability among painters (Markowitz & Rosner, 2002). For the most part, unhealthy levels of lead exposure are avoidable and easily diagnosed using blood diagnostic tests (Sanborn, Abelsohn, Campbell, & Weir, 2002). Although lead levels have declined considerably as the result of national and global legislation and education, lead poisoning continues to be a globally environmental issue, and lead is a common substance in today's ambient and indoor air, dust, soil, and water (EPA,

BOX 19-2 A Self-Care Guide to Air Quality: Selected Strategies

INDOOR AIR QUALITY IN THE HOME

- Do not permit smoking in the house or car.
- Do not use pesticides in the home. If the problem is severe, consult experts about alternatives.
- Air dry-cleaned items in the garage or outside before wearing.
- Ventilate while cooking. For a gas stove, use an overhead range hood that vents outdoors.
- Cook meats, poultry, and fish well, but slowly, to prevent burning, which releases carcinogenic chemicals into indoor air.
- Inspect furnaces, gas water heaters, and clothes dryers regularly to ensure proper ventilation. Never use a kerosene heater without proper ventilation.
- Check ventilation of woodstoves, fireplaces, and fuel-burning appliances, which can be important sources of indoor air pollution if ventilation is poor. If you smell smoke, you have a problem.
- Reduce the indoor humidity and sources of mold and dust mites.
- Use high-efficiency particulate air (HEPA) filters in heating and cooling units and portable air cleaners.
- Clean air conditioners, humidifiers, and heat exchangers regularly to prevent a buildup of mold and bacteria.
- Test the home to determine whether radon is a problem.
- Install and regularly test fire alarms and carbon monoxide detectors in the home.
- Remove contaminated clothing immediately after yard work and use of pesticides and after exposure to hazardous chemicals in occupational settings before returning home.
- Never idle the car in the garage.
- Limit the amount of carpeting in the home. When possible, use wool or cotton rugs, and clean them well. Carpets are reservoirs for chemicals, molds, and animal dander.
- Use water-based (low or zero volatile organic chemical [VOC] content) paints, wood finishes, and sealants.
- Minimize the use of air fresheners, fragrances, deodorizers, and harsh cleansers and ventilate areas where they are used.
- Ventilate always when paints, solvents, or strong cleaning solutions are used; and do not use these products around children.
- Avoid exposure of pregnant women and young children to home renovations and construction areas.
- Store fuels, automotive supplies, and solvents in air-tight and childproof containers.
- Have cars and trucks inspected regularly for exhaust leaks.

OUTDOOR AIR QUALITY

- Pay attention to daily air quality reports.
- Avoid intensive exercise and play outdoors during periods of high air pollution and near heavily traveled highways.
- Drive with auto widows up in heavy traffic with recycled air vents closed.
- If you live adjacent to farmland, golf courses, or recreational areas or have neighbors who routinely apply pesticides, learn about the timing of application. Be certain to keep children and pets inside during that time, and close your windows and doors.
- Learn strategies to reduce exposure to outdoor pollens that cause allergies during seasons when the pollen count is extremely high.

WORKPLACE AIR QUALITY

- Advocate and work with others to establish a smoking policy that eliminates involuntary exposure to environmental tobacco smoke.
- Talk with your own physician and report problems to the company physician, nurse, or health and safety officer.
- Obtain a copy of *An Office Building Occupant's Guide to Indoor Air Quality* (EPA-402-K-97-003, October 1997) from Indoor Air Quality Information at 1-800-438-4318.
- Call the National Institute for Occupational Safety and Health (NIOSH) for information on obtaining a health hazard evaluation of your office (800-35NIOSH), or contact the Occupational Safety and Health Administration (202-219-8151).

Adapted from Environmental Protection Agency and Consumer Product Safety Commission. (1995). *The inside story: A guide to indoor air quality* (EPA Document No. 402-K-93-007). Washington, DC: Author.

2003c, Tong, von Schirnding, & Prapamontol, 2000). Unfortunately, in the twenty-first century, lead products remain at unhealthy levels in the interior of many North American homes and in the soil. For example, an estimated 3 million tons of lead persists in the paint of kitchen cupboard and woodwork in more than 57 million (85%) U.S. homes constructed before 1978 (EPA, 1998).

A highly toxic natural element, lead is a heavy, soft metal with a bluish metallic look. It can be found in all parts of the world. It is indestructible and nonbiodegradable. Initially, it was thought to be harmless in low doses, but a myriad of health problems have been linked to lead ingestion by children and adults. The efforts of the World Health Organization, other organizations, and U.S. health policy (the U.S. Lead Based Poisoning Prevention Act of 1971) have successfully reduced the amount of lead released into the environment (Knestrick & Milstead, 1998). Proactive activities include (1) nearly halting the production of paint with lead content of more than 0.06%, (2) reducing the lead content in food cans and plumbing, and (3) planning for phasing out leaded gasoline. Although some underdeveloped countries lag behind in this endeavor, more than 60 nations have created laws to outlaw lead-based fuels (WHO, 2002).

Lead is released into the environment through manufacturing processes, battery recycling, fuel (coal and oil) emissions, vehicle emissions from leaded gasoline, and some hobby materials (see Box 19-3). Microscopic lead particles are inhaled from air containing lead dust, absorbed through the skin (e.g., contact with lead products), or ingested through drinking water, using dishes containing lead, or ingesting paint dust or chips. Although blood lead levels have decreased from 16.5% in children ages 1 to 5 years in 1972 to 2.2% in 1999, low-income and African American, Hispanic, and Native American children are disproportionately affected. The greatest disparity is among African American children, whose families are impoverished (EPA, 2003c). Despite the steady decline of blood lead levels (BLLs), 5% of the world's children have high BLLs, and more than 500,000 adults have dangerously high BLLs (WHO, 2002). In the United States approximately 1,000,000 children ages 1 to 6 years have BLLs that are greater than the recommended level of 10 micrograms of lead per deciliter (mg/dl) of blood (EPA, 2003c). In Canada, 5% to 10% of the children are reported to have higher than normal BLLs (Sanborn et al., 2002).

Markowitz and Roser (2002) suggest that children are constantly exposed to lead. Over 1 million children younger than 6 years in the United States are reported to have BLLs of at least 10 mg/dl, a level high enough to adversely affect their intelligence, behavior, and development (CDC, 2003). Children tend to absorb 5 to 10 times more lead than adults or 50% of lead that they ingest, whereas adults tend to absorb about 10% (Sanborn et al., 2002). The blood lead poisoning reaches higher levels in children because of their body size and more frequent exposure to pesticides from hand-to-mouth play on the floor or with soil. The effects of lead on children are more pronounced, and they are affected by lower doses of ingestion than adults are. Although lead poisoning is more common among inner-city low-income children living in substandard housing, no socioeconomic level is exempt. For example, children living in restored expensive historical homes are vulnerable to lead poisoning from paint chips and refinishing dust. In children with long-term exposure, the reported results of low levels of lead poisoning are learning disabilities, impaired growth, and hearing loss (Cohen, 2001; Sanborn et al., 2002) and at very high levels, mental retardation, behavioral problems, seizures, coma, and even death (EPA, 2003c). Lead also is transmitted to the fetus if the mother is exposed to high levels of lead from the ambient air or contaminated skin or clothing of others.

Lead poisoning can affect nearly every system in the body and may frequently have unrecognizable symptoms. *Minute lead particles can travel long distances, creating problems far from their source.* Artisans and workers who manufacture or repair products containing lead are at risk for short- and long-term health problems caused by lead, and their family members can become affected by the workers transporting particles of lead to their homes on clothes and skin (*Morbidity and Mortality Weekly Report* [MMWR], 2001; Sanborn et al., 2002). Children who play near traffic and are exposed to vehicle exhaust from lead fuel are also vulnerable to toxic levels of lead through inhalation.

Long-term low-level exposure generally does not produce acute, toxic reactions in adults, and there may be a long latency period between exposure and the onset of symptoms. Examples of illnesses resulting from a long latency period include occupationally and environmentally related asthma, cancers, chronic musculoskeletal disease, chronic heart and lung diseases (e.g., emphysema and other chronic obstructive pulmonary diseases), infertility in both men and women, and adverse pregnancy outcomes. In children with lead levels as low as 10 mg/dl, symptoms can include mental retardation, coma, seizures, and death. Long-term low levels of lead exposure are the most common and can lead to anemia, learning and reading disabilities, behavior changes, insomnia and hyperactivity, impaired growth, hearing loss, and upper extremity weakness (Cohen, 2001). Long-term exposure can also affect the blood, kidneys, the central nervous system, and the skeletal system.

A major goal of *Health People 2010* is the reduction of elevated blood levels among children and at-risk adults. The most reliable and valid measure of recent lead exposure is assessing blood levels. Sanborn et al. (2002) suggest that summer, when lead exposure peaks, is an optimal time to test children's levels. BLLs should be less than 0.50 mg/dl. Each child with levels greater than 0.75 mg/dl should be referred to a clinician with expertise in treating lead poisoning. Children with levels higher than 2.0 mg/dl require urgent attention and possibly hospitalization for management and treatment (Sanborn et al., 2002).

Critical recommendations to further reduce BLLs include primary prevention, case finding, health teaching, and treatment. Key interventions include the following (NCEH, 2003; Sanborn et al., 2002):

- Act before children are poisoned by preventing exposure.
- Lead hazards in a child's environment must be removed.
- Educate parents living in older homes about risks, screening, and treatment.
- Educate parents about risks of lead poisoning from herbal medicine, water, book bags, paint, soil, hobbies, jewelry, and cosmetics.

- Create safe areas outside for children to play in sand rather than in soil and away from vehicle exhaust.
- Educate public and health care professionals about lead poisoning and how to prevent it.
- Test children who are at risk for lead poisoning and, if necessary, treat and follow up in 2 years.

Common sources of lead exposure are listed in Box 19-3. Strategies to help families and communities reduce exposure to lead are listed in Box 19-7 later in the chapter.

Water Quality

Water is essential to life. Plants, animals, and humans cannot continue to survive without clean and safe sources of water. According to WHO

BOX 19-3 Sources of Lead Exposure

THE HOME

Batteries, lead paint, drinking water from lead pipes, dust, plastic window blinds, solder from lead plumbing, ceramic ware, food stored in lead crystal, lead candle wicks, soil, costume jewelry, cosmetics, ink pigments

OCCUPATIONAL SITES

Auto repair, chemically stripping furniture, lead mining and refining, plumbing and pipefitting, glass manufacturing, printing, battery manufacturing and recycling, construction work, firing range instruction, plastic manufacturing, and working as a gas station attendant

HOBBIES

Glazed pottery making, target shooting on firing ranges, lead soldering, preparing lead shot for fishing sinkers, stained-glass making, painting, car or boat repair

OTHER

Folk remedies (such as "greta" and "azarcon"), selected Mexican candies, gasoline sniffing, cosmetics, antique furniture refinishing

(2002) and NCEH (1998), water quality, sanitation, and hygiene are among the greatest health risks and global priorities for the twenty-first century. Sources of water include rain, surface water, groundwater, oceans, and recycled water (EPA, 2000). Desalination of ocean water is costly and is therefore reserved for extreme circumstances. Rain is a difficult resource to collect for large populations and is vulnerable to contamination by suspended particulate matter and organic chemicals.

Groundwater and surface water have been easily accessible and economical resources for humankind and make up about 80% of the water source in the United States. Early evidence of microbial epidemics also demonstrates the vulnerability of surface water and dependent populations. Common pollutants in groundwater include carbon, hydrogen, sulfur, chlorine, nitrogen, sulfur, and phosphorus. Other pollutants include solvents, degreasers, petroleum components, pesticides and certain industrial by-products, and viral and bacterial pathogens (Zublena, Cook, & St. Clair, 1997). Eighty-five percent of industrial waste is introduced untreated into deep wells (Sattler, 2003). Health problems caused by polluted water include diarrhea, upset stomach, vomiting, stomach cramps, fever, headache, muscle pain, bloodstream infections, meningitis, and encephalitis—all of which may result in death.

Humankind has learned that direct contamination of proximal waters may adversely affect the health of those consuming water downstream. The epidemic of cryptosporidiosis that occurred in Milwaukee, Wisconsin, in 1993 is evidence of the excessive morbidity and mortality that can occur when water resources are contaminated with harmful agents (CDC, 1995). More than 400,000 people became ill when filtered, treated public water supplies were contaminated (CDC, 1995).

Groundwater, which may be drawn from springs or wells, is more mineralized than rainwater and is less vulnerable to direct contamination than surface water. Direct toxic discharges or leaching, however, may cause an aquifer to become polluted. If groundwater becomes polluted, it may take many years to recover naturally, if detoxification occurs at all (Water Environment Federation [WEF], 2003). In rural areas, groundwater may become polluted by household disposal of waste and other chemicals. For example, in North Carolina, more than 1 million homes in the state use onsite septic systems to dispose of waste water (Cook, Zublena, & Naderman, 1997). In addition, runoff water from fields and surface water contain harmful levels of nitrogen that affect both animals and humans. Adults usually excrete nitrogen without harm to their systems. However, high levels of nitrates, toxins, and bacteria in drinking water can cause diarrhea that may result in death in young children. Therefore when the nitrate level is higher than 44 ppm, health officials recommend that young children and infants be given bottled distilled water (Cook, Zublena, & Naderman, 1997).

The adoption of drinking water standards in the early part of the twentieth century promoted potable water and prevented disease transmission. Federal controls were enacted in 1974 with the passage of the Safe Drinking Water Act. Additionally, Congress amended the Safe Drinking Water Act in 1986 and 1996 to substantially increase the number of regulated substances in drinking water (Okun, 1992; EPA, 2000). The microbial content of water is monitored by the Environmental Protection Agency through two regulations: The Total Coliform Role and Surface Treatment Requirements (CDC, 1993b). The maximum contaminant levels for total coliforms and the turbidity of drinking water are specified by these policies.

Although federal and state efforts have been directed at regulating and ensuring the public of a clean water supply, the shortcomings must be stressed. Water resources in communities numbering fewer than 10,000 and in rural areas are more vulnerable. Rural families may also draw their water directly from aquifers that are contaminated by toxic substances, pesticides, or pathogens. Indirectly reused water (i.e., wastewater that has been partially treated and discharged into surface water) may also transmit heavy metals, toxicants, and pathogens. An example of the long-term effects of toxic substances is shown in the case study on dioxin in Box 19-4 later in the chapter.

Families should be taught to prevent contamination of groundwater and surface water by properly disposing of chemicals, pesticides, batteries, and workshop liquid solutions. For example, they should be taught that pouring toxic chemicals down the drain could be hazardous to fish and other humans. The family nurse could refer families to the EPA and CDC websites or their local health department's registered "sanitation expert" regarding the disposal of hazardous chemicals and products.

More than 23 million households in the United States use wells that are not protected by the Clean Air Act. Families who use wells for drinking water should be aware of the risks and should learn ways to keep their drinking water safe. For example, well water quality should be tested annually for nitrates and coliform bacteria, and a regular schedule for checking the myriad aspects specific to "well hygiene" should be in place. One valuable "well health" resource is the EPA pamphlet *Drinking Water from Household Wells*, which can be obtained from the EPA website, the Farm*A* Syst website (see the Website Resources box at the end of the chapter), or a local health department. Also, the EPA has a Safe Drinking Water Hotline that provides immediate answers to questions about water quality (the number can be found on the EPA's website). Families and children should be encouraged to be advocates for and protectors of surface water and groundwater for themselves, for humankind, and for future generations.

Soil Quality

Soil is essential for growth of plants, which provide nourishment, oxygen, shelter, and beauty. Cultivation of plants has been radically altered by modern technology and the use of chemicals for pest control and fertilization. In addition, modern manufacturing processes and chemicals may alter the soil. The leakage of chemicals and toxicants from landfills is a hazard to the safety of soil. In rural areas, soil may be polluted by inadequate sewage systems, leaking septic systems, and animal waste from pork and poultry farms. Also, the by-products of vehicle fuel pollute the soil for an undetermined amount of time. Pesticides continue to be used, even though contemporary society does not favor their presence in foodstuffs. This may be related to fears of both immediate toxic effects and long-term, unknown biological effects. Residues may result from internal treatments, external treatments, or the accidental contamination of soil by spillage or previous application. Acute, high-level exposures to pesticides typically occur with accidental contamination and produce a constellation of symptoms related to the toxicological properties of the substance. Long-term exposure, generally associated with ongoing occupational contact, produces a more diffuse pattern of illness. The Research Synopsis details a study of pesticide exposure in children.

RESEARCH SYNOPSIS

ORGANOPHOSPHORUS PESTICIDE EXPOSURE OF URBAN AND SUBURBAN PRESCHOOL CHILDREN WITH ORGANIC AND CONVENTIONAL DIETS

Researchers assessed organophosphorus (OP) pesticide exposure from diet by biological monitoring among preschool children in a northwestern coastal state in the United States. Parents of the children kept food diaries for 3 days before urine collection, and they distinguished organic and conventional foods according to label information. Children were then classified as having consumed either organic or conventional diets based on analysis of the diary data. Residential pesticide use was also recorded for each home. Twenty-four–hour urine samples were collected from 18 children with organic diets and

21 children with conventional diets and analyzed for five OP pesticide metabolites.

Median concentrations of total dimethyl alkyl phosphate metabolites were found to be significantly higher than total concentrations of diethyl alkyl phosphate metabolites (0.06 and 0.02 µmol/L, respectively; $p = 0.0001$). The median total dimethyl metabolite concentration was approximately six times higher for children with conventional diets than for children with organic diets (0.17 and 0.03 µmol/L; $p = 0.0003$); mean concentrations differed by a factor of 9 (0.34 and 0.04 µmol/L).

Continued

RESEARCH SYNOPSIS

ORGANOPHOSPHORUS PESTICIDE EXPOSURE OF URBAN AND SUBURBAN PRESCHOOL CHILDREN WITH ORGANIC AND CONVENTIONAL DIETS—cont'd

The data showed that the median total dimethyl metabolite concentration was approximately six times higher for the children eating conventional diets than for the children eating organic diets. The dose estimates suggest that consumption of organic fruits, vegetables, and juice can reduce children's exposure levels from above to below the U.S. Environmental Protection Agency's current guidelines, thereby shifting exposure from a range of uncertain risk to a range of negligible risk. Consumption of organic produce appears to provide a relatively simple way for parents to reduce their children's exposure to OP pesticides.

Curl, C. L., Fenske, R. A., & Elgethun, K. (2003). Organophosphorus pesticide exposure of urban and suburban preschool children with organic and conventional diets. *Environmental Health Perspectives, 111*, 377-382.

Families would potentially benefit from removal of pesticide residue from foods. Proper application of chemicals to home-grown vegetables and fruits—with adherence to the manufacturer's suggested dose, application, and timing—would minimize potential exposures. Thorough washing of fruits and vegetables before use significantly reduces the amount of toxicant present (Awad & el Shimi, 1993). Also, the purchase of foods not grown with pesticides (organic) is a useful strategy to reduce pesticide ingestion.

Hantavirus (a recently identified human pathogen) has been detected in a southwestern U.S. population and rural regions. It was found to result from direct or indirect contact with excreta from indigenous rodents. Most disease occurs in adults and is associated with domestic, occupational, or leisure activities that bring humans into contact with infected rodents. To protect themselves from diseases carried by rodents and their waste products, families should be instructed to eliminate rodent infestations, reduce rodent food sources, and destroy nesting sites within homes or outbuildings. Also, rodent infestation sites should be cleansed thoroughly with disinfectants and detergents, and inhalation of dust that may contain particles of excreta should be avoided by wearing a mask (CDC, 1993a).

Occupational Hazards

The workplace can be a site of environmental hazards. Most members of society perform some type of work. Regardless of whether this occurs in a factory, a shop, an institution, or a home, most people spend a significant portion of their day in the performance of their occupation. In the decade of 2000 to 2010 the U.S. workforce is expected to increase by 15% (17 million) to reach approximately 158 million (U.S. Bureau of Labor Statistics [BLS], 2001). By 2005, approximately 28% of workers will be from varied ethnic groups, and 48% will be women.

The trend that is expected to continue in the United States is the shifting of jobs from manufacturing to service and the reduction of expenses. Resultant changes for the workforce that are expected to continue are longer hours; compressed work week; rotating shifts; uncertainty in the permanence of the job; and part-time, temporary, and contract status (National Institute of Occupational Safety and Health [NIOSH], 2002). An unfortunate reality of the workplace is the myriad of occupational hazards that may result in fatal occupational injuries, fatal occupational illnesses, nonfatal injuries, or nonfatal occupational illnesses (NIOSH, 2002). In the United States in 2001, "approximately 5.2 million injuries and illnesses were reported in private industry workplaces" (U.S. BLS, 2002, para. 1). Excluding the 2886 work-related fatalities from the events of September 11, 2001, the overall workplace fatality number was 5900 in 2001 (U.S. Bureau of Labor Statistics, 2002). In addition, approximately 16 workers were fatally injured on the job in 2000 (U.S. BLS 2002). The following sections discuss selected occupational hazards.

An alarming and too often common phenomenon of the last decade is workplace violence. According to NIOSH (1996), homicide is the second leading cause of occupational death in the United States (see the discussion later in the chapter on environmental violence).

Many occupational hazards have characteristics that make their presence more noticeable to the average person. Color, mist, vapor, taste, odor, and tactile properties may act as clues. Hazards common to the workplace include physical dangers such as mechanical, chemical, electrical, thermal, vibration, radiation, and auditory threats. Biological dangers encompass exposure to viruses, rickettsia, bacteria, fungi, and parasites. Chemical dangers include naturally occurring toxins and synthetically manufactured toxicants. Work-related stress may be global or specific in nature, manifesting itself during work or leisure time.

Noise

According to the 1998 report *Criteria for a Recommended Standard for Occupational Noise Exposure* (NIOSH, 1998), noise is an increasing public health problem in the workplace, as well as in recreational and residential settings. Noise can have adverse health effects such as tinnitus, sleep disturbances, cardiovascular and psycho-physiological problems, performance reduction, annoyance responses, and adverse social behavior. Prolonged exposure to workplace noise (e.g., machinery and hammers) and residential noise (e.g., loud music, appliances, and power tools) can cause hearing loss. Niskar et al. (2001) found that approximately 12.5% of children between the ages of 5 and 19 years in the United States (5.2 million) have hearing loss caused by exposure to continual excessive noise. NIOSH (1998) estimates that more than 13.3% of American workers are exposed to noise levels of 85 decibels (dB) or more. According to NIOSH, hearing loss is the second most frequent occupation-related disease and affects more than 30 million workers per year.

Sound at high decibel levels is injurious to health. The frequency of sound refers to the rate at which each sound wave cycles; amplitude is a measure of sound intensity or "loudness." A single, high-amplitude, high-frequency sound may cause pain and temporary or permanent hearing loss. "Noise" is generally a mixture of frequencies, intensities, pressures, and durations of sound waves. Protracted exposure to noise levels exceeding 90 dB can cause immediate or latent hearing loss. The Occupational Safety and Health Administration (OSHA) requires employers to develop and implement a noise monitoring program when information indicates that any employee's exposure may equal or exceed an 8-hour average exposure of 85 dB. When engineering controls have not eliminated hazardous noise, OSHA also requires employers to provide hearing protectors and to ensure that workers wear them.

Workers and their family members should be taught the proper use of hearing protectors. They should be encouraged to ask the following questions:

- Is the noise at my workplace so loud that I have to raise my voice significantly for someone an arm's length away to hear me?
- When I leave work or a workshop and am in a quieter environment, do my ears feel plugged?
- Do I hear a mild ringing or whooshing noise that goes away after an hour or two?

If a person answers yes to any of these questions, his or her hearing needs to be checked.

Radiation

Ionizing radiation is but one of many levels of energy in the electromagnetic spectrum. Absorption may cause physiological damage by excitation or ionization of body tissues. Radiation may either pass through the human body or become internalized by ingestion, inhalation, or surface absorption of radioactive particles. Nausea, fatigue, blood dyscrasias, intestinal compromise, alopecia, central nervous system disorders, and death are short-term sequelae of toxic doses of ionizing radiation. Genetic mutation, infertility, and malignancies are potential long-term side effects (Johnson, 1984; Talbott, Youk, McHugh-Pemu, & Zborowski, 2003).

The biological effects of non-ionizing radiation are related to the energy source, duration of exposure, and penetrating power. Short-term effects of excessive ultraviolet (UV) light exposure include pigment changes, changes in cell growth, and burns. Long-term adverse outcomes associated with excessive exposure to UV light include skin cancers.

Biological Occupational Hazards

Biological hazards exist where direct or indirect contact between workers and viruses, rickettsia, bacteria, fungi, and/or parasites is possible. Common vehicle contact and air droplet and vector contamination are modes of transmission. The efficiency of the transmission and the likelihood of resultant infection are related to host characteristics and the directness of the inoculation. Blood splashing into the eyes or into an open wound of a worker is an example of direct contamination. Needle sticks and mouth pipetting require an intermediate object (i.e., a needle and a pipette, respectively) between the contaminated substance and the new host and are therefore considered indirect. The probability of infection diminishes as the contaminated body substance becomes more removed from the reservoir of infection.

Infections

The current epidemic of HIV infection and related diseases has led to a heightened and warranted awareness of biological hazards among health care workers. The CDC continues to recommend adoption of appropriate, routine precautions and use of personal protective devices to limit the contact between the (infectious) agent and a potential host (consult the CDC website).

Although HIV infection is of concern, it is not the only type of infection that may be transmitted to humans and result in significant illness or death. Precautions to prevent infection should extend to all persons who risk exposure to microorganisms. Persons who treat or handle animals, manage sewage waste, or process body substance specimens should avoid unprotected contact. Body substance isolation is one example of a systematic approach to avoiding direct or indirect contact between biological hazards and workers. The body substance isolation system requires

appropriate personal protective devices or barriers between workers and potentially infected fluids; all body secretions, excretions, and fluids are assumed to contain potentially harmful agents. The diagnosis-independent system of isolation shifts traditional isolation procedures from depending on diagnosis of a specific entity before protective measures are initiated to a system driven by the potential for interaction between agent and host.

Other forms of infectious agent transmission present less severe risk of infection. Classical "common vehicle transmission" generally occurs when a group of individuals have common contact with a contaminated substance. Outbreaks are typically related to ingestion of contaminated foods or beverages. Airborne transmission occurs when contaminated droplets remain suspended in the air. Not only must the droplet remain suspended, but the host must then inhale a sufficient dose of infectious material to cause illness. More than 50% of tuberculosis cases in the United States are identified among immigrants from developing countries. Tuberculosis remains a concern for developing nations and for new U.S. residents from developing nations (MMWR, 2003). In 2002, 15,078 cases were reported in the United States, which is a decline of 43.5% from 1992 (CDC, 2002). Families are encouraged to follow CDC guidelines for tuberculosis skin testing for screening and prevention.

Toxicant Exposure

Workers come into contact with a variety of synthetic and organic substances and may be exposed to toxicants through inhalation, skin diffusion, or ingestion. Environmental dust, fumes, mists, vapors, and gases may be indicators of possible pulmonary contaminants. Liquid and solid toxicants may pose dangers to the worker if diffusion or direct ingestion occurs. Warnings may be used to protect workers from harmful agents and may include labels, signs, and company policies or procedures.

The Agency of Toxic Substances and Disease Registry (ATSDR) implemented a limited, active, state-based Hazardous Substance Emergency Events Surveillance System in 1989 to monitor the public health consequences of hazardous substance releases (CDC, 1994). The ATSDR data indicate that 77% of the 3125 hazardous substance emergency events reported by participating states from 1991 through 1992 were from fixed facilities and 23% were related to transportation. Most emergencies occurred on weekdays between 6:00 AM and 6:00 pm. Volatile organic compounds, herbicides, acids, and ammoniac comprised almost 58% of the reported hazardous substance releases. Although 3500 injuries were reported to the ATSDR during the surveillance period, approximately 60% were reported as respiratory or eye irritation (CDC, 1994).

Dioxin is one of the most toxic chemicals known. Since 1994 the EPA has clearly described dioxin as a serious public health threat. According to the EPA there appear to be no safe level of exposure to dioxin. Levels of dioxin and dioxin-like chemicals that are at or near levels associated with adverse health effects have been found in the general U.S. population. The EPA report confirms that dioxin is a cancer hazard to people, that exposure to dioxin can also cause severe reproductive and developmental problems (at levels 100 times lower than those associated with its cancer-causing effects), and that dioxin can cause immune system damage and interfere with regulatory hormones. Dioxin is a by-product of incineration and is found in meat and dairy projects, soil, water, and the chlorine-based solution used in paper production (EPA, 2003d). It is reported to cause cancer, reduce sperm count, and increase breast and prostate cancer rates; and it has been detected in breast milk. The primary concern is that long-term exposure to dioxin may cause cancer. In lower doses it may cause skin rashes, acne, excessive body hair, and mild liver damage. Box 19-4 presents a case study on the effects of dioxin exposure in one town.

BOX 19-4   A Chemical Case Study: Times Beach, Missouri

Before the environmental justice movement, Times Beach, Missouri, an ecological "experiment," illustrates a relationship between primary pollution of land and the secondary contamination of streams and rivers. Dioxin, a toxic by-product, was produced by a pharmaceutical and chemical company in Missouri between 1970 and 1972. Storage at the plant site appears to have been safe, and direct detoxification conducted by the company followed recommended guidelines. Unfortunately, 18,000 gallons of the toxic oil was removed by a waste oil hauler and sprayed on eastern Missouri roads, including those in Times Beach, as an anti-dust treatment (Powell, 1984).

The immediate effect of dioxin spraying was truly disastrous. Shenandoah Stables, the first site of documented human illness, was sprayed with approximately 6 pounds of dioxin (Powell, 1984). Many animals died or were destroyed, and one child was hospitalized shortly after the contamination. Times Beach was a contaminated area with multidimensional problems. Like the Shenandoah Stables, it was directly contaminated with dioxin.

Times Beach was further postulated to contain more than 60% of dioxin-contaminated soil in Missouri (Powell, 1984). Its soil was first tested in early December 1982, and residents were ordered to evacuate shortly thereafter. Two natural floods have occurred in Times Beach since the evacuation, and yet no appreciable change in the dioxin concentration of the Meramec River, on which Times Beach is located, has occurred. Erosion and flooding still pose significant problems because they potentiate the transfer of stored dioxin from soil to potable water and river-bottom soil over time.

The long-term effects of existing and potential dioxin contamination in Times Beach, Missouri, are only postulated. This example, though, highlights the issue of the interaction between general soil contaminants and groundwater pollution. Chemicals and waste products may also be transmitted to the water supply through purposeful or accidental spillage. Sewage treatment plants, manufacturers, small business, and agricultural enterprises all handle and dispose of toxic chemicals that cause water pollution. The long-term effects of low-dose exposure on family health and well-being are unknown.

From Powell, R. L. (1984). Dioxin in Missouri: 1971-1983. *Bulletin of Environmental Contamination and Toxicology, 33,* 648-654.

Effects of Toxicant Exposure. The effects of toxicant exposure may include immediate toxicosis, mutagenesis, oncogenesis, or teratogenesis. The effects on a family may include altered reproduction, cancer, and immediate development of disease. Early detection of exposure to a known toxicant may minimize the effect and may guide families in decisions about lifestyle, reproduction, and health surveillance.

The biological effects of toxicant exposure may be reversible or irreversible. For example, lead poisoning, an occupational illness of battery factory workers, may produce classic symptoms of lassitude, hematological disturbances, sleep disorders, and weight loss. Unlike other disorders, lead poisoning may be treated, and its effects may be reversed when it is discovered early. In contrast, prolonged occupational exposure to 1,2-di-bromo-3-chloropropane (DBCP), a nematocide, rendered male factory workers infertile (Whorton, Krauss, Marshall, & Milby, 1977).

Stress

Occupational stress and nonoccupational stress are difficult to describe because of the difficulty of quantification. Stress may be either positive or negative and requires an organism or system to adapt within an environment (Neuman, 2002). It is crucial for nurses practicing in occupational health settings to recognize that whether primary or secondary to the work setting, hazardous stressors may induce illness, disability, or violence.

Information and Regulation for Occupational Hazards

Workers may or may not have access to information about the potentially harmful agents within their environment. Interpretation of the information provided by material safety data sheets is difficult for many workers, and administrators fear that misinterpretation may breed distrust and unnecessary worry among employees. Those industries producing potentially toxic substances may additionally fear increased lawsuits from workers exposed to their products. Disclosure of chemical makeup may also jeopardize commerce if trade secrets are revealed.

The regulation of the industrial environment has been a controversial issue since before the inception of OSHA. The 1970 legislation that established OSHA aimed to ensure that no employee would experience impairment as a result of occupational exposure. OSHA regulations are enforced by consultation, inspection, and citation. Many states have developed individual occupational safety and health administrations, some of which hold industry more accountable than their federal counterpart.

NIOSH promotes workplace research, consultation, and standard setting. This agency was created to complement OSHA. Although its mission is noble, the number of potentially harmful substances are many, and its resources are limited. Recent history has demonstrated both successes and failures attributable to OSHA and NIOSH.

Paraoccupational Hazards

Paraoccupational hazards are related to indirect exposure of nonworkers to the hazardous substances present within a work setting. The children and spouses of workers and social contacts within the home may be at risk for disease when hazardous dust, residues, liquids, or solids are transported by the worker outside the occupational environment. Soiled clothing and residue on the skin are examples of means by which a toxic agent may be brought into the home. Diseases related to paraoccupational exposure are dependent on the dose received, the duration of exposure, and the physiological and genetic makeup of the individual.

One example of a growing concern about risk associated with paraoccupational exposures recently surfaced. OSHA has drafted regulations designed to protect the family and social contacts of workers employed at Superfund cleanup sites. The regulations require that decontamination of clothing and equipment be conducted on site. Personal protective equipment and decontamination procedures must be explained in detail to the workers and are designed to protect the workers, peers, and off-site contacts. Examples of these procedures might include use of disposable impermeable clothing, on-site showers, separate decontamination "rooms," and impenetrable gloves.

Although monitoring family members for illness is costly and cumbersome, it is imperative that specific industries assume some account-ability for family health. However, caution and wisdom should be used in surveys of at-risk populations because all illness may not be related to paraoccupational exposures.

Avocational Hazards

Hazards that result from recreational activities are difficult to estimate. Toxicants may be found in materials used for hobbies such as leaded-glass window construction, model airplane assembly, furniture refinishing, and automobile restoration. Safety controls are generally limited to user knowledge and general regulation of substances by government agencies. For example, the sale of toluene, a chemical solvent, is regulated in some states because of both its potential for abuse and its toxic properties. The more stringent controls and inspections related to OSHA and state regulations on industry are absent in home and recreation settings.

Recreational activities may pose additional environmental threats. Injuries related to auto-mobiles, motorcycles, and bicycles are ever-present. The financial and emotional burdens individuals and families endure from such injuries are great. Automobile crashes are the single greatest cause of death for persons 5 to 32 years of age in the United States, and it is esti-mated that nearly half are alcohol-related (Minino, Arias, Kochanek, Murphy, & Smith, 2002). The national focus on drunk driving has stimulated widespread public education and discussion.

Unintentional injuries from recreation and the family's home environment cause a significant number of injuries and death in the home and during leisure. Injuries include those resulting from bicycle-related accidents; falls, particularly by seniors; fireworks; dog bites; drowning; resi-dential falls; poisonings; playground accidents; alcohol-related deaths (fires and drownings) (CDC, 2003). The studies further indicate that risk of a "bed disability" caused by injury or ill-ness is highest among those persons older than 45 years.

Although adults are more likely to be involved in recreation that results in injury and illness, it is imperative that the nurse consider children in the assessment of environmental hazards. Tradi-tional safety measures have long been a part of home nursing practice and must be continued. Toxicant exposure of young children caused by improper handling and storage of chemicals and preparations continues to be a problem in modern society. Many states have poison control centers. More information about these centers can be found in the Website Resources box at the end of the chapter, which includes the URL for the American Association of Poison Control Centers. Rural communities and those not served by an official poison control center are usually dependent on a less formal system of physicians and nurses practicing in ambulatory care centers, emergency departments, and home settings. Health care professionals practicing in these settings need to be cognizant of the resources of nearby centers and should know how to intervene when poison-ings and accidents occur.

Terrorism and Unexpected External Environmental Disasters

As the world enters the early part of the twenty-first century, the peril of terrorism is experienced on nearly a daily basis by some populations. Devastating acts, such as the September 11, 2001, terrorist attacks on the World Trade Center and the Pentagon have left many people concerned about the possibility of future attacks and their potential severity. The world's political climate has escalated uncertainty about what types of permanent changes might take place in the years ahead. Social stress is encountered to various degrees by both the family unit and individual members. Nevertheless, there are things families can do to prepare themselves for the unexpected and reduce their level of stress now and the risk of injury should disastrous events occur. Families should ordinarily be prepared for both natural and human-initiated disasters.

Natural disasters include events such as earth-quakes, tornados, and floods. Human-initiated disasters include events such as arson, power outages, riots, sabotage, and terrorism. The basic preparations are similar for each category. Although there is no way to predict what will happen or what an individual's personal circumstances might be, there are simple protective measures that people can take now to prepare themselves and their families. (One source to consult is the Federal Emergency Management Agency's booklet, *Are You Ready: A Guide to Citizen Preparedness* [2002]; see the website at the end of the chapter.)

With regard to continuing threats of terrorism, the U.S. Department of Homeland Security (see website at the end of the chapter) warns the public that terrorists are working to obtain biological, chemical, nuclear, and radiological weapons and that the threat of an attack is a real possibility. Further, the Department advises all Americans to begin learning about potential threats and developing disaster plans, to be better prepared to react during an attack.

Families can prepare themselves for disasters by doing the following:

- Being informed about what might happen to assist in taking the appropriate actions
- Making family and individual plans for home, workplace, or school for effective responses
- Making emergency kits for the home, workplace or school, and vehicles to reduce stress and inconvenience

Families must be informed about the possible types of threats so that they can reduce loss and provide for basic needs during and immediately after a disaster. Box 19-5 summarizes types of unexpected terrorist disasters. A detailed description of threats and appropriate responses can be found on the Department of Homeland Security's website. Box 19-6 contains the essential components of a family disaster plan and presents elements of a family communication plan that provides for effective responses during an unexpected environmental disaster. Families should create disaster kits for the home, office, school, and family vehicle that contain items needed for a period of 3 to 5 days. In-depth information on preparation for disasters, disaster kits, and external environmental threats to family safety can be obtained from the websites and offices of the American Red Cross, the Department of Homeland Security, the Federal Emergency Management Agency, the CDC, the Center for Food Safety and Applied Nutrition, and local emergency management agencies. The website URLs for these federal agencies are presented in the Website Resources box at the end of the chapter.

BOX 19-5 Types of Unexpected Terrorist Disasters

Preparedness must take into account the possibility of human-initiated disasters, as well as natural ones. Families should understand the types of disasters. Knowing what to do in an emergency is a critical part of being prepared and can be vital when seconds count.

SPECIFIC TERRORIST THREATS

A *biological attack* is the deliberate release of germs or other substances that can make humans sick. Agents may be inhaled, may enter through a cut in the skin, or may be eaten.

A *chemical attack* is the deliberate release of a toxic gas, liquid, or solid that can poison people and the environment.

An *explosion* is a sudden blowing up of structure, and one often hears a loud noise caused by a bomb or other devices. The result may be fire, falling debris, or collapse of structures.

A *nuclear blast* is an explosion with intense light and heat, a damaging pressure wave, and widespread radioactive material that can contaminate the air, water, and ground surfaces for miles around.

A *radiation threat* or "dirty bomb" is the use of common explosives to spread radioactive materials over a targeted area.

For more in-depth information on the threats and related symptoms and how to recognize these threats, consult the website cited below.

Adapted from Preparing makes sense. *Get ready now*. Retrieved February 28, 2003, from http://www.ready.gov/readygov_brochurev3.pdf

Environmental Health across the Life Span

Congenital and Reproductive Hazards

Exposure to potential reproductive hazards poses problems for men, women, and children. The expression of altered reproductive capacity includes changes in libido and potency; altered fertility; menstrual disturbances; alterations in sperm structure, number, and chemical makeup; chromosomal disturbances; teratogenesis; fetal

---

BOX 19-6   Creating a Family Plan for Unexpected Environmental Disasters

Families may not be together when disaster strikes, so they need a plan for how to contact one another and what members will do in different situations. Families should talk about this in advance and do the following:

- Create an emergency communication plan.
  - —Designate an out-of-town contact whom the family or household will call or e-mail to check on each other.
  - —Be sure every member of the family knows the phone number and has coins or a prepaid phone card to call the emergency contact.
  - —Make sure all family members have essential phone numbers, e-mail addresses, cell phones, and/or pagers. Leave contact numbers at schools and workplaces.
- Establish a meeting place. Have two predetermined meeting places if the home area is affected or evacuated: one in town and another out of state.

- Create a disaster supply kit.
- Make a plan for pets, since shelters and hotels do not allow pets.
- Obtain emergency information from the American Red Cross, safety agencies, or the Department of Homeland Security.

Find out what kinds of disasters, both natural and man-made, are most likely to occur in your area and how you will be notified. One common method is to broadcast emergency information by radio and television. You might hear a special siren or get a telephone call, or emergency workers may go door to door.

CREATE EMERGENCY PLANS

You may also want to inquire about emergency plans at places where your family spends time: work, day care centers, and schools. If no plan exists, consider volunteering to help create one. Talk to your neighbors about how you can work together in the event of an emergency.

Adapted from the U.S. Department of Homeland Security. *American Red Cross disaster safety.* http://www.ready.gov/family_plan_text.html Retrieved February 28, 2003; http://www.redcross.org/services/disaster/keepsafe/unexpected.html

---

death; cancer; and developmental delays or disabilities. Although a woman's exposure to hazardous materials is more likely to cause an adverse pregnancy outcome, a man's exposure may also affect the fetus. Congenital defects may be related to chemical exposure during pregnancy or to sperm damage caused by the father's exposure to hazardous materials before conception (Smith et al., 1999). Globally, up to 10% of maternal deaths are attributed to unhealthy environments in the home and workplace. For the purposes of understanding and reducing adverse environmental effects on human genetics, the Environmental Genome Project (EGP) was initiated by the National Institute of Environmental Health Sciences (NIEHS) in 1998. The mission of the EGP is to improve understanding of human genetic susceptibility to environmental exposures. Health care professionals can assist at-risk women, men, and families by encouraging them to be cognizant of the potential adverse effects of

pollutants in their homes, neighborhoods, communities, and workplace environments.

Primary prevention of adverse reproductive outcomes includes family and community education programs and activities to prevent contact between hosts and harmful agents (Box 19-7). Secondary prevention activities would include early screening, diagnosis, and treatment; and tertiary prevention activities would involve attempts to restore reproductive function.

Childbearing and Childrearing Years

Many couples today express concerns about the effects of toxicants on their unborn children. In both home and work settings, direct effects on the fetus are frequently difficult to ascertain. Adverse reproductive outcomes are related to known and unknown risk factors. Reproductive history, age, parity, and preexisting medical conditions are known to be associated with poor

---

BOX 19-7   Ten Tips to Protect Children from Pesticide and Lead Poisoning around the Home

These simple steps can save children from environmental hazards around the home:

1. Always store pesticides and other household chemicals, including chlorine bleach, out of children's reach—preferably in a locked cabinet.

2. Always first read directions carefully because pesticide products, household cleaning products, and pet products can be dangerous or ineffective if too much or too little is used.

3. Before applying pesticides or other household chemicals, remove children and their toys, as well as pets, from the area. Keep children and pets away until the pesticide has dried or as long as is recommended on the label.

4. If use of a pesticide or other household chemical is interrupted (perhaps by a phone call), properly close the container and remove it from children's reach. Always use household products in child-resistant packaging.

5. Never transfer pesticides to other containers that children may associate with food or drink (such as soda bottles), and never place rodent or insect bait where small children can get to it.

6. When applying insect repellents to children, read all directions first; do not apply over cuts, wounds, or irritated skin; do not apply to eyes, mouth, or hands or directly on the face; and use just enough to cover exposed skin or clothing, but do not use under clothing.

7. Wash children's hands, bottles, pacifiers, and toys often. Regularly clean floors, window sills, and other surfaces to reduce potential exposure to lead dust. Wash work clothes or other clothes coming in contact with lead or chemicals separately from family laundry.

8. Get your child tested for lead poisoning if you suspect he or she has been exposed to lead in either your home or neighborhood.

9. Inquire about lead hazards. Before you buy or rent a home or apartment built before 1978, the seller or landlord is now required to disclose known lead hazards.

10. If you suspect that lead-based paint has been used in your home or if you plan to remodel or renovate, get your home tested. Do not attempt to remove lead paint yourself. Call 1-800-424-LEAD for guidelines. For more information about pesticides, call the National Pesticide Information Center (NPIC) at 1-800-858-7378.

From U.S. Environmental Protection Agency. (2003). *10 tips to protect children from pesticides and lead poisonings.* Retrieved March 7, 2003, from http://www.epa.gov/oppfead1/cb/10_tips/

---

pregnancy outcome. The influence of specific products or work settings is much more difficult to ascertain. The occupational settings that have been clearly linked to poor reproductive outcomes have had dramatic effects on specific, sizable groups of individuals over time (NCEH, 2002; Whorton, Milby, Krauss, & Stubbs, 1979). Hemminki, Kyyronen, Niemi, Koskinen, Sallmen, and Vainio (1983), for example, reported an increased rate of spontaneous abortion among textile workers in Finland. Further, Kierkegaard and Kristiansen (1992) found that women who were textile workers had a greater risk of sick leave associated with the threat of miscarriage and pain in the locomotor system than other surveyed women of childbearing age. In general,

advice to families during the childbearing years includes seeking early prenatal care and avoiding unnecessary pharmaceutical, toxicant, or pathogen exposures (Sharara, Seifer, & Flaws, 1998).

Childhood

During childhood, environmental effects on health may be especially serious. Children are vulnerable to pesticide and lead poisoning for the following reasons:

- Children eat more food and drink more water than adults because of their relative body weight. In addition, the ambient and indoor air they breathe is twice that per unit of body weight compared with adults.

- Children play on the floor and ground and put their hands in their mouths.
- Children's developing bodies and brains are more sensitive to poisons.
- Children's bodies have immature immune systems and are physiologically less efficient in detoxifying and excreting drugs, pesticides, and toxicants.
- Children are often exposed at school and play to toxicants and pesticides because adults are not cognizant of the risk to children.

Asthma affects 5 million children. Since 1980, the biggest growth in asthma cases has been in children younger than 5 years. The disease is a leading cause of childhood hospitalizations and school absenteeism, accounting for 100,000 child hospital visits a year, at a cost of almost $2 billion and causing 10 million school days missed each year (EPA, 2003b). In a typical day, children may be exposed to a wide array of environmental agents at home, in day care centers, at school, and while playing outdoors (EPA, 2003b). Common indoor household environmental triggers of asthma include the following:

- Secondhand (cigarette) smoke
- Cockroaches
- Dust mites
- Molds
- Pets and other animals with fur or feathers
- House dust
- Ozone
- Combustion by-products
- Pollen (tree, grass, and weed)

Primary prevention of asthma exacerbations includes avoidance of exposure to allergens. Family activities include preventing exposure to secondhand smoke, cleaning to remove dust mites and mold, lowering household humidity, and removing roaches. Families can be referred to multiple websites and resources on asthma prevention and treatment. Examples of these are the IOM (2000) book *Cleaning The Air: Asthma and Indoor Education*; the National Heart, Lung, and Blood Institute's website; and several websites listed in the Website Resources box at the end the chapter.

Adulthood

Environmental effects on health reach far beyond the early developmental years. Health risks to adults include acute, chronic, and latent illness or injury. Adults may encounter a myriad of chemical, physical, or biological substances; some are innocuous, and some are hazardous to health. Factors to consider in evaluation of the effects of specific agents include the type of exposure, known associated toxicity and health risks, intensity and duration of exposure, and associated latency.

Environmental agents and conditions often affect individuals beyond their working years. Human beings are products of all previous experiences and exposures, genetic predispositions, and current circumstances. Many agents and conditions have long latency periods between exposure and effect. A thorough history of both work and nonwork environmental exposures is helpful in counseling, diagnosis, education, and treatment of the older person.

Macrosystem Environmental Violence

In the United States, violence in the macrosystem environment of families and individuals is a threat to their well-being and a priority health concern of the *Healthy People 2010* initiative. For example, homicide is the second leading cause of death among youth ages 15 to 19 years. The three major arenas in which violence is a critical concern are schools, the workplace, and the home as a consequence of lifestyle behaviors. Violence is a concern for children, parents, educators, justice professionals, nurses, social workers, physicians, psychologists, and public health professionals. Therefore the interventions are complex and often require collaborative efforts. The following section highlights the key issues of macrosystem violence for families and individual members.

School Violence

Prinz (2000) observes that the term *school violence* encompasses a range of behavior including the use of firearms on school grounds and youth misconduct, as well as community and societal influences on such behavior. Although crime decreased in schools and elsewhere during recent years, the amount of crime committed in U.S. schools continues to be a concern. In 1999, students ages 12 through 18 years were victims of about 186,000 serious violent crimes at school and about 476,000 away from school (Kaufman, Chen, Choy, Peter, Ruddy, Miller et al., 2001). Risk factors associated with either aggressive students or victimized students may occur in the environment, in the individual, or in the demand-response aspects in the environment and the individual's ability to respond (Kellam, 2000; Doerner & Lab, 1998). Internationally, a crucial concern in the area of school violence is bullying among school-age children and adolescents (Drake, Price, and Telljohann, 2003). More than 16% of U.S. children report they were bullied in the past term (Nansel, Overpeck, Pilla, Ruan, Simmons-Morton, & Scbeidt, 2001). The negative outcomes of school bullying have received increased public attention and scrutiny amid reports that peer harassment may have been a contributing factor to the shootings at Columbine High School in Littleton, Colorado, in 1999 and at Santana High School in Santee, California, in early 2001 and in other acts of juvenile violence including *suicide* (Ericson, 2001).

A report by National Institute of Child Health and Human Development (NICHD) researchers on the U.S. contribution to the WHO's Health Behavior in School-Aged Children survey revealed that 17% of the respondents had been victims of bullying "sometimes" and "weekly," 19% had bullied others sometimes or weekly, and 6% had both bullied others and been victims of bullying (Nansel et al., 2001). The researchers estimated that 1.6 million children in grades 6 through 10 in the United States are bullied at least once per week and that 1.7 million children are victimized by bullies frequently. High risk for involvement in violent behaviors by children and adolescents (as victims or perpetrators) is indicated by the following (Thornton, Craft, Dahlberg, Lynch, & Baer, 2002):

- A history of early aggression
- Social or learning difficulties
- Exposure to violence in the home or through the media
- Friends who engage in problem behaviors
- Academic failure or poor commitment to school
- Poverty
- Recent family divorce, relocation, or other family disruptions

- Access to firearms
- Use of alcohol and drugs
- Recent immigration
- Homelessness
- Family unemployment

Ordinarily, school bullying comprises a variety of negative acts carried out repeatedly over time. It involves a real or perceived imbalance of power, and the powerful take advantage of the weak. Bullying can take three forms: physical, verbal, and psychological. The outcomes of all incidents of bullying are not fatal. However, its presence on school campuses can create a climate of fear among students, inhibiting their ability to learn and leading to other antisocial behavior. The NICHD study indicated that bullying also has long-term and short-term psychological effects on both bullies and those who are bullied. Victims experience loneliness and report having difficulty making social and emotional adjustment. Evidence suggests that the impact of being frequently bullied often accompanies victims into adulthood (Ericson, 2001). Also, Olweus (1993) observed that school bullies are also at increased risk for criminal behavior in adulthood. Prinz (2000) states that approaches to modify the risk for antisocial behavior and violence that focus exclusively on processes internal to the child have limited effectiveness. Providing families with skills to recognize risk factors and to use appropriate protective measures should begin early and move beyond the individual child to also take into account larger contexts. At a minimum, family, classroom, and peer contexts are integrally related to a child's functioning and should be considered in developing protective measures. Likewise, several protective measures and strategies that complement one another should be pursued (Thornton et al., 2002).

Health care professionals should become skilled in interventions that increase the capacity of parents and youth, as well as the community and schools, to deal with bullying or potentially violent social situations. Numerous resources can be found on the websites of organizations such as the CDC, the National Institute of Justice, and the Office of Juvenile Justice and Delinquency Prevention. Authorities recommend the following strategies and interventions (Prinz, 2000; Thornton et al., 2002):

1) Parent-child family strategies (e.g., establish rules and role modeling)
2) Home visits by professionals to empower families with parenting skills and use of community resources
3) Social-cognitive strategies (e.g., finding alternatives to violence and aggression and anticipating consequences of aggressive behavior)
4) Community and school strategies (e.g., setting and reinforcing limits and conflict resolution)
5) Mentoring of parents, children, and adolescents

In summary, strategies to reduce violence and bullying in schools consist of a holistic approach involving families, schools, and community agencies. From the family perspective, the best strategy is to improve family interactions and family well-being, beginning during pregnancy.

Workplace Violence

Within the past several decades, workplace violence has emerged as a serious threat to the safety and health of workers, customers, clients, and innocent bystanders (Baron, 1993). According to the NIOSH (1996), "violence is a substantial contributor to occupational injury and death, and homicide has become the second leading cause of occupational injury death. Each week, an average of 20 workers are murdered and 18,000 are assaulted while at work or on duty. Nonfatal fatal assaults result in millions of lost work days and cost workers millions of dollars in lost wages" (p. iv). Between 1993 and 1999, workplace violence accounted for 18% of all the violent crimes committed in the United States (Duhart, 2001).

Workplace violence can be defined as any violent act directed against persons or property in an occupational setting including threats, intimidation, harassment, or other inappropriate behaviors that arouse fear for personal safety at the worksite or off site during the performance of an employee's duties. An act of workplace violence can affect or involve strangers, customers or clients, co-workers, and personal relations. Associated risk factors may be viewed from three broad perspectives: environment, work practices, and perpetrator/victim profile (State of California, 1993). From the environment perspective, some workers may be increasingly vulnerable to violence because of negative episodes in the political, social, or economic system. The work practices perspective focuses on the management style, antisocial behaviors, staffing requirements, design of safe and productive work stations, and other personal safety and security practices. Perpetrator and victim profiles encompass psychological and personal traits of both the victims and offending individuals. Occupational stress of a family member often affects family well-being and the quality of family relationships.

Olson (1994) contends that occupational nurses are the critical link between workers and management. As such, nurses can play a vital role by advocating for workers and balancing the concerns of management in the design of violence prevention programs. They have direct access to the worker populations and should be involved in policy making and every phase of the prevention model. During the primary prevention phase, nurses will be instrumental in designing and implementing protective measures in three major strategy areas: administrative controls, engineering, and behavioral modifications. Administrative controls consist of policies and procedures for minimizing acts of violence in specific workplaces. Examples of these types of controls include the following protective measures (NIOSH, 1996):

- Developing and selecting a multidisciplinary team to assess the potential for violence
- Establishing a policy authorizing the violence protection program and goals
- Establishing policies and procedures for actions to be taken before, during, and after the occurrence of a violent event
- Setting policies and procedures governing employees' conduct, staffing levels, and escorts
- Developing procedures for assessing and reporting violent incidents
- Developing procedures for describing work practices (such as escorting clients and prohibiting unsupervised movement with and between clinic areas (State of California, 1993)

- Establishing policy and procedures for equitable layoff of employees

Attention to the environment is also a component of primary prevention. Commonly implemented engineering controls include the following (NIOSH, 1996):

- Design of buildings, landscaping, parking lots, lighting systems, and barrier systems
- Security control systems including closed circuit television
- Increasing height and depth of interior service counters
- Card-key access control systems
- Geographic locating devices in mobile workplaces

Behavior modifications include providing all employees with training in hazard awareness, management of assaults, conflict resolution, and employee assistance programs (EAPs). Training in recognizing the signs of troubled employees and nonviolent responses has been suggested to reduce the risk that volatile incidents will escalate to physical violence. The strategy of supporting a troubled employee through the EAP ordinarily deals with a broad range of factors related to antecedent conditions, intervening processes, and behavior responses.

Secondary prevention requires early recognition and prompt intervention to control the potential severity of an incident. The nurse and a multidisciplinary team such as members of the human resources, safety, security, and legal departments can act as first responders to stabilize the situation and determine the need for appropriate management of the incident and individuals involved.

In cases of workplace violence, tertiary prevention includes minimizing the severity and negative effects after an act has occurred. A post-incident analysis may be undertaken to examine what elements of the environment or operations could be modified to reduce the possibility of another similar incident. It is of paramount importance that victims receive immediate medical and psychological care and continuing support. This assures the victim of management's interest in his or her welfare and rehabilitation. Successful rehabilitation means the worker is returned to the workplace sooner, disability payments are discontinued, and the worker's full lost wages are restored. Aside from the places where family members attend school and work, other environmental elements such as where they live, play, and spend leisure time affect their risk of being a victim or perpetrator of violence.

Violence and Lifestyle

Some criminologists argue that families or individuals possibly become victims of violent crimes because they maintain lifestyle behaviors and patterns that increase their exposure to criminals. Semi-annual *National Crime Victimization Surveys* (NCVS) and the Federal Bureau of Investigation's annual *Uniform Crime Reports* reveal that the risk of victimization is increased by such behaviors and qualities as living alone, being unmarried, associating with high-risk young males, going to public places at night, and residing in highly populated urban areas (Siegel, 1998)

Siegel (1998), in his examination of the lifestyle and the *proximity hypothesis,* suggests that some adults simply place their families in jeopardy by choosing or being forced by economics to reside in physical proximity to criminals. Victims are targeted because they share similar backgrounds and circumstances. For example, families living in socially disorganized high-crime areas have the greatest risk for contact with criminals, regardless of their own behavior or lifestyle. Thus the proximity hypothesis suggests that victims do not encourage crime; they are merely in the wrong place at the wrong time. Therefore there may be little motivation for families and individuals residing in low-income areas to alter their lifestyles or use protective measures because personal behavior choices may not effectively influence the likelihood of victimization.

The former perspective implies that the only effective intervention is for practitioners to facilitate and motivate their clients to increase the earning capacity of the family, so they can relocate out of the area. However, given the fact that families cannot always relocate, professionals can empower families to reduce the risk of macrosystem violence by (1) suggesting that parents provide loving and careful supervision of children and adolescents, (2) initiating neighborhood or block watch programs, (3) encouraging parents to instill moral judgment in their children,

(4) empowering parents of children and youth to relate to their children in positive ways, (5) providing social and economic support, (6) suggesting avoidance of high-risk public places at night, (7) teaching environmental safety awareness to children, and (8) using an interdisciplinary holistic approach for this complex issue. The reader is encouraged to consult agencies and websites such as the CDC's Division of Violence and the National Center for Injury Prevention and Control for resources. In addition, there are numerous books on parenting; the CDC source book *Best Practices of Youth Violence Prevention: A Sourcebook for Community Action* (Thorton et al., 2002) is an excellent resource for family professionals.

Nursing Process Related to Environmental Health

Whether family health nurses function within an acute-care setting, ambulatory care clinic, or public health agency, their role must include holistic assessment of and collaboration with families in the area of environmental health (King & Harber, 1998). Usual practice dictates that a history of present and past illness, developmental milestones, and family strengths and risks be reviewed. Incomplete assessment may leave a nurse without key pieces to a complex puzzle. Nurses and family professionals are key to primary prevention of environmental risks. Box 19-8 summarizes the role of the health professional in capacity building of families in the realm of environmental health.

A complete nursing assessment must take occupational, paraoccupational, avocational, home, and general environmental variables into consideration. Appendix 19-1 presents an environmental health assessment guide for the home and family. Selected nursing diagnoses for environmental health include the following (Gordon, 2002):

- Risk for Poisoning
- Risk for Physical Injury
- Risk for Latex Allergy
- Risk for Allergy Response
- Late Allergy Response
- Knowledge Deficit
- Impaired Home Maintenance
- Risk for Trauma

The role of the nurse includes assessment of the family, diagnosis of the issue, creation of a plan for intervention, and a follow-up evaluation. Key aspects of nursing intervention include teaching the family, appropriate treatment, referral, advocacy, and case management. A dominant feature of the twenty-first century is the myriad of printed materials and websites available for health care professionals and families on the topic of environmental health (Nastoff et al., 2002). For examples of national sources of in-depth information on environmental health issues and assessment of the home, school, workplace, and community, the reader is encouraged to consult (1) *Environmental Health and Nursing Practice* (Sattler, Lipscomb, & Nelson, 2003), (2) the University of Maryland School of Nursing Community Health Nursing *EnviRN*, and (3) other websites specific to the family's environmental noted at the end of the chapter. The EnviRN site also includes numerous credible websites for family education and training.

Workplace Interventions

Neuman (2002) emphasizes the use of primary, secondary, and tertiary prevention as an integrative tool with which to attain and maintain client stability. Primary prevention of illness within the work setting requires that contact between workers and hazardous substances be prevented. Education, industrial hygiene, and safety techniques are three classic ways used to promote primary prevention. Secondary prevention requires early diagnosis and screening for active disease. Rehabilitation and promotion of worker reentrance into the employment setting are essential to tertiary prevention techniques. Members of the industrial hygiene team must be sensitive to known hazards present within the work setting, and their work should include active surveillance of the site, periodic and thorough review of the literature, and consultation with known experts. Although they are employed by the industry, nurses and other professionals have an ethical responsibility to develop and enhance worker awareness of safety techniques.

The assessment phase of primary prevention requires the professional to recognize potential hazards to workers that are directly related to

---

BOX 19-8   Role of the Health Professional in Family Environmental Health Care

ASSESSMENT TASKS

- Obtain an exposure history of the individual, family, or community. A visual inspection, site visit, or "walk-through" should be attempted whenever possible to increase the amount of assessment data.
- Complete family and individual risk assessments. Review the existing health effects information about the hazards that are identified.
- Identify patterns of comorbidity among family and community members that suggest environmental causes.
- Be alert for sentinel events in microsystems, macrosystems, and suprasystems.
- Obtain continual input from individuals, families, and communities.
- Make a diagnosis by using the North American Nursing Diagnosis Association (NANDA) nursing diagnoses for individuals, families, and communities. Nurse practitioners may use medical terminology.

PLANNING/OUTCOME TASKS

- Establish optimal health outcomes for individuals, families, and communities.

INTERVENTIONS

- Education: Provide information about hazards and increase families' capacity to protect themselves from hazards. The nurse should make sure that families have the following:
  —Access to information such as right-to-know laws
  —Knowledge of local resources such as poison control center and disposal of toxic substances

  —Ability to access resources
  —Information about risks
  —Knowledge of how to use ipecac and other antidotes for poisoning
  —Access to community education
  —Internet and printed consumer resources
  —Ability to assess their environment
- Advocacy Tasks
  —Enforce existing regulations
  —Encourage new protections or regulations
  —Provide testimony to policy makers
  —Invoke precautionary principle
- Referrals
  —Occupational/environmental medicine experts for verification of medical diagnosis
  —Nursing colleagues: occupational health nurses
  —Environmental engineers/industrial hygienists
  —Public health agencies
  —Legal organizations
  —Social services
- Case Management Tasks
  —Coordinate activities to reduce or eliminate exposure.
  —Assist families in locating resources.
- Evaluation Tasks
  —Determine family and individual health outcomes.
  —Evaluate hazard abatement: Has hazard been removed?
  —Determine effectiveness of interventions.
  —Evaluate preventive measures in place to prevent future occurrences.
  —Determine level of family/community satisfaction.

Adapted from EnviRN. *Interventions/nursing actions.* Retrieved March 10, 2003, from http://envirn.umaryland.edu/interventions/interventions.htm#grad

---

industry. It further requires the assessment of behaviors and risk factors unique to the worker that might potentiate illness. The care plan and nursing actions then focus on intervention aimed at preventing contact between the worker and the

hazard and maximizing personal behaviors that promote health and minimize risk for disease.

Health promotion techniques might include education in the use of personal safety equipment, smoking cessation programs, physical fitness activities for sedentary workers, and stress recognition and management. Families benefit from primary prevention programs when the health and fitness of wage earners are enhanced, stressors are minimized, and family wellness and integrity are promoted.

Nurses and industrial hygienists have a responsibility to enhance worker awareness of safety techniques. Personal protective equipment provided within specific environments requires knowledge of its proper use, limitations, regulations, and protective qualities. For example, health care professionals exposed to chemotherapeutic drugs within their occupational settings may be unaware that gloves exist that are impermeable to the harmful chemicals they use. More important, they may be using gloves that provide a false sense of security, thus indirectly increasing risk. Nurses and industrial hygienists have a responsibility to educate managers and advocate personnel policies that ensure worker safety. For example, magnesium foundry workers receiving health and safety education may pay little heed to what they have learned if line supervisors fail to wear personal protective equipment in appropriate areas. Combined strategies of manager education and increased management awareness of liability for these behaviors may encourage change in a relatively nonthreatening manner.

Health teaching and anticipatory guidance by nurses provide a heightened awareness of vulnerability and a list of alternative behaviors that may increase workers' adherence to proper technique and protective devices. Other aspects of primary prevention include conducting EAPs; monitoring noise and dust levels, temperature variations, and levels of toxicants; assessing risk factors (e.g., smoking, overweight, absenteeism, hypertension); and assessing the impact of a factory on the air, soil, and water of the community. Nurses may also introduce new information into the workplace. Vigilance of pertinent literature; participation in local, state, and national organizations; and advocacy for responsible regulation are all methods of providing managers and workers with complete and up-to-date information. It is crucial to know the appropriate community, state, and national resources. Box 19-9 and Box 19-10 provide examples of such resources.

Secondary prevention requires early diagnosis and treatment of illness. Periodic and thorough histories and physical examinations are essential to diagnosis of industrial diseases. Special attention should be paid to prior employment patterns, exposures, and illnesses associated with work.

The use of biochemical profiles to monitor vulnerability and illness among workers has resurged in recent years. Special laboratory tests are of questionable value for the detection of disease or measurement of risk for potential illness. Screening programs may be expensive, and the yield of accurate information is limited, even when highly sensitive and specific laboratory tests are used. Therefore implementation of mass screening tests should be undertaken with caution.

Screening and case finding should be planned and continuous rather than singular or episodic in nature. Screening programs should limit themselves to tests that determine or implicate worker exposure to harmful agents and should further stipulate that tests be developed that monitor the environment rather than the worker. This approach suggests that primary prevention measures be used rather than waiting until some physiological or psychological abnormality develops within the individual.

Tertiary prevention seeks to maximize rehabilitative efforts and return the individual to work. This not only benefits workers but directly affects the economic outcome of their families. Injured or disabled workers are subject to compensation regulations, which vary from state to state. A maximum weekly disability payment is frequently far below the usual earning capacity of the worker. Wage loss may impose great stress on both the employee and the family. Continuity of care by public health nursing referral may enhance family coping and worker reentry.

Interventions for the Home

The home setting is complex. It is the occupational environment of homemakers, the recreational setting for family members at a variety of developmental levels, and the site of many potential paraoccupational exposures. As discussed previously, children are particularly at risk for poisoning with seemingly innocuous household substances.

BOX 19-9 Selected City and County Official Government Agencies

Animal Control (sometimes listed with "Dead Animal Removal")

This agency will generally remove dead animals that are not the property of the caller.

Building Inspection/Building and Housing Department

This agency has regulatory functions but also may become involved in disputes between landlords and tenants when housing is unsafe or not in compliance with health/building codes.

Board of Supervisors/City Council/Town Council

Elected body of local government officials who govern the municipality, county, or town. This group is generally responsive to the electorate and may be especially instrumental in getting changes made in local codes, regulations, and laws that pertain to environmental health and safety.

District Attorney

Official of local government assigned to prosecute those who break the law.

Health Services/Health Department

This agency generally has a broad scope of practice. It generally monitors vital statistics, epidemiological changes, drug and alcohol programs, adult and child health, tuberculosis, mental health, and environmental health.

Hazardous Materials Department

This department may be subsumed by the local health department under the division of environmental health. It generally responds to hazardous spills and emergency situations. It has some regulatory functions.

Noise Control/Noise Abatement

This department may be subsumed by the local health department or may be a separate entity. It monitors noise levels in accordance with local regulations/codes when requested or investigates a noise complaint.

Permits Department

This department issues many types of permits as directed by local codes and regulations. Some of interest to the family health practitioner might include refuse disposal, explosives, and sewers.

Public Works Department

This agency generally includes flood control and drainage, construction inspection, sanitation/sewer, and solid waste disposal.

BOX 19-10 Selected United States Government Departments, Offices, and Agencies Specific to Environmental Health

On February 11, 1994, President Bill Clinton signed Executive Order 12898 "Federal Actions to Address Environmental Justice in Minority Populations and Low-Income Populations." This order directed federal agencies to develop environmental justice strategies to identify and address disproportionately high and adverse human health or environmental effects of their programs, policies, and activities on minority and low-income populations.

One provision of the order established an Interagency Working Group (IWG) on environmental justice chaired by the EPA Administrator and composed of the heads of federal departments or agencies and five White House offices. The members of the IWG are listed below.

1. Office of Environmental Justice
2. Environmental Protection Agency
3. The Department of Justice
4. Department of Defense
5. Department of Energy
6. Department of Labor
7. Department of the Interior
8. Department of Transportation
9. Department of Agriculture
10. Housing and Urban Development
11. Department of Commerce
12. Department of Health and Human Services
13. Council on Environmental Quality
14. The Office of Management and Budget
15. Office of Science and Technology Policy
16. Domestic Policy Council
17. Council of Economic Advisors

NOTE: These agencies can be reached by consulting their websites for up-to-date telephone numbers and contact information.

Environmental family health nurses must focus on potential risk during evaluation of family wellness and health promotion.

Information about potential risks is essential for family members, particularly information about risks related to reproduction and child health. Families and health care professionals can together become more aware of the connections between their environment and health risks. Careful assessment is essential to discovery of environment-related health issues. Boxes 19-2, 19-3, and 19-7 provide guides for empowering families in reducing and preventing environmental threats to personal and family health.

Substandard, aging structures present risks for physical injury. In addition to lead poisoning, radon, and roaches, poorly maintained dwellings may increase the risk of falls or crushing injuries for all family members. Nurses may need to advise clients who live in old, inner-city areas or in rural settings to assess their homes for structural dangers. Also, as nurses work with homeless populations, they may need even greater awareness of the physical structures their clients use to seek shelter from the elements. All homes, new and old, may present dangers related to loose rugs, cluttered stairways, overloaded electrical circuits, and unstable furniture. Nurses should be keenly aware of the structural environmental dangers of every patient's dwelling.

Water presents a danger to families with children. Unfenced pools, streams, and lakes may lure children to unsupervised play and increase the risk of drowning. Parents should be made aware of the need for proper fencing of pools and natural swimming areas. Adults should be encouraged to learn cardiopulmonary re-suscitation in all circumstances, but especially if the home has easy access to water. Though this is seemingly simple advice, adults should be cautioned to supervise dependent children constantly around family pools or lakes or during bath time. The risk of drowning while unsupervised is greater for toddlers, preschoolers, and children with significant developmental delays. Researchers also suggest that the disinfection by-products in tap water produce a fine aerosol that pregnant women may inhale. Studies suggest a strong association with birth defects. After women showered, high levels of the trihalo-methanes were found in their blood (Lynberg et al., 2001).

Interventions for Recreation and Play

Environmental stressors present within the avocational setting may be related to personal behaviors or external factors. Individuals may choose pastimes that increase their exposure to environmental threats. Increasing the capacity of clients to use safe conduct rules, follow regulations and codes, and avoid solitary work or play is an important task. Health teaching to parents should include teaching children of all ages safety rules for play, recreational equipment, and vehicles. In addition, parental role modeling of appropriate safety behaviors helps to foster patterns of safety wellness behaviors in children.

Animal care, travel with animals, and ordinary human contact may pose an increased risk of infection. Up-to-date immunization will promote immunity against illnesses such as measles, mumps, rubella, polio, and diphtheria. Foreign travel may necessitate special vaccinations and should be undertaken with the knowledge of endemic diseases and risk reduction behaviors. Animal handling should include proper personal protective equipment, knowledge, and appropriate pet vaccinations (CDC, 2003). Families should cautiously consider the purchase of rare or exotic wild animals as pets.

Wood refinishing, model airplane assembly, automobile restoration, and leaded-glass assembly are but a few of a myriad of hobbies that may increase the risk of toxicant exposure. Adults and children should be encouraged to read and follow instructions closely. Those working with volatile substances should do so in well-ventilated areas where the danger of spark or fire is limited. Protective clothing, eyewear, and/or masks should be worn when substances that are abrasive, caustic, defatting, or irritating to mucous membranes are used. However, users should be aware of the limitations of protective equipment. Gloves permeable to toluene, for instance, are of little use to the wearer during contact with the toxicant.

One interpersonal factor that affects families during recreation is the responsible conduct of others. Adults and children should be aware of dangers imposed on others when toxic substances are improperly used or stored. More global, extra-personal variables might include locations of toxic dump sites near recreational areas, contamination of streams and lakes, natural disasters, and improper labeling and marketing of recreational products. These variables are beyond the control of the family and may represent significant danger. Families should be encouraged to use areas specifically marked for recreational use. Hikers should filter water to remove impurities and pathogens, and adults should be aware of and prepared for weather conditions before embarking on a journey. Families may wish to purchase products that are well known to them and should be aware of any illness or discomfort experienced during their use.

Fostering Self-Care in Environmental Health

Using the Neuman Health-Care Systems Model (Neuman, 1982, 2002), the nurse can encourage clients to determine intrapersonal, interpersonal, and extrapersonal variables that affect personal and family health. Family environmental self-care is a dynamic process that requires the family to perceive vulnerability to accidents, injury, or illness and to use self-responsibility to prevent environmental hazards and to protect and promote the family's environmental health and safety. The family is required to recognize and anticipate potential and actual threats to their health from the environmental variables that exist in ecosystems.

Using the self-care perspective to assist clients to improve their environmental health requires that the nurse (1) assess, with families, their potential and actual hazards, (2) collaborate with and educate families about primary and secondary prevention strategies to minimize hazards in their environment and to plan for unexpected disasters, (3) empower families who have children to teach them about environmental hazards and risk reduction behaviors, and (4) evaluate the outcome of their plan.

Role of the Twenty-First Century Family Nurse in Environmental Health

Until the previous decade, except for occupational health nursing, environmental issues as they relate to families were seldom a concern in nursing practice, education, and research. With the increase in global migration, expansion of cities, and increased production of toxins, environmental health is a paramount concern for health care professionals collaborating with families. Environmental health is a specialized field, and diagnosis and treatment often require a team of specialists. As primary care providers and primary prevention case finders, nurses and social service professionals in the new millennium must be competent in the following areas (IOM, 1999):

1) Understanding of basic environmental scientific principles and their relationship to vulnerable populations and individuals in places where they work, live, and play.

2) Assessment and referral of families and individuals at risk, particularly children. This includes obtaining a history and making appropriate referrals.

3) Teaching students, families, and individual clients about environmental risks and prevention strategies and encouraging them to stay informed.

4) Advocacy, ethics, and risk communication for global, national, and local environmental justice; staying informed of environmental issues and policies.

5) Research on environmental issues for all specific cases and for groups known to have disparities in environmental health.

6) Knowledge, which of legislative rules and regulations, is essential to provide a frame work for capacity building and nursing interventions.

It is beyond the scope of this chapter to discuss each of these areas in depth. The websites and references at the end of the chapter provide valuable resources.

Nurses need to be knowledgeable about potential and actual environmental threats. Staying informed about the varied print and Internet resources that provide current information on rapidly changing issues such as food contamination, bioterrorism, and local issues will assist family nurses and other health care professionals. For example, regularly consulting the CDC and FDA websites for updates and current issues is essential for twenty-first century health professionals. Families should also be encouraged to stay informed about new developments in environmental issues.

One role of the health care professional in environmental health is to be an advocate for families and individuals at risk or adversely affected by environmental issues. For example, advocacy is needed for legislation regarding reduction and removal of harmful chemicals in the air, soil, and water and in older homes. Although there is considerable environmental legislation, such as the Clean Air Act, more specific legislation and regulation to protect children and pregnant women and racial and ethnic populations from toxic chemical exposures may be needed (Sattler, 2003). Nurses should be aware of the ethics of environmental disparities and be willing to take action by recording and communicating the environmental health issues of all clients.

Environmental Justice

It is vital that nurses become advocates for environmental justice for individuals and families from all socioeconomic and ethnic groups. *Environmental justice* denotes principled and fair policies and behaviors that promote health in the realms of physical, cultural, and social systems in relation to the distribution of environmental benefits and burdens, particularly in degraded and hazardous physical environments occupied by low-income groups, people of color, and tribal communities (IOM, 1999; Lee, 2002). At the policy level in the United States,

> Environmental justice is the goal to be achieved for all communities and persons. … Environmental justice is achieved when everyone, regardless of race, culture, or income, enjoys the same degree of protection from environmental and health hazards and equal access to the decision-making process to have a healthy environment in which to live, learn, and work (EPA, 2003d, para. 2).

According to Lee (2002), environmental justice may be derived through undertaking the challenge of long-term strategies to educate the nation's leaders about the goal of environmental justice that is already embedded within the nation's existing environmental, public health, transportation, housing, and other legislation.

Fostering capacity building and consensus building with families and communities is paramount for a collaborative model of environmental justice to develop beyond merely being a good suggestion. Health care and environmental practitioners can play a vital role in nurturing and promoting a unifying vision of health and the environment within the community and family unit where support for this new paradigm may find its political nourishment and growth (Lee, 2002).

Nursing Education and Environmental Health

The International Council of Nursing and the IOM (1999) have advocated more emphasis on environmental health in nursing education (Pope et al., 1995). As a result, there is a renewed interest in environmental health in both undergraduate and graduate nursing education. For example, the University of Maryland and University of California Schools of Nursing offer master's degrees and doctorates in occupational and environmental heath nursing. A major goal of these programs is prevention and management of illnesses that occur in the workplace from toxicants or hazards. In 1999, the CDC and the Agency for Toxic Substances and Disease Registry funded the Howard University Division of Nursing's development of "Environmental Health Nursing: The Mississippi Delta Project," an environmental curriculum for undergraduate nursing education. To facilitate holistic care for families and communities, faculty are encouraged to incorporate environmental concepts into twenty-first century nursing education curricula.

Environmental Health Research

Research specific to families and environmental heath conducted by nurses is sparse but is a twenty-first century imperative. There is a dearth of descriptive, epidemiological, and intervention research with a goal of reducing economic, racial, and ethnic disparities in environmental health (Northridge, Stover, Rosenthal, & Sherad, 2003). Another crucial aspect of nursing's role in environmental health is the tracking and reporting of family environmental health issues, particularly those pertaining to children (Anderko, 2003). Research in these realms is crucial to provide population-specific knowledge about disparate environmental health issues, treatments, and appropriate interventions to prevent exposure.

In addition, nurses should be vigilant of global environmental health issues specific to families and vulnerable family members such as children and pregnant women. During the twenty-first century, global migration of families seeking improvement in their quality of life will continue. As a result, some immigrant families and individuals may have existing environmental health issues related to previous exposure or continued use of home remedies or foods from their country of origin. For example, in the United States immigrant families from Mexico and South America may use herb and candy products that contain toxicants. Other examples of global environmental health risks include tourism, military service, imported food and herbs, and air pollution.

In summary, individuals and families are intricately connected to the macrosystems and suprasystems outside family boundaries. Overwhelming evidence compels nurses to strive toward strengthening and increasing the capacity of families and individuals of all ages, cultures, races, and social classes to improve and monitor the quality of their environmental health. Lastly, nurses, in collaboration with colleagues from other disciplines and various agencies and organizations, must be vigilant in supporting environmental health assessment, treatment, and surveillance systems locally, regionally, nationally, and globally.

CASE SCENARIO

One cool day in February in a southern state, Garland, 85 years old, and his 70-year-old wife, Rosa, were doing their usual chores. They live in a rural county about 10 miles from town. Rosa worked inside cleaning and cooking, while Garland worked in the yard or on other outside projects. When Garland came in for a break around 10:00 AM, Rosa told him she nearly fainted an hour before and wanted him to take her to the doctor. Rosa then fainted in the doorway of the home as Garland was driving the car up to the side door to take her to their family physician. Unable to move Rosa, Garland left the door open because she was lying in the doorway and called 911.

When the paramedics arrived, Rosa was responding but could not move. The paramedics gave her oxygen immediately and started intravenous fluids. They took her to the regional hospital where the medical history revealed chronic diabetes, hypertension, and congestive heart failure. Her blood pressure was normal, and glucose and electrolyte levels were normal. After receiving oxygen in the emergency department, Rosa seemed to be stabilized and was admitted for observation because of her congestive heart failure. Her husband, Garland, returned home to rest after the excitement of admitting Rosa to the hospital. Later in the day, Rosa talked to her husband and he was relaxing, watching television, but told her he would call her later. Garland began to feel chilly, turned up the oil stove that heated the family room, and reclined to snooze as he usually did in the afternoon. When he awoke and tried to get up out of the chair, he could hardly get out. He began to feel so sleepy that he thought he would faint. Using the telephone near the chair, he called 911 and told them he needed help. The operator told him to stay on the line until the paramedics arrived. When they arrived, he was so disoriented that he had to crawl to the door to open it. After a brief time in the emergency department receiving oxygen and an intravenous infusion, Garland was admitted to the hospital and shared a room with Rosa.

The same team of paramedics had provided care for each of them. In their training, the paramedics were taught about the hazards of overheating and carbon monoxide buildup in the winter. The incident was reported to the fire department and the health department.

INFORMATION FROM THE HISTORY

Rosa tells the nurse that she felt lethargic and was sleeping a lot during the day for about 5 days. She explained, "I just couldn't get enough sleep and it was hard for me to wake up. I have been taking all my pills and insulin." Rosa and Garland noted no unusual odors in the home. Garland is healthy, slim, energetic, weighs about 150 pounds, and seems to be cold all the time when inside during the winter. He keeps the family room very warm with a wood-burning stove. The remainder of the home is heated by the gas furnace. The kitchen stove and hot water heater are

CASE SCENARIO—cont'd

gas. Garland and Rosa were following their usual routine. After breakfast, she does inside household chores and he completes outside farm-related chores. He works outside most of the day, comes in for lunch, rests an hour, and then goes back outside until dinner. When the temperature gets cooler in the evening during the winter, Garland makes a fire in the wood-stove despite having a gas furnace. Rosa usually spends most of the day inside while Garland spends most of the day outside.

INTERVENTION

The staff in the emergency department and the paramedics reported the incident to the fire department and the health department. After Garland was admitted to the hospital, public health officials and the fire inspector checked the home for gases and carbon monoxide. They found dangerously high levels (nearly at the explosive level) of carbon monoxide. The deadly gas was produced by the furnace and a wood stove having the same chimney. The wood stove was removed and a carbon monoxide detector was installed. The officials believed that if the levels had been that high at night, the results would have been fatal for both Rosa and Garland. Later, a public health environmental inspector assisted the couple with a home inspection and helped them create an annual checklist for air pollution. The family nurse taught them signs of carbon monoxide poisoning and to perform a regular inspection of their alarm systems.

WEBSITE RESOURCES

ORGANIZATION	WEBSITE ADDRESS
Federal Agencies	
Agency for Toxic Substance and Disease Registry	http://www.atsdr.cdc.gov
Centers for Disease Control and Prevention (CDC)	http://www.bt.cdc.gov/
National Center for Environmental Health	http://www.cdc.gov/nceh/
Environmental Protection Agency (EPA)	http://www.epa.gov
Bioterrorism Preparedness and Response	http://www.fda.gov/oc/bioterrorism/bioact.html
National Institute of Environmental Health	http://www.niehs.nih.gov/
Environmental Health of America's Children 2003	http://www.epa.gov/envirohealth/children/ace_2003.pdf
Department of Homeland Security	http://www.dhs.gov/dhspublic/
Department of Agriculture	http://www.usda.gov/
Food and Drug Administration	http://www.fda.gov
Federal Emergency Management Agency	http://www.rris.fema.gov
Department of Energy (DOE), Environment, Health and Safety Information Portal	http://www.tis-hq.eh.doe.gov/portal/
Occupational Safety and Health Administration	http://www.osha.gov/
Office of Environmental Justice	http://www.epa.gov/compliance/about/offices/oej.html
Medlineplus: Occupational Health	http://www.nlm.nih.gov/medlineplus/occupationalhealth.html
National Heart, Lung, and Blood Institute, National Asthma Education and Prevention Program	http://www.nhlbi.nih.gov/about/naepp/index.htm

Continued

WEBSITE RESOURCES—cont'd

Department of Housing and Urban Development, Office of Healthy Homes and Lead Hazard Control	http://www.hud.gov/offices/lead/index.cfm/leadsaferule/
Agency for Toxic Substances and Disease Registry (ATSDR)	http://www.atsdr.cdc.gov/about.html
Consumer Product Safety Commission	http://www.cpsc.gov/
National Institute of Occupational Safety and Health (NIOSH)	http://www.cdc.gov/niosh/homepage.html
National Center for Toxicological Research	http://www.fda.gov/nctr/index.html
Department of Justice, Office of Juvenile Justice and Delinquency Prevention	http://www.ncjrs.org/pdffiles1/ojjdp/fs200127.pdf
National Center for Injury Prevention and Control	http://www.cdc.gov/ncipc
Health Canada	http:www.hc-sc.gc.ca/
Nonprofit Environmental Health Agencies	
American Association of Poison Control Centers	http://www.aapcc.org/
American College of Occupational and Environmental Medicine	http://www.acoem.com/
American Red Cross	http://www.redcross.org/
American Association of Occupational and Environmental Health Nurses	http://www.aaohn.org/
EnviRN: Environmental health and nursing website from the University of Maryland School of Nursing	http://www.envirn.umaryland.edu/
Clean Air Council	http://www.cleanair.org/index/index_1.ht
Children's Environmental Health	http://www.cehn.org/cehn/resourceguide/pesticides.html
Water Environment Federation (WEF)	http://www.wef.org
Physicians for Social Responsibility, Environment, and Health	http://www.psr.org/home.cfm?id=environment
National Rural Water Association	http://www.nrwa.org
Farm*A*Syst	http://www.uwex.edu/farmasyst/
World Health News	http://www.worldhealthnews.harvard.edu/#environ_health
Protection of the Human Environment	http://www.who.int/peh/

■ CHAPTER HIGHLIGHTS

- Diverse environmental concerns influence or have the potential to influence the health of individuals and families across the life span.
- Biological, physical, and chemical environmental hazards can be found in homes, workplaces, schools, and play or leisure settings.
- Occupational and recreational exposure to chemical and biological hazards can result in genetic mutations, fetal malformation, and exposure of other household members.
- The family nurse's role in environmental health for individuals and families includes preventing contact by anticipatory guidance and health teaching, performing early screenings and diagnosis, and offering appropriate preventive or rehabilitative measures.
- Primary prevention of environmental hazards includes public and family education and activities to reduce contact between people and harmful agents.

- Secondary prevention activities provide for early screening, diagnosis, and treatment of harmful environmental agents.
- Tertiary prevention includes attempts to remove harmful agents from the environment and to restore the host to normal functioning.
- Families should be aware of the potential for unexpected environmental disasters and violence in their macrosystem environment. The role of the family nurse is to increase the capacity of families and their members to prepare for unexpected disasters and to prevent and deal with conflictual social situations in schools, the workplace, and the community.
- The role of health care professionals in environmental health includes supporting and being knowledgeable about environmental justice; assessment and referral; advocacy of ethical practices; risk communication; a new emphasis on environment in teaching, research, practice, and service; and remaining current regarding environmental legislation and policy.

⫼ CRITICAL THINKING ACTIVITIES

You are a nurse in an emergency department and a Hispanic mother brings in her 10-year-old daughter who has complained of diarrhea, lethargy, and stomachache for about a week. The child was also upset because the family cat had died. You find nothing specifically wrong with the child, and she is sent home. Later, the mother brings the child back to the emergency department because she is having difficulty waking the child, who has a slight wheeze, is clammy, and has pinpoint pupils. You note that the family lives in a neighborhood where the homes were built in the 1950s.

Refer to the case above in answering questions 1 to 3.

1. What family and individual assessment questions would you ask the parents and the child?
2. Explain what actions you would take after your assessment if you suspect the problem is related to toxic substances.

3. Discuss what immediate referrals might be necessary.
4. Explain to your colleagues why low-income African Americans, Hispanic and Latino Americans, and American Indians are more at risk for environmental hazards. Discuss why environmental justice activities are so important.
5. Explain why environmental assessment is a crucial aspect of family assessment and teaching.
6. Explain why the home is not always a safe haven from environmental hazards. What are potential products or items that may cause indoor air pollution in the home?
7. Visit the websites of two government and two private environmental organizations. List their missions and determine whether you would refer a family to the websites you evaluated.

CRITICAL THINKING ACTIVITIES—cont'd

8. Conduct an assessment of the indoor air quality in your home using the self-assessment tool in Appendix 19-1.
   - Examine the various chemicals and solutions used in your home for personal care, cleaning, and pest control.
   - Are health problems present in your family? Who in your family is at risk for health

problems caused by inhalation of or skin contact with air pollutants? Make a list of the various solutions. Write down the ingredients of five of the solutions.
   - Read the warning labels on these solutions. What do they say? Is any specific age group targeted?

REFERENCES

Abelsohn, A., Stieb, D., Sanborn, M., & Weir, E. (2002). Identifying and managing adverse health effects: 2. Outdoor air pollution. *Canadian Medical Association Journal, 166*(6), 1161-1168.

Aday, L. A. (1993). *At risk in America: The health and health care needs of vulnerable populations in the United States.* San Francisco: Jossey-Bass.

Anderko, L. (2003). Protecting the health of our nation's children through environmental health tracking. *Policy, Politics & Nursing Practice, 4,* 14-22.

Awad, O. M., & el Shimi, N. M. (1993). Influence of different means of washing and processing removal of acetellic residue from spinach and eggplant and its in-vivo action on mice hepatic biochemical targets. *Journal of Egyptian Public Health Association, 68,* 671-686.

Baron, S. A. (1993). *Violence in the workplace.* Ventura: CA: Pathfinder.

Blain, P. G. (1990). Aspects of pesticide toxicology. *Adverse Drug Reactions and Acute Poisoning Reviews, 9*(1), 37-68.

Carson, R. (1962). *Silent spring.* New York: Houghton Mifflin.

Centers for Disease Control and Prevention. (1994). Surveillance of emergency events involving hazardous substances—United States 1990-1992. *Mortality and Morbidity Weekly, 43*(55), 1-6.

Centers for Disease Control and Prevention. (1995). Assessing the public health threat associated with cryptosporidiosis. *Mortality and Morbidity Weekly, 44*(21), 404-406

Centers for Disease Control and Prevention. (2002). *CDC's response to ending neglect: The elimination of tuberculosis in the United States.* Atlanta, GA: U.S. Department of Health and Human Services, Centers for Disease Control.

Centers for Disease Control and Prevention. (2003). *Intentional injury prevention.* Atlanta, GA: Centers for Disease Control, National Center for Injury Prevention and Control. Retrieved June 20, 2003, from http://www.cdc.gov/ncipc/duip/duip.htm

Cohen, S. M. (2001). Lead poisoning: A summary of treatment and prevention. *Pediatric Nursing, 27,* 125-129.

Cook, M. G., Zublena, J. P., & Naderman, G. C. (1997). Soil and water quality. *Soil facts* (North Carolina Cooperative Extension Service Publication No. AG-439-1). North Carolina State University. Retrieved March 3, 2003, from http://www.soil.ncsu.edu/publications/soilfacts/ag-439-01

Doerner, S., & Lab, S.P. (1998). *Victimology.* Cincinnati, OH: Anderson.

Drake, J. A., Price, J. H., Telljohann, S. (2003). The nature and extent of bullying at school. *Journal of School Health, 73*(5), 173-180.

Duhart, D. T. (2001). *National crime victimization survey: Violence in the work place, 1993-1999* (Bureau of Justice Statistics Special Report). Washington, DC: U.S. Justice Department.

Eggleston, P. A., Buckley, T. J., Breysse, P. N., Wills-Karp, M., Kleeberger, S. R., Jaakkaola, J. J. K. (1999). The environment and asthma in U.S. inner cities. *Environmental Health Perspectives, 107*(Suppl. 3), 439-450.

Environmental Protection Agency. (1998). *Lead in your home: A parent's reference guide* (EPA Publication No. 747-B98-002). Retrieved March 4, 2003, from http://www.epa.gov/lead/leadrev.pdf

Environmental Protection Agency. (2000). *Drinking water past, present and future.* Office of Water: U.S. Environmental Protection Agency EPA816-F-00-002. Retrieved March 8, 2003, from http://www.epa.gov/safewater/consumer/dwppf.pdf

Environmental Protection Agency. (2002). *A citizen's guide to radon: The guide to protecting yourself and your family from radon* (4th ed.). Washington, DC: U.S. Government Publishing Office. EPA Document 402-K02-006. Retrieved March 1, 2003, from http://www.epa.gov/iaq/radon/pubs/citguide.html#overview

Environmental Protection Agency. (2003a). *Acid rain.* Retrieved March 1, 2003, from http://www.epa.gov/airmarkets/acidrain/index.html

Environmental Protection Agency. (2003b). *Asthma fact sheet.* Retrieved March 1, 2003, from http://www.epa.gov/iaq/asthma/introduction.html

Environmental Protection Agency. (2003c). Concentrations of lead in blood. *America's children and the environment: A first view of available measures.* Retrieved February 27, 2003, from http://yosemite.epa.gov/ochp/ochpweb.nsf/content/blood_lead_levels.htm

Environmental Protection Agency. (2003d). *Environmental justice.* Retrieved March 7, 2003, from http://www.epa.gov/compliance/environmentaljustice/index.html

Ericson, N. (2001). *Addressing the problem of juvenile bullying.* Washington, DC: U.S. Department of Justice.

Federal Emergency Management Agency. (2002). *Are you ready? A guide to citizen preparedness.* Washington, DC: Author.

Friedeman, M. M., Bowden, V. R., & Jones, E. G. (2003). *Family nursing research, theory and practice* (5th ed.). Upper Saddle River, NJ: Prentice Hall.

Gordon, M. (2002). *Manual of nursing diagnosis* (10th ed.). St. Louis, MO: Mosby.

Gore, A. (1992). *Earth in balance: Ecology and the human spirit.* Boston: Houghton Mifflin.

Hemminki, K., Kyyronen, P., Niemi M. L., Koskinen, K., Sallmen, M., & Vainio, H. (1983). Spontaneous abortion in an industrialized community in Finland. *American Journal of Public Health, 73*(1), 33-37.

Higgins, I. (1986). Air pollution. In J. M. Last (Ed.), *Maxcy-Rosenau: Public health and preventative medicine* (pp. 576-586). Norwalk, CT: Appleton-Century-Crofts.

Institute of Medicine. (1999). *Toward environmental justice: Research, education, and health policy needs.* Washington, DC: National Academy Press.

Institute of Medicine. (2000). *Clearing the air: Asthma and indoor exposure.* Washington, DC: National Academy Press.

Johnson, C. J. (1984). Cancer incidence in an area of radioactive fallout downwind from the Nevada test site. *Journal of the American Medical Association, 25*(1), 230-236.

Johnson, D. E. (1990). The behavioral system model or nursing. In M. E. Parker (Ed.), *Nursing theories in nursing practice* (pp. 23-32). New York: National League for Nursing.

Kaufman, P., Chen, X., Choy, S. P., Peter, K., Ruddy, S. A., Miller, A. K., et al. (2001). *Indicators of school crime and safety: 2001.* Washington, DC: US Departments of Education and Justice. NCES-2002-113/NCU-190075.

Kellam, S. G. (2000). Community and institutional partnerships for school violence prevention. In S. G. Kellam, R. Prinz, & J. F. Sheley (Eds.), *Preventing school violence. Plenary Papers of the 1999 Conference on Criminal Justice Research and Evaluation-Enhancing Policy and Practice through Research, Volume 2* (pp. 1-22). U.S. Department of Justice, National Institute of Justice: Washington, DC.

Kierkegarrd, O., & Kristiansen, J. L. (1992). Sick leave during pregnancy. *Ugeskrift for Lager, 154*(34), 2305-2308.

King, C., & Harber, P. (1998). Community environmental health concerns and the nursing process: Four environmental health care plans. *American Association of Occupational Health Nursing Journal, 46,* 20-27.

King, I. (1981). *A theory of nursing: Systems, concepts and process.* New York: Wiley.

Knestrick, J., & Milstead, J. A. (1998). Public policy and child lead poisoning: Implementation of Title X. *Pediatric Nursing, 24,* 37-41.

Lee, C. (2002). Environmental justice: Building on a unified vision of health and the environment. *Environmental Health Perspectives, 110*(Suppl. 21), 141-144.

Lynberg, M., Nuckols, J. R., Langlois, P., Ashley, C., Singer, P., Mendola, P., et al. (2001). Assessing exposure of disinfection by-products in women of reproductive age living in Corpus Christi, Texas and Cobb County, Georgia. *Environmental Health Perspectives, 109,* 597-604.

Markowitz, G., & Rosner, D. (2002). *Deceit and denial: The deadly politics of industrial pollution.* Berkeley: University of California Press.

Minino, A. M., Arias, E., Kochaenk, K. D., Murphy, S. L., Smith, B. L. (2002). Deaths: Final data for 2000. *National Vital Statistics Reports, 50*(15), 1-6.

Morbidity and Mortality Weekly Report. (2001). Occupational and take-home lead poisoning associated with restoring chemically stripped furniture—California, 1998. *Morbidity and Mortality Weekly Report, 50,* 246-249.

Morbidity and Mortality Weekly Report. (2003). Trends in tuberculosis morbidity—United States, 1902-2002. *Morbidity and Mortality Weekly Report, 52*(21), 217-222.

Nansel, T. R., Overpeck, M., Pilla, R. S., Ruan, W. J., Simons-Morton, B., Scbeidt, P. (2001). Bullying behavior among U.S. youth. *Journal of American Medical Association, 285,* 2094-2100.

Nastoff, T., Drew, D. M., Wigington, P. S., Wakefield, J., Philips, J., & O'Fallon, L. R. (2002, August). *Nursing and environmental health roundtable: Final report.* Agency for Toxic Substances and Diseases Registry and National Institute of Environmental Health Sciences. Retrieved March 22, 2003, from http://www.niehs.nih.gov/translat/murseRT_rpt.pdf

National Center for Environmental Assessment. (2003). *Dioxin exposure initiative.* Environmental Protection Agency. Retrieved March 7, 2003, from http://cfpub.epa.gov/ncea/cfm/recordisplay.cfm?deid=15239

National Center for Environmental Health. (1998). *FY 1998, NCEH Global Health Activities.* Atlanta, GA: Author. Retrieved March 8, 2003, from http://www.cdc.gov/nceh/globalhealth/GHAR/exec_summ.htm

National Center for Environmental Health. (2002). *Environmental health 2002: National Center for Environmental Health fact book.* Centers for Disease Control and Prevention. Atlanta, GA: Author. Retrieved March 8, 2003, from http://www.cdc.gov/nceh/publications/factbook/2002/EHResourceBook.pdf

National Center for Environmental Health. (2003). *Childhood lead poisoning. A fact sheet.* Retrieved February 27, 2003, from http://www.cdc.gov/nceh/lead/factsheets/childhoodlead.htm

National Center for Health Statistics. (2003). *Asthma prevalence, health care use and mortality, 2000-2001.* Retrieved March 1, 2003, from http://www.cdc.gov/nchs/products/pubs/pubd/hestats/asthma/asthma.htm

National Institute of Occupational Safety and Health. (1996). *Current intelligence bulletin 57: Violence in the workplace: Risk factors and prevention strategies.* (DHHS [NIOSH] Publication No. 96-100). Retrieved March 10, 2003, from http://www.cdc.gov/niosh/violcont.html

National Institute of Occupational Safety and Health. (1998). *Criteria for a recommended standard: Occupational noise exposure* (Revised 1998 DHHS [NIOSH] Publication No. 98-126). Cincinnati, OH: Author.

National Institute of Occupational Safety and Health. (2002). *Worker health chartbook, 2000, non-fatal injury.* Cincinnati, OH: Centers for Disease Control: National Institute of

Occupational Safety and Health. (NIOSH Publication #2002-119).

Neuman, B. (1982). *The Neuman Systems Model: Application to nursing education and practice.* Norwalk, CT: Appleton-Century-Crofts.

Neuman, B. (2002). The Neuman Systems Model. In B. Neuman & J. Fawcett (Eds.), *The Neuman Systems Model* (4th ed., pp. 3-33). Upper Saddle River, NJ: Prentice-Hall.

Nightingale, {F. (1859/1992). *Notes on nursing: Commemorative edition with commentaries by contemporary nursing leaders.* Philadelphia: Lippincott.

Niskar, A. S., Kieszk, S. M., Holmes, A., Easebaun, E., Rubin, C., & Brody, D. J. (2001). Estimated prevalence of noise-induced hearing threshold shifts among children 6-19 years of age: The third National Health Survey and Nutritional Survey. 1988-94 United States. *Pediatrics, 108,* 40-43.

Northridge, M, E., Stover, G. N., Rosenthal, J. E., & Shepard, D. D. (2003). Environmental equity and health: Understanding complexity and moving forward. *American Journal of Public Health, 93,* 209-215.

Okun, D. A. (1992). Water quality management. In J. M. Last (Ed.), *Maxey-Rosenau: Public health and preventive medicine* (pp. 807-842). Norwalk, CT: Appleton-Century-Crofts.

Oleweus, D. (1993). *Bullying at school: What we know and what we can do.* Cambridge, UK: Blackwell.

Olson, N. K. (1994). Workplace violence: Theories of causation and prevention strategies. *AAOHN Journal, 42,* 447-482.

Pope, A., Snyder, M. A., & Mood, L. H. (1995). (Eds.). *Nursing, health, & the environment: Strengthening relationship to improve the public's health.* Washington, DC: National Academy Press.

Prinz, R. (2000). Research-based prevention of school violence and youth antisocial behavior: A developmental and educational perspective. In S. G. Kellam, R. Prinz, & J. F. Sheley (Eds.), *Preventing school violence: Plenary paper of the 1999 Conference on Criminal Justice Research and Evaluation-Enhancing Policy and Practice through Research, Volume 2* (pp. 23-36). Washington, DC: U.S. Department of Justice, National Institute of Justice.

Roy, C., & Roberts, S. L. (1984). *Theory construction in nursing: An adaptation model.* Englewood Cliffs, NJ: Prentice-Hall.

Sanborn, M. D., Abelsohn, A., Campbell, M., Weir, E. (2002). Identifying and managing adverse environmental health effects: 3. Lead exposure. *Canadian Medical Association Journal, 166*(10), 1287-1292.

Sattler, B., & Lipscomb, J. (Eds.). (2003). *Environmental health and nursing practice.* New York: Springer.

Sharara, F. I., Seifer, D. B., & Flaws, J. A. (1998). Environmental toxicants and female reproduction. *Fertility and Sterility, 70,* 613-620

Siegel, L. J. (1998) *Criminology* (6th ed.) Belmont, CA: West/Wadsworth.

Smith, K. R., Corvalan, C. F., & Kjellstrom, T. (1999). How much global ill health is attributable to environmental factors? *Epidemiology, 10,* 573-584.

State of California. (1993). *Guidelines for security and safety of health care and community service workers.* Sacramento, CA: Division of Occupational Safety and Health, Department of Industrial Relations.

Talbott, E. O., Youk A. O., McHugh-Pemu, K. P., & Zborowski, J. V. (2003). Long-term follow-up of the residents of the Three Mile Island accident area: 1979-1999. *Environmental Health Perspectives, 111,* 341-348.

Thornton, T. N., Craft, C. A., Dahlberg, L. L., Lynch, B. S., Baer, K. (2002). *Best practices of youth violence prevention: A source book for community action (rev.).* Atlanta, GA: Centers for Disease Control and Prevention. National Center for Injury Prevention and Control.

Tong, S., von Schirnding, Y., & Prapamontol, T. (2000). Environmental lead exposure: A public health problem of global dimensions. *Bulletin of the World Health Organization, 78*(9), 1068-1077.

U.S. Bureau of Labor Statistics. (2001). BLS releases 2000-2010 employment projections. *News bureau of labor statistics* (December 3, 2001). Retrieved online July 14, 2003, from ftp://ftp.bls.gov/pub/news.release/ecopro.txt

U.S. Bureau of Labor Statistics. (2002). *Census of fatal occupational injuries summary.* Retrieved March 10, 2003, from http://www.stats.bls.gov/news.release/cfoi.nr0.htm

U.S. Bureau of Labor Statistics. (2002). Workplace injuries and illness in 2001. *News United States Department of Labor* (December 19, 2002). Retrieved online July 14, 2003, from http://www.bls.gov/iif/oshwc/osh/ os/osnr0016.pdf

U.S. Department of Health and Human Services. (2000). *Healthy People 2010.* Washington, DC: U. S. Government Printing Office. Retrieved September 20, 2002, from http://www.health.gov/healthypeople/Document/tableofco ntents.htm

U.S. Department of Labor. (2001). *Workplace injuries and illness in 2001.* Washington, DC: U.S. Department of Labor, Bureau of Labor Statistics. Retrieved online June 20, 2003, from http://www.bls.gov/iif/oschwc/osh/os/ osnr0016.pdf

Water Environment Federation. (2003). *Guard your ground-water!* Alexandria, VA: Author.

Webster-Stratton, C., & Hammond, M. (1997). Treating children with early-onset conduct problems: A comparison of child and parent training interventions. *Journal of Consulting and Clinical Psychology, 65*(1), 93-109.

Whorton, D., Krauss, R. M., Marshall, S., & Milby, T. H. (1977). Infertility in male pesticide workers. *The Lancet, 2,* 1259-1261.

Whorton, D., Milby, T. H., Krauss, R. M., & Stubbs, H. A. (1979). Testicular function in DBCP exposed pesticide workers. *Journal of Occupational Medicine, 21,* 161-166.

World Health Organization. (1999). *Air quality guidelines, WHO, 1999.* Geneva: Author. Retrieved March 6, 2003, from http://www.who.int/environmental_guidelines/Air/ GuidelinesAQGUIDEEXECSUM.htm

World Health Organization International. (2002). *World health report 2002.* Geneva: Author. Retrieved March 1, 2003, from http://www.who.int/peh/burden/ burdenindex. htm

Zublena, J. P., Cook, M. G., & St. Clair, M. B. (1997). *Pollutants in ground water: Health effects. Soil facts* (North Carolina Cooperative Extension Service Publication No. AG-439-14). Retrieved March 8, 2003, from http:// www.soil.ncsu.edu/publications/Soilfacts/AG-439-14/

For a complete resourse guide for use in conjunction with this assessment tool, with links to appropriate pages of websites, see www.envirn.umaryland. edu → assessment.

*When using websites cited in this document, the following paths will be helpful:
- www.cpsc.gov → consumer → publications → specific topics (incl. "air quality")
- www.oehha.ca.gov → education → guidelines for safe use of art & craft material
- www.lungusa.org → air quality → indoor air quality
- www.epa.gov/iaq → introduction to indoor air quality
- www.epa.gov/pesticides → concerned citizens
- www.ace.orst.edu → NPIC → Extoxnet
- www.sis.nlm.nih.gov → toxnet
- www.atsdr.cdc.gov → toxicological profiles
- www.cdc.gov → health topics → headlice
- www.aapcc.org → poison prevention education
- www.epa.gov/mercury → fact sheets
- www.nsf.org → information for consumers → drinking water treatment
- www.cdc.gov.nceh → NCEH topics
- www.cdc.gov/niosh → safety and health topics

Year home built/age of home: _____

Condition of paint on:
  Walls: _____
  Window sills: _____

Paint dust present? ____ yes ____ no
Where? _____

Has paint, dust or outdoor soil sample been tested for lead? ____ yes ____ no
If yes, ask to see report.

Recent renovations ("home repair projects")? ____ yes ____ no

If yes, what and when:

_____

_____

_____

Potential health effect: lead poisoning
Related to:
- house built before 1978
- paint chips, dust, contaminated soil
- recent renovations
- arts and crafts materials

Resources:
www.atsdr.cdc.gov
www.cpsc.gov, www.aeclp.org
www.acminet.org,
www.oehha.ca.gov

Potential health effect: asbestos related illness
Related to:
- recent renovations
- house built before 1978

Resources:
www.atsdr.cdc.gov
www.cpsc.gov, www.lungusa.org
www.epa.gov/iaq

Copyright © 2002 University of Maryland School of Nursing. All rights reserved. This material was developed at the Environmental Health Education Center of the University of Maryland School of Nursing. Used with permission. For more information, see envirn.umaryland.edu

Continued

New furniture or other furnishings (i.e., carpeting, curtains)?
____ yes ____ no

Unusual or strong odor?
____ yes ____ no

Hobbies, arts and crafts activities?
____ yes ____ no

Type of hobbies: _____

_____

What materials are used?

_____

_____

General appearance:
    Visible dust? ____ yes ____ no
    Pet hairs on furniture? ____ yes ____ no
    Food covered? ____ yes ____ no
    Surfaces clean? ____ yes ____ no
    Water accumulation? ____ yes ____ no
    Where are problems found? ____

    _____

Pets: ____ yes ____ no
Types and numbers: _____

Roaches:
    Observed? ____ yes ____ no
    Reported by family? ____ yes ____ no

Rodents:
    Observed? ____ yes ____ no
    Reported by family? ____ yes ____ no

Indications of mold or mildew:
    Odor? ____ yes ____ no
    Visible? ____ yes ____ no
    Description (including location): _____

Potential health effect: volatile organic compound (ex.: formaldehyde) related illness
Related to:
- ➤ construction materials (such as particleboard, laminated wood products)
- ➤ carpeting, textiles
- ➤ paints and other surface treatments
- ➤ arts and crafts supplies

Resources:
www.atsdr.cdc.gov
www.epa.gov/iaq
www.cpsc.gov
www.lungusa.org
www.acminet.org
www.oehha.ca.gov

Potential health effect: asthma, allergy
Related to:
- ➤ dust (dust mites)
- ➤ pet hairs and body fluids
- ➤ roaches
  - ○ feed on grease, food crumbs, water deposits
- ➤ rodents
- ➤ mold, mildew

Resources:
www.epa.gov/iaq
www.lungusa.org (incl. "biological pollutants")
www.cpsc.gov

Pesticides ("roach/insect sprays," "mouse/rat poison," "weed killers") used in home or yard? _____ yes _____ no

Pesticides used on pets (flea baths, collars, etc.)?
_____ yes _____ no

Lice or scabies treatments used?
_____ yes _____ no

Insect repellants used?
_____ yes _____ no

Name(s) of pesticide products used*, used on whom, where, duration and frequency of use:

_____

_____

*obtain name(s) of active ingredients (and other ingredients, if listed) from product labels

---

Potential health effect: pesticide poisoning
Related to:
  ➤ use of pesticides (including lice treatments and insect repellants)
  ➤ storage of pesticides
Resources:
www.epa.gov/iaq
www.lungusa.org
www.epa.gov/pesticides
www.ace.orst.edu
www.sis.nlm.nih.gov
www.atsdr.cdc.gov
www.hsph.harvard.edu/headlice
www.cdc.gov
www.cpsc.gov ("poisoning")
www.aapcc.org

Where are pesticides stored (both inside and outside house):

_____

_____

What household cleaning and home maintenance products (paints, strippers, glues, etc.) are used*?

_____

_____

*obtain name(s) of active ingredients (and other ingredients, if listed) from product labels

Where are these products stored?

_____

_____

Where are medications stored (including over-the-counter and topical medications)?

_____

_____

Potential health effect: multiple (see resources)
Related to:
  ➤ use of cleaning and home maintenance products
  ➤ storage of these products (unintentional exposure of children)
Resources:
www.atsdr.cdc.gov
www.epa.gov/iaq
www.cpsc.gov (incl. "poisoning")
www.greenseal.org
www.aapcc.org

Potential health effect: medication overdose
Related to:
  ➤ storage of medications (unintentional exposure of children)
Resources:
www.cpsc.gov ("poisoning")
www.aapcc.org

Continued

What kind of fever thermometer is used?
____ mercury ____ digital
____ other: _____

Where is the thermometer stored?
_____

Potential health effect: mercury poisoning
Related to:
➢ elemental mercury spilled from broken thermometer
Resources:
www.epa.gov/mercury

Drinking water source:
____ public (pay for service) ____ private well

If public system, request copy of most recent Consumer Confidence Report (CCR).

If private well, when was water last tested for contaminants? _____
Request copy of report.

Potential health effect: multiple (see resources)
Related to:
➢ water contamination
Resources:
www.nsf.org
www.epa.gov/safewater

Heating Sources:
Primary: ___ oil ___ gas ___ electric
____ other
Secondary (space heaters, fireplaces):
___ oil ___ gas ___ electric ___ kerosene
___ wood ___ other: _____

Location of space heaters: _____
_____

When was the furnace last serviced? _____
When was the chimney last cleaned and serviced? _____

Potential health effect: carbon monoxide (CO) poisoning, injury
Related to:
➢ fuel burning appliances that are not adequately vented, maintained or situated
Resources:
www.cdc.gov/nceh
www.cpsc.gov (incl. "space heaters")
www.epa.gov/iaq
www.lungusa.org

Types of cooking equipment (check all that apply): ___ electric ___ gas ___ other:_____

Is oven ever used as a secondary source of heat? ("Do you ever use the oven to heat the house?") ___ yes ___ no

CO (carbon monoxide) detectors present? ___ yes ___ no
Located where? _____
Working? ___ yes ___ no
Tested how frequently: _____

In past year, have multiple family members developed flu-like symptoms ("gotten sick from flu") at the same time? ___ yes ___ no
Symptoms relieved ("Did you feel better?") when away from home? ___ yes ___ no

Smoke detectors present?
____ yes ____ no
Located where? _____
Working? ____ yes ____ no
Tested how frequently? _____

Potential health effect: injury, burns *Related to:*   ➢ fire **Resources:* www.cpsc.gov

Odor of cigarette smoke in house?
____ yes ____ no
Do family members or regular visitors smoke?
____ yes ____ no
Where do they smoke?
____ inside house ____ outside only ____ car

Potential health effect: cancer,
  respiratory disease
Related to:
  ➢ secondhand smoke
*Resources:
www.atsdr.cdc. gov
www.lungusa.org, www.epa.gov/iaq

Does the family utilize living space in the basement?
____ yes ____ no

Has radon testing been done? ____ yes ____ no
Ask to see report.
What remediation has been performed?
_____

Potential health effect: cancer
Related to:
  ➢ radon entering house from under-
    ground sources
*Resources:
www.lungusa.org
www.epa.gov/iaq

Family Interview Questions:

What are the ages of household members?
_____

Are any household members pregnant, or anticipating pregnancy? ____ yes ____ no

How many servings of fish (including tuna) do family members eat per week? _____
_____

Do family members (especially children) take vitamin and mineral supplements (esp. iron and calcium)? ____ yes ____ no

How many servings/day of foods high in calcium and iron (ex.: dairy, cereal, beans)? _____
_____

Potential health effect: mercury
  poisoning
Related to:
  ➢ consumption of fish
  ➢ increased risk for fetus and
    children
*Resources:
www.epa.gov/mercury ("fish
advisories")

Potential health effect: lead poisoning
Related to:
  ➢ increased GI absorption of lead in
    children
  ➢ increased absorption of lead with
    inadequate iron, calcium intake
*Resources:
www.aeclp.org
www.nal.usda.gov.fnic

Continued

What are the household handwashing practices? (i.e.: Hands washed after returning from work, school, outdoor play? Before meals? During food preparation? After toileting?) _____

_____

Occupation(s) of household teens and adults: _____

_____

(If appropriate for occupations): Do household members change out of work clothes and shower before returning home? _____ yes _____ no

Potential health effect: Poisoning from multiple sources (lead, pesticides, etc.), infectious disease
Related to:
  ➢ transmission of substances from outside environment to home
  ➢ transmission of substances from hand to mouth
*_Resources:_
  www.cdc.gov/niosh (incl. "construction safety and health")
  www.cpsc.gov ("lead")
  www.aeclp.org

Health Promotion of Families in Rural Settings

20

Janice M. Wiegmann

As the family goes, so goes the nation and so goes the whole world in which we live.

— Pope John Paul II

OBJECTIVES

On completion of this chapter, the reader will be able to do the following:

1. *Examine various ways to define rural.*

2. *List characteristics of rural families.*

3. *Describe rural family life.*

4. *Identify health issues for rural families across the life span.*

5. *Analyze nursing interventions to enhance the health promotion capacity of rural families.*

More than 80% or four fifths of the land area in the United States is considered rural. About 55 million people or one fifth of the U.S. population lives in nonmetropolitan areas, which have come to be known as *rural America*. For many people, life in rural America evokes pictures of small communities where everyone knows each other. Surrounding these small communities are small, family-owned farms where family members work together milking the cows, gathering eggs, shearing the sheep, feeding the hogs, caring for the horses, and tilling the ground. For others, living in a rural area means miles and miles of flatlands with the nearest neighbors and city several hours away. Rural living could also mean mountainous frontier. Yet for others, anything outside the city limits of a metropolitan area is considered rural. For some, rural life is represented by migrant workers or families living in run-down housing and working long hours for little economic benefit. Even though a rural area is often regarded as a better location for family life, living in rural communities presents special challenges to families (Whitener, 1995). These challenges include poverty, limited access to health care, and a shortage of health care professionals.

This chapter begins by discussing the meaning of rurality and provides various definitions of the term *rural*. Issues that rural families face throughout the life span are identified. Strategies used to assess, diagnose, and intervene to meet the needs of rural families are discussed. Problems and concerns that nurses face working in rural settings are explored.

Definitions of Rurality

Just as various images of rural life exist, so do various definitions of *rural*. The term *rural* has been difficult to define and is subjective in nature, in part because it evokes different images for different people (Bushy, 2000a; Johnson-Webb, Baer, & Gesler, 1997). A cattle ranch, a migrant farm camp, a coal mining community, a logging camp, a grain farm, and a mountain frontier each bring to mind a different conceptualization of life in rural America. Population density, population size, and distance from health care facilities have been criteria frequently used in differentiating rural and urban areas (Bushy, 2000b). *Rural* has been defined in terms of geographic location, distance in miles from an urban area, distance in time needed to commute to an urban area, and farm versus nonfarm residence (Bushy, 2000a). The numerical values and terms used to describe and define rural areas are varied; and descriptions of the rural-urban continuum include fewer than six persons per square mile, fewer than 99 persons per square mile, community with less than 2500 residents, community with less than 20,000 residents, and county with a central city of less than 50,000

residents (Bushy, 2000a). In articles published in *The Journal of Rural Health* between 1993 and 1995, Ricketts and Johnson-Webb (1997) report that they found 26 different definitions of *rural* used.

Three commonly used and cited federal definitions of rural are the definitions from the U.S. Bureau of the Census, the White House Office of Management and Budget, and the Economic Research Service of the U.S. Department of Agriculture (USDA). These definitions have often been used as the criteria to determine eligibility for funded programs, grants, special services, or other economic community benefits specifically designated for rural areas. Each definition is discussed in more depth.

The 2000 U.S. Census Bureau used population density to differentiate urban and rural areas. An urbanized area consists of a central city and the surrounding area that together have a population of 50,000 or more and a population density of greater than 1000 people per square mile. An urban cluster is an area that has a population of

TABLE 20-1   Economic Research Service Rural-Urban Continuum Codes

Code	Description
METRO COUNTIES:	
0	Central counties of metro areas of 1 million population or more
1	Fringe counties of metro areas of 1 million population or more
2	Counties in metro areas of 250,000 to 1 million population
3	Counties in metro areas of fewer than 250,000 population
NONMETRO COUNTIES:	
4	Urban population of 20,000 or more, adjacent to a metro area
5	Urban population of 20,000 or more, not adjacent to a metro area
6	Urban population of 2,500 to 19,999, adjacent to a metro area
7	Urban population of 2,500 to 19,999, not adjacent to a metro area
8	Completely rural or less than 2,500 urban population, adjacent to a metro area
9	Completely rural or less than 2,500 urban population, not adjacent to a metro area

NOTE: New Rural-Urban Continuum Codes based on the 2000 Census are not expected to be available until 2003. The development of the updated codes requires journey-to-work commuting data from the long form of the 2000 Census and delineation of the new metropolitan area boundaries by the Office of Management and Budget (OMB). OMB's work is not scheduled to be completed until 2003.
From U. S. Department of Agriculture, Economic Research Service. (1993). *Measuring rurality: Rural-urban continuum codes.* Retrieved May 27, 2002, from http://www.ers.usda.gov/briefing/rurality/RuralUrbCon/

at least 2500 people but less than 50,000 people. Anything outside an urban area is considered rural (U.S. Census Bureau, 2002).

The Office of Management and Budget classifies areas as metropolitan or nonmetropolitan. A metropolitan area is a city of at least 50,000 residents or an area of 50,000 residents in a county of at least 100,000. An area meeting these criteria is considered a standard metropolitan statistical area (SMSA) or urban area. Counties that do not meet SMSA criteria are considered to be rural (Office of Management and Budget, 2000).

The Economic Research Service has developed several classifications to measure rurality and has used them to determine the economic conditions of a rural area and to determine whether that area is eligible for federal programs. The three most commonly used are the Rural-Urban Continuum Code (Table 20-1), the Urban-Influence Codes (Table 20-2), and the Rural-Urban Commuting Areas (Economic Research Service, 2000a).

Not only do variations in quality of life exist between rural and urban locations, great vari-ations exist even within rural settings themselves. Several authors (Farmer, Clark, & Miller, 1993; Goins & Mitchell, 1999; Hewitt, 1992; Smith, 2002; Weinert & Burman, 1994) have recommended using a more detailed measure, even within a pre-dominantly rural area, to acknowledge differences among persons living on a farm, living in a non-farm residence outside city limits, in communities of less than 500 people, in communities of 500 to 2500 people, and in towns of 2500 to 4000 people. When a person's place of residence is considered on a continuum rather than in one of two categories (rural vs. urban), a more precise picture may be obtained, especially when research that may affect health policy and health services planning is conducted. One such example is the MSU Rurality Index developed by the Montana Family Cancer Project research team at Montana State University. Weinert and Boik (1995) describe the development of the index, its validity and reli-ability, and the usefulness of the index in taking into account the problems caused by the wide differences in other definitions of *rural* and *urban*.

TABLE 20-2   Economic Research Service Urban Influence Codes

Code	Description
	METRO COUNTIES:
1	Large—in a metro area with at least 1 million residents or more.
2	Small—in a metro area with fewer than 1 million residents.
	NONMETRO COUNTIES:
3	Adjacent to a large metro area and contains a city of at least 10,000 residents.
4	Adjacent to a large metro area and does not have a city of at least 10,000 residents.
5	Adjacent to a small metro area and contains a city of at least 10,000 residents.
6	Adjacent to a small metro area and does not have a city of at least 10,000 residents.
7	Not adjacent to a metro area and contains a city of at least 10,000 residents.
8	Not adjacent to a metro area and contains a town of 2,500- 9,999 residents.
9	Not adjacent to a metro area and does not contain a town of at least 2,500 residents.

NOTE: New Urban Influence Codes based on the 2000 Census are not expected to be available until 2003. The development of the updated codes requires journey-to-work commuting data from the long form of the 2000 Census and delineation of the new metropolitan area boundaries by the Office of Management and Budget (OMB). OMB's work is not scheduled to be completed until 2003.

From U. S. Department of Agriculture, Economic Research Service. (1993). *Measuring rurality: Urban influence codes.* Retrieved May 27, 2002, from http://www.ers.usda.gov/briefing/rurality/UrbanInf/

However, questions still remain regarding what geographic areas to include and how to best define the smallest and most remote areas of America that some call *the frontier* (Frontier Education Center, 2000).

Health Issues of Rural Families across the Life Span

Rural Family Life and Characteristics of Rural Families

The family, as an important unit of society, has a powerful influence on the health and well-being of its members. Some people hold the view that life in a rural setting is much more peaceful and calm and thus provides a healthier environment for living. Some associate rural life with a feeling of connection with one's neighbors and with the land (Pierce, 2001). Another belief is that it is easier to raise a family in a tranquil rural setting because children are less likely to be exposed to drugs, gangs, violence, sexual promiscuity, and other "city life" troubles. Bushy (2000b) has summarized some of the differences between rural and urban lifestyles (Table 20-3).

Research on the characteristics and health care needs of rural families is limited because only a few researchers have methodically studied rural families. People living in rural settings are considered to be tough and extremely independent, with fewer years of formal education and poorer communication skills when compared with persons living in urban settings (Bushy, 1997). In general, rural people have been described as being hesitant to ask for help from others. Thus they may tend to wait longer to seek care for a health problem (Bushy, 1990). For many rural residents, having the ability to carry out day-to-day activities is important (Long, 1993). Thus

---

TABLE 20-3   Selected Lifestyle Features of Rural-Urban Residency

Feature	Rural	Urban
Population density	Lower	Higher
Distances between places and services	Great/further Few options	Closer More options to choose from
Social interactions	Residents often related or acquainted Interactions tend to be less formal, more face to face Preference for interacting with local persons Mistrust of outsiders Difficult to maintain anonymity Church and school are centers for socialization	Social interactions tend to be more formal Wider array of designated places for socialization, business, and recreation
Occupations	Cyclical and seasonal work and recreational activities More high-risk occupations (e.g., agriculture, mining logging, fishing) Higher proportion of occupation-related injuries without immediate access to health services Less available information technology	More likely to be year-round, with cyclical fluctuations in intensity and production Workers in high-risk occupations probably have faster and better access to health care if injured Greater access to information technology
Predominant industries	Fewer industries in a small community More family-owned, smaller enterprises Town is center of trade	Economic diversity More large employers/industries Wider array of places designated for business and trade interactions
Economic orientation	Based on extraction from land and nature (agriculture, mining, logging, fishing, tourism)	Varied—wider range of economic enterprises

NOTE: There are wide variations among and between rural and urban communities. These are general characteristics, and each community exhibits varying degrees of each particular trait.

health is often viewed as being able to continue to work (Brown, 1990; Long & Weinert, 1989; Weinert & Long, 1990). Rural residents often may not allow themselves to be sick when there is work to be completed or a job to be done. Because of this close connection between health and the ability to work and maintain their way of living, rural older adults may put up with failing health rather than admit that they have problems (Goins & Mitchell, 1999). For African American families in rural southern communities, staying healthy is reported to be a process of surviving whatever health and illness experiences they face (Smith, 1995). The families believe that as they learn from these events, they become more aware of their own abilities to deal with crises. These findings are similar to those of a study conducted by Pierce (2001). In another study, Wiegmann (2000) interviewed rural mothers and fathers in a Midwest county to determine their descriptions of the meaning of family health and the behaviors they perform to promote health and well-being in their families. For these mothers and fathers, physical health meant the family lived in a clean, safe environment; had no major illnesses or health problems; ate balanced meals; exercised regularly; and had proper rest. Emotional health or well-being meant that family members were there for each other in times of need, were happy, and got along. Garrison (1998) studied 150 rural farm and nonfarm families to examine what impact gender, race, marital status, employment status, residence, age, income, and household size had on quality of life. The most important predictor of subjective well-being was household size. Persons from larger family households were less content with their financial circumstances.

However, the agricultural restructuring that has been occurring in the Midwest over the past 20 years and the changes in the mining and timber industries in the West have greatly affected the typical picture of rural life in the United States. As families encourage their children to seek employment elsewhere and more nonfarm newcomers move into rural areas, the quality of life that has drawn people to these areas may be threatened. Further research of these developments and their impact on rural American family life needs to be conducted (Effland, 2000; Purdy, 1999).

Rural Poverty and Homelessness

Economic trends during the 1990s introduced many questions about the effects of the economy on family well-being (Wallace, Green, Jaros, Paine, & Story, 1999; White & Rogers, 2001). A major family expense is childrearing. The cost of childrearing is typically divided into seven categories: housing, food, transportation, clothing, health care, childcare/education, and miscellaneous expenses (Walker & Reschke, 2003). Figure 20-1 shows the childrearing expenses of rural families. In general, the amount of money that families in rural areas spend on their children is less than the amount of money that families in urban areas spend on children (Lino, 2002). However, transportation, health care, and childcare and education expenses for a child are higher in rural areas than in urban areas (Table 20-4). The reasons are probably that families in rural areas have longer distances to drive; may need a second vehicle and so have extra automobile insurance and car maintenance expenses, especially when teenagers begin

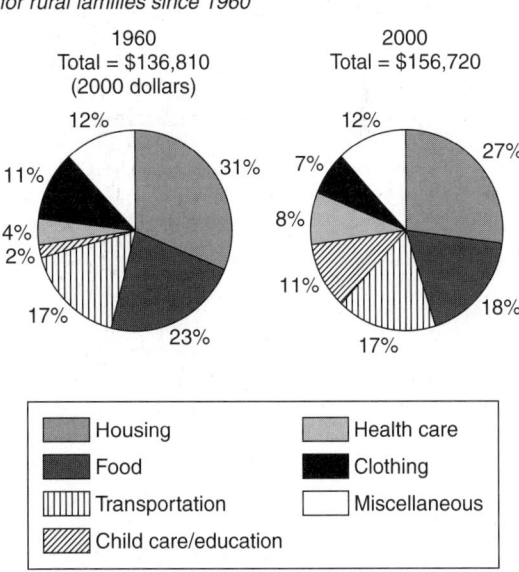

Expenditures on a rural child, 1960 and 2000
Childrearing expenses have increased in real terms for rural families since 1960

Figure 20-1   Lino, M. (2002). Expenditures on children by rural families. *Rural America, 17,* 26-33. Retrieved August 29, 2002, from http://www.ers.usda.gov/publications/ruralamerica/ra171/ra171.pdf

TABLE 20-4   Expenses on a Child up to Age 18 by Rural and Urban Families, by Income and Budgetary Component, 2000

Housing expenditures on children are less in rural than urban areas, but transportation expenditures are greater in rural areas.

	Lower income	Middle income	Higher income
Rural families:			
Housing	$ 29,310 (27%)	$ 44,190 (27%)	$ 76,230 (33%)
Food	22,920 (20%)	27,750 (18%)	34,470 (15%)
Transportation	19,440 (17%)	26,580 (17%)	35,100 (15%)
Clothing	9,030 (8%)	10,650 (7%)	13,620 (6%)
Health care	9,690 (9%)	12,630 (8%)	14,580 (6%)
Child care/education	9,450 (8%)	16,650 (11%)	26,790 (12%)
Miscellaneous	12,090 (11%)	18,270 (12%)	29,670 (13%)
Total	$111,930	$156,720	$230,460
Urban families:			
Housing	$ 43,880 (36%)	$ 58,790 (35%)	$ 90,950 (38%)
Food	24,530 (20%)	29,270 (17%)	35,870 (15%)
Transportation	16,730 (13%)	23,890 (14%)	32,360 (13%)
Clothing	9,170 (7%)	10,780 (6%)	13,780 (6%)
Health care	8,570 (7%)	11,350 (7%)	13,200 (5%)
Child care/education	9,260 (7%)	16,370 (10%)	26,360 (11%)
Miscellaneous	12,530 (10%)	18,710 (11%)	30,080 (12%)
Total	$124,670	$169,130	$242,600

NOTES: Budgetary shares in parentheses. Estimates of 2000 family expenditures on the younger child in husband-wife households with two children by rural-urban residence. The expenses are for a child up to age 18 and for lower, middle, and higher income groups of households (approximate before-tax income under $38,000, between $38,000 and $64,000, and over $64,000).
From U. S. Department of Agriculture. *Expenditures on children by families, 2000 annual report.*

to drive; and pay more out of pocket for health care because they have less health insurance coverage.

Even though, in general, rural family income has increased and the poverty rate for rural persons has declined, the rural poverty rate still exceeded the urban poverty rate by 2 percentage points in 1998 (Economic Research Service, 2000b). The percentage of rural poor families with at least one full-time, year-round worker in the home has increased since 1996. The changes in the criteria for national welfare assistance may have contributed to this situation (Whitener, Weber, & Duncan, 2001).

However, the economic changes resulting from welfare reform have made it increasingly difficult for rural families to "make ends meet" (Katras, Dolan, Braun, & Seiling, 2002). The types of jobs available to the rural poor, especially rural women in female-headed, single-parent families, are low-paying with few benefits and limited opportunities for promotion. These include jobs in housecleaning or housekeeping, fast-food restaurants, factories, and health care settings (e.g., nurse's aide) (Dolan, Seiling, Braun, & Katras, 2002). In addition, the number of uninsured and under-insured persons in rural and frontier areas is greater than that in urban areas. According to the National Rural Health Association (NHRA), a study by the Agency for Health Care Policy and Research indicated that the number of persons uninsured is more than 20% higher in rural areas than in urban areas (National Rural Health Association, 1999). Some of the reasons for these differences are that rural and frontier areas have a greater percentage of persons who do seasonal work; are self-employed in agriculture; or own and operate small businesses that are directly related to the mining, fishing, and agricultural activities of the area. Employers in rural and frontier areas are less likely to provide health insurance as a benefit. If health care benefits are available, premiums for family coverage are often rather expensive.

Overall, when compared with the urban poor populations, the rural poor are more likely to have intact families, be non-Hispanic white, and live in the South. However, racial or ethnic characteristics, as well as geographic location, have been associated with rural poverty (Nord, 1997). In the Black Belt, defined by Nord as the southeast area of the United States extending from the Carolinas to Alabama and the lower Mississippi River Valley, the poor population is predominantly African American. In the Appalachian, Ozark, and Ouachita mountains, the majority of the poor are white. In the Rio Grande Valley and the Southwest, the majority of the poor are Hispanic. In the central Southwest, the northern Great Plains, and western Alaska, the rural poor are primarily American Indians. Nord found that poverty rates have been greater than 20% since 1960 in 535 rural counties of these geographic areas. Such counties have been defined as "persistent-poverty" counties. In addition to having a high proportion of African Americans, Hispanic Americans, and American Indians, most of these persistent-poverty counties have towns with populations less than 2500 and tend to be far from urban centers, with the majority of the people employed in agriculture, forestry, or fishing.

The challenges of low-income ethnic minority women in rural areas are particularly discouraging. Although these women experience the same health disparities as ethnic minority women in urban areas, health problems of rural ethnic minority women are often more severe. This is probably due not only to the problems facing rural women in general (e.g., geographic isolation, educational limitations, fragmented services) but also to culturally different health beliefs; language barriers; gender bias; racism; and political, economic, and access inequalities (Hargraves, 2002). For example, rural nonwhite women have greater morbidity and mortality rates associated with cardiovascular disease than do white women (Taylor, Hughes, & Garrison, 2002).

Migrant and seasonal farm worker families are particularly more vulnerable to complex health problems related to poverty than families in the general population. According to the National Center for Farmworker Health (n.d.), 58% of all households in migrant home-base areas are below the nationally defined poverty levels. In general, the farm workers themselves tend to have infectious diseases, contact dermatitis, and eczema more frequently. Children ages 1 to 4 years are seen in the clinics mostly because of otitis media and nutritional problems. As children grow older (ages 5 to 9 years), dental problems begin to appear, as well as problems with infections, as stated previously. For children ages 10 to 14, dental problems continue to be a significant concern. In the female adolescent population, pregnancy is the major health concern; whereas for the male adolescent population, dental disease, as well as skin rashes and dermatitis, remain significant health concerns. As persons move into young adulthood, the problems of diabetes, hypertension, and arthritis begin to surface. These problems become significant as persons age. Community-based, nurse-managed clinics provide education for health promotion and disease prevention, as well as interventions for health problems (Guasasco, Heuer, & Lausch, 2002).

As a result of poverty and a lack of affordable housing, homelessness among rural families is increasing. According to the National Coalition for the Homeless (1999), rural homelessness is more likely to occur in agricultural regions; in areas where the declining mining, timber, and fishing industries are greatly affecting the economic stability of the community; and in areas that are trying to attract and develop new industries and businesses, thus attracting more workers than available jobs or attracting higher-income residents, with the result being increased taxes and living expenses. Homelessness for rural families is complicated by the fact that there are fewer shelters in rural areas. Often, homeless rural families live with relatives in crowded, substandard housing or in a car or camper rather than in the street or in a shelter. This "doubling up" can mask the seriousness of homelessness in rural areas (Bushy, 2000b). Enrolling homeless rural children in school can be difficult because of missing health and academic records. In addition, the emotional turmoil and day-to-day uncertainty can chip away at educational success (Vissing, 1999). The Research Synopsis details a study comparing Appalachian and urban family coping during a critical illness.

Maternal and Infant Health

The availability of obstetrical services can have an impact on pregnancy outcomes, increase hospital length of stay, and thus increase hospital charges and costs. Women living in rural parts of the country who have limited access to local prenatal services are less likely to deliver term healthy babies. One reason for this may be that problems during pregnancy are not detected early. The increased stress of having to travel for services may also negatively affect the birthing process; thus more intense treatment and longer stays for delivery of the baby and postpartum care for the mother may be required (Nesbitt & Larson, 1997).

Rural mothers of low birth weight (LBW) babies may be at risk for health problems of their own for a couple of reasons. As explained earlier, rural persons tend to wait longer to seek help from health care providers. These women may be more concerned with seeking care for their children than for themselves. Also, the stress of having to travel greater distances for follow-up care for the infant may add to the perceived economic and financial burden of caring for an LBW infant. Health care providers in rural communities should pay particular attention to support services that may be needed, as well as parent education programs focusing on growth and development of LBW babies (Sachs, Hall, Lutenbacher, & Rayens, 1999) and childcare (Walker & Reschke, 2003).

RESEARCH SYNOPSIS

COPING WITH CRITICAL ILLNESS

Coping with a family member's critical illness can be stressful. The family's response can affect the course and outcome of the patient's illness and the family unit's functioning over time. Rural Southern Appalachia has been identified as having a distinct culture, yet research relevant to critically ill patients and their families in rural settings is nearly nonexistent. Practitioners in rural areas must rely on urban-based research. Generalizing research across cultures may result in inappropriate care.

In this study, 30 family members of patients in two critical care units in rural Appalachian hospitals participated in structured interviews to determine their coping strategies as compared with the coping strategies used by family members of patients in a major metropolitan area in the northern United States. Seven of the 10 top-ranked coping strategies used by the families in the rural setting were also in the 10 top-ranked coping strategies used by the families in the urban setting. The rankings of the coping styles were almost identical for the two groups.

Findings of the study reflected descriptions of Appalachian people contrary to some characteristics previously noted in the literature. When the coping styles of the rural and urban populations in this study were compared, the similarities outweighed the differences. Both groups used supportive and optimistic coping styles most frequently. Findings also indicated that families need help in identifying strategies to effectively cope with a member's critical illness, and family assessments should be used to provide more appropriate family-focused nursing care.

Hunsucker, S., Flannery, J., & Frank, D. (2000). Coping strategies of rural families of critically ill patients. *Journal of the American Academy of Nurse Practitioners, 12,* 123-127.

School-Age Children

Agriculture has been identified by the National Safety Council as one of the most dangerous occupations in America. Children can be at risk for a farm-related accident or injury while playing or working. McNab (1998) divided children's farm injuries and deaths into three categories: accidents involving machinery, accidents involving livestock, and accidents involving recreation and play.

Children in rural, agricultural areas are often put to work to instill in them a sense of responsibility or a work ethic. Sometimes they are required to work out of economic necessity, either because childcare is too expensive or paying an employee is not economically feasible. Many times rural children are given chores that exceed their physical, mental, and emotional abilities (Lee, Jenkins, & Westaby, 1997). Parents should be aware of their children's developmental capabilities and take action to protect them from unnecessary risks. Shutske (2002) has outlined typical stages of child development, safety risks associated with each stage, and protective measures for parents to take to keep their children safe from harm (Table 20-5). The North American Guidelines for Children's Agricultural Tasks are available on the Internet through the National Children's Center for Rural and Agricultural Health and Safety website. The National Agricultural Safety Database website also lists several informational topics and prevention tips pertaining to child safety. The Website Resources box at the end of the chapter contains the URLs for these and other websites related to rural families.

Hohman (1994) has identified several existing health education curricula that discuss usual topics such as fire safety, traffic safety, water safety, bicycle safety, personal safety, and first aid. However, he notes that farm safety content is not included. He recommends that agricultural safety be added to rural school health education programs. McNab (1998) also recommends that parents and school health professionals work together to provide farm safety instruction in the school health education curriculum to help prevent or reduce many farm-related injuries and deaths.

In addition to accidents and injuries, rural children are at risk for lead poisoning, partly because of a lack of parental knowledge about prevention (Polivka, 1999). Objective 8-11 of *Healthy People 2010* is to eliminate elevated blood lead levels in children. Although progress has been made in reducing blood lead levels in children in the United States, information that is appropriate in terms of culture, language, and level of education is needed to eliminate elevated blood lead levels, especially in rural, poor, minority children (U.S. Department of Health and Human Services [DHHS], 2000).

Children with special needs present unique challenges to their families. These challenges are even greater for rural families because access to specialty services and support groups may be limited. Objective 16-14 of *Healthy People 2010* is to reduce the occurrence of developmental disabilities. Although specific disabilities will be monitored among school-age children, it is important that community-based services be available for rural and underserved children. Telehealth programs show promise for integration of in-patient specialty care with follow-up care for children with special needs, once they and their families leave the tertiary care center and return to the local health care providers for management of their needs (Farmer & Muhlenbruck, 2001; Karp et al., 2000). However, the cost of developing such programs and inadequate reimbursement for services could be barriers to the future of telehealth programs for these children and their families.

Adolescence

Since the mid 1990s, many education and health agencies in several states have used the Youth Risk Behavior Survey (YRBS) from the Centers for Disease Control and Prevention (CDC) to examine health behaviors of adolescents. The YRBS measures priority health-risk behaviors among a nationally representative sample of ninth- through twelfth-grade students. Although a great deal of useful information has been obtained from the YRBS, Puskar, Tusaie-Mumford, Sereika, and Lamb (1999a) believe that little is known about the health concerns of rural teens.

Puskar et al. (1999a) used the Adolescent Health Inventory developed by Nelson, Barnard, King, Hassanein, and Rapoff (1991) to determine

TABLE 20-5 Child Developmental Stages, Risks, and Protective Measures

Characteristics	Typical Risks	Protective Measures
Toddler/preschooler		
Unable to understand cause and effect	Drinking or eating poison	Careful supervision at home or in childcare
Illogical, "magic" thinking	Falling off farm equipment or pickup truck	Physical barriers such as locks & fences
Fascinated by movement or moving parts	Drowning in pond or manure pit	Safe distractions
May love to climb	Wandering into highway	Prohibiting riding on farm machinery
Curious		
Early School Age (5-9)		
Inconsistent use of logic	Livestock kicks or crushing	Consistent rules
Wishes to appear competent	Entanglements in augers or other moving machinery	Discussion of safe behaviour
Wants adult approval	Falling out of tractor or pickup	Assignment of simple farm chores, with careful supervision
Not aware of realistic dangers—more fearful of kidnapping or war than of much more likely farm accident		Bike safety training and use of bike helmet
Older School Age (10-13)		
Greater physical and mental skills	Operating machinery designed for adults	Consistent rules, with consequences for infractions and rewards for safe behavior
Physical development may outstrip mental or emotional maturity	Being struck by a car while riding bicycle	Bike safety classes, use of bike helmet
Wants social and peer acceptance	Falling from hay loft or ladder	Deliberate, planned increases in chores and responsibilities
Wishes to practice new skills without constant adult supervision		Special education on farm hazard avoidance
Adolescent (13-16)		
Desire to experiment		
Strong need for peer acceptance	Machinery rollover or roadway accident	Education from peers who have experienced injury or illness themselves
Resistance to adult authority	Hearing loss from exposure to loud machinery	Consistent rules, with predictable consequences for infractions and rewards for safe behavior
	Head or spine injury from motorcycle or all-terrain vehicle (ATV) accident	Motorcycle and ATV safety education and use of helmets
		Involvement in farm safety projects through 4-H, FFA and other groups
Young Adult (16-18)		
Increasing sense of adult responsibility and competence	Same as adult risks: respiratory illness, tractor or machinery rollover or entanglement, hearing loss, muscle or bone injuries	Clear and consistent rules regarding drugs and alcohol
Desire to be supportive, take on adult share of farm work		Rewards for acceptance of adult responsibilities
Need to take risks	Additional risk from experimentation with alcohol or drugs	Opportunity to be role model, teaching younger children about farm safety
Feeling of "immortality"		

Reprinted with permission from John Shutske, PhD, Associate Professor and Workplace Safety and Health Specialist, Department of Biosystems and Agricultural Engineering, University of Minnesota, St. Paul, Minnesota, http://safety.coafes.umn.edu

the health concerns of adolescents in rural Pennsylvania. The major health concerns reported by these adolescents were feeling tired, having frequent headaches, concern about weight, depression, and confusion about the future. Use of alcohol and use of tobacco were the most frequently reported risk behaviors. Overall, the findings were consistent with national statistics when compared with information from the YRBS and the National Longitudinal Study of Adolescent Health databases. However, the rural adolescents surveyed reported more alcohol and tobacco use than those in the YRBS. Also, boys reported more use than girls in both the YRBS and the Pennsylvania study. Further study revealed that the most frequent substances abused were alcohol, painkillers, and marijuana (Puskar, Sereika, Lamb, & Tusaie-Mumford, 2000). As alcohol and drug use among teens rises, there is growing concern that drug use and abuse will begin at younger ages (Finke & Williams, 1999).

Realizing that adolescence is recognized as a time for sexual exploration, Puskar et al. (1999a) examined sexual behaviors of rural youth. Although the Adolescent Health Inventory had no specific questions about the number of students having had sexual intercourse, 30% of the rural adolescents in the Pennsylvania study reported having access to birth control. In addition, the rural adolescents' concern about contracting AIDS or venereal disease was minimal. This is consistent with data from the YRBS. However, according to a report by Monts and Bufalini (2002), there are more than 45,000 people in rural communities who are diagnosed with HIV. Because rural communities are typically seen as close-knit communities, rural teens may wait until the disease has progressed rather than seeking treatment early, simply because they are afraid someone will find out and they will face rejection (Monts & Bufalini, 2002).

Hawkins et al. (2002) wanted to know how rural youth defined the terms *abstinence* and *sexual activity*. The researchers asked 311 students in grades 7 through 12 in a southern rural school to write their own definitions. The students' answers were vague and showed no uniform agreement on the meaning of the terms. Although the generalizability of the study is limited because the sample was one of convenience with no ethnic diversity, the authors caution educators not to assume that students will understand what is meant by these terms when they are used in sex education classes.

Much has been documented about the increase in sexual activity among teens and the occurrence of first sexual encounter at increasingly younger ages. As a result, parents have been urged to talk to their children about the risks involved in sexual behavior. Jordan, Price, and Fitzgerald (2000), discovering that research on parent-teen communication about sexual issues had been done only with urban and suburban populations, studied the communication of rural parents with their teens. Ninety-four percent of the parents reported that they had talked to their teens about sex, but 65% reported being "somewhat uncomfortable" or "very uncomfortable" in doing so. Results indicated that most of these rural parents believed that the family should have the major responsibility for children's sex education with additional help from the school, beginning during sixth or seventh grade. Surprisingly, most of the parents believed that information about the use of condoms should be included in formal sex education classes.

Rural Older Adults

Rural older adults face many challenges. In general, health promotion services and support services for the disabled, chronically ill, or terminally ill rural elderly are limited. Most rural physicians are generalists and family practice physicians. As rural primary care providers, these physicians are often required to provide specialty care and rehabilitation, as well as fundamental care. Sometimes they collaborate with specialists in distant, urban areas (Rosenthal & Fox, 2000). Access to specialists in urban areas may be further complicated by the older patient's inability to drive or find transportation.

In some small rural communities, the children of older adults have moved to larger metropolitan areas for employment. This leaves elderly parents with no one to act as a caregiver or to assist them in managing a chronic illness. Many rural aging couples also have fixed incomes that hinder their ability to hire someone to help them. Changes in Medicare reimbursement have also limited the number of home health visits to the elderly. In the rural South, many single parents also relocate to urban areas for higher-paying jobs, leaving their minor children with older parents. Caring for minor children adds additional stress to the life of rural older adults, particularly women.

Gender Issues

As a result of low income, inadequate access, and isolation, there are significant differences in the health of men and women living in rural areas compared with urban residents. Hispanic and African American women are more likely to lack cancer screening, have advanced cancer at initial diagnosis, smoke, and be obese (CDC, 1999; U.S. DHHS, 2002). In addition, men who live in rural areas have poorer health status and often perform hazardous work such as farming and mining. Suicide rates are reported to be higher in rural areas. From 1979 to 1997, the suicide rate for rural men was twice the national rate and was significantly higher for American Indian men, particularly in the western United States (CDC, 2002; Singh & Siahpush, 2002).

Ethnicity and Rural Health

A disparity in the health status of racial and ethnic minorities is noted by rural health policy researchers. More than 8,750,000 members of racial and ethnic minority groups live in rural areas of the United States. The majority of rural-dwelling minorities are African Americans and Hispanic Americans who are often underserved in health care because of poverty or low income and less access to transportation to health care. The majority of rural-dwelling African Americans live in the South, and the majority of rural-dwelling Hispanic Americans live in the southwestern United States. Historically, health care providers prefer to locate their practices in settings other than the rural South and Southwest (Slifkind, Goldsmith, & Ricketts, 2000). Researchers at the North Carolina Cecil G. Sheps Center for Health Services Research (2001) reported that the travel time and distance for rural minorities is twice that for people living in urban areas (Pathman, Konrad, & Schwartz, 2001). Also, the disparities in the health status of low-income minorities are

evidenced by pronounced higher incidences of cardiovascular disease and diabetes and underuse of well-woman examinations (mammograms and Pap smears). In some areas of the rural South, the incidence of prostate cancer is twice the national average. The reported death rate from HIV infection for African Americans was higher in rural areas (Slifkin et al., 2000). Rural-dwelling American Indians also tend to have higher rates of poverty and higher incidences of chronic diseases, low birth weight, and alcoholism. The central goal of the United States' health promotion and disease prevention agenda, *Healthy People 2010*, is the reduction of health disparities for all by providing access to health care services. In light of the economic decline in the United States in the early twenty-first century, states that are primarily rural will be faced with a considerable challenge to meet the 2010 goal of reducing health disparities and improving health care access.

The Canadian Perspectives box presents information about the unique health care issues related to the aboriginal people who live in rural areas of Canada.

Mental Health Care in Rural Areas

With the economic changes occurring in rural areas, mental health can be greatly affected. A recent public policy forum, sponsored by the Illinois Rural Health Association (Cooksey, 2002), addressed the health care issues of rural residents and the availability of health care providers in rural parts of the state. Primary care providers need more training in managing the mental health of their patients. Patients frequently display symptoms of depression and anxiety disorders. At the forum, family practice physicians in rural health clinics reported that sometimes as many as 80% of patient visits are related to these mental health concerns. Adolescents, especially girls, are at risk (Puskar, Tusaie-Mumford, Sereika, & Lamb, 1999b). With a lack of mental health specialists in rural areas, particularly child and adolescent behavioral mental health specialists, primary care providers are caught trying to manage care with the help of a few counselors and social services.

Once a diagnosis of mental illness is made, finding available mental health services for persons living in rural settings is difficult. There

CANADIAN PERSPECTIVES
ABORIGINAL PERSPECTIVES IN RURAL HEALTH PROMOTION PRACTICE

P. Gaye Hanson, RN, SCM, BScN, MPA
Aboriginal Nurses Association of Canada

Aboriginal people of Canada include the First Nations and the Inuit. Primary care and health promotion are provided by the Canadian First Nations and Inuit Health Branch on-reserve and in Inuit communities. Recent developments in the theory and practice of aboriginal health nursing in Canada have begun to describe the unique perspectives held by nurses working in rural and remote areas with aboriginal communities. Fundamental to the aboriginal perspective is the concept of the "four aspects of self," specifically the spiritual, physical, emotional, and mental (intellectual) dimensions of human development. A "whole and balanced" approach to health promotion is one in which all four aspects of self are addressed within the social context of the family, extended family, and community.

The internal interdependence of these four aspects of self in supporting health-promoting behaviour is well understood by aboriginal people. Impediments to health-promoting ways of living are seen through the interrelationships of these elements. The external interdependence of the individual, family, and community is also important in understanding the implementation of effective health promotion initiatives. Both strengths and weaknesses identified within the community must be con-sidered in developing programs to improve social support systems directed toward improving health. Working from individual, family, and community strengths—while addressing weaknesses—provides a positive perspective in health promotion and moves the focus toward seeing and building capacity, not becoming trapped in the incapacity.

Aboriginal people living in rural and remote settings have an increased likelihood of holding a more traditional aboriginal world-view as described previously, although there is a great deal of diversity within rural and urban aboriginal populations (Smylie, 2001). In addition, individuals and families experience unique challenges to high-level wellness such as the high cost of healthy foods, lack of options for physical exercise in cold climates, higher smoking rates, high rates of chronic disease, limited employment opportunities, low incomes, limited access to health services, and social problems such as violence, alcohol and drug use, and gambling addiction (Dumont-Smith, 2001; Hanson, 2001). Many aboriginal communities also experience the intergenerational effects of colonization, including the specific effects of residential school syndrome. The legacy of this history contributes to the disproportionate burden of ill health in aboriginal populations. The loss of language, culture, and traditional lands had a significant impact on many aboriginal populations. In addition, the "culture of dependency" needs to be considered in developing health promotion activities directed toward empowering individuals and families to take personal responsibility for creating health for themselves and contributing to the health of others. Community development methods are essential in assisting families and communities to rebuild their capacity to positively affect the health of their members.

Rates of diabetes among aboriginal people in Canada are three to five times higher than those of the general Canadian population. Aboriginal children are also now being diagnosed with type 2 diabetes, a condition that in the past occurred mainly in older persons. Inuit rates of diabetes are not as high as those of other aboriginal populations; however, there is concern that the rates of type 2 diabetes are increasing among Inuit as well. The Canadian Diabetes Strategy, announced in the 1999 federal budget, created a 5-year, $115 million strategy to begin to deal with the issue of diabetes. Over the 5 years, $58 million has been allocated to the Aboriginal Diabetes Initiative (ADI) to begin to address the epidemic of diabetes in aboriginal communities (Aboriginal Diabetes Initiative, 2002).

Continued

CANADIAN PERSPECTIVES
ABORIGINAL PERSPECTIVES IN RURAL HEALTH PROMOTION PRACTICE—cont'd

Advances in health promotion that have begun to address these challenges include the use of information systems to track health status and create community-based health promotion plans directed toward the most pressing problems. In addition, community nurses are using traditional aboriginal knowledge in the design of health promotion programs. One result is a return to programs based on traditional views of human healing and development and the role of a land base in contributing to health. Traditional knowledge also encourages the rebuilding of the family as a "unit of strength" in the community and a move away from health promotion programs directed primarily toward individuals. Increasing self-determination among aboriginal governments provides for increased governance authority within communities. Various forms of aboriginal self-government create opportunities for healthy public policy development that reflects the realities and priorities of their members. Aboriginal communities are also taking more control over local health service delivery, which allows for more precise direction of health services toward the needs of the communities. Limited funding levels and a population base growing at rates in excess of the overall Canadian population add significant pressure to the health service delivery mechanisms (National Aboriginal Health Organization, 2002). Communities must make difficult decisions in directing limited health care resources away from "illness care" to "health promotion" in the face of an increasing demand caused by the excess burden of ill health and injury.

References

Aboriginal Diabetes Initiative. (2002). Retrieved from http://www.hc-sc.gc.ca/fnihb-dgspni/fnihb/cp/adi/introduction.htm

Dumont-Smith, C. (2001). *Exposure to violence in the home: Effects on aboriginal children: Discussion Paper.* Aboriginal Nurses Association, Ottawa, Ontario, Canada.

Hanson, P. G. (2001). *Submission to the Commission on the future of health care in Canada.* Ottawa, Ontario, Canada: Aboriginal Nurses Association of Canada.

National Aboriginal Health Organization. (2002). *Discussion paper on end of life/palliative care for Aboriginal people.* Ottawa, Ontario, Canada: Author.

Smylie, J. (2001). A guide for health professionals working with aboriginal people. *Journal of the Society of Obstetricians and Gynecologists of Canada, 23*(4), 6-7.

Canadian spelling is used.

---

is also a need for increased opportunities for vocational activities for rural clients with mental illness (Dottl & Greenley, 1997). One goal of *Healthy People 2010* is to improve mental health and ensure access to appropriate, quality mental health services (U.S. DHHS, 2000). Developing specialized mental health programs in rural areas is not always economically feasible, but figuring out how to provide continuity of traditional psychiatric services to patients and families in rural settings should be a priority issue for practitioners and policy makers (Bjorklund & Pippard, 1999).

Oral Health Care in Rural Areas

In general, dental caries is the most common chronic, yet preventable, disease in children (Heer, 2002). According to Surgeon General David Satcher, as stated in the article by Heer, dental disease in children causes 52 million hours of missed school every year. As mentioned earlier, children in migrant families begin to experience problems with their teeth as early as 5 years of age.

Access to oral health care is a major health issue for rural families, particularly for those with poverty level incomes and inadequate transportation. One reason for the lack of access is that it is difficult to attract dentists to such remote areas (Gordy, 2001). Also, family wage earners in low-income jobs often do not receive dental insurance benefits. Even if these benefits are offered, the employee's portion of the premiums for preventive dental coverage for a family plan tends to be expensive (Beetstra et al., 2002). In general, approximately 27 million children have no dental insurance. In low-income families, almost 50% of tooth decay in children remains untreated (Heer, 2002).

Fluoridated water is considered to be one of the most important factors in eliminating dental caries (Banks, 2001). Yet many rural family homes receive their water supply from their own untreated wells. A key objective of *Healthy People 2010* is to increase the proportion of persons served by community water systems who receive a supply of drinking water that meets the regulations of the Safe Drinking Water Act. Until then, some rural counties have begun to use mobile dental units as a method of intervention. The mobile dental unit is a specially built van, bus, recreational vehicle, or large truck that can hold portable dental equipment such as exam chairs and x-ray machines. Staffed by dentists, dental hygienists, dental assistants, and dental students, the units can travel to rural areas to perform dental screenings as well as preventive and treatment services (Burger, Boehm, & Sellaro, 1997; Lopez, 1998).

Agricultural Health Issues

Although the emphasis on farming and agriculture has diminished in the past 2 decades, a considerable number of safety and health issues remain for farm families and agricultural workers. Farmers must handle a variety of chemicals and other toxic and irritating substances and must operate many types of equipment. Exposure to chemicals is addressed in Chapter 19 of this text. The major

safety issue for farm families, children, and their employees is injury caused by farm machinery. According to the Occupational Safety and Health Administration (OSHA), every year, farm accidents claim as many as 1400 lives and cause 140,000 farm-related injuries, most of which are preventable (U.S. Department of Labor, OSHA, 1995). The majority of persons killed in farm accidents are men and children younger than 15 years, and the majority of accidental deaths involve tractors. In fact, in 1992, farm accidents claimed the lives of 300 children in the United States (Adekoya & Pratt, 2001). The second cause of death among children who live on farms is drowning, and the third cause is firearms (Adekoya & Pratt, 2001).

The role of the nurse is to provide families with information about equipment and chemical safety and the use of protective equipment. In addition, because children are at high risk for injury, families should be taught to be cognizant of the dangers of chemicals and machinery for children. The following OSHA recommendations for accident and illness prevention should be taught to families who live on farms (U.S. Department of Labor, OSHA, 1995):

- Make accident prevention a goal for employees, oneself, and one's children.
- Prevent the risk of injury or illness by using preventive measures. Follow instructions in manuals for equipment and chemicals.
- Learn cardiopulmonary resuscitation (CPR), have first aid equipment and emergency numbers readily available, and have a plan for obtaining professional emergency assistance.
- Conduct routine inspection of equipment and inventory of chemicals.
- Conduct regular family and employee meetings to assess safety hazards and potential hazardous situations and outline emergency procedures.
- Be alert to hazards for children and the elderly.
- Use seat belts when riding farm equipment.
- Provide roll-over protective structures and other safety devices on farm tractors.
- Communicate hazard and safety procedures to workers. Provide protective equipment and information to workers to prevent acute

pesticide poisoning and dermatitis. Make sure all chemicals are labeled properly.

- Use guards and safety features for farm equipment and put them back on after use to protect workers and children from machinery moving parts.
- Take the necessary precautions to prevent entrapment or suffocation by grain storage bins, silos, or hoppers.
- Be aware that methane gas, carbon dioxide, ammonia, and other gases can be present in unventilated grain silos and manure pits in sufficient quantities to cause asphyxiation or explosion.

Strategies to Provide Rural Health Care

Community Partnerships

In an effort to help small, rural hospitals afford to provide primary care, as well as emergency services, to families in their communities, the Medicare Rural Flexibility Program was established by the Balanced Budget Act (BBA) of 1997 (Public Law 105-33). Through this program, rural hospitals that meet certain criteria are classified as critical access hospitals (CAHs) and receive enhanced Medicare reimbursement. Several states—including Illinois, Minnesota, Nebraska, Oklahoma, Oregon, Wisconsin, and Washington—have taken steps to implement such programs through their state rural health associations and/or state hospital associations. As part of the BBA of 1997, and as amended by the Balanced Budget Restoration Act (BBRA) of 1999, CAHs were established by Congress. CAHs are rural community hospitals that provide outpatient, emergency, and inpatient services and receive cost-based reimbursement. To be designated a CAH, a rural hospital must meet defined criteria outlined by the BBRA and the Benefits Improvement and Protection Act (BIPA) of 2000 (American Hospital Association, 2002; Stensland, Moscovice, & Christianson, 2002).

The Office of Rural Health Policy (ORHP) was established in 1987 as part of the Health Resources and Services Administration. The ORHP works with the DHHS on behalf of rural health care providers regarding matters that affect rural health care and rural hospitals. These activities include developing and implementing rural health policy, promoting rural health research, funding innovative rural health programs, and serving as a clearinghouse for rural health information.

One strategy that has been recommended through the *Healthy People 2010* and the Healthy Communities initiatives is development of community partnerships. This strategy is particularly lucrative for rural communities. For example, at a conference in Eastern Kentucky, parents of LBW babies were asked to share their concerns and stories about the adjustments they had to make in caring for their infants after discharge (Sachs & Hall, 1998). Although many of the concerns of the rural parents were similar to those expressed by urban parents, more creative solutions were needed in this rural area because of the differences in resources, as well as the fact that, overall, fewer families in rural areas have LBW babies. Using information gathered at the conference, the local county health department and the perinatal and neonatal providers developed a support program. A local community health worker assists the families in communicating with providers, coordinates services, informs the parents about financial and transportation resources, and provides some basic childcare advice. This method will be evaluated for its value in improving health care to families with LBW babies in rural areas.

It is well known that education is an important method to improve people's health, and farm family focus groups in Wisconsin recommended that their children be taught about healthy lifestyles and cancer risks. Through the combined efforts of the Wisconsin Division of the American Cancer Society, state representatives from the Future Farmers of America (FFA) organization and members from 39 FFA chapters throughout Wisconsin, 2007 third graders learned about sun protection and skin cancer (Reding et al., 1996). The project was judged to be a great success. The high school student facilitators were effective in improving the third graders' knowledge about skin cancer prevention.

School-based clinics could also be a means of delivering needed health services to rural youth. Such clinics could provide an avenue for distributing valuable information to youth about their risk behaviors. Further research is needed to determine whether rural adolescents would use the clinics and to determine what services would be used most (Crosby & St. Lawrence, 2000; Hanson et al., 1999; Rickert, Davis, O'Riley, & Ryan, 1997). School-based dental programs are being developed throughout the United States. (Heer, 2001a, 2001b; Pinkelman, 2001).

Telehealth and Telemedicine

Another innovative method of intervening in health care problems of rural persons who are geographically isolated from major medical centers is through the initiation of telehealth programs. Telehealth is defined by Thede (2001) and Russo (2001) as the use of electronic communication networks to transmit data or provide education and information to patients and their families to increase their awareness of health promotion and disease prevention practices, diagnosis, consultation, and therapy.

Access to computers in rural settings is increasing, not only for use in business and agricultural operations, but also for personal use for home budgets and entertainment. Computers also have the potential to offer social support to persons in rural settings. For example, in a study to test the use of a computer to provide diabetes education and social support to 30 rural women, Smith & Weinert (2000) used a type of software that had four components. One component, called *the Conversation Area* served as a chat room, where the women could talk with each other via the computer about what was going on in their lives. The "Mailbox" area allowed for private conversation between two women or between a patient and the nurse. The HealthChat area was designed for education, and the "Resource Rack" allowed posting of informational items of interest. The women used the "Conversation" and "Mailbox" areas the most and said these areas provided them with a great deal of contact and a feeling of connectedness with women who are experiencing the same issues and concerns. Even though this study was small, it demonstrated that computer technology might be a valuable resource for social support in rural areas. Other authors agree that using technology in remote areas can improve access to health care information, as well as provide support (Archambault, 2002; Buckwalter, Davis, Wakefield, Kienzle, & Murray, 2002).

Research Implications for Rural Health

As mentioned earlier, research on the characteristics and health care needs of rural families is limited because only a few researchers have methodically studied rural families. The majority of current research consists of descriptive statistics and studies from policy centers. Research studies that provide understanding of the phenomenon of rural family health at varied developmental stages, of different ethnic groups, and specific health issues are needed. For example, reliable and valid scales for rural families are needed. Gragert and Ide (2002) tested the validity and reliability of the Family Disruption from Illness Scale with rural families and found the scale to be reliable to measure disruption of families during illness of family members. Specific, regionally and ethnically sensitive health promotion and prevention and intervention studies are needed for rural families.

Practicing Rural Nursing

During the 1980s and 1990s, economic conditions precipitated a course of events in rural America that came to be known as *the farm crisis*. Financial problems caused economic hardship for many rural families. At the same time, health care expenditures were found to be out of control, creating enormous pressures on health care facilities in rural areas and limiting access to quality care. Strategies to resolve the cost-access dilemma included mandated cost constraints, cost shifting, and foundation-funded community programs.

A significant result of the turmoil was a growing interest in rural health care regarding availability of, access to, and use of health care services. In addition, the labor force accessible to serve rural populations was investigated (Morris & Palmer, 1994). The education, recruitment, and retention of health care providers in sparsely populated areas were examined (Moscovice, 1989). Communities lacking resources were designated as *underserved* or *shortage areas*, with primary health care provided by mid-level providers such as nurse practitioners (Stratton, Gibbens, Dunkin, & Juhl, 1993).

As rural health clinics emerged and outreach programs were developed, the special challenges of practicing nursing in a rural environment became evident (Bigbee, 1993; Bushy, 1994).

Through scholarly inquiry, nurses began developing a body of knowledge about the unique aspects of rural health and rural health nursing (Bushy, 1991; Thobaden & Weingard, 1983; Winstead-Fry, Tiffany, & Shippee-Rice, 1992). Bigbee (1993) defines rural nursing as the practice of professional nursing in sparsely populated communities and characterizes rural nursing as requiring a multiplicity of functions carried out with a generalist orientation. The types of practice and settings encountered by rural nurses include prenatal care, infant and child care, hospice, schools, faith-based health care, mental health care, migrant health care, caregiver support, home health care, and nurse-managed centers.

Rural health care continues to pose unique challenges for nurses because of the diversity of rural communities and rural families. Nurses who practice in rural settings need a wide range of knowledge and skills (Davis & Droes, 1993; Weinert, 1994). As generalists, nurses working in rural settings must be able to collaborate with families to assess their strengths and health issues and to prioritize needs, plan care, and evaluate outcomes simultaneously for a variety of patients and health problems (Long, Scharff, & Weinert, 1997). The nursing shortage at the beginning of the twenty-first century has created significant problems for rural health care facilities. Just as people in general have different images of rural life, nurses themselves have misconceptions about what it is like to work in a rural setting. Replacing nurses who quit or retire can be challenging (Trossman, 2001a). Schools of nursing and other professional schools can play an important role in rural health care by including curricular content about rural family issues. Also, students from disciplines such as nursing, social

work, and psychology have clinical exposure to rural families in rural settings.

Many advanced practice nurses enjoy the challenges, as well as the opportunities, of functioning as primary care providers in rural settings (Trossman, 2001b). Rural communities have been identified as ideal settings for advanced practice nurses to coordinate health promotion activities and research (Anderson & Yuhos, 1993; Doty, 1996). Nurses continue to play an important role in providing primary health care to families in rural communities (Anderko, Uscian, & Robertson, 1999; Bushy 1998). Rural nurses must have integrity and a strong sense of purpose (Scharff, 1998). In addition, they must be committed to working with diverse families who have a wide variety of cultural, socioeconomic, gender, family type, and family history issues.

Nurses working with rural families must be "expert generalists" (Henson, Chafey, & Butterfield, 2001). One aspect of being an expert generalist is being aware of the subtle cultural differences in rural communities. Henson et al. point out that expert nurses should be cognizant of the independence, self-reliance, and hardiness that characterize rural families. Rural persons sometimes can be mistrusting of health care providers new to the community and often are hesitant to accept care from them. Weinert and Long (1987) described this as the "insider versus outsider" or "newcomer" phenomenon. Nurses should be aware of the social resources and the health care policies that are salient to the quality of health for rural families. Lastly, educators and researchers should be cognizant of and incorporate rural family health and social issues into twenty-first century curricula and research studies.

CASE SCENARIO

Dennis (age 43) and Susan (age 41) have four children: Peter (age 17), Cathy (age 15), Brian (age 12), and Tommy (age 10). They live on a grain and cattle farm, located about 5 miles from a small-town community with a population of 1500. The nearest major city is about 100 miles away. Dennis farmed with his father until 4 years ago when his father retired. At that time, Dennis and Susan refinanced their loans and purchased the cattle and land. Dennis' parents kept a few acres of the land and built a small home. They live just down the road from Dennis and Susan. Dennis' father comes by every day to see whether Dennis needs help with anything, but his arthritis limits his ability to perform a great deal of physical labor at this time.

In the past 2 years, both grain and beef prices have decreased, and the family began having some economic concerns. To supplement the family's income, Susan took a job as a secretary for a printing company in a slightly larger community about 30 miles from their home. This also provided some basic health care coverage for the family.

Dennis and Susan were both reared in the Lutheran faith and have continued to attend church regularly. The children all participate in religious education at their church and in youth group activities. Dennis' father has been a lifelong member of that same church.

Dennis was last seen at the nearby rural health clinic more than a year ago, at which time he had a broken wrist. Dennis' blood pressure was a little high, but nothing out of the ordinary. The doctor suggested he watch his diet, try to lose a little weight, and come back in 6 months for a follow-up visit. Dennis lost 5 pounds and has felt fine so he hasn't returned to the doctor. He has been very busy since Susan started working and is not available to help him out by running errands and doing other chores. Susan recently had a Pap smear and a mammogram. Since she started working, Susan has not been feeling well. She thinks it is related to adjusting to the changes in their lives in the past couple of years. However, her family has a history of diabetes. The children are all up to date on their immunizations. Peter has asthma and eczema, a skin condition that some of Susan's siblings have. The grain dust and hay and straw for the cattle seem to aggravate both conditions. Because of this, Peter tends to get Brian to help him with chores more than a child of Brian's age should. Cathy has had anemia since she was born.

MAJOR FAMILY STRESSORS

A major stressor for this family is the financial burden resulting from the decline in agricultural economy just after the purchase of the land and cattle from Dennis's parents. The decision to have Susan work off the farm to relieve some of the financial strain has led to a second stressor. Family roles have had to be reorganized since someone has to run the errands and complete the chores previously performed by Susan. A third stressor relates to the ages of the children. As Peter and Cathy struggle with the developmental tasks of adolescence, Dennis and Susan are faced with the challenges of setting limits that maintain family stability yet allow for individual growth and development. At the same time, they must enable Brian and Tommy to progress through preadolescence.

FAMILY STRENGTHS

The family seems to share a religious core as evidenced by its regular attendance at church services and involvement in church activities. This may be a valuable resource to the family as it copes with problems and crises. The church community may be a source of social support to individual members, as well as to the family as a whole. The family members also seem to share responsibility and work together. Keeping the balance of interaction among family members will be important as they adjust to the role changes. Hopefully, they will be able to communicate their concerns to each other. The intergenerational connection with Dennis's parents, especially his father, may be a source of support for Dennis.

LIFESTYLE CHANGES INDICATED

Changes in physical health for both Dennis and Susan may warrant some needed lifestyle changes. Dennis's hypertension and Susan's family history of diabetes indicate a need to pay attention to diet, exercise, and the impact of stress on general health and well-being. The risk for farm injury may be even greater for Brian and Tommy now that Suan is working off the farm and Brian and Tommy may have more chore responsibilities at home. Being cognizant of farm safety issues is especially important at this time. Also, as the family becomes busier and busier, they will need to make a concerted effort to spend family time and leisure time together.

WEBSITE RESOURCES

ORGANIZATION	WEBSITE ADDRESS
National Children's Center for Rural and Agricultural Health and Safety	http://www.research.marshfieldclinic.org/children/
Economic Research Service (ERS)	http://www.ers.usda.gov/Topics/View.asp?T=104000
Frontier Education Center	http://www.frontierus.org/
National Agricultural Safety Database (NASD)	http://www.cdc.gov/niosh/nasd.html
National Center for Farmworker Health, Inc.	http://www.ncfh.org
Office of Rural Health Policy (ORHP)	http://www.ruralhealth.hrsa.gov
Online Journal of Rural Nursing and Health Care	http://www.rno.org/Journal/org
National Rural Health Association (NHRA)	http://www.nrharural.org
Rural Family Medicine	http://www.ruralfamilymedicine.org
Rural Information Center Health Service (RICHS)	http://www.nal.usda.gov/ric/richs
Rural Nurse Organization	http://www.rno.org

CHAPTER HIGHLIGHTS

- Defining rurality is difficult because no universally accepted definition is used.
- A clearer distinction between varying degrees of rurality, including the meaning of the term *frontier,* is needed.
- Research on characteristics of rural families and health promotion practices of rural families is limited.
- Health care, childcare/education, and transportation expenses are greater for families in rural areas than for families in urban areas.
- Low-paying jobs and seasonal jobs with few benefits place many rural families at risk for living in poverty and for being uninsured or underinsured.
- The health problems and disparities faced by rural minority families, especially migrant and seasonal farmworker families and single-parent families headed by minority women, are greater and more severe than those faced by their urban counterparts.
- Rural families have limited access to specialty health services.
- Rural nursing is a unique branch of nursing that provides challenges, as well as opportunities, for nurses to provide primary health care to families living in remote areas.
- Community outreach programs developed through community partnerships between small rural clinics or hospitals and college or university health science centers represent one strategy that can be used to address access to care.
- Telehealth electronic communications systems are emerging to provide support and follow-up care for families in remote areas.

CRITICAL THINKING ACTIVITIES

Note: Refer to the family presented in the Case Scenario to answer the following questions.

1. Analyze some of the behaviors or characteristics of this family that fit the lifestyle features of rural families.

2. What are some of the health issues and concerns this family is currently facing? What

other issues and concerns are they likely to be confronted with in the future?

3. How might you as the nurse in the rural health clinic encourage this family to practice health-promoting behaviors?

REFERENCES

Adekoya, N., & Pratt, S. G. (2001). *Fatal unintentional farm injuries among persons less than 20 years in the United States.* U.S. Department of Health and Human Services, Centers for Disease Control and Prevention. Cincinnati, OH: National Institute of Occupational Safety and Health.

American Hospital Association. (2002). CAH roll grows by 64 in 2002. *American Hospital Association News, 38,* 8-12.

Anderko, L., Uscian, M., & Robertson, J. F. (1999). Improving client outcomes through differentiated practice: A rural nursing center model. *Public Health Nursing, 16,* 168-175.

Anderson, J., & Yuhos, R. (1993). Health promotion in rural settings: A nursing challenge. *Nursing Clinics of North America, 28,* 145-155.

Archambault, D. (2002). Telemedicine and telehealth programs in rural health care. *Community Health Forum, 3,* 12-14.

Banks, M. (2001). Fluoridated water: Nature's cavity fighter. *Community Health Forum, 2,* 13-15.

Beetstra, S., Derksen, D., Ro, M., Powell, W., Fry, D. E., & Kaufman, A. (2002). A 'health commons' approach to oral health for low-income populations in a rural state. *American Journal of Public Health, 92,* 12-14.

Bigbee, J. L. (1993). The uniqueness of rural nursing. *Nursing Clinics of North America, 28,* 131-144.

Bjorklund, R. W., & Pippard, J. L. (1999). The mental health consumer movement: Implications for rural practice. *Community Mental Health Journal, 35,* 347-359.

Brown, K. (1990). Connected independence: A paradox of rural health? *Journal of Rural Community Psychology, 11,* 51-64.

Buckwalter, K. C., Davis, L. L., Wakefield. B. J., Kienzle, M. G., & Murray, M. A. (2002). Telehealth for elders and their caregivers in rural communities. *Family & Community Health, 25,* 31-40.

Burger, A. D., Boehm, J. M., & Sellaro, C. L. (1997). Dental disease prevention programs in a rural Appalachian population. *Journal of Dental Hygiene, 71*(3), 117-122.

Bushy, A. (1990). Rural determinants in family health: Considerations for community nurses. *Family and Community Health, 12,* 29-38.

Bushy, A. (1991). *Rural nursing* (Vols. 1-2). Newbury Park, CA: Sage.

Bushy, A. (1994). When your client lives in a rural area: Rural health care delivery issues. *Issues in Mental Health Nursing, 15,* 253-266.

Bushy, A. (1997). Case management in rural environments: An emerging opportunity for counselors. *Guidance and Counseling, 12,* 28-31.

Bushy, A. (1998). Rural nursing in the United States: Where do we stand as we enter the new millennium? *Australian Journal of Rural Health, 6,* 65-71.

Bushy, A. (2000a). Community health nursing in rural environments. In M. Stanhope & J. Lancaster (Eds.), *Community and public health nursing.* (5th ed., pp. 330-348). St. Louis, MO: Mosby.

Bushy, A. (2000b). *Nursing in the rural community.* Thousand Oaks, CA: Sage.

Centers for Disease Control and Prevention, National Center for Health Statistics. (1999). *Health, United States, socioeconomic chart book.* Hyattsville, MD: Author.

Centers for Disease Control and Prevention. (2002). *Suicide in the United States.* Retrieved October 26, 2002, from http://www.cdc.gov/ncipc/factssheets/suifacts.htm

Cooksey, J. (2002 March). *The rural health workforce: Challenges ahead for this valuable community resource.* Presented at the Public Policy Forum of the Illinois Rural Health Association, Springfield, IL.

Crosby, R., & St. Lawrence, J. (2000). Adolescents' use of school-based health clinics for reproductive health services: Data from the longitudinal study on adolescent health. *Journal of School Health, 70,* 22-27.

Davis, D. J., & Droes, N. S. (1993). Community health nursing in rural and frontier counties. *Nursing Clinics of North America, 28,* 159-169.

Dolan, E., Seiling, S., Braun, B., & Katras, M. J. (2002). Rural families speak: The challenge of employment. In *Family Focus On...Section of Report of the National Council of Family Relations, 47*(3), F4-F5.

Dottl, S., & Greenley, J. R. (1997). Rural-urban differences in psychiatric status and functioning among clients with severe mental illness. *Community Mental Health Journal, 33,* 311-321.

Doty, R. E. (1996). Alternative theoretical perspectives: Essential knowledge for the advanced practice nurse in the promotion of rural family health. *Clinical Nurse Specialist, 10*, 217-219.

Economic Research Service. (2000a). *Measuring rurality: Overview*. Retrieved May 10, 2002, from http://www.ers.usda.gov/briefing/rurality/overview.htm

Economic Research Service. (2000b). Rural poverty rate declines, while family income grows. *Rural Conditions and Trends, 11*(2), 62-67. Retrieved May 10, 2002, from http://www.ers.usda.gov/publications/rcat/rcat112/rcat112

Effland, A. B. (2000). When rural does not equal agricultural. *Agricultural History 74*, 489-501.

Farmer, J. E., & Muhlenbruck, L. (2001). Telehealth for children with special health care needs: Promoting comprehensive systems of care. *Clinical Pediatrics, 40*, 93-98.

Farmer, R., Clark, L., & Miller, M. (1993). Consequences of differential residence designations for rural health policy: The case of infant mortality. *Journal of Rural Health, 9*, 17-26.

Finke, L., & Williams, J. (1999). Alcohol and drug use of inter-city versus rural school age children. *Journal of Drug Education, 29*, 279-291.

Frontier Education Center. (2000). *The geography of frontier America*. Retrieved April 27, 2002, from http://www.nal.usda.gov/ric/richs/frontierinventory.htm

Garrison, M. E. B. (1998). Determinants of the quality of life. *Journal of Rural Health, 14*, 146-153.

Goins, R. T., & Mitchell, J. (1999). Health related quality of life: Does rurality matter? *Journal of Rural Health, 15*, 147-156.

Gordy, A. (2001). The impact of declining dentist-to-population ratios. *Community Health Forum, 2*, 28-31.

Gragert, M., & Ide, B. A. (2003). Reliability and validity of a revised family disruption from illness scale in a rural sample. *Online Journal of Rural Nursing and Health Care*. Retrieved April 19, 2003, from http://www.rno.org/journal/issues/Vol-2/issue-2/Ide.htm

Guasasco, C., Heuer, L. J., & Lausch, C. (2002). Providing health care and education to migrant farmworkers in nurse-managed centers. *Nursing Education Perspectives, 23*, 166-171.

Hanson, C. L., Kittleson, M., Welshimer, K. J., Ritzel, D. O., Woehlke, P. L., & Isberner, F. R. (1999). Rural school health services: An assessment of adolescents' felt needs. *International Electronic Journal of Health Education, 2*, 18-27.

Hargraves, M. (2002). Elevating the voices of rural minority women. *American Journal of Public Health, 92*, 514-515.

Hawkins, M. I., Davis, M., Eady, C., Rausch, S., Donnelly, J., & Young, M. (2002). Meanings of abstinence and sexual activity for rural youth. *American Journal of Health Education, 33*, 140-145.

Heer, E. (2001a). Promoting good oral health: Outreach programs teach the basics. *Community Health Forum, 2*, 20-23.

Heer, E. (2001b). School-based dental programs. *Community Health Forum, 2*, 24.

Heer, E. (2002). What's ailing our children? *Community Health Forum, 3*, 12-14.

Henson, D., Chafey, K., & Butterfield, P. G. (2001). Rural and migrant health. In M. A. Nies & M. McEwen (Eds.), *Community health nursing: Promoting the health of populations* (3rd ed., pp. 548-582). Philadelphia: Saunders.

Hewitt, M. (1992). Defining "rural" areas: Impact on health care policy and research. In W. M. Gesler & T. C. Ricketts (Eds.), *Health in rural North America: The geography of health care services and delivery* (pp. 25-54). New Brunswick, NJ: Rutgers University.

Hohman, S. (1994). Farm safety: A missing topic in comprehensive school health education. *Wellness Perspectives, 10*, 26-37.

Johnson-Webb, K. D., Baer, L. D., & Gesler, W. M. (1997). What is rural? Issues and considerations. *Journal of Rural Health, 13*, 253-256.

Jordan, T. R., Price, J. H., & Fitzgerald, S. M. (2000). Rural parents' communication with their teen-agers about sexual issues. *The Journal of School Health, 70*, 338-344.

Karp, W. B., Grigsby, R. K., McSwiggan-Hardin, M., Pursley-Crotteau, S., Adams, L. N., Bell, W., et al. (2000). Use of telemedicine for children with special health care needs. *Pediatrics, 105*, 843-847.

Katras, M. J., Dolan, E. M., Braun, B., & Seiling, S. (2002). Rural families speak: Making ends meet after welfare reform. In *Family Focus On…Section of Report of the National Council of Family Relations, 47*(3), pp. F3-F4.

Lee, B. C., Jenkins, L. S., & Westaby, J. D. (1997). Factors influencing exposure of children to major hazards on family farms. *Journal of Rural Health, 13*, 206-215.

Lee, H. J. (1991a). Definitions of rural: A review of the literature. In A. Bushy (Ed.), *Rural nursing* (Vol. 1, pp. 7-20). Newbury Park, CA: Sage.

Lee, H. J. (1991b). Relationship of hardiness and current life events to perceived health in rural adults. *Research in Nursing and Health, 14*, 351-359.

Lee, H. J. (1993). Health perceptions of middle, "new middle," and older rural adults. *Family and Community Health, 16*, 19-27.

Lino, M. (2002). Expenditures on children by rural families. *Rural America, 17*, 26-33. Retrieved August 29, 2002, from http://www.ers.usda.gov/publications/ruralamerica/ra171/ra171d.pdf

Long, K. A. (1993). The concept of health: Rural perspectives. *Nursing Clinics of North America, 28*, 123-130.

Long, K. A., Scharff, J. E., & Weinert, C. (1997). Advanced education for the role of the rural nurse generalist. *Journal of Nursing Education, 36*, 91-94.

Long, K. A., & Weinert, C. (1989). Rural nursing: Developing the theory base. *Scholarly Inquiry for Nursing Practice, 3*(2), 113-127.

Lopez, K. (1998, November 9). Mobile dental unit benefits children in western Kentucky. *University of Kentucky Chandler Medical Center News*. Retrieved June 18, 2003, from http://www.mc.uky.edu/mcpr/news/1998/Nov/mobnileental.htm

McNab, W. L. (1998). Incorporating farm safety into the health education curriculum. *Journal of School Health, 68*, 213-215.

Monts, R. D., & Bufalini, M. (2002). HIV & AIDS in rural America. *Community Health Forum, 3*, 17-19.

Morris, L. V., & Palmer, H. T. (1994). Rural and urban differences in ten allied health professions. *Journal of Allied Health, 23*, 143-153.

Moscovice, I. (1989). Strategies for promoting a viable rural health care system. *The Journal of Rural Health, 5*, 216-230.

National Center for Farmworker Health, Inc. (n.d.). *Fact sheet about farm workers.* Retrieved September 30, 2002, from http://www.ncfh.org/factsheets_05.shtml

National Coalition for the Homeless. (1999). Rural homelessness (Fact Sheet No. 13). Retrieved July 1, 2002, from http://www.nch.ari.net/rural.html

National Rural Health Association. (1999). Access to health care for the uninsured in rural and frontier America. Retrieved September 27, 2002, from http://www.nrharural.org/dc/issuepapers/ipaper15.html

Nelson, L. R., Barnard, M. U., King, C., Hassanein, R., & Rapoff, M. A. (1991). Instrument development for the determination of adolescent health needs. *Journal of Adolescent Health, 12,* 164-172.

Nesbitt, T. S., & Larson, E. H. (1997). Access to maternity care in rural Washington: Its effect on neonatal outcomes and resource use. *American Journal of Public Health, 87,* 85-90.

Nord, M. (1997, June 1). Overcoming persistent poverty— and sinking into it: Income trends in persistent-poverty and other high poverty rural counties 1989-94. *Rural Development Perspectives, 12(3),* 2-10. Retrieved May 10, 2002, from http://www.ers.usda.gov/publications/rdp/htm

Office of Management and Budget. (2000). Standards for defining metropolitan and micropolitan statistical areas (NTIS No. PB83-218891). *Federal Register, 65,* 82227-82238.

Pathman, D. E., Konrad, T. R., Schwartz, R. (2001). *The proximity of rural African American and Hispanic/Latino communities to physicians and hospital services* (North Carolina Rural Research and Health Policy. Working Paper, Series No. 72.) Retrieved November 21, 2002, from http://www.shepscenter.unc.edu/research_programs/rural_program

Pierce, C. (2001). The impact of culture on rural women's description of health. *The Journal of Multicultural Nursing & Health, 7,* 50-56.

Pinkelman, M. A. (2001). Talking 'bout a revolution. *Community Health Forum, 2,* 4-8.

Polivka, B. (1999). Rural residents' knowledge of lead poisoning. *Journal of Community Health, 24,* 393-408.

Purdy, J. S. (1999). The new culture of rural America. *American Prospect, 11,* 26-31.

Puskar, K. R., Sereika, S., Lamb, J., & Tusaie-Mumford, K. (2000). Substance use among high school students in rural Pennsylvania. *Journal of Addictions Nursing, 12,* 55-63.

Puskar, K. R., Tusaie-Mumford, K., Sereika, S., & Lamb, J. (1999a). Health concerns and risk behaviors of rural adolescents. *Journal of Community Health Nursing, 16,* 109-119.

Puskar, K. R., Tusaie-Mumford, K., Sereika, S., & Lamb, J. (1999b). Screening and predicting adolescent depressive symptoms in rural settings. *Archives of Psychiatric Nursing, 13,* 3-11.

Reding, D. J., Fischer, V., Gunderson, P., Lappe, K., Anderson, H., & Calvert, G. (1996). Teens teach skin cancer prevention. *The Journal of Rural Health, 12,* 265-272.

Rickert, V. I., Davis, S., O'Riley, A. W., & Ryan, S. (1997). Rural school-based clinics: Are adolescents willing to use them and what services do they want? *Journal of School Health, 67,* 144-148.

Ricketts, T. C., & Johnson-Webb, K. D. (1997). *What is "rural" and how to measure "rurality": A focus on health care delivery and health policy.* Chapel Hill, NC: Federal Office of Rural Health Policy, North Carolina Rural Health Research and Policy Analysis Center, Cecil G. Sheps Center for Health Services Research.

Rosenthal, T. C., & Fox, C. (2000). Access to health care for the rural elderly. *Journal of the American Medical Association, 284,* 2034-2036.

Russo. H. (2001, September 30). Window of opportunity for home care nurses: Telehealth technologies. *Online Journal of Issues in Nursing, 6,* Manuscript 4. Retrieved June 18, 2002, from http://www.nursingworld.org/ojin/topic16/tpc16_4.htm

Sachs, B., & Hall, L. A. (1998). Developing community partnerships to enhance care for rural families with low birth weight children. *The Journal of Rural Health, 14,* 51-58.

Sachs, B., Hall, L. A., Lutenbacher, M., & Rayens, M. K. (1999). The physical health of rural mothers and their low birth weight children. *Journal of Community Health, 16,* 209-222.

Scharff, K. E. (1998). The distinctive nature and scope of rural nursing practice: Philosophical bases. In H. J. Lee (Ed.), *Conceptual basis for rural nursing.* New York: Springer.

Shutske, J. (2002). *Keeping farm children safe.* University of Minnesota Extension Service Fact Sheet No. FS-06188-GO. Retrieved September 1, 2002, from http://www.extension.umn.edu/distribution/youthdevelopment/DA6188.html

Slifkin, R., Goldsmith, L., Ricketts, T. (2000). *Race and place: Urban-rural differences in health for racial and ethnic minorities* (North Carolina Rural Research and Health Policy. Working Paper, Series No. 66). Retrieved November 21, 2002, from http://www.shepscenter.unc.edu/research_programs/rural_program

Singh, G. K., & Siahpush, M. (2002). Increasing rural-urban gradients in U.S. suicide mortality, 1970-1997. *American Journal of Public Health, 92,* 1161-1167.

Smith, C. A. (1995). The lived experience of staying healthy in rural African-American families. *Nursing Science Quarterly, 8,* 17-21.

Smith, L., & Weinert, C. (2000). Telecommunication support for rural women with diabetes. *The Diabetic Educator, 26,* 645-655.

Smith, S. (2002). Defining the "rural" in health care. *Community Health Forum, 3,* 5-7.

Stensland, J., Moscovice, I., & Christianson, J. (2002). Future financial viability of rural hospitals. *Health Care Financing Review, 23,* 175-188.

Stratton, T. D., Gibbens, B., Dunkin, J. W., & Juhl, N. (1993). How states respond to the rural nursing shortage. *Nursing & Health Care, 14,* 238-243.

Taylor, H. A., Hughes, G. D., & Garrison, R. J. (2002). Cardiovascular disease among women residing in rural America: Epidemiology, explanations, and challenges. *American Journal of Public Health, 92,* 548-541.

Thobaden, M., & Weingard, M. (1983). Rural nursing. *Home Healthcare Nurse, 1,* 9-13.

Thede, L. Q. (2001, September 30). Overview and summary: Telehealth: Promise or peril? *Online Journal of Issues in*

Nursing, 6. Manuscript 4. Retrieved June 18, 2002, from http://www.nursingworld.org/ojin/topic16/tpc16ntr.htm

Trossman, S. (2001a, July/August). Rural nursing anyone? Recruiting nurses is always a challenge. *The American Nurse,* pp. 1, 18, 19.

Trossman, S. (2001b, July/August). Fueling two passions: NP role, rural nursing. *The American Nurse,* p. 19.

U.S. Census Bureau. (2002). Census 2000 urban and rural classification. Retrieved April 30, 2002, from http://www.census.gov/geo/www/ua/ua_2k.html

U.S. Department of Health and Human Services. (2000). *Healthy People 2010* (Vols. 1-2). Washington, DC: Author.

U.S. Department of Health and Human Services, Health Resources and Services Administration, Maternal and Child Health Bureau. (2002). *Women's health USA 2002.* Rockville, MD: Author.

U.S. Department of Labor Occupational Safety and Health Administration. (1995). *Farm safety* (U. S. Department of Labor Fact Sheet OSHA 95-39). Retrieved November 21, 2002, from http://www.osha.gov/pls/oshaweb/owadis.show_document?p_table=FACT_SHEETS&p_id=174

Vissing, Y. M. (1999). *Homeless children: Addressing the challenge in rural schools.* Retrieved August 29, 2002, from http://www.ael.org/eric/digests/edorc981.htm

Walker, S. K., & Reschke, K. (2003). Child-care issues facing contemporary rural families. *National Council on Family Relations Report, 48*(1), F5-F6.

Wallace, H. M., Green, G., Jaros, K. J., Paine, L. L., & Story, M. (1999). *Health and welfare for families in the 21st century.* Sudbury, MA: Jones and Bartlett.

Weinert, C. (1994). Rural nursing: Legacy, science, trajectory. *Communicating Nursing Research, 27,* 63-77.

Weinert, C., & Boik, R. J. (1995). MSU rurality index: Development and evaluation. *Research in Nursing & Health, 18,* 453-464.

Weinert, C., & Burman, M. E. (1994). Rural health and health seeking behaviors. In J. J. Fitzpatrick & J. S. Stevenson (Eds.), *Annual review of nursing research* (Vol. 12, pp. 65-92). New York: Springer.

Weinert, C., & Long, K. A. (1987). Understanding the health care needs of rural families. *Family Relations, 36,* 450-455.

Weinert, C., & Long, K. A. (1990). Rural families and health care: Refining the knowledge base. *Journal of Marriage and Family Review, 15,* 57-75.

White, L., & Rogers, S. J. (2001). Economic circumstances and family outcomes: A review of the 1990s. In R. M. Milardo (Ed.), *Understanding families into the new millennium: A decade in review* (pp. 254-270). Minneapolis, MN: National Council on Family Relations.

Whitener, L. (1995). Families and family life in rural areas. *The Journal of Rural Health, 11,* 217-223.

Whitener, L. A., Weber, B. A., & Duncan, G. J. (2001). Reforming welfare: Implications for rural America. *Rural America, 16*(3), 2-11. Retrieved August 29, 2002, from http://www.ers.usda.gov/publications/ruralamerica/ra163/ra163b.pdf

Wiegmann, J. (2000, July). *Health and well being of rural families.* Paper presented at the 5th International Family Nursing Conference, Chicago, IL.

Winstead-Fry, P., Tiffany, J. C., & Shippee-Rice, R. V. (Eds.). (1992). *Rural health nursing.* New York: National League for Nursing Press.

UNIT IV

Social and Family
Policy and the
Future of Family
Health

Influences of Social and Health Policy on Family Health

Susan E. Scheuring

The final great issue is this: What do we owe each other, not simply as individuals, but as a community or nation?

— Michael Katz (1996) *In the Shadow of the Poorhouse*, p. 332

OBJECTIVES

On completion of this chapter, the reader will be able to do the following:

1. *Understand the significance of social and health polices that influence family health.*
2. *Explain the U.S. policy-making process.*
3. *Analyze policies using a framework.*
4. *Describe the policies developed that have affected American families historically.*
5. *Identify the current health and social issues affecting families in the United States.*
6. *Analyze the nurse's role as a shaper of policy for family health.*
7. *Understand future family policy issues.*
8. *Use critical thinking to apply the steps of policy making to a family policy situation.*

Family life and family health take place in a complete and dynamic socioeconomic, ethical-legal, physical, psychological, and political environment. As the twenty-first century begins, families are experiencing unprecedented changes and challenges (Mason, Skolnick, & Sugeraman, 1998). Many families in North America have comfortable lifestyles. However, the increasing issues of insecurities and inequities in employment, social status, and health care for individuals and families threaten their well-being (Blau, 1999; Gebbie & Gebbie, 2001). Contemporary nursing practice occurs in conjunction with an

unparalleled shifting in the global, national, and local milieu that affects families. Therefore it is paramount that the realms of social and health policy are a component of nursing practice (Chooporian, 1986). This environment, then, is the context in which contemporary health and social policy are formulated. All policy that affects health, social, and economic indicators affects families.

Internationally, 1994 was declared the "Year of the Family" by the World Health Organization. Valuing the family is the first step in raising awareness for policy focus. This declaration resulted in an international advocacy and support for family policies. The attempt at health care reform in the United States in 1996 and its defeat highlighted the need for family-focused policy, especially the need for women's and children's access to health care (Sidel, 1992). Because the populace would not support wide-range changes for universal health care, a partial or incremental plan (Wilensky, 1998) for improved access for children finally evolved. Currently, in the United States, many interest groups are competing for the attention of a policy maker, while foremost is cost control on existing policies. When resources are dwindling and costs are escalating, the competition intensifies among the myriad of interest groups for their cause to remain in the forefront. U.S. policies are set in this context of market competition. Without authorization of funds to accompany a policy or proof of cost savings, policy is not viable. The topic of family-focused policies is broad, and it is beyond the scope of this chapter to discuss the varied topics thoroughly. The purpose of this chapter is to highlight social, health, and family policies as they relate to the well-being and health of twenty-first century families.

Basic Policy Terms

It is important to differentiate among social, health, and family policy. A major challenge is a clear definition of the term *family policy* (Bogenschneider, 2000). The following list of terms clarifies policy concepts used in this chapter.

- *Policy* is the manifestation of values and priorities for distribution of financial resources. It is the action toward a given means and end that is publicly proclaimed.
- *Health policy* is the prioritizing of a political action for a health outcome to which finances are directed.
- *Family policy,* broadly, is a coherent set of principles and practices that has direct consequences for family life. Specifically, it is the planning and implementing of legislation, regulations, rules and codes, and judicial decisions that affect family entitlements (such as housing, nutrition, and maternal and child benefit programs), family formation, family preservation, economic support, childbearing and parenting, and family caregiving (Lawson,

Briar-Lawson, Hennon, & Jones, 2001). The goal of family policy is to stabilize and strengthen the functioning of the family.
- *Family perspective in policy making* is a view that analyzes the consequences of any policy and its impact on the roles, resources, and well-being of families (Bogenschneider, 2000; Lawson et al., 2001; Ooms, 1990).
- *Politics* consists of the interactions among the key actors in the agenda-setting and policy-making process that result in an outcome either in favor or not in favor of various interests or groups in society. Families are one of these groups.
- *Social justice* is a belief framework that includes the view of equitable distribution of health care as a social responsibility. Health is a social entity. Shi & Singh (2001), Chooporian (1986), and Chafey (1995) point out that ethics must be part of nursing practice in the care of families and community, which includes proposing policy.
- *Market justice* is the opposite of social justice. Market justice favors distribution of health care according to the market forces in a free economy (Shi & Singh, 2001). The market justice view prevailed in the United States in the mid 1990s, when President Clinton's plan for health care reform was defeated.
- *Employer-sponsored compensation for health care* is the mandatory health plan that evolved in the United States after World War II. Currently, the directive is that companies of a certain size must provide health benefits for full-time employees.
- *Managed care* is the cost control measure or system that combines the functions of health insurance and the actual delivery of care, in which the cost and use of services are controlled through gate-keeping, case management, and utilization review.

Historical Background of Policy Development

Many important policies have shaped the social and health environments for families. As can be seen in Table 21-1, the twentieth century marked the beginning of regulation and standard setting based on the values and assumptions of the time.

TABLE 21-1   Historically Significant Health and Social Policies in the United States

Year	Policy
1912	Child Welfare Law
1914	Worker's Compensation
1935	Social Security Act: provided maternal-child care; aid to crippled children, blind persons, and health-impaired persons; and old age benefits
1937	Congress passes unemployment compensation.
1939	Old Age and Survivors Insurance
1944	Public Health Service Act: consolidated all Public Health Service authorities into a single statute
1946	National School Lunch Act: authorized a national school lunch program
1950	Post-war era of health benefits being a part of employee benefits
1950	Aid to Families with Dependent Children
1956	Old Age Survivors and Disability Insurance
1960s	
1962	National Institute of Child Health and Human Development and General Medical Sciences: Institute to study childhood diseases and human growth
1963	Community Mental Health Center Construction Acts
1964	Food Stamp Act: authorized food stamp program for low-income persons to buy nutritious food for a balanced diet
1965	Housing and Urban Development Act
1965	Vocational Rehabilitation Act
1965	Water Quality Act
1965	Clean Air Act
1965	Federal Cigarette Labeling and Advertising
1965	Heart Disease and Stroke Amendments
1965	Medicare: A-hospital, B-physician, outpatient
1965	Medicaid
1966	Comprehensive Health Planning Act
1970s	
1970	Community Mental Health Centers Amendments: extended grants for centers and facilities for alcoholics and narcotic addicts and established programs for children's mental health
1970	Family Planning Services and Population Research Act
1971	Exceptional Children's Act for Free Access to Equal Education
1972	Supplemental Security Income
1974	Health Planning and Resource Development Act
1974	Child Abuse Prevention and Treatment Act
1977	Rural Health Clinic Acts: amendment to Medicaid to include rural health clinic services by nurse practitioners
1980s	
1983	Diagnosis-Related Groups (DRGs) to control governmental spending on health care
1984	First state (New York) makes safety belt use mandatory in cars.
1988	Medicaid Catastrophic Act: state option to cover families at 185% of poverty guidelines
1989	Mandated coverage for pregnant women and infants in families with incomes below 133% of poverty guidelines and children up to age 6

Continued

TABLE 21-1   Historically Significant Health and Social Policies in the
United States—cont'd

Year	Policy
1990s	
1990	Americans with Disabilities Act
1990	*Healthy People 2000* set national health priorities and goals to reduce disparities in high-risk populations.
1990	Patient Self-determination Act: Patient has the right to make decisions about future medical care and preferences.
1990	Healthy People National Guidelines to Reduce Disparities
1990	Tobacco-Free Environments
1993	Family and Medical Leave Act
1993	Family Preservation and Support Act
1993	Clinton proposal for health care reform
1994	Declaration of International Year of the Family
1994	Child Support Orders Act
1996	Personal Responsibility and Work Opportunity Reconciliation Act
1996	Temporary Assistance for Needy Families (TANF): replaces Aid to Families with Dependent Children (AFDC)
1996	Health Insurance Portability and Accountability Act (HIPAA)
1996	Mental Health Parity Act
1997	Supplemental restraint systems (airbags) mandated for automobiles
1997	Balanced Budget Act: provided direct reimbursement for American nurse practitioners
1998	Child Health Insurance Plan: to provide universal health care for children
1998	Deadbeat Parents Act
1998	Third-Party Reimbursement for Medicare Part B services for clinical nurse specialists and nurse practitioners
1999	Surgeon General reports on mental health.
2000s	
2000-01	Surgeon General reports on mental health of children.
2001-02	Bush administration proposes tax cut spending for Medicare prescription drug plan.
2002	Bush administration instituted tax cut for top 1% wealthy and decreased spending on public schools and programs known to improve poverty indicators for children such as Head Start, child care, after-school care, nutrition, "welfare to work," and health programs.
2002	Legislation to prohibit tobacco from school premises and limit age to purchase cigarettes

By the beginning of the twenty-first century, the focus of policy was the preservation of the eroding health care system. Some question whether the term *system* can be used for the form of health care that currently exists (Shi & Singh, 2001). Table 21-1 highlights some of the major legislation that demonstrated efforts to introduce policies that affect the family.

Zimmerman (2001), in a content analysis, delineates categories of family-related policies dealt with by the U.S. Senate in a 7-year period from 1990 to 1997. The categories are as follows:

- Childcare and child welfare
- Domestic abuse
- Postsecondary education and training
- Employment and work force development
- Family farms
- Health (e.g., senior health, teen and reproductive issues)
- Immigration
- Marriage

- Military families
- Taxes
- Welfare, welfare reform

These categories relate to the economic, health, and social functioning of the family but are not specific family-focused policies. These legislative policies tend to represent an individualist philosophy rather than a family perspective, demonstrating in the United States, that most recent policies are not viewed from a family perspective. In the future, the policy model may evolve so that family policies are developed in a holistic way in which individual rights are respected yet the family system is strengthened (Ooms, 1990).

Models to Explain the Policy-Making Process

There are several models that explain policy (Hanley, 1998). One is Kingdon's (1995) Stream Model, with three streams of activities: the problem stream, the policy stream, and the political stream. The streams interact when windows of opportunities appear. For example, crossing of the problem and the political streams provides an opportunity for policy stream, producing change.

An awareness of the problem can be brought forward into policy, if the topic fits the political agenda. Figure 21-1 shows the Kingdon Streams Model.

In the United States welfare reform began in 1996. An example is the Temporary Assistance for Needy Families (TANF) policy. The *problem* was the shrinking federal government budget. The policy was introduced because the *political stream* of the U.S. Congress believed that persons on welfare were remaining unemployed and remaining on public assistance too long.

The Policy Systems Model, as described by Ripley (1996), explains the policy process as a systems process. In this model, functional activities occur in sequential stages as input with outcomes or systems as output. Agenda setting, formulation of goals and programs, program implementation, and evaluation are the stages of the systems model (Figure 21-2). The process results in a government agenda with policy statements, actions, and program evaluation of impacts.

Kingdon's (1995) framework is more dynamic, whereas the Policy Systems Model is linear. One model may be easier to understand than the other, depending on one's style of learning.

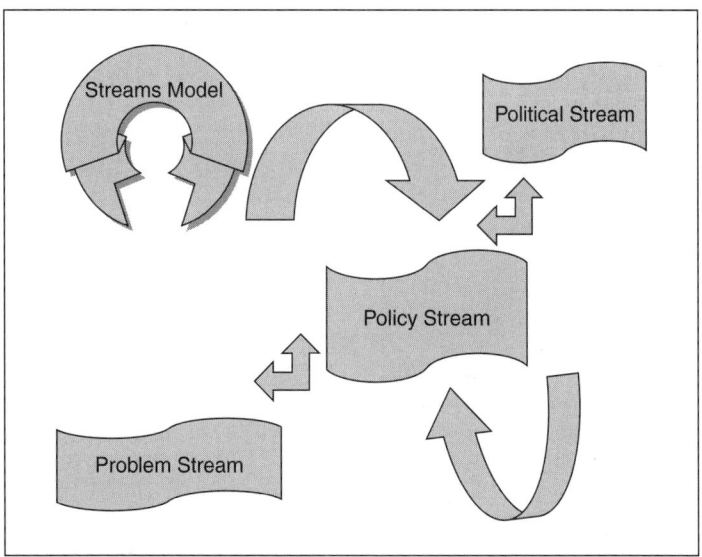

Figure 21-1   The Streams Model. (Adapted from Kingdon, J. W. (1995). *Agendas, alternatives, and public policy*. Boston: Little Brown).

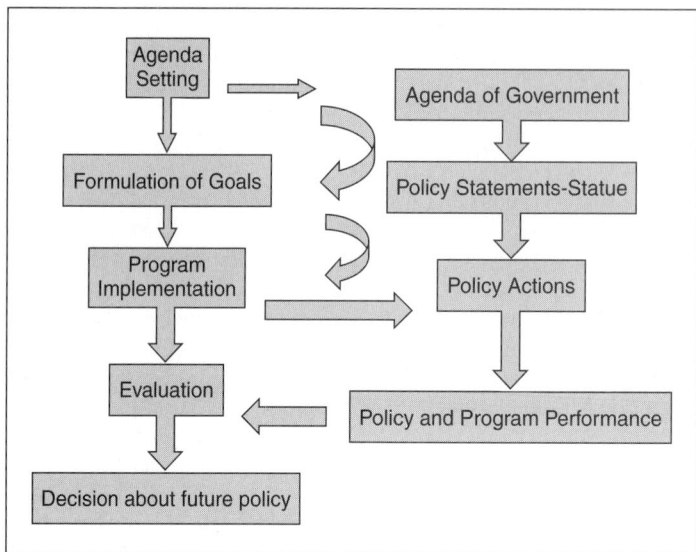

Figure 21-2 Policy Systems Model. (Adapted from Ripley, R. B. (1996). Stages of the policy process. In D. C. McCool (Ed.), *Public policy theories, models and concepts: An anthology* (pp. 157-162). Englewood Cliffs, NJ: Prentice-Hall).

The Purpose of Policy As It Relates to Families

Ideally, family policy functions as a protective, prioritizing, and advocacy action for families. In the twenty-first century, these ideal values conflict with the realities of budget constraints. Thus begins the perceived nonsupport by policy makers by families in American society. Policy is created in this conflicting context. The ideal purposes either are or are not valued over the cost control function by policy makers and the electorate. In the twenty-first century, the primary focus on health policy in the United States continues to be cost control and affordability of health care. Access and accountability continue as the secondary focus of health policy.

The health status of families affects American society financially, and conversely, cost containment in health policy affects the health status of families. With the protective function of health policy, having access to affordable health care can strengthen families. Doherty (2002) proposes that families are instrumental in producing health in family members, in addition to being consumers of health care. He also states that plans for

managed care should include a family perspective and consideration of the consequences of stress and illness for families as a whole. If families are lacking in adequate health care supports, the risk for expensive health care outcomes is great. Supported families can be influential in preventing disease and promoting health. Waller (2003) reports that U.S. mayors are opposed to reauthorization of the 1996 Temporary Assistance for Needy Families, welfare-to-work legislation because funding is inadequate for the work programs. Therefore support for working poor families may be eliminated in many cities.

Conceptualizations of health care as either an economic good (the market model) or a social resource (the social justice model) are the opposing American values (Shi and Singh, 2001). Health care, then, is distributed according to the prevailing view. These polar views conflict with and influence attempts to improve access and reduce disparities in health outcomes. Families benefit from affordable, convenient, and quality health care, which is slowly dwindling because of the rising costs. Health policy focuses on cutting these increasing costs. It is difficult to develop policy that protects both the financial resources of the United States and families, positive assets in U.S. society. However, having healthy families is protective to American society because it contributes to increased societal functioning.

According to Eichler (1997), American family policy tends to be the individual responsibility model rather than the social responsibility model. In the individual model, family members are equally responsible for providing for each member, whereas in the social responsibility model, the public shares in the responsibility of raising and providing essential resources for children. In light of the American value system of rugged individualism and the constraints of budget deficits, the conflict between the proponents of the two models is apparent. Value systems underlie all health and social policies. Persons making policies and the voting public are forces that move policy along, and they have different value systems that influence policy. Family policy is health and social policy that aims to strengthen the family, and values the family as an important component of society (Bogenschneider, 2002; National Council on Family Relations, 2000; Zimmerman, 2001). Bogenschneider (2002) and Kimball (1999) categorize areas of family life needing societal support as family and work conflicts, long-term care, family poverty, and marriage and family diversity. The purpose of family policy, then, is to advocate for solutions to specific social, health, and well-being issues of families.

As the consumers of health care and receivers of dwindling social resources, families become enmeshed in these issues by nature of participation in American society. Families with low income, children, and elderly members need protection and advocacy because resources are declining.

Young Families

Even though U.S. policy is based on an economic model rather than a social model, in the late 1990s there was a movement to ensure access for all children by providing health insurance to those who were not eligible for Medicaid. The health of children was made a priority in the United States. The Children's Defense Fund's policy advocates (1989) and Sherman (1997), among many, concur that children in poverty have poor health and social outcomes. The dilemma of reducing health care costs while providing more services for more children remains. However, if the health care system cannot support universal health care, at least children can be covered.

For example, *Health Choice* is North Carolina's plan to cover all children through the Child Health Insurance Plan (CHIP) program. The main characteristics of *Health Choice* are as follows:

- Children qualify if they have had no comprehensive health insurance for the past 6 months.
- Families of four qualify if they have incomes of less than $2742 per month (March 1999) and adjustments are made periodically.
- Families pay an enrollment fee of $50.00 per child, but no more than $100.00 per family for two or more children.
- There is a $5.00 fee per physician visit, $6.00 for each prescription, and $20.00 for an emergency department visit.
- No family pays for well-child visits or immunizations.

The *Health Choice* policy is family friendly because it promotes access to health care for children who, with their families, can have a better quality of life. The CHIP policy is an example of a policy that is protecting, advocating for, and prioritizing the health of children. Other policies, however, are reducing government spending for young family supports and protection, as will be seen later in the chapter.

In the second half of the 1990s, U.S. social welfare policy such as Temporary Assistance for Needy Families (TANF) was created for families living in poverty to have time-limited support and time to find a job. Many of the low-income families in the United States are single-parent families. Under TANF, parents are expected to train for new skills, obtain jobs, and find affordable day care in 2 years, or their social welfare income will be stopped. A major challenge for policy makers is creating viable funding streams to keep vulnerable families together. The assumption of this policy is that limited subsidies for day care and job training will be available for the qualifying families. In the twenty-first century, funds for these programs are being curtailed.

Earned income credits were given to low-income families as a break on income taxes owed the federal government, but programs promoting affordable childcare or flexible work schedules are being reduced (Bartfeld, 2003). In the 1980s and the 1990s, the bottom fifth percentile of the population experienced a 6% loss of income, whereas the top fifth percentile of the population saw their income improve 30%. Concurrently, policies such as TANF attempted to curtail government spending within the context of shrinking income. In addition, families living in poverty were negatively affected as the economy began to fall in 2001. Expanded comprehensive policies are needed to strengthen impoverished families who are affected by welfare reform.

The new working families produced by the TANF policy will need an additional policy to keep them out of poverty. Hogan (2000) supports widening the goals of welfare reform. Families still need improved access to health care, economic shoring up, tax credits, and childcare. "Promoting equity building in housing policy, micro-enterprise with matching savings accounts, restructuring of training and education programs, greater insight into the role of technology as a leveler and potential lifter, and the 'skilling up' of the working poor are all emerging strategies to help move low-income families to contribute to and benefit from our nation's rapidly changing new economy" (Hogan, 2000, p. 4). In 2002 President Bush's administration cinched the belt on spending for families in transition from welfare to work by freezing states' income for transition and education and by dropping childcare supplements. In 2003 the Bush administration eliminated provisions of tax credits for the very poor with the rationale that they do not pay much federal income tax and are not entitled to a tax rebate. Consequences of the TANF policy, in light of budget reduction, are not favorable because supports for families in transition are less available through the lack of tax rebate for economically challenged families.

Older Adult Families

Since the initiation of the Medicare program, only 1% of U.S. senior citizens older than 65 years are not covered by some form of health insurance (U.S. Census Bureau, 1999). However, disparities continue to exist in access and health status among low-income U.S. older adults (particularly minorities). Low-income seniors also have higher incidences of diabetes, heart disease, hypertension, and cancer. Many of these diseases and accidents, such as falls by seniors, can be prevented by health teaching and self-care or support for family caregivers. In addition, many low-income seniors receive the minimal Social Security financial support. As a result, inadequate finance decreases their access to affordable housing and adequate food. Unfortunately, except in some instances for diabetes education, the U.S. health care system and insurers do not reimburse nurses for health promotion and health education. Although the U.S. Department of Housing and Urban Development supports access to low-income housing for seniors and low-income families, the demand exceeds the resources, and many seniors live alone in substandard housing.

In 1966 several incremental changes emerged for health care delivery and managed care to assist with cost containment and quality (Wilensky, 1998). Two examples are the Health Insurance Portability and Accountability Act (HIPAA) of 1996, and the Patients' Bill of Rights Act. HIPAA allows families to purchase their same health care plan for 180 days after a job is lost. The assumptions are that continuing health insurance will provide stability for families (Wilensky, 1998). The Patients' Bill of Rights Act was passed in 1996. This bill gives patients the right to sue their health insurance company for denial of care. These two incremental changes in policy affecting health care delivery were possible because the large-scale Clinton health plan was not approved

Also, managed care organizations proliferated to control costs in health care as a further incremental change. Each of these incremental changes, while not simple, seem to fit the U.S. culture and beliefs about reforms of the health care delivery system. Meanwhile, health services for the elderly are shrinking, while their incomes do not increase.

In the first decade of the twenty-first century, it is apparent that costs for long-term care for elderly and disabled persons are escalating out of control in the United States. An attempt was made in 2002 to plan for assistance with the cost of medications for the elderly. To date, only minimal assistance is available under the states' budget to provide for medications.

However, a Bush administration policy in 2002 stipulated that Medicare beneficiaries can no longer be denied reimbursement for mental health, hospice, or home health care because of Alzheimer's disease. When research-based practice demonstrated that clients with Alzheimer's disease can benefit from special services, Medicare policy was changed to include reimbursement for these services.

In summary, health and family policies that provide holistic support to the elderly and their families are necessary to eliminate these disparities and to promote family well-being.

Special Populations: Families at Risk

Examples of families at risk, and in need of ongoing progressive policies to protect their health and social welfare, include families who are coping with mental health problems, HIV and AIDS, inadequate health care access in rural or urban settings, and homelessness. Families battling drug abuse, homelessness, and chronic mental illness are affected negatively when policies fail to provide funding for rehabilitation, halfway houses, and family supports. These are challenges that future policies must address to strengthen families.

According to the Streams Model (Kingdon, 1995), the social issues of underserved families often are not championed by lobbyists. Their problem stream may or may not join with policy or political streams to institute policy. Conflict with other problem streams for prioritization may disenfranchise vulnerable families. The timing, advocacy, and awareness by policy makers about the need of special populations are required for their issues to rise to the top of the political agenda.

Understanding the Legislative Process

It is important for health care professionals to understand the influence of their family advocacy activities on the legislative process and also models for policy analysis. In general, at either the state or national level, nurses can be an integral part of the policy-making process. Examples include planning grassroots efforts to support families and running for elected office. The legislative process is a lengthy one (Aiken & Catalano, 1994).

BOX 21-1   Summary of the United States Legislative Process

1. Idea emerges for legislated change.
2. Group of initiators develops a proposal.
3. Proposal is discussed with members of a professional organization and committee sponsors of the bill.
4. Support is garnered from organization board of directors and sponsors.
5. Public information dispersal is promoted by coalition.
6. Final sponsors are selected.
7. Sponsor brings bill to House or Senate for initial presentation.
8. Senate President or House Speaker refers bill to Health Committee for review.
9. Health Committee holds public hearings and health care and family professionals testify to importance of bill.
10. Health Committee recommends bill to House or to Senate.
11. Bill passes first in one congressional arena and then is sent to the other.
12. Bill is heard by second congressional body's Health Committee.
13. Second congressional body holds public hearings and health care and family professionals testify.
14. Second chamber (congressional body) recommends bill.
15. Bill passes with changes or bill is rejected with changes.
16. Conference Committee of both chambers irons out difficulties.
17. Bill accepted by both House and Senate with Conference Committee recommendations.
18. Bill sent to either Governor or President for signature.
19. Signing of bill, letting it become law; vetoing and sending back; or tabling for a non-vote occurs.

Adapted from Kalisch, B., & Kalisch, P. (1982). *Politics of nursing.* Philadelphia: Lippincott; Ripley, R. B. (1996). Stages of the policy process. In D. C. McCool (Ed.), *Public policy theories, models and concepts: An anthology* (pp. 157-162). Englewood Cliffs, NJ: Prentice-Hall; Clark, M. J. (2003). *Community health nursing: Caring for populations* (4th ed., pp. 61-78). Upper Saddle River, NJ: Prentice Hall.

As presented in Box 21-1, the legislative process is similar to the first column of stages in the Policy Systems Model. Family nurses should understand that they can get involved at any point of the U.S. legislative process. Gebbie, Wakefield, and Kerfoot (2000) report that once nurses involved themselves in the policy-making process, they continued to remain actively engaged in the political arena.

Other means by which family nurses can advocate for specific family policies include letter writing, voting, monitoring legislation, and inviting a legislator or reporter to visit them on the job. The key suggestions described earlier apply to these processes also.

Policy Analysis Framework

Policy analysis is the systematic description and explanation of the context and structure of decision making as the policy is developed (Hanley, 1998). Policy is not merely a goal-oriented activity with outcomes (Dye, 1987), but is a systematic, problem-solving activity. Background, assumptions, values, beliefs, prior legislation, resources, affordability, access and accountability, and outcomes or implications are the components of a policy analysis framework that can be used to view policy influencing family health and social arenas (Haskins & Gallagher, 1981).

Background of the Policy

A multiplicity of variables are in the background of the health, economic, and social dilemmas of families and individuals within a family context. An understanding of these background variables is essential before bringing forth a recommendation for policy development and implementation. Data for the background can be obtained from case histories, clinical practice reports, family observation and interviews, and review of related research reports. Background data can assist in creating an issue paper that is based on reliable information.

Values and Beliefs

Historically, Americans have had an aversion to higher taxation for health and welfare reform, as evidenced at election time when candidates campaign against taxes. In some instances, there is a stalemate between policy makers, which is described as *conflicting values*.

Conflicting Values

Universal health care coverage has always had significant opposition in the United States to prohibit movement forward. The failure of the Clinton health care reform plan is an example of unreconciled conflicting values. As these conflicting values enter the political arena, policy either reflects a negotiated compromise or is tabled because support is not strong enough to see an issue through. These conflicting values, or debatable views, must be analyzed to understand the context in which policy occurs or fails. The debatable views that are impeding forward movement of family health and social policy in the United States are as follows:

- Is health care a right or a professionally granted privilege?
- To what extent is society committed to the ethical concept of equality or distributive justice?
- With limited resources, when should policy decisions determine who shall live and who shall die?
- What is the nature of the relationship between a health care system and a profit-driven economy? Market justice or social justice?
- How much influence should stakeholders, especially groups of health care professionals, be allowed in regulation and determination of health care policy?

Besides conflicting values among U.S. citizens, several shortsighted myths also contribute to the foundation for the fragmented health and social policy regarding families of all ages (Kimball, 1999). When myths are believed, progress toward holistic familial policy with positive outcomes for families is deterred. Examples of myths that influence health and social policy are as follows (Hogan, 2000):

- The health and social policy in the United States is supportive of families and children.
- Work and family life are not connected.
- Parenting is solely a private issue, not a social one.

- Only those who fail ask for help.
- Home issues are female; work issues are male.

Assumptions

Policies have inherent assumptions. For example, policy to provide health care to children who do not qualify for Medicaid includes the assumption that all children need health care because they are future citizens.

Stakeholders

Stakeholders play a pivotal part in policy analysis, as political forces in the Policy Streams Model, and as they influence policy as it responds to a problem. The stakeholders are those with vested interests in the consequences of a policy enactment. The three primary stakeholders are the consumers, the providers, and the payers. Some specific stakeholders are as follows:

- Federal and state governments
- Employers
- Private insurers
- Practitioners
- Provider organizations
- Technology producers

Design of Policy

The design of a policy encompasses access, affordability, and accountability. When a policy is analyzed, the following components of the framework are integral.

Access

Health care access is the ability of special populations or any group as needed in a timely manner to receive affordable, convenient, acceptable, and culturally sensitive health care (Chang, 2001). A predominant theme in access to health care is income. When the primary breadwinner is unemployed, underemployed, underinsured, or uninsured, a major outcome is inadequate or lack of health care access. Key factors affecting access to health care are increasing health care costs, the shifting of the health care sector to for-profit policies, reducing of funding for public health services, and reforming welfare in the late 1960s (Clark, 2003). An example of this is CHIPs.

The goal of the child health plans is to improve children's health care access or entry into the U.S. health care system. During the first years of the nationwide program, the maximum number of targeted enrollees was not met, in part because many parents were not aware of the benefits. Strategies that states used to improve enrollment included improving the point of entry contact with eligible consumers, increasing program advertising, and training registration technicians at community sites.

Affordability

The cost of the child health plans to consumers is minimal so that cost is not a barrier to admission to the program. Federal and state funds maintain the program. The other stakeholders will determine whether the program is affordable to the state budget and to providers who receive reimbursement.

Accountability

The oversight of quality outcome indicators is spelled out in varying degrees through Health Care Financing Authority (HCFA) audits, managed care plan audits, and HIPAA. States are required to monitor funds allotted to the CHIP and to monitor the health status of children receiving care in the program as part of the evaluation of each plan.

Consequences of the Policy

A positive consequence of the child health plan is that children in 30 of the 50 states were given assigned primary providers to enter the health care system where there had been none. This improved access will improve the health of families and communities as healthy families raise healthy citizens. As members of the family unit, children are now guaranteed access to preventive care and to illness care. Other consequences to the enactment of the CHIPs were the lack of assigned personnel to broadcast the mechanism for enrollment and the low percentage (only 30 state plans) of states approved to enroll successfully proposed monitoring the plans.

Besides the framework for analyzing policy mentioned earlier, another more family-specific framework for analyzing policy was proposed.

Ooms and Preister (1988) specifically devised the framework, and it was further refined by a Family Criteria Task Force (1988). The analysis of a family-specific policy can be assessed by answering the following questions, which are the main categories devised by the Family Criteria Task Force:

1) Do the policies and programs aim to support and supplement family functioning and provide substitute services only as a last resort?

2) Do the policies and programs encourage and reinforce marital, parental-child, and stable family commitment?

3) Do the policies and programs recognize that families are an asset to society?

4) Do the policies and programs recognize the family as a partner in planning, providing, and evaluating services?

5) Do the policies and programs value diversity in families?

6) Do the policies and programs include the most vulnerable family population?

If family nurses are trying to decide whether they should support or vote against a family policy enactment or a policy change, answers to these questions should help them make decisions in advocating for U.S. family policy.

Frameworks, in general, are helpful to appreciate the multiple forces at play when a policy is brought forth for consideration. Policies should be family-friendly; should strengthen, not weaken, family structure; and should enhance, not impede, family roles. Family nurses can use the two described frameworks to determine whether policies are family-friendly and whether they can advocate for these policies.

Barriers to Family Policy

Besides conflicting values and myths about families impeding enactment of family policy, Bogenschneider (2000) cites several barriers in the U.S. policy process. The first is the founding U.S. value of rugged individualism. This value refers to the U.S. immigrants who "pulled themselves up by their bootstraps." She perceives this philosophy as hindering the study of family problems and solutions, because this value fosters individualistic versus familial policy direction. Persons with this value view families as being responsible for taking care of themselves instead of receiving government-funded health and social service assistance. American society must change this predominant value to have policy with a family perspective because all families cannot be "rugged individuals." Bogenschneider (2000) suggests that change will take coordinated education, research, and practice by family nurses and other family professionals.

Bogenschneider (2000) also proposes that diverse family values pose barriers for a concerted effort leading to family policy. Competing values about family decision making create bipolar opinions regarding abortion, contraception, childrearing, and sex education in schools, for example. In addition, the rights and responsibilities of the parent-child, mother-father, and caregiver-dependent dyads are frequently debated.

The dialectic of shrinking family supports when more are needed makes improved comprehensive family policy difficult. The U.S. health and social systems need improved services in the midst of rising health and social costs, concurrent with dwindling finances. These financial conditions impede forward movement toward comprehensive family policy. Dwindling resources mean budget cuts, not expansion. Day care subsidies are disappearing and coverage for health care for adults is shrinking. Recently, Congress failed to renew funding for unemployment benefits for several months at the end of 2002. Some families lost more than they gained with the loss of social and health services. Where is the support some families need to become independent of TANF? The mobilization of defense funds for the war against terrorism will further deplete health and social funds. All in all, U.S. systems present many barriers to arriving at family-strengthening policies, which necessitates family nurses joining forces with other pro-family professionals to advocate for family policy

Mechanic and Reinhard (2002) note that nurses can create barriers to significant involvement in policy formation. They cite an isolating and less collaborative presence of nurses in the political arena because of an effort to elevate the individual status of the nursing profession. Family nurses must not miss opportunities to use their expertise and be central in the problem, political, and policy streams of the Kingdon (1995) model.

Twenty-First Century U.S. Family Health and Social Policy Issues

Young Families: Women's and Children's Issues

The National Council on Family Relations (2002) recommends several policies addressing issues that families with children face in the twenty-first century, for example, raising the minimum wage, providing more housing assistance, health care coverage for all family members, improved day care and after-school programs, and better school-to-home connections. Inclusion of women's health screenings by private insurance plans is being legislated on a state-by-state basis to include coverage for birth control pills and mammograms.

Recently, as demonstrated in the national news, the foster care system has come under scrutiny because it requires better supervision. Decreased caseloads for social workers, frequent on-site inspections, and monitoring of foster parents are recommended. Social service agencies will need overhauling for these recommendations to be fulfilled.

Family and work conflict is an issue to be resolved in the future of family policy. For example, flexible work hours and childcare at the work-place are future policies that would strengthen families. Some corporations have recognized that being family-focused results in better productivity.

Family poverty will remain a focal point for family policy in the future, as income disparity increases between the indigent and the wealthy (Altman, Reinhardt, & Shields 1998; Bogenschneider, 2000). Further, TANF evaluation, more state earned income tax incentive plans, and inclusion of education mobility plans are future agendas proposed by these family advocates. Hildebrandt (2002) supports a more holistic response to poverty than the current attempt with TANF to respond economically. This is another market justice policy for individuals versus families.

Ooms and Preister (1988) and Ooms (1990) cited marriage-strengthening policy as an important future family policy issue. There have been attempts to obtain child support payments from absent fathers, but the marriage-strengthening policy is a proposal that provides more incentives to stay married rather than to get out of a marriage (i.e., to reduce marriage tax penalties).

Family makeup in the twenty-first century is more diverse than the traditional nuclear family of the previous century. Providing a good start for families regardless of gender, race, and ethnicity is an issue that should continue to be to addressed in family policy and research (Bogenschneider, 2002). She further highlights the disparity of family outcomes based on race as being tied to income. Research on the similarities of families is as important as research on diversity to sort out the complexity of family issues in the twenty-first century. Including the topics of work, poverty, diversity, marriage, and family developmental stage is a goal for research that is in the best interest of future young families and communities.

Family Mental Health Issues

Mental health has not fared as well as physical health in the U. S. health care delivery system. Mental illness requires more health services than any other illness except cardiovascular disease. Issues for families with mental health problems are parity or equal coverage, placement choices, services from the public to the private sector, declining public funding for care, escalating cost of care, medications, and decreasing benefits in most insurance plans.

In 1999 the Surgeon General issued a report on the state of affairs of mental health diagnosis and treatment (Satcher, 1999). It was the first time that such a report was issued with recommendations for improving delivery of care for patients with mental illness. Reduction of barriers and use of evidence-based treatment modalities were highlighted. Families with members who have mental health problems are under a great deal of stress with the current gaps in health and social services. The national report focuses on programs that work and funding research projects to prevent and intervene with mental health conditions.

The Mental Health Parity Act (1996) was passed as an attempt to have sufficient and equitable coverage for mental health issues, as there is for physical problems. The limited coverage and capitated limited lifetime service costs for inpatient mental health care have proven to be a problem. If a family member exhausts his or her lifetime benefit for mental health hospitalization, there is no other insurance coverage available. However, there are usually more physical health benefits than mental health benefits. Minority populations have less insurance coverage than the majority of U.S. citizens. If 16% of the U.S. population is not covered by health insurance, then minorities have a higher rate of no insurance, especially for mental health issues (Shi & Singh, 2001). Families with assistance from governmental or private health insurance for mental health issues will be empowered to fulfill family roles in society.

States are experimenting with turning management of clients over to the lowest bidder for mental health managed care contracts. These plans are not completely thought out; as Smith (2002) states, "scheming entrepreneurs are looking to reap a financial windfall from dollars accompanying clients with either Medicaid or private insurance . . . the reform plan for mental health is an air castle without a foundation" (p. 9A).

An attempt to offer benefits to clients with substance abuse problems under the Americans with Disabilities Act was passed in 2000. If these clients meet the criteria, they will have access to health and social benefits. This legislation will expand services to family members, and at the same time, will increase costs of mental health services to the health care system.

A major role for family nurses is to advocate for and direct families with service gaps to local and national coalitions dealing with mental health problems. For example, clinicians could take part in programs such as Friends of Public Mental Health of North Carolina.

Older Families

Families that include older adults are witnessing the investigation of more cases of elder abuse The laws that began in the mid 1970s for child protection have been updated to cover elder abuse. Other policy issues for the elderly are medication plans, coverage of Alzheimer's disease and hospice care under Medicare and Medicaid, advanced directives for end-of-life issues, and legislation to grant public assistance to biological and step-relatives such as grandparents who are raising children of their children. Also, caretakers of the elderly need to receive assistance to keep older adults in their own homes instead of in nursing homes, if their conditions are manageable. With more family members aging and living longer and technology prolonging life, the numbers of older family members are increasing. Future health and social policy needs to have a family perspective relating to elder care. Today's families are called the "sandwich generation" because they have children preparing to launch their own lives while grandparents are living longer and need assistance.

Family Safety

Gun violence is prevalent in American culture. As yet, the United States has no policies, only recommendations, regarding limiting firearms in families (Darras, 2001). Family nurses can inform families of these firearm risks and work toward community awareness by using organizations such as PAX: Real Solutions to Gun Violence as a resource. Its website URL is available in the Website Resources box at the end of the chapter.

The Brady Bill, passed in 1994, restricts firearm sales in the United States by requiring a background check before purchase of a gun. The purpose of this legislation was to reduce the numbers of firearms circulating in society. Besides screening for firearms in homes and in community health settings, family nurses can assess families by asking questions such those in Box 12-1 in Chapter 12 to identify those at-risk for domestic violence, so they can refer them for intervention (Ashur, 1993). Community grassroots efforts must take place to enact preventive policy; family nurses can play a significant part in these efforts.

Family Nurses' Roles in Family Social Policy

Nurses and family professionals in family and social policy were initially voters, then advocates for issues related to the profession, and then coalition builders to address and resolve family or societal issues. More recently they have begun to assume leadership roles in creating support for developing and implementing policies (Clark, 2003).

Family Nurses as Advocates

Nurses and family professionals are in a position to see the influence of and to act for families in the health and social policy realms or arenas (Mason & Leavitt, 1998; Seidel & Seidel, 1998). Nurses can join coalitions in communities to affect legislation at any point on the policy-making continuum. Earlier in the chapter, Box 21-1 lists the steps in the legislative process for policy making.

Activities for an advocacy role for family nurses include working with lobbyists, interest groups, and varied policy institutes that advocate for family strengthening by studying poverty and similar issues. Guidelines for accomplishing effective lobbying are presented by Aiken and Catalano (1994). Presentations should be polished, succinct, and based on research and practice. It may take time to get into the legislator's office to present an idea for legislation, so one must remain patient and courteous. One recommendation is to develop a coalition that is broad-based, but not too large, and will support an idea with a good rationale. After meeting with or receiving contact with a legislative lobbyist, be sure to follow up with a thank you letter including a summary of the lobbyist's main points and the lobbyist's availability to promote the idea and answer questions as needed.

Family Nurses as Family Educators

Family nurses plan, implement, coordinate, and evaluate home visitation educational programs for families from the prenatal period through early childhood. Private foundations, such as the Robert Wood Johnson Foundation, fund the programs. However, these are not yet mandated by policy. Evaluation studies have indicated that home interventions for families are effective in

---

RESEARCH SYNOPSIS

RESEARCH WITH POLICY IMPLICATIONS

The purpose of this study was to present current prevalence estimates and descriptive characteristics of children with unmet health needs by using the National Health Interview Survey data. Unmet need for health is a measure of access to health services. The significance of children's lack of access to health services is important for prevention of future short-term and long-term problems. The researchers analyzed 4 years of nationally representative data, from 1993 through 1996. The analysis included 97,206 children younger than 18 years. An adult household member provided measures of unmet need for medical care, dental care, prescription medications, and vision care. Bivariate and multivariate analyses were used to assess demographic and socioeconomic factors related to specific unmet needs.

The results showed that 7.3% (4.7 million) of U.S. children experienced at least one unmet need. Dental care was the most prevalent need. An adjustment was made for confounding variables. Near-poor and poor children were three times more likely to have an unmet health need as nonpoor children,

with a 95% confidence interval ratio. The researchers found that uninsured children were also three times more likely to have an unmet need than privately insured children.

The researchers said that implications demonstrate that it is imperative for financial and non-financial barriers to be removed through enactment of public policy. Despite the wealth of the United States and the creation of Child Health Insurance Plans in each state aimed at covering children not qualified for Medicaid programs, many families in the United States have difficulty obtaining preventive health care for children.

The Clinton health care reform plan was defeated during this time, which demonstrated the public's lack of readiness for universal health care. Nurses need to analyze policies regarding the values and assumptions underlying family policy. The data in this study show that children have unmet health care needs, and the enactment of child health insurance policy shows that it is time to have a universal approach to children's health care.

Newacheck, P. W., Hughes, D. C., Hung, Y. Y., Wong, S., & Stoddard, J. J. (2000). The unmet needs of America's children. *Pediatrics, 105,* 989-997.

improving parenting and decreasing child abuse. Home programs that have positive outcomes may be the basis for future family policy that would implement a national prevention plan (Kitzman, Olds, Sidora, Henderson, Hanks, Cole, et al., 2000; Olds, Eckenrode, Henderson, Katzman, Powers, Cole, et al., 1997).

Family Nurses as Leaders

Except for voting, many nurses and professionals are not involved in policy analysis or policy making. Davis (1979), looking forward to the 1980s, noted that only a small sector of nurses, administrators, and educators were functioning as policy makers and dedicated to professionalism. Nurses must be knowledgeable about the future trends and anticipate where to put energy to direct changes through local and national levels. Except through their professional organizations, such as the American Nurses Association or a specialty organization, most nurses are not organized to influence reform and policy making. The untapped resources of the sheer volume of nurses could be harnessed to influence expanding and improving policies. Family nurses also need to be aware of the power bases that drive policy. Some believe that the local grass-roots level is the most effective level to begin the work of politicking and choose to be leaders at that level.

Clark (2003) suggests the following strategies for nurses to influence policy development and implementation (p. 75):
1. Creating support for the policy
   • Coalition building
   • Creating media support
   • Community organizing
   • Lobbying
   • Presenting testimony
2. Traditional political activities
   • Voting
   • Campaigning
   • Holding office

Family Nurses as Planners and Organizers

Many family nurses engage in planning coalitions to improve the health status of families, such as those that promote immunization of children before entry into school. Looking for members of the coalition who will be supportive of promoting immunization legislation is an example of planning for family policy. Searching for possible opponents is also a useful strategy for planning and organizing promotion of health policy.

Family Nurses as Resource Networkers

As part of U.S. policy to guarantee universal access to health care for children, nurses and other health care professionals refer families to the appropriate point of entry to enroll in the Child Health Insurance Plans in their community. Another example of family nurses as resource workers is referring families to programs for improved access to health care and social services. An example of this method is presented in Box 21-2, which describes a program in Hawaii in which home visiting reduces the risk for unhealthy starts for families. Other programs are the Colorado-originated program, Nurse-Family Partnership (part of the National Center for Children, Families and Communities), and the REACH-Futures Program in Chicago (Barnes-Boyd, Fordham, Norr, & Nacion, 2001).

Family nurses should know of these services and make referrals to qualifying families. Nurses can interact with families in the community and can identify at-risk families who could benefit from this family protective program.

Education of Health Professionals

Health, family, and social policy should be incorporated into each nursing and health professions curriculum. Lawson (2000) suggests that in the realm of family and social policy for the twenty-first century helping professional, the roles of social trustee and civic professional are entwined. The new professional is caring, is trusted, and builds networks with families, individuals, and other professionals. The new millennium family professionals should be active citizens in their society, and families and clients should be the center of their work (Briar-Lawson, Lawson, & Hennon, 2001). One strategy to educate new health professionals is to first include content on the topics discussed in this

---

BOX 21-2   Components of *Hawaii's Healthy Start* Home Visiting Program

- Family identification in a statewide home visiting program for at-risk families of newborns
- Paraprofessional home visiting to improve family functioning, promote child health and development, and prevent child maltreatment
- Cross-sectional study and longitudinal study to define characteristics of families and to describe home visiting process and family characteristics associated with continued enrollment
- High-risk families, such as young mothers with limited schooling and families with infants at biological risk, were most likely to enroll

- One half of families continued in the program for 1 year for an average of 22 visits
- Families with a father with multiple risk factors and a mother with substance abuse problems were more likely to have less than or equal to 12 visits
- Most families were linked with a medical home (or primary entry into health care system) and linked to other community services

From Duggan, A., Windham, A., McFarlane, E., Fuddy, L., Rohde, C., Buchbinder, S., et al. (2000). Hawaii's healthy start program of home visiting for at-risk families: Evaluation of family identification, family engagement and service delivery. *Pediatrics, 105*, 250-259.

---

chapter as a separate course or module, in addition to providing students with an opportunity to engage in activities of advocacy for the well-being of families. For example, students might write letters to a legislator or attend a legislative assembly. For example, annually, the North Carolina Nurses Association sponsors a legislative day at the North Carolina legislature. Statewide, hundreds of nurses, students, and faculty visit selected legislators and attend a brief legislative session. Also, periodically, nurses volunteer to serve as the "nurse of the day" when the legislature is in session.

The recent community-campus partnership and the service-learning movements include beliefs that communities, families, and individuals are partners in their health care. A purpose of these two initiatives is to encourage advocacy and the support of allies of family well-being through collaboration and empowering families by stakeholders, health professionals, families, faculty, and students. A common feature of service-learning and community-campus partnerships is collaborative assessment of community and family health and social issues. The findings can be used to provide data for legislators to create needed family or social policies.

There is a dearth of data on the health, family, and social policy contents of curricula of professional schools. *The Essentials of Graduate Education in Nursing* published by the American Association of Colleges of Nursing recommends that health policy is a core component of graduate curricula. However, there is no mention of family policy. Therefore research is needed on the knowledge and proficiency of graduates of the helping professions in advocacy, civic responsibility, family-centered practice, and participation in policy making.

Research and Family Policy

The research generated by family professionals in the clinical field builds the case for more effective policy for families. For example, nurses are working in and researching the effects of home visitation. These programs may be used as models by other states to implement their own programs (Barnes-Boyd, 2001; Kitzman et al., 2000). Family nurses and family clinicians can use research findings to strengthen a rationale for supporting or developing a program or policy that takes into account the context in which families are functioning.

The Future of Family-Focused Policies in the Twenty-First Century

In 1987 the American Nurses' Foundation and the Annenberg Center for Health Services of the Eisenhower Medical Center forecast trends for nursing practice in the twenty-first century. That time is here, and the health care system has drastically changed with dynamic responses to economic factors.

After the defeat of the Clinton health plan in 1996, several predicted market trends followed. Managed care, increased cost constraints, and emphasis on data for outcomes measurement occurred as incremental changes in the policy arena (Raffel, Raffel, & Barsukiewicz, 2002). Children benefited from the initiation of the CHIPs. More reforms are needed for adult family members to have access to health care. Looking to the future, Salmon (1995) suggests that the public health and the personal care systems' agendas must merge for implementation, suggesting a more universal plan. The base of reform must be a broader collaboration than the last time reform was attempted during the Clinton administration to arrive at Salmon's proposal. If population-based approaches are taken, families and communities will be the target. The American Public Health Association's (1993) proposal for eight essentials for health reform, which concurs with Salmon's recommendation for streamlining the system to improve access for all families, is as follows:

1) Universal coverage for comprehensive health care
2) Incentive system that rewards improved health of populations
3) Monitoring of performance indicators that measure health of populations
4) Revision of information systems so that duplication is eliminated and usefulness is primary
5) Properly trained and geographically distributed workforce
6) A new focus away from crisis focus to prevention research, preventive health services, epidemiological and behavioral interventions
7) Improved access to health care to improve services to the underserved
8) Strengthening of components of public health by means of federal, state, and local assessments

Families are considered part of communities. Therefore measures that strengthen communities strengthen families. Safety-net reforms (providing measures for families on the verge of falling out of the system) will attempt to meet the essential goals of reforming the health care system in incremental ways. The Safety-Net Act of 1993 attempts to preserve federally funded community health centers (FFCHCs) by facilitating Medicaid funding measures for them. These FFCHCs are centers that serve the underserved and meet some of the essential goals of health care reform. These clinics provide services to promote family health and social roles.

Another key to reforming the health care system is the distribution of health care providers to rural and urban underserved areas. The Omnibus Funding Act of 1992 improved nurse practitioners' funding sources for reimbursements, which will assist in placing nurse practitioners in underserved areas for improved health care outcomes. This act will promote the American Public Health Association's proposal for improved distribution of the health care workforce. Wilensky (1998) predicts that incremental change will drive legislation in the United States, the uninsured will need separate plans, and HIPAA will continue as a complement to employer-sponsored insurance. There is much work to be done to reform the health care system, and family nurses need to see how their contributions can fit into local and state plans. Coile (2001), another future predictor, states that health policy will affect families across the age span in the following ways:

- Congress will mirror the divided nation, politically, after the split during the 2000 election to develop health policy.
- Health care reform will start with children and may broaden to the 45 million uninsured in small increments, but there will be no major reform by the Bush administration.
- Relief ($11.35 billion)—in the form of more Medicaid, Medicare, and state health insurance programs (SHIPs)—will go to community hospitals, academic hospitals, and rural hospitals over 5 years as a result of the Benefits and Improvement Act (2000).

- HIPAA cost for compliance will increase.
- Congressional control of the prescription drug process for seniors may be the next phase of pharmaceutical regulation.
- State legislation may overcome the Washington, DC, inertia and take the initiative in health care reform.

"How much change can occur in the health sector without major changes in the larger social system and its power structure?" (Davis, 1979, p. 6). This question still remains. Because change is such a slow process, nurses must persist and play the roles of family advocate and change agent regarding health and social policy. It is hoped that the United States will overcome its barriers and enact family policy. This question motivates family nurses who have a social contract with clients to use professional knowledge, practice, and research for the good of change for families and communities.

First, nurses must realize their position in relation to dominant power bases and gender status in society. Second, they must understand the health policy process as a socioeconomic-political process. Women have been predominant in the nursing profession historically; however, power has traditionally been assumed by men in our society. Social, health, and economic policy makers are still predominantly males. Nurses must understand the theories about power and politics, especially relating to marginalized and disenfranchised persons in the health care system. Family nurses understand the complex context in which families exist. Families, especially indigent families, have few advocates. Nurses make excellent allies for families because they share marginal status (Krueger, 2001).

Nurses are poised to wield power, based on knowing what families face in the changing health and social arenas. Nurses must help families to understand the policy process. After they share that baseline knowledge, nurses and families must become partners and make the choice to be active in advocating for and with disenfranchised families, recognizing that the power bases need to shift for any true change to occur.

Many changes in health and social policy will continue to occur, even if they are incremental.

Employer-based health care may be less inclusive for families, and other sources may have to emerge. Families with health insurance may have to spend more money out of pocket. More sacrifice will be inevitable for families to budget for health care. Managed care may continue to provide incentives for wellness and preventive care, beyond cost management.

The *Healthy People 2010* national health goals will continue to serve as the policy agenda toward decreasing health disparities, but the public health system officials must expand collaboration and the numbers of profamily policy proposals. Further health reform will be more successful if the focus is not solely on individuals, but also on families. The progress made through CHIPs must be preserved. Welfare reform must be evaluated in a holistic way to include a family perspective for further improvement. It behooves nurses as family proponents to establish a visible, consistent, rational, broad-based presence with legislators and to work with legislators from the grassroots level up to the level of budget committees (Zimmerman, 2001). The Canadian family health-promoting policy and policy making are summarized by Virginia E. Hayes from the University of Victoria.

Families with adequate support are contributing to the health and social systems by enacting the health and social functions of a strong family. Policy makers should value the importance of the contributions that families make to society and include them as partners in the formation of profamily policies. The stakeholders in insuring families for comprehensive health coverage must work in a collaborative manner toward the social justice model that recognizes health care as a right for all citizens. Family policy practice, education, and research can strengthen the infrastructure in which families are protected. Change will occur, then, with (1) a shift to social justice, (2) recognition of the power health professionals can exert as advocates of family-centered policy, and (3) a holistic approach to welfare reform. Davis' question can then be answered—that incremental changes in the larger system have been made. Family nurses are integral to that change (Krueger, 2001; Mechanic & Rheinhard, 2002).

CANADIAN PERSPECTIVES
FAMILY HEALTH-PROMOTING POLICY AND POLICY MAKING IN CANADA

Virginia E. Hayes, RN, PhD
University of Victoria

Policy related to the "social safety net," health, and the economy is essentially all *family* policy because families are the major socializing unit of society—and the social unit in which Canadians develop the basic beliefs, values, and practices that are essential to health and well-being (Schor, 1995). Though we see the hospital and support agency dollars being spent on health and social services, it is actually within the family that illness is managed. In Canada, the health cost–containing measure of shifting more and more care to the community is an example of governmental policy that profoundly affects families. Family policy—as process, product, or instrument (Clarke, 2003)—is complex and sometimes mystifying; this is no different in Canada. The complexities of governments, geography, health and social service funding and delivery, community organizations, and families themselves render family health-promoting public policy difficult to trace, make, implement, evaluate, and change.

Although Canadians' assurance of universal, comprehensive, accessible, portable, and publicly funded health care was established by law with the *Canada Health Act* in 1984, there have been many changes and erosions since then. The Act focused on individuals' health through a health care system, not on the health of the population (Glass & Hicks, 1995) or on health promotion. The Lalonde Report (1974) that

preceded it laid health and well-being at the feet of the individual, and the Epp (1986) *Framework for Health Promotion,* despite taking a broad and forward-looking stance about health promotion, argued that the three mechanisms intrinsic to health promotion are *self*-care, mutual aid, and health environments. Further, Epp recommended fostering public participation, strengthening community services, and coordinating healthy public policy as implementation strategies, but these were interpreted as *individual*-related approaches, such as immunization, individual lifestyle and behaviour change, prenatal health, and dealing with stress.

To date, there has been little or no overt policy focus on the role of families in health promotion, nor on how families themselves become and remain healthy *as families*. Canadian family health and social policy initiatives are a patchwork of economic, health, social, and mental health services; education, recreation, and culture; child and senior protection; and justice decisions, laws, and regulations (Mahon & Beauvais, 2002). A very real problem is that an integrated, coordinated system of care and support of families is not currently possible in Canada because each of the "patches" in the patchwork is independently financed, in silos (Spalding, Hayes, Williams, & McKeever, 2002).

However, significant efforts are currently being expended on behalf of families' health and well-being and in support of the

work that families do to promote and maintain individuals' health. Below are just a few examples.

Health and social policies are developed at all three levels of government and within the departments and agencies to which the implementation of major policies is delegated, such as "In-School Supports," "Women's Directorate," Centres Locales de Sante Communitaire (CLSGs or Local Community Health Centers), or "Parks and Recreation," hence, the "silos." Government bureaucrats, policy makers, and senior agency personnel do form interministerial committees (often multidisciplinary) to identify, address, and resolve issues that cross jurisdictions; and a Federal/ Provincial/ Territorial Advisory Committee has been in existence since 1973 to coordinate and advise Deputy Ministers of Health (McKay, 2001). Recently, in the proceedings of this Committee, there has been a shift toward the integration of health promotion and community and public health, and further, toward research and advocacy, possibly driven by fiscal problems and federal provincial differences about health strategies (McKay, 2001). In these, the family is frequently assumed, taken for granted in health care delivery and health promotion. For example, "several jurisdictions are using indicators of child and family well-being or 'outcomes' as part of . . . [the policy] performance measurement process" (Thompson, Maxwell, & Stroick, 1999).

CANADIAN PERSPECTIVES
FAMILY HEALTH-PROMOTING POLICY AND POLICY MAKING IN CANADA — cont'd

Periodically, health and health promotion have been surveyed in Canada (Health Canada, 1999; Rootman, Warren, Stephens, & Peters, 1988). Current health statistics measure and report individual health characteristics, disease and disability incidences, and so on. Family health-related indicators are evident only through extrapolation.

Two means of communicating with Canadians about their health are the Internet and media. Another is through regular symposia on health and health promotion. "Think tanks" and the health and social policy background research work of the Canadian Policy Research Networks hold promise for movement toward a perspective of health promotion that recognizes the interaction between an individual and his or her environment (Glouberman, 2001), the unarguably essential component of which is the family. The Canadian Institute of Child Health has been a stalwart advocate for child and family health, striving to keep health policy at the forefront of policy makers' agendas. Family caregiving has been the focus of the Canadian Home Care Association and the Canadian Association for Community Care, each doing its part to foster improved resources and policy change in support of family caregiving.

Two recent waves in health policy development have been the involvement of Canadians in health and social policy planning and the emphasis on research-based policy. The Commission on the Future of Health Care in Canada (Romonow Commission) illustrates only one of many recent attempts to involve the public in health policy development.

Another significant recent trend is the increasing use of research in the formulation and evaluation of health policy. In this, the role of Canadian Policy Research Networks has been a major one. Made up of Health, Family, and Work Networks, its objective has been to conduct a series of research studies to provide "a new and richer basis for the direction of health policy in the 21st century" (Canadian Policy Research Networks, 1998, p. 5), within its mandate to create knowledge and lead public debate on social and economic issues important to the well-being of Canadians (see its website at http://www.cprn.org/cprn.html). In addition, the major Canadian research funders have been conscientious and consistent in providing leadership for the creation of solid, research-based policy. Researchers are encouraged or required to demonstrate the policy applications of their proposed work. Research in which the family is the unit of analysis, however, still receives little focus in these institutes; the complexity of both family study and community-based health-promoting policy are both significant challenges!

Is there health-promoting family policy in Canada? Yes. Is there a widely-agreed-upon, pinned-down definition of what constitutes a full range of family policy? Have Canadians penetrated the complex interplay among health, health promotion, families, individuals, and policy? There is a beginning, but family policy is currently a patchwork, and much of our effort in family policy is so far reactive rather than proactively health-promoting. Like those in the United States, Canadian nurses have a huge role to play in advocating for, developing, implementing, and evaluating health-promoting family policy.

References

Canadian Policy Research Networks. (1998, Summer). "Towards a new perspective on health policy": Planning a Health Network project. *Health Newsletter, 5,* 3.

Clarke, H. F. (2003). Health and nursing policy: A matter of politics, power, and professionalism. In M. McIntyre & E. Thomlinson (Eds.), *Realities of Canadian nursing: Professional, practice, and power issues* (pp. 60-82). Philadelphia: Lippincott.

Epp, J. (1986). *Achieving health for all: A framework for health promotion.* Ottawa: Minister of Supply and Services Canada.

Glass, H., & Hicks, S. (1995). Health public policy, political structure, and health care organizations. In M. J. Stewart (Ed.), *Community nursing* (pp. 200-218). Toronto: Saunders.

Continued

CANADIAN PERSPECTIVES
FAMILY HEALTH-PROMOTING POLICY AND POLICY MAKING IN CANADA—cont'd

Glouberman, S. (2001). *Towards a new perspective on health policy.* Toronto: Health Network: Canadian Policy Research Networks.

Health Canada. (1999). *Toward a healthy future: Second report on the health of Canadians.* Ottawa: Author.

Lalonde, M. (1974). *A new perspective on the health of Canadians.* Ottawa: Information Canada.

Mahon, R., & Beauvais, C. (2002). *School-aged children across Canada: A patchwork of public policies.* Canadian Policy Research Networks. Retrieved November 5, 2002, from http://www.cprn.org/Release/Black/bsac_e.htm

McKay, L. (2001, January). *Changing approaches to health: The history of a Federal/Provincial/Territorial Advisory Committee.* Toronto: Health Network: Canadian Policy Research Networks.

Rootman, I., Warren, R., Stephens, T., & Peters, L. (Eds.). (1988). *Canada's health promotion survey: Technical report.* Ottawa: Health and Welfare Canada; Minister of Supply and Services Canada.

Schor, E. L. (1995). The influence of families on child health. *Pediatric Clinics of North America, 42,* 89-102.

Spalding, K. L., Hayes, V. E., Williams, A. P., & McKeever, P. (2002). *Services for children with special needs and their families: Analysis of interfaces along the continuum of care* (Report to Funder Technical Report 5). Victoria, British Columbia: Hollander Analytical Services Ltd.

Thompson, S., Maxwell, J., & Stroick, S. M. (1999). *Moving forward on child and family policy: Governance and accountability issues* (pp. 50). Toronto, Ontario, Canada: Family Network: Canadian Policy Research Networks.

Canadian spelling is used.

CASE SCENARIO

Amy is a 23-year-old single mother of three children: Mathew (age 6), Mark (age 2), and Luke (age 1). Amy's husband of 2 years left her and obtained custody of the children by getting a restraining order against Amy. When he left his girlfriend, he turned the children over to Social Services. Amy petitioned the court and recently obtained a new house trailer through a Section 8 housing assignment. She was permitted to have the children on an increasing number of weekends, progressing until she could have them full-time.

Amy has limited work experience, including hotel cleaning. Her jobs pay minimum wage and provide no health benefits. She could not pay childcare costs and meet all her expenses for the month. With the help of a social worker, Amy enrolled in a technical college to learn how to be a beautician. As part of the Temporary Assistance for Needy Families (TANF) program in her state, Amy will receive the cost of childcare, health insurance, child welfare, rent, and tuition for trade school. After 2 years, she will receive no more childcare assistance, health benefits, or food stamps. She will be expected to be self-supporting. Amy will have to apply for child support from the children's father through the court system. If they can locate him and he has a job, he will have his wages garnished for the amount of child support determined by the courts.

The influence of health and social policy on Amy's and her children's lives can be remedied by the provision of job training, low-income housing, health benefits, food supplements, and rent until her job training is completed. In 2 years, Amy will be weaned from public assistance and supposedly self-sufficient. In theory, this is appropriate; however, the reality is that Amy has not had consistent work experience and has not proved capable of raising three children on her own. Mathew was diagnosed with attention-deficit/hyperactivity disorder (ADHD) and wears glasses. Mark was recently fitted with eyeglasses. Luke

CASE SCENARIO—cont'd

has had frequent ear infections. Medical visits for these conditions could interfere with Amy's work attendance.

Amy has some support from her divorced parents, but they work full-time themselves. When the children cannot attend childcare because of illness, she has an older sister who can take care of them. Amy has to maintain a car in working order and pay the insurance and repairs for it. There is no reliable public transportation in her city. Her future is fuzzy at best.

To date, the experience of families having to be self-sufficient is mixed. Zimmerman (2001) notes that people tend to evaluate the outcome of policy in keeping with their beliefs. If people view aid to families as an individual responsibility, they may think

the results of TANF are successful. If they believe that family aid is a social responsibility, then TANF results are not successful because some families cannot be self-sufficient with the financial assistance cap and limited childcare and job training (Waller, 2003). Some families need more services, especially single-parent families. Family policies need to be flexible and comprehensive to have meaningful results. Not all policymakers are willing to support comprehensive family policy. Some policy makers may believe the current reform is all that is affordable and is good enough. Family education and research will have to inform future policies for substantive change to occur.

WEBSITE RESOURCES

ORGANIZATION	WEBSITE ADDRESS
National Center for Children in Poverty	http://www.nccp.org
Institute for Child Health Policy	http://www.ichp.edu
National Center for Education on Maternal and Child Health	http://www.ncemch.georgetown.edu
Children's Defense Fund	http://www.childrensdefense.org
National Campaign to Prevent Teen Pregnancy	http://www.teenpregnancy.org
Child Maltreatment: Reports from the States to the National Child Abuse and Neglect Data Systems	http://www.cdc.gov/nccdphp/dash.gov/programs/cb/stats/ncands
Centers for Disease Control and Prevention, Division of Adolescent and School Health	http://www.cdc.gov/nccdphp/dash
Campaign for Tobacco-Free Kids	http://www.tobaccofreekids.org
Bright Futures: Maternal Child Health and Medicaid	http://www.brightfutures.org
National Center for Families	http://www.nationalcenter.com/
Brookings Institution: Center on Urban and Metropolitan Policy	http://www.brook.edu/es/urban/urban.htm
National Center for Policy	http://www.ncp.com/
Thomas full-text legislative guide	http://www.localthomas.gov/
Couples & Marriage Policy	http://www.clasp.org/Pubs/Pubs_Couples
The Heritage Foundation Policy, Research and Analysis, Health Care Reform: Medicare, Federal Employee Health Benefits Program, and Policy Archives	http://www.heritage.org/
Firstgov.gov: Search this site to track legislation.	http://www.firstgov.gov/

W EBSITE RESOURCES—cont'd

National Health Service	http://www.biblio.org/nhs
PAX: Real Solutions to Gun Violence	http://www.pax.com/
Violence Policy Center	http://www.vcp.org/
National Safe Kids Campaign	http://www.safekids.org/
Children's Safety Network	http://www.edc.org/HHD/csn
National Council on Family Relations	http://www.ncfr.org
Patient Bill of Rights	http://www.npaf.org/provisions.htm
Healthy People 2010	http://www.healthypeople.gov/
Youth Risk Behavior Survey	http://www.cdc.gov/nccdphp/dash/yrbs/index.htm

■ CHAPTER HIGHLIGHTS

- All policy affects families at some point on the health and social service continuum.

- Implementation of policy for families has been disjointed and fragmented because of the U.S. culture's emphasis on crisis rather than prevention until the *Healthy People* National Guidelines.

- The tension between market justice and social justice philosophies exemplifies conflicts evident in American policy arenas.

- More family members are aging and living longer, putting a strain on social and health programs, necessitating cost control policies.

- Historically, the 1960s marked a period of many social and heath policies.

- The 1990s marked a resurgence of policy to improve cost, access, and quality of health care for vulnerable populations

- Until the 1990s, families headed by women had poor health outcomes as the health data accumulated. The national guidelines for *Healthy People 2000* and *Healthy People 2010* were developed to address disparities of health outcomes.

- Congressional legislation followed in the late 1990s, prioritizing resources for programs for women and children.

- The employed are primarily covered by voluntary insurance jointly funded by employee and employer contributions.

- The elderly are insured through a combination of coverage financed by Social Security tax revenues (Medicare, Part A) and self-pay for physician and supplemental coverage.

- Current policy issues affect U.S. families with young and old members, because comprehensive health coverage is proving too costly and is spiraling out of control.

- Managed care is a U. S. cost control phenomenon that is not always satisfactory.

- Family nurses play multiple roles in affecting and promoting health and social policy for families.

- Policy with a family perspective is imperative so that families are valued and strengthened as assets to society.

- In the future, there will be incremental changes in health and social policy because American culture will not support major sweeping changes.

CRITICAL THINKING ACTIVITIES

1. Investigate the nutritional supplement program in your state, such as the Women, Infants, and Children (WIC) program, and discover the rate of funding and sources of funding for it.

2. Determine where your state ranks in financing of the nutritional supplement program. Find out whether there are any alternative programs to supplement the WIC programs, such as breast-feeding programs.

3. What did your state develop for a universal child health plan during the late 1990s? Develop a summary and analysis of it to report in class. Analyze it according to the framework provided in the chapter.

4. Use the steps for policy making and apply them to the following situation:

   State nursing, health, and education leaders have met to determine the best ways to help children learn. It has been decided to focus on a comprehensive health curriculum consisting of the eight components of physical and mental health, nutrition, exercise, safety, environmental protection, counseling, and stress management.

   • What would be some probable goals and objectives for the planning process?

   • Who would be the members of a coalition that would be important to include in planning?

   • Who has a power base that would benefit the plan?

   • What steps would you take to set up a legislative agenda?

   • What legislation would be appropriate to secure support for a statewide comprehensive school health program?

REFERENCES

Aiken, T. D., & Catalano, J. (1994). *Legal, ethical, and political issues in nursing.* Philadelphia: F. A. Davis.

Altman, S. A., Reinhardt, U., & Shields, A. (1998). *The future U.S. healthcare system: Who will care for the poor and uninsured?* Chicago: Health Administration Press.

American Nurses' Foundation & the Annenberg Center. (1987). *Forum on nursing practice in the 21st century.* Kansas City, KS: Author.

American Public Health Association. (1993). *Predictions for the future.* Washington, DC: Author.

Ashur, M. L. (1993). Asking about domestic violence. SAFE questions. *Journal of the American Medical Association, 269,* 2367.

Barnes-Boyd, C., Fordham Norr, K., & Nacion, K. (2001). Promoting infant health through home visiting by a nurse-managed community worker team. *Public Health Nursing, 18,* 225-235.

Bartfeld, J. (2003). Falling through the cracks: Gaps in the child support among welfare recipients. *Journal of Marriage and Family, 65,* 72-90.

Blau, J. (1999). *Illusions of prosperity: America's working families in an age of economic insecurity.* New York: Oxford University Press.

Bogenschneider, K. (2000). Has family policy come of age? A decade review of the state of U.S. family policy in the 1990s. *Journal of Marriage and Family, 62*(4), 1136-1159.

Bogenschneider, K. (2002). *Family policy matters: How policymaking affects families.* Mahwah, NJ: Lawrence Erlbaum Associates.

Briar-Lawson, K., Lawson, H. A., & Hennon, C. B. (2001). *Family-centered policies and practices.* New York: Columbia University Press.

Chafey, K. (1995). Caring is not enough. *Nursing and Health Care, 17,* 10-15.

Chang, C. F. (2001). Access to health care: In C. F. Chang, S. A. Price, S. K. Pfoutz (Eds.), *Economics and nursing: Critical professional issues* (pp. 335-363). Philadelphia: Davis.

Children's Defense Fund. (1989). *A vision for America's future: An agenda for the 1990's.* Washington, DC: Author.

Chooporian, T. J. (1986). Reconceptualizing the environment. In P. Moccia (Ed.), *New approaches to theory development* (pp. 39-54). New York: National League for Nursing.

Clark, M. J. (2003). *Community health nursing: Caring for populations* (4th ed., pp. 61-78). Upper Saddle River, NJ: Prentice Hall.

Coile, R. (2001). *Futurescan 2001: Millennium forecast of healthcare trends 2001-05.* Chicago: Administration Press.

Darras, K. (2001). Firearm safety: An essential primary care issue. *Advances for Nurse Practitioners, 10,* 51-54.

Davis, A. (1979). *Nursing's influence on health policy for the eighties.* Kansas City, KS: American Nurses Association.

Doherty, W. (2002). Can family-focused approach benefit health care? In K. Bogenschneider (Ed.), *Family policy matters* (pp. 67-77). Mahwah, NJ: Erlbaum Publishing.

Duggan, A., Windham, A., McFarlane, E., Fuddy, L., Rohde, C., Buchbinder, S., et al. (2000). Hawaii's healthy start program of home visiting for at-risk families: Evaluation of family identification, family engagement and service delivery. *Pediatrics, 105,* 250-259.

Dye, T. (1987). *Understanding public policy.* Englewood Cliffs, NJ: Prentice-Hall.

Eichler, M. (1997). *Family shifts: Families, policies, and gender equality.* Toronto, Ontario, Canada: Oxford University Press.

Family Criteria Task Force. (1998). In National Council on Family Relations. *Families are our strength.* Minneapolis, MN: Author.

Gebbie, K., & Gebbie, E. (2001). Families, nursing and social policy. In S. M. H. Hanson (Ed.), *Family health nursing care: Theory, practice, and research* (pp. 364-385). Philadelphia: F. A. Davis.

Gebbie, K., Wakefield, M., & Kerfoot, K. (2000). Nursing and health policy. *Journal of Nursing Scholarship, 32*(3), 307-315.

Hanley, B. E. (1998). Policy development and analysis. In D. Mason & J. Leavitt (Eds.), *Policy and politics in nursing and health care* (3rd ed., pp. 125-138). Philadelphia: W. B. Saunders.

Haskins, R., & Gallagher, J. (1981). *Models for analysis of social policy: An introduction.* Norwood, NJ: Ablex Publishing.

Hildebrandt, E. (2002). The health effects of work-based welfare. *Journal of Nursing Scholarship, 34,* 363-368.

Hogan, C. (2002). Beyond welfare to work: Strategies to help low-income working families. *News and Issues: National Center for Children in Poverty, 10,* 4-5.

Kalisch, B., & Kalisch, P. (1982). *Politics of nursing.* Philadelphia: Lippincott.

Katz, M. (1996). *In the shadow of the poorhouse: A social history of welfare in America.* New York: Basic Books.

Kimball, G. (1999). *21st century families: Blueprints to create family-friendly work-places, schools, and governments.* Chico, CA: Equality Press.

Kingdon, J. W. (1995). *Agendas, alternatives, and public policy.* Boston: Little Brown.

Kitzman, H., Olds, D. L., Sidora, K., Henderson, C. R., Hanks, C., Cole, R., et al. (2000). Enduring effects of nurse home visitation on maternal life course: A 3 year follow-up of a randomized trial. *Journal of the American Medical Association, 238,* 1983-1989.

Krueger, B. J. (2001). Title V-CSHCN: A closer look at the shaping of the national agenda for children with special health care needs. *Policy, Politics, & Nursing Practice, 2,* 321-330.

Lawson, H. A. (2000). Back to the future: New century professionalism and collaborative leadership for comprehensive, community based systems of care. In A. Salle, H. A. Lawson, & K. Briar-Lawson (Eds.), *Innovative practices with vulnerable children and families* (pp. 393-418). Dubuque, IA: Eddie Bowers.

Lawson, H. A., Briar-Lawson, K., Hennon, C. B., & Jones, A. R. (2001). Key sensitizing concepts, a family policy continuum and example from the IYF. In K. Briar-Lawson, H. A. Lawson, & C. B. Hennon, with A. R. Jones (Eds.), *Family-centered policies and practices.* New York: Columbia University Press.

Mason, D., & Leavitt, J. (1998). *Policy and politics in nursing and health care* (3rd ed.). Philadelphia: Saunders.

Mason, M., Skolnick, A., & Sugeraman, S. (1998). *All our families: New policies for a new century.* New York: Oxford University Press.

Mechanic, D., & Reinhard, S. (2002). Contributions of nurses to health policy: Challenges and opportunities. *Nursing and Health Policy Review, 1,* 7-15.

Mezey, J. (2003). Threatened progress: U.S. in danger of losing ground on child care for low-income working families. *CLASP Policy Brief,* Brief Number 2.

National Council on Family Relations. (2000). *Public policy through a family lens: Sustaining families in the 21st century.* Minneapolis, MN: Author.

National Council on Family Relations. (2002). *Executive summary: Public policy through a family lens: Sustaining families in the 21st century.* Minneapolis, MN: Author.

Newacheck, P. W., Hughes, D. C., Hung, Y. Y., Wong, S., & Stoddard, J .J. (2000). The unmet needs of America's children. *Pediatrics, 105,* 989-997.

Nurse Family Partnership. (2001). Evaluation update. Retrieved June 30, 2001, from http://www.nccfc.org

Olds, D., Eckenrode, J. Henderson, C. R., Katzman, H., Powers, J., Cole, R., et al. (1997). Long-term effects of home visitation on maternal life course and child abuse and neglect: Fifteen year follow-up of a randomized trial. *Journal of American Medical Association, 278,* 637-643.

Ooms, T. (1990). Families and government: Implementing a family perspective in public policy. *Social Thought, 16,* 61-78.

Ooms, T., & Preister, S. (Eds.) (1988). *A strategy for strengthening families: Using family criteria in policymaking and program evaluation.* Washington, DC: Family Impact Seminar.

Pratt, L., Runyan, C., Cohen, L., Margolis, P. (1998). Home visitors' beliefs and practices regarding childhood injury prevention. *Public Health Nursing, 15,* 44-49.

Raffel, M., Raffel, N., & Barsukiewicz, C. (2002). *The U.S. health system origins and functions.* (5th ed.). Albany, NY: Delmar.

Ripley, R. B. (1996). Stages of the policy process. In D. C. McCool (Ed.), *Public policy theories, models and concepts: An anthology* (pp. 157-162). Englewood Cliffs, NJ: Prentice-Hall.

Salmon, M. (1995). Public health policy: Creating a healthy future for the American public. *Family and Community Health, 18,* 1-11.

Satcher, D. (1999). *Mental health: A report of the Surgeon General.* Retrieved December 13, 2002, from http://www.surgeongeneral.gov/library/mentalhealth/home.html

Seidel, B., & Seidel, P. (1998). *Politics in nursing.* Philadelphia: J. B. Lippincott.

Sherman, A. (1997). *Poverty matters: The cost of child poverty in America.* Washington, DC: Children's Defense Fund.

Shi, L., & Singh, D. (2001). *Delivering health care in America* (2nd ed.). Gaithersburg, MD: Aspen Publications.

Sidel, R. (1992). Women and children first: Towards a US family policy. *American Journal of Public Health, 82,* 664-665.

Smith, T. (2002, June 19). Mental health reform risky. *Wilmington Morning Star,* p. 9A.

U.S. Census Bureau. (1999). *Statistical abstracts of the United States, 1999.* (119th ed.). Washington, DC: Author.

Waller, M. (2003). *Welfare, working families, and reauthorization: Mayor's views*. Washington, DC: Brookings Institution Center on Urban and Metropolitan Policy.

Wilensky, G. (1998). Incremental reform: The Health Insurance Portability and Accountability Act of 1996. In S. Altman, U. Reinhardt, & A. Shields (Eds.), *The future US healthcare system: Who will care for the poor?* Chicago: Health Administration Press.

World Health Organization. *Definition of health*. Retrieved December 13, 2002, from http://www.who.int/about/definition/en/

Youth Risk Behavior Survey (YRBS). Retrieved June 9, 2003, from http.www.cdc.gov/nccdphp/dash/yrbs/about_yrbss.htm

Zimmerman, S. (2001). *Family policy: Constructed solutions to family problems*. Thousand Oaks, CA: Sage.

22

Family Health Promotion and Family Nursing in the New Millennium

Perri J. Bomar

Ambiguity is the warp of life and cannot be eliminated. We must help families find coherence within complexity.

— Forma Walsh, 2003

Nursing encompasses autonomous and collaborative care of individuals of all ages, families, groups and communities, sick or well and in all settings. Nursing includes the promotion of health, prevention of illness, and the care of ill, disabled and dying people.

— International Council of Nurses

OBJECTIVES

On completion of this chapter, the reader will be able to do the following:
1. *Examine the changing structures and emerging issues of families.*
2. *Discuss emerging factors that will affect family nursing in the next decade.*
3. *Identify factors that may impede the implementation of family health promotion and family nursing.*
4. *Discuss current and future family health promotion issues in family theory and research, nursing education, practice, and family policy.*

As the new millennium begins, families throughout the world are confronted with unprecedented economic, political, social, and environmental changes that are unpredictable and complex. These changes have the potential to significantly diminish the health and social well-being of families in all nations of the globe (World Health Organization [WHO], 1997, 1998). Also evident is a paradox that exists. Traditionally, societal values in the United States espouse high values for the health and quality of family life for all families and citizens. However, in actuality, at the beginning of the twenty-first century, the economic, social, health, and family policies do not adequately and holistically support the well-being of each family. For example, the wealthy nation of the United States is experiencing unprecedented economic growth and leads the world in health care expenditures, but at the same time, millions of its families live in poverty and their members have poor health status (Institute of Medicine [IOM], 2002b). Although the U.S. Department of Health and Human Services promotes improved quality of health for all citizens in the United States, approximately 74.7 million individuals in the country are uninsured themselves or live with a family member who is uninsured (Families USA, 2003; IOM, 2002a, 2003). Authorities anticipate that the number of medically uninsured and the continuing increases in health care costs will be persistent issues in the current decade. Concurrently, disparities in health care confronting racially and ethnically diverse families in the United States remain a major issue for policy makers, providers, and families (IOM, 2002a, 2002b). As discussed in Chapter 3, the social determinants of health are crucial factors in the multidimensional phenomenon of family health. Therefore reducing the impact of these determinants on the well-being of vulnerable families should be the major mission for policy makers, the health care system, and health professionals in the twenty-first century.

Major health-related issues for families in the twenty-first century are as follows:

- Diverse family forms
- Changing gender roles
- Cultural diversity and socioeconomic disparity
- Varying and expanded family life cycle course
- Increased expectations of self-responsibility for health care and disease prevention
- Technology and scientific advances
- Health care reform

These issues are discussed in the remainder of the chapter.

Diverse Family Forms

Amid periodic chaos and uncertainty, health care professionals in the new millennium will encounter varied family structures including a traditional nuclear dyad, domestic partnering of couples as young as 16 years of age, same-sex partnering, and domestic partnering of seniors in their eighties. As described in Chapter 2, the structure of the majority of twenty-first century families is no longer primarily a two-parent family with a male wage earner and a female homemaker. Currently, this family structure is found in only about 3% of American families. The "postmodern" American family is a "salad bowl" that includes a variety of family structures and patterns such as dual-earner couples, working parents, single adults with children, and domestic partners. Other diverse family structures and issues such as same-sex couples with or without children, extended networks, discrimination, and

gender roles will be encountered by nurses working with families in the new millennium.

Divorce

According to Gerlach (2003), a social worker, there is a "silent American epidemic" of unprecedented divorce (56%) and re/divorce (more than 50%) in the United States. In the twenty-first century, the majority of individuals and families that professionals encounter will have experienced divorce in at least one generation of the family. From observations of his clinical practice of more than 20 years, Gerlach has determined that the most vulnerable family members in divorce are the children. Gerlach posits that children are the most at risk for inner pain, economic deprivation, poor health status, and emptiness from inadequate childhood emotional and spiritual nurturance. The mental and physical health of children of divorced families will need particular attention.

Stepfamilies

Lou Everett*

Family nurses have a responsibility to become educated about key concepts related to the structure and function of stepfamily life, as well as legal concepts related to stepfamilies. Knowledge of these concepts is crucial if nurses are to teach and empower stepfamilies who are coping with stressors of health and illness. Without knowledge specific to stepfamilies such as what defines a stepfamily, the tasks of a stepfamily, developmental stages of the stepfamily, legal rights of stepparents, and resources available for stepfamilies, how can the nurse assess the needs of such families, intervene, or make appropriate referrals?

It may take 5 years or longer before a stepfamily perceives itself as having completed the normal stages that all remarried families experience. Family nurses and family professionals need to know how to normalize

---

*This section is written by Lou Everett, EdD, LMFT, Professor and Associate Dean, School of Nursing, East Carolina University, Greenville, North Carolina.

experiences of stepfamilies instead of perceiving them as dysfunctional because stepfamily needs and experiences differ from those of "non-blended" families. Also, family nurses can be advocates for stepfamilies by recognizing that from preschool through college, school officials need to know that *all* of the children's parents should be invited to school and social events. Children should not have to decide which parents to invite when they are given "two tickets" for events.

With so many Americans watching television and surfing the Internet, family nursing experts can offer the public an avenue through which to identify characteristics of healthy families, including stepfamilies, a topic that, when compared with other disciplines such as psychology or social work, is often an "ostrich" concept in nursing literature (Everett, 1998a). Some family nurse scientists are beginning to conduct nurse-hosted, family-focused talk shows, which increase public awareness of the contributions nurses make to families and society, while providing viewers with education that enhances the psychological, physical, and spiritual health of their families. Such programs with nursing expertise also provide supportive information for those experiencing illnesses.

A *healthy* stepfamily shares with other families the traits of effective communication and listening skills. However, it is essential to remember that a marriage often ends in divorce because of ineffective communication patterns. Remarriages, too, may end in divorce because an individual does not learn what he or she has contributed to the demise of the first marriage or because of unhealthy patterns that have developed in communication styles. Twenty-first century challenges for family nurses will be to serve as advocates to prevent or reduce the cycles of divorce and re/divorce. Family nurses who understand that *effective communication* and *listening* are key characteristics of all healthy families will facilitate communication by doing the following:

- Encouraging couples to discuss their problems with a certified or licensed professional counselor before making a decision to divorce
- Encouraging each spouse to examine what he or she contributed to the relationship

Even though divorce may be inevitable, when communication is effective, each spouse will be better prepared to be cordial to each other in the future and more successful in the next relationship. When children are involved, effective communication becomes even more imperative as the parents complete unfinished business with each other, let go of each other emotionally, and learn how to co-parent. These are essential tasks for future healthy adjustments to occur between the separating parents and between the children and each of the parents.

As noted in Chapter 7, family nurses need keen assessment skills as they listen for patterns of communication in families. Some schools of nursing are offering elective courses on step-family life in their undergraduate curricula, and some states are beginning to recognize that bullying behaviors in elementary school may be early symptoms of patterns of aggression that may result in assaultive behavior or domestic violence later in life. States and universities are beginning to direct more attention and time to conflict resolution in the preparation of teachers.

Family nurse scientists can do much to reinforce these primary prevention strategies by serving as resource persons and workshop leaders or lecture presenters for these modules or courses. Modules that begin with instruction on effective communication and follow with practice in conflict resolution may do more than reduce "bullyism" in the schools. They may enhance better communication in couples and families, increasing the potential for healthy families (Everett, 1998a, 1998b, 1995).

Changing Gender Roles

As discussed in Chapter 5, families who have family structures and processes different from those of the traditional two-parent model should be considered "normal" rather than abnormal. The key issue for the health care professional is to help the family to assess their unique strengths and to promote strategies and activities that increase family resilience and the capacity to adapt to a rapidly changing society. As a result of the evolving gender roles of the past 30 years, women of the twenty-first century may experience increased stress because of multiple roles and responsibilities that may include childcare, care for aging parents, and making decisions as a chief executive officer of a major organization. Families can benefit from collaborating with family nurses and family scientists to co-create family lifestyles that reduce stress, increase resilience, promote flexibility and adaptability to change, encourage supportive and caring family relationships, and increase family social support and economic resources (Olson & Olson, 2000; Walsh, 1998; Walsh, 2003).

Cultural Diversity and Socioeconomic Disparity

Cultural Diversity

Substantial global migration will continue throughout the twenty-first century as a result of natural disasters, political upheavals, armed conflicts, and persecution (WHO, 1998). Many developed nations are experiencing social and economic challenges brought about by foreign-born low-income or impoverished immigrants. For example, in Canada, Toronto, Montreal, and Vancouver are among the top five multicultural cities, with Vancouver having a reported 35% foreign-born population. Vancouver has the highest proportion of Asians of any city in North America. In 1997, 10% of the population of the United States, a total of 25.8 million people, was foreign-born—a 30% rise since the 1990 census, and the largest proportion since 1930. Between 1990 and 2000, 1.7 million people migrated to the United States from other countries. One quarter of Californians are foreign-born, the largest figure in the nation (U.S. Census Bureau, 2000). Between 1970 and 2000, the number of European-born immigrants dropped by 47%, and the portion of foreign-born Asian Americans grew from 9% to 25%. Concurrently, the number of Hispanic Americans increased from 19% to 51% (U.S. Census Bureau, 2000). The U.S. Census Bureau projects that the migration of people around the globe to more affluent countries will continue in the twenty-first century. With the expected increase in cultural pluralism in these countries, health care professionals and family and social scientists are cautioned to avoid making generalizations about these new families

based on white middle-class standards and beliefs (Walsh, 1998; International Council of Nursing [ICN], 2003). Nurses will be called on to learn about the culture of the new pluralism of families that they encounter in their practice, research, and service. In addition, families from diverse cultures should become informed partners in health care decisions and should be empowered to use self-care behaviors to prevent disease and reduce the severity of disease. Also, children from diverse ethnic groups should be taught, in their language if possible, approaches to improve their quality of life and to become accustomed to the predominant culture. Lastly, in the new millennium, nurses can contribute to improving the quality of life for displaced families, refugees, or immigrants by doing the following (ICN, 2003):

- Increasing public awareness of the needs of new immigrants
- Lobbying for the health, nursing, and social needs of immigrants
- Assisting with mobilization of resources specific to the new immigrant groups
- Assisting with planning and implementation of emergency and resettlement programs, particularly for vulnerable populations such as children, pregnant women, the disabled, and older adults
- Implementing appropriate educational programs for nursing and family professionals about the health and socioeconomic needs of refugees, immigrants, and displaced persons

Economic Disparities

Economic status and social well-being are significant contributors to family well-being. As a result, health is determined by families' economic and social status (Marmot & Wilkinson, 1999). In the United States in 2000, 31,000 million people were reported to live in poverty (U.S. Census Bureau, 2002). Poverty was greatest among female head-of-household families (25%), children younger than 18 years (37%), and African Americans (22%), Hispanic Americans (21%), and inner-city low-income African American and Hispanic American males. Families who live at, near, or below the poverty line (particularly people of color and single older women) experience inequities in access to quality health care and financial burdens that affect the quality of their health care, living conditions, and safety (IOM, 2002a, 2003; Henderson, Yasgur, & Warhowsky, 2002).

Poor families often have inadequate or no health care; live in substandard housing; are often uninsured; and live in neighborhoods with poor schools, high crime and substance abuse rates, significant environmental pollution, and random violence. Their lives are a continuous struggle to survive the challenges of a rapidly changing society and an economy with escalating costs (IOM, 2002a). Among the 73 million individuals who are uninsured, extremely high levels of disparity are noted for women and children (Barnett & Rivers, 1996; Dixon, 2000). Around the globe, the chasm between the wealthy and poor continues to widen (Zigler, Kagan, & Hall, 1996).

A challenge for nurses and family social scientists in this decade will be to collaborate with impoverished families to gain and maintain resiliency and to obtain access to health-promoting and health protection services and support for the family and individual members, particularly children, mothers, and older adults (Clear, 1999). Participatory and intervention research with larger and more diverse groups of families needs to be done. Lastly, research and clinical findings about the lived experiences of families must be made available to legislators, colleagues, and others who make decisions that influence family well-being.

Varying and Expanded Family Life Cycle Course

Demographic projections for the next two decades suggest that the number of older adults is increasing globally (U.S. Census Bureau, 2000). In the United States, a child born in 1900 was expected to live 47 years. By the end of the twentieth century, life expectancy had risen to 74 years for men and 79 years for women. In addition, in 2000, the population older than 55 years consisted of 25 million men and 31 million women. Another phenomenon is that 32% of women older than 55 years are widowed; 41% of those are ages 65 to 84, and 79% of women are

age 85 and older. In the 2000 census, the poverty rate for women of all ages was higher than that for men.

Because of changing social and economic conditions and related factors such as substance abuse, HIV deaths, and increased stress for young parents, many low-income women older than 55 years are unemployed, uninsured, and caregivers for young children, aging parents, and spouses. In addition, they have poor health status and a high incidence of chronic disease. In some families, because of the early deaths of parents from HIV or substance abuse, grandparents are the primary caregivers for young children. The health issues of the aging population will be political, social, and economic in nature. Family nurses should be able to assist families to anticipate aging and retirement and to plan and implement health-promoting lifestyles. Collaborating with families and multidisciplinary professionals to create social and economic support and a network of resources for low-income seniors is crucial.

Increased Expectations of Self-Responsibility for Health Care and Disease Prevention

As noted throughout this text, for the past 30 years, the emphasis on health promotion and self-responsibility has been a focus of the U.S. and Canadian governments, as well as WHO (Pender, Murdaugh, & Parsons, 2002; Young & Hayes, 2002). *Healthy People 2010* lists 10 leading indicators of the health status of individuals, families, and communities in the United States for the next decade (Table 22-1). This document suggests that health care professionals, families, communities, faith communities, schools, and workplaces collaborate on interventions, using the indicators as a guide to prioritize and design programs for reducing disparities and improving the quality of life of all individuals and families in the next decade.

As health care costs escalate, families and individuals will be expected to be more accountable for health promotion and health protection for themselves and family members. In addition, as discussed in Chapter 18, many families, including

TABLE 22-1   Leading Health Indicators for 2000-2010

Health Indicator	Health Promotion and Prevention
Physical activity	Promote regular physical activity
Obesity and overweight	Promote healthier weight and good nutrition
Tobacco use	Prevent and reduce tobacco use
Substance abuse	Prevent and reduce substance abuse
Responsible sexual behavior	Promote responsible sexual behavior
Mental health	Promote mental health and well-being
Injury prevention	Promote safety and reduce violence
Environmental quality	Promote a healthy environment
Immunizations	Prevent infectious disease through immunizations
Access to health care	Increase access to quality health care

The leading health indicators are a set of 10 high-priority public health issues in the United States for 2000-2010. Motivating individuals and families to act on even one of the indicators can have a profound effect on enhancing their quality of life. Also, making these indicators a high priority in health care systems will significantly reduce health disparities. The indicators can be used as a tool to develop comprehensive health-promoting and disease prevention activities that work simultaneously to improve many aspects of health for families and individual family members.

From Office of Health Promotion and Disease Prevention. (2001). *Healthy people in healthy communities.* U.S. Department of Health and Human Services. Retrieved March 20, 2003, from http://www.healthypeople.gov/publications/HealthyCommunities2001/healthycom01hk.pdf

those in which the caregiver works full-time, are providing home health care for chronically ill family members. Similarly, one of four families (23%) will be confronted with home care issues related to caregiving for members with dementia and Alzheimer's disease (Covinsky et al., 2001) or children with long-term disabilities (such as ventilator dependency) and problems associated with HIV and other sexually transmitted diseases (STDs), mental illness, an aging generation, poverty, and environmental pollution. In the twenty-first century, individuals, families, and health care professionals will continue to be interested in self-care for chronic diseases such as asthma, hypertension, diabetes, heart disease, and cancer (Adams & Corrigan, 2003).

Many of the health issues of families and chronic illness in individuals can be prevented or reduced in severity by self-care behaviors. Family nurses will have the opportunity and challenge to empower families to perform self-care activities. A discussion of each of these issues is beyond the scope of this chapter; however, family professionals should be aware of the issues and resources for each. Many of the decisions and

support are family-focused. For example, the twenty-first century STD that is reaching epidemic proportions is human papillomavirus (HPV) (Henderson et al., 2002). HPV is nearly ignored by health care professionals, and therefore women and families remain uninformed about it. Families need health literature that includes sex education and information on prevention of STDs such as HPV and HIV, as well as unplanned pregnancies.

Another health problem overlooked by the health care delivery system and society is the impact of mental illness of a family member. For example, what is the impact of mental illness, HIV, medication safety, and adherence on the quality of family life? Collaborating with families to increase their capacity for problem solving to promote medication adherence might be better accomplished if the interventions are family-focused rather than targeted to individual behaviors. The Research Synopsis discusses a study designed to identify factors that influence adherence to medication regimens.

Improvement in dental health is a *Healthy People 2010* priority. Dental caries is a preventable infectious disease that is five times more common

RESEARCH SYNOPSIS

ANTIRETROVIRAL ADHERENCE IN PERSONS WITH HIV AND CHRONIC MENTAL ILLNESS

The objective of this study was to identify the factors that influence adherence to antiretroviral medication regimens in persons with HIV/AIDS and severe mental illness (SMI). The critical incident technique was used to identify factors determining adherence. Through a series of brief, focused interviews, participants were asked to recall specific incidents that affected their adherence to HIV medications. Participants' responses were grouped into categories by using a qualitative software program. Two nurse experts, with 94% agreement, determined the reliability of the category listings. A chi-square analysis was used to compare the proportion of participants reporting each adherence factor across sociodemographic characteristics, including psychiatric diagnosis.

The total sample included 46 males and females receiving care through a day care program in San Francisco that treats patients with dual diagnoses of HIV/AIDS and SMI. The interviews yielded a total of 311 incidents. Eight major categories were identified, and a taxonomy of critical factors determining antiretroviral adherence was developed. The categories included planning (20%), interacting with others (19%), using reminders and cues (18%), responding to HIV/AIDS and treatment (11%), dealing with HIV medication characteristics (9%), dealing with lifestyle characteristics (8%), dealing with the effects of mental illness (7%), and associating HIV medicines with HIV (6%).

A comparison of adherence factors across participant groups indicated that planning was more likely to be reported by older persons taking HIV medications over longer periods. The second largest category, interacting with others, reflects the key role that supportive involvement of family, friends, or health care providers plays in maintaining adherence to HIV treatment regimens. Nonwhite persons and those living alone were more apt to rely on the use of reminders and cues. Persons with bipolar disorder reported substantially more incidents that demostrated the impact of their symptoms on adherence to HIV therapies than persons with other psychiatric diagnoses. The taxonomy of adherence factors provides important information for developing relevant adherence education programs and an essential foundation for developing future studies.

Written by Jeanne K. Kemppainen. Abstracted from Kemppainen, J. K., Levine, R., Buffum, M., Holzemer, W., Finley, P., Jensen, P., & Garcia, G. (2001). *Antiretroviral adherence in persons with HIV and chronic mental illness.* Minneapolis: MN. Paper presented at the Proceedings of the 14th Annual American Association of Nurses in AIDS Care.

than asthma (U.S. Department of Health and Human Services, 2000). Dental caries and other dental diseases are more common among individuals living in poverty, particularly children. Although the major issues in dental health are being uninsured, having low income, and a lack of access, families often lack knowledge about appropriate dental self-care. Families can reduce their health care costs and health problems by teaching children good self-care behaviors such as healthy nutritional choices to reduce obesity and improve health status, proper brushing of teeth, good hand washing techniques, stress management, resilient behaviors, and physical activity. Family nurses and family professionals have a unique opportunity to assist families with the challenges of a dynamic and rapidly changing, uncertain social, economic, and ecological environment (Denham, 2003; IOM, 2002a). In addition to health teaching, other goals are to strive for health literacy of families and communities and to influence policy for health promotion (Nutbeam, 2000).

Technology and Scientific Advances

Telehealth

The use of telehealth was initiated in the 1950s as a method of communicating with individuals who were geographically separated (e.g., rural families). The equipment can range from a telephone or fax machine to setups for live video conferencing. In a review of the literature on telehealth, Siden, Young, Starr, and Tedwell (2001) note that telehealth is used as a method for communicating and follow-up with a variety of families and individuals experiencing varied health issues. Examples of health concerns suited for telehealth are postdischarge procedures, remote consultation, mental health counseling, pediatric follow-up, geriatric care, cardiology, and rehabilitation. Telehealth can be used by nurses, physicians, social workers, family therapists, and other health care professionals to provide access to health care for families. Siden et al. (2001) found a paucity of research about family-centered telehealth and a lack of clarity on what constitutes family telehealth. The major advantage is the savings in time, cost, and travel. Once the initial cost of setting up the system is met, a savings can be realized.

Also, family nurses should be prepared to increase the capacity of families to operate the myriad of technologies used for chronically ill persons (e.g., ventilators, intravenous and tube feedings, respirators, and other sophisticated equipment). The use of telehealth and technology for health care with families of diverse cultures and with low literacy will be a challenge of the twenty-first century. However, there is a dearth of literature about the topic and research about the relationship of technology and its cultural implications, as well as an inadequate number of culturally sensitive guidelines.

Genetics and Family Nursing Practice

Research in the area of clinical genetics (the study of possible genetic factors in clinical disorders) and the mapping and sequencing of the human genome (the full set of human genes) will revolutionize "our understanding of biomedical science in clinical applications" (Grady & Collins, 2003, p. 69). After 50 years of research, in 2003 the National Human Genome Research Institute completed the production of a highly accurate gene sequence. As a result, more than ever before in history, twenty-first century clinicians will be able to use genetics for (1) identification of the specific mechanism of a disease, (2) selection of diagnostic tests, (3) predicting risks for diseases, and (4) deciding on therapies specific to the

explicit disease rather than symptoms. The use of genetics will be commonplace for the diagnosis and treatment of many chronic health problems and reproduction issues. Families of the twenty-first century will be more aware of the use of genetics and asked to make decisions about its use for family health issues. The informed consumer will increasingly make inquiries of nurses about testing, decision making, ethics, legal issues, and genetic therapy. Family decisions about genetics and the health of family members will no longer be related only to reproduction, but will also be made in oncology and critical care units (Williams, 2002).

National and international nursing organizations such as the American Nurses Association (ANA, 2002) and the International Society of Nurses in Genetics (n.d.) (see the Website Resources box for the URLs of these organizations) recommend that nurse clinicians, researchers, and educators do several things related to genetics:

- Keep abreast of recent developments in genome research and therapy
- Empower families in decision making about genetic testing and therapy
- Keep abreast of the economic, ethical, legal, and access issues of genome research and therapies
- Keep current about research priorities and reports
- Attend conferences and institutes on genetics as it relates to nursing practice, education, research, and family policy
- Integrate guidelines for genetics into nursing practice
- Serve as advocates for client/family autonomy, privacy, and confidentiality
- Conduct and disseminate genetics research

For example, in 2003, University of Iowa School of Nursing researchers had studies underway that addressed the psychosocial aspects of genetics testing, genes' involvement in hypertension, genetic markers of pain, and functions and behaviors in persons with Alzheimer's disease (University of Iowa, School of Nursing, n.d.). In a study in which the plasma leptin gene (the obesity gene) was compared with measures of obesity, gender, and race in a sample of 124 mother-offspring pairs, Harrell, Bomar, McMurray, Bradley, and Deng (2001) report that heredity plays a minor role in determining leptin levels in children. They suggest that obesity in children might be determined more by environment than by heredity. The study of leptin and related obesity variables in family members is an area of research that will assist scholars in determining whether obesity is related to family genetics or lifestyle.

Minimal genetics competencies for each health professional include the following (National Coalition for Health Professional Education in Genetics, n.d.):

- Appreciating the limitations of his or her genetics expertise
- Understanding the social, ethical, and psychological implications of genetic services
- Knowing how and when to make a referral to a genetics professional

Lastly, health care professionals should attain the core proficiencies in genetics suggested by the National Coalition for Health Professional Education in Genetics (n.d.). (See their website for details; the URL is listed in the Website Resources box.) The broad categories of the competences in genetics health include knowledge, skills, and attitudes. Professional and lay resources on genetics can be found on the website of the National Human Genome Research Institute (n.d.) (see the Website Resources box for the URL).

Health Care Reform

In the past 10 years, families have experienced the results of unprecedented health care reform and changes in the health care system. Each year, insured families assume more of the cost of their health care and premiums (IOM, 2003). Other problems in the health care system include continually rising health care costs, increasing reliance on managed health care plans, a shortage of nurses, limited health care access for vulnerable families, increased consumer prescription drug costs, increased need for consumers to pay for more of their health care costs, increasing chronic illness, and families who are uninsured (Families USA, 2003; IOM, 2003).

Lack of insurance causes individuals to delay health care for minor illnesses, to forego immunizations, and to do without regular medications for chronic health problems such as hypertension, diabetes, heart disease, and asthma. As a result, these family members often seek treatment in emergency departments while in acute distress. In addition, uninsured adults often go without cancer screening tests, which results in higher cancer mortality rates. Families with uninsured members often do without or delay preventative care, and their children do not receive routine well-child care. The cost of health care is increasing, whereas the wages of many workers have remained the same since 1999, and others are without jobs. In addition, despite having the highest health care expenditures in the world, after a review of national documents, the Committee on Health Education Summit reports that the United States is experiencing the following challenges (Greiner & Knebler, 2001):

- Poor health care system designs are leading to errors in care, poor quality of care, and dissatisfaction among clients and heath care professionals.
- The needs of persons who are chronically ill are being inadequately met by all health care professionals.
- Technological advances and information technology are not being harnessed to effectively improve the health status of clients.
- Clients and consumers are more informed than in the past. Therefore heath professionals need to believe their role is to collaborate with clients and families while being cognizant of each client's values, culture, and preferences.
- The shortage of health care professionals and workforce issues in the health care system may affect the quality of health of families and clients.
- There is a gap between the education contemporary health professionals receive and what they are actually called on to do in practice.

For example, according to the American Lung Association (2003), the prevalence of asthma continued to increase in the last decade and is the leading cause of chronic illness in children in the United States (6.5 million). This chronic, preventable disease is best treated by using an interdisciplinary, caring, culturally sensitive, family-centered, empowering, and community-participatory approach. However, the incidence of asthma in low-income children, particularly African American and Hispanic American children, in U.S. inner cities continues to escalate (American Lung Association, 2003).

These sobering health statistics raise questions for nursing. What is the role of the nurse with uninsured families and healthy families? Do the majority of nursing education curricula include content on the self-management strategies for children and families, for example, the prevention of asthma? Do schools of nursing teach the implications of family literacy and problem-solving ability for removing asthma triggers? Family nurses can improve the quality of life for patients with asthma and reduce health care expenditures by teaching children and families self-management approaches to reduce asthma-related hospitalizations and emergency department visits.

The report *Crossing the Quality Chasm: A New Health Care System for the 21st Century* (Institute of Medicine Committee on Quality Care in America, 2001) states that the U.S. health care system should be safe, effective, client-centered, timely, efficient, equitable, and efficient. Twenty-first century family nurses will have an opportunity to take part in health care reform by (1) keeping informed of public policy changes and social, economic, and health challenges of families; (2) keeping abreast of changes in the health care system; (3) collaborating with the health care delivery system, community employers, and policy makers to improve the quality of health care for families; (4) advocating for vulnerable families and for diverse family health issues at each systems level; (5) providing, to policy makers, regular data that influence policies that affect the quality of family life and health for diverse and vulnerable families; and (6) being willing to make professional and educational commitments to improve and promote health for individuals, families, and communities.

International Family Nursing

Although family nursing has been implicitly practiced internationally, the intentional incorporation of family health nursing concepts into nursing practice in the twenty-first century will remain an international trend (Bell, 1999). For example, in 1997, the Family Nursing Network was established in Edinburgh, Scotland, with the

purpose of promoting family nursing practice, research, and education (Claveirole, Mitchell, & Whyte, 2001). Also in the United Kingdom, the Stationary Office established a policy commitment to family health and established that health visitors are the key health professionals to provide health care to the entire family (Baggaley & Kean, 1999). The Department of Nursing at the University of Tampere in Finland established the Department of Family Nursing in 1997. WHO reports that in Botswana, family nursing was organized more than 20 years ago. The Canadian Perspectives box presents issues relevant to Canadian families in the twenty-first century. WHO's *Health 21 Policy* document established family nursing as an integral component of community health care (WHO, 1998). An outcome of this policy statement was the *Munich Declaration: Nurses and Midwives: A Force for Health, 2000* (WHO, 2000). In this declaration, European nurses and nurse-midwives made a commitment to family-focused care and to the support of family health nursing. Pioneering nurses have begun international research studies in family health (Brooten et al., 1997).

In the twenty-first century, family nurses throughout the world have the opportunity and challenge to make significant contributions to the quality of family health through advocacy, research, practice, and nursing education. Twenty-first century forums for family nursing will be venues such as the International Family Nursing Conference to be held in 2005 in Vancouver, British Columbia, Canada, and in other national and international forums.

Advocacy, promotion of a safe environment, research, participation in shaping health policy and in patient and health systems management, and education are also key nursing roles.

— International Council of Nurses (2003)

Priorities, Practice, Research, and Education

The following section lists implied priorities for family nurses in the next 10 years as they collaborate with families and other professionals to improve the quality of life for families.

CANADIAN PERSPECTIVES
CANADIAN FAMILIES IN THE 21ST CENTURY

Megan Aston, PhD, RN
Dalhousie University

Canadian families can be characterized by their diversity. For nurses, there are multiple ways to define and understand a family in order to effectively provide health care. First, there is a simple but profound definition put forth by two Canadian authors, Wright and Leahey (2000), who note that the family is who they say they are. When nurses use this definition, they can encourage families to express freely who they believe they are. This practice follows the concept of primary health care within Canada (Anderson 2001) where families are to be the center of care and acknowledged as relevant stakeholders within health care (Canadian Nurses Association, 1997). Relying on families to define themselves encourages nurses to look beyond stereotypes associated with families. It also allows nurses to understand how individuals are situated both inside and outside of families in order to address family health issues and societal supports on many levels.

Canada's 13 provinces and territories provide a variety of settings for health care. For example, families who live in large cities and suburbs will have different health concerns than families who are living in rural areas. Access to hospitals and community health facilities is often more challenging for those who live in rural areas. Aboriginal families who live both on and off reserves will have their own unique health issues and health practices. The way in which nurses are including environmental issues as part of caring for families has changed over the years as more is learned about environmental hazards. Family health services in Canada are guided by documented determinants of health, which may include income, social status, education, employment, social environment, healthy child development, gender, and culture. Social structures organize families personally, socially, and politically into income categories (Statistics Canada, 2002). Although this is meant to assist individuals who are poor, it also creates stereotypes and barriers for families. Families may be labeled as *working poor, on social assistance,* or *homeless.*

Changes in job security and the hope for work opportunities encourage Canadian families to migrate within Canada, as well as outside it. This creates a situation in which many individuals may be separated from their immediate or extended families. Family feelings of stress and isolation are two important health concerns that result from this phenomenon. Numerous families continue to immigrate into Canada (Statistics Canada, 2002), many of whom are refugees. Families from around the world add to the diverse and unique profiles of Canadian families. Being a newly immigrated family may involve long-distance relationships with family members in other countries. There may be difficulties for these families and feelings of isolation caused by cultural, language, or racial barriers. It is important for health care professionals to be knowledgeable about unique populations of families that exist in Canada.

Canada's publicly funded health care system follows the World Health Organization's mandate that people are to be supported to take responsibility for their own health. For example, the concept of primary health care in Canada focuses on promoting health and preventing illness of families (Wright & Leahey, 2000). This relates to the concept of population health that suggests that both health care workers and the public must address inequities in the health of identified populations (Anderson, 2001; Pyra, 2001). All of these ideas inform the way health care professionals understand and interact with families.

Keeping the family at the center of health care, whether in the hospital or in the community, will support comprehensive assessments and effective interventions. Canadian families are diverse, which demands that nurses and other health care professionals be both flexible and knowledgeable in their interactions with families.

References

Anderson, S. (2001). *Canada/international review of primary health care.* Halifax, Nova Scotia, Canada: Nova Scotia Department of Health.

CANADIAN PERSPECTIVES
CANADIAN FAMILIES IN THE 21ST CENTURY—cont'd

Canadian Nurses Association. (1997, September). The family connection. *Nursing Now: Issues and Trends in Canadian Nursing, 3,* 1-5.

Pyra, K. (2001). *Report on the Vision Workshop on Primary*

Health Care Renewal. Prepared for the Nova Scotia Department of Health, Halifax, Nova Scotia, Canada.

Statistics Canada. (2002). Retrieved from http://www.statscan.ca

Wright, L. M., & Leahey, M. (2000). *Nurses and families: A guide to family assessment and intervention* (3rd ed.). Philadelphia: F. A. Davis.

Canadian spelling is used.

Priorities for Practice

- Provide family-centered, community-based, and culturally competent care (McCorskey & Meezan, 1998).
  - Identify family strengths and increase family resilience (Walsh, 1998; Denham, 2003).
  - View families as resources to their own members.
  - Provide interventions that affirm and strengthen families' cultural, racial, and ethnic identities.
  - Seek multidisciplinary solutions to family issues.
  - Promote activities that mobilize family and individual resources, increase family resiliency, meet the needs of each family member, and enhance the growth and development of family members.
- Promote the well-being and health promotion of each family member.
  - Support couples in maintaining marital health and family resilience.
  - Support families in childrearing and child development and health care.
- Encourage health literacy and health promotion and prevention education for families and assist them in navigating the vast amount of health literature to select the most appro-

priate information (Nutbeam & Kickbusch, 2000).
  - Teach parents about health promotion, so that by the process of "diffusion" they in turn empower their children to choose health-promoting behaviors and lifestyles.
  - Encourage families to remain vigilant of the external environment and factors that might affect the quality of health for each member, particularly children.
  - Increase the capacity of families to "think family health promotion" and to create rituals and routines that foster connections and closeness and build memories.
  - Promote quality improvements such as safety in medication use by providers, families, clients, and parents (IOM, 2001).
  - Advocate for family health and health promotion in multiple arenas: health care, schools, clinics, health centers, and health care agencies.
- Provide accessible and affordable health care.
  - Provide nurse-managed centers in proximity to families (Anderko & Uscian, 2001; Clear, 1999).
  - Advocate for affordable, accessible, and comprehensive health care.

- Design nursing and health care programs that acknowledge the unique needs of vulnerable populations.
  — Seniors
  — Children, particularly low-income children
  — Families and women in poverty from varied ethnic groups
  — Clients with HIV infection and their family caregivers
  — Caregivers of the disabled, seniors, and the dying
  — Disabled persons
  — Displaced, immigrant, and refugee families
  — Families with members who have mental health issues
- Advocate for the family issues, programs, access, and policy at multiple levels: organizational/agency, local, regional, state/provincial, national, and international.
- Collaborate with other health care professionals to promote the mental, spiritual, social, sexual, and environmental health of families (Campbell, 1993; IOM, 2001).
- Use evidenced-based practice to promote family health and well-being (Greiner & Knebler, 2001).

Priorities for Research

- Design research that strengthens family health promotion, well-being, economic development, and environment.
- Create, test, and disseminate intervention- and evidenced-based family-focused studies.
- Test and develop family health promotion theories on diverse families and their issues, processes, and challenges.
- Design international research interventions and evidence-based, qualitative studies to illuminate and provide solutions to improve the health of families and their members.
- Create research to illuminate the family factors that are important in health promotion for families from diverse cultures.
- Design intervention research that tests family-centered heath promotion strategies to reduce obesity, violence, and substance abuse and assist in smoking cessation programs and other health-promoting activities.

- Create research to focus on vulnerable families and individuals (Leeman, Harrell, & Funk, 2002).
- Design intervention research to assess issues of health care technology and telehealth with ethnic families.

Priorities for Nursing Education

- Teach that family is who that client says is his or her family.
- Instruct students at each educational level about the family context for health, health promotion, disease prevention, health maintenance, health teaching, and care of the ill and dying.
- Incorporate safety practices in medications, genetics, ethics, health care, environmental health, informatics, telehealth, health care technology, and health literacy in all levels of nursing education.
- Provide experiences for students to teach and collaborate with families.
- Include the use of informatics and technology in nursing practice for family health promotion and family well-being.
- Incorporate family nursing and family-centered concepts that include family as context, individual in the family context, family as the unit of care, and families in the community and society in curricula at all levels.
- Provide clinical experiences with diverse families, health promotion and disease prevention, self-care and prevention lifestyle practices for prevention and control of chronic disease from an individual and family context.
- Provide interdisciplinary learning experiences with families (IOM, 2001).
- Teach the importance of the use of evidence-based clinical practice strategies by using published family research studies.

Summary

In the United States, nurses are the largest group of health care professionals. However, at the beginning of the new millennium, there is a nursing shortage of crisis proportion. At the same time, nurses are the "frontline providers in long term care, home care, primary and preventative care health promotion and public health" (ANA, 2002, p. 5). The future access and quality of family health promotion and the health of family members will depend considerably on an adequate number of nurses, nurses knowledgeable about the health needs of twenty-first century families, who are considerably different from families in the twentieth century.

Incorporation of concepts of family health promotion and family well-being into twenty-first century family routines means that families will depend on caring, knowledgeable, and committed nurses and family scientists who continually learn about evolving social, economic, and policy issues that influence family health (ANA, 2000). Families will need professionals who view them as partners in the health and illness experience. For this to be accomplished, family health and health promotion concepts must become an integral part of all levels of nursing education, practice, theory, and research in the next decade. Only then will we be able to fully support the diverse families living in the twenty-first century to find coherence in our ambiguous and complex society and health care delivery system.

WEBSITE RESOURCES

ORGANIZATION	WEBSITE ADDRESS
Alliance for Health Care Reform	http://www.allhealth.org/
Families USA	http://www.familiesusa.org
Kaiser Family Foundation	http://www.kff.org
Public Citizen	http://www.citizen.org/congress/reform/index.cfm
International Society of Nurses in Genetics	http://www.globalreferrals.com/about/default.htm
Core Competencies in Genetics Essential for All Health Care Professionals	http://www.nursingworld.org/aan/expert/genet2.htm
National Human Genome Research Institute	http://www.genome.gov/
Institute of Medicine	http://www.iom.gov
Stepfamily Association of America	http://www.saafamilies.org/
Stepfamily Associates	http://www.stepfamilyboston.com/aboutstep.htm
Stepfamily Foundation	http://www.stepfamily.org/
World Health Organization	http://www.who.org
Office of Minority Health	http://www.hrsa.gov/OMH
National Institute of Mental Health	http://www.nimh.nih.gov
Fogarty International Center	http://www.fic.nih.gov

CHAPTER HIGHLIGHTS

- New millennium families will be characterized as complex and by varied family structures, changing gender roles, increasing ethnic diversity and socioeconomic disparities, increasing self-care responsibility for health, new technology and scientific advances, and new sexual issues. Family nurses will need to keep abreast of the dynamic family issues and determinants of family health and remain advocates for family health in families from diverse structures, socioeconomic levels, and ethnicities.

- As the chasm between the wealthy and those who live in poverty widens, a major task of family professionals will be to collaborate with other professionals, families, and communities to improve the health status of impoverished children, women, and families.

- Families will become more responsible for their disease prevention and health promotion as health care costs increase. Family nurses will need to increase the health literacy of families in terms of disease prevention, health promotion, and family well-being.

- Family nurses and other family professionals will be called upon to be cognizant of the stepfamily lifestyle and transition issues that family members and the family system must transcend for healthy stepfamily living. Stepfamilies can benefit from empowerment strategies to prevent re/divorce and strengthen families in ways that nurture each family member, especially vulnerable children.

- Improving the capacity of families in promoting healthy family life and the health of each family member is the role of nurses internationally.

CRITICAL THINKING ACTIVITIES

1. Interview a parent or a family member and determine his or her major health issues and what he or she believes are the issues for families in the next 10 years. Share your findings with your classmates and create a list of common themes.

2. Interview a nurse and determine his or her major health issues and what he or she believes are the issues for families in the next 10 years. Share your findings with your classmates and create a list of common themes.

3. Compare the commonalties and differences in the issues identified by nurses and by families.

4. Discuss with your peers examples of nursing interventions to empower uninsured families in self-care management for health promotion and disease prevention.

5. List the priorities for family professionals in the next 10 years based on your understanding of the current dynamics in their social, economic, ethnic, environmental policy, religious, and health care delivery systems.

REFERENCES

Adams, K., & Corrigan, J. M. (2003). *Priority areas for national action: Transforming health care quality.* Washington, DC: National Academies Press.

American Lung Association. (2003). *Trends in asthma morbidity and mortality.* American Lung Association. Retrieved April 26, 2003, from http://www.lungusa/data/asthma/asthma/pdf

American Nurses Association. (2000). *Achieving access for all Americans. A proposal from the American Nurses Association for Health Coverage 2000.* Retrieved September 20, 2002, from http://www.nursingworld.org/readroom/rwjpaper.htm

American Nurses Association. (2002). *Nursing's agenda for the future.* American Nurses Association. Retrieved September 21, 2002, from http://www.nursingworld.org.naf

Anderko, L., & Uscian, M. (2001). Quality outcome measures at an academic rural nurse-managed center: A core safety net provider. *Policy, Politics, & Nursing Practice, 2,* 288-294.

Baggaley, S., & Kean, S. (1999). Health visitors as family nurses: A discussion of research, policy and practice in the United Kingdom. *Journal of Family Nursing, 5,* 388-403.

Barnett, R.C., & Rivers, C. (1996). *She works/he works*. San Francisco: Harper-San Francisco.

Bell, J. M. (1999). Family nursing network: Family nursing in Japan—A firsthand glimpse. *Journal of Family Nursing, 5,* 236-238.

Brooten, D., Thompson, J., Makoza, J., Koponda, C., Mede, E., Kachapila, L., et al. (1997). Collaborating for international research development in Malawi, Africa. *Journal of Nursing Scholarship, 29,* 369-375.

Campbell, T. L. (1993). Health promotion/disease prevention and the family. In S. J. Price & B. A. Elliot (Eds.), *Vision 2010: Families and health care.* (pp. 4-6). Minneapolis, MN: National Council on Family Relations.

Claveirole, A., Mitchell, R., & Whyte, D. (2001). Family care: Family Nursing Network: Scottish initiative to support family care. *British Journal of Nursing, 10,* 1142-1147.

Clear, J. B. (1999). Nursing centers and health promotion: A federal vantage point. *Family and Community Health.* Retrieved September 21, 2002, from http://www.findarticles.com/cf_0/m)FSP/4_21/53475162/print.jhtml

Covinsky, K. E., Eng, C., Lui, L. Y., Sands, L. P., Sehgal, A. R., Walter, L. C., et al. (2001). Reduced employment in caregivers of frail elders: Impact of ethnicity, patient clinical characteristics, and caregiver characteristics. *Journal of Gerontology: Series A—Biological Sciences and Medical Sciences, 56,* 707-713.

Denham, S. A. (2003). *Family health: A framework for nursing.* Philadelphia: F. A. Davis.

Dixon, J. (2000). Resource reviews. Social determinants of health. *Health Promotion International, 15,* 87-89. Retrieved September 7, 2002, from http://www.heapro.oupjournals.org/cgi/content/full/15/1/87

Everett, L. (1995). Stepfamilies: An 'ostrich' concept in nursing education. *Nurse Educator, 20,* 29-35.

Everett, L. (1998a). Paths to successful stepfamily living. In A. Burgess (Ed.), *Advanced practice psychiatric nursing* (pp. 445-453). Stamford, CT: Appleton and Lange.

Everett, L. (1998b). Factors that contribute to satisfaction or non-satisfaction in stepfather-stepchild relationships. *Perspectives in Psychiatric Care: The Journal for Nurse Psychotherapists, 34,* 25-34.

Families USA. (2003). Going without health insurance: Nearly one in three non-elderly Americans. In *Cover the uninsured week.* Released by the Robert Wood Johnson Foundation. Retrieved April 26, 2003, from http://www.familiesusa.org

Gerlach, P. K. (2003). *The silent American re/divorce epidemic.* Stepfamily in Formation. Retrieved April 18, 2003, from http://www.stepfamilyinfo.org/pop/epidemic.htm

Grady, P. A., & Collins, F. S. (2003). Genetics and nursing science. *Nursing Research, 52,* 69.

Greiner, A. C., & Knebel, E. (Eds.). (2001). *Health professions education: A bridge to quality.* Washington, DC: National Academies Press.

Harrell, J. S., Bomar, P. J., McMurray, R. G., Bradley, C. B., & Deng, S. (2001). Leptins and obesity in mother-child pairs. *Biological Research in Nursing, 3,* 55-64.

Henderson, G. S., Yasgur, B. S., & Warshowsky, A. (2002). *Women at risk.* New York: Avery.

Institute of Medicine. (2002a). *The future of the public's health in the 21st century.* Washington, DC: National Academies Press. Retrieved April 18, 2003, from http://www.iom.gov

Institute of Medicine. (2002b). *Unequal treatment: Confronting and understanding racial and ethnic disparities in health care.* Washington, DC: National Academies Press.

Institute of Medicine. (2003). *A shared destiny: Effects of uninsurance on individuals, families, and communities.* Washington, DC: National Academies Press.

Institute of Medicine, Committee on Quality Health Care in America. (2001). *Crossing the quality chasm: A new health care system for the 21st century.* Washington, DC: National Academies Press.

International Council of Nursing. (2003). *ICN on displaced persons: A global challenge.* Retrieved March 29, 2003, from http://www.icn.ch/matters_displacedpersons.htm

International Society of Nurses in Genetics. (n.d.). *Position statement: Informed decision-making and consent: The role of the nurse.* Retrieved April 26, 2003, from http://www.globalreferrals.com/about/position_statements/consent.htm

Leeman, J., Harrell, J. S., & Funk, S. G. (2002). Building a research program focused on vulnerable people. *Western Journal of Nursing Research, 24,* 103-111.

Marmot, M., & Wilkinson, R. (1999). *Social determinants of health.* Oxford: Oxford University Press.

McCorskey, J., & Meezan, W. (1998). Family-centered services: Approaches and effectiveness. *The Future of Children, 8,* 54-71.

National Coalition of Health Professional Education in Genetics (NCHPEG). (n.d.). *Core competencies in genetics essential for all health-care professionals.* Retrieved April 3, 2003, from http://www.nchpeg.org

National Human Genome Research Institute. (2002). *National Human Genome Research Institute fact sheet.* Retrieved April 22, 2003, from http://www.genome/gov

Nutbeam, D. (2000). Health literacy as a public health goal: A challenge for contemporary health education and communication strategies into the 21st century. *Health Promotion International, 15,* 259-267.

Nutbeam, D., & Kickbush, I. (2000). Advancing health literacy: A global challenge for the 21st century. *Health Promotion International, 15,* 183-184. Retrieved September 7, 2002, from http://www.heapro.oupjournals.org/content/vol16/issue1/

Olson, D. H., & Olson, A. K. (2000). *Empowering couples: Building on your strengths* (2nd ed.). Minneapolis, MN: Life Innovations, Inc.

Pender, N. J., Murdaugh, C. L., & Parsons, M. A. (2002). *Health promotion in nursing practice* (4th ed.). Upper Saddle River, NJ: Prentice Hall.

Siden, H. B., Young, L. E., Starr, E., & Tredwell, S. J. (2001). Telehealth: Connecting with families to promote health and healing. *Journal of Family Nursing, 7,* 315-327.

University of Iowa, School of Nursing. (n.d.). *Postdoctoral fellowship in clinical genetics research.* Retrieved May 20, 2003, from http://www.nursinguiowa.edu/areas/ parentchild/geneticresearch.htm

U.S. Census Bureau. (2000). *Population profile of the United States* (Internet Release). Retrieved December 10, 2002, from http://www.census.gov/population/pop-profile/2000/profile2000.pdf

U.S. Census Bureau. (2002). *Direct measures of poverty*

as indicators of economic need. Retrieved November 29, 2002, from http://www.census.gov/population/www/documentation/twps0030/ twps0030.html

U. S. Department of Health and Human Services (DHHS). (2000). *Oral health in America: A report of the Surgeon General.* Rockville, MD: DHHS, National Institutes of Health, National Institute of Dental and Craniofacial Research.

Walsh, F. (1998). *Strengthening family resilience.* New York: The Guilford Press.

Walsh, F. (Ed.). (2003). *Normal family processes: Growing diversity and complexity.* New York: The Guilford Press.

Williams, J. K. (2002). Education for genetics and nursing practice. *AACN Clinical Issues: Advanced Practice in Acute and Critical Care, 13,* 492-500.

World Health Organization. (1997). *Health promotion after Jakarta: What are the implications for health for all in the 21st century?* Retrieved February 8, 2003, from http://www.who.int/archives/hfa/techsem/970922.htm

World Health Organization. (1998). World Health Report. *Life in the 21st Century—a vision for all.* World Health Organization. Retrieved February 8, 2003, from http://www.who.int/inf-pr-1998/en/pr98-WHA4.html

World Health Organization. (2000). *Munich Declaration: Nurses and midwives: A force for health, 2000.* Retrieved February 25, 2003, from http://www.euro.who.int/AboutWHO/Policy/200108284

Young, L. E., & Hayes, V. (2002). *Transforming health promotion practice: Concepts, issues and applications.* Philadelphia: F. A. Davis.

Zigler, E. F., Kagan, S. L., & Hall, N. W. (1996). *Children, families, and government: Preparing for the twenty-first century.* Cambridge, United Kingdom: Cambridge University Press.

Index

Figures denoted by *f*; tables denoted by *t*.